Routledge
Encyclopedia of
PHILOSOPHY

General Editor
E D W A R D   C R A I G

London and New York

First published 1998
by Routledge
_____ /ew Fetter Lane, London EC4P 4EE
Simultaneously published in the USA and Canada
by Routledge
29 West 35th Street, New York, NY 10001

©1998 Routledge

Typeset in Monotype Times New Roman by
Routledge

Printed in England by
T J International Ltd, Padstow, Cornwall, England

Printed on acid-free paper which conforms to ANS1.Z39, 48-1992 and ISO 9706 standards

British Library Cataloguing-in-Publication Data
A catalogue record for this book is available from the British Library

The Library of Congress Cataloguing-in-Publication data is given in volume 10.

ISBN: 0415-07310-3 (10-volume set)
ISBN: 0415-18706-0 (volume 1)
ISBN: 0415-18707-9 (volume 2)
ISBN: 0415-18708-7 (volume 3)
ISBN: 0415-18709-5 (volume 4)
ISBN: 0415-18710-9 (volume 5)
ISBN: 0415-18711-7 (volume 6)
ISBN: 0415-18712-5 (volume 7)
ISBN: 0415-18713-3 (volume 8)
ISBN: 0415-18714-1 (volume 9)
ISBN: 0415-18715-X (volume 10)

ISBN: 0415-16916-X (CD-ROM)
ISBN: 0415-16917-8 (10-volume set and CD-ROM)

Contents

Using the *Encyclopedia*

List of entries

Using the *Encyclopedia*

The *Routledge Encyclopedia of Philosophy* is designed for ease of use. The following notes outline its organization and editorial approach and explain the ways of locating material. This will help readers make the most of the *Encyclopedia*.

SEQUENCE OF ENTRIES

The *Encyclopedia* contains 2,054 entries (from 500 to 19,000 words in length) arranged in nine volumes with a tenth volume for the index. Volumes 1–9 are arranged in a single alphabetical sequence, as follows:

Volume 1: A posteriori *to* Bradwardine, Thomas

Volume 2: Brahman *to* Derrida, Jacques

Volume 3: Descartes, René *to* Gender and science

Volume 4: Genealogy *to* Iqbal, Muhammad

Volume 5: Irigaray, Luce *to* Lushi chunqiu

Volume 6: Luther, Martin *to* Nifo, Agostino

Volume 7: Nihilism *to* Quantum mechanics, interpretation of

Volume 8: Questions *to* Sociobiology

Volume 9: Sociology of knowledge *to* Zoroastrianism

Alphabetical order

Entries are listed in alphabetical order by word rather than by letter with all words including *and*, *in*, *of* and *the* being given equal status. The exceptions to this rule are as follows:

- biographies: where the forenames and surname of a philosopher are inverted, the entry takes priority in the sequence, for example:

Alexander, Samuel (1859–1938)
Alexander of Aphrodisias (*c.* AD 200)
Alexander of Hales (*c.* 1185–1245)

- names with prefixes, which follow conventional alphabetical placing (see Transliteration and naming conventions below).

A complete alphabetical list of entries is given in each of the Volumes 1 to 9.

Inverted titles

Titles of entries consisting of more than one word are often inverted so that the key term (in a thematic or signpost entry) or the surname (in a biographical entry) determines the place of the entry in the alphabetical sequence, for example:

Law, philosophy of *or*
Market, ethics of the *or*
Hart, Herbert Lionel Adolphus (1907–93)

Conceptual organization

Several concerns have had a bearing on the sequence of entries where there is more than one key term.

In deciding on the sequence of entries we have tried, wherever possible, to integrate philosophy as it is known and studied in the USA and Europe with philosophy from around the world. This means that the reader will frequently find entries from different philosophical traditions or approaches to the same topic close to each other, for example, in the sequence:

Political philosophy [signpost entry]
Political philosophy, history of
Political philosophy in classical Islam
Political philosophy, Indian

Similarly, in entries where a philosophical tradition or approach is surveyed we have tried, whenever appropriate, to keep philosophical traditions from different countries together. An example is the sequence:

Confucian philosophy, Chinese
Confucian philosophy, Japanese
Confucian philosophy, Korean
Confucius (551–479 BC)

Finally, historical entries are usually placed with contemporary entries under the topic rather than the historical period. For example, in the sequence:

Language, ancient philosophy of
Language and gender
Language, conventionality of
Language, early modern philosophy of
Language, Indian theories of
Language, innateness of

DUMMY TITLES

The *Encyclopedia* has been extensively cross-referenced in order to help the reader locate their topic of interest. Dummy titles are placed throughout the alphabetical sequence of entries to direct the reader to the actual title of the entry where a topic is discussed. This may be under a different entry title, a synonym or as part of a larger entry. Wherever useful we have included the numbers of the sections (§§) in which a particular topic or subject is discussed. Examples of this type of cross-reference are:

AFRICAN AESTHETICS *see*
AESTHETICS, AFRICAN

CANGUILHEM, GEORGES *see*
FRENCH PHILOSOPHY OF SCIENCE §§3–4

TAO *see* DAO

GLOSSARY OF LOGICAL AND MATHEMATICAL TERMS

A glossary of logical and mathematical terms is provided to help users with terms from formal logic and mathematics. 'See also' cross-references to the glossary are provided at the end of entries where the user might benefit from help with unfamiliar terms. The glossary can be found in Volume 5 under L (LOGICAL AND MATHEMATICAL TERMS, GLOSSARY OF).

THE INDEX VOLUME

Volume 10 is devoted to a comprehensive index of key terms, concepts and names covered in Volumes 1–9, allowing readers to reap maximum benefit from the *Encyclopedia*. A guide to the index can be found at the beginning of the index. The index volume includes a full listing of contributors, their affiliations and the entries they have written. It also includes permission acknowledgements, listed in publisher order.

STRUCTURE OF ENTRIES

The *Routledge Encyclopedia of Philosophy* contains three types of entry:

- 'signpost' entries, for example, METAPHYSICS; SCIENCE, PHILOSOPHY OF; EAST ASIAN PHILOSOPHY. These entries provide an accessible overview of the sub-disciplines or regional coverage within the *Encyclopedia*; they provide a 'map' which directs the reader towards and around the many entries relating to each topic;
- thematic entries, ranging from general entries such as KNOWLEDGE, CONCEPT OF, to specialized topics such as VIRTUE EPISTEMOLOGY;
- biographical entries, devoted to individual philosophers, emphasizing the work rather than the life of the subject and with a list of the subject's major works.

Overview

All thematic and biographical entries begin with an overview which provides a concise and accessible summary of the topic or subject. This can be referred to on its own if the reader does not require the depth and detail of the main part of the entry.

Table of contents

All thematic and biographical entries over 1000 words in length are divided into sections and have a numbered table of contents following the overview. This gives the headings of each of the sections of the entry, enabling the reader to see the scope and structure of the entry at a glance. For example, the table of contents in the entry on HERACLITUS:

1 Life and work
2 Methodology
3 Unity of opposites and perspectivism
4 Cosmology
5 Psychology, ethics and religion
6 Influence

Cross-references within an entry

Entries in the *Encyclopedia* have been extensively cross-referenced in order to indicate other entries that may be of interest to the reader. There are two types of cross-reference in the *Encyclopedia*:

1. 'See' cross-references

Cross-references within the text of an entry direct the reader to other entries on or closely related to the topic under discussion. For example, a reader may be directed from a conceptual entry to a biography of the philosopher whose work is under discussion or vice versa. These internal cross-references appear in small capital letters, either in parentheses, for example:

Opponents of naturalism before and since Wittgenstein have been animated by the notion that the aims of social science are not causal explanation and improving prediction, but uncovering rules that make social life intelligible to its participants (see EXPLANATION IN HISTORY AND SOCIAL SCIENCE).

or sometimes, when the reference is to a person who

has a biographical entry, as small capitals in the text itself, for example:

> Thomas NAGEL emphasizes the discrepancy between the objective insignificance of our lives and projects and the seriousness and energy we devote to them.

For entries over 1,000 words in length we have included the numbers of the sections (§) in which a topic is discussed, wherever useful, for example:

> In *Nicomachean Ethics*, Aristotle criticizes Plato's account for not telling us anything about particular kinds of goodness (see ARISTOTLE §§ 21–6).

2. 'See also' cross-references

At the end of the text of each entry, 'See also' cross-references guide the reader to other entries of related interest, such as more specialized entries, biographical entries, historical entries, geographical entries and so on. These cross-references appear in small capitals in alphabetical order.

References

References in the text are given in the Harvard style, for example, Kant (1788), Rawls (1971). Exceptions to this rule are made when presenting works with established conventions, for example, with some major works in ancient philosophy. Full bibliographical details are given in the 'List of works' and 'References and further reading'.

Bibliography

List of works

Biographical entries are followed by a list of works which gives full bibliographical details of the major works of the philosopher. This is in chronological order and includes items cited in the text, significant editions, dates of composition for pre-modern works (where known), preferred English-language translations and English translations for the titles of untranslated foreign-language works.

References and further reading

Both biographical and thematic entries have a list of references and further reading. Items are listed alphabetically by author's name. (Publications with joint authors are listed under the name of the first author and after any individual publications by that author). References cited in the text are preceded by an asterisk (*). Further reading which the reader may find particularly useful is also included.

The authors and editors have attempted to provide the fullest possible bibliographical information for every item.

Annotations

Publications in the 'List of works' and the 'References and further reading' have been annotated with a brief description of the content so that their relevance to readers' interests can be quickly assessed.

EDITORIAL STYLE

Spelling and punctuation in the *Encyclopedia* have been standardized to follow British English usage.

Transliteration and naming conventions

All names and terms from non-roman alphabets have been romanized in the *Encyclopedia*. Foreign names have been given according to the conventions within the particular language.

Arabic

Arabic has been transliterated in a simplified form, that is, without macrons or subscripts. Names of philosophers are given in their Arabic form rather than their Latinate form, for example, IBN RUSHD rather than AVERROES. Arabic names beginning with the prefix 'al-' are alphabetized under the substantive part of the name and not the prefix, for example:

> KILWARDBY, ROBERT (d. 1279)
> AL-KINDI, ABU YUSUF YAQUB IBN ISHAQ
> (d. *c*.866–73)
> KNOWLEDGE AND JUSTIFICATION, COHERENCE
> THEORY OF

Arabic names beginning with the prefix 'Ibn' are alphabetized under 'I'.

Chinese, Korean and Japanese

Chinese has been transliterated using the Pinyin system. Dummy titles in the older Wade–Giles system are given for names and key terms; these direct the reader to the Pinyin titles.

Japanese has been transliterated using a modified version of the Hepburn system.

Chinese, Japanese and Korean names are given in Asian form, that is, surname preceding forenames, for example:

> WANG FUZHI
> NISHITANI KEIJI

The exception is where an author has chosen to present their own name in conventional Western form.

Hebrew

Hebrew has been transliterated in a simplified form, that is, without macrons or subscripts.

Russian

Cyrillic characters have been transliterated using the Library of Congress system. Russian names are usually given with their patronymic, for example, BAKUNIN, MIKHAIL ALEKSANDROVICH.

Sanskrit

A guide to the pronunciation of Sanskrit can be found in the INDIAN AND TIBETAN PHILOSOPHY signpost entry.

Tibetan

Tibetan has been transliterated using the Wylie system. Dummy titles in the Virginia system are given for names and key terms. A guide to Tibetan pronunciation can be found in the INDIAN AND TIBETAN PHILOSOPHY signpost entry.

European names

Names beginning with the prefixes 'de', 'von' or 'van' are usually alphabetized under the substantive part of the name. For example:

BEAUVOIR, SIMONE DE
HUMBOLDT, WILHELM VON

The exception to this rule is when the person is either a national of or has spent some time living or working in an English-speaking country. For example:

DE MORGAN, AUGUSTUS
VON WRIGHT, GEORG HENRIK

Names beginning with the prefix 'de la' or 'le' are alphabetized under the prefix 'la' or 'le'. For example:

LA FORGE, LOUIS DE
LE DOEUFF, MICHÈLE

Names beginning with 'Mc' or 'Mac' are treated as 'Mac' and appear before Ma.

Historical names

Medieval and Renaissance names where a person is not usually known by a surname are alphabetized under the forename, for example:

GILES OF ROME
JOHN OF SALISBURY

List of entries

Below is a complete list of entries in the order in which they appear in the *Routledge Encyclopedia of Philosophy*.

An alphabetical list of contributors, their affiliations and the entries they have written can be found in the index volume (Volume 10).

IRIGARAY, LUCE (1930–)

Luce Irigaray holds doctorates in both linguistics and philosophy, and has practised as a psychoanalyst for many years. Author of over twenty books, she has established a reputation as a pre-eminent theorist of sexual difference – a term she would prefer to 'feminist'. The latter carries with it the history of feminism as a struggle for equality, whereas Irigaray sees herself more as a feminist of difference, emphasizing the need to differentiate women from men over and above the need to establish parity between the sexes.

*Speculum de l'autre femme (1974) (*Speculum of the Other Woman, *1985), the book that earned her international recognition, fuses philosophy with psychoanalysis, and employs a lyrical 'mimesis', or mimicry, that parodies and undercuts philosophical pretensions to universality. While adopting the standpoint of universality, objectivity and uniformity, the philosophical tradition in fact reflects a partial view of the world, one which is informed by those largely responsible for writing it: men. Without the material, maternal and nurturing succour provided by women as mothers and homemakers, men would not have had the freedom to reflect, the peace to think, or the time to write the philosophy that has shaped our culture. As such, women are suppressed and unacknowledged; femininity is the unthought ground of philosophy – philosophy's other.*

1　Life and works
2　'Luce' and 'Irigaray'
3　*Speculum of the Other Woman*
4　Lips that speak together

1　Life and works

Born in Belgium, Luce Irigaray first studied literature, focusing on Paul Valéry, and her early training was at Louvain. She completed her Doctorate of Letters at the University of Paris VIII, and has lived in France since that time. Her thesis was later published in 1974 as *Speculum de l'autre femme* (1974) (*Speculum of the Other Woman*, 1985). In 1977 a collection of articles and interviews, *Ce sexe qui n'est pas un* (1977) (*This Sex Which is Not One*, 1985), appeared. Translations of both books were published in 1985, and these are the two early works for which she is still best known in the English-speaking world. She is better known in Italy, where she has established a large following, has contributed frequently to a Communist Party paper, and has engaged with public dialogues with Renzo Imbeni, an Italian politician to whom her book *J'aime à toi* (1992) is dedicated.

While at times she insists on the importance of her philosophical contribution, her work is also heavily indebted to Jacques LACAN, whose psychoanalytic theory remains an important influence in her more recent work, such as *Sexes et parentés* (1987) (*Sexes and Genealogies*, 1987) – despite the break with Lacan after the appearance of *Speculum* in 1974. Luce Irigaray is the Director of the Centre National de la Recherche Scientifique, where she established an international team to work on linguistic patterns in relation to gender, the focus of her most recent work.

In a 1994 interview (Hirsh and Olson 1995) Luce Irigaray divides her work into three periods. The first stage includes *Speculum of the Other Woman* and *This Sex Which is Not One*, and is characterized as a critique of the way in which 'a single subject, traditionally the masculine subject, had constructed the world and interpreted the world according to a single perspective' (see SUBJECT, POSTMODERN CRITIQUE OF THE §2). The second stage, in which one might include *Sexes and Genealogies*, was one in which she defined 'a second subject', that of a 'feminine subjectivity'. The third phase, represented by *Je, tu, nous* (1990) (*Je, Tu, Nous: Toward a Culture of Difference*, 1993), is one in which she constructs 'an intersubjectivity respecting sexual difference'. Here I shall focus on the first phase of Irigaray's tripartite division, as the most overtly philosophical period of her work, noting only that the third phase contains some more accessible works such as *Je, tu, nous*. It is also the period during which Irigaray began to receive a more sympathetic hearing from critics, who in the 1980s tended to dismiss her, with Julia KRISTEVA, as an essentialist.

2　'Luce' and 'Irigaray'

Luce Irigaray prefers to be referred to by her given name, Luce, as well as her paternal name, Irigaray. This preference reflects several fundamental issues with which her work is centrally concerned, the most obvious of which is a rejection of the primacy of the name of the father, and an insistence upon the distinction between femininity and masculinity. By insisting on the difference between her first name and her surname, Luce Irigaray draws attention to the act of naming and its presuppositions, and calls for a thoughtful relation to the language and traditions that we often unthinkingly inhabit. At the same time, she reclaims authority from the paternal law that governs language, refusing to capitulate to the dictates of a system of representation that has repressed and marginalized women. In doing so, she recreates and transforms the significance that we usually assume in the process of naming, in a gesture that is both negative and positive. On the one hand Luce Irigaray

1

challenges the traditional place of women as defined by mainstream Western society, and on the other she offers a new interpretation of women's roles. This double gesture opens the way for a third contribution, namely the re-enactment of sexual difference as a relationship between men and women that is not governed by a privileging of masculinity.

3 *Speculum of the Other Woman*

In *Speculum*, Luce Irigaray provides close textual readings of philosophical figures ranging from Plato to Freud, and including Descartes, Hegel and Plotinus. In her own words, *Speculum* treats 'the problem of the Other as woman in Western culture'. In 1985, along with *This Sex Which is Not One*, the English translation of *Speculum* appeared, marking the beginning of what has proved to be a turbulent relationship between Luce Irigaray and her critics. One reason for the controversial reception her work has elicited from English-speaking readers is the difficulties her writing – which is full of word play – poses for translators. By the word 'speculum' Luce Irigaray intended an allusion not only to 'the mirror in a simple sense', in which 'one sees oneself', but also to works that speak of '"*speculum mundi*" – that is, the "mirror of the world"'. Thus, says Luce Irigaray, at issue is how 'it's possible to give an account of the world within a discourse'.

The problems of translation that Luce Irigaray's work precipitates are not limited to her sometimes elliptical allusions. The translation of *Speculum: de l'autre femme* as *Speculum of the Other Woman* led to the assumption, says Luce Irigaray, that she was concerned with 'the image of the other woman', or with 'an empirical relation between two women, for example. This is absolutely not the project of Speculum. . . . it should have been put, *Speculum* on *the Other Woman* or *On the Other: Woman*. That would have been best' (Hirsh and Olson 1995).

By documenting the ways in which diverse texts of the Western philosophical tradition adhered to a systematic representation of women as other, Luce Irigaray demonstrated the sense in which the tradition achieved a certain unity and coherence on the basis of that which it excluded: women. Disparate in other respects, the philosophers she explores in *Speculum* share in common their dismissal, neglect and denigration of women.

Deploying a strategy of mimicry, imitating the methods of the very texts she examines, Luce Irigaray exhumes what remains of women, once the tradition has had its say, putting together the disparate parts, the shattered remnants, in order to create for the first time an image of women that goes beyond the mirroring function they have served in order to 'constitute a masculine subject' and knowledge.

Thus, for example, she retrieves the tragic and mythical figure of Antigone from the hands of Hegel ([1807] 1952) not by repudiating from the start the Hegelian analysis of this Sophoclean heroine, but precisely by taking his analysis to its limits, pushing the boundaries of his own presuppositions until they pass into their opposite, and yielding conclusions that contradict Hegel's own premises. Thus Hegel, the master of dialectic, is dialectically forced to say what he both says and cannot say: that women are 'the eternal irony of the community', and that their disruption of the ethical system of the state is to be celebrated and desired, rather than contained and repressed. Luce Irigaray thus sublates the conclusions of his absolute knowledge. She perfects and masters Hegel's own methods, even as she undermines and erases their results.

Antigone represents for Hegel the purest tragic figure, but she is not conscious of the meaning of her own deed. Hegel will grant Antigone only an immediate and intuitive understanding of ethical action, denying her the ability to reflect rationally on the significance of her action in the state as a whole. He thereby privileges the community over the individual, rationality over intuition, and abstract political duty over the exigencies of body, blood, and kinship. He upholds Creon's male claim to represent the *polis*, over Antigone's female adherence to the only tasks that ancient Thebes allows her as a woman – the care of the body and allegiance to family. Insisting on performing the rites of burial for her traitorous brother, Antigone will care for her family members in death, as in life. But whereas Hegel, along with Creon, upbraids her for this, Luce Irigaray rejoices in her refusal to obey an edict that forbids her to do the only task that is truly hers as a woman – banned from public life as her sex is.

4 Lips that speak together

Luce Irigaray is best known for the image that she presents in her essay 'When Our Lips Speak Together' (in *Ce sexe qui n'en est pas un*, 1977). Read as an ironic counterpart to Lacan's 'phallus', Luce Irigaray's view of the subject is what one critic calls 'lipcentric', but in a way that seeks to uncover multiple 'phalluses' rather than make any foundational or univocal claims for its own privilege. Luce Irigaray's work creates a 'feminine imaginary' to counteract that of the dominant culture, a masculine imaginary. A feminine or female imaginary can be understood both as the shards or fragments that remain of woman in the Western philosophical unconscious, and the creative space that these open for future re-mapping of women's identification. Luce Irigaray's texts flout academic conventions, insisting on a plurality of meanings, and blurring the boundaries separating commentary from the original texts she interprets, in order to make the point that the authority of the canon often derives from a source of unacknowledged sustenance, namely the work of women.

List of works

Irigaray, L. (1974) *Speculum de l'autre femme*, Paris: Éditions de Minuit; trans. G.C. Gill, *Speculum of the Other Woman*, Ithaca, NY: Cornell University Press, 1985. (Exposes the phallogocentric mythology pervading philosophical texts of the Western tradition from Plato to Freud.)

—— (1977) *Ce sexe qui n'en est pas un*, Paris: Éditions de Minuit; trans. C. Porter with C. Burke, *This Sex Which is Not One*, Ithaca, NY: Cornell University Press, 1985. (A collection of essays and interviews expounding the ways in which women have functioned as objects of exchange among a male economy, as the unacknowledged resource that supports a phallic symbolic, and suggesting an alternative view of interaction both among women and between women and men.)

—— (1980) *Amante marine. De Friedrich Nietzsche*, Paris: Éditions de Minuit; trans. G. Gill, *Marine Lover of Friedrich Nietzsche*, New York: Columbia University Press, 1991. (A study of the ways in which Nietzsche's work operates by excluding one of the four elements, water.)

—— (1982) *Passions élémentaires*, Paris: Éditions de Minuit; trans. J. Collie and J. Still, *Elemental Passions*, New York: Routledge, 1992. (A poetic meditation on the role of earth, air, fire and water, emphasizing the fluidity of these categories.)

—— (1983) *L'Oubli de l'air: chez Martin Heidegger*, Paris: Éditions de Minuit. (A study of Heidegger's work in the light of his repression of air as an element, which is sacrificed in favour of the other elements.)

—— (1984) *Ethique de la différence sexuelle*, Paris: Éditions de Minuit; trans. C. Burke and G. Gill, *An Ethics of Sexual Difference*, Ithaca, NY: Cornell University Press, 1993. (Irigaray's most philosophical work since Speculum, containing essays on Plato, Aristotle, Merleau-Ponty and Levinas, among others.)

—— (1985) *Parler n'est jamais neutre*, Paris: Éditions de Minuit. (Argues against the neutrality of language in relation to gender, and includes discussion of Derrida among others.)

—— (1987) *Sexes et parentés*, Paris: Éditions de Minuit; trans. G. Gill, *Sexes and Genealogies*, New York: Columbia University Press, 1993. (Psychoanalytic studies of feminine sexuality in relation to myth and religion.)

—— (1989) *Le Temps de la différence*, Paris: Éditions Générale Française; trans. A. Martin, Thinking the Difference, New York: Routledge, forthcoming.(Accessible essay on cultural and political measures that need to be taken in order to ensure the recognition of sexual difference.)

—— (1990) *Je, tu, nous*, Paris: Grasset & Fasquelle; trans. A. Martin, *Je, Tu, Nous: Toward a Culture of Difference*, London: Routledge, 1993. (Comprised of essays first presented in oral form, this brief text provides a useful introductory text to Irigaray's recent thought.)

—— (1991) *The Irigaray Reader*, ed. M. Whitford, Oxford: Blackwell. (Offers a collection of representative essays and abridged versions of texts from Irigaray's early and middle periods.)

—— (1992) *J'aime à toi: esquisse d'une félicité dans l'histoire*, Paris: Bernard Grasset; trans. A. Martin, I Love To You, London: Routledge, 1996. (Explores positive ways in which men and women can establish relationships based upon respect for each other in their difference.)

References and further reading

* Berg, M. (1991) 'Luce Irigaray's "Contradictions": Poststructuralism and Feminism', *Signs* 17 (1). (One of the best discussions of Luce Irigaray, particularly good on the relationship between the phallus and the figure of the lips.)

Chanter, T. (1995) *Ethics of Eros: Irigaray's Rewriting of the Philosophers*, London: Routledge. (Concentrates on Luce Irigaray's relation to de Beauvoir, Derrida, Hegel, Heidegger and Levinas.)

* Hegel, G.W.F. ([1807]1952) *Phänomenologie des Geistes*, ed. J. Hoffmeister, Hamburg: Felix Meiner; trans. A.V. Miller, *Phenomenology of Spirit*, Oxford: Clarendon Press, 1979. (Classic text in the history of philosophy which includes a discussion of Sophocles' Antigone, the text that forms the basis of Irigaray's essay on women as, in Hegel's phrase, 'the eternal irony of the community' in Speculum.)

* Hirsh, E. and Olson, G.A. (1995) '"Je – Luce Irigaray": A Meeting with Luce Irigaray', *Feminist Ethics and Social Policy*, Part II, special issue of *Hypatia* 10 (2). (A useful interview covering the tripartite division of Luce Irigaray's work and the difficulty of translation.)

Whitford, M. (1991) *Luce Irigaray: Philosophy in the Feminine*, London and New York: Routledge. (The first monograph on Luce Irigaray's work to appear in English; a comprehensive and scholarly discussion of her work, focusing on its psychoanalytic aspects. Very good bibliography.)

TINA CHANTER

ISAAC BEN MOSES LEVI
see DURAN, PROFIAT

ISAAC ISRAELI *see* ISRAELI, ISAAC BEN SOLOMON

ISAAC OF STELLA (d. *c*.1177)

Like other twelfth-century Cistercians, Isaac of Stella was well versed in secular learning. Centrally engaged with the contemplative life, he expresses his spiritual insights in terms of the science of his day, and combines a spiritual psychology derived from Johannes Scottus Eriugena and Hugh and Richard of St Victor with an anthropology grounded in Stoic physics, Greek and Arab medicine, and a cosmic model derived from Plato's Timaeus. *A unifying theme of his writings is the relation between the physical and spiritual dimensions of human experience.*

Born in England in the early twelfth century, Isaac studied in France. Though he speaks of the boldness and brilliance of his teachers, he mentions no names, but his writings reveal the influence of THIERRY OF CHARTRES, GILBERT OF POITIERS and WILLIAM OF CONCHES, and indicate a solid grounding in the liberal arts and the writings of secular authors. He was also throughly versed in the Augustinian tradition represented by HUGH OF ST VICTOR (see AUGUSTINIANISM), and in Greek patristic thought as transmitted by ERIUGENA. He had presumably been a monk for some time when, in 1147, he became abbot of the monastery of l'Étoile (Latin *Stella*), near Poitiers, which had recently been joined to the Cistercian Order. After twenty years during which he helped to found further Cistercian houses, and apparently aided Thomas Becket in his exile from England in the mid-1160s, Isaac removed, probably in 1167, to the island of Ré near La Rochelle. Here he assisted in founding a new monastery, Notre-Dame des Chateliers, where he evidently remained until his death around 1177.

Isaac's secular training appears plainly in his sermons, which are in effect brief theological essays dealing, frequently in technical language, with human nature, the relation of God to the universe, the Trinity and the stages of the soul's ascent to God. The distinctive features of his thought are synthesized in his *Epistola de anima* (Letter on the Soul), a short treatise which considers the soul as an intermediary between the material world and the divine. Like PLATO in the *Timaeus*, Isaac develops the idea that human nature in its complexity mirrors the universe at large, but a human being is more than a 'lesser universe', for the human soul has the power to comprehend its cosmic environment and consider it in relation to the divine Wisdom it manifests. The soul is the eye of the cosmic body, and at the same time bears a unique relation to God. Its three fundamental faculties, the rational, concupiscible and irascible (*rationabilitas, concupiscibilitas, irascibilitas*), correspond to the Persons of the Trinity conceived as Wisdom, Love and Power.

Set between God and the material world, the soul, sustained and inspired by divine grace, has the capacity to resolve the opposition between body and spirit. *Rationabilitas*, in which the soul resembles the divine Wisdom, and *conscupiscibilitas*, which emulates the all-embracing love of the Holy Spirit, reach out to the created world by means of the senses, whose perceptions are adapted to spiritual understanding by reason and imagination. When intimately engaged with the material world, the soul's imagining power (*phantasticum animae*) conceives images that are 'almost bodily', while sensory imagination for its part can form images of an 'almost spiritual' purity. At this level, Isaac declares, drawing on the Stoic concept of a 'fiery' power which informs physical and mental activity at all levels (see STOICISM), bodily and spiritual perception can collaborate, 'joined in a personal union without confusion of nature'. This linkage, through which material reality becomes accessible to the divine faculties of the soul, is analogous to the relationship whereby the soul itself bears the likeness of God and has the capacity to be 'taken up even into personal oneness' with him. From this analogy, Isaac proceeds to consider other ways in which the 'likeness' between physical and spiritual allows perception to transcend the limits of bodily existence by bringing all levels of our nature into collaboration with 'the gift of creating grace'.

Though the circulation of Isaac's writings seems to have been limited, the *Letter on the Soul* had a considerable influence through its contribution to the widely circulated treatise *On the Spirit and the Soul*. This compilation, wholly unoriginal and occasionally confused, nonetheless exercised a wide influence, partly because of its attribution to AUGUSTINE, and brought elements of Isaac's spiritual psychology to bear on the *summae* of the thirteenth-century pioneers of systematic theology, as well as the contemplative writers of the later Middle Ages.

See also: CHARTRES, SCHOOL OF; SOUL, NATURE AND IMMORTALITY OF

List of works

Isaac of Stella (before 1177) *Opera* (Works), ed. B. Tissier, Bibliotheca Patrum Cisterciensum, Bonnefontaine, 1664; repr. in J.-P. Migne (ed.) Patrologia Latina 194, Paris, cols. 1689–1786. (Edition of collected works.)

—— (before 1177) *Epistola de anima* (Letter on the Soul); trans. B. McGinn, *Three Treatises on Man: A Cistercian Anthropology*, Cistercian Fathers Series 24, Kalamazoo, MI: Cistercian Publications, 1977, 155–77. (This collection also contains the anonymous treatise *On the Spirit and the Soul*, 181–288.)

—— (before 1177) *Sermones* (Sermons), ed. A. Hoste, G. Raciti and G. Salet, Sources Chrétiennes nos. 130, 207, 339, Paris: Éditions du Cerf, 1967–87, 3 vols. (With French translation. English versions of Sermons 1–26 appear in *Isaac of Stella: Sermons for the Christian Year*, vol. I, trans. H. McCaffrey, introduction by B. McGinn, Cistercian Fathers Series 11, Kalamazoo, MI: Cistercian Publications, 1979.)

References and further reading

McGinn, B. (1969) *The Golden Chain. A Study in the Theological Anthropology of Isaac of Stella*, Cistercian Studies Series 15, Washington, DC: Cistercian Publications, Consortium Press. (Places Isaac's writings in the context of twelfth-century thought and learning.)

Raciti, G. (1971) 'Isaac de l'Étoile', in *Dictionnaire de Spiritualité*, Paris: Beauchesne, vol. 7, cols. 2011–38. (A careful review of the evidence for Isaac's life and work, and a lucid summary of his theology and anthropology.)

WINTHROP WETHERBEE

ISHRAQ *see* ILLUMINATIONIST PHILOSOPHY

ISIDORE OF SEVILLE
see ENCYCLOPEDISTS, MEDIEVAL

ISLAM AND KNOWLEDGE
see EPISTEMOLOGY IN ISLAMIC PHILOSOPHY

ISLAM, CONCEPT OF PHILOSOPHY IN

There is no generally accepted definition of what Islamic philosophy is, and the term will be used here to mean the sort of philosophy which arose within the culture of Islam. There are several main strands to Islamic philosophy. Peripatetic philosophy follows broadly the Greek tradition, while Sufism uses the principle of mystical knowledge as its leading idea. Some would argue that Islamic philosophy has never lost its concentration on the Qur'an and other significant Muslim texts, and that throughout its history it has sought to understand the essence of the realities both of the Sacred Book and of the created world. The decline of Peripatetic philosophy in the Islamic world did not mean the decline of philosophy as such, which continued to flourish and develop in other forms. Although it is sometimes argued that philosophy is not a proper activity for Muslims, since they already have a perfect guide to action and knowledge in the Qur'an, there are good reasons for thinking that Islamic philosophy is not intrinsically objectionable on religious grounds.

1 **Nature and origins of Islamic philosophy**
2 *Falsafa* **and** *hikma*
3 **Heresy and the decline of Peripatetic philosophy**
4 **Reason and revelation**

1 Nature and origins of Islamic philosophy

One of the interesting features of Islamic philosophy is that there is controversy as to what it actually is. Is it primarily the sort of philosophy produced by Muslims? This is unsatisfactory, since many Muslims who work as philosophers do not deal with Islamic issues in their philosophical work. Also, there are plenty of philosophers who are not Muslims and yet whose work is clearly in the area of Islamic philosophy. Could we call 'Islamic philosophy' philosophy which is written in Arabic? Certainly not, since a great deal of Islamic philosophy, perhaps the majority of it, is written in other languages, in particular Persian. Is Islamic philosophy then philosophy which examines the conceptual features of specifically Islamic issues? Not necessarily, since there are many thinkers whose work on logic and grammar, for example, is part of Islamic philosophy, even though there is no direct religious relevance in their work. Some commentators have tried to develop a central agenda which everyone who can be called an Islamic philosopher must share; they then have the difficulty of fitting everything in Islamic philosophy into that framework, a task which ultimately tends to fail (Leaman 1980). Perhaps the best way of specifying the nature of Islamic philosophy is to say that it is the tradition of philosophy which arose out of Islamic culture, with the latter term understood in its widest sense.

When did Islamic philosophy start? This is also a difficult question to answer, since from the early years of Islam a whole variety of legal and theological problems arose which are clearly philosophical, or at least use philosophical arguments in their elucidation. For example, there were heated debates about the acceptability of anthropomorphic language to describe the deity, and about the roles of free will and determination in the lives of human beings. Philosophy in its fullest sense began in the third century of the *hijra*. (The *hijra* was in 622 AD, when the Prophet Muhammad moved to Medina and set up a political community there; it is the first year according to the Muslim calendar, represented as AH 1.) The supremacy of the Abbasids over the Umayyads had led to an eastward movement of the Islamic empire, with the capital moving from Damascus to Baghdad. By this time also, Islam dominated such areas as Egypt, Syria and Persia, all places which were thoroughly immersed in Greek culture. The new rulers sought to apply the learning which existed in the empire to their own purposes. Much of this knowledge was very practical, being based on medicine, astrology, astronomy, mathematics and engineering. The caliph al-Ma'mun founded in Baghdad the *bayt al-hikma*, the House of Wisdom, in AH 217/AD 832, which served as an observatory and, more importantly, as a library and centre for the translation of Greek texts into Arabic. Many of the translators were Christians, who translated texts first from Greek into Syriac and then into Arabic (see GREEK PHILOSOPHY: IMPACT ON ISLAMIC PHILOSOPHY). In addition to the influence of the many translations of Greek texts, there was also an important transmission of Indian and Persian literature into Arabic, which undoubtedly had an influence on the development of Islamic philosophy.

It should not be thought that these translations were uncontroversial. Many Muslims questioned the necessity for Muslims to study philosophy at all. After all, Islam presents a complete practical and theoretical model of the nature of reality, and the 'first sciences' of the Greeks often seemed unnecessary and even opposed to Islam. Muslims had not only the Qur'an to help them regulate their lives and theoretical queries, they had also the *hadith*, the traditional sayings of the Prophet and the righteous caliphs (his immediate successors and companions) and the *sunna*, the practices of the community. There was further the system of *fiqh*, Islamic law, which discussed particular problems concerning how Muslims ought to behave, and the science of grammar, which explained how the Arabic language ought to be understood. There was also by this time a well-developed system of *kalam*, theology, which dealt with the less obvious passages of the Qur'an, and which sought conceptual unity in apparent difficulties arising from the combinations of different canonical texts (see ISLAMIC THEOLOGY). What need was there then for the sort of philosophy which existed in Greek, which originated with non-Muslims and was initially transmitted into Arabic by non-Muslims?

This would not have been such a heated issue had philosophy not seemed to be so antagonistic to Islam on so many points. The philosophy that was transmitted into Arabic at this time was profoundly Neoplatonic (see NEOPLATONISM IN ISLAMIC PHILOSOPHY); it tended to agree with ARISTOTLE (§16) that the world is eternal, that there is a hierarchy of being with the intellect at the summit and the world of generation and corruption at the bottom, and recommended a rather ascetic system of ethics (see NEOPLATONISM §3). Even more crucial was the criterion of validity which the philosophers used. This was based on reason, as opposed to revelation, and naturally brought into question the significance of religious revelation. Thus philosophy came to be seen not so much as an alternative formulation of religious truths but as a rival and competing system of thought, one which required opposition by Islam. Those Muslims who worked as philosophers had to justify themselves, and they did so in a number of ways.

The first philosopher of the Arabs, AL-KINDI, tended to argue that there is no basic inconsistency between Islam and philosophy, just as there is no basic inconsistency between Plato and Aristotle. Philosophy helps the Muslim to understand the truth using different techniques from those directly provided through Islam. Once philosophy became better established, however, it managed to sever the link with religion altogether, as we can see from AL-FARABI onwards. Religion is then taken to represent the route to truth available to the unsophisticated and simple believer; when compared to philosophy it is seen as a version of the truth, albeit perhaps of poorer conceptual quality. The most determined defender of this view is undoubtedly IBN RUSHD (Averroes), with whom this form of philosophy largely came to an end in the sixth century AH (twelfth century AD).

2 *Falsafa* and *hikma*

Peripatetic philosophy in the Islamic world came to have considerable importance for a fairly limited period, from the third to sixth centuries AH (ninth to twelfth centuries AD). Sometimes the distinctness of this form of reasoning from traditional Islamic methodologies was emphasised by the use of the term *falsafa*, an Arabic neologism designed to represent the Greek *philosophia*. Often, however, the familiar Arabic term *hikma* was used. *Hikma* means 'wisdom', and has a much wider meaning than *falsafa*. A good deal of *kalam* (theology) would be classed as *hikma*, as would mysticism or Sufism (see MYSTICAL PHILOSOPHY IN ISLAM §1). Whereas much *falsafa* is defined as the knowledge of existents, wider conceptions of the discipline tend to use the term *hikma*. AL-SUHRAWARDI, the creator of illuminationist philosophy, called it *hikmat al-ishraq*, a title which was taken up later by MULLA SADRA, and which is often translated in English as theosophy (see ILLUMINATIONIST PHILOSOPHY; THEOSOPHY). This sort of philosophy involves study of reality which transforms the soul and is never really separated from spiritual purity and religious sanctity.

Philosophy as *hikma* has the advantage of referring to a wide range of conceptual issues within Islam. Philosophy can then deal both with the exoteric aspects of the Qur'anic revelation and the esoteric dimensions which lie at the heart of religion. Both the Qur'an and the universe are often viewed as aspects of divine revelation which require interpretation, and philosophy in its widest sense has a vital role here. Western commentators have tended to overemphasize the Greek background of Islamic philosophy, yet most of the major Islamic philosophers wrote extensively on the Qur'an and saw the role of philosophy as lying chiefly in the hermeneutic investigation of holy texts. This is particularly the case with the philosophers in Persia and India, who continued the philosophical tradition after it largely came to an end in its Peripatetic form. Islamic philosophy is then essentially 'prophetic philosophy', since it is based on the interpretation of a sacred text which is the result of revelation. It deals with human beings and their entelechy, with the One or Pure Being, and the grades of the universal hierarchy, with the universe and the final return of all things to God. An important aspect of this view is that it sees Islamic

philosophy not as a transitory phenomenon but as a continuing tradition in the Islamic world, not as something largely imported from an alien culture but as an essential aspect of Islamic civilization.

A good example of this wider notion of philosophy lies in the controversy over the 'oriental philosophy' (*al-hikmat al-mashriqiyya*) of Ibn Sina (Avicenna). IBN SINA is well known as a creator of a Peripatetic philosophical system, one which came to have considerable significance within both Islamic and Western philosophy. His book *Mantiq al-mashriqiyyin* (Logic of the Orientals) deals largely with logical differences between him and Aristotle, but also includes a reference to other of his own works in which he claims to have gone in an entirely different direction from that of the Peripatetic (*mashsha'i*) thinkers. This book is not extant; perhaps the *Mantiq* is the first part of it. From what we find in his surviving works, a picture of the 'oriental philosophy' can be constructed. The Aristotelian universe becomes transformed, reason is linked to the intellect, the external universe becomes interiorized, facts become symbols and philosophy itself becomes a type of gnosis or *sophia*. The aim of philosophy is not only the theoretical knowledge of the substances and accidents of the universe, but also the experience of their presence and instantiation in such a way as to enable the soul to free itself from the confines of the universe. The universe is experienced not as something external to be understood but rather as a succession of stages along a path on which one is travelling. The notion of this 'oriental philosophy' has played an important part in the development of future illuminationist and Sufi forms of philosophy which not only seek to understand the universe rationally but also analyse the wonder we feel when we contemplate the divine mystery of that universe.

An advantage of seeing Islamic philosophy as broadly *hikma* rather than as the more narrow *falsafa* is that it avoids the danger of regarding it as predominantly an unoriginal and transmitted form of thought. This has often been the form of interpretation favoured by Western commentators, who are interested in seeing how originally Greek (and sometimes Indian and Persian) ideas reach the Islamic world and then form part of alternative systems of philosophy. There is no doubt that an important part of Islamic philosophy does follow this path, and the study of it is perhaps more appropriately a part of the history of ideas than of philosophy. Yet it should not be forgotten that by far the larger part of Islamic philosophy does not deal with the concerns of Peripatetic philosophy as such, but is firmly directed to the issues which arise within the context of an Islamic perspective on the nature of reality. Peripatetic philosophy, *falsafa*, may well enter this process, but it is far from the uncritical application of Greek ideas to Islamic issues. Although the central principles of *falsafa* have their origin in Greek philosophy, they were so radically transformed and developed within Islamic philosophy that there is no justification in thinking that the latter is merely a result of the transmission of ideas from outside Islam.

3 Heresy and the decline of Peripatetic philosophy

A highly influential attack on the role of philosophy as part of Islam was carried out by AL-GHAZALI in his *Tahafut al-falasifa* (The Incoherence of the Philosophers). According to al-Ghazali, the Peripatetic philosophers (he was thinking in particular of Ibn Sina) present as truths theses which are often either heretical (*kufr*) or innovatory (*bid'a*). One might have expected him to go on to argue that these philosophical theses are therefore unacceptable on those grounds alone, but he does not do so. Instead, al-Ghazali criticizes these theses because, he argues, they do not follow from the arguments which the philosophers themselves give. These arguments are philosophically weak, and so need not be accepted. It is a happy consequence of the failure of these arguments that the principles of Islam are seen to rest on solid rational principles, at least in the sense that their contraries are untrue. Although al-Ghazali is often regarded as the archenemy of philosophy, it is evident on closer inspection of many of his texts that he himself seems to adhere to many of the leading principles of Ibn Sina's thought. Also, in common with many other opponents of philosophy, he had a high regard for logic (which was regarded as a tool of philosophy rather than a part of it) and insisted on the application of logic to organized thought about religion. Some opponents of philosophy such as IBN TAYMIYYA even went so far as to criticize logic itself, but on the whole as the Peripatetic tradition of philosophy declined in the Sunni Islamic world it nonetheless entered other areas of Islamic life, such as theology and jurisprudence, and continued to have an influence until it was revived within the last century as part of the Islamic renaissance (*nahda*) (see ISLAMIC PHILOSOPHY, MODERN §1).

Philosophy persisted in the Shi'i world far more easily, and there has been a continuing tradition of respect for philosophy in Persia and other Shi'i communities up to today. Sunni Muslims tend to accept that the door to *ijtihad* (independent judgment) is now closed, and we must seek resolution of any theoretical and practical difficulties by referring to a series of canonical texts and to the consensus of the community. Shi'i Muslims appeal also to the authority of the imams, and especially in the case of some Shi'is to the 'hidden' or twelfth imam, as being in the continuing line of religious descent from the Prophet and from his son-in-law Imam 'Ali. Since the bases of religious authority are more fluid for the *shi'a*, it tends to be more receptive to philosophy than is the case with the Sunnis. The legal definitions of what constitutes heresy and unbelief are sometimes much looser (as with the Isma'ilis, for example), and the openness to a diversity of ideas and approaches has marked many Shi'i communities and countries. While Peripatetic philosophy went into a sharp decline in the Sunni world after the sixth century AH/twelfth century AD, it continued as part of a variety of philosophical approaches in the Shi'i world, either on its own or combined with elements of illuminationist (*ishraqi*) philosophy, and developed into more and more complex theoretical systems. Of course, philosophy continued to flourish in both the Sunni and Shi'i worlds in the sense of mystical philosophy or Sufism, which has been a persistent aspect of Islamic philosophy throughout its life.

4 Reason and revelation

Many Western commentators on Islamic philosophy take the conflict between reason and revelation as its central issue. This is often symbolized as the struggle between Athens and Jerusalem, or between philosophy and religion. While this is far too crude to be an accurate description, it does raise an important issue which has been discussed ever since Islamic philosophy began and which is still a live issue today in the Islamic world. If revelation tells believers everything they need to know, why bother to explore the same topics with reason? There are a number of answers to this question. First of all, the Qur'an itself speaks not only to Muslims, but to everyone who is able to read and understand it. It constantly urges the reader to consider rationally the evidences for Islam, and so places a high value on reason (Leaman 1985). This is not to suggest that there is no role for faith, nor that faith will not be necessary at some stage in order to approach God, but the Qur'an does offer rational indications of the truth of what it is advocating in terms of signs and proofs. This is certainly not an argument for free enquiry in the modern sense of the term, but it is an approach which places high value on the notion of independent reason, which might be seen as sympathetic also to the practice of philosophy itself.

According to Islam, the Prophet Muhammad is the last prophet. This implies that from that time on, no messenger can claim divine authority. We are reliant upon the correct interpretation of the *ayat* (signs) in both the Qur'an and in the universe. The ending of prophecy means that God expects human beings to use their reason to seek to understand the nature of reality, albeit reason which is guided by the principles of Islam. As the Qu'ran has it, 'We will show them our signs in all the parts of the earth and in their own souls, until they clearly see what is true' (Surah 41: 53). It is not as though there is competition between prophecy and philosophy, since the latter should be seen as supplementing and explaining the former. There are good grounds, then, for thinking that there is no basic incompatibility between the pursuit of reason and the pursuit of religion, at least not in Islam.

See also: Aesthetics in Islamic philosophy; Aristotelianism in Islamic philosophy; Causality and necessity in Islamic thought; Epistemology in Islamic philosophy; Ethics in Islamic philosophy; Faith; Hellenistic philosophy; Illuminationist philosophy; Islamic fundamentalism; Islamic theology; Logic in Islamic philosophy; Meaning in Islamic philosophy; Islamic philosophy, modern; Mystical philosophy in Islam; Neoplatonism; Law, Islamic philosophy of; Science in Islamic philosophy; Platonism in Islamic philosophy; Political philosophy in classical Islam; Revelation; Greek philosophy: impact on Islamic philosophy

References and further reading

Akhtar, S. (1995) 'The Possibility of a Philosophy of Islam', in S.H. Nasr and O. Leaman (eds) *The History of Islamic Philosophy*, London: Routledge, 1162–9. (Defence of the view that there is scope for philosophy within an Islamic context.)

Corbin, H. (1993) *History of Islamic Philosophy*, trans. L. Sherrard, London: Kegan Paul International. (Very important defence of the significance of mysticism and Persian thought as key aspects of Islamic philosophy.)

* al-Ghazali (1095) *Tahafut al-falasifa* (Incoherence of the Philosophers), in S. Van Den Bergh (trans.) *Averroes' Tahafut al-tahafut*, London: Luzac, 1978. (The classic attack on Peripatetic philosophy in Islam.)

* Leaman, O. (1980) 'Does the Interpretation of Islamic Philosophy rest on a Mistake?', *International Journal of MidEastern Studies* 12: 525–38. (Critique of the view that all Islamic philosophy is about the reason versus revelation issue.)

* —— (1985) 'Introduction', in O. Leaman (ed.) *An Introduction to Medieval Islamic Philosophy*, Cam-bridge: Cambridge University Press, 1–21. (Account of the relationship between Islam and rationality.)

—— (1992) 'Philosophy vs. Mysticism: An Islamic Controversy', in M. McGhee (ed.) *Philosophy, Religion and the Spiritual Life*, Cambridge: Cambridge University Press, 177–88. (A discussion of two different ways of interpreting Islamic philosophy.)

—— (1996a) 'Introduction', in S.H. Nasr and O. Leaman (eds) *History of Islamic Philosophy*, London: Routledge, 1–10. (Elucidation of different definitions of Islamic philosophy.)

—— (1996b) 'Orientalism and Islamic philosophy', in S.H. Nasr and O. Leaman (eds) *History of Islamic Philosophy*, London: Routledge, 1143–8. (Critique of Western approaches to Islamic philosophy.)

Nasr, S.H. (1996c) 'Introduction', in S.H. Nasr and O. Leaman (eds) *History of Islamic Philosophy*, London: Routledge, 11–18. (Nasr has also produced a number of important chapters in this work, including 'The Meaning and Concept of Philosophy in Islam', 21–6; 'The Qur'an and *Hadith* as Source and Inspiration of Islamic Philosophy', 27–39; and 'Ibn Sina's "Oriental Philosophy"', 247–52.)

OLIVER LEAMAN

ISLAMIC FUNDAMENTALISM

The philosophical roots of Islamic fundamentalism are largely the result of a conscious attempt to revive and restate the theoretical relevance of Islam in the modern world. The writings of three twentieth-century Muslim thinkers and activists – Sayyid Qutb, Ayatollah Ruhollah al-Khumayni and Abu al-'Ala al-Mawdudi – provide authoritative guidelines delineating the philosophical discourse of Islamic fundamentalism. However, whereas al-Khumayni and al-Mawdudi made original contributions towards formulating a new Islamic political theory, it was Qutb who offered a coherent exposition of Islam as a philosophical system.

Qutb's philosophical system postulated a qualitative contradiction between Western culture and the religion of Islam. Its emphasis on Islam as a sui generis and transcendental set of beliefs excluded the validity of all other values and concepts. It also marked the differences between the doctrinal foundations of Islam and modern philosophical currents. Consequently Islamic fundamentalism is opposed to the Enlightenment, secularism, democracy, nationalism, Marxism and relativism. Its most original contribution resides in the formulation of the concept of God's sovereignty or lordship. This concept is the keystone of its philosophical structure.

The premises of Islamic fundamentalism are rooted in an essentialist world view whereby innate qualities and attributes apply to individuals and human societies, irrespective of time, historical change or political circumstances. Hence, an immutable substance governs human existence and determines its outward movement.

1 **Essentialism and dualism**
2 **The fundamental principles of Islam**
3 **Islam's attributes**
4 **Knowledge, causation and faith**

1 Essentialism and dualism

Paganism (*jahiliyya*) is the generic designation given to all systems of thought other than Islam, both ancient and modern. According to Islamic fundamentalism, since the dawn of history human society has been a battleground between belief and unbelief, right and wrong, religious faith and idolatry. Individuals and their beliefs may carry different names in different ages, but this duality remains essentially the same.

The definition of paganism is thus stretched to encompass Greek philosophy in the ancient world as well as utilitarianism and existentialism in the modern age. To Sayyid Qutb, for example, paganism is deemed to be present wherever 'people's hearts are devoid of a divine doctrine that governs their thought and concomitant legal rules to regulate their lives' (Qutb 1982: 510). Moreover, although outward manifestations may differ from age to age, the nature and attributes of paganism remain permanent. On the other hand, religion operates throughout the ages within constant perimeters, rotating around a fixed axis. Furthermore, religion and the cosmic order reflect God's will in its harmonious design (see COSMOLOGY).

In this scheme of things, human nature and the cosmos are substances which retain their identities while undergoing change. A substance generates properties and assigns them a function peculiar to their qualities. Properties inhere in substances and are dependent for their existence and persistence on them. Such properties are not incidental, but form an identifiable structure quite distinct from other structures. These properties are therefore not transferable, in that once transferred they lose their function or significance (see SUBSTANCE).

According to Islamic fundamentalism, the essential nature of human beings is religious and atheism is an aberration. Throughout human history there have been only two methods of organizing human life: one

that declares God to be the sole sovereign and source of legislation, and another that rejects God, either as a force in the universe or as the lord and administrator of society. These two methods are irreconcilable: the first denotes Islam, the second paganism. Once human beings accept legislation to be dependent on the will of an individual, a minority or a majority, and not as the prerogative of God alone, they lapse into a type of paganism, be it a dictatorship, capitalism, theocracy or communism.

However, human history is an emanation of a doctrinal concept that is implanted by God in human beings in their capacity as his designated lieutenants on this earth. The lieutenancy (*khilafa*) of a human being is to carry out the commands of God. According to this line of reasoning, most human societies in the twentieth century resemble in their way of life the state of affairs that existed before the rise of Islam. In order to re-establish Islam as a system of government, it is thus of primary importance to discover anew the fundamental constituents of its doctrine. Such an honourable task falls to a well-disciplined group of believers. These pioneers, dubbed 'the vanguard' by Qutb, 'the Revolutionary Party' by Abu al-'Ala al-Mawdudi and 'the holy warriors' by Ayatollah Ruhollah al-Khumayni, are called upon to undertake the reinstatement of Islam in both its doctrinal and political dimensions. The method of struggle is often referred to as *jihad*, or holy war launched in the path of God.

2 The fundamental principles of Islam

The fundamental principles of Islam and the injunctions of its laws are one seamless garment woven by God for his creatures. Whereas Greek thought, particularly Aristotelian thought, asserted that we are political animals by nature, Islamic fundamentalism contends that the basic instinct of human beings is intrinsically religious. Religion is understood in this context to be Islam itself (see ISLAMIC THEOLOGY).

Islam has its own constant, immutable and clearly defined nature. Its underlying aim is to change the process of history and create a new human being, unfettered by subservience to other human beings or institutions. To be a Muslim is to believe in the fundamental principles of Islam in their entirety. Moreover, the doctrinal principles of Islam are not to be studied theologically, metaphysically or philosophically. Their study is primarily a practical endeavour aimed at discovering the base on which an all-embracing system is to be erected for the benefit of humanity. Theory and praxis go hand in hand; knowledge is simply a prelude to social action and political engagement.

For Qutb, al-Mawdudi and al-Khumayni, the doctrine of Islam forms an organic unity. A description of its constituent parts is therefore a mere analytical device, which should under all circumstances indicate the interdependence and complementarity of these parts. Once a part is detached and treated on its own it loses its significance, depriving the harmonious totality of its beauty and truth. The true nature of divinity, for example, cannot be understood apart from its direct efficacy in regulating the movement of the universe and in all its physical and spiritual connotations. Thus God's divinity ensures the harmonious essence of cosmic laws: God sustains, guards and regulates the universe according to fixed laws. Nevertheless, his absolute will fashions every movement or event without being bound by them. These laws are not self-regulatory in that they persist as a result of the immediate act of God, and are thus created anew every moment. The world was created in time, a fact denoting a temporal beginning rather than an eternal existence.

In classical Islam, God's attributes were enumerated and discussed by a number of theologians and philosophers, but his essence was deemed to lie beyond human knowledge. Islamic fundamentalism, as represented by Qutb's system, shifted the debate to Islam's essence and attributes. Hence the fundamental principles of Islam were considered by Qutb to consist in their delineation of God's divinity as well as human servitude in carrying out the tenets of the message as handed down to the seal of the prophets, Muhammad. These fundamentals spell out God's divinity (*uluhiyya*) and the servitude of animate and inanimate objects to God (*'ubudiyya*), in addition to the true essence of the cosmos, life and humanity (see GOD, CONCEPTS OF). Moreover, the visible and invisible worlds are both an integral part of this doctrine and should be present in treating the vicissitudes of human existence.

These fundamentals are not the result of an exertion by the human mind. Rather, the human mind receives them in their entirety once it is freed of its *a priori* conceptions. One does so by adhering to the sound linguistic or conventional meaning of the text in which such principles are propounded. The human mind has no function other than to understand the exact meaning of the text, irrespective of its conformity to the axioms of reason. Hence, one must accept the existence of angels, *jinns*, resurrection, hell and paradise without equivocation.

According to Qutb, the principle of divinity is the primary and most efficacious essence in the formation of the Islamic doctrine. The existence of such an essence, being absolute and eternal, does not stand in need of external evidence. The innate nature of

human beings recognizes this existence, unless it is encumbered by corrupt beliefs that render it incapable of receiving this single fact. Furthermore, the methodology of the Qur'an itself is not concerned with affirming the existence of divine power. Rather, it concentrates on describing its true quality in order to rectify the distorted views of other creeds. This rectification is not confined to distortions which prevailed before the rise of Islam; its scope covers all deviant beliefs down to the present. It thus shows the aberrance or the negativity of Aristotle's God (see ARISTOTLE §16), that of Plato's Forms and their adoption in Schopenhauer's unconscious will (see PLATO; SCHOPENHAUER, A.), and the series of emanations elaborated by PLOTINUS and taken over by so-called Islamic philosophy (see NEOPLATONISM IN ISLAMIC PHILOSOPHY). It also rectifies the dualism of DESCARTES as well as Bergson's vital power (see BERGSON, H.-L. §7), in addition to the materialism of PARMENIDES in the ancient world and that of Karl MARX in our modern period (see MATERIALISM). The Qur'anic methodology is first and foremost concerned with the question of monotheism rather than existence (see MONOTHEISM). Its main aim is to show the simple, indivisible and unique essence of God; it also asserts the attributes of God in their utter uniqueness and splendour.

3 Islam's attributes

Whereas orthodox Islamic philosophy and theology (*'ilm al-kalam*) were largely concerned with defining and elaborating God's attributes, Islamic fundamentalism shifted its focus to the attributes of Islam itself. In other words, Islam became a substantive quality with certain characteristics which could rival in their structures and functions other modern ideologies, such as fascism and Marxism. This is not to say that the divine attributes were ignored, but their significance was made a function of the predicative characteristics of a new Islamic theory.

It is well known that in mainstream Islamic theology, as propounded in the tenth century AD by Abu al-Hasan al-Ash'ari, only those attributes denoting God's acts are considered to lie within human knowledge (see ISLAMIC THEOLOGY §§2–3; ASH'ARIYYA and MU'TAZILA §1). These acts were held by al-Ash'ari to be seven in number. It is in this context that Qutb's doctrinal work, *Khasa'is al-tasawwur al-islami* (The Characteristics of the Islamic Conception), gains in significance. Although Qutb contended that Islamic theology and philosophy were outdated modes of knowledge, tainted by their reliance on categories derived from classical Greek thought, he aspired to inaugurate a new Islamic vision using an amalgamation of ancient and modern ideas. He claimed, for example, that his new interpretation consisted of a direct act of understanding the Qur'an. This receptivity is said to be unmediated and based on an immediate grasp of Qur'anic verses.

However, Qutb's binary division of Islam into 'characteristics' and 'fundamentals' is reminiscent of orthodox debates on the essence and attributes of God. It is also worth mentioning that in enumerating the characteristics of Islam, Qutb devised a new list which nevertheless, in a manner reminiscent of al-Ash'ari, included seven attributes: lordship, constancy, comprehensiveness, balance, positivity, realism and absolute unity or monotheism. These attributes of Islam emanate from God's will and specify certain rules and modes of behaviour incumbent on all believers.

4 Knowledge, causation and faith

In Islamic fundamentalism, the affinity between philosophy and natural science, an axiom of classical and medieval thought (see NATURAL PHILOSOPHY, MEDIEVAL), is ruptured and deemed to be unwarranted. Scientific knowledge is then confined to technical details and superficial alterations, a fact that renders its concepts temporary, relative and liable to change. Science is linked with experimental knowledge rather than the discovery of underlying principles.

Islam continues to be credited with stimulating the promotion of experimental methodologies that were appropriated by European scholars after the Renaissance. Nevertheless, Islamic fundamentalism, while placing the Qur'an outside the scope of modern science and philosophical debates, persists in alluding to the shortcomings of Western theories and trends of thought. Qutb, for example, highlights the fact that life itself is not inherent in the nature of matter or the universe (see LIFE, ORIGIN OF); rather, it was infused by God into dead substances. This statement allows him to refute Darwin's theory of evolution in so far as it leaves aside supernatural factors in explaining the emergence of living beings (SEE DARWIN, C.R.). He also calls Karl Marx's interpretation of social progress by means of purely economic laws an arbitrary idea; so also is Bergson's concept of life as a willed or vital creation (see MARX, K. §8; BERGSON, H-L. §7).

While Islamic fundamentalism rejects the atomist theory of orthodox Muslim theologians, it retains the idea of God as the real cause of events (see ISLAMIC THEOLOGY). Thus the connection between a cause and its effect is assumed to be the result of God's action. The metaphor used by AL-GHAZALI to show that combustibility, in the case of a flame coming into

contact with a piece of cotton, has no other cause but God, is reiterated by Qutb. A piece of cotton is not set alight because of an act performed by a flame, but as a result of God's will to render the piece of cotton combustible. Moreover, God may decide to suspend the common course of nature, and miracles occur as an indication of the divine interruption of fixed laws. Such a miracle, Qutb points out, is mentioned in the Qur'an in relation to Abraham when a burning flame failed to set him alight. It is for this reason that the use of empirical evidence in order to demonstrate causality becomes an arbitrary human construct.

See also: ASH'ARIYYA AND MU'TAZILA; CAUSALITY AND NECESSITY IN ISLAMIC THOUGHT; AL-GHAZALI; ISLAMIC PHILOSOPHY, MODERN; ISLAMIC THEOLOGY; MONOTHEISM

References and further reading

Choueiri, Y.M. (1990) *Islamic Fundamentalism*, London: Pinter Publishers; 2nd revised edn, London and Washington, DC: Cassell-Pinter, 1997. (An essential guide to the philosophical and political discourse of al-Mawdudi, al-Khumayni and Qutb.)

al-Khumayni, Imam R. (1981) *Islam and Revolution*, trans. and annotated H. Algar, Berkeley, CA: Mizan Press. (An essential collection of articles, essays and speeches outlining the theoretical and political background to Khumayni's contribution.)

al-Mawdudi, S. (1932) *Towards Understanding Islam*, Beirut: The Holy Koran Publishing House, 1980. (A succinct exposition of the theoretical foundations of Islamic fundamentalism. The work was originally published in Urdu under the title *Risala-e-Diniyat*.)

Qutb, S. (1978) *Ma'alim fi al-tariq* (Milestones), Beirut: The Holy Koran Publishing House. (One of the most powerful accounts of the doctrine of Islamic fundamentalism.)

* —— (1980) *Khasa'is al-tasawwur al-islami* (The Characteristics of the Islamic Conception), Beirut: Dar al-Shuruq. (One of the most comprehensive accounts of the theoretical assumptions of Islamic fundamentalism.)

* —— (1982) *Fi zilal al-Qur'an* (Under the Aegis of the Qur'an), Beirut: Dar al-Shuruq, vol. 1: 510. (This work forms part of a multi-volume exegesis that is considered the essential theoretical work on modern Islamic fundamentalism.)

—— (1986) *Muqawimat al-tasawwur al-islami* (Foundations of the Islamic Conception), Beirut: Dar al-Shuruq. (An indispensable work on the philosophy of Islamic fundamentalism.)

YOUSSEF CHOUEIRI

ISLAMIC MEDICINE *see* AL-RAZI, ABU BAKR MUHAMMAD IBN ZAKARIYYA'

ISLAMIC PHILOSOPHY

Islamic philosophy may be defined in a number of different ways, but the perspective taken here is that it represents the style of philosophy produced within the framework of Islamic culture. This description does not suggest that it is necessarily concerned with religious issues, nor even that it is exclusively produced by Muslims (see ISLAM, CONCEPT OF PHILOSOPHY IN*).*

1 The early years of Islamic philosophy
2 Philosophy in Spain and North Africa
3 Mystical philosophy
4 Islamic philosophy and the Islamic sciences
5 Islamic philosophy in the modern world

1 The early years of Islamic philosophy

Islamic philosophy is intimately connected with Greek philosophy, although this is a relationship which can be exaggerated. Theoretical questions were raised right from the beginning of Islam, questions which could to a certain extent be answered by reference to Islamic texts such as the Qur'an, the practices of the community and the traditional sayings of the Prophet and his Companions. On this initial basis a whole range of what came to be known as the Islamic sciences came to be produced, and these consisted largely of religious law, the Arabic language and forms of theology which represented differing understandings of Islam.

The early conquests of the Muslims brought them into close contact with centres of civilization heavily influenced by Christianity and Judaism, and also by Greek culture. Many rulers wished to understand and use the Greek forms of knowledge, some practical and some theoretical, and a large translation project started which saw official support for the assimilation of Greek culture (see GREEK PHILOSOPHY: IMPACT ON ISLAMIC PHILOSOPHY). This had a powerful impact upon all areas of Islamic philosophy. Neoplatonism definitely became the prevalent school of thought (see NEOPLATONISM IN ISLAMIC PHILOSOPHY), following closely the curriculum of Greek (Peripatetic) philosophy which was initially transmitted to the Islamic world. This stressed agreement between Plato and Aristotle on a range of issues, and incorporated the work of some Neoplatonic authors. A leading

group of Neoplatonic thinkers were the Ikhwan al-Safa' (Brethren of Purity), who presented an eclectic philosophy designed to facilitate spiritual liberation through philosophical perfection (see IKHWAN AL-SAFA'). However, there was also a development of Aristotelianism in Islamic philosophy, especially by those thinkers who were impressed by the logical and metaphysical thought of Aristotle, and Platonism was inspired by the personality of Socrates and the apparently more spiritual nature of Plato as compared with Aristotle (see ARISTOTELIANISM IN ISLAMIC PHILOSOPHY; PLATONISM IN ISLAMIC PHILOSOPHY). There were even thinkers who seem to have been influenced by Greek scepticism, which they turned largely against religion, and IBN AR-RAWANDI and Muhammad ibn Zakariyya' al-RAZI presented a thoroughgoing critique of many of the leading supernatural ideas of Islam.

AL-KINDI is often called the first philosopher of the Arabs, and he followed a broadly Neoplatonic approach. One of the earliest of the philosophers in Baghdad was in fact a Christian, Yahya IBN 'ADI, and his pupil AL-FARABI created much of the agenda for the next four centuries of work. Al-Farabi argued that the works of Aristotle raise important issues for the understanding of the nature of the universe, in particular its origination. Aristotle suggested that the world is eternal, which seems to be in contradiction with the implication in the Qur'an that God created the world out of nothing. Al-Farabi used as his principle of creation the process of emanation, the idea that reality continually flows out of the source of perfection, so that the world was not created at a particular time. He also did an enormous amount of work on Greek logic, arguing that behind natural language lies logic, so that an understanding of the latter is a deeper and more significant achievement than a grasp of the former. This also seemed to threaten the significance of language, in particular the language – Arabic – in which God transmitted the Qur'an to the Prophet Muhammad. A large school of thinkers was strongly influenced by al-Farabi, including AL-'AMIRI, AL-SIJISTANI and AL-TAWHIDI, and this surely played an important part in making his ideas and methodology so crucial for the following centuries of Islamic philosophy.

IBN SINA went on to develop this form of thought in a much more creative way, and he presented a view of the universe as consisting of entirely necessitated events, with the exception of God (see CAUSALITY AND NECESSITY IN ISLAMIC THOUGHT). This led to a powerful reaction from AL-GHAZALI, who in his critique of Peripatetic philosophy argued that it was both incompatible with religion, and also invalid on its own principles. He managed to point to some of

13

the major difficulties with the developments of Neoplatonism which had taken place in Islamic philosophy, and he argued that while philosophy should be rejected, logic as a conceptual tool should be retained. This view became very influential in much of the Islamic world, and philosophy came under a cloud until the nineteenth century.

2 Philosophy in Spain and North Africa

A particularly rich blend of philosophy flourished in al-Andalus (the Islamic part of the Iberian penninsula), and in North Africa. IBN MASARRA defended a form of mysticism, and this type of thinking was important for both IBN TUFAYL and IBN BAJJA, for whom the contrast between the individual in society and the individual who primarily relates to God became very much of a theme. The argument was often that a higher level of understanding of reality can be attained by those prepared to develop their religious consciousness outside of the framework of traditional religion, a view which was supported and became part of a highly sophisticated account of the links between religion and reason as created by IBN RUSHD. He set out to defend philosophy strenuously from the attacks of al-Ghazali, and also to present a more Aristotelian account than had been managed by Ibn Sina. He argued that there are a variety of routes to God, all equally valid, and that the route which the philosopher can take is one based on the independent use of reason, while the ordinary member of society has to be satisfied with the sayings and obligations of religion. IBN SAB'IN, by contrast, argued that Aristotelian philosophy and logic were useless in trying to understand reality since those ideas fail to mirror the basic unity which is implicit in reality, a unity which stems from the unity of God, and so we require an entirely new form of thinking which is adequate to the task of representing the oneness of the world. A thinker better known perhaps for his work on history and sociology than in philosophy is IBN KHALDUN, who was nonetheless a significant philosophical writer; he presents an excellent summary of preceding philosophical movements within the Islamic world, albeit from a conservative (Ash'arite) point of view.

3 Mystical philosophy

Mystical philosophy in Islam represents a persistent tradition of working philosophically within the Islamic world (see MYSTICAL PHILOSOPHY IN ISLAM). Some philosophers managed to combine mysticism with Peripatetic thought, while others saw mysticism as in opposition to Peripateticism. Al-Ghazali had great influence in making mysticism in its Sufi form

respectable, but it is really other thinkers such as AL-SUHRAWARDI and IBN AL-'ARABI who produced actual systematic mystical thought. They created, albeit in different ways, accounts of how to do philosophy which accord with mystical approaches to reality, and which self-consciously go in opposite directions to Peripateticism. Ibn al-'Arabi concentrated on analysing the different levels of reality and the links which exist between them, while al-Suhrawardi is the main progenitor of Illuminationist philosophy (see ILLUMINATIONIST PHILOSOPHY). This tries to replace Aristotelian logic and metaphysics with an alternative based on the relationship between light as the main principle of creation and knowledge, and that which is lit up – the rest of reality. This tradition has had many followers, including AL-TUSI, MULLA SADRA, MIR DAMAD and AL-SABZAWARI, and has been popular in the Persian world right up to today. SHAH WALI ALLAH extended this school of thought to the Indian subcontinent.

4 Islamic philosophy and the Islamic sciences

Islamic philosophy has always had a rather difficult relationship with the Islamic sciences, those techniques for answering theoretical questions which are closely linked with the religion of Islam, comprising law, theology, language and the study of the religious texts themselves. Many theologians such as IBN HAZM, AL-JUWAYNI and Fakhr al-Din AL-RAZI presented accounts of Islamic theology which argued for a particular theory of how to interpret religious texts (see ISLAMIC THEOLOGY). They tended to advocate a restricted approach to interpretation, rejecting the use of analogy and also the idea that philosophy is an objective system of enquiry which can be applied to anything at all. Most theologians were Ash'arites (see ASH'ARIYYA AND MU'TAZILA), which meant that they were opposed to the idea that ethical and religious ideas could be objectively true. What makes such ideas true, the Ash'arites argued, is that God says that they are true, and there are no other grounds for accepting them than this. This had a particularly strong influence on ethics (see ETHICS IN ISLAMIC PHILOSOPHY), where there was much debate between objectivists and subjectivists, with the latter arguing that an action is just if and only if God says that it is just. Many thinkers wrote about how to reconcile the social virtues, which involve being part of a community and following the rules of religion, with the intellectual virtues, which tend to involve a more solitary lifestyle. IBN MISKAWAYH and AL-TUSI developed complex accounts of the apparent conflict between these different sets of virtues.

Political philosophy in Islam looked to Greek

thinkers for ways of understanding the nature of the state, yet also generally linked Platonic ideas of the state to Qur'anic notions, which is not difficult given the basically hierarchical nature of both types of account (see POLITICAL PHILOSOPHY IN CLASSICAL ISLAM). Even thinkers attracted to Illuminationist philosophy such as AL-DAWANI wrote on political philosophy, arguing that the structure of the state should represent the material and spiritual aspects of the citizens. Through a strict differentiation of role in the state, and through leadership by those skilled in religious and philosophical knowledge, everyone would find an acceptable place in society and scope for spiritual perfection to an appropriate degree.

Particular problems arose in the discussions concerning the nature of the soul (see SOUL IN ISLAMIC PHILOSOPHY). According to the version of Aristotle which was generally used by the Islamic philosophers, the soul is an integral part of the person as its form, and once the individual dies the soul disappears also. This appears to contravene the notion of an afterlife which is so important a part of Islam. Even Platonic views of the soul seem to insist on its spirituality, as compared with the very physical accounts of the Islamic afterlife. Many of the philosophers tried to get around this by arguing that the religious language discussing the soul is only allegorical, and is intended to impress upon the community at large that there is a wider context within which their lives take place, which extends further than those lives themselves. They could argue in this way because of theories which presented a sophisticated view of different types of meaning that a statement may have in order to appeal to different audiences and carry out a number of different functions (see MEANING IN ISLAMIC PHILOSOPHY). Only the philosopher really has the ability to understand this range of meanings, and those who work in the Islamic sciences do not know how to deal with these issues which come outside of their area of expertise. While those skilled in dealing with the law will know how to adjudicate between different legal judgements, we need an understanding of the philosophy of law in Islam if we are to have access to what might be called the deep structure of law itself (see LAW, ISLAMIC PHILOSOPHY OF). Similarly, although the Qur'an encourages its followers to discover facts about the world, it is through the philosophy of science that we can understand the theoretical principles which lie behind that physical reality (see SCIENCE IN ISLAMIC PHILOSOPHY).

Many of the problems of religion versus philosophy arose in the area of aesthetics (see AESTHETICS IN ISLAMIC PHILOSOPHY). The rules of poetry which traditionally existed in the Arabic tradition came up against the application of Aristotle's *Poetics* to that poetry. One of the interesting aspects of Islamic aesthetics is that it treated poetry as a logical form, albeit of a very low demonstrative value, along the continuum of logical forms which lie behind all our language and practices. This is explained in studies of both epistemology and logic (see EPISTEMOLOGY IN ISLAMIC PHILOSOPHY; LOGIC IN ISLAMIC PHILOSOPHY). Logic came to play an enormous role in Islamic philosophy, and the idea that logic represents a basic set of techniques which lies behind what we think and what we do was felt to be very exciting and provocative. Many theologians who attacked philosophy were staunch defenders of logic as a tool for disputation, and IBN TAYMIYYA is unusual in the strong critique which he provided of Aristotelian logic. He argued that the logic entails Aristotelian metaphysics, and so should be abandoned by anyone who wishes to avoid philosophical infection.

However, the general respect for logic provides the framework for the notion that there is a range of logical approaches which are available to different people, each of which is appropriate to different levels of society. For the theologian and the lawyer, for instance, dialectic is appropriate, since this works logically from generally accepted propositions to conclusions which are established as valid, but only within the limits set by those premises. This means that within the context of theology, for example, if we accept the truth of the Qur'an, then certain conclusions follow if we use the principles of theology; but if we do not accept the truth of the Qur'an, then the acceptability of those conclusions is dubious. Philosophers are distinguished from everyone else in that they are the only people who use entirely certain and universal premises, and so their conclusions have total universality as well as validity. When it comes to knowledge we find a similar contrast. Ordinary people can know something of what is around them and also of the spiritual nature of reality, but they are limited to the images and allegories of religion and the scope of their senses. Philosophers, by contrast, can attain much higher levels of knowledge through their application of logic and through their ability to perfect their understanding and establish contact with the principles which underlie the whole of reality.

5 Islamic philosophy in the modern world

After the death of Ibn Rushd, Islamic philosophy in the Peripatetic style went out of fashion in the Arab world, although the transmission of Islamic philosophy into Western Europe started at this time and had an important influence upon the direction which medieval and Renaissance Europe was to take (see AVERROISM; AVERROISM, JEWISH; TRANSLATORS;

ISLAMIC PHILOSOPHY: TRANSMISSION INTO WESTERN EUROPE). In the Persian-speaking world, Islamic philosophy has continued to follow a largely Illuminationist curriculum right up to today; but in the Arab world it fell into something of a decline, at least in its Peripatetic form, until the nineteenth century. Mystical philosophy, by contrast, continued to flourish, although no thinkers matched the creativity of Ibn al-ʿArabi or Ibn Sabʿin. AL-AFGHANI and Muhammad ʿABDUH sought to find rational principles which would establish a form of thought which is both distinctively Islamic and also appropriate for life in modern scientific societies, a debate which is continuing within Islamic philosophy today (see ISLAMIC PHILOSOPHY, MODERN). Iqbal provided a rather eclectic mixture of Islamic and European philosophy, and some thinkers reacted to the phenomenon of modernity by developing Islamic fundamentalism (see ISLAMIC FUNDAMENTALISM). This resuscitated the earlier antagonism to philosophy by arguing for a return to the original principles of Islam and rejected modernity as a Western imperialist instrusion. The impact of Western scholarship on Islamic philosophy has not always been helpful, and Orientalism has sometimes led to an overemphasis of the dependence of Islamic philosophy on Greek thought, and to a refusal to regard Islamic philosophy as real philosophy (see ORIENTALISM AND ISLAMIC PHILOSOPHY). That is, in much of the exegetical literature there has been too much concern dealing with the historical conditions under which the philosophy was produced as compared with the status of the ideas themselves. While there are still many disputes concerning the ways in which Islamic philosophy should be pursued, as is the case with all kinds of philosophy, there can be little doubt about its major achievements and continuing significance.

See also: ANCIENT PHILOSOPHY; JEWISH PHILOSOPHY; MEDIEVAL PHILOSOPHY; RENAISSANCE PHILOSOPHY

References and further reading

Corbin, H. (1993) *History of Islamic Philosophy*, trans. L. Sherrard, London: Kegan Paul International. (An authoritative account of most Islamic philosophy, stressing in particular the illuminationist and mystical trends.)

Gibb, H. *et al.* (eds) (1960–) *Encyclopaedia of Islam: New Edition*, Leiden: Brill. (A continuing project which provides exhaustive accounts of all the main philosophical figures and concepts.)

Nasr, S. and Leaman, O. (eds) (1996) *History of Islamic Philosophy*, London: Routledge. (A comprehensive account of the different schools of thought, thinkers and concepts.)

OLIVER LEAMAN

ISLAMIC PHILOSOPHY IN SPAIN *see* IBN AL-ʿARABI, MUHYI AL-DIN; IBN BAJJA, ABU BAKR MUHAMMAD IBN YAHYA IBN AS-SAʾIGH; IBN RUSHD, ABUʾL WALID MUHAMMAD; IBN TUFAYL, ABU BAKR MUHAMMAD

ISLAMIC PHILOSOPHY, MODERN

There are a number of major trends in modern Islamic philosophy. First, there is the challenge of the West to traditional Islamic philosophical and cultural principles and the desire to establish a form of thought which is distinctive. From the mid-nineteenth century onwards, Islamic philosophers have attempted to redefine Islamic philosophy; some, such as Hasan Hanafi and Ali Mazrui, have sought to give modern Islamic philosophy a global significance and provide an agenda for world unity.

Second, there is a continuing tradition of interest in illuminationist and mystical thought, especially in Iran where the influence of Mulla Sadra and al-Suhrawardi has remained strong. The influence of the latter can be seen in the works of Henry Corbin and Seyyed Hossein Nasr; Mulla Sadra has exercised an influence over figures such as Mahdi Haʾiri Yazdi and the members of Qom School, notably Ayatollah Ruhollah Khomeini. The philosopher Abdul Soroush has introduced a number of concepts from Western philosophy into Iran.

Finally, there have been many thinkers who have adapted and employed philosophical ideas which are originally non-Islamic as part of the normal philosophical process of seeking to understand conceptual problems. This is a particularly active area, with a number of philosophers from many parts of the Islamic world investigating the relevance to Islam of concepts such as Hegelianism and existentialism. At the same time, mystical philosophy continues to exercise an important influence. Modern Islamic philosophy is thus quite diverse, employing a wide variety of techniques and approaches to its subject.

1 Reactions to the West

There has been a tendency in the Islamic world since the late nineteenth century to explore the issue of the relative decline or decadence of Arabic intellectual thought and science as compared with its Western equivalent. During the Christian medieval period the Islamic world was in its cultural and political ascendancy, and was at the centre of theoretical work in both science and philosophy. However, by the nineteenth century an enormous gap had opened between the Islamic world and the West. A wide variety of explanations for this decline have since been sought.

The realization that this gap existed led to the *Nahda* (rebirth or renaissance) movement between 1850 and 1914. Beginning in Syria but developed largely in Egypt, the movement sought to incorporate the main achievements of modern European civilization while at the same time reviving classical Islamic culture which predated imperialism and the centuries of decadence.

The main problem facing the *Nahda* thinkers had was how to interpret the Islamic cultural tradition, including philosophy, in an environment dominated by the West. Jamal al-Din AL-AFGHANI and Muhammad 'ABDUH both argued that Islam is inherently rational and need not be abandoned in the face of the encroachment of Western forms of scientific and cultural thought. The Egyptian philosopher Mustafa 'Abd al-Raziq also argued that it is possible to demonstrate the authenticity of traditional Islamic philosophical work and its modern relevance within Islamic society. He posits an inseparable link connecting rationalism and revelation in Islam, and he defends the traditional Islamic sciences as compatible with science and rationality. In this he constitutes what might be thought of as a more conservative position than his predecessor 'Abduh, who was more dubious about the values of some of the Islamic schools of thought, in particular of Sufism (see MYSTICAL PHILOSOPHY IN ISLAM).

Muhammad 'Abid al-Jabiri suggests that a viable Arab future can only come about through a deconstruction and critique of the reasons for the decline of the Arab world. He criticizes the dichotomy between the Islamicists, who hark back to a Golden Age in the past, and the liberal Westernizers, who praise the principles of the European Renaissance from which colonialism originated. The solution he offers is the freeing of modern Arabic thought from both the language and the theological limitations of the past. The Arab mind has become very much part and parcel of traditional ways of exploring the world, and is restricted in its potential if it remains too closely wedded to its Islamic heritage.

Fu'ad Zakariyya' argued that the Arab world declined due to its inability to historicize the past and its dependence on tradition, while Zaki Najib Mahmud brought out the importance of philosophy in taking us from the known to the unknown, and was critical of the ability of religion to interfere with this movement in thought. Hasan Hanafi presents a form of phenomenology which argues that a new concept of *tawhid* (divine unity) should be developed which will involve a principle of unity and equality for all people. Hanafi also throws the charge of decadence back at the West, suggesting that the West is now entering a period of decadence and will require an infusion of ideas and energy from the East. He uses the language of liberation theology, which holds that revelation is adaptable to the language of each age (see LIBERATION THEOLOGY). The original revelation was suited to the time and place of the Prophet and not necessarily of the current world. Modern Muslims should reinterpret revelation in modern language and in accordance with present demands; fossilized conservatism is a misinterpretation of the true dynamic and dialectical spirit of Islam.

Fazlur Rahman also contends that Islamic conservatism contradicts the essence of Islam. Islam's aims are economic reform and the establishment of a just social order (see ISLAMIC THEOLOGY §6). According to the Qur'an, he argues, moral and economic decline are related events. Therefore Islamic societies should turn away from petrified conservatism and educate their children in the new technologies. Islam should not be limited to communities of the faithful, but should seek a prominent place in the new ethical and social world order.

Another movement in Islamic political philosophy depicts Muslims not as the antagonists of Western culture, but rather as being in the vanguard of the globalization of peace and social justice. The most popular thinker of this school in the USA is Malcolm X, who began his career as an isolationist minister for the Nation of Islam movement. At first he used Islam to separate African-Americans from white people, but later he preached an internationalized Islam that reaches beyond racial and national differences.

An important African thinker in this tradition is Ali Mazrui, who tries to harmonize several interdependent factors in Islamic theology with current global realities. Mazrui proposes a marriage between the Islamic monotheistic *jihad* (universal struggle), Islam's anti-racist and humanist agenda, and the need for global economic cooperation; he employs culture as a vehicle for social change through his integration of multiculturalism, the politics of pan-Islamicism and the need for globalism. He takes Islam to be the first Protestant revolution in Christianity. Moreover, he suggests that Islam's economic message turns monotheism from isolated spirituality to communitarian humanism – in the form of a Muslim world order among a community of faithful (*umma*) – through global economic cooperation, social justice and the brotherhood of all. The essence of a multicultural perspective implies the acknowledgement that cultures project their own biases onto their perceptions of other societies. In a world which demands global economic policy-making and increasing interdependency, Mazrui believes that Muslims should see their religion of 'all is Godism' as a type of globalism. His innovation (*ijtihad*) interprets the Islamic *jihad* as an agenda of global peace and justice, thereby transforming what is taken to be a negative image of Islam into a signal for economic unity and world peace.

2 The Persian approach to philosophy

The area of the Islamic world which continued most forcefully the Islamic tradition in philosophy after the decline of Peripateticism is undoubtedly Persia (see ISLAM, CONCEPT OF PHILOSOPHY IN §§3–4). Interestingly, one of the most staunch advocates of the form of thought which might be called neo-Illuminationism, and which stems from the *ishraqi* principles of al-Suhrawardi, is Henry Corbin (1903–78), a French philosopher who worked in Iran. Corbin was active in translating and interpreting post-Avicennan Islamic philosophy with an emphasis on shi'ism, *ishraqi* thought and the mysticism of IBN AL-'ARABI. He posited the existence of a perennial school of philosophical wisdom, which can be detected through the recurrence of archetypal symbols such as the icon of light. Such icons exist in the works of Shihab al-Din AL-SUHRAWARDI in the early twelfth century AD, and have their source in Eastern (*ishraqi*) traditions such as Zoroastrianism, Hermeticism and Manicheism. (The term *ishraq*, which signifies 'light', also means 'East' or 'Orient'.)

For Corbin, '*ishraq*' designates not only a static spatial direction but a prescriptive invitation for a hermeneutic reorientation, whereby persons scrutinize their spiritual needs and points of return to archetypal origins. Corbin also discusses the role of the imagination, a faculty which exists between the senses and the intellect. While the senses perceive discrete data and the intellect categorizes, imagination is concerned with the world of archetypes ('*alam at-mithal*). For example, the notion of the perfect person (*al-insan al-kamil*) is an icon for the psychic centre. This centre signifies peace and the perfection of the self-realization process. Corbin asserts that by means of a series of epistemic states – which include revelation (*kashf*) and recollection (or archetypal memory) (*dhikr*) – one may return to the eternal origin. This process describes a cycle, thereby reasserting the Islamic theme of the unity of being (*al-wahdat al-wujud*).

Corbin's followers, such as Hermann Landolt, William Chittick and Seyyed Hossein Nasr, have developed his ideas in a variety of different ways. The latter is the best known contemporary Islamic philosopher. According to him, people share a spiritual component that cannot be actualized by either descriptive or pragmatic accounts of nature. Nasr's world perspective includes a normative element which integrates people in the same way as earlier religions and cosmologies (Nasr 1993). In the past, everyone considered their religion to be the true religion; today, however, we are confronted with a plurality of religions. How can a Muslim attain a workable relation with the sacred in such an environment? Nasr employs Sufism to refer to the archetypal dimensions common to all religions; it is through the realm of mysticism that different forms of spirituality meet. The contemporary world creates the need for followers of different creeds and cultures to communicate.

Islam must coexist with the Western world, but this does not imply an Islamic surrender to all the practices of Western society. Nasr's views on Western scientific progress show his dissatisfaction with many Western perspectives. Citing the ecological disasters of overpopulation and pollution, Nasr criticizes the value of Western technological advances. According to him, the fault lies in the mistaken metascientific presupposition that an innate nature exists which is disconnected from humanity and can be investigated separately and controlled. Moreover, the increasingly pervasive quantitative perspective supplied by units of measurement – like that by which the size of a building might be described – is an incomplete outlook because it does not articulate the qualitative effects of what it describes on the surrounding environment. By contrast, Nasr holds that Islamic and Eastern perspectives on science and technology are integrative and harmonious. They stress unity in their studies of nature, thereby acknowledging the long-term ecological significance of development. Unless religious and spiritual values are embedded in a technological agenda, ecological disasters as well as a general lack of a sense of meaning in life are inevitable. Western science and its technological consequences are of ecological import to modern civilization. Consequently, neither science nor technology can consider itself irrelevant to environmental ethics (see ENVIRONMENTAL ETHICS). Philosophy along Neoplatonic lines should be pursued, since only this form of analysis does justice to the spiritual wholeness of humanity.

The main emphasis in recent Persian philosophy has been on the thought of MULLA SADRA and al-Suhrawardi. Islamic philosophy has moved from the *madrasa* (traditional school) system and became an important part of the university curriculum. One of the most interesting thinkers is Mahdi Ha'iri Yazdi, whose work on knowledge by presence (*'ilm al-huduri*) provides an example of the fruitful combination of ideas from Western analytical philosophy and the *ishraqi* tradition in order to elucidate metaphysical and epistemological problems (Ha'iri Yazdi 1992). Recent Shi'ite theologians, as students of the work of Mulla Sadra, were versed in the dialectics of time and change. 'Ali Shari'ati, another student of Corbin, is an important social thinker whose work advocates a social process of Islamization. He rejects both the Peripatetic philosophers and the mystical thinkers, claiming that the existential being of each person contains a determination formed through mutual trust and compassion between them and God as their essence. This presumption is the ground for each person's being and the very core of each subject's potential for therapeutic unity (*tawhid*); its purpose is justice in both the providential and the social contexts. Islamization is achieved through an existential empathy and a phenomenological assimilation of exemplary people – such as the Imam Hossein (the Prophet's grandson) or Fatima (his daughter and the wife of Imam 'Ali) – into archetypal memory. The martyrdom of 'Ali or Hossein is a paradigmatic message, not for sorrow but for the assimilation of their characters into the self. Further, Shari'ati depicts history as a dialectical process which does not exclude economic and material realities, Islam as a practical religion or people as potential agents of justice. He replaces the Platonic theory of epistemic recollection with a theory of normative archetypal recollection. One may gain normative knowledge through the archetypal recollection of a religion's most exemplary mythical figures. Religion provides social ideals, and yet it demands not a withdrawal to a secret realm but a social revolution in the everyday world.

A creative commentary on Mulla Sadra was produced by Ruhollah Khomeini, who argues that people are primarily social as well as private citizens. Thus religious teachings relate not only to the personal morality of individuals but also to their social responsibilities and political actions (see SOCIAL SCIENCES, PHILOSOPHY OF). In practice, these ideas imply a theocracy that does not distinguish between politics and religion. Bringing such a dominion into existence, he claims, requires an internal revolution from the masses directed against the existing ruling class, but this revolution must be guided by the directives of the religious authorities. He modifies Islamic theology with the notion of the religious jurist-ruler's guardianship (*velayat-e-faqih*), whose role is to guide the community of faithful in their universal struggle (*jihad*). This *jihad* is not essentially military, but is largely educational and seeks the expansion of monotheistic (that is, Islamic) ethics (see ETHICS IN ISLAMIC PHILOSOPHY).

Khomeini was a member of the School of Qom, based on the college in that city, which also produced Muhammad Hossein Tabataba'i, Murtaza Mutahheri and Muhammad Taqi Misbah Yazdi, all of whom have directed their influential thought at confronting the challenge to Islamic philosophy coming from the West. It should not be thought that this is an essentially reactionary strategy, however; Misbah has encouraged many of his students to study in the West and to take seriously scientific and logical thought as practised in the West. Also, although much of Misbah's work has been on Mulla Sadra, he has been far from uncritical of the latter. In particular, he criticizes the notion of prime matter, which MULLA SADRA (§§1–2) identifies as the pure potentiality for existents. He questions the principle that a potentiality for existents exists prior to existents themselves; after all, there is nothing but existents. Misbah argues further that many relations are not truly essences. For example, in the mind-dependent realm, we may ascribe 'below' as a relation between a table and book, but this subject-directed ascription does not imply that below is an essence in the actual world.

An interesting and quite recent controversy in Persian philosophy has been that between Abdul Soroush on the one hand, and the philosophers of the school of Qom, as well as those influenced by the Corbin school, on the other. Soroush introduced a number of concepts from Western philosophy into Iran, in particular the leading ideas of POPPER, MOORE, BERLIN and WITTGENSTEIN. This led him to suggest that we should use a notion like that of collective reason to understand and interpret religious ideas. Collective reason is the best way of dealing with theoretical and practical problems, and is preferable to relying solely on solutions attainable through the efforts of the jurisprudents and religious authorities. Not surprisingly, this aroused the ire of the school of Qom philosophers, and their representative Sadiq Larijani engaged Soroush in a debate which largely dealt with the correct interpretation of thinkers such as Popper, Watkins and Stalnaker, and in particular Hempel's paradoxes of confirmation (see HEMPEL, C.G. §2). Soroush was also attacked by the Corbin circle, whose basic philosophical approach relies very much on HEIDEGGER along with traditional Islamic philosophy, and who were quite out of sympathy with the analytical nature of Soroush's books. This controversy is interesting in that it brings out the fact that philosophers in Iran are generally familiar now not only with traditional forms of Islamic philosophy but also with the current philosophical ideas of the West. Modern philosophers do not entirely reject Western views, but neither are they completely taken over by the West; they are prepared to examine Western views with a critical sympathy.

3 Modern trends

A very vibrant area in Islamic philosophy is the history of philosophy, in particular the Greek tradition in Islamic philosophy. There exists both in the West and in the Islamic world a large number of scholars who have developed accounts of this close relationship and who continue to edit, translate and work on important texts in order to get some idea of the nature of the philosophical material which was produced in the early centuries of Islam. In addition, many philosophers in the Islamic world have adapted Western philosophy so as to make sense of the philosophical problems in which they are interested. C.A. Qadir in Pakistan developed an account of Islamic philosophy which he thought was in line with logical positivism, while 'Abd al-Rahman Badawi applied existentialism to Arab society. Zaki Najib Mahmud followed William JAMES in presenting a pragmatic account of philosophy. Some thinkers applied particular techniques in the Islamic tradition to philosophy, so that 'Ali Sami al-Nashshar for example based his work on Ash'arite theology (see ASH'ARIYYA AND MU'TAZILA), while Muhammad 'Aziz Lahbabi (1954) used Hegelianism to develop a theory of being which is quite unusual within the context of Islamic ontology. Hichem Djait (1986) combines Hegelianism with existentialism. He argues that only dialectical epistemology can be used to understand the modern situation of the Arab world, and that the apparent opposites of decadence/renaissance, Arab/non-Arab, orthodox/heterodox, tradition/modernity need to be transcended if we are to understand the present nature of Islamic culture. Abdallah Laroui (1976) and Muhammad Arkoun (1985) both stress the contrast between Islam and modernity, and the former advocates the adoption of Westernization as the appropriate strategy for the Islamic world. In his approach to the Qur'an, Arkoun uses the semiotic ideas current in modern French literature to argue that Islam has always been changing and developing, so that there is no point in referring to a particular constant orthodoxy.

While many of these thinkers are hostile to mysticism and its Islamic form, Sufism, there can be little doubt that the latter represents a very potent framework for a good deal of present Islamic philosophy. The tradition of Sufism presents both a way of life which avoids many of the rigidities of traditional Islam and also a complex conceptual system which enables the philosopher to develop ideas and arguments which are intellectually satisfying. Modern Islamic philosophy employs a wide variety of different techniques and approaches to the subject.

See also: 'ABDUH, M.; AL-AFGHANI; ILLUMINATIONIST PHILOSOPHY; ISLAM, CONCEPT OF PHILOSOPHY IN; ISLAMIC FUNDAMENTALISM; ISLAMIC THEOLOGY; MYSTICAL PHILOSOPHY IN ISLAM

References and further reading

* Arkoun, M. (1985) *La pensée arabe* (Arab Thought), Paris: Presses Universitaires de France. (Account of how theoretical concepts in the Arab world have changed in response to influences from the West.)

Brown, S., Collinson, D. and Wilkinson, R. (eds) (1995) *Biographical Dictionary of Twentieth-Century Philosophers*, London: Routledge. (Contains information on a number of modern Islamic philosophers. Relevant entries include 'Arkoun, Mohammed' (30–1), 'Corbin, Henry' (159–60), 'Hanafi, Hasan' (305–6), 'Lahbabi, Muhammad Aziz' (431), 'Nagib Mahmud, Zaki' (562), 'Nasr, Seyyed Hossein' (563–4), 'Qadir, C.A.' (641), 'Rahman, Fazlur' (645–6), and 'Yazdi, Mehdi Hairi' (859). These and many other thinkers are also discussed in Nasr and Leaman (1996).)

Corbin, H. (1993) *History of Islamic Philosophy*, with the collaboration of S.H. Nasr and O. Yahya, trans. P. Sherrard, London: Kegan Paul International. (Discussion of the links between Islamic philosophy and contemporary Persian thought.)

Clarke, J.H. (1993) *Malcolm X: The Man and his Times*, Trenton, NJ: Africa World Press. (Study of the Nation of Islam leader and his thought.)

* Djait, H. (1986) *Europe and Islam: Cultures and Modernity*, Berkeley, CA: University of California Press. (Discussion of how the Islamic renaissance came about through contact with the West, and how it has revived Arab culture.)

* Ha'iri Yazdi, M. (1992) *The Principles of Epistemology in Islamic Philosophy: Knowledge by Presence*, Albany, NY: State University of New York Press.

(A combination of modern Western epistemology with illuminationist philosophy into a creative and interesting synthesis, representing the openness of modern Islamic philosophy to Western thought.)

Khomeini, R. (1981) *Islam and Revolution: Writings and Declarations*, trans. H. Algar, Berkeley, CA: Mizan Press. (An account of the theological and philosophical bases of the Shi'i notion of the Islamic state.)

* Lahbabi, M. (1954) *Le personalisme musulman* (Muslim Personalism), Paris: Presses Universitaires de France. (The application of Hegelianism and existentialism to Islamic thought, together with the argument that the latter has to develop in accordance with changing cultural and material trends.)

* Laroui, A. (1976) *The Crisis of the Arab Intelligentsia: Traditionalism or Historicism?*, Berkeley, CA: University of California Press. (Argument for the replacing of traditional Islamic issues with Western ones, since the Islamic world needs to transcend its past to come into real contact with modernity.)

Morewedge, P. (1990) 'The Onyx Crescent: Ali A. Mazrui on the Islamic–Africa Axis', in O.H. Kokole (ed.) *The Global African: A Portrait of Ali A. Mazrui*, Trenton, NJ: Africa World Press, 217–65. (On Mazrui's African–Islamic philosophy.)

—— (1995a) *Essays in Islamic Philosophy, Theology and Mysticism*, Oneonta, NY: Oneonta Philosophy Series. (Interesting account of the basic ideas of Islamic philosophy, theology and mysticism.)

—— (1995b) 'Theology', in J.L. Esposito (ed.) *The Oxford Encyclopedia of the Modern Islamic World*, Oxford: Oxford University Press, vol. 4, 214–24. (Description of modern theological issues, with their underlying assumptions from Islamic philosophy.)

* Nasr, S.H. (1993) *The Need for a Sacred Science*, Albany, NY: State University of New York Press. (Defence of the notion of a firm of knowledge which is thoroughly based on contact with the sacred.)

—— (1996) 'Islamic Philosophical Activity in Contemporary Persia: A Survey of Activity in the 50s and 60s', in M.A. Razavi (ed.) *The Islamic Intellectual Tradition in Persia*, Richmond, VA: Curzon. (Useful account of the forms of philosophical thought in Iran during this period.)

Nasr, S.H. and Leaman, O. (eds) (1996) *History of Islamic Philosophy*, London: Routledge. (See the section 'The Modern Islamic World', 1037–1169, in particular M. Aminrazavi, 'Persia', 1037–50; M. Suheyl Umar, 'Pakistan', 1076–80; I. Abu-Rabi', 'The Arab World', 1082–1114; M. Campanini, 'Egypt', 1115–28; Z. Moris, 'South-East Asia',
1134–40; P. Lory, 'Henry Corbin', 1149–55; S. Akhtar, 'The Possibility of a Philosophy of Islam', 1162–69. This section contains discussions of all the thinkers mentioned in this entry.)

Rahman, F. (1982) *Islam and Modernity: Transformation of an Intellectual Tradition*, Chicago, IL: University of Chicago Press. (A defence of modernism and the importance of independent judgment, and an emphasis on ethics as opposed to metaphysics in philosophy.)

Shari'ati, A. (1980) *Marxism and Other Western Fallacies: An Islamic Critique*, trans. H. Algar, Berkeley, CA: Mizan Press. (An advocate of the significance of the people of the Third World using their culture to overthrow imperialism, arguing for an Islamic state on different and more liberal principles as compared to Khomeini.)

PARVIZ MOREWEDGE
OLIVER LEAMAN

ISLAMIC PHILOSOPHY: TRANSMISSION INTO WESTERN EUROPE

The Arabs took on the mantle of late antique philosophy and passed it on to both Latin scholars and Jewish scholars in Western Europe in the Middle Ages. The debates among Islamic scholars between rationalism and fideism also provided texts and models for Christian and Jewish debates. In this assimilation of Islamic thought, several stages can be observed. First, there was an interest in Neoplatonic cosmology and psychology in the latter half of the twelfth century, which fostered the translation of texts by al-Kindi, al-Farabi, the Ikhwan al-Safa' and, especially, Avicenna (Ibn Sina). Second, the desire to understand Aristotle's philosophy resulted in the translation of the commentaries and epitomes of Averroes (Ibn Rushd) in the second quarter of the thirteenth century. Jewish scholars participated in both these movements, and from the second quarter of the thirteenth century they took the initiative in translating and commenting upon Arabic texts. Thus when, in the late fifteenth century, a renewed interest in the ancient texts led scholars to search out the most accurate interpretations of these texts, it was to Jewish scholars that they turned for new translations or retranslations of Avicenna and, in particular, Averroes. From the early sixteenth century, Arabic philosophical texts were again translated directly into Latin, Arabic speakers began to collaborate with Christian scholars and the foundations for the teaching of Arabic were being laid. With the establishment of Arabic chairs in European universities, the rich variety of Islamic thought began to be revealed. This process has lasted until the present day.

1 Early translations: twelfth century
2 Thirteenth-century translations
3 The contribution of Jewish scholars
4 The beginnings of Arabic scholarship

1 Early translations: twelfth century

Some seventy works were translated from Arabic by GERARD OF CREMONA, nicknamed 'the Master' (*dictus magister*), at the cathedral of Toledo. These included Aristotle's *Posterior Analytics, Physics, On Generation and Corruption* and *Meteorology* I–III (see ARISTOTLE), as well as four short tracts on natural science by ALEXANDER OF APHRODISIAS. To these originally Greek works, Gerard added four philosophical letters of AL-KINDI, a letter on proof by the Ikhwan al-Safa' and al-Farabi's *Kitab ihsa' al-'ulum* (On the Classification of the Sciences) (see AL-FARABI).

Also at this time, the importance of the *al-Shifa'* (Healing) of Avicenna (Ibn Sina) was brought to the notice of Archbishop John of Toledo by a Jewish scholar called 'Avendauth' (perhaps the same as Abraham IBN DAUD, the author of *al-'Aqida al-rafi'a* (The Exalted Faith)). Portions of the text, including those on universals, physics (in part), the soul and metaphysics, were translated by Avendauth, Dominicus Gundissalinus (an archdeacon in the cathedral, *fl.* 1161–81) and a certain '*magister* John of Spain'. Members of this team also translated Algazel's *Maqasid al-falasifa* (The Aims of the Philosophers) (the first part of a two-part work, the second part being *Tahafut al-falasifa* (Incoherence of the Philosophers)) (see AL-GHAZALI); the *Mekor Hayyim* (Fountain of Life) of the Jewish philosopher IBN GABIROL, translated into Latin as *Fons vitae*; and the *Liber de causis*, a cento of propositions from the *Elements of Theology* of Proclus, assembled in Arabic (see LIBER DE CAUSIS). Unattributed are translations of *On the Rise of the Sciences* (said in the Latin version to be by al-Farabi), and a compendium of sixteen questions on Aristotle's *On the Heavens* made by Hunayn ibn Ishaq and added to the selections from the *al-Shifa'* in the Latin tradition (*Collectiones expositionum ab antiquis grecis in libro Aristotelis De mundo qui dicitur liber caeli et mundi*).

Many of these works have a distinctly Neoplatonic tone, which is reflected in the original works of Gundissalinus and the anonymous author of the *Liber de causis primis et secundis et ... qui consequitur eas* (Book of the First and Second Causes and ... Which

Follows Them), who joins Avicenna to the radically Neoplatonic John Scottus ERIUGENA. Some of these works were being read in the late twelfth century at Oxford University, amongst whose scholars was, in all probability, the translator Alfred of Shareshill (responsible for the translation from Arabic of Nicholas of Damascus' *De plantis* and the sections from *al-Shifa'* on mineralogy, on inundations and, perhaps, on botany) whose commentaries influenced the style of philosophical teaching in the embryonic university (see TRANSLATORS §3).

2 Thirteenth-century translations

The translation of *al-Shifa'* continued in the thirteenth century: Aristotle's *Zoology* was translated by Michael Scot, and the *Physics* (starting from the point where the earlier translation left off), *On the Heavens, On Generation and Corruption, On Actions and Passions, Meteorology* and perhaps the *Botany* were translated by Juan Gonsalvez de Burgos and a Jew called Salomon for Gonsalvez García de Gudiel, Bishop of Burgos (1275–80), apparently from a single manuscript deposited in Toledo cathedral.

However, with the exception of the *Zoology*, these translations were hardly read. Rather, a new climate in which Aristotle's texts were on the one hand being accepted as the foundation for the arts curricula in the newly-founded universities, but on the other hand appeared to present some views dangerous to Christianity, made the interpretative works of Averroes (see IBN RUSHD) particularly relevant (see ARISTOTELIANISM, MEDIEVAL). Many of the latter's commentaries on Aristotle's texts were translated. Michael Scot (d. before 1236), who moved from Toledo to the court of Frederick II in Sicily, translated Averroes' 'large commentaries' on the *On the Heavens* and probably those on the *On the Soul, Physics* and *Metaphysics* and others as well. Theodore of Antioch, the court philosopher, translated Averroes' *Proemium to the Physics*, and William of Luna, perhaps another member of Frederick II's circle, translated the 'middle commentaries' on the *Isagōgē* of Porphyry, and on Aristotle's *Categories* and *De interpretatione*.

Hermann the German (see TRANSLATORS §3) translated the 'middle commentaries' on the *Rhetoric* (partial, together with excerpts on rhetoric from *al-Shifa'* and by al-Farabi), *Poetics* (in 1256) and *Nicomachean Ethics* (in 1240) in Toledo, but may also have been patronized by Frederick II's son Manfred, if he is the same as the 'translator Manfredi' mentioned by Roger BACON (*Opus tertium*, cap. 25). Hermann's translation of Averroes' 'middle commentary' on the *Poetics* was the only form in which Aristotle's *Poetics* was known to Latin readers in the

Middle Ages: William of Moerbeke made a Greek–Latin translation in 1278, but this was lost until the 1930s. The letter of Manfred to the philosophers of Paris, accompanying translations of 'Aristotle and other philosophers from Greek and Arabic', indicates one route by which these texts may have been transmitted, although the 'large commentaries' on *On the Soul*, *Physics* and *Metaphysics* were already known in Paris and Oxford in the late 1220s.

The fact that only authors whose writings have been translated from Arabic are included amongst the philosophers whose errors are listed by GILES OF ROME – who mentions Aristotle, Averroes, Avicenna, Algazel, al-Kindi and Maimonides – gives some idea of the extent of the penetration of these texts. The margins of manuscripts of Aristotle's works on natural science from Oxford University in the same period, which are crammed with citations from Averroes' commentaries, also testify to this penetration.

The Arabic contribution to the Latin rationalist–fideist controversy began with the translation of Algazel's introduction to his double volume *Maqasid al-falasifa* and *Tahafut al-falasifa* by Gundissalinus' circle (see AL-GHAZALI). This introduction only survives in one manuscript, but was known to Roger BACON. Maimonides' *Dalalat al-ha'irin* (Guide to the Perplexed), originally written in Arabic (see MAIMONIDES), which was read by and was most likely translated in the circle of Frederick II, provided material for the debate; both Algazel's work and Averroes' *Tahafut al-tahafut* (Incoherence of the Incoherence), along with other texts, were used in the Arabic original by the Franciscan Ramón LLULL, and in the polemical work *Pugio fidei* (The Dagger of Faith), written in 1278 by the Dominican Ramón Martí. The doctrines of the Mu'tazila and Ash'ariyya, and especially the dialectical theologians (*mutakallimun*) were reported in the *Dalahat al-ha'irin* and the *Tahafut al-tahafut*, and Averroes' 'large commentary' on the *Physics* included the ideas of IBN BAJJA as well as of the Greek philosophers THEMISTIUS, ALEXANDER OF APHRODISIAS and John PHILOPONUS.

If the edict promoted by Llull at the Church Council of Vienne in 1312, calling for chairs in Arabic to be set up in four universities and the Papal curia, had been put into effect, Arabic studies in Europe might have had a different history. As it is, the teaching of Arabic in the Dominican mission schools and the use of newly-translated Arabic philosophical works by Dominican preachers against the Cathar heresy may have contributed to the interest in Arabic authorities shown by the Dominican masters, Albert Magnus (see ALBERT THE GREAT) and Thomas AQUINAS.

3 The contribution of Jewish scholars

Jewish scholars had often acted as interpreters of the Arabic texts for Christian translators or patrons. This practice continued in the fourteenth century when Calonymus ben Calonymus ben Meir translated Averroes' *Tahafut al-tahafut* from Arabic for Robert of Anjou, King of Naples. However, from the late thirteenth century onwards, most of the Latin translations of Arabic authors were made from Hebrew versions. When Jewish scholars in the West started to use Hebrew rather than Arabic as the language of learning, they began to translate a large number of Arabic philosophical texts into Hebrew. At least thirty-eight of Averroes' commentaries were translated into Hebrew; the earliest of these is the 'middle commentary' on *De interpretatione*, translated at the court of Frederick II by Jacob Anatoli at the same time as William of Luna translated it into Latin. Thereafter in the thirteenth and fourteenth centuries several scholars in the south of France, Catalonia and Italy, including Moses ibn Tibbon, Shem Tov IBN FALAQUERA, Levi ben Gerson (see GERSONIDES) and Moses of Narbonne translated Averroes' commentaries and other works, and wrote 'super-commentaries' on them. It was to these Hebrew versions that humanist scholars turned in the late fifteenth century, just at the time when the works of Aristotle, Avicenna and Averroes were being set in print (see HUMANISM, RENAISSANCE).

The new translations, patronized especially by PICO DELLA MIRANDOLA, Cardinal Domenico Grimani and Pope Leo X, were made by Elias del Medigo ('middle commentary' on *Meteorology* I–II, *Quaestiones* on *Prior Analytics*, the preface to Book Lambda of the *Metaphysics*, the 'middle commentary' on *Metaphysics* I–VII and the 'middle commentary' on Plato's *Republic*) (see DELMEDIGO, E.); by Paulus Israelita ('middle commentary' on *On the Heavens*); Abram de Balmes (epitomes of the Organon, 'middle commentaries' on *Topics*, *Sophistical Refutations*, *Rhetoric* and *Poetics*, the 'large commentary' on the *Posterior Analytics* and the *Epistola expeditionis* of Avempace (see IBN BAJJA)); Johannes Burana (epitome and 'middle commentary' on *Prior Analytics*, 'middle' and 'large commentary' on *Posterior Analytics*); Vitalis Nissus (epitome on *On Generation and Corruption*) and above all, Jacob Mantinus. This hard-working Jewish doctor from Tortosa had apparently been charged by Girolamo Bagolino, Romolo Fabi and Marco degli Oddi, the ambitious editors of Aristotle's complete works with Averroes' commentaries (finally published by Tommaso Giunta in Venice in 1550–2), with the complete overhaul of the translations of Averroes' commentaries. However, having made ten new translations of Averroes' texts (including another translation of the 'middle commentary' on Plato's *Republic*) and of Levi ben Gerson's 'super-commentary' on the Organon, he died in 1549 on a journey to Damascus. From the late 1530s onwards, the old translations were replaced or at least printed side by side with the new, as can be seen especially in the Giunta printing of 1550–2 and the subsequent Aristotle – Averroes editions of 1562 and 1573–6.

4   The beginnings of Arabic scholarship

The early sixteenth century also saw the beginning of a revival of the study of Arabic texts directly and, of providing the means to do this. A grammar and dictionary of Granadan Arabic by Pedro Alcalà was published in 1505. The kidnapped Arab scholar who took the name Leo Africanus, from Pope Leo X, provided biographies of Arabic authors after 1518. An Arabic manuscript of the so-called *Theology of Aristotle* (in reality parts of Plotinus' *Enneads* 4–6) (see PLOTINUS) was found in Damascus and, in the translation by Moses Arovas and Pier Nicolas Castellani, was published in Rome in 1519. Also in Damascus, Andrew Alpago revised the medieval translation of Avicenna's medical *Canon*, introduced two new works on the soul by Avicenna and described Sufi rituals from first-hand experience. In 1584, an Arabic press was set up in Rome by Giovan Battista Raimondi under the aegis of the Medici. Arabic studies became established through the efforts of Guillaume Postel, who took the first European chair in Arabic in Paris in 1535, and wrote a grammar, Franciscus Raphelengius, the author of the first dictionary of classical Arabic, Thomas Erpenius, the first to hold a chair in Arabic in Leiden in 1613 and the author of what became the standard grammar of Arabic, Jacob Golius and Edward Pococke. Pococke's *Specimen historiae Arabum* (including sketches of the ideas of a wide range of Islamic philosophers) and translation of Ibn Tufayl's philosophical novel, *Hayy ibn Yaqzan* (to which his son, of the same name, added an edition of the Arabic text), are indicative of the new, academic study of Arabic philosophy which was to flourish in European universities and which has culminated in the multi-volume publications of the Egyptian Academy's edition of the Arabic Avicenna, Simone Van Riet's *Avicenna Latinus* and the *Corpus Averroicum*. But at the same time, these works mark the end of a period in which Arabic authors were regarded as important for assimilating the knowledge which made humanity wise.

See also: ARISTOTELIANISM, MEDIEVAL; ARISTOTELIANISM, RENAISSANCE; AVERROISM; AVERROISM, JEWISH; al-FARABI; GERARD OF CREMONA; al-GHAZALI; GREEK PHILOSOPHY: IMPACT ON ISLAMIC PHILOSOPHY; IBN RUSHD; IBN SINA; LIBER DE CAUSIS; TRANSLATORS

References and further reading

Bertola, E. (1962) 'Le traduzioni delle opere filosofiche arabo–giudache nei secoli XII e XIII' (The Translations of Arabic–Jewish Philosophical Works in the Twelfth and Thirteenth Centuries), in *Studi di filosofia e di storia della filosofia in onore di Francesco Olgiati*, Milan: Società editrice vita e pensiero. (A useful list of works translated and their manuscripts or printed editions.)

Butterworth, C.E. and Kessel, B.A. (1994) *The Introduction of Arabic Philosophy into Europe*, Leiden: Brill. (Articles deal respectively with Spain (before 1200), Paris in the thirteenth century, British schools in the Middle Ages, Oxford in the seventeenth century, Louvain from the sixteenth century to the present day, Budapest, Cracow and Kiev, and with the reception of Sufism in the West.)

Callus, D.A. (1943) 'Introduction of Aristotelian Learning to Oxford', *Proceedings of the British Academy* 29: 229–81. (Shows the influence of Avicenna and Averroes on the doctrine and format of Latin philosophical texts.)

Cranz, F.E. (1976) 'Editions of the Latin Aristotle Accompanied by the Commentaries of Averroes', in E.P. Mahoney (ed.) *Philosophy and Humanism: Renaissance Essays in Honor of Paul Oskar Kristeller*, Leiden: Brill, 116–28. (Explores the motives for making new translations of Averroes in the fifteenth and sixteenth centuries and the publication of the Aristotle – Averroes editions of 1550–2, 1562 and 1573–6.)

D'Alverny, M-T. (1993) *Avicenne en Occident* (Avicenna in the West), Paris: Vrin. (Articles concerning both the medieval and the Renaissance translations of Avicenna.)

Halkin, A. (1971) 'Translation and Translators (Medieval)', *Encyclopedia Judaica* 15: 1318–29. (Summarizes in English the monumental research of M. Steinschneider.)

Hamesse, J. and Fattori, M. (eds) (1990) *Rencontres de cultures dans la philosophie médiévale: traductions et traducteurs de l'antiquité tardive au XIVe siècle* (Meetings of Cultures in Medieval Philosophy: Translations and Translators from Late Antiquity to the Fourteenth Century), Louvain: Brepols. (See especially the articles by A.L. Ivry on 'Philosophical Translations from the Arabic in Hebrew during the

Middle Ages', and H. Daiber, 'Lateinische Über-setzungen arabischer Texte zur Philosophie und ihre Bedeutung für die Scholastik des Mittelalters', the latter of which includes a comprehensive bibliography.)

Jolivet, J. (1988) 'The Arabic Inheritance', in P. Dronke (ed.) *A History of Twelfth-Century Western Philosophy*, Cambridge: Cambridge University Press, 113–47. (Expertly covers the period discussed in §1 above.)

L'Averroismo in Italia (Averroism in Italy) (1979), Atti dei convegni Lincei 40, Rome: Accademia nazionale dei Lincei. (Includes discussions on the court of Frederick II by R. Manselli, the introduction of Averroes into the West by F. Van Steenberghen and Averroism in the Renaissance by C.B. Schmitt.)

Leaman, O. (1996) 'Jewish Averroism', in S.H. Nasr and O. Leaman (eds) *History of Islamic Philosophy*, London: Routledge, ch. 46, 769–80. (An account of the influence of Ibn Rushd on Jewish philosophy in the Middle Ages.)

Marenbon, J. (1996) 'Medieval Christian and Jewish Europe', in S.H. Nasr and O. Leaman (eds) *History of Islamic Philosophy*, London: Routledge, ch. 58, 1001–12. (Short survey of the transmission and interpretation of Islamic philosophy in medieval Europe.)

Russell, G.A. (1994) *The 'Arabick' Interest of the Natural Philosophers in Seventeenth-Century England*, Leiden: Brill. (On the beginnings of academic research into Arabic learning.)

Stroumsa, G.G. (1992) 'Anti-Cathar Polemics and the *Liber de duobus principiis*', in B. Lewis and F. Niewöhner (eds) *Religionsgespräche im Mittelalter*, Wolfenbütteler Mittelalter-Studien 4, Wiesbaden: Harrassowitz, 169–83. (Discusses the use of new translations from Arabic and Hebrew in combatting the Cathar heresy.)

Wilson, C. (1996) 'Modern Western Philosophy', in S.H. Nasr and O. Leaman (eds) *History of Islamic Philosophy*, London: Routledge, ch. 59, 1013–29. (Intriguing account of the ways in which modern Western philosophy came into contact with Islamic philosophy, and the impact which this contact may have had.)

Wolfson, H.A. (1961) 'The Twice-Revealed Averroes', *Speculum* 36: 373–92. (A readable introduction to the thirteenth century Arabic–Latin and fifteenth/sixteenth-century Hebrew–Latin translations of the commentaries of Averroes, and the main doctrinal debates that they fuelled.)

Zonta, M. (1996) *La filosofica antica nel medioevo ebraico* (Ancient Philosophy in the Hebrew Middle Ages), Brescia: Paideia. (An authoritative survey of all the forms in which ancient philosophy was transmitted in the Hebrew language.)

CHARLES BURNETT

ISLAMIC THEOLOGY

'Ilm al-kalam (literally 'the science of debate') denotes a discipline of Islamic thought generally referred to as 'theology' or (even less accurately) as 'scholastic theology'. The discipline, which evolved from the political and religious controversies that engulfed the Muslim community in its formative years, deals with interpretations of religious doctrine and the defence of these interpretations by means of discursive arguments.

The rise of kalam came to be closely associated with the Mu'tazila, a rationalist school that emerged at the beginning of the second century AH (seventh century AD) and rose to prominence in the following century. The failure of the Mu'tazila to follow up their initial intellectual and political ascendancy by imposing their views as official state doctrine seriously discredited rationalism, leading to a resurgence of traditionalism and later to the emergence of the Ash'ariyya school, which attempted to present itself as a compromise between the two opposing extremes. The Ash'arite school gained acceptability within mainstream (Sunni) Islam. However, kalam continued to be condemned, even in this 'orthodox' garb, by the dominant traditionally-inclined schools.

In its later stages, kalam attempted to assimilate philosophical themes and questions, but the subtle shift in this direction was not completely successful. The decline of kalam appeared to be irreversible, shunned as it was by traditionalists and rationalists alike. Although kalam texts continued to be discussed and even taught in some form, kalam ceased to be a living science as early as the ninth century AH (fifteenth century AD). Attempts by reformers to revive it, beginning in the nineteenth century, have yet to bear fruit.

1   **The pre-Mu'tazilite groups**
2   **Mu'tazila and rise of *kalam***
3   **Main themes**
4   **Methodological tendencies**
5   **Later evolution and decline**
6   **Conclusion**

1   The pre-Mu'tazilite groups

The term *kalam* has usually been translated as 'word' or 'speech', but a more appropriate rendering in this context would be 'discussion', 'argument' or 'debate'.

Those who engaged in these discussions or debates were referred to as *mutakallimun* (those who practise *kalam* or debate). The term has special significance in that traditionalists disapproved of these discussions, arguing that the early Muslims were not known to have indulged in them. Those who dabbled in such debates were said to have 'spoken about' or 'discussed' (*takallma fi*) 'forbidden' topics. The proponents of *kalam* also liked to refer to it as *'ilm al-usul* (the science of basic principles) or *'ilm al-tawhid* (the science of [affirming God's] unity), and it is under this latter name that some of its topics continue to be taught and discussed in Muslim educational institutions today.

The rise of *'ilm al-kalam* was a result of the many controversies that had divided the Muslim community in its early years. Although the emergence of Islam was characterized by polemics with polytheists and followers of earlier revelations, controversies over fundamental religious questions were deemed irreverent by early Muslims, especially during the lifetime of the Prophet. However, disputes (mainly political) broke out immediately following the death of the Prophet, and again following the tragic events that led to the murder of the third Caliph Othman in AH 35/AD 656, this time heralding the breakdown of the political system established after the Prophet's death.

In a community that defined itself in terms of its religious identity, political disputes inevitably turned into theological ones. The political struggles over who should lead the Muslim community gave rise to three major competing groups: the Khawarij, who opposed the fourth Caliph 'Ali and rejected the compromises he made with his opponents; the Shi'a, who supported 'Ali; and the Murjiya, who tried to remain neutral. These groups attempted to influence a wider Muslim community dominated by a loose grouping of mainstream schools, mainly conservative or traditionalist, known collectively as *ahl al-sunna wa'l-jama'a* (the proponents of the [Prophet's] traditions and consensus).

The term *khawarij* (literally 'rebels') first referred to a group of dissidents who rebelled against the leadership of 'Ali following the inconclusive battle of Siffin (AH 37/AD 658) between 'Ali and his challenger, Mu'awiya, and later evolved into a distinct antiestablishment tendency. The Khawarij had neither a unified leadership nor a settled doctrine, and was primarily a militant political tendency with an uncompromising attitude. The core of their views revolved around the nature of legitimate leadership and the conditions for salvation. Although the Khawarij's uncompromising views condemned them to a marginal existence, their impact on the general body of the Muslim community was significant. Most of the major schools of thought that emerged did so in response to one or other of their assertions, especially on the issues of leadership and the 'status of sinners'.

At the opposite pole stood the Shi'a (party) of 'Ali. Unlike the Khawarij, who defied all authority, the Shi'a believed in the undisputed authority of the divinely ordained *imam* (leader). The position of 'Ali as *imam* and successor to the Prophet was vouchsafed by revelation and was not a matter of opinion. Each *imam* would then designate his successor by virtue of the divine authority vested in him. In theory, Shi'ism should not have encouraged much theological speculation, since it sought to perpetuate and reproduce the authority of the Prophet and vest it in the person of the living *imam*, who had direct access to the divine truth. In practice, however, Shi'ism did indulge in theological speculation, especially with the emergence of the doctrine of the Absent *Imam*, which referred the burden of seeking the truth back to the community.

In between these two extremes, a large number of intermediary positions were espoused, notably that of the Murjiya. This group refused to condemn the perpetrators of grave sins (a euphemism for usurpers of power) as unbelievers, but neither did it want to absolve them, arguing that the matter should be left to God to judge in the hereafter. Murjiism was also associated with political neutrality, and an implied tacit support for the *status quo*.

While the above three groups were political in origin, adopting theological arguments to support their politics, there were also groups of which the primary focus was on theology. The earliest of these was the Qadariyya (the name, meaning proponents of *qadar*, or predestination, was a misnomer for this school which supported freedom of the will). This school argued for the absolute freedom of the will. God, its members said, would not put us human beings under obligation to act righteously if we did not possess the power to choose our course of action.

Diametrically opposed to this school were the Jabriyya (determinists). Their most prominent spokesman was Jahm ibn Safwan (d. AH 128/AD 746), who taught that no attributes could be predicated of God except for creation, power and action, since any attribute that could be predicated of creatures was not fit to be predicated of the Creator. As God is the sole Creator and actor, our actions are also authored by him alone; therefore, we as persons have no control over our actions and no free will. Jahm also said that since God could not be described as a speaker, the Qur'an could not be said to be his word, except in the sense of having been created by him.

2   Mu'tazila and rise of *kalam*

These earlier schools were amorphous groupings, very fluid both in membership and doctrine. With the exception of the Shi'a, who later developed into a number of coherent sects, these tendencies either faded away or merged into other tendencies. The rise of a systematic theological discourse had to await the emergence of the Mu'tazila. The association of *kalam* with the Mu'tazila, who were characterized by their elitism and their militant rationalism, determined its course and its eventual fate. The Mu'tazila attempted to systematize religious doctrine into a rational schema centred on the affirmation of God's absolute unity and absolute justice (see ASH'ARIYYA AND MU'TAZILA).

However, the Mu'tazila's elitism and their irreverent quest for 'a reason for everything,' to paraphrase al-Shahrastani, alienated the more conservative mainstream tendencies. The latter questioned the very possibility of a theological discourse of the type advocated by the Mu'tazila, regardless of content, viewing such discourse as at best superfluous and at worst a heretical deviation. This attitude was expressed succinctly by Malik ibn Anas (d. AH 179/AD 795), the leading jurist of Medina, when asked to explain how God could be said to have 'established himself on the Throne' as mentioned in the Qur'an: 'The establishment is known, the modality is unknown, the belief in it is obligatory and asking questions about it is an unwarranted innovation.' On the question of divine justice, the traditionalists rejected the Mu'tazila's attempts to impose human and rational concepts of justice on God. It would be meaningless to speak of justice in this context, since God was the absolute sovereign and absolute master of all His creation, which meant that anything which He did was by definition just (see OMNIPOTENCE §5).

The struggle between the two trends came to a head in the 'creation of the Qur'an' controversy which erupted in the first half of the third century AH (ninth century AD). The 'Inquisition' which the Mu'tazila instigated with the help of the ruler of the day, the Caliph al-Mamun (AH 198–218/AD 813–33), to enforce this and related doctrines proved disastrous, not only for the Mu'tazila but also for the discipline of *kalam* itself. In spite of being reclaimed for orthodoxy by Abu'l-Hassan al-Ash'ari and others, the science and art of arguing matters of faith with appeal to unaided human reason fell into disrepute and went into a decline from the start of the sixth century.

3   Main themes

Classical definitions tended to emphasize the apologetic function of *kalam*, probably in order to appease traditionalist critics. Al-Iji speaks of 'a science which makes it possible to prove the truth of religious doctrines by marshalling arguments and repelling doubts' (*al-Mawaqif*: 7). *Kalam*, however, has also been the arena on which battles over what constituted true religious doctrine were fought between rival schools.

The subject of *kalam*, to quote al-Iji again, was 'knowledge on which the proofs of religious doctrines depend, directly or indirectly' (*al-Mawaqif*: 7). It was also said to deal with *'usul* (basics), as opposed to *furu'* (subsidiary issues). These included the fundamentals of religious belief, such as God, his attributes and acts, the proofs of religious doctrines, the nature of the universe and our place in it.

The first issue that divided Muslims into opposing schools was the question of political authority and its legitimacy. Most traditionalist and mainstream schools accepted the actual procedures adopted to elect the first four caliphs as normative, thus affirming that a ruler gains legitimacy by being freely elected by the influential members of the community. The Khawarij accepted the procedures up to the election of the third caliph, but then added that even an elected caliph should be removed if he deviated from his mandate. The Khawarij also held that any qualified individual was fit to be caliph, provided the community at large approved of him. The traditionalists narrowed the field of selection to the Prophet's tribe, Quraysh, while the Shi'a narrowed it still further to the Prophet's family, in particular his son-in-law 'Ali and the latter's descendants. Shi'ism argued that political leadership, being the most important religious institution, could not be left for human reason to determine.

The second major issue to be discussed within *kalam* was the status of the grave sinner. The Khawarij started this debate by arguing, contrary to mainstream opinion, that any person who committed a grave sin automatically became a non-believer, thus forfeiting all rights and protections afforded by Islamic law. The Murjiya argued for the withholding of judgment while tending to widen the interpretation of who could qualify as a believer; the Mu'tazila held that such a person was in an intermediate position, being neither a Muslim nor an unbeliever.

The third major issue discussed in *kalam* was freedom of the will. The Mu'tazila and Qadariyya both came out unequivocally in support of freedom of the will. They held that we are the creators of our own acts, for otherwise God would be committing a grave injustice if he were to punish those who had no choice in what they did (see EVIL, PROBLEM OF §3; FREE WILL). At the other extreme, the Jabriyya held that man could not have any control over his actions, since God was the sole creator and actor. Most other groups tried to strike a balance between these two poles. The Shi'a tended to affirm the freedom of the will and some of them, such as the Zaydiyya, agreed completely with the Mu'tazila on this. Some Shi'a factions, however, qualified their stance by affirming that we are in part compelled because of the chain of causation that triggered our acts. The Khawarij accepted the idea of predestination, holding that God was the Creator of the acts of people, and that nothing occurs which he did not will.

This was also the view of mainstream orthodox and traditionalist groups, who affirmed that the will of God was supreme and that he was the creator of all human acts, whether evil or good; nothing could happen on earth that contradicted his will. This position was later given some nuances by al-Ash'ari, who argued that God created human acts, but we acquired (*kasaba*) these acts by willing them prior to their creation.

The fourth major issue discussed in *kalam* was the question of divine attributes. The Jabriyya used the affirmation of the uniqueness of God's attributes to deny the existence of free will. The Mu'tazila developed the idea further, arguing that God could not have attributes in addition to his essence, for this would mean a multiplicity of eternal entities. Later Mu'tazilites, such as Abu'l-Hudhayl al-'Allaf (d. AH 227/AD 842), added that the divine attributes are identical with the divine essence. God's knowledge is not an attribute added to his essence, but is identical with that essence.

Early Shi'ite theologians opposed the Mu'tazila, affirming God's immanence in space and denying his immutability and transcendence of time and space. They held that God's will was also mutable, and ascribed motion to him. God could also be the locus of accidents (*hawadith*) and was corporeal in some sense. God's knowledge and will could not be eternal, for this would negate human freedom and make accountability redundant. It could also imply the eternal existence of things. Later Shi'ite theologians, however, especially the Zaydiyya, repudiated most of the anthropomorphisms of their predecessors and veered towards Mu'tazilite positions.

Traditionalists (who include the Ash'ariyya) affirmed the reality of God's eternal attributes, which they said were neither identical with his Essence nor distinct from it. They also affirmed the literal sense of apparently anthropomorphic Qur'anic references, such as those to God's 'face', 'hands' and 'eyes', adding that the exact nature of these limbs could not be known.

Related to the issue of divine attributes was the issue of the Qur'an's creation. The Mu'tazila denied that God's words were eternal and affirmed that the Qur'an had to be created; this idea was accepted also by the Khawarij. However, the bulk of the traditionalists (and Ash'ariyya) rejected this view, arguing that one could not describe God's speech as created because this would mean that God was subject to changing states. Speech (*kalam*) was one of God's eternal attributes, and the Qur'an, being God's word, could not be said to be created or uncreated. Some early Shi'i theologians, in particular Hisham ibn al-Hakam (d.c. AH 200/AD 816), developed a more sophisticated version of the latter argument, saying that the Qur'an (or God's word) could not be described as creator, created or uncreated, because an attribute, being an adjective, could not have another adjective predicated of it. Similarly, one could not say about God's attributes that they were eternal or contingent.

Besides these main themes, *kalam* touched on related issues such as whether God could be seen in the hereafter (with the Mu'tazila rejecting this, while their opponents affirmed beatific vision), the nature and limits of faith, whether hellfire and paradise were everlasting, and the nature and limits of God's knowledge, will and power. Starting with 'Allaf, some philosophical themes were introduced into *kalam*, in particular the discussion of such questions as the nature and classification of knowledge and the nature of movement, bodies and things. It even went on to discuss questions belonging to other sciences, such as biology, psychology and chemistry, as well as various logical investigations. However, this expansion of the scope of *kalam* coincided with its decline and did not lead to significant advances in any of these areas.

4 Methodological tendencies

Kalam generally dealt either with attempting to justify religious beliefs to reason, or with employing reason to draw new conclusions and consequences from these beliefs. Its doctrines comprise three major components: the articulation of what a school regarded as fundamental beliefs; the construction of the speculative framework within which these beliefs must be understood; and the attempt to give coherence to these views within the accepted speculative framework.

The various schools of *kalam* agreed with the traditionalists in accepting the authority of texts as the basis of the first component. They disagreed, however, about the extent to which these texts should be subjected to 'rational' analysis. Traditionalists had always suspected that the 'reason' being referred to was in fact the suspect intellect of infidel heretics; why else would a believer want to drag the articles of faith in front of the court of human reason, fallible and limited as it was? The traditionalist suspicion of non-Islamic influences behind every early *kalam*-ist 'heresy' has been reproduced by modern researchers, who seek an alien origin for every idea expressed in *kalam* (see ORIENTALISM AND ISLAMIC PHILOSOPHY). However, the impact of non-Islamic influences on the evolution of the schools of *kalam*, though undeniable, could easily be exaggerated. Many of *kalam*'s early themes, such as the status of the sinner or the question of political legitimacy, appear to have arisen within a purely Islamic context.

Regarding the second component, the speculative framework, the early groups did not erect elaborate systems. It is with the Mu'tazila that we find the first attempt to construct such a system, based on their five principles (divine unity, divine justice, divine warnings, the intermediary status and the enjoining of virtue and discouragement of vice). The Mu'tazila also brought with them an attitude of absolute confidence in human reason and a consequent lack of reverence for the authority of texts, which they regularly challenged.

The third component, the cohesion of views within the speculative framework, also came into prominence with the Mu'tazila, who tried to systematize the body of religious beliefs and harmonize its components, provoking intense controversy as they attempted to reinterpret key elements of orthodoxy in order to achieve this. The attempts at systematization inevitably led to the raising of philosophical questions. Later Mu'tazilite thinkers, such as al-'Allaf and Ibrahim al-Nazzam (d. AH 231/AD 846), reflected in their theses the influence of translated Greek philosophical texts and propagated a worldview influenced by Hellenistic speculation (see GREEK PHILOSOPHY: IMPACT ON ISLAMIC PHILOSOPHY). The Ash'arite school, especially AL-JUWAYNI and AL-GHAZALI, formally introduced the tools of Aristotelian logic into the methodology of *kalam* (see LOGIC IN ISLAMIC PHILOSOPHY).

This introduction of philosophical themes and methods and the employment of formal logic in the Aristotelian tradition represented a significant development in *kalam*. Prior to that, *kalam* arguments had used textual and linguistic analysis as their central tools. However, in spite of these forays into philosophical speculation and the employment of Aristotelian logic, *kalam* remained firmly anchored in a specifically Islamic framework. Authoritative texts were routinely cited to clinch an argument, while an accusation of heresy was thought to be a conclusive refutation of any argument.

Even without the help of philosophy, however, Ash'arism brought to *kalam* a trenchant scepticism that had a healthy impact on the field of rational argument. This scepticism was carried to great lengths by al-Ghazali, who used it to demolish the confused Neoplatonism of the Hellenizing philosophers. This approach had the potential to contribute much more to the advancement of knowledge than the dogmatic reiteration of philosophical theses, but that potential was not to be realized because the *kalam* practitioners were more interested in demolishing their opponents' arguments than in constructing viable alternatives.

5 Later evolution and decline

The decline of *kalam* proceeded apace from the fifth century AH (eleventh century AD), settling by the ninth century AH (fifteenth century AD) into ossified dogmatic texts that, to paraphrase al-Ghazali, taught the dogma as well as its formal 'proof', which was not the same thing as proving it to be true. This decline of *kalam* became too apparent to ignore even by its practitioners. Al-Iji comments that the aversion to the discipline in his time meant that engaging in it had become 'among the majority a reprehensible thing' (*al-Mawaqif*: 4). IBN KHALDUN, another Ash'arite writing during the same period (c. AH 779/AD 1377), deplored the fact that *kalam* had deteriorated and become confused with philosophy, on top of being redundant because the heresies it was meant to combat had become extinct.

However, *kalam*'s problem was not so much its fusion with philosophy as its failure to evolve into a fully-fledged philosophical system with its own complete frame of reference. The possible evolution in this direction had been interrupted by a number of factors. First, there was the rift that developed between *kalam* as a discipline and philosophy proper; this was caused in part by the decline of the Mu'tazila, the natural allies of philosophy. In addition, the failure of the Mu'tazila to develop a common language with their opponents, thus turning *kalam* into a kind of sectarian pursuit rather than a discipline, was duplicated by the philosophers. The quasi-religious reverence shown by early Muslim philosophers to Greek texts put them at odds with mainstream thought, causing them to behave like just another sect. This limited the interaction between *kalam* and philosophy, as each treated its basic principles and texts as 'sacred' rather than as theses which could themselves be questioned. The rise of philosophy thus came both at the expense of *kalam* and in opposition to it, and this antagonism damaged both.

Kalam was also undermined by the rise of pro-traditionalist tendencies within the discipline itself. It was difficult to reconcile vigorous rationalist discourse with the traditionalist position, which discouraged questioning in many key areas and even counselled the acquiescence in apparent contradictions. At another level, the resurgence of traditionalism under Ahmad ibn Hanbal and subsequent revivals under IBN TAYMIYYA and his disciples was anti-*kalam*, rejecting not only its theses but its methods as anathema. Rearguard actions fought by Ash'arite and Maturidi scholars of the fifth to eighth centuries AH (eleventh to fourteenth centuries AD), failed to stem this tide and revive *kalam*. Finally, complementing the effect of traditionalism was the rise and popularity of Sufi mysticism (see MYSTICAL PHILOSOPHY IN ISLAM). Although opposed by traditionalism, Sufism was also anti-rationalist and had also grown at the expense of *kalam* and philosophy.

With all these powerful forces deployed against it, the decline of *kalam* was inevitable. The early schools of *kalam* all became extinct, but traces of their teachings remain embedded within the doctrines of the six main schools of Islamic jurisprudence. The two main Shi'a schools (the Ithna 'Ashriyya and Zaydiyya) have inherited some aspects of Mu'tazilite rationalism and doctrines. Shi'ism has also been more successful in assimilating Sufi tendencies and more reconciled to philosophical discourse. The Hannafiyya became closely associated with the Maturidi school of *kalam*. The Shafi'iyya espoused Ash'arism as a general rule, as did the Malikiyya, although with less enthusiasm. The Hanbalites favoured an anti-rationalist and anthropomorphic position, distrusting *kalam* altogether.

6 Conclusion

The manifest failure by the various schools of *'ilm al-kalam* either to create for itself a secure niche among the religious sciences, or to attain the status of a philosophical system independent of religious dogma, was not merely the result of the arrogant elitism of the Mu'tazila and their political opportunism. A deeper malaise afflicted the rationalist schools, reflected in their methodological confusion and, simultaneously, their militant dogmatism. Ironically, it was left to the traditionalist theologians, notably al-Ash'ari, al-Ghazali and Ibn Taymiyya, to introduce some healthy scepticism into the discourse by revealing some of the more glaring self-contradictions of the rationalist dogmas. However, the traditionalists not only inherited some of the confusion of their opponents, they also added some of their own.

An interesting example of this confusion was the uncritical acceptance by all schools of *kalam* of the Neoplatonic premise that the perfection of God as an eternal being meant that he could not be the locus of accidents (*hawadith*), while rejecting its logical consequence: God's remoteness from his creation and the impossibility of his day-to-day involvement with it. The confusion which this self-contradiction generated was then cited by many as a proof of how inadequate reason was in dealing with matters of faith. The choice offered the community was thus between rationalists who discredited themselves by their manifest errors, and traditionalists who exploited these errors and confusion to discredit rational thought as such.

The attacks of self-doubt brought by turmoil of modern times have created an atmosphere for a revival of Islamic theology and philosophy (see ISLAMIC PHILOSOPHY, MODERN). The pioneers of the modern Islamic revival, such as Jamal al-Din AL-AFGHANI and Muhammad 'ABDUH, tried to revive Islamic philosophy and *kalam*; al-Afghani indeed insisted that the revival of philosophy was an indispensable precondition for any Islamic revival. A century later, the tides of revival have drowned all attempts at philosophizing. On the face of it, the vibrancy and capacity for self-regeneration of the Islamic faith seem to be proportionately resistant to the emergence of systematic theologies and philosophies.

However, in spite of the self-satisfaction on the part of orthodoxy, on the grounds that history has condemned the systems rejected by Islam as fatally flawed and confused, there can be no substitute for setting up a viable worldview and a defensible theology, which would remain fallible and incomplete but still an essential guide for life. It would seem that if Islam is to continue as a living system, *'ilm al-kalam* (or something like it) may need to be revived, so that progress towards Muslim self-understanding, interrupted some six centuries or so ago, can be resumed.

See also: ASH'ARIYYA AND MU'TAZILA; GREEK PHILOSOPHY: IMPACT ON ISLAMIC PHILOSOPHY; ISLAMIC FUNDAMENTALISM; MYSTICAL PHILOSOPHY IN ISLAM; POLITICAL PHILOSOPHY IN CLASSICAL ISLAM; RELIGION, HISTORY OF PHILOSOPHY OF; RELIGION, PHILOSOPHY OF; REVELATION; SOUL IN ISLAMIC PHILOSOPHY

References and further readings

Abdel Haleem, M. (1996) 'Early *Kalam*', in S.H. Nasr and O. Leaman (eds) *History of Islamic Philosophy*, London: Routledge, ch. 5, 71–88. (Description of some of the variety among early theologians in Islam.)

'Abduh, M. (1954) *Risalat al-tawhid* (Treatise on Divine Unity), Cairo: Dar al-Manar; French trans.

by B. Michel and M. Abdel Razik, Paris: Librairie Orientaliste Paul Gauthner, 1925. (An early modern attempt at reformulating *kalam* textbooks.)

Anawati, G. and Gardet, L. (1950) *Introduction à la théologie musulmane* (Introduction to Muslim Theology), Paris: Vrin. (One of the most thorough discussions of *kalam* in a Western language.)

Corbin, H. (1993) *History of Islamic Philosophy*, trans. L. Sherrard, London: Kegan Paul International. (While most introductions tend to neglect Shi'i contributions to *kalam*, this one redresses the imbalance, with an extensive bibliography.)

al-Farabi (*c.*870–950) *Ihsa' al-'ulum (Enumeration of Sciences)*, ed. A. González Palencia, with Spanish translation (*Catálogo de las ciencias*), Madrid: Maestre, 1932. (A survey of the state of learning in the fourth century AH (tenth century AD), offering an assessment of *kalam* in its heyday from a philosophical perspective.)

Farrukh, O. (1979) *Tarikh al-fikr al-'arabi ila ayyam Ibn Khaldun* (The History of Arab Thought up to the Time of Ibn Khaldun), Beirut: Dar al-'Ilm li'l-Malayin. (A general introduction to *kalam* and Islamic philosophy with a comprehensive bibliography of Arabic sources.)

al-Ghazali (*c.*1107) *al-Munqidh min al-dalal* (The Deliverer from Error), ed. and trans. F. Jabre, *Erreur et délivrance*, Beirut: al-Lajnah al-Lubnaniyyah li-Tarjamat al-Rawai', 1965; trans. W. Montgomery Watt, *The Faith and Practice of al-Ghazali*, London: George Allen & Unwin, 1953. (A celebrated intellectual autobiography by the most famous Ash'arite author, telling of how he had sought salvation in *kalam*, in vain.)

—— (*c.*1111) *Iljam al-'awam 'an 'ilm al-kalam* (Restraining Commoners from *Kalam*), ed. M. al-Baghdadi, Beirut: Dar al-Kitab al-'Arabi, 1985. (Al-Ghazali's final attacks on *kalam*, arguing that it would be harmful for most people to indulge in it.)

Goldziher, I. (1910) *Vorlesungen über den Islam* (Introduction to Islam), Heidelberg; trans. A. Hamori and R. Hamori, *Introduction to Islamic Theology and Law*, Princeton, NJ: Princeton University Press, 1981. (An early introduction that still stands out in spite of minor flaws that are a feature of its times.)

Hallaq, W. (1993) *Ibn Taymiyya Against the Logicians*, Oxford: Clarendon Press. (A translation of a summary of Ibn Taymiyya's *al-Radd 'ala al-mantiqiyyin* with a good introduction to the latter's crusade against logic and philosophy.)

* al-Iji (before 1355) *Al-mawaqif fi 'ilm al-kalam* (Book of Stations on *Kalam*), Cairo: Dar al-'Ulum. (Textbook which reflects the culmination of the

rapprochement between philosophy and *kalam* in later Maturidi thought.)

Macdonald, D. (1903) *Muslim Theology, Jurisprudence and Constitutional Theory*, New York: Scribner's. (A scholarly introduction that deserves its status as a classic in the field.)

Madelung, W. (1985) *Religious Schools and Sects in Medieval Islam*, London: Variorum Reprints. (A reprint of essays published by the author over many years covering various aspects of *kalam* and the evolution of religious thought in Islam.)

Montgomery Watt, W. (1948) *Free Will and Predestination in Early Islam*, Edinburgh: Edinburgh University Press. (A discussion of the beginning of theological thinking in Islam.)

—— (1962) *Islamic Philosophy and Theology*, Edinburgh: Edinburgh University Press. (A broader introduction to *kalam* and Islamic philosophy.)

Morewedge, P. (ed.) (1979) *Islamic Philosophical Theology*, Albany, NY: State University of New York Press. (A collection of essays by leading writers in the field.)

Muhajarani, A. (1996) 'Twelve-Imam Shi'ite Theological and Philosophical Thought', in S.H. Nasr and O. Leaman (eds) *History of Islamic Philosophy*, London: Routledge, ch. 8, 119–43. (Discussion of the main principles of Shi'ite theologians.)

al-Nashshar, A. (1984) *Manahij al-bahth 'ind mufakkiri al-Islam* (The Research Methodologies of Muslim Thinkers), Beirut: Dar al-Nahda al-'Arabiyyah. (An attempt to shed light on the evolution of methodological approaches in philosophy, theology and science in medieval Islam.)

Pavlin, J. (1996) 'Sunni *Kalam* and Theological Controversies', in S.H. Nasr and O. Leaman (eds) *History of Islamic Philosophy*, London: Routledge, ch. 7, 105–18. (Account of some of the most important Sunni theologians.)

al-Tusi (*c.*1270) *Talkhis al-muhassal* (Summary of [al-Razi's] *Muhassal*), ed. T.A. Sa'd, Beirut: Dar al-Kitab al-'Arabi. (A summary and commentary on al-Razi by a leading Shi'ite scholar who favoured Neoplatonist philosophy more than did al-Razi and other practitioners of *kalam*.)

Wensinck, A. (1932) *The Muslim Creed*, Cambridge: Cambridge University Press. (An early introduction which influenced a large number of writers on the subject.)

ABDELWAHAB EL-AFFENDI

ISRAELI, ISAAC BEN SOLOMON (*c*.855–955)

A pioneering Jewish philosopher and a physician, Isaac Israeli was among the very first medieval Jewish writers to formulate a philosophy employing Greek sources. He based his metaphysics chiefly on the Neoplatonic theory of emanation. However, like many later Jewish philosophers, Israeli understood God as a voluntary agent who acted through power and will. He combined a commitment to the traditional doctrine of creation ex nihilo *with the idea of emanation: the first level of the ontic hierarchy was formed by divine creation but lower levels emerged by emanation. This original synthesis was Israeli's most prominent philosophical innovation.*

Israeli's anthropology was at base largely Neoplatonic, teaching that the soul can ascend the emanatory ladder back to God. The first Jew to give a psychological account of prophecy, Israeli, unlike later Jewish thinkers, did not discuss at length the relation between his philosophical ideas and traditional sources. His pioneering work did not have a decisive impact on later generations of Jewish thinkers; he was known in Latin Europe, but mainly for his medical writings.

1 Life and career
2 Metaphysics
3 Anthropology

1 Life and career

Little is known about the life and background of Isaac ben Solomon Israeli, a Jewish philosopher and physician who lived in North Africa. He was one of the earliest medieval Jewish philosophers and a distinguished physician in the court of the Fatimid caliph in Kairouan (modern Tunisia). His disciple, Dunash ibn Tamim, mentions a philosophical correspondence with Saadiah, later known as SAADIAH GAON – who, like Israeli, was of Egyptian origin – in which Saadiah presented questions to his older contemporary.

In spite of his long life, Israeli never married. He is said to have remarked that his books would be a greater guarantor of immortality than children. His numerous writings include such philosophical works as the *Kitab al-hudud wa 'l-rusum* (Book of Definitions), *Kitab al-ustuqussat* (Book on the Elements), *Kitab al-jawahir* (Book of Substances), *The Book on Spirit and Soul* and the *Chapter on the Elements*, and such medical works as *Kitab al-Hummayat* (Book of Fevers), *Kitab al-adwiya al-mufrada wal-aghdiya* (Book of Foodstuffs and Drugs), and *Kitab al-baul* (Book of Urine). Although written

in Arabic, these books are known to us mainly in Hebrew and Latin translations.

Israeli was not on the whole an original philosopher; he tended to the eclectic, but he was one of the first Jewish thinkers to recognize the value of the Greek philosophical tradition, known to him through Arabic translations. Adopting ideas from both ARISTOTLE and PLATO, he assumed agreement between the two, as did his Muslim contemporary AL-FARABI. Israeli was most directly influenced by AL-KINDI, the first major Muslim philosopher, and by an unknown Neoplatonic work, traces of which are found in later Jewish philosophical writings. He made concerted efforts to integrate ideas from his sources into a unified, rational outlook, but did not attempt explicitly and systematically to reconcile philosophical methods with Jewish tradition, as Saadiah later sought to do.

Despite his varied sources and his quest to bridge opposing viewpoints, Israeli is clearly an early Jewish Neoplatonist, as can be seen in his emanationism, his ideas of illumination and unification with the divine light, and the general Neoplatonic cast of his imagery (see NEOPLATONISM). When Jewish thought turned toward Aristotelianism, Israeli's views were largely forgotten. MAIMONIDES dismissed him as 'only a physician', and called his books 'futile and vain'.

2 Metaphysics

The central questions of Neoplatonism, as laid out by Plotinus, were first, how and why plurality entered the world from the One, that is, God; and second, what was the source of matter if the One is absolutely incorporeal (for if it were corporeal, it would not be absolutely One). The Neoplatonists found their answer in the idea of emanation: the One timelessly produces a series of hypostases. Each flows from that which precedes it in a procession that transcends the limits of any merely natural process, and seemingly any volitional process as well. The further a hypostasis is from the Source, the more plurality enters into it until, ultimately, the level of sheer matter is reached. Plotinus follows emanation from the One, to the divine and universal Mind, to the world Soul, and then to Nature. However, the Neoplatonic tradition that reached Israeli proposed a more complex scheme, partly as a result of efforts to introduce a dimension of voluntarism into the process of emanation (see VOLUNTARISM, JEWISH).

Israeli envisioned the following series:

The Creator (with will and power);

First form (wisdom) and first matter – intellect;

The rational soul;

The animal soul;

The vegetative soul;

Nature (= sphere = heavenly bodies);

The four elements.

God acts as a voluntary creator. Power and will are aspects of God, not independent hypostases (as contrasted with the view of the later Jewish Neoplatonist Solomon IBN GABIROL). In traditional Neoplatonism, all entities emanate from the One (see NEOPLATONISM), but Israeli taught that the first form and the first matter were created *ex nihilo*. The remaining spiritual substances arise by emanation from these. Hence there is a double creation: a voluntary act of God at the start of creation, and emanation as its continuation. This unconventional and original theory clearly seeks to to unite Neoplatonic premises with Jewish tradition.

Israeli deviated from other Plotinian ideas in describing the remaining hypostases too, although these deviations were generally not original to Israeli but were derived from the Neoplatonic tradition. For example, Israeli located matter in the beginning of creation. He also identified the first form with the divine wisdom which together with the first matter, forms the intellect. He divided the hypostatic soul, in accordance with the Aristotelian scheme, into rational, animal and vegetative souls (see ARISTOTLE), and replaced Plotinian nature, with the Sphere, that is, the heavenly bodies from which the four elements proceed.

3 Anthropology

Israeli adopted the Neoplatonic doctrine of the return of the soul through purification and illumination. The goal of the ascent is unification with the supernal light, not directly with God. Some human beings, whose evil nature and impurity prevent them from ascending to the spiritual substances, are left below the sphere, tormented by heat and fire. Thus Israeli combines rabbinic teachings concerning heaven and hell with Neoplatonic doctrines about the destiny of noble and base souls.

Analysing the nature of prophecy, without direct reference to the Bible or the rabbinic sources, Israeli used Neoplatonic accounts of the intellect and the soul to forge the first Jewish psychological account of prophecy (see PROPHECY). A prophet, who is also a philosopher, seeks to direct people toward righteousness. Prophetic inspiration is manifested mainly in dreams, when the powers of the soul apprehend spiritual objects. Prophets transmit what they receive to the people, sometimes clearly, sometimes through obscure expressions which need to be explained. Although he did not explicitly discuss such distinctively Jewish topics as the commandments or the revelation at Mount Sinai, Israeli does obliquely indicate his sensitivity to these theological themes.

The Jewish Neoplatonists who followed Israeli were to a certain extent influenced by him, as were the Kabbalists of the school of Gerona (see KABBALAH). Yet it is difficult to conclude that Israeli had a decisive influence on later Jewish thought. His work did not address the core issues of theology that occupied so many other Jewish thinkers, and his Neoplatonism came to seem irrelevant or primitive. He did, however, win the immortality he sought through his books, which are still studied a thousand years after his death.

See also: NEOPLATONISM; SAADIAH GAON; VOLUNTARISM, JEWISH

List of works

Israeli, Isaac ben Solomon (before 955) Collected Works, ed. A. Altmann and S.M. Stern, *Isaac Israeli. A Neoplatonic Philosopher of the Early Tenth Century: His Works Translated with Comments and an Outline of his Philosophy*, London: Oxford University Press, 1958. (English translations of Israeli's major philosophical works, and a thorough discussion of his philosophy, with extensive bibliography.)

—— (before 955) *Kitab al-hudud wa 'l-rusum* (Book of Definitions), German and Hebrew edition in *Festschrift zum 80. Geburtstag M. Steinschneiders*, Leipzig: Hartwig Hirschfeld, 1896. (An early, not entirely accurate edition.)

—— (before 955) *The Book on Spirit and Soul*, ed. M. Steinschneider in *Ha-Karmel*, 1871, 400–5. (An early edition.)

—— (before 955) *Chapter on the Elements*, ed. A. Altmann, 'Isaac Israeli's "Chapter on the Elements" (Ms. Mantua)', *Journal of Jewish Studies* 7, 1956: 31–57. (Relatively recent edition of this short work.)

—— (before 955) *Kitab al-jawahir* (Book of Substances), ed. S.M. Stern, 'The Fragments of Isaac Israeli's "Book of Substances"', *Journal of Jewish Studies* 7, 1956: 13–29. (Only fragments of this work have survived.)

—— (before 955) (The Book on the Elements), ed. S. Fried, *The Book on the Elements (Sefer Ha-Yesodot)*, Drohobycz, 1900. (A Hebrew version of Israeli's longest philosophical work.)

References and further reading

Altmann, A. (1979) 'Creation and Emanation in Isaac Israeli: A Reappraisal', in I. Twersky (ed.) *Studies in Medieval Jewish History and Literature*, Cambridge, MA: Harvard University Press, 1–15. (Rebuts an attack on Altmann's understanding of Israeli's doctrine of creation.)

DANIEL J. LASKER

IS/OUGHT CONTROVERSY
see LOGIC OF ETHICAL DISCOURSE

ITALY, PHILOSOPHY IN

Since the Renaissance, Italian philosophy has been rooted in the humanist and historical tradition, stemming from the rediscovery of Greek philosophy in the fifteenth century and the resumption of classical studies at that time. However, the momentous cultural and religious transformations of sixteenth-century Europe caused a reaction which greatly restrained the innovative impact of Renaissance thought. Living through these two periods, Bruno, Campanella and Galileo experienced all the conflicts of the Counter-Reformation, when philosophy especially felt the weight of the Roman Catholic Church which exercised a tight control on the culture of the time. The best traditions of the Renaissance were inherited and maintained solely by Vico, the most important figure of this latter period.

As the spirit of the Counter-Reformation declined, Italian philosophy acquired a new vigour in the eighteenth and nineteenth centuries. This occurred especially in the north of the country where contacts with modern European culture influenced a political situation dominated by the question of national unity (a problem debated since the time of Machiavelli). Philosophical thought during this period tended to be strongly political (as in the philosophy of Cattaneo), although it also assumed a deeply religious tone (for example, Mazzini and Gioberti). These themes were united in Hegelian Idealism, promoted by Spaventa among others. The neo-Idealists of the early twentieth century, such as Croce and Gentile, distinguished themselves by assuming a political role and by opposing empiricism and positivism, philosophical heirs of the Enlightenment which were traditionally considered alien although popular at that time.

The aftermath of the Second World War brought to gradual dissolution both philosophical and political neo-Idealism, a movement which was rooted especially at the universities of Rome and Naples; it also saw the rise of Marxist thought (Gramsci) and Existentialism, especially at the universities of Bologna, Milan and Turin. Among the most important figures in contemporary Italian philosophy we find Bobbio (political philosophy), Pareyson, Vattimo and Eco. While both French and German philosophy still play a major role in the philosophical debate, in recent years increasing attention has been paid to Anglo-Saxon philosophy.

1   **From Counter-Reformation to Enlightenment**
2   **The nineteenth century**
3   **The twentieth century**

1   From Counter-Reformation to Enlightenment

The great philosophical blossoming of the fifteenth and sixteenth centuries, which in Italy had started with the revival of the *humanae litterae*, came to a decisive and lasting halt with the Counter-Reformation movement which began with the Council of Trent (1545–63). The new cultural climate – inspired by an idea of humanity and human destiny which bore little resemblance to the spirit of liberty, creativity and loyalty typical of philosophers and artists such as Pico della Mirandola, Marsilio Ficino, Leonardo da Vinci and Michelangelo – prevailed in the second half of the sixteenth century and especially in the seventeenth century. Indeed, the general lack of cultural confidence expressed itself as censorship, especially of the three main philosophers of the sixteenth and seventeenth centuries: Bruno and Campanella (both heirs to Telesio's naturalistic tradition, combined with Neo-Platonist, magical and cabalistic ideas), and Galileo.

Having fled Italy to avoid being persecuted by the Church for his philosophical ideas, Giordano BRUNO lived in England between 1583 and 1585, where he wrote and published works which were later gathered under the title of *Dialoghi Italiani* (Italian Dialogues). When he returned to Italy, he was condemned by the Church authorities to die at the stake in 1600. Central to his philosophy is the idea of the unity and infinity of nature which the Copernican system, through Neo-Platonist metaphysics, attempts to demonstrate. The universe is one, open and infinit, and may contain many worlds. The unity of nature means that it contains within itself the principle of its own movement. Bruno thus adapts, and uses against Aristotle, the hylozoistic idea of the Presocratics to which he often refers. Corresponding to this naturalistic concept is an ethical vision that unites contemplation and activity through a radical criticism of medieval virtues and the defence of worldly virtues. The *eroico furore* (heroic fury) is the synthesis of theoretical knowledge and practical activity which allows the individual to grasp the dynamical unity of nature, a composition of opposing tensions (*coincidentia oppositorum*) that Cusano had previously attributed solely to God.

Tommaso CAMPANELLA, a contemporary of Bruno, further undermined the influence of Aristotelian philosophy (still prominent at the University of Padua). His epistemology is a combination of Augustinism and empiricism: knowledge is sensation, but its justification is grounded on the internal awareness of self (*sensus inditus*) By referring to AUGUSTINE (§§4, 5), Campanella anticipates DESCARTES. His naturalism is full of references to magic (*De sensu rerum et magia* 1620), on which he builds his religious, ethical and political vision – the ultimate goal of magic is 'to give laws to men'. In his *Città del sole* (City of the Sun) (1623) Campanella describes the organization of an ideal city (like Thomas More's *Utopia* or Plato's *Republic*). The three principal officers (Captain, Wisdom and Love) and supreme head (Metaphysic or Sun) are personifications of metaphysical and religious principles derived from the synthesis of Christianity with a natural religion of a strongly naturalistic and magical character, which in its essence tries to be 'rational'. The extent of Campanella's awareness of the developments in scientific thought is evident from his *Apologia pro Galilaeo* (1622).

Galileo is credited with having been the first to formulate what has gone down in history as the 'Galilean scientific method' (see GALILEI, GALILEO). However, unlike Bacon, he never actually explicitly formulated this method – it was derived from his scientific treatises, including the *Saggiatore* (The Verifier) (1623), the *Dialogo sui massimi sistemi* (Dialogue on the Chief World Systems) (1632), and *Discorsi e dimostrazioni matematiche intorno a due nuove scienze* (Dialogues and Mathematical Demonstrations about Two New Sciences) (1638). As a result of this method, using some fundamental concepts (such as causality) and ideas from the traditions of Ockham and of Naturalism (which had undermined medieval ways of thought), Galileo made scientific discoveries of enormous importance in both astronomy and in physics. Unlike Bruno and Campanella, he based his study of nature on mathematics and excluded anything metaphysical or magical. Only what is measurable (what Locke was to call 'primary qualities') can be the subject of investigation: this establishes a distinction between religion/philosophy and science, and guarantees the autonomy of the latter from the former.

While Galileo was not a philosopher in the strict sense of the word, the cultural importance of his personal vicissitudes, and his trial and conviction by the Inquisition, is especially significant. Bruno and Campanella remained isolated in the tragedy of their personal circumstances because the philosophy of each of them was closely tied to his personality. In the case of Galileo, the condemnation did not manage to stem the spread of his ideas, because they were based on a new methodology which was destined to dominate on its own merits. The immediate influence of Galileo was therefore mainly confined to the scientific sphere, where his pupils initiated an important series of studies, especially in the field of mathematics. Bonaventura Cavalieri, for example, sought to replace the method of indivisibility with the method of exhaustibility in the calculation of volumes and areas: Evangelista Torricelli, possibly Galileo's greatest pupil, built on these discoveries. Vincenzo Viviani is known for his work on geometry, and Michelangelo Ricci was the author of a book on the problem of tangents and of maxima and minima.

The Counter-Reformation movement sought to reunite philosophy, science and religion, whose compartmentalization had given rise to the new science based on experimentation (Galileo himself tried throughout his life to show that the three disciplines were compatible with each other). Campanella more than anybody had tried to achieve this goal: the *Città del Sole* is in fact the idealization of a world in which religion, science, philosophy and politics find a harmonious synthesis. Less idealistic, on the other hand, is the political thought of the Jesuit Giovanni Botero, author of *Della ragion di stato* (About the Reason of State) (1589). In this work he opposes Machiavelli by attempting to bring ethics back into politics, believing justice to be the prince's supreme virtue and claiming that politics is ultimately subordinate to the counsels of religion. At this time Alberico Gentili, professor at Oxford and one of the first theoreticians of natural law, maintained in his *De jure belli* the existence of rights that apply even in times of war (respect for prisoners, women and children and so on), holding that the only just war is carried on in self-defence.

Continuing Counter-Reformation preoccupations meant that Italian philosophy of the seventeenth and eighteenth centuries was limited to repeating scholastic arguments. The thought of Descartes, Hobbes (who had visited Galileo during his exile at Arcetri), as well as that of Leibniz and Berkeley (both of whom had also visited Italy), had little impact (but see FARDELLA, M.). The first figure of note in this period took an open stance *against* European thought, continuing in that tradition of historical Humanism typical of Italian thought (especially of the Neapolitan school down to the present day). Gianbattista VICO was a seventeenth-century humanist who, like all other humanists, regarded the Middle Ages a time of barbarism and considered the main path of knowledge to lie in the synthesis of philology and philosophy. In contrast to Descartes, Vico denies that evidence is the criterion of truth or that the *Cogito* could convince sceptics. In fact, one can only know what one has done oneself. Just as God knows the universe because he created it, humans can know their own works, but they cannot know nature or know themselves, only their history.

The identity between explanatory knowledge of *x* and direct experience of the causes that have brought about *x* (the *Verum et factum convertuntur* hypothesis) is the great principle of the *nuova scienza* (new science) which justifies including Vico in the history of the contemporary hermeneutic movement. In his main works *De antiquissima Italorum sapientia* (1710), and in *Scienza nova* (which went to three editions), Vico outlines the foundations of historical science. Against Descartes' followers, he extols the superiority of both historical-juridical studies and of the rhetoric over the exact sciences. History he divides into three eras: the age of gods (when imagination plays an important part in the origin of language), the age of heroes, and the age of humans. These three phases are cyclical, so human history is a repetition of historical phenomena, guided by a providence that makes it 'a reasoned civil theology of the divine providence'.

Mario Pagano, a follower of Vico, was representative of the Neapolitan Enlightenment that opened up to European culture from the middle of the eighteenth century. Traces of Rousseau are evident in his *Saggi politici* (Political Essays), just as echoes of Montesquieu can be found in Gaetano Filangieri's *Scienza della legislazione* (Science of Legislation). The high opinion in which these men are held by J. SCHUMPETER (he gives a place of honour in the field of pre-Smith systemizers to Italian economists of the eighteenth century), is due to their analytical capacity and to their interest in a civil economy which reconciles 'public good' and 'utilitarian happiness' in the concept of 'public happiness'. Many of these economists were in public employment as ambassadors and administrators, for example L.A. Muratori, author of *Della pubblica felicità* (Concerning Public Happiness); Antonio Genovesi, who in his *Meditazioni filosofiche sulla religione e sulla morale* (Philosophical Meditations on Religion and Morals) expounded an ethical concept inspired by Condillac and Helvetius; and Ferdinando Galiani, author of the treatise *Della moneta* (On Money).

The influence of the French Enlightenment was strong in the Neapolitan School (see ENLIGHTENMENT, CONTINENTAL). The Italian translation of the Encylopédie was published in Lucca and Livorno between 1758 and 1779. Lombardy was another centre for the diffusion of Enlightenment thought. Its geographical position and economic and political situation (it was part of the Austro-Hungarian Empire, whose rulers Maria Theresa and Joseph II were among the more enlightened sovereigns), placed it in a strategic position for contact with the rest of Europe. Gathered around the 'Società dei Pugni' (Society of Fists) founded in 1761, whose mouthpiece was 'Il Caffé' (a newspaper inspired by England's 'Spectator'), the exponents of the Enlightenment in Lombardy were, like those in Naples, mainly interested in economic and political studies. Pietro Verri's *Discorso sulla felicità* (Discourse on Happiness) (1763) proposed an ethical theory which merged sensationalistic and utilitarian themes; Cesare Beccaria, author of the well-known *Dei delitti e delle pene* (On crimes and punishments) (1764) which was condemned and banned by the Catholic Church in 1766, questioned the justice and use of the death penalty and of torture. For him punishment must defend public welfare – punishment is just only when it guarantees the inviolability and freedom of the people.

2 The nineteenth century

During the nineteenth century, philosophy in Italy was closely connected to political events in which most philosophers played an active part. The influence of Vico was especially strong and, due to Vincenzo Cuoco, permeated even the Milanese school which traditionally tended more towards the Enlightenment. The attention to historical detail and to Italian tradition which are evident in Cuoco's work *Platone in Italia* (Plato in Italy) (1805) was also characteristic of the work of Carlo CATTANEO, a proponent of Federalism along with Giuseppe Ferrari. But Cattaneo's work is more philosophically aware of wider issues in European culture. He was the author of historical and economic studies (in 1844 he predicted the famine that was to hit Ireland during 1845–8) and the driving force behind the group based around the journal 'Il Politecnico', which he also managed on many occasions. His original theory of knowledge, outlined in the *Psicologia delle menti associate* (Psychology of associated minds) (1859–66), justifies Kant's theory of phenomena in terms of historical development and the efficacy of science. Works closer to Enlightenment thought from this time include those of Francesco Soave, critic of Kantianism; Melchiorre Gioia who, in *Filosofia della statistica* (Philosophy of Statistics) (1826), worked out an economic theory influenced by Bentham; and Giandomenco Romagnosi who put forward a naturalistic conception of society.

The major European philosophies of the time – Kantianism and Idealism – were combined in Italy with elements derived from the long-standing humanist and religious traditions. Pasquale Galluppi contributed to the spread of the philosophy of Kant, especially in Naples (which later became an important centre for Hegelian philosophy). In his *Saggio filosofico sulla critica della conoscenza* (Philosophical essay on the critique of knowledge) (1819), Galluppi maintained the necessity of going beyond sensationalism (such as that of Condillac) and Kantian subjectivism, but his critics charged him with falling into an idealism more inconsistent than that of Kant.

Strongly spiritualistic elements are found in the romantic idealism of authors such as Giuseppe Mazzini, Antonio Rosmini and Vincenzo Gioberti. Mazzini advocated ideas that inspired the struggle for national unity (*Risorgimento*), and the slogan '*Dio e popolo*' (God and the people) summarizes his thought: supreme authority is of the people, but the aims they pursue are inspired by God. The Italian people, he believed, had been called to begin a new era founded not on rights, like the French Revolution, but on duties, on the awareness that each person belongs to Humanity. Mazzini, an opponent of Socialist International, proposed a lay spiritualist philosophy and attempted to give it European significance by creating an association called '*Giovane Europa*' (Young Europe), following the domestic '*Giovane Italia*' movement. The philosophy of Antonio Rosmini is even more strongly spiritualist (see ROSMINI-SERBATI, A.). A priest, he elaborated a philosophy (suspected of being heterodox) which was meant to supersede that of Kant. He developed an ontology founded on the primacy of the idea of being as prior to any other knowledge or category. The sole category is possibility and knowledge is rooted in consciousness of self (*Nuovo saggio sull'origine delle idee* (New essay on the origin of ideas) (1830); *Logica* (Logic) (1854)).

If, in spite of his polemics, Rosmini is considered the Italian Kant, Vincenzo GIOBERTI is the Italian Hegel. A critic of Rosmini, Gioberti summarized his own philosophy with the formula '*L'ente crea l'esistente, l'esistente ritorna all'ente*' (being creates existence, existence returns to being). This describes a process of imitation and participation clearly inspired by Neoplatonism, which brought accusations of immanentism. Also a priest, Gioberti like Rosmini was motivated by an apologetical intention, but his Catholic philosophy does have some original points. Apart from strictly philosophical works such as *Degli errori filosofici di A. Rosmini* (On the philosophical errors of A. Rosmini) (1841) and *Protologia* (Protology) (1857), Gioberti is also remembered for his

civil commitment and political theories. In *Del primate morale e civil degli italiani* (On the moral and civic superiority of the Italians) (1842–3) he supports a neo-Guelphian idea which sees the Roman Catholic Church as the guide of the Italian people, helping them to regain their historical pre-eminence. Rosmini's and Gioberti's Catholic spirituality met with hostility from the Church which, in the 1879 encyclical *Aeterni Patris* of Leo XIII, declared the philosophy of Thomas Aquinas to be the orthodox doctrine of the Roman Catholic Church. This date marks the beginning of neo-scholastic philosophy which became widespread in the twentieth century, especially at the Pontifical University of Rome and Catholic University of Milan.

The legacy of the Enlightenment continued, particularly in the positivist school in the North which comprised more scientists than philosophers, and which was interested in the 'sciences of life', by which was meant anthropology, psychology, sociology and so on. The major figure of this movement was Roberto Ardigò, an ex-priest and academic at Padua (a well-known centre for heterodoxy since the Renaissance). He wrote an essay on POMPONAZZI and maintained a naturalistic positivism which was a cross between Spencer's Evolutionism (SPENCER was the best-known positivist philosopher in Italy) and Bruno's Naturalism. For Ardigò, the fact is divine, the absolute to which every theory must be referred. Although not without a certain dogmatism, this theory is more radical than Spencer's because it refuses to recognize the unknowable. Ardigò's work on ethics, *La morale dei positivisti* (The morality of positivists) (1879), met with great success, especially in the field of criminal law, while his *Psicologia come scienza positiva* (Psychology as a positive science) (1870) is important in the development of psychology as an autonomous science.

Naples was the centre of Hegelianism in Italy, and two of the most influential Italian philosophers of the beginning of the twentieth century, CROCE and GENTILE, were educated there. Hegelianism in Italy is not regarded as an imported school of thought – rather, the roots of European philosophy are sought in the Italian and especially the Neapolitan tradition. Bertrando Spaventa's theory of the circulation of ideas, outlined in his *La filosofia italiana nelle sue relazioni con la filosofia europea* (Italian philosophy and its relation to European philosophy) (1862), maintains that the origin of modern philosophy is to be found in the Italian Renaissance: Spinoza, Kant, Fichte and Hegel he regards as disciples of Bruno, Campanella and Vico. This interpretation of history, in spite of its one-sidedness (it ignores Galileo and the Enlightenment), stimulated important historical studies, especially on the Renaissance and on German philosophy which was seen as the link with the Renaissance. Such one-sidedness is typical of Italian philosophy of the nineteenth century, where Positivists and Idealists alike viewed theoretical progress in science with indifference, leaving thinkers of European stature practically isolated: these included Giuseppe Peano, for instance, who completed the work of Weierstrass and whose discoveries in mathematics and geometry place him among the greatest scientists of the century; and Federigo Enriques, the greatest representative of the Italian school of algebraic geometry and supporter of an epistemological theory similar to that of Lakatos (see LAKATOS, I.).

3   The twentieth century

In the early twentieth century, Italian philosophy was dominated by a lively anti-positivist controversy, led by Idealist, Marxist and by Pragmatic thinkers. The major figures of neo-Idealism were Benedetto Croce and Giovanni Gentile, both committed to reforming Hegelianism. Initially close to Marxism, Croce later embraced a philosophy of Spirit clearly of Hegelian stamp. For the triad of the dialectic movement (thesis, antithesis and synthesis), Croce substituted a dialectic of opposites articulated in four distinct categories: aesthetics, theoretics, economics and ethics. The first two make up theoretical activity, the others the practical (*Logica come scienza del concetto puro* (Logic as the science of pure concept) (1905); *Filosofia della pratica, economia e etica* (Philosophy of practice, economics and ethics) (1909)). The distinct categories are mutually irreducible, though they are not independent. Croce is especially famous for his aesthetic theory, outlined in *Estetica come scienza dell'espressione e Linguistica generale* (Aesthetics as the science of expression and general linguistics) (1902), which was founded on the identification of both intuition and expression. He also provoked philosophical debate through the journal 'La Critica', a forum for cultural, civil and social discussion which was open to European influences.

If the Idealism of Croce is characterized by a devaluation of scientific thought (whose concepts he regarded as 'pseudo-concepts'), the Idealism of Giovanni Gentile classified science in the dogmatic manner of Fichte. The reform of Hegelianism proposed by Gentile in his *Teoria generale dello spirito come atto puro* (General theory of the spirit as pure act) (1916) and *Sistema di logica* (System of logic) (1917–22) eliminates any presupposition (both logic and philosophy of nature) of the life of the spirit. The life of the spirit is consequently reduced to pure act – beyond the actuality of thought there is nothing.

As in Fichte, the ego is self-creation. Whereas Croce viewed philosophy as history in a wide sense (economic, political and so on), for Gentile philosophy is merely the history of thought, it is the history of philosophy and the history of the spirit is its own education. As Minister for Education in the Fascist Government Gentile had enormous influence on Italian culture. He was instrumental in the education reforms of 1924 and directed the *Enciclopedia Italiana*, one of the greatest productions of Italian culture from that time. Gentile's involvement with Fascism, however, caused a bitter rift with Croce, who had distanced himself from Mussolini. Similarly, Piero Martinetti was strongly anti-Fascist. He reinterpreted Kant's philosophy in Platonic and Spiritualistic terms and, arguing against positivism, he maintained the superiority of a philosophy whose result is faith, which he regarded as the most radical fruit of reason. Giovanni Vailati also argued against positivism: his pragmatism is independent of the corresponding American movement and is original in its attention to language through the study of semantic and syntactic structure, and the demand for logical rigour as a tool for conceptual clarification.

The prevailing climate of Idealism at the beginning of the twentieth century meant that Marxism had little support in Italy. It is thanks to Antonio LABRIOLA that the philosophies of Marx and Engels became known, thereby opening a debate with Positivism and Idealism. A pupil of Spaventa, Labriola developed a philosophy whose central element is a social psychology which considers the ego not in an abstract sense but in the context of its historical condition. Only after the Second World War did Marxism permeate cultural life more deeply due to the publication of the works of Antonio GRAMSCI. A vigorous opponent of Fascism and a founder of the Italian Communist Party, Gramsci was imprisoned and wrote the majority of his works while thus incarcerated. These were published posthumously under the title *Quaderni dal carcere* (Notebooks from Prison) (1948–51). His philosophy is a philosophy of practice – in opposition to the speculative historicism of Croce, it eliminates all transcendency and thus is absolute Historicism and Humanism. The intellectual is not separated from the rest of society (a renaissance ideal still valid for Croce and Gentile), but rooted in it, an 'organic intellectual' with a fundamental role to play in the revolution. Gramsci reversed the Marxist relation between structure and superstructure. He regarded it as the duty of intellectuals to guide the masses to the revolution, to permeate civilian society, and to undertake a role of cultural hegemony in the awareness that the Party is the 'modern Prince'.

Unlike Machiavelli, for Gramsci this prince is merely a body expressing a collective will. The influence of Lenin is evident in the demand for a synthesis between theory and practice, the duty to inaugurate a new society falling on intellectuals and on the Party (see LENIN, V.I.).

After the Second World War, Italian philosophy became more open to contemporary European culture, especially to German phenomenology and hermeneutic existentialism. This phase was dominated by the Turin school, where some of the major present-day Italian philosophers taught or were educated. Nicola Abbagnano was among the first Italians to develop existentialist themes, but was also known for his historical studies on ancient scepticism and Hume. His 'positive' existentialism, which is strongly influenced by Dewey's Pragmatism, regards existence as a possibility or project within a finite horizon. The existentialism of Luigi Pareyson has personal and hermeneutical elements as outlined in his *Verità e Interpretazione* (Truth and interpretation) (1970): the human person is an organ of truth, which is interpretation, although not exhausting itself in interpretation. These themes were developed towards a theory of 'formativeness' in Pareyson's aesthetics, whereby artistic activity becomes object and manner of its own action (*Estetica, Teoria della formatività* (Aesthetics: A Theory of Formativeness) (1954)). The final phase of his philosophy is strongly religious, offering a meditation on mythical and revelatory language.

Norberto BOBBIO, a political philosopher initially closer to phenomenology, has moved towards Anglo-American trends, from the analytical philosophy expressed in his *Giusnaturalismo e positivismo giuridico* (Natural law doctrine and legal positivism) (1964) to the formalism of KELSEN which he revised in a functionalist manner more appropriate to the description of democratic societies in *Dalla struttura alla funzione* (From structure to function) (1977). Well-known for his anti-Fascist views and for his civic commitment (he was made a senator for life), Bobbio represents a new spirit of enlightenment. He has contributed to widening the horizons of political studies in Italy, freeing them from Idealism, and has contributed greatly to the theory of law with works such as *Teoria della norma giuridica* (Legal Theory) (1968), *La teoria delle forme di governo* (Theory of the forms of government) (1976), and *Destra e sinistra* (Right and left) (1994).

The founder of the phenomenological school in Italy is Enzo Paci whose thought centres mainly on Husserl's ideas, trying to bridge the gap between the categorial and pre-categorial world. Umberto Eco, a pupil of Pareyson and professor of semiotics at Bologna, is well-known not only as a philosopher but also as a writer (*Il nome della rosa* (*The Name of the Rose*) is his most famous novel). Applying Pareyson's aesthetic theories to modern art, Eco has developed a semiological theory which sees meaning as indefinite and open (*Opera aperta* (Open Work) (1962)), which does not mean absent, as he particularly points out in his recent works against American deconstructionism, including *I limiti della interpretazione* (The Limits of Interpretation) (1990).

Another pupil of Pareyson is Gianni Vattimo, a professor in Turin and Italy's most important representative of hermeneutic philosophy based on Heidegger and Gadamer. In works such as *La fine della modernità* (The end of modernity) (1985), Vattimo regards hermeneutics as the philosophy consequent upon the end of metaphysics and modernity. The acknowledgement of the end of foundational systems is seen to bring a liberating and emancipating effect (*La società trasparente* (Transparent society) (1989)). His hermeneutic way of thinking follows Nietzsche and Heidegger: *Pensiero debole* (Weak Thought) (1983) posits the end of the stable structure of being, noting that any relation to being is within linguistic boundaries which are historically determined.

The philosophies of Emanuele Severino and Massimo Cacciari (both professors at Venice) are developed on original lines. Severino criticizes the nihilism of Western philosophy which, by reducing being to nothing (going from being to becoming), creates a philosophical justification for its project of domination, whose final outcome is technology (*Essenza del nichilismo* (The Essence of Nihilism) (1972)). Against this tendency Severino proposes a return to PARMENIDES, to an ontology of identity that unmasks the illusion of becoming and makes it possible to act free from domination. Through an original interpretation of Nietzsche, Heidegger and Wittgenstein, Cacciari sees in 'negative thought' (technology and conventionalism) the origin of the modern crisis of foundations, whose outcome is disenchantment and whose theoretical premises are found in the religious tradition of the West. His works include *Krisis* (1976), *L'angelo necessario* (The necessary angel) (1986), and *Dell'inizio* (On origins) (1990).

Italian philosophy has always considered philosophical movements and fields such as empiricism, analytical philosophy, logic and philosophy of science to be of minor importance, its strong humanist and historical tradition aligning more with French and German thought. This has become less true in recent times. The example of Ludovico Geymonat, who held the first chair of Philosophy of Science in Milan, is indicative. Having studied with Reichenbach, Schlick and Carnap, Geymonat developed an epistemological theory sensitive to the historical evolution of science, attempting to bridge the traditional gap between humanist and scientific culture. His studies of Galileo and of philosophical and scientific thought are also directed to this end.

See also: HUMANISM, RENAISSANCE; RENAISSANCE PHILOSOPHY

References and further reading

* Ardigò, R. (1870) *Psicologia come scienza positiva* (Psychology as a positivist science), Mantova: Guastalla. (Outlines Ardigò's idea of psychology as a science. Includes a chapter about the relationship between positivist psychology and philosophy.)

* —— (1879) *La morale dei positivisti* (The morality of positivists), ed. G. Giannini, Milan: Marzorati, 1973. (The ethical doctrine of Ardigò, in open debate with idealism, with an introduction and bibliography by the editor.)

Bausola, A. *et al.* (1985) *La filosofia italiana dal dopoguerra a oggi* (Italian philosophy from the end of the Second World War to today), Rome and Bari: Laterza. (Essays by Garin, Dal Pra, Pera, Bedeschi, Bausola and Verra on the most significant movements in contemporary Italian philosophy.)

* Beccaria, C. (1764) *Dei delitti e delle pene* (On crime and punishment), ed. F Venturi, Turin: Einaudi, 1992. (Introduction and bibliographical notes by the editor. Includes an appendix of letters and documents relating to the composition of the work and to the arguments it gave rise to in eighteenth-century Europe.)

* Bobbio, N. (1964) *Giusnaturalismo e positivismo giuridico* (Natural law and legal positivism), Milan: Comunità, 1977. (Collection of essays from 1958 to 1964 on the difference between natural rights and positivist rights.)

* —— (1968) *Teoria della norma giuridica* (Theory of judicial standards), Turin: Giappichelli. (University lectures on the theory of rights from the normative viewpoint.)

* —— (1976) *La teoria delle forme di governo* (Theory of forms of government), Turin: Giappichelli. (University of Turin lectures, 1975–6, on political theories from Plato to Marx.)

* —— (1994) *Destra e sinistra* (Right and left), Rome: Donzelli. (Brief essay on the causes and significance of the political distinction between right and left, with a bibliography by P. Polito following the debate about the left in Italy.)

* Bruno, G. (1584–5) *Dialoghi italiani* (Italian dialo-

gues), ed. G. Aquilecchia, Florence: Sansoni, 1958, repr. 1985. (Critical edition of Bruno's metaphysical and moral dialogues, with a note on the translations into foreign languages in the preface by G. Gentile.)

* Botero, G. (1589) *Della ragion di stato* (The reason of state), ed. L. Lirpo, Turin: U.T.E.T., 1948. (Critical edition with an introduction, biographical note and list of all Botero's works with an annotated list of essential reading.)

* Cacciari, M. (1976) *Krisis*, Milan: Feltrinelli. (An examination of negative and critical-radical thought in contemporary culture, with particular reference to the German-speaking world, especially Nietzsche and Wittgenstein.)

* —— (1986) *L'angelo necessario* (The necessary angel), Milan: Adelphi. (The angel in Western culture regarded as a hermeneutic bridging the visible and the invisible.)

* —— (1990) *Dell'inizio* (On origins), Milan: Adelphi. (Cacciari's most important and difficult theoretical work which re-examines the philosophical problem of origins through a combination of philosophy and theology.)

* Campanella, T. (1620) *Del senso delle cose e della magia* (On material things and magic), ed. A. Bruers, Bari: Laterza, 1925. (Unedited Italian text with a critical introduction.)

* —— (1622) *Apologia di Galileo* (Apology for Galileo), ed. L. Firpo, Turin: U.T.E.T., 1968. (Useful for understanding the relation between Campanella and Galileo. Text, with a copy of the 1632 Latin edition and a brief historical-bibliographical note.)

* —— (1623) La *Città del sole* (The city of the sun), ed. N. Bobbio, Turin: Einaudi, 1941. (Latin text with historical-critical note on the different editions of this work in which Campanella sets out his political doctrine. Extensive introduction and essential reading list.)

* Cattaneo, C. (1859–66) *Psicologia delle menti associate* (Psychology of associated minds), in *Scritti filosofici* (Philosophical writings), vol. 1, 407–479, ed. N. Bobbio, Florence: Le Monnier, 1960. (Introduction and critical notes by the editor. There is a psycho-sociological interpretation of Kantianism which re-evaluates the latter's idealistic-transcendental aspect.)

* Croce, B. (1902) *Estetica come scienza dell'espressione e Linguistica generale* (Aesthetics as the science of expression and general linguistics), ed. G. Galasso, Milan: Adelphi, 1990. (Systematic exposition of aesthetics, divided into theoretical and historical parts. Extensive bibliography and critical note by the editor.)

* —— (1905) *Logica come scienza del concetto puro*

(Logic as the science of pure concept), Bari: Laterza, 1971. (Fundamental text on historical idealism in which Croce sets out his idea of philosophy as Logic and its relationships with experience and history. Not for beginners.)

* —— (1909) *Filosofia della practica. Economia e etica* (Philosophy of practice, economics and ethics), Bari: Laterza, 1945. (Sets out Croce's systematic theory of the forms of spiritual, economic and ethical activity.)

* Cuoco, V. (1805) *Platone in Italia* (Plato in Italy), ed. F. Nicolini, Bari: Laterza, 1969. (Translated from the Greek, this describes a hypothetical journey by Plato to Italy.)

* Eco, U. (1962) *Opera aperta* (Open work), Milan: Bompiani. (Essays, 1958–60, examining form and indeterminism in contemporary poetics.)

* —— (1990) *I limiti dell'interpretazione* (The limits of interpretation), Milan: Bompiani. (Collection of essays about his own hermeneutic anarchism, and in particular of American deconstructionism. The interpretation is free, but follows a principle of falsification which is its limit.)

* Filangieri, G. (1784) *Scienza della legislazione* (The science of legislation), in *Scritti* (Writings), ed. F. Venturi, Turin: Einaudi, 1976, 3–109. (Sets out Filangieri's political and economic theory. Introduction and good bibliography.)

* Galiani, F. (1780) *Della moneta* (On money), ed. F. Nicolini, Bari: Laterza, 1915. (Work of economic theory on the value of money.)

* Galilei, G. (1964) *Opere* (Works), ed. F. Brunetti, Turin: U.T.E.T., 2 vols. (Critical edition of Galileo's scientific works and scientific-philosophical polemics, including *Saggiatore* (vol. 1), *Dialogo sui massimi sistemi* and *Discorsi e dimostrazioni matematiche intorno a due nuove scienze* (both vol. 2). Each work has introductory notes and biographical and bibliographical references. Useful on Galileo's scientific discoveries but rather specialized.)

* Galluppi, P. (1819) *Saggio filosofico sulla critica della conoscenza* (Philosophical essay on the critique of knowledge), ed. N. Abbagnano, Turin: Paravia, 1943. (Attempts to reduce the sceptical aspects of previous theories, from Berkeley and Hume to Condillac and Kant. Introduction and critical notes by the editor.)

Garin, E. (1970) *Dal Rinascimento all'Illuminismo. Studi e Ricerche.* (From the Renaissance to the Enlightenment. Studies and research), Pisa: Nistri-Lischi. (Essays giving an overview of Italian philosophy in the 1500s to 1700s. Attention is drawn particularly to the essays on the period from Campanello to Vico and to that on the reception of Hobbes in the 1700s.)

* Genovesi, A. (1977) *Scritti* (Writings), ed. F. Venturini, Turin: Einaudi. (Economic writings and letters on various subjects, with an introduction and good bibliography.)

* Gentile (1916) *Teoria generale dello spirito come atto puro* (General theory of the spirit as pure act), in Scritti, vol. 3, Florence: Sansoni, 1959. (Fundamental text of Gentile's actualism in which the influence of Berkeley and Fichte is evident.)

* —— (1917–22) *Sistema di logica* (System of logic), in Scritti, vol. 5, Florence: Sansoni, 1964. (Systematic exposition of Gentile's logic as the logic of the Identical; difficult text.)

* Gentili, A. (1877) *Del diritto di guerra* (On the rules of war), ed. A. Fiorini, Livorno: Vigo. (Italian translation of *De jure belli*, holding that the only just war is carried out in self-defence.)

Geymonat, L. (1970–2) *Storia della pensiero filosofico e scientifico* (History of philosophical and scientific thought), Milan: Garzanti, 6 vols. (University-level manual with particular reference to the history of scientific thought, structured by topic, with specific chapters on Italian philosophy and a bibliography up to the 1970s.)

* Gioberti, V. (1841) *Degli errori filosofici di A. Rosmini* (On Rosmini's philosophical errors), in *Opere* (Works), vols 9 and 10, ed. U. Redano, Milan: Bocca, 1939. (Documents the dispute between Rosmini and Gioberti; with introduction and bibliographical notes.)

* —— (1842–3) *Del primato morale e civile degli italiani* (On the moral and civil superiority of the Italians), in *Opere* (Works), vols 1, 2 and 3, ed. E. Castelli, Milan: Bocca, 1938. (Gioberti sets out his political ideas recalling the Italians to their historic mission; preface and essential reading list.)

* —— (1857) *Protologia* (Protology), 4 vols, ed. G. Bonafede, Padua: Cedam, 1983–4. (Essential for understanding Gioberti's idealism. Extensive introduction by the editor.)

* Gioia, M. (1826) *Filosofia della statistica* (Philosophy of statistics), Turin: Tip. Economica, 1852. (The first Piedmontese edition of Gioia's work. Contains brief historical notes on his life and works.)

* Gramsci, A. (1948–51) *Quaderni dal carcere* (Notebooks from prison), ed. V. Gerratana, Turin: Einaudi, 1975, 4 vols. (Critical edition from the Gramsci Institute with introduction and biography by the editor. The fourth volume provides an index.)

* Muratori, L.A. (1749) *Della pubblica felicità* (On public happiness), ed. B. Brunelli, Bologna: Zanichelli, 1941. (Muratori's ethical-political theory,

with an introduction and brief bibliographical note by the editor.)

* Pagano, F.M. (1800) *Saggi politici* (Political essays), ed. F. Collotti, Bologna: Cappelli, 1936. (Political essays on the origins and differences between different societies with an introduction and brief bibliographical note.)
* Pareyson, L. (1954) *Estetica. Teoria della formatività* (Aesthetics: a theory of formativeness), Turin: Edizioni di Filosofia. (Sets out Pareyson's aesthetic theory in which art is not form but formativity, a doing which gives form. The discussion develops in the context of different modern theories of aesthetics, in particular from Kant onwards.)
* —— (1970) *Verità e interpretazione* (Truth and interpretation), Milan: Mursia, 1971. (Collection of essays from 1964–70 on the hermeneutic concept of truth and the relationship between religion, science and philosophy.)
* Rosmini, A. (1830) *Nuovo saggio sull'origine delle idee* (New essay on the origin of ideas), ed. F. Orestano, Rome: An. Romana editor, 3 vols, 1934. (Systematic account of Rosmini's epistemology and ontology, with a preliminary critique of previous philosophers from Plato to Kant.)
* —— (1854) *Logica* (Logic), ed. V. Sala, Centro Internazionale di Studi Rosmini, Strese: Città Nuova Editrice, 1984. (Critical edition of Rosmini's work centred on the relative and innate nature of the idea of being, and on the objectivity of knowledge as opposed to Kantian and idealistic subjectivity.)
* Severino, E. (1972) *Essenza del nichilismo* (The essence of nihilism), Brescia: Paideia. (The idea of being as becoming. Severino proposes a 'return to Parmenides', rethinking his fundamental idea. Not an easy text.)
* Spaventa, B. (1862) *La filosofia italiana nelle sue relazioni con la filosofia europea* (Italian philosophy and its relation to European philosophy), ed. G. Gentile, Florence: Sansoni, 1943. (Account of Italian philosophy in an idealistic key from Bruno to Gioberti, tracing its roots in European philosophy up to Hegel.)
* Vattimo, G. (1985) *La fine della modernità* (The end of modernity), Milan: Garzanti. (Essays from 1981–4 on nihilism and hermeneutics in postmodern culture, with particular reference to Nietzsche and Heidegger.)
* —— (1989) *La società trasparente* (Transparent society), Milan: Garzanti. (Analysis of contemporary postmodern society as the society of communication in which the mass-media, with its pervasive, complex and chaotic qualities, provides a possibility of emancipation.)
* Vattimo, G. and Rovatti, P.A. (eds) (1983) *Il pensiero debole* (Weak thought), Milan: Feltrinelli. (Collection of essays by various authors including Vattimo, Rovatti, Eco, Marconi and Carchia, on the 'crisis of reason' in contemporary philosophy which sees in the end of 'strong reason' the emergence of a more flexible and tolerant truth.)
* Verri, P. (1763) *Discorsi... sull'indole del piacere e del dolore, sulla felicità...* (Discourses... on the balance of pleasure and pain, on happiness...), ed. A. Plebe, Milan: Marzorati, 1972. (Brief text illustrating Verri's concept of ethics. Introduction, critical interpretation and bibliographical note by the editor.)
* Viano, C.A. and Rossi, P. (1991) *Filosofia italiana e filosofie straniere nel dopoguerra* (Italian philosophy and foreign philosophies in the period following the Second World War), Bologna: il Mulino. (Collection of essays by various authors, on topics such as phenomenology, existentialism, hermeneutics, pragmatism, positivism, Marxism and structuralism. Provides a clear and coherent view of contemporary Italian philosophy.)
* Vico, G. (1710) *De antiquissima Italorum sapientia* (On the ancient knowledge of the Italians), in *Opere filosofiche* (Philosophical works), ed. P. Cristofolini, Florence: Sansoni, 1971, 55–131. (Advances Vico's principal doctrine in which truth and fact are mutually interchangeable, thus founding the new historical science.)
* —— (1744) *Scienza nova* (New science), in *Opere filosofiche* (Philosophical works), ed. P. Cristofolini, Florence: Sansoni, 1971, 377–702. (Advances Vico's philosophy of history.)

Translated by Anna Gannon

CHIURAZZI GAETANO

ITŌ JINSAI (1627–1705)

Itō Jinsai, along with his contemporary Yamaga Sokō, pioneered the kogaku*, or 'Ancient Learning', philosophical movement of Tokugawa Japan. Kogaku reacted against the allegedly stifling and excessively metaphysical ideas of Zhu Xi's neo-Confucianism. In making his call for a return to the ancient Confucian teachings, Jinsai produced one of the first and most systematic visions of Confucian philosophy.*

A lifelong resident of Kyoto, the imperial capital, Jinsai made his call for a return to the ancient Confucian teachings of the *Analects* and the *Mengzi* (see CONFUCIUS; MENCIUS) in isolation from the *samurai* regime based in Edo (now Tokyo). He published little in his day, being content with a life of dignified poverty teaching numerous students, including townspeople and court nobles, at his *Kogidō*, or 'School of Ancient Semantics'. Nevertheless, Jinsai's ideas circulated nationally through pirated editions of his writings. One such unauthorized publication sparked the interest of OGYŪ SORAI, then living in Edo, in *kogaku*. Ogyū Sorai wrote to Jinsai, praising his ideas and requesting a teacher–disciple relationship, but Jinsai, then within a year of his own death, never responded. About a decade later, Ogyū Sorai formulated his own *kogaku* system, which systematically attacked Jinsai's ideas even as it advanced upon the trail Jinsai had blazed. Despite Ogyū Sorai's critiques, Jinsai's ideas, as popularized and published by his son and successor Itō Tōgai, prevailed in the eighteenth century as the most humane variety of classical Confucianism.

Jinsai's philological methodology derived largely from the *Xingli ziyi* (The Meanings of Neo-Confucian Terms) of Chen Beixi (1159–1223), a philosophical lexicon systematically defining some twenty-five key concepts as understood by ZHU XI, the master synthesizer of neo-Confucian philosophy in East Asia. The *Xingli ziyi*, first promoted in Japan by Hayashi Razan (1583–1657), appeared in several seventeenth-century editions as Tokugawa scholars sought to fathom the new metaphysical philosophy of neo-Confucianism. No sooner had Chen Beixi's lexicon conveyed the essence of Zhu Xi's ideas, than its philologico-lexicographical methodology gave rise to systematic critiques of Zhu Xi's philosophical semantics by Sokō, Jinsai and then Sorai.

Jinsai's *Gomō jigi* (The Meanings of Terms in the *Analects* and the *Mencius*) was patterned after the *Xingli ziyi*. The word *jigi* in Jinsai's title is the Japanese for *ziyi* (the meanings of terms), part of Chen Beixi's title. However, the *Gomō jigi* repeatedly criticizes Chen Beixi, taking issue with him even as it appropriates his methods. Themes developed in the *Gomō jigi* owe much to the ideas of Luo Qinshun (1465–1547), a Ming dynasty scholar who espoused loyalty to Zhu Xi's neo-Confucianism even while criticizing it. The critiques of Luo Qinshun and Jinsai in turn reflected Zhu Xi's open-minded call for critical scrutiny in philosophy. The *Jinsilu* (Reflections on Things at Hand), edited by Zhu Xi, quips, 'By doubting the indubitable, one greatly advances.'

Jinsai's ideas ultimately transcended their Chinese sources, producing one of the first and most systematic, philologically-based visions of Confucian philosophy ever articulated in East Asian intellectual history. Japanese scholars often note that Jinsai's ideas predated, by nearly a century, those of DAI ZHEN, the famed Qing dynasty scholar of 'Evidential Learning' whose critiques of Zhu Xi took much the same form as those of Jinsai.

Breaking with the neo-Confucian dualism of principle and material force, Jinsai proclaimed that all things consist of a unitary, primal material force, and that alone. His metaphysics assumed vivacious activity, unlike Zhu Xi who claimed that the original nature of humanity could only be glimpsed in quietistic meditation (see XING). Jinsai saw the human mind as an energetic, active endowment, not as a quiescent, motionless entity (see MIND, PHILOSOPHY OF; XIN). He valued human feelings, contending that they are the innate roots of moral behaviour. He praised *jin*, or empathetic moral concern, along with other ancient Confucian virtues as integral elements of *michi*, or the true Way of human conduct. Perfection of the latter made one a gentleman, the ideal proffered by Jinsai in place of Zhu Xi's notion of sagehood. Religiously, Jinsai did affirm the neo-Confucian line in explaining ghosts and spirits as the activities of the psycho-material forces of *yin* and *yang* (see YIN–YANG). Though generally a tolerant and broadminded thinker, Jinsai argued in a famous essay that the *Daxue* (Great Learning) was not an authentic Confucian text because it devalued the emotions in ways that Confucius never had (see DAXUE).

See also: CONFUCIAN PHILOSOPHY, JAPANESE; DAI ZHEN; JAPANESE PHILOSOPHY; NEO-CONFUCIAN PHILOSOPHY; OGYŪ SORAI; ZHU XI

List of works

Itō Jinsai (1683–1705) *Gomō jigi* (The Meanings of Terms in the *Analects* and *Mencius*), in Yoshikawa Kōjirō and Shimizu Shigeru (eds) *Itō Jinsai/Itō Tōgai*, Nihon shisō taikei vol. 33, Tokyo: Iwanami shoten, 1971. (This source includes annotated Japanese texts of not only the *Gomō jigi* but also of Jinsai's other major work, *Kogaku sensei bunshū* (Collected Prose Works of the Master of Ancient Learning) along with explanatory essays. Itō Tōgai's *Kokin gakuhen* (The Shift in Learning from Ancient to Modern Times) is also included.)

References and further reading

de Bary, W.T. and Bloom, I. (eds) (1979) *Principle and Practicality: Essays in Neo-Confucianism and Practical Learning*, New York: Columbia University Press. (Contains several well-researched essays pertaining to Jinsai.)

Ishida Ichirō (1960) *Itō Jinsai*, Tokyo: Yoshikawa Kōbunkan. (A somewhat dated but useful biography of Jinsai in Japanese.)

Katō Nihei (1940) *Itō Jinsai no gakumon to kyōiku* (The Scholarship and Education of Itō Jinsai), Tokyo: Meguro shoten. (The only book-length study of Jinsai's pedagogical practices.)

Kimura Eiichi (ed.) (1970) *Itō Jinsai shū* (The Works of Itō Jinsai), Nihon no shisō vol. 11, Tokyo: Chikuma shoten. (Includes major texts by Jinsai and an analytic essay by Kimura.)

Koyasu Nobukuni (1982) *Itō Jinsai–jinrinteki sekai no shisō*, Tokyo: Tokyo daigaku shuppankai. (A biography in the style of intellectual history.)

—— (1986) *Itō Jinsai kenkyū* (A Study of Itō Jinsai), in *Osaka daigaku daigaku kiyō*, vol. 26. (A concept-by-concept study of Jinsai's thought.)

Miyake Masahiko (1987) *Kyōto chōshū Itō Jinsai no shisō keisei*, Tokyo: Shibunkaku shuppan. (Explores Jinsai's relations as a thinker to Kyoto and its populace. Also pioneers textual studies distinguishing Jinsai's thought from that of Tōgai.)

Sakai Naoki (1992) *Voices of the Past: The Status of Language in Eighteenth-Century Japanese Discourse*, Ithaca, NY: Cornell University Press. (Argues that from the late-seventeenth century, Japanese discourse began conceptualizing the world in diverse ways, all of which had political consequences.)

Spae, J.J. (1948) *Itō Jinsai*, New York: Paragon; repr. 1967. (The only biography of Jinsai in English.)

Yamashita, S. (1983) 'The Early Life and Thought of Itō Jinsai', *Harvard Journal of Asiatic Studies* 43: 453–80. (Surveys Jinsai's transition from neo-Confucianism to Ancient Learning philosophy.)

Yoshikawa Kōjirō (1983) *Jinsai, Sorai, Norinaga: Three Classical Philologists of Mid-Tokugawa Japan*, Tokyo: Tōhō Gakkai. (Presents an English translation of Yoshikawa's seminal 'Jinsai gakuan'.)

JOHN ALLEN TUCKER

J

JACOBI, FRIEDRICH HEINRICH (1743–1819)

Polemicist and literary figure, Jacobi was an outspoken and effective defender of individualism. He accused philosophers of conceptualizing existence according to the requirements of explanation, thus allowing no room for individual freedom or for a personal God. In a series of polemics that influenced the reception of Kant, Jacobi applied his formula, 'Consistent philosophy is Spinozist, hence pantheist, fatalist and atheist', first to Enlightenment philosophy and then to idealism. Jacobi was not however opposed to reason; in 'faith' and 'feeling' he sought to recover the intuitive power of reason philosophers ignored.

Jacobi also criticized the literary movement spearheaded by the young Goethe, because of its latent fatalism. He dramatized in two novels the problem of reconciling individualism with social obligations. An exponent of British economic and political liberalism, Jacobi was an early critic of the French revolution which he considered the product of rationalism.

1   **Life and work**
2   **Critique of philosophy**
3   **Critique of idealism**
4   **Positive doctrine**
5   **Literary work**
6   **Political ideas**
7   **Influence**

1 Life and work

Born in Düsseldorf, of well-to-do merchant family, Jacobi studied in Geneva where he became acquainted with Rousseau and Bonnet. Destined to a business career, after marrying Elisabeth (Betty) von Clermont he entrusted his affairs to his brother-in-law and dedicated himself to literary and social activities. Together with Betty he made his villa at Pempelfort a meeting place for the personalities of the day and a centre of liberal ideas. He was instrumental to the founding of the journal der Teutsche Merkur. In the 1770s he held political positions in the duchies of Julich-Berg and, briefly in 1779, in Bavaria. In 1805 he moved to Munich to take up the post of president of the

Academy. He spent his last years there, supervising the edition of his works.

Widely regarded as an anti-Enlightenment figure in his own lifetime and afterwards, Jacobi in fact sought to defend individualistic values which were just as much part of the Enlightenment as the rationalism he fought all his life. He claimed that philosophy artificially abstracts from the individuality of existence yet takes its empty conceptual artifacts to define reality itself. For the sake of explanation philosophy subordinates conditions of existence to conditions of thought, thereby subverting the possibility of choice and action. Hence Jacobi accused philosophy of 'nihilism' (a term he popularized).

2 Critique of philosophy

In a masterstroke of philosophical propaganda, Jacobi propelled his position (and himself) to the centre of attention in 1785, by publishing with commentary letters he had recently exchanged with Moses Mendelssohn (*Concerning the Doctrine of Spinoza in Letters to Herr Moses Mendelssohn*; second, much enlarged edition, 1789) (see MENDELSSOHN, M.). The purpose of the correspondence had been to clarify Lessing's declaration, allegedly made to Jacobi in a conversation shortly before Lessing's death, that he was a Spinozist (see LESSING, G.E.; SPINOZA, B. DE). In that conversation Jacobi had claimed that philosophy inexorably leads to Spinoza's 'substance', and this abstract concept, when set up as first principle, undermines individual distinctions, most of all the distinction between God and creatures. Lessing had responded by declaring his sympathy for Spinoza, and Jacobi had thereupon urged him to perform a *salto mortale* – a spiritual somersault in virtue of which, through an act of faith, Lessing would simply declare himself for a personal God, and for freedom, and thereby rejoin common sense.

The book caused an uproar. Jacobi had succeeded in dramatizing his cause against philosophy by identifying the latter with Spinozism (widely regarded at the time as synonymous with atheism), and, by associating Spinoza with Lessing, he had cast doubt on Lessing's typical Enlightenment belief that reason can save the essential truths of religion and morality. Jacobi had at the same time challenged the authority of Mendelssohn, universally acknowledged as Lessing's intimate friend and a witness to reason's ability to establish truths transcending ethnic and religious differences. The equation Jacobi then drew, 'Consistent philosophy=Spinozism=pantheism=fatalism=atheism', is one he defended to the end, although he soon had to adapt it to the idealism of Kant and his followers.

3   Critique of idealism

Jacobi's objections to Kant's critique of reason became commonplace in the sceptical reaction to KANT (see the Appendix to *David Hume on Faith, or Idealism and Realism: A Dialogue*, 1787). Jacobi argued that it is inconsistent to accept the 'thing in itself' yet disclaim knowledge of it; that in a priori 'space-time' the individuality of determination is a mere illusion; that the categories are empty forms artificially imposed upon experience, and the transcendental 'I' a counterfeit subject. His later negative reactions to FICHTE and SCHELLING were even stronger. Jacobi accused Fichte of inverted Spinozism – of parading as 'subject' and 'subjectivity' an indeterminate source of activity (the self-positing 'I') in fact just as anonymous and impervious to individuation as Spinoza's substance. He made this accusation in *Jacobi to Fichte* (1799), at a time when Fichte was under suspicion of atheism. The attack on Schelling – fellow member of the Munich Academy whose views on art and nature Jacobi feared would corrupt the young – came in 1811 (*Of Divine Things and Their Revelation*). The ensuing bitter public debate is known as the 'pantheism dispute'.

4   Positive doctrine

Despite his polemics, Jacobi insisted that he was not against reason but that, on the contrary, his aim was to unmask the irrationalism latent in rationalistic philosophy. In *David Hume* – philosophically his most interesting work – he claimed that he used 'faith' in the sense of Hume's 'belief' (both *Glaube* in German). He however rejected Hume's phenomenalism and in the same work defended a realism of the senses not unlike that of Thomas REID (by whom he was influenced, as also by Adam FERGUSON). He concluded with the suggestion that reason is a higher and more reflective form of sensibility – a position which Jacobi associated with LEIBNIZ and which had obvious vitalistic implications. Yet Jacobi later rejected the vitalism of HERDER because of its pantheism (Appendices IV–V to *Doctrine of Spinoza*, 1789).

Jacobi's ambiguity towards philosophy – to which

he was attracted but which he feared because of its possible nihilistic effects – was reflected in his attitude to the philosophers he criticized. He admired Spinoza for his consistency and his recognition that truth is selfrevelatory (hence transcends ratiocination). He felt kinship with Kant, with whom he shared belief in the priority of existence over thought and in the finitude of reason. Retrospectively he used Kant's distinction between reason and understanding to define what he had always meant by 'faith' or the 'feeling for truth'. He identified the 'reason' he had criticized as Kant's 'understanding'– a faculty by nature bent on cataloguing and exploiting finite, sensible things. But above understanding there is true reason with its intuitive power to apprehend higher moral truths. By 'faith', Jacobi claimed, he had always meant this true reason. Kant had rightly distinguished it from understanding but had failed to recognize its intuitive power, thereby subordinating it to understanding ('On the Undertaking of Critique to Reduce Reason to the Understanding', 1802). Jacobi also hinted that in his *David Hume* he had offered an alternative to Kant's deduction of the categories, and that Kant had based his refutation of idealism on his own early claim that no 'I' is possible without a 'Thou'. Despite ambiguities and fluctuations, Jacobi always defended his two fundamental theses: (1) Existence is radically individualized and precedes thought possibilities; (2) Truth is selfrevelatory and is best intuited in the relations between individuals and between individuals and their God.

5   Literary work

Inspired by GOETHE, with whom he had a long but uneven relationship, Jacobi wrote two novels which he published, beginning in 1775, under various forms: *Allwill*, (final form 1792) and *Woldemar* (final form 1796). Goethe had also figured in Jacobi's report of his controversial conversation with Lessing and, implicitly, was just as much a target of attack in the ensuing controversy as Mendelssohn. Jacobi feared Goethe's enthusiasm for Spinoza, and the literary glorification of nature he promoted. In *Allwill* he portrayed the seductive and ultimately destructive effects of a lively poetic imagination undisciplined by social and moral constrains. In *Woldemar* he explored the problem of balancing nature with art and virtue, and of establishing social bonds between individuals richly endowed with subjectivity. The man-woman relationship theme is central to both novels.

6   Political ideas

In early essays Jacobi defended free trade and

attacked the theorists of state absolute power. Passionately interested in anything political, he criticized the French revolution which he regarded as an unrealistic attempt to reshape human institutions to suit abstract reason, without regard for history or nature.

7 Influence

Jacobi's personalism and his religiosity (which drew inspiration from many sources, notably HAMANN) had wide influence. In his early *Kantian Letters* REINHOLD cast Kant in the role of mediator between Mendelssohn's reason and Jacobi's faith, with far-reaching consequences for the reception of Kant. Jacobi's influence also spread through personal contacts and a voluminous correspondence. Although not himself a product of pietism, late in his life Jacobi inspired pietist educated writers such as SCHLEIER-MACHER and FRIES, and through their writings his influence passed on to the nineteenth century (see PIETISM).

See also: ENLIGHTENMENT, CONTINENTAL

List of works

Jacobi, F.H. (1785) *Über die Lehre von Spinoza an den Herrn Moses Mendelssohn* (Concerning the Doctrine of Spinoza in Letters to Herr Moses Mendelssohn), Breslau: Löwe; 2nd edn, 1789; repr. in H. Scholz (ed.) *Die Hauptschriften zum Pantheismusstreit zwischen Jacobi und Mendelssohn*, Berlin: Reuther & Reichard, 1916. (1789 edition is much enlarged. 1916 edition also contains other writings relating to the Jacobi-Mendelssohn controversy.)
—— (1787) *David Hume über den Glauben, oder Idealismus und Realismus. Ein Gespräch* (David Hume on Faith, or Idealism and Realism: A Dialogue), Breslau: Löwe; 2nd edn, 1815; 1st edn repr. New York and London: Garland, 1983. (1815 edition was part of the *Werke* and was significantly edited, with a new lengthy introduction. 1983 edition includes this 1815 new Preface, with an English introduction by Hamilton Beck.)
—— (1792) *Eduard Allwills Briefsammlung, herausgegeben von Friedrich Heinrich Jacobi, mit einer Zugabe von eigenen Briefen* (Edward Allwill's Collection of Letters, edited by Friedrich Heinrich Jacobi, with an Addition from Letters of His Own), Königsberg: Nicolovius; repr. J.U. Terpstra (ed.), Groningen: Djakarta, 1957. (This is the final text of a novel, parts of which had previously been published starting from 1775. 1957 edition is a critical edition.)
—— (1796) *Woldemar*, Königsberg: Nicolovius. (This is a somewhat edited version of the 1794 final text of a novel, parts of which had previously been published starting from 1779.)
—— (1799) *Jacobi an Fichte* (Jacobi to Fichte), Hamburg: Perthes; repr. in R. Lauth and H. Gliwitzky (eds) (1972) *Fichte-Gesamtausgabe*, Stuttgart and Bad Cannstat: Frommann, series 3, vol.3. (An open letter to Fichte publicly rejecting his idealism. 1972 edition is a critical edition.)
—— (1802) 'Über das Unternehmen des Kriticismus, die Vernunft zu Verstande zu bringen, und der Philosophie überhaupt eine neue Absicht zu geben' (On the Undertaking of Critique to Reduce Reason to the Understanding, and to Give a New Purpose to Philosophy in General), in *Beyträge zur leichtern übersicht des Zustandes der Philosophie beym Anfange des 19. Jahrhunderts* 3: 1–110. (The Beyträge were a series of volumes edited by K.L. Reinhold.)
—— (1811) *Von den Göttlichen Dingen und ihrer Offenbarung* (Of Divine Things and Their Revelation), Leipzig: Fleischer; repr. in W. Weischedel (ed.) (1967) *Streit um die göttlichen Dinge. Die Auseinandersetzung zwischen Jacobi und Schelling*, Darmstadt: Wissenschaftliche Buchgesellschaft. (Jacobi's attack on Schelling. 1967 edition includes other writings relating to the Jacobi–Schelling controversy.)
—— (1812–25) *Friedrich Heinrich Jacobi's Werke*, eds J.F. Köppen and C.J.F. Roth, Leipzig: Fleischer, 6 vols; easily available in photo-mechanical reproduction, Darmstadt: Wissenschaftliche Buchgesellschaft, 1968. (1812–25 edition was supervised by Jacobi before his death. It is not reliable as a document of Jacobi's earlier production.)
Brüggen, M. and Sudhof, S. (eds) (1981–) *Briefwechsel*, Stuttgart and Bad Constatt: Frommann-Holzboog. (The first volumes of a projected critical edition so far covering the early correspondence. Published to date: part 1, vols 1–3, part 2, vol. 1.)
di Giovanni, G. (ed. and trans.) (1994) *The Main Philosophical Writings and the Novel 'Allwill'*, Kingston and Montreal: McGill-Queen. (It includes complete translations of *Concerning the Doctrine of Spinoza* (1785), *David Hume* (1787), *Allwill*, *Jacobi to Fichte*, the introduction to the *David Hume* of 1815, and excerpts from other works. It also includes a long study on Jacobi and his age, and a detailed bibliography.)

References and further readings

Baum, G. (1969) *Vernunft und Erkenntnis. Die*

Philosophie F.H. Jacobis, Bonn: Bouvier. (A study of Jacobi's epistemology.)

Beiser, F.C. (1987) *The Fate of Reason*, Cambridge, MA: Harvard University Press. (Includes a very readable interpretation of Jacobi as proto-existentialist.)

di Giovanni, G. (1989) 'From Jacobi's Philosophical Novel to Fichte's Idealism: Some Comments on the 1798–99 "Atheism Dispute"', *Journal of the History of Philosophy* 27 (1): 75–100. (Readable and informative.)

Ford, L.S. (1965) 'The Controversy Between Schelling and Jacobi', *Journal of the History of Philosophy* 3 (1): 75–89. (Readable and informative.)

Hammacher, K. (ed.) (1971) *Friedrich Heinrich Jacobi. Philosoph und Literat der Goethezeit*, Frankfurt: Klostermann. (A collection of important but highly specialized studies.)

—— (1969) *Kritik und Leben II. Die Philosophie Friedrich Heinrich Jacobis*, Munich: Fink. (A scholarly treatment of all aspects of Jacobi's philosophy.)

Hammacher, K. and Hirsch, H. (1993) *Die Wirtschaftspolitik des Philosophen Friedrich Heinrich Jacobi*, Amsterdam and Atlanta, GA: Editions Rodopi. (A study of Jacobi's economic policy.)

Lévy-Bruhl, L. (1894) *La philosophie de Jacobi*, Paris: Alcan. (A dated but still very readable study.)

Nicolai, H. (1965) *Goethe und Jacobi, Studien zur Geschichte ihrer Freundschaft*, Stuttgart: Metzler. (A fascinating study of Jacobi's relationship to Goethe; it throws light on the whole period.)

Verra, V. (1963) *F.H. Jacobi. Dall'Illuminismo all'Idealismo*, Turin: Edizioni di 'Filosofia'. (Still the best introduction to Jacobi and his age.)

GEORGE DI GIOVANNI

JAINA PHILOSOPHY

The issues in Jaina philosophy developed concurrently with those that emerged in Buddhist and Hindu philosophy. The period from the second century BC to about the tenth century AD evinces a tremendous interaction between the schools of thought and even an exchange of ideas, borne out especially in the rich commentary literature on the basic philosophical works of the respective systems. Jaina philosophy shares with Buddhism and Hinduism the aim of striving, within its own metaphysical presuppositions, for absolute liberation (mokṣa or nirvāṇa) from the factors which bind human existence. For the philosophical systems of Indian thought, ignorance (of one's own nature, of the nature of the world and of one's role in the world) is one of the chief such factors, and Jainism offers its own insights into what constitutes the knowledge that has the soteriological function of overcoming ignorance. Jainism is not exempt from the problem of distinguishing the religious and/or mystical from the 'philosophical'; the Indian tradition has no exact equivalents for these categories as they are usually employed in Western thought.

The significance ascribed to knowledge is reflected in the attention given to epistemology and logic by Jaina philosophers. The first systematic account was given by the fourth- or fifth-century philosopher Umāsvāti, who distinguished two types of knowledge: partial knowledge, which is obtained from particular standpoints, and comprehensive knowledge, which is of five kinds – sensory knowledge, scriptural knowledge, clairvoyance, telepathy and omniscience. Of these, the first two are held to be indirect (consisting in, or analogous to, inference) and the remainder are direct; Jainism is unique among Indian philosophies in characterizing sensory knowledge as indirect. The aim of the treatises on knowledge is to present what the Jainas believe would be known in the state of omniscience, as taught by Mahāvīra. Omniscience is an intrinsic condition of all souls; however, due to the influence of karma since beginningless time this essential quality of the soul is inhibited.

The Jaina interest in logic arose, as with the other schools, through a consideration of inference as a mode of knowledge. The methods and terminology of the Nyāya school were heavily drawn upon; this is evident in Siddhasena Divākara's Nyāyāvatāra (The Descent of Logic) (c. fifth century), one of the first detailed presentations of Jaina logic. The Jainas used logic to criticize other schools and defend their own. The acquaintance with other traditions that this implies is a notable aspect of classical Jainism; their interest in other schools, coupled with their belief in collecting and preserving manuscripts, makes the Jaina corpus very important for the study of classical Indian thought.

According to Jaina ontology, reality is divided into the two basic principles of sentience and non-sentience, neither of which is reducible to the other. The former is manifested in souls, of which there are an infinite number, and the latter in the five basic substances, which are matter, dharma and adharma (factors posited to explain movement and rest), space and time. Matter consists of atoms; as it becomes associated with the soul, it gets attached to it, becomes transformed into karma and thereby restricts the functions of consciousness. This pernicious process can only be reversed through ascetic practices, which ultimately lead to liberation.

Ascetic practices constitute the basis of Jaina ethics, the framework of which are the 'five great vows', according to which the ascetics vow to live. These are: nonviolence towards all forms of life, abstinence from lying, not taking what is not given, celibacy and renunciation of property. Nonviolence is strongly emphasized, since violence produces the greatest amount of karma. Hence great care has to be exercised at all times, especially because injury of life forms should be avoided also in plants, water, fire, etc. The minimization of physical activity to avoid injury is therefore an important ideal of Jaina asceticism. Inspiration for constant ethical behaviour is provided by a contemplation of the lives of the twenty-four Jinas, of whom Mahāvīra was the last. Though human, these 'conquerors of the passions' are worshipped as divine beings because of their conduct in the world and knowledge of the nature of ultimate reality.

1   **Ontology and metaphysics**
2   **Epistemology and logic**
3   **Ethics**
4   **Kundakunda, Umāsvāti and Siddhasena Divākara**
5   **Other notable philosophers**

1   Ontology and metaphysics

Jaina thought has retained several elements of ancient natural philosophy, such as the theory of atoms, explaining the nature of the universe without recourse to a creator god, and the interpretation of karma as particles of subtle matter (see KARMA AND REBIRTH, INDIAN CONCEPTIONS OF §6). The Jainas hold an ancient theory in which ultimate reality is divided into two basic categories, one which represents the principle of sentience or consciousness as such, usually translated as 'soul' (*jīva*), and one which represents the non-sentient principle (*ajīva*). In their intrinsic natures they are exclusive categories in the sense that, despite their coexistence (as in human beings), the one cannot take on the nature of the other. Both are ontological substances (*dravya*) in that reality or existence as such can ultimately be reduced to these two eternal, uncreated and indestructible categories (see ONTOLOGY IN INDIAN PHILOSOPHY §1). The soul is best described as a monad, of which there are a countless number, each independent but with the same principle of sentience as its chief characteristic, and each able to expand or contract according to the size of the body which it inhabits. Souls intrinsically possess unlimited qualities of bliss and energy, and are omniscient.

The non-sentient principle is a generic term for the following five substances. First, matter (*pudgala*) represents the basic stuff or raw material out of which the universe is composed. Matter is made up of atoms, each of which occupies one point of space, and which can be with or without form and can be inhabited by souls. Objects come into being through a combination or aggregation of atoms and change is explained not through destruction or creation of atoms but as a rearrangement of the basic stuff. Together with the view that atoms can have the qualities of colour, taste, touch and smell, Jaina philosophy evolved the theory of substance, quality and mode (see §4) to explain the world in terms of identity and difference, depending on the standpoint and purpose. Matter is crucial for the philosophical anthropology of Jainism because it is matter that directly affects the nature of the soul in the sense that, by becoming converted into karma, it restricts the intrinsic functions of the soul, inhibiting right faith, right knowledge and right conduct. Precisely how this operates is explained later in this section with reference to the so-called 'seven basic truths' which form the basis of Jaina metaphysics.

The second and third substances, called *dharma* and *adharma*, are posited for technical reasons. They stand respectively for the factors that assist movement and rest, without themselves being set into motion or coming to rest. They are formless, coextensive with worldly space and without qualities. The function of these two substances is usually explained on the analogy of water and fish. Just as water is not responsible for the fish's movement or its being stationary but makes these possible, so too *dharma* and *adharma* offer the condition for the possibility of movement or rest to souls and matter.

The fourth substance, ether or space (*ākāśa*), does not itself occupy space but is space itself, giving the other substances the place they require in which to exist. According to Jaina cosmology, space is the only substance that encompasses both the world (*loka*) and the nonworld (*aloka*). The world is divided into the underworld or hells, in which souls reap the fruits of their unmeritorious deeds, the middle world, which corresponds to our world and in which only human beings can perform the necessary austerities for absolute freedom, the world of different kinds of heaven, in which souls reap the fruits of their meritorious acts and, finally, the world above the heavens, to which a liberated soul (one that has completely rid itself of the burden of all its positive and negative karma) rises, to remain there in its pristine nature. The nonworld serves no purpose at all and is described as being empty. However, it demarcates the area along which liberated souls eternally exist (see COSMOLOGY AND COSMOGONY, INDIAN THEORIES OF §3).

Time (*kāla*) is the fifth non-sentient substance; it

has no spatial points, its smallest unit being called a moment (*samaya*), out of which the other units of time – minutes, hours, and so on – are then derived. Time enables change to take place without itself changing. On the absolute level, time exists as an undifferentiated continuum for the liberated souls. On the cosmological level, it has two broad phases or eras, and is described on the analogy of a wheel with twelve spokes. The world goes through six phases of gradual descent, representing the decline of values, then through six phases of gradual ascent, representing a steady improvement of values. Both phases involve fantastic spans of time. The Śvetāmbara tradition hesitates to accord time the status of an independent substance, though it uses it as a category necessary to explain the course of the world. The Digambaras and the Śvetāmbaras, the two main groups of Jainism, differ in several philosophically minor issues.

What the above ontological structure of reality does not do is explain the original cause of the association of the souls with the other substances, and especially how karma originally attaches itself to the soul to its detriment. This problem applies *mutatis mutandis* to all schools of Indian thought which speak of the possibility of liberation from the bondage of karma, where the basic issue is simply presupposed and is either left unanswered or euphemistically avoided by saying, as the Jainas also do, that the association between the souls and the world has been so since beginningless time (*anādi*). The karma theory was accepted a priori without the need to explain a first cause and the issue does not seem to be regarded as a problem. Moreover, Jainism shares with Buddhism and Hinduism the basic assumption that the human situation is characterized by suffering and pain; more important than seeking the first cause is what can be done to free oneself from this predicament. Past deeds cannot be undone, but once the basic presuppositions are accepted – especially that the process of karma, which is responsible for the cycles of existence, can be interfered with – the individual is free to opt for the path that promises the goal of absolute freedom. The Jainas do not have recourse to a creator god who sets the universe and life in the world in motion. Everything operates through its own inner dynamics and the role of the individual is to meditate on the basic truths of reality.

Jaina metaphysics is based on seven truths or fundamental principles (*tattva*) which are an attempt to explain the human predicament. The first two are the two ontological categories of the soul and the non-soul discussed above, namely the truth that they exist. For the remaining five truths the factor of karma has to be brought into play because all are

connected to it. The third truth is that through the interaction, technically called *yoga*, between the two substances, soul and non-soul, matter flows into (*āsrava*) the soul, clings to it, becomes converted into karma and – the fourth truth – acts as a factor of bondage (*bandha*), restricting the manifestation of the consciousness intrinsic to it. The fifth truth states that a stoppage (*saṃvara*) of new karma is possible through asceticism. An intensification of this burns up the existing karma – this sixth truth is expressed by the word *nirjarā*. The final truth is that when the soul is freed from the influence of karma, it reaches the goal of Jaina teaching, which is liberation (*mokṣa*).

It must be noted that the later tradition included two more categories after bondage (*bandha*), namely *puṇya* and *pāpa*, which may be translated as 'good' and 'bad'. They refer to two kinds of bondage caused by one's deeds. The ethical implications of these terms underscore the significance of Jaina ethics for Jaina soteriology.

2 Epistemology and logic

Epistemology and logic are closely linked in the Indian tradition because logical issues are largely associated with problems related to inference which, in turn, is regarded as a means or instrument of knowledge. The occupation with abstract, logical ideas related to inference was the favourite topic of the Nyāya school, particularly in its Navya-Nyāya form, which flourished between about the thirteenth and the seventeenth century. Jaina logic adopts much of the Nyāya language and method (see NYĀYA-VAIŚEṢIKA §6).

The history of Indian logic can be traced back at least to pre-Christian works on Indian medicine in which physicians are advised to know about a long list of categories, epistemological and logical, when participating in public debates. In the commentary literature to the basic philosophical treatises, especially after the third century AD, epistemology takes a prominent position, each school presenting its own theory of knowledge after criticizing other views. Jainism made its own unique contribution to this mainstream development by also occupying itself with the basic epistemological issues, namely, with those concerning the nature of knowledge, how knowledge is derived, and in what way knowledge can be said to be reliable. These issues feature in the Indian context in the form of the consistent attention paid to what exactly constitutes cognition, the means of cognition, and the validity of cognition. The problems dealt with in epistemology broadly served two functions. They represented an attempt to provide the basis for an intelligible discourse on matters of common, everyday experience and, albeit indirectly, to distinguish this area of discourse from what constitutes the knowledge of ultimate reality. Thus Indian epistemology entails an implicit metaphysical concern when it is employed in the context not only of the knowledge of one's intrinsic nature but also of reality as such.

Knowledge for the Jainas takes place in the soul, which, without the limiting factor of karma, is omniscient. Human beings have partial knowledge – the object of knowledge is known partially and the means of knowledge do not operate to their full capacity. The Jainas have an intricate theory of knowledge concerning the fundamental principles (*tattva*), and the first systematic presentation of it was given by Umāsvāti (see §4) in the first chapter of his *Tattvārthasūtra* (fourth or fifth century). The following is a summary of his theory; the bracketed numbers are the relevant aphorisms. The knowledge of the basic Jaina truths is said to be obtained through means or instruments of knowledge (*pramāṇa*) which can yield a comprehensive knowledge of an object, and through particular standpoints which yield a partial knowledge (*naya*; 6) (see MANIFOLD-NESS, JAINA THEORY OF). The first type of knowledge is of five kinds: sensory knowledge, scriptural knowledge, clairvoyance, telepathy and omniscience (9–10), among which again the first two are described as being indirect means of knowledge (*parokṣa*), with the others furnishing direct knowledge (*pratyakṣa*; 11–12), by which it is meant that the object is known directly by the soul (not, for example, as with inferring fire through the cognition of smoke). Jainism is unique in the Indian tradition in regarding sensory perception as an indirect means of knowledge, because it does not take place directly through the soul, although some notable Jaina thinkers (such as Akalaṅka and Māṇikyanandin) are exceptions.

Synonyms for sensory knowledge are remembrance, recognition, 'induction' and 'deduction', all caused by the senses and the mind (13–14). Scriptural knowledge, which is based on sensory knowledge, is of two, several or twelve kinds (20), depending on which scriptural works are taken as authoritative. The range of sensory and scriptural knowledge extends to all the six substances (soul and the five non-sentient substances), but not in all their modes (26). Clairvoyance is possessed by divine and infernal beings, and can be obtained by human beings and animals through a destruction and/or subsidence of the karma which hinders it (21–2). Its scope is all entities that have form (27). Telepathy is of two kinds, which are distinguished on the basis of purity and infallibility (23–4). Its scope is infinitely greater than that of clairvoyance (28). The scope of omniscience, on the other hand, extends to all substances in all their modes simultaneously (29). Sensory knowledge, scriptural knowledge and clairvoyance are explicitly referred to as means of knowledge that may also be erroneous (31).

The basic division of knowledge into the direct and indirect types is generally retained by all Jaina thinkers, though with differences in the way in which they are further classified. For example, Akalaṅka (*c.* eighth century) regarded sensory knowledge as a direct means of knowledge, and Māṇikyanandin (*c.* ninth century) evolved a much more complex system with several more subvarieties. When a description of inference as a means of knowledge is given, the occasion is used to discuss logical issues in detail. Jaina logic applies the Nyāya language within its own metaphysical presuppositions. Some of the basic features of Indian logic which the Jainas also adopt involve: (1) the use of inference in the accepted standard form, to convince others of the validity of an argument, clearly distinguishing the three basic terms of the major, the middle and the minor; (2) an example or instance, which can also be in a negative form, based on the invariable concomitance of or inseparable connection between the middle term of an argument and all cases in which the major term obtains; and (3) a concern with types of fallacies based not only on pervasion but also on the relation of the different terms with each other and the locus in which they apply (see INFERENCE, INDIAN THEORIES OF).

With his *Nyāyāvatāra* (The Descent of Logic), Siddhasena Divākara (*c.* fifth century) is perhaps the first Jaina thinker who deals with these and other issues in Jaina logic. A few selected examples will show how Jainism imbibed the logic of the Nyāya school, the structure of which it applied to prove its own arguments and to show errors in the arguments of others. The classical example for an understanding of the abstract ideas expressed here is that of smoke and fire, the basic elements of which, as they feature in a five-step inferential argument, are: (1) the theory – the hill (minor term) possesses fire (major term); (2) the cause or reason – because of smoke (middle term); (3) the example based on invariable concomitance – wherever there is smoke there is fire (as in a kitchen); (4) the application of the theory – similarly the mountain has smoke; and (5) the conclusion – therefore it is the same, that is, has fire.

A statement expressive of the reason (*i.e.*, the mark or the middle term, called *hetu*) which is inseparably connected with that which is to be proved (*i.e.*, the major term, called *sādhya*) having been composed of the minor term (called *pakṣa*, signifying a side or place), etc., is called an inference for the sake of others (*parārthānumāna*). (*Nyāyāvatāra*, stanza 13; trans. S.C. Vidyabhusan)

Where the inseparable connection of the major term (*sādhya*) and the middle term (*sādhana* or *hetu*) is shown by homogeneousness (*sādharmya*), the example is called a homogeneous one, on account of the connection (between those terms) being recollected.

(stanza 18)

The reason (*i.e.*, the middle term called *hetu*) has been defined as that which cannot exist except in connection with the major term (*sādhya*); the fallacy of the reason (*hetvābhāsa*) arises from nonconception, doubt or misconception about it (the middle term).

(stanza 22)

The Indians did not develop a system for presenting their abstract ideas symbolically; natural language (pre-eminently Sanskrit), used in such a technical way that only the specialist can decipher the arguments, served the function. However, there have been several successful contemporary attempts to translate Indian logic into the terminology of modern Western logic (Ingalls 1951; Matilal 1968, 1971; Staal 1960).

3 Ethics

Jaina ethics evolved out of the rules for the ascetic, which served as the model, with necessary changes, for the laity as well. The basic ascetic rules are encapsulated in the so-called five great vows (*mahāvratas*) ascribed to Mahāvīra, which seem to be a summary of Indian asceticism as a whole from ancient times. The first and foremost of these is nonviolence, which entails total abstinence in thought, word and deed from injury to all life forms. The principle of life is the souls which inhabit atoms, so Jainism emphasizes extreme care with reference not only to plant and animal life forms but also to those in earth, water, fire and air. The vow of nonviolence is extended to include not making another perform acts of violence and not approving them in any way. Further, ascetics, who are usually wandering mendicants, are required to stay in one area during the monsoon to avoid unintentionally disturbing and harming life forms in and as a result of the abundance of water. To avoid inadvertently injuring insects, certain groups of ascetics even cover their mouths and noses, and carry a whisk to keep insects away. The vow of not eating after sunset for the same reason is an ascetic rule and one which is considered to be ethically meritorious when practised by householders.

The other vows are: to abstain from lying, and to take care not to use violent or harmful speech; not to take what is not given; to lead a life of celibacy; and to renounce attachment to the objects of the world, that is, to renounce possession of property.

Jainism's extreme emphasis on nonviolence is grounded in its metaphysics. Violence is responsible for the maximum amount of karma that can be accumulated by the soul, and since liberation is possible only when karma is completely destroyed, the task is reduced through an avoidance of violent deeds. Physical activity *per se* is responsible for the accumulation of karma; abstinence from it is symbolized by the famous iconic representations of ascetics standing upright over such long periods that vines grow up their legs – physical control represents the mental control that is also necessary to avoid subtle, inner movement. With the axiom 'nonviolence is the highest religion', Jainism summarizes the basis of its ethics and religious life.

The ascetic vows are mirrored in the rules for what the laity should do to exemplify an ethical life. The vow of chastity is relaxed for householders, with sexual contact restricted to the married partner; bearing in mind the ascetic's great vow of chastity, however, restraint is enjoined as a virtue. Other vows which are included in the religious life of devotees include: nonattachment to property and possessions, and the aim of leading a simple life; religious giving or donation; eschewing excessive and unnecessary travel; fasting on auspicious days of the Jaina calendar.

The mutual reliance of ascetics and laity is evident throughout the history of Jainism. The ascetics do not cook, and rely on the devotees for their daily subsistence, and the laity require the ascetics for their religious teaching and advice. Confession of ethical transgressions belongs to the religious life of both ascetics and laity, who atone for them by penances of religious purification, the aim being to reduce or even completely annihilate the karmic effect of the infringement.

Jainism, together with Buddhism, shows how a religious and virtuous life is possible without the idea of a creator god to whom one can turn, one who is ultimately made responsible for the human condition. Models for ethical life in Jainism are provided by the biographies of the twenty-four Jinas, the conquerors of the passions, of whom Mahāvīra was the last. Indeed, they are worshipped as divine beings, even though the tradition represents them as human beings who through their extreme asceticism gained an insight into the nature of reality, on account of which they are regarded as omniscient. Their lives serve as a guiding principle and, according to the tradition, an emulation of their virtues can lead one to the same goal of liberation that they achieved.

Under the rubric of ethics the issue of voluntary death may be mentioned. Inscriptional evidence records its occurrence throughout the history of Jainism and even in contemporary times, though it has been rare since about the twelfth century. This kind of death, open to both ascetics and laity, is a death that literally makes 'the physical body and the internal passions emaciated' (*sallekhanā*; Pūjyapāda on *Tattvārthasūtra* V, 22); often it serves to accelerate the death process already in progress. Jainism contrasts this with death that occurs through suicide, which the Jainas eschew because passions such as 'attachment, aversion or infatuation' are involved in suicidal death. By virtue of its excellence, the passionless death (which is performed under strict conditions), is regarded as the most effective ascetic practice to rid the soul of binding passions and to terminate an ethical life.

4   Kundakunda, Umāsvāti and Siddhasena Divākara

These three thinkers are the pioneers of Jaina philosophy whose basic ideas set the trend for most later thinkers. Biographical details of all of them are mixed with legend and there are differences of opinion as to whether they really wrote all the works ascribed to them; there is also a lack of consensus about their dates.

Kundakunda. If recent research is correct in considering him to have belonged to the second or third century AD, then this would make him the first significant and independent thinker of the post-canonical period whose views are accepted as representing the essence of Jaina thought. Although he was a pioneering Digambara thinker, probably from South India, appreciation for his views also comes from the Śvetāmbara sect of Jainism. He was also known as Padmanandi. The name Gṛdhrapiccha, erroneously used for him since about the fourteenth century, has led to confusion because it is also an alias for Umāsvāti.

A total of eighty-four works on various themes are ascribed to Kundakunda, of which fifteen are extant and three may be said to be philosophical master-pieces, all written in the Prakrit language. These are the *Pañcāstikāyasāra* (Essence of the Five Existents), the *Pravacanasāra* (Essence of the Scripture) and the *Samayasāra* (Essence of the Doctrine). The *Pañcāstikāyasāra* is an elementary work dealing with the Jaina substances (excluding time because it does not occupy any spatial points) and the fundamental truths, to which two additional categories are added,

namely the meritorious and demeritorious acts related to karma (*puṇya* and *pāpa*). The *Samayasāra* emphasizes, among other things, two standpoints mentioned in the canonical literature which seem to have no relation to the standard sevenfold standpoint (see MANIFOLDNESS, JAINA THEORY OF). These are the 'definitive' standpoint (*niścayanaya*), used synonymously with the 'pure' or 'transcendental' (*śuddha* or *paramārtha*) standpoint, and the 'mundane' standpoint (*vyavahārikanaya*). It is an illuminating work dealing with the nature of the soul and its contamination by matter, and whether the soul's intrinsic nature is in any way affected or changed through karma bondage in so far as it is the doer and enjoyer of activities. An attempt is made to reconcile these problems, solutions to which depend on the standpoint from which one approaches the issues. The *Pravacanasāra* is an insightful work whose three sections clearly delineate its scope: knowledge, the objects of knowledge, and conduct. The problem of substance, quality and mode, is one of the pivotal issues in Jaina philosophy and a few points are outlined below in order to show how Kundakunda deals with it. It forms the subject matter of the second section of the *Pravacanasāra*, which the tenth-century commentator Amṛtacandra says Kundakunda 'properly discusses'.

The problem is basically that of how change in the world may be explained given the permanent, eternal nature of the two basic substances of ultimate reality; this has obvious implications for the essential nature of the soul. Kundakunda begins the section with the statement: 'The object of knowledge is made up of substances, which are said to be characterized by qualities, and with which, moreover, are (associated) the modifications' (*Pravacanasāra* II, 1; trans. A.N. Upadhye). The basic problem is then evident when he says: 'There can be no origination without destruction, nor is there destruction without origination; origination and destruction are not possible in the absence of permanent substantiality' (II, 8). How 'origination' and 'destruction', which in fact refer to change, are to be understood is expressed by Kundakunda in typical Jaina language in II, 19: 'The substance forever retains its position, its own nature, as endowed with positive and negative conditions according as it is looked at from the substantial and the modificational viewpoints.' This is further elaborated:

All substances are nondifferent from the substantial viewpoint, but again they are different from the modificational view-point, because of the individual modification pervading it for the time being. According to some modification or the other it is stated that a substance exists, does not exist, is indescribable, is both or otherwise.

(II, 22–3)

What Kundakunda means by origination and destruction is distinctively Jainist and is clarified later in the same section: 'In this world, in which modifications originate and pass away at every moment, nothing is absolutely produced or destroyed; what is the production of one modification is the destruction of another; and thus origination and destruction are different' (II, 27). The change that occurs in matter is understandable on the analogy of objects and colour. Just as gold (regarded here as a substance), for example, can have not only different shades of colour (with colour being its basic quality) but also different forms (with the object made out of gold being its modification), so too all substances retain their substantiality despite the apparent destruction of their qualities and modes. The situation is more complicated with the soul substance. The problem is technical, and relates to two 'operations' (*upayogas*) ascribed to the soul, namely 'indeterminate intuition' and 'determinate knowledge'; these operations are described as two qualities (*guṇas*) of the soul. The concern is with the unity or identity of the soul and involves the question of whether the two *upayogas* operate in the soul simultaneously or in succession, and if in succession, which is first, and whether they maintain their distinctness in the state of omniscience. Kundakunda maintains that they operate successively at the mundane level and simultaneously at the transcendental level of omniscience. His view, which is also held by Umāsvāti, represents the attitude of the Digambara sect and is opposed, for example, by Siddhasena Divākara, who, in regarding quality and mode as synonyms, says that they are not separate operations in the state of omniscience. His view represents the general Śvetāmbara standpoint, based on the fact that the canonical literature distinguishes only substance and quality, without mentioning the standpoint connected with the modifications of a substance.

Umāsvāti. He is famous for the first Jaina work written in Sanskrit, called the *Tattvārthasūtra* or *Tattvārthādhigamasūtra* (Mnemonics on the Meaning of the Fundamental Principles). Again, biographical details are scanty and both the sects of Jainism claim him as one of their own (with the Digambaras also calling him Umāsvāmī) and regard his work, in traditional Indian manner, as authoritive for Jaina thought. His dates vary from the second to the fifth centuries AD, with recent preference for the fourth or fifth centuries. Of the five works ascribed to him, the *Praśamaratiprakaraṇa* (Treatise on the Love for

Tranquility) – a popular work dealing with ethical issues and addressed to ascetics and householders – and the *Tattvārthasūtra* are philosophically important. There is an ongoing debate about whether, as the Śvetāmbaras believe, a commentary on the *Tattvārthasūtra* was written by Umāsvāti himself, or whether, as the Digambaras believe, the first commentary on it is Pūjyapūda's fifth-century *Sarvārthasiddhi* (Attainment of the Meaning of Everything). There are two versions of the work by the two sects, with hardly any philosophically significant differences.

The *Tattvārthasūtra* contains a series of aphorisms, divided into ten chapters, which are understandable only with a commentary. The value of the work is evident from the fact that throughout the history of Jaina philosophy, every major thinker has written a commentary on it. Until around the tenth century, the Digambara thinkers, such as Akalaṅka (*c.* eighth century) and Vidyānandin (*c.* ninth century), took centre stage. They wrote in a difficult style and hardly any research related exclusively to their writings has been done.

Commentators often took the opportunity to criticize other views and defend the Jaina standpoint. For example, in his commentary on Umāsvāti's aphorism on the means of knowledge and the standpoints (*Tattvārthasūtra* I, 6), Vidyānandin enters into an interestingly detailed debate with the Buddhists (even quoting from Dharmakīrti's seventh-century work on the means of knowledge, *Pramāṇavārttika*) regarding the knowledge of an object, namely, whether an object is cognized as a whole or in parts. The issue is raised in the context of the Buddhist view that an object as a whole does not exist, against which it is asserted that a part of an object, which can be understood to be a whole in itself, cannot then be cognized, putting the Buddhist standpoint in jeopardy. Vidyānandin, applying the Jaina theory of standpoints, says that both a part of an object and the object as a whole are cognized from different standpoints.

Umāsvāti's contribution lies in presenting the basic issues in Jaina philosophy in a systematic form, so much so that his work usually forms the standard for Jaina thought as a whole. The ontology, metaphysics and epistemology summarized in §§1–2 are based on his *Tattvārthasūtra*.

Siddhasena Divākara. It seems certain that Siddhasena lived in the fifth century AD and that he wrote in Sanskrit and Prakrit. He is generally considered to have belonged to the Śvetāmbara sect, although he is claimed by both the sects of Jainism as one of their own, serving as the first Jaina logician for both. Apart from the canonical literature, there seems to be little influence from other sources in his writings, despite similarities of ideas between him and, for example, Kundakunda. Reference to Siddhasena's work on logic, the *Nyāyāvatāra*, has been made in §2. His second most important work on philosophy, written in Prakrit, is the *Sammaisutta* (Mnemonics on Proper Understanding; Sanskrit, *Sanmatisūtra*), dealing with the seven Jaina standpoints, knowledge and the objects of knowledge. It is in the last section that he clearly discusses the issue of the standpoints, taking into consideration the quality of a substance, which according to him is not sanctioned by Jaina scripture as a separate category.

Siddhasena is also credited with having written twenty-one short compositions, each consisting of thirty-two verses (and simply called the 'thirty-twos'), on a variety of themes, including eulogies to Mahāvīra, critiques of Buddhist and Hindu schools, and an exposition of Jaina concepts. The work on logic is also written in this form.

5   Other notable philosophers

A host of philosophers, some already referred to, have followed Kundakunda, Umāsvati and Siddhasena. Suffice it to make a few remarks on the contribution of five further thinkers, to cover the period until the seventeenth century. Haribhadra, perhaps of the eighth century, belongs to the Śvetāmbara sect and is praised as a great teacher of Jainism. Apart from works on classical yoga as a system of meditational practice, which he applies in the Jaina context, he is famous for his compendium of six systems, the *Saḍḍarśanasamuccaya*, in which he includes Jaina philosophy together with Buddhism and four Hindu systems. He evinces a trait common among Jaina thinkers and evident already in Akalaṅka, namely an excellent acquaintance with other systems of Indian thought so as to enter into authentic debate with them. Some scholars (notably Halbfass 1981) have seen a connection between this and the emergence of the theory of manifoldness which became the hallmark of Jainism.

There is a relative consensus about the dates of the polyhistor Hemacandra (1089–1172), whose contribution lies especially in systematizing and upholding the Śvetāmbara tradition of Jainism. Although his influence is stronger in the field of Jaina literature, insightful attacks on other philosophical views are also evident, for example, in his *Anyayoga-vyavacchedikā* (Critique of Other Schools). His treatise on yoga (*Yogaśāstra*), dealing with Jaina ethics, is still an exemplary work.

Abhayadeva, active in the eleventh century, needs to be mentioned for his commentaries on the Jaina canonical works. The value of the commentary literature in India lies not only in the explication and clarification of basic texts, but also in the fact that commentators often present views which they might not otherwise have found occasion to express. In his commentary on the *Sthānāṅgasūtra*, for example, a canonical text which is a compendium of Jaina doctrine, ethics and cosmology, Abhayadeva takes the opportunity to discuss epistemological issues.

Vādidevasūri (twelfth century) is not only famous as a Śvetāmbara thinker who defeated in a public debate the Digambara thinker Kumudacandra, but for his excellent *Syādvādaratnākara* (The Ocean of Manifoldness). This is a commentary on his own work on knowledge and standpoints, inspired by the work of the ninth-century Digambara thinker Māṇi-kyanandin.

Yaśovijaya (1624–88) is perhaps the last intellectual giant of Jainism, praised not only for his acumen as a logician, but also for his vast knowledge of Jainism and other traditions. This erudite Śvetāmbara scholar is credited with up to a hundred works, including an attack on the great logician of Navya-Nyāya, Raghunātha Śiromaṇi (early sixteenth century), and a commentary on a work by Vidyānandin.

Jaina philosophy never really took the centre of the philosophical stage in India, but that does not reduce its significance. Royal patronage from Mahāvīra's time till about the sixteenth century, especially in Gujarat and Karnataka, and the architectural masterpieces of its temples bear witness to the social impact it has had throughout its history. Jaina monasteries were and are centres of learning, and research undertaken since the early 1980s is gradually reaping the benefit of the Jaina virtue of collecting and copying manuscripts of all disciplines for the sake of acquiring religious merit. It is thanks to this that a Jaina scholar, Sukhlalji Sanghvi, was able to publish in 1940 an original eighth-century work on Indian materialism by one Jayarāśi, based on the only extant manuscript. Further, the European Indologist Erich Frauwallner, in a posthumously published work (Frauwallner 1984), convincingly proves the original atheistic beginnings of the Vaiśeṣika system on the basis of the information about it from Haribhadra. The Jaina libraries contain a wealth of information relevant not only to philosophy but also to various aspects of Indian studies which have yet to be researched. Unfortunately, studies in Jainism suffer from a lack of published texts, though an earnest attempt has been made in the West and by the various Jaina institutions in India to make available critical editions, translations and studies. Clearly this has important implications for the study of the history of Indian philosophy.

See also: MAHĀVĪRA

References and further reading

Bhatt, B. (1974) 'Vyavahāra-naya and Niścaya-naya in Kundakunda's Works', *Zeitschrift der Deutschen Morgenlandischen Gesellschaft*, supplementary vol. 2: 279–91. (Deals with the two standpoints mentioned in §4.)

Folkert, K.W. (1933) *Scripture and Community: Collected Essays on the Jains*, ed. J.E. Cort, Atlanta, GA: Scholars Press. (Deals not only with aspects of Jaina philosophy, but also Jaina scripture, monastic praxis, lay–monastic relations, rituals and community.)

* Frauwallner, E. (1984) *Nachgelassene Werke I. Aufsätze, Beiträge, Skizzen* (Posthumous Works I. Essays, Contributions and Outlines), ed. E. Steinkellner, Vienna: Verlag der österreichischen Akademie der Wissenschaften; trans. J. Soni, *Erich Frauwallner's Posthumous Essays*, New Delhi: Aditya Prakasan, 1994. (Frauwallner refers to the Jaina polyhistor Haribhadra to establish the original atheism of Vaiśeṣika philosophy.)

* Halbfass, W. (1981) *Indien und Europa. Perspektiven ihrer geistigen Begegnung*, Basle and Stuttgart: Schwabe & Co.; *India and Europe: An Essay in Philosophical Understanding*, Delhi: Motilal Banarsidass, 1990. (See the chapter on doxography for his view described in §5; the 1990 edition contains additional material.)

* Haribhadra (c. 8th century) *Saḍḍarśanasamuccaya* (Compendium of Six Systems), ed. M.K. Jain, Delhi: Bharatiya Jnanpith Publication, 1970, 3rd edn 1989; trans. K.S. Murphy, *A Compendium of Six Philosophies*, Tenali: Tagore Publishing House, 1957. (The Jain edition includes an explanatory translation of the text, and the commentaries of Guṇaratna and Somatilaka.)

* Hemacandra (1089–1172) *Anyayogavyavacchedikā* (Critique of Other Schools), Sanskrit with Hindi trans. by P. Sāhityācārya, Agas: Rājacandra Jaina Śāstramālā, 1970; trans. F.W. Thomas, in *The Flower-Spray of the Quodammodo Doctrine*, Delhi: Motilal Banarsidass, 1968. (This work was made famous in the thirteenth century through Mallisena's commentary on it, the *Syādvādamañjarī*, and is usually published with it.)

* —— (1089–1172) *Yogaśāstra*, trans. A.S. Gopani, *The Yoga Shastra of Hemchandracharya (A 12th Century Guide to Jain Yoga)*, Jaipur: Prakrit Bharti Academy, 1989. (Gopani's edition also includes the Sanskrit text.)

* Ingalls, D.H. (1951) *Materials for the Study of Navya-Nyāya Logic*, Harvard Oriental Series 40, Cambridge: Harvard University Press; repr. Delhi: Motilal Banarsidass, 1987. (One of the earliest serious attempts to present Indian logic in terms of Western logic.)

Jaini, P.S. (1979) *The Jaina Path of Purification*, Delhi: Motilal Banarsidass. (An authoritative work dealing with the nature of reality, the mechanism of bondage, the mendicant path and the attainment of the goal, among other matters.)

Jayarāśi (c. 9th century) *Tattvopaplavasiṃha* (The Lion that Destroys Philosophical Categories), ed. S. Sanghavi and R. Parikh, Gaekward Oriental Series 87, Baroda: University of Baroda, 1940; trans. E. Franco, *Perception, Knowledge and Disbelief: A Study of Jayarāśi's Scepticism*, Wiesbaden: Franz Steiner Verlag, 1987; 2nd edn, Delhi: Motilal Banarsidass, 1994. (The only extant text of the Indian materialist school called Cārvāka, known for its radical scepticism.)

* Kundakunda (2nd or 3rd century) *Pravacanasāra* (Essence of the Scripture), ed. and trans. A.N. Upadhye, Gujarat: Shrimad Rajachandra Ashrama, 1984. (The Prakrit text, critically edited with Sanskrit and Hindi commentaries, together with an English translation and a scholarly introduction on the linguistic and philosophical aspects of this and other works by Kundakunda.)

* —— (2nd or 3rd century) *Pañcāstikāyasāra* (Essence of the Five Existents), ed. A.N. Upadhye, *Pañcāstikāyasāra: The Building of the Cosmos*, Delhi: Bharatiya Jnanpith Publication, 1975. (Contains the Prakrit text, a Sanskrit translation by the tenth-century commentator Amṛtacandra, an English translation by A. Chakravartinayanar, and an introduction to Jaina philosophy.)

* —— (2nd or 3rd century) *Samayasāra* (Essence of the Doctrine), ed. Pannalāla Sāhityācārya, Varanasi: Śrī Gaṇeśaprasāda Varṇī Granthamālā, 1969. (Prakrit text with Hindi translation and commentary, with an introduction including Kundakunda's biography.)

Māṇikyanandin (9th century) *Parīkṣāmukham* (Gateway of Investigation), trans. and ed. S.C. Ghosal, *Parīkṣāmukham by Māṇikyanandī*, Lucknow: Ajitasram, 1940. (The text of this influential ninth-century Jaina thinker is translated into English, with comments; the introduction contains an excellent survey of Jaina epistemology.)

* Matilal, B.K. (1968) *The Navya-Nyāya Doctrine of Negation: The Semantics and Ontology of Negative Statements in Navya-Nyāya Philosophy*, Harvard

Oriental Series 46, Cambridge, MA: Harvard University Press. (Presents Indian logic in terms of Western logic.)

* —— (1971) *Epistemology, Logic and Grammar in Indian Philosophical Analysis*, The Hague: Mouton. (Presents Indian logic in Western terms, but not restricted to one school as in Matilal 1968.)

Ohira, S. (1982) *A Study of the Tattvārthasūtra with Bhaṣya. With Special Reference to Authorship and Date*, Ahmedabad: L.D. Institute of Indology. (Deals with the issues of date and authorship of Umāsvāti's pioneering work on Jaina philosophy, including the debate over the authorship of an auto-commentary.)

* Pūjyapāda (*c.* 5th century) *Sarvārthasiddhi* (Attainment of the Meaning of Everything), trans. S.A. Jain, *Reality*, Madras: Jwalamalini Trust, 1960, repr. 1992. (This is the first commentary, according to the Digambara sect, on Umāsvāti's *Tattvārthasūtra*, the standard work on Jaina philosophy.)

Settar, S. (1986) *Inviting Death: Historical Experiments on Sepulchral Hill*, Dharwad: Karnatak University. (Deals with the 'passionless death' mentioned in §3.)

—— (1990) *Pursuing Death: Philosophy and Practice of Voluntary Termination of Life*, Dharwad: Karnatak University. (Deals with the 'passionless death' mentioned in §3.)

* Siddhasena (5th century) *Nyāyāvatāra* (The Descent of Logic), trans. S.C. Vidyabhusan, in A.N. Upadhye (ed.) *Siddhasena's Nyāyāvatāra and Other Works*, Bombay: Jaina Sāhitya Vikāsa Maṇḍala. (A collection of works containing the text of the *Nyāyāvatāra*, with English translation and notes, the texts of two other works by Siddhasena, *Twenty-one Dvātriṃśikās* and the *Sammaisuttam* (Mnemonics on Proper Understanding), an informative introduction and a bibliographic survey.)

Sikdar, J.C. (1991) *Theory of Reality in Jaina Philosophy*, Varanasi: P.V. Research Institute. (Deals with Jaina ontology on the basis of original texts, comparing the Jaina view with other schools of Indian thought.)

Singh, R.J. (1974) *The Jaina Concept of Omniscience*, Ahmedabad: L.D. Institute of Indology. (Examines the traditional arguments for and against omniscience.)

Soni, J. (1991) '*Dravya, Guṇa* and *Paryāya* in Jaina Thought', *Journal of Indian Philosophy* 19: 75–81. (Places in philosophical context the issue of substance, quality and mode in Jainism; a more detailed discussion of the question of change and permanence according to Kundakunda described in §4.)

—— (1996a) *Aspects of Jaina Philosophy*, Madras: Research Foundation for Jainology, for University of Madras Department of Jainism. (Deals with karma theory and Jaina ethics, the Jaina theory of manifoldness and Vidyānandin's commentary on *Tattvarthasūtra* I, 6, on the means of knowledge.)

—— (1996b) *The Notion of Āpta in Jaina Philosophy*, Toronto, Ont.: University of Toronto, Centre for South Asia Studies. (Discusses the Jaina view that a trustworthy person (*āpta*) is a source of knowledge and compares the Jaina view of reality with that of the Śaiva Siddhānta tradition.)

—— (forthcoming) 'Aspects of Jaina Epistemology with Special Reference to Vidyānandin', paper presented at conference 'Approaches to Jain Studies', Toronto March 31–April 2 1995, to be published in conference volume. (Deals especially with Vidyānandin's debate with the Buddhists – in which he even quotes Dharmakīrti – over the issue of parts and wholes, or universals and particulars, as mentioned in §3.)

* Staal, J.F. (1960) 'Correlations Between Language and Logic in Indian Thought', *Bulletin of the School of African and Oriental Studies* 23: 109–22. (Presents Indian logic in terms of Western logic, as do some of Staal's subsequent articles.)

Suklalji, P. (1974) *Tattvārthasūtra of Vācaka Umāsvāti*, trans. K.K. Dixit, Ahmedabad: L.D. Institute of Indology. (A modern commentary by a renowned authority on Jaina philosophy, with an introduction about the original author and commentaries on the work.)

Tatia, N. (1951) *Studies in Jaina Philosophy*, Varanasi: P.V. Research Institute. (A systematic interpretation of Jaina philosophy based on a critique of other schools.)

* Umāsvāti (*c.* 2nd century) *Tattvārthādhigamasūtra* (Mnemonics on the Meaning of the Fundamental Principles), trans. and ed. J.L. Jaini, Sacred Books of the Jainas 2, Arrah: The Central Jaina Publishing House, 1920; repr. New Delhi: Today and Tomorrow's Printers and Publishers, 1990; trans. N. Tatia, *Tattvārtha Sūtra: That Which Is*, London: HarperCollins, 1994. (The first work in Sanskrit which summarizes the whole of Jaina philosophy in traditional, classical style. Jaini's edition supplies the differences between the Digambara and Śvetāmbara versions of the text. Tatia's translation takes into consideration the commentaries of Umāsvāti, Pūjyapāda and Sīddhasenagaṇi.)

* —— (*c.* 2nd century) *Praśamaratiprakaraṇa* (Treatise on the Love for Tranquility), trans. and ed. Y.S. Shastri, Ahmedabad: L.D. Institute of Indology, 1989. (A popular and simple work presenting the basics of Jaina thought.)

* Vādidevasūri (12th century) *Syādvādaratnākara* (The

Ocean of Manifoldness), Delhi: Bhāratīya Book Corporation, 1988. (Sanskrit text. An influential Śvetāmbara thinker deals with various aspects of Jaina philosophy.)

Yaśovijaya (17th century) *Jaina Tarka Bhāṣā* (The Language of Jaina Logic), trans. and ed. D. Bhargava, *Mahopādhyāya Yaśovijaya's Jaina Tarka Bhāṣā*, Delhi: Motilal Banarsidass, 1973. (A critical edition of a popular treatise on Jaina epistemology serving also as a manual of Jaina logic.)

Zydenbos, R.J. (1983) *Mokṣa in Jainism According to Umāsvāti*, Wiesbaden: Franz Steiner Verlag. (Deals with liberation, the subject of chapter 10 of Umāsvāti's *Tattvārthasūtra*; includes text and translation, a commentary attributed to Umāsvāti and an introduction to the problem.)

JAYANDRA SONI

JAMES OF VITERBO
(*c.*1255–1308)

James of Viterbo's writings reveal a loyalty to Augustine combined with an interest in Neoplatonic sources such as Proclus, Pseudo-Dionysius and Boethius. He also reveals a strong interest in the Greek commentators on Aristotle, in Simplicius as regards predication and language and in Themistius and John Philoponus as regards the nature of the intellect and intellectual cognition. Frequently, after presenting various positions on a topic and noting how they differ, he proposes to state what seems probable to him. He thus proposes, for example, a theory of innatism. In contrast, he shows no little certitude in his De regimine christiano *(On Christian Rule), where he presents a markedly papalist political theory.*

James entered the Order of the Hermits of Saint Augustine around 1272, and studied at Paris from 1275 to 1282 and again after 1285. He later succeeded to the chair of his teacher, GILES OF ROME, which he held until 1300. He then taught at the Augustinian *studium generale* in Naples until 1302. He ended his career involved in active ministry as the Archbishop of Naples.

The major source for our knowledge of James' philosophical views is his *Disputationes de quolibet* (Quodlibetal Disputations), written some time between 1293 and 1297 at Paris. James accepts Augustine's concept of seminal reasons present in matter. He takes them to be the beginning (*inchoatio*) of or aptitude (*aptitudo*) for the form that will actually exist when something is generated. Nonetheless,

James emphasizes that the human soul, unlike other forms, comes to exist through its direct creation by God. He does not consider Aristotle's position on the origin of soul, that is, whether or not it comes from outside the fetus, to be evident (see SOUL, NATURE AND IMMORTALITY OF THE).

When James analyzes the nature of the agent intellect, he adopts a theory of innate knowledge that resembles his theory of seminal reasons. He sets forth the positions presented by PHILOPONUS and THEMISTIUS, as well as views taken from AUGUSTINE, BOETHIUS and his own contemporaries. Although James accuses ancient and recent interpreters of Aristotle of attempting to shape his words to suit their own positions, he then does the same. He proposes that when God creates the soul he endows the human intellect, which is itself a general aptitude, with special aptitudes or fitnesses (*idoneitates*) that are only incomplete actualities. These are the potential contents of the cognitive acts of our intellect. Sense experience simply excites the human intellect, which then moves itself to actual knowledge. James sets forth a similar theory regarding special aptitudes in the human will, which is itself a general aptitude, in order to explain individual acts of volition and to maintain that the will, too, is fundamentally active in nature and not passive to anything external.

Some of James' metaphysical views merit attention. In his early *Quaestiones de divinis praedicamentis* (Questions on Divine Categories), he discusses problems concerning language and predication regarding the Trinity, referring constantly to Simplicius' commentary on Aristotle's *Categories* (see SIMPLICIUS). James opts for his own version of analogical language. In his *Disputationes de quolibet*, after analyzing the differing views of Giles of Rome, HENRY OF GHENT and GODFREY OF FONTAINES on essence and existence, he proposes to put forth what appears probable to him. Basically, essence and existence are related as the abstract to the concrete. Although they are identical as regards the principal thing that they signify, namely the essence, they differ by a real composition, since existence signifies secondarily and concretely all the things that are joined to the essence and that essence needs in order to exist (see EXISTENCE). In like fashion, James pursues a question which also much interested Henry and Godfrey as well as John DUNS SCOTUS, namely whether all beings comprise an essential order which must come to a stop (*status*). James appears to favor the view that the series stops with a highest creature.

James occasionally alludes to a widely adopted scheme of metaphysical hierarchy. Many of his contemporaries held that both God and matter (or non-being) serve as measures of all the grades within the order of things according as things approach to or recede from them. James appears to concentrate almost exclusively on God as the measure. None the less, the concept of metaphysical hierarchy enables him to account for the destiny of human beings. In order to communicate and represent divine goodness, God established different grades among created things. The human being is the one creature that is composed of both the spiritual and the bodily and that thereby serves, as it were, as the medium and bond (*medium et vinculum*) of both. The human soul perfects the body rather than being perfected by the body. Indeed, the end of the soul is not the perfection of the body but union with something better than either the body or the soul, namely God.

See also: ARISTOTELIANISM, MEDIEVAL; AUGUSTINIANISM; HENRY OF GHENT; LANGUAGE, MEDIEVAL THEORIES OF; NEOPLATONISM

List of works

James of Viterbo (c.1255–1308) *Disputationes de quolibet* (Quodlibetal Disputations), ed. E. Ypma, Cassiciacum, Supplementband I–IV, Würzburg: Augustinus-Verlag, 1968–75, 4 vols. (The major source for James' views.)

—— (c.1255–1308) *Prima quaestio disputata de verbo* (First Disputed Question on the Word), in C. Scanzillo, 'La prima quaestio disputata "De verbo" del Codice A. 971 della Biblioteca dell'Archiginnasio di Bologna', *Asprenas* new series 19, 1972, 25–61. (Disputed question on language.)

—— (c.1255–1308) *Quaestiones de divinis praedicamentis* (Questions on Divine Categories), q. I–X and XI–XVII ed. E. Ypma, *Corpus Scriptorum Augustinianorum*, Vol. V, Parts 1–2, Rome: Augustinianum, 1983, 1986. (Ypma has continued to publish the remaining questions in *Augustiniana*: q. XVIII, *Augustiniana* 38, 1988, 67–98; q. XIX, *Augustiniana* 39, 1989, 154–85; q. XX, *Augustiniana* 42, 1992, 351–78; q. XXI, *Augustiniana* 44, 1994, 177–208; q. XXII, *Augustiniana* 45, 1995, 299–318; q. XXIII, *Augustiniana* 46, 1996, 147–76; q. XXIV, *Augustiniana* 46, 1996, 339–69. There are thirty-two questions in the work.)

—— (c.1255–1308) *De regimine christiano* (On Christian Rule) in H.-X. Arquillière, *Le plus ancien traité de l'Église: Jacques de Viterbe 'De regimine christiano' (1301–1302). Étude des sources et édition critique*, Paris: Gabriel Beauchesne, 1926; ed. and trans. R.W. Dyson, *On Christian Government: De Regimine Christiano*, Woodbridge: The Boydell Press, 1995. (James' work on political philosophy.)

References and further reading

Casado, F. (1951–3) 'El pensiamento filosófico del Beato Santiago de Viterbo' (The Philosophy of the Blessed St James of Viterbo), *La Ciudad de Dios* 163, 437–54; 164, 301–31; 165, 103–44, 283–302, 489–500. (Informative general overview.)

Mahoney, E.P. (1973) 'Themistius and the the Agent Intellect in James of Viterbo and Other Thirteenth Century Philosophers (Saint Thomas, Siger of Brabant and Henry Bate)', *Augustiniana* XXIII: 422–67. (Discusses James's use of Greek commentators on Aristotle, Themistius, Simplicius and Philoponus, and also his innatism.)

—— (1980) 'Metaphysical Foundations of the Hierarchy of Being according to Some Late Medieval and Renaissance Philosophers', in P. Morewedge (ed.) *Philosophies of Existence: Ancient and Medieval*, New York: Fordham University Press, 165–257. (Conceptual scheme for the Great Chain of Being.)

—— (1995) 'Duns Scotus and Medieval Discussions of Metaphysical Hierarchy: The Background of Scotus's "Essential Order" in Henry of Ghent, Godfrey of Fontaines and James of Viterbo', *Via Scoti: Methodologica ad mentem Joannis Duns Scoti, Atti Congresso Scotistico Internazionale Roma 9-11 marzo 1993*, vol. 1, ed. L. Sileo, Rome: PAA–Edizioni Antonianum, 359–74. (Evidence that others besides Scotus worried about the notion of an "essential order" and whether it must come to a stop.)

Phelps, M. (1980) 'The Theory of Seminal Reasons in James of Viterbo', *Augustiniana* 30: 271–83. (Clear statement of his theory together with medieval criticisms.)

Ruello, F. (1974–5) 'Les fondements de la liberté humaine selon Jacques de Viterbe O.E.S.A. Disputatio 1ᵃ de Quolibet, q. VII (1293)' (The Foundations of Human Freedom According to James of Viterbo), *Augustiniana* 24, 283–347; 25, 114–42. (Close detailed analysis.)

Wippel, J.F. (1982) 'The Relationship between Essence and Existence in Late Thirteenth-Century Thought: Giles of Rome, Henry of Ghent, Godfrey of Fontaines, and James of Viterbo', in P. Morewedge (ed.) *Philosophies of Existence: Ancient and Medieval*, New York: Fordham University Press, 131–64. (Shows importance of James's theory in context of contemporary discussions.)

Ypma, E. (1974) 'Recherches sur la carrière scolaire et la bibliothèque de Jacques de Viterbe 1308' (The Scholarly Career and Library of James of Viterbo), *Augustiniana* 30: 247–82. (Fundamental examination of problem of dating and sources.)

—— (1975) 'Recherches sur la productivité littéraire de Jacques de Viterbe jusqu'à 1300' (The Literary Productivity of James of Viterbo Before 1300), *Augustiniana* 25: 223–82. (Further on dating.)

EDWARD P. MAHONEY

JAMES, WILLIAM (1842–1910)

The American William James was motivated to philosophize by a desire to provide a philosophical ground for moral action. Moral effort presupposes that one has free will, that the world is not already the best of all possible worlds, and, for maximum effort, according to James, the belief that there is a God who is also on the side of good.

In his famous, often misunderstood paper 'The Will to Believe', James defended one's right to believe in advance of the evidence when one's belief has momentous consequences for one's conduct and success, and a decision cannot be postponed. One such belief is the belief in objective values. Generally, a belief is objective if it meets a standard independent of the believer's own thought. In morals, objective values emerge from each person's subjective valuings, whatever their psychological source, when these valuings become the values of a community of persons who care for one another. Still, even in such a community there will be conflicting claims, and the obligations generated by these claims will need to be ranked and conflicts resolved. James' solution is to say that the more inclusive claim – the claim that can be satisfied with the lesser cost of unsatisfied claims – is to be ranked higher. This is not to be mistaken for utilitarianism: James is not a hedonist, and it is not clear what he means by the most inclusive claim.

A concern for others makes sense only if there are others who inhabit with us a common world. Pragmatism, which he co-founded with C.S. Peirce, and radical empiricism provide James' answer to those who would be sceptics concerning the existence of the common-sense world. Pragmatism is both a theory of meaning and a theory of truth. As a theory of meaning it aims at clarity; our thoughts of an object are clear when we know what effects it will have and what reactions we are to prepare. As a theory of truth, pragmatism makes clear what is meant by 'agreement' in the common formula that a belief is true if it agrees with reality. Only in the simplest cases can we verify a belief directly – for example, we can verify that the soup is too salty by tasting it – and a belief is indirectly verified if one acts on it and that action does not lead to unanticipated consequences. Contrary to a widespread misunderstanding, this does not mean that James defines truth as that which is useful; rather, he points out that it is, in fact, useful to believe what is true.

James rejects the dualism of common sense and of many philosophers, but he is neither a materialist nor an idealist, rather what he calls a 'pure experience' (for example, your seeing this page) can be taken as an event in your (mental) history or as an event in the page's (physical) history. But there is no 'substance' called 'pure experience': there are only many different pure experiences. You and I can experience the same page, because an event in your mental history and an event in mine can be taken to be events in the same physical history of the page; James may even have been tempted to say that a pure experience can be taken to belong to more than one mental history.

According to James, pragmatism mediates the so-called conflict between science and religion. James took religious experiences very seriously both from a psychologist's perspective and as evidence for the reality of the divine.

1   Life
2   Psychology
3   Moral philosophy
4   Religion
5   Pragmatism
6   Radical empiricism

1   Life

William James, brother of the novelist Henry James, Jr, was the oldest child of Henry James, Sr, a man of independent means, who in early manhood experienced a major psychological crisis. Under the influence of the writings of the eighteenth-century Swedish mystic Emanuel Swedenborg, Henry Sr came to see redemption in self-surrender, allowing an inflowing of divine love that led to a concern with social justice, an interest in Fourierist socialism, and a large number of writings and public lectures. William experienced a similar crisis in 1870, but for him the return to normality was stimulated by reading the French philosopher Charles RENOUVIER; it consisted not in self-surrender but in affirming his belief in free will and in the resolve to acquire intellectual habits that would lead to daring acts of thought. However, James shared his father's concern for social justice. The effects of this experience are to be seen in many of James' writings, from the long discussion of the will and the emphasis on habit in *The Principles of Psychology* (1890), and the often misunderstood essay 'The Will to Believe', to his widely read *The Varieties of Religious Experience* (1902) and *A Pluralistic Universe* (1909).

After an unorthodox but rich education at home and in Europe, William found it difficult to decide on a career. Eventually he earned an MD, but never practised. In 1873 he taught a course in physiology at Harvard, where he was to continue to teach until his retirement in 1907. In 1875, James set up the first psychological laboratory in America and taught his first seminar in psychology; in 1878 he married and, in the same year, published his first articles in philosophy. James taught both psychology and philosophy, advancing to a full professorship, and in 1890 published the monumental, justly renowned two-volume *Principles of Psychology*; in abridged form, it became a widely used text.

From 1879 on James presented single lectures before a variety of audiences, some of which were published in 1897 in *The Will to Believe, and Other Essays in Popular Philosophy*. In its preface, James announces that he regards all claims concerning matters of fact as hypotheses subject to revision in the light of subsequent experience, and extends this empirical attitude to metaphysical hypotheses. *Talks to Teachers on Psychology and to Students on Some of Life's Ideals* appeared two years later. He concludes the preface to that volume, after condemning American imperialism, 'Religiously and philosophically, our ancient national doctrine of live and let live may prove to have a far deeper meaning than our people now seem to imagine it to possess'.

James retired in January 1907 having just given the Lowell lectures. These were published under the title *Pragmatism: A New Name for Some Old Ways of Thinking* and brought together virtually all of James' philosophical concerns. While the term 'pragmatism' was first introduced by James' friend C.S. Peirce in 1878 and reintroduced by James in a lecture given at Berkeley in 1898, after which it became widely used, it is fair to say that in *Pragmatism* this philosophy receives its full elaboration, at any rate as it is understood and embraced by James (see §5 below). The central idea is James' account of truth; its acceptance, James thought, would bring about a revolution in epistemology. Instead it met with misunderstanding and opposition to which James responded in 1909 in *The Meaning of Truth: A Sequel to 'Pragmatism'*, a collection of articles, the first of which was written as early as 1884 but several of which were composed specifically for that volume.

William James died on the 26 August 1910. There were several posthumous publications, in particular *Essays in Radical Empiricism* (1912) which contains James' most technical philosophy (see §7 below). While James claims in the preface to *Pragmatism* that the doctrine of radical empiricism is logically independent of that of pragmatism, John J. McDermott is surely correct when he claims that one will misunderstand James' views in the works published in his lifetime unless one takes his radical empiricism into account (introduction to *Essays in Radical Empiricism*).

2 Psychology

Although he taught both subjects, James is one of those to be credited with the separation of psychology from philosophy. In the preface to *The Principles of Psychology* (1890), James attempts to distinguish sharply between metaphysics and psychology. 'I have kept to the point of view of natural science throughout the book. Every natural science accepts certain data uncritically.... Psychology, the science of finite individual minds, assumes as its data (1) *thoughts and feelings*, and (2) *a physical world* in time and space with which they coexist and which (3) *they know*. Of course, these data are themselves discussible; but the discussion of them (as of other elements) is called metaphysics and falls outside the province of this book' (1890: v–vi). Yet James cannot avoid metaphysics entirely and admits as much. Psychology, he holds, accepts the mind–body dualism of common sense but rejects the metaphysical dogma that there can be no mind–body interaction. For if mind and body are radically different, the biological evolution of mind can be explained only on the hypothesis that there have been 'mental atoms' as well as physical ones at the origin of the universe, and that the former must be able to form complex aggregates just as physical atoms do. But in *The Principles of Psychology*, James denies precisely this: 'We cannot mix feelings as such, though we may mix the objects we feel, and from *their* mixture get new feelings' (1890: 157). Moreover, feelings, sensations and thoughts cannot combine themselves; they form new wholes only from the perspective of an outside observer. Confusing one's own standpoint with that of the mental fact observed is, for James, the 'Psychologist's Fallacy' (1890: 196). Of course, James does not deny the existence of 'higher' states of mind, say, understanding a five-word sentence, but what he asserts is that understanding the sentence is a mental fact other than, and in addition to, the five facts of understanding each word separately. But on this James was to change his mind. In his presidential address to the American Psychological Association in December 1894, 'The Knowing of Things Together', he concludes that mental contents can be complex, that we can speak of the parts of a field of consciousness, though such parts are not separable. In the same lecture he also rejects the dualism that had been a working assumption of *The Principles of Psychology* (see §6 below). Always, however, the mind is not a mere knower: we know in order to act.

Two chapters of *The Principles of Psychology* are of particular philosophical interest, namely, 'The Stream of Thought' (later called 'stream of consciousness') and 'The Consciousness of Self'. In the former, James offers five facts. (1) Every thought (taking thought to include feelings and sensations) appears to belong to some self. (2) No state of mind can recur in exactly the same way. Although we may experience the same object again, the sensation will be different the second time, for the condition of the brain will have been modified by the earlier sensation. (3) Introspection shows that consciousness does not jump from one discrete content to the next, but changes in a continuous manner. Even after interruptions, such as in sleep, we are aware of being the same person, and no sudden change in sensation comes as a total break; it is only a more rapid change. Another element in the continuity of consciousness is what James called 'fringe'. The fringe is what leads one's mind from thought to thought, rejecting this one and accepting another until one reaches a conclusion. Later James identified the 'fringe' with the subconscious, and that was to play an important role in his explanation of religious experience (see §4 below). (4) We take it that our thoughts refer to independently existing objects because many thoughts (both of one person and of different persons) appear to have the same object. (5) We pay selective attention to some parts of the field of consciousness, and over the millennia we and our ancestors have in this manner 'extracted' the everyday world out of 'the primordial chaos of sensations' (1890: 277) (see §5 below).

While we agree to a remarkable degree in what we find interesting, our own selves are for each of us of unique importance. James distinguishes several senses of self. The material self consists of one's body and at least some of one's material possessions. The social self, or rather the social selves, are the various personalities one presents to various others; these, to a large extent, dictate one's behaviour. One's spiritual self is not the whole of one's inner life but that portion of which we say that it *has* the thoughts, feelings, etc. that make up our stream of consciousness. Although James calls this self 'spiritual', he does not identify it with a continuous soul substance. Introspection reveals only a stream of thoughts, of which the present one is the judgment that I am the same self I was yesterday, a judgment based on resemblance of present bodily feelings to past ones and on the continuity of this thought with its predecessors. The present thought appropriates (selectively!) past thoughts of the stream; it is the 'thinker'.

It is pointless to appeal to a Kantian pure ego or a Cartesian soul, for no one has explained how such an entity would hold the stream of thought together (see KANT, I. §6; DESCARTES, R.).

3 Moral philosophy

James' writings in moral philosophy, though sparse, provide the best entrance into his thinking. These writings fall into two categories: those that address directly some relatively concrete problem and those of a more systematic nature. The former range from letters to newspapers protesting against America's policy in the Philippines, to essays like 'The Moral Equivalent of War', suggesting a struggle against nature as a substitute for the senseless struggle of nations against nations, and 'The Social Value of the College-Bred', seeking to allay the ennui of young women who saw no use for the education they had acquired. 'What Makes a Life Significant' and 'On a Certain Blindness of Human Beings' are essays that speak to a precondition of the moral life – the ability to appreciate what another's life is like, what makes it worth living or intolerable – and form a bridge to the ethical theory found in the essay 'The Moral Philosopher and the Moral Life' (1891) and in various passages in *The Principles of Psychology*.

Leading a moral life requires, according to James, a purpose that gives the life significance, will, courage and determination, a belief in objective values and a belief in free will; here I shall concentrate on the last two items. In 'The Moral Philosopher and the Moral Life', James distinguished three questions: (1) where do our moral ideas come from? (2) To what do they refer? (3) How do we weigh various goods and evils, various obligations against one another?

Our valuings have multiple psychological sources: some can be traced back to bodily pains and pleasures, others are the result of habituation or indoctrination, while still others are due to an inborn higher moral sensibility that varies somewhat from person to person. Examples of the last are the demand that like cases be treated alike and the abhorrence with which we respond to the thought of sacrificing an innocent child for the happiness of many. These subjective valuings become objective, that is, coercive, whenever there are creatures who care about one another or acknowledge the claims they make upon each other. Our sympathetic instincts are not only the source of our higher moral sensibilities, but the basis of objectivity in ethics. Conflicts of claim are, however, unavoidable; how are they to be resolved?

Moral agents encounter conflicts of serious claims in moments of crisis. In *The Principles of Psychology*,

James emphasizes the loneliness of such moments and also their momentous nature. What one chooses in such a moment is not so much what one is to do as what sort of person one is to become, and what guides one here is the inner voice of one's higher moral sensibilities. That voice, according to 'The Moral Philosopher and the Moral Life', will tell us to 'seek incessantly, with fear and trembling, so to vote and to act as to bring about the very largest total universe of good which we can see' (1897: 209). Analogously, moral philosophers are to fashion out of the values they find in the world the most inclusive coherent system. And to this task they are to bring no value of their own (this is how the philosopher differs from the ordinary moral agent) other than these 'logical' values of coherence and inclusiveness. But this, surely, is an impossible task. Since there is no common unit to which all goods can be reduced and yet all goods cannot be jointly realized, moral philosophers must appeal to their own moral sensibilities in weighing one ideal against another. The impossible task seemingly given to moral philosophers is perhaps an ironic description of what other philosophers have attempted, rather than a task for us, or James, to accomplish. Ethics, like physics, is for James an empirical science. It rests on claims actually made, and what the most inclusive realizable good will be depends both on that and on the nature of the universe; finally, since we are fallible, we must be prepared at all times to revise our judgments in response to complaints from those whose demands have gone unmet. When James demands that we pursue ideals that can be realized at least cost to other ideals, he does not simply say that in our own lives we must be prepared to sacrifice lesser goods for greater ones, nor that a minimal sympathy and a minimal sense of justice suggest that we are at times to sacrifice our own lesser goods to the greater goods of a larger community. He articulates here his commitment to democracy and liberalism, to tolerance of anything other than intolerance, and his struggle against that blindness in human beings mentioned above.

The moral life consists not only of moments of crisis; for the most part, guided by our aspirations that give it significance, it runs along in quite habitual ways. James provides a series of maxims on how to acquire and keep good habits, for good habits are what make up a moral character. There is nothing so repulsive, he thought, as a sentimental character who never acts forthrightly.

All the above assumes that we can and do choose among alternatives that make a real difference to the world. As a psychologist, James simply records that deliberation usually comes to an end when one has only one idea of one action before one's mind; action follows. But when one's moral impulses conflict with more habitual or instinctive ones, countervailing reasons and motives tend to be still before the mind; one has a sense of effort and we speak of moral victories. What has been said so far is compatible both with the hypothesis of free will and its denial. Indeed, neither logic nor empirical evidence can decide the question, and since for James it seem to have momentous consequences, he opts for free will, for a universe of alternative possible futures. James rejects both a facile optimism that believes nothing in the world needs fixing and a pessimistic resignation that believes nothing can be fixed. Indeed only in an open world are there objectively good and bad actions, and only someone believing in such a world will be able to lead the strenuous moral life. Additional moral energy, James holds, flows from the belief that the help of a God makes the victory of good over evil possible.

4 Religion

The question of the nature of God and of His existence occupied James' thought throughout his life. Although he was not a conventional Christian and quite anticlerical, he was a deeply religious person. In *The Varieties of Religious Experience*, he wrote with regret regarding mystical states, 'my own constitution shuts me out from their enjoyment almost entirely' (1902: 299). Yet twice in his life he suffered the sense of utter worthlessness and despair, indeed panic-fear, that often precedes a religious experience.

James took seriously the question whether, or to what extent, religious experiences provide evidence for the existence of the divine. In reply to positivistic scientists who claim a priori that religious experience is non-veridical and impugn it by pointing to its organic bases, he notes that all experience has an organic basis, and maintains that a religious experience's 'spiritual value' depends on its 'immediate luminousness', on how it fits into the rest of our beliefs and on its 'moral helpfulness' (1902: 33). All our conceptual systems are fashioned by us to deal with experience from the perspective of some interest or sets of interests; we have no reason to think that only one of them agrees with reality. In particular, both science and religion (better: particular sciences as well as particular religious beliefs and practices) are 'genuine keys to unlocking the treasure-house of the universe to him who can use either of them practically', and the use of one does not exclude that of the other (1902: 110).

After a rich and detailed survey of religious personalities and religious experiences, James then turns to the questions of spiritual value and practical moral consequences.

> What I then propose to do is, briefly stated, to test saintliness by common sense, to use human standards to help us decide how far the religious life commends itself as an ideal kind of human activity. If it commends itself, then any theological beliefs that may inspire it, in so far forth will stand accredited. If not, then they will be discredited, and all without reference to anything but human working principles.
>
> (1902: 264)

James' conclusion is well modulated. In a world in which not everyone is a saint, saintly turning of the other cheek will lead to the victory of evil. Yet both the faith of saints in a kingdom of heaven already here and the utopias of socialists and anarchists 'help to break the edge of the general reign of hardness and are slow leavens of a better order' (1902: 285).

There remains the question whether the religious person's sense of a divine presence is objectively true. Because mystical experiences are intensely private and vary from person to person, and because the arguments of philosophers and theologians are unconvincing, James concludes that any attempt to demonstrate the existence of a deity is hopeless. Philosophy can distinguish, however, between a common religious core and the various 'over-beliefs' found both in institutionalized creeds and in the faith of individuals. The core is objectively true and consists in an awareness that one's conscious self is part of a wider self. That wider self is understood as the source of one's higher moral ideals and of one's religious experiences, but may be merely one's subconscious. However, James' own over-beliefs include a belief in a God who is not only the source of our highest ideals but can produce real changes in us. He makes the victory of good over evil possible but (here James differs from most religious persons) not certain. This over-belief is a hypothesis and entails predictions – in a world with such a God, miracles will happen, and a different conduct is required than would be in a godless world; for, James speculates, it may well be that our efforts aid God in His tasks as He aids us in ours. Finally, James notes, religious experience requires neither that the deity be infinite nor that there be only one.

5 Pragmatism

James' major contributions to philosophy are pragmatism and radical empiricism. Pragmatism for James consists in both a theory of meaning, which he ascribes rightly to C.S. PEIRCE, and a theory of truth, which he ascribes too generously to John DEWEY and F.S.C. SCHILLER (see TRUTH, PRAGMATIC THEORIES OF §2).

James gives in one paragraph two formulations of the Pragmatic Maxim: '... to develop a thought's meaning, we need only determine what conduct it is fitted to produce: that conduct is for us its sole significance'. And, virtually quoting Peirce,

> To attain perfect clearness in our thoughts of an object, then, we need only consider what conceivable effects of a practical kind the object may involve – what sensations we are to expect from it, and what reactions we must prepare. Our conception of these effects, whether immediate or remote, is then for us the whole of our conception of the object, so far as that conception has positive significance at all.
>
> (1907: 26)

This maxim must not be confused with the verifiability criterion of meaning of the logical positivists (see MEANING AND VERIFICATION). Neither Peirce nor James used the maxim to reject metaphysics, although, as noted in §2, James used it to point out that the metaphysical hypothesis of a substantial soul merely reasserts, but fails to explain, one's sense of being a continuous self. Again, unlike the logical positivists, James includes among sensations all kinds of feelings and emotional reactions; 'experience' would have been a less misleading choice of word. Thus, as mentioned in §4, religious hypotheses have meaning for James: believing them makes a difference to one's moral energy, and some religious experiences are, for those who have them, overwhelmingly evidential. Finally, unlike the logical positivists, James, as discussed in §3, takes it that value judgments, in particular moral judgments, are true or false, not mere expressions of the speaker's state of mind, nor mere attempts to sway an audience (see EMOTIVISM; PRESCRIPTIVISM).

As a form of empiricism, pragmatism emphasizes the fallibility of all knowledge claims, but unlike other empiricisms it does not conceive of the mind as a passive receptacle. Rather, guided by our interests and the concepts we already have, we pay selective attention to our sensory inputs. Since human beings have, through evolution and through upbringing, to a very large extent identical interests, we have come to share a conceptual framework, the framework of common sense. Our common conceptual scheme makes our common lives possible, though we tend to notice our disagreements rather than the larger-scale agreements in which they are embedded. But we could not even disagree, nor would our disagreements matter, if we did not live in a common world, if any one person's beliefs and actions did not have practical consequences for others.

We move, with greater or lesser ease, between conceptual systems: in addition to those of common sense and of religion, there are multiple scientific frameworks. These ways of ordering experiences were developed in response to pressing interests and are modified or rejected if they fail to be useful. Seen in this light, scientific theories are not transcriptions of reality but rather 'instruments' that summarize old facts and lead us to new ones. They are true in so far as the new facts we are led to expect do in fact materialize, or, as James would prefer to say, they *become* true in so far as they become verified. Does he really mean that there are no unverified truths? According to James' student and biographer, Ralph Barton Perry, while he often defends the existence of an unexperienced reality, he fails to explain what this existence consists in (Perry 1935: 591–2).

James points out that all our knowledge of the world is a product of the world and the human mind. Most of us take the basic concepts of common sense to correspond to reality, while physicists and some philosophers say this rather of the concepts of relativistic quantum physics. But these and any other conceptual frameworks are all equally human contributions to our knowledge. There is no reason to think that one of these will emerge as ultimately triumphant, nor that all of them will prevail as our knowledge grows. Some philosophers find this idea, the idea that the trail of the human serpent is over every knowledge claim, distressing, as if we 'made up' the world. But we only make up the concepts, and whether our beliefs using these concepts are true depends on the world.

Pragmatists accept the traditional view that truth is an agreement between our beliefs or propositions and reality but try to clarify the notion of agreement by asking how agreement is verified. I can see (verify directly) that there is a clock on the wall. But my belief that it tells the time correctly is taken 'on credit'; it will be verified if I act on it and that action does not lead to surprises, for example, a missed appointment. The vast majority of our beliefs are verified even more indirectly. Yet truth is tremendously important. Our existence in the world is precarious; true beliefs lead us to avoid dangers and take advantage of opportunities, while false beliefs may prove fatal. Thus true beliefs are useful and good to believe, but that does not mean that any belief that proves temporarily useful or makes us feel good is true. Not only must any one of our beliefs harmonize with the whole body of beliefs already held – past experience and logic between them leave very little play to the mind – but our new beliefs must prove themselves not merely at the present moment but for the indefinite future. Both common sense and scientific beliefs may have to be modified radically in response to future experiences.

Although James held that the truth is useful to believe, critics who accuse him of identifying truth with usefulness are careless readers. The misreading is, perhaps, encouraged by a hasty reading of his essay 'The Will to Believe' as well as by its unfortunate title. There are certain times when one has to decide to believe 'ahead of the evidence'. We must decide to trust a new acquaintance before we have any basis for trust, else the opportunity of forming a friendship will be lost for ever. What characterizes such situations is that the alternatives before us are equally 'live' for us (we can see ourselves making either choice), that the choice is 'momentous' (much hangs on it; we would not care to toss a coin), and that there is no time to wait for further evidence (waiting is making the choice; in the example, it is to lose the opportunity for friendship). In such cases, and only in such cases, James insists that we have the right to believe. He exercised that right when he chose to believe in free will; as do scientists who commit themselves to investigate as yet untested hypotheses and political reformers who stake their lives on realizing their programmes. It is perhaps worth mentioning that beliefs thus chosen are nevertheless subject to the same verification/falsification processes as are any other beliefs.

6 Radical empiricism

Radical empiricism, found primarily in the posthumously published *Essays in Radical Empiricism* (1912), is James' ontology, his theory of perception and his theory of intentionality. Although James claimed, rightly, that one could be a pragmatist without being a radical empiricist, pragmatism must be able to explain how it is that we live in a world about which we can communicate, which we can change by joint actions, and which any one person's action can change for everyone. The question is urgent because philosophy since Descartes tends to lead to 'a congeries of solipsisms, out of which in strict logic only a God could compose a universe even of discourse' (1912: 37–8). Beliefs in the existence of other minds and of bodies are instinctive, noninferential beliefs, part of the common-sense framework within which we infer what another thinks or what kind of bodies there are. These common sense beliefs do not, however, survive philosophical criticism unaltered. James holds that there is 'one primal stuff or material in the world, a stuff of which everything is composed' but 'there is no *general* stuff of which experience at large is made' (1912: 4, 14). This is not simply a rejection of mind–matter dualism, even talking of a 'stuff' out of which everything is made is misleading; pure experience – the 'primal stuff' – has no essential properties. While the word 'experience' tempts one to understand radical empiricism as a version of Berkeleyan idealism, the view resembles rather a neutral monism, but that it is a label James would have abhorred (see NEUTRAL MONISM). In all his writings James emphasized pluralism: a plurality of possible futures, a plurality of irreducible values, a plurality of useful conceptual schemes, a plurality of pure experiences.

Radical empiricism attempts to answer two related questions: how is it that what I take to be my percept of this page of this book is indeed *of* this page (and not of any one of the thousands of exactly similar pages of this book elsewhere), and how is it that my percept and your percept are of the same page when, as we normally say, we are looking at the same page? Analogous questions arise with respect to objects merely thought about. When I see a pen, the experience (call it E) taken in itself, apart from all conceptualization – to the extent that that is possible – is what James calls a 'pure' experience, and the crucial claim made by James is that E is as much an event in the pen's history as it is an event in mine. If we take E with what James calls its 'energetic associates' – with how the pen came to be here and what happens to it hereafter – we have the pen, and if we take E with my prior and subsequent thoughts, feelings, etc. we have my stream of consciousness. This is, first of all, a direct realism. I do not have a sense datum (idea, impression, representation) from which I infer (or 'construct') the pen: I see the pen. And I see its surroundings, I handle it, etc. That is how the mystery of how I can 'mean' this pen rather than any one of the thousands of virtually identical other pens is answered. But who does the 'taking'? It can only be a later item in the stream of consciousness, but just what that item would be is unclear.

To say, as James does, that the context defines the referent when you and I are talking about some absent person presupposes that we live in a common world – that we experience, for example, the same pen as you hand it to me. But how is this possible? No experience of mine is an experience of yours. My-seeing-the-pen is an experience of mine, hence it is not an experience of yours. How then can the-pen-being-seen-by-me be the-pen-being-seen-by-you? James responds that thinking of the pen as my percept (or yours) is a later experience; it is not the 'pure experience' that James calls 'the pen'. *That* pure experience may be appropriated by you as well as by me. As if he realized that this answer might not convince his readers, James

adds that 'the decisive reason in favour of our minds meeting in *some* common objects at least is that, unless I knew that supposition, I have no motive for assuming that your mind exists at all . . . and for me to speak of you is folly' (1912: 38). And, he continues, these objects would be there even if one or more of our minds were destroyed. Indeed, James agrees with common sense that the earth existed before there were any sentient beings and that there will be stars after the last human being has vanished. Once again we are driven to wonder what James can mean by an unexperienced reality. We can easily grasp the idea of a pure experience that does not 'belong' to a physical object (for instance, a hallucination), but what can we make of the idea of a pure experience that is not experienced at all? James himself, perhaps due to this difficulty, toyed with the idea of panpsychism, but this appears to be an unnecessary concession to idealism.

See also: EMPIRICISM; IDEALISM; PANPSYCHISM; PRAGMATISM; PRAGMATISM IN ETHICS; PSYCHOLOGY, THEORIES OF §§1–2; RELIGIOUS EXPERIENCE; RELIGION AND MORALITY

List of works

James, W. (1975–88) *The Works of William James*, Cambridge, MA, and London: Harvard University Press, 17 vols. (This edition includes all previously published as well as many previously unpublished writings by James. Several of his writings are, however, readily available in paperback. References in the text are to the editions listed below.)

—— (1878) 'Remarks on Spencer's Definition of Mind as Correspondence', in *Essays in Philosophy*, Cambridge, MA and London: Harvard University Press, 1978. (The first statement of James' view that the mind is not a passive recipient but actively contributes to what is known.)

—— (1890) *The Principles of Psychology*, New York: Dover, 1950, 2 vols. (A monumental work; when it was published and for many years thereafter, it was widely used as a text in psychology courses. Today it is of interest for its many philosophical reflections.)

—— (1891, 1897) 'The Moral Philosopher and the Moral Life' and 'The Will to Believe' in *The Will to Believe and Other Essays in Popular Philosophy*, New York: Dover, 1956. (A collection of essays almost all of which were originally delivered as lectures to student audiences. This is one of James' most accessible books, and the second essay mentioned is one of his best known.)

—— (1895) 'The Knowing of Things Together', in *Psychological Review* 2; repr. in *Essays in*

Philosophy, Cambridge, MA, and London: Harvard University Press, 1987. (This volume contains 21 essays from 1876–1910 covering a wide range of topics.)

—— (1898) 'Philosophical Conceptions and Practical Results', Appendix to *Pragmatism*, Cambridge, MA and London: Harvard University Press, 1975, 255. (In this lecture to the Philosophical Union at the University of California, Berkeley, James reintroduced Pragmatism twenty years after Peirce's original essays on the subject.)

—— (1899) 'What Makes a Life Significant' and 'On a Certain Blindness in Human Beings', in *Talks to Teachers on Psychology and to Students on Some of Life's Ideals*, Cambridge, MA, and London: Harvard University Press, 1983. (The talks to teachers cover topics discussed in *The Principles of Psychology* that are of particular interest to school teachers, but the two essays mentioned are of enduring human interest and do not presuppose any knowledge of either philosophy or psychology.)

—— (1902) *The Varieties of Religious Experience*, New York: Collier Books; repr. London: Collier Macmillan Publishers, 1961. (James' most popular book is a careful account and analysis of the various types of religious experience and religious personality, mostly Christian.)

—— (1907) *Pragmatism: A New Name for Some Old Ways of Thinking*, Indianapolis, IN, and Cambridge: Hackett Publishing Company, 1907. (A series of eight lectures for educated laypersons; an exuberant presentation of the essentials of pragmatism as James understood it.)

—— (1908) 'The Social Value of the College-Bred', in *Essays, Comments and Reviews*, Cambridge, MA, and London: Harvard University Press, 1987. (An address to a meeting of the Association of American Alumnae at Radcliffe College, the essay was published in McClure's Magazine in 1908. The volume is of interest primarily because it contains all of James' writings on matters of political concern.)

—— (1909) *The Meaning of Truth*, Cambridge, MA, and London: Harvard University Press, 1975. (This sequel to *Pragmatism* consists of replies to critics and attempts at clarification. *Pragmatism* and *The Meaning of Truth* were published bound together and with an introduction by A.J. Ayer by Harvard University Press in 1978; this is available in paperback.)

—— (1910) 'The Moral Equivalent of War', in *Essays in Religion and Morality*, Cambridge, MA, and London: Harvard University Press. (The essay was published in various journals and magazines in 1910 and reprinted in *Memories and Studies* (ed.

Henry James, Jr) in 1912. The volume contains twelve essays on various topics.)

—— (1912) *Essays in Radical Empiricism*, Cambridge, MA, and London: Harvard University Press, 1976. (This volume, first published posthumously, contains James' most sustained attempt to deal with epistemology, ontology and the theory of intentionality. It is difficult reading, but intellectually highly rewarding.)

References and further reading

Barzun, J. (1983) *A Stroll with William James*, New York: Harper & Row. (An easy-to-read, loving introduction to James, the man and the thinker.)

Bird, G. (1987) *William James*, London and New York: Routledge & Kegan Paul. (A volume in the *Arguments of the Philosophers* series; an excellent and very readable introduction to James.)

Edie, J.M. (1987) *William James and Phenomenology*, Bloomington, IN, and Indianapolis, IN: Indiana University Press. (An approach to James' philosophy from a phenomenological (Husserlian) perspective.)

James, H. (ed.) (1920) *The Letters of William James*, Boston, MA: Atlantic Monthly Press, 2 vols. (These letters, edited by James' son Henry, provide an opportunity to become acquainted with William James, the man, as well as offering some insights into his philosophizing.)

Levinson, H.S. (1981) *The Religious Investigations of William James*, Chapel Hill, NC: University of North Carolina Press. (A thorough but readable examination of James' inquiries into religious matters.)

Lewis, R.W.B. (1991) *The Jameses: A Family Narrative*, New York: Doubleday. (A thorough and thoroughly enjoyable biography of the family, from William James' grandfather to his children.)

Myers, G.E. (1986) *William James: His Life and Thought*, New Haven, CT, and London: Yale University Press. (A monumental scholarly study of all of James' writings. A worthy successor to Perry (1935).)

* Perry, R.B. (1935) *The Thought and Character of William James*, Boston, MA: Little, Brown, 2 vols. (Perry uses hundreds of unpublished letters by James and scores addressed to him as well as many manuscripts (then unpublished) in this masterly account of James' life and thought.)

—— (1938) *In the Spirit of William James*, New Haven, CT: Yale University Press. (A brief, thoughtful, appreciative yet critical exposition and discussion of James' main ideas.)

Putnam, R.A. (ed.) (1997) *The Companion to William*

James, Cambridge: Cambridge University Press. (Eighteen informative and provocative articles on various aspects of James' thought provide a thorough but accessible introduction to his thought. An extensive bibliography is provided.)

Skrupskelis, I.K. and Berkeley, E.M. (eds) (1992–4) *The Correspondence of William James, vols 1–3: William and Henry*, Charlottesville, VA, and London: University Press of Virginia. (All the extant letters exchanged by these famous brothers provide a wonderful insight into their personalities and relationship.)

Sprigge, T.L.S. (1993) *James and Bradley: American Truth and British Reality*, Chicago and La Salle, IL: Open Court. (An excellent, quite technical, sympathetic but critical examination of the views of these important philosophers.)

Wilshire, B. (1968) *William James and Phenomenology: A Study of the Principles of Psychology*, Bloomington, IN: Indiana University Press. (A thorough study of James' *The Principles of Psychology* for advanced readers.)

RUTH ANNA PUTNAM

JANSENIUS *see* PORT-ROYAL

JAPANESE PHILOSOPHY

The most distinctive characteristic of Japanese philosophy is how it has assimilated and adapted foreign philosophies to its native worldview. As an isolated island nation, Japan successfully resisted foreign invasion until 1945 and, although it borrowed ideas freely throughout its history, was able to do so without the imposition of a foreign military or colonial presence. Japanese philosophy thus bears the imprint of a variety of foreign traditions, but there is always a distinctively Japanese cultural context. In order to understand the dynamics of Japanese thought, therefore, it is necessary to examine both the influence of various foreign philosophies through Japanese history and the underlying or continuing cultural orientation that set the stage for which ideas would be assimilated and in what way.

The major philosophical traditions to influence Japan from abroad have been Confucianism, Buddhism, neo-Confucianism and Western philosophy. Daoism also had an impact, but more in the areas of alchemy, prognostication and folk medicine than in philosophy. Although these traditions often overlapped, each also had distinctive influences.

In its literary forms, Japanese philosophy began about fourteen centuries ago. Confucian thought entered Japan around the fifth century AD. Through the centuries the imprint of Confucianism has been most noticeable in the areas of social structure, government organization and ethics. Philosophically speaking, the social self in Japan has its roots mainly in Confucian ideals, blended since the sixteenth century with certain indigenous ideas of loyalty and honour developed within the Japanese samurai *or warrior class.*

The philosophical impact of Buddhism, introduced around the same time as Confucianism, has been primarily in three areas: psychology, metaphysics and aesthetics. With its emphasis on disciplined contemplation and introspective analysis, Buddhism has helped define the various Japanese senses of the inner, rather than social, self. In metaphysics, Buddhist esotericism has been most dominant; through esoteric Buddhist philosophy, the Japanese gave a rational structure to their indigenous beliefs that spirituality is immanent rather than transcendent, that mind and body (like humanity and nature) are continuous rather than separate, and that expressive power is shared by things as well as human thought or speech. This metaphysical principle of expression has combined with the introspective psychology and emphasis on discipline to form the foundation of the various aesthetic theories that have been so well developed in Japanese history.

Neo-Confucianism became most prominent in Japan in the sixteenth century. Like classical Confucianism, it contributed much to the Japanese understanding of virtue and the nature of the social self. Unlike classical Confucianism in Japan, however, neo-Confucianism also had a metaphysical and epistemological influence. Its emphasis on investigating the principle or configuration of things stimulated the Japanese study of the natural world. This reinforced a tendency initiated with the very limited introduction of Western practical sciences and medicine in the sixteenth century.

Western philosophy, along with Western science and technology, has had its major impact in Japan only since the middle of the nineteenth century. The process of modernization forced Japanese philosophers to reconsider fundamental issues in epistemology, social philosophy and philosophical anthropology. As it has assimilated Asian traditions of thought in the past – absorbing, modifying and incorporating aspects into its culture – so Japan has been consciously assimilating Western thought since the early twentieth century. The process continues today.

What in all this is distinctively Japanese? On the superficial level, it might seem that Japan has drawn eclectically from a variety of traditions without any inherent sense of intellectual direction. A more careful analysis, however, shows that Japanese thinkers have seldom adopted any foreign philosophy without simultaneously adapting it. For example, the Japanese philosophical tradition never fully accepted the emphasis on propriety or the mandate of heaven so characteristic of Chinese Confucianism. It rejected the Buddhist idea that impermanence is a reality to which one must be resigned, and instead made the appreciation of impermanence into an aesthetic. It criticized the neo-Confucian and Western philosophical tendencies toward rationalism and positivism, even while accepting many ideas from those traditions. In short, there has always been a complex selection process at work beneath the apparent absorption of foreign ideas.

Both historically and in the present, some Japanese philosophers and cultural critics have tried to identify this selection process with Shintō, but Shintō itself has also been profoundly shaped by foreign influences. The selection process has shaped Shintō as much as Shintō has shaped it. In any case, we can isolate a few axiological orientations that have seemed to persist or recur throughout the history of Japanese thought. First, there has been a tendency to emphasize immanence over transcendence in defining spirituality. Second, contextual pragmatism has generally won out over attempts to establish universal principles that apply to all situations. Third, reason has often been combined with affect as the basis of knowledge or insight. Fourth, theory is seldom formulated in isolation from a praxis used to learn the theory. Fifth, although textual authority has often been important, it has not been as singular in its focus as in many other cultures. Thus, the Japanese have not typically identified a single text such as the Bible, the Analects, *the Qur'an or the* Bhagavad Gītā *as foundational to their culture. Although there have been exceptions to these general orientations, they do nonetheless help define the broader cultural backdrop against which the drama of Japanese philosophy has been played out through history.*

1   Archaic spirituality

The earliest accounts of Japan by Chinese visitors, archaeological remains of the prehistoric culture and the earliest recorded prayers and songs all suggest that Japan was originally an animistic culture with shamanistic qualities. The world was understood to be full of *kami*, sacred presences in the form of awe-inspiring natural objects, personal deities, ghosts and clannish guardian spirits. The ancient rituals were apparently designed for appeasing the *kami* so that humans might live in harmony with them and benefit from their powers. The early poems, recorded in such court-sponsored compilations as the *Man'yōshū*, indicate an internal relationship between humanity and nature. That is, the ancients understood humanity and nature to be parts of each other, not independently existing entities related as subject and object. The ancient myths describe the creation of Japan through the fortuitous actions of the deities. For this reason, the world is infused with *kami* or sacred presence.

According to the myths, natural objects such as rocks and streams were originally endowed with speech, a power taken from them because of their noisy bickering and querulous nature. Although natural things lost their voice, they did not necessarily lose their expressiveness. Human beings, if properly attuned to the natural world, could voice that expressiveness in thoughts, words and artefact. In ancient Japanese, the term for this expressive possibility was *kotodama*, the 'spirit' (*dama*) of 'word' (*koto*) and/or 'thing' (also *koto*).

In short, the ancient Japanese worldview understood the gods, the natural world and humanity to be an ontological continuum. It is not precise to say that rocks and trees were the dwelling place of spirits, because that would establish a bifurcation between the spiritual and material instead of a continuity. The term *kami*, therefore, applied to any object where a sacred presence was particularly manifest or concentrated: the Sun Goddess Amaterasu, Mount Fuji, a special tree or waterfall, the emperor or the vengeful spirit of a fallen warrior. Even the sword of that warrior might be treated as *kami*. This represents one enduring idea in Japanese culture, the emphasis on spiritual immanence instead of transcendence: the sacred permeates the everyday world.

2   The importation of Confucianism and Buddhism

The Chinese writing system was introduced into Japan at about the beginning of the fifth century AD, but it was not until the eighth century that a viable adaptation was devised for rendering Japanese in written form. Therefore early Japanese thought was expressed in Chinese, and in fact many philosophical intellectuals continued to write in Chinese (or a Japanized version of Chinese) as late as the nineteenth century.

When the Chinese writing system was first introduced, the various clans had begun to form a central government under the leadership of what would become the imperial family. The government coalesced in Yamato, a large plain adjoining what is today Kyoto, Nara and Osaka. With the introduction of Chinese literacy, the Japanese elite gained access to more than a millennium of Confucian and Buddhist philosophy. These ideas were immediately put to use in organizing the state.

Confucianism gave Japan a hierarchical model for social and political order. It focused on personal interaction, explaining the responsibilities and duties relevant to the five basic dyadic relations: master–servant, parent–child, husband–wife, elder sibling–younger sibling and friend–friend. When the dyadic relationships are hierarchical, the person in the superior position is to care for the person in the lower and the person in the lower position is to be loyal to the superior. The imperial family used this system to institute a vertical bureaucracy. Although Confucianism supplied a social structure to the state, the ancient Japanese showed little interest in developing Confucian philosophy *per se* (see CONFUCIAN PHILOSOPHY, JAPANESE).

Buddhism, on the other hand, was initially most attractive to the Japanese for its aesthetic and thaumaturgic qualities. Buddhist artisans, often immigrants from Korea, brought new techniques of grand architecture, painting, sculpture and music. Using these elegant accoutrements in its rituals for healing, prosperity and protection of the state, Buddhism sometimes competed with the indigenous religious practices addressed to the *kami*.

From the philosophical perspective, however, the most important impact of Buddhism was its psychology. Through its meditative techniques and advanced analyses of the human predicament, Buddhism heightened the Japanese awareness of the workings of heart and mind. Buddhism teaches that egoism is the primary cause of human anguish and dissatisfaction. The ego seeks permanence and control in a world of continuing flux. By controlling the desires and eliminating egoism, one can achieve peace and inner harmony. These Buddhist teachings brought a dimension of inner awareness and psychological analysis to a culture that had formerly operated only within the concepts of taboo, purification and animistic appeasement (see BUDDHIST PHILOSOPHY, JAPANESE).

At the same time, the indigenous religion began to define itself in relation to its rival, Buddhism. It took the name *kami no michi or shintō*, the 'way of the *kami*'. The state helped to systematize a series of myths in the eighth century, explaining the relationships among the tutelary *kami* of the various powerful clans and, presumably, the political relationships among the clans themselves. Most critically, through its familial relation with the chief *kami*, the Sun Goddess Amaterasu, the throne established itself as the blood tie between the celestial *kami* and the Japanese people (see SHINTŌ).

A major goal of philosophy in the seventh and eighth centuries, therefore, was to integrate the available ideas, both foreign and native, into a systematic worldview in the service of political stability. In this light the Seventeen Article Constitution of AD 604 is one of the first philosophical documents of ancient Japan (see SHŌTOKU CONSTITUTION). Attributed to Prince Shōtoku (574–622), the Constitution is really more a set of guidelines for bureaucrats than a set of laws defining political structure. In it, however, we find the early impact of Chinese thinking and its adaptation to the Japanese context of the time.

The Constitution's first article opened with a quotation from CONFUCIUS about the importance of maintaining 'harmony'. As noted already, in traditional Confucianism one achieves harmony primarily through performing actions appropriate to one's relationships in the society. Rather than discussing such Confucian principles, however, a large portion of the Constitution discussed human frailty and the need to develop a sympathetic attitude. The Constitution admonished against hypocrisy, preferential treatment, envy and egocentric motives. On the positive side, it advocated consensus and open-mindedness. In short, while the document aimed for a harmonious Confucian social order, it also drew on Buddhist psychology to explain the obstacles to harmony and to suggest an introspective understanding of personal motivations. Although the Constitution itself lacked any detailed philosophical argument, it marks an early attempt to draw on multiple philosophical traditions in a coherent manner. In effect, it advocated a Confucian social and government order (see CONFUCIAN PHILOSOPHY, JAPANESE) supported by Buddhist practice and the insights of Buddhist psychology. This philosophy of government remained dominant in Japan for at least a millennium.

In the Nara period (710–94), Japanese scholar-monks secured court support to accumulate and study more texts in Buddhist philosophy. They organized themselves loosely around major traditions from the mainland, and became the Six Nara Schools of Buddhism: Ritsu, Kusha, Jōjitsu, Hossō, Sanron and Kegon (see BUDDHIST PHILOSOPHY, JAPANESE). The first primarily concentrated on the study of Vinaya, the precepts and regulations for ordering monastic life. The Kusha and Jōjitsu were schools of Abhidharma Buddhism emphasizing the detailed analysis of dharmas, the basic constituents of reality or consciousness (see BUDDHISM, ABHIDHARMIKA SCHOOLS OF). The Hossō was primarily based in the Indian Yogācāra tradition and Sanron in the Mādhyamika (see BUDDHISM, YOGĀCĀRA SCHOOL OF; BUDDHISM, MADHYĀMIKA: INDIA AND TIBET). Kegon represented the tradition known in China as Huayan. Although the Six Nara Schools played an important role in both education and court politics, there is little evidence that they were philosophically creative centres. Their historical role was mainly to introduce Buddhist analysis and doctrine into Japanese culture. They provided the intellectual raw material for the later philosophical developments of the Heian period.

3 Metaphysical vision of ancient Japanese esoteric Buddhism

Although already a significant presence in the Nara period, only in the Heian period (794–1185) did Buddhism undergo a profound process of philosophical development and Japanization. Two Buddhist thinkers were particularly influential: KŪKAI (774–835; posthumous title, Kōbō Daishi) and Saichō (767–822; posthumous title, Dengyō Daishi). Of the two, Kūkai's philosophical contribution was the more comprehensive. He went to China in 804 to study esoteric Buddhism and, upon his return two years later, founded Japanese Shingon Buddhism. The analytic and systematic character of Kūkai's writings may well qualify him as the first true philosopher in Japanese history.

For Kūkai, reality is fundamentally a person. The entire cosmos is no more than the thoughts, words and deeds of the Buddha called Dainichi (literally the 'Great Sun'). Dainichi is not the creator of the universe; Dainichi is the universe. In a perpetual state of enlightened meditation, Dainichi performs the three great practices of esoteric Buddhism: the chanting of sacred syllables (mantras), the visualization of geometrical arrays of symbols (mandalas) and the performance of sacred postures or hand gestures (mudras). These three activities define the nature of the universe. The mantras are microcosmic resonances or vibrating states of matter–energy that constitute the basic elements. The mandalas define the essential structure, and the mudras constitute the patterns of change. By performing the rituals of mantra, mandala

and mudra, a person achieves immediate insight into the nature of the cosmos. By introspection on the nature of their own thoughts, words and deeds, the Shingon Buddhist is said to achieve insight into the thoughts, words and deeds of the Buddha, Dainichi. By understanding one's own person, one understands the person that is all of reality.

Within the framework of this metaphysical system, Kūkai developed a comprehensive philosophy addressing several major philosophical issues. For example, he criticized the idea that insight or enlightenment could be purely mental or intellectual. Because the universe itself consists of thought, word and deed (or structure, resonance and patterned change), it can only be grasped by unified praxis of the whole person: mind, speech and body. To know reality is to participate in it fully, in all three of its dimensions.

Another philosophical issue of interest to Kūkai was the nature of expression. Because the cosmos is a person, reality is the expressive style of that person. Every entity is, therefore, a symbol or imprint of Dainichi's mental, somatic and verbal activity. Yet, because we contain the element of volitional consciousness, we humans can also ignore the true source of all activity, construing ourselves as independent entities. We can interpret things through the superimposition of our own imprints, covering over their (and our) more fundamental nature. This delusion is the source of human anguish and ignorance. The escape from delusion lies in recognizing and participating in the self-expressive nature of reality.

Kūkai's contemporary and major competitor, Saichō, founded Japanese Tendai Buddhism. Although Saichō's primary goal in visiting China was to bring back to Japan the teaching of the Tiantai Buddhist tradition (see BUDDHIST PHILOSOPHY, CHINESE §7), he also had a chance encounter with a teacher of esotericism. When he returned to Japan, therefore, his Tendai school incorporated esoteric Buddhist elements as well as exoteric Tiantai teachings. Through the exchange of Shingon and Tendai disciples in Japan, some of Kūkai's esoteric teachings also found their way into Tendai. The result was that by the end of the ninth century, the two dominant forms of Japanese Buddhism were both at least partially esoteric in nature.

We can explain the influence of the esoteric Buddhist theory of reality from both the standpoint of cultural history and the history of philosophy. Culturally, it is important that esoteric Buddhism did not either doctrinally or politically oppose the presence of the indigenous religion, Shintō. Esoteric Buddhism reinforced rather than challenged many aspects of the indigenous religious worldview: the ubiquity of the sacred, the expressiveness of nature and the nonduality of matter and spirit, for example. Furthermore, both Kūkai and Saichō correlated the various buddhas of esotericism with the various *kami* of the traditional Japanese religion. By this process, Japanese archaism was, in effect, defended by a philosophically sophisticated system of Buddhist thought imported from the mainland and adapted to the Japanese context. Buddhism and Shintō could therefore be practised alongside each other without contradiction.

This development set the metaphysical backdrop against which later Japanese thought would develop. One might say that esoteric Buddhism did for Japanese philosophy what Plato and Aristotle did for Western philosophy. It laid out a set of assumptions and a *Problematik* that had a profound influence on the thought to follow. Two assumptions were particularly influential.

First, esotericism has a distinctive view of the relation between part and whole. The whole is recursively manifest or reflected in the part. It is not that the parts constitute the whole nor that the whole is more than the sum of its parts; rather, since the part is what it is by virtue of the whole, if we truly understand the part, we find the whole imprinted in it. In Shingon's case, for example, since any individual thing is an expression of the cosmos as Dainichi, when we truly understand the part (the individual thing), we encounter the whole (Dainichi) as well.

With this orientation as a cultural presupposition, later Japanese philosophers would seldom endorse either atomistic analysis or individualism (see ATOMISM, ANCIENT; METHODOLOGICAL INDIVIDUALISM). Atomistic analysis had been introduced into Japan via the Nara Schools of Jōjitsu and Kusha. Kūkai explicitly ranked them as philosophical 'mindsets' far below Kegon and Tendai, in part because only the latter endorsed this theory of whole-as-part. Individualism, with attendant theories of social contract, entered Japan via the West only in the late nineteenth century. Since it viewed the social whole as constituted by the parts, it ran counter to this esoteric assumption. Not surprisingly, individualism has never taken hold in Japan as a basis for social, ethical or political theory.

Second, esotericism's metaphysics argued that reality is self-expressive. Human beings are, of course, part of reality. When humans speak authentically or truly, therefore, they do not refer to reality, but rather are part of its self-expression. This position undermines any philosophical tendencies toward idealism (reality as a production of mind), realism (reality as pre-existing our expressions and truth as matching our expressions with that reality) or radical nomin-

alism (expressions refer primarily to other expressions without necessary connection to non-linguistic reality) (see IDEALISM; REALISM AND ANTIREALISM; NOMINALISM). In the Nara Schools there were variants of idealism (Hossō), realism (Kusha and Jōjitsu) and nominalism (Sanron). Again Kūkai ranked them all below Kegon and Tendai, and certainly below what he believed to be the only comprehensive mind-set, esotericism.

This presupposition about the self-expressive nature of reality underlies most Japanese aesthetic theories as well. The Heian period was the first to develop a detailed set of aesthetic terms, for example, *miyabi* (cultured, refined elegance) and *mono no aware* (the 'ah-ness of things' or the aesthetic tinge of sadness arising from an appreciation of the evanescent). In later periods, other aesthetic terms such as *yūgen* (hidden sublimity or depth), *sabi* (the 'loneliness' of an elegance allowed to age) and *wabi* (rusticity) came to the fore. These terms have rich connotations not readily translated into English. In general, though, they signify equally a quality of the object and the response of the aesthete or artist. The aesthetic is understood to be a self-expressive resonance between the object and artist. The world expresses itself through the artist as the work of art (see AESTHETICS, JAPANESE).

4 Medieval philosophical anthropology: Pure Land Buddhism

During the Heian period the highly literate and elegant culture of the Kyoto court was at its peak. The aesthetically pleasing rituals of esoteric Buddhism found a receptive audience among the aristocrats and clergy. They alone enjoyed the leisure time, education and resources to devote their lives to its study and practice. The general populace were left to their folk religions, an amalgamation of practices with roots in Buddhism, Shintō and Daoist alchemy.

By the early twelfth century, the court had become so politically effete that the provincial aristocracy began to vie for power and the newly risen *samurai* fought for control of territory. Plagues, famines and earthquakes were also unusually devastating. In short, to any sensitive observer of the times, it was easy to see the decadence of the social order, the harshness of nature and the corruption of the human spirit. There was little time for, or consolation in, metaphysical speculations. The philosophers turned their analyses to this world and their imaginations to wondering what failing in humanity had caused such suffering. By 1185 the Minamoto clan was victorious and in 1192 Yoritomo became *shōgun*, establishing his centre of government in Kamakura. Thus began the

Kamakura period (1185–1333) and a new set of philosophical and religious orientations.

The Kamakura period philosophers such as Hōnen (1133–1212), SHINRAN (1173–1262), Yōsai or Eisai (1141–1215), DŌGEN (1200–53) and NICHIREN (1222–82) responded to the decay and suffering of their times. Each developed his own interpretation of the human predicament with an accompanying solution. All had originally trained as Tendai monks, but these reformers eventually left the establishment and founded new Buddhist sects that served the masses as well as the elite echelons of Japanese society. Of the Kamakura schools of Buddhism, Pure Land and Zen have been the most influential in their theories of human being. Shinran was the founder of Shin Buddhism or the 'True Pure Land School; Dōgen was the founder of Sōtō Zen. Each developed most fully the philosophical foundations for his own tradition (see BUDDHIST PHILOSOPHY, JAPANESE).

These two schools differ radically in their philosophical anthropologies. As Buddhists, both Shinran and Dōgen accepted the general Buddhist analysis about the source of ignorance: egoism. Egoism defines the self as an independent agent that initiates actions and has experiences. The Buddhist view, on the other hand, maintains that 'I' is no more than a name for related actions and events, not something that lies behind them. This implies that the boundaries of the self are fuzzy rather than sharply delineated. For example, from a distance we can readily identify the general course of a river, but if we move up close enough, we cannot specify exactly where the river ends and the river bank begins. If the river were self-conscious and tried to specify for itself 'my' boundaries as opposed to 'its' boundaries, the river would lose sight of the very processes that bring it into being and help define it. Analogously, Buddhists generally maintain that egoism, by attempting to define, delineate and protect the self, ignores the self's broader context. It overlooks the self's dependence on what egoism considers to be outside and separate from it.

As a disciple of Hōnen, the founder of the Japanese Pure Land School, Shinran also accepted the specific ideas of that tradition, including the theory that humanity had entered a degenerate period in history. Left to our own devices, we are presumed to be doomed to live and relive an existence of anguish, dissatisfaction and despair. Pure Land Buddhists believe, however, that a celestial buddha called Amida has seen our situation and taken pity on us. He has vowed that if we entrust ourselves totally to his compassion and call on his name, we can be assured rebirth in his Pure Land where the conditions are conducive to Buddhist practice. In his Pure Land we can perform the necessary spiritual disciplines and then return to this world to attain enlightenment. In so doing, we can be a spiritual aid to others in this world. Such was the basic tradition of Pure Land Buddhism that Shinran accepted. Within that traditional framework, however, he developed his own distinctive philosophical analysis of human being.

Shinran believed he had found a contradiction in how most Buddhists understood practice. Specifically, they self-consciously undertook various disciplines (meditation, reading texts, chanting mantras) as a means of eliminating egoism and attaining insight into reality. The implication is that one can overcome egoism by one's own power, by 'self-power.' People believed they were 'earning merit' by their religious practices. Shinran argued that if people practice as a means of achieving merit, then the actions only feed, rather than eradicate egoism: discipline is understood as a means by which *I* can improve *myself*. Shinran considered this emphasis on self-power to be the psychological foundation of the degenerate age in which he believed he lived. Because people misunderstood the relation between self and Buddhist practice, the teachings of Buddhism had indeed become unintelligible and the prospect for insight had disappeared.

Although Shinran did not explicitly deny the ontological reality of the Pure Land or the account of Amida's vow as historical, his philosophy focused more on the psychological and logical implications of the Pure Land position. For him the fundamental point was that people must surrender their egoistic senses of self by adopting an 'entrusting heart-and-mind' (*shinjin*). By completely abandoning the ego, people can have faith in the power of Amida's vow to help. They turn from 'self-power' to 'other-power.' Assured birth in the Pure Land, the realm devoid of egoism, the sense of a discrete or independent self will disappear. Yet, Shinran reasoned, if there is no self at that point, logically there can be no discrete 'other' either. There is just 'naturalness' and Amida in effect disappears as well. *Shinjin* continues as the entrusting that opens itself to this naturalness. In that egoless state, one can spiritually help other people. It can be said that one returns from the Pure Land to be reborn in this world. Yet, by assisting others in this world, the ego may once again be constituted as the 'I' who self-consciously helps 'others.' As soon as one begins to think that good deeds are done by virtue of one's own power, the whole process must be renewed. One must again see the delusion of the ego, again turn oneself over to Amida's power, again be reborn in the Pure Land, again allow self and Amida to disappear, and again return to this world from the Pure Land .

In short, Shinran agreed that to eliminate ignorance one must eliminate egoism. This can be accomplished, he believed, only by the complete renunciation of the notion that one can help oneself. Only by despairing of the efficacy of self-power and by entrusting oneself to Amida's power can one become naturally what one truly is (see SELF-REALIZATION). In that egoless state one can understand reality for what it is and act freely in the world as a compassionate being. In addressing the same issue, Zen Buddhism took an almost diametrically opposed approach, however.

5 Medieval philosophical anthropology: Zen Buddhism

Like the Pure Land Buddhists, Zen Master Dōgen believed there is a fundamental flaw in the usual interpretation of Buddhist practice as the means to enlightenment. Rather than arguing that practice must be abandoned, however, he instead maintained that practice or self-discipline is an end in itself. He rejected the popular theory that his was a degenerate age in which enlightenment was no longer possible. Instead, Dōgen maintained everyone is already enlightened, but that enlightenment was not being manifested or expressed in their actions. The goal, therefore, is to authenticate what we already are.

Trained in the Zen (Chan) Buddhist tradition in China, Dōgen was sensitive to the limitations of language and mistrustful of certain types of thinking. Like other Buddhists, he understood the problem to be egoism. By hypostatizing the ego, one falls into a desire for reality to be a specific way. One seeks permanence in both self and in one's own worldview. Therefore, it is easy to project interpretations on experience, interpretations that shape the experience to meet our presuppositions, expectations and desires.

Dōgen believed that experiential immediacy is possible. In Zen meditation, one quiets the mind and merely lets phenomena appear. Dōgen called this a state of 'without-thinking' as opposed to either 'thinking' or 'not-thinking'. Thinking, for Dōgen, included any form of sustained conceptualization whether fantasy, cogitation, believing, denying, wishing, desiring or whatever. Not-thinking is the effort to blank the mind and empty it of all awareness. In without-thinking, however, there is the awareness of brute phenomena but no sustained act of bestowing meaning. There is no consciousness of a self having an experience. Furthermore, since no meaning at all is projected on the event, it is free of the distortions found in ordinary, ego-driven forms of experience. Dōgen simply called this 'the presencing of things as they are'.

Dōgen claimed this form of meditation was not a means to enlightenment. Instead, precisely because it is egoless, it is enlightenment itself. Yet, this meditation–enlightenment event is always accessible. It is, as it were, at the root of all experience, even thinking and not-thinking. In this respect we are all already enlightened but we have not authenticated that fact. Of course, to authenticate it, we must return to a state of without-thinking.

Without-thinking is, therefore, a not-yet-conceptualized immediacy. Since it is without concepts, however, it is intrinsically meaningless; but it is impossible for humans to live a life without meanings. Enlightenment must not only be authenticated in meditation. It must also be expressed in everyday life. How can this be possible?

Dōgen claimed that meaning is always contextual. He noted that the ocean has a different meaning to a fish swimming in it, a person in a boat out at sea and a deity looking down at it from the heavens. To the fish, the ocean is a translucent palace; to the person it is a great circle extending to the horizon in all directions; to the deity it is a string of jewel-like lights glittering in the sunshine. If the deity were to interpret the ocean as a circle or the person in the boat were to interpret it as a palace, however, they would not be expressing what is actually in front of them. Their interpretation would be false. Therefore, the key to truth in meaning is the appropriateness of the context.

According to Dōgen, meditative without-thinking is the 'touchstone' for determining whether the context is appropriate. Context is continually shifting and giving rise to new meanings as we live out our lives. What is 'tree branch' at one point may be 'firewood' at another and 'weapon' in a third. Dōgen referred to these points as 'occasions' of 'being-time'. For Dōgen, the problem with egoism is its resistance to accepting flux. Egoism tries to make a set of previous meanings into a fixed worldview, into *my* reality. Therefore, one projects contexts that are not actually present in the current phenomena. Through meditation, however, one can break the closed cycle of self-verifying projections. One can return to the presence of things as they are before meaning, before they are embedded in any particular context. Then, as one returns to the expressive world of everyday action, it is easier to verify the appropriateness of the contextualizing process that generates meaning (see MEANING AND VERIFICATION).

The philosophical anthropologies of Pure Land and Zen address the common problem of egoism, but their solutions to the problem are fundamentally different. In Pure Land Buddhism, recognizing the inefficacy of egoism leads to a psychodynamic of despair, entrusting and naturalness. In the Pure Land philosophy of human being, the ego is rejected in favour of a model of dependence or interdependence. It is a process of self-effacement and surrender. By contrast, Zen overcomes the negative effects of egoism not by self-effacement, but by self-analysis. One studies the dynamics of consciousness and grounds oneself in pure, but meaningless, presence. Pure Land and Zen agree that self-discipline is not a means to enlightenment. Yet, for Pure Land this entails the rejection of self-discipline; in Zen, on the other hand, it entails the acceptance of self-discipline as an end in itself.

These two philosophical anthropologies exemplify how Kamakura philosophers generally focused on the nature of praxis as part of an analysis of human existence. In the Heian period, the pressing philosophical question seems to have been the nature of the cosmos. In the Kamakura period it shifted to the nature of the self. Shinran and Dōgen produced particularly impressive analyses of human motivation and the structure of consciousness, and their models of the self remain influential in Japanese culture up to the present. It is significant, however, that their focus was primarily on the inner self instead of the social self. The social dimension was to become a major concern in the next major period in the development of Japanese philosophy.

6 Neo-Confucianism, the *samurai* code and Tokugawa society

Following the Kamakura period there were more periods of intermittent warfare and internal strife. A long lasting, nationwide peace arrived only with the establishment of the Tokugawa family's regime as *shogun*s. For nearly all of the Tokugawa period (1600–1868) Japan closed itself off from most interaction with outside world. For example, Christianity, which had been introduced by missionaries in the sixteenth century, was formally proscribed. The Tokugawa *shogun*s established a highly bureaucratic government, giving them unprecedented control over Japanese society from its system of education to its business practices and religious institutions. In this context, much of philosophy turned to the interests of the state and the definition of social responsibility.

During the fifteenth and sixteenth centuries, Japan had again received a strong infusion of foreign thought. In particular, Zen Buddhist monks who had visited the mainland brought back to Japan texts of the neo-Confucian traditions established in China by ZHU XI and WANG YANGMING. Since Japanese Buddhist philosophy taught little about social responsibility in secular contexts, the ethical dimension of these texts attracted increasing attention. Neo-Confucianism went further than traditional Confu-cianism by adding a metaphysical level to explain the natural world and how it could be known (see NEO-CONFUCIAN PHILOSOPHY).

From ancient times Confucianism had played a major role in the social, bureaucratic and ethical structures of Japanese culture. In trying to organize and stabilize the government after centuries of warfare, the Tokugawa *shogun*s were naturally intrigued by this new and more comprehensive form of the social philosophy that had already served Japan in the past. Furthermore, wary of Buddhism's popularity, they probably welcomed neo-Confucianism's challenge to the near hegemony that Buddhism had established in Japanese philosophy. In any case, from early in the seventeenth century, the Tokugawa *shogun*s gave special status and support to neo-Confucianism, especially to the school called Shushigaku, the Japanese school of Zhu Xi.

With the increased peace and prosperity of the Tokugawa period, there was a new market for philosophical education, especially in the great urban centres of Kyoto, Osaka and Edo (now Tokyo). The rising merchant class wanted the social polish of an upper class education. Furthermore, because it was peacetime, many unemployed *samurai* wanted a classical education to qualify for positions in the government bureaucracy. The result was an increase in independent schools and a proliferation of teachers with different philosophical approaches.

Generally we find major philosophical development during the Tokugawa period in two areas: naturalistic metaphysics and social philosophy or ethics. The Shushigaku school introduced a theory of reality or metaphysics foreign to the Buddhist theories so entrenched in Japanese thought. In particular, it analysed reality in terms of the dynamic between 'configuration' or 'principle' (*ri*; in Chinese, *li*) and 'material energy' or 'vital force' (*ki*; in Chinese, *qi*) (see LI; QI). According to Shushigaku, *ri* gives the universe its structure and, since *ri* is also in the mind, it is the foundation of knowledge. By 'investigating the nature of things' we come to know *ri*, both in ourselves and in the things we study. *Ki*, on the other hand, was considered the basic stuff that is ordered by *ri*.

Although the notion of *ri* was known to the Japanese through Tendai and Kegon Buddhism, the neo-Confucians gave the term a distinctive emphasis. They embedded it into the broader enterprise of understanding of the natural world. During the Tokugawa period there was a practical interest in better understanding nature; in the sixteenth-century traders, and missionaries from Europe had introduced some Western science. With the closure of Japan this contact was severely limited, although the occasional

Dutch treatise on practical science or medicine did find its way into Japan.

For the most part, Japanese philosophers found the Shushigaku emphasis on *ri* to be overly abstract. To many, it seemed that *ri* was an unnecessary transcendent realm behind physical reality that could be known only through some mysterious half-contemplative, half-empirical study. In response, many Japanese thinkers took a more phenomenalistic approach. KAIBARA EKKEN (1630–1714), for example, argued for the primacy of *ki*. To him, *ki* was the basic constituent of reality and should be studied directly; *ri* was no more than the name for the patterns one could abstract from the behaviour of *ki*. Certainly from the perspectives of both medicine and the martial arts, *ki* became the more important category in Japan.

Other naturalistic philosophers such as Miura Baien (1723–89) developed intricate systems of their own for categorizing natural phenomena. Such indigenous concerns for observation and classification of the natural world may not have developed into a full-blown science in the Western sense, but the orientation did show an increasing Japanese concern for observing and understanding the natural world. This phenomenalist tendency would serve Japan well in the nineteenth century when Western science and technology were reintroduced.

In the field of social or moral philosophy, an important development was the emergence of the school of 'Ancient Learning'. Led by Yamaga Sōkō (1622–85), ITŌ JINSAI (1627–1705) and OGYŪ SORAI (1666–1728), these philosophers rejected the metaphysical speculations of the neo-Confucianists and tried to return to the early classics of the Confucian tradition, especially the *Analects* (see CHINESE PHILOSOPHY; CONFUCIAN PHILOSOPHY, CHINESE; CONFUCIUS). They developed sophisticated philological and exegetical skills as tools for attempting to discover the original meanings of those texts. Their goal was to clarify traditional Confucian social philosophy so that it could become the basis for Japanese society. In this regard, the school of Ancient Learning put its emphasis on the nature of virtue and the development of character. Ogyū Sorai had an especially broad impact on society for his theories about education and moral training.

Some philosophers, like Yamaga Sōkō of the Ancient Learning School, mixed Confucian values with warrior values about loyalty and honour. Yamaga tried to develop a warrior mentality for service to the state that would be appropriate to peace time. Furthermore, in their unemployment, many *samurai* entered the various Buddhist orders, especially Zen, where they found a familiar emphasis on discipline and regimentation. The combined result

was an idealized code of the warrior (*bushidō*) as a way of life, even for non-*samurai* and even in times of peace (see BUSHI PHILOSOPHY).

7 Native studies: religio-aesthetic foundation of the Shintō state

The school of Ancient Learning's return to the original classics of Chinese Confucianism was mirrored in a movement to return to the early texts of Japan, the school of 'Native Studies' or 'National Studies' (*kokugaku*). Originally a literary and philological group, Native Studies scholars like Keichū (1640–1701), Kada no Azumamaro (1669–1736) and Kamo no Mabuchi (1697–1769) analysed the language and worldview of Nara and Heian poetry and prose. The school expanded beyond these literary goals, however, as it turned to questions of religion and national identity. In this development the philosophy of MOTOORI NORINAGA (1730–1801) played a pivotal role.

The major shift in Native Studies began with Motoori's decision as a philologist to decode the antiquated writing system of the *Kojiki* (The Record of Ancient Matters). An eighth-century text, the *Kojiki* was supposedly the written version of what had formerly been an oral tradition. Mixing myth and history, it discussed the origins of the world, the formation of Japan and the succession of Japanese emperors from the beginning of time up to its present. There was a twin work in Chinese written at the same time, *Nihon shoki* (The Chronicle of Japan). Because the orthography of the *Kojiki* died out as a writing system for Japanese shortly after the Nara period, the *Nihon shoki* became the more used text, supposedly containing the same information. The *Kojiki* had in fact become virtually unintelligible even to the educated Japanese of Motoori's time. By decoding the text, therefore, Motoori hoped to bring to light the original Japanese worldview.

A devout follower of Shintō, Motoori's task assumed a profoundly religious dimension as well. He believed the *Kojiki* was a written account of what had been orally transmitted word for word from the time of creation. The Kojiki contained the very words of the deities who had created the world. Furthermore, since the text was written in an orthography that had soon fallen into disuse, Motoori believed the written text was uncorrupted by later interpreters, making it superior to the adulterated cosmogonies of other cultures. This firm belief sustained Motoori's lifelong devotion to the enormously complex task of decoding the text.

Based on his readings of Japanese classics, Motoori also developed a philosophy of poetic or religious expression: his theory of 'heart' (*kokoro*). As a technical term, kokoro designates the seat of thinking and feeling; it is the basis of sensitivity (see KOKORO). Heart is not, however, limited to people; things and words also have heart. If poets have 'genuine heart,' they will be touched by the heart of things and the heart of words. The poetically or religiously expressive act, therefore, is an act of the heart, something shared by the things, the person and the words. Since the genuine heart is also a goal of Shintō purification, Motoori saw in this theory the basis of religious language as well. This in turn influenced his understanding of the significance of the *Kojiki*.

If the *Kojiki* represents the original words of the deities at the time of creation, to read or study the text is virtually a ritualistic re-enactment of creation. The implication for Motoori was that the ancient Japanese language of the text is not only the language of the deities, but also the most pure intimation of the heart of things. By this line of reasoning, Motoori made the *Kojiki* into the sacred scripture of Shintō. Based on his reading of the text, Motoori founded a philosophy of Shintō supposedly free of Buddhist influence. For virtually the first time, Shintō could develop a formal doctrinal system of its own (see SHINTŌ).

This line of thought readily supported a nationalist ideology. If the ancient Japanese language was the protolanguage of all languages, if that language were most purely resonant with the heart of things and if the Japanese emperor was the special link between the deities and humanity, obviously Japan would have a special place in the world. This sense of national superiority became especially strong in the next generation of Native Studies scholars such as Hirata Atsutane (1776–1843) and helped contribute to the movement to overthrow the Tokugawa shogunate and restore the emperor as the true leader of Japan. In this effort, it found an intellectual ally in the Mito School, a Shintō–Confucian synthesis, that argued for the centrality of the emperor as the 'body of the state'. The restoration of the emperor was completed in 1868, the beginning of Japan's modern era.

In summary, the introduction of neo-Confucianism from China and the establishment of a stable state under Tokugawa rule created a new fertile environment for Japanese philosophy. Ultimately, neo-Confucianism itself did not become a dominant philosophy in Japan, but its presence challenged the dominant Buddhist philosophies. In this new context Japanese philosophy grew more concerned with social ethics, the study of the natural world and cultural identity. In this period developed the idea of the warrior-turned-bureaucrat, as fiercely loyal to the organization as formerly to the lord. As there was more interest in studying and classifying the physical processes of nature, there was also a newly defined aesthetic of sensitivity and poetic expression (see AESTHETICS, JAPANESE). For the first time, Shintō became a major intellectual force in Japanese thought and there was an attendant sense of the uniqueness and superior quality of Japanese culture. All these factors became the intellectual background for the emergence of the modern era after 1868, and its related philosophies.

8 Modern Japanese philosophy and its critique of Western philosophy

The Tokugawa policy of seclusion ended with the appearance of US gunboats in 1854 and their demand that Japan open itself to international trade. To protect its sovereignty from infringement by the Western powers, Japan believed it had to become a modern industrial and military power in its own right. The government sent its brightest young intellectuals to Europe and the United States to study what was needed for modernization, such as medicine, engineering, agriculture, postal systems and education. This effort included the study of Western thought as a means to understanding Western society and the ideas behind its science and technology. Although there was some sustained interest in American pragmatism (see PRAGMATISM), most Japanese philosophers turned toward Germany for their inspiration (see GERMAN IDEALISM).

Throughout the nineteenth century, most Japanese leaders hoped Japan could superimpose Western science and technology on a society that remained true to Asian cultural values. By the first decade of the twentieth century, Japan had successfully developed the technology and military might needed to defeat both Russia and China in wars. Many Japanese intellectuals feared, however, that this was at the expense of traditional values. The ideal of detached objectivity in Western science threatened the tradition of apprenticed learning through imitation of the master. The Buddhist and Confucian theories of reality were in jeopardy of being overwhelmed by Western scientism. The new egalitarian ideals of education so helpful in developing a technological society were also part of a democratic worldview that emphasized the individual as basic unit of society and threatened the traditional Confucian virtues and social hierarchy. How to negotiate the differences between traditional Asian and modern Western values became a major concern among Japanese philosophers in the first half of the twentieth century.

The most influential development in modern Japanese philosophy was the emergence of the Kyoto School of thought (see KYOTO SCHOOL). By the early twentieth century, philosophy had become an academic study in Japanese universities. An influential circle of philosophers clustered around NISHIDA KITARŌ (1870–1945), a professor at Kyoto University. This group tended to address problems about the meaning of self, the nature of knowledge, the role of spirituality and the place of both ethical and aesthetic value.

Nishida was the single most influential philosopher in the prewar period. His philosophical goal was to locate empiricism and scientific thinking within a larger system that would also give value judgements a non-subordinate place. *Zen no kenkyū* (An Inquiry into the Good), his first major work, developed the notion of 'pure experience', an idea adapted from William JAMES and perhaps developed in light of Nishida's own Zen Buddhist practice. The book's theme is that there is a thrust toward unity in all experience. Thought arises out of the disruption of the unity of immediacy and serves as a means to establishing a more comprehensive unity. In Nishida's phrase, pure experience is the 'alpha and omega of thought'.

Nishida himself subsequently decided this early effort was too 'psychologistic' and 'mystical', and developed a different philosophical system in the 1920s and 1930s that emphasized the 'logic of place (or *topos*)'. According to Nishida, every judgement is restricted by the logic of its context, which in turn derives from a broader experiential domain that it cannot explain in its own terms (see LOGIC IN JAPAN). An empirical judgement, for example, excludes the subject of the experience (see EMPIRICISM). Its internal logic precludes the consideration of the self. Yet, of course, there can be no empirical data without an experiencing subject; so, the logical place within which empirical judgements are made is within a broader experiential context that assumes the function of the self. If that broader context is then made the logical domain for judgements, we have idealism. In turn, according to Nishida, the experiential locus that makes idealist judgements possible cannot be spoken of logically within the domain of idealism. Nishida calls this experiential locus 'place of absolute nothingness', the ground of 'acting-intuiting'. This region cannot be expressed in any logical form, but is the basis of all logical expression. It is also the ground of value: spiritual, ethical and aesthetic.

In this way, Nishida argued that the realm of empirical judgement is necessarily grounded experientially in a realm of value that it cannot analyse from its own standpoint. Nishida's system attempted to grant Western science its logical place while showing that its experiential ground was what traditional Asian values had affirmed all along. Religion, at least

in its Asian forms, was not antagonistic to science, nor was it endangered by science. On the contrary, Nishida argued that spiritual experience is what makes science logically possible.

Nishida argued for the synthesis of Eastern values and Western values by analysing the logic of epistemology. He was joined in this logical or epistemological approach by other philosophers connected in some way with the Kyoto School such as TANABE HAJIME (1885–1962) and NISHITANI KEIJI (1900–90). Other Kyoto School philosophers addressed the issue from the other direction, by analysing values. Hisamatsu Shin'ichi (1889–1980), for example, analysed the religio-aesthetic worldview of Zen Buddhism, advocating it as the basis for a style of life. MIKI KIYOSHI (1897–1945), on the other hand, developed a 'logic of creativity' inspired by both Buddhist and Marxist theories of praxis.

Among the modern Japanese ethicists, the most influential was WATSUJI TETSURŌ (1889–1960), a professor at Tokyo University and not technically a member of the Kyoto School. Watsuji explained that Western ethics takes the individual for its prime locus. Western ethics is constituted *vis-à-vis* individual needs and the focus of morality is the individual agent. In contrast, Watsuji said, Confucian ethics takes the social as its prime locus, being constituted out of the primary social relations. Watsuji maintained both traditions are faulty in seeing only one dimension of the whole. As an alternative, he developed a philosophical anthropology emphasising 'betweenness', a dialectical tension between the individual and the collective. The collective establishes norms within which one can act in a given society, whereas the individual serves as the locus of freedom. If unqualified by the opposing pole, the collective suppresses freedom and the individual rejects the objective validity of norms.

Watsuji concluded, therefore, that true ethical behaviour is possible only as a 'double negation' that rejects both poles without settling in either. In this 'betweenness' we find the dialectical tension between the social and the individual, the fundamental definition of our human being. So, the nature of ethics follows from the definition of human being, and ethics is the fundamental way of realizing our humanity. Watsuji developed these ideas first in his *Ningen no gaku to shite no rinrigaku* (Ethics as the Study of Human Being) (1934) and then more fully in his magnum opus, a three-volume work called simply Rinrigaku (Ethics) (1937–49).

9   Postwar developments

The defeat in the Second World War caused many

philosophers to rethink their positions. Tanabe and Watsuji, for example, explicitly repented some of the nationalistic implications of their earlier writings. In his *Zangedō to shite no tetsugaku* (Philosophy as Metanoia) in 1946, Tanabe developed an intricate, self-critical dialectical method to check the emergence of philosophical ideologies. In conceiving this method he drew inspiration from the philosophical analysis of Shinran's thought done by one of his students, Takeuchi Yoshinori. The connection with religious philosophy has become a recurrent theme in the further development of the Kyoto school as exemplified in the works of Nishitani, Takeuchi and Ueda Shizuteru. In a spirit reminiscent of the Kamakura Buddhist thinkers, many of the postwar philosophers have turned inward to re-examine the nature of human existence, now able to be formulated in relation to the problematics of existentialism as well as Buddhism.

At the same time some Japanese philosophers have continued to specialize in the scholarly study of Western philosophy. In many Japanese universities there are departments of philosophy where much of the work is indistinguishable from what might find in a philosophy department in Europe or North America. In general, the Continental traditions of philosophy, rather than the British analytic traditions, continue to dominate.

Lastly, and especially since the 1960s, there are individuals and groups of philosophers who have explored new provocative directions, drawing their ideas from a wide variety of sources including Western science, psychoanalysis and phenomenology as well as traditional Asian thought and medicine. This phenomenon is another example of a recurrent pattern in the history of Japanese philosophy: the assimilation and adaptation of foreign ideas against the background of an ongoing tradition.

See also: AESTHETICS, JAPANESE; BUDDHIST PHILOSOPHY, CHINESE; BUDDHIST PHILOSOPHY, JAPANESE; BUSHI PHILOSOPHY; CONFUCIAN PHILOSOPHY, CHINESE; CONFUCIAN PHILOSOPHY, JAPANESE; LITERATURE, PHILOSOPHY IN MODERN JAPANESE; KOKORO; KYOTO SCHOOL; LOGIC IN JAPAN; SHINTŌ

References and further reading

Maruyama Masao (1952) *Nihon seiji shisō shi kenkyū*, trans. Mikiso Hane, *Studies in the Intellectual History of Tokugawa Japan*, Tokyo: University of Tokyo Press, 1974. (English translation of Maruyama's classic study of the relation between Tokugawa thought and politics, including good summaries of the basic philosophical positions.)

Matsunaga Daigan and Matsunaga, A. (1974–6) *Foundation of Japanese Buddhism*, Los Angeles, CA: Buddhist Books International, 2 vols. (A technical, detailed exposition of the Buddhist philosophical systems of Nara, Heian and Kamakura Japan.)

Moore, C.A. (ed.) (1967) *The Japanese Mind: Essentials of Japanese Philosophy and Culture*, Honolulu, HI: University of Hawaii Press. (A provocative, but somewhat uneven, collection of fifteen essays by Japanese philosophers who participated in East–West Philosophers' Conferences during 1939–64.)

Nakamura Hajime (1969) *A History of the Development of Japanese Thought*, Tokyo: Kokusai Bunka Shinkokai (Japan Cultural Society), 2 vols, 2nd edn. (Not an integrated book but a set of seven excellent essays on different periods of Japanese philosophy. Out-of-print, but still one of the most insightful discussions available in English.)

* Nishida Kitarō (1911) *Zen no kenkyū* , trans. Masao Abe and C. Ives, *An Inquiry into the Good*, New Haven, CN: Yale University Press, 1990. (Translation of Nishida's first major work; probably the most famous philosophical work of modern Japan.)

Piovesana, G.K. (1969) *Contemporary Japanese Philosophical Thought*, New York: St John's University Press. (Good survey of major Japanese philosophers 1862–1962. Includes a good, but dated, bibliography.)

* Tanabe Hajime (1946) *Zangedō to shite no tetsugaku*, trans. Takeuchi Yoshinori *et al.*, *Philosophy as Metanoetics*, Berkeley, CA: University of California Press, 1987. (Translation of Tanabe's dense but profound reflection on the nature of philosophy.)

Tsunoda, R., de Bary, W.T. and Keene, D. (eds) (1964) *Sources of Japanese Traditions*, New York: Columbia University Press, 2 vols. (Extensive collection of short excepts from philosophical texts in translation, including brief but useful introductions to each writer.)

* Watsuji Tetsurō (1937–49) *Rinrigaku* (Ethics), Tokyo: Iwanami shoten, 3 vols. (Watsuji's fully developed ethical system with critiques of other systems, East and West. The best available edition is in vols 10–11 of *Watsuji Tetsurō zenshū* (Watsuji's Collected Works), Tokyo: Iwanami shoten, 1961–3, 20 vols.)

* —— (1934) *Ningen no gaku toshite no rinrigaku* (Ethics as the Study of Human Being), Tokyo: Iwanami shoten. (The best source is vol. 9 of *Watsuji Tetsurō zenshū* (Watsuji's Collected Works), Tokyo: Iwanami shoten, 1961–3, 20 vols. About

half of this work has been translated by S. Yamamoto and R.E. Carter, *Watsuji Tetsuro's Rinrigaku: Ethics in Japan*, Albany, NY: State University of New York Press, 1996.)

THOMAS P. KASULIS

JASPERS, KARL (1883–1969)

Karl Jaspers is generally known as an existentialist, but he also developed interesting conceptions in other fields of philosophy: in philosophy of religion, the concepts of Transcendence, cipher and philosophical faith; in philosophy of history, the thesis of an Axial Period in history; in political philosophy, the idea of a new, reasonable politics. His existentialism deals mainly with personal moral attitudes and private aspects of individual self-realization in boundary situations and intimate interpersonal communication. His political philosophy concentrates on controversial political affairs and some of the urgent problems of his age (for example, the possibility of extinguishing all life on earth by the atom bomb, or of establishing a world-wide totalitarian regime).

1 **Life**
2 **Existentialism**
3 **Metaphysics and philosophy of religion**
4 **Philosophy of reason and political thinking**
5 **Philosophy of history and history of philosophy**

1 Life

Karl Jaspers studied medicine and became a psychiatrist and psychologist before turning to philosophy at the University of Heidelberg in 1920. His first major book, *Allgemeine Psychopathologie* (General Psychopathology) (1913), is a study in the methodology of psychiatry focusing on the relevance of phenomenological and hermeneutical approaches for the methods of psychopathology, while his second major book, *Psychologie der Weltanschauungen* (1919), sets forth a psychology of worldviews. This book shows clearly how much he was influenced by Immanuel Kant, Søren Kierkegaard, Friedrich Nietzsche and Max Weber. Other formative influences on his philosophy stem from Plato, Plotinus, Friedrich Hegel, Friedrich Schelling, Wilhelm Dilthey and Edmund Husserl. Jaspers' existentialism is developed extensively in the three-volume *Philosophie* published in 1932. During the Nazi regime in Germany he was denied the right to teach and forbidden to publish. In 1948 he moved from Heidelberg to Switzerland where he earned a

professorship at the University of Basel. The experience of Nazi terrorism led to a break in the continuity of his philosophizing: he no longer understood his philosophy as an existential philosophy, but as one of reason, reflecting on actual political concerns. This change in Jaspers' philosophical perspective becomes evident in his major book in political philosophy, *Die Atombombe und die Zukunft des Menschen* (The Atom Bomb and the Future of Man) (1958). During this period, Jaspers also published his main works in philosophy of religion, *Der philosophische Glaube* (The Perennial Scope of Philosophy) (1948) and *Der philosophische Glaube angesichts der Offenbarung* (Philosophical Faith and Revelation) (1962) and began developing a new and original conception of world-philosophy. When he died, only a single volume of a history of world-philosophy had been published.

2 Existentialism

Jaspers' existentialism is grounded on a conception of the human being as a dual project of self-realization. Combining some ideas of KANT and KIERKEGAARD, he sees a human being as an empirical phenomenon and as a phenomenon with a non-empirical dimension. In the empirical dimension he distinguishes three modes of human being or self-realization: (1) vital existence or naive vitality (*bloßes Dasein*); (2) consciousness-as-such (*Bewußtsein überhaupt*), that is, the dimension of logical thinking and rationality; (3) spirit (*Geist*), that is, the dimension of ideas which becomes manifest in personal ideals, creative conceptions of the arts, and so on. These three modes of self-realization are the empirical media for another mode which is non-empirical and non-objective, which Jaspers calls '*Existenz*'. *Existenz* is the authentic ground of human being, the intimate dimension of personal autonomy, existential freedom and true selfhood. No empirical studies or doctrines of ontology, philosophical anthropology, or ethics can give an adequate understanding of this dimension of subjectivity and humanity. Such an understanding is possible only by realizing this dimension in one's own life or by elucidating it through philosophizing.

But how can one realize one's personal autonomy and *Existenz*? Jaspers' answer is that *Existenz* cannot be planned or managed at all because it is a gift from a non-objectifiable being which he calls 'Transcendence'. Furthermore, realization of *Existenz* in specific moments of life is possible only under two conditions: first, the experience of boundary situations and, second, the experience of mutual existential communication with a partner. Boundary situations like death, suffering, struggle, and guilt cannot be overcome by using the objective and rational knowledge that helps us solve everyday problems. They require a radical change in our attitudes and common ways of thinking. In *Psychologie der Weltanschauungen* and volume 2 of *Philosophie* Jaspers presents a remarkable range of deep psychological insights into boundary situations drawn from his experience as a psychiatrist and psychologist. He shows that many of the usual reactions to such situations prevent us from realizing our *Existenz*. The boundary situation of death, for example, can be the source of fear, anxiety and nihilistic despair, but it can also evoke the urgency of living authentically without delay and self-deception.

Jaspers distinguishes four types of communication operative in the four modes of being by which we exist. In the dimension of naïve vitality a human being lives in primitive communities with other human beings using other people only to reach vital ends. The second dimension, consciousness-as-such, is linked to a type of intellectual communication based on logical and rational categories. In the third dimension, spirit, a human being experiences communication in the close community of an 'idea of a whole', a religion, family, university, party, society, state and so on. The highest and most valuable form of communication, where the human being realizes *Existenz*, is existential communication. This is a non-objective, very intimate personal relationship between two persons, friends, lovers, a married couple, parent and child, or teacher and student. This type of communication cannot be adequately described and verbally communicated in an objectifying language. In Jaspers' subtle analyses of different reactions to boundary situations, as well as in his reflections on existential communication, a number of moral attitudes are mentioned which are highly significant for his concept of *Existenz*: courage without self-deception, composure, self-possession, dignity, fidelity, existential solidarity, responsibility, autonomy. These values constitute a specific ethos of humanity in Jaspers' existentialism (see EXISTENTIALISM).

3 Metaphysics and philosophy of religion

Self-realization as *Existenz* is experienced as a gift from a transcendent source. This experience directs the subject to a dimension of being which Jaspers calls 'Transcendence', absolute being, being-as-such, God and the Encompassing. His metaphysics rejects every type of metaphysical system or speculation that aims to bridge the gap between immanence and Transcendence. The task of metaphysics is instead to appeal to every human being to 'read' the cipher-script or the 'language' of Transcendence for its own sake. A cipher is a subjective and intuitive symbol that always

remains open in its meaning and functions as a signpost to Transcendence. Everything in the world is able to become a cipher. Jaspers explicitly mentions: nature, creations of the arts, metaphysical systems, myths and religions. He emphasizes the experience of foundering (*Scheitern*) as a special cipher and signpost to Transcendence.

Jaspers' philosophy of religion does not accept an objective historical revelation of God. God is hidden forever and cannot speak to us in an objectifying language through mediators. We can only be aware of Transcendence as *Existenz* in a non-objective act of cipher-'reading'. But no cipher can give any information about Transcendence beyond the horizon of historicity. It is a necessary consequence of this position that Jaspers understands Jesus as one of the 'examplary men' in human history alongside Confucius, Buddha and Socrates. Because of the paradigmatic way that Jesus realized existential possibilities, such as the ability to love and capacity for suffering, he is relevant to human beings at all times. In place of any religious faith grounded on a revelation of God, Jaspers holds out the conception of philosophical faith. This sort of faith has no objectively guaranteed proof of the existence of Transcendence and is not bound to rituals, churches, priests and theologians, who claim to be the interpreters of God's revelation. Philosophical faith is an optimistic credo involving confidence in the possibility of freedom and humanity and in the existence of a meta-empirical dimension of being (Transcendence, God, the Encompassing). It claims neither absolute certainty with respect to the possession of moral truth, nor an absolutely true knowledge of this dimension of being (see EXISTENTIALIST THEOLOGY).

4 Philosophy of reason and political thinking

The concept of reason became increasingly dominant in Jaspers' later philosophy. His comprehensive book, *Von der Wahrheit* (1947), is an extensive study of the dimensions of reason explicated in the context of the doctrine of the Encompassing. Reason is the bond of all modes of the Encompassing, a dynamic principle that expresses an anti-dogmatic and pluralistic intention, on the one hand, and a universalizing and communicative intention, on the other. These basic intentions of reason influenced Jaspers' political philosophy after the Second World War. During this period, he was concerned with the nature of German guilt for the rise of the Nazi movement in *Die Schuldfrage* (The Question of German Guilt) (1946), and with the problem of German reunification, as well as with global problems such as an emerging world order, the dangers of totalitarianism, the chance for worldwide communication among different nations in the face of the atom bomb and the cold war, the importance and deficiencies of the United Nations Organisation, and the necessary conditions of world peace. Reason works in this context as a dynamic principle to prevent the dogmatization of political worldviews. It is also the task of reason to give normative impulses to traditional politics, that is, 'Realpolitik', as a means for gaining power and domination over others. Reason transfers the ethos of humanity and moral ideals characteristic of Jaspers' concept of *Existenz* from the private sphere of life to the public sphere. In this way a new reasonable politics based on moral attitudes (for example, intellectual integrity, open-mindedness, tolerance, respect for other persons, groups and people in their cultural and ethnic diversity) may help overcome the two universal political-boundary situations of the modern age: the possibility of annihilating all life on Earth with the atom bomb and the possibility of establishing a worldwide totalitarian regime.

5 Philosophy of history and history of philosophy

Jaspers' philosophy of history, which he develops in *Vom Ursprung und Ziel der Geschichte* (The Origin and Goal of History) (1949), argues for the existence of an Axial Period in history (800–200 BC). During the Axial age the basic categories of human thought, culture and religion were developed in China, India and the West. Those categories have enabled the self-understanding of mankind to continue up to the modern period. The historical consciousness of the Axial Period reminds us not only of certain cultural highlights of mankind (in China, the thoughts of Confucius and Laozi; in India, the Upanishads and Buddha; in Palestine, the prophets; in Greece, the great philosophers and tragedians), but also of the threefold origin of the culture of mankind and of the importance of pluralism in universal history. This historical consciousness provides impulses for a worldwide communication beyond all differences of creed and political opinion in our time. Jaspers' philosophy of history is nondeterministic: history is not a teleological process whereby individuals are determined by historical laws, inevitable fate, or socioeconomic mechanisms immune from human will and intention. Rather, human beings help direct the historical process through their freedom without ever being able completely to predict future tendencies by means of total planning.

For Jaspers, studying the history of philosophy entails an existential act of encounter with great human beings in the history of mankind. Great philosophers can influence life orientations and modes of thinking in all times because they make us aware of basic existential possibilities and fundamental attitudes of thinking as such. Jaspers intended to write a world history of philosophy based on five distinct approaches to the history of philosophy (historical, thematic, genetic, practical, dynamic). This project remained unfinished. During Jaspers' lifetime, only the book *Die Großen Philosophen* (The Great Philosophers) (1957) appeared; but two volumes with fragments of this immense project were published in 1981, long after his death.

List of works

Jaspers, K. (1913) *Allgemeine Psychopathologie*, Berlin: Springer; 7th edn, trans. J. Hoenig and M.W. Hamilton, *General Psychopathology*, Chicago, IL: University of Chicago Press, 1963. (A methodological work which focuses on the hermeneutic approach in psychiatry.)

—— (1919) *Psychologie der Weltanschauungen* (Psychology of Worldviews), Berlin: Springer; 6th edn, Munich, 1985. (A psychological analysis of worldviews which anticipates basic ideas of Jaspers' later existentialism.)

—— (1932) *Philosophie,* Berlin: Springer, 3 vols; trans. E.B. Ashton, *Philosophy*, Chicago, IL: University of Chicago Press, 3 vols, 1969–71. (Jaspers' main work in existentialism, comprising three volumes: World-Orientation, Existential Elucidation and Metaphysics.)

—— (1935) *Vernunft und Existenz*, Groningen: J.W. Wolters; trans. W. Earle, *Reason and Existenz,* London: Routledge & Kegan Paul, 1956. (A collection of five lectures concerning the relation between Existenz and reason.)

—— (1946) *Die Schuldfrage*, Heidelberg/Zurich; trans. E.B. Ashton, *The Question of German Guilt*, New York: Dial Press, 1947. (This book treats the question of German guilt in relation to the rise of the Nazi regime.)

—— (1947) *Von der Wahrheit* (On Truth), Munich: R. Piper. (In this book Jaspers' conception of the Encompassing and his philosophy of reason are developed.)

—— (1948) *Der philosophische Glaube*, Zurich; trans. R. Manheim, *The Perennial Scope of Philosophy*, London: Routledge & Kegan Paul, 1950. (The first explication of Jaspers' conception of philosophical faith.)

—— (1949) *Vom Ursprung und Ziel der Geschichte*, Zurich: Artemis; trans. M. Bullock, *The Origin and Goal of History*, London: Routledge & Kegan Paul, 1953. (A representation of Jaspers' philosophy of history in which he sets forth his idea of an Axial Age in world history.)

Jaspers, K. and Bultmann, R. (1954) *Die Frage der Entmythologisierung*, Munich; trans. N. Guterman, *Myth and Christianity*, New York: Noonday Press, 1958. (The question of the inevitable function of myth in Christianity is discussed in opposition to Bultmann's call for demythologization.)

Jaspers, K. (1957) *Die Großen Philosophen Erster Band*, Munich; ed. H. Arendt, trans. R. Manheim, *The Great Philosophers*, New York: Harcourt Brace, 2 vols, 1962, 1966. (The first volume of Jaspers' enormous project of a world history of philosophy.)

—— (1958) *Die Atombombe und die Zukunft des Menschen*, Munich; trans. E.B. Ashton, *The Future of Mankind* (also as *The Atom Bomb and the Future of Man*), Chicago, IL: University of Chicago Press, 1961. (Jaspers' basic work in political philosophy which gives a thorough analysis of the implications of human existence after the advent of atomic weapons.)

—— (1962) *Der philosophische Glaube angesichts der Offenbarung*, Munich: R. Piper; trans. E.B. Ashton, *Philosophical Faith and Revelation*, Chicago, IL: University of Chicago Press, 1967. (A critical engagement of Jaspers' conception of philosophical faith with religious faith based on revelation.)

—— (1981) *Die Großen Philosophen Nachlaß 1 und 2*, Munich; ed. M. Ermarth and L.H. Ehrlich, trans. E. Ehrlich and L.H. Ehrlich, *The Great Philosophers Vol. III*, New York: Harcourt Brace, 1993. (Fragments of Jaspers' project of a world history of philosophy.)

—— (1986) *Karl Jaspers: Basic Philosophical Writings; Selections*, ed., trans. and with intro. by L.H. Ehrlich, E. Ehrlich and G.B. Pepper, Athens, Ohio and London: Ohio University Press; 2nd edn, Atlantic Highlands, NJ: Humanities Press, 1994. (An excellent selection of key texts with competent introductions and translations.)

References and further reading

Ehrlich, L.H. (1975) *Philosophy as Faith*, Amherst, MA: University of Massachusetts Press. (Focusing on Jaspers' philosophy of religion.)

Ehrlich, L.H. and Wisser, R. (eds) (1988) *Karl Jaspers Today: Philosophy at the Threshold of the Future*, Lanham, MD: University Press of America. (A collection of papers initially presented on the occasion of the centenary year of Jaspers' birth at the 17th World Congress of Philosophy.)

Hersch, J. (1986) *Karl Jaspers: Eine Einführung in sein Werk*, Munich: R. Piper. (An introduction to the main ideas of Jaspers' philosophy.)

Köhler, L. and Saner, H. (eds) (1985) *Hannah Arendt Karl Jaspers Briefwechsel 1926–1969*, Munich; trans. R. Kimber and R. Kimber, *Hannah Arendt Karl Jaspers Correspondence 1926–1969*, New York: Harcourt, 1992. (Gives fruitful insights into the close relationship and friendship of both philosophers.)

Olson, A.M. (1979) *Transcendence and Hermeneutics: An Interpretation of Karl Jaspers*, The Hague: Nijhoff. (Focuses on hermeneutical aspects of Jaspers' philosophy that are relevant to the philosophy of religion.)

—— (ed.) (1994) *Heidegger and Jaspers*, Philadelphia, PA: Temple University Press. (A collection of essays that incorporates the results of investigations into the Jaspers–Heidegger relationship presented at conferences of the Jaspers Society of North America.)

Penzo, G. (1985) *Il comprendere in Karl Jaspers e il problema dell' ermeneutica*, Rome: Armando editore. (Points out the hermeneutical dimension of Jaspers' philosophizing.)

Salamun, K. (1985) *Karl Jaspers*, Munich: C.H. Beck. (A general introduction with critical arguments concerning methodological positions in Jaspers' existentialism.)

—— (ed.) (1991) *Karl Jaspers – Zur Aktualität seines Denkens*, Munich: R. Piper. (A collection of articles demonstrating the continuing importance of Jaspers' philosophy for the present age.)

Salamun-Hybasek, E. and Salamun, K. (eds) (1988–95) *Jahrbuch der Österreichischen Karl-Jaspers-Gesellschaft* (Yearbook of the Austrian Karl-Jaspers-Society) 1–8, Innsbruck, and Vienna: Österr. Studienverlag. (Periodical concerning Jaspers published by the Austrian Karl-Jaspers-Society.)

Samay, S. (1971) *Reason Revisited: The Philosophy of Karl Jaspers*, Notre Dame, IN: University of Notre Dame Press. (Treats the relevance of Jaspers' concept of reason for his conceptions of philosophy, science and metaphysics.)

Saner, H. (1970) *Karl Jaspers in Selbstzeugnissen und Bilddokumenten*, Reinbeck: Rowohlt. (Chronological introduction stressing also biographical facts.)

—— (ed.) (1970) *Karl Jaspers in der Diskussion*, Munich: R. Piper. (A collection of articles and reviews dealing with several fields of Jaspers' philosophical thinking from a critical point of view.)

Schilpp, P.A. (ed.) (1981) *The Philosophy of Karl Jaspers*, La Salle, IL: Open Court. (The essays in this collection address a wide range of basic ideas in Jaspers' philosophizing. Includes a 'Reply' by Jaspers to his critics.)

Schrag, O.O. (1971) *Existence, Existenz, and Trans-*

cendence, Pittsburgh, PA: Duquesne University Press. (Discusses Jaspers' position in philosophy of religion, especially his concept of cipher.)

Tilliette, X. (1959) *Karl Jaspers: Theorié de la vérité, Metaphysique des chiffres, Foi philosophique*, Paris: Aubier. (Provides fruitful insights into the metaphysical components of Jaspers' philosophy.)

Walraff, C.F. (1970) *Karl Jaspers: An Introduction to His Philosophy*, Princeton, NJ: Princeton University Press. (A short and clear introduction to basic themes of Jaspers' existential philosophy, his conception of philosophy, and his idea of the Encompassing.)

Walters, G.J. (1988) *Karl Jaspers and the Role of 'Conversion' in the Nuclear Age*, Lanham, MD: University Press of America. (An interesting application of Jaspers' existentialist and political idea of 'conversion' to the problems of nuclear war and disarmament.)

—— (ed.) (1995) *The Tasks of Truth: Essays on Karl Jaspers' Idea of the University*, Frankfurt and New York: Peter Lang. (A collection of articles about Jaspers' philosophy of education.)

Wisser, R. and Ehrlich, L.H. (eds) (1993) *Karl Jaspers: Philosopher among Philosophers*, Würzburg: Königshausen & Neumann. (A collection with contributions concerning the relation of Jaspers to other philosophers.)

Young-Bruehl, E. (1981) *Freedom and Karl Jaspers' Philosophy*, New Haven, CT: Yale University Press. (An analysis of the various aspects of Jaspers' concept of freedom.)

KURT SALAMUN

JEFFERSON, THOMAS (1743–1826)

Thomas Jefferson came from a privileged background, began his public career as a lawyer, and rose to hold the governorship of his home state of Virginia and to serve his country successively as minister to France, secretary of state, vice-president and president. His proudest declared achievements were to have been author of the Declaration of Independence, and of the Statute of Virginia for religious freedom, and founder of the University of Virginia. An architect, inventor, scientist, educator and writer, he was one of the most versatile and brilliant men of his generation. In philosophy his main contribution was to political theory, where he supported a social contract theory and a doctrine of natural rights.

1 Life
2 Philosophical outlook

1 Life

Thomas Jefferson was born on 13 April 1743 at Shadwell in Virginia, heir of a wealthy family. Educated (1760–62) at William and Mary College, he became a lawyer, served (from 1769) in the Virginia House of Burgesses, and in 1775 and 1776 in the Continental Congress. In June 1776 he was appointed head of a committee of five to prepare the Declaration of Independence, of which he was the principal author. From 1779 onwards he held a number of major political posts, including that of US minister to France (where he succeeded Benjamin FRANKLIN in 1785), the vice-presidency of the USA from 1796 to 1800, and the presidency from 1800 to 1808.

2 Philosophical outlook

Jefferson's intellectual debts were particularly to John LOCKE, Isaac NEWTON, Dugald STEWART, Destutt de Tracy, Pierre-Jean CABANIS, and J.P. Flourens. He was a materialist whose model of reality derived from Newton, but also a deist who considered Jesus a great moral teacher but not divine. From Stewart and the Scots he absorbed the moral sense theory, but his realism owed more to the French Ideologues than the Scots (see ENLIGHTENMENT, CONTINENTAL; FRENCH PHILOSOPHY OF SCIENCE).

Jefferson's philosophical contribution was in political philosophy. He was a firm believer in the social contract theory and in natural rights, which he believed were based in the biological constitution of the individual and God's benevolence in making possible the satisfaction of those needs with which individuals were created. Jefferson's view of the political order was normative rather than descriptive, but it was empirical in that it was founded on the moral sense – violations of natural rights are immediately known to be wrong. Majority rule, while essential to democracy, cannot therefore involve infringement of the natural rights of the minority. Believing that sovereignty lay undivided in the people, he thought the people could employ multiple political agents to perform their will. This led to a hierarchy of political units – individual, local, state, and Federal – on the principle that each should be responsible for those functions which it can perform alone, delegating to the larger unit those which it cannot.

Although concerned with the machinery of government and the methods of balancing the units to prevent concentration of power, Jefferson believed that structure was not enough; the success of democracy lay in the values and attributes of the people. But these in turn, he thought, were influenced by society and education. For Jefferson, a free society had to be one in which people were independent, not only politically but also economically, through the ownership of property. In the society of yeomen farmers he saw the nearest realization of his ideal of a nation of free, responsible, and moral individuals. Free elections, he believed, would result in leadership being furnished by the 'natural aristocracy' of talent and virtue, for the cultivation of which he proposed a system of public education. But Jefferson's democracy did not include blacks; although he condemned slavery, he held slaves and regarded blacks as inferior.

See also: AMERICAN PHILOSOPHY IN THE 18TH AND 19TH CENTURIES; ENLIGHTENMENT, SCOTTISH; FRANKLIN, B.

List of works

Jefferson, T. (1892–9) *The Writings of Thomas Jefferson*, ed. P. Leicester Ford, New York: Putnam, 10 vols. (An older edition, but covering the span of Jefferson's life.)
—— (1950–92) *The Papers of Thomas Jefferson*, vols. 1–19 ed. Julian Boyd et al, vols. 20–23, ed. C. Cullen, vols. 24–6 ed. J. Catanzariti, Princeton, NJ: Princeton University Press. (The best modern scholarly edition, done in chronological order, but still in progress.)
—— (1984) 'The Declaration of Independence' in *Thomas Jefferson: Writings*, ed. M. D. Peterson, New York, Library of Classics of the United States Inc., 19-24. (This text gives the original version of the Declaration as Jefferson wrote it, together with the changes made before its adoption and promulgation on July 4, 1776. The Declaration of Independence is, together with the Constitution, the most important state paper in American history.)

References and further reading

Boorstin, D. (1948) *The Lost World of Thomas Jefferson*, New York: Holt. (Excellent study of the Jeffersonian intellectual world.)
Flower, E. and Murphey, M.G. (1977) *A History of Philosophy in America*, New York: Putnam, vol. 1, chap. 5. (A brief study of Jefferson's philosophy.)
Koch, A. (1943) *The Philosophy of Thomas Jefferson*, New York: Columbia University Press. (Dated but useful study of Jefferson's thought.)
Sheldon, G.W. (1991) *The Political Philosophy of*

Thomas Jefferson, Baltimore: John Hopkins Press. (Relying on the recent work of J.G.A. Pocock, Joyce Appleby and others, Sheldon attempts to fit Jefferson's thought into the current debates over Republicanism, Liberalism and Classicism.)
Wills, G. (1978) *Inventing America: Jefferson's Declaration of Independence*, Garden City, NY: Doubleday. (Particularly good on the Scottish influence on Jefferson.)

MURRAY G. MURPHEY

JEN *see* CONFUCIAN PHILOSOPHY, CHINESE; CONFUCIUS

JEWISH PHILOSOPHY

Jewish philosophy is philosophical inquiry informed by the texts, traditions and experiences of the Jewish people. Its concerns range from the farthest reaches of cosmological speculation to the most intimate theatres of ethical choice and the most exigent fora of political debate. What distinguishes it as Jewish is the confidence of its practitioners that the literary catena of Jewish tradition contains insights and articulates values of lasting philosophical import. One mark of the enduring import of these ideas and values is their articulation in a variety of idioms, from the mythic and archetypal discourse of the Book of Genesis to the ethical and legislative prescriptions of the Pentateuch at large, to the admonitions of the Prophets, the juridical and allegorical midrash and dialectics of the Rabbis, and to the systematic demonstrations, flights of imagination, existential declarations and apercus of philosophers in the modern or the medieval mode.

1 The nature of Jewish philosophy
2 Strengths and weaknesses
3 Movements and important figures
4 Movements and important figures (cont.)

1 The nature of Jewish philosophy

Students of Jewish philosophy, especially those who aspire to contribute a window or a wing to the edifice, must learn many languages, to read and listen to voices very different from their own. Just as the writers of the Genesis narratives or of the Pentateuch had to recast and reinvent the ancient creation myths and the ancient Babylonian laws to express the distinctively universal ethical demands and aesthetic standards of their God, and just as the Deuteronomist had to rediscover the ethical core in the original Mosaic legislation, hearing God's commands now as urgent reminders through the very human voice of Moses, so in every generation new interpreters are needed, to rediscover what is essential and living in the tradition. Such interpreters have always needed to negotiate the rapids of historical change – not just with regard to idiom but also with regard to content, refocusing and restructuring the living tradition, sculpting it philosophically with their own moieties of reason. Such thinkers have worked always with a view to the continuity of the tradition; that is, to the faithfulness of its future to its past, but also to the vitality and vivacity of what they found timeless in the tradition and therefore capable of acquiring new meanings and new spheres of application in the present.

The confidence of the practitioners of Jewish philosophy in the conceptual vitality and continually renewed moral and spiritual relevance of the tradition is typically the reflex of an existential commitment to that tradition and to the people who are its bearers. That confidence, and its repeated vindication by the richness of the tradition itself, is also a wellspring of renewal and encouragement for the commitment that energizes it – even, and especially, in times of historical crisis and external pressures, which have rarely confined themselves to sheerly intellectual challenges. Symptomatic of that commitment is the prominence and recurrence of the philosophy of Judaism among the concerns of Jewish philosophy. However, the two should not be confused. The philosophy of Judaism is inquiry into the nature and meaning of Jewish existence. Its questions address the sense to be given to the idea of a covenant between the universal God and the people of Israel, the meaning of that people's mission, their chosenness, their distinctive laws, customs and rituals and the relation of those norms to the more widely recognized norms of humanity, of which the Prophets of Israel were early and insistent messengers.

The philosophy of Judaism wants to understand Zionism, the Holocaust, the Jewish Diaspora and the historical vicissitudes that gave shape to Jewish experience over the millennia, from the age of the biblical patriarchs to the destruction of the first and second temples in Jerusalem, to the exile of the Jewish people and the return of many, after a hundred generations, to the land they had been promised and in which they had prospered, a land which some had never left but which most, for centuries, had pictured only through the sublimating lenses of sacred history, apocalypse and philosophy. The philosophy of Judaism wants to understand the ancient Jewish liturgy,

the exegetical practices and hermeneutical standards of the Jewish exegetes. Like Freud, it wants to understand Jewish humour. Like Pico della Mirandola, it wants to understand Kabbalah, Jewish mysticism, and like Buber, it wants to understand Hasidism. The concerns of the philosophy of Judaism touch every aspect of Jewish experience, just as the concerns of philosophy at large touch every aspect of experience in general. But the concerns of Jewish philosophy, like those of general philosophy, do not confine themselves to Jewish experience. They are, in fact, the same concerns as those of general philosophy, rendered distinctively Jewish by their steady recourse to the resources of the tradition, and sustained as philosophical by an insistence on critical receptivity, responsible but creative appropriation of ideas and values that withstand the scrutiny of reason and indeed grow and give fruit in its light.

2 Strengths and weaknesses

There are two weaknesses in Jewish philosophy as practised today. One is a tendency to historicism, that is, the equivocal equation of norm with facticity and facticity with norm that leads to an abdication of philosophical engagement for a detached clinical posture or an equally unwholesome surrender of judgment to the flow of events. Historicism is a natural by-product of respect for tradition, or of expectation of progress. It becomes particularly debilitating under the pressure of positivism, whether of the logical empiricist sort that dominated philosophy for much of the early twentieth century, or of the more endemic sort that thrives on the sheer givenness of any system of law and ritual or that allows itself to be overwhelmed by the press of history itself. It is not unusual, even today, when logical positivism is widely thought to be long dead, to find scholars of Jewish thought who substitute historical descriptions for philosophical investigations, often in the process begging or slighting the key philosophical questions. Nor is it unusual among those of more traditional stamp for scholars to be found who imagine that a faithful description of the contents of authentic Jewish documents constitutes doing Jewish philosophy – as though faithfulness to the tradition were somehow a substitute for critical grappling with the issues and problems, and as though the question as to what constitutes faithfulness to the tradition, conceptually, historically, morally and spiritually, were not itself among the most crucial of those issues and problems.

The second weakness is a narrowing of the gaze, a tendency to substitute philosophy of Judaism for the wider discourse of Jewish philosophy, as though the resources of the tradition had nothing (or nothing more) to contribute to ethics, or natural theology, or metaphysics and logic, for that matter. The work of the great practitioners of Jewish philosophy has repeatedly given the lie to such narrow expectations. In every epoch of its existence, Jewish philosophy has played an active role in the philosophical conversation of humankind – which is a universal conversation precisely because and to the extent that those who take part speak every language and bring to the conversation experiences that are universal as well as those that are unique.

But if two weaknesses are to be mentioned here, at least one strength should be cited as well: Jewish philosophy, although intimately engaged throughout its history with the philosophical traditions of the West, has also been a tradition apart. The open access of most of its practitioners to the Hebrew (and Aramaic) Jewish sources has afforded a perspective that is distinctive and that can be corrective of biases found in other branchings of the tree of philosophical learning. The early access of medieval Jewish philosophers to Arabic philosophical and scientific writings, and to the Greek works preserved in Arabic, enriched and broadened their philosophical repertoire. The scholastic learning of later medieval Jewish philosophers and their collaboration with scholastic thinkers made them at once participants and observers of in the lively philosophical debates of their day. The immersion and active participation of Renaissance and Enlightenment Jewish philosophers in the movements that spawned modernity gave them a similar philosophical vantage point. All philosophers must be, to some degree, alien to their society – Socrates and Nietzsche, and for that matter even Plato, Aristotle and Descartes were, to some degree, intellectual outsiders in their own times – not so alien as to have no word or thought in common with their contemporaries, but not so well integrated as to become mere apologists, or complacent and unquestioning acquiescors in the given. Jewish philosophy has long made and continues to make a distinctive, if today underutilized, contribution to cosmopolitan philosophical discourse in this regard. It shares the problematic of Western philosophy but typically offers a distinctive slant or perspective that calls into question accepted verities and thus enhances the critical edge of philosophical work for those who study it.

3 Movements and important figures

Jewish philosophy has over the course of its history been the source of a number of different types of study based on the philosophically relevant ideas of the Hebrew Bible, Rabbinic Law (Halakhah), Rabbinic theology and Rabbinic homiletics, exegesis and hermeneutics (midrash) (see BIBLE, HEBREW; HALAKHAH; THEOLOGY, RABBINIC; MIDRASH). The anti-Rabbinical, biblicist movement known as Karaism and the mystical tradition of the Kabbalah are examples of differing types of movements which have emerged (see KARAISM; KABBALAH), while Jewish voluntarism and Jewish Averroism were fields for the rivalry between intellectualist and less deterministic, more empiricist views of theology as it was played out among Jewish thinkers (see VOLUNTARISM, JEWISH; AVERROISM, JEWISH). More modern movements include the Jewish pietist movement founded by Israel Baal Shem Tov and known as Hasidism, the Jewish Enlightenment movement known as the Haskalah, and Zionism, the movement that led to the establishment of the modern State of Israel (see HASIDISM; ENLIGHTENMENT, JEWISH; ZIONISM).

The first exponent of Jewish philosophy was PHILO OF ALEXANDRIA, a major contributor to the synthesis of Stoicism, Middle Platonism and monotheistic ideas that helped forge the tradition of scriptural philosophy in the West. Other early figures include Daud AL-MUQAMMAS and Isaac ISRAELI, two of the first figures of medieval Jewish philosophical theology. Al-Fayyumi SAADIAH GAON (882–942), the first systematic Jewish philosopher, was also a major biblical translator and exegete, a grammarian, lexicographer and authority on Jewish religious law and ritual. The rationalism, pluralism and intellectual honesty evident in his work made it a model of Jewish philosophy for all who came after him. Solomon IBN GABIROL (c. 1020–c. 1057), long known as a Hebrew poet, was discovered in the nineteenth century to have been the author as well of the famous Neoplatonic philosophical work, preserved in Latin as the *Fons Vitae*. Moses IBN EZRA (c. 1055–after 1135) is notable for his poetic and philosophic conributions. Abraham IBN EZRA (c. 1089–1164) is likewise noted for his hermeneutical ideas and methods; his forthright approach to the Hebrew Bible was a critical influence on the thinking of Jewish philosophers from the Middle Ages to SPINOZA and beyond. A less familiar figure is Abu 'L-BARAKAT AL-BAGHDADI (*fl. c.* 1200–50), a brilliant Jewish thinker who converted to Islam late in life. He developed highly independent views about the nature of time, human consciousness, space, matter and motion. His work undercuts the notion that the medieval period was simply an age of faith and static commitment to a faith community.

A polymath of rather different spirit was Abraham BAR HAYYA in the eleventh century, who wrote on astronomy, mathematics, geography, optics and music as well as philosophy and who collaborated on scientific translations with the Christian scholar Plato of Tivoli, the transmitter of the Ptolemaic system to the Latin world. Bar Hayya's *Meditation of the Sad Soul* expresses the forlornness of human life in exile from the world of the divine, a forlornness tinged with the hope of future glory. Joseph IBN TZADDICK (d. 1149) similarly developed Neoplatonic ideas around the theme of the human being as a microcosm.

Bahya IBN PAKUDA (early twelfth century) wrote as a pietist philosopher. He placed philosophical understanding and critical thinking at the core of the spiritual devotion called for by the sincerest form of piety. Judah HALEVI (before 1075–1141), probably the greatest Hebrew poet after the Psalms, wrote a cogently argued philosophical dialogue best known as the *Kuzari*, but more formally titled, *A Defence and an Argument in behalf of the Abased Religion*. Set in the Khazar kingdom, whose king, historically, had converted to Judaism, the work mounts a trenchant critique of the intellectualism of the prevalent philosophical school and the spiritualizing and universalizing ascetic pietism that was its counterpart. Calling for a robust recovery of Jewish life and peoplehood in the Land of Israel, the work is not only a striking anticipation of Zionist ideas but a remarkable expression of the need to reintegrate the spiritual, intellectual, moral and physical dimensions of Jewish life.

Abraham IBN DAUD (c.1110–80), a historian as well as a philosopher, used his historiography to argue for the providential continuity of the Jewish intellectual and religious tradition. His philosophical work laid the technical foundations that made possible the philosophical achievement of Moses MAIMONIDES (1138–1204), the greatest of the philosophers committed to the Jewish tradition. Besides his medical writings and his extensive juridical corpus, which includes the authoritative fourteen-volume code of Jewish law, the *Mishneh Torah*, Maimonides was the author of the famous *Guide to the Perplexed*. Written in Arabic and intended for an inquirer puzzled by the apparent discrepancies between traditional Judaism and Aristotelian-Neoplatonic philosophy, the *Guide* is a paradigm in the theology of transcendence, addressing questions ranging from the overt anthropomorphism of the scriptural text to the purposes of the Mosaic legislation, to the controversy over the creation or eternity of the world, the problem of evil, and the sense that can be made of the ideas of revelation, providence, divine knowledge and human perfectibility. Like Halevi's *Kuzari* and Bahya's *Duties of the Heart*, the *Guide to the Perplexed* continues to be studied to this day by Jews and non-Jews for its philosophical insights.

Abraham BEN MOSES MAIMONIDES (1186–1237),

the son of the great philosopher and jurist, began his scholarly life as a defender of his father's work against the many critics who feared Maimonidean rationalism. In his mature work he became the exponent of a mystical, pietist and ascetic movement, largely influenced by Sufism. Moses NAHMANIDES (1194–1270), exegete, theologian and a founding figure of the Kabbalistic theosophy, championed Judaism in the infamous Barcelona Disputation of 1263 and played a leading role in the Maimonidean controversy. He struggled to harmonize his conservative and reactive tendencies with his respect for reason and the unvarnished sense of the biblical text.

IBN KAMMUNA (d. 1284) was a pioneer in other areas. Besides his work in the Ishraqi or Illuminationist tradition of theosophy, laid out in commentary on the Muslim philosopher IBN SINA (Avicenna), he wrote a distinctively dispassionate study of comparative religions, favouring Judaism but fairly and unpolemically presenting the Christian and Muslim alternatives.

Shem Tov IBN FALAQUERA (c.1225–c.1295) was a warm exponent of Maimonidean rationalism and an ardent believer in the interdependence of faith and reason. His selections in Hebrew from the lost Arabic original of Ibn Gabirol's magnum opus allowed modern scholars to identify Ibn Gabirol as the Avicebrol of the surviving Latin text, the *Fons Vitae*.

Hillel BEN SAMUEL OF VERONA (c.1220–95), physician, translator, Talmudist and philosopher was a Maimonist who introduced numerous scholastic ideas into Hebrew philosophical discourse. IMMANUEL OF ROME (c.1261–before 1336) was a prolific author of philosophical poetry and exegesis, often praising reason and intellectual love. Judah BEN MOSES OF ROME (c.1292–after 1330), known as Judah Romano, was an active bridge person between the Judaeo-Arabic and the scholastic tradition of philosophical theology.

Levi ben Gerson, known as GERSONIDES (1288–1344), was an important astronomer and mathematician as well as a biblical exegete and philosopher. His *Wars of the Lord* grappled with the problems of creation, providence, divine knowledge, human freedom and immortality. Aiming to defend his ancestral faith, Gersonides followed courageously where the argument led, often into radical and creative departures from traditional views.

Hasdai CRESCAS (1340–1410), an ardent defender of Judaism against Christian conversionary pressures, was among the most creative figures of Jewish philosophy, challenging many of the givens of Aristotelianism, including the idea that the cosmos must be finite in extent. Crescas' student Joseph ALBO (c.1360–1444) sought to organize Jewish theology into an axiomatic system, in part to render Jewish thought defensible against hostile critics.

Profiat DURAN (d. c. 1414), also known as Efodi, used his extensive understanding of Christian culture to criticize Christianity from a Jewish perspective. Deeply influenced by Moses Maimonides and Abraham ibn Ezra and by Neoplatonic and astrological ideas, he sought to balance the practical with the intellectual aspects of the Torah. Simeon BEN TZEMACH DURAN (1361–1444) contributed an original approach to the project of Jewish dogmatics and an implicit critical examination of that project.

The Shem Tov family included four thinkers active in fifteenth century Spain (see SHEM TOV FAMILY). Their works follow the persecution of 1391 and the ensuing mass apostasy of Spanish Jews and seek to rethink the relations of philosophy to Judaism. Shem Tov, the *paterfamilias*, criticized Maimonides and endorsed Kabbalah, but his sons Joseph, a court physician and auditor of royal accounts at Castile, and Isaac, a popular teacher of Aristotelian philosophy, and Joseph's son, again named Shem Tov, wrote numerous Peripatetic commentaries. These offspring charted a more moderate course that enabled Jewish intellectuals to cultivate philosophy and the kindred arts and sciences while asserting the ultimate primacy of their revealed faith.

Isaac BEN MOSES ARAMA (c.1420–94), like Nahmanides, was critical of Maimonidean and Aristotelian rationalism but did not discard reason, seeing in it a crucial exegetical tool and an avenue toward understanding miracles and providence. Isaac ABRAVANEL (1437–1508), leader of the Jews whom Ferdinand and Isabella exiled from Spain in 1492, like Arama criticised Maimonidean rationalism in the interest of traditional Judaism as he saw it, but at the same time put forward a theistic vision of history and strikingly modern views about politics and the state. His son, Judah BEN ISAAC ABRAVANEL, also known as Leone Ebreo (c.1460–c.1521), wrote the *Dialoghi d'amore*. Couched in the language of courtly love, the work explores the idea that love is the animating force of the cosmos. The work stands out as a brilliant dialectical exploration of the differences and complementarities of the Platonic and Aristotelian approaches to philosophy.

Judah MESSER LEON (c.1425–c.1495) was a philosopher, physician, jurist, communal leader, poet and orator. Awarded a doctorate in medicine and philosophy by the Emperor Frederick III, he could confer doctoral degrees in those subjects on the students in his *yeshivah*. He saw logic as the key to harmonizing religion and philosophy and favored scholastic logic over the Arabic logical works. His encyclopedia became a popular textbook, and his systematic elicitation of Hebrew rhetoric from the biblical text, in *The Book of the Honeycomb's Flow*, one of the first Hebrew books to be printed, was a masterpiece of cross-cultural humanistic scholarship. But Messer Leon failed to curb the spread of Kabbalah, whose underlying Platonic metaphysics he abhorred and whose appropriation by Christian Platonists he held in deep suspicion. Indeed, his own son turned toward the Kabbalah and sought to combine its teachings with the Aristotelianism favored by his father.

Yohanan BEN ISAAC ALEMANNO (1433/4–after 1503/4) brought together in his thinking Averroist, Kabbalistic, Neoplatonic and Renaissance humanist themes. He instructed PICO DELLA MIRANDOLA in Hebrew and in Kabbalah, bringing to birth what became a Christian, syncretic Kabbalism. Elijah DELMEDIGO (c.1460–1493) was an Aristotelian and Averroist. He translated works into Latin for Pico della Mirandola and developed a subtle critique of the kabbalistic ideas that in his time were rivaling and often displacing what he saw as more disciplined philosophical thinking. Abraham Cohen de HERRERA (c.1562–c.1635) was a philosophically oriented kabbalist of Spanish origin. His Spanish writings, in Latin translation, were blamed for inspiring Spinoza's views.

4 Movements and important figures (cont.)

Moses MENDELSSOHN (1729–86), a leading figure of the European Enlightenment, spread Enlightenment ideas to Hebrew literature, fought for Jewish civil rights and did pioneering conceptual work on political theory, especially with regard to religious liberty in his Jerusalem. Solomon MAIMON (1753/4–1800) took his name in honour of Moses Maimonides. Trained as a rabbi, he pursued secular and scientific learning and became an important and original critic of the philosophy of Kant. Nachman KROCHMAL (1785–1840), a leader of the Jewish Enlightenment in Galicia, found anticipations of Kant, Hegel and Schelling in the ancient Jewish writings. His work shows how a thinker whose underlying assumptions differ from those of the idealist philosophers could take their views in quite a different direction from the one they chose.

Hermann COHEN (1842–1918), a major Kantian philosopher and one of the first non-baptized Jews to hold an important academic post in Germany, applied his own distinctive version of critical idealism to the understanding of Judaism as a spiritual and ethical system. Franz ROSENZWEIG (1886–1929), an important Hegelian thinker, went on to formulate a Jewish existential philosophy that deeply influenced many of the most prominent Jewish thinkers of the twentieth century. Martin BUBER (1878–1965), Zionist advocate of accommodation with the Palestinian Arabs and an admiring student of Hasidic traditions, added his own stamp to the continental tradition of Jewish philosophy by developing a widely influential dialogical philosophy that privileged relationships experientially and celebrated the I–thou, a mode of relation that allows for authentic encounter.

A number of twentieth century philosophers of Judaism have grasped at diverse threads of the Jewish experience, illustrating both the attractions of the tradition and the fragmentation produced by centuries of persecution that would culminate in the Holocaust, only to be accentuated by the centrifugal tendencies of Jewish life in post-Holocaust liberal societies. Ahad HA'AM, the pen name of Asher Ginzberg (1856–1927), was an essayist who argued that the creation of a 'spiritual centre' of Jewish culture in Palestine would provide the sustenance needed to preserve the diaspora Jewry from the threat of assimilation. No state was needed. David BAUMGARDT (1890–1963) was a philosopher who sought to reconcile ethical naturalism with the ideals he found in the Jewish sources, but, unlike Hermann Cohen, Baumgardt did not explore those sources in close detail. Mordecai KAPLAN (1881–1981) sought to devise a social mission and communal identity for Jews without reliance on many of the core beliefs and practices that had shaped that identity in the past. Abraham Joshua HESCHEL (1907–72) sought to salvage the spiritual dimensions of Jewish experience, which found expression both in ritual and in ethical and social action. Joseph SOLOVEITCHIK (1903–93) gave canonical expression to Orthodox ideals by focusing on the intellectual and ritual rigours of his archetypal figures, Halakhic man and the Lonely Man of Faith. Yeshayahu LEIBOWITZ (1903–94), an influential Israeli thinker, struggled for the disengagement of authentic and committed religious observance from the toils of governmental officialdom. Jews are mandated, he argued, to observance, as a community. That imperative is not to be put aside. Neither can the observant pretend to ignore the State of Israel. But the State can give no mandate to religious observance, and religious faithfulness can impart none of its aura to the State. For it is essential not to place God in the service of politics. Emil FACKENHEIM (1916–) seeks an authentic response to the Holocaust, which he formulates in an intentionally inclusionary way, as a '614th' commandment, not to hand Hitler a posthumous victory but to find some way, that might vary from individual to individual, of keeping alive Jewish ideas, practices and commitments.

See also: ANTI-SEMITISM; BIOETHICS, JEWISH; ENLIGHTENMENT, JEWISH; HOLOCAUST, THE; ISLAMIC PHILOSOPHY; JEWISH PHILOSOPHY IN THE EARLY NINETEENTH CENTURY; JEWISH PHILOSOPHY, CONTEMPORARY; MEDIEVAL PHILOSOPHY; RENAISSANCE PHILOSOPHY; RELIGION, PHILOSOPHY OF; ZIONISM

L.E. GOODMAN

JEWISH PHILOSOPHY, CONTEMPORARY

Jewish philosophy is pursued by committed Jews seeking to understand Judaism and the world in one another's light. In this broad sense, contemporary Jewish philosophy maintains the central focus of classical, medieval and Enlightenment Jewish philosophy. But a certain kind of traditionalism distinguishes many contemporary Jewish philosophers from their predecessors: an effort to show how Judaism maintains continuity and coherence despite historical change. Jewish thinkers who are traditionalists in this sense are no longer preoccupied with showing non-Jewish philosophers how Judaism fares when evaluated by universal reason, as their classical, medieval and modern predecessors were. Nor is their chief concern with exhibiting the good reasons for remaining Jewish and not converting to Christianity or Islam, as was that of many earlier Jewish thinkers. One work that sets an agenda for many of these traditionalists is Franz Rosenzweig's Der Stern der Erlösung *(The Star of Redemption) (1921). Like Rosenzweig, (1) they often reject the Enlightenment demand for a transcendental propaedeutic as a prelude to asking substantive questions. Instead, they address Jewish thought, ethics and experience head on. (2) None among this group thinks of his work as beholden primarily and inevitably to standards of thought articulated first and foremost outside distinctively Jewish experience. (3) The six points of* Der Stern der Erlösung *(The Star of Redemption) – Creation, Revelation, Redemption, God, Israel, and the World – mark the large themes they aim to define or the categories through which they propose, explore and defend their claims. Besides traditionalism thus understood, contemporary Jewish philosophy, particularly among philosophers with analytic training, is marked by efforts philosophically to reanimate the classic texts of medieval Jewish philosophy, especially the work of Moses Maimonides.*

1 **Classical and medieval background**
2 **Modern background**
3 **Characteristics of contemporary Jewish philosophy**
4 **Contemporary problems and prospects**

1 Classical and medieval background

What counts as contemporary Jewish philosophy? Posing the question historically is virtually inevitable, because the discipline recurrently contends with its own past. Locating Jewish philosophy in the context of classical and medieval thought seems relatively easy, especially with the aid of hindsight: We might describe such philosophy as a reasoned and disciplined investigation by committed Jews of humankind-in-God's-world, or as their search 'for the deepest truth the world has to offer' (Novak 1995: 6). Typically, the philosophers engage extensively with traditional Jewish texts, especially the Hebrew Scriptures and Talmud. PHILO OF ALEXANDRIA, Al-Fayyumi SAADIAH GAON, Judah HALEVI and Moses MAIMONIDES are salient examples.

For most classical and medieval Jewish philosophers, the confluence of Jewish with non-Jewish sources – for example, PLATO and ARISTOTLE – is decisive. Thus Jewish philosophy is syncretistic all the way down. With the destruction of an independent Jewish state and the emergence of the cosmopolitan imperial cultures in which the key figures of classical and medieval Jewish philosophy typically wrote, a central question motivating many Jewish philosophers well versed in the philosophical canon of the cosmopolitan culture was this: how can learned and reasoning people embrace the claims that Jewish texts seem to make? A tension was all but inevitable between views rooted in Jewish history and tradition and what non-Jewish philosophers typically saw and presented as universal truths. Are Jewish claims about humankind-in-the-world compatible with, even deducible from, the principles and claims of universal reason, as articulated, say, in the Graeco-Roman philosophical tradition?

2 Modern background

Classical and medieval Jewish philosophers, living in cosmopolitan Alexandria, in Muslim-governed countries, or the ghettoes of Catholic Europe, saw themselves as free to pursue their basic questions in ways that allowed them to live, act and think openly as Jews. Their concerns over possible tensions between particularity and universality persist into the modern period. But the writing of many modern thinkers takes a new turn, under the threat of a Protestant theocracy, as in the case of Spinoza, or under what might be called the tyranny of liberal Protestant civility, as with MENDELSSOHN, COHEN, ROSENZWEIG, BUBER and others.

Responding to his intellectual and spiritual environment, SPINOZA treated both Judaism and Christ-ianity as significant, but human, cultural constructions with no privileged authority vis-à-vis the universe. He could thus lay conceptual foundations for a liberal republic welcoming to a plurality of reasonable religions that would benefit the public welfare by inculcating moral constraints and, as Jefferson would later put it, 'neither pick [our] pocket[s] nor break [our] leg[s]'.

Much influenced by Spinoza, Mendelssohn (1783) shared a liberal, republican agenda with many of the Protestant thinkers of his day. But he could not share a vision of grace and law that is so heavily laden as theirs often is with ancient anti-Hebraic grudges and disparaging misreadings of Judaism. He had to rebuff his Protestant admirers when they urged him, in the name of his own philosophy, to abandon Judaism for Christianity. He demanded separation of church and state and dismissed claims to political control over the human mind and spirit. Jewish life and thought, he argued, are compatible with universal reason and at least as conducive to liberal republican polity and culture as Christianity. But they depend necessarily on freedom of conscience.

Cohen went a step further. In *Die Religion der Vernunft aus den Quellen des Judentums* (Religion of Reason out of the Sources of Judaism) (1919) he argues that Judaism, more than other religious options, offers the morality, piety and spirituality that a thinking, liberal person requires. Buber's *Ich und Du* (I and Thou) (1923) similarly celebrates the Jewish covenant as central to the universal values of human life at its best. He actually dismisses any vestige of Jewish law, so as to render Judaism a paradigm of the 'grace-ful' existential attitude that is conducive to a liberal democratic community, open to divinity – the ultimate Thou – and capable of thriving among the nations (see BUBER, M.).

Franz Rosenzweig was at first attracted to liberal Protestantism but ultimately rejected its blandishments. He turned the tables on Buber's Jewish existentialism, arguing for a religious philosophy that renders any and every humanism, including every kind of liberal or socialist doctrine, dependent on a prior theology. The core of this theology is the conception of God's word, embodied eternally, outside the historical life of the nations, by the Jewish people, even as it is embodied historically in the Christian Church(es) and their militant quest for peace and understanding among the nations.

Rosenzweig presents himself as a *ba'al teshuvah*, a penitent returning to Judaism from the theologically liberal tradition that runs from Spinoza through Mendelssohn to his own teacher, Hermann Cohen. Rosenzweig's stance as a returning Jew is crucial in understanding contemporary Jewish philosophy. At least for many paradigm cases, a similar attitude of return sets the tone and orients much of the programme – certainly for Fackenheim (1973, 1982), Levinas (1969, 1990), Novak (1995) and Wyschogrod (1983). How is this so?

3 Characteristics of contemporary Jewish philosophy

First, philosophers as diverse as Fackenheim, Hartman, Leibowitz, Levinas, Soloveitchik and Wyschogrod have learned the lesson Rosenzweig taught: that it is possible to drop the Kantian (or Lockean) transcendentalist demand for a philosophical propaedeutic before first-order questions can be asked. None of them takes the transcendental turn before turning to traditional religious issues – as Rosenzweig himself still did in Part One of *Der Stern der Erlösung* (1921), seeking to refute, not simply reject, transcendentalism. None of these figures asks such Lockean or Kantian questions as 'What are the conditions for the possibility of thought, language, knowledge, science, ethics, or experience' in general, or of religious thought, language, knowledge, ethics, or experience in particular (see LOCKE, J.; KANT, I.)? Rather, each investigates Jewish thought, ethics and experience head on, asking in particular the following questions. How good are these things? How can they help us shape our lives? What resources do they give us to conceptualize problems of meaning that threaten our human capacity to endure or triumph, physically, cognitively, morally, in the face and wake of suffering, absurdity and evil? How do they fare when compared with challengers or competitors, opposers, or nay-sayers? Perhaps most often addressed is this question: how did Enlightenment philosophy thin out the rich tradition of Judaism that once gave Jews conceptual and practical tools for understanding and acquitting themselves with grace, mercy and justice in God's vexed and vexing world? Even more significantly, how can Jewish thought, ethics, and experience be restored to their cultural, social and personal thickness, their traditional complexity, profundity and open-ended creative dynamic?

These preoccupations mark many contemporary Jewish philosophers as traditionalists in the sense that they are seeking, as William JAMES might have put it, 'a minimum of jolt and a maximum of continuity' in Jewish ways of thinking and living. As David Novak puts it in his own case (1995), they embrace a traditionalism that tends to avoid both historicism and fundamentalism, two orientations that had already rejected the Enlightenment project. Historicism, as they see it, undercuts the coherence of Jewish tradition by rendering it into discrete, ultimately incommensurable epochal, or time-sliced, cultures.

Fundamentalism, by contrast, assumes too much invariance in the tradition. It transforms Jewish continuity and coherence into a monolith and blunts its vital and vibrant diversity – just as what we might call Enlightenment fundamentalism assumed too much invariance in rationality.

Historicists are left with many Judaisms but no tradition. Fundamentalists are left with a purportedly essential Jewish tradition that lacks historical dynamic or nuance. Traditionalists, seeking a way between this Scylla and Charybdis, contend that the task for a living Jewish philosophy is to discover how Judaism maintains continuity and coherence through all the vicissitudes it has suffered and all the changes it has undergone – not merely despite them. This approach, they claim, reflects the open-textured character of Judaism; it also permits a full-fledged philosophy of Judaism and clarifies Judaism's contributions to philosophy at large.

If this characterization of such thinkers as Fackenheim, Hartman, Leibowitz, Novak, Soloveitchik and Wyschogrod makes sense, a second Rosenzweigian characteristic of their work readily comes into view: None among these contemporary traditionalists thinks of his work as beholden, primarily or inevitably, to standards of thought and action articulated first and foremost outside distinctively Jewish experience. To be sure, like Rosenzweig, each learns from mentors and gleans arguments where or when he finds them; and, like him, some, at least, will be much concerned with relations between Judaism and Christianity – although none will adopt Rosenzweig's duplex theology, dividing the work of true religion between Jewish spirituality and Christian worldliness. There is no sense among them that Jewish ideas, as such, must be checked for their validity, as a matter of sound principle, against any purportedly universal philosophical standard, whether Greek, Cartesian, Kantian, Hegelian, or existentialist. They abandon any variety of Enlightenment fundamentalism. This marks a departure from the practice of Jewish philosophers from Philo to Buber. Indeed, much of the Jewish philosophical writing of these contemporary traditionalists reflects on and continues the work of Jewish sources, often using commentary with a marked family resemblance to Jewish midrashic and *aggadic* discourse.

Third, as we have suggested, for these traditionalists, Rosenzweig's *Der Stern der Erlösung* outlines the basic points of concern. The six points of this work – (1) Creation, (2) a Revealed Covenant for an elect People, (3) the promise of Redemption, (4) God as the Creator and Revealer of Covenant, (5) Israel as God's Elect and (6) the World as the beneficiary of God's Promise of Redemption – mark out the ground they aim to defend and provide the categories through which they explore, discover and urge their claims.

Fourth, and linked with this agenda, if this group shares *bêtes noires*, they are thinkers who despoil or reject any of the above six points. Thus, perhaps no *bête* is more *noire* than Spinoza (see Fackenheim 1982; Hartman 1985; Levinas 1969; Novak 1995). Spinoza here is the great and baleful alternative to Rosenzweig's return. He is the classic renegade who abandons Judaism and rejects its deepest truths. And he is the father of academic anti-Hebraism, the watershed figure who teaches the likes of Kant and Hegel to portray Judaism as spiritually crippled, fanatically nationalistic, and superstitiously, slavishly loyal to 'the Law'.

For the contemporary traditionalists, SPINOZA was the first and perhaps most challenging philosopher to attempt a complete dismantling of transcendence; he directly attacks all six points of *Der Stern der Erlösung*. Where Judaism contends that we live in a created world, Spinoza argued that the idea of creation explains nothing. Where Judaism contends that the world is governed by a God who especially cares for humankind and reveals that care in the covenant by which he elects the people Israel, Spinoza maintained that the world is explainable through natural principles that relate only randomly to human wish and will (see Fackenheim 1982; Hartman 1985). For Spinoza, although everything is grounded in divine power, God has no particular role in establishing the Hebrew covenant. The Hebrews legislated that covenant for their own local purposes, in essence electing God (see Novak 1995). Where Judaism finds in God's world profound reasons for hope or the expectation of redemption, since God, in cooperation with Israel and all humankind, works to realize, in due time, the good life and the establishment of his kingdom, Spinoza seems to picture humankind as an incident within and among the many incidents of a self-perpetuating and unending process, a motiveless but all-encompassing system of physical or natural cause and effect (see Fackenheim 1982; Hartman 1985; Levinas 1969; Soloveitchik 1944).

Finally, like Rosenzweig, the modern traditionalists turn the tables on the mainly Protestant liberal philosophical theologies that emerged in the intellectual and cultural wakes made by Kant and Hegel: Paradigmatically, they reject the anthropologizing of religion they find apparent in Kant's *Die Religion innerhalb der Grenzen der blossen Vernunft* (Religion within the Limits of Reason Alone) (see KANT, I. §14) (see Fackenheim 1973; Hartman 1985; Leibowitz 1992; Novak 1985; Soloveitchik 1944; Wyschogrod 1983). Parallel with neo-orthodox Protestant thinkers like Karl BARTH, they are confident of reaching perfectly reasonable religious decisions and conclusions out of unabashedly covenantal sources and theocentric lines of thinking (for parallels with Barth, see Novak 1985 and Wyschogrod 1983). As part of this aspect of their 'return', they reject Kant's insistence on the self-legislation – and in that sense, autonomy – of ethics, attempting to restore what might be described as Micah's view, that justice and mercy towards the neighbour and stranger are grounded in the humble love of God and are virtually inseparable from it (see Fackenheim 1973, 1982; Levinas 1969).

Naturally, they find in Kant's academic anti-Hebraism an unappreciative and distorted reading of Jewish sources that reduces the mutuality of the covenant to tyrannical legalism and that caricatures the *mitzvot* as onerous and alienating obedience (see Fackenheim 1973; Soloveitchik 1944). They reject the Protestant/Hegelian triumphalist history-of-religions narratives at work in liberal theology, the Hegelian presumption picked up by such writers as Otto, Wach, and Eliade, that irreversible, unidirectional progress from religious particularism to religious universalism (of a decisively Christian incarnational kind) is either somehow historically inevitable or normatively optimal for genuinely religious people or peoples (again, see Fackenheim 1973, but also Soloveitchik 1944).

The contemporary traditionalists barely bother to contend any longer with Enlightenment attacks on transcendence or demands for epistemological or metaphysical propaedeutics. The theological liberalisms that emerged out of the German Enlightenment, which reduced full-bodied – and fully bodied – Jewish tradition to some thin, vague, relatively nondescript and typically secularized confession are hardly engaged, even as straw men. The single issue emerging from the German Enlightenment that still divides traditionalists is that of religious pluralism (see RELIGIOUS PLURALISM). Some, like Fackenheim, Hartman and Novak, construe an appreciation for other religious traditions as a kind of moral, social, or intellectual requirement. Others, like Soloveitchik, find such appreciations tangential to *halakhic* life. Still others, like Leibowitz, find such pluralism actually beside the point, covenantally speaking.

Most exponents of contemporary traditionalism find four episodes in twentieth-century Jewish history decisive in the emergence of their outlook: the Nazi destruction of European Jewry, the wartime abandonment of the Jews by the North Atlantic democracies, the re-establishment of the State of Israel in the wake of the Second World War, and the disaffection of increasing numbers of American Jews from traditional Jewish life, in response to the attractions of secular affluence and assimilation. These events locate

Jewish philosophy socially and culturally in a context vastly different from that of its classical, medieval, or Enlightenment counterparts. They seem to render almost irrelevant the particularist/universalist, faith/reason problematics of the medievals and the more distinctively modern challenges of liberal Christian civility. It is widely supposed that if the First World War did not render the German Enlightenment tradition quaint, then surely the Third Reich's Final Solution and the moral abdication of the North Atlantic republics exposed in its implementation a depth of hypocrisy that soured the entire enterprise (see HOLOCAUST, THE).

Liberal, secular and assimilationist paths seem to many clearly to spell the extinction of the ancient tradition. And many, especially in the United States, suppose that cultural Zionism, or a diaspora sensibility centred on Israel can alone render appealing the commitments of Jewish traditional life (see ZIONISM). But these assumptions are highly debatable, if rarely argued pro or con with much rigour. In fact, Jewish philosophers, like virtually all other philosophers as the century ends, have barely begun to come to grips with the profound events affecting Jewish life throughout the twentieth century.

4   Contemporary problems and prospects

Many characteristics of contemporary traditionalism reflect the course philosophy itself has taken, especially in western Europe, notably, with the emergence of existential, phenomenological, hermeneutic, Marxist, feminist and other cultural critiques of the Enlightenment. The works of Fackenheim, Levinas, Soloveitchik, Wyschogrod and others must be read in this context. So too must Israelis like Halbertal and Margalit (1992), who address traditional Jewish concepts like idolatry and worship in analytically and phenomenologically rigorous ways. Here, too, we have philosophers abandoning the Enlightenment thinning of tradition and reduction of religion to, say, the presumptive categories of science (error and accuracy), ethics (duties and inclinations), and aesthetics (appropriateness and inappropriateness). For many of the new traditionalists, authenticity means giving a full-blooded religious culture an honest and appreciative hearing in something like its own terms.

Paralleling the Continental developments, English-speaking philosophers, especially Wittgensteinians, and analytic pragmatists like Quine, Sellars, Davidson, Putnam and Rorty, have subjected basic Enlightenment assumptions (such as that about 'the given' or 'the very idea of a conceptual scheme') and distinctions (such as those between analytic and synthetic judgments, or between things and phenomena) to severe criticism. Many of the English-speaking philosophers have themselves essayed what might be construed as forms of traditionalism. But no contemporary Jewish philosopher has attempted to construct a Wittgensteinian philosophy of Judaism, and virtually none has come to grips with the pragmatists – despite Harry Austryn Wolfson's pronouncement (1912) that the tangles between the Halevian and Maimonidean approaches in philosophy prefigure what Wolfson considered the major philosophical debate of his time (which surely overlaps with ours): the debate between pragmatism and eternalism – or what we might now call realism.

Among English-speaking religious philosophers, the vacuum left by the collapse of modern Enlightenment projects has been filled largely by analytically trained thinkers, many of whom study classical, medieval, or scholastic texts and issues. Here an asymmetry must be noted between the works of Christian and those of Jewish philosophers. Christian philosophers like Alvin Plantinga, William Alston, or James Ross engage in historical studies of Christian scholasticism (broadly construed) but go on to converse about various issues in the wider Christian intellectual community, and finally to contribute variations on scholastic Christian arguments to current epistemological, semantic and metaphysical debate. Analogous Jewish philosophers, by and large, have not followed suit. Unlike their traditionalist Jewish peers, most have focused on reorienting and reanimating the history of medieval Jewish philosophy itself, especially as represented in the work of Moses Maimonides, treating his thought with the philosophical sophistication it deserves and opening up avenues for renewed philosophical engagement with it. Such engagement may both reflect and stimulate a constructive turn in Jewish philosophy that is more appreciative of the role of (a restrained, chastened, or more epistemically catholic) reason in religious thought and more sanguine about the light it can shed on Judaism and on the world – witness the recent ambitious work by Lenn Goodman (1991, 1996). Still it remains true that few have yet sought to help revitalize or heighten the tenor of intellectual concern and philosophical conversation in the general Jewish community; and few have yet contributed arguments to current epistemological, semantic, or metaphysical debate out of distinctively Jewish sources or commitments. How this asymmetry between Jewish and Christian philosophy is to be explained – by the negligence or diffidence of the potential practitioners or their marginalization by the intellectual community – and whether it will disappear in years to come are questions that remain to be answered.

See also: ENLIGHTENMENT, CONTINENTAL;
ENLIGHTENMENT, JEWISH; JEWISH PHILOSOPHY IN
THE EARLY 19TH CENTURY; MAIMONIDES, M.

References and further reading

* Buber, M. (1923) *Ich und Du*, Leipzig: Insel Verlag; trans. R.G. Smith, *I and Thou*, New York: Charles Scribner's Sons, 2nd edn, 1958; trans. W. Kaufman, *I and Thou*, New York: Charles Scribner's Sons, 1970. (The classic exposition of Buber's dialogical philosophy.)
* Cohen, H. (1919) *Die Religion der Vernunft aus den Quellen des Judentums*, Leipzig: Fock; trans. S. Kaplan with an introduction by L. Strauss, *Religion of Reason out of the Sources of Judaism*, New York: Frederick Ungar, 1972. (A systematic exposition of Judaism by the founder of German Neo-Kantianism.)
 Cohen, A. and Mendes-Flohr, P. (eds) (1987) *Contemporary Jewish Religious Thought*, New York: Charles Scribner's Sons. (Original essays on critical concepts, movements and beliefs of contemporary Jewish thinkers.)
* Fackenheim, E. (1973) *Encounters between Judaism and Modern Philosophy*, New York: Basic Books. (Critical consideration of modern philosphers from Hume through Heidgger in terms of Fackenheim's own construal of Judaism.)
* —— (1982) *To Mend the World*, New York: Schocken. (A neo-Hegelian philosophy of Judaism which emerges out of criticism of Spinoza, modern empiricism, Kant, Hegel, Sartre and Heidegger.)
* Goodman, L.E. (1991) *On Justice: An Essay in Jewish Philosophy*, New Haven, CT: Yale University Press. (An ontological theory of justice based on the biblical idea of deserts.)
* —— (1996) *God of Abraham*, New York: Oxford University Press. (Reflections on the nexus between natural theology and the values represented in the Jewish tradition.)
* Halbertal, M. and Margalit, A. (1992) *Idolatry*, Cambridge, MA: Harvard University Press. (Philosophically sophisticated conceptual and historical account of Jewish understandings of idolatry.)
* Hartman, D. (1985) *A Living Covenant*, New York: Free Press. (A neo-Maimonidean defence of Jewish covenantalism in dialogue with Soloveitchik and Leibowitz.)
* Leibowitz, Y. (1992) *Judaism, Human Values, and the Jewish State*, Cambridge, MA: Harvard University Press. (Collection of provocative occasional pieces on Jewish religion and politics.)
* Levinas, E. (1969) *Totalité et infini*, The Hague: Martinus Nijhoff; trans. A. Lingis, *Totality and Infinity*, Pittsburgh, PA: Duquesne University Press, 1969. (The classic expression Levinas' views of ethics, rather than of metaphysics, as first philosophy.)
* —— (1990) *Nine Talmudic Readings*, trans. A. Aronowicz, Bloomington, IN: Indiana University Press. (Seminal works by the leading French Jewish phenomenologist, concerned to replace ontology with ethics.)
* Mendelssohn, M. (1783) *Jerusalem, oder über religiöse Macht und Judentum* (Jerusalem, or on Religious Power and Judaism), trans. with notes by A. Arkush, *Jerusalem*, Hanover, NH: University Press of New England, 1983. (Inaugural work of German Enlightenment Jewish philosophy.)
* Novak, D. (1995) *The Election of Israel*, Cambridge: Cambridge University Press. (Systematic effort to retrieve philosophically the biblical notion of election.)
 Pines, S. and Yovel, Y. (eds) (1986) *Maimonides and Philosophy*, Dordrecht: Martinus Nijhoff. (Collection of philosophical essays on Moses Maimonides.)
* Rosenzweig, F. (1921) *Der Stern der Erlösung*, Frankfurt: Kauffmann; trans. W.W. Hallo, *The Star of Redemption*, Boston, MA: Beacon Press, 1970. (The highly influential twentieth-century philosophy of Judaism opposing all Enlightenment Jewish philosophy.)
 Seeskin, K. (1991) 'Jewish Philosophy in the 1980's', *Modern Judaism* 11: 157–72. (A helpful summary and enumeration of recent work on Jewish Philosophy.)
* Soloveitchik, J. (1944) *Ish ha-Halakhah*; trans. L. Kaplan, *Halakhic Man*, Philadelphia, PA: Jewish Publications Society, 1983. (An existentialist presentation of *halakhic* Judaism.)
 Spinoza, B. (1985) *Collected Works*; trans. E. Curley, Princeton, NJ: Princeton University Press, 2 vols. (Includes Spinoza's celebrated naturalistic account of salvation as the intellectual love of God, the inaugural work in modern biblical criticism, and an early defence of political and religious liberalism.)
* Wolfson, H.A. (1912) 'Maimonides and Halevi', in I. Twersky and G.H. Williams (eds) *Studies in the History of Philosophy and Religion*, vol. 2, Cambridge, MA: Harvard University Press, 1977. (An exposition of Maimonidean and Halevian attitudes towards Greek philosophy with allusions to contemporary debates in philosophy.)
* Wyschogrod, M. (1983) *The Body of Faith*, New York: Harper & Row. (Exceptionally well-written account of the relationship between philosophy and Judaism; includes a spirited defence of the election of

Israel and an attack on liberal tendencies to spiritualize Judaism.)

HENRY S. LEVINSON
JONATHAN W. MALINO

JEWISH PHILOSOPHY IN THE EARLY 19TH CENTURY

Although Jewish philosophy flourished in the Middle Ages, it underwent a serious decline in 1492, when the Jews were expelled from Spain. The period following Kant and Mendelssohn witnessed an attempt to reintegrate Jewish philosophy into the mainstream of Western culture. The strategy of reintegration consisted of two elements: (1) showing that there is more to Judaism than the study of Scripture; and (2) arguing that some of the ideas that won favour in the Enlightenment were anticipated by Jews centuries earlier.

The most central idea that Jewish thinkers claimed as their own is a shift in focus from theoretical issues to practical ones. As important features of the medieval worldview fell into disrepute, many philosophers began to ask whether there are limits to what human reason can know. Can it really prove that God exists or that the soul is immortal? One response was to argue that even if no proof can be found, there are still grounds for believing, particularly if our understanding of ourselves as moral agents makes no sense without them.

But it did not take long for people to argue that moral agency requires not just a God but a free and transcendent God capable of issuing commands to free agents created in the divine image. Here too, Jewish thinkers claimed that the idea of a God who is not limited by nature and insists on mercy and justice for all people was an integral part of monotheism as understood by the Hebrew prophets.

1 **The legacy of Mendelssohn and Kant**
2 **S.D. Luzzatto**
3 **Moritz Lazarus**
4 **Solomon Ludwig Steinheim**
5 **Solomon Formstecher**
6 **Samuel Hirsch**
7 **Conclusion**

1 The legacy of Mendelssohn and Kant

It is generally agreed that Jewish Emancipation and modern Jewish philosophy began with Moses MEN-DELSSOHN. A product of, and participant in, the Enlightenment, Mendelssohn saw no incompatibility between his commitment to Judaism and his integration into modern European society (see ENLIGHT-ENMENT, CONTINENTAL). According to Mendelssohn (1783), the truths on which religion is based – the existence of God, divine providence, and the immortality of the soul – can be grasped by all people through the aid of reason. Since these truths are required for the pursuit of happiness, revelation is not only unnecessary but unjustifiable. Why would God reveal the secrets of happiness to one nation and leave the rest of humanity in the dark? Thus Mendelssohn recognizes no eternal truths other than those comprehensible to human reason and capable of being verified by it. With respect to Judaism, Mendelssohn points out that the Torah contains no commandment that says 'Thou shalt believe...'. Rather than articles of faith, Judaism is based on revealed legislation. Although this legislation presupposes truths accessible to all humanity, the only thing incumbent on Jews alone is a system of behaviour.

Mendelssohn's stress on the practical nature of Jewish spirituality bears a strong resemblance to the critical philosophy of Immanuel KANT. While Kant is often credited with the destruction of metaphysics, it would be more accurate to say that he attempts to move metaphysical ideas from a theoretical context to a practical one. Though reason cannot prove the existence of God, the immortality of the soul, or personal freedom, we must presuppose these foundational ideas if we are to make sense of our duties under the moral law. The result is that our idea of God is not a 'demonstrated dogma' but a necessary postulate. As Kant says in the introduction to the *Critik der Reinen Vernunft* (Critique of Pure Reason), his intention is to limit knowledge in order to make room for faith (*Glaube*).

Not surprisingly, Kant concludes that the only content we can ascribe to our idea of God is moral. Even if we could prove that a necessary Being exists, we could not get a satisfactory idea of divinity because the crux of that idea is the notion of a perfect or holy will. It could be said, therefore, that Kant's view of God is much closer to the prophetic model of a judge and law-giver than it is to the idea of a first cause. This is important because scientific speculation is not indigenous to Judaism. The prophets sought God not by reasoning from effect to cause but by trying to awaken people's conviction that the world could be better and that it is our obligation to make it so. In short, they sought God in ideas like commandment and repentance, both of which play a central role in Kant's understanding of morality.

Kant argues for an idealized form of Christianity, which is to say a religion which recognizes all moral duties as divine commands. Looking beyond sectarian quarrels, he stresses the importance of trying to overcome the propensity of the human heart to do evil. Religion becomes spurious when people believe they can please God in ways that do nothing to improve behaviour, that simply wearing the right clothes or performing the right ritual is more important than purifying one's motives. Kant's picture of a religion that rejects intolerance and dogmatic pronouncements could not help but appeal to Jews, even though Kant himself did not think much of Judaism as a religion. Yet Kant's attempt to formulate an idealized form of Christianity raised the question of whether the same could be done for Judaism.

2   S.D. Luzzatto (1800–65)

Luzzatto agrees with Mendelssohn that Judaism is not based on articles of faith but carries this conclusion much further. Sharply critical of the medieval philosophers who tried to justify the principles of Judaism with rational arguments, Luzzatto argues that metaphysics is impossible and trust in human reason, unfounded. In fact, the whole attempt to view Judaism as a source of truth about God is characteristic of what Luzzatto terms 'Atticism'. In his view, Greek ethics was an attempt to achieve happiness through wisdom. But experience shows that the Greek view of human behaviour is fundamentally flawed: intelligence alone will not yield lasting well-being or cure human ills. Luzzatto therefore proposes that we understand wisdom not as contemplation of abstract truths but as a condition in which people act with care and thoughtfulness, trusting in the saving grace of God (see GRACE).

The positive side of Luzzatto's thought is his emphasis on compassion. All that is abiding in human life is the joy of performing acts of kindness and love, putting aside self-interest to help others. In Luzzatto's view (1880), these emotions, ignored by rationalist philosophers, permeate every aspect of the legislation of the Torah. In the days of Abraham, Isaac and Jacob, Luzzatto claims, religion was not enforced by a system of rewards and punishments. People understood the difference between right and wrong and invariably chose the former. Without proofs or arguments, they believed in God and worshipped in a natural, self-initiated fashion. It was only when the Israelites became a nation and began to mix with other nations that they needed the laws, rituals and educational imperatives revealed to Moses. Thus Judaism is autonomous before and heteronomous after Sinai.

Luzzatto's scepticism about human reason goes well beyond anything found in Mendelssohn and Kant. In fact, his emphasis on moral emotions and natural religion is suggestive of ROUSSEAU. Although his influence was not nearly as great as Mendelssohn's, Luzzatto was one of the first Jewish thinkers to break with medieval Jewish rationalism.

3   Moritz Lazarus (1824–1903)

Closer in spirit to Mendelssohn and Kant is the thought of Moritz Lazarus. In a two volume work entitled *Die Ethik des Judentums* (The Ethics of Judaism) (1901), he argues that the Bible does not expound dogmatic teachings about the nature of God. Obedience to God is not based on omnipotence or omnipresence but on God's moral perfection. God commands an act because it is right; it is not right because God commands it. It is not God's command but its own moral necessity that makes a law binding. 'Law' and 'morality' here mean Kant's categorical imperative. In Lazarus' view, this principle underlies all the commandments, sayings and moral insights scattered through the Torah and Talmud.

Lazarus argues that Judaism is committed to the autonomy of the moral subject. When Kant says that morally we are subject only to a law of which we can regard ourselves as author, the point is not that we have created the law ourselves but that our moral self recognizes and accepts the validity of the law. God may be the one who gives the law, but it is the recognition of its validity that determines its moral character. Sanctification, as Lazarus says several times, is moralization. Not surprisingly, Lazarus goes to great length to stress the universal features of Jewish law. All people are created by God and formed in the image of God. Thus the Bible commands the Israelite to 'love thy neighbour as thyself' (Leviticus 19: 18) and to ensure that there is 'one law for you and for the stranger in your midst' (Leviticus 24: 22; Numbers 15: 15). The election of Israel has nothing to do with blood or moral superiority but with the fact that Israel was commanded to follow a universal moral law.

Book Two of *Die Ethik des Judentums* is mainly a study of the psychological foundations of Jewish ethics. The purpose of ethics is not to negate human nature and promote asceticism but to assign boundaries to the various instincts clamouring for satisfaction and to harmonize the opposing claims that arise in social intercourse. Lazarus maintains that Jewish teachings foster sympathy, charity and love of one's fellow human beings. His focus on the psychological foundation of Jewish ethics is both the strong point and the weak point of his system. The strong point, because he sheds considerable light on Jewish ritual: each practice either curbs an instinct or fosters a virtue (see RITUAL). The weak point, because Kantian ethics is supposed to be based on the objective necessity of the moral law, not on the feelings it engenders or the social harmony it promotes.

4 Solomon Ludwig Steinheim (1789–1866)

A very different reaction to Kantian philosophy can be found in the thought of Solomon Ludwig Steinheim, whose major work, *Die Offenbarung nach dem Lehrbegriffe der Synagoge* (Revelation according to the Doctrine of the Synagogue) (1835), is a critique of all attempts to justify religion with arguments derived from philosophy. The crux of Steinheim's argument is that it would be silly and superfluous for God to reveal a doctrine that we are capable of discovering on our own. Steinheim therefore rejects scholastic attempts to argue that reason and revelation are alternative ways of arriving at the same truth. This does not mean that the contents of revelation are secret, ineffable, or unfathomable. On the contrary, Steinheim insists that revelation offers us a doctrine that is both communicable and comprehensible. His point is that it must give us something new, something beyond what our reason, conscience, or feelings already provide.

By 'revelation', Steinheim means a historical event, not an evolutionary process or rational discovery (see REVELATION). Although our understanding of revelation may change and grow over time, the contents do not. Revelation is needed because reason cannot free itself from antinomies regarding freedom and necessity. Reason conceives of the world according to necessary connections. Whether God is understood as the first member of a causal chain or as a being whose essence implies existence, it is still true that the God of reason must submit to the rule of necessity. According to Steinheim, this means that the God of reason is not a free and spontaneous agent who creates the world but a mechanical force that resides within it. The problem is that reason has no choice but to uphold the principle *ex nihilo nihil fit*, from nothing comes nothing. If this principle is true, every event must be preceded by a cause. It follows that reason cannot conceive of anything that is spontaneous, least of all a creation that is genuinely *ex nihilo*. The only creation it can subsume under causal laws is the ordering of an eternal, formless matter. But, in Steinheim's opinion, this sort of creation is no creation at all. So reason cannot account for the existence of the world in time.

What is true of creation is also true of human action. If every event must be preceded by a cause, individual moral responsibility is impossible. Like creation, the initiation of action requires spontaneity, a coming into being from nothing. Freedom is an undeniable fact, the basis of all ethical judgments. But without the teaching of revelation, this fact also would be simply an event without a cause.

In Steinheim's view, we have no choice but to admit the superiority of revelation: that is, a creating God, human agents made in the image of God, and the immortality of the soul. Although Steinheim is sometimes read in light of KIERKEGAARD, the comparison is wide of the mark. We do not give up reason in order to embrace absurdity but go beyond reason in order to avoid determinism. Note, however, that Steinheim's view of the contents of revelation corresponds to Kant's idea of the postulates of pure practical reason. So while Steinheim may be right in saying that reason, understood as a faculty that moves from cause to effect, cannot account for spontaneity, it does not follow that we have no choice but to affirm revelation as a historical fact. The Kantian retort is that reason also has a practical employment compatible with freedom.

5 Solomon Formstecher (1808–89)

If the thought of Lazarus and Steinheim is a reflection on Kant, that of Formstecher is a reflection on HEGEL and SCHELLING. In *Die Religion des Geistes* (The Religion of Spirit) (1841), Formstecher emphasizes that Judaism is based not on the apprehension of timeless truths given to Moses but on an evolving conception of spirit that achieves greater clarity over time.

Formstecher's philosophy begins with the idea of a world soul (*pneumatikon*) that manifests itself either as spirit or as nature. The world soul is a unity that underlies the world and exists independently in the sense that the world soul could exist without the world but not vice versa. Formstecher insists, however, that the world is not created by a necessary causal process but by free choice. Put otherwise, God, the bearer of the world soul, is a free, self-conscious, self-determining entity, separate from the world but responsible for its existence. Formstecher thus rejects any form of pantheism. Of the two spheres of reality, only spirit is conscious both of itself and of nature. Thus the world soul can be conceived only under the guise of spirit.

The duality of nature and spirit gives rise to two forms of religion: one based on necessity, the other on freedom. Formstecher identifies the first type with paganism; the second, with Judaism. Paganism deifies nature by worshipping objects within it or identifying God with the forces that control it. The outgrowth of paganism is detached contemplation of the beauty of nature and the attempt to decipher its secrets. But a religion of spirit stresses freedom over necessity and goodness over beauty. It is here that knowledge becomes more than awareness of an external object and attains self-consciousness in the true sense. The essence of Judaism is ethical monotheism: God stands apart from nature, and our purpose in life is not to achieve unity with God but to emulate God's ways by striving for the moral ideal.

Formstecher treats revelation not as a single event but as the process by which spirit becomes aware of itself. A liberal, he looks forward to the day when Judaism will de-emphasize ritual and stake its claim on greater understanding of the process of spiritual development. In Formstecher's view, Christianity is an attempt to bring the religion of spirit to the nations of the world. But where Hegel saw the doctrine of incarnation as an attempt to bridge the gap between an infinite creator and finite creation, Formstecher sees it as a concession to paganism.

6   Samuel Hirsch (1815–89)

Like Formstecher, Hirsch interpreted the history of religion in terms of the historical development of spirit. His major work, *Die Religionsphilosophie der Juden* (The Religious Philosophy of the Jews) (1842), argues that while European society has begun to tolerate Jews, it has failed to recognize the unique contribution of Judaism to world culture. Thus Kant did not regard Judaism as a religion at all, and Hegel thought of it as an inferior religion superseded by Christianity.

At the root of Hirsch's philosophy is the act of self-consciousness or recognition of the self as an 'I'. It is in this act that we separate ourselves from nature and come to experience freedom. But, being abstract, this freedom is empty. Religious life is the process by which true freedom is realized. For freedom to become concrete, it must acquire content by facing the choice between real freedom, which implies virtue, and illusory freedom, which implies sin (see FREEDOM AND LIBERTY).

According to Hirsch, freedom is experienced as a gift, so there must be a divine dispenser of freedom who is absolutely free. Humans are the image of God, and history is the human quest for perfect freedom. Hirsch took strong exception to the Pauline doctrine of original sin, on the grounds that it compromises the idea of freedom. I am not guilty of sin until I exercise my own free choice (see SIN). Like Formstecher, Hirsch sees Christianity as an attempt to bring the truth about God to the nations of the world. But, unlike Formstecher, he does not argue for the inherent superiority of Judaism. In his view, both religions are evolving and will reach their perfect or absolute state in the days of the Messiah. With respect to Judaism, Hirsch played a decisive role in the founding of the Reform movement.

7   Conclusion

Despite their differences, all the philosophers discussed in this article tried to integrate Judaism into Western culture or what Formstecher called 'the universal religion of civilized people'. All stress the importance of human freedom, the need to undertake moral action, and the existence of a transcendent God. As the nineteenth century drew to a close, the influence of Hegel began to wane and rationalist thinkers returned to Kant. After the First World War, the primary debate in Jewish philosophy became that between Kantians like Hermann COHEN and existentialists like Martin BUBER and Franz ROSENZWEIG.

See also: JEWISH PHILOSOPHY, CONTEMPORARY; KANT, I.; MENDELSSOHN, M.

References and further reading

Cohen, H. (1919) *Die Religion der Vernunft aus den Quellen des Judentums*, Leipzig: Fock; trans. S. Kaplan, *Religion of Reason out of the Sources of Judaism*, New York: Frederick Ungar, 1972. (Cohen was the greatest of the Jewish Neo-Kantians. His work can be viewed as the culmination of nineteenth-century Jewish philosophy or the beginning of the twentieth.)

* Formstecher, S. (1841) *Die Religion des Geistes* (The Religion of Spirit), Frankfurt: Hermann'sche Buchhandlung. (Emphasizes the idea of spirit and historical evolution. Although clearly in the Hegelian tradition, Formstecher still believed in a God who is separate from the world but responsible for its existence.)

Guttmann, J. (1933) *Die Philosophie des Judentums*; trans. D.W. Silverman, *Philosophies of Judaism*, New York: Schocken, 1973. (The best one-volume history of Jewish philosophy available. Keep in mind, however, that Guttman was sympathetic to Kant and Cohen.)

* Hirsch, S. (1842) *Die Religionsphilosophie der Juden* (The Religious Philosophy of the Jews), Leipzig: Hunger. (Like Formstecher, Hirsch was influenced by Hegel. Also like Formstecher, he emphasized the idea of freedom and believed in a God who is separate from the world.)

* Lazarus, M. (1901) *Die Ethik des Judentums*, Frankfurt: J. Kauffman; trans. H. Szold, *The Ethics of Judaism*, Philadelphia, PA: Jewish Publication Society of America, 1900. (Lazarus was one of

the first of the Jewish Neo-Kantians, but his work was overshadowed by that of Cohen.)

* Luzzatto, S.D. (1880) *Yesodei ha-Torah*; trans. N.H. Rosenbloom, 'The Foundation of the Torah', in N.H. Rosenbloom (ed.), *Luzzatto's Ethico-Psychological Interpretation of Judaism*, New York: Yeshivah University, 1965. (Luzzatto was one of the first people to break with scholasticism, particularly the thought of Maimonides.)
* Mendelssohn, M. (1783) *Jerusalem, oder über religiöse Macht und Judentum* (Jerusalem, or on Religious Power and Judaism), trans. with notes by A. Arkush, *Jerusalem*, Hanover, NH: University Press of New England, 1983. (A religious and rhetorical masterpiece. This is the book that launched modern Jewish philosophy and made pioneering contributions to the theory of the separation of Church and state.)
Rotenstreich, N. (1968) *Jewish Philosophy in Modern Times*, New York: Holt, Rinehart & Winston. (A critical study of Jewish philosophy from Mendelssohn to Rosenzweig.)
Schwarzschild, S. (1990) *The Pursuit of the Ideal*, ed. M. Kellner, Albany, NY: State University of New York Press. (A collection of distinguished essays written by a modern philosopher in the Kantian tradition.)
* Steinheim, S.L. (1835) *Die Offenbarung nach dem Lehrbegriffe der Synagoge* (Revelation according to the Doctrine of the Synagogue); trans. J.O. Haberman, 'The Revelation according to the Doctrine of Judaism: A Criterion', in J.O. Haberman (ed.) *Philosopher of Revelation: The Life and Thought of S.L. Steinheim*, Philadelphia, PA: Jewish Publication Society of America, 1990. (An excellent translation and commentary on Steinheim's work. Steinheim emphasized the superiority of revelation to reason in order to preserve the idea of human freedom.)

KENNETH SEESKIN

JHERING, RUDOLF VON (1818–92)

Jhering saw law as a mechanism for achieving current purposes, supplying the compulsion needed where other levers were insufficient to secure the conditions of social life. In this, he took issue with those other nineteenth-century German jurists who regarded law as a settled hierarchy of rules and concepts. He had considerable influence on the development of jurisprudential thought both in Germany and in the USA.

Born in Aurich, a lawyer by education, Jhering taught at various universities, including Basle and Vienna, spending sixteen years at Giessen and twenty at Göttingen, where he died in 1892. He was a gifted lecturer, a prolific and often entertaining writer, a robust debater, an enthusiastic supporter of Bismarck, a once-failed parliamentary candidate and a twice-married family man who enjoyed social life.

Jhering's first research was in Roman law, which remained a lifelong interest. Soon, however, he was concentrating on its evolutionary and comparative aspects, publishing, from 1852–8, several volumes on *Geist des römischen Rechts* (The Spirit of Roman Law). The work was never completed, as he turned to the development of his own philosophical approach.

This was largely a reaction to the views of two allied and influential schools of German thought. One saw law as something that grew unconsciously, reflecting the spirit of a people (see JURISPRUDENCE, HISTORICAL; SAVIGNY, F.K. VON). The other treated it as a settled hierarchy of rules and concepts, the terms used being sufficient to resolve any problem that might arise. Jhering also took issue with English utilitarianism. Though espousing the notion that law has a purpose and certain of their ideas about human motivation (Jhering expresses these in ways also reminiscent of Adam Smith), he rejected BENTHAM and Mill's individualism.

Jhering's own views are found in *The Struggle for Law* (1872), arguing that law develops as the result of a 'conscious struggle for claims', and in *Law as a Means to an End* (1877–83). Also unfinished, this presented law as directed to the fulfilling of human interests or purposes, which involve securing 'not merely the conditions of physical existence, but all those goods and pleasures which in the judgment of the subject give life its true value' (1877–83: 331). This requires cooperation, individuals connecting their own interests with those of others and 'the converging of all interests at the same point'. Certain social levers are needed to bring this about. Where duty, love or economic reward prove insufficient, the law steps in to provide the compulsion required.

The connections Jhering made between law, social utility and interests were influential for, though not entirely endorsed in, US thought (see POUND, R.) and for the development of *Interessenjurisprudenz* (the jurisprudence of interests) in Germany, while his analysis of legal coercion seems to foreshadow the ideas of Hans KELSEN.

Some sociologists, however, maintain that his statist and coercive conception of law inadequately reflects social facts. He is also criticized for endorsing such a conception, for taking relativistic views of social utility and justice, and for subordinating individual to social interests. On another understanding, he was actually arguing that it is only possible to secure individual interests in a 'realized partnership of the individual and society'.

See also: LAW, PHILOSOPHY OF; LEGAL IDEALISM §3; ROMAN LAW/CIVILIAN TRADITION §3

List of works

Jhering, R. von (1852–8) *Geist des römischen Rechts* (The Spirit of Roman Law), Leipzig: Breitkopf und Härtel; repr. Aalen: Scientia Verlag, 1968. (Usually referred to as 'The Spirit of Roman Law', there is no English version but it has been translated into various other languages.)
—— (1869) *Über den Grund des Besitzesschutzes* (On the Reason for the Protection of Possession), Jena: Mauke; repr. Aalen: Scientia Verlag, 1968. (Analysing Roman law on possession.)
—— (1870) *Die Jurisprudenz des tägliches Lebens*, Jena: H. Dufft; trans. H. Goudy, *Law in Daily Life*, Oxford: Clarendon Press, 1904; repr. Littleton, CO: F.B. Rothman, 1985. (A collection of questions and cases for discussion.)
—— (1872) *Der Kampf um's Recht*, Vienna: G.J. Manz; trans. from 5th edn by J.J. Lalor, *The Struggle for Law*, 2nd edn with intro. by A. Koucourek, Chicago, IL: Callaghan and Co., 1915. (Regarded as one of his two main jurisprudential works.)
—— (1877–83) *Der Zweck im Recht*, Leipzig: Breitkopf und Härtel; trans. I. Husik, *Law as a Means to an End*, New York: Macmillan, 1924. (Regarded as the second of his two major jurisprudential works.)
—— (1879) *Vermischte Schriften juristischen Inhalts* (Miscellaneous Writings with a Legal Content), Leipzig: Breitkopf und Härtel; repr. Aalen: Scientia Verlag, 1968. (Includes his 1842 doctoral dissertation in Latin on the possession of an inheritance.)
—— (1882) *Das Trinkgeld* (On Gratuities), Braunschweig: G. Westermann. (In which he argues that gratuities are a form of organized begging.)
—— (1885) *Scherz und Ernst in der Jurisprudenz* (Jest and Earnest in Jurisprudence), Leipzig: Breitkopf und Härtel, repr. Darmstadt: Wissenschaftliche Buchges, 1992. (Collection of essays and articles of which the most famous is 'Im juristischen Begriffshimmel: ein Phantasiebild', for which see trans. C.L. Levy, 'In the Heaven for Legal Concepts: a Fantasy', in *Temple Law Quarterly* 58 (1985): 799.)
—— (1889) *Der Besitzwille* (On Intention to Possess), Jena: G. Fischer; repr. Aalen: Scientia Verlag, 1968. (With a critique of prevailing juristic method.)

—— (1894) *Vorgeschichte der Indo-Europaër und die Entwickelungsgeschichte des römischen Rechts* (A Prehistory of the Indo-Europeans and an Account of the Historical Development of Roman Law), Leipzig: Breitkopf und Härtel, trans. A. Drucker, *The Evolution of the Aryan*, London: S. Sonnenschein & Co., 1897. (Posthumously published.)
—— (1913) *Rudolph von Jhering in Briefen an seine Freunde* (Jhering in Letters to his Friends), Leipzig: Breitkopf und Härtel; repr. Aalen: Scientia Verlag, 1971. (With an introduction by Helene Ehrenberg, née Jhering.)
—— (1988) *Briefe an Windscheid* (Letters to Windscheid), Göttingen: Vandehoeck & Ruprecht Verlag. (Of interest to theorists; in German.)

References and further reading

Dreier, R. (1993) 'Jherings Rechtstheorie – eine Theorie evolutionärer Rechtsvernunft' and the response by O. Behrends, 'War Jhering ein Rechtspositivist?', in *Privatrecht heute und Jherings evolutionäres Rechtsdenken* (Private Law Today and Jhering's Evolutionary Legal Thought), Cologne: Dr Otto Schmidt. (A collection of essays by contemporary scholars of Jhering; in German.)
Jenkins, I. (1960) 'Rudolph von Jhering', *Vanderbilt Law Review* 14: 169–90. (Suggesting an interpretation of Jhering that places him closer to idealism than understood by his followers.)
Losano, M.G. (1984) *Studien zu Jhering und Gerber* (Studies on Jhering and Gerber) and *Der Briefwechsel zwischen Jhering und Gerber* (The Correspondence between Jhering and Gerber), Ebelsbach: Verlag Rolf Gremer. (Both volumes reviewed by S.L. Paulson *American Journal of Comparative Law* 37 (1989): 171–84.)
Macdonell, Sir J. and Manson E. (eds) (1914) 'Rudolph von Jhering', in *Great Jurists of the World*, Continental Legal History Series, vol. 2, Boston, MA: Little, Brown and Co.; repr. New York: Augustus M. Kelley, 1968: 590. (A brief biography.)
Smith, M. (1895) 'Four German Jurists', *Political Science Quarterly* 10: 664. (On Bruns, Windscheid, Jhering, Gneist.)
Stone, J. (1965) *Human Law and Human Justice*, London: Stevens & Co., esp. 147–59. (An account and assessment of Jhering, with many useful references.)
Wieacker, F. (1942) *Rudolph von Jhering*, Leipzig: Kohler & Ameling; repr. Stuttgart: Kohler, 1968. (A remembrance on the 50th anniversary of Jhering's death, in German.)
Wieacker, F. and Wollschlägen, C. (eds) (1969)

Jherings Erbe: Göttinger Symposium zur 150 Wiederkehr des Geburtstags von Rudolph von Jhering, Göttingen: Vandenhoeck & Ruprecht Verlag. (The proceedings of a symposium celebrating the 150th anniversary in 1968 of Jhering's birth, to which the contribution of H.L.A. Hart on 'Jhering's Heaven of Legal Concepts and Modern Analytical Jurisprudence' is reprinted in his *Essays in Jurisprudence and Legal Philosophy*, Oxford: Clarendon Press, (1983), and that of K. Zweigert in an extended English version by Zweigert and Siehr in *American Journal of Comparative Law* 19 (1971): 215.)

ELSPETH ATTWOOLL

JIA YI (201–169 BC)

Jia Yi, in forging a brilliant synthesis of classical Legalist, Daoist and Confucian doctrines, fashioned a coherent political and educational philosophy in support of strong central government. Jia's impact on Chinese history can hardly be overestimated; his philosophy significantly shaped the imperial institutions of the Han dynasty (202 BC–AD 220), which became the models for successive dynasties of imperial China.

Jia Yi's writings show him to have been a forceful, often iconoclastic thinker. At 20, in recognition of his remarkable erudition, Jia was appointed academician (*boshi*), the highest scholastic honour usually reserved for senior teachers, at the court of Emperor Wen of Han (179–157 BC). By that time, Han rule had been established for some twenty years. Fearing that the court had been lulled into a false sense of security by self-serving advisors, Jia insisted that the empire was neither at peace nor well-ruled. According to Jia's most famous essay, 'Faulting the Qin', an empire may be won by arms but it can only be preserved by 'benevolent government' for: 'The common people in every single case are the basis for the state. ... Calamity and good fortune [for the ruler] does not depend upon Heaven, but upon the [will] of the people.' To win their support, good government should (1) establish more lenient penal, tax and *corvée* codes; (2) encourage the 'basic' occupations of farming and weaving, while prohibiting the wasteful production of luxury items; and (3) adopt a new calendar and new ritual standards to further distinguish Han rule from that of the Qin, the previous dynasty, which was widely regarded as oppressive. Once the ruler has won the approval of the masses, Jia argued, he can then inculcate in them the social values

that make for stable community. In the process, the ruler maximizes the number of trustworthy subjects from whom he may gather necessary information and advice.

To reduce the likelihood of civil and foreign wars, which inevitably impose the greatest hardship upon the common people, Jia proposed a series of daring initiatives. In effect, the semi-feudal institutions adopted by the Han founder would be dismantled and replaced with centralized institutions. At the same time, Jia devised an insidious plan by which to sap the strength of China's nomadic enemies: Chinese luxury goods, rather than crack troops, would be sent deep into Xiongnu territory. Though senior advisors at court, stung by Jia's criticisms and jealous of his undeniable charisma, persuaded Emperor Wen to send him into virtual exile, most of Jia's policy proposals were implemented soon after his untimely death.

Jia's masterwork, the *Xinshu* (New Book) contains a number of chapters that are less overtly political. For example, the essay 'Arts of the *Dao*' builds upon early Mohist attempts to define systematically fifty-six ethical terms and their antonyms. Three essays identify and consider six patterns inherent in human nature that will lead to virtue if fostered by a classical education: the Way (*dao*), grace, disposition, divine charisma, brilliance and destiny. In addition, several chapters devoted to education attribute the development of the moral sense less to human nature than to intelligent social engineering. Therefore, the skilled use of ritual precepts (especially sumptuary regulations) designed to counter the profit motive can promote a society in which 'no man who is treacherous will benefit, and so all will be good'. Convinced that the single most effective educator in the state is the ruler, whose suasive example in turn insures the survival of the dynasty, Jia Yi also details the proper training of the heir apparent in the ritual and legal precedents that make for strong, yet benevolent government.

Jia's work shows a philosophical coherence far beyond mere rhetorical skill, despite a fundamental tension between his desire to consolidate imperial power and his drive to inculcate ethical values in order to maintain a workable balance of power within the state. With Jia's sophisticated analysis tracing the success of public policy to the quality of the contemporary ritual and educational systems, his writings in these areas are still of considerable interest today.

See also: LEGALIST PHILOSOPHY, CHINESE; CONFUCIAN PHILOSOPHY, CHINESE; DAOIST PHILOSOPHY; LOGIC IN CHINA; MOHIST PHILOSOPHY

List of works

Jia Yi (207–169 BC) *Xinshu* (New Book), ed. and trans. Tsuruda Kyūsaku, *Kokuyaku kambun taisei*, Tokyo: Kokumin bunko, 1924, vol. 18. (A collection of essays attributed to Jia. A review of the grammar, vocabulary and content of the received text supports the traditional attribution, despite objections regarding its content and style posed by certain sceptics.)

References and further reading

Emmerich, R. (1991) *Untersuchungen zu Jia Yi (200–168 v.Chr.)*, PhD. thesis, University of Hamburg. (General introduction, with an emphasis on Jia Yi's political thought.)

Hsiao Kung-ch'üan (1979) *A History of Chinese Political Thought*, trans. F.W. Mote, Princeton, NJ: Princeton University Press, vol. I, 469–83. (Still the standard overview on Jia Yi's political programmes.)

Qi Yurang (1974) *Jiazi Xinshu jiaoshi* (Collated Explanations for Jia Yi's *Xinshu*), Taibei: Dongya. (Provides background information on the life and works of Jia Yi.)

Satō Akira (1981), 'Shinsho yōkei hen ni tsuite' (On the 'Rongjing' Chapter in the Xinshu), *Chūgoku kankei ronsetsu shiryō* 23: 309–16. (Argues the authenticity of the 'Rongjing' (Classic on Demeanour) chapter in the *Xinshu*).

Svarverud, R. (1992) *The Art of Defining Ethical Terms in Ancient China*, Oslo: Serica Osloensia, no. 5. (A preliminary study of the 'Daoshu' (Arts of the *Dao*) chapter in the *Xinshu*.)

Wang Zhouming (1982) 'Xinshu fei weishu kao' (An Investigation into the Authenticity of the *Xinshu*), *Wenxue yichan* 2: 17–28. (Defends the authenticity of the *Xinshu*).

MICHAEL NYLAN

JINA *see* MAHĀVĪRA

JOACHIM OF FIORE (*c.*1135–1202)

Joachim was a charismatic monastic reformer and inventive scriptural exegete whose study of the Bible led him to propound complex theories of history. Especially interested in the Apocalypse as a guide to history, he believed that the advent of the Antichrist and a violent end of the age were imminent. Contemporaries considered him a prophet, and this reputation – furthered by spurious works attributed to him – endured for four centuries. His theology, however, was widely criticized by such authoritative thinkers as Aquinas, Bonaventure and Bradwardine.

Joachim was born near Cosenza in Calabria, Italy. Educated as a notary, he began his career at the court of the Norman Kingdom of Sicily. An interior conversion around 1167 prompted him to devote himself to religious life. After false starts as a hermit, itinerant preacher and ordained priest, in 1171 Joachim became a monk (and later abbot) at the Benedictine monastery of Corazzo, where he began his intensive study of the Bible and the Church Fathers. From 1184, he became increasingly preoccupied with his writing, and with the pursuit of a more rigorous monasticism, eventually founding a new monastic order and monastery, San Giovanni in Fiore, around 1190.

Joachim's four major works – *Liber de concordia novi ac veteris testamenti* (The Book on the Concord of the New and Old Testaments), *Expositio in apocalypsim* (Commentary on the Apocalypse), *Psalterium decem chordarum* (The Ten-Stringed Psaltery) and *Tractatus super quatuor evangelia* (Treatise on the Four Gospels) – all begun in or after 1183, interweave novel principles of exegetical theory with the exegesis itself. Except for the *Psalterium*, a study of the Trinity in the form of a commentary on the Psalms, each of these works shows his concern with the patterns of history. The *Liber de concordia* expounds the correspondence of persons and events in the Old Testament to those in the New; the *Expositio* charts the history of the church in the events of the Apocalypse; and the *Tractatus* shows the correspondence of events in the Gospels with events in the shared history of the Jews and the Greek and Latin churches. The premise of all three works is that an understanding of relations between past and present, as read through Scripture, reveals something of future history.

Joachim simultaneously adhered to several theories of history, including the Augustinian seven-age scheme (see AUGUSTINIANISM) and the division of all history into two periods, one before Christ's incarnation and one after. His own theory, informed by Trinitarian theology, divides all history into three overlapping ages (*status*). Each age, in order, is identified with one person of the Trinity – Father, Son and Holy Spirit – and the relations between the ages reflect relations within the Trinity (see TRINITY). Thus, the second age arises out of the first, and the third has its sources in both the first and the second. In the fullness of the third age, the Holy Spirit is to bring peace and religious perfection to the world through a new type of monks, a renewed church and a perfect 'spiritual understanding' of the Old and New Testaments. Joachim believed that tribulations traditionally associated with the end of human history and Christ's return would instead mark the transition to the third age, which he expected by the mid-thirteenth century.

Though he was an idiosyncratic exegete, Joachim's doctrinal polemic against Peter LOMBARD shows that he was not entirely isolated from the scholastic currents of his day. Joachim's *De unitate et essentia trinitatis* is no longer extant, but we know he accused Lombard of transforming the Trinity into a 'quaternity' by making the divine essence into something really distinct from the three persons. According to Lateran Council IV (1215), which vindicated Lombard and condemned *De unitate*, Joachim erroneously explained the divine essence as a composition of the three persons, thereby compromising divine simplicity (see SIMPLICITY, DIVINE).

Joachim's two other important theological treatises, *De prescientia Dei et predestinatione electorum* (On the Foreknowledge of God and the Predestination of the Elect) and *De articulis fidei* (On the Articles of Faith), contrast strikingly with his four major works. Setting aside his theories of history, he concentrates on explaining Christian doctrine. *De prescientia* attempts to show that human freedom is compatible with divine grace and foreknowledge. Salvation is impossible without grace, but grace is available to all. It is a matter of free choice whether a person accepts and remains in grace, or rejects it. He emphasizes humility as the virtue by which one can best see and accept God's offer of grace (see GRACE; SALVATION). Joachim carefully distinguishes between divine foreknowledge and predestination, arguing that God foreknows, but does not predestine, all things. Foreknowledge, he argues, does not compromise human freedom, because God's knowledge is not the antecedent cause of a future human action, but is itself dependent on that future action's being chosen (see OMNISCIENCE).

See also: HISTORY, PHILOSOPHY OF; MYSTICISM, HISTORY OF

List of works

Joachim of Fiore (1183–?) *Liber de concordia novi ac veteris testamenti* (The Book on the Concord of the New and Old Testaments), ed. E.R. Daniel, *Transactions of the American Philosophical Society* 73 (8), 1983. (Books I–IV only. For Book V, see the Venice edition, 1519, reprinted Frankfurt: Minerva, 1964. An English translation of Book II, Part 1, Chapters 2–12 can be found in B. McGinn, *Apocalyptic Spirituality*, New York: Paulist Press, 1979. The *Liber de concordia* includes a systematic development of Joachim's two chief theories of history.)

—— (1183–?) *Expositio in apocalypsim* (Commentary on the Apocalypse), Venice, 1527; repr. Frankfurt: Minerva, 1964. (The most important source for his ideas about the imminent end of the age.)

—— (1183–?) *Psalterium decem chordarum* (The Ten-Stringed Psaltery), Venice, 1527; repr. Frankfurt: Minerva, 1965. (Essential for understanding Joachim's trinitarian thought.)

—— (1183–?) *Tractatus super quatuor evangelia* (Treatise on the Four Gospels), ed. E. Buonaiuti, *Fonti per la Storia d'Italia* 67, Rome: Tipografia del Senato, 1930. (The last of his major exegetical works, left unfinished at his death.)

—— (1183–?) *De articulis fidei* (On the Articles of the Faith), ed. E. Buonaiuti, *Scritti minori di Gioacchino da Fiore, Fonti per la Storia d'Italia* 78, Rome: Tipografia del Senato, 1936. (Briefly analyses and explains central Christian doctrines, including the Trinity, the Incarnation and the sacraments; also shows his practical interest in the pursuit of religious perfections.)

—— (1183–?) *De prescientia Dei et predestinatione electorum dialogi* (Dialogues on the Foreknowledge of God and the Predestination of the Elect), ed. P. De Leo, *Gioacchino da Fiore: Aspetti inediti della Vita e delle Opere*, Soveria Manelli: Rubbettino Editore, 1988. (The most philosophical of Joachim's works; makes original contributions to longstanding debates over divine foreknowledge and predestination.)

References and further reading

Baraut, C. (1974) 'Joachim de Flore', *Dictionnaire de Spiritualité*, Tome VIII, Paris: Beauchesne, 1179–1201. (The best short introduction to Joachim's thought.)

McGinn, B. (1985) *The Calabrian Abbot: Joachim of Fiore in the History of Western Thought*, New York: Macmillan. (Useful chapters on Joachim's exegesis, Trinitarian theology and treatment by Aquinas and Bonaventure.)

Reeves, M. (1969) *The Influence of Prophecy in the Later Middle Ages: A Study in Joachimism*, Oxford: Clarendon. (Indispensable as a study of Joachim's influence, though very brief in its exposition of his thought and works. Reprinted with an updated bibliography, Notre Dame, IN: University of Notre Dame Press, 1993.)

West, D.C. and Zimdars-Swartz, S. (1983) *Joachim of Fiore: A Study in Spiritual Perception and History*, Bloomington, IN: Indiana University Press. (A good introduction to Joachim because it assumes no prior knowledge and follows the texts very closely.)

SEAN EISEN MURPHY

JOHN OF ALEXANDRIA
see PHILOPONUS

JOHN OF DAMASCUS
(*c*.675–*c*.750)

John of Damascus, who lived in the seventh and eighth centuries, is known for his Fount of Knowledge, *which became the standard textbook of theology in the Eastern Orthodox tradition, and his opposition to the Iconoclasts, who opposed the use of images in Christian worship. The* Fount of Knowledge, *which drew heavily on patristic sources, was translated in the West by Robert Grosseteste, where it had an influence on writers such as Peter Lombard.*

John Mansur, also known as Chrysorrhoas (Golden-tongued), was born of a well-to-do Christian family in Damascus about 675 AD. He was educated by Cosmas, a ransomed Sicilian prisoner. The city was under Arab rule, but John rose in the Muslim administration until the anti-Christian Caliph Malik came to power in 685, when John retired with Cosmas to become a monk at Mar Saba near Jerusalem. He died about 750.

John composed a summa of theology, the *Fount of Knowledge* (after 743), divided into three parts. The first part, translated in the West by Robert GROS-STESTE as the *Dialectica*, is a philosophical diction-ary intended as an aid to the study of theology. It defines key terms in logic and metaphysics, many with theological implications, and generally follows the Eastern patristic tradition and responds to its concerns. The logical definitions draw heavily on Porphyry's *Isagōgē*, Ammonius Hermeae's commen-tary on the same and Aristotle's *Categories* (see AMMONIUS; ARISTOTLE; PORPHYRY). The second part, also translated by Grosseteste, is a history of heresies, following verbatim the *Panarion* of Epipha-nius of Constantia in most of it, and some other work for more recent heresies. In the last three chapters, which are of John's own composition, he discusses the Muslims, the Iconoclasts and a sect, otherwise unknown, that rejected the sacraments and the priesthood. The third part, the *Exposition of the Orthodox Faith*, was highly regarded in the East, where it has the same status as Aquinas' *Summa theologiae* in the West. Four translations were made of the work in the medieval West, where it was known as *De fide orthodoxa* (On the Orthodox Faith), the most popular being those of Burgundio (1153–4), and Grosseteste's revision of Burgundio's translation (1235–40). Peter LOMBARD used Burgun-dio's translation in his *Sentences*. John also wrote polemical tracts against the Muslims, Manichees and various Christian heretics, and *Sacred Parallels*, a collection of biblical and patristic texts chiefly on moral questions, arranged in alphabetical order by topic. Of his devotional and ascetic works, the three sermons on the Assumption of Mary are most famous.

John's writing is a patchwork of selections, generally uncredited, from earlier authors, though his own opinion usually emerges in his selection, omissions and commentary. The lost *Apology* of Aristides was discovered as a speech in his hagio-graphical romance, *Barlaam and Josaphat*. His philo-sophical and theological convictions are essentially those of the Cappadocian Fathers (see PATRISTIC PHILOSOPHY) and PSEUDO-DIONYSIUS. Thus he em-phasizes the incomprehensibility of God's nature, particularly in connection with the Trinity, where the distinction of Persons is only thought, but nonetheless objective. He shows no knowledge of AUGUSTINE, or any other Western writer except Leo the Great. In the West, Walter of St Victor identified John as an opponent of the Augustinian *filioque* doctrine, which holds that the Spirit proceeds from both the Father and the Son, and John did hold, with Gregory of Nyssa, that the Son and the Spirit 'co-originate' from the Father, and though the Son is first-born, the nature of this priority cannot be grasped intellec-tually. In particular, though the Spirit proceeds from ((*k*) the Father ('from' indicating a causal relation), it arises and is manifested through ((((() the Son (see TRINITY).

John is most noted for his role in the Iconoclastic controversy, supporting the veneration of images in three *Discourses Against the Iconoclasts* (726–30) that formed the basis for the orthodox view in the Eastern Church. He could oppose the Iconoclastic Emperor Leo III in part because he lived outside the Byzantine Empire. Though condemned in the Iconoclastic Synod of 754, John was vindicated by the second

Nicaean Council of 787, and has been considered a saint since the ninth century. He argued that God is beyond both being and knowledge, and so before the Incarnation it was suitable that he not be represented by any earthly image. However, he is now just as suitably worshipped in his manifestation as Jesus Christ, for just as Christ is truly God and truly man, and even the fleshly man Jesus is worthy of worship, so an image of this man is truly an image of God. It represents the now visible God, even when it represents suffering and ignominy. Therefore, whoever confesses the genuineness of the Incarnation ought to accept the veneration of images.

See also: ARISTOTLE COMMENTATORS; BYZANTINE PHILOSOPHY; GOD, CONCEPTS OF; PATRISTIC PHILOSOPHY

List of works

John of Damascus (*c.*675–*c.*750) Collected Works, ed. P.B. Kotter, *Die Schriften des Johannes von Damaskos*, Patristische Texte und Studien, Bd. 7, 12, 17, 22, 29, Berlin: de Gruyter, 1969–87, 5 vols. (This is the standard edition in Greek.)
—— (726–30) *Apologetic Discourses Against Those who Slander the Holy Images*, ed. P.B. Kotter in *Die Schriften des Johannes von Damaskos*, Berlin: de Gruyter, vol. 1; trans. D. Anderson, *On the Divine Images*, Crestwood, NY: St. Vladimir's Seminary Press, 1980; trans. M.H. Allies, *St. John Damascene on Holy Images: Followed by Three Sermons on the Assumption*, London: T. Baker, 1898. (John's most notable polemic work.)
—— (after 743) *Fount of Knowledge: The Philosophical Chapters*, ed. P.B. Kotter in *Die Schriften des Johannes von Damaskos*, Berlin: de Gruyter, vol. 1; medieval Latin translation ed. O.A. Colligan, *Dialectica, Version of Robert Grosseteste*, St Bonaventure, NY: The Franciscan Institute, 1955; trans. F.H. Chase in *John of Damascus: Writings*, Fathers of the Church 37, New York: Fathers of the Church, 1958; trans. G. Richter, *Philosophische Kapitel*, Stuttgart: Anton Hiersemann, 1982. (Richter contains a German translation embedded in extensive scholarly notes on John's sources.)
—— (after 743) *Fount of Knowledge: On Heresies*, ed. P.B. Kotter in *Die Schriften des Johannes von Damaskos*, Berlin: de Gruyter, vol. 4; trans. F.H. Chase in *John of Damascus: Writings*, Fathers of the Church 37, New York: Fathers of the Church, 1958. (This is largely taken verbatim from earlier writers and provides no independent information about heretical movements, but John is also interested in attacking contemporary hereies, and Islam, and the

last chapters of the work are interesting and original.)
—— (after 743) *Fount of Knowledge: An Exact Exposition of the Orthodox Faith*, ed. P.B. Kotter in *Die Schriften des Johannes von Damaskos*, Berlin: de Gruyter, vol. 2; medieval Latin translation ed. E.M. Buytaert, *De Fide Orthodoxa, Versions of Burgundio and Cerbanus*, St Bonaventure, NY: The Franciscan Institute, 1955; trans. F.H. Chase in *John of Damascus: Writings*, Fathers of the Church 37, New York: Fathers of the Church, 1958. (An extremely influential work in the Eastern Church.)
—— (*c.*675–*c.*750) *Dialogue Between a Saracen and a Christian*, trans. D.J. Sahas, Leiden: Brill, 1972. (An interesting attack on Islam. Sahas also includes a translation of Chapter 100 of *Fount of Knowledge: On Heresies*.)
—— (*c.*675–*c.*750) *Encomium on the Assumption of Holy Mary, Mother of God*, ed. P.B. Kotter in *Die Schriften des Johannes von Damaskos*, Berlin: de Gruyter, vol. 5; trans. M.H. Allies, *St. John Damascene on Holy Images: Followed by Three Sermons on the Assumption*, London: T. Baker, 1898. (Perhaps John's most important contribution to more popular religious thought.)

References and further reading

Florovsky, G. (1987) *The Byzantine Fathers of the Sixth to Eighth Century*, trans. R. Miller and A.M. Dollinger-Labriolle, Collected Works of Georges Florovsky, Vaduz: Bücher vertriebs anstalt, vol. 9, 254–92. (An excellent discussion of John's theology.)

JOHN LONGEWAY

JOHN OF FIDANZA
see BONAVENTURE

JOHN OF JANDUN
(*c.*1280/9–1328)

John of Jandun was the most important medieval philosopher in the Latin West to consider Averroes the true interpreter of the thought of Aristotle. He considered Aristotle to be 'the prince of philosophers', and Averroes to be the best philosopher after him. Jandun's defense of Averroes' attributing to Aristotle the doctrine that the intellect is one for all humans, and his own interpretation of various doctrines of Averroes, were much debated and criticized in Italy during the late fifteenth and the sixteenth centuries.

John of Jandun was a native of the small town of Jandun, near Rheims. Since he was a master of arts at Paris by the year 1310, he must have been born sometime before 1290, probably between 1280 and 1289. His earliest work was a question on the agent sense written in reply to a sophisma on the subject by Bartholomew of Bruges. He taught at the new College of Navarre from 1315 onwards. Jandun was closely identified with MARSILIUS OF PADUA, and fled Paris with him in 1326 when Marsilius' authorship of the *Defensor pacis* became known. Both went to the court of Emperor Ludwig of Bavaria. Excommunicated in 1327, Jandun died the following year.

In his questions on Aristotle's *Physics*, which were finished in 1315, Jandun insists that philosophical reasoning must be based on self-evident principles that agree with what is experienced by the senses. The first part of natural philosophy, namely physics, has as its subject matter mobile being or mobile body. It treats of things in motion, motion itself and the principles of motion. This science is in no way subordinated to metaphysics. Indeed, it is necessary for human happiness, since without it humans cannot know God perfectly in this life. It belongs to the natural philosopher and not to the metaphysician to demonstrate the existence of God and separated substances (the Intelligences), and to prove that they and God are immaterial (see NATURAL PHILOSOPHY, MEDIEVAL). The metaphysician's proper task is to determine the quiddity of God and the separated substances. Jandun denies that philosophers such as ARISTOTLE and Averroes (see IBN RUSHD) could have known creation from nothing, since their knowledge starts with what can be known through the senses. That all things were created by God, including the first man, must be held both according to Christian faith and according to truth. In like fashion, while the resurrection of numerically the same individual human being is impossible according to the philosophers, it should be asserted on the basis of faith.

Jandun's psychological views are to be found especially in his questions on Aristotle's *De anima*. (There are two versions of Books I and II but only one of Book III.) However, he also discusses psychological topics in other question-commentaries on Aristotle and in independent questions. Although he does take Aristotle and Averroes to be the best and the next best philosopher and spends much effort on explicating their common position on the soul and intellect, he makes clear that he does not think that they knew the truth. Against their views, Jandun proclaims that he accepts as true that the human soul is created from

nothing by God, is the form of the human body that gives existence to the body, and has immaterial powers of an agent intellect and a potential possible intellect. However, he insists that none of these things was held by Aristotle, nor can any of them be demonstrated by natural reason. On the contrary, since the miraculous is involved, these things are held only on faith.

Against ALBERT THE GREAT and Thomas AQUINAS, he maintains the plurality of forms in the human being. Jandun is insistent that if the intellective soul were the act of the body, giving it existence (*esse*) and united to it in existence – as Aquinas held – it would be corruptible. There are in fact two forms of the human body. The one is the sensitive or cogitative soul which gives existence to the body; the other is the intellective soul that is a single separate substance and one for all humans. It is a form only in an extended meaning of the term. Borrowing from the *de anima intellectiva* of SIGER OF BRABANT, whom he mentions by name, Jandun explains that the intellective soul is an active cause that operates within the body (*operans intrinsecum*). It is united to the body in its operation as a sailor is united with his ship. Jandun attempts to answer two objections, namely that his account of Aristotle and Averroes would mean that the individual human being (a) does not really think and (b) lacks unity. The latter objection he admits to be the greatest difficulty and the strongest point of those who attack Averroes (see SOUL, NATURE AND IMMORTALITY OF THE).

The intellective soul is itself composed of two different essential parts, an agent intellect and a potential (possible) intellect. Jandun denies that the agent intellect is God for Averroes, and against Thomas Wilton's proposal that the potential intellect is active, Jandun insists that it is not. He takes the phantasm to be the immediate active principle of the intelligible species produced in the potential intellect, while the agent intellect is simply the immediate active principle of the act of thinking. The agent intellect's 'abstracting' is not a process of universalizing the content of the phantasm, but rather simply causes the act of thinking. Jandun's attributing the notion of intelligible species to Averroes was later attacked by Renaissance Aristotelians such as Agostino NIFO.

Jandun maintains that after the human being has developed its speculative intellect and has been united to all the intelligible species in the possible intellect, it knows the separate agent intellect intuitively and then ascends through the different separate substances until it enjoys an intuitive knowledge of God.

In the realm of metaphysics, Jandun shows his allegiance to Averroes in his denial that there is any distinction of essence and existence. Unlike Siger of

Brabant, he does not appear to accept the doctrine of participation as central to his metaphysics. In various writings, Jandun accuses Aquinas of attempting to contradict Averroes but considers his labours to have been in vain (*Physics* VII, q.2). Jandun's different treatises on the agent sense would mark him as one of the major sources of the long discussion of this topic that lasted until the end of the sixteenth century.

See also: ARISTOTELIANISM, MEDIEVAL; ARISTOTELIANISM, RENAISSANCE; AVERROISM; IBN RUSHD; MARSILIUS OF PADUA; SIGER OF BRABANT; SOUL, NATURE AND IMMORTALITY OF

List of works

John of Jandun (before 1328) *In libros Aristotelis De coelo et mundo quae estant quaestiones subtilissimae* (Commentary on Aristotle's On the *Heavens and Earth*), Venice: Iuntas, 1552. (This edition also contains a work on the *De substantia orbis* that is not by Jandun.)

—— (before 1328) *Quaestio de habitu intellectus* (Question on the Disposition of the Intellect), in Z. Kuksewicz, 'Les trois "Quaestiones de habitu" dans le ms. Vat. Ottob. 318. Editions des textes de Jean de Jandun, Guillaume Alnwick et Anselme de Côme (?)', *Mediaevalia philosophica Polonorum* 9, 1961: 3–30. (Edition of one of Jandun's Questions.)

—— (before 1328) *Quaestio de infinitate vigoris Dei* (Question on God's Power), in Z. Kuksewicz, '*De infinitate vigoris Dei* des Pariser Averroisten Johannes de Janduno', *Manuscripta* 9, 1965: 167–70. (Edition of one of Jandun's Questions.)

—— (before 1328) *Quaestio de notioritate universalium* (Questions on Universals as Better Known [than Particulars]), in Z. Kuksewicz, 'La *quaestio de notioritate universalium* de Jean de Jandun', *Mediaevalia philosophica Polonorum* 14, 1970: 87–97. (Edition of one of Jandun's Questions.)

—— (before 1328) *Quaestio de principio individuationis* (Question on the Principle of Individuation), in Z. Kuksewicz, '*De principio individuationis* de Jean de Jandun', *Mediaevalia philosophica Polonorum* 11, 1963: 93–106. (Edition of one of Jandun's Questions.)

—— (before 1328) *Quaestio utrum aeternis repugnet habere causam efficientem* (Question: Is Having an Efficient Cause Incompatible with Eternal Things), in A. Maurer, 'John of Jandun and the Divine Causality', *Mediaeval Studies* 17, 1980: 198–207; repr. in A. Maurer, *Being and Knowing: Studies in Thomas Aquinas and Later Medieval Philosophers*, Toronto, Ont.: Pontifical Institute of Mediaeval

Studies, 1980, 275–308. (Edition of one of Jandun's Questions.)

—— (before 1328) *Quaestio utrum forma substantalis perficiens materiam sit corruptibilis* (Question: Is the Substantial Form that Perfects Matter Corruptible?), in Z. Kuksewicz (ed.) *Averroïsme bolonais au XIVe siècle: Edition des textes*, Ossolineum: Editions de l'Academie Polonaise des Sciences, 1965. (Edition of one of Jandun's Questions.)

—— (before 1328) *Quaestiones in duodecim libros Metaphysicae iuxta Aristotelis et magni Commentatoris intentionem disputatae* (Disputed Questions on Aristotle's *Metaphysics* and the Great Commentator's Intention), Venice: Hieronymus Scotus, 1553; repr. Frankfurt: Minerva, 1966. (Edition of the disputed questions.)

—— (before 1328) *Quaestiones super metaphysicam* (Questions on the *Metaphysics*), (Book IV, q. 6, Book VI, q. 8 and Book VII, q. 6, are reprinted in R. Lambertini and A. Tabarroni, 'Le *Quaestiones super Metaphysicam* attribuite a Giovanni di Jandun. Osservazioni e problemi', *Medioevo* 10, 1984: 41–104. (Questions on Aristotle.)

—— (before 1328) *Sophisma de sensu agente* (Sophisma on the Agent Sense), in A. Pattin (ed.) *Pour l'histoire du sens agent: La controverse entre Barthélemy de Bruges et Jean de Jandun, ses antécédents et son évolution*, Louvain: Presses Universitaires de Louvain, 1988, 118–65. (Jandun on the intellect.)

—— (before 1328) *Super libros Aristotelis De anima subtilissimae quaestiones* (Questions on Aristotle's *On the Soul*), Venice: Heirs of Hieronymus Scotus, 1587; repr. Frankfurt: Minerva, 1966. (Questions on Aristotle, Jandun's major psychological work.)

—— (before 1328) *Super octo libros Aristotelis de physico auditu subtilissimae quaestiones* (Questions on Aristotle's *Physics*), Venice: Iuntas, 1587; repr. Frankfurt: Minerva, 1969. (Questions on Aristotle.)

—— (before 1328) *Super parvis naturalibus Aristotelis quaestiones perutiles ac eleganter discussae* (Questions on Aristotle's *Parva naturalia*), ed. M. Zimara, Venice: Heirs of Octavianus Scotus, 1505. (Questions on Aristotle.)

—— (before 1328) *Tractatus de laudibus Parisius* (A Treatise on the Praises of Paris), in *Paris et ses historiens aux XIVe et XVe siècles*, ed. Le Roux de Lincy and L.M. Tisserand, Paris: Imprimerie Impériale, 1867, 32–79. (Jandun on the city of Paris.)

—— (before 1328) *Tractatus de sensu agente* (A Treatise on the Agent Sense), in A. Pattin (ed.) (1988) *Pour l'histoire du sens agent: La controverse entre Barthélemy de Bruges et Jean de Jandun, ses antécédents et son évolution*, Louvain: Presses

Universitaires de Louvain, 166–222. (Jandun on the intellect.)

References and further reading

Duhem, P. (1954) *Le système du monde*, VI, Paris: Librairie Scientifique Hermann, 534–75. (A systematic summary of Jandun's thought.)

Ermatinger, C.J. (1969) 'John of Jandun in His Relations with Arts Masters and Theologians', in *Arts libéraux et philosophie au moyen âge*, Montreal, Que.: Institut d'études médiévales, and Paris: Vrin, 1173–84. (Indicates topics that Jandun debated with such contemporaries at Paris as Bartholomew of Bruges, Thomas Wilton and William Alnwick.)

Grignaschi, M. (1958) 'Il pensiero politico e religioso di Giovanni di Jandun' (The Political and Religious Thought of John of Jandun), *Bullettino del'Istituto Storico Italiano per il Medio evo e Archivio Muratoriano* 70: 425–96. (Bases himself on the questions on the *Metaphysics* and *Rhetoric*.)

Jung-Palczewska, E. (1987) 'Jean de Jandun, a-t-il affirmé la nature active de l'intellect possible? Problème d'un contradiction dans la question 6 du livre III "De anima" de Jean de Jandun' (Did John of Jandun Posit an Active Nature for the Possible Intellect? The Problem of Contradiction in Qu. 6 of Book III of John of Jandun's Questions on Aristotle's *On the Soul*), *Mediaevalia philosophica polonorum* 27: 15–20. (Solves seeming contradiction in Jandun's remarks about whether the possible intellect is active.)

Kuksewicz, Z. (1968) *De Siger de Brabant à Jacques de Plaisance: La théorie de l'intellect chez les averroïstes latins des XIIIᵉ et XIVᵉ siècles* (From Siger of Brabant to Jacques de Plaisance: The Theory of the Intellect among the Latin Averroists of the Thirteenth and Fourteenth Centuries), Wroclaw: Editions de l'Academie Polonaise des Sciences, 202–43, 292–310. (A detailed overview of Jandun's psychology.)

MacClintock, S. (1956) *Perversity and Error: Studies on the 'Averroist' John of Jandun*, Indiana University Publications, Humanities Series 37, Bloomington: Indiana University Press. (Study of Jandun's position on the soul, the intellect and the agent sense. Many references to manuscripts.)

Mahoney, E.P. (1986) 'John of Jandun and Agostino Nifo on Human Felicity (*status*)', in C. Wenin (ed.) *L'homme et son univers au moyen âge*, Philosophes médiévaux 26, Louvain-la-Neuve: Editions de l'Institut Superieur de philosophie, vol. I, 465–77. (Compares Jandun's and Nifo's views on union of the human being to the separate intellect.)

—— (1987) 'Themes and Problems in the Psychology of John of Jandun', in J.F. Wippel (ed.) *Studies in Medieval Philosophy*, Studies in Philosophy and the History of Philosophy 17, Washington DC: The Catholic University of America, 273–88. (A synthesis of Jandun's remarks in different works regarding the nature of the soul, the intellect and cognition.)

Maurer, A. (1955) 'John of Jandun and the Divine Causality', *Mediaeval Studies* 17: 185–207, repr. in Maurer (1980) *Being and Knowing: Studies in Thomas Aquinas and Later Medieval Philosophers*, Toronto, Ont.: Pontifical Institute of Mediaeval Studies, pp. 275–308. (On efficient causality, creation and divine causality.)

Pacchi, A. (1958–60) 'Note sul commento al "De anima" di Giovanni di Jandun' (Notes on John of Jandun's Commentary on *On the Soul*), *Rivista critica di storia della filosofia* 13: 372–83, 14: 437–57, 15: 354–75. (A comprehensive summary of Jandun's psychological views including the agent sense.)

Schmugge, L. (1966) *Johannes von Jandun (1285/89–1328): Untersuchungen zur Biographie und Sozialtheorie eines lateinischen Averroisten* (John of Jandun: Studies in the Biography and Social Theory of a Latin Averroist), Pariser Historische Studien 5, Stuttgart: Anton Hiersemann. (Close study of Jandun's life and the chronology of his writings, his relation to Marsilius of Padua, and his views on virtue, the social community and political structures.)

Vitali, M.C. and Kuksewicz, Z. (1984) 'Notes sur les deux rédactions des "Quaestiones de anima" de Jean de Jandun' (Notes on the Two Versions of John of Jandun's Questions on Aristotle's *On the Soul*), *Mediaevalia Philosophica Polonorum* 27: 3–24. (Careful and detailed examination of this work that includes a dating of various of Jandun's writings.)

EDWARD P. MAHONEY

JOHN OF LA ROCHELLE (d.1245)

John of La Rochelle was one of the first generation of Franciscan theologians at the University of Paris. What little is known of his life places him as a close partner to the greatest of the early Franciscan teachers, Alexander of Hales. John collaborated with Alexander not only in steering the Franciscan order towards some sort of institutional equilibrium, but also in the elaboration of the first synthesis of Franciscan theology, the Summa

Fratris Alexandri *(Summa of Brother Alexander)*. *Whole sections of the* Summa *were written by John, most notably the treatment of moral law. John wrote in his own voice a number of theological works and two books on the soul, the* Tractatus de divisione multiplici potentiarum animae *(Treatise on the Multiple Division of the Soul's Power) and the* Summa de anima *(Summa on the Soul)*.

John seems to have entered the Franciscan order around 1230. He then studied theology at Paris, perhaps under ALEXANDER OF HALES, the most important Franciscan theologian. John became a Master of Theology in 1236, but he remained associated with Alexander in his work and in the public imagination. Indeed, he joined with Alexander in helping to depose Brother Elias as minister general of the Franciscans. He then collaborated with Alexander and two other Franciscans to write an important commentary on the Franciscan rule in 1240–1. John was also, and more influentially, a member of the team of editors that composed a massive summa of theology, which was attributed as a whole to Alexander, from affection or filial piety, under the title *Summa Fratris Alexandri* (Summa of Brother Alexander). Significant sections of the *Summa* were written by John, most notably the treatment of moral law. He also wrote in his own name in the genres typically used by Parisian masters of theology, producing sermons, a treatise on preaching, disputed questions and various short treatises (on grace, the articles of faith, the sacraments and topics in moral theology). John was praised by his contemporaries for his gift of clarifying inherited material by organizing it around central theological themes.

John's interest in philosophical topics seem to have been focused on the human soul, its nature and its moral dispositions. In this interest, John shows himself the heir of several twelfth-century genres, most notably treatises on natural philosophy, summaries of virtues or vices and handbooks of spiritual psychology. John also inherits Aristotle's *On the Soul* and the annexed biological books, as well as the ample erudition of newly translated Arabic medicine. He is, like his contemporary Vincent of Beauvais, within reach of an ever-expanding philosophical library. The temptation merely to accumulate citations was real, but not fatal. Indeed, John's two works on the soul move from encyclopedism to a more disciplined consideration of the soul. The first work, the *Tractatus de divisione multiplici potentiarum animae* (Treatise on the Many Divisions of the Soul's Powers), is encyclopedic in its selection and handling of authorities. The second work, the *Summa de anima* (Summa on the Soul), excludes a number of topics

and precedent texts in order to present a tighter arrangement of its teaching. Unfortunately, only the *Tractatus* is readily available in a modern edition. Fortunately, it shows more clearly than the *Summa* how John appropriates and begins to transform his philosophical sources.

According to John's own explanation, the *Tractatus* is divided into three parts that correspond to three ways of considering the soul: according to definition, according to division and according to completion or perfection. The parts are not equal in length nor, one presumes, in importance. The division of the soul's powers is by far the longest; the consideration according to definition by far the shortest. There is also marked variety in the complexity of internal organization. The first part proposes and explains in linear sequence eleven different definitions of the soul. The second part can be broken into five sections: philosophical divisions of the soul's powers, with special attention to Avicenna (see IBN SINA); medical divisions; a division by John Damascene (see JOHN OF DAMASCUS); a division by AUGUSTINE; and a review of some individual powers. These powers include what John distinguishes as reason, intellect, spirit (in both intellectual and physiological senses), will, intelligence and imagination. His third part can be understood as treating three large topics: grace and its divisions; the virtues, both philosophical and theological; and beatitude.

Even this brief summary will suggest that John has luxuriant vocabularies for discriminating among internal 'faculties'. His problem is rather to simplify than to complicate the resulting descriptions. John's typical procedure in each of the three parts of the *Tractatus* is to assemble authoritative texts on the point at hand and then to analyze their competing vocabularies. These authorities cover an enormous range, and are by no means exclusively philosophical. Definitions of the soul are taken from PLATO, ARISTOTLE, SENECA, the Book of Genesis, NEMESIUS of Emesa (cited as 'Remigius'), John Damascene and the anonymous Cistercian work *On Spirit and Soul*. Among the five different divisions of the soul considered, there are medical schemata taken from Johannitius (Hunayn ibn Ishaq) and Avicenna's *Canon of Medicine*. Even when John moves on from these schemata to consider some of the soul's powers individually, he seems principally concerned to catalogue various descriptions of each. But John is no mere copyist, even in the *Tractatus*. He often uses one or another text to provoke an extended discussion in the style of a disputed question. For example, a definition taken from BOETHIUS occasions a string of questions on what kind of existence ultimate happiness can have in the soul. John replies with careful distinctions among virtue, passion, habit and power, as well as with technical efforts to situate the gift of blessedness with respect to each power's sphere of action. In this way, John's *Tractatus* shows the labour of conceptual clarification required during the first half of the thirteenth century as masters of theology read their ways into the flood of newly translated philosophy.

See also: ALEXANDER OF HALES; ARISTOTELIANISM, MEDIEVAL

List of works

John of La Rochelle (1233–9) *Tractatus de divisione multiplici potentiarum animae* (Treatise on the Many Divisions of the Soul's Powers), ed. P. Michaud-Quantin, Paris: Vrin, 1964. (A critical edition of John's *Treatise*.)

—— (1240?) *Summa de anima* (Summa on the Soul), ed. T. Domenichelli, *La Summa de anima di Frate Giovanni della Rochelle dell'Ordine de'minori*, Prato: Giachetti, 1882. (An uncritical edition of John's *Summa*.)

—— (before 1245) *Quaestiones de gratia* (Questions on Grace), ed. L. Hödl, *Die neuen Quästionen der Gnadentheologie des Johannes von Rupella OM (†1245)*, Munich: M. Hüber, 1964. (Contains on pages 51–81 a critical edition of John's disputed questions on grace.)

References and further reading

Bougerol, J.-G. (1994) 'Jean de la Rochelle – les oeuvres et les manuscrits' (John of La Rochelle – Works and Manuscripts), *Archivum Franciscanum Historicum* 87 (3–4): 205–15. (A survey of some aspects of the transmission of John's works.)

Glorieux, P. (1943) *Répertoire des Maîtres en Théologie de Paris au XIIIe siècle*, Paris: Vrin, no. 302, vol. 2: 27. (A list of John's works, both philosophical and theological.)

Lottin, O. (1942–60) *Psychologie et morale aux XIIe et XIIIe siècles*, Louvain: Abbey of Mont César, vol. 6: 181–223. (On John's definitions and divisions of the soul.)

Michaud-Quantin, P. (1949) 'Les puissances de l'âme chez Jean de la Rochelle', *Antonianum* 24: 489–505. (A summary of John's several discussions of the soul's powers.)

Salman, H.D. (1947–8) 'Jean de la Rochelle et l'averroïsme latin', *Archives d'histoire doctrinale et littéraire du Moyen Age* 16: 133–42. (Shows John's dependence on intermediate sources for his knowledge of Aristotle's natural works.)

Smalley, B. (1985) *The Gospels in the Schools, c.1100–c.1280*, London: Hambledon Press, 171–190. (On John's Gospel commentaries, with particular attention to their Franciscan elements.)

—— (1974) 'William of Auvergne, John of La Rochelle, and St. Thomas Aquinas on the Old Law', in *St. Thomas Aquinas, 1274–1974: Commemorative Studies*, Toronto, Ont.: Pontifical Institute of Medieval Studies, vol. 2: 11–71. (On John's role in the constitution of the debate about the rationality of Old Testament Law.)

MARK D. JORDAN

JOHN OF MIRECOURT (*fl. c.*1345)

The traditional view that John of Mirecourt was condemned because he was a radical sceptic has been brought into question by more extensive research on his writings. For example, it appears that he did not doubt the existence of God as he was accused of doing. John was, however, greatly interested in describing as accurately as possible the kinds of evidence that lead to knowledge and the means by which they are produced.

John of Mirecourt, a Cistercian monk, lectured on the *Sentences* of Peter LOMBARD at the University of Paris during 1344–5. Propositions drawn from his *Sentences* commentary were condemned by the chancellor of the university in 1347. Against an initial list of condemned propositions, Mirecourt issued an apology in 63 articles, and then later, in reply to the official list of condemned propositions, he issued a further apology in 41 articles. Study of Mirecourt's thought has been hampered by the lack of a critical edition of the full Sentences commentary. The edition of the two apologies includes brief excerpts from the commentary, and questions I 2–6 (on knowledge) and I 13–16 (on enjoyment of God) have been edited. In addition, a few scholars have based their discussions of specific issues on examinations of unedited questions. However, as the table of contents printed in Tessier (1974) indicates, much more remains to be done before Mirecourt's thought may be properly assessed.

As is true of several of his contemporaries at Paris, Mirecourt's areas of special interest and the methods of inquiry he uses to pursue them show the influence of debates at Oxford earlier in the century. For example, Mirecourt displays interest in specifying and carefully describing the kinds and sources of human knowledge. He distinguishes suspicion or opinion (based on 'inevident assent' given with some concern about actual or potential error) from knowledge proper, relying on 'evident assent' given without fear of actual or potential error. Two sorts of evidence lead to evident assent: 'special' and 'natural'. Only the principle of non-contradiction, conclusions based upon it and propositions reducible to it are specially evident. Propositions derived from experience are nearly always proven only by natural evidence; the only exceptions (an example Mirecourt derives from AUGUSTINE) are those referring to the speaker's own existence, since one who doubts such a proposition would contradict one's intuitive awareness of one's own existence.

Mirecourt's careful investigation of the cognitive processes by which we acquire natural evidence shows not scepticism about the reliability of natural compared with special evidence, but deep interest in the debates at Oxford about the mechanism and respective priority of intuitive and abstractive cognition. His familiarity with these debates is revealed as a result of his style of argument: he tends to include a wide range of possible positions and to give detailed arguments for and against each one. While it is not always easy to determine Mirecourt's own view – he does not always indicate which side (if either) of an argument he prefers – on the whole it appears that Mirecourt tightens up the conditions for the acts of cognition that precede assent to natural evidence so as to reduce or eliminate intermediaries between the object of cognition and its subject. Like Adam WODEHAM, Mirecourt rejects any extension of intuitive cognition to cover cases other than simple apprehension in the presence of its object: he ascribes Scotus' and Ockham's imperfect intuitive cognition (the cognition of an existent object not present at the time) to memory, and appears also to reject any intuitive cognition of non-existents (see DUNS SCOTUS, J.; WILLIAM OF OCKHAM). While Mirecourt agrees with the usual view that abstractive cognition does not depend on the existence and presence of its object, he advances a number of arguments that propose (as Ockham did) that it does not rely on intermediary *species*, but instead results more directly from a prior intuitive cognition or from a *habitus* (that is, a disposition produced by one or several cognitions in the past).

Besides the compendious tendency of his questions, another characteristic of fourteenth-century English philosophy found in Mirecourt is his interest in using new logical and scientific techniques in order to discuss theology. For example, he uses proportional analysis to explain the conventional distinction between *usus* and *fruitio*, the 'use' and 'enjoyment'

of an achieved end, and discusses questions of human will and merit using theories of intension and remission and of extrinsic limits (see NATURAL PHILOSOPHY, MEDIEVAL; OXFORD CALCULATORS). It may have been the style and methodology of Mirecourt's commentary more than the views it expressed that got him into trouble with the authorities at Paris: if, indeed, the condemnation was motivated by anything other than the simple malice to which Ceffons and d'Ailly attribute it (for the suggestion that the real controversy producing the Paris condemnations was over methodology, and references to the remarks of Peter Ceffons and Pierre d'Ailly, see Tachau (1988): 379–80, and Courtenay (1973): 173).

See also: OXFORD CALCULATORS

List of works

John of Mirecourt (1344–6) *In I librum Sententiarum* (Commentary on Book I of the Sentences). (Portions appear in A. Franzinelli (1958) 'Questioni inedite di Giovanni di Mirecourt sulla conoscenza (Sent I q. 2–6)' (Unedited Questions by John of Mirecourt on Cognition), *Rivista Critica di Storia della Filosofia* 13: 319–40, 415–49; and M. Parodi (1978) 'Questioni inedite tratte dal I libro del Commento alle Sentenze di Giovanni di Mirecourt (q. 13–16)' (Unedited Questions Drawn from Book I of the Commentary on the Sentences by John of Mirecourt), *Medioevo* 3: 237–84.)

—— (1347) *Apologiae*, ed. F. Stegmüller, 'Die zwei Apologien des Jean de Mirecourt' (The Two Apologies of John of Mirecourt), *Recherches de théologie ancienne et médiévale* 5, 1933, 40–78, 192–204. (Includes both *apologiae*, the *Iohannes de Mercuria Apologia Prima* and *Iohannes de Mercuria Apologia Altera*. Excerpts from the relevant passages of the *Sentences* commentary are included in the notes.)

References and further reading

Copleston, F.C. (1963) *A History of Philosophy*, Garden City, NY: Image Books, vol. 3, 127–34. (An introductory account largely based on the two apologies.)

* Courtenay, W. (1972–3) 'John of Mirecourt and Gregory of Rimini on Whether God can Undo the Past', *Recherches de théologie ancienne et médiévale* 39: 224–56; 40: 147–74a. (Discusses I 39, suggesting Mirecourt was not as radical as he has often been considered.)

Murdoch, J.E. (1978) '*Subtilitates Anglicanae* in

Fourteenth Century Paris: John of Mirecourt and Peter Ceffons', in M.P. Cosman and B. Chandler (eds) *Machaut's World: Science and Art in the Fourteenth Century*, New York: New York Academy of Science. (Examines the use of scientific concepts derived from Oxford in III 4, 6–11 and I 10.)

Parodi, M. (1984) 'Il linguaggio delle proportiones nella distinctio prima di Giovanni di Mirecourt (The Language of Proportions in the first distinction of John of Mirecourt)', *Rivista Critica di Storia della Filosofia* 39 (4): 657–86. (Shows how I 13–15 use mathematical ratios.)

* Tachau, K. (1988) *Vision and Certitude in the Age of Ockham*, Leiden: Brill, 365, 371–3 and *passim*. (The best guide to the intellectual background to Mirecourt's theory of cognition in late thirteenth- and early fourteenth-century Oxford. Examines the situation in Paris only briefly and in conclusion. Shows the influence of Wodeham on I 3–5.)

* Tessier, G. (1974) 'Jean de Mirecourt, Philosophe et Théologien' (John of Mirecourt, Philosopher and Theologian), *Histoire Litteraire de la France* 40: 1–52. (Discusses I 21 of the *Sentences* commentary, and prints a table of contents for the whole work.)

Van Neste, R. (1976) 'The Epistemology of John of Mirecourt: A Reinterpretation', *Citeaux* 27: 5–28. (The only commentary on I 3–5 available. To be used with caution, preferably in conjunction with Tachau (1988).)

FIONA SOMERSET

JOHN OF PARIS (*c.*1260–1306)

John of Paris was a prominent Dominican theologian at Paris at the end of thirteenth century. He began his career with polemical works in defense of Thomist positions. In them, he asserts the distinction between essence and existence, the unity of substantial form and the function of matter as principle of bodily individuation. John later took part in wider controversies, including those between the French crown and the papacy. His best known work is a treatise on the mutual independence of secular and spiritual authority.

John of Paris (or John Quidort) spent much of his life as a controversialist. After the deaths of Thomas AQUINAS in 1274 and ALBERT THE GREAT in 1280, the Dominicans were pressed to explain their appropriation of Aristotelian doctrines in theology (see ARISTOTELIANISM, MEDIEVAL). However, the strife between Thomists and anti-Thomists, or 'Aristotelians' and 'Augustinians', was symptomatic of deeper

tensions in the theological use of philosophy. The controversies produced by these tensions dominated John's career as a teacher and writer.

The year of John's birth is uncertain. Probably he was studying as a Dominican in Paris by the end of the 1270s. What is certain is that John's first large-scale work, written in the early 1280s, was a work by a Dominican on behalf of Dominicans. It had its origin in a controversy that threatened the standing of the order generally and of its Parisian house in particular: the controversy over Thomas Aquinas' adaptations of Aristotle.

After March 1277 and before August 1279, the Franciscan William de La Mare wrote his *Correctorium fratris Thomae* (Correctory of Brother Thomas), a collection of about 118 passages from Aquinas's works, mostly from the first part of the *Summa theologiae*. William described, criticized and refuted each passage by authoritative texts drawn from the Bible and other authorities. In 1282, the Franciscan order decreed that Aquinas' *Summa* was not to be read in Franciscan houses except when it was accompanied by William's 'declarations'. However, the Dominicans, who dubbed William's work the 'Corruptory', had already begun to produce rebuttals. John of Paris undertook to write one of these, which is known by its opening word as *Sciendum*. His eclectic defence of Thomas is marked by an emphasis on the logic of terms and demonstrations, and is concerned primarily with showing flaws in the complaints of his opponents.

In 1292, John began his commentary on the *Sentences* of Peter LOMBARD, in which he takes up and augments Thomist positions. It is perhaps not surprising, then, that sixteen theses in it were singled out as heterodox. John's point-by-point replies to the charge seem scattered and pusillanimous. Still, John also defended himself in a public disputation on the distinction between essence and existence. His defence contains several striking passages of metaphysical analysis.

John's best known and most influential work is the short treatise *De potestate regia et papali* (On Royal and Papal Power), his contribution to the quarrel between Philip IV of France and Pope Boniface VIII. The quarrel began in 1296 over the crown's right to tax clerical property without seeking permission from the papacy. The resolution of the immediate dispute did not settle its principles, the most pertinent of which was the king's claim that in the temporal regimen of his kingdom he was not subject to the rule of the pope. Boniface asserted the papacy's right to judge the actions of all, kings included. The French party replied with a call for Boniface's trial before a general council of the Church on charges of heresy and simony. In this atmosphere, but before agents of the French king finally arrested the pope, John wrote his measured defence of the separation of royal and papal power.

The treatise traces something like the dialectic of a medieval disputed question. Its first ten chapters describe general principles of secular and ecclesiastical power, including the principle that bishops have as such no civil jurisdiction. In the eleventh chapter, John rehearses forty-two arguments for the opposing, papal side. He then turns in Chapters 12 and 13 to deciding the question, to weigh the merits of the two sides. He argues that God gave to the Church a spiritual power comprising the capacity to perform its sacraments, the authority to teach the faithful and to coerce those who despise the sacraments, and a proper provision both for the differentiation and support of its ministers. God did not give the Church as such any direct temporal power or jurisdiction. Having set forth this determination, John proceeds in Chapters 14–20 to reply to each of the forty-two arguments advanced from the other side. He then adds five chapters in something like an appendix, addressing the so-called 'donation of Constantine', the claim that the papacy was immune from criticism and the issue of papal abdication. John's treatise proved quite influential, especially in the Gallican movement of the seventeenth century.

Determinatio de modo existendi corporis Christi in sacramento altaris (Determination on the Manner of Existing of Christ's Body in the Sacrament of the Altar), John's last and in some ways most controversial work, was an attempt to offer an alternative to Aquinas' understanding of the transubstantiation of bread and wine in the celebration of the Eucharist, namely that Christ assumes the bread and wine as he assumed a human body. This view was immediately contested. In 1305, John was censured by an episcopal commission for his alternative teaching. He died at Bordeaux in September 1306 while awaiting a ruling on his appeal to the papacy.

See also: AQUINAS, T.; ARISTOTELIANISM, MEDIEVAL; POLITICAL PHILOSOPHY, HISTORY OF

List of works

John of Paris (1283–4) *Correctorium corruptorii* (Correctory of the Corruptory), ed. J.-P. Muller, *Le Correctorium corruptorii 'Circa' de Jean Quidort de Paris*, Rome: Herder, Studia Anselmianum, 1941. (This is John's detailed rebuttal of charges against the teaching of Thomas Aquinas.)

—— (1292–6) *Super Sententias* (Commentary on the Sentences), ed. J.-P. Muller, *Commentaire sur les Sentences*, Rome: Herder, Studia Anselmianam, 1961–4. (Books 1–2 only.)

—— (1296–9) *Apologia*, ed. J.-P. Muller, 'À propos du Mémoire justificatif de Jean Quidort', *Recherches de théologie ancienne et médiévale* 19, 1952: 344–51. (On John's reply to the charges against his commentary on the *Sentences*.)

—— (1296–9) *Quaestio de unitate esse et essentiae* (Question on the Unity of Being and Essence), ed. P. Glorieux, 'Jean Quidort et la distinction réelle de l'essence et de l'existence', *Recherches de théologie ancienne et médiévale* 18, 1951: 156–7. (The 'real distinction' was a characteristic position for Thomists.)

—— (1302–3) *De potestate regia et papali* (On Royal and Papal Power), ed. and trans. F. Bleienstein, *Johannes Quidort von Paris Über königliche und päapstliche Gewalt*, Stuttgart: Klett, 1969; trans. J.A. Watt, *On Royal and Papal Power*, Toronto, Ont.: Pontifical Institute of Mediaeval Studies, 1971. (Watt's translation contains a full and helpful introduction.)

—— (1304–5) *Determinatio de modo existendi corporis Christi in sacramento altaris* (Determination on the Manner of Existing of Christ's Body in the Sacrament of the Altar), ed. and trans. J.H. Martin, 'The Eucharistic Treatise of John Quidort of Paris', *Viator* 6, 1975: 214–40. (This had been one of the most contested topics in the dispute between Thomists and anti-Thomists.)

References and further reading

Coleman, J. (1983) 'Medieval Discussions of Property: *Ratio* and *Dominium* according to John of Paris and Marsilius of Padua', *History of Political Thought* 4: 209–28. (Connects John's discussions with the more notorious and influential views of Marsilius of Padua.)

Kaeppeli, T. (1975) 'Ioannes Parisiensis Quidort (Monoculus)', in *Scriptores ordinis praedicatorum medii aevi* 2: 517–24. (The most comprehensive bio-bibliography.)

* La Mare, William de (1277–9) *Correctorium fratris Thomae* (Correctory of Brother Thomas), in P. Glorieux (ed.) *Les premières poléemiques thomistes 1: Le Correctorium corruptorii 'Quare'*, Bibliothèque Thomiste 9, Kain, 1927. (William's text is found *passim*, interspersed among the replies to his various articles.)

Leclercq, J. (1942) *Jean de Paris et l'écclésiologie du XIIIe siècle* (John of Paris and the Ecclesiology of the Thirteenth Century), Paris: Vrin. (Still the standard introduction to John's teaching on the relations of ecclesiastical and secular authority.)

Roensch, F.J. (1964) *Early Thomistic School*, Dubuque: Priory Press, 98–104. (The most synoptic treatment in English.)

MARK D. JORDAN

JOHN OF SALISBURY (1115/20–1180)

John of Salisbury is one of the most learned and penetrating of twelfth-century Latin writers on moral and political matters. In his style as in his teaching, John represents a style of medieval philosophy heavily indebted to Roman models of rhetorical education. His interests in grammar, dialectic, politics and ethics are subordinated to an over-arching concern for moral formation. Three of John's works stand out. The Entheticus de dogmate philosophorum *(Entheticus of the Teaching of the Philosophers) is a satire on the pretensions and immoralities of those who divorce eloquence from philosophy in order to pursue power. The* Metalogicon *defends the traditional arts of the* trivium *and asserts the unity of eloquence and the other verbal arts with philosophy. By far the most important is the* Policraticus, *a sustained argument for philosophic wisdom against the vanities of worldly success, especially in politics.*

1 Life
2 Works

1 Life

John of Salisbury is one of the most learned, acerbic, reactionary and penetrating of twelfth-century Latin writers of moral and political philosophy. His writing and teaching represent the culmination of a style of medieval philosophy heavily indebted to Roman models of rhetorical formation, especially to CICERO and SENECA. His discussions of grammar, dialectic, politics and ethics are subordinated to an over-arching concern for moral formation. Indeed, John may well be considered one of the pre-eminent figures for the history of moral philosophy in the Latin West before the re-introduction of Aristotle's *Nicomachean Ethics*.

Little is known of John's early life. He traveled in 1136 to Paris to study at Mont-Saint-Geneviève, then the site of numerous schools of the liberal arts and theology. From the *Metalogicon* we learn that John studied with Peter ABELARD, WILLIAM OF CONCHES, THIERRY OF CHARTRES, Adam of Petit-Pont and GILBERT OF POITIERS. In 1147, John joined the household of Theobald, Archbishop of Canterbury, traveling as his envoy to the Continent and managing his complex domestic affairs. Among Theobald's other aides, and so among John's friends, the most notable figure was Thomas Becket. In 1156, Henry II banished John from the English court for two years for being over-loud in defence of Church rights against the crown. He regained favour, only to lose it again by supporting Becket's cause after 1162. He spent much of the 1160s in exile on the Continent, lobbying for the rights of the English church and trying to find some middle ground between the arrogance of the crown and the recalcitrance of his friend, the archbishop. After Becket's murder, John returned to England and to new ecclesiastical offices. In 1176, he was called back to the Continent as bishop of Chartres, where he died in 1180.

John complained of the pressures of his ministerial occupations, but found time for a brilliant literary career. His writings fall into two classes. Before the struggles of the 1260s, John wrote a number of works in the liberal arts and philosophy. Three of these are notable for their philosophic teaching: *Entheticus de dogmate philosophorum* (Entheticus of the Teaching of the Philosophers), completed probably in 1156, the *Metalogicon* in 1159, and the *Policraticus*, also in 1159. Later, John turned to ecclesiastical history, writing his memoirs of the papal court, the *Pontifical History*, and very polished lives of Anselm of Canterbury and Becket.

2 Works

The *Entheticus* is the earliest of John's major works, and it sketches out in poetic form some of the concerns that would preoccupy him in all of them. There is evidence that the *Entheticus* was never finished and, hence, never intended for circulation outside a small circle of friends. It is hard to imagine a satire of such specific ferocity ever being offered to the public. The work begins by defending the alliance of reason and eloquence against the decadence of John's contemporaries. It next extols philosophy, bringing forward the principal teachers of antiquity. The conclusion of the hortatory argument is the superiority of Christian wisdom and the folly of an exclusive infatuation with logic. The poem then breaks off to describe, in harsh terms, the little book's imagined voyage to the royal court. It ends with a brief epilogue on grace. Readers have found it hard to discern any single plan in the *Entheticus*; John took his patterns of composition from the dialectical, digressive masters of Roman oratory. He is less concerned with demonstration or analysis than with producing rhetorical effects by which the reader may be persuaded to a virtuous life.

The *Metalogicon* is often pillaged for what it records of the Parisian schools in the twelfth century. It deserves better. With the *Metalogicon*, John first achieves the kind of scope needed for his pedagogical project. The work presents itself as a reply to unnamed opponents who have, once again, arrogantly denied the importance of eloquence to philosophy, thereby upending the whole order of liberal arts and so wrecking the foundation of philosophy. John undertakes to show what unites the verbal arts with each other and why they are all necessary for philosophy. Much of what follows in the *Metalogicon* is an erudite rehearsal of lessons about the interrelations of grammar and logic, including all of the pieces of Aristotle's *Organon*. Shorter, more elliptical lessons are recalled about philology and eloquence. However, John interrupts or enriches his rehearsal with explanations of the sources of cognition, the nature of moral virtue and the limitations of philosophy in regard to faith. The *Metalogicon* is not so much a handbook of the verbal arts, then, as an extended argument for the instrumental use of a unified *trivium* in the service of moral philosophy.

The *Policraticus*, John's last and most famous philosophical book, is typically studied as a work of political philosophy, best known for some remarks on the justice of killing tyrants, but the work is considerably more. John intends it as an extended invitation to take up philosophic life, by which he means the pursuit of the moral good. The basic contrast of the *Policraticus* is between the 'frivolity of courtiers' and the 'traces of the philosophers', between the evident emptiness of lives squandered on worldly ambition and the alluring reminders of lives devoted to the pursuit of truth. For example, Book 1 shows how the talented are corrupted by cheap gifts into the pursuit of any number of unsuitable ends: hunting, gambling, theatre and especially the shams of magic. Book 2 then distinguishes useless superstition from the pious interpretation of natural phenomena as signs of divine will. This dialectical progression, of invective and instruction, of misuse and right use, runs throughout the *Policraticus*.

For that reason, the work cannot be mapped in a small space. Indeed, John takes different maps for different parts of his text. *Policraticus* 4, for example, is loosely ordered as a commentary on Deuteronomy 17: 14–20, a passage introduced to support the claim that princes ought to be subservient to the divine law. John not only dilates the commentary over eight chapters, he omits, perhaps deliberately, certain parts of the biblical text, such as its prescriptions for the selection of rulers. Book 5 develops an analogy between the human body and human government:

the prince is the head, the senate the heart, and so on. Present throughout the work are bits of moral invective, poetic quotations and historical examples, both pagan and biblical. The examples are probably the most important element in John's notion of moral teaching. He seems to find in these carefully chosen tales not just colour or incident, but the deeper logic of moral consequences.

If John's larger structures are loose, they are not negligible. In one crucial case, the structure of his argument settles a vexed problem of interpretation: whether John does or does not advocate the killing of tyrants. The claim that he does usually relies on an extended discussion of tyranny in *Policraticus* 8, though the text seems very unsatisfying as a guide to assassination. It is a description of tyranny as a moral anti-type, as a negation of what should be sought in a philosophically ordered life. Tyrants live deformed lives and so meet with hideous deaths, which they deserve because their lives deform what is fundamental in human morality. The discussion of tyranny is a striking and even terrifying depiction of the anti-type of morality. The reader can learn this from Book 8's rhetorical structure. It begins with a critique of the Epicureans, who, John says, taught self-love and self-indulgence, the fundamental vices from which tyranny springs and also, not coincidentally, the typical vices of courtiers. Hence the critique of Epicureanism, the antithesis of philosophy, is properly followed by the depiction of the tyrant and then by a moral peroration in which the reader is asked for a last time to reject the failed life of Epicureanism, the vanity of courtiers, in favour of the morally good life taught by philosophy (see EPICUREANISM).

What remains truly puzzling in the *Policraticus* is John's integral appropriation of pagan philosophy even as he professes the Christian faith. He is fond of juxtaposing the two: he compares Christ with Odysseus, and supplements Socrates with the Bible. He does sometimes stop to justify at least a piece of his practice, as when he argues that he can use pagan examples because Paul used them. However, John seems most often to proceed as if Christianity could complete pagan philosophy without conflict and without remainder. If he censures pagan superstition, he immediately praises pagan wisdom, and he frequently quotes the Roman poets as moral authorities. In these details as much as in his professed teaching, John shows a characteristic confidence in the unity of human learning. He also shows his antipathy to the separation of philosophy either from the liberal arts that lead to it or from the Christian theology that completes it.

See also: CHARTRES, SCHOOL OF; POLITICAL PHILOSOPHY, HISTORY OF

List of works

John of Salisbury (1155–9) *Entheticus de dogmate philosophophorum (Entheticus major)*, ed. and trans. J. van Laarhoven, Leiden: Brill, 1987. (A critical edition with a well-annotated and well introduced translation.)

—— (1159) *Metalogicon*, ed. J.B. Hall and K.S.B. Keats-Rohan, Turnhout: Brepols, 1991; ed. and trans. K.S.B. Keats-Rohan, Oxford: Clarendon, 1990. (Discusses the *trivium* and asserts the unity of the verbal arts with philosophy.)

—— (1159) *Policraticus*, ed. C.C.J. Webb, Oxford: Clarendon Press, 1909; *Policraticus* I–IV, ed. K.S.B. Keats-Rohan, with the *Entheticus minor*, Turnhout: Brepols, 1993. (Salisbury's major work of political philosophy. A translation of the whole of the *Policraticus* can be pieced together from J. Dickinson, *Policraticus: The Statesman's Book*, New York: Knopf, 1927, and J.B. Pike, *The Frivolities of Courtiers and the Footprints of the Philosophers*, Minneapolis: University of Minnesota Press, 1938. Selections have been translated by C.J. Nederman, Cambridge: Cambridge University Press, 1990.)

References and further reading

Liebeschütz, H. (1968) *Mediaeval Humanism in the Life and Writings of John of Salisbury*, revised edn, Nendeln: Kraus. (A standard intellectual biography, now somewhat dated.)

Nederman, C.J. (1988) 'Nature, Sin, and the Origins of Society: The Ciceronian Tradition in Medieval Political Thought', *Journal of the History of Ideas* 49: 3–26. (The impact of Cicero on medieval philosophy.)

—— (1991) 'Aristotelianism and the Origins of 'Political Science' in the Twelfth Century', *Journal of the History of Ideas* 52: 179–94. (The development of political philosophy in the Middle Ages.)

Wilks, M. (ed.) (1984) *The World of John of Salisbury*, Oxford: Blackwell. (An anthology of twenty-four papers, with a bibliography of works on John for 1953–82 on pages 445–57.)

MARK D. JORDAN

JOHN OF ST THOMAS (1589–1644)

The seventeenth-century Portuguese Dominican, John of St Thomas or John Poinsot, was a major figure in late scholastic philosophy and theology. Educated at Coimbra and Louvain, he taught both disciplines in Spain: at Madrid, Plasencia and Alcalá. Aspiring to be a faithful disciple of Thomas Aquinas, he published a three-volume Cursus philosophicus thomisticus *(Thomistic Philosophical Course) and before he died began the publication of a* Cursus theologicus *(Theological Course). His philosophical writing was explicitly on logic and natural philosophy. However, in both his philosophical and theological works, he treated many metaphysical, epistemological and ethical issues. His logic is divided into two parts, formal and material. Of particular interest is his semiotic doctrine which appears in the second part. In natural philosophy, he explained Aristotle with a Thomistic slant. While following Aquinas in theology, John at times developed his master's doctrine along new lines. Both in his own time and after he has had considerable authority within scholasticism, especially for Thomists. Among those whom he has influenced in twentieth-century Thomism are Joseph Gredt, Reginald Garrigou-Lagrange, Santiago Ramirez, Jacques Maritain and Yves Simon.*

1 Life and works
2 Logic
3 Natural philosophy
4 Metaphysics

1 Life and works

John of St Thomas was born John Poinsot in Lisbon. He studied humanities and philosophy at the University of Coimbra, where in 1605 he received a bachelor of arts degree. While studying philosophy, he probably attended lectures given by the Jesuits who directed the College of Arts at Coimbra and whose course in philosophy was published in five volumes which appeared successively between 1562 and 1606 (see COLLEGIUM CONIMBRICENSE). In October 1605, John began the study of theology at Coimbra and the following year he continued this at Louvain where in 1608 he gained his bachelor's degree in biblical studies. On 17 July 1609, he entered the Order of Preachers (the Dominicans) at the Convent of Our Lady of Atocha in Madrid, where he spent the next year. On 17 July 1610, he made his formal profession as a Dominican and at this time chose the name by which he would be known in religion: John of St Thomas. From 1610 to 1615 he studied philosophy and theology at the Atocha convent where from 1615 to 1620 he taught arts. In 1620, he went as lecturer in theology to the Dominican priory at Plasencia. Between 1625 and 1630 he was a lecturer in arts and theology at the Dominican College of St Thomas in Alcalá. In 1626, he became regent of studies there and in 1627 was appointed as a consultant for the Supreme Tribunal of the Spanish Inquisition. From 1630 to 1640, he held the *cátedra de vísperas* (chair of vespers) in theology at the University of Alcalá. During this period he received his doctorate in theology in 1633 and he published, at Alcalá and Madrid, his logic and natural philosophy, which, printed together at Rome in 1637–8 and at Cologne in 1638, became his *Cursus philosophicus thomisticus* (Thomistic Philosophical Course). At Alcalá in 1637, he began to publish his *Cursus theologicus* (Theological Course), which was completed posthumously from its author's manuscripts edited by Diego Ramirez, Jacques Quetif and Francis Combefis. In 1641 he attained at Alcalá the theological *cátedra de prima* (chair of prime), which he held until 1643. In that year, he was appointed confessor to King Philip IV. Accompanying the king on an expedition to Catalonia, John was stricken by fever at the siege of Lerida and died at Fraga in Aragon.

Most of all, John of St Thomas aimed at being a true disciple of Thomas AQUINAS. As he tells us in his *Cursus theologicus* (I d.2 a.5), this entailed two things: (1) to follow Aquinas' doctrine as true and Catholic, and (2) to develop it as much as possible. Since beyond Aquinas in philosophy there was ARISTOTLE, John's own philosophical work was also very much in the vein of Aristotelian commentary (see ARISTOTELIANISM, RENAISSANCE). Explicitly, as published, that work was in logic and natural philosophy. However, in both his philosophical and theological writings, he covered numerous issues in metaphysics, epistemology and ethics. On such issues he almost invariably sought to defend Thomistic doctrine against its adversaries. Chief among these, as John saw them, were the Jesuits, Gabriel Vásquez (1549–1604) and Francisco SUÁREZ.

2 Logic

John of St Thomas' logic is divided into two parts. In the first part, his concern is with the formal theory of correct thinking. This part, which includes such medieval items as supposition, exponibles and consequences, corresponds especially to the *Summulae Logicales* of PETER OF SPAIN and the *Prior Analytics* of ARISTOTLE. In the larger second part, which corresponds to the *Isagōgē* of PORPHYRY, plus the *Categories* and the *Posterior Analytics* of Aristotle, he deals with material logic, which is a general theory of scientific demonstrations and the necessary connections they involve depending upon their content. Organized according to the three operations of the intellect (simple apprehension, judgment and reasoning) the first part treats of terms, propositions, consequences and syllogisms, along the way attending to definitions, divisions and their various facets. In the second part, John reflects upon the nature of logic itself, which he thinks is at once an art and a science. As science, he says, 'logic is essentially and absolutely in virtue of its own principles speculative, but it takes on the manner of a practical science in so far as it offers rules and direction for speculation itself' (*Ars Logica*, II q.1 a.4). The object of logic is beings of reason, such as species, genus, subject, predicate, antecedent, consequent and so on, formed by the mind's reflections upon its own operations. Such beings of reason, which have some foundation in reality outside the mind, fall under a wider notion that includes beings of reason like chimeras. These last lack such a foundation because they are impossible (that is, self-contradictory) objects. Contrasted with both sorts of beings of reason are real beings which are divided into the various Aristotelian categories (see LOGIC, MEDIEVAL §4).

The categories are the central concern of the second part of John's logic. He rejects Duns Scotus' teaching that *ens* (being) is said univocally of the categories (see DUNS SCOTUS, J. §5). Rather, as CAJETAN (§2) thought, 'being' as said of the categories is 'formally analogous with an analogy of proper proportionality' (*Ars Logica*, II q.14 a.3). Passing through each category in succession he concurs with Cajetan's interpretation of Aquinas (*Summa theologiae* Ia.28.1) to the effect that relation is unique because it can be found in the order either of real being or being of reason. Only relation, since it is not just 'in' something but also 'towards' something, can transcend categorial status and be conceived apart from real existence either in itself (that is, the mode of existence proper to a substance) or in something else (the mode proper to an accident). This thought was to be central to John's doctrine of signs.

The doctrine of signs itself, which in part at least reflects the influence of John's Jesuit teachers at Coimbra, forms a treatise which runs over questions 21–3 in the second part of his logic. Essentially relational, signs are divided first into formal and instrumental, and second into natural, conventional and customary. All signs make something else known: formal signs (for example, a concept or an impressed species) do so without themselves first being known; instrumental signs (such as smoke or a spoken word) are themselves first known and then lead to the knowledge of something else. Natural signs (smoke) differ from conventional signs (words) inasmuch as the former simply arise from causal connections in the natural order while the latter result from human choice. Customary signs also result from choice but can be natural when a custom leads us naturally to its cause. Signs involve two non-reciprocal relations: between the sign and the significate (as in the relation of measured to measure) and between the sign and the cognitive power of a knower (as in the relation of measure to measured). Considered just as such, these relations are not in the line of physical causality but rather in that of intentionality in which the sign substitutes for the significate. Within this line of intentionality the ability of relation to transcend real being and being of reason becomes the basis of a unified semiotic doctrine respecting all signs of whatever sort they are (see COLLEGIUM CONIMBRICENSE; LANGUAGE, RENAISSANCE PHILO-SOPHY OF §1).

3 Natural philosophy

John originally planned his natural philosophy in parts corresponding to four subject areas: mobile being in general, incorruptible mobile being, corruptible mobile being and animated mobile being. The second part, a tract on astronomy, may have existed in manuscript but was never published. The first part contains twenty-six questions principally expounding the matter of Aristotle's *Physics*. Thus after a question about the science of natural philosophy, its formal object (mobile being), its unitary character and way of proceeding, he proceeds to explain the principles of natural things (matter, form and privation). Going beyond ARISTOTLE, he here (*Naturalis philosophiae*, I q.7) discusses subsistence and existence, and he defends the Thomistic real (*a parte rei*) distinction of essence and existence in creatures. Continuing with natural philosophy, he follows Aristotle to explain nature versus art and what is forced or unnatural, causality in general, the four basic causes (material, formal, efficient and final), motion, the infinite, place, the void and time. Near the end of this part (*Naturalis philosophiae*, I q.24 a.3) he treats Aristotle's Prime Mover. This he identifies with God whose attributes of infinity, immateriality, intelligence, ubiquity, eternity and unity he deduces from the fact that God is pure act. The third part corresponds to Aristotle's *On Generation and Corruption* and *Meteorology*. Through twelve questions on the *On Generation*, it deals with such topics as substantial generation, corruption, alteration, intension, remission, action and reaction, mixing, con-

densation and rarefaction, nutrition and growth. This last provokes the question: 'How does a living thing remain the same during the whole time of its nutrition and growth?' (*Naturalis philosophiae*, III q.9 a.6). To this John replies with Aquinas that living flesh remains the same not according to that within it which is material but according to that which is formal, that is, according to a disposition continuing over time to retain a certain figure, temperament, and order in respect of other parts and the form of the whole. The fourth part contains John's philosophical psychology. After a brief summary of Book 1 of Aristotle's *On the Soul*, it discusses issues raised in Books 2 and 3 about the soul in general, the vegetative soul, the sensitive soul with its external and internal sense powers, and finally the rational soul. In a more Thomistic than Aristotelian way, he defends (*Naturalis philosophiae*, IV q.9 a.1) the immortality of this last on the basis of Scripture and with two philosophical arguments. These are, first, that the operational independence of the soul from the body indicates its ability to survive the death of the body, and second, that a need for ethical sanctions here and now suggests the soul's survival to receive reward or punishment in an afterlife (see NATURAL PHILOSOPHY, MEDIEVAL §§8–9).

4 Metaphysics

In his *Cursus theologicus* John addressed a variety of metaphysical questions about the existence, nature and operations of God. Like AQUINAS (§13), he rejects the assertion that God's existence is self-evident. Instead, a demonstration must be mounted from creatures as effects to God as their cause. In this, he retraces and explains the famous 'five ways' of Aquinas. He also follows Aquinas in his general deduction of the attributes of God. Distinctive, however, is his interpretation of Aquinas to the effect that it is the very act of intellection itself which is 'formally constitutive of the divine nature' (*Cursus theologicus*, I d.16 a.2). Also distinctive, but perhaps more a matter of updating, is John's elaborate confrontation, here (d.18 a.4) as well as earlier in his logic (*Ars Logica*, II q.2 a.4), of the late scholastic question of whether God knows impossible beings of reason. In contrast with Vásquez, he maintains that while God may not form such beings of reason, he can know them as formed by us. Both the question itself and his discussion of it have an important bearing on scholastic intentionality teaching. Finally in his moral doctrine, yet another difference with Aquinas which John most likely saw as an updating was in his embrace of 'probabilism', the theory that one may resolve a moral doubt by accepting any opinion proposed by a prudent moral authority (*Cursus theologicus*, IV d.12 a.3) (see GOD, CONCEPTS OF).

See also: AQUINAS, T.; ARISTOTELIANISM IN THE 17TH CENTURY; ARISTOTELIANISM, RENAISSANCE; COLLEGIUM CONIMBRICENSE; LANGUAGE, RENAISSANCE PHILOSOPHY OF; LOGIC, RENAISSANCE

List of works

John of St Thomas (1631–2) *Cursus philosophicus: Ars Logica* (Philosophical Course: Logical Art), ed. B. Reiser, vol. 1, Turin: Marietti, 1930; trans. F.C. Wade, *Outlines of Formal Logic*, Milwaukee, WI: Marquette University Press, 1955; trans. Y.R. Simon, J.J. Granville and G.D. Hollenhorst, *The Material Logic of John of St Thomas*, Chicago, IL: University of Chicago Press, 1955. (Contains the two parts of John's formal and material logic. The 1955 editions are partial translations.)
—— (1632) *Tractatus de Signis: The Semiotic of John Poinsot*, trans. and ed. J.N. Deely with R. Austin Powell, Berkeley, CA: University of California Press, 1985. (A translation and interpretative arrangement of passages from the *Ars Logica*, including Part II, Questions 21–3.)
—— (1633–5) *Cursus philosophicus: Naturalis philosophiae partes I, III, et IV* (Philosophical Course: Natural Philosophy), ed. B. Reiser, Turin: Marietti, vol. 2, 1933; vol. 3, 1937. (Contains John's natural philosophy, including his philosophical psychology in volume three.)
—— (1637–45) *Cursus theologicus* (Theological Course), ed. Solemnes, vols 1–4, Paris: Desclée, 1931–46; vol. 5, Matiscone: Protat Frères, 1964. (Contains John's commentary questions on Aquinas' *Summa theologiae*.)
—— (1649–67) *Cursus theologicus* (Theological Course), vols 6–8, ed. D. Ramirez and F. Combefis, Paris: Louis Vivès, 1885. (Completed posthumously from John's manuscripts, this edition continues his commentary on Aquinas' theology.)

References and further reading

Ashworth, E.J. (1988) 'The Historical Origins of John Poinsot's *Treatise on Signs*', *Semiotica* 69: 129–47. (A critical review of Deely's translation and interpretation of the *Tractatus de Signis*.)
Deely, J. (1983) 'Neglected Figures in the History of Semiotic Inquiry: John Poinsot', in A. Eschbach and J. Trabant (eds) *History of Semiotics*, Amsterdam: John Benjamins Publishing Company, 115–26. (Treatment of John's doctrine of signs.)

—— (1994) *New Beginnings. Early Modern Philosophy and Postmodern Thought*, Toronto, Ont.: University of Toronto Press. (John's semiotic doctrine as central to a new approach to the history of philosophy.)
—— (ed.) (1994) 'John Poinsot', special issue of *American Catholic Philosophical Quarterly* 67 (3). (Contains articles on various aspects of John's work.)
Lohr, C.H. (1987) *Latin Aristotle Commentaries. II Renaissance Authors*, Florence: Olschki, 204–5. (Contains biographical and bibliographical information on John.)
Maritain, J. (1938) 'Signe et symbole', *Revue Thomiste* 44: 299–330; trans. H. Binsse, 'Sign and Symbol', in *Redeeming the Time*, London: Geoffrey Bles, 1943, 191–224, 268–78. (Presents John's doctrine of signs.)
Ramirez, J.M. (1924) 'Jean de St Thomas', *Dictionnaire de théologie catholique*, Paris: Letouzey & Ane, vol. 8, cols 803–8. (Contains information on John's life, writings and theological doctrine.)

JOHN P. DOYLE

JOHN THE GRAMMARIAN
see PHILOPONUS

JOHNSON, ALEXANDER BRYAN (1786–1867)

Johnson was a self-taught philosophic genius who, completely alone, set out in the 1820s to analyse the nature and limits of language. He was the first thinker who consciously and systematically based his whole approach to philosophical problems on a critique of language. According to Johnson, a knowledge of the nature of language is important because it 'bears the same relation to all speculative learning as a knowledge of the qualities of drugs bears to the practice of medicine or as a knowledge of perspective and colours bears to painting' (1854).

Johnson tried to show that most of the propositions and questions of speculative philosophers are neither true nor false, but 'insignificant'. They arise from our 'misunderstanding of the nature of language'. He found the source of the misunderstanding in our tendency to interpret nature by language. 'My lectures', Johnson wrote, 'will endeavour to subordinate language to nature – to make nature the expositor of words, instead of making words the expositor of nature. If I succeed, the success will ultimately accomplish a great revolution in every branch of learning' (Rynin 1947: 300). Johnson's work did not attract any attention until the 'linguistic turn' in philosophy in the twentieth century made his rediscovery possible.

Born in 1786 in Gosport, England, of Dutch-Jewish ancestry, Johnson emigrated to the USA in 1801 and settled in Utica, New York, where he embarked on a long and successful career in banking. He published books on banking, on politics, and on religion and morality. However, what engrossed him most was language and philosophy. He published three books on language: *The Philosophy of Human Knowledge* (1828), *A Treatise on Language* (1836) and *The Meaning of Words* (1854). He also published two books on the theory of knowledge: *The Physiology of the Senses* (1856) and *Deep Sea Soundings and Explorations of the Bottom* (1861). In his unpublished autobiography Johnson briefly summarized what he thought his writings had accomplished:

The verbal systems of speculative philosophy are as interminable as the different tunes that can be formed out of the notes of a piano, and realizing how barren such philosophies have ever been for the settlement of the questions for which such philosophies are employed, I have essayed the new system as an ultimate and fixed limit of all speculative knowledge; and which will in time...cause an abandonment of the old and endless speculations of the verbal philosopher.

(Johnson's unpublished autobiography, date of writing unknown)

Johnson conceived of his philosophical task as that of setting limits to our knowledge: in *The Physiology of the Senses*, the limits of what we can perceive; in his books on language, the limits of what we can say; and in *Deep Sea Soundings*, the limits of what we can think. These limits are determined by the nature of reality and the nature of human beings. Human beings, according to Johnson, are physical, emotional and intellectual (he called it 'Man's Triplicity') and reality as it appears to us is divisible into three irreducible classes: the physical (sights, sounds, tastes, feels and smells), the emotional (the emotions of joy, pain, fear, awe, and so on) and the intellectual (concepts such as cause, identity, infinity, and so forth, which Johnson called 'intellections'). Johnson considered the failure to discriminate clearly these three irreducible classes the main cause of philosophical confusions.

Properly discriminated into its organic classes, all

our knowledge is free from mystery, or equally mysterious if we prefer to esteem it mysterious; but we add an unnecessary mystery at our inability to discover sensibly what is not sensible. Human knowledge can be analyzed no farther than into the organisms to which it pertains; and all attempts to delve below or beyond this boundary are founded in ignorance of the inconvertibility into each other, of the information yielded by our several organisms.

(Johnson 1861: 10)

Johnson's conception of the nature and tasks of philosophy is amazingly similar to that of WITTGEN-STEIN. According to Johnson, speculative philosophers are 'misled by language', or 'deceived by the forms of language'; they 'play bo-peep with words', and their 'misuse of language' causes intellectual 'perplexity', 'amazement' and 'mystery'. Thus, Johnson's verdict on previous philosophy is: 'much of what is esteemed as profound philosophy is nothing but a disputatious criticism on the meaning of words' (1836: 282) and 'Nearly all the perplexing questions of speculation are produced by verbal equivokes... Such equivokes pass usually for profound mysteries; but all mystery vanishes' when we understand the nature of language correctly (1854: 231–2). Like Wittgenstein, Johnson's goal in philosophy is to make philosophical problems 'vanish' or to 'terminate the mystification'.

To make all philosophical perplexities 'vanish', Johnson concentrated much of his efforts on the study of language, especially its inherent defects. On the title page of *The Meaning of Words* we find the statement: 'Four ineradicable fallacies are concealed in the structure of language: it identifies what unverbally are diverse, assimilates what unverbally are heterogeneous, makes a unit of what unverbally are multifarious, and transmutes into each other what unverbally are untransmutable'. This structural defect is one of the main causes of philosophical problems. Language consists of a limited number of words, but they are used to talk about an infinite number of things. And because we use one word to refer to many things, we assume there must be something in common among these things. As Johnson puts it, 'In all our speculation, we estimate created existences by the oneness of their name' (1836: 47). For example: 'I am speaking, I am standing, several persons are present. Each of these assertions is a truth. But if we seek among these truths for truth itself, believing it to be a unit, we are seeking a nature for what is merely a contrivance of language' (1836: 73).

Johnson used his insights on language to throw light on a whole host of traditional philosophical puzzles and in the process anticipated many ideas which became fashionable one hundred years later. For example: 'Words have no inherent signification; but as many meanings as they possess applications to different phenomena' (1836: 73); and 'If we wish to know the meaning of the word truth in any given case, we must examine the circumstances to which the word is applied' (1836: 73); another example: 'After hearing all that he can adduce in proof of the earth's sphericity, consider the prepositions significant of these proofs. If you deem it significant beyond them, you are deceived by the forms of language' (1836: 129). Similarly, a theory 'is significant of nothing but the data which are adduced in proof of the theory' (1836: 236).

List of works

Johnson, A.B. (1828) *The Philosophy of Human Knowledge, or a Treatise on Language*, New York: G. & C. Carvill. (A version of this treatise, collated with *A Treatise on Language*, was reprinted in Rynin 1947.)
—— (1836) *A Treatise on Language, or The Relation which Words Bear to Things*, New York: Harper & Bros. (Reprinted in Rynin 1947, in a version collated with *Philosophy of Human Knowledge*.)
—— (1854) *The Meaning of Words*, New York: Appleton & Co.
—— (1856) *The Physiology of the Senses*, New York: Derby & Jackson.
—— (1861) *Deep Sea Soundings and Explorations of the Bottom: or The Ultimate Analysis of Human Knowledge*, Boston, MA. (This work was published privately by the author.)

References and further reading

* Rynin, D. (ed.) (1947) *Alexander Bryan Johnson: A Treatise on Language*, ed. D. Rynin, Berkeley, CA: University of California Press, 1947. (A collated version of Johnson's *Treatises* of 1828 and 1836, with a critical essay on his philosophy of language.)
Todd, C.L. and Blackwood, R.T. (eds) (1969) *Language and Value: Proceedings of the Centennial Conference on the Life and Works of Alexander Bryan Johnson*, New York: Greenwood Publishing Co.

K.T. FANN

JOHNSON, SAMUEL (1709–84)

Famous as a man of letters and lexicographer, Johnson was no formal academic philosopher – indeed he was suspicious of abstractions. His works perfectly embody the darker side of the eighteenth-century mind, with its distrust of theoretical reason and system-mongering, and a profound sensitivity to the imperfections of a human existence in which there was more to be endured than to be enjoyed.

Born on 18 September 1709 in Lichfield, Staffordshire, the child of ill-matched parents, Samuel Johnson was a sickly child. At the age of three he was taken by his mother to Queen Anne in London to be cured of a scrofula through the 'royal touch'.

He matriculated at Pembroke College, Oxford, but poverty forced him to leave after only two years. For the next two decades his life was a struggle with penury and with psychological traits (awkwardness, anxiety, anger) that left him prey to melancholy, and which manifested themselves in a profusion of personal eccentricities. His melancholy coloured his views of human nature and destiny. A pious, even superstitious Anglican, he found little solace in a faith that left him with a profound sense of the misery of human existence in general, and of his personal shortcomings and culpability.

Having moved to London in 1737, he obtained employment on the *Gentleman's Magazine* as a parliamentary reporter and hack writer. His poem *London*, a satire on the great city, appeared anonymously in 1738. In 1747 he was commissioned by London's main booksellers to prepare a *Dictionary of the English Language*, in two volumes. It was eventually published in 1755. Johnson had no belief in any such thing as an ideal language; nevertheless, in his view it was one of the lexicographer's duties to regulate and stabilize language.

Meanwhile in January 1749 he published *The Vanity of Human Wishes*, an imitation of the tenth satire of Juvenal and an expression of his own vision of human folly. Around the same time, his tragedy, *Irene*, was finally staged by his erstwhile pupil, David Garrick.

About a year later, he began to publish *The Rambler*, a magazine in the manner of the *Spectator* containing short essays on morals, manners and literature. This was followed in 1758 by *The Idler*. Johnson's essays were sober, moralistic and instructive, commenting insightfully on human failings. In the meantime, he published a review of Soame Jenyns' *A Free Enquiry into the Nature and Origin of Evil* (1757). Jenyns had argued, in a rather Leibnizian way, in favour of the doctrines of cosmic optimism and plenitude: all evils (for example, illness and disability) were only apparent, part of a larger scheme of benevolence created by a superfecund Deity. Johnson countered that Jenyns' views were specious rationalizations that trivialized pain and suffering and discredited philosophy.

Meditations on malevolence and the vanity of human wishes formed the core of Johnson's only extended work of fiction, *Rasselas*, published in 1759. Its protagonists, Rasselas and Imlac, Nekayah and Pekuah, leave their 'happy valley' in Abyssinia to see the world, but find only suffering, pride, fatuity and self-deception in a series of exploits that parallel *Candide*, the contemporary work by VOLTAIRE. Johnson's work ends in a 'Conclusion, in which nothing is Concluded'. For rather traditional Christian reasons, Johnson could not easily subscribe to Enlightenment notions of human goodness and progress.

From the 1760s, Johnson was befriended by the Scot James Boswell. Thanks to Boswell, Johnson is remembered as a conversationalist, famous for his trenchant, peremptory, but often deeply humane, sentiments.

In the 1770s Johnson wrote as a political polemicist, first in defence of the British title to the Falkland Islands, and then on the side of the Crown in the dispute with the American colonies. *Taxation no Tyranny* shows Johnson as an authoritarian Tory, though in his off-the-cuff remarks he often supported the underdog against authority. In 1765 his edition of Shakespeare had appeared; the first four volumes of the *Lives of the Most Eminent English Poets* were published in 1779, the remaining six in 1781.

List of works

Johnson, S. (1750–52) *The Rambler*, London: Payne & Bouquet; ed. W.J. Bate and A.B. Strauss, New Haven, CT: Yale University Press, 1969, 3 vols. (Magazine containing short essays on morals, manners and literature.)
—— (1755) *A Dictionary of the English Language*, London: Strahan, 2 vols. (Not, as sometimes imagined, the first major English dictionary, but the first with copious instances from literature of the proper use of the words in question.)
—— (1757) 'A Review of Soame Jenyns' *A Free Enquiry into the Nature and Origin of Evil*', in B. Bronson (ed.), *Samuel Johnson, Rasselas, Poems and Selected Prose*, San Francisco, CA: Rinehart Press, 1971, 219–28. (Johnson's attack on Jenyns was perhaps the most biting and devastating attack on the vacant moral optimism in fashion in the mid eighteenth century.)
—— (1758–60) *The Idler*, London: Newbery; ed. W.J. Bate, J.M. Bullitt and L.F. Powell, New Haven, CT: Yale University Press, 1963. (Together Johnson's *The Rambler* and *The Idler* essays take the form of the brief essay earlier pioneered by Addison and Steele and give the genre an altogether more serious moral twist.)
—— (1759) *The Prince of Abissinia: A Tale*, London: Dodsley; repr., ed. J.P. Hardy, Oxford: Oxford University Press, 1988. (Popularly known today as *Rasselas*. Rightly regarded as the English equivalent to Voltaire's exactly-contemporaneous *Candide*, Johnson's moral tale poses the question of the choice of life before ending with a conclusion in which nothing is concluded.).)
—— (1779–81) *The Lives of the Most Eminent English Poets*, London: Bathurst; repr. ed. A. Waugh, London: Oxford University Press, 1952. (Johnson's book helped to establish the 'canon' of great English poetry while offering sometimes provocative judgments, as with his rather negative verdicts on Milton.)
—— (1968) *Selected Writings*, ed. P. Cruttwell, Harmondsworth: Penguin. (Includes Johnson's 1738 poem *London*, published anonymously and his *Vanity of Human Wishes* of 1749.)

References and further reading

Boswell, J. (1791) *The Life of Samuel Johnson*, ed. G.B. Hill, 6 vols, Oxford: Clarendon Press, 1934–50. (The classic biography.)
Chapman, R.W. (ed.) (1984) *The Letters of Samuel Johnson*, 3 vols, Oxford: Clarendon Press. (Though no copious correspondent, Johnson's letters convey the personal sources of his wider moral philosophy.)
Gross, G.S. (1992) *This Invisible Riot of the Mind: Samuel Johnson's Psychological Theory*, Baltimore, MD: University of Pennsylvania Press. (Explores Johnson's view of human nature as well as his own psychological weaknesses.)
Pierce, C. (1983) *The Religious Life of Samuel Johnson*, London: Athlone. (Emphasizes Johnson's strong religious guilt.)
Reddick, A. (1990) *The Making of Johnson's Dictionary 1746–73*, Cambridge: Cambridge University Press. (Contains useful material on the philosophical writings rifled by Johnson in compiling his *Dictionary*.)
Schwarz, R.B. (1975) *Samuel Johnson and the Problem of Evil*, Madison, WN: University of Wisconsin Press. (Contextualizes Johnson's attack on Jenyns.)
Wain, J. (1980) *Samuel Johnson*, London: Macmillan. (A lively and readable modern biography.)

ROY PORTER

JOHNSON, SAMUEL (1696–1772)

Johnson was the first important philosopher in colonial America and author of the first philosophy textbook published there. He derived his views largely from others, combining in one system elements from diverse sources. He followed the empiricists in holding that knowledge begins with sensations but held the Augustinian view that knowledge of necessary truths comes only from the mind's illumination by divine light. With Berkeley, he denied matter's existence, viewing bodies as collections of ideas. He held that these ideas are 'faint copies' of God's archetypal ideas, which he thought of in much the same way as had Malebranche and John Norris. His ethical views, influenced by William Wollaston, take happiness to be the supreme good, stressing that human beings should seek a happiness consonant with their nature as rational, immortal and social beings.

1 Life
2 Epistemology and metaphysics
3 Ethics

1 Life

Born at Guilford, Connecticut in Colonial America, Johnson was brought up as a Calvinist and educated at Yale in the Ramist philosophy favoured by the Puritans. At eighteen, he wrote 'An Encyclopedia of Philosophy', a compendium of learning set forth in 1,271 propositions. At this stage of his intellectual development he considered the masters of modern philosophy to be RAMUS and his followers Richardson and Ames. While still a student at Yale, Johnson's outlook underwent a twofold revolution: after reading works of BACON, LOCKE, NEWTON and John NORRIS, he became a keen defender of the 'new philosophers'; and after reading works of Anglican apologetics, he converted to Anglicanism and became, in 1722, a priest. During the next four decades, he produced successive versions of his compendium of philosophical learning (not all appeared in print), first revising his 'Encyclopedia' in light of his new views (1716), then composing a 'Logic' (1720), several versions of *An Introduction to the Study of Philosophy* (1731) and finally *Elementa philosophica* (1752). The *Elementa*, his most important work, consists of two parts, 'Noetica: Or the First Principles of Human Knowledge' and 'Ethica: Or the First Principles of Moral Philosophy' (the latter a revision of his 1746 *A New System of Morality*). Locke and Newton were important influences on Johnson once he was 'wholly

changed to the New Learning'. But from 1730 onwards, his dominant influence was BERKELEY, whom he visited during the latter's residence in Rhode Island, with whom he carried on a notable correspondence, and to whom he dedicated *Elementa philosophica*. Johnson was a founder of King's College (today Columbia University) and its first president.

2 Epistemology and metaphysics

With Locke, Johnson held that knowledge begins with 'ideas' received from the senses, ideas that are either simple (for example, red, sweet, hard) or complex (such as our idea of an apple). But he followed Berkeley in insisting that these ideas do not *represent* bodies to the mind; rather, a complex idea of sensation – for example, a certain combination of colour, shape, odour and so on – *is* a body; again like Berkeley, he held that, since bodies are combinations of ideas and ideas cannot exist without a mind that perceives them, bodies exist only if perceived.

Having got ideas from sensation, the mind, reflecting on its own operations and states, gets 'simple notions' of perceiving, remembering, willing and the like, and the complex notion of itself as a 'spirit' (mind). Self-reflection further discloses to the mind that, although it passively receives ideas from the senses, it is essentially active and capable of self-determination – a view that led Johnson to attack belief in predestination (see PREDESTINATION). From sensation and reflection we thus get notions of two kinds of being: bodies (passive beings that exist only because they are perceived) and spirits (active, perceiving beings). Only an active being can be a causal agent, so spirits are the sole true causes. We are immediately aware only of our own minds and of the ideas we perceive, but we infer, from their bodily behaviour, the existence of other finite spirits. Further, we have abundant evidence of the existence of God, the infinite spirit. (Johnson gave several arguments for God's existence, one inspired by Locke's argument in *Essay concerning Human Understanding* IV.10; one taken from Berkeley's *Principles of Human Knowledge* §§146–7; and one a version of the Augustinian argument that infers, from the existence of 'eternal and necessary truths', the existence of an eternal mind that knows them – see AUGUSTINE.)

Johnson acknowledged Berkeley as his chief inspiration, but he also expressed high regard for Locke, WOLLASTON, Norris, MALEBRANCHE and FÉNELON. By the last three he was persuaded of the Augustinian doctrine that we can know 'eternal truths' of logic, mathematics, metaphysics and morality only because God, by 'divine light', directly illuminates our 'pure intellect', disclosing to it an 'intelligible realm'. To Johnson, the doctrine that God immediately causes our knowledge of the intelligible order seemed the complement of Berkeley's doctrine that God immediately causes our perception of the sensible order. And he found a use for Malebranche's and Norris' doctrine that there is in the divine mind an 'ideal world' – the intelligible, non-sensuous model of which the natural or sensible world is a copy. Berkeley had held that there are, in God's mind, archetypal ideas that are somehow correlated with our sensible ideas, but he never gave a very full account of his theory of archetypes, though Johnson several times, in his letters, asked him to do so. With Johnson, the doctrine of archetypes became part of a theory of representative perception: our impermanent, private sensible ideas are 'faint copies or images' that represent to us a stable, ideal world that exists, independently of our minds, in the divine mind.

3 Ethics

Happiness, for Johnson, is the 'natural good', the end all conscious beings strive for; but the happiness we seek should be consonant with our nature. Hence, ethics must begin with the study of human nature. We have senses like the animals, argued Johnson, but we also have reason; our bodies will perish after a time, but our souls are immortal; we have private interests but are also by nature social and mutually dependent. We must seek, therefore, a happiness consonant with our rational, immortal, social nature. Hedonists fall into error not in taking happiness to be our natural end but in failing to discover our true nature. These considerations led Johnson to a threefold account of duty: we have duties to ourselves, to God and to our fellow creatures. To ourselves, our duty is to pursue a kind of happiness befitting our nature; we fail in this duty if we gratify our senses at the expense of reason, temporal interests at the expense of eternal ones, private interests at the expense of public ones. Our duty to God is to love and worship him, both because we owe that to the being from whom our existence derives and because it is in his power to make us happy. To others, our duty is to increase their happiness and relieve their suffering when we can, both because reason shows us that happiness is also their natural end, and because our own happiness is bound up with theirs. One who fulfils each of these duties has the *virtues*, respectively, of temperance, piety and benevolence; one who fulfils them all has the virtue of justice, rendering to all persons what is their due.

Elementa philosophica was the philosophy textbook used at the colonial colleges that became the University of Pennsylvania and Columbia University.

With his pupil Jonathan EDWARDS, Johnson was one of the earliest American defenders of idealism, a species of philosophy that, in one form or another, has been a recurring motif in American thought.

See also: IDEALISM

List of works

Johnson, S. (1929) *Samuel Johnson: President of King's College, His Career and Writings*, ed. H.W. Schneider and C. Schneider, New York: Columbia University Press, 4 vols. (The standard edition of Johnson's works; volume 2 includes his previously unpublished 'Encyclopedia of Philosophy' and 'Logic', and his philosophical correspondence with Berkeley and others.)

—— (1731) *An Introduction to the Study of Philosophy*, London; 2nd edn, London, 1744. (A short work first published in the periodical *Republic of Letters*, May 1731; the second edition is an enlarged version published as a small volume for use of students at Yale. Excerpts are included in *Samuel Johnson* (1929), volume 2.)

—— (1746) *A New System of Morality*, Boston. (Also bears the title *Ethices elementa. Or, the First Principles of Moral Philosophy*; a revised version of this work became Part II of *Elementa philosophica*.)

—— (1752) *Elementa philosophica*, Philadelphia. (Johnson's chief work, setting out his metaphysical, epistemological, and ethical views, and incorporating material from the two preceding works. It is included in its entirety in *Samuel Johnson* (1929), volume 2.)

References and further reading

* Berkeley, G. (1949) *The Works of George Berkeley, Bishop of Cloyne*, vol. 2, ed. A.A. Luce and T.E. Jessop, Edinburgh: Thomas Nelson. (This volume contains the two philosophical works that most deeply influenced Johnson, *A Treatise concerning the Principles of Human Knowledge* and *Three Dialogues between Hylas and Philonous*; it also contains the philosophical correspondence between Berkeley and Samuel Johnson (1729–30), in which Berkeley replies to a number of penetrating questions asked by Johnson about those works.)

Carroll, P.N. (1978) *The Other Samuel Johnson: A Psychohistory of Early New England*, Rutherford, NJ: Fairleigh Dickinson University Press. (A psychoanalytically-oriented biography in the manner of Erik Erikson.)

Ellis, J. (1973) *The New England Mind in Transition:*

Samuel Johnson of Connecticut, New Haven, CT: Yale University Press. (A good general account of Johnson's life and thought.)

Flower, E. and Murphey, M.G. (1977) *A History of Philosophy in America*, vol. 1, New York: G.P. Putnam's Sons, 81–99. (A brief, accurate account of Johnson's philosophy.)

* Locke, J. (1689) *An Essay concerning Human Understanding*, ed P.H. Nidditch, Oxford: Clarendon Press, 1975. (Johnson's early 'Logic' closely followed the Essay's account in Book 2 of the origin and kinds of ideas, and in Book 4 of the degrees of knowledge and of probable assent. The Essay's influence is still evident much later in *Elementa philosophica*.)

Schneider, H.W. (1958) *The Puritan Mind*, Ann Arbor, MI: University of Michigan Press. (Chapter 5 contains a good account of Johnson's development by a leading historian of American philosophy.)

CHARLES J. McCRACKEN

JOURNALISM, ETHICS OF

It is sometimes suggested that ethical principles, even fundamental ones like nonmaleficence and beneficence, are totally out of place in journalism, and that it should be shaped solely by market forces. This suggestion should be resisted. One reason why journalism should be ethical is that in a democracy it is expected to serve the public interest, which means that it should accept the responsibility to circulate the information and opinion without which a democracy could not operate, and to enable it to do this the freedom of the press is acknowledged.

If journalism is to serve the public interest, then a commitment to truth-telling is fundamental. Journalists should also be fair and accurate in reporting news, should publish corrections, should offer a right of reply. They should avoid discrimination, deception, harassment, betraying confidences and invasions of privacy. But ethical journalism is more than lists of requirements and prohibitions. In investigative journalism, for example, some deception or intrusion into privacy could be justified in order to uncover corruption. Ethical journalism is therefore reflective understanding of the underlying principles of harm and benefit and the public interest, and an ability to apply them in particular cases.

1 The very idea of ethics in journalism
2 Journalism and democracy
3 The ethics of journalism

1 The very idea of ethics in journalism

There are good reasons why journalism should be regarded as a practice governed by ethics, but also good reasons why this is problematic. It is expected of any group of practitioners who aspire to professional status that they base their practice in ethics, often by adhering to an explicit code of practice that specifies the expected behaviour in accordance with an acknowledged set of ethical principles ruled by the twin principles of nonmaleficence (do no harm) and beneficence (do good) (see PROFESSIONAL ETHICS). Those in breach of the professional code may be penalized in some way, with expulsion from the profession as the ultimate sanction. Clear examples are regulated professions like medicine, nursing, social work, law and teaching, in which the practitioner provides care or service for the client (patient, student) with individual and identifiable needs (see MEDICAL ETHICS; NURSING ETHICS).

But can journalism be fitted into this model? Whereas it is easy to say that journalism too should be governed by nonmaleficence and beneficence – because these principles are all-encompassing – it is not so easy to see further analogies between journalism and the traditional professions, for two related reasons.

First, journalism is not a regulated profession, and perhaps not a profession at all: anyone who can get a relevant job in the media industry is a journalist. Second, even if it is a profession, journalism is certainly not a 'caring' profession with individual 'clients', but an occupation that takes place within a very competitive commercial framework. Journalists increasingly work for organizations which seek power and profits, and which are concerned with quantitative measures like audience figures and advertising revenue rather than with qualitative issues of ethics.

As a result the professional advancement of journalists depends (with rare exceptions) not on their adherence to ethical principles but on their contribution to the commercial success of their organization. Indeed, the 'scoop' is all, so success is more likely to follow from ignoring ethical considerations like confidentiality or privacy. This leads to the sceptical claim that there simply is no place for ethics in journalism. Even the principles of nonmaleficence and beneficence would be ludicrously out of place, because on this view journalism is motivated and shaped solely by market forces (see MARKET, ETHICS OF THE).

2 Journalism and democracy

But before the irrelevance of ethics to journalism can

be confirmed, we need to look at the traditional political justification of ethical journalism, as this is ignored rather than refuted by the sceptics.

Liberal theory places a high value on freedom of thought and freedom of speech (see FREEDOM OF SPEECH). One argument for this is in terms of *rights*: rational individuals have a right to think as they find and to speak as they think. Another argument, due especially to Mill, is in terms of *consequences*: truth is beneficial to individuals and society, and it is most likely to be arrived at through free expression and open discussion, through the unfettered critical clash and contention of ideas (see MILL, J.S. §12).

Democratic theory adds to these goals and arguments (see DEMOCRACY). An informed citizenry is a necessary condition of democracy, and this gives the media their special role with both rights and responsibilities. The rights are the privileges of press freedom, and the responsibilities are the duties to provide the accurate information and balanced comment without which people cannot fulfil their roles as rational citizens.

This link between free speech, freedom of the press and liberal democracy famously appears in the First Amendment to the Constitution of the United States of America: 'Congress shall make no law… abridging the freedom of speech, or of the press'. It has since become enshrined in international charters such as the Universal Declaration of Human Rights: 'Everyone has the right to freedom of opinion and expression; this right includes freedom to hold opinions without interference and to seek, receive and impart information and ideas through any media regardless of frontiers' (Article 19).

To the extent that there is anything in this democratic justification of journalism, the abandonment of journalism to market forces must be rejected, and journalism emerges as an ethical practice. This is because it can serve the required democratic role only if it constitutes itself on the basis of ethical concepts like truth, objectivity and fairness. Journalism which is ethical in this sense rejects a purely commercial ethos and recognizes a commitment to serving the public interest.

The more specific principles of journalistic ethics, concerning objectivity, confidentiality and the like, follow from this overall commitment that journalism should do no harm to but should further the interests of a democratic polity and its individual citizens. Although there is scope for a legal framework on such matters as defamation, obscenity and privacy, legislation has a merely restrictive effect on freedom of expression and does not actively promote journalism of high quality. It is ethical engagement by journalists,

and not legally backed censorship, which is a necessary condition of journalistic quality.

3 The ethics of journalism

Although ethical issues in journalism can be classified in various ways, the most straightforward is to distinguish between what is ethically required and what is forbidden. (This is not, however, an absolute distinction, and some injunctions, depending on how they are worded, can be in either category.)

On the side of what is required, it follows from the democratic justification that truth is fundamental, and this leads to the often-made claim that truth-telling is constitutive of journalism (see TRUTHFULNESS). Therefore, honesty and accuracy in presenting factual information is required, and, since no one is free from error, a commitment to publish corrections and to offer a right of reply to those who are criticized. In practice it is not as simple as this, as there is often no agreement about what is a factual matter or about what the facts in a particular case are, and a right of reply could easily be abused by anyone with a trivial complaint against the press.

There is also the problem that although journalists might have a commitment to the truth and nothing but the truth, it is impossible to publish the whole truth. Selection of material is always necessary, and so further principles like objectivity and impartiality, fairness and balance, are called up. It follows that there is never an algorithmic solution to ethical problems in journalism. The broad principles of honesty, objectivity, fairness and the like require both further specification and detailed consideration in the context of particular cases, and journalists must exercise ethically-informed judgments in the light of a commitment to the public interest.

The difficulties are compounded if we turn from factual journalism to comment and opinion, and especially to political journalism. Whereas public service broadcasting is expected to conform to the principles of impartiality and balance, the commercial press normally has a political commitment or 'bias'. There is nothing wrong with individual journalists being partisan so long as they are honestly and openly partisan, but when does partisanship become manipulation or propaganda? And to what extent do editors have a responsibility to try to ensure that all varieties of opinion are represented in their paper? To what extent does the press as a whole have such a responsibility? It is in this area that the ethical ideals that lie behind the democratic justification of press freedom are diminished by commercial realities.

What is ethically forbidden in journalism includes sexism, racism and other forms of discrimination, deception, harassment, invasions of privacy, exploiting children who are in the news, and buying the stories of criminals (see DISCRIMINATION). Again, in practice these prohibitions are problematic, and a good deal of reflection on fundamental principles of good, harm and the public interest is required.

This is so especially in the area of the relations between journalists and their sources or potential sources. The confidentiality of willing sources, including whistle-blowers, should be respected, but investigative journalism presents special difficulties. Journalists often want to find out things which those who are involved prefer to keep hidden. Investigative journalism is part of the truth-telling function of journalism, and journalists have a responsibility to uncover scandal and corruption, especially where harm is being done to innocent victims. So investigative journalism can serve the public interest, and in doing so there may be justification for some deception or intrusion into privacy. But where in such cases to strike a balance is the most difficult issue in the ethics of journalism.

Privacy is especially problematic. Whereas it is easy to agree that journalists should not invade privacy, it is not at all easy to draw a satisfactory boundary between private and public (see PRIVACY). The truly private citizen who lives a life of public insignificance is in little danger from intrusive journalists, but sometimes such citizens are forced by good fortune (winning a lottery) or bad (being a disaster victim) into the public eye. In such cases requests for privacy should be respected and harassment frowned on. There is a difference between the public interest and what the public is interested in.

But should public figures in politics, business, entertainment, sport, be entitled to privacy? There is more than one issue involved here. Many such figures choose to live by publicity and are not in a morally strong position to object if the publicity is not exactly what they want. But are politicians, for example, entitled to a private life? The usual answer is to say that those areas of their lives that do not affect the performance of public duties are properly private, and that therefore financial scandals can legitimately be exposed in the media, but not sexual scandals. But it is doubtful whether this distinction, which involves dividing one person into two separate parts, the private and the public, is satisfactory on psychological or ethical grounds. And there is a further problem, in that appeals to 'privacy' can be question-begging. Investigative journalism often shows that what the corrupt politician claims is private is not private at all but is legitimately a matter of public concern.

What this brief survey of ethics in journalism shows is that there are no easy answers. Although it is

possible to talk of what is required and what is forbidden in ethical journalism, more than a list of positive and negative injunctions is necessary. This is one reason why various formulations of codes of practice for journalists have not proved satisfactory. What is needed is a rational understanding of the underlying principles of harm and benefit, of individual rights and the democratic public interest. What is needed is the incorporation of reflective ethical practice into journalism, so that, as Klaidman and Beauchamp so well express it (1987), every journalist becomes 'the virtuous journalist'.

See also: APPLIED ETHICS; RESPONSIBILITIES OF SCIENTISTS AND INTELLECTUALS

References and further reading

Belsey, A. and Chadwick, R. (eds) (1992) *Ethical Issues in Journalism and the Media*, London: Routledge. (A collection of introductory essays on various aspects of media ethics.)
—— (1995) 'Ethics as a vehicle for media quality', *European Journal of Communication* 10: 461–73. (Part of a special issue on media ethics.)
* Klaidman, S. and Beauchamp, T.L. (1987) *The Virtuous Journalist*, New York: Oxford University Press. (Discusses ethical journalism and its democratic justification in the context of the American Constitution's guarantee of press freedom. The best introduction to media ethics.)
Lee, S. (1990) *The Cost of Free Speech*, London: Faber & Faber. (A close critical examination of the usual justifications of free speech.)
Stephenson, H. (1994) *Media Freedom and Media Regulation: An Alternative White Paper*, Birmingham: Association of British Editors, Guild of Editors and International Press Institute. (Argues against further legal restrictions on the press in Britain, especially a privacy law.)

ANDREW BELSEY

JUDAH BEN MOSES OF ROME (*c.*1292–after 1330)

Judah Romano, translator and Maimonidean philosopher, participated in the intellectual climate of Latin scholasticism, introducing a large number of the ideas of the Christian philosophers into Hebrew. He gained his knowledge in the various branches of philosophy through meticulous study of the writings of Aristotle and the scholastic commentaries to his works (particu-

larly those of Albert the Great, Aquinas and Giles of Rome), of the Maimonidean-Tibbonian school, and of some Arabic philosophical treatises in Latin translation. Influenced by Albert the Great, Aquinas and Maimonides, he discussed all the major philosophical topics, and especially the idea of creation through intermediaries, the origins of the human soul, the cognitive process, which represents the real purpose of man, the nature of prophecy and prayer.

1   Creation
2   Prophecy
3   Prayer and the universe

1   Creation

Judah may well have held an official position at Naples, at the court of Robert II of Anjou. Since Robert was then Senator of Urbe, one cannot exclude the possibility that he actually worked in Rome. The terminology of his exegetical writings almost entirely Aristotelian, but Judah fuses Aristotle's doctrines with others of Neoplatonic origin. His *Be'ur Ma'aseh Be-re'sit* (Commentary on Genesis) interprets philosophically the verses which open the Bible and argues that the creation cannot be proven apodeictically. Judah adopts the doctrine of creation through intermediaries: creation is seen as a process of emanation from the First Cause. The first emanation is light, identified with existence, which is the first perfection of a being (see NEOPLATONISM).

Judah goes on to develop a fully-fledged metaphysics of light and to discuss a number of astronomical questions regarding such as matters as the stellar motions, the positions and dimensions of the planets, and solar and lunar eclipses. The First Cause is called the subsisting Being. It is the simplest being, differing from created beings, which are compounded of essence and existence (in the case of the separate Intelligences) or of matter and form (in the case of the creatures of the sublunar world).

Judah also expounds on the creation of the vegetative, sensitive and rational souls, following the approach of ALBERT THE GREAT: the rational soul represents the ultimate and most elevated degree of a dynamic process which starts from the active element, present in the potentiality of the prime matter. The creation of the rational soul, unlike that of the vegetative and sensitive souls, the causes of which are organic and natural factors joined to celestial virtue, takes place as a result of the direct intervention of the First Cause, through the influence of the 'active intellect'. It is because of the intellect, which is the substantial form of man, that man belongs to the superior world of the Intelligences. It is for this reason

that man is said to be created 'in the image of God'. In agreement with Moses MAIMONIDES, and contrary to the teachings of the Latin scholastics, Judah does not hold the active intellect to be the active element intrinsic in the the human rational soul, but rather the tenth separate Intelligence.

Adam, once created and endowed with an intellect capable of receiving the *intelligibilia*, was put under the dominion of the active intellect. Knowledge attained with the aid of the active intellect represents the ultimate purpose of man. Even after the expulsion from Eden, the purpose of man is to devote oneself to the *intelligibilia*, in order to be able to conjoin oneself with the active intellect in the highest degree of the cognitive process.

2   Prophecy

In *Sa'arim* (Gates to the Books of Prophecy), Judah fuses Maimonides' and Aquinas' doctrines of prophecy, claiming for prophecy the character of a science on a par with other philosophical disciplines (see AQUINAS, T.). He analyses its properties and assigns to it the peculiarities attributed by the Latin scholastics to theology, at the service of which the secular sciences are placed. The science of prophecy, which emanates from God's knowledge, differs from the natural sciences by its supernatural source of inspiration. It is the most elevated among the intellectual and ethical sciences with regard to veracity. The content of some prophetic revelations is superior to that of metaphysics, the highest science, although its final purpose, the ultimate realization of the human being, is not superior to that of ethics. Prophetic revelations were necessary in order to reveal supernatural truths to humanity. as well as certain natural truths, which would otherwise have remained concealed from the majority of mankind.

Judah analyses the content of the prophetic revelations and the purpose and nature of prophecy. He reaches a conclusion at a middle position between that of Maimonides and that of Aquinas: the prophet is a philosopher, prepared in all the branches of knowledge, whose rational and imaginative faculties are perfect. The preparation of the prophet is a prerequisite for prophecy, but prophecy is not a purely natural phenomenon. Some prophecies are natural and others miraculous: in the natural revelations the prophet perceives the content of the revelation, which is similar to that of the various branches of science, by means of a cognitive intellectual–imaginative process. The content of the miraculous revelations, however, surpasses human capacities, or the prophetical cognitive process takes place without the mediation of the imagination.

Prophecy consists of: (1) intellection, (2) transmission of the prophetic message to others (3) the performing of miracles. Only the first element, however, is necessary; by means of the other two elements, the prophet functions as a guide. For Judah, influenced by Maimonides, prophecy is an inspiration from the First Cause, through the mediation of the active intellect, to the intellect and then to the imaginative faculty of the prophet (see PROPHECY).

3 Prayer and the universe

In *Be'ur ha-Qaddis we-ha-Qedusah* (Commentary to the Liturgy), Judah interprets philosophically the key-words of prayer, using the *Liber de Causis* (Book of Causes) as his guide. The First Cause is the universal, infinite, most simple and transcendent cause, beyond all definition; all beings, according to their nature, are influenced and 'preserved' by it. The universe is organized hierarchically, and the world of the Intelligences exerts a real causal impact on the sublunar world. The First Cause is the cause of eternity; the Intelligences are eternal – that is, timeless and motionless – and the human soul, identified by Judah as the 'noble soul', belongs by nature to the eternal intellectual world, although operating within time.

Through a rationalistic analysis in which he is influenced by Aquinas, Judah discerns two components of prayer: (1) the uplifting of the human intellect to God by means of the cognitive process and (2) the 'request of suitable things': the content of the prayer expresses the agreement of the will of the human being with his intellectual representation, whereby the individual renders his words ('the external language') suitable and asks God for suitable things. Through prayer supplicants reach the point where their intellect conforms to the divine will and, thanks to the perfection of their intellection, are the cause of the acceptance of their own prayer. Concerning the distinction between individual prayer and public prayer, Judah asserts that the former is not necessarily expressed in words: for one who has reached a high level of perfection, prayer is an intellectual act, superior to any form of prayer expressed by means of the voice. Individual prayer, in its most elevated expression, is then a cognitive and contemplative act. Public prayer, however, is necessarily 'vocal', since the officiant in the synagogue prays for the whole community. Such prayer has the 'political' function of strengthening the faith of the masses.

Following Albert the Great, Judah stresses repeatedly that the individual must advance gradually in the acquisition of the *intelligibilia*, in order to achieve the highest level of intellection. The most elevated intelligible concepts are, in fact, God and the separate Intelligences. The real purpose of man is to 'purify' his intellection. This purpose can be partially realized starting in this life, while the soul is united to the body. It is completely attainable, however, only in the hereafter. Then the human rational soul, free from corporeal bonds, will unceasingly enjoy the *intelligibilia* gleaned during this life. This will constitute its eternal happiness. For its condition, at that point, will be like that of the separate Intelligences.

See also: ALBERT THE GREAT; AQUINAS, T.; MAIMONIDES, M.; NEOPLATONISM; PRAYER; PROPHECY

List of works

Judah Ben Moses of Rome (*c.*1320–50) 'Sancti Thomae de Aquino *Opusculum de ente et essentia* a Rabbì Jehudàh ben Mosèh ben Dani'èl Romano primum hebraice redditum (saec. XIV incipiente)', ed. G. Sermoneta, in A.Z. Bar-On (ed.) *From Parmenides to Contemporary Thinkers: Readings in Ontology*, Jerusalem, I: The Magnes Press, 1978, vol. 1: 184–214. (Judah's version of an Aquinas text.)

—— (*c.*1320–50) 'Il *De substantia orbis* di Averroè: edizione della versione latino-ebraica con commento di Yehudah b. Mosheh Romano', ed. with introduction and commentary by C. Rigo, Ph.D. dissertation, Turin: Università degli Studi di Torino, 2 vols, 1989–92. (Critical edition of Judah's translation of Averroes' *De substantia orbis*.)

References and further reading

Rigo, C. (1993a) 'Un antologia filosofica di Yehuda b. Mosheh Romano', *Italia* 10: 73–104. (A philosophical anthology of Judah ben Moses.)

—— (1993b) 'Yehudah b. Mosheh Romano traduttore di Alberto Magno (commento al *De Anima* III, II, 16)', *Henoch* 15: 65–91. (A critical edition and analysis of two different translations of a passage from Albert the Great's commentary on Aristotle's *De Anima*.)

—— (1993c) 'Le traduzioni dei commenti scolastici al *De Anima* eseguite da Yehudah b. Mosheh nella tradizione filosofica ebraico-italiana dei secoli XIII–XIV', in F. Vattioni (ed.) *Atti della VII settimana (Roma, 25–30 novembre 1991): Sangue e antropologia nel Medioevo*, Rome: Pia Umione Preziosissimo Sangue, 1073–95. (Account of his translations of scholastic commentaries to Aristotle's *De Anima*.)

—— (1994) 'Egliolio Romano nella cultura edraica: le versioni di Yehudah b. Mosheh Romano', *Documenti e studi sulla tradizione filosofica medievale* 5: 397–437. (Examines Judah's role as a translator of Giles of Rome.)

—— (1995) 'Yehudah b. Mosheh Romano traduttore degli Scolastici latini', *Henoch* 17: 141–70. (Focuses on Judah as a translator of Latin scholastics.)

—— (1996) 'The Be'urim on the Bible of R. Yehudah Romano: the Philosophical Method which comes out of them, their sources in the Jewish Philosophy and in the Christian Scholasticism', Ph.D. dissertation, Jerusalem: The Hebrew University of Jerusalem, 2 vols. (A study of Judah's philosophical interpretations of biblical verses.)

Sermoneta, G. (1965) 'La dottrina dell'intelletto e la "fede filosofica" di Jehudàh e Immanuel Romano', *Studi Medievali*, series 3, 6 (2): 3–78. (Comparison of his doctrine of conjunction with the active intellect with that of Immanuel of Rome.)

—— (1969) 'The Commentary to the First Weekly Reading in *Genesis* by Judah Romano', *Fourth World Congress of Jewish Studies* 2: 341–3. (An analysis of Judah's commentary to the first weekly portion in Genesis.)

—— (1976) 'Yehudah and Immanuel ha-Romi, "Rationalism Culminating in Mystical Faith"', in M. Hallamish and M. Schwarz (eds) *Revelation, Faith, Reason*, Ramat Gan: Bar Ilan University, 54–70. (Analyses Judah's doctrine of conjunction with the active intellect.)

—— (1980) 'Jehudah ben Moše ben Danìel Romano, traducteur de Saint Thomas', in G. Nahon and Ch. Touati (eds) *Hommage à Georges Vajda: Études d'histoire et de pensée juive*, Louvain: Éditions Peeters, 235–62. (Looks at Judah's role as a translator of Aquinas.)

—— (1984) 'Prophecy in the Writings of R. Yehuda Romano', in I. Twersky (ed.) *Studies in Medieval Jewish History and Literature*, Cambridge, MA: Harvard University Press, vol. 2, 337–74. (A study of Judah's doctrine of prophecy.)

—— (1990) '"Thine Ointments Have a Goodly Fragrance": Rabbi Judah Romano and the Open Text Method', in 'Shlomo Pines Jubilee Volume on the Occasion of his Eightieth Birthday', *Jerusalem Studies in Jewish Thought* special issue 9 (2): 77–113. (Discussion of his hermeneutical approach.)

—— (1994) 'The Light – its Definition and Function in the Commentary to the First Reading in Genesis by R. Yehudah ben Mosheh ben Daniel Romano', M. Oron and A. Goldreich (eds) *Massu'ot: Studies in Kabbalistic Literature and Jewish Philosophy in memory of Prof. Ephraim Gottleib*, Jerusalem: The Bialik Institute, 343–60. (Examines Judah's metaphysics of light.)

Steinschneider, M. (1870) 'Guida Romano', *Il Buonarroti*, series 2, 5: 3–12. (Account of his works.)

CATERINA RIGO

JUDAH BEN YEHIEL MESSER LEON *see* MESSER LEON, JUDAH

JUDAH HALEVI *see* HALEVI, JUDAH

JUDAEO-ARABIC PHILOSOPHY IN SPAIN
see ABRAVANEL, ISAAC; ABRAVANEL, JUDAH BEN ISAAC; ALBO, JOSEPH; ARAMA, ISAAC BEN MOSES; BAR HAYYA, ABRAHAM; CRESCAS, HASDAI; DURAN, PROFIAT; HALEVI, JUDAH; IBN DAUD, ABRAHAM; IBN EZRA, ABRAHAM; IBN EZRA, MOSES BEN JACOB; IBN FALAQUERA, SHEM TOV; IBN GABIROL, SOLOMON; IBN PAQUDA, BAHYA; IBN TZADDIK, JOSEPH BEN JACOB; MAIMONIDES, MOSES; SHEM TOV FAMILY

JUDAISTIC PHILOSOPHY
see JEWISH PHILOSOPHY

JUDGMENT, MORAL
see MORAL JUDGMENT

JUNG, CARL GUSTAV (1875–1961)

Jung was among the leaders in the development of depth psychology at the beginning of the twentieth century. An early follower of Sigmund Freud, he broke with the founder of psychoanalysis in 1913 and established his own school of analytical psychology.

Jung's theoretical development originated in his work on the word association test and the theory of feeling toned complexes. As he continued to explore the workings of the unconscious, he postulated the existence of instinctual patterns of cognition and behaviour which he termed 'archetypes'. Archetypal patterns are, according to Jung, common throughout the human species and constitute an inherited 'collective unconscious'.

Jung's approach to psychology was eclectic. He accepted the psychological importance of any phenomenon, even if it conflicted with current thinking in other fields. This attitude led to a deep investigation of the psychological significance of occult phenomena and alchemy, which Jung viewed as expressions of the unconscious that anticipated modern psychology. Later in life, Jung turned increasingly to considerations of the contemporary cultural expressions of psychological forces, writing extensively on what he viewed to be a deepening spiritual crisis in Western civilization.

1   **Early work and relationship with Freud**
2   **The theory of archetypes and personality theory**
3   **Occultism, alchemy and projection**
4   **The critique of culture**

1   Early work and relationship with Freud

Jung's father was a Protestant minister and Hebraist, while his paternal grandfather had been a distinguished physician and university reformer. On his mother's side, Protestant theologians predominated. Given this milieu, Jung was exposed, from an early age, to the main currents of nineteenth-century theology and philosophy, most notably the works of Kant, Schopenhauer and Nietzsche. Jung attended gymnasium in Basel and went on to medical school at the University of Basel. Following graduation, he undertook postgraduate training in psychiatry at the Burghölzli Hospital in Zurich, under the direction of Eugen Bleuler. At about the same time, Jung married Emma Rauschenbach, the daughter of a wealthy German industrialist. They had five children together. From 1906 to about 1913, Jung was deeply involved with Sigmund FREUD in the development of psychoanalysis. Following their break, Jung undertook to

develop his own theories about the workings of the psyche. The theory of archetypes and the collective unconscious, for which he is best known, prompted Jung to travel widely, after the First World War, in search of evidence to support his understanding of the commonality of psychological functioning throughout the species. In the 1930s, Jung was briefly in contact with figures connected to the National Socialist takeover of German medicine. He soon broke contact, however, and deeply regretted having had any relationship with them.

Jung was surrounded, throughout his adult life, by a large circle of students and admirers. Eventually, this circle developed into the C.G. Jung Institute at Kusnacht, outside Zurich, where Jung had his home.

Although Jung is best known for his theories of the archetypes of the collective unconscious, he first attracted international attention for his work on the word association test. The test was conducted by reading off a list of stimulus words and noting the characteristics of the responses on the part of the subject. Jung significantly refined the measurement of the anomalies in association, such as delayed response, cardiopulmonary function, and galvanic skin response. These refinements allowed for more precise interpretation of test responses. Out of this experimental work, but also under the influence of Pierre Janet in France and Théodore Flournoy in Switzerland, Jung developed the theory of 'feeling toned complexes', or affect-laden automatisms within the larger psychic structure of the individual. This theory formed the foundation for all subsequent developments in Jung's system of psychology.

The refined word association test provided the first experimental evidence supporting Sigmund Freud's theory of repression. In 1906, Jung wrote to Freud, sending copies of his most recent work on the test, only to learn that Freud already had the papers. Thus began one of the most famous and ill-fated collaborations in modern science.

Although a host of factors contributed to the eventual break between Jung and Freud, several points of theory distinguished the two from the beginning. Freud based his work on a definition of libido that was exclusively sexual in nature, and the conviction that psychopathology derived from infantile sexual conflicts. The task of psychoanalysis was to uncover the sexual etiology of the disorder and thereby dissipate its effect. Jung's work with the association test, however, had convinced him that libido was not exclusively sexual and that not all complexes could be reduced to a single etiologic source.

Other points of theory further separated the two. Based on work done in his doctoral dissertation on a case of somnambulism or mediumship, Jung argued that at least some of the workings of the unconscious were motivated by the anticipated development of the individual. This teleological view of the unconscious prompted Jung to question the role of *repression*, which for Freud was the fundamental mechanism of psychodynamics, in the psychic economy. For Jung, *projection* of psychic contents from the unconscious, without prior repression, took on increasing significance. Finally, based on his extensive experience with dementia praecox (schizophrenia) at the Burghölzli hospital, Jung concluded that there were what he termed 'psychological dominants' at work in all individuals, and that these dominants were evolutionary in origin, and relatively consistent throughout the species. Although Freud believed that the Oedipus complex was common throughout humanity, he resisted the notion that there could be other complexes with equal status.

2   The theory of archetypes and personality theory

Following the break with Freud in 1913, Jung went into a period of self-analysis and theory building. At this time, Jung developed his method of active imagination which used the images presented in dreams and waking reveries to explore the individual psyche. Out of this work with the imagination he developed his characteristic vocabulary for the structure of the psyche, and his more refined understanding of the psychological dominants, now referred to as 'archetypes'. The consciously presented personality was referred to as the 'persona', from the mask worn by actors in the ancient Greek theatre. Those parts of the personality that were not allowed into conscious presentation formed the individual's 'shadow'.

In addition to persona and shadow, Jung posited the existence of images of the counter-sexual in both men and women. These he referred to as 'anima' and 'animus', respectively. The images of the counter-sexual formed a bridge between the individual unconscious and the 'collective unconscious' which contained the archetypes. The term collective unconscious refers to the inherited instinctual substrate of human psychological functioning.

The theory of archetypes has been the subject of various interpretations, and Jung was not always precise in his application of the term to a psychological event. One common misconception, however, is that Jung thought of the archetypes in purely Platonic terms, as existing in some transcendent realm of ideas. Much of the confusion arises from a failure to recognize Jung's distinction between *archetypes* and *archetypal images*. Although there are places where Jung appears to discuss the archetypes in transcendental terms, perhaps informed by his extensive reading of Kant, his most consistent position is that the archetypes are biologically inherited, instinctual patterns of cognition and behaviour. It is this level of shared cognitive and behavioural patterns that constitutes the *collective unconscious*.

'Archetypal images', on the other hand, are more or less conscious representations of the archetypal or instinctual structures. Thus, instinctual seeking of the breast in the new-born infant demonstrates an archetypal form of behaviour associated with the mother. The instinctual relationship to the mother, however, also drives the formation of individual fantasies and images representative of the infant's experience of the mother, and the culture at large contributes to the further elaboration of these fantasies by means of myths, rituals, fairy tales and other forms of collective representation associated with the mother.

Jung was also at work on a theory of personality or 'psychological types'. Jung posited two essential orientations toward the world, introversion and extroversion, to which were added the functions of thinking, feeling, intuiting and sensing. In essence, the extrovert focuses on the outside world for information and inspiration, while the introvert focuses on interior states. By the same token, the functions are paired in such a way that one operates consciously while the other works unconsciously. Thus a thinking type will have an unconscious feeling function that attaches itself to contents of the unconscious.

3   Occultism, alchemy and projection

Jung had a lifelong interest in occultism and esoteric traditions. He was by no means alone in this interest, as research on spiritualism was widespread at the time. Jung and Freud both met with William JAMES during a trip to the USA in 1909, and James came away deeply impressed by Jung, in part, no doubt because of their shared interest in spiritualism. For his part, Jung considered James to be a profound influence on his development.

Interest in how causally unrelated events could be meaningfully connected, as when a series of numbers seem to repeat themselves several times during a single day, led Jung to develop his theory of synchronicity. As with many of Jung's theories, it is difficult to distinguish empirical research from the formulation of a theory of psychological functioning. Thus, on its surface, the theory of synchronicity attempts to provide statistical measures of some paranormal phenomena. By and large, however, these measures are not significant. On the other hand, the role of projection in the formation of meaningful associations is clearly demonstrated. This understanding of the primacy of projection in psychic functioning laid the foundation for the development of such standard projective tests as the Rorschach and the Thematic Apperception Test (TAT).

Jung's long-standing fascination with esoteric traditions, particularly Gnosticism (see GNOSTICISM), led him into an extensive study of alchemy. Alchemy was not, on Jung's reading, a precursor to modern natural science. Rather, it was essentially a Western form of psychological and spiritual discipline resembling the great meditative traditions of India and East Asia. The operations of the alchemists in their work and writings were manifestations of psychic projection, and the search for a means to transform base metals into gold was a spiritual quest for self-perfection (see ALCHEMY).

The investigation of projection eventually led Jung to consider the epistemological implications of his system of psychology. To the extent that projection from the unconscious informed his interpretation of cognitive phenomena, it became increasingly difficult to maintain a purely empirical view of those phenomena. In the end, Jung spoke of a 'psychoid world' where the boundaries between psychic events and objective reality break down.

4 The critique of culture

While implicit in some aspects of his early work, Jung's late work (1939–61) focused increasingly on what he saw as a crisis in Western civilization. In many respects, Jung's critique resembles those of HUSSERL and HEIDEGGER, although it focuses more on issues of spiritual collapse and renewal. Additionally, Jung thought that it was possible to assume a therapeutic stance in relation to the cultural crisis.

Jung focused his critique of culture, to a substantial degree, on the historical role of Christianity. He approached this problem from within the frame of his psychological theories, however, rather than from either a historical or theological standpoint. This meant that the body of historical and textual materials that make up the Christian tradition were treated, by Jung, much as he would treat the dreams and fantasies of a patient. Jung viewed the tradition as increasingly maladaptive, and therefore in need of therapy. At the same time, he viewed such doctrinal moves as the proclamation of the bodily assumption of the Virgin as attempts to overcome maladaptive aspects of dogmatic Christianity by incorporating previously denigrated aspects of human experience such as the female body.

Jung exercised an influence on the practice of psychotherapy and on fields ranging from literature to industrial psychology that far exceeds what is usually recognized. The circumstances surrounding his break with Freud, as well as his brief association with the Nazis, did considerable damage to his reputation. An idiosyncratic vocabulary added to his image as an undisciplined thinker. Nevertheless, his system of psychology, beginning as it does with the word association test, and emphasizing the biological foundations of cognition and behaviour, thereby anticipating more recent developments in cognitive theory and evolutionary psychology, rests on far stronger empirical foundations than most other depth psychologies.

See also: INDIAN AND TIBETAN PHILOSOPHY; PSYCHOANALYSIS, METHODOLOGICAL ISSUES IN; PSYCHOANALYSIS, POST-FREUDIAN; PSYCHOLOGY, THEORIES OF; REDUCTIONISM IN THE PHILOSOPHY OF MIND

List of works

Jung, C.G. (1953–91) *The Collected Works of C.G. Jung*, eds G. Adler, M. Fordham, and H. Read, executive ed. W. McGuire, trans. R. Hull, Princeton, NJ: Princeton University Press, and London: Routledge. (The standard collection of Jung's works.)

—— (1973) *Memories, Dreams, Reflections*, recorded and edited by A. Jaffé, trans. R. and C. Winston, New York: Pantheon Books. (Jung's autobiography, important not only for the light it sheds on his life, but also as a study in autobiographical technique.)

—— (1974) *The Freud/Jung Letters: The Correspondence Between Sigmund Freud and C.G. Jung*, ed. W. McGuire, trans. R. Manheim and R. Hull, Princeton, NJ: Princeton University Press. (The indispensable source on the relationship between Jung and Freud.)

—— (1988) *Nietzsche's Zarathustra: Notes on the Seminar Given in 1934–1939 by C.G. Jung in Two Volumes*, ed. J. Jarrett, Princeton, NJ: Princeton University Press. (A transcription of Jung's Nietzsche seminar. Of interest mainly as an example of Jung at work on a text and in dialogue with his students.)

References and further reading

Brome, V. (1978) *Jung*, New York: Atheneum. (The most reliable survey of Jung's life.)

Brooke, R. (1991) *Jung and Phenomenology*, London: Routledge. (A clear and compelling view of Jung in relation to the phenomenological tradition.)

Franz, M.-L., von (1975) *C.G. Jung: His Myth in Our Time*, trans. W. Kennedy, New York: G.P. Putnam's Sons. (An intellectual biography of Jung by one of his closest followers. While often hagiographic, it nevertheless captures the more spiritual aspects of Jung's work.)

Hogenson, G. (1994) *Jung's Struggle with Freud*, Wilmette: Chiron Publications, revised edn. (A view of the philosophical implications of the conflict between Jung and Freud with particular emphasis on the problem of authority.)

Homans, P. (1979) *Jung in Context: Modernity and the Making of a Psychology*, Chicago, IL: University of Chicago Press. (A view of Jung's development in light of modern psychoanalytic theory, particularly Kohut's self-psychology.)

Kerr, J. (1993) *A Most Dangerous Method: The Story of Jung, Freud, and Sabina Spielrein*, New York: Alfred A. Knopf. (A historical overview of the conflict between Jung and Freud which also provides a discussion of the important role played by Sabina Spielrein in the early development of psychoanalysis. Contains an excellent annotated bibliography.)

Maidenbaum, A. and Martin, S. (eds) (1991) *Lingering Shadows: Jungians, Freudians and Anti-Semitism*, Boston, MA: Shambhala. (A collection of essays concerned with Jung's alleged anti-Semitism and his relation to the Nazis.)

Samuels, A. (1985) *Jung and the Post-Jungians*, London: Routledge & Kegan Paul. (A survey of Jung's theories and of subsequent developments in Jungian psychology. Contains a comprehensive bibliography.)

Stein, M. (1985) *Jung's Treatment of Christianity: The Psychotherapy of a Religious Tradition*, Wilmette: Chiron Publications. (An analysis of Jung's hermeneutics and his critique of culture.)

Young-Eisendrath, P. and Dawson, S. (eds) (1997) *The Cambridge Companion to Jung*, Cambridge: Cambridge University Press. (A comprehensive set of essays on Jung and developments in Jungian theory.)

GEORGE B. HOGENSON

JUNGIUS, JOACHIM
(1587–1657)

Joachim Jungius was one of the most important seventeenth-century reformers of Aristotelian logic. Through critical assessment of Suarez and by recourse to Ramus, Zabarella and Melanchthon, he tried to replace Aristotelian syllogistics with a logic based on empirical judgment. This differed sharply from other contemporary attempts to reform logic in Protestant Europe. Jungius was a pioneer in the development of the modern concept of 'element' in chemistry, and made an important contribution to the classification of plants.

1 **Life and works**
2 *Logica Hamburgensis*
3 **Writings on natural history**

1 Life and works

As a schoolboy in the German city of Lübeck, Jungius showed his exceptional talent by teaching his classmates the dialectic of Petrus RAMUS. Thus in 1606, when he began to study logic and metaphysics in Rostock, his stance towards the neoscholastic system of SUÁREZ and the logic of Coimbra was already influenced by his thorough knowledge of Ramus (see COLLEGIUM CONIMBRICENSE). Soon he turned to mathematics and continued his studies at the recently-founded University of Giessen, receiving a Master's degree in 1608. Having taught there as a professor of mathematics, he moved back to Rostock in 1616, began to study medicine, and – after a scholarly tour through Europe – qualified as *Doctor medicinae* in Padua. There he worked mainly on botany and zoology before returning to Rostock in 1619. He joined Johann Valentin Andreae's circle and helped to found the *societas ereunetica/zetetica* (*c*.1623). However, this society lasted only until 1625 because of the Thirty Years' War. Its aims were on the one hand the rejection of Jesuit metaphysics and the critique of sophistics, on the other the promotion of mathematical studies and a natural science regulated by observation and experience. The relation between *ratio* and *experientia* should be determined in such a way that the sciences could be based on demonstrable certainty. After professorships in mathematics in Rostock (1624) and medicine in Helmstedt (1625), work as a doctor in Braunschweig and return to his professorship in Rostock (1626), Jungius took up simultaneously the rectorships at the Johanneum and the academic *Gymnasium* in Hamburg. Disputes with the politically influential Lutheran orthodoxy about the style of New Testament Greek forced him to retire as rector of the Johanneum in 1640.

Jungius did not publish much during his lifetime, but his ideas were promoted to a certain extent by COMENIUS and by the British mathematician Charles Cavendysshe. His immediate influence was in part based on the disputations and dissertations he supervised when rector at the academic *Gymnasium* (for example on stoicheiometry, doctrine of physical principles, theory of motion and other subjects). In 1691 all but about a quarter of Jungius' originally voluminous posthumous papers were destroyed by fire (Meinel 1984b).

2 *Logica Hamburgensis*

Written in the early 1630s as a textbook for the academic *Gymnasium*, the *Logica Hamburgensis* is based on the idea of a continuous improvement of the sciences. In this respect it directly follows Francis Bacon's concept of science and the pedagogical-utopian ideas of Johann Valentin Andreae (see BACON, F.). According to Jungius, one can discern a progress in the sciences despite the Deluge, the migration of nations and the Thirty Years' War, and this progress is due to the improvement of logic. As the editor of the second edition explained, the aim of the *Logica Hamburgensis* was to complete and amend Aristotelian logic – a very accurate description of the syncretistic character of Jungius' logic, which links up conceptually with Zabarella's definition of logic as 'habitus mentis organicus (instrumentalis)' (see ZA-BARELLA, J. §2) and with Ramus' concept of logic as the art of proper reasoning. Accordingly, the structure of the *Logica Hamburgensis* follows the Ramistic distinction between *inventio* and *iudicium* which Jungius relates to the three activities of the human mind, namely (1) *notio* or *conceptus*, (2) *enuntiatio* and (3) *discursus* or *ratiocinatio*. Following this basic structure, Jungius deals in the first three books (*Logica generalis*) with the doctrine of the predicables (*De notionibus*), the doctrine of the predicables' modes of expression (*De enuntiatione*), and finally their application to syllogistic figures (*De ratiocinatione*). Books 3 to 6 (*Logica specialis*) deal with the range of our a posteriori cognition within the limits of apodictic certainty (*Logica apodictica*), with dialectics, and sophistics (particularly the theory of fallacies). Given this heterogeneous internal structure, the merit of the *Logica Hamburgensis* lies certainly in its strongly epistemological concept of logic and the value it ascribes to empirical concepts. Although Jungius' logic was sometimes harshly criticized for its attempt at a moderate reform of Aristotelian syllogistics, it remained the basis for the teaching of logic at the academic *Gymnasium* in Hamburg for many decades and even influenced Leibniz's studies of logic.

3 Writings on natural history

Jungius' writings on natural history, based on lectures and published posthumously, are of an even more didactic nature than his logic textbook. Unlike Descartes, who had tried to found philosophy anew seemingly without any presuppositions, Jungius apparently thought that progress in philosophy through the study of nature could be achieved only by examination of traditional doctrines. By critically assessing the physics of Zabarella, Jean Fernel, Daniel Sennert and others, Jungius defined natural science in the *Doxoscopiae physicae minores* (1662) as a mode of cognition which does not adjust the phenomena to preconceived opinions but the hypotheses to the phenomena. In the Aristotelian-Theophrastic-Galenic tradition, on which he explicitly based his methods, he replaced – in contrast to the metaphysics of Coimbra – the question of the essence of things with that of their function and mode of action. According to Jungius, the natural scientist does not define 'change' or 'motion', but rather what it means 'to be changed' or 'to be moved'. Therefore he focused on the concept of a *materia substantialis* which, together with a critical assessment of the ancient doctrine of principles, Anaxagoras' homoeomeries, Democritus' theory of atoms, and other theories, led him to the discovery of material 'elements'. This theory of elements was not only different from the ancient doctrine of the four elements and the hermetic doctrine of the three principles, but also from Robert Boyle's corpuscular theory, and was a major step towards the modern notion of element.

Among his contributions to almost every aspect of natural history and its applications, from mineralogy to entomology, chemistry, mining, mechanics and so on, Jungius established a classification of plants into classes, genera and species according to a uniform principle (*ratio constans*). He made a distinction between specific differences (for example, leaves) and accidental differences which have no influence on the definition of the species (such as spines, smell, medical use, place, time of germination, number of petals and so on), thereby anticipating Linnaeus' system of classification.

See also: ARISTOTELIANISM IN THE 17TH CENTURY

List of works

Jungius, J. (1613) *Kurtzer Bericht von der Didactica, oder Lehrkunst Wolfgangi Ratichii* (Short treatise concerning the Didactica, or Art of Learning, according to Wolfgang Ratichius), Frankfurt. (Written with Christoph Helvich, this is a positive assessment of Wolfgang Ratichius' inductive method of teaching; at least five editions were published up until 1621.)

—— (1627) *Geometria empirica* (Empirical geometry), Rostock. (Early work on geometry.)

—— (1638) *Logica Hamburgensis, hoc est, institutiones logicae in usum scholae Hamburgensis consciiptae* (Logica Hamburgensis, that is institutions of logic, written for the use of the Academic Gymnasium in Hamburg), Hamburg: Barthold Offermans; 2nd edn, ed. J. Vagetius, Hamburg, 1681; German trans. R.W. Meyer, Hamburg: Augustin, 1957. (Books 1–3 had already been published in 1635.)

—— (1662) *Doxoscopiae physicae minores, sive isagoge physica doxoscopica. In qua praecipue opiniones in physica passim receptae breviter quidem, sed accuratissime examinantur* (The Pupils of physical doctrine, or, Introduction to the physical doctrines, in which the traditional opinions in physics are shortly, but accurately examined), ed. M. Fogel, Hamburg: Johannes Nauman. (Reprinted Hamburg 1679.)

—— (1678a) *Harmonica* (Harmony). (Investigates the doctrines of harmony and introduces the theory of music.)

—— (1678b) *Isagoge phytoscopica* (Introduction to the doctrines and the theory of plants), Hamburg. (Investigates the received doctrines of plants on the basis of empirical observations).

—— (1691) *Historia vermium* (Natural history of worms and insects), ed. J. Vagetius, Hamburg. (Contains mainly contributions to entomology.)

—— (1747) *Opuscula botanico-physica* (Short treatises on botany and natural history), ed. M. Fogel and J. Vagetius, Coburg: Georg Otto. (Collection of Jungius' botanical studies, based on his private lectures. Reproduces some pieces already published in his *Doxoscopiae physicae minores.*)

—— (1863) *Briefwechsel mit seinen Schülern und Freunden. Ein Beitrag zur Kenntniß des großen Jungius und der wissenschaftlichen wie sozialen Zustände zur Zeit des dreißigjährigen Krieges, aus den Manuscripten der Hamburger Stadtbibliothek zusammengestellt* (Correspondence with his pupils and friends. Information on Jungius and the scientific and social circumstances at the time of the Thiry Years' War, compiled from manuscripts in the Hamburg City Library), ed. R.C.B. Avé-Lallemant, Lübeck: Friedrich Asschenfeldt. (Contains an essential part of Jungius' correspondence.)

—— (1977) *Logicae Hamburgensis additamenta*, ed. W. Risse, Veröffentlichungen der Joachim-Jungius-Gesellschaft der Wissenschaften, BD 25, Göttingen:Vandenhoeck & Ruprecht. (Unpublished additions to the *Logicae Hamburgensis.*)

—— (1982) *Praelectiones physicae*, ed. C. Meinel, Veröffentlichungen der Joachim-Jungius-Gesellschaft der Wissenschaften, BD 45, Göttingen:Vandenhoeck & Ruprecht. (Critical edition of Jungius' lectures on physics.)

—— (1988) *Disputationes Hamburgenses*, ed. C. Müller-Glauser, Veröffentlichungen der Joachim-Jungius-Gesellschaft der Wissenschaften, BD 59, Göttingen:Vandenhoeck & Ruprecht. (Critical edition of Jungius' disputations and dissertations.)

References and further reading

Avé-Lallemant, R.C.B. (1882) *Das Leben des Dr. med. Joachim Jungius aus Lübeck* (The life of Doctor of medicine Joachim Jungius from Lübeck), Breslau: Hirt. (Interesting work on Jungius' Life.)

Fogel, M. (1657) *Memoria Joachimi Jungii* (Memorial to the late Joachim Jungius), Hamburg. (First biographical survey, published at the time of Jungius' death.)

Guhrauer, G.E. (1850) *Joachim Jungius und dein Zeitalter. Nebst Goethe's Fragmenten über Jungius* (Joachim Jungius and his time; including Goethe's fragments on Jungius), Stuttgart and Tübingen: J.G. Cotta. (Thorough study of Jungius' life, work and its reception.)

Kangro, H. (1968) *Joachim Jungius' Experimente und Gedanken zur Begründung der Chemie als Wissenschaft. Ein Beitrag zur Geistesgeschichte des 17. Jahrhunderts* (Joachim Jungius' experiments and thoughts to found chemistry on scientific grounds. A contribution to the intellectual history of the seventeenth century), Boethius, Bd. VII, Wiesbaden: F. Steiner. (Important work with a very helpful bibliography.)

—— (1969) 'Joachim Jungius und Gottfried Wilhelm Leibniz. Ein Beitrag zum geistigen Verhältnis beider Gelehrten'(Joachim Jungius and Gottfried Wilhelm Leibniz. A contribution to the intellectual relationship between them), *Studia Leibnitiana* 1: 175–207. (Study of the influence of Jungius on Leibniz.)

Meinel, C. (1982) 'Der Begriff des chemischen Elementes bei Joachim Jungius' (The concept of the chemical element in Joachim Jungius' thought), *Sudhoffs Archiv* 66: 313–38. (Important contribution to the notion of a chemical element.)

—— (1984a) *In physicis futurum saeculum respicio. Joachim Jungius und die Naturwissenschaftliche Revolution des 17. Jahrhunderts* (In physics I see the coming age. Joachim Jungius and the scientific revolution in the seventeenth century), Veröffentlichungen der Joachim Jungius-Gesellschaft der Wissenschaften, Bd. 52, Göttingen: Vandenhoeck & Ruprecht. (Investigates Jungius' contribution to the history of science.)

—— (1984b) *Der handschriftliche Nachlaß von Joachim Jungius in der Staats- und Universitätsbibliothek Hamburg* (The manuscript heritage of Joachim Jungius in the State and University

Library of Hamburg), Katalog der Handschriften der Staats- und Universitätsbibliothek Hamburg, Bd.IX, Stuttgart: Hauswedell. (Catalogue of Jungius' remaining manuscripts.)

—— (1992) *Die Bibliothek des Joachim Jungius. Ein Beitrag zur Historia litteraria der frühen Neuzeit* (The library of Joachim Jungius. A contribution to the *historia litteraria* in the early modern period), Veröffentlichungen der Joachim Jungius-Gesellschaft der Wissenschaften, Bd.67, Göttingen: Vandenhoeck & Ruprecht. (Study of Jungius' library.)

Meyer, R.W. (1957) 'Joachim Jungius und die Philosophie seiner Zeit' (Joachim Jungius and the philosophy of his age), in *Die Entfaltung der Wissenschaft. Zum Gedenken an Joachim Jungius*, Hamburg: Augustin. (Examines the position of Jungius within the seventeenth-century philosophical tradition.)

Trevisani, F. (1978) 'Geometria e logica nel metodo di Joachim Jungius' (Geometry and logic as contained in the method of Joachim Jungius), *Rivista critica di storia della filosofia* 33: 171–208. (Interesting work on the mathematical basis of Jungius' scientific method.)

Translated by Peter Schnyder

RALPH HÄFNER

JURISPRUDENCE, HISTORICAL

Historical jurisprudence is the title usually given to a group of theories, which flourished mainly in the nineteenth century, that explain law as the product of predetermined patterns of change based on social and economic change. It is thus opposed both to theories that see law as essentially an expression of the will of those holding political power (positivist theories) and to those that see it as an expression of principles that are part of man's nature and so applicable in any kind of society (natural law theories). The writers of the Scottish Enlightenment first connected the historical development of law with economic changes. In the nineteenth century, Savigny and Maine postulated grand evolutionary schemes, which purported to be applicable universally. They were, however, based on the development of ancient Roman law and could only with difficulty be applied to other systems. These schemes are now discredited, but in the twentieth century more modest studies have successfully related particular kinds of law to particular sets of social circumstances.

1 The historical school of law

Montesquieu in his influential *The Spirit of the Laws* (1748) first showed the connection between law and the circumstances of society. He accepted the natural lawyers' view that law must reflect the nature of things but insisted that the nature of things is not the same in every society. Rather law reflects the spirit of each society, which is an amalgam of various components, some physical, such as its climate and the qualities of its land, and some moral, such as religion and social customs. Montesquieu recognized that some societies were more developed than others and that therefore their laws had to be more sophisticated, but he imposed no scheme of historical progression on his material. Adam Smith in his *Lectures on Jurisprudence* (1762–3) argued that a society's law changes according to the progress of society through four stages based on the prevailing mode of subsistence, namely, hunting, pastoral, agricultural and commercial. The first three were reflected in developments in the law of property and the last in the law of contract. The writers of the Scottish Enlightenment accepted as axiomatic that as a society's mode of subsistence varies, so its laws must be different, and thus established the connection between legal and economic development.

In the nineteenth century these ideas formed the basis for theories of legal evolution, which held that law develops on predetermined lines from its own internal forces. The implication was that changes should be left to these natural social mechanisms and therefore that reform legislation and codification were contrary to the nature of law. Its theorists generalized from the history of ancient Roman law, which had a continuous development of over a thousand years, and appeared to be relatively unaffected by legislation. From its infancy as the law of a tribal society in the sixth century BC, it grew into the law of a world empire, reached its technical peak in the second and early third centuries AD and thereafter declined until its codification by the Emperor Justinian in the sixth century AD.

The main German protagonist of historical jurisprudence was F.K. von SAVIGNY, whose view was published in 1814 as a polemic against the proposal to codify German law on the model of the Code Napoléon. Eighteenth-century proponents of codes had combined the positivist and the naturalist traditions by arguing that what would make the codes law was legislation but their substance would be dictated by what was congruous with man's nature. Savigny insisted that a people's law must fit its particular circumstances. He took over the idea that the history of Roman law was divided into three periods, dressed it in the metaphor of organic growth, which Edmund Burke had used to describe the unwritten constitution of Britain, and declared that law among the 'nobler' nations (by which Savigny meant essentially the Roman and the German) goes through three periods: growth, maturity and decline. In the first period it is manifested directly in the practices of the people. As society grows, some parts of law become more technical and are adapted by expert jurists, acting as delegates of the people; but whether it is based on custom or on juristic discussion, it is developed not by legislation but through silent forces within itself. In its infancy it is not technical enough for legislation and in its decline it is not worthy to be codified. The only suitable period for codification would be the period of maturity, but then, with the maximum participation of the people and juristic science at its zenith, legislation would be an unnecessary intrusion.

Savigny's followers in the German Historical School accepted the organic and inevitable connection between the special character of a people and its language and its law. For them the spirit of a particular people (*Volksgeist*) was something more than Montesquieu's spirit. The latter comprised a number of quantifiable components. The *Volksgeist* had a mystical dimension, much in tune with the romanticism of the first half of the nineteenth century. The enthusiasm generated by the historical school produced a series of distinguished studies of legal history, both in the Roman law and in the Germanic law area.

2 Maine's ancient law

In France Charles Comte (1827) produced *Traité de legislation ou exposition des lois générales suivant lesquelles les peuples prospèrent, dépérissent ou restent stationnaires* (Treatise on Legislation or Exposition of the General Laws According to which Peoples Prosper, Decline or Remain Stationary). He put special emphasis on geographical and racial factors as accounting for the progress of some societies and lack of progress of others and their effect on such societies' law. Relying on the lectures of the English physiologist William Lawrence, he asserted the superiority of people of Caucasian race.

Comte's distinction between progressive and stationary societies was combined with Savigny's scheme of legal evolution by the principal English exponent of historical jurisprudence, Sir Henry Maine, in *Ancient Law* (1861). Maine was concerned to provide a theory which would explain the law of 'progressive' societies (principally ancient Rome and England) and act as a counterweight to the positivism of Bentham and Austin, which held that all true law was the product of legislation by a political sovereign. He was equally concerned to refute those who based law on a priori abstractions such as the law of nature, and sought to offer an explanation of law which was both empirical and universally true in the sense that natural science was true.

> If it be truth at all, it must be scientific truth. There can be no essential difference between the truths of the Astronomer, of the Physiologist and of the Historian. The great principle that underlies all our knowledge of the physical world, that Nature is ever consistent with herself, must also be true of human nature... if indeed history be true, it must teach that which every other science teaches – continuous sequence, inflexible order, and eternal law.
>
> (Maine 1876: 265–6)

Maine's starting point was sound. By viewing all law as legislation, Bentham and his followers obscured the nature of legal change. As Maine insisted, the farther back in time we go, the farther we are removed from the Benthamite notion that law is made expressly by legislation. Rather it evolves imperceptibly. The science which Maine used as his model was geology: the rudimentary ideas of law found in the literature of early societies 'are to the jurist what the primary crusts of the earth are to the geologist' (Maine 1861: 3).

Ancient Law, however, although purporting to be concerned with 'the early history of society', was not concerned with primitive societies, such as Native Americans. It was essentially limited to Indo-European societies and was structured round the development of the institutions of Roman law. Thus the account of the law of the earliest period of society starts with divinely inspired kings handing down isolated judgments, or 'themistes'. Later they lose their sacred power and are replaced by a small group of aristocrats who have a monopoly of knowledge of the traditional customs. They abuse their power and popular agitation demands the recording of the customs in 'Ancient Codes'. This is a generalization of what happened in Rome when the monarchy gave way to the Republic and the plebeians demanded the enactment of the Twelve Tables. The scheme is not readily discernible elsewhere and in particular it has little application to England.

On the other hand Maine introduced certain ideas

which have entered the common currency of jurisprudential discourse. Examples are the recognition of fictions and equity as early 'agencies of legal change', which precede legislation; the predominance of procedural rules over substantive rules in early law; and especially his famous generalization: 'the movement of progressive societies has hitherto been a movement from Status to Contract' (Maine 1861: 170).

Maine's work fitted the mood of the age of biological evolution, produced by Darwin's *Origin of Species* (1859), but its ideas were challenged both by anthropologists, who showed that they did not apply to early non-Indo-European societies, and by legal historians, who objected to the inaccuracies of his generalizations. Politically Maine's ideas led to a legal conservatism that saw the movement from status to contract as leading to ever greater self-determination for the individual, so that the imposition of any form of strict liability on someone without fault was condemned as contrary to the principles of legal evolution.

Loss of faith in the applicability of the methods of the natural sciences to social phenomena and in the idea of the progress of society reduced interest in Maine's theories. However, the notion that a society's law must be viewed as closely related to its social and economic circumstances and should be studied not in isolation but in comparison with the laws of other societies with similar or different circumstances became permanently rooted in legal thought and is now commonplace.

3 Maine's heirs

Two followers of Maine, James BRYCE and Sir Paul Vinogradoff, attempted modifications of his ideas. Bryce (1901) developed the comparative method. For him the law of any society is always a compromise between tradition and convenience. The study of similarities and differences in different legal systems can lead to the identification of frequently recurring phenomena, which can be treated as universals and thus in turn elucidate the nature of law in general. Vinogradoff (1920–22) more ambitiously extrapolated from the history of European societies six stages of legal progress, from totemistic law through medieval law, marked by the tension between feudal and canon law, to individualistic jurisprudence and finally socialist jurisprudence.

The immediate heirs of historical jurisprudence can be found in various disciplines. In the area of social theory, its influence can be seen in the work of two significant writers. Ferdinand Tönnies (1887), starting from the movement from status to contract, devel-oped the idea of two contrasting forms of social grouping, the *Gemeinschaft*, or community of those sharing to some degree a common way of life, and the *Gesellschaft*, a more limited relationship, based on the parties' will to achieve a particular purpose, usually by contract. In the same tradition Max Weber (1922) introduced a typology of legal authority, contrasting rational authority with traditional and charismatic types of authority. He popularized the notion of 'ideal' model types, in the sense of social constructs, not actually found in reality, but useful as hypotheses to enable the scholar to highlight similarities and differences in actual systems. These types provide a way of coping with the theorists' perennial dilemma of achieving their need to generalize while at the same time maintaining fidelity to accuracy (see SOCIAL THEORY AND LAW §§1–3).

4 Historical jurisprudence today

Although much of what would once have been called historical jurisprudence is now carried on under such labels as legal anthropology or comparative legal history, there are signs of a revival of the traditional search for general patterns of legal change, but with more modest objectives than those of the nineteenth-century theorists. Progress is no longer seen in terms of continuous improvement, but recurring patterns of legal change, corresponding to social and economic changes, can be identified. By shifting the notion of causal connection from one of necessity to one of probability, one can postulate likely connections between forms of society and the kinds of law they have and this process can result in some, albeit provisional, general propositions. Hitherto theories were concerned almost exclusively with the institutions of private law, but it is possible fruitfully to use model types to relate the growth of a distinct public law to a society with particular characteristics (such as France) and so criticize its introduction in a society (such as England) which lacks those features (Allison 1996).

Roberto Unger (1976) has emphasized the need to identify the different conceptions of the law and of what may be expected from it that characterize different types of society. This has enabled him to distinguish various types of society on the basis of such interpretive explanations. Thus in 'savage' societies customary patterns of interaction among individuals and groups are based on a recognition that such patterns produce reciprocal expectations of conduct. In 'bureaucratic' societies, the state has become the controlling institution, in which the dominant hierarchy begins to take a critical attitude to social customs and seeks to control them through the publication of express rules, seen as emanations of the human will. The idea that such rules should apply equally to all members of the society only emerges, however, in societies of the 'legal order', as exemplified by the liberal societies of post-feudal Europe. Such societies are composed of different groups with different interests, no one of which is dominant, so that the law is seen as a cohesive force, binding all groups equally.

Another manifestation of what may be called historical jurisprudence concentrates on the identification of recurring patterns in the technical development of law, irrespective of their social context. Such studies emphasize similarities between the legal techniques of the laws of different societies, in such matters as the relations between procedure and substantive law, for example, the effect of use of laymen, such as civil juries, on the nature of the law, or the relations between written law, in which the text is fixed but subject to recurring techniques of interpretation, and unwritten law, in which the rules are not finally formulated but elucidated on a case by case basis by authoritative judges or jurists.

See also: EVOLUTION AND ETHICS; EVOLUTIONARY THEORY AND SOCIAL SCIENCE; LAW, PHILOSOPHY OF

References and further reading

* Allison, J.W.F. (1996) *A Continental Distinction in the Common Law: A Historical and Comparative Perspective on English Public Law*, Oxford: Oxford University Press.
* Bryce, J., Viscount (1901) *Studies in History and Jurisprudence*, 2 vols, Oxford: Clarendon Press.
* Comte, C. (1827) *Traité de legislation ou exposition des lois générales suivant lesquelles les peuples prospèrent, dépérissent ou restent stationnaires* (Treatise on Legislation or Exposition of the General Laws According to which Peoples Prosper, Decline or Remain Stationary), 4 vols, Paris.
  Diamond, A. (ed.) (1991) *The Victorian Achievement of Sir Henry Maine: a Centennial Re-appraisal*, Cambridge: Cambridge University Press. (Various studies of Maine's influence, of which those of J.W. Burrow, E. Shils and C. Woodard are specially relevant.)
  MacCormack, G. (1985) 'Historical Jurisprudence', *Legal Studies* 5: 251–60. (Current state of the movement.)
* Maine, H.S. (1861) *Ancient Law*, London: Murray.
* —— (1876) *Village Communities in the East and West*, 3rd edn, London: Murray.
* Montesquieu, C. Baron de (1748) *De l'esprit des lois* (*The Spirit of the Laws*), trans. T. Nugent, 2 vols, London, 1750.
* Savigny, F.K. von (1814) *Zum Beruf unsrer Zeit für Gesetzgebung und Rechtswissenschaft*, trans. A. Hayward, *On the Vocation of Our Age for Legislation and Jurisprudence*, London: Littlewood, 1831.
* Smith, A. (1762–3) *Lectures on Jurisprudence*, R.L. Meek, D.D. Raphael and P.G. Stein (eds), Oxford: Oxford University Press, 1978.
  Stein, P. (1980) *Legal Evolution: The Story of an Idea*, Cambridge: Cambridge University Press. (General survey of theories of evolution of law through successive stages.)
  —— (1986) 'The Tasks of Historical Jurisprudence', in N. MacCormick and P. Birks (eds), *The Legal Mind: Essays for Tony Honore*, Oxford: Clarendon Press. (A possible future for historical jurisprudence.)
* Tönnies, F. (1887) *Gemeinschaft und Gesellschaft*, trans. C.P. Loomis, *Community and Society*, London: Routledge, 1955.
* Unger, R. (1976) *Law in Modern Society*, New York: Free Press.
* Vinogradoff, Sir P. (1920–22) *Outlines of Historical Jurisprudence*, 2 vols, Oxford: Oxford University Press.
* Weber, M. (1922) *Wirtschaft und Gesellschaft* (*Max Weber on Law and Society*), M. Rheinstein (ed.), Cambridge, MA: Harvard University Press, 1954.

PETER STEIN

JUSTICE

The idea of justice lies at the heart of moral and political philosophy. It is a necessary virtue of individuals in their interactions with others, and the principal virtue of social institutions, although not the only one. Just as an individual can display qualities such as integrity, charity and loyalty, so a society can also be more or less economically prosperous, artistically cultivated, and so on. Traditionally defined by the Latin tag 'suum cuique tribuere' – to allocate to each his own – justice has always been closely connected to the ideas of desert and equality. Rewards and punishments are justly distributed if they go to those who deserve them. But in the absence of different desert claims, justice demands equal treatment.

A common division of the topic distinguishes between corrective and distributive justice. Corrective justice covers that which is due to a person as punishment, distributive that which is due by way of benefits and burdens other than punishments. Within the sphere of corrective justice there is disagreement about the justification of punishment itself. But there has been – and is – widespread agreement on the criteria for just punishment: just punishments must be properly imposed and the quantum of punishment must reflect the seriousness of the offence.

There has been no such agreement about the content of just principles for the distribution of benefits and (non-punitive) burdens. Conventionalists claim that what is due to each person is given by the laws, customs and shared understandings of the community of which the person is a member. Teleologists believe that an account can be given of the good for human beings and that justice is the ordering principle through which a society (or humanity) pursues that good. Justice as mutual advantage proposes that the rules of justice can be derived from the rational agreement of each agent to cooperate with others to further their own self-interest. Theorists of what may be called justice as fairness believe that justice is a thin concept which provides a fair framework within which each person is enabled to pursue their own good.

1   **Corrective justice**
2   **Conventionalism**
3   **Teleology**
4   **Justice as mutual advantage**
5   **Justice as fairness**
6   **Critics of justice**

1   Corrective justice

There is general agreement that a just punishment should meet the following criteria. First, it should be imposed only on a properly convicted wrongdoer. Second, the quantum of suffering should satisfy the principle of ordinal proportionality. This means, as Hirsch (1990) has put it, that 'persons convicted of crimes of comparable gravity should receive punishments of comparable severity' except where mitigating or aggravating circumstances alter the culpability of the offender. Third, the quantum of suffering should satisfy the principle of cardinal proportionality: there should be a vertical ranking of crimes and penalties by seriousness.

There is, however, disagreement over the justification for punishment, and this makes it controversial how 'seriousness', 'severity' and 'culpability' are assessed and how the scale of penalties should be fixed. Those who appeal to deterrence may regard a widespread and socially disruptive crime as serious (whatever its degree of moral wrongness), and favour a scale of penalties designed to deter criminality. Those who favour retribution, however, have traditionally regarded seriousness as a factor of moral culpability

and the scale of penalties as being derived from some notion of desert (see CRIME AND PUNISHMENT).

2   Conventionalism

Turning to social, or distributive, justice, the attraction of some form of conventionalist approach is clear. Since there are institutions, conventions and systems of law that determine what is due to whom, resolving issues of justice may be thought merely to require reading off the correct answer from such sources. The earliest extant statement of a conventionalist view of justice is offered by Socrates' interlocutors, Cephalus and Polemarchus, in Book I of Plato's *Republic*. Polemarchus states that justice is giving a man his due, or what is appropriate to him, and it is clear that for Polemarchus what is appropriate to each person is dictated by the conventions prevalent in contemporary Athenian society.

A more complicated statement of conventionalism has been offered by Michael Walzer (1983). He argues that every social good (for example, health care, wealth, income and political rights) has an appropriate criterion of distribution which is internally related to how that good is understood by society. For example, in the UK (as elsewhere), health care is understood essentially to concern itself with illness and the restoration of health. This shared understanding of health care seems to entail a distributive criterion: medical need. Anyone, therefore, who claims that health care in the UK (and many other societies) ought to be distributed in accordance with, say, status has either failed to grasp the nature of the good of health care or falls outside the community which is united and defined by its shared understandings. The only universal principle of distributive justice is the demand that respect be given to different shared understandings: no community ought to impose its own understanding of a given good, and its criterion for the distribution of that good, on any other community with different views.

The dependence of this theory on shared understandings has led to its being criticized on both empirical and theoretical grounds. Empirically, it is doubtful that any society is so homogenous as to boast a single, coherent and uncontested understanding of each of its social goods. (Is the freezing of embryos so that women might have children later in life, after they have established themselves in a career, meeting a medical need?) Theoretically, the account is flawed because the proposed universal principle of justice is not found in any society. A belief may be 'ours' in that it defines justice *according* to us; but it does not follow that we believe it is 'ours' in the sense of *applying* only to us. If justice is internally related to social understandings, there can be no perspective from which anyone might, from outside a given set of understandings, condemn the understandings or practices of a society as unjust. Yet there clearly is such a perspective. For example, in a hierarchical society it may be that the local conception of justice would require gross inequalities based on ascription at birth; this could be regarded as unjust.

The *prima facie* attraction of conventionalism is immediately undone when one asks why any given set of conventions, laws, or shared understandings should determine the distribution of benefits and burdens. Once this question is asked there is no reason why the answer has to flow from within the narrow resources of the community. It is at this point, when one asks why things are as they are, that the philosophical problem of justice really begins.

3 Teleology

In the history of thought about justice, the most common justification of any given set of laws, conventions or practices has been to appeal to an external, usually divine, authority. In the natural law tradition, to make an act just it is not enough that it complies with the society's positive law. The positive law must itself be in accordance with a natural law which is knowable through the faculty of human reason (see NATURAL LAW). This tradition, owing its origins to the Greek Stoics, found its most lucid interpreter in CICERO (§§2,4) and was given its definitive Christian form by AQUINAS (§13). 'True law', writes Cicero, 'is right reason in agreement with nature; it is of universal application, unchanging and everlasting'(c.54–51 BC: III, XXII, 211). The link to human nature via human reason is important, for it then follows that human beings reach their true end, or realize their true natures, only by living in accordance with natural law. What justice is and why it is a good are, thus, answered at the same time.

A major problem for this account is its reliance on an external source. Cicero is typical in claiming in the same passage that it is God who 'is the author of this law, its promulgator, and its enforcing judge'. Natural law theory faces the difficulty of having to give an account of the existence and verifiability of the 'true and unchanging' moral order. Commonly, the natural law was conveniently said to underwrite the existing positive law: this may reflect the role of the powerful both in formulating positive law and defining natural law.

Suppose we are attracted to the notion that human institutions are to be justified by their contribution to human good, but do not believe that human reason is capable of discerning a divine plan. Then we may naturally arrive at the secular alternative embodied in utilitarianism: the idea that the ground of justification is human wellbeing, happiness or 'utility'. When the utility of different people conflicts, the criterion for bringing their interests into relationship with one another is that aggregate utility is to be maximized (see UTILITARIANISM).

Utilitarianism can be characterized as a theory of justice if we simply define justice as the principal virtue of institutions. Utilitarians claim that, in the last analysis, there is only one virtue that matters: maximizing utility. However, utilitarianism is liable to violate elementary demands of justice as they are commonly understood: two people with identical deserts will be treated very differently if the utilitarian calculus happens to produce the finding that utility would be maximized by so doing. The common belief is that what is due to a person ought to be related to something about that person, not derived from a calculation about what would most effectively further some overall desirable state of affairs.

An important line of thought within utilitarianism has attempted to head off such criticisms by arguing that in practice the dictates of utilitarianism would underwrite the practices and institutions that are usually thought of as being required by justice. Thus, David HUME (§4), in *A Treatise of Human Nature* (1739–40), described justice as an 'artificial virtue' in that individual acts of justice contributed to utility not directly (as an act of benevolence would) but indirectly *qua* adherence to an institution that was on the whole beneficial. Hume's examples were respect for property, chastity (in women), allegiance to the government and promise-keeping. For Hume, then, justice was a convention – but it made sense to ask what good was served by following it. On somewhat parallel lines, J.S. MILL (§11) argued in 'Utilitarianism' (1861) that 'justice' is the name we give to those precepts whose strict observance is important for the furtherance of the utilitarian end. Thus, utilitarians argue that the arbitrary departures from social rules summoned up by anti-utilitarians as an implication of the doctrine are, in the long term, not really for the general good. Opponents of utilitarianism however have claimed that situations might still arise in which injustice (as normally understood) would be for the general good. Further, they complain that the foundations of the theory remain unsatisfactory because it does not (in John Rawls' phrase) 'take seriously the separateness of persons'.

4 Justice as mutual advantage

Utilitarianism is based on the assumption that the

good of different individuals can be in some sense lumped together, and the pursuit of aggregate utility proposed as the objective of everyone. But, in the absence of an external lawgiver, how can an (not naturally benevolent) individual be encouraged to adopt the maximization of total utility as a binding demand? If we doubt that any satisfactory answer can be given, we may be tempted by a theory of justice that takes as its starting point the assumption that each person has a conception of their own good, and that justice must be shown to contribute to the attainment of that good. Justice is thus the terms of a *modus vivendi*: it gives everyone the best chance of achieving their good that they can reasonably expect, given that others are simultaneously trying to achieve their (different) good. Versions of 'justice as mutual advantage' can be found in Thrasymachus' 'might is right' argument in Book I of Plato's *Republic* and in the fraudulent social contract identified by Rousseau (1755: Part II) as having been perpetrated by the rich on the poor. But the *locus classicus* of this theory is undoubtedly *Leviathan* by Thomas HOBBES (§7).

If the terms of agreement are to be to the advantage of each (compared with unrestrained conflict), they must reflect the relative bargaining strengths of the cooperators. The strong and talented have little to gain (or to fear) from the weak or infirm, and the latter may even 'fall beyond the pale' of morality if the strong have no reason for taking their interests into account (Gauthier 1986: 268). Intuitively, it may seem perverse to call this a theory of justice. It is true that justice as mutual advantage has much of the structure of a theory of justice in that it results in rules that constrain the pursuit of self-interest. But the content of those rules will correspond to those of ordinary ideas of justice only if a rough equality of power holds between all the parties.

Even if this objection is not regarded as decisive, the theory suffers from internal problems. These concern the determinacy of the rules and their stability. The determinacy problem arises because of the necessity for all to start from a common view of the relative bargaining strengths of the participants. This is an immensely demanding condition, given the information about resources required and the different predictions that are liable to be made about the outcome of conflict. Even after rules have been agreed, some parties will have reason to press for changes if their bargaining power increases. Justice as mutual advantage results in rules which are no more than truces and, like truces, they are unlikely to be stable if there are changes in the balance of power between the sides (Barry 1995: 41).

Stability will also be challenged by the problem of non-compliance. Justice as mutual advantage appeals to the self-interest of each and does so by establishing rules that, if generally complied with, will further the interests of all individuals. However, this gives the agent no reason to comply with a given rule when there is greater advantage to be had by breaking it. This applies especially when the agent can free ride on the compliance of others. All that can be attempted is to increase the costs of non-compliance by increasing the sanctions if the agent is detected. To run a society using only self-interest and sanctions, however, would mean using a degree of coercion and of 'policing' hitherto unthought of in even the most totalitarian society.

5 Justice as fairness

Theories of justice as fairness start, like those of justice as mutual advantage, from the premise that the role of justice is to provide a framework within which people with competing ideas of the good can live together without conflict. However, justice as fairness seeks a framework that can be said to be fair to all the parties. It aspires to allocate to each person a fair set of opportunities to pursue their idea of the good life. The problem is that if what is due to each person is not determined by convention, by some overarching theory of the good, or by mutual advantage, how is it to be determined? On this question there is widespread disagreement. What is agreed is that there is an initial equal claim to consideration (see Kymlicka 1990). The root of disagreement lies in determining the scope, grounds and nature of this equality.

The range of accounts of the content of justice which is compatible with justice as fairness is very great: Robert Nozick's entitlement theory and John Rawls' theory of justice, for example, come to very different conclusions about what justice demands, even though both start with the basic idea that justice is to regulate the interactions of free and equal persons. Nozick believes that 'individuals have rights, and there are things no person or group may do to them (without violating their rights)' (1974: ix). From this starting point he generates what he calls an entitlement theory of justice (see NOZICK, R. §2). The just pattern of distribution is that which would result from voluntary transfers, given that holdings were justly acquired in the first place (by just transfer or by an appropriation that makes no one else worse off). Nozick, then, regards the claim to an equal set of absolute rights as defining the limits of justice: any actions which interfere with those rights (such as redistribution) are unjust no matter what the pattern or outcome of the entitlement theory. Nozick does not, however, offer any account of the existence of such robust rights, and his arguments from intuition to show that any interference with individual rights is unjust are unconvincing. It is plausible that injustice may result from a large number of individual transactions each of which taken separately seems just.

John Rawls (1971) has argued that justice requires the provision of equal basic liberties and fair opportunities for all, and that social and economic inequality can only be justified where it is to the benefit of the least advantaged. These principles are derived by arguing that they would be chosen by free persons in an 'original position', the specifications of which prevent people from making unfair use of their natural and social advantages (see CONTRACTARIANISM §7; RAWLS, J. §1). Rawls then, in contrast to Nozick, believes that justice requires us to do much more for each agent than merely provide them with absolute property rights. Rather, the pattern of distribution is set at that which will maximally benefit the worst off. The question is one of determining the content of justice: when is it appropriate to move away from the concept of equality? 'when have we done enough' for a person to be able to say that variations in outcome are 'deserved'? (Scanlon 1988: 187) (see EQUALITY; DESERT AND MERIT)

Recent work in Anglo-American political theory has been dominated by the development of theories between these positions. Ronald Dworkin (1981), for example, has argued that Rawls goes too far in treating all characteristics that make people more or less productive as 'morally arbitrary', and thus fails to allow for the justice of rewarding enterprise and ambition. Dworkin, in his own work, seeks to accommodate differences in ambition while retaining the feature of endowment insensitivity (see DWORKIN, R.).

A different line of argument is that Rawls' original position is not a bargaining environment because the veil of ignorance entails that the participants are identical. Moreover, Rawls secures the two principles only by building in a number of ad hoc requirements (for example, that the participants are risk averse). The alternative proposed is to posit participants who are aware of their identities and *morally* motivated to seek agreement. Such a position has been proposed by the philosopher Thomas Scanlon (1982) and developed into a theory of justice by Brian Barry (1995) (see CONTRACTARIANISM §9).

All theories of justice as fairness face the problem of grounding the commitment to the fundamental equality of persons and giving an account of each agent's motivation to behave justly. Rawls offers two justifications for his principles. The first is that the principles match our 'considered moral judgements' about justice: we come to a 'reflective equilibrium' in which the principles reflect and organize our moral intuitions. The second justification is offered as a Kantian interpretation. On this account the original position provides a 'procedural interpretation' of Kant's realm of the 'kingdom of ends' (see KANT, I. §9). The original position and the choice of the principles are viewed as an attempt to replicate Kant's reduction of morality to autonomy and autonomy to rationality. Thus, by living in accordance with justice we realize our true natures as autonomous beings. This provides the motivation required.

In later papers and in his second book, *Political Liberalism* (1993), Rawls has moved away from the Kantian interpretation on the grounds that it requires a controversial metaphysics and that it commits him to a particular view of the good life as autonomy. Instead Rawls now emphasizes that his theory relies on nothing more than ideas 'latent in the public political culture' of modern Western democratic states. This move aligns him with the conventionalist position discussed in §2, and is open to the criticisms raised there. Without the Kantian interpretation it is also difficult for Rawls to give an account of moral motivation. What is left is a theory that claims to give a content to the idea of justice but which cannot, when the demands of justice conflict with the self-interest of the agent, provide the agent with a reason to be moral (Nagel 1991).

Scanlon's and Barry's accounts assume morally motivated individuals who are concerned to find terms of agreement which reflect the equality of persons. Barry has argued that the demands of fairness can be generated from the lack of an authoritative account of the good; but this argument still relies on a prior commitment to freedom and equality. There is, however, no reason why such theories should not claim that such a commitment has universalist implications: an appeal to what we believe does not mean that what we believe applies only to us. Similarly, theorists of justice as fairness need not make the illegitimate claim (much more often attributed to them than made by them) that justice as fairness is neutral between all ways of life (no matter how illiberal) (see NEUTRALITY, POLITICAL).

Justice as fairness can claim to give a content to the idea of justice by telling us what is justly due to whom, and can do so in a way that matches our fundamental intuitions about the nature not only of justice but of morality generally – namely, that each agent is a locus of equal value. That they cannot provide the agent with a decisive reason to behave morally when to do so conflicts with the agent's self-interest or conception of the good may not reflect a defect of justice as fairness. Rather, it may be an inevitable aspect of moral theorizing without recourse to a divine order or a single, comprehensive, idea of the good (see MORAL MOTIVATION).

6 Critics of justice

The discussion so far has proceeded on the assumption that justice is the principal virtue of institutions. The theories of justice examined here would explain this primacy in different ways; by appealing to the most important shared understandings, the most stringent demands of Nature or God, the conduciveness of justice to utility or civil peace, or the role of justice in providing a fair framework for the pursuit of different conceptions of the good. But all agree that, where justice conflicts with other values, those other values must give way.

This consensus has been challenged on the grounds that under ideal conditions justice would be unnecessary, and appeals to it would actually destroy valuable social relationships. Thus, a marriage in which the spouses were constantly arguing in terms of rights and duties would be less good than one in which mutual love created spontaneous harmony. By an extension of this sentimental line of thought, an ideal community would be one in which justice had been transcended by a spirit of what used to be called (until feminist scholars objected) fraternity. This is one strand in the thought of Marx, and it recurs in the work of some contemporary feminist and communitarian writers (see COMMUNITY AND COMMUNITARIANISM; FEMINIST POLITICAL PHILOSOPHY §4).

The theorists of justice discussed above would not necessarily dispute such claims. Both Hume and Rawls argued that there are 'circumstances of justice' that make justice necessary. These are precisely the conditions – conflicting demands for material goods and unreconcilable aspirations – that the critics of justice believe would be transcended by a sufficiently strong community spirit. The disagreement is not analytical but turns on the view taken of the possibility and the desirability of creating a community in which justice ceased to be the first virtue. The partisans of justice can point out that the theoretical assault on 'bourgeois morality' has provided the supposed justification for the most appalling violations of rights (for example, in China, Cambodia and the former USSR), and ask if there is any reason to suppose that other social experiments driven by the same animus would be any more benign.

References and further reading

Aristotle (*c*.mid 4th century BC) *Nichomachean Ethics*, trans. D. Ross, revised J.L. Ackrill and J.O. Urmson, Oxford: Oxford University Press, 1980. (Famous discussion of ethics. Book V contains an extended analysis of justice including its division into distributive and rectificatory.)

* Barry, B. (1995) *Justice as Impartiality*, vol. 2, *A Treatise on Social Justice*, Oxford: Clarendon Press. (Author's work. Develops the approach introduced by Scanlon and also contains useful discussions of justice as mutual advantage and of Rawls' theory. Referred to in § 4 and 5.)

* Cicero, M.T. (*c*.54–51 BC) *De Re Publica*, trans. C.W. Keyes, Cambridge, MA: Harvard University Press and London: Heinemann, 1928. (Parallel Latin text and English translation. Important statement of neo-Stoic and natural law theory. Referred to in §3.)

D'Entrèves, A.P. (ed.) (1948) *Aquinas: Selected Political Writings*, Oxford: Blackwell. (Standard English edition of Aquinas' political theory, relevant to the natural law position discussed in §3.)

* Dworkin, R. (1981) 'What is Equality? Part 1: Equality of Welfare; Part 2: Equality of Resources', *Philosophy and Public Affairs* 10 (3 and 4): 185–246, 283–345. (Quite difficult discussion of whether equal treatment requires equality of welfare or of resources. Also contains Dworkin's theory of justice referred to in §5.)

* Gauthier, D. (1986) *Morals By Agreement*, Oxford: Clarendon Press. (Modern neo-Hobbesian account of justice as mutual advantage. Referred to in §4.)

* Hirsch, A. von (1990) 'Proportionality in the Philosophy of Punishment: From "Why Punish?" to "How Much?"', *Criminal Law Forum* 1 (Winter): 259–90. (Referred to in §1.)

* Hobbes, T. (1651) *Leviathan*, ed. R. Tuck, Cambridge: Cambridge University Press, 1991. (Referred to in §4.)

* Hume, D. (1739–40) *A Treatise of Human Nature*, ed. L.A. Selby-Bigge, Oxford: Clarendon Press, 1978. (Referred to in §3. See especially Book 3 Part 2 for a discussion of justice.)

—— (1748 and 1751) *Enquiries Concerning Human Understanding and Concerning the Principles of Morals*, ed. L.A. Selby-Bigge, Oxford: Clarendon Press, 1975. (Published originally as two works, hence the dates.)

* Kymlicka, W. (1990) *Contemporary Political Philosophy: An Introduction*, Oxford: Clarendon Press. (Very useful introductory work covering many of the positions dealt with here. Referred to in §5.)

Marx, K. and Engels, F. (1968) *Marx/Engels: Selected Works in One Volume*, London: Lawrence & Wishart. (Contains extracts of many of Marx's most famous tracts. For a denunciation of the whole idea of justice see the 'Critique of the Gotha Programme', 311–31.)

* Mill, J.S. (1861) 'Utilitarianism', *Collected Works of John Stuart Mill*, vol. X, *Essays on Ethics, Religion and Society*, ed. J.M. Robson, Toronto: University of Toronto Press, 1969. (Discussion of utilitarianism. Chapter V contains the argument for a utilitarian theory of justice referred to in §3.)

* Nagel, T. (1991) *Equality and Partiality*, New York: Oxford University Press. (Referred to in §5.)

Noddings, N. (1984) *Caring: A Feminine Approach to Ethics and Moral Education*, Berkeley, CA: University of California Press. (Leading feminist theorist who argues for the replacing of the ethic of justice with an ethic of care.)

* Nozick, R. (1974) *Anarchy, State, And Utopia*, New York: Basic Books. (Discussed in §5.)

* Plato (*c*.380–367 BC) *Republic*, trans. R. Waterfield, Oxford: Oxford University Press, 1993. (Classic discussion of justice. Book 1 is referred to in §2.)

* Rawls, J.B. (1971) *A Theory of Justice*, Cambridge, MA: Harvard University Press. (Discussed in §5.)

* —— (1993) *Political Liberalism*, New York: Columbia University Press. (Rawls' revised theory, referred to in §5.)

* Rousseau, J.-J. (1755) *A Discourse on Inequality*, trans. M. Cranston, Harmondsworth: Penguin, 1984. (Referred to in §4.)

Sandel, M.J. (1982) *Liberalism and the Limits of Justice*, Cambridge: Cambridge University Press. (A communitarian critique of Rawls and of the centrality of justice.)

* Scanlon, T.M. (1982) 'Contractualism and Utilitarianism', in A. Sen and B. Williams (eds) *Utilitarianism and Beyond*, Cambridge: Cambridge University Press, 103–28. (Discussed in §5.)

* —— (1988) 'The Significance of Choice', in S.M. McMurrin (ed.) *The Tanner Lectures on Human Values*, vol. 8, Salt Lake City, UT: University of Utah Press, 151–216. (Referred to in §5.)

Waldron, J. (ed.) (1987) *Nonsense on Stilts*, London: Methuen. (Reprints some attacks on rights and contains a valuable discussion of these critiques by Waldron.)

* Walzer, M. (1983) *Spheres of Justice: A Defence of Pluralism and Equality*, New York: Basic Books; London and Oxford: Blackwell. (Discussed in §2.)

BRIAN BARRY
MATT MATRAVERS

JUSTICE, EQUITY AND LAW

Laws are intended to achieve justice, but the application of an otherwise just law may yield an injustice in the circumstances of a particular case. This is because laws are framed in terms of general rules which cannot adequately provide in advance for all possible variations in relevant circumstances. Equity modifies the rigid application of the law in such cases in order to secure justice in the light of all the relevant circumstances. So, in Aquinas' example, the law may justly require the closure of the city gates after a certain hour, but officials may equitably decree the opening of the gates during the legal hours of closure in order to save fighters defending the city who are being pursued by an enemy. In this sense, the equitable decision is not distinct from justice, but rather secures justice in the particular case by remedying the deficiencies of positive law retrospectively at the point of application. The question of the proper relationship between justice, equity and law has been explored both by a rich philosophical tradition that finds its classic statement in the writings of Aristotle, and by the world's major legal traditions.

At least two major problems arise for this complex of ideas. First, that of the 'decadence' of equity. As equity is incorporated into formal processes of legal adjudication, for instance in the form of 'maxims' of equity or equitable 'doctrines', it comes to acquire the generality of positive law. This creates the problem that the so-called equitable maxims or doctrines may themselves then be applied in a strict way that leads to injustice in the particular case, which is precisely the problem equity is meant to remedy. Second, in securing justice by the deployment of discretion in the particular case equity also threatens an injustice. For it seems to involve a departure from the principle of legality, that is, the duty to apply pre-existing laws declared beforehand to those subject to them. In being adversely affected by the retrospectively operative discretion of the adjudicator, the party who would have benefited from the strict application of the law may regard the resort to equity as itself unjust.

1 **Positive law and justice**
2 **Equity between law and justice**
3 **Contemporary influence**
4 **The 'systematization' and 'decadence' of equity**
5 **The conflict with legality**
6 **Responses to the conflict**

1 Positive law and justice

A fundamental objective of positive law is widely thought to be that of achieving justice. Even contemporary legal positivists hold that it is an essential feature of law that it claims to conform with precepts of justice (see LEGAL POSITIVISM §4). In its broadest sense, justice refers to those moral requirements that apply in any interpersonal context. It is that part of morality that governs the relations and interactions between morally significant beings. It is in this vein that John Rawls refers to an abstract *concept* of justice – understood as a 'set of principles for assigning rights and duties and for determining...a proper distribution of the benefits and burdens of social cooperation' (Rawls 1971: 5) – that is shared by most people who engage in discourse about justice, but regarding which there may be vastly divergent and competing specific interpretations or *conceptions*.

However justice is understood, it is a further widely held belief that positive laws may fail to achieve justice. Those who deny the moral fallibility of law are the proponents of a rarely held version of normative ethical relativism, according to which the laws of one's community are always just or according to which justice is to be identified with the standards enshrined in those laws. But this sort of relativism conflicts with the pervasive fact that people do submit laws to critical scrutiny in terms of independent standards of justice and often intelligibly purport to find those laws to be unjust for breaching those standards.

Given that positive laws are morally fallible, injustice can arise in various ways (Finnis 1980: 352–4). The lawmaker may have been motivated by improper considerations; the law may have been made outside the scope of the lawmaker's authority; the law may have been enacted in contravention of the formal requirements of the rule of law, for example, publicity, generality, prospectivity, and so on; and, finally, the law may be substantively unjust, because it posits a morally defective assignment of rights and duties or benefits and burdens.

2   Equity between law and justice

The study of the relationship between justice, equity and law belongs in a normative theory of legal adjudication (see LEGAL REASONING AND INTERPRETATION). This is concerned with articulating the nature of ethically sound legal adjudication. One of its central aims is to determine whether and how a judge or other legal decision-maker may rely on the deliverances of their sense of justice in order to adjust, or depart from, the strict application of a law to avoid doing injustice in the circumstances of a particular case. It is in responding to this question that the nexus between justice, equity and law has been invoked, both by an illustrious philosophical tradition and by the world's major legal systems.

Equity is a form of judgment that remedies the injustice of positive law at the point of application by attending to the particular features of the persons and circumstances involved. Thus, equity is not concerned with defects in intention, author and form or with the substantive injustice of the general rule itself. Even if a positive law avoids these kinds of injustice it may still yield a result that is substantively unjust when it is applied to a particular set of facts. The source of the injustice is the inherent generality of legal rules. We can trace the philosophical elaboration of the idea of equity back to ancient Greece. The canonical text is Aristotle's *Nicomachean Ethics*, especially Book V, as supplemented by his discussion in the *The Art of Rhetoric*, although Aristotle's account is prefigured in earlier writings both literary and philosophical, for example by Plato (see ARISTOTLE; PLATO).

For Aristotle justice, both as an individual virtue and as an ordering of social life, is only possible within the context of the institutional arrangements, especially the laws, of a political community. He attributes three general characteristics to laws (see Yack 1993: 180–4). First, laws are expressed in the form of general rules intended to apply to an indefinite multiplicity of future situations. This is what distinguishes them from decrees (*psephismata*) about specific individuals and circumstances. Second, they apply to all members of the political community, including its leaders. Third, laws originate in the practical wisdom (*phronēsis*) of individuals and communities. The latter feature does not mean that laws are inherently good or just, but rather that they represent a fallible attempt on the part of humans' practical reason to cope with the problems of establishing a morally sound ordering of social life.

Aristotle introduces his analysis of equity (*epieikeia*) by means of an apparent paradox: equity seems neither the same as justice nor different from it in kind. On the one hand, we regard equity as a praiseworthy quality in both individuals and judgments. But it seems odd to value the equitable if it does not coincide with the just. Hence the dilemma: either we must cease regarding the just or the equitable as good; or, if they are both good, we must regard them as identical. Aristotle's solution is to define equity as a kind of justice, but a kind that is superior to and often opposed to another kind, strict legal justice. So, equity is not generically different from justice. But it is ideal justice – taking into account all the relevant circumstances of a given case – as opposed to justice strictly according to law.

The need for equity arises because the law is framed in general rules that apply prospectively to a vast number of future situations picked out by their general features. Only the general features thus identified (for example, regarding the type of person to which the rule applies, the type of activity it regulates, and so on) are relevant to the application of the rule. These comprise the only material facts to be taken into account in applying the rule, with all other facts being ignored. But, when applied to a particular situation in accordance with its terms, such a general rule may work an injustice. This will be either because the general rule is silent with respect to a particular situation, so that a just resolution is not secured, or because its application leads to an unjust result. This deficiency is not the fault of the lawmaker, but resides in the inherent variability of the circumstances of human life, which are such that the demands of practical wisdom (*phronēsis*) cannot be adequately captured in any set of general rules capable of a mechanical and unerring application.

In such cases equity justifies a departure from the strict letter of the legal rule, and a resort to its animating purpose or intention, in order to secure justice. Equity thus mediates between positive law and justice by importing an element of flexibility and context-sensitivity into legal adjudication. Hence the essential nature of equity as 'a rectification of law in so far as law is defective on account of its generality' (*Nicomachean Ethics* 1137b26–7; or 'right going beyond the written law', *The Art of Rhetoric* 1374a27–8).

The benefits of equity go beyond the attainment of justice in the particular case. On the one hand, equitable discretion admits into the adjudicative process ameliorative values such as mercy that mitigate the harshness of legal rules (see FORGIVE-NESS AND MERCY §3). The emergence of equity is therefore historically bound up with a heightened sensitivity to the plight of individuals, as opposed to an unbending concern with the maintenance of an impersonal moral order (Nussbaum 1993: 87–92). On the other hand, where the unforeseen situations to which equity responds reflect important changes in society generally, equity can be seen as a mechanism for the progressive and piecemeal adaptation of law to evolution in social conditions and moral belief. This reforming process is augmented by the tendency of the grounds on which equitable judgments are made to be 'systematized' into rules of positive law (see Maine 1930: 15).

It is clear that Aristotle regards equity as consti-tuting a general virtue of character that also operates outside the context of formal legal adjudication. The equitable person 'is not unduly insistent upon his rights, but accepts less than his share, although he has the law on his side' (*Nicomachean Ethics* 1137b34–1138a3; *The Art of Rhetoric* 128). He also differentiates crimes from errors and misfortunes,

since the latter are not a product of human wicked-ness; forgives human failings; judges actions in terms of the purposes of their agents and the entire context in which they occur; and recollects the good rather than the bad treatment they have received and endures being wronged. But the connection between equity and mercy is not yet fully established in Aristotle's analysis, for the latter can involve a leniency in assigning and exacting punishment that tempers the demands of particularized justice itself. Aristotle's concern is that such leniency may express an unacceptable self-depreciation in the face of injustices committed by others. A fuller elaboration of the connection between equity and mercy is, instead, given by the Roman Stoics (see STOICISM), especially Seneca, and the medieval canonists.

3   Contemporary influence

Although Aristotle is the key figure in the equity tradition in philosophy, this general complex of ideas has a line of inheritance that includes the Greek and Roman Stoics, the Roman orators, St Thomas Aquinas and the medieval canonists and casuists. In contemporary jurisprudence, however, this tradition has been somewhat sidelined by a preoccupation with the logically prior question of whether in fact judges ever do, or should, possess discretion. There are, however, three contemporary movements which embody essential themes of the equity tradition. Despite their many differences, they are united by a rejection of the merely mechanical application of general legal rules as an adequate normative account of legal adjudication and by an emphasis on the need for sound legal reasoning to be attentive to the normative significance of the constituent features of the parti-cular case.

First, there is the neo-Aristotelian approach to legal reasoning (for example, Kronman 1993: Part 1). This portrays legal reasoning as a matter of Aristo-telian practical wisdom, a mode of judgment that implicates the character of the legal reasoner in response to the salient particularities of the situation they are adjudicating upon, and not as the expert manipulation of a body of legal norms in a merely 'technical' or 'scientific' fashion. More generally, the emergence of neo-Aristotelian theories of practical reasoning illustrates the same line of thought. These urge the inadequacy of a purely rule-bound concep-tion of practical reasoning – commonly associated with the Kantian and utilitarian traditions (see KANTIAN ETHICS; UTILITARIANISM) – and defend instead a model of practical reasoning as involving a quasi-perceptual appreciation of the normative de-mands generated by the particular context of agency and deliberation. Proponents of neo-Aristotelian theories of practical reasoning include John McDowell (1979), Martha Nussbaum, David Wiggins (1975–6) and Alasdair MacIntyre. The latter explicitly contends that Aristotle's account of the need for equity in purely legal contexts holds of practical life and reasoning in general (MacIntyre 1988: 120).

Second, the equity tradition resonates with key themes in feminist legal theory. For much feminist theory posits a stark opposition between a 'masculine' approach to legal reasoning, one that prizes the rigorous application of general rules that inevitably abstract from the rich complexity of concrete situations, and a 'feminine' approach that is highly particularistic, arriving at a judgment of substantive justice that reflects the totality of the circumstances (see Gilligan 1982). Feminist theory tends to employ this opposition in an antinomian way, privileging the substantive justice attainable through the exercise of unconstrained discretion over the idea of rule-following. Here it departs from the equity tradition, which views equitable discretion as a supplement to rule-governed reasoning in law (see FEMINIST JURISPRUDENCE).

Third, the 'law and literature' movement advances the reading and appreciation of literary texts as a model for legal adjudication. In the hands of one of its major exponents – Martha Nussbaum – the connection with the equity tradition is made central. Nussbaum stresses the importance Aristotle accords to *sungnome*, or 'judging with', in his analysis of equity. This is the sympathetic understanding of 'human things' which is tied up with the disposition to appraise actions in relation to the motives and intentions that animate them as well as the broader personal and social context in which they occur. Nussbaum associates this account of equitable judgment with Aristotle's theory of tragedy, which involves the spectator attending to the particular features of a tragic hero's narrative and, by doing so, sympathetically identifying with their plight. In Nussbaum's own analysis, however, the paradigmatic model of equitable judgment is not that of the spectatorship of tragic plays, but rather the sensitive reading of a novel, since the latter genre exceeds tragic drama in its formal commitment to 'following complex life histories, looking at the minute details of motive and intention and their social formation' (Nussbaum 1993: 105).

4 The 'systematization' and 'decadence' of equity

The equity tradition in philosophy has had an impact on the two major Western legal traditions: Roman law and English common law. Equity is recognized in Roman law in the distinction between *ius* (law) and *aequitas* (equity), in the Roman orators' maxim *summum ius summa iniuria* (extreme right is extreme injury), and, most importantly, in the role of the *praetor*, an official empowered to grant a remedy where no legal remedy previously existed by exercising an equitable discretion. But perhaps the most conspicuous attempt formally to incorporate the notion of the equitable mediation between legal rules and justice is provided by the English common law.

From the fifteenth century until the late nineteenth century the English legal system was unique in maintaining an institutional distinction between courts that administered the common law, and those that administered equity (since then the bifurcated system has been abolished, and all courts are empowered to apply both law and equity). The court dispensing equity – the Court of Chancery – dealt with petitions from those claiming that the common law system was not capable of achieving a just result in their particular case. Equity was viewed as supplementing the common law and remedying some of its imperfections by developing discretionary remedies to deal with situations where the rigorous application of common law rules would lead to an injustice. By the sixteenth century, the dominant justification for this sort of modification of the application of general legal rules in specific cases was sought in Aristotle's writings on equity.

As in the Roman case, a chief concern of English equity was to give effect to the substance of transactions, despite failures of legal form. This coheres with the Aristotelian notion that equity looks to the substance of the law and to the intentions of the parties. So, for example, the Court of Chancery could relieve a party from meeting a legal requirement that a contract be put in writing if it would be against conscience for the other party to rely on the lack of writing, for example, when the first party has already carried out his part of the bargain. Equity also recognizes that the common law remedy for breach of contract – monetary damages – does not yield a just result in certain cases, and allows for an order that the contract be performed specifically. Similarly, equity intervened in other situations where strict reliance on legal rules was productive of injustice: for example, where there is fraud or mistake in formal transactions, to protect people incapable of looking after their own interests, or to protect relationships of trust and confidence. In addition to these doctrines, a number of principles were formulated – 'maxims of equity' – to underwrite and justify the use of equitable discretion, for example, 'he who comes to equity must have clean hands', 'equity regards the substance and not the form', 'equity is equality'.

With the systematization of equity into doctrines – such as that of specific performance, trusts and so on – and maxims that came to have the force of general rules of law, the Court of Chancery in turn came to be almost as rule-bound in its activities as the common law courts. Equity thereby ceased to be – as on the Aristotelian model – a discretionary modification of the application of legal rules in response to the particular circumstances of the case, and became instead a separate body of law itself expressible in general rules.

But with this systematization there arises the danger of what Roscoe Pound called 'the decadence of equity' (Pound 1905: 25). As equity becomes a system of legal rules, those rules are susceptible to being applied in a strict way that leads to injustice in the particular case, which is precisely the problem equity was meant to remedy. Pound's prescription was not to resist systematization, but rather to adopt an attitude of vigilance (see POUND, R.).

5   The conflict with legality

The idea of equity as a discretionary rectification of positive law at the point of application in the interests of substantive justice has, however, been subjected to a number of criticisms (see Lucas 1966: 214–22). Most of these come down to the objection that equity conflicts with the principle of legality. This is a normative principle requiring adjudicators to resolve disputes by applying legal rules that have been declared beforehand, and not to alter the legal situation retrospectively by discretionary departures from established law. The principle of legality, therefore, provides a basis for claiming that the deployment of equitable discretion, although intended to secure justice in the particular case, in fact produces injustice to the party adversely affected by it. But whence derives the normative force of the principle of legality itself?

Most importantly, it derives from the fact that it expresses a requirement of the rule of law as it bears on adjudicators (see RULE OF LAW (RECHTSSTAAT)). The rule of law requires that people – including the legal officials of a state – be ruled by the law and obey it. But this whole ideal will be undercut if adjudicative bodies fail to apply pre-existing law in accordance with its clear and settled meaning. The sort of retrospective modification of pre-existing legal rules that is authorized by equity threatens this principle. The rule of law itself is upheld because it secures a number of central values. First, it achieves certainty and predictability in legal administration, so that people will know to what laws (and, in particular, what legal penalties) they will be subject.

This enables them to plan their affairs, which is itself a key manifestation of a form of 'negative' liberty. Second, it protects human dignity. General legal rules create rational expectations among those subject to them. For an adjudicator to frustrate those expectations retrospectively seems akin – as Bentham argued – to the arbitrary way in which a man makes law for his dog: not declaring beforehand what conduct is required but rather waiting until the animal has done something he thinks wrong, and beating it. That equity is in tension with the rule of law, that its essentially discretionary and retrospective character imports an unacceptable element of uncertainty and arbitrariness into the legal system, is a common complaint, one expressed famously in the English legal context by the jibe that equity varied with the length of the Lord Chancellor's foot.

It is the attraction of the principle of legality which explains in large part the tendency to crystallize the grounds of equitable intervention into general legal rules, which in turn leads to the problem of the 'decadence' of equity mentioned above. More generally, it seems that we are confronted here with a conflict between 'formal' legal justice (which may be expressed in the injunction to 'treat like cases alike', where the criterion of likeness is determined by features picked out in advance by general legal rules) and 'substantive' justice in the particular case, which is the concern of equity. The sense of a clash between basic values is heightened by the realization that the 'generality' of legal rules – which is the structural source of the injustice that equity is meant to correct – is itself a requirement of the rule of law as it bears on the activities of legislatures (disallowing Acts of Attainder, for example).

6   Responses to the conflict

The classical equity tradition does not provide us with a ready response to such criticisms, mainly because the rule of law (in its connection with certainty and autonomy, at least) is a distinctively modern value that did not have a prominent role in the classical tradition represented by Aristotle and Aquinas. However, a response to such criticism might be to argue that the notion of equity can be understood as grounded in existing law, and therefore not discretionary in any way that seriously impugns the rule of law. There are at least two versions of this reply.

First, it might be claimed that in dispensing equity, the adjudicator is not departing from existing law nor making new law, but rather complying with the intention (as opposed to the letter) of existing law, which is its true meaning. This in fact is Aristotle's construal: the equitable adjudicator decides the case as the legislator would have decided it had he been aware of those particular circumstances. This response suffers from two main defects. On the one hand, it may be unworkable, given that it may not be possible to find any, or the right kind of, underlying legislative intention in a given case. In particular, all the serious difficulties involved in constructing a counterfactual intention arise here. On the other hand, to seek to avoid this problem through a presumption that legislators always intend to secure justice is to fall into vacuity, for what will then be at work will be a discretionary judgment dressed up as the realization of the legislator's intention.

The second version holds that the equity is grounded in ethical principles which are part of the law. One might here deploy Dworkin's theory of adjudication, according to which judges must strive to identify the set of ethical principles that provide the best interpretation of the back letter legal rules (Dworkin 1977). These principles are for Dworkin part of the law, and yield a single right answer in each case, thus eliminating the need for extra-legal discretion (see DWORKIN, R.). But again there are at least two problems. First, if they are part of the law, it is not at all clear that these principles really perform the classic function ascribed to equity. Indeed, the principles to which Dworkin refers are not usually thought of as equitable but rather as expressing the rationale behind a series of more particular rules, and hence legitimately controlling the application of those rules in particular cases. Second, in so far as principles are legal standards with a determinate content, they fall victim to the possibility of the 'decadence' of equity.

A more promising line of response is to reject the demand to make an all-or-nothing choice between legality and equity (formal justice and substantive justice, rule and discretion) as posing a false dilemma. What is needed in any ethically sound legal system is an appropriate mix of both of these values, not a decision single-mindedly to pursue one at the complete expense of the other. Indeed, the equity tradition conceives of equity as a crucial supplement and corrective to legality in certain circumstances, not something that licenses the substitution of an unfettered and arbitrary discretion for the application of legal rules. Further, combining both legality and equity, rule and discretion, in a legal system seems practically unavoidable. This is because the idea of pure legality, of a legal code so determinate in its meaning that it calls for no discretionary judgment on the part of the adjudicator, seems illusory. The leeway for discretion will

arise from at least two sources, in addition to the source (generality) already mentioned as giving rise to equity. These are: (1) indeterminacy in the interpretation of rules; and (2) indeterminacy in the proper characterization of the fact situation to which it will apply (see Lucas 1966: 24–5).

What is more difficult to ascertain is how the institutional balance between legality and equity is to be rightly struck. There is no reason to believe that there is a single best solution to this problem. But the equity tradition as discussed here does offer guidance on the reasonable solution in concrete circumstances (see Tasioulas 1996: 462–6); the rule of law tradition and the equity tradition need to be read together and held in balance.

See also: JUSTICE; LAW, PHILOSOPHY OF

References and further reading

Aquinas, T. (1266–73) Law and Political Theory, in *Summa theologiae*, vol. 28, IaIIae 90–97, London: Eyre and Spottiswoode, 1966.

* Aristotle (c. mid 4th century BC) *Nicomachean Ethics*, trans. J.A.K. Thomson and revised with notes and appendices H. Tredennick, Harmondsworth: Penguin, 1976. (Canonical text, especially Book V, on the idea of equity.)

* —— (c. mid 4th century BC) *The Art of Rhetoric*, trans. with intro. and notes H. Lawson-Tancred, Harmondsworth: Penguin, 1991. (Supplement to Aristotle's discussion of equity in *Nicomachean Ethics*.)

* Dworkin, R.M. (1977) *Taking Rights Seriously*, London: Duckworth. (Chapter 2 contains a classic exposition of the role of principles in legal reasoning.)

* Finnis, J. (1980) *Natural Law and Natural Rights*, Oxford: Clarendon Press. (A major contemporary restatement of natural law theory.)

* Gilligan, C. (1982) *In a Different Voice: Psychological Theory and Women's Development*, Cambridge, MA: Harvard University Press. (Extremely influential psychological analysis of gender differences in ethical reasoning.)

* Kronman, A.T. (1993) *The Lost Lawyer: Failing Ideals of the Legal Profession*, Cambridge, MA: Harvard University Press. (Presents a neo-Aristotelian approach to legal reasoning.)

* Lucas, J. (1966) *The Principles of Politics*, Oxford: Oxford University Press. (A very effective discussion of the inter relations of justice, equity and law.)

* McDowell, J. (1979) 'Virtue and Reason', *The Monist* 62: 331–50. (Defends an Aristotelian approach to practical reasoning.)

* MacIntyre, A. (1988) *Whose Justice? Which Rationality?*, Notre Dame, IN: University of Notre Dame Press. (Defends a broadly Aristotelian-Thomistic approach to practical reason and justice.)

* Maine, H.S. (1930) *Ancient Law: Its Connection with the Early History of Society and its Relation to Modern Ideas*, ed. F. Pollock, London: John Murray. (Chapters 2 and 3 contain a classic account of the history and social function of equity.)

Newman, R.A. (1973) *Equity in the World's Legal Systems: A Comparative Study*, ed. R.A. Newman, Brussels: Établissements Émile Bruylant. (Contains an exhaustive historical and comparative survey of the role of equity in the world's major legal systems.)

Nussbaum, M. (1990) 'The Discernment of Perception: An Aristotelian Conception of Private and Public Rationality', in *Love's Knowledge: Essays on Philosophy and Literature*, Oxford: Oxford University Press. (Defends an Aristotelian conception of practical rationality as involving 'perception' of what is rationally required in particular situations.)

* —— (1993) 'Equity and Mercy', *Philosophy and Public Affairs* 22: 83–125. (A discussion of the classical roots of the equity tradition and of its contemporary relevance, from the point of view of both neo-Aristotelianism and the law and literature movement.)

* Pound, R. (1905) 'The Decadence of Equity', *Columbia Law Review* 5: 20–35. (Relates to the discussion of 'decadence' in §4.)

—— (1954) *An Introduction to the Philosophy of Law*, New Haven, CT: Yale University Press. (Chapter 3 is particularly effective in stressing how the appropriateness of equitable judgment varies according to the area of law in question.)

* Rawls, J. (1971) *A Theory of Justice*, Oxford: Oxford University Press. (The classic contemporary discussion of justice.)

Stein, P. and Shand, J. (1974) *Legal Values in Western Society*, Edinburgh: Edinburgh University Press. (Chapters 3 and 4 present a general account of justice, equity and law with illuminating legal illustrations.)

* Tasioulas, J. (1996) 'The Paradox of Equity', *Cambridge Law Journal* 55: 456–69. (See discussion §6.)

* Wiggins, D. (1975–6) 'Deliberation and Practical Reason', *Proceedings of the Aristotelian Society* 76: 29–51. (Defends an Aristotelian account of practical reason.)

* Yack, B. (1993) *The Problems of a Political Animal: Community, Justice, and Conflict in Aristotelian Political Thought*, Berkeley, CA: University of California Press. (Chapters 5–6 are a vigorous presentation of the Aristotelian understanding of justice, equity and law that distances it from the concerns of classical natural law theory.)

JOHN TASIOULAS

JUSTICE, INTERNATIONAL

Although it has been denied (by, for example, F.A. Hayek 1976) that the concept of distributive justice has application within states, it is not controversial that there can be unjust laws and unjust behaviour by individuals and organizations. It has, however, been argued that it makes no sense to speak of justice and injustice beyond the boundaries of states, either because the lack of an international sovereign entails that the conditions for justice do not exist, or because the state constitutes the maximal moral community. Both arguments are flawed. Without them, we are naturally led to ask what are the implications of the widely-held idea of fundamental human equality, the belief that in some sense human beings are of equal value. This cannot be coherently deployed in a way that restricts its application to within-state relations. In either a utilitarian or Kantian form it generates extensive international obligations. An objection that is often made to this conclusion is that the obligations derived are so stringent that compliance cannot reasonably be asked under current political conditions. But this shows (if true) that current political conditions are incompatible with international justice.

1   The scope of international justice
2   Scepticism about international justice
3   Cosmopolitan justice
4   Problems with cosmopolitan justice

1   The scope of international justice

In its most literal sense, 'international justice' refers to justice between nations – 'nations' in this context being equivalent to 'states', as in 'international law', 'national sovereignty', and so on. Following common usage in political philosophy, it will here be understood in a more extended sense. In this sense, 'international justice' refers to justice in any context other than that of the purely internal affairs of a state.

It is possible that an inquiry into international justice will yield the conclusion that justice can be predicated properly only of relations between states. But formulating the scope of the inquiry in this way leaves open a variety of other possibilities. Thus, for example, it may be concluded that states have obligations of justice to individuals outside their borders (for example, to give asylum), that individuals have obligations of justice to states other than their own (for example, not to engage in terrorism), and that international organizations, transnational corporations and collective actors other than states have obligations of justice that should constrain their behaviour. The conclusion may also be that a world organized into states is inherently incapable of satisfying the demands of justice, and that only a single worldwide state holds out any possibility of realizing global justice.

2 Scepticism about international justice

International justice has in common with some other topics (for example, theology) the peculiarity that there is some controversy about the existence of its object. One reason for scepticism is that international agreements, including those setting up international organizations, are (in Hobbes' words) 'covenants without the sword'. However, granting the premise that the international arena is a Hobbesian 'state of nature' (see HOBBES, T.§6), it still does not follow that considerations of justice are irrelevant to it. We should bear in mind the conclusion that Hobbes himself drew from the insecurity of a 'state of nature': that a sovereign was needed to supply the security that would render it safe to keep covenants and thus ensure their validity. This, as Hobbes recognized, leaves the sovereigns in a 'state of nature' with one another. But a more thoroughgoing Hobbesian might plausibly derive the conclusion that the lack of an international sovereign threatens precisely the calamities that states were supposed to protect against: violent death in war and lack of the conditions of 'commodious living'. Even if the threat of war is receding, military expenditure diverts resources away from life-saving alternative uses. Moreover, the faltering international response to such issues as global warming and biodiversity may suggest that only international-level coercion is capable of maintaining the long-term conditions of life on the planet.

It is also worth recalling that, according to Hobbes, there can be obligations of justice even in a 'state of nature', since one of the 'laws of nature' is 'that men perform their covenants made' and justice consists in keeping covenants. Admittedly, the obligation is said to hold only when the other party has performed its part and there is no 'new cause of fear' arising subsequent to the making of the covenant. But this is enough to establish that, in general, states behave unjustly in reneging on an

international agreement that the other signatories have adhered to.

A second line of argument derives from the romantic nationalist movement of the nineteenth century. This assumes that each state is the home of a community whose members share a certain view of the world which gives meaning to their lives (see NATION AND NATIONALISM). In its strongest (and most logically coherent) form, this doctrine concludes that, since there is no moral community beyond the state, there is no basis for saying that anything a state does can be unjust. A weaker version (especially associated with Michael Walzer (1977)) maintains that the notion of distributive justice makes sense only within each community, since this consists in the distribution of each kind of good in accordance with the meaning that the community attributes to that good (see JUSTICE §2). Clearly, there is no global community with shared understandings of the meanings of goods, so it follows that the notion of distributive justice has no application outside a state.

An obvious objection to both versions is that scarcely any states are moral communities of the postulated sort. Moreover, many people do in fact have views (albeit often somewhat inchoate) about what international justice requires. It is not necessary to have very sophisticated ideas about the shared meanings of goods to arrive at the view that there is something fundamentally wrong with a world in which millions of people are starving to death and dying of easily preventable diseases while others are reduced to buying jewelled necklaces for their pets to find a way of disposing of their incomes.

3 Cosmopolitan justice

The American Declaration of Independence, the French Declaration of the Rights of Man and the Citizen and the Universal Declaration of Human Rights all proclaim the equal value of all human beings. The two main strands of modern moral philosophy, Kantianism and utilitarianism, are likewise based on an axiom of equal value: for Kant everyone is a participant in the 'kingdom of ends' and entitled to equal respect, while for Bentham 'everybody counts for one' in the sense that all units of utility are given the same weight regardless of the identity of their owners.

In practice, however, many philosophers operate as if the axiom's validity extended only to fellow citizens, and much popular discourse follows the same lines. Yet a universal principle cannot simply have its application arbitrarily truncated at a state boundary. In revulsion against this, it is tempting to adopt an equally absolutist cosmopolitan line, according to which each of us should regard ourselves as citizens of the world, with no special obligations to the fellow citizens of our own state. But if (see §2) justice entails keeping covenants, may we not be said to be bound to our fellow citizens by innumerable implicit covenants? If you have contributed throughout your adult life to the national system of social insurance, for example, you have a claim on your fellow citizens for support in old age or in the event of becoming disabled and incapable of working. Your co-nationals owe this to you in virtue of a formal system of mutual aid: they do not have the same obligation to somebody (perhaps equally deserving or needy) who has not participated in the scheme.

There is nothing in this which is inconsistent with cosmopolitanism, understood as the extension to all human beings of the axiom of fundamental equality. Utilitarians normally recognize that the universal good is likely to be most effectively pursued indirectly. Similarly, a Kantian can agree that an element of particularism may consistently be willed as a universal law. The limits of this particularism are, however, quite tightly drawn. The value of a family to its members depends on a certain material base: formal autonomy without adequate resources is a cruel cheat. In a similar way, the picture of a world in which people have special obligations to compatriots loses its moral attractiveness unless each country has enough material resources to provide at least the basic essentials in the way of food, shelter, sanitation and medical care to its inhabitants (see INTERNATIONAL RELATIONS, PHILOSOPHY OF §§3, 4).

A utilitarian will have little difficulty in recognizing that, however inefficient the transfer process might be, a situation in which the richest fifth of the world's population is sixty times better off than the poorest fifth must be one in which utility would be increased by a shift in resources. The Kantian legacy leaves more room for interpretation. All that can be said here is that contemporary neo-contractarianism seems naturally to lead to an equally pressing obligation to shift resources from the richest to the poorest countries. Thus, if we imagine people from everywhere in the world, ignorant of their personal identities, meeting in a Rawlsian 'original position' to choose principles of global justice, we must regard it as inconceivable that they would not seek to guard against suffering the fate of the majority of inhabitants of the poorest countries (see RAWLS, J. §1). And if we follow Thomas Scanlon's (1982) proposal that we ask what principles could not reasonably be rejected by people seeking agreement with others under conditions that ruled out the exercise of bargaining power, we would have to say that those from the poorest countries could reasonably reject principles giving rise to a world order that left so many living in degrading deprivation (see CONTRACTARIANISM; JUSTICE).

4 Problems with cosmopolitan justice

The absorptive capacities of poor countries set severe limits on the amount of global redistribution that would be possible. Nevertheless, let us suppose that cosmopolitan principles would require rich countries to transfer ten per cent of their incomes to poor ones. This would imply a tenfold increase in aid from the Scandinavian countries, and an increase of fifty times and more from the current laggards such as the UK and USA. It is widely assumed not only that this is 'politically infeasible' but that this infeasibility somehow casts doubt on either the premises or the reasoning process leading to the conclusion about what justice demands. Yet many countries must on the same criteria be judged grossly unjust domestically, and this is not normally felt to cast doubt on the conclusion. Is there any rationale for the difference in attitude?

Thomas NAGEL, in *Equality and Partiality*, has argued that lying behind the 'political infeasibility' is a moral consideration: that people in rich countries 'have sufficient reason to resist if they can' a 'radical drop in the standard of living of [themselves] and [their] famil[ies]' (1991: 174). Nagel denies that this reason amounts only to 'pure selfishness', but all he claims is that 'personal interests and commitments' are relevant (1991: 172). It is, however, hard to see how any morally compelling commitments could not be met with a modestly reduced standard of living, so 'personal interests' (that is, the unwillingness to do what is just) seems to be all that is left. Even if some commitments such as private schooling or a car as a graduation present had to be abandoned, it seems grotesque to mention this in the same breath as the plight of parents in poor countries who have to watch helplessly while their children die of diseases caused by malnutrition and lack of sanitation.

For Nagel, international redistribution does not create problems that are distinctive in principle: 'some poor countries such as India and Mexico have wealthy minorities' who can, apparently, equally legitimately resist redistribution (1991: 170). Other people, however, seem to regard the problem of international justice as different. A possible rationale might run as follows. States have a coercive apparatus at their command which *could* be used to bring about justice even if it is not so used and (given the constellation of political forces) is in many cases not likely to be so used. There is no international agency with the coercive power to create international justice, even under ideal political conditions. This means that moves towards international justice will require voluntary action by governments. We cannot reasonably expect the electorates of rich countries to vote for politicians who promise if elected to take steps to reduce their standard of living significantly. But if we cannot reasonably expect somebody to do something, we can scarcely mount a serious criticism of that person for not doing it. This must suggest that failing to do it is not appropriately described as unjust.

This argument is manifestly a close cousin of the Hobbesian one dissected in §2 in the link it makes between motivation, institutions and justice. As before, we can respond that the correct conclusion to draw is that justice requires appropriate coercive institutions. If domestic taxation were purely voluntary, it would no doubt be regarded as unreasonable to expect people to pay a large proportion of their incomes to the government, yet nobody thinks much of governments taking in over forty per cent of the national income for the provision of public services and cash benefits. If rich countries could be coerced by an international organization, there would, similarly, be no reason for a tax rate of, say, ten per cent to be regarded as extraordinary.

The absence of such a coercive institution has meant that the populations of rich countries have had little self-interested motivation to correct the situation. However, as Annette Baier has argued, 'people grow more reckless of the lives of others as their own lives become more wretched, insecure, and intolerable' (1991: 34). And while it would be better in every respect if rich countries acted under their own momentum to transfer resources to poor countries, the development and proliferation of devastating nuclear and (relatively portable) chemical and biological weapons means that not to do so 'may be not just inhumanity [but] *folly* if the excluded do feel resentment and have power to make it felt' (1991: 54; original emphasis).

References and further reading

* Baier, A. (1991) 'Violent Demonstrations', in R.G. Frey and C.W. Morris *Violence, Terrorism, and Justice*, Cambridge: Cambridge University Press, 33–58. (One of a several essays discussing the problem of terrorism; referred to in §4.)

Barry, B. (1989) *Theories of Justice*, vol. 1, *A Treatise on Social Justice*. Hemel Hempstead: Harvester Wheatsheaf, Berkeley and Los Angeles, CA: University of California Press, 183–9. (Discussion of Rawls, with special reference to international justice.)

—— (1995a) *Justice as Impartiality*, vol 2, *A Treatise on Social Justice*, Oxford: Clarendon Press. (Develops the approach introduced by Scanlon; see 67–72 for initial exposition.)

—— (1995b) 'Spherical Justice and Global Injustice', in D. Miller and M. Walzer (eds) *Pluralism, Justice, and Equality*, Oxford: Oxford University Press, 67–80. (Discussion of Walzer, including implications for international justice.)

Beitz, C. (1979) *Political Theory and International Relations*, Princeton, NJ: Princeton University Press, part III, 125–76. (Contains an argument for the global application of Rawls' 'difference principle', which prescribes making the worst-off group as well off as possible.)

Brown, C. (1992) *International Relations Theory: New Normative Approaches*, Hemel Hempstead: Harvester Wheatsheaf. (A lucid explanation of the 'liberal versus communitarian' theme in relation to international normative issues; good discussion of Kant and Hegel.)

Brown, C. (ed.) (1994) *Political Restructuring in Europe: Ethical Perspectives*, London: Routledge. (Part II, pp. 69–184, contains a useful and accessible cosmopolitan/anti-cosmopolitan debate, with contributions by O. O'Neill, T.W. Pogge, C.R. Beitz, D. Miller and C. Brown.)

* Hayek, F.A. (1976) *The Mirage of Social Justice*, vol. II, *Law, Legislation and Liberty*, Chicago, IL: University of Chicago Press. (Referred to at the beginning of the entry.)

* Hobbes, T. (1651) *Leviathan*, ed. R. Tuck, Cambridge: Cambridge University Press, 1991, ch. 13. (Justice in the 'state of nature', referred to in §2.)

Honderich, T. (1994) *Hierarchic Democracy and the Necessity of Civil Disobedience*, London: South Place Ethical Society. (The 69th Conway Memorial Lecture, this argues that the scale of inequality within and between countries demands civil disobedience and would justify violence if there were any prospect of its succeeding.)

* Nagel, T. (1991) *Equality and Partiality*, New York: Oxford University Press, ch. 15, 169–79. (Quoted in §4.)

O'Neill, O. (1986) *Faces of Hunger: An Essay on Poverty, Development and Justice*. London: George Allen & Unwin. (A Kantian argument for the redistribution of material resources.)

Pogge, T.W. (1989) *Realizing Rawls*, Ithaca, NY: Cornell University Press, part III, 211–80. (Discussion of possible international application of Rawls' principles.)

* Rawls, J. B. (1971) *A Theory of Justice*, Cambridge, MA: Harvard University Press, ch. 3, 118–92. (Sets

out the idea of an 'original position' mentioned in §3.)

* Rogers, P. (1995) 'Security Means More Now Than Defence'. Parliamentary Brief 3, no. 5: 30–1. (Makes the point about 'suitcase bombs' and their implications for the security of rich countries in line with the end of §4.)
* Scanlon, T.M. (1982) 'Contractualism and Utilitarianism', in A. Sen and B. Williams (eds) *Utilitarianism and Beyond*. Cambridge: Cambridge University Press, 103–28. (Discussed in §3.)
Shue, H. (1995) 'Avoidable Necessity: Global Warming, International Fairness and Alternative Energy', in I. Shapiro and J.W. DeCew *Theory and Practice*, NOMOS XXXVII. New York: New York University Press, 239–64. (To avoid potentially catastrophic global warming, sharp reductions in the emission of 'greenhouse gases' are required. What would be a fair distribution of the burden internationally, and how does 'political feasibility' enter in to it?)
Singer, P. (1972) 'Famine, Affluence and Morality', *Philosophy and Public Affairs* 1 (3): 229–43. (Famous article making a strong case on utilitarian premises for large-scale global redistribution.)
UNICEF (1992) *The State of the World's Children*, Oxford: Oxford University Press. (New editions each year; this one includes the estimate of global military expenditures in relation to the national incomes of poor countries given in §2.)
* Walzer, M. (1977) *Spheres of Justice: A Defense of Pluralism and Equality*. New York: Basic Books; Oxford: Blackwell. (This contains the theory of distributive justice associated with Walzer and discussed in §2.)

BRIAN BARRY
MATT MATRAVERS

JUSTIFICATION AND KNOWLEDGE, COHERENCE THEORY OF *see* KNOWLEDGE AND JUSTIFICATION, COHERENCE THEORY OF

JUSTIFICATION, EPISTEMIC

The term 'justification' belongs to a cluster of normative terms that also includes 'rational', 'reasonable' and 'warranted'. All these are commonly used in epistemology, but there is no generally agreed way of understanding them, nor is there even agreement as to whether they are synonymous. Some epistemologists employ them interchangeably; others distinguish among them. It is generally assumed, however, that belief is the target psychological state of these terms; epistemologists are concerned with what it takes for a belief to be justified, rational, reasonable or warranted. Propositions, statements, claims, hypotheses and theories are also said to be justified, but these uses are best understood as derivative; to say, for example, that a theory is justified for an individual is to say that were that individual to believe the theory (perhaps for the right reasons), the belief would be justified.

Historically, the two most important accounts of epistemic justification are foundationalism and coherentism. Foundationalists say that justification has a tiered structure; some beliefs are self-justifying, and other beliefs are justified in so far as they are supported by these basic beliefs. Coherentists deny that any beliefs are self-justifying and propose instead that beliefs are justified in so far as they belong to a system of beliefs that are mutually supportive. Most foundationalists and coherentists are internalists; they claim that the conditions that determine whether or not a belief is justified are primarily internal psychological conditions (for example, what beliefs and experiences one has). In the last quarter of the twentieth century, externalism emerged as an important alternative to internalism. Externalists argue that one cannot determine whether a belief is justified without looking at the believer's external environment. The most influential form of externalism is reliabilism.

Another challenge to traditional foundationalism and coherentism comes from probabilists, who argue that belief should not be treated as an all-or-nothing phenomenon: belief comes in degrees. Moreover, one's degrees of beliefs, construed as subjective probabilities, are justified only if they do not violate any of the axioms of the probability calculus. Another approach is proposed by those who advocate a naturalization of epistemology. They fault foundationalists, coherentists and probabilists for an overemphasis on a priori theorizing and a corresponding lack of concern with the practices and findings of science. The most radical naturalized epistemologists recommend that the traditional questions of epistemology be recast into forms that can be answered by science.

An important question to ask with respect to any approach to epistemology is, 'what implications does it have for scepticism?' Some accounts of epistemic justification preclude, while others do not preclude, one's beliefs being justified but mostly false. Another issue is the degree to which the beliefs of other people *affect what an individual is justified in believing. All theories of epistemic justification must find a way of acknowledging that much of what each of us knows derives from what others have told us. However, some epistemologists insist that the bulk of the history of epistemology is overly individualistic and that social conditions enter into questions of justification in a more fundamental way than standard accounts acknowledge.*

1   Epistemic and non-epistemic justification

Decisions, actions, policies, procedures, punishments, laws, rules and host of other things can be justified or unjustified. They are justified only if there are adequate reasons for them, and unjustified if there are not. Epistemic justification is concerned with the justification of beliefs, and hence with reasons for believing. However, being epistemically justified is not simply a matter of having adequate reasons for believing, since there can be reasons for believing a claim that are not epistemic. If I offer you a million dollars to believe that the earth is flat, I have given you a reason to have this belief, but it is not an epistemic reason. The most controversial use of this point was made by Pascal and James, each of whom argued that we have such reasons to believe in God (see JAMES, W. §4; PASCAL, B. §6).

A straightforward way to understand the distinction between epistemic and non-epistemic reasons for belief is in terms of the end, or goal, that the reason aims at promoting. If X is a valuable end and if bringing about Y increases the likelihood of X occurring then, all else being equal, one has a reason to bring about Y. Different kinds of reasons are distinguished in terms of different kinds of ends. If X is an economic end, one has an economic reason to engage in Y. If X has broader pragmatic value – it improves your health, enhances your friendships and so on – one has a more broadly pragmatic reason to engage in Y. Analogously, if X is epistemically valuable, one has an epistemic reason for Y (see REASONS FOR BELIEF).

The question of what makes a reason an epistemic reason thus reduces to the question of what constitutes an epistemic end. A commonly accepted answer is that an end is epistemic in so far as it is concerned with believing what is true and not believing what is false. Once epistemic reasons are distinguished from non-epistemic ones, a question arises as to whether the latter can ever override former in cases where the two conflict. W.K. Clifford (1879), arguing against William James, said that they can not, claiming that we have an absolute obligation to believe only that for which we have adequate evidence. This is a difficult position to defend, however. Suppose a catastrophe could be avoided by believing a claim for which there is little or no evidence – for example, a terrorist threatens to detonate a bomb that will kill thousands of people unless you somehow get yourself to believe that the earth is flat. Clifford is committed, implausibly, to saying that under such conditions you have an obligation not to believe that the earth is flat.

Although it may be possible for non-epistemic reasons for belief to override epistemic ones, it is also rare. One explanation of its rarity is that even if we become convinced that we have non-epistemic reasons to believe a claim, this is ordinarily not enough to prompt belief. By contrast, if we become convinced that there is good evidence (that is, good epistemic reasons) for a claim, we usually automatically come to believe it. This suggests that if we are to acquire beliefs for which we realize we lack adequate evidence, we may have to go to extraordinary lengths. For example, one might have to resort to post-hypnotic suggestion or some equally extreme measure. However, such measures will typically have unfortunate consequences, especially since beliefs cannot be altered in a piecemeal fashion. Believing the earth is flat, for instance, will involve dismissing as misleading or fabricated a huge amount of information that on the face of it indicates that the earth is spherical. Dismissing such information in turn will adversely affect the overall accuracy of one's belief system and with it the overall effectiveness of one's decision making, with the likely result that one will be less able to achieve one's goals in a wide variety of contexts. The lesson, then, is that except in the most unusual kinds of cases – the case of the terrorist, for example – the costs associated with an effort to get oneself to believe that for which one lacks adequate evidence will not be worth the effort. Thus, what we have reasons to believe all things considered – that is, when all our ends are taken into account – is usually identical with what we have epistemic reasons to believe.

2   Foundationalism and coherentism

According to foundationalists, epistemic justification has a hierarchical structure. Some beliefs are self-justifying and as such constitute one's evidence base. Others are justified only if they are appropriately supported by these basic beliefs. Foundationalists differ among themselves as to what conditions have to be met in order for a belief to be basic and what conditions have to be met in order for other beliefs to be appropriately supported by basic beliefs. The strictest versions of foundationalism require that a belief be infallible, indubitable or incorrigible if it is to be self-justifying. A belief is infallible if it is impossible to have the belief and for it to be false; a belief is indubitable if it is impossible to doubt whether it is true; and a belief is incorrigible if it is impossible to have good reasons for thinking it is false. The strictest versions of foundationalism also impose stringent constraints on the support relation, restricting it to logical implication and enumerative induction; a non-basic belief is justified only if it is implied or inductively supported by one's basic beliefs. Many of the most influential figures in the history of epistemology are strict foundationalists (for example, Descartes, Hume, Berkeley and Locke) as are many of the most important epistemologists in the twentieth century (for example, Russell, Ayer and Carnap).

Modest versions of foundationalism relax the requirements of justification. For a belief to be basic, it does not have to be infallible, indubitable or incorrigible, but it does have to be intrinsically probable; the fact that one has the belief must itself make it likely that the belief is true. Similarly, the support relation is broadened beyond logical implication and enumerative induction to include inferences to the best explanation and other support relations (see INFERENCE TO THE BEST EXPLANATION; THEORETICAL (EPISTEMIC) VIRTUES).

Another distinction is between those foundationalists who insist on objective conditions of justification and those who permit subjective conditions. For example, Foley (1993) argues that one's basic beliefs are those that are noncontroversial for one to use as evidence, given one's other beliefs and one's own deepest epistemic standards. He adds that one's other beliefs are justified in so far as one would agree on ideal reflection that one's basic beliefs make them probable. This is a version of foundationalism, but it is a subjective version.

For the foundationalist, the reigning metaphor for epistemology is that of a building whose foundation of basic beliefs supports additional stories of non-basic beliefs. For the coherentist, the reigning metaphor is that of a web made up of, and deriving its strength from, mutually supportive beliefs.

According to coherentists, the primary objects of justification are not individual beliefs but, rather, belief systems. A belief system is justified if its component beliefs cohere in an appropriate way.

Individual beliefs are justified by virtue of belonging to such a set of beliefs. Thus, for the coherentist, epistemic justification is a holistic notion rather than a hierarchical one. The picture is not of basic beliefs being intrinsically justified and then passing on their justification to other beliefs; it is, rather, of justification emerging when one's belief system hangs together, or coheres.

Nineteenth-century philosophers such as Hegel and Bradley were coherentists, and in the twentieth century it was critiques of foundationalism that led to a resurgence of coherentism. Especially influential was the work of Wilfrid SELLARS, who argued that no belief is self-justifying; beliefs can be justified only by appeal to other beliefs. Sellars was particularly forceful in his criticism of what he called the 'myth of the given', which is the notion that beliefs about our own sense experiences cannot be mistaken, since these experiences are directly presented, or given, to us.

It was then a small step from the claim that no belief is self-justifying to a coherence theory of epistemic justification. The step was made with the help of the observation that at least some beliefs are justified by reference to other beliefs that are themselves justified. This observation invites the question 'what justifies these latter beliefs?', and if the answer is 'still other justified beliefs', we can ask of the latter, 'what justifies them?' If pursued, this line of questioning suggests there are only three different ways of thinking about the structure of epistemic justification. The first is that there is an infinite regress of justifiers. Belief A is justified by belief B, B is justified by C and so on *ad infinitum*. However, most philosophers have thought that if there is no way to stop this regress, none of the early members of the series is justified and scepticism is the result; nothing is epistemically justified (see SCEPTICISM). A second option is the one endorsed by foundationalists; belief A is justified by belief B, B by C and so on until a self-justifying belief ends the regress. The critiques of Sellars and others caused many to reject this second option, and thus they seemed to be left with no option but to endorse circular justification of some sort. Belief A is justified by belief B, B by C and so on until we reach a belief that is justified by A and other beliefs early in the series. In other words, the set of beliefs is mutually supportive, with belief A being justified by beliefs that A itself helps to justify.

Coherence among beliefs is at least a matter of consistency. If a set of beliefs is inconsistent, it is impossible for all the beliefs in the set to be true, and hence they are not mutually supportive. However, consistency is not enough for coherence; beliefs that are altogether unrelated to one another are consistent, but they are not mutually supportive. Some coherentists, F.H. BRADLEY for example, suggest that mutual entailment is required for coherence; every member of a coherent set should be deducible from other members of the set. However, most coherentists propose far less stringent conditions. BonJour (1985), for example, thinks of coherence as more than mere consistency but less than mutual entailment; it comes in degrees, with the degree increasing with the number of inferential connections among the component beliefs of the set and decreasing with the number of unexplained anomalies.

An objection to coherentism is that even the minimal condition of coherence – namely, consistency – is not an absolutely necessary condition of justification. It is ordinarily epistemically desirable to avoid inconsistency, but sometimes the costs are too high. The case of the lottery can be used to illustrate this.

Imagine a lottery of a million tickets, and suppose you are justified in believing that the lottery is fair and as such has only one winning ticket. Suppose also you have no reason to distinguish among the tickets concerning their chances of winning. So, the probability of ticket number 1 losing is .999999, the probability of ticket number 2 losing is .999999, and similarly for each of the other tickets. Thus, you have extraordinarily strong reasons to believe of ticket number 1 that it will not win, and accordingly it seems that you are justified in believing this. If we deny that you are justified, we will be hard-pressed to claim that very many of your other beliefs are justified, since the chances of their being in error are at least as great. However, your position with respect to ticket number 2, ticket number 3 and right through to ticket number 1,000,000 is the same as your position with respect to ticket number 1. So, if you are justified in believing that number 1 will lose, it seems that you are justified in believing this of each of the other individual tickets as well. But then, if you also justifiably believe that one ticket (you know not which) will win, you have justified but inconsistent beliefs. Hence, consistency is not an absolutely necessary condition of epistemic justification, contrary to what coherentists claim (see PARADOXES, EPISTEMIC §1).

3 Internalism and externalism

Most foundationalists and coherentists share a commitment to internalism. In its strongest form, internalism is the view that one can always determine by careful introspection whether one's beliefs are justified. A motivation for strong internalism – found in epistemologists as otherwise diverse as Descartes, Locke, Chisholm and BonJour – is that we have a *prima facie* duty to have epistemically justified beliefs.

If so, we are *prima facie* blameworthy if we have unjustified beliefs. But then, internalists argue, we must have access to the conditions that determine whether our beliefs are justified. Otherwise, we could do our epistemic best and hence be blameless but still have unjustified beliefs (see EPISTEMOLOGY AND ETHICS).

Modest internalism is any view that has epistemic justification supervening upon internal psychological conditions, whether or not these conditions are introspectively accessible to the believer. To say that epistemic justification supervenes on psychological conditions is to say that whenever a belief p is epistemically justified, there is a set of psychological properties β such that necessarily if one has β and believes p, then one's belief is justified (see SUPERVENIENCE).

A number of epistemologists (for example, BonJour 1985; Chisholm [1966] 1989; Foley 1993 and Lehrer 1974) propose conditions of epistemic justification that are internal psychological conditions but that are also complex enough for it to be implausible to think that we can always determine by introspection whether or not they obtain. Such epistemologists are best regarded as modest internalists. By contrast, externalists insist that some of the key prerequisites of epistemic justification obtain outside the skin of the believer, for example, those concerning the believer's environment, history or social context.

Externalist accounts of epistemic justification are encouraged by the presupposition that when epistemic justification is added to true belief, knowledge is the result if there are no Gettier problems present (see GETTIER PROBLEMS). Alvin Goldman (1986) is an especially instructive figure in this regard. He was one of the earliest champions of a reliabilist account of knowledge. According to reliabilists, one knows that p, at least in the simplest cases, if one has a true belief p that is the product of a generally reliable cognitive process (see RELIABILISM). With this account of knowledge in hand, Goldman argued that because epistemic justification is by definition that which has to be added to true belief to get knowledge, epistemic justification must essentially be a matter of one's beliefs having been produced by highly reliable cognitive processes. Since the reliability of a cognitive process is in part dependent on the external environment in which one is operating, this is an externalist account of epistemic justification.

Reliabilism is the most influential form of externalism, and the most influential reliabilists include Goldman, Dretske (1981), Armstrong (1973) and Sosa (1991). Despite their differences, these epistemologists share a commitment to the view that justification is basically a matter of there being a correct fit between one's environment on the one hand and one's cognitive processes and intellectual practices on the other, where a fit is correct if it has a tendency to produce true beliefs and not produce false beliefs. An offshoot of reliabilism is a view, championed by Alvin Plantinga (1992), that makes epistemic justification a matter of having beliefs that are the products of a properly functioning cognitive system, where a system is properly functioning if it is functioning in the way it was designed to function (either by natural selection or God) in the environment that it was designed for.

The disputes between internalists and externalists illustrate that the notion of epistemic justification is used by epistemologists in different senses. One way to determine how the notion is being used is to inquire whether the epistemologist is assuming that justification is by definition what has to be added to true belief in order to get a serious candidate for knowledge. Many externalists have been explicit about defining justification in this way. For others it is an implicit working assumption; if a proposed account of justification is such that justified true beliefs are not always good candidates for knowledge, the proposed account is for that reason inadequate. By contrast, many internalists understand justification in some independent way, leaving it an open question whether justification when added to true belief generates a serious candidate for knowledge.

Confusion can occur when epistemologists use the notion in more than one way. For example, they may want to think of epistemic justification in terms of what a responsible believer would believe and also in terms of what has to be added to true belief to get knowledge. Confusions of this sort are not entirely unexpected, given that some of the most influential figures in epistemology have thought that one and the same notion could capture both ideas. Descartes and Locke, for example, were concerned with what is involved in being a responsible believer, and each thought that this was in large part a matter of believing only that for which we have adequate (internal) evidence. However, they also thought that by being responsible believers, we can be assured of acquiring knowledge.

Few epistemologists are so sanguine any more, but the lesson is not that the one or the other aspect of Cartesian and Lockean projects have to be abandoned. The lesson, rather, is that there are different projects for epistemologists to pursue. One project, roughly put, is to explore what is required for us to put our own intellectual house in order. Another is to explore what is required for us to stand in a relation of knowledge to our environment. It is not unnatural to report the results of both kinds of exploration using the language of justification and rationality, given the history of these terms. But this means, in turn, that the terms have distinct senses, one tending to be externalist, objective and closely connected with knowledge, the other tending to be internalist, more subjective and closely connected with responsible believing.

4 Probabilism

Whereas reliabilism is an externalist alternative to traditional foundationalism and coherentism, probabilism is an internalist alternative. Probabilists note that one's doxastic options with respect to a proposition are not limited to believing it, disbelieving it or withholding judgment on it. Rather, one can have varying degrees of belief, or confidence, in the truth of a proposition. Probabilists often add that these degrees of belief can be represented as subjective probabilities, with a subjective probability of 1 representing maximum confidence in the truth of a proposition, a subjective probability of 0 representing no confidence in its truth, and the numbers in the interval $(0,1)$ representing degrees of confidence between the two extremes. Probabilists then argue that one's degrees of belief must be coherent if they are to be justified, and that they are coherent if they obey the probability calculus.

Consider some simple examples. According to the probability calculus, a proposition can be no more probable than a proposition it implies. Thus, if P implies Q and if one believes P with more confidence than Q, one's degrees of belief are incoherent and hence unjustified. Similarly, if P and Q are mutually exclusive propositions – that is, if it is not possible for both to be true – the probability of $(P$ or $Q)$ is equal to the probability of the first disjunct plus the probability of the second disjunct. Suppose, then, that one believes P with degree of confidence x, Q with degree of confidence y, and the disjunction $(P$ or $Q)$ with degree of confidence z. If $z \neq x + y$, one's degrees of belief are incoherent and as a result unjustified.

'Dutch book arguments' are sometimes used by probabilists to illustrate the undesirability of having incoherent degrees of belief. These arguments establish that if you are willing to post betting odds on the truth of propositions in accordance with your degrees of belief – for example, if you are twice as confident of the truth of P as you are of its negation, you are willing post 2:1 odds on the truth of P, giving an opponent the option of betting on P or against it – you will be vulnerable to having someone make a dutch book against you if your degrees of belief are incoherent. A dutch book is made against you when your opponent makes a series of bets such that you will suffer a net loss no matter how the events you are betting on turn out.

The most influential form of probabilism is Bayesianism, which proposes both an account of synchronic rationality (what is required for one's degrees of belief to be justified at any given moment) and also an account of diachronic rationality (what is required for one's degree of belief to change rationally over time). With respect to former, Bayesians insist on coherence. With respect to the latter, they insist that one should modify one's beliefs over time, in response to new information, in accordance with Bayes' Theorem (see PROBABILITY THEORY AND EPISTEMOLOGY).

One advantage of probabilism is that it sidesteps the lottery problem. Probabilists simply observe that it is rational to have a high degree of belief in the individual propositions in the lottery – that ticket number 1 will lose, that ticket number 2 will lose and so on – but an extremely low degree of confidence in the conjunction of these propositions, a conjunction that is equivalent to the proposition that no ticket will win. They are then free to leave the matter at that, without having to decide whether it is rational to believe *simpliciter* the individual propositions.

Nevertheless, the most persistent objection against probabilism is analogous to the objection that the lottery problem raises for traditional coherentism. Most generally expressed, the objection against traditional coherentism is that sometimes we can be justified in having beliefs that we know are less than ideally accurate. In particular, we can be justified in having beliefs that we know to be inconsistent and hence that we know cannot all be true. Similarly, we sometimes can be justified in having degrees of belief that we know are incoherent and hence cannot possibly reflect the objective probabilities. The clearest examples are non-contingent propositions, whose objective probability we know is either 1 or 0. For example, Goldbach's conjecture, which asserts that every even number can be expressed as the sum of two primes, is either necessarily true or necessarily false. If the former, it has an objective probability of 1, if the latter, it has an objective probability of 0. But since the conjecture has never been proven or disproven, we can be justified in having a degree of belief in the conjecture that is neither 1 nor 0.

5   Naturalized epistemology

Naturalized epistemology is the name given to a cluster of views that insist upon a close relationship between epistemology and the practices and findings of science. Naturalized epistemologists criticize foundationalists, coherentists and probabilists for their overemphasis on a priori theorizing. If we want to know how cognition actually works, why it is usually reliable, and when it has a tendency to go wrong, they say we need to turn to science. Psychology and neurobiology can tell us how cognition works; biology and especially evolutionary theory can provide us with an explanation as to why cognition is generally reliable; and cognitive psychology can give us information about the kinds of intellectual mistakes we have a tendency to make, so that we can guard against them.

Quine (1969) coined the phrase 'naturalized epistemology' and is one of its most influential proponents. In his most trenchant moments, he recommends that epistemology should become a chapter of psychology. This is to be accomplished by recasting the traditional questions of epistemology into forms that can be answered by psychology. For example, the question 'Does sensory experience give us good reasons to have beliefs about the external world?' is replaced with 'How do sensory experiences in fact cause us to believe what we do about the external world?'. The idea is to make epistemology a part of natural science and hence, in Quine's view, respectable.

In this radical form, naturalized epistemology threatens to become non-normative. It describes how a relatively restricted sensory input produces a rich array of beliefs, but it does not assess which procedures, methods and practices we are justified in using. Naturalized epistemologists, including Quine himself, have been eager to respond that they are not abandoning the normative element within epistemology. One response, emphasized by Alvin Goldman (1986), is that a naturalized approach to epistemology can coexist comfortably with a reliabilist account of epistemic justification. Epistemology, on this conception, is normative, since it tells us we are justified in employing an intellectual procedure, method or practice in so far as the practice is reliable; but it is also naturalized, since science that tells us which procedures, methods and practices are reliable.

6   Scepticism

One way of marking differences among various epistemological theories is to ask what, if anything, does the theory imply about radical sceptical hypotheses, which imply that most of one's beliefs are mistaken, not just in detail but seriously mistaken. For example, the evil demon hypothesis, which Descartes tried to refute, is that unknown to me I am under the control of a demon who is manipulating me and my environment in such a way that almost all my beliefs about the external world are false. Such hypotheses seem far-fetched, but they do illustrate in a dramatic way what seems to be a legitimate question, namely, whether or not our beliefs might be largely in error.

In so far as naturalized epistemologists feel free to bring the findings of science to their epistemologies, they are presupposing the falsity of such sceptical worries. By contrast, reliabilists can be neutral about sceptical hypotheses. They assert that our beliefs must be the products of reliable cognitive processes in order to be justified, but they need not take a stand on whether the cognitive processes we actually employ are reliable. Strong foundationalism purports to provide a refutation of sceptical hypotheses. Descartes, for example, thought that his method of doubt could establish with certainty a set of truths, including the existence of a benevolent and omnipotent God, which could then be used to disprove the evil demon hypothesis and other such sceptical hypotheses (see DESCARTES, R. §4). Modest versions of foundationalism are usually regarded as more plausible than Descartes' version, but they also provide correspondingly weaker responses to the sceptic. The same is true of coherentism; it is difficult to argue that it is altogether impossible for coherent beliefs to be drastically mistaken.

One stance to take towards sceptical worries, available to coherentists, moderate foundationalists and reliabilists alike, is to concede that it is part of our human intellectual predicament that such worries cannot be definitively banished; we have no choice but to live with them and the uncertainty they entail. It has proved difficult for epistemologists to be content with this uncertainty, and this in turn has motivated attempts to show that sceptical worries are self-referentially incoherent. The argument is that, in raising radical worries, would-be sceptics inevitably make use of the very intellectual faculties and methods about which they are raising doubts. In doing so, they are presupposing the general reliability of these faculties and methods. Hence, it is incoherent for them to entertain the idea that they might be unreliable. An objection against this anti-sceptical argument is that it fails to appreciate that the argumentative strategy of sceptics can be entirely negative. Their aim need not be to establish any positive thesis, not even the thesis that our faculties and methods are untrustworthy. Rather, their strategy can be to assume for the sake of argument that our favourite faculties, procedures and methods are reliable, and then to illustrate that these faculties, procedures and methods, if applied rigorously, will generate evidence that undermines their pretence of reliability.

Another anti-sceptical position is that sceptical hypotheses are metaphysically impossible. For example, Davidson (1986) argues that the nature of belief is such as to rule out the possibility that our beliefs are largely in error since, at least in the most simple cases, the objects of our beliefs are the causes of them. Hence, our beliefs must be largely true (see DAVIDSON, D.). In a similar spirit, Putnam (1987) argues that, in thinking about the world, it is impossible to separate our conceptual contributions from what is 'objectively there', and that plausible theories of reference and truth must acknowledge this impossibility. But in turn, Putnam says, this implies that the world cannot be entirely different from what our beliefs represent it to be (see PUTNAM, H.).

Such theories of truth, belief and reference are interesting and debatable as metaphysical positions, but for the purpose of laying sceptical worries to rest they are of limited value, especially since the intricate arguments used to defend these theories are themselves subject to sceptical doubts. Regardless of how we marshal our intellectual resources, there can be no non-question-begging assurances that the resulting inquiry is reliable, and this applies to metaphysical inquiries into the nature of truth, belief and reference as much it does to any other kind of inquiry.

7 Testimony and social epistemology

Another issue that marks differences among various approaches to epistemology is the degree to which the beliefs of other people enter into questions of what an individual is justified in believing. It is not seriously debatable that much of what each of us believes derives from others. So, all theories of epistemic justification must find a way to acknowledge the social interdependence of knowledge and justification. What separates epistemologists is how to do justice to this interdependence.

One way is to focus on the importance of testimony in our intellectual lives. A historically important approach to testimony, associated with Hume, claims that we all have good inductive reasons for thinking that others are reliable. Hence, we are generally justified in relying on what others tell us. There are at least two problems with this approach. First, it does not seem adequate to the breadth and depth of our dependence on others. As children, we acquire a huge set of beliefs from others, mostly without thought and long before we have the capacity to judge whether we have inductive reasons to trust them. Second, it is notoriously difficult to reconstruct the good inductive reasons we are supposed to have for trusting others. We rely on the testimony of strangers whose track record for truthfulness is unknown to us. Similarly, we rely of the opinions of experts in fields of inquiry about which we know so little that we are unable to verify reliability of the experts.

Another approach is to claim that we are always *prima facie* justified in accepting the testimony of others, even when we do not have good inductive reasons for trusting them. This approach is associated with Thomas Reid, who said that we all have a sense of credulity which disposes us to believe what others tell us. Reid regarded credulity as a cognitive faculty, analogous to vision, hearing, touch and memory. We are born with this faculty and, like other native cognitive faculties, we are justified in relying on it unless problems arise, that is, unless we have concrete reasons to distrust it (see REID, T.).

A third approach is that, in so far as I am entitled to trust in general my own cognitive functioning, I am also entitled to trust in general the cognitive functioning of others, since their cognitive faculties are broadly similar to mine and likewise their environment is similar to mine. This is not to deny there are important differences among people and their environments, but the differences arise against an enormous backdrop of similarity. Thus, it would be incoherent for me to trust my cognitive functioning unless I am also willing to trust that of others; consistency demands this.

Some epistemologists insist that all the above approaches are overly individualistic, since they try to account for the social interdependence of justification by focusing on how individuals should treat the testimony of others. Social conditions enter into questions of justification in a more fundamental way than this, these critics say. For example, a position hinted at by both Wittgenstein and Rorty is that one is justified in believing *p* only if the manner in which one comes to believe *p* is intellectually acceptable in one's community (see WITTGENSTEIN, L. §12; RORTY, R.M.).

A claim that has even more radical implications for epistemology is that the target states of epistemic justification are not the beliefs of individual people but rather the opinions of social groups, where these opinions cannot be reduced to the opinions of the individuals comprising the group. The beliefs of individuals are justified only in a derivative sense. Either they belong to the set of opinions justifiably held by one's community, or they are appropriately related to this set of opinions.

See also: EPISTEMOLOGY, HISTORY OF; INDUCTION, EPISTEMIC ISSUES IN; INTERNALISM AND EXTERNALISM IN EPISTEMOLOGY; KNOWLEDGE AND JUSTIFICATION, COHERENCE THEORY OF; KNOWLEDGE, CONCEPT OF; NATURALIZED EPISTEMOLOGY; RATIONAL BELIEFS; REASONS FOR BELIEF; SCEPTICISM; SOCIAL EPISTEMOLOGY; TESTIMONY

References and further reading

Alston, W. (1989) *Epistemic Justification*, Ithaca, NY: Cornell University Press. (Collection of important essays on foundationalism, externalism and internalism, reliabilism and other epistemological issues.)

* Armstrong, D.M. (1973) *Belief, Truth, and Knowledge*, Cambridge: Cambridge University Press. (Early defence of a reliabilist theory of knowledge.)

* BonJour, L. (1985) *The Structure of Empirical Knowledge*, Cambridge, MA: Harvard University Press. (Clear, concise criticism of foundationalism and a defence of coherentism.)

* Chisholm, R. (1966) *The Theory of Knowledge*, Englewood Cliffs, NJ: Prentice-Hall, 3rd edn, 1989. (Influential and detailed defence of foundationalism and internalism.)

* Clifford, W.K. (1879) 'The Ethics of Belief', in *Lectures and Essays*, vol. 2, London: Macmillan. (Defence of the view that it is always wrong to believe something for which there is insufficient evidence.)

* Davidson, D. (1986) 'A Coherence Theory of Truth and Knowledge', in E. LePore (ed.) *The Philosophy of Donald Davidson*, London: Blackwell. (The most accessible of several articles in which Davidson argues that the nature of belief and reference makes it impossible for our beliefs to be radically incorrect.)

* Dretske, F. (1981) *Knowledge and the Flow of Information*, Cambridge, MA: MIT Press. (Information-theoretic defence of reliabilism.)

* Foley, R. (1993) *Working Without A Net*, New York: Oxford University Press. (Discussions of subjective foundationalism, epistemic and non-epistemic reasons for belief, coherentism, probabilism and scepticism.)

* Goldman, A. (1986) *Epistemology and Cognition*, Cambridge, MA: Harvard University Press. (Influential and detailed defence of reliabilism.)

Kornblith, H. (ed.) (1994) *Naturalizing Epistemology*, Cambridge, MA: MIT Press. (Collection of influential articles by proponents of naturalized epistemology plus a helpful introduction by Kornblith.)

* Lehrer, K. (1974) *Knowledge*, Oxford: Oxford University Press. (Important defence of coherentism and attack on foundationalism.)

* Plantinga, A. (1992) *Warrant: The Current Debate*, New York: Oxford University Press. (Discussions of foundationalism, coherentism, probabilism and reliabilism, and a defence of Plantinga's own proper functioning account.)

* Putnam, H. (1987) *The Many Faces of Realism*,

LaSalle, IL: Open Court. (Defence of Putnam's internal realism and its anti-sceptical implications.)

* Quine, W.V. (1969) 'Epistemology Naturalized', in *Ontological Relativity and Other Essays*, New York: Columbia University Press. (The article most responsible for beginning the naturalized epistemology movement.)

* —— (1990) *The Pursuit of Truth*, Cambridge, MA: Harvard University Press. (The first chapter contains a succinct and accessible account of Quine's epistemology.)

Schmitt, F. (ed.) (1994) *Socializing Epistemology*, London: Rowan & Littlefield. (Collection of articles on testimony and the social epistemology.)

Sellars, W. (1963) *Science, Perception, and Reality*, London: Routledge & Kegan Paul. (Difficult but influential statement of Sellars's epistemological and metaphysical positions.)

* Sosa, E. (1991) *Knowledge in Perspective*, Cambridge: Cambridge University Press. (Collection of essays on justification, knowledge, reliabilism, foundationalism and coherentism.)

RICHARD FOLEY

JUSTIFICATION, MORAL

see MORAL JUSTIFICATION

JUSTIFICATION, RELIGIOUS

Justification is about the restoration of human beings after Adam's Fall, by the life, death and resurrection of Jesus, and the beginning of a new life that anticipates the glory of heaven. According to the Roman Catholic Church, justification has two aspects: forgiveness of sin and the infusion of grace that makes Christians just (innocent). It is the beginning of a new life of grace, in which the gifts of faith, hope and charity enable one to perform meritorious works. However, the restoration is never complete in this life and concupiscence remains; a fall from the state of grace is thus possible, but this is reversible through penance.

A central feature of the Protestant Reformation was a dispute with the Roman Catholic Church over how justification should be understood. According to Luther, one does not become renewed (innocent) in justification. Rather, one is forgiven because the righteousness or justice of Christ is imputed to those who have faith in God's promise of redemption; however, one remains a sinner. More recent thought, however, has pointed to the fact that in both Lutheran and Catholic conceptions of

justification, there is a sense of incompleteness, that it is just part of the process of redemption. There has also been interest in the idea of justification involving an indwelling of God rather than a gift from God to the individual; this has interesting affinities with Eastern Orthodox beliefs.

1 **The Bible**
2 **Augustine**
3 **Medieval theology**
4 **Luther**
5 **Possible reconciliation**

1 The Bible

In the Old Testament the word 'justification' has a juridical connotation. It refers to the obtaining of justice for one who is unjustly accused, whereby they are vindicated or shown to be not guilty. Quite often the context is one in which the innocence of a person before God is made plain by God through a public tribunal.

One exceptional but important use is in Isaiah: 'The righteous one, my servant, shall make many righteous, and he shall bear their iniquities' (53: 11). A servant by his suffering death obtains pardon and remission of sin for others. His suffering justifies, makes the guilty righteous. If this passage is interpreted in terms of the juridical understanding of justification, it must mean that the guilty are actually made innocent. In the New Testament, Jesus is identified as the suffering servant, whose life, death and resurrection justify the sinner.

Jesus used the term 'just' in a very wide sense to mean a life of innocence or holiness before God. For him, the righteousness of the kingdom of God was very different from that of the Pharisees. In one parable, a Pharisee thanks God for his freedom from sin, while a tax collector prays for God to have mercy for his sinfulness; 'I tell you, this man went home justified rather than the other; for all who exalt themselves will be humbled, but all who humble themselves will be exalted' (Luke 18: 9–14). In the parable of the prodigal son (Luke 15: 11–32), Jesus made it clear that God seeks a deep bond of love, not just external conformity, as the basis of his relationship with both the prodigal and the conventional son. Covenant, a sacred relation established by God, precedes law, and is the foundation of life with God, rather than conformity to law apart from the covenantal relation.

According to Paul, who explicated Jesus' teaching on justification more systematically than any other biblical writer, the insistence that Gentiles (non-Jewish converts) should observe the Jewish law threatened to destroy the new covenant established by Jesus. The controversy forced Paul to explore more deeply the significance of Jesus' death and resurrection: 'We ourselves are Jews by birth and not Gentile sinners; yet we know that a person is justified not by the works of the law but through faith in Jesus Christ' (Galatians 2: 15). Life in God is the acceptance of the gratuitous gift of justification through faith in Christ. The justified believer lives a new life because they are united with the risen Lord.

2 Augustine

Augustine's teaching on justification had far-reaching influence in the Latin (Western) Church (see AUGUSTINE §6, 13). It was occasioned by the teachings of Pelagius, who denied that one needed divine grace to do good and right (see PELAGIANISM). This denial of original sin, and hence of the need of redemption through Christ, aroused Augustine to reaffirm that all are born in sin and cannot become just except through the grace of Christ. God saves those who would justly be condemned. All the initiative in justification comes from God, so that free cooperation with God in justification (manifest in faith, hope and charity) is possible only by God's grace. Later, Augustine rejected semi-Pelagianism, in which it was taught that God's justification awaits a person's good action. Augustine stressed that a person's very assent to the message of salvation is God's gift. Grace is necessary to restore free will (see GRACE).

Augustine set the terms for the discussion of justification in the Western Church. The way the medieval Church developed Augustine's views on the remission of sin and good works led Luther to reject its teaching on justification. Augustine's stress on the total gratuity of justification led to controversy among Calvinists and to a deep division between Calvinists and Methodists over the role of free will; it also gave rise to the Jansenist controversy within Roman Catholicism in the seventeenth century.

3 Medieval theology

Medieval theologians agreed with Augustine that there are two aspects of justification: forgiveness of sin and an infusion of grace that overcomes one of the effects of the Fall, so that one becomes in fact just or innocent. The gift of integrity, whereby appetites are fully controlled by reason, is not given. Concupiscence therefore remains, but, as Augustine taught, it is not itself sin and there is room for growth in the gifts of faith, hope and charity; one can move towards integrity. Justification can be lost by mortal sin, but can be regained through the sacrament of penance.

Divisions occurred over the relation between the two aspects of justification, forgiveness of sin and the infusion of grace. They were prompted, in part, by the scholastic desire for precision, and this discussion of justification has the flavour of academic speculation, rather than of practical and pastoral concerns as in Augustine. The application of Aristotelian philosophy, particularly the notion of change in terms of formal and material causality, to theological issues shaped the way the question of the two aspects of justification was treated.

There were two primary schools of thought regarding the changeover from the state of sin to the state of grace. According to Aquinas, there is a necessary connection between the forgiveness of sin and the infusion of grace, or between forgiveness and restoration to a condition of justice or innocence. This stems from Aristotle's notion of one form replacing another form: the change involves the form of grace expelling the form of sin. Both aspects of justification occur together because they are necessarily connected to the reception of the form of grace.

The other school of thought rejected this Thomist intellectualism in favour of the primacy of divine will. Duns Scotus said that forgiveness of sin and infusion of grace are connected in fact because of God's will, but not by their nature. William of Ockham went even further by saying that not only is God's decree or will the only reason for the actual connection of forgiveness of sin and the condition of grace, but that there would be no logical contradiction if they were not connected, so that God could decree one without the other (see WILLIAM OF OCKHAM § 10; VOLUNTARISM).

It is generally held by Roman Catholic theologians that Duns Scotus' voluntarism and Ockham's nominalism, by rejecting any intrinsic connection between remission of sin and grace, enabled Martin LUTHER to claim that in justification people remain sinners. That is, when forgiven by God, people remain sinners, but God declares that they are just. However much Luther may have been influenced in his theology by voluntarism and nominalism, he appealed to Scripture for his views on justification. This is also true of later reformers, such as John CALVIN (§4).

The sixteenth-century Council of Trent by and large endorsed the Thomistic view of justification. Justification implies an actual removal of sin, not a pardon of sin only (a mere forensic declaration by God that one is forgiven, but with sin still remaining). There is an interior renewal by the infusion of grace, whether or not it is experienced psychologically.

4 Luther

Luther's view that in justification one is *simul iustus et peccator* (both just and sinner) does indeed mean that for him justification is forensic (not an actual regeneration). Because of Christ, God does not impute one's sins to one and so remits punishment. One is not internally renewed or made pure, but is saved by faith in God's promise in Christ to bring his followers into his eternal kingdom. Since one is saved unconditionally, there is no role for good works in the attainment of salvation. Good works flow from one's faith.

Luther's views on justification can easily be misconstrued by both Roman Catholics and Protestants if his approach is not kept firmly in mind. Luther believed that he was following Paul in stressing that one is not justified *according* to the law, but *apart* from the law. According to the law, all are sinners. But by imputing Christ's righteousness to sinners, God forgives them and declares them to be just. In relation to God, but not according to the law, they are just. *Simul iustus et peccator* is to be understood in the context of a justification *apart* from the law. If one retains the framework of justification according to the law, then one can understand the reasoning that insists that one must have undergone a total inner transformation, for only so can one actually be just according to the law. But for Luther this means retaining the Old Testament principle noted in §1 above, namely that in justification the person who is justified is found to be innocent of sin. For Luther, to claim that in justification one becomes inherently innocent of sin by the infusion of grace is to remain within the context of justification according to the law. None the less, he insists that the law is not abolished and that one is not to become lawless; rather, one is justified apart from the law.

Luther's approach does not settle the question of whether the two aspects of justification, forgiveness of sin and total renewal, can be separated, as he and Ockham (for different reasons) claimed. But to understand Luther's approach enables one to see more accurately the differences between the Roman Catholic Church and Luther. According to the Roman Catholic Church, one is made pure (innocent) by infused grace, and one is just or justified because one is innocent. According to Luther, one is saved or justified by faith in God's forgiveness in Christ, not because one is innocent. He claimed that the need to insist that one is actually innocent is because justification is conceived within the framework of the law, even though the alleged innocence is achieved by infused grace. For both Luther and the Roman Catholic Church, good works are only possible because of divine grace, but for the Church, good works are needed because one must actually be good to deserve justification. For Luther, good works flow from our justification.

Protestants have frequently failed to grasp properly Luther's approach. The stress that justification is by faith alone, a completely gratuitous gift, led Protestants to wrestle in various ways with the question raised by Paul in Romans 6: 1. After Paul has explained that one is justified apart from the law, he asks 'Should we continue in sin in order that grace may abound?' If God has done everything for one's salvation, what is there for one to do? Why should one obey the law? Protestants have oscillated between laxity, on the ground that justification is apart from good deeds, and rigorism, on the ground that since good works flow from one's faith, unless one performs them, one cannot have been saved.

The tendency to laxity stems from a failure to see that, for Luther, justification is the *beginning* of renewal or inner transformation by the Holy Spirit. (Seeberg (1961) and Forde (1984) insist that, for Luther, justification is the beginning of holiness.) To infer from justification apart from the law that one is to be lawless is to repudiate justification itself, since justification is the beginning of the reception of God's promise in Christ eventually to establish his kingdom or rule in his followers. Rigorism, in its reaction to lawlessness, lapses into the framework of justification according to the law.

5 Possible reconciliation

Recent post-Tridentine and ecumenical thought has softened the opposition between Roman Catholicism and the Protestants who, in various denominations, follow Luther's teaching on justification. In the Roman Catholic view, justification does not deliver one wholly from the effects of the Fall because concupiscence, which inclines one to sin, remains. It is also clear that Luther's claim that in justification one is *simul iustus et peccator* includes the notion that justification is the beginning of one's renewal (holiness). Since in both views of justification there is newness and incompleteness, the difference is not absolute.

The Roman Catholic Church is now raising into prominence the teaching of the indwelling or the presence of God in one's salvation. The earlier stress on infused grace tended to overlook the fact that such grace is relative to or linked to the divine presence (uncreated grace). The stress on infused grace enabled one to focus on one's condition in isolation, so that even though one's state of grace and good works are possible only because of infused grace, one's state and deeds are one's own and are meritorious. The indwelling of God mitigates such an overly external relation between God and those whom God sanctifies. One's state and one's good works are the result of the continuing presence of God, so that one can never attend to oneself apart from God.

Among the Fathers of the Eastern Orthodox Church, for whom the indwelling of God and one's elevation into the life of God are central, there are no controversies over justification. Some Roman Catholic theologians (such as Garrigou-Lagrange 1957 and Congar 1962) are aware that their recent emphasis on the central concerns of the Orthodox Fathers has important ecumenical promise, not only for their relation to Orthodoxy, but also for their relation to those Protestants who are increasingly aware that Luther's view of justification may be harmonious with that of the Fathers. In time, there may be a growing convergence of opinion, not only on justification, but also on the nature of the Christian life.

See also: ATONEMENT; FAITH; FORGIVENESS AND MERCY; SALVATION; SANCTIFICATION

References and further reading

Aquinas, T. (1266–73) *Summa theologiae*, New York: McGraw-Hill, 1964. (Aquinas' views on the necessary connection of forgiveness and regeneration; section 4 of book III is particularly useful.)

Augustine (412–15; 428–9) *The Nicene and Post-Nicene Fathers*, vol. 5, *Saint Augustine: Anti-Pelagian Writings*, ed. P. Schaff, Grand Rapids, MI: Eerdmans, 1956. (A collection of Augustine's influential views on justification; the earlier writings are against Pelagianism, the later ones against semi-Pelagianism.)

Cassirer, H. (1988) *Grace and Law*, Grand Rapids, MI: Eerdmans. (A study of Paul, Kant and the Hebrew prophets by a Kantian scholar.)

* Congar, Y.M.J. (1962) *The Mystery of the Temple*, London: Burns & Oates. (Treats of divine indwelling.)

* Forde, G.O. (1984) 'The Christian Life', in C.E. Braaten and R.W. Jensen (eds) *Christian Dogmatics*, vol. 2, Philadelphia, PA: Fortress. (A thorough discussion of Luther and Lutheranism on justification and sanctification.)

Froude, J.A. (1896) *Lectures on the Council of Trent*, New York: Scribners. (A classic, sympathetic Protestant account.)

* Garrigou-Lagrange, R. (1957) *Grace*, St Louis, MO: B. Herder Book Co. (Treats of how we are partakers of the divine nature.)

Küng, H. (1964) *Justification*, New York: Thomas Nelson & Sons. (A careful comparison of Karl Barth's work and Roman Catholic teaching on justification; includes an ample bibliography.)

Luther, M. (1515–16) *Commentary on the Epistle to the Romans*, ed. J. Theodore Mueller, Grand Rapids, MI: Zondervan, 1954. (A major account of Luther's development of what became the Protestant view of justification.)

McGrath, A. (1986) *Iustitia Dei*, New York: Cambridge University Press, 2 vols. (A history of work on the doctrine of justification and sanctification.)

* Seeberg, R. (1961) *Textbook of the History of Doctrines*, trans. C.E. Hay, Grand Rapids, MI: Baker Book House. (A brief, valuable account of the Augsburg Confession of 1530, the main Lutheran confession.)

Stump, E. (1989) 'Justification and Atonement', in R. Feenstra and C. Plantinga (eds) *Trinity, Incarnation, and Atonement*, Notre Dame, IN: University of Notre Dame Press. (An examination of the connection between justification by faith and atonement.)

DIOGENES ALLEN

JUSTINIAN (AD 482–565)

There was a late Roman renaissance during Justinian's reign in the sixth century AD. Its high point was the compilation by his minister Tribonian of a huge restatement of Roman law in four works, the Institutes, Digest, Code *and* Novels, *preserving a selection of its achievements. Called by medieval lawyers the* Corpus iuris civilis, *it is the basic material for studying Roman law and the source of much of Europe's legal thinking.*

Born Petrus Sabbatius in Macedonia, Justinian (Iustinianius Flavius) became Emperor at Constantinople in 527. Eager for fame, he wanted to restore and renew the Roman world. His generals reconquered the western empire while his architects adorned the capital with buildings such as St Sophia. Roman law, too, represented the glorious past: his minister Tribonian was put in charge of an elaborate programme for its restatement.

This began in 529 with the first *Code*, a collection of earlier imperial enactments, superseded in 534 by the second and only existing version. Subsequent legislation by Justinian and others is preserved in a sixth-century compilation called the *Novels*. The *Digest*, begun in 530 and completed, according to Bluhme's theory (1820), by three committees working furiously in parallel in only three years, was Justinian's largest work, about one and a half times the size of the Bible. An anthology of excerpts from the great jurists of the classical age (*c.* 50 BC to AD 250) such as Papinian, Paul, Ulpian and Gaius, it contains virtually all that has survived of them (see GAIUS).

However, its compilers could and did change the original texts: scholars have been pointing out these 'interpolations' for centuries.

Though providing a ready-made law library in one book, the *Digest* was a vast and shapeless collection, in which the detailed rules on any topic were hard to find and fit into an overall pattern. Justinian's *Institutes*, a short introductory textbook published in 533, was an attempt to solve this problem for first-year law students at Constantinople. It was largely a second edition of the classical *Institutes* of Gaius, from which it took its so-called institutional order and much of its contents, with later reforms tacked on to each section.

Justinian intended his restatement to be final, with further commentary banned. But medieval and later scholars in Europe called it the *Corpus iuris civilis*, the basic source-material for an enormous body of secondary literature on Roman law (see LEGAL HERMENEUTICS §1). These studies were the starting point for much of Europe's legal thinking. Through them most European countries experienced a 'reception' of Roman law, becoming what are called civil law systems. Typically the *Digest*, *Code* and *Novels* supplied them with many specific rules and institutions, while the *Institutes* provided a clear scheme for systematizing and later codifying their law. Whatever its imperfections, Justinian's compilation gave the world Roman law (see ROMAN LAW).

See also: LAW, PHILOSOPHY OF

List of works

Justinian (533) *The Digest of Justinian*, T. Mommsen, P. Krueger and A. Watson (eds), Philadelphia, PA: University of Pennsylvania Press, 1985. (The Latin text by Mommsen and Krueger with a readable translation by various writers edited by A. Watson.)

—— (533) *Justinian's Institutes*, P. Birks and G. McLeod, London: Duckworth, 1987. (The Latin text by Krueger with a good modern translation and useful introduction.)

—— (534) *Codex Iustinianus*, in *Corpus iuris civilis*, vol. 2, ed. P. Krueger, 13th stereotype edn, Berlin, 1954. (The Latin and Greek text of Justinian's *Code*; there is no English translation.)

—— (after 578) *Iustiniani Novellae*, in *Corpus Iuris Civilis*, vol. 3, eds R. Schoell and G. Kroll, 6th edn, Berlin, 1954. (The predominantly Greek text of the *Novels* of Justinian and his successor; there is no English translation.)

References and further reading

Honoré, T. (1978) *Tribonian*, London: Duckworth. (A brilliant though sometimes technical account of the whole of Justinian's work.)

Stein, P.G. and Lewis, A.D.E. (eds) (1983) *Studies in Justinian's Institutes in Memory of J.A.C. Thomas*, London: Sweet and Maxwell. (A collection of detailed studies on aspects of the *Institutes*.)

GRANT McLEOD

AL-JUWAYNI, ABU'L MA'ALI (1028–85)

Al-Juwayni rose to great prominence as a theologian in the Islamic world, and his theoretical discussions of philosophical issues played a significant role in the development of Islamic philosophy. He provided a stout defence of the Ash'arite theory that emphasizes the power of God and the insignificance of human beings. His work on the meaning of scriptural texts provided Muslims with a sophisticated and productive series of concepts with which to discuss issues of interpretation.

1 Life and works
2 Ethics

1 Life and works

Born in Juwayn in Persia, al-Juwayni spent his life defending the principles of Ash'arism (see ASH'AR-IYYA AND MU'TAZILA). By the time of his death he was widely known as the Imam al-Haramayn, the imam of the two great mosques of Mecca and Medina. This gives some indication of the influence of his thinking in the Islamic world. He worked in an interesting time of transition between the original Ash'arite *kalam* (theology) (see ISLAMIC THEOLOGY) and the more radical developments which were to be undertaken by AL-GHAZALI.

Al-Juwayni argued that there are some forms of knowledge which are available to contingent beings such as ourselves, yet this knowledge is itself irretrievably contingent and should be distinguished from the sort of knowledge which God has. Although God is not a body and is neither a spatial nor temporal being, it is nonetheless possible for him to be seen, in the next life, through beatific vision. God is completely free, acting for no reason other than that which he gives himself. There is nothing necessary about causality, and the possibility of miracles is based upon the fact that there is nothing fixed about nature. God is not only the creator of the universe in the sense of being the first cause, but he is also the agent who is the cause of its continuous existence. The existence of the world at every moment depends upon God's will. God is the sole creator, and even our actions do not really originate with us but are acquired from God.

The route to an understanding of the Qur'an is through a thorough grounding in the Arabic language. Al-Juwayni distinguishes between different kinds of text. Some texts are obvious and clear, some are accurate, some are concealed and yet others are obscure. Texts which are clear do not change their sense, whatever context they appear in. Those which are accurate have a sense which is clearly linked to a particular state of affairs which the text describes, and present no difficulties. Concealed texts have two sorts of meaning, one which requires interpretation by a prophet and his followers, or one which is capable of explanation by a body of readers who really understand the difficulties of what is before them. Obscure texts require *ta'wil* or analogical interpretation, in accordance with which the correct meaning will be carefully extended from the actual forms of words which are used. This form of interpretation should only be used as a last resort, and it is replete with dangers in that it can lead to a loose and undisciplined approach to understanding the meaning of scripture. Al-Juwayni presents in his work a highly organized system of hermeneutics designed to make scripture accessible and yet also restricted within particular theological boundaries.

2 Ethics

Al-Juwayni was a staunch defender of the Ash'arite view of the basis of value judgments, which is entirely scriptural. What is good is what is said to be good in scripture, and what is bad is what scripture condemns, and there is no other basis to such judgments. Any attempt at finding a rational foundation is flawed, and it can be assumed that here he had the Mu'tazilites in mind. He suggests that the Mu'tazilites are wrong in thinking that there are basic rational moral truths, since if this were the case there would be no possibility of widespread moral disagreement, something which quite clearly does arise. Similarly, the idea that particular forms of behaviour are absolutely right or wrong is difficult to establish, given that we often base our judgments here on the context surrounding those actions and the precise nature of the agent (see ETHICS IN ISLAMIC PHILOSOPHY). For example, an adult and a child may perform a similar action; the former action may be called evil, but this is not appropriate as a description of the child's action.

In his account of what it means for God to be obliged to act in certain ways, al-Juwayni totally rejects such language. He argues that it is mistaken to talk about God being under any obligation to his creatures at all. He often pokes fun at the very idea of explaining the sometimes tragic events of this world as part of an objective divine plan. God does not need to operate in accordance with such a plan; this would be to deny the uniqueness of God and his radical separation from his creatures. Al-Juwayni argues that his thesis has the advantage of not needing to provide implausible explanations of why things are as they are in the world. The world is as it is because of the decisions of the deity, but we cannot fathom his reasons for those decisions and it is entirely inappropriate to hold him liable to adhere to an essentially human system of justice.

See also: ASH'ARIYYA AND MU'TAZILA; OMNIPOTENCE

List of works

al-Juwayni (1028–85) *Kitab al-irshad ila qawati 'al-adilla fi usul al-i'tiqad* (The Guide to the Cogent Proofs of the Principles of Faith), ed. M. Musa and A. 'Abd al-Hamid, Cairo, 1950. (A detailed account of al-Juwayni's theological principles.)
—— (1028–85) *al-Burhan fi usul al-fiqh* (The Proofs of Jurisprudence), ed. A. al-Dib, Cairo: Dar al-Ansar, 1980. (Al-Juwayni's doctrine of legal judgement.)

References and further reading

Allard, M. (1965) *Le problème des attributs divins dans la doctrine d'al-Ash'ari et de ses premiers grands disciples* (The Problem of Divine Attributes in the Doctrine of al-Ash'ari and His First Major Disciples), Beirut: Recherches publiées sous la direction de l'Institut de Lettres Orientales de Beyrouth. (A classic introduction to Ash'arite thought.)
Gardet, L. and Anawati, G. (1948) *Introduction à la théologie musulmane* (Introduction to Muslim Theology), Paris: Études de philosophie médiévale. (Excellent account of al-Juwayni's place in Ash'arite thought.)
Hourani, G. (1985) 'Juwayni's criticisms of Mu'tazilite ethics', in G. Hourani (ed.) *Reason and Tradition in Islamic Ethics*, Cambridge: Cambridge University Press, 124–34. (Al-Juwayni's critique of Mu'tazilite ethics.)

OLIVER LEAMAN
SALMAN ALBDOUR

K

KABBALAH

Kabbalah is the body of Jewish mystical writings which became important at the end of the twelfth century in Provence and has been taken up with varying degrees of enthusiasm in an attempt to explore the esoteric side of Judaism. There are two main forms of Kabbalah: one which concentrates on gaining knowledge of God through study of his name, and a theosophical tradition that approaches God through his impact on creation. On both accounts God is linked to the world through ten Sefirot, *hypostatic numbers which mediate between the Infinite and this world and thus (among other functions) help to explain how a being who is entirely ineffable can produce so much variety as is observed in nature. God's willingness to relate to the world gives his creatures the possibility of personal knowledge of him, although this can be acquired only through difficult and strenuous spiritual exercises. The variety of works which the Kabbalists produced are a blend of philosophical and mystical ideas which attempt to explore the inner meaning of faith and represent a creative and influential stream that both draws upon and contributes to Jewish philosophy.*

1   **The nature of Jewish mysticism**
2   **Merkavah and Hekhalot mysticism**
3   **God as a physical being**
4   **Esoteric cosmology**
5   **German pietism**
6   **Kabbalah in Spain and Provence**
7   **Light and darkness**
8   **Abraham Abulafia and prophetic Kabbalah**
9   **Jewish mysticism and Sufism**

1   The nature of Jewish mysticism

There are broadly two types of mysticism within the Jewish tradition. One identifies mysticism with esoteric knowledge and links mysticism with philosophy. This provides the adept with access to a level of understanding unavailable to ordinary believers. The mystical knowledge is passed on from teacher to student, generally orally. In some cases, however, there is a gnosis that is achieved through some variety of divine revelation. Reliance on esoteric teachings and privileged gnosis is not taken to show that the traditional Jewish texts such as the Torah are not themselves sources of deep insight into the nature of reality. But the Kabbalistic tendency is to assume that such texts need to be interpreted in the right way if their inner essence is to be extracted. For this the reader needs a key, which Kabbalah (literally, tradition) can provide, through the appropriate training, to those capable of grasping it.

The other type of mysticism places the emphasis on experience, in particular ecstatic experience. The route to this experience is frequently allied to magic. It may involve the recitation of the divine name, specific rituals or particular types of meditation.

Study of the Kabbalah has often been controversial. Some who saw the Torah as consisting of secrets felt that once they understood these secrets they need no longer obey the laws. And there were a variety of heresies that challenged orthodoxy by the interpretations that they put on mystical experience. Yet within certain Jewish communities of great piety the Kabbalah became widely popular, especially because of its claim to elucidate (and facilitate) the linkage between this world and the divine. The ideas of the Kabbalah were also taken up by a variety of Christian thinkers who were interested in mysticism. These included Ramon Lull, PICO DELLA MIRANDOLA, AGRIPPA VON NETTESHEIM and Henry MORE.

2   Merkavah and Hekhalot mysticism

Merkavah (chariot) and Hekhalot (palace) mysticism have a common form. They deal with accounts of the ascent of the individual through the celestial realms, and end with the attainment of an ecstatic vision of the throne in the seventh palace of the seventh heaven. The reference to the chariot comes originally from the Book of Ezekiel, where the prophet describes his vision of the glory of the enthroned Godhead. Descriptions of this experience frequently refer to the experiencing (or perhaps better, the experiencing again) of God at Sinai, one of the crucial revelatory episodes in Judaism. There are two linked features of this form of mysticism. There is the ascent which results in a mystical experience, and there is also the acquisition of the angelic powers, perhaps through the adept's clothing himself with the divine name.

The notion of experiencing God is problematic in a religion like Judaism, with its frequent emphasis on God's transcendence. Thus there arises an interesting tension in Jewish mysticism, with its aim of seeing a God who at the same time cannot be seen. One way of addressing this tension is through poetic discourse that characterizes the mystical experience in erotic terms. Thus, the throne is often represented as female and the glory on it as male, so that the successful mystic makes contact with the holy union that lies at the core of reality.

What is the process by which mystics attain their experience? They progress through the seven heavens of Jewish cosmology and the six palaces of the last and seventh heaven, and then enter the seventh palace, where the last throne exists. They stand before the enthroned glory and repeat the appropriate words with the angels. This may give them access either to the throne of glory itself or to a neighbouring throne. There they have a vision of the shining form of God. Although they never become the same as God, they do acquire some of the divine characteristics – spiritual or angelic properties. Angels participate in both divinity and humanity and thus permit the mystic to approach God without becoming God. Once mystics acquire angelic properties (through purification and asceticism), they can understand the hidden nature of reality, which was not available to them in their mundane existence.

3 God as a physical being

One of the aspects of God which the mystic is, in principle, capable of grasping is his physicality. Usually this is not expressed in terms of the asciption to God himself of physical proportions. But such proportions are ascribed to a secondary power, sometimes called the Metatron. This device enabled mystics to provide a visionary interpretation of the Talmudic notion, for example, that God wears phylacteries (Berachot 6a). It also allowed them to weave a visual symbolism on verses such as 'Let us make man in our image' (Genesis 1: 26). Such verses could not apply unproblematically and literally to God himself, since God transcends physicality. But they could be applied to a lower, angelic being who shares some physical characteristics with creatures. There were many different calculations of the size of God and the Metatron, based on the numerical values of Hebrew letters in crucial biblical passages (see GOD, CONCEPTS OF).

4 Esoteric cosmology

The outstanding Kabbalistic work that deals with cosmology is the *Sefer Yetzirah* (The Book of Creation). The work has obviously experienced changes and accretions over the centuries, but it seems to have been constructed between the third and ninth centuries. Its main assertion is that the scope for divine creativity involves the thirty-two paths of wisdom which make up ten basic forces (Sefirot) and the twenty-two letters of the Hebrew language. The Sefirot are to be seen as the attributes of God. They are sometimes identified with the heavenly creatures who support the throne. The notion of Sefirot helps the mystic understand the concept of God as enthroned, surrounded by his power. The Sefirot have a neo-Pythagorean origin, so it is natural for them to be identified with numbers, but they are also the basic constituents of physical matter; and they can be equated with other elemental notions, such as east, west, south, north, height, depth, good, evil, the end and the beginning. They are thus the underlying principles of the temporal, spatial and moral order of the world. Accordingly, they are sometimes seen as the four directions, spirit, water, fire, height, depth and the divine spirit. A common representation of the Sefirot takes the form shown in the figure.

Keter (crown)
Binah (understanding)   Chochmah (wisdom)
Din (judgment)   Chesed (mercy)
Tiferet (beauty)
Hod (splendour)   Netzach (victory)
Yesod (foundation)
Malchut (kingdom)

The first triad of the Sefirot represent thought, understanding and wisdom, the three intellectual aspects of the first emanation. The first nine are regarded as masculine, while the last, kingdom, is identified with the *shekhinah*, the divine presence, immanence, or indwelling, and is feminine. The divine powers present in the Sefirot are part of the continuous process of emanation, by which the world is created.

The Sefirot represent the expressivity of divine creation. Tzimtzum (contraction) is the divine self-contraction – for the differentiation brought about by God also implies not only emanation but also limitation. The Sefirot represent the capacity to create. But Tzimtzum is the precondition of that creation. For without self-limitation, God would not be able to enter into relationship with us. Sometimes this idea of divine self-limitation is expressed in terms of the divine light's having to go into vessels in order to be weak enough to make contact with mortal creatures. Unless God were prepared to limit the extent of the light, it would not be suitable for the finitude of creation but would overwhelm all that was to be with the divine effulgence. Creation and revelation are parallel here. So the specificity of the divine Law is another outcome made possible only by divine self-limitation. Furthermore, since God is infinite, when God creates he does not create something outside of himself. Rather, he makes room within his own self for a greater diversity. Isaac Luria (1534–72) argued that the vessels in which the light is restricted represent the commandments (*mitzvot*) of the Torah. God's restricting himself to the commandments does not bring him into the power of human beings, nor does it confine him under the categories which apply to our notion of how things are. His self-limitation is an internal action, and the appropriate response of human beings is to carry out his laws in order that we may become colleagues with God in an inner sphere of activity. As an ineffable and infinite being, God transcends multiplicity while at the same time linking himself to everything through the Sefirot. He freely chooses, through self-contraction to allow multiplicity to emerge. This gave the Kabbalists an interesting route to reconciling freedom with divine omniscience. God could know what was going to happen in the future, but he wills not to, in order to allow human beings to make their own decisions freely (see OMNISCIENCE).

One intriguing aspect of the *Sefer Yetzirah* is its discussion of letter symbolism as both the form of divine creativity and the content of reality. A thing is brought to life through the appropriate combination of letters, since the letters both represent the potentiality of things and the materiality of existence. Each letter has an effect on three levels: space, time and the microcosm. The human body, like everything else, is composed basically of letters.

5 German pietism

Although Jewish mystical thought has a long history, it received a fresh impulse from the thinkers in the Rhineland in the twelfth and thirteenth centuries. Judah ben Samuel ben Kalonymus of Regensburg (d.1217) and his pupil Eleazar ben Judah ben Kalonymus of Worms (d.1240) combined the Kabbalah with the contributions of philosophers such as Al-Fayyumi SAADIAH GAON and Abraham IBN EZRA to concentrate on the nature of divine glory. This concept was felt to be problematic, in that prayer implies that God has characteristics which Judaism in other places denies, and yet for prayer to be possible (it often seemed) there should be some scope for visualization of the object of prayer. Rhineland mystics distinguished between a lower and a higher glory, the latter being the *shekhinah* (presence or indwelling) while the former is to be identified with the prophetic or mystical imagination. The lower

glory varies in its images, depending on the will of God and the capacities of the individual worshipper. There is certainly likely to be a heavy use of anthropomorphic imagery, in particular the notion of enthronement, with the proviso that the one who sits on the throne should not be regarded as a body. This point is emphasized by the tendency to apply the measurements which previously had been applied to God to the form which is constituted within the imagination, the lesser glory. How is the mystical experience to be achieved? Of great importance here is contemplation of the divine name, which progresses via a series of rituals of purification, and the recitation of the divine and angelic names and combinations of letters in order to bring about a state of religious ecstasy similar to prophecy.

6 Kabbalah in Spain and Provence

Kabbalistic thought developed at much the same time in Provence and Spain, although the lines of transmission are not clear. The main text here is the *Sefer ha-Bahir* (Book of Bahir), which interprets biblical and rabbinic language into images of divine activity. The Sefirot in this work are seen as either like a tree or a human figure. We again need to return to Genesis 1: 26 and the idea of humanity being created in God's image, and this produces the notion of the divine body as paralleling the human frame – often characterized as Adam Kadmon, the primordial man. Through obeying the religious law, the individual strengthens the divine limb, while disobeying the law weakens it. Some Kabbalists see the Torah itself as the shape of God, so that each of the laws corresponds to, or is derived from, a particular limb in the perfect form of man, the form of Adam. On the other hand, they frequently warned against taking this imagery too literally, insisting that language about divine limbs was really about the divine powers, the Sefirot. Such language is entirely symbolic, and we cannot know the nature of divine reality. On the other hand, it must be admitted that much Kabbalistic writing is intensely anthropomorphic, and some Kabbalists were not frightened by the prospect of the interpretation of their language as more than exercises of imagination.

7 Light and darkness

The Sefirot are frequently identified with light, and are seen as the ten spiritual lights which emanate from the Eyn Sof, the Infinite. Although the Sefirot are many, they all originate in the One and indeed constitute a unity, expressed in an image popular in a variety of mystical philosophies. Light comes from one thing, and enables many things to be noticed, yet it is essentially just one thing. Neoplatonic language dominates here, and the emanation of the Sefirot from the Infinite One resembles the rays of light from the sun (see NEOPLATONISM). Like such rays, their production does not in any way diminish the power or the unity of the source. This sort of language led to an interesting debate between Kabbalists as to whether the Sefirot represent the essence of the deity or rather are the instruments into which God pours his ineffable light.

Questions about the nature of the opposite of light, namely, darkness, naturally arose within the Kabbalah. The *Zohar: Mishnat ha-Zohar* (The Book of Splendour) is the work that has the most detailed account of the struggle between the holy and the unholy. Sometimes this is represented as a battle between the forces of light and the forces of darkness, and sometimes both good and evil are seen as existing along a continuum of reality. On the latter view it is probably a mistake to see evil as a force which is in principle eradicable from the world, since it is a formal feature of reality and the best that can be achieved is to contain it.

The notion of light served as more than just a metaphysical notion; it is also a guide to the view of the Kabbalists as to how to achieve enlightenment. The divine form can be visualized through study of the Torah, and the esoteric approach to the latter as containing secrets means that these need to be elucidated, lit up as it were, so as to reveal what they hide. It was not regarded as coincidental that the Hebrew for 'secret' (*raz*) and 'light' (*or*) have the same numerical value. The letters of the Torah are literally luminous to those who know how to read them. The techniques of the Kabbalists often involved imagining colours while praying or meditating upon particular passages of the Bible, and the role of light is clearly of the first importance here.

8 Abraham Abulafia and prophetic Kabbalah

Abraham Abulafia (*c*.1240–*c*.1291) produced a different account of Kabbalah, which sees as the purpose of mysticism union with the deity. Abulafia criticizes the Kabbalists who see the Sefirot as divine powers, since such a view seemed to limit our access to the divine. If the Sefirot are seen as Neoplatonic separate intellects then we can, through perfecting ourselves, make contact with them, and thus become one with the emanation of reality and truth that flows from God. The route to this end is, among other activities, contemplation of the divine name. This sort of approach is called prophetic because it uses the language of prophecy made popular by the writings of Moses MAIMONIDES and heavily relied upon in

Islamic philosophy. For the authors who relied on these Neoplatonic themes, the overflow from the 'active intellect' leads to prophecy, and the prophet as a result comes into contact with the active intellect, the lowest of the ten separate intellects below God. It is when the prophet transcends his materiality and fulfills his spirituality that he may be able to rise to the level of the active intellect. Unlike the Islamic philosophers and Maimonides, who set forth an intellectual path for those who would attain prophecy, Abulafia recommended concentration on the permutations of the names of God and the letters constituting those names. The prophet has succeeded when he is able to see both the letters of the divine name and the being of God simultaneously.

Prophetic Kabbalah exercised much influence from the end of the thirteenth century in Palestine. Kabbalists in both Safed and Jerusalem derive much of their doctrine from Abulafia. They range from Isaac of Acre to Solomon Alkabetz, Moses Cordovero, Elijah de Vidas and Chayyim Vital, and even extend up to the eighteenth century and the works of the Hasidim (see HASIDISM).

9 Jewish mysticism and Sufism

There can be little doubt that Sufism had a powerful impact on Jewish mysticism and Kabbalah (see MYSTICAL PHILOSOPHY IN ISLAM). In the Iberian peninsula there were often close intercultural exchanges between Jews and Muslims, and both IBN MASARRA (886–931) and his disciple Sahl al-Tustari placed great importance on the mystical significance of the Arabic alphabet. As we have seen, there was a long-standing interest among Jewish thinkers in the arithmetical properties of Hebrew letters, and while this certainly predated Islam itself in the Talmud, it could well have been encouraged when Jewish philosophers became involved with Islamic Neoplatonism (see NEOPLATONISM IN ISLAMIC PHILOSOPHY). Bahya ibn Pakudah's *Fara'id al-qulub* (Duties of the Hearts) contains an individualistic description of a spiritual journey, leading the soul through contemplation and love to union with the divine light, very much following the progressive spiritual stages of the path as described in Sufi pietistic books (see IBN PAQUDA, BAHYA). Bahya replaces Qur'anic motifs with Jewish ones and does not advocate extreme asceticism, as do some of the Sufis, yet the Sufi influences on his work are quite clear.

Sufism became important as a part of Islamic religious life in Egypt, which country was a haven for many Jews fleeing the Almohad persecution in the West and the Crusaders in the East. There are many Sufi works in the Cairo Genizah, the room in an old synagogue which contained thousands of writings going back to the Middle Ages. They were not destroyed, since it is forbidden to destroy anything on which the divine name may be written. There are many manuscripts of Muslim Sufi writings either in Arabic characters or in Hebrew (obviously translated for Jewish readers), or Sufi-inspired works written by Jews. The latter often include works on traditional Jewish themes, describing biblical figures as masters of the Sufi way. The most famous Jewish mystic in Egypt was undoubtedly the son of Moses Maimonides, Abraham (1186–1237) who is quite explicit in his use of Sufi material and authors in his *Kifayat al-'Abidin* (Complete Guide for Devotees) (see MAIMONIDES, A.). Abraham stressed the spiritual significance of the Torah and the mysteries it contains, claiming that the Sufis had managed to hold on to these mysteries which then needed to be rediscovered by the Jews, who had lost them during the tragedy of the exile. Abraham seems to have initiated ceremonial practices in synagogues which were closely linked with Muslim practices in the mosque. He also advocated solitary meditation in a dark and isolated place, and reliance on the guidance of a spiritual master. Abraham's son, Obadyah, even went so far as to write rather disparagingly of marriage and family responsibilities, which is to go very far from the mainstream Jewish view of social responsibilities and the importance of family life.

The Kabbalist communities in Palestine were also close in their practices to Sufism, which was no doubt present in the wider community of the area. They advocated meditation and breath control in quiet dark places in order to attain illumination of the soul. The system of techniques used during these retreats included ritual purity, silence, fasting, restrictions of sleep and food, deep trust in God and the constant repetition of the divine name as aspects of the path to ecstasy and personal fulfilment. Sufism may even have influenced the types of mysticism followed in the Hasidism of the eighteenth century, which, it must be remembered, first developed in what had been a Turkish province of Poland. Shabbetai Zvi (d.1675) came into close contact with the Sufis even before his conversion to Islam, and his followers in the Ottoman empire continued to follow a form of worship which incorporated many Sufi practices. The close contact between Islamic and Jewish culture, which existed over a long and especially rich period, undoubtedly played its part in defining the specific character of Jewish mysticism.

See also: FICINO, M.; HASIDISM; HERMETISM; MYSTICAL PHILOSOPHY IN ISLAM; MYSTICISM, HISTORY OF; PLATONISM, RENAISSANCE

References and further reading

Dan, J. (1986a) *The Early Kabbalah*, New York: Paulist Press. (Standard introduction to the early Kabbalah.)

—— (1986b) *Jewish Mysticism and Jewish Ethics*, Seattle, WA: University of Washington Press. (An account of the link between mysticism and ethics.)

Fenton, P. (1995) 'Judaism and Sufism', in S. Nasr and O. Leaman (eds) *History of Islamic Philosophy*, London: Routledge, 755–68. (Excellent account of the many links between Jewish and Islamic mysticism in the Middle Ages.)

Gikatilla, J. (*c*.1300) *Sha'arey Orah*, Mantua, 1561; trans. with introduction by A. Weinstein, *Gates of Light*, London: HarperCollins, 1994. (An important Kabbalistic work by a thirteenth-century thinker who tried to make Kabbalah more accessible).

Idel, M. (1988a) *Kabbalah: New Perspectives*, New Haven, CT: Yale University Press. (The best account of the Kabbalah as a whole.)

—— (1988b) *Studies in Ecstatic Kabbalah*, Albany, NY: State University of New York Press. (Standard text on the ecstatic school of Kabbalah.)

—— (1989) *Language, Torah, and Hermeneutics in Abraham Abulafia*, Albany, NY: State University of New York Press. (Excellent account of the significance of Abulafia as a Kabbalistic thinker.)

Schafer, P. (1992) *The Hidden and Manifest God: Some Major Themes in Early Jewish Mysticism*, Albany, NY: State University of New York Press. (An acute discussion of the controversies about the precise nature of Kabbalah.)

Scholem, G. (1961) *Major Trends in Jewish Mysticism*, New York: Schocken. (Very influential text in the modern history of Kabbalah scholarship.)

—— (1969) *On the Kabbalah and its Symbolism*, trans. R. Manheim, New York: Schocken. (A definitive guide to the language of the Kabbalah.)

—— (1973) *Sabbatai Sevi: The Mystical Messiah*, trans. R. Werblowsky, Princeton, NJ: Princeton University Press. (A magisterial account of his links with Kabbalah and general influence on Jewish thought.)

—— (1991) *On the Mystical Shape of the Godhead: Basic Concepts in the Kabbalah*, New York: Schocken. (Summary of the views of this century's most famous Kabbalah scholar.)

* *Sefer Yetzirah* (3rd–6th century AD) trans. I. Friedman, *The Book of Creation*, New York: Schocken, 1977. (The outstanding Kabbalistic work that deals with cosmology. Its main assertion is that the scope for divine creativity involves the thirty-two paths of wisdom which make up ten

basic forces (Sefirot) and the twenty-two letters of the Hebrew language.)

Wolfson, E. (1994) *Through a Speculum that Shines: Vision and Imagination in Medieval Jewish Mysticism*, Princeton, NJ: Princeton University Press. (Exploration of some of the main concepts used in medieval Kabbalah.)

—— (1996) 'Jewish Mysticism: a Philosophical Overview', in D. Frank and O. Leaman (eds) *History of Jewish Philosophy*, London: Routledge, 450–98. (Clear survey of the area.)

* *Zohar: Mishnat ha-Zohar* (*c*.13th century) ed. I. Tishby, Jerusalem: Mosad Bialik, 1957; trans. and ed. G. Scholem, *Zohar, Book of Splendour: Basic Readings from the Kabbalah*, New York: Schocken. (One of the main Kabbalistic texts.)

OLIVER LEAMAN

KAIBARA EKKEN (1630–1714)

*Kaibara Ekken was a leading Japanese scholar in the school of neo-Confucianism established by the renowned twelfth century Chinese synthesizer, Zhu Xi. As a thinker and a scholar Ekken embraced a wide variety of topics from highly specialized neo-Confucian philosophy to the need to popularize Confucian ethics and to assist the society through practical learning (*jitsugaku*).*

Born in Fukuoka in southern Japan, Ekken studied for seven years in Kyoto with the principal scholars of the period. He spent much of his life as an advisor and teacher to the Kuroda *daimyō* family in Fukuoka, but traveled frequently to Kyoto and the capital, Edo (Tokyo). Although Ekken did not establish his own school as did other neo-Confucian scholars, he became through his writings one of the most influential figures in early modern Japan. He lived during a period when Japan isolated itself from the rest of the world while developing a rich complex of Confucian, neo-Confucian, Shintō and Buddhist schools of thought. Neo-Confucianism in particular made a significant contribution to education during this period with the spread of schools and a curriculum largely based on Confucian and neo-Confucian texts and commentaries (see CONFUCIAN PHILOSOPHY, JAPANESE; NEO-CONFUCIAN PHILOSOPHY). It was in this context that Ekken's ideas had a particular impact in both their breadth and depth of concerns.

Ekken was especially concerned to spread neo-Confucian moral teachings and self-cultivation to society at large, and he encouraged the education of all classes. He felt that neo-Confucian ideas could contribute to harmony of both self and society. To accomplish this, he wrote numerous popular treatises on learning for women, for children and for the family. Many of these treatises were reprinted frequently throughout the Tokugawa period (1603–1868). He also wrote on such practical subjects as healthcare, botany, agriculture, topography and history. His work on healthcare is still consulted, and his botanical studies and classification earned him the title of 'the Aristotle of Japan'.

These broad interests in both education and practical learning were based on a carefully developed philosophical position. By the age of thirty he had rejected Buddhism as tending toward quietism, and Wang Yangming's neo-Confucianism as potentially antinomian (see WANG YANGMING). He argued for the importance of Zhu Xi's neo-Confucianism (see ZHU XI) but with some significant adaptations. Philosophically, Ekken embraced the unity of principle (*li*) and material force (*qi*) (see LI; QI). His position, which was indebted to the Chinese neo-Confucian Luo Qinshun, is described as a monism of *qi*. In a significant treatise, the *Taigiroku* (Record of Grave Doubts), Ekken demonstrated strong support for Zhu Xi while taking issue with Zhu Xi's apparent dualism of principle and material force.

Ekken's position came to advocate a dynamic naturalism that was both the basis of his studies of nature and medicine as well as of moral self-cultivation. His monism of *qi* in his philosophical writings was paralleled by a position of filiality in his popular treatises. Ekken suggested that just as reverence and respect are due to parents for their care and support, so also because humans are 'children of heaven and earth' they should encourage a filial response to heaven's mandate and care for nature's abundance.

See also: CONFUCIAN PHILOSOPHY, JAPANESE; EDUCATION, PHILOSOPHY OF; LI; NEO-CONFUCIAN PHILOSOPHY; QI; ZHU XI

List of works

Kaibara Ekken (1665–1714) *Ekken zenshu* (Collected Works of Kaibara Ekken), Tokyo: Ekken zenshū kankōbu, 1910–11, 8 vols. (This is the definitive body of Ekken's collected works, which includes his philosophical essays, his educational treatises, his botanical classification work, his travelogues and his records of local geography.)

—— (1665–1714) *Ekken jikkun* (Ekken's Ten Moral Treatises), ed. Tsukamoto Tetsuzō, Tokyo: Yūhōdō shoten, 1927. (A selection of ten significant moral and educational treatises which represent Ekken's efforts to make Confucian ideas understood by ordinary Japanese.)

—— (1708) *Yamato zokkun* (Precepts for Daily Life in Japan), Tokyo: Kiyomizu Kakujirō, 1967; trans. M.E. Tucker in *Moral and Spiritual Cultivation in Japanese Neo-Confucianism: The Life and Thought of Kaibara Ekken (1630–1714)*, Albany, NY: State University of New York Press. (One of Ekken's more important educational treatises.)

—— (1714) *Taigiroku* (Record of Grave Doubts), in *Kaibara Ekken, Muro Kyūsō*, Nihon shisō takei vol. 34, Tokyo: Iwanami shoten, 1970, 10–64; German trans. O. Graf in *Kaibara Ekken*, Leiden: Brill, 1942. (Supports Zhu Xi, but takes issue with the latter's apparent dualism of principle and material force.)

References and further reading

Graf, O. (1942) *Kaibara Ekken*, Leiden: Brill. (This lengthy work in German consists of a biography of Ekken, a discussion of his philosophy, and a translation of the *Taigiroku* into German.)

Inoue Tadashi (1963) *Kaibara Ekken*, Tokyo: Yoshikawa kōbunkan. (Extensive biographical account (in Japanese) of Ekken's life, emphasizing in particular his role as advisor to the Kuroda *daimyō*.)

Inoue Tadashi and Araki Kengo (eds) (1970) *Kaibara Ekken, Muro Kyōsō*, Nihon shisō taikei vol. 34, Tokyo: Iwanami shoten. (In Japanese, this book provides a strong introductory essay on Ekken's thought and gives annotated selections from some of his major works.)

Irizawa Sōju (1954) *Kaibara Ekken*, Nihon kyōiku sentetsu soho, Tokyo: Bunkyō shoin. (Written in Japanese, this book emphasizes Ekken's contributions to the educational needs of his time, in particular through discussion of his educational treatises written in a more simplified Japanese.)

Ishikawa Matsutaro (ed.) (1968) *Kaibara Ekken, Muro Kyusō shū*, Sekai kyōiku hōten, Nihon kyōiku hen vol. 3, Tokyo: Tamagawa Daigaku shuppanbu. (Written in Japanese as part of a series on educational issues in Japanese history, this book discusses Ekken's educational philosophy and gives some selections from his moral treatises.)

Komoguchi Isao and Okada Takehiko (1985) *Andō Seian; Kaibara Ekken*, Tokyo: Meitoku shuppansha. (In Japanese, this work provides a general discussion of Ekken's philosophy, his moral teachings and his contributions to the practical learning of his day.)

Matsuda Michio (ed.) (1969) *Kaibara Ekken*, Nihon no meicho vol. 14, Tokyo: Chūō koronsha. (Part of a series on major figures in Japanese history, this work provides a biographical introduction to Ekken's life and thought and gives selections in modern Japanese from some of his major works.)

Najita Tetsuo (1975) 'Intellectual Change in Early Eighteenth-Century Tokugawa Confucianism', *Journal of Asian Studies* 34 (4): 932–44. (A short essay in English which provides a penetrating analysis of Ekken's thought in relation to other trends in Tokugawa Confucianism.)

Okada Takehiko (1979) 'Practical Learning in the Chu Hsi School; Yamazaki Ansai and Kaibara Ekken', in W.T. de Bary and I. Bloom (eds) *Principle and Practicality*, New York: Columbia University Press, 231–305. (This articles provides an insightful overview of some of the key elements of Ekken's thought, especially his contributions to 'practical learning'.)

—— (1992) *Kaibara Ekken*, Fukuoka: Nishi nihon shinbunsha. (In Japanese, this is a helpful treatment of Ekken's life and thought by a leading Confucian scholar still living in the area of Ekken's birthplace.)

Tucker, M.E. (1989) *Moral and Spiritual Cultivation in Japanese Neo-Confucianism: The Life and Thought of Kaibara Ekken (1630–1714)*, Albany, NY: State University of New York Press. (The only book-length work in English on Ekken, this monograph provides an introduction to Ekken's life, thought and times as well as a translation and discussion of one of his major ethical treatises.)

MARY EVELYN TUCKER

KALAM *see* ISLAMIC THEOLOGY

KAMES, LORD *see* HOME, HENRY (LORD KAMES)

KANT, IMMANUEL (1724–1804)

Immanuel Kant was the paradigmatic philosopher of the European Enlightenment. He eradicated the last traces of the medieval worldview from modern philosophy, joined the key ideas of earlier rationalism and empiricism into a powerful model of the subjective origins of the fundamental principles of both science and morality, and laid the ground for much in the philosophy of the nineteenth and twentieth centuries. Above all, Kant was the philosopher of human autonomy, the view that by the use of our own reason in its broadest sense human beings can discover and live up to the basic principles of knowledge and action without outside assistance, above all without divine support or intervention.

Kant laid the foundations of his theory of knowledge in his monumental Critique of Pure Reason *(1781). He described the fundamental principle of morality in the* Groundwork of the Metaphysics of Morals *(1785) and the* Critique of Practical Reason *(1788), in the conclusion of which he famously wrote:*

> *Two things fill the mind with ever new and increasing admiration and awe, the more often and steadily reflection is occupied with them:* the starry heaven above me and the moral law within me. *Neither of them need I seek and merely suspect as if shrouded in obscurity or rapture beyond my own horizon; I see them before me and connect them immediately with my existence.*

> *(5: 161–2; see* **List of works** *for method of citation)*

Kant tried to show that both the laws of nature and the laws of morality are grounded in human reason itself. By these two forms of law, however, he is often thought to have defined two incommensurable realms, nature and freedom, the realm of what is and that of what ought to be, the former of which must be limited to leave adequate room for the latter. Kant certainly did devote much space and effort to distinguishing between nature and freedom. But as he also says, in the Critique of Judgment *(1790), it is equally important 'to throw a bridge from one territory to the other'. Ultimately, Kant held that both the laws of nature and the laws of free human conduct must be compatible because they are both products of human thought imposed by us on the data of our experience by the exercise of our own powers. This was clearly stated in his last book,* The Conflict of the Faculties *(1798):*

> *Philosophy is not some sort of science of representations, concepts, and ideas, or a science of all sciences, or anything else of this sort; rather, it is a science of the human being, of its representing, thinking, and acting – it should present the human being in all of its components, as it is and ought to be, that is, in accordance with its natural determinations as well as its relationship of morality and freedom. Ancient philosophy adopted an entirely inappropriate standpoint towards the human being in the world, for it made it into a machine in it, which as such had to be entirely dependent on the world or on external things and circumstances; it thus made the human being*

into an all but merely passive part of the world. Now the critique of reason has appeared and determined the human being to a thoroughly active *place in the world. The human being itself is the original creator of all its representations and concepts and ought to be the sole author of all its actions.*

> *(7: 69–70)*

Thus, Kant derived the fundamental principles of human thought and action from human sensibility, understanding, and reason, all as sources of our autonomy; he balanced the contributions of these principles against the ineliminable inputs of external sensation and internal inclination beyond our own control; and he strove both to demarcate these principles from each other and yet to integrate them into a single system with human autonomy as both its foundation and its ultimate value and goal. These were the tasks of Kant's three great critiques. In the Critique of Pure Reason, *the essential forms of space, time and conceptual thought arise in the nature of human sensibility and understanding and ground the indispensable principles of human experience. He then argued that reason, in the narrow sense manifest in logical inference, plays a key role in systematizing human experience, but that it is a mistake to think that reason offers metaphysical insight into the existence and nature of the human soul, an independent world, and God. In the* Critique of Practical Reason *and* Groundwork, *however, he argued that reason as the source of the ideal of systematicity is the source of the fundamental law of morality and our consciousness of our own freedom, which is the source of all value, and that we can postulate the truth of the fundamental dogmas of Christianity, our own immortality and the existence of God, as practical presuppositions of our moral conduct but not as theoretical truths of metaphysics. In the* Critique of Judgment, *Kant argued that the unanimity of taste and the systematic organization of both individual organisms and nature as a whole could be postulated, again not as metaphysical dogmas but rather as regulative ideals of our aesthetic and scientific pursuits; he then went on to argue that it is through these ideals that we can tie together the realms of nature and freedom, because aesthetic experience offers us a palpable image of our moral freedom, and a scientific conception of the world as a system of interrelated beings makes sense only as an image of the world as the sphere of our own moral efforts. In many of his last writings, from* Religion within the Limits of Reason Alone *(1793) to his final manuscripts, the* Opus postumum, *Kant refined and radicalized his view that our religious conceptions can be understood only as analogies for the nature of human reason itself.*

The Enlightenment began by attempting to bring even God before the bench of human reason – at the turn of the eighteenth century, both Shaftesbury in Great Britain and Wolff in Germany rejected voluntarism, the theory that God makes eternal truths and moral laws by fiat, and argued instead that we ourselves must know what is right and wrong before we could even recognize supposedly divine commands as divine. Kant completed their argument, concluding that the human being 'creates the elements of knowledge of the world himself, a priori, from which he, as, at the same time, an inhabitant of the world, constructs a world-vision in the idea' (Opus postumum, 21: 31).

1 Life and works

Immanuel Kant was born on 22 April 1724 in Königsberg, the capital of East Prussia. He was the child of poor but devout followers of Pietism, a Lutheran revival movement stressing love and good works, simplicity of worship, and individual access to God. Kant's promise was recognized by the Pietist minister Franz Albert Schultz, and he received a free education at the Pietist gymnasium. At sixteen, Kant entered the University of Königsberg, where he studied mathematics, physics, philosophy, theology, and classical Latin literature. His leading teacher was Martin KNUTZEN (1713–51), who introduced him to both Wolffian philosophy and Newtonian physics, and who inspired some of Kant's own later views and philosophical independence by his advocacy of physical influx against the pre-established harmony of LEIBNIZ and Wolff. Kant left university in 1746, just as the major works of the anti-Wolffian Pietist philosopher Christian August CRUSIUS were appearing. Kant's upbringing would have made him

receptive to Crusius, and thus he left university imbued with the Enlightenment aims of Wolffian philosophy but already familiar with technical criticisms of it, especially with Crusius's critique of Wolff's attempt to derive substantive conclusions from a single and merely formal first principle such as the logical principle of non-contradiction (see WOLFF, C.).

On leaving university, Kant completed his first work, *Thoughts on the True Estimation of Living Forces* (1746, published 1749), an unsuccessful attempt to mediate between Cartesian and Leibnizian theories of physical forces. Kant then worked as a tutor, serving in households near Königsberg for the next eight years. When he returned to the university in 1755, however, he had several works ready for publication. The first of these was *Universal Natural History and Theory of the Heavens*, a much more successful scientific work than his first in which Kant argued for the nebular hypothesis, or origin of the solar system out of a nebular mass by purely mechanical means. The book was scarcely known during Kant's lifetime, however, so the French astronomer Pierre Laplace (1749–1827) developed his version of the nebular hypothesis (published 1796) independently, and the theory became known as the Kant-Laplace hypothesis only later. In 1755, Kant also published two Latin works, his MA thesis *A brief presentation of some thoughts concerning fire*, and his first philosophical work, *A new elucidation of the first principles of metaphysical cognition*, which earned him the right to offer lectures at the university as a *Privatdozent* paid directly by his students. The following year Kant published *The employment in natural philosophy of metaphysics combined with geometry, of which sample I contains the physical monadology*, which made him eligible for a salaried professorship, although he was not to receive one until 1770. In these years, Kant also published four essays on earthquakes and winds.

Kant began lecturing in the autumn of 1755, and to earn a living lectured more than twenty hours a week. His topics included logic, metaphysics, ethics, and physics, and he subsequently added physical geography, anthropology (Germany's first lectures so entitled), pedagogy, natural right and even the theory of fortifications. Except for one small essay on optimism (1759), he did not publish again until 1762, when another burst of publications began. He then published, all in German: *The False Subtlety of the Four Syllogistic Figures* (1762); *The Only Possible Argument in support of a Demonstration of the Existence of God* and *Attempt to Introduce the Concept of Negative Magnitudes into Philosophy* (1763); *Observations on the Beautiful and Sublime* and *Inquiry concerning the Distinctness of the Principles of Natural Theology and Morality* (1764), the latter of which was his second-place entry in a competition won by Moses MENDELSSOHN; *Dreams of a Spirit-Seer, elucidated by Dreams of Metaphysics* (1766); and *Concerning the Ultimate Ground of the Differentiation of Directions in Space* (1768). These publications earned Kant widespread recognition in Germany. During this period, Kant was deeply struck by the work of Jean-Jacques ROUSSEAU, especially by his *Social Contract* and the paean to freedom in *Émile* (both 1762). By this time Kant was also acquainted with the philosophy of David HUME, whose two *Enquiries* and other essays, but not *A Treatise of Human Nature*, were published in German as early as 1755.

Having unsuccessfully applied for several chairs at home while declining offers elsewhere, Kant was finally appointed Professor of Logic and Metaphysics in Königsberg in 1770. This event occasioned his inaugural dissertation, and last Latin work, *On the form and principles of the sensible and intelligible world*. Following correspondence about this work with Johann Heinrich LAMBERT, Johann Georg Sulzer, and Mendelssohn, however, Kant fell into another decade-long silence, broken only by a few progress reports to his recent student Marcus Herz and a few minor essays. Yet during this 'silent decade', Kant was preparing for his enormous body of subsequent works. Beginning in 1781, with the first edition of the *Critique of Pure Reason*, Kant unleashed a steady torrent of books. These include: *Prolegomena to Any Future Metaphysics that shall come forth as Scientific*, an attempted popularization of the first *Critique*, in 1783; two essays, 'Idea for a Universal History from a Cosmopolitan Point of View' and 'What is Enlightenment?' in 1784; *The Groundwork of the Metaphysics of Morals* and four other essays in 1785; *The Metaphysical Foundations of Natural Science*, essays on 'The Conjectural Beginnings of Human History' and 'What Does it mean to Orient Oneself in Thinking?' and two other pieces in 1786; a substantially revised second edition of the *Critique of Pure Reason* in 1787; in 1788, the *Critique of Practical Reason* and an essay on 'The Use of Teleological Principles in Philosophy'; the *Critique of Judgment* as well as an important polemic 'On a discovery according to which any new Critique of Pure Reason is rendered dispensable by an older one' in 1790; the political essay 'On the Common Saying: "That may be right in theory but does not work in practice"' and the controversial *Religion within the Limits of Reason Alone* in 1793; *Towards Perpetual Peace* in 1795; the *Metaphysics of Morals*, comprising the 'Doctrine of Right' and the 'Doctrine of Virtue',

in 1797, as well as the essay 'On a putative Right to Lie from Love of Mankind'; and his last major works in 1798, a handbook on *Anthropology from a Pragmatic Point of View* and his defence of the intellectual freedom of the philosophical faculty from religious and legal censorship in the restrictive atmosphere of Prussia after Frederick the Great, *The Conflict of the Faculties*. (With Kant's approval, some of his other lecture courses were also published, including *Logic* in 1800 and *Physical Geography* and *Pedagogy* in 1804.) Kant retired from lecturing in 1797, at the age of seventy-three, and devoted his remaining years to a work which was to be entitled 'The Transition from the Metaphysical First Principles of Natural Science to Physics', but which was far from complete when Kant ceased working on it in 1803. (Selections from his drafts were first published in 1882–4, and they were first fully published as *Opus postumum* in 1936–8). After a lifetime of hypochondria without any serious illness, Kant gradually lost his eyesight and strength and died on 12 February 1804.

2 Kant's work to 1770

In his first work, *Living Forces*, Kant tried to mediate a dispute about the measurement of forces between DESCARTES and Leibniz by employing a distinction between 'living' or intrinsic forces and 'dead' or impressed ones to argue that Leibniz's measure was correct for the former and Descartes's for the latter. This distinction could not be maintained in a uniform mechanics, and the young Kant remained ignorant of the mathematically correct solution, which had been published by D'ALEMBERT in 1743. Nevertheless, the work already showed Kant's lifelong preoccupation with the relation between scientific laws and metaphysical foundations. It also included the observation that the three-dimensionality of physical space is a product of actually existing forces, not the only geometry that is logically possible (10, 1: 24).

Kant's works of 1755 reveal more of his originality and his enduring themes. *Universal Natural History*, deriving the present state of the planets from postulated initial conditions by reiterated applications of the laws of Newtonian mechanics, manifests not only Kant's commitment to those laws, for which he was subsequently to seek philosophical foundations, but also his commitment to thoroughly naturalistic explanations in science, in which God can be the initial source of natural laws but never intervenes within the sequence of physical causes. *New Elucidation*, while not yet a methodological break from the rationalism of Leibniz, Wolff and Alexander Gottlieb BAUMGARTEN (1714–62) (whose textbooks on metaphysics, ethics and aesthetics Kant used for decades), breaks with them on several substantive issues. Kant begins by rejecting Wolff's supposition that the principle of non-contradiction is a single yet sufficient principle of truth, arguing instead that there must be separate first principles of positive and negative truths; following Crusius, Kant was always to remain suspicious of programmes to reduce all truth to a single principle. Kant then criticized previous proofs of the Principle of Sufficient Reason, although his own proof was also a failure. More importantly, he argued that the principle of sufficient reason does not entail the theory of pre-established harmony drawn from it by the Leibnizians: the need for a sufficient reason for any change in a substance proves the necessity rather than impossibility of real interaction among a plurality of substances. Transposed into an epistemological key, this argument was to become central in the first *Critique*. The work is also noteworthy for the first suggestion of Kant's critique of Descartes's ontological argument for the existence of God (see GOD, ARGUMENTS FOR THE EXISTENCE OF), and for a first treatment of the problem of free will as well. Here Kant defended against the indeterminism of Crusius the determinism of Leibniz (see DETERMINISM AND INDETERMINISM), although he was later to criticize this as the 'freedom of a turnspit' (5: 97). Kant's later theory of free will, however, attempts to reconcile Crusius and Leibniz.

In the *Physical Monadology* (1756), Kant tries to reconcile the infinite divisibility of space in geometry with the need for simple, indivisible substances in metaphysics – the subsequent theme of the first *Critique*'s second Antinomy (see §8). Kant does not yet appeal to a metaphysical distinction between appearance and reality, but instead argues that because bodies in space are not ultimately composed of particles but of attractive and repulsive forces (1: 484), they may be physically indivisible even when space itself is still mathematically divisible.

Kant's works of the 1760s introduce some of the methodological as well as substantive assumptions of his mature philosophy. *The Only Possible Argument* details Kant's attack upon the ontological argument, the paradigmatic rationalistic argument because of its presupposition that an existence-statement can be derived from the analysis of a concept. Kant argues that 'existence is not a predicate or a determination of a thing' (2: 72), but rather the 'absolute positing of a thing' (2: 73); that is, the existence of its subject is *presupposed* by the assertion of any proposition, not inferred from the concepts employed in it. Kant also maintains that the other rationalist argument for theism, the argument from the contingency of the world to a necessary cause of it, as well as the

empiricists' favourite, the argument from design, fail to prove the existence of a necessary being with all the attributes of God. However, Kant still holds that the existence of God can be proved as a condition of the *possibility* of any reality. Finally, Kant further develops his argument that scientific explanation cannot allow divine intervention in the sequence of events, and that God must only be seen as the original ground of the laws of nature.

Negative Magnitudes announces a fundamental methodological break from rationalism. Inspired by both Crusius and Hume, Kant argues that *real opposition* (as when two velocities in opposite directions or a pleasure and a pain cancel each other out) is fundamentally different from *logical contradiction* (as between a proposition and its negation); he then applies this to causation, arguing that the *real ground* of a state does not entail its existence logically, but is connected to it in an entirely different way. This precludes any proof of the principle of sufficient reason from merely logical considerations alone (2: 202).

The *Inquiry into the Distinctness of the Principles of Natural Theology and Ethics* continues Kant's attack upon rationalism. The question for this essay was whether metaphysics could use the same method as mathematics, which Kant firmly denied: mathematics, he argues, can prove its theorems by constructing its objects from their very definitions, but metaphysics can only use analysis to tease out the definitions of its objects from given concepts, and cannot construct the objects themselves (2: 276). The claim that the method of philosophy is analysis may sound like rationalism; however, Kant insists that in both metaphysics and ethics philosophy needs *material* as well as *formal* first principles, again precluding any purely logical derivation of philosophical theses. Kant does not yet have a clear account of material first principles – he is sympathetic to Crusius's account of indemonstrable cognitions and to the suggestion of the moral sense theorists SHAFTESBURY and HUTCHESON that the first principles of ethics arise from *feeling*, but not satisfied with either. Without yet naming it, Kant also introduces his distinction between hypothetical and categorical imperatives (2: 298).

Still in 1764, however, the book *Observations on the Beautiful and Sublime* already announces Kant's departure from moral sense theory and introduces the most fundamental theme of Kant's ethics. Virtue cannot depend merely on benevolent inclination, but only on general principles, which in turn express 'a feeling that lives in every human breast and extends itself much further than over the particular grounds of compassion and complaisance... the *feeling of the beauty and dignity of human nature*' (2: 217). In notes in his own copy of this work, Kant went even further, and first clearly stated his enduring belief that 'freedom properly understood (moral, not metaphysical) is the supreme principle of all virtue as well as of all happiness' (20: 31).

In *Dreams of a Spirit-Seer*, Kant ridicules traditional metaphysics by comparing it to the fantasies of the Swedish theosophist Emmanuel SWEDENBORG; Kant argues instead that metaphysical concepts cannot be used without empirical verification, and that therefore metaphysics can at most be 'a science of the *boundaries of human reason*' (2: 368). The work also contains further thoughts on morality, suggesting that the two forces of egoism and altruism define the structure of the moral world in much the way that the forces of repulsion and attraction define that of the physical world (2: 334). But Kant does not yet argue that postulates of practical reason may be a valid alternative to the delusions of metaphysics.

Finally, the brief essay on *Directions in Space* argues that incongruent counterparts, such as right- and left-handed gloves, which have identical descriptions but cannot occupy the same space, prove that the qualities of objects are not determined by concepts alone but also by their relation to absolute space. Kant did not yet raise metaphysical questions about the nature of absolute space or epistemological questions about how we could know it, but this essay can be seen as introducing the distinction between intuitions and concepts which was to be a cornerstone of Kant's subsequent thought (see §5).

3 The *Inaugural Dissertation* of 1770 and the problem of metaphysics

Kant's *Inaugural Dissertation* of 1770 consolidated many of the gains he had made during the 1760s and introduced a fundamentally new theory about the metaphysics and epistemology of space and time which was to remain a constant in his subsequent thought, but also left open crucial questions about the source of our most fundamental concepts. Although Kant hoped to proceed quickly to his projects in the philosophy of science and in moral and political theory, it was to take him all of the next decade to answer these preliminary questions.

Taking up where *Directions in Space* left off, Kant begins the dissertation with the distinction between intuitions (singular and immediate representations of objects) and concepts (general and abstract representations of them) as distinct but equally important elements in the *'two-fold genesis'* of the concept [of a world] out of the nature of the mind'. The intellect (Kant does not yet divide this into understanding and reason) provides abstract concepts, under which

instances are subordinated; the 'sensitive faculty of cognition' provides 'distinct intuition[s]' which represent concepts 'in the concrete' and within which different parts may be coordinated (2: 387). Kant goes on to claim that 'whatever in cognition is sensitive is dependent upon the special character of the subject', that is, the knower, so that sensation, through intuitions, represents things *'as they appear'* (*phenomena*), while the intellect, through concepts, represents things *'as they are'* (*noumena*) (2: 392). Kant then presents the 'principles of the form of the sensible world': time and space are the forms of the intuition of all objects (time is the form for all representation of objects, inner or outer, while space is the form for the representation of all outer objects) which do not arise from but are presupposed by all particular perceptions; they are singular rather than general, that is, particular times or spaces are parts of a single whole rather than instances of a general kind; and they must each be 'the subjective condition which is necessary, in virtue of the nature of the human mind, for the coordinating of all things in accordance with a fixed law', or a *'pure intuition'* rather than *'something objective and real'* (2: 398–400, 402–4). Only thus can we explain our knowledge of both these general claims about space and time as well as particular claims about their structure, such as the theorems of geometry (2: 404). In other words, we can explain the certainty of knowledge about space and time only by supposing that it is knowledge of the structure of our own minds, and thus of how objects appear to us, rather than knowledge about how things are in themselves. This necessarily subjective origin and significance of certainty, which Kant was later to name 'transcendental idealism', is the foundation for the active role of the human mind in knowledge of the world.

Kant has little to say about the source of intellectual concepts, but continues to believe that they give us knowledge of how things are independently of the structure of our own minds. His main claim, still Leibnizian, is that in order to conceive of things as genuinely distinct substances, yet as collectively interacting in a single world, we must conceive of them as contingent beings all depending upon a single necessary being (2: 407–8). Kant then argues that metaphysical error arises when the principles of sensitive and intellectual cognition are confused, but more particularly when 'the principles which are native to sensitive cognition transgress their limits, and affect what belongs to the intellect' (2: 411) – the opposite of what he will argue later when he claims that metaphysical illusion arises from thinking that human reason can reach beyond the limits of the senses (see §8). Finally, Kant introduces as mere 'principles of convenience' the principles of universal causation and of the conservation of substance as well as a more general 'canon' of rationality, that *principles are not to be multiplied beyond what is absolutely necessary*' (30, 2: 418). A better account of these principles will occupy much of Kant's later work (see §7).

Early readers of Kant's dissertation objected to the merely subjective significance of space and especially time, but Kant was never to surrender this theory. What came to bother him instead was his inadequate treatment of metaphysical concepts such as 'possibility, existence, necessity, substance, cause, etc.' (2: 395). In a famous letter of 21 February 1772 to Marcus Herz (10: 129–35), Kant claimed that the 'whole secret' of metaphysics is to explain how intellectual concepts which neither literally produce their objects (as God's concepts might) nor are merely produced by them (as empirical concepts are) nevertheless necessarily apply to them. But Kant did not yet know how to answer this question.

His first progress on this issue is found in fragments from 1774–5 (Reflections 4674–84, 17: 643–73). Two key ideas are found here. First, Kant finally formulates the problem of metaphysics as that of 'synthetic' rather than 'analytic' propositions: how can we know the truth of propositions in which the predicates clearly go beyond anything contained in their subject-concepts but yet enjoy the same universality and necessity as propositions which are mere tautologies, whose predicates are contained in their subject concepts (17: 643–4, 653–5)? Second, Kant here first states that the answer to this question lies in recognizing that certain fundamental concepts, not just the intuitions of space and time, are 'conditions of the concrete representation [of objects] in the subject' (17: 644) or of the unity of *experience in general*' (17: 658). Kant's idea is that in order to ground any determinate ordering of either subjective or objective states in temporal succession, we must use the concepts of substance, causation, and interaction, and that these must therefore be categories which originate in the understanding just as the pure forms of space and time originate in the sensibility.

4   The project of the *Critique of Pure Reason*

In spite of this progress in 1775, six more years passed before the *Critique of Pure Reason* finally appeared in 1781. In an unmistakeable reference to Locke's *Essay concerning Human Understanding* (see LOCKE, J.), Kant began the work with the promise to submit reason to a critique in order to obtain a 'decision about the possibility or impossibility of metaphysics in general and the determination of its sources, its

scope and its boundaries' (A xii). The 'chief question' would be 'what and how much can understanding and reason know apart from all *experience*?' (A xvii). Answering this question would require discovering the fundamental principles that human understanding contributes to human experience and exposing the metaphysical illusions that arise when human reason tries to extend those principles beyond the limits of human experience.

But Kant's project was even more ambitious than that, as he was to make clear in the revised edition of the *Critique* six years later. There, in addition to more explicitly describing his strategy for explaining the certainty of the first principles of human knowledge as one of supposing that 'objects must conform to our knowledge' rather than vice versa (B xvi), Kant described his whole project in broader terms: 'I therefore had to offset *knowledge* in order to make room for *belief*' (B xxx). Kant did not mean to return to the sceptical fideism of earlier thinkers such as Pierre BAYLE, who simply substituted religious belief for theoretical ignorance. Instead, Kant argues first that the human mind supplies necessary principles of sensibility and understanding, or perception and conception; next, that if human reason tries to extend the fundamental concepts and principles of thought beyond the limits of perception for purposes of theoretical knowledge, it yields only illusion; but finally that there is another use of reason, a practical use in which it constructs universal laws and ideals of human conduct and postulates the fulfilment of the conditions necessary to make such conduct rational, including the freedom of the will, the existence of God, and the immortality of the soul. This use of reason does not challenge the limits of theoretical reason but is legitimate and necessary in its own right.

In the Introduction, Kant defines his first task as that of explaining the possibility of synthetic a priori judgments. This notion is grounded in two distinctions. First, there is a logical distinction between analytic and synthetic propositions: in analytic propositions, the predicate-concept is implicitly or explicitly contained in the subject-concept (for example, 'A bachelor is unmarried' or 'An unmarried male is male'), so the proposition conveys no new information and is true by identity alone; in synthetic propositions, the content of the predicate is clearly not contained in the subject-concept (for example, 'Bachelors are unhappy') (A 6–7/B 10–11), so the proposition conveys new information and cannot be true by identity alone. Second, there is an epistemological distinction between propositions which are a posteriori, or can be known to be true only on the basis of antecedent experience and observation, and those which are a priori, or known to be true independently of experience, or at least any particular experience (A 1–2/B 1–3). Kant maintains that anything which is known to be universally and necessarily true must be known a priori, because, following Hume, he assumes that experience only tells us how what has actually been observed is, not how everything must be (A 1–2/B 3–4). Combining these two distinctions yields four possible kinds of judgments. Two of these obviously obtain: analytic a priori judgments, in which we know a proposition to be true by analysis of its subject-concept and without observation; and synthetic a posteriori judgments, in which we know factual statements going beyond subject-concepts to be true through observation. Equally clearly, a third possibility is excluded: there are no analytic a posteriori judgments, for we need not go to experience to discover what we can know from analysis alone. What is controversial is whether there are synthetic a priori judgments, propositions that are universally and necessarily true, and thus must go beyond experience, but which cannot be reached by the mere analysis of concepts. Both rationalists and empiricists had denied such a possibility, but for Kant only it could ground an informative science of metaphysics at all.

Kant's notion of synthetic a priori judgment raises various problems. Critics have long complained that Kant provides no unequivocal criterion for deciding when a predicate is contained in a subject, and twentieth-century philosophers such as W. QUINE argued that there are no analytic truths because not even definitions can be held entirely immune from revision in the face of empirical facts. Lewis White Beck showed, however, that this did not affect Kant's project, for Kant himself, in a polemic with the Wolffian Johann August EBERHARD, argued that analysis always presupposes synthesis, and that the adoption of any definition itself has to be justified, either by construction or observation; so even conceding that all judgments are ultimately synthetic, Kant's question remains whether any of these are synthetic a priori.

Another issue is just what synthetic a priori judgments Kant intended to justify. In the 'Prolegomena' and the 'Introduction' to the second edition of the Critique, Kant suggests that it is obvious that synthetic a priori judgments exist in what he calls 'pure mathematics' and 'pure physics', and that his project is to show that what explains these also explains other such propositions, in metaphysics. Elsewhere, however, Kant suggests that metaphysics must show that there are any synthetic a priori judgments, even in mathematics and physics. While much of the content of the Critique suggests that

Kant's considered view must be the latter, he is far from clear about this.

5 Space, time and transcendental idealism

The first part of the Critique, the 'Transcendental Aesthetic', has two objectives: to show that we have synthetic a priori knowledge of the spatial and temporal forms of outer and inner experience, grounded in our own pure intuitions of space and time; and to argue that transcendental idealism, the theory that spatiality and temporality are only forms in which objects appear to us and not properties of objects as they are in themselves, is the necessary condition for this a priori knowledge of space and time (see SPACE; TIME).

Much of the section refines arguments from the inaugural dissertation of 1770. First, in what the second edition labels the 'Metaphysical Exposition', Kant argues that space and time are both *pure forms of intuition* and *pure intuitions*. They are pure *forms* of intuition because they must precede and structure all experience of individual outer objects and inner states; Kant tries to prove this by arguing that our conceptions of space and time cannot be derived from experience of objects, because any such experience presupposes the individuation of objects in space and/or time, and that although we can represent space or time as devoid of objects, we cannot represent any objects without representing space and/or time (A 23–4/B 38–9; A 30–1/B 46). They are pure *intuitions* because they represent single individuals rather than classes of things; Kant tries to prove this by arguing that particular spaces and times are always represented by introducing boundaries into a single, unlimited space or time, rather than the latter being composed out of the former as parts, and that space and time do not have an indefinite number of instances, like general concepts, but an infinite number of parts (A 24/B 39–40; A 31–2/B 47–8).

Next, in the 'Transcendental Exposition', Kant argues that we must have an a priori intuition of space because 'geometry is a science which determines the properties of space synthetically and yet a priori' (B 40). That is, the propositions of geometry describe objects in space, go beyond the mere concepts of any of the objects involved – thus geometric theorems cannot be proved without actually constructing the figures – and yet are known a priori. (Kant offers an analogous but less plausible argument about time, where the propositions he adduces seem analytic (B 48).) Both our a priori knowledge about space and time in general and our synthetic a priori knowledge of geometrical propositions in particular can be explained only by supposing that space and time are of subjective origin, and thus knowable independently of the experience of particular objects.

Finally, Kant holds that these results prove transcendental idealism, or that space and time represent properties of things as they appear to us but not properties or relations of things as they are in themselves, let alone real entities like Newtonian absolute space; thus his position of 1768 is now revised to mean that space is epistemologically but not ontologically absolute (A 26/B 42; A 32–3/B 49–50; A 39–40/B 56–7). Kant's argument is that 'determinations' which belong to things independently of us 'cannot be intuited prior to the things to which they belong', and so could not be intuited a priori, while space and time and their properties *are* intuited a priori. Since they therefore cannot be properties of things in themselves, there is no alternative but that space and time are merely the forms in which objects appear to us.

Much in Kant's theory has been questioned by later philosophy of mathematics. Kant's claim that geometrical theorems are synthetic because they can only be proven by construction has been rendered doubtful by more complete axiomatizations of mathematics than Kant knew, and his claim that such propositions describe objects in physical space yet are known a priori has been questioned on the basis of the distinction between purely formal systems and their physical realization.

Philosophical debate, however, has centred on Kant's inference of transcendental idealism from his philosophy of mathematics. One issue is the very meaning of Kant's distinction between appearances and things in themselves. Gerold Prauss and Henry Allison have ascribed to Kant a distinction between two kinds of *concepts* of objects, one including reference to the necessary conditions for the perception of those objects and the other merely leaving them out, with no ontological consequences. Another view holds that Kant denies that things in themselves, and not merely their concepts, are spatial and temporal, and that spatial and temporal properties are, literally, properties only of our own representations of things. Kant makes statements that can support each of these interpretations; but proponents of the second view, including the present author, have argued that it is entailed by both Kant's argument for and his use of his distinction, the latter especially in his theory of free will (see §8).

The debate about Kant's argument for transcendental idealism, already begun in the nineteenth century, concerns whether Kant has omitted a 'neglected alternative' in assuming that space and time must be *either* properties of things as they are in themselves or of representations, but not both,

namely that we might have a priori knowledge of space and time because we have an a priori subjective representation of them while they are also objective properties of things. Some argue that there is no neglected alternative, because although the *concepts* of appearances and things in themselves are necessarily different, Kant postulates only one set of *objects*. This author has argued that the 'neglected alternative' is a genuine possibility that Kant intends to exclude by arguing from his premise that propositions about space and time are *necessarily* true: if those propositions were true *both* of our own representations and of their ontologically distinct objects, they might be necessarily true of the former but only contingently true of the latter, and thus not necessarily true throughout their domain (A 47–8/B 65–6). In this case, however, Kant's transcendental idealism depends upon a dubious claim about necessary truth.

6 Pure concepts of the understanding

The 'Transcendental Analytic' of the *Critique* breaks new ground, arguing that the most fundamental categories of thought as well as the forms of perception are themselves human products which are necessary conditions of the possibility of experience. Like the 'Transcendental Aesthetic', its first section, the 'Analytic of Concepts', is also divided into a 'metaphysical' and a 'transcendental deduction' (B 159).

In the metaphysical deduction Kant intends to provide a principle to identify the most fundamental concepts of thought, the categories of the understanding, and then to show that our knowledge of any object always involves these categories. The key to his argument is the claim that knowledge is always expressed in a *judgment* (A 68–9/B 93–4); he then argues that there are certain characteristic forms or 'logical functions' of judgment, and that in order for our judgments to be about objects, these logical functions of judgments must also provide the basic concepts for conceiving of objects. Thus Kant first produces a table of the logical functions of judgment, based on the premise that every judgment has a *quantity*, *quality*, *relation* and *modality*, and then produces a table of categories, under the same four headings, showing how objects of such judgments must be conceived. Thus, judgments may be universal, particular, or singular, and then their objects must be unities, pluralities, or totalities; judgments may be affirmative, negative, or infinite, and objects manifest either reality, negation, or limitation; judgments may relate a predicate to a subject (categorical judgment), or else relate one predicate-subject judgment to another as antecedent and consequent (hypothetical judgment) or as alternatives (disjunctive judgment), and objects may correspondingly manifest the relations of inherence and subsistence, causality and dependence, or community or reciprocity; finally, judgments may be problematic, assertoric, or apodeictic, thus their objects either possible or impossible, existent or non-existent, or necessary or contingent (A 70/B 95; A 80/B 106).

Kant's scheme is intuitively plausible, and he makes use of it throughout his works. But philosophers as diverse as HEGEL and Quine have questioned its coherence and necessity. What is troubling for Kant's own project, however, is that he does not show why we must use all the logical functions of judgment, hence why we must use all the categories. In particular, he does not show why we must make not only categorical but also hypothetical and disjunctive judgments. Without such a premise, Kant's arguments for causation, against Hume, and for interaction, against Leibniz, are not advanced.

Kant's aim and his strategy in the transcendental deduction remain debatable, despite his complete revision of this section in the second edition of the *Critique*. Some view the transcendental deduction as a 'regressive argument' aimed at empiricism, meant to show only that *if* we make judgments about objects then we must use a priori concepts. But if Kant already established this in the metaphysical deduction, the transcendental deduction becomes redundant. It seems more natural to see the latter as intended to fix the *scope* of our use of the categories by showing that we can have *no* experience which is immune from conceptualization under them, thus that the categories enjoy universal objective validity. Because these categories originate in the logical structure of our own thought, Kant holds, we must conceive of ourselves as the autonomous lawgivers for all of nature (A 127–8, B 164).

There are many differences between the two versions of the transcendental deduction, but both employ the fundamental idea that we cannot have some form of *self*-consciousness, or 'transcendental apperception', without also having consciousness of *objects*, which in turn requires the application of the categories; then, since Kant holds that we can have no experience at all without being able to be conscious that we have it, he can argue that we can have no experience to which we cannot apply the categories. The success of this strategy is unclear. The first-edition deduction begins with a debatable analysis of the necessary conditions for knowledge of an object, which slides from the conditional necessity that we must use rules if we are to have knowledge of objects to an absolute necessity that we must have knowledge of objects, and then introduces transcendental apperception as the 'transcendental ground' of the latter

necessity (A 106). In the second edition, Kant begins directly with the claim that self-consciousness of our experience is always possible, which has not met with much resistance, but then makes the inference to the necessity of knowledge of objects conceived of through the categories by equating transcendental apperception with a notion of 'objective apperception' that is equivalent to judgment about objects (B 139–40). This makes the connection between self-consciousness and the categorial judgment of objects true by definition, and undermines Kant's claim to provide a synthetic rather than analytic proof of the objective validity of the categories.

In spite of these problems, the idea that self-consciousness depends upon knowledge of objects and thus on the use of the categories to conceive of objects has remained attractive; and some of the most interesting recent work on Kant has been reconstructions of the transcendental deduction, such as those by Peter Strawson, Jonathan Bennett and Dieter Henrich. Others have concluded that Kant only establishes a convincing connection between self-consciousness and categorial thought of objects once he shows that making judgments about objects, using the categories, is a necessary condition for making judgments about the *temporal* order of our experience. This is Kant's project in the next section of the *Critique*.

7 The principles of judgment and the foundations of science

Kant proceeds from the categories to the foundations of natural science in several steps. First, he argues that the categories, which thus far have merely logical content, must be made 'homogeneous' with experience, or be recast in forms we can actually experience. Since time, as the form of both outer and inner sense, is the most general feature of our sensible experience, Kant argues that the categories must be made homogeneous with experience by being associated with certain determinate temporal relations or 'schemata' (A 138–9/B 177–8). For example, the pure category of ground and consequence, thus far understood only abstractly as the relation of the states of objects that makes them fit to be objects of hypothetical ('if–then') judgments, is associated with the schema of rule-governed temporal succession, something closer to what we can actually experience. Focused as he is on the universality of time, Kant seems to de-emphasize spatiality unduly in the 'Schematism': for example, it would seem more natural to say that the schema of causality is the rule-governed temporal succession of states of objects within an appropriate degree of spatial contiguity.

Next, in the 'System of all Principles of Pure Understanding', Kant argues for the necessity of certain fundamental principles of all natural laws. Following the division of the categories, this chapter is divided into four parts. In the first, the 'Axioms of Intuition', Kant argues that 'All intuitions are extensive magnitudes' (B 202), and thus that all objects of experience are subject to the mathematics of discrete quantities. In the second, the 'Anticipations of Perception', Kant proves that 'In all appearances, the real that is an object of sensation has intensive magnitude, that is, a degree' (B 207), and is thus subject to the mathematics of continuous quantities; here he argues that because our sensations manifest varying degrees of intensity we must also conceive of the objects they represent as manifesting a reality that varies in degree. The first of these two 'mathematical' principles (A 162/B 201) does not add to results already established in the Transcendental Aesthetic, however, and the second depends upon an empirical assumption.

In the next section, the 'Analogies of Experience', dealing with the first of two kinds of 'dynamical' principles, Kant offers some of the most compelling and important arguments in the *Critique*. In the First Analogy, Kant argues that we can determine that there has been a change in the objects of our perception, not merely a change in our perceptions themselves, only by conceiving of what we perceive as successive states of enduring substances (see SUBSTANCE). Because we can never perceive the origination or cessation of substances themselves, but only changes in their states, Kant argues, the sum-total of substances in nature is permanent (B 224). In the Second Analogy, Kant argues for a further condition for making judgments about change in objects: because even when we undergo a sequence of perceptions, there is nothing in their immediate sensory content to tell us that there is an objective change, let alone what particular sequence of change there is, we can only distinguish a '*subjective sequence* of apprehension from the *objective sequence* of appearances' (A 193/B 238) by judging that a particular sequence of objective states of affairs, *a fortiori* the sequence of our perceptions of those states, has been determined in accordance with a rule that states of the second type can only follow states of the first type – precisely what we mean by a causal law. Finally, the Third Analogy argues that because we always perceive states of objects successively, we cannot immediately perceive states of two or more objects to be simultaneous, and can therefore only judge that two such states simultaneously exist in different regions of space if they are governed by laws of interaction dictating that neither state can exist without the other (A 213/B 260).

Kant's arguments have been assailed on the basis of relativity theory and quantum mechanics. But since they are epistemological arguments that our ability to make temporal judgments about the succession or simultaneity of states of affairs depends upon judgments about substance, causation and interaction, it is not clear that they are open to objection from this quarter. If relativity tells us that the succession or simultaneity of states of affairs may depend upon the choice of inertial frame, then Kant's theory is not refuted, but just predicts that in that case our own judgments about temporal sequence must also vary. If quantum mechanics tells us that causal laws are merely probabilistic, then Kant's theory is again not refuted but just predicts that in that case our temporal judgments cannot be entirely determinate.

In the last section of the 'Principles', Kant assigns empirical criteria to the modal concepts of possibility, actuality and necessity. The main interest of this section lies in the 'Refutation of Idealism' which Kant inserted into it in the second edition. Here Kant argues that temporal judgments about one's own states require reference to objects which endure in a way that mental representations themselves do not, and therefore that consciousness of oneself also implies consciousness of objects external to oneself (B 275–6; also B xxxix–xli). There has been controversy not only about the precise steps of the proof, but also about whether it is supposed to prove that we have knowledge of the existence of things ontologically distinct from our own representations, which seems to undercut Kant's transcendental idealism. However, the argument of 1787 was actually just the first of many drafts Kant wrote (Reflections 6311–16, 18: 606–23), and these suggest that he did mean to prove that we know of the existence of objects ontologically distinct from ourselves and our states, although we cannot attribute to them as they are in themselves the very spatiality by means of which we represent this ontological distinctness.

Finally, in the *Metaphysical Foundations of Natural Science*, published between the two editions of the *Critique* (1786), Kant carried his a priori investigation of the laws of nature one step further by introducing not only the empirical notion of change itself but also the further empirical concept of matter as the movable in space (4: 480). With this one empirical addition, he claims, he can deduce the laws of phoronomy, the vectorial composition of motions in space; of dynamics, the attractive and repulsive forces by which space is actually filled; of mechanics, the communication of moving forces; and of phenomenology, which in Kant's sense – derived from J.H. Lambert, and very different from its later senses in Hegel or HUSSERL – means the laws for distinguishing apparent from real motions. This work is not an essay in empirical physics but rather an exploration of the conceptual framework into which the empirical results of physics must be fitted.

8 The illusions of theoretical reason

In the 'Transcendental Dialectic', Kant argues that the doctrines of traditional metaphysics are illusions arising from the attempt to use the categories of understanding to gain information about objects beyond the horizon of our forms of intuition. What makes such illusions inevitable is the tendency of human reason to seek the unconditioned, that is, to carry a chain of ideas to its assumed completion even when that lies beyond the bounds of sense. For example, understanding may tell us that wholes consist of parts, and sensibility may allow us to find a smaller part for any given whole; but only reason suggests that decomposition into parts must come to an end in something absolutely simple, something we could never perceive by sense. In its practical use, reason may produce ideas of the unconditioned, such as the idea of the universal acceptability of maxims of action, which do not tell us anything misleading about the world because they do not tell us anything about how the world is at all, only how it ought to be; but in its theoretical use reason appears to tell us things about the world that cannot be confirmed by our senses or are even incompatible with the forms of our perception.

This diagnosis of metaphysical error makes good sense of Kant's procedure in the 'Antinomy of Pure Reason', where he presents a series of conflicts between the form and limits of sensibility as structured by the understanding, on the one hand, and the pretensions of unconditioned reason, on the other. In early sketches of the *Dialectic* (Reflections 4756–60, 1775–7, 17: 698–713), Kant diagnosed all of the illusions of traditional metaphysics in this form. In the *Critique*, however, Kant singled out some metaphysical beliefs about the self and about God for separate treatment in the 'Paralogisms of Pure Reason' and 'Ideal of Pure Reason'. These sections offer powerful criticisms of traditional metaphysical doctrines, but require a more complex explanation of metaphysical illusion than the single idea of reason's search for the unconditioned.

In the 'Paralogisms', Kant diagnoses the doctrines of 'rational psychology' that the soul is a *substance* which is *simple* and therefore incorruptible, *numerically identical* throughout the experience of any person, and necessarily *distinct* from any external object (this is how he reformulates the Fourth Paralogism in the second edition (B 409)), as a tissue

of ungrounded assertions mistaking the logical properties of the *representation* 'I' or the *concept* of the self for the properties of whatever it is in us which actually thinks (A 355, B 409). Kant's criticism of the traditional metaphysics of the soul is convincing, but does not depend on reason's postulation of the unconditioned; instead, Kant's demonstration that these doctrines arise from confusion between properties of a representation and what is represented showed that they were not inevitable illusions by destroying their credibility once and for all.

The four metaphysical disputes that Kant presents in the 'Antinomy of Pure Reason' are often read as straightforward conflicts between reason and sensibility; but Kant characterizes them as disputes engendered by pure reason itself, so a more complex reading is required. In fact, both sides in each dispute – what Kant calls the 'thesis' and 'antithesis' – reflect different forms of reason's demand for something unconditioned, and what conflicts with the limits of sensibility is the assumption that these demands give rise to a genuine dispute at all. Kant again uses the contrast between 'mathematical' and 'dynamical' to divide the four disputes into two groups, and resolves the disputes in two different ways.

In the first antinomy the dispute is between the thesis that the world has a beginning in time and a limit in space and the antithesis that it is infinite in temporal duration and spatial extension (A 426–7/B 454–5). In the second antinomy, the dispute is between the thesis that substances in the world are ultimately composed of simple parts and the antithesis that nothing simple is ever to be found in the world, thus that everything is infinitely divisible (A 434–5/B 462–3). In each case, thesis and antithesis reflect reason's search for the unconditioned, but in two different forms: in the thesis, reason postulates an ultimate *termination* of a series, and in the antithesis, an unconditional *extension* of the series. In these 'mathematical antinomies', however, Kant argues that *neither* side is true, because reason is attempting to apply its demand for something unconditioned to space and time, which are always *indefinite* in extent because they are finite yet always extendible products of our own cognitive activity (A 504–5/B 532–3).

In the two 'dynamical antinomies' Kant's solution is different. In the third antinomy, the thesis is that 'causality in accordance with laws of nature' is not the only kind of causality, but there must also be a 'causality of freedom' underlying the whole series of natural causes and effects, while the antithesis is that everything in nature takes place in accord with deterministic laws alone (A 444–5/B 462–3). In the fourth antinomy, the thesis is that there must be a necessary being as the cause of the whole sequence of contingent beings, either as its first member or underlying it, while the antithesis is that no such being exists inside or outside the world (A 452–3/B 480–1). Again, the theses result from reason's desire for closure and the antitheses result from reason's desire for infinite extension. But now the theses do not necessarily refer solely to spatio-temporal entities, so the claims that there must be a non-natural causality of freedom and a necessary being can apply to things in themselves while the claims that there are only contingent existents linked by laws of nature apply to appearances. In this case both thesis and antithesis may be true (A 531/B 559). This result is crucial to Kant, because it means that although theoretical reason cannot prove that either freedom or God exist, neither can it disprove them, and room is left for the existence of freedom and God to gain credibility in some other way.

The last main part of the 'Dialectic' is Kant's critique of rational theology. Here Kant reiterates his earlier critique of the ontological argument as well as his claim that the arguments for the existence of God from contingency and from design – the 'cosmological' and 'physico-theological' proofs – can only get from their ideas of a first cause or architect to the idea of a *perfect* being by the supposition of the ontological argument, and thus fall along with that. But he now precedes this argument with a critique of the argument for God as the ground of all possibility that he had earlier accepted: the very idea that there is an *ens realissimum*, an individual being containing in itself the ground of 'the sum-total of all possibility' (A 573/B 602), is another of the natural but illusory ideas of reason.

Kant does not, however, conclude the first *Critique* with an entirely negative assessment of pure reason. In an appendix to the 'Transcendental Dialectic', he argues that even though reason in its theoretical use cannot yield metaphysical insight, it does supply us with indispensable 'regulative' principles, of both the maximal simplicity of natural laws and the maximal variety of natural forms, for the conduct of empirical research; and in the 'Canon of Pure Reason', he argues that practical reason supplies an ideal of the highest good, the union of virtue and happiness and ultimately the union of freedom and nature, which is indispensable for moral conduct, not as its direct object but as a necessary condition of its rationality – which in turn gives ground for the practical postulation if not theoretical proof of the existence of God. Kant expands on both of these ideas in subsequent works (see §11 and §13).

9 The value of autonomy and the foundations of ethics

In his theoretical philosophy, Kant argued that we can be certain of the principles that arise from the combination of the forms of our sensibility and understanding, as products of our own intellectual autonomy; but he also argued that any attempt to see human reason as an autonomous source of metaphysical insight valid beyond the bounds of human sensibility leads to illusion. But in his practical philosophy, Kant argues that human reason is an autonomous source of principles of conduct, immune from the blandishments of sensual inclination in both its determinations of value and its decisions to act, and indeed that human autonomy is the highest value and the limiting condition of all other values.

Traditionally, Kant has been seen as an ethical formalist, according to whom all judgments on the values of ends must be subordinated to the obligatory universality of a moral law derived from the very concept of rationality itself. This interpretation has drawn support from Kant's own characterization of his 'paradoxical' method in the *Critique of Practical Reason*, where he holds that the moral law must be derived prior to any determination of good or evil, rather than vice versa (5: 62–3). But this passage does not do justice to the larger argument of Kant's practical philosophy, which is that rationality itself is so valuable precisely because it is the means to freedom or autonomy. Kant expressed this in his classroom lectures on ethics, when he said that 'the inherent value of the world, the *summum bonum*, is freedom in accordance with a will which is not necessitated to action' (27: 1482), and even more clearly in lectures on natural right given in the autumn of 1784, the very time he was writing the *Groundwork of the Metaphysics of Morals*, where he said that 'If only rational beings can be ends in themselves, that is not because they have reason, but because they have freedom. Reason is merely a means' (27: 1321). Kant makes the same point in the *Groundwork* when he says that the incomparable dignity of human beings derives from the fact that they are 'free with regard to all laws of nature, obeying only those laws which' they make themselves (4: 435).

The strategy of the *Groundwork* is by no means obvious, and the real character of Kant's view emerges only gradually. In Section I, Kant tries to derive the fundamental principle of morality from an analysis of 'ordinary rational knowledge of morality.' The key steps in his analysis are: virtue lies in the good will of an agent rather than any natural inclination or any particular end to be achieved;

good will is manifested in the performance of an action for the sake of fulfilling duty rather than for any other end; and what duty requires is the performance of an action not for the sake of its consequences but because of its conformity to law as such; thus the maxim, or subjective principle, of virtuous action can only be that 'I ought never to act except in such a way *that I can also will that my maxim should become a universal law*' (4: 402). In Section II, Kant apparently tries to reach the same conclusion from more philosophical considerations: by arguing on the one hand that a moral or practical law must be a categorical rather than hypothetical imperative, that is, one commanding unconditionally rather than depending upon the adoption of some antecedent and optional end, and on the other hand that happiness is too indeterminate an end to give rise to such an imperative, Kant concludes that a categorical imperative can contain 'only the necessity that our maxim should conform to this law', thus that 'there remains nothing to which the maxim has to conform except the universality of a law as such' (4: 421). This version of the categorical imperative is known as the Formula of Universal Law.

Kant then furnishes further formulations of the categorical imperative, especially the Formula of Humanity as an End in Itself – '*Act in such a way that you always treat humanity, whether in your own person or in the person of any other, never simply as a means, but always at the same time as an end*' (4: 429), which at the very least requires the possibility of rational consent to your action from any agent affected by it – and the formula of the kingdom of ends, the requirement that any proposed course of action be compatible with 'a whole of all ends in systematic conjunction (a whole both of rational beings as ends in themselves and also of the personal ends which each may set before himself' (4: 433). The usual interpretation is that these two formulations are supposed to follow from the Formula of Universal Law. However, several factors suggest that Kant did not mean the derivation of that formula from either common sense or 'popular moral philosophy' to be self-sufficient, and it is only with the introduction of the notion that humanity is an end in itself because of its potential for freedom, that the real 'ground of a possible categorical imperative' is discovered (4: 428). If so, then this is Kant's theory: the ultimate source of value is human freedom as an end in itself, manifested in interpersonal contexts in the possibility of freely given consent to the actions of others; conformity to the requirement of universal law is the way to ensure that this value is preserved and fostered; and the ideal outcome of the observation of such a law would be a kingdom of ends as a system of freedom, in which all

agents freely pursue their freely chosen ends to the extent compatible with a like freedom for all.

10 Duties of right and duties of virtue

In the *Groundwork*, Kant's principle of morality gives rise to a fourfold classification of duties, resulting from the intersection of two divisions: between duties to oneself and to others, and between perfect and imperfect duties. Perfect duties are proscriptions of specific kinds of actions, and violating them is morally blameworthy; imperfect duties are prescriptions of general ends, and fulfilling them is praiseworthy. The four classes of duty are thus: perfect duties to oneself, such as the prohibition of suicide; perfect duties to others, such as the prohibition of deceitful promises; imperfect duties to oneself, such as the prescription to cultivate one's talents; and imperfect duties to others, such as the prescription of benevolence (4: 422–3, 429–30). It is straightforward what a perfect duty prohibits one from doing; it requires judgment to determine when and how the general ends prescribed by imperfect duties should be realized.

In the later *Metaphysics of Morals*, Kant works out a detailed budget of duties that is generally based on this scheme, but with one key distinction: duties of justice (*Recht*) are those of the above duties that can appropriately be enforced by means of coercion, and the remainder are duties of virtue, which are fit subjects for moral assessment but not coercion (6: 213, 219). Since freedom is Kant's chief value, coercion is permitted only where it is both necessary to preserve freedom and possible for it to do so. This means that only a small subset of our duties, namely some but not all of our perfect duties to others, are duties of justice, thus proper subjects for public legislation; the majority of our moral duties are duties of virtue which are not appropriate subjects for coercive legal enforcement.

Kant's treatment of the duties of virtue is less complicated than that of the duties of justice, and will be considered first. Kant does not explicitly characterize these as duties to preserve and promote the freedom of oneself and others, as he does in the *Groundwork*, but instead characterizes them as duties to promote one's own perfection and the happiness of others: while one can directly perfect one's own freedom, one can avoid injuring but not directly perfect the freedom of another. On close inspection, however, Kant's duties of virtue require precisely that one perfect both the internal and external conditions for the exercise of one's own freedom and at least the external conditions for the exercise of the freedom of others. Thus, ethical duties to oneself include the prohibition of injury to the physical and mental bases of one's free agency, as by suicide or drunkenness, and the prescription of efforts to improve both the physical and mental conditions for the exercise of one's freedom, as by the cultivation of talents and of one's spiritual and moral faculties themselves; and ethical duties to others include both the prohibition of injuries to the dignity of others as free agents, for example by insulting or ridiculing them ('duties of respect'), and the prescription of efforts to improve the conditions for others' exercise of their own freedom, as by beneficience and sympathy ('duties of love').

Kant's foundation of his political philosophy on the duties of justice is more complicated. From the ultimate value of freedom, Kant derives the universal principle of justice, that an action is right only if 'on its maxim the freedom of choice of each can coexist with everyone's freedom in accordance with a universal law' (6: 230). Kant then argues that coercion is justified when it can prevent a hindrance to freedom, since a hindrance to a hindrance to freedom is itself a means to freedom (6: 231). This is too simple, since coercion might only compound the injury to freedom. Kant needs to add that coercive enforcement of the law is not itself a hindrance to freedom, since the threat of juridical sanction does not deprive a would-be criminal of freedom in the way that his crime would deprive its victim of freedom: the criminal exercises the choice to risk sanction, but deprives his victim of a like freedom of choice.

Kant goes on to argue that the only proper aim of coercive juridical legislation is the prevention of injury to the person and property of others; this is 'Private Law', while 'Public Law' concerns the proper form of the state, whose function is the enforcement of private law. Kant takes the prevention of injury to persons to be an obvious requirement of duty, needing no special discussion, but the right to property receives extended discussion.

Kant recognizes three classes of property: property in things, property in contracts, and contract-like property in other persons, such as marital rights. His discussion of property in things is the most important for his political theory. The gist of Kant's account is that it would be irrational to deprive ourselves of the right to place physical objects, above all land, at our own long-term disposal, since we are rational agents who may need to use such things to realize our freely chosen ends, while the things themselves are not free agents and have no rights. But since the earth is initially undivided, specific property rights are not innate but must be acquired. Since the claim to any particular thing would limit the freedom of others who might also be able to use it, however, property

rights cannot be claimed unilaterally, but can only be claimed with the multilateral consent of those others, which they can reasonably give only if they too are accorded similar rights necessary for the successful exercise of their own agency (6: 255–6). For Kant, the right to property is thus not a natural right of isolated individuals, but a social creation depending upon mutual acceptability of claims. The state, finally, exists primarily to make claims to property rights both determinate and secure, and anyone claiming property rights thus has both the right and the obligation to join in a state with others (6: 256–7, 306–8). Since property exists only by mutual consent, and the state exists to secure that consent, the state necessarily has the power to permit only those distributions of property rights sufficiently equitable to gain general consent.

Both claims to property and expressions of philosophical and religious opinions, for example, are expressions of human autonomy. But while one person's property claims may directly limit the freedom of others, his beliefs do not, and thus do not require the consent of any other. The state therefore has no right to intervene in these matters. This fundamental difference between the state's proper concern with property and its improper concern with personal belief defines Kant's liberalism. It is only implicit in the *Metaphysics of Morals*, but becomes explicit in more purely political writings.

11 Freedom of the will and the highest good

Having considered some practical implications of Kant's conception of autonomy, we now turn to its metaphysical consequences.

In Section III of the *Groundwork*, Kant attempts to prove that the categorical imperative, derived in Section II by the analysis of the concept of free and rational beings, in general actually puts us under an obligation by proving that we are indeed free and rational beings. In his terminology, he wants to show that it is not merely an analytic but a synthetic a priori proposition that our wills are constrained by this imperative. Both the interpretation and the assessment of the arguments by which he proposes to accomplish this remain controversial.

The first claim that Kant makes is that 'every being who cannot act except under the idea of freedom is just on that account really free in a practical respect, that is, all laws that are inseparably bound up with freedom are valid for it just as if its will were really declared to be free in itself and in theoretical philosophy', and that every being with a will must indeed act under the idea of freedom (4: 448) (see WILL, THE). This seems to mean that agents who conceive of themselves as choosing their own actions, whether or not they conceive of themselves as subject to determinism, do not or perhaps even cannot consider any antecedent determinants of their actions in deciding what to do, but only what now seems most rational to do; thus they must govern their actions by rational and therefore moral laws. This seems right for agents considering their own future actions, but leaves unclear how we are to assess the freedom of the actions of others or even our own past actions.

However, Kant goes on to offer what seems to be a theoretical and therefore general proof of the existence of human freedom. He argues that theoretical philosophy has shown that we must distinguish between considering ourselves as phenomena and noumena, or members of the sensible and the intelligible worlds. From the first point of view, we must consider our actions to be governed by the causality of nature, while in the second, since we cannot consider our actions there to be governed by no law at all, we must consider them to be governed by another kind of causality, namely causality in accord with laws of reason (4: 451–3). Thus while our actions appear to be determined by natural causes, in reality they not only can but in fact must accord with laws of reason, hence with the categorical imperative.

There are two problems with this argument. First, it flouts transcendental idealism by assuming positive knowledge about things in themselves. Second, as Henry SIDGWICK was to object a century later, it precludes moral responsibility for wrong-doing: if the real laws of our behaviour are necessarily rational and hence moral, any wrong-doing could only show that an agent is not rational, and therefore not responsible, at all.

Whether consciously aware of these objections or not, Kant radically altered his argument for freedom of the will in the *Critique of Practical Reason*. Here he does not argue from a theoretical proof of our freedom to the fact of our obligation under the moral law, but conversely from our consciousness of that obligation – the 'fact of reason' – to our freedom as the necessary condition of our ability and responsibility to fulfil it (5: 29–31). This argument first assumes that transcendental idealism has left open at least the theoretical possibility of freedom of the will, and then depends upon the famous principle 'ought implies can' ('Theory and Practice', 8: 287). Transcendental idealism, of course, seems problematic to many; and although the 'ought implies can' principle seems an intuitive principle of fairness, Kant does not actually argue for it. Nevertheless, since this argument assumes only that 'ought' implies '*can*', it does not imply that any agent who is obliged under the moral law necessarily *will* act in accordance with it, and thus

avoids Sidgwick's problem about the very possibility of wrong-doing.

Kant depends upon this result in his next major treatment of freedom, in *Religion within the Limits of Reason Alone*, although there he seems to go too far by assuming that evil-doing is not just *possible* but even necessary. Kant begins this discussion with an elegant account of wrong-doing, arguing that because no human being is simply unaware of the demand of morality – that is implied by the 'fact of reason' – acting immorally never comes from mere ignorance of it, but rather from deciding to exempt oneself from this obligation. This position is compatible with the argument for freedom in the second *Critique*, although not with that of the *Groundwork*. However, Kant goes on to argue that an evil rather than virtuous choice of fundamental maxim, or 'radical evil', is not only *possible* but inevitable, to be escaped from only by a moral conversion. This doctrine hardly follows from Kant's previous argument, and seems instead to rest on an odd mixture of empirical evidence and the lingering grip of the Christian doctrine of original sin.

The reality of freedom is only the first of Kant's three 'postulates of pure practical reason'; the other two are the existence of God and the immortality of the soul. Again Kant's argument is that, as the first *Critique* showed, neither of these can be proven by theoretical metaphysics, but they can nevertheless be postulated as necessary conditions of something essential to morality. In this case, however, they are conditions not of our obligation under the categorical imperative but for the realization of the 'highest good.' This is another complex and controversial concept. Kant typically defines it as happiness in proportion to virtue, which is worthiness to be happy (5: 110), but suggests different grounds for the necessity of this conjunction. In the *Critique of Practical Reason*, Kant sometimes treats happiness and virtue as two separate ends of human beings, one our natural end and the other our moral end, which we simply seek to combine (5: 110). In other places, however, beginning with the 'Canon of Pure Reason' in the first *Critique*, he holds that since what virtue does is precisely to coordinate our mutual pursuit of ends, and happiness arises from the realization of ends, maximal happiness would inevitably follow maximal virtue under ideal circumstances (A 809/B 837). Of course, circumstances are not always ideal for morality: as far as we can see, no one achieves perfect virtue in a normal lifespan, and such virtue as is attained is hardly always rewarded with happiness. To counter this, Kant holds that we may postulate immortality, in which to perfect our virtue, and the existence of God, who can legislate a nature in which the ends of virtue are achieved.

This theory has seemed to many to be Kant's vain attempt to save his personal faith from his own scathing critique of metaphysics. Before such a claim could even be discussed, we would have to know what Kant really means by a postulate of practical reason. Kant gives several hints about this which have not been adequately explored. In the first *Critique*, he discusses the practical postulates in a section where he considers readiness to bet as a measure of belief, thus suggesting that what he actually has in mind is Pascal's wager (see PASCAL, B.): since there is no theoretical disproof of these postulates, and nothing to lose if they are false, but their value to happiness is great, it is rational to act as if they were true. In a later essay, a draft on the 'Real Progress of Metaphysics from the Time of Leibniz and Wolff' from the early 1790s (posthumously published), Kant makes an even more striking suggestion. There he says that in the assumption of the practical postulates 'the human being is authorized to grant influence on his actions to an idea which he, in accord with moral principles, has made himself, just as if he had derived it from a given object' (20: 305). Here the suggestion is that the practical postulates are nothing less than another expression of human autonomy: not theoretical beliefs at all, let alone religious dogmas, but ideas which we construct for ourselves solely to increase our own efforts at virtue. This idea, that God is in fact nothing but an idea of our own making for use within our moral practice, is a thought Kant repeatedly expressed in his very last years (see §14).

12 Taste and autonomy

Under the rubric of 'reflective judgment', defined as that use of judgment in which we seek to find unknown universals for given particulars rather than to apply given universals to particulars (5: 179–80), the *Critique of Judgment* deals with three apparently disparate subjects: systematicity in scientific concepts generally, natural and artistic beauty, and teleology or purposiveness in particular organisms and in nature as a whole (see TELEOLOGY). Even more than the idea of reflective judgment, however, what ties these subjects together is again the idea of autonomy.

In the the first *Critique*, Kant had suggested, with but few exceptions, that the search for systematicity in scientific concepts and laws – the subordination of maximally varied specific concepts and laws under maximally unified general ones – is an ideal of reason, not necessary for empirical knowledge but still intrinsically desirable. In the third *Critique*, he reassigns this search to reflective judgment, and argues

that we must adopt as a transcendental but indemonstrable principle that nature is adapted to our cognitive needs (5: 185; 20: 209–10). By this reassignment Kant indicates that systematicity is a necessary condition for the acceptance of empirical laws after all, and thus a necessary condition for experience itself. Kant thereby suggests that our empirical knowledge is neither passively received nor simply guaranteed, but dependent on our active projection of the unity of nature.

Kant next turns to judgments of taste as both a further expression of human autonomy and further evidence that the adaptation of nature to our own cognitive needs is both contingent yet reasonably assumed. Judgments of taste, beginning with the simplest such as 'This flower is beautiful' and progressing to more complex ones such as 'This poem is beautiful' and 'This landscape is sublime', are connected to autonomy in two ways: while they claim universal agreement, they must always be based on individual feeling and judgment; and while they must be made free of all constraint by theoretical or moral concepts, they are ultimately symbols of moral freedom itself.

Kant begins from an analysis of the very idea of an 'aesthetic judgment'. As aesthetic, judgments of taste must both concern and be made on the basis of the most subjective of human responses, feelings of pleasure, but, as judgments, they must still claim interpersonal agreement (5: 203, 212–16). To retain their link to feelings, judgments of taste can never simply report how others respond, but must be based on one's own free response to the object itself; in this way they express individual autonomy (5: 216, 282–5). But to claim universal agreement, they must be based on cognitive capacities shared by all, yet by a condition of those faculties that is pleasureable because it is not constrained by rules (5: 187). Such a state is one of 'free play' between imagination and understanding, in which the imagination satisfies understanding's need for unity by presenting a form that seems unitary and coherent without any concept, or, even where a concept of human use or artistic intention is inescapable, that seems to have a unity going beyond any such concept – artistic genius lies precisely in such transcendence of concepts (5: 317–18). With debatable success, Kant argues that this 'free play' must occur under the same circumstances in all human beings (5: 238–9, 290), and thus that judgments of taste can have the 'quantity' of universality and the 'modality' of necessity while retaining the 'quality' of independence from direct moral interest and 'relation' to merely subjective, cognitive interests rather than objective, practical ones.

How does aesthetic judgment so understood both express autonomy in a moral sense and also give further evidence of the contingent adaptation of nature to our own needs? Kant answers the latter question with his idea of 'intellectual interest': the very fact that beauty exists, he argues, although it cannot be derived from any scientific laws, can be taken by us as evidence that nature is receptive not only to our cognitive needs but even to our need to see a possibility for success in our moral undertakings (5: 300). Kant's answer to the first question, how taste expresses autonomy in its moral sense, is more complex but also more compelling than this.

Like other eighteenth-century authors such as Edmund BURKE, Kant draws a fundamental distinction between the beautiful and the sublime (see SUBLIME, THE). Beauty pleases us through the free play of imagination and understanding. In our response to the sublime, however – which for Kant is not paradigmatically a response to art, but to the vastness of nature – we enjoy not a direct harmony between imagination and understanding, which are rather frustrated by their inability to grasp such immensities, but a grasp of them which reveals the power of reason within us (5: 257). And this, although it would seem to involve theoretical reason, symbolizes the power of practical reason, and thus the foundation of our autonomy, in two ways: our power to grasp a truly universal law, such as the moral law, and our power to resist the threats of mere nature, and thus the blandishments of inclination (5: 261–2).

In this way, the sublime symbolizes the sterner side of moral autonomy. But the experience of beauty is also a symbol of morality, precisely because the freedom of the imagination that is its essence is the only experience in which any form of freedom, including the freedom of the will itself, can become palpable to us (5: 353–4). Kant thus concludes his critique of aesthetic judgment with the remarkable suggestion that it is in our enjoyment of beauty that our vocation as autonomous agents becomes not just a 'fact of reason' but a matter of experience as well.

13 Design and autonomy

Kant's critique of teleological judgment in the second half of the *Critique of Judgment* has an even more complicated agenda than his aesthetic theory. The work has roots in both eighteenth-century biology – which began the debate, lasting until the twentieth century, whether organisms could be understood on purely mechanical principles – and natural theology – that is, the great debate over the argument from design that culminated in Hume's *Dialogues concerning Natural Religion*. Yet again Kant's motive is to show that even our understanding of nature ultimately drives us to a recognition of our own autonomy.

The work is divided into three main sections: an examination of the necessary conditions for our comprehension of individual organisms; an examination of the conditions under which we can see nature as a whole as a single system; and a restatement of Kant's moral theology. First, Kant argues that an organism is a system of whole and parts manifesting both 'regressive' and 'progressive' causality: the whole is the product of the parts, but the parts in turn depend upon the whole for their own proper functioning and existence (5: 372, 376). But our conception of mechanical efficient causation includes only progressive causation, in which the state of any system depends upon the prior state of its parts (see CAUSATION). The only way we can understand the regressive causation of the whole with respect to its parts is by analogy to intelligent design, in which an antecedent *conception* of the object as a whole determines the production of the parts which in turn determine the character of the resultant whole. However, Kant insists, we have absolutely no justification for adopting a 'constitutive concept' of natural organisms as a product of actual design; we are only entitled to use an analogy between natural organisms and products of design as 'a regulative concept for reflective judgment to conduct research into objects in a remote analogy with our own causality in accordance with purposes' (5: 375). In other words, seeing organisms as products of intelligent design is a purely heuristic strategy.

However, Kant next argues that if it is natural for us to investigate organisms as if they were products of intelligent design, then it will also be natural for us to try to see nature as a whole as manifesting a purposive design (5: 380–1); and only by seeing the whole of nature as a product of intelligent design – of course, only regulatively – can we satisfy our craving to transform every particularity of nature, which must always be left contingent by our own general concepts, into something that seems necessary (5: 405–7). However, from a merely naturalistic viewpoint the ultimate purpose of nature as a system must remain indeterminate – grass might exist to feed cows, or cows exist to fertilize the grass (4: 426). Nature can be seen as a determinate system only if it can be seen as collectively serving an ultimate end that is itself an intrinsic end. This can only be humanity itself (4: 427) – but not humanity merely as a part of nature, seeking happiness, which is neither a determinate end nor one particularly favoured by nature (4: 430), but only humanity as the subject of morality, able to cultivate its freedom (5: 435–6). Thus the urge to see nature as a systematic whole, an inevitable concomitant of our research into the complexities of organic life, can only be satisfied from the moral point of view in which human autonomy is the ultimate value.

Kant is still careful to remind us that this doctrine is regulative, furnishing us with a principle for our own cognitive and practical activity, not constitutive, pretending to metaphysical insight into the nature of reality independent from us. It is therefore particularly noteworthy that the last part of the critique of teleological judgment is a restatement of Kant's moral theology, the argument for belief in the existence of God as a postulate of practical reason. This restatement in a general theory of reflective judgment, the principles of which are meant above all else to guide our own activity, confirms the view that in the end the theory of practical postulates is not meant to support any form of dogma but only to serve as another expression of our own autonomy.

14 The final decade of Kant's public and private career

German intellectuals were drawn to political issues after the French revolution in 1789, and Kant was no exception. Key elements of his political philosophy were presented in essays such as 'Theory and Practice' (1793) and *Perpetual Peace* (1795) before its formal exposition in the *Metaphysics of Morals* (1797). As was argued above (§10), the foundation of Kantian liberalism is the idea that coercion is justifiable only to prevent hindrances to freedom, and thus to protect personal freedom and regulate property, every claim to which represents a potential constraint of the freedom of others unless they can reasonably agree to that claim as part of a system of property rights; but individual beliefs and conceptions of the good, whether religious or philosophical, do not directly interfere with the freedom of others and are therefore not a proper object of political regulation. Kant's development of this basic principle into a political philosophy, however, is complex and controversial.

On the one hand, Kant argued from this premise to a firm rejection of any paternalistic government, even benevolent paternalism. Government exists for the protection of the freedom individuals have to determine and pursue their own ends to the extent compatible with the like freedom of others; so a '*paternalistic government*, where the subjects, as minors, cannot decide what is truly beneficial or detrimental to them, but are obliged to wait passively for the head of state to judge how they *ought* to be happy... would be the greatest conceivable *despotism*' (8: 290–1). Further, Kant held that the sovereignty of any government derives solely from the possibility of those who are governed rationally consenting to it,

and thus that it is a necessary test of the legitimacy of all laws 'that they can have arisen from the united will of an entire people' (8: 297). These constraints could best be met in a republic, without a hereditary monarchy or aristocracy pitting proprietary privilege against public right. Finally, Kant argued in *Perpetual Peace*, only in a world federation of republics, where no proprietary rulers could identify the forcible extension of their domains with the aggrandizement of their personal property, could a cessation of warfare ever be expected.

On the other hand, Kant accompanied these liberal doctrines with a denial of any right to violent revolution, which has seemed surprising to many. But Kant's thought here is complex. Underlying his position as a whole is his view that in any situation in which different persons are bound to come into contact with each other we have not merely a moral right but a moral obligation to found or uphold a state. But one could easily argue that a tyranny is a state in name only, and that our moral obligation with regard to a tyranny is precisely to replace it at any cost with a legitimate state. Kant offers several reasons why this is not so. One claim is that violent revolution does not leave time for genuine reform in principles (8: 36), and another argument is that people revolt for the sake of greater happiness, which is an illegitimate reason for the overthrow of a state (8: 298). But these are empirical claims, and do not prove that people cannot revolt solely to remove illegitimate constraints to their freedom. Another argument Kant makes is that a constitution granting a legal right to rebel against the highest authority it creates would thereby not create a single highest authority after all, and would thus be self-contradictory (6: 319). This has seemed to many to be a sophism; but it may have been Kant's attempt to get his liberalism past the Prussian censorship, denying a *legal* right to rebel without ever explicitly denying a *moral* right to rebel.

Kant had been battling censorship even before the death of Frederick the Great in 1786. In 'What is Enlightenment?' (1785), he argued that while persons in an official capacity have to obey orders (in what he confusingly calls the 'private use of reason'), no official, not a professor or even a military officer, has to surrender his right to address his views to 'the entire *reading public*' (the 'public use of reason') (8: 37). But Kant's attack on the necessity of an established church in *Religion within the Limits of Reason Alone* (1793), even though legally published with the imprimatur of a non-Prussian university (Jena), outraged the conservative Frederick William II and his minister Wöllner, and Kant was threatened with punishment if he published further on religion. With an oath of loyalty to his sovereign, Kant promised to desist, but after the death of this king in 1797 he regarded himself as freed from this promise, and the next year issued his most spirited defence of intellectual freedom yet, *The Conflict of the Faculties*. Here Kant argued that while the theological faculty might have the obligation to advance certain dogmas approved by the state, it was nothing less than the official function of the philosophical faculty to subject all views to rational scrutiny; and in any case, a government genuinely concerned with its people's welfare would not want them to base their morality on fear or dogma but only on the free exercise of their own reason. The new government had no stomach for further suppression of the aged philosopher, and Kant was able to publish this defence of intellectual freedom without incident.

Privately, Kant's last years were devoted to the project of closing the gap between the metaphysical foundations of natural science and actual physics, begun about 1796. He never published the work, leaving behind only the notes later published as the *Opus postumum*. Here Kant tried to show that by using the categorial framework and the concept of force we can derive not only the most general laws of mechanics, as he had argued in 1786, but a much more detailed categorization of the forms of matter and its forces. Kant also argued that an imperceptible, self-moving ether or 'caloric' is a condition of the possibility of experience. In the latest stages of this work, however, Kant returned to the broadest themes of his philosophy, and tried to develop a final statement of transcendental idealism. Here he argued that 'The highest standpoint of transcendental philosophy is that which unites God and the world synthetically, under one principle' (21: 23) – where that principle is nothing other than human autonomy itself. God and the world are 'not substances outside my thought, but rather the thought through which we ourselves make these objects' (21: 21): the world is our experience organized by categories and laws of our own making, and God is the representation of our own capacity to give ourselves the moral law through reason. The moral law 'emerges from freedom ... which the subject prescribes to himself, and yet as if another and higher person had made it a rule for him. The subject feels himself necessitated through his own reason ...' (22: 129). This is a fitting conclusion to Kant's philosophy of autonomy.

See also: A PRIORI; ANALYTICITY; AUTONOMY, ETHICAL; EMPIRICISM; FREE WILL; KANTIAN ETHICS; NEO-KANTIANISM; PRACTICAL REASON AND ETHICS; RATIONALISM; TRANSCENDENTAL ARGUMENTS

List of works

Citations to Kant, with the exception of the *Critique of Pure Reason*, are standardly located by the appropriate volume and page number in Kant (1900–). This practice has been followed in this entry by giving the arabic volume number followed by the arabic page number. Citations to the *Critique of Pure Reason* are given with the pagination of the first (A) and/or second (B) editions, according to whether the passage occurred in one or both editions.

German editions

Kant, I. (1900–) *Kant's gesammelte Schriften* (Kant's Collected Works), ed. Royal Prussian (subsequently German) Academy of Sciences, Berlin: Georg Reimer, subsequently Walter de Gruyter, 29 vols, in 34 parts. (27 volumes are published so far. The edition is divided into four parts: *Werke* (Works) (vols 1–9), *Briefe* (Letters) (vols 10–13), *Handschriftlicher Nachlaß* (Handwritten remains) (vols 14–23), and *Vorlesungen* (Transcriptions of lectures by other hands) (vols 24–29, no volumes 25 and 26). This edition, referred to as the 'Akademie' edition, is the most complete collection of Kant's works. While some of its texts of Kant's published works have been superseded, it remains the only source for most of Kant's unpublished notes and lectures.)

—— (1956–62) *Immanuel Kant: Werke in sechs Bänden* (Immanuel Kant: Works in Six Volumes), ed. W. Weischedel, Wiesbaden: Insel; repr. (in 12 vols but with original pagination) Frankfurt am Main: Suhrkamp Verlag, 1968. (A more modern edition of Kant's published works only, also including German translations of Kant's Latin works. Orthography is modernized, but the texts are more reliable than in the older Akademie edition.)

—— (1990) *Kritik der reinen Vernunft* (Critique of Pure Reason), ed. R. Schmidt, with bibliography by Heinrich Klemme, Hamburg: Felix Meiner, 3rd edn. (Published in the Philosophische Bibliothek series. This edition was the basis for N. Kemp Smith's translation)

—— (1996) *Kritik der reinen Vernunft Reclam* (Critique of Pure Reason), ed. I. Heidemann, Stuttgart: Philipp Reclam Jun. (Published in the Universal-Bibliothek series. The best modern edition of the work)

English translations

Only the most important translations currently in widespread use are included. The Cambridge Edition of the *Works of Immanuel Kant*, currently in production under the general editorship of P. Guyer and A.W. Wood, will provide new or revised translations of all of Kant's published works and selections from his correspondence, notes, and lectures. The following volumes of this series have thus far appeared:

Kant, I. (1992) *Theoretical Philosophy, 1755–1770*, trans. and ed. D. Walford, in collaboration with Ralf Meerbote, Cambridge: Cambridge University Press. (Contains all of Kant's writings up to 1770 except for scientific works and *Observations on the Feeling of the Beautiful and Sublime*.)

—— (1992) *Lectures on Logic*, trans. and ed. J.M. Young, Cambridge: Cambridge University Press. (Contains the authorized handbook edited by G.B. Jäsche in 1800, and three complete sets of lecture notes from the early 1770s, 1780s and 1790s.)

—— (1993) *Opus postumum*, ed. E. Förster, trans. E. Förster and M. Rosen, Cambridge: Cambridge University Press. (The first English translation, it includes about one-third of the highly repetitive German text, arranged chronologically.)

Individual works

Kant, I. (1911) *Critique of Aesthetic Judgement*, trans., with analytical indexes, J.C. Meredith, Oxford: Clarendon Press.

—— (1928) *Critique of Teleological Judgement*, trans., with analytical indexes, J.C. Meredith, Oxford: Clarendon Press.

—— (1933) *Critique of Pure Reason*, trans. N.Kemp Smith, London: Macmillan, 2nd ed. (Following Schmidt, Kemp Smith, perspicuously displays all the material from both editions, but accepts too many emendations and is also too loose with Kant's sentence structure. But his translation of Kant's technical terminology has become canonical, and his elegance has made it the standard translation for sixty years.)

—— (1948) *The Groundwork of the Metaphysics of Morals (originally The Moral Law)*, trans. H.J. Paton, London: Hutchinson (now Harper & Row). (The most elegant translation of this work, although it does insert subheadings not to be found in the original.)

—— (1950) *Prolegomena to Any Future Metaphysics*, trans. L.W. Beck, Indianapolis and New York: Bobbs-Merrill (now Macmillan). (A reliable revision of the Paul Carus translation of 1902.)

—— (1952) *Kant's Critique of Judgement*, trans. J.C. Meredith, Oxford: Clarendon Press. (Reprint of Kant (1911) and (1928), without indices. While

loose, Meredith's remains the most felicitous translation of *Critique of Judgment*.)

—— (1956) *Critique of Practical Reason*, trans. L.W. Beck, Indianapolis and New York: Bobbs-Merrill. (Takes some liberties with Kant's paragraphing, but otherwise reliable.)

—— (1959) *Foundations of the Metaphysics of Morals and What is Enlightenment?*, trans. L.W. Beck, Indianapolis and New York: Bobbs-Merrill (now Macmillan). (The texts from Beck's 1949 collection, still basically reliable.)

—— (1960) *Observations on the Feeling of the Beautiful and Sublime*, trans. J.T. Goldthwait, Berkeley and Los Angeles: University of California Press.

—— (1960) *Religion within the Limits of Reason Alone*, trans. T.M. Greene and H.H. Hudson, with a new essay on 'The Ethical Significance of Kant's Religion' by J.R. Silber, New York: Harper & Row, 1960. (A fine translation, with an extensive introduction by an important Kant scholar of the 1960s who never published a book.)

—— (1963) *Lectures on Ethics*, trans. L. Infield, London: Methuen; repr. with introduction by L.W. Beck, New York: Harper & Row (now Hackett Publishing Company). (Based on a 1924 edition by Paul Menzer superseded by the Collins and Mrongovius texts in Akademie edition, volume 27, remains a source of tremendous insight into Kant's ethical thought just before the publication of his major works.)

—— (1965) *First Introduction to the Critique of Judgment*, trans. J. Haden, Indianapolis and New York: Bobbs-Merrill. (Better than Pluhar's translation, but now hard to find.)

—— (1967) *Kant: Philosophical Correspondence 1759–99*, trans. A. Zweig, Chicago, IL: University of Chicago Press. (A selection of the most philosophically interesting letters with useful annotations.)

—— (1969) *Universal Natural History and Theory of the Heavens*, trans. W. Hastie, with new introduction by M.K. Munitz, Ann Arbor: University of Michigan Press. (Antiquated translation.)

—— (1970) *Metaphysical Foundations of Natural Science*, trans. J. Ellington, Indianapolis and New York: Bobbs-Merrill; repr., with *Prolegomena*, in *Philosophy of Material Nature*, Indianapolis, IN: Hackett, 1985. (The only translation currently available.)

—— (1973) *The Kant-Eberhard Controversy: An English translation together with supplementary materials and a historical-analytical introduction of Immanuel Kant's On a New Discovery According to which Any New Critique of Pure Reason Has Been*

Made Superfluous by an Earlier One, trans. H.E. Allison, Baltimore: The Johns Hopkins University Press. (Kant's polemical defense of the idea of the synthetic a priori from the Wolffians, with valuable supplementary material.)

—— (1974) *Anthropology from a Pragmatic Point of View*, trans. M.J. Gregor, The Hague: Martinus Nijhoff.

—— (1978) *Lectures on Philosophical Theology*, trans. A.W. Wood and G.M. Clark, Ithaca and London: Cornell University Press. (Valuable supplement to the Transcendental Dialectic.)

—— (1979) *The Conflict of the Faculties*, trans. M.J. Gregor, New York: Abaris Books.

—— (1983) *What Real Progress Has Metaphysics Made in Germany since the Time of Leibniz and Wolff?*, trans. T. Humphrey, New York: Abaris Books. (Only English translation of this unfinished competition entry, posthumously published by Rink in 1804.)

—— (1987) *Critique of Judgment: Including the First Introduction*, trans. W.S. Pluhar, Indianapolis, IN: Hackett Publishing Company. (While the English is infelicitous and the editorial intervention excessive, this does include the only translation of the 'First Introduction' still in print.)

—— (1991) *The Metaphysics of Morals*, trans. M.J. Gregor, Cambridge: Cambridge University Press. (The first single-volume translation of both the Rechtslehre and Tugendlehre, supersedes all earlier separate translations.)

References and further reading

Multi-author anthologies and general background

Beck, L.W. (1969) *Early German Philosophy: Kant and his Predecessors*, Cambridge, MA: Harvard University Press. (Detailed history of German philosophy from the middle ages to Kant, the only work of its kind.)

* —— (1965) *Studies in the Philosophy of Kant*, Indianapolis, IN: Bobbs-Merrill Company. (Contains Beck's essays on analytic-synthetic distinction and on political philosophy.)

—— (1978) *Essays on Kant and Hume*, New Haven and London: Yale University Press. (Contains noteworthy essays on causation.)

Beiser, F.C. (1987) *The Fate of Reason: German Philosophy from Kant to Fichte*, Cambridge, MA: Harvard University Press. (A detailed study of the reception of Kant; contains extensive bibliography of primary sources.)

Chadwick, R. (ed.) (1992) *Immanuel Kant: Critical Assessments*, London: Routledge, 4 vols. (One volume of classical critiques from Friedrich Schiller to Strawson and Bennett, followed by three volumes of recent articles.)

De Vleeschauwer, H.J. (1934–7) *La Déduction Transcendentale dans l'œvre de Kant* (The Transcendental Deduction in the Work of Kant), Antwerp, Paris, and the Hague: De Sikkel, Champion, and Martinus Nijhoff, 3 vols. (More general than its title suggests, it is still the most detailed study of Kant's philosophical development available.)

—— (1962) *The Development of Kantian Thought: The History of a Doctrine*, trans. A.R.C. Duncan, London: Thomas Nelson. (An abridgement of De Vleeschauwer (1934–7).)

Förster, E. (ed.) (1989) *Kant's Transcendental Deductions: The Three 'Critiques' and the 'Opus postumum'*, Stanford: Stanford University Press. (Includes noteworthy essays by Dieter Henrich and John Rawls.)

Guyer, P. (ed.) (1992) *The Cambridge Companion to Kant*, Cambridge: Cambridge University Press. (Specially written chapters surveying the whole of Kant's philosophy and an extensive bibliography.)

* Henrich, D. (1994) *The Unity of Reason: Essays on Kant's Philosophy*, ed. R. Velkley, Cambridge, MA: Harvard University Press. (Translations of Henrich's important monograph on the transcendental deduction from 1976 and several of his essays on Kant's ethics.)

Höffe, O. (1994) *Immanuel Kant*, trans. M. Farrier, Albany: State University of New York Press. (The best recent German survey of Kant's philosophy.)

Walker, R.C.S. (1978) *Kant*, London: Routledge & Kegan Paul. (A well-informed, argumentative overview.)

Wolff, R.P. (ed.) (1967) *Kant: A Collection of Critical Essays*, Garden City: Doubleday Anchor. (Includes Lewis White Beck's papers on the analytic-synthetic distinction.)

Individual topics

* Allison, H.E. (1983) *Kant's Transcendental Idealism*, New Haven and London: Yale University Press. (Influential presentation of the 'two-aspect' theory, includes extensive bibliography.)

Ameriks, K. (1982) *Kant's Theory of Mind: An Analysis of the Paralogisms of Pure Reason*, Oxford: Clarendon Press. (Using Kant's lectures on metaphysics, argues that Kant's departure from traditional rational psychology is not as radical as is usually assumed.)

Beck, L.W. (1960) *A Commentary on Kant's Critique*

of Practical Reason, Chicago, IL: University of Chicago Press. (Only detailed commentary on the second *Critique*, defends a perspectival approach to freedom.)

Beiser, F.C. (1992) *Enlightenment, Revolution and Romanticism: The Genesis of Modern German Political Thought, 1790–1800*, Cambridge, MA: Harvard University Press. (Places Kant's political thought in detailed historical context.)

* Bennett, J. (1966) *Kant's Analytic*, Cambridge: Cambridge University Press. (Together with Bennett (1974) constitutes one of the most influential analytical studies of Kant; the 1966 work remains more successful.)

—— (1974) *Kant's Dialectic*, Cambridge: Cambridge University Press. (Together with Bennett (1966) constitutes one of the most influential analytical studies of Kant; the 1966 work remains more successful.)

Brittan, G.G., Jr. (1978) *Kant's Theory of Science*, Princeton, NJ: Princeton University Press. (A contemporary assessment of Kant's philosophy of mathematics and physics.)

Brook, A. (1994) *Kant and the Mind*, Cambridge: Cambridge University Press. (A study of Kant's philosophy of mind aimed at contemporary philosophers.)

Cohen, T. and Guyer P. (eds) (1982) *Essays in Kant's Aesthetics*, Chicago, IL: University of Chicago Press. (Includes important papers by R. Aquila, D. Crawford and D. Henrich as well as the editors; includes extensive bibliography.)

Crawford, D.W. (1974) *Kant's Aesthetic Theory*, Madison: University of Wisconsin Press. (The first important analytical study of Kant's aesthetics, it argues for a moral completion of the deduction of taste.)

Dryer, D.P. (1966) *Kant's Solution for Verification in Metaphysics*, London: George Allen & Unwin. (Overshadowed by Strawson (1966) and Bennett (1966), remains a wordy but valuable study of Kant's theory of the synthetic a priori.)

Ewing, A.C. (1924) *Kant's Treatment of Causality*, London: Routledge & Kegan Paul. (Old but still insightful.)

Galston, W.A. (1975) *Kant and the Problem of History*, Chicago, IL: The University of Chicago Press. (A wide-ranging survey focusing on history and political progress.)

Gregor, M. (1963) *Laws of Freedom: A Study of Kant's Method of Applying the Categorical Imperative in the Metaphysik der Sitten*, Oxford: Basil Blackwell. (The standard English commentary on the *Metaphysics of Morals*.)

Guyer, P. (1979) *Kant and the Claims of Taste*, Cambridge, MA: Harvard University Press. (A controversial critical scrutiny of Kant's analysis and deduction of judgments of taste.)

* —— (1987) *Kant and the Claims of Knowledge*, Cambridge: Cambridge University Press. (After a study of Kant's development in the 1770s, separates Kant's theory of categories from transcendental idealism.)

—— (1993) *Kant and the Experience of Freedom: Essays on Aesthetics and Morality*, Cambridge: Cambridge University Press. (A collection of essays placing Kant's aesthetics in its historical context and exploring connections with Kant's moral philosophy.)

Howell, R. (1992) *Kant's Transcendental Deduction: An Analysis of Main Themes in his Critical Philosophy*, Dordrecht and Boston: Kluwer. (A detailed study influenced by Hintikka's philosophy of language.)

Kemp Smith, N. (1923) *A Commentary to Kant's Critique of Pure Reason*, London: Macmillan, 2nd edn. (The classical English presentation of the 'patchwork theory' of the composition of the first *Critique*, it remains stimulating and the only important English commentary on every part of the *Critique*.)

Kitcher, P.(1990) *Kant's Transcendental Psychology*, Oxford: Oxford University Press. (A defense of Kant's cognitive psychology.)

Melnick, A. (1973) *Kant's Analogies of Experience*, Chicago, IL: University of Chicago Press. (Indispensable interpretation of the Analogies.)

—— (1989) *Space, Time, and Thought in Kant*, Dordrecht: Kluwer. (Immensely complicated reconstruction of the genesis and content of Kant's theory of empirical judgment.)

Nell, O. (O'Neill) (1975) *Acting on Principle: An Essay on Kantian Ethics*, New York: Columbia University Press. (The most important interpretation of the categorical imperative.)

O'Neill, O. (1989) *Constructions of Reason: Explorations of Kant's Practical Philosophy*, Cambridge: Cambridge University Press. (Papers on both the interpretation and application of Kantian ethics.)

Paton, H.J. (1936) *Kant's Metaphysics of Experience: A Commentary on the First Half of the Kritik der reinen Vernunft*, London: George Allen & Unwin, 2 vols. (Extensive rebuttal of Kemp Smith's 'patchwork theory'; like the contemporary work by De Vleeschauwer, makes much use of Kant's notes.)

—— (1947) *The Categorical Imperative: A Study in Kant's Moral Philosophy*, London: Hutchinson. (The classical English commentary on the *Groundwork*.)

* Prauss, G. (1974) *Kant und das Problem der Dinge an*

sich (Kant and the Problem of the *Ding an sich*), Bonn: Bouvier. (An influential presentation of the 'two-aspect' interpretation of the distinction between appearances and things in themselves.)

Reich, K. (1992) *The Completeness of Kant's Table of Judgments*, trans. J. Kneller and M. Losoncy, Stanford: Stanford University Press. (Influential defense of the metaphysical deduction.)

* Strawson, P.F. (1966) *The Bounds of Sense: An Essay on Kant's Critique of Pure Reason*, London: Methuen. (An elegant reconstruction, based on Strawson's theory of meaning, that stimulated much of the best work on Kant in the 1960s and 1970s.)

Vaihinger, H. (1881–92) *Commentar zu Kants Kritik der reinen Vernunft* (Commentary on Kant's *Critique of Pure Reason*), Stuttgart: W. Spemann and Union Deutsche Verlagsgesellschaft, 2 vols. (The most detailed study of the Introduction and Transcendental Aesthetic ever produced.)

Ward, K. (1972) *The Development of Kant's View of Ethics*, Oxford: Basil Blackwell. (The only modern study of this topic in English.)

Williams, H. (1983) *Kant's Political Philosophy*, New York: St. Martin's. (A general survey.)

—— (ed.) (1992) *Essays on Kant's Political Philosophy*, Chicago, IL: University of Chicago Press. (Contains essays by O. Höffe, W. Kersting and O. O'Neill among others.)

* Wolff, R.P. (1963) *Kant's Theory of Mental Activity: A Commentary on the Transcendental Analytic of the Critique of Pure Reason*, Cambridge, MA: Harvard University Press. (Valuable commentary on the first-edition deduction and the second Analogy.)

Wood, A.W. (1970) *Kant's Moral Religion*, Ithaca and London: Cornell University Press. (A valuable study of Kant's moral theology.)

—— (1978) *Kant's Rational Theology*, Ithaca and London: Cornell University Press. (A study of Kant's critique of the traditional arguments for the existence of God, drawing heavily on Kant's lectures.)

PAUL GUYER

KANTIAN ETHICS

Kantian ethics originates in the ethical writings of Immanuel Kant (1724–1804), which remain the most influential attempt to vindicate universal ethical principles that respect the dignity and equality of human beings without presupposing theological claims or a metaphysical conception of the good. Kant's systematic, critical philosophy centres on an account of reasoning about action, which he uses to justify principles of duty and virtue, a liberal and republican conception of justice with cosmopolitan scope, and an account of the relationship between morality and hope.

Numerous contemporary writers also advance views of ethics which they, and their critics, think of as Kantian. However, some contemporary work is remote from Kant's philosophy on fundamental matters such as human freedom and reasoning about action. It converges with Kant's ethics in claiming that we lack a substantive account of the good (so that teleological or consequentialist ethics are impossible), in taking a strong view of the equality of moral agents and the importance of universal principles of duty which spell out what it is to respect them, and in stressing an account of justice and rights with cosmopolitan scope.

Both Kant's ethics and contemporary Kantian ethics have been widely criticized for preoccupation with rules and duties, and for lack of concern with virtues, happiness or personal relationships. However, these criticisms may apply more to recent Kantian ethics than to Kant's own ethics.

1   **Kant's ethics**
2   **Contemporary Kantian ethics**
3   **Criticisms of Kantian ethics**
4   **Back to Kant?**

1   Kant's ethics

Kant's main writing on ethics and politics can be found in *Grundlegung zur Metaphysik der Sitten (Groundwork of the Metaphysics of Morals)* (1785), *Critik der practischen Vernunft (Critique of Practical Reason)* (1788), *Die Metaphysik der Sitten (The Metaphysics of Morals)* (1797) and numerous sections of other works and free-standing essays. Throughout these writings he insists that we cannot derive ethical conclusions from metaphysical or theological knowledge of the good (which we lack) or from a claim that human happiness is the sole good (which we cannot establish). We lack the basis for a teleological or consequentialist account of ethical reasoning, which therefore cannot be simply a matter of means-ends reasoning towards some fixed and knowable good (see CONSEQUENTIALISM; TELEOLOGICAL ETHICS).

Yet if reasoning about action, that is practical reasoning, is not means-end reasoning, what can it be? Kant's alternative account proposes simply that reasons for action must be reasons for all. He insists that we can have reasons for recommending only those principles of action which could be adopted by all concerned, whatever their particular desires, social identities, roles or relationships. Correspondingly, practical reasoning must reject any principles which cannot be principles for all concerned, which Kant characterizes as *non-universalizable* principles (see UNIVERSALISM IN ETHICS §5).

Kant gives this rather limited modal conception of practical reasoning some grand names. He calls it the 'supreme principle of morality' and the 'categorical imperative'. He formulates this fundamental principle of ethics in various ways. The formulation most discussed in the philosophical literature runs 'act only on that maxim [principle] through which you can at the same time will that it become a universal law' ([1785] 1903: 421). The formulation that has had and still has the greatest cultural resonance requires us to treat others with impartial respect. It runs 'treat humanity... never simply as a means, but always at the same time as an end' ([1785] 1903: 429) (see RESPECT FOR PERSONS §2). The equivalence of these two formulations of the categorical imperative is far from obvious. One way of glimpsing why Kant thought they were equivalent is to note that if we treat others as persons rather than as things then we must not destroy or impair their abilities to act, indeed must leave it open to them to act on the same principles that we act on; hence we must act on universalizable principles. On Kant's view, one of the worst features of consequentialist ethics is that it not merely permits but requires that persons be used as mere means if this will produce good results.

Kant claims that the categorical imperative can be used to justify the underlying principles of human duties (see DUTY §2). For example, we can show by a *reductio ad absurdum* argument that promising falsely is not universalizable. Suppose that everyone were to adopt the principle of promising falsely: since there would then be much false promising, trust would be destroyed and many would find that they could not get their false promises accepted, contrary to the hypothesis of universal adoption of the principle of false promising. A maxim of promising falsely is not universalizable, so the categorical imperative requires us to reject it. Parallel arguments can be used to show that principles such as those of coercing or doing violence are not universalizable, and so that it is a duty to reject these principles.

Kant calls duties such as these *perfect* (namely, complete) duties. These are duties which can observed by each towards all others. He also provides arguments to establish the principles of certain *imperfect* (namely, incomplete) duties, such as those of helping others in need or developing one's own talents. One way in which imperfect duties are unavoidably incomplete is that they cannot be observed towards all others: nobody can help all others, or develop all possible talents. Kant calls these

imperfect duties 'duties of virtue' (see VIRTUES AND VICES §§2–3).

The derivation of principles of duty from his conception of practical reason is the core of Kant's ethics, and provides the context for his discussion of many other themes. These include: the difference between internalizing principles and merely conforming to them in outward respects ('acting out of duty' versus 'acting according to duty'); the place of happiness in a good life; the need for judgment in moving from principle to act (see MORAL JUDGMENT §2); the justification of state power; and the justification of a cosmopolitan account of justice. He also develops the connections between his distinctive conceptions of practical reason and of freedom and his equally distinctive view of religion, which he sees as a matter not of knowledge but of reasoned hope for a future in which morality can be fully realized. In some works Kant articulates reasoned hope in religious terms; in others he articulates it in political and historical terms as a hope for a better this-worldly human future (see HOPE §3).

2 Contemporary Kantian ethics

Much contemporary work on ethics is labelled Kantian, in the main because it does not derive an account of right action from one of good results, but rather sees the right as prior to the good (RIGHT AND GOOD). In contemporary Kantian work obligations and rights are the fundamental ethical notions. Such work is often called *deontological ethics* (the term derives from the Greek word for *ought*) (see DEONTOLOGICAL ETHICS). Deontological ethical theories are contrasted with teleological or consequentialist theories, which treat the good as prior to the right. Deontological theories are concerned with ethically required action, hence with principles, rules or norms, with obligations, prohibitions and permissions, and with justice and injustice, but not with virtues, good lives, moral ideals and personal relationships (see Fried 1978; Gewirth 1978).

Deontological ethics have many distinct forms. Many versions endorse one or another interpretation of the Kantian demand to respect persons, and think that moral principles should be universal; few mention Kant's minimalist strategy for justifying certain universally binding principles as those we must live by if we reject non-universalizable principles. Indeed, many deontological ethical theories rely on conceptions of freedom, reason and action which are unlike Kant's, and resemble those typically used by consequentialists.

One prominent range of deontological positions seeks to justify principles of justice by showing that they would be agreed to by all concerned under certain hypothetical conditions. They draw on the thought that agreements and contracts are good reasons for action, and suggest that all ethical claims are to be justified by showing that they are based if not on actual then on hypothetical agreements or contracts. These sorts of deontological theories are often called *contractarian* or *contractualist*; they are contemporary versions of social contract theories (see CONTRACTARIANISM).

Some contractualists take a Hobbesian rather than a Kantian approach. They argue that principles of justice are those on which instrumentally rational persons, guided by their individual preferences, would agree (see HOBBES, T. §§6–7). Other contractualists take a more Kantian approach. They argue that principles of justice are those which would be accepted or agreed to by persons who are not merely instrumentally rational but can use certain reasonable procedures.

The best known exponent of Kantian contractualism is John RAWLS, whose *A Theory of Justice* (1971) identifies principles of justice as those that would be agreed by rational and self interested beings in circumstances which ensure that their choosing will be reasonable as well as rational (see Rawls 1980, 1993). He argues that principles of justice would emerge if they were chosen by all concerned in a hypothetical situation devised to ensure impartiality and hence agreement. Rawls calls this hypothetical situation 'the original position', and represents it as one in which persons are ignorant of their own social position and personal attributes, hence of their own advantage, hence cannot but be impartial.

Rawls claims that rational persons in this hypothetical situation would choose principles of justice that prescribe equal rights for all and the highest attainable level of wellbeing for the worst off. Since everything that differentiates individuals, and could thus provide a basis for disagreement, for bargaining, or for a need to seek agreement, is carefully excluded from the original position, it is not obvious why principles chosen in it should be thought of as matters of *agreement*, or why the parties to the original position should be thought of as *contracting* with one another. Nor is it clear why the fact that certain principles would be agreed to under these conditions justifies those principles to those in other situations. Why are principles which would be agreed to under conditions that do not obtain binding under conditions that actually obtain?

In *A Theory of Justice* Rawls argues that principles that would be so agreed are binding in other situations because they cohere, or form a 'reflective equilibrium' with 'our considered judgments' (see

MORAL JUSTIFICATION §2). Principles are justified not merely because the instrumental reasoning of the hypothetically ignorant would select them, but because we would reasonably judge them congruent with our most carefully considered moral views. In his later *Political Liberalism* (1993) Rawls depicts these principles as the outcome not of hypothetical agreement in an original position, but as the hypothetical agreement of persons who are not only rational but reasonable, in the sense that they are willing to abide by principles given assurance that others will do so too (1993: 49). Principles and institutions are just if they are the focus of reasonable agreement by all concerned.

Jürgen HABERMAS has also advocated versions of Kantian ethics which stress agreement between agents. In earlier work he argued that the test of justification or legitimation is that a proposal would be agreed in a hypothetical 'ideal speech situation', in which communication was undistorted. In more recent work (1993), he has argued that legitimation of norms is achieved through processes of public discourse, to which each can contribute and in which all can agree.

3 Criticisms of Kantian ethics

Both Kant's ethics and contemporary Kantian ethics have been criticized from many quarters. The critics evidently include those who advocate one or another form of teleological or consequentialist theory, who believe that it is possible to establish an account of the good, from which a convincing account of the right, and specifically of justice, can be derived. However, they also include a variety of writers who reject consequentialist thinking, including communitarians, virtue ethicists, Wittgensteinians and feminist thinkers (see COMMUNITY AND COMMUNITARIANISM; VIRTUE ETHICS; WITTGENSTEINIAN ETHICS; FEMINIST ETHICS).

The most common and general criticisms are that, because it concentrates on principles or rules, Kantian ethics is doomed to be either empty and formalistic or rigidly uniform in its prescriptions (the complaints cannot both be true). The charge of empty formalism is based on the correct observation that principles underdetermine action; it is usually countered with the equally correct observation that quite indeterminate principles (such as 'Stay within the budget' or 'All religions are to be tolerated') may set significant constraints on action, so are not empty. The charge of rigidly uniform prescriptivity is based on the thought that rules prescribe, so must regiment. It is usually countered by the reminder that since rules can be indeterminate, they need not regiment: universal principles need not be uniformly prescriptive. An ethical theory that applies to principles can be more than empty and less than rigid.

Other critics object that since Kantian ethics focuses on obligations and rights, and in good measure on justice, it either must or does neglect other ethical categories, and in particular the virtues, good character or good lives; that 'natural and human rights...are fictions' (MacIntyre 1981: 67); and that obligations inevitably conflict in ways that render all deontological ethics incoherent. Some critics have laid particular stress on the point that in requiring impartial respect for all, Kantian ethics wholly ignores the place of happiness, of the emotions, of personal integrity and above all of personal relationships in the good life (see MORALITY AND EMOTIONS §§2, 4). They have claimed that we must choose between an ethics of justice and one of care, an ethic of rules and one of relationships, an ethic of duty and one of virtue, and that the latter term of each pair is to be preferred.

4 Back to Kant?

Some of these criticisms are accurately aimed at significant features of various forms of contemporary Kantian writing in ethics; many of them are less apt as criticisms of Kant's ethics. Several recent writers have suggested that Kant's ethics is the most convincing form of Kantian ethics, and that its distinctive features are strengths rather than weaknesses. Many of these writers accept much of the critique of deontological ethics, but think that not all the criticisms apply to Kant's ethics, of which they offer detailed interpretations. Part of their effort has gone into work on Kant's conceptions of action, reason and freedom, and part into work on his ethics. They have pointed out that Kant's account of practical reason and of its vindication does not assume either that all reasoning about action is instrumentally rational pursuit of preferred ends, or that ethical vindication is located in hypothetical agreements or contracts reached by reasonable procedures. They have stressed that Kant's conception of practical reason is based on universalizability rather than impartiality or reciprocity and that he views obligations rather than rights as basic to ethics. They have insisted that impartial respect for persons and a cosmopolitan approach to justice are not morally negligible matters, and have criticized communitarians, virtue ethicists and some feminist thinkers for not taking justice seriously. They have also pointed out that Kant offers accounts of the virtues, of the role of happiness in the good life, and of judgment, and argued that his position is not damagingly individualistic and that he acknowledges the importance of institutions and of social and personal relationships in human life (see Hill 1992; Korsgaard 1996; Herman 1993; O'Neill 1989).

See also: AUTONOMY, ETHICAL; KANT, I. §§9–11; PRACTICAL REASON AND ETHICS

References and further reading

* Fried, C. (1978) *Right and Wrong*, Cambridge, MA: Harvard University Press. (Forthright defence of deontological ethics.)
* Gewirth, A. (1978) *Reason and Morality*, Chicago, IL: University of Chicago Press. (Rational justification of deontological ethics.)
* Habermas, J. (1993) *Between Facts and Norms: Contributions to a Discourse Theory of Law and Democracy*, trans. W. Rehg, Cambridge: Polity Press. (Habermas' most recent extended discussion of questions of normative justification.)
* Herman B. (1993) *The Practice of Moral Judgement*, Cambridge, MA: Harvard University Press. (Essays on the use of Kantian ethical reasoning; argues that it can be sensitive to context.)
* Hill, T.E., Jr (1992) *Dignity and Practical Reason in Kant's Moral Theory*, Ithaca, NY: Cornell University Press. (Essays on Kant's ethics, and especially on respect for persons.)
* Kant, I. (1785) *Grundlegung zur Metaphysik der Sitten*, in *Kants gesammelte Schriften*, ed. Königlichen Preußischen Akademie der Wissenschaften, Berlin: Reimer, vol. 4, 1903; trans. with notes by H.J. Paton, *Groundwork of the Metaphysics of Morals* (originally *The Moral Law*), London: Hutchinson, 1948; repr. New York: Harper & Row, 1964. (References made to this work in the entry give the page number from the 1903 Berlin Akademie volume; these page numbers are included in the Paton translation. This is Kant's classic, short, if difficult, introduction to ethics.)
* —— (1788) *Critik der practischen Vernunft*, trans. L.W. Beck, *Critique of Practical Reason*, New York: Macmillan, Library of Liberal Arts, 1993. (Kant's most abstract account of his ethics; particular stress on reason and the highest good.)
* —— (1797) *Die Metaphysik der Sitten*, trans. M.J. Gregor, *The Metaphysics of Morals*, Cambridge: Cambridge University Press, 1991. (Kant's accounts of justice and of the virtues.)
* Korsgaard, C.M. (1996) *Creating the Kingdom of Ends*, Cambridge: Cambridge University Press. (Essays on the categorical imperative and its implications.)
MacIntyre, A. (1981) *After Virtue: A Study in Moral Theory*, London: Duckworth. (Vigorous criticism of

Kantian ethics from a distinctive neo-Aristotelian viewpoint.)

* O'Neill, O. (1989) *Constructions of Reason: Explorations of Kant's Practical Philosophy*, Cambridge: Cambridge University Press. (Essays on Kant's vindication of reason and its implications for ethics.)

—— (1996) 'Kant's Virtues', in R. Crisp (ed.) *How Should One Live?: Essays on the Virtues*, Oxford: Oxford University Press, 77–97. (Critical account of Kant on virtue.)

* Rawls, J. (1971) *A Theory of Justice*, Cambridge, MA: Harvard University Press. (Very influential work on liberal political philosophy; many Kantian aspects.)

* —— (1980) 'Kantian Constructivism in Moral Theory' (The Dewey Lectures), *Journal of Philosophy* 77: 515–72. (Rawls' reconsideration of his theory of justice; discusses the importance of pluralism and the impossibility of justifying a conception of the good to all.)

* —— (1993) *Political Liberalism*, New York: Columbia University Press. (Reworks Rawls' theory of justice, grounding it in a distinctive conception of public reason.)

Williams, B. (1985) *Ethics and the Limits of Philosophy*, Cambridge, MA: Harvard University Press and London: Fontana. (Varied and thoughtful criticism of Kantian ethics.)

ONORA O'NEILL

KANZE MOTOYOSHI *see* ZEAMI

KAPLAN, MORDECAI (1881–1983)

Kaplan argued that Judaism was the evolving religious civilization of the Jewish people. He attempted to recast an inherited faith in rational and natural terms. His advocacy of Jewish communalism, Jewish cultural expression in literature and art, and creativity and experimentation in liturgy had a pronounced impact on wide circles of US Jews. He took seriously the challenge to the traditional interpretation of religious values from science and modernity, and sought to establish a form of religion that was both intellectually respectable and communally responsible. Kaplan's distinctive analysis of Jewish peoplehood and the Jewish religion responsed to a wide variety of philosophical and theological perspectives and challenges.

1 Crisis and challenge
2 The response of reconstructionism

1 Crisis and challenge

Reconstructionism, the movement in Judaism founded by Mordecai Kaplan, grew out of his perception that the modern era posed a unique threat to the continuity of Judaism and the Jewish people. The corporate political character of the medieval European Jewish community had ceased to exist and Jews no longer constituted an *imperium in imperio*. Instead, with the rise of modern political structures, Jews, like others, were enfranchised as individual citizens of a modern nation-state. Judaism had to adapt to the demands of a democratic national order where the status of the Jews as a discrete political entity was lost.

Kaplan contended that the rise of naturalism undermined a number of foundational beliefs that had sustained Jewish solidarity during the Middle Ages (see SOLIDARITY). Modern men and women, he held, could no longer entertain belief in a supernaturalistic God who would miraculously intervene in the affairs of persons and the processes of nature. Nor could they affirm the idea of otherworldly reward and punishment. The dogma that God had revealed eternal written and oral laws to Moses at Sinai, as well as the belief that the rabbis had received a divine mandate as the legitimate expositors of those laws, were in his view no longer tenable. As a result of the collapse of these beliefs, Kaplan observed, most Jews no longer asserted that God had chosen the Jews from among all peoples for a special relationship, nor did they contend that the observance of Jewish law would allow the individual to attain otherworldly salvation after death.

All this led the Jewish masses to abandon their fidelity to Jewish law. As the strength of the rabbis diminished and the observance of Jewish law faltered, the bond that tied Jews together became increasingly looser. Judaism was endangered because no convincing rationale for justifying the existence of the Jews as a distinct and vital community obtained in the present day. The forces of modern nationalism and naturalism had combined to destroy the structure and rationale that had promoted Jewish group survival for centuries, forcing a crisis of continuity upon the Jewish people.

As Kaplan acknowledged, others had recognized and attempted to respond to this crisis. Yet, in his opinion, all previous attempts had failed. Kaplan condemned both the Reform movement and neo-orthodoxy for overly intellectualizing and spiritualizing Judaism. Each had forsaken Jewish peoplehood and each – in its own way – had consigned Judaism to the status of a religious confession. Nor did the political Zionism of Herzl fare better in Kaplan's analysis (see ZIONISM). Its truncated vision of the Jewish past was inauthentic, for it made no room for the religious elements of Jewish civilization. Kaplan maintained that only a reconstructionist conception of Judaism, and the course of action that flowed from it, could preserve Judaism and the Jewish people from the impairments brought on by the modern age.

2 The response of reconstructionism

Kaplan's reconstructionism was a mixture of philosophical, sociological and religious elements. He drew eclectically from thinkers as diverse as Matthew Arnold, John DEWEY, Emile DURKHEIM, William JAMES and George Herbert MEAD. He also drew upon the ancient rabbis and the contemporary cultural Zionist Ahad HA'AM. His aim was to formulate an ideology that would preserve the identity, unity and continuity of the Jewish people and its religion in the modern world. At the core of his thought lay a social existentialism: the existence of the Jewish people must be set prior to any attempt to define its essence (see EXISTENTIALISM).

Kaplan's reconstructionism focused on the proposition that Judaism was the creation of the Jewish people and, as such, existed for the people's sake. Underpinning all of his teaching was his conviction that religion, like all human life, was subject to change. Reflecting his sociological bent, Kaplan contended that the Jewish people, as the authors of their own religious forms, had engaged throughout history in a process of definition and redefinition of these forms. Judaism was conceived as the evolving religious civilization of the Jewish people. The meaning attached to the various rites of Judaism, as well as the concepts of God and Torah, had to be understood and evaluated only in relation to the reality of a living Jewish people. Theology and abstract ideas had a place in Judaism, but that place was a pragmatic one, designed to enhance the life of the group and the individuals who constituted it. In keeping with this agenda, Kaplan set out to redefine Jewish beliefs and rituals in a manner consonant with what he identified as the modern spirit.

This led him to foster a 'Copernican Revolution' in Jewish thought, placing the people of Israel, not its God, at the centre of Jewish religious reflection. Kaplan refused to countenance any notion of God as a supernatural being and advanced instead a naturalistic conception of God as that process in the universe which makes for human salvation. He contended that God was that power in the universe,

not ourselves, which makes for order, justice and goodness, and which helps men and women to achieve self-fulfilment in this world (see GOD, CONCEPTS OF).

Kaplan rejected the idea that God had chosen the people of Israel. For him, the idea of divine election was unacceptable both in its traditional supernatural form and in various modern reformulations. The concept of a chosen people served no functional purpose in contemporary society, for it failed to promote Jewish survival in any meaningful way. Indeed, the exclusivity of the concept raised serious questions about the morality of a God who would display such divine favouritism and was incompatible with modern democratic universalism. Indeed, the idea of chosenness entailed a claim to superiority that could only inflame rivalry and heighten tensions between Jews and their non-Jewish neighbours. Accordingly, Kaplan replaced the idea of a chosen people with that of 'vocation', the calling by which every individual and nation seeks to develop and use its powers for the benefit of humanity.

Kaplan affirmed the importance of religious ritual in Jewish life. He recognized that rites and rituals provided for structure and stability in Jewish life (see RITUAL). However, he would not countenance rituals as part of a supernaturally revealed code of Jewish law, nor would he envisage them as divine commandments. Instead, he identified Jewish rituals and rites as 'folkways' and 'sancta', and asserted that they embodied the sacred values of Judaism and served as the cement which bound the Jewish people together across time and space. Nevertheless, in a growing and evolving civilization such as Judaism, old forms at times become obsolete and new forms of religious expression must be developed to take their place. Kaplan, in a famous aphorism, asserted 'The past has a vote, but not a veto'. Kaplan ceded Zionism and the State of Israel a major place in his thought. Like Ahad Ha'am, he believed that Zionism would serve to unify and awaken the Jewish people to its particular destiny, and he contended that the State of Israel would serve to regenerate the Jewish people in its contemporary state of disintegration and dissolution.

Kaplan believed that his thought would provide a basis for a modern-day expression of Judaism which would foster the establishment of an 'organic community' where all the elements that constitute a civilization could play a role in the life of the Jew. He viewed the synagogue as central to this process of community-building, and asserted that it had to function as more than a house of prayer and study. Kaplan therefore set out to 'reconstruct' the synagogue to meet the challenge of the day. He proposed that this institution be converted into an all-embracing centre of Jewish cultural and social activity. The synagogue building would become a Jewish centre, complete with swimming pool, gym, library and other facilities, the primary purpose of which would no longer be worship, but 'social togetherness'. The large number of contemporary synagogues which follow this pattern, either wholly or in part, provides ample testimony to the influence of Kaplan's ideals on the US Jewish landscape. His programme of Jewish reconstructionism transcended denominational affiliations. While Kaplan had more than his share of theological and philosophical critics, there is no doubt that his death at the age of 102 brought to a close the life of one of the seminal figures in US Jewish religious history.

See also: HA'AM, AHAD; JEWISH PHILOSOPHY, CONTEMPORARY

List of works

Kaplan, M.M. (1934) *Judaism as a Civilization: Toward a Reconstruction of American Jewish Life*, New York: Schocken, 1967. (This book is Kaplan's magnum opus and has been reissued many times. It represents his classical synthesis between Jewish tradition and modern civilization.)

—— (1956) *Questions Jews Ask: Reconstructionist Answers*, New York: Reconstructionist Press. (Kaplan here responds to basic questions concerning Judaism from his own reconstructionist perspective.)

—— (1958) *Judaism Without Supernaturalism: The Only Alternative to Orthodoxy and Secularism*, New York: Reconstructionist Press. (Indicates how Judaism can be revitalized and enhanced by being freed from the shackles of a supernaturalistic theology.)

—— (1960) *The Greater Judaism in the Making: A Study of the Modern Evolution of Judaism*, New York: Reconstructionist Press. (Kaplan explains how Judaism is to respond to the twin challenges of naturalism and nationalism.)

—— (1962) *The Meaning of God in Modern Jewish Religion*, New York: Reconstructionist Press. (Argues that only a Judaism devoted to what Kaplan terms a 'this-worldly salvation' can be relevant to the modern Jew.)

—— (1964) *The Meaning and Purpose of Jewish Existence*, New York: Reconstructionist Press. (Novel in its devotion to, and presentation of, the thought of the famed German Neo-Kantian philosopher Hermann Cohen.)

—— (1970) *The Religion of Ethical Nationhood*, New York: Macmillan. (Sets forth the idea that the only hope for the survival of humanity resides in the creation and ascendancy of a spiritual political leadership devoted to the eradication of humanly created evils.)

References and further reading

Eisen, A.M. (1983) 'Mordecai Kaplan and the New Jewish "Vocation"', in *The Chosen People in America*, Bloomington, IN: Indiana University Press, chapter 4. (A particularly insightful study of Kaplan's thought.)

Eisenstein, I. and Kohn, E. (eds) (1952) *Mordecai M. Kaplan: An Evaluation*, New York: Reconstructionist Press. (A collection of essays by critics and admirers of Kaplan's thought.)

Gurock, J.S. and Schachter, J.J. (1997) *A Modern Heretic and a Traditional Community*, New York: Columbia University Press. (A fascinating study of Kaplan's life and thought from the perspective of his involvement in, and ultimate estrangement from, the US Orthodox community.)

Liebman, C. (1970) 'Reconstructionism in American Jewish Life', *American Jewish Year Book* 71: 3–99. (Remains the best summary overview of Kaplan's thought and the movement it spawned.)

Scult, M. (1994) *Judaism Faces the Twentieth Century: A Biography of Mordecai M. Kaplan*, Detroit, MI: Wayne State University Press. (The definitive and comprehensive intellectual portrait of Kaplan – his life, times and thought.)

DAVID ELLENSON

KARAISM

*The Karaites (*qara'im*, or* benei miqra*) take their name from the Hebrew word for Scripture. The sect's scripturalism originated in its rejection of the 'Oral Law' embodied in rabbinic literature. Like earlier scripturalist groups – notably the Sadducees – Karaites sought to derive their practices directly from the biblical text. While Karaism is usually traced to mid-eighth-century Iraq, the early history remains murky. The sect crystallized in the Islamic East during the late ninth and early tenth centuries, calling forth stern reactions from the leaders of mainstream rabbinic Judaism. Although harsh at times, the ensuing polemics stimulated both Karaite and Rabbanite scholarship in the fields of biblical exegesis, Hebrew grammar and lexicography, jurisprudence and religious philosophy. The two groups differed sharply over points of law and practice – the calendar, dietary laws, Sabbath regulations – but typically concurred on questions of theology.*

1 The Mu'tazilite phase
2 The post-Maimonidean phase

1 The Mu'tazilite Phase

Early medieval Jewish thinkers of both Rabbanite and Karaite persuasion found the *kalam* (speculative theology) of the Muslim rationalistic school known as the Mu'tazila congenial to their outlook and adopted many Mu'tazilite ideas (see ASH'ARIYYA AND MU'TAZILA). The Mu'tazilites' uncompromising definitions of God's unity and justice inform the writings of leading Rabbanites like SAADIAH GAON (d. 942) and Samuel ben Hofni Gaon (d. 1013). During the mid-tenth to mid-twelfth centuries, their Karaite contemporaries also produced works closely modelled upon Mu'tazilite patterns.

Widespread knowledge of Arabic facilitated the appropriation of Islamic theology by Eastern Jewish thinkers. Paralleling the doxographic interests of his Muslim contemporary, the *mutakallim* al-Ash'ari (d. 935), Ya'qub al-Qirqisani (d. after 938) betrays a lively interest in the history of Jewish sects. His *Kitab al-anwar wa'l-marakib* (Book of Lights and Watchtowers), a comprehensive Karaite code, incorporates discussions of epistemology, philosophy of law, and theology. In this, it resembles the codes of later thinkers active in the Islamic world such as AL-GHAZALI (d. 1111) and MAIMONIDES (d. 1204).

While al-Qirqisani lived in Iraq, the main centre of Karaite spiritual and intellectual activity during the tenth and eleventh centuries was Jerusalem. Ascetic and apocalyptic in outlook, the Karaite Mourners for Zion preached a strict regime of repentance, prayer and Bible study. Their writings evince a certain hostility to 'alien wisdom' but do endorse some Mu'tazilite teachings. The commentaries of Japheth ben Eli – originally covering the entire Bible and largely extant in manuscript – include long speculative excursuses and strikingly apply *kalam* doctrines to the explication of such passages as Genesis 1–2, Genesis 22 and Job.

Karaism became truly scholastic with the assimilation of works emanating from the Mu'tazilite school of Basra. The writings of the Mu'tazilite theologian 'Abd al-Jabbar (d. 1025) powerfully influenced such leading Karaites as Yusuf al-Basir (Joseph ben Abraham, d. 1040) and Abu'l-Furqan ben al-Asad (Yeshu'ah ben Judah, d. after 1065). Structured around the doctrines of divine unity and justice, Yusuf's *al-Kitab al-muhtawi* (Comprehensive Treatise) is a compendium of Karaite *kalam*. Its forty chapters grapple with most of the salient issues confronting Jewish (and Muslim) *mutakallimun*. Under the rubric of divine unity we find discussions of epistemology and the obligation to engage in speculative theology (chapters 1–2), physical theories (3), existence of the Creator (4), the divine attributes – omnipotence, omniscience, existence and eternity – and their essential nature (5–11), divine incorporeality and unity (12–14) and the createdness of God's speech (15). Under the second major heading of Mu'tazilite theology, divine justice, we find discussions of God's will and self-sufficiency (chapters 16–17), theodicy (18–26), human free will (27–31), revelation and divine obligation (32–36) and reward, punishment, merits and repentance (37–40).

Like 'Abd al-Jabbar, Yusuf was a jurist. Theology naturally impinged on his juridical writings. In discussing circumcision, for example, he considers such questions as intention, compensation for suffering and the nature of obligation. His disciple Yeshu'ah ben Judah prefaces a treatise on marriage law with an elaborate epistemology. His Bible commentaries show a much greater interest in *kalam* problems than is evident in those of his predecessor Japheth ben Eli.

Like the Mu'tazilites – but unlike the Rabbanites – both Yusuf and Yeshu'ah believed that all bodies are composed of atoms, in which accidents reside (see ATOMISM, ANCIENT; OCCASIONALISM). Among Muslims, atomism was typically linked with occasionalism, continuous creation and the rejection of natural causality. The Karaites, however, seem to have affirmed a form of natural causality as a corollary of their theory of creation.

Karaite teachings found a receptive audience among eleventh-century Byzantine Jews, some of whom studied in Jerusalem. They produced the earliest Hebrew translations of Arabic speculative writings over a century before the famous translations of the Ibn Tibbon family in Provence. Despite their odd renderings of technical terms and slavish adherence to Arabic syntax, these Hebrew versions, epitomes and anthologies linked later Byzantine Karaites to the earlier tradition. The transmission process culminated in 1148–9 with the completion of Judah Hadassi's *Eshkol ha-Kofer* (Cluster of Henna), an encyclopedic code in rhymed Hebrew acrostics. Although more original in form than in content, the work notably includes a creed – a mark of Islamic influence – anticipating Maimonides' Thirteen Principles by a decade. Hadassi's ten articles address: (1) God's existence, unity and wisdom; (2) divine eternity and uniqueness; (3) the world's createdness; (4) the revelations to Moses and other Hebrew prophets; (5) the truth of the Torah; (6) the distinctiveness of the Hebrew language; (7) the unique and eternal sanctity of the Temple site; (8) the resurrection of the dead; (9) divine judgment; and (10) reward and punishment.

Most of these articles align with positions developed in Kalam treatises like the *al-Kitab al-muhtawi* (Comprehensive Treatise).

Numerous harsh, anti-sectarian remarks in the writings of twelfth-century Andalusian Rabbanites indicate the spread of Karaism to Islamic Spain. In an autograph letter, Judah Halevi (d. 1141) reveals that he began his *Kuzari* in response to questions from a Karaite. The third part contains an informed attack on Karaite practice and a staunch defence of rabbinic tradition. In *Sefer ha-Kabbalah* (The Book of Tradition), Abraham IBN DAUD (d. *circa* 1180) chronicles the history of Rabbanite scholarship in order to prove the validity of the Oral Law. In documenting the heresy of Spanish Karaites, he even mentions how Rabbanite Jews were given license to persecute them. The great exegete Abraham IBN EZRA polemicizes against numerous Karaite legal positions and records his disputations with the sectarians (for example, in commenting on Leviticus 7: 20). While a vigorous Karaite community clearly existed in twelfth-century Spain, neither the names nor works of Spanish Karaites have survived. And although the Andalusian Rabbanites seem to be implacable foes of the sectarians, Ibn Ezra, at least, regularly cites the commentaries of Japheth ben Eli and Yeshu'ah ben Judah in non-polemical contexts; their philological, rationalistic approach clearly appealed to him.

2   The post-Maimonidean phase

Later Byzantine Karaites similarly admired the clarity, erudition and rationalism of IBN EZRA and MAIMONIDES. Writing in fluent Rabbinic Hebrew, Aaron ben Joseph (d. *circa* 1320) and Aaron ben Elijah of Nicomedia (d. 1369) engage, criticize and frequently borrow from them and other Rabbanite authors. The latter Aaron is remarkable for his trilogy: *'Ets Hayyim* (The Tree of Life), a theological *summa*; *Gan Eden* (The Garden of Eden), a code; and *Keter Torah* (The Crown of the Law), a commentary on the Pentateuch. Modelled on the *Guide to the Perplexed*, *'Ets Hayyim* is the first substantial Karaite work of religious philosophy composed in Hebrew. Its technical vocabulary is largely Tibbonid, although the older Karaite terminology also persists. Like Maimonides, Aaron clearly deems religious philosophy an authentic and original component of Judaism. But while Maimonides hails Aristotelianism as the soundest speculative system, Aaron clings to the *kalam* of his ancestors. Where Maimonides subjects *kalam* theories to rigorous criticism (*Guide to the Perplexed* 1: 73–6), Aaron defends Mu'tazilite teachings or seeks to harmonize them with Aristotelianism – sometimes through terminological sleights of hand. Consequently, *'Ets*

Hayyim is more a *kalam* response to Aristotelianism than a Karaite critique of Rabbanism.

During the fifteenth century, Byzantine Karaites and Rabbanites reached an intellectual rapprochement. Increasingly, Karaite disciples incorporated the scholarship of their Rabbanite teachers into their own compositions. However, while Rabbinic writing began to take new turns, Karaite literary activity became increasingly derivative, and though small sectarian communities still flourished (notably in Poland, Lithuania, the Crimea and Egypt), the great age of Karaite intellectual achievement and innovation had effectively come to an end. Today, Karaites in Israel, Europe and the USA face the challenge of establishing their own communal identities as minorities within minorities. The old philosophical problems that exercised their ancestors are all but forgotten.

See also: ASH'ARIYYA AND MU'TAZILA; ISLAMIC THEOLOGY; THEOLOGY, RABBINIC

References and further reading

Ankori, Z. (1959) *Karaites in Byzantium*, New York: Columbia University Press, 1959. (Focuses on the activities of eleventh- and twelfth-century sectarians; comprehensive bibliography on pages 461–84.)

* al-Basir, Y. (before 1040) *al-Kitab al-muhtawi* (Comprehensive Treatise), ed. and trans. G. Vajda, *Al-Kitab al-Muhtawi de Yusuf al-Basir*, Leiden: Brill, 1985. (Reprints articles containing a virtually complete French translation of the text and extensive analyses adducing Jewish and Islamic parallels.)

Ben-Shammai, H. (1985) 'Studies in Karaite Atomism', *Jerusalem Studies in Arabic and Islam* 6: 243–97. (Full presentation of this central Kalam problem.)

Frank, D. (1991) 'The Religious Philosophy of the Karaite Aaron ben Elijah: The Problem of Divine Justice', Ph.D. dissertation, Harvard University, Ann Arbor, MI: University Microfilms International. (Contains an annotated translation of *'Ets Hayyim*, chapters 79–90.)

Husik, I. (1940) *A History of Mediaeval Jewish Philosophy*, Philadelphia, PA: Jewish Publication Society of America. (See especially Chapter 4 on Joseph al-Basir and Jeshua ben Judah, and Chapter 16 on Aaron ben Elijah of Nicomedia.)

Lasker, D.J. (1992) 'Karaism in Twelfth-Century Spain', *Journal of Jewish Thought and Philosophy* 1: 179–95. (Overview with reference to virtually all known sources.)

Nemoy, L. (1952) *Karaite Anthology*, New Haven, CN: Yale University Press. (Well-chosen collection illustrating seven hundred years of Karaite thought.)

Sirat, C. (1985) *A History of Jewish Philosophy in the Middle Ages*, Cambridge: Cambridge University Press, 37–56; repr. 1990. (A useful survey with bibliography: see pages 418–21, 459–60.)

Sklare, D.E. (1995) 'Yusuf al-Basir: Theological Aspects of His Halakhic Works', in D. Frank (ed.) *The Jews of Medieval Islam: Community, Society, and Identity*, New York and Cologne: Brill, 249–70. (Comprehensive survey of his works and discussion of the interplay between law and *kalam*.)

Wieder, N. (1962) *The Judean Scrolls and Karaism*, London: East and West Library. (Excellent monograph on apocalyptic aspects of sectarian exegesis.)

Wolfson, H.A. (1979) *Repercussions of the Kalam in Jewish Philosophy*, Cambridge, MA: Harvard University Press. (Includes concise analyses of such topics as divine attributes, divine speech and causality as treated by Karaite scholars.)

DANIEL FRANK

KARMA AND REBIRTH, INDIAN CONCEPTIONS OF

The combined beliefs in karma and rebirth, that is, the retributive power of actions and decisions and a beginningless, though not necessarily endless, succession of births and deaths for living beings, constitute a fundamental premise of the great majority of India's religious and philosophical traditions. The suggestion first made by the great Muslim scholar al-Biruni (973–1048) that they are the fundamental creed of Indian religious thought in general may be questionable, but it is certainly understandable. Although such notions are by no means exclusively Indian, they have played a far more central and pervasive role in India than in any other cultural domain.

In a sense, the idea of karmic retribution postulates that the act itself will hold its originator responsible and accountable. Acts of moral or ritual significance will bring about their own reward or punishment, that is, favourable or unfavourable experiences. On the other hand, favourable or unfavourable experiences and conditions are forms of reward or punishment for past actions and decisions. Karmic retribution takes place through a sequence of countless existences and may involve a movement through a vast variety of forms of life. More specifically, this implies that birth into a particular species, physiological and psychological features, sex, social status, life span, exposure to pleasant or unpleasant experiences, and so on, appear as results of previous actions (usually acts committed in previous lives), and that current actions are expected to have a corresponding influence on future existences. In Sanskrit, the realm of rebirth and karmic retribution is known as saṃsāra. Its precise scope has been subject to some debate. The most common assumption is that it coincides with sentient existence and includes the entire hierarchy of living organisms from the gods down to the plants. While later Buddhism tends to exclude the plants from this domain, Jainism finds forms of life and sentience even in the elements water, earth, and so forth. Most schools of philosophy view being in saṃsāra as a condition of bondage, suffering and alienation; even karmic ascent is ultimately undesirable. The ability to transcend this condition by transforming and eventually eliminating the power of karma is often associated with human existence and considered a rare privilege. Most forms of life are just forms of karmic retribution, without any capacity for karmic initiative.

The historical origins of the doctrine of karma and rebirth cannot be determined with certainty and precision. While the Vedas and Brāhmaṇas provide significant antecedents, they do not show any clear recognition of the doctrine as such. Even in the older Upaniṣads (prior to 500 BC), its formulations are still tentative, partial and more or less isolated. It seems that the teachings of the Buddha added a new and stricter notion of causality and a far more explicit sense of moral responsibility and universal applicability to the older versions. The other important reform movement of this period, Jainism, showed an early commitment to a systematic elaboration of karmic factors and processes. Unlike the Buddhists, the Jainas developed a reified, even substantialist notion of karma. In Hindu literature, such texts as the great epic the Mahābhārata (beginning around 400 BC) give clear evidence of a fully developed and generally recognized doctrine of karma and rebirth. Subsequently, the doctrine was adopted and variously interpreted by most schools of philosophical and religious thought. It served, moreover, as a basic premise of law texts, popular narratives and mythologies, and a wide array of traditional 'sciences', such as medicine, embryology and astrology. Significant disagreements and debates occurred with regard to the status and character of the karmic agent and the subject of transmigration and rebirth (most conspicuously in connection with the Buddhist denial of a durable 'self' or ātman). The moral relevance and metaphysical qualities of acts and decisions, the nature of karmic causality and the mechanism of rebirth, the possibility of a transfer of karma, the compatibility of knowledge and action, and the prospects of and problems concerning the elimination of karma and the ultimate transcendence of rebirth provided further topics of debate.

In its various contexts and applications, the doctrine of karma and saṃsāra *has at least three different yet interrelated functions and dimensions: it is used to provide causal explanations (especially in the realm of life); it serves as a framework for ethical discipline and religious orientation; and it provides the rationale for a fundamental dissatisfaction with worldly existence and a commitment to final liberation from such existence. The ways in which these functions have been balanced or correlated with one another reflect fundamental trends and tensions in the Indian tradition in general.*

1   **Terminology**
2   **Sources**
3   **Beginnings and early developments**
4   **Applications and interpretations in Hindu thought**
5   **Buddhism**
6   **Jainism**
7   **Applications and reinterpretations in modern Indian thought**
8   **General and concluding observations**

1   Terminology

The word 'karma', one of the most familiar Indian loan words in colloquial English and other Western languages, is the nominative of the Sanskrit noun *karman*, which is a derivative of the verbal root *kṛ*, 'to do', 'to make'. The literal and primary meanings of *karman* are 'deed', 'work', 'action', 'act' (often with ritual connotations), but also 'object' in a grammatical sense. The semantic linkage with an inherent retributive power of acts and decisions, or with an accumulation and preservation of their effects, occurs in some Upaniṣads and, much more clearly and explicitly, in early Buddhism   (Pāli: *kamma*). A familiar alternative for *karman* in this sense, especially in Hindu literature, is *adṛṣṭa*, 'unseen', that is, the 'invisible' results of our actions. In closer association with ritual acts, we also find the term *apūrva*. Good karma is often referred to as *dharma* or *puṇya* ('merit'), bad karma as *adharma* or *pāpa* ('demerit', 'evil', 'guilt'). The term *karmavipāka* refers, primarily in Buddhism, to the 'ripening' or 'fruition' of the karmic potential, while *karmāśaya* refers to the 'karmic residue' or the 'accumulation of karma'.

The English term 'rebirth' has its literal equivalent in *punarjanma*, but this does not carry much terminological weight. In the Brāhmaṇas, it is preceded by *punarmṛtyu*, 'redeath', 'recurrent death', and *punarāvṛtti*, 'return' from an otherworldly realm to life on this earth. In Buddhism, which does not recognize a durable self, we find *punabbhava/punarbhava*, 'repeated existence'; more specifically, the Pāli term *paṭisandhi* (Sanskrit: *pratisaṃdhi*) refers to the

causal linkage between successive lives. In the middle Upaniṣads as well as in old Buddhism and Jainism, *saṃsāra*, 'roaming through' (successive states or existences), 'transmigration', emerges as a fundamental notion. It refers to worldly existence as an aimless recurrence of life and death, and to the world itself as a karmic stage. Karma and rebirth are inseparable in this concept.

As far as English terminology is concerned, it should be noted that 'rebirth' is ontologically more neutral than 'transmigration', 'metempsychosis' or even 'reincarnation', which may suggest the existence of a durable entity and would thus seem inappropriate in Buddhism. The common phrase 'law of karma' has no terminological equivalent in traditional Indian thought, where there is no use for the modern concept of 'natural laws', nor any commitment to their systematic empirical verification. 'Law of karma' is not only a terminological innovation, but, in many of its usages, also a conceptual reinterpretation.

2   Sources

References to karma and rebirth are to be found in Indian texts of the most diverse types and genres, from the late Vedic to the modern period. The doctrine appears in popular mythology and philosophical thought as an unquestioned presupposition and a topic of explicit theoretical efforts. But except for Jainism, comprehensive and systematic presentations are rare.

Various suggestions and tentative statements are found in the old Upaniṣads, for instance in Bṛhadāraṇyaka Upaniṣad 6.1– and 4.4, and Chāndogya Upaniṣad 5.1–. The great epic the *Mahābhārata* contains a large number of casual references, but also some relatively systematic and coherent presentations. In the 'law books' (Dharmaśāstras), the most coherent and significant survey is provided by the twelfth chapter of the *Manusmṛti*. The Purāṇas and other more popular religious texts add much relevant material (see, for instance, the *Pretakalpa* of the Garuḍa Purāṇa). Among the traditional sciences, the medical texts (Āyurveda) provide the most extensive discussions. Various works compile and summarize older statements on karma and its effects, especially karmic punishments, in the form of digests. Among these, the popular and anonymous *Karmavipākasaṃhitā* and the more scholarly *Madanamahārṇava* (fourteenth century) by Viśveśvara Bhaṭṭa are available in printed editions.

More or less explicitly, the doctrine appears throughout the literature of the classical systems (*darśanas*) of Hindu philosophy; one of the more coherent treatments is found in the Yoga system (see

Yogasūtra 2.13 with commentaries). Nyāya and Vaiśeṣika add more basic arguments concerning rebirth and the existence of the self. Advaita Vedānta has produced one of the rare philosophical monographs on karma, the *Vijñānadīpikā*, falsely attributed to Śaṅkara's disciple Padmapāda. In a more theological fashion, the numerous schools of 'sectarian' (Śaivite and Vaiṣṇava) thought continue the debate.

The basic acceptance of karma and rebirth in Buddhism is obvious in its most ancient documents; its full realization is associated with the enlightenment of the Buddha. However, relatively few texts in the oldest parts of the Theravāda canon, for instance the *Mahā-* and *Cūḷakammavibhaṅgasutta* of the Majjhimanikāya, deal with it in a thematic fashion. The Jātaka texts describe the future Buddha's path through more than five hundred existences. The Abhidhamma/Abhidharma part of the canon produces elaborate conceptual schemes in its analysis of karma and rebirth. Numerous details were debated among the Buddhist schools and sects; from a Theravāda perspective, these debates are documented in the *Kathāvatthu*. The popular *Milindapañha* (Questions of Menander) pays special attention to reconciling the postulate of personal accountability with the Buddhist 'no-self' doctrine.

For the Sarvāstivāda views on karma, the *Mahāvibhāṣā* and the *Abhidharmakośa* (which also includes Sauntrāntika ideas) are exemplary documents. Vasubandhu's *Karmasiddhiprakaraṇa* combines Sautrāntika and Yogācāra ideas on karma. The spread of Buddhism beyond South Asia also led to a dissemination of the ideas of karma and rebirth. The fact that the basic premises of the doctrine were less familiar in the non-Indian traditions which adopted Buddhism sometimes led to the production of auxiliary or explanatory materials, for instance, the *paralokasiddhi* texts in Tibet, which are supposed to establish the basic facts of rebirth and life after death.

The most elaborate treatises on karma and rebirth are found in Jainism. The oldest extant sources already indicate an extraordinary scholastic commitment to this doctrine. A concise summary of the oldest developments is given in Umāsvāti's *Tattvārthasūtra*, produced around the fourth or fifth centuries CE and accepted as authoritative by the Digambara and Śvetāmbara schools of Jainism. The systematic elaboration of the karma theory continues through a large number of works, including Śivaśarman's *Karmaprakṛti*, the anonymous *Saptatikā*, Candrarṣi's *Pañcasaṃgraha* and a group of nine texts known as Karmagranthas. In addition to the Prakrit and Sanskrit originals of these works, we

also find adaptations and commentaries in vernaculars, especially Gujarati.

3 Beginnings and early developments

The absence of any clear evidence for karma and rebirth in the older Vedic documents has led to extensive speculations concerning potential extra-Vedic or 'non-Aryan' origins of the doctrine. The possibility of such origins cannot be excluded. On the other hand, we have no historical documents to support and substantiate it. For the time being, the philologist and historian of ideas will have to work with those materials that *are* available, even if they do not answer the question of the origin, but provide only more or less relevant antecedents and approximations. For this endeavour, it is essential not to presuppose and impose the standards of a unified theory of *saṃsāra*, or of any other kind of systematic theory.

Different ideas about life after death coexist in Vedic thought. Among them we find such beliefs as a reappearance of the dead in the form of animals (birds or snakes), but also as their own descendants or relatives. While this may pave the way for the later concept of rebirth, it does not imply that reappearance or survival after death was taken for granted in Vedic times. Other, less popular, notions suggest that the continuation of existence after death had to be accomplished through specific, primarily ritual, activities and techniques and was by no means accessible to all living beings. Side by side with such ideas we find concepts of cosmic balance and justice (most significantly *ṛta*) which may foreshadow certain aspects of the karma theory.

Against this general Vedic background, some of the oldest Upaniṣads provide us with more specific approximations and anticipations of the later concept of *saṃsāra*. The cyclical explanation of life and death found in the combined doctrines of the 'two paths' and the 'five fires' (Bṛhadāraṇyaka and Chāndogya Upaniṣads) is among the most significant examples. This theory does not assume a direct transition from one living organism to another, but an intermediate residence in a heavenly realm, as determined by the amount of ritual merit accumulated during the preceding lifetime. The cyclical 'way of the fathers' is contrasted with the 'way of the gods', which transcends all cycles, and an enigmatic 'third condition' for creatures without access to the 'two paths' and possibly without any capability of rebirth and permanent survival. Other ancient texts speak of a transfer of ritual merit or 'works' (*karman*) from one person to another, for instance, from a dying father to his son (Kauṣītaki Upaniṣad 2.15). Bṛhadāraṇyaka

Upaniṣad 3.2.13 proclaims, in a brief and elusive reference, *karman* as the decisive factor for the continuation of existence after death, but does not give any further details. Other relevant passages suggest various possibilities concerning the nature of acts, their inherent retributive power and the modalities of rebirth. The ritual dimension is supplemented by notions of moral behaviour (such as *caraṇa*; see Chāndogya Upaniṣad 5.10.7) in a wider sense. Concepts of 'desire' (*kāma*) and 'decision' or 'commitment' (*kratu*) appear in some competition with *karman* itself. The identity and nature of the agent, the mechanism of retribution, and the scope and limits of the field of transmigration remain ambiguous. The process is not governed by strict causality; there is always room for chance.

Clearer formulations of what may be called (in the sense of a convenient label) a 'standard version' of karma and rebirth emerge in the *Mahābhārata* and other texts of the period beginning around 400 BC (for instance, the 'law texts', with their elaborate catalogues of different acts and their karmic compensation). The *Mahābhārata* itself recognizes the two basic postulates which define the 'classical' karma theory: 'deeds' require the appropriate retribution as their effect; and positive or negative experiences and modes of being require a karmic cause. We may assume that the anti-Vedic reform movements of Buddhism and Jainism played a significant role in this consolidation of the doctrine of karma and rebirth.

4 Applications and interpretations in Hindu thought

During the centuries preceding the beginning of the Common Era, the concepts of karma and *saṃsāra* became pervasive, almost universally accepted premises of Indian thought and literature, from religion, philosophy and the traditional sciences to poetry, mythology and popular narratives. Only the materialistic Cārvākas and a few other groups that denied life after death and the moral and retributive implications of actions rejected these concepts (see MATERIALISM, INDIAN SCHOOL OF §3). Karma was, moreover, projected into the most ancient layers of the tradition and appeared as the indispensable background and presupposition of the most ancient texts, including the Vedic hymns. Older doctrines and ideas, such as the conceptions of fate (*daiva*) or time (*kāla*) as cosmic powers, were reinterpreted in the light of the karma theory and included in the comprehensive notion of *saṃsāra*. Early developments in some of the philosophical systems (*darśanas*) exemplify and illustrate these general observations.

There is little evidence that karma played any significant role in the cosmology of ancient Sāṅkhya, probably the oldest of the classical systems of Hindu philosophy. It was absent from the original conception of the periodic manifestation and unfolding of the basic matter and matrix (*prakṛti*). With the consolidation of the karma theory, the power of deeds and the need for retributive experiences were invoked as a catalyst for the actualization of the cosmic energy of the 'matrix' and thus for the initiation of a new world cycle. However, karma remains insignificant in so far as its ethical and soteriological role is concerned. Actions as such are relegated to the realm of *prakṛti*, that is, to objective 'material' processes. They do not affect the essence of the pure subject or spirit (*puruṣa*). The acting and transmigrating entity itself is a mere product and configuration of *prakṛti* and will ultimately be dissolved in it (see SĀṄKHYA §§2, 6).

The allied Yoga system of Patañjali offers a more integrated, coherent and explicit explanation of karma and rebirth, which suggests an early interaction with Buddhism. Karma functions within the 'wheel of *saṃsāra*' (*saṃsāracakra*), which is kept in motion by pleasure and pain, desire and aversion, merit and demerit. The production and operation of karma depends on the presence of the five 'afflictions' (*kleśa*); the most fundamental item in this group, which includes desire and aversion, is 'nescience' (*avidyā*), a radical misconception of oneself and the world. As long as this nescience has not been eliminated, the other afflictions will remain in place, and new karma will be produced. As a rule, the karma accumulated during one lifetime will determine the conditions of the immediately following existence, that is, birth in a particular species (*jāti*), life span or 'life-quantum' (*āyus*), and affective potential, or the balance of favourable and unfavourable experiences (*bhoga*). However, this basic rule of 'karmic ripening' (*karmavipāka*) is subject to innumerable qualifications and exceptions, so that the incompatibility with such texts as the *Manusmṛti*, which do not recognize the 'one life' rule at all, may be less severe than it appears.

The treatment of karma and rebirth is somewhat different in Nyāya and Vaiśeṣika. Unlike Sāṅkhya and Yoga, both Vaiśeṣika and Nyāya consider the soul or self (*ātman*, *puruṣa*) to be the originator of acts and decisions and, accordingly, as the substrate of karma. In their assessment of the moral quality of acts, they are more committed to the orthodox 'law books' than Sāṅkhya and Yoga. Also, they do not advocate the 'one life' rule of karmic ripening.

According to Nyāya, the effects of actions are stored as 'dispositions' (*saṃskāra*) in the soul. Sooner or later, they will initiate the formation of a new organism, which will provide the appropriate karmic retribution. Elaborate arguments are devised to demonstrate the distinctness and immortality of the soul and the indispensability of its stored karma for the explanation of biological and physiological processes. With the general alliance and amalgamation of the two systems, the Nyāya teachings on karma and rebirth were combined with those of Vaiśeṣika and became virtually indistinguishable. However, there are obvious differences in the oldest texts. While old Nyāya shares its use of the term 'karma' with Yoga and Buddhism, Vaiśeṣika prefers *adṛṣṭa* (and assigns a different terminological role to *karman*). *Adṛṣṭa*, the 'unseen' result of our actions, includes 'merit' and 'demerit' (*dharma* and *adharma*), two of the twenty-four 'qualities' (*guṇa*) that constitute the second ontological category (*padārtha*) of the system. It inheres in the 'souls' or 'selves' (*ātman*), which are conceived as omnipresent spiritual substances. Accordingly, its retributive potential is all-pervasive, and it can influence or direct events anywhere in the world. The preceding exposition follows Praśastapāda's presentation of the Vaiśeṣika system (*c.*500 CE). There are significant and historically symptomatic differences in the older *Vaiśeṣikasūtra*. Here, *adṛṣṭa* is not even listed among the 'qualities' of the soul, and the cosmological role of karma remains generally more ambiguous (see NYĀYA-VAIŚEṢIKA §§4–5, 7).

Because of its commitment to the proto-karmic ritualism of the Brāhmaṇas, the contributions of classical Mīmāṃsā to the karma theory are more limited. However, in its complex and highly technical theory of the Vedic ritual, it offers significant general perspectives concerning the motivation to act, the capacity to act ritually and produce ritual merit (which it restricts, in an exemplary and influential manner, to upper-caste Hindus), the connection between actions and their results, and the formation and structure of complex acts or clusters of action. Kumārila's theory of *apūrva*, the latent power produced by rituals, deserves special attention in this context.

In the school of Advaita Vedānta, as represented by ŚAṄKARA and his followers, the role of karma and rebirth is very significant, but also ambiguous and elusive. On the one hand, Upaniṣadic notions of the recurrence of life and death live on in Advaita Vedānta. On the other hand, later systematic and scholastic views concerning the accumulation and elimination of karma are adopted and developed in a somewhat eclectic fashion. For instance, the division of karma into that which is being accumulated (*sancīyamāna*), that which has been accumulated but may still be neutralized (*sañcita*), and that which has started producing its results (*prārabdha*) is a familiar item. But although karma is a basic premise in Advaita Vedānta, it is ultimately irrelevant. It is confined to the level of conventional, provisional truth (*vyavahāra*). In the end, karma and rebirth have only one meaning and function: to expose the ontological and soteriological deficiency of our world of time and space. Good karma is as vacuous as bad karma. The entire domain of karma and causality is a realm of ignorance and illusion (*avidyā*, *māyā*) and needs to be transcended.

The radical monism and illusionism of Advaita Vedānta was criticized by numerous schools of theistic Vedānta, especially those that flourished among the devotees of Viṣṇu (for instance, Rāmānuja's Viśiṣṭādvaita and Madhva's Dvaita Vedānta). According to these groups, karma was real; but it could be neutralized and superseded through loving devotion to God (*bhakti*) and divine grace, and was thus relegated to a lower level of relevance (see VEDĀNTA §3; RĀMĀNUJA; MADHVA). Corresponding materials are found in the rich philosophical and theological traditions of the devotees of Śiva, such as the South Indian Śaiva Siddhānta and the Pratyabhijñā school of Kashmir.

5 Buddhism

In the oldest extant sources of Buddhism, there is far less ambiguity about karma and rebirth than in the Upaniṣads, not to mention the older Vedic texts. In the legendary accounts of his enlightenment, the BUDDHA himself (*c.*500 BC) is credited with the discovery of a pervasive causality and with the realization that living beings are causal series of acts and results which extend over countless successive existences. Although the number of older canonical texts which deal with the doctrine in greater detail is relatively small, its central significance cannot be questioned. It is, in fact, inseparable from the quintessential Buddhist formula of 'dependent origination' (*pratītyasamutpāda*; Pāli: *paṭiccasamuppāda*). In the emerging sectarianism, debates on karma play an important role; different conceptions and interpretations of karma are among those factors that define the doctrinal identity of the various schools.

The basic contributions of ancient Buddhism to the development of the karma theory relate, above all, to the following five areas:

1 a stricter notion of causality which postulates a pervasive coherence of karmic events, but insists on the feasibility of choice and responsibility, that is, of acts which are not themselves karmic effects (thus avoiding the karmic determinism associated with the Ājīvika school);

2 a notion of agency which defines the act as rooted

in, or even as essentially identical with, volition and decision (*cetanā*) and interprets its vocal or physical implementation as a secondary phenomenon;

3 a process ontology which interprets the connection between act and experienced result strictly and exclusively as causal continuity and tries to avoid the assumption of an identical subject or substrate of act and result;

4 a comprehensive ethicization which replaces Vedic-Brahmanic notions of ritual correctness and caste-bound aptitude with more open and universal ideas of moral obligation and value;

5 a more radical notion of final liberation (*nirvāṇa/ nibbāna*) and the commitment to achieve it by eliminating the roots of karmic existence, that is, selfish desire and the illusion of the self.

All these areas leave room for further analysis and debate. What, more precisely, is the nature of the mental act or intention, and how does it relate to speech and physical action? How is karmic causality transmitted, and how does it interact with other causes? Is there an intermediate existence between death and rebirth? How does karma influence the external, material world, and how does it determine the physiological or psychological constitution of sentient beings? What is the special karmic situation of a *buddha* or an *arhat*, whose selfish desire has been eliminated? Such and similar issues are discussed in detail in the Abhidharma texts and the commentarial literature of the Theravāda tradition, and analysed in the context of their complex theories of causal conditions (*pratyaya/paccaya*) and the ultimate constituents of reality (*dharma/dhamma*). The *Kathāvatthu* defends the Theravāda views against numerous alternatives.

Among the other great schools of Buddhist thought, Sarvāstivāda made significant and influential contributions to the *dharma* theory, the classification of causal factors, and the analysis of the person as a 'series' (*santāna*) of *dharmas*. Its reifying conception of 'acquisition' (*prāpti*) is supposed to explain the way the series is affected by the moral and karmic implications of decisions and actions. It also deals with the relation between mental acts and their vocal and physical manifestations and in general with the question of how latent actions (*avijñapti*) relate to their manifest counterparts (*vijñapti*). To provide a basis for causality and especially for the durable retributive power of acts in an impermanent world, Sarvāstivāda developed its distinctive theory of time, which postulates an irreducible state of nonactual being or subsistence for past and future entities, side by side with the actual existence of present entities (see BUDDHISM, ĀBHIDHARMIKA SCHOOLS OF §3).

In the teachings of the Vātsīputrīya-Sāṃmatīya school, we find the peculiar and seemingly 'heterodox' concept of a durable 'person' (*pudgala*), that is, a common basis of act and result. However, this *pudgala* is described, in a somewhat elusive fashion, as neither different from nor identical with the impersonal factors that are supposed to constitute the person. It should not be identified with the Hindu notion of the 'soul' or 'self' (*ātman*).

The Sautrāntika school adds various qualifications to the Sarvāstivāda analysis of volition, action and the transition from the initial impetus to the intended act itself (*cetayitvā karman*). But most significant is its explanation of the process that leads from the act to the retributive result: any intentional act or decision affects the subsequent series of mental events (*cittasantāna*) in a particular fashion and impregnates it with a certain potential. It initiates, in collaboration or competition with other acts, a process of evolution or transformation (*pariṇāma*) within the series which will lead to a mental state of fruition or retribution. It is a kind of mental seed or germ (*bīja*) which is transformed into its appropriate fruit.

The Yogācāra-Vijñānavāda school adopts these and other Sautrāntika ideas and develops them in the context of its 'consciousness only' theory, a subjective idealism which reduces reality to states of awareness or mental occurrences. Reality in this sense, as mental and experienced reality, is *eo ipso* a medium of retribution. As a basis and matrix for the generation of retributive – favourable or unfavourable – experiences, the school postulates a 'warehouse consciousness' (*ālaya-vijñāna*), which contains the potential, or the stored 'seeds', for all actual awareness (*pravṛttivijñāna*) (see BUDDHISM, YOGĀCĀRA SCHOOL OF §§5–8).

The most radical treatment or rather transcendence of karma and rebirth is found in the Mādhyamika school of NĀGĀRJUNA. Here (as centuries later in Śaṅkara's Advaita Vedānta), karma and rebirth are relegated to the level of provisional, pragmatic and conventional truth (*saṃvṛti* or *vyavahāra*), to an understanding of oneself and the world which needs to be transcended. Neither the accumulation of good karma nor the attempt to eliminate all karma will lead to *nirvāṇa*. Karma is inseparable from a false commitment to means and ends, to acquisition, ownership and selfhood. From the standpoint of absolute truth, it is as essenceless and 'void' (*śūnya*) as the self or soul (*ātman*) itself. Realizing this voidness is liberation.

In general, the transfer of karmic merit plays a much greater role in the Mahāyāna schools than in old Buddhism; it is a defining characteristic of the *bodhisattva* ideal.

6 Jainism

The ancient movement of Jainism, founded or perhaps reorganized by the Jina MAHĀVĪRA, an older contemporary of the Buddha, is small as far as the number of its followers (3–4 million) is concerned. But in quantity and speculative technicality, its literary contribution to the doctrine of karma and rebirth surpasses those of both Hinduism and Buddhism.

There can be no doubt that some form of the doctrine, probably with a certain degree of technical elaboration, was part of the teachings of the founder himself. However, because of problems of transmission and documentation, it is difficult to determine with precision their nature and contents. We may assume that the following features were present already in the most ancient period of Jaina thought: the conception of karma as a material or quasi-material substance that is attached to the soul (*jīva*) and suppresses its inherent potential; an extremely wide-ranging notion of life and *saṃsāra* which finds souls and the potential for rebirth and retribution not only among humans, animals and plants, but also in such substances as earth and water (though not all souls may have the capacity for final liberation); a strong emphasis on ethical practice and asceticism; a peculiar technical terminology concerning the attraction, accumulation, exclusion and elimination of karmic matter (which was later supplemented, but not replaced by, terms borrowed from the Hindu and Buddhist schools).

A very concise, highly authoritative presentation of the Jaina theory of karma in its developed form is found in Umāsvāti's *Tattvārthasūtra* (perhaps fourth century or even earlier). Numerous later commentaries, digests and systematic treatises, produced by both the Digambara and Śvetāmbara sects, add a vast amount of technical and speculative detail to this version of the doctrine, but they do not question or alter its basic premises. It can be summarized as follows. The basic framework is provided by the division of reality into living and lifeless entities (*jīva* and *ajīva*) and the karmic categories of influx (*āsrava*) of karmic matter into the soul, subsequent bondage (*bandha*), stoppage (*saṃvara*) and expulsion (*nirjarā*) of karma, and final liberation (*mokṣa*). A soul defiled by confusion, passion and selfish desire attracts particles of potentially karmic matter floating in space; and through the 'vibrations' produced by volitional activities, it binds or glues these particles to itself and converts them into actual karma. The activities relate to body, speech or mind, and the

'vibrations' vary accordingly. A soul which is thus associated with karmic matter will inevitably be an embodied soul, and will be unable to extract itself from the cycle of transmigration.

The Jainas pay special attention to preventing the influx of new karmic particles and to expelling karma that has already been accumulated. To achieve these objectives, they invoke a complex set of ethical rules and regulations, which are supplemented by practices of asceticism and meditation. The principle of nonviolence (*ahiṃsā*) constitutes the core of Jaina ethics. Classifications and subdivisions of the types and functions of karma are highly elaborate. Basically, they distinguish 'ruinous' (*ghātin*; Prakrit: *ghāi*), from 'nonruinous' (*aghātin/aghāi*) karmas. The first category, which impedes or obscures the internal cognitive and soteriological potential of a soul, comprises 'perception-obscuring', 'knowledge-obscuring', 'affective' (*vedanīya*) and 'confusing' karmas. The second group relates to the conditions and circumstances of a soul's embodiment; it includes those karmas which account for certain basic limitations of the soul's potential, membership of a particular species and physiological setup (*nāman*), social position (*gotra/goya*) and life span (*āyus/āuya*). Numerous subdivisions and specifications supplement these general categories.

The proliferation of speculative and scholastic details is a most conspicuous feature of the Jaina literature on karma and rebirth. But there are also other developments, such as the tradition of more basic philosophical arguments concerning the existence of the soul (as the condition of the possibility of rebirth) which is affiliated with Jinabhadra's *Viśeṣāvaśyakabhāṣya* (about sixth century). Even more significantly, we also find an orientation which tends to relegate the entire domain of karma and rebirth, and of causal interaction between soul and matter, to a level of conventional and provisional truth which needs to be transcended. The *Samayasāra* of Kundakunda, possibly an older contemporary of Umāsvāti and one of the most authoritative teachers in the Digambara tradition, exemplifies this orientation, which combines a traditional Jaina perspectivism with the Mādhyamika Buddhist notion of 'two truths'.

7 Applications and reinterpretations in modern Indian thought

With the dissemination of Indian ideas beyond South Asia, chiefly through the spread of Buddhism, the doctrine of karma and rebirth was adopted by such traditions as China, Japan and Tibet and adjusted to various cultural contexts and presuppositions. These developments had no visible repercussions in India itself. Likewise, the encounter with those foreign religions that had their own presence in India and were generally opposed to karma and rebirth, above all Islam and later on Christianity, did not lead to any explicit defence or reconsideration of the doctrine. However, the Indian attitude to the foreign, especially Western, world began to change during the early nineteenth century, which can be described as the beginning of modern Indian thought. Western ideas gained an increasing significance for the Indian self-understanding. Traditional concepts and doctrines were reinterpreted in the light of modern Western thought; quite naturally, this included revisions and transformations in the theory of karma and rebirth. Western interpretations and reinterpretations of karma, for instance those by the theosophists and anthroposophists, contributed to and interacted with these revisions (see THEOSOPHY §2).

Exemplary modernist statements on karma and rebirth may be found in the works of such Neo-Hindu thinkers as Vivekananda (1863–1902), AUROBINDO GHOSE (1872–1950) and RADHAKRISHNAN (1888–1975). Numerous authors continue the debate in contemporary India, both in English and in Indian vernaculars. The most distinctive features of the modernist interpretation can be described as follows:

1 Karma is, more or less radically, dissociated from the traditional mythological implications of *saṃsāra*, which include heavens, hells and other transempirical realms of existence; rebirth itself is treated as a less essential adjunct of karma.
2 Karma is presented as a fundamentally scientific notion, a comprehensive 'law' and principle of explanation, which supersedes all merely physical causality and regularity.
3 There is a stronger commitment to empirical evidence, to 'case studies', to the collection and analysis of 'reports' and personal claims concerning rebirth; research in this sense is foreign to the traditional treatment of karma and rebirth.
4 The doctrine is associated with modern Western concepts of evolution and progress; the world of karma and rebirth appears not so much as the realm of aimless wandering (*saṃsāra*) which calls for transcendence and ultimate liberation (*mokṣa*), but rather as a sphere of potential self-perfection and spiritual growth.
5 In response to European criticism, any fatalistic implications of karma are strongly and passionately rejected, and its compatibility with action, initiative and social responsibility is emphasized.
6 The notions of 'collective karma', 'group karma' or even 'national karma', which have no place in traditional thought, but seem to be taken for granted in theosophy, emerge in Neo-Hindu thought and discourse, although their uses are somewhat elusive and in some cases merely rhetorical.

Such concepts appear also in modern Buddhism, together with other reinterpretations and transformations of the traditional concepts. An important trend is exemplified by the work of the modern Theravādin M.W.P. de Silva, for whom the theory of karma is primarily a theory of psychological and characterological development, and who de-emphasizes its 'judicial' or retributive implications. Even more radical forms of 'demythologizing' karma and rebirth may be found in modern Japanese Buddhism. In both Buddhism and Hinduism, reinterpretations coexist with more traditional and traditionalistic versions. There has even been a certain resurgence of mythical and esoteric ideas concerning intermediate stages and the like, most conspicuously among Western proponents of Hindu or Buddhist traditions.

8 General and concluding observations

Karma and rebirth are among the most important regulative ideas in the history of Indian thought. But there has never been one identical theory (and certainly no scientific theory) of karma to which a majority of thinkers could have agreed. The expression 'the doctrine of karma and rebirth' is only a convenient label. To be sure, there are certain shared premises – above all, the twin postulates that there should be no undeserved suffering or wellbeing and that no effect of a past deed should be lost. But apart from such rather formal premises (which may be derived from the even more fundamental postulate that justice should be inherent in the universe), there has been a wide variety of interpretations and manifestations and much room for debate. The twin postulates themselves may be applied more or less strictly. In fact, their rigid implementation would hardly be compatible with the element of freedom and initiative which is implied in the notion of karmic action.

Furthermore, the familiar association and correlation of karma and rebirth is itself problematic. While the two concepts have become virtually inseparable in the idea of *saṃsāra*, their historical roots may, in fact, be quite different. There are also significant conceptual differences between karma and rebirth, and their relation is not a symmetrical one. While karma requires rebirth as the condition of its own inescapability, rebirth does not require karma. It could just be a merely factual continuation of existence, without subjection to retributive justice. In this sense, and in spite of its wide-ranging mythical ramifications, the concept of rebirth would, in principle at least, be more easily compatible with a 'scientific' worldview which understands the universe in terms of facts, not values or judicial standards. A world in which rebirth had a place could still be our 'natural' world, the domain of science, while a world in which karma operated would have to be a structurally different universe. Explanation in such a universe would involve justification in the sense of 'theodicy' or rather 'cosmodicy'.

However, karmic causality does not always imply a judicial order of deeds and corresponding rewards or punishments. There is also an ancient and recurrent tendency to explain the functioning of karma as a natural sequence of mental states and events, a psychological, not retributory or quasi-legal, process which links acts and decisions with the formation of dispositions, instincts, character attributes or other internal modes of being. This may, indeed, be the case in some of the oldest statements on karma, which appear in the Bṛhadāraṇyaka Upaniṣad (3.2.13; 4.4.5). Here, Yājñavalkya does not propose reward and punishment (that is, pleasant and painful experience) as the result of karma, but the formation of a good or bad person. Similar ideas are documented in ancient Buddhism. Most later schools distinguish the formation of dispositions, especially of mental 'defilements' (kleśa, doṣa, anuśaya) such as attachment and hate, from the accumulation of retributive karmic potential (karmāśaya). The 'defilements' are often presented as a condition for the perpetuation of karma; in some texts (for instance, Vasubandhu's Abhidharmakośabhāṣya), the fundamental disposition of existential craving (tṛṣṇā) appears as the cause of rebirth per se, while karma is said to regulate its specific circumstances. But there has also been much overlap and ambiguity (for instance, in the Jaina notion of 'ruinous' karmas).

What is an act in a karmically relevant sense? What is the significance of intention? What distinguishes good and bad deeds? How does an act produce its 'unseen' power (adṛṣṭa), and what is the ontological status of this power? Who or what acts? What connects the karmic agent and the subject of retribution? What is the scope and nature of karmic causality? How does it affect the mental and the physical realm? How do we know about karma and rebirth? Do we have valid arguments for their existence, or is it a matter of authoritative tradition and superhuman modes of awareness (such as 'yogic perception')? Are there basically different types of karma, and how can they be classified?

Our preceding survey has shown a wide variety of answers to these and similar questions. But this multitude of theoretical answers does not describe the breadth and complexity of the phenomenon in its entirety. In the history of Indian thought and life, karma has functioned at various levels of understanding and interpretation, as an unquestioned presupposition and a topic of theoretical inquiry, in popular mythology and in philosophical thought. In its various contexts and applications, it has at least three clearly separable, but interrelated, functions and dimensions:

1 It provides causal explanations of factual occurrences and correlates the present with the past (for instance, in traditional medical literature).
2 It provides perspectives on and incentives for actions and decisions and correlates the present with the future (most conspicuously in the normative Dharmaśāstra literature).
3 It provides a soteriological point of departure, a view of the causal and temporal world which calls for detachment, transcendence and final liberation.

In the philosophical traditions of Hinduism, Buddhism and Jainism we find all of these meanings of karma. But the third one clearly overshadows the other two, and it accounts for the pervasive sense of soteriological commitment in Indian philosophical thought.

See also: Buddhist philosophy, Chinese; Buddhist philosophy, Japanese §6; Duty and virtue, Indian conceptions of; Hindu philosophy §5; Jaina philosophy §§1, 3–4

References and further reading

Collins, S. (1982) *Selfless Persons*, Cambridge: Cambridge University Press. (A clear and attractive exposition of the Buddhist 'no-self' doctrine and its implications for karma and rebirth.)

Glasenapp, H. von (1915) *The Doctrine of Karman in Jain Philosophy*, trans. G.B. Gifford, Bombay: Bai Vijibai Jivanlal Panalal Charity Fund, 1942. (A good survey of texts and teachings, but no philosophical analysis; translated from a German original.)

Horsch, P. (1971) 'Vorstufen der indischen Seelenwanderungslehre' (Early Stages of the Indian Theory of the Transmigration of Souls), *Asiatische Studien* 25: 99–157. (A survey of Vedic antecedents of karma and rebirth.)

Jaini, P.S. (1979) *The Jaina Path of Purification*, Berkeley, CA: University of California Press. (Discusses karma and rebirth in the general context of Jainism.)

Krishan, Y. (1983) 'Karma Vipāka', *Numen* 30:

199–214. (A useful collection of quotes and references concerning the notion of 'karmic ripening'.)

Lamotte, É. (1936) 'Le traité de l'acte de Vasubandhu: *Karmasiddhiprakaraṇa*', *Mélanges chinois et bouddhiques* 4: 151–288; trans. L.M. Pruden, *Karmasiddhiprakaraṇa: The Treatise on Action by Vasubandhu*, Berkeley, CA: Asian Humanities Press, 1988. (Contains a valuable introduction concerning different Buddhist theories of karma.)

McDermott, J.P. (1984) *Development in the Early Buddhist Concept of Kamma/Karma*, New Delhi: Munshiram Manoharlal. (A survey and analysis of relevant debates in Theravāda literature and Vasubandhu's *Abhidharmakośa*.)

Neufeldt, R.W. (ed.) (1986) *Karma and Rebirth: Post-Classical Developments*, Albany, NY: State University of New York Press. (A collection of articles discussing reinterpretations of the doctrine in modern Hindu, Buddhist and Western thought.)

Oetke, C. (1988) *'Ich' und das Ich: Analytische Untersuchungen zur buddhistisch–brahmanischen Āmankontroverse* ('I' and the Self: Analytical Investigations into the Buddhist–Brahmanic Controversy about *Ātman*), Stuttgart: Franz Steiner Verlag. (A pioneering analytical study of the Hindu and Buddhist arguments concerning personal identity, the existence of the self, and the meaning of rebirth.)

O'Flaherty, W.D. (ed.) (1980) *Karma and Rebirth in Classical Indian Traditions*, Berkeley, CA: University of California Press. (Twelve representative essays on karma in traditional Indian thought; a revised and updated version of the contribution by W. Halbfass was published in his *Tradition and Reflection*, Albany, NY: State University of New York Press, 1991, 291–345.)

* Patañjali (*c*.2nd century BC) *Yoga Sūtras* with the commentary of Vyāsa and the gloss of Vachaspati, trans. R. Prasāda, New Delhi: Oriental Books, 1978. (A standard and readily available translation.)

Prasad, R. (1989) *Karma, Causality and Retributive Morality*, New Delhi: Indian Council of Philosophical Research. (A discussion of ethical and meta-ethical issues; see especially chapter 13.)

Reichenbach, B.R. (1990) *The Law of Karma: A Philosophical Study*, Honolulu, HI: University of Hawaii Press. (A clear presentation of major philosophical issues, but on a limited textual and philological basis.)

Schmithausen, L. (1991) *The Problem of the Sentience of Plants in Earliest Buddhism*, Tokyo: The International Institute for Buddhist Studies. (A penetrating study of early Buddhist ideas concerning life and *saṃsāra*.)

—— (1995) 'Mensch, Tier und Pflanze und der Tod in den älteren Upaniṣaden' (Man, Animal, Plant and Death in the Earlier Upaniṣads), in G. Oberhammer (ed.) *Im Tod gewinnt der Mensch sein Selbst* (In Death Man Wins Himself), Vienna: Akademie der Wissenschaften, 43–74. (A careful examination of the beginnings and early developments of the idea of *saṃsāra*; on pages 75–96 of the same volume, W. Halbfass discusses the relation between karma and death.)

Steinkellner, E. (1985) 'Paralokasiddhi Texts', *Buddhism and its Relation to Other Religions: Essays in Honour of Dr Shozen Kumoi on His Seventieth Birthday*, Kyoto: 215–22. (On the Indo-Tibetan tradition of proofs for rebirth.)

Tull, H.W. (1989) *The Vedic Origins of Karma*, Albany, NY: State University of New York Press. (This book contains some interesting suggestions, but has to be used with caution; see the review by L. Schmithausen, *Indo-Iranian Journal* 37: 151–58 (1994).)

* Viśveśvara Bhaṭṭa (14th century) *Madanamahārṇava*, E. Krishnamacharya and N.M. Nambiyar (eds), Baroda: Oriental Institute, 1953. (A detailed presentation of karmic punishments, especially diseases.)

WILHELM HALBFASS

KATHARSIS

One of the central concepts of Aristotle's Poetics, *katharsis* ('purgation' *or* 'purification'; *often spelled* catharsis) *defines the goal of the tragic poet: by depiction of human vicissitudes so to provoke the spectators' feelings of pity and fear that such emotions in them are finally purged.*

Aristotle's doctrine of *katharsis* is a response to a familiar problem in aesthetics (see ARISTOTLE §29): why do audiences take pleasure in watching tragedies, with their depictions of terrible crimes and sufferings? Plato, who divided the human psychological system into mutually antagonistic rational and irrational components, had a ready answer: he argued that the irrational impulses enjoyed receiving stimulation and nurture from the opportunity tragedy provided them to indulge themselves in such emotions as pity and fear, which were normally kept under tight rein but which thereby became harder to control. This was one reason Plato felt obliged to exclude the tragic poets from his ideal city (see PLATO §14).

Against such an accusation, Aristotle merely

implied in a single sentence a defence of poetry in terms of *katharsis*: his definition of tragedy in chapter 6 of his *Poetics* culminates in the words 'by means of pity and fear performing the *katharsis* of emotions of this sort'. Because Aristotle never fully explains or justifies this phrase, the term *katharsis* has proven to be endlessly controversial – and also extremely fruitful for all European literary theory since the Renaissance. Scholars are divided on whether *katharsis* means 'purgation' or 'purification', whether the term is derived from medicine or religion, whose emotions undergo the process described, and whether it is moral or psychological, temporary or permanent. The following reconstruction is necessarily tentative.

According to Aristotle, the ultimate goal of every poet is to produce in the audience a kind of pleasure which is peculiar to the kind of poetry in question; all of the constituents of the poem are means towards that end, though not all contribute to the same degree. The production of the kind of pleasure peculiar to tragedy, involving pity, fear and the *katharsis* of such emotions, is the goal to which all the constitutive elements of a tragedy – above all the structure of its plot – are subordinated. Pity is our reasonable response to the sight of someone's undeserved suffering and fear implies our judgment of a similarity between the sufferer and us such that the same kind of suffering could befall us. To provoke these responses, the tragic poet must deploy the appropriate means: a central hero whose fate interests us strongly, who suffers (hence the better tragedies move from happiness to suffering), who is neither too evil (for then his suffering would not seem undeserved) nor too good (for then we would not consider him similar to us), and whose suffering is the result not of his culpability, nor of the gods or fate, which Aristotle ignores, but of some error of judgment he makes.

For Aristotle, pity and fear are not pleasures, but kinds of pain. If tragedy is to procure pleasure, it cannot do so by 'purifying' or 'refining' emotions such as pity and fear – a purer pain is not a greater pleasure – but only by 'purging' or 'discharging' them. In medicine, normally healthy fluids such as bile or blood can put the body at risk when they exceed a certain level; when this happens, the body restores its endangered equilibrium by a purging of these substances. The sufferings in any tragedy provoke pity and fear. But the best kind of tragedy astonishes its viewers by what Aristotle calls *peripeteia*, a sudden change in the expected outcome such that events turn out otherwise than anticipated but still retain a logical concatenation which we recognize afterwards. This shock enhances the viewers' pity and fear so strongly that these emotions and similar states of disturbance end up discharging themselves; as a result, the viewers are left free of them and are restored to their normal state after having been temporarily upset. They enjoy both the restorative pleasure that derives from liberation from pain and the intellectual pleasure that accompanies their delayed recognition of the logical concatenation of the events of the plot.

On this view of *katharsis*, tragedy does not permanently make us better people, refine our emotions or provide a profound insight into the tragic nature of the human condition. Aristotle is simply countering Plato's attack upon tragedy by agreeing with him that tragedy does provoke pity and fear and that such emotions are indeed unpleasant, but objecting that they are not entirely irrational after all and that the effect of the best tragedies is first to provoke them, then to enhance them, but finally to free us of them.

See also: EMOTION IN RESPONSE TO ART; MIMĒSIS; TRAGEDY

References and further reading

* Aristotle (*c.* mid 4th century BC) *Poetics*, trans. S. Halliwell, Loeb Classical Library, Cambridge, MA: Harvard University Press and London: Heinemann, 1995. (Greek text with an English prose translation on facing pages.)

Belfiore, E.S. (1992) *Tragic Pleasures: Aristotle on Plot and Emotion*, Princeton, NJ: Princeton University Press, esp. 257–360. (A detailed defence of the medical interpretation of *katharsis*.)

Bernays, J. (1857) *Grundzüge der verlorenen Abhandlung des Aristoteles über Wirkung der Tragödie* (Features of Aristotle's lost treatise on th effect of tragedy), Breslau: Trewendt; repr. Hildesheim: Olms, 1970; partially trans. in J. Barnes, M. Schofield and R. Sorabji (eds) *Articles on Aristotle*, vol. 4, *Psychology and Aesthetics*, London: Duckworth, 1979, 154–65. (The single most important and influential study of *katharsis* ever written; the first to argue cogently for a medical interpretation of the term.)

Else, G.F. (1957) *Aristotle's Poetics: The Argument*, Cambridge, MA: Harvard University Press. (A provocative and original critique of views still widely shared.)

—— (1986) *Plato and Aristotle on Poetry*, ed. P. Burian, Chapel Hill, NC, and London: University of North Carolina Press. (A more generally accessible presentation of some of the arguments in Else (1957).)

Golden, L. (1992) *Aristotle on Tragic and Comic Mimēsis*, Atlanta, GA: Scholars Press. (An eloquent defence of a more cognitive view of *katharsis* than the one presented here.)

Halliwell, S. (1986) *Aristotle's Poetics*, London: Duckworth. (A general introduction to the treatise with a full treatment of *katharsis*, pages 168–201.)

Lucas, D.W. (ed.) (1968) *Aristotle: Poetics*, Oxford: Clarendon Press, 273–90. (The standard English commentary, with a good discussion of *katharsis*.)

* Plato (*c.*370s BC) *Republic*, trans. G.M.A. Grube, Indianapolis, IN: Hackett, 1974. (See especially books III and X for Plato's treatment of tragedy.)

Rorty, A.O. (ed.) (1992) *Essays on Aristotle's Poetics*, Princeton, NJ: Princeton University Press. (A stimulating collection of recent articles on *katharsis* and many related issues; good bibliography.)

GLENN W. MOST

KAUTILYA (*fl. c.*321–*c.*296 BC)

Kautilya is famous as the author of the Arthasastra, *a political treatise often compared with Machiavelli's* The Prince. *Although its influence on subsequent political and literary writers is noteworthy, tradition has remained somewhat ambivalent about it, especially because of its seemingly ruthless prescriptions for efficacious government. On a closer reading, however, Kautilya is assiduously concerned to secure the welfare and wealth of the citizens of a state under a just government, of which the king, although the sovereign, is just one among seven institutes. Upon the king falls the duty of safeguarding the good of the people in as* dharma-*sanctioned a way as possible; the 'rule of the rod', intrigues and stratagems are reserved for combatting internal and external threats.*

Kautilya did not leave behind any information about himself, but it is generally believed that he was a minister in the kingdom of Maurya Candragupta, who ascended to power after defeating the Nandas in Magadha country. Since Candragupta promulgated the Gupta Empire *circa* 320 BC, Kautilya (which is a nickname; his real name was Cānakya) is believed to have lived and written the *Arthasastra*, the work for which he is famed, around 321–296 BC. A number of Western scholars have, however, proffered a much later date, closer to the early years of the Common Era or even later.

The *Arthasastra* is a comprehensive treatise on statecraft that gives cohesion to the political thinking of Kautilya's predecessors. It is tersely written, and organized into fifteen books comprising 150 chapters. Like most classical Indian writings on politics, it is mostly instructional in content and lacks theoretical depth on questions such as the ideal state, the origin of the state, and so on. Kautilya gives no arguments to ground his political precepts, or to explain why he makes the pursuit of wealth the principal end. He emphasizes the significance of sensual pleasure (for both king and people), and upholds *dharma* (law) as the beacon of socially ordered conduct; but *moksa* (spiritual enlightenment and escape from the material world) warrants no place in the *Arthasastra*. Kautilya's apparent advocacy of the 'rule of the rod' has traditionally been controversial; nevertheless certain of his important teachings were appropriated by the Dharmasastras (for centuries the basic legal/moral canons deferred to in India) and, on a close reading, he is mainly concerned to guarantee the citizens' wellbeing. Kautilya's sovereign king is just one of seven institutes of the ideal body politic; the others are the ministers, the territory and its subjects (*janapada*), the fort, the treasury, the rod-bearing army, and strategic allies.

The *Arthasastra* creates a secular ethos, but religious life and wisdom are given prominence by the appointment of the *purohita*, a Brahmanical priest-chancellor who is to be consulted by the monarch at every decisive step in the affairs of the state. Kautilya also describes laws restricting forms of marriage, the urban location of the major caste-groups, the duties of caste-groups, and inter-caste mixing. But beyond this, he cannot be said to be an advocate for the sort of inward-looking Hindu state that has been a feature of post-independence Indian political thought. To be sure, the idea of a nation-state, loosely federated or unified, or even of a representative democratic state, never took root in pre-modern Indian political thinking.

Kautilya is quite conscious of the diversity from ancient days of the Indian regions and accordingly allows for a degree of flexibility in matters of law and justice. The king is expected to attend each morning to pleas and petitions from subjects who may come from all walks of life and from different castes or regions. When meting out justice, the king or the state is not in a position to make laws; rather, the sovereign court's jurisdiction is to negotiate between (1) *dharma*, (2) custom or settled community law, and (3) commercial and personal transactions and written edicts. The king may overrule the latter two sources of law, but he cannot put himself above *dharma*, in accordance with which all disputes and contradictory judgments are to be decided (*Arthasastra* 3.1.40–4). This precept entails that the king should maintain detailed codes of law, judge each case on its legal merit and mete out punishment proportionate to the offence, not in whimsical excess. The king's ministers, the *purohita*, the ascetics, the queen and prince, the gods and, above all, *dharma* are a check to any possible deviation. (Note that these are broadly ancillary to the principal institutes: the queen is married to the king; the *purohita*, independently of the ministers, counsels the king; ascetics and leading citizens echo the territory's subjects; the gods are the heavenly guards of the fort and the treasury; and *dharma* is the impersonal rule and codes of transcendental ethics symbolized in the rod.) Kauṭilya is credited with having been among the first to set down codes of law, as distinct from listing desirable prescriptions and customary rules regardless of their moral or philosophical merits.

Kauṭilya accorded an unusually important role to philosophy in the training of the king. He called this art *anvīkṣīki*, understood as the art of reasoning and learning in traditional disciplines (notably Sāṅkhya, Yoga and Lokāyata), alongside the Vedas, economics and politics. The king is expected to maintain a regime of study of this material throughout his life. The study of reasoning is undertaken more for its applications in matters of law than for its employment in speculative philosophy (*tarka*). Despite this positive register for philosophy, Kauṭilya does not employ philosophy *per se* in thinking through moral issues and problems in politics. Perhaps the idealistic tendencies of philosophy in the Upaniṣadic tradition made him cautious about philosophy's true worth in the more realistic pursuits of state-making. A life of detached asceticism is not worthy of the philosopher, whose life of practical activity is accomplished if it culminates in providing further instruments by which the state can ensure the protection, prosperity and sovereign stability of the people; there is no state without happy people.

Following a comprehensive treatment of topics connected with internal administration, Kauṭilya devotes a substantial discussion to foreign policy and diplomacy. The king, through his emissaries and envoys, should maintain harmonious relations with neighbouring kingdoms; however, he should be vigilant and alert to possible threats to his kingdom. To this end he is advised to deploy spies and secret agents disguised as ascetics, who, through magical spells and propaganda can create dissension among neighbouring populations, and eventually insurgency. In case an enemy should prove to be powerful, the king should enlist the help and sanction of other neighbours, in a roulette of diplomacy common in international relations anywhere.

See also: POLITICAL PHILOSOPHY, INDIAN

List of works

Kauṭilya (*c.*320 BC) *Arthaśāstra*, ed. and trans. R. Shamasastry, *Arthaśāstra of Kauṭilya*, Mysore: University of Mysore Oriental Library, 1915; 3rd edn, 1929; repr. as *Kauṭilya's Arthaśāstra*, Mysore: Mysore Printing and Publishing House, 1967. (The *Arthaśāstra* first came to the notice of Dr R. Shamasastry, a curator with the Government Oriental Library in Mysore, when he unexpectedly received a palm-leaf manuscript; this he began painstakingly to edit, translate and publish in fragments from 1905, culminating in the first ever English work on Kauṭilya in 1915.)

—— (*c.*320 BC) *Arthaśāstra*, ed. R.P. Kangle, Bombay: University of Bombay Press, 1960, 1965; repr. Delhi: Motilal Banarsidass, 1986. (This critical edition of the Sanskrit text takes cognizance of commentaries in various vernaculars and editions issued by European Indologists that have appeared since the work's first discovery.)

—— (*c.*320 BC) *Arthaśāstra*, ed. and trans. R.P. Kangle, *The Kauṭiliya Arthaśāstra*, Delhi: Motilal Banarsidass, 3 vols, 1986, 1988, 1992. (This erudite English translation in the idiom of Enlightened Western political philosophy is known for utilizing the text of a translation by the Russian Indologist Kalyanov (Moscow 1959), lending at once further clarity but also some confusion over the difficult passages in Kauṭilya's treatise. Part I presents the Sanskrit text, Part II is an English translation, and Part III is a study of the work.)

—— (*c.*320 BC) *Arthaśāstra*, ed. and trans. L.N. Rangarajan, *The Arthaśāstras*, New Delhi: Penguin Books India, 1992. (This is a substantial reworking of Kangle's and Shamasastry's editions and translations in the style of a modern treatise on political economy, and has an informative introduction.)

References and further reading

Breloer, B. (1927, 1928) *Kauṭaliya Studien*, Bonn, 2 vols. (This voluminous study is a good example of early European/German interest in the discovery of the *Arthaśāstra*, which was seen as one of the earliest systematic Indo-Iranian treatises on the state.)

Krishna Rao, M.V. (1953) *Studies in Kauṭilya*, Delhi: Munshiram Manoharlal, 1979. (An early attempt at a philosophical treatment of Kauṭilya, which seeks parallels with Aristotle on conceptions of the republic and statecraft in ancient political thought.)

Radhakrishna, C. (1971) *Kauṭilya's Political Ideas and Institutions*, Varanasi: Chowkhamba Sanskrit Series Office. (This Marxian rendering of the *Arthaśāstra* locates Kauṭilya in the history of Indian political thought, and is inspired by the Indian Marxist critic D.D. Kosambi.)

Winternitz, M. (1920) *Some Problems of Indian Literature*, Delhi: Motilal Banarsidass, 1969. (Useful for discussions of dating and linkages with other texts on ancient Indian polity. Although Winternitz is an unusually reliable and balanced Indologist with no Aryan axe to grind, this work is limited by the fact that the definitive work on the Dharmaśāstras had not been done at the time of writing.)

PURUSHOTTAMA BILIMORIA

KAUTSKY, KARL JOHANN (1854–1938)

Karl Johann Kautsky became the leading German socialist theoretician at the time of the Second International and the authoritative exponent of 'orthodox Marxism'. He was a close associate of Engels, editor of Die Neue Zeit *from 1883 until 1917, and author of numerous political, historical and theoretical works. He clashed with Bernstein in the 'revisionist debate' in the late 1890s and with Lenin during the Russian Revolution.*

1 Beginnings
2 The consolidation of Kautsky's position
3 Later controversies

1 Beginnings

Karl Johann Kautsky was born in Prague. His family moved to Vienna where he went to school (the Benedictines at Melk) and then to university (although he dropped out before finishing his degree). The rise and fall of the Paris Commune helped steer his early romantic radicalism in the direction of socialism. At this time, he also began to take an interest in Darwinist evolutionary theory and in the application of science to the study of human societies (Haeckel and Büchner being particularly influential). In 1875 he joined the nascent Austrian Social Democratic Workers' Party and, over the next few years, he wrote extensively for various socialist papers. His first theoretical work, *Der Einfluss der Volksvermehrung auf den Fortschritt der Gesellschaft untersucht* (The Influence of Population Growth on Social Progress) appeared in 1880.

In 1880 he moved to Zurich where he established contact with Karl Höchberg and Eduard Bernstein

and, a year later, with MARX and ENGELS in London. Indeed, it is from around this time that it would be fair to describe Kautsky as a Marxist. In 1882 he returned to Vienna, where he collaborated with the publisher, Dietz, in founding *Die Neue Zeit*, a journal which established itself as the most influential theoretical organ of the Second International. He was to be its editor until 1917. His editorship, together with his many other published works, established him as the leading Marxist theoretician of his time.

2 The consolidation of Kautsky's position

Broadly speaking, Kautsky endorsed Engels' analysis that, while capitalism was undoubtedly heading for a terminal economic crisis, this crisis would be forestalled by a political crisis in the course of which social democracy would be called upon to seize political power and use it to transform the failing capitalist economy into a socialist order of society. This meant, according to Engels and Kautsky, that social democracy would have to prepare for its forthcoming task by employing all legal means to improve its organizational strength and increase its popular support. Kautsky underpinned this view by emphasizing the determinist aspects of Marx's materialist conception of history. This emphasis was reinforced in the course of a long and bruising controversy (largely in the pages of *Die Neue Zeit*) with the English socialist, Ernest Belfort Bax, during the mid-1890s.

In 1885 Kautsky moved to London where he worked closely with Engels. Marx's materialist conception of history provided the perspective, and the British Museum the resources, for a number of historical studies; notably, *Thomas More und seine Utopie* (Thomas More and His Utopia) (1888) and *Die Klassengegensätze von 1789: Zum hundertjähren Gedenktag der Grossen Revolution* (Class Struggles in the Age of the French Revolution) (1889). He was to pursue his historical interests in later years in a series of studies in which he attempted to identify the socialist element in Western civilization, particularly in early Christianity.

In 1890 he moved to Stuttgart and, in the following year, he played a major part in drafting the new programme for the German Social Democratic Party (SPD), subsequently known as the Erfurt Programme. It established the SPD as a party fundamentally Marxist in orientation. Indeed, Kautsky's own analysis and justification of the programme, *Das Erfurter Programm in seinem grundsätzlichen Teil erläutert* (The Class Struggle: Erfurt Programme) (1892), played a major role in the propagation of

Marxism within the German socialist movement. During the 1890's he continued his activities as editor and publicist with characteristic vigour and growing popular success. His study of 'parliamentarianism' was published in 1893, and his thoughtful critique of the policy pursued (mainly) by Georg von Vollmar and his supporters, *Die Agrarfrage* (The Agrarian Question), appeared in 1899. However, most of his energy in the later years of the decade were devoted to the 'revisionist debate'.

3 Later controversies

Shortly after the death of Engels in 1895, Eduard BERNSTEIN had launched a campaign urging social democrats to abandon their revolutionary aspirations and set about achieving socialism by piecemeal parliamentary reform. Kautsky was slow to react. However, at the party conference at Stuttgart in 1898, he came out against Bernstein and, in the following year, engaged Bernstein in a lengthy controversy which culminated with the publication of his *Bernstein und das sozialdemokratische Programm: Ein Anti-Kritik* (Bernstein and the Programme of Social Democracy) (1899b). The effect of all this was to consolidate his position as chief guardian and exponent of what since came to be known as 'orthodox Marxism'. He won the admiration of LENIN and even the grudging respect of Rosa LUXEMBURG. His position at this stage in his career is exemplified in his *Die soziale Revolution* (The Social Revolution) (1902), described by the then Chancellor, Prince Bernhard von Bülow, as 'a Baedeker for the state to come'.

During the turbulent years preceding the First World War, Kautsky developed an increasingly cautious approach to the question of violent revolutionary activity. His ambitious *Ethik und materialische Geschichtsauffasung: Ein Versuch* (Ethics and the Materialist Conception of History) (1906) was an attempt to vindicate a materialist approach to ethics against the arguments of the neo-Kantians. And in his *Der politische Massenstreik* (The Political Mass Strike) (1914) he sought the middle ground between the revolutionary left and the reformist right within the SPD. When war broke out, he maintained his 'centrist' position and tried unsuccessfully to preserve party unity.

The Bolshevik seizure of power in 1917 brought Kautsky once more into the forefront of debate. In his view, a socialist society was one in which all exploitation and oppression had been abolished, and this meant that its political form had to be a full democracy. The Bolshevik regime, he argued, could not be described as democratic and was therefore not, properly speaking, a socialist regime. Furthermore, Russia was a relatively backward agricultural economy with only a small industrial sector. The social and economic preconditions for the establishment of socialism were therefore absent, and the Bolshevik 'revolution' was bound to fail, with disastrous consequences for the socialist movement as a whole. Kautsky embodied these and other thoughts in his *Die Diktatur des Proletariats* (The Dictatorship of the Proletariat) (1918). It elicited a furious response from Lenin in his book *Proletarskaia revoliutsiia i renegat Kautskii* (The Proletarian Revolution and the Renegade Kautsky) (1918) and provoked a controversy which lasted for several years.

In 1927 Kautsky published his *Die Materialistische Geschichtauffassung* (The Materialist Conception of History) in which he gathered together his thoughts on Marx's basic theory. Many regard it as his major work.

See also: MARXISM, WESTERN; SOCIAL DEMOCRACY; SOCIALISM

List of works

Kautsky, K. (1880) *Der Einfluss der Volksvermehrung auf den Fortschritt der Geschellschaft untersucht* (The Influence of Population Growth on Social Progress), Vienna: Bloch und Hasbach. (His first significant socio-economic work.)

—— (1888) *Thomas More und seine Utopie*; trans. *Thomas More and His Utopia*, London and New York: International Publishers, 1927. (His most enduring contribution to the history of social and political thought.)

—— (1889) *Die Klassengegensätze von 1789: Zum hundertjähren Gedenktag der Grossen Revolution* (Class Struggles in the Age of the French Revolution), Stuttgart: Dietz. (An interpretation of the French Revolution from the standpoint of historical materialism.)

—— (1892) *Das Erfurter Programm in seinem grundsätzlichen Teil erläutert*; trans. *The Class Struggle: Erfurt Program*, Chicago, IL: Kerr, 1910. (An exposition and defence of the Erfurt Program of 1981)

—— (1899a) *Die Agrarfrage* (The Agrarian Question), Stuttgart: Dietz. (His main contribution to the debate on whether the SDP should revise its programme to accommodate the agrarian or 'peasant' interest.)

—— (1899b) *Bernstein und das sozialdemokratische Programm: Eine Anti-Kritik* (Bernstein and the Programme of Social Democracy), Stuttgart: Dietz. (A systematic statement of his objections to Bernstein's revisionist views.)

—— (1902) *Die soziale Revolution*; trans. *The Social Revolution*, Chicago, IL: Kerr, 1903. (A good statement of Kautsky's socialist vision of the future at the high point of his career.)

—— (1906) *Ethik und materialische Geschictsauffassung: Ein Versuch*; trans. *Ethics and the Materialist Conception of History*, Chicago, IL: Kerr, 1907. (Kautsky's main attempt to deal with a fundamental problem in the materialist conception of history.)

—— (1914) *Der politische Massenstreik* (The Political Mass Strike), Berlin: Vörwarts. (His main contribution as to how the SDP should react to the anticipated outbreak of war in Europe.)

—— (1918) *Die Diktatur des Proletariats*; trans. *The Dictatorship of the Proletariat*, Ann Arbor, MI: University of Michigan Press, 1964. (A critique of the Bolshevik revolution and the direction in which it was going.)

—— (1927) *Die Materialistische Geschichtsauffassung*; trans. *The Materialist Conception of History*, New Haven, CT: Yale University Press, 1988. (His final and definitive statement of what was called orthodox.)

References and further reading

Geary, D. (1987), *Karl Kautsky*, Manchester: Manchester University Press. (A detailed analysis of Kautsky's theoretical position.)

* Lenin, V.I. (1918) *Proletarskaia revoliutsiia i renegat Kautskii*; trans. *The Proletarian Revolution and the Renegade Kautsky*, New York: Contemporary Publishers Association, 1920. (Lenin's counterblast to Kautsky's *The Dictatorship of the Proletariat*.)

Salvadori, M. (1976) *Kautsky e la revoluzione socialista 1880–1938*, Milan: Feltrinelli; trans. J. Rothschild, *Karl Kautsky and the Socialist Revolution 1880–1938*, London: New Left Books, 1979. (An analytical study of Kautsky's contribution by an eminent Italian political scientist.)

Steenson, G.P. (1978) *Karl Kautsky 1854–1938: Marxism in the Classical Years*, Pittsburgh, PA: University of Pittsburgh Press. (A good intellectual biography of Kautsky.)

H. TUDOR

KAVELIN, K. *see* HEGELIANISM, RUSSIAN; LIBERALISM, RUSSIAN; POSITIVISM, RUSSIAN; RUSSIAN LITERARY FORMALISM

KAYDRUP GELEK BELSANGBO *see* MKHAS GRUB DGE LEGS DPAL BZANG PO

KECKERMANN, BARTHOLOMEW (1571/3–1609)

Calvinist philosopher and theologian, Bartholomew Keckermann wrote textbooks in logic, ethics and metaphysics which were widely read and in which he advanced his notion of a system of knowledge. Like so many of his contemporaries in the late sixteenth and early seventeenth centuries, Keckermann was interested in methodological matters. As professor of philosophy in Danzig, Poland, he implemented a new curriculum intended to give students an encyclopedic education within three years. His proposals had considerable influence on subsequent educators and philosophers, especially in northern Europe.

Born and brought up in Danzig (now Gdansk), Poland in 1571/3, Keckermann was given a strict Calvinist education before studying in Wittenberg, Leipzig and Heidelberg. After receiving his MA in Heidelberg in 1594, he taught philosophy first at Studentenburse Paedagogium and then at Collegium Sapientiae where he acquired the chair of Hebrew in 1600 and received his doctorate of divinity in 1602. His growing reputation resulted in an invitation from the Danzig senate to return to the city's Gymnasium, which he did in 1602. As professor of philosophy in Danzig, Keckermann developed a new educational programme intended to give students an encyclopedic education within three years: the first year was devoted to logic and physics, the second to mathematics and metaphysics, and the third to ethics, economics and politics. Several of his textbooks, which were widely used throughout northern Europe, were published posthumously.

In the sixteenth century many philosophers were engaged in a re-evaluation of the methodological and educational assumptions inherent in the scholastic universities of Europe. Progressive Aristotelians like Jacopo Zabarella re-examined the structure of knowledge and science (see ZABARELLA, J.), and anti-Aristotelians like Peter Ramus proposed a reformation of scholastic logic (see RAMUS, P.). Keckermann drew upon Aristotelian and Ramist ideas in his own methodological proposals. With Zabarella, Keckermann believed that the scholastics' intense occupation with the texts of Aristotle should be diverted to the development of new methods and analytic systems. With Ramus, he thought that the teaching of the liberal arts should be made more systematic so that each 'art' would have a precisely delimited field and method of exposition.

Like many progressive Aristotelians of his day, Keckermann was a critical rather than dogmatic follower of Aristotle. As opposed to what he called the 'textual' Aristotelians, who laboured over every word of the ancient texts without introducing any thought of their own, Keckermann placed himself among the 'methodical' Peripatetics, who were concerned 'to develop absolute Methods and Systems of disciplines from Aristotle's font'. According to Keckermann, methodological Aristotelians like himself (and Zabarella) would first delineate a discipline and then accommodate the text of Aristotle to it.

Keckermann was probably the first philosopher to develop a theory about systems of knowledge, and it was in his writings that the term 'system' acquired its technical sense of a body of knowledge unified by a single idea or principle. His theory emphasized the orderly presentation of doctrine. For each genuine discipline or liberal art, there was a set of precepts and rules which characterized it and through which, if properly ordered, one could gain knowledge. Therefore, when the precepts and rules of a discipline were correctly presented, any student with the requisite skill and practice could master that body of knowledge. To become learned one only needed to master all the disciplines.

Keckermann adapted his theory about systems to all the liberal arts. In his lectures and textbooks, he applied his method to logic, physics, politics, metaphysics, ethics, medicine, jurisprudence, mathematics and theology. As a good 'methodological' Aristotelian, his philosophical proposals relied heavily on the texts of Aristotle and yet went beyond them. For example, *Systema ethicae* (1607), his important and large-scale work on ethics, provides a comprehensive treatment of the major issues in the field and uses Aristotle as its primary source; it also presents its topics in a framework and order different from Aristotle's.

One of the important implications of Keckermann's theory of systems is that, when taken together, they would form a unified whole which would constitute all of knowledge and which could be imparted to students. In the conception of this encyclopedia of the 'arts' Keckermann differed significantly from Aristotle in the role he assigned to metaphysics. For Keckermann metaphysics was no longer an Aristotelian science, but a liberal art which had the task of attributing to each of the other arts or disciplines its proper domain and place in the encyclopedia. It is also noteworthy that Keckermann placed theology among the liberal arts so that it too became part of the encyclopedia of knowledge.

See also: ARISTOTELIANISM IN THE 17TH CENTURY; ARISTOTELIANISM, RENAISSANCE; CALVIN, J.; MEDIEVAL PHILOSOPHY

Lists of works

Keckermann, B. (1614) *Opera Omnia*, Geneva, 2 vols. (The standard edition of his work.)
—— (1600) *Systema logicae*, Hanau.
—— (1607) *Systema ethicae*, London.
—— (1607) *Praecognita philosophica*, Hanau.
—— (1609) *Scientiae metaphysicae compendiosum systema*, Hanau. (Posthumously published.)
—— (1610) *Systema physicum*, Danzig. (Posthumously published.)
—— (1612) *Praecognitorum philosophicorum libri duo; naturam philosophiae explicantes et rationem eius tum docendae tum discendae monstrantes*, Hanover. (Posthumously published.)

References and further reading

Ayers, M. and Garber, D. (eds) (forthcoming) *The Cambridge History of Seventeenth-Century Philosophy*, Cambridge: Cambridge University Press. (Includes various remarks on Keckermann's place in seventeenth-century logic and a more complete bibliography.)

Gilbert, N. (1960) *Renaissance Concepts of Method*, New York: Columbia University Press. (Chapter 10 provides a brief account of Keckermann's concept of method.)

Schmitt, C. and Skinner, Q. (eds) (1988) *The Cambridge History of Renaissance Philosophy*, Cambridge: Cambridge University Press, 632–7. (A brief discussion of Keckermann's conception of system and its relationship to metaphysics.)

CHRISTIA MERCER

KELSEN, HANS (1881–1973)

Hans Kelsen was one of the foremost (positivist) legal theorists of the twentieth century. He taught in Vienna, Cologne, Geneva and Paris, and finished his life in America, teaching in Chicago, Harvard and Berkeley. He wrote widely, on legal philosophy, constitutional and international law, and political philosophy. Kelsen is best known for his Pure Theory of Law *(Reine Rechtslehre) (1934). This is the basis of a theory which, with many changes, he espoused till he died.*

Kelsen wanted to purify the study of law by ridding it of all unnecessary distortion or bias, to produce a science of law that would study what the lawyer did as legal scientist without asking sociological, political, or moral and value questions. He first distinguished legal science from the sociology of law (which asked questions as to what were the causes of law and how it operated in society; see SOCIAL THEORY AND LAW §2). Here Kelsen makes a distinction between normative and causal science. Legal science is a branch of normative science whereas the sociology of law is a branch of natural science concerned with the study of causes. The mode of explanation in natural science, the way in which we make sense of the world, takes the form 'if A then B will follow'. Normative science tries to make sense of the world in terms of the principle of imputation, 'if A, then B ought to follow' (see NORMS, LEGAL §3).

What does Kelsen think a legal norm is? Its form is that of a direction to officials to apply a sanction if someone does something that is forbidden. Thus, 'Thou shalt not kill' would be a prescription addressed to a judge (a direction to an official) to sentence someone to life imprisonment (to apply a sanction) if they unlawfully kill someone (if they commit a wrong). For Kelsen the norm is the meaning of a natural act and not the natural act itself – it is an act of will. The norm is the product of an interpretation of the act. But this interpretation itself implies a norm and that is why Kelsen calls the norm a scheme of interpretation. What does this mean? I see someone standing in a large hall talking to themselves. However I can also interpret this physical act in the normative world as praying. This is the normative meaning of that particular natural act of talking. That is what that person meant by the act and what I understand by it. We both use 'a scheme of interpretation' instantiated here by the norm 'one ought to ask God for help in living in a dangerous world' to make sense of the natural act. But this raises a problem. Is the fact that the people standing in the hall interpret the person's natural act as praying definitive?

For legal science, says Kelsen, it is not. This would be merely the subjective meaning of the act and legal science is interested in the objective meaning of the act. That meaning is one from the point of view both of the individual who receives the direction and of third parties, not only from that of the individual issuing direction. When the policeman waves a car down the meaning of that act is objective because a police official is recognized as having that right by the individuals concerned and third parties. This is so because there is a valid norm, 'drivers ought to obey policemen', and the mode of existence of a norm is its validity. The validity or otherwise of a norm of the positive law is to be found by reference to another superior norm. This superior norm will likewise be validated by another, more general, norm. But we do not go up an infinite ladder. We finally get to the historical starting point of norm-creation, the historically first constitution. To know this is valid we have to ask whether the natural acts of, say the first Parliament, can have the objective meaning of law-making behaviour (whether their meaning is that coercive acts ought to be carried out under conditions determined by them). All the original founders are dead so we have to suppose that their activity was some form of law-making behaviour. It is only if we assume this basic norm (the *Grundnorm*) that we can say that the norms created in the system had an objective validity. It is this *Grundnorm* that enables us to recognize all the laws belonging to a particular system. So legal science is concerned with those norms that can be traced back to the *Grundnorm* that is valid because presupposed. These form a legal system that is coterminous with the state.

It is the concept of system that enables Kelsen to differentiate law from other branches of normative science, especially morals. Validity in law depends upon the pedigree of the norm, on being able to trace it back to the *Grundnorm*. Any content whatsoever can be a legal norm as long as it has been constituted in the correct fashion and can be traced up the chain of validation. The content of law is not relevant to its validity for the purpose of legal science. And any content can be a legal norm as long as it is valid. This is not the case with morals (see LAW AND MORALITY).

Also the law comprises a 'dynamic system' as opposed to the static one of morals. In a moral system the norms are deduced from some *Grundnorm* such as 'Love thy neighbour'. In a dynamic system the derivation does not quite work like that. The norm is concretized as it goes down the hierarchy. Thus, the Road Traffic Act will end up as the judge fining a particular person for a particular act. The judge's action will have the meaning of a norm which will be the concretization of the norm made by Parliament and called the Road Traffic Act. The judge creates here an individual norm. Within limits the judge has a choice and the judge's action is valid because it has been validly authorized by the norm above. This expresses Kelsen's view that there is always the possibility of choice in the law because the system ultimately depends upon authorized choice. Thus morals and law differ in that they are separate normative systems and that one is static and deducible and the other dynamic and undeducible.

For Kelsen validity comes from the presupposition of the *Grundnorm*. But this presupposition is not made by reason of the efficacy or moral rightness of the *Grundnorm*. The former is a sociological question and the latter a moral question; both are distinct from legal science. According to Kelsen we can presuppose the validity of the *Grundnorm* because the system is by and large effective. But this does not mean that validity is equal to effectiveness. Rather it is saying that the condition for making judgments about validity is effectiveness. This is a fine distinction, as can be seen in revolutionary cases where the *Grundnorm* appears to have been changed. Which legal system is valid? Kelsen's attempt to postulate this *Grundnorm* as a pure hypothesis, the content of an act of thought, detached from both morals and sociology, has been very controversial and must probably be deemed a creative and interesting failure.

See also: BOBBIO, N.; HART, H.L.A.; LAW, PHILOSOPHY OF; LEGAL POSITIVISM; WEYR, F.

List of works

Kelsen, H. (1925) *Allgemeine Staatslehre*, Berlin: Springer; trans. A. Wedberg, *The General Theory of Law and State*, Cambridge, MA: Harvard University Press, 1945. (One of his two major works.)

—— (1934) *Reine Rechtslehre*, Leipzig and Vienna: Deuticke; trans. B. Litchewski Paulson and S. Paulson, *Introduction to the Problems of Legal Theory*, Oxford: Oxford University Press, 1995. (One of his two major works.)

—— (1957) *What is Justice?*, Berkeley, CA: University of California Press. (A translation of essays on law, politics and justice.)

—— (1960) *Reine Rechtslehre*, completely rewritten and expanded 2nd edn, Vienna: Deuticke; trans. M. Knight, *Pure Theory of Law*, Berkeley, CA: University of California Press, 1967. (Rewritten and expanded edition of one of his two major works.)

—— (1973) *Essays in Legal and Moral Philosophy*, Dordrecht: Reidel. (Translated essays by P. Heath.)

—— (1979) *Allgemeine Theorie der Normen*, ed. R. Ringhofer and R. Walter, Vienna: Manz, trans. M. Hartney, *General Theory of Norms*, Oxford: Oxford University Press, 1991. (A translation of his last work, which was left in manuscript when he died.)

References and further reading

California Law Review (1971) Essays in Honour of Hans Kelsen 59 (3). (Special issue on Kelsen.)
Ebenstein, W. (1969) *The Pure Theory of Law*, New York: Kelley. (A clear introduction.)
Tur, R. and Twining, W. (eds) (1986) *Essays on Kelsen*, Oxford: Clarendon Press. (A good collection of essays.)

ZENON BAŃKOWSKI

KEMP SMITH, NORMAN (1872–1958)

Norman Kemp Smith is now most widely known for his translation of Kant's Critique of Pure Reason. *This was begun in 1913 while Kemp Smith was completing his* Commentary on Kant's Critique of Pure Reason *which, together with his classic studies on Descartes and Hume, established his reputation as the greatest British philosophical scholar of his day. But he was also an outstanding member of the now forgotten British 'Critical Realist' movement, much respected by A.N. Whitehead, which also included among others Kemp Smith's mentor Robert Adamson, Adamson's English pupil G. Dawes Hicks, James Ward, and his pupil G.F. Stout. Science and scientist fallacies, psychology, including developmental psychology and the histories of science and philosophy were alike concerns of a group of independent thinkers. Their work was obscured by subsequent English philosophers' lack of attention, and the prevailing false assumption that the work of those antecedent thinkers was dominated comprehensively by views mistakenly attributed to 'Hegel' or 'Idealism'.*

1 **Life**
2 **Philosophy and the history of philosophy**
3 **Nature contra 'Naturalism'**
4 **Critique of 'Enlightenment'**
5 **Hume, Descartes and rediscovery**

1 Life

Born in Dundee in 1872, Norman Smith grew up in Cupar Angus (only in 1910 did he add his wife's maiden name 'Kemp' to his own). He studied at the

University of St Andrews, and on graduation in 1894 won a Ferguson scholarship which enabled him to undertake further studies in Germany, Switzerland and France. He became a Teaching Assistant at Glasgow University in 1894, where he was acting Professor of Logic in 1901–2 after Robert Adamson's untimely death. He became Professor of Psychology at Princeton in 1906 and, in 1914, McCosh Professor of Philosophy there. He returned to London in 1915 for war work until 1918, and in 1919 was appointed to the Edinburgh chair of Logic and Metaphysics. He held this position until 1945, the Second World War delaying his retirement and adding the duties of the Moral Philosophy Chair for the period 1941–4.

2 Philosophy and the history of philosophy

Kemp Smith believed that much twentieth-century British philosophy simply rehearses long-refuted views. His view was that advance in philosophy is dependent on dialogue with earlier thinkers, which requires study of their cultural contexts, including the history of science, as well as of philosophy.

While accurate learning and historical insight distinguish his early work, *Studies in the Cartesian Philosophy* (1902), this book was also, for thinkers as diverse as Ryle, Lovejoy and Macmurray, both influential and modernizing. Although Kemp Smith was no Hegelian, he insisted that the criterion of truth is the systematic coherence of mutually related viewpoints *in the light of all appearances*. Hence axioms are illicit in philosophy, and Kemp Smith criticizes Descartes' *Cogito* by showing how it implies untenable doctrines concerning perception and mind–body dualism.

Dedicated as the book Adamson did not live to write, Kemp Smith's *Commentary on Kant's Critique of Pure Reason* (1918) has become a classic. Kemp Smith goes beyond exegesis to critical dialogue. Giving new attention to the first edition of Kant's *Critique*, Kemp Smith's account of this as a patchwork, with parts from the pre-critical phases of Kant's thinking, is much more than a simple completion of Vaihinger's work. Against subsequent tendencies of English analytic philosophy Kemp Smith insists that Kant's terminology retains a provisional character due to its having originated in different contexts. Hence one cannot assume that the same word always bears the same signification, and Kant's work is further contextualized by viewing it as an attempt not at finality but at making an advance towards greater coherence and adequacy.

3 Nature contra 'Naturalism'

Although described in the 1930s as a leading figure in the new 'Realist' philosophy, Kemp Smith characterized his thought as 'Idealist' in his 1919 Inaugural address ('*The Present Situation in Philosophy*'), by contrast with 'Naturalism', not Realism. He later described this position as one which regards ethical and aesthetic (spiritual) valuations as real determining factors in the physical world.

Kemp Smith's 1905 critique of Avenarius' misleadingly named doctrine of *reine Erfahrung* ('*Pure Experience*') relates not to any contemporary prominence of AVENARIUS' work, but to his having given the most thorough working out of the view that perception and the attainment of truth consist in a direct physical conforming of the brain to the external world's particularity. In opposition to this view, Kemp Smith argues against all doctrines, including that implied by Bradley's conception of 'feeling', which allege that the brain or mind has access to sheer particularity. According to Kemp Smith, the sciences of anthropology and psychology show that the development of mind, including perception, requires the initial operation of animistic notions, theologies, myths, all of which involve the identification of general patterns; and any development of the mind towards a greater objectivity proceeds by criticism of the mutually contradictory beliefs to which these early operations give rise. Furthermore, Kemp Smith argues, the origin and function of these early operations cannot be accounted for in a physicalist theory such as that of Avenarius; the hypothesis would be of a species programmed with a tendency to self-deception while also capable of desiring and possessing truth. In fact, theologies, myths and so forth are not the sheer obstructions to knowledge Avenarius supposes; they arise from confrontations with practical needs and remain subject to challenge by further practical needs. Avenarius has obscured the truth by imposing a methodology which, by parroting categories from a currently fashionable science, mistakenly fancies itself to be scientific.

Kemp Smith (1923) further develops his position in a response to Whitehead's conception of nature (see WHITEHEAD, A.N. §§3–4). 'Nature' is no mere scheme of abstract physical laws; instead it is of such a complexity that the richness of sense-experience, far from being a mere subjective colouring, manifests only the structures that human practical needs have revealed. Thus 'subjectivism' is rejected as missing the real complexity of reality, and it is affirmed that the routes to insight into reality may be various, with none that can be presumed exhaustive. In his *Prolegomena to an Idealist Theory of Knowledge*

(1924) Kemp Smith proceeds by way of a phenomenology of mind as a 'patchwork' which takes account of the problem of illusion and its recognition. 'Intuition' is the capacity which results from the developing mind's transactions with reality and the variously mythical and generalizing schemata that have come into being within the mind's development. It comes into being through the lifetime operation of practical needs and of that gradual getting beyond them which constitutes the capacity for knowledge. Biological evolution and the development of the individual organism have equipped it to deal with 'sensa'. These sensa are the data of the senses, and also elements of the presentations witnessed when, for instance, thinking or dreaming. That actual things are seen, says Kemp Smith, is the result of the operation of 'intuition', as understood above. Thus the particular is not the basis of knowledge but the objective of a complex, lengthy pursuit.

In 'The Nature of Universals' (1927) Kemp Smith criticizes the positions of Bradley and Bosanquet, and also that of his friend G.F. Stout, and advances an account of universals which echoes that of Reid. It is not the white of any existing thing which is the universal (for that cannot be whiteness of another thing). The universal 'white' comes into being by way of contrasts made between different characteristics of things, of characteristics identified by contrast as 'colours'. Universals access reality by representing kinds and characters as these have been identified by way of contrasts, both in one's own experience and in that of others from whom one learns them. Linguistic terms are general too, but for Kemp Smith they differ from universals *qua* logical terms as a result of the different context of investigation in which logical terms arise and are applied. This difference between language and logic is crucial for Kemp Smith's friend and former assistant, John Anderson (see UNIVERSALS §2).

4   Critique of 'Enlightenment'

Kemp Smith conceives of original sin as human limitedness compounded by delusions of self-sufficiency which ignore the unconscious and unwilled aspects of the development of mind and knowledge. Calvin, he held, was a 'Copernicus of psychology', his theology a pioneering scientific criticism of naive voluntarism. Yet Kemp Smith is also a critic of sophistical relativism. He argues that different viewpoints, such as those of religion, manifest different bases in the development of mind, the different perspectives consequent on different minds addressing a complex reality. In the 1920s Kemp Smith contemplated a book-length study of Romanti-

cism, but this was not written; the critique of 'Enlightenment' in his protégé A.A. Bowman's *Studies in the Philosophy of Religion* (1938), however, follows Kemp Smith in emphasizing the reliance of shallow, optimistic naturalism in ethics on a decontextualized, ahistorical, frame of reference (see ENLIGHTENMENT, CONTINENTAL §2; NATURALISM IN ETHICS §2).

5   Hume, Descartes and rediscovery

While editing his late close friend F. von Hugel's *The Reality of God* (1927), Kemp Smith seems to have reconceived the project of a critique of Enlightenment, von Hugel's clichéd depiction of HUME as smiling villain being so much at odds with the seriousness and reverence for nature that Kemp Smith traced in 'The Naturalism of Hume' (1905). Kemp Smith's introduction to what has on occasion been referred to as his 'flawless edition of a flawless work', Hume's *Dialogues on Natural Religion* (1935), identifies the 'delusion' and 'sham' of a famous quote with the ratiocinatory 'Federal' perversion of neo-Calvinist religion on which Hume was raised. Opening a new era in study of that towering figure, *The Philosophy of David Hume* (1941) shows Hume rejecting a Hobbesian self-interest doctrine but also directly criticizing Francis Hutcheson's moral intuitionism and the doctrine of design on which it is founded. Deepening his perspective by reference to continental Hume studies, Kemp Smith refutes the conception of an 'associationist' Hume beloved of the Mills and their followers, and on the same misreading anathema to their adversaries. According to Kemp Smith, Hume's later work is no falling-away from his *Treatise*; Hume had rather abandoned his false hopes for what might be accomplished by associationist theory. His writings from the *Enquiries* onwards represent Hume's initial and abiding project of a comprehensive scientific account of human beings founded on the Newtonian observational approach to 'moral questions'. His abiding merit is in his application of the approach of natural history to the study of man and society, making observations inconsistent with that very crude associationism which has often mistaken him for an ally.

This commitment to comprehensive critical-historical exegesis was for Kemp Smith not a retirement into the 'history of philosophy', but a way of advancing philosophy. In his *New Studies in the Philosophy of Descartes* (1954) Kemp Smith expounds the range of Descartes' interests and the development of his doctrines within the historical contexts which shaped their formulation. Half a century after his early challenge to Descartes' *Cogito*, Kemp Smith reconsiders the fruitful complexities of his views on mind–body dualism and perception, especially in relation to later scientific developments.

In returning to Descartes, Kemp Smith addresses the 'two cultures' problem raised by Alois Riehl, whom Princeton had honoured during Kemp Smith's time there. In his *Der Philosophische Kriticismus* (1876–87), Riehl followed the one-sided emphasis of Kant's immediate successors on literary and humanistic studies and suggested a loss of that close relation to the physical sciences which Kant shared with Descartes, a loss which imperilled subsequent philosophy. Furthermore, Riehl thought that philosophy, by way of reaction, mightequally lose itself in an exclusive pursuit of a scientistic methodology. In response, Kemp Smith maintained that in order to avoid these errors, manifest time and again in the history of philosophy, philosophers need to remain open to the history and context of philosophy, both as a warning and as a source of still unappreciated insights. The history of philosophy is an essential element of the dialogue which is philosophy's continuing project.

List of Works

Smith, N. (1902) *Studies in the Cartesian Philosophy*, London: Macmillan. (Decisive for its critique of the *Cogito*, this discusses Descartes' medieval inheritance and examines his influence on Malebranche, Leibniz, Berkeley and Hume.)
—— (1905) 'The Naturalism of Hume', *Mind* 14: 149–73, 335–47. (Counters notions of Hume as an impious mischief-maker by reference to an account of Nature which echoes Calvin and foreshadows Wordsworth.)
—— (1906) 'Avenarius's Philosophy of Pure Experience', *Mind* 15: 13–31, 149–60. (William James declared this paper to have dealt a death-blow to Avenarius' theory.)
Kemp Smith, N. (1918) *A Commentary on Kant's Critique of Pure Reason*, London: Macmillan; 2nd enlarged edn, 1923. (Includes a thorough account of previous commentaries; invaluable resource for explication of Kant's terminology in general.)
—— (1919) *The Present Situation in Philosophy*, Edinburgh: Thin; repr. in *The Correspondence of Baron Friedrich von Hugel with Professor Norman Kemp Smith*, New York: Fordham University Press, 1981. (Incidentally valuable in exposing implications of doctrines pretending to be all-comprehendingly scientific. The *Correspondence* sheds light on wider references not represented in Kemp Smith's published work.)
—— (1923) 'Whitehead's Philosophy of Nature', *Issues and Tendencies in Contemporary Philosophy*, Berke-ley, CA: University of California Publications in Philosophy, 4, 197–224. (Emphasizes the limitation of any theory in relation to the complexity of subject-matter.)
—— (1924) *Prolegomena to an Idealist Theory of Knowledge*, London: Macmillan. (Emphasizes the complexity of mind and seriously criticizes pretences of theory to exclusiveness. Apparent simplicities of relations between mind and reality are founded on mental processes of intense complexity.)
—— (1927) 'The Nature of Universals' *Mind* 36: 137–57, 265–80, 393–422. (Criticizes Bosanquet and Stout, maintaining that universals are abstract terms in debate rather than psychological representations.)
—— (1935) 'Introduction' to *David Hume: Dialogues on Natural Religion*, Edinburgh: Nelson; 2nd augmented edn, 1947. (Draws particular attention to Hume's restricted definition and limited experience of religion.)
—— (1941) *The Philosophy of David Hume*, London: Macmillan. (Notes contemporary references not identified in Hume's arguments and maintains that Hume's *Treatise* and *Enquiries* were preparatories to the later historical and political studies.)
—— (1954) *New Studies in the Philosophy of Descartes: Descartes as Pioneer*, London: Macmillan. (Presents the immense range of Descartes' scientific studies, insisting on the importance of mind–body dualism in identifying questions liable to be raised by future scientific developments.)
—— (1967) *The Credibility of Divine Existence*, ed. A.J.D. Porteous, R.D. MacLennan and G.E. Davie, London: Macmillan. (This is Kemp Smith's own selection from his papers – including 1905, 1906, 1923, 1927 above – which covers topics such as Locke, Bergson, progressivism in ethics and fear.)

References and further reading

* Bowman, A.A. (1938) *Studies in the Philosophy of Religion*, ed. N. Kemp Smith, London: Macmillan. (Criticism of the Enlightenment project by a friend, much influenced by Kemp Smith.)
Calder, R.R. (1997) *A School of Thinking*, Edinburgh: Polygon. (Devotes a chapter to Kemp Smith in an account of his Scottish contemporaries as well as of Robert Adamson and the Critical Realist background.)
Ewing, A.C. (1959) 'Norman Kemp Smith', obituary in the *Proceedings of the British Academy* 45: 297–306. (Biographical account by a contemporary, mostly in sympathy and usually tentative regarding any disagreement.)
* Kant, I. (1781/1787) *Immanuel Kant's Critique of Pure*

Reason, trans. N. Kemp Smith, London: Macmillan, 1929; 2nd corrected impression, 1933. (The second edition of the first *Critique*, supplemented with translation of the passages from the first edition which were altered or replaced in the second. Numerous reprints.)

Merz, J.T. (1896) *History of European Thought in the Nineteenth Century*, Edinburgh: Blackwood, vols 3 and 4; repr. New York: Dover, 1965. (An authoritative work by an Anglo–German, with a full appreciation of the very different context in which Kemp Smith's thought developed.)

Metz, R. (1938) *A Hundred Years of British Philosophy*, London: Routledge. (Includes accounts of Kemp Smith, Adamson, *et al.*, with an informative depiction of the variety of British philosophy c.1930.)

Passmore, J. (1968) *A Hundred Years of Philosophy*, Harmondsworth: Penguin. (A useful supplement to Metz.)

* Riehl, A. (1876–87) *Der Philosophische Kriticismus und seine Bedeutung für die positive Wissenschaft*, Leipzig: W. Engelmann, 1924–5. (Presentation of Kantian method which emphasizes Kant's continuity with preceding philosophy and physical science.)

ROBERT CALDER
GEORGE DAVIE

KEMPIS, THOMAS À

see THOMAS À KEMPIS

KEPLER, JOHANNES
(1571–1630)

Kepler's mathematical analysis of Brahe's observations of the motions of Mars enabled him to formulate the descriptive 'laws' of planetary motion, thus giving heliocentric astronomy an empirical basis far more accurate than it had before. He insisted that astronomy had to discover the causes *of the motions that the laws described, in this way becoming a 'physics of the sky'. In the pursuit of this goal, he formulated the notion of distance-dependent forces between sun and planet, and guessed that gravity could be explained as an attraction between heavy bodies and their home planets, analogous to magnetic action, thus pointing the way for Newton's theory of gravity.*

Kepler was introduced to the work of COPERNICUS while at the University of Tübingen. In 1596 he completed the *Mysterium cosmographicum*, explaining the spacing and the periods of the planets in the Copernican system along broadly Neoplatonic lines. The orbits of the six planets were to be separated by the five regular polyhedra, and the increase in the planetary periods with distance from the sun would be explained by the diminution of a driving force from the sun. Since all of this was contingent upon the Copernican planetary ordering, the treatise constituted an explicit (if unconventional) defence of that ordering, the first since the *De revolutionibus orbium coelestium* in 1543.

In 1600, the astronomer Tycho Brahe asked Kepler to defend Brahe's work against the criticisms of Nicolaus Ursus (Baer), who dismissed mathematical astronomy generally as no more than convenient fiction. In a short work, the *Apologia pro Tychone contra Ursum* (1600), Kepler drew on the history of astronomy to construct a perceptive analysis of hypothetical reasoning in astronomy. He argued that astronomers must not be content with geometrical description, since two such 'hypotheses' might very well save the phenomena equally well. One could not in that case decide between them on geometrical-empirical grounds. What is needed is a causal analysis, a physics of the motions that explains why they occur as they do. Not published until 1858, the *Apologia* has come to be recognized as one of the more acute contributions to philosophy of science from the seventeenth century.

Kepler succeeded Brahe as imperial mathematician in 1601 and began intensive work aimed at establishing the shape of Mars' orbit. He could not avail himself of the convenient device that both Ptolemy and Copernicus had relied on of using different orbits for the calculation of the planet's longitudes and latitudes. The seemingly irreducible error of 8′ that resulted would not have been significant were it not for the unprecedented accuracy of Brahe's data. Kepler asked himself what physical causes could make the planet move in its evidently non-circular path. Gilbert's theory of the earth as a vast magnet led him to propose that magnetic forces between the two great magnets, sun and planet, could account for both the varying distance between planet and sun, and the variations in orbital velocity of the planet. Finally, in chapter 58 of the *Astronomia nova* (1609), he announced triumphantly: 'Reasoning from physical principles agreeing with experience, there is no figure left for the orbit of the planet except a perfect ellipse'. His second law, that the planet's radius vector sweeps out equal areas in equal times, is tucked away in the massive book also, but even Kepler himself did not recognize its significance until later.

In 1618, he published the *Harmonice mundi*. Applying the principles of harmony to the universe, he tried to explain the distances and periods of the planets and discovered what would come to be known later as his third law (the squares of the periods of any two planets are proportional to the cubes of their mean distances from the sun). In this work he also attempted to formulate an elaborate theoretical basis for astrology. The zodiac, he asserts, is a projection of the human soul; the positions of the planets at a person's birth mark the soul for the remainder of life. Kepler constructed horoscopes and prognostications throughout his professional career; astrology was an important source of income for him. Yet he also expresses doubt about its claims, warning that it may be a matter of luck when astrological prognostications turn out to be correct.

His next work, the *Epitome astronomiae Copernicanae* (1618–21), was widely influential. It presented the case for Copernican astronomy in textbook fashion, laying out the evidence for the earth's motions and discussing, though not as fully as Galileo would later do, the imperceptibility of shared uniform motion. Much of the work was devoted to the technical geometrical detail required for practical computation of the planetary orbits. But the emphasis of the argument was, as always, on causal reasoning; this time he proposed a swirl of magnetic 'species' that would move planets along in their paths. (Lacking the principle of inertia, he had to find a cause for continuing onward motion.) But as in his earlier works, he did not confine himself to efficient causes only, and found a motive for Copernicanism in the symbolism of God's Trinitarian relation with the universe, the centre of the universe representing God the Father. He also sought final causes for every major feature of the planetary system, even down to the relative sizes and densities of the planets.

Kepler sought order and harmony in the universe, a conviction that guided him in his successful search for the true orbits of the planets. And it prompted him to see astronomy itself as a causal science and not merely a saving of the phenomena. His assurance that harmonies discoverable by the human mind were embodied in the cosmos derived in the first instance from his theology of creation and Neoplatonic metaphysics. Yet his achievements in astronomy, particularly his unconventional notion of a sun-centred force controlling the movement of the planets, showed the way to a self-contained quasi-mechanistic worldview.

See also: CAUSATION; COSMOLOGY; EXPLANATION; GALILEI, G.; NEWTON, I.

List of works

Kepler, J. (1600) *Apologia pro Tychone contra Ursum* (A Defence of Tycho against Ursus); in N. Jardine (ed.), *The Birth of History and Philosophy of Science*, Cambridge: Cambridge University Press, 1984, 134–207. (The *Apologia* in English, with the addition of the Latin text and eight chapters detailing the circumstances of the work's composition and its significance in terms of contemporary philosophical concerns.)

—— (1609) *Astronomia nova* (New Astronomy); trans. W.H. Donahue, Cambridge: Cambridge University Press, 1992. (Kepler's most important work, available for the first time in English translation. A challenge to the translator because of its convoluted style as well as its author's habit of retracing every blind alley taken.)

—— (1618) *Harmonice mundi* (The Harmony of the World); trans. E.J. Aiton, A.M. Duncan and J.V. Field, Philadelphia, PA: American Philosophical Society, 1995. (With an introduction and notes.)

—— (1937–) *Gesammelte Werke*, eds M. Caspar *et al.*, Munich: Beck. (The definitive edition, of twenty-two volumes, under the guidance of a series of devoted editors.)

References and further reading

Beer, A. and Beer, P. (eds) (1975) *Kepler: Four Hundred Years*, New York: Pergamon; vol. 18 of the series *Vistas of Astronomy*. (Large set of scholarly essays on every aspect of Kepler's life and legacy.)

Caspar, M. (1993) *Kepler*, trans. C.E. Hellman, New York: Dover. (The standard biography of Kepler, with a new introduction and references by O. Gingerich.)

Koyré, A. (1961) *The Astronomical Revolution: Copernicus, Kepler, Borelli*; trans. R.E.W. Maddison, Ithaca, NY: Cornell University Press, 1973. (The central section of this work, *Kepler and the New Astronomy*, 117–464, gives an admirably clear account of Kepler's unique contribution: a new ideal of astronomy that would require not only accurate prediction of planetary motions but an explanatory account of the forces responsible for them.)

Stephenson, B. (1987) *Kepler's Physical Astronomy*, Princeton, NJ: Princeton University Press. (A detailed account of the physical theories with which

Kepler complemented his mathematical analysis of the planetary motions.)

—— (1994) *The Music of The Heavens: Kepler's Harmonic Astronomy*, Princeton, NJ: Princeton University Press. (A sympathetic analysis of Kepler's use of harmonies and archetypes to construct a planetary cosmology.)

ERNAN MCMULLIN

KEYNES, JOHN MAYNARD (1883–1946)

Keynes is best known as an economist but, in the tradition of John Stuart Mill and William Stanley Jevons, he also made significant contributions to inductive logic and the philosophy of science. Keynes' only book explicitly on philosophy, A Treatise on Probability *(1921), remains an important classic on the subject. It develops a non-frequentist interpretation of probability as the key to sound judgment and scientific reasoning. His* General Theory of Employment, Interest and Money *(1936) is the watershed of twentieth-century macroeconomics. While not, strictly speaking, a philosophical work, it nonetheless advances distinct readings of rationality, uncertainty and social justice.*

1 **Probability and induction**
2 **Political economy**

1 Probability and induction

Born in Cambridge, England, Keynes was educated at Eton and Cambridge University where his father Neville lectured on logic and economics. After studying mathematics and economics and working briefly in the India Office, Keynes was elected, in 1908, a fellow of King's College Cambridge. During his twenties and thirties, Keynes undertook an informal study of philosophy in the company of the Cambridge 'Apostles' – G.E. Moore, John McTaggart, Bertrand Russell, Alfred North Whitehead, Frank Ramsey and Ludwig Wittgenstein – from whom he forged his own unique matrix of rationalist and empiricist beliefs. Perhaps the most colourful episode of Keynes' fascinating life was his founding association with the Bloomsbury Group of artists and intellectuals. He also served as an advisor to the British Treasury, most notably on the Treaty of Versailles (1919), which he repudiated, and on the early negotiations for the Bretton Woods Agreement (1946). Keynes' prophetic grasp of the political and economic transformations of his world will undoubtedly be valued for generations to come.

In his *Treatise on Probability* (1921), Keynes sought to draw out the logical foundations of probability and to graft these onto the mathematical calculus of probability. This complemented the logicist programme of Russell and Whitehead, particularly the common aim of grounding knowledge in a limited set of intuitions. Keynes viewed probability as a species of logical inference, as the degree of rational belief about a given proposition which extant knowledge authorizes us to entertain. Propositions are known by direct acquaintance with the world and may be true or false, but probability, as a property of an argument, has no bearing on the question of truth. As more evidence comes to light, the probability might increase in value. It does not, however, approximate truth in the straightforward correspondence sense. For Keynes, 'probability begins and ends with probability'.

Probability is objectively determined in the sense that it is transindividual and thus not a function of personal history. A rational person, such as a magistrate or actuary, will arrive at the correct probability judgment and use this as the guide to right action. Nevertheless, in most areas of life we must be content with a qualitative estimate. A numerical measure is only possible in the case of a set of exclusive and exhaustive equiprobable alternatives, and such cases are the exception rather than the rule. Keynes thereby contracts rather than expands the domain of numerical probability assertions. There are for him four possible options when confronted with a non-deductive argument:

(1) there is no probability;
(2) the probabilities do not all belong to a single set of magnitudes measurable in terms of a common unit;
(3) there are existing measures but they must remain unknown; or
(4) the probabilities can be measured and belong to the same set, and are thus capable of comparison.

As for constructing a scale of probabilities, Keynes grants that the end points of the series, certainty and impossibility $(1,0)$, always exist and that, if there is a given probability, it will lie between them. But in the majority of cases it is not possible to provide a measure of that probability, let alone compare it to others.

Keynes appreciated statistics for its fact-gathering function but was sceptical about its potential for hypothesis testing. Accordingly, he did not extend the rich linkages between probability and statistics. The theorems of Bernoulli and Laplace were discredited, as was any statistical inference that presupposed a probability distribution. John Venn's frequency interpretation of probability was also misguided, in part because of its ascription of numerical measures, in part because of its contingent character and in part because large and stable samples are difficult to obtain (see VENN, J.). Moreover, the frequency interpretation entails a commitment to natural kinds and to the belief that probabilities are features of the external world rather than of the human mind. For Keynes, probability is a purely logical relationship between the propositions of an argument. In response to criticisms from Ramsey, Keynes later equivocated on the degree of consensus required for objective probability assertions, but he remained steadfast to his rationalist interpretation.

Laplace and a number of followers endorsed the principle of indifference, which stipulated that, in the case of complete ignorance, the a priori probability of a given proposition would be 1/2. Keynes found this suspect because of its ready ascription of a number to what is, at best, known qualitatively. Furthermore, he recognized that one could always break the class of objects denoted by the predicate term into further subdivisions and thus grant that what were treated as equivalent classes before may now contain a different or an indefinite number of more elementary groupings.

One of Keynes' innovations is a property that he calls the weight of an argument, which measures the absolute amount of knowledge and ignorance respectively. Hence, in the case of gathering more relevant yet unfavourable evidence, one would increase the weight while lowering its probability. One might also have a proposition with a high probability and a low weight. The question Keynes leaves us with is whether or not one should always set out to acquire a high weight. Clearly, there comes a point where it is no longer worthwhile to acquire further information, but what principle will determine this threshold is a matter left unresolved. In his economic analysis of investment, however, Keynes made use of this property in order to highlight the ever-present uncertainty of business forecasting.

A hue of uncertainty is also cast over science in general. Inductive arguments are fundamentally probabilistic and thus do not serve to approximate the ideal state of complete certainty. Moreover, pure induction is for Keynes relatively pointless if the confirming instances do not differ except with respect to their spatiotemporal properties. It is analogical reasoning that matters the most. In order to strengthen a scientific hypothesis, it is important to vary the instances, particularly to increase the negative analogies. We are impressed with Newton's law of universal gravitation because of the variety of circumstances it fulfils rather than the mere number of them. Furthermore, prediction in itself is of no consequence since it is essentially a case of pure induction and plays into a dispositional weakness for the temporal ordering of scientific discoveries. Proper grounds for accepting a hypothesis are built up from objective logical relations as elucidated by the theory of probability.

Previous solutions to the problem of induction, such as J.S. MILL's appeal to the uniformity of nature, are discarded as spurious. Keynes concentrates rather on a probabilistic justification of analogical inference. Our convictions about the existence of other people and about the causal links between beliefs and actions are both ample evidence of the support we hold for analogizing. More importantly, we would only be in a position to draw analogies if the universe was not infinitely varied. A priori, we require a finite probability in favour of the inductive hypothesis that there is an upper limit to the independent variety of the objects that comprise our generalizations. Once we grant this so-called principle of the limitation of independent variety, we find that our experience of the world, rather than diminishing its probability, has in fact increased it. In this respect, Keynes maintains that induction is non-circular, even if it is not fully justified. He has provided a probabilistic argument for a principle that he assumes to have an initial probability.

2 Political economy

Keynes viewed economics as a moral science and unfolded one of the most detailed pictures of human agency since David HUME and Adam SMITH. By distinguishing different motives for investment and different capacities to discern the flux of the business cycle, and by recognizing that individual motives and actions are rarely synchronized due to ignorance and uncertainty, he broke with the classical conviction that economies are self-equilibrating. Claiming as his forebears the mercantilist economists of the seventeenth century, he argued that the state alone had the monetary and fiscal means to achieve economic stability. But he stopped short of state socialism. With an eye to preserving individual liberty, Keynes proposed a nation of semi-autonomous bodies serving the public good, on the scale of corporations, universities or the central bank.

Keynes was sanguine that the solution to economic scarcity lay in capital accumulation guided by science, technology and the state. But capitalism as a system, while the most efficient means to this end, is grounded in cupidity and thus is morally reprehensible. Moreover, it tolerates high levels of unemployment and unwarranted inequalities of wealth. Genuine social justice would be possible only if and when humankind freed itself from its animal passion for money and expanded its ambit of altruism. This, he hoped, would come about gradually, with the euthanasia of the *rentier* class and the redistribution of wealth through sound fiscal policy. It was conceivable to Keynes that within approximately 100 years, citizens of the developed economies would no longer be bound by economic necessity and that such abundance would unleash a new form of human flourishing and morality. Keynes' biographical essays on great minds (1933), and his lifelong devotion to the arts leaves little doubt as to what form these higher goods would take.

See also: ECONOMICS, PHILOSOPHY OF; INDUCTION, EPISTEMIC ISSUES IN; INDUCTIVE INFERENCE; PROBABILITY, INTERPRETATIONS OF

List of works

Keynes' early philosophical essays are unpublished, and are housed in the Keynes Papers, King's College, Cambridge University.

Keynes, J.M. (1921) *A Treatise on Probability*, in D. Moggridge and A. Robinson (eds) *The Collected Writings of John Maynard Keynes*, vol. 8, London: Macmillan, and New York: Cambridge University Press, 1971–89. (Keynes' one philosophical treatise. Developed an analysis of probability that complements the logistic programme of Russell and Whitehead.)

—— (1931) *Essays in Persuasion*, in D. Moggridge and A. Robinson (eds) *The Collected Writings of John Maynard Keynes*, vol. 9, London: Macmillan, and New York: Cambridge University Press, 1971–89. (Keynes as policy advisor on the Treaty of Versailles, the gold standard, free trade and liberal ideals. Also offers a vision of the future in 'Economic Possibilities for our Grandchildren'.)

—— (1933) *Essays in Biography*, in D. Moggridge and A. Robinson (eds) *The Collected Writings of John Maynard Keynes*, vol. 10, London: Macmillan, and New York: Cambridge University Press, 1971–89. (Keynes the master stylist captures the personalities of Isaac Newton, Stanley Jevons, Frank Ramsey and Winston Churchill, among others.)

—— (1936) *The General Theory of Employment, Interest and Money*, in D. Moggridge and A. Robinson (eds) *The Collected Writings of John Maynard Keynes*, vol. 7, London: Macmillan, and New York: Cambridge University Press, 1971–89. (The most important treatise on macroecononics of the twentieth century. Maintained that economies are not self-regulating and require government intervention in periods of high unemployment.)

References and further reading

Bateman, B.W. (1987) 'Keynes's Changing Conception of Probability', *Economics and Philosophy* 3: 97–119. (Argues that Ramsey's criticisms prompted Keynes to shift to a frequentist interpretation of probability prior to the publication of the *General Theory*.)

Carabelli, A.M. (1988) *On Keynes's Method*, New York: St Martin's Press. (Detailed study of Keynes' probability and its links to economics.)

Davis, J.B. (1994) *Keynes's Philosophical Development*, Cambridge: Cambridge University Press. (Places Keynes' thought within the context of the Cambridge philosophers G.E. Moore, L. Wittgenstein and F. Ramsey.)

Moggridge, D.E. (1992) *Maynard Keynes, An Economist's Biography*, London: Routledge. (A fine biography with detailed chapters on his probability and economic philosophy.)

O'Donnell, R.M. (1989) *Keynes: Philosophy, Economics and Politics*, London: Macmillan. (Highlights the unity of Keynes' philosophy and political economy.)

Runde, J. (1994) 'Keynes After Ramsey: In Defense of *A Treatise on Probability*', *Studies in History and Philosophy of Science* 25: 81–96. (Argues, contra Bateman, that Keynes did not significantly alter his views on probability after Ramsey's criticisms. Nice summary of the debate.)

MARGARET SCHABAS

KHAI-DUB *see* MKHAS GRUB DGE LEGS DPAL BZANG PO

KHOMIAKOV, A.

see SLAVOPHILISM; HEGELIANISM, RUSSIAN

KIERKEGAARD, SØREN AABYE (1813–55)

Although Kierkegaard's name has come to be chiefly associated with writings on philosophical themes, his

235

various publications covered a wide range that included contributions to literary criticism, discourses on specifically religious topics and forays into polemical journalism. Born in Copenhagen in 1813, he led an outwardly uneventful existence there until his death in 1855. None the less much that he wrote drew upon crises and turning points in his personal life; even his theoretical works often had an autobiographical flavour.

Kierkegaard held that the philosophy of his time, largely owing to the influence of Hegelian idealism, tended to misconstrue the relation of thought to reality, wrongly assimilating the second to the first; in doing so, moreover, it reflected an age in which habits of abstract reflection and passive response had blinded people to their true concerns as self-determining agents ultimately accountable for their own characters and destinies. He sought to counter such trends, exploring different approaches to life with a view to opening his reader's eyes both to where they themselves stood and to possibilities of opting for radical change. He implied that decisions on the latter score lay beyond the scope of general rules, each being essentially a problem for the individual alone; even so, his portrayal of the religious mode of existence presented it as transcending limitations experienced in alternative forms of life. Kierkegaard, himself an impassioned believer, was at the same time crucially concerned to articulate the Christian standpoint in a fashion that salvaged it from recurrent misconceptions. Rejecting all attempts to provide objective justifications or proofs of religious claims, he endorsed a conception of faith that eschewed rational considerations and consisted instead of subjective self-commitment maintained in the face of intellectual uncertainty or paradox. His account was set within a psychological perspective that laid stress upon freedom as an inescapable condition of action and experience. The complex implications he believed this to possess for the interpretation of pervasive human emotions and attitudes were discussed in works that later proved highly influential, particularly for the growth of twentieth-century existentialism. Here, as in other areas of his writing, Kierkegaard made a significant, though delayed, impact upon the course of subsequent thought.

1 **Life**
2 **The limits of objectivity**
3 **Aestheticism and the ethical**
4 **The religious consciousness**
5 **Faith and subjectivity**
6 **Psychological themes and influence**

1 Life

Kierkegaard was the youngest son of a prosperous and largely self-made Danish businessman. The father was a deeply religious but exacting and guilt-ridden individual who communicated his feelings of melancholy and anxiety to other members of his family; they certainly left a lasting impression on Kierkegaard's own character and development, causing him later to describe his upbringing as having been 'insane'. It was perhaps largely from a desire to please his father, towards whom he tended to exhibit an ambivalent mixture of love and fear, that at the age of seventeen he enrolled at the University of Copenhagen with the object of taking a degree in theology. Nevertheless, after passing his preliminary examinations he found himself increasingly attracted to other spheres of intellectual interest, particularly those involving developments in contemporary philosophy and literature; at the same time he cultivated a fashionably sophisticated lifestyle, following pursuits sharply at variance with the austere precepts that had been inculcated upon him at home. But in his journals, which he began during his protracted period as a student and continued to keep for the rest of his life, he is already to be found recording a growing dissatisfaction with the wayward mode of existence he had adopted, and the death of his father in 1838 appears finally to have prompted him to return to his academic studies with a view to settling down to a professional career. Thus by July 1840 he had been awarded his degree, and two months later he announced his engagement to marry Regine Olsen, the daughter of a highly placed civil servant. This, however, was not to be.

The story of Kierkegaard's abortive engagement is familiar from his journals, where he provided a detailed account of how he eventually broke off the relationship after an uneasy year during which he harboured regrets about his proposal. While his actual motives for making the final breach are left somewhat obscure, there can be no doubt as to its significance for his later thought and writings, allusions to it – often only lightly disguised – occurring in a variety of his works. In any case it certainly constituted a turning point. Henceforward he withdrew into a bachelor existence; moreover, although by now firmly committed to Christianity, he effectively abandoned any further thought of a clerical career and devoted himself instead to living as a writer on the very comfortable income he had inherited from his father's estate. The initial period of his authorship was in fact remarkably productive. He took less than a year over his master's dissertation *Om Begrebet Ironi* (The Concept of Irony), successfully submitting it to the university faculty in 1841, and he followed it with a series of books, all issued under pseudonyms, which were largely concerned with philosophical or psychological aspects of ethical and religious belief. The first, entitled *Enten-Eller* (Either/Or), came out in two substantial volumes in 1843 and was succeeded later in the same year by *Frygt og Baeven* (Fear and Trembling) and *Gjentagelsen* (Repetition); in 1844 *Philosophiske Smuler* (Philosophical Fragments) and *Begrebet Angest* (The Concept of Anxiety) appeared, and these in turn were followed by *Stadier paa Livets Vej* (Stages on Life's Way) in 1845 and by *Afsluttende uvidenskabelig Efterskrift* (Concluding Unscientific Postscript) in 1846. Two further pseudonymous works on connected themes, *Sygdommen til Døden* (The Sickness unto Death) and *Indøvelse i Christendom* (Training in Christianity), were published in 1849 and 1850 respectively.

Although it is the writings listed above that have chiefly attracted the attention of subsequent philosophers and commentators, they by no means exhaust the total of Kierkegaard's literary output during the 1840s. Apart from some critical pieces, he also produced – this time under his own name – a number of directly religious discourses in which he aimed to present the essentials of Christian teaching; thus such works as his *Opbyggelige Taler i forskjellig Aand* (Edifying Discourses in Various Spirits) of 1847 were expressly designed to communicate and illustrate the true nature of the Christian message and the demands it imposed upon the individual. In their uncompromising emphasis on the severity of these requirements, and in their manner of stigmatizing the complacency and 'double-mindedness' imputable to contemporary representatives of the faith they professed to serve, the latter books can be said to foreshadow the standpoint from which, in the culminating phase of his career, he launched a violent assault upon the established Church of Denmark. The occasion for this was the death of the Danish primate, Bishop Mynster, in 1854. Kierkegaard had increasingly come to regard Mynster as exemplifying in his own person many of the shortcomings of the church as a whole, and he was therefore incensed by hearing the dead prelate pronounced instead to have been a 'witness to the truth'. As a result he set out in the following months to denounce the covert worldliness and hypocrisy that permeated the clerical establishment, first through articles in the public press and subsequently in a broadsheet printed at his own expense. The ferocity of his attacks, appearing after a spell when he had published relatively little, caused surprise and some consternation. The controversy they stirred up was, however, abruptly interrupted by Kierkegaard's sudden collapse in October 1855 and his death a few weeks later.

2 The limits of objectivity

In an early entry in his journals, written when he was still a student, Kierkegaard gave vent to the dissatisfaction he felt at the prospect of a life purely devoted to the dispassionate pursuit of knowledge and understanding. 'What good would it do me', he then asked himself, 'if truth stood before me, cold and naked, not caring whether I recognized her or not?' Implicit in this question was an outlook which was to receive mature articulation in much of his subsequent work, being particularly prominent in his criticisms of detached speculation of the kind attributable to those he called 'systematists and objective philosophers'. To be sure, and notwithstanding what has sometimes been supposed, he had no wish to be understood as casting aspersions on the role played by impersonal or disinterested thinking in studies comprising scholarly research or the scientific investigation of nature: such an approach was quite in order when adopted within the limits set by determinate fields of enquiry. But matters were different when philosophical attempts were made to extend it in a manner that purported to transcend all particular viewpoints and interests, this conception of the philosopher's task leading to the construction of metaphysical theories which sought to comprehend every aspect of human thought and experience within the disengaged perspective of objective contemplation. Kierkegaard considered Hegel to be the foremost contemporary representative of the latter ambition, the famous system to which it had given rise being in his opinion fundamentally misconceived.

Kierkegaard's general reaction to what he found unacceptable in the Hegelian theory is in fact crucial to an understanding of his own philosophical position. On his interpretation Hegel's philosophy ultimately rested upon a central error, one that involved the illicit identification of essence and existence, thought and reality. The German writer had endeavoured to exhibit the world, and the place of humanity within the world, in terms of an evolving sequence of logical categories that rendered its overall structure fully intelligible from the impersonal standpoint of pure reason (see HEGEL, G.W.F. §§4–8). Kierkegaard disclaimed any desire to dispute the considerable ingenuity of the Hegelian metaphysic when this was regarded simply as an 'experiment in thought'. He insisted, however, that thought was not the same as reality, nor could anything real be validly deduced from it; in particular, it was altogether mistaken to suggest that changes and developments in the sphere of actual existence were assimilable to dialectical transitions between timeless concepts – it was one thing to construct a self-contained logical or formal system, quite another to entertain the project of producing an existential one. In raising such objections, moreover, he was especially concerned to stress their relevance to Hegel's treatment of specifically human existence. The Hegelian world-picture presupposed the possibility of adopting an absolute, God-like point of view from which everything was seen as contributing to an interlocking and rationally determined totality; as a result, human nature tended to be reduced to a philosophical abstraction, the individual to a representative of the species, and the significance of a particular person's life and actions to their role in forwarding an all-encompassing historical process that overshadowed and transcended them. At the same time, Kierkegaard suggested that the notion of an impersonal 'knowing subject' of the type postulated by thinkers of the Hegelian school was symptomatic of a corresponding inclination to forget that the speculative philosopher was himself an 'existing human being' whose status and situation imposed necessary limits upon his outlook and cognitive credentials. Far from his viewpoint on the world being from nowhere within it, such a philosopher inescapably belongs to it in his capacity as a finite empirical individual who 'sleeps, eats, blows his nose' and who has 'to face the future'.

Although Kierkegaard's attitude to Hegel is most extensively displayed in the polemical references that enliven the pages of his *Concluding Unscientific Postscript*, scattered allusions to the faults and weaknesses of 'the System' also appear in many of his other writings. The number and variety of the contexts in which they occur indicate that he regarded the current vogue of Hegelianism as having more than a purely academic significance, the popularity it enjoyed at once reflecting and helping to promote a contemporary ethos in which what he termed the 'illusions of objectivity' exercised a pervasive and corrupting influence. Thus he conceived the age to be one wherein people had lost a clear sense of their identity as individuals ultimately responsible for their own characters, outlooks and modes of living. Instead it was customary for them to take refuge in the anonymity provided by membership of collective movements or trends and to envisage themselves as being inevitably circumscribed by the social roles they occupied in a manner that absolved them from personal accountability for their pronouncements or actions. In Kierkegaard's view, they had largely forgotten what 'it means for you and me and him, each for himself, to be human beings', succumbing to a 'quantitative dialectic' in which a bemused preoccupation with large-scale historical events and a passive submission to the levelling influence of 'the crowd' took precedence over the vital constituents of

human life and experience – 'the inner spirit, the ethical, freedom'.

Confronted by such tendencies, Kierkegaard considered it to be a primary part of his task as a writer to challenge habits of thought that smothered spontaneous feeling and obstructed active commitment. He held that these had had a particularly deleterious effect in the religious sphere; the widespread belief that the fundamental tenets of Christianity could be rationally interpreted and objectively justified within the framework of the Hegelian system was symptomatic of a more general disposition to treat both religion and morality alike in a blandly contemplative spirit that detached them from the contexts of inward conviction and practical engagement to which they essentially belonged. With this in mind it was necessary in the first instance to 'make people aware', bringing home to them the limitations of their present condition and awakening them to the possibility of subjective self-determination and change.

3 Aestheticism and the ethical

Kierkegaard maintained that in his early writings he had aimed to arouse and enlarge the self-understanding of his readers by eschewing abstract instruction and by employing in its place an avowedly therapeutic method he referred to as 'indirect communication'. This meant delineating particular ways of life in a fashion that enabled people to grasp concretely and from within the distinct types of outlook and motivation involved, such a procedure being a characteristically literary or 'poetic' one. Not only were alternative positions imaginatively presented as if in a novel or play; the books in which this was done were attributed to different personages in the shape of pseudonymous authors or editors. He intended thereby to avoid the kind of *ex cathedra* didacticism he associated with standard philosophical texts of his time. Instead he favoured an undogmatic approach in which competing views and attitudes were 'allowed to speak for themselves', it being left to his readers to decide where they stood in relation to these and to make up their own minds about the practical conclusions to be drawn.

Either/Or was the first of Kierkegaard's works to be published under a pseudonym and was a book he later alluded to as clearly exemplifying his use of the above method. It purports to portray two radically dissimilar modes of existence, one characterized as 'aesthetic' and the other as 'ethical'. Both are presented through the medium of allegedly edited papers or letters, the first set being ascribed to an individual referred to as 'A' and the second to an older man who is said to be by profession a judge. Aestheticism as exhibited in A's loosely related assortment of papers is seen to take on a lively variety of forms and guises; among other things, it is held to find expression in the characters of legendary figures like Don Juan and Faust, and it is also illustrated by an account in diary form of a step-by-step seduction. By contrast, the position of the ethicist is set out in two somewhat prosaic letters which are addressed by the Judge to A and which include detailed critical analyses of the younger man's motives and psychological prospects.

What did Kierkegaard understand by the categories he distinguished? From the text the aesthetic life emerges as one in which the individual is essentially concerned with exploring means to his own satisfaction and where there is a consequent absence of overall continuity in the course he follows. As has been indicated, however, the picture drawn is complex and multi-faceted. While in general outline it is suggestive of a person in pursuit of transient pleasures rather than following any long-term aim, there are passages where attention is chiefly focused on the aesthetic individual's dependence upon unpredictable vicissitudes of mood or circumstance, and others again where emphasis is laid on his need to guard against the threats posed by ennui or melancholy. Not unexpectedly, it is the problematic possibilities inherent in A's lifestyle that the Judge singles out for criticism in his comprehensive survey of the aesthetic position. Whereas the aestheticist typically allows himself to be swayed by what he conceives to be the unalterable constituents of his natural disposition, the ethically orientated individual is prone to look at himself in an altogether different light. Both his motivation and behaviour are responsive to a self-image 'in likeness to which he has to form himself', his particular aptitudes and propensities being seen as subject to the control of his will and as capable of being directed to the realization of demanding projects that reflect what he truly aspires to become. It is commitment to such projects which endows the ethical life with a coherence and self-sufficiency that its aesthetic counterpart conspicuously lacks (see EXISTENTIALIST ETHICS).

Kierkegaard's treatment in *Either/Or* of the aesthetic/ethical contrast is frequently thought to echo the Kantian distinction between inclination and duty (see KANTIAN ETHICS). But although there may be discernible affinities, there are also significant differences. Thus Kant's predominantly schematic accounts of sensuous motivation are devoid of both the psychological penetration and the literary sophistication that characterize Kierkegaard's wide-ranging portrayals of the aesthetic stance. And comparable divergences are apparent in the case of the ethical. Kierkegaard's judge may be said to follow the

German philosopher in highlighting the role of the will, underlining its independence of contingent circumstances and stressing its capacity to manage the sphere of natural inclination in a way that is conformable to the ethical individual's paramount concerns. Yet while he shares Kant's belief in and respect for the latter's autonomy, he differs in not presenting moral requirements in terms of the purely formal prescriptions of practical reason. The self which it is the task of each individual to choose and develop is not an 'abstract' but a 'concrete' self; it stands in 'reciprocal relations' with its actual social and cultural surroundings, things like marriage, having a job and undertaking civic and institutional responsibilities being intrinsic to personal fulfilment in the requisite sense. It is implied, moreover, that such active participation in communal affairs, involving an unconstrained and inward adherence to standards presupposed by a shared form of life, reinforces the contrast already drawn with the unreflective or wayward 'experimentalism' typified by certain manifestations of the aesthetic outlook. Thus the Judge insists upon the conceptual exclusion from the ethical of whatever savours of the arbitrary or the merely capricious. At the same time, however, he indicates that this should not be thought of as circumscribing in any fundamental fashion the subjective freedom and independence of the individual. For although moral requirements must of necessity be treated as authoritative, they are not apprehended as deriving from a source 'foreign to the personality' but are instead experienced as springing or 'breaking forth' from the latter's essential nature.

Even so, it is arguable that the internal tensions between individualistic and socially conformist strains discernible in the Judge's representation of the ethical sphere cannot always be easily or satisfactorily resolved. Kierkegaard discussed one context in which they might be said to arise in a critical form when he went on to consider a way of life that constituted an alternative to the possibilities so far portrayed. This stage of existence, transcending the other two, was the religious.

4 The religious consciousness

Central to Kierkegaard's account of religion is his treatment of the concept of faith, a treatment that throws into relief the most distinctive features of his philosophical standpoint. There are two main areas in which these manifest themselves and in which it is the crucial inadequacies of human reason, practical as well as theoretical, that are emphasized.

The first concerns limitations in the outlook of accepted morality that make themselves felt at certain levels or junctures of experience and are held to call for what is termed a 'teleological suspension of the ethical'. The implications of this *prima facie* puzzling notion are explored in *Fear and Trembling*, an intricately wrought study in which Kierkegaard's pseudonymous author – Johannes *de silentio* – treats as his central theme the biblical story of Abraham and Isaac. Johannes portrays Abraham as being ostensibly called upon to set aside ethical concerns in deference to a higher *telos* or end that altogether transcends them. Such a situation is contrasted with the predicament of what he terms the 'tragic hero', the latter being someone who is forced to make a choice between conflicting moral requirements but who in doing so still remains within the bounds of the ethical domain. Thus although the decisions taken there may be at an agonizing cost, the fact that they can none the less be seen to conform to universally recognized norms renders them rationally acceptable to others and capable of gaining their respect. This, however, is not so in the case of Abraham, who, as a solitary 'knight of faith', responds to a divine command supposedly addressed to himself alone and having a content – the killing of his own son – that must inevitably strike ordinary thought as being both outrageous and incomprehensible. No attempt is made to soften the paradoxical character of such points. On the contrary, Kierkegaard's pseudonym sets out to underline, indeed to dramatize, the disturbing nature of the demands which religious faith can impose on the life and conduct of an individual. At the same time, he takes practising churchmen severely to task for paying lip service to a phenomenon whose awesome significance they fail to appreciate, and he also criticizes contemporary theorists of religion for construing an intrinsically transcendent category in terms drawn from social and essentially secular conceptions of ethics. This was not to suggest that from a religious point of view moral standards and principles could in general be abrogated or overruled. It did mean, on the other hand, that within that perspective they took on a radically different aspect, one where they possessed a relative rather than an absolute status and where it was the individual's own relation to God that was paramount, assuming precedence over all other considerations.

The claim that faith in the religious sense pertains to what exceeds the limits of human rationality and understanding recurs in the two subsequent writings that Kierkegaard referred to as his 'philosophical works' – *Philosophical Fragments* and *Concluding Unscientific Postscript*. Here, however, it is discussed within a wider setting and in connection with theoretical questions concerning the proper interpretation of religious assertions. Although once again

ascribed to a pseudonym, albeit a different one, both books appeared under Kierkegaard's imprint as their 'editor' and in any case may be taken to have expressed views that were basically his own. Thus in each of them it is made apparent that the author totally rejects the feasibility of trying to provide religious tenets with an objective foundation. The belief that the existence and nature of God could be conclusively established from resources supplied by pure reason might have enjoyed a long philosophical career; none the less it was demonstrably unacceptable, Kierkegaard largely echoing – though in a summary form and without attribution – some of the objections that Kant had levelled against arguments traditionally advanced by theologians and metaphysicians. Nor was he any more receptive to the suggestion that religious claims of a specifically historical character, such as those relating to the doctrines of Christianity, were susceptible to justification on straightforwardly empirical grounds; it was impossible to regard them as representing ordinary historical facts of the sort to which standard appeals to inductive inference and evidence would normally be considered appropriate. As he acknowledged, Lessing and Hamann were thinkers who in different ways had already underlined the problematic issues raised by the latter. But it was perhaps Hume's contention in his first *Enquiry* that only a 'miracle in his own person', subverting all the principles of his understanding, could bring a reasonable individual to embrace the Christian religion which most strikingly foreshadowed Kierkegaard's approach to the subject. No doubt Hume himself had intended his words to be taken in a strictly ironical sense. Even so, Kierkegaard implied that it was open to believers to look at sceptical asides of the type cited in a different light. For by exposing the vanity of attempts to encompass within its grasp matters that lay beyond the scope of reason, such remarks could be said to provide salutary reminders of what was really at stake. It was not to the spheres of impersonal judgment and dispassionate assent that the religious consciousness rightfully belonged, but on the contrary to those of individual choice and inner commitment.

5 Faith and subjectivity

Kierkegaard was certainly not alone in suggesting that writers who tried to justify religious belief on cognitive grounds were more confused about its true nature than some of their sceptically minded critics and to that extent posed a greater threat to it; indeed, Kant himself had virtually implied as much when he spoke of denying knowledge to make room for faith, as opposed to seeking to give religious convictions a theoretical foundation that could only prove illusory (see KANT, I. §4). The question arose, however, of what positive account should be given of such faith, and here Kierkegaard's position set him apart from many thinkers who shared his negative attitude towards the feasibility of providing objective demonstrations. As he made amply clear, the religion that crucially concerned him was Christianity, and far from playing down the intellectual obstacles this ostensibly presented he went out of his way to stress the particular problems it raised. Both its official representatives and its academic apologists might have entertained the hope of making it rationally acceptable to a believer, but in doing so they showed themselves to be the victims of a fundamental misapprehension. From an objective point of view, neither knowledge nor even understanding was possible here, the proper path of the Christian follower lying in the direction, not of objectivity, but of its opposite. It was only by 'becoming subjective' that the import of Christianity could be grasped and meaningfully appropriated by the individual. Faith, Kierkegaard insisted, 'inheres in subjectivity'; as such it was in essence a matter of single-minded resolve and inward dedication rather than of spectatorial or contemplative detachment, of passion rather than of reflection. That was not to say, though, that it amounted to a primitive or easy option. On the contrary, faith in the sense in question could only be achieved or realized in the course of a person's life at great cost and with the utmost difficulty (see FAITH).

To understand what lay behind this claim it is important to recognize that Kierkegaard broadly distinguished between two levels or stages of development at which religious belief manifested itself. In his account of the first of these, in which he specified the criteria that any standpoint must conform to if it was to count as a religious one, he was at pains to emphasize the element of 'objective uncertainty' surrounding assertions about the transcendent, such uncertainty deriving from the absence of rational support previously alluded to. So construed, faith essentially involved personal venture or risk, preserving it being figuratively compared to 'remaining out upon the deep, over seventy thousand fathoms of water'. But to hold fast to a conviction in the face of a lack of objective justification or grounds was not the same as giving assent to something that appeared to be intrinsically contrary to reason, an 'offence' to the understanding itself. And it was in the latter terms that Kierkegaard referred to the Christian conception of the incarnation, this being an 'absolute paradox' that required the believer to 'risk his thought' in embracing its reality. Moreover, it was in the light of such a requirement that the level of faith aspired to in

Christianity could be said to constitute 'the highest passion in the sphere of human subjectivity', exceeding other forms of religious belief in virtue of the unique nature of the demands it made upon an individual's mind and outlook.

According to Kierkegaard, the paradox of the incarnation lay in the notion that the eternal or timeless had entered the sphere of finite and temporal existence: this amounted to uniting contradictories in a fashion that meant a 'breach with all thinking'. Such a feature precluded treating it as if it could be vouchsafed by ordinary historical enquiry, and he set aside the scholarly pursuit of biblical research and criticism as altogether irrelevant to what was here at issue; quite apart from the specifically 'approximative' status he assigned to history as a branch of knowledge, the content of the particular 'hypothesis' under consideration defied logic in a way that contravened the principles governing any kind of accredited cognitive discipline. Furthermore, he regarded its paradoxical character as having another crucial consequence, namely, that there was no basis for the common assumption that the contemporary witnesses of what was recorded in the Gospels were in a better position to authenticate the reality of the incarnation than subsequent generations who had only the testimony of others to rely on. To suppose that in the present case the evidence of direct observation was superior to testimony was to fail to see that neither could ever function as more than an 'occasion' for belief of the sort of question. With both, a volitional leap of faith was necessary, one that involved a 'qualitative transition' from the realm of rational thought into that of the intellectually inaccessible or 'absurd'.

Kierkegaard's stress on the gap separating faith from reason, which it could need divine assistance to surmount, was reflected in the controversial account he offered of religious truth; this likewise received a subjective interpretation. Thus in a well-known passage in the *Postscript* he contrasted two distinct ways of conceiving of truth, one treating it as a matter of a belief's corresponding to what it purported to be about and the other as essentially pertaining to the particular manner or spirit in which a belief was held. And it was to the second of these conceptions that he ostensibly referred when he declared that 'subjectivity is the truth', genuineness of feeling and depth of inner conviction being the decisive criterion from a religious point of view. Admittedly he has sometimes been criticized here for a tendency to shift from construing religious truth along the above lines to doing so in terms of the objective alternative, with the questionable implication that sheer intensity of subjective acceptance was sufficient to authenticate the independent reality of what was believed. But however that may be, it is arguable that in this context – as is often the case elsewhere – his prime concerns were conceptual and phenomenological in character, rather than epistemic or justificatory. Kierkegaard's central aim was to assign Christianity to its proper sphere, freeing it from what he considered to be traditional misconceptions as well as from the falsifying metaphysical theories to which there had more recently been attempts to assimilate it. If that meant confronting what he himself called 'a crucifixion of the understanding', the only appropriate response from the standpoint in question lay in a passionate commitment to the necessarily paradoxical and mysterious content of the Christian religion, together with a complementary resolve to emulate in practice the paradigmatic life of its founder (see EXISTENTIALIST THEOLOGY §§1, 2).

6 Psychological themes and influence

Kierkegaard's preoccupation with the category of subjectivity that ran like a continuous thread through his theoretical writings was integrally linked to his conception of human beings as individual and self-determining participants in the 'existential process'. The view that freedom and the possibility of change constituted fundamental conditions of human life and fulfilment was delineated in his so-called 'psychological works', *The Concept of Anxiety* and *The Sickness Unto Death*. In both books the structure of human personality is portrayed in developmental and volitional terms; individuals exist in the mode, not of being, but of becoming, and what they become is something for which they themselves are ultimately responsible. In this connection certain pervasive attitudes and emotions can be seen to possess a special significance, Kierkegaard giving priority of place to a form of anxiety or dread (*Angst*) which differed from sentiments like fear in lacking any determinate object and in being directed instead to 'something that is nothing'. Such a state of mind might manifest itself in a variety of ways, but he made it clear that his fundamental concern was with its relation to the consciousness of freedom. Thus he referred to the particular kind of dizziness, or vertiginous ambivalence between attraction and repulsion, that was liable to afflict us when, in certain circumstances, the realization dawned that there was nothing objective that compelled us to opt for one course of action rather than another; in the last analysis what we did was up to ourselves alone, freedom being said to 'look down into its own possibility' as though into a yawning abyss or void. Kierkegaard believed that the psychological phenom-

enon so identified had momentous consequences, not least for its bearing on the religious alternatives of sin and salvation. On the one hand, the story of Adam represented a mythical illustration of how the awakened consciousness of freedom could arouse an anxiety whose occurrence in this case was the precursor of sin. On the other hand, however, such an emotion might also arise when there was a possibility of making a qualitative leap, not into sin and alienation from God, but towards the opposite of this, namely, faith and the promise offered by Christianity. But here Kierkegaard reiterates the point that a presentiment of the difficulties and sacrifices entailed made the latter a course which there were strong temptations to resist; it followed that people were only too prone to conceal from themselves their potentialities as free beings, such self-induced obscurity serving as a convenient screen for inaction and a failure to change. Self-deception of this sort in fact formed a component of many of the varieties of spiritual despair which Kierkegaard picked out for analysis, as well as underpinning his diagnosis of some of the broader types of malaise he detected in the social and cultural climate of his time.

In his insistence upon the ultimacy of human freedom and his correlative attention to the devices and strategies whereby people may seek to protect themselves from a recognition of some of its disturbing implications, Kierkegaard anticipated themes that were taken up, albeit much later and often in an explicitly secular setting, by a number of leading twentieth-century writers (see EXISTENTIALISM). Subjectivity and the primacy of the individual, the 'burden' of freedom, the contrast between authentic and inauthentic modes of existence – these and associated topics became familiar through the works of existentialist philosophers such as Jean-Paul SARTRE and Martin HEIDEGGER as well as figuring in the wider field of imaginative literature. Nor were those the only areas in which his ideas eventually made an impact. In the sphere of ethics his emphasis on radical choice indirectly contributed to the growth of non-cognitivist theories of value, while in religion his conception of faith had a profound influence on the development of modern Protestant theology, notwithstanding understandable reservations about some of his more extreme claims regarding its paradoxical character.

See also: HEGELIANISM §4; RELIGION AND EPISTEMOLOGY; RELIGION AND SCIENCE

List of works

Kierkegaard, S.A. (1962–4) *Samlede Vaerker*, ed. A.B.

Drachmann, J.L. Heiberg and H.O. Lange, Copenhagen: Gyldendalske Boghandel, 20 vols. (The definitive edition of Kierkegaard's complete works.)

—— (1841) *Om Begrebet Ironi*, trans. H.V. Hong and E.H. Hong, *The Concept of Irony*, Princeton, NJ: Princeton University Press, 1989. (Kierkegaard's university dissertation. Though principally concerned with Socratic irony, he also discusses the concept in relation to writers associated with German romanticism.)

—— (1843a) *Enten-Eller*, trans. H.V. Hong and E.H. Hong, *Either/Or*, Princeton, NJ: Princeton University Press, 1987, 2 vols. (Presents contrasting lifeviews, one aesthetic and the other ethical, in the form of papers and letters attributed to two imaginary characters.)

—— (1843b) *Frygt og Baeven* and *Gjentagelsen*, trans. H.V. Hong and E.H. Hong, *Fear and Trembling* and *Repetition*, Princeton, NJ: Princeton University Press, 1983. (Two pseudonymous writings: the first an extended meditation on the implications of the biblical story of Abraham and Isaac; the second a portrayal in fictional form of psychological, ethical and religious issues raised by a problematic love-affair.)

—— (1844) *Philosophiske Smuler*, trans. H.V. Hong and E.H. Hong, *Philosophical Fragments*, Princeton, NJ: Princeton University Press, 1985. (A concise and complex study in which idealist and rationalist approaches to truth are contrasted with ones fundamental to Christian belief.)

—— (1844) *Begrebet Angest*, trans. R. Thomte and A.B. Anderson, *The Concept of Anxiety*, Princeton, NJ: Princeton University Press, 1980. (An analysis of a pervasive attitude of mind (*Angst*) chiefly evoked by an awareness of human freedom and of possibilities involving radical choice.)

—— (1845) *Stadier paa Livets Vej*, trans. H.V. Hong and E.H. Hong, *Stages on Life's Way*, Princeton, NJ: Princeton University Press, 1988. (The stages in the title are identified as aesthetic, ethical and religious, Kierkegaard's treatment of the last of these drawing indirectly but graphically on his own life and experience.)

—— (1846) *Afsluttende uvidenskabelig Efterskrift*, trans. D.F. Swenson, L.M. Swenson and W. Lowrie, *Concluding Unscientific Postscript*, Princeton, NJ: Princeton University Press, 1941. (The book most central to an understanding of Kierkegaard's philosophical position, both in its critique of objective or speculative approaches to religion and in its correlative stress on the irreducibly subjective character of authentic religious faith.)

—— (1849) *Sygdommen til Døden*, trans. H.V. Hong and E.H. Hong, *The Sickness Unto Death*, Prince-

ton, NJ: Princeton University Press, 1980. (Contains intricate accounts of various forms of spiritual malaise seen as reflecting specific failures in individual self-development.)

—— (1850) *Indøvelse i Christendom*, trans. W. Lowrie, *Training in Christianity*, Princeton, NJ: Princeton University Press, 1944. (Kierkegaard's final pseudonymous work. Strongly critical of contemporary interpretations of Christianity, it anticipates the uncompromising virulence of his open attacks on the clerical establishment in the last year of his life.)

—— (1967–78) *Journals and Papers*, trans. H.V. Hong and E.H. Hong, Bloomington, IN: Indiana University Press, 7 vols. (A comprehensive and scholarly edition in English of assorted writings unpublished in Kierkegaard's lifetime.)

References and further reading

Arbaugh, G.B. and G.H. (1967) *Kierkegaard's Authorship*, Rock Island, IL: Augustana College Library. (Contains summaries and concise discussions of the main publications.)

Collins, J. (1983) *The Mind of Kierkegaard*, Princeton, NJ: Princeton University Press. (A clear and informative account of Kierkegaard's thought.)

Edwards, P. (1973) 'Kierkegaard and the "Truth" of Christianity', in P. Edwards and A. Pap (eds) *A Modern Introduction to Philosophy*, New York: The Free Press, Macmillan. (Criticizes a central aspect of Kierkegaard's account of religious belief.)

Gardiner, P. (1988) *Kierkegaard*, Oxford: Oxford University Press. (Introduction to Kierkegaard's philosophical writings and their historical background.)

Green, R.M. (1992) *Kierkegaard and Kant: The Hidden Debt*, New York: State University of New York Press. (Investigates the extent of Kantian influence on Kierkegaard's treatment of ethical and religious themes.)

Hannay, A. (1982) *Kierkegaard*, London: Routledge & Kegan Paul. (Comprehensive study of the structure and contemporary implications of Kierkegaard's thought.)

Law, D.R. (1993) *Kierkegaard as Negative Theologian*, Oxford: Clarendon Press. (Discusses Kierkegaard's place in the tradition of thinkers who have stressed the unknowability of God.)

Mackey, L. (1971) *Kierkegaard: A Kind of Poet*, Philadelphia, PA: University of Pennsylvania Press. (A subtle appraisal stressing the literary aspects of Kierkegaard's work.)

Malantschuk, G. (1971) *Kierkegaard's Thought*, ed. and trans. H.V. and E.H. Hong, Princeton, NJ: Princeton University Press. (Wide-ranging exploration of the presuppositions and interrelations of Kierkegaard's leading ideas.)

Michalson, G.E. (1985) *Lessing's 'Ugly Ditch': A Study of Theology and History*, University Park, PA: Pennsylvania State University Press. (Includes lengthy discussion of Kierkegaard's relation to Lessing.)

Rudd, A. (1993) *Kierkegaard and the Limits of the Ethical*, Oxford: Oxford University Press. (Relates Kierkegaard's contributions to problems in moral and religious philosophy to modern analytical work in these fields.)

Thompson, J. (1974) *Kierkegaard*, London: Gollancz. (A penetrating critical biography.)

Thulstrup, N. (1980) *Kierkegaard's Relation to Hegel*, trans. G.L. Stengren, Princeton, NJ: Princeton University Press. (Provides detailed account of the historical connections.)

Weston, M. (1994) *Kierkegaard and Modern Continental Philosophy*, London and New York: Routledge. (Relates Kierkegaard's critique of traditional forms of philosophy to the work of such later thinkers as Nietzsche, Heidegger and Derrida.)

PATRICK GARDINER

KILVINGTON, RICHARD (d. 1361)

Richard Kilvington, an English philosopher and theologian, was born near the beginning of the fourteenth century and died in 1361. His academic career in Oxford (1320–38) was followed by diplomatic service and an ecclesiastical career that culminated in his serving as dean of St Paul's Cathedral, London. His known works (besides a couple of sermons) are commentaries or 'questions' (philosophical inquiries) regarding three works by Aristotle, a commentary on the Sentences *of Peter Lombard (a standard academic requirement for theologians in the later Middle Ages) and the* Sophismata. *Only his* Sophismata *has been edited, translated and studied. An ordered collection of philosophical puzzles designed to raise and settle issues in natural philosophy and epistemology, it is one of the earliest and subtlest contributions to the literature associated with the Oxford Calculators.*

Judging from his *Sophismata*, Kilvington's other works are very likely to be ingenious, with some importance for the history of philosophy and of science. However, because they survive only in medieval manuscripts and have not been studied

since the Middle Ages, our present appraisal of him as a philosopher is confined to that one work.

Kilvington's *Sophismata* was written in Oxford in the early 1320s. Like other medieval works with that title, it grew out of disputations *de sophismatibus*, which had an established place in the fourteenth-century curricula of the universities of Oxford and Paris. A sophisma is a sentence puzzling simply as it stands or on the basis of some hypothesis, designed to bring some abstract issue into sharper focus – the medieval ancestor of 'The present king of France is bald', or 'The morning star is the evening star'. Medieval university disputations based on sophismata were designed to advance a student's training in logic even when the sophisma sentences presented issues in other subject matter. Thus although the first forty-four of Kilvington's forty-eight sophismata are especially concerned with problems regarding change, motive power, velocity or strength, his analysis of the puzzles is always conceptual rather than mathematical; and his solutions, though they often seem to be preparing the ground for a mathematical approach, are always found by applications of logic rather than by calculations. His interest is in *the logic of* change, velocity, knowing and doubting, or any other of the topics investigated in this treatise.

In dealing with his topics chosen from natural philosophy and epistemology, Kilvington employs almost all the devices of fourteenth-century logic, occasionally criticizing their standard use. In each of his sophismata he generates an apparent paradox by presenting what he takes to be at least plausible arguments for both sides of a contradiction, after which he undertakes to resolve the paradox. Opposition and resolution are familiar features of the standard scholastic method, in which the opposition is patently substantive, presenting immediately understandable disagreement over recognizable issues. In Kilvington's use of the method, however, the substantive issues are almost always masked by the (frequently fantastic) examples around which he develops them; as in Sophisma 16, which focuses on the Aristotelian analysis of a sphere's traversal of a proportionally divided plane in order to ask whether the dominant continuist account of space and time violates the principle of non-contradiction. Kilvington clearly intends to make quite general theoretical points about important issues via this oblique approach, although he often leaves it to the reader to recognize that those points have been made.

Kilvington seems to have arrived in Oxford soon after WILLIAM OF OCKHAM left in 1317. Ockham's teachings had generated strong opposition in the university even before its chancellor, John Lutterell, had charged him with heresy, and it seems very unlikely that Kilvington could have been unaffected by Ockham's views and the official reaction to them. In the *Sophismata* there is no explicit reference to any philosopher besides ARISTOTLE, but the orthodox Aristotelian positions Kilvington takes there regarding physical and epistemological problems suggest that he may be counted among those who rejected Ockhamism.

Kilvington was personally associated with Thomas BRADWARDINE and Walter BURLEY. Bradwardine and Kilvington (and perhaps Burley in some of his later writings) constituted the first academic generation of the Oxford Calculators (see OXFORD CALCULATORS). William HEYTESBURY, the most prominent member of the second generation, seems to have been one of Kilvington's students and to have written his own *Regulae solvendi sophismata* (Rules for Solving Sophsimata) with Kilvington's *Sophismata* uppermost in his mind. Toward the end of his life Kilvington, with his friend Richard FitzRalph, played a prominent role in the anti-mendicant controversy.

See also: ARISTOTELIANISM, MEDIEVAL; LANGUAGE, MEDIEVAL THEORIES OF; LOGIC, MEDIEVAL

List of works

Of Kilvington's works, only the *Sophismata* has been edited; the other works exist in medieval manuscripts, identified in the introduction of the translation and commentary on the edition. Like most other unedited medieval treatises, these last four works are variously titled in the manuscripts.

Richard Kilvington (1321–6) *Sophismata*, ed. N. Kretzmann and B.E. Kretzmann, *The Sophismata of Richard Kilvington*, Oxford: Oxford University Press for the British Academy, 1990. (The critical edition of the Latin text, with an index. A translation is also available in N. Kretzmann and B.E. Kretzmann, *The Sophismata of Richard Kilvington: Introduction, Translation and Commentary*, Cambridge: Cambridge University Press, 1990.)

—— (1324–6) Questions on Aristotle's *On Generation and Corruption*. (Questions on Aristotle; exists in manuscript form only.)

—— (1324–6) Commentary on Aristotle's *Physics*. (Questions on Aristotle; exists in manuscript form only.)

—— (1324–6) Questions on Aristotle's *Nicomachean Ethics*. (Questions on Aristotle; exists in manuscript form only.)

—— (*c.*1333) Commentary on Peter Lombard's *Sentences*. (Sometimes titled *Quaestiones theologi-*

cae, this work is confined to just a few of Lombard's topics.)

References and further reading

d'Ors, A. (1991) '"Tu scis regem sedere" (Kilvington, S47 [48])', *Anuario Filosofico* 24: 49–74. (A careful examination of Kilvington's Sophisma 47 in the context of the doctrine of obligations, with attention to recent literature.)

Kretzmann, N. and Kretzmann, B.E. (1990) *The Sophismata of Richard Kilvington: Introduction, Translation, and Commentary*, Cambridge: Cambridge University Press. (Historical introduction, complete translation and philosophical commentary, with extensive bibliography and indexes.)

Stump, E. (1981) 'Roger Swineshead's Theory of Obligations', *Medioevo* 7: 135–74. (Shows the importance of Kilvington's work for understanding later developments in obligational disputation.)

—— (1982) 'Obligations: From the Beginning to the Early Fourteenth Century', in N. Kretzmann, A. Kenny and J. Pinborg (eds) *The Cambridge History of Later Medieval Philosophy*, Cambridge: Cambridge University Press, 315–41. (See especially 329–32, 'Richard Kilvington'. This chapter puts Kilvington's work on obligational disputation into its historical context.)

NORMAN KRETZMANN

KILWARDBY, ROBERT (d. 1279)

Robert Kilwardby is one of the most remarkable thinkers of the thirteenth century. He is the champion of the traditional approach to philosophy and theology, which developed the body of doctrines worked out by Augustine. His activity is set in the very crucial period of middle scholasticism, when the diffusion of Aristotle's philosophical system and its utilization for Christian theology caused a sharp conflict between the followers of the Patristic tradition, such as Kilwardby or the members of the Franciscan school, and the new theologians, such as Thomas Aquinas, who tried to express the contents of divine revelation within the Aristotelian paradigm. Kilwardby used all of his intellectual resources and ecclesiastical authority in fighting against this new trend and in defending Augustinianism, whose main theses (for example, a plurality of substantial forms in composite substances, the presence of seminal reasons in matter, universal hylomorphism, individuation by matter and form, a conceptual distinction between the soul and its faculties, and the necessity of divine illumination in order to grasp the eternal truths) he supports in his writings.

1 Life and works
2 Grammar and logic
3 Metaphysics
4 Ethics

1 Life and works

The English Dominican Robert Kilwardby was a master of arts in the University of Paris during the years 1237–45, and later a student and master of theology at Blackfriars, Oxford. Prior Provincial of the English Dominicans in 1261, he became Archbishop of Canterbury in 1272 and a cardinal in 1278. He died in the papal service at Viterbo on 10 September 1279.

No listing of Kilwardby's writings and the surviving manuscripts is wholly satisfactory, since in many instances works have been attributed to him on insufficient grounds and their attribution has not yet been the subject of critical study. It is known that while he was teaching in the Faculty of Arts in Paris, Kilwardby wrote a set of *Sophismata grammaticalia* and *Sophismata logicalia*, and commentaries on *Priscianus minor* (Books 17 and 18 of Priscian's *Institutiones grammaticae*; the commentary on *Priscianus maior* is spurious), *De accentibus* and *Barbarismus Donati*, covering syntax, prosody, solecism and figurative speech (see LANGUAGE, MEDIEVAL THEORIES OF). In addition, he commented on seven works of ARISTOTLE: *Categories, Perihermeneias, Prior* and *Posterior Analytics, Topics, Sophistical Refutations* and the first three books of the *Nicomachean Ethics* (the only ones available in Latin around 1240; Kilwardby is perhaps the earliest Latin commentator whose name can be firmly attached to an exposition of that text). His impressive series of commentaries concludes with works on Porphyry's *Isagōgē*, Boethius' *Liber divisionum* and the anonymous *Liber sex principiorum* (see PORPHYRY; BOETHIUS, A.M.S.).

At Oxford around 1250, Kilwardby wrote the *De ortu scientiarum* (On the Origin of Sciences), a classification of sciences, which is intended to be a general introduction to philosophy. His questions on the *Sentences* of Peter LOMBARD, probably connected with teaching at Blackfriars, was written perhaps around 1256. Around 1256–61 Kilwardby produced the treatises *De natura relationis* (On Relation), *De tempore* (On Time) and *De spiritu fantastico* (On Imagination).

To these works must be added two *epistulae*, the *Responsio de 43 quaestionibus Iohannis Vercellensis* (Response to the 43 Questions of John of Vercelli) and the *Epistula ad Petrum de Confleto* (Letter to Peter Conflans). In these, Kilwardby states his position on many important issues concerning physics and ontology and clarifies his attitude towards Aristotle. The *Responsio* is Kilwardby's reply to the questions asked by John of Vercelli, Master of the Dominicans, of himself, Thomas AQUINAS and ALBERT THE GREAT on a number of physical and metaphysical topics that were then widely discussed. The letter to Peter Conflans is connected with the Oxford condemnation of 18 March 1277, which was begun at the instigation of Kilwardby himself. Many of the thirty condemned theses were peculiar to Thomistic thought, such as those concerning the merely potential nature of matter and the unicity of the substantial form. Peter Conflans, Archbishop of Corinth, had written a letter to Kilwardby in defence of the Thomistic theories. Kilwardby's response enables us to measure the distance and appreciate the conflict between the Augustinianism in Kilwardby's system and Aquinas's Aristotelianism, the two main philosophical trends of middle scholasticism (see ARISTOTELIANISM, MEDIEVAL; AUGUSTINIANISM).

2 Grammar and logic

Kilwardby's logico-linguistic theories are among the most important pre-modistic medieval accomplishments. According to him the disciplines of the *trivium* (grammar, logic and rhetoric) fall outside the Aristotelian division of speculative philosophy into physics, mathematics and metaphysics. They are concerned with signs rather than realities, and they constitute the most convenient introduction to philosophy, teaching the skills of correct speech, writing and reasoning. Grammar comes first, since it deals with the understanding and expression of ideas; then logic, which provides all sciences with a method and is corrective of the reasoning of other disciplines; and finally rhetoric, which serves ethics but is not subordinate to it. Rhetoric is a part of civic studies, because the rhetorician's aim is to devise reasoning appropriate for settling questions arising in civil disputes.

In his commentary on the *Categories*, Kilwardby states that the main difference between grammar and logic consists in the different points of view from which they look at language. The grammarian starts with the utterance and goes on to the thought; the logician starts with the thought and ends with the utterance. So the intentions or concepts that characterize grammar are applied to signs, while those characteristic of logic are applied to the essences of things. As a consequence, logic is concerned not only with speech and reasoning, but also with reality itself. However, the logician's treatment of reality is not that of the metaphysician, who studies the primary classes of being as parts of being. The logician, on the other hand, studies them in regard to their function as predicates or subjects in sentences. Consequently, logic is intended to be the theory of mental discourse concerning being and is therefore ontologically grounded in a correspondence between the structural connections in thought and the framework of reality (see LOGIC, MEDIEVAL).

In the commentary on the *Perihermeneias*, Kilwardby specifies his theory of meaning. Like every other physical entity, a word (*dictio*) is composed of matter (the utterance, *vox*) and form. What gives a word its form is the act of signifying, which makes it a *significant* utterance, with its meanings as accidental qualifications. Meaning is impressed on the word as a whole. It depends on the mind, which can abstract the common features of individuals and thus produce a conceptual likeness of what is thought about. It is just this conceptual likeness which is conveyed to another person through utterance, while the sign itself is what affects the hearer's perception and evokes thought (see LANGUAGE, MEDIEVAL THEORIES OF).

3   Metaphysics

Kilwardby's metaphysical doctrine is very different from those that many other authors of his time drew from Aristotle's system. He is faithful to Augustine's thought, even if some understanding of the Aristotelian metaphysics of being is reflected in his theory when, for example, he distinguishes between *ens* (being) and *esse* (existing) and considers *esse* as the act of *ens* (see EXISTENCE). Furthermore, he maintains that from a metaphysical point of view the term 'being' is analogically predicated of everything. Therefore, he can regard the categories as classes of being, excluding a narrowly linguistic study of them.

Regarding universals and individuals, Kilwardby adopts a moderate realism in which the Platonist view is preserved for the divine ideas (exemplars of universals in the created order) and individuals are conceived of as their instantiations. This reconciliation of Plato and Aristotle includes a continuing existence of the likeness of the universal in the divine mind even when all the instantiating individuals have perished. However, in addition to this primary existence in the divine mind, universals have a substantial reality in their individuals. Kilwardby argues that if universals were not real (*in re*), our knowledge of the world would be empty, since knowledge is of the universal (see REALISM AND ANTIREALISM; UNIVERSALS).

Kilwardby denies that the universal *in re* is numerically one in all its individuals. In his commentary on the *Sentences*, he proposes a modal unity based on an agreement in essence of all individuals of one type. (Thus, utilizing Boethian terminology, he maintains that the universal is that by which something is (*quo est*), rather than that which is (*quod est*)). This agreement in essence is considered either according to its concreteness – the existence it has in the many – or according to its essence in abstraction, as a construct of our mind. Taken in the first way, the universal form, despite its essential unity, has an existence that differs according to the different matter of the numerically distinct individuals, like the many images of one thing in the fragments of a splintered mirror. Taken in the second way, the form most properly has the status of a universal, that is, something common shared as a whole by a multiplicity of objects.

Since real universals rather than singulars properly correspond to the ideas in the divine mind, how can individuals be obtained from such forms? In his commentary on Porphyry's *Isagōgē*, Kilwardby answers that it is the material aspect of substance that is the cause of individuation, so that the individual is constituted by its substantial components – form and matter – rather than by its properties, as Porphyry had thought. In his later questions on the *Sentences*, Kilwardby claims that the intrinsic causes of individuation are the form – which plays the active role in designating the matter as that of this or that individual and consequently designating itself as the form of the individual – and the matter, which plays the passive role of being designated as the individual's matter by receiving the form. The language of 'designation' (*signatio*), which had not been used in Kilwardby's earlier treatment of this topic, stems from Avicenna (see IBN SINA); the influence of Bonaventure's *Sentences* commentary has also been suggested (see BONAVENTURE).

Between the *Isagōgē* commentary and the questions on the *Sentences*, Kilwardby's thought underwent a development in which more stress is placed on the role of form in individuation, and in which the aspects under which matter and form are to be considered as belonging to a particular individual are specified more exactly. Even in Kilwardby's later treatment of individuation, however, there is still no preoccupation with quantity and dimensions, which already feature in Aquinas' *Sentences* commentary.

Nor is this the only important difference between Kilwardby's ontology and that of Aquinas. It is clear even from an early work such as the *Isagōgē* commentary that he holds that there is some kind of materiality in angelic intelligences, thus adopting the doctrine of universal hylomorphism that he defends in his *epistulae*.

Another important difference lies in the notion of matter. According to AQUINAS, who follows Aristotle, prime matter is pure potentiality; Kilwardby, following AUGUSTINE, maintains on the contrary that there are active powers in matter. Matter 'strives' for form, such a powerful appetite is an action, and there is no action without a form which performs it. Therefore active powers, or seminal reasons, must be present in matter as a kind of germinal existence of the fully actualized creatures, containing the principles of their subsequent development.

As a further consequence of the rule that there is no action without a form which performs it, there must be a plurality of substantial forms in a composite substance. Thus Kilwardby denies the unity of the substantial form and admits that even the human soul is not simple but is compounded of essentially different parts. On the other hand, he recognizes only a conceptual distinction between the rational soul and its faculties (see SOUL, NATURE AND IMMORTALITY OF THE).

4 Ethics

Kilwardby's moral system is based on an accurate definition of the proper domain of ethics – human goods which belong to this life and are subject to rational inquiry and civic studies – and is aimed at a reconciliation of Aristotle and Augustine.

The achievement of the highest earthly human good constitutes the first step towards reaching blessedness. There are not two ends of human existence in keeping with the created/uncreated distinction, but a single highest uncreated good in God, to which human happiness is subordinated. He defines the happiness which is the end of civic studies as an act of the rational practical soul consisting in perfect studious activities or the best and most pleasurable perfections of the soul. This is the only kind of happiness Aristotle knew. Whether the soul or the whole human being is happy after death is not settled by Aristotle. In the *De ortu scientiarum*, Kilwardby draws a distinction between the happiness which most philosophers call *felicitas* and the one which Catholics call *beatitudo*. He draws a corresponding distinction between Aristotle's saying that there is happiness in completely virtuous activity and Augustine's claim that there is no possibility of being fully happy in this life without the beatific vision. According to Kilwardby, Aristotle is speaking of habitual (moral) and not theological virtues, and the philosophers who follow him give a diminished but not false account of virtue, since habitual virtue is a large part of virtue in this life, contributing further to the disposition to a more perfect life.

List of works

Robert Kilwardby (*c.*1237–45) *In Donati Artem maiorem III* (Commentary on Donatus), ed. L. Schmücker, Brixen/Bressanone: Typographia A. Weger Fund, 1984. (Commentary on the grammatical work of Donatus.)

—— (*c.*1237–45) *Notule libri Prisciani de accentibus* (Commentary on *De accentibus*), ed. P.O. Lewry, 'Thirteenth-Century Teaching on Speech and Accentuation: Robert Kilwardby's Commentary on *De accentibus* of Pseudo-Priscian', *Mediaeval Studies* 50, 1988: 96–185. (Commentary on Priscian.)

—— (*c.* 1250) *De ortu scientiarum* (On the Origin of Sciences), ed. A.G. Judy, Auctores Britannici Medii Aevi 4, London: British Academy, 1976. (Kilwardby on natural philosophy.)

—— (*c.*1256) *Quaestiones in librum primum Sententiarum* (Questions on the First Book of the *Sentences*), ed. J. Schneider, Veröffentlichungen der Kommission für die Herausgabe ungedruckter Texte aus der mittelalterlichen Geisteswelt, Band 13, Munich: Verlag der Bayerischen Akademie der Wissenschlaften, 1986. (Questions on the *Sentences* of Peter Lombard.)

—— (*c.*1256) *Quaestiones in librum secundum Sententiarum* (Questions on the Second Book of the *Sentences*), ed. G. Leibold, Veröffentlichungen der Kommission für die Herausgabe ungedruckter Texte aus der mittelalterlichen Geisteswelt, Band 16, Munich: Verlag der Bayerischen Akademie der Wissenschlaften, 1992. (Questions on the *Sentences* of Peter Lombard.)

—— (*c.*1256) *Quaestiones in librum tertium Sententiarum* (Questions on the Third Book of the *Sentences*), Part I, *Christologie* (Christology), ed. E. Gössmann, Veröffentlichungen der Kommission für die Herausgabe ungedruckter Texte aus der mittelalterlichen Geisteswelt, Band 10, Munich: Verlag der Bayerischen Akademie der Wissenschlaften, 1982; Part II, *Tugendlehre* (Virtue), ed. G. Leibold, Veröffentlichungen der Kommission für die Herausgabe ungedruckter Texte aus der mittelalterlichen Geisteswelt, Band 12, Munich: Verlag der Bayerischen Akademie der Wissenschlaften, 1985. (Questions on the *Sentences* of Peter Lombard.)

—— (*c.*1256) *Quaestiones in librum quartum Sententiarum* (Questions on the Fourth Book of the Sentences), ed. R. Schenk, (Veröffentlichungen der Kommission für die Herausgabe ungedruckter Texte aus der mittelalterlichen Geisteswelt, Band

17, Munich: Verlag der Bayerischen Akademie der Wissenschaften, 1993. (Questions on the *Sentences* of Peter Lombard.)

—— (*c*.1256–61) *De natura relationis* (On Relation), ed. L. Schmücker, Lenggries: L. Schmücker. (One of Kilwardby's later works.)

—— (*c*.1256–61) *De tempore* (On Time), ed. P.O. Lewry, *On Time and Imagination: De tempore, De spiritu fantastico*, Auctores Britannici Medii Aevi 9, Oxford: Oxford University Press for the British Academy, 1987. (Later work, on the nature of time.)

—— (*c*.1256–61) *De spiritu fantastico* (On Imagination), ed. P.O. Lewry, *On Time and Imagination: De tempore, De spiritu fantastico*, Auctores Britannici Medii Aevi 9, Oxford: Oxford University Press for the British Academy, 1987. (Later work, on the imagination.)

—— (1271) *Responsio de 43 quaestionibus Iohannis Vercellensis* (Responses to the 43 Questions of John of Vercelli), ed. H.-F. Dondaine, 'Le *De 43 questionibus* de Robert Kilwardby', *Archivum Fratrum Praedicatorum* 47, 1977: 5–50. (Reply to questions asked by John of Vercelli on a number of physical and metaphysical topics.)

—— (1277–8) *Epistula ad Petrum de Confleto* (Letter to Peter Conflans), ed. A. Birkenmajer, 'Der Brief Robert Kilwardbys an Peter von Konflans und die Streitschrift des Aegidius von Lessines', Beiträge zur Geschichte der Philosophie 20.5, *Vermischte Untersuchungen zur Geschichte der mittelalterlichen Philosophie*, Münster: Aschendorff, 1922, 36–69; an edition can also be found in F. Ehrle, 'Der Augustinismus und der Aristotelismus in der Scholastik gegen Ende des 13. Jahrhunderts', *Archiv für Literatur und Kirchengeschichte des Mittelalters* 5, 1889: 614–32. (Response to a letter from Conflans defending Thomistic theories.)

References and further reading

Braakhuis, H.A.G. (1985) 'Kilwardby versus Bacon? The Contribution to the Discussion on Univocal Signification of Beings and Non-Beings found in a Sophism attributed to Robert Kilwardby', in E.P. Bos (ed.) *Medieval Semantics and Metaphysics*, Artistarium supplementa 2, Nijmegen: Ingenium, 111–42. (An introduction to Kilwardby's theory of signification.)

Chenu, M.D. (1930) 'Les réponses de s. Thomas et de Kilwardby à la consultation de Jean de Verceil (1271)', in *Mélanges Mandonnet*, Paris: Vrin, vol. I, 191–222. (A comparison between Kilwardby's answers to John of Vercelli and those of Aquinas, with *excerpta* from Kilwardby's *epistula*.)

Gál, G. (1953) 'Robert Kilwardby's Questions on the *Metaphysics* and *Physics* of Aristotle', *Franciscan Studies* XIII: 7–28. (On the attribution to Kilwardby of a set of metaphysical and physical questions extant in ms. 509 of Gonville and Caius College, Cambridge.)

Lewry, P.O. (1975) 'The Commentary on *Priscianus Maior* Ascribed to Robert Kilwardby: The Problem of the Authorship', *Cahiers de l'Institut du Moyenage Grec et Latin* XV: 12*–17*. (Demonstrates the spuriousness of the commentary on books 1–16 of Priscian's Institutiones grammaticae.)

—— (1978) 'Robert Kilwardby's Writings on the *Logica Vetus* Studied with Regard to Their Teaching and Method', D.Phil. thesis, Oxford University. (The standard exegesis of Kilwardby's contribution to the logic of terms and proposition, with a careful discussion of the authorship of his commentary on the *Logica vetus*.)

—— (1981a) 'Robert Kilwardby on Meaning: a Parisian Course on the *Logica Vetus*', in J.P. Beckmann *et al.* (eds) *Sprache und Erkenntnis im Mittelalter*, Miscellanea mediaevalia 13.1, Berlin: de Gruyter, 376–84. (A survey of Kilwardby's theory of meaning.)

—— (1981b) 'The Oxford Condemnation of 1277 in Grammar and Logic', in H.A.G. Braakhuis, C.H. Kneepkens and L.M. de Rijk (eds) *English Logic and Semantics From the End of the Twelfth Century to the Time of Ockham and Burleigh*, Artistarium supplementa 1, Nijmegen: Ingenium, 235–78. (An account of the grammatical and logical implications of the Oxford condemnation of 1277.)

—— (1983) 'Robert Kilwardby on Imagination: the Reconciliation of Aristotle and Augustine', *Medioevo* IX: 1–42. (A clear account of Kilwardby's theories of soul and knowledge.)

—— (1986) 'Robert Kilwardby's Commentary on the *Ethica nova* and *Vetus*', in C. Wenin (ed.) *L'homme et son univers au moyen-âge*, Philosophes médiévaux 27, Louvain-la-Neuve: Editions de l'Institut Superieur de Philosophie, 799–807. (A summary of Kilwardby's ethical system, with a discussion of the authorship of the *Nicomachean Ethics* commentary.)

ALESSANDRO D. CONTI

AL-KINDI, ABU YUSUF YA'QUB IBN ISHAQ (d. *c.*866–73)

Practically unknown in the Western world, al-Kindi has an honoured place in the Islamic world as the 'philosopher of the Arabs'. Today he might be viewed as a bridge between Greek philosophers and Islamic philosophy. Part of the brilliant ninth-century 'Abbasid court at Baghdad, composed of literati of all types, he served as tutor for the caliph's son. He gained insights into the thought of Greek philosophers, especially Aristotle, through the translation movement; although he did not make translations himself, he corrected them and used them advantageously in his own thought.

Al-Kindi is notable for his work on philosophical terminology and for developing a vocabulary for philosophical thought in Arabic, although his ideas were superseded by Ibn Sina in the eleventh century. The debate about the allowability of philosophy in terms of orthodox Islam also began with al-Kindi, a battle that is usually considered to have been won for religion by al-Ghazali. Like other innovators, his ideas may no longer appear revolutionary, but in his own day, to push for the supremacy of reason and for the importance of a 'foreign science' – philosophy – as opposed to an 'Arab science' – grammar, Qur'anic studies – was quite astonishing. When the Khalif al-Mutawwakil came to power and sought to restore traditionalism, al-Kindi suffered a reversal of fortunes.

1   **Logic and translation**
2   **Metaphysics**
3   **Ethics**

1   Logic and translation

Abu Yusuf Ya'qub ibn Ishaq al-Kindi was an ethnic Arab (died in Baghdad between AH 252–60/AD 866–73), with an illustrious lineage going back to such near-mythic Arabian families as Qays. Al-Kindi was known as 'the philosopher of the Arabs' in contrast to the later Islamic philosophers who, though Muslim, were not Arabs and often learned Arabic as a second language. The early bio-bibliographers gave his ancestry and a long list of works, many of which are no longer extant, but his personal life remains unknown. Although he is remembered for introducing philosophy to the 'Abbasid court, his skills covered many fields including medicine, mathematics, music, astrology and optics. He also served as tutor to the son of the Khalif al-Mu'tasim. Al-Qifti, one of the medieval Islamic bio-bibliographers, pointedly as-serted that al-Kindi was skilled in the arts of the Greeks, the Persians and the Hindus.

Al-Kindi used early, Arabic-language translations of Greek philosophy, which enabled him to add part of the Hellenistic tradition to his programme. The founding of the *bayt al-hikma* (house of wisdom), for the large-scale translation of documents from Greek, in the early ninth century meant both that the 'foreign sciences' were available wholesale to Arabophone scholars and that there was serious interest in the knowledge they contained. Al-Kindi was occasionally credited (in the title inscription) with correcting the translation, but it is generally accepted that he did not read Greek himself. The pursuit of 'foreign sciences' was also politically acceptable at this juncture, which ceased to be the case later. A study of his terminology shows that al-Kindi was aware of particular terms used in Hellenistic philosophy, and of which Arabic word best expressed the same idea.

Al-Kindi may be thought of as a stage-setter for philosophy in the Islamic world, laying out terms *qua* terms and redirecting the metaphysical concerns suggested by the *mutakallimun* (theologians) from the realm of religion to that of philosophy. His lack of interest in religious argument can be seen in the topics on which he wrote. These topics were ontological, but he generally refrained from eschatological discussions on topics such as the resurrection, the last day and the last judgment. Even in his ethical treatise he dealt with the disciplined life in which a person might find interior serenity in their current life, rather than an emphasis on reward in the hereafter. Scholars have sometimes thought of al-Kindi as a Mu'tazili sympathizer, but this has not been proved; he appears rather to coexist with the worldview of orthodox Islam.

Al-Kindi's work on definition is *Fi hudud al-ashya' wa-rusumiha* (On the Definitions of Things and their Descriptions). Through the terms he chose to define – finitude, creation, the first cause – we can see where the constructs of Islamic philosophy diverged from their Greek predecessors. In the eleventh century the *Kitab al-hudud* (Book of Definitions) of IBN SINA replaced al-Kindi's work; this was considerably more advanced, both in its definitions and in its organization of the world into a concise ontological schema.

2   Metaphysics

Al-Kindi's best known treatise is the metaphysical study, *Fi al-falsafa al-ula* (On First Philosophy). Aristotelian influence can be seen in certain elements, such as the four causes. However he is Aristotelian only up to a point. The point of divergence is reached over the question of the origin of the world. Aristotle teaches the eternity of the world; Al-Kindi propounds creation *ex nihilo*. The later philosophers, such as AL-FARABI, are usually considered to understand Aristotle more accurately; they had the advantage of better translations and a greater number of works. In *Fi al-falsafa al-ula*, al-Kindi described the first philosophy, which is also the most noble and highest philosophy, as the knowledge of the first truth, including the cause of every truth (the first cause). The first cause is prior in time because it is the cause of time. By the study of philosophy, people will learn the knowledge of things in reality, and through this the knowledge of the divinity of God and his unity. They will also learn human virtue. Throughout many of his treatises, al-Kindi emphasizes the importance of the intellect (*'aql*) and contrasts it with matter.

He also discusses the One Truth, which is another name for God, and states that it does not have any attributes, predicates or characteristics. This view is consonant with the Mu'tazili declaration of the unity of God as being strictly without attributes, and consequently al-Kindi has sometimes been deemed to be a Mu'tazili by scholars.

Other aspects of his position include emphasis on the absolute unity of God, his power – particularly as creator – and creation *ex nihilo*. The Eternal, that is God, is not due to another; he has no cause and has neither genus nor species. There is no 'before' for the Eternal. The Eternal is unchanging, immutable and imperishable. In human terms, death is the soul's taking leave of the body, which it employed during life. For al-Kindi, the intellect continues. Perhaps the soul is primarily the locus of the intellect. He reiterated in his ethical treatise the idea that humans must choose the world of the intellect over the material world (see §3).

Al-Kindi differs from the Hellenistic philosophical tradition primarily in espousing the belief that the world was created *ex nihilo*. In Aristotelian metaphysics the Prime Mover set the world in motion, but in the Hellenistic tradition, time and motion are intrinsically linked. Matter set in motion is eternally existing, since it exists before motion (and therefore before time). In this system, time is defined as the extension of the series of movements. Thus time begins with movement. In al-Kindi's system, matter, time and movement are all finite, with a beginning and a cessation at some future point. Other subjects that concern al-Kindi can be seen from his titles, including *Fi wahdaniya Allah wa tunahiy jirm al-'alam* (On the Unity of God and the Limitation of the Body of the World), and *Fi kammiya kutub Aristutalis wa ma yahtaj ilahi fi tahsil al-falsafa* (The Quantity of the Books of Aristotle and What is Required for the Acquisition of Philosophy).

In his philosophical writings, al-Kindi does not so much direct arguments to the concerns of religion as avoid them altogether, instead describing a parallel universe of philosophy. He consistently tries to show that the pursuit of philosophy is compatible with orthodox Islam. The *mutakallimun* had previously speculated on questions about matter, atoms and substance, which he also considers. Another reason for the claim that he was a Mu'tazili was his persecution by the Khalif al-Mutawwakil, who instigated a reactionary policy against the Mu'tazili and a return to traditionalism (see ASH'ARIYYA AND MU'TAZILA). Al-Kindi was caught in the general net of the Khalif's anti-intellectualism; the Kindian emphasis is always on rationalism, an attitude which the orthodox establishment of a revealed religion is bound to find inimical.

3 Ethics

Al-Kindi's ethics and practical philosophy are most discussed in a treatise *Fi al-hila li-daf' al-ahzan* (On the Art of Averting Sorrows), of questionable authenticity. Fehmi Jadaane (1968) argues that al-Kindi was strongly influenced by the Stoic tradition, particularly the thought of EPICTETUS, which was known throughout the Islamic world at the time through contact with Syriac Christian scholars, if not through specific texts. Epictetus emphasized the importance of freedom from the world and human beings' status as agents, who through their ultimate independence were responsible for their own happiness and independent of others. His last logical step, however, was that suicide was permissible if life was no longer worth living. This last idea is not repeated in al-Kindi.

Like the writings of the Stoics, al-Kindi's treatise, which is of the 'consolation of philosophy' type, exhorts readers to concentrate on the life of the mind and the soul, not of the body (see STOICISM). Al-Kindi says that human beings are what they truly are in the soul, not in the body. Again, on the futility of looking for eternities in the visible world, he says that whoever wishes for what is not in nature wishes for what does not exist. The reader is admonished that unhappiness follows such an attitude. In this treatise, al-Kindi advocates maintaining an internal balance through the mechanism of the individual's interior autonomy. If worldly property becomes a concern and is then lost or damaged, this will upset an individual's mental equilibrium. Stoic ideas about the ephemeral nature of earthly goods are recalled; al-Kindi warns against attachment to favourite worldly goods, using an example from Plutarch's *On Moral Virtue*. In that story, Nero receives a gift of a gorgeous, elaborate crystal tent, with which he is obviously smitten. A philosopher who is present in the crowd advises him that he has already been impoverished through his keen attachment to this object. If Nero were to lose it, the philosopher says, he will suffer because it is irreplaceable. Later when the rare object is lost at sea during transport, Nero is devastated. Scholars have argued that this treatise appears to be a mélange of wisdom literature from various Hellenistic sources, with no ideas that sound Kindian. IBN MISKAWAYH refers to the ideas of al-Kindi in his treatise on ethics, *Tahdib al-akhlaq*.

Some ethical remarks are contained in other treatises. The virtues discussed in the treatise on definitions are wisdom, courage and temperance. A reflection of each virtue which exists in the soul is seen in the body. Virtue exists as a focal point between two extremes. Bravery, for example, is both mental and physical; it is midway between rashness and timidity.

Some reverberations of al-Kindi's thought also continued in the twelfth-century Christian Latin West, as certain of his treatises were translated into Latin by the Scholastics, notably *De intellectu* (On the Intellect). In the thirteenth century GILES OF ROME criticized 'Alkindus' with other philosophers in his work *Errores philosophorum* (Errors of the Philosophers). Only a portion of al-Kindi's work survives, so judgment of him must necessarily be imperfect. However, al-Kindi's influence endured longer in the Western Islamic tradition than in the Eastern, as reflected in the writings of the twelfth-century mystic IBN AL-'ARABI. With al-Kindi, who pursued reason against the background of revealed religion, begins the Islamic philosophical tradition which continues with the works of IBN SINA and IBN RUSHD.

See also: ARISTOTELIANISM IN ISLAMIC PHILOSOPHY; ETHICS IN ISLAMIC PHILOSOPHY; ISLAM, CONCEPT OF PHILOSOPHY IN; LOGIC IN ISLAMIC PHILOSOPHY

List of works

al-Kindi (before 873) *Rasa'il al-Kindi al-falsafiya* (Philosophical Treatises of al-Kindi), ed. M.A. Abu Ridah, 2 vols in 1, Cairo, 1953. (The standard collection of al-Kindi's treatises, with introductory notes in Arabic.

—— (before 873) *Fi al-falsafa al-ula* (On First Philosophy), ed. and trans. A.L. Ivry, *Al-Kindi's Metaphysics: A translation of Ya'qub ibn Ishaq al-Kindi's Treatise 'On First Philosophy'*, Albany, NY:

State University of New York Press, 1974. (A clear account of al-Kindi's metaphysics with English translation.)

—— (before 873) *Risalah fi al-hilah li-daf' al-ahzan* (On the Art of Averting Sorrows), ed. and trans. H. Ritter and R. Walzer, 'Uno scritto morale inedito di al-Kindi', *Memorie della Reale Accademia nazionale dei Lincei*, Rome, Series VI, 8 (1), 1938, 47–62. (Text and Italian translation.)

—— (before 873) *Fi hudud al-ashya' wa-rusumiha* (On the Definitions of Things and their Descriptions), ed. M.A. Abu Ridah in *Rasa'il al-Kindi al-falsafiya*, Cairo, 1953; trans. D. Gimaret in *Cinq épîtres*, Paris: Centre National de la Recherche Scientifique, 1976. (Al-Kindi's treatise on definitions.)

—— (before 873) *Fi wahdaniya allah wa tunahiy jirm al-'alam* (On the Unity of God and the Limitation of the Body of the World), ed. M.A. Abu Ridah in *Rasa'il al-Kindi al-falsafiya*, Cairo, 1953. (Al-Kindi on the nature of God.)

—— (before 873) *Fi kammiya kutub Aristutalis wa ma yahtaj ilahi fi tahsil al-falsafa* (The Quantity of the Books of Aristotle and What is Required for the Acquisition of Philosophy), ed. M.A. Abu Ridah in *Rasa'il al-Kindi al-falsafiya*, Cairo, 1953. (Writings on Aristotle.)

References and further reading

Gimaret, D. (1976) *Cinq Épîtres* (Five Treatises), Paris: Centre National de la Recherche Scientifique. (An excellent French translation with commentary of five treatises by al-Kindi. There are unfortunately very few English translations of al-Kindi's works.)

* Jadaane, F. (1968) *L'Influence du stoïcisme sur la pensée musulmane* (The Influence of Stoicism on Muslim Thought), Beirut: Dar el-Machreq. (An interesting argument for Stoic, rather than merely Aristotelian and Neoplatonic influence, on the Islamic philosophers.)

Jolivet, J. (1971) *L'Intellect selon Kindi*, Leiden: Brill. (A classic work: extensive commentary and French translation of al-Kindi's treatise on the intellect.)

Klein-Franke, F. (1996) 'Al-Kindi', in S.H. Nasr and O. Leaman (eds) *History of Islamic Philosophy*, London: Routledge, ch. 11, 165–77. (Account of the role of al-Kindi as the first Muslim philosopher, and in particular the links between his philosophy and contemporary theology and understanding of Greek thought.)

Moosa, M. (1967) 'Al-Kindi's Role in the Transmission of Greek Knowledge to the Arabs', *Journal of the Pakistan Historical Society* 15 (1): 3–18. (Good discussion of 'The Quantity of the Books of Aristotle'.)

Rosenthal, F. (1940) Review article of 'Uno scritto morale', *Orientalia* IX: 182–91. (An interesting review of the Ritter–Walzer treatise, still important despite its age.)

Stern, S.M. (1959) 'Notes on al-Kindi's Treatise on Definitions', *Journal of the Royal Asiatic Society* parts 1 and 2: 32–43. (Considered a classic.)

KIKI KENNEDY-DAY

KIRCHHEIMER, OTTO

see FRANKFURT SCHOOL

KIREEVSKY, I. *see* HEGELIANISM, RUSSIAN; SLAVOPHILISM

KNOWABILITY PARADOX

see PARADOXES, EPISTEMIC

KNOWLEDGE AND BELIEF

see BELIEF AND KNOWLEDGE

KNOWLEDGE AND JUSTIFICATION, COHERENCE THEORY OF

Coherence theories of justification represent one main alternative to foundationalist theories of justification. If, as has usually been thought, possessing epistemic justification is one necessary condition (along with truth and perhaps others) for a belief to constitute knowledge, then a coherence theory of justification would also provide the basis for a coherence theory of knowledge. While some proponents of coherence theories have restricted the scope of the theory to empirical justification, others have applied it to all varieties of epistemic justification. (There are also coherence theories of meaning and of truth, as well as coherence theories of ethical or moral justification.)

The initial contrast between coherence theories and foundationalist theories arises in the context of the epistemic regress problem. It is obvious that the justification of some beliefs derives from their inferential relations to other, putatively justified beliefs, and that the justification of these other beliefs may depend on inferential relations to still further beliefs, and so on, so that a potential regress of epistemic justification looms, with scepticism as the threatened outcome. The foundationalist solution to this problem is that one arrives sooner or later at basic or foundational beliefs: beliefs that are epistemically justified, but whose justification does not derive from inferential relations to any further beliefs and so brings the regress to an end. The defining tenet of a coherence theory of justification is the rejection of this foundationalist solution, the coherentist insisting that any belief (of the kinds to which the theory is applied) depends for its justification on inferential relations to other beliefs and eventually to the overall system of beliefs held by the believer in question. According to the coherentist, the justification of this system of beliefs is logically prior to that of its component beliefs and derives ultimately from the coherence of the system, where coherence is a matter of how tightly unified or interconnected the system is by virtue of inferential connections (including explanatory connections) between its members.

Contrary to what this might seem to suggest, coherence theories do not deny that sensory observation or perception plays an important role in justification. What they deny is that this role should be construed in a foundationalist way, insisting instead that the justification of observational beliefs ultimately derives also from considerations of coherence. Specific coherence theories may also add other requirements for justification, thereby departing from a pure coherentism, while still avoiding foundationalism.

While the idea of a coherence theory has often played the role of a dialectical foil, developed theories of this kind are relatively rare and are often in serious disagreement among themselves. In this way, coherentism is much less a unified view with standard, generally accepted features, than is foundationalism.

1   History
2   The regress problem and non-linear justification
3   The concept of coherence
4   Coherence and observation
5   The standard objections
6   The problem of access

1   History

In contrast to foundationalism, the coherence theory of justification is a relatively recent innovation in the history of philosophy. Although it is possible, albeit with some strain, to construe Spinoza and Kant as advocating versions of coherentism, the first relatively clear-cut coherentist positions are those of the late nineteenth and early twentieth century absolute idealists, especially F.H. Bradley (1914) and Bernard

Bosanquet (1920) (see BRADLEY, F.H.; BOSANQUET, B.). Unfortunately, however, the views of these philosophers are marked by a pervasive failure to distinguish epistemological and metaphysical issues, making it hard to separate their coherence theories of justification from their distinct, though related, advocacy of coherence theories of the nature of truth. (A more recent version of essentially the same position, in which this distinction is clearly drawn, is found in the work of Brand Blanshard (1939).)

Coherentism was also advocated in the 1930s by some of the logical positivists, mainly Otto Neurath (1933) and Carl Hempel (1934), in response to the foundationalist views of Moritz Schlick (1934) (see NEURATH, O.; HEMPEL, C.G.; SCHLICK, F.A.M.). NEURATH identifies coherence with mere logical consistency; he also, while retaining something like a justificatory appeal to observation, in effect identifies observational beliefs solely by reference to their content. He thus has no apparent response to what is perhaps the most central and obvious objection to coherence theories: that there will always be indefinitely many different coherent systems between which a coherence theory will provide no basis for a reasoned choice (see further below). Hempel avoids this problem to some extent by simply identifying observational beliefs as those beliefs with the right sort of content that are accepted by 'the scientists of our culture circle', but is able to offer no real rationale for such an identification. He also, like the idealists, fails to distinguish in any clear way between a coherence theory of justification and a coherentist account of the nature of truth.

More recent coherentist positions, in contrast, generally repudiate the coherence theory of truth entirely and are more explicitly and narrowly epistemological in their character and motivation. The main arguments offered in their favour almost always derive from perceived objections to foundationalism, perhaps the central one being the charge that the foundationalist can account for the status of the allegedly basic or foundational beliefs as genuinely justified (in the sense of there being some reason or basis for thinking them to be true) only by appealing to justificatory premises of some sort and so destroying the status of such beliefs as foundational (see FOUNDATIONALISM). Thus coherentists insist that there is no way to appeal for justification to anything outside of one's system of beliefs because any such supposed source of justification would have to be apprehended by the person in question in a belief or belief-like state before it could play any justificatory role, and then it would be the belief rather than the external item that was the immediate source of justification.

As this suggests, coherentist positions are virtually always internalist rather than externalist in character, in that they insist that the basis for epistemic justification must be cognitively accessible to the believer in question; while an externalist version of coherentism is theoretically possible, it would have little philosophical point, since a foundationalist view would be vastly more straightforward if externalism were otherwise acceptable (see INTERNALISM AND EXTERNALISM IN EPISTEMOLOGY).

These recent coherentist views differ from each other in a wide variety of ways, and often seem to have little in common beyond their rejection of foundationalism and their invocation in some fashion of the idea of coherence (and indeed there is often room for doubt in a particular case about how thoroughgoing the former of these two aspects really is). Coherentism is one ingredient, though never developed in a fully systematic way, in the comprehensive and difficult philosophical system of Wilfrid Sellars (1963) (see SELLARS, W.S.). The epistemological position of W.V. Quine is also frequently described as coherentist in character, though other features of Quine's position, especially his claim that epistemology should be naturalized (reduced to psychology), make it difficult to decide whether his view is genuinely a version of coherentism, as opposed to a qualified version of foundationalism (see NATURALIZED EPISTEMOLOGY). More overtly coherentist positions have been advocated by Gilbert Harman (1973) (influenced especially by Quine), Nicholas Rescher (1973, 1974, 1977), Keith Lehrer (1974, 1990), and Laurence BonJour (1985) (influenced especially by Sellars).

As the foregoing suggests, coherence theories first arise as dialectical alternatives to foundationalism, rather than as views that are claimed to be initially plausible on their own. Their defence and elaboration must confront a number of standard problems and objections, with which any such view must seemingly deal in some fashion, and it is around these that the present entry is organized.

2 The regress problem and non-linear justification

The first standard problem arises from the epistemic regress problem itself. If foundationalism is repudiated (and if a genuinely infinite regress of justification is also rejected as psychologically impossible and in any case tantamount to scepticism), then the only remaining possibility for the outcome of the initial regress of epistemic justification seems to be a circle in which the chains of justification eventually loop back upon themselves. Incautious advocates of coherentism have sometimes seemed to endorse the idea that such a result is acceptable if only the circles are 'large enough'. But the obvious objection to circular chains of justification, to which the size of the circle seems irrelevant, is that they involve circular reasoning and hence have no genuine justificatory force. This is essentially the reason that foundationalists give for rejecting the coherentist alternative and taking the regress problem to constitute a decisive argument for foundationalism.

Perhaps the most standard coherentist response to this issue, stemming originally from Bosanquet (1920), is to reject the idea, implicit in most presentations of the regress problem, that relations of justification must involve a linear, asymmetrical order of dependence among the beliefs in question. They insist instead that justification, when properly understood, is ultimately holistic and non-linear in character, with all of the beliefs in the system standing in relations of mutual support, but none being epistemically prior to the others. In this way, it is alleged, any true circularity is avoided. Such a view amounts to making the system itself the primary unit of justification, with its component beliefs being justified only derivatively, by virtue of their membership in an appropriate sort of system. And the property of the system, in virtue of which it is justified, is of course specified as coherence.

3 The concept of coherence

But what exactly is coherence? A second obvious problem for a coherence theory is to explicate and clarify this central concept. Intuitively, coherence is a matter of how the beliefs in a system of beliefs fit together or dovetail with each other, so as to constitute one unified, organized, and tightly structured whole. And it is clear that this fitting together depends on a wide variety of logical, inferential and explanatory relations among the components of the system. But spelling out the details of this idea, particularly in a way that would allow unproblematic assessments of comparative coherence, turns out to be extremely difficult, in part at least because of its obvious dependence on more specific and still unsettled topics, such as induction, confirmation, probability and explanation.

The strongest and most demanding conception of coherence, advocated by the idealists, specifies a coherent system of beliefs as one in which each member entails and is entailed by all of the others. It seems clear, however, that this strong conception is both unrealizable by any actual system of beliefs imaginable and also of dubious cognitive value, since it would seem to make all of the beliefs but one redundant and dispensable. (These problems may be mitigated somewhat, though certainly not eliminated, by remembering that the idealists have a quite broad conception of entailment, one in which, for example, relations of nomological necessity are regarded as a kind of entailment).

At the opposite extreme, it seems equally mistaken to follow Schlick (1934) and some others in identifying coherence with mere logical consistency, since the beliefs of a logically consistent system might be entirely unrelated to each other, thus yielding no real degree of mutual support and no apparent reason for thinking that any of them are true. Somewhat more surprisingly, it also seems to be a mistake to make complete logical consistency even an absolutely *necessary* condition for any degree of coherence, as many coherentists have done. In light of such things as the preface paradox and general human fallibility, this would probably mean that few if any actual systems of belief are coherent to any degree at all, a result that seems unacceptably paradoxical (see PARADOXES, EPISTEMIC).

If there is a tenable conception of coherence along these general lines, it must seemingly fall somewhere between the two extremes just discussed. Coherence will be a matter of degree, with logical consistency being a highly relevant but not absolute criterion. Coherence will also require a high degree of inferential interconnectedness in the system, involving relations of necessitation, both strictly logical and otherwise, together with probabilistic connections of various kinds. An important aspect of this is what might be called probabilistic consistency, that is, the absence of relations between beliefs in the system in virtue of which some are highly unlikely to be true in relation to others. A further important ingredient of coherence that is much emphasized in recent discussions is the presence of explanatory relations among the components of the system, thus reducing the degree to which the beliefs of the system portray unexplained anomalies. (If 'inference to the best explanation' is accepted as one species of inference, then such explanatory relations can be viewed as a kind of inferential relation – see INFERENCE TO THE BEST EXPLANATION.) Indeed, some positions such as that of Harman (1973), and perhaps also Sellars (1963), go so far as to virtually identify coherence with the presence of such explanatory relations.

The foregoing is an approximate account of the historically standard conception of coherence. While some proponents of coherentism have employed essentially this conception, others have in effect devised more idiosyncratic conceptions of coherence, conceptions whose connection to the historical concept is often quite tenuous. In particular, Rescher (1973, 1977) in fact employs both the standard conception of coherence, for certain purposes, and also a quite different concept that involves forming maximally consistent subsets of initially conflicting 'data' or 'truth-candidates', and then choosing among these subsets in a variety of ways that involve no appeal to standard coherence. And Lehrer (1974, 1990) has offered two subtly different versions of a general view that defines coherence in relation to the believer's own subjective conception of probability or relative likelihood of truth; for a belief to cohere with the person's system of beliefs is roughly for it to be judged to be more probable or more reasonable than any relevant competitor.

The precise nature of coherence remains a largely unsolved problem. It is important to see, however, that difficulties in this area cannot yield anything like a decisive argument against coherence theories and in favour of their foundationalist rivals. This is so because the concept of coherence, or something so similar to it as to be capable of playing essentially the same role, is also an indispensable ingredient in virtually all foundationalist theories: coherence must seemingly be invoked to account for the relation between the basic or foundational beliefs and other non-foundational or 'superstructure' beliefs, in virtue of which the latter are justified in relation to the former. For this reason, giving an adequate account of coherence should not be regarded as exclusively or even primarily the responsibility of coherentists, despite the central role that the concept plays in their position.

4 Coherence and observation

As mentioned above, few if any coherentists have wished to deny the seemingly obvious fact that sensory observation or perception plays a crucial role in justification (although they have not always been fully explicit on this point). It is thus incumbent on a coherence theory to explain how such observation can be construed in a non-foundationalist way. The central idea is that a belief that is produced by the senses, rather than being arrived at inferentially, might still depend for its justification on coherence with the background system of beliefs. But it is crucial here that the justification in question should still depend also in some way on the fact that the belief was a result of perception, since justification that depended only on the coherence of the belief's propositional content with the rest of the cognitive system would make the observational status of the belief irrelevant.

One way to develop this idea is to focus on the fact that observational or perceptual beliefs are *cognitively spontaneous*; they simply strike the observer in an involuntary, coercive, non-inferential way, rather than

as a product of any sort of inference or other discursive process, whether explicit or implicit. That a belief has this status, however, says nothing so far, according to the coherentist, about whether or how it is justified. Indeed, there is no reason to think that all cognitively spontaneous beliefs *are* justified, or even necessarily that most of them are, since the category would include hunches and irrational spontaneous convictions, as well as beliefs resulting from perception. But suppose that, as seems to be the case with most ordinary systems of belief, the system includes a belief to the effect that specific kinds of cognitively spontaneous beliefs (identified by their general subject matter, by their apparent mode of sensory production as reflected in the content of the belief, and by concomitant factors of various kinds) are, under specified (or perhaps 'normal') conditions, highly likely to be true. It then becomes possible to give a justifying reason for such a belief that appeals to its status as cognitively spontaneous and putatively observational, but still does so in a way that depends on the coherence with the background system of beliefs of the claim that a belief of this kind and produced in this way is true. Such a belief would be arrived at non-inferentially, but still justified by appeal to inference relations and coherence. (This view of observation is most explicit in BonJour (1985), but something like it seems implicit in Blanshard's (1939) talk of 'beliefs about the technique of acquiring beliefs', in Sellars's (1963) talk of 'language-entry transitions', in Quine's talk of the 'observational periphery' of the 'web of belief', in Rescher's (1973, 1974, 1977) idea of 'data', and in Lehrer's (1974, 1990) discussion of a person's trustworthiness in acquiring certain kinds of information).

The foregoing provides at best only the beginning of a coherentist account of observation, leaving various problems to be solved that can only be touched on here. First, the other beliefs needed to give a justifying reason for a particular observational belief must themselves be justified in some fashion, without relapsing at this point into foundationalism. These beliefs will include at least (1) beliefs about the conditions; (2) the general belief about the reliability of the kind of cognitively spontaneous belief in question; and (3) beliefs about the occurrence of that particular belief, including the belief that it was indeed cognitively spontaneous. The justification for (1) will presumably have to include other observational beliefs, themselves justified in the same general fashion, so that any case of justified observation will normally or perhaps always involve a set of mutually supporting observations. The justification for (2) will appeal inductively to other cases of correct observation, as judged from within the system, as well as to more theoretical reasons for thinking that beliefs of the kind in question are generally produced in a reliable way. The justification for (3) will appeal to introspective beliefs, themselves constituting a species of observation, and ultimately to the believer's comprehensive grasp of their overall system of beliefs – a grasp whose status poses one of the main problems to be considered below.

Second, it is not enough for the justification of an observational belief that a reason of the foregoing sort should merely be present in a person's system of beliefs, since such an individual might completely fail to notice that this was so, and might hold the belief on some other basis or for no reason at all. Thus even though the observational belief is not arrived at by inference, the availability of the inferential justification in question, even if never explicitly rehearsed, must be the reason why the believer continues to accept the belief and to appeal to it for further purposes. A full account of coherentist observation would have to spell out exactly what this requirement amounts to and how it can be satisfied.

Third, the bare possibility of coherentist observation seems insufficient to accommodate the role that observation plays in our cognitive lives. Given the convictions that observation is not only possible but pervasive and that an appeal to observational evidence, whether direct or indirect, is essential for the justification of at least contingent beliefs about the world, an intuitively adequate coherence theory must somehow *require* and not just allow that a substantial observational element should be present in any justified system that includes such contingent beliefs. A view that insisted on such a requirement would thereby depart from a pure coherence theory, but might still avoid foundationalism if the coherentist account of observation is otherwise successful. (Such a requirement is relevant to several of the objections examined below.)

5 The standard objections

In considering objections to coherence theories, we may begin with the three that are historically most standard and familiar. The first of these is what is commonly referred to as 'the isolation problem' or 'the input objection': an account of justification that appeals entirely to coherence within a system of beliefs seems to have the consequence that the justificatory status of the beliefs in the system will not depend in any way on the relation of the system to the world that it purports to describe, or on any sort of information derived from that world. This would seem to mean in turn that the truth of the component beliefs, if they happened to be true, could only be an

accident, and thus that there is no reason to think that they are true and so no epistemic justification. The coherentist account of observation sketched above, if it can be successfully fleshed out, provides the beginning of an answer to this objection by showing how observational beliefs that are apparently generated by the world might none the less be given a coherentist justification. In this way, a coherent system that involves a putatively observational component will at least seem from the inside to have input from the world and thus not to be isolated. Whether this seeming is likely to be veridical will depend, however, on the more general issue, discussed below, of whether and why coherentist justification should be regarded as conducive to finding the truth.

The second familiar objection, already briefly alluded to earlier, is what may be called the alternative coherent systems objection: even given a relatively strong account of coherence, there will still be indefinitely many different possible systems of beliefs, each of which is as internally coherent as the others, and so all of which will be equally justified on a coherentist view – surely an absurd result. The response to this objection also depends crucially on the idea of observation. If, as suggested earlier, it will be a requirement for justification in an adequate coherence theory that there be a substantial observational component (that is, a substantial proportion of cognitively spontaneous beliefs that the system itself certifies as likely to be true and hence worthy of being accepted), then such alternative systems can no longer be freely invented and it is no longer obvious why they should be thought to exist. Only a system that is actually accepted and employed in cognitive practice can contain cognitively spontaneous beliefs and thus satisfy the requirement for observation. There is no way to guarantee that the acceptance of such beliefs will not lead quickly to incoherence in an arbitrarily devised system, even if it is initially coherent. (As this suggests, it is coherence over a period of time and not just at a moment that is ultimately the basis for justification in all coherence theories that have been seriously advocated.)

The third of the standard objections is in effect a challenge to the coherentist to give a reason for thinking that adopting beliefs on the basis of coherentist justification is likely to lead to believing the truth. Different coherentists give very different responses to this crucial question, each problematic in its own way. These can only be briefly sketched here: (1) The absolute idealists in effect solve the problem by adopting a coherence theory of truth as well, thus reducing the gap between coherentist justification and truth (though only Blanshard is very explicit about this strategy). On such a view, truth is essentially identified with long-run justification, making it relatively easy to argue that seeking justified beliefs is likely to lead eventually to finding true ones – but at the significant cost of adopting an extremely implausible conception of truth. (2) Rescher (1973, 1974, 1977) attempts to give a pragmatic argument to the effect that the practical success which results from the employment of the coherent system makes it likely that the beliefs of the system are at least approximately true (in the sense of corresponding to independent reality). Unfortunately, however, the need for justification for the claims of practical success, which must presumably also be coherentist in character, threatens the project with vicious circularity. (3) BonJour (1985) attempts to give an a priori 'metajustificatory argument', relying on a rationalist and foundationalist conception of a priori knowledge, for the conclusion that a system of beliefs that remains coherent over the relatively long run, while receiving apparent observational input, is likely to be approximately true (again in the correspondence sense of truth). The main reason offered is that only approximate truth could explain continued coherence in the face of new observations. In addition to defending the general account of a priori justification presupposed, such an approach must also claim that sceptical explanations of one's beliefs (for example their being produced by a Cartesian demon), are a priori less likely than the preferred explanation of correspondence with reality, a claim that many have found highly implausible. (4) Lehrer's approach is to construct alternative conceptions of justification that involve the hypothetical replacement of erroneous beliefs in a person's system of beliefs with their corrected alternatives, and then require that the person's initially justified beliefs remain justified after such replacements in order for such beliefs to constitute knowledge. The main difficulty here is that such an approach seems to concede that 'personal justification' – the sort of justification which exists before the hypothetical replacements – is not in itself conducive to finding the truth, even though such personal justification is the only sort that the believer is in general ever actually aware of.

6   The problem of access

In addition to the foregoing objections, there are a number of further problems with which an adequate coherence theory would have to deal. Perhaps the most urgent of these is that of whether coherentist justification is accessible to the believer in the way that it must be if an internalist position is to result. Assuming for the moment, as is the case with all the positions discussed here, that coherentist justification

is taken to require coherence with the believer's entire system of beliefs, then there are three aspects to this problem: (1) whether the believer has adequate access to their system of beliefs; (2) whether the believer has an adequate grasp of the concept of coherence; and (3) whether the believer is able to apply the concept of coherence to their system of beliefs in a way that will yield a definite assessment. All these aspects pose serious problems, and (3) in particular is anything but trivial, even given satisfactory solutions to (1) and (2). But (1) is the most difficult and will accordingly be the main focus here.

A believer's access to their own system of beliefs is in fact seriously problematic in two quite different ways. First, there is the problem of the epistemological status of the result of such access if it were achieved, which we may think of as a reflective meta-belief describing the entire contents of the system. Such a meta-belief would be clearly contingent and empirical and hence one that on any coherence theory of the sort under consideration here ought to be itself justified by appeal to coherence. But since any coherentist justification that is to be accessible to the believer must appeal to such a meta-belief in order to characterize the system of beliefs with which the belief to be justified must cohere, a coherentist justification of that meta-belief itself appears to be totally and irrevocably circular (and no appeal to non-linear justification will help here, since what is being explained is how the very sort of non-linear justification advocated by the coherentist is possible).

The most explicit discussion of this issue is given by BonJour (1985), who responds by invoking what he calls 'the Doxastic Presumption'. The idea is that coherentist justification must *presume* that the believer's grasp of their overall system of beliefs is at least approximately correct (small corrections being possible by appeal to coherence). This has the consequence that the resulting justification is contingent upon the presumed correctness of this grasp, and hence that there is no possible answer on the part of a coherence theory to the specific variety of scepticism that questions whether this presumption is indeed correct. This has seemed to many to be a very drastic result, but it is unclear what the alternative might be, so long as foundationalism is eschewed.

Even if the foregoing issue were resolved in a satisfactory way, there is still the second aspect of the present problem: the quite sticky issue of whether ordinary believers ever in fact possess or could possess anything like the reflective grasp of the entire contents of their systems of beliefs that a coherence theory seems to require. On this issue, it seems likely that a coherence theory will have to concede that ordinary cases of justification are at best only an approximation, and perhaps a fairly distant one, to the ideal justification that a coherence theory portrays.

One further problem is worth a brief mention. If, as is almost always the case, a coherence theory appeals to coherence over the relatively long run, then the issue arises of how the memory beliefs upon which any access to the fact of continued coherence must seemingly rely, are themselves to be justified. Many philosophers have offered coherence theories of the justification of memory beliefs, but such a view is again threatened with vicious circularity if the only reason for thinking that coherentist justification is conductive to truth – and so that the memory beliefs in particular are true – relies on coherence over time, and so on those very memory beliefs themselves.

See also: JUSTIFICATION, EPISTEMIC; KNOWLEDGE, CONCEPT OF; TRUTH, COHERENCE THEORY OF; TRUTH, CORRESPONDENCE THEORY OF

References and further reading

Bender, J. (ed.) (1989) *The Current State of the Coherence Theory*, Dordrecht: Kluwer. (Critical essays on the coherence theories of Lehrer and BonJour, with replies.)

* Blanshard, B. (1939) *The Nature of Thought*, London: Allen & Unwin. (An updated version of the absolute idealist coherence theory, referred to in §§1 and 4.)
* BonJour, L. (1985) *The Structure of Empirical Knowledge*, Cambridge, MA: Harvard University Press. (The author's version of coherentism, discussed especially in §§4 and 6 above but containing elaborations of material in other sections as well; also contains an appendix discussing the views of the positivists, the absolute idealists, Lehrer, and Rescher.)
* Bosanquet, B. (1920) *Implication and Linear Inference*, London: Macmillan. (Bosanquet's critique of the linear view of justification and defence of coherentism, referred to above in §§1 and 2.)
* Bradley, F.H. (1914) *Essays on Truth and Reality*, Oxford: Oxford University Press. (Essays criticizing the correspondence theory of truth and defending coherentism with respect to both justification and truth; referred to in §1 above.)
Harman, G. (1967) 'Quine on Meaning and Existence 1', *Review of Metaphysics* 21 (1): 124–51. (An account of Quine's theory of knowledge, including a discussion of his coherentism, as discussed in §§1 and 4 above: Quine's own works discuss epistemological themes in passing, but there is no single unified discussion that can be cited.)

* —— (1973) *Thought*, Princeton, NJ: Princeton University Press. (A coherentist position influenced by Quine, referred to in §1 above.)
* Hempel, C. (1934) 'On the Logical Positivist's Theory of Truth', *Analysis* 2 (4): 49–59. (A reply to Schlick's 1934 work; referred to in §1 above.)
Lehrer, K. (1974) *Knowledge*, Oxford: Oxford University Press. (The first statement of Lehrer's coherentism, somewhat superseded by his 1990 work, but still worth comparing.)
* —— (1990) *Theory of Knowledge*, Boulder, CO: Westview Press. (A revision of Lehrer (1974); referred to in §§1, 3 and 4 above.)
* Neurath, O. (1933) 'Protokollsätze', *Erkenntnis* 3; trans. as 'Protocol Sentences', in A.J. Ayer (ed.) *Logical Positivism*, New York: Free Press, 1959, 199–208. (Neurath's early, rather simplistic version of coherentism; referred to in §1 above.)
* Rescher, N. (1973) *The Coherence Theory of Truth*, Oxford: Oxford University Press. (Should be read together with Rescher (1977); referred to in §§1, 3 and 4 above.)
* —— (1974) 'Foundationalism, Coherentism, and the Idea of Cognitive Systematization', *Journal of Philosophy* 71 (19): 695–708. (A useful summary of Rescher's coherence theory.)
* —— (1977) *Methodological Pragmatism*, New York: New York University Press. (Restates and completes the view expressed in Rescher's 1973 work.)
* Schlick, M. (1934) 'Uber das Fundament der Erkenntnis', *Erkenntnis* 4; trans. as 'The Foundation of Knowledge', in A.J. Ayer (ed.) *Logical Positivism*, New York: The Free Press, 1959, 209–27. (A succinct statement of Schlick's foundationalism, which was the target of both Neurath and Hempel; referred to in §§1 and 3 above.)
* Sellars, W. (1963) *Science, Perception and Reality*, London: Routledge & Kegan Paul. (A collection of papers. Chapters 5 and 11 present some of the coherentist ideas discussed in §§1 and 4 above.)

LAURENCE BONJOUR

KNOWLEDGE BY ACQUAINTANCE AND DESCRIPTION

The attempt to distinguish knowledge by acquaintance from knowledge by description is most closely associated with Bertrand Russell. The distinction is also crucial to one way of trying to develop a plausible foundationalist theory of justification and knowledge.

According to Russell one can distinguish the two kinds of knowledge in terms of their respective objects. Put crudely, one has knowledge by acquaintance of things, and one has knowledge by description of propositions (representations of reality that are either true or false). But this crude characterization of the two kinds of knowledge is misleading. Russell also seemed to believe that one can have knowledge by acquaintance of properties and even facts (where a fact is a complex consisting of a thing's exemplifying a quality or standing in a relation to another thing). The distinction, then, might be better put in terms of a kind of knowledge which has as its object something that is neither true nor false (knowledge by acquaintance) and a kind of knowledge which has as its object a bearer of truth value (knowledge by description).

According to Russell, all knowledge of truths ultimately rests on knowledge by acquaintance. The traditional foundationalist in epistemology holds that although I can know one truth by inferring it from something else I know, not everything I know can be inferred in this way. We can avoid a regress of knowledge by holding that at least some truths are known as a result of direct awareness of or acquaintance with those aspects of the world that make the corresponding propositions true.

1 **Acquaintance**
2 **Additional criteria of acquaintance, and an initial problem**
3 **Criticisms**

1 Acquaintance

To distinguish between two *objects* of knowledge is not by itself to say anything very informative about the nature of the respective knowing relations. What is it to know something (a thing, a property or a fact) by acquaintance? Unfortunately, a proponent of the view that such knowledge exists is likely to take the relation of acquaintance to be a primitive. To be sure one can invoke metaphors. When one knows a particular shade of colour by acquaintance, for example, the colour is directly and immediately 'before' one's consciousness. There is nothing 'between' the colour and oneself. By contrast, one might know truths about Julius Caesar but one's access to such truths is only through inference from other things one knows about the contents of history books and the like. A huge expanse of time stands 'between' us and the man, Caesar. The spatial metaphors of 'before' and 'between' are, however, just that – metaphors. As such they are as misleading as they are helpful. More often than not, philosophers who think that there is such a thing as acquaintance do not even take the objects of

acquaintance to be in physical space. Classical acquaintance theorists were usually either dualists who took the objects of acquaintance to be properties of a non-spatial mind, or sense-datum theorists for whom sense-data, if in space at all, were in a two-dimensional space. The relational concepts of 'before' and 'between' are clearly most at home in the conceptual framework of three-dimensional space.

If one cannot define the relation, one might attempt to make the concept of acquaintance clear by giving examples of things with which one can be acquainted. Even proponents of the view that there is such a relation as acquaintance do not, however, agree on what one should take the objects of acquaintance to be. The radical empiricists held that the prime candidates for objects of acquaintance include the contents of consciousness (see EMPIRICISM §2). Thus when I am in severe pain, the pain I feel is said to be directly and immediately 'before' my mind. The contents of my visual field, the sensory character of tactile, olfactory, auditory and gustatory sensations, my thoughts and emotions are all held by most radical empiricists to be items with which I can be directly acquainted. In addition, one might hold that the mind is capable of directly encountering such abstract entities as numbers and universals (properties which can be exemplified in more than one thing and are often thought to exist even when not exemplified by anything). The radical empiricists typically denied that one can be directly acquainted with physical objects, items in the past or items in the future. To return to the metaphor, between us and the physical world is the 'veil' of subjective fleeting sensation. Our access to the world of physical objects is always through belief in propositions which can be known only as a result of inference from what we can know about the character of the sensations with which we are acquainted. Likewise, the past (at least the distant past) can be known only through present memory experience, and the future can be known only through our knowledge of the past and present.

2 Additional criteria of acquaintance, and an initial problem

How is one to know whether or not one is acquainted with something? Here the plot gets difficult to follow. According to at least some philosophers, one is directly acquainted with something only if one can know without inference that the thing in question exists or exemplifies some contingent property. The test of whether or not one can know without inference that something exists is itself sometimes described in terms of the conceivability of error. On this view, one sign that I cannot be directly acquainted with the physical table before me now is that my evidence for believing that the table exists does not logically guarantee its existence. My evidence is said to consist of what I know about my sensations, knowledge that would be no different were I dreaming or hallucinating the table's existence. I am directly acquainted with my severe pain because the justification I now have for believing that I have this pain precludes the possibility of my being wrong – I cannot hallucinate the existence of severe pain.

Some critics complain that making the impossibility of error the mark of direct acquaintance is in tension with other things philosophers want to say about the relation of acquaintance. Specifically, acquaintance is not even supposed to involve bearers of truth value. Let us explore this alleged tension.

In addition to giving examples of things with which we can be acquainted, Russell and others also gave negative characterizations of knowledge by acquaintance. When one knows a thing by being acquainted with it, that knowledge does not involve the application of concepts to the thing – one does not categorize the thing. Presumably, knowledge by acquaintance does not even presuppose linguistic or conceptual capacity on the part of the knower. To know a *truth*, on the other hand, one must explicitly or implicitly apply a concept to a thing or property. To think that this colour with which I am acquainted is red is to apply the concept red to the thing with which I am acquainted. According to some philosophers it is only with the application of concepts that it makes sense to talk of truth and error. I can correctly or incorrectly categorize something with which I am acquainted, but the prior act of my being acquainted with the thing does not involve the possibility of error, because acquaintance does not by itself involve an attempt to categorize the thing in question.

But if knowledge by acquaintance does not even involve representations or characterizations which introduce the elements of truth and falsehood, then what has knowledge by acquaintance got to do with knowledge by description? According to Russell, all knowledge by description ultimately depends upon knowledge by acquaintance. But if knowledge by acquaintance does not even involve a bearer of truth value, how can knowledge by acquaintance yield knowledge by description (knowledge of truths)? In a famous argument against those philosophers who seek to find foundations for knowledge in elements of the world that are simply *given* to one, Wilfred Sellars (1963) claimed that proponents of the view face a dilemma (see SELLARS, W.S. §3). On the one hand, they want to hold that one needs no concepts to have something given to one. Presumably, even the lower animals have qualities given to them in sensory experience. On the other hand, the given is supposed to end a regress of justification. The foundationalist argues that one cannot infer everything one knows from something else one knows, and thus that there must be a kind of knowledge that does not depend on any other knowledge and which can give us the 'first truths', the 'foundational' premises from which we can infer all other truths (see FOUNDATIONALISM). But if knowledge by acquaintance does not involve the possibility of error because it does not have as its object something that can be true or false, how can it give us first truths? How can it give us *premises* (which by their very nature must be true or false) from which to infer other truths? Either knowledge by acquaintance does not involve the application of concepts and cannot therefore furnish premises for inference, or it does involve the application of concepts and cannot be distinguished from knowledge by description.

Although Russell is not as clear as he might be about the relationship between knowledge by acquaintance and knowledge by description, it seems that one might offer the following characterization of the way in which the latter depends on the former. The view itself depends on a controversial conception of truth as 'correspondence'. Roughly, the idea is that a bearer of truth value is true when it corresponds to some aspect of reality. On one view, the world contains facts (things having relational and non-relational properties) whether or not those facts are *represented* by conscious beings. Without representations of facts there are neither truths nor falsehoods. But true propositions are made true by virtue of their accurately 'picturing' facts (see TRUTH, CORRESPONDENCE THEORY OF §1). One can be directly and immediately acquainted with the nonlinguistic (representation-independent) complexes we have called facts. We can call such acquaintance knowledge, but we must be careful to emphasize that having a fact before one in this way does not by itself give one knowledge of a truth. One can be acquainted with a fact without having the capacity to represent the fact, without having a 'picture' of the world that can be made true or false by the fact. But when one does have a representation of the world and one is directly acquainted with the picture, the fact that makes the picture true and the correspondence between the picture and the fact, one has a kind of propositional knowledge that does not depend on any other propositional knowledge. One has foundational propositional knowledge created by direct acquaintance with features of the world. Furthermore, if my belief that I am in pain, for example, is justified by my standing in a relation of acquaintance to the very fact that makes what I believe true, it seems that my justification would (trivially) guarantee the truth of what I believe (see RUSSELL, B.A.W. §§11–14).

3 Criticisms

This view of the way in which knowledge by acquaintance provides foundations for knowledge seems to rely on a highly controversial correspondence conception of truth. Many philosophers reject the basic idea behind the view that truth consists in representations of the world corresponding to facts. Some of these philosophers will reject the metaphysical category of fact (construed as truth-maker) as an illusion. There are no facts that are independent of conceptual frameworks, some philosophers argue. The world is not divided into things, their properties and relations. Indeed the only distinctions that exist are distinctions that we 'carve out' of the world with our concepts and categories. An extreme version of this view would hold that referring to a fact is just another way of talking about a proposition's being true. To say that the world contains the fact, snow's being white, is just another way of saying that it is true that snow is white. If such a view were plausible, then it would be a serious, almost pathetic, mistake to suppose that we could ground knowledge of truths in some relation we bear to the facts that make propositions true.

Notice that the attempt (discussed above) to understand foundational propositional knowledge as resting on knowledge by acquaintance, must make intelligible the concept of being acquainted with a *fact*. It is only if we can stand in some direct unproblematic relation to a *truth-maker* that such a relation might be thought of as yielding knowledge of a *truth-bearer*. Consequently, any philosophical misgivings one has about the metaphysical category of fact, and with it the concept of being acquainted with a fact, might translate into misgivings about the epistemic utility of the concept of knowledge by acquaintance. That we might stand in some kind of direct relation to a thing or property seems neither here nor there when it comes to gaining non-inferential, direct knowledge of truths. Only a *structured* reality could make propositions true and only acquaintance with such structure would be a plausible candidate for the source of foundational knowledge.

Even if one embraces the metaphysical category of fact construed as something that is distinct from representations of it, one might still have qualms about the intelligibility of this relation of direct acquaintance that we are supposed to bear to some, but not all, facts. Many contemporary philosophers argue that the very nature of justification precludes the possibility of having justification for believing empirical propositions that eliminates the possibility of error. Some of these arguments rely on thought experiments which describe sources of error even when one has the best imaginable evidence. Others invoke theoretical models about the nature of judgment which require us to recognize always the possibility of error with respect to empirical judgment. If, for example, judgment always involves relating something present to something past, then it seems doubtful that our justification for accepting such judgments could ever preclude the possibility of error.

Even if the acquaintance theorist can respond to criticisms, what positive reason could one give for supposing that the relation of direct acquaintance exists? Here, the dialogue is likely to reach an impasse. Proponents of the view that there is such a thing as direct acquaintance are quite likely to claim that they are directly acquainted with the fact that they are directly acquainted with certain facts. Such a claim is unlikely to make their critics happy, but then a proponent of the view probably does not care much about making critics happy. After all, if the concept of direct acquaintance with a fact is intelligible, why should one not use the concept in the course of justifying a belief that the relation exists?

See also: CERTAINTY; PERCEPTION; SENSE PERCEPTION, INDIAN VIEWS OF; SENSE-DATA

References and further reading

BonJour, L. (1985) *The Structure of Empirical Knowledge*, Cambridge, MA: Harvard University Press. (Chapter 4 is most relevant. Heavily influenced by Sellars, Bonjour presents a clear argument against the doctrine of the given, an argument that includes an attack on the idea that empirical knowledge can be grounded in direct acquaintance.)

Fumerton, R. (1985) *Metaphysical and Epistemological Problems of Perception*, Lincoln, NB: University of Nebraska. (Chapter 2 is an attempt to combine a specific correspondence conception of truth with the concept of acquaintance to present a plausible version of foundationalism.)

Russell, B. (1912) *The Problems of Philosophy*, London: Oxford University Press, 1959. (Chapter 5 is probably the clearest of Russell's attempts to explain the distinction between knowledge by acquaintance and knowledge by description. Accessible to readers with widely varying philosophical backgrounds.)

—— (1914) 'On the Nature of Acquaintance', *Monist,*

24: 1–16, 161–87, 435–53. (This three-part article contains a more extensive treatment of the distinction discussed in *The Problems of Philosophy*.)

* Sellars, W. (1963) 'Empiricism and the Philosophy of Mind', in *Science, Perception and Reality*, London: Routledge & Kegan Paul, 127–96. (Wide-ranging and in parts very difficult. The argument referred to in the text is contained in section 1 of the article.)

RICHARD FUMERTON

KNOWLEDGE, CAUSAL THEORY OF

Epistemologists have always recognized the importance of causal processes in accounting for our knowledge of things. In discussions of perception, memory and reasoning, for example, it is commonly assumed that these ways of coming to know are fundamentally causal. We perceive things and thus come to have knowledge about them via complex causal processes; memory is, at least in part, the retention of previously gained knowledge through some sort of causal process; and reasoning is a causal process that takes beliefs as inputs and generates beliefs as outputs.

A causal theory of knowledge is a form of externalism and is based on the fundamental idea that a person knows some proposition, p, only if there is an appropriate causal connection between the state of affairs that makes p true and the person's belief in p. Although this kind of theory has roots that extend to ancient times, contemporary versions attempt to make more precise the nature of the causal connections required for knowledge. The causal theory is closely related to other forms of externalist theories, such as the conclusive reasons theory, information-theoretic views and the various forms of reliabilism.

1 **Formulation of the causal theory of knowing**
2 **The Gettier examples**
3 **Problems for the causal theory**
4 **Successors to the causal theory of knowing**

1 Formulation of the causal theory of knowing

In the internalist-oriented environment which dominated epistemology from the time of Descartes until the middle of the twentieth century, it was not considered appropriate to refer to the causal history of a belief in providing an analysis, or definition, of the positive epistemic status of that belief (see INTERNALISM AND EXTERNALISM IN EPISTEMOLOGY).

Rather, the epistemologist's job was to provide definitions of concepts such as justification and knowledge independently of any assumed causal connections with the external world, and then to show how, from such analyses, one could argue ('internally') that such causal connections exist. To do otherwise would be to beg the question against scepticism about the external world.

Since the 1960s, there has been a shift away from the internalist position in epistemology. The causal theory of knowing is one of the early versions of externalism, introduced by Alvin Goldman (1967) and conceived primarily as a response to the Gettier problem which had appeared only a few years earlier (see GETTIER PROBLEMS). In Gettier examples, a person, *S*, has a justified belief in something that is only coincidentally true. This element of coincidence, which is perhaps the most salient feature of Gettier cases, is very difficult to explain without introducing some element of external connection between the individual's belief, the justification for that belief and the state of affairs which is the object of the belief. Goldman's original proposal was to focus on the causal connections that typically obtain between these various epistemically relevant items when a person has knowledge.

Goldman expressed his proposal as a set of truth-conditions for knowledge, in the following schematic form:

[A person] *S* knows that *p* if and only if the fact *p* is causally connected in an 'appropriate' way with *S*'s believing *p*.

The ways that are 'appropriate' include perception, memory, various other kinds of causal chains and forks, and combinations of these. Goldman adds to this the further condition that the relevant causal connections obtaining between the state of affairs *p* and one's belief must be 'correctly reconstructed by inferences, each of which is warranted'. This further condition is designed to accommodate the fact that causal chains can sometimes take very unexpected routes. If the route is unusual enough, then even though it results in a true belief that *p*, it does not provide knowledge. For example, suppose that Sally is perceiving an object only through a complex network of mirrors, or via some holographic imaging device which produces a very realistic image of the object. Then, she might come to believe that the object is in front of her when in fact it is, but she might fail to know that it is there, as she knows nothing about the unusual causal mechanism. If she were in a position to correctly reconstruct the causal chain, however, then she would have knowledge.

One example developed by Goldman that illustrates the intuitive appeal of his proposal involves a person, Smith, who perceives solidified lava lying around a mountain. On the basis of beliefs about this lava, and background beliefs, Smith inferentially comes to believe, correctly, that the mountain erupted many centuries ago. Assuming that Smith's inferences are warranted, does he know? To answer this, we must ask what sort of causal ancestry obtains between the eruption of the mountain and Smith's belief that it has erupted. If the lava that he sees resulted from the eruption, as he imagines, then Smith does have knowledge. However, suppose that unknown to Smith the lava has been placed there by promoters who wish to make it look as though the area was once volcanic. The lava actually produced by the eruption has been completely covered by years of sedimentation, and cannot be seen. Then, there is no appropriate causal connection between eruption and perceived lava, and Smith does not know. The naturally intuitive appeal of such an example is confirmation that Goldman's causal theory captures at least part of what we require for knowledge.

2 The Gettier examples

In Gettier examples, the requirement that there be an appropriate causal connection between the fact p, and S's (warranted) belief, is not satisfied, very much along the lines illustrated in the lava case. This can be seen by considering a specific (Gettier-style) example, introduced by Keith Lehrer (1965). Suppose Smith correctly infers that someone in his class owns a Ford, from some true evidence that justifies the false belief that a student, Mr. Nogot, owns a Ford. It so happens that another student in Smith's class, Mr. Havit, does own a Ford, but Smith has no evidence one way or the other for this proposition. The causal theory clearly explains the lack of knowledge in this example, since the state of affairs making it true that someone in Smith's class owns a Ford (namely, Havit's owning a Ford) is not causally related in any of the appropriate ways with Smith's belief. Rather, Smith's belief is caused by states of affairs which make true the evidence on which his belief that Mr. Nogot owns a Ford is based. And, these states of affairs, whatever they are, have nothing to do with Mr. Havit's ownership.

It should also be noticed that if this case were redescribed so that Smith does have evidence that Havit owns a Ford, then it would be clear (all else being equal) that he does have knowledge that someone in his class owns a Ford, for then the required causal connection would obtain. It can be concluded that in Gettier examples, as well as 'ordinary' cases in which we would tend to ascribe

knowledge to individuals, the causal theory provides a clear and intuitively appealing account of knowledge.

3 Problems for the causal theory

Despite its merits, there are a number of examples that raise serious difficulties for the causal theory. One class of examples is generated by the phenomenon of causal overdetermination. Suppose Alfred comes to believe that there is a sheep in the field by hearing a recording of the sounds normally produced by sheep while also looking at a distant boulder that looks like a sheep in the field. Even if there is a sheep somewhere in the field not seen by Alfred, he does not know that one is there. Later, should he come to perceive the real sheep, he would come to know that there is a sheep in the field. The problem for the causal theory is that Alfred's later perception of the real sheep would not cause his belief in an appropriate way, because his belief already exists. The causal theory would incorrectly deny that Alfred has knowledge. This kind of case can be accommodated within the general spirit of the causal theory by allowing as 'appropriate' the relation of causal sustaining, a very weak form of causal connection.

More difficult to accommodate are overdetermination cases in which an individual is acquainted with some state of affairs which is causally sufficient for the state of affairs p, but which is not in fact any part of the cause of p. Abigail might, for example, be aware that Jones has taken a fatal dose of poison, with no antidote, and thereby come to know that Jones is dead even though in fact (but unknown to her) Jones died of other causes. The only way to accommodate such an example is to further extend the scope of 'appropriate causal connections' to include cases in which one infers p from something which is causally sufficient for p even though not the cause or any part of the cause of p. It is not obvious, however, that this kind of modification is in the spirit of the causal theory, for it abandons the idea that knowledge requires a causal *connection* between belief and known fact.

Equally troubling for the causal theory are situations involving logical and/or mathematical facts. One kind of situation is very similar to the example just given. Suppose Mark observes that an owl is on top of a flagpole, which he already knows to be 15 feet high. He also observes a mouse to be 12 feet from the bottom of the flagpole. Mark correctly infers that the mouse is a little over 19 feet from the owl. But, the mouse's being a little over 19 feet from the owl is no part of the cause of Mark's belief in that fact, nor are the facts from which he makes the inference themselves causes of the mouse's distance from the owl. Rather, this is a case in which the fact concluded follows logically from the observed premises. To take another example, suppose that the object of belief is itself a logical or mathematical truth, such as '$2 + 2 = 4$'. Surely a theory of knowledge should allow for knowledge of such truths, but the causal theory faces serious obstacles in attempting to provide an account. Whatever the nature of the facts which make true logical and mathematical truths, they do not seem to be the sorts of facts that are parts of causal chains. If not, then there can be no appropriate causal connection of any kind between such facts and one's beliefs. It should be noted, however, that there have been some serious efforts, particularly by Mark Steiner (1973) and Philip Kitcher (1984), to accommodate mathematical and logical knowledge within the framework of a causal theory.

In his own effort to accommodate examples involving inferences based on logical connections, such as the one concerning the owl and mouse, as well as knowledge of mathematical and logical truths, Goldman (1967) proposed that the scope of 'appropriate causal connection' be extended even further to include logical and mathematical connections. Even those philosophers who are inclined to be sympathetic with the previously mentioned extensions of the notion of a causal connection have baulked at this idea. Peter Klein (1976) argues that there is no adequate way of formulating a version of the causal theory which allows logical and mathematical connections to be counted as causal.

The problematic examples discussed thus far have raised questions about the necessity of the 'appropriate causal connection' requirement. There are also difficult examples that raise doubts about the sufficiency of the 'appropriate causal connection' requirement, even in its most refined forms. Perhaps the most famous of these examples is one introduced by Goldman himself (1976), leading to his own ultimate abandonment of the early version of his causal theory.

In this example, we are to suppose that Henry is driving through the countryside looking at the scenery. One of the things he sees is a barn, and on the basis of this perfectly ordinary perceptual evidence, along with his background beliefs about barns, Henry comes to believe that there is a barn there. Unknown to him, however, the region is populated by papier-mâché barn facsimiles, of the sort found on movie-studio lots. These facsimiles, which are propped up by sticks from behind, would be mistaken by Henry, or anyone else, for real barns when sighted casually from the road. It is only by good fortune, or coincidence, that Henry has perceived a real barn rather than a facsimile. Given this,

Henry cannot be said to have knowledge that the object he sees is a barn, for he could just as well have been perceiving a facsimile. The problem is that Goldman's causal theory of knowledge is satisfied: Henry's belief that there is a barn there is caused in a perfectly straightforward way by the presence of the barn, and we may suppose that Henry has correctly reconstructed through warranted inferences the causal chain leading to this belief. So, if Henry does not have knowledge, the conditions of the causal theory do not appear to be sufficient for knowledge.

In light of these and other difficult counterexamples to both the necessity and the sufficiency of the causal theory, it has largely been abandoned, at least in the form originally suggested by Goldman in which a causal connection between state of affairs and belief is required.

4 Successors to the causal theory of knowing

The causal theory of knowing still survives in many of the externalist theories which have arisen since Goldman's early proposal. Among the more prominent theories in this category are the 'conclusive reasons' approach, exemplified in the works of Dretske and Armstrong, and various versions of Reliabilism, exemplified in the later works of Goldman, and in works by Swain, Alston and Plantinga.

Goldman (1976) proposed a modification of the early causal theory in which it is required not only that the individual's belief that p be caused in an appropriate way by the state of affairs p, but also that the individual be a reliable discriminator with respect to p and other, alternative states of affairs that might causally substitute for p. When this discriminatory capacity is lacking, or is not functioning properly, then the individual fails to know even if the causal connection requirement is met. In this way, examples such as the one involving Henry can be accounted for.

But even with this modification, the causal theory cannot handle examples in which there is no causal connection of the required sort, such as the mathematical and logical cases illustrated above. Ultimately, the requirement that there be an actual causal chain linking the state of affairs that makes p true with the belief that p must be abandoned. Taking its place is the notion of an 'appropriate causal *ancestry*' of a belief. A belief is an instance of knowledge, according to this kind of causal theory, provided it is produced in an appropriate manner, where the manner of production is appropriate just in case it is *reliable*. A theory which holds this is called a 'reliability theory', and is the main kind of successor to the early causal theories (see RELIABILISM).

See also: CAUSALITY AND NECESSITY IN ISLAMIC THOUGHT; INFORMATION THEORY AND EPISTEMOLOGY

References and further reading

Alston, W. (1989) *Epistemic Justification: Essays in the Theory of Knowledge*, Ithaca, NY: Cornell University Press. (In this collection of essays, items 8, 9 and 12 present the author's externalistic position.)

Armstrong, D. (1973) *Belief, Truth, and Knowledge*, Cambridge: Cambridge University Press. (Presentation of a form of reliabilism which requires for knowledge a 'lawlike' connection between belief and state of affairs; very closely related to the causal theory.)

Carrier, L.S. (1976) 'The Causal Theory of Knowledge', *The Southern Journal of Philosophy* 9: 3–11. (Critique of Goldman's causal theory and presentation of an alternative view.)

Dretske, F. (1971) 'Conclusive Reasons', *The Australasian Journal of Philosophy* 49: 1–22. (Classic presentation of the conclusive reasons view, which is closely related to the causal and reliability views.)

Foley, R. (1987) *The Theory of Epistemic Rationality*, Cambridge, MA: Harvard University Press. (Chapter 4 has interesting arguments and examples which challenge the fundamental premise of the causal theory, namely, that at least some appropriate causal history is necessary for knowledge.)

* Goldman, A. (1967) 'A Causal Theory of Knowing', *The Journal of Philosophy* 64 (12): 355–72; repr. in G.S. Pappas and M. Swain (eds) *Essays on Knowledge and Justification*, Ithaca, NY and New York: Cornell University Press, 1978. (The original article in which Goldman presents the causal connection view.)

* —— (1976) 'Discrimination and Perceptual Knowledge', *The Journal of Philosophy* 73: 771–91; repr. in G.S. Pappas and M. Swain (eds) *Essays on Knowledge and Justification*, Ithaca, NY and New York: Cornell University Press, 1978. (Presentation of the Barn-facsimile example, and development of an early version of a reliabilist view as a successor to the early causal theory.)

—— (1986) *Epistemology and Cognition*, Cambridge, MA: Harvard University Press. (Some historical tracing of the causal theories, and presentation of the author's reliabilist views.)

* Kitcher, P. (1984) *Mathematical Knowledge*, Oxford and New York: Oxford University Press. (A thorough discussion of mathematical and logical knowledge, including an effort to accommodate such knowledge within a causal/reliability theory.)

* Klein, P. (1976) 'Knowledge, Causality, and Defeasibility', *The Journal of Philosophy* 73 (20): 792–812. (A detailed critique of the causal theory of knowing, in which it is argued that no theory of this kind can succeed in the face of examples involving logical and mathematical connections.)

* Lehrer, K. (1965) 'Knowledge, Truth, and Evidence', *Analysis* 25: 168–75. (The 'Nogot-Havit' example can be found in this early discussion of Gettier problems.)

Plantinga, A. (1994a) *Warrant: The Current Debate*, Oxford: Oxford University Press. (See chapter 9 for a critical discussion of reliabilism and related theories.)

—— (1994b) *Warrant and Proper Function*, Oxford: Oxford University Press. (Development of the author's version of externalism.)

Shope, R. (1983) *The Analysis of Knowing*, Princeton, NJ: Princeton University Press. (See especially chapter 5 for a good survey of causal theories of knowing and related theories.)

Skyrms, B. (1967) 'The Explication of "X knows that p"', *The Journal of Philosophy* 64: 373–89. (An early discussion of Goldman's view, raising problems having to do with overdetermination.)

* Steiner, M. (1973) 'Platonism and the Causal Theory of Knowledge', *The Journal of Philosophy* 70 (3): 57–66. (An attempt to provide for mathematical knowledge within the framework of a causal theory of knowing.)

Swain, M. (1972) 'Knowledge, Causality, and Justification', *The Journal of Philosophy* 69 (11): 291–300. (Discussion and revision of Goldman's early theory, and of examples raised by Skyrms and others.)

—— (1979) *Reasons and Knowledge*, Ithaca, NY: Cornell University Press. (See especially chapters 2 and 6 for a detailed development of a causal theory of knowing designed to avoid many of the problems with Goldman's view.)

MARSHALL SWAIN

KNOWLEDGE, CONCEPT OF

The branch of philosophy concerned with the nature and extent of human knowledge is called epistemology (from the Greek epistēmē *meaning knowledge, and* logos *meaning theory). Knowledge seems to come in many varieties: we know people, places and things; we know how to perform tasks; we know facts. Factual knowledge has been the central focus of epistemology.*

We can know a fact only if we have a true belief about it. However, since only some true beliefs are knowledge (consider, for example, a lucky guess), the central question asked by epistemologists is 'What converts mere true belief into knowledge?'. There are many, and often conflicting, answers to this question. The primary traditional answer has been that our true beliefs must be based upon sufficiently good reasons in order to be certifiable as knowledge. Foundationalists have held that the structure of reasons is such that our reasons ultimately rest upon basic reasons that have no further reasons supporting them. Coherentists have argued that there are no foundational reasons. Rather, they argue that our beliefs are mutually supporting.

In addition to the constraints upon the overall structure of reasons, epistemologists have proposed various general principles governing reasons. For example, it seems that if my reasons are adequate to affirm some fact, those reasons should be adequate to eliminate other incompatible hypotheses. This initially plausible principle appears to lead directly to some deep puzzles and, perhaps, even to scepticism. Indeed, many of the principles that seem initially plausible lead to various unexpected and unwelcome conclusions.

Alternatives to the primary traditional answer to the central epistemic question have been developed, in part because of the supposed failures of traditional epistemology. These alternative views claim that it is something other than good reasons which distinguishes (mere) true beliefs from knowledge. Reliabilists claim that a true belief produced by a sufficiently reliable process is knowledge. Good reasoning is but one of the many ways in which beliefs can be reliably produced. The issue of whether the objections to traditional epistemology are valid or whether the proposed substitutes are better remains unresolved.

1 **The varieties of knowledge**
2 **Propositional knowledge is not mere true belief**
3 **Warrant**
4 **Foundationalism and coherentism**
5 **Defeasibility theories**
6 **Externalism**
7 **Epistemic principles**
8 **The epistemic principles and scepticism**
9 **The epistemic principles and some paradoxes**
10 **Some challenges to traditional epistemology**

1 The varieties of knowledge

Knowledge comes in many varieties. I can know *how* to adjust a carburettor. I can know a person. I can know *that* mixing bleach and ammonia is dangerous. In the first case, I possess a skill. In the second, I am acquainted with someone. In the third, I know a fact.

Epistemologists have differed on the relationships between these types of knowledge. On the one hand, it could be held that knowing a person (place or thing) should be construed as nothing more (or less) than knowing certain facts about that someone and possessing the skill of being able to distinguish that person from other objects. On the other hand, it has been held that knowing facts depends upon being acquainted with particular objects. Whether the reduction of one form of knowledge to another is ultimately successful is an area of contention among epistemologists (see KNOWLEDGE BY ACQUAINTANCE AND DESCRIPTION).

Nevertheless, it is knowledge of facts, so-called *propositional knowledge*, as opposed to knowledge by acquaintance or the possession of skills, that has been the central concern of epistemologists. The central question can be put this way: which beliefs of mine are to be counted as knowledge? This question presupposes that knowledge is a species of belief, but some might think that knowledge and belief are mutually exclusive: for example, we say such things as 'I do not *believe* that; I *know* it'. But we also say such things as 'I am not *happy*; I am *ecstatic*'. A suggested paraphrase of this expression seems to capture what is meant without denying the obviously true claim that ecstasy is a form of happiness. The paraphrase is: I am not *merely* happy, I am ecstatic. The parallel is: I do not *merely* believe it; I know it. Thus, this type of linguistic evidence does not support the suggestion that belief and knowledge are mutually exclusive. In general, epistemologists have held that propositional knowledge is a species of belief.

2 Propositional knowledge is not mere true belief

Propositional knowledge is a species of belief; but which beliefs are knowledge? The first thing to note is that a belief must be true in order for it to count as knowledge. But that is obviously not enough. First, true beliefs can be based upon faulty reasoning. Suppose that I believe that smoking is a leading cause of fatal lung cancer because I infer it from the fact that I know two smokers who died of lung cancer. The generalization is true, but my evidence is too meagre for my belief to count as knowledge. Second, true beliefs can be based on false beliefs. Modifying an example used by Bertrand Russell, suppose that I believe truly that the last name of the President of the United States in 1996 begins with a 'C'. Also suppose this belief is based upon the false belief that the President is Winston Churchill. My true belief that the President's name begins with a 'C' is not knowledge because it is based on a false belief.

Third, even some true beliefs resulting from good

reasoning based upon true beliefs are not knowledge. Suppose that I believe (truly) that my neighbours are at home. My belief is based upon good reasoning from my true belief that I see lights on and that, in the past, the lights have been on only when they were at home. But suppose further that this time the lights were turned on by a guest and that my neighbours had just entered the house and would not have had time to turn on the lights. In this case, I fail to know that my neighbours are home. So, the central question becomes: what must be added to true belief to convert it into knowledge?

3 Warrant

The property, whatever it is, that, if added to true belief converts it into knowledge, we may refer to as 'warrant'. Knowledge, then, is true, warranted, belief. But simply to name the missing property does not bring us closer to understanding it and we must be careful not to think of 'warrant' as a sophisticated synonym for 'justified'. Let us say that a belief is *justified* just in case we are entitled to hold it on the basis of suitable reasons available to us. In the neighbour/lights case mentioned above, we have already seen that justification is not sufficient for warrant. Whether it is even necessary will be important in the discussion that follows, especially in §6.

Given the great variety of approaches to an account of warrant, is there any common, underlying starting point embraced by epistemologists? Yes: a warranted belief is one that is not held on the basis of mere cognitive luck. Plato appeals to that intuition in the *Theaetetus*; Aristotle's account of the transition from ignorance of the first principles in science to knowledge of them in the *Posterior Analytics* is designed to demonstrate that there are reliable cognitive mechanisms whose output is not the result of chance; Descartes (1641) proposes methods for acquiring beliefs that would (he thinks) necessarily lead to truth; Locke (1689) suggests that even if persons arrive at a true belief by accident, they are not thereby free from criticism.

Let us start with the assumption that a proposition is known just in case it is not an accident, from the cognitive point of view, that it is both believed and true. Hence the task becomes one of developing an account of warrant that accurately portrays what it is that makes a belief non-accidentally true from the cognitive point of view.

4 Foundationalism and coherentism

There are two main, traditional approaches to the account of justification: foundationalism and coherentism. Both are *normative* views about rules in virtue of which propositions *ought* to be accepted or *ought* to be rejected or *ought* to be suspended (see KNOWLEDGE AND JUSTIFICATION, COHERENCE THEORY OF; FOUNDATIONALISM; NORMATIVE EPISTEMOLOGY). In order to characterize these approaches, recall how the ancient Pyrrhonian Sceptics divided the possible structures of reasons that provide a basis for accepting a belief (see EPISTEMOLOGY, HISTORY OF; PYRRHONISM). Suppose you hold a belief and offer another belief as the reason for the first – for example, suppose you believe that Ford cars are generally less expensive than BMWs. Your reason could be your belief that you were told so by a reliable person. An obvious question arises: what is your basis for believing that the person is reliable? You could answer with another reason and that reason could, itself, be supported by a further reason, and so on.

This process of providing reasons for your beliefs can have only three possible structures:

Foundationalism: The process of giving reasons could be such that not every reason is supported by another reason because there are *basic reasons* which have no need of further reasons supporting them.

Coherentism: The process of giving reasons could have no reason that is not supported by another reason, but there is not an infinite number of reasons. Thus, beliefs are mutually supporting.

Infinitism: The process of giving reasons could have no reason that is not supported by another reason, but there is an infinite number of reasons.

Foundationalism and coherentism have both been developed and defended, and there are well-known objections to each view. In contrast, the *prima facie* objections to infinitism have seemed so overwhelming that it has not been investigated carefully. Infinitism *seems* to require that a person should have an infinite number of beliefs (which *seems* on its face to be false). In addition, it *seems* to lead inevitably to the conclusion that no belief could ever be justified, since the process of justification would never come to an end.

The standard objections to foundationalism are several. First, as the Pyrrhonians would point out, there must be a distinction between what makes a belief *properly* basic and what makes it simply one for which no other reason is, in fact, given. Otherwise, the offered 'basic' reason is arbitrary. But if there is some further reason for thinking that an offered reason is not arbitrary, then there is a reason for accepting it, and the offered reason is, thereby, not basic. Hence, there can be no foundational propositions.

Second, some preferred candidates for properly basic reasons seem not to be properly basic on closer inspection. Consider perceptual judgments – the source of most of our knowledge of the external world according to many philosophers (see EMPIRICISM; A POSTERIORI). A reason for believing that there is a tree before me is that I see a tree before me. But the latter proposition does not appear to be properly basic because one could be required to explain what it is about what is seen that leads one to believe that it is a *tree* that one sees (as opposed to an illusion). Thus, some foundationalists have retreated to sensation-beliefs (so-called sense-data propositions) as their candidates for properly basic beliefs: for example, 'I seem to see a green, brown, tallish object' (see AYER, A.J.; BROAD, C.D.; MOORE, G.E.). But although these propositions might seem to be properly basic, there are notorious problems with the sense-data view (see PERCEPTION, EPISTEMIC ISSUES IN; SENSE-DATA). First, the proffered basic beliefs seem to be too meagre to provide a sufficient basis for the rich scope of things we seem to know. For example, how can my knowledge that objects persist when not being perceived be traced to particular sense-data? Second, it appears that our knowledge of the way in which to characterize our sensations (private sensations accessible only to the individual having them) depends upon our knowledge of public objects (see CRITERIA; WITTGENSTEIN, L.J.J.). How could we know, for example, that we have a throbbing pain without first recognizing what it is for a public object (say, a muscle) to be throbbing?

Foundationalists have developed answers to these objections in part by liberalizing the requirements either for being properly basic or for being an acceptable pattern of inference from the foundational propositions to the non-foundational ones (see INFERENCE TO THE BEST EXPLANATION). For example, *contextualist* accounts of knowledge have been developed that hold that a proposition is properly basic just in case it is accepted by the relevant community of putative knowers. In a discussion with a friend I could offer as my reason for believing another moon of Jupiter had been discovered that 'I read it in the newspaper'. I would not need further reasons for believing that I read it. In contrast, at a convention of astronomers that reason would not be accepted. Hence, contextualists claim, what counts as a basic reason is context-dependent.

There are two obvious responses to contextualism. The first is that it might be an accurate description of some aspects of our epistemic practices, but the fundamental Pyrrhonian question remains: what distinguishes a properly basic proposition from one that is merely offered and accepted by a community of putative knowers? The issue concerns what beliefs, if any, *ought* to be offered and accepted without further reasons. The question is not what beliefs *are* offered and accepted without further reason. The second response is a corollary of the first. Knowledge seems to be a highly prized state of belief (as PLATO put it). But, if the contextualists were right, I would gain knowledge by joining a community of rather epistemically gullible and permissive folk. That hardly seems right! (See CONTEXTUALISM, EPISTEMOLOGICAL.)

In sum, it remains a subject of dispute among epistemologists whether the stock of purported foundational propositions can be made sufficiently rich and abundant without including too many that clearly require evidential support, or whether the patterns of inferences can be liberalized sufficiently without allowing patterns that are not sufficiently truth-conducive.

The historical rival of foundationalism is coherentism. Coherentists deny that there are basic reasons and claim that all propositions derive their warrant, at least in part, from other propositions. The fundamental objection is this: Typically, we recognize that arguing in a circle is not an acceptable pattern of inference, so what makes it acceptable in some cases? Suppose I believe that apples contain vitamin C, at least in part because I believe that fruits contain vitamin C. I would surely be appropriately accused of circular reasoning if I believed, in part, that fruits contain vitamin C because apples do.

Coherentists would be quick to point out that they are not really suggesting that one should argue in a circle. Rather, they would point to the fact that our beliefs come in bunches with a web-like structure (see QUINE, W.V.). They are 'mutually supporting' just as the poles in a tepee are mutually supporting. A belief is warranted just in case it is a member of a set of coherent beliefs.

But whether these colourful analogies answer the basic objection is not clear. Presumably, circular reasoning is not acceptable because although it might be the case that if you believe b_1 it might be reasonable to believe b_2, and if you believe b_2 it might be reasonable to also believe b_1, their mutual support gives you no reason for believing them both. Thus, the fundamental question is this: What makes one total set of coherent beliefs, say T_1, any more acceptable than an alternative total set of coherent beliefs, say T_2?

The Pyrrhonian Sceptics would point out that coherentists either have an answer for that question or they do not. If they do, then they seem to have abandoned their central view, since there now seems to be a reason for adopting the set of beliefs, T_1, that is not one of the beliefs in T_1. Indeed, if they provide an answer, they have embraced foundationalism. If they do not have an answer, then it seems that adopting T_1 is arbitrary. Coherentists have attempted to answer this objection by giving a 'meta-justification' for thinking that certain kinds of coherent belief systems are likely to contain true members. Indeed, some have argued that coherent beliefs are, by their very nature, likely to be true (see DAVIDSON, D.). But whether that strategy will suffice to answer the objections remains an open question in epistemology.

5 Defeasibility theories

A basic objection to the foundationalist's and coherentist's accounts of justification is that neither seems to be able to show that a true belief which satisfied their accounts would be non-accidentally true. First, as the neighbour/lights case showed, a true belief could be fully justified on their accounts, but not be knowledge. Second, as the Pyrrhonians pointed out, either the beliefs seem to rest upon arbitrary foundations or they seem to be only one of many, equally coherent sets of beliefs. The defeasibility theory was developed, in part, to address these issues. It holds, roughly, that it is not only the evidence that one possesses that makes a belief warranted; it is equally important that there is no defeating evidence that one does not possess. That is, in order for a belief to be warranted it must not only be justified (in the sense required by either the foundationalists or the coherentists) but its justification must be such that there is no truth which, if added to the reasons that justify the belief, is such that the belief would no longer be justified (see KNOWLEDGE, DEFEASIBILITY THEORY OF).

The defeasibility theory can explain why it is not a cognitive accident that the warranted belief is true. If any of the important supporting reasons (those that if removed would destroy the justification) were false, then adding the denial of those reasons (in other words, adding the truth) to one's beliefs would undermine the justification. In addition, if there is evidence that one does not possess such that it makes it an accident that the belief is true, the propositions describing that evidence would undercut the justification.

A well-known case will help to illustrate this (see GETTIER PROBLEMS). Suppose that I know Tom Grabit well and I see what appears to be Tom stealing a library book: I come to believe that Tom stole a library book. And, let us suppose that Tom did indeed steal the book. Foundationalists and coherentists could deploy their accounts in order to show that the belief is justified. Nevertheless, suppose that, unknown to me, Tom has an identical twin, John, who is

a kleptomaniac and was in the library on the day in question and stole a copy of the same book. Even though I arrived at a true belief as a result of good reasoning based upon true propositions, I do not know that Tom stole the book since it is accidental, from the cognitive point of view, that I arrived at the truth. I could just as easily have based my belief on having seen John stealing the book.

The defeasibility theorists would point out that the belief that Tom stole the book is defeated; if the true proposition describing John were added to my beliefs, I would no longer be justified in believing Tom stole the book. In general, the defeasibility theory can rule out accidentally true beliefs as warranted because those beliefs would not be able to stand up to the truth.

Nevertheless, the defeasibility theory has its problems. The primary one is that it seems to exclude too much from what we know. Returning to the Grabit Case, suppose that everything is as it was except that Tom does not have a twin but that Tom's mother sincerely avows the claims about John. Now, there is a true proposition (Tom's mother has said sincerely that Tom has an identical twin, John) that defeats the original justification. Hence the belief that Tom stole the book would be defeated. But if Tom's mother were demented and there never was a twin, it seems that I knew all along that Tom stole the book.

Defeasibility theorists have tried to answer this objection by suggesting ways to distinguish between so-called misleading defeaters (for example, Mrs Grabit sincerely avows that Tom has an identical twin, John) and genuine ones (for example, Tom has an identical twin, John), but there is no agreement among epistemologists that any of these suggestions has succeeded in correctly capturing the distinction between genuine and misleading defeaters.

6 Externalism

Partly in response to the difficulties with foundationalism and coherentism even as supplemented by the defeasibility theory, epistemologists have developed a variety of alternative accounts of warrant. They have been called 'externalistic' because their accounts of warrant focus on features of the world other than the knower's reasons for belief. Two important ones are the causal theory and the reliabilist theory (see KNOWLEDGE, CAUSAL THEORY OF; RELIABILISM).

In their purest forms, these accounts begin with the view that knowledge, and hence warrant, does not require justification. The foundationalists had already conceded that there are no reasons for properly basic beliefs. This seemed to create a problem for foundationalism only because it was assumed that all beliefs needed to be justified and the 'basic' reasons appeared to be arbitrary. But drop the requirement that beliefs need to be justified in order to be warranted, and this problem immediately disappears.

Roughly, the causal theory of warrant holds that a belief is warranted if and only if the state of affairs represented in the belief is appropriately causally related to the belief. For example, suppose I come to believe that there is a bird in a tree as a causal consequence of seeing the bird in the tree. Sometimes the causal connection is more complex; but this direct type of causal connection between the belief and what it represents will suffice for our purposes.

This theory is initially appealing because it appears to satisfy the basic requirement that a warranted belief be non-accidentally true since the state of affairs represented in the belief is a cause of my belief. However, it is easily seen to be both too weak and too strong; and there seem to be some deep problems with it as a general account of warrant. It is too weak because it would count some true beliefs as warranted that clearly are not known. Recall the Grabit case. My belief that I see Tom stealing the book is caused by Tom's stealing the book, but if he has an identical twin, I do not know that Tom stole the book. It is too strong because there seem to be many beliefs that count as knowledge which can not be appropriately *causally* related to what they represent. Suppose I know that there is no elephant smaller than a kitten: what possible *causal* connection could there be between there being no elephant smaller than a kitten and my belief? In addition, potential difficulties arise about knowledge of a priori propositions (such as $2 + 2 = 4$) and counterfactuals (such as, if it were raining today, we would have called off the picnic). It looks as though there is no possible way to produce a causal connection between my belief and what is represented in the belief – at least as 'cause' is usually understood (see A PRIORI).

Nevertheless, a basic tenet of the causal theory might still be correct: Not all beliefs need to be based on reasons in order to count as knowledge. The reliabilist theory of warrant can be seen as the successor of the causal theory. Instead of requiring an appropriate causal connection between the states of affairs represented in the belief and the belief itself, a typical form of reliabilism holds that a belief is warranted just in case the process resulting in the belief produces true beliefs sufficiently often.

Thus, the non-accidental nature of the true belief receives a very straightforward analysis. The belief is non-accidentally true because the process that produces the belief produces true beliefs sufficiently often. This view has many advantages over the causal theory. My belief that elephants are larger than kittens need not be caused by that state of affairs. All that is required is that the process by which I come to believe that proposition typically (often enough) results in true beliefs. A priori or counterfactual propositions present no problem since there could be reliable processes that produce those beliefs.

Nevertheless, there are problems confronting this view. Suppose that you require that the process should produce true beliefs on 100 per cent of the occasions on which it arises. That is a very stringent condition; but it is not stringent enough! For if the belief that Tom Grabit stole a book arises only once in the history of the world – the time I saw him stealing the book – the actual process produced a true belief 100 per cent of the times it arose; but it is not knowledge. The obvious move for the reliabilist is not only to include the actual occasions when the particular belief is produced but rather to consider whether the type of process that produced this belief would produce true beliefs of this type sufficiently often. But correctly characterizing those types has not proved easy. Is the type of belief one in which Tom is involved? Or identical twins? Or libraries? That seems too narrow. Is the type of process one in which there is first a perception and then some inferences? That seems too broad. It remains an open question whether reliabilism can produce an acceptable account of the types of processes and the types of beliefs.

Finally, there is one further objection that some epistemologists have brought against reliabilism. Perhaps it is best illustrated in a case presented by Keith Lehrer (1990: 163) that can be summarized as follows: a certain Mr Truetemp has a thermometer-with-temperature-belief-generator implanted in his head so that within certain ranges of temperatures he has perfectly reliable temperature beliefs. When it is 50 degrees, he comes to believe that it is 50 degrees. When it is not 50 degrees, he does not come to believe that it is 50 degrees. He holds these beliefs without knowing why he does.

Such beliefs would satisfy all of the requirements suggested by the reliabilists, but many epistemologists would hold that although Mr Truetemp has true beliefs and they are not accidentally true because his thermometer-with-temperature-belief-generator is reliable, they are accidentally true *from the cognitive point of view*, as he has no reasons at all for his beliefs. Indeed, some would say that what Mr Truetemp possesses is a skill (of telling the temperature) and not propositional knowledge at all.

Here we can detect a fundamental clash of intuitions. The reliabilists would hold that Mr Truetemp does know; the traditional normativists would hold that he does not. There appears to be no way to satisfy both. But this much seems clear: There are some situations in which the steps in the process that brings about a belief include the holding of reasons. In those cases in which there is no automatic true-belief-generator (as in the Truetemp case) and in which we must rely upon our reasoning to arrive at a belief, the questions asked by the traditional normativists are crucial: what must the structure of our reasons be so as to make a true belief acceptable? Are there foundational reasons? Can mutually supporting reasons be offered without begging the question? (Could reasons be infinite in number?) And need those reasons be such that they are not undermined by the truth, as the defeasibility theorists would hold? At least in some cases, it seems that normative standards for belief-acquisition apply and their satisfaction will determine whether a belief ought to be accepted. Thus, it appears that an evaluation of the conditions under which beliefs ought to be accepted, denied or suspended is inescapable (see INTERNALISM AND EXTERNALISM IN EPISTEMOLOGY; JUSTIFICATION, EPISTEMIC).

7 Epistemic principles

Epistemic principles describe the normative epistemic status of propositions under varying conditions (see EPISTEMIC LOGIC). It is generally agreed that if a person, S, is justified in believing any proposition, x, then S is not at the same time justified in believing that not-x. Foundationalists and coherentists alike can, and typically do, accept this principle. Other principles are more controversial. They are intuitively plausible but they seem to provide a basis for scepticism and for some deep epistemic puzzles. Here are three of the more interesting principles.

Conjunction Principle (CON-P): If S is justified in believing that x, and S is justified in believing that y, then S is justified in believing that (x and y).

Closure Principle (CLO-P): If S is justified in believing x, and x entails y, then S is justified in believing that y.

Evidence Transfer Principle (ET-P): If there is some evidence, e, that justifies S in believing that x, and x entails y, then e justifies S in believing that y.

In each principle and with suitable grammatical modifications 'justified' could be replaced by other epistemic terms, such as 'reasonable', 'plausible', 'evident', 'certain'. Furthermore, each principle is designed to capture a basis upon which a positive normative epistemic status of a proposition can be transferred to another proposition. As a corollary, 'S is justified in believing x' is not taken to entail 'S does believe that x, justifiably'. For S may not form the belief because of a failure to see the connection between the propositions. Finally, with regard to CLO-P and ET-P, since a tautology is entailed by every proposition, the entailment must be restricted to some form of relevant entailment and/or the range of propositions must be restricted to contingent ones (see RELEVANCE LOGIC AND ENTAILMENT). Other restrictions are no doubt necessary; but these three seemingly intuitive principles have been challenged at their core.

It is important to see some of the relationships between these principles. CLO-P does not entail CON-P since the CLO-P is about *one* proposition that S is justified in believing, not *sets* of propositions. In addition, CLO-P does not entail ET-P because CLO-P does not require that it is the *very same evidence*, e, that S has for x that justifies y for S. Thus, one can accept CLO-P without accepting either of the other principles.

8 The epistemic principles and scepticism

Scepticism – the view that we lack knowledge in those areas commonly thought to be within our ken – comes in many varieties. The most extreme view is global scepticism. It holds that we have very little, if any, knowledge. That view seems preposterous at first glance. Indeed, some epistemologists think that any theory that leads to global scepticism should, *ipso facto*, be rejected (see COMMONSENSISM; SCEPTICISM). Yet there are many arguments for global scepticism that are difficult to answer. In addition, more modest forms of scepticism about particular subject matters (for example, other minds or the future) have been developed. But since the more modest sceptics employ strategies similar to those employed by the global sceptics, I here consider only the most extreme form of scepticism – global scepticism (see OTHER MINDS).

We have already seen the basis for one such argument for global scepticism that can be gleaned from the Pyrrhonians, namely:

(1) All knowledge requires having reasons that are neither arbitrary nor question-begging nor infinitely many.

(2) The only structures for reasons are such that reasons are either arbitrary (foundationalism), question-begging (coherentism) or infinitely many (infinitism).

Therefore, there is no knowledge.

There are at least four possible responses to this argument: (1) the foundational, basic propositions are not arbitrary; (2) coherentism does not necessarily lead to question-begging arguments; (3) requiring infinitely many reasons for a belief does not entail that a belief cannot be justified; (4) not all knowledge entails having reasons. All but (3) have been systematically developed by epistemologists.

Pyrrhonism does not rely directly upon the epistemic principles discussed in the preceding section. But there are other important forms of scepticism that do. Consider this argument that can be traced to Descartes (see DESCARTES, R. §4):

(1) If I am justified in believing that there is a table before me, then I am justified in believing that I am not in one of the sceptical scenarios (evil demon worlds, for example) in which there is no table but it appears just as though there were one.

(2) I am never justified in believing that I am not in one of the sceptical scenarios in which there is no table but it appears just as though there were one.

Therefore, I am never justified in believing that there is a table before me.

Premise 1 is a clear instance of CLO-P. Since the argument is valid (if the premises are true, the conclusion must be true), there are only three plausible responses: (1) CLO-P is false; (2) the second premise is false; (3) the argument begs the question. Responses (1) and (2) are relatively easy to envisage; the third is not so obvious. Roughly, the argument goes as follows: since one of the potentially available grounds for my being justified in believing that I am not in a sceptical scenario is any proposition that entails that I am not in such a scenario, every good argument for the second premise would have to establish that I am not justified in believing that there is a table before me. But that, of course, is the very conclusion.

It is important to note that there is an apparently similar argument for scepticism employing the stronger epistemic principle, ET-P:

(1) If the evidence, e, that I have for believing that there is a table before me is adequate to justify that belief, then it is adequate to justify the belief that I am not in one of the sceptical scenarios.

(2) The evidence, e, is not adequate to justify that I am not in one of the sceptical scenarios.

Therefore, the evidence, e, is not adequate to justify that there is a table before me.

Of course, it is open to epistemologists to deny ET-P. Since one can deny ET-P without abandoning CLO-P (because CLO-P does not entail ET-P), that certainly seems to be a strategy worth considering. The discussion in the next section provides additional reasons for considering that strategy.

9 The epistemic principles and some paradoxes

There are many epistemic paradoxes (see PARADOXES, EPISTEMIC). I here consider two in order to show how they depend upon some of the epistemic principles considered earlier.

The Lottery Paradox: Suppose that enough tickets (say n tickets) have been sold in a fair lottery for you to be justified in believing that the one ticket you bought will not win. In fact, you are justified in believing about each ticket that it will not win. Thus, you are justified in believing the following individual propositions: t_1 will not win. t_2 will not win. t_3 will not win.... t_n will not win.

Now if the conjunction principle is correct, you can conjoin them, ending up with the obviously false but apparently justified proposition that no ticket will win. So, it seems that you are in the awkward position of being justified in believing each of a series of propositions individually, but not being justified in believing that they are all true. Some philosophers have thought that this seemingly awkward position is not so bad after all, since there is no outright contradiction among any of our beliefs as long as the conjunction principle is rejected. But others have thought that making it rational to hold, knowingly, a set of inconsistent beliefs is too high a price to pay.

Others have suggested that we are not actually justified in believing of any ticket that it will lose; rather what we are justified in believing is only that it is highly likely that it will lose. But the lottery can be made as large as one wants, so that any level of probability (below 1) is reached. Thus, this suggestion seems to rule out our being justified in believing any proposition with a probability of less than 1. That is a very high price to pay! There is no generally agreed-upon solution for handling the Lottery Paradox (see PROBABILITY THEORY AND EPISTEMOLOGY; CONFIRMATION THEORY).

The Grue Paradox: The so-called 'Grue Paradox' was developed by Nelson Goodman and has been recast in many ways (see GOODMAN, N.). Here is a way that emphasizes the role of ET-P:

All of the very many emeralds examined up to the present moment, t_{now}, have been green. In fact, one would think that since we have examined so many of them, we are justified in believing that (G): all emeralds are green. But consider another proposition, namely that all emeralds examined up to t_{now} are green, but otherwise they are blue. Let us use 'grue' to stand for the property of being examined and green up to t_{now} but otherwise blue. It appears that the evidence which justifies us in believing that all emeralds are green does not justify us in believing that (N): no emerald is grue.

What are we to make of this version of the paradox? First, note that it depends upon ET-P. Although (1) our inductive evidence (the many examined green emeralds) justifies (G), and although (2) (G) does entail (N), the inductive evidence does not justify (N). In other words, this version of the paradox arises because the evidence does not transfer as the principle would require. Second, note that CLO-P is not threatened by this paradox since it is the evidence for (G) that is inadequate for (N). (The issue is not whether we are justified in believing (N) whenever we are justified in believing that (G).)

But if ET-P were not valid, then the sting of this version of the paradox can be pulled. Recall the original Grabit case. In that case, I had adequate evidence for being justified in believing that Tom stole the book, that is, the person stealing the book looked just like Tom. It seems clear that this evidence is not adequate to justify the proposition that it was not Tom's identical twin who stole the book. If it were the twin, things would appear to be just as they did appear to be. But this tends to show that we do not typically impose ET-P on our evidence.

There are other versions of the Grue Paradox that do not make explicit use of ET-P. For example, since 'all emeralds are green' and 'all emeralds are grue' are alternative hypotheses, it seems paradoxical that the very same evidence that justifies believing the first alternative also seems to support the second. But perhaps, like the version considered above, this apparent paradox rests on a mistaken intuition. Consider the Grabit Case once again. Here, the evidence which justifies the belief that Tom is the thief would also support the claim that Tom's identical twin stole the book. To generalize further, consider any hypothesis, say h, that is justified by some evidence that does not entail h. It is always possible to formulate an alternative hypothesis that is supported by that very evidence, namely (not-h, but it appears just as though h because of . . .). Thus, an intuitively plausible epistemic principle similar to ET-P might be invalid. That principle is: if there is some evidence, e, that justifies S in believing that x, and x is an alternative hypothesis to y, then e does not support y.

To sum up, if ET-P and similar epistemic principles do not accurately capture our normative epistemic practices and if the argument for scepticism that depends upon CLO-P begs the question, then the sting of Cartesian scepticism (considered in the previous section) is numbed and the Grue Paradox

can be addressed. But those are big 'ifs', and the issue remains open (see INDUCTION, EPISTEMIC ISSUES IN).

10 Some challenges to traditional epistemology

A traditional question asked by epistemologists is 'what ought we to believe?' Typically, the answer is given by (1) describing the types of reasons that contribute to warranting a belief, and (2) developing a set of necessary and sufficient conditions for knowledge in which the types of reasons depicted in (1) play a prominent role. But there are many challenges to this answer.

We have already seen the challenge developed by the causal theorists and the reliabilists. Roughly, they hold that our beliefs need not be the result of proper reasoning to be counted as knowledge. Sufficiently reliable belief-acquisition methods are all that is required. Indeed, some have held that epistemology, when done correctly, is a branch of psychology because the primary issue is the study of reliable belief-acquisition methods. This programme has often been referred to as 'naturalized epistemology' and, in one form, its basic tenet is there are no a priori knowable epistemic principles (see NATURALIZED EPISTEMOLOGY; QUINE, W.V.).

Another challenge to traditional epistemology comes from 'virtue epistemology', which makes the primary object of epistemic evaluation traits of persons rather than properties of beliefs or belief-forming processes. The virtue approach has been taken farthest by Linda Zagzebski (1996) who proposes an epistemic theory modelled on virtue ethics and argues that such a theory permits the recovering of such neglected epistemic values as understanding and wisdom (see VIRTUE EPISTEMOLOGY).

A further type of challenge is that of Edward Craig (1990). While allowing that the debate has been shaped by real features of the concept of knowledge, he rejects the project of analysing it in necessary and sufficient conditions. Instead, he tries to 'synthesize' the concept by deriving these features from a pragmatic hypothesis about its purpose, thus explaining the debate rather than joining it.

Even more radical challenges have been developed. First, some have argued that there is no unique method of acquiring and revising beliefs that ought to be employed by all people (see COGNITIVE PLURALISM). Second, it has been argued that the proposed conditions of good reasoning (for example, objectivity and neutrality) tacitly aim at something other than truth. They are developed to prolong entrenched power (see FEMINIST EPISTEMOLOGY). Finally, it has been argued that successful belief acquisition occurs when the future can be adequately anticipated and controlled (see PRAGMATISM).

The defenders of traditional epistemology have two basic types of reply. First, they can examine the particular arguments developed by the critics to determine whether any one of them is sound. Second, they can point out that the critics will have to defend the reasonableness of their views by at least tacitly employing the very principles of good reasoning investigated by traditional epistemologists. Of course, this would not show that the critic's position is false, but it does at least illustrate the universality of the question 'what ought we to believe?'.

See also: DAOIST PHILOSOPHY §5; KNOWLEDGE, INDIAN VIEWS OF; KŪKAI; LINJI; WANG YANGMING

References and further reading

Alston, W. (1989) *Epistemic Justification*, Ithaca, NY: Cornell University Press. (Develops and defends a theory of knowledge containing elements of internalism and externalism.)

Annis, D. (1978) 'A contextualist theory of epistemic justification', *American Philosophical Quarterly* 15 (3): 213–19. (A non-technical contextualist account of justification.)

* Aristotle (3rd century BC) *Posterior Analytics*, ed. and trans. J. Barnes, Oxford: Clarendon Press, 1975. (Aristotle proposes and defends an empirical foundationalist account of knowledge. It can be viewed as containing a basis for a reliabilist account of knowledge of first principles in science.)

Armstrong, D. (1973) *Belief, Truth and Knowledge*, Cambridge: Cambridge University Press. (One of the first carefully developed reliabilist accounts of knowledge.)

Audi, R. (1993) *The Structure of Justification*, Cambridge: Cambridge University Press. (Develops and defends a version of foundationalism.)

Ayer, A.J. (1940) *Foundations of Empirical Knowledge*, London: Macmillan. (Develops and defends a foundationalist account of the structure of reasons.)

BonJour, L. (1985) *The Structure of Empirical Knowledge*, Cambridge, MA: Harvard University Press. (Contains a sophisticated defence of coherentism.)

Broad, C.D. (1965) 'The Theory of Sensa' in R. Swartz (ed.) *Perceiving, Sensing and Knowing*, Berkeley, CA: University of California Press. (Develops the sense-data theory of knowledge. The collection contains many of the most important papers on perception written in the early- and mid-twentieth century.)

Chisholm, R. (1966) *Theory of Knowledge*, Englewood Cliffs, NJ: Prentice Hall; 2nd edn, 1977; 3rd edn, 1989. (The successive editions contain increasingly complex foundationalist accounts of knowledge along with versions of the defeasibility account.)

Code, L. (1991) *What Can She Know? Feminist Theory and the Construction of Knowledge*, Ithaca, NY: Cornell University Press. (Contains a sophisticated feminist challenge to traditional epistemology.)

* Craig, E. (1990) *Knowledge and the State of Nature*, Oxford: Oxford University Press. (The concept of knowledge approached by asking 'why do we have it?' Assumes some familiarity with the current debate. Mentioned in §10 above.)

Davidson, D. (1983) 'A coherence theory of truth and knowledge', in E. LePore (ed.) *Truth and Interpretation: Perspectives on the Philosophy of Donald Davidson*, Oxford: Blackwell, 1986. (Contains an account of the coherence theory of knowledge, as well as arguments for the claim that coherent beliefs must be true in the main.)

DeRose, K. (1995) 'Solving the Skeptical Problem', *Philosophical Review* 104 (January): 1–52. (Develops a contextualist theory of knowledge and uses it to address the problem of scepticism.)

* Descartes, R. (1641) *Meditations on First Philosophy*, in E. Haldane and G.R.T. Ross (eds) *The Philosophical Works of Descartes*, vol. 1, Mineola, NY: Dover Publications, 1955. (Contains a classic formulation of rationalistic foundationalism. Meditation I contains the 'Cartesian' argument for scepticism which he rejects in the following five meditations; Mediation IV employs the notion of warrant requiring non-accidentally true beliefs – see especially paragraphs 11–13 on page 176 of this edition.)

Dewey, J. (1929) *The Quest for Certainty: Gifford Lectures 1929*, New York: Capricorn, 1960. (Contains a contextualist account of doubt and justification.)

Dretske F. (1981) *Knowledge and the Flow of Information*, Cambridge, MA: MIT Press. (Contains a reliabilist account of knowledge employing information theory.)

Foley, R. (1987) *A Theory of Epistemic Rationality*, Cambridge, MA: Harvard University Press. (Develops and defends a sophisticated version of subjective justification.)

Gettier, E. (1963) 'Is justified true belief knowledge?', *Analysis* 23 (6): 121–3. (This article was responsible for focusing attention on the inadequacies of characterizing warrant in terms of justification alone.)

Goldman, A. (1967) 'A causal theory of knowing', *Journal of Philosophy* 64 (12) 357–72. (The first careful statement of the causal theory of warrant.)

—— (1986) *Epistemology and Cognition*, Cambridge, MA: Harvard University Press. (Contains a sophisticated development and defence of reliabilism.)

* Goodman, N. (1965) *Fact, Fiction and Forecast*, New York: Bobbs-Merrill, 2nd edn. (Contains the formulation of the Grue Paradox discussed in §9 above.)

Klein, P. (1981) *Certainty: A Refutation of Scepticism*, Minneapolis, MN: University of Minnesota Press. (Examines various forms of scepticism and develops the defeasibility theory of knowledge as a response to scepticism.)

—— (1996) 'Skepticism and closure: why the evil genius argument fails', *Philosophical Topics* 23 (1) spring 1995: 215–38. (Develops the 'question-begging' reply to scepticism briefly discussed in §8 above.)

* Lehrer, K. (1990) *Theory of Knowledge*, Boulder, CO: Westview Press. (An accessible introduction to the fundamental questions in epistemology that defends a version of coherentism and contains arguments against externalism including the True-Temp example cited in §6 above; see especially pages 163–75.)

* Locke, J. (1689) *An Essay Concerning Human Understanding*, ed. A.C. Fraser, Mineola, New York: Dover Publications, 1959. (Contains the classic defence of empirical foundationalism conforming to the constraint that knowledge cannot be accidentally true belief. See especially Book XI, chapter 23, section 28 – pages 413–14 of this edition.)

Lucey, K. (1996) *On Knowing and the Known*, Buffalo, NY: Prometheus Books. (A comprehensive and accessible collection of essays on the concept of knowledge.)

Moore, G.E. (1953) *Some Main Problems of Philosophy*, New York: Collier Books, 1962. (The text of lectures given in 1910–11. See especially chapter 2 which develops the sense-data foundationalist theory of knowledge.)

Moser, P. (1989) *Knowledge and Evidence*, Cambridge: Cambridge University Press. (Contains a sophisticated development of foundationalism.)

Nozick, R. (1981) *Philosophical Explanations*, Cambridge, MA: Harvard University Press. (Develops and defends a reliabilist account of knowledge.)

Plantinga, A. (1993) *Warrant: The Current Debate*, Oxford: Oxford University Press. (A good source for discussions of various accounts of warrant.)

* Plato (4th century BC) *Theaetetus*, in *The Collected Dialogues of Plato*, ed. E. Hamilton and H. Cairns, Princeton, NJ: Princeton University Press, 1961. (Suggests that knowledge cannot be mere true belief even with a justification; but Plato does not suggest what the missing feature is.)

Pollock, J. (1986) *Contemporary Theories of Knowledge*, Totowa, NJ: Rowman & Littlefield. (Examines various contemporary accounts of knowledge and justification and develops a sophisticated version of the defeasibility theory.)

Prichard, H.A. (1950) *Knowledge and Perception*, Oxford: Clarendon Press. (Defends the view that knowledge is not a species of belief. See page 88 and following.)

Quine, W.V.O and Ullian, J. (1978) *The Web of Belief*, 2nd edn, New York: Random House. (A very accessible defence of coherentism.)

Radford, C. (1966) 'Knowledge – by examples' *Analysis* 27 (1): 1–11. (Defends the view that belief is not a necessary condition of knowledge.)

Sextus Empiricus (c.200) *Outlines of Pyrrhonism*, trans. R.G. Bury, Cambridge, MA: Harvard University Press and London: Heinemann, 1976. (See especially book I, chapter 15, for the argument that the three logically possible theories of justification lead to scepticism.)

Shope, R. (1983) *The Analysis of Knowing*, Princeton, NJ: Princeton University Press. (A thorough discussion of the Gettier Problem and the various approaches to solving it.)

Sosa, E. (1991) *Knowledge in Perspective*, Cambridge: Cambridge University Press. (Contains an interesting version of reliabilism that is designed to address issues generated by traditional normative epistemology.)

—— (ed.) (1994) *Knowledge and Justification*, vols 1 and 2, Brookfield, VT: Ashgate Publishing Company. (Contains a comprehensive set of essays on knowledge and justification.)

* Zagzebski, L. (1996) *Virtues of the Mind*, Cambridge: Cambridge University Press. (Develops an account of virtue epistemology based on virtue ethics.)

PETER D. KLEIN

KNOWLEDGE, DEFEASIBILITY THEORY OF

Based upon an analogy with the legal and ethical concept of a defeasible, or prima facie, *obligation, epistemic defeasibility was introduced into epistemology as an ingredient in one of the main strategies for dealing with Gettier cases. In these cases, an individual's justified true belief fails to count as knowledge because the justification is defective as a source of knowledge. According to the defeasibility theory of knowledge, the defect involved can be characterized in terms of evidence that the subject does not possess which overrides, or defeats, the subject's* prima facie *justification for belief. This account holds that knowledge is indefeasibly justified true belief. It has significant advantages over other attempts to modify the traditional analysis of knowledge in response to the Gettier examples. Care must be taken, however, in the definition of defeasibility.*

1   Chisholm's account

The concept of epistemic defeasibility was introduced into epistemology as an ingredient in one of the main strategies for dealing with Gettier cases and other instances in which an epistemic justification for a belief fails to provide the believer with knowledge, even though the resulting belief is true (see GETTIER PROBLEMS). An early discussion by Roderick Chisholm noted that the problems raised by Gettier cases are analogous to problems that arise in ethical contexts. In the ethical case, we have the concept of a *prima facie* obligation, one that might be overridden. When there is a conflict between circumstances that create a *prima facie* obligation and special additional circumstances that override them, the original obligation is defeated and is no longer actual.

Building upon this notion, Chisholm defines an epistemic version of defeasibility, a concept that applies by analogy to justification for a belief. When a person's belief that *h* is *prima facie* justified by the evidence they possess, it is possible that additional evidence would undermine that justification. If this were to happen, the original justification would be defeated. Chisholm (1964: 148–9) defines epistemic defeasibility in two steps:

(1) There is a justification for *h* which has been overridden =df. There is a body of evidence *e* and a body of evidence *e'* such that *e* is true and *e* justifies *h*, and *e'* is true and the conjunction of *e* and *e'* does not justify *h*.

(2) A justification for *h* is defeasible =df. There is a body of evidence *e* such that *e* is true and *e* justifies *h* and this justification may be overridden.

The opposite of defeasibility is *indefeasibility*, which is then defined as justification which cannot be overridden.

In these definitions, it is assumed that epistemic justification is of the 'linear' variety normally associated with foundational theories of justification. This assumption is not necessary for an account of defeasibility. Defeasibility conditions can be incorporated into a coherence theory of justification (as is done by Lehrer 1990) or into a reliabilist account (as is done by Swain 1981) (see JUSTIFICATION, EPISTEMIC §§2–3). For ease of exposition, the linear notion of justification will be assumed here.

2   The traditional analysis and Gettier cases

The traditional analysis of knowledge maintains that a person has knowledge provided they have a justified true belief (see KNOWLEDGE, CONCEPT OF). In the kind of counterexample introduced by Gettier, an individual has a justification for some true belief, but this justified true belief is not knowledge because the justification is defective as a source of knowledge. In all such cases, the individual has arrived at the justified true belief by reasoning which depends upon an essential intermediate premise which, though justified, is false. Were the falsity of this essential intermediate premise brought forth as the additional evidence *e'* in the definition (1) above, the resulting conjunction of *e* with *e'* would not justify the proposition *h*. Hence, the justification that the individual has in a Gettier case is defeasible, and this is taken to explain why the individual does not have knowledge. Specifically, the proposal is to modify the traditional definition of knowledge as justified true belief to include an additional requirement: knowledge is *indefeasibly* justified true belief. On this proposal, known as the defeasibility theory of knowledge, a justified belief will count as knowledge only if the justification cannot be overridden by the unpossessed evidence.

Consider a specific example, introduced by Keith Lehrer (1965). Suppose Smith correctly infers that (*h*) someone in his class owns a Ford from some true evidence (*e*) that justifies the false belief (*q*) that a student, Mr Nogot, owns a Ford. It so happens that another student in Smith's class, Mr. Havit, does own a Ford, but Smith has no evidence one way or the other for this proposition. Smith's justification for *h*, which consists of *e* and his inference to *h* through the false but justified proposition (*q*) that Mr. Nogot owns a Ford, is nevertheless rendered defeasible by the true proposition *e'*, which asserts that 'Nogot does not own a Ford'. Because Smith's justification is defeasible, he does not know that someone in his class owns a Ford. All Gettier cases have essentially this same structure, and so the defeasibility theory provides a general solution to the problem they pose for the traditional analysis of knowledge.

3 Advantages of the defeasibility approach

The defeasibility theory has advantages over other, simpler, proposals for modifying the traditional analysis of knowledge in response to Gettier cases. For example, the traditional definition can be revised to require that one's justification not involve or depend essentially upon any false intermediate premises. Or, the definition of epistemic justification can be strengthened to require that only true beliefs can be epistemically justified, blocking the move through (q) in the above example. However, these alternative solutions, which are aimed at specific features exemplified by Gettier cases, do not result in an acceptable general account of knowledge. There are examples which show that the traditional analysis fails even when all the evidence, essential intermediate lemmas and final conclusions involved in the justification of a belief, are true. The defeasibility analysis of knowledge has the merit of providing an adequate account even in these additional examples.

One illustration of the merits of the defeasibility account of knowledge over others is the well-known 'Barn Facsimile' example introduced by Alvin Goldman (1976). A subject, S, is looking at a barn under normal conditions of perception. S comes to believe, correctly, that there is a barn there on the basis of the perceptual evidence gained by looking at the barn. It may be assumed that all of S's essential evidence is true, S correctly infers that there is a barn present in a manner that does not depend upon any false propositions, and S arrives at a true belief. Even so, S does not know that there is a barn there because of unusual surrounding circumstances. Unknown to S, the neighbourhood is populated by a number of structures which consist only of barn facades propped up by sticks. The only real barn in the neighbourhood is the one that S happens to see, and it is just by chance that S is perceiving that structure rather than one of the façades. Had S perceived a façade rather than a barn, S would have mistaken it for a real barn. All efforts to modify the traditional analysis of knowledge by disallowing justifications that depend essentially upon false beliefs will fail to rule out this example, since there are no false beliefs involved. The defeasibility account gives the right answer, however, for in this case the subject's justification is rendered defeasible by the availability of the true proposition e', which asserts that 'Virtually all the things in this neighbourhood that look like barns are actually barn facades'.

4 Problems facing the defeasibility approach

Perhaps the most serious problem facing the defea-sibility account, as it is expressed in the definitions (1) and (2) above, is the existence of examples in which there are special circumstances that would override a subject's justification even though that justification is not defeasible. As formulated, the account of defeasibility is too strong. This phenomenon is illustrated in the well-known example of Tom Grabit, presented by Lehrer and Paxson (1969). Suppose you observe your friend, Tom Grabit, in the act of stealing a book from the library. You know Tom well, and have no doubt whatever that it is Tom who stole the book. Your belief is true, your evidence is true, and your justification does not essentially involve any false beliefs. It would seem obvious that you have knowledge. Unknown to you, however, Tom's mother, upon hearing that her son has been arrested, fabricates a lie: she tells the police that it could not have been Tom, for Tom is in some other city. Instead, she says, it was almost certainly Tom's twin brother Tim, who is a kleptomaniac. But there is no twin brother; it was in fact Tom who stole the book. Given this scenario, your justification will be rendered defeasible by the availability of the true proposition e', which asserts that 'Tom's mother says Tom was out of town at the time of the theft'.

Several modifications of the defeasibility theory have been suggested that would make it sensitive to such examples of apparent or pseudo-defeasibility. Gilbert Harman (1973) suggests that we make a distinction within the class of potentially undermining counter-evidence – evidence that would qualify as overriding by (1) above – between that which is genuinely defeating and that which is not. Then, undermining evidence will prevent knowledge only if it is genuinely defeating, as it is not in the case of Tom Grabit. Unfortunately, Harman left the distinction between genuine and non-genuine defeating counter-evidence undefined.

Another proposal, made by David Annis (1973), suggests a distinction between genuinely defeating and 'merely misleading' counter-evidence. In the Grabit example, the mother's testimony is merely misleading and not genuinely defeating. Although this proposal has considerable intuitive appeal, Annis was not able to provide a generally accepted account of the key notion of 'merely misleading' counter-evidence. An attempt to make this distinction precise was made by Peter Klein (1980 and 1981), who suggests that the misleading effect of a defeater such as the one in the Grabit example is explained by the fact that it depends essentially on a false proposition. In genuine defeat, the defeater does not so depend. This proposal may prove to be adequate, although there is some debate about the notion of essential dependence.

Yet another proposal, suggested by Barker (1976), Swain (1974, 1981), Lehrer (1990) and Pollock (1990), attempts to take into account the defeasible nature of the defeasibility relation itself. In judging whether a subject's justification is defeasible, it is a mistake to consider isolated members of the total body of unpossessed evidence which is available to the subject, as is encouraged by (1) and (2). In many cases, such as the Grabit example, a justification's apparent defeat is itself only *prima facie*. It is itself defeated by further unpossessed evidence or special circumstances. The apparently defeating effect of the mother's testimony is itself overridden by the additional circumstance that she is lying. The final answer to the question of defeasibility of a justification in a given situation can only be arrived at when all of the relevant available counter-evidence, countervailing counter-evidence and so on, is taken into account. If a justification still holds when all the special circumstances are taken into account, it is said to be 'ultimately undefeated'. In the Gettier cases, the barn-facsimile example and other cases in which the subject genuinely lacks knowledge, their justification is ultimately defeated. In genuine cases of knowledge, even if some isolated undermining counter-evidence is available, the subject's justification will be ultimately undefeated.

This final proposal has also come under critical attack. Klein has argued (1980, 1981), for example, that even in cases of genuine defeat it will turn out that the justification is ultimately undefeated, since the 'original', or target proposition is true. Given these various disagreements, it seems fair to say that the defeasibility theory remains one of the most viable alternative approaches to the analysis of knowledge, but that there is no unanimity concerning the best way to handle the misleading defeater cases.

References and further reading

All these items involve intricate argument and moderate use of technical terminology.

* Annis, D.B. (1973) 'Knowledge and Defeasibility', *Philosophical Studies* 24: 199–203; repr. in G.S. Pappas and M. Swain (eds) *Essays on Knowledge and Justification*, Ithaca, NY and New York: Cornell University Press, 1978. (Introduces the distinction between genuinely defeating and 'merely misleading' counter-evidence, and suggests an account of both notions.)

* Barker, J. (1976) 'What You Don't Know Won't Hurt You?', *American Philosophical Quarterly* 13: 303–8. (Early discussion of the complications involved in defeasibility.)

* Chisholm, R. (1964) 'The Ethics of Requirement', *American Philosophical Quarterly* 1: 147–53. (Introduces the analogy between ethical and epistemological defeasibility.)

* Goldman, A. (1976) 'Discrimination and Perceptual Knowledge', *Journal of Philosophy* 73: 771–91; repr. in G.S. Pappas and M. Swain (eds) *Essays on Knowledge and Justification*, Ithaca, NY and New York: Cornell University Press, 1978. (Presentation of the 'barn facade' example and other well-known considerations.)

* Harman, G. (1973) *Thought*, Princeton, NJ: Princeton University Press. (Chapter 9 provides a sustained discussion and defence of the suggestion that reasoning through false premises cannot provide one with knowledge.)

* Klein, P.D. (1980) 'Misleading Evidence and the Restoration of Justification', *Philosophical Studies* 37 (1): 81–99. (A self-contained discussion of the 'merely misleading defeaters' solution.)

* —— (1981) *Certainty: A Refutation of Scepticism*, Minneapolis, MN: University of Minnesota Press. (See especially pages 137–70 for a sustained discussion of defeasibility.)

* Lehrer, K. (1965) 'Knowledge, Truth, and Evidence', *Analysis* 25: 168–75. (The 'Nogot-Havit' example can be found in this early discussion of Gettier problems.)

* —— (1990) *Theory of Knowledge*, Boulder, CO: Westview Press. (Chapters 1 and 7 provide a detailed discussion of defeasibility and knowledge. Excellent bibliography to 1990.)

* Lehrer, K. and Paxson, T. (1969) 'Knowledge: Undefeated Justified True Belief', *Journal of Philosophy*, 66: 225–37; repr. in M. Roth, and L. Galis (eds) *Knowing: Essays in the Analysis of Knowing*, New York: Random House; also repr. in G.S. Pappas and M. Swain (eds) *Essays on Knowledge and Justification*, Ithaca, NY and New York: Cornell University Press, 1978. (Early discussion of defeasibility theory, containing several important examples.

* Pollock, J. (1986) *Contemporary Theories of Knowledge*, Lanham, MD: Rowman & Littlefield, 1991. (The appendix contains a discussion of defeasibility theory.)

Shope, R.K. (1983) *The Analysis of Knowing: A Decade of Research*, Princeton, NJ: Princeton University Press. (Chapters 1 and 2 provide a thorough survey of defeasibility theories. The remainder of the book is a survey of attempts to analyse knowledge, and there is an excellent bibliography to 1983.)

Swain, M. (1974) 'Epistemic Defeasibility', *American Philosophical Quarterly* 11: 15–25; repr. in G.S. Pappas and M. Swain (eds) *Essays on Knowledge and Justification*, Ithaca, NY and New York: Cornell University Press, 1978. (Early discussion of defeasibility, with a detailed proposal and several important examples.)

* —— (1981) *Reasons and Knowledge*, Ithaca, NY and New York: Cornell University Press. (See especially chapter 5 for an extended discussion of defeasible justification.)

MARSHALL SWAIN

KNOWLEDGE, INDIAN VIEWS OF

Classical Indian epistemology centres on a complex of terms for knowledge, knower and the known or knowable, including pramāṇa, *'means to knowledge' or 'source of knowledge'. Views about perception, inference, testimony and a few additional candidate sources are the topics of core proposals of competing epistemological theories. Certain types of scepticism are also addressed, but explaining how it is possible that we know anything has been less central than other issues. Debates about knowledge – and doubt as well – are often caught up in larger war plans concerning the nature of awareness.*

The various classical schools typically bring views about awareness with them to the epistemological arena, but a neutral, common touchstone for and important constraint on all pramāṇa *theorizing is what is called speech behaviour,* vyavahāra, *reflecting, it is presumed, bits of everyday knowledge. Verbalizations of perception, for example, 'That is a pot', of inference, for example, 'There is fire on yonder mountain' (made on the basis of the sight of smoke and an understanding of the general rule that wherever there is smoke, there is fire), of information acquired through testimony, and so on, are the givens for which a successful theory has to account.*

Principal candidate sources proposed in addition to perception and inference are testimony, analogy, circumstantial implication and negative perception. Mystical experience as a pramāṇa *for spiritual matters is viewed as a variety of perception by its advocates, and scripture as a variety of testimony. With stock examples of bits of knowledge agreed upon, disagreement typically centres on what the source is for a particular example and whether admission of any source in addition to perception and inference is ever required. Or, in some cases, a stock example is slightly modified, better to align with a stance taken on a putatively additional* pramāṇa.

With regard to what the sources make known, some argue that each pramāṇa *works within a range of possibilities unique to itself, with no overlap. Thus what is known by perception cannot be known by inference. Others dispute such contentions, although at least a few such restrictions on individual knowledge sources are usually recognized. Buddhists and some others appear to be motivated to deny* pramāṇa *status to testimony because appeal to testimony is used to justify what they see as objectionable religious theses. Similarly, the Cārvāka materialist denies inference, apparently out of fear of its power to prove the existence of spiritual entities such as God or the soul.*

The Buddhist Nāgārjuna and others challenge the pramāṇa *programmes proffered by epistemologists of all stripes, and provoke what may be called meta-epistemological responses that bring out connections between* pramāṇa *proposals and a logic of presumption. In particular, the Nyāya response to Nāgārjuna and company is by any light an admirable effort of philosophy.*

1   **Awareness, knowledge and doubt**
2   **Candidate sources**
3   **Object-wise restrictions**
4   **Scepticism and epistemology**

1   Awareness, knowledge and doubt

In the classical Indian context, knowledge is treated as a species of awareness or cognition (*jñāna*), not of belief. A common opinion is that only a verbalizable or propositional awareness can be a bit of knowledge, and the examples of bits of knowledge talked about by classical epistemologists are expressed as sentences. For instance, the sensory awareness 'That is a pot', when a cognizer is perceptually presented with a pot, would, on most views, count as a bit of knowledge, although some theorists would object to this way of framing the matter. Awarenesses normally form beliefs in that there is – again, most would agree – a causal relation between an awareness and a memory or, more precisely, a 'disposition', *saṃskāra*. This reverberates with contemporary dispositional analyses (roughly: *A* is *S*'s belief if and only if *S* would answer certain questions in certain ways or behave in certain ways). Still, the bits of knowledge focused upon by classical Indian epistemologists are not beliefs but cognitions or awarenesses – right cognitions and veridical awarenesses.

Inferential knowledge is also an awareness, as too is knowledge acquired from any of the more exotic (and disputed) sources. Those who have become accustomed to talking about arguments in terms of propositions or sentences have to guard against imposing a nonpersonal understanding upon Indian discussions of logic in particular. Unlike in Western treatments, inference is not abstracted wholesale out of the context of persons who make inferences. The result of a good inference is an inferential awareness, a proposition-laden cognitive event arrived at by a process of understanding that such-and-such is the case because such-and-such else is the case. In practice – that is to say, in the context of philosophical discussion and debate – there is, to be sure, abstraction from actual situations of knowing; otherwise, epistemology would be impossible since it is, at least normally, a discourse about cognitive events other than those provoked or reflected by the discourse itself (although self-referential, or meta-, epistemological discourse does occur: see §4). But the personal context is not lost sight of.

Another presupposition of classical Indian epistemology that is often missed or considered strange by those weaned on Western materials is the assumption that awareness, and thus knowledge, is episodic in character. In Plato's *Meno*, Socrates argues that part of the value of knowledge is its steadfastness: *justifiable* true belief cannot be easily unpegged. One must keep in mind that 'knowledge' as used in the present entry renders a Sanskrit term, *pramā*, whose meaning has been the focus of extensive probing and controversy, comparable to the amount of philosophical attention knowledge has received in the West. There is no single English term or phrase that captures precisely the meaning of any of the family of Sanskrit words rendered here as 'knowledge', 'knower', 'source of knowledge', and so on. Many contemporary philosophers have detailed opinions about just what knowledge is, and so to render *pramā* as 'knowledge', for example, or *pramāṇa* as 'source of knowledge' may be especially to invite misunderstanding. The classical Indian approach to epistemology and translations such as 'knowledge', 'knower', and so on, have, however, been ably defended by several scholars and philosophers, most notably by Bimal Matilal (1986), who argues that to have knowledge in the episodic sense is a necessary (though not a sufficient) condition for knowledge in the sense of (roughly) a justified true belief. A belief not acquired through a reliable means will not count as knowledge. Classical Indian epistemologists focus on the event that is, one might say, the first formation of a bit of knowledge. With many, *pramāṇa* is to be understood both as evidence and as proximate cause of the first formation of any bit of knowledge – to use the term 'knowledge' in the nonepisodic sense. The dispositions required for reactivation or later use of a knowledge episode are not ignored by classical epistemologists. But

again, the primary focus is on knowledge as an episode.

Doubt is also a cognitive episode or awareness, and it arises in specific situations whose general features we may become apprised of – this is another task of epistemology as practised in classical India. The *Nyāyasūtra* (*c.* AD 150; although it did not reach its present form until about 400), for example, says that doubt arises when, about the same object or topic, (a) there is insufficient information to determine what something is among things sharing common characteristics (for example, a post or a person in the distance), (b) there is insufficient information to determine what something is among things fundamentally distinct (for example, whether sound is a substance, quality or motion), (c) contradictory assertions are made and (d) there is inconstant information (for example, there seems to be water in the distance and then there does not). In this way, the *Nyāyasūtra* embraces a project of articulating conditions of meaningful doubt, a project that becomes much advanced during the following centuries. Philosophers of the Nyāya school take it to be a knockdown argument against a position that it provokes irresolvable doubt, and no school, not even Nāgārjuna's Mādhyamika, which is famed for its scepticism about philosophy (see §4), holds doubt to be anything like a foundational, or natural, philosophical position. Doubt is a cognitive event that arises under certain conditions.

2 Candidate sources

Perception, inference and testimony are treated elsewhere (see SENSE PERCEPTION, INDIAN VIEWS OF; INFERENCE, INDIAN THEORIES OF; TESTIMONY IN INDIAN PHILOSOPHY). So also is the issue of how negative facts are known (for example, Devadatta's not being at home or the absence of my glasses on the table), and whether they are known through a special *pramāṇa* (see NEGATIVE FACTS IN CLASSICAL INDIAN PHILOSOPHY). The present entry will air arguments surrounding the candidate sources of analogy and circumstantial implication. The question of mystical experience as a possible source of knowledge about spiritual matters is assimilated in classical discussions to the epistemology of perception.

An example commonly used of knowledge acquired through *upamāna*, 'analogy', is, according to Nyāya, as follows. A knower *S* has been informed by a forester that a *gavaya* (a kind of ox, *Bos gavaeus*), a species with which *S* has had no prior acquaintance, is similar to a cow except for certain differences that the forester spells out. *S* proceeds into the forest and encounters a *gavaya*, recognizes it as the animal the forester said was similar to a cow and shows the recognition by saying 'Hey, a *gavaya*!' Philosophers of the Nyāya school hold that *S* acquired a new piece of vocabulary (a bit of knowledge) through the analogy drawn by the forester, as shown by *S*'s correct use of the word *gavaya* to designate the animal commonly referred to by that name.

Two principal contrary positions are, first, that what is known in such cases is not a new piece of vocabulary but a similarity, which, according to some but not all those who so endorse the *pramāṇa* status of *upamāna*, is a distinct category of the real. A second camp denies *pramāṇa* status to analogy no matter how understood; that is to say, analogy is no additional source of knowledge and the cited examples of knowledge from analogy are to be understood as examples of knowledge from testimony (in so far as testimony is itself an irreducible source) or perception or inference or a combination of these.

According to the Mīmāṃsā school, which is intent on explaining and defending Brahmanical rituals, *upamāna* is the source for knowing the similarity of two things – a particularly useful bit of information when a substitute has to be found to complete a sacrifice or other ritual performance. For example, wild rice (*nīvāra*) can be substituted for domestic rice (*vrīhi*) because of their similarity. Also, when scripture does not elaborate the details of the performance of a particular rite *X* that is similar to rite *Y*, then rite *Y* can be used as a model for the performance of *X*. In the Mīmāṃsaka version of the stock example (which probably predates that in Nyāya), a knower *S* sees a *gavaya* and is reminded of a cow: 'Similar to this is my cow.' Analogy is said to be the proximate cause of knowledge of such a similarity. Against the arguments of Buddhists and others who hold that no special source need be postulated, Mīmāṃsakas respond by pointing out peculiar features of what is made known, along with strictures (some recognized by their opponents) on the range of operation of perception and inference.

It is difficult to see what motivates the Nyāya endorsement of analogy, since, as some of that very persuasion (such as the tenth-century philosopher Bhāsarvajña) insist, testimony and perception appear sufficient to account for vocabulary acquisition, at least in the stock example. Advaita Vedāntins, in contrast, have clear and substantial motives for endorsing analogy as understood roughly in the Mīmāṃsaka fashion: the true Self (*ātman*), as declared in scripture, is known as eternal, all-pervasive and unattached *like the sky*, and not as perishable, limited and prone to attachments – that is, it is known to be *unlike the body*. Such comparisons are grounded in facts that only the special source of

analogy is capable of conveying. The Self is best or directly known in a meditative or mystical experience; no knowledge source, not even the testimony of scripture, operates except within the conditions of spiritual ignorance, *avidyā*, that are transcended in direct Self-experience. Nevertheless, scripture does refer to similarities and dissimilarities to help the mystic aspirant. So convinced, some late Advaitins speculate at length on the peculiar power of analogy.

Circumstantial implication, *arthāpatti* (sometimes rendered 'presumption'), is held to be another special and irreducible source according to Mīmāṃsakas and Vedāntins, and a type of inference according to most other disputants. Two stock examples are: (a) from discovery that Devadatta is not in his house it is known by implication that he is outside, and (b) from testimony about fat Devadatta that he does not eat during the day it is known by implication that he eats at night.

Kumārila (*c.*650), a Mīmāṃsaka with an extraordinary breadth of interest and the founder of one of two principal Mīmāṃsā subschools, is often cited for his views on *arthāpatti* by philosophers of all persuasions. He lists six types of circumstantial implication according to how the critical circumstances are known, that is, according to the six sources identified by his school: perception, inference, analogy, circumstantial implication (making known the crucial circumstances in the present case, although the circumstances leading to it may be known differently), negative perception (the source for knowledge of absences) and testimony.

As comes to be common practice for wide-ranging philosophers of almost all points of view, Kumārila finds use for *arthāpatti* in establishing positions in ontology and metaphysics. Some modern commentators have seen *arthāpatti* as a pattern of reasoning commonly employed in the system-building typical of both Western and Eastern metaphysics, namely, reasoning to a vaunted best explanation. The best explanation of the information that fat Devadatta fasts by day is that he is a glutton at night, though there are other possibilities. Similarly, a Nyāya philosopher will argue against a Buddhist nominalist that postulation of real universals does a better job of explaining certain generalities or recurrences of experience than the Buddhist theory does. However, Kumārila and others seem to hold (it is probably Prabhākara, Kumārila's pupil and rival, and founder of the second principal Mīmāṃsā subschool, who had the insight originally) that what makes *arthāpatti* effective is the absence of all other (live?) explanatory possibilities. (Prabhākara adds a proviso, disputed by the Kumārila camp: the absence of other explanatory possibilities in a given context of inquiry.) In reasoning to the best explanation, on the other hand, alternatives are presumably admitted. Of course, there is no modal logic in classical Indian thought informing such reflections (until in a sense in very late New Logic, according to Sibajiban Bhattacharyya (1987)); we should avoid reading too much into classical discussions of albeit interesting examples. In any case, controversies in other domains, such as the basic categories of reality, come to bear on philosophers' understanding of *arthāpatti* – as they do too in particular with perception among other candidate sources.

Nyāya philosophers and others argue that circumstantial implication is a form of inference: roughly, from the premises (1) Devadatta is fat, (2) whoever is fat eats either at night or during the day, and (3) Devadatta does not eat during the day, one infers (4) Devadatta eats at night. In terms closer to the Sanskrit locutions used to express inferences, the invariable concomitance or pervasion, *vyāpti*, between occurrences of properties *F* and *G* that would underpin inference in this case would be: any person not eating at night or during the day exhibits absence of fatness (whatever is not-*G* is not-*F*).

3 Object-wise restrictions

Another important feature of classical Indian epistemology is the tendency to find restrictions governing the operations of individual knowledge sources, restrictions tied to the nature of the objects the sources reveal. Although objects are made known only by sources, knowing them we are apparently led to a view of epistemic limitations. And the individual sources themselves, it should be pointed out, can be objects of knowledge, at least according to the most prominent views.

Mīmāṃsāsūtra 1.1.4 presents an argument against perception's being the source of ethical knowledge: perception apprehends only what *already exists*, whereas ethics – *dharma* in Sanskrit, 'right practice' – is comprised of what one *should do*. The nature of *dharma* precludes perception as the knowledge source. Thus in so far as ethical knowledge is presumed, its source must be other than perception. It is, according to Mīmāṃsā, scripture, the Veda, interpreted as a list of injunctions prescribing what we should do. In this way, a limitation of perception concerning something presumed knowable (*prameya*, 'object of knowledge', in this case *dharma*) is used as a way to defend the authority, the *pramāṇa* status, of scripture.

Disputes between Nyāya realists and Buddhist Yogācāra idealists centre on conflicts over perception and inference. Object-wise distinctions shore up a Yogācāra partitioning of the two *pramāṇa*: there are

unconceptualizable individuals on the one hand, and concept-fused generalities on the other. The Yogācārin DIGNĀGA (§1) says:

> Now the means of cognition are [immediate and mediate, namely] perception and inference. They are only two, because the object to be cognized has [only] two aspects. Apart from the particular and the universal there is no other object to be cognized, and we shall prove that perception has only the particular for its object and inference only the universal.
>
> (*Pramāṇasamuccaya* 1.B)

And he goes on to present several considerations that bear on – or that elaborate – a rather trenchant division (see BUDDHISM, YOGĀCĀRA SCHOOL OF §§1–4). Nyāya, in contrast, finds universals such as cowhood as well as individuals such as Bessie the cow to be known perceptually. Inference is seen as dependent on perception in specified ways but also as filling out what is perceptually known, and a single object, such as a fire, can be known by perception or by inference or by both (or, indeed, by testimony) (see NYĀYA-VAIŚEṢIKA §§5–6). Inference is dependent on perception both in that it is perception that establishes a required general thesis (paradigmatically, wherever there is *F*, there is *G*) and in that every inference, in providing knowledge of the world, is said to have to have – to get started, so to speak – a perceptually warranted premise. For example, from the sight of smoke rising from a hill, it is known by inference that there is fire there, too. (Several Nyāya philosophers point out that testimony can substitute for perception here, since, for example, we can be told that there is smoke on a hill and infer fire.) Dignāga and his school view inference as operating in a world of concepts or generalities all of its own, with the role of perception in concept formation as negative, as excluding (*apoha*) or ruling out what proves unpragmatic. To label Bessie a cow is to impose a generality of the mind on her unique particularity, a generality that, all things considered, is nevertheless better than its negation, a non-cow, with the opposition of cow and non-cow understood as a law of logic, not, as in Nyāya, a natural opposition, an incompatibility in the world (see EPISTEMOLOGY, INDIAN SCHOOLS OF §1).

The topic of object-wise restrictions on individual sources looms large in still other schools. ŚAṄKARA (*c*.700) presents an argument (probably inspired by the Mīmāṃsaka move respecting *dharma*) to shore up an Advaita absolutist metaphysics: proclamations of scripture (the Upaniṣads) have exclusive authority within their own province, namely, the reality and nature of Brahman, the Absolute (*Brahmasūtrabhāṣya* 2.1.1). Thus no evidence derived from perception, for example, could conflict with what the Upaniṣads say of Brahman. Similarly, the Upaniṣads cannot dispute perceptual evidence about objects in the world. Indeed, Saṅkara holds that 'It is not the case that one source of knowledge (ever) opposes another source, for the one source makes something known that is not at all an object of the other' (*Bṛhadāraṇyakabhāṣya* 2.120). One wonders, however, whether Saṅkara intends a position, like that of Yogācāra, according to which the perceptible and the inferable are distinct realities, or whether he intends only to stress (by exaggeration) the separate domain of scriptural authority.

Later Advaitins follow Saṅkara's apparent endorsement of partition, at least in part. Dharmarāja (*c.*1600), the author of a popular Advaita textbook with an epistemological slant, holds for instance that the inferential cognition 'The hill is fiery' is perceptual and immediate with respect to the 'hill portion' but conceptual and mediate with respect to the 'fiery portion' (*Vedāntaparibhāṣā* 1.31). In Nyāya, it is insisted that we can touch what we see, and that even a cognition such as 'I see fragrant sandalwood' is legitimately deemed perceptual with respect to the property of being fragrant as well as with respect to the sandalwood. The relation between the grasping organ and the grasped property is said to be 'extraordinary'. The relation, or process, involves memory, as in the case of illusion, but the property is none the less perceived. Dharmarāja says, in contrast, that the sense of sight is not capable of grasping what is smelled. Nyāya philosophers agree with their adversaries that the organs of hearing, taste and smell are confined to sounds, tastes and odours respectively, and that depending on the precise nature of what is to be known there are restrictions on the other faculties. But they maintain that sight and touch range rather unrestrictedly over most properties most things exhibit, as do also the knowledge sources of inference and testimony.

4 Scepticism and epistemology

Focused, as explained, on the nature and number of knowledge sources, classical Indian epistemology met with scepticism practically from its inception. The Buddhist NĀGĀRJUNA (*c.* AD 150) asks how – supposing that the known becomes known through *pramāṇas* – the *pramāṇas* themselves are established: 'If the *pramāṇas* are established through other *pramāṇas*, then there is an infinite series [and] neither the beginning nor the middle nor the end can then be established' (*Vigrahavyāvartani* 32–3). Next he explores two metapositions, finding neither satisfactory: (a) a foundationalist stance and (b) a view of a

reciprocal making-known, with objects taken to be sources for knowing the usual sources as well as the reverse. Against the former view, which is expressed by an analogy to fire's illuminating itself along with other things, Nāgārjuna argues that, first, fire does not illuminate itself – as though it existed in darkness – and, second, if *pramāṇas* are self-established, without relation to objects made known (*prameyas*), then they are *pramāṇas* of nothing. Against the latter view, which specifies that the *pramāṇas* are established as *pramāṇas* in relation to the objects they make known (*prameyas*), he says that without being first established itself, nothing could establish another. A son is incapable of begetting his father. Thus all *pramāṇa* programmes are bankrupt.

In the *Nyāyasūtra* and commentaries, a response to such epistemological scepticism is forged whose linchpin is a view about the burden of proof and the relevance of citing *pramāṇas* varying according to specific contexts of inquiry. Consider what you would do if you were worried about the correctness of a scale used to weigh gold, says VĀTSYĀYANA (5th century) in commenting on *Nyāyasūtra* 2.1.16, 'as a scale can be an object of knowledge as well'. According to this earliest *Nyāyasūtra* commentator, you would take a piece of gold to another scale, or to two or three other scales, determine its precise weight and bring it back to calibrate the scale in question. What was formerly an instrument for determining the weight of gold – thus a *pramāṇa*, in the sense that the scale is what is consulted about weight – becomes what is to be made known, *prameya*, in this special instance. Similarly, a piece of gold, which was the object of knowledge, becomes a source of knowledge. There is no rule that a specific instance of operation of a knowledge source – whether perception or inference or whatever – may not itself become the object of inquiry. In that case, some other instrument or knowledge source would be employed.

The complete Nyāya response to Nāgārjuna includes four further points. First, the threat of an infinite series is faced by a purported willingness to try to provide answers as long as there are meaningful questions. Second, infinite series, it is pointed out, do occur, for example, a seed, a sprout, a seed, and so on. If you want us to answer the question as to what stands at the end of the series, say Nyāya philosophers, then we say that your question is framed in confused terms, that there is no possible answer: infinite series have no ends. We will consider issues of justification as far back as you wish, but – and here is the first point again – doubt has to be meaningful (see §1). Thus Nyāya philosophers assume that the balance of *reasonable* doubt is not tipped against them. Third, if the question is what justifies the entire *pramāṇa* programme, the answer is inference based on an invariable concomitance which itself is known from wide experience of the success of action guided by awarenesses whose sources are perception, testimony, and so on. If the basis of this and all inference is challenged, it is pointed out – fourth and finally – that to argue against *pramāṇas* is self-defeating, for what could be the source of one's argument? In particular, GAṄGEŚA (*c.*1325) counters that the sceptic who opens his mouth to attack the foundation of inference, namely invariable concomitance (or *vyāpti*, 'pervasion'), commits a pragmatic contradiction, for his behaviour shows that he assumes that there is such a concomitance between speaking and communicating to another. Similarly, the sceptic who presents an argument against inference as a *pramāṇa* cannot be in good faith.

See also: AWARENESS IN INDIAN THOUGHT; ERROR AND ILLUSION, INDIAN CONCEPTIONS OF

References and further reading

* Bhattacharyya, S. (1987) *Doubt, Belief and Knowledge*, New Delhi: Indian Council of Philosophical Research and Allied Publishers. (Contains excellent analyses of a range of cognitive phenomena, drawing on classical views of awareness as an episode in a temporal series; also introduces some of the reflections of the latest New Logicians, including their development of modal and cognitive logics.)

Datta, D.M. (1932) *Six Ways of Knowing*, London: Allen & Unwin. (Lucid exposition of the late Advaita Vedānta understanding of knowledge sources.)

* Dharmarāja (*c.*1600) *Vedāntaparibhāṣā*, ed. and trans. S.S. Suryanarayana, *Vedāntaparibhāṣā by Dharmarāja Adhvarin*, Madras: Adyar Library and Research Centre, 1971. (An excellent translation of an important late classical Advaita text.)

* Dignāga (*c.*500) *Pramāṇasamuccaya* (Collected Writings on the Acquisition of Knowledge), chapter 1 trans. Masaaki Hattori, *Dignāga, On Perception*, Cambridge, MA: Harvard University Press, 1968. (This important Yogācāra Buddhist philosopher was eclipsed in his own school by the great Dharmakīrti; Hattori's translation is quoted in §3.)

Kumar, S. (1980) *Upamāna in Indian Philosophy*, Delhi: Eastern Book Linkers. (Comprehensive concerning the classical debate about analogy as a *pramāṇa*.)

Kumārila (*c.*650) *Ślokavārttika*, trans. G. Jha, Delhi: Sri Satguru, 1983. (This is a reprint of the 1908 edition; although difficult to read, it is the only available English translation of the work of the important Mīmāṃsaka philosopher.)

* Matilal, B.K. (1986) *Perception: An Essay on Classical Indian Theories of Knowledge*, Oxford: Oxford University Press. (A modern classic by a premier scholar and philosopher; referred to in §1 for a defence of knowledge as episodic.)

* *Mīmāṃsāsūtra* (*c.* AD 100) trans. Mohan Lal Sandal, *Mīmāṃsā Sūtras of Jaimini*, Delhi: Motilal Banarsidass, 1923–5, repr. 1980, 2 vols. (An introduction to Mīmāṃsā philosophy accounts for a large portion of the first volume; the author's running commentary is, he says, based on the oldest extant, Śabara's.)

* Nāgārjuna (*c.* AD 150) *Vigrahavyāvartani*, trans. K. Bhattacharya, *The Dialectical Method of Nāgārjuna*, Delhi: Motilal Banarsidass, 1978. (An annotated translation, quoted in §4, of a work in which the Buddhist philosopher attacks *pramāṇa* programmes.)

* *Nyāyasūtra* (*c.* AD 150), trans. M. Gangopadhyay, *Nyāya-Sūtra with Vātsyāyana's Commentary*, Calcutta: Indian Studies, 1982. (A readable and accurate translation.)

* Śaṅkara (*c.*700) *Bṛhadāraṇyakabhāṣya*, ed. E. Roer, Osnabrück: Biblio Verlag, 1980. (Reprint of the 1849–56 edition; the translation of the quote in §3 is mine.)

* —— (*c.*700) *Brahmasūtrabhāṣya*, ed. J.L. Shastri, Delhi: Motilal Banarsidass, 1980. (Referred to in §3.)

Sundaram, P.K. (1968) *Advaita Epistemology*, Madras University Philosophical Series 11, Madras: University of Madras. (A continuation and advance of Datta's exposition with a special focus on the *Iṣṭasiddhi* of Vimuktātman.)

STEPHEN H. PHILLIPS

KNOWLEDGE, INNATE
see INNATE KNOWLEDGE

KNOWLEDGE, JUSTIFICATION OF
see JUSTIFICATION, EPISTEMIC

KNOWLEDGE, MORAL
see MORAL KNOWLEDGE

KNOWLEDGE, SOCIOLOGY

OF *see* SOCIOLOGY OF KNOWLEDGE

KNOWLEDGE, TACIT

Tacit knowledge is a form of implicit knowledge we rely on for both learning and acting. The term derives from the work of Michael Polanyi (1891–1976) whose critique of positivistic philosophy of science grew into a fully developed theory of knowledge. Polanyi believed that the 'scientific' account of knowledge as a fully explicit formalizable body of statements did not allow for an adequate account of discovery and growth. In his account of tacit knowledge, knowledge has an ineliminable subjective dimension: we know much more than we can tell. This notion of tacit knowing in science has been developed by Thomas Kuhn, has figured prominently in theoretical linguistics and has also been studied in psychology.

POLANYI maintained that at each stage of scientific inquiry, from discovery to confirmation, a crucial role is played by experience, skill and expertise, each of which involves a kind of knowing on the part of the practitioner which is implicit and unformalizable. His distinction between tacit and explicit 'knowledge' is grounded in his distinction between subsidiary and focal 'awareness'. Drawing on Gestalt psychology's account of perceptual integration, whereby we are perceptually aware of the coherent whole to which we are attending on the basis of a subsidiary awareness of details or clues to which we are not attending, Polanyi develops a general account of awareness wherein our focused awareness of *B* is a function of our subsidiary awareness of *A* (see GESTALT PSYCHOLOGY). The tacit integration of the subsidiary elements that makes possible our explicit recognition of the perceptual object becomes a model of a kind of implicit knowing that lies at the heart of our cognitive orientation to the world. This generalization is driven by the conviction that such tacit knowledge is basic to our understanding of language and to comprehending any complex situation. For Polanyi, tacit knowledge is not just one kind of knowing we are capable of; it is absolutely fundamental: 'all knowledge is either tacit or rooted in tacit knowledge' (1969: 144).

The feature of tacit knowledge that bears on knowing more than we can tell is both crucial and ambiguous. The distinction between subsidiary awareness and focal awareness seems to be merely functional in that items of subsidiary awareness in this experience can be objects of focal awareness in the next. Is the same true of the tacit–explicit distinction? Is it simply the case that all explicit knowing is rendered possible by a shifting background of implicit knowing, or are there some kinds of knowledge which are (at least for us) in principle non-explicit? On the weak interpretation 'knowing more than we can tell' is time-indexed and seems uncontroversial, whereas the strong interpretation invokes a species of knowledge shrouded in mystery. Recent attempts to construct computer programmes that would replicate the skills that involve tacit knowledge could shed light on the '*de facto*' versus 'in principle' character of the tacit–explicit distinction.

The basic notion that there is a dimension of scientific knowledge that is acquired only through practice and that cannot be (or is not) articulated explicitly has been developed in Thomas Kuhn's account of both normal and revolutionary science (see KUHN, T.S. §§2–3). The recognition of what is significant in theoretical and experimental situations so fundamental to the conduct of science is learned in actually doing science rather than by the acquisition of rules for doing it. In these basic procedures the scientist has no direct access to what is known, nor generalizations in which to express it, but inasmuch as it is an ability that is transmitted through education it seems appropriate to categorize it as knowledge, albeit of the tacit variety. The distinction invoked here encompasses but is not exhausted by that articulated by Gilbert Ryle (1949) in terms of 'knowing how' and 'knowing that'. This tacit knowing which functions so pervasively in normal science also plays a critical role in those creative advances characterizable as scientific revolutions (see KNOWLEDGE, CONCEPT OF §1).

The notion of tacit knowledge also figures prominently in theoretical linguistics. The debate in this area has been between the empiricist tradition (which construes language as an adventitious construct built up in a basically inductivist manner by elementary data-processing procedures) and the rationalist tradition (which maintains that behind these processing mechanisms there must be innate formal and substantive linguistic universals built into the language user to account for both acquisition and competence). The principal figure in the rationalist tradition has been Noam CHOMSKY and his theory invokes the notion of tacit knowledge. He argues that since the knowledge of a language involves the implicit ability to understand indefinitely many sentences, it seems reasonable to attribute to the competent speaker the grasp of a system of linguistic rules that can generate an indefinitely large number of structures. These rules are obviously not explicitly known by the speaker, but the tacit knowledge of them seems necessary to explain not only competent performance but, in particular, the ability to learn any natural language (see LANGUAGE, INNATENESS OF).

Much work has also been done in experimental psychology bearing on the notion of tacit knowledge. This research usually goes under the rubric 'implicit versus explicit cognitive processing' and is normally construed as mapping on to the unconscious–conscious distinction. Implicit learning and implicit memory have been the subjects of numerous studies and there seems to be considerable evidence, particularly from the study of amnesia patients, that implicit cognitive processes are more robust than their explicit counterparts. Given the emergence of cognitive science as a basic research programme, both in experimental psychology and philosophy, there has been a recent cross-fertilization of the inquiry into notion of tacit knowledge.

See also: INNATE KNOWLEDGE

References and further reading

Chomsky, N. (1965) *Aspects of the Theory of Syntax*, Cambridge, MA: MIT Press. (Chapter 1 contains a general discussion of the differences between the empiricist and the rationalist accounts of language learning.)

Kuhn, T. (1962) *The Structure of Scientific Revolutions*, Chicago, IL: University of Chicago Press, enlarged 2nd edn, 1970. (The postscript employs the concept of tacit knowledge in an account of science.)

Polanyi, M. (1958) *Personal Knowledge: Towards a Post-Critical Philosophy*, Chicago, IL: University of Chicago Press. (The preface to this very expansive work contains brief but important observations on tacit knowledge.)

—— (1966) *The Tacit Dimension*, New York: Doubleday. (The first two lectures in this short book present an overview of Polanyi's account of tacit knowledge.)

* —— (1969) *Knowing and Being*, Chicago, IL: University of Chicago Press. (Part 3 of this collection contains some of Polanyi's most important essays on tacit knowing.)

Reber, A. (1993) *Implicit Learning and Tacit Knowledge*, Oxford: Oxford University Press. (A good overview of recent empirical research bearing on implicit learning and implicit knowledge.)

* Ryle, G. (1949) *The Concept of Mind*, London: Hutchinson's University Library. (Chapter 2 of this classic work articulates the distinction between 'knowing how' and 'knowing that', and also

provides a positive account of what is involved in 'knowing how'.)

C.F. DELANEY

KNUTZEN, MARTIN (1713–51)

Martin Knutzen was a follower of Christian von Wolff. His work is the result of an effort to reconcile Wolff's system, more persuasively than Wolff himself had, with common sense, Christian faith and the latest results in the natural sciences. Because Wolff had come under fire from Christian Pietists for apparently trying to resurrect Leibniz' system of pre-established harmony, thereby possibly flirting with Spinozism and therefore atheism, Knutzen argued from Leibnizian premises that real interaction is at work in the world at large and is constitutive of the mind–body union. Knutzen was Kant's teacher.

Knutzen was born in Königsberg, East Prussia, the only child of a humble Danish merchant. Orphaned at the age of six, he was cared for by a relation who saw to his education. At fifteen, Knutzen entered the University of Königsberg where he developed an interest in the natural sciences and made two lifelong and apparently incompatible commitments: to PIETISM, and to the philosophy of Christian von WOLFF. Much of Knutzen's later philosophical work can be understood as an effort to reconcile these two commitments. At twenty one, he became professor extraordinary of logic and metaphysics at Königsberg. In spite of this brilliant debut, he never rose to the higher rank of professor ordinary. Knutzen was said to be an engaging lecturer. At any rate, he was a very busy one, teaching as many as six hours a day. In addition, he wrote much on philosophy, the natural sciences and theology.

Wolff had made the philosophy of LEIBNIZ fashionable again by packaging it as an easy-to-digest system. The system was appealing, because it offered a comprehensive picture of God, the world, the human soul and things in general by elaborating the consequences of two principles: the law of contradiction and the principle of sufficient reason. As the system won followers, it came under critical scrutiny. Pietists attacked it for blasphemy, arguing that it reduced to Spinozism and thus to atheism (see SPINOZA, B. DE). Friends of common sense within and without the school reacted against the eccentric aspects of Leibniz' thought. Wolff's followers set out to reconcile the system more persuasively with

Christian faith, common sense, and the latest results in the natural sciences. Knutzen was one of the most eminent of these innovating Wolffians.

A great stumbling block in Leibniz philosophy for common sense, and, in the eyes of some, for Christian faith, is the doctrine of pre-established harmony. According to this, no real interaction occurs among created substances. Every monad is itself the author of every change it ever undergoes. The appearance of interaction is the effect of God's having arranged things so that change in one substance would always arise in concert with change in every other. The doctrine also denies real interaction between body and soul (see DUALISM). Their intimate union is the effect of selfproduced change in each, harmoniously pre-established by God. This doctrine was attacked by pietists, who complained that it represents the soul as a spiritual automaton, fatalistically spinning out its future under the principle of sufficient reason, and impiously absolves us of responsibility for our sins. But the doctrine met with hesitation even within the school, notably from Knutzen who tried to show, from Leibnizian premises, that interaction must be at work in the world, not pre-established harmony.

Knutzen's argument for real interaction borrows the following ideas from Leibniz as understood by Wolff: every body is composed of monads; every monad produces change in itself; by reason of their changing inner states, monads externally relate to one another. Since selfproduced change in one monad alters its external relations with other monads, they are also affected by such change; real interaction must therefore take place among the monads. There must also be real interaction between body and soul, argues Knutzen, because the soul is a simple substance. We may therefore expect the soul to interact with the monads, constitutive of the human body, just as these monads interact with one another. Real interaction of soul and body is properly understood as real interaction of soul and monads.

Leibniz had also argued that body–soul interaction would disturb the order of nature determined by the laws of motion, given that the total quantities of motion and 'living forces' in the world are always conserved. Knutzen agrees that we must reject any system of mind–body union which can be shown to disturb the order of nature. But he denies that, properly understood, this would ever be disturbed by real interaction. The order of nature, he says, is established by the set of rules that govern different forces in the world. But any given rule operates only under certain conditions. Knutzen says that the law of conservation of living forces holds only for bodies mechanically interacting amongst themselves. If a body interacts with a soul, neither it nor the soul,

which is immaterial, is subject to this conservation law. Interaction may therefore take place between them without disturbing the order of nature. Furthermore, Knutzen draws a parallel between the law of conservation of living forces and the law of conservation of motion. Like the former, the latter operates only under certain conditions, namely in the ideal case of collision between perfectly elastic bodies, which never obtains in the world. Since both conservation laws are restricted in important ways, their jurisdiction over nature is curtailed, leaving open the possibility of real interaction.

Perhaps due to the isolation of Königsberg, Knutzen was not renowned even in his day, though he was well known to figures more familiar to us than he himself is, such as HAMANN and KANT. Knutzen's philosophy and lectures apparently influenced the latter, to whom they may have suggested the idea of reconciling Leibnizian metaphysics and Newtonian natural philosophy, as, for example, in Kant's dissertations of 1755–6.

List of works

Knutzen, M. (1744) *Philosophische Abhandlung von der immateriellen Natur der Seele* (Philosophical Treatise of the Immaterial Nature of the Soul), Königsberg: Hartung. (An attempt to refute materialism. Copies can be found in the libraries of Harvard University and the University of Chicago. They are bound with a German translation of William Warburton's Divine Legation of Moses, Frankfurt and Leipzig, 1751.)

—— (1745) *Systema causarum efficientium seu commentatio philosophica de commercio mentis et corporis per influxum physicum explicando* (System of Efficient Causes or Philosophical Treatise on the Interaction of Mind and Body Explained through Physical Influence), Leipzig: Christian Langhem. (An attempt to refute pre-established harmony and establish real interaction. Copies can be found in the British Museum and the library of the Georg-August-Universität, Göttingen.)

—— (1747) *Elementa philosophiae rationalis logicae cum generalis tum specialis mathematica methodo in usum auditorum suorum demonstrata a Martino Knutzen*, Königsberg and Leipzig: Hartung. (A work of philosophical logic. Copies can be found in the libraries of Harvard University and the University of Chicago. A reprint is now available from Olms.)

References and further reading

Erdmann, B. (1876) *Martin Knutzen und seine Zeit*,

Leipzig: Voss. (A very informative book about Knutzen, his work and the philosophical and historical context of his work.)

Euler, L. (1746) 'Enodatio quaestionis utrum materiae facultas cogitandi tribui possit necne ex principiis mechanicis petita', repr. in A. Speiser *et al.* (eds) *Opera omnia*, Zurich: Orell Füssli, 3rd series, vol. 2, 1911–. (A discussion of the question whether we can attribute a faculty of thought to matter. Euler explicitly refers to Knutzen.)

Kant, I. (1755) *Principiorum primorum cognitionis metaphysicae nova dilucidatio*, repr. in *Gesammelte Schriften*, vol. 1, Berlin: De Gruyter, 1968. (One of Kant's earliest writings. May show Knutzen's influence, inasmuch as Kant can be understood as trying to reconcile what he takes to be fundamental commitments of Leibniz and fundamental commitments of Newton.)

—— (1756) *Metaphysicae cum geometria iunctae usus in philosophia naturali, cuius specimen I. continet monadologiam physicam*, repr. in *Gesammelte Schriften*, vol. 1, Berlin: De Gruyter, 1968. (One of Kant's earliest writings. May show Knutzen's influence, inasmuch as Kant can be understood as trying to reconcile fundamental commitments of Leibniz and his followers in metaphysics with a fundamental commitment held by Newton and his followers concerning the nature of space.)

Wolff, C. von (1720) *Vernünfftige Gedancken von Gott, der Welt und der Seele des Menschen, auch allen Dingen überhaupt* (Sensible Thoughts on God, the World and the Human Soul, and Indeed on Everything), Hildesheim: Olms, 1983. (A comprehensive statement of Wolff's metaphysics.)

A. LAYWINE

KŌBŌ DAISHI *see* KŪKAI

KOJÈVE, ALEXANDRE (1902–68)

Alexandre Kojève developed an idiosyncratic and widely influential reading of G.W.F. Hegel in a seminar in Paris from 1933 to 1939. Kojève read Hegel as having discovered that truth was the product of history, and that history was the product of the human desire and struggle for recognition. Kojève emphasized that once this desire was satisfied, history, properly so-called, was over. He claimed that for all essential purposes this human desire had been satisfied in the modern period, and thus that we had experienced (and Hegel had come to know) the end of history. The notes from this seminar were published in 1947 and continued to have an important impact on French philosophy throughout the post-war period.

1 Life
2 The end of history
3 Later works

1 Life

Kojève (born Kojèvnikoff) left Moscow at the age of 18, and spent most of the 1920s in Berlin and Heidelberg. During his years in Germany, he was strongly affected by the teaching of Martin HEIDEGGER and by his fellow students in philosophy, Jacob Klein and Leo STRAUSS. By 1927 he had come to Paris, where he would give his Hegel seminar as a replacement for his friend, Alexandre KOYRÉ. After the Second World War, Kojève worked as a negotiator and advisor for the French Ministry of Economic Affairs (especially on world trade matters). He continued to write on philosophy in his spare time.

2 The end of history

Kojève's early writings, especially those on the mystical philosophical texts of Vladimir SOLOV'ËV, show a concern with finding legitimate criteria for making sense of historical change. If these criteria were themselves the product of historical change, how could stable philosophical knowledge be possible? Kojève's idea of the 'end of history' (which he attributed to HEGEL) was meant to answer this question.

Kojève acknowledged his departure from Hegel in his sharp separation of the natural from the historical. Kojève was interested only in the latter, and used the master–slave dialectic as a schema for understanding the stages of work and struggle in history. In this schema the human is defined by the desire for recognition – a desire that could be satisfied only with the conservation of its object (the person who provides love, honour, respect) – and the will to risk one's life in order to satisfy that desire. The realm of the human and of history is defined specifically in contradistinction to the realm of the animal and of nature.

The desire for recognition is the motor of history, and Kojève used the master–slave dialectic as an allegory of human development: bloody battles for recognition were followed by the rule of the masters over the working slaves. Slaves were those whose animal desires for self-preservation led them to surrender and to recognize the masters. The masters, however, could not satisfy their human desire, because they were recognized by *mere* slaves. Eventually the slaves deposed the masters through revolution but they remained in servitude in relation to their work. This is the bourgeois condition. Real freedom would come only through the universal recognition of each and every one as a citizen.

The final synthesis of the master–slave dialectic is the freedom of universal recognition because it provides full (human) satisfaction. It also represents the end of history, since once the desire for recognition is satisfied there will be no force to create historical (human) change. There would be merely the activity of beings seeking to satisfy animal (nonhuman) desires. In other words, rather than engaging in action to achieve freedom and recognition, after the end of history 'people' would find ways of acquiring toys of various sorts. For Kojève, the end of history was the 'definitive reality' that served as a transhistorical standard of judgment.

3 Later works

In the 1930s, Kojève situated his reading of Hegel just before a revolution that would be a final confirmation of the interpretation itself. History was ending in universal recognition, and Kojève was contributing to the self-consciousness that would be part of the final state. Perhaps in response to some important criticism of his views by Leo Strauss, and certainly in response to the increasingly congealed political situation of the early 1950s, I have argued that Kojève abandoned his 'heroic Hegelianism'. He continued to believe that the culmination of world history would define the truth of all previous events, but in his later work claimed that the end of history had occurred at the beginning of the nineteenth century. This left the mid-twentieth-century philosopher in the ironic position of having nothing left to say, except to repeat that everything of importance had already been said in order to make sense of what had already been done.

The idea of the 'end of history' in Kojève's later work no longer refers to the triumphant ascension of humanity, but instead, for those who see that we live on the other side of it, signals a final decadence in which humans are distinguished from other animals only by their snobbery. Kojève's early combination of MARX, Hegel and Heidegger in the service of claiming the future of the world is thus incorporated into a perspective reminiscent of WEBER on the routinization of life. The closure of the end of history is an iron cage in which human animals can engage in a variety of activities without struggle because their essential drives have been satisfied. Kojève takes an ironic

stance towards this condition in which the struggle for recognition is replaced by conspicuous and endless consumption; historical change is replaced by animalistic or snobbish repetition.

Kojève's idea of the end of history spoke to the dissatisfaction of those on the left and right who thought that liberalism and modernity left no possibility either of genuine human life or of greatness. The philosopher continued his work among the bureaucrats until his death, helping to work out trade policies that might be suitable for the end of history.

See also: HEGELIANISM §4; HISTORY, PHILOSOPHY OF

List of works

Kojève, A. (1946) 'Hegel, Marx et le christianisme', *Critique* 1: 339–66; trans. H. Gildin, 'Hegel, Marx and Christianity', *Interpretation* (1970) 1: 21–42; repr. in Stern (ed.), vol. 2: 359–82. (Argues for what he describes as an atheistic reading of Hegel.)

—— (1947) *Introduction à la lecture de Hegel*, Paris: Gallimard; partly trans. J.H. Nichols, Jr as *Introduction to the Reading of Hegel*, ed. A. Bloom, New York: Basic Books, 1969. (Text of Kojève's influential lectures at l'École des Hautes-Études from 1933 to 1939.)

—— (1968–73) *Essai d'une histoire raisonnée de la philosophie païenne* (Attempt at a Systematic History of Pagan Philosophy), Paris: Gallimard, 3 vols. (An attempt to provide access to Hegelian wisdom by re-collecting the history leading up to it, from the Presocratics through Aristotle and the Neoplatonists.)

—— (1973) *Kant*, Paris: Gallimard. (Kant after Hegel. In light of the latter's completion of philosophy in absolute knowing, the former's important contribution to bringing philosophy into relation with time is discussed.)

—— (1981) *Esquisse d'une phenomenologie du droit* (Sketch of a Phenomenology of Right), Paris: Gallimard. (Originally written during the Second World War.)

—— (1991) 'The Political Action of Philosophers', in *Leo Strauss, On Tyranny*, ed. V. Gourevitch and M.S. Roth, New York: The Free Press. (Originally published in 1950; this edition also includes the correspondence between Strauss and Kojève.)

References and further reading

Auffret, D. (1990) *Alexandre Kojève: La philosophie, l'état, la fin de l'histoire*, Paris: Bernard Grasset. (A sketchy biography with some philosophical interpretation.)

Butler, J.P. (1987) *Subjects of Desire: Hegelian Reflections in Twentieth-Century France*, New York: Columbia University Press. (A contemporary perspective on how Hegel resonates throughout French philosophy from existentialism onwards.)

Cooper, B. (1984) *The End of History: An Essay on Modern Hegelianism*, Toronto, Ont.: University of Toronto Press. (A thoughtful account of Kojève's relevance to modernity.)

Drury, S. (1994) *Alexandre Kojève and the Roots of Postmodern Politics*, New York: St Martin's Press. (An attempt to link Kojève to a nihilistic, desperate brand of contemporary thinking about politics.)

Fukuyama, F. (1992) *The End of History and the Last Man*, New York: The Free Press. (Uses Kojève and Leo Strauss to proclaim the end of the cold war as the end of history.)

Gourevitch, V. (1968) 'Philosophy and Politics I', 'Philosophy and Politics II', *Review of Metaphysics* 22 (1): 58–84; 22 (2): 281–328. (A philosophical account of what is at stake in Kojève's thinking about politics, history and truth.)

Roth, M.S. (1988) *Knowing and History: Appropriations of Hegel in Twentieth-Century France*, Ithaca, NY: Cornell University Press. (A discussion of Kojève as part of the Hegelian investment in the historical from the 1930s to the 1950s.)

—— (1995) *The Ironist's Cage: Memory, Trauma and the Construction of History*, New York: Columbia University Press, chaps 5, 8 and 9. (Discussions of Kojève, Strauss, Fukuyama and the idea of the end of history in relation to contemporary cultural criticism.)

MICHAEL S. ROTH

KOKORO

Kokoro is a comprehensive term in Japanese religion, philosophy and aesthetics often translated as 'heart', whose range of meanings includes mind, wisdom, aspiration, essence, attention, sincerity and sensibility. In Buddhist texts and in philosophy, kokoro *(or* shin *in its Sino-Japanese reading) denotes mind, heart or inner nature, the site of human sentience or delusion. By extension, in pre-modern theories of art,* kokoro *signifies simultaneously the emotional capacity of the artist to respond to the natural world, which ideally catalyzes the act of creation; the parallel ability of an audience to respond to such a work of art and thus indirectly to the experience of the artist; and finally the evaluation of such a work as possessing the 'right conception',* kokoro ari *or alternatively* ushin.

While the specific implications of *kokoro* changed in the context of cultural development, its far-ranging meanings, which additionally include intention, vitality, knowledge, sentiment, wholeheartedness, reason, state, appearance, spirit, will and duty, imply both a dynamic potentiality and a fundamental concern with the authenticity of human being as well as its integrity. This integrity precludes any dualistic mind–body distinctions. Ultimately, *kokoro* serves as the foundation for almost all pre-modern Japanese theories of art, which may be described as expressive-affective in their orientation (see AESTHETICS, JAPANESE).

In Buddhist writings we often encounter *kokoro*, especially in its compound form *shin*, as in the well-known Buddhist dictum *ishin denshin* (transmission from mind to mind), alluding to the ideal transmission of spiritual truth that is intuitive in nature and does not rely on verbal and other explicit means. In Buddhism, *kokoro* or *shin* is not simply the faculty for apprehending truth, but can also be the site of delusion and desire within human being, as suggested in the phrase *kokoro no yami* (the darkness of the heart), in other words, the spirit of the unawakened being still wallowing in the mire of the phenomenal world. In seeming contrast to the usage of the terms *ushin* and *mushin* in aesthetics, in Buddhism, *ushin* (having heart or mind) and *mushin* (lacking heart or mind) represent respectively the deluded state of being attached to the world (that is, possessing desires) and the liberating state of awareness that has eschewed the heart and hence all desire.

In the realm of pre-modern artistic theories, *kokoro* receives not only extensive theoretical treatment as a crucial artistic component, but becomes a term of aesthetic approbation as well. In the often quoted Japanese preface to the *Kokinwakashū* (The Anthology of Japanese Poetry Ancient and Modern), *circa* 905, Ki no Tsurayuki conjoins the concept of *kokoro* with a parallel concept *kotoba* (words), and begins 'Japanese poetry has the human heart (*kokoro*) as its seed and burgeons forth into myriad words (*kotoba*) as its leaves.' He traces the genesis of poetry to the fact that all living beings respond to the natural world around them in the form of song, like the cries of birds in the midst of blossoms or frogs croaking in the water. Hence, *kokoro* is that faculty within us which hearkens to the world outside and poetry is what results when we give utterance to the feelings and thoughts in our hearts in the form of words. However, he also offers a secondary understanding of *kokoro* when he goes on to imply that *kokoro* (heart, conception, treatment) and *kotoba* (words, diction, materials) are the two constituent elements of any poem, which may be used to evaluate the success of any poetic endeavour. He criticizes, for example, a verse by a well-known poet of a former age Ariwara no Narihira with the comment *kokoro amarite, kotoba tarazu* (too much heart and too few words). Ideally, we infer, the poem must have a balance of *kokoro* and *kotoba*.

This interest in *kokoro* and *kotoba* is echoed and developed by the twelfth-century poet-critic Fujiwara Shunzei, who in surveying what he perceived as the second-rate nature of the poetry of his age, issues the challenge, *kotoba furuku, kokoro atarashi* (old words, new heart). He argues for the need to retain the traditional diction and materials, but to infuse them as well with a new spirit that would revitalize them. Apart from regarding *kokoro* as merely the resonant capacity within all living beings to feel and respond as well as one of the constituent components of poetry, Shunzei goes further and elevates *kokoro* into an aesthetic ideal known as *ushin*. His son Fujiwara Teika develops his father's theory still further, describing *ushin*, which may be translated as 'having heart', as signifying an intensity or conviction of feeling which is paramount. *Ushintei* (the style of *ushin*), as he comments, is the overarching style of the so-called ten styles of poetry; all great poetry for him must possess this intensity of feeling, whose articulation is influenced by the Tendai Buddhist contemplative practice of *shikan*, or concentrated meditation.

The Buddhist notion of *ushin* as still being mired in the desires of the phenomenal world, and *mushin* as a release from such delusion, stands in sharp contrast to the role of *kokoro* in poetry, which is composed in response to the beauties of the natural world, and thus itself is illusory and deluded. Hence, a conflict emerges between poetry and religion in which poetry is seen to represent as well as encourage attachment to the phenomenal world, and doctrinally is both deceived and deceptive. The medieval poet Saigyō illustrates this predicament in his poem in the *Shinkokinwakashū* (The New Anthology of Japanese Poetry Ancient and Modern) (IV, 362), when he mentions that though a priest, he 'lacks a heart' (*kokoro naki*); in other words he has renounced the world. Nevertheless, as a human and as a poet, he remains beguiled by the natural realm and hence is trapped. This dilemma is mediated by a new understanding of poetry itself as a religious path or *michi* in the form of *shikan*, disciplined contemplation, as *kadō* (the way of poetry). Paradoxically, delusion can be an instrument of awakening as in the Buddhist notion of *hōben*, or expediency, as illustrated by the use of parables.

During this period *kokoro ari* (having heart), apart from its Buddhist implications, came to mean also decorous, or worthy of the canonical stamp of approval, in contradistinction to *mushin*. Poetry that

adhered to the conventions was labelled *ushin*, and aberrant poetry that deviated too much from the norms was termed *mushin* or substandard. These terms subsequently came to be applied not only to *tanka* (the classical form of poetry) but also to the newer form of linked verse known as *renga*, which was subdivided into two kinds, serious and comic (or careless).

The *Nō* playwright and critic ZEAMI (c. 1363–1443), whose theatre was grounded in the beliefs and practices of Zen Buddhism, further expands the significance of *kokoro* when he remarks cryptically in his treatise known as the *Fūshi kaden* (Teachings on Style and the Flower), 'The flower is the heart (*kokoro*), the seed is the performance', an inversion of Tsurayuki's original assertion some centuries before. Now the heart no longer functions as the seed of poetry, but becomes instead the culmination of *Nō*, aesthetically and spiritually, as emblemized by Zeami in the metaphor of the flower. Ironically, the performance, while seminal, is secondary ultimately to the epiphanic awareness blossoming in the hearts of those expressing their feelings and those affected by it.

Kokoro also proved central to perspectives outside Buddhism, as in the commentaries of the classics written by the *kokugakusha* (scholars of national learning) in the eighteenth century, who sought to elevate indigenous traditions in opposition to imported philosophies such as Confucianism and Buddhism. MOTOORI NORINAGA, for example, rather than merely seeing *kokoro* as either a capacity of the perceiver or the place of moral conflict within an individual, stresses the idea of *kokoro* as the intrinsic or essential nature of objects themselves, in the form of *koto no kokoro* 'the essence of abstract things', such as the sadness of an experience, and *mono no kokoro*, 'the essence of natural things', such as the beauty of blossoms.

See also: AESTHETICS; AESTHETICS, CHINESE; AESTHETICS, JAPANESE; BUDDHIST PHILOSOPHY, JAPANESE; ZEAMI

References and further reading

Hisamatsu Sen'ichi (1970) *The Vocabulary of Japanese Literary Aesthetics*, Tokyo: Center for East Asian Cultural Studies. (Useful and comprehensive summary of various terms and their interrelations.)

* Ki no Tsurayuki (c. 905) 'Kanajo' (Kana Preface), in *Kokinwakashū*, ed. Umetomo Saeki, Tokyo: Iwanami Shoten, 1958; trans. L.R. Rodd and M. Henkenius, *Kokinshū*, Princeton, NJ: Princeton University Press, 1984. (First imperially commis-

sioned anthology of Japanese poetry whose chief compiler was Tsurayuki; his well-known preface raises crucial concerns alluded to by later theorists.)

Suzuki, D.T. (1959) *Zen and Japanese Culture*, Princeton, NJ: Princeton University Press. (An imaginative and insightful explanation of how Zen permeates Japanese art by one of the great proponents of our century; the section on 'Zen and Swordsmanship' (89–117) is especially pertinent.)

Ueda Makoto (1967) *Literary and Art Theories in Japan*, Cleveland, OH: The Press of Western Reserve University. (A rich survey of the ideas of thirteen pre-modern theorists of art from such perspectives as literature, theatre, tea ceremony, painting and calligraphy.)

* Zeami (1400–02) *Fūshi kaden* (Teachings on Style and the Flower) [alternatively known as *Kadensho*, (Writings on the Transmission of the Flower)], in *Nōgakuronshū* (Collection of Treatises on the Art of *Nō*), ed. Minoru Nishio, Tokyo: Iwanami, 1961; trans. J.T. Rimer and Yamazaki Masakazu, *On the Art of the Nō Drama*, Princeton, NJ: Princeton University Press, 1984. (Zeami's first treatise in which he discusses elements of theatre in terms of the underlying perspectives and values of classical poetry.)

MEERA VISWANATHAN

KOLLANTAI, ALEXANDRA

see FEMINISM (§4)

KOREAN PHILOSOPHY

see BUDDHIST PHILOSOPHY, KOREAN; CHINUL; CHŎNG YAGYONG (TASAN); CONFUCIAN PHILOSOPHY, KOREAN; EAST ASIAN PHILOSOPHY; HAN WŎNJIN; SIRHAK; SŎSAN HYUJŎNG; TONGHAK; ÛISANG; WŎNCH'ŬK; WŎNHYO; YI HWANG; YI KAN; YI YULGOK

KOTARBIŃSKI, TADEUSZ (1886–1981)

Kotarbiński was one of the founders and main representatives of the Polish philosophical school known as the Lvov–Warsaw School and akin to, though independent of (and less radical than), the Vienna Circle; an anti-metaphysical, pro-scientific, rationalistic school of philosophy, which was very active and influential between the First and the Second World Wars.

Kotarbiński's programme for philosophy was a minimalistic and a practical one: he stressed the need to purify the field of philosophy of questions and concepts that lack factual content or logical coherence. According to him, the term 'philosophy' should be used, if at all, to denote only logic (understood as the philosophy of cognitive thought) and the philosophy of action, including moral philosophy. His numerous (more than 500) works are devoted to logic and philosophy of action in this broad sense. One of his main original ideas is the doctrine of reism or concretism, a special version of nominalism.

Kotarbiński was admired by several generations of his pupils for his unusual pedagogical gifts, his integrity and his moral courage.

1 Ontological reism
2 Semantic reism
3 Independent ethics
4 Praxiology

1 Ontological reism

Tadeusz Kotarbiński studied philosophy and classics at the University of Lwów (Lvov). From 1918 he was a professor of philosophy at the University of Warsaw. After the Second World War he was the president of the University of Lódż and from 1951 to 1956 a chairman at the University of Warsaw. When he retired from the University he was elected president of the Polish Academy of Science and from 1960 to 1963 he was the chairman of the International Institute of Philosophy.

His main subject of inquiry and teaching was logic in a broad sense of the term, comprising formal logic as well as semiotics and methodology of science. He wished to reconstruct the conceptual apparatus of logic in this sense to make it an exact discipline which would fulfil the rigorous criteria of intelligibility and soundness. One of the results of this project was the reduction of all categories to the category of things, known as his doctrine of *reism* or *concretism*.

In its original formulation (Kotarbińsky 1929) the

doctrine of reism was the ontological thesis, answering the question 'What is there?'. According to this doctrine, all objects are things, that is, only concrete, physical objects (including sentient bodies) exist. There are no so-called abstract objects: properties, relations, states of affairs, and so on. Things can be white or black, but there is no such being as whiteness or blackness; two things can be similar to each other or – if they are sentient bodies – can be friends with each other, but there is no such being as similarity or friendship. The apparent existence of beings of these kinds is an illusion which has its origin in our use of the corresponding abstract terms in the same syntactic role as names of things. To avoid the illusion one has to realize that this usage is a metaphorical one: when translated into the literal mode of speaking, sentences containing abstract terms (apparent names or *onomatoids*) turn out to refer to concrete, physical individuals.

In its old ontological version the doctrine of reism can be (and was) objected to as one which cannot be consistently formulated. For to deny the existence of properties, relations and so on, one has to use apparent names as subjects in sentences (for example, 'Properties do not exist') which – according to reism itself – cannot be literally interpreted. On the other hand, the thesis 'Whatever exists is a thing' is nothing more than a decision concerning the choice of language: namely, the decision to use a language allowing only things as values of variables which can be bound by the existential operator (see NOMINALISM).

2   Semantic reism

For this reason Kotarbiński reinterpreted his reism as the semantic thesis according to which any sentence having cognitive value is (or can be translated into) a sentence referring only to things; in other words, apparent names of properties, relations and so on can always be eliminated from sentences without any loss of content.

To prove this thesis one should be able to formulate methods of transforming all kinds of sentences which are generally accepted as meaningful – especially all scientific theorems – into sentences which do not contain apparent names. Yet lack of such a method does not falsify the thesis: one can argue that if, for example, in physics there is no method of translating sentences which contain the term 'field' (which does not seem to be the name of a thing) into sentences containing names of things only, this is because the concept of field is not sufficiently clear; physicists should seek its explication.

However, there is a discipline which does have a clear and exact conceptual apparatus while including abstract terms which seem to be irreducible: mathematics. The most troublesome case is the concept of class (in the distributive, set-theoretical sense). The simplest contexts containing this term can be replaced by contexts which do not contain it (for example, the sentence 'x is a member of the class of dogs' by the sentence 'x is a dog'); but there seems to be no method of eliminating the term 'class' from more complex contexts ('x is a member of the class of the classes of . . .' and so on).

Thus, as a semantic thesis, reism is not a theorem but a postulate or a suggestion. The reason for accepting this postulate is that speaking – if possible – only in terms of things is the best way of avoiding Bacon's *idola fori*: illusions and confusion in thinking caused by the traps of language. Kotarbiński had his predecessors (such as, LEIBNIZ and BRENTANO), but his reism was more radical as concerns the mind–body problem in the light of his thesis that only physical objects exist (pansomatism).

3   Independent ethics

As a young student, Kotarbiński began to look for a replacement for the religious justification of morality, considering the suggestions of Stoicism, Epicureanism and utilitarianism. After many unsatisfactory trials he came to the conclusion that

> ethics . . . , just as medicine or administration, does not need a justification derived from an outlook on life. Its rules are invariable no matter whether a rational person is a materialist, an idealist or a spiritualist. . . . What, on the other hand is needed is to avoid using fantasy in justifications.
>
> (Kotarbiński 1952)

In the light of this he formed an ethical system which he called independent ethics

As the main parameters for the moral evaluation of actions he distinguished the following antitheses of what he called motives: kindness – cruelty; honesty – dishonesty; courage – cowardice; competence – indolence; composure – succumbing to temptation. Further, he described the moral ideal as a trustworthy guardian: a person on whom one can count, in a difficult situation, 'not an egoist but a kind person, a reliable, courageous, competent, and composed man'. In striving for this ideal one has to establish a hierarchy of persons and needs, and to complement the evidence of one's consciousness with suitable extra-ethical assumptions.

Kotarbiński's system of ethics is independent in a double sense: first, because it is free of any religious or philosophical assumptions, and second, because according to it, the conscience of a human being is the supreme judge of their actions, and cannot be replaced by that of anyone else.

4 Praxiology

As early as his first work Kotarbiński stressed the necessity of elaborating the conceptual apparatus for practical philosophy in a broad sense; first he called it general practice, then general methodology or praxiology. The programme of general methodology was outlined by Kotarbiński at the IX International Congress of Philosophy held in Paris, in 1937. He defined it as the investigation of 'rules of intentionality in action which are of value regardless of what material is being worked upon and to which a division of labour of arts or skills belongs'.

The programme was carried out in his main exposition of praxiology, *Traktat o dobrej robocie* (1955). The book contains numerous conceptual distinctions, definitions and rules which afford the basis for the utilitarian evaluation of actions according to their effectiveness and efficiency. Kotarbiński considered it to be a closed canon of praxiology.

Some ideas of praxiology can be found in writings of earlier thinkers (A. Bogdanov, G. Hostelet), but Kotarbiński's work in this field was both pioneering and systematic.

See also: POLAND, PHILOSOPHY IN; VIENNA CIRCLE

List of works

Kotarbiński, T. (1929) *Elementy teorii poznania, logiki formalnej i metodologii nauk*, Lwów: Ossolineum; Wrocław, Warsaw and Cracow: Ossolineum, 1961, 2nd edn; trans. *Gnosiology: The Scientific Approach to the Theory of Knowledge*, Oxford: Pergamon Press, 1966. (Extensive handbook of logic, semantics and theory of knowledge.)

—— (1952) 'Zagadminia etyki mizateznij' (Problems of Independent Ethics), *Kronika* (Lódż) No. 21. (Kotarbiński's statement of an ethics that is to be independent of religion, metaphysics and politics.)

—— (1955) *Traktat o dobrej robocie*, Lódż: Ossolineum; trans. O. Woitasiewicz, *Praxiology: An Introduction to the Sciences of Efficient Action*, Oxford: Pergamon Press, and Warsaw: PWN, 1965. (The fullest exposition of praxiology.)

—— (1957a) *Wykłady z dziejów logiki* (Lectures on the History of Logic), Lódż: Ossolineum; French trans. *Leçons sur l'histoire de la logique*, Warsaw 1964. (A survey of the history of logic from a nominalist point of view.)

—— (1957b) *Myśli o działaniu* (Reflections on

Action), vol. I of *Wybór pism* (Selected Writings), Warsaw: PWN. (Includes the most important essays and articles on different topics of practical philosophy, written between 1913 and 1954.)

—— (1958) *Myśli o myśleniu* (Reflections on Thinking), vol. II of *Wybór pism* (Selected Writings), Warsaw: PWN. (Includes the most important essays and articles on the theory of knowledge, 1913–54.)

——(1987) *Pisma etyczne* (Ethical Writings), Wrocław: Ossolineum. (A collection of Kotarbiński's ethical writings.)

References and further reading

Ajdukiewicz, K. (1935) 'Der Logistische Antiirrationalismus in Polen', *Erkenntnis* 5: 151–61. (Historically the first account of the contribution of the Polish School in philosophy – the 'Lwów–Warsaw School' – of which Kotarbiński was co-founder and one of the main representatives. Ajdukiewicz was another eminent representative of this school.)

Gasparski, W. (1993) 'A Philosophy of Practicality: A Treatise on the Philosophy of Tadeusz Kotarbiński', *Acta Philosophica Fennica*, 53 Helsinki. (A monograph devoted to Kotarbiński's philosophy seen as the philosophy of practicality in all its parts – in praxiology as well as in ethics, metaphilosophy, philosophy of language and philosophy of science.)

Gasparski, W. and Pszczołowski, T. (eds) (1983) *Praxiological Studies: Polish Contribution to the Science of Efficient Action*, Dordrecht. (An account of the Polish contribution to praxiology as conceived by Kotarbiński, written by his closest co-workers in this field.)

Kotarbińska, J. (1989) 'Droga Tadeusza Kotarbińskiego do prakseologii' (Tadeusz Kotarbiński's Route to Praxiology), *Praxiology* 4; trans. in *Praxiology: The International Annual of Practical Philosophy and Methodology*, vol. I, New Brunswick, NJ, 1992. (A short account of the evolution of Kotarbiński's views and interest in practical philosophy, given by his wife, who was his successor as the chairman of the Department of Logic at the University of Warsaw.)

Szaniawski, K. (1984) 'Philosophical Ideas of Tadeusz Kotarbiński', *Reports on Philosophy* 8: 25–32, Kraków: Uniwersytet Jagielloński. (A summary of Kotarbiński's philosophical views, written by one of his most eminent students and followers.)

Woleński, J. (1985) *Filozoficzna szkoła lwówsko-warszawska*, Warsaw: PWN; trans. *Logic and Philosophy in the Lvov–Warsaw School*, Dordrecht: Kluwer, 1989. (Extensive monograph on the contribution to logic and analytic philosophy of the Polish school between the First and Second World Wars.)

B. STANOSZ

KOYRÉ, ALEXANDRE (1892–1964)

The scope of his research and his effort to give civilization meaning make Alexandre Koyré one of the boldest and most influential of twentieth-century historians of scientific thought. He was Russian of origin, German by philosophical training, French by adoption, and chose the USA as his second intellectual homeland. From the mysticism of the Renaissance to Romantic philosophy, from Copernican theory to Newtonian synthesis, he interpreted modern cosmology in the light of 'the unity of human thought' and of mathematical realism, as both effect and origin of a 'spiritual' revolution.

After the Russian Revolution of 1905 Koyré was arrested and is said to have read Husserl's *Logical Investigations* in prison. From 1908 to 1914 he studied in Paris with Bergson, Lalande and Brunschvicg and in Göttingen with Husserl, Hilbert and Reinach. His made his debut with an essay on Zeno's paradoxes, centred on the concept of movement, leitmotif of his later work as a historian of science. Realist phenomenology led him to study scholastic theology with Gilson and Picavet. In 1914 he enrolled as an officer in the Foreign Legion and was posted on the Russian front, taking part in the February Revolution and fighting in the October Revolution.

Having emigrated to Paris in 1919, he taught philosophy in Montpellier and from 1931 was in charge of the *direction d'études* of 'History of Religious Ideas in Modern Europe' at the École Pratique. In 1929, an important doctoral dissertation on Boehme and an essay on Russian Romantic philosophy showed his capacity to unite the 'profound intuitions' of metaphysics with cultural contexts like Renaissance spirituality or Russian nationalism by means of 'conceptual analysis'. He studied the terminology of Russian mysticism, of Spinoza and reinterpreted Hegel phenomenologically, in a way decisively influential for the Hegelianism of KOJÈVE and Sartre. It was largely thanks to the journal *Recherches philosophiques* (1931–7), edited by Koyré, Puech and Spaier, that phenomenology and existentialism were promulgated in French philosophy between the wars. At the conference on phenomenology of the Société Thomiste at Juvisy in 1932, Koyré

criticized Husserl's evolution towards the transcendental idealism of the *Cartesian Meditations*, of which he had reviewed the French edition in 1931. He believed in phenomenology, in its ontological meaning, as a method for studying essences, not as a metaphysic, as he observed with regard to Heidegger.

At the same time Koyré began a history of science with studies of Nicolas of Cusa, Paracelsus and Copernicus. For Paracelsus he adopted Lévy-Bruhl's notion of 'mentalité': 'what is most difficult and most necessary when we tackle the study of thought that is no longer ours, is to forget what we know' (1955: 46). It was not philosophy of history that interested Koyré, but the uncertain adventures of Western philosophy before its issues had become stable: *itinerarium mentis in veritatem* (the mind's journey toward the truth). Scientific doctrines, like theological ones, belonged to 'structures of thought', which is what he called Dilthey's *Weltanschauungen* and Hoffding's 'concepts of the world'. Koyré was moved towards science by the epistemological circle of MEYERSON, Lévy-Bruhl and Hélène Metzger: 'Have I remained faithful to Meyerson? Not completely, because in my studies I have striven to show not the identical basis of human thought, but the differences of its structures in different historical periods. I have remained faithful to his precept of studying the reasons for mistakes with the same attention accorded to successes' (1986: 139).

In his masterpiece *Études galiléennes* (1939), dedicated to Meyerson and inspired by Burtt (1925), Koyré studied the difficulties and failures with regard to the concept of movement as a state and to the principle of inertia, 'paradoxes' contrary to experience, conceivable only through ideal experiments on nature made mathematical. Making space geometrical and the universe infinite defined the 'scientific revolution' as a 'revenge of Plato upon Aristotle'.

This polemically antipositivist representation of modern science became known when his essay 'Galileo and Plato' (1943) was published by the History of Ideas Club, while Koyré was in New York to found the prestigious École Libre des Hautes Études with Maritain, directing the review *Renaissance* and lecturing on Plato at Columbia University. After the war, his project for a chair in 'History of Scientific Thought' at the College de France having failed, Koyré became a member of the Institute for Advanced Study in Princeton in 1955. He continued teaching in Paris with the history of religious ideas and of scientific thought at the Department of Economic and Social Sciences at the École Pratique.

Acceleration, heliocentricity, attraction and the Newton–Leibniz controversy are the themes of the 'scientific revolution' developed by Koyré. In the course of his research, this category turned out to be unstable and the length of the work problematic. In *From the Closed World to Infinite Universe* (1957), his main work of synthesis, he went as far as Laplace, though he intended to extend it to Maxwell and Einstein.

'Scientific thought does not develop in a vacuum but always within a frame of ideas, of fundamental principles, of self-evident axioms which have usually been considered as belonging properly to philosophy' ([1961b] 1971–2: 256). By opening science to the interaction of other collective representations and recreating the language of the past with the coherence of his terminology, Koyré put the history of science on a footing with anthropological history and established a historical methodology as a new way of analysing science. His influence on KUHN and FOUCAULT renewed epistemological controversy, though in ways often distant from and even opposed to his own work.

See also: ANTHROPOLOGY, PHILOSOPHY OF; GALILEI, G.; MECHANICS, CLASSICAL; NEWTON, I.

List of works

Koyré, A. (1938) *Trois leçons sur Descartes* (Three Lectures on Descartes), Le Caire: Éd. de l'Universite du Caire; repr. in *Entretiens sur Descartes*, New York: Brentano, 1944. (Published in French and Arabic while a visiting professor in Egypt, these lectures on the *Discourse on Method* introduced his notion of 'revolution' through the geometrical and infinite universe of Cartesian physics.)

—— (1939) *Études galiléennes*, Paris: Hermann; trans. by J. Mepham, *Galileo Studies*, Atlantic Highlands, NJ: Humanities Press, 1978; Hassocks: Harvester Press, 1978. (Three essays on the problem of the law of falling bodies and the principle of inertia in Galileo and Descartes' physics. Arguing polemically, Koyré introduced Galileo's experiments and the discovery of inertia as belonging to Descartes.)

—— (1943) 'Galileo and Plato', *Journal of the History of Ideas* 4: 400–28. (Galileo's mathematical physics as a 'Platonic revenge' against the traditional positivist view of the history of science. Republished in 1968.)

—— (1945) *Discovering Plato*, New York: Brentano. (Presented at Columbia University and also published in a French edition, these lectures applauding democracy through a commentary of Plato's *Republic* had been composed in Beirut after the fall of France in 1940.)

—— (1955) 'A Documentary History of the Problem of Fall from Kepler to Newton', *Transactions of the American Philosophical Society* 45: 329–95. (An

exemplary case study of the ramifications of a physical problem through an anthropological approach.)

—— (1957) *From the Closed World to the Infinite Universe*, Baltimore, MD: Johns Hopkins University Press. (In this best-known work he traced the relation of God to the world from Nicolas of Cusa's cosmology to Newtonian natural theology.)

—— (1961a) *La révolution astronomique*, Paris: Hermann; repr. ivi 1974; *The Astronomical Revolution*, London, Methuen, 1980. (His last book on Kepler's astronomical metaphysics situated between Copernicus' geometrical cosmos and Borelli's celestial mechanics.)

—— (1961b) *Études d'histoire de la pensée philosophique* (Studies in History of Philosophical Thought), Paris: A. Colin; repr. ivi, Gallimard, 1970. (Contains the three most important essays by Koyré on Hegel: 'Note sur la langue et la terminologie hégélienne' (Note on Hegelian Language and Terminology) 1931, 'Rapport sur l'état des études hégéliennes en France' (Report on the State of Hegelian Studies in France) 1931 and 'Hegel à Jena' (Hegel in Jena) 1934. Instead of the prevailing image of the young Hegel diffused in France by Jean Wahl, these essays dealt with the problems inherent to Hegelian language, philosophy of time and *Logik*.)

* —— (1986) *De la mystique à la science. Cours, conférences et documents, 1922–1962* (From Mystical Theology to Science. Courses, lectures and documents 1922–62), Paris: Éditions de l'EHESS. (This collects Koyré's course abstracts, unpublished lectures on theology and science and documents on his teaching and biography.)

Koyré, A. and Cohen I.B. (eds) (1971–2) *Isaac Newton's Philosophiae Naturalis Principia Mathematica*, Cambridge, MA: Harvard University Press, 2 vols.

References and further reading

* Burtt, E.A. (1925) *The Metaphysical Foundations of Modern Physical Science*, New York: Harcourt Brace, and London: Routledge & Kegan Paul. (A seminal book on the relationships between philosophical and religious ideas underlying the early modern science.)

Clagett, M. and Cohen, I.B. (1966) 'Alexandre Koyré', *Isis* 57: 157–66. (An obituary essay attesting the role played by Koyré in the growth of the history of science as an academic discipline in the USA.)

* Gillispie, Ch.C. (ed.) (1973) 'Koyré', *Dictionary of Scientific Biography*, New York: Charles Scribner's

Sons, vol. 7, 482–90. (A relevant biographical source.)

Hering, J. (1964–5) 'In memoriam', *Philosophy and Phenomenological Research* 25: 453–4. (A useful source on the spread of phenomenology in France through Koyré.)

* Kuhn, T. (1970) 'A. Koyré and the History of Science', *Encounter* 34: 67–9. (The document of the intellectual encounter between the main historian of the 'révolution scientifique' and the author of *The Structure of Scientific Revolutions*.)

Redondi, P. (ed.) (1987) 'Science: The Renaissance of a History, Proceedings of the International Conference Alexandre Koyré, Paris 10–14 June 1986', *History and Technology* 4. (Among the contributors: G. Canguilhem, 'Preface', 7–10; K. Schuhmann, 'Koyré et les phénoménologues allemands', 149–68; Y. Elkana, 'Alexandre Koyré: Between the History of Ideas and Sociology of Disembodied Knowledge', 115–48; E. Couumet, 'Alexandre Koyré: la révolution scientifique introuvable?', 497–530.)

Salvadori, R. (ed.) (1980) '"Introduzione"', J. Hyppolite, A. Kojève, A. Koyré, J. Wahl', *Interpretazioni hegeliane*, Florence: La Nuova Italia, VII–XVIII. (A presentation of the main texts of the Parisian debate on Hegel in the 1930s.)

Speilberg, H. (1960) *The Phenomenological Movement. A Historical Introduction*, The Hague: Nijhoff, 2 vols. (A classical historical presentation of Husserl and his disciples' work.)

Vinti, C. (ed.) (1994) *A. Koyré. L'avventura intellettuale*, Naples: ESI. (Among the contributors to this conference held at the University of Perugia in 1992; F. Barone, E. Berti, M. Biagioli, P. Galluzzi, G. Jorland, E. Mirri, P. Redondi, P. Rossi, P. Zambelli.)

Wahl, J. (1965) 'Le rôle d'Alexandre Koyré dans le développement des études hégéliennes en France', *Archives de philosophie* 23: 323–36. (The scope and impact of Koyré's phenomenological reading of Hegel in the 1930s.)

Zambelli, P. (ed.) (1967) '"Introduzione", A. Koyré', *Dal mondo del pressappoco all'universo della precisione*, Turin: Einaudi. (An overview on the sociological and cultural insight of Koyré's history of scientific thought.)

—— (1995) 'Alexandre Koyré versus Lucien Lévy-Bruhl. From Collective Representations to Paradigms of Scientific Thought', *Science in Context* 13: 531–55. (A contextual analysis of the influence of Lévy-Bruhl's notion of mentalité on Koyré's historical method.)

PIETRO REDONDI

KOZLOV, A.A. *see* LOSSKY, NICHOLAS ONUFRIEVICH

KRAUSE, KARL CHRISTIAN FRIEDRICH (1781–1832)

Krause sought an overall explanation of reality in the manner of the post-Kantian idealists; the key elements of his thoughts are the concepts of organism and harmony, involving the incorporation of opposing elements rather than their annihilation. Three main themes characterize his philosophy: the doctrine of science, together with the equivalence of knowledge and being, or rational realism; the religious doctrine of panentheism which proclaims, 'everything in God'; and the social doctrine of the League of Humanity.

1 Life
2 The System
3 Influence

1 Life

Krause was born in Eisenberg, in the region of Thuringia. He studied theology, mathematics and philosophy at the University of Jena, with Fichte and Schelling. There he habilitated as a *Privatdozent* in 1802, having written his dissertation, *Dissertatio philosophico-matematica de philosophiae et matheseos notione et earum intima coniunctione* (Philosophico-Mathematical Dissertation on Philosophical and Mathematical Ideas and Their Close Relation). With increasing success, he taught logic, natural law, the philosophy of nature and his system of philosophy, as well as music. In 1803, the Napoleonic wars forced him to move twice: first to Rudoldstadt, then to Dresden. During this period he wrote *Grundlage des Naturrechts* (Basis of Natural Law) and continued working on *System der Philosophie* (System of Philosophy). In 1805 he joined the Archimedes Lodge of the Brotherhood of Freemasons, and studied the history of Freemasonry. Five years later he published *Die drei ältesten Kunsturkunden der Freimauererbruderschaft* (The Three Oldest Documents of the Brotherhood of Freemasons), in which he tried not only to prove that the masonic law of secrecy contradicted two of the Brotherhood's most ancient documents, but also called for its abolition. His expulsion from the Brotherhood of Freemasons was immediately decreed, and he would always attribute his subsequent penury to his Masonic enemies. In 1811 he published *Das Urbild der Menschheit* (The

Ideal of Humanity), in which he set out his doctrine concerning the social structure of humanity. In 1813 the war reached Dresden and he had to move to Tharand; six months later he went to Berlin, where he habilitated again with *Oration de scientia humana* (Oration on Human Science). He set up the *Berlinische Gesellschaft für Deutsche Gesprache* (Berlin Society of the History and Grammar of the German Language), although he did not succeed in obtaining a post as a teacher. In 1817 he went on a study visit to Italy, France and Germany, and wrote *Aesthetik* (Aesthetics). In 1825 he moved to Göttingen, where Heinrich Ahrens became his student. It was Ahrens who made his master's philosophy more widely known in Spain. In 1831, student riots forced Krause to move again, this time to Munich, where Schelling opposed his appointment as a professor. Krause died the following year.

2 The System

The first part of Krause's philosophical system is a process of 'analysis' which starts from a subjective perspective, both from knowledge and feeling, and which reveals the essential self (*Ur-Ich*) through intuition (*Anschauung*). This is an expression of individual substantiality, which is still not the thinking self – although this substantiality is one of its main activities – but the real self, unified, alive, different from any other entity. The doctrine of science deals with the cognitive self. However, knowledge does not just involve the logical knowledge of the intellect, but also comprises the areas of feeling and will as parts of the concept of Reason; moreover, the three of them are essential for each other and for their complete development.

Contrary to the Fichtean view, while Krause's 'self' is a foundation of the subjective realm, it is not enough to explain either knowledge of the other or that of the self in relation to the other. Also, the self is considered as a human being, made up of body and soul, finite essences which therefore belong to two universal ones: Nature and Spirit, both of which are contained in the concept of Humanity. And these three beings, infinite in themselves, are limited by each other, that is, in the Krausean language, they are 'relative infinites' and they require a 'Foundation' which comprehends and explains them: a basic and original essence, the absolute Being or metaphysical God (*Ur-Wesen*). From this point Krause moves on to the second part of the System, the Synthesis. He begins by studying the absolute, necessary Foundation and in reverse order reconstructs the whole process of knowledge, objectively and not only in the subjective aspect of analysis.

The 'Real Intuition' of the Absolute is the culmination of the process of analysis witnessed by the self: logical knowledge finds the absolute, necessary Foundation for its own intellectual knowledge. This 'intuition' – originating from the Latin word '*tuitio*' – has two modes of access to the absolute Foundation through the two aforementioned elements of Reason: the path of feeling, which produces religion's Real Intuition of the Supreme Being, God; and the path of will to the absolute God, which is the foundation of goodness and morality. These three paths integrate the panentheist doctrine, or 'everything in God', which is opposed to pantheism, in which all idealisms come together.

With this discovery, two important problems which idealistic pantheism did not solve are now avoided: human freedom and determinism in history. God is the absolute principle of the world, life and thought: he creates what is finite together with Man. However, this does not constitute a foundational and causal relation in time, but only in a metaphysical sense. The act of creation happened once and for all: Man, who was created like God, has, like him, infinite freedom, which is only limited by the condition that he is a finite being, but not by his essential, vital capacity. Likewise, God is the lord of history from its beginning but he does not intervene either in its temporal evolution or in its end. Contrary to the Hegelian view of history, Krause does not conclude with a fusion of all beings in the Absolute, but in a 'League of Humanity' with God. This alliance is brought about by a free and autonomous decision by both parties.

This explains the importance of the process of analysis and synthesis of the fundamental science from which all individual sciences evolve: psychology, or the analysis of the self's faculties; physics, or the science of nature; and anthropology, or the science of Man. They are all contained in history, which is the expression of Man's action and God's revelation.

The most interesting discovery of Krause's philosophy from the perspective of nineteenth-century idealistic thought is the focus on Man as a living being, that is, Man and environment temporally determined as philosophy's authentic objective. The formal process of science's doctrine of analysis and synthesis, together with the discovery of the self, do not adequately explain the reality of Man considered as a living being, determined in time. There are two essential levels of reality: the permanent and the changeable. Time distinguishes these levels, while Man contains both, inseparably. With this, Krause overcomes the dichotomy between Man and History, ideas and facts. Nature and Spirit are entwined as a supreme synthesis, and this should be their role in the science of life: to establish unions and to propitiate them, since Man is the being of union *par excellence*.

3 Influence

This extremely optimistic thought, which emphasizes the essential goodness of human beings as well as of values such as freedom and equality, made a significant impression in emerging bourgeois societies with new constitutional governments, such as Spain and the Latin American countries. For them, Krausean pedagogy, in conjunction with the ideas of F.W.A. Froebel, was especially attractive and influential as an agent of social change beginning from the full education of the individual, and not from a purely scientific education. Also influential was the philosophy of law, which establishes principles for the union of human beings. It regulates mutual relationships among individuals and social groups, not only in order to achieve their freedom but also for each individual to attain moral perfection. Societies are determined by organic functions (scientific, artistic, moral and religious society) and also by personal ones (individual, family, nation, country).

These disciplines – pedagogy and the philosophy of law – together with the Theory of Science, were extensively elaborated and developed by Krause's immediate followers. They were seen as a part of a continuous process of development which individuals elaborate throughout life when they enter into relationship with all the realities around them, and are indissolubly linked to the concepts of ethics, freedom and autonomy in every social group and in every individual. They both enabled this idealism to connect with the multiplicity of scientific disciplines and research areas which positivism generated in the later nineteenth century. Thus, in an apparent paradox, the German spiritualist current of thought became united with French positivism, combining the main concerns of ethics with the strict determinism of science. In the same way, Krause's emphasis on the concept of harmony between Nature and Spirit confirms him and all his followers as pioneers of ecological thought in its main postulate of harmony and balance between science and the natural world.

See also: ABSOLUTE, THE; GERMAN IDEALISM; SPAIN, PHILOSOPHY IN §4

List of works

Krause, K.C.F. (1802) *Dissertatio philosophico-matematica de philosophiae et matheseos notione et earum intima coniunctione* (Philosophico-mathematical Dissertation on Philosophical and Math-ematical Ideas and Their Close Relation), Jena: Voigtium. (Krause's Ph.D. thesis, which puts forward the philosophy and mathematics he uses to construct a system which explains reality.)

—— (1803) *Grundlage des Naturrechts* (Basis of Natural Law), Jena and Leipzig: Christian Ernst Gabler. (Krause's first attempt to formulate a world state as a social organization upon which a federation of nations could be established.)

—— (1810) *Die drei ältesten Kunsturkunden der Freimauererbruderschaft* (The Three Oldest Documents of the Brotherhood of Freemasons), Dresden: Arnoldischen Buchhandlung. (Krause's attack on the Freemasons, in which he called for their abolition.)

—— (1811a) *Das Urbild der Menschheit* (The Ideal of Humanity), Dresden: Arnoldischen Buchhandlung. (Krause's most translated work, which contains his concept of society determined by organic functions – religious, scientific, the state and art – and by personal functions, such as family, friendship and nationality.)

—— (1811b) *Versuch einer wissenschaftlichen Begründung der Sittenlehre* (Attempt at a Scientific Foundation of Ethics), Leipzig: Reclam. (This work concerns practical philosophy, considered as an essential component in the construction of a philosophical system.)

—— (1825) *Abriss des Systemes der Philosophie* (Outline of his System of Philosophy), Göttingen: Dieterischen Buchhandlung. (Sets out the development of the analysis and synthesis process in Krause's philosophical system.)

—— (1828) *Abriss des Systemes der Rechtes, oder der Naturrechtes* (Outline of the System of Right, or of Natural Law), Göttingen: Dieterischen Buchhandlung. (The philosophy of law is based on the individual's freedom and participation in society through associations, one of them being the estate, which is equal to the rest.)

—— (1829) *Vorlesungen über die Grundwahrheiten der Wissenschaft* (Lectures on the Basic Principles of Science), Göttingen: Dieterischen Buchhandlung. (Sets out the Krausean theory of knowledge.)

—— (1837) *Abriss der Aesthetik oder Philosophie des Schönen und der schönen Kunst* (Outline of Aesthetic and the Philosophy of Beauty and Fine Arts), Göttingen: Dieterischen Buchhandlung. (Contains the definition of beauty as the perfect union between Nature and Spirit. This idea is central to Krause's pedagogic project.)

—— (1848) *Vorlesungen über die psychische Anthropologie* (Lectures on Psychical Anthropology), Göttingen: Dieterischen Buchhandlung. (Presents the doctrine of Man and life, based on the

Krausean concept of the union of both the material and the spiritual part of being, as well as the need of a harmonious development for being.)

—— (1900) *Der Menschheitbund* (On the League of Humanity), Berlin: Felber. (Apart from developing the theory of a world state, this work offers a federal account of the government of nations.)

References and further reading

Abrahamson, M.R. (1991) 'Krausism, Pepita Jiménez and the Divinization of Life', *Letras Peninsulares* 4 (1): 225–43. (Emphasizes the importance of Krause's philosophy of life in the Spanish novel at the end of the nineteenth century.)

Davies, H.E. (1984) 'Alejandro Deustúa: His critique of the Aesthetic of the Vasconcelos', *International Philosophy Quarterly* 24: 69–78. (A discussion of the aesthetic theory of the Krausean, Deustúa.)

Dendle, B.J. (1991) 'Armando Palacio Valdés, the Revista Europea and the Krausist movement', *Letras Peninsulares* 4 (1): 25–34. (The writer Armando Palacio Valdés sarcastically criticizes Krausean thinkers, especially Sanz de Río and Francisco de Paula Canalejas, from a philosophical as well as from a literary viewpoint.)

Diaz, E. (1989) *La filosofía social del krausismo español* (The Social Philosophy of Spanish Krausism), Madrid: Debate, 3rd edn. (A comparative study of three Spanish Krausean thinkers: Sanz del Río, Giner and Azcárate.)

Garcia Mateo, R. (1982) *Das deutsche Denken und das modernen Spanien* (German thought and modern Spain), Frankfurt: Lang. (The importance of the Krausean social doctrine, which was promulgated in Paris and Brussels by Krause's follower H. Ahrens.)

Kodalle, K. (ed.) (1985) *K.Ch.F. Krause (1781–1832) Studien zu seiner Philosophie uns zum Krausismo* (Studies of Krause and Krausism), Hamburg: Meiner. (Contains various studies on Krause by specialists on Krausism and on idealist philosophy in general: the theory of knowledge, philosophy of religion and practical philosophy.)

Lipp, S. (1985) *Francisco Giner: A Spanish Socrates*, Waterloo, Ont.: Laurier University Press. (An account of the Krausean thinker F. Giner de los Ríos' pedagogical theory and its effects on modernization in contemporary Spain.)

Lopez Morillas, J. (1981) *The Krausist Movement and Ideological Change in Spain: 1854–1874*, trans. J. López Morillas, Cambridge: Cambridge University Press. (Offers an excellent description of the various areas of influence of the Krausean movement in Spain.)

Ríos Urruti, F. de los (1916) *La Filosofía del Derecho en don Francisco Giner y su relación con el pensamiento contemporáneo* (Francisco Giner's Philosophy of Laws and its Relation to Contemporary Thought), Madrid: Corona. (An important comparative study of Krause's philosophy of law and his contribution to this discipline.)

Rodriguez de Lecea, T. (ed.) (1983) *Reivindicacion de Krause*, Madrid: Fundación F. Ebert. (Contains various contributions about Krause and Spanish Krausism during the second half of the nineteenth century, such as the theory of knowledge, philosophy of religion, philosophy of law and social philosophy.)

—— (1987) *El Krausismo y su influencia en América Latina* (Krausism and its Influence in Latin America), Madrid: Fundación F. Ebert. (Various contributions on the influence of Krausean books and doctrines in countries such as Argentina, Brazil, Cuba, Mexico and Puerto Rico.)

—— (1991) *Antropología y filosofía de la historia en Julián Sanz del Río* (Anthropology and Philosophy of History in Julián Sanz del Río), Madrid: Centro de Estudios Constitucionales. (A study of the Krausean process of analysis considered as a theory of man and history.)

Ureña, E.M. (1991) *Krause, educador de la humanidad* (Krause: Educator of Humanity), Madrid: Unión Ed. (A detailed intellectual biography of Krause.)

Willm, J. (1849) *Histoire de la philosophie allemande depuis Kant jusqu'à Hegel* (History of German Philosophy from Kant to Hegel), Paris: Lagrange. (An important study on German philosophers contemporary to Krause, and his situation among them. Despite its age, it is still useful, though difficult to find.)

Translated by Isabel Venceslá

TERESA RODRÍGUEZ DE LECEA

KRIPKE, SAUL AARON (1940–)

Saul Kripke is one of the most important and influential philosophers of the late twentieth century. He is also one of the leading mathematical logicians, having done seminal work in areas including modal logic, intuitionistic logic and set theory. Although much of his work in logic has philosophical significance, it will not be discussed here.

Kripke's main contributions fall in the areas of metaphysics, philosophy of language, epistemology, philosophy of mind and philosophy of logic and mathematics. He is particularly well known for his views on and discussions of the following topics: the concepts of necessity, identity and 'possible worlds'; 'essentialism' – the idea that things have significant essential properties; the question of what determines the referent of an ordinary proper name and the related question of whether such names have meanings; the relations among the concepts of necessity, analyticity, and the a priori; the concept of belief and its problems; the concept of truth and its problems; and scepticism, the idea of following a rule, and Ludwig Wittgenstein's 'private language argument'. This entry will be confined to the topics of identity, proper names, necessity and essentialism.

1 Life
2 Identity, proper names and possible worlds
3 Necessity and essentialism

1 Life

Saul Kripke was born in Bay Shore, New York, the son of a rabbi and a teacher. The family soon moved to Omaha, Nebraska, where Kripke spent the rest of his childhood. At a very early age, he began to display prodigious mathematical ability and intense curiosity about philosophical questions. At the age of 15 he developed a semantics for quantified modal logic and his proof of the completeness of the semantics appeared in *The Journal of Symbolic Logic* when he was 18.

Kripke received his bachelor's degree in mathematics from Harvard in 1962 and was appointed to the Harvard Society of Fellows in 1963. There followed appointments as Lecturer at Princeton (1965 and 1966) and Harvard (1966–8). He was appointed Associate Professor at The Rockefeller University in 1968 (then Professor in 1972), and McCosh Professor of Philosophy at Princeton in 1977, which is the position he currently holds. Kripke was the youngest person ever chosen to give the John Locke Lectures at Oxford (1973) and he has been the recipient of many prestigious honours and accolades.

2 Identity, proper names and possible worlds

Kripke began working on these topics in the early 1960s and developed a number of positions that initially met with surprise and suspicion, but eventually became widely accepted. The most comprehensive presentation may be found in *Naming and Necessity* (1980), which is an edited transcript of three lectures given at Princeton in January 1970, together with a preface and addenda.

Kripke maintains that identity is a relation that holds between each thing and itself, never holds between any two things, and always holds (or fails to hold) of necessity (see IDENTITY). The 'necessity of identity' is a theorem of quantified modal logic (with identity), but some philosophers nevertheless thought certain examples cast doubt upon the doctrine (see MODAL LOGIC). For example, the identity of the inventor of bifocals with the first Postmaster General can easily seem contingent. But Kripke observed that what is contingent here is that one person attained both of these (separately contingent) distinctions, and that this contingency in no way undermines the necessity of that person's identity with himself – Benjamin Franklin would have been identical with himself even if he had never been Postmaster General or worked with lenses.

This last point reflects a fundamental Kripkean doctrine about the behaviour of ordinary proper names such as 'Franklin'. It is that when we utter a sentence such as 'Franklin might never have become Postmaster General', we are describing a way in which things might have gone differently for the very person who, in actual fact, was the first Postmaster General. We are describing a 'counterfactual situation' or 'possible world' involving Franklin himself, but in which he is not Postmaster General.

Kripke does not offer a detailed ontological account of possible worlds (though he does explicitly reject the 'counterpart' account favoured by David LEWIS (1968)). He does not see worlds as offering a useful analysis of our modal notions, but rather as reflecting pre-existing modal intuitions, and thinks that for most philosophical purposes we need no precise notion of possible worlds. It is normally sufficient to think in an everyday way of counterfactual situations or alternative possibilities, and this can help relieve any worry that we are trading on a technical notion of possible worlds without first defining it. Now invoking the terminology of worlds, the idea of the previous paragraph generalizes to the claim that an ordinary proper name always designates the same thing 'in other possible worlds' that it designates in the actual world. Kripke introduced the term 'rigid designator' for singular terms that behave in this way, allowing his thesis to be compactly expressed as the claim that proper names are rigid designators. But this rather technical-sounding formulation is intended as little more than a generalization of the hardly controversial idea that 'Franklin invented bifocals' and 'Franklin might not have invented bifocals' both concern the same person.

Now consider the sentence 'Cicero is Tully', which seemingly asserts a true identity and which involves two proper names. If these names are rigid designators, then each designates the same entity in every possible world – the entity that each designates in the actual world. But in the actual world both names designate the same person. It follows that they both designate this person in every possible world, and so it must be a necessary truth that Cicero is Tully. But it has often been thought that because such a fact is not knowable a priori, but rather requires empirical investigation, it could not be necessary. Kripke sees this as a fundamental error, stemming from a confusion of the epistemic notion of a prioricity with the metaphysical notion of necessity. For Kripke, 'Cicero is Tully' expresses an a posteriori, necessary truth (see A POSTERIORI; A PRIORI).

The idea that 'Cicero is Tully' is merely contingent is also fostered by theories of proper names in the tradition of Frege and Russell, according to which the referent of a name is determined by a definite description (or, in more recent versions, a 'cluster' of descriptions) associated with the name. Such theories often hold that the description gives the meaning (or sense) of the name. Because the description associated with 'Cicero' might be utterly different from the one associated with 'Tully', and because these descriptions might have distinct referents in some other world, it would be natural to think that 'Cicero is Tully' is contingent in much the same way that 'The first Postmaster General is the inventor of bifocals' is contingent. But Kripke argued that such theories of proper names are incorrect. His view is more in the spirit of J.S. Mill's and Ruth Barcan Marcus's, according to which names are mere 'tags' which lack senses and serve only to pick out their referents. Kripke held that a name is explicitly linked to its referent when it is first introduced, and that subsequent uses of the name refer to that entity because they trace backwards through an appropriate causal chain of uses to that initial introduction of the name. Subsequent uses do not achieve their reference to that entity as a result of its satisfying any specific descriptions associated with the name.

3 Necessity and essentialism

Essentialism is the view that things have certain of their significant properties necessarily – that they could not have existed without possessing those properties (see ESSENTIALISM). In the early 1960s the very notion of necessity was often thought to be incoherent. But even philosophers who granted the meaningfulness of the notion and conceded the existence of certain necessary truths typically found essentialism unacceptable.

Much of the antipathy towards necessity and essentialism may be traced to a confusion of necessity with analyticity (see ANALYTICITY). Just as Kripke urged that a prioricity and necessity are distinct

notions, so did he insist that analyticity is a third notion, not to be confused with the others. But such a confusion appears to underlie one of the main arguments against essentialism. It was claimed that the idea that a thing has a property necessarily makes no sense absolutely, but only relative to a specific way of designating the thing. For example, if the number nine is designated by 'the number of the planets', then it has the property of numbering the planets necessarily, but if it is designated by 'nine', it does not. So the idea of attributing a necessary property to the object independently of any designation makes no sense (see QUINE, W.V.).

This may seem correct if we have not carefully distinguished necessity from analyticity. For 'The number of the planets numbers the planets' seems analytic while 'Nine numbers the planets' does not. But when we set aside analyticity and focus clearly on necessity, the question no longer concerns sentences of our language. Instead we are asking whether a certain object had to have a certain property. If the object is the number nine and the property is numbering the planets, the answer must be 'no', for we can imagine a world in which the solar system developed differently. And if the property is being a square, the answer must be yes. There is no world in which nine is not a square. (Of course it could be that the name 'nine' did not refer to nine. But, in such a world, nine – whatever it might be called there – would still be a square.)

Kripke argued that ordinary entities also have nontrivial essential properties. Suppose a specific table, T, is made of wood. According to Kripke, although it is possible for tables to be made of other materials, no such possibility exists for T. Of course it is an empirical matter whether T has this property at all. But this merely means the matter is a posteriori, not that it is contingent. We know that such properties as T's location or finish are contingent because we can imagine a world in which T is somewhere else or differently finished. According to Kripke, we cannot imagine a world in which T is not made of wood. When we think we have imagined such a world, closer consideration reveals it is really a world in which some other table has been switched with T (or made instead of T, and so on).

Kripke relies heavily on 'intuition' here and in his other philosophical work. But he is not invoking a special power or sense. Rather, he is insisting that the concepts that concern us in philosophy are, after all, our own concepts, and accordingly that the best evidence for how they fit together can only come from thinking as carefully as we can about them. In this entry we have managed a glimpse at some of the results of this approach in Kripke's work on reference and modality. Comparably powerful and compelling results are to be found throughout the full range of his remarkable work.

See also: SEMANTIC PARADOXES AND THEORIES OF TRUTH; SEMANTICS

List of works

Kripke, S.A. (1959) 'A Completeness Theorem in Modal Logic', *Journal of Symbolic Logic* 24 (1): 1–14. (Proves that a formula is a theorem of quantified modal logic if and only if it is valid in Kripke's semantics. Very technical.)

—— (1963) 'Semantical Considerations on Modal Logic', *Acta Philosophica Fennica* 16: 83–94; 53–355. (Presents Kripke's semantics for modal logic. Partly informal, partly technical.)

—— (1971) 'Identity and Necessity', in M.K. Munitz (ed.) *Identity and Individuation*, New York: New York University Press, 135–64. (An early presentation of key ideas treated in Kripke 1980.)

—— (1972) 'Naming and Necessity', in D. Davidson (ed.) *Semantics of Natural Language,* Dordrecht: Reidel, 2nd edn, 253–355. (Treats the topics of Kripke 1980.)

—— (1975) 'Outline of a Theory of Truth', *Journal of Philosophy* 72 (19): 690–716. (Sketches a theory of truth designed to avoid paradox while minimizing truth-value gaps. Very technical.)

—— (1976) 'Is There a Problem about Substitutional Quantification?', in G. Evans and J. McDowell (eds) *Truth and Meaning*, London: Oxford University Press, 325–419. (Discussions of the substitutional interpretation of quantification and evaluation of its philosophical significance. Difficult, often technical.)

—— (1977) 'Speaker's Reference and Semantic Reference', *Midwest Studies in Philosophy* 2: 255–76. (On the potential divergence of what a speaker intends to refer to from what the speaker's words refer to, and whether the words are ambiguous. Largely nontechnical.)

—— (1979) 'A Puzzle About Belief', in A. Margalit (ed.) *Meaning and Use*, Dordrecht: Reidel, 239–83. (Discusses a vital problem concerning the interplay of reference and belief. Difficult, not very technical.)

—— (1980) *Naming and Necessity*, Oxford: Blackwell, and Cambridge, MA: Harvard University Press. (The key source for Kripke's views on proper names, reference, identity, necessity, essentialism and related topics. Difficult but largely nontechnical.)

—— (1982) *Wittgenstein on Rules and Private Language*, Oxford: Blackwell, and Cambridge, MA: Harvard University Press. (Discusses scepticism, rule-following and Wittgenstein's 'private language argument'. Nontechnical.)

—— (1986) 'A Problem in the Theory of Reference: The Linguistic Division of Labor and the Social Character of Naming', in *Philosophy and Culture (Proceedings of the 17th World Congress of Philosophy)*, Montreal: Editions du Beffroi, Editions Montmorency, 241–7. (Discusses a problem about how proper names refer.)

References and further reading

Branch, T. (1977) 'New Frontiers in American Philosophy', *The New York Times Magazine*, August 14. (Evidence of Kripke's popular fame, with discussion of his early work.)

French, P.A., Uehling, T.E., Jr. and Wettstein, H.K. (eds) (1986) *Studies in Essentialism, Midwest Studies in Philosophy* 11. (A valuable collection of twenty-six essays on essentialism and related topics by noted authors. Includes an abundance of useful references. The essays vary in techicality and difficulty.)

Jubien, M. (1993) *Ontology, Modality, and the Fallacy of Reference*, Cambridge: Cambridge University Press. (Offers a theory of proper names and an account of essentialism that differ sharply from Kripke's, despite a fundamental agreement at the intuitive level. Difficult but not overly technical.)

* Lewis, D.K. (1968) 'Counterpart Theory and Quantified Modal Logic', *Journal of Philosophy* 65: 113–26. (A rather technical presentation of an account of modality criticized in Kripke 1980. Requires an understanding of quantified modal logic.)

—— (1986) *On the Plurality of Worlds*, Oxford: Blackwell. (A philosophical elaboration of the key ideas of Lewis 1968, and related topics. Difficult but not overly technical.)

Marcus, R.B. (1993) *Modalities*, New York: Oxford University Press. (Collects Marcus's essays on modality, modal logic, and other topics. Of special interest are essays 1, 14, and appendix 1A, a discussion among the author, Quine, Kripke, T. McCarthy, and D. Follesdal, which followed a 1962 presentation of essay 1. Essay 1 is quite technical, essay 14 and appendix 1A are less so.)

Plantinga, A. (1974) *The Nature of Necessity*, Oxford: Oxford University Press. (Contains an influential account of possible worlds and a general theory of modality. Difficult and fairly technical.)

Quine, W.V. (1960) *Word and Object*, Cambridge, MA: MIT Press. (Offers criticisms of modal notions that are responded to in Kripke 1980. Difficult and sometimes technical.)

MICHAEL JUBIEN

KRISTEVA, JULIA (1941–)

Born in Bulgaria, Kristeva entered the Parisian scene of avant-garde intellectuals in the 1960s. Her earliest work in linguistics was shaped by the post-Stalinist communism of eastern Europe, a political climate that exerts its influence on her entire corpus, even as she distanced herself from it, to embrace an increasingly psychoanalytic perspective. Dissatisfied with scientific models of language, conceived as a mere means of communicating preconceived ideas, where words simply function as isolated symbols that represent discrete concepts, Kristeva analyses language as a signifying process. As such, language is not a static and closed system of signs, but a mobile, fluid process that implicates bodily and vocal rhythms in the generation of symbolic meanings. In La Révolution du langage poétique *(1974) (*Revolution in Poetic Language, 1984*) Kristeva fuses linguistic insights with psychoanalytic inquiry as she presents two distinct yet interrelated aspects of the signifying process, the semiotic and the symbolic. The semiotic aspect of language is vocal, pre-verbal, rhythmic, kinetic and bodily. The symbolic aspect of language is social, cultural, and rule-governed. Focusing on the interplay between the semiotic and the symbolic, Kristeva is able to analyse literary and historical texts, works of art and cultural phenomena in a way that thematizes the complex relationship between materiality and representation.*

1   Life and works
2   Linguistics
3   *Revolution in Poetic Language*
4   Kristeva and feminism
5   Psychoanalysis

1   Life and works

Although Kristeva has come to be known to a large portion of her English readership as a French feminist, the label is misleading. Bulgarian by birth, Kristeva moved to Paris in 1966, and her engagement with feminism has been nothing if not polemical. After an early training in the sciences, she worked as a journalist while pursuing her literary studies. In France, having received a doctoral fellowship, she followed the advice of Tzvetan Todorov, and attended the seminar of Lucien Goldmann. She embarked on a career that is distinguished by its breadth and interdisciplinary approach, the main strands of which – in addition to philosophy – can be identified as linguistics, literature, and psychoanalysis. A research assistant at Claude Lévi-Strauss's Laboratory of Social Anthropology, she also took advantage of the resources offered by the Centre National de Recherche Scientifique, and the École Pratique des Haute Études. As an associate of the *Tel Quel* review, edited by Philippe Sollers, Kristeva quickly took her place at the centre of French intellectual life (see TEL QUEL SCHOOL). She joined the faculty of the University of Paris VII, and became a practising psychoanalyst.

Among the early influences on her work, in addition to Marxism, Mikhail BAKHTIN stands out, as does her engagement with structuralism. Semiotics, or the science of signs, provided the focus of her first published works, *Semeiotiké: Recherches pour une sémanalyse* (1969) and *Le Texte du roman* (1970). Adapting and building upon the work of Roland BARTHES, Ferdinand de SAUSSURE and Charles S. PEIRCE, Kristeva began to develop a theoretical framework that would be more fully elaborated in the landmark text *La Révolution du langage poétique* (1974) (*Revolution in Poetic Language*, 1984).

By 1980, with the publication of *Pouvoirs de l'horreur: essai sur l'abjection* (*Powers of Horror: An Essay on Abjection*, 1982) Kristeva's growing interest in psychoanalysis had become decisive. The impact of Jacques Lacan's *Écrits* (1971), and the psychoanalytic training that Kristeva had undergone continued to inform her approach in *Histoires d'amour* (1983) (*Tales of Love*, 1983), *Soleil noir* (1987) (*Black Sun*, 1989), *étrangers à nous-même* (1988) (*Strangers to Ourselves*, 1991) and *Les Nouvelles Maladies de l'âme* (1993) (*New Maladies of the Soul*, 1995). Her work also includes novels.

2   Linguistics

Language, for Kristeva, has transformative capacities. In order to unearth the heterogeneous character of language, considered as in process, Kristeva departs from the 'generative grammar' of Chomsky that gained popularity in the 1970s (see CHOMSKY, N.). The Chomskian view that 'surface' structures derive from 'deep' structures appeared to reduce the 'speaking subject' to a series of translinguistic generalities that privilege systematic structures. In its search for truth, its emphasis on logic, and its adoption of scientific procedures Saussurean linguistics fared no better than Chomsky's innatist belief in linguistic universals. Although Kristeva would rehabilitate de Saussure's interest in semiology, she found his implementation of it inadequate to the subject of enunciation, or to what she called the 'speaking subject'. Kristeva's desire to attend to the exigencies of the speaking subject is not a matter of returning to a Cartesian self, or a transcendental ego, but rather takes account of the disruptive and disturbing qualities that invade the equilibrium of linguistic frameworks that reduce language to a series of rules, or contain it within a formal system of signs.

Kristeva calls for linguistics to change its object of study. It is no longer the theoretical rules governing language, whether these are conceived as grammatical, or semiological, that should be studied, but rather – and it is here that the influence of Roman Jakobson (see RUSSIAN LITERARY FORMALISM) makes itself felt – 'poetic language'. Far from harnessing or fixing language by establishing its foundational structures, or stabilizing it within a system, Kristeva focuses on a 'speech practice' that involves a dialectic between its 'signified structure (sign, syntax, signification)', and a 'semiotic rhythm'. Although Kristeva uses the term 'dialectic' to describe the struggle that takes place between 'language and its rhythm', she depends on post-Hegelian and post-Marxist resonances to give meaning to the term. It is Heidegger's vision of the strife of world and earth as the origin of the work of art, and the work of Mallarmé and Artaud, Lautréamont and Bataille, as well as that of the Russian poets Mayakovsky and Khlebnikov, that Kristeva draws on when she observes, in 'The Ethics of Linguistics' (in *Desire in Language*, 1977), that the poet 'wants to make language perceive what it doesn't want to say'.

Wary of neutralizing the specificity of the speaking subject, Kristeva wants to find a way to recapture the 'rhythm of the body', to reclaim the 'semiotic materials' that other linguistic models tend to obliterate in their fascination with the technical elements of language.

3 Revolution in Poetic Language

By refusing to restrict the significance of language to its meaning – to see in it only a system of representation – Kristeva insists on the materiality of language, on its emergent conditions. In *Revolution in Poetic Language*, she thematizes the divergent modalities of language under the heading 'the semiotic and the symbolic'. Kristeva's analysis of the semiotic is informed by Freud's notion of instinctual drives or impulses, the unconscious, and the pre-Oedipal. The symbolic is associated with the Freudo-Lacanian notion of post-Oedipal relations, with the function of representation, and with language as a sign-system.

The semiotic drives articulate what Kristeva calls the *chora*, a term she inherits from Plato's account of the creation of the universe in his dialogue the *Timaeus* (1975). The *chora* is a maternal receptacle, a generative matrix, an eternal place that, Plato tells us, is neither visible nor partakes of form, but is in some way intelligible. Amorphous and formless, Plato calls it the nurse of becoming, a kind of wet-nurse. Kristeva retains the paradoxical quality she sees in Plato's account of the *chora* as formless and undetermined, yet capable of receiving form and determination. The *chora* is neither sign nor signifier, neither model nor copy. It is pre-symbolic, not yet posited, and yet it can be named and spoken of – a process that converts the semiotic into the symbolic, conferring on the semiotic precisely the order, constraint, or law of culture that it resists. Just as Plato's *chora* resists definition, although it can be spoken of as if it were identifiable as an entity, so Kristeva constitutes the semiotic by naming it, even as its mobile forces elude conceptualization. In both cases the very utterance involves a loss, a betrayal of what language attempts to say. Yet this is a necessary betrayal, since the semiotic relies upon the symbolic for its articulation – one might say for its very existence – even if it suffers a transformation in the process of coming to representation.

If the semiotic needs the symbolic to represent it, the register of the symbolic requires the irruption and influx of the semiotic if it is to remain capable of change. If, in the interests of the very integrity of the semiotic, the subject cannot repudiate the symbolic, neither can it do without the semiotic. The need that the symbolic has for the excesses of poetic motion, or for the otherness of musical rhythm that marks the semiotic rupturing of the symbolic might be described as an ethical and political exigency.

4 Kristeva and feminism

A visit to China which resulted in the book *Des Chinoises* (1974) (*About Chinese Women*, 1977) set the tone for Kristeva's uneasy relationship with feminism. The book caused controversy, and Kristeva was accused of being 'romantic' and 'utopian' in her figuring of the Orient as other. Given to dramatic statements, such as 'a woman cannot "be"', Kristeva's often dismissive remarks about other versions of feminism – what she calls in an interview 'sociological protest' (Marks and de Courtivron 1981) – did little to curry favour with her detractors. In her defence, it should be pointed out that Kristeva's work has shared the same fate as that of Luce IRIGARAY and Hélène CIXOUS, with whom she is so often compared. The reception of their work has been plagued by a failure to take account of their intellectual heritage, political contexts and personal biographies. The misshapen versions of their work that critics have handed down to their English-speaking readers made it easy for readers of the 1980s to accuse these three so-called French feminists (Irigaray is Belgian, and Cixous is Algerian) of 'essentialism'. Afraid that Kristeva's caution about totalizing politics, her attempt to reintroduce the body into analyses of language, and the Lacanian influence on her work amounted to a male-identified conservative and reactionary elitism, feminist critics shunned her work. Instead of understanding her insistence upon sexual difference as a refusal to neutralize the specific material conditions of the production of language, conditions which include the sexed body, her attempt to reintroduce the body into feminism was hailed as detrimental to the progress of women's quest for equality.

In the 1990s, Kristeva began to receive a fairer hearing in English-speaking feminist circles, and this was in large part due to the fact that critics began to equip themselves with the conceptual tools that Kristeva's diverse intellectual endeavours required. Not least among these is the importance of phenomenology, psychoanalysis and post-structuralism – specifically Ferdinand de Saussure's structural linguistics and its post-structuralist modifications by figures such as Roland Barthes.

5   Psychoanalysis

When Kristeva denies being to a woman, her assertion takes account of Heidegger's ontological distinction – the difference between a being and Being (or existence) as such (see HEIDEGGER, M.) – and Lacan's notorious statement in *Seminar* XX (1972–3) that 'There is no such thing as *The* woman.' Understood in this light, rather than as a merely polemical statement, it can be read as a way of insisting upon the relevance of sexual difference, the limitations of ontological language, and the need to interrogate the possibilities of situating a woman's subjectivity on a level that does not simply conform to the position of male subjectivity. The position adopted by the female subject is thus one in excess of the boundaries of language, outside the order of being – at least in so far as language and existence are sanctioned as male.

It was Kristeva's abiding interest in language that drew her to psychoanalysis. Interested in the underside of language, Kristeva's work of the late 1980s and 1990s is preoccupied with the exploration of borderlines, marginal existence, outlawed subjectivities, and what it means to be a foreigner, an outsider. While the significance of these themes is by no means limited to sexual difference – the question of nationality, the issue of psychosis, and the desire for abjection are a few of the concerns that Kristeva pursues by focusing upon the limits and borders of subjectivity and consciousness – the question of feminine and masculine identity is a central one.

The symbolic, a Lacanian term that Kristeva invests with a new significance in counterposing it to the semiotic, interprets the father of Freud's Oedipal drama in terms of language. Since the semiotic *chora* has maternal connotations, there is a sense in which the distinction between the semiotic and the symbolic is sexually marked. This does not mean that Kristeva discerns semiotic energies only in the work of women artists. On the contrary – and this has provoked consternation to some feminists – she points more often to the works of Bellini and Giotto, Baudelaire and Proust for their capacity to evoke the sexual pleasure that she calls corporeal '*jouissance*'. This term, like so much of her work, reflects the influence of Lacan, whose impact on Kristeva's corpus is decisive, despite the critical distance she inserts between her own writing and Lacan's *oeuvre*.

List of works

Kristeva, J. (1969) *Semeiotiké: Recherches pour une semanalyse*, Paris: Éditions du Seuil. (Early work on semiotics.)

—— (1970) *Le Texte du roman*, The Hague: Mouton. (Semiotic theory and linguistic literary analysis.)

—— (1974a) *La Révolution du language poétique*, Paris: Éditions du Seuil; trans. M. Waller, *Revolution in Poetic Language*, introduction L.S. Roudiez, New York: Columbia University Press, 1984. (Fusing insights from the diverse sources of linguistics, Bahktin, Hegel, Lacan and others, this central text firmly established Kristeva's reputation as an original theorist, mobilizing the distinction between the semiotic chora as a motile rhythmic sensible aspect of language and the symbolic realm of meaning that has become the hallmark of her work.)

—— (1974b) *Des Chinoises*, Paris: Éditions des Femmes; trans. A. Barrows, *About Chinese Women*, London: Marion Boyars, 1977.

—— (1977) *Polylogue*, Paris: Éditions du Seuil. (Of the twenty essays comprising this collection, eight are translated in *Desire in Language: A Semiotic Approach to Literature and Art*, ed. L.S. Roudiez, trans. T. Gora, A. Jardine and L.S. Roudiez, 1980.)

—— (1980) *Pouvoirs de l'horreur: essai sur l'abjection*, Paris: Éditions du Seuil; trans. L.S. Roudiez, *Powers of Horror. An Essay on Abjection*, New York: Columbia University Press, 1982. (Psychoanalytic work exploring abjection, perversion and defilement in the context of Céline's novels, the Oedipal myth and biblical semiotics.)

—— (1983) *Histoires d'amour*, Paris: Denoël; trans. L.S. Roudiez, *Tales of Love*, New York: Columbia University Press, 1987. (Freudian inspired theoretical and historical theory of love drawing on religious and literary conceptions of agape and eros, from Plato to Bataille.)

—— (1987) *Soleil noir: dépression et mélancolie*, Paris: Gallimard; trans. L.S. Roudiez, *Black Sun: Depression and Melancholia*, New York: Columbia University Press, 1989. (Analysis of melancholia and depression as different ways of mourning the lost maternal object.)

—— (1988) *étrangers à nous-mêmes*, Paris: Fayard; trans. L.S. Roudiez, *Strangers to Ourselves*, New York: Columbia University Press, 1991. (Cultural, political and psychoanalytic analysis of the phenomenon of foreignness, nationality and individuality.)

—— (1993) *Les Nouvelles maladies de l'âme*, Paris: Fayard; trans. R. Guberman, *New Maladies of the Soul*, New York: Columbia University Press, 1995. (A meditation on the function of psychoanalysis in relation to the soul, approached as the 'psyche' by the ancients.)

References and further reading

* Baruch, E. Hoffamn and Serrano, S.J. (ed.) (1988) *Women Analyze Women: In France, England, and the United States*, New York: Columbia University Press. (Contains an interview with Kristeva.)

Fletcher, J. and Benjamin, A. (ed.) (1990) *Abjection, Melancholia and Love: The Work of Julia Kristeva*, London and New York: Routledge. (A useful collection, focusing on the literary and feminist aspects of Kristeva's corpus.)

* Lacan, J. (1971) *Écrits*, Paris: Éditions du Seuil; trans. A. Sheridan, *Écrits: A Selection*, New York: Norton. (Lacan's major collection of essays containing seminal pieces, such as the essay on the 'mirror stage'.)

* —— (1972–3) 'God *and the* Jouissance *of The* Woman', in *Seminar XX, Encore*, Paris: Éditions du Seuil; trans. J. Rose, in J. Mitchell and J. Rose (eds) *Feminine Sexuality: Jacques Lacan and the école freudienne*, London: Macmillan, 1982. (The translation is in a collection of essays focusing on the question of woman, with two very helpful introductory essays by the editors.)

Lechte, J. (1990) *Julia Kristeva*, London and New York: Routledge. (A general introduction, helpful for situating Kristeva's semiotics in its linguistic context.)

* Marks, E. and de Courtivron, I. (eds) (1981) *New French Feminisms: An Anthology*, Brighton, Sussex: Harvester Press. (The first collection of essays to introduce Kristeva to an English speaking feminist audience. Includes an extract from an interview, 'Woman Can Never be Defined', first published in 1974 by *Tel Quel*, conducted by the radical feminist group known as 'Psych & Po'.)

* Oliver, K. (ed.) (1993) *Ethics, Politics, and Difference in Julia Kristeva's Writing*, New York: Routledge. (To date the best collection of essays, representing the diverse elements of Kristeva's work, including an article by Lisa Lowe concerning Kristeva's work on Chinese women.)

* —— (1993) *Reading Kristeva: Unraveling the Doublebind*, Bloomington and Indianapolis, IN: Indiana University Press. (Particularly useful for readers interested in psychoanalysis and feminism.)

* Plato (1975) *Timaeus, Critias, Cleitophon, Menexenus, Epistles*, trans. R.G. Bury, Loeb Classical Library, vol. IX, London: Heinemann. (Plato's *Timaeus* is a classic ancient text that presents a myth of creation and concerns the themes of space, place and time. Kristeva borrows the term which plays an organizing role in the crucial distinction between the semiotic and the symbolic from Plato's discussion of place: chora, translated as matrix or receptacle, and associated with maternal giving.)

TINA CHANTER

KROCHMAL, NACHMAN (1785–1840)

Nachman Krochmal was leader of the Jewish Enlightenment or Haskalah in Galicia, eastern Europe. An astute observer of the German philosophical environment, Krochmal provided one of the first Jewish responses to, and adaptations of, elements of the philosophical work of Spinoza, Kant, Herder, Schelling and Hegel. His posthumously published Moreh Nevukhei ha-Zeman *(Guide to the Perplexed of Today) (1851) adapted Kantian epistemological methods to interpret the Jewish religious sources with an eye to discovering their inner, philosophical meaning. Krochmal argued that at that their deeper level these sources, both ancient and medieval, anticipated the discoveries of the German Idealist philosophers. Thus, for example, the Jewish belief in a personal God who created the world and revealed a desired way of life could remain philosophically fruitful. For, when properly interpreted, such ideas were concrete representations of the truths laid bare in the metaphysics of Hegel and Schelling.*

Krochmal answered the regnant philosophy of history, which considered Jewish culture to have been sublated, by arguing that Jewish religion, by its apprehension of the absolute, stood outside the historical 'laws' that mandate the eventual cultural demise of all nations and states.

Although he was an important model for aspiring Jewish intellectuals in eastern Europe, Krochmal's work was of limited philosophical influence. His lasting contribution may be his implicit exposure of the unstated cultural biases of modern idealist philosophy. For his work shows that alternative cultural assumptions would turn idealist philosophy towards philosophical and religious conclusions significantly different from those of the German Idealists themselves.

1   **Life and times**
2   *Moreh Nevukhei ha-Zeman*

1   Life and times

Nachman Krochmal was born in the city of Brody in Galicia, eastern Europe, then under Austrian rule and lived in Brody and the Galician cities of Zollkiew, Lemberg (Lwów) and Tarnopol. His birth came in the middle of the decade-long reign of the Austrian Emperor Joseph II, whose ideals committed him to modernizing the educational institutions of the Jews and instilling in them German language skills. Krochmal himself remained largely untouched by the Emperor's educational programme, but the penetration of German language and culture profoundly challenged his Galician-Jewish environment. The movement to bring 'enlightenment' to the Jews, known in Hebrew as the Haskalah (see ENLIGHTENMENT, JEWISH), was strongly centred in Galicia and deeply affected Krochmal, who emerged there as its leader. But its programme of cultural modernization was of extremely limited reach and was not accompanied, in his lifetime, by significant political or social change. The small coterie of modernist Jewish intellectuals in Galicia experienced 'modernity' mainly in the form of cultural challenges that came, in part, from an ongoing philosophical discussion in a distant land, whose intellectuals they did not know and could not engage with in any immediate way. The medieval Jewish philosophical tradition was of limited help in facing the new challenges, for the medieval Jewish philosophers typically addressed the challenge of Aristotelian thought. In Krochmal's view, Jewish intellectuals needed a new guide, to replace Maimonides' *Guide to the Perplexed* (see MAIMONIDES, M.), if they were to find continued philosophical vitality in the Jewish tradition.

2   *Moreh Nevukhei ha-Zeman*

Roughly one-third of Krochmal's *Moreh Nevukhei ha-Zeman* addresses philosophical themes. He begins his philosophical discussion by noting the incoherence of both philosophical scepticism and religious fideism. Staking out a middle ground between these two extremes required an epistemological foundation that would explain how and why religious thinkers formulate their ideas. Drawing on KANT – as he would have to do to be convincing – Krochmal notes that the path to clear philosophical ideas moves from sensory stimuli to preliminary concepts or representations (*Vorstellungen*), and on to concepts of the understanding (*Begriffe*), and the purely intellectual ideas of reason (*Ideen*). Most people never rise beyond the level of the *Vorstellung*, or representational thought. But any successful religious community must address a broad base. So religious communication is naturally formulated representationally. Diverging from Kant, Krochmal insists that religious representations differ from the more abstract *Ideen* descriptively and linguistically, but are no less apprehensions of truth. Religions always communicate representationally, but they focus on speculative concerns and convey philosophical truths, albeit less clearly than abstract philosophical discourse. Krochmal, then, sees religions as suffused with esoteric speculation. The task of the interpreter is to uncover the hidden speculative content. Accordingly, traditional Jewish sources and Western philosophical thinking are drawn into a lengthy philosophical dialogue in Krochmal's work.

The Jewish sources traditionally saw a purpose in created existence. Their teleological conception sustained their affirmation of the existence of God. Modern philosophy formidably challenged this view. Spinoza for one dismissed such teleology as illusory (see SPINOZA, B. DE §4). Kant reaffirmed the logic of teleological judgments, drawing on the interdependent and organic character of nature; but his reaffirmation allowed us to use teleology only as a regulative, not as a constitutive, idea. HEGEL developed Kant's argument into a metaphysical claim, affirming the organic nature of existence. Krochmal, too, adapted Kant's argument and, like Hegel, moved the organic characterization of nature beyond the realm of regulative ideas and into metaphysics. He went on to assert that teleology presupposes a willing and thus a personal God as creator. The traditional Jewish sources, then, with their affirmation of divine teleology, communicated, by way of representations, the speculative truth of organic nature and the reality of its purposing creator.

Reliance on a teleological proof that led to a

creator God raised a second of the philosophical challenges that faced modern Jews. Hegel, in his 'Lectures on the Philosophy of Religion', had identified creation – *creatio ex nihilo* – as the source of the fundamental defect of Jewish religion, its sublimity. In Hegel's view the vision of a world created from nothingness by a transcendent being symbolized the absolute and unbridgeable gulf that the Jewish religion opened up between the infinite and the finite. Christianity, the consummate religion, by rejecting the transcendent otherness of God and relying on the symbolism of the incarnation, overcame that gap, sublated the finite/infinite antinomy, and so reached a more advanced stage of religion and a closer approximation to the truth (see HEGEL, G.W.F. §7).

Turning to the work of the medieval Bible commentator and thinker Abraham IBN EZRA among others, Krochmal argued that Hegel's was not an accurate portrayal of Jewish theology. Creatively drawing on Ibn Ezra and other Jewish Neoplatonists, he reconstructed a vision of a protracted divine drama, in which God begins the process of coming to self-consciousness through a purposeful act of self-limitation. The world is created not from nothingness but from God's very being. Thus it is suffused with divinity or spirit (*Geist*); the gulf between God and the world is illusory. Traditional Jewish images and representations anticipate the fundamental insights of German Idealism. The modern idealist philosophers contribute conceptual vocabulary and conceptual clarity; but it was the ancient Jewish texts that first communicated, however imperfectly, the fundamental insights into the relationship of the finite and infinite.

The awareness that the world and all that it contains, including human intellect, is suffused with *Geist* meant for Krochmal that Judaism was the first, and as yet the only, religion to recognize that nothing exists apart from God. God represents the ultimate unity of all existence, and the God of traditional Judaism corresponds to the absolute spirit of Hegelian philosophy. All other religions and cultures have only partial appreciations of the spirituality represented in the idea of God. Their fragmentary visions of spirit may elevate aesthetics or politics as a bearer of spirit, but only Jewish culture is based on a recognition of the absolute nature of spirit.

This claim of Krochmal's is no mere religious triumphalism. It would, if accepted, contribute to Judaism's continued viability in its confrontation with modern philosophy. But its implications affect the philosophy of history profoundly. Despite the substantial differences between Herder and Hegel (and some would insist that Vico is relevant here as well), each views history as a process in which cultures – represented concretely in the *Volk* or the state – emerge, mature and decay. Whether this process is organic or dialectical, the cultures perish, passing on to the next world-historical culture some central legacy. Modern Europe is the culmination (or at least the latest culmination) of this process. For Hegel, this is because the modern European state stands closer than any of its predecessors to the realization of the absolute in its historical self-consciousness (see HISTORY, PHILOSOPHY OF).

Krochmal accepted the idea that history is a process moving towards the realization of the absolute within human consciousness and culture. But his reading of the Jewish sources led him to insist that Judaism has already achieved self-conscious awareness of the absolute. Thus the bearers of the Jewish religion stand clear of the central 'law' of the regnant philosophy of history. Unlike other ancient and medieval cultures, the Jews do not wither and perish. To be sure, Jews have an external history like any other people; but their absolute God is not limited by place or historical circumstance. Thus, when Jews are vanquished militarily, their culture and religion retain their self-evidence; the Jews undergo cultural rebirth and begin a new cycle of growth and maturity. The laws of history proposed by Herder and Hegel apply to other cultures but misrepresent the place of the Jews in history by radically misunderstanding Jewish metaphysics and its historical repercussions.

Krochmal's original contributions to philosophy are limited. Almost all of the central philosophical ideas of *Moreh Nevukhei ha-Zeman* originated elsewhere. And its philosophical sections, written in a difficult Hebrew idiom, were beyond the reach of most of his intended audience. But his implicit exposure of the unstated cultural biases of modern idealist philosophy are an enduring achievement. Readers are quickly brought to the realization that idealist philosophy, as Hegel himself understood, represents its own age, apprehended in thought. A comparison of Krochmal with Schelling or Hegel, among others, brings the Christian, Lutheran roots of idealist thought into sharp relief. Krochmal's reversal of many of the cultural and historical judgments familiar in idealist philosophy, and his elicitation of the central metaphysical claims of idealism from Jewish sources show that a philosopher using different assumptions could develop and apply idealist metaphysical concepts to reach philosophical and religious conclusions significantly different from those of the German Idealists themselves. Krochmal's efforts to reconcile Judaism and idealism provided new insight into Judaism and demonstrated new possibilities within idealism.

See also: CULTURAL IDENTITY; ENLIGHTENMENT, JEWISH; HEGEL, G.W.F.; HISTORY, PHILOSOPHY OF

List of works

Krochmal, N. (1851) *Moreh Nevukhei ha-Zeman* (Guide to the Perplexed of Today), ed. with Hebrew introduction by S. Rawidowicz, Berlin: Einot, 1924; repr. Waltham, MA: Ararat, 1961. (Adapts Kantian epistemological methods to interpret the Jewish religious sources with an eye to discovering their inner, philosophical meaning. Krochmal argues that at that their deeper level these sources, both ancient and medieval, anticipated the discoveries of the German Idealist philosophers.)

References and further reading

Guttmann, J. (1964) *Philosophies of Judaism*, New York: Schocken, 365–90. (A learned treatment of Krochmal's thought in a classic one-volume history of Jewish philosophy.)

Harris, J.M. (1991) *Nachman Krochmal: Guiding the Perplexed of the Modern Age*, New York: New York University Press. (The only book-length treatment of Krochmal's work; it treats Krochmal's thought as a response to idealism.)

* Hegel, G.W.F. (1832–45) 'Lectures on the Philosophy of Religion', in *Werke. Vollständige Ausgabe durch einen Verein von Freunden des Verewigten*, vols 11–12, Berlin: Duncker & Humblot; trans. C.P. Hodgson and R.F. Brown, *Lectures on the Philosophy of Religion*, Los Angeles, CA: University of California Press, 1984–7. (Translation of manuscripts based on student notes of Hegel's lecture courses on the philosophy of religion.)

Rotenstreich, N. (1984) *Jews and German Philosophy: The Polemics of Emancipation*, New York: Schocken, 138–59. (A discussion of Krochmal's philosophy of history and its philosophical difficulties.)

JAY M. HARRIS

KRONECKER, LEOPOLD (1823–91)

Leopold Kronecker was one of the most influential German mathematicians of the late nineteenth century. He exercised a strong sociopolitical influence on the development of mathematics as an academic institution. From a philosophical point of view, his main significance lies in his anticipation of a new and rigorous epistemological perspective with regard to the foundations of mathematics: Kronecker became the father of intuitionism or constructivism, which stands in strict opposition to the methods of classical mathematics and their canonization by set theory.

One of the most influential mathematicians in Germany of his time, Leopold Kronecker exercised a strong sociopolitical influence on the development of mathematics as an academic institution. He was a member of the Academy of Science in Berlin and editor of *Crelle's Journal* (the *Journal für die reine und angewandte Mathematik*), and tried to control the future development of pure mathematics as a supreme science by his superb and original contributions to arithmetic, algebra and the theory of functions.

Kronecker became the father of intuitionism or constructivism, anticipating a new and rigorous epistemological perspective with regard to the foundations of mathematics. In his 'Neubegründung der Mathematik' (New Foundations of Mathematics, 1922), Hilbert compares the views of the two outstanding intuitionists of his own time, Brouwer and Weyl, with those of Kronecker and remarks:

> I believe that as little as Kronecker succeeded in abolishing irrational numbers in his day, just as little will Weyl and Brouwer succeed today. No, Brouwer is not, as Weyl suggests, the revolution, but only the repetition of an attempted Putsch by old means, which in former times, were applied much more resolutely, but wholly without success.
> (1922: 160)

Why is Hilbert, the head of the mathematical establishment in the twentieth century, so hostile – and at the same time so respectful – towards Kronecker? One must remember that in 1886 – at a time when Kronecker's influence was still dominant – Hilbert had given a 'solution' to Gordan's problem (to prove the existence of a finite basis for the infinite system of invariant forms) which had perplexed the mathematical world. Instead of constructing a finite basis for the infinite system of invariant forms, Hilbert proved its existence by proving that the assumption of its nonexistence leads to a contradiction.

Such an indirect existence proof was against the basic methodological principles of mathematics that Kronecker had tried to establish. Hence, in Hilbert's opinion, Kronecker's sin was his attempt to restrict mathematical reasoning by setting up arbitrary prohibitions regarding the admissible means of developing and proving certain propositions. This, in turn, leads to an intolerable restriction of mathematical knowledge. But is Hilbert's assessment of Kronecker fair and accurate?

There are very few places in Kronecker's published work where he expresses his philosophical attitude with respect to foundational issues. But in his late essay 'Über den Zahlbegriff' (On the Concept of Number), 1887 he is quite explicit. Elaborating a remark by Gauss that just as mathematics is the queen of sciences, so, too, arithmetic is the queen of mathematics, he writes:

> Indeed, arithmetic stands in a relation to the other two mathematical disciplines, geometry and mechanics, that is similar to that in which mathematics as a whole stands to astronomy and the other sciences of nature.... Here, however, the word 'arithmetic' should not be taken in its usual restricted sense, but in a broader sense according to which all mathematical disciplines, with the exception of geometry and mechanics, have to be included – in particular algebra and analysis. And I also believe that we will succeed some day in 'arithmetizing' the entire content of all these mathematical disciplines, so that they will be based purely and simply on the conception of number taken in its narrowest sense. Hence, all modifications and extensions of this concept [Footnote: 'I mean, in particular, the inclusion of the irrational as well as the continuous quantities.'], which in most cases were prompted by its application to geometry and mechanics, will once again be stripped off.
>
> (1887: 252–3)

What Kronecker envisages here is in essence nothing other than basing the whole of mathematics, including analysis, on the concept of positive integers without any further existential assumption; in particular without assuming the existence of irrational numbers and continuous quantities. Consequently, he tries to eliminate all numbers 'alien to proper arithmetic' by giving definitions in terms of positive integers and functions thereof. For example, negative numbers can be eliminated by replacing the factor -1 with the indeterminate x and replacing the equality sign with the Gaussian symbol for congruence modulo $(x+1)$. The equation $7-9=3-5$ then becomes transformed into the congruence $7+9x=3+5x(\mathrm{mod.}\ x+1)$. Although no one took this particular proposal any more seriously than other proposals to eliminate the rational and irrational numbers, not only Weyl and Brouwer but also Hilbert shared the basic epistemological convictions behind Kronecker's proposals (at least after 1920, when Hilbert developed his finitism). These convictions can be summarized in two statements.

First, the infinite exists nowhere in actuality; neither in nature nor in our thinking. It is a mere potentiality. Therefore it has to be eliminated as an actual object from mathematics and be treated as a mere instrument (Kronecker) or an idea (Hilbert) to facilitate mathematical reasoning. Second, objects or functions, such as irrational numbers or continuous quantities, which presuppose infinite sequences of objects or operations have to be replaced by their proper meaning in arithmetic (Kronecker) or be treated as 'ideal elements' (Hilbert).

See also: INTUITIONISM; MATHEMATICS, FOUNDATIONS OF; LOGICAL AND MATHEMATICAL TERMS, GLOSSARY OF; PROOF THEORY §2

List of works

Kronecker, L. (1895–1930) *Werke*, ed. K. Hensel, Leipzig: Teubner, 5 vols. (The most complete edition of Kronecker's work.)

—— (1887) 'Über den Zahlbegriff' (On the Concept of Number), *Journal für die reine und angewandte Mathematik* 101: 337–55; repr. in *Werke*, ed. K. Hensel, Leipzig: Teubner, 1895–1930, vol. 3, part 1, 249–74. (Perhaps Kronecker's most important contribution to the foundations of arithmetic.)

References and further reading

Biermann, K.-R. (1981) 'Kronecker, Leopold', in *Dictionary of Scientific Biography*, vol. 7, ed. C.C. Gillispie, New York: Charles Scribner's Sons, 1984. (A good, readable biography.)

Edwards, H. (1987) 'An Appreciation of Kronecker', in *The Mathematical Intelligencer*, New York: Springer, vol. 9, 28–35. (A sympathetic reading of Kronecker's work.)

—— (1989) 'Kronecker's View on the Foundations of Mathematics', in D. Rowe and J. McCleary (eds) *The History of Modern Mathematics*, vol. 1, *Ideas and Reception*, San Diego, CA: Academic Press. (A proposal to make Kronecker's algebraic point of view intelligible.)

* Hilbert, D. (1922) 'Neubegründung der Mathematik' (New Foundations of Mathematics), *Abhandlungen aus dem mathematischen Seminar der Hamburgischen Universität* 1: 157–77; repr. in *Gesammelte Abhandlungen*, vol. 3, Berlin: Springer, 1935. (The first paper in which Hilbert formulated his programme to prove the consistency of arithmetic by finite means.)

—— (1926) 'Über das Unendliche', *Mathematische Annalen* 95: 161–90; repr. in *Gesammelte Abhandlungen*, vol. 3, Berlin: Springer; trans. 'On the

Infinite', in P. Benacerraf and H. Putnam (eds) *Philosophy of Mathematics*, Cambridge: Cambridge University Press, 2nd edn, 1983. (The most important paper in defence of finitism.)

Kneser, A. (1925) 'Leopold Kronecker', *Jahresbericht der Deutsche Mathematiker-Vereinigung* 33: 210–28. (An excellent biography.)

Majer, U. (1993) 'Das Unendliche – eine bloße Idee?', *Revue internationale de Philosophie* 47: 319–41. (A critical analysis of Hilbert's finitist point of view.)

Weyl, H. (1921) 'Über die neue Grundlagenkrise der Mathematik', *Mathematische Zeitschrift* 10: 39–79; repr. in *Gesammelte Abhandlungen*, vol. 2, ed. K. Chandrasekharan, Berlin: Springer, 1968. (The work which triggered Hilbert's response.)

—— (1925) *Die heutige Erkenntnislage in der Mathematik*, Erlangen: Weltkreis; repr. in *Gesammelte Abhandlungen*, vol. 2, ed. K. Chandrasekharan, Berlin: Springer, 1968. (The best defence of intuitionism/constructivism in Kronecker's sense.)

ULRICH MAJER

KROPOTKIN, PËTR ALEKSEEVICH (1842–1921)

A founder of anarchist communism and guiding spirit of the international anarchist movement after the death of Bakunin, Kropotkin was also a distinguished geographer, a scientist and a positivist. He saw the development of anarchism as one aspect of the whole movement of modern science towards an integrated philosophy. He believed that the dominant phenomenon in nature was harmony, arrived at by a continuous process of adjustment between contending forces. In human, as in animal societies, the dominant phenomenon was mutual aid: thus once metaphysics, law and state authority had been shaken off, harmony could be realized.

Born into an aristocratic Moscow family close to the Russian Imperial throne, Pëtr Kropotkin was educated at an exclusive military academy, but at 20, filled with the desire to be useful, he renounced a brilliant career to serve for five years as a military administrator in Eastern Siberia.

His hopes for liberal reform by Alexander II, the tsar who had abolished serfdom, were soon disappointed. He also lost any faith in the virtues of state discipline in society and began to move slowly towards an anarchist position (see ANARCHISM). He now turned to scientific exploration, leading geographical expeditions and achieving distinction as a geographer. His observations laid the foundations of his theory of mutual aid among animal species.

Abandoning military service in 1867, he joined the Russian revolutionary movement in the early 1870s, and after a sensational escape from prison to the West in 1876 became a leading figure in the International, participating in the congress debates between the Marxist and anarchist wings of the movement, which led to the theory of anarchist communism.

After the death of BAKUNIN in 1876 he became, through his writings and propagandist journalism in *Le Révolté* and *La Révolte*, the guiding spirit of the movement. At the same time, during his years in the West, in England, France and Switzerland, he came to enjoy high esteem as a geographer, publishing in learned journals. He returned to Russia in 1917.

Kropotkin's anarchist communism aimed at a society without government, where harmony would be obtained

> not by submission to law, or by obedience to any authority, but by free agreements between the various groups, territorial and professional, instituted for the sake of production and consumption as also for the satisfaction of the infinite variety of needs and aspirations of a civilized society.
>
> (1927: 284)

In such a society, as in organic life, Kropotkin believed harmony would result from 'an ever-changing adjustment and readjustment of equilibrium between a multitude of forces and influences'.

The individual would not be limited in the free expression of his powers in production by a capitalist monopoly, or by obedience, which only led to the sapping of initiative. On the contrary, he would be able to obtain the complete development of all his faculties: the fullest individuation.

Like socialists, anarchist communists combated the monopolization of land and capital. But they also combated the state, which, Kropotkin argued, as the instrument for establishing monopolies in favour of ruling minorities, was the main support of the capitalist system. Anarchist communists finally believed, said Kropotkin, that the era of revolutions was not closed. Periods of revolution must be taken advantage of to reduce the powers of the state.

Kropotkin's anarchist communism was also inspired by his scientific studies: indeed he saw the development of anarchist social theories and the growth of nineteenth-century philosophies deriving from scientific study as simply two branches of the same movement. Anarchism itself was for him a world concept based on a mechanical explanation of all phenomena and embracing the whole of nature, including human societies. Its aim was actually 'to construct a synthetic philosophy comprehending in one generalization all the phenomena of nature' (1927: 150). Kropotkin shared the optimism of the positivists of his time with regard to the limitless possibilities of the inductive–deductive method of scientific inquiry. He went perhaps further than Proudhon, or even Elisée Reclus, in rejecting as unscientific all metaphysics and the justification it offered for the power of Church and state, whether that power emanated from the Christian belief in an all-powerful God or from the Hegelian concept of the Universal Spirit. He went so far, in 1913, as to attack Bergson savagely for denigrating science by arguing that intuition played an important part in scientific discovery.

Kropotkin's own scientific work had convinced him that, in human as in animal societies, the instinct of mutual aid aimed at the preservation of the species was stronger than the instinct for the self-preservation of the individual, the notion of a struggle for life between competing individuals being based on an incorrect interpretation of the work of Darwin. Instead, the fundamental struggle for each species was that of the species as a whole against external forces.

Within human societies therefore, once the monopolization of capital and rule by minorities through their instrument, the state, had been shaken off, harmony could be achieved by a continuous series of adjustments among contending forces.

The central concept in Kropotkin's thinking is that of harmony in nature, a harmony which he himself had observed both in animal species and throughout human history, and which he believed would become possible in the new anarchist communist society. Such harmony is not the result of anything preconceived, but a

> temporary adjustment established among all forces acting upon a given spot – a provisional adaptation. And that adjustment will only last on the condition that it is continually modified; that it represents at every moment the resultant of all conflicting actions. If one force is hampered in its actions, harmony will disappear, force will accumulate its effect and a new equilibrium will emerge.
> (1927: 121)

Kropotkin drew an analogy here between the intermittent disruption of harmony in nature by earthquakes and that brought about in societies by revolutions.

He finally believed that the fundamental phenomenon of mutual aid in human societies provided a foundation for a new scientific morality independent of religion. In his *Ėtika* (Ethics) (1922), which remained unfinished, he surveyed the historical development of ethics, pointing to the fact that Darwin, after Bacon, had provided the basis for a new morality. However, that new morality had not yet been worked out. Kropotkin did not live long enough to develop a non-religious morality himself.

List of works

Kropotkin P.A. (1892) *La Conquête du Pain* (The Conquest of Bread), Paris: Stock. (Includes a chapter on anarchist communism.)
—— (1899) *Fields, Factories and Workshops*, London: Hutchinson. (Foreshadows economic tendencies in industry and agriculture.)
—— (1902) *Mutual Aid: A Factor of Evolution*, London: Heinemann. (Collects Kropotkin's articles of the 1890s on mutual aid in the animal kingdom and human society.)
—— (1922) *Ėtika* (Ethics), ed. N. Lebedev, Petrograd and Moscow: Golos Truda. (Historical examination of the development of ethics.)
—— (1927) *Kropotkin's Revolutionary Pamphlets*, ed. R.N. Baldwin, New York: Dover. (Includes *La Morale anarchiste* (Anarchist Morality) (1891), *L'Anarchie: sa philosophie, son idéal* (Anarchism: Its Philosophy and Ideal); *Modern Science and Anarchism*; and 'Anarchism', from the *Encyclopaedia Britannica* (11th edn). These all provide a clear outline of Kropotkin's anarchist communism and its relation to contemporary science and philosophy.)

References and further reading

Cahm, C. (1989) *Peter Kropotkin and the Rise of Revolutionary Anarchism 1872–1886*, Cambridge and New York: Cambridge University Press. (Includes introduction on Kropotkin's political and philosophical ideas.)
Marshall, P. (1993) *Demanding the Impossible: A History of Anarchism*, London. (Contains a very clear and readable chapter on Kropotkin the Revolutionary Evolutionist.)
Miller, M.A. (1976) *Kropotkin*, Chicago, IL and London: University of Chicago Press. (Well-documented account of life and work.)
Woodcock, G. and Avakumovic, I. (1950) *The Anarchist Prince*, London: Boardman. (Good introduction to life and ideas but no documentation.)

CAROLINE CAHM

KUAN TZU *see* GUANZI

KUHN, THOMAS SAMUEL (1922–96)

The early 1960s saw substantial turmoil in the philosophy of science, then dominated by logical empiricism. Most important was the confrontation of the prevailing philosophical tradition with the history of science. Whereas the philosophy of science was mainly normatively oriented, that is it tried to delineate what good science should look like, historical studies seemed to indicate that the practice of science both past and present did not follow those prescriptions.

Thomas S. Kuhn was educated as a theoretical physicist but soon turned to the history and philosophy of science. In 1962, he published The Structure of Scientific Revolutions *(SSR). This book was the single most important publication advancing the confrontation between the history and the philosophy of science; it is now a classic in science studies. SSR was most influential not only in the discussion within philosophy but also in various other fields, especially the social sciences. The central concepts of* SSR, *like scientific revolution, paradigm shift and incommensurability, have been in the focus of philosophical discussion for many years, and the term 'paradigm' has even become a household word (although mostly not in Kuhn's intended sense). After* SSR, *Kuhn continued to develop his theory; apart from minor modifications it is mainly the explication of* SSR's *more intricate philosophical topics, especially of incommensurability, which is characteristic of his later work.*

1 **Life and works**
2 *The Structure of Scientific Revolutions*: survey
3 *The Structure of Scientific Revolutions*: **philosophical significance**
4 **Further developments**

1 Life and works

Kuhn received his Ph.D in theoretical physics from Harvard University in 1949. While working on his dissertation he became interested in the history of science. His first book-length publication in this field was *The Copernican Revolution* (1957). From the late 1950s, Kuhn started to publish in the philosophy of science, leading to the appearance of *The Structure of Scientific Revolutions* (*SSR*) (1962). This work is now a classic; it has been controversially discussed in extremely diverse fields, and translated into some

twenty languages. Kuhn's historical work after *SSR* concerned mainly the genesis of quantum mechanics. *Sources for the History of Quantum Physics* (1967) contains an inventory of relevant material including interviews with many of the contributors to quantum mechanics; *Black Body Theory and the Quantum Discontinuity, 1894–1912* (1978) is a controversial account of the introduction of the quantum hypothesis. Some of Kuhn's papers both on the history and the philosophy of science are contained in *The Essential Tension* (1977).

Kuhn taught at Harvard University until 1956 when he joined the University of California at Berkeley to teach history of science. In 1964, he left for Princeton University. Finally, he became professor for philosophy and history of science at MIT, from where he retired in 1992. He died in 1996.

2 The Structure of Scientific Revolutions: survey

Kuhn's *SSR* was probably the most important single work in bringing out the turmoil in philosophy of science in the early 1960s. The table of contents of *SSR* displays a developmental scheme for scientific fields in the basic sciences. This sort of structuring makes its philosophical reading difficult since, for a particular topic, passages scattered around the whole book must be considered.

The first chapter opens with a much-quoted sentence that describes concisely what *SSR* is all about: 'History, if viewed as a repository for more than anecdote or chronology, could produce a decisive transformation in the image of science by which we are now possessed' ([1962] 1970: 1).

Kuhn refers here to two modes of doing history of science. For the older historiographic tradition, the predominant goal was to reach a deeper understanding of *contemporary science* by displaying its historical evolution. This was to be done by discovering the elements of today's science, for example, its concepts, theories, experimental methods and so on, in older texts and by arranging them in a chronological narrative. The resulting picture of scientific development was necessarily a *cumulative* one: science grows step by step by adding new pieces of knowledge to those already in place. But this form of historiography invariably introduces distortions into the presentation of the older science by projecting today's science into the past. Instead, following especially Alexandre KOYRÉ's model, the 'new historiography of science' attempts a display of the historical integrity of a science in its own time. More specifically, the concepts, the research problems and the standards of evaluation of an older science must be reconstructed in a historically adequate way. The aim of *SSR* is to

315

delineate a new image of science 'by making explicit some of the new historiography's implications' ([1962] 1970: 3).

The picture of science that emerges from this historiography contains a developmental scheme for scientific disciplines. Before reaching maturity, nascent scientific fields are typically characterized by controversies between competing schools; there is no consensus among the practitioners of the emerging field. This competition may eventually end when one group produces an exemplary solution to a preeminent research problem with two characteristics: it is sufficiently unprecedented to attract the members of the other schools, and it is sufficiently open-ended to leave enough interesting problems for further scientific work. These model solutions are called paradigms; they serve to guide research in an implicit way in the following period. This period is called 'normal science'. It is characterized by a broad consensus of the practitioners of the field about fundamental questions, and, consequently, by a particular mode of research. This mode of research can be described by a five-dimensional analogy to puzzle-solving where exemplars of puzzles include chess problems and crossword puzzles. The analogy concerns:

- the existence of regulations constraining acceptable approaches to and solutions of problems;
- the expectation of the solubility of appropriately chosen problems;
- no fundamental changes in the guiding regulations;
- absence of test or confirmation of the guiding regulations;
- individual motivations: to prove oneself an expert puzzle solver.

Normal science is always confronted with anomalies, that is, with phenomena or problems that behave contrary to the expectations supplied by the paradigm. Usually, anomalies do not call into question the validity of the guiding regulations of normal research. But under special circumstances they may, and then they become 'significant anomalies'. Then, the practice of science changes again into 'extraordinary science' or 'science in crisis'. Extraordinary science aims at amending or even overthrowing the binding regulations. Its research focuses on the significant anomalies and their context. If this research leads to a new theory that is accepted by the scientific community because it can lead to a new phase of normal science, a scientific revolution has occurred. In Kuhn's sense scientific revolutions are 'the tradition-shattering complements to the tradition-bound activity of normal science' ([1962] 1970: 6). More specifically, in a scientific revolution an accepted theory is rejected in favour of a new one. This rejection is accompanied by a change of the problem-field and its related standards of solution, and by a sometimes subtle change in basic scientific concepts. Revolutions can even be described as transformations of the world in which scientific work is done. Kuhn compresses these features of revolutions into the concept of 'incommensurability': this relation holds between successive traditions of normal science. In *SSR*, the concept of incommensurability was not entirely clear; it was therefore subject to much criticism and also misunderstanding, and most of Kuhn's philosophical work after *SSR* aims at a clarification and further explication of the concept of incommensurability (see §4) (see INCOMMENSURABILITY).

Because of incommensurability, we must, according to Kuhn, rethink the concept of scientific progress. First, progress is not cumulative, because there are conceptual changes during revolutions. Furthermore, Kuhn denies that scientific progress is an approach to truth. Instead of conceiving of scientific progress as a teleological process, that is, one that is goal-directed, we should think of progress as Darwinian evolutionary theory does. Accordingly, there is no 'set goal, a permanent fixed scientific truth', but 'an increase in articulation and specialization' ([1962] 1970: 172, 173).

3 *The Structure of Scientific Revolutions*: philosophical significance

Why is Kuhn's theory of scientific development philosophically significant? Why did philosophers take notice of a theory that appears essentially historical? The reason is that Kuhn's theory ran counter to many philosophical convictions about science in the early 1960s. I have already mentioned Kuhn's altered view of scientific progress (§2). This view implies the untenability of those forms of realism that assert that science at least approximately describes what is really 'out there', independently of any observer (see SCIENTIFIC REALISM AND ANTI-REALISM §1). Instead, theories describe the world in terms of concepts which are historically contingent and which may change in the future. Furthermore, because of this change of basic scientific concepts, the classical conception of reductionism is hardly tenable. According to this conception, theories may be reduced to more fundamental theories by redefining their concepts by means of the concepts of the reducing theory, and then deriving their laws from the laws of the reducing theory, supplemented by the redefinitions and, possibly, boundary conditions (see REDUCTION, PROBLEMS OF §2). But if incommensurability prevails between the pair of theories in question, the reduction relation cannot hold, since some of the required redefinitions are blocked by meaning shifts. In fact, as has become clearer in Kuhn's work after *SSR*, mutual untranslatability of some of the key terms is the hallmark of incommensurability between theories.

Many of *SSR*'s assertions stood in marked opposition to the Popperian philosophy of critical rationalism (see POPPER, K.R.). For instance, the practice of normal science as described by Kuhn may look like bad science, because it is not directed at a critical test of the guiding assumptions, but at a quasi-dogmatic exploitation of their potential. Yet, in Kuhn's view, the task of critical evaluation of fundamental theories is restricted to the period of extraordinary science, and even then scientific practice is not simply an attempt to falsify theories by confrontation with basic statements about nature, as Popper would have it. Rather, theory evaluation is always a comparative procedure in which two (or more) theories are assessed with respect to their cognitive abilities, especially, whether they can cope with the significant anomalies from which the crisis state originated (see §2). From this view, theory falsification as described by Popper is a stereotype not found in the actual history of science.

Another consequence of Kuhn's theory is to abolish the idea that science is guided by a scientific method, a set of rules rigorously to be followed (see SCIENTIFIC METHOD §2). Due mainly to Bacon and Descartes' initial influence, this idea has dominated the understanding of modern science from its very beginning. But according to Kuhn, what chiefly guides scientific research in its normal phase are exemplary problem solutions. Their cognitive potential for research is exploited not by explicit (or fully explicable) rules but rather by implicit analogies; new problems are identified in the light of achieved ones, and new solutions are judged as legitimate in a like manner.

4 Further developments

It is not only that Kuhn opposed many doctrines of established philosophy of science; an additional factor for the sometimes vehement reactions to *SSR* was a deep and widespread misreading of its main theses. Kuhn has thus constantly been challenged to articulate his main theses more fully and to refine them, in the course of which his position has also shifted in some respects.

During the early reception of *SSR*, the main target of criticism was the paradigm concept, which was seen as equivocal. Kuhn responded by distinguishing a narrow sense of paradigm, meaning exemplary problem solutions, from a wide sense which comprises all the components of scientific consensus, the 'disciplinary matrix'. The latter includes, among other elements, scientific values (like accuracy, consistency, fruitfulness, scope and simplicity) which operate constantly but which are especially visible during theory choice. Since these values only guide and do not dictate theory choice, individual scientists can disagree in matters of theory evaluation without any of them being irrational. The latter would be a consequence if theory choice were determined by some fixed set of rules which defined the canon of scientific rationality.

The most important change in Kuhn's position has been a shift from the predominant description of scientific revolutions in *SSR* in terms of visual metaphors to a description by means of a linguistic framework. In *SSR*, revolutions were depicted as something like visual gestalt switches, and their outcome as a changed way of seeing the world. Though meaning shifts played some role in *SSR*, meaning becomes increasingly the dominant theme of Kuhn's later work. But what is the meaning of a term? How is a term connected with its referents? Kuhn does not deal with these profound questions in complete generality but only with kind terms, for example, mass nouns like 'gold' or count nouns like 'cat'. In the sciences, the meanings of kind terms are usually not specified by explicit definitions; rather, they are established by processes involving ostension of typical examples of the kind in question. When objects of the same kind are ostended, they are declared similar, and those not belonging to the same kind are declared dissimilar. By this procedure, a taxonomy of objects can be built up and transmitted. Kind terms involved in the taxonomy can stand in two relations only, namely, either exclusion or inclusion. Partial overlap between contrasting kind terms is forbidden: something is either a planet or a star but not both. Kuhn refers to the net of relations in such a taxonomy as the 'structure of the [respective] lexicon'. It is now characteristic for scientific revolutions, and hence for incommensurability, that the structure of the lexicon changes, resulting in partial untranslatability between propositions articulated by means of different lexicons. Changes of this kind may be initiated by the discovery of objects violating the no-overlap principle, that is, objects that seem to belong to mutually disjoint kinds. Objects of this sort cannot be described with the given lexicon nor can the lexicon simply be extended or refined in order to make description possible; rather a partial reordering of the categories involved is inescapable.

See also: FEYERABEND, P.K.; INCOMMENSURABILITY

List of works

Kuhn, T.S. (1957) *The Copernican Revolution. Planetary Astronomy in the Development of Western Thought*, Cambridge, MA: Harvard University Press. (A widely read historical textbook foreshadowing some of *SSR*'s theses.)

—— (1962, 1970) *The Structure of Scientific Revolutions*, Chicago, IL: University of Chicago Press. (Kuhn's classic work; the second edition, to which citations refer, contains an important Postscript.)

—— (1977) *The Essential Tension. Selected Studies in Scientific Tradition and Change*, Chicago, IL: University of Chicago Press. (Contains historical and philosophical articles.)

—— (1978) *Black Body Theory and the Quantum Discontinuity, 1894–1912*, Oxford: Clarendon Press. (Kuhn's controversial narrative about the introduction of the quantum into physics.)

—— (1991) 'The Road Since Structure', in A. Fine, M. Forbes and L. Wessels (eds) *PSA 1990*, East Lansing, MI: Philosophy of Science Association, vol. 2, 2–13. (Summarizes Kuhn's development since *Structure of Scientific Revolutions*.)

—— (1993) 'Afterwords', in P. Horwich (ed.) *World Changes. Thomas Kuhn and the Nature of Science*, Cambridge, MA: MIT Press, 1993, 311–41. (Kuhn's reaction to papers presented at a conference on his work in 1990.)

Kuhn, T.S., Heilbron, J.L., Forman, P. and Allen, L. (1967) *Sources for the History of Quantum Physics. An Inventory and Report*, Philadelphia, PA: American Philosophical Society.

References and further reading

Barnes, B. (1982) *T.S. Kuhn and Social Science*, London: Macmillan. (A book about the sociology of scientific knowledge taking Kuhn's work as its point of departure.)

Gutting, G. (ed.) (1980) *Paradigms and Revolutions. Applications and Appraisals of Thomas Kuhn's Philosophy of Science*, Notre Dame, IN: University of Notre Dame Press. (A collection of articles, mainly from the 1970s, documenting Kuhn's impact in various fields.)

Hacking, I. (ed.) (1981) *Scientific Revolutions*, Oxford: Oxford University Press. (Essays by influential writers on scientific revolutions.)

Horwich, P. (ed.) (1993) *World Changes. Thomas Kuhn and the Nature of Science*, Cambridge, MA: MIT Press. (Proceedings of a conference about Kuhn's work, held in 1990 at MIT; includes Kuhn's reaction to the papers presented.)

Hoyningen-Huene, P. (1993) *Reconstructing Scientific Revolutions. Thomas S. Kuhn's Philosophy of Science*, trans. A.T. Levine, foreword by T.S. Kuhn, Chicago, IL: University of Chicago Press. (A critical reconstruction of Kuhn's theory and its development; contains the most complete bibliography of his writings.)

Lakatos, I. and Musgrave, A. (eds) (1970) *Criticism and the Growth of Knowledge*, London: Cambridge University Press. (Contains some of the most influential papers discussing Kuhn's work in the 1960s.)

Popper, K. (1975) 'The Rationality of Scientific Revolutions', in R. Harré (ed.) *Problems of Scientific Revolutions*, Oxford: Clarendon Press, 72–101. (Popper's answer to Kuhn's supposedly irrationalist view of scientific revolutions.)

Scheffler, I. (1967) *Science and Subjectivity*, Indianapolis, IN: Hackett; enlarged 2nd edn, 1982. (Representative of the reception and criticism of Kuhn in the 1960s.)

Shapere, D. (1984) *Reason and the Search for Knowledge. Investigations in the Philosophy of Science*, Dordrecht: Reidel. (Contains several highly influential papers criticizing Kuhn.)

PAUL HOYNINGEN-HUENE

KŪKAI (774–835)

Kūkai, also known by his posthumous honorific title Kōbō Daishi, was the founder of Japanese Shingon ('truth word' or 'mantra') Buddhism and is often considered the first comprehensive philosophical thinker in Japanese history. Building on the Buddhist esoteric tradition first developed in India and then in China, where Kūkai encountered it, he maintained that reality is a cosmic person, the Buddha Dainichi. Dainichi's cosmic thoughts, words and deeds form microcosmic configurations, resonances and patterns of change. By performing Shingon rituals, one can supposedly accord with the microcosmic constituents and know the foundational structures of reality that compose the sensory world in which we ordinarily live.

Kūkai was an aristocrat born on the island of Shikoku, far from the major cultural centres. Trained in the Chinese classics, he went to the capital area of Nara-Nagaoka at the age of eighteen to study for qualification in the court bureaucracy. Within a few years, however, he left the college and isolated himself in the mountains, practising austerities. In 804 he left for China to study the texts and practices of esoteric

Buddhism, which had been only unsystematically and partially introduced to Japan. In China Kūkai studied under Huiguo, the seventh patriarch of Zhenyan (Shingon) Buddhism. He returned to Japan in 806 as the eighth patriarch of the tradition and the first in Japan.

Kūkai devoted his efforts in Japan to establishing Shingon as a major school or sect. He founded a monastic community and temple complex on Mt. Kōya and a major temple, Tōji, in the new capital of Kyoto. He wrote poems, copied sacred texts, painted *mandalas* and undertook civil works such as establishing a public school for boys and girls of all classes, engineering irrigation projects and performing rituals for the relief of plagues and famines. Popular culture reveres Kūkai as a great thaumaturgist of ancient Japan.

Kūkai's philosophical contributions were no less impressive. A prolific writer, he wrote many treatises to explain and justify the basic Shingon position. His philosophical works generally concentrated on two themes, his critique of other philosophical schools and his elaboration of the relation between the nature of reality and the participation in that reality through Shingon ritualistic practice.

On the first point, he developed his theory of the 'ten mindsets' as explained in his *Jūjūshinron* (Treatise on the Ten Mindsets) and *Hizō hōyaku* (Precious Key to the Secret Treasury). In those works he analysed the limitations of the philosophies known in Japan at the time, including Confucianism and Daoism as well as exoteric forms of Buddhism. Although it was then common in Chinese Buddhism to classify the teachings of the various schools, Kūkai's innovation was to study the teachings as an expression of specific mindsets; he was as interested in the experiential basis of the ideas as in what they said about reality and to whom they said it. This allowed him simultaneously to see their appropriateness and to criticize their incompleteness.

Kūkai's typical critique of the mindsets outside Shingon Buddhism was that they could not adequately justify the basis for their worldviews. For example, the lowest mindset understands its own human existence to be controlled by animal desires. Yet no animal desire could itself lead one to that conclusion; therefore, the mindset is based in something it cannot explain within its own terms. Towards the other end of Kūkai's scale, the ninth mindset, that associated with Kegon (Huayan) Buddhism, understands reality as a web of interdependence in which each thing reflects every other thing. Kūkai basically agreed with that metaphysical model, but questioned whether Kegon could adequately explain how that fact is known. Indeed, what would 'knowledge' even

mean in such a context? Kūkai insisted that only the tenth mindset, that of Shingon's esoteric Buddhism, could adequately assert a metaphysical theory and ground that theory within its own parameters. This claim points to Kūkai's theory about knowledge as the self-aware participation in reality.

According to Shingon the cosmos as a whole is a person, the Buddha Dainichi. Like any other person, Dainichi's behaviour can be analysed in terms of thought, word and deed, the respective functions of mind, speech and body. On the cosmic level these functions give reality its configuration, resonance and patterns of change. Specifically, Dainichi's geometric contemplative visualisations (*mandala*) shape reality, Dainichi's intoning of sacred syllables (*mantra*) fill the universe with resonant states of matter–energy, and Dainichi's ritualistic gestures (*mudra*) give the universe its patterns of movement. Therefore, according to Kūkai's analysis, each thing in the universe is ultimately an expression of Dainichi's enlightened activity.

Of course to our human senses, the universe does not ordinarily appear that way. Because the senses cannot experience the cosmos as a whole, how could Kūkai ground his metaphysical position? His argument was that, like every other thing in the universe, human beings are the product of Dainichi's self-expression. Unlike most other expressions of Dainichi, however, human beings are also persons, beings who express themselves through the activities of thought, word and deed. Hence, the basic functioning of the cosmos is recursively manifest or reflected in each human being. If we delude ourselves into thinking that our actions are strictly our own, separate from all the rest of reality, we cannot justify our metaphysics. What knows metaphysics must itself be metaphysically explainable.

On the other hand, Kūkai argued, if our everyday actions mirror the basic functions of the universe, we can recognize that our own actions are also expressions of Dainichi's activity. The knower and the known are part of the same metaphysical system. Yet how can one become fully aware of this mirroring? The answer is, by enacting the same three activities as Dainichi: contemplating the *mandalas*, intoning the *mantras* and gesturing the *mudras*. Through ritualization, one's own self-expression becomes consciously the same as the cosmos' self-expression. To know reality is to self-consciously participate in it as its own self-expression. Religious praxis and religious knowledge become, in the end, identical. According to Kūkai, that insight was the unique contribution of esoteric Buddhism.

See also: BUDDHIST PHILOSOPHY, JAPANESE; JAPANESE PHILOSOPHY; KNOWLEDGE, CONCEPT OF; METAPHYSICS

List of works

Kūkai (774–835) *Kōbō Daishi zenshū* (Complete Works of Kōbō Daishi), ed. Inabe Yoshitake *et al.*, Koya-san: Mikkyō bunka kenkyū-sho, 3rd edn, 1965; trans. Hakeda Yoshito, *Kūkai: Major Works*, New York: Columbia University Press, 1972. (Inabe is the standard critical edition of the complete works in the original Chinese. Hakeda is an abridged translation of the eight treatises generally considered to be the core of Kūkai's philosophy, including a helpful introduction about Kūkai's life and thought.)

—— (830) *Jūjūshinron* (Treatise on the Ten Mindsets), in *Kōbō Daishi zenshū*, Koya-san: Mikkyō bunka kenkyū-sho, 3rd edn, 1965, vol. I. (First develops his theory of the ten mindsets.)

—— (830) *Hizōhōyaku* (Precious Key to the Secret Treasury), in *Kōbō Daishi zenshū*, Koya-san: Mikkyō bunka kenkyū-sho, 3rd edn, 1965, vol. I; abridged trans. in Hakeda Yoshito, *Kūkai: Major Works*, New York: Columbia University Press, 1972. (Compares various other philosophies to Buddhism.)

References and further reading

Kasulis, T.P. (1982) 'Reference and Symbol in Plato's *Cratylus* and Kūkai's *Shōjijissōgi*', *Philosophy East and West* 32 (4): 393–405. (Cross-cultural comparison of two early works on language and philosophy in ancient Greece and Japan.)

—— (1988) 'Truth Words: The Basis of Kūkai's Theory of Interpretation', in D.S. Lopez, Jr (ed.) *Buddhist Hermeneutics*, Kuroda Institute Studies in East Asian Buddhism 6, Honolulu, HI: University of Hawaii Press, 257–72. (A general study of Kūkai's theory of truth and its application to his evaluation of the ten mindsets.)

—— (1990) 'Kūkai: Philosophizing in the Archaic', in F. Reynolds and D. Tracy (eds) *Myth and Philosophy*, Albany, NY: State University of New York Press, 131– 50. (A general overview of Kūkai's philosophy within its historical and cultural setting.)

Kiyota Minoru (1978) *Shingon Buddhism: Theory and Practice*, Los Angeles, CA: Buddhist Books International. (A detailed, scholarly and highly technical explanation of the system of Shingon doctrine, mainly as developed by Kūkai.)

Shaner, D.E. (1985) *The Bodymind Experience in Japanese Buddhism: A Phenomenological Study of Kūkai and Dōgen*, Albany, NY: State University of New York Press. (A good comparative analysis of Kūkai's theory of the oneness of body and mind using Western phenomenological categories.)

Yamasaki Taikō (1988) *Shingon: Japanese Esoteric Buddhism*, Yasuyoshi Morimoto and D. Kidd (eds), Boston and London: Shambhala Publications. (Excellent introduction to Shingon doctrine and practise in a readable format for a general audience.)

THOMAS P. KASULIS

KUKI SHŪZŌ (1888–1941)

Kuki's philosophical project was focused on the issues arising from dualistic thinking. He incorporated into his work a cross-cultural, historical perspective, while applying Heidegger's hermeneutical ontology and exhibiting bold, systematic, speculative acumen.

Kuki Shūzō was born in Tokyo as the fourth son of Baron Kuki Ryūichi. He graduated in 1921 from Tokyo Imperial University, where he majored in Western philosophy and found Raphael von Köbel and Okakura Tenshin particularly inspirational. His graduation thesis dealt with mind–body correlativity. In 1922 he went to Europe to study under Rickert, Oskar Becker, HUSSERL and HEIDEGGER in Germany, and had an association with BERGSON in France. (It was Kuki who introduced Sartre to the philosophies of Husserl and Heidegger.) While in Europe, Kuki acquired extensive and detailed knowledge of Western philosophy. He returned to Japan in 1929, and in 1935 became a professor at Kyoto Imperial University, where he lectured on the history of Western philosophy (see KYOTO SCHOOL).

Of his complete works – almost all of which attempt to go beyond modern European philosophy – the three best known in Japan are *Iki no Kōzō* (The Structure of Iki) (1930), *Gūzensei no mondai* (The Problem of Contingency) (1935), and *Ningen to jitsuzon* (The Human and Human Existence) (1939). In Heidegger's *Unterwegs zur Sprache* (On the Way to Language), Kuki's *iki* is thematized in the dialogue between *iki* and a Japanese interlocutor.

Kuki's concern for dualism is expressed in *Iki no kōzō*, wherein he thematized an aesthetic mode of living [*iki+ru*] uniquely found in the intersexual dealings between man and woman that were cultivated in the 'pleasure quarter' as an expression of 'being-of-the-people', in contrast to Heidegger's

Dasein. He analyzed this mode of living as a phenomenon of consciousness embracing three constitutive momenta: coquetry, liveliness and resignation. It is through the spiritualization of coquetry via the idealism of *bushidō* (see BUSHI PHILOSOPHY) and the appropriation of destiny via Buddhism (in other words, resignation) that *iki* is lived aesthetically as 'liveliness'. Kuki's general thesis is that aesthetics must be sought in the phenomenon of consciousness as it is historically nurtured and articulated in language *vis-à-vis* the 'being-of-the-people'.

In *Gūzensei no mondai*, his *magnum opus*, Kuki brought his concern for dualism to a metaphysical height. He scrutinized in 'metaphysical solitude' the problem of contingency, focusing on: (1) propositional (that is, logical) contingency, which arises from the encounter between particulars ('eidetic singularity'); (2) hypothetical contingency (which encompasses the empirical causal and the teleological); and (3) metaphysical contingency, arising from the playful discrepancies within the one-many relationship. Contingency, or lack of necessity, arises where there is a duality between the necessary one (being or Being) and the contingent other *qua* the many (non-being). Only when there is a concrete interiorization of the other within the one can the logic of life be understood. Herein can be discerned Kuki's effort to resurrect life in the otherwise empty, abstract universals devoid of the humanly constitutive elements.

See also: CONTINGENCY; HEIDEGGER, M.; KYOTO SCHOOL; LOGIC IN JAPAN

List of works

Kuki Shūzō (1930–39) *Kuki Shūzō zenshū* (The Complete Works of Kuku Shūzō), Tokyo: Iwanami shoten, 1980–82, 12 vols. (Posthumous collection of Kuki's philosophical and literary works.)
—— (1930) *Iki no Kōzō* (The Structure of Iki), Tokyo: Iwanami shoten; trans. Maeno Toshikuni, *Structure de l'Iki*, Tokyo: Maison Franco-Japonaise, 1984. (An aesthetic evaluation of the phenomenon of *iki* in the being of Japanese people, relative to the other Japanese aesthetic values.)
—— (1935) *Gūzensei no mondai* (The Problem of Contingency), Tokyo: Iwanami shoten; trans. Omodaka Hisayuki, *Le problème de la contingence*, Tokyo: L'Université de Tokyo, 1966. (An attempt to resurrect a logic of life through a philosophical reflection on the problem of contingency.)
—— (1939) *Ningen to jitsuzon* (The Human and Human Existence), Tokyo: Iwanami shoten. (A philosophical probe into the 'primitive contingency'

in regard to the 'here and now' of human existence in an attempt to gain a primordial understanding of both being and nothingness.)

References and further reading

Light, S. (ed.) (1987) *Shūzō Kuki and Jean-Paul Sartre: Influence and Counter-Influence in the Early History of Existential Phenomenology, Including the Notebook 'Monsieur Sartre' and Other Parisian Writings of Shūzō Kuki*, Carbondale, IL: Southern Illinois University Press. (A recounting of Kuki's stay in Europe including his association with Sartre, and a commentary on two of his essays in French, 'La notion du temps et la repreise sur le temps en Orient' and 'L'expression de l'infini dans l'art japonais'.)
Pincus, L. (1996) *Authenticating Culture in Imperial Japan*, Berkeley, CA: University of California. (A recasting of Kuki's cultural specificism surrounding the *Iki no Kōzō vis-à-vis* a postmodern, cultural and literary criticism.)
Sakabe Megumi (1990) *Fuzaino uta* (The Songs of Absence), Tokyo: TBS Buritanika. (An in-depth and comprehensive summary of Kuki's major works.)
Viswanathan, M. (1989) 'An Investigation into Essence: Kuki Shūzō's 'Iki' no kōzō', *Transactions of the Asiatic Society of Japan* 4 (4): 1–22. (A balanced summary of *Iki no kōzō*.)
Yuasa Yasuo (1987) 'The Encounter of Modern Japanese Philosophy with Heidegger', in G. Parkes (ed.) *Heidegger and Asian Thought*, Honolulu, HI: University of Hawaii Press,155–74. (A brief introduction to Kuki, along with other prominent Japanese philosophers who studied in France and Germany in the 1920s and 1930s.)

NAGATOMO SHIGENORI

KUMAZAWA BANZAN (1610–91)

Trained under Nakae Tōju, the founder of the Wang Yangming school (Yōmeigaku) of Confucian idealism during the Tokugawa era in Japan, Kumazawa Banzan is known for his eclectic and pragmatic philosophy emphasizing political and economic reforms. For example, he recommended that the shogunate take greater responsibility for promoting economic equity and prosperity by supporting rice production and storage as well as the use of rice as the medium of exchange. He advocated a form of government dedicated to the Confucian ideal of benevolence.

Kumazawa Banzan is generally regarded as the second leading figure in the Japanese Wang Yangming school of Confucian idealism, following his teacher Nakae Tōju (1608–48), founder of the movement during the Tokugawa era (see CONFUCIAN PHILOSOPHY, JAPANESE). Whereas Nakae stressed Wang's ideal of the unity of knowledge and action from the standpoint of personal discipline and cultivation, thereby setting an example that greatly inspired his student, Kumazawa, a leaderless samurai (*rōnin*), emphasized the application of this theory to the political and economic realms. He achieved great success and fame as a reformer in the service of Ikeda Mitsumasa, the lord (*daimyō*) of Bizen Province from 1645–56. However, his unorthodox views and outspoken criticism of what he considered a somewhat oppressive and ineffective government led to his resignation and a life of semi-exile in official disfavour.

His main works are two collections of dialogues on moral philosophy and social problems, commentaries on the Confucian classics, a commentary on the *Tale of Genji*, and the *Daigaku Wakumon* (Dialogues on Learning), a series of dialogues on contemporary social, political and economic issues which was long suppressed by the Tokugawa authorities. The latter text, the title of which refers to questions concerning the Confucian classic *Daxue* (Great Learning), actually consists of Kumazawa's recommendations for restoring vitality to government, prestige to the ruling *samurai* class, self-identity and fairness to the peasant farmers and protection for the isolated and vulnerable Japanese nation at risk from possible attacks by the Mongols.

Although a follower of the idealist school, Kumazawa was also influenced by the rival Zhu Xi school of Confucian realism (see ZHU XI), and he combined a belief in the innate capacity of humanity to grasp truth and choose the correct conduct with an emphasis on the value of empirical knowledge of external reality. In particular, he opposed the shogunate's strict adherence to Confucian ritualism and instead advocated a government dedicated to the genuine pursuit of the Confucian philosophical ideal of *jinsei* (benevolence) and the recognition of individual merit based on performance rather than rank in the conventional class hierarchy. Kumazawa sought to eliminate class discrimination which he considered counter-productive for the shogunate, and he proposed the resettlement of *samurai* on the land, the relaxing of restrictions on the *daimyō* (especially the requirement that they divide their time between their home town and the capital in Tokyo), and the combining of warriors into one class with farmers. In addition, Kumazawa recommended for the proposed *samurai*-farmer class a partial return to rice as the medium of exchange, the storing of rice against drought or invasion, and the construction of flood basins and the afforesting of mountains.

A critic on religious issues as well as a political dissenter, he stressed the abolition of methods for suppressing Christianity and the institution of strict tests for men aspiring to become Buddhist priests. Kumazawa's views exerted a great influence on thinkers and reformers near the end of the Tokugawa shogunate in the mid-nineteenth century.

See also: CONFUCIAN PHILOSOPHY, JAPANESE; DAXUE; POLITICAL PHILOSOPHY, HISTORY OF; WANG YANGMING; ZHU XI

List of works

Kumazawa Banzan (1610–91) *Kumazawa Banzan zenshū* (Collected Works of Kumazawa Banzan), Tokyo: Banzan zenshū kankōkai, 1940–3, 6 vols. (The collected works of Kumazawa Banzan.)

—— (1610–91) *Daigaku Wakumon* (Dialogues on Learning) trans. G.M. Fisher, 'Dai Gaku Wakumon: A Discussion of Public Questions in the Light of the Great Learning', *Transactions of the Asiatic Society of Japan* 16, 1938: 259–356. (Translation of the main text, emphasizing social, political and economic reform.)

References and further reading

McMullen, J. (1983) 'Kumazawa Banzan', *Kodansha Encyclopedia of Japan*, Tokyo: Kodansha, vol. 4, 307. (A concise, insightful account of his life and thought.)

Ryūsaku Tsunoda, de Bary, W.T. and Keene, D. (eds) (1958) 'Kumazawa Banzan, A Samurai Reformer', in *Sources of Japanese Tradition*, New York: Columbia University Press, vol. 1, 375–88. (An historical overview with translations of selected passages.)

STEVEN HEINE

KUNDAKUNDA *see* JAINA PHILOSOPHY

KYOTO SCHOOL

The Kyoto school of philosophy pivots around three twentieth-century Japanese thinkers who held chairs of philosophy or religion at Kyoto University: Nishida Kitarō (1870–1945), Tanabe Hajime (1885–1962) and Nishitani Keiji (1900–91). Its principal living representatives, who also held chairs at Kyoto until their retirement, are Takeuchi Yoshinori (1913–) and Ueda Shizuteru (1926–). The keynote of the school was struck by Nishida in his attempt, on the one hand, to offer a distinctively Eastern contribution to the Western philosophical tradition by bringing key Buddhist concepts to bear on traditional philosophical questions, and on the other, to enrich Buddhist self-understanding by submitting it to the rigours of European philosophy.

The name 'Kyoto school' was coined in 1932 by the Marxist philosopher Tosaka Jun (1900–45) to denounce what he saw as a bourgeois ideology – which he characterized as 'hermeneutical, transhistorical, formalistic, romantic, and phenomenological' – that had grown up around Nishida, Tanabe and their immediate disciples at the time. These latter included Miki Kiyoshi (1897–1945), Kosaka Masaaki (1900–69) and Koyama Iwao (1905–93) as well as the young Nishitani. At the time the Japanese state had taken its first definitive steps in the direction of a militaristic nationalism that would involve it in the 'fifteen-year war' with Asia and finally the West over the period 1930–45. As the leading philosophical movement in Japan, the Kyoto school was caught up in this history, although there was little unanimity among the responses of the principal figures.

Postwar criticisms and purges of the Japanese intelligentsia attached a certain stigma to the school's name, but later and more studied examination of those events, as well as the enthusiastic reception of translations of their works into Western languages, has done much to ensure a more balanced appraisal. Today, the philosophy of the Kyoto-school thinkers is recognized as an important contribution to the history of world philosophy whose 'nationalistic' elements are best recognized as secondary, or at least as an unnecessary trivialization of its fundamental inspirations.

As a school of thought, the common defining characteristics of the Kyoto school may be seen in an overlap of four nodal concerns: self-awareness, the logic of affirmation-in-negation, absolute nothingness and historicity.

1   Survey

The story of Western philosophy in Japan began just over one hundred years ago with the general opening up of Japan after more than two centuries of isolation from the rest of the world. As young scholars went to Europe to study, and philosophical literature became available, the currents of neo-Kantian and neo-Hegelian thought (see NEO-KANTIANISM; HEGELIAN-ISM) opened a gateway to Greek, medieval and modern philosophy, almost all of which was read in the Western languages. These ideas were taken over by Buddhist thinkers anxious to update their self-understanding. While most of the work of these early pioneers was premature and uncritical, they charted a course which within a generation would produce its first original thinker in the person of NISHIDA KITARŌ.

Like others of his age, Nishida's initial interests were in British empiricism and positivism, but by the time he began at Tokyo University, German philosophy was in vogue (even though the medium of instruction for foreign professors was English). After graduating in 1894 and before taking up employment, he had the idea of writing a book to introduce the ethical theory of the British philosopher T.H. GREEN to the general Japanese reading public. Although much of the subtlety of Green's language and thought was lost on the young Nishida, leading him to abandon the project in mid-stream, the association of theories of the good and the Hegelian dialectic struck a chord that resonated in him for the next fifteen years, culminating in the publication of his maiden work, *Zen no kenkyū* (A Study of the Good), in 1911.

In general, the most important intellectual influences during these years were BERGSON, William JAMES and HEGEL. However, the critical catalyst that convinced Nishida to strike out creatively in his own direction came from quite another quarter. For at least ten years, beginning in 1896, he practised meditation under a Zen master and was assigned the koan *mu*, or 'nothingness'. While there is little evidence that the variety of Zen systems of thoughts as such influenced the maturation of his philosophical ideas, the discipline of meditation was decisive. On the one hand, it convinced him that philosophy does not begin in knowing *about* things through the medium of objective logic, but in the knowing *of* things through the medium of direct experience. On the other, it showed him that philosophy does not end there, in ineffability, but only begins its work of expressing as clearly as possible the structure of reality and the place of human meaning and action within it. For if the pure ideas transplanted from Western philosophy needed to sink roots in the lived experience of Japan, so did the kind of pure experiencing cultivated in Buddhist meditation need to mature into self-expression under the critical eye of philosophical thinking (see BUDDHIST PHILOSOPHY, JAPANESE).

This ideal of bringing pure experience and clear understanding to bear on one another was the hallmark of the *Zen no kenkyū* and runs throughout all Nishida's philosophy. If Nishida's thinking straddles East and West, it does not do so on the naive supposition that the one can be made to supply what the other lacks. The fact that he chose the term 'pure experience' from James to express the direct experience he had come to know through Zen, and the Buddhist idea of 'nothingness' to clarify Western ideas about the ultimate ground of understanding, shows that the standpoint he sought was finally philosophical in the proper sense of the term. It was a standpoint that transcended East and West, not in the sense that it bleared distinctions of culture and tradition, but in the sense that it pointed to the aim of clear thinking in all culture and tradition as a lived 'religious' expression, in word and deed, of universal ideas. Through his disciples Tanabe Hajime and Nishitani Keiji, this standpoint distanced itself from Nishida's person and mode of expression to become a forum for thought of great variety, but never lost the religious-philosophical stamp that Nishida had given it.

Although Nishida himself never left Japan, he encouraged TANABE to go to Germany. There the latter studied HUSSERL, COHEN and Natorp, and became close to HEIDEGGER. The religious character of Tanabe's philosophic concerns was not associated with any particular Buddhist sect, though he favoured the Sōtō Zen of Dōgen more than the koan-centred Zen of the Rinzai sect, and later turned enthusiastically to Pure Land Buddhism and Christianity for philosophical inspiration. The unifying factor for him was Hegelian logic and dialectic. NISHITANI, who also later studied in Germany, took an early interest in NIETZSCHE, whose thought had an enduring impact on him. Like Nishida, Nishitani's primary connection with Buddhism was Zen, both Rinzai and Sōtō; but like Tanabe, Nishitani wrestled with Christian ideas through most of his mature years, mainly through his reading of the mystics and the European existentialists.

Takeuchi's religious frame of reference has consistently been that of Pure Land Buddhism (it was through his influence that his teacher, Tanabe, took to reading Shinran), seasoned by a studied reading of modern Christian theologians such as BULTMANN and TILLICH. With encouragement from Nishitani, Ueda studied in Germany and wrote a doctoral thesis on MEISTER ECKHART. During his teaching career he wrote mainly on Zen and Christian mysticism, but since retirement has concentrated on invigorating interest in Nishida's philosophy as such. In both Takeuchi and Ueda we find less of the kind of direct engagement with Western philosophical ideas that we find in Nishida and Tanabe, and practically none of the sort of textual analysis we see in Nishida's struggles with neo-Kantian thought or Nishitani's studies on Aristotle and Descartes. In their case, the influence of Western philosophy has been filtered through their reading of Nishida and Tanabe, who are now recognized as world-class philosophers in the Western sense of the term. Far from indicating a dilution of Nishida's original inspiration, their relative distance from the West shows the sense in which the Kyoto school has turned in the direction of thought that can be approached philosophically on its own merits, without the need to establish credibility through the study of major Western thinkers.

Despite the constant presence of Western intellectual history in the writings of the Kyoto school philosophers and their insistence on the role that Japanese thought has to play in the world philosophical forum, dialogue with their philosophical contemporaries outside Japan played a surprisingly insignificant role in the development of their thought. Differences between their respective positions and debate over those differences neither solicited nor attracted the attention of the philosophical community of Europe and the United States, let alone of other Asian countries. In part this was due to the inaccessibility, until quite recently, of their works in Western languages. In part it was also due to the largely tacit assumption that only the Buddhist East, and perhaps only Japan, as the sole country to engage in modernization freely and without the pressures of colonial rule, was equipped to produce a philosophy that can bridge East and West.

The launching of the Kyoto school, and hence Japanese philosophy, into the world philosophical forum was not the result of determined efforts by the philosophers themselves, but of initiatives from their Western counterparts in philosophy and religious studies. A flurry of translations, as well as a wave of young scholars from Western countries trained to read the original texts and converse in Japanese, not only brought their philosophy to the attention of the world community but prompted a revival of interest in the Kyoto school philosophers in Japan. Ironically, it has only been after the passing of Nishida, Tanabe and Nishitani that the philosophy of the Kyoto school has passed from the stage of being a Japanese event witnessed by a privileged few who knew the language, to a common forum of ideas in which philosophers from around the world can discuss and debate.

Given the relative isolation of the writings of the Kyoto school philosophers from direct criticism by their contemporaries abroad, their thought was free to take new directions that might not have occurred to them under the monitoring of foreign tutors. Similarly, the lack of affinities between their own language and ancient Greek and Latin, and the lack of popular currency to the vocabulary created to translate Western philosophical terminology, gave an entirely different flavour to the linguistic frame within which they worked. The borrowed vocabulary was generally translated taking only the flat, surface meaning, with no thought to associations of feeling or history or literary allusion. Despite its claims to indigenous thinking, their language is barely less alien to those untrained in its meanings than was the rest of Western philosophy.

On the positive side, the etymology and historical resonances of the Chinese characters suggested different associations, and led them in directions that the retranslation of their works back into Western languages all but entirely gloss over. Well before Heidegger's works were translated into English, and even while the battles over how to render his wordplays into acceptable idiom were raging in the West, the Japanese showed their natural affinity for his attempts to disclose the wonderful world within worlds of language.

At the same time, their inheritance of modern philosophical questions – from epistemology and the philosophy of science to existentialism and the overcoming of metaphysics – allowed certain questions to pass by unnoticed. In this regard, one thinks particularly of the question of criteria for distinguishing literal truth from symbolic truth. Their failure to concern themselves with symbolic theory in general, and with demythologizing religious truth or distinguishing faith from rationalism in particular, made it possible for them to work from a standpoint of 'philosophy-religion' that is not so easily taken by theologians or philosophers in the West.

2 Self-awareness

As noted above, Nishida's concern with Western philosophy stemmed from the need for an objective standpoint from which to rethink, systematically and rigorously, the experience of being rational within an Eastern, and in particular a Japanese, culture. Though his writings make few direct references to Zen, in his lectures he is reported to have defined his philosophical aim as seeking a rational foundation for the Zen experience of enlightenment. The term he chose

for this, 'self-awareness' (*jijaku*), is an ordinary word in Japanese which had loose ties to Buddhist and Western philosophical thought but had not been preempted as technical jargon by either of them. On this term he laid the burden of resisting the self-understanding being urged on Japan from the outside world and at the same time of submitting vernacular patterns of self-understanding to as serious a critique as possible. In this sense, it was less a clearly defined concept than a kind of bridge that allowed him to move back and forth freely between two worlds of ideas and forge a philosophy of his own. Moreover, because of its inherent ambiguity, the term provides a kind of symbolic connection between Nishida and his disciples, even when other differences of opinion seem to pull them far apart.

The designation of awareness as *self*-awareness is more than the result of literal translation. It draws attention to two important traits of enlightened consciousness for Nishida. First, it was an awareness that comes about *of itself*, without the interposition of judgment or discursive knowing on the part of the individual. It is an event, not the result of any systematic technique of reflection; it is the foundation of the philosophic enterprise, not the aim. Second, the awareness is without any 'object' that distinguishes it from the 'subject' of the awareness. It is, one might say, an awareness of awareness itself, not of any one that is aware or about any thing that is the focus of consciousness. In other words, it is the state of pure experience prior to the distinctions and judgments that begin with the distinction of any experiencing subject and an experienced object.

In his early writings, Nishida spoke of this refinement of everyday subjectivity into self-awareness as the discovery of the 'true self', a no less ambiguous yet symbolically important term that appears commonly in the work of both Tanabe and Nishitani as well. The more he threw himself into the Western intellectual tradition, the more he recognized cognates there for the notion of a self that loses itself in being aware of itself, and thus gradually gave up allusions to its distinctively Buddhist quality. His focus shifted rather to seeing the knowing, feeling and experiencing self of ordinary consciousness as the maidservant of self-awareness, in effect inverting Western philosophy as he knew it.

NISHITANI took up this concern with the true self and the attainment of an awakened subjectivity in serious confrontation with Western philosophical texts. At the same time, he delved deeper into Zen Buddhist literature in search of connections between self-awareness of one's true self and the enlightenment experience. For Nishitani, self-awareness consisted of a 'realization' that entailed both *really* coming to one's senses and a coming to *reality* just as it is. Awakening to this self means that consciousness 'sees' itself as an event in reality even as it 'sees through' any attempt to set itself over against the incessant change and interdependence of all things that are in the world of being. It is not ordinary consciousness, which sets itself up as a knower of the world to be known and hence puts itself in a position to change it, but a sort of consciousness of being conscious in the world. In this sense, as Nishitani points out, self-awareness is not the awareness of a self set up in opposition to another, but of a true self in which self and other are no longer two. He contrasted this self as a 'letting go of ego', by which he meant not simply ridding oneself of selfishness or uncluttering the everyday mind, but of 'breaking through' of ego in its highest form (for Nishitani, this is the Cartesian ego) (see DESCARTES, R.). The latter term, adopted from MEISTER EC-KHART, shows how Nishitani did not hesitate to point out equivalent critiques of the ego in the Christian tradition and to apply them to clarifying classical Buddhist notions.

In TANABE, the use of the terms 'self-awareness' and 'true self' was less self-conscious than it was in Nishida and Nishitani until he came to his project of revitalizing philosophy as a 'metanoetics'. There self-awareness is seen less as an immediately accessible, primordial state than as the disciplined, deliberate letting go of the 'self that is not a self' through reason exhausting itself on its own principles. In his later writings he used the notion deliberately to stress his differences from Nishida, but the basic meaning, and the fact that it was the lodestone of true philosophical thought, were never questioned.

3 The logic of affirmation-in-negation

In giving self-awareness a central place and all but identifying it with religious experience, NISHIDA distanced himself from the classical Western distinction between faith and reason. At the same time, he rejected the hasty appeals to the transrational or paradox in which Zen and other Eastern philosophies have often found a convenient retreat from criticism. Rather, he recognized the need to introduce a new logic to complement the two-valued logic of affirmation-or-negation that he found in his Western counterparts. His aim was, as he said, to give 'philosophical moorings' to the centuries-old preoccupation of Eastern cultures with such things as the 'form of the formless' or the 'voice of the voiceless'. This new logic was one of affirmation-in-negation and negation-in-affirmation (see LOGIC IN JAPAN).

The grammatical index of this logical relationship was the Sino-Japanese copula *soku* (rendered here as

'a-*in*-b') which Nishida used freely but did not assign an explicit place in formal logic. The most succinct statement of the *soku* logic is given by D.T. Suzuki, Nishida's friend from high school days: '*A* is not *A*, therefore *A* is *A*'. The point is not to deny the principle of contradiction by claiming that '*A* is *A*' and '*A* is not *A*' mean the same thing; nor is it simply to assert that ultimately there is nothing in the complexity of the real world that corresponds to the logical form '*A* is *A*'. Nishida did not mean to reject the need for abstract and logically regulated thinking. His point was rather to insist that the 'identity' of a thing is not contained within a thing itself, as a kind of self-subsistent fact waiting for the mind to discover it, but is always a function of its interaction with what it is not. This identity is therefore not something that can be grasped by a logically thinking subject passing judgment on a perceived object, but only in an act of self-awareness in which the logical affirmation of the thinking subject is taken up into an experience that erases the distinction between subject and object, between affirmation and negation. It is only after one has seen that '*A* is not *A*' that one is able to return to subjective judgment to understand what is meant by the claim that '*A* is *A*'.

This act of seeing that '*A* is not *A*' preoccupied Nishida for several years during which he concentrated his attentions on a process he called 'acting intuition'. Briefly put, his idea was that pure intuition needs to be deliberately *cultivated* as a way of acting on the world, participating in the world's dynamic by expressing it in creative form, without interposing the subject–object dichotomy on it. Nishida describes this as a 'seeing without a seer' and of 'knowing a thing by becoming it'. Later he used the term 'self-identity of absolute contradictories' as a general index of the *soku* logic and its corresponding epistemological theory.

TANABE took up the *soku* logic as a way for him to appropriate the Hegelian dialectic without succumbing to its assumptions about an unfolding of Being and consciousness in which the opposites are subsumed into a higher unity. (In fact, one of his points of disagreement with Nishida was what he saw as the reintroduction of a quasi-Plotinean One in the idea of the self-identity of absolute contradictories (see PLOTINUS §3).) Tanabe set the *soku* relationship in the context of a broader logic of what he called 'absolute mediation', his own alternative to the logic of non-contradiction. Like Nishida, he insisted that logic is a way of seeing that only makes sense when it is engaged in the seen, but he went further to see affirmation-in-negation as a function of a reality that is always in the making. The mutual mediation among things, their *soku* relationship, propels them through time and gives the lie to simple noncontradiction, but is also itself a part of the process. It is 'absolute' precisely in the sense that it does not stand above the process it enables. Hence while it governs contradictories like death-in-life, the *soku* relationship also applies to identities that do not involve contradiction, such as God-in-love.

While NISHITANI was never persuaded that Tanabe's idea of absolute mediation corrected a fault in Nishida's logic of *soku* and tended to use it as a copula between absolute contradictories, neither did he adopt the latter's terminology in his own philosophical writings. Moreover, like Nishida, he tended to see the *soku* statement as an index of a realization which precludes the working of the objectifying ego and its principle of noncontradiction.

4 Absolute nothingness

If there is one idea that has been associated with the Kyoto school of philosophy more than any other, it is that of absolute nothingness. Nishida's introduction of the notion into philosophy seems to have been motivated by his wish to remove traces of psychologism or idealism that were present in his early writings (see NISHIDA KITARŌ). Rather than have recourse to the Western notion of Being as a universal that would embrace both mind and the reality that it perceives or expresses, he turned to the Buddhist idea of nothingness and moulded it into an absolute that could answer philosophical questions generated outside of the Buddhist tradition (see BUDDHIST CONCEPT OF EMPTINESS).

In the Western philosophical heritage, nothingness has been defined in terms of Being and for the most part made subservient to Being as a privative (see BEING). Its positive side is most often caught by notions of nonexistent potentialities, ideals or aims. Wherever becoming is stressed as the correlative of being, at least a minimal idea of nothingness is present. None of this contradicts Nishida's use, but neither does it come close to exhausting it.

As an idea, the designation of nothingness or emptiness (*kū* in Japanese; in Sanskrit, *śūnyatā*) as 'absolute' is nothing new to Zen or to Mahāyāna Buddhism in general, and related ideas can be found in Daoist classics as well. However, the particular term (*zettai*) that Nishida used was a translation of the Hegelian 'Absolute', and is not found in the Chinese Buddhist canon. The term means literally 'without an opposing other', while the classical Chinese term found in Sanlun meant 'without dependency'. As a pure logical relation, Nishida's absolute does not contradict its use in Schelling and Hegel, through whom the notion of the Absolute was introduced into philosophy, although he uses it differently and does not arrive at the ontological conclusions of these latter (see ABSOLUTE, THE; HEGELIANISM). Indeed, the notion is not ontological at all, since that would reintroduce it as a subsidiary of being; rather, it is a principle that belongs to self-awareness. It is not a being or state of being or even the absence of them; it is a transcendence of the perspective of being that is meant to forfeit none of the possibility of being found in Being.

In the Kyoto philosophers, then, the idea of nothingness is cut off – that is, 'absolutized' – from its dependency on the idea of Being and set up in its place as the supreme ontological principle. The roles are thus reversed: nothingness takes over the centrality of Being, which is always dependent on an 'other' defined in terms of nothingness. To carry out this reversal in the context of philosophy, the thinkers of the Kyoto school were obliged to turn to Eastern thought, particularly Buddhism, for guidance. In this way it developed variously in each of them, suggesting that absolute nothingness can produce the same plurality of philosophies as being is able to.

For Nishida, absolute nothing belonged to his overall logic of place, a model of ever widening concentric contexts aimed at 'locating' self-awareness in reality. The first context inverts the fundamental bias of Western logic, which focuses judgment on the substantial individual, the particular (grammatical subject) that cannot become a universal (predicate) (see UNIVERSALS). For Nishida, self-awareness begins in focusing on the universal that deabsolutizes the existence of the individual. This horizon widens when self-awareness turns attention to the basic locus of universals, which is no longer in the world of individuals but only in the nothingness of consciousness. The only 'being' universals retain is that of events in consciousness. Thus the need to open the perspective still further, to deabsolutize consciousness by locating it in a wider context. This final, circumferenceless circle transcends the contents of consciousness altogether and opens into a universal of all universals. This is absolute nothingness. It is not any relative thing or any relative state of consciousness, but the ultimate homeground of reality itself, beyond being and our conscious judgments about it. In the logic of place, absolute nothingness is the crowning context in which everything else is 'located'. It is none other than the locus of enlightenment itself, and in that sense becomes part of a single philosophy the religious-experiential and the philosophical-reflective.

Like Nishida, TANABE accepted absolute nothingness as the final ground of reality, but for him this ground was essentially dynamic. That is, it is the actual 'working' of absolute mediation, known not by direct intuition but through its effects, namely the interdependency of the haphazard items that make up reality as we experience it. In other words, without the world of being, absolute nothingness would be static; and the world of being can only function because it is *not* nothingness. This was for Tanabe the principle behind all transformation, both personal and historical, which is always a form of being-in-nothingness.

The absoluteness of nothingness is not merely a logical quality but, for Tanabe, points to the religious dimension of the fundamentally social nature of all reality. This religious dimension was decidedly not mystical, but always practical. Positively, this meant that for the dynamism of absolute nothingness to be truly salvific required the cooperation of the individual conscience in the social world. Negatively, it meant that the progress of virtue in human society was ultimately not the work of the members who make it up or of particular structures that govern it, but of an absolute nothingness functioning as what Pure Land Buddhism calls 'Other-power'.

Nishitani's work represents a major advance in the idea of absolute nothingness (see NISHITANI KEIJI). This appears in two principal forms. On the one hand, he drew the idea closer to its Buddhist background by relating it directly to the Buddhist idea of emptiness, particularly in its Zen formulations. Throughout his mature writing he speaks of the 'standpoint of emptiness' as the locus from which self-awareness comes to realization. On the other, he was at pains to locate absolute nothingness squarely in the existential struggle of contemporary consciousness. The course of this struggle is laid out most clearly in his major work, *Shūkyō to wa nani ka* (Religion and Nothingness). There the ordinary, pre-awakened self is described as the ego of self-consciousness that sets itself up outside the world of things as a knowing subject. This is the standpoint of 'egoity'. Driven by death and an awareness of the impermanence of all things to see the empty abyss that yawns underfoot of ordinary egoity, one awakens next to an initial sense of the vanity of self and world. This is what Nishitani calls the standpoint of 'nihility', whose philosopher-saint was NIETZSCHE (see NIHILISM). It represents a conversion to a standpoint of nothingness, but only a *relative* nothingness. By facing this abyss of nihility squarely and yet not clinging to it as ultimate, we open up a final standpoint, that of 'emptiness' as such in which things appear just as they are, in their 'suchness', and in which the true self is seen to reside not in the workings of egoity but in a letting go of ego. The awareness of the relative nothingness of nihility is converted spontaneously and of its own – it is, as noted above, a *self*-awareness

– to an awareness of absolute nothingness as the ground of reality.

Using this model of religious conversion, Nishitani took up key notions of self and self-nature in Zen Buddhism, as well as their conceptual counterparts in Western philosophy and theology. His reflections on the impersonality of God, the kenosis of God in Jesus, and even the immaculate conception of the Virgin Mary draw freely on the Western mystical tradition, but in the end rest on his Buddhist strategy of emptying language into self-awareness of the true self.

5 Historicity

At the time that Nishida was producing his major work, the notion of historicity most dominant in Japanese philosophy was that of Marxism (see MARX, K.; HISTORY, PHILOSOPHY OF). The influence of Marxist thought was perhaps mostly immediately associated with the person of MIKI KIYOSHI, who enjoyed amicable relations with Nishida. Nishida did not employ Marxist-style analysis in his own thought, and seems to have considered it something of a distraction. His own position offered an alternative on two fronts. First, on the abstract level, he saw the actual production of history as the self-identity of the temporal opposites of past and future and the spatial opposites of the bodily self and the natural environment, both of which are a kind of continuity-in-discontinuity. Second, on the concrete level, he saw the need for something like an Eternal Now or absolute present to synthesize the contradictions of history as a self-expression of reality in the making (not yet) on the one hand, and as a self-negation of reality (has been) on the other. This he gathered under the rubric of 'tradition', in which the specific *ethnos* of particular peoples would be made manifest, and the combination of these specific peoples would constitute a global world. In Japan's case, this tradition centred on the Imperial Throne.

Whatever consolation the subtlety of his language afforded Nishida personally during the heavy censorship of the war years (the emperor's place in Japanese self-consciousness was referred to as a 'self-identity of contradictories', omitting the qualifier 'absolute'), it was lost on nearly everyone else, particularly on his postwar critics. At the height of the war his prestige gave him access to leading political figures, some of whom had studied under him, and although they protected him, in the end he despaired of their ability to act objectively.

TANABE was still less drawn to struggle with Marxist thought, but more than Nishida – or at least earlier than Nishida – he struggled with bringing the element of historicity into philosophy through his notion of 'the specific'. In the context of history, this meant that the universal (humanity) and the particular (the human individual) are related to one another concretely in the form of particular cultures, languages and ethnic particularity. For Tanabe, this specific substratum, insofar as it was functional, was nonrational; and insofar as it was unreflected, was susceptible to manipulation by rational ideologies. At the same time, even though he made it clear that the ultimate foundation of the specific was not any particular historical relative situation, but absolute nothingness, he also saw that this latter needs expression in the specific in order to be known.

More than anything Nishida had written, this idea of Tanabe's seemed to suit Japan's growing imperialistic ideology insofar as it stressed the specific as the most real experience of history and even regarded the emperor as a unifying symbol of its foundations in an absolute, with the result that concern for the wider human community and broader humanitarian questions tended to be relegated to a more abstract and ahistorical plane. Tanabe himself yielded to this tendency in the early years of the Pacific war. Later, as the war was drawing to a close, he publicly repented in his *Zangedō to shite no tetsugaku* (Philosophy as Metanoetics), in which he spoke of the need to historicize philosophy by first negating it as a powerless, weak-willed enterprise that has nothing to say in time of crisis, and then reaffirming it as a letting go of self. That step having been taken, he later returned to his notion of the specific, but was never quite able to remove the shadow that the war experience had cast over this important idea for the history of philosophy.

Nishitani's ideas on the philosophy of history developed in the opposite direction from those of Nishida. As a young professor thrust into the thick of the debate over Japan's philosophy of 'all-out war', recorded in the pages of the journal *Chūōkōron* in 1941 and 1942, he had not yet worked out a mature position of his own and lapsed into remarks that seem to smack of the very nationalism that was at the heart of the militarist ideology. After the war, having suffered censorship and a temporary purge from his post in Kyoto University, he wrote a number of essays on nationalism, adopting a position close to the globalism of Nishida and the critique of the specific found in Tanabe. It was only when this was behind him, however, that he was able to forge a view of history more properly in line with his standpoint of emptiness, and without the spectre of nationalism lingering in the background. Nishitani offered Zen as a corrective to what he called the 'optical illusion' of Western linear notions of history, which look backwards to an absolute beginning or forward to an absolute end of history. It is only in the self-awareness of the ground of history as resting underfoot in the direct immediacy of the present that we can shake off the anthropocentric myths of scientific progress, special election and irreligious secularism that infect modern consciousness.

Whether or not the approach of the Kyoto school philosophers to Western philosophy will have the lasting, positive effect on Buddhist self-understanding they intended it to, and whether or not their revision of classical philosophical themes from a Buddhist perspective will have any lasting impact on philosophical thought outside Japan, are questions too large to pronounce on summarily. No doubt many of their ideas need to be broken down for scholars to assess and examine in further detail. However, their vision remains an important contribution, indeed the first important contribution, of Japan to world philosophy.

See also: BUDDHIST PHILOSOPHY, JAPANESE; HEGELIANISM; HISTORY, PHILOSOPHY OF; JAPANESE PHILOSOPHY; LOGIC IN JAPAN; MIKI KIYOSHI; NISHIDA KITARŌ; NISHITANI KEIJI; TANABE HAJIME

References and further reading

Heisig, J. and Maraldo, J. (eds) (1994) *Rude Awakenings: Zen, the Kyoto School, and the Question of Nationalism*, Honolulu, HI: University of Hawaii Press. (A multi-faceted look at the political dimensions of the Kyoto-school philosophers.)

* Nishida Kitarō (1911) *Zen no kenkyū* (An Inquiry into the Good), trans. Masao Abe and C. Ives, New Haven, CN: Yale University Press, 1990. (First work by Nishida, the founder of the Kyoto School.)

—— (1917) *Jikaku ni okeru chokkan to hansei* (Intuition and Reflection in Self-Consciousness), trans. V. Viglielmo with Takeuchi Yoshinori and J. O'Leary, Albany, NY: State University of New York Press, 1987. (Later important work by Nishida.)

* Nishitani Keiji (1985) *Shūkyō to wa nani ka* (Religion and Nothingness), trans. J. Van Bragt, Berkeley, CA: University of California Press, 1985. (Nishitani's major work on religion.)

—— (1949) *Nihirizumu* (The Self-Overcoming of Nihilism), trans. G. Parkes and Setsuko Aihara, Albany, NY: State University of New York Press, 1990. (Nishitani's work on nihilism.)

—— (1985) *Nishida Kitarō*, trans. Yamamoto Seisaku and J.W. Heisig, Berkeley, CA: University of California Press, 1991. (Nishitani's biography of his teacher.)

Ohashi Ryosuke (ed.) (1990) *Die Philosophie der*

Kyoto-Schule: Texte und Einführung (The Philosophy of the Kyoto School: Texts and Introduction), Munich: Karl Alber. (A selection of writings translated into German with brief introductions and a solid bibliography.)

Takeuchi Yoshinori (1983) *The Heart of Buddhism: In Search of the Timeless Spirit of Primitive Buddhism*, New York: Crossroad. (Exploration of Buddhist philosophy.)

* Tanabe Hajime (1986) *Zangedō to shite no Tetsugaku* (Philosophy as Metanoetics), trans. Takeuchi Yoshinori and J.W. Heisig, Los Angeles, CA: University of California Press, 1986. (Tanabe's best-known work.)

Ueda Shizuteru (1965) 'Die Gottesgeburt in der Seele und der Durchbruch zu Gott: Die mystische Anthropologie Meister Eckharts und ihre Konfrontation mit der Mystik des Zen-Buddhismus' (The Birth of God in the Soul and Breakthrough to God: The Mystical Anthropology of Meister Eckhart and its Confrontation with the Mysticism of Zen Buddhism), Ph.D. dissertation, Gütersloh. (Ueda's dissertation on Meister Eckhart.)

Unno Taitetsu (ed.) (1990) *The Religious Philosophy of Nishitani Keiji*, Berkeley, CA: Asian Humanities Press. (A series of essays devoted to a critical appraisal of Nishitani's thinking.)

Unno Taitetsu and Heisig, J.W. (eds) (1990) *The Religious Philosophy of Tanabe Hajime*, Berkeley, CA: Asian Humanities Press. (A series of essays devoted to a critical appraisal of Tanabe's philosophy.)

JAMES W. HEISIG

L

LA BARRE, POULAIN DE

see FEMINISM (§§2, 3)

LA FORGE, LOUIS DE (1632–66)

Louis de la Forge, a medical doctor by profession, was an important champion of Cartesian philosophy in mid-seventeenth century France. Through his work on the first published edition of Descartes' Traité de l'homme, *as well as in his own* Traité de l'esprit de l'homme, *La Forge sought to complete Descartes' project of giving a full and detailed account of the human being as a union of two essentially distinct substances: mind and body. His analysis of causation introduced occasionalist elements into his otherwise orthodox Cartesian system, and he is credited with being one of the originators of occasionalism.*

Louis de la Forge was born in November 1632 in La Flèche, France. As a young man he was captivated by Descartes' philosophy. When, in 1653, he moved to the intellectually lively environment of Saumur (with its schools and academies) to set up his medical practice, he quickly became known primarily as a fervent champion of Cartesian thought. In his published works he assumed the task of faithfully completing Descartes' unfinished project of giving a full and detailed account of the human being, considered particularly as a union of two radically distinct substances: mind and body (see DESCARTES, R. §8). At the request of Claude Clerselier, Descartes' friend, he helped to edit and draw the figures for the first published edition of Descartes' *Traité de l'homme*, which appeared in 1664 with La Forge's own critical notes. To supplement this work (which considers only the physical functions and processes of the human body, treated in purely mechanistic terms) La Forge composed his own *Traité de l'esprit de l'homme* (1665), in which he considers the soul itself, its union with the body, and all the phenomena that derive from their mutual interaction. This gained him an international reputation as one of the originators of occasionalism (see OCCASIONALISM). His philosophical career, however, was cut short by his death in 1666.

While La Forge was not a particularly original thinker, he was not, on the other hand, an uncritical or unimaginative disciple of Descartes. His figures and notes to the *Traité de l'homme* occasionally correct his mentor. His most important philosophical contribution lies in his discussion of causation, both as it relates to bodies and in connection with the interaction of mind and body. While modest about his accomplishments and eager to remain as faithful as possible to Descartes' doctrines, La Forge went deeper than did Descartes himself into certain metaphysical problems facing Cartesian mechanism and dualism.

La Forge begins the *Traité de l'esprit de l'homme* by considering the soul itself, including its immateriality, its cognitive and volitional functions and its immortality. He then turns to the soul's union with the body. Any union between two substances consists in a certain mutual dependence of their states, a relative correlation of action and passion. In the case of bodies, it is their local contact that establishes this dependence. In the case of minds, love accounts for the fact that one mind wills what another mind wills. A mind and a body are united when thoughts in the former depend upon motions in the latter, and vice versa. The immediate explanation of these mutual dependencies is causal. In the case of bodies and of minds, where the effect resembles the cause, it is a matter of what (employing a medieval distinction) he calls 'univocal causation'. In the mind–body case, since the effect does not resemble the cause, it is 'equivocal causation'. But La Forge then considers the nature of causality itself, and here he turns to God. *Prima facie*, causal relations between bodies appear to have an intelligibility that is lacking in the body-mind case, since we think that we can understand how one body can communicate motion to another body. In fact, genuine body–body causation is no more intelligible or possible than body–mind causation, and all species of causal relationship have their ultimate ground in the divine will.

With respect to body–body relations, La Forge adopts an occasionalist solution. A body, according to the orthodox Cartesian schema that La Forge follows, is nothing more than pure extension, devoid of any spiritual properties (thoughts, desires, will). Thus, a body is, by nature, inert and passive, and has absolutely no active motive force, no power to put itself in motion. This is particularly clear when we

331

consider that all the properties of body must be understood in terms of its underlying essence: extension. And while this is possible for such properties as size, shape, internal figure and mobility, it is clearly not possible for active force. But if bodies cannot move themselves, then they cannot move other bodies. Moreover, the motion of a body is simply a modification of its substance, and (on the Cartesian ontology) modes cannot pass from the substance to which they belong to some other substance. Thus, real transitive causation – whereby one body would communicate its motion to another – is ruled out.

La Forge's strongest argument on this issue is based on principles concerning divine sustenance that he inherits from Descartes (see DESCARTES, R. §6). God, he insists, is required not just to create the world *ex nihilo*, but to sustain it in existence from moment to moment by a kind of continuous production. This applies, as well, to all the particular substances in the world. When God creates or sustains a body at a given time, he must do so in some relative place or another. But it follows, then, that the motion of a body is just its being sustained or recreated by God from one moment to the next in different successive relative places. The force that moves a body can only be the will of God, and the local contact of a body in motion with another that is at rest is only an occasion for God to modify the motion of the first body and to put the second body into motion, as dictated by the laws of nature.

While La Forge does bring God into the picture in the other two causal contexts, it is not in such an occasionalist manner. The body plays a causal role in the generation of sensations in the mind, but only in so far as the motions communicated to the brain 'occasion' the mind to bring about a sensory idea. Thus, while the body is the occasional cause of the idea, the mind is the real efficient cause. God is required in order to institute this causal body–mind relationship in the first place (and, subsequently, to sustain it), but not to be the direct efficient cause of the mental event on the occasion of the bodily event. God has also given to the soul – an active substance – the power to move the body by its volitions, without the need of constant divine involvement. In each of these cases, La Forge appears to be entirely faithful to Descartes.

La Forge's analysis of causation was of great importance in the development of occasionalism, and some of his arguments reappear without acknowledgement in Malebranche's deeper and more systematic occasionalist doctrine (see MALEBRANCHE, N. §4). LEIBNIZ, for one, recognized La Forge's originality here, and ascribed to him (along with

CORDEMOY) significant modifications to the Cartesian system.

List of works

La Forge, L. de (1665) *Traité de l'esprit de l'homme* (Treatise on the mind of man), in P. Clair (ed.) *Oeuvres philosophiques*, Paris: Presses Universitaires de France, 1974. (La Forge's completion of Descartes' account of the human being.)

References and further reading

Balz, A.G.A. (1951) *Cartesian Studies*, New York: Columbia University Press. (Contains a chapter on La Forge's critique of substantial forms.)

Clair, P. (1974) 'Étude Bio-Bibliographique' (Bio-bibliographical study), in La Forge *Oeuvres philosophiques*, Paris: Presses Universitaires de France. (The most complete account available of La Forge's life and writings.)

—— (1976) 'Louis de la Forge et les origines de l'occasionalisme' (Louis de la Forge and the origins of occasionalism), *Recherches sur le XVIIème siècle* 1: 63–72. (A brief study of La Forge's role in the development of occasionalism.)

* Descartes, R. (1664) *Traité de l'homme* (Treatise on man), Paris. (A mechanist account of the human body.)

Nadler, S. (1993) 'The Occasionalism of Louis de la Forge', in S. Nadler (ed.) *Causation in Early Modern Philosophy: Cartesianism, Occasionalism, and Pre-established Harmony*, University Park, PA: The Pennsylvania State University Press. (An examination of the nature and extent of La Forge's occasionalism.)

Prost, J. (1907) *Essai sur l'atomisme et l'occasionalisme dans la philosophie cartésienne* (Essay on atomism and occasionalism in Cartesian philosophy), Paris: Henry Paulin. (One of the best studies of occasionalism, with several chapters on La Forge's arguments and his role in the doctrine's development.)

STEVEN NADLER

LA METTRIE, JULIEN OFFROY DE (1709–1751)

La Mettrie is best known as the author of the eighteenth-century materialist manifesto, L'Homme machine (1747). His interest in philosophical issues grew out of his preoccupation with medicine, and he developed a tradition of medical materialism within the French Enlightenment. Born in St Malo, into the family of a prosperous textile merchant, La Mettrie pursued a medical career in Paris. He also studied for two years with the renowned Hermann Boerhaave in Leiden. After a brief period of medical practice, La Mettrie devoted his efforts to his translations and commentaries on Boerhaave's medical works. He also began to publish the works that made him a pariah to both the Faculty of Medicine of Paris and to the orthodox – that is, his medical satires and his first work of materialist philosophy, L'Histoire naturelle de l'âme (1745). Because of the outrage provoked by these works, he was exiled to Holland in 1745. But L'Homme machine, the text in which he applied his materialism thoroughly and explicitly to human beings, was too radical even for the unusually tolerant Dutch, and La Mettrie was forced to seek asylum at the court of Frederick the Great where he later died. His willingness to publish ideas his contemporaries considered too dangerous led the philosophes to repudiate him.

1   Medical roots of materialism
2   Materialist philosophy
3   Moral philosophy
4   Role in the Enlightenment

1   Medical roots of materialism

La Mettrie's best known work, L'Homme machine (1747), has sometimes been construed, largely because of its title, as a simple application to man of Descartes's bête machine hypothesis (see DESCARTES, R. §12). But his materialism is richer, less mechanistic, and more embedded in the scientific and medical traditions of the eighteenth century than this narrow appreciation has suggested.

La Mettrie's interest in philosophical issues grew out of his preoccupation with medicine. His medical works include translations and commentaries on Boerhaave's principal works, five medical treatises on specific diseases and public health, and seven volumes of medical satires lampooning the ignorance and venality of the medical profession. His work manifests the hostility to metaphysics and commitment to an empiricism typical of many medical writers in the eighteenth century. His awareness of the divergent manifestations of disease in different individuals led him to emphasize the importance of the physiological constitution in his philosophical works. La Mettrie built upon Boerhaave's tentative correlations between Lockean epistemology and the physiology of mental process to develop a materialist philosophy. That is to say, he not only adopted Lockean psychology as the best framework within

which to discuss brain functions but also made the easy transition from LOCKE to materialism; in all of his philosophical writings, he emphasized the physiological evidence for taking this step.

2   Materialist philosophy

La Mettrie's first philosophical work, L'Histoire naturelle de l'âme (1745), appears to be a conventional metaphysical treatise in style and vocabulary. But he deliberately subverted conventional philosophical arguments to argue for materialism, perhaps attempting to legitimate materialism by placing it within the established philosophical canon (see MATERIALISM IN THE PHILOSOPHY OF MIND). For example, he claimed that Aristotelian substantial forms – defined as the power of matter to acquire form, force, and the faculty of sensation – prefigured his materialism. He used the Aristotelian sensitive soul as a fruitful way to discuss mental processes and cited, as an epistemological rallying cry, the Aristotelian maxim, 'nothing in the intellect which is not first in the senses'. He wielded his materialist reading of Locke as a weapon against seventeenth-century metaphysicians, especially LEIBNIZ and Descartes, to argue that the soul could be completely identified with the physical functions of the body and that any claims about its existence or function must be substantiated through physiology. Without the impediment to research and understanding that the notion of the immortal soul posed, one could come to a more realistic assessment of human nature by studying all available scientific data. Writing as a physician committed to the practical application of empirical physiology to investigations of human nature and the soul, La Mettrie reappraised philosophical issues with the evidence and methods of medicine and physiology.

In L'Homme machine (1747), La Mettrie adopted a freer and more polemical style to canvass all the scientific issues of his day for empirical evidence for materialism. He provided lengthy and elaborate discussion of the physical basis of human behaviour in order to demonstrate that the effects of the body on the soul are so striking that one cannot reasonably assume that a soul controls the body; thus one must ultimately conclude that the soul, if the term has any meaning, must be considered part of the body. He used evidence drawn from anatomy, physiology, and psychology to assert the complete dependence of the soul on the body. Albrecht von Haller's findings on muscular irritability were particularly attractive to La Mettrie as the most conclusive evidence against those who refused to admit that matter was capable of selfmovement, particularly the Cartesians. Making no qualitative distinction between conscious and voluntary and involuntary or instinctual, La Mettrie posited an active, organic, and selfmoving 'man machine'. With his materialist theory of man substantiated by physiological experiments, La Mettrie thoroughly compared human beings to animals, despite the implicit disparagement of conventional notions of man's place in the universe which those comparisons entailed. Furthermore, he suggested that atheism was the logical outcome of his notion of an active, selfcreating and sustaining nature.

La Mettrie's other works on the philosophy of nature, *L'Homme plante* (1748) and *Système d'Epicure* (1750), further integrate human beings in nature by comparing them to lower creatures, like plants, and by placing them in the context of the unfolding of matter and motion in an evolutionary process.

In these works, La Mettrie empowered the physician, at the expense of the theologian and metaphysician, because he maintained that the physician's physiological understanding of human beings was the most sound and most likely to yield productive results. The close connections he was able to draw between physical and mental processes demonstrated the utility of knowledge gleaned by his method, which was unsystematic, incautious and unconstrained by standards of orthodoxy, bound instead by stringent empirical standards – the method, he suggested, of the reform-minded, empiricist physician. La Mettrie then turned his attention to an area where the authority of the metaphysician or the theologian traditionally prevailed over that of the physician, ethics.

3 Moral philosophy

La Mettrie's *Discours sur le bonheur* (1750) used his materialist notion of man and his place in nature to examine the implications of materialism for moral systems and for the individual in society. He raised the question of the effect society can have on the individual or the degree to which education can countervail physiological determinants.

He sought to determine whether our notions of virtue and vice correspond to human nature as revealed by physiology. The evidence of comparative anatomy led him to conclude that society was not only unnatural but also arbitrary, and that its notions of virtue and vice, while socially useful, were fundamentally at odds with nature and simply the result of socialization. Therefore, just as the physician must acknowledge the effects of the individual constitution on health and disease, La Mettrie insists, so too must the moral reformer recognize the limits that the individual constitution imposes on one's ability to behave in the ways society has defined as

virtuous. The brunt of La Mettrie's moral argument is the hope that society, recognizing that its notions of virtue and vice are relative and designed merely to further its interests, will be persuaded to reward a greater range of human behaviour; thus, more individuals will be able to aspire to social virtues. In light of his understanding of human nature and morality, La Mettrie critically appraised other moral systems; he indicted Christianity and Stoicism, in particular, for their distorted views of human nature (see VIRTUES AND VICES).

4 Role in the Enlightenment

La Mettrie was more pessimistic than other *philosophes* about the possibility of social reform; for him, reform efforts were severely circumscribed by the sway that the physiological constitution exercises over the individual. His specific claim that virtue and vice are completely relative put him at odds with the aspirations of other Enlightenment moralists writing within the natural law tradition, and his hedonistic ethic put him beyond the pale as far as many of his contemporaries were concerned. But despite the fact that virtually all of the *philosophes*, even those like DIDEROT and d'Holbach who were indebted to him, found it dangerous to be associated with his radical materialism, La Mettrie himself was eager to proclaim his adherence to them. In his last philosophical work, the *Discours préliminaire*, written in 1751 just as the philosophic movement was beginning to coalesce around the *Encyclopedia*, La Mettrie claimed to speak for the *philosophes*. He explicitly identified his work in both medicine and philosophy with their concerns for reform. Where medicine offered hope for a more naturalistic understanding of human nature, the *médecin-philosophe* (a term he coined) might be able to reform social institutions in accord with that understanding. La Mettrie's medical materialism is his distinctive contribution to the French Enlightenment and the history of philosophy.

See also: ENLIGHTENMENT, CONTINENTAL; MEDICINE, PHILOSOPHY OF

List of works

La Mettrie, J.O. de (1747–51) *Oeuvres philosophiques* (Philosophical Works), Berlin: Etienne de Bourdeau, 1750, 3 vols; repr. Paris: Fayard, 1987. (Contains all of the major philosophical works.)
—— (1747) *L'Homme machine*, trans. and ed. A. Thomson, *Man Machine and other writings*, Cambridge: Cambridge University Press, 1996.

References and further reading

Thomson, A. (1981) *Materialism and Society in the Mid-Eighteenth Century: La Mettrie's 'Discours preliminaire'*, Geneva: Librairie Droz. (Critical edition of text with monographic introduction. Advanced introduction to philosophical context.)

Vartainian, A. (1960) *La Mettrie's 'L'Homme Machine': A Study in the Origins of an Idea*, Princeton, NJ: Princeton University Press. (Critical edition of text with monographic introduction.)

Wellman, K. (1992) *La Mettrie: Medicine, Philosophy, and Enlightenment*, Durham, NC: Duke University Press. (Intellectual biography.)

KATHLEEN WELLMAN

LABRIOLA, ANTONIO (1843–1904)

Antonio Labriola was the founder of Italian theoretical Marxism. Generally situated in the Marxism of the Second International, he was more questioning than others in that movement. He profoundly influenced the development of Italian thought, constantly challenging the influential idealism of Benedetto Croce and Giovanni Gentile. His attempt to maintain a place for human creativity within a deterministic Marxist view of history influenced Antonio Gramsci and helped give Italian Eurocommunism its distinctive flexibility. His concepts of 'genetic method', 'social morphology', 'philosophy of praxis' and 'social pedagogy' are indications of this attempt.

Labriola was born in Cassino (near Naples) and studied at the University of Naples. He became Professor of Moral Philosophy and Pedagogy at Rome University in 1874 and remained there until his death. In 1887 he gave lectures in the philosophy of history and two years later began a series of lectures on the French Revolution which had to be suspended when right-wing students demonstrated.

Labriola was taught by Bertrando Spaventa, leader of the Neapolitan Hegelians, who was, however, critical of Hegel's deterministic interpretations (see HEGELIANISM §4). Labriola adopted a similar position and began to borrow the social psychology of Johann Friedrich HERBART while eschewing his metaphysics. Later, under the impact of reading Karl MARX, Herbart's social psychology was reconceived in terms of class consciousness.

Once he perceived that the Italian middle class in the 1870s were incapable of creating an Italian state which could provide unifying cultural leadership, Labriola rejected the Hegelian notion of the 'Ethical State' (see HEGEL, G.W.F. §8) and came to regard class conflict as necessary to social advancement. He leaned towards socialism from 1879, and in 1889 discovered Marx's writings, which were almost unknown in Italy at the time. Everything he had previously learned was now reshaped in Marxist categories.

He corresponded extensively with Friedrich Engels, as well as with Eduard Bernstein and Karl Kautsky attempting to engage Italy with German social democracy. He expounded Marxism in four highly original essays. His third and most insightful essay is composed from correspondence with Georges Sorel, and his final essay was incomplete at his death. Outside Italy his work was ignored, except in Russia, where his essays were applauded by Plekhanov, Lenin and Trotsky. Labriola's work generally re-entered histories of philosophy only as a result of widespread interest in Gramsci's prison notebooks.

Labriola introduced the concepts of 'genetic method', 'social morphology' and 'philosophy of praxis' in an attempt to characterize Marx's method in such a way as to avoid, on the one hand, a rigid materialist determinism and, on the other, the risk of appropriation by Italian Hegelianism. The three concepts are not really new, however, since they correspond to 'materialist method', 'social structure' and 'Marx's dialectic' in the works of Engels and others (see ENGELS, F. §3).

He saw Marx as having developed a systematic study of specific societies and of their modes of thought as distinctive and coherent wholes. Such study was carried out with the genetic method, which involved laying bare the complex of particular conditions (social morphology) which gives rise to the whole. Although Labriola wanted an empirical Herbartian approach, and was reluctant to speak of a dialectical method, his genetic method closely approximates the method promoted by Engels (see DIALECTICAL MATERIALISM).

Labriola took the philosophical kernel of Marxism to be 'the philosophy of praxis', that is, 'the reversal of the Hegelian dialectic', so that thought must be understood in terms of the practice in which it is embedded. For him this implied an entirely novel way of looking at things. Although he understood that thought could shape practice, he failed to avoid the determinism inherent in a metaphysics of history which insisted on the inevitability of the proletarian revolution. It was this same naturalistic evolutionism (albeit distinct from social Darwinism, which he criticized) which led him to advocate Italian colonialism in Africa as a means of raising Italy to the stage necessary for revolution (see EVOLUTIONARY THEORY AND SOCIAL SCIENCE).

Prior to his adoption of Marxism, Labriola for some years held a government position with responsibilities for the direction of public education. He came to prefer lecturing to workers. He always emphasized progressive popular education ('social pedagogy') and the creation of the cultural conditions for a society more civilized than capitalism, regarding Marxism as having a central role as a new conception of the world.

GRAMSCI took his Marxism in large part from Labriola, but rejected his evolutionism. He tried to resolve the methodological difficulty Labriola had encountered with deeper explorations of 'praxis' and 'social pedagogy'.

See also: MARXISM, WESTERN

List of works

Labriola, A. (1959) *Opere complete di Antonio Labriola* (Complete Works), ed. L. Dal Pane, Milan: Feltrinelli. (The definitive collection of Labriola's writings.)

—— (1895) *In memoria del Manifesto dei comunisti* (In Memory of *The Communist Manifesto*), Rome. (This first essay presents the theory of historical materialism as a product of its time.)

—— (1896) *Del materialismo storico: Dilucidazione preliminare* (Historical Materialism: Preliminary Exposition), Rome. (Labriola's analysis of ideologies and the structure–superstructure relation.)

—— (1898) *Discorrendo di socialismo e di filosofia* (Discourse on Socialism and Philosophy), Rome; 3rd essay, trans. in *Socialism and Philosophy*, trans. and with intro. by P. Piccone, St. Louis, MO: Telos Press, 1980. (This innovative essay examining class consciousness comprises letters to Georges Sorel. The translation contains a useful long introduction.)

—— (1903) *Essays on the Materialist Conception of History*, trans. C.H. Kerr, Chicago, IL. (The first English translation of Labriola's first three essays.)

—— (1904) *Da un secolo a un'altro* (From One Century to the Next), Rome. (Unfinished essay, published posthumously, mainly about the 'liberal age' and imperialism.)

—— (1976) *Scritti filosofici e politici* (Philosophical and Political Writings), ed. F. Sbarberi, Turin: Einaudi. (Contains all four Marxist essays, plus many articles and letters in political philosophy. Good bibliography of Italian editions.)

References and further reading

Hunt, G. (1987) 'Antonio Labriola, Evolutionist Marxism and Italian Colonialism', *Praxis International* 7 (3, 4): 340–59. (Draws out the connections between Labriola's method and his espousal of Italian colonialism.)

Mastroianni, G. (1976) *Antonio Labriola e la filosofia in italia* (Antonio Labriola and Philosophy in Italy), Urbino: Argalia. (A short survey of the entire trajectory and influence of Labriola's thought.)

Ragionieri, E. (1976) *Socialdemocrazia tedesca e socialisti italiani: 1875–1895* (German Social Democracy and Italian Socialists), Feltrinelli: Milan. (The best work for relating Labriola's thought to the Second International.)

GEOFFREY HUNT

LACAN, JACQUES (1901–81)

Jacques Lacan was a French psychoanalyst and philosopher whose contribution to philosophy derives from his consistent and thoroughgoing reinterpretation of Freud's writings in the light of Heidegger and Hegel as well as structuralist linguistics and anthropology. Whereas Freud himself had disparaged philosophical speculation, claiming for himself the mantle of the natural scientist, Lacan demonstrates psychoanalysis to be a rigorous philosophical position. Specifically, Lacan suggests that the Freudian unconscious is best understood as the effect of language (what he calls, 'the symbolic') upon human behaviour.

Lacan gives the name, 'unconscious' to what necessarily disrupts conscious life. In order to remain true to this disruptive effect, Lacan rejects the falsely reassuring clichés with which the idea of the unconscious has been popularized. He develops an understanding of the unconscious (doubtless strongly influenced by Hegel) that is based upon the difference implied in every identity – a difference conceivable as the 'gap' between the subject and any object that provides an identity to it. Since, according to Lacan, any such space or gap in some sense *belongs to* the object, identification is always imperfect. The effects that Freud associates with the unconscious derive from this imperfection.

Lacan developed his theory of the unconscious in three historical stages and corresponding to three 'fields' that define subjectivity – 'imaginary', 'symbolic' and 'real'. Lacan's major exposition of the idea of the imaginary came (while he was still in training as a psychoanalyst) in the 1936 paper later published as

'The Mirror Stage as Formative of the Function of the I' (in Lacan 1966). In that paper, Lacan posited an imaginary field dramatized by events of mirror identification (with 'images') in pre-verbal infants. The prematurity of human infants – their incapacity, compared with the young of other species, to control their own actions – creates the need for an external model for intentional unity; such is Lacan's explanation of the 'jubilation' of pre-verbal children from 6 months old onwards upon discovering their image either in a mirror or, more typically, in the mimicking gestures of another person.

But the same image that provides the site for jubilation also becomes the object of what Lacan calls 'aggressivity' – a proto-agression directed at the object of identification. For Lacan, such aggressivity results from the 'alienation' of that locus – the ego – where imaginary identification forms intentional unity. That is, in Lacanian theory the ego is first of all an object, the object in which the subject finds a 'self.' Because the ego can only appear as an object – as an other – its emergence also, according to Lacan, occasions the formation of a primordial violence directed against it.

Lacan's work in the 1950s, starting with the so-called, 'Rome Discourse' – the essay later published under the title of 'Function and Field of Speech and Language in Psychoanalysis' (in Lacan 1966) – elaborates a new dimension in his thought, the symbolic. Lacan's immersion in the structuralist linguistics of Ferdinand de SAUSSURE and anthropology of Claude LÉVI-STRAUSS helps him to reveal the alternative to the imaginary. Whereas the imaginary offers the exclusive either/or of obsessive identity through representation or aggressive destruction of the object of identity, the symbolic partially satisfies both impulses.

The symbolic is able to have such success based upon the structure of the sign. If, for Saussure, the sign combines a material element (the signifier) and the 'idea' which it indicates (the signified), then Lacan sees this structure as representing precisely the split condition of all human representation. That is, because the sign can only make present a signified through the mediation of a signifier, there is an absence in every presence; the idea can only be present through what represents it but is not it. Moreover, to speak a language is implicitly to accept this limitation. It is to partially master absence – the absent signified is always to some extent present – but at the price of the implicit admission that there can be no transparent presence. Language is a representation, then, that always represents the necessity of alienation (in the 'bar' dividing signifier and signified) along with a specific object or state of affairs. Lacan's reinterpretation of the Freudian Oedipal and castration dramas

as the acceptance of this prohibition implicit in language (for example, the 'Name-of-the-Father' for the father) allows him to divide off the Freudian developmental schema from any culturally specific view of the family.

To address the symbolic more concretely demands one more observation. If the bar between signifier and signified represents to the subject its own 'gap' or 'want-to-be' ('manque-à-être)', then it does so in a movement, the process that Lacan identifies with 'desire'. Within desire, language concretely demonstrates the impossibility of complete, unmediated presence. It does so by producing an ongoing process of 'identifications' mediated by language and always presenting themselves, therefore, as inadequate. Desire involves an ongoing movement which destroys identity (the ego) in favour of a metonymic 'sliding' from one signifier to another – but always by producing a new identity in the place of the old one.

It is this sliding that Lacan valorizes over and against the obsessive identification or aggressive demolition allowed by the imaginary. Lacan thus finds the efficacy of psychoanalysis in its ability to release desire from the limitations of the imaginary. It is possible to see how far a Freudianism based upon such an 'ethics' of pure desire, departs from almost all psychoanalytic orthodoxy. For most Freudians the purpose of analysis is at least partly to strengthen the ego. For Lacan the purpose of analysis is to allow the subject's desire to overcome the imaginary grip of the ego – to make identity fluid (see ALTERITY AND IDENTITY, POSTMODERN THEORIES OF §2; SUBJECT, POSTMODERN CRITIQUE OF THE).

In the 1960s and 1970s, Lacan's work concentrates on Freud's least accepted thesis. As (Boothby 1991) shows, Lacan takes the Freudian hypothesis of a 'death drive', strips it of its biological trappings and then places it at the centre of psychoanalysis: what the dynamism of symbolic desire sustains within the subject's world is precisely the release of those energies which, within the imaginary, could only gain expression through aggression – energies that necessarily evade the stasis of imaginary representation. The symbolic sublimates these energies, the energies of the death drive, by putting them to work in the process by which language erodes identity. With these ideas, Lacan devotes his latest work to what he calls the 'impossible real', to that which is forbidden entry into representation.

See also: FREUD; PSYCHOANALYSIS, POST-FREUDIAN §3; STRUCTURALISM; STRUCTURALISM IN SOCIAL SCIENCE §3

List of works

Lacan, J. (1966) *Écrits*, Paris: Éditions du Seuil; selections trans. A. Sheridan. *écrits: A Selection*, New York: W.W. Norton, 1977. (Lacan's major collection of writings, while containing such seminal pieces as the essay on the 'mirror stage' and the 'Rome Discourse', is extraordinarily difficult. Beginners are advised to start with Le Séminaire.)

—— (1974) *Télévision*, Paris: Éditions du Seuil; trans. D. Hollier, R. Krauss, A. Michelson and J. Mehlman, *'Television' and 'A Challenge to the Psychoanalytic Establishment'*, ed. J. Copjec, New York: W.W. Norton, 1990. (Texts relating to the institutionalization of psychoanalysis including docments from Lacan's secession from the Societé Psychanalytique de Paris and his foundation of the École Freudienne de Paris.)

—— (1975-94) *Le Séminaire de Jacques Lacan*, texte établi par Jacques-Lacan à Jacques-Alain Miller, vol. 1, *Les Écrits techniques de Freud*, vol. 2. *Le Moi dans la théorie de Freud et dans la technique de la psychanalyse*, vol. 3, *Les Psychoses*, 1955-6, vol. 4, *La Relation d'objet*, 1956-7, vol. 7, *L'éthique de la psychanalyse*, 1959-60, vol. 8, *Le Transfert*, 1960-1, vol. 11, *Les Quatre Concepts fondamentaux de la psychanalyse*, vol. 17, *L'Envers de la psychanalyse*, 1969-70, vol. 20, *Encore*, Paris: Éditions du Seuil; vol. 1 trans. J. Forrester, *Freud's Papers on Technique*, vol. 2 trans. S. Tomaselli, *The Ego in Freud's Theory and in the Technique of Psychoanalysis*, 1954-5, vol. 3 trans. R. Grigg, *The Psychoses*, 1955-6, vol. 7 trans. D. Porter, *The Ethics of Psychoanalysis*, all ed. J.-A. Miller, New York: W.W. Norton. (Transcriptions of Lacan's weekly public teaching seminar which ran, with a few breaks, from 1953 until 1979–80. Far more accessible for the beginner than *Écrits*.)

—— (1980) *De la psychose paranoïque dans ses rapports avec la personnalité* (On Paranoid Psychosis in its Relationship with the Personality), Paris: Éditions du Seuil. (Lacan's 1932 doctoral thesis in psychiatry.)

—— (1981) *The Four Fundamental Concepts of Psycho-Analysis*, trans. A Sheridan, New York: W.W. Norton. (Lacan's seminar for 1963 in an early translation.)

Lacan, J. and the École Freudienne (1982) *Feminine Sexuality*, New York: W.W. Norton. (Late writings on feminine sexuality by Lacan and various disciples.)

References and further reading

* Boothby, R. (1991) *Death and Desire: Psychoanalytic Theory in Lacan's Return to Freud*, New York: Routledge. (Boothby's approach provides an excellent introduction to Lacan; by using the Freudian death drive, he ties together all of Lacan's work in an extremely convincing and clear way.)

Weber, S.M. (1991) *Return to Freud*, Cambridge and New York: Cambridge University Press. (Weber's introduction to Lacan, translated from lectures originally delivered in German, locates his work within the context of French post-structuralism.)

Zizek, S. (1991) *For They Know not What They Do: Enjoyment as a Political Factor*, London and New York: Verso. (Zizek, perhaps the most brilliant interpreter of Lacan today, uses Lacan as a tool for interpreting political ideology.)

THOMAS BROCKELMAN

LACHELIER, JULES (1832–1918)

Lachelier is, along with Octave Hamelin, one of the foremost French metaphysicians of the nineteenth century. An idealist, he was a major figure in the neo-spiritualist movement, which opposed the materialism dominating scientific thought at the time. For all that, Lachelier did not set up a division between consciousness and life, but, following the example of Maine de Biran and Ravaisson, he rather saw in mind the inwardness of life, at work in the whole of nature.

As a student, Lachelier graduated top in the *agrégation* in philosophy, and in 1871 he defended his doctoral theses, 'Du fondement de l'induction' (On the Basis of Induction) (1871) and 'De natura syllogismi' (On the Nature of the Syllogism). In the former, he showed that the real inductive process assumes not only the principle of causality but also a principle of persistence for essences, which are perceived through the individual, and which orientate themselves in relation to one another in a hierarchy. 'Harmony is in some way the supreme interest of nature' ([1902] 1871: 70). Nature cannot be completely external to thought, since then it would be as if it did not exist for us. It is therefore necessary to find some way of both 'making thought real, and making nature intelligible' ([1902] 1871: 74).

The article 'Psychologie et métaphysique' (Psychology and Metaphysics) (1885) is perhaps Lachelier's greatest work, in which he goes far beyond the dogmatism of Victor Cousin. He begins by remarking that to be extended and to perceive extension are two distinct things, and neither of them is sufficient to define a consciousness. Extension appears to be outside us, but this externality is our work. Extension cannot exist in itself, because its parts, which are infinitely divisible, would be without continuity if separated from thought. Extension is 'a whole, whose parts divide but do not constitute it' (1902 [1885]: 188). Its continuity comes to it from the mind, and the perception of depth, for example, is nothing more than 'a spontaneous product of our thought'; it represents a beyond.

Consciousness is therefore primary. Further, instead of saying with the materialists that it progresses from perception to will, the contrary is true, in that it descends from will to perception. In sensation, there is always something affective. Sensibility senses itself; at the same time, it feels some quality. Thus, the subject is given to itself, and distinguishes itself from the external world.

However, we cannot say that our affections are ourselves. We ourselves *make* our feelings through our own love or hatred. The awareness of each feeling includes the operation of some tendency and ultimately the will to live. And 'if we do not feel our will, this is not because it is nothing, but because it is ourselves' (1902 [1885]: 194). Will is the principle and the hidden source of everything. Man is the only being which fixes qualities in extension and composes 'this permanent mirage which he calls the external world' (1902 [1885]: 195). But the pure will – which is closer to that envisaged by SCHOPENHAUER than MAINE DE BIRAN (§3) – goes beyond individual existence. The self is the will refracted in the affective state whose form expresses one's character. It is found only to be lost.

From psychological analysis, Lachelier moves towards synthesis, where the primary place is given to the idea of truth. Even at the level of physical pain, it is necessary to say that 'consciousness of pain is not painful, but true' ([1902] 1885: 201). This is an elegant idea, with a hint of stoicism, for which Lachelier has often been criticized, since if the feeling of pain is not painful, how can it be true, that is to say, conform to its object? Moreover, it is above all the property of pain to be essentially present, so that no memory or idea can affect it; it is an existential shock that one also finds at the height of physical joy. But Lachelier wants to say that psychological consciousness is based on an *intellectual* consciousness, which gives it the seal of objectivity. Therefore consciousness resides in the final analysis in the truth of being, and the idea of being, being itself of being, can construct itself, from the sphere of logical necessity right up to that of living things.

The final word is given to a dialectic of liberty, through which the being that supports us produces itself. The subject is not an act, but a form, and Lachelier eloquently puts away 'any idea of a special and mysterious subject, the transcendent I in the sensible consciousness. Such a subject would in fact be only one more object', 'To know something one must in some manner *be* that very thing, and to accomplish this one must not in the first instance be other than oneself' ([1902] 1885: 206). Besides, if by some supernatural act the self of another person was put in place of one's own, it would be absolutely impossible for us to see this. In short, individuality is based on the simple connection of memories. On the other hand, the 'light of thought' is infinitely greater than the individual self and escapes its grasp, because it is of the order of having to be rather than being. The progress of thought ends when, after seeking for itself in necessity as in its shadow, then in the will as in its body, it finally finds itself in freedom. There is not a fourth idea of being, because there is no fourth dimension of extension.

List of works

Lachelier, J. (1902) *Oeuvres*, vol. 1, Paris: Alcan, 4th edn. (The standard complete works, containing 'Du fondement de l'induction' (On the Basis of Induction) (1871), 'Psychologie et Métaphysique' (Psychology and Metaphysics) (1885) and 'Note sur le pari de Pascal' (Note on Pascal's Wager) (1907).)

—— (1907) *Oeuvres*, vol. 2, Paris: Alcan, 4th edn. (This second volume of the complete works contains 'Études sur le syllogisme' (Studies on the Syllogism) (1876, 1906), 'L'observation de Platner' (The Observation of Platner) (1903) and 'Note sur le Philèbe' (Note on Philebus) (1902).)

—— (1960) *The Philosophy of Jules Lachelier*, The Hague: Martinus Nijhoff. (An English translation of Lachelier's main works.)

References and further reading

Bouglé, C. (1937) *Les maîtres de la philosophie universitaire en France* (Masters of Academic Philosophy in France), Paris: Maloine. (A penetrating book in the mainstream university tradition.)

Duméry, H. (1957) *Philosophie de la religion* (Philosophy of Religion), Paris: Presses Universitaires de France. (An interesting and accessible work, written by a specialist in religious thought.)

Jolivet, R. (1934) 'Lachelier et l'idéalisme contemporain' (Lachelier and Contemporary Idealism), *Revue thomiste* (July–October). (A thorough article, but more ready to criticize than to understand.)

Millet, L. (1959) *Le Symbolisme dans la philosophie de Lachelier* (Symbolism in the Philosophy of Jules

Lachelier), Paris: Presses Universitaires de France. (A relatively recent and important study, which locates Lachelier in what is called 'reflexive' French philosophy.)

Séailles, G. (1920) *La philosophie de Jules Lachelier* (The Philosophy of Jules Lachelier), Paris: Alcan. (A basic study by a thinker under the influence of Ravaisson.)

Translated by Robert Stern

MICHEL PICLIN

LACOUE-LABARTHE, PHILIPPE (1940–)

Philippe Lacoue-Labarthe is Professor of Philosophy at the universities of Strasbourg and Berkeley. At the centre of his thought is philosophy's ostracism of literature, which in his view characterizes the foundational scene of philosophy itself. Lacoue-Labarthe demonstrates how all Western thought, including Heidegger (perhaps its most faithful deconstructor) lies within a conception of mimesis which is still metaphysical in that it remains bound to the opposition between truth and mimesis: an 'imitation' alters (or falsifies) its original, thus contrasting with that which is 'true'. The non-metaphysical thought of mimesis proposed by Lacoue-Labarthe, by contrast, shows how a mimetic aspect structures the concept of truth itself, making it impossible to distinguish between truth and verisimilitude, model and copy. Thus a new area of investigation is laid open concerning fictional modes of thought: the manner in which myths and figures are produced.

Lacoue-Labarthe's thought is largely a rereading of the history of philosophy, from the Greeks to the present day. In Plato's *Republic*, the affirmation of philosophy's superiority runs parallel to a devaluing of literature (*mythopoïesis*, telling of myths). Mytho-poetical activity is devalued because *mimesis* (see MIMĒSIS), imitation, pertains, not to truth, but to verisimilitude (myths are fiction, falsifications of the original). Such activity, Lacoue-Labarthe argues, necessitates a passive, and so unfree, attitude on the part of the subject.

A similar bias against literature characterizes the whole Western tradition, at least up to what Lacoue-Labarthe calls the 'Romantic moment', which continues down to the present. With early German Romanticism, literature (poetry, in particular) starts to be re-evaluated as a place of truth. Traces of this re-evaluation can be found in Hölderlin, Heidegger and Celan (see HÖLDERLIN, J.C.F.; ROMANTICISM, GERMAN). Lacoue-Labarthe's own thought is situated, in a rather peculiar way, inside this 'anti-Platonic' tradition: hence his interest in early German Romanticism (*L'Absolu littéraire*, 1978, with Jean-Luc Nancy), idealism, Nietzsche and Heidegger.

In this, Lacoue-Labarthe attributes a particularly important role to HEIDEGGER, whose thought constitutes the most extreme and complete attempt at deconstruction of the metaphysical tradition. Such thought was also responsible, however, for Heidegger's calamitous association with National Socialism in 1933. Many of Lacoue-Labarthe's works seek to explain this unsettling combination of totally different aspects in Heidegger's thought.

First, in the key work *Typographie* (1975) (*Typography*, 1989), Lacoue-Labarthe demonstrates how in Heidegger a Platonic conception of *mimesis* – thus truth – still persists and is to a large extent undisputed. Truth is, in fact, conceived as a static determination of Being, the erection of a 'pedestal', or 'stele' (translation of *Ge–stell*, a key term in Heidegger's later works). For this reason Lacoue-Labarthe proposes setting the term *onto–theo–logy* (used by Heidegger to indicate Western metaphysics) side by side with the term *onto–typo–logy*, which would characterize the tradition of Western metaphysics *and*, at least partially, Heidegger's own thought. The concept of *onto–typo–logy* restates Heidegger's 'onto-logical difference' in light of the question about *mimesis*: Being is considered in the fixed quality of a *typos* (type, seal, stamp) from which beings originate as traces or imprints which resemble the *typos* itself. This means that Heidegger thinks, as is the case in the Platonic model, that the mimetic relationship between Being and beings corrupts the truth of Being.

Second, in *La Fiction du politique* (1988) (*Heidegger, Art and Politics: The Fiction of the Political*, 1989), *L'Imitation des modernes* (1986a) as well as, in other, new ways, *La Poésie comme expérience* (1986b, dedicated to Paul Celan), and *Musica ficta (figures de Wagner)* (1991) (*Musica Ficta: Figures of Wagner*, 1995), Lacoue-Labarthe demonstrates how the figural immutability characterizing thought in general is again found, with notable force, in Heidegger's reflection on art after 1933, in which the work of art is thought of above all as shape and support (*Gestalt* and *Ge–stell*) of truth. This way of thinking reveals, according to Lacoue-Labarthe, the 'mythical' nature of National Socialism. For, as he argues in 'The Nazi Myth' (1989, with Jean-Luc Nancy), Nazi ideology repeats the constitutive traits of the mythic process. By means of the creation of great ideal figures (leader as figure *par excellence*), it attempts to respond to the demand for identity on the part of the German people: the community identifies itself with the figure and fashions itself as would a work of art. In reality, National Socialism is, for Lacoue-Labarthe, a National *Aestheticism*. Entirely apart from his adhesion to the Nazi Party in 1933, then, Heidegger's thought would appear to demonstrate both a pronounced proximity *and* a total distancing from National Socialism.

Lacoue-Labarthe's complex relationship with Heidegger places him in a position within post-Romantic and anti-Platonic thought which is unique in three ways. First, he opens a new conception of *mimesis*, according to which it does not corrupt truth but rather is co-originating. The two conceptions of truth pointed out by Heidegger are articulated together: *aletheia*, truth as 'revealing', always tends towards *adaequatio*, truth as adequation, but each time finds itself only to be inadequate to itself. Second, he presents a new image of the subject. In essays such as 'L'Écho du sujet' (in *Le Sujet de la Philosophie*, 1979) and 'Le Titre de la lettre' [1973, with Jean-Luc Nancy], Lacoue-Labarthe confronts psychoanalysis, which itself is based on a mimetological mythography (for example, Oedipus). Against the speculative dream of a subject capable of theorizing about its own conception, Lacoue-Labarthe sets up an image of a subject which is constitutively incomplete. The truth of the subject is captured by its verisimilitude: by the inexhaustible tension of resembling itself, which must always surrender and fail. The subject can therefore never become a figure, because every figure of the origin of the subject falls back to an engendering of the figure itself. This deconstruction of the concepts of origin and dichotomous conceptuality draws Lacoue-Labarthe's thought close to that of Jacques DERRIDA. Third, he produces an esthetic and ethical-political position which is unique, though in certain aspects close to that of Maurice BLANCHOT. In Lacoue-Labarthe's view, the incompleteness of the subject tends towards a state of impotence which must not be thought of as passivity. It is rather more a *désistance*, a stoic, active existence/resistance. The human being, by actively protecting its own passivity and the lack of a figure capable of identifying it, can thus oppose itself to any form of totalization and totalitarianism.

See also: HEIDEGGER, M.; NANCY, J.-L.

List of works

Lacoue-Labarthe, P. (1975) *Typographie*, Paris: Aubier-Flammarion; trans. *Typography: Mimesis, Philosophy, Politics*, Cambridge, MA: Harvard University Press, 1989. (Collection of essays on mimesis, art and politics, Nietzsche, Heidegger, Diderot, Hölderin and others.)

Lacoue-Labarthe, P. with J.-L. Nancy (1978) *L'Absolu littéraire: théorie de la littérature du romantisme allemand*, Paris: Éditions du Seuil; trans. *The Literary Absolute: The Theory of Literature in German Romanticism*, Albany, NY: State University of New York Press, 1988. (Anthology of writings on literary theory in German Romanticism – in particular from the *Atheneum* – with full introdcution and comments.)

Lacoue-Labarthe, P. (1986a) *L'Imitation des modernes (Typographies 2)*, Paris: Galilée; trans. in *Typography: Mimesis, Philosophy, Politics*, Cambridge, MA: Harvard University Press, 1989.

—— (1986b) *La Poésie comme expérience*, Paris: Christian Bourgois.

—— (1987) *La Fiction du politique*, Paris: Christian Bourgois; trans. C. Turner, *Heidegger, Art and Politics: The Fiction of the Political*, Oxford: Blackwell, 1989. (Heideggerian allegiance to national socialism and what it shows about modern politics; modern politics is based on the imitation of the classical ideal ('the Greek model') and on art and myth insofar as they are the means of a people's cultural identity.)

Lacoue-Labarthe, P. with Nancy, J.-L. (1989) 'The Nazi Myth', *Critical Inquiry* 16 (2): 291–312.; trans. into French as *Le Mythe nazi*, La Tour d'Aigues: Éditions de l'Aube, 1991. (Nazi ideology as a process of the constitution of the myth, an extreme symptom of the treatment of the political as aesthetics.)

Lacoue-Labarthe, P. (1973) *La titre de la lettre: une lecture de Lacan*, Paris: Galilée; trans. *The Title of the Letter: A Reading of Lacan*, Albany, NY: State University of New York Press, 1992. (A deconstructive reading of Lacan.)

—— (1979) *Le Sujet de la philosophie*, Paris: Aubier-Flammarion; trans. *The Subject of Philosophy*, Minneapolis, MN: University of Minnesota Press, 1993. (Collection of essays on literature and philosophy, music and philosophy, and Nietzsche, Heidegger and Reick.)

—— (1991) *Musica ficta (figures de Wagner)*, Paris: Christian Bourgois: trans. F. McCarren, *Musica Ficta: Figures of Wagner*, Stanford, CA: Stanford University Press, 1995. (Four readings of Wagner (Baudelaire, Mallarmé, Heidegger and Adorno) show how the political can be treated as aesthetics and explain the split between Nietzsche and Wagner.)

References and further reading

Derrida, J. (1989) 'Désistance', in P. Lacoue-Labarthe, *Typography: Mimesis, Philosophy, Politics*, Cambridge, MA: Harvard University Press. (A rereading of Lacoue-Labarthe's thought starting from a term (désister) which alludes to a condition of dispossession of the subject.)

Translated by William Finley Green

GIOVANNI SCIBILIA

LAKATOS, IMRE (1922–74)

Imre Lakatos made important contributions to the philosophy of mathematics and of science. His 'Proofs and Refutations' (1963–4) develops a novel account of mathematical discovery. It shows that counterexamples ('refutations') play an important role in mathematics as well as in science and argues that both proofs and theorems are gradually improved by searching for counterexamples and by systematic 'proof analysis'. His 'methodology of scientific research programmes' (which he presented as a 'synthesis' of the accounts of science given by Popper and by Kuhn) is based on the idea that science is best analysed, not in terms of single theories, but in terms of broader units called research programmes. Such programmes issue in particular theories, but in a way again governed by clear-cut heuristic principles. Lakatos claimed that his account supplies the sharp criteria of 'progress' and 'degeneration' missing from Kuhn's account, and hence captures the 'rationality' of scientific development. Lakatos also articulated a 'meta-methodology' for appraising rival methodologies of science in terms of the 'rational reconstructions' of history they provide.

1   Life
2   'Proofs and Refutations': contributions to philosophy of mathematics
3   The 'methodology of scientific research programmes': contributions to philosophy of science

1   Life

Imre Lakatos was born Imre Lipschitz in Hungary in 1922. His early life was turbulent even by the remarkable standards of the time. He was a member of the resistance during the Second World War, fortunately evading arrest (unlike his mother and grandmother, both of whom were murdered in Auschwitz). After the war he pursued a political

career and by 1947 had become a powerful figure within the Hungarian Ministry of Education; in 1950, however, he was arrested and spent over three years in a Stalinist jail. Informed of the likelihood of rearrest, he fled in 1956 to Vienna, and eventually to Cambridge, where he studied for a (second) doctorate under the supervision of R.B. Braithwaite.

In the course of these studies, he became a regular attender of Karl POPPER's seminar at the London School of Economics, and Popper's thought and approach had a major influence on him. Lakatos was appointed to a Lectureship at the LSE in 1960, and spent the rest of his life there, being awarded a personal chair in 1970. For unrevealed reasons, the British Home Office rebuffed two impressively supported attempts to obtain British citizenship and Lakatos remained officially 'stateless'. He died suddenly, from a heart attack, in February 1974. He had a vivid personality, strong political views and a sharp wit: he inspired intense loyalty and opposition in roughly equal measures.

2   'Proofs and Refutations': contributions to philosophy of mathematics

Lakatos published some philosophical articles (mostly book reviews) before coming to the West, and some commentators discern the influence of his Marxist and Hegelian education throughout his career, but his significant contributions to philosophy were all made after arriving in the West. His doctoral studies at Cambridge eventually formed the basis for his 'Proofs and Refutations' (originally published as a series of four journal articles in 1963–4, and in book form with further material only posthumously in 1976). Perhaps his major work, it consists of an imaginary discussion between a teacher and a group of his (frighteningly bright) students. The first part reconstructs the history of the attempts to prove the Descartes–Euler conjecture about polyhedra (that the number of vertices minus the number of edges plus the number of faces is equal to two for any polyhedron). The real history is told in the many footnotes. A second part of the discussion reconstructs the discovery of uniform convergence as the result of the 'refutation' of one of Cauchy's results. Aside from its philosophical and historical interest, the dialogue is a literary *tour de force*.

Lakatos argued that the standard picture of the development of mathematics is seriously faulty. On that picture, either an assertion is conjectured to hold and after a time a proof of it is produced, or mathematicians simply set out to 'prove' from some agreed axiomatic basis, recording as a 'theorem' any result which they hit upon that happens to interest them. Lakatos suggested that in fact theorems are invariably conjectured ahead of proof, and the proof process is a protracted affair in which initial attempts are criticized and gradually improved, along with the 'theorem' itself. At first this is trial-and-error, involving searches for counterexamples both to the original 'theorem' and to the 'hidden assumptions' that are articulated in the course of initial attempted proofs.

This trial-and-error phase of conjecture followed by undirected search for proof and/or counterexample is eventually superseded, however, by a more systematic phase – that of 'proof analysis'. Lakatos – inspired by his countryman Polya – argued that the process of mathematical discovery is not a 'merely' psychological affair to be studied by trying to delve into the minds of the great mathematicians, but can be shown instead to be governed by articulable heuristic principles. Hans REICHENBACH, Popper and the Logical Positivists all saw an unbridgeable divide between – in Reichenbach's terminology – the 'context of justification' and the 'context of discovery'; and all asserted that philosophy or logic of science is concerned only with the former 'context'. Questions of discovery were alleged neither to call for logical analysis nor to be susceptible of it. Lakatos argued that, in the case of mathematics at least, this view is importantly mistaken, and that there is a realm of logically analysable, mathematical heuristic outside the two traditional 'contexts'. This claim forms an important link with Lakatos's later contributions to the philosophy of science (see DISCOVERY, LOGIC OF §2).

One of the intriguing (but often frustrating) aspects of 'Proofs and Refutations' is that its dialogue form, although used to brilliant effect, sometimes makes it difficult to discern what thesis is actually being propounded: not even 'Teacher' is always right. This has resulted in some obscurity about the underlying view of the nature of mathematical knowledge. Lakatos himself believed that his message was fundamentally Popperian – that he was extending Popper's fallibilism into the area of mathematics. Another view – indicated in the book's editorial footnotes – is that Lakatos simply described (in fascinating detail) the fallible *process* by which essentially infallible, logically true, knowledge is created in mathematics. These editorial footnotes have themselves been attacked as a 'betrayal' of the real 'anti-formalist' message of the book (Davis and Hersch 1981).

3 The 'methodology of scientific research programmes': contributions to philosophy of science

After 'Proofs and Refutations', Lakatos turned his attention to the philosophy of science. Although his 1968 paper 'Changes in the Problem of Inductive Logic' defends a broadly Popperian line against Carnapian 'inductive logic', Lakatos soon came to see major defects in the Popperian approach. 'Popper on Demarcation and Induction' (1974) contains a detailed criticism of Popper's claim to have solved Hume's problem. Popperian corroboration appraisals are simply summaries of how the available theories have stood up to testing *so far*. Those appraisals, therefore, can have no consequences for the comparative future reliabilities of the various theories, nor for the reasonableness of relying on one theory rather than a rival in future applications, unless some assumption is made that – in Popperian terms – links corroboration appraisals to claims about overall 'verisimilitude'. Such an assumption amounts to a reformulation in Popperian terms of a uniformity-of-nature assumption, linking past test results to an overall judgment of the theory's truth-likeness and hence its reliability in past *and* future tests. That (merely posited) principle has, therefore, seemed to most commentators much stronger than a mere 'whiff' of induction, as Lakatos represented it.

Although argued in a new way, Lakatos's point here is similar to arguments against Popper already produced by Reichenbach, Ayer, Salmon and others. Lakatos's views on 'demarcation' were altogether more innovative. Thomas KUHN had pointed out (1962 and elsewhere) that many aspects of the development of science seem at direct odds with Popper's falsificationist account. For example, the typical response of a theoretician to an experimental 'refutation' of his favoured theory is not, as Popper seemed to suggest, to reject that theory and look for an alternative, but instead to treat the experimental result as an 'anomaly' which could and should be accommodated within the theory. Lakatos saw his 'methodology of scientific research programmes' (further developed and defended in his 1970 paper) as a synthesis of the views of Popper and of Kuhn. He agreed with Kuhn that the correct unit of analysis in science is much broader than that of a single theory. A Lakatosian research programme is characterized by a 'negative heuristic' principle specifying its 'hard core' (the set of basic propositions that will be implied by every theory that issues from it), and by a 'positive heuristic' (a set of directives, possibly deriving from some broad metaphysical principle, governing the construction of specific theories within the programme, and governing their modification in the light of experimental difficulties that may arise). Specific theories produced by a programme *are* experimentally refutable (or would be if fully articulated), but the standard response to an actual refutation will be to look for a further specific theory within the same programme. Since this successor theory will also entail the same central ('hard core') claims, this process will seem like 'holding onto' a theory by 'modifying' it in the light of experimental difficulties, rather than rejecting it.

This sounds like Kuhn's idea of 'articulating the paradigm' and treating experimental difficulties as 'anomalies'. According to Lakatos, the main problem with Kuhn's account is that it seems not to be able to explain scientific change as a rational process. What distinguishes a proper, scientific further articulation of a paradigm or programme from a defensive nonscientific one? If it was good scientific practice for Newtonians to defend their basic 'paradigm' or 'hard core' against their failure to explain Uranus's orbit by postulating a hitherto unknown planet, was it not equally good scientific practice for phlogistonists to defend their theory – that combustion always involves release of phlogiston – against the fact that burning mercury in air produces a heavier 'ash' by postulating negative weight for phlogiston (or by postulating that burning mercury involves both the release and the absorption of material)? A second, related problem is that the distinction between real science and pseudoscience seems to be endangered by Kuhn's account. Kuhn seems committed to the view that there are no articulable 'logical' rules of good science or of correct response to evidence. Priestley was not 'wrong or unscientific' to hold on to the phlogiston theory, he was simply outvoted.

Lakatos argued that there is in fact a clear-cut distinction here – one based on the old idea of independent evidence, but given a new slant. The difference between, for example, the Newtonian shift and that involved in defending phlogistonism is the difference between a 'progressive' and a 'degenerating problem shift'. The postulation of a further planet to explain the anomalous motion of Uranus within Newtonian theory not only solved the problem of Uranus's motion but also led to further independently testable predictions – the new planet could after all be observed. On the other hand, the shift in phlogistonist assumptions simply *at best* resolved the known anomaly, while making no further testable predictions.

Lakatos was always interested in the relationship between the philosophy of science (and mathematics) and its history and felt that philosophy of science in the post-war period had suffered from its paying too

little attention to actual scientific practice. In his 1971 paper 'History of Science and its Rational Reconstructions', he proposed a general method for the evaluation of rival philosophies or methodologies of science in terms of the 'rational reconstructions' they provide of the history of science and especially of historical episodes of major changes in accepted theories. His basic idea was that there is a range of historical cases in which, speaking intuitively, the 'scientifically correct' decisions were clearly made (for example, the acceptance of Newtonian theory or of Maxwell's theory). A methodology should endorse (and so give a general explanation of) these cases; and should, in cases where it implies that the 'wrong' decision was made, be able to point to independent evidence for the operation of 'external factors' (political or religious interference, for example). He argued that his own methodology did better on these terms than other accounts, such as inductivism, conventionalism or Popperian falsificationism.

See also: EXPERIMENT §2; FEYERABEND, P.K. ; SCIENTIFIC METHOD §2; THEORIES, SCIENTIFIC §8

List of works

Lakatos, I. (1963–4) 'Proofs and Refutations', *The British Journal for the Philosophy of Science* 14: 1–25, 120–39, 221–43, 296–342; repr. with editorial footnotes in Lakatos 1976. (The original published version of Lakatos's major work in the philosophy of mathematics.)

—— (1968) 'Changes in the Problem of Inductive Logic', in I. Lakatos (ed.) *The Problem of Inductive Logic*, Amsterdam: North Holland; repr. in Lakatos 1978. (Lakatos's account of the dispute between Carnap and Popper over probabilistic, inductive logic.)

—— (1970) 'Falsificationism and the Methodology of Scientific Research Programmes', in I. Lakatos and A.E. Musgrave (eds) *Criticism and the Growth of Knowledge*, Cambridge: Cambridge University Press, 1970; repr. in Lakatos 1978. (The definitive account of Lakatos's views on scientific research programmes and their development.)

—— (1971) 'History of Science and its Rational Reconstructions', in R.C. Buck and R.S. Cohen (eds) *PSA 1970, Boston Studies in the Philosophy of Science 8*, Dordrecht: Reidel; repr. in Lakatos 1978. (This paper contains Lakatos's views about 'meta-methodology': how to evaluate rival theory-appraisal criteria.)

—— (1974) 'Popper on Demarcation and Induction', in P.A. Schillp (ed.) *The Philosophy of Karl Popper*, Library of Living Philosophers, La Salle, IL: Open

Court; repr. in Lakatos 1978. (Lakatos's appeal to Popper for a 'whiff of induction' and a systematic comparison of his views on science with those of Popper.)

—— (1976) *Proofs and Refutations: The Logic of Mathematical Discovery*, ed. J. Worrall and E. Zahar, Cambridge: Cambridge University Press. (This book contains extra material on Cauchy and uniform convergence as well as the original 1963–4 papers.)

—— (1978) *The Methodology of Scientific Research Programmes: Philosophical Papers vol. 1*, ed. J. Worrall and G. Currie, Cambridge: Cambridge University Press. (Volume 1 of Lakatos's collected papers.)

—— (1978) *Mathematics, Science and Epistemology: Philosophical Papers vol. 2*, ed. J. Worrall and G. Currie, Cambridge: Cambridge University Press. (Volume 2 of Lakatos's collected papers, including some hitherto unpublished material.)

References and further reading

* Davis, P.J. and Hersh, R. (1981) *The Mathematical Experience*, Brighton: Harvester. (Contains an endorsement of some of Lakatos's views on mathematics and criticism of the editorial footnotes in Lakatos 1976.)

Hacking, I. (1983) *Representing and Intervening: Introductory Topics in the Philosophy of Natural Science*, Cambridge: Cambridge University Press. (Contains an important chapter on Lakatos's methodology of research programmes.)

Howson, C. (ed.) (1976) *Method and Appraisal in the Physical Sciences*, Cambridge: Cambridge University Press. (Contains several 'case studies' of important episodes of theory-change in the history of science analysed from the point of view of the methodology of scientific research programmes.)

* Kuhn, T.S. (1962) *The Structure of Scientific Revolutions*, Chicago, IL: University of Chicago Press, 2nd edn, 1970. (The most influential contemporary account of theory-change in science.)

Lakatos, I. and Musgrave, A.E. (eds) (1970) *Criticism and the Growth of Knowledge*, Cambridge: Cambridge University Press. (Contains an outline of Kuhn's account of science, together with a range of commentaries and Kuhn's replies.)

Newton-Smith, W.H. (1981) *The Rationality of Science*, London: Routledge. (Contains a sympathetic, but critical analysis of the views of Lakatos and of related authors on scientific progress.)

Zahar, E.G. (1989) *Einstein's Revolution: A Study in Heuristic*, La Salle, IL: Open Court. (A critical account of the methodology of scientific research

programmes, including a significant elaboration of the idea of rationally analysable heuristic, together with an extended case study of the relativistic revolution.)

JOHN WORRALL

LAMBDA CALCULUS

The lambda calculus presents a delimited formal setting for expressing and studying properties of mathematical operations and computer programs. Its syntactical unit is the term. Application terms tu represent supplying argument u to routine t. Abstraction terms λx.t (in which λx binds x in t) represent the explicit definition of an operation from a routine t. Term computation is by reduction: (λx.t)(u) reduces to t[x/u], the result of substituting u for x in t; this corresponds to operating with t on u. Terms are equal either when they differ only in bound variables or when one converts to the other via a finite chain of reductions and counter-reductions. There are two main varieties of lambda calculi: typed and untyped (or type-free). Any untyped term is applicable to any other and equality between such terms is undecidable. In the typed case, terms are indexed by types and application is permitted only when types conform. Here, equality is decidable. A. Church proposed formalisms for both varieties during the 1930s. He and his students S. Kleene and J. Rosser proved the early syntactical metatheorems linking the untyped calculus with computability theory. In 1969, D. Scott gave the first set-theoretic construction of a functional model of the untyped calculus; since then, many other models have been devised. As for the typed calculus, Gödel's Dialectica *interpretation inspired many of its applications to proof theory. Also, the idea, due to H. Curry and W. Howard, of using logical formulas as types reveals a close correspondence between typed terms and derivations in intuitionistic formal systems. In the last decades of the twentieth century, the lambda calculus and its models have been put to many uses in computer science, with functional programming and denotational semantics deserving special mention.*

1   **Abstraction, application and currying**
2   **A formal calculus of terms**
3   **Computations, reductions and normal terms**
4   **Arithmetic and undecidability**
5   **Models**
6   **Typed lambda calculi**
7   **Computers and the lambda calculus**

1 Abstraction, application and currying

Gottlob Frege's doctrine of concepts and objects (1893) put abstract mathematical functions, including higher-order functions taking functions as inputs or yielding functions as outputs, at the centre of logic (see FREGE, G. §3). He insisted that adequate notation for functions must distinguish them from their values. For example, the expression $x^2 + 3x + 7$, for x a natural number, is ambiguous, denoting both the value of the expression at fixed input x and the function that yields $n^2 + 3n + 7$ for every value n of x. Frege realized that, to disambiguate, it suffices to bind x with a prefix operator, such as λx, to yield

$$(1) \qquad \lambda x . x^2 + 3x + 7.$$

(Frege's own notation did not employ λ but the Greek symbol for smooth breathing.) These expressions, conveniently displaying both independent variable and a recipe for computation, Frege took to denote functions (in *extension*). Such terms as (1), now called 'abstraction terms', reflect a Fregean notion of function as grasped by abstraction from its values: $0^2 + 3 \cdot 0 + 7$, $1^2 + 3 \cdot 1 + 7$ and so on. Those values are retrievable from (1) by application: the term

$$(\lambda x . x^2 + 3x + 7)(0)$$

denotes the value of the function on the input 0, which we compute by dropping λx and substituting 0 for x in $x^2 + 3x + 7$ to obtain $0^2 + 3 \cdot 0 + 7 = 7$.

In effect, Frege also recognized that lambda notation renders binary or multiary functions as combinations of unary ones, a conversion known as 'currying' after the logician H. Curry. For instance, a lambda term for addition, $\lambda x \lambda y . x + y$, denotes a function taking its arguments one at a time: first x and then y. Its evaluation at 2 yields a unary function

$$(\lambda x \lambda y . x + y)(2) = \lambda y . 2 + y,$$

which can be evaluated at 3:

$$(\lambda y . 2 + y)(3) = 2 + 3 = 5$$

to yield the desired result.

Alonzo CHURCH was the first to devise formal systems, which he called 'calculi of lambda-conversion' (1941), devoted primarily to codifying such properties of functions. He introduced lambda notation as a variant of the caret (⌢) employed in Whitehead and Russell's *Principia Mathematica* (1910–13) as abstraction operator. Church intended his calculi to capture an operational conception of function distinct from the extensional notion enshrined in set theory. Set theory conceives of functions as collections of ordered pairs with domain and range so delimited that application of arbitrary function to arbitrary input is prohibited. Hence, set theory does some injustice to operations which apply universally, such as identity, which maps anything to itself, or that operation taking each entity a to the constantly a-valued function. By Church's lights, expressions of the lambda calculus were to denote operations or 'functions in intension': mathematical rules, routines or programs for computing outputs from inputs which may apply universally, even applying to themselves.

2 A formal calculus of terms

There are two general varieties of lambda calculi: 'typed' and 'untyped' (or 'type-free'), both devised by Church. In either case, the basic syntactic category is that of the 'term' (or λ-term). Atomic terms are either variables or constants. Compound terms are of two kinds. There are 'application' terms: if t and u are both terms, so is tu, denoting the input of u to routine t. And, for explicit functions, there are 'λ-abstractions': if t is a term, so is $\lambda x . t$, where x is a variable and λ binds all occurrences of x. In typed systems, each term is also assigned a type and applications tu are well-formed only if the types of t and of u are suitable. (Further discussion of typed systems is postponed to §6). The untyped lambda calculus suffers no such restriction: self-applications such as xx and $(\lambda x . xx)(\lambda x . xx)$ are permitted. Sample untyped terms include $\lambda x . x$, $\lambda x . a$, $\lambda x \lambda y . x$, $\lambda y . y$. The first gives the identity function, the second (with a a constant) the constant a-valued function and the third the first projection function, mapping each item a to the constantly a-valued function $\lambda y . a$. The last yields the same function as the first: terms differing only in bound variables, known as 'α-congruent terms', are identified.

Closed abstraction terms without constants are called 'combinators'. Conventionally, combinators $\lambda x . x$, $\lambda x \lambda y . x$ and $\lambda x \lambda y \lambda z . xz(yz)$ are abbreviated I, K and S, respectively, where I stands for 'identity', K for the *Konstanzfunktion* yielding constant functions, and S for a general composition function or *Verschmelzungsfunktion*. This nomenclature derives from M. Schönfinkel's combinatory logic and signals that these lambda terms perform the same operations as their combinatory namesakes (see COMBINATORY LOGIC §1).

3 Computations, reductions and normal terms

It is in no way inaccurate to see lambda calculi as rudimentary programming languages, with terms representing computing recipes and their values. As a programming language, unrestricted application in the untyped lambda calculus realizes von Neumann's idea that programs serve also as data (see NEUMANN, J. VON). There is a notion of lambda calculus computation, which may, like real-life computation, lead to non-terminating 'infinite loops'. As will be apparent (see below) the lambda calculus programming language is rich enough to express all possible algorithms on the natural numbers and is illuminated by respectable concepts of program meaning or denotation.

The notion of 'reduction' (properly, β-reduction) is the principal analogue within the lambda calculus of finitary computation. It affords an analysis of a process of stepwise evaluation obeying a series of atomic, rule-governed steps. Every such step takes its start from the idea of abstraction term exploited above: $\lambda x.t$ names the recipe which begins computation when λx is removed and a name for an input is substituted where x appears free in t. In the lambda calculus, every atomic reduction step begins with a 'redex', an application term of the form $(\lambda x.t)u$ – setting us the project of evaluating recipe $\lambda x.t$ at input u. One replaces the redex with its 'contractum', term $t[x/u]$, the result of substituting u for all free occurrences of x in t (with bound variable changes to avoid clashes). 'Computing' in the lambda calculus is iterated reduction: term v reduces to w if w results from v via a finite number of one-step reductions or replacements of contractum for redex.

Terms are equal when they are interconvertible via computation. If u is derivable from t via a finite sequence of reductions and counter-reductions (perhaps with changes in bound variables) t β-equals (or β-converts to) u; symbolically, $t = u$. A lambda theory T is a set of formal equations between terms that extends β-equality: whenever t β-equals u, then $t = u$ belongs to T. Intuitively, correct reductions preserve the meanings of the terms involved; hence, β-equal terms share the same meaning. Lambda theories, as sets of equations, respect those meanings. (Lambda models make rigorous sense of these intuitions about meaning. See §5.)

A series of reductions terminates when no further reduction is possible. Irreducible terms are said to be in 'normal form'. It follows that any variable or constant is in normal form, as is any term $\lambda x.t$ in which t itself is normal. But, just as some computer programs loop infinitely, some untyped terms never reduce to a normal form: $(\lambda x.xxy)(\lambda x.xxy)$ reduces to $((\lambda x.xxy)(\lambda x.xxy))y$ and further reductions always reproduce the original redex. Though some untyped terms lack a normal form, when a term does so reduce, its normal form is unique, at least up to bound variables. This is a corollary of the crucial 'Church–Rosser theorem', which states that, if t reduces to u and to v, then there is a term w to which u and v both reduce.

Notions of equality alternative to β-equality are studied, among them $\beta\eta$-equality. This relation respects the 'η-rule': that $\lambda x.tx$ reduces to t when t does not contain x free.

4 Arithmetic and undecidability

Church and his students S. Kleene and J. Rosser showed, in effect, that, as a programming system, the untyped lambda calculus is comprehensive in that one can define any computable function within it, once natural numbers are represented. Let 0 be $\lambda x \lambda y.y$, 1 be $\lambda x \lambda y.xy$, 2 be $\lambda x \lambda y.x(xy)$, 3 be $\lambda x \lambda yx(x(xy))$, and so on. These 'Church numerals' possess the attractive property, exemplified by 3, that $3ab$ reduces to $a(a(ab))$. Also, all Church numerals are in normal form. Let $[[n]]$ stand for the Church numeral of n. A natural number function f, which may be partial, is λ-defined by t just in case, whenever $f(n)$ exists, $t[[n]]$ reduces to $[[f(n)]]$, and, if $f(n)$ is undefined, then $t[[n]]$ does not reduce to a normal form. A function is λ-definable when it has a λ-defining term.

During 1933, Church speculated that the λ-definable functions coincide with the algorithmically computable functions. This speculation came to be known as 'Church's thesis'. If Church's thesis is true, then every possible recipe for computing with the integers is λ-defined by a term in the untyped lambda calculus and every computation with that recipe appears as a reduction sequence involving that term. Church and Kleene were able to confirm Church's thesis by proving that every function which is Gödel–Herbrand general recursive is λ-definable. One proof of this requires the construction of fixed-point combinators: terms which, given t, yield u such that tu β-equals u. Y, the 'paradoxical combinator' discovered by Curry,

$$\lambda x.(\lambda y.x(yy))(\lambda y.x(yy))$$

is one such; applied to any t, Yt β-equals $t(Yt)$.

As befits a programming system, the untyped lambda calculus exhibits undecidability. In 1936, Church used the calculus to prove the undecidability of first-order logic, resolving Hilbert's *Entscheidungsproblem* ('decision problem'; see HILBERT'S PROGRAMME AND FORMALISM). A general undecidability theorem for the lambda calculus, first proved by D. Scott in 1963 and rediscovered by Curry in 1969, can be stated in terms of recursive separability. Two sets of terms are 'recursively separable' if there is a decidable set containing one and disjoint from the other. The 'Scott–Curry theorem' asserts that no two non-empty sets of terms closed under β-equality are recursively separable. A corollary is that untyped β-equality and normalizability are both undecidable.

5 Models

Until the late 1960s, syntactic study dominated research on the untyped lambda calculus. Term models were constructed but their elements were syntactic: equivalence classes of terms under such relations as β-equality. An obstacle to building models in set theory, models which capture Church's vision of a calculus of functions, was self-application. In standard set theory, self-application of functions is not permitted, since no set-theoretic function lies in its own domain.

In 1969, Scott constructed D_∞, the first recognizably functional model for the untyped case. Scott realized that terms can be interpreted successfully as continuous (rather than arbitrary) functions on complete partial orders. Here, a complete partial order is a partially ordered set with a least element and with least upper bounds for all directed subsets. A continuous function is one whose output values are determinable by finite approximations. D_∞ is a complete partial order enabling self-application, since it is isomorphic to the space of continuous functions from D_∞ into itself. Each element of D_∞ then plays two roles: as element of the model and as function on the model's domain.

Other models, some simpler in design, were soon forthcoming. G. Plotkin, in 1972, discovered the fundamental idea behind (what is now called) the graph model $P\omega$. The elements of $P\omega$ are subsets of the natural numbers. $P\omega$ is not isomorphic to its space of continuous functions but, since that space is embedded within $P\omega$, it interprets self-application. A general notion of lambda model, due to A. Meyer (1982) and Scott (1976), which both D_∞ and $P\omega$ exemplify, is tripartite, comprising non-empty domain D, binary application $\circ$ on D and a unary operation Λ. $\circ$ creates on D a model of combinatory logic while Λ serves as a 'functionalizer' mapping each d in D to the function taking a into $d \circ a$ (see COMBINATORY LOGIC §2). Soundness and completeness theorems confirm the adequacy of this general notion: every lambda model satisfies all basic principles of β-equality and every lambda theory has a lambda model. Intuitively, then, the meanings preserved by reductions are respected in every lambda model.

6 Typed lambda calculi

In the typed lambda calculus, inputs to a function given by a term, as well as its outputs, are restricted to a particular domain or type. For example, to say that term t has type $A \Rightarrow B$ will mean that its inputs are restricted to members of type A and its outputs to B. Hence, if $\mathbb{N}$ is the domain of natural numbers, the successor function on $\mathbb{N}$ is of type $\mathbb{N} \Rightarrow \mathbb{N}$. Typing renders formal two informal ideas. The first is the notion that every well-defined mathematical function bears a specific domain of inputs and range of outputs. The second is that underlying programming languages in which allowable inputs to a program are restricted to members of a particular type, say, natural numbers or integers. With respect to decidability, typing lambda terms makes for notable differences.

Types are defined inductively: there are atomic types and, whenever α and β are types, so is $\alpha \Rightarrow \beta$. One may interpret atomic types to include the natural numbers or the truth-values and compound types $\alpha \Rightarrow \beta$ as containing functions from type α to type β. Types are then used to index terms. Variables and constants, if any, are assumed typed. Application terms must accord with typing: if t is of type $\alpha \Rightarrow \beta$ and u is of type α, then (tu) is of type β. For abstraction terms, when x is of type α and t of type β, $\lambda x.t$ is of type $\alpha \Rightarrow \beta$.

It is straightforward to define natural concepts of reduction, equality and normality for typed terms. There are no self-applications or paradoxical combinators in typed systems. As A. Turing first proved, every typed term reduces to a normal form. Typed reduction also satisfies a Church–Rosser theorem. In fact, a strong normalization theorem obtains: given a typed term, every legitimate way of reducing it eventually ends in the same normal term. It follows that, in contrast with the untyped calculus, typed equality is decidable. Suitable Church numerals are constructible; the natural number functions definable by typed terms are, as discerned independently by H. Schwichtenberg and R. Statman, precisely the extended polynomials. These include integer polynomials such as $\lambda n.3n^2 + 6n + 4$, and functions defined from them using definitions by polynomial cases, for example, $3n^2 + 6n + 4$ if $n = 3$ and n^4 otherwise.

Proof-theoretic applications of typed lambda calculi are prominent. The calculus is extendible to a formalism T for describing the constructive functionals Gödel used in his *Dialectica* interpretation and proof of arithmetic's consistency (see INTUITIONISM §6). Terms in T admit a natural reduction relation which is Church–Rosser and terms are strongly normalizable.

In the typed calculus, if A, B and C are types, then compound types such as $A \Rightarrow (B \Rightarrow A)$ and

$$[A \Rightarrow (B \Rightarrow C)] \Rightarrow [(A \Rightarrow B) \Rightarrow (A \Rightarrow C)]$$

resemble formulas in implicational logic. Curry and R. Feys (1958) noted that these formulas, which are intuitionistically valid, are types suitable for the combinators *K* and *S*, respectively. Indeed, the correspondence is general: typed terms accord precisely with correct derivations in the implicational part of intuitionistic propositional logic with application mirroring *modus ponens* and abstraction conditional proof. Moreover, reductive simplifications in logical derivations coincide with reductions in the lambda calculus. This correlation of terms with proofs, known as the 'Curry–Howard isomorphism' or 'formulas as types', was successfully extended to first-order logic by W. Howard (1980) and to second-order logic by J.-Y. Girard.

7 Computers and the lambda calculus

Research on the lambda calculus is now closely allied with machine computation. For one thing, lambda calculi exhibit, in pure form, issues of decidability, non-termination and typing which face computer theorists. Also, the lambda calculus formalism has inspired a range of functional programming languages, including J. McCarthy's LISP and J. Reynold's GEDANKEN. Third, model theory for the lambda calculus gave rise to both operational and denotational semantics for programming languages. A semantics for a programming language is 'operational' when it explains the meaning of a program in terms of its effect upon the state of an abstract machine; it is 'denotational' when the meaning of a program is a mathematical function denoted by that program. P. Landin, in 1965, employed translation into the lambda calculus to give an operational semantics for the language ALGOL. In the early 1970s, Scott and C. Strachey used the ideas behind Scott's lambda calculus models to give denotational semantics for programming languages exhibiting such phenomena as recursion and non-termination.

See also: LOGICAL AND MATHEMATICAL TERMS, GLOSSARY OF

References and further reading

Barendregt, H. (1981) *The Lambda Calculus: Its Syntax and Semantics*, Amsterdam: North Holland, 2nd edn, 1984. (A bible of lambda calculus research; authoritative and detailed.)

* Church, A. (1941) *The Calculi of Lambda Conversion*, Princeton, NJ: Princeton University Press. (The original monograph on the lambda calculus.)

* Curry, H. and Feys, R. (1958) *Combinatory Logic*, vol. 1, Amsterdam: North Holland. (Once the premier work on the subject; it remains an excellent reference.)

* Frege, G. (1893) *Grundgesetze der Arithmetik: begriffsschriftlich abgeleitet*, vol. 1, Jena: Pohle; part 1 trans. and ed. M. Furth, *Basic Laws of Arithmetic: An Exposition of the System*, Berkeley, CA: University of California Press, 1964. (Furth's introduction is extremely helpful.)

Hindley, J. and Seldin, J. (1986) *Introduction to Combinators and λ-Calculus*, London Mathematical Society Student Texts no. 1, Cambridge: Cambridge University Press. (An excellent brief introduction to the subject. Highly recommended for beginners.)

* Howard, W. (1980) 'The Formulas-As-Types Notion of Construction', in J. Hindley and J. Seldin (eds) *To H.B. Curry: Essays on Combinatory Logic, Lambda Calculus and Formalism*, New York: Academic Press, 479–90. (The first publication of notes circulated informally in 1969.)

Kleene, S. (1981) 'Origins of Recursive Function Theory', *Annals of the History of Computing* 3: 52–67. (A fascinating eyewitness account of the birth of the lambda calculus and computability theory at Princeton in the early 1930s.)

Martin-Löf, P. (1984) *Intuitionistic Type Theory*, Naples: Bibliopolis. (Among the most influential contemporary developments of typed lambda calculus and formulas-as-types.)

* Meyer, A. (1982) 'What is a Model of the Lambda Calculus?', *Information and Control* 52: 87–122. (A brilliant and highly readable article on a unitary general semantics for the lambda calculus.)

Rosser, J.B. (1984) 'Highlights of the History of the Lambda Calculus', *Annals of the History of Computing* 6: 337–49. (Another fine memoir on the early days of lambda calculus research at Princeton and later developments.)

* Scott, D.S. (1976) 'Data Types as Lattices', *SIAM Journal of Computing* 5: 522–87. (A characteristically charming exposition of results by Scott, Plotkin and others on the graph model.)

Stenlund, S. (1972) *Combinators, λ-Terms and Proof Theory*, Dordrecht: Reidel. (Remains one of the best and most lucid introductions to the proof-theoretical applications of the lambda calculus; highly recommended.)

Stoy, J. (1977) *Denotational Semantics: The Scott–Strachey Approach to Programming Language Theory*, Cambridge, MA: MIT Press. (The first book-length introduction to Scott–Strachey semantics for programs.)

* Whitehead, A.N. and Russell, B.A.W. (1910–13) *Principia Mathematica*, Cambridge: Cambridge University Press, 3 vols; 2nd edn, 1925–7; repr. 1994. (The section 'Propositional Functions' in the

introduction's chapter 1 describes functional abstraction.)

DAVID CHARLES McCARTY

LAMBERT, JOHANN HEINRICH (1728–1777)

Lambert was a German mathematician, physicist, astronomer and philosopher, who was among the leading figures of German intellectual life in the late eighteenth century. As a practising scientist, who made important discoveries in many areas, Lambert was interested in philosophical questions regarding the methods of scientific knowledge. In his philosophical works he sought to reform metaphysics by subjecting it to the procedures and standards of mathematics, advocating a combination of conceptual analysis and deductive construction in philosophy. With Lambert the tradition of German rationalist thought reaches directly into the time of Kant, who had great esteem for his analytic skills.

Lambert was born in Mühlhausen, Alsace (then under Swiss dominion). Having received no regular schooling beyond the age of twelve, he was almost entirely self-taught. He undertook his studies and research activities in mathematics and the natural sciences while working in various auxiliary positions in Switzerland and Southern Germany. From 1748 to 1758 he served as tutor to a Swiss family. During the final two years of that appointment he accompanied two of his pupils on their grand tour of Western Europe, which led through the major university towns and allowed him to meet some of the leading scientists of his time. In 1759 he became a member of the newly founded Munich Academy, an association that was terminated in 1762 because Lambert failed to take up residency in Munich. In 1764 he travelled to Berlin, ostensibly on his way to St Petersburg, where he hoped to gain an appointment as member of the Academy. Rather than travelling on, he stayed in Berlin for the rest of his life, becoming a member of the Berlin Academy in 1765 and assuming the post of surveyor of public works in Prussia in the same year.

Lambert was one of the leading mathematicians and natural scientists of his time. In mathematics he proved the irrationality of pi, introduced hyperbolic functions into trigonometry and made contributions to probability theory and the development of non-Euclidean geometry. In physics, Lambert mainly worked on light, heat and humidity of the air. He founded the science of photometry and also made contributions to acoustics and meteorology. In his *Cosmologische Briefe über die Einrichtung des Weltbaues* (Cosmological Letters about the Structure of the Universe, 1761) he developed a hypothesis about the nebular origin of the universe akin to the one developed by Kant in his *Allgemeine Naturgeschichte und Theorie des Himmels* (Universal Natural History and Theory of the Heavens) of 1755, which was not known to Lambert at the time.

Lambert was first and foremost a mathematician and scientist and only second a philosopher. His philosophical works all date from the 1760s and are mainly concerned with questions of method. The major influences on Lambert's philosophical views were MALEBRANCHE, WOLFF and LOCKE. Lambert sought to improve the scientific standing of philosophy in general and metaphysics in particular by emulating mathematical procedures in philosophical reasoning. Like LEIBNIZ before him, he was intrigued by the idea of a universal characteristic that would allow the formal presentation and definite solution to problems of all kinds. Unfortunately Lambert did not pursue this project in the last ten years of his life, effectively abandoning philosophy in favour of mathematics and the physical sciences (see UNIVERSAL LANGUAGE).

The first of Lambert's two main philosophical works is the *Neues Organon oder Gedanken über die Erforschung und Bezeichnung des Wahren und dessen Unterscheidung vom Irrthum und Schein* (New Organon or Thoughts on the Investigation and Designation of the True and its Distinction from Error and Appearance) which appeared in 1764. The work is a treatise on logic in the Pietist tradition of Hoffmann and CRUSIUS, but also reflects the influence of Leibniz, Wolff and Locke. In line with contemporary practice, the more strictly logical core of the *New Organon* is enriched by psychological and methodological considerations. The work is organized in four parts. Part One, which is by far the most extensive, is the 'Dianoiology or Doctrine of the Laws of Thinking' and contains the traditional logical doctrines concerning concepts, judgments and syllogistic inferences. Important innovative topics include the discussion of the methodological status of questions and problems, the role of ordinary as well as scientific, experimental experience, and the distinction between historical and scientific knowledge. Moreover, Lambert introduces a linear symbolism for the representation of judgments, which is then employed in his syllogistic logic.

Part Two of the *Neues Organon* is the 'Alethiology or Doctrine of Truth'. Lambert's key concern here is with the nature and function of the simple concepts that serve as the building blocks for the logical construction of true propositions. Part Three, the 'Semiotics or Doctrine of the Designation of Thoughts and Things', features the traditional distinction between word, concept and thing but also includes interesting considerations on linguistic confusion. The work concludes with the 'Phenomenology or Doctrine of Appearance' (*Schein*), in which Lambert distinguishes between true and false appearance, discusses probable knowledge and investigates the role of appearance in various forms of cognition.

Lambert went on to apply the logical canon set forth in the *New Organon* in his second main contribution to philosophy, *Anlage zur Architectonic, oder Theorie des Einfachen und des Ersten in der philosophischen Erkenntniß* (Plan for the Architectonic, or Theory of What Is Simple and First in Philosophical Knowledge), which was published in 1771 but had been finished in 1764. The work provides the propaedeutic for a foundational philosophical science in the tradition of Wolff's ontology or general theory of being. Lambert analyses the basic philosophical concepts and principles with an eye to their eventual use in the edifice of philosophical knowledge. Most of the work consists of detailed, often very subtle examinations of philosophical terms and distinctions. In the procedure of philosophy, as envisioned by Lambert, the analysis of the basic concepts is followed by the axiomatic construction of a body of propositions, which is then applied to experience in the manner of applying mathematics to physical reality. Lambert's own work did not extend significantly beyond the initial, analytic phase of the project.

While Lambert's analyses of philosophical concepts and principles exercised some influence on TETENS and KANT, it was not until some two hundred years after his death that his contributions to the theory of scientific reasoning were properly recognized.

See also: SCIENTIFIC METHOD

List of works

Lambert, J.H. (1965–9) *Philosophische Schriften* (Philosophical Writings), ed. H.-W. Arndt, Hildesheim: Olms, 10 vols.

—— (1761) *Cosmologische Briefe über die Einrichtung des Weltbaues* (Cosmological Letters on the Structure of the Universe), Augsburg; repr. in G. Jakisch (ed.) *J.H. Lamberts 'Cosmologische Briefe' mit Beiträgen zur Frühgeschichte der Kosmologie*, Berlin: Akademie-Verlag, 1979.

—— (1761) *Abhandlung vom Criterium veritatis* (Treatise on the Criterion of Truth), ed. K. Bopp,

Berlin: Reuther & Reinhard, 1915. (Published posthumously.)

—— (1762) *Über die Methode die Metaphysik, Theologie und Moral richtiger zu beweisen* (On the Method of Proving Metaphysics, Theology and Morals More Correctly), ed. K. Bopp, Berlin: Reuther & Reinhard. (Published posthumously.)

—— (1764) *Neues Organon oder Gedanken über die Erforschung und Bezeichnung des Wahren und dessen Unterscheidung vom Irrthum und Schein* (New Organon or Thoughts on the Investigation and Designation of the True and its Distinction from Error and Appearance), Leipzig, 2 vols; repr. in *Philosophische Schriften*, vols 1–2; repr. and ed. G. Schenk, Berlin: Akademie-Verlag, 1990, 3 vols.

—— (1771) *Anlage zur Architectonic, oder Theorie des Einfachen und des Ersten in der philosophischen Erkenntniß* (Plan for the Architectonic, or Theory of What Is Simple and First in Philosophical Knowledge), Riga; repr. in *Philosophische Schriften*, vols 3–4.

—— (1781–7) *Johann Heinrich Lamberts deutscher gelehrter Briefwechsel*, ed. J. Bernoulli, Berlin, 5 vols; vol. 1 repr. in *Philosophische Schriften*, vol. 9. (Lambert's scientific correspondence conducted in German.)

—— (1782–7) *Logische und philosophische Abhandlungen* (Logical and Philosophical Essays), Berlin, 2 vols; repr. in *Philosophische Schriften*, vols 6–7.

—— (1988) *Texte zur Systematologie und zur Theorie der wisssenschaftlichen Erkenntnis* (Writings on the Theory of Systems and the Theory of Scientific Knowledge), ed. G. Sigwart, Hamburg: Meiner. (Includes selections from Neues Organon and Anlage zurArchitectonic, with bibliography.)

References and further reading

Baensch, O. (1902) *Johann Heinrich Lamberts Philosophie und seine Stellung zu Kant*, Tübingen and Leipzig: Mohr; repr. Hildesheim: Gerstenberg, 1978. (An account of Lambert's philosophy and his relation to Kant; Baensch rejects the then current view of Kant's indebtedness to Lambert.)

Beck, L.W. (1969) *Early German Philosophy. Kant and his Predecessors*, Cambridge, MA: Harvard University Press, 402–12. (Places Lambert in the context of German rationalist tradition in metaphysics.)

Debru, C. (1977) *Analyse et représentation. De la méthodologie à la théorie de l'espace: Kant et Lambert*, Paris: Vrin. (A study of Lambert's contribution to the formation of Kant's philosophy.)

Hinske, N. (ed.) (1983) *Lambert-Index. Stellenindex zu*

Johann Heinrich Lamberts 'Neues Organon', Stuttgart and Bad Cannstatt: Frommann-Holzboog, 2 vols. (Word index to Lambert's New Organon.)

—— (ed.) (1987) *Lambert-Index. Stellenindex zu Johann Heinrich Lamberts 'Anlage zur Architectonic'*, Stuttgart and Bad Cannstatt: Frommann-Holzboog, 2 vols. (Word index to Lambert's *Plan for an Architectonic*.)

Peters, W.S. (1968) 'I. Kants Verhältnis zu J.H. Lambert', *Kant-Studien* 59: 448–53. (A documentation of the references to Lambert in Kant's writings and correspondence.)

Steck, M. (1970) *Bibliographia Lambertiana. Ein Führer durch das gedruckte und ungedruckte Schrifttum und den wissenschaftlichen Briefwechsel von Johann Heinrich Lambert. 1728–1777*, Hildesheim: Olms. (A guide through Lambert's published and unpublished writings and his scientific correspondence, with bibliography of literature on Lambert.)

Université de Haute-Alsace (ed.) (1979) *Colloque international et interdisciplinaire Jean-Henri Lambert Mulhouse, 26–30 septembre 1977*, Paris: Ophrys. (Conference proceedings with eight contributions on Lambert's philosophy.)

Wolters, G. (1980) *Basis und Deduktion. Studien zur Entstehung und Bedeutung der Theorie der axiomatischen Methode bei J.H. Lambert (1728–1777)*, Berlin and New York: De Gruyter. (Focuses on Lambert's importance as a philosopher of science; includes bibliography.)

GÜNTER ZÖLLER

LANDMARKS MOVEMENT
see SIGNPOSTS MOVEMENT

LANGE, FRIEDRICH ALBERT (1828–75)

A German philosopher, social scientist and political activist, Lange was best known for his study of the history of materialism. He was a leading proponent of Neo-Kantianism, a critic of speculative metaphysics, and a defender of the view that philosophy should incorporate the findings of the exact sciences. As a social scientist, Lange described the emergence of a social Darwinian 'struggle for existence' in modern times due to the rapid advancement of industrialization and a growing conflict of interest among social classes.

Cognizant of the scientific trends of his time, Lange anticipated some of the central ideas of pragmatism and adopted a form of conventionalism in regard to scientific principles and concepts. Although sympathetic to materialism, Lange also saw the inevitability of an idealist element in interpretations of natural phenomena and insisted on the importance of projecting ethical, social and aesthetic ideals.

1   Life
2   Philosophical writings
3   Social thought and influence

1   Life

Lange was born at Wald and died near Zurich. He was educated at the University of Bonn and later became a university instructor there in 1851. In 1870, he was appointed professor of inductive logic at Zurich. Accepting a professorship at Marburg in 1873, Lange established an influential Neo-Kantian orientation there. By 1861 he became actively involved in politics, working for constitutional reform along democratic socialist lines.

2   Philosophical writings

Lange's most important philosophical work is his impressive *Geschichte des Materialismus und Kritik seiner Bedeutung in der Gegenwart* (*History of Materialism*), published in a one-volume edition in 1866 and a two-volume edition in 1873–5. The two-volume edition included references to contemporary scientific theories. A supplementary study, *Neue Beiträge zur Geschichte des Materialismus* (New Contributions to the History of Materialism), was published in 1867. Two years earlier, he had presented *Die Grundlegung der mathematischen Psychologie* (The Foundation of Mathematical Psychology). His last work, *Logische Studien* (Logical Studies), appeared posthumously in 1877.

The *History of Materialism* is a detailed and informative study of the development of materialism from ancient Greece to the scientifically supported modes of materialism emerging in the 1870s. More than a scholarly history, Lange's major work presents perceptive commentaries on physical and biological theories, political economy and ethical naturalism. There is also an extensive discussion of the critical philosophy of Kant in relation to nineteenth-century scientific thought. Lange adopts a restrained positivism in regard to scientific theory and a conventionalist orientation towards scientific principles and posits. He also advocates the construction of aesthetic conceptions of 'the All' from what he called 'the standpoint of the ideal'.

Lange avoids a reductive materialism and argues that a critical analysis of materialism reveals ideal-theoretical principles, concepts and assumptions that cannot be interpreted materialistically. Hence, his considered philosophical position is a form of materio-idealism. Anticipations of pragmatism, scientific conventionalism, instrumental fictionalism and a phenomenalism in regard to scientific concepts can all be discerned in his *History of Materialism*. In terms of his critical commentaries on a variety of scientific theories and their conceptual foundations, Lange anticipated the approach later adopted in the philosophy of science.

Under the influence of Kant, Lange criticized speculative metaphysical claims to a knowledge that transcends experience. He viewed traditional metaphysics as akin to religion and art, as a form of conceptual poetry. The projection of ideals beyond the 'fragments of truth' discovered by the exact sciences was, however, construed as a basic human need. Space, time and causality, as well as the fundamental posits of science, were conceived of as human inventions or, in effect, useful fictions. Lange insisted that the discoveries in the exact sciences must be incorporated into philosophical thought in so far as they are directly relevant to our concept of actuality and theory of knowledge.

3 Social thought and influence

Though less well-known than his study of materialism, Lange's writings on social science were insightful. In *History of Materialism* he already predicted that there would be 'earthquakes' in the sociopolitical realm due to the decline of the power of religion, the advance of science and the tensions generated by the 'social problem'. In a neglected study of 1865, *Die Arbeiterfrage in ihrer Bedeutung für Gegenwart und Zukunft* (The Problem of the Worker and its Meaning for the Present and Future), he analysed the implications of the increasingly rapid industrialization in Europe and its need for an army of workers and skilled technicians. He foresaw a coming social (Darwinian) struggle for existence that would generate radical sociopolitical change. A champion of workers' rights and sympathetic to democratic socialism, Lange envisaged the emergence of a new class of technically proficient workers who would soon attain a position of leadership among European nations.

In another work of 1865, *J. St. Mills Ansichten über die sociale Frage und die angebliche Umwälzung der Socialwissenschaften durch Carey* (J.S. Mill's Views on the Social Problem and Carey's Supposed Social-Scientific Revolution), Lange displayed his knowledge of J.S. Mill's liberal-democratic ideas, as well as of Henry Carey's defence of a capitalist national-economic theory (see MILL, J.S. §12). He was a perceptive analyst, aware of the 'egoism' and social atomism that the drive to accumulate capital can produce. Lange held that the rapid economic changes in Europe would lead both to social conflict and radical political oppositions. These views helped shape his socialist sentiments (see SOCIALISM).

The influence of Lange on subsequent philosophers and philosophical trends, though generally indirect, is traceable in some instances. The Neo-Kantianism he inaugurated had a long-range effect on German thought and influenced a number of philosophical scientists (see NEO-KANTIANISM §§1–2). In social thought he was a forerunner of the conception of social Darwinism, not as an advocate but as a predictor of it. The fictionalist and pragmatic theory of Hans VAIHINGER was shaped by Lange's post-Kantian conventionalist theory of the use and meaning of categories, scientific postulates and theory-construction. Friedrich NIETZSCHE considered Lange's *History of Materialism* 'a real treasure-house, to be looked into and read repeatedly'. He was strongly influenced by him in regard to his own general philosophical goal of uniting philosophy, science and art, as well as in his critical analysis of knowledge.

List of works

Lange, F.A. (1863) *Die Leibesübungen* (Physical Training), Gotha: Besser. (An early work, perhaps the earliest, on the importance of 'body-training' or physical education for students.)

—— (1865) *Die Arbeiterfrage in ihrer Bedeutung für Gegenwart und Zukunft* (The Problem of the Worker and its Meaning for the Present and Future), Duisburg: Falk & Volmer. (An analysis of the rising problem of a Darwinian struggle for survival in European society as a consequence of the new social classes emerging out of increasing industrialization with emphasis upon the impact of the class of skilled workers and technicians on the balance of power in society.)

—— (1865a) *J.St. Mill's Ansichten über die sociale Frage* (J.S. Mill's Views on the Social Problem and Carey's Supposed Social-Scientific Revolution), Duisburg: Falk & Volmer. (A sympathetic analysis of Mill's democratic liberal ideals and socialist programmes, and a critique of Henry Carey's nationalist political economic theory.)

—— (1865b) *Die Grundlegung der mathematischen Psychologie* (The Foundation of Mathematical

353

Psychology), Duisburg: Falk & Volmer. (An attempt to place psychology on an experimental, empirical basis in terms of a mathematical model.)

—— (1866) *Geschichte des Materialismus und Kritik seiner Bedeutung in der Gegenwart*, Iserlohn: Baedeker; 2nd edn, Iserlohn and Leipzig, J. Baedeker, 1873– 5, 2 vols; trans. E.C. Thomas, *History of Materialism*, Boston, MA, Osgood, 1877, 3 vols. (A detailed, then-comprehensive study of the history of materialism from the ancient Greeks to 1872 (in the 2nd edition) with special emphasis on recent developments in physics, biological theory and social theory, and their impact on a Neo-Kantian epistemology, as well as ethics. A pioneering work in what was later designated philosophy of science.)

—— (1867) *Neue Beiträge zur Geschichte des Materialismus* (New Contributions to the History of Materialism), Iserlohn: Baedeker. (An updating of his work of 1866, primarily in the areas of the sciences. Most of this material was incorporated into his 2nd edition of the *History of Materialism*.)

—— (1877) *Logische Studien* (Logical Studies), Iserlohn: Baedeker. (An analysis of logic in terms of a nominalism that conceives of language as comprised of 'arbitrary signs' that refer to particulars. Logic should focus on the logical aspects of language, as well as its diachronic features.)

References and further reading

Ellissen, O.A. (1891) *F.A. Lange*, Leipzig: Baedeker. (Interesting biographical material in the form of letters.)

Salaquarda, J. (1978) 'Nietzsche und Lange', *Nietzsche-Studien* 7: 236–60, Berlin and New York: De Gruyter. (A concise discussion of some aspects of Lange's impact on Nietzsche.)

Stack, G.J. (1983) *Lange and Nietzsche*, Berlin and New York: De Gruyter. (A comprehensive study of the influence of Lange on Nietzsche's philosophical project, as well as on his critique of knowledge.)

Vaihinger, H. (1902) *Die Philosophie des 'Als-Ob'*, Berlin: Reuther & Reichard; trans. C.K. Ogden, *The Philosophy of 'As-if'*, London: Routledge & Kegan Paul, 1924. (Contains a substantial discussion of Lange's thought with special emphasis on his idea of the use of fictions in philosophy and science, as well as the value of edifying cultural ideals.)

—— (1876) *Hartmann, Dühring and Lange*, Iserlohn: Baedeker. (A summary of the central conceptions of Hartmann's philosophy of the unconscious, Dühring's social and scientific theories, and Lange's phenomenalism.)

GEORGE J. STACK

LANGER, SUSANNE KATHERINA KNAUTH (1895–1985)

With roots in logic, philosophy of language and philosophy of mind, Susanne Langer sought to explicate the meaning and cognitive import of art works by developing a theory of symbolism that located works of art at the centre of a network of relations based firmly on semantic theory. Art works were non-discursive, presentational symbols that expressed an artist's 'life of feeling', by which observers, through a process of immediate apprehension (or intuition) came to acquire knowledge.

Langer was educated at Radcliffe College and briefly attended the University of Vienna. She held the post of tutor at Radcliffe from 1927 to 1942, followed by positions at the University of Delaware (1943), Columbia University (1945–50), the Connecticut College for Women (1954–62), and a number of visiting positions.

Langer's early writings prefigure her later theorizing on art. *The Practice of Philosophy* was influenced by work on symbolism by Whitehead and the early Wittgenstein. For Langer, the relation between a symbol and the symbolized object depended solely upon analogy of form; only by studying the structure of an entity and its comparable analogue could the symbolic relationship be established. The logical analysis of symbols – as analogues to one's concrete experiences – admitted of meanings that were incommunicable by ordinary, public discourse. Symbols, through non-discursive form, achieved cognitive weight and force equal to the original experience. As such, they transmitted knowledge of the ineffable. Her second text, *An Introduction to Symbolic Logic*, moved beyond a presentation of standard techniques in symbolic logic to an exploration of its conceptual foundations.

Her explicit theory of art began with *Philosophy in a New Key: A Study in the Symbolism of Reason, Rite and Art*. Combining her interest in the nature of knowledge with a long-standing wish to actualize a complete theory of mind (realized decades later with the publication of *Mind: An Essay on Human Feeling*), she expanded her discussion of symbols by focusing on the role of human reason in ritual acts and the creation of art objects. Challenging traditional philosophical approaches, which had previously located the focus of attention in theories of taste, beauty or notions of aesthetic value, she sought to alter radically the most basic questions in the philosophy of art. Symbolism was the 'new key' to understanding how the human mind transformed the primal need to express oneself. All forms of human activity, including 'speech and gesture, song and sacrifice' were seen as expressive. The mental work of symbolic transformation resided in abstracting a gesture or an object from reality. Symbols, in contrast to signs (later called signals), gave expression to thoughts that went beyond what could be expressed in language. Therefore, a wide range of symbols evolved over time: simple ones became complex; ritual (or convention) became art. Art became the conveyor of inner life: artists expressed 'ideas of feeling' – 'formulation and representation of emotions, moods, mental tensions and resolutions' – not their own actual or personal feelings. The artistic significance of music, for instance, consisted in pure form – 'the sensuous percept' – apart from its literal content (what, if anything, it represented).

In *Feeling and Form*, written eleven years later as a sequel to *Philosophy in a New Key*, art was characterized as the creation of forms symbolic of human feeling. Every work of art involved (1) abstraction from actuality, thereby becoming mere semblance, a created realm of illusion, (2) plasticity (the capacity of being manipulated in the interests of expression), and (3) expressiveness whereby the symbol became transparent. A focus on the meaning of art works was replaced by a discussion of their import or significance. Intuition became the link between the qualities of the art work that constituted it a symbol and the import the work of art held for the observer. Through intuition, we perceive the 'felt life' of the artist's expression.

In *Problems of Art*, a collection of essays originally delivered as lectures, Langer refined her views: a work of art was a form expressive of human feeling, created for our aesthetic perception through sense or imagination. Emphasizing the role that artistic intention played in creative activity, she traced the unity of the arts to their semblance of organic form. Insight (understanding of the essential life of feeling) was designated the aim of art. *Reflections on Art*, a collection of twenty-six essays ranging over music, art, dance, poetry, film and architecture, focused on two main issues: expressiveness and semblance. Her list of contributors included artists and 'lay aestheticians', as well as professional philosophers. Her final work, *Mind*, ambitiously sought to explicate the role feelings play as the mind functions uniquely in humans, and in particular how an artist projects an idea of feeling by means of art.

See also: ANTHROPOLOGY, PHILOSOPHY OF §1; ARTISTIC EXPRESSION; MUSIC, AESTHETICS OF §§6, 9

List of works

Langer, S.K.K. (1930) *The Practice of Philosophy*, New York: Holt. (An early general analysis of symbols, not related to art.)

—— (1937) *An Introduction to Symbolic Logic*, Boston, MA: Houghton Mifflin. (Conceptual foundations of how logic is needed to clarify semantics.)

—— (1942) *Philosophy in a New Key: A Study in the Symbolism of Reason, Rite and Art*, Cambridge, MA: Harvard University Press. (Art is a nondiscursive symbol that conveys an artist's expressed 'ideas of feeling'.)

—— (1953) *Feeling and Form: A Theory of Art*, London: Routledge. (Extends *Philosophy in a New Key* to a characterization of art as the creation of forms symbolic of human feeling.)

—— (1957) *Problems of Art: Ten Philosophical Lectures*, New York: Charles Scribner's Sons. (Published lectures extending Langer's theory to discussions of artistic intention, the unity of the arts, and insight.)

—— (1958) *Reflections on Art: A Source Book of Writings by Artists, Critics, and Philosophers*, Baltimore, MD: Johns Hopkins University Press. (An edited interdisciplinary collection of essays focusing on expressiveness and semblance.)

—— (1962) *Philosophical Sketches*, Baltimore, MD: Johns Hopkins University Press. (A collection of essays that are studies towards the philosophy of mind presented in *Mind: An Essay on Human Feeling*.)

—— (1967, 1972, 1982) *Mind: An Essay on Human Feeling*, 3 vols, Baltimore, MD: Johns Hopkins University Press. (An exploration of the biological foundations of human mentality as the site of source of the artistic expression of 'living' form.)

References and further reading

Ahlberg, L.-O. (1994) 'Susanne Langer on Representation and Emotion in Music', *British Journal of Aesthetics* 34 (1): 69–80. (Compares Langer's views to those of Peter Kivy and Jerrold Levinson.)

Bertocci, P.A. (1970) 'Susanne K. Langer's Theory of Mind and Feeling', *Review of Metaphysics* 23: 527–51. (A critique of Langer's form of naturalism, her attempt to escape dualism, and her account of the unity and continuity of mind.)

Binkley, T. (1970) 'Langer's Logical and Ontological Modes', *Journal of Aesthetics and Art Criticism* 28: 455–64. (Argues that music is not an essentially significant form because music has an ontological, not a logical, function.)

Bufford, S. (1972) 'Susanne Langer's Two Philosophies of Art', *Journal of Aesthetics and Art Criticism* 31: 9–20. (Detects a 'perceivability theory' in Langer's writings in addition to her well-known expression theory.)

Davies, S. (1983) 'Is Music a Language of the Emotions?', *British Journal of Aesthetics* 23: 222–33. (Rejects Langer's theory in favour of his own, in which music is naturally meaningful.)

Hagberg, G. (1984) 'Art and the Unsayable: Langer's Tractarian Aesthetics', *British Journal of Aesthetics* 24 (4): 325–40. (Reconsidering Langer's theory on a Wittgensteinian model of meaning.)

Hansen, F. (1968) 'Langer's Expressive Form: An Interpretation', *Journal of Aesthetics and Art Criticism* 27: 165–70. (Interprets and extends Langer's original concept of 'symbol' beyond her own presentation.)

Lang, B. (1962) 'Langer's Arabesque and the Collapse of the Symbol', *Review of Metaphysics* 16: 349–65. (The failure of Langer's theory based on the cognitive content of a symbol.)

Price, K. (1993) 'Philosophy in a New Key: An Interpretation', *The Philosophy of Music Education Review* 1 (1): 34–43. (Reasons for Langer's immediate popularity upon publishing *Philosophy in a New Key* and her lasting importance; some questions her works raise.)

Reichling, M.J. (1993) 'Susanne Langer's Theory of Symbolism: An Analysis and Extension', *The Philosophy of Music Education Review* 1 (1): 3–17. (A concise overview of Langer's theory and its critics, and an analysis and extension of the theory into music.)

—— (1995) 'Susanne Langer's Concept of Secondary Illusion', *The Journal of Aesthetic Education* 29 (4): 39. (Short note on 'secondary Illusion'.)

Reimer, B. (1993) 'Langer on the Arts as Cognitive', *The Philosophy of Music Education Review* 1 (1): 44–60. (Seeks to clarify Langer's position as to how the arts are cognitive, and why education in the arts is essential (and often ignored by scholars in cognitive science).)

Yob, I. (1993) 'The Form of Feeling', *The Philosophy of Music Education Review* 1 (1): 18–33. (Focuses on the metaphorical nature of a non-discursive symbol.)

PEG BRAND

LANGUAGE, ANCIENT PHILOSOPHY OF

The earliest interest in language during the ancient Greek period was largely instrumental: presumed facts about language and its features were pressed into service for the purpose of philosophical argumentation. Perhaps inevitably, this activity gave way to the analysis of language for its own sake. Claims, for example, about the relation between the semantic values of general terms and the existence of universals invited independent inquiry into the nature of the meanings of those general terms themselves. Language thus became an object of philosophical inquiry in its own right. Accordingly, philosophers at least from the time of Plato conducted inquiries proper to philosophy of language. They investigated:

(1) how words acquire their semantic values;
(2) how proper names and other singular terms refer;
(3) how words combine to form larger semantic units;
(4) the compositional principles necessary for language understanding;
(5) how sentences, statements, or propositions come to be truth-evaluable;

and, among later figures of the classical period,

(6) how propositions, as abstract, mind- and language-independent entities, are to be (a) characterized in terms of their constituents, (b) related to minds and the natural languages used to express them, and (c) related to the language-independent world.

1   Pre-Platonic figures
2   Plato
3   Aristotle
4   The Stoics and other Hellenistic movements

1   Pre-Platonic figures

Before Plato, evidence for inquiries into the semantic and syntactic features of language is sketchy, if suggestive. Even so, there is clear interest in language among pre-Platonic philosophers, rhetoricians and Sophists. In some cases this interest is motivated by a concern for developing persuasive speech, primarily for forensic or political use (see RHETORIC §1). In other cases, it has a more philosophical orientation. Thus, quite early, Parmenides (early to mid-5th century BC) sought to exploit a putative fact about language when defending an improbable form of monism: he argued that 'what is for saying and thinking must be' (fr. 6) and concluded that it is impossible to speak or think of what does not exist, with the consequence that it is equally impossible to speak or think of generation, change, or plurality, since each of these is implicated, directly or indirectly, in what is not. With the additional thesis that it is possible to speak and think of everything which exists (fr. 3), Parmenides concludes that the universe is an eternal undifferentiated unity, altogether remote from the appearances of plurality, change and generation delivered by the senses (see PARMENIDES §2). When Plato and Aristotle later exposed the fallacy in this argument, it was mainly by distinguishing syntactic and semantic features of the verb *to be* which Parmenides had failed to mark.

The Sophist Gorgias (late 5th century BC) similarly appealed to features of language when attempting to establish the nihilistic theses that:

(1) nothing exists;
(2) even if something did exist, it would be unknowable;
(3) even if something did exist and were knowable, it would be incommunicable.

On behalf of the odd counterfactual (3), in particular, he appealed to a subjectivist form of meaning: if something were perceived, it could be communicated only by means of a sign, which, even on the untenable assumption that it could be made to represent the supposed object of perception perfectly, could not be shared by more than one mind. Hence, communication about objects perceived is impossible (see GORGIAS §3). However implausible this argument may sound, it is worth remarking that it appeals to a thesis about meaning that many find natural and attractive; indeed, many centuries later, Frege still felt the need to mount positive arguments against just its kind of semantic subjectivism (see FREGE, G. §4).

The atomist DEMOCRITUS (mid 5th–4th century BC) reportedly composed a treatise *On Words*. In this or another work he inaugurated an important discussion, taken up with great earnestness by later philosophers, concerning the signification of names. Democritus thus stakes out what appears to be the first case for a dedicated semantic theory. He thus moves beyond the primarily instrumental interest in the semantic features of language displayed by his predecessors.

Democritus evidently argued for a form of *conventionalism*, according to which the relation between names and things named is determined by agreement or legislation. He argues that there cannot be a natural relation which ties a word to the world, since:

(1) there are homonyms, that is one name for different entities (for example, 'bank');

(2) there are synonyms, distinct names for the same thing;
(3) entities can change names in the course of their existence.

Consequently, it would be wrong to suppose that a name is determined by anything other than an arbitrary designation.

In arguing this way, Democritus means to reject *naturalism*, a view according to which names and things named are related by some non-conventional relation. A first approximation of naturalism might be the view that all naming is at root onomatopoetic or somehow pictographic. Put thus crudely, naturalism may seem a non-starter. But other forms of naturalism, loose by comparison with these simpler versions, appeal instead to natural descriptions, with the result that names, especially proper names, all turn out to be disguised definite descriptions. Making naturalism more tenuous still, a fair number of naturalists were in the habit of appealing to the origin of names and other words, thereby confusing genetic and semantic questions.

Although in these varying contexts, the varieties of 'naturalism' were unhelpfully conflated, the contrast between conventionalism and naturalism is important for the history of classical semantics for three related reasons. First, the ensuing debate, much of it quite subtle and sophisticated, is initially couched in terms of a contrast between conventionalism and naturalism, and even in late antiquity data to which naturalists appeal appear in a surprisingly forceful way. Second, part of the motivation for naturalism turns out to be reasonable: naturalism, unlike some varieties of conventionalism, seemed to capture the normativity of language. Some names are correct and fitting, while others are incorrect or otherwise inappropriate. It is hard to specify precisely how this can be the case if spoken sounds are applied to things in a purely conventional manner, especially when conventions may be generated quite locally. Third, whatever its ultimate faults, naturalism at least attempts to explain how reference occurs. In some of its ancient forms, conventionalism had difficulty even broaching a suggestion on this point.

2 Plato

The opposition between conventionalism and naturalism dominates Plato's most explicit and extended treatment of language, the *Cratylus* (see PLATO §15). The dialogue opposes equally untenable naturalist and conventionalist theories of naming, while at the same time promoting the virtues of each. Plato focuses initially on proper names, but it is clear that his interest extends to other singular terms and to general terms as well. Perhaps Plato means to explore facts about reference by laying out extreme forms of views which, though incompatible, each have some merit. At any rate, in the course of the dialogue he sets aside the most implausible features of conventionalism and naturalism without detailed comment.

These implausible features are, however, fully present in the initial presentations of each theory. Cratylus opens the dialogue, arguing on behalf of naturalism that it is possible for someone not to be named *n* even if 'all people were to call' him *n* (383b6–7, cf. 429b12–c2). This is because, as we later learn, '*n*' is the name of something only if it bears a natural relation *R* to that thing, where *R* is specified by Cratylus only incompletely as a kind of mimetic or imitative relation (423b–428a, 430a10–b1). Thus, something qualifies as a name *n* only if it is correct, that is, only if it imitates the thing named and indeed indicates what that thing is (428e1–2).

Hermogenes responds on behalf of conventionalism:

> I cannot be persuaded that there is some correctness (*orthotēs*) of names other than convention and agreement. For it seems to me that whatever name someone gives to something, this is the correct one.... For no name is suited by nature to anything, but rather by the custom and habit of those in the habit of using it and calling things by that name.
>
> (*Cratylus*, 384c10–d9)

Hermogenes' conventionalism may seem initially more plausible than any variety of naturalism. Yet he is taken to task for failing to consider external constraints on convention. More importantly, names have the dual function of conveying information and distinguishing real natures in the world (388b7–11); if a name misses or obscures these real natures, then it will not succeed as a name, or at any rate will be at best only a sub-optimal name. Plato suggests that even this degree of normativity is incompatible with the version of conventionalism Hermogenes espouses.

In opposing this kind of conventionalism, Plato does not adopt Cratylus' naturalism. On the contrary, the Socrates of the dialogue, who evidently represents Plato's point of view, is equally critical of a naturalism which fails to distinguish between the correct name of an entity and the name which people actually employ when designating that entity. Socrates thus twice embarrasses Cratylus by forcing him to allow that his theory cannot distinguish between successfully referring to an object and referring to it correctly (429c3–5 and 429e8–430a5). The point, updating Plato's example a bit, is this: if a child points to a whale,

exclaiming, 'That fish is bigger than our house!', the child has evidently successfully referred to the whale, but only incorrectly. Cratylus must allow that not only has the child failed to designate the whale, but also may have produced a false sentence by referring to a minnow in the whale's neighbourhood.

Plato, in the end, agrees with the naturalist that there must be some relation *R* which in a direct or indirect way relates a name to a thing named; but he denies that *R* can be specified in a way which wholly ignores convention. So, he equally agrees with the conventionalist that convention is relevant to determining names; but he denies that convention by itself can determine *R*. For he believes that names are information-bearers which, if correct, reflect the structure of the extra-linguistic world. Thus, the argument of the *Cratylus* has the effect of distilling what is right from both conventionalism and naturalism, and of laying down the constraints for a semantically and metaphysically adequate account of reference. It also advances the debate by distinguishing different ways in which a name may be said to be correct or incorrect: a name may be correct in a pragmatic way by fulfilling its reference-fixing function, or correct in a descriptive way by carrying information which accurately reflects the world. Plato appreciates that these functions may come apart in ways which make the job of specifying *R* exceedingly difficult. He himself does not, however, offer an articulated account of the no doubt complex relation *R*. Instead, the dialogue ends in perplexity.

Although it contains his most self-conscious and sustained treatment, the *Cratylus* hardly exhausts Plato's views on naming or language more generally. Of special note are his complex discussions of the various syntactic and semantic functions of the verb *to be*, conducted most thoroughly in the *Parmenides* and *Sophist*, both late dialogues. In the *Parmenides* (142a, 161e–162b), raising a puzzle about saying truly '*a* is not' (we cannot predicate something of *a* unless *a* is; but then we cannot do what we plainly can do, namely deny the existence of something), Plato takes up a discussion about negative existentials which continues even today (see EXISTENCE). When, in the *Sophist*, he responds to the Parmenidean argument for monism, Plato quite rightly focuses on distinct uses of 'is'. The distinction remains an important philosophical tool for recognizing and diagnosing fallacies.

3   Aristotle

ARISTOTLE approaches the study of language with a logician's eye. He seeks to determine how terms relate in syntactic structures of various sorts, mainly to determine and regiment the correct and incorrect forms of inference-drawing. Accordingly, he investigates the nature of meaning, the difficulties of reference, and the errors which result from failing to attend to what he calls the *homonymous* uses of words, that is the uses of words with a plurality of distinct but connected meanings, including especially core philosophical terms whose non-univocity may initially elude us. He thinks that when they seek unified definitions of these sorts of terms – at any rate, non-disjunctive definitions given as necessary and sufficient conditions – philosophers ignore the complexity of the concepts or properties they are used to express. Natural language sometimes reflects this complexity; at other times, it obscures it.

Aristotle investigates linguistic phenomena primarily in the *Categories* and *De Interpretatione*, but also in the *Metaphysics*, the *Topics*, the *Sophistical Refutations*, and the *Prior* and *Posterior Analytics*. He does not always explicitly connect these investigations, but there are several bridge passages that indicate how he takes his views in these areas to be related. Perhaps the single most important such passage opens the *De Interpretatione*, where Aristotle draws a fairly complete analogy between words and sentences on the one hand and types of affections (*pathēmata*) in the soul on the other.

According to this analogy, there is a reasonably straightforward relation between thoughts and spoken sounds: individual words are to assertoric sentences as individual thoughts are to compound thoughts. The first members of these pairs are without truth value, being in some sense semantically atomic. The second members are by contrast necessarily either true or false. That is, Aristotle claims that bivalence obtains for all simple assertoric sentences and their mental analogues, compound thoughts.

Partly in virtue of this analogy, the opening of the *De Interpetatione* contains the seeds of four related Aristotelian semantic theses, each of which is developed in various places in the corpus:

(1) *Compositionality.* The semantic value of assertoric sentences is a function of their sub-sentential semantically relevant parts (semantically relevant, because, as he points out (*De Interpretatione* 16a20–22), neither 'ton' nor 'dent' contributes anything to the meaning of 'Clinton was unusually well educated for an American president.');

(2) *Conventionality.* The written and spoken symbols used to stand for thoughts are conventional, whereas the thoughts themselves and that for which they stand are not;

(3) *Relationalism.* Conventional semantic units (written marks and spoken sounds) receive their semantic significance from those things of which they are symbols;

(4) *Signification.* The relationship in virtue of which they receive their semantic significance consists in or involves what Aristotle calls signification (*sēmainein*).

Of these, (2) and (4) merit special attention.

The second thesis, conventionalism, indicates where Aristotle stands on the question explored in the *Cratylus*. He explicates his contention thus:

> I say < a name is a significant sound > according to convention (*kata sunthēkēn*) because no name is by nature < significant >, but only when it has become a symbol. Even though inarticulate noises, e.g. those belonging to wild beasts, do reveal something (*dēlousi ti*), none of them is a name.
> (*De Interpretatione* 16a26–29)

He rejects naturalism, but without endorsing any simple version of conventionalism. Instead, he lays down the constraint that a sound becomes a name only when it has become a symbol, where something is a symbol only when it stands in an appropriate relation to a non-conventional mental representation.

With respect to Aristotle's approach to language and meaning, the fourth thesis, regarding signification (*sēmainein*), is easily the most central and important. It is also the most complex and difficult. Aristotle often writes as if signification were a simple meaning-relation: words signify things, even when they lack referents. Thus, for example, after distinguishing sharply between assertoric expressions, which alone have truth-value, and their constituents, which are not yet truth-evaluable, he imagines someone objecting that the word 'goatstag' (*tragelaphos*) is already false, since there are no such creatures. He responds that although 'goatstag' signifies something, it is not yet true or false, precisely because it is not yet part of an assertoric sentence (*De Interpretatione* 16a16–18). Aristotle's response correctly drives a wedge between vacuous reference and falsity; it also seems to treat signification as closely akin to sense expression: 'goatstag' has sense, but lacks reference (see SENSE AND REFERENCE).

Still, a complication arises for two related reasons:

(1) Aristotle sometimes appeals to signification where it seems unlikely that it can be understood in terms of sense expression;

(2) Aristotle sometimes denies signification to vacuous singular terms.

In the first case, Aristotle surely maintains that not only words signify: the word 'man' signifies rational animal, but the entity man signifies rational animal as well (*Categories* 3b10–23; *Topics* 122b16–17, 142b27–29; *Posterior Analytics* 85b18–21; *Metaphysics* 1017a22–27, 1028a10–16); further, clouds signify rain and smoke signifies fire (*Posterior Analytics* 70a10–38).

Elsewhere, he denies that a single word made to mean 'manandhorse' has signification (*De Interpretatione* 18a19–27). The probable resolution is that the signification relation is for Aristotle in some contexts semantic and in some contexts not; further, in some contexts, signification is more akin to reference and in others more akin to sense expression. In some more technical contexts, Aristotle introduces signification as a sort of essence-specification: man signifies rational animal because humans are essentially rational. Perhaps in this sense, though, 'signification' behaves all the more like the English word 'meaning': smoke means fire; 'ghoul' means 'a spirit that robs graves and devours the corpses'; and we say that although he speaks of piety, Euthyphro does not even know the meaning of the term. In some philosophical contexts, we are appropriately technical about how we understand the concept of meaning; in some other contexts, we are comparatively relaxed. This practice mirrors Aristotle's treatment of signification (see SEMIOTICS).

4 The Stoics and other Hellenistic movements

The Hellenistic schools which flourished after the death of Aristotle became increasingly technical and specialized in their treatments of language. This is especially true of the Stoics, whose interests in logic, grammar and syntax led them to offer deeply subtle theories replete with technical vocabularies capable of an unprecedented richness and precision. The most intricate and important innovations were most likely introduced by CHRYSIPPUS.

It is difficult to recapitulate elements of the Stoic system briefly. To begin, the evidence is fragmentary, deriving from many different sources, some of them hostile and most of them secondhand. Moreover, there is a fair amount of divergence within the Stoic camp itself; it is worth remembering that we are dealing with the data of several centuries of philosophy. That said, the doxographer DIOGENES LAERTIUS provides a serviceable overview of the main features of Stoic semantic theory:

Utterance (*phōnē*) and speech (*lexis*) differ, because while vocal sound is also an utterance only articulate sound is speech (*lexis*). And speech differs from language (*logos*), because language is always significant (*sēmantikos*) whereas speech < can > also lack significance, for example,

'blityri'; language can in no way < lack significance >. Moreover, saying (*to legein*) differs from voicing (*to propheresthai*). For while utterances are voiced, what is said are states of affairs – which turn out to be things said (or things which can be said, *lekta*).

(Diogenes Laertius 7.57)

The initial view here is straightforward. Animals, including humans, make noises; but only some of these noises are meaningful. Those noises which express *lekta* are meaningful, or *sēmantikos*, and those which do not are mere sounds. If I speak German and you do not, the utterance '*verkehrt*' will be meaningful for me, but not for you; but even if we both speak German, the nonsense utterance 'blityri' will be meaningless for us both. The Stoics suggest, then, because some noises are significant and others are not, we must suppose that some noises have meanings, namely express *lekta*, while others do not. Hence, it is necessary to postulate the existence of *lekta*.

The primary motivation for the introduction of *lekta* is, then, semantic. For better or worse, with the Stoics we have the first self-conscious reification of meanings as such. Unsurprisingly, the Stoics were quick to exploit a second semantic function of *lekta*. Some *lekta*, called by the Stoics *axiōmata*, are the principal bearers of truth and falsity. According to the Stoics, then, one species of *axiōmata* can be true or false, evidently in a primary way. Our speaking truly or falsely, that is our uttering sentences with truth values, depends upon our uttering a sentence which expresses a complex of meanings, an *axiōma*. Hence, the sentence 'Dion is walking' is true just in case it expresses the proposition, held by the Stoics to be noncorporeal, *that Dion is walking* and that proposition is true. Just as words are correlated with meanings or significates, which the Stoics regard as incomplete *lekta*, so the complete sentence 'Dion is walking' gains its meaning and truth-evaluability by expressing the complete *lekton*, the *axiōma* or proposition which is true independent of its being expressed. Just how determinate Stoic thinking about propositions is remains disputed, since some reports have the Stoics introducing propositions which change truth-values and which, though noncorporeal, can perish, or go out of existence. Often enough, though, in these cases the Stoics turn out to be grappling with quite subtle problems generated by indexicals and demonstratives. Indeed, they often show more sensitivity to these problems than their critics and later expositors display when discussing their views (see STOICISM §8).

The Stoics are by no means alone in offering

important advances in thought about language during the Hellenistic period. SEXTUS EMPIRICUS certainly develops semantic themes. Additionally, the Epicureans, and to a lesser extent the Academics, offer treatments of meaning and language understanding, often reverting to earlier debates about natural versus conventional signification. Later, the eclectic physician and philosopher Galen (AD 129–c.210) returns to the naturalism–conventionalism debate, ridiculing the naturalist propensity for etymology as 'fine friend' which is also an 'impostor'. No other Hellenistic school rivals the Stoics, however, in their genuinely innovative and impressively technical handling of semantic and syntactic matters.

See also: DIALECTICAL SCHOOL; LANGUAGE, INDIAN THEORIES OF; LANGUAGE, PHILOSOPHY OF; NATURE AND CONVENTION; PROPER NAMES; PROPOSITIONS, SENTENCES AND STATEMENTS; REFERENCE

References and further reading

Annas, J. (1982) 'Knowledge and Language: the *Theaetetus* and the *Cratylus*', in M. Schofield and M. Nussbaum (eds) *Language and Logos*, Cambridge: Cambridge University Press. (An exploration of some overlooked connections between Plato's approach to naming in the *Cratylus* and the difficult dream passage of the *Theaetetus*.)

* Aristotle (c. mid 4th century BC) *The Complete Works of Aristotle*, ed. J. Barnes, Princeton, NJ: Princeton University Press, 1984, 2 vols. (Although the focus of several works, Aristotle's attention to semantic matters pervades much of the corpus.)

Atherton, C. (1993) *The Stoics on Ambiguity*, Cambridge: Cambridge University Press. (A comprehensive treatment of Stoic approaches to ambiguity, with a special emphasis on Stoic classifications of forms of ambiguity and their role in fallacious argumentation.)

Bolton, R. (1976) 'Essentialism and Semantic Theory in Aristotle', *Philosophical Review* 85: 514–44. (An investigation into Aristotle's approach to nominal definition and the semantics of natural-kind terms.)

Brown, L. (1986) 'Being in the *Sophist*, a Syntactical Enquiry', *Oxford Studies in Ancient Philosophy* 4: 49–70. (A clear and accessible investigation into Plato's treatment of being in the *Sophist* which challenges some orthodox interpretations.)

Everson, S. (ed.) (1994) *Companions to Ancient Thought 3: Language*, Cambridge: Cambridge University Press. (An extremely useful anthology of papers on many aspects of ancient philosophical thought about language, with a special emphasis on continuities between ancient and contemporary concerns. This work should be consulted for additional bibliography.)

Fine, G. (1977) 'Plato on Naming', *Philosophical Quarterly* 27: 289–301. (An exceptionally clear and forthright account of Plato's approach to naming.)

Irwin, T. (1982) 'Aristotle's Concept of Signification', in M. Schofield and M. Nussbaum (eds) *Language and Logos*, Cambridge: Cambridge University Press. (A challenge to the widely held view that signification in Aristotle is a kind of meaning-relation; instead, Irwin argues, signification is a technical relation of essence-specification.)

Kretzmann, N. (1971) 'Plato on the Correctness of Names', *American Philosophical Quarterly* 8: 126–38. (A detailed and highly nuanced investigation of Plato's *Cratylus*.)

* Long, A. and Sedley, D. (1987) *The Hellenistic Philosophers*, Cambridge: Cambridge University Press, 2 vols. (The first volume contains translations of the principal fragments of Hellenistic philosophy, together with commentary. The second volume contains original texts and a very useful bibliography.)

Nuchelmans, G. (1973) *Theories of the Proposition: Ancient and Medieval Conceptions of the Bearers of Truth and Falsity*, Amsterdam: North Holland. (A full assessment of the evidence for the introduction of propositions in ancient thought.)

* Plato (390s–347 BC) *Plato: Complete Works*, ed. J.M. Cooper, Indianopolis, IN: Hackett Publishing Company, 1997. (This edition contains the best translation of the *Cratylus*, together with the rest of Plato's works, many of which contain sub-sections relevant to his views on language.)

Shields, C. (1998) *Order in Multiplicity: Homonymy in the Philosophy of Aristotle*, Oxford: Oxford University Press. (A full account of Aristotle's approach to homonymy, discussed within the broader context of his semantic theory.)

CHRISTOPHER SHIELDS

LANGUAGE AND DISCRIMINATION
see LINGUISTIC DISCRIMINATION

LANGUAGE AND GENDER

How do language and gender interact? This can be interpreted as asking about sexual difference in relation to language-use. How do the sexes speak, how do we speak of the sexes? And could or should these patterns change?

Not surprisingly, understanding language-gender interactions solely in terms of sexual difference yields a static and polarized picture. Men insult and swear, women flatter and wheedle, women draw others out while men monopolize conversations, men are direct and women beat around the bush, women gossip whereas men lecture. Linguistic conventions and familiar vocabulary equate humanity with males (note, for example, so-called generic uses of 'he') and sexuality with females ('hussy', for instance, once meant 'house-wife'). Men are linguistically represented as actors and women as acted upon, passive. Men control the institutions controlling language – such as schools, churches, publications, legislatures. Children of both sexes, however, learn a 'mother tongue' at a mother's knee.

Such generalizations contain a few grains of truth, at least if restricted to so-called mainstream contemporary America or England. But they completely obscure the differences among women and among men and the varied forms of social relations so important to gender. One is never just a woman or a man: sexual classifications are inflected by age, class, race and much else. And gender involves not only women in relation to men as a group but also more specific cross-sex and same-sex relations ranging from egalitarian heterosexual marriages and same-sex partnerships through intense friendships and enmities among adolescent schoolgirls to camaraderie among boys on a football team. All such relations are partly constituted by people using language to and of one another; all are informed by and inform larger social arrangements. On the more linguistic side, these include dictionaries, the language arts curriculum and editorial guidelines; arrangements with a gender focus include marriage, high-school dances and gay rights legislation.

Emphasizing large-scale sex difference ignores cross-cultural and historical variation and makes change in language, in gender, or in their interaction appear mysterious. And such an emphasis erases the linguistic dynamics of a particular society's construction of gender. Yet it is in such dynamics that, for example, language shapes and is shaped by sexual polarization and male dominance. This entry highlights approaches to language and gender that root each in historically situated social practice. Linguistic change and gender change then become inseparable.

1   Recent background
2   Gender and language in social practice
3   Connecting two different conceptions of discourse
4   Changing language, changing gender

1   Recent background

In the early 1970s, feminist-inspired interest in sex and gender revived venerable philosophical and linguistic questions about how language, culture and thought interact. During the 1980s and 1990s, feminist scholarship in the USA and Europe took an increasingly linguistic turn, not only in philosophy and linguistics but also in history, literary theory, psychology, politics and sociology. From many different viewpoints, scholars argue that language – and more generally, discourse (see §3) – shapes gender identities and relations and supports male and heterosexual privilege. Outside the academy as well, language figures prominently in gender discussions. Mass circulation publications report that the sexes speak 'different languages'; feature writers complain about feminist 'word police' (and often two sentences later about 'misuses' or 'abuses' of words like rape); anti-sexist and gay rights activists invent new terminology (sexism or homophobia) or renovate the old (using queer in positive self-reference or she as a generic pronoun).

Language-gender debates, however, include participants with different conceptions both of language and of gender. This section touches on three recent kinds of work: the Anglo-American empirically oriented tradition, psychoanalytic theorizing from French philosophers and linguists, and work on discourse and gender construction from feminist philosophers and other theorists in literary and cultural studies.

Linguist Robin Lakoff's widely read Language and Woman's Place (1975) framed much subsequent discussion by American linguists and social scientists and some philosophers. Lakoff argued that women face a double-bind. To sound feminine they must speak indirectly and euphemistically; that style, however, is derided as ineffective in public arenas. She argued also that women were systematically derogated when spoken of, that language used of women conventionally implied that they were less worthy and important than men. Although she did not join in the widespread critique of masculine generics (for example, man for humans generally or he with a general antecedent; see the introduction to Frank and Treichler (1989) for a discussion of this topic), she noted instructive examples of asymmetries in linguistic resources for speaking of men and of women: cleaning lady, for instance, versus the non-occurring garbage gentleman or the metaphorical extension of animal or food terms to refer to women, such as cow or tart.

Others challenged Lakoff's ideas. Linguists such as Janet Holmes (1995) pointed to the multiple functions of linguistic forms. For example, rising intonation on a statement, a form Lakoff interpreted as signalling women's uncertainty or insecurity, can facilitate effective communicative interaction, inviting others to speak. Tag questions ('he's pathetic, *isn't he*?') have a similar range of functions. Lakoff's critics also noted the cultural specificity of speech styles (for example, many African-American women reported Lakoff's characterizations inapplicable to their everyday speech). Furthermore, some (most notably, Penelope Brown (1980) and Marjorie Harness Goodwin (1990)) argued that sex-differentiated rhetorical strategies are not arbitrary cultural conventions. They arise as strategic responses to general social constraints and the specific demands of particular communicative contexts. Women's linguistic agency began to be explored, not just their victimization.

During the same period, some French thinkers began to articulate feminist perspectives on post-structuralist or postmodern views of language. The post-structuralist stance does not take language as a closed system for representing a pre-existing reality (see POSTMODERNISM §2). To speak or write is never a neutral act of encoding, as dominant Anglo-American views of language seem to suggest, but always enacts a self; language is constitutive of subjectivity.

Psychoanalysis, Freud's 'talking cure', has always given language a prominent place, and French psychoanalyst Jacques LACAN made it central in his interpretation of Freud. Linguistic communication, he proposed, is an attempt to erase the first and most traumatic psychic pain, the wrenching separation of birth. To speak is to try to reconnect with the mother, or, more generally, to connect to another; this attempt at (re)connection is inherently phallic. Moreover, to speak and be understood requires one to submit to patriarchal social laws, to place oneself under the Law of the Father. None of this is a matter of being male or female: women can and do speak and write but linguistic communication remains phallic, not feminine, at a deep psychosexual level (see FEMINISM AND PSYCHOANALYSIS).

Then is silence the only feminine linguistic move? The linguistic and social *status quo*, though powerful, are not stable closed systems. Breaks in the discourse, slips of the tongue, puns, parody and repetition, all bespeak psychic difference and potential resistance, and offer a glimpse beyond the Law of the Father. Such moves disturb and destabilize the patriarchal *status quo*; they can render audible a feminine voice outside the phallic linguistic order. Again it is not sex that is at issue: a man's speech or writing may inscribe a de-centring feminine voice, exposing the instability of the ruling order and threatening its hegemony. Although the French postmodern turn does not

necessarily promote the dismantling of male privilege, there is a strong feminist strain in such thinking. The feminine and masculine within each person – a kind of bisexuality – is the fulcrum on which Luce IRIGARAY and Hélène CIXOUS, for example, balance femin*ist* politics. Although their specific projects differ, both make femin*ine* outside voices more prominent, and they subvert in varied ways established patriarchal assumptions and values.

Both early American emphasis on sex-differentiated modes of speaking and sexist linguistic resources, and the French focus on the psychosexual significance of language, seemed to take sexual difference and male dominance as given, as prior to linguistic practices. Women and men, the feminine and the masculine – these were unequal poles existing outside language. During the mid-1980s and early 1990s, however, a number of English-speaking feminist philosophers and other cultural and social theorists explicitly questioned the 'naturalness' of heterosexuality and of polarized and hierarchized gender oppositions. They reread thinkers like Irigaray (1977) and emphasized the role of discourse in constructing gender identities and relations, noting that linguistic abstractions and other symbolic practices are central to constructing categories of sex and sexuality. Queer theory especially emphasized the instability of those categories, their emergence from performance, and thus the possibility of alternative forms of gender and sexuality (see, for example, Butler 1990). In a related move, thinkers with a more empirical bent began to conceptualize gender as emerging from social practice (see, for example, Connell 1987).

2 Gender and language in social practice

Much early empirical work took gender and language each as independent structured systems. Researchers asked whether these systems were correlated or connected but not how such connections might arise or why they might matter. Social practice theory suggested a different strategy. Do not look at language and gender as macrosystems; look instead at the microlevel of social activities and conventions for understanding and regulating them. Both gender and language systems can be seen as rooted in social practice; because a single activity often has both gender and language implications, these roots intertwine. Even shared roots do not, however, guarantee that the separate structures supported will connect at higher levels.

What does it mean to say that language is rooted in social practice? Natural language grammars have been argued (most notably by Chomsky and followers) to be tightly constrained by the nature of human minds, seen in this respect as sexless – and likewise unaffected by race, class and geographical origins (see CHOMSKY, N.; LANGUAGE, INNATENESS OF). From this perspective, fruitful for much linguistic inquiry, social life seems inconsequential to the forms of language. Specifying grammatical possibilities, however, does not tell us everything about language in human history.

At the simplest level, people aim at coordinating their grammars so that communication works reliably within a community. They also talk like those around them simply in order to mark themselves as a social collectivity. Thus controversial questions arise: which grammar(s) or language(s)/dialect(s) should a particular community use? Who adjusts to whom? How do male-dominated institutions affect choice among linguistic possibilities? And (nearer the periphery from a grammatical viewpoint but central for language-users) which words with which meanings are part of shared resources? What difference can vocabulary make to thought and social interaction?

This latter question moves us beyond the form of a community's linguistic resources to the functions those resources serve. What are norms for using language? Are women supposed to listen to men more than men to women? Is it mostly men's linguistic formulations of ideas that enter common currency and serve as background when others speak and write? Who jokes and when? Who swears and when? Who is polite to whom and why? Who suggests and who orders? In which situations and to which addressees? Which meanings are contested? When, where and for whom is silence or talk prescribed? In most communities, doing things with words is highly inflected by gender relations – and also by class, race, age and other dimensions of social difference and hierarchy.

Even more than language, gender is assumed to be built on a biological foundation. Virtually all cultures sort people at birth into one of two sex categories – female and male. External genitalia, which generally predict potential reproductive roles, mark sex at birth. Thereafter, however, other socially constructed markers take precedence. In most social groups sexual classification is associated with power relations, division of labour and regulation of many other areas of life including erotic activity (heterosexism and racism, for example, dictate that desire should be directed only towards someone of the other sex and the same race). Even what we think of as most 'biological' – the roles played in species reproduction – can be affected by social activity. Consider such historical developments as bottle-feeding, frozen sperm and test-tube babies. Just as strikingly, cultures differ dramatically in the range of gendered identities they offer (not all, for instance, stop with two sexes) and the kinds of gender relations that prevail.

The substantive content of gender derives from social practices and the attitudes and expectations that drive and support them. Some areas of gender practice seem independent of language: for example, styles of dress and other kinds of bodily adornment and demeanour, conventions regulating who touches whom when and where and what the reaction should be, participation in competitive sports, food preparation and serving. Even these, however, connect to linguistic practices. A person's clothes and visual style may get them dubbed 'slutty' or 'elegant', silence is deemed consent to sexually charged touch, locker-room talk is judged unsuitable for female ears, a group of women talks in the kitchen while their male partners trade comments about the football game on the living room television.

Writing is also important. Teen magazines have articles on lip gloss and diet, self-help books advise on female orgasm, newspapers devote much of their space to sports stories and use sports metaphors even in articles about business or politics, women's but not men's magazines include many pieces on food for family and for entertaining. Of course neither speech nor writing is just words. Teen magazines, for example, link to huge cosmetics and fashion industries and to the myriad of institutions and practices pushing teenage girls towards (exclusively heterosexual) romance. But the bottom line is that social practices of all kinds have rich linguistic texture: language is central to social life.

3 Connecting two different conceptions of discourse

The emphasis of much recent feminist thinking has been on discourse as a global feature of culture, what I will call cultural discourse. We might, for instance, talk about the (cultural) discourse of romance in which talk, writing, clothing, photographs, film and much else present romance as normatively heterosexual, females' primary aspiration in life, the only important form of cross-sex relations, and so on. Cultural discourse covers background assumptions, favoured rhetorical strategies, vocabulary, and non-linguistic activities and representations that highlight some perspectives on a particular domain (for example, intimate interpersonal relations) and obscure others.

Linguists and many philosophers of language use a notion of discourse more narrowly linguistic and less global. What I will call a situated discourse consists of a historically located series of connected utterances or inscriptions – for example, a conversation or a written narrative. For analytic purposes we can identify a (situated) discourse with a string of sentences together with relevant aspects of the contexts in which the sentences are produced and interpreted. Cultural discourse can be seen as grounded in situated discourses, whose detailed analysis may shed light on the microstructure of larger discursive constructions of gender.

Studies of language in use give concrete linguistic content to claims about the discursive production of sex, sexuality and gender. For example, names and styles of address start forming sexed identities early on (nurses in one hospital were heard calling baby girls 'sweetheart' or 'beautiful', but using 'Jones' for the baby boy with that surname). Adolescents draw on categorizing practices that link sex and sexual decorum with social class when they label someone 'slut'. Engagement in same-sex verbal tussles (direct insults, often overlaid with humour, or 'he-said/she-said' tales about absent parties), heterosexual harassment (street comments on a woman's body) or the discourse of romance (identifying four-year-olds' opposite-sex playmates as their 'sweethearts') – such everyday language-use helps shape and sustain particular forms of gender identity and relations.

Less everyday language-use is also, of course, critically important. Sermons or scriptures may enjoin women's silence in places of worship or other forms of sex-differentiation and hierarchy. And social scientists write about gender, often equating it with statistically significant sex differences (and ignoring its inseparability from matters of class, race, gender and even age). We find, for instance, sweeping and dichotomizing claims about how women and men speak. Such work is popularized and becomes enormously influential. It gets used not only for interpreting but for regulating gender-language connections: not only is this 'on average' how women and men speak but this is how 'real' or 'nondeviant' women and men speak or ought to speak. (Although Tannen (1990) herself avoids such normativizing, her many readers have not.)

Social life depends on social interaction, whether face-to-face or more diffuse and larger in scale. Interactions are made up of more than situated discourses, of course, but language is central to most of them and virtually essential to large-scale and long-distance social exchange. Situated discourses are the primary ingredient of social life: cultural discourses derive much of their substance from situated discourses.

All situated discourses are constrained by conventions and institutions predating them. All, however, have potential effects on subsequent discourses and, more generally, on social structural constraints

affecting talk and understanding, on cultural discourses and other macro-level social arrangements. For example, when talking about people in general, saying 'Each must do what she thinks best' will startle many listeners: English classes have prescribed 'Each must do what he thinks best' in such contexts. The feminine generic goes against familiar conventions, yet its increasing use (notably in American philosophical writing) begins to establish an alternative convention. The more it is used the less it shocks.

4 Changing language, changing gender

'Sticks and stones may break my bones but words will never hurt me', chant children trying to defuse the sting of labels like 'sissy', 'faggot' or 'bitch'. They seek to convince themselves and their tormentors of the view, widely endorsed in one form or another, that language has no force, is causally inert. As formal objects on their own, of course, words (more generally, languages) do not hurt people or do anything else to them. But words in use do indeed affect people in many ways: they convince, persuade, enlighten, frighten, humiliate, amuse, disgust, titillate. Words link to social arrangements on the one hand (see SPEECH ACTS), and to causally relevant features of courses of events on the other (see REFERENCE). These links give them many kinds of power in human affairs and thinking, both individual and collective. Thus it is not surprising that language and social change might go hand in hand.

Take a simple example. Labelling people affects how those people and their labellers then enter into a host of social practices. Until recently most communities using American-English conventionally assigned adult women social titles on the basis of marital status ('Mrs' or 'Miss'), whereas men's social titles were not so differentiated ('Mr' being the only option other than occupational and professional titles). The introduction of 'Ms' offered women a title option supposedly neutral as to marital status. This option was adopted by a diverse group including advertisers who did not want to offend by making mistaken assumptions about marital status, young unmarried women wishing not to advertise themselves as single, and self-described feminist women claiming a status equivalent to that of male peers (whether husbands or not). There have been other changes in linguistic practice connected to marriage, sexuality and family: for example, more women retain a pre-marriage surname or hyphenate surnames, some couples create a new shared surname, and some use the mother's surname for a child; even women who have adopted a husband's surname frequently favour 'Ms/Mrs Jane Doe' over the formerly dominant 'Mrs

John Doe' form; employers and others now inquire about a 'spouse' (or even a 'partner', finessing both marital status and sexual preference) rather than a 'wife'; marriage ceremonies much less often ask a woman to 'obey' a husband, and those officiating frequently pronounce the couple 'husband and wife' rather than 'man and wife'; same-sex couples go through marriage-like rituals and adopt common surnames; 'parent' has acquired a use as a verb (which is semantically far closer to the verb 'to mother' than to the verb 'to father').

Such changes in sociolinguistic practice have accompanied nonlinguistic changes in the institutions of marriage and family and practices associated with them. Middle-class women are less likely than they used to be to assume their economic welfare and social position will derive from husbands' income and status. Not only do young women see divorce as a real possibility, they also see themselves as capable of significant earnings and professional achievement, whether or not they opt to marry or to have children. Some men see caring for children – parenting – as a central role for part of their lives. Heterosexual marriage of the traditional hierarchical and strongly sex-differentiated kind, though still in many ways the default option for middle-class Americans, is increasingly seen as not the only choice open, not even for women who want to bear children. Adding 'Ms' as a title option for women and changing laws about surnames of married women and their children could not have increased women's participation in high-level careers if all else had remained the same, just as having available the sex-neutral verb 'to parent' does not suffice to get men more actively engaged in the activity it denotes. But changes in linguistic practice have been (and continue to be) part and parcel of changes in gender practices – the linguistic and nonlinguistic developments reinforce one another.

Linguistic practices change all the time. For example, new words or terms are introduced. 'Surrogate mother' designates a kind of relation of woman and child not earlier envisaged (and carries with it certain assumptions about the social weightiness of that relation); 'sexual harassment' groups together, on the basis of similar effects, kinds of situations previously either ignored or seen as very different in kind ('sexual teasing', for instance, and 'seduction'). Of course, new expressions draw on associations with existing ones: 'sexism', for example, developed meaning in part through the implied analogy with the word 'racism'. Sometimes an existing form is altered in its uses, as when 'partner' comes to designate the person with whom one lives in a sexually intimate relationship, whether that relationship is sanctioned by the state or religious authorities, whether the person so

designated is a woman or a man, and whether of the same sex as, or opposite sex to, oneself. But the implication of equality remains from other uses of the term 'partner'.

Customary usage may change while reference stays fixed. Some have begun to say 'my child' or 'my kid' in contexts where most people still say 'my daughter' or 'my son', to say 'kids' rather than 'girls and boys', and in other ways to resist identifying everyone always in sex-specific terms. The linguistic system and its interpretation are not thereby changed, but patterns of language-use are and with them what is implicated when people speak, what we take them to mean above and beyond what their words literally say (see IMPLICATURE). There are no explicit norms that say adults must identify a person to children by using 'that woman' or 'that man' or similar sex-specific forms, yet this is standard practice: 'Say thank you to the nice lady' rather than 'Say thank you to the nice person who gave you that sweet'. Changes in such practices might ultimately help effect major shifts in gender polarization and emphasis on sexual difference, an emphasis important for enforcing heterosexuality.

Could some group impose what might seem desirable linguistic and related social changes? Should they? History shows that some regulation is possible: for more than a century, schools and editors, for example, have proscribed singular 'they' (used by Shakespeare, Jane Austen and many others, including me and the authors of other *Routledge Encyclopedia of Philosophy* entries) and prescribed a supposedly sex-indefinite 'he'. Simply removing institutional sanctions (poor grades, having an article rejected) from the use of singular 'they' would almost certainly greatly reduce use of supposedly generic 'he'. But of course some people might continue its use, and even those who have dropped it might nonetheless speak in other ways indicating a view of humans as normatively male: 'During the night the villagers left in canoes, leaving us behind with the women and children.'

Linguistic conventions, both those that narrow the range of linguistic systems on which community members can draw and expect to be understood and those that promote certain patterns of usage (for instance, when to say 'thank you'), only constrain and never completely determine what community members will say. People can in various ways challenge and resist such conventions or exploit indeterminacy in them as to form and meaning. And other people can make countermoves as in the charges of a silly 'political correctness' hurled at those who have drawn attention to social biases implicit in existing linguistic conventions and have proposed alternatives. No social standpoint monopolizes all moves; subordinated interests can find expression. This does not mean that social advantage confers no linguistic advantage (it does) or that linguistically aided social change is not possible (it is). But total control of language use (and therefore of the patterns of thought and action it might facilitate) is only an Orwellian nightmare, not a real possibility. And, as many feminist thinkers have reminded us, quick linguistic fixes for sexism and heterosexism are just pipedreams (see the guidelines in Frank and Treichler 1989).

See also: FEMINISM; LINGUISTIC DISCRIMINATION

References and further reading

* Brown, P. (1980) 'How and Why are Women More Polite: Some Evidence from a Mayan Community', in S. McConnell-Ginet, R.A. Borker and N. Furman (eds) *Women and Language in Literature and Society*, New York: Praeger, 1980, 111–36. (Draws on Grice-style pragmatic theory and her own ethnographic work to develop a strategic view of politeness and, more generally, speaker style. Reprinted in Coates 1997.)
* Butler, J. (1990) *Gender Trouble*, London and New York: Routledge. (Develops her view of the performativity of gender and its base in discourse.)
  Cameron, D. (1985) *Feminism and Linguistic Theory*, London: Macmillan, 2nd edn, 1992. (Argues that linguists' limited conceptions of language and their inattention to feminist theory have impeded their understanding of language and gender.)
  —— (ed.) (1990) *The Feminist Critique of Language: A Reader*, London and New York: Routledge. (Extracts from a variety of sources, both literary and social scientific, including Lakoff's early writing and an interview with Irigaray.)
  Coates, J. (1996) *Women Friends Talking*, Oxford: Blackwell. (Situated discourses and their detailed analysis.)
  —— (ed.) (1997) *Language and Gender: A Reader*, Oxford: Blackwell. (Reprints many of the hard-to-get 'classics' on the topic.)
* Connell, R.W. (1987) *Gender and Power*, Stanford, CA: Stanford University Press. (A social practice theory of gender; see especially chapter 4, 'The Body and Social Practice'.)
  Eckert, P. and McConnell-Ginet, S. (1992) 'Think Practically and Look Locally: Language and Gender as Community-based Practice', *Annual Review of Anthropology* 21: 461–90; repr. in C. Roman, S. Juhasz and C. Miller (eds) *The Women and Language Debate: A Sourcebook*, New Brunswick, NJ: Rutgers University Press, 1994. (Develops

social practice view of language and of gender discussed in §2.)
* Frank, F.W. and Treichler, P.A. (eds) (1989) *Language, Gender and Professional Writing: Theoretical Approaches and Guidelines for Nonsexist Usage*, New York: Modern Language Association. (Includes several articles on how meanings develop in discourse and are sanctioned institutionally, as well as intelligent and detailed guidelines accompanied by discussion of the complexities of language-use.)
* Goodwin, M.H. (1990) *He-Said-She-Said: Talk as Social Organization among Black Children*, Bloomington, IN: Indiana University Press. (Draws on ethnomethodological theory to argue that social structure is constituted in large part by the conversational structures community members produce in their daily interactions, examples of which are analysed in detail.)
  Hall, K. and Bucholtz, M. (eds) (1995) *Gender Articulated: Arrangements of Language and the Socially Constructed Self*, London and New York: Routledge. (Papers are all written for this volume and include Lakoff's recent work, an excellent anthropological essay by S. Gal, an essay by Eckert and McConnell-Ginet developing and applying the theoretical framework introduced in their 1992 article, and many other diverse and detailed studies of language-use.)
* Holmes, J. (1995) *Women, Men and Politeness*, London: Longman. (Draws on empirical studies she and others have done of politeness and gender in language-use, noting especially multiple functions of linguistic forms.)
* Irigaray, L. (1977) *Ce Sexe Qui N'En Est Pas Un*, Paris: Éditions de Minuit; trans. C. Porter with C. Burke, *This Sex Which is Not One*, Ithaca, NY: Cornell University Press, 1985. (The essay by the same name gives a short and relatively accessible introduction to her thinking.)
* Lakoff, R. (1975) *Language and Woman's Place*, New York: Harper & Row. (An influential argument that women are victimized by language.)
  McConnell-Ginet, S., Borker, R.A. and Furman, N. (eds) (1980) *Women and Language in Literature and Society*, New York: Praeger; repr. New York: Greenwood, 1994. (First collection to bring together empirical and theoretical work from social sciences, literature and philosophy: see especially article on defining 'anger' by N. Scheman.)
  Roman, C., Juhasz, S. and Miller, C. (eds) (1994) *The Women and Language Debate: A Sourcebook*, New Brunswick, NJ: Rutgers University Press. (Collects a number of papers from literary, psychoanalytic and social scientific authors.)

* Tannen, D. (1990) *You Just Don't Understand: Women and Men in Conversation*, New York: William Morrow. (An anecdotal best-seller focusing on supposed sex differences in communicative styles.)

Vetterling-Braggin, M. (ed.) (1981) *Sexist Language: A Modern Philosophical Analysis*, Totowa, NJ: Littlefield, Adams & Co. (This collection contains many philosophical discussions of language-gender issues, including a debate on the ethics of 'Ms', along with more linguistic contributions, such as V. Valian's critique of Lakoff's failure to distinguish a language system from its uses.)

Wright, E. (ed.) (1992) *Feminism and Psychoanalysis: A Critical Dictionary*, Oxford: Blackwell. (See especially the entry 'Language', by J.F. MacCannell, and its accompanying bibliography.)

SALLY McCONNELL-GINET

LANGUAGE, CONVENTIONALITY OF

When we say that smoke means fire or that those spots mean measles, we are noting how the presence of one thing indicates the presence of another. For these natural relationships to continue, it is enough that the laws of nature remain the same. The connection between the two states is strictly causal. By contrast when we say, 'In English, "gold" means this stuff', pointing at some metal, we are insisting on an arbitrary connection between a piece of language and part of the world. We might have used another word, as other languages do, or have used this word for something else. But, for a word to have the literal meaning it does in a language, this arbitrary connection must be sustained on subsequent occasions of use. What is needed to sustain the connection is an intention on our part, not just the continued operation of natural laws.

Of course, some connections between words and things are based on natural relations; there is, for example, onomatopoeia. However, few words have this feature. For the majority of words it is quite arbitrary that they have the meanings they do, and this has led many to suppose that the regularities needed to sustain the connections between words and what they stand for are conventional rather than causal. But there are also those who deny that convention is an essential feature of language.

1 **Language as governed by conventions**
2 **Problems with convention-based accounts**
3 **Language without conventions**

1 Language as governed by conventions

Words do not have intrinsic meanings. They mean what they do because speakers have given them this meaning (see MEANING AND COMMUNICATION). But how do they do this? At first we might focus on what a speaker means by their use of words on a given occasion. This may be fixed by their communicative intentions. But for words to have a literal meaning in a public language they must have the same meaning from one occasion to the next, and many have supposed that this can be established only by conventional practice. Conventions, it is claimed, establish the regularities that give words the meanings they have for groups of speakers. So while a speaker may succeed in communicating something by their utterance of an expression on a given occasion, its literal meaning among a population of speakers is what it is conventionally used to communicate on each occasion of use.

Among those who think the appeal to conventions is essential in the study of language, there is room for disagreement about the precise explanatory role they play. Conventions are arbitrary practices that can be defined nonlinguistically; and for some this provides a reason to think they can serve in an analysis of the concept of literal meaning. The analysis proceeds in two stages. If we can explain how a speaker succeeds in meaning something by their use of words on a particular occasion then we can try to explain how this is established as the conventional meaning of those words in the common language of a given population.

An example of this programme is provided by Stephen Schiffer (1972). Schiffer begins with Grice's analysis of speaker-meaning in terms of the speaker's beliefs and intentions to explain what an expression means on a single occasion of use (see GRICE, H.P.; COMMUNICATION AND INTENTION). He then argues that we must appeal to conventions to show how speaker-meaning can give rise to the regular and literal meaning of expressions in a public language. A sequence of sounds or marks will have the literal meaning it does among a group of speakers when there is a convention to use those sounds or marks with a particular speaker-meaning. It will no longer be necessary to work out the speaker's meaning each time; the prevailing conventions among a population of speakers will make certain sounds and marks meaningful to them but not necessarily to others, and languages will be patterns of conventional regularities sustained by the practices of particular groups.

A different explanatory role for conventions is proposed by David Lewis (1975). Conventions governing use do not constitute language or determine meaning but they do establish which language is the actual language used by a population. For Lewis, *languages* are well-defined abstract objects – sets of expression-meaning pairs – which exist independently of speakers. We can characterize a language as a function which maps strings of signs to meanings. Among populations of humans there will exist conventions of *language* (in a second and more general sense of the term). These will be regularities in verbal behaviour depending on the beliefs and actions of people in those populations. These conventional regularities determine which of these abstract objects is the actual language used by that population. A population of speakers can be said to use a given language L just in case the meaning an expression has in L is the meaning it is conventionally taken to have in that population. The account is not reductive, however, for it assumes that speakers already know the meaning of sentences in a given language and choose to conform to these. But it does offer an analysis of the conventions needed for members of a population to speak the same language. This goes via Lewis' general analysis of conventions which runs as follows.

A regularity R is a convention in a population P if and only if:

(1) Everyone in P conforms to R.
(2) Everyone in P believes the others are conforming to R.
(3) The belief that the others are conforming to R gives each person in P a good reason to conform to R.
(4) People in P prefer general conformity to R to less than general conformity to it.
(5) R is not the only regularity it would be possible for everyone in P to conform to.
(6) Conditions (1) to (5) are mutually known to members of P.

On this model it is in our common interest to conform to the regularities and abide by the conventions of using a given language. This facilitates cooperation and secures communication. We can coordinate our activities by communicating reliable information to one another by using the same words. This gives us a motive for wanting the regularities to be upheld.

The actual language relation is specified as follows. For a language L to be the actual language used in P is for there to be a convention of truthfulness and trust in L; that is, a convention of using particular sentences in L to make statements only if members of P believe them to be true, and to take statements other people make in L to be a basis for forming beliefs about what is true. To do this speakers must use sentences in accordance with their meanings in L

just so long as other members of P do so. In this way Lewis seeks to reconcile the formal study of languages with activities of particular populations of human language-users.

Followers of Wittgenstein would reject both of the above accounts, criticizing as mysterious the idea of conventions correlating expressions with meanings *qua* entities, and rejecting the idea that meaning in a speech community can be explained in terms of a prior account of what individuals mean by their words on particular occasions. Once we accept that the meaning of expressions is determined by communal use, no appeal to Platonic entities is necessary. But since the rules that govern linguistic practice are determined by the community as a whole, an individual's understanding of language must be parasitic on communal practice. In contrast to the attempted reduction of literal meaning to conventions and speaker-meaning, an individual can only use language meaningfully when participating in the shared practices of a linguistic community. Thus Michael DUMMETT (1991) thinks that in using words individual language-users must hold themselves responsible to the standards of use of the language to which those words belong. On this view, a language is constituted by the conventional practices and agreed standards of usage. In addition, Dummett believes there are overarching conventions governing the overall aim of language-users to aim at the truth, as well as conventions governing the force (for example, assertoric, interrogative, imperative, and so on) with which they make their utterances.

Dummett offers an argument for the view that language must be governed by communal conventions. It concerns use of terms where we rely on experts to determine their precise meaning. The claim is that I can use the words 'fullback' or 'leveraged buyout' meaningfully while knowing little about football or finance because I rely on there being others who can use these words with greater precision. This is the phenomenon Hilary Putnam (1975) calls the division of linguistic labour (see PUTMAN, H. §3). It depends on a speaker making use of a word that has both an everyday and a more technical meaning, deferring to experts to fix the precise application of the term. However, this feature of language, although pervasive, is not essential to the existence of meaningful speech and we could get by without it. It does not show that there must be conventions of use among, or deference to, a set of experts for me to use words meaningfully.

2 Problems with convention-based accounts

In a revision to his earlier thinking, Schiffer (1987)

argues that the reductive analysis of literal meaning is unlikely to succeed since every account of the notion of speaker-meaning we have devised fails. He makes powerful criticisms of Lewis' account of the actual language relation. Speakers can understand sentences of their language they have never heard before: there are potentially infinitely many of these. Clearly, there are no conventions governing the 'still to be used' part of a language. So unless the part we use fixes the unused part there will be nothing to determine which language is the actual language of a group of speakers. It is implausible that speakers know a function which maps an infinity of sentences onto meanings. But perhaps what they know about the conventionally governed part of the language provides the resources to use and understand the rest. This would require a convention-based account of the expression-meaning of subsentential items, and the rules for their combination. Yet it is equally unlikely that speakers knowingly subscribe to conventions governing each word and grammatical construction ever used. A more plausible suggestion is that speakers have internalised a grammar of the language and this provides the semantic and syntactic resources to comprehend any sentence belonging to it. If this is correct, then why should we think it is conventions rather than psychological mechanisms that relate speakers to their languages? Schiffer argues that just as many difficulties confront us in attempting to relate speakers to grammars as to particular languages.

3 Language without conventions

Objections in principle have been raised to the idea that conventions have an essential role to play in the analysis of language. Donald DAVIDSON and Noam CHOMSKY have both denied that language requires the existence of conventions. Davidson (1986) rejects the idea that conventions are necessary for linguistic competence. Chomsky (1986) rejects the idea that they are sufficient. For Davidson, Lewis-style conventions are too restrictive to explain successful communication. For Chomsky, they are insufficiently systematic to explain a speaker's knowledge of language. (This was the basis of the criticism in §2.)

Both Chomsky and Davidson have opposed the idea of language as a social practice bound by a shared set of rules or conventions. Instead they argue that the fundamental notion of language is that of an individual's language, or idiolect. For Chomsky, language has no existence outside the mind of the individual language-user. It is a body of knowledge represented in the mind/brain of the speaker. Davidson, on the other hand, views language as necessarily social, requiring the existence of others with whom we

communicate. Despite their differences, neither accepts that we need to share a language in order to communicate.

For Davidson, meaning something by one's words depends on one's intention to be understood in a particular way and whether one succeeds. What we mean depends on what we can be understood to mean. This is possible even when speaker and hearer do not share the same meaning for a word, as the case of malapropism makes clear. Davidson goes further in conjecturing that there is no reason in principle why speakers who understand each other have to share any aspects of their language. What they would rely upon instead are general principles for interpreting one another's behaviour: principles for ascribing meanings to each other's words, so as to make rational sense of someone's utterance given the beliefs and desires that best explain that person's behaviour. This is not to deny that there are conventional aspects to language use, or that in actual speech situations people will make use of similar syntactic devices and enjoy overlapping vocabularies. But none of this is essential for communication. Even where conventions do exist in a language, it is possible to depart from them and still be understood. How far we can depart cannot be determined in advance nor settled by another set of conventions. Thus, Davidson argues, we need neither appeal to conventions nor stick to them to be understood, so they cannot play an essential role in linguistic understanding.

Chomsky agrees with Davidson that for a speaker and hearer to understand one another they do not need to agree on the meaning of words or abide by shared conventions. He departs from Davidson in rejecting the idea that success in communication is a condition of significant language use. Communication is never guaranteed and it does not enter into the conditions for something's being a language. For Chomsky, language is determined by the cognitive psychological facts internal to the speaker's language faculty. No two speakers will share the same idiolect; each will have their own internalized grammar and lexicon. If anything is shared it is the initial state of the language faculty characterized by the principles of universal grammar. For Chomsky, universal grammar, which comprises a set of structural principles true of all human languages, is a genetic endowment (see LANGUAGE, INNATENESS OF). Speakers have no conscious or explicit knowledge of it, so cannot choose to conform to it. Nor, if Chomsky is right, is there any alternative to relying on it. Its operation cannot count, therefore, as a convention of language according to Lewis' definition. For Chomsky it is universal grammar, and not the existence of conventions, that explains the possibility of human languages.

Whether one accepts Chomsky's view of languages, his empirical findings point to difficulties for Lewis' proposal. For if no two speakers ever share the very same vocabulary items or observe exactly the same rules of grammar there will be no formally precise, syntactic and semantic characterization of the language spoken by a given community. On the other hand, what the regularity account of conventions correctly stresses is the social and public aspect of linguistic use and meaning, although in insisting on shared practices, or conformity to communal standards, it goes beyond what is necessary to ensure these. Davidson's arguments show that meanings can be established publicly without having to be conventional. Conventions of language may abound but they have not been shown to play an essential role in language.

See also: Language, social nature of

References and further reading

* Chomsky, N. (1986) *Knowledge of Language*, New York: Praeger. (Chapters 1 and 2 offer a clear exposition of his psychological conception of an individual's language.)
* Davidson, D. (1986) *A Nice Derangement of Epitaphs*, in E. Lepore (ed.) *Truth and Interpretation*, Oxford: Blackwell. (Presents the case against conventions and shared public languages.)
  Davies, M. (1981) *Meaning, Quantification, Necessity*, London: Routledge. (Chapter 1 presents a clear and detailed account of the analytical programme discussed in §1.)
* Dummett, M.A.E. (1991) *The Logical Basis of Metaphysics*, Cambridge, MA: Harvard University Press. (Chapter 4 summarizes Dummett's views about language, arguing against Davidson and Chomsky and in favour of a communal conception of language.)
* Lewis, D.K. (1975) *Languages and Language*, in A. Martinich (ed.) *The Philosophy of Language*, Oxford: Oxford University Press, 2nd edn, 1990. (Key paper expanding on material discussed in §1.)
  Loar, B. (1981) *Mind and Meaning*, Cambridge: Cambridge University Press. (A well-argued account of the project to define semantic notions in psychological terms with good observations of the difficulties noted in §2 for convention-based accounts of meaning.)
* Putnam, H. (1975) 'The Meaning of "Meaning"', *Collected Papers*, vol. 2, Cambridge: Cambridge University Press. (An important paper covering many themes beyond the scope of this entry. Of use here for the account of the division of linguistic labour.)
* Schiffer, S. (1972) *Meaning*, Oxford: Oxford University Press. (A densely argued book with elaborate discussion of the analytic programme described in §1. Not elementary.)
* —— (1987) *Remnants of Meaning*, Cambridge, MA: MIT Press. (A closely argued rebuttal of his earlier views and of any attempt to provide a theory of meaning. Challenging but not for beginners.)
  —— (1993) 'Actual Language Relations', *Philosophical Perspectives* 7: 231–58. (A thorough assessment of attempts to define these relations.)

BARRY C. SMITH

LANGUAGE, EARLY MODERN PHILOSOPHY OF

Philosophical interest in language during the seventeenth and eighteenth centuries was strong but largely derivative. Most thinkers shared Leibniz's view 'that languages are the best mirror of the human mind, and that a precise analysis of the significations of words would tell us more than anything else about the operations of the understanding'.

The three most important areas of philosophical discussion about language in the modern period were the nature of signification, the origin of human language and the possibility of animal language. Signification was generally viewed as a relation between linguistic signs and ideas. There was no agreement whether signification is entirely conventional or contains a natural element, but the view is that it is entirely natural virtually disappeared. Even those who retained the belief in the possibility of a philosophically perfect language insisted that such a language should be constructed anew, rather than rediscovered as the lost language of Adam. The traditional biblical account of the origin of language was more and more contested but, as more naturalistic theories emerged, the problem of why other animals cannot talk became especially pressing.

Debates about language in the seventeenth and eighteenth centuries were highly speculative; participants in these debates often relied on simplistic biological theories, inadequate grammars or anecdotal evidence from travellers. What makes these discussions important is less their scientific contribution than their engagement with the philosophical problems concerning the relationship between the human mind and the natural world.

1   The biblical and Lucretian accounts

Two classical accounts provided the intellectual background for modern philosophical debates about language. The first is the biblical story according to which the original names of beasts and birds were given by Adam. Renaissance speculation contends that these names were inspired by God, bore a natural relation to the creatures, and captured their essences. After the confusion at Babel, Adam's universal language was scattered into mutually unintelligible forms of speech, each of which began to decay. The second influential ancient story comes from Lucretius' *On the Nature of Things* (V.1028–90). According to Lucretius, language is an institution created by a community of humans, rather than a single name-giver. People came to form articulate sounds out of a need to coordinate their actions. At the beginning, the ability to communicate by words differed little from children's ability to indicate the object they desire by means of gestures, or animals' ability to indicate fear or pain by cries. As language developed, its structure became more complicated and its uses more diverse.

Perhaps the most criticized point of the biblical account is the claim that language originates with the naming act of a single person. Ideas from Hobbes' *Leviathan* (1651), Locke's *Second Treatise on Government* (1690) and Rousseau's *Du contrat social* (The Social Contract) (1762) provide the paradigm of how a social account of the origin of language might be framed. According to the contractarian view, social norms – whether they are laws of property or laws of meaning – are the result of explicit or tacit agreements among human beings. There is a striking parallel between Locke's criticism of the natural origin of the title to sovereignty in the *First Treatise on Government* (1690) and his opposition to the natural foundation of categorization in the *An Essay Concerning Human Understanding* (1689). Who is to be the heir is not to be decided through the study of the line of inheritance from Adam; what is to be gold is not to be decided through the study of how the word 'gold' descended from the original naming act of Adam. It is rationally grounded convention that settles these matters. Philosophers of the Enlightenment followed Locke's analysis and brushed away the biblical account. Condillac, Rousseau and Herder argued that even if language happens to be a divine creation, human beings had to reinvent it after the Flood or after they scattered over large uninhabited areas, leaving the biblical story at best irrelevant.

The most controversial point of the Lucretian account is the claim that the difference between the primitive signalling of animals and human languages is only a matter of degree. Descartes argued that the ability to understand an unlimited variety of expressions is distinctive of a mind, something that the smartest animal could never do, but which is no challenge for even the dullest human being. This shows 'not merely that beasts have less reason than men, but that they have no reason at all' (Descartes 1637: 58). In his objections, Gassendi protested against this conclusion, and insisted that animals do in fact speak. The Cartesian response – analysing animal signalling and the bodily aspects of human communication in physiological terms – was accomplished in great detail by Géraud de Cordemoy. The conclusion was that since such an analysis provides a full account of animal signalling, but not of human language, the latter but not the former presupposes a mind (see ANIMAL LANGUAGE AND THOUGHT).

2   Empiricism: Hobbes

Although not primarily concerned with philosophy of language, Thomas Hobbes presented an influential and distinctively empiricist account of language in Chapter 4 of *Leviathan* (1651) and Part 1 of his *De corpore* (On the Body) (1655).

According to Hobbes, the purpose of speech is to 'transferre our Mentall Discourse, into Verbal; or the Trayne of our Thoughts, into a Trayne of Words' (1651: I.4). There are two reasons we make such a transfer: to record our thoughts for ourselves, and to communicate our thoughts to others. Words employed as mnemonic devices are *notae* (marks); words employed as means of communication are *signa* (signs) (1655: II.1–2). Hobbes holds that the first use of words is primary: if a person were alone in the world, he could create a private language and use words as marks, but not as signs (1655: II.3).

Hobbes' philosophy of language has two main parts. The first is the account of the relationship between words and what they stand for, or the theory of *names* (1655: II); the second is the account of the connections names bear to each other, or the theory of *propositions* (1655: III).

Names signify conventionally: Hobbes thinks that even if the original names of animals come from God himself, he nevertheless chose those names arbitrarily (1655: II.4). What a name signifies is a *cogitatio* (thought), for the claim that a word like 'stone' is a sign for stones can only be understood as saying that 'he that hears it collects that he that pronounces it thinks of a stone' (1655: II.5). (Nonetheless, Hobbes often speaks of names as signifying things without the mind.) Hobbes is committed to the empiricist thesis that all human thinking is based on imagination. Since imagination itself is nothing but decaying sense, we cannot meaningfully speak of things that cannot be thought of as combinations of sensory images we had previously. Hence, for example, we cannot think of actual infinity: saying that something is infinite means merely that we are 'not able to conceive the ends, and bounds of the thing named' (1651: III.12).

Hobbes' semantics is purely nominalistic (see NOMINALISM §3). General terms do not pick out properties, but signify disjointedly every individual to which they apply (1655: II.9). In a proposition, both terms 'raise in our mind the thought of one and the same thing', and the copula 'makes us think of the cause for which those names were imposed on that thing' (1655: III.3). The proposition *man is a living creature* raises but one idea in us, though in that idea we consider that first, for which he is called man, and next that, for which he is called living creature' (1655: V.9).

Conventionalism about signification and nominalism in semantics prepare the ground for conventionalism about truth. Truth is ascribed only to propositions, and it consists in the fact that the predicate is a name of everything that the subject is a name of. According to Hobbes, 'the first truths were arbitrarily made by those that first of all imposed names upon things, or received them from the imposition of others. For it is true (for example) that man is a living creature, but it is for this reason, that it pleased men to impose both those names on the same thing' (1655: III.8). It is controversial whether Hobbes consistently adhered to this radical view (see HOBBES, T. §3).

3 Rationalism: Port-Royal

Grammaire générale et raisonnée (*General and Rational Grammar: The Port-Royal Grammar*) (1660) and *La logique ou l'art de penser* (*Logic or the Art of Thinking*) (1662) articulate a rationalist conception of language sharply opposed to Hobbes' empiricism. Following Descartes, Arnauld and his collaborators (Claude Lancelot in *Grammar* and Pierre Nicole in *Logic*) reject not only empiricism, but conventionalism and nominalism as well.

The empiricist claim that all our thoughts originate in perception leaves unexplained how we attain ideas like those of being and thinking. Since – the authors of *Logic* insist – we do have such ideas, it follows that 'the soul has the faculty to form them from itself, although often it is prompted to do so by something striking the senses' (1662: I.1). The element of truth in conventionalism is that the association between a word and an idea is arbitrary. However, since the connections among ideas and between ideas and things are natural, we reason not about words but 'about the nature of things by considering ideas of the mind that people chose to mark by certain names' (1662: I.1). Finally, while nominalists are right to claim that all existent things are singular, some entities are not things, but rather modes of things. Modes exist only in virtue of being instantiated in things, but they can be thought of independently of the things in which they inhere (1662: I.2, I.6, II.1).

The semantic terminology of *Grammar* and *Logic* is often loose. The authors talk about words signifying (*signifier*), expressing (*exprimer*) or marking (*marquer*) both things and ideas. (The relationship between ideas and things, however, is consistently called *représentation* (representation).) The principal meaning (*signification principale*) of a word or a sentence is the idea or proposition it expresses, but in order to capture its full meaning connotations must also be taken into account. These connotations are called *auxiliary ideas* (*idées accessoires*). For example, the principal meaning of the sentence 'You are lying' is simply 'You know that the contrary of what you say is true', but in addition to the principal meaning, these words also convey the idea of contempt (1662: I.14).

The principal meaning of a word can often be presented by an explicit definition. Following Aristotle's distinction and scholastic terminology, Arnauld and Nicole distinguish between *nominal definition* and *real definition* (1662: I.12). A nominal definition captures a connection between a word and an idea; a real definition captures a connection between ideas, which in turn corresponds to a connection between real entities. Therefore, nominal definitions – at least in their purest form – are arbitrary and are not subject to rational criticism. On the other hand, real definitions in their purest form 'do not depend on us at all, but on what is contained in the true idea of a thing' (1662: II.16). But there are impure definitions as well. *Lexical* definitions are intended to capture the ordinary meaning of the word and are consequently discovered and not stipulated by lexicographers (1662: I.14). As lexical definitions are atypical nominal definitions, *descriptions* are atypical real definitions. Descriptions list a number of accidents which are sufficient to specify the extension of an idea, but not the common nature of things within the extension (1662: II.16).

According to Arnauld and Lancelot there are two major categories of words: those that signify the objects of thoughts and those that signify the manner of thoughts (1660: II.1, II.13). The most important subcategory within the first is that of nouns; within the second, verbs. Concrete substantival nouns (such as 'sun') signify substances, abstract substantival nouns (such as 'whiteness') signify modes (1662: II.1). An adjectival noun has two significata: 'white' signifies distinctly the mode of whiteness, and confusedly signifies white things. A verb is a word whose principal function is to indicate assertion, and the copulative verb 'to be' has only this principal function (1660: II.13). Other verbs also have a secondary role: they express ideas and thereby refer to entities, and they indicate the time with respect to which the assertion is made. For instance, the verb 'lives' in the sentence 'Peter lives' expresses the mode of being alive and indicates the assertion that this mode belongs to Peter at the time of the assertion (1660: II.13).

The mind judges by uniting or separating two ideas. The product of judging is a proposition. Propositions are *simple* if they have a single subject and a single predicate, and *compound* otherwise. Compound propositions include among others conjunctions, disjunctions and conditionals. Not all complexity in the subject or predicate terms indicates that the proposition is compound. For example, 'The invisible God has created the visible world' – or equivalently, 'God who is invisible created the world which is visible' – is a *simple but complex* proposition. For although it contains three propositions – 'God is invisible', 'God created the world' and 'The world is visible' – only the second of these is asserted, while the others are assumed or taken for granted (1662: II.5; 1660: II.9). By contrast, the proposition 'God is invisible and he created the visible world' is compound, since it ascribes two different predicates to the same subject (see ARNAULD, A.; PORT-ROYAL).

4 Locke's *Essay*

Although remaining firmly in the empiricist tradition, John Locke's *An Essay Concerning Human Understanding* (1689) incorporates some of the insights of Cartesian rationalism. This synthesis makes the *Essay* the essential point of reference for all philosophy of language in the eighteenth century.

According to Locke, the primary purpose of language is communication. God or nature made our organs fit to produce articulate sounds, and through arbitrary imposition we are capable of making these sounds 'Signs of internal Conceptions' (Locke 1689: III.i.2; see also III.ii.1). At first glance, this view resembles Hobbes', but – as Leibniz remarks at the beginning of Book III of his *Nouveaux essais sur l'entendement humain* (*New Essays on Human*

Understanding) (posthumously published in 1765) – there is an important difference: for Hobbes the private use of words is fundamental, whereas for Locke it is their use as signs for others.

The main thesis of Locke's theory of signification is that 'Words in their primary or immediate signification, stand for nothing, but the Ideas in the Mind of him that uses them' (1689: III.ii.2). Since the purpose of words is to invoke in the hearer's mind an idea identical (or at least sufficiently similar) to the idea the speaker has in mind, a word is bound to be intimately connected to an idea of the speaker. To say that primary signification is nothing but the speaker's idea does not mean that the word refers to that idea, or that in using a certain word the speaker is talking about the idea his word primarily signifies. Besides the primary signification of words, men often 'in their Thoughts give them a secret reference to two other things': the ideas in the minds of other speakers, and the reality of things (1689: III.ii.4). This supposition of *secondary signification* is indispensable for human beings, since 'without this double Conformity of their Ideas, they find, they should both think amiss of Things in themselves, and talk of them unintelligibly to others' (1689: II.xxxii.8). Locke apparently condemns only the assumption that words can directly signify the ideas of others and the reality of extramental things, without the mediation of their primary signification.

In accordance with the Cartesian tradition, Locke emphasizes that a genuine language cannot contain only singular names. We need signs which stand for more than one thing, since without these there would be too many (perhaps infinitely many) words to learn (1689: III.i.3; III.iii.2–4). With regard to the signification of these general terms Locke was a conventionalist. His primary target is the doctrine that general terms signify substantial forms, genuine universals in the things themselves that provide the ground for an objective classification of things. Since, he argues, our ideas are made up exclusively from the materials provided by experience (1689: II.xii.1), and since we cannot form ideas of substantial forms in this manner (1689: III.vi.10), substantial forms cannot be the significata of general words. The general term 'horse' signifies the *abstract general idea* of a horse, an idea that represents actual horses in virtue of representing certain sensible qualities they have in common. According to Locke, when we categorize things, we use the significata of our general terms. Fixing the significata of these terms is not a matter of discovering determinate species that exist independently of us, but rather a matter of reasonable choice from among the innumerable objective similarities of things (1689: III.iii.13).

In the case of ideas of substance, which represent natural unions of qualities, our forming of the appropriate abstract idea is independent of our linguistic abilities. The case is more complicated in the case of ideas of mixed modes, which represent collections of qualities that are not necessarily united in the same subject. For such complex ideas, although it is 'the Mind that makes the Collection, 'tis the Name which is, as it were the Knot, that ties them fast together' (1689: III.v.10). In the case of simple modes, like those of number, the dependence on naming is even more explicit: according to Locke, we could not have ideas of large numbers for which we have no names (1689: II.xvi.5).

Locke subscribes to the Port-Royal view that syncategorematic words – terms like 'is' and 'but', which he calls *particles* – stand not for ideas but for operations of the mind by which the ideas signified by other words are put together into a proposition. The truth of a proposition consists in the 'joining or separating of Signs, as the Things signified by them, do agree or disagree with one another' (1689: IV.v.2). Whether for Locke truth consists always in agreement and disagreement between ideas, or whether he allows for agreement and disagreement between an idea and what it represents, is a controversial question of Locke interpretation (see LOCKE, J. §§3–5).

5 Critique of Locke: Berkeley and Leibniz

The main tenets of Lockean philosophy of language were widely accepted among philosophers in the eighteenth century, but they did not remain unchallenged. The most important objections to the Lockean theory were made by George Berkeley and Gottfried Wilhelm Leibniz. Berkeley's critique was sketched in his *Philosophical Commentaries* (written between 1707 and 1708), and elaborated in *A Treatise Concerning the Principles of Human Knowledge* (1710), and his dialogue *Alciphron* (1732). Leibniz's objections take the form of a line-by-line critical commentary in his *New Essays on Human Understanding* (1765).

Berkeley's critique focuses on three major areas: the purpose of language, the semantics of general terms, and the nature of signification. He denies that communication is the chief end of discourse. Besides conveying our thoughts to others, language is also used in 'the raising of some passion, the exciting to, or deterring from an action, the putting the mind in some particular disposition' (Berkeley 1710: Introduction 20). These are direct effects of speech, possibly achieved without the mediation of ideas. Berkeley's remark concerning the use of the expression 'good thing' prefigures later emotivist treatments: the function of such expressions is to excite the appropriate feelings in us (1710: Introduction 20) (see EMOTIVISM). Even expressions that – unlike 'good thing' – do signify ideas, can do so in the way the letters of algebra signify, where 'though a particular quantity be marked by each letter, yet to proceed right it is not requisite that in every step each letter suggest to your thoughts, that particular quantity it was appointed to stand for' (1710: Introduction 19).

Berkeley harshly criticizes a view he associates with Locke concerning the generality of words and ideas. For Berkeley, a general word stands for a class of particulars by signifying 'an idea, which considered in itself is particular, [but] becomes general, by being made to represent or stand for all other particular ideas of the same sort' (1710: Introduction 12). There is no need to assume that a single abstract idea is signified by each general term: by the mechanism of *selective attention* we can consider one or another feature of a particular idea, and then use it as a sign for all particular ideas that share the given feature. Berkeley's criticism may miss its target. When Locke talks about abstraction, he also uses the language of considering certain features within a particular idea (for example, Locke 1689: II.xi.9). Still, it remains unclear whether Locke thinks that abstract ideas are made from particulars via selective attention, or whether he in fact agrees with Berkeley that abstract ideas simply are particular ideas considered selectively.

Berkeley rejects the thesis that certain words have a secondary signification without the mind; things without the mind could be either material or immaterial, and Berkeley denies the existence of the former and the imaginability of the latter. Words like 'horse' or 'white' signify an idea without indicating anything beyond the idea; words like 'soul' or 'God' signify a substance without the mediation of an idea. A language is a network of signification relations between ideas which obtain in virtue of some customary connection. If the connections are the result of human imposition (for example, associating the idea of the letter 'a' with the idea of the corresponding sound, or associating the idea of the word 'apple' with some idea of an apple), the system of significations is an *artificial language*. If the connections result from divine imposition (for example, the connection between the ideas of fire and smoke, or between the visual idea of a square and a tactile idea of a square), the system is a *natural language* (Berkeley 1733: 40; see also Berkeley 1709: 140, 147). For Berkeley, the study of nature is the study of grammar for the divine language. Natural phenomena – which, of course, are merely collections of ideas – can signify one another, but they cannot stand in genuine causal relations to one another: it is God's creating and sustaining act that causes everything to exist and be the way it is (1733: 13; 1710: 65, 108) (see BERKELEY, G. §§5–6, 11).

Leibniz's two main targets in the Lockean theory are claims wholeheartedly endorsed by Berkeley: that signification of words is arbitrary and that categorization is the work of the mind. According to Leibniz, signification is 'settled by reasons – sometimes natural ones in which chance plays some part, sometimes moral ones which involve choice' (Leibniz 1765: III.2). To support this thesis, Leibniz presents etymological links connecting contemporary words with earlier forms, and sometimes ultimately with onomatopoeia. What grounds these explanations is the principle of sufficient reason: brute accidents are as unacceptable in semantics as in physics.

Leibniz defends the semantic relevance of real definitions against Locke. Although 'gold' can be given a number of different nominal definitions, only a few of these will be in agreement with the genuine conceptual analysis. A real definition is grounded in a real species, and has the characteristic mark that it 'displays the possibility of the definiendum' (1765: III.3). Since he rejects the view that ideas we have must be completely transparent to us, he can resist Locke's claim that our words cannot signify unknown features: 'the name "gold"... signifies not merely what the speaker knows of gold, e.g. something yellow and very heavy, but also what he does not know, which may be known about gold by someone else, namely: a body endowed with an inner constitution from which flow its color and weight, and which also generates other properties which he acknowledges to be better known by the experts' (1765: III.11). If pressed, we would have to come up with nominal definitions for substances; but these do not fix the meaning of the corresponding terms, since we recognize that 'our definitions are all merely provisional'. We know that something that passes all our current tests for being gold may nevertheless fail to be gold, since 'one might... discover a new assaying method which would provide a way of distinguishing natural gold from this artificial gold' (1765: III.4, 6).

What underlies this insistence on real definitions is Leibniz's commitment to the ideal of a *universal characteristic*, a written language which could be understood by any rational being and which could perfect human reasoning itself. Corresponding to each complex concept or proposition, there is a complex symbol in the universal characteristic whose structure is the same as the structure of the concept or proposition signified. Occasionally, Leibniz talks about the primitive symbols of the universal characteristic as geometrical figures – like Egyptian

hieroglyphs or Chinese characters – which bear some similarity to what they represent (Liebniz 1875–90: IV.72–3). He also made attempts to assign numerical values to various concepts and to represent conceptual analysis as analogous to prime factorization (Couturat 1903: 245–6). But – as Leibniz himself realized – our concepts are so complex that we have no reason to believe that the process of resolving them into primitive constituents is a finite one. This does not mean that the system of numerical characteristic is useless. Since logic imposes constraints on possible assignments of numerical values to concepts, and since these constraints are expressible in the form of Diophantine equations, the system of numerical characteristic without the analysis of concepts can be used as a *formal calculus* to check the validity of inferences (1875–90: VII.205) (see LEIBNIZ, G.W. §10).

6 The origin of language: Condillac and Rousseau

Questions about the origin of language were widely discussed in the seventeenth century but the views proposed did not go much beyond the biblical or the Lucretian accounts. This changed radically in 1746 with the publication of Étienne Bonnot de Condillac's *Essai sur l'origine des connaissances humaines* (*An Essay on the Origin of Human Knowledge*).

Condillac was an enthusiastic but critical follower of Locke. His disagreement with Locke concerns two issues related to language. Condillac's first criticism is that Locke's theory about the mind is merely descriptive and fails to explain how understanding originates from sensation. The second is that Locke underestimates the role language plays in a theory of ideas. The two points are connected, since the 'the consideration of words, and of our manner of using them, might give some light into the principle of our ideas' and could yield 'a far better explication of the springs of the human understanding' (introduction to Condillac 1746).

Condillac claims that human beings can attain control over their thoughts solely in virtue of the use of *instituted signs*. Animals lack the ability to establish a conventional relation between an object and its sign, they cannot recall ideas at will, and therefore cannot prudently direct their behaviour. Animals are driven by instinct, which is 'no more than the imagination, as independent of our command, though by its activity, completely concurring to the preservation of our being' (1746: I.ii.95). In *Traité des sensations* (*Treatise on Sensation*) (1754), Condillac imagines a statue gradually brought to life by obtaining its five senses one by one. According to Condillac, the fully sensitized statue will be able to recognize its basic needs, remember things and learn from experience but, because it lacks speech, it will have only 'the habit of directing itself by ideas for which it does not know how to account' (1754: II.viii.35).

But it seems that in order to make use of instituted signs, we must already have sufficient reflection to choose them and to establish the conventional link between the signs and their significata (1746: I.ii.49). This is the problem that Condillac's account of the origin of language is supposed to answer. The explanation begins with natural signs – cries and gestures: these constitute the *language of action* (1746: II.i.1). The development of reflection and the development of language are intertwined: since both require the other, they evolve through a process of bootstrapping. Communicative intentions first arise due to the recognition of the accidental success of the language of action. From that point on, reflection and language interact to the mutual expansion and sophistication of both (see CONDILLAC, É.B. DE §§2, 3).

In the years following the appearance of Condillac's *Essay*, DIDEROT, Maupertuis and Turgot in France, Adam SMITH and Lord MONBODDO in England, Moses MENDELSSOHN and Johann Gottfried HERDER in Germany each expressed their views on the origin of language. But perhaps the most significant contributions to the debate initiated by Condillac were Jean-Jacques Rousseau's *Discours sur l'origine et les fondements de l'inégalité parmi les hommes* (*Discourse on the Origin and Foundations of Inequality among Mankind*) (1755) and *Essai sur l'origine des langues* (*On the Origin of Languages*) (published posthumously in 1781). Rousseau replaces Condillac's relatively harmonious conception of the course of development with his emphasis on the conflict between human nature and social existence. He agrees that languages arise because of human needs, but he rejects the idea that these are physical needs. Physical needs would never have forced us to abandon the language of gesture (Rousseau 1781: 1). What stimulated the first words were *moral needs*, passions. 'As man's first motives for speaking were of the passions, his first expressions were tropes' (1781: 3). That is, language and art were not separated at the beginning of history. As savage man turned into barbarian man and finally into civilized man, human needs changed, and as a consequence human languages lost their connection to music, becoming more and more rational and less and less passionate (1781: 19). And as societies assumed their final form, where 'no longer is anything changed except by arms and cash', languages have also become less favourable to liberty (1781: 20) (see ROUSSEAU, J.-J. §2).

See also: LANGUAGE, PHILOSOPHY OF; LANGUAGE, RENAISSANCE PHILOSOPHY OF; UNIVERSAL LANGUAGE

List of works

Arnauld, A. and Lancelot, C. (1660) *Grammaire générale et raisonnée de Port-Royal*, repr. Geneva: Slatkine, 1968; trans. J. Rieux and B.E. Rollin, *General and Rational Grammar: The Port-Royal Grammar*, The Hague: Mouton, 1975. (The Port-Royal account of the principles of grammar.)

Arnauld, A. and Nicole, P. (1662) *La logique ou l'art de penser*, ed. P. Clair and F. Girbal, Paris: Vrin, 1981; trans. J.V. Buroker, *Logic or the Art of Thinking*, Cambridge: Cambridge University Press, 1996. (The Port-Royal account of the principles of logic.)

Berkeley, G. (1707–8) *Philosophical Commentaries*, in A.A. Luce and T.E. Jessop (eds) *The Works of George Berkeley, Bishop of Cloyne*, London: Nelson & Sons, 1948–57, 9 vols. (Berkeley's previously unpublished early notebooks.)

—— (1709) *An Essay towards a New Theory of Vision*, in A.A. Luce and T.E. Jessop (eds) *The Works of George Berkeley, Bishop of Cloyne*, London: Nelson & Sons, 1948–57, 9 vols. (Berkeley's first published work: its subject matter is visual perception.)

—— (1710) *A Treatise Concerning the Principles of Human Knowledge*, in A.A. Luce and T.E. Jessop (eds) *The Works of George Berkeley, Bishop of Cloyne*, London: Nelson & Sons, 1948–57, 9 vols. (Berkeley's main philosophical work.)

—— (1732) *Alciphron, or the Minute Philosopher*, in A.A. Luce and T.E. Jessop (eds) *The Works of George Berkeley, Bishop of Cloyne*, London: Nelson & Sons, 1948–57, 9 vols. (Dialogue of philosophical, moral and theological content.)

—— (1733) *The Theory of Vision, Vindicated and Explained*, in A.A. Luce and T.E. Jessop (eds) *The Works of George Berkeley, Bishop of Cloyne*, London: Nelson & Sons, 1948–57, 9 vols. (Reply to criticism of Berkeley 1709.)

Condillac, É.B. de (1746) *Essai sur l'origine des connaissances humaines*, in G. Le Roy (ed.) *Oeuvres philosophiques*, Paris: Presses Universitaires de France, 1947–51, 3 vols; trans. T. Nugent, *An Essay on the Origin of Human Knowledge*, Gainesville, FA: Scholar's Facsimile and Reprints, 1971. (Condillac's main philosophical work.)

—— (1754) *Traité des sensations*, in G. Le Roy (ed.) *Oeuvres philosophiques*, Paris: Presses Universitaires de France, 1947–51, 3 vols; trans. G. Carr, *Treatise on Sensations*, Los Angeles: University of Southern

California Press, 1930. (A treatise on the nature of sense perception.)

Descartes, R. (1637) *Discours de la méthode*, in C. Adam and P. Tannery (eds) *Oeuvres de Descartes*, Paris: Vrin/C.N.R.S., 1964–76, 11 vols. (The standard edition of Descartes' writings.)

Hobbes, T. (1651) *Leviathan*, ed. R. Tuck, Cambridge: Cambridge University Press, 1991. (Hobbes' main work in political philosophy.)

—— (1655) *De corpore*, in W. Molesworth (ed.) *The Latin works of Thomas Hobbes of Malmesbury*, London: John Bohn, 1845, 5 vols; trans. W. Molesworth, *The English Works of Thomas Hobbes of Malmesbury*, London: John Bohn, 1839–45, 11 vols. (Hobbes' main work in natural philosophy.)

Leibniz, G.W. (1765) *Nouveaux essais sur l'entendement humain*, in German Academy of Sciences (ed.) *G.W. Leibniz: Sämtliche Schriften und Briefe*, Berlin: Akademie, 1923–; trans. P. Remnant and J. Bennett, *New Essays on Human Understanding*, Cambridge: Cambridge University Press, 1981. (A paragraph-by-paragraph commentary and critical discussion of Locke 1689.)

—— (1875–90) *Die Philosophische Schriften von Leibniz*, ed. C.I. Gerhardt, Berlin: Weidmann, 7 vols. (One of the standard editions of Leibniz's writings.)

—— (1903) *Opuscules et fragments inédits de Leibniz*, ed. L. Couturat, Paris: Alcan. (A collection of smaller, previously unpublished pieces by Leibniz.)

Locke, J. (1689) *An Essay Concerning Human Understanding*, ed. P.H. Nidditch, Oxford: Clarendon Press, 1975. (Locke's main philosophical work.)

—— (1690) *Two Treatises of Government*, ed. P. Laslett, Cambridge: Cambridge University Press, 1960. (Locke's main work in political theory.)

Lucretius (*c.*55 BC) *On the Nature of Things*, ed. C. Bailey, *Titi Lucreti Cari De rerum natura libri sex*, Oxford: Oxford University Press, 3 vols, 1947. (Bailey is the monumental standard edition, with text, translation and commentary, still highly informative and not fully superseded.)

Rousseau, J.-J. (1755) *Discours sur l'origine et les fondements de l'inégalité parmi les hommes* (Discourse on the Origin and Foundations of Inequality among Mankind), in B. Gagnebin and M. Raymond (eds) *Oeuvres Complètes de Jean-Jacques Rousseau*, vol. 3, Paris: Pléiade, 1964; trans. D.A. Cress, *Jean-Jacques Rousseau: Basic Political Writings*, Indianapolis, IN: Hackett Publishing Company, 1987. (Rousseau's prize-winning essay on the origins of inequality.)

—— (1762) *Du contrat social* (The Social Contract), in B. Gagnebin and M. Raymond (eds) *Oeuvres Complètes de Jean-Jacques Rousseau*, vol. 3, Paris:

Pléiade, 1964; trans. D.A. Cress, *Jean-Jacques Rousseau: Basic Political Writings*, Indianapolis, IN: Hackett Publishing Company, 1987. (Rousseau's most famous political writing.)

—— (1781) *Essai sur l'origine des langues*, ed. C. Porset, Bordeaux: Ducros, 1968; trans. in J.H. Moran and A. Gode (eds) *On the Origin of Languages*, Chicago, IL: University of Chicago Press, 1966. (Rousseau's main contribution to the debate about the origin of language in the eighteenth century.)

References and further reading

Aarsleff, H. (1982) *From Locke to Saussure*, Minneapolis, MN: University of Minnesota Press. (Collection of essays on Wilkins, Locke, Leibniz, Condillac, Herder and lesser figures.)

Bertman, M. (1978) 'Hobbes on Language and Reality', *Revue Internationale de Philosophie* 32: 536–51.

Buroker, J.V. (1993) 'The Port-Royal Semantics of Terms', *Synthèse* 96: 455–75.

Chomsky, N. (1966) *Cartesian Linguistics*, New York: Lanham. (Controversial account about the connections between modern generative grammar and the Port Royal.)

Ducret, M. and Lannay, M. (1967) 'Synchronie et diachronie: *L'essai sur l'origine des langues* et le second *Discours*', *Revue Internationale de Philosophie* 21: 421–42. (On Rousseau's views about the origin of language. The entire issue of the journal is devoted to philosophy of language in the eighteenth century.)

Flage, D. (1987) *Berkeley's Doctrine of Notions: A Reconstruction Based on his Theory of Meaning*, London: Croom Helm.

Guyer, P. (1994) 'Locke's Philosophy of Language', in V. Chappell (ed.) *The Cambridge Companion to Locke*, Cambridge: Cambridge University Press. (Survey article. The volume contains a detailed bibliography.)

Heinekamp, A. (1975) 'Natürliche Sprache und Allgemeine Charakteristik bei Leibniz', *Studia Leibnitian Supplementa* 15: 257–86. (Looks at natural language and the *universal characteristic* in Liebniz.)

Hungerland, I. and Vick, G.R. (1973) 'Hobbes's Theory of Signification', *Journal of History of Philosophy* 11: 459–82.

Ishiguro, H. (1972) *Leibniz's Philosophy of Logic and Language*, Cambridge: Cambridge University Press. (Includes discussion of the connections between Leibniz's views on language and his metaphysics.)

Juliard, P. (1970) *Philosophies of Language in Eight-*

eenth Century France, The Hague: Mouton. (Discusses the philosophy of language of Condillac, Maupertuis, La Mettrie, Turgot and Rousseau.)

Kremer, E.J. (ed.) (1994) *The Great Arnauld and Some of His Philosophical Correspondents*, Toronto, Ont.: University of Toronto Press. (A collection of papers with detailed bibliography.)

Kretzmann, N. (1968) 'The Main Thesis of Locke's Semantic Theory', *Philosophical Review* 77: 175–96.

Land, S. (1986) *The Philosophy of Language in Britain*, New York: AMS Press. (Discussion of the philosophy of language of Hobbes, Locke, Berkeley, Harris, Reid, Monboddo and Smith.)

Nuchelmans, G. (1983) *Judgment and Proposition from Descartes to Kant*, Amsterdam: North Holland.

Porset, C. (1977) 'Grammatista philosophans. Les sciences du langage de Port-Royal aux Idéologues (1660–1818)', in A. Joly and J. Stefanini (eds) *La Grammaire générale. Des Modistes aux Idéologues*, Lille: Presses Universitaires de France, 11–95. (Bibliography of works in the philosophy of language and grammar between 1660 and 1818. Also covers the secondary literature before 1976.)

Ricken, U. (1984) *Linguistics, Anthropology and Philosophy in the French Enlightenment*, London: Routledge. (General survey, includes a detailed bibliography.)

Rousseau, N. (1986) *Connaissance et langage chez Condillac*, Geneva: Libraire Droz. (Monograph on Condillac with a detailed bibliography.)

Rutherford, D. (1995) 'Philosophy and Language in Leibniz', in N. Jolley (ed.) *The Cambridge Companion to Leibniz*, Cambridge: Cambridge University Press, 224–69. (Survey article. The volume contains a detailed bibliography.)

Sgard, J. (ed.) (1982) *Condillac et les problèmes du langage*, Geneva: Slatkine. (Collection of critical essays.)

Slaughter, M. (1982) *Universal Languages and Scientific Taxonomy in the Seventeenth Century*, Cambridge: Cambridge University Press.

Winkler, K.P. (1989) *Berkeley: An Introduction*, Oxford: Clarendon Press. (Chapters 1 and 2 deal with questions of language and abstraction in Berkeley.)

ZOLTÁN GENDLER SZABÓ

LANGUAGE, INDIAN THEORIES OF

Language is a much debated topic in Indian philosophy. There is a clear concern with it in the Vedic texts, where efforts are made to describe links between earthly and divine reality in terms of etymological links between words. The earliest surviving Sanskrit grammar, Pāṇini's intricate Aṣṭādhyāyī (Eight Chapters), dates from about 350 BC, although arguably the first explicitly philosophical reflections on language that have survived are found in Patañjali's 'Great Commentary' on Pāṇini's work, the Mahābhāṣya (c.150 BC). Both these thinkers predate the classical systems of Indian philosophy. This is not true of the great fifth-century grammarian Bhartṛhari, however, who in his Vākyapadīya (Treatise on Sentences and Words) draws on these systems in developing his theory of the sphoṭa, a linguistic entity distinct from a word's sounds that Bhartṛhari takes to convey its meaning.

Among the issues debated by these philosophers (although not exclusively by them, and not exclusively with reference to Sanskrit) were what can be described as (i) the search for minimal meaningful units, and (ii) the ontological status of composite linguistic units. With some approximation, the first of these two issues attracted more attention during the early period of linguistic reflection, whereas the subsequent period emphasized the second one.

1   **Historical sketch**
2   **The search for minimal meaningful units**
3   **The ontological status of composite linguistic units**
4   **Early *sphoṭa* theory**
5   **Later *sphoṭa* theory**

1   Historical sketch

Linguistic science in India started soon after the Vedic period. The earliest grammarian whose work has survived is Pāṇini (c. 350 BC), author of the *Aṣṭādhyāyī* (Eight Chapters). This work consists of some 4,000 aphoristic statements (*sūtras*) which describe the Sanskrit language in considerable detail, but leave no space for explicit reflections about the nature of language. Such reflections make their appearance in the voluminous *Mahābhāṣya* (Great Commentary) of PATAÑJALI (c. 150 BC). The *Mahābhāṣya* is a commentary on the *Aṣṭādhyāyī* (but not on all of its *sūtras*), and on the aphoristic *vārttikas* of Kātyāyana, which comment upon Pāṇini's *sūtras*. Another linguist whose work has been preserved and who, like Kātyāyana, appears to belong to the period between

Pāṇini and Patañjali, is Yāska, author of the *Nirukta* (Etymological Explanation).

All these authors precede the formation of the classical systems of Indian philosophy; their reflections on language are therefore largely unaffected by them. This changes with BHARTṚHARI (*c.* fifth century), perhaps the first commentator on Patañjali's *Mahābhāṣya*, and the author of the *Vākyapadīya* (Treatise on Sentences and Words). Bhartṛhari is well aware of the philosophies of his time, and makes ample use of them to construct his own system, which he presents as the philosophy of grammar. The subsequent Pāṇinian tradition accepts this philosophy (or what it preserves of it) as its own, but there are remarkably few grammarians who write treatises on it. Apart from the three principal commentators on the *Vākyapadīya* – Helārāja (tenth century), Puṇyarāja and Vṛṣabhadeva (dates unknown) – by far the most important among them are Kauṇḍa Bhaṭṭa and Nāgeśa Bhaṭṭa, both belonging to the most recent period of grammatical studies (after 1600). Some authors belonging to different schools of thought, however, adopt and defend some of the points of view of the grammarians. The ontological status of composite linguistic units is a subject that evokes special interest.

2 The search for minimal meaningful units

The different linguistic sciences of ancient India – and in particular grammar and etymological explanation – have to be understood against the background of the practice, common in the Vedic Brāhmaṇas (before Pāṇini), of giving etymological explanations of names of gods and of other terms, usually related to the sacrifice and often occurring in sacred formulas (*mantras*). Unlike those of modern linguistics, the etymologies of ancient India have nothing to do with the origin or the history of the words concerned. They cannot, because language, and the Sanskrit language in particular, was looked upon as stable in time; from the subsequent period we know that many even believed Sanskrit to be eternal, that is, without beginning. These etymologies establish links between things and the mythological reality that hides behind them. The god Agni ('fire'), for example, is thus called because he was created first (*agre*). There are countless etymologies of this kind in the Brāhmaṇas. These texts frequently add that the gods have obscured a number of the etymological links. The god Indra, for example, is 'really' called Indha ('the kindler') because he kindled the vital airs. However, people call him Indra because the gods are fond of the cryptic, and dislike the evident.

Knowledge of the links revealed by etymologies is important in reaching one's religious goals.

Yāska's *Nirukta* takes the validity of such etymologies for granted, but secularizes their use. It presents etymologizing as a way to arrive at the meaning of unknown words. Moreover, only nouns and adjectives can be etymologically explained, and then only in terms of verbal forms: verbs explain nominal words, and show the (or an) activity that characterizes the object named. Yāska illustrates his method with the help of known words. One might expect that this procedure would lead to the identification and isolation of the common parts found in different words (such as the common part *ag* of *agni* and *agre* in the above example), and would determine their meanings. But Yāska's demands with regard to the semantic adequacy of etymological explanations are so stringent that this turns out to be impossible. He insists, for example, on two different etymological explanations for words that have two meanings. This rigour forces Yāska to be very undemanding with respect to the phonetic similarity required in etymological explanations. With the help of a number of examples from grammar, he shows that phonemes may disappear, be modified, change position, and so on. The same applies, *a fortiori*, to etymology. Similarities between words in etymological explanations may, as a consequence, be minimal: one single phoneme in common may have to do. The main thing is that one should not be discouraged; one should not stop looking for an etymological explanation simply because one does not find similar words.

It is interesting to observe that Patañjali's *Mahābhāṣya* contains a passage which, like Yāska's *Nirukta*, shows how phonemes may undergo change of position, elision and modification in grammatical derivations. Unlike Yāska, Patañjali concludes from this quite explicitly that phonemes by themselves cannot have meaning, although it seems likely that Yāska, even though he does not state it in his *Nirukta*, drew the same conclusion as Patañjali. It appears that Yāska's semantic rigour prevented him from trying to identify the ultimate meaningful constituents of Sanskrit (as we see for ancient Greek in Plato's *Cratylus*, for example). This task, but on a far less ambitious scale, is left to the grammarians, among whom Pāṇini is the most famous. His grammar is not an analysis of Sanskrit but a synthesis: it produces the words and sentences of the language, starting from their ultimate meaning-bearing constituents, essentially stems and affixes. To be precise, Pāṇini's grammar first furnishes stems and affixes on the basis of a semantic input, and these stems and affixes are subsequently joined together, and modified where necessary, so as to yield words and sentences (see Bronkhorst 1980).

In view of the background of Vedic etymologies, discussed above, one may legitimately conclude that Pāṇini considers these ultimate meaningful constituents to be really meaningful, more so perhaps than the 'surface forms' they help produce. The search for 'really meaningful' ultimate constituents of language is clearly present in the efforts of the grammarians. Pāṇini's *sūtra* 1.2.45, which recognizes but three meaningful entities, namely verbal roots, nominal stems and suffixes, indicates that words and sentences are considered to have at best a composite meaning. This search manifests itself later in the attribution by a number of Tantric thinkers of metaphysical meanings to individual phonemes. They can afford to go further than Pāṇini and Yāska in their analysis, continuing all the way to the individual phonemes, owing to the fact that they are less limited by semantic considerations. This in its turn is no doubt linked to the circumstance that sacred formulas (*mantras*) in Tantrism (unlike the Vedic ones) have shed their connection with ordinary language and its semantic constraints.

Returning to Pāṇini and grammatical analysis, later grammarians, mainly under the influence of Patañjali and Bhartṛhari, reject the position according to which the ultimate meaningful constituents presented by grammar are somehow more real than the words they produce. For them, stems and affixes are conventions, or rather inventions of grammarians. This reaction is to be understood in the light of the ontological concerns to be discussed below. The semantic analysis underlying Pāṇini's procedure, on the other hand, came to be generally accepted (albeit sometimes with slight modifications). Later thinkers use this analysis as the basis for deliberations on the relative importance of the various 'semantic elements' that Pāṇini assigns to a sentence in the understanding obtained by a hearer (*śābdabodha*). In a sentence like *caitraḥ pacati* ('Caitra cooks'), to take a simple example, the grammatical elements are: *caitra-s pac-a-ti*. Of these, the following are expressive: *caitra, pac* and *ti*. Thinkers of the new Nyāya school (Navya-Nyāya) consider the grammatical subject (in this case *caitra*) most important, and give (approximately) the following semantic analysis of the sentence: 'Caitra characterized by the activity of cooking'. The grammarians look upon the meaning of the verbal root (*pac*) as central, and paraphrase the sentence (again approximately) as: 'The activity of cooking whose agent is Caitra'. The Mīmāṃsakas, finally, put emphasis on the verbal suffix (here *ti*); since they are primarily interested in Vedic injunctions, and conse-quently in imperative and optative verbal forms, we shall not enter into the details of their analyses.

3 The ontological status of composite linguistic units

To appreciate the importance of the debate on the ontological status of composite linguistic units, one has to be aware of the great interest in ontological questions that characterizes much of Indian philosophy. In the realm of language this leads to questions like: Do words and sentences really exist? If so, how can they, given that the phonemes that constitute them do not occur simultaneously? Since, moreover, simultaneous occurrence is a condition for the existence of collective entities, do individual phonemes exist? They, too, have a certain duration, and consist therefore of parts that do not occur simultaneously.

Perhaps the first to address these questions were Buddhists of the Sarvāstivāda school. These Buddhists were active in the first centuries BC in drawing up lists of elements – the so-called *dharmas* – which were considered to constitute all there is (see BUDDHISM, ĀBHIDHARMIKA SCHOOLS OF). The list accepted by the Sarvāstivādins contains three elements which correspond to phonemes (*vyañjana-kāyas*), words (*nāmakāya*) and sentences (*padakāya*) respectively. This means that these Buddhists postulated phonemes, words and sentences as existing entities which, like virtually everything else in their ontology, are momentary. Little is known about the way they visualized the mutual relationship between these entities, or how they would answer the questions formulated above.

The grammarian Patañjali may have been influenced by these ideas. He certainly knew the notion of an individual phoneme and of a word conceived of as a single entity. For Patañjali, these phonemes and words are not momentary; they are, on the contrary, eternal. One should not, however, attach too much importance to this difference: for the Buddhists, everything is momentary; for many Brahmans, the Veda, and therefore also its language, is eternal. It is more important to observe that these notions play a relatively minor role in Patañjali's expositions. They acquire major significance in Bhartṛhari's *Vākyapadīya*, where they are made to fit his general philosophy that more comprehensive totalities are more real than their constituent parts.

It appears that in the period between Patañjali and Bhartṛhari a major shift of emphasis took place in the discussion of linguistic units. The discussion became centred on the linguistic unit as meaning-bearer. The problem of individual phonemes, which have no meaning, came to be separated from that of words, grammatical elements (stems and affixes) and sentences, which do. In the context of Bhartṛhari's philosophy this is understandable, for here linguistic units and the 'objects' they refer to are treated in a parallel fashion. But this shift of emphasis was not confined to the grammatical tradition. Śabarasvāmin, the author of the oldest and most important surviving commentary on the *Mīmāṃsāsūtra*, and who may be an approximate contemporary of Bhartṛhari, cites (1.1.5; see Frauwallner 1968: 38–) an earlier commentator who rejects the notion of a word as different from its constituent phonemes. This does not, however, prevent him from proclaiming that phonemes are single and eternal. In other words, phonemes and words undergo a different treatment altogether. Moreover, the author of the *Yogabhāṣya* (whose name was probably Patañjali, like the author of the *Mahābhāṣya*, although he was certainly different from the latter; recent tradition calls him Vyāsa) speaks about the single word which is without parts, without sequence, without constituent phonemes, and which is mental (on *Yogasūtra* 3.17). This Patañjali may have lived around 400 AD, and therefore perhaps before Bhartṛhari.

4 Early *sphoṭa* theory

Patañjali (the grammarian) and Bhartṛhari use the word *sphoṭa* to refer to linguistic entities conceived of as different from the sounds that reveal them. For Patañjali, the *sphoṭa* does not necessarily convey meaning; he uses the term also in connection with individual phonemes. For Bhartṛhari, the *sphoṭa* is a meaning-bearer. The *sphoṭa*, he points out, is different from the sounds which manifest it, and he makes several suggestions as to what constitutes it. It might be a mental entity. Or one might take it to be the universal residing in the manifesting sounds. One could even look upon the material basis of words, for example, wind, as being the *sphoṭa*. Bhartṛhari presents these options, but his perspectivism allows him to avoid choosing between them.

Arguments claiming to prove the existence of the *sphoṭa*, as well as arguments which try to refute it, henceforth concentrate heavily, even exclusively, on the *sphoṭa* as meaning-bearing unit. The primary question is not 'What exactly is the *sphoṭa*?' but rather 'How can a sequence of phonemes, each without meaning and not even occurring simultaneously, express meaning?' According to some, a sequence of sounds can express meaning; they have to show how it does so. Others hold that this is not possible; they solve the problem by postulating the existence of the *sphoṭa*. These two positions find their classical expositions in Kumārila Bhaṭṭa's critique of the

sphoṭa doctrine in his *Ślokavārttika* (Commentary in Verse) (seventh century), and in Maṇḍana Miśra's (c. 700?) defence against these attacks in his *SphoṚasiddhi* (Demonstration of the *Sphoṭa*). Neither Kumārila nor Maṇḍana were grammarians: the former belonged to the school of Vedic hermeneutics called Mīmāṃsā; the latter, too, had links with this school.

Kumārila, elaborating the opinions of Śabarasvāmin (see §3), on whose *Mīmāṃsābhāṣya* he comments, accepts the eternal existence of individual phonemes. But he combats the notion that more than phonemes are required to understand the meaning-bearing function of language. It is true that the phonemes constituting a word are not pronounced simultaneously. But there are situations where everyone agrees that a series of activities that succeed each other in time can none the less jointly produce an effect. He gives the example of a Vedic sacrifice, whose constituent activities are performed at different times, but which produces a single result, namely heaven. Another example concerns counting: we can count objects in sequence, one after the other, and arrive at one result, their number. Furthermore, the fact that individual phonemes are without meaning does not exclude the possibility that they can express a meaning when pronounced in sequence. The parts of a cart, too, cannot fulfil the functions that a cart can fulfil. Last but not least, though the constituent phonemes of a word are not pronounced simultaneously, they are remembered together the moment the last phoneme is (or has just been) uttered.

Maṇḍana answers Kumārila's arguments one by one. He protests against the idea of the combined memory of the phonemes that constitute a word. First of all, one does not remember phonemes, but the word as a whole. Second, memory impressions can only present to us their contents, in this case phonemes, not something else, such as the meaning of the word. And third, two words may consist of the same phonemes, say 'pit' and 'tip' (a Sanskrit example is the pair *saraḥ/rasaḥ*, 'lake'/'taste'), so that the memories that combine their phonemes should be the same, yet they are recognized as different. Perhaps Maṇḍana's most interesting contribution to the discussion is his claim that the *sphoṭa* is directly perceived: it is gradually revealed by the phonemes.

The *sphoṭa* constitutes the central element of what came to be called the philosophy of the grammarians. All thinkers who deal with the issue, including Maṇḍana Miśra, refer in this connection to Bhartṛhari's *Vākyapadīya*. But the more encompassing ideas in the context of which Bhartṛhari worked out his ideas on the nature of linguistic entities largely escaped the attention of those who so faithfully cited him.

5 Later *sphoṭa* theory

After a lull, a revival of interest in the *sphoṭa* and related issues took place from the sixteenth century onward. Of the various authors who wrote treatises on the philosophy of grammar, Nāgeśa Bhaṭṭa (*c.*1700) was the most famous. He wrote a large number of treatises on various subjects, among them the *Sphoṭavāda* (Exposition on *Sphoṭa*), the *Laghumañjūṣā* (Small Casket) and the *Paramalaghumañjūṣā* (Extremely Small Casket) (written in this order), which deal with the philosophy of grammar. These books show that Nāgeśa changed his mind several times with regard to the *sphoṭa* doctrine.

The *Sphoṭavāda* enumerates eight types of *sphoṭa*: (1) phoneme, (2) word, (3) sentence, (4) indivisible word, (5) indivisible sentence, (6) phoneme-universal, (7) word-universal, (8) sentence-universal. These *sphoṭas* are primarily meaning-bearers. The first and sixth ones, in spite of their misleading names, refer to grammatical elements (stems and affixes) rather than to phonemes. Nāgeśa's reasons for postulating these eight types are not always clear. This early work gives the impression that he collected various ideas without being able to combine them into one overarching vision.

This changes with the *Laghumañjūṣā*, which opens with the words: 'In this [work] the sentence-*sphoṭa* is most important.' Other parts of the work make it clear that Nāgeśa has been converted – no doubt under the influence of Bhartṛhari, whose *Vākyapadīya* he frequently cites – to the idea that only sentences really exist, that words and grammatical elements are no more than imaginary. He is particularly fierce with regard to grammatical stems and affixes.

Surprisingly, the *Paramalaghumañjūṣā*, meant to be an abbreviated version of the *Laghumañjūṣā*, begins, like the *Sphoṭavāda*, with an enumeration of the eight kinds of *sphoṭa*. Immediately following this it repeats the opening statement of the *Laghumañjūṣā*, according to which the sentence-*sphoṭa* is most important. Closer study reveals that Nāgeśa has been confronted with cases where the sentence-*sphoṭa* view comes into conflict with grammatical derivations. There is a grammatical meta-rule which states that a grammatical derivation evolves in the order in which the expressive elements arise. Expressive elements acquire in this way importance, and it will not do to say that their expressiveness is merely imaginary. The issue is all the more important in view of the fact that there were different opinions as to whether the final substitutes of the grammatical elements – which appear in the 'surface forms' – are expressive, or whether the substituends are. This disagreement can have an effect on the correct derivation of words and sentences. Nāgeśa's final position is chosen in awareness of these complications. He still maintains that the sentence-*sphoṭa* is most important. But he no longer treats the other, 'imaginary', entities as lightly as he did earlier.

Nāgeśa is often thought of as the last great author in the Pāṇinian tradition. His vacillations where the *sphoṭa*-doctrine is concerned illustrate the conflict that exists between the two major issues of grammar distinguished in this entry: the search for minimal meaningful units on the one hand, and the ontological status of composite linguistic units on the other. His final position tries to give both their due: the idea inherited from Bhartṛhari that only the sentence is 'real', rather than words and smaller grammatical elements; and the idea inherited from Pāṇini that grammar is concerned with the smallest identifiable meaningful elements and the way they combine to form larger units.

See also: INTERPRETATION, INDIAN THEORIES OF; MEANING, INDIAN THEORIES OF; MĪMĀṂSĀ §3

References and further reading

Most of the ancient works listed here are highly technical and voluminous, and apt to be unrewarding for those who are not specialists in this field. Reliable translations are nonexistent in most cases.

* Bhartṛhari (5th century) *Vākyapadīya* (Treatise on Sentences and Words), ed. W. Rau, Wiesbaden: Franz Steiner, 1977. (A very difficult work that has occasioned a lot of controversy among scholars.)
* Bronkhorst, J. (1980) 'The Role of Meanings in Pāṇini's Grammar', *Indian Linguistics* 40 (1979): 146–57. (Shows that meanings are the input of Pāṇini's grammar.)
—— (1981) '*Nirukta* and *Aṣṭādhyāyī*: Their Shared Presuppositions', *Indo-Iranian Journal* 23: 1–14. (Analyses the aims and procedures of Yāska's *Nirukta*.)
—— (1984) 'Patañjali and the Yoga Sūtras', *Studien zur Indologie und Iranistik* 10: 191–212. (§2 deals with the authorship of the *Yogabhāṣya*.)
—— (1986) *Tradition and Argument in Classical Indian Linguistics*, Dordrecht: Reidel. (On Nāgeśa Bhaṭṭa; see especially chapters 10 and 11, and appendix 3.)
Coward, H.G. and Raja, K.K. (eds) (1990) *Encyclopedia of Indian Philosophies*, vol. 5, *The Philosophy of the Grammarians*, Delhi: Motilal Banarsidass. (Contains bibliography up to 1983.)
Deshpande, M.M. (1992) *The Meaning of Nouns. Semantic Theory in Classical and Medieval India. Nāmārtha-nirṇaya of Kauṇḍabhaṭṭa*, Dordrecht:

Kluwer. (Richly annotated translation of a chapter of Kauṇḍa Bhaṭṭa's *Vaiyākaraṇabhūṣaṇa*; the long introduction contains useful discussions of concepts of linguistic philosophy.)

* Frauwallner, E. (1968) *Materialien zur ältesten Erkenntnislehre der Karmamīmāṃsā* (Materials on the Oldest Karmamīmāṃsā Epistemology), Vienna: Hermann Böhlaus. (Contains text and translation of an important portion of Śabarasvāmin's *Mīmāṃsābhāṣya*.)

Gaurinath Sastri (1980) *A Study in the Dialectics of Sphoṭa*, Delhi: Motilal Banarsidass, revised edn. (Presents various arguments for and against the *sphoṭa* that were used in classical India.)

Houben, J. (1997) 'The Sanskrit Tradition', in W. van Bekkum *et al.*, *The Emergence of Semantics in Four Linguistic Traditions: Hebrew, Sanskrit, Greek, Arabic*, Amsterdam/Philadelphia, PA: John Benjamins, 49–145. (Survey of semantics in classical India.)

* Kumārila Bhaṭṭa (7th century) *Ślokavārttika* (Commentary in Verse), ed. Dvārikādāsa Śāstrī, Varanasi: Ratna Publications, 1978. (The most important commentary by the founder of the Bhaṭṭa school of Mīmāṃsā.)

* Maṇḍana Miśra (*c.*700?) *Sphoṭasiddhi* (Demonstration of the *Sphoṭa*), ed. and trans. M. Biardeau, *La Démonstration du Sphoṭa*, Pondicherry: Institut Français d'Indologie, 1958. (A response to Kumārila's *Ślokavārttika*.)

Matilal, B.K. (1988) '*Śabdabodha* and the Problem of Knowledge-Representation in Sanskrit', *Journal of Indian Philosophy* 16: 107–22. (On *śabdabodha*, mentioned in §2 of the present entry.)

—— (1990) *The Word and the World: India's Contribution to the Study of Language*, Delhi: Oxford University Press. (Discusses various issues in Indian linguistic philosophy.)

Padoux, A. (1990) *Vāc: The Concept of the Word in Selected Hindu Tantras*, Albany, NY: State University of New York Press. (See especially chapter 5, on the meaning attributed to individual sounds.)

* Pāṇini (4th century BC) *Aṣṭādhyāyī* (Eight Chapters), ed. and trans. O. Böhtlink, Leipzig, 1887; repr. Hildesheim/New York: George Olms, 1997. (The earliest surviving Sanskrit grammar.)

* Patañjali (2nd century BC) *(Vyākaraṇa-)Mahābhāṣya* (Great Commentary), ed. F. Kielhorn, 1880–5, 3 vols; 3rd edn, ed. K.V. Abhyankar, Poona: Bhandarkar Oriental Research Institute, 1972. (A commentary on Pāṇini's grammar and Kātyāyana's *vārttikas*.)

Raja, K.K. (1969) *Indian Theories of Meaning*, Madras: The Adyar Library and Research Centre; 2nd edn, 1977. (Useful but generally nonhistorical survey of fundamental concepts.)

Scharfe, H. (1977) *A History of Indian Literature*, vol. 5, fasc. 2, *Grammatical Literature*, Wiesbaden: Harrassowitz. (Historical survey of technical linguistic literature; pays little attention to philosophical issues.)

JOHANNES BRONKHORST

LANGUAGE, INNATENESS OF

Is there any innate knowledge? What is it to speak and understand a language? These are old questions, but it was the twentieth-century linguist Noam Chomsky who forged a connection between them, arguing that mastery of a language is, in part, a matter of knowing its grammar, and that much of our knowledge of grammar is inborn.

Rejecting the empiricism that had dominated Anglo-American philosophy, psychology and linguistics for the first half of this century, Chomsky argued that the task of learning a language is so difficult, and the linguistic evidence available to the learner so meagre, that language acquisition would be impossible unless some of the knowledge eventually attained were innate. He proposed that learners bring to their task knowledge of a 'Universal Grammar', describing structural features common to all natural languages, and that it is this knowledge that enables us to master our native tongues.

Chomsky's position is nativist *because it proposes that the inborn knowledge facilitating learning is* domain-specific. *On an empiricist view, our innate ability to learn from experience (for example, to form associations among ideas) applies equally in any task domain. On the nativist view, by contrast, we are equipped with special-purpose learning strategies, each suited to its own peculiar subject-matter.*

Chomsky's nativism spurred a flurry of interest as theorists leaped to explore its conceptual and empirical implications. As a consequence of his work, language acquisition is today a major focus of cognitive science research.

1   **The development of Chomsky's nativism**
2   **The poverty of the stimulus**
3   **Other arguments for nativism**

1   The development of Chomsky's nativism

In a review of Skinner's *Verbal Behavior*, Chomsky (1959) rejected the behaviourist view that mastery of a language, or 'linguistic competence', consists in complexes of 'dispositions to verbal behaviour' instilled in our minds by 'operant conditioning' during childhood (see SKINNER, B.F.; BEHAVIOURISM, METHODOLOGICAL AND SCIENTIFIC). First, children neither need nor receive the careful linguistic training that the behaviourist acquisition-theory requires. Second, our use of language is both *stimulus-independent* (not determined by the inputs we receive) and *productive* (we can utter and understand indefinitely many novel sentences). Hence competence must be more than a congeries of 'verbal habits'. Both language acquisition and linguistic competence involve complex systems of psychological states and processes.

But how to characterize these states and processes? In the early 1960s, Chomsky's 'generative' approach to linguistics challenged the 'taxonomic' approach of American structuralists such as Bloomfield and Harris (see STRUCTURALISM IN LINGUISTICS §4). He urged that linguists abandon the structuralist aim of elucidating 'discovery procedures' (that is, mechanical methods which, when applied to a corpus of sentences in a language, will deliver a grammar descriptive of that language) and focus instead on the development of rigorous, formalizable syntactic theories for particular languages. The linguist's goal should be to develop *generative* grammars for natural languages, that is, sets of rules that will produce all and only the sentences in a language, together with their syntactic-structural descriptions (see SYNTAX §3).

Much of Chomsky's work in linguistics has aimed at refining the generative programme. Of particular interest here, however, is his contention that a grammar's usefulness outruns its ability to characterize a language. Its real importance, he argued, is psychological. Since speakers' grammatical intuitions (their judgments as to the well-formedness of sentences) constitute the data for a grammatical theory, that theory is in some sense descriptive of what speakers know about their language. Thus, Chomsky inferred, grammars supply (partial) accounts of the psychological structures underpinning language use, so providing a timely replacement for the ousted behaviourist account of linguistic competence. (Chomsky distinguishes theories of linguistic competence from theories of linguistic performance. Competence theories describe our capacity for language in a way that abstracts from the question of how that capacity results in the production and comprehension of sentences. Performance theories explain how the system of knowledge postulated in a competence theory interacts with other psychological systems such as memory, perception and the articulatory systems, in order to produce actual linguistic behaviour.)

But if grammars are competence theories, the question of how language is *learned* becomes acute. Normal children master language by about the age of eight. On Chomsky's view, this mastery entails, among other things, the 'internalization', 'cognizance' or 'tacit knowledge' of their language's grammar. But a grammar is a highly complex body of syntactic, semantic, morphological and phonological rules, employing concepts and constructs far removed from experience. How do children internalize so complex a grammar at so tender an age, with apparently no conscious effort or instruction?

Chomsky argues that children's acquisition of grammar is explicable only on the assumption that a substantial portion of the knowledge eventually attained is innate. On his view, a 'Universal Grammar' (UG), which specifies information about 'linguistic universals' (features common to all natural languages), is embodied in the language-learning mechanism itself. Thus, children need not *learn*, for instance, that declarative sentences must have a noun phrase as their subject: that fact they bring with them to the learning task. All they need do during learning is determine those facts (such as that, in English, the subject precedes the verb) that are *specific* to their language.

Chomsky is notable in that he does not rest content with the claim that we have innate knowledge of UG. Unlike his nativist predecessors, such as Plato, Descartes and Leibniz (see NATIVISM §2), he has offered two concrete proposals as to how that knowledge is realized.

Up to the late 1970s, he defended a 'hypothesis-testing' model of learning according to which children unconsciously project hypotheses about the grammar of their language, testing them against the data provided by experience. Their innate knowledge of UG, on this view, takes the form of constraints on the kinds of hypotheses they can entertain: they must be formulated in a particular language; they must have a certain form; and, in cases where the evidence is insufficient to arbitrate between two competing hypotheses, the language-learning mechanism itself will supply a decision.

More recently, Chomsky has embraced a picture of language learning as involving 'parameter-setting'. On this view, which is as yet only partially developed, the principles of UG are encoded in the mind of the neonate, each principle containing one or more variables or 'parameters'. A parameter's possible values are extremely limited and are fixed by experience, different parameter-settings resulting in competencies in different languages. The 'null subject parameter', for example, governs whether one may omit the grammatical subject of a spoken sentence.

Exposure to a language, like Spanish, where subjects may be omitted, sets the parameter one way; exposure to a language, like English, where subjects must be phonologically realised, will cause it to be set differently. Thus, children's linguistic experience does not function as *evidence* for or against their grammatical hypotheses. Rather, and in much the same way as their hormones trigger the bodily changes that take place at puberty, exposure to the language of their community 'triggers' the mental changes that eventually result in linguistic competence.

Evaluating the merits of these models is in large part an empirical task and is outside the scope of this article. We will consider instead the case for linguistic nativism itself; that is, for the view that language-learning requires a task- or domain-specific mechanism of some kind.

2   The poverty of the stimulus

The commonest motivation for nativism is the argument from the poverty of the stimulus (POS). It contends that there is a 'gap' between the rich stock of linguistic knowledge that competent speakers acquire and the meagre supply of information about language that their experience during learning provides. This gap is so wide, the nativist contends, that no child endowed only with an empiricist-style, general-purpose learning mechanism could hope to bridge it. Language learning, therefore, requires a special-purpose device, one that embodies at the start some of the information about language that is ultimately attained.

This basic argument is elaborated in two ways. There are several a posteriori versions, due mainly to Chomsky; and a rather more a priori version with roots, seemingly, in Formal Learning Theory, a branch of mathematical linguistics.

A posteriori POS arguments are based on specific empirical claims about the inputs to and outputs of learning. In *Reflections on Language* (1975: 31 and following), for example, Chomsky claims that (1) competent speakers know the auxiliary fronting rule for question-formation; and that (2) the information available to children does not reliably distinguish the correct rule from incorrect but equally plausible alternatives. Hence, he infers, the learner's choice of the correct rule is driven not by any general principles of theory-construction (such as the empiricist envisages), but is due rather to the fact that the acquisition device itself is biased towards grammatical rules of certain kinds, namely those conforming to UG.

Note that a posteriori POS arguments rely on specific empirical assumptions about the nature of linguistic competence and the data accessible to children. If it were discovered, for example, that speakers had *not* in any interesting sense internalized the rule in question, or that data disconfirmatory of incorrect rules were readily available, Chomsky would have failed to locate a gap – and hence to have supported his nativism. Hence, the success of a posteriori arguments turns on the degree to which their factual premises can be empirically sustained. But while some steps have recently been taken towards furnishing the supporting (for example, developmental) data required by arguments like this, their overall bearing on the nativism–empiricism controversy remains undecided.

In contrast to the preceding, the a priori POS argument (often called the Logical Problem of Language Acquisition) seeks to infer the existence of a gap from a consideration of the logical structure of the acquisition-task itself. Take some state in the learning process at which a child has acquired a grammatical hypothesis. Call the set of sentences (the language) generated by their hypothesised grammar H. Call that generated by the correct grammar (the target language) L. Then the learner is in one of five situations: (1) H is disjoint from L; (2) H overlaps L; (3) H is a subset of L; (4) H is a superset of L; (5) H is equivalent to L.

Situation (5) represents the end point of the learning process: the child has learned the target language. Situations (1), (2) and (3) are relatively unproblematic: the learner will be forced to revise their hypothesis if they hear a sentence in L that is not in H. Thus, they can converge on the correct grammar by exposure to 'positive evidence', evidence (as is provided by someone's uttering a sentence) that a given string of words is a sentence of the target language. But, crucially, if they are in situation (4) – if their grammar 'overgenerates', that is, generates all of L and also some sentences that are *not* in L – they cannot discover *this* by exposure to further sentences of the target language. For, every sentence of L is equally a sentence of H. What this learner needs is the information that a sentence that is generated by their grammar – a sentence in H – is *not* a sentence of L; only then can they 'shrink' their hypothesis so that it converges on the correct one.

This latter kind of evidence, that a sentence is *not* in the target language, is called 'negative evidence'. And case (4) is of interest because negative evidence is in general unavailable to children. *Explicit* negative evidence is scarce: children are not provided with lists of ungrammatical sentences; their errors are rarely corrected; nor do parents typically notice their own ungrammatical utterances. And *indirect* negative evidence is hard to find too. The non-occurrence of a sentence in the data, for example, is not negative evidence. For, there are infinitely many sentences of L that *de facto* will never be uttered. Hence from the mere fact that they have not heard a certain string of words in the data to date, the child cannot infer that it is not a sentence of the target language.

Thus learners who find themselves in situation (4) have no systematic access to evidence that would enable them to correct their overgeneral hypotheses. Which means, since children *do* eventually converge on the correct grammar, that they must never be in situation (4); the learning mechanism must be constrained such that they *never* hypothesize a grammar that is 'too large'.

Nativists contend that the general-purpose constraints on hypothesis-formulation envisaged by empiricists are insufficient to ensure that overgeneration will not occur. Hence, they conclude, the space of possible grammars must be constrained by further, linguistically-specific principles such as are provided by UG: the poverty of negative evidence in the data requires a nativist approach to language acquisition.

The a priori POS argument is at first sight much more compelling than its empirically undersupported a posteriori relatives. It is not, however, without points of weakness. First, one may question whether negative evidence is really as scarce as it seems. For example, while the non-occurrence of a particular sentence in the data may not be evidence that it is not grammatical, perhaps the repeated non-occurrence of certain syntactic forms could be evidence that sentences of that form are not grammatical. (That there must be at least *some* negative evidence available is evident from the fact that children do, as a matter of fact, recover from overgeneral grammatical hypotheses: they learn, for example, that you do not *always* add /d/ to the stem to form the past tense of a verb).

Second, one may question the nativist's contention that general-purpose constraints are insufficient to prevent a learner's making incorrigible overgeneralizations. Not only is this contention to my knowledge unargued, there is reason to believe that in at least *some* cases, general-purpose learning strategies *are* efficacious in the face of what seem to be identical 'negative evidence' problems. For, negative evidence – evidence as to what things are *not* – is *quite generally* unavailable. When we learn what cars are, for example, we are not systematically informed about the countlessly many things that are not members of that class. Yet, and despite this paucity of negative evidence, we do manage to converge on the correct hypothesis about 'car-bonnet'. So, assuming that it is implausible to postulate a task-specific 'automotive faculty' that facilitates our learning in this domain, it must be the case that whatever general-purpose

learning strategies we possess are in at least some contexts able to function successfully in the (near) absence of negative evidence.

In sum, arguments from the POS alone cannot compel nativism about language. We need additional reasons to think that there is something *special* about language acquisition – features it does not share with learning about, say, cars – such that nativism is plausible in the former case, while being clearly implausible in the latter.

3 Other arguments for nativism

Language acquisition has been held, by Chomsky and others, to be special in a number of ways that support linguistic nativism. Examples of these claims, and of the empiricist responses to them, are:

(1) *Species specificity.* Only human beings, so far as we know, speak a language. We thus possess a special biological affinity for language, an affinity which may amount to an innate language-learning faculty. Response: only human beings build cars, too, but that does not make for an innate automotive faculty. What our species possesses that others do not is general intelligence – an ability to learn from experience in a wide variety of contexts.

(2) *Critical period.* Language acquisition displays 'critical period effects': the ability to learn language declines drastically after puberty. This resemblance to other biologically-controlled developmental processes suggests that the acquisition of language too is determined more by our genes than our environment. Response: perhaps *all* learning declines after puberty. There are no data supporting the view that language-learning is special in this regard.

(3) *Facility of acquisition.* Language is acquired with remarkable speed and ease at a very early age. Processes distinct from those underpinning other kinds of learning are therefore at work. Response: given that we lack anything to compare language learning with, it is unclear that it is either notably fast, or especially easy.

(4) *Linguistic universals.* There are deep syntactic and semantic similarities among all known natural languages. Since there is no evidence to support the view that now-current languages descended from a common ancestor, these commonalities must be consequences of the way the language faculty is structured. Response: of course languages are shaped by the minds that use them. But linguistic universals may be due to constraints on what can be learned via a general-purpose

learning strategy, rather than arising out of the structure of an innate language faculty.

(5) *Linguistic complexity.* Linguists, using *exactly* the 'general principles of theory-construction' beloved of the empiricist, spend entire careers laboriously constructing grammars for tiny corners of a language. But children can learn *all* of the grammar of *any* language simply by hearing it spoken around them. Surely some special faculty is at work here? Response: this argument assumes that there *is* an interesting sense in which speakers know – hence must learn – the grammar of their language. This assumption, however, may be challenged. First, there are conceptual difficulties involved in understanding what it is for a speaker to know a grammar. Thus, it is unclear whether children's ability to learn one is remarkable or not. Second, it has proved difficult to find empirical confirmation for the claim that grammars are implicated in any straightforward way in on-line linguistic processing. Thus it is unclear in what sense, if any, grammars need to be learned. And finally, one might question whether the linguist's methodology is appropriate for investigating the psychology of language use and understanding. Thus, while it is remarkable that the linguist's task in characterizing the language the child knows is dauntingly complex, this is of unclear relevance to the child's task in learning it.

In conclusion, Chomsky's claim that knowledge of language is largely innate has renewed the interest of linguists, philosophers and psychologists in the problem of explaining language acquisition. It remains, however, an open empirical question whether that explanation requires the postulation of a special-purpose learning mechanism embodying innate knowledge of language; and, if it does, what the nature of that mechanism and that knowledge is.

See also: CHOMSKY, N.; INNATE KNOWLEDGE; LANGUAGE, PHILOSOPHY OF; SEMANTICS §1

References and further reading

* Chomsky, N. (1959) 'Review of Skinner's *Verbal Behavior*', *Language* 35: 26–58. (Chomsky's critique of behaviourism; discussed in §1.)

* —— (1975) *Reflections on Language*, Glasgow: Fontana/Collins. (Seminal presentation of *de facto* POS argument (in §2) and the hypothesis-testing model of learning discussed in §1.)

—— (1988) *Language and Problems of Knowledge: The Managua Lectures*, Cambridge, MA: MIT Press. (Chomsky's current views about the innateness of language. Discussion of parameter-setting (in §1). References to earlier works.)

Hornstein, N. and Lightfoot, D. (eds) (1981) *Explanation in Linguistics: The Logical Problem of Language Acquisition*, London: Longman. (Sympathetic exploration of a priori POS argument; discussed in §2.)

Katz, J.J. (ed.) (1985) *The Philosophy of Linguistics*, Oxford: Oxford University Press. (Chomsky's nativism is a major focus of this collection.)

Matthews, R.J. and Demopoulos, W. (eds) (1989) *Learnability and Linguistic Theory*, Amsterdam: Kluwer. (Implications of the a priori POS argument (discussed in §2) for the theories of language learning.)

Newmeyer, O. (ed.) (1988) *Linguistics: the Cambridge Survey*, vol. 3, *Language: Psychological and Biological Aspects*, Cambridge: Cambridge University Press. (Empirical approaches to language acquisition. More up-to-date than Wanner and Gleitman (1982), but less focused on the nativism issue.)

Piattelli-Palmarini, M. (1989) 'Evolution, Selection and Cognition: From "Learning" to Parameter Setting in Biology and in the Study of Language', *Cognition* 31: 1–44. (Introduction to parameter-setting discussed in §1, with references.)

Pinker, S. (1979) 'Formal Models of Language Learning', *Cognition* 7: 217–82. (Survey of formal learning theory literature discussed in §2.)

—— (1994) *The Language Instinct*, New York: William Morrow. (An excellent and highly readable summary of the case for linguistic nativism.)

Sells, P. (1985) *Lectures on Contemporary Syntactic Theories: An Introduction to Government-Binding Theory, Generalized Phrase Structure Grammar and Lexical-Functional Grammar*, Stanford, CA: Center for the Study of Language and Information. (Introduction to formal syntax, including a chapter on generative grammar relevant to §1.)

Wanner, E. and Gleitman, L.R. (eds) (1982) *Language Acquisition: The State of the Art*, Cambridge: Cambridge University Press. (Collection of psychologists' writings on language acquisition, with special emphasis on nativism.)

FIONA COWIE

LANGUAGE, ISLAMIC PHILOSOPHY OF *see* MEANING IN ISLAMIC PHILOSOPHY

LANGUAGE, MEDIEVAL THEORIES OF

*A great deal of theorizing about language took place in western Europe between 1100 and 1400. The usual social context of this theorizing was the teaching of grammar, logic or theology. Rhetoric was traditionally counted as one of the language disciplines (*scientiae sermocinales*) together with grammar and logic, but in practice it received little attention. Medieval thinkers produced a vast literature on aspects of linguistic theory, but they did not write books with such titles as 'A Theory of Language'. The theories that have come down to us today have been reconstructed from a large number of sources, even when they are attributed to a single person.*

Although the medieval writers on language were very innovative, they owed some key ideas to ancient Greek and Latin authors, for example: (1) words acquire their meaning by an act of 'imposition' when a sound is chosen as the label of some thing; (2) there are three key ingredients in signification: the word, a concept and the thing signified; (3) concepts can be thought of as mental words; (4) the grammaticality of a sentence cannot be explained purely in terms of morphology; and (5) words have different contents when used as predicates of creatures and when predicated of the Creator.

The medieval thinkers disagreed as to whether words signify things directly or only through concepts. The latter view ran the danger of making concepts a screen between language and reality, but it had the advantage of being able to explain why different words can signify the same object without being quite synonymous. Many thought that general terms signify universal things, but there were also nominalist schools which held that the general terms themselves are the only universal things. Fourteenth-century nominalists located universality in concepts, also called mental terms, and only secondarily in spoken words. The language of thought had gained priority over that of speech.

The theory of grammar known today as modism was developed in the thirteenth century. This theory assumed that there are only two contributors to the sense of an expression, lexical meaning and grammatical features, and that only the latter belong to the province of grammar, which thus became a purely formal science that could claim applicability to all languages irrespective of their surface differences. The problem with modism was that it had no tools for dealing with even slightly deviant, yet intelligible expressions. Thus it would have to reject a statement such as 'the crowd are rushing' because of the lack of concord of number.

A number of medieval scholars focused on the various forms of metaphorical language and ambiguity, which were more appropriate for dealing with deviant expressions of the type mentioned above. It was realized that speaker, listener and context must be taken into account in order to explain how words can communicate something different from their primary sense, and how it is possible for a listener to grasp the intended sense of an ambiguous message. One motivation for this study was a need to understand how theological discourse functions. Theology also lay behind a heated debate about the ontological status of the meanings of propositions, and sacramental theology joined grammar in developing a notion of performative locutions.

The study of syntax yielded many new concepts, including those of government and dependence. Much less work was done on the evolution of languages, but Roger Bacon and Dante did offer some perceptive observations. Though never creating fully fledged artificial languages, logicians did develop a semi-artificial Latin.

1 Sources

The most important source for grammar in the Middle Ages was Priscian's *Institutiones grammaticae* (Institutions of Grammar), a comprehensive Latin morphology and syntax composed in the early sixth century AD. Priscian not only describes and prescribes but also reasons about linguistic problems, using a theoretical framework borrowed from the second-century Greek grammarian Apollonius Dyscolus. Priscian transmitted to posterity the notion that the grammaticality (*congruitas*) of a sentence depends on a proper fit among the conceptual elements signified by its constituent words. Also important were his classifications of words, including the eight-fold partition of constituents of sentences as partes orationis (parts of speech). These eight parts were known from other sources, but Priscian provided the best discussion of the subject. Matters left untouched by Priscian, such as tropes and figures, were treated in Chapter 3 of Donatus' *Ars Maior*, composed in the fourth century. Under the name of *Barbarismus*, this chapter became a focus around which investigations of deviant expressions developed.

In logic, ARISTOTLE was the main source of inspiration. His *Sophistical Refutations* made it clear that an argument does not always carry its validity on its surface, and his explanations of why a bad argument may look good gave impetus to the development of studies in semantics, and to a lesser degree in the pragmatics of linguistic communication. In *Peri hermeneias* (On Interpretation) 1, Aristotle briefly sketches which relations hold between corresponding items in writing, speech, thought and external reality. According to the standard interpretation of this text, Aristotle says that written words signify spoken ones, which in turn signify concepts, while concepts signify things. This reading can support the notion that truth, validity and their opposites are not primarily properties of spoken or written sentences and arguments, but of their mental counterparts. If the Aristotelian level of concepts is equated with that of Priscian, grammatical and logical correctness (congruity and truth) have the same primary bearers, that is, mental propositions whose 'words' are concepts. Aristotle's definitions of noun and verb in *Peri hermeneias* 2–3 differ from those of the Latin grammatical tradition, and this tension between grammar and logic created fruitful discussion. In *Categories* 1, Aristotle introduces the notion of paronymy or denomination: for example, the just (person) is denominated from justice. From this seed, theories of primary and secondary signification developed (to continue with the example, 'just' primarily signifies justice and secondarily signifies a person).

The logical works of BOETHIUS provided the notion of imposition (*impositio*). Following POR-PHYRY, Boethius taught that words acquire their meaning by an act by which a human 'impositor' decides to use a certain sound to name some thing. He distinguished a first imposition, by which features of the physical world acquire names ('tree', 'green', 'three cubits long' and so on), from a second one by which names acquire names ('noun', 'verb' and so on). He further suggests that a word such as 'species' is a name of names, so that 'man is a species' is a statement not about man but about the word 'man'. This suggestion helped to fuel early nominalism.

In theology, some essays by Boethius were influential until about 1200, but the principal authority was always AUGUSTINE. These two authorities inculcated in medieval writers the conviction that ordinary words do not have their ordinary meanings when used of God. For God to be high and just is not the same as his having big quantity and the quality of justice. God in his absolute simplicity cannot be analysed in terms of the Aristotelian categories. This doctrine was particularly important in the twelfth century when,

according to a widely accepted analysis, ordinary predication was thought to consist in the ascription of a certain form to some bearer or bearers. Any such form was supposed to belong to some Aristotelian category. Thus, 'Socrates is a man' ascribes the substantial form 'humanity' to Socrates, 'Socrates is just' ascribes the quality of justice to him, and so on. Since the truth of 'God is just' was uncontroversial, the Augustinian–Boethian doctrine forced medieval writers to deny one or both of the claims that (a) a predicate term always signifies some categorial form, and (b) in propositions of the type '*X* is *Y*', the form signified by *Y* is always attributed to the referent(s) of *X*. Usually, some combination of the two solutions was advanced. In the first place it was claimed that 'divine terms' ('God' in particular) never signify categorial forms; in the second place it was claimed that true propositions of the type 'God is *Y*' never ascribe categorial forms to God, but either indicate a sort of total identity between God and *Y* or actually ascribe a categorial form to his creation, so that 'God is just' may be paraphrased as 'there is justice in the created world, and it derives from God'.

Augustine (*De trinitate* XV) also contributed to the theory of mental speech his notion of a soundless 'speech in the mind' (*verbum mentis*) prior to any language in the phonic medium. He further gave a definition of a sign as that which, besides presenting itself to the senses, also makes the mind think of something other than the sign itself. In somewhat different wordings, this definition also occurs in Augustine's *De doctrina christiana* 2.1.1 and *De dialectica* 5. The last-named work had few readers; one, Roger BACON, developed from Augustine's work an unusual awareness that signification is a three-term relation involving not only sign and *significatum* but also someone to whom the sign signifies the *significatum*.

The whole patristic tradition of Biblical exegesis provided another rich source for medieval speculation about linguistic matters, not least about metaphorical language.

2 Words, concepts and things: introduction

Words were said in the Middle Ages to signify (*significare* or *designare*). A special terminology was developed for reference, but it remained a matter for debate what sort of entities significates actually were.

Few writers of the period were very concerned about written words, which they considered as mere 'stand-ins' for spoken words, although Pierre d'AILLY pointed out that a written message can be understood directly without recourse to sound. Concerning spoken words, late ancient sources suggested that they signify things through concepts. Typological interpretation of Biblical passages introduced the further notion of words signifying things which in turn signify other things, but this model was relevant only in Biblical studies. Some, such as John BURIDAN, took the word–concept–thing model to mean that words signify concepts which in turn signify things, so that words signify things only thanks to the transitivity of signification. Others, notably several late-thirteenth-century authors as well as WILLIAM OF OCKHAM in the fourteenth century, took it in the sense that for words to have the relation of signification to things, they must also be related in a certain way (subordinated) to concepts.

Those who took words to signify things directly usually did so because they felt that otherwise the concepts would become an impenetrable screen between language and external reality. If concepts were what our words signify, then it seemed we would always be talking about mere psychological entities. Buridan preferred the alternative model, *inter alia* because it can explain how two words can have the same extramental referents without being strictly synonymous. It suffices that the two words have different concepts for their direct significates.

The link between word and significate was generally held to be conventional (*ad placitum*), as Aristotle had said, but this was understood more in the sense that the link was the result of a free choice than in the sense that it depended on agreement between the users of the language. This link was supposed to have been established by 'the impositor', a figure who can trace his ancestry through Boethius and Porphyry back to the 'giver of names' in Plato's *Cratylus*. Some authors seem to have understood the 'impositor' very literally as some wise man who at some time had decided what things were to be called. Others took 'the impositor' to be a collective designation of the people who had introduced new words in course of time, so that in practice 'word *X* was imposed to mean *Y*' equalled 'the traditional meaning of *X* is *Y*'. Still others distinguished between the original wise impositor(s) who devised the phonology and other grammatical features of the language and laid down a basic vocabulary, and later users of the language who added to the vocabulary through new acts of imposition while not introducing major systematic changes.

Boethius operated with a first imposition to produce words for natural phenomena, and a second one to introduce words predicable of words (such as 'noun' or 'trisyllabic'). Early nominalists included terms such as 'species' among those of the second imposition, but after the thirteenth century the vocabulary of logic was more often described as words of second intention, 'second imposition' being reserved for the vocabulary of grammar. Neither the distinction according to imposition nor that according to intention was designed to cover the whole of a language's vocabulary, but only such items as are predicable (*categore(u)mata*). The understanding of what sort of entities first and second 'intentions' are changed over time. To Ockham, a word of the second intention is one that signifies mental *intentiones* (concepts), which are natural signs of other things (the individuals falling under the concept). By contrast, words of the second imposition signify things which are conventional signs, namely words.

While most medieval writers ascribed freedom of choice to 'the impositor', they also assumed that sounds had not been selected at random. Thus there was a justification for etymology, the art of revealing which properties of some thing the impositor paid special attention to when selecting a sound to name it. For example, many found it probable that the Latin word for 'stone', the accusative form of which is *lapidem*, had been chosen because it is characteristic of stones to hurt one's foot, and in Latin 'hurting the foot' is *laedens pedem*, which is somewhat similar to *lapidem*. Moreover, this aggressive feature of stones could be alleged as a reason for the masculine gender of *lapidem*. Theologians commenting on Genesis 2: 19–20, where Adam appears as the first giver of names, stressed that he selected appropriate names on the basis of his understanding of the nature of the things to be named. This conventionality of language was particularly emphasized by a number of four-teenth-century thinkers, who felt that the previous age had tended to produce overly rich ontologies by assuming some real distinction corresponding to every linguistic distinction they saw.

The act of imposition could be understood as one of uniting the material aspect of a word (sound) with a formal aspect (informational content). Thirteenth-century scholastics worried about how this could be possible. One proposal was that just as the formal features of a material thing can be transferred to the mind as an immaterial likeness (species), so the intelligible species can be communicated to other people by means of a material vehicle, the mind impressing a sort of copy of the relevant species on any particular token of a type of the sound conventionally associated with some sort of thing. Roger Bacon took this mechanism to be the explanation of magic and, apparently, of ordinary persuasion. He thought that if the speaker's mind and body cooperate to emit sound carrying some species, the species may act as a force (*virtus*) capable in favourable conditions of producing changes in both material and spiritual things. However, many thinkers of the next century were to deny material words the ability to carry information; instead, they located the information in the concepts to which words correspond.

3 Words, concepts and things: nominalism

Shortly before 1100, some philosophers began to define universals as words (*voces*) or names (*nomina*), and to consider predication a linguistic phenomenon: words are predicated of words, not things of things. Logic thus became a genuinely linguistic discipline (see LOGIC, MEDIEVAL). Porphyry's five predicables (genus, species and so on), Aristotle's ten categories (substance, quantity and so on), and Boethius' topical differences (genus, opposite and so on) could all be viewed as names applicable to certain classes of words, that is, as words of the second imposition.

Early representatives of this 'vocalism' apparently did not make it sufficiently clear that the voces that are the bearers of universality are not mere articulated sounds without regard to their meaning, and thus they laid themselves open to the objection that, in their theories, the Greek *anthropos* and the Latin *homo* would be two different universals even though they both mean 'man'. Likewise, *homo* uttered at one time would not be identical with the equiform sound uttered at another time. The supposed universal would thus dissolve into a host of individual sounds.

This problem in early 'vocalism' was solved when Peter ABELARD, the father of a school of *nominales*, made it clear that the criterion of identity for a universal was its signification: several voces with a shared signification make up one *sermo*, he held, and *sermones* are the bearers of universality. The signification of a universal term consists first in naming (picking out) individual things, and second in a relation to mental acts (*intellectus*). The individuals that a universal (such as 'man') picks out share a circumstance (*status*), for example *esse hominem* (being a man), but a *status*, Abelard held, is no thing. Some of his followers seem to have taken a *status* to be what a universal signifies; thus terms acquired significates of a type similar to those of whole propositions, for 'Socrates is a man' was supposed to signify the *dictum* that-Socrates-is-a-man (*Socratem esse hominem*) (see NOMINALISM).

About 1200, nominalism almost disappeared and only returned after 1310 with William of Ockham and John Buridan as its leading figures. Both the latter operated with three types of language, written, spoken and mental, and of these the mental language was considered logically most important. According to Ockham, terms of the written language are 'subordinated' to terms of the spoken language, and they in turn are subordinated to terms of the mental language. A mental term is a natural sign of some set of individuals. Its subordinate spoken and written terms are conventional signs of exactly the same individuals, so signification always links a term to individual things. Buridan sometimes uses Ockham's terminology, but more often he assumes that written terms signify spoken terms which in turn signify mental terms, which finally signify individual things, the 'ultimate significates'.

To both Ockham and Buridan, mental terms are concepts, and they are the primary bearers of universality. Oral and written terms are so derivatively. Similarly, 'true' and 'false' are primarily predicates of mental propositions. In Ockham's mature theory, a concept is identical with an act of intellection, and its ontological status is therefore that of an accidental characteristic of a soul. The ability of a concept C to signify every member of some set S derives from a combination of (1) a causal history reaching back from C to some member x of S encountered in direct cognition (intuition), (2) an isomorphism between C and x, and (3) a maximal similarity between x and any other member of S.

Ockham's mental language was almost a duplication of spoken language, but sometimes, at least, he thought of it as a language purified of the ambiguities and redundancies of its spoken counterpart and held that spoken language has two strictly synonymous terms, mental language has only one. Similarly, he claimed that grammatical features of spoken language lack mental counterparts if they are irrelevant to the truth of a proposition. Thus mental language does not have grammatical gender, but it does have tense.

Ockham and Buridan assumed multiple denotation for general terms whether they be in the subject or the predicate position, and co-reference of subject and predicate term was their fundamental criterion of truth for a categorical proposition. According to them, an affirmative categorical proposition is true if and only if the subject and the predicate term each refer to (*supponit pro*) at least one individual, and any individual to which the subject term refers is also referred to by the predicate term. The occurrence of an empty term like 'chimera' renders any affirmative proposition false and any negative proposition true (see PROPOSITIONS, SENTENCES AND STATEMENTS).

Thirteenth-century thinkers typically took signification to be a relation linking words with universal concepts, common natures or the like. The technical term for the relation between word and individual things was 'supposition' (see §12). For fourteenth-century nominalists, however, both signification and supposition terminate in individuals, but a word supposits only when occurring as a term in a proposition whereas it signifies even when uttered in isolation. Generally, a word's supposita will be a subset of its significates. The exception is the case when a word supposits for itself (or equiform words), whether in the mental, the spoken or the written variant, such as 'man' in 'man is an absolute concept', 'man is a monosyllabic word' or 'there are three letters in man'. In such cases, the term was said to be used non-significatively.

Whereas the verb's tense and modality define the relevant set of supposita, quantifiers affect the way a term supposits and thus the way to spell out the truth conditions of the proposition by means of the technique known as exposition. Exposition replaces the original proposition by an equivalent conjunction or disjunction of propositions, or by one proposition with a conjunct or disjunct subject or predicate. Thus 'every man runs' → 'this man runs, and that man runs, and so on', 'some man runs' → 'this man runs, or that man runs, and so on'.

In the early fourteenth century, the dominant grammatical theory was based on the notion that words possess 'modes of signifying' from which they derive their grammatical properties. It took some time for nominalist philosophers to work out an alternative, but by 1400 a new grammar had developed which took mental language to be the primary bearer of grammatical as well as of logical predicates. Mental terms were said to signify 'nominally' or 'verbally' the grammatical categories built into the concepts. Well-formedness was claimed to belong to spoken strings of words only thanks to their 'subordination' to grammatical strings of mental terms, not thanks to any grammatical properties inherent in the spoken words themselves, for how could sounds bear such properties, which obviously have an origin in the mind? Proponents of such views on grammar included ALBERT OF SAXONY, Pierre d'Ailly and one Marsilius (possibly MARSILIUS OF INGHEN). Some fifteenth-century thinkers also accepted modes of signifying, but held that they resided in concepts, not in words.

One strange result of late medieval nominalism was that thought was often considered to be more genuinely language than speech.

4 Words, concepts and things: realism

Taking universality to be a predicate only of concepts and/or words was not the prevailing view in the Middle Ages; more often, universality was held to reside somehow in things, though requiring a mental operation to be brought out into the open. This is not the place for a history of realist theories (see REALISM AND ANTIREALISM), but two points need to be

mentioned. First, the naïve Platonism in which universal Forms, residing in a world of their own, are the principles of being and of understanding for perishable things, while being also the significates of general terms, never had currency during this period. Second, probably the most influential variant of realism was one that arose in the thirteenth century and owed much of its inspiration to the Persian philosopher Avicenna (see IBN SINA). While accepting the reality of universals, this theory did not make them the significates of general terms. Instead, it held that such words signify 'common natures' transcending the distinction between universal and particular, existence and non-existence. As the common nature was generally identified with quiddity and essence, it was considered a principle of the understanding and being of things, but not one that would bestow either universality, particularity or existence on them. Particularity and universality were considered different manifestations, as it were, of the same underlying common nature or *res* (thing). Such 'things', the theory held, may have being in many alternative 'ways' or *modi essendi* (modes of being), in a static and in a dynamic way, in a universal or a particular way and so on, and this is reflected in human understanding and language. Thus the distinction between nouns and verbs brings out the distinction between the static and the dynamic modes of being of things.

5 Words, concepts and things: modism

About 1260–80 a grammatical theory of high generality was developed, known as *grammatica speculativa* (theoretical grammar); today the standard term for this theory is 'modism'. The first generation of 'theoretical grammarians' included BOETHIUS OF DACIA, Martin of Dacia and John of Dacia. Radulphus BRITO and Thomas of Erfurt, both active around 1300, belong to the second generation. Few theoretical advances seem to have been achieved after about 1310, though the works of Martin and Thomas continued to be used for about two centuries.

The term *modus significandi* (way/mode of signifying) had been in use since the twelfth century, typically to explain why an abstract and a concrete word for the same thing are not interchangeable *salva veritate*. Stephen Langton, for example, claimed that *deus* (God) and *deitas* (godhood) have the same signification and the same referent, and yet the truth of *deus est in lapide* (God is in a stone) does not entail the truth of *deitas est in lapide* (godhood is in a stone) because *deus* and *deitas* do not signify in the same way. The first proposition is true because of God's ubiquity, the second is false because it amounts to a claim that the stone is divine. By the mid-thirteenth century, it had become common to call grammatical properties of words 'modes of signifying', and a distinction had been introduced between a word's 'general' (lexical) signification and the 'special signification' due to its grammatical form.

In a further development, the notion, inspired by Avicenna, of common natures and their modes of being provided a suitable metaphysics for a linguistic theory with 'modes of signifying' as the key concept. It was assumed that the structure of human language reflects a correct understanding of the structure of external reality. Each of the traditional grammatical categories reflects one way of thinking, a *modus intelligendi* (way/mode of understanding) of items of reality – *res* or *natura communis* – and each way of understanding corresponds to one of the ways in which such items are, a *modus essendi* (way/mode of being). For a word thus to belong to some grammatical category means that it signifies some thing in a certain way, as having a certain mode of being: for a word to be a noun means that it signifies some thing in the way things are signified under their static aspect (mode), and for a word to be a verb means that it signifies some thing in the way things are signified under their dynamic mode. The noun *dolor* (pain) and the verb *dolere* (to ache) signify the same *res*, but in different ways.

While the modes of signifying are derived from correct understanding of the modes of real things, once they have been found and have found morphological expression, nothing prevents humans from inventing a word such as 'chimera' and furnishing it with a noun's mode of signifying. That mode of signifying indicates that if reality has a match for the word 'chimera', that thing must have static being. No particular facts about the external world can be deduced from grammar, only some general structural features.

Modes of signifying were divided into two types, *essential* and *accidental*. The essential modes establish the eight parts of speech, while the accidental modes establish moods, tenses, numbers, genders, cases and so on. Like the essential modes, accidental modes are derived from features of reality. Thus in reality things can have an active, passive or neutral way of being; this is the origin of the modes of signifying traditionally called masculine, feminine and neuter gender. A word must not be marked for masculine gender if the intended significate can have only feminine being, for that would make it the sign of another sort of thing than the one intended. However, for a word to be comprehensible it is only required that the mode of being indicated by the mode of signifying is compatible with the actual modes of being of the thing in question. Hence for things neutral with respect to action and passion, the choice of gender is arbitrary.

According to several modists, any particular word-form may be analysed as follows. First, it is a vocal sound (*vox*), endowed with a significative function (*ratio significandi*), one essential mode of signifying and some accidental modes of signifying. Having a significative function makes it into a sign, and having articulated sound (*vox*) for the vehicle of its significative function makes it into the sort of sign called a *dictio*. Having an essential mode of signifying makes it a *pars orationis* (part of speech, or in other words, a constituent of a sentence).

A fundamental, and controversial, thesis of modism was that the significative function linking a particular type of sound to some specific significate (*significatum, res*) is irrelevant for the grammaticality of constructions. Grammaticality is the result of licit combinations of modes of signifying. Thus {[+ noun + substantive + plural + nominative] + [+ verb + plural + third person]} is a licit combination, and any two words having those modes of signifying make a grammatical construction, no matter what their lexical meanings are. Thus 'stones speak' is as correct as 'men speak'. (In the schema shown above, the terms 'verb' and so on replace the cumbersome names of the corresponding modes of signifying.)

Modists assumed that external reality is accessible to human understanding, and that whatever can be understood can be expressed. Different peoples may choose different ways of encoding their understanding of reality in sound, but reality is the same for all and is understood in the same way by all peoples. Consequently, all languages must be structurally identical; they must all have the same grammar, surface differences notwithstanding. Greek (the modists wrongly assumed) has lexicalized 'number' as far as nouns are concerned and indicates it by means of special words called articles instead of using endings as in Latin, but what matters is that both languages can express 'number'. If the underlying grammatical system is the same for all languages, it follows that there is total translatability between them, and modists thought as much. Indeed, they found empirical evidence for the thesis in the well-known fact that logic was first developed in a Greek context and written down in Greek, then successfully translated into Latin. If logic is international and translatable, then surely nothing is untranslatable.

Among medieval thinkers, the modists presented the most articulate theory of the universality of grammar. Fourteenth-century opponents of modism, such as John Aurifaber, sometimes explicitly denied the universality thesis.

6 Multiple signification: proper and improper locutions

A pervasive theme in the thought of ANSELM OF CANTERBURY is that people often use improper locutions, and that these must be recognized as such and replaced by the proper ones if truth is to be found. A typical example of his use of this technique concerns the argument that for any thing (A) existing at t_1, it was true at $t_{<1}$ that A could come into being, and so any actual thing has a potential predecessor. For Anselm, potency and power were not distinct concepts, and the argument thus became a claim that at $t_{<1}$, A had the power to come into being. It follows that the actual A may have generated itself; thus the created world needs no creator, as it has its own principle of existence. Anselm's way of countering this line of thought is to claim that 'Before A came into being, A could come into being' is a colloquial way of saying 'Before A came into being, God had the power to bring A into being.' The improper locution leaves the false impression that at $t_{<1}$ A is the holder of the power to produce A, when in fact that power is held by God. This distinction between a more and a less proper meaning of words recurs in many guises in medieval thought.

7 Multiple signification: metaphor, allegory and author's intention

Language with one surface meaning and another one hiding beneath the surface was of particular concern to the theologians. For one thing, it was agreed that 'God is just' cannot be interpreted in the same way as 'Peter is just'. For another, it was commonly assumed that not only does the Bible sometimes use expresions that are only meant to be understood metaphorically (for example, 'sprout from the root of Jesse' as a metaphor for Christ), but often a Biblical text carries several senses besides the one apparent on the surface (*sensus historicus*). Thus 'heaven and earth' in Genesis 1:1 could be said to signify heaven and earth on one level of interpretation, angel and man on another, spirit and flesh on a third. In such cases we are dealing with *allegoria in verbis*, that is, words having another meaning than or besides their *prima facie* meaning.

However, following a suggestion from AUGUSTINE in *De trinitate*, medieval writers also assumed an *allegoria in factis* (allegory in deeds), in which the words do not directly have any but their surface meaning, but the thing meant in turn means something else. This occurs in the Bible when words directly signify some event (*factum*) from the time of the Old Covenant, but indirectly also signify some fact belonging to the time of the New Covenant. Thus

if the text says that the people of Israel were delivered from Egypt, the words primarily refer to the liberation of the Israelites from the Egyptian captivity; but this event in turn was a sign of the future liberation from evil of the members of the Church, which is then indirectly signified by the text. Interpreting in terms of *allegoria in factis* was later called 'typological exegesis'.

The assumption of simple *allegoria in verbis* was a way to make sense out of apparent nonsense, and was just one of many strategies used in the interpretation of authoritative texts, secular and sacred alike. After the thirteenth century, a distinction was often made between what a text means *de virtute sermonis* (in virtue of its wording), that is, the meaning the text conveys to anyone knowing the vocabulary and grammar of the language in question, and what it means *ex intentione auctoris* (in accordance with the intention of the author). By identifying the latter meaning with his own favourite view, a medieval author could avoid declaring his disagreement with an old authority.

In 1340, the Faculty of Arts at the University of Paris forbade its masters to call an authoritative utterance false in virtue of its wording if they thought the author had intended it in a true sense. Instead, teachers were required to say that the text had two senses, one of which was false and the other true, though both senses were 'in virtue of the wording' of the text. According to the reasoning behind the decree, it constitutes no violation of the 'virtue' (force) of the wording if an author intends the words to carry an unusual sense, for words have no semantic 'virtue' independent of their users. The explicit motive for the 1340 prohibition was fear of the consequences of accepting the judgment 'false by virtue of the wording' passed on a Biblical passage, as there might then appear to be a mismatch between the Bible's wording and truth.

8 Multiple signification: systematic use of metaphors (Gilbert and the Porretans)

Gilbert de la Porrée, Bishop of Poitiers from 1142–54 and father of a school of *Porretani*, barely escaped a condemnation for heresy (see GILBERT OF POITIERS) for his claim that the proposition *Deus est Deitas* (God is Godhood) is false, while *Deus est Deus Deitate* (God is God in virtue of Godhood) is true. He appeared to be violating the doctrine of divine simplicity (see SIMPLICITY, DIVINE). The Porretans were also ridiculed for tripling the Aristotelian categories. These two pieces of unusual doctrine were in fact part of one theory.

As Augustine and Boethius had made clear, words

cannot function the same way when used about creatures and about God. Christian theologians know that 'God is just' is a true proposition because it has the support of Scripture, but they do not fully know what its terms mean. What God is cannot be fully grasped by a human mind, at least not in this life. Nor is it clear what it is for God to be; used about creatures 'is' indicates temporal being, but this cannot be so with the Creator (see GOD, CONCEPTS OF). For a creature to be just is to have a certain property, but the doctrine of divine simplicity forbids this interpretation of 'just' in the case of 'God is just'. To speak about God implies transferring terms from the known realm of creatures into the unknown realm of the divine.

Starting from this problem, Gilbert and his followers developed a general theory about transferred language. In their theory, language was originally instituted to deal with the direct results of creation. The terms of this primary language describe the members of natural classes with their substantial and accidental forms. The ten Aristotelian categories are ten classes of words which may be used to describe a subject by signifying a predicate; a predicate in turn is a form that constitutes the subject's being something or in-some-way. In other words, a categorial term signifies a substantial or an accidental form. Only natural things have genuine forms. Hence, properly speaking, the ten categories pertain only to this primary language, that of the *naturalis facultas* (natural domain).

Artifacts, social institutions, values and other consequences of human activity constitute an ontologically secondary group of things to be named, but the *moralis* (behavioural) language used for the purpose is not structurally different from the one used for natural entities. People speak as if houses, prices and moral values were constituted by substantial and accidental properties in the same way as trees and colours. Propositions still have the shape '*x* is *F*', although '*F*' does not signify a genuine form. Most of the words of behavioural language are also loans from the primary language: thus 'high' has been borrowed from the category of quantity to be used in a transferred sense about prices. The semantic contents of the words are of different sorts, but the vocabulary still falls into ten groups, ten quasi-categories, and quite generally the structure of the language remains the same. The behavioural language owes its intelligibility to its retention of the structural features of the natural language.

The second-order language of logic and grammar (*rationalis facultas*) similarly retains the structure of the primary language. There is no real form of equivocation, yet '*x* is equivocal', which has the

structure of a genuine predication, may be true; and if it is so, we are justified in talking about the equivocation of *x*.

Finally, there is theological discourse. Words are transferred to new and fundamentally unknown senses. The only way to retain some sort of intelligibility is by obeying the same structural laws, the same syntax, as our primary language. One of the relevant laws might be stated as follows: if '*X*' and '*Y*' are concrete terms, and '*Y*-hood' the abstract term corresponding to '*Y*', then (1) '*X* is *Y*' implies '*X* is *Y* by virtue of *Y*-hood', and (2) '*X* is *Y*-hood' is nonsensical or false. Applied to the case of 'God is...' the rule yields the result that 'God is God' implies 'God is God by virtue of Godhood', while 'God is Godhood' is an unacceptable proposition. Gilbert did not intend to undermine the doctrine of divine simplicity. His discovery was that no intelligibility at all is left if one changes syntax and the meaning of the vocabulary at the same time.

9 Multiple signification: metaphor as a key tool in ordinary communication (Roger Bacon)

The mainstream tendency in the thirteenth century was to treat a word's meaning as an unchangeable companion of its sound once the word had been 'imposed' to mean something. This view implied, *inter alia*, that a word does not lose its meaning if such things as it signifies cease to exist; 'donkeys are animals' would be a meaningful (and, most would say, true) proposition even if donkeys had become extinct, and 'donkeys' would signify the same as when donkeys did exist. Similarly, while recognizing a difference between 'the donkey' used to refer to the asinine species and to a particular donkey, most philosophers would deny that a switch from one use to the other amounts to a change of signification.

Around the 1260s, Roger BACON developed a radically different view. According to Bacon, there is no way in which a word can be imposed simultaneously as the name of an existing and of a non-existing thing, of a universal and of a particular, and so on. Words are instituted and learned with some definite meaning, but it is in every speaker's power to change that meaning. In fact, this is done all the time, and generally tacitly. People are continually confronted with the task of expressing something they have not thought of or talked about before. They habitually solve the problem by means of metaphors, using a term whose meaning is somehow similar to what they now need to express. For example, to someone 'John' may signify a certain animate being. Standing in front of John's dead body, this person may identify the body with the words 'This is John', without intending to say that the corpse is an animate being. Tacitly, 'John' has been given a new meaning (body that used to be the material component of a human being called John). The speaker has performed a new imposition and has rendered the term equivocal.

The correct interpretation of the term in each particular case depends on the speaker's intention. The hearer may not grasp it, but generally the ability of speakers to create metaphors is matched by the ability of listeners to grasp them. To Bacon, metaphor was the individual person's fundamental tool for communicating new thoughts, and we have new thoughts all the time.

10 Multiple signification: the intentionalist current in grammar

Modistic grammar was intended to be an Aristotelian science, with principles of its own. In this the modists had been anticipated by others, but they were particularly insistent on the point that grammar cannot allow the use of information obtainable only from other sources than its own principles. According to the modists, grammar is concerned with grammaticality, not with truth or reality, and a string of words is grammatically well-formed (*congrua*) if it exhibits no mismatched modes of signifying. For this string to be a complete (*perfecta*) sentence, it must fulfil the further requirements of containing a subject (*suppositum*) and a predicate (*appositum*), and of leaving no relations of grammatical dependence between the ingredient words unsaturated. In modism, the lexical content of the sentence's constituent words is grammatically irrelevant, and so are non-linguistic circumstances that might influence the interpretation of an utterance. It follows that *turba ruunt* (the crowd are rushing) is ill-formed, whereas *capa categorica* (a categorical cloak) and *Socrates curret heri* (Socrates will run yesterday) are well-formed expressions.

By contrast, many twelfth-century thinkers had held that such expressions are ill-formed because they are unintelligible. Congruity was required both on the vocal level and on the level of sense. This meant that many putative propositions could be dismissed as not even being grammatically correct sentences. Even lack of referents for an ingredient term could rob an otherwise good sentence of sentencehood and propositionhood.

Constructions such as *turba ruunt* violate rules of concord (in this case, the rule that a verb agrees in number with its subject). However, such constructions could be found in authoritative writers and were generally classed as 'figurative'. For an 'error' to qualify as a figure instead of a mere error, it must have

some reasonable excuse: *figura est vitium ratione excusatum*, as the saying went. Moreover, the reasons excusing the deviant use of words were held to be twofold: there are reasons why the deviation is possible, and there are reasons why it is demanded, *ratio qua potest fieri* and *qua oportet fieri*, respectively. Reasons of the first type explain why the deviant expression is intelligible to an audience (for example, *turba ruunt* strongly resembles the correct *turba ruit* and *turba*, though of singular number, signifies a plurality of people, so somehow the plurality required by *ruunt* is present to the hearer's mind). Reasons of the second type explain why a speaker would choose the deviant formulation rather than a regular one (for example, the use of a plural verb is needed to give a vivid impression of the many individuals that compose the crowd); that is, such reasons appeal to the speaker's intentions in formulating the message.

Figurative and incomplete constructions invited grammarians to take the situation of communication into account. Further, as in the case of metaphors, appeal could be made to the speakers' intentions as a major factor in deciding the meaning attributable to an utterance. This ran counter to modist principles, but since modism did not have any good tools for dealing with deviant yet intelligible expressions, even modists would sometimes adopt 'intentionalism', as this context-sensitive grammar has been called. Robert KILWARDBY and Roger Bacon were among the foremost intentionalists.

In theology, there was an ongoing debate whether the verbal components of the sacraments were in some sense bearers of a power to sanctify along with their power to signify. The less inclined a theologian was to accept this, the more it would be stressed that the sacrament's efficacy depends on the intention of its original institutor and of its administrator (the priest).

11 Multiple signification: primary and secondary signification

ANSELM, in his *De grammatico*, introduced a distinction between what a word signifies by itself (*per se*) and what it signifies via something else (*per aliud*). By itself *grammaticus* (literate) signifies literacy plus having (or having literacy); indirectly it signifies a human being to whom having literacy applies. The human being is not directly signified by the word, but anyone who understands it can supply the information that literacy requires a human possessor. Anselm also uses the expression *appellare* as a synonym of *significare per aliud*.

In the twelfth century, it became common to distinguish a word's signification from its appellation or nomination. The things 'called' or 'named' (*appellata*, *nominata*) were whatever things the term applies to considered in their own right, whereas the term was said to 'signify' also or exclusively a concept, a form or the things qua carriers of some form. Thus 'white' might be said to name white things but to signify whiteness. In the thirteenth century, 'nomination' disappeared and 'supposition' replaced 'appellation' as the general term in descriptions of the varieties of reference.

Thirteenth-century writers worked not only with the distinction between signification and supposition, but also with a distinction between primary and secondary (*secund(ari)a* or *ex consequenti*) signification. A concrete accidental term (white) was said to signify primarily a form (whiteness) and secondarily whatever has that form (the thing that is white). Similarly, a substance-term like 'man' might be said to signify primarily human form (humanity) and secondarily the 'aggregate' of matter and form (man). A relative (such as 'parent') could be said to signify one relative thing (the parent) primarily and its correlative (the child) secondarily. Excessive use of the distinction led some to hold that a proposition could be true or false *per se* on account of the primary significates of its terms and have the opposite truth value *per accidens* on account of their secondary significates.

In the next century, WILLIAM OF OCKHAM used the distinction as a means to keep his ontology lean. He operated with (a) *absolute* terms such as 'dog', which signifies individual dogs and nothing else, and (b) *connotative* terms such as 'white' or 'parent', which directly signify whatever individual things are white or parents but connote (that is, secondarily signify) their whitenesses and children. By treating all terms in categories other than substance and quality as connotative, Ockham could avoid positing special quantitative entities, relative entities and the like.

BURIDAN made very similar use of the concept of connotation although, confusingly, he stood the twelfth-century terminology on its head, saying that 'white' directly signifies and supposits for something white but connotes or *appellat* its whiteness. Similarly, 'rich' supposits for a man and *appellat* his possessions. Names of fictitious entities (for example, 'chimera') signify nothing directly, but they connote the real entities such monsters are mistakenly supposed to consist of (a snake's tail, a lion's head and so on). Oblique cases of nouns are limited to connoting; thus in 'Plato's donkey is running', Plato is only connoted whereas a donkey is directly signified. Buridan calls what a connotative term supposits its 'matter' and what it connotes its 'form', but the latter does not imply that his *connotata/appellata* are supra-individual things.

12 Multiple signification: properties of terms (supposition, ampliation and restriction)

Handbooks of logic from the later Middle Ages generally devote much space to the so-called 'properties of terms'. The most notable of these are signification, supposition, ampliation, restriction and distribution.

The twelfth-century notion of supposition may have part of its background in Trinitarian theology, which distinguished between *suppositio personalis* and *suppositio essentialis* according to whether a term stands for one of the divine persons or the divine essence. However, the further development of supposition theory took place in the context of logic. The core idea of the theory is that a term does not always represent the same objects, even though it retains its meaning. In different contexts, the term refers to different subsets of the totality of objects of which it may be truly predicated. The proposition 'all the doctors will dispute next year' is ambiguous as to whether it claims that all presently existing doctors will dispute next year or that all the doctors existing next year will be disputing then. This was expressed in the rule that a general term acting as subject for a verb of future tense supposits for things present or future. Sometimes this rule comes in the form 'things present and future'. The first formulation shows an understanding of the term's *supposita* as the minimal set of objects that will verify the proposition; the second formulation takes the term's *supposita* to be the conjunction of those sets.

Another core idea was that a term's *supposita* are the individuals falling under it in some particular sentential context, but from the very beginning this idea was somewhat obfuscated by attempts to allow the notion of supposition also to cover other variations in the way a term may be understood. A distinction between personal and material supposition was commonly accepted. In personal supposition, the word 'donkey' stands for members of the asinine species; in material supposition, 'donkey' stands 'for itself', that is, for the word 'donkey', as in 'donkey is a noun'. Counting material use as a sort of supposition was a complication of the theory, and it was often unclear what exactly was meant by 'itself' in the formula 'standing for itself'. Another complication was the acceptance in the thirteenth century of a 'natural supposition': lifted out of any sentential context, a term was said to have natural supposition for the totality of objects falling under its signification. This could only make sense in an age when signification was not taken as a relation between a word and extramental particulars but between a word and some non-particular entity. Many authors further accepted a *suppositio pro significato* or *suppositio simplex*, claiming that in 'the donkey is a species', 'donkey' stands for the universal signified by 'donkey'.

The notion of supposition was most successful as a tool for dealing with tense, quantification and the effects of intentional verbs (such as 'know' and 'promise'). In the fourteenth century, Ockham and Buridan removed many of the inconsistencies in the knowledge inherited from the previous century. The notion of supposition was inextricably linked to those of ampliation (widening) and restriction. The idea is this: the set of objects for which a term would otherwise stand can be made bigger or smaller by the occurrence of some other word. Typically the neutral situation was taken to be that of a subject of a present-tense proposition containing neither modal nor intentional verbs – for example, 'every man is running' – in which 'man' was said to supposit for presently existing men. The addition of an adjective ('every young man is running') will restrict the set of verifiers by excluding old men. Saying 'may be running' instead of 'is running' extends the range of the term by adding an alternative set of verifiers, that of men who are yet to be (according to some authors) or that of possible men (according to others).

Fourteenth-century logic usually operated with four domains (sometimes called 'tenses'): the past, the present, the future and the possible. MARSILIUS OF INGHEN proposed to add a fifth 'tense' or domain, that of the imaginable, in order to provide verifiers for propositions of the type '*X* is imagined', in which '*X*' refers to an object that is indeed imaginable even though it may not be physically possible. According to his proposal, the verb 'is imagined' ampliates its subject so that it supposits not only for actually existing things but also for imaginable ones. This was a considerable step in the direction of developing a theory of the language of fiction, a subject to which scholastic philosophers had paid little attention save for one much-discussed example: propositions about chimeras. Chimeras were supposed to be impossible entities, though it was often unclear what sort of impossibility was involved. Marsilius' master, John Buridan, had sided clearly with logical impossibility, and to underline this he had ended up changing the medieval standard definition of a chimera, 'animal composed of lion, cow and young woman', into 'animal composed of parts that cannot possibly be put together'. However this invited the question of what to do about logically possible, and hence imaginable, things that nature does not allow. This was the background of Marsilius' proposal of an 'imaginable tense'.

13 Multiple signification: ambiguity

After about 1150, Aristotle's *Sophistici Elenchi* provided the general framework for most discussions of ambiguity. ARISTOTLE used six fallacies 'in speech'. Following Galen, medieval writers usually took these six fallacies to be due to three types of ambiguity (*duplicitas*), occurring in two types of expressions, single words (*dictiones*) or complexes of words (*orationes*). The resulting system is described in Table 1:

Table 1

Expression	Duplicity		
	actual	potential	imaginary (*fantastica*)
Simple	equivocation	accent	figure of speech
Complex	amphiboly	composition and division	

An actual ambiguity was supposed to be present any time the expression is uttered. The standard example of equivocation was *canis*, which can refer to (1) a dog, (2) a dogfish, or (3) the Dog Star. According to late thirteenth-century doctrine, such a term could be disambiguated only by the immediate addition of a determination suitable to only one of the significates. Thus 'dog' was supposed to have only sense (1) in 'a barking dog' while keeping all three senses in 'a dog is barking'. Aristotelian equivocation was designed primarily for nouns, but medieval writers sometimes used equivocation in all parts of speech, even pronouns and prepositions. For example, some held that 'this' is equivocal with respect to all things that may be pointed at, and the preposition *de* was considered equivocal because it can indicate local origin or material composition, as in *Socrates est de terra*, which can mean (1) 'Socrates is *from* a country' or (2) 'Socrates is *composed of* earth'.

In genuine equivocation, one sense cannot be derived from another. Each sense derives from an independent imposition when a sound was chosen, without concern for whether it had already been selected to label some other thing. According to the principles of modist grammar, this would mean that there could not strictly be such a thing as an equivocal noun. There could be one phonetic entity common to three significates, but then there would be as many nouns as there are significates. When this was realized in the 1270s, an attempt was made to save the essentials of the theory while preserving the intuition that *canis* is exactly one noun with the same grammatical properties no matter which sense is intended by the speaker or needed to make the proposition true in which the word occurs. It was proposed that there are both active and passive modes of signifying, with the active ones residing in the word and their passive counterparts (indistinguishable from modes of being) in the things signified. One active mode may correspond to three different passive ones, it was claimed, and syntactic properties depend on the active modes. This was not a happy solution, since it introduced two levels of grammatical structure with the surface structure determining syntax. As so often in the history of linguistics, ambiguity had proved a hard test for a theory (see AMBIGUITY).

In the principal type of equivocation, the different senses of the word are not ordered. However, standard doctrine also accepted types of equivocation in which one sense could be described as primary or proper and the other(s) as secondary, improper or transferred, as when 'running' primarily describes fast foot-propulsion, but metaphorically describes the movement of a river. Thirteenth-century writers adopted the name 'analogy' for equivocation in which one thing is signified primarily and one or more others secondarily. If a term signifies all its significates, equally it always needs a determination in order to be disambiguated. An analogical term unaccompanied by any determination was held to represent only its primary significate. An Aristotelian example was often used: 'healthy' primarily signifies a property of animate beings, while secondarily it signifies (a) a property of animal excretions, namely that of indicating that the animal they come from enjoys good health, and (b) a property of food and drugs, that of being conducive to the health of some animate being. To actually signify (a) or (b), 'healthy' needs to be joined with words like 'urine' or 'potion'. This particular type of analogy was called *analogia attributionis*. A considerable debate arose concerning another example, 'man', which some held to signify primarily a compound of body and rational soul and secondarily a mere body. In this view, the primary significate is represented by 'man' in 'this is a man' and the secondary one by the 'man' of 'this is a dead man', and so the latter proposition does not entail the former.

Some modists assumed that the significative function (*ratio significandi*) assigned to an analogical term on its imposition was a complex one selecting different significates in different contexts. Radulphus BRITO gave up considering the multiple meaning a property of the word itself prior to its actual use. The secondary signification comes about, he claimed, when a speaker uses a word improperly and a listener catches his intention thanks to a charitable inter-

pretation of an utterance that would make little sense if taken literally. In so claiming, however, Brito sacrificed the modist axiom that only two factors contribute to the sense of an utterance: lexical (imposition-given) meaning and modes of signifying.

In the thirteenth century, it became standard doctrine that *ens* (being) is analogical as to substance and accidents. Attempts were made to use this distinction as a model for the relation between the use of terms for both creatures and the creator, and a long debate about the analogy or univocity of being ensued (see BEING).

The notion of potential ambiguity led to a theory according to which the *litterae* (letters, phonemes) are the matter of an expression, which can be actualized only by the addition of a form, the 'way of pronouncing' (*modus pronuntiandi*), consisting in stress, pauses and the like. For example, in English the letters 'i-n-v-a-l-i-d' are the common matter of two distinct actual words, '*in*valid' and 'inva*lid*'. The fallacy of composition and division was used, *inter alia*, to explain cases in which a string of words can be interpreted either as an atomic or as a molecular proposition; thus *falsum est Socratem esse hominem si est animal* can be read as an atomic proposition ('that-Socrates-is-a-man-if-he-is-an-animal is false') or a molecular proposition ('that-Socrates-is-a-man is false, if he (or: there) is an animal'). The distinction between a 'composite' and a 'divided' sense also played a central role in the analysis of modal propositions. Often, *possibile est sedentem stare* was said to mean 'that-a-man-stands-while-sitting-is-possible' in the composite (or *de dicto*) sense, and 'a sitting man has the possibility of standing' in the divided (or *de re*) sense.

The notion of imaginary ambiguity was always somewhat unclear, but 'figure of speech' became a head under which the scholastics could examine the relation between (onto)logical and grammatical categories, for example, action versus active voice, substance versus substantive and individual versus singular number.

Use–mention ambiguity was usually dealt with in terms of supposition. In 'man is an animal', 'man' supposits personally (that is, for things signified by the word 'man'), while in 'man is monosyllabic', 'man' supposits materially (for phonetic entities equiform with the word pronounced). On the other hand, ambiguous supposition was often classified as a mode of either equivocation or figure of speech.

Logicians classified words as either categorematic (roughly = nouns + verbs) or syncategorematic (mostly quantifiers, modal terms, prepositions and conjunctions). There were few ancient precedents for inquiry into the contribution of syncategoremata to the sense of a proposition, but a major research effort was made in the later Middle Ages, especially with regard to ambiguity traceable to the occurrence of such logical operators, including scope ambiguity.

14 The significate of propositions

Any syntagm could be called an *oratio*, whether a sentence fragment such as 'a white horse' or a whole sentence (see PROPOSITIONS, SENTENCES AND STATEMENTS). Among the different types of sentences, the declarative was both the grammarians' preferred and the logicians' sole object of study. In logic, the technical term was *propositio*, and the standard definition (from Boethius) was *propositio est oratio verum vel falsum significans* (a proposition is a syntagm that signifies a truth (or some true thing) or a falsehood (or some false thing)). Propositions were said to be either categorical (that is, atomic) or hypothetical (that is, molecular; in medieval terminology, conditionals are only one among several types of hypothetical propositions). The Boethian definition suggests that there are entities – truths and falsehoods – signified by propositions. In the twelfth century, the significate of a proposition was usually called *enuntiabile* (statable) or *dictum (propositionis)*, (what is said (by the proposition)). Thus 'Socrates is running' (*Socrates currit*) signifies the *dictum* that-Socrates-is-running (*Socratem currere*), and the string of words 'that Socrates is running' is the name of the *dictum* (*nomen dicti*). It was commonly, though not universally, assumed that the objects of knowledge and belief are *dicta*.

The ontological status of *dicta* was controversial. Nominalists could not give them full reality, for that would be a repetition of the error of hypostatizing the significates of single words. On the other hand, a *dictum* is either a truth or a falsehood, and some truths at least might seem to be eternal; but if *dicta* were eternal, there were other eternal things than God, which was scarcely an acceptable thought. The majority view seems to have been that *dicta* are a sort of quasi-thing.

Controversy also surrounded the nominalist thesis *quod semel est verum semper est verum* (what is true at one time is always true). This thesis was theologically motivated. The pre-Christian patriarchs were assumed to have believed that Christ would be born, and that was a truth; Christians believe that Christ has been born, and that is a truth. Do Christians believe in the same truth as did the patriarchs? Or did the truth in which the patriarchs believed cease to be a truth when Christ was born? In the nominalist view, 'Christ will be born' and 'Christ has been born' express the same truth supposing that they are pronounced before and after his birth, respectively. The same true *dictum* has two differently tensed names, 'that Christ will be born' and 'that Christ has been born'. The nominalist thesis amounts to a claim that the class of linguistic expressions that are verified by the same event or events express the same *dictum*. Non-nominalists replied that the differently tensed 'that' clauses are or signify different statables; some tried to escape unfortunate theological consequences by denying that statables are what knowledge and belief have for their objects.

After the twelfth century, interest in statables abated somewhat, but it came back strongly in the fourteenth. Most authors then shared the belief that propositions, whether mental or spoken, are individual entities existing in time. Previously there had been a tendency to neglect the difference between proposition token and proposition type, but now the distinction came into the foreground, especially thanks to John Buridan. He also contributed to the popularity of a three-part analysis of propositions into subject, copula and predicate, with the copula treated as a term in its own right. The copula of a mental proposition could be described as a 'complexive concept' uniting the extremes. Pierre d'Ailly, while accepting the three-part analysis, insisted that ontologically a mental proposition is a unity; it is tripartite only in the sense that it is a cognition equivalent to the conjunction of three other cognitions.

Philosophers influenced by Ockham often held that the objects of knowledge and belief are mental propositions. According to Ockham, a proposition's truth is nothing other than the proposition itself, and it has no other significate than the individual things to which its terms refer. Some found this implausible, *inter alia* because truth would then seem to depend on the existence of propositions in human minds rather than on external reality. Instead, they (most famously GREGORY OF RIMINI), took the object of knowledge and bearer of truth to be a state of affairs, *complexe significabile (tantum)* (something that can (only) be signified in a complex way, for example by a proposition, not by a term). The same quasi-entity could also be called *totale* (or *adaequatum*) *significatum propositionis* (the total (or: adequate) significate of a proposition), as opposed to the significates of each of its ingredient terms. Gregory vigorously denied that total significates are existing entities, whether mental or extramental. Consequently, he thought, God's uniqueness as an eternal being is not compromised by claiming that even before the beginning of the world 'complexly signifiables' were true or not true in virtue of the sign and source of all truth, God himself.

Walter BURLEY held the unusual view that just as

vocal terms have real things as their ultimate significata, so vocal propositions ultimately signify propositions in external reality. However, he seems never to have reached a satisfactory answer to the question of what sort of thing such a *propositio in re* is. In one of his formulations, a real proposition has the things signified by its subject and predicate for its matter and a composition or division of that matter (in affirmation or negation) contributed by the mind for its form.

15 Syntax

The explicit aim of all medieval grammar was to spell out the rules of grammaticality (*congruitas*), or in other words, syntactical rules. The key term in grammatical syntax was *constructio*, standardly defined as *congrua dictionum ordinatio* (congruous linking of words), and most attention was paid to the pairwise linking of words rather than to more complex linguistic entities. The elementary rules of concord were easily describable in terms of grammatical accidence; thus substantive nouns and adjectives were both said to have the accidents of gender, number and case, and the rule 'a substantive and its adjective must agree in gender, number and case' was thus a rule on how to match the accidents of one word with those of another. In modistic grammar, such concord could be described as a 'proportionality of modes of signifying', with the idea being the same, that certain secondary semantic features of one of the words to be construed require or forbid certain semantic features of the other word.

The relationship between the words to be construed was most often described in terms of determination, government (*regimen*), demand (*exigentia*), or dependence with the last term dominating in modistic grammar. In about 1300, a construction was taken to be the union of a *dependens* (dependent, unsaturated constituent) and a *dependentiam terminans* (a constituent that saturates the dependence). Just as in logic a proposition is a union or composition of subject and predicate, most simply expressed in the form 'noun + verb', so in grammar a sentence is a union of *suppositum* and *appositum*, most simply expressed as 'noun + verb', with the verb being the dependent constituent requiring saturation such as can be provided by the noun that signifies *per modum per se stantis* (purports that its significate is a self-sufficient entity). In the complex sentence 'Socrates goes to the church' the verb 'goes' has two relations of dependence, one being saturated by 'Socrates', another by '(to) the church'. As far as the verbs are concerned, the medieval notion of dependence had

approximately the same function as the modern notion of valency.

16 Informative and performative locutions

While most medieval linguistic thought concentrated on descriptive propositions, a conceptual apparatus for talking about performative locutions did exist, at least since the early thirteenth century. This was provided by a distinction between *actus significatus* (or *conceptus*) and *actus exercitus*, act(ion) signified or conceived versus act(ion) performed. The distinction was used in several ways.

First, if *A* says 'Bravo!' when hearing *B* say 'They sacrificed themselves', the exclamation may either comment on the act of self-sacrifice signified by *B*'s statement or on the act performed by *B* in uttering the statement. This raises the question of whether in the first case 'Bravo' is construed as an adverb with the word 'sacrificed' but in the second case with an event, not with a word.

Second, some words signify what others perform. The words 'I address you' signify an action that is performed by saying 'Hello'; 'or' and 'every' perform – or are means of performing – what 'disjoins' and 'distributes' signify. Some logicians held that syncategoremata (that is, logical operators) were purely performative, having no signification besides their function (*officium*). According to Ockham, '*B* is predicated of *A*' should not be confused with '*A* is *B*': in the former proposition predication is signified, in the latter it is performed.

Third, in some situations words which are usually informative (signify an action) become performative: when a priest says 'I baptize you', his words are instrumental in performing what they describe. Finally, some thought a confusion of signification with performance was the source of the Liar paradox, the act of saying signified by 'I am saying a falsehood' being confused with the act of saying performed by uttering those words.

17 The diversity of languages

Medieval theoreticians were aware of the possibility of non-vocal sign systems fulfilling the same role as ordinary languages, but spent little time on the investigation of any other non-vocal communication than that between angels, who were supposed to use no material signs because of their immateriality. The theoreticians were, of course, aware of the diversity of human languages but usually merely acknowledged the phenomenon, noting that different peoples can use different conventional signs for the same things. The modists of the late thirteenth century produced an account of how the shared human rationality and shared external reality resulted in one common linguistic structure (grammar), capable of accidental diversification through the arbitrary choice of material (sounds) to carry the sign function. Modists did not typically raise the question of a possible common origin of the different languages' phonetic manifestations. Medieval writers who did raise the question usually agreed that the first human language, that of Adam, was Hebrew, and that there was some sort of connection linking Hebrew to the many languages spoken after the Babylonian confusion, but few apart from Roger Bacon and Dante had any clear ideas of linguistic development.

Dante ALIGHIERI presented a remarkably well-developed theory of linguistic change in his *De vulgari eloquentia*. Dante operates with two types of language: (a) such as is the maternal tongue of certain people, (b) such as is no-one's primary language. Languages of type (a), the vernaculars, are subject to change, while type (b) languages, the 'grammatical' ones such as Latin and classical Greek, are exempt from change, their form having been determined once and for all by codified rules. The 'grammatical' languages are artificial; they have been created to avoid the breakdown of communication that spatial and temporal distances cause in natural languages. Contrary to the humanists of later periods, Dante did not see Latin as Cicero's maternal tongue, though he was clearly aware that it was based on ancient Roman vernacular.

To Dante the natural languages, the vernaculars, are the nobler ones. All derive from the language that Adam acquired on acquiring his soul. Thus far it might appear as if Dante followed modist teaching, for if Adam's acquisition of language was inseparable from his acquisition of soul, language is innate in humans. However, whereas the modists only claimed that all languages share an abstract structure, Dante saw them all as historical developments of one original language, that of Adam, which was not just an abstract structure but a fully fledged language with phonetics, vocabulary and syntax. He tried to make sense of the Babylonian confusion by taking it to represent the emergence of sociolects, each craft developing its own way of speaking. However, his finest observations concern the way language changes with time and how geographical isolation can make two branches of a language develop in different ways. Applying his theory to European languages, he assumed that all derive from three languages that must have arrived in very ancient times. One of these was the ancestor of Northern and Eastern European languages (about which Dante obviously knew little;

Roger Bacon had been better informed), the second of the Romance languages, and the last of Greek.

Since Dante's purpose was to persuade his readers that Italian could serve as a language of refined literature, he had to face the argument that is always brought up when a new literary language is being formed, namely that there is no such common language with a describable form of its own but only a large number of local dialects. His counterclaim was that it makes sense to have a supra-regional Italian language, identical with no particular dialect but acceptable to educated people everywhere.

18 An artificial language

No medieval author envisaged an artificial, uninterpreted language. Nevertheless, some developments in logic pointed in that direction. The use of variables was known from Aristotelian syllogistics and was employed by medieval writers in the same way as Aristotle had done. Moreover, a number of standard examples developed into quasi-variables, the name 'Socrates' having any human proper name for its value, 'Caesar' representing any proper name of a human being from the past, 'currit' any present-tensed active verb, and so on. Thus, if a logician asked whether the proposition 'Caesar is a man' is true, he was asking about propositions with the proper name of a no-longer-existing individual for their subject term. Buridan explicitly recognized that the standard examples in jurisprudence, 'Titius' and 'Bertha', were not genuine proper names; they do not elicit singular concepts, but common ones.

Logicians also came close to creating an artificial language when they stated rules of supposition, often reflecting tendencies rather than hard and fast rules of Latin. Thus according to many logicians, *asinus cuiuslibet hominis currit* equals 'there is a donkey such that it belongs to just any man, and this donkey is running' while *cuiuslibet hominis asinus currit* means 'for just any man it is true that his donkey runs'. Though not quite aware of the fact, these logicians had created fragments of an artificial disambiguated language. This was to earn them much scorn from humanists, who could see no good in unnatural Latin.

See also: ARISTOTELIANISM, MEDIEVAL; LANGUAGE, PHILOSOPHY OF; LANGUAGE, RENAISSANCE PHILOSOPHY OF; LOGIC, MEDIEVAL; NATURAL PHILOSOPHY, MEDIEVAL §8; NICHOLAS OF AUTRECOURT; NOMINALISM; SEMANTICS; WILLIAM OF OCKHAM §6

References and further reading

Biard, J. (1989) *Logique et théorie du signe au XIVᵉ siécle*, Paris: Vrin. (Especially valuable as an introduction to some lesser-known thinkers from the fourteenth century.)

Bursill-Hall, G.L., Ebbesen, S. and Koerner, K. (eds) (1990) *De ortu Grammaticae: Studies in medieval grammar and linguistic theory in memory of Jan Pinborg*, Studies in the History of the Language Sciences 43, Amsterdam: Benjamins. (Articles on medieval logic and grammar.)

Ebbesen, S. (1987) 'The Way Fallacies Were Treated in Scholastic Logic', *Université de Copenhague. Cahiers de l'Institut du Moyen Age Grec et Latin* 55: 107–34. (Survey article with extensive bibliography.)

—— (ed.) (1995) *Sprachtheorien in Spätantike und Mittelalter*, Geschichte der Sprachtheorie 3, Tübingen: Narr. (Articles in English, German and French on a broad variety of themes. Also useful as a bibliographical guide.)

Kneepkens, C.H. (1987) *Het iudicium constructionis. Het leerstuk van de constructio in de 2de helft van de 12de eeuw*, 4 vols, Nijmegen: Ingenium. (On twelfth-century grammarians' theories of syntax. Discussion in vol. I followed by text editions in vols II–IV.)

—— (1990) 'On Medieval Syntactic Thought with Special Reference to the Notion of Construction', *Histoire Épistémologie Langage* 12: 139–76. (Can be used as a guide to the scarce literature on medieval syntactic theory.)

Kretzmann, N. (ed.) (1988) *Meaning and Inference in Medieval Philosophy: Studies in Memory of Jan Pinborg*, Synthese Historical Library 32, Dordrecht: Kluwer. (Contains several relevant papers.)

Kretzmann, N., Kenny, A. and Pinborg, J. (eds) (1982) *The Cambridge History of Later Medieval Philosophy*, Cambridge: Cambridge University Press. (Several relevant articles.)

Libera, A. de (1996) *La querelle des universaux. De Platon à la fin du Moyen Age*, Paris: Éditions du Seuil. (Provides an up-to-date account of medieval theories of universals.)

Marmo, C. (1994) *Semiotica e linguaggio nella scolastica: Parigi, Bologna, Erfurt 1270–1330*, Roma: Istituto Storico Italiano per il Medio Evo. (A thorough study of modistic theory; uses both grammatical and logical sources.)

Nuchelmans, G. (1973) *Theories of the Proposition: Ancient and Medieval Conceptions of the Bearers of Truth and Falsity*, North-Holland Linguistic Series 8, Amsterdam: North Holland. (A classic with strong impact on later research.)

Panaccio, C. (1991) *Les mots, les concepts et les choses*, Montreal, Que.: Bellarmin, and Paris: Vrin.

(A penetrating analysis of Ockham's theory of language.)

Pinborg, J. (1967) *Die Entwicklung der Sprachtheorie im Mittelalter*, Beiträge zur Geschichte der Philosophie und Theologie des Mittelalters, Texte und Untersuchungen 42.2, Münster: Aschendorff, and Copenhagen: Frost-Hansen. (The classic on modistic grammar.)

—— (1972) *Logik und Semantik im Mittelalter. Ein Überblick*, Stuttgart: Frommann–Holzboog. (Survey with extensive quotations of original texts.)

—— (ed.) (1976) *The Logic of John Buridan*, Copenhagen: Museum Tusculanum. (Somewhat outdated, but still useful as an introduction to Buridan's semantics.)

—— (1984) *Medieval Semantics, Selected Studies on Medieval Logic and Grammar*, ed. S. Ebbesen, London: Variorum. (Several relevant papers.)

Rijk, L.M. de (1962–7) *Logica Modernorum*, 2 vols in 3 parts, Assen: Van Gorcum. (The richest single collection of twelfth-century logic texts with extensive discussion by the editor; partly outdated, but still invaluable.)

—— (1989) *Through Language to Reality: Studies in Medieval Semantics and Metaphysics*, ed. E.P. Bos, Northampton: Variorum. (Several relevant papers.)

Rijk, L.M. de and Braakhuis, H.A.G. (eds.) (1987) *Logos and Pragma: Essays on the Philosophy of Language in Honour of Professor Gabriel Nuchelmans*, Nijmegen: Ingenium. (Several papers about the meanings of terms and propositions.)

Rosier, I. (1983) *La Grammaire spéculative des Modistes*, Lille: Presses Universitaires de Lille. (Valuable survey of modist doctrine.)

—— (1994) *La parole comme acte. Sur la grammaire et la sémantique au XIIIᵉ siècle*, Paris: Vrin. (On the 'intentionalist' current in grammar and on a wide range of linguistic topics in medieval grammar, philosophy and theology, with special attention paid to Roger Bacon; rich bibliography.)

Vineis, E. and Maierù, A. (1990) 'La linguistica medioevale', in G.C. Lepschy (ed.) *Storia della linguistica* II, Bologna: Il Mulino, 11–168. (A good introduction to the grammatical tradition in particular, with rich bibliography.)

STEN EBBESEN

LANGUAGE OF THOUGHT

The 'language of thought' is a formal language that is postulated to be encoded in the brains of intelligent creatures as a vehicle for their thought. It is an open question whether it resembles any 'natural' language spoken *by anyone. Indeed, it could well be encoded in the brains of people who claim not to 'think in words', or even by intelligent creatures (for example, chimpanzees) incapable of speaking any language at all. Its chief function is to be a medium of representation over which the computations posited by cognitive psychologists are defined. Its language-like structure is thought to afford the best explanation of such facts about animals as the productivity, systematicity and (hyper-) intensionality of their thought, the promiscuity of their attitudes, and their ability to reason in familiar deductive, inductive and practical ways.*

1   The language of thought hypothesis (LOTH)
2   Arguments for LOTH
3   Some common objections to LOTH

1   The language of thought hypothesis (LOTH)

One of Descartes' greatest challenges to the materialist theory of the mind was that it was impossible to imagine a physical device capable of the diverse intelligent behaviour often exhibited by human beings. Frege's development of formal logic, and then Turing's conception of a Turing machine offered the promise of a serious reply to this challenge, since they showed how at least deductive reasoning could be realized as a form of mechanically realizable computation (see TURING MACHINES; MIND, COMPUTATIONAL THEORIES OF). Their proposals were an inspiration for the development of computational formalisms for various forms of non-deductive reasoning: induction, abduction, practical reason and decision theory.

But computations presuppose representations (Fodor 1975): the computations of Turing machines and many computers are, for example, often defined over *numerals* that represent *numbers*. A suggestion that has been advanced by a variety of philosophers and cognitive scientists (Harman 1973; Newell and Simon 1972; Fodor 1975, 1987) is that thinking requires precisely the sort of representations that are standardly used to *identify* thoughts, namely *sentences*: representations with logico-syntactic structure, of the sort defined recursively in logic texts in terms of names, predicates ('is bald'), variables ('x', 'y'), connectives ('and', 'only if'), quantifiers ('all', 'some') and various operators ('probably', 'necessarily'). Thus, the thought that 'Necessarily God does or does not exist' is normally identified by using that sentence (or a translation of it).

The language of thought hypothesis (LOTH) is then the hypothesis that thinking consists in performing computations on sentences whose logico-syntactic

parts are causally efficacious, for example, by being encoded in a creature's brain. The process is akin to theorem-proving in logic, except that, where the rules of logic are ordinarily applied by us *consciously following* the rules, according to LOTH the rules are applied by virtue of the causal structure of the brain. For example, where, in elementary logic, we follow the rule *modus ponens* – 'From 'p' and 'If p then q' derive 'q'' – for LOTH the brain is so constructed that, if it is in a state that represents the premises, then it is (sometimes) caused to enter a state that represents the conclusion.

'Thinking' here is a generic word for processes involving propositional attitudes, and these are distinguishable in at least two ways that are often blurred in ordinary talk: by their *contents* (the sentence complement, for example, the that-clause, that follows the attitude verb) and by the different *relations* the agent may have to the same such contents, for example, *believing* or *hoping* that God exists (see PROPOSITIONAL ATTITUDES). According to LOTH, different propositional attitudes of an agent involve different computational relations borne by the agent to sentences in a language of thought (LOT) that express the various thought contents of the agent. To a first approximation (see also Field 1981):

> For any agent, x, and propositional attitude, A that p, there exists some computationally definable relation C_A such that:
>
> x A's that p iff   for some σ: $(xC_A\sigma \,\&\, \sigma)$ means that p

For example, actively judging or desiring that God exists might be defined in terms of different computational relations, J or D, that an agent, x, might bear to a sentence, '$(\exists x)Gx$', that expresses the proposition 'God exists'.

LOTH must, of course, specify the computational relations for specific attitudes, as well as provide an account of how a symbol in the brain can have a specific meaning. For the first task it appeals to the familiar flow-charts of cognitive psychology. Judgment, for example, might be the output of perceptual and reasoning systems that is the input to a decision-making one. For a theory of meaning, LOTH has turned to (combinations of) 'informational' approaches (Fodor 1987), teleological approaches (Neander 1995) and 'computational role' approaches (Field 1981).

Note that, *pace* Searle (1984; see also CHINESE ROOM ARGUMENT), LOTH does not entail that syntactically defined sentences in a LOT do not have many real and important semantic properties; all that is claimed is that the relational clause and the causal

405

processes of thinking are specifiable syntactically. However, there are some LOTH proponents (for example, Jackendoff 1987) who do seem to think that syntax would be enough to determine semantics, and others (for example, Stich 1983) who argue that the semantic clauses are not in principle determinate.

2 Arguments for LOTH

Although some philosophers (for example, Davies 1991) have ventured a priori arguments for LOTH, the chief arguments for it are that it provides the best explanation of at least the following phenomena (see Rey 1997: chaps 8–9 for a longer list).

The productivity of attitudes. People seem to be able to think a potential infinitude of thoughts, that is, to a first approximation, people can (in principle) think all permissible combinations of the primitive syntactic elements. For example, they can understand a conjunction of $n + 1$ sentences if they can understand n of them. Some theorists have baulked at the substantial idealization (from memory, mortality) that this involves, and so Fodor (1987) proposed a related, but more modest claim:

The systematicity of attitudes. Anyone who can think p can think any logical permutation of p: for example, if someone can think that 'Ann hates Bob only if Charles loves Di', they can also think that 'Charles loves Di only if Ann hates Bob', 'Di loves Charles only if Bob hates Ann' and so on for all permissible logical permutations. LOTH captures both productivity and systematicity by presuming that any system in which the logico-syntactic elements of sentences are causally efficacious is one in which they are readily available for recombination.

Rational and irrational relations among attitudes. Both deductive reasoning and many common fallacies are 'structure-sensitive', involving the scopes of operators, for example, negations, conditionals and quantifiers (see SCOPE). Quantifier scope is what distinguishes, for example, 'Everyone loves someone' form 'There is someone whom everyone loves'. Standard treatments of logic capture such structural facts in the terms of logical syntax. By insisting that that syntax is causally efficacious, LOTH is able to explain people's ability to reason, and why they are prone to certain errors (for example, misrepresenting a scope).

The (hyper-)intensionality of attitudes. Propositional-attitude ascriptions are 'intensional': terms that (even necessarily) refer to the very same thing cannot be substituted for one another without risking a change in the truth-value of the whole. There is a difference between thinking 'Water is wet', thinking 'H_2O is wet', and thinking 'The stuff of rain is wet', despite the fact that water = H_2O = the stuff of rain. LOTH distinguishes these attitudes by distinguishing syntactically between different symbolic structures to which an agent can be related (it can even distinguish them when the structures have the same 'meaning', as in *hyper*-intensional cases such as remembering that a fortnight is a fortnight as compared with remembering that a fortnight is two weeks).

The multiple roles of attitudes. Different attitudes can be directed at the same thoughts. People often *wish* for the *very same thing* that they *believe* does not presently obtain; they often come to *think* what they previously only *feared*. LOTH captures this by positing different computational relations to the same internal representation (or ones with the same content).

3 Some common objections to LOTH

Many people claim introspectively not to 'think in words', but, rather, for example, in mental images (see IMAGERY). Now, in the first place, LOTH is not meant to be establishable by introspection; it is purely an *explanatory* hypothesis. Moreover, by careful delineation of the different computational roles of specific representations, some (for example, Pylyshyn 1981) have argued that it can capture imagistic experiences, and even subjectivity and sensation (for example, Lycan 1990; Rey 1992).

But, second, it is difficult to think of a non-linguistic representational system with anything like the expressive power of a linguistic one. *Purely* imagistic systems, for example, do not seem adequate to represent logically complex thoughts – for example, negations, conditionals, nested quantifications – nor to distinguish thoughts about a general category (for example, cow) from ones about a particular instance (Elsie), for which the same image might serve.

Note that LOTH is not committed to the language of thought being confined only to creatures that speak a natural language, much less to the language of thought actually *being* a natural language. According to LOTH, any creature that *thinks* (as, for example, chimpanzees seem to do) will need a LOT, whether it *speaks* or not.

Wittgenstinians often object that LOTH presupposes the very sorts of processes it purports to explain: if there is a LOT, do we not need an 'homunculus' in the brain to read it? LOTH answers this objection by emphasizing Turing's proposal for computation in general, whereby brute causation replaces human calculation.

But did Wittgenstein's 'private language' argument not show that languages are necessarily public? (See

Philosophical Investigations §§243–; PRIVATE LAN-GUAGE ARGUMENT; WITTGENSTEIN, L. §13.) Wittgenstein was concerned, however, only with languages whose references could not be publicly ascertained (for example, because they referred to 'private sensations'). LOTH makes no such commitment.

Dennett (1987: ch. 3) argues that many attitude ascriptions are merely 'interpretations' of behaviour that do not commit us to a corresponding sentence in the head. For example, we might say of a chess-playing computer that 'It likes to get its queen out early', even though there might be no corresponding sentence manipulated by the computer's program. However, LOTH is not committed to the literal truth of *every* ordinary ascription; only ones that figure in a causal explanation of such phenomena as those mentioned above.

The chief rival to LOTH is the so-called 'radical connectionist' models of cognition (in contrast to connectionist models that are merely implementations of 'classical' ones such as LOTH). Defenders of radical connectionism complain that LOTH models are too rigid, inefficient and not as neurophysiologically realistic as connectionist networks (see Smolensky 1988). However, the cognitively relevant physical properties of the brain have yet to be sufficiently identified to pass judgment on such a claim, and it has yet to be shown that radical connectionist theories can explain all the above phenomena as well as a language of thought does (see CONNECTIONISM).

See also: MIND, COMPUTATIONAL THEORIES OF

References and further reading

* Davies, M. (1991) 'Concepts, Connectionism, and the Language of Thought', in W. Ramsey, S. Stich and W. Rumelhart (eds) *Philosophy and Connectionist Theory*, Hillsdale, NJ: Erlbaum. (An a priori argument for the language of thought.)
* Dennett, D.C. (1987) *The Intentional Stance*, Cambridge, MA: MIT Press. (Essays critical of LOTH, presenting a less realistic, more 'instrumental' theory of mental states instead.)
* Field, H. (1981) 'Mental Representation', in N. Block (ed.) *Readings in Philosophy of Psychology*, vol. 2, Cambridge, MA: Harvard University Press. (An extremely lucid presentation of the essential claims of LOTH, as well as of a conceptual role semantics for it.)
* Fodor, J. (1975) *The Language of Thought*, New York: Crowell. (The most influential defence of LOTH as a psychological hypothesis.)
* —— (1987) *Psychosemantics*, Cambridge, MA: MIT Press. (A defence of LOTH on the basis of systematicity, as well as a development of a specific version of informational semantics for it.)
* Harman, G. (1973) *Thought*, Princeton, NJ: Princeton University Press. (An early statement of a language of thought view, more from a philosophical than a psychological point of view.)
* Jackendoff, R. (1987) *Consciousness and the Computational Theory of Mind*, Cambridge, MA: MIT Press. (A linguist's attempt to work out in some detail a LOTH view, incorporating research in vision and language.)
Loewer, B. and Rey, G. (1991) *Meaning in Mind: Fodor and his Critics*, Oxford: Blackwell. (Collection of papers reacting to Fodor's defence of LOTH, with replies by Fodor and an extended introduction by the editors.)
* Lycan, W. (1990) 'What is the 'Subjectivity of the Mental'?', in J.E. Tomberlin (ed.) *Philosophical Perspectives*, vol. 4, *Action Theory and Philosophy of Mind*, Atascadero, CA: Ridgeview, 109–30. (An attempt to account for subjective experiences by means of LOTH.)
Maloney, J. (1989) *The Mundane Matter of the Mental Language*, Cambridge: Cambridge University Press. (A clear and very readable defence of LOTH, with replies to many critics and consideration of problems outside its normal range, such as sensations and moods.)
* Neander, K. (1995) 'Misrepresenting and Malfunctioning', *Philosophical Studies* 79: 109–41. (An evolutionary (teleosemantic) approach to the problem of assigning content to expressions in a language of thought.)
* Newell, A. and Simon, H. (1972) *Human Problem Solving*, Englewood Cliffs, NJ: Prentice Hall. (An influential statement of the 'classical' LOTH approach in artificial intelligence.)
* Pylyshyn, Z. (1981) 'The Imagery Debate: Analog Media vs. Tacit Knowledge', in N. Block (ed.) *Imagery*, Cambridge, MA: MIT Press. (Argues that LOTH can capture imagistic experiences.)
* Rey, G. (1992) 'Sensational Sentences Switched', *Philosophical Studies* 67: 77–103. (An attempt to account for sensory experience, and the puzzle of inverted qualia, by means of LOTH.)
* —— (1997) *Contemporary Philosophy of Mind: A Contentiously Classical Approach*, Oxford: Blackwell. (An introduction to recent work and an attempt to show that LOTH handles traditional problems in philosophy of mind.)
* Searle, J. (1984) *Minds, Brains and Science*, Cambridge, MA: Harvard University Press. (A well-known attack on LOTH.)
* Smolensky, P. (1988) 'A Proper Treatment of

Connectionism', *Behavioral and Brain Sciences* 11: 1–23. (Influential critique of LOTH and suggestion of a connectionist alternative.)

* Stich, S. (1983) *From Folk Psychology to Cognitive Science: The Case Against Belief*, Cambridge, MA: MIT Press. (A clear discussion of LOTH, and a defence of it as a purely syntactic account of thought.)

GEORGES REY

LANGUAGE, PHILOSOPHY OF

Philosophical interest in language, while ancient and enduring (see LANGUAGE, ANCIENT PHILOSOPHY OF; LANGUAGE, MEDIEVAL THEORIES OF; LANGUAGE, RENAISSANCE PHILOSOPHY OF; LANGUAGE, EARLY MODERN PHILOSOPHY OF), has blossomed anew in the past century. There are three key historical sources of the current interest, and three intellectual concerns which sustain it.

Philosophers nowadays often aspire to systematic and even mathematically rigorous accounts of language; these philosophers are in one way or another heirs to Gottlob FREGE, Bertrand RUSSELL, Ludwig WITTGENSTEIN and the logical positivists, who strove to employ rigorous accounts of logic and of meaning in attempts to penetrate, and in some cases to dispel, traditional philosophical questions (see LOGICAL POSITIVISM). Contemporary philosophers, too, are often attentive to the roles that philosophically interesting words (like 'know', 'true', 'good' and 'free') play in ordinary linguistic usage; these philosophers inherit from 'ordinary language philosophers', including G.E. MOORE, J.L. AUSTIN and again Wittgenstein, the strategy of finding clues to deep philosophical questions through scrutiny of the workaday usage of the words in which the philosophical questions are framed (see ORDINARY LANGUAGE PHILOSOPHY).

Philosophical interest in language is maintained by foundational and conceptual questions in linguistics, quintessentially philosophical problems about the connections between mind, language and the world, and issues about philosophical methodology. These springs sustain a rich and fascinating field of philosophy concerned with representation, communication, meaning and truth.

1 Philosophy of linguistics

Language is an impressive and fascinating human capacity, and human languages are strikingly power-ful and complex systems. The science of this capacity and of these systems is linguistics. Like other sciences, and perhaps to an unusual degree, linguistics confronts difficult foundational, methodological and conceptual issues.

When studying a human language, linguists seek systematic explanations of its *syntax* (the organization of the language's properly constructed expressions, such as phrases and sentences; see SYNTAX), its *semantics* (the ways expressions exhibit and contribute to meaning; see SEMANTICS), and its *pragmatics* (the practices of communication in which the expressions find use; see PRAGMATICS).

The study of syntax has been guided since the 1960s by the work of Noam Chomsky, who, in reaction to earlier behaviourist and structuralist movements in linguistics (see BEHAVIOURISM, ANALYTIC; BEHAVIOURISM, METHODOLOGICAL AND SCIENTIFIC; STRUCTURALISM IN LINGUISTICS; SAUSSURE, F. DE), takes an unapologetically cognitivist approach. Human linguistic capacities, he holds, issue from a dedicated cognitive faculty whose structure is the proper topic of linguistics. Indeed, Chomsky construes at least the study of syntax and (large parts of) semantics as attempts to uncover cognitive structures. Finding impressive commonalties among all known natural languages, and noting the paucity of evidence and instruction available to children learning a language, Chomsky suggests that surprisingly many features of natural languages stem from innate characteristics of the language faculty (see CHOMSKY, N.; LANGUAGE, INNATENESS OF).

Whereas contemporary philosophers have tended to stay at a remove from work in syntax, discussing rather than doing it, semantics is another matter entirely. Here many of the great strides have been made by philosophers, including Gottlob FREGE, Bertrand RUSSELL, Ludwig WITTGENSTEIN, Rudolf CARNAP, Richard MONTAGUE and Saul KRIPKE. (However, quite a number of linguists and logicians who do not call themselves philosophers also have contributed heavily to semantics.) One major strand in semantics in the past century has consisted in the development and careful application of formal, mathematical models for characterizing linguistic form and meaning (see SEMANTICS, GAME-THEORETIC; SEMANTICS, POSSIBLE WORLDS; SEMANTICS, SITUATION).

Pragmatics, at least as much as semantics, has benefited from the contributions of philosophers. Philosophical interest in pragmatics typically has had its source in a prior interest in semantics – in a desire to understand how meaning and truth are situated in the concrete practices of linguistic communication. The later WITTGENSTEIN, for instance, reminds us of the vast variety of uses in which linguistic expressions participate, and warns of the danger of assuming that there is something aptly called their *meanings* which we might uncover through philosophy. J.L. AUSTIN seeks in subtleties of usage clues to the meanings of philosophically interesting terms like 'intentional' and 'true'. Austin keeps a careful eye to the several different things one does all at once when one performs a 'speech act' (for instance: uttering a sound, voicing the sentence 'J'ai faim', saying that one is hungry, hinting that one's companion might share their meal, and causing them to do so). His taxonomy has provided the basis of much subsequent work (see SPEECH ACTS; PERFORMATIVES). H.P. GRICE, while critical of some of Austin's methods, shared the aim of distilling meaning from the murky waters of use. Grice portrays conversation as a rational, cooperative enterprise, and in his account a number of conceptions of meaning figure as central strategies and tools for achieving communicative purposes. Grice's main concern was philosophical methodology (see §3), but his proposals have proven extremely popular among linguists interested in pragmatics (see COMMUNICATION AND INTENTION; MEANING AND COMMUNICATION). Recently, philosophers and linguists have become increasingly persuaded that pragmatic concerns, far from being mere addenda to semantics, are crucial to the questions of where meaning comes from, in what it consists, and how the many incompletenesses and flexibilities in linguistic meaning are overcome and exploited in fixing what speakers mean by their words on particular occasions (see PRAGMATICS; IMPLICATURE; METAPHOR).

Our focus on language should not omit a field of study with a rather broader scope, namely *semiotics*, which is the study of signs and signification in general, whether linguistic or not. In the view of the scholars in this field, the study of linguistic meaning should be situated in a more general project which encompasses gestural communication, artistic expression, animal signalling, and other varieties of information transfer (see SEMIOTICS; ANIMAL LANGUAGE AND THOUGHT).

2 Meaning: language, mind and world

Philosophy aims at intellectually responsible accounts of the most basic and general aspects of reality. Part of what it is to provide an intellectually responsible account, clearly, is for us to make sense of our own place in reality – as, among other things, beings who conceive and formulate descriptions and explanations of it.

In framing issues about our roles as describers and explainers, philosophers commonly draw a triangle in which lines connect 'Language', 'Mind' and 'World'. The three lines represent relations that are keys to understanding our place in reality. These relations in one or another way constitute the *meaningfulness* of language.

Mind ↔ World. Between Mind and World there are a number of crucial relations studied by philosophers of mind. Among these are perception, action, the mind's bodily constitution and intentionality (the mind's ability to think *about* what is in the world) (see MIND, PHILOSOPHY OF).

Mind → Language. Using and understanding language is a heavily mental activity. Further, this activity seems to be what the real existence of meaningful language consists in. In short, mind invests *meaning* in language.

Theorists of language focus on the Mind/Language connection when they consider *understanding* to be the cornerstone concept, holding, for instance, that an account of meaning for a given language is simply an account of what constitutes the ability to understand it (see MEANING AND UNDERSTANDING). Philosophy has seen a variety of accounts of wherein understanding consists. Many have been attracted to the view that understanding is a matter of associating the correct ideas or concepts with words (see, for instance, LOCKE, J.; FREGE, G.; LANGUAGE OF THOUGHT). Others have equated understanding with knowing the requirements for accurate or apt use of words and sentences (see, for instance, DAVIDSON, D.; DUMMETT, M.A.E.). Still others find the key to understanding in one's ability to discern the communicative goals of speakers and writers (see, for instance, GRICE, H.P.), or more directly in one's ability to 'pass' linguistically, without censure (see, for instance, WITTGENSTEIN, L.J.J.). Certainly, these approaches do not exclude one another.

Some philosophers focus more on production than consumption – on the speaker's side of things – analysing linguistic meaning in terms of the goals and practices of speakers, and in terms of relations among communities of speakers (see GRICE, H.P.; COMMUNICATION AND INTENTION; LANGUAGE, CONVENTIONALITY OF; LANGUAGE, SOCIAL NATURE OF).

Many of the philosophers who see understanding and use as the keys to linguistic meaning have held that the meaningfulness of language in some sense derives from mental content, perhaps including the contents of beliefs, thoughts and concepts. This enhances the interest of *cognitive semantics*, which is a thriving field of study (see SEMANTICS; SEMANTICS, CONCEPTUAL ROLE; SEMANTICS, INFORMATIONAL; SEMANTICS, TELEOLOGICAL; CONCEPTS).

It has not gone unquestioned that mind indeed can assign meaning to language, and in fact scepticism about this has figured quite prominently in philosophical discussions of language. Wittgenstein has been read as at least flirting with scepticism that there is anything our minds *can* do that would constitute meaning one thing rather than another (see WITTGENSTEIN, L. §§10–12; MEANING AND RULE-FOLLOWING; PRIVATE STATES AND LANGUAGE). W.V. Quine, starting from the thought that meaning is whatever good translation captures, and on arguments that good translation is not squarely dictated by any real facts, concludes that meaning is highly indeterminate. Quine is not alone in the view that linguistic and mental meaning are best seen not as 'out there' to be discovered, but rather as partly constituted or constructed by our practices of interpreting and translating (see QUINE, W.V.O.; DAVIDSON, D.; DENNETT, D.C.; LEWIS, D.K.; RADICAL TRANSLATION AND RADICAL INTERPRETATION).

Language → Mind. If mind assigns meaning to language, so also language *enables* and *channels* mind. Acquiring and trafficking in a language brings one concepts, thoughts and habits of thought, with all sorts of consequences (see SAPIR-WHORF HYPOTHESIS; LINGUISTIC DISCRIMINATION; LANGUAGE AND GENDER). Indeed, having language is so crucial to our ability to frame the sophisticated thoughts that appear essential to language-use and understanding, that many doubt whether mind is 'prior' to language in any interesting sense (see MEANING AND COMMUNICATION; DAVIDSON, D.).

Language ↔ World. Since language is the vehicle of our descriptions and explanations of reality, philosophers are concerned about what if anything makes for a *true* or *apt* characterization of reality. Philosophers have these concerns for reasons of philosophical methodology (which we will come to in a moment), but also owing to the naturalness and plausibility of a certain picture of meaning.

According to this picture, the key to meaning is the notion of a *truth-condition*. A statement's meaning determines a condition that must be met if it is to be true. For example, my statement 'Ireland is larger than Manhattan', given what it means, is true just in case a certain state of affairs obtains (namely, a certain island's being larger than a certain other island). According to the truth-conditional picture of meaning, the core of what a statement *means* is its truth-condition – which helps determine the way reality is *said to be* in it – and the core of what a word means is the contribution it makes to this (perhaps, in the case of certain sorts of word, this would be what the word *refers* to) (see SEMANTICS; MEANING AND TRUTH; REFERENCE).

While the truth-conditional picture of meaning has dominated semantics, a serious challenge has been presented by philosophers, including Michael Dummett, who urge that the key to meaning is a notion of *correct use*. According to this alternative picture, the core of a sentence's meaning is the rule for its appropriate utterance. Of course, the two pictures converge if sentences are correctly used exactly when they are true. The interest of the distinction emerges only when (a 'realist' conception of) truth is dislodged from this role, whether because of scepticism about truth itself, or because truth is seen as too remote from the crucible of social practice to be the meaning-relevant criterion for correct use (see REALISM AND ANTIREALISM; INTUITIONISTIC LOGIC AND ANTIREALISM; MEANING AND VERIFICATION; DUMMETT, M.A.E.; TRUTH, PRAGMATIC THEORY OF; TRUTH, DEFLATIONARY THEORIES OF; TRUTH, COHERENCE THEORY OF; TRUTH, CORRESPONDENCE THEORY OF). The challenge illustrates a sense in which the Mind/Language and Language/World connections can seem to place a tension on the notion of meaning (meaning is whatever we cognitively *grasp*, but the meaning of language just is its bearing on the world).

3 Linguistic philosophy

Apart from language's interest as a target of science and its centrality to our self-conception as describers of reality, language plays a key methodological role in philosophy. It is this role perhaps more than anything else that has explained the continued close attention paid to language in the past century by philosophers working in such varied areas as epistemology, aesthetics, ethics, metaphysics, the philosophy of science and the philosophy of mind.

The methodological role of language in philosophy is most easily explained by example. A philosopher is interested in the nature of value; they want to know *what goodness is*. Language enters when they observe that goodness is what is attributed when we *say* of a thing that it 'is good'. So the philosopher focuses on certain statements, and seeks an understanding of what such statements *mean* and in general of how they work. They explore whether such statements are ever objectively true or false, whether their truth or aptness varies from speaker to speaker, whether a satisfying explanation of them entails that the word 'good' refers to or expresses a genuine characteristic (of actions, states of affairs, persons, and so on), and how their meaning relates to the distinctive sorts of *endorsement* that such statements commonly convey (see ANALYTIC ETHICS; EMOTIVE MEANING).

The pattern exhibited in the example of value is apparent throughout philosophy. We are interested in knowledge, fiction, necessity, causation, or sensation, so we find ourselves studying statements *about* what interests us: statements attributing knowledge, describing fictions, asserting necessities, assigning causes and reporting sensations. Tools from the philosophy of language make available quite a number of views about what these statements mean and in general about how they do their expressive and communicative work; and these views inform and support philosophical positions on the real objects of philosophical interest. There have been dramatic and no doubt exaggerated claims about such techniques – for instance, that philosophy should simply *consist* in this sort of study of language. But it is if anything an understatement to say that linguistic sophistication has deepened philosophical understanding and has advanced debate in nearly all areas of philosophy (see CONCEPTUAL ANALYSIS).

See also: ADVERBS; AMBIGUITY; ANALYTICITY; ANAPHORA; COMPOSITIONALITY; COUNTERFACTUAL CONDITIONALS; DECONSTRUCTION; DEMONSTRATIVES AND INDEXICALS; DESCRIPTIONS; DISCOURSE SEMANTICS; FICTION, SEMANTICS OF; INDICATIVE CONDITIONALS; INDIRECT DISCOURSE; LANGUAGE, INDIAN THEORIES OF; LOGIC IN CHINA; LOGIC, PHILOSOPHY OF; LOGICAL FORM; MASS TERMS; MEANING IN ISLAMIC PHILOSOPHY; MEANING, INDIAN THEORIES OF; MOSCOW-TARTU SCHOOL; PROPER NAMES; PROPOSITIONAL ATTITUDE STATEMENTS; PROPOSITIONS, SENTENCES AND STATEMENTS; QUESTIONS; RELIGIOUS LANGUAGE; SCOPE; SEMANTICS; SEMIOTICS; SENSE AND REFERENCE; VAGUENESS

References and further reading

Devitt, M. and Sterelny, K. (1987) *Language and Reality*, Oxford: Blackwell. (A brief and readable introduction to some central issues, with useful references and bibliography.)
Martinich, A. (1990) *The Philosophy of Language*, Oxford: Oxford University Press, 2nd edn. (A collection of many key writings – often quite difficult – in philosophy of language.)

MARK CRIMMINS

LANGUAGE, RENAISSANCE PHILOSOPHY OF

Renaissance philosophy of language is in its essentials a continuation of medieval philosophy of language as it developed in the fourteenth century. However, there were three big changes in the fifteenth and sixteenth centuries. First, humanism led to a much greater interest in the practical study of languages, including Greek, Hebrew and vernacular languages, as well as classical Latin. Literary analysis and eloquent discourse were emphasized. Second, there was a loss of interest in such medieval developments as supposition theory, which meant that there was little discussion in logic texts of how words relate to each other in propositional contexts, and how sense and reference are affected by the presence of such logical terms as 'all', 'none', 'only', 'except' and so on. Only in early sixteenth-century Paris were these issues pursued with any enthusiasm. Third, the fourteenth-century insistence that both words and concepts were signs had several effects. There was a new interest in the classification of different sorts of signs, both linguistic and non-linguistic, particularly in the work of some early sixteenth-century Spaniards. Naturally significant mental language was emphasized in a way that diverted the attention of logicians from spoken languages and their imperfections. Finally, concepts themselves came in for more attention, so that many of the topics discussed by logicians overlapped with what would now count as philosophy of mind, as well as with metaphysics. For instance, philosophers in the late scholastic tradition made much use of an early fourteenth-century distinction between the formal concept, which is a representative act of mind, and the so-called objective concept, which is whatever it is that is represented by a formal concept. The discussion of these issues by such writers as Pedro da Fonseca and Francisco Suárez has an obvious bearing on developments in early modern philosophy.

1   **Signs and signification**
2   **Mental, spoken, natural and conventional languages**
3   **Intentional contexts and beings of reason**
4   **Analogy**
5   **Humanism**

1   Signs and signification

The central semantic claim of Renaissance thinkers was that the word or term is a sign, and the central semantic notion was that of signification. Frequent reference was made to Aristotle's remark (*De interpretatione* 16a3–4), 'Spoken words are signs of concepts' (see ARISTOTLE §4); and there was widespread use of Pierre d'Ailly's definition, 'To signify is to represent some thing or some things or in some way (*aliqualiter*) to a cognitive power' (see AILLY, P. D'). Since categorematic terms such as 'cow' (unlike the categorematic terms 'concept' or 'mermaid') are intended to point to things in the world, a three-place relation of word, concept and thing was established. This account raises several problems: how syncategorematic terms (for example, 'all', 'none') can be signs; how non-referring categorematic terms are to be explained (see §3); and the precise nature of the word–concept–thing relation.

The problem of syncategorematic terms was much discussed by the nominalists of early sixteenth-century Paris (see MAJOR, J. §2), and, following d'Ailly's definition, it was agreed that such terms signified in some way. That is, a syncategorematic term performs a function rather than pointing to an object, and this function is not itself signified by the term, though it can be in a separate locution. If I say 'No dogs are running', the act of negation is exercised; if I say 'That sentence is negative', the act of negation is signified.

The notion of signifying in some way was also extended to propositional signification by some authors, notably Fernando de Enzinas, who argued that a proposition (in the then-standard sense of an occurrent declarative sentence) does not signify things, whether ordinary things in the world or propositional complexes enjoying a special kind of existence, but performs a function. This discussion of propositional signification was linked with discussion of such issues as whether the proposition is the object of knowledge and judgment (assent and dissent) (see TOLETUS, F. §5), and whether it is the bearer of truth-values. These topics were still of interest to early seventeenth-century scholastics.

The precise nature of the word–concept–thing relation was the focus of the long-standing debate whether spoken words signify concepts or things. This question first became popular in the late thirteenth century, and it was still discussed by such late sixteenth- and early seventeenth-century authors as Franciscus Toletus, Sebastian de Couto (see COLLEGIUM CONIMBRICENSE) and JOHN OF ST THOMAS (§2). All the participants in the debate agreed on certain points. They agreed that concepts play an essential role in the significative process, for we cannot refer to objects we have no notion of. They also agreed that words are typically used to pick out things in the world rather than our own concepts. The debate concerned the way in which the role of concepts in the significative process was to be described. Some authors, following such disparate figures as AQUINAS and John BURIDAN, held that words primarily signified concepts and only secondarily signified things. Others, following WILLIAM OF OCKHAM, held that words signified things alone in virtue of being subordinated to concepts. Sebastian de Couto preferred to say that while the signification of

things had a certain primacy, both concepts and things were made known by words, which thus enjoy a double signification. John of St Thomas held that words signify concepts more immediately and things more principally.

What has been said so far applies equally well to medieval and Renaissance treatments of the word as sign. There was, however, an important development in the fourteenth century which helps differentiate the later period from the earlier, and which stems from Ockham's insistence that the concept itself must be regarded as a sign. This notion (while foreign to Augustine) was not new, but Ockham made it central. In doing so, he made mental language (see §2) rather than spoken language the paradigm of signification.

Once the concept had come to be regarded as a sign, we find in some early sixteenth-century authors, especially Domingo de SOTO (§2), a careful classification of signs, both linguistic and non-linguistic. In relation to the speaker, spoken words were said to be instrumental signs, because they were used as instruments of communication, and mental terms were said to be formal signs, because they represented by their very nature. In relation to the things signified, spoken words were said to be conventional signs, and mental terms were said to be natural signs, since their signification did not depend on choice or convention. In the various editions of his *Summulae*, Soto asked whether one should add a category of customary signs, such as napkins on the table as a sign of lunch. In the end he concluded that these signs were natural, albeit founded on a convention. Soto's classifications were elaborated by many later authors, including Sebastian de Couto and John of St Thomas; though at least one late sixteenth-century Spaniard, Domingo BÁÑEZ, did explicitly reject the view that the concept was a formal sign.

2 Mental, spoken, natural and conventional languages

The doctrine that the concept is a formal sign went hand-in-hand with the notion of mental language, a language of thought that is naturally significant and common to all human beings. Such a notion is present at least from AUGUSTINE on, but it was fully developed in the fourteenth century, first by William of Ockham and then by Pierre d'Ailly (see WILLIAM OF OCKHAM; AILLY, P. D'). Mental propositions were thought of as having syntactic structure and mental terms were thought of as having supposition, so that the notion of a language system was internalized. As a corollary, the place of grammar in the study of logic and philosophy of language was devalued. Some of the problems raised by the notion of mental language, such as the difficulty of identifying the mental correlates of demonstratives and pronouns, or of impersonal verbs such as *pluit* ('It is raining'), were still the object of lively debate in early sixteenth-century Paris. Later, the discussion of the structure of mental language disappeared, but the notion of an inner language remained. For instance, in his *Scholae* (Lectures) Petrus RAMUS (§2) argued that logic or dialectic deals directly with thought, with *ratio* (reason) rather than *oratio* (discourse).

Whether mental language was seen as some kind of ideal language is unclear. Mental language certainly provided some kind of universality in that all spoken language was subordinated to it. However, it did not necessarily provide a common syntactic structure, for logically equivalent spoken propositions could turn out to be subordinated to different mental propositions. Nor was mental language necessarily thought of as being ideal in the sense of reproducing the structure of the world. On the other hand, it was supposedly ideal in the sense of being a language which was free of ambiguous terms and which contained only as much structure as was required for the formulation of judgments.

The discussion of spoken language was often related to two key episodes in the Bible: Adam's naming of the animals, and God's inflicting different languages on human beings as a punishment for building the Tower of Babel. One issue had to do with the nature of the original language and its relation to later languages. If the first language was Hebrew, as Isidore of Seville had held, in what form did it survive? If it was not Hebrew, did it completely disappear, or did it contribute at least some structure to the post-Babel tongues? A second issue had to do with the original institution of language: did Adam form it, or did God give him his language (as Sebastian de Couto, among others, held)? This in turn raised a third issue. Was the language instituted by Adam, or by God through Adam, a natural language in the sense of one that enabled users to grasp essences by virtue of a natural relationship between spoken words and the things named?

While this issue became more important in the seventeenth century with the work of such authors as Jacob Boehme and Francis Mercurius van Helmont, there was considerable discussion in the sixteenth century. The interest was due not only to biblical studies but also to the rediscovery of Plato's *Cratylus* and other classical sources, as well as to the strong Renaissance interest in magic and the Kabbalah, with the concomitant hope that a knowledge of natural language would enable one to exercise some control over the objects signified. The consensus, particularly among logicians, was that Aristotle was right, and

spoken language is indeed conventional, whether it is directly God-given or not. On the other hand, the belief that language was conventional was seen as compatible with the belief that the institution of language is guided by reason (as Pseudo-Kilwardby had argued in the thirteenth century). To say that spoken words have signification *ad placitum* (by convention or agreement) does not mean that their signification is random and unmotivated. This point was emphasized by the Spanish grammarian Sanctius (Francisco Sánchez de la Brozas) in his *Minerva*, published in 1587. He felt that Aristotle, Plato and the Bible could be reconciled; and he also argued that the rational origin of language provided an underlying system of regularities in conventional languages.

3 Intentional contexts and beings of reason

Given the focus on spoken and mental terms as signs, one must ask what is referred to in intentional and modal contexts, or by fictional terms such as 'chimera'. Authors who worked within the medieval logical tradition, particularly the nominalists of early sixteenth-century Paris, attempted to treat both problems within the framework of supposition theory. There are elaborate discussions of the reference of 'horse' in such contexts as 'I promise you a horse', 'A horse is necessary for riding', 'A horse is imaginarily a chimera'. In particular, people asked whether it was legitimate to postulate reference to imaginary and impossible objects, or whether the reference of terms in special contexts could be explained solely in terms of reference to ordinary past, present, future and possible objects. In the later sixteenth century, this type of discussion disappeared from most logic texts, though there are still references in Pedro da FONSECA.

What did survive, at least in the scholastic tradition, was the discussion of beings of reason (*entia rationis*). This investigation, which can be traced back to the thirteenth century, did not focus on the problem of reference in special propositional contexts, but on the reference of terms in general. There were said to be two types of being, real beings which (with the exception of God) fall under Aristotle's ten categories, and beings of reason (*entia rationis*), which include negations, privations and relations of reason. The latter included the logical second intentions (that is, higher-order concepts used to organize first-order concepts) such as 'genus' and 'species'. Beings of reason are non-categorial and exist only because of the work of the human mind, though they may have some foundation in reality. 'Nonbeing', for instance, is a term which is significant as referring to a pure negation; and 'blindness' is a term which is significant as referring to a privation, the absence of a capacity that animals normally have; yet neither pure negations nor privations can be literally parts of the world. They must be conceptual entities. Genus and species terms (as opposed to the terms 'genus' and 'species' themselves) were often included among the terms whose significance involves relations of reason. As Domingo de SOTO (§2) indicated, the point here is that when we say 'A human being is an animal' our general terms do not refer to special universal things, humanity and animality, but they imply a well-founded relation between particular individuals in the world and the concepts we use to classify them into groups. There was general agreement that chimeras should be classified as negations, and some people held that they were the most proper examples of beings of reason since, as impossible, they must be completely mind-dependent (see JOHN OF ST THOMAS §§2, 4; SUÁREZ, F. §2).

4   Analogy

Analogy as a theory about a certain sort of linguistic usage has thirteenth-century roots, and involves three problems. First, there is the problem of equivocal terms as Aristotle introduces it at the beginning of his *Categories*. Equivocal terms (for example, 'bank') are those which can be used in two quite different senses, and it seems natural to extend the notion of an equivocal term to cover terms that are used in different but related senses. Second, there is the metaphysical problem of how to discuss being (*ens*) in general when the being of a substance is so different from the being of an accident. Third, there is the problem of religious language. How can words normally used of humans, such as 'just' or 'good', be meaningfully used of God, when God is so different from human beings? In answer to these problems, logicians and theologians developed a theory which divided words into three sorts, independently of context. Some were univocal (always used with the same sense), some were purely equivocal (used with totally different senses), and some were analogical (used with related senses).

The term 'analogy' itself had two senses. In the original (Greek) sense, it involved a comparison of two proportions or relations. Thus 'principle' was said to be an analogical term when said of a point and of a spring of water because a point is related to a line as a spring is related to a river. This type of analogy came to be called the analogy of proportion, proportionality, or (by Cajetan) proper proportionality. In the second sense, analogy involved a relation between two things (or one pair of things and a third), of which one

is secondary and the other primary. Thus 'healthy' was said to be an analogical term when said of a dog and its food because while the dog has health directly, its food is healthy only as contributing to or causing the health of the dog. This second type of analogy became known as the analogy of attribution.

One of the main subjects of debate was how to classify types of analogy, and how to apply the various types to the different metaphysical and theological cases mentioned above. Although in *De veritate* (On Truth) AQUINAS said that religious language must be interpreted by means of the analogy of proportionality, in other writings he appealed to the analogy of attribution. During the fourteenth and fifteenth centuries most logicians and theologians, including CAPREOLUS, appealed to the analogy of attribution (if they discussed the topic at all). At the end of the fifteenth century, however, Thomas de Vio, Cardinal Cajetan argued that the analogy of proportionality was the only true analogy (see CAJETAN §2). Cajetan's view was not always accepted, but there was much discussion of the issue by the later scholastics, including Soto, FONSECA (§3) and SUÁREZ (§2) (see SILVESTRI, F.).

The other main subject of debate is very closely related to philosophy of mind, and springs mainly from the work of early fourteenth-century philosophers, particularly DUNS SCOTUS. Latin translations of Aristotle maintained that the difference between a univocal term and an equivocal term was that the latter was subordinated to more than one *ratio*. The *ratio* soon came to be identified with a concept, and the question then was how many concepts are involved when an analogical term is used. There were three views among logicians and theologians. Analogical terms could be seen as straightforwardly equivocal terms subordinated to two distinct concepts; they could be seen as subordinated to an ordered cluster of concepts (possibly but not necessarily described as a disjunction of concepts), or they could be subordinated to a single concept which represents in both a prior and a posterior manner (*per prius et posterius*). Scotus and his followers rejected all these possibilities, and argued that the word *ens* was univocal, but a lively discussion continued (especially among Thomists) until the time of Suárez.

Many of these thinkers made a distinction between formal and objective concepts. The formal concept was the act of mind or conception that represented an object, and the objective concept was the object represented. If the spoken word 'being' corresponds to just one formal concept (a point on which there were some differences of opinion), the focus of discussion shifts to the status of the objective concept. Is it the actual thing in the world which is thought about; is it a common nature or some other kind of intermediary entity which is distinct from the external object without being mind-dependent; or is it a special kind of mind-dependent object which has only objective being, the being of 'being thought' (*esse objective, esse cognitum*)? It is at this point that philosophy of mind and ontology take over from philosophy of language.

5 Humanism

Humanists, including VALLA, ERASMUS and VIVES, were more concerned with the description of language as a literary phenomenon and with the cultivation of eloquence than with philosophy of language proper. The late fifteenth and sixteenth centuries saw an explosion of practical language studies. New humanist grammars appeared which prepared students for literary analysis rather than philosophy and theology; Greek and Hebrew studies expanded; there was an increasing use of and interest in vernacular languages; biblical studies and translations flourished; the widespread use of printing focused attention on problems of spelling and grammatical norms; and there was new interest in forms of writing, including Hebrew characters and Egyptian hieroglyphs. This last interest was often combined with a belief in magic. Agrippa, for instance, discussed how one might manipulate the numerical values of the letters of the Hebrew alphabet in order to make contact with the spirit world.

See also: HUMANISM, RENAISSANCE; LANGUAGE, MEDIEVAL THEORIES OF; LOGIC, MEDIEVAL; LOGIC, RENAISSANCE; UNIVERSAL LANGUAGE

References and further reading

Ashworth, E.J. (1985) *Studies in Post-Medieval Semantics*, London: Variorum. (A collection of articles including studies of reference in intentional contexts, propositions and mental language.)

—— (1988) 'Traditional Logic', in C.B. Schmitt, Q. Skinner and E. Kessler (eds) *The Cambridge History of Renaissance Philosophy*, Cambridge: Cambridge University Press, esp. 153–62. (A useful general account with plenty of references.)

—— (1990) 'Domingo de Soto (1494–1560) and the Doctrine of Signs', in G.L. Bursill-Hall, S. Ebbesen and K. Koerner (eds) *De Ortu Grammaticae: Studies in Medieval Grammar and Linguistic Theory in Memory of Jan Pinborg*, Amsterdam and Philadelphia, PA: John Benjamins, 35–48. (Discussion of how signs were classified.)

—— (1995) 'Suárez on the Analogy of Being: Some Historical Background', *Vivarium* 33: 50–75. (How analogical terms were classified; formal and objective concepts; bibliography.)

Coudert, A. (1978) 'Some Theories of a Natural Language from the Renaissance to the Seventeenth Century', in *Studia Leibnitiana, Sonderheft 7*, Wiesbaden: Franz Steiner, 56–114. (A clear overview.)

Demonet, M.-L. (1992) *Les Voix du signe: Nature et origine du langage à la Renaissance (1480–1580)* (Voices of the Sign: the Nature and Origins of Language in the Renaissance), Paris and Geneva: Champion-Slatkine. (A full, fascinating account of all aspects of language based on both philosophical and literary sources.)

Jardine, L. (1988) 'Humanistic Logic', in C.B. Schmitt, Q. Skinner and E. Kessler (eds) *The Cambridge History of Renaissance Philosophy*, Cambridge: Cambridge University Press, 173–98. (A useful general account, though controversial on Lorenzo Valla; shows how humanist logic was used in textual exegesis.)

Nuchelmans, G. (1980) *Late-Scholastic and Humanist Theories of the Proposition*, Amsterdam, Oxford and New York: North Holland. (Discusses mental language, the significate of the proposition, and the terminological innovations of Melanchthon and Ramus.)

—— (1983) *Judgment and Proposition from Descartes to Kant*, Amsterdam, Oxford and New York: North Holland. (First chapter discusses Renaissance Thomism, including material on formal and objective concepts.)

Padley, G.A. (1976) *Grammatical Theory in Western Europe, 1500–1700. The Latin Tradition*, Cambridge: Cambridge University Press. (Generally good, but to be used with caution where logic is concerned.)

Percival, W.K. (1982) 'Changes in the approach to language', in N. Kretzmann, A. Kenny and J. Pinborg (eds) *The Cambridge History of Later Medieval Philosophy*, Cambridge: Cambridge University Press, 808–17. (Discussion of humanist grammar teaching.)

Roncaglia, G. (1995) 'Smiglecius on *entia rationis*', *Vivarium* 33: 27–49. (Useful introduction to the notion of beings of reason, with good bibliography.)

E.J. ASHWORTH

LANGUAGE, SOCIAL NATURE OF

Language is mostly used in a social setting. We use it to communicate with others. We depend on others when learning language, and we constantly borrow one another's uses of expression. Language helps us perform various social functions, and many of its uses have become institutionalized. But none of these reflections settle the question of whether language is an essentially social phenomenon. To address this we must consider the nature of language itself, and then ask which social elements, if any, make an essential contribution to its nature.

While many would accept that language is an activity that must take place in a social setting, others have gone further by arguing that language is a social practice. This view commits one to the claim that the meanings of an individual's words are the meanings they have in the common language. The former view need not accept so strong a claim: meaning depends on social interaction because it is a matter of what one can communicate to others but this does not require the existence of communal languages. A competing conception which rejects the social character of language in either of these versions is the thesis that language is mentally represented in the mind of an individual.

1   Linguistic Platonism
2   Communal languages and idiolects
3   Language as a psychological or a social phenomenon
4   Idiolects as social phenomena

1   Linguistic Platonism

Languages can be used in many ways and for many purposes, but a dispute about the nature of language concerns language in its most fundamental sense. Is it fundamentally social or do individual speakers have their own languages?

One view of language, which will not be discussed in any detail in this entry, is linguistic Platonism. This is the view that languages are formally characterized abstract entities existing independently of all speakers. Platonists then seek to define a relation between these abstract objects and speakers to determine which is the actual language of an individual or a population. The actual language relation may be defined either in terms of the conventional practices adopted by a population, or the psychological make-up or linguistic intuitions of the individual language-user. Thus Platonism does not settle the issue of whether

languages are properties of individuals or social groups.

2   Communal languages and idiolects

A broad division exists between those philosophers and linguists who think the fundamental conception of language is that of a shared public language, and those who consider the fundamental notion to be that of an individual's language or idiolect. Within each of these schools there is room for disagreement about the precise nature of languages and idiolects. These differences will be reviewed below.

Michael DUMMETT (1989), following the ideas of Ludwig WITTGENSTEIN (1953), offers a number of arguments for the communal conception of language. One of these goes via his rejection of Platonism. For Dummett, the objectivity of meaning requires the meaning of a word to be independent of any given speaker's judgment of it. But if the meaning of words were independent of all speakers, as the Platonist suggests, this would open up the sceptical possibility that all speakers could be in ignorance about the actual meaning of words in their language. Rejecting this possibility, Dummett insists that what an expression means among a community of language-users must be determined by the publicly observable conventions governing its use.

Dummett also argues that the publicity of meaning is required to ensure successful communication. Because speakers hold themselves responsible to the conventional meanings of words in taking themselves to be speaking a given language, what they say when uttering certain words is what those words mean in the communal language to which they belong. It is only because there are such conventional practices that meaning is shared and communicable; and for Dummett, were it not for such standards of use, speakers could not know they attached the same significance to their words. Meanings would be private and incommunicable, hidden in the minds of each individual speaker. But if this were the case, we could never learn a language, or know if someone else understood it. But we can work out what people mean by the observable use they make of their expressions; and to learn or understand a language is simply to participate in these shared linguistic practices. However, no speaker will be fully competent in the conventions governing the use of words and rules for grammatically compounding them; at most speakers will have a partial mastery of the public language. Nevertheless, for Dummett communication depends on the standards of the communal practice.

Similar considerations have been advanced by John McDowell (1988) who regards the possibility of thought and of knowing the minds of others as depending on our speaking a communal language. We arrive at our thoughts by finding the words to express them, and so in virtue of the language in which we do this we make our minds immediately available to one another. The words you use to express a thought will express the same thought for me and so, just in virtue of hearing you speak sincerely, I can know what you think. This is possible because the meanings of a speaker's words lie open to view on the surface of his practice. But they are recognizable only to those who share those practices. These ideas hail from the later work of Wittgenstein, who saw language as a social practice governed by rules of use (see MEANING AND RULE-FOLLOWING). Along with Wittgenstein, Dummett and McDowell assume that in the absence of shared languages, or observable conventions of use, our knowledge of others' meanings would be a matter of psychological speculation about what goes on in a private realm concealed behind behaviour. And, given the doubtful coherence of a private language, McDowell thinks the absence of shared languages would de-stabilize communication, meaning and thought.

Not every defender of communal languages accepts the publicity of meaning. It is possible to argue that private language states are involved in the meanings of public language items so long as speakers have sufficiently similar responses to the situations in which those words are used. On this view, it would be enough for the purposes of communication that speakers attached the same significance to terms in the language: they would not also have to know that they did. Success in communication would be a contingent matter and could never be guaranteed (see PRIVATE STATES AND LANGUAGE).

The strongest opposition to the communal view of language comes from those advocating the idiolectic conception of language, although there is deep disagreement amongst the protagonists over the extent to which an idiolect is social or psychological in nature. However, all proponents of the idiolectic view resist the assumption made by Dummett and McDowell that if a language is not shared then the meaning of an individual's words would have to be subjective and private. It does not follow from the fact that meanings are publicly discoverable that they are shared. I can work out the meaning someone attaches to a word without attaching that meaning to it myself. Donald DAVIDSON (1986) stresses malapropisms as providing cases of this kind (see §4). The denial of shared language does not entail the privacy of meaning and the publicity of meaning does not require a communal language. The arguments of McDowell and Dummett designed to show that the

language of an individual would be necessarily private remain inconclusive. Facts about my idiolect may be knowable by those I interact with, and linguists studying me scientifically may know more about my idiolect than I do.

3 Language as a psychological or a social phenomenon

Noam CHOMSKY (1986) is a vigorous opponent of the notion of shared public languages. He argues that there is no empirically respectable way to define such a notion. According to Chomsky there is no such thing, for example, as English, or Dutch, or Chinese. In each case there is no single set of grammatical rules, shared vocabulary items, or rules for pronunciation which characterize the language in question. Whether we include every idiosyncratic use of every word and rule of grammar by a particular population of speakers, or select only the intersection of those uses, what is specified is a language nobody knows or speaks. The same problems beset attempts to delimit a dialect. For this reason, Chomsky abandons the everyday use of 'language', which he calls E-language: this being an ill-assorted set of overlapping practices, patterns of deference, power relations among speakers, and so on. He replaces it with the notion of a speaker's I-language: an internal component of the individual's mind/brain which assigns meaning and structure to the sounds and signs the speaker encounters. The I-language is a cognitive psychological entity – a state of the language faculty – which together with a lexicon of word-like items determines the extent of the speaker's idiolect.

According to Chomsky, language is essentially defined by its meanings and structures, but these exist only as mental representations in the mind of the speaker – as part of the speaker's knowledge of language – and have no reality in the external or social world. Linguistically, the world contains only sounds and marks: it is creatures equipped with a language faculty who assign them meaning and structure. At first, this is achieved without reference to others. Our earliest interactions will of course influence our acquisition of vocabulary and the particular grammar we attain although, in the case of the latter, Chomsky regards this as environmental triggering: a prompt from one's surroundings to set the parameters of a system that is already in place. Thus the development of one rather than another I-language is the result of interaction between the linguistic environment and the innate linguistic system (see LANGUAGE, INNATENESS OF).

After we attain mature linguistic competence, we often defer to others in positions of authority in their use of words and assessments of grammar. But Chomsky points out that this is social behaviour undertaken after we have acquired a language, and so it does not constitute an essentially social contribution to it. On the notion of language Chomsky favours, the study of language becomes a branch of individual cognitive psychology. The study of group behaviour has no impact on it. Communication is not, on this picture, essential to language. Language is primarily a means of expressing thought. Speakers and hearers do have the means to try to make sense of one another's talk and the closer their I-languages and vocabularies are to one another, the more chance they will have of success. However, for Chomsky, communication is risky and success is never guaranteed so it cannot provide the basis for linguistic competence.

Where he is willing to acknowledge a pervasive social aspect of language is in the case of the division of linguistic labour: a phenomenon Hilary Putnam (1975) drew attention to. This occurs where there are words having an everyday sense and a more technical meaning without being ambiguous. The words 'gold' and 'carburettor' provide examples for those with little knowledge of chemistry or cars. Speakers can use these words without knowing their precise meanings because they defer to experts in their community who know how to fix the meaning and reference of those terms precisely (see PUTNAM, H. §3). Chomsky points out that the entries for such words in a speaker's mental lexicon will specify the meaning of the terms as far as the speaker's (partial) knowledge carries him, but they would also include an indication that further details are to be filled out by others. The meanings specified in this way do not go beyond what can be studied in an individual's knowledge of language. It is not to concede that language includes any essentially social elements. The phenomenon Putnam alludes to, while extensive, is not fundamental to the use of language. People could cease to use terms they did not fully understand without ceasing to speak or understand a language. What this shows is that the division of linguistic labour provides the weakest claim for the social character of language. Other reasons are needed to conclude that language is necessarily social in character.

4 Idiolects as social phenomena

Arguments for this are provided by Donald Davidson and Tyler Burge, although they differ in their conceptions of what makes an idiolect social.

Davidson rejects the idea of language as 'a clearly defined shared structure' which language-users learn and deploy in communicative exchanges. The appeal

to conventions is neither necessary nor sufficient for linguistic communication, since speakers and hearers need not attach the same meanings to their words nor stick to the conventions they have established in order to make sense of one another's remarks. All that is required is that the hearer know what the speaker means; it is not additionally required that the hearer attach the same significance to their own use of those words. The cases of malapropism and slips of the tongue serve to make the point. I can know that someone uses 'debated' as I use 'abated' when they say 'The rain has debated'. But there is no reason for me to adopt their use of that word. So long as I can work out, by means of interpretation, what significance the speaker intends their words to have, I can understand them without having to share their language. Communication does not require speaker and hearer to belong to the same linguistic community, or to share a set of linguistic practices; it requires them to share an ability to interpret one another's utterances as part of a larger project of making sense of one another's behaviour in rational terms through the attribution of beliefs, desires and intentions. Part of this project will consist in assigning meanings to people's utterances that make sense of what they say against the background of the mental states we take them to be in. Clues of all kinds can figure in the evidence an interpreter draws upon to work out the meaning of someone's remarks, and no single set of shared conventions will be necessary or sufficient for this task.

While it is unlikely that any two speakers will ever speak the same language – minor differences in their vocabularies or grammar will always distinguish their idiolects – what they must share, according to Davidson, is the method of interpreting one another's speech. It is this condition which ensures the notion of idiolect has a social dimension since speakers can only mean what others can recognize or interpret them as meaning. The meanings of the words and sentences of their idiolects are fixed by others' publicly determined interpretations. For Davidson, the possibility of meaning anything depends on successful communication with another: having one's words interpreted as one intends them to be interpreted. In this way, meaningful speech, although it demands nothing more than a variety of idiolects, is necessarily social (see RADICAL TRANSLATION AND RADICAL INTERPRETATION §§7–10).

Burge (1989), in contrast, argues that social factors beyond the scope of local communicative interactions play an essential role in the meaning of words in the individual's idiolect. He takes language to be a partly social phenomenon not just because it is learned and used in a social setting but because the meanings of a person's words depend on the way others in their linguistic community use them. He agrees with Chomsky that the study of language is a project for individual psychology, but he argues the semantic facts about an individual's idiolect depend essentially on their relations to other language-users. To establish that meaning must be individuated nonindividualistically and that idiolects are to some extent social, Burge (1982) constructed a famous thought-experiment in which there is an individual who uses the word 'arthritis' to express a number of thoughts about pain in their joints. One day they declare 'I have arthritis in my thigh'. Since the community the individual belongs to uses the word to apply only to inflammation of the joints, what the individual says is false. Burge then asks us to consider a counterfactual situation in which the community the subject belongs to uses 'arthritis' to apply both to inflammations of the joints and to other rheumatoid ailments. In this counterfactual situation there is no change in the individual's physical history or nonintentionally characterized experiences, and yet the statement they make there is true not false. Burge invites us to share the intuition that the truth-value of what is said differs in the two situations because something different is meant in each context. He concludes that meaning of the word 'arthritis' on the speaker's lips is different in each of these situations because of the different linguistic communities to which they belong. By this argument Burge hopes to show that the meanings of someone's words are individuated not just by facts about the individual but also partly by facts about the uses of words in the wider linguistic community (see CONTENT: WIDE AND NARROW). In this way, the meanings of many words in a person's language are not just up to him but depend essentially on the linguistic practices of others around him. But what is it for a speaker to belong to a particular linguistic community? For Burge it is a matter of his deferring to members of that community to explicate the meanings and determine the reference of his words on what are cognitive and not just pragmatic grounds. If Burge is right, facts about the meaning of our words supervene not only on facts about our use of words but also on facts about other people's usage. This amounts to a strong claim that social factors are constitutive of meaning and hence of language and that, although language is a matter of individual psychology, it is also partly a social phenomenon.

See also: LANGUAGE, CONVENTIONALITY OF; METHODOLOGICAL INDIVIDUALISM; LANGUAGE AND GENDER; MEANING AND COMMUNICATION

References and further reading

* Burge, T. (1982) 'Individualism and the Mental', *Midwest Studies* 4: 73–121. (The source of the famous thought experiment discussed in §4, containing objections to it and responses.)
* —— (1989) 'Wherein is Language Social', in A. George (ed.) *Reflections on Chomsky*, Oxford: Blackwell, 1989. (A demanding paper which contains his exposition of the partly social, partly psychological conception Burge has of idiolects.)
* Chomsky, N. (1986) *Knowledge of Language*, New York: Praeger. (Chapters 1 and 2 contain a clear statement of Chomsky's conception of I-language discussed in §3.)
* Davidson, D. (1986) 'A Nice Derangement of Epitaphs', in E. Lepore (ed.) *Truth and Interpretation*, Oxford: Blackwell, 1986. (An important paper challenging the need for conventions and rules of language, but defending the social nature of communicative exchanges.)
* Dummett, M.A.E. (1989) 'Language and Communication', in A. George (ed.) *Reflections on Chomsky*, Oxford: Blackwell, 1989. (Careful discussion of many of the issues raised in §§2–3, including critical discussions of Davidson and Chomsky.)
* McDowell, J. (1988) 'In Defence of Modesty', in B. Taylor (ed.) *Michael Dummett: Contributions to Philosophy*, Dordrecht: Martinus Nijhoff, 1988. (A subtle and penetrating account of McDowell's views on language and mind.)
* Putnam, H. (1975) 'The Meaning of "Meaning"', in *Collected Papers*, vol. 2, Cambridge: Cambridge University Press. (A seminal paper containing the notion of the division of linguistic labour among many other influential ideas.)
* Wittgenstein, L. (1953) *Philosophical Investigations*, Oxford: Blackwell. (A difficult read but taken to be the origin, and the most powerful sustained defence of, the philosophical conception of language as a social practice.)

BARRY C. SMITH

LAO TZU/LAOZI *see* DAODEJING

LASSALLE, FERDINAND (1825–64)

Ferdinand Lassalle was one of the principal founders of German social democracy and a strong advocate of state socialism. He was associated with Marx, although he was not himself a Marxist but rather a radical philosophical idealist in the Hegelian tradition.

Ferdinand Lassalle was born in Breslau, the son of a wealthy Jewish merchant. He was involved in the abortive revolution of 1848 and was imprisoned for six months. A restlessly active man, he devoted much of his life to political agitation and to prosecuting the case of his friend, the Countess Sophie Hatzfeld, against her estranged husband. In 1863 he founded the General German Workingmen's Association, a political party unmistakably socialist in orientation. In 1864 he was killed in a duel.

Lassalle was acquainted with MARX and ENGELS and was influenced by their work, although not to the exclusion of other thinkers. Indeed, the doctrine he finally advocated was a collection of points drawn from a variety of sources and welded together to produce what many regarded as a strikingly original result. The centrepiece of his economic theory was 'the iron law of wages': market forces would inexorably depress wages to the 'physiological minimum' necessary to keep the workers alive. The solution to this unsatisfactory situation was, he argued, to establish producers' cooperatives through which the workers, by becoming their own employers, could remove themselves from the labour market, thus nullifying the effect of the 'iron law'. For this, and for his other economic doctrines, Lassalle was indebted chiefly to Malthus and Ricardo. His political views, however, he drew from the German philosophical idealists. From FICHTE he took the idea of a German nation, now divided, but destined to become a single state with a unified territory; and from HEGEL he took his view of the state as the necessary instrument for 'the elevation and development of the human race into freedom'. It followed from this that the real enemy of the industrial proletariat was not the state but the liberal bourgeoisie, together with all those who, by endorsing the capitalist market economy, had ranged themselves against the proletariat as 'one reactionary mass'. The party of the proletariat should, therefore, form a tactical alliance with the Prussian state. The basis of the alliance would be that the party would support the state against liberal opposition and help promote a 'Prussian' solution to the problem of German unification, in return for which the state would implement democratic reforms, in particular universal franchise, and provide financial support for the establishment of producers' cooperatives. In short, the ultimate objective would be a united German state with a democratic constitution and a socialist economy. It was an ingenious strategy, much of which commended itself to Bismarck, and most of which infuriated Marx.

Lassalle's earliest significant work was a study of Heraclitus (1858). It was basically a Hegelian interpretation and caused something of a stir at the time. However, it is no longer referred to by classical scholars. His other major works include his *Das System der erworbenen Rechte* (System of Acquired Rights) (1861), which features an attempt to show that, in certain cases, retrospective legislation is compatible with the idea of right as such, and his *Bastiat-Schulze* (1864), a polemic against the liberal economist Franz Hermann Schulze-Delitzsch.

See also: SOCIALISM

List of works

Lassalle, F. (1858) *Die Philosophie Herakleitos des Dunklen von Ephesos* (The Philosophy of Heraclitus, the Dark One from Ephesus), Berlin. (Lassalle's most ambitious philosophical and scholarly work; although a sensation at its time, it failed to make a lasting impression.)

—— (1861) *Das System der erworbenen Rechte* (System of Acquired Rights), Leipzig: J.A. Brockhaus. (An essay in jurisprudence with particular reference to rights, the most notable feature of which is Lassalle's attempt to show the legitimacy of retroactive legislation.)

—— (1864) *Herr Bastiat-Schulze von Delitzsch*, Berlin: R. Schlingmann. (Lassalle's most celebrated work on social and economic policy.)

—— (1962) *Ausgewählte Texte* (Selected Texts), trans. and ed. T. Ramm, Stuttgart: Koehler. (A useful selection from Lassalle's principal writings.)

References and further reading

Bernstein, E. (1893) *Ferdinand Lassalle as a Social Reformer*, New York: Greenwood Press, 1969. (The most important study of Lassalle available in English.)

Footman, D. (1946) *The Primrose Path: A Life of Ferdinand Lassalle*, London: Cresset Press. (Includes extensive quotations, in English, from Lassalle's writings.)

Knapp, V.J. (1971) 'Ferdinand Lassalle on the State and Society: A Legacy to Welfare Statism', *The*

Australian Journal of Politics and History XVII: 377–85. (A helpful study of the main point in Lassalle's political programme.)

Ramm, T. (1956) *Ferdinand Lassalle als Rechts- und Sozialphilosoph* (Ferdinand Lassalle as Legal and Social Philosopher), Meisenheim am Glan, 2nd edn. (A good and searching analysis by an eminent Lassalle scholar.)

H. TUDOR

LATIN AMERICA, ANALYTIC PHILOSOPHY IN

see ANALYTICAL PHILOSOPHY IN LATIN AMERICA

LATIN AMERICA, COLONIAL THOUGHT IN

Colonial refers to Spanish and Portuguese sovereignty in America from the arrival of Columbus in 1492 up to the emergence of modern Latin American states in the nineteenth century. The intellectual life of the colonies and their mother countries at that time falls into two phases: traditional and modern. The traditional phase includes the siglo de oro, *or the Golden Age of the sixteenth and seventeenth centuries. This was a time when literature and the arts flourished, along with Scholastic philosophy, jurisprudence and theology. During the eighteenth century, traditional thought gradually gave way to modern movements, particularly from France.*

The universities founded in the mid-sixteenth century, notably those of Mexico and Peru, as well as colleges and seminaries, were impressively productive in the area of philosophy. The pressure of events such as the clash between European and Native American cultures in the sixteenth century and the struggle for independence from Spain and Portugal in the nineteenth century brought about numerous nonacademic works with philosophic content. Authors wrote in both Latin and Spanish or Portuguese and often knew native languages, such as Nahuatl and Quechua as well. Many operated in several different areas, such as the nun, Sor Juana Inés de la Cruz, one of the greatest poets in the Spanish language, who wrote a book on logic in Latin, which has since been lost.

Students studied philosophy first, then specialized in medicine, law, or theology. The core philosophy
curriculum was logic, natural philosophy or physics and metaphysics. In the eighteenth century Scholastic logic, similar to what has come to be known as formal logic, was weakened and natural philosophy began to incorporate experimental science. The bulk of philosophy was affected by modern thinkers such as René Descartes.

Eighteenth-century savants were critical of Scholasticism and later Latin American intellectuals tended to disavow the entire colonial past. However, historians since the 1940s have stressed the currency of modern scholarship, especially in science and since the 1960s have been rediscovering the sophisticated philosophy of the Golden Age.

1 **Issues of the conquest**
2 **Philosophy in the colonies**
3 **Philosophers**
4 **Formal logic**
5 **A theory of science**
6 **A defence of Plato**
7 **Natural philosophy in the eighteenth century**

1 Issues of the conquest

Contact between Spain and the Indies gave rise to a vast body of literature, including accounts of the conquest from both the Spanish and Indian viewpoints, studies of native culture, language and history and plans for new types of communities. Mexican bishop Vasco de Quiroga, for example, used ideas from Thomas More's *Utopia* (1516) to design settlements, or *congregaciones* for Indians dispersed or decimated by disease or mistreatment. These settlements became a model for later communities in Peru, known as *reducciones* and Brazil, known as *aldeias*.

An extraordinary body of writing on ethics, jurisprudence, politics and anthropology developed around the bitter controversies over relations between Spaniards and Indians. The most important figure was Dominican friar Bartolomé de Las Casas. Early in the settlement period a concession system, or *encomienda*, developed allowing Spaniards to force Indians to work on farms and in mines in return for fair treatment, which they usually did not receive. Las Casas, a Spanish landholder, or *encomendero*, in Cuba, heard a sermon denouncing this injustice which led him to free his Indians. He spent the next half of the century defending the rights of both native and African people. In carefully reasoned writings in Latin and Spanish he stressed that cultural differences do not suppress human rights. He questioned whether natural law supported the claims of the Crown, which caused him to advocate Spain's withdrawal from the Indies. Along with his fellow Dominican Francisco de

VITORIA in Spain, Las Casas made an important contribution to international law.

2 Philosophy in the colonies

The bulk of colonial philosophy was done by members of religious orders. Each of these orders pursued its own traditions. Franciscans followed John DUNS SCOTUS, while Dominicans, Augustinians and Jesuits developed their interpretations of Thomas AQUINAS. In the eighteenth century, Jesuits and Oratorians were key figures in bringing modern philosophy and science to America. American Scholastics remained in close contact with their European colleagues, although seventeenth-century Peruvians complained that Europeans paid their works scant attention.

The most important philosophical sources in the colonies were textbooks published by professors and manuscript classnotes taken down by their students. Other materials included academic programmes which listed the *theses* participants defended publicly. These are useful in tracing the progress of modern ideas. (A thesis on methodic doubt, for example, showed that Descartes was being discussed.) Theological works also contained philosophical material. A work on theology by Chilean Franciscan Alfonso Briceño included a series of excursuses on metaphysics.

Philosophy textbooks were known as commentaries or (from the seventeenth century) *cursus philosophici* (philosophy courses). Authors mostly used Aristotle's works as a framework to cover the assigned subject and to contribute to debates current at that time. In the eighteenth century, headings were added in modern works to accommodate new interests in methodology, science, mathematics and ethics.

Logic was taught in two parts. Formal, or the 'lesser' logic was called *summulae*, since it surveyed the *Summulae logicales* (Summary of Logic) of thirteenth-century logician PETER OF SPAIN. The 'greater' logic followed the structure of Porphyry's *Isagōgē* on universals and the 'predicables', of Aristotle's *Categories* and *Posterior Analytics*, and often of his *Topics* and *Sophisms* (see ARISTOTLE §§1, 7; PORPHYRY).

3 Philosophers

Augustinian friar Alonso de la Vera Cruz began teaching philosophy in Mexico in 1540 and published the first work (1554) on the subject in the western hemisphere, a two-volume logic book. He also wrote on natural philosophy and current issues and studied the Tarascan language. Dominican Tomás Mercado

included in his logic his own translation of Greek texts of Aristotle (see MEXICO, PHILOSOPHY IN).

After teaching in Mexico for sixteen years, Jesuit Antonio Rubio wrote what he hoped would become standard university textbooks in the three core areas of philosophy. His greater work of logic appeared in eighteen editions, between 1603 and 1641, seven of which were dubbed the *Logica mexicana* and became the official textbook in the Spanish University of Alcalá. Four of his works on natural philosophy went through over thirty-five editions. His metaphysics was never published (and is lost). It was, perhaps, eclipsed by Francisco Suárez's *Disputationes metaphysicae* (Metaphysical Disputations) (1597) (see SUÁREZ, F.). Rubio's works appeared in over fifty editions in six European countries. He also found time to study the language of the Aztecs.

The logic of Franciscan Jerónimo de Valera, published in Peru in 1610, was the first philosophy book printed in South America. Peruvian Jesuits Alonso Peñafiel, Nicolás de Olea and José de Aguilar published full courses on logic, natural philosophy and metaphysics.

Juan de Espinosa Medrano (c.1633–88), known as El Lunarejo, was professor of philosophy and theology in Cuzco, Peru. In his day, he was active in literary and philosophical controversies. His defence of poet Luis de Góngora holds a place in Spanish literary criticism. He was also famous for his eloquence not only in Spanish and Latin, but Quechua, the language of the Incas, in which he composed a biblical play set in Peru. He wrote his (lesser and greater) logic to defend traditional positions against a philosophical rebellion in seventeenth-century Spain which reflected modern impatience with conventional thought. His logic contains an unusual defence of Platonic ideas (see PLATO).

Although eighteenth-century philosophers were critical of previous Scholasticism, they usually blended it with modernism. Franciscan José Elías del Carmen Pereira in Argentina is an example of this eclecticism. The Jesuits had founded the University of Córdoba early in the seventeenth century and taught traditional Scholasticism using Rubio's logic as a textbook. By the mid-eighteenth century, conservatives complained that 'anti-Scholastic' doctrines were being taught. After the Jesuits were expelled from the region in 1767, the Franciscans, including Pereira continued their modern tendencies. The manuscripts of his course on natural philosophy dating from 1784 are extant.

Other representatives of the modern movement are José Agustín Caballero in Cuba, Isidoro de Celis in Peru, Jesuit Diego José Abad in Mexico and Oratorian Juan Benito Díaz de Gamarra y Dávalos.

Well-known scientists, mathematicians and historians included Carlos de Sigüenza y Góngora in Mexico and Pedro Peralta Barnuevo in both Mexico and Peru.

4 Formal logic

Sixteenth-century Scholastic logicians at the time of Alonso de la Vera Cruz analysed sentences in several ways. One way, still used in logic, would be to see a sentence like 'Bossy is a cow' as attributing the feature of being a cow, signified by the general term 'cow', to the thing denoted by the name 'Bossy'. However, they often took what logicians of the twentieth century would term a 'many-sorted' approach, wherein they reduced sentences containing general terms to sentences having only terms for things. 'Bossy is a cow', therefore, would be equivalent to a disjunction (a sentence made up of smaller ones joined by 'or'): 'Bossy is this cow *or* Bossy is that cow'. Deictic terms like 'this cow' they called 'wander terms'. Alonso took the disjunction to be true when at least one of the sentences it comprised was true, so that 'Bossy is a cow' is true when at least one cow is Bossy. On the other hand, 'Bossy is not a dog' would be analysed as a conjunction (a sentence made up of smaller ones joined by 'and'): 'Bossy is not this dog *and* Bossy is not that dog'. A conjunction is true when every sentence it is made up of is true. A universal sentence like 'every cow is an animal' is analysed as a conjunction of disjunctions: 'this cow is this animal *or* this cow is that animal... *and* that cow is this animal *or* that cow is that animal... *and*'.

Alonso (1554) and his colleagues formulated rules to expand general sentences into disjunctions and/or conjunctions ('descent') and from these to derive general sentences ('ascent' or 'induction'). In fact, they defined quantification (words like 'every', 'any', 'some') by means of these rules. They used such procedures to study many kinds of sentences: non-standard quantification ('Fido is not every dog'), relations ('Peter and Paul are discussing', 'every cow belongs to some man'), modality, the notions of possibility and necessity ('Fido need not wag his tail') and many others.

Alonso's definition of conjunctions and disjunctions is truth-functional: the truth of a compound sentence depends on the truth or falsehood of its parts. He takes the normal case of a conditional sentence like 'if Bossy is a cow, she is an animal' as 'strict implication', to use a twentieth-century expression, that is, it implies necessity: 'Fido cannot be a dog without being an animal'.

In general, Golden Age logic was quite similar to logic today and is often especially interesting where it differs (see Logical and mathematical terms, glossary of).

5 A theory of science

In his *Commentarii in universam Aristotelis dialecticam* (Logica mexicana) (1603), Rubio worked out a partially original theory of the relation of logic to science. Ideally, a science is an axiom system, a structured network of inferences resting ultimately on axioms. Science is general: it is not merely about *this* animal but about *animal* as such. Science is necessary in the sense that it seeks to describe physical law. A science aims at identifying the properties, or *passiones*, of its subject matter. In biology, for example, a statement would attribute the property, say, of *having DNA* to animals. Scientists must also be logicians, who use logic in two complementary ways. From a stock of terms, they construct sentences, link them together to form inferences and finally shape the inferences into a system. This is the practical or constructive (*compositorius*) side of logic. Its theoretical or analytic (*resolutorius*) function comes into play when they trace the paths of inference back to the axioms and break up statements into their constituent terms.

Logic itself is a science, hence an axiom system comprising terms, sentences, inferences, as well as a necessary structure. But to Rubio, it is unique because its subject matter is ultimately the same as that of all the sciences and is constructed without any subject matter. (Later logicians use variables to bracket out what is not of logical interest.)

Rubio defined the entities logic deals with in terms of relations and converse relations. The above construction and analysis, for example, are the two sides of a *making up* relation. In construction, terms make up statements, statements inferences and inferences are bound together into a system. Analysis is the converse relation of *being made up of*: the network is made up of inferences, these of statements and statements of terms. Another example of relations and converse relations is the predicate and subject of a sentence. A predicate is the relation of *being stated of* and a subject is the converse relation of *being what something is stated of*. These relations are the properties that logic as a science studies and seeks to identify in scientific discourse. The scientist says 'animals have DNA', but the logician says '*having DNA* is a predicate', that is, '*having DNA* is stated of something (animal)'. In other words, the scientist attributes the logical property of *being a predicate* to the 'thing' *having DNA*. However, science and logic deal with different sorts of properties. *Having DNA* is a real property since it belongs to things in the world like Bossy and Fido. But a logical property like *being stated of* applies only to 'things' in the mind, like *having DNA*. Logical properties are 'of second intention' ('higher level' would be a twentieth-century expression), since they apply to things as known and they are 'mental constructs' (*entia rationis*) in the sense that they do not really apply to them.

Rubio's theory of logic can be formulated in the following way: logic studies and in some sense constructs higher-level relations and attributes them to entities studied by other sciences. In turn, these entities apply to concrete things.

6 A defence of Plato

Juan de Espinosa Medrano (1688) developed an original defence of Plato with regard to his treatment of the problem of universals. The issue, then as now, has to do with explaining the nature of the general features of things. Logicians say that Fido and Bossy have the universal feature of *having DNA*. Fido and Bossy are concrete things, but what is *having DNA* the universal quality that they share? Thomists (followers of Thomas AQUINAS) and the Scotists (followers of John DUNS SCOTUS), grouped together by Espinosa as *peripatetics*, usually rejected nominalist and psychologistic solutions that universals were simply the words or the thoughts of a person. Peripatetics held several varieties of realism, according to which universals, or essences, are somehow more than mere words or private thoughts. However, all peripatetics routinely rejected what they took to be Plato's theory, which claimed that universals, or ideas, exist *apart* from the concrete, singular things which embody them.

Espinosa wanted to know what peripatetics meant by realism. He carefully isolated the elements found in both Thomist and Scotist theories and came up with a common peripatetic definition of essence. Both theoretical branches claimed, for example, that universals have essential being, that is, they exist as essences, that they do not change, are independent of time and space and, most importantly, that they differ both from concrete things and from God. Espinosa went on to analyse Plato's position. First, he questioned the usual Neoplatonic and Aristotelian interpretations of ideas: that they are (an aspect of) God or they exist by themselves apart from things. Espinosa believed that, if we judge by Plato's aim, which was to identify the object of knowledge, then he had only to describe his ideas as the peripatetics described their essences; in other words, what Plato said about his ideas was already *included in* what peripatetics said about their essences. Therefore, if peripatetic essences do not exist apart from things,

neither do Platonic ideas. Espinosa did not infer from Plato's words that ideas do or do not exist apart. What is clear is that 'the peripatetics, willing or not, have platonized and wounded themselves as they attacked Plato' (1688: 67) (see NEOPLATONISM). Espinosa stressed that his interesting claim 'has not been put forward until now, as far as I know, although (fifteenth-century Dominic of) Flanders and (contemporary Francisco) Araujo have favoured it in part' (1688: 62). The essences he described are not unlike twentieth-century abstract entities. Although Espinosa was aware of their ambiguous ontological status, he thought the objections against them could be resolved.

Scholastic rebels of his time, especially a group of Spanish Jesuits, had nominalistic tendencies which Espinosa attacked fiercely. His arguments, he believed, finally put nominalism to rest, after outbreaks of the doctrine during the Greek period (Heraclitus (*c*.540–480 BC)), in the twelfth and fourteenth centuries (Roscelin (*c*.1050–after 1120) and Ockham (*c*.1287–1347)) and during the seventeenth century, in Espinosa's own time (see HERACLITUS; WILLIAM OF OCKHAM; ROSCELIN OF COMPIÈGNE). Indeed, it was he who wrote nominalism's epitaph:

Thrice slain and then revived, I, Ockham's sect,
A fourth time now follow Euridice;
Lo, here I helpless lie among the shades:
A word, a concept, sans reality.

(1688: 128)

7 Natural philosophy in the eighteenth century

In his course on natural philosophy or physics Elías del Carmen Pereira (1784) blended modern science and traditional philosophy. He took his ideas from Scholastics such as ANSELM OF CANTERBURY, Aquinas, Duns Scotus, Suárez, modern philosophers, such as, Francis BACON, René DESCARTES, Pierre GASSENDI, Baruch SPINOZA and G.W. LEIBNIZ, modernizing Scholastics, such as, Benito Jerónomo Feijoo, Teodoro Almeida and Tomás Vicente Tosca and scientists, such as, Robert BOYLE and Torricelli. Pereira's favourite topics were scientific: the vacuum, capillary action, motion, gravity and light. However, he continued to work within the traditional conception of science, as can be gathered from his definition of general physics as the natural body and its properties.

Pereira's use of the traditional categories of matter and form was an example of an old theory disguised as a new one. He claimed to be following the example of the more cultivated nations in his refusal to quibble over prime matter, defining matter as extended particles, which, 'whatever they are', are physically, but not mathematically indivisible, and are formed in various sizes and shapes. The form of a material thing became the manner in which material particles combined, with their relationship giving rise to the specific properties of the material thing.

Pereira framed his theory of light in traditional terms of substance and accident, matter and form. Light, he believed, was not an accident of matter as the Scholastics thought, but a substance and that the effluence theory of Newton and Gassendi was also wrong (see NEWTON, I.). Taking his lead from Nicolas MALEBRANCHE, Pereira claimed that the 'matter' of light is the medium wherein it is propagated, that is, the ether which consists of tiny contiguous elastic globules. Its 'form' is the rapid vibratory motion transmitted instantaneously from one particle to another in straight lines. In this particle-wave theory, the globules themselves do not move away from the light source and their vibration has frequency, but little or no amplitude.

Despite his Scholastic vocabulary, Franciscan Friar Elías del Carmen Pereira's world was no longer that of the Scholastics.

See also: ARGENTINA, PHILOSOPHY IN; BRAZIL, PHILOSOPHY IN; LATIN AMERICA, PRE-COLUMBIAN AND INDIGENOUS THOUGHT IN

References and further reading

* Aristotle (*c.*mid 4th century BC) *Categories*, trans. J.L. Ackrill, Oxford: Oxford University Press, 1963. (One of Aristotle's works on logic.)
* —— *Posterior Analytics*, ed. W.D. Ross, trans. J. Barnes, Oxford: Oxford University Press, 2nd edn, 1993. (Formulates an account of rigorous scientific knowledge.)
* Espinosa Medrano, J. de (1688) *Philosophia Thomistica seu Cursus Philosophicus*, Rome. (His defence of Plato on pages 52–73 appeared in Spanish translation in W. Redmond, 'Juan de Espinosa Medrano: Sobre la naturaleza de los universales', *Humanidades* 3, Catholic University of Peru, 1969: 131–85.)
Hanke, L. (1965) *The Spanish Struggle for Justice in the Conquest of America*, Boston, MA: Little, Brown & Co. (A readable account of the controversies in which Bartolomé de Las Casas was involved.)
Irving, L. (1929) *Don Carlos de Sigüenza y Góngora, A Mexican Savant of the Seventeenth Century*, Berkeley, CA: University of California Press. (The most complete work on Sigüenza in English.)
Lanning, J.T. (1940) *Academic Culture in the Spanish Colonies*, Oxford: Oxford University Press. (A classic study of philosophy theses tracing the prompt arrival of modern ideas in Latin America.)
Navarro, B. (1948) *La Introducción de la filosofía moderna en México* (The Introduction of Modern Philosophy in Mexico), Mexico: El Colegio de México. (A study of the influence of modern philosophy in eighteenth-century Mexico.)
* Pereira, E. del Carmen (1784) *Physica generalis* (General Physics), Facultad de Ciencias Jurídicas y Sociales, La Plata University; trans. in J. Chiabra (ed.) *La enseñanza de la filosofía en la Época Colonial* (Philosophy Teaching in the Colonial Period), Buenos Aires: Coni Hermanos, 1911: 173–333. (This book blends Scholasticism with modernism.)
* Porphyry (mid 3rd century AD) *Introduction Isagōgē*, ed. A. Busse, *Isagoge et in Aristotelis categorias commentarium*, CAG 4.1, Berlin: Reimer, 1887; trans. E. Warren, *Porphyry the Phoenician: Isagōgē*, Toronto, Ont: Pontifical Institute of Medieval Studies, 1975. (English translation.)
Redmond, W. (1972) *Bibliography of the Philosophy in the Iberian Colonies of America*, The Hague: Nijhoff. (The standard bibliography of source material and secondary literature.)
—— (1974) 'Latin American Colonial Philosophy: The Logic of Espinosa Medrano', *The Americas* 30 (4): 192–212, Washington, DC: Academy of American Franciscan History. (The logic of Espinosa in its historical setting.)
—— (1979) 'Formal Logic in New Spain: The Work of Fray Alonso', *International Philosophical Quarterly* 19 (3): 331–51. (A history of colonial logic and a nontechnical description of its content.)
—— (1984) 'Lógica y ciencia en la *Logica mexicana* de Rubio' (Logic and Science in Rubio's *Mexican Logic*), *Quipu: Revista Latinoamericana de Historia de las Ciencias y la Tecnología* (Quipu: Latin American Journal of the History of Science and Technology) 1 (1): 55–82. (A full account of Rubio's concept of logic and science and their interrelation.)
—— (1991) 'El Lunarejo on Abstract Entities', *Concordia: Internationale Zeitschrift für Philosophie* (Concordia: International Journal of Philosophy) 20: 91–8, Aachen, Germany: Augustinus-Buchhandlung-Verlag. (Espinosa's defence of Plato.)
—— (1993) 'Logik, Wissenschaft und Literatur' (Logic, Science and Literature), *Concordia: Internationale Zeitschrift für Philosophie* (Concordia: International Journal of Philosophy) 24: 24–33, Aachen, Germany: Augustinus-Buchhandlung-Verlag. (Interesting discussion on logic and literature.)
Redmond, W. and Beuchot, M. (1985) *La lógica*

mexicana del Siglo de Oro (Mexican Logic in the Golden Age), Mexico: National University of Mexico. (Historical and technical aspects of the logic of de la Vera Cruz, Mercado and Rubio.)

—— (1995) *La teoría de la argumentación en el México colonial* (Argumentation Theory in Colonial Mexico), Mexico: National University of Mexico. (Analysis of logical argumentation in Mexico from the sixteenth to eighteenth centuries.)

* Rubio, A. de la Rueda (1603) *Commentarii in universam Aristotelis dialecticam* (Logica mexicana), Alcalá; Cologne, 1605; Valencia, abridged edn, 1606. (The author's original theory of the relation of logic to science.)

* Suárez, F. (1597) *Disputationes metaphysicae* (Metaphysical Disputations), in *Opera omnia*, vols 25–6, Paris: Louis Vivès, 1856–66; repr. Hildesheim: Olms, 1965. (Suárez's systematic presentation of metaphysics.)

* Vera Cruz, A. de la (1554) *Recognitio Summularum* (Examination of the *Summulae* (of Peter of Spain)), vol. 1, *Dialectica Resolutio* (Analysis of Logic), vol. 2, Mexico City. (Suárez's work on metaphysics perhaps eclipsed that of Rubio.)

—— (1557) *Physica speculatio* (Speculation on Physics), Mexico City. (The author speculates on physics.)

WALTER B. REDMOND

LATIN AMERICA, PHILOSOPHY IN

Geographically, Latin America extends from the Mexican–US border to those regions of Antarctica to which various Latin American countries have laid claim. It includes the Spanish-speaking Caribbean. Philosophy in Latin America dates from pre-Columbian (before 1492 in Hispanic America) and pre-cabralian times (before 1500 in Brazil). Autochthonous cultures, particularly the Aztecs, Mayas, Incas and Tupi-Guarani, produced sophisticated thought systems centuries before the arrival of Europeans in America.

Academic philosophy began in the sixteenth century when the Catholic church began to establish schools, monasteries, convents and seminaries in Latin America. The seventeenth century saw little philosophical activity as effort was made to use academic thought to maintain the status quo, which reinforced a basically medieval worldview. Intellectually, the eighteenth century perpetuated this calm traditionalism until mid-century when a generation of

Jesuits tried to break with the thought of Aristotle in order to modernize it. Political turmoil prevented academic philosophy from broadening in the early part of the nineteenth century. Later in the nineteenth century and into the early twentieth, positivism eventually became entrenched in most Latin American countries. In the early twentieth century new intellectual movements began as a backlash against anti-positivism.

1 Latin American philosophy up to the nineteenth century

Indigenous cultures, particularly the Aztecs, Mayas, Incas and Tupi-Guarani, produced interesting and sophisticated thought systems centuries before the arrival of Europeans in America. Many cultural artefacts were lost or destroyed so that study of this period involves many challenges in deciphering the subtleties and complexities of the earliest thought in Latin America. Indigenous cosmologies were often linked to phenomena in the natural world (see LATIN AMERICA, PRE-COLUMBIAN AND INDIGENOUS THOUGHT IN; BRAZIL, PHILOSOPHY IN).

Academic philosophy grew up in the sixteenth century when the Catholic church began to establish schools, monasteries, convents and seminaries in Latin America. If the encounter with the New World had significant impact on the European mind, this was not initially reflected in the philosophy being taught and written in the sixteenth and seventeenth centuries, which tended to restate and reinforce medieval values. However, intriguing writings on ethics and jurisprudence grew out of the contact between Spain and Latin America. Essentially, these writings analysed the relationship between cultural differences and human rights. The Dominican friar Bartolomé de las Casas was a pivotal figure who defended the rights of native and African peoples living in the Indies in the sixteenth century (see LATIN AMERICA, COLONIAL THOUGHT IN; MEXICO, PHILOSOPHY IN).

With a few notable exceptions, the seventeenth century was largely moribund philosophically because most efforts were directed towards using academic thought to maintain the status quo, which reinforced a fundamentally medieval worldview. The main philosophical task involved justifying and protecting the Catholic faith against Protestantism and science. Scholasticism was the dominant trend. However, there were some exceptions to the dominant practices in the form of several remarkable historical and philosophical figures. Antonio Rubio's studies on logic are remarkably advanced. Juana Inés de la Cruz had a brilliant philosophical mind and is usually considered one of the earliest feminist thinkers in America (see LATIN AMERICA, COLONIAL THOUGHT IN; FEMINIST THOUGHT IN LATIN AMERICA).

Intellectually, the eighteenth century continued this calm traditionalism until mid-century when a generation of Jesuits tried to break with the thought of Aristotle and bring philosophy into 'modernity'. They were primarily influenced by post-Renaissance Italian and French philosophy. However, the Jesuit order was expelled from the Spanish-speaking world in 1767. This delayed the introduction of proto-modern European philosophy in Latin America. The eighteenth century has become the subject of much revisionist philosophical study, particularly in Mexico (see MEXICO, PHILOSOPHY IN).

Academic philosophy still did not broaden in the early nineteenth century because of political turmoil both in various Latin American countries and in Europe. Universities occasionally closed. This inhibited academic philosophical progress as universities were the locus of much philosophical activity. A more productive forum for philosophy was often the political arena in which thoughtful essays of ideas were written by nonacademics on themes such as constitutional government, progress and autonomy (see LITERATURE, PHILOSOPHY IN LATIN AMERICAN; ARGENTINA, PHILOSOPHY IN).

Later in the nineteenth century and into the early twentieth, positivism eventually became entrenched in most Latin American countries. This movement claimed to be an objective methodology of the sciences. It was widely believed that scientific doctrines could provide the most efficient management of society through educational and political reforms. Auguste COMTE and Herbert SPENCER were the primary positivist influences in Latin America (see POSITIVIST THOUGHT IN LATIN AMERICA; ANALYTICAL PHILOSOPHY IN LATIN AMERICA; BRAZIL, PHILOSOPHY IN).

2 Latin American philosophy in the twentieth century

In the early twentieth century new intellectual movements began. Arising from these was a strong, thoroughgoing anti-positivist backlash. Ideas that positivists had promoted as 'scientific' were rejected by anti-positivists for being scientist (see ANTI-POSITIVIST THOUGHT IN LATIN AMERICA; ARGENTINA, PHILOSOPHY IN). Philosophers entertained idealism, vitalism, pragmatism and various political and social philosophies (see PHENOMENOLOGY IN LATIN AMERICA; EXISTENTIALIST THOUGHT IN LATIN AMERICA). Neo-Thomist thought continued to be widely studied, primarily in the Catholic universities.

A focus on regional thought in Latin America was an outgrowth of anti-positivist thought and a consequence of the arrival of Spanish philosophers who were exiled after the fall of Republican Spain. The writings of the Spaniard, José ORTEGA Y GASSET, were widely influential in shaping Latin American philosophical reflections. Philosophers addressed the question of authenticity as they explored whether Latin Americans were simply adopting European philosophies, or whether they themselves had any authentic philosophy to offer. Many concluded that Latin Americans were adapting, rather than adopting European philosophies to their own reality (see EXISTENTIALIST THOUGHT IN LATIN AMERICA; PHENOMENOLOGY IN LATIN AMERICA; ANTI-POSITIVIST THOUGHT IN LATIN AMERICA).

This process of critical self-examination, or 'autognosis', was twofold. First, philosophers in individual countries and regions of Latin America sought to identify what was unique or distinctive about their thought or being. Later, philosophical contributions made by Latin America as a whole were compared and contrasted with those of other regions in the world (see ARGENTINA, PHILOSOPHY IN; BRAZIL, PHILOSOPHY IN; MEXICO, PHILOSOPHY IN). Studying Latin American thought in comparative perspective engendered a debate of considerable longevity over whether 'Latin American philosophy' exists or whether 'philosophy in Latin America' is a more accurate denotation. Every Latin American country, including Puerto Rico, can be argued to possess unique philosophical traditions. At the same time there exists an extensive body of argument and commentary on what kind of philosophy, if any, can claim to be 'universal'.

Since analytical philosophy presents perspectives, methods and projects which claim to have universal appeal and applicability, it is often embraced in academic circles and is most frequently entrenched institutionally in Mexico, Brazil and Argentina. Analytical philosophy in these countries, while not obviously a response to immediate regional social, political or economic circumstances, serves to include and validate its adherents in international circles by adopting a style widely practised and accepted by mainstream Anglo-American academic philosophy. Attracted to the linguistic 'rigour' of analytical philosophy, some adherents claim that it is the only way to do 'real philosophy'.

The late twentieth century reveals that it is possible to speak of both 'Latin American philosophy' and 'philosophy in Latin America'. Some areas of philosophical research imbued with regional and cosmopolitan appeal are cultural identity, feminist thought, liberation philosophy, marginality and Marxist thought in Latin America (see CULTURAL IDENTITY; FEMINIST THOUGHT IN LATIN AMERICA; LIBERATION PHILOSOPHY; MARGINALITY; MARXIST THOUGHT IN LATIN AMERICA). Many of these areas are profoundly engaged with Latin American realities in historical context. Rather than blindly adopting canonical Western philosophical paradigms, writers in these traditions seek to broaden the definition of what is human by convincingly articulating and incorporating Latin American experience and values into both the crucial discourses of philosophy and the pressing themes of the modern world (see MARGINALITY).

Marxist philosophy has been and most likely will continue to be significant in Latin America partly because of continuing problems of economic disparities. Concerns with retributive justice, human rights and issues of power and truth, as well as the belief that Marxist theory more accurately describes reality, contribute to the vitality of this thought. Despite the collapse of the Soviet Union and the passing of Maoism in China, for many the Cuban Revolution of 1959 is still idealized because it continues to threaten the US 'monster' to the north, while advancing the notion of a supportive, egalitarian and responsible community. The Peruvian José Carlos Mariátegui was an original Latin American Marxist thinker whose thought has generated interest and respect internationally (see MARXIST THOUGHT IN LATIN AMERICA).

One of the best known and most interesting contributions of modern Latin American intellectual life is liberation philosophy. The philosophical movement originated in Argentina, although many of its practitioners reside in other Latin American countries (see ARGENTINA, PHILOSOPHY IN; MEXICO, PHILOSOPHY IN). Philosophy of liberation should not be confused with liberation theology (see LIBERATION THEOLOGY). Philosophy of liberation attempts to explain philosophically the theoretical underpinnings of social and political phenomena, such as dependency, and reinforces theology of liberation. These movements are responses to significant events in twentieth-century Latin America such as the Cuban Revolution (1959), the Argentine 'Dirty war' (1976–1983) and repressive regimes which began in Guatemala in 1954, Brazil in 1964 and Chile in 1973. Other political topics for these writers included populism, Marxism and Peronism. Philosophy of liberation differs from theology of liberation, Latin Americanist philosophy and Marxist philosophy especially in terms of its more limited accessibility. Philosophers of liberation employ a complex and specialized vocabulary which requires initiation on the part of readers. In addition, philosophy of liberation is not a unified movement: it is more appropriate to speak of philosophies of liberation. Such fragmenta-

tion in this field can be partly explained by the political orientations of thinkers whose views range from the extreme left to the extreme right. Their philosophical influences vary widely and include Francophone, German and other Latin American thinkers.

Philosophical activity in Latin America is characterized by a tremendous diversity of focus and methodologies. Latin Americans are keenly aware of philosophical developments in the rest of the world and thus entertain a variety of philosophical stances: progressive and conservative, pragmatist and idealist, materialist and spiritualist. Numerous philosophical interests and projects exist in Latin America because of a diversified and active philosophical profession, an interested public, some government support, a cultural awareness of other continents among the educated and noneducated alike and a widespread faith in education as a key to development.

AMY A. OLIVER

LATIN AMERICA, PRE-COLUMBIAN AND INDIGENOUS THOUGHT IN

The term 'pre-Columbian thought' refers to the set of beliefs and ideas held by the civilizations existing in Latin America prior to the arrival of Columbus in 1492. Research in pre-Columbian thought poses several questions linked to language, interpretation, chronology and cultural diversity. They can roughly be organized according to the three main regions in which the indigenous cultures flourished upon the arrival of the Spanish invaders: Nahuatl/Aztec *in central and southern Mexico,* Quiché/Maya *from Yucatan in southern Mexico to Honduras in central America and* Quechua/Inca, *from Ecuador to northern Chile. They each correspond to an empire into which previously many diverse, distinguishable peoples were assimilated. Since the Spanish invaders had destroyed most of their 'heretical' cultural objects by 1550, the question arises whether an accurate knowledge of their thought can be obtained.*

Some ethnohistorians believe that each of the aforementioned cultures developed a hieroglyphic system of codification and documentation, called Codices, *to preserve their theocosmogony, history and wisdom. Since the sixteenth century, however, it is known with certainty that only the Aztec and Mayan cultures developed such a system. According to some historians, the Incan culture did not use any kind of writing. They probably created 'paintings', as the Spaniards called their hieroglyphs, but these were totally destroyed.*

It is known that all pre-Columbian religions worshipped the events and forces of nature. The term used to name them was translated into Spanish as 'gods' when they were acceptable, or 'demons' when they seemed heretical – the indigenous peoples were polytheistic. The gods did not dwell in a region beyond our world, but rather populated it and were actively intertwined with it. All pre-Columbian cultures believed the sun to be the highest deity. The universe was conceived as a holistic structure in which human life, society and the gods were parts of an interrelated universe. Beyond these, however, the three cultures believed in an intangible, abstract deity, or principle, which ruled above all others.

The sun, being the highest tangible deity, led the priests of these cultures to observe the skies. Based on a highly developed knowledge of astronomy and mathematics, they established an accurate solar calendar.

1   **Sources**
2   **Worldviews**
3   **Three sages**

1   Sources

In opposition to the colonizers of the USA and Canada, the Spanish invaders of the first generation (up to 1550 AD) described in great detail the cities, temples and well-organized commerce and transport systems they encountered. They were awed by the magnificence of the civilizations they discovered in Mexico, as expressed by Hernán Cortés (*c*.1485–*c*.1547) and Bernal Díaz del Castillo (d. *circa* 1560). Since they did not know the pre-Columbian languages and were both biased by the beliefs of their own age and culture and blinded by their greed for gold and silver, they did not collect direct information about the beliefs and thought of the original inhabitants. The recording of these beliefs became the task of some of the first Franciscan missionaries in Mexico and Guatemala. Bernard Sahagún (d. *circa* 1590) termed this set of beliefs 'philosophy' and Diego de Landa (1524–79 [1978]) called them 'heresy'.

Contemporary research on the pre-Colombian cultures relies on a variety of sources: first, archaeological excavations of ancient cities, temples and reliefs, sculpture, figurines and pottery; second: with regard to the Aztec and Mayan culture, codices, which are figurative, polychromatic manuscripts drawn by Indian priests; third: manuscripts dictated by converted Indian nobility, which then were translated into Latin, or else they were transliterated by Indians from the indigenous languages with the

use of the Latin alphabet. (The Aztecs spoke, among other languages, Nahuatl or Mexica; the Mayas spoke, among other languages, Maya-Quiché.) All the codices depict themes inherited by the oral tradition: theocosmogony, history, religious ceremonies and social mores. Other sources include chronicles and histories written in Spanish by missionaries.

Research on Mayan thought differs from that on the Aztecs and Incas in that many of the codices depicting texts have not been completely deciphered. However, their numerical system (which was not decimal but vigesimal) has been well understood. Mayan priests, who were also mathematicians, conceived of the number zero prior to the arrival of the Spaniards. Remaining texts, such as the *Popol Vuh* (*c*.1600 [1996]) and *The Book of Chilam Balam of Chumayel* (*c*.1600 [1967]), were written in the Maya/Quiché language using the Latin alphabet. They have since been translated into Spanish and other languages. They record Mayan cosmogony, the history of their cities, astronomy and astrology.

The only Inca codex to be found was the *quipu*, a sort of rosary or abacus made from hemp and beads. This was designed for purposes of numerical information. Research on Inca culture has mainly been obtained from massive monuments, such as the old cities of Macchu Picchu and Cuzco, with their observatories for recording the movement of the sun, moon and stars. Archaeological digs have led to the retrieval of pottery, jewellery and mummies that escaped the Spanish destruction. The oral tradition has also helped to maintain Inca history. In its technical capability, Incan culture has been compared to that of the Roman Empire. The Incas built an elaborate system of channels to capture the melting snow from the slopes of the Andes and to transport it to the valleys where they had settled, some of which are still in use in the 1990s. Similarly, they built a road system extending from the sacred city of Cuzco, which for the Incas was the centre of the universe, to the four cardinal points – north, south, east and west. In the coastal plains huge geometrical figures have been found, whose shape and size can be appreciated only from the air and no one has been able to interpret their function and meaning. In addition and most important, are several manuscripts written in Spanish by converted Inca noblemen, for example Diego de Castro Tito Cussi Yapanqui (*c*.1529–71) and Felipe Guamán Poma de Ayala (*c*.1550–*c*.1615 [1977]). They tell us that the last Incan emperor Atahualpa, ruler at the time of the arrival of the Spaniards and killed in 1533 by the conqueror Pizarro, established a 'clock' by which he determined the period of preparing the soil, seeding and harvesting.

2 Worldviews

As to the thoughts and worldviews of these cultures, it is difficult to form a clear and distinct conception due to the problem of language. The first translators, the Spanish Catholic friars, came to the New World to convert the original peoples to the 'true religion' during the century when Spain was dominated by the Counter-Reformation. These friars had been trained in the medieval Aristotelian view of both the true God and the world, and their descriptions mirrored this background. For instance, Bernabé Cobo, a missionary travelling in Peru, appalled by the Indians' idolatry, referred to the sacred sculptures and figurines as 'demons'. Newly converted Indians and several friars used the term 'god' as a translation of the names given to the various images representing the forces and events of nature.

According to Miguel León-Portilla (1963), the Aztec peoples had a precise conception of a metaphysical God despite their belief in a variety of deities corresponding to natural recurrent events, such as the recurrence of the moon and the sun and the cycles of planting and harvesting. All the deities, both feared and revered, were thought to be manifestations of a single supreme intangible, immaterial principle endowed with diverse attributes and present in all phenomena. Its name was Ometeotl, the god of duality and wisdom. As duality, he was partially male and female. His male name was Ometecutli, 'he... who is activity on earth' and his wife Omecihuatl, she who 'gives stability to (our) earth', as translated by León-Portilla (1963). These two notions are conceived as a unity which comprises everything by virtue of being dual: dark and light, masculine and feminine, life and death. One of Ometeotl's attributes is *tloque nahuaque*, or owner of proximity in time and space, who rules over the earth. As a representation of activity and stability, Ometeotl can be interpreted as a dialectical principle which, as activity, is the principle of destruction and recreation, but which, by giving stability to the earth, maintains the world's continuity. One of the main scholars of Nahuatl culture, Angel María Garibay (1892–1967), translates Ometeotl as 'two-god' (*c*.1930 [1965]).

A similar notion of duality can be found in the Mayan religion, where duality is called Hunab-Ku. In its masculine form, it is Itzamna, whose wife is Ix-Chel, or mother earth. They are the ancestors of all other gods and of humans. Reliefs show Itzamna as an old man representing wisdom, life-giving forces and writing. Since Itzamna is wisdom, he 'knows something about time'. Therefore, he also is the patron of astronomical and mathematical knowledge. Similar to Ometeotl for the Aztecs, Itzamna and Ix-Chel, were conceived as a unity, or single metaphysical principle.

The Incan religion was different. Ticci Viracocha, also called Pachayachachic, was thought to be the creator and ruler of all things. According to Garcilaso Inca de la Vega (1539–1616) in *Royal Commenatries of the Incas and General History* (*c*.1600 [1966]), Pachayachachic is the world's origin and soul, the giver of life and the mover of the universe. Since this deity is incorporeal, the mind cannot have an image of its being. A person who makes contact with this god does so through the heart. Therefore it was forbidden to pronounce its name, to build temples dedicated to it and to offer up sacrifices to it. In a sense, Pachayachachic was a hidden god. Below this deity were the diverse Viracochas: the sun, representing agriculture, the earth, representing our mother and minor deities, such as rocks and earthquakes. The Incan emperor and his dynasty were also considered to be divine, but below the higher ranking Viracochas. According to Bernabé Cobo (*c*.1550 [1990]), one of the early missionaries in Peru, Ticci Viracocha was the highest deity, or as Cobo states, the first cause.

There is the question of whether the pre-Columbian peoples were polytheistic. Some interpreters claim that the Aztec and Mayan gods are images and should not be understood as personifications of natural events and forces, but rather as ideas of them. The Aztecs called the regular appearance of the sun *tonatiuh*, meaning the main star in the sky; the Quechuas called it *apu inti*. The idea of the sun as the giver of life and the deity which keeps the sun, understood as the soul of the world moving, amounts to the same unique first metaphysical principle. Therefore, the first bishop of Guatemala and Chiapas, Fray Bartolomé de las Casas called these religions monotheistic.

With regard to their view of the universe, the three cultures have astonishing similarities. None of them knew of the existence of other continents. They viewed the universe as divided into four regions, each corresponding to the four cardinal directions. They believed in the existence of a region below our earth, where the dead are buried and survive in the dark. The Aztecs and Mayas, but not the Incas, believed in a recurrent cycle of creation and destruction. The Aztecs measured the universe's time in cycles, known as suns, equal to fifty-two years after which, due to a cosmic cataclysm, the universe would be destroyed, and accordingly recreated.

3 Three sages

León-Portilla (1963) translated works from Nahuatl into Spanish. He interpreted the poems of the most representative sages and priests, or *tlamatimine*, meaning 'he who knows something'. Counted among these sages were Quetzalcoatl, or the 'plumed serpent' (ninth century AD), probably king of Tula, Tlacaelel, advisor to the king (*c.*1398) and Netzahualcoyotl, king of Texcoco (1402–72).

From Quetzalcoatl we know how the Nahuas, and later the Aztecs, viewed the universe. It was imagined as an enormous is land divided horizontally into four regions surrounded by enormous waters. The four regions converge at the world's centre. East is the region of light, of fertility and of life, symbolized by the colour white; north is the universe's black region, where the dead are buried; west is the sun's house, its colour red; and south is the region of seeds, its colour blue. Vertically, the universe is built in layers, some above, others beneath the earth. Above the earth the sky forms a blue dome covered by a network of paths on which the sun, stars and moon move. At the highest level is Ometeotl, other gods are on lower levels. Beneath the surface of earth there are other levels, the deepest being the region of death, or Mictlan.

Netzahualcoyotl's thought is the best known. Some texts thought to be by Netzahualcoyotl remain, such as *Anales de Cuauhtitlan* (*c.*1402–72). One of the recurrent themes refers to the world's constant flow of time and the never ending change and futility of being. The often used expression *cachuitl*, or 'what is left behind', also refers to death and the sorrow of human mortality. This concern explicitly leads Netzahualcoyotl to reflect on the unique value of human life. Being aware of the inevitability of death, he reflects upon the possibility of overcoming it. He searches for a fixed point which does not change or perish. He sees it in the mystery of *tloque nahuaque*, or 'owner of proximity in time and space', but the mystery can only be invoked, not resolved. This fixed point can only become real if it grows roots in our hearts and the sorrow about death can only be silenced in one's heart, through *flor y canto*, or poetry. As king of Texcoco, Netzahualcoyotl unsuccessfully tried to oppose the practice of human sacrifice, a ritual brought to the land by the Aztecs, also known as Mexicas, the last indigenous group who had conquered the whole region by 1325 AD.

Tlacaelel's thought was the expression of an ideology that justified Aztec political practices. He was an outspoken advocate of the glorification of Huitzilopochtli, the god of war. In order to create the new cycle of life on earth following the last cataclysm, the gods gave their own blood as the elixir of life and strength. To correspond to this sacrifice it was necessary to offer them human blood. In order to have access to this elixir, Tlacaelel supported the practice of regular warfare, or *guerras floridas* against their neighbours for the explicit purpose of obtaining prisoners. This ideology became acceptable because human sacrifices made it impossible for the next cataclysm to happen. Hence, the Aztecs saw themselves as the chosen people who could overcome the inevitable destruction of the universe.

When the missionaries arrived in the New World, they were appalled by the immorality of the indigenous peoples. Not only were they shocked by the practice of human sacrifices, but also disgusted by the purported custom of eating the flesh of victims. However, cannibalism has been a controversial issue among historians who think it was alleged by the conquerors to justify the appropriation and plundering of the whole territory. In addition, most sixteenth-century chronicles report a variety of 'sins' attributed to biblical Babylon from prostitution and incest to homosexuality. It is true that the Incas worshipped fertility and many remaining *huacas*, or sacred figures in clay, are endowed with phallic forms.

Most recently, the opposite view has been taken. As the great empires required the rule of law and discipline, all three cultures were based on similar moral values. The main virtues were courage, fortitude, sobriety and obedience. Drunkenness was regarded as the source of all vices. Monogamy seems to have been the correct relationship between man and woman, since under the Incas adultery, like theft, was punished with death. Greed was condemned and riches in gold, silver and precious stones (and among the Aztecs and Mayas, the quetzal's colourful feathers), belonged to the gods, their temples and the courts of emperors and priests.

Sahagún (*c.*1550 [1970]) outlined the many virtues an Aztec father taught his children. Both sons and daughters had to worship the gods daily, be diligent in their tasks so that time would not be wasted, be meticulous when carrying out their craft, act friendly and respectfully towards others, keep peace with them, be honest and never steal from them. He taught his daughter to practise chastity and modesty before marriage, to be obedient to her father or husband and to do the work of women, such as cooking, weaving and painting.

In addition, he taught his sons not to act arrogantly, not to sow disharmony, to cultivate the land, to learn an honourable trade or art, to be always modest and enduring and always be responsible for his wife and family.

See also: LATIN AMERICA, COLONIAL THOUGHT IN

References and further reading

* Anonymous (*c.*1600) *Popol Vuh*, trans. D. Tedlock, New York: Simon & Schuster, 1996. (An excellent translation of the myths and history of the Quiché/Mayan peoples.)
* Anonymous (1600) *The Book of Chilam Balam of Chumayel*, Oklahoma, OK: University of Oklahoma Press, 1967. (Another translation of an anonymous text written in the Maya/Quiché language using the Latin alphabet.)
* Cobo, B. (*c.*1550) *Inca Religion and Customs*, Austin, TX: University of Texas Press, 1990. (Part of a more extensive work and shows the animosity felt by the many missionaries for the pagan Incan religion and mores.)
  Coe, D.M. (1992) *Breaking the Maya Code*, New York: Thames & Hudson. (An important book with regard to deciphering Mayan hieroglyphs.)
  —— (1993) *The Maya*, New York: Thames & Hudson. (One of the best books in English discussing Mayan culture).
  Cortés, H. (*c.*1523–27) *Letters From Mexico*, New York: Grossman Publishers, 1971. (Letters to Charles I of Spain. A historical document in which Cortés tries to prove the glory of his conquest.)
  Díaz del Castillo, B. (*c.*1570) *The Conquest of New Spain*, New York: Penguin, 1963. (Memoirs by Cortés's captain. Probably one of the most interesting introductions to the adventures of the conquest.)
* Garibay, A.M. (*c.*1930) *Teogonía e historia de los mexicanos* (The Family Tree of Pagan Gods), Mexico: Universidad Nacional Autónoma de México, 1965. (The translation of Nahuatl texts and commentaries on their origins.)
* Guamán Poma de Ayala, F. (*c.*1550– *c.*1615) *Letter to a King: A Picture History of the Inca Civilization*, trans. C. Dilke, London: Allen & Unwin, 1977. (A good translation from the Spanish. The translation reproduces Guamán Poma de Ayala's irony and his profound moral sense. It includes his drawings.)
* Inca de la Vega, G. (*c.*1600) *Royal Commentaries of the Incas and General History*, Austin, TX: University of Texas Press, 2 vols, 1966. (An excellent source of Inca history and mores.)
* Landa, D. de (1524–79) *Yucatan Before and After the Conquest*, trans. W. Gates, New York: Dover Publications, 1978. (Description of religion, mores and bleeding practices of the Mayan peoples. Source for deciphering the written Maya code.)
* León-Portilla, M. (1963) *Aztec Thought and Culture: A Study of the Ancient Nahuatl Mind*, Oklahoma City, OK: Oklahoma University Press. (The main source for philosophers who do not read Nahuatl and who are interested in interpreting indigenous thought.)
  Morley, S. (1946) *The Ancient Maya*, Stanford, CA: Stanford University Press, 1983. (The story of the author's research into the Mayan past.)
* Netzahualcoyotl (*c.*1402–72) *Anales de Cuauhtitlan* (Review of Cuauhtitlan), in *Chimalpopoca Codex: Noticias históricas de México y sus contornos* (Chimalpopoca Codex: Historical Notices of Mexico and it Surroundings) Mexico: Imprenta de Escalante, 1885; trans. P.F. Velázquez, Mexico: Imprenta Universitaria, 1945. (The paleography of this text was also published in German in 1938.)
* Sahagún, B. de (*c.*1550) *General History of the Things of New Spain*, trans. C.E. Dibble and A.J.O. Anderson, Santa Fe, NM: School of American Research, 1970. (The complete translation of the Aztec text recording the pre-Colombian history of Mexico, written with the Latin alphabet by indigenous sages known as Sahagún's informers.)

LAURA MUES DE SCHRENK

LATIN AMERICAN LITERATURE, PHILOSOPHY IN *see* LITERATURE, PHILOSOPHY IN LATIN AMERICAN

LATITUDINARIANISM

The term 'Latitudinarianism' designated, initially abusively, the attitudes of a group of late seventeenth-century Anglican clergy who advocated ecclesiastical moderation, voiced broad if heavily qualified support for religious toleration, and emphasized an undogmatic probabilism, 'moral certainty', a reasoned faith and moral performance over against infallibility, dogma, ritual performance and 'unreasoning' faith. They attempted to construct a 'reasonable' faith, with some emphasizing belief in carefully evaluated miracles to attest to the central truths of Christianity. The Latitudinarians had considerable influence on the thought of John Locke, among others, although Locke's anti-clericalism, tolerationism and reticence on the Trinity went beyond their positions. The most important of the Latitudinarians, listed from the most eirenic to the least, were Edward Fowler, Benjamin Whichcote, John Wilkins, John Tillotson, Gilbert Burnet, Joseph Glanvill and Edward Stillingfleet; they were particu-

larly influenced by the thought of William Chilling-worth, the Cambridge Platonists and Hugo Grotius.

1 Lives, fallibility and attitudes towards toleration

The Latitudinarians were mainly educated during controversies between Catholics and Protestants over the 'Rule of Faith', during the attempts by many puritans in the English civil wars to impose their own brands of religion on others, backed by the certainties of 'conscience', and during a time when there was a proliferation of sects emphasizing the roles of illumination, grace and private revelation. The Latitudinarians' heroes of this period were eirenic Anglicans such as William CHILLINGWORTH and Viscount Falkland who had stressed, in contrast to both Puritans and Roman Catholic controversialists, humankind's fallibility, the need to proportion assent to the evidence, the limited number of fundamentals of Christianity and the legitimacy of differing opinions. Several of the Latitudinarians were, further-more, taught by the leading Cambridge Platonists and influenced especially by their emphases on reason and morality (see CAMBRIDGE PLATONISM).

The Latitudinarians reiterated many of the posi-tions of Chillingworth, Falkland and the Cambridge Platonists, stressing that the fundamentals of Christ-ianity were clear but should not be specified 'too forwardly', that differing opinions on other issues within Christianity were unavoidable, and that no particular form of church government was required by divine or natural law. They supported accommo-dating 'a latitude' of different practices and beliefs in a broad church, which they saw as a form of religious toleration, combined – with varying degrees of reluctance – with toleration for those few to be left outside. They supported the toleration provided by the Revolution of 1689 and rose at that point to occupy the highest offices in the Church of England. As Whichcote argued, 'our fallibility and the Short-ness of our Knowledge should make us peaceable and gentle: because I may be mistaken I must not be dogmatical' (Ashcraft *et al.* 1992: 236). For Burnet, it was from their allowance of 'great freedom both in philosophy and divinity' that they received the name of Latitudinarians. Their argument that no particular form of church was required by Christianity, their confidence that in fact they reasoned correctly and others were 'enthusiastic' and unreasonable, and their emphasis on peace and the authority of the civil

magistrate, were, however, often combined before 1689 with a preference for episcopacy and with an emphasis on the duty to unite in the civilly established church, limiting their tolerationism. The most im-portant works of the Latitudinarians enunciating these principles were Stillingfleet's *Irenicum* (1660) and, far less eirenic, his *Unreasonableness of Separa-tion* (1681), the *Brief Account of the New Sect of Latitude-Men* by 'S.P.' (1662), Tillotson's sermons and especially Edward Fowler's *Principles and Practices of Certain Moderate Divines* (1670).

2 Epistemology: certainty, 'moral certainty' and miracles

In a series of works and sermons John Tillotson, Edward Stillingfleet and John Wilkins refined and extended the arguments about knowledge made by Chillingworth earlier in the century. 'Absolute' infall-ibility was declared possible only for God. For Tillotson, however, a kind of 'conditional' infallibility was possible for humans. Immediate sense perception gave the highest assurance attainable by man alone. A similarly high level of certainty attached to demon-stration, most notably possible in the field of math-ematics. For demonstration, the denial of the conclusion necessarily involved a contradiction. Wilkins similarly described conditional 'infallible certainty' as associated both with the physical certainty derived from sense-data, the 'highest kind of Evidence, of which humane nature is capable' and with the mathematical certainty of matters of self-evidence, basic principles of logic, and deductions from these principles (Shapiro 1983: 85).

In most matters of religion, however, only the 'moral certainty' of belief and no higher level of certainty was possible. It was none the less sufficient. For Tillotson, such belief excluded 'reasonable cause' for a 'considerate Man' to doubt, but not 'all possibility of Mistake'. It thus involved a probability sufficiently high to call for 'a firm and undoubted assent' on grounds 'fit fully to satisfy a prudent man' (Van Leeusen 1970: 37). As Wilkins put it, there was an 'indubitable certainty' the objects of which did not compel assent but which were so plain, 'that every man whose judgment is free from prejudice will consent to them' (Shapiro 1983: 85–6). God was declared to be good, and so had created humans in such a way that they assented to evidence properly; only an unreasonable person would require more than the appropriate level of certainty. As Stillingfleet put it, God 'doth not require us to believe any thing without sufficient grounds for our believing it, and those grounds do bear a proportionable evidence to the nature of that assent which he requires' (Carroll 1975: 68).

These arguments were designed to counter those who were too dogmatic and those who were too sceptical. Dogmatists were unreasonable because many beliefs needed a far more careful assessment of testimony and evidence and a far more careful interpretation of the words of Scripture than they produced. Many beliefs could not reach the level of certainty that dogmatists claimed. Human knowledge was limited, and humans were subject to error. Sceptics were unreasonable because they wished for more certainty than was required, focused on 'subtilties', and ended with more doubt than was appropriate. Atheists were particularly unreasonable because they required more evidence for belief in the existence of God than was necessary, and neglected the testimony of the intelligent creation in the 'book of the world'. According to Tillotson, atheists were also unreasonable because, in quasi-Pascalian terms, they were imprudent in ignoring the 'danger' of choosing a few base pleasures when God might exist and if so would punish them exceedingly (see PASCAL, B. §6). Tillotson and Wilkins focused on the pursuit of happiness as a motivation to be religious, with man's dominant interest being happiness in the next life. As Wilkins put it, the 'rational and prudent man' should 'order his actions in favour of that way which appears to be most safe and advantageous for his own interest' (Shapiro 1983: 89). Emphasizing the morality taught in Revelation and by natural reason, and the role of God's rewards and punishments to motivate moral performance, the Latitudinarians effectively identified evangelical righteousness with natural righteousness.

For several of the Latitudinarians miracles had been crucial to generating appropriate belief: 'to confirm a Divine Testimony to the World, and to make that appear credible which otherwise would have seemed incredible' (Stillingfleet, cited in Carroll 1975: 68). Belief in such miracles depended on the credibility of their witnesses. Such credibility therefore needed to be assessed carefully in order to yield appropriate moral certainty. Writing many works against Roman Catholicism in his early years, Stillingfleet particularly sought to distinguish true miracles from false wonders, and to repudiate Catholic claims about the continued performance of miracles. He therefore set out a series of criteria to distinguish miracles from frauds: that miracles were wrought to confirm a divine testimony; that miracles did not contradict revelation; that they left divine effects on believers; that they tended to overthrow the devil's power; that the circumstances and manner of operation of the true differed from the false; and that

they evidently exceeded created power. For Stillingfleet, once Christianity was established, further miracles were unnecessary. Catholic claims were therefore false (see MIRACLES).

The arguments of Tillotson, Stillingfleet and Wilkins on proportioning assent to the evidence, the limitations of knowledge, the dependence of men upon appearances and the rejection as 'unreasonable' of scepticism, atheism, and dogmatism in favour of a reliance on 'moral certainty' were paralleled and extended in the fields of scientific enquiry and defences of natural religion in many other works by Latitudinarians and their associates, including Joseph Glanvill's *Vanity of Dogmatizing* (1661) and *Essays on Several Important Subjects in Philosophy and Religion* (1676), and many of the scientific works of Robert Boyle (see GLANVILL, J.; BOYLE, R.).

3 Locke and Latitudinarianism

LOCKE knew several Latitudinarians well, especially Tillotson and Fowler, and he indicated support for 'latitudinism' in his *Essay on Toleration*. The *Essay Concerning Human Understanding* (1689) presented a generalized philosophic statement significantly influenced by many elements of the Latitudinarians' account of the limitations of the human mind and proportioning of assent. Many of Locke's emphases on moralism, on God's rewards and punishments, and on the limited number of fundamentals of Christianity, were shared with the Latitudinarians. However, Locke restricted the term 'certainty' to that which is known to be true, and refused to apply it to that which was probable or 'morally certain'. Moreover, he argued that the idea of substance could not come from sensation or reflection, and made the idea of substance an idea of 'I know not what', effectively undercutting some of the Latitudinarians' attempts in the 1690s to defend the Trinity against the claims of deists and unitarians that the application of reason to religion supported their own more radical rejections of the Trinity or of Christianity itself (see DEISM). In reply to Locke, Stillingfleet utilized scholastic metaphysics in defence of the mysteries of religion, holding that substance was a 'rational idea' emanating from the soul itself. Other Latitudinarians, such as Tillotson, in general preferred to stress that the Trinity was to be believed as 'above' but not contrary to reason; Tillotson defended the Trinity in the 1690s. For their emphases on reason, morality and toleration, the Latitudinarians were often accused of Socinianism; Locke was closer to it (see SOCINIANISM).

See also: RELIGION, HISTORY OF PHILOSOPHY OF

References and further reading

* Ashcraft, R., Kroll, R. and Zagorin, P. (eds) (1992) *Philosophy, Science and Religion in England 1640–1700*, Cambridge: Cambridge University Press. (Especially useful are essays by Rogers on ignorance and toleration; Ashcraft on Latitudinarians and intolerance; Hutton on Stillingfleet and More; and Marshall on Locke and Latitudinarianism.)
* Carroll, R.T. (1975) *The Commonsense Philosophy of Religion of Bishop Edward Stillingfleet*, The Hague: Martinus Nijhoff. (Especially good on Stillingfleet's analysis of 'moral certainty', criteria for miracles, scholastic rationalism, and relative intolerance. See §2 above.)
* Fowler, E. (1670) *Principles and Practices of Certain Moderate Divines*, London. (A general statement of the eirenic principles of Latitudinarians.)
* Glanvill, J. (1661) *The Vanity of Dogmatizing: or Confidence in Opinions. Manifested in a Discourse of the Shortness and Incertainty of our Knowledge, and its Causes, with some reflections on Peripateticism; and an Apology for Philosophy*, London; repr. New York: Facsimile Text Society, Columbia University Press, 1931. (A work supporting proportioning assent to the evidence in the comprehension of nature.)
* —— (1676) *Essays on Several Important Subjects in Philosophy and Religion*, London. (Essays further articulating the ideas of *The Vanity of Dogmatizing*.)
* Locke, J. (1667) *Essay on Toleration*, in *John Locke: Writings on Politics, Law and Religious Toleration 1667–1683*, ed. J.R. Milton and P. Milton, Oxford: Oxford University Press, forthcoming. (An early tolerationist essay.)
* —— (1689) *An Essay Concerning Human Understanding*, ed. P.H. Nidditch, Oxford: Oxford University Press, 1975. (Locke's *magnum opus*, significantly influenced by latitudinarians' ideas.)
  Shapiro, B. (1983) *Probability and Certainty in Seventeenth- Century England*, Princeton, NJ: Princeton University Press. (A very useful survey of the relationships between issues of probability and certainty in natural science, religion, history, law and literature in seventeenth-century England.)
* S.P. (1662) *Brief Account of the New Sect of Latitude-Men*, London; repr. William Andrews Clark Library, University of California, 1963. (A defence and definition of ecclesiastical moderation against Roman Catholicism, fanaticism, atheism, enthusiasm and superstition.)
* Stillingfleet, E. (1660) *Irenicum*, London. (An eirenic early work emphasizing civil authority)
* —— (1662) *Origines Sacrae*, London. (A defence of the primacy and authenticity of Scripture.)
* —— (1681) *The Unreasonableness of Separation*, London. (A uniformitarian attack on nonconformist separation.)
* —— (1696) *A Vindication of the Doctrine of the Trinity*, London. (A scholastic metaphysical defence of the Trinity against deism, unitarianism and, less directly, against Locke's account of the limits of the understanding.)
  Tillotson, J. (1664) *The Wisdom of Being Religious*, London. (A quasi-utilitarian defence of religiosity.)
* —— (1666) *The Rule of Faith*, London. (Against Roman Catholics on standards of judgment in religious controversy.)
  Tulloch, J. (1966) *Rational Theology and Christian Philosophy*, Germany: Georg Olms Verlagsbuchhandlung, 2 vols. (Reprint of a nineteenth-century general survey of philosophy and theology; dated but still useful.)
  Wilkins, J. (1672) *Of the Principles and Duties of Natural Religion*, London. (A defence of natural religion; identifying natural morality and evangelical morality and emphasizing rewards.)
* Van Leeuwen, H. (1970) *The Problem of Certainty in English Thought 1630–90*, The Hague: Martinus Nijhoff. (A precise study of epistemology and certainty in the period leading up to and including the latitudinarians; excellent on the similarities and divergences of Locke and the latitudinarians.)

JOHN MARSHALL

LAVROV, PĚTR LAVROVICH (1823–1900)

*Pětr Lavrov was one of the main theorists of Russian populism (*narodnichestvo*) – a trend of thought and a movement which crystallized after the abolition of serfdom in Russia in 1861.*

There were many different currents within this broad trend but all of them concentrated on the possibility and desirability of securing a non-capitalist way of development for Russia. This was so because the populists, having perceived (often with the help of Marx's Capital*) the contradictions of capitalist development, lost their confidence in 'European' progress, recognized in capitalism only a regression and chose therefore an adamantly anti-capitalist stand, combined, as a rule, with backward-looking idealization of the peasant commune.*

The dominant Western theories of social evolution – from Spencerian liberalism to Marxism – strongly emphasized the 'objective' character of the laws of social development and defined capitalism as a necessary phase of progress. Russian populist socialists deeply felt that in Russia's backward condition such theories offered a convenient tool for apologists of capitalist progress, who sanctioned and justified the suffering of the masses by referring to the 'objective laws of history' or 'the iron laws of political economy'. This led them to a demonstrative rejection of the 'objectivist' conception of progress. Lavrov was the first populist theorist who set against 'objectivism' a conscious and systematic vindication of 'subjectivism'. He was supported in this by another populist thinker, Nikolai Mikhailovskii. The common features of their views have been labelled 'subjective sociology' or the 'subjective method'.

1 **Anthropologism**
2 **'Subjective method' and theory of history**
3 **Sociological conceptions**

1 Anthropologism

Pëtr Lavrovich Lavrov, the son of a wealthy Russian landowner, embarked in his youth on a military career. By 1858 he had already attained the rank of colonel. He was also interested in philosophy and sociology, and in 1860 published his first book, *Ocherki voprosov prakticheskoi filosofii* (Sketches in the Domain of Practical Philosophy), in which he defined his position as 'anthropologism'. In 1862 he became a member of the underground revolutionary organization Land and Freedom. In 1866 he was arrested and sentenced to exile in Vologda province. In February 1870 he managed to flee abroad, made contacts with the International Workingmen's Association and, in the next year, took part in the Paris Commune. From 1873 to 1876 he published, in Zurich and in London, an influential revolutionary periodical *Vperëd* (Forward).

Lavrov's initial philosophical position, as presented in *Ocherki voprosov prakticheskoi filosofii* and in his lectures 'On the Contemporary Significance of Philosophy' (1860), was directly connected with the antitheological and anti-Hegelian anthropologism of Ludwig FEUERBACH: it was conceived as the radical overcoming of speculative idealism, which reduced individuals to mere tools of Absolute Spirit, and as a philosophical vindication of really existing human beings, creatures of flesh and blood. The human person as an indivisible physical-psychological individual was for Lavrov the only indisputable datum and the necessary starting-point for a scientific philosophy. This entailed commitment to a sort of anthropocentric scientism and anthropological relati-

vism. Philosophical questions were interpreted as pertaining ultimately to man, to the human experience, while 'things-in-themselves' were excluded from the sphere of legitimate scientific knowledge. The relativistic component, inherent in this view, effectively undermined metaphysics but did not apply to ethics. Lavrov saw man as an ethical being and, following Kant, argued for the possibility of non-relative judgments in the sphere of 'practical reason'.

Lavrov took care to distinguish his position from positivistic scientism, based on the natural sciences. In the essay 'Zadachi positivizma i ikh reshenie' (The Tasks of Positivism and their Solution) (1868) he discussed different variants of positivist thought, recognized the centrality of positivism in contemporary intellectual life and fully endorsed the positivist commitment to strictly scientific methods. At the same time he criticized the one-sided 'objectivism' of contemporary positivism, setting against it the positivism of Auguste COMTE, which recognized the legitimacy of the 'subjective method'. His conclusion was that positivism proved incapable of solving its own problems because it lacked a unifying philosophical principle. This principle was man as a feeling and thinking being, a symbol of the true unity of mind and body. Thus, the historical role of positivism was only to pose problems – their solution would be provided by an anthropological philosophy whose germ could be found in Feuerbach, Proudhon and J.S. Mill.

2 'Subjective method' and theory of history

Lavrov's preoccupation with legitimizing the 'subjective method' reached a new level in his *Istoricheskie pis'ma* (*Historical Letters*) (first published, under the pseudonym 'Mirtov', in a Russian periodical, in 1868–9). This short book gained him immense popularity among young radicals, tormented by feelings of social guilt and eager to sacrifice their personal interests for the good of the masses.

Historical Letters owed this enormous success mainly to one chapter, 'The Price of Progress'. The possibility of talking about progress, argued Lavrov, has been dearly bought by the human race. The personal development of some members of the privileged classes has been purchased with the labour and suffering of many generations of heavily exploited people. The 'conscious minority' should never forget its debt and should make every effort to discharge it.

Lavrov's conviction that the 'debt to the people' must be paid off now was incompatible with the theory of progress as an objective and inevitable law of development. The 'objectivist' conception of progress had to be replaced by a 'subjectivist', ethical conception, based upon 'subjective sociology'.

The basic assumptions of Lavrov's 'subjectivism' can be embraced in three points. First, it was a defence of ethicism, a standpoint derived from a strong conviction that values are independent of facts, that moral evil cannot be 'scientifically' explained away, and that moral protest against suffering is valuable and obligatory irrespective of any 'objective' condition. Second, it was an epistemological and methodological position, which denied or disputed the possibility of 'objective' methods in the social sciences: it claimed that historical and sociological knowledge can never be value-free because it always depends upon the unconscious emotions or (much better) on the consciously chosen ideals of scholars. Third, it was a philosophy of history which maintained that the 'subjective factor' – human thought and will – can effectively oppose the spontaneous tendencies of development and play a decisive part in historical process. Lavrov based upon it his 'practical philosophy' which proclaimed that 'critically thinking individuals', having united in a party, could become a social force and change the existing state of affairs in the direction indicated by their 'subjective' aims.

In its application to methodological problems Lavrov's 'subjectivism' yielded an interesting epistemology of history, anticipating, to a certain extent, the revolt against positivism in the humanities. The so-called 'laws of history', he claimed, do not exist; historical events are always unique and unrepeatable. Historians cannot limit their task to the description of facts, since 'facts' are not something given; they have to be selected and endowed with meaning, which presupposes a creative activity on the part of the knower. In looking at history, therefore, the main problem is one of selection, of finding a criterion that will make it possible to pick out 'what is important and meaningful' from the amorphous mass of historical data. Such a criterion must be subjective because it depends on the social ideal adopted by a particular scholar. All facts are classified and all historical events interpreted according to how they relate to this ideal. Progress is a category required to impose order on the raw material of history. In itself, history has no meaning: there are many meanings to be found in it, but all of them are imparted to it by human individuals. Imposing a meaning on history presupposes an ideal not only in the sphere of historical understanding but also in the sphere of historical action. Human history begins therefore with the emergence of critically thinking individuals trying to shape society by means of 'criticism' and 'idealization'.

Lavrov formulated his own ideal as follows: 'The physical, intellectual, and moral development of the individual; the incorporation of truth and justice in social institutions'. Progressive approximation to this ideal was defined by him as a process that is being accomplished by means of the critical thought of individuals who aim at the transformation of their culture. By 'culture' Lavrov meant a static social structure based on religion, tradition and folk ways; by 'civilization' he meant a dynamic social structure in which religion was replaced by science, and custom by law. These two concepts were further developed in his sociological theory.

3   Sociological conceptions

With the decline of revolutionary populism in the 1880s Lavrov returned to scholarly work and produced several books in the field of historical sociology, such as *Opyt istorii mysli novogo vremeni* (Essay on the History of Modern Thought) (1888–94), *Zadachi ponimaniia istorii* (Problems in the Interpretation of History) (1898), and the posthumously published *Vazhneishie momenty istorii mysli* (Stages of Great Importance in the History of Thought) (1903). All these works reflect an influence of positivist evolutionism and thus appear to make considerable concessions to 'objectivism'. On closer examination, however, it turns out that it was only a change in emphasis. In *Historical Letters* Lavrov made a distinction between history, which deals with what is unique, and sociology, which aims at discovering certain overall laws of development. Later, in an article, 'O metode v sotsiologii' (On Method in Sociology), he clearly stated that in sociology, in contrast to history, both methods – the subjective and the objective – were justified and applicable. Recognizing the legitimacy of the 'objectivist' approach did not change this view that conscious, subjectively motivated actions were axiologically infinitely superior to 'natural' processes, assuming the form of 'objective laws'.

Lavrov defined sociology as a science dealing with the forms of social solidarity, which he divided into three main types. The first was the unconscious solidarity of custom; the second was a purely emotional solidarity, based on impulses not controlled by critical reflection; the third was 'conscious historical solidarity' resulting from a common effort to attain a consciously selected and rationally justified goal. This third type represented the highest and most important form of human solidarity. It evolved later than the first two types and heralded the process of the transformation of static 'culture' into dynamic 'civilization'.

In his conception of the motive force of history

437

Lavrov consciously avoided reductionism. Social evolution, he thought, was stimulated by the individual's diverse needs. Among biological needs the most important was the need for food, which stimulated economic development. But apart from biological needs, characterizing humanity as an animal species, there were also specifically historical needs, constituting the historical dimension of human existence. The most important of these was the disinterested 'need for development' typical of 'critically thinking individuals'. Lavrov believed that this need was becoming more and more important.

Lavrov's overall conception of social evolution was tied to the Saint-Simonian and Comtian notion of history as a succession of 'organic' and 'critical' phases. Historical progress moved along a spiral in an accelerating rhythm – its successive stages were growing shorter, and the difference between organic and critical periods was constantly diminishing. This was because historical evolution offered growing opportunities to achieve a harmonious fusion of solidarity and development, order and progress.

Regardless of their scholarly value, Lavrov's sociological conceptions are of great interest as a historical document. They reveal Lavrov as an ideologist of the intelligentsia, the author of an extremely influential and truly classical conception of the intelligentsia's historical mission. Some scholars have suggested that his writings were an expression of a specific 'intellectual aristocratism', or even of certain characteristic aspects of the gentry mentality (the view of the masses as an inert herd, combined with a sense of guilt). Such views were being formulated even within the populist movement; their most extreme exponent was Pëtr Tkachëv (1844–86), a 'Jacobin' populist, who accused Lavrov of betraying egalitarianism and paving the way for the transformation of the intelligentsia into a new ruling class. In fact, however, Lavrov consciously distanced himself from the theories of intelligentsia as a 'new class', such as the Comtian theory of an intellectual elite that would govern the hierarchically stratified society of the future. For him the intelligentsia was first and foremost the *moral* elite, the conscience of society, not an aristocracy of intellect; intellectually bright and educated people who were selfishly indifferent to the fate of the suffering masses were defined by him as 'cultural savages', not members of the intelligentsia. He was therefore a leading theorist and spokesman of the intelligentsia as an ethical category, that is, in the nineteenth-century Russian meaning of the term.

See also: MIKHAILOVSKII, N.K.; POSITIVISM IN THE SOCIAL SCIENCES; POSITIVISM, RUSSIAN

List of works

—— (1860) *Ocherki voprosov prakticheskoi filosofii* (Sketches in the Domain of Practical Philosophy), St Petersburg: Glazunov. (Lavrov's first book, in which he defined his position as 'anthropologism'.)

—— (1870) *Istoricheskie pis'ma*; trans. and introduced by J.P. Scanlan, *Historical Letters*, Berkeley, CA, 1967. (Lavrov's best-known work, first published under the pseudonym P.L. Mirtov.)

—— (1965) *Filosofiia i sotsiologiia: izbrannye proizvedeniia*, Moscow: Mysl', 2 vols. (Provides a representative selection of Lavrov's philosophical and sociological works in Russian.)

References and further reading

Copleston, F.C. (1986) *Philosophy in Russia. From Herzen to Lenin and Berdyaev*, Kent: Search Press and Notre Dame, IN: University of Notre Dame, ch. 6.

Hecker, J.F. (1915) *Russian Sociology: A Contribution to the History of Sociological Thought and Theory*, New York. (A good outline of Lavrov's philosophical sociology.)

Kareev, N.I. (1907) *Teoriia lichnosti P.L. Lavrova* (P.L. Lavrov's Theory of Personality), St Petersburg. (The classic work on Lavrov's philosophy of man from pre-Revolutionary Russia.)

Ladokha, G. (1927) 'Istoricheskie i sotsiologicheskie vozzreniia P.L. Lavrova', in M.N. Pokrovskii (ed.), *Russkaia istoricheskaia literatura v klassovom osveshchenii*, Moscow. (An interesting Marxist analysis of Lavrov's sociology and philosophy of history.)

Pomper, P. (1972) *Peter Lavrov and the Russian Revolutionary Movement*, Chicago.

Sorokin, P.A. (1922) 'Osnovnye problemy sotsiologii P.L. Lavrova' (Main Problems in Lavrov's Sociology), in *P.L. Lavrov. Stat'i, vospominaniia, materialy*, Petrograd: Kolos. (A detailed analysis.)

Walicki, A. (1979) *A History of Russian Thought From the Enlightenment to Marxism*, Stanford, CA: Stanford University Press, ch. 12; Oxford: Clarendon Press, 1980. (Provides a general outline of Lavrov's philosophy and sociological theory.)

ANDRZEJ WALICKI

LAW AND MORALITY

Within the tradition of natural law thinking which finds its roots in the philosophies of Aristotle and Aquinas, the political community has generally been understood

in terms of a fundamental goal: that of fostering the ethical good of citizens. Law, on this conception, should seek to inculcate habits of good conduct, and should support a social environment which will encourage citizens to pursue worthy goals, and to lead valuable lives. Pragmatic considerations may sometimes suggest the wisdom of restraint in the pursuit of these goals, and citizens may therefore, on appropriate occasions, be left free to indulge depraved tastes or otherwise fall short of acceptable standards. Such pragmatic arguments for the freedom to engage in vice, however, do not call into question the legitimacy of the state's concern with individual morality.

By contrast the liberal tradition has tended to place constraints of principle upon the scope and aims of the law. The most influential such attempt was J.S. Mill's advocacy of 'the harm principle': that the law may forbid only such behaviour as is liable to cause harm to persons other than the agent. Many difficulties surround this and other, more recent, attempts to formulate and defend constraining principles. For instance, should one take into account only the immediate effects of behaviour, or more remote and diffuse effects as well? Thus it is argued that immoral behaviour which in the short term 'harms nobody' may, in the long run, lead to a decline in morality in society at large and thereby to diffuse harmful effects.

1 **Two traditions**
2 **Mill's 'harm principle'**
3 **The Hart/Devlin debate**
4 **Dworkin on 'external preferences'**

1 Two traditions

The attempt to delimit principles which confine and constrain the proper scope of legal and governmental interference is inseparable from the liberal tradition: one need only think of Locke's attempt to define such a sphere of legitimacy by reference to a body of natural rights. Yet the attempt to delineate such principles has not always focused in a clear and circumscribed way upon the particular problem of an allegedly private sphere of morality. Thus when Locke, in his *Letter Concerning Toleration* (1689), seeks to defend religious toleration, he seems to do so not by reliance on his theory of natural rights and social contract, but by means of a pragmatic argument which would have sat comfortably within the assumptions of the Thomist natural law tradition: intolerance is, for Locke, pointlessly ineffectual rather than a violation of a distinct constraining political principle (see LOCKE, J. §1). Debate began to focus clearly on the idea of constraining principles precluding the state from interference with private immor-

ality only in consequence of essays such as Wilhelm von Humboldt's *The Sphere and Duties of Government* (published posthumously in 1852) and J.S. Mill's *On Liberty* (1859) (see §2 below). The latter work has exerted the most fundamental influence in English-speaking countries.

Before we examine Mill's claims, however, it is worth making a couple of preliminary points. In particular, we should reflect upon the diverse motivations which may underpin rejection of the Aristotelian tradition of political thought, and may lead to the search for principles constraining the community's entitlement to enforce 'private' moral standards. It is often thought that the liberal is committed to a 'subjectivist' or noncognitivist understanding of moral judgment, and that the liberal concern for tolerance is simply a consequence of such subjectivism (see MORAL JUDGMENT §1). Such an interpretation must, however, be a mistake: for, if moral judgments are simply expressions of subjective emotion or attitude, this must apply to moral judgments about the importance of tolerance along with all other moral judgments. A better reading of liberalism would see it as flowing from the inability to reach *agreement* on moral questions, rather than from the supposedly 'subjective' character of moral judgments. This reading does not succumb to the self-subverting character of an appeal to subjectivism, but it does have its problems. In some versions, for example, it can seem to imply that the need for consensus among those who disagree is the rationale for restricting the state's role; but this seems to make the argument for tolerance dependent upon the existence of a balance of power between contending factions.

Finally, one popular line of defence claims that liberalism is reliant neither upon moral subjectivism nor upon the inconclusive nature of moral argument, but upon the value of autonomous choice: it is good that people choose their own projects and lifestyles, even when they choose degrading or unworthy options (see AUTONOMY, ETHICAL). The problem posed by this approach is that it is not wholly clear that the approach can be contrasted in any very fruitful way with the concerns of the Aristotelian tradition. After all, the Aristotelian might claim that *being freely chosen* is an essential condition of a good life, so that the state's concern to encourage good lives itself dictates a concern to protect autonomy. Viewed from this perspective, the debate with liberalism would seem to be a pragmatic argument within the parameters of the Aristotelian tradition.

Such a reconceptualization of the terrain might well be viewed as damaging by many liberals. For many of the critics of Mill and of more recent liberals have directed their fire at the very idea of abstract principles constraining legitimate interference with a realm of supposedly 'private' conduct. They have been less concerned to oppose the concrete applications of these principles advocated by the liberals themselves. A characteristic example is James Fitzjames Stephen, who, in his book *Liberty, Equality, Fraternity*, wrote as follows:

> I object rather to Mr. Mill's theory than to his practical conclusions....The objection which I make to most of his statements on the subject is, that in order to justify in practice what might be justified on narrow and special grounds, he lays down a theory incorrect in itself and tending to confirm views which might become practically mischievous.
>
> (1873: 74)

2 Mill's 'harm principle'

Mill proposes what he describes as a 'very simple principle' as being 'entitled to govern absolutely the dealings of society with the individual in the way of compulsion and control'. The principle asserted that 'The only purpose for which power can rightfully be exercised over any member of a civilised community, against his will, is to prevent harm to others' ([1859] 1956: 13).

Mill's 'harm principle' has sometimes been taken to suggest an atomistic view of society such that there is an area of private conduct which does not impinge on others at all, and which falls outside the law's proper domain for that reason. As his critics were quick to point out, only the most trivial actions are devoid of effects upon others. In spite of the encouragement that Mill gives to this interpretation in some of his language, however, he explicitly conceded that 'self-regarding' actions may nevertheless affect other people. His principle is not intended to demarcate an area of conduct that is beyond the law's remit, so much as a type of reason to which the community should restrict itself: in considering whether an action should be prohibited, only *some* of the effects of an action should be taken into account. In particular, the action's effects in 'harming' others may be taken account of, while the effects upon the actor himself must be disregarded, as must the disapproval of unaffected third parties who consider the act immoral (see PATERNALISM §2).

In other ways, however, the suggestion that Mill adopts an unduly 'atomistic' view might seem to have some validity. For, if the harm principle is construed as prescribing a focus on fairly immediate and individuated harms, it may lead us to neglect the importance of sustaining social institutions that may be undermined in more oblique ways by the law's failure to uphold conventional moral standards. One reply to this line of attack might be that nothing in the harm principle compels such a narrowly individuated focus: if the erosion of some social institution *is* a probable consequence of liberalization in an area of conduct, and if that erosion would be harmful, the harm principle legitimates our taking such considerations into account. The reply is problematic, however, in so far as a harm principle which invites us to take account of quite remote and diffuse effects threatens to prove empty and insubstantial in application. Mill himself is quite ready to accept that highly diffuse effects upon others can constitute 'harm' (he is, for example, critical on this ground of the unrestricted right to procreate) but the concession does represent an erosion of the integrity of the principle.

A number of other serious problems are associated with the harm principle. One question concerns the compatibility of the principle with Mill's commitment to utilitarianism (see UTILITARIANISM). For should not a utilitarian legislator take account of *all* of the effects of an action, before deciding upon its prohibition? If some people suffer deep unhappiness at the very thought of acts of which they disapprove being performed in private, how can this unhappiness be justifiably *ignored* from the viewpoint of utility? It has been suggested that a utilitarian legislator should disregard such unhappiness in so far as it flows from the adoption of nonutilitarian moral views. But even if this argument could be sustained, it would not go far enough: I may be upset by the thought of acts which I consider simply disgusting rather than immoral; and, in any case, the exclusion of harm to the actor himself remains unexplained by this approach.

It is likely that Mill saw the harm principle as an intermediate maxim, by which utilitarians should regulate their conduct, with the ultimate objective of advancing overall happiness in the long run. Such a view avoids inconsistency, however, only at the price of rendering the entire case dependent on largely empirical claims about the long-term effects of individual liberty. Mill's defence of the harm principle could in this way be thought to manifest an undue and ungrounded optimism. Given the aggregative conception of the common good espoused by utilitarianism, it would be remarkably fortunate if the best way of advancing the collective welfare was invariably to protect individual freedoms.

Quite apart from the compatibility or otherwise of the harm principle with Mill's utilitarianism, however, is the question of the meaning of 'harm' itself. For it has been repeatedly and justifiably pointed out that the question of what constitutes harm is an evaluative question which cannot in the end be separated from our wider ethical beliefs. Attempts, such as that of Joel Feinberg (1984), to analyse harm in terms of setbacks to interests simply reformulate the problem as one concerning the nature and content of our interests. Yet, without some morally neutral account of harm, Mill's principle seems to do little to exclude criminal prohibitions which are simply based upon moral disapproval of the actor's conduct. Consider, for example, the harm principle in its application to the debate about pornography. One issue concerns the suggestion that pornography fosters a social environment within which violent crimes against women are more likely: this argument appeals to an uncontroversial instance of harm, but makes the issue depend upon highly contestable empirical theses about the effects of pornography. What then if someone suggests that women are harmed *intrinsically* by pornography, in the sense that all women are harmed when some women are depicted as being objects available for sexual gratification? This suggestion employs a notion of harm which might not be universally accepted, but it challenges us to articulate criteria for what is to be regarded as harm (see PORNOGRAPHY).

A relevant suggestion has been made (in a slightly different context) by Brian Barry. He suggests (1995) that 'harm' might be defined in terms of what the great majority of people, having divergent conceptions of the good, would nevertheless agree upon as 'bad'. The suggestion builds upon the sound insight that people may have divergent ethical conceptions which nevertheless have an extensive area of overlap; but in requiring something short of complete universality and unanimity, Barry's approach seems in danger of making the scope of the harm principle itself depend upon majoritarian politics of a kind that Mill was concerned to constrain.

The above arguments may or may not be fatal to Mill's position. They do not render the harm principle wholly vacuous, because that principle serves, at a minimum, to direct our attention to an action's effects on others, rather than on the actor himself; but, if sound, the arguments dramatically reduce the value of the principle as a limitation upon the proper scope of the state's coercive power.

Even the requirement that we should have regard only to effects upon others may be a less substantial constraint than it seems, for we must remember Mill's acceptance of diffuse effects as 'harm'. Acts which are widely considered to be immoral may, in the first instance, affect only the actor himself; but, by creating a communal environment in which such acts are tolerated, they may make it harder (for example) to educate children into moral standards of conduct.

When combined with the impossibility of offering a morally neutral account of the nature of 'harm', such diffuse effects seem to reduce the significance of Mill's principle to vanishing point.

3 The Hart/Devlin debate

A concern for such diffuse effects of immoral conduct lies at the bottom of an argument presented by Lord Devlin in 1959, in a British Academy Maccabean Lecture in Jurisprudence. Lord Devlin was then a judge of the Queen's Bench Division of the High Court, becoming a Lord of Appeal in 1961. His Maccabean Lecture arose out of the Wolfenden Report on Homosexual Offences and Prostitution, which had been published in 1957, and which had articulated the principle that 'private immorality' should not be the concern of the criminal law. Devlin criticized this approach, on the ground that society depends for its survival upon the existence of a shared morality, and that it was therefore in principle possible for grossly immoral conduct to threaten the survival of the society. Consequently, society has a right to enforce its shared morality as a measure of self-protection. Devlin was concerned, not with the truth or falsehood of the relevant moral views, but solely with the fact that they were widely shared and fundamental to the society's stability (Devlin 1965).

H.L.A. HART responded to Devlin's assault by pointing to the absence of empirical support for Devlin's claims that immorality could lead to social breakdown (Hart 1963). But it has more recently been suggested (George 1993) that Devlin had in mind not a breakdown in social order so much as a loss of social cohesion, where people relate to each other purely on a basis of self-interest rather than on a basis of moral principle. If this interpretation is correct, it would make Devlin's claim both more plausible and less open to empirical refutation or confirmation.

Devlin acknowledged a debt to the Victorian judge and jurist James Fitzjames Stephen, whose book *Liberty, Equality, Fraternity* (1873) was a forceful attack upon Mill's theory. Stephen's approach was utilitarian in character, but he regarded Mill as having departed from the consistent utilitarianism of Bentham and James Mill. Hart described the works of Stephen and Devlin as revealing 'the outlook characteristic of the English judiciary' (Hart 1963).

4 Dworkin on 'external preferences'

The 'goal-based' approach of utilitarianism is rejected by Ronald DWORKIN in favour of what he calls a 'rights-based' approach; but, in reality, there are good grounds for considering his position to be a modified form of utilitarianism, rather than a radical rejection of that approach. Dworkin takes the view that, in so far as utilitarianism possesses any genuine moral appeal, that appeal is a consequence of the extent to which it expresses our belief in a 'right to equal concern and respect'. He argues, however, that the notion of equal concern and respect receives inadequate expression within utilitarianism to the extent that the utilitarian takes account not only of 'personal preferences' (preferences for what I myself do and receive) but also of 'external preferences' (my preferences about what others do or receive). A proper concern for equality would exclude the influence of external preferences by recognizing a 'right to moral independence': the right not to suffer disadvantage simply on the ground that others consider one's conceptions of a good life to be ignoble or wrong (Dworkin 1985).

Dworkin believes that rights are best understood as 'trumps' over collective goals, and that, consequently, their philosophical justification is in part relative to the goals which have been adopted. The problem with taking account of external preferences (if a utilitarian goal has been adopted) is that the external preferences 'purport to occupy the same space' as the utilitarian theory itself: utilitarianism must be neutral between pushpin and poetry, but it cannot be neutral between itself and Nazism (for example) (Dworkin 1985: 363).

Dworkin insists that this argument holds even when the external preferences are not based on any general moral or political theory: they still 'invade the space claimed by neutral utilitarianism'. It is difficult to see how this argument can be sustained, however. One cannot argue, for example, that a preference 'invades the space of utilitarianism' simply because, if fully satisfied, it would necessitate a distribution not recommended by utilitarianism. Such an approach would prescribe a decision procedure which was viciously circular: for one would have to decide upon the requirements of utility before one could say whether any particular preference should be taken into account in calculating those requirements.

In any case, could it not be said that Dworkin's approach fails to show equal concern for those whose wellbeing or utility is a function of their external preferences? Suppose that my sole concern is your welfare, and my life will be a failure if your happiness is not secure. How can equality of concern dictate that my wellbeing should be disregarded?

Many will consider that the proposed 'right to moral independence' is more attractive than is the justification which Dworkin proposes for it; but then, few if any theorists have argued that people should be disadvantaged simply in consequence of a widely held disapproval of their lifestyles, so perhaps the 'right' is not very substantial after all.

See also: LAW, LIMITS OF §4; LIBERALISM; NATURAL LAW; PRIVACY; RULE OF LAW (RECHTSSTAAT); TOLERATION

References and further reading

* Barry, B. (1995) *Justice as Impartiality*, Oxford: Oxford University Press. (An intelligent development of some recent liberal political theory.)
* Devlin, P. (1965) *The Enforcement of Morals*, Oxford: Oxford University Press. (A vigorously argued and provocative work.)
* Dworkin, R. (1985) *A Matter of Principle*, Cambridge, MA: Harvard University Press. (Parts Three and Six are particularly helpful.)
* Feinberg, J. (1984) *Harm to Others*, Oxford: Oxford University Press. (Feinberg attempts to explain 'harm' in terms of setbacks to 'interests'.)
—— (1990) *Harmless Wrongdoing*, Oxford: Oxford University Press. (A clear and helpful survey of many of the basic issues.)
* George, R.P. (1993) *Making Men Moral*, Oxford: Oxford University Press. (A clear and accessible discussion, which could form a good starting point for the beginner, in spite of being written from a standpoint which is quite critical of liberalism.)
* Hart, H.L.A. (1963) *Law, Liberty, Morality*, Oxford: Oxford University Press. (A work of elegance and clarity that repays detailed study.)
* Locke, J. (1689) *A Letter Concerning Toleration*, J. Horton and S. Mendys (eds), London: Routledge, 1991. (A classic text in the early development of liberal thought.)
* Mill, J.S. (1859) *On Liberty*, Indianapolis, IN: Bobbs-Merrill, 1956. (A classic work which has shaped the character of modern liberalism.)
* Stephen, J.F. (1873) *Liberty, Equality, Fraternity*, intro. by R. Posner, Chicago, IL: University of Chicago Press, 1991. (A robust and colourful period piece.)

N.E. SIMMONDS

LAW AND RITUAL IN CHINESE PHILOSOPHY

The contrast between li, *conventionally translated as 'rites' or 'rituals', and* fa, *conventionally translated as 'law', marks a distinction in Chinese political theory as to the nature of political order and the preferred means* of achieving such order. Lizhi, traditionally associated with Confucianism, refers to political order predicated on and achieved primarily by reference to the li or 'rites', that is, traditional customs, mores and norms. In contrast, fazhi, associated with Legalism, refers to political order attained primarily through reliance on fa or 'laws', that is, publicly promulgated, codified standards of general applicability backed up by the coercive power of the state.

The tension between these two dominant strategies for achieving social and political order – lizhi and fazhi – is a theme that began in the classical tradition and has persisted down to the present day, even though the understanding of li and fa and the relation between them has changed and evolved over the years. For example, some thinkers saw li as context-specific, flexible norms or standards of a particular culture. Others saw li as more permanent, general standards. Some objected to the codification of li and fa; others favoured it. Some saw li and fa as interdependent, equally important and mutually reinforcing; others relied predominantly on one to the detriment, if not total exclusion, of the other.

Accordingly, it is not possible to speak of a single conception of li (lizhi) or fa (fazhi). Nevertheless, one must extract or highlight certain general or dominant features that tend to characterize lizhi and fazhi and to distinguish the one from the other, if one is to make use of this important contrast as a hermeneutical tool for interpreting, explaining and understanding a central debate in Chinese political philosophy. In reflecting on the importance of the lizhi versus fazhi distinction, five salient points emerge.

First, advocates of lizhi have tended to favour less formal means of conflict resolution than advocates of fazhi. The former believe that informal methods foster more particularized justice; the latter believe such methods provide excessive discretionary authority to those in power and thus foster abuse. Accordingly, publicly promulgated rules or laws are necessary.

Second, and a corollary to the first, fa or 'laws' are more formal norms of greater general applicability than the li, which in most instances consist of the web of informal context- and culture-specific rules that provide guidance for appropriate civil interaction in daily life among the various members of a certain community. Fazhi, therefore, is more of an externally imposed order that requires of the individual compliance more than participation. In contrast, lizhi proponents view order as emerging out of a particular context, a particular community of people. Society is what those who comprise it choose and make it to be. Participation rather than mere compliance is central.

Third, and again a corollary, lizhi and fazhi mark a contrast in the goals and aspirations of society.

Advocates of lizhi tend to be more optimistic about human kind and the possibility of achieving a harmonious social order in which each person is able to find their place and play their chosen role. They tend to see society, social order, humanity, as an achievement. If human beings are willing to put aside narrowly selfish and provincial concerns, if they are willing to defer to the excellence of others and to cooperate in the project of creating a harmonious social order in which each has a place, then such an order is possible. In the process, one becomes a better person. Put differently, one's potential for individual and personal growth is inextricably bound up with the fate of society.

In contrast, many of the fazhi persuasion take a dimmer view of human nature. Humans are by and large self-interested beings. Left to their own devices, the strong will exploit the weak; the powerful will abuse the powerless. Impartial rules are necessary to limit what one person can do to another. Laws provide this minimum layer of protection, this floor below which society cannot sink and remain a peaceful, and arguably just, society. Of course law may play a more positive role as well; recourse to general laws may simply be an efficient way to ensure an equitable distribution of social resources, for example. At the end of the day, however, advocates of fazhi have been primarily concerned with the use of fa as a corrective to the abuses and weaknesses of li. Thus law's role in ensuring a minimal floor of protection, a base equality, has been underscored, explaining in part the rather negative image of law in China through the ages. In contrast, the positive side of law, the empowering aspect of rights, the ability to use law as a vehicle for social change, has been central to many Westerners' conception of law.

Fourth, as might perhaps be expected, there has been no clear victor in the lizhi versus fazhi controversy. No system is perfect; no one has yet achieved the perfect means for realizing social order. Many of the same issues confront every society: how to achieve fairness and justice for all while at the same time recognizing the uniqueness of each person and each situation, and thereby achieve justice for each; how to provide those in power the necessary discretionary authority to mete out a particularized justice without falling prey to personal prejudice, bias, corruption and abuse; how to ensure that individuals have sufficient rights to shield themselves against each other and the state, and yet simultaneously encourage people not to wield those rights as weapons in endless litigation aimed at maximizing one's own personal interests to the detriment of society's interests; how to ensure that law will be a tool of the disempowered to effect social change and not simply a tool for exploitation and legitimation by those in power; how to implement a formal rule of *law with institutional integrity and independence, overseen by professionals, and yet prevent the institution from becoming overly bureaucratic and law the esoteric province of the professional lawyer. The* li *versus* fa *distinction, although not a perfect fit, is useful as a way to organize Chinese thinking on, and approaches to, these and similar issues.*

A fifth and final introductory point is that both lizhi *and* fazhi, *as they have developed in China, have failed in two important respects. First, they have failed to provide effective restraints on the power of the ruler, especially institutional restraints. Second, they have failed to adequately address the need to protect the individual against the state. Again, this failure is largely institutional, although like the failure to adequately restrain the power of the ruler, it can also be traced back to certain underlying philosophical assumptions common to both the* lizhi *and* fazhi *traditions. These assumptions include the rejection of three key assumptions of the western liberal tradition: (1) that someone to treat someone with respect and as one's equal requires that one refrain from imposing one's view on them (the normative equality premise); (2) that each person knows what is best for themselves and/or people reasonably disagree about what constitutes the good (the epistemic equality premise); and (3) that the interests of the individual and state may not be, and arguably are not, reconcilable.*

1   Context

Chinese philosophical thinking has always been elitist. Few Chinese thinkers would accept the liberal assumption (the epistemic equality premise) that no person or group possesses superior moral insight. From the pre-historical mythical ancestors of China, Yao and Shun, to the Confucian sage-rulers of the Warring States period, to Mao Zedong and Deng Xiaoping in the twentieth century, Chinese leaders have been credited with an uncanny ability to fathom what is in the best interests of society and its individual members. Indeed, much of their authority to rule is predicated on their claim to special ethical

insight and unique political knowledge of the way of rulership.

The rejection of the epistemic equality premise calls into question the normative equality premise (for liberals, the latter also follows as the conclusion of the former): in other words, that to treat someone with respect is to refrain from imposing one's normative views on them. In China, the government has pursued a substantive moral agenda defined in large part by the particular normative vision of the ruler. Chinese governments have been and continue to be paternalistic (much to the dismay of Americans who find, for example, Singapore's public flogging of juvenile delinquents and prohibitions on chewing gum objectionable). The image of the father dominates the political rhetoric of China. To be sure, the specifics of the image vary by school. The Confucian (*lizhi*) father-ruler is kind and compassionate and more of a facilitator of order than a dictator, whereas the Legalist father-ruler (*fazhi*) is the tough disciplinarian who well understands that to spare the rod is to spoil the child. Nevertheless, the image remains the same: the father, knowing what is best, takes care of his children.

Paternalism is on the whole antithetical to individual rights (see PATERNALISM). Not surprisingly, individual rights have not been and are not a prominent feature of the political landscape of China. There are of course many reasons for China's lack of a strong tradition of individual rights – which, we do well to recall, is a singular phenomenon, until this century virtually unique to the Enlightenment and post-Enlightenment West. One of the reasons for the lack of a strong rights tradition in China is the assumption that the interests of the state and the individual can be brought into harmony, an assumption particularly prevalent among *lizhi* thinkers but also present in many *fazhi* proponents. Given this assumption, it is suggested there is no need for rights to protect the individual against the state.

Ironically, even among contemporary Chinese rights advocates, few have taken note of, much less celebrated, the anti-majoritarian role of rights as 'trumps' on the collective good and the interests of society as a whole. Indeed, it is not at all clear that even the most ardent Chinese rights advocates would agree with Ronald DWORKIN that individual rights trump the overall social good or with John RAWLS that 'each person possesses an inviolability founded on justice that even the welfare of society as a whole cannot override.' In fact, it is not at all clear that Chinese rights thinkers conceive of rights as anything other than a kind of interest, to be weighed against other interests, including the interests of the majority, the collective, society and the nation. In contrast, most Western rights proponents conceive of rights as moral ends in themselves, deontic in character, and thus different in kind from interests, which are consequentialist or utilitarian in character (see RIGHTS). The difference between rights understood instrumentally as interests versus rights as trumps, moral principles or ends in themselves is not only theoretically fundamental but of utmost practical importance. Translating rights into the language of interests generally has the effect of decreasing the likelihood that rights will be taken seriously. When weighed against the interests of society as a whole, or against the state, the interests of society and the state will usually prevail. This is probably all the more likely in China, given the historical tendency to privilege the interests of the group and the state over the interests of the individual when those interests conflict.

The *li* and *fa* systems as developed to date in China have yet to adequately address the twin issues of restraints on the ruler and individual rights (which set restraints on the state and the majority *vis-à-vis* the individual). Arguably, *fazhi*, with its emphasis on impartial laws of general applicability, provides a more likely source for both effective restraints on the those in power and effective individual rights. Thus it is not surprising that one increasingly sees raised the banner of *fazhi*, which increasingly represents a rule of law along Western lines, with an institutionally independent and professionalized judiciary assigned the role of checking the legislative and executive branches and safeguarding individual rights. Nevertheless, the weight of the past continues to be felt. It is important therefore to understand the *li–fa* debate, and to understand the *li–fa* debate, one must return to the source.

2 Confucius' classical conception of *lizhi*

The *locus classicus* for *lizhi* is the *Analects* of Confucius:

Lead the people with government regulations and organize them with penal law (*xing*), and they will avoid punishments but will be without shame. Lead them with virtue and organize them through the *li*, and the people will have a sense of shame and moreover will become humane people of good character.

(*Analects*)

Confucius maintained that to rely solely or even predominantly on law to achieve social order was folly. Laws, backed up by punishments, may induce compliance in the external behaviour of individuals, but they are powerless to transform the inner character of the members of society.

Confucius' goal was not simply a stable political order in which everyone coexists in relative harmony and isolation, with each afraid to interfere with the other for fear of legal punishment. Rather, Confucius set his sights considerably higher. He sought to achieve a harmonious social order in which each person is able to realize their full potential as a human being through mutually beneficial relations with others.

For Confucius, society is the medium through which one becomes a human being. That is, one becomes a human being, a humane person, by virtue of participation in society. Personhood and humanity are functions of socialization. At birth, before the process of enculturation, of becoming humane, humans are not different from the other beasts. If one does not or is not willing to participate in society and enter into harmonious relations with others, one remains at the level of a beast; one is human *qua* member of a biological species. By turning their back on society, the bestial person (literally *xiaoren*, 'small person') fails to utilize the cognitive, aesthetic and spiritual powers which distinguish humans from other species. It is just the engagement of these capacities in joining with others to shape a new world, to create a significantly different and better society and to overcome one's natural conditions in achieving innovative resolutions to conflicts, that is distinctive about humans. If one cannot overcome the passions, instincts and desires that one shares with other beasts, if one wars against all and resorts to violence and brute strength to fulfil one's narcissistic wants, then one fails to become truly human, to achieve humanity.

Of course there will always be those who turn their back on society, who refuse to participate in creating a harmonious order and insist on pursuing their narrow self-interest in any manner possible. For such people, law and punishments are necessary. Confucius, ever practical, did not advocate the complete abandonment of laws. Nevertheless, the goal is to foster an environment in which laws need to be imposed as little as possible: 'In hearing litigation I am much the same as anyone. If you insist on a difference, it is perhaps that I try to get the parties not to resort to litigation.' For Confucius, the ethical and political challenge is to inspire in the many members of society the desire to achieve a humane society and to encourage them to direct their energies toward the attainment of a harmonious social order. What is being required is a willingness to participate in collective living, to search for a cooperative solution, to become humane (*ren*) (see CONFUCIAN PHILOSOPHY, CHINESE §5).

For Confucius, the codification and public dissemination of laws sends the wrong kind of message. Laws are designed to protect the minimum interests of the members of society and to provide a mechanism for dealing with and removing those individuals who are not only unwilling to participate in fostering a harmonious social order, but whose behaviour threatens the well-being of others and the ability of society to function. Making the laws public focuses attention, not on the achievement of the highest quality of social harmony possible, but on the lowest level of participation required by society. Consequently, it may encourage some persons to look only to manipulate the system for their own advantage. Thus we find Confucius criticizing the state of Jin for publicly promulgating laws: 'Jin is going to ruin. It has lost its proper rules.... But now when those rules are abandoned and tripods with penal laws on them are cast instead, the people will study the tripods, and not care to honour men of rank.' The proto-Confucian *Shu Xiang* adds:

> In antiquity, the former kings considered the particular circumstances in regulating affairs. They did not make public general laws of punishments and penalties, fearing that this would foster a contentious attitude among the people that could not be stopped or controlled. For this reason, they used their discretionary judgment (*yi*) to keep the people in bounds... and guided them in their behaviour through the rites (*li*)...
>
> (*Shu Xiang*)

Confucius rejects law as a means for attaining social order because law focuses on external compliance. Since one is merely expected to conform one's behaviour to the given legal norm, one is denied the opportunity to fully participate in the creation of a social order more reflective of one's individual character. Laws, as standards of general applicability, do not allow for sufficient individual expression or particularity.

The formal character of a legal proceeding further diminishes the opportunity for a more contextualized justice able to account for the particular circumstances of the individuals involved. By its very nature, a formal legal system elevates procedural justice relative to, if not at the expense of, substantive justice. In fact, one of the motivations for the development of a formal legal system is to provide a procedural means of resolving interpersonal conflicts that cannot be resolved on a more informal, personal level. While substantive justice has always remained the primary goal of the legal system in China, the formal character of the process and the emphasis on predetermined procedures for resolving conflict have often been seen as obstacles to a more personalized and creative approach, to interpersonal conflict.

Confucius' politics of harmony require the voluntary participation of the individuals who collectively comprise society. If conflicts arise, as they inevitably will, each person must evidence a willingness to look for a mutually acceptable solution. Of course a willingness to cooperate is not enough to overcome all conflicts. There must also be sufficient common ground to provide a basis for discussion, understanding and potential mutually agreeable solutions. The *li* provide this essential communally owned repository of shared meaning and value on which to draw in times of conflict. One is inextricably a part of one's tradition. However different one may be from one's neighbour, there are still deep chords of affinity that bind one to other members of one's community. By tapping the areas of commonality, one may be able to find the ground upon which to build a consensus to forge a new harmony. It is the *li* that provide this common foundation for Confucius, and it is in this sense that the *li* are, in the apt description of the contemporary philosopher A.S. Cua, mutual accommodations of differing attitudes, beliefs and values in social intercourse (see CONFUCIAN PHILOSOPHY, CHINESE).

The *li* have often been construed as universal ethical principles. As a result, Confucius' *lizhi* has been depicted as a kind of natural law. However, the *li* are better understood as customary norms that gain favour within a particular historical tradition at a particular time and that constitute not unchanging, determinant rules of behaviour but culturally valued, though negotiable, guidelines for achieving harmony in a particular context. There is nothing sacred about the *li* in the manner of the Ten Commandments; the *li* are merely culturally and historically contingent norms. As such, to depict them as eternal, universal norms is to render them unduly static and determinate.

Although the *li* derive their normative force in part from the fact that they have withstood the test of time and as such represent the amassed wisdom of the ages, they nevertheless must be interpreted in the light of present circumstances to retain their currency and relevance in shaping behaviour. If the *li* are not invested with new meaning and value, reinterpreted in the light of current circumstances, they will degenerate into irrelevant and trivial formal rules of etiquette.

Traditionally, Confucians were members of the *shi* (literati) class, charged with the responsibility of interpreting the *li* and making it applicable to the times. When called upon to resolve conflicts, they attempted to interpret and apply the *li* in such a way as to give effect to a particularized justice that was amenable to all parties and thus restored harmony. Accordingly, they had a vested interest in the *li* and the informal system of mediating conflict that relied heavily on their individual wisdom and judgment. In a system without formal means of appeal, each individual charged with mediation wielded considerable power, a power that could be abused in the absence of the kinds of procedural protections afforded by a formal legal system. On a grander sociopolitical level, the ruler was charged with generating and maintaining social order. Living as he did during the Warring State period, Confucius realized that society was comprised of persons with diverse interests. To bring diverse interests into harmony requires a unifying agent. The ruler was the unifying agent – the Pole Star – responsible for providing the pivotal note.

Yet the Confucian ruler was more of a facilitator of order than a dictator – at least in theory. Using persuasion rather than force, he was to inspire in others a willingness to become humane, to put aside narrow self-interest and form a harmonious society. The ruler was to lead by example. His virtue was to sweep over the people and transform them just as the wind blowing over long stalks of grass bends them as it passes. Ideally, the ruler would not have to impose his way; rather, the people would naturally defer to his example, to his superior moral cultivation. With everyone participating willingly in the collective project of creating a humane society, social order was sure to result. There was no need for the heavy hand of the law. The ruler merely set himself aright, assumed his position at the centre, and let society follow his lead. This was the ideal of the *wuwei* ruler: 'The Master said: "If there ever was a ruler who could be said to have achieved proper order while refraining from actively imposing his way on others (*wuwei*), it was Shun. What was there for him to do? He simply made himself respectful and took up his position facing due south."'

While the ideal Confucian ruler at least in theory sought not to impose his way, he nevertheless played a pivotal role in setting a course for society, particularly in times of conflict or trouble. It was his ability to perceive creative solutions to the problems facing society that enabled him to lead (see DAOIST PHILOSOPHY §6).

In the end, the Confucian ruler ruled by virtue of his moral vision. His authority to lead was a function of his ability to know the way (*dao*). *Dao* refers to the patterns in the world, the ways in which things are related and the possible ways in which they might be related (see DAO). To 'know dao' is to perceive these patterns and relations. As a moral achievement,

knowing the way requires that one overcome the limited perspective of one's narrow self-interest to see oneself in relation to others. The more truly cultivated one is, the more relations and possible relations one sees. For Confucius, knowing *dao* also meant understanding tradition and how the past informed and shaped the present. Accordingly, knowledge of the *li* was an essential component of the education of the ruling class.

Confucianism is, as noted above, decidedly elitist and, as a result, paternalistic. In theory, the ruler is the one able to see things other people do not, to see a way (*dao*) to bring harmony out of diversity, to turn disorder into order and to persuade others to join in the realization of that harmonious social order by virtue of his moral vision, character and the example he set. But vision is at bottom personal. As a consequence, political order was (and has remained) largely dependent of the quality of those in power.

The absence of effective institutional checks on the power of the ruler charged with achieving sociopolitical order on a macro level mirrored the absence of procedural constraints of the Confucian literati charged with resolving conflict on an interpersonal level. The combination of the lack of effective restraints and the elitist fallacy – that the Confucian literati/sage/ruler possessed superior normative insights – left the disempowered largely at the mercy of those in power.

3 The evolution of *li*: increased codification and stratification

The hierarchical nature of society was further reinforced by the *li*, which reflected differences in personal cultivation and social accomplishment and in so doing inevitably fostered such differentiation. Confucius maintained that humans are by nature similar. Each person has the potential to become a sage. At the same time, however, he realized that not all people will become sages. As a practical matter, people will achieve different levels of cultivation and accomplishment. A properly functioning society recognizes excellence and harmoniously integrates the varying roles of its members. Thus it was essential for Confucius that each person fulfilled their role, as delineated by the *li*: a ruler was to act as a ruler, a minister as a minister, a father as a father, a son as a son, a friend as a friend and so on.

To be sure, neither one's role nor the rules (*li*) delineating one's role were predetermined for Confucius. One could escape one's class through personal cultivation. Indeed, as one moved through life, one's role naturally changed. First a son, one later becomes the father; first the subordinate, one later assumes positions of increasing authority. Further, as noted above, Confucius insisted that the *li* required personal investment, interpretation and adaptation, lest they become ossified and outdated rules of petty etiquette.

Confucius' words, however, were not heeded. Over time, the *li* became increasingly codified and rigid. One finds in many classic texts, the *Liji* (Book of Rites), the *Xunzi*, even in the *Analects* of Confucius, painstakingly detailed expositions of the proper behaviour for the various strata: the ruler was to use a *jian* cup, the ministers a *jia* cup; a ruler used a decorated bow, a feudal lord a red bow, a high officer a black bow, and so on. More important than the exhaustive detail of these works, however, is the underlying theory. There is a marked change in emphasis from Confucius' own view of the *li* as flexible and adaptable and of society as a continually evolving, open-ended project. Increasingly, the primary function of the *li* is taken to be class differentiation. Thus we find the Confucian XUNZI asserting:

> The ancient kings invented the *li* and standards of rightness (*yi*) for humans in order to divide them; causing them to have the classes of noble and base, the disparity between elderly and young, the distinction between wise and stupid, the able and the incompetent; all to cause people to assume their duties and each to get his proper position.
>
> (*Xunzi*)

Similar sentiments were echoed in a wide variety of classical texts, from the *Liji* to the eclectic Daoist text the *Huainanzi* to the dynastic history of the Han, the *Hanshu* (History of the Former Han Dynasty) (see HUAINANZI; CHINESE CLASSICS).

As the *li* became more rigid, so did the social classifications. Confucians were privileged in the social hierarchy; they wielded considerable power in their role as the mediators of conflict and as keepers and interpreters of the *li*. The establishment of the Imperial University in the Han, with an examination system based on the Confucian classics as the core curriculum, further solidified the role and position of the Confucian literati in the social hierarchy.

4 The Legalist response

Not surprisingly, there were those who objected to the power granted the literati (and the ruler) in a Confucian *li*-based order. To the Legalists, the Confucian system of *lizhi* was nothing more than 'rule of man' (*renzhi*). The Confucian sage determined what was best in a given situation based on his own judgment and interpretation of the *li* rather than by appeal to fixed standards or laws of general applic-

ability. Accordingly, *lizhi* strengthened the hand of the elitist class by ceding to the literati the discretionary authority to interpret and apply the *li* as they saw fit. In response, the Legalists advocated clearly codified, publicly promulgated laws applicable to commoner and noble alike as a means of undermining the dual class system in which 'the *li* do not reach down to the common people; penal law does not reach up to the great official'.

While advocating the impartial application of publicly codified laws, Legalism was hardly a 'rule of law', which, as applied to contemporary legal systems, at minimum refers to the existence of an institutionally independent and professionalized judiciary that interprets and applies laws construed as general commands, publicly known, clearly stated, legitimately enacted and altered, and backed up by the coercive power of the state (see LAW, PHILOSOPHY OF). Accordingly, the Legalist *fazhi* is better characterized as rule by law. Law was simply a pragmatic tool for obtaining and maintaining political control and social order. In the Legalist view, humans are self-interested. To avoid conflict and achieve order, they must be manipulated through a reliable and impartial system of rewards and punishments. Clear, codified, public law lets every person know what is expected and what the consequences of their actions will be.

Law was also a pragmatic tool in the sense that the Legalists understood that reliance on the personal qualities and judgment of the ruler would in many instances, if not most, lead to disarray. According to HAN FEIZI, most rulers are simply average in their abilities: the truly exemplary ruler such as Yao or Shun is as rare as the truly evil and incompetent ruler such as Jie or Zhou. Thus the Legalists sought to design a system that would work even with – or despite – a ruler who is neither exceptionally bright, morally good or politically adept. To do this, they had to conceal the weaknesses of the ruler by erecting a screen of institutional mechanisms, political strategies and techniques (*shu*). Law was one such mechanism. Once the system of laws with their attendant punishments was made known, the laws were to be impartially applied. Neither the ruler nor the bureaucrat who applied the law on a daily basis was to allow personal bias or relationships to sway the outcome. In fact, Han Feizi encouraged the ruler to remain behind the scenes and allow his ministers to carry out the day to day functions of governance. This was the Legalist understanding of *wuwei* – literally, non-action – that is so central to Laozi's Daoist philosophy (see DAOIST PHILOSOPHY §6).

Nevertheless, the ruler remained the ultimate authority, both in theory and practice. In the final analysis, law was what pleased the ruler. Accordingly, the ruler retained the authority to promulgate and change laws. Further, although the Legalists advised the ruler against lightly changing the laws, they did allow that laws should be changed when their costs outweighed their benefits. In a direct attack on the importance invested by the Confucians in the *li*, the Legalists cautioned against undue reverence toward outdated norms.

In sum, Legalist law was positive law, not natural law. It was a pragmatic tool for effecting social order. While law was intended as a means to limit the arbitrary power of the ruling class and the ruler, Legalist *fazhi* or rule by law ultimately failed, as did Confucius' *lizhi* or rites-based order, to impose effective checks on the ruler. By allowing the ruler the final word, Legalism lent theoretical legitimacy to the excesses of the first Emperor of the Qin, the first emperor to unite China whose reign, marked by strict laws and draconian punishments, was short-lived.

5 Huang–Lao: a natural law alternative

There arose in response to the deficiencies of both Confucianism and Legalism a new school, the Huang–Lao school, which flourished during the early Han period (*circa* 200 BC). Huang–Lao attempted to limit the power of the ruler and provide a theoretical and moral foundation for a law-based rule (*fazhi*) by grounding the sociopolitical order in a normatively predetermined natural order. Ultimate authority lies not with the ruler but with the Way (*dao*). The Way/ *dao* gives rise to or determines the laws (*dao sheng fa*); the ruler is merely the medium who by overcoming personal, subjective biases is able to apprehend the objectively given Way. Laws are therefore determinate normative standards to be discovered by the sage-ruler: 'There is a distinction between right and wrong: use the law to adjudicate between them. Being empty, tranquil and listening attentively, take the law as the tally.'

Just as the sage is responsible for discovering the law but not for creating it, so is he responsible for impartially applying the law but not for interpreting it. In the legal empire of Huang–Lao, the scales of justice are finely calibrated objective standards. Discretion is eliminated. It is neither the sage's duty nor his role to balance the arguments pro and con in light of the particular circumstances or the culturally and historically contingent norms, attitudes and beliefs of a particular community (in other words, the *li*). Unlike his Confucian (and Daoist) counterpart, the Huang–Lao sage is not called upon to build a consensus out of dissension, to realize a harmony amenable to all concerned parties. He is a judge, not a mediator. His task is to decide who is right and who is wrong, nothing more, nothing less. On one side of the scales of justice goes the deed, on the other the Way. The burden on the sage is to eliminate subjective bias so that he is able to apprehend the deed as it actually is and the Way as it should be.

Thus, like the Legalists and contra Confucius, Huang–Lao advocates an impartial application of publicly promulgated, codified laws of general applicability. However, unlike the Legalists, Huang–Lao attempts to constrain the power of the ruler. Whereas the Legalist ruler was the ultimate authority as to what the law is and how it should be interpreted and thus 'above the law', in the Huang–Lao universe the Way is the ultimate authority and thus the ruler, like all others, must abide by the laws. Accordingly, law for Huang–Lao is not merely a political tool to be used by the ruler to further his own ends. The ruler cannot change the law at will, nor can he circumvent it by issuing pardons.

In sum, whereas law for the Legalists was positive law, a pragmatic means of attaining social order, law for Huang–Lao is natural law, grounded in the normatively predetermined natural order or Way. By grounding law in the Way, Huang–Lao attempted to circumscribe the power of the ruler and thereby avoid the evils of the despotic first emperor of China. However, while there may have been limits on the ruler in theory, there were no such limits in practice. Given that there is no way to verify the ruler's claim to have discovered the Way and hence the correct laws, the ruler's power remains as unchecked in practice as that of either the Confucian or Legalist ruler.

6 The evolution of *li* and *fa*: Xunzi's synthesis

In the absence of a clear victor, the *lizhi–fazhi* debate evolved over time, surfacing in slightly altered forms, in different combinations. On a theoretical level, there have been attempts to synthesize *li* and *fa*, as in the writings of XUNZI.

Xunzi, like HOBBES, portrays the human condition as a struggle to overcome self-interest. In antiquity, people lived in a state of nature. Dominated by their inherent tendencies toward self-interestedness, they competed one with the other for the scarce goods available, giving rise to strife and social disorder. To rectify the chaos and set the social order aright required some system of laws or normative guidelines. In explaining the origin of this system, Xunzi turned to the mythical Ancient Kings (whereas Hobbes turned to the myth of the social contract):

> What is the origin of the *li*? I reply, man is born with desires. If his desires are not satisfied for him, he cannot but seek means to satisfy them himself. If

there are no limits and degrees to his seeking, then he will inevitably fall to wrangling with other men. From wrangling comes disorder and from disorder comes exhaustion. The Ancient Kings hated such disorder, and therefore they established the *li* in order to curb it, to train men's desires and to provide for their satisfaction.... This is the origin of the *li*.

(Xunzi)

Faced with divergent interests and conflicting claims among the members of society, Xunzi turns to the *li* as a mechanism for adjudication and social control. But the *li* do not function alone; they form part of a larger complex of *li yi fa du* (rites, normative judgment, law and statutes). To rule effectively requires use of both *li* and *fa*.

Xunzi differed from Confucius not only in the importance he attached to *fa* but in his conception of *li*. Xunzi saw the *li* as a means of differentiating the various classes or society not just socially but economically. That is, the *li* provided a principle for determining an equitable distribution of the scarce resources available to society: the nobility (including Confucian literati) received more than those at the bottom of the hierarchy. In contrast, Confucius emphasized the integrative, social aspect of the *li* rather than the divisive, economic aspect. The *li* made possible harmonious interaction among the various social groups by providing a common network of behavioural norms. Civil interaction was possible because all shared the *li*.

Furthermore, in synthesizing *li* and *fa*, Xunzi tended to remake the *li* in the image of *fa*. Xunzi's *li* are similar to *fa* in that they require less participation and more compliance than in the case of Confucius. *Li* for Xunzi are norms created and imposed by those in power on those without power, albeit with the interests of the disempowered in mind. The lower classes are not required to participate in generating the *li* or investing the *li* with personal meaning so much as they are required to comply. Hence one finds Xunzi placing great emphasis on moral training and habituation. The goal is to drill on the *li* until one can comply without reflection. To be sure, once one has thoroughly internalized the *li*, one may experiment with them and be flexible in their application. But for most mere compliance is all that is expected.

Another difference is that whereas Confucius' *li* were context-specific, Xunzi's *li* are less so. For Xunzi, the *li* arose as a response to the unchanging nature of humans as self-interested beings. In his view, the ancient sages were able to take the measure of human nature and design the network of *li* accordingly.

Because human nature is relatively stable, so also

are the *li*. This is not to say, however, that the *li* are universal, eternal truths. For Xunzi, the particular laws and *li* by which one adjudicates conflicts and achieves social order are human products, human artifacts. The process by which the sage generates the *li* is one of pragmatic experimentation: 'The sage gathers together his thoughts and ideas, experiments with various forms of conscious activity, and so produces *li* and sets forth laws and regulations.'

Xunzi realized that circumstances change and that the *li* and laws must change as well. Nevertheless, he was concerned that there be some basic guidelines, a single agreed set of standards, laws and norms for guiding behaviour and resolving conflicts. To change the *li* and laws without regard to whether change is desirable would be both inefficient and unfair in that it would make it impossible for people to plan their futures. When essential, the *li* and laws could be changed. But given the constancy of human nature, there is as a rule little call to do so.

Although differing from Confucius in some respects, Xunzi remains true to his Confucian roots in others. Perhaps most importantly, he allows the sage the ultimate discretion to determine and apply *li* and *fa* based on his own best judgment:

> Just as there are disorderly rulers, but no such thing as a disorderly state, so there are exemplary persons who effect proper order but no such thing as laws that can effect it.... The laws cannot establish themselves and cases cannot determine themselves. Where there is the right person, they exist; where the right person is lost, they perish. Law is the beginnings of proper order, but the exemplary person is the source of laws.

(Xunzi)

Xunzi's goal was clear: to synthesize Legalism's impartial application of generally applicable laws with Confucius' concern for a particularized justice achieved through the discretionary judgment of a mediator who looks to the nuanced norms, attitudes and beliefs of the particular parties and community. Problems remained, however. The emphasis on informal means of resolving conflict ceded considerable power to the mediator. On the formal side, the ruler remained largely unchecked. There were no effective institutional impediments to limit the ruler's power. Finally, like his predecessors, Xunzi offered no protection to the individual against the state.

7   The Confucianization of law and Legalization of Confucianism

Xunzi's attempt to synthesize *li* and *fa* on a theoretical level was mirrored in practice by the so-called

Confucianization of law and, conversely, the Legalization of Confucianism. The Confucianization of law has been discussed and documented by Ch'ü T'ung-Tsu (1961). It refers to the way in which the legal system came to adopt and reflect the important values of Confucianism. No doubt the formal legal system did incorporate and reflect many Confucian values. For example, the legal system paid particular attention to familial relations and filial piety. One of the unpardonable 'ten offences' was unfilial behaviour. Another was the murder of one's parents. But while it was unpardonable for a son to murder his father, the father was permitted to kill or mutilate his unfilial son, as long as he first petitioned the court. Similarly, in keeping with the deference owed to parents, a son could be punished for simply accusing his father. As a result, the law officially permitted a son to conceal the crimes of the parent. One also had a legal duty to support one's parents (as is still the case). In fact, the legal codes allowed for the non-execution of a criminal so that the criminal could look after his parents.

The influence of Confucianism and the *li* was also reflected in the hierarchical nature of the legal system and the concern for particularized justice. Punishments were meted out in accordance with one's status and the status of the victim. Officials were treated more favourably than commoners. They could not be arrested, investigated or sentenced without permission of the emperor. Some were exempt from torture for certain crimes. All benefitted from sentence reductions, and could redeem certain punishments either by paying a fine or accepting a demotion. Status was also important for the official *qua* victim. Generally speaking, the higher the status of the victim and the lower the status of the offender, the more severe the punishment.

The law also drew a distinction between free persons and slaves. Slaves and members of the inferior class were punished more severely for killing, injuring, marrying or engaging in illicit sex with a free person or member of superior class than the contrary. Gender, age and moral character were also factors expressly incorporated into the legal codes' scheme of punishment.

The influence of Confucianism on the legal system is equally apparent in the seriousness with which the system treated homicide and personal injury. Such crimes were punished with particular severity because they undermined the Confucian *lizhi* system. The Confucian approach to conflict resolution is one of persuasion, not force. Disputes are handled outside the courts through informal mediation. To be successful, the parties must be amenable to persuasion, willing to engage in discussion and compromise

if necessary. If the situation has deteriorated to the point of violence, the parties will most likely be hostile to each other and less willing to listen to reason and compromise. Violence and killing, therefore, constitute a rejection of the Confucian mediation process. Once they occur, the state is forced to intervene and to mete out a severe punishment as a deterrent.

Of course, the continued reliance on extrajudicial means such as mediation to settle disputes is itself a product of the Confucian *lizhi* tradition. Another product of that tradition is the legal system's enduring tendency to pursue substantive justice at the cost of procedural justice. Perhaps the best indicator of the concern for substantive justice is the ready availability of appeal. Litigants could continue to press their case all the way up to the emperor if they so desired.

More generally, the influence of Confucianism and *lizhi* continued to be felt in the people's attitudes toward law. Most people felt it was a disgrace to be involved in a lawsuit. At trial, one would be forced to kneel and often subjected to torture. Litigation was also expensive, as captured by the Chinese proverb 'win your lawsuit but lose your money'. Thus most people attempted to resolve conflicts through extrajudicial channels if at all possible.

Although much has been made of the Confucianization of the law, equally important, though less discussed, is the 'Legalization' of Confucianism. Perhaps this phenomenon has drawn less attention because law has always played some role in a Confucian world. As noted above, Confucius saw a role for penal law. By the time of Xunzi, the role of law had expanded considerably. The importance of law is even more evident when one turns away from theory and the ideal society envisaged by Confucius and Mencius toward the real world. Recent archeological discoveries reveal, for instance, that contract law existed as early as the Han. In addition, each dynasty had its own legal code, which was often quite developed and intricate, and provided not just a finely calibrated system of punishments, but procedures for appeal and review of cases. The importance of law in pre-modern China is better appreciated if one considers not just the formal legal system, which was predominantly penal, but the full range of legal norms, including clan regulations and the rules of a particular guild or profession, which served at least to some extent as a form of civil law.

It would, therefore, be a mistake to portray pre-modern China according to some idealized Confucian stereotype that discounts the importance of law and minimizes the role of the formal legal system. At the same time, it would be a mistake to present the pre-modern Chinese state as a rule of law in a contemporary Western sense, at least if that is understood to entail equality before the law and the impartial administration of justice by an independent and professional judiciary. The pre-modern legal system continued to reflect the tension between *li* and *fa*, between the goal of a particularized justice that fully accounts for each person's circumstances and role in society and the goal of impartial justice meted out in accordance with rules of general applicability. It was, however, no more successful in its attempt to combine the best of *li* and *fa* in practice than Xunzi was in his attempt to synthesize the two in theory. The problems that threatened to undermine Xunzi's theoretical synthesis surfaced in practice. Corruption was rampant; the wealthy and powerful used their wealth and connections to circumvent justice. The ruler remained unchecked. Individuals were left at the mercy of the powerful state. As a result, the legal system was often feared more than respected, and reformers continued to press for change.

8   *Li* and *fa* in the modern era

The *li*–*fa* debate has continued in the modern era. With modernization as their slogan, turn-of-the-century reformers such as Liang Qichao declared ideological war on Confucianism, arguing for *fazhi* over and against *lizhi* and *renzhi* (rule by man). In the early years after the communist victory, the new regime was forced to turn to legal specialists, most of whom were Nationalist supporters, to design and implement a legal system. At the same time, however, many important positions within the legal system were filled by 'new cadres' appointed not for their legal skills but for ideological dependability. The specialists favoured a rule of law; the new cadres, supported by the central authorities, a more *li*-based 'rule of man'.

Ironically, the politics of the Cultural Revolution provided an interesting twist to the debate, with the post-Mao government siding with 'revolutionary' Legalism and rule of law and opposing 'revisionist' Confucianism and rule of man. After the lawlessness of the Cultural Revolution and Mao's death, Deng Xiaoping then made reform of the legal system a top priority. For the time being, advocates of rule of law and a formalized legal system continue to have the upper hand.

The ongoing theoretical battle between the supporters of *li* and *fa* has meant in practice wide oscillation between formal and informal means of conflict resolution. During the Mao era, China lacked a formal criminal procedure law. Although the courts remained responsible for punishing major criminals, less informal channels for dispensing justice were equally if not more important. Work and residential units handled minor offences, and the police imposed administrative sanctions ranging from warnings to fines to re-education through labour. Mediation remained popular.

It is important to realize, however, that during the socialist period the state has controlled and continues to control both the formal and informal means of resolving conflict. Mediation committees, even at the neigbourhood level, are part of the state. The goal is to impart socialist ideology, raise the level of political consciousness of the disputants and resolve disputes in a way consistent with the policies of the Communist Party. Thus in many instances, mediation is far from the voluntary process envisaged by many Western advocates of alternative dispute resolution. Participation is often mandatory; there is often little choice but to accept the solution proposed by the mediator.

Furthermore, contemporary mediation and other informal or extrajudicial means of resolving conflict remain subject to abuse. Before, the Confucian literati were responsible for mediating an informal, particularized justice; now it is the *ganbu* (political cadres) that wield authority. When these cadres put their own interests first, the process breaks down and corruption becomes rampant as the parties seek to exercise their connections (*guanxi*) to influence the 'neutral' arbitrator or judge. Accordingly, many reformers have suggested that less emphasis be placed on informal techniques such as mediation and, conversely, the role of the formal legal system expanded. Their belief is that a formal legal process affords one greater procedural rights and protections, whereas more informal approaches too often subject one to abuse by those in power.

On the formal side, however, law and the judiciary remain firmly under the control of the state. The official view continues to be that law is to serve the Party. Ren Jianxin, President of the Supreme Court, recently stated: 'The independent exercise of judicial power by the people's courts occurs under the leadership of the Party. In order to adhere to [that principle] the independent exercise of judicial power by the people's courts must be supervised and supported.... Courts at all levels must consciously keep aligned with the central Party line, obey orders, listen to commands.'

Ironically, recourse to law has often meant harsh punishments in accordance with the latest Party dictates. Normally, the first official reaction to deviant or criminal behaviour is to attempt to informally persuade the violator to reform. Only if the deviant behaviour persists is the violator subject to the formal legal system and increasingly harsh punishments. However, during periods of political instability when the Party feels the need to address a particular pressing issue such as corruption or the outbreak of political demonstrations, the Party will insist that any violators be subject to the full force of the law. Accordingly, law, as for the Legalists, has remained a pragmatic tool to be exploited by those in power.

Despite the turn toward formal law, the influence of the past and *lizhi* thinking remains strong. One indicator is the ongoing concern for mediation and informal, extrajudicial means of conflict resolution. Perhaps most fundamentally, however, *li*-consciousness continues to shape the very understanding of the nature of law. Law, for most, is not understood as a universal norm. Rather, laws are culturally contingent, albeit generally applicable, norms. This understanding of law explains in part the difficulties in US–China discussions of 'human rights'. The US side considers such rights, if not self-evident, at least universally applicable regardless of time and place, historical traditions or level of economic development. In contrast, the Chinese view human rights, and particularly the civil and political human rights championed by the US, as the contingent product of Western Europe's Enlightenment traditions and the current economic and political circumstances of the US itself (see RIGHTS). Although such rights may be worthy goals, they are predicated on assumptions about the nature of the individual, the relationship of the individual to the state, and the normative value of the individual and individual freedom *vis-à-vis* the good of the community and society as a whole. Accordingly, when China complains that the US is interfering in China's domestic affairs, it is reflecting an understanding of laws, including human rights, as culturally contingent. When China conditions discussion of rights on the other's willingness to 'seek common ground while reserving differences, maintain mutual self-respect and promote understanding and cooperation', as is China's official policy, it is merely reflecting a traditional understanding of the nature of ethical norms and laws and the proper way to resolve conflict, whether interpersonal or international.

Conversely, China's human rights problems are emblematic of long-existing internal tensions in both China's political theory and practice. The human rights problem results in part from a lack of institutional restraints on those in power, which today means the Communist Party. The lack of effective institutional constraints – a professionalized and truly independent judiciary, for example – has been a characteristic of *lizhi* and *fazhi* throughout the ages.

The human rights problem also results from the lack of a constitutional tradition that looks to the constitution as a source of legally enforceable rights. China has had many constitutions: twelve since 1908. Many of these constitutions have set forth an impressive array of individual rights. However, Chinese citizens do not enjoy such rights in practice because the constitution is not justiciable. Rather, the constitution is hortatory: it sets forth the aspirations and goals of society. In that sense, the constitution reflects the Confucian tradition of emphasizing the development of the moral character of people and the role of the government as a provider of moral guidance and a vision of the good life.

Further, the fact that constitutions come and go is consistent with the traditional *lizhi* concern for context-specificity. Chinese constitutions do not set forth universal principles, eternal truths. Rather, they provide a snapshot of the cultural, political, economic and social values important at that particular time to that particular society. For instance, China has recently amended its constitutions to reflect significant changes in the economic system: socialist commodity economy is out, socialist market economy is in. If the political situation changes, and the conservatives and hardliners regain power, the constitution would probably be amended once again: socialist market economy would be out, socialist commodity economy back in.

9 Conclusion

Socialist China has continued to debate the merits of an informal *li*-based type of political order and a more formal *fa*-based political order. Increasingly, the institutional components of a formal legal system are being developed and implemented: a professional judiciary is being trained, new laws are being codified, programs aimed at educating people about the legal system and their rights are beginning to have effect, as evidenced by the dramatic rise in the number of lawsuits.

Nevertheless, critics abound, and many of these continue to raise the banner of *fazhi*. Increasingly, however, *fazhi* is understood as 'rule of law' in the sense of a professionalized and independent judiciary with the institutional integrity and authority to constrain the Party and safeguard individual rights. Whether such a system can be achieved, and how the traditional concern with *li* and informal justice will affect such a system, remains to be seen.

See also: CHINESE CLASSICS; CHINESE PHILOSOPHY; CONFUCIAN PHILOSOPHY, CHINESE; DAOIST PHILOSOPHY; FA; LAW, PHILOSOPHY OF; LEGALIST PHILOSOPHY, CHINESE; MARXISM, CHINESE; PATERNALISM; SOVEREIGNTY; XUNZI

References and further reading

Ames, R.T. (1988) 'Rites as Rights: The Confucian Alternative', in L.S. Rouner (ed.) *Human Rights and the World's Religions*, Notre Dame, IN: University of Notre Dame Press. (Contrasts the two concepts of rites and rights.)

Bodde, D. and Morris, C. (1967) *Law in Imperial China*, Cambridge, MA: Harvard University Press. (Survey of the history of law in China.)

* Ch'ü T'ung-tsu (1961) *Law and Society in Traditional China*, Paris: Mouton. (Survey of the history of law in China.)

Cohen, J.A. (1966) 'Chinese Mediation on the Eve of Modernization', *California Law Review* 54: 1201–26. (Discusses the Chinese legal practice of mediation.)

Edwards, R.R. *et al.* (1986) *Human Rights in Contemporary China*, New York: Columbia University Press. (Looks at the issue of human rights in a Chinese context.)

Fu Hualing (1992) 'Understanding People's Mediation in Post-Mao China', *Journal of Chinese Law* 6: 211–46. (Another examination of the concept of mediation.)

Hall, D. and Ames, R.T. (1987) *Thinking Through Confucius*, Albany, NY: State University of New York Press. (Study of the impact of Confucius on Chinese thought.)

Hulsewe, A.F.P. (1955) *Remnants of Han Law*, Leiden: Brill. (Discussion of law in the Han period.)

Leng Shao-chuan and Chiu Hungdah (1985) *Criminal Justice in Post-Mao China*, Albany, NY: State University of New York Press. (A look at recent and current law in China.)

Li, V.H. (1978) *Law Without Lawyers*, Boulder, CO: Westview Press. (A look at Chinese attitudes to law and legal practice.)

MacCormack, G. (1990) *Traditional Chinese Penal Law*, Edinburgh: Edinburgh University Press. (Study of traditional Chinese law.)

Nathan, A. (1986) *Chinese Democracy*, Berkeley, CA: University of California Press. (Looks at the concept of democracy as understood in China.)

Peerenboom, R.P. (1993) *Law and Morality in Ancient China: The Silk Manuscripts of Huang–Lao*, Albany, NY: State University of New York Press. (Detailed study of law in the ancient period.)

—— (1993) 'What's Wrong with Chinese Rights? Toward a Theory of Rights with Chinese Characteristics', *Harvard Human Rights Journal* 6: 29–57. (Looks at Chinese approaches to the concept of human rights.)

Tay, A. (1987) 'The Struggle for Law in China', *University of British Columbia Law Review* 561.

(Study of changes in the law in China following the end of the Maoist period.)

R.P. PEERENBOOM

LAW, ECONOMIC APPROACH TO

The development of an economic approach to legal practice has been the most important jurisprudential development in the last third of the twentieth century. Economic analysis has been offered as both a positive and a normative jurisprudence: as an analysis of important features of existing legal practices and as an ideal against which these practices ought to be evaluated. For some, economic analysis has a narrow explanatory range (in various fields of private law, corporations and taxation, and anti-trust law, for example), while others make broader claims for its ability to illuminate any area of law. Finally, there is a difference between those who focus on one explanation and those who focus on prediction, but all offer positive economic analysis of law based on the concept of economic efficiency as defined in welfare economics and applied to law by Coase, Posner, Calabresi and others.

1　The concept of economic efficiency
2　The 'Coase Theorem'
3　The Coase Theorem in action: contracts and torts

1　The concept of economic efficiency

Economics, and social sciences generally, in the early part of this century was under the influence of both utilitarianism and logical positivism. The correct course of conduct would be that which maximized utility (utilitarianism) (see UTILITARIANISM); the correct social science methodology required that claims be empirically verifiable or testable (logical positivism) (see POSITIVISM IN THE SOCIAL SCIENCES §2). This was not an altogether happy marriage, largely because judgments about which course of action are utility-maximizing required judgments of interpersonal utility which were viewed as unverifiable. Because there exists no common metric against which the gains to one person can be compared with the losses others might suffer, social policy assessment of utilitarian terms in particular is thus called into question.

The sociologist Vilfredo Pareto introduced a mechanism for ordering social states that did not require interpersonal comparisons of utility but did allow policy-makers to favour some policies over others as utility-maximizing. This ordering relationship is known as 'Pareto superiority': one state of the world, W, is preferable to another, S, provided no one prefers S to W and at least one person prefers W to S (see PARETO PRINCIPLE). Put slightly differently: W is Pareto superior to S if and only if no one is better off in S than in W and at least one person is better off in W than in S. (These two characterizations are sometimes mistakenly equated on the grounds that the only reason why a person would have a preference for one state to another is that they would be better off in one or the other.)

The concept of Pareto optimality is then defined in terms of Pareto superiority. A state, W, is Pareto optimal if there exists no state, S_i, that is Pareto superior to it. The world is Pareto optimal when there are no ways of rearranging holdings (or anything else redistributable) to make at least one person better off without making someone else worse off.

There are obvious limitations to the Pareto rankings. Very few interesting real-world policy choices produce only winners (or, more weakly, produce no losers). Second, Pareto optimality can be extremely indiscriminate. Assuming a starting point in which A has ten units of some resource and B has none, any reallocation can improve B's standing by harming A's. Pareto superiority is almost never satisfied in practice, while Pareto optimality is too easily satisfied.

To help alleviate the first problem, several economists have introduced related ranking relationships, the most famous of which is the Kaldor-Hicks criterion: a state of the world, W, is Kaldor-Hicks superior to another state, S, provided that those who gain in going from S to W could compensate those who lose in such a way that, were compensation to occur, W would be Pareto superior to S. In principle, Kaldor-Hicks allows us to compare states that create winners and losers without making interpersonal comparisons, thus extending the Pareto rankings.

Kaldor-Hicks employs a notion of 'hypothetical compensation'. In contrast, Pareto superiority requires actual compensation (so that losers, when compensated, are no longer losers). Actual compensation may be costly, and in some cases these costs might suffice to eliminate the gains associated with reallocation. From a utilitarian point of view compensation may be self-defeating. But, if the point of the ranking relationship is simply to have a reliable indicator that a policy is utility-increasing, then hypothetical compensation may be all that is required.

Kaldor-Hicks is not, however, a transitive ordering relationship. Two social states may be Kaldor-Hicks superior to one another. In that case, it is impossible to infer that either has more total utility than the other. Thus Kaldor-Hicks cannot be used to judge the utilitarian merits of various policy options. Numerous variants on the Kaldor-Hicks criterion have been introduced to overcome the intransitivity problem. Tibor Scitovsky, who first established the intransitivity paradox that beset Kaldor-Hicks, developed his own variant, which was shown also to be intransitive by Kenneth Arrow. Of course, one way of obviating the problem would be to make interpersonal comparisons of relative utility, but doubts as to the meaningfulness of such comparisons were precisely what led to the alternative ranking systems.

2 The 'Coase Theorem'

Ronald Coase's seminal piece 'The Problem of Social Cost' (see Coleman and Lange 1992) established the so-called 'Coase Theorem'. In a well-functioning market, individuals trade with one another in ways that benefit all concerned. These exchanges are Pareto superior or Pareto improving (barring adverse third-party effects). In a perfect or idealized market, such exchanges occur until no further mutually advantageous exchanges can be made. At that point the outcome would be Pareto optimal. There are many barriers to successful exchange, however. If property rights are uncertain, then exchange will be difficult. Take the familiar case of the rancher and the farmer. The rancher believes he can raise cattle and the farmer believes he has the right to grow corn. The relevant uncertainty concerns whether, if the rancher's cows eat the farmer's corn, the rancher will be liable in damages to the farmer.

In his essay Coase argues that, under certain conditions, it will not matter from the point of view of efficiency whether the rancher is free to raise as many cows as he would like without being liable to the farmer or whether, instead, the farmer can prohibit the rancher from raising cows altogether. The argument has two parts. First, what would be the efficient allocation of cows and corn?

Suppose the rancher and the farmer were one person, rancher-farmer, then the answer is simple. Each cow imposes costs in terms of corn that will be destroyed by roaming cows. The rational rancher-farmer will continue raising cows until the marginal costs of doing so exceed the marginal benefit. When the rancher-farmer can earn more from the corn their cows would destroy than they would from the cows, then they will stop raising cows. That is the efficient allocation of cows and corn. Any additional cows will be more costly than beneficial.

The second part of the argument is that when rancher and farmer are two individuals they will raise the same allocation of cows and corn they would have as rancher-farmer. This is so no matter which party has relevant right. Suppose that the rancher and the farmer are fully rational, informed about each other's preferences and, finally, that the transaction costs between them are trivial. Then suppose that the farmer is entitled to prohibit the rancher from raising cows altogether. We know from the above discussion that the value of the last bit of corn to the farmer is less valuable than is the first cow to the rancher. Thus, the rancher can afford to offer the farmer a sum of money equal to, or somewhat greater than, the value of the lost corn to the farmer (and less than the value of the first cow to the rancher). Accepting that sum will make the farmer better off and the rancher will have his first cow. This will apply right until that point at which the rancher will be unwilling to pay the farmer an amount of money equal to the value of the corn the farmer will lose. This is just another way of saying that the value of the next cow will fall below the value of the forgone corn. When that occurs, no further transactions will occur. The net effect will be an efficient allocation of cows and corn.

Conversely, it is easy to see that this same line of argument would work were we to begin with the assumption that the rancher had a right to raise as many cows as he would like free from liability to the farmer. The last cow is less valuable to him than is the first bushel of corn to the farmer. The farmer would be in a position to offer the rancher a mutually advantageous exchange: cows for corn. This will go on until it is no longer rational for the farmer to purchase rights from the rancher. And that will be the efficient point at which no more mutually advantageous trades can be made.

One way of looking at the Coase Theorem is that when there are barriers to market exchange that would otherwise be mutually advantageous or efficient, then the best first option is to see if a secondary market can be set up that allows individuals to contract around their problem. In this case, the barrier to efficiency is an *externality*, that is, the social costs cows impose on corn; the solution is transactions (themselves made possible by the absence of transaction costs). Always look to the contract or the market solution. Why? Simply because such a process assures Pareto improvements: rational, fully informed agents make mutually advantageous exchanges.

But when the market fails and it is too costly to create secondary markets, then look to the law to establish legal rights and duties that mimic the outcome the market process would have come to had the transaction costs been less troublesome. When it is not possible completely to mimic the efficient outcome, the law should do what it can to reduce transaction costs and encourage private solutions.

3 The Coase Theorem in action: contracts and torts

In a fully specified contract, all the parties would anticipate and respond to all possible contingencies. Nothing could happen in the future that the parties had not contemplated and responded to. For a variety of reasons, no contract is fully specified. Some contingencies are not accounted for in a normal contract. That does not mean, unfortunately, that none of those unlikely events will come about. How should the costs of such an event be allocated among parties who have not determined in advance how they would allocate the risks between or among themselves?

There is always a possibility that the parties could work it out privately. Suppose they cannot, and the matter comes to a court. What should the court do? What rule should the court apply in *default* of the parties having an explicit arrangement? One answer, suggested by the Coase Theorem, is that the court should impose the allocation of rights and responsibilities the parties would have come to themselves had transaction costs not made it impossible for them to contract such an arrangement. There is another alternative that also has links to the original Coase article. The court should forget about the two parties currently before it. Instead it should focus on future contracting parties. In doing so it should set default provisions that will encourage future contractors to reveal information that it would be socially desirable for them to reveal but which neither party would normally have a rational self-interest in revealing. So we can use the default rule to promote efficiency in at least two different ways: either by minimizing transaction costs so that the parties can spend the resources they have in areas that are more important to them, or by promoting *socially* efficient revelation of information by future contracting parties.

Now to torts. A injures B. Should A be made to pay B's costs or should they be required to shoulder their own costs? Should a rule of fault or of strict liability be applied? If A has to bear B's costs whether or not A is at fault (strict liability), that would be just like making A be the 'owner' of both activities, by making A the owner of B's costs. Even if A has to bear B's costs, it does not mean that A will no longer injure B. Rather, A will decide whether it is worth it to injure B and bear the costs or whether it is better to forego the injurious activity. That, in turn, depends on the relative costs and benefits. In economics, this practice of forcing A to bear the costs he imposes on B is referred to as *internalizing externalities*. A rule of strict liability appears to lead to efficient outcomes in just the way the rancher-farmer example does.

The goal of tort law is not to eliminate accidents altogether. After all, the costs of preventing an accident may exceed the costs of the accident itself. It may cost $100 to prevent a $50 accident, and that would not be rational. If it would have cost A that much to prevent a similar injury to B, he would not have prevented the injury. Instead he would have risked the injury and saved $50.

The goal is not to avoid accidents but to minimize the sum of the costs of accidents and the costs of avoiding them. Sometimes minimizing costs means reducing the probability of an accident's occurrence. Sometimes reducing the probability requires that precautions be undertaken by both injurers and victims. A rule of strict liability will not give a victim any incentive to take precautions, because the victim is fully compensated for his loss. Why would he accept any additional costs? A rule of strict liability will not be efficient under such circumstances.

Consider the alternative. Under a rule of negligence, an injurer will not be liable unless he is at fault or negligent in causing another harm. What do we mean by negligence? In economic analysis, negligence is the failure to take cost-justified precautions. Precautions are cost-justified when incurring them is less costly than the injury they are designed to prevent, discounted by the probability of its occurrence. So failure to take precautions would be negligent if it would cost $50 to prevent a $100 accident – but not if it would cost $150 to prevent the same accident.

It will always be rational for an injurer to take all cost-justified precautions under a negligence rule. If he does, he escapes liability; if he does not, he will bear the full costs of the accident which, *ex hypothesi*, exceed his prevention costs. Thus, rational agents will not be negligent. Because the injurer always takes rational precautions, the accidents that occur are not his fault. That means the victim will have to bear his own costs under a negligence rule, and hence will always have a similar incentive to take all cost-justified precautions. If he can reduce the probability of his incurring costs by taking precautions that are less costly than the harm, then he will do so; and so on. Thus, there will be cases when it would make sense to have a rule of negligence, and other times when a rule of strict liability will be in order.

See also: Economics and ethics §4; Law, philosophy of; Market, ethics of the §2

References and further reading

Coleman, J. (1992) *Risks and Wrongs*, Cambridge: Cambridge University Press. (Expansion of the material in §4 of this entry.)

* Coleman, J. and Lange, J. (1992) *Law and Economics*, Aldershot: Dartmouth. (Wide-ranging collection of essays, including R. Coase's 'The Problem of Social Cost', with an introduction by the editors.)

Posner, R. (1972) *Economic Analysis of Law*, Boston, MA: Little, Brown. (Seminal work for modern Chicago-based economic analysis, particularly influential in US legal thought.)

JULES L. COLEMAN

LAW, ISLAMIC PHILOSOPHY OF

*One of the principles of Islam which precedes juristic discussion proper is that God, the creator and lord of the world, has commissioned humanity to believe, confess and act in particular ways. The details of this commission (*taklif*) were handed down through a sequence of prophets, culminating in Muhammad, and were then embedded in two literary structures which together constitute revelation (*wahy*): the Qur'an, which is the word of God, and the* hadith, *short narratives of the prophet's life and sayings which give expression to his (and his community's) ideal practice or* sunna. *The totality of beliefs and rules that can be derived from these sources constitutes God's law or* shari'a.

Juristic literature has generated two major literary genres. One, known as usul al-fiqh *(roots of jurisprudence), deals with hermeneutical principles that can be used for deriving rules from revelation; it represents, in part, something like a philosophy of law. The other, dominant genre,* furu' al-fiqh *(branches of jurisprudence), is an elaboration of rules which govern ritual and social activities. An overall philosophy of law in Islam, not fully articulated in the pre-modern tradition, can only be discovered through consideration of both genres.*

1   **Revelation**
2   *Usul al-fiqh*
3   *Furu' al-fiqh*
4   **Contemporary trends**

1 Revelation

In Islamic belief there are a number of principles, derived from the exercise of the intellect or from history, which precede juristic discussion proper. These include, for example, that God exists, that he is creator and lord of the world, and that he has commissioned humanity to believe, confess and act in particular ways. The details of God's commission (*taklif*) have been mediated through a sequence of prophets culminating in the seal of all the prophets, Muhammad, whose message abrogates previous messages and is for all peoples. With the death of the Prophet, the divine command has been embedded in two literary structures which together constitute revelation (*wahy*): the Qur'an, which is the word of God, a miracle, and the *hadith*, short narratives of the Prophet's life and sayings which give expression to his (and his community's) ideal practice or *sunna*. The totality of beliefs and rules that can be derived from these sources constitute God's law or *shari'a* (see ISLAMIC THEOLOGY).

The Qur'an is usually deemed to contain no more than about 500 verses of legal import. The body of *hadith* was immensely larger. It was contained in a number of admired collections, the core of which included, for the mainstream Sunni community, the pre-eminent collections of Bukhari (d. AH 256/AD 870) and Muslim ibn al-Hajjaj (d. AH 261/AD 875). Beyond these, there were a number of collections that might be brought into the play of juristic discussion; the major sectarian group, the Shi'is, also had their own collections. The vast bulk of *hadith* material, as contrasted with the modest quantity of juristic material in the Qur'an, ensured that *hadith* was in practice the dominant element of revelation in hermeneutical discussions. The Book is more in need of the *sunna* than the *sunna* of the Book, said the Syrian jurist Awza'i (d. AH 157/AD 774), echoing the efforts of other scholars to articulate the controlling effects (judging, abrogating and explaining) of *sunna* on the Qur'an.

2 *Usul al-fiqh*

The literary tradition of *usul al-fiqh* (roots of jurisprudence) is usually thought to begin with the Risala of Muhammad ibn Idris al-Shafi'i in the third century AH (ninth century AD). However, there is then a hiatus between this work and the emergence, some two centuries later, of other works of the same kind. Modern scholars have put this down to pseudepigraphy, or to the community's engagement with theological and intellectual problems. Once established, this tradition, although it developed in a variety of ways, showed remarkable structural and conceptual unity over the centuries, with individual books always including a presentation of hermeneutical principles and an elaboration of the theory of *ijtihad* (independent judgment).

Since revelation was constituted by written texts, a primary bundle of hermeneutical techniques related to linguistic and rhetorical structures. These were usually presented under simple antithetical headings (the general and the particular, commands and prohibitions, the clear and the ambiguous, the absolute and the qualified, truth and metaphor and so on), which might or might not be integrated into a general theory of language and rhetoric. Consideration was given to the principle of abrogation (*naskh*), a result of diachronic revelation, and (with reference to *hadith* only) to the mode of transmission, which was either general report (*tawatur*, giving rise to certain knowledge) or isolated report (*ahad*, giving rise to uncertain knowledge or opinion). Consensus (*ijma'*), whether of the community or of scholars, on the meanings of revelation was discussed, as was the operation of analogy (*qiyas*) as a means (variously qualified) to permit extrapolation of rules from a finite body of revealed texts. These, together with a limited number of extra items, either of substance (such as the opinions of the Prophet's companions) or of judgment (such as the relevance of *maslaha*, or social welfare) represented the major focuses of analysis and discussion within a single and more or less unified literary tradition for about a thousand years. The hermeneutical loyalties of the mainstream Sunni community were summarized by reference to the four principles (*usul*) of Qur'an, *sunna*, consensus and analogy.

The whole bundle of interpretative devices and principles of judgment was acknowledged to lead to conflicting possibilities (*ta'arud*) and to the necessity for rational and justified preference (*tarjih*). The context and the significance of juristic preference depended on the theory of *ijtihad*, the expression of which was a culmination and a kind of resolution for all other arguments in a work of *usul*. *Ijtihad* literally means effort; technically, it means the exertion of the utmost possible effort by a trained jurist, taking into account all the relevant texts of revelation and principles of interpretation, in order to discover, for a particular human situation, a rule of law. Underlying this definition there is an important epistemological principle. It concedes that most of the details of the law are not known (not certain) but are a matter of skilled (and preferably pious) deduction on the basis of principles that are themselves subject to debate and incapable of providing certainty.

Within this area, the jurists were committed to

acknowledging the views of other jurists, if adequately defended, and to the elaboration of systematic arguments to defend their own views. Committed in this respect to debate and uncertainty, the jurists (in this context *mujtahids*, those who undertake *ijtihad*) also acknowledged a need for final decisions in particular cases. This was provided by asserting that the result of an act of *ijtihad* was binding both on the *mujtahid* himself and, where relevant, on those who were not experts in the law and could not participate in juristic debate (*muqallids*). These, by an exercise of choice (which was itself an act of *ijtihad*), were required to commit themselves to a particular *mujtahid* and to accept his rulings. The theory of *ijtihad* thus provides both an epistemology (permitting and encouraging debate and intellectual play) and a structure of authority. In its former aspect it accounts (in part) for the vitality of the tradition of *furu' al-fiqh*, and in its latter aspect it justifies the participation of the jurists in positions of authority, notably as judges (*qadis*) and the jurisconsults (*muftis*).

The structures set out above, which were capable of considerable and diverse development, represent the main features of *usul* literature for both the Sunni community and for the Shi'is. The latter differed from the Sunnis in rejecting most forms of analogical argument. Summarizing their *usul*, they substituted for the Sunni principle of analogy that of intellect (*'aql*) deemed by them (but not by the Sunnis) to be capable of independent moral judgment. The Shi'i community was initially suspicious of the theory of *ijtihad* (perhaps because it too easily acknowledged plurality and uncertainty in the law), but it was integrated into their works of *usul* from the time of 'Allamah al-Hili in the eighth century AH (fourteenth century AD). Amongst the standard classics of the Sunni tradition are the *Mustasfa* of AL-GHAZALI (§2) and the *Muwafaqat* of Shatibi (d. AH 790/AD 1388), showing an original foregrounding of the principle of *maslaha*. One of the outstanding *usul* writers of the Shi'i tradition after 'Allamah is the nineteenth-century Shaykh Murtada ibn Muhammad Ansari.

3 Furu' al-fiqh

The other major genre of juristic literature, *furu' al-fiqh* (branches of jurisprudence), is constituted primarily by rules (positive law). It might be expected that individual writers in this genre were, from generation to generation, engaged in the process of *ijtihad*. However, this is not quite the case. In the course of the ninth and tenth centuries AD, the Islamic community became committed to a pattern of juristic loyalties whereby, in the end, all Muslims identified

themselves with particular schools (*madhahib*) of the law. Within the Sunni tradition there were four dominant schools, the Maliki, Hanafi, Shafi'i and Hanbali schools, each named after its founder. These acknowledged each other and also gave qualified acknowledgment to a number of minor schools, and to the Shi'is. The vast majority of significant jurists belonged to one of the major schools, usually by virtue of birth and geography, only rarely by choice and adoption. When they wrote a work of *furu' al-fiqh*, they gave expression to the rules (with the attendant patterns of dispute and debate) that they had inherited within their school. The fundamental acts of *ijtihad* were thus projected back to the founder and to the early masters. By an ongoing act of loyalty, commitment and preservation, successive generations of jurists rediscovered and restated the rules of the tradition to which they belonged.

Works of *furu'* therefore show a dominant hermeneutical orientation towards earlier works in their own tradition, and not towards revelation. This is reflected in the characteristic patterns of citation, which invariably recall the opinions and judgments of earlier masters within the school, and the literary forms of such works (epitome, commentary, super-commentary), all marks of hermeneutical commitment to a particular school. In so far as writers in this tradition actually deployed arguments of the type described in works of *usul*, they did so in order to demonstrate that the inherited structure of rules could be aligned with revelation and not for the purposes of *ab initio* deduction of the law. Developments in the law, manipulation of its concepts and their application to new cases were always carried out in the light of the inherited structure. The inconcinnity between the principles of jurisprudence as set out in a work of *usul* and the practice of a writing jurist was eventually acknowledged with the recognition that, in relation to the school founders, these were principles of discovery while, in relation to later jurists, they were principles of justification. Hermeneutical thinking within the tradition (based on juristic texts, not texts of revelation) was known as *ijtihad fi 'l-madhhab* or school-*ijtihad* and distinguished from the independent *ijtihad* of the founding figures.

4 Contemporary trends

Muslim thinkers of the twentieth century, committed to various programmes of legal reform or political action, have developed a number of theoretical props which take them away from the traditional modes of juristic expression. They have often abandoned the particularity of school loyalties; instead, they have adopted law-drafting techniques that reflect the realities of modern nation-states, borrowed legal and social principles from a variety of sources, and argued strenuously that the door of independent *ijtihad* is open, meaning that they can again make independent legal judgments based on direct confrontation with revelation (often using a definition of revelation, at least in relation to *hadith*, which is more limited than that of the past). The major, and certainly the most obvious, modern responses to the juristic tradition have been practical, either in the service of state law or in the service of political opposition. There has been a corresponding lack of interest in the philosophy that is articulated in the traditional forms of juristic discourse, especially those of *furu'*. In different ways, both of the traditional genres, *usul* and *furu'*, acknowledge the exploratory nature of the effort of defining God's law and situate themselves in a flexible and pluralist system of rules. They may have more relevance to contemporary problems than is generally conceded (see ISLAMIC PHILOSOPHY, MODERN).

The modern linguistic calque *falsafat al-tashri'* (philosophy of legislation) or its equivalent is currently used in several Islamic countries to designate a variety of academic activities. These range from conservative scholarship, drawing heavily on the tradition of *usul al-fiqh*, to analytic descriptions of legal developments in modern Islamic states and something like the Western discipline of philosophy of law.

See also: EPISTEMOLOGY IN ISLAMIC PHILOSOPHY; ETHICS IN ISLAMIC PHILOSOPHY; ISLAMIC PHILOSOPHY, MODERN; ISLAMIC THEOLOGY; LAW AND RITUAL IN CHINESE PHILOSOPHY; LAW, PHILOSOPHY OF

References and further reading

Calder, N. (1993) *Studies in Early Muslim Jurisprudence*, Oxford: Clarendon Press. (The most recent substantial effort to describe the early stages of Islamic juristic thinking.)

—— (1996a) 'Islamic Law', in S.H. Nasr and O. Leaman (eds) *History of Islamic Philosophy*, London: Routledge, 979–98. (Offers a general account of Muslim juristic literature, initiating a literary description of the tradition of *furu' al-fiqh*.)

—— (1996b) 'Al-Nawawi's Typology of *mufti*s and its Significance for a General Theory of Islamic Law', *Islamic Law and Society* 3 (2): 137–64. (Demonstrates the emergence and elaboration of a clear theoretical distinction between independent *ijtihad* and *ijtihad fi 'l-madhhab*.)

Hallaq, W. (1994) *Law and Legal Theory in Classical and Medieval Islam*, London: Variorum. (An important reassessment of scholars' approaches to the history of *ijtihad*.)

—— (1992) '*Usul al-fiqh*: Beyond Tradition', *Journal of Islamic Studies* 3 (2): 172–202. (The bibliography of this article contains an up-to-date list of Hallaq's substantial and important body of studies related to *usul al-fiqh*.)

Masud, M.K., Messick, B. and Powers, D. (1996) *Islamic Legal Interpretation: Muftis and their Fatwas*, Cambridge, MA: Harvard University Press. (An important and wide-ranging collection of articles representing some of the most recent thinking about the theory and practice of Islamic law.)

Schacht, J. (1950) *Introduction to Islamic Law*, Oxford: Clarendon Press. (Still the classic introduction to the subject, with an excellent but now dated bibliography.)

NORMAN CALDER

LAW, LIMITS OF

Questions concerning the proper limits of law are of particular interest to thinkers in the Western political tradition of individualism. In this tradition the law is regarded primarily as an instrument of coercion and the problem is to define the scope of law in such a way that it fulfils its necessary purposes at minimum cost to individual liberty. Debate therefore centres on the proper ends of legal coercion. Two law-limiting strategies are commonly adopted; the practical and the moral. As the most important ends of human life (salvation of the soul, or its secular equivalent, moral integrity) are taken to require the uncoerced, 'inward', assent of the individual, the effective scope of the law is significantly limited on practical grounds to the regulation of 'outward' behaviour. On the moral question concerning which behaviour ought to fall within the purview of the law, conservatives contend that society has a right to enforce its moral values by criminalizing whatever behaviour its members regard as 'sinful'. The characteristic strategy of liberals is to respond by arguing that unorthodox or unpopular activities must clearly be shown to be 'harmful' before they may properly be outlawed. Much debate focuses upon the interpretation of this principle (the 'harm principle'), particularly what is to count as 'harm' for purposes of legislation, and whose harm is properly in question. Dissatisfaction on these crucial issues has led some liberals to reject what they consider to be the fruitless attempt to draw the line between liberty and law by balancing individual against social harm in favour of various theories of individual rights, while it has led others (communitarians and some feminists) to question the individualist assumptions in terms of which the problem of the limits of law gains its especial urgency.

1 Individualism and the limits of law
2 Practical limits to law
3 Moral limits to law
4 Law-limiting principles and the crisis of liberalism

1 Individualism and the limits of law

Should the law be used to promote religion, regulate trade and 'enforce morals'? Or, should it be narrowly confined to the bare essentials of preserving the peace and preventing violence? The question of the proper limits of law was at best a marginal one for the ancient Greeks and the medievals, and remains so today for many non-Western thinkers. It is, however, an issue which has been of particular concern within the modern (post-sixteenth century) Western tradition of political thought, a preoccupation reflecting the importance accorded to individual liberty in this tradition, together with the marked cultural diversity of modern Western societies and the unprecedented growth in the power of the state. The conceptual background against which the question of the proper limits of law is most naturally raised is one of 'individualism', according to which society is composed of independent individuals who associate politically on the basis of a mutual sacrifice of liberty in return for the various benefits of social cooperation. This view encourages a search for reasons or principles which may be used to assess the appropriateness both of existing laws and of proposed legislation by defining the proper balance between individual liberty and state power. 'Appropriateness' may, however, mean either practical efficiency or moral rightness (see LIBERALISM §3).

2 Practical limits to law

It is manifestly desirable that laws be efficient; the proposed ends of the law should be achievable by the means available to the law. Now the law, broadly understood as a system of rules established by a legal authority requiring us to do or forbear on pain of punishment, ultimately relies upon coercion for its enforcement (see LAW, PHILOSOPHY OF). Consequently, the scope of the law is limited to those ends which can be attained by regulating *behaviour* by playing upon *fear*. LOCKE deployed the efficiency argument against the state enforcement of religion. Beginning from the proposition that the main

purpose of religion is the salvation of souls, which requires an unforced act of faith on the part of the individual believer, he argued that legislators who set out to enforce religion can at best compel 'outward conformity' rather than genuine conviction of belief (see TOLERATION §1). Hence the legal enforcement of religious orthodoxy commits a practical error – it mismatches means and ends. The efficiency argument thus sets limits to the scope of law by dividing society into separate spheres, in Locke's case the religious and the secular, legal coercion being confined strictly to the latter. Later liberals confine the scope of state action even within the secular sphere itself, especially in respect of morality and economics (see SMITH, A.). In regard to morality the argument focuses upon the conditions for the attainment of moral virtue. Thus, Kant argued that a morally good person is someone who not only does the right thing, but does it for morally the right reasons (see KANT, I. §10). As the freely adopted intentions of the agent are of paramount ethical concern, the (positive) promotion of virtue is assigned to education and placed permanently beyond the reach of the rough coercive engine of the law, which is restricted to the more modest role of the (negative) prevention of vice.

The efficiency argument well reveals the twin poles around which liberal individualism revolves: reverence of individual freedom of choice and a corresponding distaste for legal coercion. The position, however, has its weaknesses. In particular, it takes a debatably narrow view of the strategies open to legislators. Thus, although 'true faith' might not be directly enforceable, it might still be produced by indirect means, for example, by banning religious competition, censorship and by controlling education. Likewise, the Kantian position on moral goodness perhaps underestimates the scope for indirect coercion by way of using the law to sustain a framework of broadly educative institutions and practices within which morally desirable motives might be elicited and encouraged. Even so, these possibilities raise in their turn difficult questions concerning the 'authenticity' of beliefs and the 'genuineness' of motives produced by such methods of 'social engineering'. At this point the efficiency argument leads on to issues connected with freedom of the will and human agency, and to questions concerning the nature of law and the educative role of the state (see FREE WILL; AUTONOMY, ETHICAL).

3 Moral limits to law

What the law *can* do is one thing; what it *ought* to do is another. A useful way of approaching the moral question is to ask how far law should go in pursuit of the essentially negative and in general perfectly feasible goal of preventing vice. Clearly, no morally defensible legal system can permit murder and rape, ignore violence and intimidation, or countenance gross dishonesty and theft. Peace and security, the basic prerequisites of any minimally tolerable social life, are universally essential moral ends. But ought the law to be narrowly confined to securing this 'moral minimum', or should it be extended to regulate those less immediately vital aspects of our relations with others which nonetheless often express passionately held convictions about right and wrong, serve to distinguish the characteristic ethos of one community from that of another, and even to define our own sense of moral identity and personal worth?

On this question two contending schools of thought may be distinguished: conservatism and liberalism. The case for legal conservatism goes as follows. Murder, rape, theft and the like are evil acts. By outlawing evil the law expresses our deep and abiding moral convictions and, by convicting and punishing the criminal, the judge and jury give emphatic vent to our community's shared sense of moral outrage and disgust. The reach of the law is thus virtually unlimited: it stretches as far as the community's sense of sin. The chief difficulty with the conservative doctrine is that, murder and the like aside, it is far from obvious that the criminal law can any longer act (if it ever did) as the legal vehicle of a commonly shared morality. Indeed, the problem of the limits of law is an acute one precisely because little general agreement is to be found on such questions as euthanasia, abortion, genetic engineering, pornography, homosexuality, the selling and consumption of addictive drugs, 'politically correct' language, or the killing or mistreatment of animals. Thus, although legal conservatism often sails under the colours of moral populism, it sanctions the dogmatic imposition of a morality which might have little support beyond the accidental prejudices of the notoriously introverted judicial mind. Hence the need, in the liberal view, for a clear and rationally defensible moral principle which affords a critical perspective on the ends of law.

4 Law-limiting principles and the crisis of liberalism

The fruits of the liberal quest for a morally justifiable law-limiting principle have taken two main forms. The first is the Principle of Equal Freedom: 'People should be legally free to do as they please providing only that they do not interfere with the like liberty of others'. This principle reflects the liberal's concern that the state should act merely as a neutral referee of people's freely chosen activities rather than determining their ends and directing their lives (see NEUTRALITY, POLITICAL). But because it fails to specify concretely what people should be free to do, a law permitting bodily assault would satisfy the rule just as well as one prohibiting it. By contrast its rival, the harm principle, has the immediate advantage of connecting substantively with the most intuitively arresting feature of our moral minimum. The advocates of the harm principle readily concede that we are properly morally outraged by murder and the like but, *pace* the conservative, it is the objective harm done, and not the subjective feelings of the community, that justifies the criminalization of these activities. In addition, the harm principle is advanced as furnishing an empirically applicable decision procedure for rationally resolving disagreements upon cases beyond the moral minimum, and especially upon the more controversial ones such as 'victimless crimes' of the kind alluded to above.

The harm principle was classically formulated by the utilitarian philosopher J.S. MILL (§12). Mill argued that the general happiness is maximized only when coercive interference with the individual is rigorously restricted to that unavoidably necessary to 'prevent harm to others'. A great deal of contemporary discussion of the limits of law is concerned with the interpretation of Mill's version of the principle. Two questions are particularly pressing: what is to count as 'harm' for the purposes of legislation? and whose harm is properly at issue?

Physical injury clearly counts as harm for the purposes of legislation, but what about injuries sustained by voluntary participants in competitive sports? We clearly need to qualify the principle with a sub-rule of non-consent to cover cases of this kind; and this in turn raises the question of what is to count as consent – explicit agreement? tacit consent? passive acquiescence? (see CONSENT). Moreover, does harm extend to psychological harm, and does that in turn stretch to emotional hurt? If so, should offensive behaviour fall under a legal ban too? And is behaviour offensive if any one person is liable to be upset by it? Clearly, if we concede too much in this direction the protected sphere of liberty is in danger of shrinking to a nullity; a line must be drawn, yet drawing it at any particular point smacks of arbitrariness. Mill himself is by no means clear on these questions but it has been argued that we can sort out the legally relevant harms in terms of 'setbacks' to *interests* (see NEEDS AND INTERESTS §1). Physical injuries, psychological traumas and the like set us back in the sense of preventing us from effectively pursuing our chosen ends; they thus harm our interests and may properly be forbidden. Lesser hurts do not set our interests back and must therefore be permitted. However, serious set-backs can occur to an individual's economic and professional interests in competitive settings which are not themselves undesirable. What is required therefore is a tenable conception of a wrongful harm or set-back, something that is unlikely to be supplied outside the context of a general and inclusive moral theory. Mill believes that he has such a thing in utilitarianism. The weakness of utilitarianism in the eyes of many liberals, however, lies precisely in its tendency to subordinate the individual to the general interest (see UTILITARIANISM).

Similar difficulties attend the question of whose harm is at issue. Mill himself takes a radical line here, rejecting all laws against self-inflicted harm on the grounds that they constitute a paternalistic interference with the freedom of adults to live their own lives and make their own mistakes; a position on the face of it scarcely consistent with the maximization of general utility and one which also implies highly controversial conclusions about drug taking, euthanasia, sadomasochistic sex, and so on (see PATERNALISM). Equally problematical is the question of whether the principle should be restricted to harm to other *individuals* (including foetuses?) or should encompass harm to *society*, including its political institutions and practices, together with basic social forms such as the family and associated values and ideals. This was the issue of a celebrated debate between the eminent English judge Lord Devlin and the influential legal philosopher H.L.A. HART concerning the legalization of homosexuality. Devlin argues that if the purpose of the criminal law were simply to protect the individual from harm the consent of the victim of an assault or a rape would be a complete defence, but quite properly the law pursues the assailant, irrespective of consent; and it does so because it represents the profound interest society has in the integrity of the rules which protect the welfare of all its members. Given that the purpose of the criminal law is thus primarily to protect society rather than the individual, Devlin infers that homosexuals enjoy no unconditional right to pursue their consensual activities, for the law may always legitimately ask whether, in so doing, they harm or undermine institutions (such as the family) or values (such as heterosexual love) essential to society's survival or wellbeing (see Devlin 1965). And the conclusion may be generalized: no socially unorthodox activity can claim to be, as a matter of principle, 'not the law's business'.

The import of Devlin's quasi-conservative argument is thus seriously to challenge the grounds of the distinction, so vital to the liberal campaign to limit the scope of law, between the private and the public

spheres of society (see PRIVACY). What is particularly significant about Hart's response (1963) to Devlin is that it reveals the vulnerability of utility-based liberal individualism. Thus, *qua* utilitarian, Hart absorbs the force of Devlin's argument concerning the social purpose of the law, extends the harm principle to society, and concentrates his defence of individual liberty upon Devlin's claim as to what in fact constitutes social danger – in his opinion, Devlin's fear that homosexuality threatens the collapse of society is no more credible than the emperor Justinian's conviction that it is the cause of earthquakes. It is not clear, however, that Devlin does, or needs to, go further than the proposition that heterodox activities might constitute a significant danger to society to make his point. In any event, the effect of the Hart–Devlin confrontation is so to shift the debate that the outcome depends on hard-to-verify conjectures about the conditions of social stability and breakdown.

Under pressures of this kind other liberals have tended to fall back upon another Millian idea, that of 'individuality', interpreted as implying that our most vital interest as human beings lies not simply in happiness *per se* but rather in the specific satisfactions associated with developing our autonomy and displaying our individual uniqueness. As individuality essentially involves the outward expression of inward convictions and needs, it entails a presumption in favour of individual liberty in respect of unpopular or unorthodox behaviour sufficiently powerful to counter all but the most overwhelming reasons for legal interference. This raises the objection from socialists, communitarians and some feminists that liberals are prepared to erode the shared practices and values which constitute our identities as social beings in favour of an atomized association of socially disconnected 'abstract' individualists (see COMMUNITY AND COMMUNITARIANISM §3; FEMINIST POLITICAL PHILOSOPHY). Other thinkers, critical of the whole utilitarian idea of aggregating and balancing individual harm against social good, maintain that the scope of law must be limited by a theory of individual rights grounded independently of utility (see RIGHTS; for prominent examples of this position, see DWORKIN, R. and RAWLS, J.). The question as to the proper limits of law therefore appears increasingly to be embraced within a broader debate as to the philosophical credentials of individualistic liberalism.

See also: FREEDOM AND LIBERTY; JUSTICE

References and further reading

* Devlin, P. (1965) *The Enforcement of Morals*, Oxford:

Oxford University Press. (Chapter 1 formulated an influential conservative view concerning the problems facing attempts to specify moral limits to law.)

Feinberg, J. (1984–1986, 1988) *The Moral Limits of the Criminal Law*, vol. 1, *Harm to Others*, vol. 2, *Offense to Others*, vol. 3, *Harm to Self*, vol. 4, *Harmless Wrongdoing*, Oxford: Oxford University Press. (A magisterial defence of a modified version of Mill's harm principle.)

* Hart, H.L.A. (1963) *Law, Liberty and Morality*, Oxford: Oxford University Press. (Response to Devlin (1965), arguing that he misrepresents the judicial process and misunderstands the relationship of the individual to society.)

Locke, J. (1689) *Locke's Letter Concerning Toleration in Focus*, ed. J. Horton and S. Mendus, London: Routledge, 1991. (Contains Locke's *Letter* and includes a number of articles discussing the tenability of his efficiency argument.)

Martin, M. (1987) *The Legal Philosophy of H.L.A. Hart*, Philadelphia, PA: Temple University Press. (Chapter 8 is a lucid discussion of the Hart–Devlin debate.)

Mill, J.S. (1859) *Mill's Essay On Liberty in Focus*, ed. J. Gray and G.W. Smith, London: Routledge, 1991. (Includes Mill's *On Liberty* together with a number of articles on the interpretation of the harm principle.)

Oakeshott, M. (1993) *Morality and Politics in Modern Europe*, ed. S.R. Letwin, London: Yale University Press. (An incisive and authoritative account of the limited 'office of government' as understood in the tradition of individualism.)

G.W. SMITH

LAW, PHILOSOPHY OF

Law has been a significant topic for philosophical discussion since its beginnings. Attempts to discover the principles of cosmic order, and to discover or secure the principles of order in human communities, have been the wellsprings of inquiry into law. Such inquiry has probed the nature and being of law, and its virtues, whether those that it is considered as intrinsically possessing, or those that ought to be cultivated by lawgivers, judges or engaged citizens. A dialectic of reason and will is to be found in philosophical speculation about the underpinning principles of law. On the one side, there is the idea that the cosmos itself, and human society too, contain immanent principles of rational or reasonable order,

and this order must be capable of discovery or apprehension by rational (or 'reasonable') beings. On the other side, there is the view that order, especially in society and in human conduct, is not found but made, not disclosed to reason but asserted by acts of will. Either there is a 'law of reason – and nature' or there is a 'law by command of the sovereign – or of God'. A third possible element in the discussion may then enter, that of custom as the foundation of law.

Implicit in the opposition of reason and will is the question of practical reason: does reason have a truly practical role concerning ultimate ends and non-derivative principles of action, or is it only ancillary to pursuit of ends or fulfilment of norms set by will? Alternatively, does reason already presuppose custom and usage, and enter the lists only by way of critique of current custom and usage? In either case, what is at issue is the very existence of such a thing as 'practical reason' (see PRACTICAL REASON AND ETHICS). For law is about human practice, about societal order enforced and upheld. If there can be a law of reason, it must be that reason is a practical as well as a speculative faculty. The radically opposed alternative sets will above reason, will oriented to the ends human beings happen to have. Norms and normative order depend then on what is willed in the way of patterns for conduct; reason plays only an ancillary part in the adjustment of means to ends.

A further fundamental set of questions concerns the linkage of the legal with the political. If law concerns good order, and if politics aims at good order in a polity, law must be a crucial part of politics; but in this case a subordinate part, for politics determines law, but not law politics. On the other hand, politics may be considered at least as much a matter of actual power-structures as a matter of speculation about their beneficial use for some postulated common good. In the latter case, we may see law as that which can in principle set limits on and control abuses of power. Politics is about power, law about the shaping and the limiting of power-structures. The issue then is how to make law a master of politics rather than its servant.

1 Law as reason

In the *Republic*, Plato depicts Thrasymachus, proponent of the thesis that justice is the will of the powerful, as being refuted comprehensively by Socrates (see PLATO §14). The refutation postulates a human capability to discern principles of right societal conduct independently of any formal enactment or legislative decision made by somebody with power. These principles in their very nature are normative, not descriptive. In Aristotle, the same general idea emerges in the form of noticing that whereas much that is observed as law is locally variable and arbitrary, there appear to be fundamental common principles across different polities. Some principles may then be legal simply 'by enactment', but others seem to be so 'by nature'. Explorations of the nature of humans as rational and political animals may then help to underpin the idea of that which is right by nature, but that exploration is more the achievement of Aristotle's successors in the Stoic tradition than of himself (see STOICISM §18). Roman jurists adapted some of the Stoic ideas of natural law in their expositions of the civil law, and subsequently, for medieval and early modern Europe, the existence of the Justinianic (see JUSTINIAN) compilation of the whole body of Roman law was held by many thinkers to embody in large measure the promise of law as 'written reason' (see ROMAN LAW; compare GAIUS; BARTOLUS OF SASSOFERRATO; POTHIER, R.J.).

In any event, the greatest flowering of the Aristotelian idea came with its fusion into the Christian tradition in the work of Thomas AQUINAS (§13), hugely influential as this has been in the developing of Catholic moral theology in the succeeding centuries. After at least a century of relative neglect among legal scholars, especially in the English-speaking world, the last quarter of the twentieth century has seen a strong revival of the Thomistic approach in the philosophy of law (see NATURAL LAW), with contemporary thinkers developing the idea of the basic goods implicit in human nature, and showing both how these can lead to the elaboration of moral principles, and then how positively enacted laws can be understood as concretizations of fundamental principles.

In the seventeenth century, other strands of essentially the same idea had led to the belief, for example, of Hugo GROTIUS, that basic principles of right conduct and hence of human rights are themselves ascertainable by intuition and reason (compare PUFENDORF, S.; STAIR, J.D.). Kant's representation of the principles of practical reason is the classical restatement of this position in its most philosophically rigorous form (see KANT, I. §§9–11; KANTIAN ETHICS §1).

In a wide sense, all these approaches may be ascribed to rationalism, as contrasted with voluntarism (see RATIONALISM; VOLUNTARISM). For they treat law, or its fundamental principles, as discoverable by rational and discursive means, independently of the intervention of any legislative will. They do not, of course, deny the need for legislative, or adjudicative or executive, will. Even if fundamental principles stand

to reason, their detailed operationalization in actual societies requires processes of law-stating, law-applying and law-enforcement. But the issue is whether these are fundamentally answerable at the bar of reason and practical wisdom (*prudentia*), or not. To the extent that they are so answerable, we have a concept of some 'higher law', some law of reason, by which to justify, to measure and to criticize the actual practice of human legal institutions. If the rational derivation of this depends in some way on a teleological understanding of human nature and its relation to the creator and the rest of the created universe, we may reasonably enough call this a 'law of nature' or 'natural law'.

2 Law as will

But there is another possible account of higher law. It can be thought of as a law laid down by God for his creation. The divine will, not the divine reason, must be the source of law. It cannot be for created reason to presume to judge of the creator's wisdom. The omnipotence of the creator entails that the law will be whatever the creator wills it to be, and to be law by virtue of that will, not by any independent reason and nature of things. Indeed, the nature of things will be just what the creator wills it to be, and the names of things will be matters of convention derived from human linguistic usage. Concepts are not essences that guide us to essential meanings. Nominalism and voluntarism are inevitable bedfellows (see NOMINALISM).

It is therefore inaccurate to suppose that the theory of natural law as a kind of higher law presupposes rationalism. There can indeed be a voluntaristic species of 'natural law', though the voluntaristic tradition will more likely speak of 'divine law' or 'God's law' than of natural law *simpliciter* (see AUSTIN, J.). Moreover, one element in the religious upheavals associated with the Reformation was an insistence on the need for unmediated regard to the (scripturally revealed) divine law, rather than to the custom or tradition of sinful human institutions such as the Church. It is not for fallen human reason to set itself above or even beside the revealed will of God. But that revealed will must be received as a law binding above all others.

In this state of things it becomes questionable whether to accept any human law at all; and, on the voluntarist hypothesis, to see how law other than God's law can have any obligatory force at all. To the saving of human law there are only two possible moves: either it must be shown that God in fact wills our obedience to the very kings and other superiors we actually have (as in the theory of 'the divine right of kings'), or it must be the case that the binding will arises from the consent of human beings themselves, expressed through some original social contract. The divine will then enters the picture only to the extent of making obligatory the fulfilment of compacts voluntarily agreed, a point to which may be added a grimly Hobbesian acknowledgement that covenants without swords are but words, so the true binding force of the obligation of the law will derive from the effective might of the very ruler whom the social compact institutes in that office (see HOBBES, T. §§6–7). In this Hobbesian form, natural law has practically reached a vanishing point (though Locke's response envisages the state of nature as governed by reason in the form of a law of nature, grounding presocietal rights of human beings to life, liberty and estate (see LOCKE, J. §§9–10). The greatest legal expression of the Lockean vision of law, applied to expounding the English common law, is in the work of Sir William BLACKSTONE. The *coup de grâce* was administered by Hume and Bentham, the latter having as his particular target Blackstone's work. They argue that the social contract is a fifth wheel on the carriage in either Hobbesian or Lockean form, since all the reasons that there are for obeying the law that we have supposedly agreed to apply with equal force even if we did not agree to it, and there is no evidence anywhere of any such agreement as a historical phenomenon (see BENTHAM, J. §6).

3 Law as custom

Whence then comes the law? Hume ascribes it to convention and custom primarily, coupled with reflection upon the pleasing quality (the utility) of rigorous observance of customary norms (see HUME, D. §5). Bentham and Austin restrict the role of custom or 'habit' to the issue of obedience. Whoever is habitually obeyed by the many in a numerous society is in a position to enforce their commands by effectively coercive sanctions up to and including death. Thus do they differentiate the positive law from other forms of so-called law such as scientific law, laws of honour, or personal moral codes. Law is such by command of a sovereign, the one habitually obeyed who habitually obeys no other (see SOVEREIGNTY).

Legal positivism of this stamp is an easy bedfellow with political utilitarianism, and programmes of legal reform. Codification of law is an associated ambition, justified on utilitarian grounds (see UTILITARIANISM). Codification is also a distinctive phenomenon of the early nineteenth century, product of the Enlightenment critique of the old customs of the *ancien régime*, though also of spadework in the exposition of

civil law partly achieved under the aegis of late legal rationalism. After the Code Napoléon, promulgated in France in 1804, there followed a century of codification and legislative modernization of law in many places, and with this characteristically went approaches in legal philosophy that stress the essential emergence of law from a sovereign's will, or the will of the state as a rational association (in Hegelian vein; see HEGELIANISM). Nevertheless, this movement produced its own counter-movements, stressing the importance of the spirit of the people as the basis of law (see SAVIGNY, F.K. VON; BRYCE, J.; JURISPRUDENCE, HISTORICAL), or more prosaically locating it primarily in custom, a view particularly popular in the context of the common law (see COMMON LAW; SELDEN, J.).

Twentieth-century critics of classical positivism accuse its authors of confusing 'commands' with 'binding commands' (see KELSEN, H.; compare WEYR, F.) or of mislocating the roots of legislative authority in mere 'habit', rather than in the 'internal point of view' of those for whom the system within which authority is exercised has normative force (see HART, H.L.A.). The Kelsenian version of positivism rests it on the necessary presuppositions for a value-free science of law, and other thinkers have pursued further the question of 'legal science' (see BOBBIO, N.); the Hartian version rests it on the customs of at least the official and political classes in a state, whose practices concerning the recognition of certain criteria for the validity of legal rules define the ultimate 'living constitution' of a state, its 'rule of recognition' (see LEGAL POSITIVISM).

A notable offshoot of or development from positivistic legal study has been the development of ever-more rigorous approaches to conceptual analysis (see LEGAL CONCEPTS) and categorization, seeking to account for the use of concepts like 'duty', 'right', 'ownership' and others in the framework of general legal norms (see NORMS, LEGAL). Hohfeld's analysis of 'fundamental legal conceptions' (see HOHFELD, W.N.) has had many followers and critics, and contemporaries in other traditions have taken a somewhat more psychologistic approach to the task (compare PETRAŻYCKI, L.). Reflection on legal concepts as institutions or 'institutional facts' has led to developing an 'institutional' theory of law that transforms what was originally a naturalistic conception into a positivistic one (see INSTITUTIONALISM IN LAW; WEINBERGER, O.).

4 Laws and values

One way or another, whether in voluntaristic versions or in those that place more weight on customary or institutional aspects of law, nearly all forms of or approaches to legal positivism have insisted on the strong value-relevance of positive law. The matter of doubt has not been 'ought laws to be just?', but whether their being just is a condition of their being genuinely legal. The 'scientific' character of pure legal analysis has indeed been contrasted with the exercise of moral judgment or moral sentiment, or the engaging in ideological argumentation, that is involved in the critique of law as unjust or otherwise unsatisfactory from the viewpoint of human needs and aspirations. Some, however, have thought that critique itself can have a scientific or at least an objective basis, grounded in the fundamentals of human nature. Classical utilitarianism and nineteenth-century law reform are a case already noted; they had successors in the 'jurisprudence of interests' (see JHERING, R. VON; POUND, R.), and, albeit with certain qualifications, in the later twentieth-century 'economic analysis of law' (see LAW, ECONOMIC APPROACH TO).

The need to subject law to critique is obvious from many points of view, none more urgently than that which takes note of the burdensome impact of legal sanctions on human happiness and liberty. If laws characteristically carry punishments for their infraction, some theory to justify penal institutions is called for (see CRIME AND PUNISHMENT). Whether there are any abstractly stateable limits to the legitimacy of interference with liberty through legal intervention has been another heated debate (see LAW AND MORALITY).

Nevertheless, the positivists' claim that they can combine an a-moralistic conceptual analysis of law and its institutions with a readiness for critique of actual laws on moral and political grounds, and with a last-resort readiness to disobey or defy the law when it is unjust to an extreme, has been doubted by some. Gustav RADBRUCH felt himself driven by his experience of the Nazi years (and also, perhaps, by the implications of the radical voluntarism of Carl SCHMITT) to abandon such a claim and to insist on a conceptually necessary minimum of basic justice in anything we can recognize as 'law' at all. The interpenetration of equity with law, and the interweaving of ideas of justice, equity and law, can be taken to point to a similar moral (see JUSTICE, EQUITY AND LAW), and idealistic approaches to legal theory give a deeper grounding for such an approach (see LEGAL IDEALISM).

5 Law as politics

However one takes one's stand on will against reason, or on natural law against legal positivism, most of the theoretical approaches so far considered give some way of accounting for the independent existence of law as a distinct social phenomenon. Law's independence, at least when underpinned by an independent judiciary, has been held to promise the possibility of effective control over arbitrary state action while at the same time guaranteeing at least the justice of formal equality to citizens and the degree of predictability allegedly desired by modern rational subjects. Here we have the 'rule of law' ideal that demands government under the forms of law and law in the form of clearly identifiable rules (see RULE OF LAW (RECHTSSTAAT); compare DICEY, A.V.; FULLER, L.L.). Yet the mere existence of some body of sacred or secular texts embodying rules of law is not enough for any socially realistic account of law, or for any politically persuasive vision of the rule of law (see SOCIAL THEORY AND LAW; compare MILLAR, J; RENNER, K.). The statute book is not self-applying or self-interpreting (compare WRÓBLEWSKI, J.). To secure the rule of law it is necessary to have prospective rules published to all. But, as L.L. Fuller points out, it is necessary that they be interpreted in a reasonable and purposive way, and faithfully carried into action by the officials of the state whose rules they are. How is this to be secured?

Many schools of thought, chief among them the realists (see LEGAL REALISM) in Europe (see OLIVECRONA, K.; ROSS, A.) and in the USA (see HOLMES, O.W., JR; LLEWELLYN, K.N.; FRANK, J.), have stressed the widely discretionary character of legal interpretation, both in relation to the general rules of the law, and in relation to the categorization of fact-situations as subsumable under the law for one purpose or another. On inspection, 'facts' can turn out as elusive as 'laws', and the study of legal processes of proof assumes a certain urgency (see LEGAL EVIDENCE AND INFERENCE). All in all, it is a serious and difficult question to discern what, if anything, can render decisions reasonably 'reckonable' given the broad discretion vested in those who interpret the law.

One form of response has been to find that law is reckonable not on the basis of the official rules and standard doctrine, but rather on the basis of the 'situation sense' of a judiciary with a common understanding of political and policy objectives underlying law. These insights of the 'realists' have been carried forward more boldly by contemporary feminist jurisprudence, one version of which finds social prejudice directing law through the biases of judges. Another version locates an inner masculinity in the legal rules themselves, even and especially at their most abstract; the asserted values of objectivity and impersonality ultimately come under question as presumptions of doubtful desirability (see FEMINIST JURISPRUDENCE).

Within more mainstream jurisprudence the developed response to realism has been to work out extended theories of the rule of law, acknowledging that law is more than positive rules but arguing for the existence of other mechanisms within law controlling the role of substantive elements in decision-making (see LEGAL REASONING AND INTERPRETATION). Such responses find a certain coherence within law, but by contrast the more developed critical (including critical feminist) approaches argue that there are central fractures and fault lines within the law, reflecting ultimately competing political visions of human association, often summed up as individualism versus community-values (see CRITICAL LEGAL STUDIES). Ronald Dworkin's argument for coherence and integrity in law evokes the idea of an interpretive community, but seems too readily to assume that for any actual legal order there can be found a single consensual interpretive project, even in principle (see DWORKIN, R.; compare LEGAL HERMENEUTICS).

Taking an overall view, the project of establishing the rule of law as an independent base for the critique and control of state action is put in serious doubt, since interpretation is through-and-through political; and appeals to the rule of law can themselves be moves in a political game, expressions of ideology rather than of higher values. It may be that in the end legal philosophy is faced, today as at its beginnings, with this dilemma: either legal reasoning and moral reasoning have that kind of in-principle objectivity proposed by natural law theory in its rationalist versions, or the theatre of law is simply a theatre presenting endlessly the power-play of rival wills and visions of the good. Many have sought a third way, not yet with acknowledged success.

See also: LEGALIST PHILOSOPHY, CHINESE; FA; HALAKHAH; LAW AND RITUAL IN CHINESE PHILOSOPHY; LAW, LIMITS OF; LEGAL DISCOURSE; LAW, ISLAMIC PHILOSOPHY OF; VILLEY, M.

References and further reading

Harris, J.W. (1980) *Legal Philosophies*, London: Butterworth. (Straightforward and well-written introduction to issues and schools of thought in philosophy of law.)

Hayek, F.A. (1973, 1976, 1979) *Law, Legislation and Liberty*, London: Routledge & Kegan Paul. (Three-volume critique of the pretensions of constructivist rationalism, whether of utilitarian positivists or of rationalistic iusnaturalists, in favour of a 'critical rationalism' reflecting on the accumulated societal wisdom implicit in an evolved and essentially customary law, and developing an account of the rule of law on this basis.)

Kelman, M. (1987) *A Guide to Critical Legal Studies*, Cambridge, MA: Harvard University Press. (Readable and sympathetic account of, and contribution to, the 'critical' approach that regards all legal activity as intrinsically political – and ideological.)

Kingdom, E. (1991) *What's Wrong with Rights?*, Edinburgh: Edinburgh University Press. (An interesting collection of essays putting a moderate feminist case against the biases inherent in received legal categories.)

Lloyd of Hampstead and Freeman, M. (1985) *Lloyd's Introduction to Jurisprudence*, London: Stevens, 5th edn. (Another useful introduction, supported by many selected texts for reading.)

Rommen, H. (1947) *The Natural Law: a Study in Legal and Social History and Philosophy*, St Louis, MO and London: Herder Book Company. (Full and careful statement of implications and applications of natural law theory from a Catholic point of view.)

Shiner, R. (1992) *Norm and Nature: the Movements of Legal Thought*, Oxford: Clarendon Press. (A more challenging text that deals with the tensions in legal thought between positivist – or voluntarist – and anti-positivist approaches, concluding that the dialectic between them contains a truth available from neither on its own; advanced reading.)

NEIL MacCORMICK
BEVERLEY BROWN

LAW, RABBINIC *see* HALAKHAH

LAW, WILLIAM (1686–1761)

William Law is popularly known for a single devotional work, A Serious Call to a Devout and Holy Life *(1728), but was the author of seventeen other treatises concerned with many of the philosophical and theological issues of the earlier eighteenth century in England. Early on he embraced the thought of Nicolas Malebranche, and later the mystical philosophy of Jakob Boehme. Law's methodology is an awkward mixture of these influences, for he wanted to find reason in the 'creaturely Spirit' of the natural life (*The Spirit of Love, *1752). He seems finally to have abandoned reason in favour of Boehme's 'metaphysical scheme', which enables him to discover meaning and coherence in a post-Enlightenment world.*

William Law lived mostly in King's Cliffe, Northamptonshire, where he was born and died. He studied at Emmanuel College, Cambridge, where he was elected a fellow in 1711, but resigned this position in 1716, being unable to take the oath of allegiance to the Hanoverian George I. He was thus one of the 'nonjurors', who believed that the Stuarts were by Divine Right the legitimate monarchs of England and consequently true heads of the Church. Accordingly deprived of his college fellowship, he passed the next years variously in study and writing and as a tutor in the Gibbon household at Putney, Surrey, where he instructed the father of the great historian. About 1740, he retired to King's Cliffe at the invitation of Hester Gibbon, the historian's aunt, and one Mrs Hutcheson. Together they formed a kind of religious community, and in these circumstances Law, who never married, continued his reflective and orderly life to the end.

Law's writing is often polemical. *Three Letters to the Bishop of Bangor* (Benjamin Hoadly) his first work, written between 1717 and 1719, was a defence of the apostolic succession of bishops, in which he asserts the spiritual authority of the Church against an Erastian prelate who urged the ecclesiastical supremacy of the state (1762, 1:15). Later Law attacked Bernard Mandeville's *Fable of the Bees* (1714), lamenting 'the miserable Fruits of *Freethinking*, which . . . tend not only to set us loose from the Regards of Religion, but to destroy whatever is reasonable, decent, or comely in human Nature' ([1723] 1762: vol. 2, 49) (see MANDEVILLE, B.). Rather belatedly, Law joined the attack on the Restoration theatre in *Absolute Unlawfulness of the Stage-Entertainment fully Demonstrated* (1726). In his work Law argues persistently for right action. Laid out in terms of lively vignettes of persons who live frivolous or arid or else pious lives, his *Serious Call to a Devout and Holy Life* (1728) provides a systematic plan for ordering one's moral and devotional life.

Given Law's devotion to the reasonable spiritual life, his development of a mystical theology may seem curious, yet he believed he was recovering deeply felt, if elusive, truths. Never systematic, Law's philosophical ideas are expressed in generalities and his theological views often lead to untraditional conclusions. From 1740 onwards, he gave himself over to the study of Jakob BOEHME, and his later writing, especially *The Spirit of Prayer* (1749) and *The Spirit of Love* (1752), is filled with a sense of cosmic goodness. The later style may be well suited to its subject; but it is the plain and straightforward Law of *A Serious Call* that Dr Samuel Johnson pronounced 'the finest piece of hortatory theology in any language' (Boswell 1791: vol. 1, 390).

See also: MALEBRANCHE, N.; TINDAL, M.

List of works

Law, W. (1762) *Complete Works*, London: Richardson; privately repr. for G. Moreton, Brockenhurst, Hants and Canterbury, Kent, 1892–3, 9 vols. (The standard edition, which collects the individual works, all but the last of them published by Richardson of London. In addition to those works mentioned in the text and below, the *Complete Works* includes *A Practical Treatise upon Christian Perfection* (1726), *The Case of Reason . . . In Answer to a Book, entitled 'Christianity as old as the Creation'* [by Matthew Tindal] (1731), *Letters to a Lady Inclined to Enter into the Communion of the Church of Rome* (1731–2), *A Demonstration of the Gross and Fundamental Errors of a Late Book, Called 'A Plain Account of the Nature and End of the Sacrament of the Lord's Supper'* [probably by Bishop Hoadly] (1737), *The Grounds and Reasons of Christian Regeneration* (1739), *An Earnest and Serious Answer to Dr Trapp's Discourse of the Folly, Sin and Danger of being Righteous Over-Much* (1740), *An Appeal to All that Doubt, or Disbelieve the Truths of the Gospel . . . To which are Added, Some Animadversions upon Dr. Trapp's Late Reply* (1740), *The Way to Divine Knowledge* (1752), *A Short but Sufficient Confutation of the Reverend Dr. Warburton's Projected Defence* (1757), *Of Justification by Faith and Works* (1760), *A Collection of Letters* (1760) and *An Humble, Earnest, and Affectionate Address to the Clergy* (1761).)

—— (1723) *Remarks upon a Late Book, Entituled 'The Fable of the Bees'*, Bristol: Thoemmes Press, 1992. (An attack on Bernard Mandeville's book.)

—— (1728) *A Serious Call to a Devout and Holy Life*, repr. in *A Serious Call to a Devout and Holy Life and The Spirit of Love*, ed. P.G. Stanwood, New York: Paulist Press, 1978. (Law's best-known work.)

—— (1752) *The Spirit of Love*, repr. in *A Serious Call to a Devout and Holy Life and The Spirit of Love*, ed. P.G. Stanwood, New York: Paulist Press, 1978. (Law sought to find reason in the 'creaturely Spirit' of the natural life.)

References and further reading

* Boswell, J. (1791) *The Life of Samuel Johnson, LL.D.*, London: Dent, 1949, 2 vols. (Quotes Samuel Johnson on Law.)

Clarkson, G.E. (1992) *The Mysticism of William Law*, New York: Lang. (Law's indebtedness to Boehme and to mystical theology.)

Cornwall, R.D. (1993) *Visible and Apostolic: The*

Constitution of the Church in High Church Anglican and Non-Juror Thought, Newark, NJ: University of Delaware Press. (Situates Law within the High Church and Nonjuring movement of the eighteenth century; includes bibliographical references.)

Grant, P. (1985) 'William Law's *Spirit of Love*: Rationalist argument and Behemist Myth', in *Literature and the Discovery of Method in the English Renaissance*, Athens, GA: University of Georgia Press. (Surveys the influences on Law's thought.)

Hopkinson, A.W. (1948) *About William Law: A Running Commentary on his Works*, London: SPCK. (Chapters on Law the man, the controversialist, the moralist, the mystic, the theologian.)

Rudolph, E.P. (1980) *William Law*, Boston, MA: Twayne. (Introductory guide to Law's life and work.)

Talon, H. (1948) *William Law: A Study in Literary Craftsmanship*, New York: Harper. (Concerned principally with Law's literary style.)

Walker, A.K. (1973) *William Law: His Life and Thought*, London: SPCK. (Comprehensive survey of Law's life, with summaries of his eighteen volumes.)

Warren, A. (1978) 'William Law: Ascetic and Mystic', intro. to *A Serious Call to a Devout and Holy Life and The Spirit of Love*, ed. P.G. Stanwood, New York: Paulist Press; repr. in *In Continuity: The Last Essays of Austin Warren*, ed. G.A. Panichas, Macon, GA: Mercer University Press, 1996. (A general survey of the life and work.).

Young, B.W. (1994) 'William Law and the Christian Economy of Salvation', *English Historical Review* 109: 308–22. (Studies Law's soteriology.)

PAUL G. STANWOOD

LAWS, NATURAL

It is widely supposed that science aims to identify 'natural laws'. But what are laws of nature? How, if at all, do statements of laws differ from 'mere' general truths which include generalizations true only 'accidentally'? Suppose, for example, it happens to be true that all iron spheres (past, present and future) are less than 1 km in diameter. Contrast this with the truth of 'all electrons are negatively charged'. There seems to be a clear intuitive distinction between these two truths, but is there any principled distinction between them that can be drawn and defended?

This has been the traditional focus of philosophical attention concerning laws of nature, and basically two

mutually opposed philosophical accounts have been developed. According to the first account, there are real necessities in nature, over and above the regularities that they allegedly produce (whether or not these regularities are held to be observable), and law-statements are descriptions of these necessities. According to the second account, there are no necessities but only regularities (correlations, patterns) and laws are descriptions of regularities (though perhaps not of any regularity but only of the most basic or most general ones). There are significantly different variants of each account; and also positions that altogether deny the existence of general laws (or deny that science should aim to describe them).

Any one of these accounts, if it is ultimately to be coherent and defensible, has to successfully address four interrelated issues: the meaning of a law statement – the semantic issue; the fact to which a law statement refers and which makes it true – the metaphysical issue; the basis on which claims to know a law are justified – the epistemological issue; the capacity to explain adequately the variety and roles of scientific laws – the explanatory issue.

In attempting this task, each of the available accounts faces its own distinct difficulties. For example, if there are necessities in nature, as the first account claims, how exactly do we identify them: how can we tell which of the inductively confirmed regularities are laws? On the other hand, if there are only regularities, as the second account claims, does this mean that our intuitions and scientific practices are awry and that there really is no distinction between laws and accidental generalizations?

The difficulties facing all extant accounts become even more marked when we face up squarely to the surprisingly wide variety of (putative) laws supplied by current science and to the complexity of the relations between those putative laws and regularities and causes.

1   **Laws in science**
2   **Two philosophical accounts**
3   **A note on laws and logical analysis**
4   **Conclusion**

1   Laws in science

Science exhibits a diversity of kinds of law (law statements). Causal laws specify succession: B causally follows A in time; sunlight causes sunburn (see CAUSATION). Laws of synchronic coexistence specify atemporal relationships: for a gas at equilibrium, temperature equals pressure times volume (in suitable measurement units). Basic structural laws specify the fundamental principles defining a theory framework: spacetime world lines of individuals neither intersect nor branch (that is, no two things can be at the same place at the same time and nothing can be at two places at once). Derived structural laws are laws of diachronic coexistence, A at time t1 = A at time t2: energy is conserved in an isolated system. Functional-analysis laws connect functional capacities of complex systems: teleological systems require negative feed-back to maintain goal orientation.

Some laws are inclusionary: all electrons have charge e; some are exclusionary: nothing travels faster than the speed of light *in vacuo*. Some laws are deterministic: $f = ma$, Newton's second law of motion, while others are statistical: given an incident UV photon, a skin cell has probability P of dying (see DETERMINISM AND INDETERMINISM; PROBABILITY, INTERPRETATIONS OF). Some laws interrelate localized individuals (for example, the gas coexistence law above, $PV = T$), others concern field states (for example, the superposition principle, which has no equivalent among individuals). Symmetries, that is, invariance constraints, ground derived structural laws and may lie behind causal laws (quantum field theories) (see CONSERVATION PRINCIPLES; FIELD THEORY, QUANTUM).

There is no single or simple relationship of laws to causes (of law statements to causal statements). The causal gravitational action of the sun directly produces the planetary motions, but while causal collision processes are ultimately responsible for gas behaviour only their statistically average behaviour at equilibrium is captured in the constraint $PV = T$. Many laws, for example that all ravens are black, are the end product of many interacting causes (constrained by specific initial conditions). Some macroscopic succession laws cannot, at present, be clearly understood theoretically as being the result of interacting microscopic causes (for example the second law of thermodynamics, because in current theory the thermodynamic, but not the microscopic dynamic, law is time-irreversible – see THERMODYNAMICS). Some laws derive from the inoperativeness of causes (the conservation laws); others have no simple relation to causes (for example, structural laws, the quantum Pauli exclusion principle).

Nor is there any single or simple relationship between laws and regularities (between law statements and descriptions of regularities). Kepler's laws of planetary motion specify simple, if empirically approximate, regularities. Newton's first law of motion, given the gravitation law, is empirically never instantiated and so has no directly associated regularities, but does specify a higher-order regularity of convergence on first-law behaviour as system forces decrease. There is evidently no analytic solution to the Newtonian gravitational three-body problem, so

there is no easily specified associated empirical regularity; yet the earth–moon–sun system exhibits a solution. Statistical relationships do not directly issue in any particular empirical regularities, only in approximate higher-order ones (laws of large numbers). Further, a nonlinear system showing chaos will never repeat its sequence of states, yet its dynamics is law-governed, indeed deterministic (see CHAOS THEORY). Here again there is no useful logical formula that describes the dynamic pattern (as a pattern); we can only explore it through computational approximation from the generating equations. Thus evolution and history might show no repeated patterns, yet unfold according to some very complex (largely unknown) nonlinear dynamic laws.

Conversely, empirical regularities have diverse relations to laws. Consider two clocks exhibiting a regular connection between the readings on their two faces. This regularity may arise from (a) a direct physical connection between them whereby the face reading of one sets (causes) the face reading of the other; (b) an immediate common cause, a single human setting both clocks to the same time; (c) a mediate common cause, two separate people separately setting their clocks to the same socially shared time, ultimately generated from a common standard clock; (d) two mutually independent random quantum events initially coincidentally setting the clocks to the same time; (e) at each second the two clocks coincidentally resetting to the same times as in (d).

There are laws (law statements) referring to (i) real systems (for example, Newton's second law of motion), (ii) idealized systems which could not be real but which approximate real systems in some respect (for example 'PV = T', which assumes a gas of point particles – see FICTIONALISM; IDEALIZATIONS; MODELS), (iii) systems which could be real but are never instantiated (for example, Newton's first law, given gravitation), or only approximately instantiated (Kepler's laws in our solar system). Groups (ii) and (iii) nonetheless both render the mathematical structure of the corresponding natural laws simpler and exhibit the structure of component causes (for example, forces).

Within the explanatory issue, then, call achieving a coherent account of the diversity of kinds of law the 'diversity problem', understanding the complex relations of laws to regularities the 'pattern problem' and understanding the diverse roles of idealization in laws the 'idealization problem'. Philosophical theories of science have often ignored or simplified the distinctions among, and rich diversity of, scientific laws; a good philosophical account of natural laws would itself bring order into these complexities.

Scientists use laws to explain both other ('less

basic') laws and particular events (see EXPLANATION §1), to deduce what will happen (predict) and what would have happened had (counter-factually) circumstances been different, to separate complex causes into their components and to distinguish between accidental and law-based empirical regularities, to decide when experimental and inductive inference procedures are justified (see CONFIRMATION THEORY §1; EXPERIMENT; INDUCTIVE INFERENCE §4), to decide what basic properties there are, and so on. An account of the role of laws is thus central to a philosophical account of science. Call providing such an account the 'roles problem'.

In sum, the explanatory issue comprises the diversity, pattern, idealization and roles problems. Responses are based on coordinated proposals for the semantic, metaphysical and epistemological issues.

2 Two philosophical accounts

Necessitarian theories. We make sense of our experience both through introducing causes which produce or necessitate their effects, and through counterfactual reasoning about possible though not actual cases governed by laws which still continue to constrain what is possible. These are the intuitive sources of necessitarian accounts, which introduce a metaphysics of necessary connections as truthmaking conditions for law statements.

Proponents of nonlogical necessitarian theories – developed earlier this century by Johnson, Kneale and von Wright, among others – hold that both laws and true accidental regularities are confirmed by factual observation, so are in that sense contingent, but the law 'all A are B' also rules out the possibility of a non-B A, in analogy to the laws of logic specifying the logically possible. The view that laws do possess logical necessity – noncontingent, logical necessitarianism – was defended earlier this century within the idealist rationalist tradition, including Blanshard, Ewing and Stout. Recently versions have been revived of both nonlogical necessitarianism, for example Armstrong (1983), and logical necessitarianism, Swoyer (1982).

The central metaphysical problem is to characterize necessity. Is it (i) an object or (ii) a relation? Does it connect (a) objects or (b) properties, powers dispositions? There is a traditional objection to (i): how can adding an object create a necessary connection? (Notice, however, that quantum theory represents forces as something like exchange of special objects, bosons.) There is a traditional objection to (ii): it involves developing a metaphysics of real universals (properties, powers, or dispositions) but this is implausible/incoherent. Will statistical laws require

the postulation of special propensities as their truthmakers, and what are these? Would basic negative laws require real negative universals? Would uninstantiated and idealized laws require unactualized and idealized universals? Arbitrary positive answers trivialize this approach; but what principled basis for response is there? (These cases are also troubling for version (i).)

The necessitarian semantic problem is to provide a meaning for law statements that renders them logically stronger than statements of regularity. Though there are many modal logics, it is controversial whether the truth conditions of their statements identify appropriate natural necessities. It has proved similarly difficult to construct a satisfying logic of counterfactual conditionals, which natural necessities distinctively support, and it is controversial whether agreement on a satisfactory formal theory could do more than describe proper inferential practice, assuming natural necessities somehow otherwise identified (see COUNTERFACTUAL CONDITIONALS).

The central necessitarian epistemological problem is that of identifying necessities: how to tell which among inductively confirmed regularities are laws? Any principle that would render inferences from evidence to laws deductively valid (for example that nature is finite and causally uniform) must itself be justified in the same way (vicious circularity) and arguably there are no observable necessitating connections. David HUME drew the sceptical conclusion that no claim to know which evidentially confirmed regularities are laws is ever justified, our scientific knowledge being confined to affirming past regularities and relying on them out of 'habit', without rational warrant. Appeal to some scientific methodology *per se* does not alleviate this problem.

Eliminative necessitarians respond by retaining necessitarianism while dismissing laws as part of the metaphysics of science. Cartwright (1983) argues that laws are so idealized and indirectly related to empirical phenomena that they cannot be regarded as real, while individual causes are real and the basis for scientific reasoning. Eliminationism faces its own difficulties with the metaphysical and semantic issues, but especially with the epistemic and explanatory issues, since it must show how scientific practice can be properly understood without effective recourse to laws, while simultaneously identifying and using causes.

Regularity theories. Historically, objections to necessitarianism, especially epistemological objections, have motivated the development of regularity theories of laws. According to these theories, laws in nature are nothing more than matter-of-fact correlated event patterns. There is no metaphysical distinction between accidental and lawful regularities. The law-likeness of accepted scientific generalizations describing these patterns is at best organizational, a matter of our attitude to, or use of, these statements as 'inference licenses' (Lange 1993), which support habitual, because pragmatically useful, practices of induction, prediction and counter-factual reasoning. Often law-like status is held to be determined by depth of entrenchment in science – (roughly) the wider the generalization, the deeper its entrenchment and the more law-like its accorded status.

The contingent, nonlogical regularity version is the simplest, most common one and its supporters include Braithwaite (1953) and Hesse (1980) among many. It has no need for special necessities in nature, and avoids special semantics for law statements by making the simple logical form '(x)(Ax → Bx)' the universal paradigm. Conversely, however, it is difficult to provide an account of our practices of counterfactual inference since, given '–Aa', '(x)(Ax → Bx)' is vacuously instantiated independently of whether or not 'Ba' holds. It is also difficult to explain how there can be uninstantiated laws, whether or not pertaining to idealized entities, since all uninstantiated extensional conditional statements are vacuously true. More generally, it is difficult to see how a simple regularitiy account could explain the complex relationship between laws and empirical regularities; regularities are neither necessary nor sufficient for laws.

In the light of the difficulties facing nonlogical regularity theories, some philosophers sought to retain their metaphysical simplicity by adopting instead the view that laws are contentless conventions, linguistic meaning definitions, and necessarily true on that account. They were held to be pragmatically useful in the organization of empirical information, in roughly the way that any other linguistic practice is, but no more. Earlier Poincaré, Mach and Reichenbach defended versions of this noncontingent, logical regularity view and later conventionalist debates echo them (see CONVENTIONALISM). This theory provides a sense of necessity to laws compatible with a regularity metaphysics, but only at the cost of eliminating their empirical content. It is then hard to explain the content of scientific theories and hence also to make sense of scientific method. How can we explain why laws are so useful, and when they are useful, if they are only conventional definitions? Why should they ever be changed? Why are there so often no viable scientific alternatives to a theory, if alternatives are created merely by linguistic redefinition?

Another, opposite, reaction to the same difficulties is to retain empiricism while dismissing laws as of no significance to an account of science; this is eliminative regularity theory. Van Fraassen (1989) argues that scientific theories are concerned with symmetry and continuity, not universality or necessity. His view is that laws are anachronisms, remains of an early modern necessitarian essentialist metaphysics, and not something at which science can, or should, aim. He recognizes the importance of theory in science but, pursuing empiricism, construes it largely pragmatically rather than realistically, rejecting all postulated modal connections as unwarranted metaphysics. While this view faces its own problems in responding to the metaphysical, semantic and epistemological issues, special interest attaches to the explanatory issue, since eliminativism needs to show how scientific practice can be properly understood without effective recourse to laws.

3 A note on laws and logical analysis

Philosophy of science in the twentieth century has been dominated by the analytic tradition deriving from logical empiricism and Frege–Hilbert–Russell logical analysis (see ANALYTICAL PHILOSOPHY §2). This tradition emphasizes syntactical logical form, and analysis as the basic tool of philosophical inquiry. In these terms, the traditional issues surrounding natural law have been: (A) What is the syntactical logical form of law statements? (B) What distinction in logical form demarcates (statements of) laws from accidental regularities? These questions have not received satisfactory answers. For example, it has generally been held that law statements have at least to be unrestricted universal claims of the form 'all A are B'. But this claim is either substantive and false, for example statistical laws are not perspicuously of this form, having instead such forms as 'probability (B, given A) = P', or it is true but uninformatively weak, since nothing is excluded (even statistical, idiosyncratic and accidental relationships can still be forced into this form). Many philosophers, representing otherwise opposing positions about laws, now reject this syntactic search as the vehicle for addressing the semantic issue, treating the semantic structure as primary; for example Suppe (1989).

Formal analysis, whether syntactic and/or semantic, continues to be applied to other related problems. The idea of accidentality, for example, may be explicated (Popper 1990) as that of logical dependence on initial conditions (in some theory): the more condition-dependent a statement is, the relatively more accidental it will be (Sklar 1990). And the idea of entrenchment has been formally elaborated in various ways. For example, according to Piaget one does not have a natural law until it specifies a true pattern that is demonstrably (that is, mathematico-logically) complete, the ultimate laws of science being those of logic and mathematics themselves. Others attribute law-likeness only to science satisfying certain conditions, for example to the system of scientific truths having the best combination of simplicity and informativeness (Lewis 1973). Galileo's law of free fall by itself would not count in either case, but Newton's laws of motion plus gravitation plausibly would.

Here also belong analyses of law-likeness in terms of probability, subjective (Skyrms 1980; Urbach 1988) and objective (Mellor 1990), along with other formal analyses aimed at transcending various distinctions (Mormann 1994).

All of these, and the many other, formal analyses are mutually conflicting and highly controversial. Their relations to the competing regularity and necessitarian positions depends on exactly how they are developed. (Lewis and Popper, for example, claim to combine possible worlds semantics for necessity with regularity theory.)

4   Conclusion

The existence and nature of laws is a complex problem. The diversity of philosophical theories in response is matched only by the diversity of laws themselves. The reader will find many further themes recurring in the literature – for example: the analysis and status of possibility and possible worlds; laws and initial/boundary conditions; causes, capacities and laws; concepts, laws and generality – which cannot be pursued here. There is no uncontroversial theory of laws: all face difficulties. As fast as we scientifically unravel nature's mysteries, so fast does the nature of that understanding become mysterious.

See also: POSITIVISM IN THE SOCIAL SCIENCES; PRAGMATISM; SCIENTIFIC METHOD; THEORIES, SCIENTIFIC

References and further reading

* Armstrong, D.M. (1983) *What is a Law of Nature?*, Cambridge: Cambridge University Press. (Good, readable review and critique of regularity, followed by defence of property nonlogical contingent necessitarian.)

Armstrong, D.M., Cartwright, N.D., Earman, J. and Fraassen, B.C. van (1993) 'Book Symposium: Laws and Symmetry', *Philosophy and Phenomenological Research* LIII, 411–44. (Critique and defence of van Fraassen's eliminativist regularity.)

Bigelow, J.C., Ellis, B.D. and Lierse, C. (1992) 'The World as One of a Kind: Natural Necessity and the Laws of Nature', *British Journal for Philosophy of Science* 43: 371–88. (Logical, noncontingent necessitarian.)

* Braithwaite, R.B. (1953) *Explanation*, Cambridge: Cambridge University Press. (Nonlogical, contingent, regularity.)

Byerly, H. (1990) 'Causes and Laws: The Asymmetry Puzzle', in A. Fine, M. Forbes and L. Wessels (eds) *PSA 1990*, vol. 1, East Lansing, MI: Philosophy of Science Association. (Complexity of relations between causes and laws.)

* Cartwright, N.D. (1983) *How the Laws of Physics Lie*, New York: Oxford University Press. (Eliminativist nonlogical, contingent necessitarian.)

Daly, C. (1994) 'Laws and Coincidences Contrasted', *Analysis* 54: 98–104. (Accidental versus law-like patterns.)

Dretske, F.I. (1977) 'Laws of Nature', *Philosophy of Science* 44: 248–68. (Nonlogical, contingent necessitarian.)

Earman, J. (1978) 'The Universality of Laws', *Philosophy of Science* 45: 173–81. (Difficulty of defining generality for laws.)

—— (1984) 'Laws of Nature: The Empiricist Challenge', in R.J. Bogdan (ed.) *D.H. Armstrong*, Dordrecht: Reidel. (Critique of nonlogical, contingent necessitarian.)

* Fraassen, B.C. van (1989) *Laws and Symmetry*, Oxford: Clarendon Press. (Good critique of necessitarian and regularity, followed by development of eliminativist regularity; model theoretic framework for semantics of law statements.)

Harré, R. and Madden, E.H. (1975) *Causal Powers: A Theory of Natural Necessity*, Oxford: Blackwell. (Powers nonlogical, contingent necessitarian.)

Hesse, M. (1967) 'Laws and Theories', in P.M. Edwards (ed.) *Encyclopaedia of Philosophy*, London: Collier Macmillan. (Contains discussion of empirical versus theoretical laws.)

* —— (1980) 'A Revised Regularity View of Scientific Laws', in D.H. Mellor (ed.) *Science, Belief and Behaviour*, Cambridge: Cambridge University Press. (Nonlogical, contingent regularity.)

Hooker, C.A. (1992) 'Physical Intelligibility, Projection, Objectivity and Completeness: the Divergent Ideals of Bohr and Einstein', *British Journal for the Philosophy of Science* 42: 491–511. (Field versus particle laws; invariance, objectivity, and laws.)

Jones, R. (1990) 'Determinism in Deterministic Chaos', in A. Fine, M. Forbes and L. Wessels (eds) *PSA 1990*, vol. 2, East Lansing, MI: Philosophy of Science Association. (Laws and regularities in nonlinear systems.)

* Lange, M. (1993) 'Lawlikeness', *Nous* 27: 1–21. (Laws

as inference licences; review of traditional formulations.)

* Lewis, D. (1973) *Counterfactuals*, Oxford: Blackwell. (Nonlogical, contingent regularity; counterfactual reasoning in possible worlds context.)
* Mellor, D.H. (1990) 'Laws, Chances and Properties', *International Studies in the Philosophy of Science* 4, 159–70; repr. and revised in *Matters of Metaphysics*, Cambridge: Cambridge University Press, 1991. (Probabilistic nonlogical, contingent regularity.)
* Mormann, T. (1994) 'Accessibility, Kinds and Laws: A Structural Explication', *Philosophy of Science* 61: 389–406. (Structural logical, noncontingent necessitarian.)
* Popper, K.R. (1990) *A World of Propensities*, Bristol: Thoemmes. (Propensity nonlogical, contingent necessitarian.)
  Ruby, J.E. (1986) 'The Origins of Scientific "Law"', *Journal of the History of Ideas* 47: 341–59. (Useful historical discussion.)
* Sklar, L. (1990) 'How Free are Initial Conditions?', in A. Fine, M. Forbes and L. Wessels (eds) *PSA 1990*, vol. 2, East Lansing, MI: Philosophy of Science Association. (Laws and initial conditions.)
* Skyrms, B. (1980) *Causal Necessity*, New Haven, CT: Yale University Press. (Probabilistic laws and invariance.)
* Suppe, F. (1989) *The Semantic Conception of Theories and Scientific Realism*, Chicago, IL: University of Illinois Press. (Model theoretic framework for semantics of law statements.)
* Swoyer, C. (1982) 'The Nature of Natural Laws', *Australasian Journal of Philosophy* 60: 203–23. (Logical, noncontingent necessitarian.)
  Tooley, M. (1977) 'The Nature of Laws', *Canadian Journal of Philosophy* 7: 67–98. (Property nonlogical, contingent necessitarian.)
* Urbach, P. (1988) 'What is a Law of Nature? A Humean Answer', *British Journal for Philosophy of Science* 39: 193–210. (Subjective probabilistic nonlogical, contingent regularity.)
  Vallentyne, P. (1988) 'Explaining Lawhood', *Philosophy of Science* 55: 598–613. (Concept nonlogical, contingent necessitarian with structure-of-histories law structure and counterfactual reasoning.)
  Walters, R.S. (1967) 'Laws of Science and Lawlike Statements', in P.M. Edwards (ed.) *Encyclopaedia of Philosophy*, London: Collier Macmillan. (General historical discussion of philosophical issues.)
  Wilson, M. (1990) 'Law Along the Frontier: Differential Equations and Their Boundary Conditions', in A. Fine, M. Forbes and L. Wessels (eds) *PSA 1990*, vol. 2, East Lansing, MI: Philosophy of Science Association. (Laws and boundary conditions.)

C.A. HOOKER

LE CLERC, JEAN (1657–1737)

Le Clerc was not a particularly original philosopher – his position was somewhat eclectic – but his journals and textbooks make him an important historical figure. He acted as an intermediary between English and Continental traditions. In religion he advocated an attitude of toleration.

The Swiss thinker Jean Le Clerc (Johannes Clericus) was born in Geneva. After his theological studies there he travelled extensively in Europe, read Spinoza and started a correspondence with the Remonstrant theologian Philippus van Limborch. In 1683 he settled permanently in Amsterdam where he became a minister of the Remonstrant Brotherhood and was given a chair in philosophy at their seminary. In 1686 he started the journal *Bibliothèque Universelle* (25 vols), which in 1703 was followed by the *Bibliothèque Choisie* (26 vols) and in 1714 by the *Bibliothèque ancienne et moderne* (29 vols). These journals were instrumental in spawning debates which involved, among others, LEIBNIZ and BAYLE. They also were a channel for the spread of English ideas to the Continent, where people learned about LOCKE, the Cambridge Platonists, BERKELEY and others by reading Le Clerc's abstracts (see CAMBRIDGE PLATONISM). Le Clerc edited the collected works of ERASMUS and a work of Hugo GROTIUS (*De veritate religionis christianae* 1709). His correspondence testifies to his friendship with numerous famous contemporaries.

Le Clerc was familiar with the philosophy of DESCARTES from his studies in Geneva with Robert Chouet. But although in physics and in metaphysics he remained basically Cartesian all his life, Cartesianism was never for him a closed system of thought. He not only modified and corrected Descartes' ideas in the light of Locke, BOYLE and NEWTON, but was also influenced by the Platonism of CUDWORTH. Thus, we see him taking issue with Descartes on topics such as the existence of innate ideas (which he rejects) and animal machines (he attributed to animals some power of thinking). He was fascinated by Cudworth's theory of 'plastic natures' – which he publicized in his journals – because he believed that they provide a better explanation of the formation of animal organisms than the one-dimensional mechanism he found in Descartes. He remained a metaphysical dualist, however, and also believed that a consistent application of Descartes' principles (more consistent at any rate than we find in Descartes himself) is of very great use in establishing the truth of the Christian religion.

According to Le Clerc, religion does not require us to abandon our reason: we can never deceive reason, nor can reason ever deceive us. Accordingly, there is fundamental agreement between reason and revelation, not in the sense that revelation can ever be replaced by reason, but rather that the right use of reason leads us to accept revelation and that revelation in turn is never contrary to reason. In religion, Le Clerc's attitude was formed by Erasmus and Grotius. He believed in the value of philosophical and critical methods in theology and was an advocate of tolerance. His opposition to 'enthusiasm' (his reason for rejecting MALEBRANCHE) and 'fanaticism' had much influence on English Latitudinarians.

List of works

Le Clerc, J. (1685) *Sentiments de quelques théologiens de Hollande sur l'Histoire critique du Vieux Testament composé par le P. Richard Simon*, Amsterdam.

—— (1686) *Défense des Sentiments*, Amsterdam.

—— (1692) *Logica sive ars ratiocinandi*, Amsterdam; many reprints.

—— (1695) *Physica sive de rebus corporeis*, Amsterdam; many reprints.

—— (1696a) *De l'incrédulité ou l'on examine les motifs et les raisons générales qui portent les incrédules rejeter la religion chrétienne*, Amsterdam; trans. as *A Treatise on the causes of incredulity*, London, 1697, 1720.

—— (1696b) *Ars critica in qua ad studia linguarum latinae, graecae et hebraicae via munitur*, 2 vols, Amsterdam; 6th edn, 1778.

—— (1698) *Opera philosophica*, 4 vols, Amsterdam.

—— (1959) *Lettres inédites de Le Clerc à Locke*, ed. G. Bonno, Berkeley and Los Angeles, CA.

—— (1984) *Arminianesimo e tolleranza nel Seicento olandese: Il carteggio Ph. van Limborch/Jean Le Clerc, a cura di Luisa Simonutti*, Florence: Olschki.

—— (1987–) *Epistolario*, ed. M. Sina, vol. 1 (1679–89), vol. 2 (1690–1705), Florence, 1991. (In progress.)

References and further reading

Barnes, A. (1939) *Jean Le Clerc et la République des Lettres*, Paris.

Bots, H. (1977) 'L'esprit de la République des Lettres et la tolèrance dans les trois premiers périodiques savants hollandais', *XVIIe siècle* 116 (1977): 43–5.

Colie, R.L. (1957) *Light and Enlightenment: A Study of the Cambridge Platonists and the Dutch Arminians*, Cambridge: Cambridge University Press.

Haag, E. and Haag, E. (1846–58) *La France protestante*, Paris, 10 vols. (Volume 6, pages 464–70 are relevant.)

Pitassi, M.C. (1987) *Entre croire et savoir: Le problème de la méthode critique chez Jean Le Clerc*, Kerkhistorische Bijdragen, vol. 14, Leiden: Brill.

Reesink, H.J. (1931) *L'Angleterre et la Littérature anglaise dans les trois plus anciens Périodiques de Hollande de 1684 à 1709*, Paris.

Verniére, P. (1954) *Spinoza et la pensée française avant la Révolution*, Paris: PUF, 2 vols. (Volume 1, pages 73 and following are relevant.)

THEO VERBEEK

LE DOEUFF, MICHÈLE (1948–)

Michèle le Doeuff has created new possibilities for philosophical writing. By working between philosophy and Shakespearean drama, social history and personal letters, she demonstrates how philosophy's concepts gather meaning by circulating between different forms of discourse. In so doing she takes up many of the main problems of philosophy, including the nature of the self, the possibility of philosophical ethics, and the place of women in society and in philosophy. She shows, too, how philosophy's proper commitment to critical reasoning represses the role of imagery in its own creative thought; philosophy seems dedicated to achieving theoretical results beyond its means, and imagery is misused to disguise its inevitable incompleteness. The spectre of women, or of some other group typified as 'irrational' is used to reassure philosophy of its own integral rationality.

Michèle le Doeuff has been employed as a philosopher at the École Normale Supérieure de Fontenay, the Centre National de la Recherche Scientifique in Paris and (1995) the University of Geneva. Her work generated discussion internationally after the publication in English in 1977 of 'Women and Philosophy' and, in 1979, of 'Operative Philosophy'. A study of the role of imagery in philosophy and science, *Recherches sur l'imaginaire philosophique* (1981) (*The Philosophical Imaginary*, 1989) was followed by translations and studies, first of Bacon's *New Atlantis* (1983b) and then of Shakespeare's *Venus and Adonis*

(1986). Her most extended work, *L'Étude et le rouet* (1989) (*Hipparchia's Choice*, 1991), written as four 'Notebooks', interweaves semi-fictional and historical anecdote, comment on the nature of philosophy, critical analysis of existentialism, and reflection upon philosophical biography and the philosophical 'subject'.

Le Doeuff exposes the male bias in the images, anecdotes and theory of Sartrean existentialism, and expresses critical astonishment at de Beauvoir's *tour de force* in adapting this system for her analysis of the position of women in *The Second Sex* (see BEAUVOIR, S. DE). She claims that de Beauvoir placed her feminism within a structure of ideas which is itself an epitome of the male fear of women. Le Doeuff emphasizes the imagery which Sartre uses in *Being and Nothingness* to connect the female body with ontological 'lack' and the threat posed by matter generally, to 'masculine' free consciousness. In *The Philosophical Imaginary* le Doeuff develops a strategy of analysing philosophy at the 'neuralgic points' signalled by its imagery. Kant, for example, writes of 'Truth' in terms of the image of a northern island separated by a stormy ocean from the southern islands of illusion where duty and pleasure can coexist. Le Doeuff characterizes Kant's rhetorical image as a classic form of parental threat and seduction. His efforts to set limits to metaphysical speculation only indicate how much lies beyond that limit to be cordonned off.

Le Doeuff's theme of the role of utopias in philosophical enterprise connects with her use of imagery in analysing the partial blindness any theory has to its own level of operation. More's *Utopia*, for instance, is not only a political ideal, but a trope of the ideal life of the individual scholar who desires a world in which nothing disturbs his inner peace. The figure of Utopus, the island whose life is reflected in its internal harbour of still water, represents the triumph of tranquil private enjoyment as an ideal life for its citizens. It is this dream of a political system in which narcissists could cooperate enough to meet their material needs which lies behind More's criticism of existing political institutions. More's political vision is argued to spring from a too limited idea of pleasure, and of what people can gain from and with each other. Le Doeuff pays similar attention to 'voice' in philosophy, showing how voice, too, operates vitally even in writing which affects to be free of affect. While being critical of the operation of voice, philosophers must accept and use it, rather than merely deploring it as an 'irrational' element in discourse.

Le Doeuff's work stresses this need for a complex attitude towards elements which help create philosophy and yet threaten its attempt at being reasonable. 'Masculinist' and 'logocentric' assumptions have been endemic in the production of philosophy and yet it is no use, she maintains, for women to attempt to redress the situation by expressing a special 'femininity' in philosophy. That femininity is a fantasy conjured up by a 'masculinity' bent on arrogating the field of reason to itself. At the same time, le Doeuff attacks the pretensions of 'masculinism' by all available means of argument and satire. Her critique of philosophy is not that it practises some excess of reason. It exhibits too *little* reason. In the name of a higher, or benignly legislative devotion to Reason, it has defined its own integrity by excluding women, or people of 'inferior' cultures, or children, as constitutionally on the other side of Reason. It is not philosophy's ideal of being logical which does the harm. Rather it is 'logocentrism', by which le Doeuff means the hardy tendency of philosophers to 'form projects beyond philosophy's means' by aiming at one 'logos' – one account of things to legitimate all other forms of discourse. A philosophy prepared to interact with the verbal interjections of unregularized 12-year-olds, she observes, 'may be a form ... that no longer considers its incompleteness a tragedy' (1989: 126).

Le Doeuff's study of the operation of imagery in philosophy leads on to a concern with various images of the natural and the philosophical 'subject'. Though scathing of Husserl's inflated agenda for re-establishing philosophy on the basis of a 'transcendental ego', she sees the trick of transcendence – the illusion of being master of everything which is consciously intimate to us – as natural to human thought. Le Doeuff does not present a *theory* of the subject in one of the standard styles of idealism, dualism or materialism. Rather, borrowing from the tradition of phenomenology whose conclusions she repudiates, she looks into the natural origins of the fantasies such excessive theories articulate. Analysis of philosophical theory is set beside studies of the speeches of Shakespearean characters in which, humorously or tragically, they engage in the fantasy of transcending their 'empirical specificities'. She shows how the narrative voice constructed by a Descartes, a Husserl or a Sartre, becomes transformed into a 'mind distinct from a body', a 'transcendental ego', or a 'totally free consciousness'.

See also: EXISTENTIALISM; FEMINISM; POSTMODERNISM; SUBJECT, POSTMODERN CRITIQUE OF THE; CONSCIOUSNESS

List of works

Le Doeuff, M. (1977) 'Women and Philosophy', *Radical Philosophy* 17; also in T. Moi (ed.) *French*

Feminist Thought, Oxford: Blackwell, 1987. (Influential discussion of the significance of women's exclusion from philosophy.)

—— (1979) 'Operative Philosophy: Simone de Beauvoir and Existentialism', *Ideology & Consciousness* 6. (Opens new discussion of de Beauvoir's transformation of existentialism in *The Second Sex*.)

—— (1980a) *Recherches sur l'imaginaire philosophique*, Paris: Payot; trans. C. Gordon, *The Philosophical Imaginary*, London: Athlone, 1989. (Argues for philosophy 'in the mode of the essay, which does not foreclose issues'; pursues the problematic role of imagery in upholding the image of philosophy as essentially free of imagery.)

—— (1980b) 'La Philosophie renseignée', in C. Delaceaupagne and R. Maggiosi (eds) *Philosopher*, Paris: Fayard. (On teaching philosophy in the lycées.)

—— (1981–2) 'Pierre Roussell's Chiasmas', *Ideology & Consciousness* 9. (Analyses 'chiasmas' in historical and contemporary socio-biology – the theorist protests scepticism about what they know best, while asserting authoritative knowledge about the moral and social scene which lies beyond their competence.)

—— (1982a) 'Spécial-femmes, un grumeau sur la langue', *Alidades*. (The perils of being published under the rubric of 'women's writing'.)

—— (1982b) 'Quelle modernité philosophique?', *La Revue d'en Face* 12. (On the displacement of women writers by 'progressive' deconstructionist and psychoanalytically oriented male reviewers.)

—— (1983a) 'Utopies scolaires', *Revue de Métaphysique et de Morale* 88 (2); trans. 'Utopias: Scholarly', *Social Research* 49 (2). (Analysis of the 'utopia' as a projection of a form of society ideal for a vision of intellectual life.)

—— (1983b) *'La Nouvelle Atlantide' suivi de 'Voyage dans la pensée baroque'*, Paris: Payot. (Translation, with Margaret Llasera, of Francis Bacon's *New Atlantis*, followed by a monograph analysing the significance of the imagery, rhetoric and narrative of Bacon's utopia.)

—— (1984a) 'L'Unique Sujet parlant', *Esprit* 89. (Studies Sartre's letters to 'Castor and some others', sketching the collapse of the ideal of freedom into that of being unique master of discourse.)

—— (1984b) 'The Public Employer', *mlf* 9.

—— (1986a) *'Venus et Adonis' suivi de 'Genèse d'une catastrophe'*, Paris: Alidades-Distique. (Translation of Shakespeare's *Venus and Adonis*, followed by analysis of a 'modern narcissism' as at the heart of the 'catastrophe' of Venus' failed love for Adonis.)

—— (1986b) 'Du sujet', in *Cross-references*, Society for French Studies, supp. pub. 8. (Analysis of the philosophical 'subject', relating Hegel, Lacan, Descartes and Freud to a project to be found in many of Shakespeare's characters, both tragic and comic. A moral for the contemporary scene.)

—— (1987) 'Ants and Women, or Philosophy without Borders', in A. Phillips Griffiths (ed.) *Contemporary French Philosophy*, Cambridge: Cambridge University Press. (Caustic analysis of how philosophers, so careful about the lives of 'ants', feel free in their pronouncement on women. Philosophy needs borders open to all forms of knowledge, rather than a special autonomy.)

—— (1989) *L'Étude et le rouet*, Paris: Éditions du Seuil; trans. T. Selous, *Hipparchia's Choice*, Oxford: Blackwell, 1991. (Comprising four 'notebooks', deals with the problems for women within philosophy, existentialism as a theory of consciousness and freedom, the possibility of a philosophical politics and ethics, and a role for utopianism.)

—— (1990) *'Woman, Reason, etc.'*, *Différences* 2 (3). (Discusses the risk of anti-intellectualism in the idea of special relation of women to reason.)

—— (1991) *Francis Bacon: du progrès et de la promotion des savoirs*, trans. and introductory essay, Paris: Gallimard.

—— (1992) 'Gens des science: essai sur le déni de "mixité"', *Nouvelles questions féministes* 13 (1). (Studies the way groups of women and men are treated as if essentially male.)

—— (1993) 'Le chromosome du crime: a propos de XY', *Futur antérieur: féminismes au présent*, Paris: L'Harmattan. (Discusses the phenomenon of the publication of books whose politics is not to be read, but to create a transient shock, thus to be quoted as exemplifying a new wave.)

—— (1995) 'Problème d'investiture (de la parité etc.)', *Nouvelles questions féministes* 16 (2). (Argues that a legal requirement of equal numbers of women and men in parliament, as sometimes suggested, could have extremely conservative effects. Suggests alternative strategies.)

References and further reading

Beauvoir, S. de (1949) *Le deuxième sexe*, Paris: Gallimard; trans. H.M. Parshely, *The Second Sex*, Harmondsworth: Penguin, 1972.

Deutscher, M. (ed.) (forthcoming) *Imagery, Self and Feminism in the Philosophy of Michèle le Doeuff*, New York: Humanities Press.

—— (1987) 'Stories, Pictures, Arguments', *Philosophy* 62 (240).

Gatens, M. (1986) 'Feminism, Philosophy and Riddles without Answers', in C. Pateman and E.

Grosz (eds) *Feminist Challenges*, Boston, MA: Northeastern University Press.

—— (1991) *Feminism and Philosophy*, Cambridge: Polity Press.

Griffiths, M. (1995) '(Auto)biography and Epistemology', *Educational Review* 47 (1).

Grimshaw, J. (1996) 'Philosophy, Feminism and Universalism', *Radical Philosophy* 76.

Grosz, E. (1987) 'Feminist Theory and the Challenge to Knowledges', *Women's Studies International Forum* 10 (5).

Grosz, E. (1989) *Sexual Subversions*, Sydney: Allen & Unwin.

Kraus, S. (1989) 'Simone de Beauvoir: Between Sartre and Merleau-Ponty', *Temps Modernes* 45 (520).

La Caze, M. (1994) 'De Beauvoir and Female Bodies', *Australian Feminist Studies* 20.

Lagree, J. (1984) 'Utopian Fantasizing and Philosophical Conceptualization', *Études Philosophiques* 4.

Lloyd, G. (1983) 'Masters, Slaves and Others', *Radical Philosophy* 34.

Mackenzie, C. (1986) 'Simone de Beauvoir: Philosophy and/or the Female Body', in Pateman and Gross (eds) *Feminist Challenges*, Boston, MA: Northeastern University Press.

Marks, E. and de Courtivron, I. (eds) (1980) *New French Feminisms*, New York: Schocken Books.

Moi, T. (1986) 'Existentialism and Feminism: The Rhetoric of Biology in *The Second Sex*', *Oxford Literary Review* 8 (1–2).

Morris, M. (1981–2) 'Operative Reasoning: Michèle le Doeuff, Philosophy and Feminism', *Ideology & Consciousness* 9.

—— (1988) *The Pirate's Fiancée*, London: Verso.

Nelson, C. (1987) 'Feminism, Language and Philosophy', *New Literary History* 19 (1).

Spivak, G. (1981) 'French Feminism in an International Frame', *Yale French Studies* 62.

MAX DEUTSCHER

LE GRAND, ANTOINE (1629–99)

Le Grand was the foremost expositor and popularizer of Cartesian philosophy in England during the seventeenth century. He wrote on ethics, politics, logic and numerous scientific topics. His Cartesian system is one of the most complete, emphasizing mind–body dualism and interaction, innate ideas, mechanism and method. His theory of signification is important in the Cartesian debate on ideas.

Born in France at Douai, Antoine Le Grand was sent as a Franciscan missionary to England where he spent most of his life, spreading Cartesian philosophy. He was well received by the Neoplatonists at Cambridge, but not so at Oxford where Cartesian philosophy was banned.

Le Grand's early writings are not principally Cartesian. In *Le sage des Stoiques ou l'homme sans passions* (*Man without Passion*) (1662) he expounds the doctrines of the late Stoic, SENECA: the principles of the passions are useless to virtue, and thus a wise man ought to live without passion. However, Le Grand later rejected this position because, like Descartes, he came to view the passions as conducive to life in their preservation of the mind–body union. In his main political work, *Scydromedia* (1669), he depicts the ideal state as one whose dominant features include autocracy limited by law, open trade, private property, education of the youth and religious unity.

Le Grand's comprehensive *Institutio philosophiae* (*An Entire Body of Philosophy*) (1672) includes applications of Cartesian principles of the sort that Descartes had only envisaged, with discourses on insects, plants, natural theology and ethics, plus expositions of many traditional Cartesian topics such as the *Cogito*, innate ideas and proofs of God's existence. Consistently anti-Aristotelian, Le Grand substitutes Cartesian principles of method for those found in ancient and scholastic logic. He rejects the law of non-contradiction as a first principle because it presupposes that something exists, and thus is dubitable. In the Cartesian order of philosophizing, first truths must be indubitable propositions; since the *Cogito* presupposes nothing, it is indubitable and hence a first principle. Similarly, Le Grand replaces Aristotelian form and matter with Cartesian substance and mode.

Le Grand defends Descartes' account of ideas as representational modes of the mind. The nature of ideas was a topic greatly debated in the latter half of the seventeenth century. A crux of the debate was to explain how ideas which do not resemble their objects can represent them. Le Grand's contribution was to explicate the subject (idea)–object relation in terms of signification: ideas are signs that acquire signification by a causal process ultimately dependent on God's will.

Like a minority of his Cartesian contemporaries, such as DESGABETS and RÉGIS, Le Grand retains the interaction of mind and body while rejecting any occasionalist solution to the problem of how two essentially different substances causally interact. Additionally, Le Grand defends Descartes' doctrine of the free creation of eternal truths – that God created all things in their essence and their existence.

MALEBRANCHE argued that this doctrine undermines the a priori basis for knowledge, although Le Grand never drew this consequence.

Against the traditional Aristotelian account of soul, Le Grand defends the Cartesian 'beast-machine' doctrine that non-human animals lack souls and hence are subjects for purely mechanical explanations. The animal soul is essentially corporeal, unlike the human soul which is essentially thinking and incorporeal. Thus the mechanizing of the sensitive soul is achieved without abandoning a spiritual account of the rational soul.

Le Grand was not an original thinker but he was instrumental in bringing Cartesian philosophy to a wide audience in England. He gave Cartesianism a scholastic form to aid its acceptance, and he was thoroughly loyal to Descartes' ideas, making him, uniquely, a complete Cartesian apologist.

See also: DESCARTES, R.; SERGEANT, J.

List of works

Le Grand, A. (1662) *Le sage des Stoiques ou l'homme sans passions, selon les sentiments de Sénèque*, The Hague; repr. *Les caractères de l'homme sans passions, selon les sentiments de Sénèque*, Paris, 1663; Lyons, 1665; trans. G. Richard as *Man without Passion: Or, the wise Stoick, according to the Sentiments of Seneca*, London, 1667. (Advances the Stoic doctrine that the passions are not useful to man, a view Le Grand later rejected.)

—— (1669) *Scydromedia seu sermo quem Alphonsus de la Vida habuit corram comite de Falmouth de monarchia liber primus* (Conversations on Scydromedia, Alphonsus de la Vida to the Earl of Falmouth), London; Nuremberg, 1680; German trans. U. Greiff, Bern: Lang, 1991. (Semi-fictional work which depicts the ideal state, which Le Grand called 'Scydromedia'. This work is available only in Latin or German, both which are found under the Latin title *Scydromedia*.)

—— (1671) *Philosophia veterum, e mente Renati Descartes more scholastico breviter digesta*, London; repr. and augmented as *Institutio philosophiae secundum principia d. Renati Des-Cartes, nova methodo adornata & explicata, cumque indice locupletissimo actua* (Institution of philosophy according to the principles of René Descartes: The new method praised and explained, with expanded index), London, 1672; Nuremberg, 1679; Geneva, 1694. (Le Grand later edited, expanded and appended two smaller works to this work, the result of which was translated into English by R. Blome and published as *An Entire Body of Philosophy*.)

—— (1672) *Institutio philosophiae secundum principia Domini Renati Des-Cartes, nova methodo adornata & explicata in usum juventutis academicae*, trans., corrected and expanded R. Blome as *An Entire Body of Philosophy, According to the Principles of the Famous Renate des Cartes, in Three Books, I The Institution; II The History of Nature; III Dissertation on Brutes*, London: Roycroft, 1694; repr. with intro. R.A. Watson, New York: Johnson Reprint Corporation, 1972. (The first comprehensive presentation of the Cartesian system, translated from the Latin and published in English to reach a wide audience, probably intended as a textbook.)

—— (1673) *Historia naturae variis experimentis & ratiociniis elucidata* (The history of nature elucidated by various experiments and reasons), London, 1680; Nuremberg, 1678. (This work, dedicated to Robert Boyle, treats of the nature of body in general and of various kinds of bodies in particular in order to demonstrate the truth of Cartesian principles.)

—— (1675) *Dissertatio de carentia sensus et cognitionis in brutis* (Dissertation on the absence of sense and knowledge in brutes), London; Lyons, 1675; Nuremberg, 1679; English trans. appended to *An Entire Body of Philosophy*, London, 1694. (A careful account of animal souls as essentially corporeal, consisting in the movement of blood through the body, and human souls as essentially incorporeal. Le Grand aligns the Cartesian account with that of Gassendi and Fabri against that of the Aristotelians. The work is available in Latin and English; the English version, *Dissertation of the Want of Sense and Knowledge in Brutes*, is appended to *An Entire Body of Philosophy*, 1964.)

—— (1679) *Apologia pro Renato Des-Cartes contra Samuelem Parkerum, S.T.P. archidiaconum cantuariensem, instituta & adornata* (A defence of Descartes against Samuel Parker), London, 1681; Nuremberg, 1682. (Samuel Parker, an Oxford theologian who condemned Descartes' philosophy on the grounds that it leads to atheism, had effected a ban on its public entrance to Oxford university. This work is only available in the original Latin editions.)

—— (1698) *Dissertatio de ratione cognoscendi et appendix de mutatione formali, contra J.S. methodum sciendi* (Dissertation on recognizing reason, with an appendix of rule exchange, against the method of knowing of J. Sergeant), London. (An impassioned defence of Descartes and Malebranche on ideas and other metaphysical matters against his English opponent, John Sergeant. This work is available only in its Latin, 1698 edition.)

References and further reading

Bouillier, F. (1854) *Histoire de la philosophie cartésienne* (A history of Cartesian philosophy), Paris, 2 vols. (General introduction to Le Grand's life and work especially with regard to his role in the popularization of Cartesianism.)

Rosenfield, L.C. (1968) *From beast-machine to man-machine; animal soul in French letters from Descartes to La Mettrie*, enlarged edn, New York: Oxford University Press. (Very readable with an excellent discussion of the 'beast-machine' doctrine found in Descartes and his successors.)

Ryan, J.K. (1935) 'Anthony Legrand, 1629–99: Franciscan and Cartesian', *The New Scholasticism* 9: 226–50. (Examines Le Grand's life and work as a Franciscan and a Cartesian, especially the dangerous political circumstances of his mission in England; thorough bibliography.)

—— (1936) 'Scydromedia: Anthony Legrand's Ideal Commonwealth', *The New Scholasticism* 10: 39–55. (Describes in detail the ideal commonwealth that Le Grand creates in his 1669 moral-political work *Scydromedia*.)

Watson, R.A. (1966) *The Downfall of Cartesianism: 1673–1712, a study of epistemological issues in late 17th century Cartesianism*, The Hague: Martinus Nijhoff. (Clear and excellent discussion of the Cartesian controversies regarding the nature of ideas, including Le Grand's theory of signification.)

PATRICIA A. EASTON

LE ROY, ÉDOUARD LOUIS EMMANUEL JULIEN (1870–1954)

Le Roy was a French mathematical physicist and Catholic modernist philosopher. Starting from a philosophy of life similar to Henri Bergson's philosophy of creative evolution, he argued that the capacity for invention was fundamental to human existence. This led him to develop a radical form of conventionalism according to which scientific facts are created rather than discovered. Henri Poincaré attacked this view, arguing that the scientist creates only the language in which facts are expressed.

Le Roy was born in Paris. His father was in the transatlantic shipping business, with his own outfitting company in Le Havre. Le Roy entered the École Normale Supérieure in 1892, passing the *agrégation* in 1895 and earning a doctorate of science in 1898. For many years, he taught mathematics at a Paris *lycée*. An assistant to Henri Bergson at the Collège de France from 1914 to 1920, he was named Bergson's successor in the chair of modern philosophy in 1921, and remained in that position until his retirement in 1941. In 1919 Le Roy was elected a member of the *Académie des Sciences Morales et Politiques*; in 1945 he succeeded Bergson as a member of the Académie Française.

Le Roy was a controversial representative of the Catholic modernist movement in France. He held a pragmatic view of religious dogma, whereby dogma has practical value as a source of moral directives in spite of its seeming inscrutability and incompatibility with positive, rational knowledge. These ideas, developed in such works as *Dogme et critique* (1906), earned Le Roy condemnation by Pope Pius X in an encyclical of 1907, and his *Le problème de Dieu* (1929) was put on the Index in 1931. At the centre of Le Roy's thinking is a vitalist philosophy of life and a spiritualist philosophy of freedom closely allied to Bergson's doctrine of creative evolution and similar in crucial respects to the ideas of Le Roy's friend, Teilhard de Chardin (see BERGSON, H.-L.; TEILHARD DE CHARDIN, P.; VITALISM). The human capacity for invention is fundamental and points us back to the critical phenomenon of 'hominization', when the noosphere emerges from the biosphere. A free, self-creative human agent becomes the basis of Le Roy's mature moral philosophy and philosophy of religion, in which central roles are played by transcendence, a quest for self-fulfilment and respect for a generalized moral obligation and spiritual need arising out of the human vital spirit.

As with Bergson, intuition is for Le Roy the way to true knowledge, which consists in a non-discursive immediacy characteristic of the primitive, authentic relationship of instinctive life to its surroundings. All discursive knowledge, however, is invention. Such invention may be necessary in the form of practical rules as a guide for human action, but, as invention, discursive knowledge can make no more claim to truth than the arbitrary rules of a game. This idea, with its emphasis on the mediating role of the senses and conceptual forms, owes an acknowledged debt to the Neo-Kantianism of Émile BOUTROUX, but Le Roy made it the basis for a radical form of conventionalism that he first presented in a widely discussed article, 'Science et philosophie' (1899–1900) (see CONVENTIONALISM). Le Roy's point of view gained considerable notoriety when it became the subject of an extended critical discussion by Henri Poincaré in 'Sur la valeur objective des théories de physiques' (1902) (see POINCARÉ, J.H. §4). The challenge of Le Roy's more radical conventionalism led Poincaré to some valuable and essential clarifications of his own, more moderate, conventionalism. Two major points were at issue. First, Le Roy had argued that scientific facts are merely the artificial creations of the scientist, citing as examples the concept of the atom, the phenomenon of the eclipse and the rotation of the earth. Poincaré responded by doubting that one could distinguish crude facts and invented scientific facts as sharply as Le Roy might think possible and by insisting that crude facts themselves play a role in science by imposing scientific facts upon us. Poincaré grants the presence of a creative moment in science, but he confines it to the conventional choice of disguised definitions, as in the choice of a unit metre stick or the choice of Euclid's parallel postulate, choices analogous to the choice of a language. Once those conventions are accepted, the remaining propositions of science have a determinate truth-value ascertainable by empirical means. Moreover, the role of such arbitrary conventions diminishes steadily as we move from the basic levels of science, such as geometry and kinematics, to mechanics and physics. The second point of difference between Poincaré and Le Roy concerned the question whether, among the conventional variants of a given scientific theory, there remained any 'universal invariant', a content common to the different formulations. Poincaré interpreted Le Roy as denying the existence of such an invariant content, but himself insisted upon it. Arguing again by analogy with translation between two languages, such as French and German, Poincaré held that one and the same proposition could be expressed equivalently in either language, with determinate rules of translation allowing us to go back and forth between the two.

In his *La théorie physique* (1906), Pierre Duhem declared his sympathy for Le Roy's conventionalism in opposition to Poincaré's critique (see DUHEM, P.M.M. §4). Two years later, in *Identité et réalité* (1908), Émile MEYERSON expressed sympathy for Le Roy's views, but identified himself more closely with what he regarded as the less radical position of Duhem. Le Roy's radical conventionalism had perhaps its most profound influence on Kazimierz AJDUKIEWICZ. By contrast, his work in the philosophy of mathematics, and his writings on microphysics and relativity theory, were of less lasting import.

List of works

Le Roy, É. (1899–1900) 'Science et philosophie' ('Science and Philosophy'), *Revue de métaphysique et de morale* 7 (1899): 375–425, 503–62, 706–31; 8 (1900): 37–72. (First statement of Le Roy's radical conventionalism.)

—— (1900) 'La science positive et les philosophies de la liberté' ('Positive Science and the Philosophies of Liberty'), in *Congrès internationale de philosophie, I Paris 1900, Philosophie générale*, Paris: Colin, vol. 1, 313–41. (A second widely read exposition of Le Roy's conventionalism.)

—— (1901) 'Un posit-visme nouveau' ('A New Positivism'), *Revue de métaphysique et de morale* 9: 143–4. (Influential proclamation of a new anti-metaphysical movement.)

—— (1906) *Dogme et critique* (Dogma and Criticism), Paris: Bloud. (Pragmatic view of dogma, condemned by Pius X.)

—— (1912) *Une philosophie nouvelle, Henri Bergson*, Paris: F. Alcan; trans. V. Benson, *The New Philosophy of Henri Bergson*, London: Williams & Norgate, and New York: Holt, 1913. (Study of Bergson.)

—— (1927) *L'Exigence idéaliste et la fait de l'évolution* (The Exigency of Idealism and the Fact of Evolution), Paris: Boivin & Cie. (Le Roy's philosophy of life.)

—— (1928) *Les origines humaines et l'évolution de l'intelligence* (Human Origins and the Evolution of Intelligence), Paris: Boivin & Cie. (On hominization and the noosphere.)

—— (1929) *Le problème de Dieu* (The Problem of God), Paris: L'Artisan du livre. (Put on the Index in 1931.)

—— (1929–30) *La pensée intuitive* (Intuitive Thought), Paris: Boivin & Cie, 2 vols. (On intuition as the source of genuine knowledge.)

References and further reading

Abelé, J. (1955) 'Le Roy et la philosophie des sciences' ('Le Roy and the Philosophy of Science') *Études* 284: 106–12. (On the debate between Le Roy and Poincaré.)

* Duhem, P. (1906) *La théorie physique. Son objet et sa structure*, Paris: Chevalier et Rivière; 2nd edn, 1914; trans. P.P. Wiener, *The Aim and Structure of Physical Theory*, Princeton, NJ: Princeton University Press, 1954. (Claims priority over Le Roy; otherwise expresses general agreement.)

Giedymin, J. (1978) 'Radical Conventionalism, its Background and Evolution: Poincaré, Le Roy and Ajdukiewicz', in J. Giedymin (ed.) *Kazimierz Ajdukiewicz: The Scientific World-Perspective and Other Essays, 1931–1963*, Dordrecht: Reidel, xix–lii; repr. in J. Giedymin, *Science and Convention: Essays on Henri Poincaré's Philosophy of Science and the Conventionalist Tradition*, Oxford: Pergamon, 1982, 109–48. (An informative study of influence of Le Roy's conventionalism.)

* Meyerson, É. (1908) *Identité et réalité*, Paris: Alcan; 2nd edn, 1912; trans. K. Loewenberg, *Identity and Reality*, London: Allen & Unwin, 1930; repr. New York: Dover, 1962. (Expresses sympathy for Le Roy's conventionalism while claiming a position closer to Duhem.)

Miranda, M. do C.T. de (1957) *Théorie de la verité chez Édouard Le Roy* (The Theory of Truth in Édouard Le Roy), Paris: Lecoffre. (The only extended study of Le Roy's theory of truth.)

* Poincaré, H. (1902) 'Sur la valeur objective des théories de physiques', *Revue de métaphysique et de morale* 10; repr. in *La valeur de la science*, Paris: Flammarion, 1905; trans. G.B. Halstead, *The Foundations of Science*, New York: Science Press, 1913; repr. separately as *The Value of Science*, New York: Dover, 1958. (Critical attack on Le Roy's claim that scientific facts are created.)

DON HOWARD

LEARNING

Learning is the acquisition of some true belief or skill through experience. Rationalist/idealist philosophers held that the very constitution of thought guarantees that fundamental laws hold of the world we experience, and that our understanding of these laws was therefore innate, not learned. The empiricist tradition, doubtful of these Rationalist claims, denied that much was innate, and held that learning occurred through associations of mental representations. This view was lent support by the nineteenth-century development of physiological psychology, which led to a view of learning as a system of adjustments in a network without any intervening representations, a perspective that led in turn, in the twentieth century, to behaviourist studies of stimulus–response associations, and eventually to contemporary neural net computational models.

Empiricism, however, had also invited, especially with Hume, doubts that the correspondence between mental representations and the world could be known. Hume believed people learn, or at least form new habits, but he did not think there could be any normative theory of learning – any way of making it 'rational'. His scepticism led to the development by Bayes and other statisticians of formal theories of how learning from evidence ought to be done. However, the standards that developed in the form of the theory of subjective probability proved impossible to apply until very fast digital computers became available.

The digital computer in turn prompted both novel normative theories of learning not considered by the statistical tradition, and also attempts to describe human learning by computational procedures. At the same time, a revolution in linguistics held that humans have an innate, specialized algorithm for learning language. Applications of computation theory to learning led to an understanding of what computational systems – possibly including people – can and cannot reliably learn. Major issues remain concerning how people acquire the system of distinctions they use to describe the world, and how – and how well – they learn the causal structure of the everyday world.

1   Eighteenth- and nineteenth-century empiricism
2   Cognitive nature of the associative process
3   Probability and learning
4   Learning and computation

1   Eighteenth- and nineteenth-century empiricism

The empiricist tradition, represented in the eighteenth and nineteenth centuries by Hume and Mill, among philosophers, and by Maudsley among psychologists, developed an associationist psychology in which mental dynamics is driven by 'associations' among 'ideas', roughly bits of images or propositional content. Associations were thought to be constituted both by internal relations among ideas – similarity, for example – and external physical relations – near simultaneity of acquisition, for example. The doctrine of ideas distinguished simples and compounds. Experience presents compound ideas (or 'impressions' from which ideas are formed) which are separated into simples by a kind of internal analysis (see EMPIRICISM; HUME, D. §2; MILL, J.S. §§2, 3).

Empiricist psychology produced foundational problems: how such can such processes lead to faithful representations of the external world, and how can we know that they do? Hume argued that they could not be known to do so. The dominant alternative answers in the eighteenth and nineteenth (and, one might argue, twentieth) centuries were forms of idealism, from the phenomenalism of Mill and Mach, which held that all reality is appearance, to the transcendental idealism of the Kantians, who agreed with Hume that we cannot know the world 'in itself', but held that the very conditions for the possibility of thought and experience guarantee the fundamental geometric, temporal and causal structure of experience (see IDEALISM; KANT, I. §§4–6; MACH, E.; PHENOMENALISM).

HELMHOLTZ read Kant as offering a (false) psychological theory rather than a logical solution to sceptical doubts about knowledge and the apparent phenomena of a prioricity. Helmholtz offered empirical analyses of the visual and auditory systems, emphasizing both their physiological mechanisms and the external conditions required for their reliability. His work represents perhaps the first really 'naturalized' epistemology, rejecting all a priori justifications of the reliability of human belief.

The network structure of the cortex, established by Cajal in the 1890s, gave new impetus to associationist theories of learning. In psychologists as varied as William JAMES and Sigmund FREUD, 'ideas' were vaguely and variously associated with states of particular cells or collections of cells, or with distributions of energy among cells. Learning was thought to be some process by which these systems were adjusted in response to inputs from sensory transducers. The network idea offered at least the skeleton of a unified account of the acquisition of both behavioural and inferential skills. Under James' influence, Edward Thorndike called himself a 'connectionist' and network talk became (and remains) both a metaphor for associations, a detailed computational model, and a theory of brain function. In the first two roles, the strengths of the connections between network nodes have commonly been assumed to be modified either by their temporal pairing or by a feedback process sensitive to a discrepancy between the output of the system and a 'teaching' signal. This discrepancy (the error in the output) is fed back into the system that maps inputs to outputs, altering the connection strengths so as to reduce the discrepancy. In the behaviourist tradition (see BEHAVIOURISM, METHODOLOGICAL AND SCIENTIFIC), the first process for modifying the strengths of connections is called classical or Pavlovian conditioning, while the second is called instrumental or operant conditioning. In more recent 'neural net' computer simulations (see CONNECTIONISM), the first process is called 'unsupervised learning', while the second is called 'supervised learning', although no real neural process is known that corresponds to propagating errors back through a network.

2   Cognitive nature of the associative process

Thorndike is often regarded as one of the fathers of (scientific) behaviourism, the psychological movement that holds that psychology should focus exclusively on causal relations between 'stimuli' and behavioural 'responses'. One stimulus became associated with another, or with a response, as a result of 'reward' or 'reinforcement'. Behaviourism permitted associationism to be put to a fairly rigorous scientific test. However, experimental results from the study of putatively associative learning in a small number of basic experimental paradigms indicate that the process is considerably more complex than was originally thought. For example, the strengths of associations do not develop independently of one another. Whether or not the temporal pairing of two stimuli – say, the appearance of a diagonal red stripe on a round plastic button followed a few seconds later by the presentation of food to a pigeon – does or does not produce an association (in this case, between the stripe and the food) depends on the strengths of other associations that have developed prior to the current training or are developing during this training. If, for example, the average interval between food presentations is as high in the absence of the diagonal stripe as it is in its presence, the experimental chamber itself becomes strongly associated with food, and this association between the chamber and food blocks the formation of an association between the diagonal stripe and the food. The dependence of changes in one associative bond on the strengths of other associative bonds reflects the ability of the associative process to pick out the best and simplest predictors from among several competing stimuli that predict the occurrence of something important to the animal (hereafter called a 'reinforcer' because it strengthens the animal's reaction to the predicting stimulus).

A second complexity is that animals 'associate' two stimuli regardless of the temporal relation between them. 'Associate' is placed in quotes because it here means something much more vague like 'learns something about the temporal relation between'. If a stimulus reliably predicts the omission of a reinforcer, the animal learns an inhibitory association, that is, it learns that one stimulus predicts the omission of the other. If the two stimuli are made to occur truly randomly, so that knowledge of the time of occurrence of one provides no information about the time of occurrence of the other, then the animal learns that one does not predict the other. This is shown by a subsequent test in which the stimuli are temporally paired, so that now one stimulus does reliably predict the other. The exposure to the early truly random phase retards the animal's 'associating' the two stimuli in this second phase.

Note the difficulty of conceptualizing the learning in the truly random phase as the establishment of a conductive link (a true association) between the two stimuli. The one stimulus neither excites nor inhibits an expectation of the other – the only possibilities in a purely associative theory of learning – and yet the animal has learned something. Thus, it is difficult to conceptualize this learning in associative terms, because it is difficult to say what has become associated with what.

The discovery of the subtleties of the associative process in simple animal learning paradigms has led many modern theorists to adopt a more cognitive interpretation of the associative process. The process seems to depend on abstract relations between stimuli such as 'contingency' rather than on simple temporal pairing. This more cognitive view has less neurobiological transparency, and seems to require something like the resources of a computational theory of mind (see MIND, COMPUTATIONAL THEORIES OF).

3 Probability and learning

In the eighteenth and nineteenth centuries, statistics developed normative theories of inference unconnected with human psychology, but bounded by human computational limitations. A typical statistical problem concerned resolving recorded observations into a function of quantities satisfying a deterministic regularity and a quantity, representing the sum of a multitude of unknown quantities influencing the observed values, satisfying a probability distribution. After Legendre's development of least squares early in the nineteenth century, that method soon dominated practice in astronomy and geodesy. Laplace and Bayes advocated methods of learning involving forming new probabilities by conditioning old (or 'prior') probabilities on new evidence. George Boole attempted to develop more general probabilistic methods for inferring causes, but his proposals had little success.

Late in the nineteenth century Pierce introduced the idea of randomization in experiments, and Fisher's elaboration of that idea early in the twentieth century led directly to almost all of modern experimental design in the non-physical sciences, establishing a norm about how causes are to be learned in subjects from biology to economics (see STATISTICS; STATISTICS AND SOCIAL SCIENCE). Roughly in the same period, the work of Galton, Pearson and Yule on regression, correlation and contingency tables led to the application of regression and association for causal inferences from non-experimental observations. Yule himself carefully investigated the limitations of such methods, which are still widely used but regarded as unreliable by experts. Beginning at the turn of the century, a number of psychologists developed the methods of factor analysis, which amounted to algorithms for generating theories of how unobserved features influenced observed quantities.

There are two approaches to probability theory, 'objective' (for example, 'frequentist') ones, which emphasize how the probability that something is G, given that it is F, is a function of the number of Fs that have been G in the past, and 'subjectivist' ones, which emphasize the degree of a person's confidence in a hypothesis (see PROBABILITY, INTERPRETATIONS OF). Introduced by Ramsey and De Finetti early in the

twentieth century, the modern formulation of subjective probability treats probability as a measure of degree of belief, utility as a measure of desire, maximum expected utility as a decision principle, and conditional probability as a (normative) mechanism of learning. This 'Bayesian' perspective offered at least the framework of a general theory of inference and decision, but its practical influence was very limited both because of the dominance of frequentist ideas in statistics, and because the calculations required by Bayesian norms in even simple problems were beyond unaided human capacities. Kahneman, Tversky, Dawes and many others have shown regularly reproducible forms of human judgment that seem to violate Bayesian norms, but others have argued that such experiments fail to capture the range and frequency of decision-making tasks in which human competence evolved, and for that range of tasks human psychology satisfies Bayesian norms (see RATIONALITY OF BELIEF). Others have offered speculations about how the nervous system may implement (unconsciously, of course) Bayesian computations (see PROBABILITY THEORY AND EPISTEMOLOGY; RATIONALITY, PRACTICAL).

Using either the calculus of probability or logical 'partial entailment' relations, or simply *modus ponens*, KEYNES, CARNAP, REICHENBACH, HEMPEL, POPPER and others proposed theories of 'confirmation' or 'corroboration' of hypotheses (see CONFIRMATION THEORY; INDUCTIVE INFERENCE). These proposals concerned themselves largely with the a priori justification of hypotheses; no attempt was made to show that the confirmation relations they defined coincided with procedures for reliably discovering the truth, that is, for learning. These were regarded as issues exclusively for psychology. Concern with capturing reliable methods has come to dominate recent theories of learning, and 'reliabilist' approaches in epistemology generally (see RELIABILISM).

4 Learning and computation

Using logical methods derived from Frege, Carnap and Russell sketched the 'construction' of concepts of properties, objects, and spatial and temporal relations from categories held to be more immediate: 'sense-data' in Russell's case, recollections of similarity between two 'elementary experiences' – Gestalt episodes – in Carnap's case (see SENSE-DATA; LOGICAL POSITIVISM). These theories of concept formation were not offered as mathematical psychology but as analyses (explications) of ordinary concepts (see CONCEPTS §§3, 5–6; CONCEPTUAL ANALYSIS). Carnap's theory had the distinction of being algorithmic, and might arguably be considered the first attempt at an artificial intelligence programme (see ARTIFICIAL INTELLIGENCE).

The advent of the theory of computation and the digital computer prompted a number of related developments in the middle of the twentieth century. Psychologists began exploring algorithmic procedures for learning. Under the guise of 'concept learning', Bruner and his colleagues, and later Hunt, developed effective versions of Francis Bacon's methods. From instances of the predicates involved, these programs learned universal biconditionals with a single predicate on one side and any logical formula not containing that predicate on the other side. The psychologists gave some rather sophisticated thought to how the representation of propositions influences the computational complexity of their application in inference. The subject of artificial intelligence was born at the same time, and it immediately focused on how to make computers simulate learning. Although none of these algorithms was an accurate description of human learning, they were used to promote the proposition that various aspects of human learning may be algorithmic or computational.

CHOMSKY revolutionized linguistics by supposing that language speakers recognize grammatical sentences, and distinguish them from non-grammatical sentences by using an unconscious algorithm. He proposed that humans acquire the algorithm for their native language by applying a highly specific learning procedure specific to language and shared by all people. Chomsky claims that the procedure ('Universal Grammar') is not, itself, learned along 'empiricist' lines, but is innate along lines he associates with the early Rationalists. The idea naturally raised many questions of a kind that still trouble cognitive science and linguistics: how can we know whether there is a special learning facility for language? If there is such an algorithm, any human language must be of a kind the algorithm can learn from the evidence available to children (see LANGUAGE, INNATENESS OF). How does that restrict the languages that are possible for humans?

The last question has been addressed in part by computational learning theory, a subject that has one of its roots in the philosophy of Hans Reichenbach. REICHENBACH had argued that the aim of inductive inference is to judge limiting frequencies, and that the simple rule of guessing that limiting frequencies equal observed frequencies converges to the correct limit if a limit exists. His student, Hilary Putnam, combined Reichenbach's long-run, reliabilist perspective with recursion theory to create one branch of the modern subject of computational learning theory. The framework for a discovery problem assumes that a set of alternative hypotheses are to be assessed, and any member of a set of (infinitely long) data streams is possible; each hypothesis is consistent with some data streams and inconsistent with other data streams. The investigator is idealized as a function from initial segments of data streams to hypotheses. The investigator succeeds on a data stream provided that the function representing the investigator has a false (for that data stream) hypothesis as its value on at most a finite number of initial segments of the data stream. The investigator solves the discovery problem provided it succeeds on every possible data stream allowed in the formulation of the problem.

The framework captures many reliabilist intuitions, and it has the further virtue of flexibility: success criteria can be altered; the relation between data streams and hypotheses can be altered; and constraints of many kinds can be imposed on the function representing the investigator. It does not represent inductive success as getting the correct answer in the infinite future, but rather as getting the correct answer after a finite amount of evidence is acquired, but without any fixed guarantee on how large 'finite' will be.

Putnam, and independently at about the same time, E. Mark Gold, characterized when a problem can be solved by an effective learner – that is, one whose learning function is a Turing machine (see TURING MACHINES). Gold subsequently adapted the framework to model language learning, where a language is represented as a set of numbers that can be listed by a computer. For some collections of possible languages, there exist algorithms that can learn any language in the collection; for other collections, no such language is possible. On the Chomskian view, the collection of possible human languages must be of the first kind, a learnable class. So, by studying algorithms, something can be learned about the structure of human language. Computer scientists investigated both the language framework and a related one in which the data streams are graphs of recursive functions.

Kelly developed the framework into topological, measure-free alternatives to statistical analyses of reliable inference, with a whole class of counter examples to standard philosophical morals about methods of inquiry. For example, there are solvable (by computable learners) problems that cannot be solved by computable learners that output only hypotheses consistent with data received and background assumptions; other solvable (again, by computable learners) problems that cannot be solved by computable learners who change hypotheses only when they are contradicted by the evidence; and still others that cannot be solved by computable Bayesian learners. For learners that do not have to be computable, traditional confirmation strategies fail to solve discovery problems that can be solved by other means. Kelly showed there is a universal strategy that succeeds whenever success is possible but is neither Reichenbach's nor Popper's. Virtually every methodological principle advanced by philosophers of science turns out to be sub-optimal or to entail some sacrifice of reliability.

Social aspects of learning have been undertaken in the context of computational learning theory, usually as studies of 'team learning' in which a number of parallel investigators process data and success requires that only one of them succeed. Recently, using very simplified reliability frameworks, Kitcher has provided an economic analysis of social gains in reliability when investigators compete and cooperate with the selfish aim of being the first to learn the truth about a scientific question.

We are still far from understanding how humans develop so that they distinguish relevant features of the world and know the causal relations among everyday circumstances. A theory about algorithms for learning causes has recently developed in philosophy and computer science, but psychologists have not yet compared it with human performance, and statistically sophisticated psychological models of human judgment of causality are only now appearing.

See also: INNATE KNOWLEDGE

References and further reading

Amsel, A. (1989) *Behaviorism, Neobehaviorism, and Cognitivism in Learning Theory: Historical and Contemporary Perspectives*, Hillsdale, NJ: Erlbaum. (A neo-behaviourist critique.)

Blumberg, M.S. and Wasserman, E.A. (1995) 'Animal Mind and the Argument from Design', *American Psychologist* 50: 133–44. (A critique of theories that posit animal consciousness from a moderately behaviourist perspective.)

Chomsky, N. (1959) 'Review of Verbal Behavior (by B.F. Skinner)', *Language* 35: 26–58. (An influential critique of behaviourist learning theory.)

Gallistel, C.R. (1990) *The Organization of Learning*, Cambridge, MA: Bradford Books/MIT Press. (Rationalist/nativist treatments of learning.)

Gould, J.L. and Marler, P. (1987) 'Learning by Instinct', *Scientific American* 256: 74–85. (Examination of ethological evidence for innate cognitive faculties.)

Hull, C.L. (1930) 'Knowledge and Purpose as Habit Mechanisms', *Psychological Review* 37: 511–25. (Classic statement of the neo-behaviourist position.)

Klein, S.B. and Mowrer, R.R. (eds) (1989) *Contemporary Learning Theories*, 2 vols, *Instrumental Conditioning Theory and the Impact of Biological Constraints on Learning* and *Pavlovian Conditioning and the Status of Traditional Learning Theory*, Hillsdale, NJ: Erlbaum. (Modern associative learning theory.)

Osherson, D.N., Stob, M. and Weinstein, S. (1986) *Systems that Learn: An Introduction to Learning Theory for Cognitive and Computer Scientists*, Cambridge, MA: MIT Press. (A contemporary rationalist approach to learning.)

Pavlov, I.V. (1928) *Lectures on Conditioned Reflexes: The Higher Nervous Activity of Animals*, London: Lawrence & Wishart. (The central work on 'classical' behaviourist conditioning.)

Pinker, S. (1994) *The Language Instinct*, New York: William Morrow. (An excellent and highly accessible summary of the Chomskian revolution in linguistics.)

Rumelhart, D.E. and McClelland, J.L. (1986) *Parallel Distributed Processing: Explorations in the Microstructure of Cognition*, vol. 1, *Foundations*, vol. 2, *Psychological and Biological Models*, Cambridge, MA: MIT Press. (Neural net approaches to associative learning by computers.)

Skinner, B.F. (1950) 'Are Theories of Learning Necessary?', *Psychological Review* 57: 193–216. (Classic statement of the radical behaviourist position.)

—— (1990) 'Can Psychology be a Science of Mind?', *American Psychologist* 45: 1,206–10. (A radical behaviourist critique of cognitive approaches.)

Watson, J.B. (1919) *Psychology from the Standpoint of a Behaviorist*, Philadelphia, PA: Lippincott. (The early, classic statement of the behaviourist programme.)

C.R. GALLISTEL
CLARK GLYMOUR

LEBENSPHILOSOPHIE

In its most general sense Lebensphilosophie denotes a philosophy which asks after the meaning, value and purpose of life, turning away from purely theoretical knowledge towards the undistorted fullness of lived experience. In the second half of the nineteenth century and the early twentieth century the concept of 'life' assumed a central role in German philosophy. Lebensphilosophie typically opposes rigid abstractions with a philosophy based on feeling and intuition, and seeks to establish the priority of 'life' as an all-encompassing whole. The central claim underlying its various mani-festations is that life can only be understood from within.

The first recorded use of the term *Lebensphilosophie* is in a 1772 collection of essays by G.B. von Schirach, *Über die moralische Schönheit und Philosophie des Lebens* (On moral beauty and the philosophy of life). In the late eighteenth and early nineteenth centuries the expression was employed to characterize a philosophy for practical life and was used synonymously with terms such as *Lebensweisheit* (wisdom of life) and *Lebenskunst* (the art of living) in order to provide general ethical and practical maxims for correct living.

While there are obvious points of continuity with this popular usage, the roots of the modern conception of *Lebensphilosophie* should, more generally, be traced back to the mid-eighteenth-century reaction against Enlightenment rationalism. The emphasis on feeling and immediacy, and the lived experience of truth in the work of figures such as HAMANN and HERDER, together with the search for a unifying principle prior to the abstractions of reason, leads to a prioritization of 'life' over 'mere understanding'. The *Sturm und Drang* mobilized a set of fundamental oppositions – between the living and the dead, the concrete and the abstract, the organic and the mechanical, the dynamic and the static – whose influence is carried through to modern *Lebensphilo-sophie* in the Idealism of SCHELLING and the early HEGEL, as well as the Romantic attempt to establish the identity of philosophy and life, poetry and thought (see ROMANTICISM, GERMAN).

However, the centrality of the concept of 'life' to German philosophy in the decades between 1870 and 1920 cannot be understood without reference to the work of SCHOPENHAUER and NIETZSCHE. Schopenhauer's concept of the will as a single, unifying principle is both a precursor and model for subsequent attempts to grasp life as an all-encompassing metaphysical category: here the critique of rationalism first takes on the form of a metaphysics of the irrational. In contrast, Nietzsche's importance resides in his attempt to explicate truth in terms of its function for life, and his insistence on the dynamic, historical and conflictual character of human claims to knowledge. A third and later figure of comparable importance is the French philosopher Henri BERGSON, whose conception of time as lived experience exercised an enormous influence on German philosophy in the late nineteenth and early twentieth centuries. Bergson's ideas were taken up as part of the vitalist opposition to scientific materialism and the attempt to show that life cannot adequately be explained in mechanical and physical terms: biology rather than physics provides the central categories for understanding life in its own terms (see VITALISM).

Lebensphilosophie must also be seen as part of a broader cultural movement which extended beyond the confines of philosophy. This movement is marked, on the one hand, by a striving to overcome, through a vitalistic affirmation of the fullness of life, the limits placed on the isolated individual, and on the other hand by a mood of pessimism and decadence which received its most powerful expression in the arts. In the work of figures as diverse as Georg SIMMEL, Ludwig Klages and Oswald Spengler, the concept of life is taken up as a critical category by means of which the conflicts and contradictions of modern society could be identified and diagnosed.

There are two principal reasons for the relative obscurity into which *Lebensphilosophie* has fallen today, despite the dominance which it exercised prior to and immediately after the First World War. The first is the extent to which some of its principal insights were taken up in a methodologically more rigorous and productive way in Husserlian phenomenology and Heidegger's 'philosophy of existence' (see HEIDEGGER, M.). The second is the extent to which the irrationalism and cultural criticism of *Lebens-philosophie* fed into the doctrines of National Socialism. Perhaps the most enduring achievement of *Lebensphilosophie* is to be found in the work of Wilhelm DILTHEY. His emphasis on the concrete fullness of lived experience and the diversity of the manifestations of social and cultural life prior to the abstractions of reason results in a new attempt to ground philosophically the human sciences and the important methodological distinction between *Erk-lärung* (explanation) and *Verstehen* (understanding) (see EXPLANATION IN HISTORY AND SOCIAL SCIENCE).

See also: ENLIGHTENMENT, CONTINENTAL

References and further reading

Bollnow, O.F. (1958) *Die Lebensphilosophie*, Berlin/Göttingen/Heidelberg: Springer Verlag. (Comprehensive survey.)

Kühne-Bertram, G. (1987) *Aus dem Leben – zum Leben. Entstehung, Wesen und Bedeutung populärer Lebensphilosophen in der Geistesgeschichte des 19. Jahrhunderts* (From life – to life. The origin, nature and significance of popular philosophers of life in the history of ideas in the 19th century), Frankfurt: Peter Lang. (An attempt to trace the influence of popular, pre-scientific writings on later, academic *Lebensphilosophie*.)

Lieber, H.-J. (1974) *Kulturkritik und Lebensphiloso-phie. Studien zur Deutschen Philosophie der Jahr-*

hundertwende (Cultural criticism and *Lebensphilosophie*. Studies in German philosophy at the turn of the century), Darmstadt: Wissenschaftliche Buchgesellschaft. (Contains essays on Dilthey and Simmel and on the relationship of *Lebensphilosophie* to National Socialism.)

Misch, G. (1930) *Lebensphilosophie und Phänomenologie. Eine Auseinandersetzung der Dilthey'schen Richtung mit Heidegger und Husserl* (*Lebensphilosophie* and phenomenology. A critical discussion of the relationship between Dilthey's approach and that of Husserl and Heidegger), Bonn: Friedrich Cohen. (Early analysis of the relationship between *Lebensphilosophie* and phenomenology which seeks to defend the superiority of Dilthey's approach.)

Rickert, H. (1920) *Die Philosophie des Lebens. Darstellung und Kritik der philosophischen Modeströmungen unserer Zeit* (The philosophy of life. A presentation and critique of the current trends in philosophy), Tübingen: J.C.B. Mohr. (Contemporary critique of *Lebensphilosophie* from the standpoint of Neo-Kantianism.)

Scheler, M. (1915) 'Versuch einer Philosophie des Lebens' ('An essay on the philosophy of life'), in *Vom Umsturz der Werte. Abhandlungen und Aufsätze* (On the overturning of values. Treatises and essays), Bern: Francke, 1955. (Identification of Nietzsche, Dilthey and Bergson as the founding fathers of contemporary *Lebensphilosophie*.)

* Schirach, G.B. von (1772) *Über die moralische Schönheit und Philosophie des Lebens. Reden und Versuche* (On moral beauty and the philosophy of life. Lectures and essays), Altenberg. (First publication to use the term *Lebensphilosophie*.)

Schnädelbach, H. (1984) *Philosophy in Germany, 1831–1933*, trans. E. Matthews, Cambridge: Cambridge University Press. (Focused history of German philosophy written for an English-speaking audience. Contains a chapter devoted to the concept of 'life'.)

Sendlinger, A. (1994) *Lebenspathos und Décadence um 1900. Studien zur Dialektik der Décadence und der Lebensphilosophie am Beispiel Eduard von Keyserlings und Georg Simmels* (The pathos of life and decadence around 1900. Studies in the dialectic of decadence and *Lebensphilosophie* through the example of Eduard von Keyserling and Georg Simmel), Frankfurt: Peter Lang. (Investigation into the broader cultural context of *Lebensphilosophie*.)

Simmel, G. (1921) *Der Konflikt der modernen Kultur*, trans. K.P. Etzkorn in G. Simmel (ed.) *The Conflict in Modern Culture and Other Essays*, New York: Teachers College Press. (Account of the centrality

of the concept of life by one of the key thinkers of the period.)

JASON GAIGER

LEEUWIS, DENYS DE *see* DENYS THE CARTHUSIAN

LEFEBVRE, HENRI (1901–91)

Henri Lefebvre was a Marxist and existential philosopher, a sociologist and a theorist of the state. His humanistic neo-Marxism has been influential throughout Europe. In the English-speaking world he is best known for his analyses of 'everyday life', his work in the sociology of urban and rural life, and his theory of social space. Lefebvre was one of the most prominent early critics of structuralism, and is considered by some to be the first post-structuralist. He was a relentless critic of academic philosophy's metaphysical tendencies.

During the 1920s, Lefebvre was associated with the surrealist movement in Paris, and his work from this period has been described as proto-existentialist. In 1929, however, he joined the Parti Communiste Français (PCF) and by the 1940s had become the PCF's leading intellectual spokesperson and a Marxist critic of Sartrean existentialism (see SARTRE, J.-P.; MARXISM, WESTERN). With Norbert Guterman, Lefebvre was the first to translate the works of the young Karl Marx into French, and his *Le Matérialisme dialectique* (*Dialectical Materialism*) (1939) earned him the title 'Father of the Dialectic' in France. He was also the first interwar writer to attempt an anti-fascist reading of Nietzsche, and one of the few to publish rigorous critiques of nationalism and National Socialism.

Lefebvre's main philosophical work, *Logique Formelle, Logique Dialectique* (Formal logical, dialectical logic) (1947a), provides a critique of formal logic and categorical reasoning. In 1957 he was excluded from the PCF for his attacks on Stalinism and his humanist unorthodoxy, and was subsequently reconciled with Sartre. In the 1960s he inspired figures in the French avant garde, including his teaching assistant Jean BAUDRILLARD and members of the Situationniste Internationale, many of whom were his students, including Michele Bernstein, Guy Debord and Daniel Cohn-Bendt, the student leader of the May 1968 demonstrations in Paris. The failure of those demonstrations to lead to substantial changes in the French way of life was seen, however, as an indictment of Lefebvre's method of revolution-through-festival, derived from the surrealists; in subsequent years his humanist Marxism came under direct attack from Althusser's 'Scientific Marxism' (see ALTHUSSER, L.P.).

Lefebvre's influential interpretation of Marxism was similar in tone to that of the young Georg LUKÁCS, emphasizing alienation as the central concept of Marx's thought. Alienation in the economic sphere was explored using the tools of historical dialectical materialism, a methodology on which Lefebvre placed great store; but he also argued that Marxism would remain incomplete so long as it was restricted to the economic sphere rather than incorporating all aspects of life. He presented three-part dialectics in order to undermine the tendency to simplistic dualisms apparent in much Marxist thought. Lefebvre's 'retro-jective' method, by which he attempted to operationalize historical materialism for research purposes, provided the basis for Sartre's regressive-progressive method.

In his *Critique de la vie quotidienne* (*Critique of Everyday Life*) (1947b) Lefebvre critically analyses the banality of life in the modern world in terms of the 'mystification' of its alienated, boring quality. His theory is a reinterpretion of Lukács' and Heidegger's notion of 'everydayness' or banality (*Alltäglichkeit*) in the more sociological terms of alienation and everyday social routines. In this, he is a precursor of the work of BOURDIEU on habitual routines ('habitus'). A 'romantic revolutionary', Lefebvre sought a 'revolution in everyday life' in which spontaneous, ludic expression would be liberated from the restrictions of authoritarian rationality and alienated routine. He was one of the first authors to theorize the malaise of everyday modern life in terms of the 'globalization' of production.

Lefebvre was a founder of rural sociology and of applied sociology in France, where he established the first Institute of Sociology at Strasbourg. In the 1960s and 1970s, as a professor at Nanterre, he concentrated on urban problems, presenting his theory in the 1974 work *La production de l'espace* (*The Production of Space*). He argued that notions of spatiality, the interaction of bodily action and the constructed environment, and theories of geography are all aspects of a social space created by people, not something which occurs naturally. This 'space' is a dialectical product of social activity which reacts back on social action to channel it in a continuous dialectic of ongoing 'spatialization'. In the English-speaking world, where Lefebvre's Marxist and existentialist theories are less well-known, his most enduring influence has been in the fields of geography, urban planning and cultural theory.

Lefebvre served as a conduit for ideas from generation to generation, including surrealists (1920s), Marxists (1930s), existentialists (late 1940s) and situationists (early 1960s), to American neo-Marxists and analysts of late-twentieth-century postmodernity, such as Fredric Jameson and David Harvey. His key ideas of autonomous self-organization and spontaneity influenced the German Green Party and East German artists' movements, and British punk-anarchist subcultures in the 1980s.

See also: EXISTENTIALISM; MARX, K.; POST-STRUCTURALISM

List of works

Lefebvre, H. (1938) *Hitler au pouvoir, bilan de cinq années de fascisme en Allemagne* (Hitler into power, a report of five years of fascism in Germany), Paris: Bureau d'éditions. (Critical essay on fascism and the working class.)

—— (1939a) *Le Matérialisme dialectique*, Paris: Alcan; trans. J. Sturrock as *Dialectical Materialism*, London: Cape, 1968. (The most widely available introduction to the subject, and to Marxism in general.)

—— (1939b) *Nietzsche*, Paris: Editions sociales internationales. (Anti-fascist study of Nietzsche.)

—— (1947a) *Logique formelle, logique dialectique* (Formal logical, dialectical logic), Paris: Editions sociales. (Volume 1 of *A la lumière du matérialisme dialectique*, 2nd volume censored and destroyed during the Second World War. Mimeo of author's proofs available at Carleton University Library, Ottawa, Canada).

—— (1947b) *Critique de la vie quotidienne, I, Introduction*, Paris: Grasset; 2nd edn trans. with preface by J. Moore, *The Critique of Everyday Life, Volume 1*, London: Verso, 1991. (First of four volumes published between 1947 and 1981.)

—— (1959) *La Somme et le reste* (Total and dividend), Paris: La Nef de Paris, 2 vols; repr. as one vol., Paris: Bélibaste, 1973. (Dialectical autobiography.)

—— (1963) *La vallée de Campan – Étude de sociologie rurale* (The Campan valley, a study in rural sociology), Paris: Presses Universitaires de France, Collection 'Bibliothèque de sociologie contemporaine'; 2nd edn, 1991. (Pioneering work on peasant life.)

—— (1968) *La vie quotidienne dans le monde moderne* Paris: Gallimard, Collection Idées; trans. S. Rabinovitch as *Everyday Life in the Modern World*,

Harmondsworth: Penguin, 1971. (Introduction to the concepts of everyday life and alienation.)

—— (1971) *Au-delà du structuralisme* (Beyond structuralism), Paris: Anthropos. (Critique of structuralism.)

—— (1974) *La production de l'espace*, Paris: Anthropos; trans. D. Nicholson-Smith as *The Production of Space*, Oxford: Blackwell, 1991. (Dialectical theory of social space.)

—— (1975a) *Hegel, Marx, Nietzsche, ou le royaume des ombres* (Hegel, Marx, Nietzsche, or the kingdom of shadows), Paris: Tournai, Casterman. Collection 'Synthèses contemporaines'. (Synthesis of dialectics and Nietzschean philosophy.)

—— (1975b) *Le temps des méprises: Entretiens avec Claude Glayman* (The era of errors – interview with Claude Glayman), Paris: Stock. (Autobiographical interviews detailing the life of Paris intellectuals in the 1920s and 1930s.)

—— (1975c) *L'Idéologie structuraliste* (The Structuralist ideology), Paris: Le Seuil, Collection Points 6. (Critique of structuralism.)

—— (1996) *Henri Lefebvre Writings on Cities*, ed. and trans. E. Kofman and E. Lebas, Oxford: Blackwell. (Introduction and selected readings.)

References and further reading

Ajzenberg, A. (ed.) (1994) *Traces de futurs. Henri Lefebvre, le possible et le quotidien* (Traces of futures. Henri Lefebvre, the possible and the banal), Paris: La Société Française. (Retrospective colloquium on Lefebvre's influence.)

Burkhard, F. (1986) *Priests and Jesters: Henri Lefebvre, the 'Philosophies' Gang and French Marxism between the wars*, Ph.D. thesis, Department of History, University of Wisconsin – Madison. (Detailed historical research on Paris intellectuals during the mid-1920s.)

Gottdiener, M. (1985) *Social Production of Urban Space*, Austin, TX: University of Texas Press. (Application of Lefebvre's theory of space to urban planning.)

Hess, R. (1988) *Henri Lefebvre: L'Aventure d'un siècle* (Henri Lefebvre: The adventure of a century), Paris. (Standard French biography.)

Jameson, F. (1991) *Postmodernism, or, the cultural logic of late capitalism*, London: Verso. (Analysis of the late twentieth century, partly inspired by Lefebvre.)

Jay, M. (1984) *Marxism and Totality – the adventures of a concept from Lukács to Habermas*, Berkeley, CA: University of California Press. (Historical study including a summary of Lefebvre's status and context of his thought.)

Martins, M. (1983) 'The theory of social space in the work of Henri Lefebvre', in R. Forrest, J. Henderson and P. Williams (eds) *Urban Political Economy and Social Theory: critical essays in urban studies*, London: Gower, 160–85. (Systematic discussion of Lefebvre's relevance to political economy.)

Meyer, K. (1973) *Henri Lefebvre: ein romantischer Revolutionnär* (Henri Lefebvre: a romantic revolutionary), Vienna: Europa Verlag. (Standard German biography.)

Poster, M. (1975) *Existential Marxism in Postwar France: From Sartre to Althusser*, Princeton, NJ: Princeton University Press. (Historical context of Lefebvre's proto-existential contributions.)

Ross, K. (1988) *The Emergence of Social Space: Rimbaud and the Paris Commune*, London: Macmillan. (Assesses and expands Lefebvre's studies of the (1848) Paris Commune (PAC) and theories of 'festive revolution'.)

Sartre, J.-P. (1956) *Being and Nothingness*, trans. H.E. Barnes, New York: Philosophical Library. (Discussion and modification of Lefebvre's dialectical methodology.)

Shields, R. (1997) *Henri Lefebvre: a critical introduction*, London: Routledge. (Intellectual biography with standard bibliography.)

Soja, E. (1985) 'The spatiality of social life: towards a transformative retheorisation', in D. Gregory and J. Urry (eds) *Social Relations and Spatial Structures*, London: Macmillan. (Exposition of Lefebvre's theory of space.)

ROB SHIELDS

LEGAL CONCEPTS

Concept-formation is an important component of law-formation. Well-developed legal orders are profoundly conceptual in nature. Throughout Western legal history, legislators have aimed at basing their law-making on concepts of a general scope (such as 'property', 'possession', 'usufruct', 'criminal intent' and many others) – and even more so legal scholars in their reconstruction and development of law. Legal thinking makes use of concepts with many different functions and varying logical status. A distinction can be made between concepts that are an integral part of law themselves (here called L-concepts) and concepts that belong to the professional vocabulary of lawyers and jurists in their handling of the law (J-concepts). Among the L-concepts there are on the one hand concepts whose meaning is totally determined by the rules of one single legal system and on the other hand concepts that pertain to two or more legal systems. The latter concepts have a comparative function.

J-concepts provide lawyers with a language enabling them to give an intellectual structure to the legal material, to characterize and discuss the professional-juridical handling of law and the methods used for performing that task, to specify the functions of law and to formulate the underlying values of (the handling of) the legal system.

There was a tendency in earlier legal philosophy to hypostasize legal concepts, for example, the concept of 'right' in classical natural-law doctrine: that is, to postulate real entities to which our concepts/terms refer. The legal philosophy of the twentieth century has to a large extent been a reaction against this tendency. This reaction has taken three different directions: (1) to reduce the abstract legal concepts to factual phenomena such as certain human behaviour or socio-psychological factors (mainly within US and Scandinavian realism); (2) to assign to legal concepts a normative ontological status, placing them in a world of norms, distinct from the world of facts; and (3) to analyse legal concepts in a contextual setting, that is, to find out how they function in actual legal discourse.

1 **Legal concept-formation: L-concepts and J-concepts**
2 **UL-concepts: further distinctions**
3 **J-concepts**
4 **Substantialism and its opponents**

1 **Legal concept-formation: L-concepts and J-concepts**

Legal orders have, historically, emerged from a need to restrain unhampered human violence. In more developed legal orders, rational argumentation has to a large extent superseded violence as a means of solving social problems. Western legal orders, based on or at least influenced by Roman law and the dogmatic study of it since the end of the eleventh century, have a strong intellectual stamp: disputes shall be solved according to general principles and vital social relationships defined with accuracy by precise legal concepts. 'Normative order...is...a hard won production of organizing intelligence' (MacCormick 1990: 557). Just as theory-formation and concept-formation in science are 'so closely interrelated as to constitute virtually two different aspects of the same procedure' (Hempel 1952: 1), there is a similarly close connection that verges on coalescence between law-formation and concept-formation. Western science and Western law equally rest on a common base – rationalism – which has its roots in the world of ideas of ancient Greece and Rome.

Well-developed legal orders are profoundly conceptual in character.

Legal thinking, in all branches and on all levels, makes use of concepts with very different functions and of varying logical status. Let us, roughly, compare the conceptual world of, for example, a zoologist and that of a lawyer. The zoologist, like all other professionals, needs in his work a professional (technical) language. This language refers in different respects to the subject matter of zoology – foxes, halibuts, wings, cells – which are mainly entities of a physical nature (things). In contrast to the zoologist's vocabulary, the lawyer's vocabulary refers to the subject matter of the law, which is a language (a product of human culture) too, with an abundance of terms signifying different concepts. Thus, in the legal sphere of life we have to allow for two, in principle distinct, languages: the legal one (in a proper sense) – the object language – and the juridical one – the meta-language. We refer to the concepts of the first category (concepts of law) as legal concepts proper (L-concepts) and to the concepts of the latter category (concepts about law) as juridical concepts (J-concepts). L-concepts have a law-stating function, while J-concepts have a juridical-operative function.

Let us start with the L-concepts. Within this category we can distinguish between L-concepts pertaining *uniquely* to one single legal system, for example, French law (UL-concepts, where 'U' indicates this kind of 'uniqueness'), and L-concepts pertaining to two or more legal systems, comparative L-concepts (CL-concepts). (A legal system is here regarded as a set of legal norms, or rules.)

A UL-concept is an L-concept that is wholly dependent, with regard to its meaning, on the content of a given legal system at a given point of time (for example, the law in force in France on 1 January 1994). If a given concept, for example, 'ownership', is a UL-concept, then the meaning of 'ownership' is completely determined by the prerequisites (descriptions of legal, or operative, facts) and the legal consequences which, in a given legal system at a given point of time, decide how ownership arises and expires, as well as what the legal effects (the legal significance) of ownership are. From this it follows, for example, that the Swedish concept of ownership differs somewhat from the Norwegian one, and also that it is changed as soon as the legal rules ('the ownership rules') are changed with respect to the above-named descriptions.

A CL-concept is an L-concept whose meaning is dependent on the content of two or more legal systems. Suppose that a jurist is interested in the concept 'marriage', not with respect to some single legal system but to all, or some family of, legal systems. This amounts to finding the 'lowest common denominators' of all rules concerning marriage – the gist, as it were, of the phenomenon of marriage. This is, in fact, not a concept of any single legal system and hence, it might be argued, not a concept of law but a concept about law. But it is, no doubt, a concept of law in the respect that it is totally dependent on the content of legal systems – it is not a purely sociological concept. For the formation of CL-concepts the logical technique of ideal-type definitions is appropriate. CL-concepts might be of both scientific (within the field of comparative legal science) and legislative value (for example, in international legislative work of the kind that aims to harmonize different national legal systems with each other or to work out international rules in some particular sphere). As we have seen, one and the same term, for example, 'marriage', might signify both a UL-concept and a CL-concept.

2 UL-concepts: further distinctions

Within the category of UL-concepts some further distinctions can be made.

Antecedent and consequent UL-concepts
Take the legal rules

(r_1) If a owns o, then a is allowed to use (sell, pawn, ...) o.

and

(r_2) If a has bought or inherited or received as a gift or... (and not sold, or...) o, then a owns o.

In r_1 'ownership' refers to legal (or operative) facts; the phrase 'if a owns o' is shorthand for 'if a has bought or inherited or received as a gift or... (and not sold or given away or destroyed or...)'; 'ownership' is a prerequisite expressed in the antecedent of r_1.

In r_2 'a owns o' is shorthand for 'a is allowed to use and sale and pawn and lease and... o'; 'ownership' here refers to the legal effects (or legal significance) expressed in the consequent of r_2.

In the Scandinavian discussion on rights in the 1940s and 1950s (initiated by Per Olof Ekelöf; see Wedberg 1951) the function of right-concepts in legal discourse (legislative, dogmatic and so on) was regarded as a shorthand-function. If we combine the antecedent of r_2 and the consequent of r_1 we get

(r_3) If a has bought or inherited or received as a gift or... (and not sold, or...) o, then a is allowed to use (sale, pawn, ...) o.

where, apparently, the concept 'ownership' is not to be found – an observation which induced Alf Ross to

the idea that right-concepts are semantically meaningless vehicles of deduction (Ross 1957).

Genuine and non-genuine UL-concepts
A UL-concept has a genuine or non-genuine function depending on whether it appears in genuine or non-genuine legal statements in the sense indicated by Ingemar Hedenius (1941). Let us explain this – now internationally accepted – distinction with the help of an example:

(r_4) Anyone who travels by car in Sweden must drive on the right-hand side of the road.

This statement can be understood in two different ways. If r_4 appears in an official statute it is natural to understand r_4 as a normative statement, a decree, which the legislator has issued with the intention of directing a certain kind of human behaviour. Understood in this way r_4 is lacking in truth-value; it is neither true nor false. Statements with this function are genuine legal statements. But suppose that a Swede visits England and is asked by an English person what the rules of the road are in Sweden, and that in reply they utter the (somewhat magisterial) statement r_4. When they make this reply it is not their intention – at least not in the first place – to steer the questioner's behaviour; their intention is merely to inform the questioner of the content of valid Swedish law in this respect. And when r_4 has this function it is a non-genuine legal statement, and has as such truth-value; it is either true or false. Statements of legal dogmatics are usually of this kind. It is to be noted that r_4 has the same linguistic formulation irrespective of whether it is used in the genuine way or the non-genuine way, and that genuine and non-genuine legal statements are often formulated alike. But the non-genuine legal statement always contains, logically speaking, an explicit or understood clause 'according to valid law in S at t', where S is some society and t is a point of time. Thus, in its non-genuine function r_4 is equivalent – so long as Swedish law is intended – to the statement

(r_5) Anyone who travels by car in Sweden must drive on the right-hand side of the road according to (now) valid Swedish law.

Official and dogmatic UL-concepts
Official UL-concepts are found in statutes, preparatory materials, judgments and other official texts. Dogmatic UL-concepts are found in legal-dogmatic works (for example, 'causality', 'proximate cause', 'right *in rem*'). Dogmatic concepts can, but need not, have equivalents among the official concepts. Legal dogmatists can quite well create their own concepts when they consider that the official battery of

concepts is insufficient, and this happens now and then. Such concepts can later be incorporated in the law. Historically speaking there are also a number of concepts which, as products of academic law, have found their way into municipal law or are implicitly contained within it. An official concept and a dogmatic one need not have the same meaning, even if they are expressed by the same term (for example, 'possession' in Swedish statutory language is not equivalent to 'possession' as it is used in Swedish doctrinal literature).

3   J-concepts

Turning to the J-concepts, the technical tools used in the legal-professional handling of legal orders (that is, of L-concepts), we may list some important functions of juridical language and distinguish between different kinds of J-concepts on the basis of those functions (the list is by no means exhaustive). We need:

1 a set of concepts helping us to structure the law in a logical and functional respect (morphological concepts);
2 a set of concepts helping us to describe in a precise manner the professional-juridical handling of the law (praxeological concepts);
3 a set of concepts helping us to speak clearly and articulately about the relations between the law and the social reality in which the law 'operates' and which it is designed to influence – in short, about the functions of law (teleological concepts);
4 a set of concepts helping us to describe in a precise manner the programmes (methods, principles, techniques) for the juridical handling of law, be it in legislation, administration of law, legal dogmatics or otherwise (methodological concepts);
5 a set of concepts helping us to articulate our ideas about the values pertaining to the juridical handling of law (ideological concepts).

As for morphological concepts, we can differentiate between two levels: micro-morphological and macro-morphological. At the former level it is the component parts of individual (types of) legal rules that are studied. Here we meet concepts such as 'prerequisite', 'legal fact', 'legal consequence', the various concepts for (Hohfeldian) legal positions (see HOHFELD, W.N.), the various normative modalities 'shall', 'may', 'must not' (expressing obligation, permission, prohibition) and so on. At the macro-morphological level we study the component parts of legal systems, that is, different types of legal rules and different kinds of relations between such rules. As an example of such a classification can be mentioned Hart's distinction (1961) between primary rules and second-ary rules (rules of recognition, rules of change and rules of adjudication) (see HART, H.L.A.). As examples of relations between rules can be mentioned the concepts (r and r' are legal rules) 'r' is analogous to r', 'r' is in an e-contrario relation to r', 'r' is an extensive interpretation of r' and so on.

As examples of praxeological concepts can be mentioned 'complying with the law', 'breaking the law', 'administration of law', 'application of law', 'interpretation', 'evaluation of evidence', 'pleading', 'statutory drafting' and so on – all concepts concerning different kinds of legal activities.

Teleological concepts (concepts about the functions of law) are, for example, those introduced by Raz (1979) – namely, 'primary', 'secondary' and 'indirect functions' – and also concepts describing the relationship between a legal rule, r, and some social aim or purpose, p, for example, 'r is expedient with respect to p' or 'r is effective with respect to p'.

The flora of methodological terms is rich and varies from country to country. The underlying concepts, however, are very much the same. Some examples are: 'objective', 'subjective', 'historical', 'intentional', 'linguistic', 'logical-grammatical', 'systematic', 'teleological' and 'pragmatical interpretation', 'reasoning by example', 'reasoning by analogy'. To the methodological arsenal of concepts also belong the concepts dealing with the factual basis of legal argumentation – the legal sources – such as 'statute', 'act', 'precedent', 'case law', 'custom', 'preparatory materials', and the concept 'legal source' itself.

Among the ideological concepts we find concepts such as 'legal certainty' (or 'predictability'), 'legality', 'equality before the law', 'the rule of law' and '*Rechtsstaat*' ('law-state').

4   Substantialism and its opponents

In the classical natural-law doctrine of the seventeenth and eighteenth centuries there is a tendency towards substantialism, that is, to Platonic hypostasizing of legal concepts (Hobbes is an exception, but he was after all not a full-fledged natural-law philosopher anyway). During the last two centuries the development of sciences and logic has contributed to a sharpened awareness among legal philosophers as to ontological matters. The reaction against substantialism has taken three, in principle different, directions.

One is reductionism. This is an idea of venerable age. It is found as early as the time of the Presocratics, in their efforts to bring the apparent variety of entities back to one single substance. Its programme is clearly stated by Ockham (*non est ponenda pluralitas sine necessitate*; a multiplicity shall not be assumed unless it is necessary). In the legal philosophy of the first half of the twentieth century reductionistic tendencies are strong, especially within the US and Scandinavian realist movements. Here the reduction consists in reducing abstract ('fictional') legal entities to a certain kind of human behaviour or to socio-psychological pressures and reactions. (We assume that abstract concepts such as 'legal order' have the same ontological status as the abstract entities to which these concepts refer, for example, legal orders (see LEGAL REALISM).)

Another one is separatism. This consists in locating legal concepts in a separate ontological realm of their own. Kelsen's *Pure Theory of Law* is an endeavour to separate normative entities (which at least must include the L-concepts) from factual entities by differentiating the world of Is (*Sein*) from the world of Ought (*Sollen*) (see KELSEN, H.).

A third reaction against substantialism is functionalism. Instead of asking about some legal concept, *c*, 'What does *c* refer to in reality?', legal scholars with a functional approach formulate the analytical question like this: 'How does *c* function in legal thinking?' Hohfeld belongs to the functionalist jurists, his classic work on jural relations is indeed entitled *Fundamental Legal Conceptions as Applied in Judicial Reasoning*. Functionalism was also the explicit starting point for the fruitful discussion on rights that took place in Scandinavia during the 1940s and 1950s (Wedberg 1951). Hart's idea (based on Bentham; Hart 1954) that legal concepts shall be defined in a contextual setting (by contextual definitions) is in the same vein.

Apart from ontological differences concerning legal concepts, we can discern different attitudes as to their importance in legal life, oscillating between extreme absolutism and extreme relativism. Absolutism is here taken to mean a tendency to regard legal concepts as perpetual (static) and also precise with regard to their meaning, and relativism as the opposite of this. The *Begriffsjurisprudenz* (conceptual jurisprudence), flourishing in Germany during the second half of the nineteenth century, is characterized by a high degree of absolutism: when confronted with some legal problem, for example, whether some clause in a contract is about an easement or a usufruct, the task of the lawyer was to ascertain whether the right in question fell under the concept 'easement' or that of 'usufruct', and when this was done the problem was solved, since the legal effects of, for example, easement were fixed beforehand and implicit in the concept itself. This kind of legal technique is, in fact, to a certain degree indispensable in any well-developed legal order, but what gave *Begriffsjurisprudenz* its bad reputation was that it grossly disregarded the social consequences of the legal decisions and overestimated the precision of the legal concepts.

See also: CONCEPTS; CONCEPTUAL ANALYSIS; LAW, PHILOSOPHY OF; LEGAL DISCOURSE

References and further reading

Frändberg, Å (1987) 'An Essay on the Systematics of Legal Concepts: A Study of Legal Concept Formation', *Scandinavian Studies in Law* 31: 83–115. (Expansion of the material of §§1–3 of this entry.)

* Hart, H.L.A. (1954) 'Definition and Theory in Jurisprudence', *Law Quarterly Review* 70: 37–60. (Develops the idea that legal concepts shall be defined in a contextual setting.)

* —— (1961) *The Concept of Law*, Oxford: Clarendon Press. (Contributes to concept-formation within legal morphology by the distinction between primary and (three kinds of) secondary rules.)

* Hedenius, I. (1941) *Om rätt och moral* (On Law and Morals), Stockholm: Tidens förlag. (Author of the well-known distinction between sentences expressing legal norms and sentences stating the existence (validity) of such norms.)

* Hempel, C.G. (1952) *Fundamentals of Concept Formation in Empirical Science*, Chicago, IL: University of Chicago Press. (Deals with concept-formation in empirical, mainly natural, sciences in general.)

* Hohfeld, W.N. (1923) *Fundamental Legal Conceptions as Applied in Juridical Reasoning and Other Legal Essays*, ed. W.W. Cook, New Haven, CT: Yale University Press. (A classic work on different right-concepts with a contextual approach.)

* Kelsen, H. (1960) *Reine Rechtslehre*, completely rewritten and expanded 2nd edn, Vienna: Deuticke; trans. M. Knight, *Pure Theory of Law*, Berkeley, CA: University of California Press, 1967. (Rewritten and expanded edition of one of Kelsen's two major works.)

* MacCormick, N. (1990) 'Reconstruction after Deconstruction: A Response to CLS', *Oxford Journal of Legal Studies* 10: 539–58. (Argumentation for the value of rational reconstruction of legal ideas within legal dogmatics, which to a large degree is a matter of concept-formation; see especially pp. 555–8.)

* Raz, J. (1979) 'The Functions of Law', in *The Authority of Law*, Oxford: Clarendon Press, 163–79. (A contribution to the elaboration of a general classification of the functions of law, a task which also to a large degree is a matter of concept-formation.)

* Ross, A. (1957) 'Tû-tû', *Harvard Law Review* 70: 812–25. (Argues that right-concepts are semantically meaningless vehicles of deduction.)
* Wedberg, A. (1951) 'Some Problems in the Logical Analysis of Legal Science', *Theoria* 17: 246–75. (Epitomizes excellently the Scandinavian discussion in the 1940s and the early 1950s about the function of right-concepts in legal discourse.)

ÅKE FRÄNDBERG

LEGAL DISCOURSE

'Legal discourse' signifies a strong interplay between law and language, linking together law as like language and law as itself language. However, unlike other linguistically modelled accounts, this approach involves a strong opposition to formalisms and their mirror-image realisms. Language as used cannot be 'deduced' from any pregiven matrix or set of propositions but must be studied in terms of its own modalities. The theory of law-as-discourse takes inspiration from the study of legal rhetoric and from socio-legal analyses of the courtroom, but was developed in its own right in the post-structuralist turn in linguistics. Law-as-discourse requires an understanding of the operation of legal talk in different registers, and gestures towards an intertwining of the social, the legal and the linguistic by focusing on the speaker–hearer situation, locution and action.

1 **Law as rhetoric**
2 **Courtroom studies**
3 **Legal discourse**

1 Law as rhetoric

While the currency of the term 'discourse' derives from post-structuralist developments in linguistics, this type of analysis was inaugurated in law by two important precursors, the New Rhetoric movement and socio-legal courtroom studies. Both, like post-structuralism, sought to break with logicist-formalist models of language and parallel models of law as a code or system of ideally transparent propositions of universal import held together by a formalizable syntax. This rethinking, in turn, posed the problem of how to reconceptualize 'the social' as both impossible to differentiate from 'the legal' yet as constitutively law's 'outside'.

The New Rhetoric movement, led by Chaim Perelman and Lucy Olbrechts-Tyteca beginning in the mid-1940s, sought to examine the process of argumentation as a way of using language, with its own prescriptions and proprieties to be understood through a return to Aristotle and the Roman jurists, discursive techniques employed to move an audience to a decision to act. But this return required the dethronement of demonstrative reasoning. 'Any theory of argumentation must break with the notion of reason and reasoning which comes from Descartes and has left its stamp on western philosophy for 300 years' (Perelman 1963: 134). For Descartes, the very existence of dispute was the sign of error, since truth was marked by transparency and intersubjective agreement. In this tradition, rhetoric had thus languished, cast at worst as a mode of duplicity, sophism and deliberate audience-manipulation involving pseudo-logic and base, populist, appeals to the emotions; or at best a source of literary stylistic flourish.

Perelman had himself begun in the logical positivist tradition, arguing that justice was an ultimately meaningless concept. Although formalizable as 'treat like persons alike', the values of what would count as like persons or as like treatment were always contested and hence arbitrary and socially contingent. Yet where did this leave law, at all levels functioning through competing arguments, in the two-party structure of the appeal court as much as the courtroom?

More radically, justice turned out to be the rule rather than the exception. *All* formalizations suffered the same fatal flaw. 'The insufficiency of the strictly formalist attitude becomes clear as soon as the question of interpreting a logistic system arises. But without attribution of meaning, axioms are not assertions' (Perelman 1963: 148) but merely arbitrary computations. Frege's conceptual Platonism, Tarski's factual correspondences, and the rise of conventionalism all testified to formalism's need for an extra-systemic semantic supplement – which, thus beyond control of the system, undermines its fundamental claim to autonomy and closure. Meaning/value was in turn (as with justice) always contestable. Thus, as it would be put subsequently, if law operates around a core of settled meaning, 'settled' does not mean pregiven and linguistically fixed but merely not currently in dispute (Jackson 1985: 156).

Shifting direction, Perelman came to see that disputation was a more orderly process that grew out of the engagement between speakers and hearers rooted in a common frame of reference, beginning with a prescribed understanding of their correlative roles and associated forms of diction (thus, teacher–pupil, fellow citizens). Assuming that all parties have a common concern to do justice, but that the audience's conceptions of this will begin in the familiar, the effective orator will tailor argument to the local audience. For every proverb there is a counter-proverb. The speakers thus lodge their recommended courses of action within contrary realms of meaning – different construals of what it is right to do – available via one or another 'locus of the preferable'. In a key example, Perelman (1979) contrasts the loci of quantity and quality respectively as asserting the durable, the useful, the accessible, constant, symmetrically ordered, that which is useful to the greater number, the eternal and the abstract, being and form, as against the unique, the original and the difficult, the natural, the irreplaceability of the moment and the individual, the instant as the figure of totality, the poetic mode that recognizes the uniqueness of the other and the particularities of love and obligation. There are also prescriptions for the temporal ordering of argument.

Rhetoric is sometimes glossed as describing 'who can make arguments and where (and in what terms)', as does Perelman (1979) when commenting that rhetoric has always been a matter of political regulation. But here a great danger lies. In emphasizing the (indubitably) political nature of the designation of who can speak and hear, the social nature of discourse tends to be cast as an externality. Correspondingly, to speak of 'what' can be said loses the fact that the 'what' of speaking consists in the 'how'.

This example also holds together a fundamental tension in Perelman's work. The drive on the side of the locus of quantity takes him to develop a normative account of argumentation as justification in relation to a universal audience and a democratic politics, in keeping with rhetoric's birth in the agora of open political debate and a broad conception of logic that encompasses probabilistic reasoning. This is what links his work to rationalist theories of legal discourse (see LEGAL REASONING AND INTERPRETATION §3; HABERMAS, J. §4).

On the other hand, Perelman also recognizes rhetoric as having a certain generic affiliation with the locus of quality, being ever about materialities rather than abstractions, audiences being always local. Rhetoric and common law reasoning share the need to cast the new in relation to tradition and customary practice and their 'crabwise' form of connection by way of analogy. Hence too law's generic conservatism and endorsement of any prevailing 'sense of normality, or likelihood' (Goodrich 1987: 181). More hopefully, others, such as Boyd White (1985), would emphasize the heterogeneity of community with its contesting hierarchies of value: what is common as merely the starting point of cultural transformation of meaning.

To follow the materialities of rhetoric is perhaps most promising. Goodrich's *Languages of Law* (1990) thus associates together rhetoric's use of place (topos/locus) and sequence with the bodily, the way that memory techniques are situated in imageries of dwelling places, or streets, the idea of patterns linking cases, with the idea of habit as images or emblems of how to live. Similarly, the figurative dimensions of texts may speak a different and more revealing story than their propositional mode, as Douzinas, following de Man, has shown most effectively by looking at Dworkin's Hercules metaphor (Douzinas *et al.* 1991). The dimension of time and sequence is equally important: moving an audience means moving them through a series of positions and differential engagements or 'identifications' in which each stage is dependent upon the former. Legal discourse becomes a kind of memory garden. Rhetoric, as Perelman constantly emphasized, is about effecting a *change* in the hearer, by contrast to the atemporal quality of demonstrative reasoning. In this mode Bernard Jackson (1988) has argued that the 'real time' of the trial process cannot be reduced to its retrospective view, in which the end is summed in the eternal nontime of legal or logical justification.

2 Courtroom studies

Socio-legal studies of the courtroom are the natural locus of legal rhetoric as forensic argumentation and, in turn, are ever in danger of lapsing into seeing rhetoric as low persuasion. However, in contributing to the study of law as discourse, they deal with two key issues: differential audience address and the relation between legal and non-legal discourse.

Law's address is multiple. Perelman considered this divided locution in terms glossed by Hart (in the introduction to Perelman 1963): the 'rhythms' of the 'natural' 'common' language are quite different from the 'technical language' common to members of a discipline or profession, language that is the 'private preserve of initiates' (1963: 156). As Pat Carlen (1976) insisted, this split address raises serious problems of legitimization, law's continuing need, internally and publicly, to be seen to be acting according to principles of justice and fairness. This is constantly under strain because of law's existence as both formal-constitutive abstract rules and situational rules determining the use of law in practice, which she links to the socio-linguistic categorization of elaborated and restricted codes. The elaborated code being characterized in terms of flexibility, the availability of many alternative expressions, abstraction, context-independence, enabling talk between strangers, and characterizes law's universalistic diction, its general language of justification. But, in its situational usage, law operates according to a restricted code, highly concrete and local, a kind of argot, highly context-dependent, indexical, non-transportable and poor in substitute expressions, a use of language typical of closed communities with fixed structures – in this case primarily the closed community of lawyers. The lay 'audience' – which includes parties to the proceedings – thus suffers a double cognitive dissonance. (Carlen then goes on to describe the 'remedial routines' by which any resulting protests are discounted.)

Bennett and Feldman's focus (1981) is closer to the concern with argumentation, now inflected in terms of the question how juries make sense of legal arguments in trial courts in reaching their verdict. They find the bridging feature to be not the classical tropes of rhetoric but, rather, the literary mode of narrative. The story-form allows legal categories to be filled in with everyday meanings. Argumentation here means, precisely, the ability of prosecution or defence to produce a properly constructed story, potentially outweighing a more 'scientific' assessment of the evidence (as well as importing social prejudice). While providing an important counter to more abstract and philosophical understandings of narrative as coherence (MacCormick 1978), they barely glimpse the significance of narration – the way of telling the story: that very I–you relationship central to rhetoric – and law as discourse.

3   Legal discourse

The official theorization of law as discourse draws directly on linguistics, in which the term 'discourse' exists as a paradox. It begins as a stated definition: any stretch of language longer than a minimal unit of meaning (conventionally, a sentence). But filling out that definition immediately puts in question the ability of any 'minimal' unit to function autonomously, to have meaning in isolation from the discursive context in which it is bedded. Any smaller unit – a sign – does not have meaning, yet a sentence is already a miniature 'environment'. This is a more sophisticated statement of Perelman's critique of formalism as always in need of a semantic supplement.

Linguistic formalism is here construed broadly to encompass both Anglophone reference-based logical positivism and Francophone code-based structuralisms. Formalism's failure is that it cannot account for the meaning or function of any particular instance of speaking, carving it up, rather, between a 'logical deduction' from the system – the actualization of one of a matrix of given possibilities – and the residue, cast as unanalysable social and psychological contingency that can be registered only diachronically

when such usage builds up sufficient critical weight to feed back into redefining the system itself. Discourse theory begins, rather, from speaking, the speaker–hearer relationship and how that is linked to its discursive context. The meaning of terms cannot be taken as transparent but is determined by its existence in different discursive formations and use in different registers.

The most ambitious attempt to theorize law in these terms is found in Peter Goodrich (1987). Drawing together a barrage of discourse theorists, but centrally Pêcheux (1982), the book offers a double attack on conventional jurisprudence (see LEGAL HERMENEUTICS). On the one hand, most of modern jurisprudence is cast into the realm of formalism with its symptomatic failings. On the other hand, those things which jurisprudence takes to be law's essential features – its unity and coherence, its singular monolithic voice of authority – can themselves be shown to be effects produced by identifiable discursive techniques and social violences. (There is a perhaps surprisingly *marxisant* tone reminiscent of exposés of the tricks of ideology.)

Law's self-representation is disposed under the category of 'intra-discourse', designated the surface level, that describes the actual discursive techniques of law's utterances. The image of law as a coherent, auto-authorizing body is thus effected by law's continuing construction of its own history, as maintained by closure mechanisms of exclusion and discursive techniques of linkage, co-reference and internal continuity yielding the sense of a location in a continuous time: all context-dependent mechanisms that found law's claims to be universal and context-independent. Unlike Perelman, who strongly contrasted law as rhetoric (as a continuous address to an audience) to dialectic and other forms of dialogue, Goodrich claims that law pretends to be a dialogue but is really a monologue.

The level of institutionalization is, similarly, presented in terms of what is excluded from visibility and, further, posited very strongly here as a social externality that determines membership conditions of law's internal point of view. Less crudely, these cultural acquisitions evoke something of Bourdieu's account of 'knowing how' as a set of dispositions or postures, or Duncan Kennedy's 'training for hierarchy' that might locate the lawyer's 'belonging' in a more properly inarticulate and generally cultural form.

Third, and finally, there is the level of inter-discourse, law's relation to other discourses. Law's univocal mode suppresses the multi-vocal heteroglossalia of the social and law's self-referentiality means that it is an impoverished language cut off from denotation. 'Far from being expressly bound by any extra-linguistic content or denotative meaning, law's terms are connotative and symbolic: they lend themselves to an obfuscating, rhetorical or symbolic usage, to figurative or analogical manipulations within which their actual menage or referent is obscure' (Goodrich 1978: 179). This is a rather puzzlingly traditional characterization.

Although this is a highly reduced account of the book, in many ways, this is not the best of Goodrich's texts to study in order to understand what it means to look at law as discourse. What he provides elsewhere is a rich and dense series of accounts of law as compacting together many different specific genres of writing, traditions of interpretation and inscriptions of memory. It is in these works, rather than theorization, that the fruitfulness of approaching law as discourse can be seen.

See also: LAW, PHILOSOPHY OF

References and further reading

* Bennett, W.L. and Feldman, M.S. (1981) *Reconstructing Reality in the Courtroom*, New Brunswick, NJ: Rutgers; London and New York: Tavistock. (A much cited attempt to consider law as narrative that, unfortunately, has a rather undeveloped account of narrative structure.)

Bourdieu, P. (1984) *Distinction: A Social Critique of the Judgment of Taste*, London: Routledge & Kegan Paul. (Seminal work on the anthropology of culture, delineating the class-differentiated formation of aesthetic taste.)

* Boyd White, J. (1985) *Heracles' Bow: Essays on the Rhetoric and Poetics of the Law*, Madison, WI: University of Wisconsin Press. (A rather literary approach to law as rhetoric that provides a good sense of moving the audience through a series of moral positions.)

* Carlen, P. (1976) *Magistrates' Justice*, Manchester: Martin Robertson. (A classic text in socio-legal studies of the courtroom that draws together a wide range of theoretical approaches applied to empirical material.)

* Douzinas, C. and Warrington, R. with McVeigh, S. (1991) *Postmodern Jurisprudence: The Law of Text in the Texts of Law*, London: Routledge. (A critical analysis of contemporary mainstream jurisprudence that gives full play to analysing texts by their metaphors. Key text for laws as discourse.)

* Goodrich, P. (1987) *Legal Discourse: Studies in Linguistics, Rhetoric and Legal Analysis*, London: Macmillan. (Theorizes legal discourse by reference to a wide range of theories of linguistics. Fundamental for exposition.)

* —— (1990) *Languages of Law: From Logics of Memory to Nomadic Masks*, London: Weidenfeld and Nicolson. (Exploration of different discursive presences in law, especially aspects of the 'symbolic' – visual, mnemonic, Christian, with an argument that the masks of contemporary law have become dislocated from their spatial locus.)

* Jackson, B. (1985) *Semiotics and Legal Theory*, London and New York: Routledge & Kegan Paul. (A serious and scholarly analysis of law in terms of structuralist (Greimasian) analysis and which also looks into questions of pragmatics and semantics.)

* —— (1988) *Law, Fact and Narrative Coherence*, Merseyside: Deborah Charles. (Beginning from courtroom studies, seeks to argue a general account of legal norms as narrative.)

Kennedy, D. (1986) 'Freedom and Constraint in Adjudication: A Critical Phenomenology', *Journal of Legal Education* 36. (Original statement of Kennedy's famous notion that the methods of legal education replicate law's ordering as a hierarchy of values and sources; hence legal education as a 'training for hierarchy'.)

* MacCormick, N. (1978) *Legal Reasoning and Legal Theory*, Oxford: Clarendon Press. (Classic modern text on jurisprudence comparable in stature to the work of Dworkin and, similarly seeking to deal with the residue of law that does not easily fit formalism-positivism.)

* Pêcheux, M. (1982) *Language, Semiotics and Ideology*, London: Macmillan. (Key example of French development of discourse theory.)

* Perelman, C. (1963) *The Idea of Justice and the Problem of Argument*, London: Routledge & Kegan Paul; Atlantic Highlands, NJ: Humanities Press. (Includes the early logical positivist article on justice and subsequent developments of the argument.)

* —— (1979) *The New Rhetoric and the Humanities: Essays on Rhetoric and its Applications*, Dordrecht, Boston and London: Reidel Synthese Library, vol. 140. (Classic text available in English outlining not only law as rhetoric but the wider project.)

BEVERLEY BROWN

LEGAL EVIDENCE AND INFERENCE

In the field of law there is a rich legacy of scholarship and experience regarding the properties, uses and discovery of evidence in inferential reasoning tasks. Over the centuries our courts have been concerned about characteristics of evidence that seem necessary in order to draw valid and persuasive conclusions from it. Thus, they have been led to consider such matters as the relevance of evidence, the credibility of the sources from which it comes, and the probative or inferential force of evidence. Court trials usually involve inferences about events in the past. The past can never be completely recovered. In addition, evidence about past events is frequently inconclusive, conflicting or contradictory, and often vague or ambiguous. The result is that inferences about past events are necessarily probabilistic in nature. Our courts have also been concerned about whether the interests of fairness require that, on occasion, evidence might be inadmissible, even though relevant and credible. Evidential and inferential issues such as the ones just mentioned are also of concern to philosophers and persons in other disciplines. This entry concerns several evidential issues of particular interest in legal contexts.

1 **Proof and admissibility**
2 **The credentials of legal evidence**
3 **Structural issues**
4 **Probability and the probative force of evidence**
5 **Inference from a mass of evidence**

1 Proof and admissibility

Evidence in legal contexts has some distinctive features. Two issues are central in modern scholarship on evidence and inference in legal contexts. The first concerns study of the properties and uses of evidence in the process of judicial proof. To be persuasive in the process of proof, evidence must have certain 'credentials' established by defensible arguments (see §2 below). The second issue concerns study of rules regarding the admissibility of evidence. Not all legal systems have such rules. In ones that do, evidence with justified proof-related credentials is still not necessarily admissible at trial. Concern about the proof credentials and admissibility of evidence has not always been as great as it is today. This concern intensified very slowly as adversarial processes for settling disputes and the concept of jury trials came into existence.

In England in the eleventh and twelfth centuries, persons accused of crown or criminal offences had the burden of proving their innocence. This burden was discharged in three stages: judgment, trial, sentence. At the judgment stage the accused was obliged to select one of three methods of 'proof': by the swearing of oaths by witnesses, by ordeals of various kinds, or by combat. The trial thus simply consisted of the implementation of one of these methods. The trial outcome depended not on any evidence but on the judgment of God. It was then believed that, if the accused was truly innocent, God would strike down anyone who gave a false oath against the accused, would heal any injury inflicted on the accused during an ordeal, and would side with the accused in a trial by battle. Sentence was then delivered in accordance with God's verdict. With the decline of proof methods based upon oaths, ordeals and combat, jury trials gradually came into existence. But in their earliest forms these juries consisted of witnesses against the accused as well as other persons having vested interests in the case. They were not seen as objective triers of facts.

Interest in evidence emerged as the jury came to be identified not as witnesses but as a body of persons who deliberate impartially upon evidence given by external witnesses for both sides of a dispute. Thus, advocates came to be concerned about the evidential merits of their own cases and how effectively they could counter the evidence and arguments given by an opponent. A landmark case occurred in 1670 regarding the role of jurors in the process of proof. Prior to this time, jurors could be attainted for giving verdicts contrary to what the court regarded as manifest evidence. In the case of Edward Bushell, Chief Justice John Vaughan ruled that jurors could not answer questions of law but courts could not answer questions of fact. Thus, in Anglo-American courts today jurors and not the court (unless it is a bench trial) assess the credibility and force of evidence during the process of proof. As the right to cross-examine opposing witnesses became established, Sir Matthew Hale could claim (in 1739) that the adversary system, involving the parties in contention, their counsels, and the court, was unmatched for 'beating and boulting the truth'. (As against this, the twentieth-century legal realist Jerome FRANK was to compare adversarial methods to throwing pepper in the eyes of a surgeon.)

Interest in rules governing the admissibility of evidence also emerged as the adversarial system developed. Concern about the admissibility of hearsay evidence, for example, arose following the trial of Sir Walter Ralegh in 1603. Ralegh was convicted of treason partly on the basis of evidence having no better status than rumour or gossip, since the source of it was never identified. Rules concerning the admissibility of hearsay date from the acknowledged injustice in Ralegh's case. Since those times, what are now termed the laws of evidence began to emerge. In one sense these laws of evidence consist of assorted exceptions to a principle of free proof (virtually all evidence admissible), as advocated by Jeremy BENTHAM and now practised, for example, in Sweden. These laws of evidence have hardly been stationary. They have changed over time and will almost certainly continue to do so in response to continuing debates about their fairness, changes in political climate, and changes in patterns of litigation.

Even if all rules of admissibility were abolished, there would still be concern about what constitutes proof. In discussing evidence and its inferential roles in proof, we encounter matters that are continuing sources of debate among legal scholars, philosophers, probabilists and others. Settlement of any dispute, however it is accomplished, rests at some stage upon arguments based on evidence. Few episodes of litigation, whether criminal or civil, actually come to trial. Thus it would be a mistake to consider the trial as paradigmatic in any study of the properties and uses of evidence. This acknowledged, bodies of evidence encountered in any litigation have certain well-known properties. The evidence is necessarily incomplete, often on important matters. Items of evidence are usually inconclusive to some degree, meaning that the evidence is consistent with more than one probandum, hypothesis or fact in issue. Evidence is often imprecise or vague; we cannot tell exactly what it means. Evidence comes to us from sources which are not perfectly credible. Finally, bodies of evidence usually reveal interesting patterns of dissonance; some items seem to favour one conclusion, others a different conclusion.

These characteristics of bodies of evidence combine to make any conclusion drawn from them probabilistic in nature. Thus, forensic standards of proof involve hedges or qualifiers (discussed in §§4–5 below) that acknowledge these omnipresent characteristics of evidence. Judicial proof, like proof based on incomplete and fallible evidence in other contexts, is probabilistic rather than demonstrative or necessary. There is no forensic standard that requires proof with certainty or beyond the possibility of doubt.

2　The credentials of legal evidence

In the Anglo-American judicial system, a rationalist-empiricist view of the nature of proof in adversarial proceedings has been predominant in the past two centuries. On this view, matters at issue in a dispute are to be proved at specified levels of probability on the basis of evidence that is both relevant and credible

or believable. Such a process seems rational, at least with respect to earlier proof methods involving oaths, ordeals or combat, as well as juries composed of adversary witnesses. The empiricism stems from the requirement that proof be based upon evidence observable in some way to those who must render verdicts in disputes. Two of the most prominent rationalist-empiricists have been Jeremy Bentham and, in the USA, John Henry Wigmore.

There is considerable dispute about what constitutes rationality in all of human inference and choice. Regarding evidence and inference, part of this controversy concerns the means by which the probative or inferential force of evidence ought to be assessed and then combined in reaching a conclusion (see §§4–5 below). Choices made by those who participate in settling disputes involve more than evidence, inference and probabilities; they also involve value-related ingredients. In any dispute there are multiple stakeholders including the parties in contention, their advocates, court officials and society at large. Settling disputes is difficult given the competing and often internally inconsistent value systems of these stakeholders. Any pretension to rationality in legal matters appears to involve a seamless integration of matters concerning both the probability and value ingredients of choice as well as the process by which they are combined.

It appears that an item of evidence must have three credentials in order for it to be in any way persuasive during the process of proof. The necessary credentials concern the relevance, credibility and probative (inferential) force of evidence. Of course, no evidence comes with these three credentials already established; they have to be justified by cogent arguments, often having many stages, and by careful judgments (see §3 below). An item of evidence is commonly said to be relevant in a legal dispute if it makes the existence of some material fact at issue 'more probable' or 'less probable' than it would be without the evidence. This is often put subjectively: evidence is relevant if it would cause anyone to change their beliefs about the likeliness of some material fact at issue. We might also say that evidence is relevant if it has some probative force in belief revision. There are no rules in law saying how much force any item of relevant evidence ought to have.

Evidence can be relevant in different ways. It is said to be directly relevant if a chain of reasoning can be formed from the evidence to a major issue in the case. There are two species of directly relevant evidence: direct and circumstantial. Direct evidence goes in one reasoning step to some fact at issue and, if credible, would settle the matter. Circumstantial evidence, even if perfectly credible, supplies only some but not complete grounds for belief in some matter. But some evidence has only indirect relevance; such evidence is said to be ancillary or auxiliary in nature. Ancillary evidence either strengthens or weakens links in chains of reasoning set up by directly relevant evidence. Generalizations are asserted to license a reasoning step or link. Ancillary evidence bears upon whether or not this asserted generalization holds in the present case in which it is being invoked. For example, we might assert the generalization: 'if a person testifies under oath to the occurrence of an event, then this event probably did occur'. Tests of this generalization, applied to a particular witness, involve ancillary evidence concerning this witness's veracity, objectivity and observational sensitivity. We might say that ancillary evidence is evidence about the strength of other evidence. The relevance-status of evidence obviously depends upon the case at hand; a datum can be relevant evidence in one situation and quite irrelevant as evidence in another.

Suppose an item of evidence whose relevance can be established. The question then is: can we believe what this evidence says? Credibility considerations form the very foundation for all arguments based on evidence; that is, they form the first links in a chain of reasoning. There are different discernible forms of evidence (see §3 below); judgments about the credibility of evidence depend upon what form evidence takes. For tangible evidence, open to direct inspection by fact-finders, such matters as the authenticity and chain of custody are of interest as well as the accuracy of the evidence if it exists in the form of some sensor record such as a photograph or radar image. For testimonial evidence involving the assertions of human witnesses, credibility assessment is quite different. We first need to establish how a person obtained the information they report: (1) by direct observation; (2) at second-hand from another source (possibly hearsay); or (3) by inference from other information (opinion evidence). Like other human characteristics, the credibility of a witness has many attributes. Among the important attributes of witness credibility are veracity, objectivity and observational sensitivity or accuracy.

Assessing the probative force of an item of evidence is a judgmental matter for which there are no legal rules. Many factors enter into such judgments such as the credibility of the source from which the evidence comes, the probabilistic strength of links in chains of reasoning from the evidence, the number of links in the chain, the rareness or improbability of the events reported in the evidence, and the possible influence of other evidence (see also §4 below).

Courts may rule on whether an item of evidence is relevant, but fact-finders must judge the credibility and probative force of evidence. Judgments about any of these three credentials of evidence will naturally depend upon a person's standpoint or frame of reference. Disagreements about the relevance, credibility and probative force of evidence are to be expected in legal and in other contexts. One major reason is that persons having different standpoints, backgrounds, objectives and values will effectively view the same evidence through different perceptual 'lenses'.

3 Structural issues

Analyses of the relevance, credibility and probative force of evidence involve both structural and probabilistic issues. Structural issues arise during the construction of arguments or chains of reasoning to justify these three credentials of evidence. There are several major structural difficulties, the first of which concerns the fact that chains of reasoning we construct often have many links. Each link inserted in a chain of reasoning from an item of evidence to some major probandum or hypothesis identifies a source of uncertainty recognized by the person constructing the chain of reasoning. Both Bentham and Wigmore recognized that there are very few inferences in which a chain of reasoning has just one link. Wigmore applied the name 'catenated' to those inferences involving two or more links. Today such inferences are said to be cascaded, multi-stage or hierarchical; the term 'inference-upon-inference' is also employed. Until recently, there has been scant reference outside the field of law to catenated or cascaded inference.

The second structural difficulty concerns arbitrariness in the construction of a reasoning chain. Two persons may justifiably construct different chains of reasoning from the same evidence to the same probanda; in other words, they take different reasoning routes. They may of course each take reasoning routes from the same evidence to different probanda. The logician John VENN noted that both the number and the labelling of stages of reasoning is often quite arbitrary. Wigmore emphasized that the form an argument takes depends upon who constructed it. In short, there are no normatively 'correct' arguments. This has a distinct bearing on the issue of rationality in inference since more than one argument may be justifiable from the same evidence. Plausibility and the avoidance of *non sequiturs* seem to be our major guides in argument construction. The construction of any argument is in fact a creative act, as is the discovery or generation of evidence and possible probanda in the first place.

In evaluating the credentials of evidence a major

structural difficulty in legal and other contexts is that we usually have masses of evidence to contend with. Arguments constructed from masses of evidence can be stunningly complex and, when depicted graphically, they resemble complex networks; they are now in fact called inference networks. Wigmore (in 1913) was the first to study complex inference networks based upon masses of evidence. He devised a graphic scheme for charting arguments from evidence to the ultimate probandum in a case. Modern analysis of Wigmore's evidence charts shows that his inference networks can be characterized mathematically as directed acyclic graphs. A network is a kind of graph structure containing two basic elements: nodes and arcs. In an inference network nodes represent evidence and interim or final probanda (propositions to be proved); arcs represent probabilistic linkages among nodes. Inference networks are directed because reasoning proceeds inductively from evidence to major or ultimate probanda. They are acyclic because there is no path of arcs from any node that brings you back to this same node; this would amount to being in an inferential loop.

Inferences involving legal disputes tend to be well-structured from the top down. To prove a major fact at issue, at some specified level of probability, certain elements must be established. These elements, called penultimate probanda, stem from substantive law concerning the legal matter at hand. For example, a case of first-degree (premeditated) murder may involve the penultimate probanda: (1) Y was killed; (2) it was defendant X who killed Y; (3) X intended to kill Y (it was not an accident); and (4) X formed this intent beforehand. In essence, each of these penultimate probanda serves as a touchstone for determining the relevance of evidence.

Attention to structural matters provides a basis for categorizing evidence without regard to its substance or content. Jurists, and perhaps historians, must be prepared to evaluate evidence having virtually any conceivable content or substance. The relevance and credibility credentials of evidence discussed above assist first in the identification of distinguishable forms of evidence. We ask two questions: (1) how does the evidence stand in relation to the person evaluating it? and (2) how does the evidence stand in relation to the major facts at issue?

Answers to the first question allow us to identify properties of evidence that govern how its credibility is to be assessed. Discussed in §2 above are two of the basic forms of evidence: tangible and testimonial; there are others. In some cases evidence expected but missing can itself be taken as evidence. Missing evidence is not the same as negative evidence, the report of the nonoccurrence of an event. It has been recognized in law for quite some time that the non-production of evidence invites the inference that the evidence is unfavourable to the interests of the person who refuses to provide it. Other evidence comes from various authoritative sources such as almanacs and various tables of physical or chemical phenomena. In addition, there are certain facts that can be accepted without further proof, such as: strychnine in sufficient doses is lethal. Information from authoritative sources and certain accepted facts may be judicially noticed by courts and accepted without further proof. Answers to the second (relevance) question above allow us to identify evidence as being direct, circumstantial or ancillary (as noted in §2 above). Combinations of answers to these two questions allow us to categorize any evidence. For example, we may have tangible evidence that is circumstantial on some matter at issue, or have testimonial evidence that is indirectly relevant or ancillary.

In purely structural terms, we may also identify recurrent combinations of evidence. Dissonant evidence comes in two basic forms: contradictory evidence and conflicting evidence. Contradictory evidence involves events that cannot happen together, in which case we naturally look to the credibility of the sources from which it comes. Conflicting evidence, however, concerns events which seem to favour different probanda or hypotheses but which could possibly occur together. In resolving such conflicts we also look to the credibility of our sources; but we must also consider the reasons why we say the evidence is conflicting. Perhaps we could explain away this apparent conflict with better understanding of the situation at hand. Harmonious evidence also has two basic forms: corroboration and convergence. Two forms of corroboration can be discerned. In one case, we have successive reports of the same event. In another case we have ancillary evidence that favours the credibility of a source reporting a certain event. Convergent evidence involves different events we believe to favour the same probandum or hypothesis. Finally, some combinations of evidence exhibit synergism in the sense that one item of evidence seems to enhance the probative force of another. In other situations, one item of evidence may seem redundant, and thus have less inferential force, when considered in light of other evidence.

4 Probability and the probative force of evidence

Evidence is relevant if it has some probative force on material facts at issue. How much probative force an item or body of evidence has can only be graded in probabilistic terms; this is a consequence of evidence being incomplete, inconclusive, imprecise and not completely credible (see §2). There are no legal rules that prescribe how the probative force or weight of evidence should be assessed; such assessment calls for judgments on the part of jurors or judges (in bench trials). The task of weighing evidence rests upon the ordinary or common-sense reasoning ability that fact-finders are credited with possessing. Since the early 1600s, when interest in probability calculations emerged, there have been intermittent attempts to determine the extent to which mathematical probability theories can offer any guidance in the task of weighing and combining evidence in legal affairs. Some of the very earliest probabilistic analyses involved study of the relation between the probative force of testimony and the credibility of its sources.

Probabilistic analyses of the task of assessing the probative force of evidence have drawn a mixed reaction on the part of evidence scholars in law. One reason is that the theory of probability stemming from the work of Blaise Pascal (§5) in the seventeenth century is rooted in enumerative processes such as those encountered in determining probabilities in games of chance or in replicable statistical analyses. Inferences in law, however, usually concern singular or unique events that are not replicable or subject to enumerative analysis. In the conventional or Pascalian theory of probability, the one most persons learn about on first exposure to the subject, probabilities are taken to be numbers between zero and one (inclusive) that are additive across mutually exclusive events. A process called conditioning allows for the revision of a probability in light of new evidence. A consequence known as Bayes' rule, consistent with the properties of Pascalian probability and the manner in which a conditional probability is defined, emerges as a canon for probabilistic reasoning based on evidence. This rule has been the subject of controversy among philosophers, probabilists and statisticians. Some, but not all, believe Bayes' rule to be the canon for inductive and probabilistic inference (see PROBABILITY THEORY AND EPISTEMOLOGY).

Pascalian probability is subject to a variety of interpretations in addition to those involving aleatory (chance) or relative frequency (statistical) situations. One alternative, congenial to the application of Bayes' rule, involves viewing Pascalian probability in an epistemic sense to indicate a person's degree of subjective or personal belief, based on evidence, that a certain proposition is true or that some event has occurred or will occur. This interpretation allows singular or unique events to be graded probabilistically. Terms in Bayes' rule called likelihoods and likelihood ratios form one very useful way of grading the probative force of evidence. Study of these ingredients of Bayes' rule allows the capture of a wide assortment of evidential subtleties that arise in the task of assessing the probative force of the various forms and combinations of evidence mentioned in §3 above. At the same time, however, various difficulties with a Pascalian interpretation of probability, and the use of Bayes's rule, have led to some well-articulated alternatives to the Pascalian system of probability. Study of the relative merits of these alternative formal systems forms one basis for the 'probability debates' now taking place among scholars of evidence in jurisprudence.

One natural question concerns why we should expect the Pascalian system, rooted in enumeration, to be necessarily adequate in capturing all observed attributes of the epistemic probability judgments so often made regarding singular or unique events? The additivity of probabilities in the Pascalian system requires a complete commitment of belief to an event and to its complement. For example, if on evidence we believe probandum H has probability 0.8, we must also say we believe that not-H has probability 0.2. In recent years a formal non-additive system of probabilistic reasoning called 'belief functions' has been developed that allows a person to be uncommitted in various ways in making epistemic probability judgments. This system, also rooted in much earlier studies, allows capture of a variety of credal states that are elusive to Pascalian probabilities. For instance, belief functions allow us to distinguish between lack of belief and disbelief, to capture the concept of ignorance as lack of evidence, and to give a more precise meaning to the term 'doubt'.

Since the time of Francis Bacon (§4), it has been recognized that inductive reasoning can involve the eliminative rather than the enumerative use of evidence. In recent years, a system of probabilities called 'Baconian probabilities' has been developed that is expressly congenial to induction by elimination. In eliminative induction alternative probanda or hypotheses are subjected to a variety of different evidential tests, each one designed to eliminate at least one of the hypotheses. A hypothesis surviving our best attempts at variative elimination has the highest Baconian probability. A distinguishing feature of Baconian probability is the importance it places on the completeness of coverage (or the sufficiency) of evidence. The weight of evidence in Baconian terms depends not only upon questions we have answered by evidence but also upon recognized questions we have not yet answered with evidence. One very important element of the current probability debates concerns the extent to which judicial proof may be eliminative in nature.

In the process of judicial proof, probability statements are made in linguistic terms rather than in numbers. Thus we have such forensic proof standards as 'beyond reasonable doubt', 'clear and convincing evidence', and 'balance of probabilities'. Attempts to cast these standards in precise numerical terms inevitably fail; these forensic standards acknowledge the imprecision latent in so much of legal reasoning. The common-sense generalizations we assert to license stages of reasoning are stated imprecisely. For example, we assert: 'persons who utter threats *often* intend to carry them out'. Since no one compiles any relevant statistics on such matters, we use imprecise linguistic qualifiers such as 'usually', 'often', 'frequently' or 'probably'. Evidence can also be imprecise; we may have evidence reporting that a witness has not very good eyesight or that it was very dark when the witness made an alleged observation. There is now in existence a well-developed formal system of fuzzy inference and fuzzy probability that permits some very precise ways of coping with the imprecise or fuzzy linguistic variables so often encountered in judicial proof. This system rests upon a multivalued logic instead of the two-valued logic forming the basis for other formal systems of probability (see FUZZY LOGIC §3).

It does appear that the task of assessing the probative force of evidence is far too rich an intellectual activity to expect that any single formal system of probability can capture all of this richness. Each one of the formal systems just discussed is informative and resonates to some but not all of the important attributes of the task of weighing evidence.

5 Inference from a mass of evidence

Inference from evidence in judicial proof is embedded in the further process of choice. Following a trial, courts and jurors render verdicts and decide upon consequences. In other forms of settlement choices are made by both sides during the process of negotiation and bargaining. The inferential element in all such decisions involves the very difficult task of drawing conclusions from masses of evidence in which all the forms and combinations mentioned in §3 above are likely to be represented. There are no laws of evidence telling fact-finders how to combine all the evidence in reaching a final conclusion. Although the various probability theories discussed in §4 offer suggestions about how such complex inference tasks might be decomposed to simplify them, the actual inferential judgments made by fact-finders are holistic and are neither decomposed nor otherwise assisted by means of any formal theory concerning the combination of evidence. There is now an abundance of empirical research on strategies that fact-finders employ in drawing conclusions from masses of evidence.

The only inferential guidelines offered in the laws of evidence concern belief intensity thresholds required for verdicts in criminal and civil cases. These belief thresholds exist in the form of the imprecise or fuzzy forensic standards of proof such as 'beyond reasonable doubt' (in criminal cases) and 'balance of probabilities' or 'preponderance of evidence' (in civil cases). One element of the current 'probability debates' concerns whether or not contemporary theories of probability offer ways of adding precision in prescribing these forensic standards.

See also: LAW, PHILOSOPHY OF; LEGAL REASONING AND INTERPRETATION; PROBABILITY, INTERPRETATIONS OF

References and further reading

Anderson, T. and Twining, W. (1991) *Analysis of Evidence: How to Do Things with Facts Based upon Wigmore's Science of Judicial Proof*, Boston, MA: Little, Brown. (Expansion of the structural matters discussed in §3 of this entry.)

Cohen, L.J. (1977) *The Probable and the Provable*, Oxford: Clarendon Press. (Comments on the necessity of alternative formal systems of probability to capture requisites of inference in legal affairs.)

Eggleston, R.E. (1978) *Evidence, Proof, and Probability*, London: Weidenfeld and Nicolson. (Comments from a legal scholar on matters discussed in §4 of this entry.)

Hastie, R., Penrod, S. and Pennington, N. (1983) *Inside the Jury*, Cambridge, MA: Harvard University Press. (Empirical studies of the processes jurors employ in drawing conclusions from masses of evidence; expansion of matters in §5 of this entry.)

Plucknett, T. (1956) *A Concise History of the Common Law*, Boston, MA: Little, Brown. (Chapter 4 concerns the emergence of the jury system as discussed in §1 of this entry.)

Schum, D. (1994) *The Evidential Foundations of Probabilistic Reasoning*, New York: John Wiley & Sons. (A study of the properties, uses, and discovery of evidence in probabilistic reasoning; particular emphasis on alternative views of the probative force of evidence. Expansion of material in §§2–4 of this entry.)

Tillers, P. and Green, E. (1986) 'Symposium: Probability and Inference in the Law of Evidence', *Boston University Law Review*, 66 (2–3): entire issue. (A record of debates concerning the application of probability theories in legal inference. Expands on §4 of this entry.)

Twining, W. (1985) *Theories of Evidence: Bentham and Wigmore*, Stanford, CA: Stanford University Press. (Expansion of the material in §§1–2 of this entry.)

DAVID A. SCHUM

LEGAL HERMENEUTICS

Legal hermeneutics studies the interpretation and meaning of written law. By way of contrast with the related discipline of forensic rhetoric, the study of oral argumentation and persuasion in court, legal hermeneutics is best defined as a textual discipline which dates back to the classical codifications of Greek and Roman law. While the term hermeneutics is derived from the messenger god Hermes and is used by Aristotle as the title of a work concerned with the logic of interpretation, Peri hermeneias, *legal hermeneutics really only developed with the growth and medieval reception of Roman law. The Roman legal tradition was pre-eminently a tradition of* ius scriptum *or written law, of codes and codifications. The custody, interpretation and transmission of the great texts of Roman law gave rise to an exemplary discipline of hermeneutics. Its task was that of preserving, collating, translating and applying the archaic, foreign (Latin) and fragmentary texts of the legal tradition to contemporary and vernacular circumstances far removed in time and space from the original contexts of the written law. In later eras and particularly in periods of crisis or renewal of the legal tradition, the problems of text, interpretation and meaning in law have led to the revival of the concerns and traditions of legal hermeneutics.*

1   **Law, philology and hermeneutics**
2   **Hermeneutics and jurisprudence**
3   **Philosophy of language, precedent and hermeneutics**
4   **Critical legal hermeneutics**

1   Law, philology and hermeneutics

The first meaning of the term 'hermeneutics' is one which derives from the function of the god Hermes, who was said to have delivered the messages of the gods to the mortal realm. Hermes translated the divine idiom into human speech and thus became, together with his Latin form Mercury, the emblem of the task of translation between different orders, times and places. In so far as Hermes carried and communicated the words, the eloquence and the authority of the gods, his task was always tied to the question of law. In its broadest definition, hermeneutics identified the problem of meaning and interpretation with that of access to the divine source and spirit of all human law. Hermeneutics thus identified the art of interpretation with that of unveiling and translating the alien or hidden message of the divine or distant author of the laws.

While the dominant model of post-classical literary hermeneutics was theological and concerned the exegesis and interpretation of the Scriptures and the canons or laws of the Church, a parallel tradition of legal hermeneutics existed. The secular model for legal hermeneutics developed initially and somewhat paradoxically around the two main codifications of Roman law, namely the Twelve Tables from the fifth century BC and the sixth-century *Corpus iuris civilis*. These codifications, although vastly different in style, both endeavoured to state a divinely inspired and absolute body of law in a written form which would preclude the need for interpretation. The Twelve Tables dealt with disputed points of law and aimed, through the use of writing, to take the resolution of such issues out of the hands of the pontiffs, the interpreters of the law. So too the Eastern Roman emperor Justinian promulgated his massive codification of Roman law with the accompanying injunction that 'no one – neither those who presently practise jurisprudence, nor those who will practise it in future – may presume to compose commentaries on these laws', a ruling which is explained slightly later by means of the equation of interpretation with perversions (*perversiones*) of law. The jurist or practitioner of legal hermeneutics was thus originally to know and obey the law rather than to construe it, precisely because its authority was far greater than that of any interpretation.

Hermes was also, however, a thief: he stole from the gods by virtue of taking their words and presenting them in secular and novel contexts. The art of legal interpretation also borrowed from this metaphor of theft of meaning in allowing that passage of time brought with it the decline or decay of law and change in the circumstances of its application. Where circumstances had changed or time had rendered the written law less appropriate to novel contexts, the jurist had to use first fiction and then later analogy to apply it. In both circumstances, whether through the fiction of treating the litigants 'as if' they fell within the written rule, or through analogy with the clear meaning of the text, the interpretation was subordinate to the text of law, the unwritten meaning an implication or logical inference from the authoritative text. The art of hermeneutics thus acted covertly to supplement the written law and to legislate new meanings in the guise of textual reconstruction. It stole the power of the lawmaker but it did so under the veil of observance or in the form of the self-effacement of the juristic interpreter.

In its classical periods, and particularly during the medieval reception of Roman law or 'twelfth-century revolution' in interpretation, legal hermeneutics took the form of a practical exercise in the philological reconstruction of the 'true' or literal meaning of the texts of law. Constrained by the prohibition upon commentary, the interpreter of the law was restricted to the task of providing grammatical glosses and word-by-word explanations of the rules of law. Their task was to harmonize and systematize the archaic and fragmentary textual inheritance of law and through understanding it in ever more profound detail find ways of applying it to the circumstances and contexts of a later age. The glossator was the ideal type of the legal interpreter, an erudite but faceless technician of meaning, a philologist of law who purported to reconstruct and harmonize the terms and rules of written law without ever interfering or interposing between the letter of the law and its destination. In this form, hermeneutics was a discipline which guarded over both tradition and text, an art of custody and of an esoteric and exclusory knowledge of ancient rules or laws.

2   Hermeneutics and jurisprudence

The figures of Hermes and Mercury are also suggestive of passage and of turnings, of sleight of hand and the flight of words: Hermes and Mercury both guard and admit, conserve and create. The other face of legal hermeneutics is associated with the speed and slippage or transition that is associated with a law that was always conceived as Janus-faced or split between its divine and human sources. Hermeneutics was thus also associated with the magic or art of legal representation and with words of law, with Coke's *vocabula artis*, which hid behind their vulgar surface a thesaurus of artistic meanings and erudite truths. Hermeneutics was in this sense also always potentially a political and interventionist practice in which the interpreter of law would create new meanings and invent new applications for the cold prose, tired words or dead letters – Bacon's *litera mortua* – of written law (see COMMON LAW §2).

This stronger and more modern sense of legal hermeneutics developed as a reaction against the glossatorial tradition and came about primarily through the rediscovery of the classical tradition and law in the Renaissance. Legal humanism pilloried the glossatorial tradition of unthinking or 'imbecilic' reverence for the post-classical compilation and interpolation of Roman law and returned rather to the surviving sources of Roman law itself. In place of the glossators' slavish observance of textual letter and rule, humanism sought to comprehend the law in terms of the context of its historical enunciation. Roman law, according to François Hotman, was not an adequate model for contemporary law; rather it represented the property interests and privileges of the Roman bourgeoisie and should be understood in terms of (and restricted to) that social and political context. The rules of legal hermeneutic method devised by the humanists and associated particularly with Jacques Cujas, Andrea Aliciato and François Hotman on the Continent and with Christopher St German and later Sir Francis Bacon and Sir Edward Coke in England, entailed a much stronger philological sensibility and rhetorical awareness.

The exemplary form of Renaissance hermeneutics was the treatise on *Digest* 50.16, *De verborum significatione* (on the meaning of words) (see ROMAN LAW §2). While such treatises were still commentaries upon the classical Roman sources of law, and upon the terms and rules of the textual tradition, they went far beyond the singular text of the earlier tradition and expounded theories of interpretation which greatly exceeded the style of the gloss both in method and in scope of disciplinary reference. The first feature of such hermeneutics lay in the conscious comprehension of law as tradition and interpretation, as both written and unwritten, as sense and reference. The key interpretive maxim in relation to this approach was *Digest* 1.3.17 (Celsus): '[t]o know the law is not to know the words of the law, but its force and power [*vim ac potestatem*]'. In other comparable formulations the words of the law were contrasted to its 'root reason', 'intention', 'cause', 'rationale', 'purpose' and 'true sense'. The radical alterity of the past and the fragmentary character of its textual remains both forced the jurist towards a critical hermeneutics which could add to the literal meaning a covert sense or spirit of law, a meaning which could only be discovered by linguistic inference or supplementation, by reading between the lines *subauditio* or *subintellectio*. In short, the function of such a hermeneutics was to supplement the paucity of the textual remains of law and to recreate a fuller meaning by use of a wide array of philological, historical and linguistic techniques of reconstruction.

The second striking feature of hermeneutic jurisprudence lay in the methodologies developed to accommodate and expound the unwritten meaning or '*labile ratio*' of the legal text. Once it was explicitly recognized that the terms and rules laid down in antique texts could never apply directly, or without interpretation or 'interposition', to the linguistic context and social circumstances of contemporary disputes, the task of hermeneutics became that of finding something more in the law than was merely written. To this end the treatises on *De verborum significatione* developed an extensive array of techniques of interpretation drawn from a wide variety of other disciplines. History, philology, logic and rhetoric were the principal sources for extension and innovation in relation to written rules and allowed for the systematic development of techniques of contextual interpretation and supplementation. While there was no one standard set of rules for the construction of legal meaning from between the lines of the law, a series of methods and contexts were developed which still play a role in the contemporary jurisprudence of interpretation. Most notably, construction of textual meaning would start from philological criticism of the text itself and would move to reconstrue it by reference to what may be classified synoptically as linguistic, legal and rhetorical contexts. The linguistic context would refer to etymological analysis as well as to grammatical rules of construction. The legal context refers not simply to the use of analogy in the extension of rules but also to the need to relate disparate rules and maxims, customs and local laws, to the specific text subjected to interpretation. The rhetorical context, finally, referred not only to the various forms of figuration by which meaning changes according to context and use but also to specifically legal senses of the intention of the author of the laws (*mens legis*) and the force or reason of their utterance.

3 Philosophy of language, precedent and hermeneutics

The various post-Renaissance revivals of legal hermeneutics have tended to coincide with crises and renewals of the legal tradition, associated most particularly with movements for codification or other reforms of law. The nineteenth century in particular witnessed a pan-European resurgence of hermeneutic method in the arts in general and in jurisprudence in particular. The peculiar concern of the new legal hermeneutics was that of the place of language and of meaning within the efflorescence of legislation and administrative regulation that accompanied the growth of the modern industrial state. While the method and models of textual understanding were still predicated upon the earlier theological and juristic conceptions of construction and interpretation, the more secular concern of legal philosophy was that of the place of meaning within the development of a science of law.

One model of hermeneutics returned to the glossator's exegetical conception of absolute and authoritative texts. The highly restrictive hermeneutics which developed around the *Code Napoléon* (1804), for example, asserted that all meaning was to be drawn from the legal text and from nowhere but the text. In a similar vein, Jeremy BENTHAM in England believed that codification of the law could take the problem of legal interpretation out of the arbitrary jurisdiction of the common law judges and return it to the people in the form of simple, clear and comprehensive textual expressions of the rules of law. Codification, however, was only ever a temporary solution to the hermeneutic problem of interpretation and passage of time, change of context and of circumstance. The indeterminacy of language inevitably raised again the problems of finding unwritten meanings which exceeded or displaced the surface sense or letter of the law. What was new about the post-Enlightenment hermeneutics was that philosophy of language and particularly phenomenology, social science, linguistics and literary criticism replaced the earlier traditions of philology and rhetoric as the principal disciplines to come to the aid of jurisprudence. It is significant, however, that when Hans-Georg GADAMER (§3) or Emilio Betti, arguably the two great hermeneutic philosophers of the twentieth century, turn to the definition of hermeneutics they place law at the heart of the discipline. In Gadamer's terms, law is exemplary of the historical problem of writing and it is as central to the proper formulation of the problem of meaning as that of the relation between historical sense and contemporary application, between text and judgment (Gadamer 1976).

The problem of hermeneutics, according to Gadamer, is the problem of law. It is that of creating contemporary meanings out of the antique and alien materials of tradition. The lawyer faces this problem in an acute form, and therefore is forced to resolve it in an exemplary way by reconciling the spirit of the tradition with the needs of contemporary communities. For Gadamer, legal hermeneutics could resolve the problem of the meaning of tradition by understanding the prejudices or pre-judgments by means of which the tradition already governed the contemporary instance. Gadamer's notion of 'the pre-schematisation of our European attitude' draws heavily upon Heidegger's conception of language, and particularly the philosophical language of the Greeks, as a code already imprinted with the metaphysics and the meanings which the subsequent tradition has lived out. For Gadamer and in a somewhat different form for Betti, the prior existence of linguistic meaning did not wholly resolve the legal problem of law-applying acts in the sense that neither linguistic tradition nor precedent could wholly determine the contemporary instance. The hermeneutic conception of understanding (*Verstehen*) also entailed an active sense of the inevitability of the creation and extension of meanings by recourse, in Gadamer's theory, to the spirit of the legal tradition through the hermeneutic unlocking of 'original' meanings and, in Betti's theory, through the use of reasoning by analogy.

4 Critical legal hermeneutics

The problem of precedent and of the frequently disjunctive relation of norms or rules to decisions and to practices has consistently troubled the various modernist attempts to construct a science of law (see LEGAL REASONING AND INTERPRETATION). Hermeneutics, and the problems of language and of writing more broadly, were a consistent threat to the jurisprudential systematizers of the common law tradition in particular. Predicated not upon a code but upon a disparate series of statutes, reported decisions, customs, maxims and other borrowings, the claim that law formed a coherent and unitary body of determinate rules was always hermeneutically precarious. While the positivist tradition of jurisprudence on occasion has recognized a certain latitude, *Verstehen* or 'internal attitude', in the interpretation of law as a system of rules, the concept of a legal system has most generally been presented, as for example in the work of the Austrian legal theorist Hans Kelsen, in such a manner as to exclude any strong conception of hermeneutics from the theory of law (see LEGAL POSITIVISM §5; KELSEN, H.).

Historicist and more properly hermeneutic reactions against positivistic and formalistic theories of law were contemporary with their original elaboration. Such reactions to legal science could be broadly speaking conservative, as for example was the German Friedrich Karl von Savigny's historicist legal hermeneutics, which endeavoured at the beginning of the nineteenth century to counter codification with a historical science of law. The other tendency of hermeneutics, however, was more critical and iconoclastic. What may be termed critical legal hermeneutics, drawing upon disciplines as diverse as sociology, linguistics and psychoanalysis, denies that there is any unitary body of law at the level of social systems and equally disputes the possibility of 'true', objective or singular legal meanings at the level of textual interpretation. The earliest political expression of a species of critical legal hermeneutics came with the US legal realist movement in the elite law schools of the USA in the early part of the twentieth century (see LEGAL REALISM §2). Concerned primarily with issues of statutory interpretation and the decisional practices of the courts, realist legal hermeneutics asserted the priority of judgment or court practice over written norms and so either implied or directly asserted the indeterminacy of legal meaning and the creative role of all law-applying acts.

Where legal realism was concerned primarily with drawing attention to the oral and contingent context of the courtroom and thereby challenged the naïve belief in a text-based science of law, subsequent developments of critical legal hermeneutics have focused almost exclusively on the indeterminacies or undecidability of written law. Variously located within critical race theory, feminist jurisprudence and critical legal scholarship, the contemporary hermeneutic challenge to the objectivity of the legal text is formulated in terms, respectively, of ethnicity, gender and politics (see CRITICAL LEGAL STUDIES). Basing itself most broadly upon theories of textual indeterminacy, one of the key goals of critical legal hermeneutics has been to politicize law by evidencing the malleable and discretionary character of its textual practice. The legal text is a species of writing, a performative use of language or *écriture*, and it should be analysed as such before or as well as being consigned to the genre or tradition of legal science. In this respect, critical legal hermeneutics is concerned to treat the legal text as a form of literature and to subject it to the disciplines and dismemberments that the arts now throw in the way of textual meaning. Following the tradition of humanistic hermeneutics, but using contemporary disciplinary idioms, the critical legal endeavour has aimed to link legal language both to the inequity and to the literal and the metaphorical violence of law. Critical hermeneutics is aimed thus at producing an ethics of legal reading and of writing law, an ethics which ideally links text to judgment, word to act and, in its broadest philosophical expression, written law to the constraints of justice.

See also: HERMENEUTICS; LAW, PHILOSOPHY OF

References and further reading

Berman, H. (1983) *Law and Revolution: The Formation of the Western Legal Tradition*, Cambridge, MA: Harvard University Press. (Accessible guide to the disciplinary development of the modern legal tradition.)

Betti, E. (1955) *Teoria della legge e degli atti giuridici (teoria generale e dogmatica)*, Milan: Guiffrà. (General statement of legal hermeneutic method.)

Douzinas, C., Warrington, R. and McVeigh, S. (1990) *Postmodern Jurisprudence: The Law of Texts in the Text of Law*, London: Routledge. (Contains a critical discussion of contemporary hermeneutics as well as an introduction to postmodern theories of legal textuality.)

* Gadamer, H.-G. (1976) *Truth and Method*, London: Sheed and Ward. (Crucial work on the history and philosophy of hermeneutics.)

Goodrich, P. (1995) *Oedipus Lex: Psychoanalysis, History, Law*, Berkeley and Los Angeles, CA: University of California Press. (Historical and critical account of common law hermeneutics, with particular attention paid to the relevance of a psychoanalytic hermeneutics of law.)

—— (ed.) (1997) *Law and the Unconscious: A Legendre Reader*, Basingstoke: Macmillan. (Translation of a selection of works by a French legal philosopher who has developed a unique theory of the historical sources of Continental legal hermeneutics.)

* Justinian (533) *The Digest of Justinian*, T. Mommsen, P. Krueger and A. Watson (eds), Philadelphia, PA: University of Pennsylvania Press, 1985. (The Latin text by Mommsen and Krueger with a readable translation by various writers, edited by A. Watson.)

Kelley, D. (1970) *Foundations of Modern Historical Scholarship: Language, Law, and History in the French Renaissance*, New York: Columbia University Press. (Classic study of Renaissance legal humanism and its role in the development of social theory.)

Levinson, S. and Mailloux, S. (eds) (1988) *Intepreting Law and Literature: A Hermeneutic Reader*, Evanston, IL: Northwestern University Press. (Critical legal reader in literature and law.)

Leyh, G. (ed.) (1992) *Legal Hermeneutics: History, Theory, and Practice*, Los Angeles and Berkeley, CA: University of California Press. (Collection of contemporary essays on legal hermeneutics from a political perspective.)

Maclean, I. (1993) *Interpretation and Meaning in the Renaissance: The Case of Law*, Cambridge: Cambridge University Press. (Excellent expansion of material in §2 of this entry.)

Schlag, P. (1996) *Laying Down the Law: Mysticism, Fetishism, and the American Legal Mind*, New York: New York University Press. (Critical Legal Studies account of the paucity of common law hermeneutics.)

Stein, P. (1966) *Regulae Iuris: From Juristic Rules To Legal Maxims*, Edinburgh: Edinburgh University Press. (Historical account of the Roman origins and subsequent developments of the concept of legal meaning.)

PETER GOODRICH

LEGAL IDEALISM

The term 'legal idealism' has various meanings. These include: the notion that laws, and the rights and duties they confer, genuinely exist, in which legal idealism is opposed to legal realism; the notion that law is intimately connected with moral or social values, in which legal idealism is opposed to legal positivism; the notion that one can move from certain premises about human reason and will to systematic principles for legal development and decision-making; and the notion that one can derive systematic principles of a similar kind from the requirements of social life. It is also sometimes used to imply too much faith in the capacity of law to solve problems. The enduring issues of legal idealism concern establishing systematic principles for legal development and decision-making.

1　The varieties of legal idealism
2　Transcendental and absolute legal idealism
3　Historical/social legal idealism
4　An overview

1　The varieties of legal idealism

Legal idealism is a particularly confusing term as it is used of different, and sometimes incompatible, approaches to law. First, and at its broadest, it covers all those theories which regard law as normative or standard-setting, as expressing what ought to be done. Such theories typically treat law as consisting of norms or rules or principles and as conferring rights and duties (see LEGAL CONCEPTS; NORMS, LEGAL). Legal idealism, here, is tied to a certain kind of philosophical idealism, since law is seen as the product of some act of mind or will. As such its norms genuinely form part of our world. For most thinkers, this is also the case with the rights and duties to which it gives rise. So understood, legal idealism embraces most, if not all, natural law thinking (see NATURAL LAW) and even certain types of legal positivism, such as that of Hans KELSEN. It stands in opposition, however, to other types of legal positivism, for which matters such as rules and duties are at best imaginary entities, with talk about them to be explained away in terms of attempts to predict or promote certain forms of human behaviour (see LEGAL REALISM §1).

Second, the term 'legal idealism' is used for theories that regard law as intimately connected with certain specified moral or social values, such as freedom, justice, democracy, cultural evolution or group solidarity. Here idealism is understood in a sense closer to that of ordinary language, where it is tied to the having of ideals. In this context, legal idealism once again covers natural law thinking and also certain other approaches that resemble it. Here legal idealism stands in opposition to legal positivism, where it is claimed that law is to be identified solely by reference to the form it takes or the source from which it comes, with no built-in restrictions as to content or purpose (see LEGAL POSITIVISM).

Third, there is what is known as transcendental legal idealism. A transcendental inquiry is concerned with investigating the conditions under which certain kinds of experience or knowledge are possible. This kind of approach, using the tradition of KANT (§5), was adopted within a group of theories of largely, although not exclusively, German origin. Such theories begin from certain premises about the nature of human reason and will and develop a legal philosophy from them. One of the objects of such a philosophy is to provide a 'scientific', largely in the sense of 'systematic', basis for the development of law and for legal decision-making. The main departure from Kant is in terms of the emphasis that is placed on the social purposes of law.

Fourth, there is what is sometimes called absolute legal idealism, following the work primarily of HEGEL (§8). This starts from the premise that there is some absolute idea and argues that history works inexorably towards its fulfilment. Law, in both form and content, reflects stages in the development of this idea.

Fifth, there is historical/social legal idealism. This differs from transcendental and absolute legal idealism mainly by taking the actual nature of social life as a given and attempting to find within it the ideas or ideals to which law-making and legal decision-making should conform if they are to serve it properly.

Sixth, and finally, legal idealism is sometimes used pejoratively for those theories that are thought to express a naïve faith in the capacity of law to solve social problems.

Various points are worth noting about these different kinds of idealism. A theorist may be an idealist of the first kind without being one of the second kind. Kelsen, for example, subscribed to the objective existence of norms but actively sought a pure, that is value-free, theory of law. On the other hand, the third, fourth and fifth kinds of idealism are all value-laden and so are really just particular versions of the second kind. They are, however, sometimes presented as if they did nothing more than restate the factual requirements of social life. Finally, some thinkers are difficult to allocate, since their theories seem to incorporate elements from more than one of the particular versions.

2 Transcendental and absolute legal idealism

The starting point is Kant's distinction between theoretical or speculative and practical uses of human reason. Both are concerned with formulating principles or laws, theoretical reason with what is and practical reason with what ought to be. Both can be pure, in the sense that the principles involved can be arrived at, not by looking to experience, but by looking for the conditions that make such experience intelligible. Pure practical reason is directed to discovering the conditions for moral action. These are found in the laws that humans should set themselves if they are to be free, that is to determine their own wills on a fully rational basis. The actions that ought to be performed under such laws are duties. When it comes to actual human behaviour, however, duties may be performed under two different sorts of motive. The first sort is internal, where the very existence of the duty is the motive for the action, in which case the law is an ethical one and the duty a matter of virtue. The second sort is external, deriving from law in the juridical or legal sense, where conformity may be brought about by other types of compulsion and the duty is a matter of right. For Kant, however, juridical law, in the form of positive or statutory right proceeding from the will of a legislator, should be confined to enforcing perfect duties. Such duties are primarily concerned with the avoidance of wrongdoing to others, in the form of interfering with their freedom. Justice is thus seen as the sum of the conditions under which individual wills can be conjoined in accordance with a universal law of freedom.

FICHTE (§4), though a disciple of Kant, departed from certain of his ideas. One such idea was that there are 'things-in-themselves' which are unknowable, our knowledge being limited to the structure we impose on what appears to us in the course of our experiences. Instead Fichte sought to construct experience from the activity of the conscious self. By discarding the possibility of any reality beyond mind and the objects of experience, he paved the way for the development of Hegelian absolute idealism. His legal philosophy, too, started from the way in which self-conscious beings 'think themselves' and, in parallel with Kant, Fichte saw this as involving them ascribing freedom both to themselves and to others. In so far as the individual respects the freedom of others as if it were absolute, the individual acts ethically and achieves spiritual freedom. Law, however, only requires individuals to limit their freedom to the extent necessary to secure the equal freedom of others. It provides the compulsion by which the duties so generated can be enforced by others as rights. Fichte went further than Kant, however, in terms of the types of rights that should be afforded, extending these into the economic sphere.

Hegel's legal philosophy concentrated on the way in which the free and rational will embodies or objectifies itself in the world in the form of institutions, so proceeding towards a reconciliation with the universal will. It does so at the level of abstract right, involving the rights and duties of human beings as such and covering property, contract and wrong (both civil and criminal); morality, which is the rational will directed towards its own development; and the ethical life, which is a product of the dialectic between abstract right and morality. The ethical life itself begins with the family. To this is counterposed civil society, involving law and the administration of justice. Both are brought together in the state, in which individuals realize their true universal wills, finding, in their duty, their substantive freedom. Much of Hegel's importance for legal theory, however, lies in his philosophy of history, according to which there is a continuing progression towards absolute freedom, stages in this progression being represented by particular states at particular times.

These thinkers, for whom legal philosophy was simply an aspect of their more general philosophy, had considerable influence on the ideas of those concerned more directly with law. For example, Stammler developed a theory of justice obviously indebted to the ideas of Kant. He distinguished between the notion of law as a particular kind of human volition, as an inviolable, sovereign, combining will, and the idea of law, which is concerned with achieving the perfect harmony of individual purposes, with attaining the social ideal of a community whose members will this freely as an end. From this Stammler derived his four principles of just law: two of respect, limiting the manner and extent to which members of the community can impose their own will on others; and two of participation, limiting the manner and extent to which any member may be excluded from the benefits of community life. The first principle in each set is to do with the avoidance of arbitrariness; the second is to do with treating others in a neighbourly way. In considering how these principles might be applied in practice, he constructed a model for just law, involving a special community whose actual regulations and the conflicting claims under them are 'laid before the judgment of the principles of just law'. Natural law thinking, he argued, erred not so much in its method as in claiming universal validity for the rules produced by that method, since this ignores the fact that everything to do with human wants and the way they are satisfied relies on experience and so is subject to constant change.

Del Vecchio also drew a distinction between the notion or concept of law and the idea of law, but developed it in a different manner. In effect he equated the concepts of law and justice and treated them, like Fichte, as derived from the need for reciprocity. He regarded the parallel ideas, however, as more than merely an expression of the preconditions for fulfilling some social end. In his view, the idea of justice has a content which springs from the human conscience. Law is to be seen, in the manner of Hegel, as the progressive realization of justice, the recognition of the absolute value of the personality and the equal freedom of all. Del Vecchio's combination of Kantianism and Hegelianism was not particularly new. It is, for example, to be found in the writings of the Scottish jurist W. Galbraith Miller in 1884. Del Vecchio's later works showed a greater move both towards the ideas of Hegel and away from Kantian individualism into corporatism and nationalism. A similar change is to be found in the ideas of Binder, both he and Del Vecchio becoming apologists for political developments in Germany and Italy respectively.

3   Historical/social legal idealism

One theorist who attempted to address both the actual nature of social life and the way in which it changed through history was Kohler. In common with JHERING he saw law as a means to a social end but differed from him by rejecting social utility as a criterion. Like Hegel, he saw history as the unfolding of an idea but argued against him that its progress was neither necessarily visible nor logical. Kohler identified the idea as that of civilization, by which he meant the increasing capacity of humans to control both external, and their own, nature. Law has the dual function of serving the needs thrown up by the current state of civilization within a society and of fostering its development. In consequence, what he calls 'jural postulates', allowing the law to cope both with differing rates of change and its own fixity, must be developed (see POUND, R.). Kohler arguably had absolutist tendencies to the extent that he identified a single ideal, civilization, and treated law as something that should foster it. (For a different view of the relation between law and cultural values, see RADBRUCH, G.)

Other thinkers concentrated directly on social life. For example, Duguit saw social solidarity as both a fact and a requirement of social life and law as both an aspect and a requirement of social solidarity. Gény was critical of Stammler for failing to show how his principles of just law might be applied to concrete problems. In a type of natural law thinking, he turned to identifying what will affect any body of positive law – namely factors of a physical or psychological and of a historical kind, general considerations of rationality, and the values embraced by the civilization concerned. The lawyer must take account of what is given in this way, applying his technique to fashion law according to the needs of social life. Interpretation is thus seen as a creative activity and the judge should be informed by *libre recherche scientifique* (free scientific research).

A parallel development in Germany was that of *Interessenjurisprudenz*, which, in the writings, for example, of Heck, argued for the application of a proper sociological method to legal problems. Following Jhering, this was held to involve the identification, classification and balancing of interests, of both a material and an intellectual kind. A much more radical approach, sponsored by theorists such as Ehrlich and Kantorowicz, was that of the *Freierecht-slehre* or 'free law' school, which advocated the maximum possible recourse to justice and equity in legal decision-making.

4 An overview

Legal idealism, in all its guises, runs up against the much broader philosophical question of the relationship between fact and value. Idealist theories are criticized, no matter which way they appear to mcve, for failing either to bridge the gap between the two or to show that there is actually no such gap to bridge. In the legal context, idealist theories follow different paths in trying to overcome these criticisms. While admitting that facts and values are of a different order, they may variously try to show either how legal norms can, none the less, form part of the world of fact or else how they are somehow required by or derivable from facts. Alternatively, they may effectively deny the distinction, arguing that legal norms, at least those comprising the natural law, exist as a matter of moral fact. Among the most interesting more recent attempts to root norms in social fact is the 'institutional theory of law' of MacCormick and Weinberger (see WEINBERGER, O.; INSTITUTIONAL-ISM IN LAW §4). Habermas' 'theory of communicative action', offering a transcendental argument anchored in the intuitive knowledge of competent members of modern societies, provides a different approach to the same problem and one of equal relevance for legal theory.

See also: JUSTICE, EQUITY AND LAW; LAW, PHILOSOPHY OF

References and further reading

Del Vecchio, G. (1905–08) *Il presupposti filosofici della nozione del diritto; Il concetto del diritto; Il concetto della natura e il principio del diritto*, 3 separate vols published together, trans. J. Lisle, preface J.H. Drake, *The Formal Bases of Law*, New York: Macmillan, 1921. (For further of his ideas on justice, in English, see his *Justice*, ed. A.H. Campbell, Edinburgh: Edinburgh University Press.)

Duguit, L. (1913) *Les transformations de droit public*, Paris: A. Colin; trans. F. Laski and H.J. Laski, with intro. by H.J. Laski, *Law in the Modern State*, London: Allen & Unwin, 1921. (The introduction gives a helpful summary of his ideas.)

Ehrlich, E. (1903) *Freierechtsfindung und Freierechtswissenschaft* (Free Law Finding and the Science of Free Law), Leipzig: C.L. Hirschfield. (For an account in English, see Gény 1917. For his ideas more generally, in English, see *Fundamental Principles of the Sociology of Law*, trans. W.L. Moll, Cambridge, MA: Harvard University Press, 1936.)

Fichte, J.G. (1796–7) *Grundlage des Naturrechts nach Prinzipien der Wissenschaftslehre*, Jena and Leipzig: C.E. Gabler; trans. A.E. Kroeger, preface W.T. Harris, *The Science of Rights*, London: Trubner & Co., 1889. (Of particular importance for those interested in the origins of the idea of the *Rechtsstaat*.)

Friedmann, W. (1967) *Legal Theory*, 5th edn, London: Stevens & Sons. (Especially chapters 15, 16 and 27. These cover most of the theorists mentioned in the entry.)

Gény, F. (1917) 'Judicial Freedom of Decision, its Necessity and Method', in *Science of Legal Method*, trans. E. Bruncken and L.B. Register, intro. by H.N. Sheldon and J.W. Salmond, Boston: Boston Book Company. (Also containing essays by Ehrlich, Kohler and Pound.)

Heck, P. von (1932) *Begriffsbildung und Interessenjursiprudenz* (The Formation of Concepts and the Jurisprudence of Interests), Tübingen: Mohr. (For a brief account of his ideas in English, see Friedmann 1967.)

Hegel, G.W.F. (1821) *Grundlinien der Philosophie des Rechts*, Berlin: Drucker & Humboldt; trans. T.M. Knox, *Philosophy of Right*, Oxford: Clarendon Press, 1942. (A closely argued text which can be difficult without some prior knowledge of Hegel's philosophy more generally.)

Kant, I. (1797) *Metaphysische Anfangsgründe der Rechtslehre*, Köningsberg: F. Nicoloumo; trans. W. Hastie, *Kant's Philosophy of Law*, Edinburgh: T. & T. Clark, 1887. (Although aspects of Kant's more general philosophy are incorporated in the text, the concentration is on its detailed implications for law.)

Kantorowicz, H. (1925) *Aus der Vorgeschichte der Freierechtslehre* (On the Antecedents of the Free Law Doctrine), Mannheim: J. Bensheimer. (For a wider view of his ideas, in English, see *The Definition of Law*, ed. A.H. Campbell, Cambridge: Cambridge University Press, 1958.)

Kohler, J. (1909) *Lehrbuch der Rechtsphilosophie*, Berlin and Leipzig: W. Rothschild; trans. A. Albrecht, preface A. Kocourek, *Kohler's Philosophy of Law*, Boston: Boston Book Company, 1914. (The preface is by a significant figure in analytical jurisprudence.)

Stammler, R. (1902) *Die Lehre von dem richtigen Rechte*, Berlin: J. Guttentag; trans. I. Husik, appendices by J.C. Wu and F. Gény, *The Theory of Justice*, New York: Macmillan, 1925; repr. New York: A. M. Kelley, 1969. (Gény's appendix is highly critical of the theory.)

Stone, J. (1965) *Human Law and Human Justice*, London: Stevens & Sons. (Especially pp. 167–92. Covering Stammler and Kohler and, also, Nelson, who has not been included in this entry.)

ELSPETH ATTWOOLL

LEGAL INFERENCE *see* LEGAL EVIDENCE AND INFERENCE

LEGAL INTERPRETATION
see LEGAL REASONING AND INTERPRETATION

LEGAL NORMS *see* NORMS, LEGAL

LEGAL POSITIVISM

Legal positivism is the approach in the philosophy of law which treats 'positive law' – law laid down in human societies through human decisions – as a distinct phenomenon, susceptible of analysis and description independently of morality, divine law or mere natural reality. It shares with philosophical positivism the aim of dealing in facts, but these are facts about legality and legal systems. Insistence on the distinctness of positive law has been integral to the 'rule of law ideal' because of the aim of clear law applied by neutral legal officials.

However, debates about positivism have been marred by a degree of conceptual confusion: positivism often appears to mean something different to its supporters and to its enemies, and many attacks are launched against straw men. Consequently, much depends on the definition of legal positivism that is used.

Attempts have been made to put some order into the discussion. Consider, for instance, H.L.A. Hart's list of meanings of legal positivism (which cumulatively count as features of positivism): (1) law as human commands; (2) absence of any necessary connection between law and morals; (3) the study of law as meaning, as distinct from sociology, history and evaluation; (4) the contention that a legal system is a closed system, sufficient in itself to justify legal decisions; (5) non-cognitivism in ethics (Hart 1958). Norberto Bobbio's list is shorter and more orderly, but at first sight not too different (Bobbio 1960): legal positivism has been conceived as: (1) a neutral, scientific approach to law; (2) a set of theories depicting the law as the product of the modern state, claiming that the law is a set of positive rules of human origin, and ultimately amounting to a set of statutes, collected in legal systems or orders; (3) an ideology of law that gives a value to positive law as such, implying that it should always be obeyed. However, in this list, unlike Hart's, the 'meanings' cannot be added together, the first and last being incompatible. The connection between the three points is as follows: for positivists the theories of Bobbio's second point (law is made up of rules produced by the state) yield a scientific and value-free approach to law; for the adversaries of legal positivism they yield only ideology, that is hidden value judgments in favour of the power of the State.

The shortest way to understand what is at issue in these abstract discussions is to proceed by contrasting legal positivism with its main critics' approach to law. It is noteworthy that on this point legal realists and natural law theorists, although starting from different and even opposite points of view, agree in concluding that legal positivism is an ideological, covertly evaluative, thesis.

1   **Positivism versus natural law theory**
2   **Varieties of legal positivism**
3   **Positivism versus legal realism**
4   **Legal systems**
5   **Interpretation and rights**

1   Positivism versus natural law theory

One of the basic ideas of legal positivism is the separation of law and morals: according to positivism defining what the law is should be kept separate from deciding whether it is just or unjust, good or evil. This is the basic conflict with the iusnaturalists (natural law theorists) who argue that describing the law necessarily requires moral value judgments and choices (see NATURAL LAW §§1, 4). Yet, positivism's other main opponents, legal realists, who accept the positivistic aim of a value-free description of law, none the less argue that the positivistic 'formalist' approach is itself contaminated by hidden unrecognized value choices, and therefore that legal naturalism and positivism are really the same. Natural law theorists, taking positivists at their word with a vengeance, often group all their adversaries, including realists, together under the common label of positivism (meaning a value-free approach to describing the law), the lack of what they believe to be a proper understanding of the vital role played by morality in the life of law (Weinreb 1978; Fuller 1958).

Therefore, a little time spent on conceptual clarification will not be wasted. Glanville Williams proffers the most radical answer to this kind of conceptual question about competing definitions: 'Everyone is entitled for his own part to use words in any meaning he pleases: there is no such thing as an intrinsically "proper" or "improper" meaning of a word' (Williams [1945] 1956: 134–6). However, while Williams' thesis is a good antidote to philosophical verbosity, it is a little too simplistic. Not all conceptual discussions can be solved merely by arbitrary definition. In fact, concepts are fragments of theories; when we examine the concept of law in legal positivism, we are looking not just for the meaning of a word but also for a theory which will offer the best approach to legal problems and eventually to the final practical problem of obedience.

So, what is at issue in positing that the 'is' of law can be identified separately from any 'ought'? It means that nearly all positivists replace the moral commitment to justice (however this is defined), which is at the basis of the iusnaturalistic account of the law, with the aim of a value-free description of effective legal systems (however this is gauged). In other words, effectiveness thus replaces justice in the positivistic conception of law (Hart 1961; Kelsen 1945). Critics of positivism may be forgiven for thinking this to be a rather perverse attitude, making it all too easy for positivistic lawyers to neglect their (moral) duty to take a moral stance towards law. This is sometimes called the '*reductio ad Hitlerum*' of positivism, which is accused of preaching acquiescence to every (effective) law, even when it is as morally evil as Nazi law. This charge is, in turn, firmly rejected by positivists, who observe that something can only be rationally judged and valued if we first know what it is. This is precisely Bentham's basic distinction (see BENTHAM, J.), which is at the origins

of legal positivism, between censorial and expository jurisprudence (Bentham 1977). Many positivists will also add that we gain nothing but confusion in insisting, as natural law theorists do, that unjust laws are not really laws (*lex iniusta non est lex*).

However, natural law theory is saying more than that; otherwise its more dismissive critics would be right in saying that naturalists are merely engaged in a vain battle of words. Iusnaturalists maintain that the law cannot be individuated, described, interpreted or applied unless we continuously make use of moral values and moral choices (Finnis 1973): a normative element is part of the basic choices in the very description of the law. Hence, some naturalists would argue that this should also be a defensible ethical choice, rather than the morally inadequate positivistic standard of effectiveness. In any case, the positivistic attitude, so its critics would argue, leads not to empirical science but, rather, to the moral choice of conformism, an attitude to which lawyers are all too easily prone and which should not be encouraged further.

The positivist might reply that this kind of conformism is indeed an essential part of the rule of law, the ideal embodied in many contemporary legal and political institutions, that power be conferred, controlled and exercised through general rules only (Scarpelli 1965; Fuller 1958). This ideal is a component of all the basic institutions of contemporary Western states, where a legislative body is supposed to make general laws (statutes), while different bodies (the judiciary, the administration) apply them, within the limits of powers granted to them by other legal rules (rules of competence, procedural rules) (see FULLER, L.L.). It is obvious that this ideal is based on, at least, judicial compliance to law and, more widely, obedience of the subjects who fall under law or seek to use it. It is equally obvious that only in so far as it is possible to have an objective knowledge of the meaning of such laws does the whole enterprise make sense; only then will law's reality match the appearances. Legal positivism purports to provide a model of such an objective knowledge, of a legal science conceived as the study of whatever rules come from the appropriate sources and authorities. The next question then must be, what exactly is a (legal) rule?

2 Varieties of legal positivism

All positivists think that the law is a set of legal rules, or norms, a belief that is strictly connected to the fundamental value of the rule of law (see §1). Law is conceived as a device for transferring authority and (political) legitimacy by means of rules; legal rules connect individual choices, such as judicial sentencing, to general decisions such as legislation. But, what is a rule? The main versions of legal positivism can be distinguished by their different accounts of what a legal rule is.

The most immediate and common answer is that a (legal) rule is a command. This thesis is typical of early positivism, as represented by the theories of John Austin (Austin 1832). The second answer is that (legal) rules are judgments as in Kelsen's mature legal positivism (see KELSEN, H.). According to Kelsen, legal rules or norms are conditional, hypothetical judgments of the form: if you committed such and such action, then you (legally) ought to be punished (Kelsen 1945). This idea also avoids the main objection to the older ('naïve') positivism of Austin's kind: that law cannot be reduced entirely to commands, which exist only as part of a direct relation between real persons (see AUSTIN, J.).

The Kelsenian version of legal positivism sees a legal rule as a conditional ought-judgment. However, this renders problematic positivism's claims to legal empiricism. The 'existence' of the sentence/proposition 'if you kill you ought to be punished' is totally unaffected both by the fact that a killing has happened and by the fact that the killer is actually punished. This loose connection with facts is a frailty of Kelsen's brand of positivism. The norms or rules in the Kelsenian sense need to be somehow anchored to social facts, so that the Kelsenian positivist may be enabled to distinguish imaginary or ideal law from real positive law. As we shall see below (§4), Kelsen and all modern positivists attempt to solve this problem with the theory of the existence of a legal system.

The later, 'analytical', versions of legal positivism, while preserving Kelsen's idea that the law is of an impersonal and conditional character, try to translate the whole into more empirical terms. Law is seen as a social phenomenon, essentially as meaning and language. These versions of legal positivism claim that a neutral description of the law, which is vital to the ideal of the rule of law, can be attained by treating the law as a language; in fact this later positivism is usually influenced by some form of linguistic philosophy. Typically, Kelsen's 'pure theory of law' is set on these new philosophical foundations; but the rest of the building is left substantially unchanged, and especially so his theory of a legal system. Legal rules and legal systems are now conceived mainly as (sets of) sentences and meanings, which can be neutrally described without having to be accepted or followed. Their empirical existence is thought to be guaranteed by their being an actually spoken language, something provided, therefore, with a social dimension.

However, there is a significant divide between the Continental and the Anglo-Saxon versions of this linguistic positivism. On the Continent, Bobbio (Bobbio 1950) claimed that jurisprudence should follow the 'modern philosophy of science' (meaning the neopositivistic version) and translate the language of the law, especially the language of statutes and codes, into a rigorous and coherent and complete language (see BOBBIO, N.). By contrast, some years later in England, H.L.A. Hart used the analytical tools of ordinary language philosophy which roots language 'rules' in social use. He claimed that legal rules are essentially an abstraction from effective social practices, characterized by a fundamental linguistic element and certain normative uses of language (the 'internal discourses') (Hart 1961).

Bobbio's theory and Continental positivism was also perhaps influenced by a tradition of statutory law (law as command from above). Its major difficulty was, accordingly, to distinguish between positive law elaborated and made rigorous by the efforts of linguistic jurisprudence, and rigorous but non-positive law (which would have meant falling into the arms of legal naturalism). For this task, subsequent Continental positivism has relied heavily on Kelsen's theory of the basic norm, which is conceived as the linchpin connecting the whole of a legal system, a huge body of words, to social effectiveness and reality. Hart's positivism is rooted in reality through its concept of rule as social practice, and its version of the basic norm theory has a much less daunting job to do: simply to recognize when rules are part of a legal system, rather than being the sole warranty of their existence.

3 Positivism versus legal realism

Discussion about the nature of legal 'reality', the role of language in legal analysis, and the issues of value-freedom are illuminated by considering the legal realist perspective (see LEGAL REALISM). This discussion shows another essential aspect of legal positivism. As the name suggests, realists strive to attain the underlying reality of law which, they say, is hidden and distorted by other approaches, such as positivism or naturalism. The European legal realists share with analytical legal positivists the idea that law is language (see §2). Both also accept that, if it is true that legal rules are language, it is also a language that is often 'misspoken', so far as official legal rules (especially statutory law) are concerned. However, they draw different conclusions from this fact based on different ideas as to how a language should be described.

The situation here is similar to that of a natural language where the official grammar and lexicon are significantly detached from the living spoken tongue. Positivists could then be compared to the members of a purist academy who, while well aware of how the language is being used, nevertheless maintain that this is not how the language is, but only the way it is (mis)spoken, and that the task of the linguists – by analogy, the positivist legal philosopher – is to tell how a language is correctly spoken and to describe the rules which make up such a language. By contrast, the legal realists are like those linguists who maintain that the only reality of a language is the actual practice of speech; that linguistic rules are, at most, a useful device for summing up these practices and instances of actual use in so far as they are inferred or induced from actual practice. As for the British positivists, while H.L.A. Hart may, at first sight, seem immune from this criticism, most realists are unhappy with his notion that the single legal rule need not be socially effective, provided it belongs to a legal system (see below) which on the whole is effective (see HART, H.L.A.). Hart's critics say that this means taking into account lawyers' image of the law as an ordered whole, rather than the often disordered reality of the law itself. They would also add that all forms of normative grammar are prescription rather than empirical description. Hence the charge that contemporary legal positivists are engaged in surreptitiously upholding official state law.

In the empiricist, language-conscious framework in which this debate is taking place today, the realist attitude looks more attractive. Before reaching this conclusion, however, a key question needs to be considered. The discussion between realists and positivists can be whittled down to the following: how far is knowing what the law is, different from knowing what the law is for its 'speakers'? To make sense of the ideal of the rule of law, how far should we be able to distinguish what the law says from what (some) people believe it says? In other words, can we say that the intellectual practices of lawyers are a set of cognitive activities with an objective content rather than superstitious beliefs with a hidden social function?

The European realists thus also take effectiveness as the criterion of law but define that in terms of actual use. They maintain that a value-free and scientific approach to law should take into account all and only the effective legal rules, be they in the official book or not, as extracted by means of the punctual observation of legal practice. While no positivist will deny that such an enterprise is legitimate, albeit very ambitious, they will, however, call it the sociology of law. Moreover positivists would insist that jurists, legal officials, as such, need a different kind of knowledge of legal rules, which is

what Kelsen called 'normative science' and Hart an approach 'from the internal point of view'. They will need to know what certain rules prescribe not in order to predict legal behaviour, but in order to know how they should behave, in case they accept them. In fact, it could be argued that neither the realistic nor the positivistic accounts of law offer a genuinely sociological empirical explanation, even though both contain some essential reference to social reality. The realist will describe all and only the legal rules which are effective with judges, the positivist will take into account only those legal systems which are effective as a whole, disregarding the fact that some rules exist only 'on paper'.

4 Legal systems

The debate between positivism and realism brings to the forefront a key concept of legal positivism, that of a legal system. To positivistic jurisprudence, legal systems are both semantic entities and social realities. Legal rules are first of all words and meanings, prescriptions which can be described and understood, interpreted and used to give a normative legal meaning to facts and actions. Legal rules, being language, are also part of the world of social facts. Legal matters are to be decided by means of arguments or reasons taken mainly from within a legal system; these arguments or reasons are, of course, the legal rules. A legal system contains not only the rules which directly govern actions (called 'primary rules' by Hart), but also the 'secondary' rules, rules about rules, by which the former are 'serviced' (recognized, made, changed, applied). Most positivists assume that every legal system implies one supreme rule, containing or summing up the criteria by which all the other rules of the system are recognized as part of the system (basic norm in Kelsen's theory, rule of recognition in Hart's) (see §3).

The notion of a legal system explains the 'formalist' aspects of legal practice, the fact that law is conceived by positivistic jurists as being both 'closed' and 'self-sufficient' or, in a sense, 'complete'. This does not mean that all legal issues must always be argued without referring to non-legal arguments, that is, moral and sociological facts or reasons. It means, rather, that only those reasons recognized by legal systems are compelling and that they should prevail over all the others, which can be used only to fill the gaps in the system (they amount to using discretionary powers).

According to this point of view, a legal system, with its enormous complexity, is not qualitatively different from a single rule. When we accept a single rule, we can use it as a reason for justifying our practical choices. However, this only postpones the problem, as now we have to justify the acceptance of the rule itself. The same happens with a legal system, but on a much wider scale, according to the positivistic conception (Raz 1975). By accepting a legal system we can put off our basic problem for quite a while, but at the end, we shall have to justify our acceptance or rejection of any particular legal system as a guide to our actions. This is sometimes neglected by people engaged in legal practice, who become, so to speak, moral hostages of the internal complexity of a legal system, thus embracing positivism in the third of Bobbio's senses mentioned above. On the contrary, as we have seen, positivistic philosophers can well claim to be innocent of this particular sin, because of the thesis of the separation of law and morals.

In fact, having substituted effectiveness for justice as a criterion for ascertaining which normative system is law in a certain society, legal positivists will argue that such a choice is made for descriptive purposes only, and is wholly compatible with rejecting such a legal system on moral grounds. Critics of positivism, to be credible, thus have to delve deeper. To be effective, an attack has to be directed against the positivistic model of legal description; thus some critics argue that a moral bias is already present whenever we try to distinguish a legal system from other kinds of moral and social rules and, equally, when we assume that in any society there is only one such legal system. Others argue that legal systems do not even exist as a social fact, being rather the product of a normative value-laden interpretation of social reality.

This is not to say that the positivist conception, if correct, is without advantages. The process consisting in the use of the mental tool of the concept of a normative system transforms, at least up to a point, the process of reaching a legal decision into a calculus based on known rules. This is precisely what is called 'the rule of law' by its supporters and 'formalism' by its critics (see RULE OF LAW (RECHTSSTAAT)). But here uncertainties and difficulties as to this representation of legal activity will crop up at many levels. First, we might doubt that the meaning of the words which make up such rules can be ascertained in any objective way at all. This is the classic problem of interpretation. Such objections usually come from non-positivists (see §5). Second, a host of problems is raised by the 'dynamic' or 'formal' nature of legal systems, and by the connections between legal rules. If a legal system has to be a calculus, then it is a strange kind of calculus which has to refer continuously to external facts – such as the fact that a statute has been enacted by the legislature or that a court has actually issued a decision – in order to complete its own calculations. This difficulty is well recognized by legal positivists themselves (Kelsen 1979). Positivism thus emphasizes that the systematicity of legal systems is different from purely deductive normative systems where the content of individual concrete rules can be deduced from first principles. On the contrary, a 'dynamic' legal system requires a continuous input from external facts and decisions; laws are made and abrogated by legislators, not deduced from first principles. Even judicial sentencing is, obviously, not the result of pure deduction from general rules; sentences have to be pronounced by a judge in the course of a trial, and if they happen to be incorrect deductions, so much the worse for logic and legal calculus. The dynamic or formal aspect of law, so it might be argued, is a matter of power and authority rather than of logic and calculus.

The point is not just that laws can be broken. This would not worry the legal positivist much. Laws are made precisely because they are capable of being violated. The point is that the law itself appears to be able to break its own rules, so to speak, as when an unconstitutional statute is considered valid in a legal system unless it is repealed through a special legal procedure, or a legally wrong sentence is legally binding unless it is reversed on appeal (Paulson 1980). That is why the positivistic autonomous 'calculation' of legal rules and decisions can conflict with facts and arguments which are not purely external, as they are considered relevant by the calculus itself (as, for instance, the wrong decision by an authority of the system). This is a powerful argument in the hands of the critics of positivism, who believe that the theory of the legal system and therefore the rule of law idea are a disguise for the exercise of naked power; while positivists try and rebut it with the theory of delegated power (Austin) and of discretion (Hart), claiming that discretionary powers are still controlled by the legal calculus, in so far as the external input is allowed and limited by the system itself (Austin 1832; Hart 1961).

5 Interpretation and rights

Uncertainty as to the real 'closure' of a legal system will crop up also at the level of words which make up such rules. This of course is the problem of interpretation. Some realists advance an entirely sceptical theory of interpretation (rule-scepticism) in which no certainty is possible. While many will dismiss such extreme arguments as bad semantics, even the most hardened of positivists will feel much less confident when it comes to certain operations within legal systems, or about certain words of legal discourse that express concepts which have a fundamental role in legal arguments, especially words designating (legal) rights.

Rights are easily identifiable as the Trojan Horse by which external material slips into an otherwise apparently closed legal system. Opponents of positivism will then say that this is because such material is not really external to the law to begin with, but is only seen as such by an overly narrow (legalistic, formalist) conception of law and the rule of law. The legal naturalists will claim that this clearly shows that certain moral ideas are a necessary part of the construction of a right (and hence that morality is necessary to the task of describing law). This argument draws formidable support from the Constitution of the USA as interpreted by their courts, which includes several moral principles and makes them justiciable (Hart 1977).

To legal positivists, wholly open-ended interpretation would make the rule of law an empty travesty, for it depends upon the end of certainty. They point to the difference between mere legality and strict legality. The rule of law requires legality in the second sense, which implies not only that legal decisions be taken according to a law, but also that the words of the law be formulated by positivistic-minded legislators in such a way as to have a relatively determined meaning; and that interpreters must make the maximum effort in good faith to extract such a meaning before resorting to discretion (Ferrajoli 1990).

All this explains the apparently perverse positivistic attempts to 'sterilize' legal rights. If the rule of law in this strict sense has to survive, then rights must be reducible to the words of positive legal rules. Rights must derive from rules and not the other way around.

Most positivist accounts of the theory of legal rights, such as Kelsen's, stress that law must be entirely reduced to legal norms, and that therefore rights and legal institutions must also be so reduced. Ross' legal realist theory of a legal right (Ross 1951) follows the same reductionist line as Kelsen's (see Ross, A.). Legal rights amount to no more than a conceptual facility which merely makes it easier to sum up the underlying legal rules. The difference is that the positivist will say that the content of a right is a set of duties and powers attributed by legal rules, usually statutes, while a realist will say that rights and duties are empty words without any reference to facts, which at most (Ross) are a useful shorthand for describing and predicting the probable behaviour of the courts, and at worst (Olivecrona 1971) are powerful irrational social factors such as people wrongly believing in the existence of rights and being conditioned by such illusions (see OLIVECRONA, K.).

The opposite position claims that rights contain more than the words of the legal rules which express them; that they contain a normative surfeit, which can be extracted out of them without making new law. In this case rights could be a source of 'new' law which is not new but already there, although sometimes previously unstated and unsuspected. In the last twenty years Ronald Dworkin has moved a brilliant attack on the tenets of legal positivism in its Hartian form. Precisely in the name of legal rights, Dworkin has formulated in a renovated form the traditional theory of normative surfeit, that law cannot or should not be reduced to a set of explicit rules (Dworkin 1978).

The forward line of defence of positivism on this specific front is today held by Neil MacCormick (MacCormick and Weinberger 1986). As all good defences, MacCormick's stance is composed of a counterattack and a retrenchment. Against Dworkin, the basic tenet of positivism, the distinction between describing and evaluating the law, is reaffirmed (in the name of Bentham); the retrenchment is MacCormick's institutional theory of law, where a theory of right still based on rules is advanced, which attempts to make sense, through the concept of institution, of the aspects of legal rights not strictly reducible to already explicit statutory words (see INSTITUTIONALISM IN LAW §5).

See also: LAW, PHILOSOPHY OF; LEGAL CONCEPTS; LEGAL REASONING AND INTERPRETATION; NORMS, LEGAL

References and further reading

* Austin, J. (1832) *The Province of Jurisprudence Determined*, London: Weidenfeld & Nicolson, 1955. (This classic text of legal positivism is from Austin's lectures: it is the basic statement of the theory of law as commands.)
* Bentham, J. (1977) A Fragment on Government, in J.H. Burns and H.L.A. Hart (eds) *A Comment on the Commentaries and a Fragment on Government*, London: Athlone Press. (This is another great classic, preceding Austin's work, though mainly unpublished till later. In many respects, a more subtle account than Austin's.)
  Beyleveld, D. and Brownsword, R. (1989) 'Normative Positivism: The Mirage of the Middle-Way', *Oxford Journal of Legal Studies* 9: 463–512. (For advanced readers: this clearly depicts relations between positivism, realism and naturalism.)
* Bobbio, N. (1950) 'Scienza del diritto e analisi del linguaggio', in U. Scarpelli (ed.), *Diritto e analisi del linguaggio* (Legal Science and Analysis of Language), Milan: Edizioni Di Comunita, 1976.

(Advanced reading on linguistic analysis and the idea of law as science – a principled and structured body of knowledge; this attempts to combine neopositivistic ideas and Kelsen's legal theory, through reflections on the analytical approach to the philosophy of law.)

* —— (1960) *Giusnaturalismo e positivismo giuridico* (Legal Positivism and Legal Naturalism), Milan: Edizioni Di Comunita. (A collection of essays: unfortunately still unavailable in English, but far clearer than anything written in English on the controversy between legal positivism and naturalism.)

—— (1961) *Il positivismo giuridico* (Legal Positivism), Turin: Giappichelli. (Adds a historical survey to the subject matter of the previous book. Unfortunately also unavailable in English, but by far the best introduction for university students to legal positivism and contemporary legal thinking.)

* Dworkin, R. (1978) *Taking Rights Seriously*, London: Duckworth. (This is a collection of essays; intriguing and currently very fashionable in English-speaking legal philosophy; brilliant and difficult writing; advanced reading.)

* Ferrajoli, L. (1990) *Diritto e ragione: teoria del garantismo penale* (Law and Reason: A Theory of Guarantees in Criminal Law), Bari: Laterza. (The general part of this excellent book on individual rights in penal law makes a powerful contribution on the theme of legal certainty. Of average difficulty, but only available in Italian.)

* Finnis, J. (1973) 'Revolutions and Continuity of Law', in A.W.B. Simpson (ed.), *Oxford Essays in Jurisprudence*, Oxford: Oxford University Press, 2nd series. (Extremely intelligent essay by a leading representative of naturalistic thought in post-Hartian philosophy of law: Hart's analytical lesson has been well learned and put to use to criticize some positivistic ideas.)

Fryer, B., Hunt, A., McBarnet, D. and Moorhouse, B. (eds) (1981) *Law, State and Society*, London: Croom Helm. (Like the following item, this collects ideas and debates of Anglo-Saxon legal philosophy after Hart; more critical of Hartian positivism than the following. Advanced reading.)

* Fuller, L.L. (1958) 'Positivism and Fidelity to Law', *Harvard Law Review* 71: 630–67. (This debate with Hart is a widely known classic, widely reprinted, constantly quoted; Fuller is passionate but confused; his later *The Morality of Law* (revised edn 1969) is a clearer and more convincing statement of the position sketched in 1958.)

Gavison, R. (ed.) (1987) *Issues in Contemporary Legal Philosophy: The Influence of H.L.A. Hart*, Oxford: Clarendon Press. (Like the previous item, this collects ideas and debates of Anglo-Saxon legal philosophy after Hart; nearer to Hartian positivism than the preceding. Advanced reading.)

Jori, M. (ed.) (1992) *Legal Positivism*, Aldershot: Dartmouth Publishing Co. (A collection of essays, adding up to a more extensive formulation of the ideas condensed in this entry. Introductory reading.)

Hacker, P. and Raz, J. (eds) (1977) *Law, Morality and Society: Essays in Honour of H.L.A. Hart*, Oxford: Clarendon Press. (The essays in this collection are largely comments on Hart's legal philosophy. Most of the positivistic ideas subsequently debated in the Anglo-Saxon world can be found here.)

Harris, J.W. (1979) *Law and Legal Science: An Inquiry into the Concepts Legal Rule and Legal System*, Oxford: Clarendon Press. (This is a very clear presentation of and critical essay on positivistic theses. The author knows his Kelsen, and writes from that point of view. This might be used as an introduction, but perhaps better as more advanced reading.)

* Hart, H.L.A. (1958) 'Positivism and the Separation of Law and Morals', in *Essays in Jurisprudence and Philosophy*, Oxford: Clarendon Press, 1983. (This is the manifesto of Hartian positivism. A well-argued classic, of medium difficulty; the other side of the debate with Fuller noted above.)

* —— (1961) *The Concept of Law*, Oxford: Clarendon Press. (This is a classic and a must; conceived as an introduction to jurisprudence for Oxford students, and apparently plain common-sense reading, it is much more complex than it looks, and has been an outstandingly influential work.)

* —— (1977) 'American Jurisprudence through English Eyes: The Nightmare and the Noble Dream', in *Essays in Jurisprudence and Philosophy*, Oxford: Clarendon Press, 1983. (The title here speaks for itself; a brilliant and witty essay, clearly positivistically biased. A must for US jurists dealing with Old England and vice versa.)

* Kelsen, H. (1945) *General Theory of Law and State*, trans. A. Wedberg, Cambridge, MA: Harvard University Press. (A mature, and excellently translated, version of Kelsen's 'pure theory', with an adaptation by the author of his thoughts to address an Anglo-Saxon audience; but still very German.)

* —— (1979) *Allgemeine Theorie der Normen* (General Theory of Norms), trans. M. Hartney, Oxford: Clarendon Press, 1991. (This is the final, posthumous, statement of the legal positivism of the most important legal thinker of the twentieth century; an excellent introduction by the translator relates the text to Kelsen's earlier work.)

MacCormick N. (1981) *H.L.A. Hart*, London:

Edward Arnold. (The best commentary on Hart's thinking in the English language. Also useful for university students.)

* MacCormick, N. and Weinberger, O. (1986) *An Institutional Theory of Law: New Approaches to Legal Positivism*, Dordrecht: Reidel. (An attempt to overcome some of the problems of positivism as a legal theory, not limited to discussion of the Anglo-Saxon theorists – hence particularly useful reading for Anglo-Saxon students.)

* Olivecrona, K. (1971) *Law as Fact*, London: Stevens & Co., 2nd edn. (A good presentation of the European version of legal realism. Useful introductory reading.)

* Paulson, S.L. (1980) 'Material and Formal Authorization in Kelsen's Pure Theory', *Cambridge Law Journal* 39: 172–93. (Advanced reading. It points out with brilliant clarity some weak points of Kelsen's conception of 'normative theory'.)

Postema, G.J. (1987) 'The Normativity of Law', in R. Gavison (ed.), *Issues in Contemporary Legal Philosophy: The Influence of H.L.A. Hart*, Oxford: Clarendon Press. (A view of the complex relation between law and social reality.)

* Raz, J. (1975) *Practical Reason and Norms*, London: Hutchinson. (Goes beyond legal theory to discuss and clarify some basic aspects of normative speech and thinking. Not as well known as it deserves. Intermediate reading.)

* Ross, A. (1951) 'Tû-tû', *Harvard Law Review* 70: 1456–67. (Caustic and amusing, the basic idea, that a legal 'world' does not exist, should be considered seriously. Necessary reading for all legal students.)

Sampford, C. (1984) 'Legal System and Legal Theory', in D. Galligan (ed.), *Essays in Legal Theory*, Melbourne: Melbourne University Press. (Impassioned piece of post-Hartian legal theory, challenging the supposed systematicity of law. Interesting symptom of what is going on among Anglo-Saxon legal philosophers.)

* Scarpelli, U. (1965) *Cos'il positivismo giuridico*, Milan: Edizioni Di Comunita. (Turning the traditional defence of legal positivism as a factual approach to law upside down, the author defends positivism as morally and politically indispensable to maintaining the rule of law. Advanced reading.)

—— (ed.) (1976) *Diritto e analisi del linguaggio* (Law and Linguistic Analysis), Milan: Edizioni Di Comunita. (This is a collection of essays belonging to the analytical school of legal philosophy, from all countries, dealing with legal theory and linguistic analysis.)

Stewart, I. (1987) 'Closure and the Legal Norm: An Essay in Critique of Law', *Modern Law Review* 50: 908–33. (A critical assessment of legal normativism. Advanced reading.)

Tur, R. and Twining, W. (eds) (1986) *Essays on Kelsen*, Oxford: Clarendon Press. (Excellent comments on various aspects of Kelsen's legal theory by mainly Anglo-Saxon authors, but containing also contributions by R. Vernengo and O. Weinberger.)

* Weinreb, L.L. (1978) 'Law as Order', *Harvard Law Review* 91: 909–59. (Balanced exposition of the natural law point of view on those points which have been particularly stressed by positivists.)

* Williams, G. (1945) 'The Controversy Concerning the Word "Law"', repr. in P. Laslett (ed.), *Philosophy, Politics and Society*, 1st Series, Oxford: Blackwell, 1956. (The earliest application of linguistic-analytical ideas to legal philosophy. Strangely neglected today.)

MARIO JORI

LEGAL REALISM

'Legal realism' is the term commonly used to characterize various currents of twentieth-century legal thought which stand opposed to idealism. (Hence, 'realism' in this context ought to be understood not as a body of thought which opposes nominalism, but as an instance of nominalism.) In the Scandinavian countries, legal realism was modelled on Axel Hägerström's critique of idealist metaphysics, and sought ways to account for legal rights and duties without presupposing or postulating the existence of ideal objects or entities. In the USA, legal realism evolved as a critique of the idealism implicit in the vision of the common law which was promoted by C.C. Langdell, first Dean of the Harvard Law School, and in the laissez-faire ideology of the late nineteenth- and early twentieth-century Supreme Court. Realist jurisprudential sentiments – primarily as articulated in terms of the so-called indeterminacy critique – continue to bear an influence on late twentieth-century critical legal thought.

1 **Scandinavian legal realism**
2 **US legal realism**
3 **The legacy of legal realism and the problem of indeterminacy**

1 Scandinavian legal realism

Within twentieth-century legal thought, the term 'legal realism' is used very broadly to describe two branches of jurisprudence which stand opposed to legal idealism (see LEGAL IDEALISM §1). These two branches of jurisprudence – Scandinavian and US legal realism – are not connected, nor do they conceive of idealism in the same fashion. In the Scandinavian countries, legal realism represents a reaction against the influence of German idealist metaphysics on jurisprudential thought. In the USA, realism constitutes a critique of idealism implicit in late nineteenth- and early twentieth-century common law teaching and doctrine.

The Scandinavian version of realist jurisprudence is both inspired and epitomized by Axel Hägerström's writings on the philosophy of law and morals (Hägerström 1953). Legal rights and duties, he contends, cannot be identified as factually existent and therefore cannot be considered 'real'. Despite their unreality, however, rights and duties clearly do exist in some sense. The question which Hägerström thus poses is that of how, if these entities do not exist empirically in the physical world, they can be known and their contents ascertained. His answer to this question is that rights and duties constitute personal feelings of entitlement and obligation (see EMOTIVISM). There exist 'feelings of duty in regard to the restrictions which affect oneself', just as there exist 'feelings of power in regard to the acquisition of advantages . . . which are regarded as rights'. Thus it is that 'an individual who infringes the right of another lays himself open to reactions from the latter which gain a special strength through feelings of power of a special kind, which are connected with the idea of rights' (Hägerström 1953: 15).

Whereas Hägerström acknowledges that the concepts of right and duty possess psychological force (even if they cannot be empirically ascertained), his friend Vilhelm Lundstedt went so far as to argue that rights and duties are merely chimeras, discussion of which is inappropriate within a science of law (Lundstedt 1957). Indeed, Lundstedt would happily have seen analysis of rights and duties banished from jurisprudence. Other writers within the Scandinavian realist tradition none the less recognized that the concepts of right and duty possess considerable intuitive appeal. While these concepts may be essentially hollow, Alf Ross noted, the very fact that legal language is so dependent on the words 'right' and 'duty' suggests that legal statements about rights and duties – as opposed to rights and duties themselves – deserve serious philosophical attention (Ross 1958 §35). Karl OLIVECRONA offered a still stronger argument in favour of the study of rights and duties. '[T]he proposition that there is a law without rights and duties', he observed, 'seems to be contradictory since it belongs to the very essence of the law that it regulates people's rights and duties' (Olivecrona 1971: 184). Furthermore, even if the argument that

rights and duties are chimeras was correct, 'the practical conclusion should not be to throw the terms overboard but to study their functions' (Olivecrona 1971: 178).

2   US legal realism

In the context of US jurisprudence, 'legal realism' is a remarkably ambiguous concept. At the beginning of the 1930s – responding to Roscoe Pound's cursory dismissal of 'the realists' (Pound named no one specifically) as a group of legal philosophers who exaggerated the jurisprudential significance of social science while underestimating the importance of legal rules, doctrines and principles (Pound 1931) – Karl LLEWELLYN endeavoured to put flesh on the bones of realist jurisprudence by identifying a 'sample' of realist legal philosophers (see POUND, R.). Since then, various excellent studies have been produced, focusing on, among other things, the political (Purcell 1969) and social-scientific (Schlegel 1979) dimensions of realist legal thought, as well as on particular realist figures (Twining 1985).

US legal realism might be described very basically as a mood of discontentment with the idealism implicit in late nineteenth- and early twentieth-century US common law thought. This discontentment was directed towards two distinct juridical tendencies.

First, legal realism represented an expression of dissatisfaction with Langdellian idealism. The appointment of Christopher Columbus Langdell as Dean of the Harvard Law School in 1870 signalled the emergence of modern legal education in the USA (LaPiana 1994). Langdell's primary pedagogic initiative was to dispense with the traditional lecture method of teaching and put in its place the so-called 'case method' of instruction. The case method is a style of teaching which emphasizes the acquisition of knowledge through Socratic dialogue. The student subjected to this method is required to read judicial decisions in advance of class so as to be prepared to answer questions about their content and their reasoning. By teaching their subject in this fashion, Langdell and his followers were able to promote a highly abstract, idealistic – what they considered to be a scientific – image of the common law as a set of logically interconnected core doctrines and principles.

Legal realists tended to object to the scientific pretensions of Langdellianism. The idea that teaching law by the case method was tantamount to teaching law as a science was considered by various realists to constitute a form of erroneous idealism. In short, Langdellianism depicted law as mere logic rather than as experience, as something to be found in books rather than in society. Certain legal realists believed that law could be conceived as a science, but not in the Langdellian sense. For these realists, social science was the key to depicting reality.

Different legal realists took the concept of social science to denote different things. Predictivism and empiricism feature prominently as social-scientific themes in realist jurisprudence. Through 'fact research', certain realists believed, it may be possible to assess the quality of particular laws as instruments of social control and to predict the likelihood of those laws being infringed or ignored in the future (see Moore and Callahan 1943). It may well be that certain laws are difficult to enforce, or, when successfully enforced, entail an inordinately weak sanction. Someone may decide to break a particular law if they believe that their chances of being caught in breach of that law are minimal, or if the profit that they will acquire by breaking that law outweighs the fine which they might incur. Legal realists, in presenting this argument in social-scientific terms, were echoing the theory of Oliver Wendell HOLMES of the 'bad man' (Holmes 1897). Other realists, in resorting to the social sciences, attempted to move realist legal thought beyond the shadow of Holmes. In this context, the work of Jerome FRANK is exemplary.

Second, just as US legal realism may be understood as a reaction against Langdellian idealism, so too it may be understood as a reaction against the idealism embodied in the economic outlook of the late nineteenth- and early twentieth-century US Supreme Court. In a number of decisions – *Lochner* v. *New York* ([1905] 198 US 45) and *Coppage* v. *Kansas* ([1915] 236 US 1) are the most illustrious – the Court basically combined *laissez-faire* with social Darwinism. All citizens, the Court argued, possess an equal right to compete in the marketplace. This does not mean, however, that all citizens in fact possess an equal capacity to do so. Some will compete more, some more successfully than others, so that the strongest economic actors will prosper at the cost of the economically weak. In other words, an inevitable corollary of a formal equality of bargaining rights is a real inequality of bargaining power. Guided by this philosophy, the Supreme Court felt justified in constitutionally invalidating state legislation that attempted to redress inequalities of bargaining power. Freedom of contract was thus constitutionally enshrined.

For certain legal realists, the constitutional philosophy of the Supreme Court served simply to highlight the impossibility of real freedom of contract. Owing to the fact that there exists inequality of bargaining power among economic agents, they argued, markets must be essentially coercive rather

than free. According to Robert Hale, one's capacity to make choices in the marketplace is determined by the extent of one's bargaining power (Hale 1923). Morris Cohen expressed the point pithily: 'The freedom to make a million dollars is not worth a cent to one who is out of work. Nor is the freedom to starve, or to work for wages less than the minimum of subsistence, one that any rational being can prize – whatever learned courts may say to the contrary' (Cohen 1933: 560). While the USA was suffering the effects of the Great Depression, the Supreme Court continued to invalidate economic regulatory statutes on the ground that they offended against the constitutional sanctity of free exchange.

This 'economic' strand of realist legal thought has sometimes been interpreted as an outright rejection of the possibility of economic freedom. But realists such as Hale and Cohen were not denying the possibility of economic freedom *per se*. They were arguing, rather, that such freedom cannot flourish in an unregulated market. Hale in particular believed that regulation may serve to facilitate rather than to inhibit market freedom. His argument was by no means as radical as has often been assumed (as, for example, by Kennedy (1993), who interprets the argument as a rejection of the possibility of market freedom).

3 The legacy of legal realism and the problem of indeterminacy

The general assumption that US legal realism was somehow radical – that it was the rebellious offspring of the modern US law school – ought to be questioned. Certainly many legal realists took issue with the Langdellian idealist belief that rules are generally certain and capable of mechanical application to legal disputes. What we do not find in the literature of US legal realism, however, is a celebration of legal indeterminacy (see CRITICAL LEGAL STUDIES §2). One of the classic realist insights – that judges may sometimes ignore rules and principles and decide cases instead on the basis of personal intuition or 'hunch' (Hutcheson 1929) – was regarded by many realists as a cause for lament rather than celebration. Very simply, indeterminacy in adjudication was regarded as a problem.

It was a problem, furthermore, to which realism offered no persuasive answer. Some legal realists believed that remedying the problem of indeterminacy in adjudication demanded the development of a new kind of legal certainty: Holmesian, predictive certainty as opposed to Langdellian, deductive certainty. This line of argument finds its most complete expression in Llewellyn's masterful study of the 'steadying factors' in the common law tradition

(Llewellyn 1960). Still other realists, however, insisted that the belief that there exist determinate patterns of regularity in adjudication was no less ill-founded than Langdellian legal science itself (see Frank 1930). These realists – figures such as Jerome Frank, Wesley Sturges and Thurman Arnold – identified, but did not know what to do about, the existence of indeterminacy in adjudication. Thus it was that the problem of indeterminacy revealed the fundamental limitation of realist jurisprudence in the USA. Harold Berman recounts an illustrative story in this context concerning Thurman Arnold delivering a seminar at the Yale Law School in 1947. In this seminar, Arnold was apparently spinning the familiar realist line about how instinct rather than rule-following is the dominant feature of adjudication when he was interrupted and asked if that is how he had decided cases while a judge on the Columbia District Court of Appeals in the early 1940s. Berman takes up the story:

> Arnold paused before answering; one had the impression that he was transforming himself from Mr Hyde to Dr Jekyll as the professor in him yielded to the judge. He replied, 'Well, we can sit here in the classroom and dissect the conduct of judges, but when you put on those black robes and you sit on a raised platform, and you are addressed as "Your Honor", you *have* to believe that you are acting according to some objective standard.'
> (Berman 1974: 30)

Arnold is certain that there is something more to the adjudicative process than what lawyers have traditionally identified. But he is unable to pinpoint what that 'something more' might be. Other realists, in confronting this problem, placed their faith in the notion of expertise: indeterminacy need not be feared, they argued, so long as legal officials are experts in what they are entrusted to do (see Frank 1949). Many legal philosophers who searched for safeguards to US democracy in the face of growing tyranny abroad were far from appeased by this argument (Duxbury 1992; Purcell 1969). Yet this is about as near as US legal realism came to offering an original theory of adjudication. One of the primary legacies of realism rests in the fact that it impressed upon US academic lawyers the importance of developing such a theory. It is to this task that US jurisprudence in the post-realist era has been overwhelmingly devoted.

See also: LAW, PHILOSOPHY OF; NOMINALISM; REALISM AND ANTIREALISM; SOCIAL THEORY AND LAW

References and further reading

* Berman, H.J. (1974) *The Interaction of Law and Religion*, London: SCM Press. (Study of the impact of religious ideas on legal thinking.)
* Cohen, M.R. (1933) 'The Basis of Contract', *Harvard Law Review* 46: 553–92. (Classic realist critique of the notion of freedom of contract.)
* Duxbury, N. (1992) 'The Reinvention of American Legal Realism', *Legal Studies* 12: 137–77. (Analysis of post-Second World War criticisms and misinterpretations of realist legal thought.)
—— (1995) *Patterns of American Jurisprudence*, Oxford: Oxford University Press. (Study of US jurisprudence from the 1870s to the present.)
* Frank, J. (1930) *Law and the Modern Mind*, Gloucester, MA: Peter Smith, repr. 1970. (Classic realist account of judicial decision-making.)
* —— (1949) *Courts on Trial: Myth and Reality in American Justice*, Princeton, NJ: Princeton University Press. (On the uncertainties surrounding the jury system and judicial decision-making.)
* Hägerström, A. (1953) *Inquiries Into the Nature of Law and Morals*, English trans. C.D. Broad, Stockholm: Almqvist and Wiksell. (Scandinavian realist critique of rights.)
* Hale, R.L. (1923) 'Coercion and Distribution in a Supposedly Non-coercive State', *Political Science Quarterly* 36: 470–94. (Realist critique of *laissez-faire* ideology.)
* Holmes, O.W. (1897) 'The Path of the Law', *Harvard Law Review* 10: 457–78. (The classic presentation of US legal realism as the jurisprudence of prediction.)
* Hutcheson, J.C. (1929) 'The Judgment Intuitive: the Function of the "Hunch" in Judicial Decision', *Cornell Law Quarterly* 14: 274–88. (Confession by a realist judge that judicial decision-making is often nothing more than reliance on intuitions.)
Kalman, L. (1986) *Legal Realism at Yale: 1927–1960*, Chapel Hill, NC: University of North Carolina Press. (Institutional history of US legal realism at the law school with which it is most famously associated.)
* Kennedy, D. (1993) *Sexy Dressing Etc.: Essays on the Power and Politics of Cultural Identity*, Cambridge, MA: Harvard University Press. (Collection of essays on critical legal studies, post-structuralism and critical race theory.)
* LaPiana, W.P. (1994) *Logic and Experience: The Origin of Modern American Legal Education*, New York: Oxford University Press. (Study of the origin of modern US legal education at Harvard in the 1870s.)
* Llewellyn, K.N. (1931) 'Some Realism about Realism

– Responding to Dean Pound', *Harvard Law Review* 44: 1222–64. (Classic attempt to identify realist jurisprudence and its prime representatives.)

* —— (1960) *The Common Law Tradition: Deciding Appeals*, Boston, MA: Little, Brown. (Late-period US legal realist study of the adjudicative process.)

* Lundstedt, V. (1957) *Legal Thinking Revised*, Stockholm: Almqvist and Wiksell. (Scandinavian realist critique of the concepts of right and duty.)

* Moore, U. and Callahan, C. (1943) 'Law and Learning Theory: a Study in Legal Control', *Yale Law Journal* 53: 1–136. (Classic example of the social-scientific dimension of US legal realism.)

* Olivecrona, K. (1971) *Law as Fact*, London: Stevens and Sons. (Study of major jurisprudential traditions by a Scandinavian jurist.)

* Pound, R. (1931) 'The Call for a Realist Jurisprudence', *Harvard Law Review* 44: 697–711. (Critique of US legal realism as an anti-legalistic jurisprudence.)

* Purcell, E.A. (1969) 'American Jurisprudence between the Wars: Legal Realism and the Crisis of Democratic Theory', *American Historical Review* 75: 424–46. (Study of how US legal realism came to be perceived in certain academic quarters as antithetical to democratic values.)

* Ross, A. (1958) *On Law and Justice*, London: Stevens and Sons. (Scandinavian realist analysis of legal rights.)

* Schlegel, J.H. (1979) 'American Legal Realism and Empirical Social Science: from the Yale Experience', *Buffalo Law Review* 28: 459–586. (Account of the empiricist dimension of US legal realism.)

* Twining, W. (1985) *Karl Llewellyn and the Realist Movement*, London: Weidenfeld and Nicolson, revised edn. (Study of a major US legal realist.)

NEIL DUXBURY

LEGAL REASONING AND INTERPRETATION

Legal reasoning is the process of devising, reflecting on, or giving reasons for legal acts and decisions or justifications for speculative opinions about the meaning of law and its relevance to action. Many contemporary writers, such as Aulis Aarnio (1987), Robert Alexy (1988), Manuel Atienza (1991) and Aleksander Peczenik (1989), propound the view that legal reasoning is a particular instance of general practical reasoning. They suppose, that is to say, that reasoning can link up with action, guiding one what to do, or showing whether or not there are good reasons for a proposed course of action or for something already done. They suppose also that in law reason links up to legal decisions in this way. Both suppositions are well founded. Law regulates what to do and how to respond to what has been done, doing so within an institutional framework of legislatures, lawcourts, enforcement agencies and the like. It is a feature of legal institutions that they are expected to have, and usually do give, good reasons for what they do, and to do this in public. Legal reasoning is therefore not only a special case of practical reasoning, but a specially public one.

Rationality in action has at least two requirements: first, attention to facts, to the true state of affairs in relation to which one acts; second, attention to reasons for action relevant to the facts ascertained. The former aspect concerns reasoning about evidence; the latter, reasoning about rules or norms as reasons for action. In law, such rules and other norms have an institutional character. But how are these applied – by some kind of deductive reasoning, or nondeductively? Behind the rules of the law, there presumably lie other reasons, reasons for having these rules. What kind of reasons are these, developed through what modes of discourse? A discourse of principles, perhaps – but then how do reasons of principle themselves differ from rules? Reasoning from either rules or principles must always involve some process of interpretation, so how does interpretive reasoning enter into the practical reason of law? Answering such questions is the business of a theory of legal reasoning. Legal reasoning is to be understood as a form of practical reasoning concerning these very issues.

1　**Legal reasoning and questions of fact**
2　**Rules as reasons: deductively applied?**
3　**Grounds for rules: appropriateness and rhetorical argument**
4　**Procedural aspects: rational discourse**
5　**Rules again: exclusionary reasons**
6　**Legal reasoning beyond deduction**

1　Legal reasoning and questions of fact

A general requirement of sound practical reasoning is that there be due consideration of the facts relevant to a decision. A decision must be appropriate or fitting to its context. Doubts about and evidence concerning questions or opinions of fact have to be weighed and conclusions reached about the facts at issue. In law, decisions have to be made in relation to procedurally formalized claims or accusations, usually concerning particular past events. Claims and accusations have to be proved by admissible evidence. But what constitutes proof? The narrative coherence of an account of events connected to reliable present testimony seems to be an essential test, but proof of this sort can never amount to absolute certainty. Hence all legal proceedings have to address some standard of proof: 'proof beyond reasonable doubt', or 'proof on the balance of probabilities', or that proof which is found 'convincing' by the trier of fact. The burden of proof has to be determined.

So far as proof demands a judgment of probabilities, it is a question of whether or how far probability should be interpreted according to a Pascalian or mathematical/statistical model, or should be interpreted as a form of 'Baconian' probability, as argued by Jonathan Cohen (1977). It is submitted that the overall probability of a case should be interpreted in Cohen's terms, but with due allowance made for the legitimacy of statistical methods when forensic-scientific analysis can cast light on some key evidential fact or facts (see LEGAL EVIDENCE AND INFERENCE).

Important though careful factual reasoning is in processes of decision-making, on its own it is insufficient to bring practical reasoning to any conclusion. Some transformation of factual reasoning into normative conclusion is called for. That is, there has to be some further reason why to act or decide in a certain way given that the situation is held to be such-and-such. Such reasons must be right-making, showing the act or decision as right for those facts.

2 Rules as reasons: deductively applied?

What kind of such reasons are there? One possible answer is 'rules'. If there were a rule that act A ought to be performed in circumstances C, then, if it were established that C, the appropriate act in the circumstances would be A. It seems straightforward to turn this line of reasoning around and express it as a *modus ponens* hypothetical argument. 'If ever C, then A is right; C, so in this case A is right.' This assimilates practical syllogisms to ordinary deductive arguments, save that the major premise is a normative rather than a factual generalization. But the view that practical reasoning can be straightforwardly assimilated to ordinary deductive reasoning is extremely controversial. And lawyers have frequently warned against the confusion of law with (deductive) logic.

There are difficulties. First, what is presupposed in appealing to a rule in such a setting? By virtue of what could a governing rule be said to exist? Two possibilities may be suggested. The first is the establishment of a rule by some form of authority, for example as a rule of a game, by the governing body of the sport in question; or as a rule of a school or university, by its governing body; or, finally, a rule

of a legal system, established by the legislature. For a rule to count as a reason in this setting, it has to be presupposed that it is right to defer to that authority, and the problem of justification thus seems to lead out beyond any established rule or rules. We therefore need to look at the second possibility: that there is some reason to follow the rule other than the fact of its being an authoritatively established rule in some rule-system. What could such reason be?

3 Grounds for rules: appropriateness and rhetorical argument

At this point, there seem to be three possibilities: that the rule is endorsed as appropriate in itself; that it derives from a principle which is appropriate in itself; or that it is a rule justified by the value of its consequences, that is, by the consequences of following it as a rule – but in that case, some principle confirming the positive value of such consequences is presupposed, and the appropriateness of the principle is also presupposed. Returning to the question of authority, it can now also be said that the reason for accepting authority must evidently be the appropriateness of following the rules and/or principles that constitute the authority.

We are forced into considering the notion of that which is 'appropriate'. One account could be in terms of some faculty of direct apprehension or intuition (see INTUITIONISM IN ETHICS), whereby we are able immediately to recognize such appropriateness or other moral qualities. But if such an appeal to intuition is sound, why is there need for appeal to a rule at all? If we are capable of intuitively grasping the appropriateness of a rule in itself, or of the following of a rule established by an authority whose appropriateness is intuitively clear, can we not then simply apply that faculty of intuition directly to the case itself? May it not be that the appropriateness of the act to its circumstances is itself the justifying reason for the act? M.J. Detmold (1984) has argued that if one were incapable of seeing the force of such reasoning from the appropriateness of a particular act to its particular circumstances, one would be equally incapable of seeing the appropriateness of a rule, and hence incapable of arguing from rules. The foundation of legal (and moral) reasoning in this view lies in our capacity to judge what is right in individual cases, including a capacity to perceive when it is right to treat a particular case as a case covered by a rule, and decide accordingly.

Whatever may be the ultimate inevitability of some appeal to intuition, it does seem that recourse to this 'black box' ought to be deferred as long as possible in the analysis of any process of reasoning. Especially in practical reasoning, and most spectacularly in the case of legal reasoning, there are possibilities of argumentation, reasoning and discussion of a quite public kind over the issue of what is here called 'appropriateness'.

Wherever there is a process of public argumentation, there is rhetoric. The modern rediscovery of rhetoric as a discipline owes much to reflection on legal reasoning. Theodor Viehweg, drawing on Aristotle, has pointed out the significance of *topoi*, or 'commonplaces', in rhetorical arguments. An argument for a particular rule or proposition can be supported by reference to some accepted *topos*, and arguments progress by working towards, or from, such commonplace positions. In law, there are maxims and long-standing principles and presumptions, such as 'no one can give a better right than they have themselves' or 'a later law derogates from an earlier one' and such like. Likewise, there are well-established argument forms such as *argumentum a fortiori*, *argumentum a maiori ad minus*, *argumentum per analogiam* and the like. An argument in such a recognized form starting from or working towards a recognized *topos* is well calculated to be persuasive in its given context.

In a not dissimilar way, Josef Esser (1970) drew attention to the importance of *Vorverständnisse*, 'pre-understandings', the taken-for-granted assumptions that enter any judgment of what is acceptable in the setting of legal argumentation – and in the preference of one method of arguing over another in a particular case. Once premises and mode of argument are settled, it is simple to produce an argument that satisfactorily justifies the conclusion reached. But the problem then becomes one about the reasonable choice of premises and method, so there must be inquiry into pre-understandings. Aulis Aarnio (1987) has suggested that in the end these may simply have to be assessed as the 'form of life' that they constitute.

Chaim Perelman's *La Nouvelle Rhétorique* (1958) emphasizes that arguments are necessarily addressed to an audience, and that persuasiveness is audience-relative. This is especially obvious in legal practice, where trained advocates put cases before courts as persuasively as possible, and judges decide after weighing their rival arguments on points of law. But persuasiveness is not the same as soundness. The issue for a theory of reasoning-as-justification is not what argument actually persuades a particular judge or jury, but what ought to convince any rational decision-maker. In this connection, Perelman postulates a 'universal audience' as providing the ultimate test; whatever argument would convince an audience of all intelligent and interested beings is a sound one. At the same time, Stephen Toulmin (1964) proposed a

reinterpretation of traditional logic as regulating argumentative moves, and supplying warrants for moves from premises to conclusions, rather than as capturing timeless truths about rational thought.

The weakness of the rhetorical turn in analysis of practical reasoning is to reduce appropriateness to persuasiveness. Appeals to the universal audience or to any actual consensus seem unhelpful, since apparently we work out what would persuade the universal audience by reference to what is sound, not vice versa. Yet again, certain 'critical' approaches to legal thought urge that the claim to an objective soundness of legal reasons is the grandest rhetorical turn of all, enabling ideology or class interest to be misrepresented as some kind of ultimately sound reason or sound reasoning (see CRITICAL LEGAL STUDIES; LEGAL DISCOURSE).

4 Procedural aspects: rational discourse

A procedural approach to practical reasoning may provide a solution to the problems posed by theorists of rhetoric and their critics. The question is what constraints upon reasoning it is rational to accept in order to come to acceptable conclusions. Here, the rhetoricians' emphasis on the interpersonal context of argumentation is reiterated. In its light, the concept of universality has two uses: first, in stipulating universalizability of reasons – for the present instantiation of C to count as a reason now for doing A, it would have to be acceptable to hold A appropriate whenever an instance of C occurs; second, in testing the acceptability of any such reason – the universalized reason has to be acceptable to any interested party, and be challengeable by reference to anyone's feelings, interests or opinions; but any opinion or feeling or interest is challengeable as to its relevancy, and so on. As Jürgen HABERMAS (§4) and followers like Robert Alexy (1988) argue, it may be possible to test practical propositions by reference, at least in principle, to the interests and views of the totality of persons in any way affected by or concerned with them. Habermas proposes a test by reference to dialogue in an 'ideal speech situation', envisaged as one in which all forms of coercion or interpersonal power or domination are put aside for the purposes of conducting (or imagining the conduct of) interpersonal discourse (see COMMUNICATIVE RATIONALITY §1). Analysis of the necessary constraints on such a discourse yields a procedural approach to testing the kinds of principles that rational discourse-partners could accept, acknowledging the types of desires and interests they actually have. Important in this is the idea that accepted principles or *topoi* should be subject to challenge, but are considered acceptable until successfully challenged, for example, on the ground that they cannot pass the test of universaliz-ability or on the ground that they owe their origins to inequalities of power irrelevant as reasons in the ideal speech situation.

It is doubtful whether this procedural approach wholly disposes of recourse to intuition. It remains a question why some principles of argument must be accepted as 'rational' after all. But the merit of the approach is that it both postpones and narrows appeals to intuition, and scrutinizes the appropriate-ness of practical principles and rules in the light of acknowledged constraints of rational discourse. Commonplace principles are still needed as starting points, but they are challengeable within the argu-mentation. One requirement of rationality is that principles and rules be shown both to be mutually consistent and also to have overall coherence, working in priority rankings and weighing procedures to resolve *prima facie* conflicts.

This discourse-theoretical evolution of the rheto-rical approach largely substitutes for without finally supplanting intuition in accounting for the idea of the appropriateness or rightness of a rule as a reason for action, and the appropriateness of other reasons in justifying either the content of a rule or the authoritative status ascribed to it. Insistence on universality in both the senses deployed here is also of value in blocking appeal to some particular ineffable intuition as a sufficient justifying reason for a particular decision in a particular case. The reason must at least be statable as 'whenever C, then A', and some reason given for that, including a testing of it for consistency and coherence with other accepted rules, principles and unchallenged common-places.

5   Rules again: exclusionary reasons

Hitherto, it has been taken for granted that rules can be justifying reasons for actions. Now we are in a position to pose the question: 'Why rules?' Why should we have started from thinking of rules as reasons for decisions, rather than principles of rational decision-making such as might emerge from a procedurally articulated practical rationality? Rules are one type of normative entity. Their distinctiveness lies in what has been called their character as 'exclusionary reasons' (Raz 1975) or 'entrenched generalisations' (Schauer 1991). These terms draw attention to the special way one appeals to a rule in reasoning, namely as a factor that excludes considera-tion of otherwise relevant features of the situation. Appealing to a rule is appealing to an 'exclusionary reason'.

Consider this: as a matter of principle, one ought to drive with due regard for the safety of others; it is a rule that one stop at red traffic lights. To respect the rule as a rule means abstaining from deliberation in particular cases whether due regard for the safety of others requires stopping at a given red light on a given occasion. The rule is a reason to stop and a reason not to reflect further on the wisdom of stopping (which does not mean that there may not be emergencies that cancel the rule). One can, by contrast, respect the principle as a principle while allowing that in a given context it can be outweighed by considerations arising from rival principles.

How then can rules belong in a theory of practical reason? How can reason mandate the exclusion of reasons? A common answer is that human coordina-tion problems may give special utility to fixed rules for application by all parties whose actions have to be coordinated. In any interpersonal context in which pure principled reasoning guided by procedures for rational practical discourse would or could lead to conflict of soundly justified opinions (and actions) on points of conduct in shared social space, recourse to a rule is the best way to achieve the least unreasonable results on the whole, even though there are occasions when application of the rule yields non-optimal results. (Traffic-light rules exemplify this clearly, and indeed in Britain the Highway Code largely comprises rules for solving coordination problems in areas where reliance on pure principle would be obviously hazardous.)

Pure recourse to unaided practical reason without recourse to rules and authority would not yield satisfactory grounds for interpersonal decision where coordination is called for. It is therefore reasonable for humans to have or to establish authorities exercising powers of rule-making and of rule-apply-ing. That is, it is reasonable to have law (in various forms), and reasonable that law comprise in large measure relatively detailed rules established through legislation (and possibly through precedent also). This is what establishes the special sphere of legal reason-ing as a separate branch of general practical reason-ing, with appropriate special principles, rules and forms of argument. Rules duly established through law are appropriate grounds for decision-making both by citizens in relation to their own conduct and by judges and other officials in decision-making in cases involving citizen–citizen or citizen–state conflict or dispute.

Earlier, it was suggested that reasoning where rules are applied is essentially deductive. To show that a rule is being applied, one states the rule 'if C then A', and states one's finding that 'C' is satisfied in this case. 'A' can then be stated to follow as the appropriate action in the circumstances that obtain. In very straightforward cases, this indeed seems to be a complete account. But cases are frequently harder, in obvious ways. First comes the problem of possible conflicting interpretations of the rule. What does the rule properly mean? How should it be interpreted for this case? Second comes the problem known to lawyers as that of 'qualification' or 'characterization' of the facts and circumstances. For example, suppose there is an acknowledged rule not to commit adultery. If a married woman wishes to have a child, but cannot become pregnant by her husband, would it count as adultery if she participated in artificial insemination by donor (AID)? Would it make a difference if the donor were unknown or known? Or if her husband objected or consented? How should we qualify these facts having regard to the assumed rule? If a wife is pregnant through AID and if adultery is a ground for divorce, is her husband entitled to a divorce on the ground of her adultery? Whenever a rule is in view, it is crucial whether or not given facts can be legitimately so characterized as to fit the rule, or be distinguished from it. A similar question can be posed in a broader way, asking which of a range of possible interpretations of the general rule should prevail, given the wording of the rule, the general legal context of its enactment, and any values at stake in its implementation.

6 Legal reasoning beyond deduction

Even in cases where rules are *prima facie* applicable in a direct way, there can be problems of qualification and of interpretation, and a part of the rhetorical training of lawyers develops their attentiveness to such problems whenever helpful to the case they must advocate. Moreover, there may be many situations which, although not covered directly and unambiguously by an established rule, do nevertheless bear some closer or remoter analogy to the situation the rule expressly covers, and to which acceptable arguments of principle favour a resolution founded in this analogy. Decisions taken to deal with such problems or to uphold or reject the analogy may themselves constitute precedents offering grounds for future resolution of like problems. There is an obvious ground of justice for paying regard to such precedents in later cases, and the more the regard that is in fact paid on that ground, the stronger becomes the justice of holding to precedent, in view of expectations founded on the practice of following them.

This shows why the (essentially deductive) rule-application paradigm of argumentation, justifying a decision simply as an application of a rule to a particular case considered to be an uncomplicated

instance of the generic case stipulated in the rule, is rarely if ever sufficient in itself fully to justify a decision. There have to be reasons for a favoured interpretation of the rule, reasons for a favoured qualification of a fact-situation, reasons in favour of pursuing or rejecting an analogy. Theories of legal reasoning have tried to elucidate its character in these areas that lie outside the simple deductive model.

Some of its features derive directly from constraints of practical reason itself. Thus reasons for interpretations or classifications have to be universalizable, as must be grounds for decision supported by analogy. There must be some explicit or implicit 'holding' or 'ruling' or 'maxim' of the case that accounts for the decision favoured, and that must be universalizable if not explicitly stated in universalistic terms: 'given that adultery requires an actual act of sexual intercourse, pregnancy by AID is not to be considered proof of adultery' would be an example. Any claim to justification through such a holding entails a commitment to its universal applicability – to every instance of AID complained of as adulterous *per se*, not only this one. This pushes the problem back a stage, but does not solve it, for the question at once arises how to justify the ruling or holding conceived in universalistic terms. There are but two possibilities. There must be deontological or teleological reasons in play ('rightness reasons' or 'goal reasons', according to R.S. Summers 1978). Either it must be shown to be in principle right to restrict 'adultery' in this way, or it must be shown to be preferable to the alternative upon consequentialist grounds.

Reasons of principle have a dual aspect here. On the one hand, since the context of decision is a legal one, and since the concepts at issue are legal, bedded in fundamental doctrines of family law, there is a necessary interpretive element: one has to establish a good account of the values that underpin the particular view of marital fidelity (or whatever, depending on the area of law in view) enshrined in the whole relevant body of law. On the other hand, there is the test of general practical reasonableness (here interpreted in the procedural model of practical rationality, though others are available). Teleological or consequentialist reasoning places the stress on the legal acceptability or unacceptability of the state of affairs represented by one or another of the rulings that come under view. Evaluation of the 'acceptable' or 'unacceptable' in the legal setting has regard to the legal-institutional framework, and to values that make sense in this framework. So the difference between deontological and teleological in this setting may be more one of presentation than one of fundamentals. In either event, an effort is made to interpret the broad sweep of the law in terms of its point or its underlying value or values, and on this account Ronald Dworkin (1986) has characterized 'law' itself as an essentially 'interpretive concept'.

However that may be, there is another aspect of interpretation rather narrower and more exact in its reference. As noted, there are frequently issues of the interpretation properly to be put upon the terms and provisions of enacted law. While it is undoubtedly the case that this proceeds under the above-noted constraint of universalizability, nevertheless reasons for interpretations are also often strongly (and legitimately) relativized to the particular statute, its particular wording, its particular legal context, and (sometimes) particular purposes imputed to it either on objective grounds or having regard to evidence of the particular aims of the legislature that enacted it. Universalizably justifiable practices of interpretation require attention to the integrity of linguistic communication through the medium of enacted law, to the overall coherence of statute law, both internally to the particular statute and externally in testing its consistency and fit with the rest of the legal system in which it takes its place. A similar principle in favour of the overall coherence of law is also in play where argument by analogy, in particular argument by analogy with settled precedents, is advanced in justification of decisions. Here too, the case for or against extending by analogy from the law as already settled to some novel formulation is subject to testing and critique both deontologically and teleologically. Interpretation of statutes and of precedents, and arguments by analogy in both contexts, have accordingly a particular part to play in legal reasoning.

Some commentators treat this as too restricted a view of the place of inductive or analogical reasoning. E.H. Levi's classic *An Introduction to Legal Reasoning* (1948) portrayed analogical development as the essential moving force of the common law, and its most characteristic style of reasoning. More recently, Steven J. Burton (1985) and Bernard S. Jackson (1988) have argued respectively that analogical reasoning has either coequal status with the deductive rule-based paradigm suggested above or (in Jackson's case) clear primacy over it, on the ground that all our reasoning has most fundamentally a narrative structure, such that the human capacity for pattern-matching among narratives accounts both for the human skill of analogical reasoning and the human capacity to make sense of rules. The present attempt to postpone recourse to and narrow the scope of appeals to intuition applies also to this essentially intuitionistic conception of pattern-matching; but it is not hostile to the claim that analogical reasoning is omnipresent in the adjustment of legal norms to social values. It is submitted that although argument

by analogy has indeed a special role in the development of law and in processes of rational 'discovery' in developing new legal doctrine, nevertheless it has to be viewed as one part of a wider conception of legal reasoning as a special case of practical reasoning.

See also: DISCOVERY, LOGIC OF; DWORKIN, R.; LAW, PHILOSOPHY OF; LEGAL DISCOURSE

References and further reading

* Aarnio, A. (1987) *The Rational as Reasonable*, Dordrecht/Boston/London: Kluwer. (Gives an account of the relationship of rationality and reasonableness to forms of life.)
* Alexy, R. (1988) *Theory of Legal Argumentation*, trans. R. Adler and N. MacCormick, Oxford: Clarendon Press. (The best statement of the case for the 'special case thesis', namely that legal reasoning is a special case of general practical reasoning; and the best English account of Habermas' theory of rational discourse as a guide to legal discourse.)
* Atienza, M. (1991) *Las Razones del Derecho* (The Law's Reasons), Cuadernos y Debates, 31, Madrid: Centro de Estudios Constitucionales. (An extremely clear and helpful discussion of most of the approaches discussed in the present article.)
* Burton, S.J. (1985) *An Introduction to Law and Legal Reasoning*, Boston/Toronto: Little, Brown. (A good differentiation of the deductive and the narrative styles of legal reasoning; also a good, reader-friendly general account of the issues covered in this article.)
* Cohen, L.J. (1977) *The Probable and the Provable*, Oxford: Clarendon Press. (Argues for a non-mathematical interpretation of probability in legal proof, and advances a theory of 'Baconian probability'.)
* Detmold, M.J. (1984) *The Unity of Law and Morality*, London: Routledge. (Contains the best version of an essentially intuitionist account of what makes a decision right.)
* Dworkin, R. (1986) *Law's Empire*, London: Fontana. (A discussion of law as an interpretive concept, and of the forms of reasoning involved in legal interpretation.)
Eggleston, R. (1983) *Evidence, Proof, and Probability*, 2nd edn, London: Weidenfeld and Nicolson. (A powerful defence of the applicability of Pascalian – or mathematical – probability in legal proof.)
* Esser, J. (1970) *Vorverständnis und Methodenwahl in der Rechtsfindung* (Pre-understanding and Choice of Method in the Search for Law), Frankfurt: Suhrkamp. (Gives an interesting account of the

'pre-understandings' always involved in acts of legal interpretation, and discusses the place of the 'acceptable' as a standard of valuation of arguments.)

* Jackson, B.S. (1988) *Law, Fact, and Narrative Coherence*, Roby: Deborah Charles. (Contains an interesting argument for reasoning as essentially narrative in structure, and a strong critique of deductivism.)

* Levi, E.H. (1948) *An Introduction to Legal Reasoning*, Chicago, IL: Chicago University Press. (A classic account of the role of analogy and induction in the development of law – how the exception can grow to become the rule.)

MacCormick, N. (1978) *Legal Reasoning and Legal Theory*, Oxford: Clarendon Press. (An introduction to many of the ideas stated above.)

MacCormick, N. and Summers, R.S. (1991) *Interpreting Statutes: A Comparative Study*, Aldershot: Dartmouth Publishing Co. (Essays on interpretation and the theory of interpretation taking account of nine major legal systems.)

* Peczenik, A. (1989) *On Law and Reason*, Dordrecht/Boston/London: Kluwer. (An excellent account of the unity of practical reason and the differences of factual, moral and legal reasoning.)

* Perelman, C. (1958) *La Nouvelle Rhétorique* (The New Rhetoric), Paris: Presses Universitaires de France. (An outstanding statement of the modern significance of rhetoric in the Aristotelian tradition, commented on, for example, in Alexy above.)

* Raz, J. (1975) *Practical Reason and Norms*, London: Hutchinson. (The classical account of rules as 'exclusionary reasons'.)

* Schauer, F. (1991) *Playing by the Rules*, Oxford: Clarendon Press. (Gives an account partly comparable with Raz (above) of the role of rules in practical reasoning.)

* Summers, R.S. (1978) 'Two Types of Substantive Reasons: The Core of a Theory of Common-law Justification', *Cornell Law Review* 63: 707–88.

* Toulmin, S.E. (1964) *The Uses of Argument*, Cambridge: Cambridge University Press. (Challenges traditional interpretations of logic and explores structures of practical arguments; hence influential in discussions of practical reasoning in law.)

NEIL MacCORMICK

LEGALIST PHILOSOPHY, CHINESE

Legalist philosophy constitutes one of the three dominant streams of Chinese philosophy along with Confucian and Daoist philosophies. It aims to establish objective, impartial and impersonal standards for human conduct. It sets forth prescriptive models using such metaphors as the builder's plumb line and carpenter's L-square. 'Modelling after' implies reshaping and remoulding of human behaviour, not by moral suasion but by the application of fa, *a term designating both prescriptive standards and promulgated penal law, designed to achieve public interest.*

The idea of remoulding by punishment and reward is predicated on the Legalist conception of human nature. Innately self-interested human nature underlies human behaviour of liking reward and disliking punishment. Hence, penal law is both natural and an objective prescriptive technique for behavioural control that seeks to harmonize both the individual and the public interest. Penal law is efficacious in so far as it is issued from an authoritative power (shi *) based on impersonal, institutionalized position of rulership and borne up, however tacitly, by the support of the people.* Shi *cannot govern effectively, Legalists argue, without the organizational power of bureaucracy under the centralized control of the ruler. For the ruler, controlling bureaucracy means mastering the technique (* shu *) of comparing 'word' (* ming *) and actual 'performance' (* xing *), not only through objective mechanisms of empirical verification but also by means of 'the two handles' of power over life and death. Hence, the technique holds bureaucracy accountable.*

The Legalist philosophy of governing by fa, shi *and* shu *was in effect a new model for sociopolitical reorganization. It became increasingly popular during the Warring States period, a time of incessant political struggle and of irreversible systemic disintegration of the Zhou feudal order. Legalists called for a radical systemic transformation through this new model in the name of historical relativism: 'There are as many situations as there are generations... and situations change, so the measures change' (* Han Feizi *49).*

Historical relativism notwithstanding, Legalist philosophy envisages a 'natural' and 'automatic' polity that, once established, accords with dao *(that is, the way the natural world operates spontaneously). The ruler practices 'non-action', 'emptiness' and 'quiescence' so as to embody* dao, *and thereby personifies objective, impersonal standards over subjective, personal preferences. Once this 'natural' polity is established, the ruler does not act while his subordinates act according to* xingming *accountability as noted above. The ruler does not act as the centre point of the scale does not move, and yet he knows which side is heavy and which side light. In the end, the ruler does not act so that he can act, that is, so he can employ 'the two handles' to control his subordinates. This seemingly 'natural' and 'automatic' polity still requires a 'sage' ruler extraordinarily adept at covert statecraft. Only such a 'sage' ruler can hope to achieve order, wealth and power for himself and for his people.*

1 **Fa as prescriptive standards and penal law**
2 **Fa and human nature**
3 **Shi: authoritative power base**
4 **Shu: the art of rulership**
5 **Historical relativism**
6 **The Legalist vision and Daoism**
7 **Enduring significance of Legalist philosophy**

1 *Fa* as prescriptive standard and penal law

The term *fa* means not only 'law' but also means 'model', 'standard' or 'method'; therefore, it needs to be understood contextually (see Fa; Law and ritual in Chinese philosophy). Hence, the conventional translation of *fajia* (school) as the 'Legalist School of Thought' is misleading in that it overemphasizes the term 'law'. Moreover, the term *fajia* is retrospectively attributed by the Han doxographers, particularly Sima Tan (d. 110 BC), to a group of thinkers and statesmen who shared a sufficient measure of common philosophy of governing but certainly did not constitute a 'school' in the sense of the Confucian and Mohist schools. They did not have master or canonical texts and they did not live a communal life.

The third of the 'Seven Standards' of *Guanzi*, attributed to the proto-Legalist Guan Zhong (d. 645 BC), defines *fa* as 'standard' and refers to the carpenter's ink and line, compasses and L-square, the scale and the volume measures, metaphors that suggest mechanical precision and impartiality. The 'Seven Standards' are set forth as the knowledge required by the ruler for effective government. The fifth is specifically designed for transforming or reforming the people: 'Giving to or taking from, endangering or securing, benefitting or harming... killing or giving life, are called "incentives" and "deterrents"' (*Guanzi* 35). The idea of 'standard' is succinctly stated by the pre-eminent Legalist HAN FEIZI: 'The [*fa*] no more makes exception for men of high station than the plumb line bends to accommodate a crooked place in the wood' (*Han Feizi* 6).

Fa, understood as 'model' or 'standard' of behavioural pattern, is not exclusively Legalist; it is clearly present in *Mozi* (canons A70, A94) and *Mencius* (4B1). These texts placed primary emphasis

on 'government by virtuous example' and held that even the benevolent heart of a virtuous ruler would not achieve good government without the aid of the carpenter's compass and L-square. While the punitive connotation of the word *fa* became more pronounced in the Warring States period, for Legalists, *fa* continued to mean a whole network of 'standardized' patterns of behaviour. Thus to the Legalist Shang Yang (d. 338 BC), 'changing *fa*' meant a call for a new 'model' of sociopolitical institutions with corollary implications for behavioural change according to the Legalist standards.

Fa is most commonly understood as penal law. Contrary to conventional wisdom, however, the Legalists did not invent 'severe punishments and strict laws'. In the proto-Confucian canonical texts such as the *Shujing* (Book of Documents), King Wu, the founder of the Zhou dynasty (*c.* 1040–256 BC), and his brother Duke of Zhou emphasized the rational role of coercive force for a righteous cause. The Duke of Zhou advises Prince Kang to administer severe punishments according to the laws and not to bend them to agree with his 'inclinations'. Those who commit '[serious] crimes... are greatly abhorred, and how much more detestable are the unfilial and unbrotherly!... You must punish them severely' (*Shujing* IX). As Schwartz (1985) observes, the enduring legacy of meting out 'the most horrendous penal sanctions' for violation of family morality, which was supposedly held together by kinship affection, was legitimized by canonical texts. The Legalist doctrine of 'severe punishments and strict laws' likewise harks back to canonical texts. In these texts, however, there exists a judicious balance between civil and coercive administration, whereas Shang Yang and Han Feizi stress Draconian penal codes under the compelling exigencies of Warring States power politics.

2 *Fa* and human nature

How do Legalists justify their claim that *fa* is both 'objective' and 'natural'? How is *fa* related to their conception of human nature? In fact, the Legalist approach to human nature is sociological. Of the goodness and badness of human nature, GUANZI observes: 'It is not a matter of man's nature, but of poverty' (*Guanzi* 35). HAN FEIZI speaks of changing values and behavioural patterns when the population increases in geometric progression while provision for it grows in only arithmetic progression (*Han Feizi* 48). As a consequence, people compete so fiercely for survival that disorder becomes rampant even if rewards are doubled and punishments multiplied. Han Feizi contends: 'The generosity with resources in ancient times was not benevolence, it was because

532

resources were ample; the competition and robbery is not dishonesty, it is because resources are sparse.' Thus the Legalist philosophy of human nature is significantly different from that of HOBBES.

Legalists argued moreover that self-interestedness does not necessarily imply harming others. Han Feizi observed that the physician sucks patients' wounds and holds their blood in his mouth not because he loves them but because he expects profit from them. It does not mean the cartwright is 'benevolent' for wishing people to be wealthy enough to buy his carriages, nor does it mean the carpenter is 'cruel' in desiring to sell as many coffins as he can. Self-interestedness is clearly differentiated from selfishness, for it is considered a natural human condition that is ethically neutral.

People are more powerfully motivated by self-interest than the sentiments of concern for each other. This is also recognized in Western philosophy. In his *The Theory of Moral Sentiments*, Adam SMITH says: 'Every man is, no doubt, by nature, first and principally recommended to his own care.' Thus, when one hears of millions of Chinese being swallowed up by a stunning and hellish earthquake, one might momentarily feel badly but would then go about one's business and sleep soundly. 'If he was to lose his little finger tomorrow, [however], he would not sleep tonight' (Smith 1759 [1976]: III.3.4). Legalists assert that *fa* must accord with human feelings of self-interest for it to be 'objective' and 'natural'. Because human feelings have likes and dislikes, reward and punishment can be effectively applied, and when prohibitions and order prevail, good government can be achieved. The critical function of *fa* is to effectively regulate and channel the general tendency of human nature toward personal welfare in order to realize the principal goals of good government.

Given the natural tendency to be self-interested, how many people would spontaneously harmonize their concern for private welfare with public interest? How is the convergence of private and public interest to be effected? Han Feizi replies that one can neither count on arrows that are straight of themselves nor count on pieces of wood that are round of themselves in a thousand generations, and 'yet how is it that people of every generation ride carts and shoot birds? It is because the tools for straightening and bending are used...' (*Han Feizi* 50). The 'tools' are, of course, *fa*. *Fa* to one who governs is like the carpenter's L-square and compass – the objective, impersonal and prescriptive instruments for 'straightening and bending' – in short, for remoulding and channelling the general tendency of self-interested human nature toward the realization of public purposes.

What is new about Legalist view of *fa* is that it is consciously designed to institute an automatic polity (see §6). Individuals are compelled to grasp the utilitarian logic of automatically and habitually moulding their behaviour in conformity with *fa*, not only as objective standards but also as prescriptive 'tools' of penal codes, so as to achieve their self-interested goals. Given self-interested human nature, once the prescriptive mechanism of penal codes is in place, human behaviour becomes automatic and predictable, just as Adam Smith's 'economic man' becomes predictable once a free market is established. Legalists envisage a habitual convergence of private and public interest which will become automatic in due course. It is clearly more in one's own interest to be rewarded for hard labour in farming and for valour in battle than to face the terrible consequence of behaving otherwise.

3 *Shi*: authoritative power base

Shen Dao (*fl. c.*310 BC), the Legalist best known for his theory of *shi* or authoritative power base, regarded *shi* as a 'natural position of advantage' *vis-à-vis* others. *Shi* is a charismatic and mysterious 'potency' (*de*) that inspires awe and obedience among the masses. It is *shi* that enables the flying dragon to ride the clouds and the soaring serpent to float in the mist. Without the *shi* of clouds and mist, the dragon and serpent might as well be earthworms (fr. 10). 'As a simple yeoman', without *shi*, even Yao, a pre-dynastic sage ruler, 'could not command his neighbours' (fr. 12), while Jie, the depraved last emperor of the Xia dynasty, because of *shi*, could wreak havoc on the whole world. In essence, Shen Dao was expounding the very phenomenon of authority, *conditio sine qua non* for an orderly and civilized society.

None the less, Han Feizi's critique of Shen Dao centres on the theory of 'natural position of advantage', obviously analogous to the Confucian view of 'superior moral qualities' of virtuous rulers (see HAN FEIZI). Confucians argue that it is the superior qualities of the dragon that enable it to soar, and it is the superior moral virtues of Yao that brought order and benefits to the world. The argument curiously ends with an observation: 'It belongs to man's essential nature that the worthy are fewer than the unworthy' (*Han Feizi* 40). If good government depends on the worthy, Han Feizi argues, the world is condemned to almost continuous disorder and misgovernment inasmuch as Yao only appears once in 'a thousand generations'. His concern is with the rulers in between the exceptionally virtuous Yao and the notoriously depraved Jie, that is, those who regularly occupy the position of *shi*.

For Han Feizi, then, good government depends not so much on 'superior moral qualities' of one who holds authority as on *shi* being 'properly ordered'; that is, *shi* securely based on clearly defined and promulgated laws that are rigorously enforced. In short, there exists a contradiction between *shi* based on 'positive' law and the imperatives of a 'higher' moral norm. Han Fei asserts that *shi* based on law and a moral code are mutually exclusive: 'A man selling spears and shields was praising his shields as so hard that nothing could penetrate them. Immediately afterwards, he said in praise of his spears "My spears are so sharp they will penetrate anything." When some one asked "What if I penetrate your shield with your spear?" he was at a loss to answer.' Han Feizi concludes: 'The two names [power and morality] cannot be made to stand [simultaneously]. The Way of the Worthy may not be forbidden, yet it is the Way of Power to forbid anything' (*Han Feizi* 40).

In Han Feizi's conception of *shi*, there is an unmistakable shift toward an institutionalized and impersonal authoritative power exclusively based on law, consciously designed by statecraft and bureaucratically administered under the ultimate sanction of 'the two handles'. Shen Dao too is aware of the human fallibility of those who wield authority and the need for objective standards: 'When one who rules men casts aside the laws and governs on his own initiative, the punishments and rewards, seizures and grants, will be measured out according to the discretion of the ruler' (fr. 61).

Shen Dao moreover affirms an important attribute of authority, namely, 'it has weight' because it 'receives aid from many' (fr. 14). 'That the power of the Three Kings [three dynasties of Xia, Shang and Zhou] and the Five Protectors [of the Spring and Autumn period] was the same order as that of Heaven and the Earth... was due to the fact that they obtained aid from all' (fr. 16). Han Feizi likewise affirms: 'When the ruler wins the hearts of the people', he elevates himself to the position of authority 'without being raised' because the ruler is 'upheld by the masses of people with united hearts' (*Han Feizi* 28). However, he asserts that the ruler's *shi* is upheld by the masses not because of 'natural position of advantage' but rather because the well-ordered system of *fa* underpinning the ruler's *shi* will in the long run bring order and benefits to the people. In the final analysis, Legalists placed greater emphasis on the impersonal and institutionalized *shi* of rulership firmly based on *fa* than on authority borne up by 'natural position of advantage' or 'virtuous qualities' of the ruler. The concept of the 'consent of the governed' as the basis of legitimate authority, of course, was never a part of Legalist elitism.

4 *Shu*: the art of rulership

As is true of any complex sociopolitical entity, the Legalist model of sociopolitical organization cannot function without authority, nor can a 'properly ordered' authority based on law govern well without an efficient bureaucracy. The ruler who wields authority must therefore master *shu*, the 'method' or 'technique' of controlling bureaucracy and its personnel.

Shen Buhai (d. 337 BC) is best known for his theory of *shu*, although *shu* as the arcanum of government had been an essential part of covert statecraft long before his theorizing about it. What is significant about Shen's theory of *shu* is that it specifically sets forth a rational paradigm for bureaucratic accountability. Furthermore, it advances a theory of bureaucracy based exclusively on merit. Shen says: '"Method" is to scrutinize achievement and [on that ground alone] to give rewards, and to bestow office [solely] on the basis of ability' (fr. 23).

Shen Buhai's theory, elaborated by Han Feizi, argues that *shu* consists in holding officials accountable by impersonal application of objective and verifiable standards, so that an official's actual 'performance' accords with the 'name' of the office held. He uses the term 'tally' to connote a method of precise calibration and verification. For instance, an official holds the debtor's portion of a tally according to his title ('name'), and he is accountable for actual performance that tallies with the creditor's portion held by the ruler. Holding firm to the 'main cord', the ruler controls subordinates by means of the tallies. Both the metaphor of 'main cord' of a tightly-knit net (fr. 1(4)) controlling the tallies and the concept of 'cutting deeply' (fr. 27) as a means of holding subordinates accountable correspond to the Legalist concept of centralized control by holding fast to 'the two handles'. Whenever a minister utters a 'word' (proposals), the ruler measures it against actual performance. If the actual performance indeed 'tallies' (*Han Feizi* 5) with the 'word', the minister is rewarded; if the performance does not 'tally' with the 'word', the minister is punished. Han Feizi's exacting theory of accountability derives from his own experience as a prince of a ruling house. The critical observations and remonstrations throughout his writings are, in effect, diagnoses of the political pathology of his time and his prescriptions for remedying them. In particular, he addresses the problem of sovereigns being deluded by irresponsible eloquence that promotes partisan interests and weakens the state.

Han Feizi also drives home the harsh consequences of violating the requirements of functional specificity:

Once in the past Marquis Chao [Zhao] of Han got drunk and fell asleep. The keeper of the royal hat, seeing that the marquis was cold, laid a robe over him. When the marquis awoke, he was pleased and asked his attendants, 'Who covered me with the robe?' 'The keeper of the hat', they replied. The marquis thereupon punished both the keeper of the royal hat and the keeper of the royal robe. He punished the keeper of the robe for failing to do his duty, and the keeper of the hat for overstepping his office. It was not that he liked the cold, but he considered the trespass of one office upon the duties of another to be a greater danger than cold.

(*Han Feizi* 7)

How does Han Feizi or Shen Buhai know that the tallies match? The ruler's *shu* is twofold: it consists of (1) empiricism and (2) purposive Daoism (see §6). While Shen Buhai speaks of 'looking into affairs by means of their names' (fr. 1(9)) and 'careful supervision' of subordinates (fr. 17(1)), he relies more heavily on the *shu* of purposive Daoism. Han Feizi emphasizes both and provides the most elaborated philosophical arguments for purposive Daoism. He stresses the need for the ruler to gather 'causes of different affairs for comparison and observation' (*Han Feizi* 17) and to follow 'the procedures of comparison and verification to judge [actual performances]' (*Han Feizi* 14), for 'to be sure of anything that has no corroborating evidence is stupid' (*Han Feizi* 50).

Fa and *shu* are different in that *fa* is overtly promulgated and primarily intended for regulating the behaviour of general public, whereas *shu* is the covert arcanum of government and primarily intended for controlling the behaviour of bureaucracy. *Fa* and *shu* are similar in that they are impersonal and objective 'tools' for controlling human behaviour. Han Feizi criticized Shang Yang for having neglected *shu* and found Shen Buhai wanting for not having unified *fa*. *Fa*, *shi* and *shu* constitute the three interdependent pillars of Legalist philosophy.

5 Historical relativism

Shang Yang relates three different historical periods and their corollary behavioural and value patterns (*Shangjunshu* 1). Since the former generations did not share the same doctrines, he asks rhetorically, 'Which antiquity shall one imitate? The emperors and kings did not copy one another, so what rites should one follow?' (*Shangjunshu* 7). He saw more than one way to govern the world and found no need to imitate antiquity. He was quite prepared to institute new *fa* to remould the people (see §1).

HAN FEIZI elaborates on Shang Yang's historical relativism. Radical in thought and perceptive of what was to emerge in the wake of the systemic disintegration of the Zhou feudal order, he advances a new philosophy of history that directly challenges the traditional and characteristically Confucian 'Return to the Time of the Ancient Sages and Early Kings' philosophy of history (see HISTORY, CHINESE THEORIES OF). His historiography divides the history of China into three eras: (1) remote antiquity, (2) the middle age and (3) the present age, each era having its distinctive character: 'Men of remote antiquity strove to be known as moral and virtuous; those of the middle age struggled to be known as wise and resourceful; and now men fight for the reputation of being vigorous and powerful' (*Han Feizi* 49). The difference between antiquity and 'the present age' is that in antiquity 'events were few' and 'measures were simple'. Because there were relatively few people, it was easier to make light of profit and to yield to others, 'But the present age is one of numerous affairs and great struggle' (*Han Feizi* 47). He succinctly summarizes his historical relativism: 'There are as many situations as there are generations' and 'situations change, so the measures change' (*Han Feizi* 49).

Han Feizi's historiography is iconoclastic in that he unmasks the irrelevance of the sacred precepts of ancient sages and early kings in and of themselves. He is primarily concerned with the effective ways of dealing with the reality of his own time according to the principle: 'situations change, so the measures change'. He confidently concludes that *fa*, understood as a new model of sociopolitical institutions with the corollary implications for behavioural change, is the most effective instrument for dealing with the reality of 'the present age' (see §6). In his historical relativism, the main emphasis is on the 'situations change', not 'measures change':

> Change or no change, the sage does not mind. For he aims only at the rectification of government. Whether or not the ancient traditions should be changed, whether or not the existing institutions should be removed, all depends upon the question whether or not such institutions and such traditions are still useful for present-day political purposes.

(*Han Feizi* 18)

Therefore, he was judicious in avoiding indiscriminate rejection of the sacred precepts of the past merely for the sake of change. Rather, his criticism was directed against those who, while oblivious as to the 'condition of the wicked and the villainous' and clueless as to the effective means of rectifying the course of the state, blindly venerate the past and bewilder the ruler. Han

Feizi's overriding concern was no less than 'to save the present age'; hence, he placed particular emphasis on 'politics of consequence', not unlike Max Weber's 'ethics of responsibility'.

6 The Legalist vision and Daoism

Despite historical relativism, the new model of Legalist institutions represents an ahistorical 'ideal type'. This paradigm of Legalist polity is consciously designed to incorporate certain aspects of Daoism so that, once established, it operates 'naturally' and 'automatically'. In short, this paradigm may be equated with the Legalist vision and response to the perennial question of 'what is the good society?' In contrast, MACHIAVELLI was primarily preoccupied with the techniques of manipulating power and was less concerned with devising a new paradigm.

The Legalist search for objective, impersonal and impartial standards goes beyond a simple rationalization to justify political power. HAN FEIZI presents the most sophisticated philosophical inquiry into the relationship between Legalism and Daoism (see DAOIST PHILOSOPHY). He comments extensively on various sections of Laozi's *Daodejing* (see DAODEJING) in chapters 20, 'Interpreting Laozi', and 21, 'Illustrating Laozi'. He writes: '*Dao* is that from which all things are as they are, and it is the collecting point of all principles [*li*]' (*Han Feizi* 20). Things are essentially what they are because of their respective principles (*li*) (see LI).

Li etymologically refers to 'venation in pieces of jade'; hence, it symbolizes natural pattern and order that are independent of human thinking, willing and behaving. Rocks are hard; dogs bark; the four seasons run their course; day follows night; people are born and they die.

Water has its own nature: one who is drowning dies as one drinks too much of it, and one who is thirsty lives as one drinks a proper amount of it. Han Feizi's *li* represents the constants or 'objective regularities' in the natural order of things. Human beings may choose to accord with *li* or go against it at their own risk.

Shen Buhai says: 'Heaven's Way has no private [concerns]; therefore, it is always correct' (fr. 8). It is the humans who must discern and conform to the constant *dao* to be 'correct', for *dao* 'embraces all opposites' and is not partial to human concerns (see DAO). It is *dao* that patterns the universe and is the source of *li*: '*dao* is the beginning of myriad things and the standard of right and wrong' (*Han Feizi* 5). Han Feizi sees the natural world and the human world in one continuum. The very same *dao* and *li* pervade both worlds, and it is by being informed by *dao* and *li*

that the ruler is able to conform to the truly objective and natural order of things and realize the fullness of one's 'potency':

> The ancients who completed the principal features of Legalism, looked upon Heaven and earth, surveyed rivers and oceans, and followed mountains and ravines; wherefore, they ruled as the sun and the moon shine, worked as the four seasons rotate, and benefited the world in the way clouds spread and winds move.
>
> (*Han Feizi* 29)

Thus, the ruler should model after *dao* and govern according to *dao*'s objective standards by not acting (*wuwei*) contrary to the natural order of things and by cultivating 'emptiness' and 'quiescence' so as to embody *dao*. In so doing, the ruler acquires the 'potency' (*de*) for governing (see DE). Han Feizi advises the ruler to be 'humble'; this means not only refraining from overindulgence in seeing and hearing but also moderating mental activity. In short, it means bringing one's sensual and heart–mind activities under control so that one knows how to 'conserve'. By knowing how to 'conserve' through restraining his subjective inclinations, the ruler is better able to accord with *dao* and *li*.

Having instituted the new model of Legalist polity according to the objective and impersonal standards of *dao* and the natural feelings of 'likes' and 'dislikes' of human nature, the sage ruler reposes in 'non-action' (*wuwei*): 'He remains empty and waits for [the subordinates'] service, and they will exert [*yuwei*] their abilities by themselves' (*Han Feizi* 8). Thus, a *wuwei–yuwei* dialectical relationship marks the functional differentiation of the ruler and the subordinates. The ruler, uniquely personifying *dao* and grasping 'the two handles', reposes in *wuwei*, while the subordinates actively engage in fulfilling their *xingming* accountability. The sage ruler, by his gnostic grasp of *dao*, knows the source of everything and, by being in accord with objective standards, knows the 'origin of good and evil'. Such a ruler, by practising *shu* of 'emptiness' and 'quiescence', waits for all 'names' to name themselves and all 'affairs' to settle themselves as though automatically (*Han Feizi* 5). Han Feizi resorts to metaphors to clarify the *shu* of 'non-action': like the stationary mirror, the ruler can see and compare the beautiful and the ugly; like the centre point of the scale, he can weigh the light and heavy without moving (*Han Feizi* 19).

Is this comparing and weighing truly automatic? However 'natural' and 'automatic' the new paradigm of Legalist polity may seem, in the final analysis, the ruler does not act *so that* he can act, and Legalist polity requires a ruler who is exceptionally adept at covert techniques of statecraft. Like the Smithean theory, the Legalist idea of 'automatic society' proved to be illusory.

7 Enduring significance of Legalist philosophy

First, Han Feizi's drawing a parallel between Heaven and the ruler is highly symbolic, for it implies the ruler's uniqueness beyond the ordinary social hierarchy. To accentuate this uniqueness, he pushes the comparison to its ultimate level, drawing an analogy between *dao* and the ruler: '*Dao* is never a pair. Hence it is called one. Therefore, the intelligent ruler esteems singleness, the characteristic of *dao*' (*Han Feizi* 8). Just as *dao* does not identify with myriad things, accordingly the ruler sets himself apart from his ministers and people. It is in this conscious personification of *dao* that the ruler transcends the rest and achieves uniqueness. This uniqueness in turn endows him with an extraordinary power to bring all affairs under control (*Han Feizi* 29). Han Feizi may well be basing his theory of the ruler's uniqueness on Chapter 25 of the *Daodejing*: 'Hence the way [*dao*] is great; heaven is great; earth is great. Within the realm there are four things that are great, and the king counts as one.' He may also base his philosophical argument for the ruler's extraordinary power to control all affairs on Chapter 14 of the *Daodejing*: 'Hold onto the *dao* of old in order to master the things of the present' (see DAODEJING).

Thus, Han Feizi provided the most sophisticated philosophical justification for autocracy. The enduring significance of Han Feizi's Legalist philosophy is the legacy of two millennia of autocracy in China. Despite the dominance of Confucian orthodoxy, the political institutional framework of autocratic, centralized power has been essentially Legalist. Further, China is and has been an eminently bureaucratic society. Shen Buhai and Han Feizi's rational paradigm for bureaucratic accountability and merit-based functional specificity – for better or worse – has shaped the Chinese pattern and rhythm of life up to the present day. Of course, there were also strong departures from the Legalist model. However, after the eighteenth-century *philosophes* took a fancy to the Legalist model of bureaucracy based on merit, Shen Buhai may be considered 'the ancestor' of a worldwide institution of bureaucracy (Graham 1989). Lastly, the covert tradition of political technique (*shu*), inspired by purposive Daoism, namely 'non-action' as well as decisive action according to 'timeliness', continues to remain a significant aspect of Chinese philosophy of governing and political culture.

See also: AUTHORITY; CONFUCIAN PHILOSOPHY, CHINESE; MARXISM, CHINESE; CHINESE PHILOSOPHY; HISTORY, CHINESE THEORIES OF; DAO; DAOIST PHILOSOPHY; FA; HAN FEIZI; LAW AND RITUAL IN CHINESE PHILOSOPHY; LI; POLITICAL PHILOSOPHY, HISTORY OF; POLITICAL PHILOSOPHY, NATURE OF

References and further reading

Chang, L. (1979) 'Metamorphosis of Han Fei's Thought in the Early Han', in H. Rosemont and B. Schwartz (eds) *Studies in Classical Chinese Thought*: *Journal of the American Academy of Religion* 47 (3): 503–47. (An exploration into the continuing influence of Han Feizi's thought in the Early Han.)

Chang, L. and Wang, H.P. (1983) *Han Fei sixiangdi lishi yanjiu* (A Research into the History of Han Fei's Thought), Taipei: Linking (Lianjing) Publishing Co.; 2nd edn, Beijing: Zhonghua Book Co., 1986. (A detailed exposition of Han Feizi's main ideas.)

Fung Yu-lan (1952) *A History of Chinese Philosophy*, trans. D. Bodde, Princeton, NJ: Princeton University Press. (Vol. 1, chapter 13 contains a clear exposition of Legalist philosophy for upper level undergraduates.)

* Graham, A.C. (1989) *Disputers of the Tao: Philosophical Argument in Ancient China*, La Salle, IL: Open Court. (Erudite and evenhanded treatment of Legalist philosophy; for advanced students.)

* Guan Zhong (d. 645 BC) *Guanzi*, trans. of twelve chapters and notes by W. Allyn Rickett, *Kuan-tzu: A Repository of Early Chinese Thought*, Hong Kong: University of Hong Kong Press, 1965; trans. of thirty-five chapters and notes by W. Allyn Rickett, *Guanzi*, Princeton, NJ: Princeton University Press, 1985. (The work attributed to Guan Zhong is a miscellaneous collection of writings probably from the fourth to the second century BC. This is the most authoritative translation, intended for scholars in the field.)

* Han Feizi (*c.*280–233 BC) *Han Feizi*, trans. W.K. Liao, The *Complete Works of Han Fei Tzu*, London: Arthur Probsthain, vol. 1, 1938; vol. 2, 1959; trans. of twelve chapters and notes by B. Watson, *Han Fei Tzu: Basic Writings*, New York: Columbia University Press, 1964. (A good introduction to Legalist philosophy for upper level undergraduates. Liao is the only complete translation.)

* —— (*c.*280–233 BC) *Han Feizi jishi* (Collected Explanations of Han Feizi), ed. Chen Qiyu, Beijing: Zhonghua Book Co., 1958. (One of the exhaustively annotated texts on Han Feizi.)

* —— (c.280–233 BC) *Zengding Han Feizi jiaoshi* (Further Revisions of Collations and Explanations of Han Feizi), ed. Chen Qitian, Taipei: Taiwan Commercial Press, 1972. (Like Chen Qiyu's work, it is one of the thoroughly annotated texts on Han Feizi. This work has an unconventional textual sequence.)

* Schwartz, B.I. (1985) *The World of Thought in Ancient China*, Cambridge, MA: Harvard University Press. (Sophisticated and insightful exposition of Legalist philosophy that transcends the stereotypical views; for advanced students.)

* Shang Yang (390–338 BC) *Shangjunshu*, trans. J.J.L. Duyvendak, *The Book of Lord Shang*, London: Arthur Probsthain, 1928; repr. Chicago: University of Chicago Press, 1963. (Attributed to Shang Yang, this work was in all probability compiled over several decades at the beginning of the third century BC. This is the only translation available.)

* Shen Buhai (d. 337 BC) Fragments, in *Shen Pu-hai: A Chinese Political Philosopher of the Fourth Century B.C.*, Appendix C: The Shen Pu-hai Fragments, trans. H.G. Creel, Chicago: University of Chicago Press, 1974. (Thoroughly researched but controversial work; advanced reading. The actual dates of the Shen Buhai fragments are unknown.)

* Shen Dao (c.310 BC) Fragments, in P.M. Thompson (trans.) 'The Shen Tzu Fragments', University of Washington thesis, 1970, 512–75. (Painstakingly researched syntactical and philological exegesis; the only available translation.)

* Smith, A. (1759) *The Theory of Moral Sentiments*, ed. D.D. Raphael and A.L. Macfie, Oxford: Clarendon Press, 1976. (Smith's major work on moral philosophy.)

Vandermeersch, L. (1965) *La formation de Légisme: recherche sur la constitution d'une philosophie politique caractéristique de la Chine ancienne* (The Foundation of Legalism: Researches on a Political Philosophy unique to Ancient China), Paris: Publications de École Française d'Extrême-orient. (A comprehensive and imaginative treatment of the central figures and their development of Legalist 'mentality' in their respective periods.)

Wang, H.P. (1991) *Xianqin fajia sixiangshi lun* (Discourses on Pre-Qin Legalist Thought), Taipei: Linking (Lienjing) Publishing Co. (The most comprehensive and lucid account of Legalist philosophy.)

Wang, H.P. and Chang, L. (1986) *The Philosophical Foundations of Han Fei's Political Theory*, Honolulu, HI: University of Hawaii Press. (An elaboration of the Legalist vision and Daoism.)

LEO S. CHANG

LEGITIMACY

Legitimacy refers to the rightfulness of a powerholder or system of rule. The term originated in controversies over property and succession, and was used to differentiate children born of a lawful marriage from those who were 'illegitimate'. From thence the term entered political discourse via controversies over the rightful succession to the restored French throne after the Napoleonic period. However, questions about what makes government rightful have been a central issue of philosophical debate since the ancient Greeks, and in this sense the concept, if not the term, 'legitimacy' is as old as political philosophy itself. Its significance lies in the moral, as opposed to merely prudential, grounds for obedience which follow for subjects where power is rightfully acquired and exercised, and in the depth of allegiance which such political authorities can call upon in times of difficulty.

What, then, makes government legitimate? Most thinkers agree that a necessary condition is that power should be acquired and exercised according to established rules, whether these are conventionally or legally defined. However, legal validity cannot be a sufficient condition of legitimacy, since both the rules and the power exercised under them also have to be morally justifiable. Two broad criteria for moral justifiability can be distinguished: (1) political power should derive from a rightful source of authority; (2) it should satisfy the rightful ends or purposes of government. Most philosophical disputes about legitimacy take place either within or between these two broad positions; any adequate account of it must embrace both however.

1   **The source and ends of political authority**
2   **Social contract theories**
3   **'Performance' criteria of legitimacy**
4   **Legitimacy and liberal democracy**
5   **Social science and legitimacy**

1   The source and ends of political authority

Historically, claims made for the rightful source of political authority have been enormously diverse, including: divine authority, mediated via religious doctrine and its interpreters; tradition and the principle of continuity with a society's past; some infallible truth, such as Marxism-Leninism, about society's future destiny and its chosen agents; and the people as a whole, and the principle of popular sovereignty. Although the first of these is still defended within parts of the Islamic world, most Western political philosophy of the modern era has sought to establish a secular source for political authority. With the authority of tradition relegated to at most a secondary plane, and Marxism-Leninism now discredited, the principle of popular sovereignty is virtually uncontested in the contemporary world. Much room for disagreement remains, however, about which constitutional arrangements best realize this principle; and – between competing conceptions of nation and nationalism – about who precisely constitutes the people that is the source of political authority (see NATION AND NATIONALISM).

The alternative idea – that legitimate authority is one which realizes the rightful ends or purposes of government – has historically produced an equally varied set of criteria, according to how these ends or purposes have been defined: whether government exists to guarantee basic societal needs for security and subsistence; to realize some ideal conception of the good society and virtuous citizenship; or to protect specified individual rights. However, a common feature of any 'performance' criterion of legitimacy, even more clearly than for the first definition, is to establish a standard against which individual rulers or regimes can be assessed, and, where need be, found wanting. That is to say, theorizing about legitimacy typically has a critical, rather than a merely apologetic purpose; and it tends to flourish when the authority of government is already uncertain or contested (see AUTHORITY).

2   Social contract theories

The two broad types of legitimating criteria considered above – the source and the ends of political authority – were brought together in the early modern period by theorists of the social contract, such as HOBBES and LOCKE. According to social contract theory, government was a product of conscious human artifice; its legitimacy derived from its authorization by the people themselves. At the same time the deficiencies of the pre-governmental 'state of nature', which led people to enter into the social contract, both defined the proper purposes of government and also set limits to its legitimacy: according to Hobbes (1651), through the provision of physical security; according to Locke (1689), through the protection of natural rights and the rule of law. Where these purposes were manifestly broken, the obligation of subjects to government was at an end. For both writers, then, where popular authorization established the grounds of legitimate rule, the true purpose of government defined its *limits* (see CONTRACTARIANISM §§2, 5).

Subsequent critics of the two writers pointed to their arbitrary characterization of the state of nature from which the ends of government were to be derived. They also questioned whether (given that one took place) a once-for-all authorization of government through the social contract could conceivably serve to legitimate political authority for subsequent generations. Locke rightly rejected Hobbes' contention that contracts made under the duress of conquest were valid. However, his own notion of 'tacit consent', whereby those who chose not to leave the country or disown their inheritance were presumed to have agreed to the existing governmental arrangements, hardly constituted a robust condition for popular consent to, or authorization of, government (see CONSENT §2).

In his work *The Social Contract*, ROUSSEAU §3 claimed to have remedied the deficiencies in previous contract theorizing (Rousseau 1762). Political authority could be legitimate, he argued, only where citizens had the right to vote in person on legislation and where the executive was directly accountable to the sovereign legislative assembly. Whereas previous consent theory offered citizens no effective choice about accepting existing governmental arrangements, the unlimited legislative authority Rousseau gave his citizen body provided it with the continuous opportunity to modify received social and political rules. It could therefore meet the most strenuous conditions for popular consent to government. However, these conditions were bought at a price: a radical inequality of citizenship status between the sexes and the impracticality of direct legislation outside small-scale societies. If people could never autonomously consent to a representative system, then where could legitimate government realistically be found? Moreover, Rousseau's implausible contention that those who voted against any legislative proposal in the sovereign assembly had in some sense really willed it enabled him to evade the need to set constitutional limits to the scope of legislation, or to guarantee protection for individual or minority rights (see GENERAL WILL §§1–2).

3   'Performance' criteria of legitimacy

The cul-de-sac which social contract theory seemed to have reached with Rousseau led most subsequent thinkers to develop the second 'performance' dimension of legitimacy. For the utilitarians, the sole test of a rightful system of government lay in its capacity to promote the 'greatest happiness of the greatest number' (Bentham 1776, 1778) (see BENTHAM, J.). Democratic arrangements were to be defended, not on the principle of popular sovereignty, but only in so far as they served to protect the interests of the large majority against the sectional interests of the few (Mill 1821), or to develop those active qualities of citizenship which would enable people to relate their own interests to those of society as a whole (Mill 1864) (see MILL, J.S.). In contrast, idealist thinkers from Hegel to Green defined the purpose of government in more exclusively ethical terms: to develop the highest moral form of life for society. The rightful form of government was that which would be most conducive to this end.

'Performance' criteria of legitimacy have also been at the fore in recent political philosophy, albeit in a modified form of social contract theory. In the work of RAWLS, J. and his followers, the idea of the social contract is purely hypothetical: it is a device for establishing what social and political arrangements people *would* agree to, if they could imagine themselves ignorant of the social positions they would occupy or the individual characteristics and preferences they might possess (Rawls 1971). From this imagined pre-political condition we can then derive a list of basic rights and freedoms and criteria for fair decisional procedures which should command universal assent. What makes government legitimate on this view is not its *actual* authorization by the people, but its conformity to standards which they *would* authorize if they were truly impartial.

4 Legitimacy and liberal democracy

Rawls' work comes close to characterizing the underlying principles of a liberal-democratic order. As a theory of legitimacy, however, it is inadequate, being too one-dimensional. To satisfy the principle of popular sovereignty, a liberal-democratic regime has to meet criteria for the *actual* authorization of government by the people: not only through the regular, free and fair election of public officials in conditions of electoral equality, but also through the realistic opportunity to modify received constitutional arrangements by means of referendum and citizens' initiative. Only the combination of these conditions could plausibly meet the criteria for popular consent and authorization which social contract theory was aiming for, but failed to achieve. At the same time, the liberal-democratic state has also to meet continually evolving standards for the protection of individual rights and guarantee of social welfare if it is to satisfy defensible performance criteria of legitimacy (see DEMOCRACY).

Any adequate philosophical account of legitimacy, therefore, has to consider both the rightful source and ends of political authority; legitimate government must meet criteria of authorization and performance standards together. To recognize this is to identify one of the characteristic dilemmas of liberal democracy: the two dimensions of legitimacy may conflict with, as well as reinforce, one another. The governments and political arrangements that people actually choose to authorize may fail to meet defensible standards of fairness or rights protection for all citizens. This is because empirical persons with definable beliefs and interests differ in practice from the disembodied agents of a hypothetical social contract; and the circumstances of actual decision making can be far removed from the impartiality or Habermas' 'ideal-speech situation' of a pure legitimacy (see HABERMAS, J.). This tension is at its most acute in the conflict between forms of ethnic and particularistic self-definition of a people as a self-governing nation, on the one hand, and the universalistic standards implicit in any justifiable defence of individual rights or democratic citizenship, on the other.

5 Social science and legitimacy

Whereas a tendency of philosophical accounts of legitimacy is to dissolve the tensions between different legitimating principles by positing a transcendental world of impartial citizens inhabiting the good society, the tendency of social science accounts lies in a different, reductionist direction: to reduce legitimacy to whatever a given people *believes* to be legitimate. Social scientists are interested in legitimacy as an explanatory rather than a normative concept: to help explain why people actually obey authority, rather than why or when they should; why regimes actually persist, rather than whether they deserve to. From this perspective legitimacy tends to become, not a quality of regimes or governments, but an attribute of subjects: their internalized 'belief in legitimacy' (Weber 1914). Regimes are legitimate if they are able to generate and maintain the appropriate state of mind in their populations (Lipset 1960). Such an account produces a radical disjuncture between the projects of political science and political philosophy; analysing the empirical processes of *legitimation* comes to replace the construction of defensible criteria for *legitimacy*.

Social scientists can only escape from this reductionist dead-end if they acknowledge the same conceptual structure to legitimate power as do philosophers – as a matter of conformity to rules which are themselves justifiable in terms of specific beliefs about the rightful source and ends of political authority – and if they see the process of legitimation to lie in the actions of relevant subjects confirming their support for the regime or its powerholders (Beetham 1991). Equipped with this conceptual structure, social science can then make its own distinctive contribution to the study of legitimacy: through a comparative analysis of different legitimating principles and processes in different societies and epochs, and of the way these are embedded in institutional structures and practices; through an identification of the gaps that may develop between the underlying principles of a regime and their supporting beliefs, on the one hand, and its actual practice on the other; and through an examination of the processes of de-legitimation which may herald its collapse.

A comparative analysis of this kind can also serve to complement a philosophical account of liberal-democratic legitimacy by exploring why it tends to win out in competition with other legitimating principles, especially once a population attains a developed level of education and literacy. At this point the explanation of why societies come to have the legitimating principles they do cannot be divorced from the defensibility of their grounds for holding them; and such principles must be recognized as legitimate in a context of international, not merely national, scrutiny and debate. In the explanation of legitimacy, in other words, the projects of normative philosophy and a non-behaviouristic social science can be seen to become one and the same.

References and further reading

* Beetham, D. (1991) *The Legitimation of Power*, Basingstoke: Macmillan. (Comprehensive review of legitimacy from a social science perspective; see §5.)
* Bentham, J. (1776, 1778) *A Fragment on Government and An Introduction to the Principles of Morals and Legislation*, ed. W. Harrison, Oxford: Clarendon Press, 1948. (Classic statement of the utilitarian criterion for rightful government; see §3.)
  Connolly, W. (ed.) (1984) *Legitimacy and the State*, Oxford: Blackwell. (Useful introductory collection.)
  Green, T.H. (1885) *Lectures on the Principles of Political Obligation*, ed. P. Harris and J. Morrow, Cambridge: Cambridge University Press, 1986. (Classic review of political obligation and its relation to state legitimacy; see §3.)
  Habermas, J. (1976) *Legitimation Crisis*, London: Heinemann. (Influential account of the criteria for political legitimacy and the conditions for legitimacy crisis in contemporary capitalist democracies; see §4.)
  Hegel, G.W.F. (1821) *Philosophy of Right*, ed. T.M. Knox, Oxford: Clarendon Press, 1952. (Classic account of legitimacy from the standpoint of philosophical idealism; see §3.)
* Hobbes, T. (1651) *Leviathan*, ed. R. Tuck, Cambridge: Cambridge University Press, 1991. (Controversial but highly influential early modern theory which derives political legitimacy from the authorization of an original social contract; see §2.)
* Lipset, S.M. (1960) *Political Man*, New York: Doubleday. (Source for a subjective account of legitimacy in popular acceptability; see §5.)
* Locke, J. (1689) *Two Treatises of Government*, ed. P. Laslett, Cambridge: Cambridge University Press, 3rd edn, 1988. (Important for a consent theory of political legitimacy, which also emphasizes the rule of law and rights protection as conditions; see §2.)
* Mill, J. (1821) 'Essay on Government', in T. Ball (ed.) *James Mill: Political Writings*, Cambridge: Cambridge University Press, 1992. (Classic utilitarian statement of the criteria for good government; see §3.)
* Mill, J.S. (1864) 'On Representative Government', in A.D. Lindsay (ed.) *J.S. Mill: Utilitarianism, Liberty, Representative Government*, London: Dent, 1964. (Important development of utilitarian theory, incorporating a more complex account of human interests; see §3.)
* Rawls, J. (1971) *A Theory of Justice*, Oxford: Clarendon Press. (This famous work on justice also offers a theory of political legitimacy and of the limits of obligation; see §3.)
* Rousseau, J.-J. (1762) *The Social Contract*, ed. M. Cranston, Harmondsworth: Penguin, 1965. (Important for the stringent criteria it sets for the legitimacy of, and popular consent to, law and government; see §2.)
* Weber, M. (1914) *Economy and Society*, ed. G. Roth and C. Wittich, New York: Bedminster Press, 1968. (The source for much discussion of legitimacy within twentieth-century social science; see §5.)

DAVID BEETHAM

LEIBNIZ, GOTTFRIED WILHELM (1646–1716)

Leibniz was one of the central figures of seventeenth-century philosophy, indeed, one of the central intellectual figures of his age. Born and educated in Germany, he travelled to Paris in 1672 and quickly entered into its lively intellectual and scientific life, acquainting himself with the most advanced ideas then in circulation. It was there that he invented the infinitesimal calculus, and laid the foundations for the philosophical and scientific programmes that were to occupy him for the rest of his life. He returned to Germany in 1676, entering the service of the House of Hanover where, except for brief absences, he remained until his death. There, along with his court duties, he had time for a wide variety of intellectual activities that eventually gained him an international reputation.

*Leibniz's philosophy, particularly his metaphysics, can appear otherworldly and complex. But there are a few simple themes and basic commitments that run through his thought. At root is his philosophical optimism, the commitment that this is the best of all possible worlds, freely created by a rational God who always chooses the best for a good reason. This best of all possible worlds, Leibniz held, is 'the one which is at the same time the simplest in hypotheses and the richest in phenomena' (*Discourse on Metaphysics *§6). For this reason, the world must be governed by a variety of general principles to which Leibniz appealed in his philosophy: there must be a sufficient reason for everything in the world; there are no jumps in nature; there must be exactly the same power in the full cause as there is in the complete effect, among many others. While such principles do not deductively determine the rest of Leibniz's philosophy, they do play a major role in shaping it; they constitute a kind of lens through which he viewed the major philosophical issues of his age.*

One such issue concerns the ultimate make-up of the world. Like many of his contemporaries, Leibniz adopted a mechanistic view, according to which everything in the physical world is explicable in terms of the size, shape and motion of the tiny bodies that make up the grosser bodies of experience. But he rejected the idea that this could be the ultimate explanation for things. Behind the mechanistic world of inanimate bodies in motion, Leibniz saw a world of living things and souls – active, genuinely individual, genuinely different from one another, the true atoms of nature, the true reality – which he eventually called monads. At the deepest level, Leibniz's world was made up of an infinity of mind-like entities, each with its own perceptions that change from moment to moment according to an internal programme by way of the faculty of appetition, all in harmony with one another so that they all reflect the same world. While the world of physics is mechanistic, it is merely phenomenal, the confused appearance of a deeper reality. A consequence of this was Leibniz's famous doctrine of pre-established harmony. In contrast to Descartes, for whom mind and body interact, and in contrast to the occasionalists, for whom God is the true cause who brings about motion in the body on the occasion of a volition and a sensation in the mind on the occasion of a stimulation of the appropriate nerves in the body, for Leibniz God created the mind (a single monad) and the body (itself a collection of monads) in perfect harmony with one another so that their mental and physical states would always correspond in the appropriate way.

*A second set of metaphysical issues of central concern to Leibniz involves the interlocking questions of necessity, contingency and freedom. In response to contemporaries such as Hobbes and Spinoza, Leibniz tried to find room for contingency and freedom in his world. He argued that even though God is, in a sense, constrained to choose the best, he does so freely. Consequently, the world he created, the best of all possible worlds, exists contingently, and at least some features of it are contingent, those whose contraries are not in themselves impossible. So for example, 2 + 3 = 5, true in every possible world, is necessary, while 'Adam sins', whose contrary is not impossible, is contingent. But over and above contingency and divine freedom, Leibniz also wanted to make room for human freedom. According to Leibniz, when God created Adam as a part of this best of all possible worlds, he knew that Adam would sin; it is part of the concept of Adam that he sins, part of his internal 'programme' that he will eat the apple, and part of the internal 'programmes' of the monads that make up his body that he will actually eat the apple. But, Leibniz argued, what God builds in is that Adam *freely *chose to sin. God builds into the world the reasons that incline Adam's will without necessitating it, correctly predicting what Adam will do, and building the rest of the world around the consequences of Adam's free actions.*

Important as they are, these two concerns constitute only a small portion of Leibniz's thought, even within the domain of philosophy. In psychology, he introduced a distinction between conscious and unconscious perceptions and tried to understand the way in which unconscious perceptions ('petites perceptions') in part determine conscious perceptions ('apperceptions'). In epistemology, he is important for his sophisticated version of the innatist hypothesis, and for appreciating the role that a mathematical theory of probability can play in understanding the world. In logic, Leibniz advanced programmes for a new formal logic more powerful than Aristotle's, and for a universal language. In ethics and political thought, he contributed to the seventeenth-century natural law tradition. In natural philosophy, he emphasized the importance of the notion of force and advanced the broadly Cartesian programme of a physics grounded in conservation laws. Outside philosophy he is well known for his work on the calculus. Though he co-discovered it with Newton, it is his notation that is still used, and his version probably had the greater influence in his day. But he was a major contributor to many other fields, including geology, natural history, linguistics and European history. Though he left no real school of followers, he deeply influenced philosophy after his death, particularly in eighteenth-century Germany.

1 Life
2 The programme

1 Life

Gottfried Wilhelm Leibniz was born in Leipzig on 1 July 1646. He later recalled how his father, who died when he was only six years old, had instilled in him a love of learning. Leibniz started school when he was seven, but more important than his formal education in those years was his reading. He taught himself Latin at an early age in order to be able to read Livy and Calvisius, and because of that was admitted into his late father's extensive library, where he read widely. At fifteen Leibniz entered University, first the University of Leipzig (1661–66), and then the University of Altdorf (1666–67), graduating with degrees in law and in philosophy. The education he received there was conservative, a mixture of traditional Aristotelian school philosophy and Renaissance humanism. Though invited to join the faculty at Altdorf, he chose instead to enter the service of the Elector of Mainz, where he stayed until he was sent to Paris in the spring of 1672 on diplomatic business.

While he had done significant work in a number of areas before going to Paris, including law, theology, mathematics and physics, the trip was crucial to Leibniz's intellectual development. In the later part of the seventeenth century, learned Europe was in the midst of a great intellectual revolution; the older Aristotelian philosophy of the schools was being challenged by a new mechanist philosophy which rejected the form, matter and qualities of the Aristotelian world, replacing them with a world in which everything was to be explained in terms of size, shape and motion. In this new world there was a special emphasis on mathematics, which was increasingly applied to problems in physics in a way quite foreign to the Aristotelian philosophy.

Though he had taken an interest in the moderns while in Germany (HOBBES was particularly influential on his early thought), it was only after he reached Paris that Leibniz was able to enter the mainstream of European intellectual life. There he came to know the important mathematician and physicist Christiaan Huygens, who introduced him to new ideas which Leibniz absorbed quickly. In those years, Leibniz laid the foundations of his calculus, his later physics and his philosophy. While there were no publications at the time, many unpublished notes survive, important for understanding the emergence of his mature thought.

Leibniz returned to Germany in December 1676, passing through Holland, where he discussed philosophy with the reclusive SPINOZA. It was then that he first entered the service of the House of Hanover. He served under Duke Johann Friedrich until his death in 1679, under Duke Ernst August from 1680 to 1698, and then, finally, under the Elector Georg Ludwig, who ascended the throne of Great Britain as King George I in 1714. Except for his travels, he remained at Hanover for the rest of his life. There Leibniz undertook a very wide variety of tasks. He served as a mining engineer (unsuccessfully supervising the draining of the silver mines in the Harz Mountains), as head librarian of a large collection of books, as a general advisor and a diplomat, and was particularly interested in finding ways for the Catholics and the Protestants to reunite. Leibniz was also given the responsibility for writing a history of the House of Hanover. While he collected and published many previously unknown historical documents and published a number of other historical writings, this project barely got off the ground. All that he seems to have completed was a geological history of the region of Lower Saxony, the *Protogaea*. While it proved to be an important work in the history of geology when it was finally published in 1749, it seems not to have pleased Leibniz's employers who had hoped for a history of somewhat more recent times.

Through the rest of his life, Leibniz continued to explore the philosophical, scientific and mathematical questions that interested him from his earliest years. The 1680s and 1690s saw some of his most important writings. In these years, he published his new infinitesimal calculus and a variety of papers outlining his new approach to physics, particularly his new science of dynamics, the science of force and its laws. The *Brevis demonstratio* of 1686 presents for the first time a refutation of Descartes' conservation law, and hints at the foundations of a more adequate physics. The details are developed in his unpublished *Dynamica* (1690), some material from which is published in the *Specimen dynamicum* in 1695, as well as in the numerous answers to attempted refutations of his argument from tenacious Cartesians. In philosophy, Leibniz published his *Meditationes de cognitione, veritate et ideis* (Meditations on knowledge, truth and ideas) in 1684, and in 1686 composed the *Discours de métaphysique* (Discourse on metaphysics), eventually published in 1846; the main arguments from the latter are discussed in a series of letters with the Catholic theologian Antoine ARNAULD, letters Leibniz contemplated publishing in later years. These same themes are found, somewhat transformed, in two important publications in the 1690s, the *Système nouveau de la nature et de la communication des sustances* (New system of the nature and the communication of substances) (1695b) and the *De ipsa natura* (On nature itself) (1698). In the first decades of the next century, Leibniz continued to be very active. Important in these years were the *Nouveaux essais* (New essays) (1704), a close examination of Locke's *Essay Concerning Human Understanding*, abandoned at Locke's death and unpublished until 1765. But he did publish his *Théodicée* (Theodicy) (1710), a compendium of philosophical and theological ideas involving further development of themes that go far back in his thought. His final philosophical works were short summaries, intended only as brief guides to his work, the *Monadologie* (Monadology) and the *Principes de la nature et de la grâce* (Principles of nature and grace), both of which probably date from 1714.

Throughout these years Leibniz kept up a vast correspondence, including exchanges with Huygens, Johann Bernoulli, Burchardus de Volder and Bartholomaeus Des Bosses, among many others. One exchange is particularly important. Leibniz had been at war with his English counterpart, Sir Isaac Newton, for many years; their rivalry went back to at least the early 1690s, and probably to their first contact in the mid-1670s. The affair was ugly, with accusations of plagiarism regarding the calculus from both sides, and bitter disagreements over the foundations of physics. The rivalry finally resulted, in 1715–16, in a correspondence between Leibniz and Samuel Clarke, the latter standing in for Newton himself (see CLARKE, S. §3). The exchange was published by Clarke in 1717.

When his employer Georg Ludwig went to London in 1714 to take the throne of Great Britain, Leibniz did not follow. He was out of favour for his failure to make progress on the history of the House of Hanover, as well as for his generally old-fashioned manner. Furthermore, it is likely that Georg feared that the dispute with Newton and the British intellectual establishment would cause difficulties. Whatever the reason, Leibniz remained in Hanover, where he died on 14 November 1716. Though celebrated in his life and considered a universal genius for the breadth of his interests and activities, in death he was virtually ignored, buried with little ceremony in a grave that was to remain unmarked for many years.

2   The programme

Leibniz never wrote a single work, book or article, that constitutes a canonical exposition of his thought, preferring the short article or letter where he presents his thought from one or another point of view, often in response to the thought of another (DESCARTES was a favourite target), or in response to questions from a correspondent. Indeed, Leibniz's complex thought seems to resist the kind of comprehensive treatment found in works like Descartes' *Meditations* or Spinoza's *Ethics*. Furthermore, it is only to be expected that Leibniz's beliefs changed over his long career, and from one presentation of his philosophy to another.

Despite its complexity, there are some themes and characteristics that run throughout Leibniz's thought, at least in the mature period that starts after his return from Paris in the late 1670s, the period on which this entry concentrates. (While there was not a radical break from the early years to the later, there is certainly a marked development.) Basic to his thought was his philosophical optimism: this is the best of all possible worlds, freely created by a rational God, who always chooses the best for a good reason, without any arbitrariness. It is because of our limited understanding that we cannot determine a priori all the general or particular features of this world. This conception of God and his creation shaped Leibniz's philosophy: the world is ultimately both rational and in every way perfect. Furthermore, though Leibniz's philosophical intelligence ranged widely, certain problems were particularly important to him. In an untitled note from the late 1680s he wrote: 'there are two labyrinths of the human mind, one concerning the composition of the continuum, and the other concerning the nature of freedom, and they arise from the same source, infinity' (Leibniz 1989: 95). The labyrinth of the composition of the continuum concerns the ultimate make-up of the world; the labyrinth of freedom concerns how freedom and contingency are possible in the world. The solution to both involves understanding the literally infinite complexity found in the world God created. Leibniz had an opinion about virtually every philosophical and scientific issue of his day, but these two issues consistently drew his attention.

3   God: creation and theodicy

Like many of his contemporaries, Leibniz thought that the existence of God could be proved, and he was particularly attracted by the so-called Ontological Argument, invented by Anselm and revised by Descartes (see GOD, ARGUMENTS FOR THE EXISTENCE

OF §§2–3). According to the Ontological Argument, as given by Descartes and paraphrased by Leibniz in *Meditations on knowledge, truth and ideas* ([1684a] 1989: 25), 'whatever follows from the idea or definition of anything can be predicated of that thing. Since the most perfect being includes all perfections, among which is existence, existence follows from the idea of God.... Therefore existence can be predicated of God'. Leibniz's contribution to the argument is the observation that, as it stands, the argument is not valid: 'from this argument we can conclude only that, if God is possible, then it follows that he exists'. For the argument to work, we must establish the self-consistency of the definition of God. But the consistency of the definition of God follows directly from the fact that God 'is without limits, without negation, and consequently without contradiction' (*Monadology* §45). In addition to this version of the ontological argument, Leibniz also used a cosmological argument for the existence of God, arguing from the existence of contingent things in the world, things whose reason lies outside of themselves, to the existence of a necessary being (*De rerum originatione radicali* (On the ultimate origination of things) (1697); *Monadology* §45). Finally, Leibniz argued from the existence of eternal truths: 'Without [God] there would be nothing real in possibles, and not only would nothing exist, but also nothing would be possible' (*Monadology* §43).

In the opening sections of the *Discourse on Metaphysics* (1686b: §6), Leibniz argued that 'God has chosen the most perfect world, that is, the one which is at the same time the simplest in hypotheses and the richest in phenomena', a formula that recurs often in his writings. While this is the main account of creation, in other texts, particularly the essay *On the ultimate origination of things*, he argued that 'there is a certain urge for existence or (so to speak) a straining toward existence in possible things or in possibility or essence itself; in a word, essence in and of itself strives for existence' (Leibniz [1697] 1989: 150). Leibniz continued: 'From this it is obvious that of the infinite combinations of possibilities and possible series, the one that exists is the one through which the most essence or possibility is brought into existence'. Such an account of creation has the apparent implication that God is not necessary for it, and that creation results from a quasi-mechanistic weighing of possibilities with respect to one another. But Leibniz emphasized that God is the ground of all possibles, and that it is God who ultimately actualizes the possibles that 'win' the 'contest'. The 'striving possibles' account of creation would seem to be a metaphorical way of expressing Leibniz's usual account in terms of God's choice of the best of all possible worlds.

Leibniz's account of creation had a number of important implications. First, against Descartes and Spinoza, it entailed that there is a standard of goodness and perfection that exists independently of God; God creates the world because it is good, a world which is good not just because it is the creation of God (*Discourse* §2). Furthermore, unlike MALEBRANCHE, Leibniz held that the world could not have been created better than it is (*Discourse* §§3–4). Leibniz's doctrine of creation can also be read as a direct attack against a conception of God argued by Spinoza. Central to Spinoza's enterprise in the *Ethics* is an attack on the view that God is like us, that he has aims and goals, that he chooses things for a reason, and that he is bound by standards of goodness that exist independently of his will. This anthropomorphic view of God, Spinoza argued, is an illusion, a projection of our own nature onto nature at large (see SPINOZA, B. DE §4). Against Spinoza, Leibniz presented his own God, who deliberately chooses to create this world for a particular reason, because it is the best of all possible worlds, a reason intelligible to us. It is on this basis that Leibniz argued against both Descartes and Spinoza for the importance of final causes in nature.

Leibniz's account of creation also addressed the problem of understanding divine justice, in particular, how sin, evil and suffering are possible in a world created by God – the 'theodicy' problem, to use the word coined by Leibniz. His answer was complex, filling many pages in *Theodicy*, the only philosophical book he published in his lifetime. Briefly, his argument was that evil is a necessary and unavoidable consequence of God's having chosen to create the best of all possible worlds. However bad we might think things are in our world, they would be worse in any other.

Leibniz's account of creation was closely connected with a number of his key principles, most prominently the Principle of Sufficient Reason. As he wrote later in the *Monadology* (§53), 'since there is an infinity of possible universes in God's ideas, and since only one of them can exist, there must be a sufficient reason for God's choice, a reason which determines Him towards one thing rather than another'. The Principle of Sufficient Reason entails that the universe is in principle rational and intelligible: God must always act for a reason, and as a consequence, there must be a reason for everything. But the account of creation was also connected with a number of other principles in Leibniz's philosophy (discussed below). In this way one can say that the doctrine of creation underlies all of Leibniz's philosophy. Had we God's intellect, we would be able to derive all of the features of this world directly from its being the best of all possible worlds.

As it is, our understanding of God's creation will enable us to fix certain general truths about this world, and set certain bounds on our hypotheses about the way things are.

Leibniz's interest in philosophical theology was not just the interest of a philosopher. He believed that his understanding of truths about God and nature would greatly assist the undertaking of uniting the Catholic and Protestant Churches under the umbrella of the true philosophy.

4 Metaphysics: substance, monad and the problem of the continuum

Leibniz is famous for his claim that he solved the problem of the composition of the continuum. In so far as the continuum (length, area, volume) is divisible, it would seem to be made up out of parts. But what parts could make it up? If the parts are extended (like atoms), then they too are divisible, and we require an account of their composition as well. On the other hand, if the parts are non-extended (like points), then it is difficult to see how they could make up an extended magnitude. Leibniz's solution was this: the mathematical continuum should not be thought of as being *composed* of parts at all; while it has parts, those parts are the result of the division of the whole, and thus are posterior to it. On the other hand, Leibniz claimed, while real physical extensions have parts, there are no physical continua. Physical extended things are at root discrete multitudes whose constituents are substances ('Remarques sur les Objections de M. Foucher' (Remarks on the objections of M. Foucher) (1696); Leibniz to de Volder, 19 January 1706). This raises one of the central problems for Leibniz's philosophy: what are these substances that constitute the metaphysically ultimate constituents of the world?

While there are many paths into his views on substance, Leibniz's critique of Descartes' notion of corporeal substance is a convenient starting place. Descartes held that the essence of body is extension. What this meant is that bodies are geometrical objects made concrete, entities that have no properties that are not grounded in extension. Colour, taste, sound and so on are not themselves in bodies, but are only sensations in minds caused by our interaction with extended substances. While Leibniz as a mechanist agreed with this last claim, he rejected the Cartesian conception of body on which it is based (see DESCARTES, R. §§8, 11).

Leibniz offered a number of arguments against the Cartesian conception of bodily substance: (1) The notion of extension presupposes some quality that is extended, like whiteness in milk or resistance to new motion in every body, and so is not the kind of thing that by itself could constitute the essence of anything (Leibniz to de Volder, 30 June 1704; 'Note on Cartesian natural philosophy', 1702). (2) In so far as extended things are divisible, they are aggregates made up out of parts. But the reality of the aggregate presupposes some genuine individuals of which the aggregate is composed; no such individuals can be found in Cartesian bodies (Leibniz to Arnauld, 30 April 1687; *Monadology* §§1–3). (3) If the world is full and there are no vacua, and if the world is filled with Cartesian extended substance, then there can be no change in the world. For any supposed change would consist in one portion of body replacing another, identical in every way ('On nature itself'). (4) If body were just extension, then it would be perfectly inert, and would have to be moved by God. If so, then God's creation would be imperfect for lacking creatures which cannot themselves carry out any of God's commands. Indeed, such a world would reduce to Spinoza's world in which finite things are just modes of God ('On nature itself'). Because of arguments like these, Leibniz wanted to take the Cartesian mechanist analysis of body back one step further, and resolve even extension into something more basic still, a world of substances that are genuinely individual, genuinely active, and which contain properties that distinguish individual substances from one another.

While there are a number of important discussions of the nature of substance in Leibniz's writings, two are especially noteworthy: the one he gave in the *Discourse on Metaphysics* at the start of his mature period, and the one he gave at the very end of his life in the *Monadology*. (There is a third important conception of substance that arises in the dynamical writings, discussed below in connection with his physics.)

Leibniz begins Section 8 of the *Discourse on Metaphysics* by noting that 'it is evident that all true predication has some basis in the nature of things, and that, when a proposition is not an identity, that is, when the predicate is not explicitly contained in the subject, it must be contained in it virtually'. (This principle, which probably derived from Leibniz's logical studies a few years earlier, was closely connected with the Principle of Sufficient Reason in Leibniz's mind; the containment of the concept of the predicate in the concept of the subject constitutes the 'sufficient reason' for the truth of a proposition. This connection with his logic has caused some commentators to see Leibniz's metaphysics as fundamentally logical in its inspiration.) And so, Leibniz claims, 'the subject term must always contain the predicate term, so that one who understands perfectly the notion of the subject would also know that the predicate belongs to it'. He concludes that 'the nature of an individual substance or of a complete being is to have a notion so complete that it is sufficient to contain and to allow us to deduce from it all the predicates of the subject to which this notion is to be attributed'. Since he held that there must be something in the substance itself in virtue of which this complete notion holds of it, he also concludes that at any given time, a substance must contain marks and traces of everything that is true of it, past, present and future – though only God could see them all. (It is not clear whether this committed Leibniz to holding that all properties of a given individual are essential to that individual, making him a kind of 'superessentialist', or whether he takes the weaker position that they are merely internal to the individual, making him a 'superintrinsicalist'. Opinions differ among the commentators.)

In the *Monadology* Leibniz offers a somewhat different characterization of substance. Using the term 'monad' that he adopted to express the notion of an individual substance in the late 1690s, he expounds: 'The monad…is nothing but a simple substance that enters into composites – simple, that is, without parts. And there must be simple substances, since there are composites; for the composite is nothing more than a collection, or aggregate, of simples. But where there are no parts, neither extension, nor shape, nor divisibility is possible. These monads are the true atoms of nature and, in brief, the elements of things' (*Monadology* §§1–3). So understood, the Leibnizian world is grounded in non-extended simple substances, whose principal property is non-divisibility and thus, Leibniz inferred, non-extension.

From these basic characterizations of the individual or simple substance (what Leibniz called a 'monad' after the mid-1690s), he inferred a number of important properties. The individual substance or monad is a genuine unity that cannot be split, something explicit in the *Monadology* account, less so on the earlier account in the *Discourse*. Consequently, it can begin only by divine creation, and can end only with divine annihilation; it is naturally ungenerable and incorruptible. On both accounts, individual substances or monads are the sources of all their activity, and cannot be altered or changed by the direct action of others; it is in this sense that Leibniz said that 'monads have no windows through which something can enter or leave' (*Monadology* §7). In the *Discourse* he derives this from the fact that a substance contains within itself all of the grounds of all its properties; there is no need – and no room – for any external causality. In the *Monadology* it is derived

directly from the fact that monads are non-extended. The apparent action of one substance on another must be analysed in terms of the relations between the internal states of the one and the internal states of the other (as discussed below). Finally, because of the relations that hold between one substance and another, Leibniz argued that each individual substance or monad reflects the entire world of which it is a part, a thesis closely connected with the hypothesis of pre-established harmony (also discussed below). Though all the individual substances reflect the same one world, they each reflect it from a different point of view, adding the perfection of variety to God's creation (*Discourse* §§9, 15; *Monadology* §§4–7). This conception of harmony can be traced back to the Paris period and, perhaps, to Leibniz's earliest writings on physics.

On Leibniz's view, substances are distinguished from one another by their momentary perceptions, and by the appetitions, the internal source of a substance's activity that lead from one perceptual state to another. In so far as a substance has such appetitions, 'the present is pregnant with the future' (*Monadology* §22). Since there can be no external influences, each monad is created by God with a kind of internal programme, as it were, which determines all of the states that it will take and the order in which it will take them. Although the Cartesian soul is an important model for the individual substance (Leibniz to de Volder, *c.*1699), there are significant differences. While the momentary states are called perceptions, not all such perceptions are conscious. (Conscious perceptions are said to be 'appperceptions' in Leibniz's terminology, though because nature makes no leaps in this best of all possible worlds, there must be a continuous gradation between the unconscious and the conscious.) In scholastic thought, appetition is the general faculty that leads to change in a substance, of which will (or rational appetite) is a special case in rational souls. For Leibniz, too, not all appetition is rational. For these reasons, he distinguished carefully between rational souls, like ours, and monads with lesser degrees of consciousness and rationality – what he sometimes calls 'bare monads' (*Monadology* §§8–24).

5 Metaphysics: monad, body and corporeal substance

Much of Leibniz's attention was focused on the level of the individual substance or monad, the atom of nature and the building-block of his world, that which in some sense underlies the world of bodies. But in addition to the simple substances, Leibniz often also recognized complex substances, corporeal substances, particularly in the 1680s and 1690s. Corporeal substances are understood on analogy with the human being, a soul (itself an individual substance) united with an organic body. Leibniz often used Aristotelian language to characterize the corporeal substance, calling the soul its form, and the organic body its matter (see ARISTOTLE §§8, 11). The organic body of a corporeal substance is itself made up of corporeal substances, each of which is a soul united to another, smaller organic body, in a sequence of tinier and tinier organisms that goes to infinity, a manifestation of the infinite variety in this best of all possible worlds that God created. Leibniz distinguished corporeal substances from corporeal aggregates, aggregates of animate corporeal substances whose unity is only mental, imposed by the mind, which perceives a group of substances together. While these corporeal substances are ultimately made up of non-extended individual substances, Leibniz's position (at least before 1704) seems to have been that these corporeal substances, as substances, are the genuine individuals whose reality grounds the aggregates that constitute inanimate bodies.

As discussed below, the soul of a corporeal substance is united to its body by virtue of pre-established harmony. However, by 1704, in response to criticism from René-Joseph de Tournemine, Leibniz came to think that this link does not produce genuine unity, and the notion of a corporeal substance becomes problematic for him. While he continued to assert that the physical world is made up of an infinite hierarchy of organisms, after this date he was not so sure that these organisms constitute genuine substances. (Nevertheless, Leibniz always thought that every monad has a body, and cannot exist without one, even if the monad together with its body does not constitute a genuine substance. Even in death the monad has a body, just a body radically smaller than the one it had had in 'life'.) The problem of constructing complex substances from monads led Leibniz in his correspondence with Des Bosses to explore the idea of a *vinculum substantiale*, or a substantial bond. While it is not clear that he ever really endorsed this idea, he does seem to have taken the problem of corporeal substance seriously in that dialogue.

However the issue of corporeal substance is treated, body had a kind of subordinate status for Leibniz. While corporeal substances may be genuine substances, genuinely individual and genuinely active, and thus genuinely real, they are still grounded in non-extended individual substances or monads. And inanimate bodies are inevitably phenomenal, whether the appearance resulting from a multitude of organic corporeal substances, or simply the appearance presented by an infinite multitude of non-extended

substances. In this way, one can see Leibniz's philosophy as an inspiration for the distinction between the noumenal and the phenomenal worlds in Kant's philosophy. But in contrast to Kant, who claimed that we cannot know the noumenal world of the thing-in-itself, Leibniz is quite confident that he knows exactly how things are in themselves: they are monads (see KANT, I. §3).

6 Metaphysics: mind, body and harmony

A basic feature of Leibniz's metaphysics was his doctrine that everything reflects the entire world in which it exists. This harmony among things derives from God at creation, who adjusts the perceptions of individual substances or monads to one another in creating a world more perfect by virtue of its variety. And so, despite the fact that individual substances cannot communicate directly with one another, and thus have no real metaphysical causal relations with one another, yet there is an extended sense in which what happens in one substance can be considered the cause of what happens in another. Leibniz wrote: 'The action of one finite substance on another consists only in the increase of the degree of expression together with the diminution of the expression of the other, insofar as God requires them to accommodate themselves to one another' (*Discourse* §15; compare *Monadology* §52). God, in creating a given substance to perform a particular action at a given time, creates all other substances in such a way as to reflect that action at that time. This is what might be called *physical* causality, as distinct from *metaphysical* causality which Leibniz denied among finite things.

While every monad or substance is related in some way to every other, there is a special relationship between the mind and the body of a living thing, such as the human being: 'Although each created monad represents the whole universe, it more distinctly represents the body which is particularly affected by it, and whose entelechy it constitutes. And just as this body expresses the whole universe through the interconnection of all matter in the plenum (that is, space without empty place), the soul also represents the whole universe by representing this body, which belongs to it in a particular way' (*Monadology* §62; compare *Discourse* §33). In this way, the mind is connected with the world by virtue of the special connection it has with the body; on Leibniz's understanding of causality, mind and body can be the 'physical' causes of changes in one another.

So Leibniz solved to his satisfaction one of the central problems in seventeenth-century metaphysics: the interaction between mind and body. Because of the special harmony between mind and body, just when my body is in the state it would be in if it were pricked by a pin, my mind is programmed to have a sensation of pain. And just when my mind is in the state of willing my arm to raise, my body is in the physical state that would result in the raising of my arm, again not because of any direct causal connection (Leibniz to Arnauld, 28 November/8 December 1686 and 30 April 1687). For that reason, Leibniz wrote: 'According to this system, bodies act as if there were no souls (though this is impossible); and souls act as if there were no bodies; and both act as if each influenced the other' (*Monadology* §81). This is what he originally called the hypothesis of concomitance, but called the hypothesis of pre-established harmony when he published it for the first time in the *New system* (1695b).

The view is summarized in an analogy he often used. The mind and the body can be compared to two clocks that keep perfect agreement. One hypothesis to explain their agreement is that of natural influence, the hypothesis that there is some physical connection between the one clock and the other. This corresponds to Descartes' view of mind–body interaction, where there is real causal influence. The second hypothesis is that someone watches over the two clocks and, by tinkering with them, always keeps them in agreement. This corresponds to the occasionalism of many of Descartes' followers, in which mind–body causality is mediated by God who causes sensations in the mind on the occasion of an appropriate bodily state, and actions in the body on the occasion of the appropriate volition in the mind (see OCCASIONALISM). Finally there is the hypothesis that the clocks are so well made that they will always remain in perfect agreement with one another. This corresponds to the hypothesis of pre-established harmony, which Leibniz thought to be the most defensible (Leibniz to Basnage de Beauval 3/13 January 1696).

Leibniz offered a number of arguments directly against occasionalism. He argued, for example, that there must be genuine activity in things themselves because a world of genuinely active things is more perfect than a world of things manipulated by God; indeed, Leibniz claimed, a world of inert things is just the Spinozistic world in which God is the only substance of which other things are modes ('On nature itself'). He also argued that occasionalism posits perpetual miracles, in so far as God is called in to do that which goes beyond the power of things to do by their own nature (Leibniz to Arnauld, 30 April 1687). As noted below, the conception of the physical world that informs Leibniz's dynamics is itself a direct challenge to occasionalism. Nevertheless, Leibniz did share at least one important doctrine with occasion-

alism: that finite substances have no real causal relations with one another. This doctrine may strike a modern reader as eccentric, but it would have been rather less so for a seventeenth-century reader.

Leibniz often presented the hypothesis of pre-established harmony as a solution to the problem of mind–body interaction. But, at the same time, it allowed Leibniz to reconcile the mechanistic conception of the world with a conception grounded in final causes. He wrote: 'The soul follows its own laws and the body also follows its own; and they agree in virtue of the harmony pre-established between all substances.... Souls act according to the laws of final causes, through appetitions, ends, and means. Bodies act according to the laws of efficient causes or of motions. And these two kingdoms, that of efficient causes and that of final causes, are in harmony with each other' (*Monadology* §§78–9). In more concrete terms, behaviour (raising one's hand, for example) can be explained either in terms of a volition and the harmony God established between mind and body, or purely in terms of the laws of motion, as applied to the physical body. By pre-established harmony, these two explanations will always agree. In this way Leibniz managed to reconcile the dualism of Descartes with the stricter mechanism of Hobbes; everything in the body can be explained in purely mechanistic terms, while, at the same time, Leibniz could also hold that human beings (and other living organisms) have souls which are the causes of much of their behaviour.

In addition to explaining the interaction between mind and body, when first introduced, Leibniz held that pre-established harmony also explains the union of mind and body, that which makes a single substance out of a mind and the collection of individual substances that constitutes its body (*Discourse* §33). In this way, pre-established harmony provided a central support for Leibniz's account of corporeal substance. Unfortunately, however, it proved inadequate to the task. In May 1703, René-Joseph de Tournemine pointed out that whatever resemblance one might suppose between two clocks, however justly their relations might be considered perfect, one can never say that the clocks are united just because the movements correspond with perfect symmetry. While it does not challenge pre-established harmony as an account of mind–body interaction, the argument is as simple as it is devastating against the somewhat different claim that pre-established harmony accounts for mind–body unity. In consequence, Leibniz came to question the place of complex corporeal substance in his philosophy, as discussed above (see MALEBRANCHE, N. §3; OCCASIONALISM).

7 Metaphysics: necessity, contingency and freedom

Central to Leibniz's philosophy were a variety of problems concerning necessity, contingency and freedom, problems which arise in a variety of ways from a variety of sources. Spinoza stood behind many of Leibniz's worries. According to Spinoza, everything in the world is necessary and nothing is contingent, so that things could not be other than they are. Indeed, everything that is genuinely possible is actual and if something does not actually exist, it is because it could not. Everything follows from the divine nature, not by choice but by blind necessity. Furthermore, Spinoza argued, everything in the world is determined and what we take to be human freedom is just an illusion. We think that we are free because we are ignorant of the causes outside us that determine us to do what we do.

Other problems came from Leibniz's own views. Some came from Leibniz's principle in accordance with which 'when a proposition is not an identity, that is, when the predicate is not explicitly contained in the subject, it must be contained in it virtually' (*Discourse* §8). If every predicate true of an individual was part of its very concept, how could it fail to be necessary? A closely related problem followed from Leibniz's claim that every individual substance contains everything that can happen to it, past, present and future, which seems to entail that everything was determined from the beginning, and there is no room for the freedom of a creature. Here the problem concerns not necessity and contingency, but determinism and human freedom. Even if it were contingent that a certain creature has a certain built-in history, given that history, there does not appear to be room for freedom.

Leibniz offered a number of approaches to this problem in his writings. His basic response to the Spinozistic attacks on contingency is the claim that God *freely* chose the best of all possible worlds. He wrote in the early 1680s in an essay entitled *De libertate* (On freedom) 'God produces the best not by necessity but because he wills it' (Leibniz [1680–2] 1989: 20). Yet, since God is perfect, it would seem that his nature necessarily determines his will to choose the best.

This led Leibniz directly to another account of contingency. In that same document, he continued by noting that 'things remain possible, even if God does not choose them'. That is, even if God *necessarily* created the best of all possible worlds (a concession Leibniz does not always make), unactualized possibles are still, in and of themselves, possible. The recognition of such unactualized possibles is what brought him back from the precipice of necessitarianism, so Leibniz wrote in another essay from the late 1680s

(Leibniz 1989: 21). Elsewhere, he characterized those possibles that God chooses to create as necessary, but only *ex hypothesi*, on the hypothesis that God chose to create them. Though necessary in this limited sense, they are contingent in so far as their contraries are not self-contradictory (*Discourse* §13).

From time to time Leibniz used the kindred notion of compossibility. Two individuals are said to be compossible when they can be actualized at the same time, and are said not to be compossible when they cannot. In this way one can say that a possible world is a maximal set of compossible individuals. The notions of compossibility and incompossibility are not, however, logical notions, taken narrowly. Two individuals may fail to fit in the same possible world because they are logically in contradiction with one another (in a sense that must be specified), or because they fail to harmonize with one another.

Leibniz sometimes also suggested that it is contingent that this particular world is the best of all possible worlds. So, even if God necessarily created the best of all possible worlds, it is still contingent that he creates *this* world. These arguments address the worries that derive from Spinoza's view that God necessarily gave rise to this world (see SPINOZA, B. DE §4). But, as noted above, there are other more Leibnizian worries to address as well. If in any true proposition the concept of the predicate must be contained in the concept of the subject, how can any truth fail to be necessary? Leibniz gave one kind of answer in the *Discourse on Metaphysics* (§13) where he simply asserts that there are two kinds of conceptual containment. While all predicates are contained in the concept of the subject, some are contained necessarily, and some contingently. But in some documents, probably from the late 1680s, he attempted a different solution. He noted first that in some cases we can demonstrate that the predicate is contained in the subject in a finite number of steps. However, in other cases this cannot be done. 'In contingent truths, even though the predicate is in the subject, this can never be demonstrated, nor can a proposition ever be reduced to an equality or to an identity, but the resolution proceeds to infinity' (Leibniz 1989: 96). To demonstrate a contingent truth, one must show that a given individual with a given property is one among an infinity of individuals in a possible world that is the best among an infinity of other possible worlds, something that cannot be shown in a finite number of steps.

Beyond the question of necessity is the issue of human freedom. Take an individual substance, which contains everything that has happened, is happening and will happen to it. Even if one can establish that the sequence of 'happenings' it contains is contingent, yet by virtue of containing all these happenings, it would seem not to be free to do anything other than what it does. Contingency is thus compatible with strict determinism, which is incompatible with human freedom.

Leibniz's solution was that while God may build certain actions into a given individual, he can build them in as *free* actions: 'God sees for all time that there will be a certain Judas whose notion or idea... contains this free and future action' (*Discourse* §30). God does make us with free will, and the ability to choose one thing over another. So, when he chooses to create a given individual with a given life-history, he will include the conditions that will lead that individual to choose one thing over another. But the actual choice is ours, and it is free, Leibniz argued. In this way, 'God inclines our soul without necessitating it' (*Discourse* §30). Furthermore, while we can choose other than the way we do, God in his omniscience can predict what we will actually choose, and build its consequences into our future programme. This divine foreknowledge does not change the character of the events themselves: 'God foresees things as they are and does not change their nature....Thus they are assured but they are not necessary' (*Dialogue effectif sur la libertate de l'homme et sur l'origine du mal* (An actual dialogue on human freedom and on the origin of evil) [1695c] 1989: 112). Thus Leibniz had no worse problems on this score than does anyone who believes in divine omniscience.

Leibniz's doctrine did raise a knotty problem about the identity conditions for individuals, however. If all properties of a given individual are programmed in from the beginning, then though some may be contingent, and though some may be free, still, they define the individual as the particular individual that it is; were they different, then we would be dealing with another individual altogether, it would seem. From time to time Leibniz acknowledged that we might want to talk about what might have happened if Judas (*our* Judas, the Judas in *this* possible world) had not renounced Christ (*Leibniz–Arnauld Correspondence*, May 1686, Leibniz 1875–90 vol. 2: 41–2); the specific example at issue there is not Judas, as in the *Discourse*, but Adam). But often Leibniz seemed quite willing to embrace a different view: 'But someone...will say, why is it that this man will assuredly commit this sin? The reply is easy: otherwise he would not be this man' (*Discourse* §30). In this way, given that every substance mirrors the entire world in which it finds itself, Leibniz often committed himself to the thesis that a person can belong to only *one* possible world.

8 Epistemology: ideas and sensation

Despite the fact that Leibniz is usually categorized as a continental rationalist, his main interest was not epistemological. At the same time, he did contribute to the discussions of his day on questions relating to ideas and knowledge.

In the *New Essays* (II.1.1), Leibniz defines an idea as follows: 'an idea is an immediate inner object [which] expresses the nature or qualities of things'. He emphasizes that we can think that we have an idea when we do not really have one. So, for example, there can be no idea of a fastest motion because the notion is incoherent. But, he notes, 'At first glance we might seem to have the idea of a fastest motion, for we certainly understand what we say; but yet we certainly have no idea of impossible things'. Mistaking our comprehension of the phrase 'fastest motion' for having a genuine idea can lead us into contradiction in this case. But in other cases, for example in mathematics, where we often use symbols without fixing ideas to them, we often must work symbolically because of the complexity of working directly with ideas themselves. In this sense one can have thought and even reasoning when we do not have ideas in the proper sense. This observation is connected with a distinction Leibniz drew between real and nominal definitions. A nominal definition is a definition in which one can doubt whether or not the notion defined is genuinely possible; a real definition is one in which the possibility of the notion defined has been established. One can thus say that it is only of real definitions that one can be sure that they correspond to a genuine idea (*Meditations* [1684a] 1989: 25–6; *Discourse* §24).

Leibniz was a supporter of innate ideas in a number of senses. First of all, he argued that there are certain particular ideas that are innate to the mind, and do not or cannot come through the senses: 'The ideas of *being*, *possible*, and *same* are so thoroughly innate that they enter into all our thoughts and reasoning, and I regard them as essential to our minds' (*New Essays* I.3.3). He made a similar claim for other notions, such as infinity (*New Essays* II.17.3). In this connection he used his celebrated marble analogy in the preface to the *New Essays*. Ideas and truths are in the mind, he argued, just as the shape of Hercules might already be in the veins of a block of marble, making that shape more likely to emerge when the sculptor begins to hammer on it, even though considerable effort may be required to expose the shape: 'This is how ideas and truths are innate in us – as inclinations, dispositions, tendencies, or natural potentialities'.

Leibniz's metaphysics, however, committed him to

a stronger position still, that *every* idea is innate, strictly speaking, since nothing can enter a mind from the outside. He wrote: 'The mind always expresses all its future thoughts and already thinks confusedly about everything it will ever think about distinctly. And nothing can be taught to us whose idea we do not already have in our mind' (*Discourse* §26). But even though all ideas are strictly innate, Leibniz could distinguish between the ideas of sensation that in a certain sense come to us from outside, and the ideas that do not and cannot do so. As with the explication of physical causality in the context of a view in which there can be no real metaphysical causality between finite things, Leibniz could say that 'we receive knowledge from the outside by way of the senses, because some external things contain or express more particularly the reasons that determine our soul to certain thoughts' (*Discourse* §27).

Sensations are distinguished from other notions not only by their causal origin (in Leibniz's somewhat extended sense), but also by the fact that they are confused, in contrast to the distinct notions one uses, say, in mathematics. A notion is distinct when one has 'marks and tests sufficient to distinguish a thing from all other similar' things; distinct notions include number, magnitude, shape and so on. A notion is confused 'when I cannot enumerate one by one marks sufficient for differentiating a thing from others, even though the thing does indeed have such marks and requisites into which its notion can be resolved'. In this sense 'colours, smells, tastes, and other particular objects of the senses' are confused (*Meditations* [1684a] 1989: 24). Indeed, they are the confused perception of the geometrical properties of bodies that, on the mechanist programme, ground the perception of sensible qualities. 'When we perceive colours or smells, we certainly have no perception other than that of shapes and of motions, though so very numerous and so very small that our mind cannot distinctly consider each individual one in this, its present state, and thus does not notice that its perception is composed of perceptions of minute shapes and motions alone' (*Meditations* [1684a] 1989: 27). Elsewhere Leibniz used the analogy of a wave to understand this phenomenon. When we hear the roar of the ocean, we are actually hearing just a large number of individual waves, lapping on the shore. But since we cannot distinguish the sounds each individual wave makes, we hear it as an undifferentiated roar. This is just the way the confused perception of the corpuscular microstructure of bodies results in our sensation of colour, taste and so on (*New Essays* 1704: preface). In this way Leibniz rejected the claim that the connection between a particular sensation and its mechanical cause is the result of a perfectly

arbitrary divine decree; by the Principle of Sufficient Reason, there can be no such arbitrariness in the world (*New Essays* II.8.13 and following, IV.6.7). Thus, it would seem, the distinction between sensations and ideas of the intellect is not a matter of kind, but a matter of degree, degree of distinctness and confusion.

An important part of this account of sensation was Leibniz's doctrine of *petites perceptions* (minute perceptions). Like Descartes, Leibniz believed that we think all the time. However, unlike Descartes, he denied that we are always conscious of what we think. He held that 'at every moment there is in us an infinity of perceptions, unaccompanied by awareness or reflection; that is, of alterations in the soul itself, of which we are unaware because these impressions are either too minute and too numerous, or else too unvarying, so that they are not sufficiently distinctive on their own' (*New Essays* preface). Though we do not apperceive (that is, consciously perceive) each of them individually, these unconscious perceptions have their effects on us. They are what underlie and explain sensation, as suggested earlier. Furthermore, they also have their effect on the conscious choices that we make (*New Essays* II.20.6).

Finally, Leibniz also had a clear position in the debate then raging in the intellectual world over Malebranche's view that we see all things in God, that is, that ideas do not exist in finite minds, but only in the mind of God, where they are seen by finite intellects without actually being in them (see MALE-BRANCHE, N. §2). Leibniz quite clearly rejected Malebranche's view: 'Even if we were to see everything in God, it would nevertheless be necessary that we also have our own ideas, that is, not little copies of God's, as it were, but affections or modifications of our mind corresponding to that very thing we perceived in God' (*Meditations* [1684a] 1989: 27; compare *Discourse* §29).

9 Epistemology: knowledge and probability

In a famous passage of the *Monadology* (§§31–2) Leibniz writes: 'Our reasonings are based on *two great principles*, *that of contradiction*, in virtue of which we judge that which involves a contradiction to be false, and that which is opposed or contradictory to the false to be true, and *that of sufficient reason*, by virtue of which we consider that we can find no true or existent fact, no true assertion, without there being a sufficient reason why it is thus and not otherwise'. These two principles correspond to two different kinds of truths, 'those of *reasoning* and those of *fact*' (*Monadology* §33).

A truth of reason can be known with certainty by a

finite demonstration consisting of a finite number of steps containing simple ideas, definitions, axioms and postulates; these truths are necessary and can be known a priori. Sensation can give us particular instances of these truths, but can never attain the kind of universality one finds in necessary truths. As Leibniz wrote in the preface to the *New Essays*: 'necessary truths, such as we find in pure mathematics and particularly in arithmetic and geometry, must have principles whose proof does not depend on instances nor, consequently, on the testimony of the senses, even though without the senses it would never occur to us to think of them'.

While Leibniz agreed with DESCARTES that such truths are innate, he distanced himself from Descartes' appeal to clear and distinct perception. Against those who appeal to Descartes' axiom that 'whatever I clearly and distinctly perceive about a thing is true or is assertable of the thing in question', Leibniz objected that 'this axiom is useless unless we use criteria for the clear and distinct, criteria which we have made explicit' (*Meditations* [1684a] 1989: 26–7). While Leibniz agreed with Descartes that we have an innate capacity to recognize these innate truths, as a practical matter, he preferred to constrain the mind by formal rules of logic, unlike Descartes, who rejected formal logic (see §10 below).

Since in all predications, the concept of the predicate is contained in the concept of the subject, all knowledge is in principle a priori; if we only had sufficient knowledge of the subject, we could see everything that is true of it, contained in its complete concept. But this is only possible for God. Humans, incapable of performing the analysis that will reveal the truth a priori must make appeal to the senses in order to discover truths of fact. In fact, Leibniz thought, 'we are all mere Empirics in three fourths of our actions' (*Monadology* 28).

Because of the importance of empirical knowledge, Leibniz called for a genuine logic of probability. The modern theory of probability was born in the 1650s with the correspondence between PASCAL and Fermat, and then with Christiaan Huygens' little treatise, *Tractus de ratiociniis in aleae ludo* (Treatise on reasoning in games of chance) (1657). The theory very quickly developed in the seventeenth century, as new practical applications were quickly found. But Leibniz was not satisfied that it had yet been applied to the most general question of all, the kind of reasoning we do about matters of fact on the basis of sensation when demonstration is impossible. And so, in the *New Essays* (IV.2.14) he called for a new science: 'I maintain that *the study of the degrees of probability* would be very valuable and is still lacking, and that this is a serious shortcoming in our treatises

on logic. For when one cannot absolutely settle a question one could still establish the degree of likelihood on the evidence, and so one can judge rationally which side is the most plausible....I suspect that the establishment of an *art of estimating likelihoods* would be more useful than a good proportion of our demonstrative sciences, and I have more than once contemplated it'. But even though Leibniz may have contemplated it, he himself never made a serious attempt to develop the logic of probability that he called for here. However, his call was heard by David HUME, who saw his *Treatise* as, in part, answering Leibniz's challenge.

10 Logic and language

From his youth, Leibniz dreamed of constructing a perfect, logical language, 'a certain alphabet of human thoughts that, through the combination of the letters of this alphabet and through the analysis of the words produced from them, all things can both be discovered and judged'. This programme, which Leibniz called the 'universal characteristic', gets its first expression in the very early work, *Dissertatio de arte combinatoria* (Dissertation on the art of combination) (1666). But it is most fully developed later, from the mid-1670s into the 1680s.

Leibniz's programme had two parts. First, one must assign characteristic numbers to all concepts that show how they are built up out of simpler concepts. Leibniz tried a number of schemes for this, but one strategy was to assign simple concepts prime numbers, and then assign complex concepts the product of the characteristic numbers of its constituent simple concepts. The second part of the programme was then to find simple mechanical rules for the truth of propositions in terms of the characteristic numbers of their constituent concepts. Leibniz's fundamental rule in his Universal Characteristic was the principle discussed above in connection with his metaphysics: a predicate is true of a subject if and only if its concept is contained in the concept of the subject. If the concepts in question can be expressed numerically, then Leibniz thought that the rule can be given a mathematical form as well, and the truth of a proposition could be established by a simple arithmetical calculation. Leibniz's project in these writings was to show how this basic intuition about truth could be extended to propositions that are not in simple subject-predicate form. He also sought to extend the programme to formalize the validity of the standard inferences in Aristotelian logic. Even if he could not assign definite characteristic numbers to particular concepts, Leibniz tried to show that for certain configurations of premises and conclusions, if the premises are true (on his definition of truth), then so too must be the conclusion.

The programme was very ambitious; it if were successful, it would allow the truth or falsity of any proposition, necessary or contingent, to be determined by calculation alone. However, it soon dawned on Leibniz that the idea of finding all the conceptual dependencies necessary to express the contents of notions numerically was utopian in the extreme, particularly given the doctrine of infinite analysis of contingent truths Leibniz came to in the late 1680s. This realization still left in place the more modest programme of validating patterns of inference. But even this more modest programme turned out to be beyond Leibniz's ability to bring to completion, and after the early 1690s he seems to have given up trying to make it work, although he returned to it from time to time.

But even though this particular programme collapsed, the idea of formalism was quite basic to Leibniz's thought. Part of the reaction against the Aristotelian philosophy of the schools was an attack on formal logic. Descartes, Locke and others in the seventeenth century argued that we all have an innate ability to recognize truth, what was often called intuition, and that we should cultivate that capacity, and not waste our time learning formal rules. While Leibniz certainly agreed that we do have the innate capacity to grasp certain truths, he still thought that formalism is very important (Leibniz to Elisabeth of Bohemia, 1678). Much of our reasoning is 'blind' or symbolic, Leibniz thought, conducted through the manipulation of symbols without having a direct hold on the ideas that underlie the symbols. For that reason we must have clear and unambiguous symbol systems, and strict rules for manipulating them (*Meditations*).

This view is evident in the papers on the Universal Characteristic. But it also underlies another project of the same period, the differential and integral calculus, one of Leibniz's greatest accomplishments, worked out by 1676 and made public from 1684. Though others before him had solved many of the particular problems his calculus could solve, problems relating to tangents, areas, volumes and so on, Leibniz invented a simple notation, still used in the calculus ('d' to represent the operation of differentiation, and '$\int$' to represent the operation of infinite summation (integration)), and worked out a collection of simple rules for applying these operations to equations of different kinds. In this way, Leibniz was able to produce simple algorithms for solving difficult geometrical problems 'blindly', by manipulating certain symbols in accordance with simple rules.

Another issue closely connected with Leibniz's logic is that of relations. In the *Primae veritates* (First truths) ([1689] 1989: 32) Leibniz wrote: '*There are no purely extrinsic denominations* [that is, purely relational properties], denominations which have absolutely no foundation in the very thing denominated . . . . And consequently, whenever the denomination of a thing is changed, there must be a variation in the thing itself'. In this way, all relations must be, in some sense, grounded in the non-relational properties of things. But it is not clear that Leibniz held that relations had to be reducible to non-relational predicates of things. In one example he gives, he paraphrased 'Paris is the lover of Helen' by the following proposition: 'Paris loves, and by that very fact [*eo ipso*] Helen is loved'. While this certainly relates the relation '*A* loves *B*' to two propositions that have the form of simple subject-predicate propositions ('*A* loves' and '*B* is loved'), it should be noted that the predicates in question ('loves' and 'is loved') would seem to be implicitly relational; whether this is an accidental feature of the example Leibniz chose or a clue to Leibniz's views is a question of some dispute. Furthermore, it is important not to ignore that which connects the two propositions ('and by that very fact'), without which one cannot say that the two non-relational propositions capture the relation '*A* loves *B*' (Leibniz 1966: 14). Other texts suggest that individuals properly speaking have non-relational properties, and that the relations between things are something imposed by the mind onto the world: 'My judgement about relations is that paternity in David is one thing, sonship in Solomon another, but that the relation common to both is a merely mental thing whose basis is the modifications of the individuals' (Leibniz to Des Bosses, 21 April 1714). But in saying that the relations between individuals are 'merely mental', Leibniz does not necessarily mean to dismiss them. He wrote: 'God not only sees individual monads and the modifications of every monad whatsoever, but he also sees their relations, and in this consists the reality of relations and of truth' (Letter to Des Bosses, 5 February 1712).

In addition to formal languages, Leibniz was also keenly interested in the study of natural languages. Like many of his contemporaries, he was interested in the controversies over the question of the Adamic language, the language spoken in Eden and from which all modern languages supposedly derive. This, among other motivations, led him to the empirical study of different languages and the etymology of words (see UNIVERSAL LANGUAGE).

11 Natural philosophy

Leibniz is read today largely for his philosophical

writings. But in his day, he was, if anything, better known for his work in mathematics and natural philosophy. Like many of his contemporaries, Leibniz was a mechanist. Indeed, he was in a sense a much stricter mechanist than the Cartesians. Because of his doctrine of pre-established harmony (see §6 above), one can always give a purely mechanistic explanation of any physical phenomenon, even in humans, unlike in the Cartesian system, where causal interaction between mind and body, direct or occasional, can disrupt the laws governing the body. However, Leibniz's version of the mechanist programme departed significantly from other main versions of the programme of his day, particularly the Cartesian version.

Leibniz rejected the Cartesian analysis of body as extended substance (see §4 above). Instead, he argued that we must go to a deeper level of analysis, behind the extension of bodies to the substances that are the ultimate constituents of reality. Below the level of inanimate extension there are tiny organisms, souls joined to organic bodies which Leibniz, in at least one period of his thought, considered genuine corporeal substances. At a deeper level still there are the non-extended simple substances or monads that ground the reality of corporeal substances. On this view, the extended bodies of the Cartesian world are phenomena, aggregates of substances that are unified by virtue of being confusedly perceived together.

Leibniz also rejected Descartes' central law of nature. For Descartes, God conserves the same quantity of motion in the world, the size times the speed of bodies taken together (see DESCARTES, R. §11). But Leibniz argued that what is conserved is not bulk times speed, but bulk times the *square* of speed, mv^y, a quantity associated with what he called *vis viva* or living force. To defend this view, he used a cluster of a posteriori arguments which assumed the Galilean law of free-fall (the distance fallen is proportional to the square of the speed acquired in free-fall) together with the Principle of the Equality of Cause and Effect, in accordance with which there is always as much ability to do work in the cause as there is in the full effect. Leibniz showed that, on these assumptions, the Cartesian conservation law entails that the ability to do work can either be gained or lost in certain circumstances, whereas on the assumption of the conservation of mv^y, this does not happen. Leibniz used this strategy in the *Brevis demonstratio* (Brief Demonstration of a Notable Error of Descartes) (1686a), where he first published this result. In addition, he offered an a priori argument in which, arguing from certain abstract notions of motion, action and effect, together with an intuitive principle of the conservation of effect, he reached the same

conclusion (*Discourse* §17; *Dynamics* preliminary specimen). This challenge to Descartes' conservation law elicited numerous responses from the Cartesian community in what came to be called the *vis viva* controversy.

Leibniz saw the replacement of the conservation of the quantity of motion by the conservation of mv^y as leading us to introduce into the world of physics something over and above the purely geometrical qualities of size, shape and motion that pertain to the extended substance of the Cartesians. This something is what he called force, the new science of which he named dynamics. While force can cause motion and is sometimes manifested in motion, Leibniz carefully distinguished the two. In emphasizing the distinction between force and motion, Leibniz was rejecting not only the Cartesian tradition, but his own early physics where, following Hobbes, he identified force with motion.

Leibniz recognized a variety of different kinds of forces in nature. At the most fundamental level, he distinguished between primitive and derivative forces, and between active and passive forces. Thus, in all, there are four basic kinds of force: primitive and derivative active force, and primitive and derivative passive force. Active force is of two sorts, living force (*vis viva*), which is associated with bodies actually in motion (a ball moving with a definite velocity), and dead force, which is associated with the instantaneous push from which actual motion results, as in gravitation or elasticity. Passive force, on the other hand, is the force that arises in reaction to the active force of another body. It also has two varieties, impenetrability (the force that prevents two bodies from occupying the same place at the same time) and resistance (the force that opposes new motion). The distinction between primitive and derivative force is quite different. Primitive force, active and passive, is the metaphysical ground of activity and passivity, that in a body by virtue of which it is capable of acting (doing work) or resisting. Derivative forces, for Leibniz, were particular states of activity and passivity that exist in a body at a particular time. In this way, primitive force is not a measurable quantity, but something in body that grounds the reality of the derivative forces, which are measurable quantities.

This notion of force was linked directly to Leibniz's notion of corporeal substance: 'Primitive active force, which Aristotle calls first entelechy and one commonly calls the form of a substance, is another natural principle which, together with matter or passive force, completes a corporeal substance' ('Note on Cartesian natural philosophy' [1702] 1989: 252). At least in the 1680s and 1690s, when Leibniz recognized corporeal substances, the primitive forces seem to have been the form and matter of the corporeal substances that ground the reality of the physical world. Derivative forces would then be interpreted as the momentary states of these corporeal substances. The position is somewhat different after Leibniz began to doubt the reality of corporeal substance (see §5 above). Then, he wrote, 'I relegate derivative forces to the phenomena, but I think that it is obvious that primitive forces can be nothing but the internal strivings of simple substances, strivings by means of which they pass from perception to perception in accordance with a certain law of their nature' (Leibniz to de Volder, 1704 or 1705). In this way, the dynamics can be regarded as another perspective on the same entities discussed in Leibniz's more metaphysical writings.

Leibniz held that these forces (or better, the motion that they cause) obey rigorous mathematical laws. These laws include the conservation of living force, mv^y, virtually equivalent to the modern law of the conservation of kinetic energy, and the conservation of bulk times the velocity (a vector quantity), mv, identical to the modern law of the conservation of momentum. (Because Leibniz's conservation of mv involved the directionality of the motion, it is distinct from the Cartesian conservation of quantity of motion, which Leibniz rejected.) While he disagreed with Descartes about the specific contents of the laws, he can be seen as advancing the Cartesian programme of building a physics grounded in mathematically expressible conservation laws. But even though Leibniz's laws are expressible in mathematical terms, they – like the forces that they govern – are grounded in certain metaphysical principles that are imposed on the world by the wisdom of God: 'Although the particular phenomena of nature can be explained mathematically or mechanically... nevertheless the general principles of corporeal nature and of mechanics itself are more metaphysical than geometrical' (*Discourse* §18).

One such general metaphysical principle was noted in connection with the establishment of Leibniz's conservation law, the Principle of the Equality of Cause and Effect. But there were others as well. Leibniz made frequent use of the Principle of Continuity, according to which nothing happens through a leap. Leibniz used this principle to refute Descartes' laws of impact, where small changes in the initial conditions (say the comparative sizes of the bodies in question, or their motion) can result in radically different results. This principle was also used to refute atomism. If there are perfectly hard atoms, not made up of smaller separable parts, then in collision their motion would change instantaneously at the moment of impact. So, Leibniz concluded, there cannot be any such atoms in nature. Indeed, he used

this argument to conclude that every body, no matter how small, is elastic. Leibniz also made appeal to the Principle of Plenitude to argue that there can be no vacuum or empty space in the world, since if God *can* create something consistent with his other creations, he *must* do so. Finally, as seen below, Leibniz used the Principle of Sufficient Reason in connection with his relativistic account of space and time.

The very fact that the world is the product of divine wisdom allowed Leibniz to appeal to final causes in his physics. This differentiates him from both Descartes and Spinoza, both of whom rejected final causes. Leibniz agreed with both that everything in nature can be explained through efficient cause alone – that is, through the laws of motion alone. But often, particularly in optics, it is much easier to solve problems by appealing to God's wisdom, and discovering the way in which a most perfect being would have created his universe (*Discourse* §22; *Specimen of dynamics* 1695a: part I). However, the appeal to final cause only supplements the understanding of nature by efficient causes, and does not replace it. It is another manifestation of divine harmony that the explanations by efficient causes and by final causes always coincides: 'In general we must hold that everything in the world can be explained in two ways: through the kingdom of power, that is, through efficient causes, and through the kingdom of wisdom, that is, through, final causes....These two kingdoms everywhere interpenetrate each other...so that the greatest obtains in the kingdom of power at the same time as the best in the kingdom of wisdom' (*Specimen of dynamics* [1695a: part I] 1989: 126–7).

So far we have been discussing Leibniz's work in relation to that of other mechanists, particularly those of the Cartesian school. But it is also important to understand Leibniz's relations with another contemporary and often bitter rival, Isaac Newton.

In opposition to Newton, who held an absolutist conception of place and space, Leibniz argued that space is 'only relations or order or orders of coexistence, both for the actually existing thing and for the possible thing one can put in its place' (*Remarks on Foucher* [1696] 1989: 146). If Newton were right, Leibniz argued, and there was absolute space, then God could create a world in which what is currently east and west are exactly reversed, for example. But if so, by the Principle of Sufficient Reason, then God could have no reason to create one such world over another. Given that he did, he cannot have been faced with such a choice. Leibniz concludes that the two purported Newtonian worlds are really just one world, a world in which space is just constituted by the relations between things (Leibniz to Clarke, 3rd paper §5). Newton's absolutist account of space was supposed to ground an absolutist account of motion as well. For Newton, motion was the change of place of a body with respect to absolute space. Leibniz rejected this too, arguing that motion is a completely relativistic notion, a matter of the relation between bodies over time and that alone (*Specimen of dynamics* part I; Leibniz to Huygens, 12/22 June 1694).

Leibniz also rejected Newton's theory of universal gravitation. He read Newton as holding that gravity is an essential property of matter as such, and he was appalled. For Leibniz, all change in body had to happen through the intermediary of contact and collision; the idea of action at a distance that seemed to underlie Newton's theory of universal gravitation was an intellectual disaster, a treasonable abandonment of the new mechanical philosophy and a return to the worst abuses of the schoolmen. Leibniz, whose early mechanism seemed so radical at the time, could not adjust to the new Newtonian philosophy, soon to take over the intellectual world (see CLARKE, S.; NEWTON, I.).

While the emphasis here has been on the aspects of Leibniz's work in physics most relevant to his philosophical programme, he was much more widely interested in the natural world. He left notes on engineering problems, on chemistry, on geology and on curious observations in natural history including the report of a talking dog, and a goat with an odd hairstyle.

12 Ethics and political thought

Although Leibniz's ethical and political writings are not widely read today, they constitute an important part of his corpus, unsurprising, given Leibniz's own involvement in politics. Leibniz's ethical and political thought, squarely within the natural law tradition, was based on the notions of justice, charity and virtue (see NATURAL LAW). Leibniz wrote: 'Charity is a universal benevolence, and benevolence the habit of loving or of willing the good. Love then signifies rejoicing in the happiness of another, or, what is the same thing, converting the happiness of another into one's own' (*Codex Iuris Gentium Diplomaticus* (The diplomatic code of the law of nations) [1693: introduction] 1988: 171). In a note on felicity (Leibniz [*c.*1694–8] 1988: 83–4), he connected justice, wisdom, and virtue to charity: 'Virtue is the habit of acting according to wisdom.... Wisdom is the science of felicity, [and] is what must be studied above all things.... To love is to find pleasure in the perfection of another. Justice is charity or a habit of loving conformed to wisdom. Thus when one is inclined to justice, one tries to procure good for everybody, so far

as one can, reasonably, but in proportion to the needs and merits of each'.

For Leibniz, human justice is the same as God's justice, though, of course, less perfect. Leibniz wrote in the *Monita quaedam ad S. Puffendorfii principia* (Observations on the Principles of Pufendorf) ([1706] 1988: 69): 'In the science of law... it is best to derive human justice, as from a spring, from the divine, to make it complete. Surely the idea of the just, no less than that of the true and the good, relates to God, and above all to God, who is the measure of all things'. Similarly, Leibniz wrote in *Méditation sur la notion commune de la justice* (Meditation on the common concept of justice) ([1702–3] 1988: 60) that 'as soon as [the concept of justice] is founded on God or on the imitation of God, it becomes universal justice, and contains all the virtues'.

In so far as charity is defined in terms of universal love and benevolence, justice is something quite distinct from power. This is true even for God. 'Justice, indeed, would not be an essential attribute of God, if He himself established justice and law by His free will'. In this sense, God is as bound by the eternal laws of justice as he is bound by truths of reason: 'Justice follows certain rules of equality and of proportion [which are] no less founded in the immutable nature of things, and in the divine ideas, than are the principles of arithmetic and of geometry' (*Observations on Pufendorf* [1706] 1988: 69). (Here, perhaps is the origin of the theodicy problem for Leibniz: if God is bound by the same ideal of justice that binds us, then we must show how the works of the all-perfect creator can be seen to conform to that ideal.) So, too, are we bound by a standard of justice that exists independently of our wills.

Leibniz recognized three degrees of justice. The lowest, a minimal sort of justice, is simply not to harm others. The second degree is to give each their due, what it is that is owed to them. The highest, though, is to behave with genuine beneficence toward others, and to do that which will promote their happiness; this is what Leibniz calls piety (Leibniz to Coste, 4 July 1706: appendix).

Leibniz's conception of justice as the charity of the wise also placed virtue and obligation outside of the scope of a contract. For Hobbes, for example, the notion of justice arises from a contract that we make with one another in forming a society, and the notion of justice has no applicability outside that framework. Commenting on Shaftesbury in 1712, Leibniz wrote: 'Our illustrious author refutes with reason... those who believe that there is no obligation at all in the state of nature, and outside government; for obligations by pacts having to form the right of government itself, according to the author of these principles, it is manifest that the obligation is anterior to the government which it must form' (Leibniz 1988: 196). Indeed, he noted, there are societies, among the native Americans for example, in which the sovereign thought necessary by Hobbes is altogether absent: 'entire peoples can be without magistrates and without quarrels, and . . . as a result men are neither taken far enough by their natural goodness nor forced by their wickedness to provide themselves with a government and to renounce their liberty'. In people sufficiently wise, then, justice and charity are sufficient to hold society together, without the need of a contract.

But Leibniz was a practical politician, as well as a theorist of politics. He generally worked for a Europe unified under the leadership of a unified church, a Christian Europe in which there are no conflicts between different Christian states. This, in part, is what was behind his plan for the reunification of the Catholics and the Protestants. It was also behind his attempt, as early as 1671, to persuade the French to attack Egypt, a non-Christian country, rather than to invade the Netherlands. In practice, however, Leibniz was an opponent of French expansionism under Louis XIV (as much as he was an admirer of French culture), and a supporter of a union of Protestant countries in Northern Europe (his *Mars Christianissimus* (1684b) was a brilliant satire directed against Louis XIV's foreign policy). He was also an active participant in the successful campaign in support of the claim of the House of Hanover for the throne of England.

13 The Leibnizian tradition

It is important to remember when considering Leibniz's influence that much of what we now know of Leibniz's writings was unknown to his readers for many years after his death. The full dimensions of Leibniz's thought emerged only slowly, as new texts came to light. Indeed, there is still no complete edition of his work.

At the time of his death, and in the decade afterwards, only a small selection of Leibniz's texts was available. There were a fair number of publications in mathematics and physics, some legal writings and some documents collected in connection with his unfinished history of the house of Hanover. In philosophy, however, there were only a few essays. During his lifetime, Leibniz had published *Meditations on Knowledge, Truth, and Ideas* (1684a), the *New System* (1695b), *On Nature Itself* (1698) and the *Theodicy* (1710). The Leibniz–Clarke correspondence was published soon after his death, and a Latin version of the *Monadology* appeared in 1721. On the other hand, the *New Essays* did not appear until 1765,

and works that we now consider central, such as the *Discourse on metaphysics*, did not appear until 1846. Many of his philosophical writings and correspondence had to await the monumental edition of C.I. Gerhardt, which appeared between 1875 and 1890. Many texts have yet to appear.

Despite the relative paucity of his available writings, Leibniz was much read and debated in the eighteenth century. One of his early supporters was the German professor Christian Wolff who had corresponded with Leibniz during his life. He composed numerous volumes expounding a Leibnizian philosophy in an ordered and orderly way. Wolff's systematic philosophy made it ideal for the academy, and his ideas were widely influential. But there were opponents, particularly a group of pietist theologians at the University of Halle, but others as well, including Maupertuis, CRUSIUS, CONDILLAC and, most famously, VOLTAIRE, who made Leibniz into the comical Dr Pangloss of his *Candide*. KANT received his philosophical education in the atmosphere of this debate between the Leibnizians and the anti-Leibnizians in the German intellectual world. His philosophy, both pre-critical and critical, shows the marks of his knowledge of Leibniz's writings.

See also: ATOMISM, ANCIENT; CONTINGENCY; FREEDOM, DIVINE; INFINITY; MENDELSSOHN, M.; PROBABILITY THEORY AND EPISTEMOLOGY; SUBSTANCE; WILL, THE

List of works

Many of Leibniz's writings, including some of the most important of them, remained unpublished during his lifetime. As a consequence, some of them can be dated only approximately.

Leibniz, G.W. (1768) *Leibnitii opera omnia* (The complete works of Leibniz), ed. L. Dutens, Geneva, 6 vols; repr. Hildesheim: Olms, 1989. (Contains a wide range of Leibniz's papers, both inside and outside philosophy, many of which have not been reprinted since the eighteenth century. It gives the best sense of what Leibniz meant to his contemporaries.)
—— (1849–63) *Mathematische Schriften* (Mathematical writings), ed. C.I. Gerhardt, Berlin and Halle: A. Asher & comp. and H.W. Schmidt, 7 vols; repr. Hildesheim: Olms, 1962. (Still the most complete collection of Leibniz's papers and letters in mathematics and physics, in the original languages, many of which are directly connected to his more philosophical interests.)
—— (1875–90) *Die philosophischen Schriften* (Philo-

sophical writings), ed. C.I. Gerhardt, Berlin: Weidmannsche Buchhandlung, 7 vols; repr. Hildesheim: Olms, 1978. (Still the most complete collection of Leibniz's philosophical papers and letters in the original languages.)

—— (1923–) *Sämtliche Schriften und Briefe* (Collected writings and letters), ed. Deutsche Akademie der Wissenschaften (before 1945, Preussische), Berlin: Akademie Verlag. (This is to be the new complete critical edition of Leibniz's writings in the original languages, edited to the highest standards. Currently still in its early stages, it must be supplemented by earlier editions. In recent years it has been supplemented by a 'Vorausedition', giving preprints of editorial work in progress.)

—— (1666) *Dissertatio de arte combinatoria* (Dissertation on the art of combinations), Leipzig; repr. in *Die philosophischen Schriften*, vol. 4; partial trans. L.E. Loemker in *Philosophical Papers and Letters*, Dordrecht: Reidel, 1969. (Leibniz's first important publication, concerning the theory of mathematical combinations, together with various philosophical digressions. It also contains a suggestion of his later concern with a universal language.)

—— (*c.*1680–2) *De libertate* (On freedom), in *Textes inédites*, vol. 1, ed. G. Grua, Paris: Presses Universitaires de France, 1948; trans. R. Ariew and D. Garber in *Leibniz: Philosophical Essays*, Indianapolis, IN and Cambridge, MA: Hackett Publishing Company, 1989. (Interesting essay on human and divine freedom and contingency, unpublished in Leibniz's lifetime.)

—— (1684a) 'Meditationes de cognitione, veritate et ideis' (Meditations on knowledge, truth and ideas), *Acta Eruditorum* (November 1684): 537–42; repr. in *Leibnitii opera omnia*, vol. 4; trans. R. Ariew and D. Garber in *Leibniz: Philosophical Essays*, Indianapolis, IN and Cambridge, MA: Hackett Publishing Company, 1989. (Important explanation of Leibniz's views on concepts, truth and knowledge.)

—— (1684b) *Mars Christianissimus* (Most Christian War-God), Cologne; trans. P. Riley in *Leibniz: Political Writings*, Cambridge: Cambridge University Press, 1988. (A satire on the diplomatic policies of Louis XIV.)

—— (1686a) 'Brevis Demonstratio erroris memorabilis Cartesii' (Brief demonstration of a notable error of Descartes), *Acta Eruditorum* (March 1686): 161–3; repr. in *Mathematische Schriften*, vol. 6; trans. L.E. Loemker in *Philosophical Papers and Letters*, Dordrecht: Reidel, 1969. (A refutation of Descartes' law of the conservation of quantity of motion in physics.)

—— (1686b) *Discours de métaphysique* (Discourse on metaphysics), 1846; ed. H. Lestienne, Paris: Alcan,

1907; trans. R. Ariew and D. Garber in *Leibniz: Philosophical Essays*, Indianapolis, IN and Cambridge, MA: Hackett Publishing Company, 1989. (Unpublished in Leibniz's time, this is a central text in which Leibniz gives an exposition of some central elements of his metaphysics as of 1686.)

—— (1686–90) *The Leibniz–Arnauld Correspondence; repr. with related letters and documents in Die philosophischen Schriften*, vol. 2: Weidmannsche Buchhandlung, 1875–90, 1956; trans. and ed. H.T. Mason, Manchester: Manchester University Press, 1967. (Very important series of letters exchanged between Leibniz and the Cartesian philosopher Antoine Arnauld just as Leibniz was setting out his mature philosophy, providing a kind of commentary on themes developed in the *Discourse*. Although unpublished in his lifetime, Leibniz probably intended it for publication.)

—— (*c.*1689a) *De libertate* (On Freedom), in *Textes inédites*, vol. 1, ed. G. Grua, Paris: Presses Universitaires de France, 1948; trans. R. Ariew and D. Garber in *Leibniz: Philosophical Essays*, Indianapolis, IN and Cambridge, MA: Hackett Publishing Company, 1989. (Another essay on contingency and freedom, unpublished in Leibniz's lifetime, which makes use of his infinite analysis account of contingency.)

—— (1689b) *Primae veritates* (First truths); repr. in *Opuscules et fragments inédits*, 1903; trans. R. Ariew and D. Garber in *Leibniz: Philosophical Essays*, Indianapolis, IN and Cambridge, MA: Hackett Publishing Company, 1989. (An important, unpublished summary of Leibniz's metaphysics as of the 1680s. Originally thought to have preceded the 1686 composition of the *Discourse*, it is now firmly dated at 1689.)

—— (1690) *Dynamica* (Dynamics), in *Mathematische Schriften*, vol. 6; partial trans. R. Ariew and D. Garber in *Leibniz: Philosophical Essays*, Indianapolis, IN and Cambridge, MA: Hackett Publishing Company, 1989. (Unpublished in Leibniz's time, this is a systematic exposition of Leibniz's physics. Apart from the translation of the preliminary discourse in Ariew and Garber, the bulk of this work has not been translated from the original Latin.)

—— (1692) *Protogaea*, 1749; French trans, ed. B. de Saint-Germain and J.-M. Barrande, Toulouse: Presses Universitaires du Mirail, 1993. (A treatise on geology and the early days of the earth, written as the first part of Leibniz's history of the House of Hanover.)

—— (1693) *Codex Iuris Gentium Diplomaticus* (The diplomatic code of the law of nations), Hanover; partial trans. P. Riley in *Leibniz: Political Writings*, Cambridge: Cambridge University Press, 1988.

(Collection of diplomatic papers, with a long introduction on political philosophy.)

—— (c. 1694–8) *La félicité* (Felicity); repr. in *Textes inédites*, vol. 1; trans. P. Riley in *Leibniz: Political Writings*, Cambridge: Cambridge University Press, 1988. (Important but unpublished note from the 1690s in which Leibniz discusses his theory of justice as the charity of the wise man.)

—— (1695a) *Specimen dynamicum* (A specimen of dynamics), Part I, *Acta Eruditorum* (April 1695); repr. (Parts I and II) in *Mathematische Schriften*, vol. 4; trans. R. Ariew and D. Garber in *Leibniz: Philosophical Essays*, Indianapolis, IN and Cambridge, MA: Hackett Publishing Company, 1989. (Important work that links the technical physics of the *Dynamica* with more philosophical themes. Only Part I was published during Leibniz's life.)

—— (1695b) 'Système nouveau de la nature et de la communication des substances' (New system of the nature and the communication of substances), *Journal des Sçavans* (27 June 1695): 294–300; repr. in *Die philosophischen Schriften*, vol. 4; trans. R. Ariew and D. Garber in *Leibniz: Philosophical Essays*, Indianapolis, IN and Cambridge, MA: Hackett Publishing Company, 1989. (A popular presentation of Leibniz's metaphysics, featuring the first public presentation of the hypothesis of pre-established harmony.)

—— (1695c) *Dialogue effectif sur la liberté de l'homme et sur l'origine du mal* (An actual dialogue on human freedom and on the origin of evil); repr. in *Textes inédites*, vol. 1; trans. R. Ariew and D. Garber in *Leibniz: Philosophical Essays*, Indianapolis, IN and Cambridge, MA: Hackett Publishing Company, 1989. (This seems to be a record of a dialogue that actually took place between Leibniz and Baron Dobrzensky, counsellor of state and war of Brandenburg.)

—— (1696) 'Remarques sur les Objections de M. Foucher' (Remarks on the objections of M. Foucher), *Histoire des ouvrages des Savans* (February 1696): 274–6; repr. in *Die philosophischen Schriften*, vol. 4; trans. R. Ariew and D. Garber in *Leibniz: Philosophical Essays*, Indianapolis, IN and Cambridge, MA: Hackett Publishing Company, 1989. (An excellent but brief account of Leibniz's view on the problem of the continuum.)

—— (1697) *De rerum originatione radicali* (On the ultimate origination of things); repr. in *Die philosophischen Schriften*, vol. 7; trans. R. Ariew and D. Garber in *Leibniz: Philosophical Essays*, Indianapolis, IN and Cambridge, MA: Hackett Publishing Company, 1989. (This important brief essay on creation and contingency remained unpublished until the nineteenth century.)

—— (1698) 'De ipsa natura' (On nature itself), *Acta Eruditorum* (September 1698): 427–40; repr. in *Die philosophischen Schriften*, vol. 4; trans. R. Ariew and D. Garber in *Leibniz: Philosophical Essays*, Indianapolis, IN and Cambridge, MA: Hackett Publishing Company, 1989. (Significant essay on the importance of introducing genuinely active individuals into the world, against the Cartesian position that bodies are bare, extended substances.)

—— (1702) 'Note on Cartesian natural philosophy'; repr. in *Die philosophischen Schriften*, vol. 4; trans. R. Ariew and D. Garber in *Leibniz: Philosophical Essays*, Indianapolis, IN and Cambridge, MA: Hackett Publishing Company, 1989. (Untitled by Leibniz and not published in his lifetime, this is an important summary of the philosophical aspects of Leibniz's dynamics.)

—— (1702–3) *Méditation sur la notion commune de la justice* (Meditation on the common concept of justice); trans. P. Riley in *Leibniz: Political Writings*, Cambridge: Cambridge University Press, 1988. (Unpublished in Leibniz's lifetime, this is an important source for understanding his political philosophy.)

—— (1704) *Nouveau essais sur l'entendement humain* (New essays in human understanding), 1765; repr. in *Sämtliche Schriften und Briefe*, series 6, vol. 6; trans. P. Remnant and J. Bennett as *New Essays on Human Understanding*, Cambridge: Cambridge University Press, 1981. (Unpublished in Leibniz's lifetime, this is a point-by-point discussion of Locke's *Essay Concerning Human Understanding*.)

—— (1706) *Monita quaedam ad S. Pufendorfii principia* (Observations on the Principles of Pufendorf); repr. in *Leibnitii opera omnia*, vol. 4, part 3; trans. P. Riley in *Leibniz: Political Writings*, Cambridge: Cambridge University Press, 1988. (Unpublished in his lifetime, these are Leibniz's comments on the political thought of Samuel Pufendorf, the seventeenth-century jurist.)

—— (1710) *Essais de Théodicée* (Essays on Theodicy), Amsterdam; trans. E.M. Huggard as *Theodicy*, La Salle, IL: Open Court, 1985. (A treatise in which Leibniz attempts to justify the ways of God to man. Much of the work is a response to the writings of Pierre Bayle.)

—— (1712) *Jugement sur les oeuvres de Mylord Shaftesbury* (Judgment of the works of the Earl of Shaftesbury); repr. in *Leibnitii opera omnia*, vol. 5; trans. P. Riley in *Leibniz: Political Writings*, Cambridge: Cambridge University Press, 1988. (Unpublished in Leibniz's lifetime, this is a free-ranging discussion of Shaftesbury's work that includes much of interest for Leibniz's political thought.)

—— (1714a) *Monadologie*, 1721; repr. in *Die philoso-*

phischen Schriften, vol. 6; critical edn, ed. A. Robinet, *Principes de la nature et de la grâce... et Principes de la philosophie ou monadologie*, Paris: PUF, 1986; trans. R. Ariew and D. Garber as *Monadology* in *Leibniz: Philosophical Essays*, Indianapolis, IN and Cambridge, MA: Hackett Publishing Company, 1989. (Central text, not published during his lifetime, in which Leibniz gives a summary of his metaphysics at the end of his life.)

—— (1714b) 'Principes de la nature et de la grâce' (Principles of nature and grace), *Acta Eruditorum* (September 1698): 427–40; repr. in *Die philosophischen Schriften*, vol. 6; critical edn, ed. A. Robinet, *Principes de la nature et de la grâce... et Principes de la philosophie ou monadologie*, Paris: PUF, 1986; trans. R. Ariew and D. Garber in *Leibniz: Philosophical Essays*, Indianapolis, IN and Cambridge, MA: Hackett Publishing Company, 1989. (Another late summary of Leibniz's metaphysics, a companion to the *Monadology*, also not published during his lifetime.)

—— (1714c) 'De ipsa natura' (On nature itself), *Acta Eruditorum* (September 1698): 427–40; repr. in *Die philosophischen Schriften*, vol. 4; trans. R. Ariew and D. Garber in *Leibniz: Philosophical Essays*, Indianapolis, IN and Cambridge, MA: Hackett Publishing Company, 1989. (Significant essay on the importance of introducing genuinely active individuals into the world, against the Cartesian position that bodies are bare, extended substances.)

—— (1715–16) *The Leibniz–Clarke Correspondence*, 1717; trans. and ed. H.G. Alexander, Manchester: Manchester University Press, 1956. (The Alexander edition has a useful introduction and notes to the translation of the exchange.)

—— (1903) *Opuscules et fragments inédits* (Unpublished short works and fragments), ed. L. Couturat, Paris: Alcan; repr. Hildesheim: Olms, 1966. (The first publication of many of Leibniz's papers on logic, language and related areas of metaphysics, published in the original languages; this collection shaped earlier twentieth-century views of Leibniz's programme as driven by his logic.)

—— (1948) *Textes inédites d'après les manuscrits de la bibliothèque provinciale de Hanovre* (Unpublished texts, following the manuscripts in the provincial library at Hanover), ed. G. Grua, Paris: Presses Universitaires de France, 2 vols; repr. New York: Garland, 1985. (The first publication, in the original languages, of a valuable selection of writings concentrating on ethical, political and theological subjects.)

—— (1966) *Logical Papers*, ed. and trans. G.H.R. Parkinson, Oxford: Oxford University Press. (A collection of Leibniz's logical papers, translated into English, with an extensive introduction.)

—— (1969) *Philosophical Papers and Letters*, ed. and trans. L.E. Loemker, Dordrecht: Reidel. (The most extensive collection of Leibniz's writings in English, with a long introduction and useful notes.)

—— (1973) *Philosophical Writings*, ed. G.H.R. Parkinson, trans. M. Morris and G.H.R. Parkinson, London: Dent; Totowa, NJ: Rowman & Littlefield. (A useful collection in English translation.)

—— (1988) *Leibniz: Political Writings*, ed. and trans. P. Riley, Cambridge: Cambridge University Press, 2nd edn. (An excellent collection of Leibniz's moral and political writings, with a useful introduction.)

—— (1989) *Leibniz: Philosophical Essays*, ed. and trans. R. Ariew and D. Garber, Indianapolis, IN and Cambridge, MA: Hackett Publishing Company. (A widely available translation of a selection of Leibniz's most important philosophical texts.)

References and further reading

Adams, R.M. (1994) *Leibniz: Determinist, Theist, Idealist*, Oxford: Oxford University Press. (An important recent monograph that focuses on questions of contingency, natural theology, substance and body in Leibniz. Highly recommended for the serious student.)

Aiton, E.J. (1985) *Leibniz: A Biography*, Bristol: Hilger. (A recent biography in English.)

Broad, C.D. (1975) *Leibniz: an Introduction*, Cambridge: Cambridge University Press. (Though somewhat dated, still a good philosophical introduction to Leibniz's thought.)

Couturat, L. (1901) *La logique de Leibniz d'après des documents inédits* (The logic of Leibniz from unpublished documents), Paris: Alcan; repr. Hildesheim: Olms, 1961. (Still the best study of Leibniz's programme for logic and related areas.)

Duchesneau, F. (1994) La *Dynamique de Leibniz* (Leibniz's Dynamics), Paris: Vrin. (A good recent study of Leibniz's programme for physics.)

Frankfurt, H. (ed.) (1972) *Leibniz: A Collection of Critical Essays*, New York: Doubleday Anchor. (Contains many classic essays, including those of Russell and Couturat.)

Gueroult, M. (1967) *Leibniz: dynamique et métaphysique* (Leibniz: Dynamics and Metaphysics), Paris: Aubier. (A classic study of the connection between Leibniz's dynamics and his metaphysics.)

Ishiguro, H. (1972) *Leibniz's Philosophy of Logic and Language*, Ithaca, NY: Cornell University Press, 2nd edn, 1990. (A good study focusing on questions relating to logic and language.)

Jolley, N. (ed.) (1995) *The Cambridge Companion to Leibniz*, Cambridge: Cambridge University Press. (A recent collection of articles surveying the various aspects of Leibniz's thought, but focusing on his philosophy.)

Mercer, C. (1998, forthcoming) *Leibniz's Metaphysics: Its Origins and Development*, Cambridge: Cambridge University Press. (A lively study of Leibniz's early philosophy and how it evolved into the mature thought.)

Müller, K. and Krönert, G. (1969) *Leben und Werk von G.W. Leibniz. Eine Chronik* (The life and work of G.W. Leibniz: a chronology), Frankfurt: Klostermann. (An exhaustive summary of what is known about Leibniz's life, whereabouts, and when he was working on what, with documentation, arranged chronologically.)

Ravier, E. (1937) *Bibliographie des Oeuvres de Leibniz* (Bibliography of the works of Leibniz), Paris: Alcan; repr. Hildesheim: Olms, 1966. (Despite some inaccuracies, the best guide to the publication of Leibniz's writings, from his lifetime to the 1930s.)

Russell, B. (1937) *A Critical Exposition of the Philosophy of Leibniz*, London: Allen & Unwin, 2nd edn. (Advances the view that Leibniz's metaphysics is grounded in his formal logic. While the main thesis is now generally rejected, it was highly influential, and the book contains many still-valuable discussions.)

Rutherford, D. (1995) *Leibniz and the Rational Order of Nature*, Cambridge and New York: Cambridge University Press. (Ascribes the systematic unity of Leibniz's thought to his vision of the best of all possible worlds.)

Sleigh, R.C. (1990) *Leibniz & Arnauld. A Commentary on their Correspondence*, New Haven, CT, and London: Yale University Press. (While it focuses on what Leibniz was thinking in the crucial mid-1680s, this is also an excellent commentary on some of the most important philosophical themes in Leibniz's thought. Highly recommended for the serious student.)

Studia Leibnitiana (1969–), Weisbaden: Steiner Verlag. (A journal that focuses on studies of Leibniz and his age. In addition to its regular issues, it also publishes numerous supplementary volumes containing collections of essays, conference proceedings, and short monographs that pertain to Leibniz and related issues in the history of philosophy.)

* Voltaire, F.M. de (1759) *Candide, ou l'optimisme* (Candide, or optimism), Paris. (A caricature of Leibniz appears in this popular tale in the person of Dr Pangloss. It is available in numerous modern editions, both in French and in English translation.)

DANIEL GARBER

LEIBOWITZ, YESHAYAHU (1903–94)

Unlike the major intellectual currents that shaped religious thought in the modern world, Leibowitz's thought is deeply anchored in the Israeli context. Both as philosopher and activist, Leibowitz lived and articulated the paradoxes of modern Israel where he lived and was best known. His reputation as a Socratic gadfly to the establishment reflected his ongoing critique of both Israeli society in the light of Judaism, and Judaism in the light of the revolutionary implications of the creation of the State of Israel.

On the one hand, he was a Jewish patriot, a fighter for Jewish independence from all forms of foreign rule; on the other hand, he was a harsh, relentless critic of national and political expressions of chauvinism in the Israeli establishment. A strictly observant Jew, Leibowitz had less impact on traditional religious Jews than on secular Israelis. His central message is that what makes Jews distinctive as a group is neither their theology nor their Bible, but the system of law with which they regulate their lives. Judaism is a communal concept, and there is no point in religious Jews ignoring the State of Israel, or expecting others to bear their civil burdens for them. Religious law has to be reconciled with life in the political reality of the state, and this necessitates changing those attitudes to the law which reflect the historical conditions of life in exile.

1 The challenge to Judaism
2 Zionism and the critique of religious Zionists
3 Israel and *halakhah*

1 The challenge to Judaism

According to Leibowitz, the essential subject of Judaism is not the individual but community. Its primary concern is not with personal sin and finitude, but with community and its commitment to serve God. He argued that the essential factor which distinguishes Jews from other nations is not theology or the Bible, but *halakhah* Jewish law (see HALAKHAH). The laws governing what Jews eat, when they work and how they worship, constitute the uniqueness of the Jewish nation. The primacy of *halakhah* in Judaism is less a value judgment than an empirical fact of history. The relative tolerance of Jewish communities for a variety of theological opinions stands in sharp contrast to their intolerance to forms of practice that deviate from *halakhah*. Jews share a distinctive form of religious life, regardless of their divergent or even contradictory conceptions of God.

Jewish life remained broadly characterizable in

terms such as these until the beginning of the Emancipation at the end of the eighteenth century. But emancipation led to the growth of movements to modify or abandon parts of *halakhah* while preserving the synagogue as a place of worship. It also led to the emergence of secular Zionism. Leibowitz argues that the secular option, which claims continuity with the Jewish people yet abandons *halakhah* and the worship of God as defining features of Jewish identity is a falsification of the facts of Jewish history.

The question of the relationship between religion and state is connected to the larger theological issue of the religious significance of historical events. To Leibowitz, God cannot be understood in personalistic theistic terms. All attempts at describing God from a human perspective are tantamount to idolatry. In this respect, Leibowitz's position is similar to Maimonides' negative theology (see MAIMONIDES, M.). One might characterize his analysis of religious language as prescriptive rather than descriptive. One cannot talk to or about God; one can only act in the presence of God. Religious language is informed by and must be limited to the worship of God. God is not to be invoked to justify ethical or political judgments; for such usage makes God subservient to human needs. Paradigmatic for Leibowitz's understanding of Judaism is the binding of Isaac, where Abraham is ready to sacrifice his only son (representing history, the self, the human) in unconditional obedience to God's will. The Jewish model for Leibowitz's religious orientation, however, is not the personalistic theistic framework of the Bible, but the religious ethos and communal framework of the talmudic tradition. The revelatory movement of God in history, as represented in the Bible, is replaced by the worshipping movement of the Jews towards God, which the talmudic tradition embodies. Leibowitz distinguished Judaism from Christianity in terms of the latter's promise of personal salvation and liberation from finitude and sin. In Judaism, the world as it is – with the promise of redemption – expresses the will and wisdom of God. All events mirror God's power, just as all nature manifests God's wisdom. No particular event can be singularly endowed with religious meaning, so there is no theology of history. Neither the rebirth of Israel nor the tragic events of the twentieth century have instrinsic religious meaning. Similarly, holiness is not something intrinsic to things, either animate or inanimate. Holiness results solely from human action in the service of God; it is a *halakhic* and not an ontological category. Judaism as represented concretely in *halakhah* is a constant effort and striving to realize God's commands in the world.

2   Zionism and the critique of the religious Zionists

Unlike the religious conservatism of the ultra-Orthodox who relegate the legitimacy of Jewish political autonomy to an eschatological future, Leibowitz participated actively in the political struggle to re-establish an autonomous, self-governing Jewish community. While believing that nothing in the past fifteen hundred years could be compared to this heroic decision of Jews to alter their political destiny, he realized that the majority of these Jews were not motivated by a religious purpose.

Leibowitz defined Zionism as the natural expression of a national community seeking to cast off political subjugation and subservience to others. This collective impulse is in itself legitimate and healthy; it has no need of religious justification (see ZIONISM).

Nevertheless, religious Zionists adopted, or rather, co-opted this nationalist impulse by redefining the State of Israel's natural – albeit remarkable – political renewal in redemptive, Messianic terms. Yet, despite their extension of religious consciousness to include this new political reality, the religious Zionists refused to acknowledge the need to change practices based on *halakhah* which reflected very different historical conditions. How can one participate religiously in statehood, asks Leibowitz, without recognizing the incongruity of practising a *halakhah* wherein Jews are not fully responsible for maintaining the overarching socio-political reality of the state?

Leibowitz presents a Jewish categorical imperative for the religious community: act in such a way that you could wish all Jews to act in a similar fashion. Leibowitz thus rejected the granting of military exemptions to yeshivah students and religious girls. He similarly rejected all other concessions to the 'special interests' of observant Jews.

3   Israel and *halakhah*

Leibowitz is a *halakhic* existentialist who believes that the decision to participate in statehood cannot find legitimization in a framework that mirrors the historical conditions of exile. Unlike *halakhic* reform movements in the diaspora which, he believed, were usually motivated by a desire for social accommodation and convenience, Leibowitz was uncompromising in his demand for individual discipline and conformity to the standards of *halakhah*.

Modernity and the desire for social integration had no normative weight in his eyes. Leibowitz believed that the impulse for change that grew out of the new Jewish political reality was legitimate and urgent, since it was indigenous to Judaism and reflected the Jewish situation itself. Given the dependence of

Judaism on the existence and the life of a Jewish society and people, it is contradictory and inauthentic for *halakhists* to ignore the need to revise Jewish law in the light of the expanded scope of Jewish social and political responsibilities. There is, then, a striking – but logically consistent – dichotomy in Leibowitz's attitude towards *halakhah*. He is conservative and authoritarian regarding the personal dimension of *halakhic* practice (for example, *kashrut* and the laws of sexual purity). But at the same time he is boldly innovative in his call for reform in areas related to public life in the State of Israel.

This dichotomy highlights the unique nature of Leibowitz's philosophic agenda in contrast to that of most other Jewish thinkers in the twentieth century. Franz ROSENZWEIG and Hermann COHEN, for example, sought ways of legitimizing Judaism in a Christian society. Rosenzweig claimed that Judaism bore witness to the eschatological moment in history; Hermann Cohen focused on the messianic impulse of universality. Mordecai KAPLAN tried to free Judaism from the problematic notions of supernaturalism and divine election and thus to facilitate the integration of Judaism into modern pluralistic societies. Joseph SOLOVEITCHIK and Abraham HESCHEL aimed at renewing Judaism as a serious option for the individual in modern society. Soloveitchik tried to enliven the *halakhic* option by presenting Judaism as a compelling existential drama; Heschel wanted to rehabilitate the theological and spiritual sensibilities of the individual Jew. For Leibowitz, by contrast, the problem was not Christianity or the philosophical critiques of religion, but whether Judaism could be a viable and authentic possibility for an autonomous political community. While in the Diaspora, Judaism has to deal with the problems of the individual and individual relations with the surrounding culture. But in Israel the community has precedence over the individual. The individual now needs to be convinced that Judaism is an acceptable framework for the whole of society. The unique character of Leibowitz's existentialism is that it is directed towards providing for the authenticity of life as a member of the community.

See also: HALAKHAH; JEWISH PHILOSOPHY, CONTEMPORARY; ZIONISM

List of works

Leibowitz, Y. (1975) *Yahudut, Am Yehudi u-Medinat Yisrael* (Judaism, The Jewish People and the State of Israel), Tel Aviv: Schocken. (An account of his views on what is politically distinctive about Judaism.)

—— (1979) *Sichot al Pirkei Avot* (Talks on The Ethics of the Fathers), Tel Aviv: Schocken. (Reflections on Talmudic themes and the philosophy of Moses Maimonides.)

—— (1980) *Emunato shel ha-Rambam*, trans. J. Gluker, *The Faith of Maimonides*, New York: Adama, 1987. (Brilliant and concise analysis of Moses Maimonides.)

—— (1992) *Yahdut, Am Yehudi v' Medinat Yisrael*, ed. E. Goldman, trans. E. Goldman, Y. Navon, Z. Jacobson, G. Levi and R. Levy, *Judaism, Human Values and the Jewish State*, Cambridge, MA: Harvard University Press. (Compilation of Leibowitz's essays on the meaning of Judaism in the modern worlds and a critique of the political structure in Israel, where religion has been coopted by the state.)

References and further reading

Hartman, D. (1985) *A Living Covenant*, New York: Free Press, 109–30. (A critique of Leibowitz's anthropology.)

—— (1990) *Conflicting Visions*, New York: Schocken, 57–107. (A sympathetic introduction to Leibowitz's philosophy; a dialogue between the author and Leibowitz on the significance of Israel.)

—— (1993) 'Yeshyahu Leibowitz', in S. Katz (ed.) *Interpreters of Judaism in the Late Twentieth Century*, Washington, DC: B'nai Brith Books, 189–204. (Short biography of Leibowitz.)

Sagie, A. (ed.) (1995) *Yeshyahu Leibowitz: Olamo Ve'haguto* (Yeshayahu Leibowitz: His World and Philosophy), Jerusalem: Keter. (A broad collection of critical essays in Hebrew.)

DAVID HARTMAN

LENIN, VLADIMIR IL'ICH (1870–1924)

Lenin, leader of the October 1917 Revolution in Russia, wrote mainly about politics and economics, but as a Marxist of his generation he assumed that ideas about society needed to rest on sound philosophical premises. He was a militant atheist. He also regarded any other version of 'materialism' than his own as being a perversion of Marxism. Initially his works proposed an epistemology based on a crude analogy with photography. But in the First World War he revised his ideas after studying Hegel, and began to emphasize provisionality in the pursuit of scientific knowledge. Nevertheless he never disowned his earlier writings. And after his death his confused philosophical oeuvre retained axiomatic status in Marxism-Leninism.

1 **Marxism and the defence of 'materialism'**
2 **The exploration of 'dialectics'**
3 **Lenin's philosophical legacy**

1 Marxism and the defence of 'materialism'

Lenin had an influence on philosophical debate and education in his country and abroad entirely out of proportion with his expertise. Born in Simbirsk in the Russian Empire, he studied Marx's writings in his adolescence and became a follower of Georgii Plekhanov, who was the leading intellectual influence upon the clandestine Marxist groups in the Russian Empire in the 1880s and 1890s. Lenin's early articles took economic development and political struggle as their main themes. But he never lacked interest in questions of philosophy. On most fundamental questions he was Plekhanov's pupil, and proud of the fact. In so far as he intervened in the Russian Marxist discussions on epistemology, he contented himself with two activities: his repudiation of all religious belief and his castigation of the growing influence of Kant's ideas upon several prominent Russian Marxist thinkers.

He was equally opposed to the attempt by a group within his own section to inject a voluntarist element into Russian Marxist theory by linking it with the empiriocriticism of MACH (see RUSSIAN EMPIRIOCRITICISM). Its main proponent, Aleksandr Bogdanov, was for some years an ally of Lenin in the Bolshevik faction which was formed after the Second Congress of the Russian Social-Democratic Labour Party in 1903. Bogdanov had always felt uneasy about central aspects of Plekhanov's philosophical work; and as Bogdanov and Lenin fell out about general political and cultural policy, so they were drawn into exposing their private dispute on epistemology. Lenin to a great extent stuck by Plekhanov's tenets. Above all, he followed Plekhanov in asserting that the 'external world' exists independently of human cognition. In treating the mind–matter dichotomy, he propounded that 'matter' imposed itself upon 'mind'. Indeed Lenin felt that Plekhanov described the process too weakly. Whereas Plekhanov imagined the mind as registering 'external reality' through a series of 'hieroglyphs', Lenin declared the process to be unmediated by any such process: instead the mind was supposedly a mechanism akin to a camera – and Lenin believed that cameras had the capacity for the exact registration of 'external reality'.

The extraordinary optimism of Lenin's epistemology is displayed in the conclusions he drew from this argument. In particular, he claimed that the Marxist mode of understanding society enabled its proponents to attain 'absolute truth'. To the counter-argument that such a claim would render obsolete any further research on economics, politics and culture, Lenin declared that *Das Kapital* (*Capital*) had yielded up only a portion of the available absolute truth. Nothing in Marx's *magnum opus* was going to be disproven; on the contrary, it would stand as a monument of unassailable verity. According to Lenin, *Capital* also laid down the necessary guidelines whereby to contribute further portions of absolute truth. Thus Marxism was 'scientific'; it was militantly 'materialistic', atheistic and began from the premise that the material and social world were in constant flux and that the study of changing phenomena was permanently required.

These opinions were stridently asserted in *Materializm i èmpiriokrititsizm* (Materialism and Empiriocriticism), the tract Lenin issued against Bogdanov in 1909. His style was overtly political. He affirmed that there were two 'parties' in philosophy: materialism (which he advocated) and idealism (which he opposed) (see PARTIINOST'). By entering into contention against Lenin, Bogdanov had removed himself from the only acceptable party – and Lenin the politician argued that by the same action Bogdanov had left the path of revolution and had abandoned organized Marxism. Lenin treated any refusal to espouse his own narrow version of Plekhanovite Marxism as a lurch into idealism that could eventually result in a resurgence of religious belief. As it happened, some among Bogdanov's political associates – notably Anatolii Lunacharskii and Maksim Gorkii – were contemporaneously developing a form of Marxism which proposed a kind of collective deification of the working class. This had become known as 'god-building', and gave Lenin his polemical opportunity to write off all his opponents among Bolsheviks as aiming to effect a *rapprochement* with religion.

Bogdanov, who was a far subtler student of contemporary philosophy than his antagonist, did not take this lying down. He pointed out that Lenin's notion of absolute truth was antiscientific and metaphysical. Lenin made obeisance to Marx and Engels in a style of ritualist religion. Bogdanov argued that Marx had never made many of the claims made by Lenin in his name, and that the basic premise of any reasonable interpretation of Marxism should be that all analyses – including Marx's own – were merely provisional. Nor did Bogdanov fail to poke fun at Lenin's primitive understanding of how a camera works.

2 The exploration of 'dialectics'

Yet it would be wrong to give the impression that Lenin was merely exploiting philosophy for political advantage. At a basic personal level, his concern about epistemology was genuinely felt. Lenin made the assumption that any 'correct' (a favourite adjective!) statement about politics or economics had to be rooted in a 'correct' philosophical position. This, for him, was essential to Marxism. It consequently seemed to Lenin that if he disagreed with rival Marxists about their politics or economics, then a philosophical discrepancy must somehow lie at the foundations of the disagreement. Never was this clearer than in the First World War, when Lenin furiously objected to the policies pursued by the German Marxist theoretician Karl Kautsky. Kautsky had refused to make a clean break with the German Social Democratic Party over its decision to vote war credits to the German government. Lenin denounced this as a betrayal of socialist internationalism, and his reaction was not only to polemicize against Kautsky politically but also to investigate the philosophical premises implicit in Kautsky's wartime writings.

And so Lenin studied not only Marx and Engels but also those earlier philosophers who might help him understand the origins of Marxist epistemology. This brought him especially to Hegel and Aristotle; for his intuition was that Kautsky had an excessively deterministic approach to Marxism and underestimated the importance of 'dialectical' thought – of which both Hegel and Aristotle were notable exponents. Lenin was pretty thorough: he read Aristotle in a bilingual text which included the original Greek. He also re-read Marx's *Theses on Feuerbach*. Lenin's studies surprised and delighted him. With more than a touch of immodesty he decided that 'not one Marxist has completely understood Marx in the past half-century'.

His wartime notebooks on philosophy were meant to provide the material for a large, convincing exposition of the need for 'dialectics' to be bedded in the core of Marxism. His various jottings, which were not published at the time, exhibit several changes of stance from *Materialism and Empiriocriticism*. He abandoned his simplistic reflectional theory of cognition. Instead he stressed that human perception was a process of interaction not only between mind and matter but also between mind and concepts. Furthermore, he urged that the validity of theory could be judged only by 'practice' (*praktika*). In this fashion he was unwittingly moving close to the philosophical stance of his old adversary Bogdanov, who held that knowledge had to be obtained experimentally and could never be more than provisional in character.

Lenin came to his new conclusions independently of Bogdanov. For whereas Bogdanov's ideas were a fusion of Marx and Mach, Lenin had refreshed his ideas by looking at Hegel – and continued to revile empiriocriticism as a reactionary doctrine.

Hegel's writings, especially those which dwelt on dialectical processes, by contrast had a strong attraction for Lenin, who contended that Hegelianism provided Marx and Engels with the key understanding that 'interruptions of gradualness', 'leaps' and 'breaks', were basic to the functioning of both the material and the social universe. Dialectics thereby became a philosophical justification for political revolution; and Lenin contended that it was precisely on this point that Kautsky had refrained from coming to terms with authentic Marxism. Lenin also argued that Kautsky had ignored the need for philosopher-revolutionaries to take chances, to speculate, to dream. Lenin had said something along these lines in his famous political treatise of 1902, *Chto delat'* (*What Is To Be Done?*); but in the First World War such an argument became virtually a credo: 'The approach of mind (man) to a particular thing is...complex, divided, zigzaggish, *including within itself* the possibility of a flight of fantasy from life. It is stupid to deny the role of fantasy even in the strictest science'.

Yet simultaneously Lenin, who was an intelligent but confused amateur in philosophy, retained much of the views expressed in *Materialism and Empiriocriticism* in 1909. As ever, he insisted that man's abstract conceptions about the world derived from 'a knowledge of the pattern of the objective links of the world'. His belief about there being two entirely separate camps in philosophy, materialism and idealism, was unshaken. And he jotted down in his notebooks that there was no reason to deny the attainability of 'living, fruitful, true, powerful, omnipotent, objective, absolute human knowledge'. In 1920, furthermore, when he fell into public dispute again with Bogdanov (and indeed with fellow-Bolshevik Party leader Nikolai Bukharin), Lenin ordered the republication of *Materialism and Empiriocriticism*.

3 Lenin's philosophical legacy

Consequently Lenin left a legacy of great contradiction. He had changed much of his thought, but had done this by adding bits without excising earlier ones. As a philosopher he would hardly deserve a footnote in the history of twentieth-century thought if it had not been for his political career as the founder of the USSR. In everything he wrote he showed greater confidence than expertise. Even in most of his apparently original interpretations of Marx, he had largely been anticipated by Bogdanov. In his analysis of Hegel and Kant he misrepresented the differences between the two. Nevertheless in death he became the object of a secular state. Lenin himself had never claimed to be more than a follower of Marx. Nor had he attempted to assemble all his various political, economic and philosophical works into a single, authoritative set of tenets. This was done for him by his successors, especially Stalin; and his writings were codified and designated as Marxism-Leninism.

For most of the ensuing decades it was *Materialism and Empiriocriticism* which was used as the supreme philosophical text of the regime (although the *Philosophical Notebooks* became more widely discussed after Stalin's death in 1953). Even so, there was enough confusion and incompleteness in Lenin's published thought for Soviet philosophers to have plenty to argue about. The practice of philosophy in the USSR, cramped and abused as it was, would have had an even harsher environment if Lenin had been a more expert epistemologist.

See also: BOGDANOV, A.A.; PLEKHANOV, G.V.; RUSSIAN EMPIRIOCRITICISM

List of works

Lenin, V.I. (1909) *Materializm i èmpiriokrititsizm*, in *Polnoe sobranie sochinenii*, vol. 18, Moscow: Gospolitizdat, 1958–69, 5th edn. (Many republications and translations in the Soviet era.)

—— (1895–1916) *Filosofskie tetradi*, in *Polnoe sobranie sochinenii*, Moscow: Gospolitizdat, 1958–69, 5th edn, vol. 29; trans. C. Dutt, *Philosophical Notebooks*, in *Collected Works*, vol. 38, Moscow: Progress and London: Lawrence & Wishart, 1968–9. (First published in Russian in the *Leninskii sbornik* series, Moscow.)

—— (1902) *Chto delat'*, in *Polnoe sobranie sochinenii*, Moscow: Gospolitizdat, 1958–69, 5th edn, vol. 5; trans. J. Fineberg, *What Is To Be Done?* in *Collected Works*, vol. 5, Moscow: Progress and London: Lawrence & Wishart, 1968–9.

References and further reading

Kolakowski, L. (1978) *The Main Currents of Marxism*, vol. 2, *The Golden Age*, Oxford. (Magisterial, hostile account of Leninist philosophy which situates Lenin's ideas in the Marxist tradition and provides a well-constructed bibliography.)

Read, C. (1979) *Religion, Revolution and the Russian Intelligentsia, 1900–1912*, London. (Useful general account of the intellectual milieu of prewar Russian intellectual discussions.)

Scanlan, J.P. (1985) *Marxism in the USSR. A Critical Survey of Current Soviet Thought*, London. (Outstanding survey of the scope of Marxism-Leninism, including its philosophy, after Lenin's death; impressive and useful bibliography.)

Service, R. (1985, 1991, 1995) *Lenin: A Political Life*, vols 1–3, London. (General analysis of Lenin's career, involving an examination of the connections between his politics and his philosophy.)

Wetter, G. (1958) *Dialectical Materialism. A Historical and Systematic Survey of Philosophy in the Soviet Union*, London. (Pioneering study of the Marxism of Lenin and Stalin; useful despite the further development of scholarship since the book's publication.)

ROBERT SERVICE

LEONE EBREO *see* ABRAVANEL, JUDAH BEN ISAAC

LEONT'EV, KONSTANTIN NIKOLAEVICH (1831–91)

One of the more original and provocative nineteenth-century Russian thinkers, Leont'ev directed a powerful intellectual attack at the dominant historical movement of his time: the process of modernization that was sweeping across Western Europe and making inroads into Russia. Leont'ev resisted the sociopolitical aspects of this process: the spread of democratic, egalitarian and constitutional principles. He also resisted its cultural and psychological aspects: the emergence of a standardized, homogenized mode of life and set of values.

Leont'ev defended the traditional values and institutions of monarchy, established Church, aristocracy and – especially – the distinctiveness and variety of national cultures. It was this distinctiveness, based on the isolation of nation states, that he saw as increasingly threatened by the advancing technologies of transport and communication.

1 Social philosophy and philosophy of culture
2 Philosophy of history
3 Philosophy of religion

1 Social philosophy and philosophy of culture

Konstantin Nikolaevich Leont'ev was born into a

gentry family in the village of Kudinovo. He studied medicine at Moscow University and served as a military surgeon during the Crimean War, 1853–6. During his first two decades of literary activity (1854–76) he wrote mostly short stories and novels. His talent was recognized by Ivan Turgenev, who helped and encouraged him. Over the next two decades (roughly, 1872–91) Leont'ev produced a flood of brilliant and disturbing philosophical and political essays. He served for a decade as a Russian diplomat in various parts of the Ottoman Empire, 1863–73; he also worked in the Censor's Office in Moscow, 1880–7. In 1871 he experienced a spiritual crisis and lived for a year in a Russian monastery on Mount Athos. His efforts to become a monk were gently, and wisely, rebuffed by his spiritual advisors, who felt that he was not yet ready to give up the 'world' of writing and publishing. He in fact took secret monastic vows a few months before his death, at the Trinity Monastery near Moscow.

Leont'ev has often been called a 'Russian Nietzsche', not in the sense of a Russian thinker influenced by Nietzsche, since he died before Nietzsche's ideas became known in Russia (see NIETZSCHE: IMPACT ON RUSSIAN THOUGHT). Rather, it is sometimes claimed that Leont'ev anticipated Nietzsche's main doctrines. This claim is seriously misleading. Leont'ev did share, in advance, Nietzsche's stress on the priority of aesthetic over moral and practical values; his 'aesthetic immoralism' dates from the mid-1860s, a time when the dominant Russian Nihilists and Realists were deriding aesthetic values (see RUSSIAN MATERIALISM: THE '1860S'; NIHILISM, RUSSIAN). For example, a leading character in an early Leont'ev novel made the shocking assertion: 'A single century-old magnificent tree is worth more than twenty faceless men; and I will not cut it down in order to be able to buy medicine [to treat] the peasants' cholera!' (1912–14, vol. 1: 306; emphases added).

Leont'ev also agreed with Nietzsche in celebrating the 'poetry of war', regarding security and comfort as deadening to cultural creativity; and of course he was entirely at one with Nietzsche in opposing the levelling and standardizing tendencies of the time. But there were a number of key differences. For Nietzsche, Christianity and democracy (and indeed socialism) were on the same side; in contrast Leont'ev spoke of the 'Antichrist of democracy'. Leont'ev embraced strong nation states and state churches, both of which Nietzsche opposed. There is no counterpart in Nietzsche's work to Leont'ev's sweeping condemnation of modern technology. Leont'ev preached what he called the 'poetry of *life*' – the social and historical life of nations and ethnic groups in all its colourful diversity. Nietzsche preached the 'poetry' or 'aesthetics' of a universal *high culture*. Nietzsche accepted, and Leont'ev rejected, a powerful orientation towards the remote historical future. Leont'ev remained a Christian, preaching 'love of one's neighbour'; Nietzsche, the 'anti-Christian', preached 'love of the far-off', that is, 'love of the high culture of the remote historical future' and endorsed 'instrumental cruelty' towards one's neighbours who are weak, sickly and uncreative. In a word, Leont'ev embraced, while Nietzsche repudiated, 'good Samaritanism'. At the same time, Leont'ev introduced a highly original corrective, one which might well be considered 'Nietzschean': he insisted that Christian charity not be one-sidedly 'democratic'. It should not be directed only at suffering workers or wounded soldiers (of whom Leont'ev had had direct experience during the Crimean War); it should include the powerful and privileged in their hour of need, for instance, defeated generals and aristocrats abused by the mob.

Leont'ev's rejection of modernity is more sweeping than Nietzsche's. In fact, the only aspect of the many-faceted process of modernization that Leont'ev accepted was its stress on the subjectivity and – with qualifications – freedom of the individual person. On this point Leont'ev went further in Hegel's direction than Nietzsche was prepared to do.

Leont'ev offers many impressive catalogues of the glories of sociopolitical and cultural diversity and vividness in ancient Greece and Rome and in medieval Europe, along with catalogues of the horrors of sociopolitical and cultural monotony and drabness in present-day Western Europe and – increasingly – Russia. The former he celebrated as 'the poetry of life'; the latter he castigated as its 'prose' or 'prosiness'. Here is one example, which sets out four kinds of differences that are being eliminated by the hated process of modernization: (1) social (the difference between a peasant, a nobleman and 'a marquis in velvet and plumes'); (2) occupational (that between a soldier and a priest); (3) national-ethnic (that between a Basque and a man from Brittany, or between a Tyrolian and a Circassian); and (4) 'intrareligious' (that between 'a Trappist in a hair shirt' and a prelate in brocade). In this fourth difference Leont'ev would appear to have overshot his mark: even in the secularizing Europe of the late nineteenth century there was still a clear distinction between a Trappist in his hair shirt and a prelate in brocade.

The violence of Leont'ev's repudiation of technology – both the principal forms already familiar in his own day (for instance railroad and telegraph) and those being introduced during his final years (telephone, electric light and so on) – is surprising.

So is his claim that such 'peaceful' technology is much more destructive than the newer technologies of war (like the machine gun). But Leont'ev's point is that these faster, more efficient, more pervasive forms of transport and communication are undermining the 'isolation of states' and national and ethnic cultural traditions, thus facilitating the general process of standardization and homogenization of culture. Like other aspects of the modernization process, technological advance is reducing the vivid poetry of life to colourless prose.

2 Philosophy of history

In 1869–71 Nikolai Danilevskii, in his influential book *Rossiia i Evropa* (Russia and Europe), set out a large-scale theory of 'cultural-historical types' intended to show that the Slavic-Russian type possessed hitherto unrecognized cultural vitality and a special promise of future cultural creativity. Leont'ev's philosophy of history was similar to, but in important ways distinct from, Danilevskii's. Like the latter, he used an essentially biological model of historical development. Historical cultures, like living organisms, develop from a stage of 'initial simplicity' to a second stage of 'flourishing complexity' and then sink, through a third process of 'levelling interfusion', to organic decay and death. Western Europe, which had achieved its stage of flourishing complexity in the Renaissance, was already far advanced in the terminal process of 'levelling interfusion'. Leont'ev estimated the life span of historical cultures at about 1,200 years and sometimes asserted – with the Slavophiles – that Russia was a younger culture than Western Europe and therefore had more of its period of flourishing complexity still ahead of it. But at other times, and more typically, he claimed that nineteenth-century Russia possessed a unique combination of institutional elements – autocracy, Russian Orthodoxy and a system of deep and stable class divisions – which would make it possible to 'freeze Russia over' and thus save it from the creeping Western European 'rot'. Note that he claimed no special superiority – as Danilevskii had – for the uniquely Slavic elements of Russian culture; indeed, he stressed that all were derived from a non-Slavic source, namely Byzantium, that was *Greek* in language and culture.

Leont'ev sometimes spoke of his own position as 'anti-European', and one of his critics accused him of pervasive 'miso-Europeanism'. Both terms are misleading. Leont'ev's animus was directed against the process of modernization that was coming to Russia from Western Europe, not against Western Europe as such. As we have seen, he admired much in Western European history up to the Renaissance,

specifically including the Roman Catholic Church and the institution of the Germanic Knights. At the same time the unifications of Italy and Germany that were under way in Leont'ev's lifetime struck him as destructive of the diversity of 'ethnic' or 'regional' cultures of the various parts of the newly unified national wholes (say, Venice and Naples, or Bavaria and Prussia). It is true that Leont'ev was enchanted by the rich cultural diversity that he encountered during his stays in Greece, Turkey and the Balkans, and credited this to their more complete isolation (than Russia's) from Western European influences. But Leont'ev's fundamental protest was against modernization, not against Europe as such.

Looking sombrely into the future, he saw the triumph of a worldwide socialist movement – not because the socialists were right but because their principal adversaries, the liberals, were wrong. Leont'ev even envisaged the possibility that such a socialist movement – 'the feudalism of the future', as he called it – might be headed by a Russian tsar!

3 Philosophy of religion

From the beginning Leont'ev's approach to religion, like his approach to secular matters, had a strong aesthetic colouring. He was charmed by the beauty of the Russian Orthodox service – the singing, the icons, the incense. But later his religious convictions took a severe 'Byzantine' turn and he came to stress the fear of God, ascetic discipline and a profound disillusionment with all things earthly as merely 'a passing dream'. In his final letters to Vasilii Rozanov Leont'ev commented bitterly that 'Christian preaching' was joining forces with the hated modernization process to 'kill the aesthetics of life on earth'. He added, in what appears to have been a tone of quiet desperation: 'We must help Christianity even at the cost of our beloved aesthetics' (letter of 27 May 1891).

Turning to the main proponents of a 'renewed' Christianity in Russia in his time, Leont'ev found both TOLSTOI (he was right in this) and DOSTOEVSKII (here he was wrong) guilty of falling into a humanistic 'rose-coloured' Christianity that verged on 'anthropolatry' – 'a new faith in *earthly man* and in earthly mankind – in the ideal *self-sufficient, autonomous* worth and dignity of the *individual person*' (1912–14, vol. 8: 160; original emphases). He was especially infuriated by Tolstoi's presumption in editing and rewriting the New Testament and by Tolstoi's reference, in a conversation with Leont'ev, to '*my* Gospel'.

The originality and depth of Leont'ev's ideas about history, society, politics, culture and religion led to his being 'heard but not heeded, read but not understood' in his own time and for many years after his death. It is only in the twentieth century, especially during its final decade (and mostly in post-communist Russia) that Leont'ev's provocative and unsettling works have been widely reprinted and seriously discussed.

List of works

Leont'ev, K.N. (1912–14) *Sobranie sochinenii* (Collected Works), 9 vols, St Petersburg: V. Sablin (vol. 9 was published by the Russkoe knizhnoe t-vo Deiatel'); xerographic repr., Ann Arbor, MI: University Microfilms, 1967. (Includes Leont'ev's early fiction, later reminiscences and essays on social, political and religious themes. Does not include his correspondence or his autobiographical essay 'Moia literaturnaia sud'ba' (My Literary Fate).)

—— (1890) 'Analiz, stil' i veianie. O romanakh Gr. L.N.Tolstogo'; trans. S.E. Roberts, 'The Novels of Count L.N. Tolstoy: Analysis, Style, and Atmosphere – a Critical Study', in *Essays on Russian Literature: The Conservative View. Leontiev, Rozanov, Shestov*, Athens, OH: Ohio University Press, 1968, 225–356. (This is the only complete English translation of a Leont'ev work in philosophy or literary criticism.)

—— (1969) *Against the Current: Selections from the Novels, Essays, Notes, and Letters of Konstantin Leontiev*, ed. G. Ivask, trans. G. Reavey, New York: Waybright & Talley. (See especially the section entitled 'Philosophy', 133–229.)

—— (1993) *Izbrannye pis' ma 1854–1891* (Selected Letters 1854–1891), ed. D.V. Solov'ëv, St Petersburg: Pushkinskii fond. (This important edition contains 700 of Leont'ev's letters, of which 478 are published for the first time.)

—— (1996) *Vostok, Rossiia i slavianstvo: Filosofskaia i politicheskaia publitsistika. Dukhovnaia proza* (The East, Russia and Slavdom: Essays on Philosophical and Political Themes. Spiritual Prose), ed. G.B. Kremnev, introduced by V.I. Kosik, Moscow: Respublika. (This lengthy collection, which includes previously unpublished and uncollected pieces, contains such philosophically important essays as 'Vizantizm i slavianstvo' (Byzantium and Slavdom) (1875), 'Srednii evropeets kak ideal i orudie vsemirnogo razrusheniia' (The Average European as an Ideal and Instrument of Universal Destruction) (1872–84), and 'Plemennaia politika kak orudie vsemirnoi revoliutsii' (The Politics of the Tribe as an Instrument of Universal Revolution) (1888). There are also essays on the religious views of Dostoevskii and Tolstoi.)

References and further reading

Berdiaev, N.A. (1926) *Konstantin Leont'ev: Ocherk iz istorii russkoi religioznoi mysli* (Konstantin Leont'ev: An Essay in the History of Russian Religious Thought), Paris: YMCA-Press, trans. G. Reavey, *Leontiev*, London: Bles, 1940; repr. Orono, ME: Academic International, 1968. (A pioneering study, which stresses Leont'ev's critique of religion and culture.)

Dolgov, K.M. (1995) *Voskhozhdenie na Afon: Zhizn' i mirosozertsanie Konstantina Leont'eva* (The Ascent of Mount Athos: Konstantin Leont'ev's Life and World View), Moscow: Luch. (This full and sympathetic account makes judicious use of Leont'ev's correspondence.)

Kline, G.L. (1968) *Religious and Anti-Religious Thought in Russia*, Chicago, IL: University of Chicago Press, 35–54. (Offers a fuller treatment of some of the topics discussed in the present essay.)

Kologriwof, I. von (1948) *Von Hellas zum Mönchtum: Leben und Denken Konstantin Leontjews* (From Greece to Monasticism: Konstantin Leont'ev's Life and Thought), Regensburg: Gregorius Verlag. (A careful and comprehensive study by a Russian Orthodox priest.)

Korol'kov, A. and Kozyrev, A. (eds) (1995) *K.N. Leont'ev. Pro et contra: Lichnost' i tvorchestvo Konstantina Leont'eva v otsenke russkikh myslitelei i issledovatelei, 1891–1917* (K.N. Leont'ev: Pro and Contra: Konstantin Leont'ev's Personality and Work as Appraised by Russian Thinkers and Scholars, 1891–1917), St Petersburg: Izdatel'stvo Russkogo Khristianskogo gumanitarnogo instituta. (Among the thinkers represented are Berdiaev, Rozanov and Vladimir Solov'ëv. Among the scholars are A.A. Aleksandrov, Father I. Fudel' and B.Z. Griftsov.)

Zenkovsky, V.V. (1948–50) *Istoriia russkoi filosofii*, vol. 1, Paris: YMCA-Press, 433–57; 2nd edn 1989; trans. G.L. Kline, *A History of Russian Philosophy*, vol. 1, London: Routledge & Kegan Paul and New York: Columbia University Press, 1953, 434–53. (A sympathetic but not uncritical account by a Russian Orthodox priest who was the leading émigré historian of Russian philosophy.)

GEORGE L. KLINE

LESBIAN ETHICS *see* FEMINIST ETHICS

LEŚNIEWSKI, STANISŁAW (1886–1939)

Leśniewski was one of the most distinguished members of the Warsaw School of Logic. His scientific development can be divided into two periods. In the first 'philosophical' period (1911–16), he worked on problems on the borderline of logic and philosophy. In the second period (1916–39), Leśniewski concentrated on mathematical logic. Together with Łukasiewicz, he established the Warsaw School of Logic. Leśniewski intended to build a comprehensive system of logic which might be the basis for all knowledge. His system, unorthodox in many points, consists of three parts: prototethic (a generalized sentential calculus), ontology (a calculus of names) and mereology (a theory of the whole/part relation).

1   Life
2   Early views
3   General remarks on Leśniewski's logical systems
4   Prototethic
5   Ontology
6   Mereology
7   Concluding remarks

1   Life

Leśniewski was born on 30 March 1886 in Serpukhova, Russia. He studied philosophy in Leipzig and Munich (where he attended courses by Cornelius, Geiger and Pfänder). In 1910 he went to Lwów to prepare his Ph.D. thesis on existential sentences under the supervision of TWARDOWSKI; he obtained his Ph.D. in 1919. In 1915–18 he lived in Moscow, where he taught mathematics in Polish schools. At that time, he was a 'leftist' in his political views and delivered several lectures on Marxist philosophy; he entirely abandoned this ideology after the October Revolution. In 1919 Leśniewski became the professor of philosophy of mathematics at the University of Warsaw. He died of cancer on 13 May 1939.

2   Early views

In his Ph.D. dissertation, Leśniewski argued that all negative existential sentences (for example, sentences of the type '*x* does not exist') are self-contradictory. This was a direct consequence of the thesis that every sentence refers to an object. Leśniewski's doctoral dissertation was written from the point of view of a very traditional grammar and logic; he was at that time very strongly influenced by Cornelius, MILL, Marty and HUSSERL.

Leśniewski's first contact with new ideas in logic took place in 1911, when he read *On the Principle of Contradiction in Aristotle* by Łukasiewicz (PAU, Kraków, 1910). Leśniewski reported his contact with this book in the following way:

> In the year 1911...I came across a book by Jan Łukasiewicz about the principle of contradiction in Aristotle.... This book became a revelation...for the first time in my life I learned of the existence of the 'symbolic logic' of Bertrand Russell as well as his 'antinomy' regarding the 'class of all classes, which are not elements of themselves'.
>
> (Leśniewski 1992: 181)

Leśniewski undertook to resolve Russell's antinomy (see RUSSELL, B.A.W. §§4–8). After some unsuccessful attempts within standard set theory, he came to the view that the concept of a class must be reinterpreted in terms of the mereological concept of an aggregate. Given this interpretation, the expression of 'the class of all classes which are not elements of themselves' has no reference and the antinomy disappears. Leśniewski's analysis of the concept of class was the starting-point for his mereology.

Leśniewski's other investigations in the first period concerned the principle of contradiction, the principle of the excluded middle, and the concept of truth. He tried to prove the principle of contradiction via a proof of the sentence 'no object contains contradictions'. But in the case of the principle of the excluded middle, Leśniewski denied its universal validity, because he maintained that sentences of the type '*a* is *b*' with empty names in the place of '*a*' are false; thus, both '*a* is *b*' and '*a* is not *b*' are false. Leśniewski also defended the absolutism of truth: every truth is eternal and sempiternal.

Leśniewski's own evaluation of his early works was decisively negative:

> I struggled with a number of problems which were beyond my powers at that time....I have mentioned those works desiring to point out that I regret that they have appeared in print, and formally 'repudiate' them herewith...affirming the bankruptcy of the 'philosophical'-grammatical work of the initial period of my work.
>
> (Leśniewski 1992: 197–8)

However, a closer analysis shows clearly that Leśniewski did not reject all of his views from the early writings. As well as the mereological conception of class, he retained the absolutist conception of truth and the view that all sentences of the type '*a* is *b*' are false if '*a*' is an empty name.

3 General remarks on Leśniewski's logical systems

Leśniewski's system of logic comprises three systems: protothetic (an extended sentential calculus), ontology (a calculus of names) and mereology (a theory of mereological classes). This succession indicates the logical order of those systems. However, Leśniewski invented his systems in just the opposite succession. Mereology appeared as the first in 1916. Then, at the beginning of the 1920s, he completed his ontology and protothetic.

There is a considerable difference in style between Leśniewski's early work and his later work on protothetic and ontology (see Leśniewski 1929 for example). A booklet of 1916 on the foundations of the general theory of classes is written in an informal manner. Then, Leśniewski, under Chwistek's influence, began to employ formal languages as tools in doing logic. His formalism was very extreme in the sense that he required a complete codification of the languages of formal systems. Hence, he regarded Russell and WHITEHEAD's *Principia Mathematica* as a very obscure work, full of linguistic confusions: for example, it conflates object-language and meta-language. Indeed, Leśniewski was probably the first person to point out that FREGE achieved much more precision than Russell did. On the other hand, Leśniewski rejected formalism understood as a view that logic and mathematics are games with symbols devoid of meaning. He called his view 'intuitionistic formalism', although this view has nothing to do with INTUITIONISM as a position in the foundations of mathematics.

Leśniewski was a radical nominalist. He took formal systems to consist of concrete expressions (symbol-tokens, to use a popular label). Thus, on his view, formal deductive systems are always finite in the number of formulas, although they are 'unfinished' or 'unbounded', because it is always possible to add further formulas. Hence, his systems are equipped with very precise directives for introducing new expressions into the body of a system. A special role is played by the rules of definition for new signs. Leśniewski was the first logician who explicitly stated the principles of correct definition in formal systems. His systems are axiomatic, but he also used techniques of natural deduction. Certainly, his logic is peculiar, if by a deductive system we understand what is typically meant. However, it is commonly recognized that his formalization is the most precise in the entire history of logic (see NOMINALISM).

4 Protothetic

Protothetic is a generalized sentential calculus. It is a sentential logic with quantifiers which bind variables of several semantic categories: sentential variables, functorial variables which range over functors forming sentences from sentential arguments, functorial variables which range over functors of functors, and so on. In general terms, quantifiers in the theorems of protothetic bind variables of an arbitrary semantic category which are definable when we start with a category of sentences.

The full system of protothetic is based on equivalence as the sole primitive term. An important result for the formalization of protothetic on the basis of equivalence was obtained by TARSKI (in 1923) who showed that equivalence and the universal quantifier suffice to define negation and conjunction. The functions of protothetic are not limited to giving rules for sentential connectives, because this system also contains rules for the quantifiers which are used in ontology and mereology. Protothetic is, in a sense, an absolute sentential logic, because the principle of bivalence and the principle of extensionality are among its theorems. Thus, protothetic can be considered as an adequate representation of the classical idea of logic. Protothetic is consistent, but the problem of its completeness is not yet fully solved. What is known is that elementary protothetic (that is, protothetic with quantifiers restricted only to sentential variables) is complete.

5 Ontology

Ontology is the system which arises when the functor 'is' is added to protothetic. This functor forms sentences from names. Ontology considers the grammatical structure 'a is b'. Such a sentence is false if its subject is empty or refers to more than one object. This meaning is captured by the axiom of ontology which says: for any a and b, the sentence 'a is b' is equivalent to the conjunction of sentences (i) for some c, c is b, (ii) for any c and d, if c is a and d is a, then c is d, (iii) for every c, if c is a, then c is b. The intuitive content of the axiom is this: 'a is b' is true if and only if 'a' is non-empty, there is only one object to which 'a' refers ('a' is a singular name), and whatever falls under 'a' also falls under 'b'.

Ontology is supplemented by several definitions of sentence-forming functors operating on names. Two examples illustrate this matter: (i) for any a, a exists if and only if for some x, x is a; (ii) for any a, a is an object if and only if for some x, a is. (i) gives a definition of existence, and (ii) of being an object. These examples show how 'is' is understood in Leśniewski's ontology. This meaning of 'is' closely corresponds to the sense of *est* in Latin as the copula in 'Socrates est homo'. 'Is' in the considered meaning has no spatiotemporal connotations and it does not indicate the membership-relation from set theory. Also, Leśniewski's 'is' is different from 'is' in 'there is justice' or 'every man is mortal'. In general, one must be very careful in translating the basic functor of ontology (symbolically denoted by 'ε') by the English 'is', because the latter is modified by articles which do not occur in Latin (or Polish).

Leśniewski's ontology is consistent, but the question of its completeness is still open. Ontology performs the role of predicate logic, but there are also important differences. For example, identity is definable in first-order ontology, whereas it is not definable in the standard first-order logic, and the theorems of ontology are true in any domain, including the empty one. Why was this system called 'ontology'? Leśniewski chose this term because he conceived ontology as a logical theory which offers a general theory of objects in the sense of Aristotle and his followers.

6 Mereology

Mereology is a theory of classes, but classes in their mereological (collective) sense, contrary to the standard set theory which considers classes in their distributive meaning. The crucial differences between these conceptions of class is that elementhood in mereology is transitive, but membership in set theory is not: if x is a mereological element of y and y is a mereological element of z, then x is also a mereological element of z, but the comparable rule does not hold for membership. Another peculiarity of mereology is that there is no empty set.

For Leśniewski, the mereological concept of class is more intuitive than the concept of set in the distributive sense. He argued that intuitions concerning collective classes are perfectly consistent with Cantor's famous statement that any manifold which can be considered as a unity is a set (see CANTOR, G.; CANTOR'S THEOREM). Naturally, a problem arises whether mereology is as strong as set theory. The answer is negative: mereology is weaker (see MEREOLOGY).

7 Concluding remarks

Leśniewski influenced the development of logic in Poland very strongly. Together with Łukasiewicz, he trained many logicians, including Tarski (who obtained his Ph.D. under Leśniewski), Lindenbaum, Wajsberg, Sobocinski, Słupecki and Lejewski. Sobocinski and Lejewski became his main followers. In spite of his unorthodoxy in logic, Leśniewski invented several ideas which belong to the standard logical

canon. For example, he initiated the theory of syntactic categories developed by AJDUKIEWICZ in the 1930s. Leśniewski revived Frege's object-language/metalanguage distinction and used it to suggest a solution to the Liar paradox (this solution was later developed by Tarski); he also stated the conditions for correct formal systems commonly accepted by Polish logicians.

His own logical ideas are on the margin of the mainstream of logic. However, an interest in Leśniewski's logical systems is an important ingredient of logical investigations, and studies on his logical systems have been undertaken in all parts of the world, particularly in Poland, in England (among Lejewski's students – the Manchester School), and in the USA (among Sobocinski's students – the Notre Dame School). These studies have concentrated on the properties of Leśniewski's systems, and their relations to standard theories, like first-order logic, Boolean algebra and set theory. There are also attempts to apply his ideas to the analysis of natural language; for example, ontology has been interpreted as a theory of plural terms. Leśniewski's logical ideas also influenced philosophy. His ontology is nominalistic, because it admits only particulars as values of variables, and this idea was an important influence on KOTARBIŃSKI. Thus, it can be said that there is a distinctive Leśniewskian paradigm in logic.

See also: POLAND, PHILOSOPHY IN

List of works

Leśniewski, S. (1992) *Collected Works*, vols I and II, eds S.J. Surma, J.T. Srzednicki, D. I. Barnett and V.F. Rickey, Dordrecht: Kluwer. (Contains translations of Leśniewski's papers published in 1911–38 as well as a bibliography of Leśniewski's and writings on him until 1977.)

—— (1911) 'Przyczynek do analizy zdan egzystencjalnych' (A Contribution to the Analysis of Existential Propositions), *Przeglad Filozoficzny* 14: 329–45. (Leśniewski's doctoral dissertation.)

—— (1912) 'Proba dowodu ontologicznej zasady sprzecznosci' (An attempt at a Proof of the Ontological Principle of Contradiction), *Przeglad Filzoficzny* 15: 202–26. (An attempt to derive the principle of contradiction from the thesis that no objects contain contradictions.)

—— (1913a) 'Krytyka logicznej zasady wylaczonego srodku' (The critique of the Logical Principle of the Excluded Middle), *Przeglad Filzoficzny* 16: 315–22. (Leśniewski argues that the principle of excluded middle fails for sentences with empty names.)

—— (1913b) 'Czy prawda jest tylko wieczna czy tez

wieczna i odwieczna?' (Is All Truth Only True Eternally or is It Also True without a Beginning?), *Nowe Tory* 18: 493–523. (A defence of an 'absolutist' conception of truth.)

—— (1916) *Podstawy ogolnej teorii mnogosci I* (Foundations of the General Theory of Sets I), Moscow: Poplawski. (An informal presentation of Leśniewski's mereological set theory.)

—— (1927–31) 'O podstawach matematyki' (On the Foundations of Mathematics), *Przeglad Filozoficzny* 30: 164–206; 31: 261–91; 32: 60–101; 33: 77–105; 34: 142–70. (Contains a general overview of Leśniewski's systems, a detailed exposition of mereology, and remarks on the meaning of an expression '*a* is *b*').

—— (1929) 'Grundzüge eines neuen Systems der Grundlagen der Mathematik', *Fundamenta Mathematicae* 14: 1–81. (Contains a detailed exposition of prototetic.)

—— (1988) *Lecture Notes in Logic*, eds J. T. J. Srzednicki and Z. Stachniak, Dordrecht: Kluwer. (Lecture notes on prototetic, ontology, arithmetic and Whitehead's theory of events, composed from students' notes.)

References and further reading

Luschei, E. (1962) *The Logical Systems of Leśniewski*, Amsterdam: North Holland. (A systematic exposition of Leśniewski's systems.)

Mieville, D. (1984) *Un developpement de systèmes logiques de Stanislaw Leśniewski*, Berne: Lang. (A recent presentation.)

Simons, P. (1992) *Logic and Philosophy in Central Europe: From Bolzano to Tarski*, Dordrecht: Kluwer. (Contains several essays on Leśniewski's ideas.)

Srzednicki, J.T.J, Rickey, V.F. and Czelakowski, J. (eds) (1984) *Leśniewski's Systems Ontology Mereology*, The Hague: Nijhoff, and Wrocław: Ossolineum. (A collection of papers on ontology and mereology.)

Stachniak, Z. (1981) *Introduction to Model Theory for Leśniewski's Ontology*, Wrocław: Wydawnictwo Uniwersytetu Wrocławskiego. (An attempt to build a model theory in the standard sense for Leśniewski's ontology.)

Surma, S.J. (ed.) (1977) *On Leśniewski's Systems*, *Studia Logica*, vol. XXXVI, 4. (A collection of papers on Leśniewski's systems.)

Wolenski, J. (1989) *Logic and Philosophy in the Lvov–Warsaw School*, Dordrecht: Kluwer. (Chapter VII contains an overview of Leśniewski's ideas.)

JAN WOLEŃSKI

LESSING, GOTTHOLD EPHRAIM (1729–81)

Gotthold Ephraim Lessing occupies a central place in eighteenth-century European belles-lettres. He was a significant religious and theological thinker whose work puzzled his contemporaries and still provokes debate. He has been variously called a deist, a concealed theist, a Spinozist–pantheist, a panentheist, and an atheist. He was a significant dramatist whose major works include Minna von Barnhelm, *known as the first modern German comedy, and* Nathan the Wise, *which places Lessing in the tradition of eighteenth-century toleration and humanism. He was an active promoter of the contemporary German theatre and an influential drama critic and theorist. He had broad classical and antiquarian interests. And he has some claims to being one of the early developers, if not a founding father, of the discipline of philosophical aesthetics.*

Philosophically, Lessing belongs to the tradition of G. W. von Leibniz and Christian Wolff and was familiar with the post-Wolffian aesthetics being developed by Alexander Baumgarten and his follower Georg Friedrich Meier. Most importantly, perhaps, Lessing was acquainted with Moses Mendelssohn, to whose work his own philosophical writings bear many similarities and who read and commented on Lessing's aesthetic writings. But Lessing cannot be identified with any of these philosophical sources and influences. His work retains many rationalist presuppositions, but Lessing also consciously sought a more inductive approach. He adhered to neoclassical standards with respect to beauty and the application of rules of art, but severely qualified those standards by justifying them empirically and appealing to emotional effects rather than to ideal forms or Cartesian clarity. Lessing's aesthetics must be inferred from his work, particularly from his Laocoon, *some of the numbers of the* Hamburg Dramaturgy, *and to a lesser extent from short works such as 'How the Ancients Represented Death' and the letter of 26 May 1769 to Friedrich Nikolai. What emerges is a sometimes inconsistent and fragmentary aesthetic, which one might describe as a critical rationalism.*

1 The interpretation of the 'Laocoon' group
2 The comparison of painting and poetry
3 Natural and artificial signs
4 Lessing and rationalist aesthetics
5 Lessing's critical practice and aesthetic principles

1 The interpretation of the 'Laocoon' group

Lessing's *Laocoon* is a complex work that embeds an even more complex aesthetic. The published text, which was projected as the first part of a longer work that Lessing never completed, interweaves two principal themes. The first is a dispute with Johann Joachim Winckelmann over the interpretation of the statue group Laocoon. Winckelmann had claimed that the expression on the face of the priest Laocoon when he is fatally entangled with the serpents is more restrained than the scream described by Virgil in the *Aeneid* when dealing with the same incident. Winckelmann attributed this restraint to the classical Greek virtues of control and dignity in adversity, and ultimately to a superior Greek sense of ideal form. Lessing had seen only engravings of the Laocoon and not the statue itself, even as a copy, and he therefore conceded to Winckelmann the interpretation of the group itself. (This would not be granted by many contemporary art historians who find the Laocoon extremely emotionally wrought compared to classical models.) But Lessing disputed the significance of Winckelmann's interpretation by pointing out that classical painting and sculpture were frequently described as depicting extreme suffering; thus it was not Greek virtue as such that restrained the artists in this case. Rather, Lessing argued, artists are constrained by their medium. The restraint shown by the Laocoon sculptors is a product of their awareness of the rules of visual media. Virgil, as a poet, is bound by different rules.

2 The comparison of painting and poetry

Comparisons between painting and poetry were a staple of eighteenth-century critical theory, and Lessing entered these debates with vigour. Fundamentally, he distinguished between the spatial properties of painting and the temporal properties of poetry. Painting and sculpture are grasped at once by visual perception. But poetry is understood sequentially. Lessing based rules about the appropriate means of imitation for each art form on this comparison. Painters and sculptors are limited to a single moment that they can capture completely. This, in turn, dictates the specific rules that give painting and sculpture access to beauty. If the Laocoon sculptors had tried to follow Virgil by depicting the distorted face of a screaming Laocoon, the viewer would have been overwhelmed with disgust by the immediate effect, and they would have failed in their attempt to show what was happening because sculpture could not hope to capture the scene's movement and action. It is limited to a 'pregnant moment', and in order to capture that moment, the sculptors had to abstract from the visual scene those parts of it that would convey the ideal beauty and restraint that was their true object. Virgil, on the other hand, could show

change and development. Poetry imitates action, not objects. The sequence of words corresponds to a sequence of events. Thus the scream and suffering are immediately qualified by what goes before and comes after. Instead of evoking disgust, the emotions are changed and qualified. In each case, Lessing insisted, it is the aesthetic whole that must be considered.

In spite of Lessing's emphasis on the difference between poetry as an imitation of action and painting as a spatial presentation, and his insistence that each has a different set of rules which cannot be reduced to a common set, he did not completely separate the art forms. They have a common object, beauty, and a common effect, pleasure. Lessing's argument is that neither can attain this common objective without restricting itself to its own rules. In principle, he granted relative equality to the different art forms. In practice, however, poetry is clearly the superior form. Painting and sculpture are limited in two ways. The doctrine of the pregnant moment limits painting and sculpture not just to certain techniques but also to certain 'objects'. Painting has a limited number of subjects available to it. And, while painting and sculpture gain a certain immediacy from their presentational forms, that very immediacy restricts them to a concrete, visual presence that makes it difficult for them to escape the present moment. When painting becomes allegorical in order to try to enhance its significance, it violates its own spatial rules. Poetry, on the other hand, is not subject to such limitations. It appeals to the imagination, not actual vision. It can depict emotions as well as objects. And it can use its extensive, moving forms to go beyond the mundane to the significance of beauty itself. The temporal forms of poetry enhance its effects while the spatial forms of painting act as limits.

3 Natural and artificial signs

In distinguishing painting and poetry, Lessing makes use of a more fundamental distinction between natural and artificial signs. This distinction was set out clearly by Mendelssohn, who distinguished natural signs from arbitrary signs. He described natural signs as those that are connected to their objects by properties of the object. Arbitrary signs have no such natural connection and are linked to their objects only by convention (1771: 1, 437). For example, a blush is a natural sign of heightened emotion, and a picture is a natural sign of its object by virtue of its resemblance. But the choice of sounds and letters in language, while it may have natural origins, is essentially arbitrary. Thus painting uses natural signs, while poetry, which depends on language, uses arbitrary signs. Lessing's dramatic theory explores ways in which arbitrary signs for the imitation of action can be converted to natural signs when they form dramatic wholes. The theory is essentially rationalist; its goal is to account for how the intuition available in art and nature can be adequate to concepts and ideas. But Lessing, by focusing on the effects, turned the theory in the direction of the critical object.

4 Lessing and rationalist aesthetics

Lessing's aesthetics is best understood in the context of the rationalist aesthetic that was being developed at that time in Germany, particularly by Alexander Baumgarten and Georg Friedrich Meier, under the influence of Christian Wolff. Lessing himself implicitly located his own position in the preface to Laocoon. The amateur is in the position of the audience while the philosopher formulates general rules, and the critic applies them – sometimes correctly, sometimes erroneously. Lessing occupied that critical position, and he took from the philosophers – Spinoza, Leibniz, Wolff, Baumgarten, Mendelssohn and others – general aesthetic rules. But in applying those rules, he modified them to an extent of which he himself may not have been aware.

In many respects, Lessing presumes an aesthetic that can be derived more or less explicitly from Leibniz. Its object is beauty, which is understood as the perfection of a whole. Ideal beauty is found in distinct ideas whose clarity comes from their uniformity. Their reflection is found in the corporeal beauty which is a harmony of parts. Moses Mendelssohn defined beauty as the intuitive cognition of perfection. A cognition is intuitive, he wrote, when its object is immediately present to our senses or when we attend to the object rather than the sign for the object (1757: 1, 170). Lessing's formulation was similar except that Lessing was more concerned with concrete, critical applications to poetry and painting. This led him to distinguish the different possibilities provided by the differences in media. Painting is adapted to material beauty (1766: 104). Poetry, on the other hand, is adapted to a different kind of description: that of the presentation of emotions (1766: 111). Ultimately, painting and poetry have the same object: beauty. Poetry, however, has the advantage of presenting effects and thus of giving an apprehension of beauty itself, while painting can only show material beauty in its outward forms.

All rationalist aesthetics implicitly denigrates both art and nature. Beauty is grasped intuitively, but there are two forms of intuition: the sensory and the rational. Rational intuition is capable of apprehending ideas distinctly without the confusion of images and parts. Thus, it is superior to the confused sensory intuition of perception and the imagination. No rationalist aesthetic completely escapes this limitation on the products of art and nature. However, Alexander Baumgarten argued that sensate intuition was the superior form if one considered its effectiveness in guiding people to beauty, and Lessing followed Baumgarten in this respect. But Baumgarten considered sensate intuition essentially quantitative. He reasoned that since description adds to the completion of an idea, the more descriptive a painting or poetic passage, the more aesthetically perfect it is, and hence the more 'poetic' and beautiful. Lessing explicitly rejected this quantitative argument in favour of a distinction based on the effects that can be achieved. Poetry, on Lessing's view, should not strive for extended descriptions; Homer limits himself to a single trait (1766: 79). Poetry's ability to focus selectively and thus enhance its effects gives it the advantage over painting.

Thus, while Lessing remains clearly within the rationalist circle if one compares him to such sentimentalists and sense-theorists as Lord Shaftesbury or Francis Hutcheson, he departs in significant ways from the syllogistic and axiomatic descriptiveness of more orthodox rationalist formulations. Art is basically imitation, but for Lessing, imitation is directed towards action and emotion as well as objects. Lessing was thus led to consider both rules and means in a more concrete, inductive way than the axiomatic, deductive procedures of rationalist metaphysics had dictated. Rules are justified not by their logical form but by their effects. Since it is pleasure which is aimed at, one must be prepared to adjust the rules to the observed results. At this point, Lessing is very pragmatic. Empiricist aesthetics in England and France developed along psychological lines; it attempted to predict how certain emotional effects followed from artistic practice and natural beauty. Rationalist aesthetics, on the other hand, began with principles of unity and harmony and attempted to derive their application as a set of rules for the production of art and aesthetic effects. Lessing trusts neither. Emotions are not really subject to rules (1766: 28). On the contrary, rules are judged by their effects. At the same time, Lessing acknowledges the superiority of science to art. The object of science is knowledge; it is not subject to control by anything other than truth. But the object of art is pleasure. Since pleasure is not absolute, it may be judged by other standards and subjected to control (1766: 14).

5 Lessing's critical practice and aesthetic principles

In a number of ways, then, Lessing, as a critic who

employs the philosophical 'rules' of his rationalist contemporaries, complicated and modified those rules and practices in ways that enhanced their critical application. In the process, he sometimes exhibited contradictory impulses. His definition of art included both his aesthetic tendencies. In the course of discussing ancient artefacts, Lessing wrote: 'I should prefer that only those be called works of art in which the artist had occasion to show himself as such and in which beauty was his first and ultimate aim' (1766: 55). The goal of art is beauty, and beauty can be understood in terms of harmony and perfection. But the other specific difference cited is that the artist had occasion to show himself, and that expressionist aesthetic is potentially at odds with the imitation implied in the reference to beauty. Lessing did not believe that imitation is pleasurable in itself. But he did hold that it produces pleasure as a result of the mental activity it stimulates. If feelings and emotions are the proper objects of imitation, Lessing was looking in a place far removed from his rationalist sources. Given his own distinction between critic and philosopher, Lessing is a critical rationalist for whom the role of the critic is central.

His aesthetic remains critically grounded, but it also universalizes:

> The purpose of art is to save us this abstraction in the realms of the beautiful, and to render the fixing of our attention easy to us. All in nature that we might wish to abstract in our thoughts from an object or a combination of various objects, be it in time or in place, art really abstracts for us, and accords us this object or this combination of various objects as purely and tersely as the sensations they are to provoke allow.
>
> (1767–8: 226)

Art is neither pure sensate representation nor absolute truth. The former is too chaotic, too confused. The latter is beyond our finite limits. Lessing's use of the theory of natural and arbitrary signs, his combination of imitation and expression, of rules and genius, of feeling and absolute form may not always be consistent, but it has as its object a middle ground which produces a critical aesthetic of considerable practical power.

See also: POETRY §2; TRAGEDY §5

List of works

Lessing, G.E. (1886–1924) *Sämtliche Schriften*, Lachmann; 3rd edn, trans. and ed. F. Muncker, Stuttgart, Berlin and Leipzig: Goschen, later De Gruyter, 23 vols. (The standard scholarly edition of Lessing's writings.)

—— (1766) *Laocoon: An Essay on the Limits of Painting and Poetry*, trans. E.A. McCormick, Indianapolis, IN: Bobbs-Merrill, Library of Liberal Arts, 1962. (A central aesthetic text; the first part of an uncompleted three-part work.)

—— (1767–8) *Hamburg Dramaturgy*, trans. E.C. Beardsley and H. Zimmern, in *European Theories of the Drama*, ed. B.H. Clark, rev. H. Popkin, New York: Crown, 1965. (Central critical texts. A series of periodical essays and a primary source for Lessing's dramatic theory and critique of Aristotle's Poetics in relation to the dramatic unities.)

—— (1769) 'How the Ancients Represented Death', in *Death and the Visual Arts*, trans. E.C. Beasley and H. Zimmern, New York: Arno Press, 1977. (Reprint of 1879 translation. Polemical reply to an attack on *Laocoon*.)

—— (1785) *The Spinoza Conversations Between Lessing and Jacobi*, trans. G. Vallee, J.B. Lawson and C.G. Chapple, Lanham, MD: University Press of America, 1988. (Includes translations and extended introductory discussion of the controversial report by F.H. Jacobi of his 1780 conversation with Lessing.)

References and further reading

Cassirer, E. (1951) *The Philosophy of the Enlightenment*, trans. F. Koelln and J.P. Pettegrove, Princeton, NJ: Princeton University Press. (Useful if somewhat exaggerated estimate of Lessing's influence on the development of aesthetics.)

McClain, J. (1986) 'Time in the Visual Arts: Lessing and Modern Criticism', *Journal of Aesthetics and Art Criticism* 44 (1): 41–58. (Discussion of Lessing's influence on critical treatment of time.)

Mendelssohn, M. (1757) 'Reflections on the Sources and Combinations of the Fine Arts and Letters', in *Gesammelte Schriften*, Stuttgart and Bad Cannstatt: Frommann, 1971. (A primary source for Hendelssoton's distinction between natural and conventional symbols and for his attempts to classify the arts.)

—— (1771) 'On the Chief Principles of the Fine Arts and Letters', in *Gesammelte Schriften*, Stuttgart and Bad Cannstatt: Frommann, 1971. (A revised version of the 1757 essay.)

Robertson, J.G. (1965) *Lessing's Dramatic Theory*, New York: Benjamin Blom. (Extended technical discussion of Lessing's stage theory.)

Rudowski, V.A. (1986) 'Lessing *contra* Winckelmann', *Journal of Aesthetics and Art Criticism* 44 (3): 235–44. (Lessing's relation to Winckelmann.)

—— (1971) *Lessing's Aesthetica in Nuce*, Chapel Hill, NC: University of North Carolina Press. (Includes text of 1769 letter to Nicolai.)

* Wellbery, D.E. (1984) *Lessing's Laocoon: Semiotics and Aesthetics in the Age of Reason*, Cambridge: Cambridge University Press. (Theory is heavily semiotic, but also includes very good discussion of philosophical background. Citations from Mendelssohn above are Wellbery's translations.)

DABNEY TOWNSEND

LEUCIPPUS (5th century BC)

The early Greek philosopher Leucippus was the founder of atomism. Virtually nothing is known of his life, and his very existence was disputed in antiquity, but his role as the originator of atomism is firmly attested by Aristotle and Theophrastus, although the evidence does not allow any distinction between his doctrines and those of his more celebrated successor Democritus. He wrote a comprehensive account of the universe, the Great World-System. *The single surviving quotation from his work asserts universal determinism.*

Leucippus was a shadowy figure even in antiquity. Virtually nothing is known of his life. His birthplace was disputed; some sources associated him with one or other of the two principal centres of early Greek philosophy, Elea and Miletus, others with Abdera, the birthplace of Democritus. The statement in a number of sources that he was a pupil of ZENO OF ELEA may be merely an inference from the Eleatic influence on the foundations of atomism (see DEMOCRITUS §2). Of his dates, all that can be said is that he lived during the fifth century BC: he was almost certainly older than Democritus, who is described by Aristotle and Simplicius as his 'associate' (*hetairos*), implying that Democritus was his pupil (as is also attested by Diogenes Laertius). In the post-Aristotelian period he was overshadowed by Democritus to such an extent that atomism came generally to be regarded as the work of the latter, while Epicurus and his successor Hermarchus are reported to have denied that Leucippus ever existed. His historicity is, however, firmly attested by Aristotle, who is the primary source for atomism. No list of Leucippus' works exists. The catalogue of works of Democritus produced by Thrasyllus in the first century AD contains two books entitled *World-System* (*diakosmos*), respectively, the *Great World-System* and the *Small World-System*, with a note that the school of Theophrastus attributed the former to Leucippus.

It is probable that that attribution is correct, the attribution to Democritus being due to the overshadowing process mentioned above. The single quotation surviving from Leucippus is said by its source, Stobaeus, to come from a work *On Mind*; it is uncertain whether that title refers to a section of the *Great World-System* or to a separate work. The pseudo-Aristotelian treatise *On Melissus, Xenophanes and Gorgias* refers to 'the so-called arguments of Leucippus', presumably a reference to a work purporting to be by Leucippus.

Aristotle, followed by Simplicius, sometimes attributes the fundamentals of atomism to Leucippus (see, for example, Aristotle, *On Generation and Corruption* 325a23, b7). Elsewhere, however, and sometimes even in the same context (for example, *On Generation and Corruption* 325a1–2) Aristotle refers to Leucippus and Democritus jointly, and not infrequently to Democritus alone (as was the standard practice of later writers). That Leucippus was in some sense the pioneer is undoubted, but it is impossible to determine what elements of the theory of atomism are to be attributed to either, or to what extent their enterprise was collaborative. (For discussion of the principles of atomism, see DEMOCRITUS (§2).) Of the two most detailed reports of the atomists' account of the formation of worlds, one is attributed by Diogenes Laertius to Leucippus (IX 30–3), and is presumably a summary of the account in the *Great World-System*. It ascribes the formation of worlds to agglomerations of atoms which, formed by chance collisions, develop a rotation in which atoms of different sizes are sifted out, the smaller being extruded into the infinity of space, the larger forming a spherical structure which gradually differentiates itself into a cosmos as the larger atoms sink to the centre and the smaller are forced to the outside. The rotation of the cosmic aggregates was apparently unexplained, and was according to some sources attributed to chance. This raises the question whether Leucippus believed that some events, such as the cosmic rotation, are objectively random, or are merely ascribed to chance in the weaker sense that their cause is undiscoverable. The single quotation, 'Nothing happens in vain, but everything from reason and of necessity' (fr. 2, Stobaeus, I 4.4), suggests the latter. While it could in isolation be understood as asserting universal purposiveness in nature, the secondary sources, including Aristotle, are unanimous that the atomists denied all purposiveness in natural events. Hence the quotation is best understood as asserting universal determinism; 'in vain' is understood as 'for no reason', and 'of necessity' specifies the reason for which everything happens – namely, the irresistible force of causation. On that interpretation, the cosmic rotation must have had some determinate cause, but a cause undiscoverable to us.

References and further reading

Aristotle (c.mid 4th century BC) *On Generation and Corruption*, ed. H.H. Joachim, Oxford: Oxford University Press, 1922; trans. C.J.F. Williams, Oxford: Oxford University Press, 1982. (This work contains extensive critical discussions of the views of earlier philosophers on the basics of physical theory, for example, the elements, change and so on.)

Bailey, C. (1928) *The Greek Atomists and Epicurus*, Oxford: Clarendon Press, 64–108. (Seeks to individuate the contribution of Leucippus.)

Barnes, J. (1984) 'Reason and Necessity in Leucippus', *Proceedings of the First International Congress on Democritus*, Xanthi: International Democritean Foundation, 141–58. (An incisive discussion of the single remaining fragment.)

—— (1987) *Early Greek Philosophy*, Harmondsworth: Penguin, 242–3. (Translates the fragment and an important text from Simplicius referring to Leucippus.)

Diels, H. and Kranz, W. (1951) Fragments, in H. Diels and W. Kranz (eds) *Die Fragmente der Vorsokratiker* (Fragments of the Presocratics), Berlin: Weidemann, 6th edn, vol. 2, 70–81. (The standard collection of the ancient sources; includes Greek texts with German translations.)

Guthrie, W.K.C. (1962–78) *A History of Greek Philosophy*, Cambridge: Cambridge University Press, 6 vols. (The most detailed and comprehensive English-language history of early Greek thought; a review of the evidence for Leucippus can be found in volume 2, pages 383–6, and a comprehensive discussion of atomism in volume 2, pages 389–507.)

C.C.W. TAYLOR

LEVI BEN GERSHOM

see GERSONIDES

LEVINAS, EMMANUEL (1906–95)

In the 1930s Levinas helped to introduce the phenomenological philosophy of Husserl and Heidegger to the French. Subsequently his work attained classic status in its own right for his attempt to explore the meaning of ethics from a phenomenological starting-point. In Totalité et infini *(1961) (*Totality and Infinity, *1969) Levinas locates the basis of ethics in the face-to-face relation where the Other puts me in question. My obligations to the Other are not contracted by me. They not only precede any debts I incur, but also go beyond anything I could possibly satisfy. In later works, most notably* Autrement qu'être *(1974) (*Otherwise than Being, *1981), Levinas explores further the preconditions of this account, most especially by investigating the I that was said to be put in question in the encounter with the Other. In analyses that stretch phenomenology to its limits and beyond, Levinas finds alterity within the self.*

1 **Life and philosophical development**
2 *Totality and Infinity*
3 *Otherwise than Being*

1 Life and philosophical development

Emmanuel Levinas was born in Lithuania. In 1923 he went to Strasbourg University where his studies included the philosophy of Henri Bergson. From 1928 to 1929 Levinas was at Freiburg University, where he studied first with HUSSERL and then with HEIDEGGER. This led him in 1930 to publish *La Théorie de l'intuition dans la phénoménologie de Husserl* (*The Theory of Intuition in Husserl's Phenomenology*, 1973) a reading of Husserl that was informed by Heidegger's criticisms of Husserl's intellectualism. Since that time almost all of Levinas's philosophical works have taken their point of departure from either Husserl or Heidegger. If the practice of a philosopher like Levinas can be summarized in a phrase, one would have to say that he works at the limits of phenomenology by investigating the enigma behind the phenomenon. Whereas what lies hidden is, for Heidegger, primarily the being of beings, for Levinas, it is the excess of being, or in Plato's phrase, the good beyond being.

Levinas first presented his own thought in his essay on 'Evasion' (1935) and two short studies published immediately after the Second World War, *De l'existence à l'existant* (1947a) (*Existence and Existents*, 1978) and 'Le temps et l'autre' (1947b) (Time and the Other, 1987). These works offer analyses of nausea, fatigue and insomnia, as well as of the alterity found in death, fecundity and eros. They were already part of an attempt to go beyond the thought of being, although it was not until 'L'ontologie, est-elle fondamentale?' (1951) ('Is Ontology Fundamental?'), which was largely a criticism of Heidegger, that it became apparent that Levinas intended to issue his challenge to the dominance of ontology within Western philosophy specifically in the name of ethics and the alterity of the other human being. During the war, Levinas had been imprisoned in Germany in a camp for French soldiers, but on his release and in response to the Nazi persecution of the Jews, which none of the members of his family left in eastern Europe survived, he renewed his involvement with the Judaism of his childhood. From that time his studies developed along two trajectories. His main philosophical works, *Totalité et infini* (1961) (*Totality and Infinity*, 1969) and *Autrement qu'être* (1974) (*Otherwise than Being or Beyond Essence*, 1981), which increasingly stretch the language of Western philosophy to its limits, were accompanied by confessional writings, such as *Nine Talmudic Readings* (1990) and *À l'heure des nations* (1994) (*In the Time of the Nations*, 1988) which translate Hebraic wisdom into the language of Greece, by which he meant the universal language of the West. Although Levinas insisted, especially at first, that the two kinds of writing were entirely distinct and appealed to different kinds of evidence, their separation is far from straightforward. Terms like 'election', 'persecution' and 'hostage' that Levinas explored in his writings on the Talmud have found their way into his philosophical studies. Although Levinas has refused to describe himself as a Jewish philosopher, the unity of his thought lies in his attempt to address the nonsectarian question of ethics after the Holocaust by employing the resources of both phenomenology and Judaism. In this entry I focus on his contribution to ethics as the portion of his work that has attracted most attention.

2 Totality and Infinity

The guiding insight of *Totality and Infinity* is that the Other human being in their separation calls me into question. In the face-to-face relation my self-assurance disappears and I find myself in bad conscience. Levinas does not look to ethics to restore good conscience. On the contrary, I never have the luxury of knowing that I did the right thing in any given situation. Nor is it simply a question of knowledge. I can never do enough. My obligations to the Other are unlimited, as well as being asymmetrical in the sense that I have no right to ask of the Other what the Other asks of me. In society, furthermore, every effort to meet my obligations to one person comes at the expense of my efforts on behalf of the others. Levinas refuses all the standard ways of diminishing the impact of these impossible demands, such as conceiving ethics in terms of intention or employing the model of legal responsibility where I am only

answerable for what is in my power. Levinas has readily conceded that he does not provide an ethics but only an account of the condition of ethics. It should be added that what he describes as ethics is very different from what has hitherto gone under that name among philosophers.

The reciprocal system of obligations that usually passes for ethics most often goes under the name of justice in Levinas's thought. Levinas finds the system of justice to be in accord with reason, but he finds that, just as the I is put in question by the Other within the face-to-face relation, so justice is put in question by the face of the Other. The ethical relation with the Other exceeds the third-party perspective of neutral reason. As a result, Levinas is quite explicit that his account of the ethical is not constrained by what he calls 'formal logic'. Since Derrida's 1964 essay on Levinas, 'Violence et métaphysique' (1967) ('Violence and Metaphysics', 1978) questions have been raised about whether such an account is possible, thinkable and sayable. These enquiries, far from being uniformly negative, have led to some of the most far-reaching developments within continental philosophy, not least in the works of DERRIDA.

The way in which ethics questions justice also serves as an answer to the frequently heard criticism that Levinas's thought has little to offer to political theory. It is true that he has not said much about society, but his challenge to the good conscience of ethics applies equally well to politics. Levinas refers in one place to the tears invisible to the bureaucrat. In this very simple way he draws attention to what grand schemes overlook. Nor is the relation between ethics and justice one-sided in favour of the former. Just as ethics in Levinas's sense keeps justice from being satisfied with itself, so justice can also serve as a corrective to ethics. If there was only one other person in the world, I could devote myself to that person, but because I live in society, I address my obligations to the Other only by neglecting the others. It is here that the place of reason and calculation becomes important also for ethics. Levinas found a formula that encapsulated the interruption of ethics by justice when he described how the third party, in the sense of the whole of humanity, looks at me in the eyes of the Other.

3 Otherwise than Being

In *Otherwise than Being* Levinas returned to the way that the Other questions the identity of the I. To be for the Other is to be without identity. This led Levinas to introduce a new structure that he calls 'substitution' and which he summarizes with Rimbaud's formula 'the I is an other'. Levinas also says that 'subjectivity is being hostage'. He means by this that subjectivity is not the isolated ego of modern philosophy, but the restlessness of being disturbed by the other. For Levinas, questions which would seem to many to be the most fundamental of ethical questions, such as 'Why does the other concern me?', 'Am I my brother's keeper?' or, with reference to Shakespeare's *Hamlet*, 'What's Hecuba to me?', have already come too late for ethics. These questions presuppose a concept of the ego which is derivative from my proximity to the Other. In this way Levinas makes more precise the goal, announced in 1951, of having ethics supplant ontology as first philosophy. In *Otherwise than Being* it is pursued largely by exploring the realm of selfhood that previous philosophy has left unmined.

There is some controversy as to whether the analyses of *Otherwise than Being* supplant or only supplement those found in *Totality and Infinity*. Certainly there are differences. The emphasis on separation in the earlier works gives way to an account of proximity which locates at the heart of selfhood a certain restlessness unconcerned with reciprocity. The foundational narratives of *Totality and Infinity*, reminiscent of social contract theory, that describe the first encounter that an I has with an Other, give way in *Otherwise than Being* to structures that are said to be 'older even than the a priori'. There is no longer an attempt to coordinate the ethical and the ontological: the former interrupts the latter. If *Totality and Infinity* describes how the ego is put in question by the Other, *Otherwise than Being* puts the concept of the ego in question, not by denying the substantiality of the subject as other continental philosophers have done, but by locating alterity within selfhood so that I can be said to be 'in myself' only through the others. Levinas himself has indicated that it was his rejection of the ontological language of *Totality and Infinity* that led to *Otherwise than Being*, but he did not renounce the earlier analyses, which he has often repeated in essays that postdate *Otherwise than Being*.

According to Levinas, the needs of the Other make demands on me that are impossible for me to fulfil. Most traditional ethical systems reject any such multiplication of my responsibilities on the grounds that it is destructive of good conscience. Traditional ethical philosophies also have no place for Levinas's insistence that one is responsible even for what took place before one was born. They would see Levinas as extending the concept of responsibility to the point that one's sense of responsibility for what is within one's power is diminished. However, Levinas regards all such attempts on my part to limit specifically my responsibility as a reduction of ethics to justice. It amounts to limiting the demands I make on myself to the same standards that it is reasonable and proper for me to apply to others. From Levinas's perspective, what ordinarily passes for ethics is an evasion of the ethical, but he is well aware that it would be impossible to live constantly according to his conception of ethics. His account of the face-to-face is a description of being obsessed by the Other that amounts to a psychosis. Even though in interviews Levinas has questioned whether his work is properly called ethics, his questioning of the ontological basis of Western philosophy has succeeded in raising the question of whether what passes for ethics in that tradition has yet got to the bottom of the call to be ethical.

See also: ALTERITY AND IDENTITY, POSTMODERN THEORIES OF §3; PHENOMENOLOGY, EPISTEMIC ISSUES IN

List of works

Levinas, E. (1930) *La Théorie de l'intuition dans la phénoménologie de Husserl*, Paris: Felix Alcan; trans. A. Orianne, *The Theory of Intuition in Husserl's Phenomenology*, Evanston, IL: Northwestern University Press, 1973. (The first major study of Husserl in French, still valued as an introduction to his work.)

—— (1935) 'De l'evasion', *Recherches Philosophiques* 5: 373–92. (Reissued under the same title in 1982 by Fata Morgana with an introductory essay and notes that extended it to a 121-page book.)

—— (1947a) *De l'existence à l'existant*, Paris: Vrin; trans. A. Lingis, *Existence and Existents*, The Hague: Martinus Nijhoff, 1978. (Studies of fatigue, indolence, effort and horror that mark the beginning of his attempt to leave the climate of Heidegger's thought without regressing to a pre-Heideggerian position.)

—— (1947b) 'Le temps et l'autre', in *Le Choix – le monde – l'existence*, ed. J. Wahl, Grenoble and Paris: Arthaud; trans. R.A. Cohen, *Time and the Other*, Pittsburgh, PA: Duquesne University Press, 1987. (The translation adds two more recent essays, including 'Diachrony and Representation' (1982), which is especially important.)

—— (1951) 'L'ontologie, est-elle fondamentale?', *Revue de Métaphysique et de Morale* 56: 88–98. (A translation can be found in *Levinas: Basic Philosophical Writings* (1996).)

—— (1961) *Totalité et infini*, The Hague: Martinus Nijhoff; trans. A. Lingis, *Totality and Infinity*, Pittsburgh, PA: Duquesne University Press, 1969. (The classic work that lays out Levinas's basic positions on ethics and alterity.)

—— (1974) *Autrement qu'être ou au-delà de l'essence*, The Hague: Martinus Nijhoff; trans. A. Lingis, *Otherwise than Being, or Beyond Essence*, The Hague: Martinus Nijhoff, 1981. (Levinas's most important and most sophisticated work but also the most difficult.)

—— (1982a) *De Dieu qui vient à l'idée*, Paris: Vrin. (The most important of over a dozen collections of essays. It includes the classic 'God and Philosophy'.)

—— (1982b) *Éthique et infini*, Paris: Fayard; trans. R. Cohen, *Ethics and Infinity*, Pittsburgh, PA: Duquesne University Press, 1985. (Interviews with Philippe Nemo that serve as an excellent introduction.)

—— (1988) *À l'heure des nations*, Paris: Minuit; trans. G.D. Mole, *In the Time of the Nations*, London: Athlone Press, 1994.

—— (1990) *Nine Talmudic Writings*, trans. A. Aronowicz, Bloomington, IN: Indiana University Press. (Contains translations of *Quatres lecture talmudiques* (1968) and *Du sacré au saint* (1977).)

—— (1996) *Levinas: Basic Philosophical Writings*, ed. A. Peperzak, R. Bernasconi and S. Critchley, Bloomington, IN: Indiana University Press. (A collection of Levinas's most important philosophical essays with introductory essays and notes added by the editors.)

References and further reading

Bernasconi, R. and Critchley, S. (eds) (1991) *Rereading Levinas*, Bloomington, IN: Indiana University Press. (Includes essays by Derrida, Irigaray and many of the major commentators on Levinas focusing especially on Levinas's later thought and his account of the feminine.)

* Derrida, J. (1967) 'Violence et métaphysique', *L'Écriture et la différence*, Paris: Éditions du Seuil; trans. A. Bass, 'Violence and Metaphysics', *Writing and Difference*, Chicago, IL: University of Chicago Press, 1978. (Revised version of the classic study from 1964 that has set the terms of subsequent discussion of Levinas and that may have influenced Levinas himself.)

Llewelyn, J. (1995) *Levinas: The Genealogy of Ethics*, New York: Routledge. (Close readings of some of Levinas's major texts that is instructive for beginners and scholars alike.)

Peperzak, A. (1993) *To the Other*, West Lafayette, IN: Purdue University Press. (Best guide to Levinas for beginners.)

ROBERT BERNASCONI

LÉVI-STRAUSS, CLAUDE (1908–)

Lévi-Strauss is one of the outstanding figures of mid-twentieth-century intellectual life, influential far beyond the boundaries of France or the French language, and he has continued to write new work well into his eighties. His name is linked above all to the structuralist movement, of which he has been probably the most single-minded and unwavering exponent, and he was one of the key figures in the experiment of applying the insights of linguistics to the material of the social sciences. Through his work, public recognition of the discipline of anthropology grew dramatically to become an important element in discussion of philosophical issues.

The philosophical environment in France, in which structuralism developed and against which it reacted, was that of Sartrean humanism. In contrast to the existentialist emphasis on individual subjectivity, structuralism expected to find objective solutions to problems in the study of human beings. It was a form of intellectual modernism, a radical break with previous theoretical models and philosophical traditions, symptomatic of post-war optimism for the global applicability of science. It was hostile to metaphysics, bracketed the search for truth and was indifferent to the human subject. And, in contrast to Bergson's emphasis on continuity and flux, structuralism took discontinuity as its founding principle.

1 Life
2 The impact of structural linguistics
3 The study of kinship
4 Totemism and *The Savage Mind*
5 The science of mythology
6 Lévi-Strauss' theory of knowledge

1 Life

Claude Lévi-Strauss was born in 1908. His grandfather was the rabbi of Versailles and his father was a painter. After studying philosophy in Paris he went to the new university of São Paulo in 1934 as professor of sociology, and during his five years in Brazil spent some time travelling in the interior. Returning for military service in 1939 he escaped to New York after the fall of France, and spent most of the Second World War lecturing at the New School for Social Research. Two decisive influences on his intellectual development derive from this period: first, contact with Roman Jakobson and second, exposure to the empirical approach of US anthropology. Since then he has lived and worked in Paris, mostly at the Collège de France, and became a member of the Académie française in 1973.

2 The impact of structural linguistics

Attending Jakobson's lectures on linguistics and phonology in 1942 seems to have been a revelation for Lévi-Strauss. Structural linguistics taught him that 'instead of being led astray by a multiplicity of terms, one should consider the simplest and most intelligible relationships uniting them' (1983, ch. 9: 139). The idea that the phoneme has no intrinsic meaning, but only acquires significance in relation to other similar elements, became the heart of his new approach to anthropological debates. The structural study of phonology emphasized two further principles that were to become fundamental to his work: the importance of unconscious mental activity in the production of language, and the fact that language is organized through discontinuous elements linked in particular ways.

Many commentators have linked Lévi-Strauss' structuralism directly to SAUSSURE. However, it is clear from more recent writings that Lévi-Strauss' source of inspiration was Jakobson's interpretation of Saussure. His own use of Saussure was highly selective, emphasizing above all the arbitrary nature of the linguistic sign, the synchronic basis to linguistic analysis, and the syntagmatic and paradigmatic relations that link linguistic signs. These involve relations of contiguity and similarity, analogous to Jakobson's distinction between metonymy and metaphor (see STRUCTURALISM IN LINGUISTICS).

3 The study of kinship

During this same period, Lévi-Strauss engaged in an extensive study of the ethnological literature, seeking to uncover the 'simplest and most intelligible relationships' that united all the wealth and diversity of the ethnographic record. His first area of interest was kin relations, a topic that linked him directly to the central concerns of anthropology and to DURKHEIM (§3) and Mauss' theories of social solidarity. His first book, *The Elementary Structures of Kinship* (1949), brought these different strands together in a vast synthetic work that transformed the way that anthropologists understood kinship.

Lévi-Strauss proposed that the incest taboo is analogous to the phoneme, in that it has no meaning of its own but serves to link two domains. This is achieved by the exchange of women between kin-groups, which constitutes the origin of culture and is its ongoing pre-condition. Like all his work, his

theory of kinship is controversial, but many of its insights have become canonical.

4 Totemism and *The Savage Mind*

Kinship led Lévi-Strauss to the theme of totemism and systems of classification, and the application of his theories to more obviously mental phenomena. He took issue with the argument, associated particularly with Lucien Lévy-Bruhl, that the thought processes of primitives are based on entirely different principles to our own. In *The Savage Mind* (1962) he showed how all human cultures employ the same principles to define and order their environment. In fact, 'the savage mind' is an unfortunate – if by now well-established – translation of *La pensee sauvage*, since the English expression implies that he is referring to some distinctive primitive mentality. All humans are alike, in his view, in the way that we rely fundamentally on sensual perception for our systems of classification and knowledge – the 'science of the concrete'. At the same time, primitives are just as capable of abstract thought as we are.

However, Lévi-Strauss does specify the significance of different levels of abstraction, expressed through his well-known contrast between the *bricoleur* and the engineer. The French *bricoleur* is a sort of jack of all trades, who puts things together with whatever materials lie to hand. Most of us for most of the time are *bricoleurs*, close to percepts, using the science of the concrete. By contrast, the 'engineer' operates at 'one remove' from observable properties, constructing concepts appropriate for the use to which they will be put.

In practice, Lévi-Strauss has devoted his life's work to studying the thought principles of *bricoleurs* rather than engineers. But implicitly his own work stands as perhaps a key example of what he means by the engineer. He believes that he has identified the abstract principles that underlie all everyday human thought processes, and that anthropology is particularly suited to the attainment of knowledge because it seeks the 'view from afar'. No civilization can think of itself unless it uses others as a basis for comparison. The importance which he attaches to detachment and distance is also at the heart of his critique of Sartre published as the final chapter of *The Savage Mind*.

5 The science of mythology

The most extensive, and probably the best-known, part of Lévi-Strauss' work is dedicated to the understanding of myth, another manifestation of the 'science of the concrete'. While myth uses the material world as means of thought, it is free from the constraints of material reality. Lévi-Strauss contrasts his own approach to myth with that of Jung, who in Lévi-Strauss' view erred by assuming that myths have stable meanings and a referential function. For Lévi-Strauss, the search for the manifest meanings of myths misses their true nature, which lies beneath the multifarious and often fantastic surface phenomena, where the human mind (*l'esprit humain*) rehearses unceasingly the opposition between nature and culture and the contradictions of human life, without offering a clear explanation or meaning.

Lévi-Strauss' approach to the analysis of myths discounts their narrative form in favour of identifying their component parts, in the spirit of the Russian Formalism of his mentor Jakobson, and others such as Vladimir Propp, author of the hugely influential *Morphology of the Russian Folk Tale*. To identify these discontinuous elements Lévi-Srauss in *The View From Afar* coined the concept of the 'mytheme' analogous to the phoneme – 'a purely differential and contentless sign' (1983: 145). These elements are linked by the principles of metaphor and metonymy, of syntagmatic and paradigmatic relations. The language of myths is, then, an unconscious one, rather similar in his view to that of the genetic code: far from being the consciously-created stories of individual narrators, 'myths operate in men's minds without them being aware of the fact' (*The Raw and the Cooked* 1964: 12).

As such, each myth is connected to others, not only within the same language and cultural group, but beyond that to myths recorded for far-away groups speaking different languages. In his four-volume *Mythologiques* (1964–71) he traces mythical themes and structures from one end of the American continent to the other. Crucial to this enterprise is the concept of transformation: in Lévi-Strauss' hands this is a relatively static concept, referring typically to the way that myths are related through inversion, that is, the underlying structure of two apparently divergent and unrelated myths contains the same elements, but arranged in a different way.

His concept of transformation – a formal rather than a dynamic one – typifies his temporal concepts. Synchrony, the suspension of temporal movement, was a guiding principle for structuralism, and for Lévi-Strauss synchrony expresses a core value. Music has provided a significant analogy, for example in *The Raw and the Cooked* where the temporal unfolding of music (and by analogy the narrative unfolding of myths) is subordinate to the structural principles which unite a piece of music, and link it to other pieces.

6 Lévi-Strauss' theory of knowledge

True knowledge for Lévi-Strauss arises from con-

templation. In this respect pre-literate societies, where mythical structures are found in their purest form, come closest to his ideal. They typically strive to negate the effects of history and change, in contrast to the modern world where these are celebrated as good in themselves. In many of his writings Lévi-Strauss emphasizes the unity of the human mind across time and culture, stressing the similarity of purpose and method between our distant ancestors who domesticated animals and plants and our own scientific concerns (especially *Structural Anthropology II* 1973, ch.18). In others he implicitly attributes cognitive superiority to the 'engineer' or indeed to the anthropologist. And yet in other respects it is clear that he admires the disappearing world of the primitives who understood the significance of synchrony.

His passionately argued belief that the primitives were as much intellectuals as we are represents a grand if flawed attempt to create a unified theory of the human mind based on detailed comparative work. It derives from a model of human nature which is grounded in intelligence (in contrast to other models which privilege the emotions and instincts, or self-interest and strategy). However for all his intellectualism, many of Lévi-Strauss' ideas have stood the test of time more for their aesthetic insights and intuitions, than for his theoretical elaborations. As a number of commentators have pointed out, the whole elaborate edifice of structural linguistics conceals as much as it elucidates his aims and methods. He is closer to literature, to music, and above all to painting, and in a late work comments that 'the suppression by chance of ten or twenty centuries would not appreciably affect our knowledge of human nature. The only irreplaceable loss would be the works of art' (1993: 176).

In his analysis of actual myths, Lévi-Strauss' rigorous formalism and implicit reductionism is complemented by an extraordinary grasp of empirical detail and a sensitive attention to the distinctive properties – visual, tactile, olfactory, chemical, aural, functional – of whatever it is that the myth purports to be about. This attention to detail partially undermines the importance which he himself attaches to the Saussurean principle of the arbitrariness of the sign. It was clearly an important notion which enabled him to get away from the referential functions of language, but it should not blind us to the fact that most of the mythical signs which he has devoted the last thirty years of his life to analysing are not arbitrary in the Saussurean sense at all.

See also: ANTHROPOLOGY, PHILOSOPHY OF; STRUCTURALISM; STRUCTURALISM IN LITERARY THEORY; STRUCTURALISM IN SOCIAL SCIENCE

List of works

Lévi-Strauss, C. (1949) *Les structures elementaires de la parente*, Paris: Presses Universitaires de France; *The Elementary Structures of Kinship*, Boston, MA: Beacon Press, 1969. (A vast synthetic work which transformed the way that anthropologists understood kinship.)

—— (1955) *Tristes Tropiques*, Paris: Plon; *Tristes Tropiques*, London: Penguin, 1976.

—— (1958) *Anthropologie Structurale*, Paris: Plon; *Structural Anthropology*, New York: Basic Books, 1963.

—— (1962) *Le Totemisme Aujourd'hui*, Paris: Presses Universitaires de France; *Totemism*, Boston, MA: Beacon Press, 1963.

—— (1962) *La pensee sauvage*, Paris: Plon; *The Savage Mind*, Chicago, IL: Chicago University Press, 1966. (Shows how all human cultures employ the same principles to define and order their environment.)

—— (1964–71) *Mythologiques: Introduction a la Science de la Mythologie* (Mythologiques: Introduction to the Science of Mythology), 4 vols; vol. 1 *Le cru et le cuit*, Paris: Plon, 1964, *The Raw and the Cooked*, New York: Harper & Row, 1969; vol. 4 *L'homme nu*, Paris: Plon, 1971, *The Naked Man*, London: Cape, 1981.

—— (1973) *Anthropologie Structurale II*, Paris: Plon; *Structural Anthropology II*, New York: Basic Books, 1976. (Examines the unity of the human mind across time and culture, stressing the similarity of purpose between our distant ancestors who domesticated animals and plants and our own scientific concerns.)

—— (1978) *Myth and Meaning*, London: Routledge.

—— (1983) *Le regard eloigne*, Paris: Plon; *The View from Afar*, New York: Basic Books, 1985.

—— (1993) *Regarder, Ecouter, Lire* (Looking, Hearing, Seeing), Paris: Plon.

References and further reading

Leach, E. (1970) *Lévi-Strauss*, Modern Masters Series, London: Fontana. (Sympathetic but not reverential account of the main principles of Lévi-Strauss' structuralism from an anthropological perspective. Early but still worth reading.)

Merquior, J.G. (1986) *From Prague to Paris. A Critique of Structuralist and Post-structuralist Thought*, London: Verso. (Locates the philosophical and intellectual environment of Lévi-Strauss' work clearly and engagingly.)

Pace, D. (1983) *Claude Lévi-Strauss: The Bearer of Ashes*, London: Routledge. (Well-written comprehensive overview of Lévi-Strauss' work and its philosophical implications.)

Pavel, T. (1989) *The Feud of Language: A History of Structuralist Thought*, Oxford: Blackwell. (An excellent highly critical account of the whole structuralist enterprise, dense and requiring some previous understanding.)

Sperber, D. (1979) 'Claude Lévi-Strauss', in J. Sturrock (ed.) *Structuralism and Since*, Oxford: Oxford University Press. (A very useful critical but sympathetic synthesis of his *oeuvre*, by one of his most gifted students.)

Todorov, T. (1988) 'Knowledge in Social Anthropology: Distancing and Universality', *Anthropology Today* 4 (2): 2–5. (A subtle and complex exploration of Lévi-Strauss' theory of knowledge.)

OLIVIA HARRIS

LEWIS, CLARENCE IRVING (1883–1964)

The American philosopher C.I. Lewis held that in all knowledge there are two elements: that which is presented to sense and the construction or interpretation which represents the creative activity of the mind. Contrary to Kant, Lewis claimed that what is fixed and unalterable is not the structure that we bring to the sensibly presented, but rather the sensibly presented itself. The categories that mind imposes do not limit experience; they determine the interpretation we place upon experience, and if too much of experience eludes our categorizations, new ones should be established. It is pragmatically necessary that we create interpretive structures which will work in getting us around in sensory experience. This important and novel doctrine, Lewis' 'pragmatic a priori', emerged through the development of ideas which took root during his study of logic. The problems of choosing among alternative logics led him to assert the need for pragmatic criteria. The way we conceptually structure or categorize experience answers to pragmatic criteria of purposes, intents and interests. Only within a context defined by a priori categorizations can empirical judgments be made. These empirical judgments proceed from apprehensions of the sensibly presented to assertions of objectivities. Moral judgments require both judgments of good and decisions of right. Judgments of value are tied to qualitative satisfactions disclosed in experience and are empirical claims. Decisions about the morally right are based on imperatives of reason.

1 Life

Clarence Irving Lewis, an American philosopher who focused on epistemology, logic and ethics, was born in 1883 in Stoneham, Massachusetts, and died in Menlo Park, California, in 1964. He was educated at Harvard, receiving his B.A. in 1905 and his Ph.D. in 1910. After receiving his Doctorate, he taught at the University of California from 1911 to 1920, and then at Harvard, where from 1930 he was the Edward Peirce Professor of Philosophy until his retirement in 1953.

2 Logic and the a priori

Lewis' important and novel doctrine of the pragmatic a priori emerged through the development of ideas which took root during his study of logic. This work in logic, combined with a healthy respect for Kantian epistemology, a long exposure to Roycean idealism and an appreciation of certain basic tenets of classical American pragmatism, produced the context from which the pragmatic a priori, the vital core of Lewis' conceptual pragmatism, took shape (see ROYCE, J. §3; PRAGMATISM §2).

Lewis spent many years in the study of logic, disturbed mainly by the conception of implication developed in the extensional logic of Whitehead and Russell's *Principia Mathematica* (1910–13) (see RUSSELL, B.A.W. §3; WHITEHEAD, A.N. §2). This 'material implication' deviated strikingly from the ordinary sense of implication. According to it, a false proposition implies any proposition, while a true proposition is implied by any proposition. The problem, Lewis held, lay in the fact that the logic of propositions formulated in *Principia* is an extensional one, while ordinary deductive inference depends upon the meanings of the propositions used, and hence is rooted in intensional relations. The solution to this problem led Lewis to the development of the system of strict implication in symbolic logic and carried him beyond logic into the field of epistemology and the development of a detailed theory of meaning and analyticity.

A second type of issue, arising out of the entertainment of the possibility of an alternative to the logic of material implication, led to his interest in the existence of various types of alternative logics such as many-valued logics (see MANY-VALUED LOGIC §1; MODAL LOGIC §1). It also carried him beyond logic to the development of a theory of knowledge asserting the free creation of and pragmatic selection among various possible a priori conceptual schemes as tools of interpretation of experience.

Lewis held that the behaviour of symbolic systems operates in the same way as the behaviour of the human mind, that there is nothing in them which we have not put in ourselves, but that they teach us the meaning of our commitments. Thus, a priori truth is independent of experience because it is purely analytic of our conceptual meanings. The line between the a priori and the a posteriori, then, coincides with the divisions between the conceptual and the empirical, between the contributions of mind and what is given in experience, between the analytic and the synthetic.

3 Meaning and analyticity

According to Lewis, the meaning or deductive significance of a proposition, which can be thought of as a kind of term, coincides with the intension of the proposition, in the sense that whatever is deducible from the proposition is contained in its intension. A proposition signifies a state of affairs. A state of affairs is not a chunk of reality to be denoted, but rather includes all that the assertion of the state of affairs as actual implies, and only what it thus implies.

All real definitions specify intensional modes of meaning. What Lewis here means by a real definition is neither symbolic convention nor dictionary definition, but rather an explicative statement which relates a meaning to a meaning. There are two types of meanings related in such real definitions: linguistic meaning and sense meaning. Linguistic meaning is the pattern formed by the relation of a term or proposition to other terms or propositions. Sense meaning is the criterion in mind which determines the application of the term or proposition; it is the criterion by which what is meant is to be recognized.

Analytic truths state relations between sense meanings and not merely between linguistic meanings. Lewis sets out to undercut the conventionalist position that analytic truth expresses nothing beyond what is or can be determined by the language system which embodies it. Although he holds that there are conventional elements in the choice of symbols, in the assignment of the symbols to the meanings and in the choice of the meanings to be considered, he insists that the interrelation of the meanings is neither linguistic nor arbitrary. The analyticity of the linguistic meaning is determined by the fixed intensional relationships of sense meanings.

Lewis' position reveals both a sympathy towards,

and yet sharp criticism of, Kant's epistemology. This critical appreciation of the insights of Kant is nowhere more in evidence than in his rejection of Kant's synthetic a priori, a rejection based directly on Lewis' own use of the Kantian concept of schematism (see KANT, I. §7). A sense meaning as a schema is a rule or prescribed routine and an imagined result of it which will determine the applicability of the word. By this means Lewis proposes to solve the epistemological problem of the nature of the necessity of analytic truth and how we know such necessity. We perform an experiment in imagination. We know that 'All squares are rectangles' because in envisaging the test which a thing must satisfy if 'square' is to apply to it, we observe that the test it must satisfy if 'rectangle' is to apply is already included. Both Lewis' theory of meaning and his notion of the test schema reveal that his theory of analyticity is basically one of inclusion or containment.

Empirical meaning, then – meaning as a criterion in mind by reference to which the applicability of a term or the believability of an empirical statement is to be attested in experience – is a mode of intensional meaning. Lewis emphatically rejects as epistemologically untenable the nominalist conception that individuals are the first knowables and are primitively determinable by ostensive reference. It is only by reference to intensional meaning as criterion in mind by which one applies or refuses to apply a term that denotation is possible.

4 The a priori and pragmatic considerations

The truth of any empirical generalization is determined by the relationship of a conceptual scheme to given experience, and remains true, relative to that scheme. Empirical truth does not literally change, nor are contexts of interpretation proven false. Rather, conceptual schemes which do not work adequately as interpretive contexts are replaced by others. The sense in which truth is 'made by the mind' and is 'relative to human interest and purpose' is the sense in which we choose the interpretive structures by which we prescribe the outlines of realities of particular types and in so doing set the context for the discovery of empirical truth. However, the analytic or a priori truth contained in the interrelationships of the interpretive structures is subject neither to the contingencies of experience nor to the whims of convention; rather, it is eternally true. Such truth is not material truth but formal truth or validity.

Lewis holds not only that our choice of an analytic, a priori conceptual scheme is conditioned by experience in that it is based on pragmatic considerations operative in the light of past experience, but also that

the logic which the conceptual schemes apply and by which they are interrelated is itself based on pragmatic considerations and hence is, in the last analysis, conditioned by experience. Lewis' pragmatism runs quite deep. Humans, for Lewis, are essentially acting beings. Meanings which mind entertains, the logic which explicates such meanings, and mind itself emerge from behavioural responses to the environment in which humans find themselves. Our ways of behaving towards the world around us which are made explicit in our accepted logic are those which have lasted because they work. The final ground, even of the validity of the principle of consistency as well as the validity of ordinary inference, is firmly rooted in a pragmatic, evolutionary-based direction of successful activity. The principle of consistency, and that ordinary inference which explicates our meanings in accordance with the principle of consistency, is rooted in a 'pragmatic imperative': if it is rejected, then thought and action themselves become stultified.

Lewis' concept of the a priori occupies a unique position in the debate concerning the nature of a priori knowledge and the very possibility of an analytic–synthetic distinction. Drawing on a fundamentally Kantian scheme made responsive to the insights of American pragmatism and adapted to fit the needs of contemporary logic, Lewis has established an a priori which is coextensive with the analytic, yet which cannot be said to be empirically vacuous. It both arises from experience and has possible reference to experience.

5 Empirical knowledge

Lewis distinguishes three levels of empirical statement which enter into the formulation of empirical knowledge: expressive utterances, terminating judgments and objective beliefs.

Expressive statements, or the expressive use of language, signify appearances or indubitable content. They neither assert nor deny any objective reality of what appears; neither do they predict anything. Because they are confined to description of the immediate content of presentation, they cannot be in error. The immediate content is not judged, it is 'had'.

Terminating judgments state the prediction of a particular passage of experience. They find their cue in what is given, but state something taken to be verifiable by some test which involves a way of acting. Since terminating judgments are expressed in expressive language, if the judgment is true, its truth is known with certitude, since there is no further means to bring it into question.

Finally, there are non-terminating judgments or

judgments of objective fact. Such judgments express objective beliefs which can never be completely verified but are always further verifiable. Because such beliefs can never be completely verified they are probable, not certain. Non-terminating judgments are expressed in the form, 'If this is a physical object O, then if S appearance and action A occur, then in all probability E appearance will occur'. The major, or first, implication relation of the non-terminating judgment expresses the logical entailment of strict implication. The second implication relation of the non-terminating judgment, or in other terms the implication relation holding within the terminating judgment, expresses what Lewis calls 'real relations'. These real relations are causal relations involving contrary-to-fact conditionals and probability relations.

Our physical-object concepts embody habits of belief, and a habit is not just a collection of possible appearances and responses to these appearances; it is a rule of organization of possible appearances and possible responses which, in its very being as a rule, contains the possibility of generating more explicit relationships than can ever be enumerated. The meaning of objectivity is something over and above a collection of related appearances, and this meaning is supplied by the fixed rule of organization. Thus, though a physical-object statement is confirmable by verifying experiences, it is not reducible to or totally translatable into the verifying experiences.

Perhaps no single aspect of Lewis' philosophy has been subject to more frequent and diverse attacks than his concept of the given element in experience. He expressed an ongoing frustration that his understanding of the given had been so misinterpreted over the years, stressing that the point he is trying to make is so obvious that he wonders how anyone could contest it. If there is nothing given, there would be no content for thought, nor could there be success or failure in action, and prediction would be incomprehensible. His emphasis on the given, as he himself stresses, is not a foundationalist or phenomenalist concern about data from which we build up a world of objects, but a pragmatic concern with the way in which we proceed to verify our beliefs. If nothing is to be counted as certain, then probable knowledge is not possible, for knowledge would be merely 'probably probable'. The probability involved in our predictive claims must be founded in something that is not subject to probability claims. The sensibly presented, as apprehended, is a 'taken', but is pragmatically certain in that it serves as the test for our various claims, but cannot itself be tested since it makes no reference to future experience.

6 Ethical writings

Lewis' moral theory is an extension of the view developed in his philosophy of knowledge. There are two dimensions involved, a given element and a priori categorization. Lewis rejects the sceptical view that evaluations are emotive and unverifiable, and asserts instead that they are a species of empirical knowledge.

What is intrinsically valuable or valuable for its own sake is the quality of an experience. An experience further has contributory value through the contribution it makes to the full quality of the life of the person having it. These are reported in expressive terms, leading to decisively verifiable terminating judgments, and moving on to objective probability statements which are judgments of extrinsic value and attribute a property of value to an objectivity of some kind. Extrinsic values may be inherent or instrumental. The former lead directly to experiences which are intrinsically valuable, while the latter arise as means to an end that is inherently valuable. Judgments about right and wrong are not empirical, but rather are determined by principles which in their prescriptive character refer to values. The fundamental rational imperative is to think and act in a way that one will not later regret. Rationality requires that actions must be in accordance with objective knowledge of relationships productive of value experience in the future for all, rather than in accordance merely with the felt quality of one's immediate experience.

See also: INTENTIONALITY

List of works

Lewis, C.I. (1970) *Collected Papers*, ed. J.D. Goheen and J.L. Mothershead, Jr, Stanford, CA: Stanford University Press. (All of Lewis' published essays and his most important unpublished papers.)

—— (1918) *A Survey of Symbolic Logic*, Berkeley, CA: University of California Press. (As far as possible, deals with diverse systems and important developments of logic within a common notation.)

—— (1929) *Mind and the World Order*, New York: Charles Scribner's Sons; repr. New York: Dover, 1956. (Conceptions presented here grew out of his interest in exact logic; includes detailed presentation of his pragmatic a priori.)

—— (1946) *An Analysis of Knowledge and Valuation*, La Salle, IL: Open Court. (A study of meaning and analytic truth, empirical knowledge and an application of these to issues of valuation.)

Lewis, C.I. and Langford, C.H. (1932) *Symbolic*

Logic, New York: Appleton Century. (A technical study of symbolic or mathematical logic.)

Lewis, C.I. (1955) *The Ground and Nature of the Right*, New York: Columbia University Press. (Fundamental issue of 'the right' in various modes as these bear upon ethics.)

—— (1957) *Our Social Inheritance*, Bloomington, IN: Indiana University Press. (Public lectures delivered at Indiana University in 1956.)

—— (1969) *Values and Imperatives (Studies in Ethics by C.I. Lewis)*, ed. and with intro. by J. Lange. (Consists of four interrelated lectures delivered in 1959, plus six others, four of which were never before published.)

References and further reading

Flower, E. and Murphey, M. (1977) *A History of Philosophy in America*, New York: Capricorn Books and G.P. Putnam's Sons, 2 vols, 891–958. (A broad overview of Lewis' position, including his moral theory.)

Kuklick, B. (1977) *The Rise of American Philosophy: Cambridge, Massachusetts, 1860–1930*, New Haven, CT, and London: Yale University Press, 533–62. (An overview of Lewis' position within the context of American philosophy and philosophy at Harvard University.)

Rosenthal, S.B. (1976) *The Pragmatic A Priori: A Study in the Epistemology of C.I. Lewis*, St Louis, MO: Warren H. Green. (Main focus on Lewis' epistemology, but broadens to include metaphysical implications; pragmatic dimension stressed throughout.)

Saydah, J.R. (1969) *The Ethical Theory of Clarence Irving Lewis*, Athens, OH: Ohio University Press. (A detailed study of Lewis' ethical position.)

Schilpp, P.A. (ed.) (1968) *The Philosophy of C.I. Lewis*, The Library of Living Philosophers, vol. 13, La Salle, IL: Open Court. (Various papers discussing Lewis' work, with a response by Lewis.)

* Whitehead, A.N. and Russell, B.A.W. (1910–13) *Principia Mathematica*, Cambridge: Cambridge University Press, 2nd edn, 3 vols, 1927. (Development based on extensional logic and the relation of material implication.)

SANDRA B. ROSENTHAL

LEWIS, CLIVE STAPLES (1898–1963)

C.S. Lewis was a British religious writer. Originally trained as a philosopher at Oxford, he combined literary scholarship and the writing of fiction with clear and persuasive argumentation for traditional Christianity. His religious works continue to be best sellers, and much of his writing is directly or indirectly of philosophical interest. For the non-philosophical public, he probably remains the best representative of the position that religion is more rational than any alternative. Lewis is regarded by his admirers as more than a philosopher: in the words of Walsh (1949), he is the twentieth century's 'apostle to the skeptics'.

The most interesting of Lewis' arguments for the existence of God is one sometimes called 'The Mental Proof'. One way of getting a preliminary insight into this argument is to ask whether nature is a product of mind, or mind is a product of nature. If God created nature, as Christians believe, then nature is understandable by reason because it is a product of reason. It sounds superficially plausible to say that if mind were the product of nature, nature would be understandable by mind as well. But in fact, there is no acceptable general rule that a product can understand what produces it.

Furthermore, if nature is seen as non-rational, as without intelligence or purpose of its own, a special difficulty arises. One thing may produce another by design, by chance or by the unfolding or development of some process already inherent in the producing agent. But if nature is without intelligence or purpose, it cannot produce mind by design, nor can it produce it as the unfolding or development of something already there. So a mindless nature can produce mind only by chance. But if mind is only a chance product of nature, how can we trust our reasoning powers, how can we expect our minds to give us the truth about anything? In fact, Lewis slightly overstates his point in the first edition of *Miracles* (1947): he says that when we find that a position has been caused by non-rational factors, such as chance, we should immediately dismiss it.

In the same work, Lewis also makes some incisive criticisms of Hume's arguments against miracles, that 'there must be a uniform experience against every miraculous event'. First, says Lewis, Hume begs the question by assuming at the outset that there is 'uniform experience' against miracles. Second, the question of whether the universe is such as to allow miracles is not a question that can be settled just on the basis of experience. The most compelling reason for the uniformity of nature is that nature was the result of design by an intelligent being. And if we admit that, then the being who designed the laws of nature can suspend them (see MIRACLES).

A number of Lewis' arguments for God exhibit the same pattern: a fact of experience is vividly described, then explained by Christian theism. For example, our experience of recognizing the claims of morality and at the same time failing to meet those demands is explained by a God who is the source of morality and a human race estranged from that God (see RELIGION, HISTORY OF PHILOSOPHY OF §5). Or our experience of longings which can be satisfied by no finite object, but which seem to indicate a real need calling out for a real object can be best explained by a God who is our final good. On Lewis' view, attempts to explain these facts of our experience without bringing in God lead to our explaining them away.

Lewis also gives an argument which has been called the 'Lewis trilemma' (see 'The Shocking Alternative' in *Mere Christianity*). He argues that the claim by Jesus to be God cannot be separated from the New Testament accounts of his life and work; for example, his claim to forgive sins on his own authority could only be made by God. Lewis then poses three alternatives: Liar, Lunatic or Lord. But Jesus is recognized by almost everyone as a great moral teacher: could such a teacher lie or be subject to an insane delusion? Lewis concludes that seeing Jesus *only* as a great moral teacher is not a possibility left open by the evidence; he must be more or less than this.

See also: GOD, ARGUMENTS FOR THE EXISTENCE OF

List of works

Lewis, C.S. (1940) *The Problem of Pain*, London: Geoffrey Bles; New York: Macmillan, 1943. (An examination of the problem of evil.)
—— (1942) *The Screwtape Letters*, London: Geoffrey Bles; New York: Macmillan, 1943. (An insightful analysis of moral psychology.)
—— (1943) *The Abolition of Man*, Oxford: Oxford University Press; New York: Macmillan, 1947. (Revives a classical approach to moral philosophy.)
—— (1945) *The Great Divorce*, London: Geoffrey Bles; New York: Macmillan, 1945. (A fresh approach to traditional religious doctrines.)
—— (1947) *Miracles*, London: Geoffrey Bles; New York: Macmillan. (Re-examines important issues in the philosophy of religion.)
—— (1952) *Mere Christianity*, London: Geoffrey Bles; New York: Macmillan. (A very popular argument for Christianity.)
—— (1955) *Surprised by Joy*, London: Geoffrey Bles; New York: Harcourt, Brace & World, 1956. (A religious autobiography exploring one kind of religious experience.)
—— (1960) *The Four Loves*, London: Geoffrey Bles; New York: Harcourt, Brace & World, 1960. (A discussion of moral psychology.)

References and further reading

Beversluis, J. (1985) *C.S. Lewis and the Search for Rational Religion*, Grand Rapids, MI: Eerdmans. (An attack on both Lewis and rational arguments for religion.)
Cunningham, R.B. (1967) *C.S. Lewis: Defender of the Faith*, Philadelphia, PA: Westminster Press. (An analysis of Lewis' apologetics by a theologian.)
Kreeft, P. (1969) *C.S. Lewis: A Critical Essay*, Grand Rapids, MI: Eerdmans. (The first analysis of Lewis' arguments by a philosopher.)
Purtill, R.L. (1981) *C.S. Lewis's Case for the Christian Faith*, New York: Harper & Row. (A favourable assessment of Lewis' arguments.)
* Walsh, C. (1949) *C.S. Lewis: Apostle to the Skeptics*, New York: Macmillan. (The first full-length study of Lewis' works.)

RICHARD L. PURTILL

LEWIS, DAVID KELLOGG (1941–)

David Lewis has made extremely important and influential contributions to many topics in metaphysics, philosophical logic, the philosophy of science, the philosophy of mind, the philosophy of language, the philosophy of probability, rational decision theory, and ethics and social philosophy. His work on counterfactuals and the philosophy of modality has been especially influential.

1 Life
2 Counterfactual conditionals
3 Modality: logic and ontology

1 Life

David Kellogg Lewis was born on 28 September 1941 in Oberlin, Ohio, where his father taught government at Oberlin College. His mother, a historian, did some teaching for the college, but did not hold a regular appointment. Lewis attended Swarthmore College, from which he received a BA in philosophy (high honours) in 1962. His postgraduate studies were at Harvard, where he received an MA in 1964 and a Ph.D. in 1967. He served as Assistant Professor of Philosophy at UCLA from 1966 to 1970, and has since taught at Princeton. Lewis has for many years had a special relationship with Australia, where he has spent two or three months of every year, usually without formal academic appointment, since 1979. In September 1995 he was awarded an honorary doctorate by the University of Melbourne.

2 Counterfactual conditionals

In 'A Theory of Conditionals' (1968), Robert Stalnaker proposed the following semantical analysis of counterfactual conditionals: the counterfactual having antecedent p and consequent q ('$p \rightarrow q$') is true if and only if either p is impossible or q is true in the possible world closest to actuality in which p is true (or 'q is true in the p-world closest to actuality'). (Stalnaker's analysis assumes that for any possible world w and any possible proposition, there is a unique world that is the closest world to w in which that proposition is true.) One important consequence of this analysis is that any sentence of the form '$(p \rightarrow q)$ or $(p \rightarrow$ not-$q)$' – for example, 'If Lincoln had not been assassinated, Hitler would (still) have invaded Poland in 1939, or else if Lincoln had not been assassinated, it would not have been the case that Hitler invaded Poland in 1939' – must be true. Lewis proposed an alternative analysis (1973a), which replaces the second disjunct of Stalnaker's analysis with the condition that there is some world w in which both p and q are true, such that every p-world at least as close to actuality as w is also a q-world.

On reflection, it seems that a counterfactual with a possible antecedent can be true even if there is no one closest world in which that antecedent is true. Suppose, for example, that there are two or more p-worlds that are equally close to the actual world, that all worlds closer to actuality than these are not-p-worlds, and that q is true in all these 'tied' p-worlds. It seems evident that $p \rightarrow q$ is true in this case. Lewis' analysis entails that a counterfactual is true if its antecedent and consequent are so related, and it avoids the counterintuitive consequence that '$(p \rightarrow q)$ or $(p \rightarrow$ not-$q)$' is a valid sentence-schema. For these reasons, it would be generally conceded that the logic of counterfactual conditionals that is generated by Lewis' semantics is much more intuitive than the logic that is generated by Stalnaker's semantics; most philosophers of logic, in fact, would probably be willing to say that Lewis' logic is the correct logic of counterfactuals.

There would be less agreement about the value of Lewis' informal, philosophical account of the basic items in his semantics: possible worlds and the 'closeness' relation. Lewis' idiosyncratic account of 'possible worlds' will be examined below. His account of 'closeness' is given in terms of comparative similarity – the concept illustrated by the comparison 'San Francisco is more like Boston than it is like Calcutta'. According to Lewis, the worlds closest to w are the worlds most similar to w. There has been considerable controversy about whether Lewis' truth-conditions for counterfactual conditionals are correct if closeness is understood in terms of similarity (see COUNTERFACTUAL CONDITIONALS).

3 Modality: logic and ontology

Possible worlds are at the centre of Lewis' philosophy of modality. By the late 1960s it had become common to appeal to 'possible worlds' in discussions of modality. But many philosophers doubted whether any coherent philosophical sense could be made of the notion, particularly if each 'possible world' was to be associated with a well-defined set of individuals, those existing in it. By what criterion, it was asked, could an individual existing in one world – say, Quine's 'as he is in the actual world' – be judged identical with an individual existing in some other world and having a set of properties very different from Quine's?

Some philosophers think of possible worlds as abstractions of some kind, perhaps as internally consistent and 'complete' stories, the actual world being the one that is true. Such philosophers reply to sceptics about the intelligibility of 'cross-world identity' in this way: Quine can 'turn up in' various stories, stories both true and false, even if the false stories ascribe to him properties very different from the properties ascribed to him by the true stories. According to Lewis, however, a world is no mere story. A world is a spatiotemporally connected and closed object (or at least an object closed under some relations that, like spatiotemporal relations, are 'external'). For Lewis, a world is a very substantial thing indeed: our cosmos is one of them, and the others differ from it 'not in kind but only in what goes on at them'. A 'possible object' like Quine is 'in' a world if it is a part of it, and no possible object is a part of more than one world. Lewis' answer to the sceptics is therefore that Quine is simply not identical with anything in any other world.

The totality of worlds, Lewis maintains, is a 'logical plenum'; there is a world for every possible arrangement of things. (He is able to state this requirement without the use of any modal terms.) Although we rightly single out one member of the logical plenum as 'the actual world', there is in an important sense nothing special about it, for 'actual' is simply an indexical term like 'now' and 'here'.

Most philosophers have found the ontology that underlies Lewis' account of modality incredible. Many doubt whether there are any 'worlds' besides our own cosmos. Many wonder how Lewis knows that, even if there are other worlds, they are numerous and various enough to form a logical plenum. Many wonder why Lewis thinks that, given that there are all these 'worlds', they have anything to do with modality, or why each of them would be, as Lewis says each of them is, a 'way things could have been'. Another sort of worry, one that can perhaps be more profitably discussed, is closely related to Lewis' answer to the sceptics about cross-world identity: how can Lewis accommodate our convictions about 'modality *de re*'? No doubt Quine could have been a geographer. In the language of possible worlds, there is a world in which Quine is a geographer. But, the worrier points out, if Lewis is right, Quine is not in any world but our own (see DE RE/DE DICTO).

Lewis replies that, although Quine is not in any other world, there are people in some other worlds who play the same role in their worlds that Quine plays in his (our) world – who are the people in those worlds who are the most similar to Quine. If there are people in the world *w* who enjoy this status, they are the counterparts of Quine in *w*. (But since the question, 'Which things are most similar to *x*?' is a pragmatic question, one that can be answered in various ways depending on one's interests, there is no unique 'counterpart relation' – no one relation that is expressed by '*x* is a counterpart of *y*'.) Lewis analyses modal statements *de re* by reference to the counterparts of the *res* they concern: to say that Quine could have been a geographer is to say that he has a counterpart who is a geographer. This analysis has been disputed on the ground that Quine's counterparts are not, after all, Quine; therefore, it is urged, no statement about their features could be equivalent to any statement about what he could have been. Lewis replies that the property 'could have been a geographer' is the property 'has a counterpart who is a geographer'. If, therefore, Quine has a counterpart who is a geographer, Quine has the property 'could have been a geographer'. But this reply requires a qualification. Since there is no one counterpart relation, there is no one property that is expressed by 'could have been a geographer'. Whether we are willing to say that Quine could have been a geographer is, in consequence, a function of the interests that we bring to our discussions of how Quine could have been different.

In 'Counterpart Theory and Quantified Modal Logic' (1968), Lewis presents his thoughts about counterparts and modality in a very general form. He presents an extensional first-order language whose primitive nonlogical vocabulary comprises only predicates – for example, '*x* is a possible world', '*x* is a counterpart of *y*' and so on – and he embodies his theory of counterparts ('Counterpart Theory') in eight axioms stated in this language. He presents an algorithm for translating sentences of quantified modal logic into this language. He goes on to make some illuminating observations about quantified modal logic by showing that certain 'famous' problematical sentences in the language of quantified modal logic correspond under the translation algorithm to theorems, and certain others to non-theorems, of Counterpart Theory; he shows that if various formal restrictions were placed on the counterpart relation – restrictions that would in his view be arbitrary – the theorems that would thereby be added to Counterpart Theory would be translations of certain of the 'famous' sentences of quantified modal logic. He shows, finally, that, although all sentences in the language of quantified modal logic can be translated into his extensional language, the converse does not hold. The latter is therefore a richer language: it has all the expressive power of the language of quantified modal logic and more besides.

An important feature of Lewis' account of modality is that, unlike most other accounts of modality, it is reductive. If Lewis is right, modal terms can be eliminated from our discourse in favour of spatiotemporal terms, 'part', and an indexical term like 'we'. (It is, moreover, arguable that if one accepts Lewis' modal ontology, one need include in one's ontology no non-individuals, but sets ultimately grounded on individuals. Propositions, for example, can be identified with sets of worlds, and properties with sets of the things in them.) Whether or not those who find Lewis' modal ontology incredible are right so to regard it, it is undeniable that a lot more can be done with it than with any other modal ontology. We have seen that it provides a reductive analysis of modality. We have not been able to discuss its astounding successes – granting only its truth – in dealing with a very wide range of philosophical problems. (The philosopher John Perry has remarked that it 'goes through philosophical problems the way a McCormick reaper goes through wheat'.) Perhaps the same feature of the ontology – the vast range of spatiotemporal objects it assumes – accounts both for its extraordinary power and the 'incredulous stares' that have been so often directed at its inventor. Lewis does not dispute the validity of the maxim 'Entities are not to be multiplied beyond necessity', but he insists that, once the content and consequences of a theory have been made as clear as they can be, whether the entities assumed by that theory lie inside or outside the bounds of 'necessity' is a matter of individual, subjective judgment.

See also: MODAL LOGIC; MODAL LOGIC, PHILOSOPHICAL ISSUES IN

List of works

Lewis, D.K. (1966) 'An Argument for the Identity Theory', *Journal of Philosophy* 63: 17–25. (An influential argument for the mind–body identity thesis.)

—— (1968) 'Counterpart Theory and Quantified Modal Logic', *Journal of Philosophy* 65: 113–26. (Lewis' first statement of his distinctive treatment of modality.)

—— (1969) *Convention: A Philosophical Study*, Cambridge, MA: Harvard University Press. (A classic account of conventions as regularities which are recognized as solutions to coordination problems.)

—— (1970a) 'Anselm and Actuality', *Nous* 4: 175–88. (Includes Lewis' indexical conception of actuality.)

—— (1970b) 'How to Define Theoretical Terms', *Journal of Philosophy* 67: 427–46. (An elegant treatment of the role of theoretical terms in scientific theories, drawing on the work of Ramsey and Carnap.)

* —— (1973a) *Counterfactuals*, Cambridge, MA: Harvard University Press. (A full statement of Lewis' 'possible-world' treatment of counterfactual conditions.)

—— (1973b) 'Causation', *Journal of Philosophy* 70: 535–67. (Causation as counterfactual dependence.)

—— (1976) 'Survival and Identity', in *The Identities of Persons*, ed. A.O. Rorty, Berkeley, CA: University of California Press. (Argues that puzzles concerning personal identity are best solved by regarding persons as suitably related aggregates of person-stages.)

—— (1979a) 'Counterfactual Dependence and Time's Arrow', *Nous* 13: 455–76. (Uses his treatment of counterfactuals to explain asymmetries in time.)

—— (1979b) 'Attitudes De Dicto and De Se', *Philosophical Review* 88: 513–43. (Uses the theory of possible worlds to provide a sophisticated treatment of propositional attitudes.)

—— (1980) 'A Subjectivist's Guide to Objective Chance', in *Studies in Inductive Logic and Probability*, vol. II, ed. R.C. Jeffrey, Berkeley, CA: University of California Press. (An attempt to provide an account of chance in terms of degrees of belief and frequencies; subsequently Lewis has acknowledged that the account is flawed – see

relevent Postscript in 1986b and Introduction xiv–xvii.)

—— (1983a) *Philosophical Papers*, New York: Oxford University Press, vol. 1. (Contains Lewis' most important pre-1981 papers on ontology, the philosophy of mind, and the philosophy of language, including 1966, 1968, 1970a, 1970b, 1976 and 1979b. Also includes Postscripts to various of the papers, and a brief but illuminating Introduction in which Lewis discusses his way of doing philosophy.)

——(1983b) 'New Work for a Theory of Universals', *Australasian Journal of Philosophy* 61: 343–77. (Discusses theories of universals.)

—— (1986b) *Philosophical Papers*, New York: Oxford University Press, vol. 2. (Contains two previously unpublished papers and Lewis' most important pre-1982 papers on the relation of counterfactual conditionals to time, probability, causation and causal explanation, causal dependence, and decision theory, including 1973b, 1979a, 1980, and 1986a. Also includes Postscripts to various of the papers.)

—— (1986c) *On the Plurality of Worlds*, Oxford: Blackwell. (A sustained exposition and defence of Lewis' ontology of possible worlds.)

—— (1991) *Parts of Classes*, Oxford: Blackwell. (A brilliant and highly original discussion of set theory, conducted from the point of view provided by Lewis' ontology.)

—— (1994) 'Reduction of Mind', in *A Companion to Philosophy of Mind*, ed. S. Guttenplan, Oxford: Blackwell. (A reformulation of his early argument for the mind–body identity thesis, drawing on 1970b, plus an extended critical discussion of theories of mental content.)

References and further reading

Armstrong D. (1989) *A Combinatorial Theory of Possibility*, Cambridge: Cambridge University Press. (In Chapters 1 and 2 Armstrong sets out his case for a 'naturalist' alternative to Lewis' theory of possibility.)

Plantinga, A. (1987) 'Two Concepts of Modality: Modal Realism and Modal Reductionism', in *Philosophical Perspectives*, ed. J. Tomberlin, Atascadero, CA: Ridgeview, vol. 1, 189–231. (Argues that because Lewis proposes to reduce possibilities to worlds, he is not the modal realist he is generally taken to be.)

* Stalnaker, R. (1968) 'A Theory of Conditionals', in *Studies in Logical Theory*, ed. N. Rescher, Oxford: Blackwell. (The paper which started current debates on counterfactual conditionals.)

—— (1984) *Inquiry*, Cambridge, MA: MIT Press. (In

Chapter 3, Stalnaker gives an alternative to Lewis' account of possible worlds, and in Chapter 7 he responds to Lewis' criticisms of his theory of conditionals.)

van Inwagen, P. (1986) 'Two Concepts of Possible Worlds', in *Midwest Studies in Philosophy* 11: 185–213. (Extended critical exposition and discussion of Lewis' position.)

PETER VAN INWAGEN

LI

Li means 'pattern' or 'principle', and as a verb can also refer to the creation of orderly pattern. Mencius believed that the human heart–mind had an inherent taste for and attraction to such 'good order'. His contemporary, Zhuangzi, was the first to use li *to refer to an underlying normative 'pattern' structuring and giving order to the entire world. This sense in turn influenced the Confucian thinker Xunzi, who employed and developed the concept to express his understanding of Confucianism. Certain Buddhist thinkers used the notion of* li *to describe first 'emptiness' and later 'Buddha-nature', the common underlying characteristic of all phenomena. A version of this idea was adopted by neo-Confucian thinkers, who believed that while each thing manifested its own particular* li, *it also contained within it the* li *of all other things. Thus there is a profound metaphysical identity between self and world.*

The earliest and most basic sense of the character *li* ('pattern' or 'principle') is derived from the simpler graph which serves as its central component: a rectangular field divided into equal quadrants to form an 'orderly pattern'. As a verb, *li* has the related meaning of creating such a pattern, thus 'to set in good order'.

The Mohists were the first Chinese thinkers to use *li* with a distinctly philosophical sense (see MOHIST PHILOSOPHY). In the *Mozi*, *li* is used to mean 'good order' (for example, in Chapter 25 it is opposed to 'chaos'). In later Mohist writings, *li* means the principles governing such order and orderly principles of thought (Graham 1978: 192). These two senses of 'good order' are both present in *Mencius* 6A7, which claims that all human minds agree in approving of *li* (good order) and *yi* (what is right).

The most important and extensive early uses of *li* occur in the *Zhuangzi*. There, *li* appears both in the sense of the grand pattern underlying all phenomena and the individual instantiations of this pattern in discrete things. The *Zhuangzi* contains the first

occurrences of 'heavenly principles', 'principles of the Way' and 'great principles', terms which connect the notion of 'pattern' to a greater cosmic scheme, lending it a wider metaphysical role and greater normative force. Being explicitly linked to 'Heaven' and the 'Way', *li* describes not only how things are but also how they should be. We also see several references to 'the principles of the myriad things' and in one case to 'the various principles of the myriad things', ideas that prove important in neo-Confucian thought (see ZHUANGZI).

XUNZI was deeply influenced by these new senses of the term and incorporated them into his Confucian philosophy. Formally, his views are remarkably similar to those in the *Zhuangzi*, but their content – what he claimed to be the underlying pattern of the cosmos – was significantly different. Xunzi's ideal was a consciously anthropocentric harmony between human needs, desires and capacities, and Nature. Zhuangzi's vision lacked this human centre; he focused on 'heavenly principles', a term which does not appear in Xunzi's writing.

The view that *li* provides both a descriptive and normative pattern for individual things, while also being part of a larger cosmic pattern, gave rise to the idea that this larger pattern 'united' the various phenomena of the world. This idea can be found in Han dynasty texts such as the HUAINANZI. It was most developed by thinkers such as Wang Bi, who speaks of 'ultimate principle' as an object of mystical contemplation and religious veneration. His contemporary Guo Xiang, who held similar views, also believed that the 'pattern' of the world was not the result of some predetermined plan but rather of 'spontaneous' processes. He insisted that the ultimate nature of the world was *wu* (non-existence) (see YOU–WU).

Chinese Buddhists adapted these later senses of *li* to express their own views. In the *Sutra in Forty-two Sections*, *li* is used to mean 'the true nature of reality', a full appreciation of which will result in complete enlightenment. ZHI DUN developed the equation of *li* with *wu* 'non-existence', understanding both in the Buddhist sense of 'emptiness'. Huayan Buddhists understood the 'emptiness' of reality – the lack of an independent, individual nature – to mean that all things are manifestations of a shared 'Buddha-nature'. Huayan works, such as the *Treatise on the Golden Lion*, argue that every 'phenomenon' contains within it all the various *li* (see BUDDHIST PHILOSOPHY, CHINESE; BUDDHIST CONCEPT OF EMPTINESS).

Like Huayan Buddhists, neo-Confucians believed that *li* describes the fundamental character of reality and that the spiritual life lies in grasping this shared, unifying principle. CHENG YI was famous for the idea

– derived from the earlier Buddhist thinker Daosheng (d. AD 434) – that 'principle is one; its manifestations many'. However, neo-Confucians believed that principle defined a classical Confucian world. Not unlike the earlier difference between Zhuangzi and Xunzi, their disagreement with the Buddhists turned largely on the content – not the formal structure – of their metaphysical views.

ZHU XI believed *li* was logically prior to, though not actually separable from existing things. It lodged in *qi* (ether) to form actual things, riding it 'as a person rides a horse' (see QI). While each thing contained all the myriad *li*, a given thing's endowment of *qi* allowed only certain *li* to be manifested. Thus while in some deep sense things were the same, in the actual world each had its own particular (manifested) principle.

Neo-Confucians such as LU XIANGSHAN and WANG YANGMING took issue with this view. They feared that Zhu's teachings, which described *li* as 'above actual things and events', would lead students away from their moral heart–minds and into quietistic contemplation. They argued that the mind did not contain but was itself principle. Later neo-Confucians such as WANG FUZHI, Yan Yuan and DAI ZHEN criticized these earlier thinkers for being infected with Daoist and Buddhist ideas. They argued for a return to the original sense of *li*: the 'good and proper order' inherent in the world (see NEO-CONFUCIAN PHILO-SOPHY §2).

See also: COSMOLOGY; DAO; LAW AND RITUAL IN CHINESE PHILOSOPHY; NEO-CONFUCIAN PHILOSOPHY; MOHIST PHILOSOPHY; QI; XUNZI; ZHUANGZI

References and further reading

Chan Wing-tsit (1964) 'The Evolution of the Neo-Confucian concept of *li* as principle', *Tsing-Hua Journal of Chinese Studies* n.s. 4.2: 123–49. (Thorough collection of examples of *li* from throughout Chinese history.)

* Graham, A.C. (1978) *Later Mohist Logic, Ethics and Science*, Hong Kong: Chinese University Press, and London: School of Oriental and Asian Studies. (Remarkable reconstruction and analysis of the later Mohist sections of the *Mozi*, which concerns the systematic study of argumentation, ethics and science.)

—— (1992) *Two Chinese Philosophers*, LaSalle, IL: Open Court, 2nd edn. (Insightful study of the two neo-Confucian thinkers, Cheng Hao and Cheng Yi; helpful discussions of *li* especially on pages 8–22.)

PHILIP J. IVANHOE

LI (RITUAL) *see* LAW AND RITUAL IN CHINESE PHILOSOPHY

LIBER DE CAUSIS

The Liber de causis *(Book of Causes) is a short treatise on Neoplatonist metaphysics, composed in Arabic by an unknown author probably in the ninth century in Baghdad. Through its twelfth-century Latin translation, it greatly influenced mature medieval philosophy in the West.*

Drawing heavily on the Greek Neoplatonist Proclus, the Liber de causis *represents a development of late Neoplatonism along two lines. On the one hand, the author modifies and simplifies Proclus' theory of causes to accord more closely with the three-part division of ultimate causes advanced by the founder of Neoplatonism, Plotinus. On the other hand, the author introduces some of the metaphysical principles of Qu'ranic or biblical monotheism. The result is a metaphysically provocative reinterpretation of Neoplatonist thought which, because it seemed to accommodate Platonist philosophy to the medieval worldview, made the* Liber de causis *a natural source text for medieval philosophers.*

1   **Form, content and origin**
2   **Philosophical context**
3   **A source for later medieval philosophy**

1   Form, content and origin

The *Liber de causis* (Book of Causes) is presented *more geometrico*, that is, it proceeds by way of thirty-one discrete propositions, or theses (often amplified by corollaries), each accompanied by passages of interconnected supporting argumentation. Despite the systematic presentation, however, the work as a whole appears somewhat fragmentary, no doubt because the author was overly ambitious. It appears that he was trying to set forth, in outline, an entire theory of how the universe has been originated by a first cause (an entity consisting in pure goodness and perfect being) and how this cause's creative activity comports with the agency of other fundamental causes such as the Neoplatonist supramundane 'mind' and universal 'soul'. In the known Arabic manuscripts, the treatise is entitled either 'The Book of Aristotle's Exposition on the Pure Good' or 'Discourse on the Pure Good' (*Kalam fi mahd al-khair*); its designation as a *kalam* (discourse, discussion or spoken account) might be taken to indicate that the work is not actually intended to be a systematic treatise but, rather, a collection of teachings or meditations. Clearly, however, the work's shortcomings as a systematic treatise do not preclude a systematic philosophical intention on the part of its author or even a coherent underlying structure. AQUINAS, in his *Super Librum de causis expositio* (Commentary on the *Liber de causis*) proposed an underlying structure in which every proposition has an identifiable expository function.

The *Liber de causis* was long thought, by Islamic as well as Western medieval philosophers, to be a work of ARISTOTLE (see NEOPLATONISM IN ISLAMIC PHILOSOPHY §1). In these philosophers' eyes, it filled out Aristotle's otherwise deficient account of the ultimate causes of the universe as presented in *Metaphysics* XII. Even before Aquinas demonstrated that the work was un-Aristotelian and indebted to Proclus' *Elements of Theology*, speculation had arisen about its authorship. Albert the Great's idea that the author might have been a twelfth century Jewish writer in Spain, Abraham IBN DAUD, has until recently been considered a plausible hypothesis. Discoveries in the 1970s and 1980s, however, have given the controversy new direction. Very likely, the author of the *Liber de causis* was a Muslim or Christian thinker writing in the Near East, probably at the intellectual centre in Baghdad, in the ninth century (in any case, no later than the last quarter of the tenth century).

2 Philosophical context

Many historians of philosophy have seen the *Liber de causis* as merely an anonymous epitome of Proclus' *Elements of Theology* (see PROCLUS). Such views, however, miss the work's recourse to certain ideas of PLOTINUS, from which Proclus had departed. The author of the *Liber de causis* rejects Proclus' version of the doctrine of 'hypostases', the levels of reality posited by Neoplatonism as beyond the physical world, or causally prior to it (see NEOPLATONISM). Proclus argues that the fundamental causes of the universe consist in a complex system of hypostases arranged in a causal series, beginning with the first cause, the absolute One, and continuing to its ultimate effects in the material world through the intermediary hypostases of Finitude/infinity, Being, Eternity, Mind, Forms, Time, Soul and so on. By contrast, the *Liber de causis* re-affirms the simpler Plotinian causal series of three hypostases, the perfectly unified and simple first cause (the One), Mind and Soul.

What is at stake philosophically in the *Liber de causis*' simplification of the Neoplatonist series of hypostases and the denial that there are intermediary hypostases between the first cause and the hypostasis of finite being as Mind? First, the *Liber de causis* breaks with Proclus' (and perhaps ultimately Plato's) principle that any common feature of things requires a special cause, or hypostasis, in which all the things possessing the feature participate. Second, the *Liber de causis* responds to one of the most basic problems of Neoplatonist metaphysics: if causal dependence involves a certain sort of similarity of effect to cause (participation of effect in cause), how can causes give rise to effects quite different from themselves? Locating a mediating factor between cause and effect in intermediate levels of reality, or hypostases, is a tendency that can be seen already in Plotinus. The *Liber de causis* represents a development of Neoplatonist metaphysics since it attempts to redress the extreme multiplication of hypostases found in later Neoplatonism.

The *Liber de causis* also exemplifies the creative interaction of Islamic and Christian thought with the legacy of Greek philosophy (especially Neoplatonism). This is illustrated by its presentation of the first cause as truly existent and as pure being (in contrast to the Neoplatonist characterization of it as in some sense beyond being), its philosophical refinement of the idea of creative causality, and its derivation from creative causality of a doctrine of universal providence. The treatise is apparently a product of the early, seminal stages of interaction between monotheistic speculation and Greek philosophy in the Islamic milieu, which took place in the latter half of the eighth century and through the ninth century (see GREEK PHILOSOPHY: IMPACT ON ISLAMIC PHILOSOPHY). Since this formative period was a time in which Christian scholars and translators strongly influenced Islamic thought, the *Liber de causis* can also be said to have arisen out of early contact between Christianity and Islam.

3 A source for later medieval philosophy

Although further research will no doubt identify more echoes of the *Liber de causis* in the writings of later Islamic and Jewish medieval philosophers, its direct and definite influence on their work appears to have been relatively slight (exceptions are IBN SAB'IN, Al-Baghdadi and IBN EZRA). Its substantial influence is to be seen more in its contribution to a general store of philosophical ideas than in its shaping of particular doctrines. In the Latin West, by contrast, the *Liber de causis* served as one of the most frequently used sources of Neoplatonist metaphysics and aided Christian medieval philosophers, even those strongly influenced by Aristotle, in building Platonist principles and ideas into the very foundations of their philosophical systems (see PLATONISM, MEDIEVAL). Translated into Latin, probably around 1180 in Toledo by GERARD OF CREMONA, and known as *Liber Aristotelis de expositione bonitatis purae* or more simply as *Liber de causis*, the work became available to Western philosophers along with the bulk of Aristotle's works (see TRANSLATORS). It made up part of the massive influx of Greek and Arabic learning into Western Europe in the latter half of the twelfth century, quickly becoming a standard text; 237 extant Latin manuscripts have been identified. While its widespread acceptance was encouraged by the attribution to Aristotle, the *Liber de causis* was studied for its intrinsic interest. Its influence continued after Aquinas established its connection with the thought of Proclus.

The influence of the *Liber de causis* can be gauged in part by the fact that a high proportion of the major philosophers of the thirteenth and fourteenth centuries, as well as many minor figures, wrote commentaries on it. Twenty-seven commentaries from before 1500 have been identified. Written in a wide variety of genres, these commentaries include works by Roger BACON, ALBERT THE GREAT, Thomas AQUINAS, SIGER OF BRABANT, HENRY OF GHENT (attribution doubtful), GILES OF ROME and others. Even more importantly, the direct influence of the *Liber de causis* shows in the frequent citations of it and the manifold adaptations of its doctrines found in major philosophical writings from the 1230s through the Renaissance.

For medieval philosophers, the *Liber de causis* represented not only a source of Neoplatonist ideas but also an adaptation of Neoplatonist metaphysics of the sort that they themselves were intent upon. Thus Aquinas, in his detailed and masterful commentary, is concerned to show how the *Liber de causis* differs from and is superior to its source in Proclus. Using a translation of the *Elements of Theology* made in 1268 by William of Moerbeke, Aquinas draws attention both to *Liber de causis*' affinities with Proclus' systematization of Neoplatonist metaphysics, and its divergences from it. In his analysis, he employs the metaphysical writings of the fifth-century Christian Neoplatonist PSEUDO-DIONYSIUS as a key to understanding the *Liber de causis* and also as a corrective when he thinks that the author has not gone far enough in re-working classical Neoplatonism. Affecting medieval philosophers' accounts of creation, divine nature and ontology, the *Liber de causis* provides them with particular ideas about creative and natural causation, the individuation of pure being and the constitution of finite being.

See also: ALBERT THE GREAT; GERARD OF CREMONA; GREEK PHILOSOPHY: IMPACT ON ISLAMIC PHILOSOPHY; ISLAMIC PHILOSOPHY: TRANSMISSION INTO WESTERN EUROPE; NEOPLATONISM; PLATONISM, MEDIEVAL; PLOTINUS; PROCLUS; ULRICH OF STRASBOURG

References and further reading

Editions and translations

Badawi, A. (ed.) (1955) 'Procli: Liber (Pseudo-Aristotelis) de expositione bonitatis purae (Liber de causis)', *Neoplatonici apud Arabes, Islamica* 19: 1–33. (A critical edition of the Arabic text, to be superseded by the edition being prepared by R.C. Taylor.)

Bardenhewer, O. (1882) *Die Pseudo-aristotelische Schrift über das reine Gute bekannt unter dem Namen 'Liber de causis'*, Freiburg: Herder'sche Verlagsbuchhandlung; repr. Frankfurt: Minerva, 1961. (The pioneering work of modern scholarship, containing an Arabic text, a Latin text and a German translation.)

Brand, D.J. (1984) *The Liber de Causis: Translated From the Latin with an Introduction*, Marquette, WI: Marquette University Press. (The best approach to the *Liber de causis* for the English reader, with a helpful introduction and select bibliography. Aquinas' analysis of the contents of the *Liber de causis* is provided in the introduction.)

Pattin, A. (1966) 'Le Liber de causis. Édition établie à l'aide de 90 manuscrits avec introduction et notes', *Tijdschrift voor Filosofie* 28: 90–203. (An edition of the Latin translation, to be shortly superseded by the nearly critical edition being prepared by R.C. Taylor.)

Zerachja B. Izsak (1916) *Pseudo-Aristotelis Liber de causis*, ed. I. Schreiber, Budapest. (An edition of a medieval Hebrew translation of the *Liber de causis*.)

Medieval commentaries

Albert the Great (1265–75) *Opera omnia [...] Tomus XVII pars II, De causis et processu universitatis a prima causa*, ed. W. Fauser, Münster: Aschendorff, 1993. (The critical edition of Albert the Great's commentary, which is a massive and philosophically rich work.)

* Aquinas, Thomas (1272) *Super Librum de causis expositio*, ed. H.D. Saffrey, Louvain: B. Nauwelaerts, Fribourg: Société philosophique, 1954; *In Librum de causis expositio*, ed. C. Pera, Torino: Marietti, 1955; trans. V. Guagliardo, C. Hess and

R.C. Taylor, *Commentary on the Liber de Causis, Thomas Aquinas in Translation* vol. 1, Washington, DC: Catholic University of America Press, 1996. (Saffrey's critical edition of Aquinas' commentary is complemented by Pera's study-edition, containing a wealth of helpful material. Guagliardo, Hess and Taylor provide an accessible translation with introduction and notes.)

Bacon, Roger (1241–5) *Opera hactenus inedita Rogeri Baconi, XII, Quaestiones supra Librum de causis*, ed. R. Steele and F.M. Delorme, Oxford: Clarendon Press, 1935. (An excellent edition.)

Giles of Rome (1280) *Opus super authorem de causis Alpharabium*, Venice: Iacob Zoppinus, 1550; repr. Frankfurt: Minerva, 1968. (A Renaissance edition, to be superseded shortly by the critical edition being prepared by F. del Punta *et al.*)

Henry of Ghent (1245–5) *Les Quaestiones in Librum de causis attribuées à Henri de Gand*, ed. J. P. Zwaenepoel, Louvain: Publications Universitaires, 1974. (A critical edition with introduction.)

Siger of Brabant (1255–85) *Les Quaestiones super Librum de causis de Siger de Brabant*, ed. A. Marlasca, Louvain/Paris: Publications Universitaires – B. Nauwelaerts, 1972. (A critical edition with introduction.)

Further reading

Beierwaltes, W. (1963) 'Der Kommentar zum *Liber de causis* als neuplatonisches Element in der Philosophie des Thomas von Aquin' (The Commentary on the *Liber de causis* as a Neoplatonic Element in the Philosophy of Thomas Aquinas), *Philosophische Rundschau* 11: 192–215. (A philosophically perceptive overview of the influence of the *Liber de causis* on Aquinas and other philosophers of his time.)

D'Ancona Costa, C. (1995) *Recherches sur le Liber de causis* (Research on the *Liber de causis*), Paris: Vrin. (The most comprehensive and thorough general study, with very extensive bibliography.)

Endress, G. (1973) *Proclus Arabus. Zwanzig Abschnitte aus der 'Institutio theologica' in arabischer Übersetzung* (Proclus Arabus: Twenty Sections of the *Instituto theologica* in Arabic Translation), Wiesbaden: F. Steiner Verlag. (A foundational study for our understanding of the sources and origin of the *Liber de causis*.)

Rowson, E. (1984) 'An Unpublished Work by Al-Amiri and the Date of the *Liber de causis*', *Journal of the American Oriental Society* 104: 193–9. (An important contribution to our understanding of the provenance of the *Liber de causis*.)

Sweeney, L. (1959) 'Research Difficulties in the *Liber de causis*', *The Modern Schoolman* 36: 109–16; repr. in L. Sweeney (ed.) *Divine Infinity in Greek and Medieval Thought*, New York: Peter Lang, 1992. (An authoritative and influential treatment of the philosophical character of the *Liber de causis*.)

Taylor, R.C. (1983) 'The *Liber de causis*: A Preliminary List of Extant Manuscripts', *Bulletin de philosophie médiévale* 25: 63–84. (A treasury of information for further research into the role of the *Liber de Causis* in medieval philosophy.)

—— (1986) 'The *Kalam fi mahd al-khair* (*Liber de causis*) in the Islamic Philosophical Milieu', in J. Kraye, W.F. Ryan and C.B. Schmitt (eds) *Pseudo-Aristotle in the Middle AgesL The 'Theology' and other Texts*, London: The Warburg Institute, 1986. (A summary discussion of the place of the *Liber de causis* in Islamic and later Jewish philosophy.)

HANNES JARKA-SELLERS

LIBERALISM

Liberal political philosophy explores the foundations of the principles most commonly associated with liberal politics: freedom, toleration, individual rights, constitutional democracy and the rule of law. Liberals hold that political organizations are justified by the contribution they make to the interests of individuals, interests which can be understood apart from the idea of society and politics. They reject both the view that cultures, communities and states are ends in themselves, and the view that social and political organizations should aim to transform or perfect human nature. People have purposes of their own to pursue, either economic or spiritual (or both). Since those purposes do not naturally harmonize with one another, a framework of rules may be necessary so that individuals know what they can count on for their own purposes and what they must concede to the purposes of others. The challenge for political philosophy, then, is to design a social framework that provides this security and predictability, but represents at the same time a safe and reasonable compromise among the disparate demands of individuals.

1   **Liberal politics**
2   **Political philosophy**
3   **Individualism**
4   **The economic side of human nature**
5   **The social contract**

1   Liberal politics

In politics, the term 'liberalism' denotes a family of

positions centred around constitutional democracy, the rule of law, political and intellectual freedom, toleration in religion, morals and lifestyle, opposition to racial and sexual discrimination, and respect for the rights of the individual.

Often these positions are associated with a suspicion of state authority, with a view that the powers of government should be constrained if not minimized, and with a confidence in the ability of individuals to organize themselves on the basis of the market, the free interplay of ideas and the loose and informal associations of civil society. Liberal support for democracy is therefore sometimes qualified by fear of 'the tyranny of the majority' and by apprehensions about the extent and intrusiveness of the power that a populist state is capable of exercising.

These attitudes are not, however, characteristic of all forms of liberalism. In Britain, in the late nineteenth and early twentieth century, a group of thinkers known as the New Liberals made a case against *laissez-faire* and in favour of state intervention in social, economic and cultural life. The New Liberals, who included T.H. GREEN and L.T. Hobhouse, saw individual liberty as something to be achieved under favourable social circumstances. The poverty, squalor and ignorance in which most people lived made it impossible in their view for freedom and individuality to flourish, and the New Liberals believed that these conditions could only be ameliorated through collective action coordinated by a strong welfare-oriented interventionist state.

In the USA, since the early part of the twentieth century, the term 'liberalism' has been associated with 'progressive' economic reform, a commitment to the modest redistribution of income that takes place in a welfare state, a suspicion of business and an abiding faith in the legal regulation of economic affairs. The more *laissez-faire* version of liberalism is called 'conservatism' in the USA, and Europeans are often disconcerted to hear 'liberal' used there as label for positions that they themselves would describe as left-wing or moderately socialist.

This is not just terminological confusion. Those in the USA who call themselves 'liberals' do also hold the positions outlined at the beginning of this article, and their disagreement with 'conservative' opponents is partly a live and unresolved issue about the implications of traditional liberal premises in so far as social and economic policy is concerned. Does individual freedom require private ownership? Is poverty compatible with liberty? Can civil and political rights be equal if economic power is not? Liberalism is a family of positions, and these remain important family disputes.

2 Political philosophy

In philosophy, 'liberalism' is not just the name of a loosely organized and quarrelsome family of substantive political opinions. It refers also to a heritage of abstract thought about human nature, agency, freedom, and value, and their bearing on the functions and origins of political and legal institutions.

That heritage takes its rise in early modern English political philosophy – most notably in the work of Thomas HOBBES and John LOCKE §10. It is also the political philosophy of the European Enlightenment, represented in its most philosophically articulate form in the writings of Jean-Jacques ROUSSEAU, François-Marie Arouet de VOLTAIRE, Henri-Benjamin CONSTANT DE REBECQUE and, a little later, Immanuel KANT. In the nineteenth century, philosophical liberalism is represented, first, in the utilitarian theories of BENTHAM and J.S. MILL, and later in the 'Idealism' of T.H. Green.

Inevitably, because of our proximity, it is harder to identify canonical works of twentieth-century liberalism. There was a long period in the twentieth century in which liberal philosophers seemed to lose their taste (or their nerve) for grand theory on the scale of Hobbes or Kant, a period during which they seemed to pride themselves on the piecemeal, analytic and unsystematic character of their thought. In a Cold War context, these were regarded as healthy signs of being 'non-ideological'. That phase seems to have passed, and more confident versions of philosophical liberalism have re-emerged in the work of late-twentieth-century writers like F.A. VON HAYEK §3, Robert NOZICK §2, Ronald DWORKIN, Joseph Raz and, most importantly, John RAWLS §4.

Some will quibble about one or two of the names on this list. Was Hobbes really a liberal? Was Rousseau? We should remember, however, that 'liberalism' has never been a label over which any group has exercised collective control. As a result, the term is at the mercy of its most casual users, and indeed the attempt to define 'liberalism' is undertaken most commonly not by its practitioners but by its opponents, with predictable caricatural results.

Even so, the challenge is not just to correct misrepresentations. The philosophical positions that we most plausibly identify as liberal often represent distinctive expressions of ambivalence about human nature and political life, rather than dogmatic formulae in a liberal catechism. We have seen this already in the values and principles which constitute liberalism in the political sense: liberals disagree about property, economic equality and the role of the state. At the more philosophical level, liberals disagree about the nature of value, the meaning of freedom and the connection between individual and social purposes.

What follows is an attempt to lay out some of those positions and controversies. But defining liberalism is, on the whole, a frustrating pastime. There are many ways of mapping this philosophical landscape, and there is no substitute for grappling with the disparate detail of the theories propounded by particular liberal philosophers.

3 Individualism

Let us begin with some basic ethical premises. The deepest commitment of liberal political philosophy is to *individualism*, as a fundamental proposition about value. Liberal individualism has four parts to it.

First, liberals believe that the individual person is what matters for the purposes of social and political evaluation. We may be interested in the fate of a culture, a language, a community or a nation, but for a liberal such interest is always secondary or derivative. Ultimate value has to do with how things are for ordinary men and women, considered one by one: their pains and pleasures, their preferences and aspirations, their survival, development and flourishing. Of course, people do care about each other: individualism is not the same as egoism. But individualism excludes social and collective entities from the realm of ultimate goods.

There is less agreement about the grounds for this individualization of value. John Locke, writing in the seventeenth century, based it on each person being the workmanship and property of God, which meant that we were 'made to last during His, not one anothers Pleasure' (1690). This relation to God was direct, unmediated and unconditional in the case of each individual. It therefore established a basis for our rights with respect to one another that did not presuppose validation by larger social structures.

Modern liberalism, however, is a secular tradition, and its history since Locke's time is largely a history of the attempt to establish this individualism without appealing to the idea of God. Utilitarian thinkers linked the notion of value analytically to desire or preference, and they inferred, from the fact that desiring and preferring were attributes of individuals, that the fundamentals of value must be individualistic too (see UTILITARIANISM). Those following in the tradition of Kant, on the other hand, linked value analytically to the lonely individualism of will, conscience and the sense of duty, and drew the conclusion that each person, *qua* moral agent, was entitled to be regarded as an end in themselves, not just a means to broader social ends. The Kantian view has perhaps fared better in modern political philosophy, although its underlying argument – that because moral thinking takes place at the level of individual minds and wills, individual minds and wills must also be the fundamental objects of moral concern – has yet to be rendered in a compelling form.

Second, liberals believe that there is something particularly important in the capacity of individuals to direct their actions and live their lives, each on their own terms. They believe in the importance of freedom – although what that belief amounts to is one of the controversies referred to earlier. Some define freedom in negative terms: their libertarianism amounts simply to a condemnation of force, coercion and interference in human life. Freedom, they say, is what flourishes when these constraints are taken away, and there is nothing apart from the removal of constraints that needs to be done politically in order for freedom to flourish. Positive conceptions of liberty allow the state a much greater role than this: they may see freedom or autonomy as something to be achieved, rather than taken for granted, in the life of an unrestrained individual, something that requires educated individual capacities and favourable social conditions (see FREEDOM AND LIBERTY).

Some conceptions of positive liberty go well beyond this, moving out of the liberal realm altogether. If freedom is identified with the performance of social duty, or attributed to individuals only by virtue of their participation in some social whole, then the resulting theory can hardly be described as liberal.

Also, if freedom is presented as the achievement of a happy few, something of which the ordinary mass of humanity is incapable, then again we are not dealing with a liberal conception. Although liberal freedom is sometimes a developmental concept, it is not an aristocratic or utopian one. The free direction of a human life is seen as something which ordinary people are capable of, under decent social and political circumstances. When Colonel Rainsborough exclaimed in the Putney Debates of 1647, 'Really, I think that the poorest he that is in England has a life to live as the greatest he', he gave voice to an egalitarianism that lies at the foundations of the liberal tradition (Wootton 1986: 286).

The third aspect of liberal individualism, then, is a commitment to equality. We have to be careful how we formulate this. Liberal philosophers are not necessarily egalitarians in the economic sense. But they are committed as a matter of the basic logic of their position to a principle of underlying equality of basic worth. People are entitled to equal concern for their interests in the design and operation of their society's institutions; and they have the right to be equally respected in their desire to lead their lives on their own terms (see EQUALITY).

Feminists have sometimes questioned whether this liberal commitment to equality extends across boundaries of gender. In the writings of Locke, Rousseau and Kant it is easy to find throwaway lines that would be described today as sexist or misogynistic. No writer in the liberal canon committed himself explicitly and at length to the emancipation of women much before J.S. Mill's essay *The Subjection of Women* in 1868. Nevertheless, the legacy of liberal carelessness on this issue does not pose any major theoretical difficulties for the position that men and women are equal in their moral and political capacities and in the respect to be accorded those capacities. Indeed, the more challenging feminist critique is that liberals exaggerate (rather than deny) the similarities between men and women – that they fail to either acknowledge or accommodate crucial elements of 'difference' in moral reasoning and ethical demeanour (see FEMINIST POLITICAL PHILOSOPHY).

A fourth element of liberal individualism involves an insistence on the rights of individual reason. This involves not just freedom of thought, conscience or discussion, but a deeper demand about justification in politics: the demand that rules and institutions of social life must be justified at the tribunal of each individual's reason.

We see here an important connection between liberal thought and the philosophical legacy of the Enlightenment. The Enlightenment was characterized by a burgeoning confidence in the human ability to make sense of the world, to grasp its regularities and fundamental principles and to manipulate its powers for the benefit of mankind. That drive to understand nature is matched in Enlightenment thought by an optimism at least as strong about the possibility of understanding society and human nature. In one aspect, this optimism is the basis of modern sociology, history and economics. But it is also the source of certain normative attitudes towards social and political justification – an impatience with tradition, mystery, awe and superstition as the basis of order, and a determination to make authority answer at the tribunal of reason and convince us that it is entitled to respect. The social world, even more than the natural world, must be thought of as a world *for us* (for *each* of us) – a world whose workings are to be understood by the active enquiries of the individual mind, not by religious dogma, mindless tradition or the hysterics of communal solidarity.

4 The economic side of human nature

Liberals accord intrinsic value to people as individuals, and attach particular importance to each individual's capacity to organize a life on their own

terms. What terms are these likely to be? What nature of beings are these whose individual freedom we value? And what are the uses to which their freedom is likely to be put?

Critics commonly associate liberal individualism with an egoistic and acquisitive view of human nature. They say the classic liberals all gave pride of place, among human motivations, to the desire for power, pleasure and material possessions. Humanity, they argue, is reduced in liberal theory to nothing more than a competitive mass of market individuals – voracious consumers with unlimited appetites, hostile or indifferent to the well-being of others, and requiring no more of their political and legal institutions than that they secure the conditions for market activity.

The picture is not entirely a distortion. Liberal individualism does recognize that individuals' interests do not necessarily or naturally harmonize with one another. Each individual has a life of their own to lead, and there is no guarantee that one person's desires will not conflict with another's. Sometimes, as in Hobbes's theory, this is represented as an inherent hostility, a competitive diffidence and a 'mutuall will of hurting', issuing in a 'war of all against all'. Sometimes, as in John Rawls' work, it is seen simply as a postulate of mutual disinterest (rather than hostility). Mostly it is seen in Immanuel Kant's words as a matter of the 'unsociable sociability of men' – that there are things we share in common, things that drive us to society, things we can only accomplish together, as well as aspects of our nature that make us prickly, adversarial and wilfully isolated individuals.

Moreover, although – as we shall see – liberals believe that there are terms on which individuals with diverse or even opposed interests can live in peace with one another, it has never been part of their political philosophy that reason, enlightenment or socialization would put an end to this basic diversity or competitiveness. (To the extent that Rousseau suggests that the social contract might produce 'a remarkable change in man', his speculations take him outside the liberal tradition.) In the nature of things, humans will inevitably come up with diverse and opposed views of what makes life worth living, while the exigencies of our situation in the world – the moderate scarcity of material resources and our vulnerability to one another – will always furnish the raw materials for anxiety, competition and conflict (see HUMAN NATURE).

A related objection is that liberals subordinate politics to economics: they see political structures merely as instruments for securing economic peace and market interaction, and they ignore the higher calling for the state outlined, for example, in the theories of Aristotle, Hegel or Hannah Arendt.

The image is accurate, but it is not clear why it should be regarded as an objection. Certainly, liberals do not regard participation in politics as an end in itself; unlike the civic humanists, they do not think that the most important virtues and activities are those oriented towards politics and the formal exercise of power over others (see REPUBLICANISM). It does not follow that they think of political participation as a narrow self-interested enterprise. In political science, the term 'liberalism' is commonly associated with interest group politics, but philosophical liberals are about equally divided on the question of whether voters in a democracy should orient their decisions to the common good or to their own interests (with the common good emerging as some sort of resultant from the political process). The point, however, is that even those who believe we should vote on our views about the common good still maintain that politics is, in the end, a means to promote the interests of individuals (*all* individuals), not an end in itself. They may believe in Rousseauian democracy, they may even hope that democratic participation can bring out the best in people (although many are dubious about that), but their firmest conviction is that individuals have interests and purposes of their own to pursue which have nothing intrinsically to do with politics or the state, and that the function of government is to facilitate those individual purposes not judge them or replace them with political or social ones.

To say that these purposes are individual is not necessarily to say that they are economic or materialistic in their content. It is surprising, in fact, how few liberal theorists have actually held the economically acquisitive picture of human nature. Hobbes did, certainly, and so did some of the eighteenth-century political economists. But many others in the liberal tradition see material motives as means to individual ends that may well be ethical, even spiritual in their content. John Locke, notorious in some circles as the apostle of possessive individualism, insisted that our primary mission in life is to ascertain what our creator requires of us in the way of conduct and worship: 'the observance of these things is the highest obligation that lies upon mankind, and ... our utmost care, application and diligence, ought to be exercised in the search and performance of them because there is nothing in this world that is of any consideration in comparison with eternity' (1689 (1991): 42). Modern liberals, too, tend to stress the ethical and cultural character of individual pursuits. We each have our own conception of happiness or the good life – a view about what makes a life worth living – and it is the diversity of individual ideals of this kind that political structures must accommodate.

In general, there is an intriguing ambivalence in the liberal tradition about whether this shift from economic to ethical individualism presents the social problem as more or less intractable. On the one hand, it seems to make the situation look better. Economic conflict is a zero-sum game: what you have I cannot have, or, worse still, what you have puts you in a better position to take what I have away from me; I therefore have an excellent reason of self-protection to deprive you of as many resources as I can. Ethical and spiritual individualism, by contrast, seems less intrinsically competitive: 'one man does not violate the right of another', wrote Locke, 'by his erroneous opinions, ... nor is his perdition any prejudice to another man's affairs' (1689 (1991): 42). The appropriate social posture for religious or ethical individualists seems to be the mutual indifference of Rawls' theory rather than the competition or conflict of Hobbes.

In fact, of course, that has not been our experience. Wars of religion have been at least as deadly as wars for territory or resources. We may think of commercial life as bland or shallow, but there is a certain sense of relief in Voltaire's comment about the London Stock Exchange: 'Here Jew, Mohammedan and Christian deal with each other as though they were all of the same faith, and only apply the word infidel to people who go bankrupt' (1734 (1980): 41). Even Hobbes, whose *Leviathan* is the *locus classicus* for the economic war of all against all, was adamant that the problem of the struggle for resources could be solved, since people would be willing to make concessions to a strong state that could keep the peace. But sectarian religious fervour he thought of as a form of madness, and he doubted whether the partisans of rival religious ideals could ever come to terms with one another (see TOLERATION).

Critics of liberalism will no doubt persevere in their charge that the tradition flatters the materialistic side of human nature at the expense of cultural and spiritual aspirations. They will say that liberals have paid too much attention to the ways in which political and legal structures can foster market economies and too little to the contribution they can make to the quality of ethical choice. A number of liberal writers have taken this criticism seriously. Joseph Raz (1986), for example, has argued that there is an aspiration towards value in the very concept of autonomy, so that a liberal commitment to freedom should not be thought of as incompatible with a social commitment to ethical perfectionism (see PERFECTIONISM).

There comes a point, however, when liberal philosophers simply have to stand up and defend the channelling of political energies towards the real (but apparently soluble) problems of famine, plague and poverty, and away from moral, cultural and religious disputes, which promise little more in the way of progress than war, sectarianism and cults of ethical correctness. The preoccupation with economics is not based on scepticism about the ethical or spiritual dimensions of human life. It is based rather on a moderate sense of what politics can and cannot accomplish in a world where people disagree about God, value and the meaning of life, but largely converge in their desire to avoid hunger and disease and to better their material conditions.

5 The social contract

To the extent that liberal philosophy emphasizes diversity and conflict among individual purposes, it seems to steer us in the direction of anarchism. For what set of actually existing or realistically practicable institutions could possibly accommodate the individualism we have outlined?

In fact, liberal theorists have always held that something like the modern state, with its familiar institutions of law and representative government, *can* be made legitimate. They reject both the anarchist view that freedom is vindicated only in the absence of state authority and obligation and the utopian premise that a just society presupposes a radical change in human nature. This puts them in a rather ambivalent position in so far as existing 'liberal' societies are concerned – meaning here the constitutional democracies of North America, Western Europe, Australasia and Japan. Liberalism has been a remarkably successful political ideology, inasmuch as its leading principles – freedom, toleration and equality before the law – have been accepted as part of the self-image or public relations of the world's most powerful and prosperous societies. Its proponents are uneasy, however, with the common inference that the social, economic and political reality of these societies is what liberal principles amount to in practice (just as Marxists were uneasy about the presentation of the Soviet Union and its satellites as 'actually existing socialism'). They insist, quite properly, that liberalism is a set of critical principles, not an ideology or rationalization, and that it provides a basis for condemning things like deepening poverty, secretive and oligarchical government, legal abuses and the continuing legacy of racism and sexism in modern democracies. Even so, the existence of the self-styled 'liberal' democracies is important. It helps sustain the sense that liberalism is a reformist rather than a revolutionary creed and that we already know, at least in outline, what a truly liberal society would be like. That sense of moderate reformism is not just a strategic ideological advantage. Liberalism claims to

respect men and women as they are. It does not require generation after generation to undergo sacrifice for the sake of an endlessly postponed utopia. It suggests instead that political structures can be set up in now a way which represents a safe and reasonable compromise among individuals' disparate demands.

In its classical form – in the writings of Hobbes, Locke, Rousseau, and to a lesser extent Kant – the argument from liberal premises to the legitimacy of something like the modern state was presented in terms of the social contract (see CONTRACTARIANISM). The argument goes something like this.

Imagine people living outside any framework of political authority, exercising the right to direct their own lives and their own dealings with one another, in what liberal philosophers have called 'the state of nature'. Using this as a baseline, try to model the development of political institutions as a way in which individuals exercise their freedom not as a way in which their freedom is abrogated.

The social contract model represents the functions of government in terms of a set of difficulties that such people would face in a state of nature. Conceptions of these difficulties vary. There may be an internecine struggle for resources (Hobbes and Hume); there may be an appreciation of others' rights, but no reliable mechanism for enforcing them (Locke); or there may be disagreement about justice, with each person seeking to do what seems right or good in their opinion (Kant). The common element is that people in the state of nature would lack a reliable sense of what they could count on in social and economic life. What they most need is a secure set of rules, impartially administered and enforced, to provide a framework in which peaceful cooperation and long-term production is possible.

Government, then, is represented in terms of an agreement by each person with all of the others (in a given territory) to cooperate in the institution and maintenance of permanent rule-making and rule-enforcing agencies. The contract is not an agreement between the government and the individual. Instead, it presents legal and governmental institutions as structures of cooperation among individuals, and it uses that idea as a basis for deriving limits on governmental powers and restraints on particular individuals' or factions' exploitation of those powers. Tyrannical exploitation and arbitrary government are ruled out on this conception, inasmuch as they cannot be represented as any sort of improvement over the situation individuals would face if they tried to live without any political institutions at all.

Some theorists, Rousseau and Rawls for example, use the social contract idea also as a way of thinking about the content of legal rules: we can discuss what rights we have and the just distribution of resources by asking what assurances would have to be given to each individual to secure their consent to the basic structure of social arrangements. In the hands of these theorists, the social contract is a test of substantive political justification. Others see it in more procedural terms: the social contract models the construction of political and constitutional mechanisms, which will then work out substantive solutions on a basis that is relatively independent of the contract idea. Hobbes's theory is the most extreme example of this: the Hobbesian contract is simply an agreement to authorize an individual or organization (a 'sovereign') to solve the problems that generate conflict in the state of nature in any way that promises improvement. The absolute authority with which the sovereign is thus endowed has led some to deny that Hobbes is a liberal. Certainly, he is not wedded to the positions identified with liberalism at the beginning of this article. But his underlying political philosophy is liberal: his value premises are individualistic, and he is unyielding in his view that political institutions (with the powers he accords them) must be justified in relation to the interests of each individual, as well as in his optimism that such justification is possible.

Not all liberal philosophers appeal to the idea of the social contract. Many prefer to develop their theories without the mediation of this model. The arguments of J.S. Mill's 1859 essay *On Liberty*, for example – which many regard as the quintessential statement of liberal principles – are presented directly as claims that individuals are entitled to make, against their society and their government, without any historical pretence that governments were set up by individuals to validate those claims (see LAW, LIMITS OF). Others use the social contract to justify some but not all of the political constraints they propose. In the theories of John Locke and Robert Nozick, the social contract argument presupposes a distribution of 'natural' property rights. For them, the function of the social contract is to support and police these rights, not reconceive or redistribute them. In other words, Locke and Nozick propose that property rights should be justified directly in moral argument, without appealing to the social contract idea. I suspect that something like this is true of all liberal theories. The social contract is an intermediate rather than a fundamental idea: one that presupposes that individuals are free, equal and rational, and that political power requires a justification which connects with the interests of each of them.

When it is understood in this way, as a method of modelling the force of certain deeper assumptions or theorems about justification, the social contract can be used as a purely hypothetical device in normative argument. As Kant and Rawls have pointed out, we need not be embarrassed by the fact that no such contract ever took place. It is still a useful test to apply to a constitution or to a set of laws. For if we conclude, even hypothetically, that our laws or our constitution would not have commanded the agreement of all those who are constrained by them, we will have discovered a significant dissonance between our political arrangements and the fundamental (pre-contract) notion of respect for each individual – a dissonance that ought to be of concern to liberal philosophers whether they are interested in the niceties of contract theory or not.

References and further reading

Arblaster, A. (1984) *The Rise and Decline of Western Liberalism*, Oxford: Blackwell. (A critique of liberal political thought from the sixteenth to the twentieth centuries.)

Bentham, J. (1789) *An Introduction to the Principles of Morals and Legislation*, eds J.H. Burns and H.L.A. Hart, London: Athlone Press, 1970. (Classic statement of utilitarian morality.)

Berlin, I. (1969) *Four Essays on Liberty*, Oxford: Oxford University Press, 118–72. (Develops the distinction between negative and positive freedom, discussed in §3.)

Bramstead, E.K. and Melhuish, K.J. (1978) *Western Liberalism: A History in Documents from Locke to Croce*, London: Longman. (A comprehensive collection of statements by liberal politicians and statesmen in the European tradition, as well as liberal political philosophers, together with a commentary by the editors.)

Dworkin, R. (1977) *Taking Rights Seriously*, London: Duckworth. (A theory of law and political morality centred on the idea that individual rights sometimes 'trump' utilitarian justifications.)

—— (1978) 'Liberalism', in S. Hampshire (ed.) *Public and Private Morality*, Cambridge: Cambridge University Press. (An argument that moral equality lies at the heart of liberalism.)

Freeden, M. (1978) *The New Liberalism; An Ideology of Social Reform*, Oxford: Oxford University Press. (A useful discussion of 'the new liberalism' referred to in §1.)

Green, T.H. (1886) *Lectures on the Principles of Political Obligation*, ed. B. Bosanquet, London: Longman, 1941. (An influential work combining liberal and Hegelian themes.)

Hayek, F.A. (1960) *The Constitution of Liberty*, London: Routledge & Kegan Paul. (A statement of the connection between liberty and the rule of law, and a critique of the modern welfare state.)

* Hobbes, T. (1651) *Leviathan*, ed. R. Tuck, Cambridge: Cambridge University Press, 1991. (Classic statement of liberal premises of economic individualism and the war of all against all, leading to the contractual institution of an absolute sovereign.)

Hobhouse, L.T. (1964) *Liberalism*, New York: Oxford University Press. (An example of 'the new liberalism' referred to in §1.)

Holmes, S. (1993) *The Anatomy of Antiliberalism*, Cambridge, MA: Harvard University Press. (A vigorous defence of liberal political theory and source of some of the arguments about economic liberalism in §4.)

Hume, D. (1739) *A Treatise of Human Nature*, ed. L.A. Selby-Bigge, rev. P.H. Nidditch, Oxford: Clarendon Press, 1978, Book III. (A classic account of the emergence of property and justice.)

Kant, I. (1991) *Political Writings*, ed. H. Reiss, Cambridge: Cambridge University Press, pp. 73–87 and 131–64. (Various writings in this volume insist both on the hypothetical nature of social contract reasoning, and – within the contract model – on the duty of individuals to enter and remain in political society with those with whom they find themselves disagreeing about justice.)

* Locke, J. (1689) *A Letter Concerning Toleration*, ed. J. Horton and S. Mendus, London: Routledge, 1991. (Referred to in the discussion of economic versus spiritual versions of liberalism in §4.)

* —— (1690) *Two Treatises of Government*, ed. R. Tuck, Cambridge: Cambridge University Press, 1988. (The paradigmatic statement of liberal contract theory.)

Manning, D. (1976) *Liberalism*. London: Dent. (A brief overview of liberal political philosophy.)

* Mill, J.S. (1859) *On Liberty*, ed. C.V. Shields, Indianapolis, IN: Bobbs-Merrill, 1956. (A defence of individuality and freedom of thought and discussion, regarded by many as the most direct statement of liberal principle.)

—— (1868) 'The Subjection of Women', in J. Mill and H. Taylor, *Essays on Sex Equality*, ed. A. Rossi, Chicago, IL: University of Chicago Press, 1970. (The first sustained statement of gender equality by a philosopher in the classic liberal tradition.)

Nozick, R. (1974) *Anarchy, State and Utopia*, Oxford: Blackwell. (A vigorous modern defence of private property and the minimal state, in the tradition of John Locke.)

Rawls, J. (1971) *A Theory of Justice*, Oxford: Oxford University Press. (Perhaps the most famous construction of liberal theory in modern times, using the idea of a hypothetical contract to explore issues of justice and fairness.)

—— (1993) *Political Liberalism*, New York: Columbia University Press. (A defence of the claim that liberal principles of justice must command support among a wide variety of ethical and philosophical conceptions in a modern pluralist society.)

* Raz, J. (1986) *The Morality of Freedom*, Oxford: Clarendon Press, 165–216 and 369–430. (An exploration of the connection between autonomy and perfectionism, mentioned in §4.)

Rousseau, J.-J. (1762) *The Social Contract and Discourses*, trans. G.D.H. Cole, London: Dent, 1955. (A version of contractarian theory that teeters on the brink between liberal and non-liberal political thought.)

Voltaire, F.-M.A. de (1734) *Letters on England*, trans. L.Tancock, Harmondsworth: Penguin, 1980.

Waldron, J. (1987) 'Theoretical Foundations of Liberalism', *Philosophical Quarterly* 37: 127–50. (A discussion of the difficulty of defining 'liberalism' and of the connection between liberalism and Enlightenment thought, mentioned at the end of §3.)

* Wootton, D. (1986) *Divine Right and Democracy: An Anthology of Political Writing in Stuart England*, Harmondsworth: Penguin, 285–317. (Includes a transcript of the Putney Debates of 1647 in which Colonel Rainsborough gave voice to the principle of liberal equality, discussed in §3.)

JEREMY WALDRON

LIBERALISM, RUSSIAN

Unlike early English liberalism which stressed individual freedom from state control and from the 'tyranny of the majority', Russian liberalism generally emphasized the importance of legality in government, the state's positive role as guarantor of civil liberty, and the gradual achievement of social justice through reform. In the century between Peter the Great's death in 1725 and the Decembrist uprising of 1825 various politicians and thinkers proposed the introduction of representative institutions into the Russian government and recommended that serfdom be abolished in the Empire. These proposals reflected admiration for Western European models of government and the impact of the Enlightenment on Russia's ruling elite. Because the autocracy ultimately rejected these proposals and made public discussion of them all but impossible, liberalism did not take root in this period. The genesis of Russian liberalism as a philosophically elaborated, politically coherent movement occurred after the death of Tsar

Nicholas I in 1855, when the government eased censorship and announced its commitment to peasant emancipation. Mid-nineteenth-century Russian liberalism owed its intellectual inspiration to Hegelianism and French juste-milieu liberalism. Russian liberals argued that social progress in the empire had almost always come about at the state's initiative; they could scarcely imagine building a just society without the cooperation of a strong state.

At the beginning of the twentieth century Russian liberals confronted what proved to be an insuperable challenge: how to establish a viable constitutional order in an empire riven by social and ethnic strife where neither government nor the powerful socialist movement favoured a rule-of-law state. Wrestling with this difficulty, the liberals split into two factions: a 'left' or 'radical' wing that valued social justice over the sanctity of property rights; and a 'right' or 'conservative' wing that valued legal equality over social equality, and therefore interpreted socialism as a species of utopianism. Between 1905 and 1917 the liberal movement reached its political zenith, as liberal politicians exercised their influence in the State Duma and opposition movement. Following the October 1917 Bolshevik Revolution liberalism was banned in the Soviet Union. It re-emerged, albeit in altered form, during communism's collapse when neo-liberals claimed for liberalism a prominent position in the 'normal' constellation of Russian political forces. The main goals of post-Soviet liberalism are the defence of civil and political rights, the establishment of the rule of law, the assertion of individual property rights and the gradual construction of a market economy.

1   Absolutism, Enlightenment and proto-liberalism
2   Mid-nineteenth-century liberalism
3   Late imperial liberalism
4   The revival of liberalism in post-Soviet Russia

1   Absolutism, Enlightenment and proto-liberalism

The post-Petrine Russian government was a unitary absolutist state that, in theory, allowed neither individual nor corporate autonomy. Until the mid-nineteenth century the state depended on a tacit alliance between the Crown and the landed nobility dedicated to the continuation of serfdom. Between 1725 and the Decembrist uprising in 1825, however, various politicians and thinkers – among them Count Dmitrii Golitsyn (1663–1738), Count Nikita Panin (1718–83), Denis Fonvizin (1744–92), Nikita Murav'ëv (1796–1843), Mikhail Speranskii (1722–1839) and Nikolai Novosil'tsov (1761–1836) – proposed to establish new agencies to limit the Tsar's personal authority or to subject the Crown to the

higher authority of a fundamental law; in certain instances, these proposals were accompanied by recommendations that serfdom be abolished. Historians have sometimes interpreted these reformist efforts as the origins of Russian liberalism.

However, only two eighteenth-century Russian thinkers elaborated philosophical justifications for liberal government, Semën Desnitskii and Aleksandr Radishchev. Desnitskii (?–1789), a professor of law at Moscow University, was influenced by the Scottish Enlightenment, particularly by Adam Smith whose lectures he heard at Glasgow and whose Theory of Moral Sentiments he often quoted. Desnitskii divided social evolution into four ascending stages – hunting, pastoral, agricultural and commercial society – each having a legal system peculiar to it. He thought that representative government was appropriate to commercial society; popular elections expressed the electorate's historically conditioned deference towards the wealthy; and that the duty of the wealthy was to serve the less fortunate, as the dictates of virtue require. Desnitskii criticized Russian absolutism as lawless and arbitrary. He proposed that the imperial government establish an elective Senate, with representatives from the commercial classes as well as the nobility, to advise the crown on legislation. He was one of the first Russian advocates of civil rights for women.

Radishchev (1749–1802) has usually been classified as a revolutionary because he rejected nobiliary privileges, noted that tyrannicide has sometimes been the penalty for despotism and predicted a peasant revolution. However, he was far from consistent and, with equal justice, may be considered a forerunner of liberalism. Radishchev's principal commitment was to equality before the law. He followed Mably in asserting that good government requires every citizen, including the sovereign, to submit to the law; like Mably and Rousseau, he thought that government should depend upon citizens' mutual consent without which the social compact dissolves. He admired the English and American systems for their devotion to legality and encouragement of an active citizenry. His famous tract, A Journey from St Petersburg to Moscow (1790), can be read as an explicit warning to the Russian government and nobility to mend their ways, lest the peasants rise in bloody revolt. Although he was a republican, Radishchev did not support the Jacobin terror, because the terrorists violated civil rights. Unfortunately for Russia, Desnitskii's work was quickly forgotten and Radishchev's tract was burned by the imperial authorities (see ENLIGHTENMENT, RUSSIAN).

2 Mid-nineteenth-century liberalism

Russian liberalism's crystallization in the 1850s owed much to external circumstances, especially the Crimean debacle, the death of Tsar Nicholas I and the accession to the throne in 1855 of the reform-minded Alexander II. However, these events only punctuated the evolutionary process in which a portion of educated society committed itself to liberal values. During the 1840s, at the height of the Westernizer–Slavophile debate over Russian national identity, the Westernizers defined Russia as a member of the European family of nations. The historian Timofei Granovskii (1813–55) claimed that, under the aegis of the modern state, European societies had been gradually advancing towards political liberty. He hinted that even in Russia this movement would culminate with a *Rechtsstaat* wherein all individuals would have the possibility to develop their potential freely. In 1847 the jurist Konstantin Kavelin (1818–85) published a Westernizer manifesto, 'A Brief Survey of Juridical Relations in Ancient Russia', asserting that Peter I's reforms represented a victory for the principle of free individuality. Kavelin hoped that the contemporary Russian state and educated society would build upon this victory by inaugurating broad new reforms. In St Petersburg during the late 1840s and early 1850s he studied the peasant question in collaboration with other junior officials interested in serfdom's abolition; his 1855 'Memorandum on the Emancipation of Peasants in Russia' was probably the most compelling justification for ending serfdom written by a Russian intellectual. By the early 1840s, Granovskii, Kavelin, the literary critics Pavel Annenkov (1813–77) and Aleksandr Druzhinin (1824–64), the historian Sergei Solov'ëv (1820–79) and the oft-derided 'philosophical tea-merchant' Vasilii Botkin (1811–69) had arrived at a consensus on the values they thought essential to free society: respect for law, individual dignity, freedom of conscience, toleration of intellectual diversity and hostility towards serfdom. All agreed that, under Russian conditions, the state would have to assume primary responsibility for realizing these values in practice. The Westernizers' worldview was underpinned by Hegelianism, a current that dominated Russian thought during the second quarter of the century (see HEGELIANISM, RUSSIAN). Hegel's evolutionary conception of history, his efforts to reconcile the thinking individual's autonomy with the *polis'* collective life, his antipathy to unmediated state power and his support for constitutional monarchy implicitly informed the Westernizers' approach to Russia's problems.

The credit for transforming the amorphous Westernism of the 1840s into a recognizable liberal programme belonged to Boris Chicherin (1828–1904), arguably the leading Russian liberal theoretician of the century. He thought that liberals should concentrate on achieving seven objectives: freedom of conscience; peasant emancipation; freedom of speech; freedom of the press; academic freedom; publicity of all government activities; and public legal proceedings. In his classic *On Popular Representation* (1866), he sharply distinguished between the civil rights mentioned above and political rights such as voting and representation in a national assembly. He criticized Western liberals such as John Stuart Mill for mistakenly identifying liberalism with the achievement of political rights. He maintained that Russians should accustom themselves to civil rights and the legal culture entailed by such rights before establishing a constitutional government. His faith in monarchy as an engine of legal reform, his hesitations about the advisability of constitutional government in Russia, his bitter opposition to socialism, and his allegedly doctrinaire Hegelianism led many contemporaries to consider him a conservative or even a reactionary. He advertised himself as a 'conservative-liberal', professing faith in the platform 'strong government and liberal measures'. Nevertheless, late in his life Chicherin laid greater stress on individual freedom and the need for a constitution. His last major work, *Philosophy of Law* (1900), was a sweeping defence of individual freedom in the spirit of what Friedrich von Hayek later called 'classical liberalism'. Chicherin's individualism profoundly affected the philosophers Nikolai Berdiaev (1874–1948), Pavel Novgorodtsev (1866–1924) and Pëtr Struve (1870–1944) who came to share his aversion to socialism and collectivism.

Westernism was also the main source of Aleksandr Herzen's 'Russian socialism', a doctrine that contributed to the birth of Russian populism and anarchism but that has sometimes been seen as affiliated with the liberal tradition. Herzen (1812–70) was a lifelong believer in individual freedom, an opponent of tyrannous abstractions and an occasional advocate of republican government. His greatest champion, Sir Isaiah Berlin, regards him as a harbinger of contemporary liberal pluralism; others have associated him with libertarianism and the Russian federalist movement. However, Herzen was famously dismissive of European *juste-milieu* liberalism. He hated the modern bureaucratic state, wished for the triumph of a 'social republic' based on the peasant commune and anticipated a new socialist age in history. His revolutionary and millenarian side had little or nothing in common with the statist liberalism of Chicherin (see HERZEN §3).

3 Late imperial liberalism

Between 1890 and 1917 Russian liberals redefined their political agenda. They pressed the government for a constitution and national elections, a concession reluctantly granted by Nicholas II in October 1905. In the State Duma from 1906 to 1917 liberal parties played a signal role, but they overcame neither the Tsar's scepticism about representative government nor socialist opposition to the legal order. During this turbulent period liberal thinkers were divided over which objective deserved priority – legality or social justice. Left-wing liberals sought the rule of law as well as social justice but generally valued the latter over the former. Their practical aims – land redistribution from the nobility to the peasantry, an eight-hour day for workers, and a social-insurance state – overlapped with the moderate socialist agenda so extensively that left liberals tended to think of socialists as their natural allies. Indeed, Pavel Miliukov (1859–1943), Russia's best-known liberal politician, boasted in 1905 that 'our programme is undoubtedly the most leftist of all those advanced by similar political groups in Western Europe'. The philosophical foundations of left liberalism derived from disparate religious and secular sources. The religious philosopher Vladimir SOLOV'ËV (1853–1900) combined social Christianity with a Kantian insistence on individual dignity and the objectivity of ethics when he argued that a good society must guarantee to each member that minimum of welfare necessary for a dignified existence. Although Solov'ëv himself cannot be counted a left liberal, his ideas developed a wide currency in the younger generation which sought in Christian egalitarianism a solution to Russia's social problems. The Ukrainian liberal Bogdan Kistiakovskii (1868–1920), influenced by the Austrian *Kathedersozialist* Anton Menger, discovered a historical continuity between liberalism and socialism: he predicted that civil rights and the liberal *Rechtsstaat* would prepare the way for social rights and a socialist rule-of-law state. After the 1917 revolutions, the liberal-socialist synthesis reached its culmination with Sergius HESSEN (1887–1950) who predicted a new type of liberal state – one that would foster conditions in which citizens might choose the good without being hindered by economic privation.

The 'right' or 'conservative' liberals followed Chicherin in stressing that cultivation of individual freedoms and respect for law must take priority over redistributing wealth and the social insurance state. In 1909 authors of the *Vekhi* (*Signposts*) symposium accused Russian radicals, including left liberals, of supporting social equality at the expense of legality and individual freedom (see SIGNPOSTS MOVEMENT). The historian Mikhail Gershenzon (1869–1925), an outspoken defender of individualism, described egoism as the 'great force' that had made of the Western bourgeoisie 'God's unconscious instrument on earth'. Struve's essay in *Signposts* attacked the radicals' proclivity to 'stand aside' from the government rather than cooperate with it, to preach revolutionary destruction rather than to seek self-perfection as true lovers of liberty ought to do. Connecting all the *Signposts* essays was the assumption that the inner, especially religious life of the individual 'is the only sound foundation for any social structure'. A devastating critique of socialism from a conservative liberal perspective came from Novgorodtsev, whose *On the Social Ideal* (1911–16) interpreted Marxism as a doomed millenarian religious movement aimed at achieving the Kingdom of God on earth; Novgorodtsev juxtaposed to Marxism belief in a transcendent God, in natural law, in a *Rechtsstaat* and in individual dignity. During the political crises of 1917–18 several conservative liberals, among them Struve and Novgorodtsev, supported a temporary military dictatorship as an alternative to socialism. This policy showed the degree to which right liberals feared socialism and 'revolutionary democracy', as well as the unpalatable choices that confronted all Russian liberals at the end of the old regime.

Of course, the lines between left and right liberals were far from absolute. Struve moved from left to right between 1902 and 1909, whereas Miliukov tried to bridge the distance between the two wings of the party. Some thinkers – Novgorodtsev is a good example – at times straddled the left–right philosophical divide. In any event, the two groups shared a central conviction, namely that a strong government is a necessary precondition of liberty, however defined. Thus, in the main Russian liberalism was state-centred rather than federalist, pluralist or libertarian.

4 The revival of liberalism in post-Soviet Russia

Soon after the Bolshevik Revolution, the Soviet government banned liberal political parties. From 1917 to 1991 the Soviets treated liberalism as an ideological deviation punishable by public obloquy, arrest, hard labour or even death. Public advocacy of liberal values was therefore out of the question; sadly, the academic study of liberalism's legacy was circumscribed. Even before 1991, however, dissident intellectuals supported certain elements of the liberal worldview, especially guarantees of civil rights and government legality. During the 1970s, the most remarkable of these thinkers, the physicist Andrei Sakharov (1921–90), sought to combine socialist welfare with civil and political rights of the 'Western' type. Between the mid-1970s and early 1980s he jettisoned his support for Soviet power; before his death in 1990 he was preparing a draft constitution the central tenets of which were guarantees of human rights and the division of government authority. Philosophically, Sakharov was a *naif*, but he succeeded in endowing his humane vision with the force of common sense. After the collapse of the USSR in 1991, self-described liberals devoted themselves to two short-term objectives: destroying the Communist Party's hold over society and demolishing the command economy. Their long-term goals were the defence of civil and political rights, the gradual construction of a market economy, and creation of a rule-of-law state. Apparently, none of these goals was perceived as inherently incompatible with revitalization of a powerful centralized Russian state. Thus, while many liberals enthusiastically supported ending the Soviet empire and permitting devolution of certain prerogatives to local or regional levels of government, they also wanted a powerful Russian presidency in Moscow. Whether post-Soviet liberalism can contribute to the diminution of economic and political strains generated by the disappearance of the communist system, whether it can bridge the gulf between a strong state and individual liberty, and whether it can manage to balance property rights with social equality remains to be seen. At the close of the twentieth century, liberalism no longer exists as it did for so long in Russia's past, clandestinely, 'behind seven seals, beneath seven locks', as an untried, mysterious and therefore badly understood alternative to absolutist government.

See also: LIBERALISM

References and further reading

* Berdiaev, N.A., Gershenzon, M.O., Kistiakovskii, B.A., Struve, P.B. *et al.* (1909) *Vekhi. Sbornik statei o russkoi intelligentsii*, Moscow; B. Shragin and A. Todd (eds) *Landmarks: A Collection of Essays on the Russian Intelligentsia*, New York: Karz Howard, 1977. (An able translation of the controversial right liberal anthology.)

Berlin, I. (1978) 'Alexander Herzen', in H. Hardy and A. Kelly (eds), *Russian Thinkers*, New York: Viking Press, 186–209. (A wonderful, sympathetic portrait of Herzen as pluralist.)

Fischer, G. (1958) *Russian Liberalism, from Gentry to Intelligentsia*, Cambridge, MA: Harvard University Press. (The only book-length overview of post-emancipation liberalism in English; argues that the 'new liberalism' was championed by liberal intelligentsia.)

Gooding, J. (1986) 'The Liberalism of Michael Speransky', in *Slavonic and East European Review* 64 (3): 401–24. (Against Raeff's portrayal of Speranskii's conservatism, this article makes a strong case for Speranskii as progenitor of Decembrism and moderate liberalism.)

Hamburg, G.M. (1992) *Boris Chicherin and Early Russian Liberalism 1828–1866*, Stanford, CA: Stanford University Press. (Examines the connection between Westernism and early liberalism.)

Karpovich, M. (1955) 'Two Types of Russian Liberalism: Maklakov and Miliukov' in E.J. Simmons (ed.), *Continuity and Change in Russian and Soviet Thought*, Cambridge, MA: Harvard University Press. (A penetrating analysis of the left–right split in liberalism, *c.* 1905–7.)

Leontowitsch, V. (1957) *Geschichte des Liberalismus in Rußland*, Frankfurt-am-Main: Vittorio Klostermann. (Controversial survey of liberalism from the eighteenth to twentieth centuries, concentrates on right liberalism in government and educated society.)

Madariaga, I. de (1984) 'Portrait of an Eighteenth-Century Russian Statesman: Prince Dmitry Mikhaiylovich Golitsyn', in *Slavonic and East European Review* 62 (1): 36–60. (A model article on Golitsyn's intellectual/political milieu.)

Mironenko, S.V. (1990) *Stranitsy tainoi istorii samoderzhaviia. Politicheskaia istoriia Rossii pervoi poloviny XIX stoletiia*, Moscow: Mysl'. (A shrewd assessment of Alexander I's and Novosiltsov's liberalism.)

Offord, D. (1985) *Portraits of Early Russian Liberals*, Cambridge: Cambridge University Press. (A vividly written but subtle study of liberalism's genesis.)

Pipes, R. (1970) *Struve. Liberal on the Left, 1870–1905*, Cambridge, MA: Harvard University Press. (A compelling portrait of Struve's intellectual odyssey from Marxism to left liberalism.)

—— (1980) *Struve. Liberal on the Right, 1905–1944*, Cambridge, MA: Harvard University Press. (A magisterial work on the leading conservative liberal of the twentieth century.)

* Radishchev, A.N. (1790) *Puteshestvie iz Peterburga v Moskvu*; trans. and ed. R.P. Thaler, *A Journey from St. Petersburg to Moscow*, Cambridge, MA: Harvard University Press, 1958. (As discussed in §1.)

Raeff, M. (1957) *Michael Speransky: Statesman of Imperial Russia, 1772–1839*, The Hague: Martinus Nijhoff. (The classic biography reading Speranskii as a conservative.)

—— (ed.) (1966) *The Decembrist Movement*, Englewood Cliffs, NJ: Prentice Hall. (Includes Muraviev's constitutional project.)

Ransel, D. (1970) 'Nikita Panin's Imperial Council

Project and the Struggle of Hierarchy Groups at the Court of Catherine II', in *Canadian Slavic Studies* 4 (3): 443–63. (A sceptical view of Panin's constitutionalism.)

Read, C. (1979) *Religion, Revolution and the Russian Intelligentsia 1900–1912: The Vekhi Debate and its Intellectual Background*, New York: Barnes & Noble. (A monograph on the *Signposts* anthology and its religious dimension.)

Reddaway, W.F. (ed.) (1931) *Documents of Catherine the Great*, Cambridge: Cambridge University Press. (A useful collection of documents on Catherine's attitude towards the Enlightenment.)

Sakharov, A. (1968) *Progress, Coexistence and Intellectual Freedom*, New York: Norton. (Sakharov's early reflections on reconciling intellectual liberty with socialism.)

—— (1975) *My Country and the World*, New York: Alfred A. Knopf. (A trenchant criticism of Soviet socialism from a liberal humanist perspective.)

Schapiro, L. (1986) 'Liberalism and the Law', in E. Dahrendorf (ed.), *Russian Studies*, New York: Viking Press, 29–130. (Sympathetic essays on conservative liberalism.)

Walicki, A. (1979) *A History of Russian Thought from the Enlightenment to Marxism*, Stanford, CA: Stanford University Press. (The finest survey of Russian intellectual history with extended treatment of liberalism.)

—— (1987) *Legal Philosophies of Russian Liberalism*, Oxford: Clarendon Press. (A brilliant exploration of six liberal legal philosophies in late imperial Russia and thereafter; very good on social liberalism.)

G. M. HAMBURG

LIBERATION PHILOSOPHY

Philosophy of liberation emerged in Argentina early in the 1970s with the explicit intention of proposing a liberating alternative to the diagnosis of structural dependence offered by the social sciences (particularly the so-called 'theory of dependence'). Some of the original intentions of liberation philosophy were to make poor and marginalized people the subjects, or authors, of philosophy and to collaborate in the process of distancing philosophy from academia and exclusively professional settings. Social conflict and pressing national needs were topics of debate at that time. All thought started with the recognition and assessment of the experience of alterity. Horacio Cerutti-Guldberg has proposed the phrase 'philosophies for liberation' as this kind of reflection deals with multiple philosophical positions and privileges the historical process over philosophy.

1   **Initial postulations**
2   **Four discursive variants**
3   **Exterior and interior exile**
4   **Latin Americanization and globalization of the debate**
5   **Work in progress**
6   **Perspectives**

1   Initial postulations

In 1973 some theses were formulated outlining the goals of an incipient philosophical programme shared by some Argentine philosophers who were the driving force behind liberation philosophy. One goal was to create a universally valid, although historically situated Latin American philosophy. The intention was also to confront the situation of structural dependency legitimized through a self-serving and academicist philosophy as well as to explain philosophically the needs of the great exploited majority and the urgencies of the poor and oppressed Latin American people. These poor people would appear as the bearers of a historical innovation to be theorized through liberation philosophy.

Shortly after this programme was enunciated, it was divided into at least four discursive variants. These products of diverse theoretical foci and political and ideological positions had an impact on the philosophy. One could no longer justifiably speak of a single liberation philosophy as a movement or common programme. These variants presented in a very coherent way their theses regarding their point of departure, subject, methodology and conception of philosophy.

2   Four discursive variants

Ontologicist philosophy postulated as its point of departure a historical zero, as if one could begin with a *tabula rasa* – the mind in its uninformed state – regarding world philosophical tradition. The task of elaborating a new nondialectical rationality was undertaken. The task was to establish the most characteristic way of being in the world for the Latin American. The contrast between the Spanish verbs, *ser*, meaning the permanent state of being, as in 'I am Bill, or Jane' and *estar*, the changing state of *being*, as in 'I am happy, or sad' was emphasized as the key to understanding reality. It was the 'people' who were spoken about within the area of ontologicist philosophy as opposed to the 'liberal individual' or the 'proletarian class'. The philosopher would translate everyday events into philosophical language. In the face of Western rationalism, this variant contrarily valued and recognized the irrational dimensions of life. Gunther Rodolfo Kusch and Mario Casalla are representatives of this position.

Analectic philosophy was rooted in a criticism of Eurocentric or North Atlantic modernity. It rejected Latin American historical memory as purely imitative and therefore justifying its own domination. The imploring face of the poor would be the point of departure which would bring about analectic behaviour capable of opening up to all that is new and beyond the dialectic totalities. The philosopher would be a prophetic teacher capable of giving form to the message of those without a voice. The otherness and exteriority of the marginalized would be secured by divinity, the absolute Other. Subscribers to this viewpoint include Juan Carlos Scannone and Enrique Dussel.

Historicism warned that the origins of a philosophy which began with the experience of alterity should recognize its foundations in Latin American history. A historiographic reconstruction of Latin American philosophical memory constitutes a valuable aid in this effort. Contrary to the Hegelian model, which reduces political freedom to freedom of thought, historicism proposed concentrating on those subjects who reformulate popular demands and the way in which they reform them starting with their own interests. It defined itself as a comprehensive philosophy of the marginal and a new way of thinking which anticipated the future. Arturo Roig has applied himself to the theory of historicism.

Problematization of philosophy was the reconceptualization of philosophy, questioning the unfounded claims of originality and the attempt to begin from a historical zero. This version favoured the liberation process over philosophy and reclaimed the express mediation of the social sciences and ideological self-criticism. It strove for the deprofessionalization of philosophy and articulated the historical dimension in conjunction with the systematic. Practitioners of this theory are Manuel Ignacio Santos, Severino Croatto and Horacio Cerutti-Guldberg.

3 Exterior and interior exile

In under three years, many people were working on the philosophy of liberation in each of its four variants. After the Argentinian military coup in 1976, a good portion of the philosophers who were adherents to the last three previously mentioned variants had already been removed from their teaching posts in the national universities. This was owing to various types of sophistry which led to

expulsion or to contracts not being renewed. Some academics had already left the country; others had to abandon academic activity in order to survive, else they altered the scope of academic production. Practitioners of ontologicist philosophy yielded to the new repressive politics imposed by the dictatorship and there was no shortage of people who softened their positions or made them more flexible in order to coexist with the new regime.

Those who left the country, particularly Roig, Dussel and Cerutti-Guldberg, continued to advance and revise their positions, bringing about a wide and generalized debate which streamlined many theses, redefined foci and enriched initial arguments. Nevertheless, it seemed as though the basic positions were maintained to the point that works which can be situated in any of the four modalities mentioned have continued to be written.

4 Latin Americanization and globalization of the debate

The tireless work of those in exile promoted debate on the diverse modalities of this philosophy throughout the Latin American region and continued adding contingents of philosophers of diverse nationalities to the production of a body of thought which acquired regional nuances. In different parts of the world, especially in the USA and Europe, the debate on these issues was prolonged. The following points have been discussed extensively: the cognitive scope of the notion of the people as a collective of exploited social sectors united against all forms of dependency, attitudes towards historical and philosophical memory, the role of the philosopher as theorist or preacher, the ideological dimension of argumentation, the political consequences of the philosophical consideration of alterity, the insufficiencies of philosophy in the face of feminist or indigenous demands, conceptual ambiguities, interpretative difficulties of the same discursive modalities, the vague boundaries of the phenomenon of liberation and the relationships between the social sciences and philosophy.

The convergence of Latin American philosophy and liberation philosophy strengthened both traditions but also led to much confusion. An example of one type of confusion was the idea that Latin American philosophy has always been a liberation philosophy. From a historiographic viewpoint, this gives the term an excessive range.

5 Work in progress

After more than two decades of development of liberation philosophy, the branches of current research can be characterized as follows: ontologicism remains stable and does not have many variants, although studies of Kusch's work are under way which would incorporate revised arguments. The progress of analectic philosophy is a little more convoluted. On the one hand, it bears a resemblance to ontologicist culturalism, while on the other hand, it is influenced by Marx whose work reveals antecedents and confirmations of the analectic version of liberation philosophy. An international and intercultural debate has arisen and has been advanced between analectic ethics of liberation and the ethics of German moral philosopher, Apel. From historicist and problematizing positions, works on the history of ideas in Latin America have increased and their methodological and epistemological connotations have been under debate. Several research projects are under way. The debate over the idea of utopia and its heuristic power has intensified and an improved theoretical formulation of the utopian is being researched. Concern grows for the rethinking of democracy, the state and connected phenomena, and an interesting debate between the theses of the philosophies of liberation, modernity and postmodernism has been outlined. After the assassination in 1989 of Jesuit Ignacio Ellacuría, a leading liberation scholar, and his companions in El Salvador, research has burgeoned to continue his effort to establish a tradition of Latin American liberation philosophy after Xavier Zuribi.

6 Perspectives

In its primary international arenas, philosophy of liberation has been identified sometimes exclusively with analectic philosophy. In reality, 'liberation philosophy' has gone beyond analectic philosophy, which is a long way from exhausting the concerns and emergent theories of the 1970s. The confusion between liberation philosophies and other variants of Latin American philosophy has not helped. A careful and nuanced division of positions and arguments should make feasible a qualitative advance in reflection.

Trapped in its formulations with an ambiguous or salvationist language without sufficient capacity to settle internal struggles, it is barely worthwhile advancing the idea of a homogeneous and unified philosophy of liberation. It would seem more fruitful to advance the progress of and research in the promotion of dialogue based on the following facts relating to Latin American and global reality: the fruitfulness of opening up to conceptual consequences of the experience of alterity, the growing increase in poverty as an almost uncontrollable phenomenon of the world economy, the intolerable injustice of the

social structures of the world in the late twentieth century, the scientific and technological revolutions that modify the very guidelines of the political agenda and the demands for participation and the dissatisfaction of the masses. Many of the questions formulated through the philosophies for liberation directly address serious economic, social, cultural, religious, ethnic and political problems of the world in the late 1990s. The challenge consists of building better conceptual weapons to confront these problems theoretically and practically.

See also: ALTERITY AND IDENTITY, POSTMODERN THEORIES OF; LIBERATION THEOLOGY

References and further reading

Castro-Gómez, S. (1996) *Crítica de la razón latinoamericana* (Criticism of the Latin American Intellect), Barcelona: Puvill Libros. (A critical analysis of the analectic and historicist variants of liberation philosophy in terms of postmodernism and postcolonialism.)

Cerutti-Guldberg, H. (1983) *Filosofía de la liberación latinoamericana* (Philosophy of the Latin American Liberation), Mexico: Fondo de Cultural Económica, 2nd edn, 1992. (The first book to examine the antecedents, foundations and initial theses of liberation philosophy from an epistemological perspective. Four discursive variants of liberation philosophy are identified.)

—— (1988–9) 'Actual Situation and Perspectives on Latin American Philosophy for Liberation', *The Philosophical Forum* 20 (1–2): 43–62. (Assessment of liberation philosophy in the late 1980s.)

Dussel, E. (1977) *Introducción a una filosofía de la liberación* (Introduction to Liberation Philosophy), Mexico: Extemporáneos. (The best introduction available to the analectic version of liberation philosophy.)

Islas (1991), special issue 99 (May–August), Havana. (Special issue on philosophy of liberation.)

Roig, A.A. (1983) 'De la historia de las ideas a la filosofía de la liberación' (From the History of Ideas to the Philosophy of Liberation), *Latinoamérica* 10: 45–72. (An article tracing the history of Latin American philosophy.)

—— (1984) 'Cuatro tomas de posición a esta altura de los tiempos' (Four Philosophical Positions at the Height of our Times), *Nuestra América* 11 (May–August): 55–9. (Four different approaches to Latin American philosophy.)

Samour, H. (1994) 'Introducción a la filosofía de la liberación de Ignacio Ellacuría' (Introduction to the Liberation Philosophy of Ignacio Ellacuría), in *El compromiso poítico de la filosofía en América Latina* (Political Compromise of Latin American Philosophy), Bogotá: El Búho, 11–37. (A discussion of Ellacuría's work in the area of liberation philosophy.)

Scannone, J.C. (1981) 'La cuestión del método de una filosofía a latinoamericana' (The Question of the Method of Latin American Philosophy), *Stromata* 1–2 (January–June): 75–192. (Discusses the otherness and exteriority of the marginalized.)

Schutte, O. (1993) *Cultural Identity and Social Liberation in Latin American Thought*, Albany, NY: State University of New York Press. (The best analysis in English of the tradition which spans from Mariátegui to Latin American philosophy and theology of liberation to philosophy of liberation.)

HORACIO CERUTTI-GULDBERG

LIBERATION THEOLOGY

Also known as theology of liberation, liberation theology is simultaneously a social movement within the Christian Church and a school of thought, both of which react against human suffering due to poverty and various forms of oppression. The essence of liberation theology consists in an interpretation of Christian salvation that retains its transcendent eschatological content and draws out its historical dimensions and their implications for personal life, the social sphere and the public action of the Church. Salvation contains various levels of liberation.

Liberation theology is most commonly associated with Latin America, where it emerged during the 1960s. As both movement and theology, it is at present a worldwide phenomenon, taking on different characteristics according to culture, situation, the kind of oppression that predominates, and concrete political and social exigencies. Although some liberation theologians have employed Marxist language as a tool for social analysis, the underpinnings of liberation theology lie in Christian faith.

Liberation theology is predominately Roman Catholic in Latin America because of the Catholic majority; but as a movement and a school of thought it unites Catholic and mainstream Protestant Churches. Evangelical Christians are often antipathetic to liberation theology because of their individualism and otherworldliness.

1 Historical development
2 Liberation theology as a movement
3 Characteristics and significance

1 Historical development

The conditions against which liberation theology is a reaction have their prehistory in colonialism and neo-colonialism. Liberation theologians and historians chart the history of colonialism and analyse the social, economic and political dependencies of developing countries upon developed nations. In varying degrees, the relation of Latin American nations to the developed nations is mirrored in each developing country by a two-class system of educated, resourceful people and the poor or destitute majority.

The most immediate explanation of liberation theology, however, lies in the actual conditions in which poor people live and the natural human reaction to them. Christian theologians, among others, came to recognize the massive poverty of the majority of people in Latin America as radically unjust and systemically supported by social institutions. As various organizations of students and workers mobilized for social justice, the moral perception of the deadly character of destitution became a condition for appreciating the liberating potential of theology. Theologians began to interpret Christian faith as responsive to the cause of justice and the poor. By the early 1960s, essays in what would come to be called liberation theology were already being written.

Two public events in the life of the Roman Catholic Church in the 1960s served as a catalyst for liberation theology. One was the Second Vatican Council (1962–5). Its *Pastoral Constitution on the Church in the Modern World* (*Gaudium et Spes*) described the Church as deeply concerned with human life in history and with the problems of poor peoples. It encouraged regional churches to internalize this message and adapt it to each local situation. The other was the Second General Conference of Latin American Bishops in 1968, in Medellín, Colombia, which produced documents describing the social situation of the poor majority, characterizing it as institutionalized violence and sin. The bishops promised that the Church would address these inhuman conditions. The corporate commitment of the hierarchy of the Latin American Church encouraged the movement of liberation theology on all levels.

The 1970s witnessed an outpouring of work in liberation theology, Gustavo Gutiérrez's *A Theology of Liberation* (1971) being the 'classic text'. The themes that dominated the discussion during this decade were the distinctive method of this theology, by contrast with theology in Europe, and the fundamental nature and role of the Church in society. This period ended with the Third General Conference of Latin American Bishops at Puebla, Mexico, in early

613

1979. Marked by heavy internal Church politics and closely watched by people outside Latin America, its documents roundly supported liberation theology while balancing it with more traditional themes.

The next period of development, through the 1980s to 1992, included developments in theology, Christian life, and ethics, as well as an effort by the Vatican to control liberation theology. Two documents were issued in 1984 and 1986, the first condemning specific extremes perceived within liberation theology, the other developing the Vatican's version of the anthropological grounds of social liberation and emancipation. Leonardo Boff, a Brazilian liberation theologian, was forbidden to lecture for one year in 1985. By the time of the fourth meeting of Latin American bishops, in Santo Domingo in 1992, which also commemorated the five-hundredth anniversary of the coming of Christianity to the Americas, the Vatican had quieted episcopal support for liberation theology.

The development of liberation theology extended well beyond Latin America. After Medellín, other parts of the developing world immediately resonated with a theological method and language which addressed their own problems of poverty and social marginalization. But in each case, liberationist themes were received into a different situation with a distinctive modality. In south Asia, liberation theology combined with the need for interreligious dialogue and cooperation; in Africa, liberation theology merged with movements of inculturation. Liberation theology is recognizably pluralistic; common formal themes take different concrete shapes around the world.

The Vatican is not hostile to the essence of liberation theology; Vatican teaching is strongly influenced by it. At the Synod of Bishops meeting in Rome (1971), in Paul VI's influential encyclical *On Evangelization in the Modern World* (1976), in the Vatican's *Instruction on Christian Freedom and Liberation* (1986), in John Paul II's encyclical *On Social Concern* (1988), the leadership of the Roman Catholic Church has endorsed the centrality of the commitment to the welfare of the poor and marginalized which is the core of liberation theology. The agenda and language of liberation theology has thus become part of Catholic theology and social teaching from the centre, so that the internalization of liberation theology has spread not only laterally but also back through the centre to the whole Church.

Liberation theology extends beyond the confines of Roman Catholicism and Latin America, and cuts across the confessional lines of the mainstream Churches; it is ecumenical. Also, the social captivity and oppression to which it responds transcend sheer poverty. The negative reality underlying the Black liberation theology in South Africa and the United States is racism. Black liberation theology in the USA developed autonomously out of the remnants of slavery in US society, the civil rights movement, and the language and spirituality of the Black Churches. This liberation theology became articulate in the 1960s through the impetus of Martin Luther King, Jr, and, more formally, the writings of James Cone, its leading theologian. Pervasive androcentrism and patriarchalism are addressed by feminist liberation theologians such as Rosemary Radford Ruether, and this theology too has its own prehistory (see FEMINIST THEOLOGY).

Although the term 'liberation theology' refers to current movements and modes of thought, these have a tradition that extends back through the whole history of the Christian Church and finds deep roots in the Jewish and Christian Scriptures. For example, the language of liberation theology is closely analogous to the discourse of the prophets and Jesus' own concern for those marginalized in his society. The term 'liberation' is thus a present-day symbol for something essential to the Christian message. A form of liberation theology appears wherever there is systematic destruction of human freedom.

2 Liberation theology as a movement

Liberation theology is generated by a social movement broader than the Church but also reflected in the Church. In Latin America, this was a people's movement based on an insight into the sheer negativity of structural poverty and injustice and a committed effort to change society. By definition, the movement that liberation theology represents is located on the left of the political spectrum. Its constituencies are rural peasants, urban squatters, the unemployed, and exploited workers. Its allies are often students, middle-class and educated people open to change, and various organizations dedicated to social amelioration. What is true in Latin America finds its analogies in other places.

Various mechanisms structure and sustain the movement. The principle-turned-slogan that supports the liberationist agenda from within the Church at large is 'the preferential option for the poor'. This principle developed in the wake of Medellín and was formally accepted at Puebla in 1979 and endorsed by Vatican documents and papal statements. The principle is not meant to be divisive but to affirm that the whole Church in all of its members should reflect the love of God that reaches out especially to those who suffer most and are marginalized. In fact, however, the principle divides because it reflects actual social divisions. In most places where liberation theology has taken hold, clear ideological differences distinguish the Churches of the wealthy and those of the poor. The parish whose constituency is the poor is the main locus of the liberation movement. This is where poor people come together, where Christian ministry is mobilized, where various organizations address specific needs, and where Christian liberation language is heard in worship and public devotion.

In some respects even more fundamental are 'basic ecclesial communities'. These are small groups of Christians, usually homogeneous so that everyone knows each other, which meet regularly for prayer and reflection. They developed simultaneously with the liberationist movement in Brazil in the 1960s and now exist worldwide. Many combine faith and the practical concerns of survival in daily life. These communities are subgroups within a parish and, when faced with clear social objectives, are animated with a liberationist spirit.

The liberationist movement is sustained by organizations that draw people together from across the lines of basic ecclesial communities, parishes and dioceses. Regional and national agencies address issues of justice. Workshops, conferences, institutes and summer schools focus reflection on liberation theology and animate the growth and social coherence of the movement. Different organizations address specific objectives.

Finally, at the core of the liberationist movement is a distinctive piety and manner of living the Christian life. This spirituality includes responsible and committed service to the poor. In its ideal form it thrives on the idea of the human solidarity of all. It acknowledges God present within the poor, animating them to take control of their lives in the face of oppression.

3 Characteristics and significance

The theology of liberation as a form of thought and a body of literature grew up out of the movement. Some representative theological leaders are: the late Juan Luis Segundo, a Jesuit from Uruguay who studied in Paris and began writing in the early 1960s; Gustavo Gutiérrez, a diocesan priest from Lima, Peru, who studied in Louvain, Lyons and Rome, and began writing in the late 1960s; José Míguez Bonino, a Methodist theologian from Argentina who after studying in the USA undertook seminary teaching in his home country; Leonardo Boff, a Brazilian and former Franciscan who completed his doctorate in Germany in the early 1970s and began teaching in a seminary in Petropolis; and Jon Sobrino, a Spanish-born Jesuit teaching in San Salvador who also studied

in Germany and began writing in the mid-1970s. This first generation of liberation theologians, still active in the 1990s, is joined by a new generation of theologians who grew up as liberationists.

Five typical characteristics of liberation theology seen in connection with some of the major topics of Christian theology define its distinctiveness; these are described below.

First, broadly conceived, liberation theology's method is hermeneutical: it interprets the past symbols of Christian scripture and history on the basis of the questions raised by the world of the suffering poor. The general goal is to make sense of the Christian message for the innocent victim of human oppression. Theological questions thus arise out of the actual situation of the people for whom liberation theology offers a voice. The option for the poor is a premise of the theology and links it with the movement of liberation praxis. Social sciences are employed to gain a critical appreciation of the situation. Some Marxist analysis is used by some liberation theologians as a tool to understand society and history, but without the philosophical premises of Marxist doctrine. The goal of the theology is a historically critical understanding of the Christian message that will engender further emancipatory praxis.

Second, liberation theology is historically conscious in dealing with Jesus Christ. Its Christological reflection begins with the human life of Jesus and not with doctrines about him. Jesus' historical mission, particularly his prophetic judgments, displayed concern for people who either suffered physically or were excluded by social censure. Liberation theologians find humanization, compassion, healing, and empowerment of freedom dramatized by Jesus. Understanding the doctrines about Jesus begins with his ministry. That Jesus was raised from death, that Jesus is divine – these classic doctrines mean that at its deepest level salvation is liberation by God from sin and final death. But they also give divine sanction to Jesus' historical ministry as representing the will and values of God for human life. Jesus embodies God's salvation in the end and God's salvific will and power within history.

Third, liberation theology proposes a doctrine of the Church that engages society. Following the lead given by Vatican II's decree on the Church in the modern world, liberation theology regards the Church as an agent of God's intentions for human life in history. It continues the mission represented in Jesus' ministry. The Church is to be a sign of God's love liberating people. Membership of the Church does not imply passivity, but a dependence on God that generates creative action on behalf of the poor.

Sacraments are interpreted as vehicles for nurturing and empowering the Christian life of service. Publicly, the Church cannot avoid being involved in social issues, as distinct from party politics, and should always be concerned for society's weakest members. The role of the Church in society is to preserve a tradition of humane Christian values as a critical context for public policy.

Fourth, liberation theology promotes a this-worldly religious life. Christian faith itself is closely connected with praxis, with a reflective, committed way of living. Christian life consists in an imitation of Christ according to the demands of society. It consists in being a member of a mission Church, which entails some active assumption of responsibility for that mission. Liberation spirituality combines contemplation and action, mysticism and politics. It relies on a notion of God's grace that does not stymie but empowers human freedom in history.

Fifth, liberation theology is intrinsically ethical. Liberation theologians have criticized the absolute right of private property, various forms of capitalism, and the national security state. The option for the poor, a bias towards socialism, and the involvement of the Church in political and social issues raise ethical questions. How can a theology that is partisan for one group be ethical? What kind of ethical discernment is needed for a Christian praxis in this or that situation? Are there general norms for an ethics of Christian liberation? These questions were addressed from the very beginning in liberation theology, but in a variety of different ways and usually within the context of broader theological analysis. Gradually a more systematically focused liberation ethics appeared, one which examines the foundations of Christian liberation ethics and its principles and norms.

Liberation theology consists in different theologies that share a number of basic principles and commitments. These principles are foundational. Liberation theology has always considered itself less a body of content, more a fundamental way of going about the discipline of theology. Within the Roman Catholic Church, liberation theology is the first developed theology that is fully historically conscious and reflectively engaged in the process of history. From the beginning, liberation theology has spontaneously bound together theology and ethics, which for various reasons were separated from each other in the modern period. Theology emerges out of praxis and leads back to it. Because of these primordial principles, liberation theology has profoundly influenced Christian theology in the last third of the twentieth century. No Christian theology today can bypass the question of its social situation and the implied beneficiaries of its understandings. The questions and themes raised by liberation theology are now part of the discipline itself.

See also: RELIGION AND MORALITY §§3–4; RELIGION AND POLITICAL PHILOSOPHY §3

References and further reading

Boff, L. (1985) *Church, Charism and Power: Liberation Theology and the Institutional Church*, New York: Crossroad. (A collection of essays at once critical of Church institutions and optimistic about the power of basic ecclesial communities.)

Cone, J.H. (1969) *Black Theology and Black Power*, New York: Seabury. (A seminal work reflecting the emergence of Black theology out of the civil rights movement in the USA.)

* Gutiérrez, G. (1971) *A Theology of Liberation*, Maryknoll, NY: Orbis Books, 1988. (Latin America's classic statement of liberation theology and still the best introduction.)

Haight, R. (1985) *An Alternative Vision: An Interpretation of Liberation Theology*, Mahwah, NJ: Paulist Press. (A synthetic essay interpreting liberation theology in a more universal theological idiom.)

Hennelly, A.T. (ed.) (1989) *Liberation Theology: A Documentary History*, Maryknoll, NY: Orbis Books. (An indispensable collection of texts charting the development of liberation theology in Latin America.)

King, M.L., Jr (1986) *A Testament of Hope: The Essential Writings of Martin Luther King, Jr*, ed. J.M. Washington, San Francisco, CA: Harper & Row. (A compendium of King's most important sermons and speeches, with selections from his books.)

McAuliffe, P. (1993) *Fundamental Ethics: A Liberationist Approach*, Washington, DC: Georgetown University Press. (A critical and constructive analysis of foundations for a liberationist ethics.)

McGovern, A.F. (1989) *Liberation Theology and Its Critics: Toward an Assessment*, Maryknoll, NY: Orbis Books. (A fair analysis of the positions of liberation theologians and an appraisal of various critiques.)

Míguez Bonino, J. (1975) *Doing Theology in a Revolutionary Situation*, Philadelphia, PA: Fortress Press. (An early work that reflects the growing self-awareness of liberation theology in terms of social context, theological method and constructive content.)

Ruether, R.R. (1983) *Sexism and God-Talk: Toward a Feminist Theology*, Boston, MA: Beacon Press. (A treatment of the method of a feminist theology and an application of it to various theological problems.)

Schubeck, T.L. (1993) *Liberation Ethics: Sources, Models, and Norms*, Minneapolis, MN: Fortress Press. (A synthetic portrayal of the ethical teaching of Latin American liberation theologians.)

Segundo, J.L. (1971–5) *Theology for Artisans of a New Humanity*, Maryknoll, NY: Orbis Books, 5 vols. (A unified series dealing with central Christian doctrines apart from Christology.)

Sobrino, J. (1978) *Christology at the Crossroads*, Maryknoll, NY: Orbis Books. (The most influential liberation Christology of the 1980s.)

ROGER HAIGHT

LIBERTARIANISM

In political philosophy 'libertarianism' is a name given to a range of views which take as their central value liberty or freedom. Although occasionally the term is applied to versions of anti-authoritarian Marxist theory (the 'libertarian left'), more commonly it is associated with a view which champions particularly pure forms of capitalism. Libertarians endorse the free market and unfettered free exchange, and oppose paternalistic or moralistic legislation (for example, laws regulating sexual behaviour or the consumption of alcohol or drugs). Liberty, on such a view, is identified with the absence of interference by the state or by others. The legitimate state exists purely to guard individual rights, protecting people and their property from force, theft and fraud. This is the 'minimal state' or 'night-watchman state' of classical liberalism. The state has no authority to engage in the redistribution of property (except to rectify the effects of theft, and so on) or, in certain versions at least, to pursue policies designed to further the common good. Such activities are viewed by the libertarian as illegitimate interferences with an individual's right to do what they wish with their own person or property.

1   **Key features of libertarianism**
2   **Antecedents of libertarianism**
3   **Philosophical foundations**
4   **Problems and criticisms**

1   Key features of libertarianism

The central issue for libertarianism is the proper nature and justification of the state. Libertarians view the state with great suspicion and are particularly opposed to its attempts to supervise and control people's lives, or to carry out policies in the name of social justice (see JUSTICE). At the same time they assign to individuals strong rights to non-interference and reject the 'collectivist' idea that people can justly be coerced into carrying out society's goals or purposes (see RIGHTS §3). However, in most versions of the theory it is recognized that some central authority – a minimal state – is required to protect citizens from each other and from the intrusions of other states.

All forms of libertarianism assume a 'protected sphere' of strong personal rights to life and liberty. Opinions differ about individual rights to property. The main libertarian camp suggests that just as we have absolute rights of self-ownership, we can also form equally strong rights over external objects. However, left-wing libertarians argue that gross inequalities of property diminish the liberty of the poor. Those who possess no property will live or die at the mercy of the owners of private property. Left-wing libertarians argue that property should be distributed much less unequally or that rights to property should be qualified to achieve this effect (see PROPERTY §3).

In response, mainstream (right-wing) libertarians have suggested that the market, insurance and, as a last resort, charity, provide alternatives to state support for the poor. But of greater weight is the libertarian claim that there are certain detrimental consequences of allowing governments to regulate and redistribute property. First, any such system is very intrusive, restricting people's freedom of choice and requiring regular investigation of individual property holdings. Second, it interrupts the efficient running of the market, distorting incentives and price mechanisms. Third, it is counterproductive: government intervention often fails to achieve its aims and has unpredicted and unwanted effects. These are all reasons to avoid state intervention.

Nevertheless a response is owed to the challenge that the poor have very little liberty. Here a distinction between liberty and ability is crucial. There are many things I am unable to do – run a mile in four minutes, for example – which cannot be said to be limitations of my liberty. For a libertarian an individual's liberty is restricted only if some person has reduced the options available, and has done so in a way which violates that individual's rights. So if a person has few options as an unfortunate side effect of the free and legitimate actions of others, then, while their ability to do certain things is restricted, their liberty is unimpeded. But if that person is forced to act at the point of a knife, then their options have been shaped by the rights-violating actions of another; thus their liberty has been violated. On this view, then, economic disadvantage affects ability, not liberty (see FREEDOM AND LIBERTY).

2 Antecedents of libertarianism

Libertarianism, while a relatively recent development, was formed out of several currents. The first is the issue of 'the individual versus the state': libertarians of all ilks clearly wish to give the state only a very narrow authority. The second is the question of what should properly count as the individual's own concern: libertarianism strongly resists the idea that the state should have a role in the regulation of possession and exchange or in the manner in which an individual chooses to live their own life. A third impetus to libertarian thinking, underlining the other two, is the classical liberal tradition, emphasizing the economic advantages of a market free from government intervention.

In tracing the development of libertarianism, it is important to see the first of these issues – the individual versus the state – as historically prior. Many of the thinkers cited as sources for libertarianism were prepared to accept great restrictions on property holdings. It is the antipathy to a powerful, centralized state that gave libertarianism its initial spur; its transformation into a defence of absolute property rights and extensive market society has been a relatively recent development.

Given these somewhat confusing origins, it is not surprising that various forebears have been claimed for libertarianism. Clearly there are affinities between Locke's defence of individual property rights and the doctrine of the inviolability of property that forms the heart of libertarianism (see LOCKE, J. §10). Equally, the classical liberal notion of the *laissez-faire* state, derived from Adam SMITH (§4), has had great impact on libertarian thinking. On similar grounds, even David HUME (§5) has, with some justice, been cited as an influence on libertarian thought.

We can also see an overtly anarchist strand in libertarianism, springing from Proudhon and Max Stirner, and reaching twentieth-century individualist thought via the US libertarian Benjamin Tucker (see ANARCHISM §2). Thus, part of the foundation of libertarianism is an emancipatory politics, formed in radical opposition to Marxism and opposed in particular to Marx's advocation of a highly structured, authoritarian period of politics prior to the withering of the state (see MARX, K. §12). The anarchist observation that such means would inevitably lead away from the intended end inspired reflection on how a broadly egalitarian society could be organized on truly voluntary grounds. It is something of an irony, then, that such ideas have

given rise to a tradition which sometimes, and with good reason, is called anarcho-capitalism.

3 Philosophical foundations

Although it is possible to state a 'core' libertarian view, many different philosophical foundations for it have been offered. Consequently the details of the views defended have significant differences too: for example, opinions differ about whether libertarians can allow people to opt out of market society into, say, socialism if that is what they prefer. The following, used alone or in combination, are perhaps the most important lines of defence of the doctrine.

The best-known approach, that associated with Robert NOZICK (§2), is to try to justify libertarianism in terms of a doctrine of natural rights to self-ownership: as I have the right to determine the course of my own life (provided I respect the similar rights of others), I have no enforceable obligations to others unless I have brought these on myself by my own voluntary action. If a government makes me contribute to the alleviation of the plight of the needy, or forces me to act against my will, then it behaves as if it is part-owner of me, and so violates my right to self-ownership. An important variant of rights-based libertarianism justifies rights not in terms of self-ownership, but in terms of human flourishing. Here the central claim is that only in a libertarian society can a life fully worthy of human beings be achieved.

A second style of justification has greater affinities with consequentialist reasoning. Libertarian society is, at least in part, justified by the economic efficiency of market society. Interventions in the free market are criticized on the grounds that they will impede enterprise, distort incentives and thus diminish the effectiveness of the market. This type of approach does, however, allow some room for guarded government intervention to ensure the smooth running of the market and to prevent the formation of monopolies. The state also has the role of supplying 'public goods', in the technical sense, such as street lighting or a pollution-free atmosphere, which the market is notoriously poor at producing. This type of consequentialist libertarianism thus has a reason for permitting certain government activities which would be prohibited by pure rights-based libertarianism.

A third approach tries to justify libertarianism by means of a hypothetical contract. First we posit a hypothetical 'state of nature' in which individuals, considered as holders of private property, subsist alone or in family groups. It is recognized, however, that social cooperation would produce benefits for all. Accordingly, individuals come together to draw up terms of association. All have a reason to accept legally enforceable rights and duties of non-interference, and, perhaps, duties of emergency aid. However, the rich and powerful, who are in the stronger bargaining position, have reason to resist any more extensive duties, and so this limits the agreement that can be achieved. Nevertheless, certain further functions of governments could be seen as agreed to in this context. In particular, governments may tax individuals to supply public goods.

A fourth approach takes as its starting point subjectivism about values. In this way libertarianism is represented as the only morally neutral society. A society which redistributes income appears to subscribe to the value of 'need-satisfaction'. But if the wealthy do not accept this value, then to engage in redistribution is to force people to live according to values they do not hold, and so is a form of tyranny. Those who do value the alleviation of others' distress are at perfect liberty to do whatever they want with their own property. But there should be no compulsion to subscribe to this value or to any other.

A fifth approach, less common, is inspired by a point from Kant's moral philosophy. It begins with Kant's distinction between actions performed *for the sake of duty* and actions performed *in accordance with duty* (see KANT, I. §10). If we believe that only the former have moral worth, then an extensive set of legally enforceable duties removes the scope of true virtue: if I am forced to transfer some money to you by law, then, while it may be an action performed in accordance with duty, it has not been done for the sake of duty, but out of coercion, and hence there is no moral worth in my action. This form of libertarianism, then, recommends a slimmed-down state to make virtue possible. (It should be noted that Kant himself did not draw these political conclusions from his moral philosophy.)

4 Problems and criticisms

Libertarians have found themselves struggling with two major problems. First, how can the state be justified? If we cannot show that everyone consents to the state, its existence seems an illegitimate interference with individual liberty. Furthermore, if people make different levels of contribution to the upkeep of the state – some may be unable to contribute, for example – then the state appears redistributive in its nature. Second, libertarianism presupposes that individuals have strong rights to property. But everything that is now owned is constructed out of materials which, once, no individual owned. How can initial appropriation be justified? While strenuous attempts have been made to solve these problems, no consensus has developed. It is worth noting that

consequentialist libertarians find themselves in less difficulty on these issues.

In addition to these problems critics have claimed that right-wing libertarians are not entitled to adopt the language of liberty in defence of their view, given the lack of liberty of the poor. This goes hand in hand with a denial that such libertarians have framed the distinction between liberty and ability correctly. Another influential criticism is that one cannot defend powerful individual rights without also accepting a duty to support the extensive social institutions that not only sustain those rights but also give them their point and value. Hence, it is claimed libertarianism is self-defeating. Suffice to say that libertarians strongly contest these points, while pointing out the disadvantages they see with all other systems.

References and further reading

Barry, N. (1986) *On Classical Liberalism and Libertarianism*, London: Macmillan. (Useful survey of a wide range of libertarian positions and some liberal antecedents.)

Buchanan, J. (1975) *The Limits of Liberty*, Chicago, IL: University of Chicago Press. (An attempt to provide contractual foundations for libertarianism.)

Cohen, G.A. (1979) 'Capitalism, Freedom, and the Proletariat', in A. Ryan (ed.), *The Idea of Freedom*, Oxford: Oxford University Press, 9–25; revised and repr. in D. Miller (ed.) *Liberty*, Oxford: Oxford University Press, 1991. (Criticizes libertarians for abusing the language of liberty.)

Friedman, D. (1973) *The Machinery of Freedom*, New York: Harper & Row. (Presents a consequentialist version of libertarianism.)

Nozick, R. (1974) *Anarchy, State, and Utopia*, Oxford: Blackwell. (Philosophically powerful and entertaining presentation of rights-based libertarianism.)

Steiner, H. (1994) *An Essay on Rights*, Oxford: Blackwell. (A defence of left-wing libertarianism.)

Taylor, C. (1979) 'Atomism', in A. Kontos (ed.) *Powers, Possessions and Freedom*, Toronto, Ont: University of Toronto Press, 39–61; repr. in *Philosophy and the Human Sciences*, Cambridge: Cambridge University Press, 1985. (Argues that the 'atomism' or individualism of libertarianism – or liberalism – cannot be sustained.)

JONATHAN WOLFF

LIBERTINS

The term 'libertin' was first used in France in the early seventeenth century as a term of abuse directed against alleged free-thinkers and atheists who were linked with radical Italian philosophers of the previous century. It subsequently came to be associated with a sceptical literary tradition and a group of scholars, philosophers and antiquarians who discreetly ensured the circulation of such doctrines as Epicureanism, Pyrrhonian scepticism, mechanical philosophy, Baconian empiricism and the 'new' astronomy. After the disappearance of this group in the middle years of the century, the term came to connote only debauchery and irreverence.

1 'Libertins'
2 The philosopher-libertins

1 'Libertins'

The term 'libertin' has been used to describe a number of disparate literary, social and philosophical groups in France from the mid-sixteenth to the late seventeenth centuries. It was at one time claimed that libertins were rationalistic atheists who derived their philosophical doctrines from the Averroists of the School of Padua, notably Pietro POMPONAZZI and, later, Cesare Cremonini (1550–1630). But this view was subsequently discredited both by those such as Charles Schmitt (1983) who argue that Paduan Aristotelianism was not Averroist in character, and those cultural historians who, like Lucien Febvre (1982), claim that the sixteenth century was an age which found the notion of God indispensable to its systems of thought (see ARISTOTELIANISM, RENAISSANCE §5). More recently, libertins have been linked to a tradition of mitigated scepticism which is said to be an essential ingredient of the scientific revolution: but even this thesis, best known through the work of Richard Popkin (1992), has now been challenged.

The word 'libertin' emerged in the late sixteenth century as a term of abuse directed at those who were thought to have rejected traditional authority and were indifferent or irreverent in matters of religion. By the 1620s, it was associated with a broad group of sixteenth-century radical thinkers including Pomponazzi, Girolamo CARDANO, Giordano BRUNO and Tommaso Campanella, many of whom were later to be linked in some way with the authorship of the *Traité des trois imposteurs* (Treatise on the three impostors, namely Moses, Jesus and Muhammed). In France, the association with scandalous religious opinions was extended to include the imputation of a debauched, hedonistic way of life, taken to be the outward expression of an indifference towards, or

denial of, the afterlife; this is the version of libertinage against which the intemperate jesuit François Garasse fulminated in his *Doctrine curieuse des beaux-esprits de ce temps* (The doctrine of the over-inquisitive wits of our time) (1623), and which the mathematician-priest Marin MERSENNE impugns in his tract *L'impieté des déistes, athées et libertins de ce temps* (The impiety of the deists, atheists and libertins of our time) (1624). These attacks were stimulated not only by the writings of Giulio Cesare Vanini, a priest who was executed in Toulouse in 1619 for spreading allegedly materialistic doctrines, but also by the behaviour of a free-living group of noblemen in Paris whose acknowledged leader was the protestant poet Théophile de Viau. In his writings, there are hints of Lucretian atomism (see LUCRETIUS), a celebration of sensuality, and, aesthetically, a linking of freedom of thought with freedom of poetic form. Théophile suffered imprisonment and trial in 1623–5; his fate heralded a greater circumspection in libertin circles, which was accentuated further by the stricter regime of the Cardinal de Richelieu (1630–42).

2 The philosopher-libertins

The more philosophical manifestation of libertinage flourished, however, under Richelieu; this is the so-called 'libertinage érudit' of the group of scientists, antiquarians, scholars and writers which included Pierre GASSENDI, François La Mothe Le Vayer, Gabriel Naudé, Marin Mersenne and Guy Patin. It developed out of the meetings of the unofficial learned academy which met at the house of the Du Puy brothers in Paris. Many of this group shared a passionate commitment to the free exchange of scientific and cultural information at a time when, outside France, the effects of the Roman index of forbidden books and the Inquisition were felt strongly. For this reason, and also because a number of the group were themselves in religious orders, great discretion was shown in their discussion of the new empirical theories of Bacon, Copernican and Galilean astronomy, Epicurean materialism, mechanical philosophy and the ideas of radical Italian thinkers of the previous century (see BACON, F.; COPERNICUS, N.; EPICUREANISM; GALILEO, G.). It may well be that certain members of this group were free thinkers. However, it now seems implausible that the group as a whole shared these convictions, even if their discreet behaviour is taken to indicate that they knew that their discussions were potentially subversive to traditional beliefs.

A number of literary figures whose works have a significant philosophical aspect are associated with this coterie, notably La Mothe Le Vayer. His

Dialogues faits à l'imitation des anciens (Dialogues in imitation of the ancients) (1630–1) are strongly influenced by Montaigne's brand of Pyrrhonism, and draw inspiration, as does MONTAIGNE, from the writings of the ancient sceptic SEXTUS EMPIRICUS. Orasius Tubero, the wise sceptical voice in these dialogues, comprehensively discredits religious dogmatism, and even may imply support for atheism: one by one he patiently destroys the traditional arguments for the existence of God, exposes the prejudices in various religious systems, shows these to be inconsistent with each other even on fundamental points (such as whether religious practice is a matter of conscience or outward observance), and deploys Lucretian arguments against the notion of providence. Like Sextus Empiricus and Montaigne, he seems to favour discreet conformism allied with suspension of judgment, which he himself was to practise subsequently when under the patronage of Richelieu and, later still, as tutor to Louis XIV between 1652 and 1660. Most of the other publications of the so-called libertins of this circle appeared in Latin: Naudé's editions of the works of Agostino Nifo and Cardano, Gassendi's life of Epicurus and account of Epicurean philosophy, Mersenne's mathematical works. Between 1648 and 1655, the principal members of the group died, bringing to an end an early but important episode in the development of the *République des lettres*.

After 1661, discussion of the issues which preoccupied these 'libertins' became much more circumspect in the new, increasingly repressive atmosphere of Louis XIV's absolutism; the revocation of the Edict of Nantes of 1685, which took away the religious privileges of Protestants in France, had a yet more drastic effect, as did the persecution of other allegedly heretical religious practices such as Jansenism and Quietism. By the end of the century, the term 'libertin' had become detached from the nexus of connotations which it possessed in 1620; atheism in itself was no longer shocking, provided that discretion was shown in its expression; and it was no longer scandalous to make public one's adherence to the 'new' astronomy. It is therefore not surprising that the term lost much of its colour, and finally slipped, by the middle of the eighteenth century, so that it was a term used only to designate rakes and voluptuaries, whose lifestyle testified to their indifference to religion.

See also: CLANDESTINE LITERATURE; RENAISSANCE PHILOSOPHY

References and further reading

All these texts are historical and expository, and do not presuppose specialist knowledge.

Adam, A. (1964) *Les libertins au XVIIe siècle* (Seventeenth-century libertins), Paris: Buchet/Chastel. (Well-selected collection of seventeenth-century texts in French, with helpful historical and literary introductions.)

* Febvre, L. (1962) *Le problème de l'incroyance au XVIe siècle: la religion de Rabelais*, Paris: Michel, 1982; trans. B. Gottlieb as *The problem of unbelief in the sixteenth century: the religion of Rabelais*, Cambridge, MA: Harvard University Press. (An entertaining but contentious general study of the 'mentality' of the sixteenth century with respect to the question of atheism by the co-founder of the Annales School of history.)

* Garasse, F. (1623) *Doctrine curieuse des beaux-esprits de ce temps* (The doctrine of the over-inquisitive wits of our time), Farnborough: Gregg, 1971. (Mentioned in §1 above.)

Godard de Donville, L. (1989) *Le libertin des origines à 1665: un produit des apologètes* (The libertin from his origins to 1665: a product of apologists), Paris: Biblio 17. (A refutation of Pintard (1943), demonstrating that the concept of the 'libertin' emerges from Counter-Reformation theologians and controversialists.)

Kristeller, P.O. (1968) 'The myth of Renaissance atheism and the French tradition of free thought', *Journal of the History of Philosophy* 6: 233–43. (Attack on the view that a strand of atheistic thought passed from sixteenth-century Italian thinkers into seventeenth-century France.)

* La Mothe Le Vayer (1630–1) *Dialogues faits à l'imitation des anciens* (Dialogues in imitation of the ancients), Paris: Fayard, 1988. (Mentioned in §2 above.)

* Mersenne, M. (1624) *L'impieté des déistes, athées et libertins de ce temps* (The impiety of the deists, atheists and libertins of our time), Paris: Billaine. (Mentioned in §1 above.)

Pintard, R. (1943) *Le libertinage érudit dans la première moitié du XVIIe siècle* (Learned libertinage in the first half of the seventeenth century), Paris: Boivin. (Still the best general study of philosophical libertinage, but to be read in the context of Godard de Donville's 1989 refutation.)

* Popkin, R.H. (1992) *The third force in seventeenth-century thought*, Leiden: Brill. (A recent study of the influence of scepticism on seventeenth-century scientific, religious and philosophical thought.)

* Schmitt, C.B. (1983) *Aristotle and the Renaissance*,

Cambridge, MA: Harvard University Press. (Includes a reassessment of Paduan Aristotelianism.)

Spink, J.S. (1959) *French free thought from Gassendi to Voltaire*, London: Athlone Press. (Clear and sensible account of its subject.)

* *Traité des trois imposteurs* (Treatise on the three impostors, namely Moses, Jesus and Muhammad); repr. Florence: Einaudi, 1991. (Attributed to Spinoza by Silvia Berti. There is no certain evidence that the work existed in the sixteenth century.)

IAN MacLEAN

LIBERTY *see* FREEDOM AND LIBERTY

LICHTENBERG, GEORG CHRISTOPH (1742–99)

Lichtenberg was a German mathematician, physicist and astronomer, a highly successful university teacher in the field of experimental physics and a prolific writer of essays on scientific and cultural issues. He was one of the leading public figures of the German late Enlightenment, much admired for his satirical and witty style. Today he is known chiefly for his posthumously published notebooks. In thousands of entries, ranging from a single word to several pages, Lichtenberg recorded observations and thoughts about himself and the world. Only a fraction of those entries belong to the tradition of aphoristic writing developed after Lichtenberg and under his influence. A good proportion of the entries are of philosophical interest. Through the radical form as well as content of the notebooks Lichtenberg has become a contemporary to generations of his philosophical readers.

1 Life
2 Works
3 Philosophical outlook

1 Life

Lichtenberg was born in Oberramstadt near Darmstadt as the seventeenth and last child of a Lutheran pastor. From 1763 until 1767 he studied mathematics, astronomy and natural history at Georgia-Augusta University in Göttingen. From 1767 until 1770 he was a private tutor to three English students, whom he accompanied on their journey home to England in 1770. That same year he was appointed to an extraordinary professorship in the philosophy faculty at Göttingen, charged with the teaching of mathematics and physics. In 1772–3 he undertook astronomical work to determine the longitudes and latitudes of three North German cities, a task carried out in the service of the English king, who was also the elector of the German principality of Hannover. During 1774–5 he spent another sixteen months in England. In 1775 Lichtenberg was promoted to an ordinary professorship at Göttingen, where he remained, with the exception of minor travels in Northern Germany, until his death from lung and heart ailments that had afflicted him for a long time as a result of a rachitic deformation of the thorax.

2 Works

Lichtenberg was not a professional philosopher but exercised considerable influence on later thinkers both within philosophy proper and within the wider sphere of intellectual life. In order to understand Lichtenberg's philosophical significance, a more detailed presentation of the form and substance of his works is indicated.

During his lifetime Lichtenberg's early notoriety and eventual fame rested on his dual activities as a practitioner and teacher of experimental physics and as a popular writer on scientific and broader cultural matters. His main contribution to physics was the discovery of electrostatic phenomena involving the geometrical arrangement of particles on electrically charged plates (known as Lichtenberg figures), a discovery that underlies the twentieth-century development of xerography. Lichtenberg was the first to install a functioning lightning rod in Germany. He took part in scientific debates in probability theory, the physics and chemistry of gases, and meteorology.

In the field of letters Lichtenberg was a prolific and widely recognized essayist. Many of his contributions were satirical treatments of contemporary fashion and foibles. He engaged in several literary polemics, one of them against the widely influential physiognomics of J.K. Lavater, who sought to decipher character traits from facial features as represented in silhouette drawings. Lichtenberg's most successful publications for the general public were the detailed explications accompanying the German and French publication of several series of copper engravings by the English painter and graphic artist, William Hogarth, which appeared between 1794 and 1799.

Lichtenberg would be just another, once highly regarded figure of the German late Enlightenment, were it not for the posthumously published notebooks, which he had kept over some thirty years and which are filled with thousands of entries of many kinds and subject matters, ranging from book excerpts and scientific notes to witty remarks and linguistically and intellectually daring pronouncements on himself and his times. Originally intended as material for future scientific and literary projects, the 'waste books' (*Sudelbücher*), as Lichtenberg ironically called them, provide the reader with a wealth of material that defies systematization and reduction to simple positions. Through their highly original form as well as content, the waste books have exercised considerable influence on the thought and writing of generations of posthumous readers, among them Schopenhauer, Nietzsche, Freud and Wittgenstein.

3 Philosophical outlook

Many of the waste book entries are philosophically interesting as scattered documents of a sustained reflection on the peculiarities, weaknesses and limitations of the human mind revealed in Lichtenberg's own experience. Unlike the writings of ancient and modern moralists, Lichtenberg's observations are not gained or formulated with reference to an overall account of human nature. Rather they should be seen in the contemporary context of the emergence of empirical anthropology and psychology and autobiographical writing with their cultivation of individuality in character and manner of thinking. Lichtenberg's highly experimental, witty as well as daring use of the German language can be regarded as a device designed to approach more successfully the ineffable character of human experience.

A considerable subset of the waste book entries contains reflections on philosophical problems and positions. Yet it would not do justice to the fragmentary nature of this material to reduce it to a body of straightforward views or doctrines. Lichtenberg's philosophical reflections do not add up to a comprehensive or even consistent picture of the world. Compared to the systematic work of academic philosophers of his time, Lichtenberg's thoughts appear eclectic and syncretistic. What is specifically philosophical about Lichtenberg's thinking is not so much its propositional content as its modality: the sceptical attitude, the avowal of a subjective perspective and the tentative character of his reflections, typically expressed by such devices as first-person voice, subjunctive mood and laconic formulation.

Several areas of philosophical inquiry attracted Lichtenberg's thinking, chiefly among those methodological issues in the scientific study of nature and the relation between mind and body. The hetero-geneous philosophical remarks are linked by a theoretical as well as practical concern with the nature and limits of human knowledge. Main philosophical influences on Lichtenberg were the German school philosophy, which was part of his university training; British associationist psychology and psychological materialism (David HARTLEY, Joseph PRIESTLEY), with which he became acquainted during his second visit to England; Spinoza's pantheistic metaphysics, which underwent a considerable revival in late eighteenth-century German thought (see SPINOZA, B. DE); and Kant's critical philosophy, whose principled limitation of human knowledge resonated with Lichtenberg's growing agnosticism about the ultimate nature of soul, world and God in the final decade of his life (see KANT, I.).

In his theory and practice of the sciences Lichtenberg worked under the assumption of the overall unity of nature. He regarded the separation of fields of inquiry and sets of phenomena as a reflection of the limits of human knowledge. He often suggested possible relations between distinct areas of inquiry and their respective domains of objects and cultivated thinking in 'paradigms', whereby the theory of one set of phenomena is used to aid thinking about a different, apparently unrelated set of phenomena. He stressed the heuristic and hypothetical character of the paradigmatic method. For Lichtenberg a systematically unified science of nature was not so much a future possibility as an idea or device for conceptual orientation in the manifold pursuit of knowledge of nature. Especially noteworthy is his sceptical attitude toward the applicability of pure mathematics to empirical reality. Lichtenberg favoured the experimental method as a way to control the unnoticed influence of subjective factors in the observation of nature. He sided with Bacon's contemporary followers (for example, A.V. Haller) and against Newton in supporting the use of hypotheses in the study of nature.

During the 1790s Lichtenberg's thinking was considerably influenced by Kant's theoretical philosophy. Lichtenberg's understanding of Kant focused on the role of human subjectivity in the constitution of knowledge and its objects. He took Kant's restriction of human knowledge to appearances as support of theoretical egoism or the view that all we can really know are our own feelings and thoughts. Lichtenberg did not deny the existence of an independent reality but insisted on its unknowability. In line with his Spinozistic leanings he favoured the thought that the apparent distinction of mind and matter might have an unknowable substratum that is neither of the two.

In further expanding upon Kant's transcendental

idealism, Lichtenberg employed different Latin propositions to articulate the distinction between the existential independence of things from us (*praeter nos*) and their spatial externality with respect to us (*extra nos*), arguing that naïve realism consists in the illicit shift from the former to the latter. He inferred that something need not be spatially outside of us in order to be independent from us, thus allowing for the possibility that something might be in us which is yet independent from us. Lichtenberg encapsulated this line of thought in his most famous and influential philosophical aphorism, in which he proposes to replace the Kantian 'I think' with the phrase, 'it thinks', to be construed along the lines of the locution 'it lightens', thus indicating that the I is not the producer but merely the observer of its own thoughts – an un-Kantian move that was not lost on critics of the autonomy and identity of the thinking subject in nineteenth- and twentieth-century philosophy.

List of works

Lichtenberg, L.C. and Kries, F. (eds) (1800–6) *Vermischte Schriften* (Various Writings), ed. L.C. Lichtenberg and F. Kries, Göttingen: Dieterich, 9 vols. (Vols 1–2 contain a first selection from the waste books; vols 3–5 contain the essays; vols 6–9 contain the physical and mathematical writings, a good part of which have never been reprinted.)

—— (1844–53) *Vermischte Schriften. Neue vermehrte, von den Söhnen veranstaltete Ausgabe*, Göttingen: Dieterich, 14 vols. (A substantially revised edition of *Various Writings*, edited by Lichtenberg's sons, with larger selections from the waste books and the essays in vols 1–2 and 3–6, respectively, and a first selection of Lichtenberg's letters in vols 7–8 and the Hogarth explications in vols 9–14.)

—— (1902–8) *Aphorismen. Nach den Handschriften herausgegeben von A. Leitzmann*, Berlin, 5 vols; repr. Nendeln and Liechtenstein: Kraus Reprint, 1968, 3 vols. (The only critical edition of the waste books, omits the entries from physics.)

—— (1968–92) *Schriften und Briefe* (Writings and Letters), ed. W. Promies, Munich: Hanser, 4 vols with 2 vols commentary. (Vols 1–2 contain the waste books, including the entries from physics, vol. 3 contains most of the works published during Lichtenberg's lifetime, vol. 4 offers a substantial selection of the letters; detailed commentary volume to the waste books.)

—— (1983–92) *Briefwechsel* (Correspondence), ed. U. Joost and A. Schöne, Munich: Hanser, 4 vols. (Most comprehensive edition of letters from and to Lichtenberg; vol. 5 with supplements and index in preparation.)

—— (1990) *Aphorisms*, trans. R.J. Hollingdale, London and New York: Penguin. (A good selection from the waste books in an excellent translation.)

References and further readings

Baasner, R. (1992) *Georg Christoph Lichtenberg*, Darmstadt: Wissenschafliche Buchgesellschaft. (A systematic survey of work on Lichtenberg; includes bibliography.)

Gockel, H. (1973) *Individualisiertes Sprechen. Lichtenbergs Bemerkungen im Zusammenhang von Erkenntnistheorie und Sprachkritik*, Berlin and New York: de Gruyter. (Relates Lichtenberg to the rhetorical tradition and earlier as well as contemporary theories of knowledge and language.)

Jung, R. (1972) *Lichtenberg-Bibliographie*, Heidelberg: Stiehm. (Bibliography of works by and on Lichtenberg published up to 1971; 15 entries on Lichtenberg and philosophy.)

Kauther, R. (1992) 'Lichtenberg und Kant', *Lichtenberg-Jahrbuch* 5: 56–77. (Stresses the difference between Lichtenberg's pragmatic anthropology and Kant's theory of reason.)

Koehne, R. (1963) 'Gedanken und Exzerpte zur Bestimmung der philosophiegeschichtlichen Stellung Lichtenbergs', in M. Horkheimer (ed.) *Zeugnisse. Theodor W. Adorno zum sechsigsten Geburtstag*, Frankfurt: Europäische Verlagsanstalt, 133–51. (Attempts to establish the systematic, proto-Hegelian nature of Lichtenberg's thinking.)

Mautner, F.H. (1968) *Lichtenberg. Geschichte seines Geistes*, Berlin: de Gruyter. (The standard comprehensive intellectual biography.)

Patzig, G. (1992) 'Über den Philosophen Lichtenberg', *Text und Kritik* 114: 23–6. (A succinct treatment of Lichtenberg as an anti-systematic philosopher.)

Promies, W. and Joost, U. (1988–) *Lichtenberg-Jahrbuch* (Yearbook of the Lichtenberg Society), 1 vol. to date. (Includes bibliography; supplants its precursor, ed. W. Promies, *Photorin. Mitteilungen der Lichtenberg-Gesellschaft*, 12 vols, 1979–87.)

Schöne, A. (1982) *Aufklärung aus dem Geist der Experimentalphysik. Lichtenbergische Konjunktive*, 2nd edn, 1983. (An examination of Lichtenberg's usage of the subjunctive mood as an expression of his experimental spirit in physics and literature.)

Stern, J.P. (1959) *Lichtenberg. A Doctrine of Scattered Occasions*, Bloomington, IN: Indiana University Press. (The most detailed general treatment of Lichtenberg in English.)

Von Wright, G.H. (1942) 'Georg Christoph Lichtenberg als Philosoph', *Theoria* 8: 201–17. (A detailed presentation of Lichtenberg as a philosopher; claims him as a precursor of logical empiricism.)

Zöller, G. (1992) 'Lichtenberg and Kant on the Subject of Thinking', *Journal of the History of Philosophy* 30: 417–41. (Places Lichtenberg's aphorism on the 'it thinks' in the context of his selective appropriation of Kant's idealist theory of self and world.)

GÜNTER ZÖLLER

LIFE AND DEATH

Problems concerning life and death are among the most dramatic and intractable in philosophy and they feature in all fundamental areas of philosophical inquiry, especially ethics. Most basic is the problem of what account to give of the value of life itself. This problem has had two main dimensions. One has been the controversy over what precise account to give of death; this has revolved around the issue of whether death is, as it is commonly perceived, an evil, and premature death a tragedy. The other has been the equally puzzling question of how to explain the positive value of life, and to resolve the problem that the more rich we make our account of the value of life, the more the value of life, and hence the nature of the wrong done by killing someone, seems to vary with the quality of the life of the person concerned.

A second set of problems concerns the definition of death and appropriate criteria for death. Death, as the most extreme consequence of violence, also leads one into psychological discussions of aggression and into issues of political violence, terrorism, war and capital punishment in political philosophy. Third, there has been concern with a number of practical moral issues, including abortion and euthanasia. Finally, issues have arisen concerning the relation of the value of the life of persons to other sorts of lives, those of animals, for example, or the life and survival of the ecosystem itself.

This discussion will concentrate on the central themes of the value of life and the harm and wrong represented by death.

1　**The value of life**
2　**Criteria for death**
3　**Persistent vegetative state**
4　**The ethics of euthanasia**
5　**Contraception and infanticide**

1　The value of life

It is not only the evil of death that presupposes that life has value and directs us to account for this value, but also everyday discriminations between lives of different sorts. Even the food of vegetarians involves the premature death of living things, and vegetarians usually accept priorities between different animals and between human individuals at different stages of development. If the hospital is on fire, should we attempt to rescue the patients before the hospital cat, and some patients before others? Should the terminally ill, the very old or those in persistent vegetative state be rescued before or after those with radically different life expectancy and degrees of richness and variety in their lives? Should those responsible for their own poor health (heavy smokers, for example) be preferred to the more prudent? Only an account of the value of life will tell us both why lives should be saved and whether and to what extent it is legitimate to choose between lives.

The chief recent attempts to provide a theory of the value of life have sought to identify those features of the most valuable creatures (humans) which might explain their peculiar value. Most theories combine autonomy, self-consciousness and intelligence as the relevant features (see AUTONOMY, ETHICAL). Creatures with such capacities have often been termed 'persons' (see PERSONS). Radically different accounts of how to apply such criteria of personhood have emerged. Philosophers of broadly consequentialist orientation have claimed that only creatures who actually possess the relevant characteristics count as persons (see CONSEQUENTIALISM). A major difficulty for such accounts is their counter-intuitive conclusion that creatures which most people do regard as valuable (foetuses and neonates, for example) either are valuable not in virtue of any intrinsic properties that they possess, but only in so far as they are valued by persons properly so called (their parents, perhaps), or will be valuable only in terms of future expected utility.

Others, accepting broadly the same criteria for personhood, have argued that creatures structured to possess such capacities or members of a natural kind that typically possesses such capacities are valuable whether or not particular individuals (foetuses, for instance) actually possess them. Another approach rests content with stipulating that humans are more valuable than others simply in virtue of their species membership. These 'natural kind' theorists cannot account for the discriminations people make between the moral importance of, say, foetuses, and other members of the same natural kind. If the life of a mother and her foetus are in danger and both cannot be saved, most would believe it right to prefer the mother.

Philosophers faced with the sorts of problems

considered so far often produce *ad hoc*, 'common-sense' modifications to their general theories to overcome difficulties with hard cases (see COMMON-SENSE ETHICS). For example, natural kind theorists often admit of grades of natural kind membership, using terms like 'fully-fledged' humans to account for differences in attitudes to foetuses and adults.

Ronald DWORKIN, in an original account of the value of life, has argued that the sanctity of life must be understood in terms of the waste of investment in life represented by death. Dworkin (1993) distinguishes two dimensions of investment that might be wasted by death: the natural and the human. Natural investment implies that nature itself makes an investment in terms of time, trouble and natural resources when life is created and that investment increases in a linear way as the life continues. In the case of human investment, there is both the investment of the human whose life it is (in terms of self-creation both conscious and unconscious) and that of the other people who invest time, effort and resources in creating and sustaining that life. On this view the wrong of causing premature death is that of squandering this natural and human investment. A conservative view of the wrong of euthanasia and abortion, for example, prioritizes natural investment, while a more liberal view will prioritize a particular interpretation of the human contribution to a life.

This and other accounts suggesting that a life is valuable in proportion to its *richness* give importance to factors which differ across lives. On these views, lives will be more valuable the more the investment in them or the more rich and varied they are. This gives rise to the major problem that no two lives will be equally valuable and huge problems of discrimination between people are inevitable.

2 Criteria for death

Since Epicurus there has been persistent philosophical interest in the problem of accounting for the evil of death (see EPICURUS §2). We have already presupposed that this problem can be solved by discussing the value of life. Epicurus' problem is in a sense paradoxical. He made substantially the same point as Wittgenstein: 'death is not an event in life'. If it is not, then there is no one to whom death happens, no one for whom death is an evil. But, of course, most people fear death for the disaster it represents. Epicurus' point turns on the necessity of a harm's being experienced, yet we are all familiar with things we rationally regard as harms whether or not we experience them. I have a rational preference not to fall into a persistent vegetative state even if I will not

be aware of this happening and thereafter will never be aware of anything again.

The more interesting and important problems concern the nature of the evil death represents and the importance of defining death, or rather of identifying appropriate criteria for the occurrence of death.

If, as most believe, death is an evil, and premature death a tragedy, and if we can say what makes this so, we will also be answering our first question, about what it is that makes life valuable. Here it is important to distinguish the question, 'What makes life valuable – for you?' from the question, 'In virtue of what is life the sort of thing that can be valuable?' The first question is likely to have as many answers as there are persons to whom it is put, the second question rather fewer.

If we move to the issue of criteria for death we can perhaps see why this is so. Death is as old as life, and people have seldom been at a loss as to when grief is appropriate. In other words, death is not a concept which required elucidation. Traditionally, permanent cessation of breath and/or heartbeat was accepted as a reliable indicator of death. While there may have been some uncertainty as to when cessation could be regarded as permanent, the onset of *rigor mortis* and the decomposition of the body could be relied upon to settle the matter in due course.

Problems arose when technology enabled the heartbeat and breathing of individuals to be maintained almost indefinitely. This was so even when the individuals concerned were otherwise so badly injured as to make it certain both that they would never regain consciousness, and that they would die if mechanical support were withdrawn. But are such individuals *dead*? Why is the question important? Why does it even arise?

Individuals on what is popularly known as 'life support' do not appear dead. They breathe, they are supple and perfused with blood, not cold and stiff like a corpse. In order to justify the cessation of life support (I continue with the popular term because it highlights the paradox we are discussing) with the inevitable consequence that the individual would die, it first had to be clear why it was appropriate to let this individual die, why their life had ceased to be valuable, in the sense of worth saving. Second, the technology of efficient life support narrowly preceded the development of organ transplants. If the individual on life support was to be eligible as an organ donor, their organs had to be in good condition. The condition of the organs was optimized by the maintenance of life support. Finally, pressure created by scarce resources meant that the intensive care beds necessary for life support were in demand and their occupation by one individual rather than another had to be justified.

The practical way out of the problem was to invent a new set of criteria for the occurrence of death. The idea was not to take individuals off life support and wait for them to die, but to declare them dead while still having their life systems sustained. This could be done if death of the brain were to be accepted as a necessary and sufficient condition for death of the organism as a whole. It is now generally accepted in many different societies and cultures that brain death is the criterion for death of the organism as a whole even though the rest of the organism can be kept 'alive' (breathing, blood circulating) after brain death. The major dispute has been over whether whole brain death is necessary for death to be declared to have occurred, or death of the brain stem, the conduit through which all electrical activity in the brain has to pass.

This agreement about brain death is significant, for it surely contains an acknowledgement that it is mental activity, and the things that mental activity supports, that are relevant to the value of life – that when the capacity for consciousness has departed permanently, all that matters has gone. The point of declaring individuals 'dead' was to mark the fact that all that matters about an individual had disappeared and that other things of importance could now be permitted. For example, organs could be made available for donation, intensive care beds released for other urgent cases, friends and relatives released from the often considerable burden of care and support, and grief could begin.

The acceptance of brain death marks a change in understanding of what matters about life and at the same time a reassertion of a traditional conception of respect for the sanctity of life and a correlated insistence that only death takes individuals beyond our moral concern. Brain death is such an attractive notion precisely because it permits the preservation of the concept of death as the crucial moral divide and at the same time allows us to think differently of human individuals who yet breathe. However, the artificiality of brain death as a criterion for the death of the entire organism should be borne in mind. There is an important sense in which brain death is at best a new conception of what it is to be dead and at worst an uneasy compromise between facing squarely the issue of what matters about life and harnessing the massive unreflective consensus about the significance of 'death'.

3 Persistent vegetative state

That this is so can be seen more clearly if we consider the condition of persistent vegetative state, and the landmark judgment by Britain's House of Lords in the case of Tony Bland. Bland sustained brain damage after being crushed in a crowd of spectators at a football match in 1989, at Hillsborough football stadium in Sheffield, England. The brain damage left him permanently and irrevocably unconscious, in what is now termed a 'persistent vegetative state' (PVS). PVS is not fatal; people like Bland can remain alive for thirty or more years. They are not 'brain dead'. In this they are akin to infants born with anencephaly (absence of a brain) or with their cerebral cortex destroyed.

Bland's parents, who accepted that their son had ceased to exist in any real – biographical – sense, although his body remained alive, were prevented from obtaining the solace of grief. In desperation, they asked the English courts to declare that it would be lawful for medical staff to withdraw feeding and other life sustaining measures so that their son would die. It is not clear why there was any necessity to take the Bland case to the courts, since it was already well established that there was no obligation to sustain a baby by feeding (*Re C* [1989] 2 All ER 782 and *Re J* [1990] 3 All ER 930).

Eventually the House of Lords ruled unanimously that such a course of action would be lawful (*Airedale NHS Trust* v. *Bland* [1993] 1 All ER 821 H.L.). The problem was, of course, that although Tony Bland had permanently ceased to have 'a life' in any meaningful sense, he was not dead and would not die unless the courts permitted doctors to take steps to that end.

A slightly later case was concluded in the Court of Appeal in January 1994. The Master of the Rolls, Sir Thomas Bingham, held, in a bizarre judgment with which the other two lord justices of appeal concurred, that it was permissible for doctors to end the life of a patient by refusing life-prolonging treatment when the consultant and 'a number of other doctors' agreed that such a course was in the patient's best interests and 'no medical opinion contradicted it' (*Frenchay Healthcare NHS Trust* v. *S*, Court of Appeal, Judgment, 14 January 1994). Tony Bland's condition resembled those with brain death in that he had irrevocably lost the capacity for consciousness. The difference is that those in PVS still have electrical activity in the brain and through the brain stem. Does this difference amount to a morally relevant difference between those in PVS and those who are brain dead? Although the House of Lords was reluctant to change the definition of death, or even address that issue, it is clear from its decision that it thought Bland's life, because he had lost all capacity for consciousness, did not retain the sort of value that required it to be sustained. In the words of Lord Keith of Kinkel in his judgment in that case, 'It is, however, perhaps permissible to say that to an individual with no cognitive capacity whatever, and no prospect of ever recovering any such capacity in this world, it must be a matter of complete indifference whether he lives or dies'.

There was no question in Bland's case of competing claims on the resources required to sustain him, so that the decision to permit a course of action designed to achieve the death his parents sought was a deliberate, conscious decision to end his life. A hotly debated question is whether such a decision constitutes a form of euthanasia. Although the House of Lords strongly denied that this is what it was doing, its decision in the Bland case was thought by many to legalize, for the first time in the United Kingdom, a form (albeit very restricted) of euthanasia. That the case of Tony Bland establishes a precedent for legally sanctioned euthanasia in the United Kingdom is confirmed by the words of Lord Mustill in his judgment in that case:

The conclusion... depends crucially on a distinction drawn by the criminal Law between acts and omissions, and carries with it inescapably a distinction between, on the one hand what is often called "mercy killing", where active steps are taken in a medical context to terminate the life of a suffering patient, and a situation such as the present where the proposed conduct has the aim for equally humane reasons of terminating the life of Anthony Bland by withholding from him the basic necessities of life. The acute unease which I feel about adopting this way through the legal and ethical maze is I believe due in an important part to the sensation that however much the terminologies may differ the ethical status of the two courses of action is for all relevant purposes indistinguishable.

The key features of Lord Mustill's judgment are, first, the acknowledgement that the course of action requested of, and approved by, the courts 'has the aim... of terminating the life of Anthony Bland'; and, second, that the supposed difference between acts and omissions relied on by the common law tradition to make moral and legal distinctions, characterizes two courses of action that are ethically 'for all relevant purposes indistinguishable'. This decision made the United Kingdom the second country in Europe to have judicially recognized the necessity of bringing to an end the lives of at least some innocent individuals who have not requested death. The Netherlands legalized euthanasia under certain conditions in a High Court case decided in 1984 and later formally enshrined euthanasia in its legal system.

It is important to emphasize the proviso 'who have not requested death', for other instances of courts defending the right to die have turned on precisely this issue. The landmark United States case concerning PVS, that of Nancy Cruzan, depended crucially on whether Cruzan had expressed a wish to die prior to falling into PVS, and indeed it is often described as a case establishing the right to die (*Cruzan* v. *Director, Missouri Department of Health* [1990] 497 US 261).

4 The ethics of euthanasia

Arguments about the ethics of euthanasia are essentially the same as, and have been coloured by, arguments about the ethics of suicide. The wrong of suicide has, since the death of Socrates, often been seen in terms of either a violation of some idea of the sanctity of life, or the wrong of depriving a sovereign or a god of the use of a body which was theirs to dispose of. Euthanasia, as essentially assisting suicide, while of contemporary relevance as we have seen, has reawakened the centuries old debate about suicide (see SUICIDE, ETHICS OF).

Those who defend the legitimacy of euthanasia have three main approaches to defending the ethics of what they propose. First, some see euthanasia (like suicide) as a dimension of human freedom and argue that the value represented by respect for autonomy is incomplete unless it encompasses the limiting case of suicide or assisted suicide. On this view, no further justification is required. The second view is based on compassion and tends to undermine this purist approach to the ethics of euthanasia. It argues that suicide and euthanasia are legitimate ways of bringing to an end suffering which cannot be adequately controlled or ended in any other way. This approach can undermine autonomy because it lapses if there is an equally effective way of controlling the pain and suffering. The third type of defence of euthanasia is exemplified by Ronald Dworkin's account (see §1), which argues that respect for the intrinsic value of life, properly understood, sees life essentially as meaningful and valuable because of the shape given to it by the individual whose life it is, and that this shaping power must include control over life's end. Unlike the first defence of euthanasia which appeals simply to autonomy, Dworkin's approach places autonomy at the service of, and hence subordinate to, a conception of the intrinsic value of life. On this view it is not all autonomous decisions to end life that are justified, but only those which conduce to the agents own conception of what it is that makes their life make sense.

Arguments against the legitimacy of euthanasia take two forms: they take a stand on principle or they attempt to undermine the cogency of the arguments in favour of euthanasia. The principled approach either harkens back to the idea that an individual's life is not theirs to dispose of, belonging to the sovereign or the deity or both (one via the other), or takes a stand on the sanctity of life. The more pragmatic approach tends to suggest that the freedom to end one's own life is not part of autonomy properly understood, or that there are other compassionate and effective ways of controlling pain, both physical and psychological.

It is difficult to resolve the differences over euthanasia when the issue is one of principle. Perhaps the most obvious reconciling strategy is to seek cases in which those opposed to euthanasia would concede the legitimacy of killing, and ask if related justifications might not hold good in the case of euthanasia. For example, not all opponents of euthanasia are pacifists, and even pacifists might understand extreme exceptions to the rule against killing the innocent.

One test might be how people feel about the following case. A lorry driver is trapped in the blazing cab of his vehicle following an accident. A policeman is on the scene and sees that the driver cannot be extracted before the flames get to him and he is burned alive. The policeman can let him be burned alive or can give him a quick and relatively painless end by shooting him in the head. The driver says, 'Please shoot me; do not let me be burned alive!' Those opposed to euthanasia in all circumstances must give one answer to the policeman's dilemma, those in favour will give the alternative.

There is one final sort of objection to euthanasia. It avoids the policeman's dilemma but has its own problems. Some people are not opposed to euthanasia on principle and would permit it in exceptional cases, like the policeman's dilemma. However, they regard it as constituting a 'slippery slope' which if permitted would lead to unacceptable forms of killing. They therefore object to the *legalization* of euthanasia, but can cope with isolated and exceptional instances, by forgiveness rather than by justification. The question advocates of the slippery slope objection must answer is whether it is reasonable and rational to criminalize behaviour they admit to be both moral and defensible, and whether or not the unacceptable levels of the slope can be guarded against in another way.

5 Contraception and infanticide

Contraception raises issues of life and death analogous to those we have discussed. First, there are methods of contraception which operate to effect early abortion by, for example, preventing implantation of a fertilized egg. Second, those who regard the potentiality argument as giving moral status to the foetus will, if they are consistent, see contraception as one way in which potential human beings have their potential frustrated. There is, of course, another dimension to the ethics of contraception which is not related straightforwardly to issues of life and death. That is where one sexual partner conceals from the other the nature, existence and/or reliability of the methods of contraception used or leads the other partner to believe a method of contraception is being used when it is not (see TRUTHFULNESS).

Since the advent of HIV/AIDS, a popular method of contraception has become more significant as a barrier to infection, and this has added to the moral responsibility of using one particular method of contraception. Questions are often raised as to whether someone who uses no method of contraception, or fails to use a condom, is willing to conceive and bear the responsibility of a child or is willing to run the risk of HIV infection.

It is sometimes suggested, particularly by Catholic thinkers, that contraception subverts the purpose of sex, which supposedly was designed by the deity for procreation. This is a curious argument, however, because if sexual relations are wrong except when they could conceivably result in procreation, then sex between infertile people or during pregnancy is wrong. If on the other hand it is practices which weaken the prospect of new people coming into existence which are to be avoided, then it looks as though it is a celibate priesthood, or the existence of nunneries, which are an affront to God's purpose.

Infanticide raises special moral problems only for those who see a morally relevant difference between the foetus and the neonate. If abortion is permissible, infanticide will surely be permissible on the same terms, unless the newborn differs in some relevant way from those foetuses the abortion of which is permissible. Attempts have been made to identify such differences in three main ways: in terms of either some capacities possessed by the newborn and not the foetus, or the newborn's supposedly greater potential for personhood, or the social relations it forms for the first time on consciously encountering other beings. All of these alleged differences are controversial, and we should note that the last, socialization, leaves unprotected any and all unloved, unwanted and unclaimed infants (see REPRODUCTION AND ETHICS).

See also: BIOETHICS, JEWISH; DEATH; LIFE, MEANING OF; MEDICAL ETHICS; NURSING ETHICS; SUICIDE, ETHICS OF

References and further reading

Beecher, H. (1971) 'The New Definition of Death,

Some Opposing Viewpoints', *International Journal of Clinical Pharmacology* 5. (Early source on the emerging debate over criteria for death.)

Committee of the Harvard Medical School (1968) 'A Definition of Irreversible Coma', *Journal of the American Medical Association* 205: 337–40. (Traces the rationale for changes in the definition of death.)

* Dworkin, R. (1993) *Life's Dominion*, London: HarperCollins, 213–14. (Sophisticated and sustained discussion of abortion and euthanasia.)

Glover, J. (1977) *Causing Death and Saving Lives*, Harmondsworth: Penguin. (Classic discussion of killing and letting die.)

Harris, J. (1980) *Violence and Responsibility*, London: Routledge & Kegan Paul. (Discussion of the moral difference between acts and omissions and our responsibility for both.)

—— (1985) *The Value of Life*, London: Routledge & Kegan Paul. (Introduction to medical ethics which discusses the value of life.)

Keown, J. (ed.) (1995) *Euthanasia Examined: Ethical, Clinical and Legal Perspectives*, Cambridge: Cambridge University Press. (Authors from various disciplines consider euthanasia.)

Kleinig, J. (1991) *Valuing Life*, Princeton, NJ: Princeton University Press. (General account of life and death issues.)

Lamb, D. (1985) *Death, Brain Death and Ethics*, London: Croom Helm. (Collection of essays on euthanasia.)

Parfit, D. (1984) *Reasons and Persons*, Oxford: Clarendon Press. (Interesting in this context for its discussion of the possibility of a human being's instantiating a number of different persons and hence 'containing' more than one life.)

Rachels, J. (1987) *The End of Life*, Oxford: Oxford University Press. (A defence of voluntary euthanasia.)

Steinbock, B. (ed.) (1980) *Killing and Letting Die*, Englewood Cliffs, NJ: Prentice Hall. (Excellent collection of essays on life and death.)

Tooley, M. (1983) *Abortion and Infanticide*, Oxford: Oxford University Press. (A controversial argument to the effect that abortion and infanticide are morally indistinguishable.)

JOHN HARRIS

LIFE, MEANING OF

This is an obscure yet central topic in philosophy. Often associated with the question whether human beings are part of a larger or divine purpose, the question, 'What is the meaning of life?' seems to invite a religious answer. Much philosophical discussion, however, questions the necessity of this association. Attention to the inevitability of death has often seemed to make life's meaning problematic, but it is not obvious how immortality could make the difference between meaning and its absence. The theme of absurdity runs through much discussion of those who believe the universe to be indifferent. Though our lives have no significance, they argue, we must live as if they do. In the face of this absurdity, some advocate suicide, others defiance, others irony. One may also turn away from the issue of cosmic significance, and look for meaning elsewhere.

1 **The meaning of 'the meaning of life'**
2 **The relevance of death**
3 **Absurdity**
4 **Subjective and objective meaning**

1 The meaning of 'the meaning of life'

The question, 'What is the meaning of life?', probably arouses both more contempt and more respect for philosophy than any other. On the one hand, the question is notoriously vague and has encouraged much pompous nonsense. On the other, the urge to understand the point of our existence is deep and pervasive, and is indicative of qualities of mind that are arguably central to being human.

A major difficulty besetting the topic is lack of clarity about the subject itself. Drawing comparisons with other contexts in which we ask for meanings tends to increase confusion. When we ask for the meanings of words or phrases, we ask what they are typically used to communicate. Life, however, is not an item in a system of communication. It does not seem to be used or intended to represent something beyond itself. In certain circumstances we also talk about the meaning of nonlinguistic items: footprints mean someone else has been here; a rash on the skin means the child has measles. Analogies with these uses of 'meaning', however, have not proved helpful.

Religion, particularly Judaeo-Christianity, provides a natural context for the question of the meaning of life (see RELIGION AND MORALITY). If one believes that a supernatural being created the world with some grand design, the question asks for the purpose of that design or the place of life within it. However, the philosophical topic of the meaning of life – or the set of overlapping topics that have come over time to be associated with the phrase – cannot be restricted to issues that make sense only on religious assumptions.

Central concerns that come under the topic include questions about whether life has a purpose, whether life is worthwhile, and whether people have any reason to live, independently of their specific circumstances and interests. Any of these questions may be asked about life, or, more commonly, about human life, but they can also be asked about individual lives, particularly about one's own life. We can search for purposes, reasons, values that are acceptable from points of view external to ourselves, or we can restrict our attention to the realm of desires and goals found in our psyches or our communities, indifferent to possible perspectives beyond the human. Although the phrase 'the meaning of life' seems to assume only one meaning to life, we may be led to reject this assumption without concluding that life is meaningless. Often, the focus of the question shifts in the very process of trying to answer it.

To inquire into the meaning of life, then, is like engaging in a search in which you are not sure quite what you are looking for until you find it. Any attempt to give an unambiguous paraphrase of 'the meaning of life' is bound, like the phrase itself, to foreclose certain options and cut off paths of inquiry that should not be ruled out in advance.

2 The relevance of death

The sense that there is a problem about the meaning of life is frequently brought on by the contemplation of death (see DEATH §8). Indeed, it is often thought, as it was by Schopenhauer (1851) and by Tolstoi (1886), that the question arises precisely because our lives will end in death (see SCHOPENHAUER, A. §6). However, as some philosophers have noticed, the connection between our finitude and life's meaning is puzzling. If the assumption that we will all die makes life seem meaningless, how would the opposite assumption – that we will live forever – make the situation any better?

A possible explanation for the connection between the thought of death and the fear that life is meaningless is that facing up to one's own mortality destroys one's prospects for happiness. If ultimate happiness were likely or even possible, we might not feel the need for meaning – one does not need a reason to live as long as living is fun, and the aim of achieving ultimate happiness, were it attainable, might be purpose enough. For some, however, the knowledge that they will die makes happiness impossible. Somewhat differently, recognition of the inevitability of the death of one's culture and one's species as well as of oneself may make the interests and goals one formerly had appear worthless or silly.

Again, belief in a God can provide relief from these concerns. The promise of an afterlife, in which at least some achieve eternal bliss, renews the possibility of working towards ultimate happiness. Independently, the existence of an eternal and superior being who cares about us and about what we make of our lives relieves the worry that our goals and our conduct are insignificant.

3 Absurdity

If God does not exist, many argue, then human life is absurd. The human condition, these philosophers claim, would then contain a fundamental and unchangeable disharmony. Albert CAMUS focused on the clash between our demand that the world be reasonable, orderly and caring and the reality of its being silent, blank and indifferent. Thomas NAGEL emphasizes the discrepancy between the objective insignificance of our lives and projects and the seriousness and energy we devote to them. How are we to respond?

Because coming to recognize the indifference of the universe can be a shattering experience, the thought of suicide arises naturally. If all your goals are founded on the assumption that your existence or your actions matter to some entity or process larger and less in need of validation than yourself, the discovery that there is no such entity leaves you stripped of all direction. If, moreover, you think that any direction you take will necessarily reintroduce the assumption you now know to be false, then it may appear that the only option that avoids contradiction is suicide. Camus (1955), however, believed that there is a noncontradictory way of life available. He described 'absurd man' as living 'without appeal', in defiance of the world's indifference to him. Such a person embraces life as fully as possible but without ever forgetting or denying the absence of any rational foundation for it.

Nagel offers a milder response (1971): the recognition of our insignificance is a function of our distinctively human ability to adopt an external view upon ourselves; as such there is no reason to try to deny it or escape from it. At the same time, if our lives are cosmically insignificant, so is the matter of how we respond to this fact. In the light of this argument, Nagel suggests, defiance seems too overblown and dramatic, and irony is more appropriate.

Richard Taylor (1970) draws a different moral from the silence of the universe: the recognition that life is, as it were, objectively meaningless, should convince us to turn our search for meaning inward. The kind of meaning in life that it makes sense to care about is meaning to us. Life has meaning if we are able to engage in activities that we find meaningful. Otherwise, not.

These philosophers all share the view that if there is nothing larger and more intrinsically valuable than ourselves to whom we may see ourselves as positively attached, then life is meaningless in at least one important sense. In this they agree with those who rest a positive view of life's meaning on the existence of a benevolent God. Because they also believe that the condition for meaning is not met and that we none the less must live as if life had meaning, they conclude that human life is absurd. As pointed out by Joel Feinberg (1992), however, there is a difference between a situation's being absurd and a person's being so. By taking a proper attitude towards our predicament, whether that be defiance or irony or some third alternative, we can at least save ourselves from being ridiculous.

It is not clear, however, that we are rationally required to make even this relatively unpessimistic concession to the view that human life is absurd. As we have seen, this view rests on the idea that there is an inescapable clash between what we demand or inevitably presume about our place in the universe and the reality of our situation. But the tendency to want or insist on our cosmic importance may be less deep and inevitable than these philosophers think. Taking life by the horns, pursuing one's projects with energy and devotion, need not rest on delusions of grandeur. It is at least not obvious that when an Olympic athlete strains to the limit in an effort to break a world record, or that when a mother forgoes sleep and comfort to nurse her child back to health, she must believe that her achievement will be of cosmic significance.

4 Subjective and objective meaning

Although discussions of the meaning of life are often associated with considerations about our place in the universe, there are also contexts in which the intelligibility of the contrast between meaningful and meaningless lives appears to be wholly independent of the cosmic issue.

We have already mentioned the view that the kind of meaning it makes sense to care about is subjective meaning. Some, like David Wiggins (1976), believe that a wholly subjective account of meaning cannot do justice to the ordinary use of the term. As Wiggins points out, the idea of a distinction between a meaningful life and a meaningless one is not equivalent to the more obvious and uncontroversial difference between a life that is subjectively satisfying or fulfilling and one that is not. When we wonder whether our lives have meaning, we are not engaged in a wholly introspective enterprise, and when we search for a way to give meaning to our lives, we are not looking for a pill that will make us happy. The life of Sisyphus, condemned by the gods perpetually to roll a stone up a hill only to see it roll down again, has been offered, at least since Camus' writings, as a paradigm of meaninglessness. If we imagine Sisyphus as perversely fulfilled by this repetitious and futile activity, it is not clear whether we would evaluate his life as more meaningful or more dreadful.

Accounts of meaning in life need not be restricted to purely subjective and purely objective alternatives, however. The most natural paradigms of meaningful lives are both abundantly fulfilling subjectively and admirable or worthwhile as judged from points of view external to the agents themselves. The kind of life most comfortably described as meaningful appears to be one in which there is a happy connection between a subject's lively interests and the range of things that are worthy of interest. Meaning seems to arise when subjective attraction meshes with objective attractiveness.

Whether and how this kind of meaningfulness relates to the concern that seems most naturally to call for a connection to some divine or cosmic purpose are difficult issues. Moreover, the notion of 'objective attractiveness' (or objective worth or value), to which this conception of meaningfulness makes reference, is notoriously controversial. Whether such a notion is ultimately intelligible, particularly in the absence of a religious metaphysics, constitutes a major philosophical question on its own (see MORAL REALISM). That the issue of the meaning of life should open onto and connect with other major philosophical issues, however, should come as no surprise. It is, after all, one of the deepest and most basic topics in all of philosophy.

See also: BUDDHIST CONCEPT OF EMPTINESS; EXISTENTIALISM; EXISTENTIALIST ETHICS; GOOD, THEORIES OF THE; NIHILISM

References and further reading

Baier, K. (1957) 'The Meaning of Life', in E.D. Klemke (ed.) *The Meaning of Life*, New York: Oxford University Press, 1981, 81–117. (Delivered originally as the inaugural lecture at the Australian National University in Canberra, this article defends the view that meaning in life is compatible with a secular worldview.)

* Camus, A. (1943) *Le Mythe de Sisyphe*, Paris: Gallimard; expanded edition, 1945; extended edition trans. J. O'Brien, 'The Myth of Sisyphus', in *The Myth of Sisyphus and Other Essays*, New York: Alfred A. Knopf, 1955, 1–102. (Classic discussion of the absurdity of the human condition and the proper response to it – defiance.)

* Feinberg, J. (1992) 'Absurd Self-Fulfillment', in *Free-*

dom and Fulfillment, Princeton, NJ: Princeton University Press. (Especially clear and accessible discussion of the idea of absurdity and of the kind of fulfilment that is possible in spite of it.)

Klemke, E.D. (ed.) (1981) *The Meaning of Life*, New York: Oxford University Press. (Anthology containing religious and secular accounts of the meaning of life, including portions of the Baier, Camus, Nagel, Taylor and Tolstoi pieces listed here.)

* Nagel, T. (1971) 'The Absurd', *Journal of Philosophy* 68 (20): 716–27; repr. in E.D. Klemke (ed.) *The Meaning of Life*, New York: Oxford University Press, 1981, 151–61. (Analyses absurdity as the clash between pretension and reality and advocates irony as the proper response.)

Nozick, R. (1981) *Philosophical Explanations*, Cambridge, MA: Harvard University Press, ch. 6. (Wide-ranging exploration of the idea of a meaning to life, analysing meaning as the transcending of limits in a wider context of value.)

* Schopenhauer, A. (1851) 'On the Sufferings of the World', trans. T.B. Saunders, in R. Taylor (ed.) *The Will to Live: Selected Writings of Arthur Schopenhauer*, New York: Ungar, 1967. (Presents a deeply pessimistic view about the misery and meaninglessness of human life, advocating suicide as a proper response. See also 'On the Vanity and Suffering of Life' and 'The Vanity of Existence' in this volume.)

* Taylor, R. (1970) *Good and Evil*, New York: Macmillan, ch. 18. (Argues that what makes life meaningful is subjects' attachments to the activities that occupy them.)

* Tolstoi, L. (1886) *Smert' Ivana Il'icha*, trans. A. Maude, *The Death of Ivan Il'ich*, New York: New American Library, 1960. (Vivid description of the sense that, in the face of death, one's life is meaningless.)

—— (1884) *Ispoved*, trans. A. Maude, *A Confession*, in *A Confession, The Gospel in Brief and What I Believe*, London: Oxford University Press, 1971. (Autobiographical account of being struck by the need to understand the meaning of life, and of finding the only acceptable answer in faith in God.)

* Wiggins, D. (1976) 'Truth, Invention, and the Meaning of Life', *Proceedings of the British Academy*, 62: 331–78; repr. in G. Sayre-McCord (ed.) *Essays on Moral Realism*, Ithaca, NY: Cornell University Press, 1988, 127–65. (Argues against a purely subjective account of meaning, in favour of a nonsubjective but anthropocentric analysis of value – difficult reading.)

Wolf, S. (1997) 'Happiness and Meaning: Two Aspects of the Good Life', *Social Philosophy & Policy* 14 (1): 207–25. (Expounds the view that

meaningfulness in life arises from active and subjectively fulfilling engagement in projects of objective worth.)

SUSAN WOLF

LIFE, ORIGIN OF

The appearance of maggots on meat or of intestinal tapeworms supported an ancient belief in the spontaneous generation of life. This idea was challenged in the seventeenth century but not abandoned before Pasteur's experiments. Scientists now agree that terrestrial life had a single origin, but differ in explanations. Some believe that life began with the onset of protein-based metabolism, supported by evidence of spontaneous abiotic amino acid synthesis and theoretical models of self-sustaining and evolving systems of enzymes. Others believe life began with the appearance of nucleic acid-based molecular replicators and have organized their research efforts around the vision of a primordial 'RNA world'.

Aristotle's observation that some life forms 'arise not from living animals but from putrescent matter' went largely unquestioned until the beginning of the seventeenth century. DESCARTES had no difficulty conceiving of spontaneous generation occurring simply on the basis of matter in motion, though subsequent Cartesian mechanists could not countenance the possibility of life arising spontaneously from nature – construed as passive and without inherent purpose. Their deistic alternative, theories of pre-existence and preformation, endeavoured to attribute all life forms to original acts of creativity. Subsequent generations were deemed to be held in miniature in the germs of their parents and new generations could 'evolve' from the old through the unfolding and elaboration of parts already in place. Committed to an extended regress of miniatures nested inside miniatures the doctrine of pre-existent germs became increasingly vulnerable. Where 'Cartesian matter' lacked the wherewithal to become self-organized, eighteenth-century scientists conceived of a 'Newtonian matter' upon which some uncharacterized force could operate (see MATTER). Natural self-organizing capacities were attributed to the existence of 'penetrating forces' shaped by an internal mould (see BUFFON, G.L.L. COMTE DE §3) or by the expansion and resistance of opposing 'vegetative' forces (Needham). Set in motion, the new theories of spontaneous generation were carried into the nineteenth century by both the French *philosophes* and the

German *Naturphilosophen* (see NATURPHILOSOPHIE §3). Where the former opposed a deistic Cartesianism that had become conservative with an uncompromised materialism that could do it all, the latter sought a romantic *rapprochement* of nature and culture, organic and inorganic, within the unity of *Geist*.

Nineteenth-century cell theory resulted in debates over whether cells could arise out of acellular protoplasm as postulated by Schwann (allowing for the possibility of spontaneous generation), or whether cells arise only from other cells (*omnis cellula e cellula*) as proclaimed by Virchow. Scientific opinion became grouped around the poles of mechanical materialism, whose adherents were committed to some form of abiogenesis (life from nonlife), and vitalism (including vital materialism) whose adherents could countenance heterogenesis (life from another form of life) but never abiogenesis (see VITALISM §2). The elucidation of the alternation of life cycles of trematodes led to the demise of any remaining belief in the heterogenesis of parasites from degenerating tissue, and Pasteur's experiments undermined belief in the abiogenetic origins of infusoria. By the end of the nineteenth century, German cytologists too had resolved that not only do cells arise by division from other cells, but even nuclei are never created *de novo*, arising only from previous nuclei. What remained of spontaneous generation was only the conviction of dedicated materialists that there *had* to have been an abiogenetic *origin of life*.

Buttressed by advances in astro-chemistry and cosmogony and a nascent biochemistry of organic catalysis, interest in theories of the origins of life re-emerged in the twentieth century with Oparin and Haldane's visions of a pre-biotic primordial soup from which self-sustaining aggregates of colloidal reactants emerged. Subsequent work proceeded along the lines of an opposition that had already begun to take shape during the 1920s. Whereas Oparin (1924, 1938) and Haldane (1929) looked to the onset of metabolism with an interpretation of life as a *process*, Muller (1929) identified the origins of life with the appearance of an entity, an as yet uncharacterized gene, distinguished by its ability to mutate and self-replicate. With metabolism associated with the catalytic activity of protein-based enzymes, and with genetic replicators (after Watson and Crick (1953)) identified with nucleic acids, that is, deoxyribonucleic acid and ribonucleic acid (DNA and RNA), which serve as templates for their own synthesis, debates about the origins of life have also been construed in terms of 'protein-first' versus 'nucleic acid-first' theories.

Replicator-first theories gained credence from

studies by Orgel and Eigen that demonstrated RNA synthesis in vitro in the absence of either an enzyme or a *prior* template, respectively, and further with the discovery by Cech (1986a, 1986b) of RNA-based catalytic activity. However strong evidence for the abiotic synthesis of nucleic acid *precursors*, or of the ability of RNA catalysts to synthesize arbitrary nucleic acid sequences, has been lacking. Metabolism-first theories gained credence from the studies by Muller that showed that amino acids, the precursors of proteins, may well have been present in an abiotic primitive soup, and from progressively more sophisticated mathematical modelling of the possible dynamics of complex autocatalytic systems.

Aspects of *both* the metabolism first and the replicator first theories can be found in a two-stage model proposed by Dyson (1985) which takes its cue from the dual activity of one small molecule. Adenosine triphosphate (ATP) functions universally in living cells as both the principal intermediary in energy metabolism and as one of the four precursors of nucleic acid synthesis. Postulating the emergence of life as protein-based metabolism, ATP (and perhaps other) nucleic acid precursors may thus be produced biosynthetically as metabolic intermediates. The first nucleic acids would then arise by the chance polymerization of accumulated ATPs. Owing to their ability to serve as templates for further nucleic acid synthesis, these polymers then emerged as intracellular parasites akin to viruses. Dyson hypothesizes a progressive symbiosis between these parasitic replicators, which become stable repositories of polymer information, and the 'host' metabolic system which continues to provide nucleic acid precursors.

This two-stage model preserves ontological implications of both points of view. Life appears, first of all, as the holistic cooperativity of complex auto-catalytic dynamics, yet remains contingently susceptible to 'selfish' short circuiting by 'born again' parasitic replicators.

See also: CHEMISTRY, PHILOSOPHICAL ASPECTS OF; EVOLUTION, THEORY OF; GENETICS; MOLECULAR BIOLOGY; UNITY OF SCIENCE

References and further reading

Aristotle (*c*.mid-4th century BC) *Generation of Animals* (De Generatione Animalium), trans. A.L. Peck, Cambridge, MA: Harvard University Press, 1942. (Spontaneous generation referred to in book one.)

Bernal, J.D. (ed.) (1967) *The Origin of Life*, London: Weidenfeld & Nicolson. (Interesting, albeit dated, discussion by the noted crystollographer and historian; includes reprints of the 1920s articles by Oparin and Haldane.)

Cairns-Smith, A.G. (1982) *Genetic Takeover and the Mineral Origins of Life*, Cambridge: Cambridge University Press. (Good summary of the crystal-as-template theory.)

* Cech, T.R. (1986a) 'A model for the RNA-catalyzed replication of RNA', *Proceedings of the National Academy of Sciences* 83, 4,360–3. (Cech received the Nobel prize for discovery of RNA catalysis.)

* —— (1986b) 'RNA as an enzyme', *Scientific American* 255: 64–75. (Accessible summary of the RNA as enzyme work which gave rise to the 'RNA world' model of the origins of life.)

Crick, F.H.C. (1981) *Life Itself*, New York: Simon & Schuster. (Crick's version of the panspermia hypothesis of life on earth derived from extraterrestrial seeds.)

Dawkins, R. (1976) *The Selfish Gene*, Oxford: Oxford University Press. (An uninhibited explication of the replicator-first ontology.)

De Duve, C. (1991) *Blueprint for a Cell: The Nature and Origin of Life*, Burlington, NC: Neil Patterson. (Contains excellent annotated bibliography.)

* Dyson, F. (1985) *Origins of Life*, Cambridge: Cambridge University Press. (Terse and clever, Dyson's book unites the protein-first and nucleic acid-first accounts into a two-stage model.)

Eigen, M. (1973) 'The Origin of Biological Information', in J. Mehra (ed.) *The Physicist's Conception of Nature*, Dordrecht: Reidel. (Detailed treatment of the hypercycle model which attempted to identify the origins of biological information in self-sustaining interactions between proteins and RNA.)

Eigen, M., Gardiner, W., Schuster, P. and Winkler-Oswatitsch, R. (1981) 'The Origin of Genetic Information', *Scientific American* 244: 88–118. (Accessible discussion of the RNA quasi-species and hypercycle ideas.)

Farley, J. (1974) *The Spontaneous Generation Controversy: From Descartes to Oparin*, Baltimore, MD: Johns Hopkins University Press. (Excellent survey of the antecedents, within modern science, to the contemporary debate about the origins of life.)

* Haldane, J.B.S. (1929) 'The Origin of Life', in *The Rationalist Annual*; repr. as an appendix in J.D. Bernal *The Origin of Life*, London: Weidenfeld & Nicolson, 1967. (Along with Oparin, one of the founding articles offering a 'protein-first' model.)

Joyce, G.F. (1993) 'Prospects for Understanding the Origin of the RNA World', in *The RNA World*, Cold Spring Harbor, NY: Cold Spring Harbor Laboratory Press. (Detailed discussion of experimental

evidence in support of the primordial RNA world hypothesis.)

Kauffman, S.A. (1993) *The Origins of Order: Self-Organization and Selection in Evolution*, New York: Oxford University Press. (Ambitious work by dynamic-systems theorist attempting to bring self-ordering phenomena into a neo-Darwinian framework.)

Lenoir, T. (1982) *The Strategy of Life: Teleology and Mechanics in Nineteenth Century German Biology*, Chicago, IL: University of Chicago Press. (An excellent account of the role of Kantian teleology in the formulation of modern embryology, physiology, cell theory and pathology.)

Margulis, L. (1970) *Origin of Eukaryotic Cells*, New Haven, CT: Yale University Press. (Fascinating account of the evolution of the eukaryotic cell through the symbiotic engulfment and association of prokaryotic cells.)

Muller, H.J. (1929) 'The Gene as the Basis of Life', *Proceedings of the International Congress of Plant Sciences* 1: 897–921; repr. in *Studies in Genetics: The Selected Papers of H.J. Muller*, Bloomington, IN: Indiana University Press, 1962. (Earliest exposition of a gene-first ontology.)

* Oparin, A.I. (1924) *Proiskhozhdenie zhizni*, Moscow: Moskovskii Rabochi; trans. A. Synge, repr. as an appendix in J.D. Bernal (ed.) *The Origin of Life*, London: Weidenfeld & Nicolson, 1967. (The article which initiated the contemporary debate on the origins of life.)

* —— (1938) *Origin of Life*, New York: Dover. (Oparin here takes dialectical materialism into account in his considerations of the origins of life.)

Roe, S.A. (1981) *Matter, Life, and Generation: Eighteenth-Century Embryology and the Haller–Wolff Debate*, Cambridge: Cambridge University Press. (Most accessible account of the eighteenth-century debate between preformationism and epigenesis.)

* Watson, J.D. and Crick, F.H.C. (1953) 'A Structure for Deoxyribose Nuleic Acid', *Nature* 4,356: 737–. (The classic paper on the structure of DNA.)

LENNY MOSS

LIMBO

According to traditional Roman Catholic teaching, limbo is the postmortem destination of those who have not been baptized, but are not guilty of sin. Lack of baptism bars such people from salvation, but their innocence means that they do not deserve the punishment of hell. They were thought to fall into two groups:

the righteous of the Old Covenant, prior to the redemption of Christ, and unbaptized children. The former were supposed to have gone to heaven after Christ's death, but the latter had to stay in limbo forever. The existence of limbo was never dogmatically defined, and it was never given as much attention as heaven, hell or even purgatory, each of which represented a fate which human beings earned in part through personal choice. Nowadays, the possibility that unbaptized babies might be consigned to hell is not widely entertained, and some thinkers hold that the requirement of baptism for salvation is open to interpretation. Consequently, the idea of limbo is not as widely discussed as it once was.

1   History of the idea of limbo
2   The status of limbo in contemporary thought

1   History of the idea of limbo

In traditional Roman Catholic theology, limbo is a place for certain of the dead who are deprived of salvation because they have not been baptized, but who do not suffer the punishment of hell. It was usually thought to consist of two distinct parts: a limbo of the fathers (*limbus patrum*), or 'bosom of Abraham', which was a place for the righteous of the Old Covenant who could not enter heaven before the redemption of Jesus Christ; and a children's limbo (*limbus infantium*), which was a place for unbaptized babies and young children prior to the age at which they could commit sin. Such children would be in a state of original sin, but innocent of personal guilt. The limbo of the fathers was said to be empty ever since Christ's descent into hell (limbo) after the crucifixion, when all its inhabitants were transported to heaven, but the babies in the children's limbo were supposed to remain there for all eternity.

There is no mention of limbo in the Bible, and the problem of the fate of unbaptized babies was not addressed until the fifth century in response to the Pelagians, who asserted that God does not deny deceased unbaptized infants eternal life, although they are not in heaven either. The Pelagians maintained that they are in a state of innocence, not damnation, where they experience no pain and have a measure of happiness. Augustine replied that these infants are condemned to hell, but their punishment is much milder than that of adults, and it is preferable to annihilation. Augustine's position seems harsh, but his primary interest in this matter was to use it to get the Pelagians to reveal the heresy at the heart of their doctrine – the denial of original sin (see PELAGIANISM; SIN §2). The Pelagians' view on infants who die without being baptized was thus a casualty of the debate over original sin. Ironically, their position is very close to the idea of limbo that developed seven centuries later.

In the Greek Church, Augustine's contemporary, Gregory of Nyssa, had written that unbaptized infants neither suffer the torments of hell nor enter the life of the blessed in heaven. Otherwise the Augustinian position was accepted for centuries and was not broken until Peter Abelard argued that unbaptized infants do not suffer the pains of hellfire, but only grief at separation from God. Peter Lombard agrees with Abelard in his *Sentences* (*c.*1145–51), saying that unbaptized infants suffer only 'darkness' in the world to come (*Sententiarum libri quatuor*, lib. II, dist. 33, cap. 2). This development was important because Lombard's *Sentences* became a kind of university textbook, with tremendous influence on subsequent theology. Bonaventure clearly distinguishes between the children's limbo and hell, saying that divine justice establishes children in a state of unchanging love and knowledge, but which is neither joyful nor sad (*Il Sent.*, d.33, a.3, q.2). On the other hand, Albert the Great, who invented the term 'limbo', combines limbo and hell (*De resurrectione*, part 3). Thomas Aquinas took Bonaventure's position, arguing that original sin is not a positive fault, but a privation. Since the punishment must fit the crime it would be unreasonable for God to give a positive punishment for something that is not a positive fault. In arguing against punishment through sensory pain, Aquinas says that if a human being's powers are to be harmed through such pain, the punishment must bear some relation to a fault in the person who used those powers. But there can be no such fault in the case of an infant, so punishment through sensory pain would be unreasonable (*De malo*, q.5, a.3).

The problem of limbo was not handled explicitly by the Council of Trent (1545–63) and subsequently it was treated as an open question. The existence of limbo subsequently became the subject of controversy, with the Augustinians and the Jansenists denying its existence and the Jesuits defending it. In this century it has been on the decline. It is not mentioned in the documents of Vatican II, the Ecumenical Council called by Pope John XXIII in the 1960s; while *Lumen gentium*, the 'Dogmatic Constitution on the Church', mentions briefly the necessity of baptism for salvation, it does not elaborate.

2   The status of limbo in contemporary thought

The limbo of the fathers has never received much attention, presumably because it is now supposed to be empty. The children's limbo, however, not only poses an obvious theological problem, but also a pastoral one: what should priests tell the grieving parents of a child who dies shortly after birth or, for that matter, in the womb? The proposal that there is a children's limbo arises out of two suppositions: that there is no salvation without baptism; and that unbaptized babies have made no personal choice whereby they would merit eternal punishment. The limbo of the fathers is predicated on the first assumption together with the assumption that the patriarchs of the Old Covenant would have gone to heaven had they lived after the time of Christ. The compromise position on the souls in these two limbos is that they are deprived of heavenly bliss (temporarily in the case of the patriarchs, and forever in the case of the unbaptized babies), but that they do not suffer. The justification for the limbo of the fathers has obvious extensions to other classes of persons who would have gone to heaven had they been in more favourable circumstances (such as the unbaptized in non-Christian countries), but these individuals were almost always placed in a different category. However, it is not at all clear why their status should not be parallel to that of the inhabitants of the *limbus patrum*. The latter were simply born at the wrong time; the former were simply born in the wrong place. An appreciation of this difficulty and admiration for the virtuous sages of antiquity led Dante, in the *Divina Commedia*, to propose a limbo of the sages, in which Socrates, Plato and Virgil were found. Dante's poetic power reflects an enduring sensibility, one which has probably outlasted the more traditional theological views on the fate of these people.

It seems odd that the tradition never questioned the assumption that there is no salvation without baptism, but only the assumption that those in limbo do not suffer the pains of hell. However, the concept of baptism was sometimes interpreted broadly enough to include some persons who had not actually gone through the sacramental rite. Aquinas proposed two categories, Baptism of Blood and Baptism of Desire, to handle some of the problematic cases, and there were frequent appeals to these categories in Catholic theology until Vatican II. It is even possible to interpret baptism so widely that it applies to everyone. For example, Bruno Webb (1953) has suggested that death itself might be a kind of sacrament from which the saving power of baptism arises. It has become increasingly common, however, simply to dispute the requirement of baptism for salvation. Among Protestant philosophers, Jonathan Kvanvig (1993) has argued that there is no good reason for the doctrine of limbo, since it arises from a combination of a very severe conception of hell and a

very restrictive conception of how it is possible to reach heaven.

The idea of limbo has therefore fallen into disuse, not because it is generally thought that the inhabitants of limbo are really in hell, but because it is often thought that they are in heaven. Moreover, the coherence of the concept has also been questioned. Ladislaus Boros argues that the notion of an exclusion from the human being's proper and intended end that is nevertheless not experienced as suffering is self-contradictory (see Hick 1976). More and more, there is doubt that baptism is essential for salvation, so there is a growing tendency to reject the primary assumption of the dilemma which the existence of limbo was intended to resolve.

See also: EVIL, PROBLEM OF; GRACE §3; HEAVEN; HELL; PURGATORY; SALVATION

References and further reading

* Aquinas, T. (1266–72) *Quaestiones disputatae de malo* (Disputed Questions on Evil), trans. J.T. Oesterle, Notre Dame, IN: University of Notre Dame Press, 1981, q.5, a.3. (Aquinas does not have a great deal to say about limbo, but his work should be consulted because of his importance in the history of Christian doctrine. See also *Summa theologiae* IIIa, q.69.)

Dyer, G.J. (1964) *Limbo: Unsettled Questions*, New York: Sheed & Ward. (A good summary of the history of the idea of limbo.)

* Hick, J. (1976) *Death and Eternal Life*, New York: Harper & Row. (An influential book, which includes a discussion of both Western and Eastern eschatologies; also discusses the position of Ladislaus Boros mentioned in the text.)

Hill, P.J. (1962) *The Existence of a Children's Limbo According to Post-Tridentine Theologians*, dissertation, Vatican City: Pontificia Universitas Gregoriana. (A good treatment of the history of the idea of the children's limbo, the limbo most discussed in theological history. Written prior to Vatican II.)

* Kvanvig, J.L. (1993) *The Problem of Hell*, New York: Oxford University Press. (This book is a philosophical treatment of the Christian idea of hell, but includes an argument against the idea of limbo on page 57.)

* Lombard, P. (*c.*1145–51) *Sententiae in IV libris distinctae* (Sentences in 4 Separate Books), 2 vols, ed. I.C. Brady, Grottaferrata: Collegi S. Bonaventura ad Claras Aquas, 3rd rev. edn, 1971–81, Libri quatuor, lib. II, dist. 33, cap. 2. (A discussion of the fate of unbaptized infants which had a strong influence on subsequent medieval theology.)

* Webb, B. (1953) 'Unbaptized Infants and the Quasi-Sacrament of Death', *The Downside Review* (Summer): 243–57. (An example of the attempt to defend the salvation of unbaptized infants by broadening the concept of baptism.)

LINDA ZAGZEBSKI

LIN-CHI *see* LINJI

LINEAR LOGIC

Linear logic was introduced by Jean-Yves Girard in 1987. Like classical logic it satisfies the law of the excluded middle and the principle of double negation, but, unlike classical logic, it has non-degenerate models. Models of logics are often given only at the level of provability, in that they provide denotations of formulas. However, we are also interested in models which provide denotations of deductions, or proofs. Given such a model two proofs are said to be equivalent if their denotations are equal. A model is said to be 'degenerate' if there are no formulas for which there exist at least two non-equivalent proofs. It is easy to see that models of classical logic are essentially degenerate because any formula is either true or false and so all proofs of a formula are considered equivalent. The intuitionist approach to this problem involves altering the meaning of the logical connectives but linear logic attacks the very connectives themselves, replacing them with more refined ones. Despite this there are simple translations between classical and linear logic.

One can see the need for such a refinement in another way. Both classical and intuitionistic logics could be said to deal with static truths; both validate the rule of modus ponens: if $A \rightarrow B$ and A, then B; but both also validate the rule if $A \rightarrow B$ and A, then $A \wedge B$. In mathematics this is correct since a proposition, once verified, remains true – it persists. Many situations do not reflect such persistence but rather have an additional notion of causality. An implication $A \rightarrow B$ should reflect that a state B is accessible from a state A and, moreover, that state A is no longer available once the transition has been made. An example of this phenomenon is in chemistry where an implication $A \rightarrow B$ represents a reaction of components A to yield B. Thus if two hydrogen and one oxygen atoms bond to form a water molecule, they are consumed in the process and are no longer part of the current state. Linear logic provides logical connectives to describe such refined interpretations.

1 **Syntax**
2 **Models**
3 **Decidability**
4 **Applications**

1 Syntax

Given these new interpretations of implication and conjunction, they are given new symbols: '⊸' and '⊗', respectively. Thus the chemical reaction mentioned above would be given symbolically as $(H \otimes H \otimes O) \multimap W$.

Despite the appeal of these refined connectives it is clear that our logic is very weak: a formula can be used once only (hence the term 'linear'). To describe situations of static truths, where formulas can be reused (that is, allowed to persist) or ignored, we introduce a new logical connective '!' where $!A$ means that the formula A may be used as many times as needed (including zero). Thus the traditional notion of implication can be simulated by $(!A) \multimap B$. This idea leads to simple translations of both classical and intuitionistic logics into linear logic.

Given two transitions $A \multimap B$ and $A \multimap C$, we clearly have the transition $(A \otimes A) \multimap (B \otimes C)$, but not $A \multimap (B \otimes C)$. However, we shall define a new transition $A \multimap (B \,\&\, C)$, which represents the superimposition of the two transitions. It represents a choice of the resulting state B or C. Despite its disjunctive feel the connective '&' is really a conjunction – both states are being offered but only one may be chosen, via one of the axioms $(A \,\&\, B) \multimap A$, $(A \,\&\, B) \multimap B$. Consequently linear logic has two forms of conjunction, one (⊗) where the initial states are disjoint and one (&) where they are identical. The former is known as a multiplicative connective and the latter as additive. Symmetrically linear logic has two forms of disjunction, the multiplicative form written '⅋' and the additive form written '⊕'.

Linear formulas are built up from a collection of (positive and negative) atomic formulas, written p and $p^\perp$, by means of the multiplicative connectives, '⊗' and '⅋', additive connectives, '&' and '⊕' and the so-called exponentials, '!' and its dual '?'. The connectives have units (in the sense that in classical logic true (T) is a unit for conjunction (∧), as $A \wedge T \equiv A$): two multiplicative units, 1 and ⊥, and two additive units, ⊤ and 0; such that $A \otimes 1 \equiv A$, $A \,⅋\, \perp \equiv A$, $A \,\&\, \top \equiv A$ and $A \oplus 0 \equiv A$. (The logical symbols used here match Girard's rather idiosyncratic selection, apart from '⅋' which Girard writes as an upside-down ampersand.)

As with classical logic, negation, written $A^\perp$, is a defined notion given inductively over a composite formula. This is given by:

$(p^\perp)^\perp$ is p

$(A \otimes B)^\perp$ is $A^\perp \star B^\perp$

$(A \star B)^\perp$ is $A^\perp \otimes B^\perp$

$(A \,\&\, B)^\perp$ is $A^\perp \oplus B^\perp$

$(A \oplus B)^\perp$ is $A^\perp \,\&\, B^\perp$

$1^\perp$ is $\perp$

$\perp^\perp$ is 1

$\top^\perp$ is 0

$0^\perp$ is $\top$

$(!A)^\perp$ is $?(A^\perp)$

$(?A)^\perp$ is $!(A^\perp)$.

Also as with classical logic, we are able to define an implication using negation and disjunction: thus $A \multimap B$ is $A^\perp \star B$.

Gentzen's sequent calculus (see NATURAL DEDUCTION, TABLEAU AND SEQUENT SYSTEMS §2) is a tool for studying various rules of logics. Sequents are written $\Gamma \vdash \Delta$, where $\Gamma (= A_1, \ldots, A_n)$ and $\Delta (= B_1, \ldots, B_m)$ are finite sets of formulas. The traditional reading of such sequents is that $A_1 \wedge \ldots \wedge A_n$ implies $B_1 \vee \ldots \vee B_m$. In the linear setting it says that $A_1 \otimes \ldots \otimes A_n$ implies $B_1 \star \ldots \star B_m$. However, we can employ a shorthand by considering only sequents of the form $\vdash \Delta$, where general sequents of the form $\Gamma \vdash \Delta$ are simulated using $\vdash \Gamma^\perp, \Delta$. The main rules are as follows.

$$\frac{}{\vdash p, p^\perp} \quad \text{(identity)}$$

$$\frac{\vdash \Gamma, A \qquad \vdash A^\perp, \Delta}{\vdash \Gamma, \Delta} \quad \text{(cut)}$$

$$\frac{}{\vdash 1} \; (1) \qquad \frac{\vdash \Gamma}{\vdash \Gamma, \perp} \; (\perp)$$

$$\frac{\vdash \Gamma, A \qquad \vdash \Delta, B}{\vdash \Gamma, \Delta, A \otimes B} \quad \text{(tensor)}$$

$$\frac{\vdash \Gamma, A, B}{\vdash \Gamma, A \star B} \quad \text{(par)}$$

$$\frac{\vdash \Gamma, A \qquad \vdash \Gamma, B}{\vdash \Gamma, A \,\&\, B} \quad \text{(with)}$$

$$\frac{\vdash \Gamma, A}{\vdash \Gamma, A \oplus B} \quad (\text{sum}_1)$$

$$\frac{\vdash \Gamma, B}{\vdash \Gamma, A \oplus B} \quad (\text{sum}_2)$$

$$\frac{\vdash \Gamma}{\vdash \Gamma, ?A} \quad \text{(weakening)}$$

$$\frac{\vdash \Gamma, ?A, ?A}{\vdash \Gamma, ?A} \quad \text{(contraction)}$$

$$\frac{\vdash \Gamma, A}{\vdash \Gamma, ?A} \quad \text{(dereliction)}$$

$$\frac{\vdash ?\Gamma, A}{\vdash ?\Gamma, !A} \quad \text{(promotion)}$$

The difference between the multiplicative and additive connectives can be seen quite clearly by comparing the 'tensor' and 'with' rules. As is the case normally, writing the sequents in a two-sided fashion, and restricting the right-hand side so as to contain at most one formula (for example, $\Gamma \vdash A$), results in the so-called intuitionistic fragment of linear logic. It should be noted that some of the connectives are not available in the intuitionistic fragment. The sequent calculus formulation enjoys the important metatheoretic property of cut elimination (Gentzen's *Hauptsatz*), that is, there is an algorithm which rewrites any proof into one which does not make use of the 'cut' rule.

Girard also showed how one may refine the sequent calculus formulation further by replacing the sequents with graphs. Thus formulas become nodes and applications of the rules become methods for transforming graphs. For example, the 'identity' rule is replaced with two nodes (p and $p^\perp$) and an arc between them, whereas the tensor rule takes the two nodes A and B and places arcs between them and a new node $A \otimes B$. These graphs are known as 'proof nets'. Several sequent proofs are represented by a single proof net and so one may think of proof nets as revealing the essential inner structure of a linear logic proof.

2 Models

An important feature of linear logic is that its models need not be degenerate, in the sense given earlier. This is in contrast to classical logic. Using the mathematical language of category theory it is relatively easy to describe abstractly which structures are necessary for a model of linear logic: essentially they form particular categories first identified in the 1970s by Barr (see Barr 1991; CATEGORY THEORY, INTRODUCTION TO). A further problem is to construct concrete models, which are ideally complete (that is, they contain only denotations of provable formulas and valid deductions).

Girard offered two models of linear logic in his seminal 1987 paper. The first, 'phase spaces', is a model based on a certain sort of algebraic structure. The second, 'coherent spaces', is a graph-theoretic model. A large number of different models have since been identified and again it should be stressed that all of these models are non-degenerate.

An appealing model was given by Blass (1992), based on earlier work on constructive logic by Lorenzen. Here the meaning of a proposition A is given by specifying a game, or dialogue, between two players, one of whom is trying to assert A and the other refute it. Thus a proposition is interpreted as a game and validity by a winning strategy. The connectives can then be understood as operations on games. For example, the connective '$\otimes$' is interpreted as an operation which interleaves two disjoint games or, in other words, plays them side by side. These refined notions of games have been the subject of some intensive work. Despite this effort, and the intuitive appeal of the approach, these models suffer from being incomplete – they validate additional axioms, mostly 'weakening': $A \multimap 1$. Some models validate an additional axiom, known as 'mix': $(A \otimes B) \multimap (A \star B)$. The status of this axiom (which can also be given as a sequent calculus rule) is uncertain but may be decided by a convincing (game) model. Indeed providing a convincing complete model still remains an open problem.

3 Decidability

One can gain a useful insight into a logic by considering how difficult it is to decide whether a given formula is provable in that logic. Most first-order logics are undecidable but there is considerable variety when considering propositional logics. Both propositional classical logic and propositional intuitionistic logic are decidable albeit with differing complexity ($\mathcal{NP}$-complete and $\mathcal{PSPACE}$-complete, respectively; see COMPLEXITY, COMPUTATIONAL §4). Given that we can encode both these logics into linear logic one might expect linear logic to be decidable. Surprisingly it has been shown that propositional linear logic is undecidable. Indeed even the intuitionistic fragment of linear logic is undecidable. A considerable amount of work exists considering the decidability and complexity of various fragments of linear logic obtained by selecting a subset of the connectives and units.

4 Applications

As linear logic is a refined version of both classical and intuitionistic logic, it is not surprising that it has been applied to many areas of mathematical logic and theoretical computer science. Linear logic's refined connectives and notion of proof offer a new understanding of classical logic's connectives and proof deductions. In particular the notion of proof dynamics – the process of cut elimination mentioned in §1 – can be studied with improved accuracy using proof nets. As there are simple translations from classical to linear logic, it is possible to use the non-degenerate models of linear logic to tease out non-degenerate models for classical logic. Many researchers refer to this process as the extraction of the 'constructive content of classical logic'.

Logic is used by computer scientists in many ways to represent computation. One method is to represent a program as a proof and computation as the process of simplifying the proof or, in other words, bringing it to a normal form (see COMPUTABILITY THEORY §3). Another method is to represent a program as a set of rules and a goal, and computation as the process of searching for a proof of the goal given the rules. Given its refined nature, linear logic sheds new light on both these methods.

Importantly, deriving from some of the ideas of the game models described in §2, linear logic appears naturally to encode a process of computation which is inherently parallel in nature. Realizing this process and relating it to existing models of parallel computation is another important open area.

See also: LOGICAL AND MATHEMATICAL TERMS, GLOSSARY OF

References and further reading

* Barr, M. (1991) '$\star$-Autonomous Categories and Linear Logic', *Mathematical Structures in Computer Science* 1: 159–78. (A summary of earlier work by Barr which is re-considered in the light of linear logic.)

* Blass, A. (1992) 'A Game Semantics for Linear Logic', *Annals of Pure and Applied Logic* 56: 183–220. (A detailed presentation of the game model discussed in §2.)

* Girard, J.-Y. (1987) 'Linear Logic', *Theoretical Computer Science* 50: 1–101. (The original paper and still essential reading.)

Girard, J.-Y., Lafont, Y. and Regnier, L. (eds) (1995) *Advances in Linear Logic*, Cambridge: Cambridge University Press, esp. 1–42, 109–22. (Essentially a collection of research papers but includes an introduction to linear logic by Girard and a survey of decidability results by Lincoln.)

Hyland, J.M.E. (1997) 'Game Semantics', in A.M. Pitts and P. Dybjer (eds) *Semantics and Logics of Computation*, Cambridge: Cambridge University

Press. (A clear tutorial on how to construct particular game models of linear logic.)

Troelstra, A.S. (1992) *Lectures on Linear Logic*, CSLI Lecture Notes 29, Stanford, CA: Center for the Study of Language and Information. (A broad but rapid treatment of linear logic.)

G.M. BIERMAN

LINGUISTIC DISCRIMINATION

'Linguistic discrimination' is a redundancy. Discriminating is at the heart of what languages do. The question, of course, is when they can be said to do it invidiously, or rather when we, in our use of language, can be said to be discriminating invidiously. In Aristotelian terms, the proper use of linguistic discriminations is to make the right sort and number of discriminations in the right ways and at the right times – that is, not to discriminate between those things that, for the legitimate purposes at hand, ought to be seen as the same; to discriminate between those things that, for the legitimate purposes at hand, ought to be seen as different; and to discriminate in ways that advance legitimate and not illegitimate purposes. Disputes about what constitutes linguistic discrimination (in the invidious sense) revolve around both the legitimacy of our purposes and, in the light of those purposes, the aptness of particular discriminations. Such disputes presume both that our language shapes our actions (that linguistic discrimination plays a role in maintaining unjust inequalities) and that our actions can shape our language (that acknowledging such discrimination can and should lead to linguistic change).

1 **Arguments for causality and remediability**
2 **Taxonomic schemes**
3 **The paradigmatic and the generic**
4 **Stereotyping and stigmatizing**
5 **Value-laden terminology**
6 **Languages and dialects**

1 Arguments for causality and remediability

Claims for the causal efficacy of linguistic discrimination range from the claim that some thoughts are made either unavoidable or impossible because of the language in which thinking occurs, to the claim that language shapes, without determining, how we think. The stronger claim, often appealing to the Sapir-Whorf hypothesis, sees language as providing the conceptual tools without which the experienced world

is inchoate and only in terms of which can sense be made (see SAPIR-WHORF HYPOTHESIS). In its strongest form, this hypothesis is surely false: language-users are inventive, and all languages have room for invention.

It is harder to refute the view that the languages we use do shape our thoughts, making some ways of thinking more 'natural', more readily comprehended by our interlocutors, harder to avoid if they come to seem problematic. Richly nuanced vocabularies exist to describe some parts of the experienced world and not others. Nor are all the differences semantic: Black English is less well suited than is Standard English for expressing the agentless passive, that is, the idea that 'it happened' without indicating that someone or other did something (Jordan 1985).

That the language we use does not absolutely constrain us is no reason not to attend to the ways in which it shapes our thinking, leading us to imply what we do not intend, or making it difficult for us to say what we mean, or what we would mean if we had the words to mean it with. It is also remediable. Languages constantly change in response to an indefinite range of social forces; and while there can be no guarantee that a suggested reform will catch on, there is no reason a priori to argue that it could not do so. One may choose to resist it, but that choice is as political as is the argument for change.

2 Taxonomic schemes

Metaphysicians have long debated the nature of kinds. Are some of them 'natural' (whatever that means)? Are only such kinds, if there are any, 'real'? What about kinds created by our taxonomizing practices? Inspired largely by the work of Michel FOUCAULT, theorists are examining the social and political contexts within which taxonomies operate and the value judgments they both depend on and reinforce (see Root 1993). Case studies explore the social construction of race (Goldberg 1990) and gender (Lorber 1994); as well as of kinds of practices such as sexual harassment (MacKinnon 1979) and child abuse (Hacking 1992), conditions such as premenstrual syndrome (Zita 1988), life stages such as childhood (Aries 1962), and persons such as homosexuals (Stein 1992) and heterosexuals (Katz 1990). Questions about invidious discrimination arise with respect to kinds that arguably rest on dubious science or on politically questionable social practices.

Thus racial classifications have been argued to be discriminatory because they are biologically unfounded, on the assumption that races, if 'real', are so because of discoverable biological differences between different racial populations. Since there appear not to be such differences, racial classifications distinguish as different those who, on the alleged basis, are in fact the same. Alternatively, it can be argued that race is best understood as a social classification, in which case the issue is whether as such race can be made coherent and, if so, whether the social practices that make it coherent are just. If racial classification cannot be made coherent, then it is discriminatory for distinguishing between people who, on its own terms, are not distinguishable; if it is coherent but grounded on unjust social practices, then racial classification would be invidiously discriminatory because it was wrong to engage in the practices that make it descriptively correct. Others argue that, although founded on racist practices, racial classification has acquired a conceptually adequate grounding in practices that include those of anti-racist resistance and positive group identification (see RACE, THEORIES OF). Similar questions are raised about the classifying of persons as homosexual or heterosexual: apart from social practices of stigmatizing homosexuality as unnatural, perverse or sick, what reasons are there for classifying persons according to whether they desire those of the same or the opposite gender (see SEXUALITY, PHILOSOPHY OF)?

The situation is somewhat different regarding discrimination by gender (see LANGUAGE AND GENDER). There is better reason than in the case of race to regard the distinction between males and females as grounded in biology, although it is a matter of dispute whether the social practices that at the very least build upon, extend and 'clean up' the biological differences are morally and politically justifiable. But there is a further question: gender ascription, in English and in many other languages, is uniquely non-optional, in particular because of the gender inflection of pronouns. This ubiquitous marking of gender is arguably discriminatory, implying that, unlike all the other equally real differences between people, gender is ubiquitously relevant. (Similarly, the argument for the use of 'Ms' rests not on the wrongness of distinguishing between unmarried and married women but on the wrongness of requiring that such a distinction be marked whenever a woman is referred to by title.) Ubiquitous gender-marking is part of the social construction of gender, both in making gender neutrality difficult to express even when it is agreed to be appropriate and in making gender ambiguity socially stigmatizing even when it is acknowledged to be possible.

3 The paradigmatic and the generic

Semantic spaces are complex: not all unquestionable members of a class are equally paradigmatic. It seems to be a feature of human cognition to learn categories by grouping members around paradigmatic exemplars, and variation in paradigms is not for the most part idiosyncratic. It is a matter of dispute how much of the contouring of semantic space is 'hard-wired', but it is clear that for at least many categories, paradigmatic exemplars owe that status to culturally variable, frequently unjust, social arrangements.

Thus, it has been pointed out (Spelman 1988) that within racist cultures, white people are paradigmatic and people of colour are variously 'different', so that even anti-racist arguments claim that for all relevant purposes, people of colour are 'just like' white people. Similarly for other forms of privilege: those who are, for example, male or middle-class or heterosexual are paradigmatic in the sense that their achievements, interests and needs are taken as the measures against which those of others are evaluated. When, however, the category is itself a subordinate one, paradigmatic exemplars are likely to be members of a relevantly subordinated group. In either case, those who conform to the paradigm are typically 'unmarked', while those who are not paradigmatic are 'marked': 'male nurse', 'gay author'.

It is a matter of controversy the extent to which such language is itself discriminatory, rather than just accurately reflecting reality. The arguments for claiming specifically linguistic discrimination point out that being in the majority and being paradigmatic are not always the same thing and, even when they are, linguistic discrimination helps to maintain, rather than innocently reflecting, social discrimination.

A limiting case of the paradigmatic is the false generic. False generics are terms for the paradigmatic members of a group improperly used to refer to all members. It has been a matter of controversy whether in English masculine nouns and pronouns are also, ambiguously, genuinely generic, or whether they should be regarded as false generics. The arguments for the latter position are both linguistic and political. Linguistic arguments (see Mercier 1995) point to the often irresolvable ambiguities that result from the employment of the masculine as generic, as well as to the anomalous and illogical rules that govern such employment. Political arguments point to the advantages that accrue to those who are taken to be generically human, rather than 'different', and to the alienation increasingly experienced by female listeners and readers uncertain of the extent to which, if at all, they are included among the 'men' under discussion.

4 Stereotyping and stigmatizing

Another type of linguistic discrimination concerns the vocabulary used to refer to members of privileged and subordinated groups and, by analogy, parts of the nonhuman world that are variously associated with them. Tropes of light and darkness, for example, are central to European discussions of reason, especially those that were articulated concurrently with the colonization of Africa – the 'dark continent' – to which Europeans had the right and duty to bring 'enlightenment'. Gender stereotypes permeate talk about 'mother' nature, the 'hard' versus the 'soft' sciences, 'active' reason versus the 'passions'. Such vocabulary relies on and reinforces stereotypes that are inextricably bound up with socially discriminatory practices and, for reasons similar to those given in §3, can be argued to constitute linguistic discrimination.

Stigmatizing vocabulary, whether used to refer directly to members of stigmatized groups or derivatively to things associated with such groups, exemplifies linguistic discrimination not so much in how the group in question is being distinguished but in how language is being used in reference to them. The clearest examples are derogatory terms applied on the basis of race, gender, sexuality, disability, national origin, religion, and so forth. A related form of linguistic discrimination is the use of terms referring to stigmatized groups as negative characterizations: 'Indian-giver' or 'Jewing someone down'. Implicitly or explicitly gendered vocabulary typically encodes problematically stereotypical views concerning, for example, the different valuations of male versus female sexuality and assertiveness. Language referring to disabilities is often problematically generalized in ways that imply, for example, that blindness stands in the way of 'seeing' what follows from a set of premises.

Even when such forms of linguistic discrimination are not blatantly bigoted, there is good reason to avoid them, given the usual desirability of communicating as clearly as possible what is intended to the intended audience. Increasingly, audiences are reading discriminatory intent in the use of discriminatory language (including the supposedly generic masculine), and such reading habits are not in the power of authors to circumvent. To the extent that it is no part of authorial intent either to communicate negative or marginalizing attitudes towards members of particular groups, or to exclude members of such groups (and their allies) from one's audience, it is wise to eschew vocabulary that will predictably have those effects.

5 Value-laden terminology

Whether or not it is in theory possible for the discriminations made by some particular language (or part of a language) to reflect only morally and

politically non-tendentious judgments of similarity and difference, it is clear that such neutrality does not characterize a large number of the distinctions made in the languages we actually use. Public discussions are significantly shaped, in ways that frequently elude explicit debate, by the language in which the issues are framed. A central tenet of moral and political thinking is that like cases ought to be treated alike; consequently the crux of many arguments lies in judgments of similarity and difference, carried out in language that can make some of those judgments nearly automatic and others virtually unthinkable.

Examples abound, from military euphemisms that draw attention towards the achievement of strategic objectives and away from killing people, to abortion debates that pit those who favour choice against those who would coerce child-bearing or those who are pro-life against those who would kill babies. Mainstream press coverage in the USA distinguishes between freedom-fighters and terrorists in ways that map not the activities in which those individuals and groups engage so much as their congruence with or opposition to US foreign policy. Large-scale violence in inner city communities is thought of in one way when called a 'riot', in another when called an 'uprising'.

The notion of an 'essentially contested concept' (Gallie 1956) raises similar questions. Such concepts are deeply value-laden, carrying strongly positive or negative connotations: 'democracy' or 'repression'. Disputants typically share a small core of paradigmatic exemplars and differ over which additional examples are relevantly similar. A discriminatory use of an essentially contested concept would be one that applied and withheld the term in ways that are argued to be either undermotivated or motivated in problematic ways.

The point is not that we ought to eschew language that encodes controversial judgments of similarity and difference. Rather, we should be aware of what is encoded in our language and ready to argue for the judgments expressed therein and to challenge those of others with which we disagree. To call a particular use of language discriminatory goes beyond the claim that it implies a disputable judgment: rather, it commits one to arguing for why and how that judgment ought to be disputed.

6 Languages and dialects

The historical development of languages has gone on in tandem with the histories of the formation of nations, the spread of and resistance to colonization and imperialism, the globalization of culture and the influence of nationalist movements, and the development and spread of communication technologies.

Language is typically bound up with national identity, often in complex and contradictory ways. For example, movements of African nationalism sometimes embrace the language of the colonizer as the language of national unity, rather than divisively choosing among a number of indigenous languages.

Questions about whether something is a language, rather than a dialect, or a dialect, rather than a degraded use of language, will always raise contentious issues concerning present usage and users, as well as about their histories. Charges of discrimination will be appropriate when such judgments appear to be ethnocentric or otherwise biased, as, for example, in the controversy over whether American Black English is a legitimate dialect. The argument that it is rests on pointing out the rule-governed nature of its syntactic, semantic and phonological differences from Standard English, and on the history of its development from the interaction of West African languages with English (Smitherman 1977).

Languages and dialects are attached to particular groups of people, who are related to other groups in frequently hierarchical ways, and those hierarchies are reflected in the ways in which the languages and dialects are thought of and treated. Attempts are sometimes made to maintain the 'purity' of a language by codifying a version of it that carries both historical and present day prestige. Educational systems typically single out certain dialects as 'standard' or 'received': as the paradigmatic exemplars of the language they tend to be regarded not as dialects, but as the language itself, unmarked. Similarly, some speech patterns count as 'accents', and different accents lead to different stereotypical ascriptions of intelligence and social standing.

Reflecting the dominance of the USA following the Second World War, English is increasingly the global language – used, for example, in commerce, electronic communications, aviation and science – a development that privileges those who speak it fluently and marginalizes or threatens the survival of other languages. To regard the globalization of English as discriminatory is to regard that situation as other than natural, inevitable or equitably beneficial. Discrimination is also an issue when it comes to the semantic, syntactic and phonological diversity of English as spoken in different countries. Britain and the USA each have large amounts of rather different sorts of clout when it comes to determining whether or not something counts as 'proper' English, while even native English speakers from elsewhere are generally regarded as speaking either incorrectly or in a substandard dialect.

See also: DISCRIMINATION

References and further reading

* Aries, P. (1962) *Centuries of Childhood*, London: Jonathan Cape. (On the 'invention' of childhood. One of the earliest discussions of how an apparently natural kind – children – can be socially constructed.)
* Christensen, F.M. (1994) '"Sexual Harassment" Must Be Eliminated', *Public Affairs Quarterly* 8: 1–17. (Argues against the legitimacy of the concept of sexual harassment.)
* Gallie, W.B. (1956) 'Essentially Contested Concepts', *Proceedings of the Aristotelian Society* 56: 167–98. (Explanation of the concept referred to in §5.)
* Goldberg, D.T. (ed.) (1990) *Anatomy of Racism*, Minneapolis, MN: University of Minnesota Press. (Includes essays on the nature of racial classification and a bibliography.)
* Hacking, I. (1992) 'World-making by Kind-making: Child abuse for example', in M. Douglas and D. Hull (eds) *How Classification Works: Nelson Goodman among the Social Sciences*, Edinburgh: Edinburgh University Press. (This volume includes other relevant essays on the nature of kinds in relation to Goodman's work on similarity.)
* Jordan, J. (1985) 'Nobody Mean More to Me than You and the Future Life of Willie Jordan', in *On Call: Political Essays*, Boston, MA: South End Press. (Discussion of the expressive resources of Black English and of the practical choices about its use.)
* Katz, J.N. (1990) 'The Invention of Heterosexuality', *Socialist Review* 20: 7–34. (Argues that heterosexuality as an identity or 'sexual orientation' – no less than homosexuality – is distinctively modern.)
* Lorber, J. (1994) *Paradoxes of Gender*, New Haven, CT: Yale University Press. (Critical overview of the social construction of gender; includes extensive bibliography.)
* MacKinnon, C.A. (1979) *Sexual Harassment of Working Women*, New Haven, CT: Yale University Press. (Germinal text for the recognition of sexual harassment as a distinctive type of activity.)
  Matsuda, M.J., Lawrence III, C.R., Delgado, R. and Crenshaw, K.W. (1993) *Words that Wound: Critical Race Theory, Assaultive Speech, and the First Amendment*, Boulder, CO: Westview Press. (Arguments for the assaultive power of language and about the legal consequences of recognizing that power, especially in light of the US constitutional protection of the freedom of speech.)
* Mercier, A. (1995) 'A Perverse Case of the Contingent A Priori: On the logic of emasculating language (A reply to Dawkins and Dummett)', *Philosophical Topics* 23: 221–59. (Arguments, some linguistically

technical, against the allegedly generic use of masculine language.)

* Root, M. (1993) *Philosophy of Social Science*, Oxford: Blackwell. (Chapter 10, 'Sorting data into kinds', discusses the ways in which kinds can be socially constructed.)

Shapiro, M. (ed.) (1984) *Language and Politics*, New York: New York University Press. (Includes Foucault's 'The Order of Discourse' as well as a number of other, methodologically diverse essays on the language of politics and the politics of language.)

* Smitherman, G. (1977) *Talkin and Testifyin: The Language of Black America*, Detroit, MI: Wayne State University Press. (Arguments for the legitimacy of Black English, an account of its history, and outlines of its syntax, semantics and pragmatics.)

* Spelman, E.V. (1988) *Inessential Woman: Problems of Exclusion in Feminist Thought*, Boston, MA: Beacon Press. (Includes a discussion of the ways in which dominant (in this case white) members of a group (women) come to be the paradigmatic or even the sole understood referent of the generic term.)

Stein, E. (ed.) (1992) *Forms of Desire: Sexual Orientation and the Social Constructionist Controversy*, New York and London: Routledge. (Philosophically framed collection of essays on what it means, and whether or not it is true to say that, in particular, homosexuality as an identity or 'sexual orientation' is distinctively modern. Includes a bibliography.)

* Zita, J.N. (1988) 'The Premenstrual Syndrome: Dis-easing the female cycle', *Hypatia* 3: 77–99. (Arguments for the role of masculine bias in the characterization of PMS and in the social construction of the 'clinical body'.)

NAOMI SCHEMAN

LINGUISTIC RELATIVITY
see SAPIR-WHORF HYPOTHESIS

LINGUISTICS, PHILOSOPHY OF *see* LANGUAGE, PHILOSOPHY OF

LINGUISTICS, STRUCTURALISM IN
see STRUCTURALISM IN LINGUISTICS

LINJI (810/15–67)

Linji was one of the most reputed, and influential Chinese Chan masters in the history of East Asian Buddhism. He belonged to a school which advocates sudden enlightenment without dependence on words: there is an extralinguistic reality that can be intuitively apprehended through the rigorous meditative training. A person with this intuition escapes dualistic thinking and has grasped the freedom to act decisively, utilizing creatively whatever is presented before him/her. Linji's method of teaching is often characterized as 'thundering shouts and showering sticks', actions which are used to effect an awakening in his disciples. His reputation rests primarily on his ability to seize on this opportunity.

Linji Yixuan, a native of Nanhua county, became a monk at an early age, and studied *vinaya*, the *sūtras* and their commentaries extensively. Unable to gain peace of mind through textual studies, however, he changed to Chan (in Japanese, Zen) Buddhism under the tutelage of Huangbo (?–850). The *Linjilu* describes his dedication to Chan meditation as pure and single-minded. He attained great enlightenment through the assistance of both Huangbo and Dayu, prior to which event he said he was 'totally in the dark'. After twenty years with Huangbo, Linji moved in 849–50 to a temple in Zhengding county of Hebei province, where he taught his disciples for some ten years until his death at the Xinghua Temple. Posthumously, he was given the title 'Chan Master of Illuminating Wisdom'. The *Linjilu*, a record of his sermons, critical examinations and a biography, was compiled in 1120 by Yuanjue Zongyan.

Linji's philosophy focuses on the affirmation of the 'here and now' in the everyday world by bringing at a stroke the transcendental world (that is, the world of *buddhas* and patriarchs) into this world by collapsing the distinction between them. For example, we find in the *Linjilu* that 'there is a true person of no rank in a red chunk of your flesh, and it always comes and goes out of your face'. The 'true person of no rank' refers to the transparent light which, though invisible to ordinary eyes, shines forth in one's daily activities ('your face'). Because the light permeates the person as they originally are, the person lacks nothing, and in order to be emancipated from the sufferings and struggles encountered while living in the world and beyond, all one has to do is to come to this awakening. However, this awakening is paradoxical in that 'if you try to seek it, it retreats into the distance, and if you don't seek it, it appears before your eyes'.

The paradox arises, Linji observed, because the ordinary person suffers from a 'dis-ease' in the pursuit of the Buddha Way. He attributed the cause mainly to the lack of self-confidence. Doubts created in the mind cause the mind to fluctuate, chasing thoughts or images one after another: the fluctuating mind operates on the basis of dependence on people, language and things, through which the mind enters a conditioning process of transformation with the external world. Unable to discern this transformational process and mistaking it to be real, the ordinary person accepts the phenomena thus presented. For Linji, however, these are simply metamorphosing illusions and delusions, and are 'self-binding without any rope'. True reality discloses itself in a clear illumination beyond any dependence upon people, language and things.

Linji's cure for the 'dis-ease' was to discover the mind that does not fluctuate by achieving the stillness of meditation, and thereby to disengage it from the dependent, conditioning process of transformation so that the mind becomes immovable. He called it the one (unified and unifying) mind. If the mind is immovable, it becomes nondependent. It may be pointed out that the mind of dependence objectifies the things of experience and substantializes them through its discursive and discriminatory activity. This renders the mind incapable of letting things disclose themselves in total transparency because it creates the distinction between the appearance of a thing, and its nature. By contrast, the nondependent mind performs none of these activities, for it does not engage an object by discriminating and objectifying it.

Linji's position of nondependent mind leads to the thesis that anything existent lacks a substantial nature that persists through time. Everything is empty of substance, including the mind which experiences its world. In the experience of emptiness where all *dharmas* are experienced as one in the transparency of pure light, the person realizes that nothing whatsoever is obtainable, even the goal of becoming a *buddha*, for if everything is empty, nothing can be obtained. The mind which realizes this is without form, that is, 'no-mind', in virtue of which its activity is capable of penetrating the whole world (see BUDDHIST CONCEPT OF EMPTINESS).

In summary, the nondependent mind frees the person from the adverse, delusory influences of the everyday world, for the conditioning process is incapable of affecting the immovable, no-mind. The person with nondependent mind is also free from the karmic destiny of birth and death, because the experience of emancipation *vis à-vis* the emptiness of things unties the person from his/her self-binding (see KARMA AND REBIRTH, INDIAN CONCEPTIONS OF). Moreover, based on this realization, the action performed by the person of nondependence does not leave any karmic residue, and therefore the freedom from karmic determination enables the person to freely engage, by way of verbal or bodily behaviour, the matters of the triple world – the experiential worlds of desire, form and formlessness. Freedom for Linji is grounded in the power of discerning 'the *buddha* from the devil, the true from the false, and the sacred from the profane'. Linji encapsulated the characteristics of the person of nondependence in his statement: 'If one becomes a master in any place, wherever he stands is true'. He called such a person the 'person of no-event'. He exhorted people to make use of the nondependent, immovable no-mind by embodying it.

See also: BUDDHIST PHILOSOPHY, CHINESE; BUDDHIST CONCEPT OF EMPTINESS

References and further reading

App, U. (ed.) (1993) *Rinzairoku ichijisakuhin* (A Concordance to the Record of Linji (Rinzai)), Kyoto: International Research Institute for Zen Buddhism. (Locates any phrase or character in the *Linjilu* in order of their occurrence.)

Dumoulin, H. (1988) 'Lin-chi', in *Zen Buddhism: India and China*, New York: Macmillan, ch.10. (A general historical introduction.)

Iriya Yoshitaka (ed. and trans.) (1989) *Rinzairoku* (The Record of Linji), Tokyo: Iwanami Shoten. (A text with accompanying translations incorporating Tang colloquialisms.)

Sasaki, R.F. (1975) *The Recorded Sayings of Ch'an Master Lin-chi Hui-chao of Chen Prefecture*, Kyoto: Institute of Zen Studies, Nanazno College. (A reliable translation of the *Linjilu*.)

Yanagita Seizan (1972) 'The Life of Lin-chi I-hsuan', *Eastern Buddhist* 5: 70–94. (A detailed account of Linji's life.)

SHIGENORI NAGATOMO

LINNAEUS, CARL VON (1707–78)

Linnaeus was educated in Sweden, and became a doctor of medicine in Harderwijk, Holland, in 1735. He visited other European countries then, but he never left Sweden after his return in 1738. After practising as a physician in Stockholm, he moved to Uppsala University as professor of medicine and botany in 1741. He articulated four different but complementary ways of understanding nature – through two kinds of classifica-

tion, and through what can be called developmental and functional/ecological interactions. Linnaeus is best known for his classificatory work, for which he received material from all over the world. His classificatory precepts are elaborated in the Philosophia botanica *of 1751, an enlarged version of the 365 aphorisms of his* Fundamenta botanica *of 1735; the other aspects of his work are diffused through his writings. His artificial classification system, initially very popular, was replaced by the 'natural' system, more slowly in botany than in zoology, and more slowly in England than in some other countries. Current biological nomenclature is based on his* Species plantarum, *edition 1 (for plants), and* Systema naturae, *edition 10 (for animals). His codification of botanical terms remains influential. Almost 200 dissertations, most written by Linnaeus, were defended by his students. In these and other less well-known works, including the unpublished* Nemesis divina *(Stories of Divine Retribution), he covered a wide range of subjects. Quinarian thinking is noticeable in Linnaeus' work – there are five ranks in systems, five years' growth in flowers – and in some of the occult works that he knew. He also shows a strong combinatorial bent and a tendency to draw close analogies between the parts of animals and plants.*

1   **Formal classification**
2   **The natural method**
3   **Developmental interactions**
4   **Functional/ecological interactions**
5   **Conclusions**

1   Formal classification

Linnaeus was educated at Lund and Uppsala universities (he was originally destined for the priesthood); his field knowledge was largely restricted to Sweden. During Linnaeus' three years in Holland, mostly in the employ of the wealthy banker George Clifford, he published extensively, including the first editions of *Systema naturae* and *Genera plantarum*. Later, his work mostly represents elaborations of his early ideas.

Linnaeus defined natural history as the classification and naming of plants, animals (including humans) and minerals according to the number, shape, position and proportion of their parts. Classification (*dipositio*) was based on system, Ariadne's thread, and was applicable to all branches of knowledge. There were five ranks, class, order, genus, species and variety, members of each rank (except the last) including several members of the subordinate rank. Successive divisions were based as far as possible on essences, 'lubricious' distinctions, such as those between herb and tree, being avoided. Classes

and orders in the sexual system of plants ('such loathsome harlotry', according to Johann Siegesbeck) were distinguished by stamen number, whether or not the stamens were joined together, and their position relative to the pistil; they were the work of nature and art.

Genera and species were the work of nature. Genera, the focus of Linnaeus' work, were defined by features of the fructification (flower and fruit), largely those of external form. Linnaeus calculated that the different parts of the fructification, when combined in all possible ways, would yield sufficient features to distinguish all plant genera. These features were often taken from Linnaeus' examination of one species per genus. Other species were added because of their agreement in *habitus*, features other than those of the fructification. Hence Linnaeus' species of *Vaccinium* (cranberries, blueberries), although similar in appearance, had different numbers of stamens in the flower – and so should have been placed in different classes. Linnaeus' contemporaries were dismayed by such inconsistencies; Linnaeus was not.

Species were the basic unit of nature, and he first thought they were all created. They were distinguished by differences in the number, shape, proportion and position of parts like the stem, leaf and inflorescence, but not by odour, length of life, and so on. Varieties, variation produced by sowing the seed of one individual, were often the result of cultivation and were rarely of importance.

The idea of 'character' anchors the system. The essential character was the essence of a genus in a natural system, while the factitious character defined the genus in an artificial system. Both were based on features of the fructification and, when combined, made a natural character. The description was the natural character of the whole plant, so it included the habitus. For species, natural characters were descriptions, essential characters were differentiae. Finally, a *naturalissima* character contained features common to many plants.

The correct naming (*denominatio*) of plants was critical. The name of a genus was a single word ideally reflecting either its habitus or an essential feature, and Linnaeus proposed extensive guidelines for naming, relegating unacceptable names to synonymy. The specific name was a polynomial, the essential character of the species. A mere twelve words could provide differentiae for all species in a genus of 100 species when the differentiae were qualified by adjectives and used synoptically (that is, dividing the genus successively in half: 50, 25, 13, 7, 3, 2, 1). Since essential characters were not known a priori, as new species were added to a genus the polynomials (differentiae) of the other species might have to be changed. Moreover, when a species was moved from one genus to another, its name would change if the differentiae in the new genus differed. Names were not linked to specimens, all individuals of a species sharing the same essence; Linnaeus treated specimens as being by and large interchangeable.

The trivial name was a single, usually adjectival, word which, with the generic noun, formed the binomial. (Linnaeus abbreviated book titles in a comparable fashion, and binomials were initially provided for convenience.) Few nomenclatural rules applied to trivial names, which did not reflect the essence, but their value was such that they pervaded biological literature after 1753 and are often described as 'Linnaean names'. Linnaeus' reform of genera and species and his nomenclature were widely influential.

2   The natural method

The natural method was 'the ultimate goal of botanists'. There genera were grouped into orders; these were named, but not described (exceptions are the early *Musa Cliffortiana* and Paul Dietrich Giseke's descriptions in the *Praelectiones* of 1792, presumably those given by Linnaeus in lectures in 1771, but never published). Linnaeus realized that natural orders could not be defined. Even the most 'natural', such as the *Umbelliferae*, the carrot family, lacked features that were unique to and constant within them. Until these were found, natural groups were 'like a bell without a clapper'; in modern parlance, they were polythetic.

Plants showed relationships on all sides, like territories on a map. (The diagram of relationships drawn by Giseke showed 'genealogical–geographical affinities'; too much emphasis should not be placed on the genealogical element, since trees of knowledge were described in similar terms.) However, plants still undiscovered caused problems in establishing both relationships and groups. When discussing such problems, Linnaeus made the oft-quoted statement, *natura non facit saltus* (nature does not make leaps); continuity made definition difficult. Thus although there is no simple *scala naturae* in Linnaeus' work, relationships form a continuum. Characters do not define groups, indeed, in the chain of variation there is no real discontinuity even between animals and plants: plants have flowers, as do animals – but only those animals like *Hydra*, with its corolla-like circlet of tentacles, immediately adjacent to plants in the series. Such continuity pervades Linnaeus' work, *Homo troglodytes*, which linked *Homo sapiens* to other animals, being another striking example.

3   Developmental interactions

Interactions between two basic tissues, the cortex and medulla, explain the development of organs, the relationship between the inside and the outside of organisms, why different characters were used at different levels of the systematic hierarchy, the general nature of organic diversity, and even ideas of disease and its cure. Organisms were made up of cortex (the male principle; responsible for form) and medulla (female; life). Form was manifest in the cortex only after a basically epigenetic interaction with the medulla. In most animals, determinate in growth, the cortex enclosed the medulla, while in most plants the medulla pushed through the cortex and growth was indeterminate; both plants and animals had definite form. Fungi, however, had only a thin layer of cortex, so their form was notably labile and their classification, which depended on constant form, consequently chaotic. Finally, in organisms like the genus *Chaos* (amoeba) itself there was neither cortex nor constant form. Linnaeus toyed with the idea of establishing a separate kingdom for such organisms.

The vegetative organs of the plant, and most of the fructification, were cortical in origin. Each organ was formed from a particular subtype of cortical tissue, thus stamens represented the innermost part of the cortex (lignum, or wood); the pistil, however, was almost pure medulla. Fertilization thus brought together male (cortical) and female (medullary) elements. If for any reason the medulla died or was used up, the plant itself died; thus in annual plants all the 'growing points' of the medulla entered the ovaries, none remaining to continue growth.

Linnaeus equated flowering in plants with metamorphosis in insects. The young stages of the organism, the outside parts, were discarded, and the adult (insect, flower), representing the insides, emerged. Hence the different parts of the plant fructification were equated with elytra (wings) and genitalia, and the butterfly with 'a flying flower'. Metamorphosis confirmed Linnaeus' use of characters of the fructification in defining genera; they were characters of the adult. Vegetative characters, external and juvenile, were useful only as specific differentiae. (He also discussed the relationship between the animal and plant kingdoms as a form of metamorphosis in which cortex was sloughed off.)

The cortex–medulla theory had numerous implications. Linnaeus drew a parallel between the growth of the vegetative bud and that of the flower: the flower, with its five main organs, representing the equivalent of five years' vegetative growth in one. Moreover, by incorporating ideas of plant nutrition, curiosities such as flowers with only a single covering that was green on the outside and coloured on the inside, and the association of doubled flowers with varying degrees of sterility, could be explained. From observations of such phenomena, including *terata* (monstrosities), Linnaeus concluded that plant structures were inter-convertible – independently of and prior to similar ideas expressed by Goethe (see GOETHE, J.W. VON §3). Leaves could change into sepals, sepals into petals, and petals into stamens. (Note that most observations Linnaeus used here were valueless for his classification; doubled flowers were at most varieties.)

Finally, the cortex–medulla theory is integral to ideas Linnaeus developed on the generation of organic diversity. His species concept – that all species were created by God – was soon amended. Hybridization, he thought, produced the new genus *Peloria* (in fact, a mutant of toadflax) and also occurred between other genera (in combinations that are patently impossible), yet it would not destroy the overall taxonomic framework. Since the cortex of the male determined vegetative form and hence the specific character, and the medulla of the female effectively determined features of the fructification and hence the generic character, hybrids were simply new species in established genera. Thus hybridization could account for variation in taxonomically difficult genera like *Rosa*. Later, Linnaeus came to think that God had created a small number of cortex–medulla combinations representing orders or even the three main groupings of plants (based on cotyledon number). Successive hybridizations then yielded the diversity of form as manifest in the classificatory hierarchy.

4 Functional/ecological interactions

Linnaeus held physico-theological ideas of balance and compensation in nature, with a series of controls, dependencies and connections existing within and between organisms. Bird colours were important in courtship; the flowers, fruits and leaves of plants were arranged to facilitate pollination and seed dispersal. Most insect larvae ate one species of plant, and often one part of that plant; some ate other insects; plant galls housed yet other larvae. Water in the pitchers of *Tillandsia* was for the use of thirsty humans, birds and beasts alike; evergreen trees grew in barren places to provide shelter for animals in winter. Food chains, from the minute *Monoculus* to gnat to frog to pike to seal, and ecological successions, from crustaceous lichens on a rock by the sea to foliose lichens to mosses to herbs and shrubs, formed other connec-tions, as did geomorphological changes.

Ultimately, reproduction had to be checked, since simple calculation showed that otherwise single species would come to dominate nature. Hence small and useful, that is, edible, animals reproduced more than large and useless animals. After caterpillar larvae devastated grasslands, more plant species could grow there. Death and life were inseparably connected; nature was in balance.

Organisms were for human use, too, although in general Linnaeus did not think that some organisms existed for the simple and unrestricted use of others. However, he argued that the study of natural history allowed humans to use natural productions more effectively (his strong cameralist inclinations are relevant here), and about one in six of Linnaeus' theses deal with this theme. The final link in the theodicy was the *Nemesis divina*; God kept humans in check.

5 Conclusions

Linnaeus' ideas owe much to those of Cesalpino, and ultimately to Aristotelian thought. Logical division yields natural groupings only in a taxonomy of analysed entities, and Linnaeus realized that he did not have such knowledge of animals and plants; his claims for the results of the a priori reasoning he applied were modest. Stamens, although important in reproduction, were not a true *fundamentum divisionis*, hence classes and orders were the work of nature and art and were only partly natural. Indeed, Aristotle had argued that logical division was an inappropriate tool for the classification of organized beings. It is difficult to relate Linnaeus' ideas of development directly to those of Aristotle, in which the male is usually the active element, shaping a passive female substance. However, Aristotle's general teleological framework bears comparison with that of Linnaeus (see ARISTOTLE §17).

Linnaeus came to believe that species were the work of time; they were not simultaneously created – although by God's combinatorial, they were foreordained. Such developments of his ideas – let alone his interest in the origin of form and the functional interconnections within and between organisms – escaped many of his contemporaries and successors, and he came to exemplify essential-ism, stasis and classification.

See also: SPECIES; TAXONOMY

List of works

Linnaeus, C. von (1735) *Systema naturae, sive regna tria naturae systematicae proposita per classes, ordines, genera, species* [...], Leiden: T. Haak.

(Broadsheet; Linnaeus' first classification of plants, animals and minerals.)

—— (1735) *Fundamenta botanica quae majorem operum prodromi instar theoriam scientiae botanica per breves aphorismos tradunt* [...], Amsterdam: Schouten. (365 aphorisms explaining Linnaeus' classificatory philosophy and practice.)

—— (1751) *Philosophia botanica in qua expicantur fundamenta botanica cum definitionibus partium, exemplis terminorum, observationibus raiorum, adjectis figuris aeneis*, Stockholm: Kiesewetter. (An elaboration of Linnaeus' classificatory philosophy and practice.)

—— (1753) *Species plantarum, exhibentes plantas rite cognitas, ad genera relatas, cum differentiis specific, nominbus trivialibus, synonymis selectis, locis natalibus, secundum systema sexuale digesta*, Stockholm: Salvius. (Full descriptions and synonymy of all species of plants. Facsimile reprint, with important essays by W.T. Stearn and J.L. Heller, London: The Ray Society, 1957.)

—— (1758–9) *Systema naturae per regna tria naturae, secundum classes, ordines, genera, species, cum characteribus, differentiis, synonymis, locis*, 10th edn, Stockholm: Salvius, 2 vols.

—— (1766–88) *Systema naturae per regna tria naturae, secundum classes, ordines, genera, species, cum characteribus, differentiis, synonymis, locis*, 12th edn, Stockholm: Salvius, 3 vols.

—— (1785–90) *Amoenitates academiae seu dissertationes variae physicae, medicae botanicae anteac seorsim editae nunc collectae et auctae cum tabulis aeneis*, ed. J.C.D. von Schreber, Erlangen: J.J. Palm, 10 vols. (Theses, most of which were written by Linnaeus and defended (and the publication paid for) by his students. The first edition, Stockholm and Leipzig: G. Kiesewetter, 1749–69, 7 volumes, is less complete. The original theses should always be consulted. Some theses have been translated; L'équilibre de la nature, translated by B. Jasmin, introduction and notes by C. Limoges. The 1972 edition, Paris: Vrin, contains translations of five important theses dealing with relationships in nature.)

References and further reading

Blund, W. (1971) *The Compleat Naturalist: A Life of Linnaeus*, New York: Viking Press. (A general biography.)

Cain, A.J. (1995) 'Linnaeus's natural and artificial arrangements of plants', *Botanical Journal of the Linnean Society* 117: 73–133. (See also references; clarification of the structure of Linnaeus' classifications.)

Frängsmyr, T. (ed.) (1983) *Linnaeus, the Man and His Work*, Berkeley, CA: University of California Press. (See especially Gunnar Brobert, 'Homo sapiens': Linnaeus' classification of man'.)

* Giseke, P.D. (1792) *Praelectiones in ordines naturales plantarum*, Hamburg: Hoffman. (Notes made by Giseke and Fabricius from lectures given by Linnaeus.)

Koerner, L. (1993) 'Nature and Nation in Linnaean Travels', Harvard: Ph.D. Thesis, Department of History. (The importance of Linnaeus' cameralist ideas).

Larson, J.L. (1971) *Reason and Experience: The Representation of Natural Order in the Work of Carl von Linné*, Berkeley, CA: University of California Press. (The relationship between Linnaeus' theory and his practice.)

Stafleu, F.A. (1971) *Linnaeus and the Linnaeans: The Spreading of their Ideas in Systematic Botany, 1735–1789*, Utrecht: A. Oosthoek. (Linnaeus' ideas and their reception.)

Stafleu, F.A. and Cowan, R. (1981) *Taxonomic Literature: A Selective Guide to Botanical Publications and Collections, with Dates, Commentaries, and Types*, vol. III, Lh–O, Utrecht: Bohn, Scheltema & Holkema. (Pages 71–111 provides an entry to the bibliographic and biographic literature on Linnaeus.)

Stevens, P.F. and Cullen, S.P. (1990) 'Linnaeus, the Cortex–Medulla Theory, and the Key to his Understanding of Plant Form and Natural Relationships', *Journal of the Arnold Arboretum* 71: 179–220. (How the cortex–medulla theory underpins much of Linnaeus' work.)

Weinstock, J. (ed.) (1985) *Contemporary Perspectives on Linnaeus*, Lanham, MD: University Press of America. (See especially articles by Wolf Lepenies and Lars Gustaffson on *Nemesis divina*.)

P.F. STEVENS

LIPS, JOEST *see* LIPSIUS, JUSTUS

LIPSIUS, JUSTUS (1547–1606)

Justus Lipsius was a Flemish humanist and classical philologist whose work on Tacitus and Seneca led him to give the first full, formal account of Stoicism as a philosophical system, and also to develop Neostoicism, an influential political and moral theory. His most popular book was De constantia *(On Constancy), an account of how to maintain steadfastness in the face of public evils. He loved gardens and dogs.*

Justus Lipsius (Joest Lips) was born near Brussels, and lived through the Protestant revolt against Spanish Catholic rule over the Netherlands. Lipsius came from a Catholic family, and attended the Jesuit college at Cologne before going to the University of Louvain. Here he studied law, but soon turned to classical philology (though he never perfected his Greek). His first published work, *Variarum lectionum libri IV* (Four Books of Mixed Readings) (1569), was dedicated to Cardinal Granvelle, who appointed him Secretary for Latin Letters. Granvelle introduced Lipsius to scholarly circles in Rome, where he spent the years 1568–70. In 1571 he went to Vienna, and then to Jena, where he held the chair of rhetoric and history from 1572 to 1574. To hold this chair, he had to profess Lutheranism. On leaving Jena in 1574, he went to Cologne, where he married a Catholic wife, then to Louvain, where he completed his law degree in 1576. Fearing difficulties with the Spanish authorities, he next went to Leiden where he was professor of history from 1579 to 1590. Here, he had to profess Calvinism. In 1591 he made his peace with the Jesuits at Mainz and returned to the Spanish Netherlands. In 1592 he was appointed to the chair of history and Latin literature at Louvain, a post he still held at his death. He was also named historiographer to the King of Spain in 1595. Lipsius, along with his dog Mopsus, appears in a famous painting, *The Four Philosophers*, by Peter Paul Rubens, whose brother had been a pupil of Lipsius at Louvain.

Lipsius' first notable achievement was the edition (1574) of the Roman historian Tacitus, whose works had been rediscovered in the late fourteenth and fifteenth centuries. Lipsius was among those thinkers who interpreted Tacitus as counselling political prudence and non-involvement in affairs of state. In 1589, Lipsius published his own work on politics, *Politicorum sive Civilis Doctrinae libri sex* (Six Books of Politics or Civil Doctrine). His treatment of military affairs stimulated Dutch army reforms, but the chief importance of the work lay in Lipsius' appeal to the political and moral values of Ancient Rome, and his acceptance of the central role of the state. The importance that Lipsius attached to political stability led him to advocate the enforcement of a state religion, but in the first edition he also counselled toleration of private belief. As a result, his work was placed on the Index.

Lipsius' advocacy of Neostoicism in political theory was supplemented by his Neostoicism in ethics and his work on Stoicism as a philosophical system. In his very popular book *De constantia* (*On Con-*

stancy), first published in 1584, and republished many times, both in Latin and in translation, Lipsius discussed the individual's attitude towards public troubles, advocating steadfastness guided by reason, freedom from the emotions, patience in adversity, and cheerful subjection to God. He recognized that Stoicism had to be modified for, contrary to Stoic views, God is not subject to destiny, but rather destiny is subject to God. Divine providence is not an impersonal fate, and it can be reconciled with both chance and human free choice.

In 1604 Lipsius published two books on Stoic doctrine in which he argued that Stoicism, while not wholly acceptable, was the philosophy best suited to Christianity. The first, *Manuductio ad Stoicam philosophiam*, is a handbook dealing with ethical questions, including friendship and suicide (which Lipsius was against), and with the sources for Stoicism. The second (*Physiologia stoicorum*) is a study of Stoic physics as providing an essential foundation for the study of Stoic ethics, given the injunction to lead one's life in accordance with nature. Lipsius was more positive about the compatibility of Stoic views on fate with Christian views about divine providence than he had been in *On Constancy*. He also took up Stoic views on God as a divine fire infused throughout nature, on eternal matter, and on soul as material. The book presents the first systematic modern account of Stoicism (see STOICISM).

Lipsius' last contribution to the knowledge of Stoicism was his 1605 edition of Seneca's *Opera omnia* which includes an unfinished commentary and essays. Seneca had always been important to Lipsius, not just as a thinker but as a stylistic model.

In a letter of 1603, Lipsius summed up his work in these words: 'I was the first, or the only one, of my time to turn my scholarship to Wisdom; out of Philology I made Philosophy' (Morford: 137).

See also: POLITICAL PHILOSOPHY, HISTORY OF §7; SENECA; STOICISM

List of works

Lipsius, J. (1569–1606) *Opera omnia* (Complete Works), Wesel, 1675, 4 vols.
—— (1569) *Variarum lectionum libri IV* (Four Books of Mixed Readings), in *Opera omnia*, Wesel, 1675, 4 vols.
—— (1584) *De constantia*, trans. J. Stradling, *Two Bookes of Constancie*, ed. R. Kirk, New Brunswick, NJ: Rutgers University Press, 1939.
—— (1589) *Politicorum sive Civilis Doctrinae libri sex* (Six Books of Politics or Civil Doctrine), in *Opera omnia*, Wesel, 1675, 4 vols.

—— (1604) *Manuductio ad Stoicam philosophiam* (Handbook for Stoical Philosophy) and *Physiologia stoicorum* (Stoic Physics), trans. J. Lagrée, *Juste Lipse et la restauration du stoïcisme. Étude et traduction des traités stoïciens: De la constance, Manuel de philosophie stoïcienne, Physique des stoïciens (Extraits)*, Paris: Vrin, 1994. (Provides extracts of *Manuductio* and *Physiologia* in Latin with French translation.)
—— (1978–87) *Justi Lipsi Epistolae* (Letters of Justus Lipsius), ed. A. Gerlo, M.A. Nauwelaerts, H.D.L. Vervliet, S. Sué and H. Peeters, Lettern en Schone Kunsten van België, Brussels: Koninklijke Akademie voor Wetenschappen.
—— (1996) *Principles of Letter-Writing. A Bilingual Text of Justi Lipsi Epistolica Institutio*, ed. and trans. R.V. Young and M. Thomas Hester, Carbondale, IL: Southern Illinois University Press.

References and further reading

Abel, G. (1978) *Stoizismus und frühe Neuzeit. Zur Enstehungsgeschichte modernen Denkens im Felde von Ethik und Politik* (Stoicism and the Early Modern Period. On the Genesis of Modern Thought in the Areas of Ethics and Politics), Berlin and New York: de Gruyter. (A recent survey of Stoicism in the early modern period, covering Lipsius as well as other major figures.)
Lagrée, J. (1994) *Juste Lipse et la restauration du stoïcisme. Étude et traduction des traités stoïciens: De la constance, Manuel de philosophie stoïcienne, Physique des stoïciens (Extraits)* (Justus Lipsius and the Restoration of Stoicism...), Paris: Vrin. (A good general account, with Latin texts and French translations of extracts from Lipsius' philosophical works.)
* Morford, M. (1991) *Stoics and Neostoics. Rubens and the Circle of Lipsius*, Princeton, NJ: Princeton University Press. (Full of detailed information, especially about Lipsius' friends and students. Useful bibliography.)
Mouchel, C. (1990) *Cicéron et Sénèque dans la rhétorique de la Renaissance* (Cicero and Seneca in Renaissance Rhetoric), Marburg: Hitzeroth. (The opposition between Cicero and Seneca as models for style.)
Oestreich, G. (1982) *Neostoicism and the Early Modern State*, ed. B. Oestreich and H.G. Koenigsberger, trans. D. McLintock, Cambridge: Cambridge University Press. (Deals with Lipsius' political thought and its influence in part 1, pages 13–131.)
Saunders, J.L. (1955) *Justus Lipsius. The Philosophy of Renaissance Stoicism*, New York: The Liberal Arts Press. (Still the standard work on Lipsius.)

E.J. ASHWORTH

LITERARY CRITICISM, FEMINIST *see* FEMINIST LITERARY CRITICISM

LITERATURE AND PHILOSOPHY *see* ALIGHIERI, DANTE; BAKHTIN, MIKHAIL MIKHAILOVICH; BARTHES, ROLAND; BAUDRILLARD, JEAN; CAMUS, ALBERT; CAVELL, STANLEY; COLERIDGE, SAMUEL TAYLOR; COMEDY; DE MAN, PAUL; DECONSTRUCTION; DERRIDA, JACQUES; DIDEROT, DENIS; DODGSON, CHARLES LUTWIDGE (LEWIS CARROLL); DOSTOEVSKII, FËDOR MIKHAILOVICH; ELIOT, GEORGE; EMERSON, RALPH WALDO; FEMINIST LITERARY CRITICISM; FICTIONAL ENTITIES; GOETHE, JOHANN WOLFGANG VON; IRIGARAY, LUCE; JOHNSON, SAMUEL; KRISTEVA, JULIA; LESSING, GOTTHOLD EPHRAIM; LITERATURE, PHILOSOPHY IN LATIN AMERICAN; LITERATURE, PHILOSOPHY IN MODERN JAPANESE; MARCEL, GABRIEL; MONTAIGNE, MICHEL EYQUEM DE; NARRATIVE; PETRARCA, FRANCESCO; POETRY; RAND, AYN; RORTY, RICHARD MCKAY; ROUSSEAU, JEAN-JACQUES; RUSSIAN LITERARY FORMALISM; SARTRE, JEAN-PAUL; SCHILLER, JOHANN CHRISTOPH

FRIEDRICH; STAËL-HOLSTEIN, ANNE-
LOUISE-GERMAINE, MME DE;
STRUCTURALISM IN LITERARY THEORY;
THOREAU, HENRY DAVID; TODOROV,
TZVETAN; TOLSTOI, COUNT LEV
NIKOLAEVICH; TRAGEDY; UNAMUNO Y
JUGO, MIGUEL DE; VOLTAIRE
(FRANÇOIS-MARIE AROUET)

LITERATURE, PHILOSOPHY IN LATIN AMERICAN

Within the Latin American intellectual community, the relationship between philosophy and literature consti-tutes one of the most interesting chapters in its development. Much Latin American literature is characterized by profound philosophical concerns, focusing on the question of identity. From the time of the conquest and colonization of the American continent in the 1500s, a debate regarding the humanity of the recently discovered inhabitants began in Spain. This debate would prove to be one of the most revealing controversies of sixteenth-century Europe. At the point of colonial expansion, Europe projected a logocentric vision which would incite a unique Latin Americanist philosophical discourse relating to the question of identity.

During the nineteenth century, philosophical dis-course was formulated principally through literary expression. At first the quest for a cultural identity was the philosophical focus, although two conflicting positions were evident: the desire to achieve cultural independence from Europe and a yearning for Latin America to become European. This latter position inspired the urge to identify with European culture and from the mid-1900s, with the political and economic success of the USA.

In the twentieth century, from the time of the University Reform of 1918, an academic philosophy emerged close to that of Europe and began to diversify the Latin American philosophical panorama. From the various philosophical stances which arose at that time, one that dominated the cultural arena, despite its occasional relegation to a secondary position in academia, was the urge to articulate a Latin American-ist philosophical discourse which would succeed in transcending its own frontiers through liberation philo-sophy, beginning in the 1960s.

1 **Philosophy as literature**
2 **Philosophy in literature**
3 **Contextualization of philosophy in literature**

1 Philosophy as literature

In the philosophical discourses of the colonial and nineteenth-century periods, two trends appear in Latin America: an academic one inspired by the European movements and practised by the Scholas-tics, such as Alonso de la Vera Cruz (1504–84) and José de Acosta (1540–1600), Scotist Alfonso Briceño (1590–1667), Neoplatonist José Manuel Peramás (1732–93), Enlightenment thinker Eugenio de Santa Cruz y Espejo (1747–95) and positivist Carlos Octavio Bunge (1875–1918). The other Latin Americanist trend articulated its philosophical discourse through literary expression, particularly the essay and the novel. This group of philosophers comprised Mex-icans José Joaquín Fernández de Lizardi (1776–1827) and Justo Sierra (1848–1912), Venezuelan-Chilean Andrés Bello (1781–1865), Argentines Juan Bautista Alberdi (1810–84) and Domingo Faustino Sarmiento (1811–88), Chileans José Victorino Lastarria (1817–88) and Francisco Bilbao (1823–65), Cubans José de la Luz y Caballero (1800–62) and José Martí (1853–95), Ecuadorian Juan Montalvo (1832–89) and Puerto Rican Eugenio María Hostos (1839–1903). Through the literature of this second trend of the nineteenth century emerge the first expressions of Latin American thought.

In 1815 during the fight for political independence from Spain, leader Simón Bolívar (1783–1830) pre-sented the plight of Latin America in the following terms:

> We are neither Indian nor European, but a species midway between the legitimate proprietors of this country and the Spanish usurpers. In short, although Americans by birth we derive our rights from Europe, and we have to assert these rights against the rights of the natives, and at the same time we must defend ourselves against the invaders.
> ([1815] 1981: 63–4)

Bolívar only succeeded in defining Latin Americans by decribing what they were not: 'We are neither Indian nor European'. His Americanism makes reference to his birth only in as much as, culturally, he believed himself to have inherited 'Our rights from Europe'. It is in this way that the identity plight became a Latin American obsession.

During the 1800s Latin America was viewed by its people as a scene of confrontation between civiliza-tion and barbarism. Argentine essayist Domingo Faustino Sarmiento (1811–88) interpreted Latin

America's social conflict as two opposing forces: 'one civilized, constitutional, European; the other barbaric, arbitrary, American'. Sarmiento felt he was dealing with 'two distinct societies that were rivals and incompatible' (1845: 58). The significance of the thought exemplified in the work of Sarmiento is manifested more precisely in novels by such authors as Ecuadorian Juan León Mera (1832–94). In Mera's *Cumandá o un drama entre salvajes* (Cumandá or Drama Among Savages) (1879) Ecuador's inhabitants separate themselves into two large groups: the foreigners and the natives. The first comprises the 'whites' (of European descent and identified as Christians) and the other group is made up of Indians or Mestizos (of mixed blood). In Mera's work Ecuador does not have a social identity. It is seen as a border of conflict which is defined, in Sarmiento's terms, as the place of confrontation between civilization (European culture) and barbarism (what is perceived as the autochthonous, native culture).

Towards the end of the 1800s the optimism which characterized the intellectuals of independence turned to pessimism. Like the initial liberalism, the conservative positions under the positivist motto *Ordem e Progresso*, or order and progress, also had failed politically, socially and economically. However, among the pessimistic voices of, for example, Bolivian Alcides Arguedas (1879–1946), a group of essayists emerged and looked to the past in order to present a new stance on the concept of identity. Peruvian Manuel González Prada (1848–1918), Uruguayan José Enrique Rodó (1871–1917), Mexican Justo Sierra (1848–1912), Cuban José Martí (1853–95) and Puerto Rican Eugenio María Hostos (1839–1903) are notable figures in the development of this new philosophy. During this period, it was recognized that large sections of the population had been and were being ignored and that, if Latin America was going to save itself, it must save its Indians. In his essay 'Our America' (*c.*1870), Martí declared, 'To know is to resolve. To know one's country and to govern it with that knowledge is the only way of liberating it' (*c.*1870).

2 Philosophy in literature

The independence in 1898 of the last Spanish colonies in America (Cuba, Puerto Rico), the construction of the Panama Canal, the intervention of the USA in the affairs of several Latin American countries and the First World War motivated Latin American philosophers to project their national concerns across the continent. The Latin Americanist philosophers emerged with the intention of reflecting on the problem of identity on a continental scale. Counted

among these were Colombian Baldomero Sanín Cano (1861–1957), Argentines Alejandro Korn (1860–1936) and Francisco Romero (1891–1962), Uruguayan Carlos Vaz Ferreira (1873–1958), Mexicans Antonio Caso (1883–1946) and Samuel Ramos (1897–1959), Bolivian Guillermo Francovich (1901–90) and Peruvian José Carlos Mariátegui (1895–1930). The University Reform initiated in Argentina in 1918 extended rapidly throughout Latin America and gave rise to the development of an academic philosophy. From the beginning of the 1930s these philosophers felt the need to recover the Latin American cultural past as a preliminary step to the formulation of an original philosophy.

In the area of literature the concern was more personal and immediate. The problems which arose from an awareness of one's own circumstances were raised in poetry, theatre, the novel and the essay. Latin American reality was analysed and deconstructed and solutions were proposed. In short, this literature dealt with thoughts which were artistically expressed and parallel with, and sometimes even crossing over into, academic philosophy. However, this literature did not concern itself with contextualizing philosophical discourse. Hence, visions of a possible utopian development in Latin America were expressed by authors such as the Uruguayan Rodó (1871–1917) and Mexican Vasconcelos. In his work Rodó defended the integral personality of the person as well as the concept of select minorities. He criticized what he considered to be the levelling propensity of democracies and the excessive concern for materialism and mercantilism in the USA. He proposed that the Latin American 'spirit' be their objective. Against the degradation levelled at the Mestizo people by the positivists, Vasconcelos recognized the Mestizo essentiality, that is, the interracial and intercultural nature of Latin American people, which he perceived to be the future of humanity. According to Vasconcelos (1925), in Latin America, a fifth race, the cosmic race (a mixed race incorporating the creative power of the other races) would emerge, called to guide the destinies of humankind.

The novel during the period up to the 1950s surpassed the philosophical debates surrounding the concepts of civilization and barbarism which prevailed during the nineteenth century. The works by Mexican Mariano Azuela (1873–1952), Argentine Ricardo Güiraldes (1886–1969) and Venezuelan Rómulo Gallegos (1884–1969) were powerful artistic creations which contributed to a profound philosophical reflection in which the cultural past and the problem of Latin American identity were embraced and deconstructed. Gallegos in *Doña Bárbara* (1929) studied the intuitions of Martí and the vision of

Vasconcelos. In this novel the problems of Latin America continued to be defined as a confrontation between civilization and barbarism. Imitation was considered barbarism as were the imposition of alien laws upon one's own reality and egoism in search of rapid enrichment. For Gallegos, the civilizing force is that which trusts in the potential of national powers and which recognizes racial and cultural miscegenation as the basis of national identity.

The novel, particularly the *indigenista* novel, became an instrument of denunciation concerning the state of the pre-Columbian descendants' population. The indigenous population gradually recognized through its exclusion, one of the basic causes of the economic, social and political underdevelopment in which some of the Latin American countries found themselves. Peruvian César Vallejo (1892–1938) and Ecuadorian Jorge Icaza (1906–78) crudely developed the consequences of a culture of oppression: one which paralysed the internal development of a country, accentuated the weakness of its oligarchy and accepted as natural imperialist impositions from the exterior. Peruvians Ciro Alegría (1909–67) and José María Arguedas (1911–69) sought to recover the excluded populations.

The question of identity continued to be the impetus of philosophical reflection within literature. The work of Argentines Eduardo Mallea (1903–82) and Ezequiel Martínez Estrada (1895–64) contained profound philosophical reflections which had repercussions that transcended national boundaries. In countries such as Mexico, where the identity crisis was precipitated by internal circumstances, authors and philosophers, such as Samuel Ramos (1897–1959), Rodolfo Usigli (1905–79), Octavio Paz (1914–) and Carlos Fuentes (1929–), shared a mutual concern.

3 Contextualization of philosophy in literature

In the early 1950s Latin American philosophers began to formulate original thought. *América como conciencia* (America as a Collective Awareness) (1953) by Mexican Leopoldo Zea, exemplified this initial stage which reached maturity in the 1960s. For the first time Latin American thought broke its own boundaries by means of 'liberation thought'. In the 1960s such thought split into three complementary fields: pedagogy, exemplified by Brazilian Paulo Freire (1921–), theology, demonstrated in the work of Peruvian Gustavo Gutiérrez (1928–) and philosophy, reflected in the work of Leopoldo Zea (1912–). All these thinkers analysed and deconstructed Western modernity. Their works emerged at the same time as the postmodern discourses of central Europe, although contrary to postmodernism, they were formulated in

an attempt to attain a new, global utopian view of humanity.

Liberation thought in literature had immediate repercussions. Its theoretical originality and rigour stimulated writers to deconstruct and contextualize philosophical discourse as well as think about its theological, pedagogical and socioeconomic consequences. In terms of artistic expression, in addition to the liberation thought which guided them, Latin American writers and central European postmodern theorists found inspiration in the deconstruction of modernity by Argentinian Jorge Luis Borges (1899–1986) and Colombian Gabriel García Márquez (1928–), or the liberation works of Salvadorean Manlio Argueta (1936–) and Nicaraguan Claribel Alegría (1924–).

The context of economic thought was also formulated in Chile by Brazilians Fernando Henrique Cardoso and Enzo Faletto and analysed and deconstructed by Colombian Manuel Mejía Vallejo. Liberation theology is given some context in works such as *El ocaso de Orión* (The Setting of Orion) (1972) by Bolivian Oscar Uzín Ferá ndez and *La cruz invertida* (The Cross Upside Down) (1970) by Argentine Marcos Aguinis. Aguinis's novel, written at the same time as Gustavo Gutiérrez's seminal work on liberation theology (1971), deals with the theological implications of the concept of the 'new man', providing for the poor and tackling the issue of celibacy, as well as analysing the Eurocentrist discourse of the Catholic church and its power structures. Its content prophesied the Vatican's subsequent confrontation with liberation theologians.

Theorists practising liberation thought did not concern themselves directly with the condition of women in Latin America, however, the deconstruction of oppression and the plan for liberation implicit in the new man concept provoked the creation of powerful feminist movements. These movements saw the struggle for women's liberation as intimately linked to that struggle for the liberation of humankind. A new literary model known as the testimonial narrative grew up at this time, pertaining to works by such authors as Mexican Elena Poniatowska (1933–) and Elizabeth Burgos's discussion of Rigoberta Menchú (1983).

The process of contextualizing liberation thought in literature is exemplified, along with more traditional themes, in the novel *Porqué se fueron las garzas* (Why the Herons Left) (1980) by Ecuadorian Gustavo Alfredo Jácome. Jácome's novel also deconstructs the trends of the so-called intercultural philosophy. This philosophy assumes intercultural relations can be established through the media of literature and philosophy to create a dialogue among equals.The author breaks with the traditional indigenous novel by presenting an Indian with a doctoral education as rector of a school. Jácome goes beyond the search for identity by showing that it is more likely obtained when issues of racial and cultural discrimination are not constantly under examination. The protagonist creatively transcends the oppression that is assumed when one's discourse is expressed in a European language (Spanish). The novel exposes the concealed oppression that carries with it the aspiration in the 1990s of establishing an intercultural dialogue. *Porqué se fueron las garzas* (Why the Herons Left) shows that the most recent state of globalization has established an intercultural dialogue which has a hierarchical diagram and a tacit schema of oppression at its base.

See also: CULTURAL IDENTITY; FEMINIST THOUGHT IN LATIN AMERICA; LIBERATION PHILOSOPHY; LIBERATION THEOLOGY

References and further readings

* Aguinis, M. (1970) *La cruz invertida* (The Cross Upside Down), Barcelona: Editorial Planeta, 1983. (The best Argentine novel on the conflict between the priests promoting theology of liberation and the Church and state.)

Alegría, C. (1941) *El Mundo es ancho y ajeno* (Broad and Alien is the World), Madrid: Alianza Editorial, 1983. (Indigenist novel that seeks to recover the excluded Indian population of Peru.)

Arguedas, A. (1909) *Pueblo enfermo: contribución a la psicología de los pueblos hispano-americanos* (Ailing People), Barcelona: Vda. de Luis Tasso, 1958. (An essay on the psychology of the Bolivian people from a positivistic perspective.)

Arguedas, J.M. (1958) *Deep Rivers*, trans. F.H. Barraclough, intro. J.V. Murra, Austin, TX: University of Texas Press, 1978. (A classic indigenist novel of Peru from the point of view of a child.)

—— (1964) *Todas las sangres* (All the Races), Madrid: Alianza Editorial, 1980. (An indigenist novel depicting the emerging voices of the indigenous population.)

Azuela, M. (1916) *Los de abajo* (The Underdogs), Mexico: Siglo Veintiuno Editores, 1970. (A first major novel of the Mexican Revolution.)

Berryman, P. (1987) *Liberation Theology*, New York: Pantheon. (A clearly written introduction to theology of liberation; it traces the origins, spread and impact.)

* Bolívar, S. (1815) *The Jamaica Letter*, in M. Pérez Vila (ed.) *Simon Bolívar: His Basic Thoughts*, Caracas: Presidency of the Republic of Venezuela, 1981. (An essay reflecting on the fight for independence and on the future of the Spanish colonies.)

* Burgos, E. (1983) *Me Llamo Rigoberta Menchú y así me nació la conciencia* (Rigoberta Menchú: an Indian Woman in Guatemala), Mexico: Siglo Veintiuno Editores, 1993. (The most widely known work of the so-called testimonial literature.)

Cardoso, F.H. and Faletto, E. (1969) *Dependencia y desarrollo en América Latina* (Dependency and Development in Latin America), Mexico: Siglo Veintiuno Editores, 1969. (The need for a social, cultural and political contextualization of the different theoretical systems of economics.)

Freire, P. (1971) *Pedagogía del oprimido* (Pedagogy of the Oppressed), Mexico: Siglo Veintiuno Editores. (Examines the contemporary structure of education as a structure of oppression.)

Fuentes, C. (1962) *La muerte de Artemio Cruz* (Death of Artemio Cruz), Mexico: Fondo de Cultura Económica, 1962. (A novel of the Mexican Revolution that examines its social ramifications.)

* Gallegos, R. (1929) *Doña Bárbara*, Madrid: Espasa-Calpe, 1990. (A twentieth-century novel discussing the Venezuelan view of the nineteenth-century conflict betweeen civilization and barbarism.)

Gómez-Martínez, J.L. (1993) 'Discurso narrativo y pensamiento de la liberación: *La cruz invertida* en la contextualización de una época' (Literary Discourse and Liberation Thought: *The Cross Upside Down* in the Contextualization of a Period), *El ensayo en nuestra América* (The Essay in Our America), Mexico: Universidad Nacional Autónoma de México. (A study of the novels cited in §3.)

Gracia, J.J.E. and Camurati, M. (eds) (1989) *Philosophy and Literature in Latin America: A Critical Assessment of the Current Situation*, Albany, NY: State University of New York Press. (An introduction to the philosophy in Latin American literature, written for the nonspecialist.)

Güiraldes, R. (1926) *Don Segundo Sombra*, Buenos Aires: Losada, 1967. (A novel that idealizes the Argentine Gaucho tradition.)

* Gutiérrez, G. (1971) *Teología de la liberación: Perspectivas* (A Theology of Liberation: History, Politics and Salvation), Salamanca: Sígueme, 1990. (A theological work in the social, economic and political context of Latin America.)

Icaza, J. (1934) *Huasipungo* (The Villagers), Buenos Aires: Losada, 1973. (Indigenist novel that explores the consequences of cultural oppression in Ecuador.)

* Jácome, G.A. (1980) *Porqué se fueron las garzas* (Why the Herons Left), Barcelona: Seix Barral. (A novel that deconstructs the trends of the so-called intercultural philosophy.)

Mallea, E. (1937) *Historia de una pasión argentina* (History of an Argentine Passion), Madrid: Espasa-Calpe, 1969. (A literary blend of the rhetoric of the essay and that of the novel, in search of an Argentine identity.)

* Martí, J. (*c.*1870) 'Our America', in *The America of José Martí: Selected Writings*, New York: Minerva Press, 1968. (An essay reflecting on the intellectual history of Latin America and its social and political consequences.)

Martínez Estrada, E. (1933) *Radiografía de la pampa* (X-ray of the Pampa), Buenos Aires: Losada, 1976. (An essay on Argentine identity through one of its regions.)

Mejía Vallejo, M. (1972) *Al pie de la ciudad* (At the Foot of the City), Barcelona: Destino. (A novel that contextualizes the impact of the economic development of the 1960s in the cities of Colombia.)

* Mera, J.L. (1879) *Cumandá o un drama entre salvajes* (Cumandá or Drama Among Savages), Madrid: Espasa-Calpe, 1967. (A novel that views the indigenous people of Ecuador from the European perspective of Romanticism.)

Muñoz, B. (1982) *Sons of the Wind: The Search for Identity in Spanish American Indian Literature*, New Brunswick, NJ: Rutgers University Press. (The *indigenista* novel as a social indicator, which interprets key issues of Latin American cultural development.)

Oliver, A.A. (1993) 'Values in Modern Mexican Thought', *The Journal of Value Inquiry* 27: 215–30. (A solid introduction to the philosophy of Zea in the context of Mexican culture.)

Paz, O. (1950) *El laberinto de la soledad* (The Labyrinth of Solitude: Life and Thought in Mexico), Mexico: Fondo de la Cultura Económica, 1963. (A classic essay.)

Poniatowska, E. (1969) *Hasta no verte, Jesús mío* (See You Never my Jesus), Mexico: Ediciones Era. (A testimonial novel depicting the social problems of the 1960s in Mexico.)

Ramos, S. (1934) *El perfil del hombre y la cultura en México* (Profile of Man and Culture in Mexico), Madrid: Espasa-Calpe, 1951. (A philosophical essay on Mexican culture and its people.)

* Sarmiento, D.F. (1845) *Facundo: Civilización y barbarie*, Madrid: Espasa-Calpe, 1967; *Civilization and Barbarism: Life in the Argentine Republic in the Days of the Tyrants*, New York: Collier-Macmillan, 1961. (A classic positivist approach to the social situation in Argentina.)

Schutte, O. (1988–9) 'Philosophy and Feminism in Latin America: Perspectives on Gender Identity and Culture', *The Philosophical Forum* 20: 62–84. (An informative essay.)

—— (1993) *Cultural Identity and Social Liberation in Latin American Thought*, Albany, NY: State University of New York Press. (A philosophical approach with an interdisciplinary context. It focuses on cultural identity, liberation and feminist thought and includes a bibliography.)

Stabb, M.S. (1967) *In Quest of Identity: Patterns in the Spanish American Essay of Ideas, 1890–1960*, Chapel Hill, NC: University of North Carolina Press. (An expression of Latin American thought. An extensive bibliography is provided.)

* Uzín Ferá ndez, O. (1972) *El ocaso de Orión* (The Setting of Orion), La Paz: Los Amigos del Libro, 1982. (A novel reflecting on the new social awareness of the priests and traditions of the Catholic church.)

Vallejo, C. (1931) *El tungsteno* (Tungsten: a Novel), Barcelona: Laia, 1981. (Indigenist novel that explores the consequences of cultural oppression in Peru.)

* Vasconcelos, J. (1925) *La raza cósmica* (The Cosmic Race), Madrid: Aguilar, 1966. (An essay on the importance of the intercultural and interracial nature of Latin American people.)

* Zea, L. (1953) *América como conciencia* (America as a Collective Awareness), Mexico: Universidad Nacional Autónoma de México, 1972. (A seminal work of Latin American philosophy.)

—— (1969) *La filosofía latinoamericana como filosofía sin más* (Latin American Philosophy as 'Philosophy'), Mexico: Siglo Veintiuno Editores, 1980. (Zea argues for a Latin American philosophy independent from European philosophy.)

JOSÉ LUIS GÓMEZ-MARTÍNEZ

LITERATURE, PHILOSOPHY IN MODERN JAPANESE

Since the last quarter of the nineteenth century, virtually all major lines of Western thought and the works of both major and minor Western philosophers have been explored and used by Japanese writers in an effort to forge a modern Japanese literature. The history of translation alone reveals a concern to bring over synoptic summaries of Western philosophy, as well as the primary works of specific thinkers. Academic philosophy as a discipline of advanced study was established in the 1880s, the decade which corresponds to the beginnings of widespread literary reform and the often-cited creation of the first modern Japanese novel, Futabatei's Ukigumo *(Floating Cloud) in 1889.*

657

However, Japanese novelists, dramatists, poets and critics did not assimilate philosophical influences naively or passively, nor was Japanese literature made over in the shape of specific Western ideas regarding the nature and function of the self, society or literary aesthetics. Indeed, the avid translation and discussion of Western ideas frequently provoked a nativist reaction or modification. The revival of traditional tropes, the language of Confucian ethics, Buddhist practice and Shintō legends, itself often reflects the pervasive presence of Western ideas on the modern literary scene.

1 Modern literature
2 The self
3 Marxism
4 Postwar period

1 Modern literature

Few Japanese literati since the Meiji period (1868–1912) have been philosophers in an academic sense. It can be difficult to isolate specific Cartesian, Kantian, Bergsonian or Heideggerian elements in a work allegedly written under their influence. As Japanese literary critics themselves have pointed out, time and again writers responded less to an idea as such than to particular imagery, or even to the biography or the historical predicament of certain thinkers. This is especially true where Modern, Enlightenment and post-Enlightenment philosophers are concerned, that is, cultural figures who were struggling to fathom intellectual, historical and social problems analogous to those confronting Japanese writers in the late nineteenth and twentieth centuries.

The beginnings of modern literature in Japan are usually traced to the 1880s, when the literary critic Tsubouchi Shōyō and the novelist Futabatei Shimei gave voice to a new style of realism and pioneered a literary language that placed greater emphasis on speech and the expression of ordinary life. Their efforts reflect a conception of literature shaped by Western modes of literary realism (in Futabatei's case, by his study of Russian and his translations of Turgenev) and by their awareness of the ascendancy of the realist novel on the Western scale of literary values. This shift in emphasis, from literature traditionally viewed in Japan as a rhetorical medium for lyrical expression to that of a transparent reflector of things as they are, paralleled shifts and reforms being undertaken in Japanese politics, law and education. Most such reforms occurred within the prevailing atmosphere of utilitarian, Enlightenment and social Darwinist thought, as it was understood through the writings of John Stuart MILL, August COMTE, Jean-Jacques ROUSSEAU, Herbert SPENCER and others.

This mid-Meiji reform of literature, making way for a realism that would transcribe modern life as it is, met with a strong idealist reaction, itself mediated by a knowledge of similar counter-Enlightenment tendencies in Western (especially German) thought and writing. HEGEL and Eduard von HARTMANN were known to Mori Ōgai, who had studied in Germany and based his earliest writings on that foreign experience. Contrary to the brand of literary realism propounded by Shōyō, Ōgai argued that literature exists in a world of ideas and ideals apart from the everyday, where writers and works of genius from anywhere in the world exist on an equal, if lofty, plane. Whether realist or idealist, these mid-Meiji reformulations of literature were calculated to raise Japanese literature to the perceived level of superiority achieved by Western writers. They also reflect a general anxiety over Japan's vulnerability *vis-à-vis* the West and ultimately, over Japanese identity in the modern world.

2 The self

By the turn of the century, when a confessional strain of 'I-novel' writing took shape as the dominant genre of modern Japanese literature – a dominance that prevails to our own day – Christianity as a system of Western thought found its way into literary expression. Anti-institutional, introspective, Calvinist and Quaker-inflected brands of Protestantism, most clearly exemplified in the life and work of the Christian convert and educator Uchimura Kanzo and his 'no-Church' movement, both justified and provided a rich vocabulary for the literary emphasis on love and the self. Training at Christian mission schools, a conversion experience or some significant exposure to Christianity, was shared by many of the most significant Japanese writers of the twentieth century, including Kitamura Tōkoku, Tayama Katai, Shimazaki Tōson, Kunikida Doppo, Masamune Hakuchō, Shiga Naoya and Arishima Takeo. Apostasy often followed a declaration of faith, which only deepened the need to confess, or the theme of betrayal, within the genre of the I-novel.

The 'discovery' of this interior self, necessitated by Christianity, has been described in Japanese criticism as either a symptom of, or a solution to, several modern problems. The self has been seen to serve a variety of cultural purposes: to fill the void left by the collapse of an orderly, neo-Confucian world view, to have satisfied psychological demands made of writers within a rapidly modernizing nation-state, and to have provided a system of 'transcendent' values to rival the predominant stress on immanence within the traditional modes of Japanese thought, Confucianism,

Buddhism and Shintoism. Still, in specific works of literature, the emphasis on the self or on the value of romantic love often gives way to its loss or rejection. For example, in Shiga Naoya's famous *Anya Korō* (A Dark Night's Passing), the afflictions of self-consciousness yield to a new found sense of harmony within nature and the dissolution of the self within a comforting, spirit-filled landscape.

The literary expression of personal experience was further reinforced by prevailing trends in academic philosophy. Neo-Kantian thought, as well as the pragmatism of William JAMES, was especially dominant in the Taishō period (1912–25), serving as a spur to NISHIDA KITARŌ, Japan's first and perhaps greatest modern philosopher. Nishida's stress on 'pure experience' at once represents a reflection of Western idealist ethics and consciousness of self, joined to an Eastern sense of meditation praxis, as in Zen Buddhism. This conjunction of foreign and native ideas is a widely observed characteristic of the literature of this period, as seen in the eclectic use of both Western and Asian imagery in the fiction of Nagai Kafū and Tanizaki Jun'ichirō. Both exhibit traces of Western decadence, which leads to their discovery of the exotic in old Japan or in tales of the disappearance and partial recovery of tradition. This tendency was further exhibited in the work of WATSUJI TETSURŌ and KUKI SHŪZŌ, influential cultural critics in the 1920s and 1930s. Close familiarity with German phenomenology in the work of HUSSERL and especially HEIDEGGER led them to explore the distinctive climate or structure of Japanese culture.

The prevailing emphasis in modern Japanese literature on expressions of self, wherein general questions of social structure or cultural identity were engaged subjectively if at all, did not go unchallenged. The great critic of the time, Kobayashi Hideo, focused on the peculiar narrowness of the Japanese I-novel and of modern writers held in sway by a welter of Western ideas and influences. To recover both greater breadth and a sense of cultural balance, Kobayashi argued for the creation of fiction whose protagonists were bound to a recognizable history and society.

3 Marxism

Marxism had considerable influence on Japanese scholarship, education and literature, and dominated literary and cultural criticism in the late 1920s, giving rise to proletarian realism and to social problem plays in the 'new theatre' movement. Notable Marxist critics include Miyamoto Kenji, whose essay 'Haiboku no bungaku' (Literature of Defeat) in 1929 represented a sharp if ultimately sympathetic critique of the subjectivist fiction and suicide of Akutagawa Ryūnosuke, and Nakano Shigeharu, whose practice as a socially conscious poet and critic spanned several decades including the crisis of recantation or *tenkō*, the phenomenon of ideological reversal that was so conspicuous a feature of Japanese intellectual life in the 1930s. Socialist realism in fiction was practised by Kobayashi Takiji, who became a martyr to the proletarian cause when he was killed in prison in 1933. Nevertheless, at this time, as well as in the immediate postwar years and later amid the political turmoil of the 1960s, Marxism offered Japanese writers both a way to criticize modernity, and a coherent account of the interconnectedness of individuals and groups within society. Confucianism had formerly provided such an account, though with an emphasis on stability and continuity that seemed increasingly remote from a modern world of unceasing change (see CONFUCIAN PHILOSOPHY, JAPANESE).

Amid the growing forces of nationalism and militarism in the 1930s and the state of total war in the 1940s, many Marxist ideologues either fell silent or subtly exchanged their leftist critique of the West and of modernity for a rightist critique of Western cultural imperialism. A renewed emphasis on the cultural differences between Japan and the West, ironically mediated by a conscious use of German romantic thought from HERDER and SCHILLER through to Heidegger, led to a revival of things Japanese at this time, and to the literary nationalism of such critics as Yasuda Yojūrō and Hayashi Fusao, and of the poets Itō Shizuo and Hagiwara Sakutarō. Their tone of lament, and their imagery of homelessness, wandering and loss, was balanced by their advocacy of Japanese tradition. In poems or impressionistic essays, they sketched provincial journeys and encounters with simple folk as they made their 'return' to the country and home, Japan.

4 Postwar period

After the Second World War, during the early period of American occupation, the intellectual atmosphere was marked by the re-emergence of suppressed or apostate Marxists, and by the philosophy of existentialism (see EXISTENTIALISM). Occupation censors took over from war-time military censors, and writers sought to account for their loss of personal autonomy and authentic experience, as well as for the zero-degree environment of incinerated cities and a society in confusion and collapse. This atmosphere of Sartrean nausea surrounded several leading postwar Japanese authors, contributing to the desert and labyrinth allegories of Kobo Abe, the descriptions of war and moral atrocity in Ōoka Shohei, the tales of deformed historical consciousness in Ōe Kenzaburō, the wasteland poetry of Tamura Ryūichi, the experimental mythology and apocalyptic tone of the dramatists Kinnoshita Junji, Terayama Shūji and Kara Jurō, and the literary criticism of Etō Jun and Yoshimoto Takaaki. These authors were concerned, for different political motives, with issues of false consciousness, bad faith and, in the 1960s, agendas for cultural and social reform. They looked for greater freedom from the influence of Western, especially American, culture.

From the 1970s through to the mid-1990s, Japanese literature registered the changes and rifts that marked Western thought over this same period, actively contributing to that critique, uncovering yet again pockets of Japanese or Asian 'difference' from the West, and highlighting characteristics that identify contemporary Japan as a model of post-modernity. Continental philosophy and cultural critique, with renewed attention to the Frankfurt school (see FRANKFURT SCHOOL), has been widely translated and discussed in literary journals. So too have Jacques DERRIDA and Michel FOUCAULT, severe critics of western metaphysics and institutional structures, whose ideas have been used to frame analogous interrogations of Japanese phonocentrism and of Japan's own coercive social structures. Some see the underlying critique of language and of meaning within post-structuralism as sharing insights with Buddhist or Daoist thought. It has also been argued that deconstruction, for example, is everywhere on display in the Japanese literary tendency toward indeterminate structures, such as elliptical verse, open-ended narratives and non-linear, polysemic theatre (see DECONSTRUCTION). There is a sense that these recent turns in Western thought, directed as they are against stable notions of the self and of linguistic and literary meaning, are oddly congruent with the most traditional assumptions behind Japanese literary practice. In this way, critics such as Karatani Kōjin and Asada Akira have sought to situate writing in Japan within a universal crisis of meaning, while taking account of the historical pressures that have provoked both this general crisis and its inflection in Japan.

Finally, it should be said that modern Japanese literature, preoccupied as it has been with the representation of the real or the expression of the personal, reveals too an anxiety that the real may be a tissue of ideas and ideologies, and that the personal may be an illusion in an environment of incessant makeover and change. Beyond any specific influence, this may be the main legacy of Western thought to modern Japanese writing: a quickened sense for the difference between material reality and our ideas about it, as well as for the power of ideas to cross local boundaries and to define human experience in universal terms.

See also: AESTHETICS; AESTHETICS, JAPANESE; POETRY

References and further reading

Anderer, P. (1995) *Literature of the Lost Home: Kobayashi Hideo – Literary Criticism, 1924–39*, Stanford, CA: Stanford University Press. (The early writings of modern Japan's foremost literary critic.)

Doak, K.M. (1994) *Dreams of Difference: The Japan Romantic School and the Crisis of Modernity*, Berkeley, CA: University of California Press. (A study of nationalist discourse in the 1930s, focusing on critics and thinkers influenced by the German Romantics and Heidegger.)

Karatani Kōjin (1994) *Origins of Modern Japanese Literature*, ed. and trans. B. de Bary, Chapel Hill, NC: Duke University Press. (A study of the impact of Christianity, Marxism and other systems of Western thought on Japanese writing since the late nineteenth century.)

Keene, D. (1984) *Dawn to the West: Japanese Literature in the Modern Era*, New York: Holt Rinehart & Winston. (A comprehensive guide to all forms of modern Japanese literature; see especially the entries under 'Criticism'.)

Miyoshi Masao and Harootunian, H.D. (eds) (1988) 'Postmodernism and Japan', *South Atlantic Quarterly* 87 (3). (A special volume dealing with post-structuralist thought, theories of national and transnational identity, and contemporary debates in Japan.)

Nishida Kitarō (1911) *Zen no kenkyū* (An Inquiry into the Good), trans. Masao Abe and C. Ives, New Haven, CN: Yale University Press, 1987. (The seminal work of modern Japan's most distinguished philosopher.)

Rimer, J.T. (ed.) (1990) *Culture and Identity: Japanese Intellectuals during the Interwar Years*, Princeton, NJ: Princeton University Press. (Useful collection of essays on cultural criticism.)

Silverberg, M. (1990) *Changing Song: The Marxist Manifestos of Nakano Shigeharu*, Princeton, NJ: Princeton University Press. (A study of a prominent Marxist critic and the impact of Marxism on Japanese cultural life.)

PAUL ANDERER

LIU AN *see* HUAINANZI

LLEWELLYN, KARL NICKERSON (1893–1962)

Karl Llewellyn was philosophically the most original of the 'American Realist' jurists. His line of argument, sometimes misleadingly called 'rule-scepticism', casts doubt on received approaches to the formulation of legal rules and traditional assumptions about the part they play in law. His approach to law is an essentially functionalist one, owing much to philosophical pragmatism.

Llewellyn was an outstanding US legal thinker, innovative both in legal theory and in approach to legal education and practice. He played a major part in drafting the Uniform Commercial Code (UCC) for the USA. He emphasized the need to appreciate the fact-situations of legal cases in their full lawyerly detail, and the need to reflect on them from sociological and anthropological standpoints, rather than simply tackling them in terms of an over-simplifying prescriptivist jurisprudence.

The target of Llewellyn's jurisprudential critique was the tradition of legal study that takes the task to be that of ascertaining, ordering and transcribing a rather abstract body of rules and principles; this he saw as connecting with a model of legal processes that deems them a straightforward application of ascertained rules and principles to fact-situations. These approaches are characteristic of 'legal formalism', which the realists, a turbulent and critical younger generation of US lawyers in the 1920s, took to be the dominant view in law schools and indeed to be something of an official legal ideology in the country at large (see LEGAL REALISM §2).

Llewellyn's intellectual mission was to show that the actual practice of the law, especially in common law systems attaching great weight to precedent, cannot be matched to or helpfully explained by the formalist model. Much more goes into constructing a case as a lawyer than adding together a formulaic rule-statement and an abstract statement of the facts of the case. Precedents do not yield simple rules; rather they have to be subjected to painstaking analysis and synthesis, and looked at in groups by judges, advocates and scholars for their several purposes. There are contexts in which it may be helpful to test the results of this process by viewing them as if they were predictions of judicial conduct rather than prescriptions. The point is that a judge's

role is to act 'reasonably' about disputes. This by no means licenses disregard for statutes and precedents, but also brings into play more intuitionistic elements described by Llewellyn as 'situation sense', which requires sensitivity to political and economic realities (see LEGAL REASONING AND INTERPRETATION §§1–3).

Behind this lies a functionalist stance in the philosophy and sociology of law, well expressed in his 'law-jobs' theory, where he analyses legal roles and legal rules in terms of jobs to be performed in society. With E.A. Hoebel, he applied this theory to anthropological study of the traditional dispute-settlement techniques of the Cheyenne. It underlies all his later work, and yet was never fully developed as a comprehensive philosophy of law, partly because of the great demands on his time taken by first drafting and then (even harder) securing acceptance for the UCC, in which his approach to drafting exemplifies his theory. His last great work, *The Common Law Tradition: Deciding Appeals* (1960), extols what is in effect a self-conscious functionalism in adjudication, the 'grand style' of judging versus the rival 'formal style'. This is an eloquent plea for acknowledgement of the rule of law as a reconciliation between legal certainty, or 'reckonability', and legal adaptiveness to changing social and economic circumstances.

See also: CRITICAL LEGAL STUDIES §2; FRANK, J.; FULLER, L.L.; LAW, PHILOSOPHY OF; POUND, R.; SOCIAL THEORY AND LAW

List of works

Llewellyn, K.N. (1933) *The Case-Law System in America*, trans. M. Ansaldi, ed. P. Gewirtz, Chicago, IL: Chicago University Press, 1989. (An early work that reminds us of Llewellyn's strong pre-Nazi German connections; the 1989 edition is a translation of his explanation of common law methods to a German audience first published in Germany in 1933 on the basis of lectures given in Leipzig in 1928–9.)

—— (1940) 'The Normative, the Legal, and the Law-Jobs', *Yale Law Journal* 49: 1355–1400. (The original and best exposition of the law-jobs theory.)

—— (1960) *The Bramble Bush*, New York: Oceana Publications. (An exuberant guide to legal study for first-year law students, containing some of the notorious overstatements often used out of context to discredit legal realism.)

—— (1960) *The Common Law Tradition: Deciding Appeals*, Boston, MA and Toronto, Ont.: Little, Brown. (The work in which Llewellyn responded to the unease about law generated by some responses to realism, and expounded his view of the 'Grand Style'.)

—— (1962) *Jurisprudence: Realism in Theory and Practice*, Chicago, IL: Chicago University Press. (A valuable, though not comprehensive, collection of Llewellyn's essays and papers on legal theory.)

Llewellyn, K.N. and Hoebel, E.A (1941) *The Cheyenne Way*, Norman, OK: Oklahoma University Press. (The application of the law-jobs theory to legal-anthropological investigations among the Cheyenne.)

References and further reading

Twining, W. (1985) *Karl Llewellyn and the Realist Movement*, London: Weidenfeld and Nicolson. (An outstanding work of intellectual biography, covering all aspects of Llewellyn's life and work in a sympathetically critical way, and with comprehensive references and bibliography.)

NEIL MacCORMICK
WILLIAM TWINING

LLULL, RAMON (1232–1316)

One of the most extraordinary figures of thirteenth-century Europe, Llull was a self-taught lay theologian and philosopher, chiefly concerned with reforming Christian society and converting unbelievers. Details of his life remain obscure, but over 200 of his writings survive. Most of these expound his personal dialectical system, the Great Universal Art of Finding Truth, an encyclopedic collation of commonplace doctrines that attempts to show how all human knowledge conforms to divine truth. Largely ignored during Llull's lifetime and denounced as heretical in the later Middle Ages, the Great Art became very popular in the Renaissance as a programme of universal knowledge.

1 Career
2 The Great Universal Art of Finding Truth
3 Llull's legacy

1 Career

Ramon Llull came from a prosperous Catalan merchant family that had helped conquer his native Majorca from the Arabs in 1230. Little information exists about his life: several letters document his contacts with civil or ecclesiastical authorities, and his writings include some autobiographical details. Most information comes from a brief *Vita* (Life) composed

in 1311 by admirers at Paris. Llull pursued secular affairs (perhaps as a royal official) until about 1263, when visions of Christ moved him to serve God instead. He dedicated himself to three goals: writing a book to refute 'the errors of the infidels', establishing schools to train Christian evangelists in Oriental languages and converting all unbelievers. He spent ten years in private study and contemplation, acquiring a Muslim slave to teach him Arabic and perhaps receiving some formal education from local religious houses. Eventually he conceived the plan for a Great Universal Art of Finding Truth, which he attributed to divine inspiration. Around 1275 Prince James of Majorca summoned Llull to Montpellier so that church authorities could examine his writings. After this he travelled constantly, presenting his plans at the courts of Aragon, France, and the papacy, visiting the University of Paris, attending meetings of religious orders and church councils, and making private missionary trips to North Africa and the Eastern Mediterranean. Llull's greatest success came apparently in 1311 at the Council of Vienne, which created chairs of Oriental languages at several major universities. However, he often complains that his contemporaries ignore him, and depicts himself as a lone 'fool'. Llull wrote some 250 works in Catalan, Latin and Arabic. None of the Arabic works has survived.

2 The Great Universal Art of Finding Truth

Nearly all Llull's writings expound his Great Universal Art of Finding Truth, which broadly constitutes a comprehensive scheme for achieving the ancient Christian ideal that BONAVENTURE called 'retracing the arts and sciences to theology'. Llull's Art synthesizes the methods of contemplation and missionary argument that he evidently absorbed during his decade of private study. Though often compared to scholastic works such as Aquinas' *Summa theologiae*, Llull's system is in fact more popularizing. He often recommends it as a simpler alternative to the complex university curricula of his day, which he characterizes as abandoning the quest for divine truth in favour of quibbling over human errors. Llull especially criticized the schoolmen of Paris as 'Averroists' (see AVERROISM (RADICAL ARISTOTELIANISM)). His spiritual and intellectual values were thus basically conservative: he sought to maintain the subordination of philosophy to theology and the primacy of cloister over classroom in Western Christian culture.

Llull's Great Art tries to show how the many truths of human learning all depend on one divine truth. It accomplishes this by tracing the manifestation of certain 'divine dignities' (attributes of the Godhead) in every entity. The mature versions of his system specify nine divine dignities (goodness, greatness, eternity, power, wisdom, will, virtue, truth and glory) as 'absolute principles' of all being and knowledge. Nine more 'relative principles' (difference, concord, contrariety, beginning, middle, end, superiority, equality and inferiority) explain the diffusion and operation of the absolute principles in various 'subjects' of existence (God, angels, heavens, humans, imagination, senses, elements, vegetal power, and skills and arts). Finally, nine 'rules' (whether? what? why? from what? what kind? how much? where? when? and how?) function as heuristic questions for guiding inquiry about the principles and subjects. Llull usually creates lists of other categories necessary for applying the Great Art to particular fields of inquiry.

The most remarkable feature of his system is its use of the letters B, C, D, E, F, G, H, I and K to symbolize each set of nine principles or rules (the letter A is reserved to symbolize the coincidence of all absolute principles in God). Llull's handling of these symbolic terms owes little to the propositional or syllogistic structures of Aristotelian logic. Instead, he employs circular or tabular charts (called 'figures') to show all possible combinations of two or three letters, in the manner of mathematical multiplication tables. These dual and triple letter combinations are intended to comprehend all possible philosophical and theological propositions. Llull develops the combinations into discursive statements and analyses their 'truth' by applying a wide range of analogical, allegorical, proportional and figural arguments. He insists that these arguments constitute 'necessary reasons' capable of 'demonstrating' the truth of Christian belief. Successfully using the combinatory figures and necessary reasons of Llull's Great Art depends almost completely on a correct understanding of the meanings assigned to the letters B through K. This understanding in turn invariably requires extensive interpretative work, guided by unswerving fidelity to Christian dogma.

Llull almost never cites any authorities but his own writings and routinely recasts all theological or philosophical questions in the vocabulary of his Great Art. Consequently, the sources for his work remain very difficult to identify. Llull's pre-eminent concern for evangelizing probably motivated his preference for commonplace doctrines (such as the divine attributes) that would be comprehensible to Christians, Jews and Muslims alike. Some scholars have sought global precedents for Llull's arguments in a single Hebrew, Latin or Arab authority, such as the *Zohar*, Bonaventure or Algazel (see AL-GHAZALI). However, his

erudition rarely exceeds the level found in widely-circulated Latin or Arab theological and philosophical compendia.

His combinatory methods and necessary reasons do generate some novel propositions. For example, his metaphysics relies heavily on broadly Neoplatonic principles of the emanation, participation and resemblance of all beings (see NEOPLATONISM). He advocates the reality of all universals and attributes both matter and form to all things, except God. Yet he does not functionally distinguish substantial from accidental forms, and rarely appeals to Aristotelian concepts of causality. Instead he refers all real or mental relationships to the 'coessential implication' of the divine dignities in the Godhead, and ascribes to every being three 'innate correlatives' of 'act', 'activity' and 'passivity' as a reflection of the divine Trinity. In psychology, he follows well-known Augustinian, Aristotelian or Avicennan doctrines, but also treats imagination as a separate level in the soul and classifies speech as a sixth sense (because it serves the exalted purpose of comprehending God). In logic, his doctrines largely correspond to the Scholastic 'old logic'. However, he simplifies sophistics by proposing a 'master fallacy of equivocation', arguing that this explains all the other fallacies identified by Aristotle as failures to distinguish the apparent sense from the true sense (that is, the Christian interpretation) of disputed propositions, such as 'The world is eternal' (see ETERNITY OF THE WORLD, MEDIEVAL VIEWS OF). He also recommends a new method of demonstration *per aequiparantiam* that will show 'coessential' relationships. In ethics, he extends a concept of moral finality to all beings, insisting that every being possesses the dual 'intention' of either serving God or contributing to this service. Ultimately, Llull's arguments make most sense if regarded as a comprehensive natural theology: his Great Art is arguably the Christian Middle Ages' most ambitious attempt to explain how all creation manifests its Creator (see NATURAL THEOLOGY).

3 Llull's legacy

In the fourteenth century, Llull's work came to attract non-academic lay people and clergy who valued its spiritual ideals, although the Aragonese Inquisition challenged their orthodoxy. NICHOLAS OF CUSA was the first of several important thinkers whose interest in Llull made the Great Art widely known in the Renaissance and early modern era. Authorities from Giordano BRUNO to LEIBNIZ praised its pansophistic method, and schools of Lullism flourished on Majorca into the eighteenth century. An extensive body of modern non-scholarly literature on Llull exists; only a few of the best critical or historical studies are in English.

See also: BONAVENTURE; NATURAL THEOLOGY; NICHOLAS OF CUSA

List of works

Llull, Ramon (1263–1316) *Opera Latina*, Palma de Mallorca: Maioricensis Schola Lullistica del CSIC, 1959–67 and Turnhout: Brepols, 1978–, 18 vols to date; *Obres de Ramon Lull*, ed. M. Obrador y Benassar, Salvador Galmés *et al.*, Palma de Mallorca: Comissió Editora Lulliana, 1906–17 and Diputació Provincial de Balears and Institut d'Estudis Catalans, 1923–50, 21 vols. (The former is the standard modern critical edition of Llull's Latin texts, while the latter is the most comprehensive edition of the Catalan texts. Many Latin texts not printed elsewhere can be found in *Opera omnia*, ed. I. Salzinger, Mainz, 1721–40, 9 vols; repr. Frankfurt: Minerva, 1965. Other Catalan editions can be found in *Nova edició de les obres de Ramon Llull*, Palma de Mallorca: Patronat Ramon Llull, 1990–, 2 vols to date, and *Obres essencials*, ed. M. Batllori *et al.*, Barcelona: Selecta, 1957–61, 2 vols, the latter being a well-prepared omnibus of Catalan texts. For English editions, see *Selected Works of Ramon Llull*, trans. A. Bonner, Princeton, NJ: Princeton University Press, 1985, an excellent English translation of selected texts with good introduction. *Doctor Illuminatus: A Ramon Llull Reader*, trans. A. Bonner and E. Bonner, Princeton, NJ: Princeton University Press, 1993, is an abridgement of *Selected Works*, but with updated introductory material.)

References and further reading

* Anonymous (*c*.1311) *Vida de Ramon Llull: les fonts escrites i la iconografia coetànies*, ed. M. Batllori and J.N. Hillgarth, Barcelona: Associació de Bibliòfils de Barcelona, 1982. (Latin and Catalan texts, with extensive notes in Catalan.)
Brummer, R. (1976) *Bibliographia Lulliana: Ramon-Llull-Schrifttum 1870–1973*, Hildesheim: H. Gerstenberg. (Complete bibliography of scholarship on Llull.)
Garcías Palou, S. (1981) *Ramon Llull y el Islam*, Palma de Mallorca: Gráficas Planisi. (Comprehensive analysis of Llull's relations with Islamic world.)
Hillgarth, J.N. (1971) *Ramon Lull and Lullism in Fourteenth-Century France*, Oxford: Clarendon Press. (Best critical study in English of Llull and his times.)

Johnston, M.D. (1990) '*Affatus*: Natural Science as Moral Theology', *Estudios Lulianos* 30: 3–30, 139–59. (Explains Llull's proposal of speech as a sixth sense and theories of spiritual psychology.)
—— (1995) *The Evangelical Rhetoric of Ramon Llull*, New York: Oxford University Press. (Comprehensive study of Llull's preaching and literary doctrines.)
—— (1981) 'The Reception of the Lullian *Art*, 1450–1530', *Sixteenth Century Journal* 12: 31–48. (Reviews rise of Renaissance enthusiasm for Llull's work.)
—— (1987) *The Spiritual Logic of Ramon Llull*, Oxford: Clarendon Press. (Detailed analysis of Llull's logical doctrines.)
Moreno Rodríguez, F. (1982) *La lucha de Ramon Llull contra el averroismo entre 1.309 y 1.311*, Madrid: Universidad Computense de Madrid. (Reviews Llull's polemic against the 'Averroist' scholars of Paris.)
Oliver, A. (1965–9) 'El Beato Ramón Llull en sus relaciones con la escuela franciscana de los siglos XIII–XIV', *Estudios Lulianos* 9: 55–70, 145–65; 10: 49–56; 11: 89–119; 13: 51–65. (Best account of Llull's relations with Franciscan thought.)
Platzeck, E.-W. (1962–4) *Raimund Lull. Sein Leben– Seine Werke. Die Grundlagen seines Denkens (Prinzipienlehre)*, 2 vols, Rome: Editiones Franciscanae and Düsseldorf: Verlag L. Schwann. (Major comprehensive study of Llull's life and work.)
Pring-Mill, R.D.F. (1973) 'The Analogical Structure of the Lullian Art', in *Islamic Philosophy and the Classical Tradition: Essays Presented to Richard Walzer*, Columbia, SC: University of South Carolina Press, 315–26. (Excellent brief explanation of Llull's methods of argumentation.)
Salleras i Carolà, M. (1986) 'Bibliografia lul.liana (1974–1984)', *Randa* 19: 153–98. (Useful update to Brummer's *Bibliographia Lulliana*.)
Studia Lulliana (1957–). (Formerly titled *Estudios Lulianos*, this journal publishes and reviews the latest specialized scholarship on Llull and his milieu.)
Urvoy, D. (1980) *Penser l'islam: les présupposés islamiques de l'Art' de Lull*, Paris: Vrin. (Most detailed and reliable account of Llull's knowledge of Islam.)
Yates, F.A. (1954) 'The Art of Ramon Lull', *Journal of the Warburg and Courtauld Institute* 17: 115–73. (Remains a seminal study of Llull's system.)

MARK D. JOHNSTON

LOCALITY *see* BELL'S THEOREM

LOCKE, JOHN (1632–1704)

John Locke was the first of the empiricist opponents of Descartes to achieve comparable authority among his European contemporaries. Together with Newton's physics, the philosophy of An Essay concerning Human Understanding *gradually eclipsed Cartesianism, decisively redirecting European thought. Neoplatonic innatism was replaced with a modest, naturalistic conception of our cognitive capacities, making careful observation and systematic description the primary task of natural inquiry. Locke saw himself as carrying out just such a descriptive project with respect to the mind itself. Theorizing is the construction of hypotheses on the basis of analogies, not penetration to the essences of things by super-sensory means. In religion Locke took a similarly anti-dogmatic line, advocating toleration and minimal doctrinal requirements, notably in* Epistola de tolerantia *(A Letter concerning Toleration) and* The Reasonableness of Christianity. *Through his association with the Earl of Shaftesbury he became involved in government, and then in revolutionary politics against Charles II and James II. The latter involvement led to exile, and to* Two Treatises of Government, *a rejection of patriarchalism and an argument from first principles for constitutional government in the interests of the governed, and for the right of the misgoverned to rebel. Locke published his main works only after the 'Glorious Revolution' of 1688. He undertook important governmental duties for a time, and continued to write on many topics, including economics and biblical criticism, until his death. The* Essay, Epistola *and* Second Treatise *remain centrally canonical texts.*

Locke held that all our ideas are either given in experience, or are complex ideas formed from simple ideas so given, but not that all our knowledge is based on experience. He accepted that geometry, for example, is an a priori science, but denied that the ideas which are the objects of geometrical reasoning are innate. 'Experience' includes 'reflection', that is reflexive awareness of our own mental operations, which Cartesians treated as a way of accessing innate ideas, but which Locke calls 'internal sense'. To have ideas before the mind is to be perceiving given or constructed sensory or quasi-sensory images – things as perceived by sense. In abstraction, however, we consider only aspects of what is presented: for example, a geometrical proof may consider only aspects of a drawn figure, allowing generalization to all figures similar in just those respects. Universal knowledge is thus perception of a relation between abstract ideas, but we also have

immediate knowledge, in sensation, that particular external things are causing ideas in us. This awareness allows us to use the idea as a sign of its external cause: for example, the sensation of white signifies whatever feature of objects causes that sensation. Representation is thus fundamentally causal: causality bridges the gap between reality and ideas. Consequently we have sensitive knowledge of things only through their powers, knowledge of their existence without knowledge of their essence. Each way in which things act on the senses gives rise to a phenomenally simple idea signifying a quality, or power to affect us, in the object. Some simple ideas, those of the 'primary qualities', solidity, extension, figure, motion or rest, and number (the list can vary) can be supposed to resemble their causes. Others, ideas of 'secondary qualities', colour, smell, taste and so forth, do not. We also form ideas of the powers of objects to interact.

Our idea of any sort of substantial thing is therefore complex, including ideas of all the qualities and powers by which we know and define that 'substance'. Additionally, the idea includes the 'general idea of substance', or possessor of the qualities, a placemarker signifying the unknown underlying cause of their union. Locke distinguishes between the general substance, matter, and the 'particular constitution' of matter from which flow the observable properties by which we define each sort of substance – gold, horse, iron and so on. This 'real constitution' or 'real essence' is distinguishable only relatively to our definition or 'nominal essence' of the species. Locke extends this conceptualist view of classification to individuation in a famous, still influential argument that a person is individuated, not by an immaterial soul, but by unifying and continuous consciousness.

Because their real essences are unknown to us, we are capable only of probable belief about substances, not of 'science'. In mathematics, however, real essences are known, since they are abstract ideas constructible without reference to reality. So too with ideas of 'mixed modes' and 'relations', including the ideas of social actions, roles and relationships which supply the subject-matter of a priori sciences concerned with law, natural, social and positive. The three legislators are God, public opinion and government. God's authority derives from his status as creator, and natural or moral law is his benevolent will for us. Locke's political theory concerns the authority of governments, which he takes to be, at bottom, the right of all individuals to uphold natural law transferred to a central agency for the sake of its power and impartiality. Economic change, he argues, renders this transfer imperative. In a state of nature, individuals own whatever they have worked for, if they can use it and enough is left for others. But with land-enclosure (which benefits everyone by increasing productivity) and the institution of money (which makes it both possible and morally justifiable to enjoy the product of enclosure) this primitive property-right is transcended, and there is need for an authority to ordain and uphold rules of justice for the benefit of all. Any government, therefore, has a specific trust to fulfil, and should be organized so as best to safeguard this role. A ruler who rules in his own interest forfeits all rights, as a criminal at war with his subjects. Then rebellion is justified self-defence.

1 **Life and main works**
2 **The structure of Locke's empiricism**
3 **Ideas of sense and reflection: their retention and abstraction**
4 **Five sorts of idea**
5 **Substances, mixed modes and the improvement of language**
6 **Knowledge and belief**
7 **Faith, reason and toleration**
8 **Personal identity**
9 **Ethics, motivation and free will**
10 **Political theory**
11 **Influence**

1   **Life and main works**

John Locke was born at Wrington, Somerset in England on 28 August 1632. His father was a small property owner, lawyer and minor official, who served on the side of Parliament in the civil war under the more influential Alexander Popham. Through Popham, Locke became a pupil at Westminster School, then the leading school in England. From Westminster he was elected in May 1652 to a Studentship at Christ Church, Oxford, conditionally tenable for life.

During the next fifteen years at Oxford Locke took his degrees (B.A. 1656, M.A. 1658) and fulfilled various college offices, becoming Tutor in 1661. Between 1660 and 1662 he wrote three manuscripts on issues of Church and State, individual conscience and religious authority, two now published together and known as *Two Tracts on Government*, and *An necesse sit dari in Ecclesia infallibilem Sacro Sanctae Scripturae interpretem?* (Is it necessary to have in the church an infallible interpreter of holy scripture?). Although his answer to the last question was predictably negative, in the *Tracts* he expressed a less-than-tolerant view of conscientious religious unorthodoxy, assigning to rulers the right to determine details of religious observance for the sake of public peace. While Censor of Moral Philosophy at Christ Church in 1664 he completed the Latin manuscript now known as *Essays [or Questions] on the Law of Nature*, which presaged his mature views –

both his general empiricism and his conception of moral obligation as an obligation to God to obey natural law. This work also rejects wayward and dogmatic appeals to conscience, in favour of reason based on experience.

The politics of religion, at the time a large part of politics, was not Locke's only extracurricular interest. His reading-notes ('commonplace books') of this time indicate an interest in Anglican theology, and by 1658 he was reading and taking lecture notes in medicine with the assiduity appropriate to a chosen career. This interest extended to chemistry and, in the 1660s, to the new mechanical philosophy as expounded, for example, by Robert BOYLE, whom Locke had met by 1660. Locke also read the main philosophical works of Descartes, and some Gassendi, but his record focuses on their versions of corpuscularianism, bypassing metaphysical and epistemological underpinnings (see DESCARTES, R. §§11–12; GASSENDI, P. §§2, 4). On the evidence, natural philosophy attracted Locke more at this time than metaphysics, although the coarse empiricism of *Essays on the Law of Nature* is close to that of Gassendi. Yet Locke could hardly have remained ignorant of the battle among the new philosophers between 'gods' and 'giants' – between those, led by Descartes, in the Platonic-Augustinian metaphysical tradition and those, headed by Gassendi and HOBBES, who developed ancient empiricist and materialist theory.

In 1665 Locke's university life was interrupted by a diplomatic mission to Brandenburg as secretary to Sir Walter Vane. About this time he decided against entering the church, but took the one way of nevertheless keeping his Studentship (without obligation to reside in Oxford) by transferring formally to medicine. In 1666 came a momentous meeting with Lord Ashley (Anthony Ashley Cooper, who became Earl of Shaftesbury in 1672), whose London household Locke subsequently joined in 1667. Here his medical and political interests alike received a more practical edge than they had previously possessed. He began collaborating closely with the pre-eminent physician, Thomas Sydenham, and in 1668 successfully supervised an operation on Lord Ashley to drain an abscess on the liver. In the years following he continued to act as medical advisor within Ashley's circle, supervising the birth of Ashley's grandson, later the philosophical Third Earl of Shaftesbury. A manuscript of this time in Locke's handwriting (but perhaps wholly or partly by Sydenham), 'De Arte Medica', is strongly sceptical of the value of hypotheses, as opposed to experience, in medicine.

During this same period, presumably influenced by his patron, Locke wrote the manuscript *Essay concerning Toleration* (1667), departing from his earlier, nervously illiberal justification of constraint and advocating toleration of any religious persuasion not constituting a positive moral or political danger – provisos excluding, respectively, atheists and Roman Catholics. In 1667 Ashley became a member of the governing 'cabal' which followed Clarendon's period as Lord Chancellor, and in 1672 became Lord Chancellor himself. Under Ashley, and for a while after Ashley's fall from office in 1673, Locke was involved in government. He began to work on economic questions, and for some years helped in the organization of the newly founded colony of Carolina. He was registrar to the commissioners of excise (perhaps a sinecure) from 1670 to 1675, secretary for presentations (in charge of ecclesiastical patronage) in 1672–3, and secretary and treasurer to the Council for Trade and Plantations (no sinecure) in 1673–4.

Nevertheless he found time for new intellectual interests. Not later than 1671 he put down for discussion by a group of friends what he later claimed (inaccurately, given *Essays on the Law of Nature*) to have been his first thoughts on the powers of the understanding. He found the topic sufficiently gripping for a more extensive treatment than such an occasion would have demanded in '*Intellectus humanus cum cognitionis certitudine, et assensus firmitate*' (The human intellect, the certainty of knowledge and the confirmation of belief), dated 1671, with a longer (and as strongly empiricist and imagist) redrafting in the same year entitled 'An Essay concerning the Understanding, Knowledge, Opinion and Assent' – the manuscripts now known as Drafts A and B of *An Essay concerning Human Understanding*.

In 1675 Locke moved to France, beginning at the same time to write his journal. He met physicians and philosophers, undertook a programme of reading in French philosophy and continued working on his 'Essay'. On returning to England in 1678, after the fabricated 'Popish plot', he was again caught up in politics and in attempts to exclude Charles' brother James from the succession. Charles dissolved Parliament in 1681, and Shaftesbury led a group of Whigs planning insurrection. During this period Locke probably wrote the bulk of the *Two Treatises of Government*; the first, at least, to support moves for James' exclusion, the second possibly later to advocate actual rebellion. He also wrote, with James Tyrrell, a long response (still unpublished, 1997) to Edward Stillingfleet's *Unreasonableness of Separation*, defending the position of nonconformists against Stillingfleet's criticisms. In 1682 Shaftesbury went into exile, dying soon after. When the Rye House plot to assassinate Charles and James was uncovered in 1683, Locke himself prudently moved to Holland, where he contacted other, more overtly active exiles. His connections provoked expulsion from his Christ Church Studentship in 1684, and at the time of Monmouth's rebellion he went into hiding to escape arrest. His intellectual activities continued unabated, the *Essay* being largely written by 1686. In 1685–6 he wrote *Epistola de Tolerantia* (Letter concerning Toleration), perhaps in response to the revocation of the edict of Nantes. He made friends, and discussed theological questions, with the remonstrant Philippus van Limborch and Jean Le Clerc, publishing various items in the latter's journal, *Bibliothèque universelle et historique*, including a review of Newton's *Principia* (1686) and a ninety-two page abridgement of the *Essay* (1688).

In 1688 the 'Glorious Revolution' brought the deposition of James, and Locke returned to England the following year. He declined the post of ambassador to Brandenburg, accepted an undemanding post as commissioner of appeals (annual salary, £200) and set about publishing his writings. *Epistola de Tolerantia* was published pseudonymously in Holland in May 1689, and Popple's English translation followed within months. The *Two Treatises* were revised and published anonymously, and the *Essay* followed in December (with authorship acknowledged), although both books were dated 1690. *A Second Letter concerning Toleration* (1690) and *A Third Letter for Toleration* (1692) were in response to attacks by an Anglican clergyman, Jonas Proast. *Some Considerations of the Consequences of the Lowering of Interest and Raising the Value of Money*, partly based on the manuscript of 1668, was published in 1691 (dated 1692) against Parliamentary measures of the time. In 1691, Locke accepted the invitation of an old friend, Damaris Masham and her husband to live with them, as far as his concerns permitted, at Oates in Essex. Country life seems to have ameliorated the asthma which dogged his last years. *Some Thoughts concerning Education* (1693, revised 1695), a significant work in the history of educational theory, was based on a number of letters of advice to his friend, Edward Clarke. In 1694 came the second edition of the *Essay*, with important additions including a controversial chapter on identity. In 1695 he published a new work, once more anonymously, *The Reasonableness of Christianity*. John Edwards' attacks on its liberal, minimalist interpretation of Christian faith were rebutted in two *Vindications* (1695b, 1697a) (see LATITUDINARIANISM).

Locke continued to be engaged on economic questions, and in 1695 he joined a committee to advise the Chancellor of the Exchequer on monetary policy. His recommendations, supported by further papers, were accepted. In 1696 came an important government appointment to the Council for Trade and Plantations, and for four years he fulfilled fairly onerous duties on the Board of Trade for the considerable annual salary of £1,000. At the same time he engaged in an extended controversy with Edward Stillingfleet, who found the Essay theologically suspect. *A Letter to the Right Reverend Edward, Lord Bishop of Worcester* was followed by two further Letters in reply to Stillingfleet's Answers. Despite its controversial style, Locke's argument is often a cogent clarification of his position. The exchange prompted significant alterations to the fourth edition of the *Essay* (1700) and long passages were included as footnotes in the posthumously published fifth edition. In June 1700 Locke resigned from the Board of Trade, a sick man, and thereafter lived mostly at Oates. Pursuing a long-standing interest in biblical criticism, he set about the work which was posthumously published as *A Paraphrase and Notes on the Epistles of St. Paul*, an important contribution to hermeneutics (see HERMENEUTICS, BIBLICAL). In 1702 he wrote the reductive *Discourse of Miracles*, and in 1704 began a *Fourth Letter on Toleration*. On October 28th 1704 he died as Damaris Masham read to him from the Book of Psalms. For the last years of his life he was generally respected as, with Newton, one of Britain's two intellectual giants, a reputation undiminished by death.

2 The structure of Locke's empiricism

Locke's mature philosophy is 'concept-empiricist', but not 'knowledge-empiricist': he held that all our concepts are drawn from experience, but not that all our knowledge is based on experience. Yet his early position, in *Essays on the Law of Nature* and the first part of *Draft A*, was 'knowledge-empiricist' in just this sense – even the axioms of geometry gain assent 'only by the testimony and assurance of our senses' (*Draft A* I: 22–3). However, according to *Draft A*, when we find that certain relations hold without exception, we assume that they hold universally and come to employ them as 'standards' of measurement embodied in the meaning of our terms. Locke sees this as implying a choice: an axiom can *either* be interpreted as an 'instructive', but uncertain summary of experience, *or* as a quasi-definition, founded on experience but 'only verbal...and not instructive'. But later in *Draft A* he discards the notion that geometrical axioms can be interpreted empirically, taking them only in a sense in which they can be known by 'demonstration' or 'the bare shewing of things or proposing them to our senses or understandings' (*Draft A* I: 50) – that is, by intuitions with perceived or imagined instances (for example, dia-

grams) as their objects. At the same time he recognizes that mathematical propositions are not plausibly regarded as merely verbal. The possibility of alternative interpretations of universal propositions, *either* as certain, but verbal, *or* as instructive, but uncertain, is now restricted to propositions about substances, such as 'Man is rational'. Locke has shifted, in effect, from knowledge-empiricism towards a concept-empiricism which allows 'instructive' a priori knowledge (the last being the acknowledged ancestor of Kant's synthetic a priori – see KANT, I. §4).

Locke's intuitionism shapes his attack on the innatism characteristic of the Platonic-Augustinian-Cartesian tradition (see INNATE KNOWLEDGE). Starting with propositions, Locke rebuts the argument from alleged universal assent, or assent by all who have come to the use of reason. But ideas are what is before the mind in thought, and propositions are ideas in relation. Locke's underlying thesis is that to take either knowledge or ideas to be innately 'imprinted on the mind' in a merely dispositional sense (and they are clearly not actual in all human beings from birth) would be contrary to any intelligible notion of being 'in the mind': 'Whatever idea was never perceived by the mind, was never in the mind' (*Essay* I.iv.20). Locke concedes dispositional knowledge and ideas, retained by the memory and capable of being revived, but he understands both intentionality and knowledge in terms of perception, and finds nonsensical the notion of perception which never has been conscious and actual. This strongly intuitionist model rules out dispositional innatism as an intelligible possibility. Rationalist intuitionism, from Locke's point of view, is simply incoherent. And since the only dispositional ideas and knowledge are what is retained in the memory, what is before the mind as the object of intuition or demonstration must be experiential or sensory.

Locke also argues that there are no general maxims of logic or mathematics to which all assent when they come to the use of reason, since many rational but illiterate people never consider such abstract principles. He does not accept that reasoning merely consonant with logical principles is equivalent to assent to them, or, for example, that distinguishing two things is tacit employment of the idea of identity. Explicit abstract principles and ideas come late and with so much difficulty that people cannot agree on ideas of impossibility, identity, duty, substance, God and the like – just the ideas most supposed innately luminous. That rational people assent to certain propositions on first proposal is beside the point, since such people will only have understood the terms of the proposition in question by abstraction from experience. Then they will assent, not because the proposition is innate, but because it is evident. To describe the bare capacity to perceive such truths as the possession of innate principles and ideas will make all universal knowledge innate, however specific or derived. Turning to practical principles and the idea of God, Locke appeals to anthropology to rebut the claim that any of these are universally recognized. The main thrust of his argument, however, is conceptual.

Locke's empiricism has another central feature. Like Gassendi and HOBBES, he expressly accords independent authority to the particular deliverances of the senses (see GASSENDI, P. §3). Descartes had argued that sensation requires interpretation employing innate, purely intellectual ideas even in order for us to conceive of its objects as independent bodies. For Descartes, moreover, natural sensory belief is defenceless in the face of sceptical argument – secure knowledge of the existence of bodies can only be achieved through a rational proof involving reflection on the role and mechanisms of sense (see DESCARTES, R.§9). This emphatic subordination of sense to reason Locke rejects just as firmly: the senses are 'the proper and sole judges' of the existence of bodies. He sees the senses as knowledge-delivering faculties in their own right, prior to any understanding of their mechanisms: 'the actual receiving of ideas from without ... makes us know, that something doth exist at that time without us, which causes that idea in us, though perhaps we neither know nor consider how it does it' (*Essay* IX.xi.2). The sceptic's doubt about the external world is a mere pretence, not to be taken seriously: 'no body can, in earnest, be so sceptical, as to be uncertain of the existence of those things which he sees and feels'. Echoing LUCRETIUS, Locke sees the reason employed in sceptical argument itself as standing or falling with the senses: 'For we cannot act any thing, but by our faculties; nor talk of knowledge it self, but by the help of those faculties which are fitted to apprehend even what knowledge is' (*Essay* IX.xi.3). Locke does identify features of sense-experience which militate against scepticism: for example, sensory ideas depend on physical sense-organs, and are systematically and unavoidably consequent on our situation; the deliverances of different senses cohere; there is a 'manifest difference' between ideas of sense and ideas of memory and imagination (most dramatically with respect to pain), as there is between acting in the world and imagining ourselves acting; and so on (*Essay* IX.xi.4–8). Yet all these considerations are simply 'concurrent reasons' which further, but unnecessarily confirm 'the assurance we have from our senses themselves' – 'an assurance that *deserves* the name of knowledge' (*Essay* IX.xi.3).

Locke's explanation of the certainty and extent of 'sensitive knowledge of existence' hinges on his view that in sensation we are immediately aware, not only of sensations or 'ideas', but of their being caused by things outside us. We are thus able to think of the unknown cause through its effect in us: 'whilst I write this, I have, by the paper affecting my eyes, that idea produced in my mind, which, whatever object causes, I call *white*; by which I know, that that quality or accident (i.e. whose appearance before my eyes, always causes that idea) doth really exist, and hath a being without me' (*Essay* IX.xi.2). This claim ties in with another, that ideas of simple sensory qualities are always 'true', 'real' and 'adequate': 'their truth consists in nothing else, but in such appearances, as are produced in us, and must be suitable to those powers, [God] has placed in external objects, or else they could not be produced in us' (*Essay* II.xxxii.14). Simple ideas are 'distinguishing marks' which fulfil their function well enough whatever unknown difference lies behind the sensible distinction. But this function fits them for another, as terms in the natural language of thought. The idea of white signifies, that is *indicates*, its unknown cause, and also signifies, that is *stands for*, that feature of things in thought. So the limited causal knowledge that sensation supplies allows us to have contentful thought and knowledge of the external world. The idea of power extends such pretheoretical knowledge: our idea of the melting of wax, joined to the idea of active or passive power, can be employed as a sign of whatever in the sun melts wax, or of whatever in wax causes its melting. Consequently Locke decides to treat ideas of powers as simple ideas, and knowledge of powers as observational. The senses do not give knowledge of the essence or nature of bodies, but they do give knowledge of their existence, and enable us to distinguish between them.

3 Ideas of sensation and reflection: their retention and abstraction

Locke's employment of the word 'idea' responds to a variety of antecedents. Like Descartes, he uses it ambiguously both for representative states (acts, modifications) of mind and, more frequently, for the represented objects as they are represented or conceived of, the so-called 'immediate' objects of perception and thought. To have an idea before the mind is generally, for Locke, to be contemplating something under a certain conception rather than contemplating a psychological state. To 'perceive a relation between ideas' is to perceive a relation between things-as-conceived-of. But Locke's account also looks back to the Epicurean view of sensations as signs of their unknown causes in the motion of atoms or 'corpuscles' (see §2), a view which points away from the Cartesian and scholastic presumption of intrinsically representative elements in thought towards a purely causal understanding of representation, treating ideas as blank sensory effects in the mind. Locke never resolves the tension between these different conceptions of an idea, although each of them is necessary to his theory.

Locke strongly opposes the Augustinian-Cartesian view that knowledge and truth consist in the conformity of human conceptions with God's conceptions, the divine ideas or archetypes employed in creation and revealed to us in our active use of reason. For Descartes, human reason is only accidentally involved with the senses, whereas for Locke there are no purely intellectual ideas. The task traditionally assigned to intellect – universal thought – Locke assigns to 'abstraction', taken to be the mind's in some sense separating out elements of raw experience and employing them as 'standards and representatives' of a class. What this means will be considered.

Although Locke sometimes writes that all words stand for ideas, ideas are the mental correlates of terms or names: that is, words that can stand in subject or predicate place. He adheres to the traditional view that 'particles', such as prepositions, conjunctions, the copula and the negative, signify, not ideas, but 'the connection that the mind gives to ideas, or propositions, one with another' (*Essay* III.vii.1). They do not *name*, but *express* 'actions of the mind in discoursing': for example, 'but' expresses various mental operations together named 'discretive conjunction'. The mental actions or operations expressed by 'is' and 'is not' are either the 'perception of the agreement or disagreement of ideas', which is Locke's definition of (at least, general) knowledge, or the 'presumption' of such a relation, which is Locke's account of belief or judgment. As commonly in earlier logic, merely considering a proposition is not distinguished from knowing or judging it to be true.

The aim of Book II of the *Essay* is to establish that all our ideas derive from experience: that is, that the way we conceive of the world (including ourselves) is ultimately determined by the way we experience the world. 'Experience' includes not only 'sense', but reflection ('reflexion') – not reflection in today's sense but reflexive awareness of our own mental operations. Platonists, Aristotelians and Cartesians all assigned the reflexive awareness of thinking to intellect rather than to sense. For Descartes, the innateness of such ideas as *substance*, *thought* and even *God* consists in the potentiality of their becoming explicit through the mind's reflecting on itself, and Leibniz argues accordingly that, simply by admitting reflection as

well as sense, Locke admits innate ideas (see LEIBNIZ, G.W. §8). Locke, however, claims that reflection, 'though it be not sense, as having nothing to do with external objects, yet it is very like it, and might properly enough be call'd internal sense' (*Essay* II.i.4). Thereafter he treats sense and reflection as theoretically equivalent (although reflexive knowledge of one's own existence is 'intuitive' rather than 'sensitive' – *Essay* IV.ix.3). This move not only extends the empiricist principle to such non-sensory notions as *willing*, *perceiving*, *contemplation* or *hope*, but also contradicts the Cartesian model of thought as transparent to itself, propounding a gap between how thinking appears to the subject and what it really is in itself – the latter being unknown. Locke also insists that reflection is second-order awareness, presupposing sense-perception as the first mental operation. And though 'ideas in the intellect are coeval with sensation' (*Essay* II.i.23), it seems that the mind must 'retain and distinguish' ideas before it can be said to 'have ideas' dispositionally, stored in the memory for employment as signifiers in thought. Ideas of reflection in particular are achieved only 'in time' – and here 'reflection' acquires some of its modern affinity with 'contemplation'. Children, Locke's accounts of both reflection and particles imply, can discern or compound ideas without having the ideas of discerning or compounding, and few of those who employ particles to *express* various mental actions ever pay them enough attention to be able to *name* them. Locke does assert that in the reception of ideas 'the understanding is merely passive', but he also allows that attention, as well as repetition, helps 'much to the fixing any ideas in the memory' (*Essay* II.x.3).

The 'retention' of ideas in the memory, therefore, is a necessary condition of discursive thought, and its description significantly echoes Hobbes' account of memory as 'decaying sense'. What decay are – 'it may seem probable' – images in the brain, and hostility to the separation of intellect from imagination pervades the *Essay*. Descartes' famous argument for such a separation – that we can accurately reason about a chiliagon although we cannot form a distinct image of it – is directly rebutted: the reasoning is made possible by our precise idea of the number of the sides (itself dependent on the technique of counting), not by a clear and distinct idea of the shape. 'Clear' ideas are, by definition, such as we receive 'in a well-ordered sensation or perception'. Locke's treatment of abstraction accords with such express sensationism. 'Abstract ideas' are particulars, universal only in 'the capacity, they are put into... of signifying or representing many particular things' (*Essay* III.iii.11). Locke means that in abstract thought the mind relates to, and employs, sensory images in a certain way, not that it manufactures sense-transcendent objects of intellect. Abstract ideas are what we have *distinctly* before the mind in general thought, but distinctness may be achieved by 'partial consideration', not absolute separation: 'Many ideas require others as necessary to their existence or conception, which are yet very distinct ideas. Motion can neither be, nor be conceived without space' (*Essay* II.xiii.11–13). The very abstract ideas of *being* and *unity* are ideas of anything whatsoever considered as existing, or as one. Geometry gave Locke his paradigm of 'perception of the relation between ideas'. But where Cartesians saw the role of geometrical diagrams to be the stimulation of intellectual ideas, for Locke, as for Hobbes, the object of reasoning and source of 'evidence' is the diagram itself, whether actual or imagined. (Kant's 'intuition' owes something to Locke.) Given these structural features of his theory, it seems undeniable, as some have denied, that Locke's ideas are essentially sensory (or reflexive) images (see HOBBES, T. §4; KANT, I. §5).

4 Five sorts of idea

Book II of the *Essay* presents an alternative to Aristotle's doctrine of categories, the traditional typology of entities capable of being named or predicated (see ARISTOTLE §7). That Locke's classification is of *ideas* rather than of *things* stresses that the categories are purely conceptual. He identifies five broad types: simple ideas, ideas of simple modes, ideas of mixed modes, ideas of substances and ideas of relations. Simple ideas come first in the Lockean order of knowledge, as substances come first in the Aristotelian order of being. Simple ideas are necessarily given in experience, whereas complex ideas can be constructed by 'enlarging' ('repeating') or 'compounding' simple ideas. Ideas of relations result from 'comparing' ideas. 'Abstracting' is more a matter of focusing on an idea or, better, an aspect of an idea, whether given or constructed, than of creating a new one (see §3). Locke sometimes acknowledges that the overarching compositional model is problematic in its application, but it is put into doubt even by his formal introduction of the notion of a simple idea. The ideas of the sensible qualities of a body, Locke claims, though produced by the same body, in some cases by the same sense, are evidently distinct from one another, each being 'nothing but *one uniform appearance*, or conception in the mind' (*Essay* II.ii.1). Yet to ascribe the conceptual distinctions between, for example, a thing's shape, its motion and its colour to a primitive articulation of *appearance* is to beg a crucial question.

Under the topic of simple ideas Locke expounds his famous distinction between primary and secondary qualities (*Essay* II.viii). Since the cause of a simple idea may be quite different in character from the idea itself, we should distinguish the idea in the mind from the corresponding quality (that is, the power to cause the idea) in bodies. Certain qualities, however, are necessary to our conception of bodies as such. These are the primary qualities, 'solidity, extension, figure, motion, or rest, and number', just those which figured in corpuscularian speculations. Locke's proposal (displaying the tension, described in §3 of this entry, between two conceptions of representation) is that in the perception of a primary quality the represented cause, the basis of the power in the object, is qualitatively *like* the idea caused: 'A circle and square are the same, whether in idea or existence' (*Essay* II.viii.18). Only this will allow that the action of external bodies on the senses is 'by *impulse*, the only way which we can conceive bodies operate in' (*Essay* II.viii.12) – an appeal to the seventeenth-century commonplace that mechanical explanations are peculiarly intelligible. But then ideas of 'colours, sounds, tastes, etc.', Locke's 'secondary qualities', must also be mechanically stimulated. Hence secondary qualities 'are nothing in the objects themselves, but powers to produce various sensations in us by their primary qualities, i.e. by the bulk, figure, texture, and motion of their insensible parts' (*Essay* II.viii.10). Ontologically they are in the same boat as the power of fire to cause pain or, indeed, its power to melt wax.

The idea of power itself Locke attributes to experience of regular patterns of change, giving rise first to expectations that 'like changes will for the future be made in the same things, by like agents, and by the like ways', and then to the thought that in one thing exists the possibility of being changed and in another 'the possibility of making that change' (*Essay* II.xxi.1). So we form the idea of power, active and passive: the power of fire to melt wax and the power of wax to be melted are aspects of fire and wax known and identified only through their joint effect. The idea of power is thus a place-marker for attributes which could in principle be known more directly.

The ideas or experiences of pleasure and pain are important simple ideas, since they are responsible for our ideas of good and evil, and are 'the hinges on which our passions turn' (*Essay* II.xx.3). (This hedonistic theory of motivation and value is examined in §9 of this entry.)

'Simple modes' constitute another problematic category. Locke starts with modes of extension, the subject-matter of geometry, with which he compares modes of duration. Here his thesis is that we acquire ideas of particular modes of extension (that is, determinate lengths and figures) or duration (that is, periods) in experience, and can then repeat (or divide) them so as to construct ideas of possible lengths, figures or periods not previously experienced. Roughly, 'modification' here is compounding like with like. The same model supplies Locke's account of ideas of numbers, achieved by the repetition or addition of units, aided and ordered by the linguistic technique of counting. Yet he also recognizes qualitative simple modes, effectively conceding that ideas of different 'shades of the same [experienced] colour' are constructible. Even with quantitative 'modes', where the 'repetition' model has some plausibility, it is problematic what is a simple idea. The idea of determinable *extension* is a plausible candidate, with its determinates as 'modes', but the repetition model presupposes simple units. Locke impatiently responds that the smallest sensible point 'may perhaps be the fittest to be consider'd by us as a *simple idea* of that kind' (*Essay* (5th edn) II.xv.5n.), but he was evidently more concerned to argue that ideas of novel determinate figures are *somehow* constructible from what has been given, and so to subvert a Platonic-Cartesian argument for innateness, than to insist on the adequacy of a rigid compositional model.

Another target in Locke's account of simple modes is Descartes' conceptual identification of space and matter in the thesis that the essence of matter is extension. For Locke, both the essence of matter and the nature of space are unknown. He argues that our idea of a vacuum is not contradictory, since our ordinary idea of body includes solidity as well as extension, but he declines to choose between relational and realist theories of space. Yet comparison of the *Essay* with earlier notes and drafts indicates that, having first held a Hobbesian relational view, Locke came gradually to favour a realism close to that of Newton (see DESCARTES, R. §§8, 11; NEWTON, I. §4).

Ideas of mixed modes arise with the combination of unlike simple ideas, as in the idea of a rainbow. But Locke's paradigms are ideas of human actions and institutions, the materials of demonstrative moral and political theory. Like ideas of geometrical figures, ideas of mixed modes can properly be formed without regard to what exists. Ethical thought is none the worse for being about a virtue or motive or political constitution which is nowhere actually instantiated. Ideas of substances are different, for they concern the real rather than the ideal: 'When we speak of *justice*, or *gratitude*... our thoughts terminate in the abstract ideas of those virtues, and look not further; as they do, when we speak of a *horse*, or *iron*, whose specific ideas we consider not, as barely in the mind, but as in things themselves, which afford the original patterns of those ideas' (*Essay* III.v.12). Moreover, whereas ideas of substances are formed on the presumption that the complex idea represents a really or naturally united thing, the unity of mixed modes is essentially conceptual. Indeed, 'Though... it be the mind that makes the collection, 'tis the name which is, as it were, the knot, that ties them fast together'. Different languages slice up the field of human life and action in different ways, determined by the practices and priorities of the communities that speak them. This thesis can be extended to natural modes such as freezing, since even here it is the term tied to a striking appearance, not a natural boundary, which slices out the particular process from the general process of nature. That, Locke plausibly assumes, is not how it is with horses.

The chief thought behind Locke's somewhat confusing account of ideas of substances is that our idea of a thing or stuff is a compound of ideas of its qualities, but the thing itself is not a compound of qualities (*Essay* II.xxiii). The substance–accident structure is a feature of our ideas and language, not a structure in reality. It is a feature which marks our ignorance of the underlying nature of things, since we always conceive and talk of a substance as a *thing* possessing certain qualities, that is, as a '*substratum*, in which [the qualities] do subsist, and from which they do result, which therefore we call substance'. The mistake of dogmatic philosophers is to think that they can form *simple* conceptions of substances matching their unitary natures. Aristotelians are so misled by language that, just because, 'for quick despatch', we employ one name, 'gold' or 'swan', they think it a 'simple term' corresponding to a 'simple apprehension'. Cartesians take the simple essences of matter and spirit to be extension and thought. Yet so far are we from catching the nature of any thing in our *complex* idea of it that, if it is asked what the subject is of the qualities by which we define it (the colour and weight of gold, for example), the best answer we can give is 'the solid extended parts', that is, the mechanistic 'corpuscularian' hypothesis as advanced by Boyle. If it is asked in turn 'what it is, that solidity and extension inhere in,' we can only say, 'we know not what'. Our idea of the substance is of 'nothing, but the supposed, but unknown support of those qualities, we find existing, which we imagine cannot subsist, *sine re substante*, without something to support them'. Such an idea is 'obscure and relative'. Ideas of specific substances are 'nothing but several combinations of simple ideas, co-existing in such, though unknown, cause of their union as makes the whole subsist of itself' (*Essay* II.xxiii.6). Locke's point is that no theory, not even the corpuscular hypothesis, gives an account of the ultimate nature of things.

Finally come ideas of relations – father, son-in-law, enemy, young, blacker, lawful and so on (*Essay* II.xxv–xxviii). Like ideas of modes, ideas of relations can properly be constructed without regard to reality, in particular if they are conventional relations. Adequate ideas even of natural relations, Locke claims, are possible without adequate ideas of the things related: we can grasp the essence of fatherhood without knowing the essence of man or even the mechanisms of reproduction. His point is that the biological details are irrelevant to the rights and duties of a father – a question rationally determined in his own attack on patriarchalism in *Two Treatises*. From this point of view, relations are theoretically close to modes. Yet Locke does allow certain relations to have peculiar ontological significance. Causal, spatial and temporal relations are universal relations which pertain to all finite beings. Identity and diversity are so too: a thing is diverse from anything existing in a different place at the same time, 'how like and indistinguishable soever it may be in all other respects', and the continuity of individual substances is spatio-temporal. The last important type of relations to be picked out for special discussion is that of moral relations, or the relations of actions to some law 'whereby good or evil is drawn on us, from the will and power of the law-maker' (*Essay* II.viii.5).

5 Substances, mixed modes and the improvement of language

On Locke's account of communication (*Essay* III.i–ii), names should, by common convention or special agreement, excite in the hearer's mind just the same ideas as they are associated with in the speaker's mind. Collaborative progress in the sciences depends on 'clear and distinct' or 'determined and determinate' ideas – that is, on consistent and agreed association of ideas and words (*Essay* II.xxix; compare 'Epistle to the Reader'). Locke's discussion of language is shaped by his belief that these conditions of the transference of knowledge were in his time commonly unsatisfied, especially in two domains. First, there was no agreed classification of 'substances' (living things and chemicals) based on careful observation and experiment. Second, the ideas associated with the names of mixed modes often varied both in the usage of different people and in that of the same person at different times. Two mistakes in particular disguise these shortcomings of language. The first is the assumption that a common set of words ensures a common language in the full sense, with a shared set of meanings. So people may argue about 'honour' and 'courage' without realizing that they mean different things, or nothing at all, by

the words. The second mistaken assumption is that words have meaning by standing for things directly, as if the meaning of 'salt', 'gold' or 'fish' were fixed demonstratively, by what is named. The first assumption chiefly corrupts our thought about mixed modes, the second relates 'more particularly, to substances, and their names' (*Essay* III.ii.5). Locke's radical and influential views about the latter will be considered first.

The 'idea of substance in general' employed in ideas of specific substances is the idea of something unknown underlying the attributes known by experience (see §4 of this entry). Many have objected, following Leibniz, that here Locke confusedly postulates ignorance of the subject of attributes which is not ignorance of attributes of the subject. Yet he holds that our ignorance of 'the substance of body' and 'the substance of spirit' is an ignorance of the *natures* of these things – ignorance manifested in our inability to understand the internal cohesion or (he adds in later writings) mutual attraction of bodies, or to explain what thinks in us, and how it does so. His approval of the corpuscularian hypothesis and Newton's mechanics is qualified – the best available physical theory leaves too much unexplained to be the whole truth (Newton did not disagree). The idea of substance is a place-marker for essences which are unknown, but knowable, if possibly not by human beings (see NEWTON, I.).

One feature of Locke's theory which has made difficulties for the present interpretation is the distinction he makes between substance and 'real essence'. The real essence of a thing, Locke says, may be taken for 'the very being of a thing, whereby it is what it is', the 'real internal, but generally in substances, unknown constitution of things, whereon their discoverable qualities depend' (*Essay* III.iii.15). Nevertheless, 'essence, in the ordinary use of the word, relates to sorts' (*Essay* III.vi.4). Species and genera, or sorts of things, Locke asserts, are creatures of the understanding, with membership determined by abstract ideas made on the basis of experienced resemblances, not by the presence in each of a specific form, or by a common derivation from a divine archetype. Ultimately it is a matter of arbitrary definition which observable resemblances we count as necessary for membership of this or that named sort. It is not just that specific real essences are unknown, since (Locke argues) even if we did know the real constitution of things as well as clock-makers know the works of clocks, it would still be up to us where to draw the boundaries between species, and what to include in our abstract ideas or 'nominal essences'. The real essence of a species can therefore only be 'that real constitution . . . which is the foundation of all those properties, that are combined in, and are constantly found to co-exist with, the *nominal essence*' of the species (*Essay* III.vi.6). Here, the model is that of a universal matter determinately modified as a variety of particles interacting mechanically so as to constitute the material things of ordinary experience. Since at the fundamental level these observable quasi-machines differ from one another merely quantitatively, and can do so by indefinite degrees, there are no absolute boundaries among them. There are only the discernible resemblances and differences consequent on their underlying mechanical differences – 'the wheels, or springs…within'. Even more certainly our actual classification is not based on knowledge of any such boundaries. Talk of the real essence of a species, and the distinction between its 'properties' and its 'accidents' ('properties' flowing from the essence), are therefore, contrary to Aristotelian assumptions, *de dicto* and relative to the nominal essence defining the name of that species (see ARISTOTLE §8; DE RE/DE DICTO; ESSENTIALISM).

This conception of a real essence assigns it a role closely related to that of substance. What, after all, is the 'unknown cause of the union' of any of the 'combinations of simple ideas' by which 'we represent particular sorts of substances to ourselves', if not the real essence underlying the nominal essence in question? Yet Locke sometimes distinguishes both the notion and knowledge of real essence from the notion and knowledge of substance. That is not, however, because the 'substance' is an irremediably unknown subject underlying even essence, but because it is the common stuff of a variety of species of things, 'as a tree and a pebble, being in the same sense body, and agreeing in the common nature of body, differ only in a bare modification of that common matter' (*Essay* II.xiii.18). The unknown modification is the specific 'real essence', and the equally unknown general nature of matter is the 'substance'. Locke also envisages deeper differences of kind between substances: 'God, spirits and body' are all 'substances' only because we think of each of them indeterminately as *something*, not because of a shared nature. But by the same token we distinguish spirit and body only because we cannot understand how matter could think, not because we can grasp their separate essences, as Descartes had supposed (see DESCARTES, R. §8). Indeed, since we are equally unable to understand how spirit and body might interact, or how spirits could occupy places, the issue between materialist and immaterialist accounts of minds is for Locke undecidable, and at best a matter for speculation.

Locke's corpuscularian conception of a world of machines, resembling and differing from one another by continuous degrees, is consonant with his independent epistemological conviction that names have meaning only through association with 'ideas', rather than directly with 'things as really they are'. Together they motivate his programme for improving natural classification which advocates, not the allegedly impossible Aristotelian ideal of identifying the natural hierarchy of genera and species, but general agreement on a practically useful way of gathering and ordering the things in the world, taking into account such dependable concomitances of qualities and powers as appear to careful observation and experiment. Locke saw the future of biology and chemistry – and even of mechanics – in descriptive 'natural history', justifiable as a useful, orderly record of dependable means to ends but falling short of systematic 'science'. Despite its apparent pessimism, his view has survived in biological taxonomy as a continuous tradition of scepticism as to the reality of our taxonomical divisions. In semantic theory, Locke's broad conception of how the names of substances have meaning has only recently been eclipsed by a quasi-Aristotelian view (see KRIPKE, S.; PUTNAM, H.).

Locke saw equal need for a programme of agreeing definitions in ethics, where his target is less the notion that moral and political terms name independent realities, than the assumption that the very existence of a word in a language ensures that it has a fixed, common meaning. 'Common use', Locke concedes, 'regulates the meaning of words pretty well for common conversation' (*Essay* III.ix.8) – for the 'civil' rather than 'philosophical' use of words. But where precision is required, as in the establishment or interpretation of a law or moral rule, reliance on ordinary usage leaves us vulnerable to the trickery of rhetoricians who prove bad qualities good by shifting the meaning of terms; or to the subtleties of interpretors, whether of civil or revealed law, who render unintelligible what started off plain. The remedy is to give the names of virtues and vices, and of social actions, roles and relations the fixed and unequivocal definitions necessary for a clear and unwavering view of right and wrong, 'the conformity or disagreement of our actions to some law'.

6 Knowledge and belief

Like Platonists and Cartesians, Locke drew a strong distinction between knowledge and belief (also called opinion, judgment, or assent), but the ground and placing of this division between two forms of propositional 'affirmation' differed from theirs fundamentally. As the distinction is expounded in Book

IV of the *Essay*, universal knowledge or 'science' does not have special objects, whether a transcendent intelligible world in the mind of God or innate intellectual ideas. Its difference from general belief lies in the way in which ideas are related in the mind. In universal knowledge, the 'connection and agreement, or disagreement and repugnancy' of ideas is 'perceived', whereas in belief it is 'presumed' on the basis of 'something extraneous to the thing I believe'. To follow a proof gives knowledge of the conclusion, whereas to accept the conclusion on the authority of a mathematician constitutes only belief. Similarly in the case of 'sensitive knowledge' of particular existence, what we ourselves perceive we know to be so, but what we infer, or accept on testimony, we merely believe.

Knowledge, as well as assent, is subject to 'degrees': there are degrees, not only of probability, but of 'evidence'. The first degree of knowledge is intuitive knowledge, in which the mind 'perceives the truth, as the eye doth light, only by being directed toward it'. Intuition 'leaves no room for hesitation, doubt, or examination'. The second degree is demonstrative knowledge, where the truth is perceived by the aid of one or a chain of 'intermediate ideas'. Doubt or mistake is possible at any point in the sequence with respect to connections not currently in view. Hence, 'Men embrace often falsehoods for demonstration'. Locke's chief model for 'intermediate ideas' is geometrical: for example, the lines employed in the intermediate steps of the Euclidean proof which allow us to see that the angles of a triangle are equal to the angle on a straight line. Although his conception of intuition can seem Cartesian, the profound difference is that, for Locke, ideas which are objects of intuition are essentially a product of sense (including reflection) and imagination. As *Draft B* puts it, the angles and figures I contemplate may be 'drawn upon paper, carved in marble, or only fancied in my understanding' (*Drafts* vol. 1: 152). Consequently Locke often talks as if we can *literally* perceive a necessary relation between ideas. Another difference from Descartes, as also from Hobbes, is that he rejects the pretensions of proposed analytical methods to uncover self-evident principles from which the phenomena can be deduced.

The third degree of knowledge is sensitive knowledge of the existence or 'co-existence' of qualities in external things. Locke's first introduction of this category seems tentative, even an afterthought, as if it is called knowledge only by courtesy. In order to fit his main definition of knowledge it has to be interpreted as the perception of the agreement of ideas of sensible qualities with the idea of existence, an analysis Locke unsurprisingly declines to develop.

Yet 'sensitive knowledge of existence' does straightforwardly satisfy his other definition of knowledge: what is known in sensitive knowledge (that is, that something external is causing an idea of sense) is known directly, 'perceived' and not inferred (see §2 of this entry). Locke was writing in a context in which, despite Gassendi's Epicurean claim that sensory knowledge is the most evident of all, it was widely assumed that knowledge in the full sense comprises only knowledge of necessary first principles, demonstrated 'science', and perhaps reflexive knowledge. Locke wanted both to concede to orthodoxy that the evidence and certainty of our sensory knowledge is not as high as that of intuition and demonstration, and to insist that, nevertheless, 'sensitive knowledge of existence' does give a degree of immediate certainty and 'deserves the name of knowledge'.

Knowledge is also categorized in terms of four propositional relations (forms of 'agreement') between ideas, namely 'identity (or diversity)', 'relation', 'necessary connection or coexistence' and 'existence' (*Essay* IV.i). By 'identity' Locke intends tautologies such as 'Gold is gold' and 'Red is not blue'. Intuitive knowledge of such identities is achieved simply by discerning ideas. The category also includes such truths as 'Gold is a metal' or 'Gold is malleable', when the property predicated is included in the thinker's definition of gold. Thus 'identity' covers all and only 'trifling' or 'verbal' propositions (see §2 of this entry).

The categories, 'relation', 'necessary connection or coexistence', and 'existence', on the other hand, together include all 'instructive' propositions. The category, 'relation', in part a response to Locke's earlier difficulty over the informativeness of mathematics (see §2 of this entry), also marks his rejection of analytical methods in science. As well as geometrical axioms and theorems, 'relation' presumably includes more exciting Lockean principles: as that, if anything changes, something must have a power to make it change; that, if anything exists, something must have existed from eternity; and that a maker has rights over his artefact. Categorical propositions about natural things, however, fall either under 'existence' or under 'necessary connection or coexistence'. Our own existence is known intuitively, God's existence demonstratively (Locke employs an idiosyncratic hybrid of the cosmological and teleological proofs), and, as discussed, the existence of bodies by sense. The category 'necessary connection or coexistence' owes its disjunctive name to a rather complicated relation between particular and universal propositions. Particular *coexistences* are perceived by sense, for example, when we simply observe that yellowness, heaviness and the metallic qualities coexist in a particular subject together with malleability (that is, that this gold is malleable), without perceiving *necessary connections* between them. Locke assumes, however, with most mechanists, that necessary connections do hold between universally coexistent properties even if we cannot perceive or grasp them. Since he contends that no natural science based on the essences of substances has been achieved, he offers only very limited examples of perceived necessary connections, as 'whatever is solid is impenetrable' and 'a body struck by another will move'. (According to the short, posthumously published *Elements of Natural Philosophy*, the laws of inertia are evidently necessary, but the law of gravity is based only on experience.) In the absence of knowledge, beliefs in universal coexistences (for example, that all gold dissolves in aqua regia), when we *presume* unperceived connections, may be inductively based on sensitive knowledge of particular coexistences. That is descriptive natural 'history', not 'science'. In general, if the idea of a particular quality is deducible from the idea of a substance, that is only because the predication of that quality is an identity: that is, universal propositions about substances, if certain, are 'trifling' and, if 'instructive', are uncertain (see §2 of this entry). In contrast, instructive a priori sciences are possible just because their objects are constructed by us: our ideas of simple or mixed modes, formed without essential reference to actuality, themselves constitute the subject-matter of mathematics and ethics. In other words, these demonstrative sciences are possible, as natural science is not, just because they deal, hypothetically, with abstractions.

The degrees of assent are 'Belief, Conjecture, Guess, Doubt, Wavering, Distrust, Disbelief, etc.' (*Essay* IV.xvi). Probability is 'the measure whereby [the] several degrees [of assent] are, or ought to be regulated'. When assent is unreasonable, it constitutes 'error'. Reasonable assent is regulated according to the proposition's conformity with the thinker's own experience or the testimony of others. The proposition may concern 'matters of fact' falling within human experience, or else unobservables lying 'beyond the discovery of our senses'. Locke identifies four broad degrees of probability with respect to 'matters of fact': (1) when the general consent of others concurs with the subject's constant experience; (2) when experience and testimony suggest that something is so for the most part; (3) when unsuspected witnesses report what experience allows might as well be so as not; and (4) when 'the reports of history and witnesses clash with the ordinary course of nature, or with one another' – a situation in which there are no 'precise rules' for assessing probability. Finally, with respect to unobservables, 'a wary reasoning from analogy' with

what falls within our experience 'is the only [natural] help we have' and the only ground of probability (see DESCARTES, R. §4). Although Locke, in striking contrast to Descartes, brings probability into the centre of epistemology, 'belief' is always treated as a practical surrogate for 'knowledge', and he takes induction itself to be grounded on the assumption of underlying, unknown necessary connections: 'For what our own and other men's constant observation has found always to be after the same manner, that we with reason conclude to be the effects of steady and regular causes, though they come not within the reach of our knowledge' (*Essay* IV.xvi.6).

Another deliberate and radical difference from Descartes relates to the role of will in cognition. For Locke, knowledge is like sense perception: we may choose where and how hard to look, but we cannot then choose what we see. Belief is similar: 'Assent is no more in our power than knowledge... And what upon full examination I find the most probable, I cannot deny my assent to' (*Essay* IV.xx.16). Yet we are morally responsible for both error and ignorance in so far as it results from our not employing our faculties as we should. In a number of chapters of the *Essay*, Locke examines the causes of error, finding them, with many writers of his time, in the same appetites, interests, passions, wayward imaginings and associations of ideas as may motivate voluntary actions. Linguistic confusion, and its deliberate exploitation (see §5 of this entry), sometimes plays a role, and sometimes, like MALEBRANCHE and others, Locke has direct recourse to physiology, explicitly merging his explanations of error with explanations of madness. In contrast to Hobbes, he places the merely habitual 'association of ideas' in the pathology of 'extravagent' thought and action: 'all which seems to be but trains of motion in the animal spirits, which... continue on in the same steps... which by often treading are worn into a smooth path, and the motion in it becomes easy and as it were natural' (*Essay* II.xxxiii.16). But culpable error arises, on Locke's official view, when we 'hinder both knowledge and assent, by stopping our enquiry, and not employing our faculties in the search of any truth' (*Essay* IV.xx.16). It is the failure to use our power to pause for 'full examination' which leaves a space for beliefs motivated by interests and passions. But this two-stage model – the first stage voluntary, the second involuntary – proves too difficult to maintain, and sometimes passions and interests are taken to act on the will *between* enquiry and judgment, by distorting our 'measures of probability' themselves. Locke's approach is more common-sensical than that of Descartes, but the psychology of motivated error is a hard nut which he also failed to crack.

7 Faith, reason and toleration

Locke's views on belief, probability and error owed much to traditional philosophy of religious belief, and to the great debate of his century about the relationship between faith and reason. He was strongly influenced by writers in the Anglican 'probabilist' tradition, who argued for toleration within the Church with respect to all but an essential core of Christian dogma. William CHILLINGWORTH had rejected as absurd the traditional conception of a moral requirement to have 'faith' in the sense of a conviction equal to that of knowledge but beyond what is rationally justified. To recognize a proposition as probable to a certain degree is to believe it just to that degree. Revelation therefore cannot be a basis for belief distinct from probability, but is something the significance of which has to be rationally assessed, capable at best of increasing the probability of certain propositions. Similarly for Locke, when revelation grounds belief that would otherwise be improbable, that is just one natural reason outweighing another: 'it still belongs to reason to judge of the truth of its being a revelation, and of the signification of the words, wherein it is delivered' (*Essay* IV.xviii.8). For if 'reason must not examine their truth by something extrinsical to the perswasions themselves; inspirations and delusions, truth and falshood will have the same measure' (*Essay* IV.xix.14).

Accordingly, like Chillingworth, MORE and others, Locke combined a purportedly reasonable acceptance of the Bible as revelation with a critical approach to its interpretation, taking into account that it was written by men in particular circumstances. An alleged revelation which conflicts with what is naturally evident loses its claim to be revelation. Certain revealed truths (such as the Resurrection) lie 'beyond the discovery of our natural faculties, and above reason', but Locke had little time for mysteries: 'to this crying up of faith, in opposition to reason, we may, I think, in good measure, ascribe those absurdities that fill almost all the religions which possess and divide mankind' (*Essay* IV.xviii.7, 11). Locke took the existence of God and the content of moral law to be demonstrable by reason, and, according to *The Reasonableness of Christianity* and its *Vindications*, the only essentially revealed truth of the New Testament is that Christ is the Messiah, promising forgiveness of sins to those who sincerely repent and do their imperfect best to keep the law of nature. The Bible also makes that law plain to those without the leisure or capacity to reason it out – a difficult enough task for anyone, as Locke ruefully acknowledges. The meaning of scripture is thus for Locke primarily moral, and the 'truth, simplicity, and reasonableness' of Christ's teaching is itself a main reason for accepting it as revelation. Saving faith involves works, not acceptance of 'every sentence' of the New Testament under this or that preferred interpretation.

Much the same goes for immediate revelation. Even the genuinely inspired would need proofs that they really were inspired, and the errors of common-place 'enthusiasm' are ascribed, as by More, to physiology, 'the conceits of a warmed or overweening brain'. The advocate of immediate personal revelation over reason 'does much what the same, as if he would persuade a man to put out his eyes the better to receive the remote light of an invisible star by a telescope' (*Essay* IV.xix.4). Divine illumination necessarily depends on, and is not separable from, the natural light – 'reason must be our last judge and guide in everything'. Locke echoes Chillingworth's basic principle: the lover of truth, unbiased by interest or passion, will not entertain 'any proposition with greater assurance than the proofs it is built upon will warrant'. The implication of this standard, in the actual circumstances of life, is toleration: 'For where is the man, that has incontestable evidence of the truth of all that he holds, or of the falshood of all he condemns; or can say, that he has examined, to the bottom, all his own, or other men's opinions?' (*Essay* IV.xvi.4).

Locke's *Letter on Toleration*, the mature fruit of considerably more unpublished writing directly on the issue, links his epistemology with his political thinking. Belief is not something that can be commanded or submitted to the authority of the government, whose concern is not with saving souls but the preservation of property. Necessarily each individual must judge as they see fit, and the truth needs no help, having its own efficacy. But the right to toleration is nevertheless viewed in the context of the right and duty to seek salvation and true doctrine without harm to others, harm which is at least threatened by all who deny the authority either of moral law or of the established government. Atheists therefore forfeit the right in principle, and Roman Catholics as a matter of political fact. (See LATITUDINARIANISM; SOCINIANISM)

8 Personal identity

The main aim of the chapter of the *Essay* entitled 'Of Identity and Diversity' (II.xxvii) is to explain how immortality is compatible with materialism. In order to maintain an agnostic neutrality on the question of the immateriality of the soul, Locke had, first, to rebut the Cartesian claim that self-awareness supplies a clear and distinct idea of a simple, continuously existing substance; and, second, to show that the metaphysical issue is irrelevant to 'the great ends of morality and religion' (*Essay* IV.iii.6). He argues that, although the moral agent is indeed the continuously existing, rational, self-aware subject of consciousness, the 'person', the identity of this subject over time is determined by the continuity of unitary consciousness itself, not the continuity of an immaterial soul. Locke can therefore accept the Resurrection and Last Judgment as tenets of his 'reasonable' Christianity, without commitment to dualism, on the supposition that the consciousness of the resurrected person is continuous, through memory, with that of the person who died. This conclusion avoids an objection to his concept of demonstrative ethics as a science of modes, that morality relates to 'man', a substance, not a mode. His response is that morality concerns, not 'man' as a biological species, but 'man' as rational, the 'moral man', indeed all rational beings. 'Person', as he puts it, is a 'forensic term'.

Locke's argument starts from the claim that questions of identity over time are always questions as to the continuous existence in space of something of a certain kind, and that difficulties may be avoided by 'having precise notions of the things to which it is attributed'. The identity of non-substances is parasitic on that of substances: 'All other things being but modes or relations ultimately terminated in substances', their identity will be determined 'by the same way' (*Essay* II.xxvii.2). Locke holds that events and processes ('actions') are not strictly identical from moment to moment, each part of what we consider one process being distinct from every other part. Substances, however, genuinely continue to exist from moment to moment. The identity of 'simple substances' – material atoms and the presumed simple 'intelligences' – is straightforward. Each excludes others of the same kind out of its place by its very existence – a principle definitive of identity. But difficulties arise with compound substances. Strictly, a body composed of many atoms is the same just as long as the same atoms compose it – yet 'an oak, growing from a plant to a great tree, and then lopped, is still the same oak'. Locke's explanation is that 'in these two cases of a mass of matter, and a living body, *identity* is not applied to the same thing' (*Essay* II.xxvii.3). Although he does not clearly distinguish the two views, he seems to hold individuation, rather than the identity-relation, to be kind-relative. A plant or animal is not just 'a cohesion of particles anyhow united', but such an organization of parts as enables the continuation of its characteristic life, for example, as an oak. In fact the *species* of the living thing is irrelevant to Locke's theory (fortunately, given his view that the definition of 'oak' will differ from speaker to speaker). The essential claim is that life is a principle of unity and continuity distinct from simple cohesion, thus allowing a living thing and the mass of matter that momentarily composes it so to differ in kind as to be capable of occupying the same place at the same time.

Locke defines *person* as 'a thinking intelligent being, that has reason and reflection, and can consider itself as itself, the same thinking thing at different times and places' (*Essay* II.xxvii.9). His thesis is that, just as life constitutes a distinct individuative principle of unity and continuity, so does reflexive consciousness. He argues for the logical independence of the continuity of consciousness from both the continuity of substance (whether supposed material or immaterial, simple or complex) and the continuity of animal life by a series of imagined cases: for example, for someone now to possess Socrates' soul would not make him the same person as Socrates, unless he remembered Socrates' actions as his own; whereas if souls are the seat of consciousness, and the soul of a prince could migrate to the body of a cobbler, 'everyone sees he would be the same person with the prince, accountable only for the prince's actions. But who would say it was the same man?' (*Essay* II.xxvii.15). Locke viewed such cases, not necessarily as real possibilities, but as compatible with our partial understanding of things, our *ideas*: 'for such as is the idea belonging to that name [namely 'person', 'man' or 'substance'], such must be the identity'. Yet in the crucial case of the Resurrection, we are left wondering how continuous existence through time – not to speak of space – is achieved simply by a fit between present consciousness and past experience and actions. Indeed, as BERKELEY and REID argued, memory-links seem both too little and too much for the continuity of a substantial thing. Yet, despite these and other difficulties for Locke's theory, it set the agenda for subsequent discussion and versions of it still have adherents (see PERSONAL IDENTITY).

9 Ethics, motivation and free will

With Locke's conviction that a demonstrative ethics is possible went a belief that what stood in its way was the deplorable slipperiness, openly encouraged by the practise of rhetoric, of a moral language in which terms are not consistently tied to ideas (see §5 of this entry). Both were consonant with his apparently early conviction that Natural Law theory, as pursued by such as HOOKER and GROTIUS, is capable of development into a full account of our duties to God and our fellows – even though he had first seen Natural Law as empirically based (see §3 of this entry). But Natural Law theory also gave him what could not be supplied by the conception of a quasi-geometrical system of rights and duties flowing from the definitions of mixed modes and relations: the conception of an unconditional obligation to act in accordance with moral principle against what we might otherwise desire (see NATURAL LAW).

In the *Essay* the argument starts, as might be expected, with the question of how our basic concepts of value are derived from experience. Locke has no doubt about what it is in experience that makes anything matter to us. Like other empiricists of his time, he is both a psychological and an ethical hedonist. Pleasure and pain supply not only our sole motives but also our ideas of good and evil: 'That we call *good* which is *apt to cause or increase pleasure*, or *diminish pain in us; or else to procure, or preserve us the possession of any other good, or absence of any evil*' (*Essay* II.xx.1). The passions are 'modes' of pleasure and pain arising from, or involving, value-judgments: thus hope is 'that pleasure in the mind, which every one finds in himself, upon the thought of a probable future enjoyment of a thing, which is apt to delight him'; fear is 'an uneasiness of the mind, upon the thought of a future evil likely to befall us' (*Essay* II.xx.9–10). Desire is the 'uneasiness a man finds in himself upon the absence of any thing, whose present enjoyment carries the idea of delight with it' (*Essay* II.xx.6). This theory of motivation faces certain problems. First, how do we get from judgments of good and evil, of what conduces to pleasure and pain, to judgments of right and wrong, of what we morally ought or ought not to do? Second, having got there, if the passions, as modes of pleasure and pain, constitute our only motives, what passion could motivate us to do what is right? Third, in what, if anything, does choice and freewill – moral agency – consist?

Locke's answer to the first question, already given in *Essays on the Law of Nature*, is that the concept of obligation comes with the relational concept of law: '*Morally good and evil* then, is only the conformity or disagreement of our voluntary actions to some law, whereby good or evil is drawn on us, from the will and power of the lawmaker; which good and evil, pleasure or pain, ... is that we call *reward* and *punishment*' (*Essay* II.xxviii.5). Locke makes it clear that the notion of obligation presupposes the right, as well as the power of the lawgiver to legislate and punish – in *Essays* Locke's 'power' is explicitly *potestas*, authority, rather than *potentia*, mere force. There are, he says in the *Essay*, three kinds of law: divine law, the measure of sin and moral duty; civil law, the measure of crimes and innocence; and the law of opinion or reputation, the measure of virtue and vice. God legislates by *ius creationis*, the maker's right over what is made, and

divine law is binding on all rational creatures capable of pleasure and pain. God's law accords with his wisdom and benevolence, so that we can know it by reflecting on what a wise and benevolent Deity would require of us. Unsurprisingly, Locke's ethics is heavily utilitarian.

The relationship between divine law and civil law, and the standing of the civil magistrate under divine law, is the subject-matter of Locke's political theory as expounded in *Two Treatises*. The notion of a 'law of reputation', sometimes called 'the philosophical law', has a more complex role in his thought. It is Locke's explanation of popular secular morality, but it also represents his view of the possibility of non-theistic philosophical systems of ethics. Roughly, the thought is that ordinary morality, sanctioned by public approval and disapproval, exists as a means to the preservation of society, itself a condition of the happiness of individuals. As arrangements differ between societies, so do their moral concepts and what counts as virtue and vice in each, although naturally there will be overlap given their shared aim of self-preservation. Since the divine law too is concerned with the good of human beings, and with self-preservation as a duty, the law of reputation will tend to coincide with divine law. In the aborted fragment of the *Essay*, 'Of Ethick in General', Locke suggests that philosophers may have some inkling of the divine law, but they confuse it with the law of reputation. Consequently their systems reduce either (like that of Hobbes) to an advocacy of what tends to the preservation of society, or (like that of Aristotle) to the elaboration of a set of definitions of the behaviour of which a particular society approves or disapproves (King [1829] 1864: 308–13). Locke does not deny the social importance of the law of reputation, however, and in *Some Thoughts concerning Education* he assigns a necessary role in a child's moral education to public esteem and shame. His complaint is that an explanation of moral obligation in terms of the value of certain actions to society, and the value of society to the individual, cannot explain how we may be morally obliged to do something contrary to our own felt interest – our interest, at least, in this world. Self-interest may commonly prescribe adherence to social rules, but it may not always do so. As Locke says in the *Essays on the Law of Nature* ([1664] 1954: 204) 'a great number of virtues, and the best of them, consist only in this: that we do good to others at our own loss'.

Locke's position is, then, that in order to explain both moral obligation and moral motivation (conflated in the usual seventeenth-century notion of obligation), we need to see morality as a system of laws prescribed by a supremely rational, just and benevolent creator to whom we owe the duty of obedience as creatures, and whose power to reward and punish in the next life is capable of motivating anyone who duly considers it (see VOLUNTARISM). Like any theistic explanation of morality's binding force, this proposal is incoherent, and in its case the incoherence lies in the combination of the view that obligation is created by law with the claim that we have a natural obligation to obey the law of our creator. Locke, however, was more exercised by the problem of why consideration of the afterlife so often fails to move theists to do their duty. Indeed, he accorded the problem wider scope, since he followed Pascal in the thought that the bare possibility of there being an afterlife, given the infinite good at stake, ought in reason to motivate the Christian life (see PASCAL, B. §6). Locke's explanation of the human capacity to know the better and choose the worse involved a refinement of his theory of motivation which echoes his theory of error. In the first edition of the *Essay*, in the long chapter 'Of Power', he held that 'the choice of the will is everywhere determined by the greater apparent good' (*Essay* II.xxi.70). By the second, he believed that mere consideration of future benefit will not move us to action unless it gives rise to 'an *uneasiness* in the want of it' – that is, to desire. Only a present passion – and, it seems, a kind of pain – can move to present action. It may require some reflection on the situation, over and above the simple recognition of probable or possible consequences for good or ill, to bring desire up to scratch, and to 'suit the relish of our minds to the true intrinsic good or ill, that is in things'. Someone who sees the good but does not pursue it has not reflected enough: 'Morality, established upon its true foundations, cannot but determine the choice of any one that will but consider' (*Essay* II.xxi.70).

Locke's increased emphasis on the role of deliberation in his hedonistic theory of moral motivation complicates his much revised account of liberty. He adopted a self-determinist view of free will – a free action is not one that is causally undetermined, but one determined by the agent's 'own desire guided by his own judgement'. He defines 'liberty' as 'the power to act or not to act according as the mind directs' (*Essay* II.xxi.71). But another power became increasingly important to him, the power 'to stand still, open the eyes, look about, and take a view of the consequence of what we are going to do, as much as the weight of the matter requires' (*Essay* II.xxi.67), and it is in this power, he often suggests, that the liberty of rational agents really consists. The tension is unresolved, for Locke never retracts the rhetorical question to which he himself seems to have given an answer: 'For how can we think anyone freer than to have the power to do what he will?' (*Essay* II.xxi.21) (see FREE WILL).

10 Political theory

Locke's mature political theory is set out in 'An Essay concerning the True Original, Extent, and End of Civil Government', the second of *Two Treatises of Government*, the first being a point-by-point rebuttal of Robert Filmer's biblically based patriarchalism (see FILMER, R.). Locke's primary contention is that the right to govern comes with a duty to govern in the interest of the governed. Failure by the government to recognize or observe this duty creates the right to rebel. Like the Natural Law theories of Hooker, Grotius and Pufendorf on which he draws, Locke's argument moves from first principles, in effect a fragment of his proposed demonstrative ethics; but much of its richness derives from links with his practical political concerns and interests. It presents attitudes and actions attributable to Charles II and James II as a betrayal of trust, hostile to those features of the British constitution most adapted to the essential purposes of government; but he also states principles relating to property, money, social conventions, taxation, punishment, family relations, inheritance, the rights of the poor, enclosure of land, the practice and justification of colonial settlement, and more.

Filmer had argued that both political authority and property rights exist only by divine institution – by God's giving Adam dominion over the creatures, by the subjection of Eve, and by Adam's natural paternal rights over his children. Monarchs are deemed natural inheritors of Adam's rights. A part of Locke's strategy, pursued in both Treatises, against this doctrine was to drive wedges between the possession and inheritance of property and the possession and conveyance of authority, and between paternal (or, as Locke prefers, parental) authority and political authority. For example, the right of children to inherit their parents' property stems from their natural right (not just that of the eldest child) to sustenance by their parents, a right which cannot be supposed to embrace either patriarchal authority or political power. The analogy of power and property in Filmer's argument, however, was not only in relation to inheritance, for it entailed that individual ownership is simply a grant of use by the king, making taxation – its partial withdrawal – his personal right. Locke was therefore concerned to give property a quite different role in his explanation of political society.

For Locke, government is a human invention, to which personal property is prior. In a state of nature, he argues in the Second Treatise, human beings have an obligation, in accordance with divine or natural moral law, 'to preserve the rest of mankind', their equals as creatures and servants of God, by a rational extension of their duty to preserve themselves. More specifically, 'no one ought to harm another in his life, health, liberty or possessions' (*Two Treatises* II.6). Yet, before government, 'everyone has a right to punish the transgressors of that law to such a degree, as may hinder its violation'. The 'state of nature' is not, for Locke, a merely ideal abstraction, but a historical situation in which members of simple societies have lived and still live, unless in time of war, and in which independent national governments always necessarily exist. For international relations are not governed by positive law prescribed and sanctioned by constituted authority. In this situation the victim of aggression – or indeed any onlooker, for the violation is of the natural law which maintains the welfare of all – has the right to destroy the aggressor until offered peace, reparation and security for the future. Within civil society itself this 'right of war' or self-defence exists whenever the law cannot be effectively exercised, whether in the immediate circumstances of threatened harm, or when the administration of the law is manifestly corrupt, and itself employed to commit violence and injury.

'Liberty' in the state of nature is freedom from any constraint but the moral law of nature. Under government, it is freedom from the 'arbitrary will of another man', and from any human rule but the 'standing rule...common to everyone of that society' (*Two Treatises* II.22). (Locke sees slavery as continuation of war – it is just if the war is just, when it is in lieu of capital punishment, the justly enslaved, like criminals, being 'outside civil society'. Yet this hardly stands as an endorsement of contemporary colonial slavery – indeed Locke denies that the children of aggressors can be justly enslaved, or even disinherited.) 'Possessions' arise in a state of nature with the act of appropriation which is a necessary condition of the use of any of the comestibles naturally available to all: 'this law of reason makes the deer, that Indian's who hath killed it' (*Two Treatises* II.30). Such appropriation is an extension of the principle that 'every man has a property in his own person', and therefore in 'the labour of his body'. Consequently whatever someone has 'mixed his labour with' is his, provided that it is for use, and 'there is enough, and as good left in common for others' (*Two Treatises* II.27). This principle applies also to the enclosure of land for agriculture, which vastly increases its productivity. With land, as in all else, 'labour makes the far greatest part of the value of things, we enjoy in this world' (*Two Treatises* II.42).

Nevertheless, before the conventional use of money, no one would have either motive or right to produce more than they could use, give to others or exchange before it spoils. To take something from the common store and let it spoil is against natural law. Money, however, is an artifice which modifies the whole nature of property-rights, since it can be stored indefinitely without spoiling. Money makes it worthwhile to exploit land fully, and supplies a just means of keeping the product. So far from wronging others, enclosure and improvement greatly increase 'the common stock of mankind', making 'a day labourer in England' better off than a king among the (Native) Americans (*Two Treatises* II.41). Significant disparity of wealth becomes both possible and morally justified, on the assumption that none will suffer absolutely (in a Board of Trade paper Locke simply asumed that everyone should have 'meat, drink, clothing and firing...out of the stock of the kingdom, whether they work or no' – Bourne 1876 vol. II: 382). But the effect is greatly to complicate the administration of the law of nature, and to render its application uncertain, as well as to encourage its breach through greed.

All this, on top of the standing need for both impartiality and sufficient force to punish malefactors, necessitates government. The chief role of such government is to determine rules to order and preserve property. Common defence is another imperative. Government with such legislative and executive powers comes into existence when people, by consent, resign their 'executive power of the law of nature...to the public' (*Two Treatises* II.89). Each individual member gives consent, but is thereafter bound to move with the majority. To the objection that no such agreement has ever taken place, Locke argues that, although 'government is everywhere antecedent to records', cases abound of new or primitive societies with elected leaders. In the first instance, this may be 'some one good and excellent man' or effective general, or indeed the father of a familial group, but experience of unrestrained monarchy encourages legislatures of 'collective bodies of men', with none above the law. In any case, consent is normally tacit, and given in the active enjoyment of the benefit of the law, whether by possession of land or 'barely travelling freely on the highway'. Such tacit consent obliges obedience to the law, although the obligation lasts only as long as the enjoyment, leaving the individual free to give up the benefit and 'incorporate himself into any other commonwealth'. Express consent, however, binds the individual to obey and assist a particular government until its dissolution (or breach of trust).

A subject's ultimate obligation is to the supreme

power, which is the legislative, itself bound by the law of nature in its choice of means, 'established and promulgated laws', for the preservation of its subjects and their property. Given this role, a government has no right to tax its subjects without their consent 'either by themselves, or their representatives chosen for them'. In order to minimize the risk of the legislative acting in its own, rather than in the public interest, it is best that it be an assembly which meets from time to time, separate from the continuously acting executive. A third, 'federative' power of war, peace and alliances is less easily directed by antecedent laws than the executive power, but falls naturally into the same hands, since both depend on public force. Locke allows some qualification of the absolute separation of powers, and subordination of the executive to the legislative, in recognition of the 'prerogative' power of the English king to dissolve and convene Parliament as circumstances require, and to employ discretion in the execution of the laws (Locke notes without express approval the power to veto legislation). Yet Locke sees prerogative as justified only as falling under 'the power of doing public good without a rule' in the face of unforeseen circumstances, and as dangerously capable of abuse. Its continuous employment contrary to the public good, for example by refusing to convene the legislative or by tampering with the rules for its election, makes the king himself a rebel and destroyer of the government, at war with his own subjects, returning them to a state of nature with a right to set up a new government.

11 Influence

Perhaps no modern philosopher has had a wider influence than Locke. His immediate achievement was, with Newton, to bring to an end the dominance within Europe of Cartesian science and philosophy, unseating the broadly Neoplatonic notion that mind and world share a common, divinely imposed structure, in favour of a modest, naturalistic conception of human capacities. Careful observation and systematic description are more valuable than the construction of hypotheses purportedly achieved by super-experiential means. Locke's own 'historical' treatment of the mind as a familiar, describable but deeply mysterious part of nature had considerable influence on European thought. His theory of classification influenced later taxonomy, and his brilliantly original theory of personal identity is still a standard text for philosophical discussion. His philosophy was one of the chief influences on Kant, but can still suggest an alternative to Neo-Kantian conceptualism. If his ethical theory appears to be the

last throes of early modern natural law theory rather than a new beginning, within that structure he enunciated a classic justification of responsible, tolerant and broadly democratic political society which has remained a major resource for political theorists ever since.

See also: EMPIRICISM; RATIONALISM

List of works

Locke, J. (1823) *The Works of John Locke*, London: T. Tegg *et al.*, 11th edn, 10 vols; repr. Aalen: Scientia, 1963. (Still, in 1997, the most complete edition of Locke's works, together with some of the more philosophically interesting correspondence.)

—— (1975–) *The Clarendon Edition of the Works of John Locke*, general eds P.H. Nidditch (to 1983), J.W. Yolton (1983–92), M.A. Stewart (1992–), Oxford: Oxford University Press. (A critical edition, planned to include all the published works and significant manuscript material, the bulk of which is in the Bodleian Library, Oxford. Volumes are available or in active preparation in 1997 as indicated under individual titles below.)

—— (*c.*1660–2a) *Two Tracts on Government*, ed. P. Abrams, Cambridge: Cambridge University Press, 1967. (Useful introduction and notes. The 'tracts', the first in English, the second in Latin, debate 'Whether the Civil Magistrate may lawfully impose and determine the use of indifferent things in reference to Religious Worship?' Contrary to his later stance, Locke argues in these early manuscripts for the right of the magistrate to regulate religious observance for the sake of public peace.)

—— (*c.*1660–2b) 'An necesse sit dari in Ecclesia infallibilem Sacro Sanctae Scripturae interpretem?' (Is it necessary to have in the Church an infallible interpreter of Holy Scripture?), ed. J.C. Biddle in 'John Locke's Essay on Infallibility: Introduction, Text, and Translation', *Journal of Church and State* 19 (1977): 301–27. (A critique of the notion of infallibility.)

—— (1664) *Essays on the Law of Nature*, ed. and trans. W. von Leyden, Oxford: Oxford University Press, 1954; ed. and trans. R. Horwitz, J. Strauss Clay and D. Clay as *Questions concerning the Law of Nature*, Ithaca, NY: Cornell University Press, 1990. (An early manuscript in Latin in scholastic form which, despite later change in Locke's conception of moral knowledge, throws light on his mature moral theory as well as the development of his thought. Von Leyden's edition includes related manuscript material.)

—— (1667) *An Essay concerning Toleration, in John*

Locke: Writings on Politics, Law and Religious Toleration 1667–1683, ed. J.R. Milton and P. Milton, Clarendon Edition, Oxford: Oxford University Press, forthcoming. (This manuscript signals Locke's change of mind to a more liberal view of religious toleration.)

—— (?) (*c.*1668) 'De Arte Medica', in H.R.F. Bourne *The Life of John Locke*, 2 vols, London: Henry S. King, 1876, vol.1, 222–7; repr. in K. Dewhurst *Dr Thomas Sydenham (1624–1689): His Life and Original Writings*, London: Wellcome Historical Medical Library, 1966. (A manuscript in Locke's handwriting, but possibly by Sydenham, expounding a strongly empirical method in medicine.)

—— (1671) *Drafts for the Essay concerning Human Understanding, and Other Philosophical Writings*, vol. 1, ed. P.H. Nidditch and G.A.J. Rogers, Clarendon Edition, Oxford: Oxford University Press, 1990–. (Volume I contains *Drafts A and B* (1671); the forthcoming volumes II and III contain *Draft C* (1685) and associated manuscript material. Together they cast considerable light on the development and significance of Locke's general philosophy, including projected, but unfinished chapters of the *Essay*.)

Locke, J. and Tyrrell, J. (1681–3) *Locke on Separation*, ed. J. Marshall, Clarendon Edition, Oxford, Oxford University Press, forthcoming. (A jointly written, hitherto unpublished response to Edward Stillingfleet's *The Mischief of Separation* (1680) and *The Unreasonableness of Separation* (1681) in which Locke and Tyrrell defend toleration of religious nonconformity.)

Locke, J. (1686) 'Newton, Is. Philosophiae naturalis principia mathematica...' (Mathematical principles of natural philosophy), *Bibliothèque universelle et historique*. (Review, by an admiring layman, of Newton's *Principia*.)

—— (1688) 'Abrégé d'un ouvrage intitulé Essai philosophique touchant l'entendement', *Bibliothèque universelle et historique*; separately published as *Extrait d'un livre anglois... intitulé Essai philosophique concernant l'entendement...*, Amsterdam, 1688; trans. as 'An Extract of a Book, Entituled, A Philosophical Essay upon Human Understanding', in *The young-students-library, containing extracts and abridgements...*, London, 1692; in *Drafts for the Essay concerning Human Understanding, and Other Philosophical Writings*, vol. 3, ed. P.H. Nidditch and G.A.J. Rogers, Clarendon Edition, Oxford: Oxford University Press, 3 vols, 1990–. (Locke's effective abstract of *An Essay concerning Human Understanding*.)

—— (1689) *Epistola de Tolerantia*, Gouda; ed. R. Klibansky *Epistola de Tolerantia: A Letter on Toleration*, trans., intro. and notes J.W. Gough, Oxford: Oxford University Press, 1968; trans W. Popple as *A Letter concerning Toleration*, London, 1689, 2nd edn, 1690, ed. J. Tully, Indianapolis, IN: Hackett Publishing Company, 1983. (Locke's classic argument for religious toleration. Popple's vigorous translation is the one through which the work has chiefly been known to English-speakers.)

—— (1689/90a) *An Essay concerning Human Understanding*, ed. P.H. Nidditch, Clarendon Edition, Oxford: Oxford University Press, 1975. (Originally published in December 1689 but carrying the date 1690. Locke's chief and greatest work, arguing comprehensively that what we can think and know is limited by the way we experience the world, attacking dogmatic pretensions to grasp the essences of things, and affirming that 'reason must be our last judge and guide in everything', including morals and religion.)

—— (1689/90b) *Two Treatises of Government*, ed. P. Laslett, Cambridge: Cambridge University Press, 1960, 2nd edn, 1967; ed. I. Harris, with associated manuscript material, Clarendon Edition, Oxford: Oxford University Press, forthcoming. (In the First Treatise 'the False Principles and Foundation of Sir Robert Filmer and His Followers are Detected and Overthrown' – that is, the patriarchal theory of monarchy. The Second Treatise, 'an Essay concerning the True Original, Extent, and End of Civil-Government', is a major classic of political theory, arguing that government is morally, and should be constitutionally, answerable to the governed. Laslett's influential introduction stimulated continuing debate as to the immediate context and purposes of *Two Treatises*, and its relation to the rest of Locke's thought.)

—— (1690) *A Second Letter concerning Toleration*, London; repr. in *The Works of John Locke*, vol. 6, London, 11th edn, 1823. (Locke defends religious toleration, and his argument of *Epistola de Tolerantia*, in response to Jonas Proast's *The Argument of the Letter concerning Toleration, Briefly Consider'd and Answer'd*.)

—— (1691/2) *Some Considerations of the Consequences of the Lowering of Interest, and raising the Value of Money*, in *Locke on Money*, ed. P.H. Kelly, Clarendon Edition, Oxford: Oxford University Press, 1991. (Advice on the coinage which became Government policy.)

—— (1692) *A Third Letter for Toleration, to the Author of the Third Letter concerning Toleration*, London; repr. in *The Works of John Locke*, vol. 6, London, 11th edn, 1823. (Continues the argument of *Epistola de Tolerantia* and *A Second Letter concerning Toleration*, against Jonas Proast).

—— (1693) *Some Thoughts concerning Education*, London; 3rd enlarged edn, London, 1695; ed. J.W. Yolton and J.S. Yolton, Clarendon Edition, Oxford: Oxford University Press, 1989. (Consciously modest in scope, but an important and interesting work in the history of educational theory.)

—— (1695a) *The Reasonableness of Christianity*, London; 2nd edn, 1696; ed. J. Higgins-Biddle, Clarendon Edition, Oxford: Oxford University Press, 1998. (Locke's latitudinarian credo, cutting articles of faith to a minimum and emphasising the moral dimension of Christianity.)

—— (1695b) *A Vindication of the Reasonableness of Christianity, etc. from Mr Edwards's Reflections*, London; repr. in *The Works of John Locke*, vol. 7, London, 11th edn, 1823. (The first of Locke's responses to John Edwards' attack on *The Reasonableness* in *Some Thoughts concerning the Several Causes and Occasions of Atheism, Especially in the Present Age*, 1695.)

—— (1697a) *A Second Vindication of the Reasonableness of Christianity, . . .* , London; in *The Works of John Locke*, vol. 7, London, 11th edn, 1823. (A reply to John Edwards' response to *A Vindication of the Reasonableness of Christianity*.)

—— (1697b) *A Letter to the Right Reverend Edward, Lord Bishop of Worcester, Concerning some Passages relating to Mr. Locke's Essay of humane Understanding: In a late Discourse of his Lordship's, in Vindication of the Trinity*, London; in *The Works of John Locke*, vol. 4, London, 11th edn, 1823; repr. in *The Locke–Stillingfleet Debate*, ed. M.A. Stewart, Clarendon Edition, Oxford: Oxford University Press, forthcoming. (Stimulated by the theological objections of Edward Stillingfleet, Bishop of Worcester, Locke explains in particular, in this *Letter* and two further *Replies* (1697/1699), his theories of substance, real and nominal essence, and personal identity, and his agnostic attitude towards the issue between dualism and materialism. M.A. Stewart's edition will contain Stillingfleet's contributions to the debate.)

—— (1697c) *Mr Locke's Reply to the . . . Bishop of Worcester's Answer to his Letter . . .* , London; in *The Works of John Locke*, vol. 4, London, 11th edn, 1823; repr. in *The Locke–Stillingfleet Debate*, ed. M.A. Stewart, Clarendon Edition, Oxford: Oxford University press, forthcoming. (Continues the argument of *A Letter to the . . . Bishop of Worcester*.)

—— (c.1699) *The Elements of Natural Philosophy*, in *The Works of John Locke*, vol. 3, London, 11th edn, 1823. (An introductory survey of natural philosophy as Locke saw it, written for the son of his hosts, the Mashams.)

—— (1699) *Mr. Locke's Reply to the . . . Bishop of Worcester's Answer to his Second Letter . . .* , in *The Works of John Locke*, vol. 4, London, 11th edn, 1823; in *The Locke–Stillingfleet Debate*, ed. M.A. Stewart, Clarendon Edition, Oxford: Oxford University press, forthcoming. (Continues the argument of *A Letter to the . . . Bishop of Worcester, and Mr Locke's Reply. . . .*)

—— (1700–4) *A Paraphrase and Notes on the Epistles of St Paul*, London, 6 vols, 1705–7; ed. A.W. Wainwright, Clarendon Edition, Oxford: Oxford University Press, 2 vols, 1987. (Locke's chief contribution to biblical hermeneutics, now published with associated manuscript material.)

—— (1702) *A Discourse of Miracles*, in *The Works of John Locke*, vol. 9, London, 11th edn, 1823. (Defines miracles as divinely purposive and contrary to common experience, but not as contrary to the unknown laws of nature).

—— (1704) *Fourth Letter on Toleration*, in *The Works of John Locke*, vol. 6, London, 11th edn, 1823. (Locke's last, unfinished shot, following those of 1690 and 1692, in defence of the position taken in *Epistola de Tolerantia* against Jonas Proast.)

—— (1976–) *The Correspondence of John Locke*, ed. E.S. de Beer, Clarendon Edition, Oxford: Oxford University Press, 8 vols, plus forthcoming index. (Around 3,650 letters from and to Locke in the period 1652–1704 supply important evidence of his life and times. A number of exchanges, for example, those with Molyneux and Limborch, are philosophically important.)

—— (1991) *Locke on Money*, ed. P.H. Kelly, Clarendon Edition, Oxford: Oxford University Press, 2 vols. (Contains all Locke's writings on economics (1668–95), with a long introduction explaining their significance.)

—— (forthcoming) *John Locke: Writings on Politics, Law and Religious Toleration 1667–1683*, ed. J.R. Milton and P. Milton, Clarendon Edition, Oxford: Oxford University Press. (Contains the 1667 'Essay concerning Toleration' and other manuscript writings from this crucial period of Locke's association with Shaftesbury.)

—— (forthcoming) *The Journals of John Locke*, ed. H.A.S. Schankula, Clarendon Edition, Oxford: Oxford University Press, 4 vols. (Important evidence of Locke's life, interests, reading and the development of his thought, 1675–1704. Some philosophically significant entries were previously published in *An Early Draft of Locke's Essay*, ed. J.I. Aaron and J. Gibb, Oxford: Oxford University Press, 1936.)

References and further reading

Aaron, R. (1937) *John Locke*, Oxford: Oxford University Press, 3rd edn, 1971. (For long one of the two standard commentaries on the *Essay*, differing from Gibson (1917) in several important respects, some, but not all, improvements.)

Alexander, P. (1985) *Ideas, Qualities and Corpuscles: Locke and Boyle on the External World*, Cambridge: Cambridge University Press. (An extended consideration of the version of corpuscularianism favoured by Locke, and of its bearing on his epistemology and metaphysics.)

Ashcraft, R. (1986) *Revolutionary Politics and Locke's Two Treatises of Government*, Princeton, NJ: Princeton University Press. (Makes strong, controversial claims about Locke's active engagement in revolutionary politics during the writing of the *Two Treatises*.)

—— (1987) *Locke's Two Treatises of Government*, London: Unwin & Hyman, 1987. (An important analysis of the arguments of *Two Treatises*.)

—— (ed.) (1991) *John Locke: Critical Assessments*, London: Routledge, 4 vols. (A large selective collection of some of the more significant articles written on Locke's thought, a volume each on political theory, general philosophy, education and economics.)

Attig, J.C. (1985) *The Works of John Locke: a comprehensive bibliography from the seventeenth century to the present*, Westport, CT and London: Greenwood. (A list of editions and translations, including abridgements and selections, of Locke's writings, together with other works, antecedent and precedent, constituting the immediate controversial context. Secondary works are cited in relation to publication details.)

Ayers, M. (1991) *Locke*, London: Routledge, 2 vols; repr. in 1 vol. as *Locke: Epistemology and Ontology*, London: Routledge, 1993. (The most comprehensive commentary on the *Essay*, interpreting and assessing Locke's arguments in their intellectual context, but also offering detailed argument with respect to their continuing philosophical significance.)

* Bourne, H.R. Fox (1876) *The Life of John Locke*, London: Henry S. King, 2 vols. (An important biography, but now largely outdated. Bourne made use of available documents, but lacked direct access to the manuscripts now in the Lovelace Collection in the Bodleian Library.)

Chappell, V. (ed.) (1994) *The Cambridge Companion to Locke*, Cambridge: Cambridge University Press. (A well-organized and useful collection of specially written articles covering Locke's main philosophical concerns, with a good selective bibliography.)

Christophersen, H.O. (1930) *A Bibliographical Introduction to the Study of John Locke*, Oslo: Jacob Dybwad; repr. New York: Burt Franklin, 1968. (A pioneering, incomplete bibliography.)

Colman, J. (1983) *John Locke's Moral Philosophy*, Edinburgh: Edinburgh University Press. (A pioneering analysis of Locke's ethical theory which is careful, judicious and comprehensive in its analysis of Locke's arguments about ethics, but Colman's view of their relation to Locke's theology is open to question.)

Cranston, M. (1957) *John Locke: A Biography*, London: Longmans; repr. Oxford: Oxford University Press, 1985. (Based rather narrowly on Locke's then-recently rediscovered correspondence and journals, this is a readable account of his life, but is inaccurate on many details and unhelpful on his intellectual development.)

Dunn, J. (1969) *The Political Thought of John Locke: An Historical Account of the Argument of The Two Treatises of Government*, Cambridge: Cambridge University Press. (A classic study, placing Locke's political theory in its historical and intellectual context and revealing some of the coherence of his thought that had escaped earlier commentators.)

* Edwards, J. (1695) *Some Thoughts concerning the Several Causes and Occasions of Atheism, Especially in the Present Age*, London. (Contains an attack on Locke's *Reasonableness* which, together with further attacks in *Socinianism unmask'd* (1696), *The Socinian Creed* (1697), and *A brief vindication of the fundamental articles of the Christian faith... from Mr. Lock's reflections upon them* (1697), stimulated Locke's own *Vindication* (1695b), and *Second Vindication* (1697c).)

Gibson, J. (1917) *Locke's Theory of Knowledge and its Historical Relations*, Cambridge: Cambridge University Press. (An intelligent, still useful commentary, despite important mistakes.)

Hall, R. and Woolhouse, R.S. (1983) *80 years of Locke Scholarship: a bibliographical guide*, Edinburgh: Edinburgh University Press. (A useful bibliography covering 1900–80.)

Harris, I. (1994) *The Mind of John Locke*, Cambridge: Cambridge University Press. (Making wide use of unpublished manuscripts, this is a complex but rewarding attempt to integrate a wide range of Locke's concerns, and to show how they informed the writing of *Two Treatises*.)

Horton, J. and Mendus, S. (eds) (1991) *John Locke: A Letter Concerning Toleration in Focus*, London: Routledge. (A useful collection of papers on this work.)

* King, P., Lord (1829) *The life and letters of John Locke*, London; new edn, 1964. (King had access to the manuscripts Locke left to his cousin, an earlier Peter King – Lord Chancellor and first Baron King – most of which are now in the Lovelace collection in the Bodleian Library, Oxford. This 'biography' is an ill-organized selection from these journals, papers and letters, but for many years was a valuable source of information otherwise inaccessible, and records some materials since lost.)

Leibniz, G.W. (*c*.1704) *New Essays on Human Understanding*, 1765; trans. and ed. P. Remnant and J. Bennett, Cambridge: Cambridge University Press, 1981. (Translation of Leibniz's *Nouveaux essais*, a great, if somewhat unsympathetic point-by-point commentary on Locke's *Essay* from a rationalist point of view.)

Locke Newsletter (1970–), ed. R. Hall, Department of Philosophy, University of York. (An unpretentious annual newsletter, with articles, notes, reviews and, very usefully, ongoing bibliography. Both articles and reviews have been of uneven quality, but it gives an overview of Locke studies.)

Long, P. (1959) *A Summary Catalogue of the Lovelace collection of the papers of John Locke in the Bodleian Library*, Oxford: Bodleian Library. (An essential tool for Locke scholars.)

Lowe, E.J. (1995) *Locke on Human Understanding*, London: Routledge. (A clear philosophical introduction to the *Essay* for students, making sensible use of recent scholarship in interpreting Locke's arguments.)

Mackie, J.L. (1976) *Problems from Locke*, Oxford: Oxford University Press. (A selective philosophical commentary which, although lacking the historical dimension which would often clarify the arguments discussed, has been influential in rekindling interest in Locke's general philosophy.)

Marshall, J. (1994) *John Locke: Resistance, Religion and Responsibility*, Cambridge: Cambridge University Press. (A contextual account of the development of Locke's political, religious, social and moral ideas, making wide use of unpublished writings. Perhaps the best study to date of Locke's religious views and their place in his thought.)

Milton, J.R. (1994) 'Locke's Life and Times', in V. Chappell (ed.) *The Cambridge Companion to Locke*, Cambridge: Cambridge University Press, 1994. (A useful summary intellectual biography, with an account of other available biographical sources.)

Parry, G. (1978) *John Locke*, London: Allen & Unwin. (A judicious introduction to Locke's political philosophy.)

* Proast, J. (1690) *The Argument of the Letter concerning Toleration, Briefly Consider'd and Answer'd*, Oxford; repr. New York: Garland, 1984. (The work which, with its sequel, *A Third Letter concerning Toleration*, stimulated, respectively, Locke's *Second Letter concerning Toleration* (1690), and *Third Letter for Toleration* (1692).)

Rogers, G.A.J. (ed.) (1994) *Locke's Philosophy: Content and Context*, Oxford: Oxford University Press. (A lively collection of papers by leading Locke scholars on subjects including Locke's life in Oxford, substance, perception, freedom of will, meaning, atomism, aboriginal rights, sin and Locke's influence abroad.)

* Stillingfleet, E. (1680) *The Mischief of Separation*, London. (Stillingfleet's argument against toleration of nonconformity in this and his subsequent *The Unreasonableness of Separation* (1681) stimulated Locke and Tyrrell to compose a point-by-point rebuttal (1681–3).)

* —— (1697) *A Discourse in Vindication of the Doctrine of the Trinity: with an Answer to the Late Socinian Objections against it from Scripture, Antiquity and Reason*, London. (Stillingfleet accused Locke of sympathy with Socinianism, in this work and in two sequential *Answers*, stimulating Locke's *Letter to the... Bishop of Worcester* (1697), and two *Replies*, (1697/1699).)

Tully, J. (1980) *A Discourse of Property: John Locke and his Adversaries*, Cambridge: Cambridge University Press. (An illuminating study of ideas about ownership, in particular about the relation between making and owning, and their role in Locke's thought.)

—— (1993) *An Approach to Political philosophy: Locke in Contexts*, Cambridge: Cambridge University Press. (A selection of papers on Locke and his context by a leading commentator on Locke's political philosophy.)

Wolterstorff, N. (1996) *John Locke and the ethics of belief*, Cambridge: Cambridge University Press. (A vigorous argument as to the philosophical and cultural significance of Locke's principle that reason should be our guide in everything, and in religion in particular.)

Woolhouse, R.S. (1983) *Locke*, Brighton: Harvester Press. (A useful short introduction to Locke's general philosophy.)

Yolton J.S. and Yolton J.W. (1985) *John Locke: a reference guide*, Boston, MA: G.K. Hall. (A useful bibliography.)

Yolton, J.W. (1956) *John Locke and the Way of Ideas*, Oxford: Oxford University Press. (This short but informative book, locating Locke's thought in its English context, was a landmark for historical study of his general philosophy.)

—— (1970) *Locke and the Compass of the Human*

Understanding, London: Cambridge University Press. (An important contribution to the interpretation of Locke's philosophy of science and moral theory.)

MICHAEL AYERS

LOGIC, ANCIENT

Western antiquity produced two great bodies of logical theory – those of Aristotle and the Stoics. Both aim to explain what distinguishes good arguments from bad. Both see that the best arguments are valid and that an argument's validity depends on its form. For both, therefore, logic's business is to identify the valid argument forms. Both theories do this by laying down a small number of basic argument forms – Aristotle's 'perfect syllogisms', the Stoics' 'indemonstrables' – and rigorously deriving other valid forms from them. Both theories also try – though in a less systematic manner – to classify the ways in which an argument can go wrong.

Here the similarities between these two logics end. Their most significant differences can be illustrated by comparing basic argument forms from each. The argument 'Every swan is an animal and every animal is moving, so every swan is moving' has the same form as the argument 'Every musician is human and every human is a substance, so every musician is a substance'. The Aristotelian expression of this form is 'A belongs to all B and B belongs to all C, so A belongs to all C'. In this form the letters 'A', 'B' and 'C' stand for any terms whatever, and 'A belongs to all B' replaces 'Every B is an A'. This represents the Aristotelian approach. Compare it with the following. The argument 'If it is day then it is light, it is day, so it is light' has the same form as the argument 'If Dion walks then Dion moves, Dion walks, so Dion moves'. This form is expressed by the Stoics as 'If the first then the second, the first, so the second'. Here the expressions 'the first' and 'the second' stand for any declarative sentences whatever.

In both cases, the validity of the argument form is tantamount to the validity of all arguments having that form (though the Stoics, unlike Aristotle, require that the precise words used in an argument should recur in its form). But the Aristotelian argument form is different in kind from the Stoic one: while it abstracts from terms, the Stoic form abstracts from sentences. Aristotelian logic is a term logic, Stoic logic a sentential one.

1   **Aristotle's logic: general**
2   **Aristotle's semantics**
3   **Aristotle's syllogistic**
4   **Theophrastus**
5   **Stoic logic and semantics**
6   **Stoic syllogistic**
7   **Modern interpretations**

1   Aristotle's logic: general

Aristotle was the first great logician (see ARISTOTLE §§4–5, 7). His logical writings are traditionally grouped together as the Organon, comprising *Categories*, *De interpretatione*, *Prior Analytics*, *Posterior Analytics*, *Topics* and *On Sophistical Refutations*.

Categories and *Topics* share a concern with distinguishing different types of predication. In *Categories* beings are classified into substances, quantities, qualities, relatives, places, times, positions, states, actions and affections. Within any one category, beings are related to one another in tree-structures linked by the 'said of' relation; for example, in the category of substance, animal is said of swan and of horse. Between categories there are relations of 'inherence': for example, colour (a quality) inheres in body (a substance). The 'said of' and inherence relations underlie all true predications. Substances are either 'primary' (for example, this horse) or 'secondary' (for example, horse). Among all beings, primary substances are basic: all others are said of or inhere in primary substances, whereas primary substances neither are said of nor inhere in anything. Though *Categories* is concerned mainly with ontological questions, it also states a few principles of inference, including the following: 'When one thing is predicated of another as subject, everything said of the predicate will also be predicated of the subject'.

Topics divides predications into four types: (1) essential and convertible, (2) essential and non-convertible, (3) non-essential and convertible, (4) non-essential and non-convertible. Any predicate thus stands to its subject as (1) a definition (for example, 'biped land-animal' is the definition of man), (2) a 'genus' or 'differentia' (for example, colour is the genus of white, biped is the differentia of man among land-animals), (3) a 'peculiarity' (for example, 'walking in the gymnasium' would be a peculiarity of a particular man if he were the sole walker there) or (4) an 'accident' (for example, evil is an accident of chance). These four types of predication are traditionally known as the 'predicables', and *Topics* formulates a large number of principles (or, commonplaces, 'topoi') concerning them, for example, 'the genus is predicated essentially of whatever the species is predicated of' (IV 2).

The ninth book of *Topics* is known by the separate title *On Sophistical Refutations*. Aristotle there distinguishes fallacies that depend on linguistic factors (such as lexical or syntactic ambiguity) from those that do not.

Fallacies not depending on linguistic factors are seven. The fallacy of 'accident' attributes to a thing what belongs only to an accident of the thing, for example, supposing Coriscus happens to be approaching, it would be wrong to infer that you do not know Coriscus, given the premise that you do not know who is approaching. The fallacy of '*secundum quid*' argues from a qualified to an unqualified statement, for example, supposing you have a belief about a non-being, it would be wrong to infer that a non-being *is*, given the premise that a non-being is-an-object-of-belief. The fallacy of '*ignoratio elenchi*' argues to the wrong point, for example, by showing that something is double in height when required to show that it is double in width. The fallacy of '*petitio principii*' or begging the question is committed when someone 'tries to prove by means of itself what is not known by means of itself' (*Prior Analytics* II 16). The fallacy of 'affirming the consequent' is committed when the direction of implication is confused, for example, by confusing the statement that whatever is created has a beginning with the statement that whatever has a beginning is created. The fallacy of 'false cause' arises from the inclusion of redundant material in a *reductio* argument, for example, arguing that the diagonal is incommensurable with the side of a square because if it were commensurable, *and if traversing a distance entailed first traversing half the distance*, then we would be committed to the absurd statement that motion is impossible. The fallacy of 'many questions' occurs when what in fact are several questions are treated as if they were just one. (See FALLACIES.)

De interpretatione contains a semantic theory of categorical statement-forms. *Prior Analytics* contains the theory of the syllogism. *Posterior Analytics* applies the syllogistic to the special case where a syllogism embodies scientific knowledge. It deals with the orderly exposition of a body of scientific knowledge in an axiomatic deductive system: the axioms of such a system will state how things are in themselves and necessarily, and the deductions' premises will explain the truth of their conclusions.

2 Aristotle's semantics

Non-modal propositions are of four forms: '*A* belongs to all *B*', '*A* belongs to no *B*' (these two are 'universal'), '*A* belongs to some *B*' and '*A* does not belong to some *B*' (these two are 'particular'). The letters '*A*' and '*B*' stand for terms, that is, nouns or noun phrases. '*A*' is predicate and '*B*' subject in these forms. The first and third forms are 'affirmative', the second and fourth 'negative' (*Prior Analytics* I 2).

Semantics for universal propositions are given in the so-called '*dictum de omni et nullo*': 'We use the expression "predicated of all" when none of the subject can be taken of which the other term cannot be said, and we use "predicated of none" likewise' (I 1).

The universal affirmative and particular negative form a pair of 'contradictories', as do the universal negative and particular affirmative. The universal affirmative and universal negative are 'contraries'. Contradictories cannot both be true, nor can they both be false; contraries cannot both be true but may both be false (*De interpretatione* 7).

'*A* belongs to no (or some) *B*' implies – Aristotle says 'converts to' – '*B* belongs to no (or some) *A*'. '*A* belongs to all *B*' converts to '*B* belongs to some *A*' (*Prior Analytics* I 2). This can be so only if the universal affirmative has 'existential import', that is, implies that something is *A* and something is *B*.

Modal propositions are of the forms '*A* belongs necessarily (or contingently) to every *B*', '*A* belongs necessarily (or contingently) to no *B*', '*A* belongs necessarily (or contingently) to some *B*' and '*A* does not belong necessarily (or contingently) to some *B*'. Aristotle does not state truth-conditions for modal propositions, but he does define the 'contingent' (*endechomenon*) as 'that which is not necessary but, being assumed, results in nothing impossible'. He also distinguishes two senses in which *A* might be said to belong contingently to all *B*: either *A* is contingent for everything to which *B* belongs or *A* is contingent for everything for which *B* is contingent (I 13).

'*A* belongs necessarily to no (or some) *B*' converts to '*B* belongs necessarily to no (or some) *A*'. '*A* belongs contingently to some *B*' converts to '*B* belongs contingently to some *A*'; but '*A* belongs contingently to no *B*' does not convert (I 3). Contingency modals are subject to the following distinctive laws: '*A* belongs contingently to all *B*' is equivalent to '*A* belongs contingently to no *B*', and analogously for particulars (I 13).

3 Aristotle's syllogistic

Aristotle defines a 'syllogism' as 'discourse in which, certain things being proposed, something other than them results of necessity from their being so' (I 1). Syllogisms have at least two premises. In a two-premised syllogism, one term (the 'middle') occurs in both premises. Any two-premised syllogism is in one of three 'figures' depending on whether the middle term is (1) once predicate and once subject or (2) twice predicate or (3) twice subject. The conclusion's predicate is the 'major' term, and its subject the 'minor'. The premises are designated as major or minor depending on which of the conclusion's terms occurs in them.

The non-modal syllogistic is based on four 'perfect' or complete syllogisms in the first figure. These (with their medieval names) are 'Barbara' (*A* belongs to all *B* and *B* to all *C*, so *A* belongs to all *C*), 'Celarent' (*A* belongs to no *B* and *B* to all *C*, so *A* belongs to no *C*), 'Darii' (*A* belongs to all *B* and *B* to some *C*, so *A* belongs to some *C*) and 'Ferio' (*A* belongs to no *B* and *B* to some *C*, so *A* does not belong to some *C*).

Modal syllogisms may be pure (with premises and conclusion all containing the same modality) or mixed. Pure modal syllogisms all derive from pure perfect first-figure syllogisms containing either the mode of necessity or that of contingency throughout. Mixed modal syllogisms all derive from mixed perfect first-figure syllogisms whose major premise and conclusion both contain the mode of necessity (or that of contingency), but whose minor premise is non-modal. Thus, Aristotle counts as perfect, not only the four non-modal syllogisms of figure one, but four pure necessity-syllogisms, four pure contingency-syllogisms, four mixed necessity-syllogisms and four mixed contingency-syllogisms – a total of twenty. Not perfect (or even valid) are those first-figure inferences in which the major premise is non-modal while the minor premise and conclusion contain an identical modality.

The perfect syllogisms function as axioms from which other syllogisms are derived (Aristotle says other syllogisms are 'reduced' to the perfect ones). Aristotle's syllogistic is thus the first axiomatized system in history (predating Euclid).

An incomplete syllogism may be perfected in one of three ways. First, by 'direct reduction':

> In the second figure, if the negative proposition is necessary, then the conclusion will be necessary.... Let *A* be possible for no *B*, and simply belong to all *C*. Then, since the negative converts, *B* is possible for no *A*. But *A* belongs to all *C*; so *B* is not possible for any *C*.
>
> (I 10)

Here the first premise is converted, thus producing a pair of premises from which the desired conclusion follows by virtue of a 'Celarent' with necessary major and non-modal minor. Second, by 'indirect reduction':

> If *A* belongs to all *C* and *B* does not belong to some *C*, it is necessary that *B* does not belong to some *A*. For if *B* belongs to all *A* and *A* to all *C*, *B* belongs to all *C*; but we supposed it did not belong.
>
> (I 6)

Here, by taking the conclusion's contradictory together with the first premise, we get the second premise's contradictory by virtue of 'Barbara'. Third, by 'ecthesis':

> when both *A* and *B* belong to all *C*, *A* will belong necessarily to some *B*.... If *A* and *B* both belong to all *C*, and we take one of the *C*s, say *D*, *A* and *B* will belong to this, so *A* belongs to some *B*.
>
> (I 6)

Here the inference's validity is explained by reference to an individual, *D*, which is supposed to be both an *A* and a *B*: there must be such an individual if *A* and *B* both belong to all *C*, but if there is such an individual then *A* belongs to some *B*.

In Book II Aristotle works out some metatheorems for his syllogistic, including the following:

(1) A syllogism with true premises must have a true conclusion.
(2) Any most general form of syllogism may have (a) all premises true, (b) some premises true and some false, (c) all premises false and the conclusion true.
(3) The falsity of all (or some) of the premises of a syllogism stated in its most general form does not necessitate the truth of the conclusion.
(4) No syllogism stated in its most general form commits a logical *petitio principii*, that is, none has the form '*p*, *q* so *r*' where *p* implies *r*. This result does not hold for all syllogistic forms: '*A* belongs to all *B*, *B* belongs to all *B*, so *A* belongs to all *B*' commits a logical *petitio*.
(5) No syllogism by virtue of its most general form commits an epistemological *petitio* in the sense that knowing or believing premises of that form implies knowing or believing the corresponding conclusion.

4 Theophrastus

Aristotle's successor Theophrastus also wrote on logic. None of his logical writings survives, but we have reports in ancient sources, notably Alexander of Aphrodisias' commentary on Aristotle's *Prior Analytics*. Theophrastus further developed his master's syllogistic in five main ways. First, he pointed out that first-figure syllogisms may have indirect conclusions, for example, from the premises '*A* belongs to all *B* and *B* to all *C*' we can deduce '*C* belongs to some *A*'.

Second, in modal semantics Theophrastus rejected Aristotle's definition of the contingent as two-way possibility, and consequently rejected the equivalence between '*A* contingently belongs to all

689

B' and '*A* contingently belongs to no *B*'. He also took '*A* contingently belongs to no *B*' to convert to '*B* contingently belongs to no *A*'.

Third, he considered Aristotle's perfect mixed necessity-syllogisms invalid, requiring instead that the modality of the conclusion be no stronger than the weakest modality in the premises.

Fourth, with regard to 'prosleptic' propositions such as '*A* belongs to all of that to none of which *B* belongs' (briefly discussed by Aristotle), Theophrastus considered them to be equivalent to ordinary categoricals.

Fifth, Theophrastus recognized 'wholly hypothetical' syllogisms such as 'If *A* then *B*, if *B* then *C*, so if *A* then *C*', and arranged them in three figures according to the position of their 'middle'. The letters '*A*', '*B*' and '*C*' here stand for sentences rather than terms.

5 Stoic logic and semantics

Among the Stoics and their predecessors, the most famous logicians were Diodorus Cronus, Philo (the Dialectician) and Chrysippus. We have only a few fragments of their work, plus reports in Sextus Empiricus' *Outlines of Pyrrhonism* and *Against the Logicians*, Diogenes Laertius' *Lives of the Philosophers* and other ancient sources.

The Stoics distinguished four causes of argumentative failure: 'incoherence', as in the argument 'If it is day it is light, wheat is being sold in the market, so Dion is walking'; 'redundancy', as in the argument 'If it is day it is light, it is day, Dion is walking, so it is light'; 'formal invalidity', as in 'If it is day it is light, it is not day, so it is not light'; and 'deficiency', as in 'Either wealth is good or bad, it is not good, so it is bad', which is said to be deficient because the first premise omits mention of the possibility that wealth is neither good nor bad. In the first three cases (but not the fourth) the argument as a whole does not instantiate a valid form, though only the first and third are cases of invalidity.

They also studied paradoxes, including the liar paradox ('If you say that you are lying, and speak the truth, then you are lying'), 'the hooded man' (which, like Aristotle's fallacy of accident, concerns an unrecognized friend concealed beneath a hood), the 'sorites' or heap (which asks how many grains it takes to make a heap; see VAGUENESS §2) and 'the horned man' ('What you haven't lost you still have, you haven't lost horns, so you still have horns' – a relative of Aristotle's fallacy of many questions).

Stoic semantics and syllogistic is a propositional logic, dealing with the ways in which one proposition may be formed from one or more propositional components. The forms of propositional composition

on which the Stoics concentrated are negation, conjunction, disjunction and the conditional. They recognized that a conjunction 'the first *and* the second' is true if and only if both conjuncts are true. A disjunction 'either the first *or* the second' they took in the exclusive sense, requiring that one and only one disjunct be true.

The semantics of conditionals was hotly debated by the Stoics and other contemporary logicians. According to Philo, a conditional proposition ('If the first then the second') is true if and only if it does not have a true antecedent and a false consequent. According to Diodorus Cronus, a conditional is true if and only if it neither is nor ever was possible for the antecedent to be true and the consequent false. A third semantics for conditionals – 'by connection' – proposed that the antecedent be 'incompatible' with the denial of the consequent. A fourth – 'by suggestion' – proposed, somewhat vaguely, that the consequent be 'potentially in' the antecedent. (See PHILO THE DIALECTICIAN §2; DIODORUS CRONUS §§3–4; CONSEQUENCE, CONCEPTIONS OF §2.)

6 Stoic syllogistic

There are five 'indemonstrables':

(1) If the first then the second, the first, so the second.

(2) If the first then the second, not the second, so not the first.

(3) Not both the first and the second, the first, so not the second.

(4) Either the first or the second, the first, so not the second.

(5) Either the first or the second, but not the second, so the first.

Further inferences were shown valid by the application of one or more rules to the indemonstrables. There were four of these rules, of which only two are now known. The first is equivalent to Aristotle's rule of indirect reduction: if two propositions imply a third, then either of these together with the negation of the third implies the negation of the remaining one. The third rule is the one which underlies Aristotle's procedure of direct reduction: if two propositions imply a third then the first, together with any propositions that imply the second, implies the third.

The third rule is used in proving the inference 'If the first and the second then the third, not the third, but the first, so not the second'. By the second indemonstrable we have 'If the first and the second then the third, not the third, so not both the first and the second'. Applying the third rule to this and the third indemonstrable we get 'If the first and the second then the third, not the third, but the first, so not the second'.

Both the first and third rules are used in the following (modern) proof of the validity of the Stoic inference 'If you know you are dead then you are not dead, if you know you are dead then you are dead, so you do not know you are dead', whose form is 'If the first then not the second, if the first then the second, so not the first'. Applying the first rule to the first indemonstrable we get (a) 'Not the second, the first, so not if the first then the second'. But, again by the first indemonstrable, we have (b) 'If the first then not the second, the first, so not the second'. Applying the third rule to (a) and (b) we get (c) 'If the first then not the second, the first, so not if the first then the second'. And applying the first rule to (c) we get 'If the first then not the second, if the first then the second, so not the first'.

The Stoics accepted the inference 'If the first then if the first then the second, but the first, so the second'. This is said to be validated by two applications of the first indemonstrable. But strictly speaking – and the Stoics were fond of speaking strictly – all that is validated by that procedure is the inference 'If the first then if the first then the second, but the first, *and the first*, so the second'. What is needed to validate the target inference is a 'rule of contraction': if an inference with a repeated premise is valid then so is the same inference without the repetition. This rule is also tacitly used in the above proof of the 'knowing you are dead' syllogism. The rule of contraction, though required by the Stoic system, is nowhere stated in the surviving sources.

The Stoics recognized that if an argument is valid then the conditional whose antecedent is the conjunction of the argument's premises and whose consequent is its conclusion is necessary. Thus, the validity of the first indemonstrable implies the necessity of the conditional 'If "the first and if the first then the second" then the second'.

Some parts of Aristotelian metatheory – namely metatheorems (2c), (3) and (5) in §3 above – do not carry over to the system of indemonstrables. (2c) Given Philonian semantics for the conditional, not both premises of the first indemonstrable can be false: if 'the first' is false then 'If the first then the second' is true. (3) Consequently, given Philonian semantics for the conditional, if both premises of the first indemonstrable are false, the conclusion must be true. (5) The first indemonstrable is epistemically question-begging on the Philonian reading of the conditional: the premise 'If the first then the second' on this reading could be known only if 'the first' were known to be false (which it could not seeing it is

known to be true) or 'the second' were known to be true. (But none of this is the case for non-Philonian readings.)

7 Modern interpretations

The 'traditional' logic books of the nineteenth and early twentieth centuries reduced categorical and hypothetical syllogistic to rules of thumb and deprived it of its systematicity and rigour. The categorical syllogism was treated as an inference, exemplified by 'All men are mortal, Socrates is a man, so Socrates is mortal', an example nowhere to be found in *Prior Analytics*. The modal syllogism, if mentioned at all, was dismissed as useless or incoherent.

Łukasiewicz (1951) was the first to interpret Aristotle's syllogistic as a formalized axiomatic system, rigorous by the highest standards. He returned to Aristotle's text, and interpreted the syllogism not as an inference but as a conditional statement whose antecedent conjoins two universal or particular (not singular) statements. He was thereby able to treat the syllogistic as an axiomatic system whose theses have the structure of conditional statements with conjunctive antecedents. Because of this structure, the system required an 'auxiliary theory' of propositional logic, specifying the logic of conditionals, conjunctions and negation. Practically none of this auxiliary theory is to be found in Aristotle. From Łukasiewicz's point of view the Stoics therefore marked an advance on Aristotle in articulating a propositional logic.

Corcoran (1972) rejected Łukasiewicz's interpretation of Aristotelian syllogistic as an axiomatic system whose theses are conditional statement-forms; instead he treated it as a natural-deduction system, thus avoiding the need for an auxiliary propositional logic. An Aristotelian syllogism is for him not just a set of premises and a conclusion but something with a deductive structure. This interpretation enabled him to give modern formal representations not only of Aristotle's syllogisms but also of Aristotle's own manner of proving them. He could view Aristotle's system 'from the standpoint of modern logic' without imputing gross oversights to him.

Smiley's independent work arrived at these same results, but went further than Corcoran in abandoning the aim that every expressible, semantically valid formula should be a thesis of the system. He did this on two grounds. First, Aristotelian syllogistic is not governed by the 'rule of expansion' (if certain premises imply a conclusion then any set that includes those premises implies the conclusion). Second, it does not obey the rule of contraction (see §6). The addition of either of these rules to Aristotle's system, Smiley showed (1973), leads to un-Aristotelian results. The rule of expansion entails that from two mutually contradictory premises every conclusion follows. Thus '*A* belongs to every *B*, *A* does not belong to every *B*, so *C* belongs to some *D*' should be a syllogism; but it is not. Since '*A* belongs to all *C*, *A* belongs to all *C*, so *A* belongs to some *A*' is a syllogism, contraction would entitle us to drop the repetition and say that '*A* belongs to all *C*' implies '*A* belongs to some *A*'. So '*A* belongs to no *A*' would imply '*A* does not belong to all *C*'. Therefore the premises '*B* belongs to no *A*, *B* belongs to all *A*' – which imply '*A* belongs to no *A*' – would also imply '*A* does not belong to all *C*'. However, '*B* belongs to no *A*, *B* belongs to all *A*, so *A* does not belong to all *C*' is not an Aristotelian syllogism. On Smiley's interpretation, a syllogism is a deduction in a sense of 'deduction' that requires all premises to be used, and which heeds the number of times a premise is used. Smiley constructed a formal system based on such a notion of deduction, proved its completeness, and constructed a decision-procedure for it. These results allowed him to formalize some of Aristotle's own metatheory, in particular metatheorem (3) (see §3 above).

Thom (1981, 1996) further developed the Smiley interpretation, showing that Aristotle's syllogistic does not include proper substitutions in theses: thus, while '*A* belongs to all *B*, *B* belongs to all *C*, so *A* belongs to all *C*' is Aristotelian, '*A* belongs to all *B*, *B* belongs to all *A*, so *A* belongs to *A*' is not. This restriction is needed if the interpreter is to construct a formalization to which all of Aristotle's metatheory applies, since some of that metatheory holds only for theses stated in their most general form (see (2)–(5) in §3 above). He also showed how to develop Aristotle's sketchy remarks about 'ecthesis' into a natural deduction system of singular syllogisms, on which the whole syllogistic (modal as well as non-modal) can be based.

Modern interpretations of modal syllogistic take their impetus from McCall (1963), who restored faith in the rigour of Aristotle's modal system by formalizing it axiomatically. Johnson (1989) provided a formal semantics for McCall's formalization. Johnson's semantics treats '*A* belongs necessarily to every (or no) *B*' as true if and only if the *B*s are among (or exclude) the *essential A*s; '*A* belongs necessarily to some *B* (or necessarily does not belong to some *B*)' he treats as true if and only if some essential *B* is an essential *A* (or is an essential non-*A*). If, as Johnson required, the truth-conditions of Aristotle's modal sentences make reference to the essential *A*s, then it seems that modal syllogistic is underpinned by some

doctrine of essentialism. This idea was developed by Patterson (1995), who explored philosophical links between the semantics of modal sentences and the doctrine of the predicables.

Modern interpretations of Stoic logic spring from the work of Mates (1953), and Kneale and Kneale (1962). The complex relationship between the Stoic and Aristotelian systems has been studied by Frede (1987).

See also: LOGICAL AND MATHEMATICAL TERMS, GLOSSARY OF; STOICISM §11

References and further reading

* Alexander of Aphrodisias (*c*.200) *In Aristotelis Analyticorum Priorum Librum I Commentarium* (Greek text), ed. M. Wallies, Berlin: Reimer, 1883; *On Aristotle's Prior Analytics 1.1–7*, trans. J. Barnes, S. Bobzien, K. Flannery and K. Ieroddiakonou, London: Duckworth, 1991. (Includes much material on the Stoics and reports of Theophrastus' logical theories as discussed in §4, but not his discussion of modal syllogisms; excellent bibliography.)

* Aristotle (*c*.mid 4th century BC) *The Complete Works of Aristotle: The Revised Oxford Translation*, vol. 1, ed. J. Barnes, Princeton, NJ: Princeton University Press, 1984. (See 'Categories' for the theory of categories, 'Posterior Analytics' for scientific syllogisms, 'On Sophistical Refutations' and 'Topics' for predicables and fallacies, all discussed in §1; 'De interpretatione' for semantics, as discussed in §§1–2; and 'Prior Analytics' for syllogistic (Book I) and metatheory (Book II) as discussed in §§2–3.)

Barnes, J. (1984) 'Terms and Sentences: Theophrastus on Hypothetical Syllogisms, Dawes Hicks Lecture on Philosophy 1983', *Proceedings of the British Academy* 69: 279–326. (Further non-technical material on Theophrastus.)

* Corcoran, J. (1972) 'Ancient Logic and its Modern Interpretations', in J. Corcoran (ed.) *Proceedings of the Buffalo Symposium on Modernist Interpretations of Ancient Logic, 21 and 22 April, 1972*, Dordrecht: Reidel. (Partly technical treatment of Aristotelian syllogistic as a natural deduction system.)

* Diogenes Laertius (early 3rd century) *Lives of the Philosophers*, trans. R.D. Hicks, *Diogenes Laertius Lives of Eminent Philosophers*, Loeb Classical Library, Cambridge, MA: Harvard University Press and London: Heinemann, 1925, 2 vols; revised H.S. Long, 1972. (Greek text with facing English translation. Volume 2 includes material on the Stoics (book VII) and a life of Chrysippus.)

* Frede, M. (1987) 'Stoic vs. Aristotelian Syllogistic', in *Essays in Ancient Philosophy*, Oxford: Clarendon Press. (Non-technical discussion.)

* Johnson, F. (1989) 'Models for Modal Syllogisms', *Notre Dame Journal of Formal Logic* 30 (2): 271–84. (Technical treatment; referred to in §7.)

* Kneale, W. and Kneale, M. (1962) *The Development of Logic*, Oxford: Clarendon Press. (Good introduction to the subject, including an extensive bibliography.)

  Lear, J. (1980) *Aristotle and Logical Theory*, Cambridge: Cambridge University Press. (Further non-technical reading on some of the topics discussed in §3.)

  Lejewski, C. (1976) 'On Prosleptic Premisses', *Notre Dame Journal of Formal Logic* 17 (1): 1–18. (Technical discussion of prosleptic propositions, mentioned in §4.)

* Łukasiewicz, J. (1951) *Aristotle's Syllogistic from the Standpoint of Modern Formal Logic*, Oxford: Oxford University Press; 2nd enlarged edn, 1957. (Partly technical treatment; the first to interpret Aristotle's syllogistic as a rigorous, formalized axiomatic system.)

* Mates, B. (1953) *Stoic Logic*, Berkeley and Los Angeles, CA: University of California Press. (A modern interpretation with a good introduction and bibliography.)

* McCall, S. (1963) *Aristotle's Modal Syllogisms*, Amsterdam: North Holland. (Axiomatic formalization of Aristotle's modal system; technical.)

  Nortmann, U. (1994) 'Does Aristotle's Modal Logic Rest on Metaphysical Assumptions?', *Analyomen* 1: 115–25. (An alternative approach to those of Johnson and Patterson; partly technical.)

* Patterson, R. (1995) *Aristotle's Modal Logic: Essence and Entailment in the Organon*, Cambridge: Cambridge University Press. (Non-technical treatment; referred to in §7.)

  Patzig, G. (1968) *Aristotle's Theory of the Syllogism: A Logico-Philological Study of Book A of the Prior Analytics*, trans. J. Barnes, Dordrecht: Reidel. (Non-technical discussions of some of the topics mentioned in §3; good bibliography on non-modal syllogistic.)

* Sextus Empiricus (*c*.200) *Outlines of Pyrrhonism*, trans. J. Annas and J. Barnes, Cambridge: Cambridge University Press, 1994. (Material on the Stoics, as discussed in §5.)

* —— (*c*.200) *Against the Logicians*, vol. 2, trans. R.G. Bury, Loeb Classical Library, Cambridge, MA: Harvard University Press and London: Heinemann, 1933–53. (Material on the Stoics, as discussed in §5.)

* Smiley, T.J. (1973) 'What is a Syllogism?', *Journal of Philosophical Logic* 2 (1): 136–54. (Technical treatment; referred to in §6.)

* Thom, P. (1981) *The Syllogism*, Munich: Philosophia. (Largely technical treatment on modern interpretations; good bibliography on non-modal syllogistic.)

* —— (1996) *The Logic of Essentialism: An Interpretation of Aristotle's Modal Syllogistic*, Dordrecht: Kluwer. (Largely technical; bibliography on modal syllogistic.)

PAUL THOM

LOGIC DIAGRAMS *see* LOGIC MACHINES AND DIAGRAMS

LOGIC, FUZZY *see* FUZZY LOGIC

LOGIC IN CHINA

Technically, classical China had semantic theory but no logic. Western historians, confusing logic and theory of language, used the term 'logicians' to describe those philosophers whom the Chinese called the 'name school'. The best known of these were Hui Shi (380–305 BC) and Gongsun Lung (b. 380 BC?). This group now also includes the Later Mohists and the term 'distinction school' (translated as 'dialecticians') has become common.

The importance of the more detailed Mohist work came to light in modern times. The Confucian tradition had lost access to it. Rescuing that text rekindled a long-lost interest in Chinese theories of language. The restored Mohist texts give us a general theory of how words work. A term picks out part of reality. Some terms are more general than others; terms like 'dobbin' or 'horse' or 'object' might pick out the same thing. When we use a term to pick something out, we commit ourselves to using the name to pick out similar things and 'stopping' with the dissimilar. Thus, for each term we learn an 'is this' and an 'is not'. 'Is not' generates an opposite for each name and marks the point of distinction or discrimination.

Chinese doctrine portrays disagreements as arising from different ways of making the distinctions that give rise to opposites. The word bian *(distinction/dispute) thus came to stand for a philosophical dispute. The Mohists argued that, in a 'distinction/dispute', one party will always be right. For any descriptive term, the thing in question will either be an 'is this' or an 'is not'.*

693

Mohists were realistic about descriptions and the world. Real similarities and differences underlie our language. They rejected the claim that words distort reality; to regard all language as 'perverse', they noted, was 'perverse'. The Mohists failed, however, to give a good account of what similarities and differences should count in making a distinction. Mohists also found that combining terms was semantically fickle. In the simplest case, the compound picked out the sum of what the individual terms did. Classical Chinese lacked pluralization so 'cat–dog' works like 'cats and dogs'. Other compound terms (such as 'white horse') worked as they do in English. The confusion led Gongsun Long to argue, on Confucian grounds, that we could say 'white horse is not horse'.

Confucius' linguistics centred on his proposal to 'rectify names'. Confucius used a code with fixed formulations, and therefore tended to treat moral problems as turning on which terms we use in stating them. The abortion dispute illustrates this well. Both sides agree to the rule 'do not kill an innocent person': the dispute becomes one of whether to use the term 'person' or 'foetus'. In contrast, Mohists argued that we should not alter normal term use to get moral results. We simply accept that guiding compounds may not follow normal use. A thief is a person, but killing a thief (executing) is not killing a person (murdering).

These results bolstered Daoist scepticism about words. We never will fashion a 'constant' dao. According to Zhuangzi, even a realistic theory of language (like that of the Mohists) will not give constant guidance. He drew from Hui Shi's approach to language, which emphasized relative terms such as 'large' and 'small'. We may talk of a large horse (relative to other horses) or a large horsefly (relative to other flies), but 'large' itself has no constant standard of comparison. From the premise, 'all such distinctions are relative', Hui Shi fallaciously concluded that 'reality has no distinctions in itself'. Zhuangzi rejected this conclusion and ridiculed Hui Shi's monism. If we say 'everything is one', then our language attempts to 'point to' everything. If it succeeds, then in addition to the 'one–everything' there is the reference to it. That makes two. The whole consisting of everything and saying so then makes three. Referring to that whole makes four, and the fact that we have referred to it makes five, and so on.

Zhuangzi shifted Hui Shi's focus slightly, and concentrated on 'this' and 'that'. These do refer to things, but each use is different. Language, he argued, is not fixed on the world but on our relationships with it. Each existing language (different ways of making guiding distinctions) is equally natural. Human debate is as natural as the chirping of birds. We cannot appeal to nature to settle our disputes about ethics. The

standards are not constant; they are historical, variable and diverse in different moral communities.

Distinctions are real, but we can never know if we have found the right ones. Zhuangzi accepts a real world in which language works. Thus, he celebrates the endless possible ways of distinguishing 'this' from 'not-this'. Some alternatives will certainly work better (assuming our present values) than the one we have now. The problem is that any standard we could use to decide about that would itself be controversial.

The final word came from Xunzi and his student Han Feizi. The former, a Confucian, understood Zhuangzi's arguments to show that the only standard of correct usage must be convention itself. Thus he renewed Confucian tradition and promoted it politically as the only viable and valid conventional system. He advocated government suppression of dissenting voices who 'confuse language' and 'create new terms'. In the end, only the ruler may change language (and then only the 'descriptive' terms). The standards of social assent and dissent come from the Confucian 'sage-kings'. We must adhere to these as the only acceptable ideals; the alternative is anarchy in moral discourse and, consequently, in society.

Han Feizi, seized on Xunzi's attitude toward coercion while discarding the appeal to ancient tradition. Han Feizi had considerable influence on the draconian Qin emperor who ruthlessly carried out his injunction to stamp out philosophical disputes about ethics. This brought the rich tradition of creative philosophy to an abrupt end; religious thought and scholasticism dominated the rest of Chinese intellectual history.

1   **Confucius: rectifying names**
2   **Mozi: language utilitarianism**
3   **Rediscovery of later Mohist theory**
4   **Later Mohists: names and distinctions**
5   **Semantic paradoxes and compound terms**
6   **Phrase matching**
7   **Gongsun Long: one name, one thing**
8   **Hui Shi: relativism and monism**
9   **Zhuangzi: sceptical perspectivalism**
10 **Xunzi: Confucian conventionalism**
11 **The aftermath: death of philosophy**

1   Confucius: rectifying names

To understand the development of theory of language, we must place it in the context of Chinese ethical thought. The central focus of ethical dispute was about *dao*, or 'guiding discourse' (see CONFU-CIAN PHILOSOPHY, CHINESE §2). Confucius championed the historical 'guiding discourse' of the sage-kings, and purportedly studied it in the ancient documents that formed the curriculum of his school. The *Liji* (Book of Rites) is the paradigm for Confucius' conception of ethics.

Confucius' semantic framework was the relation between language and action, not between language and objects or reality. The implicit role of language was prescriptive rather than descriptive. Confucius, oblivious to ethical criticism of his discourse-based guide, addressed mainly problems in practical interpretation. His theory implied a pragmatic relation between language and objects. In order for a discourse to guide us, we must correctly pin names on the world's 'stuff'.

Confucius argued for imitation as the way to achieve this. Social leaders model the proper use of names in publicly practising the 'ritual'; the people learn from these examples and are then able to follow the code as it applies to them. Confucius called this 'rectifying names', and treated it as the key to good government:

> Zilu said, 'The ruler of Wei awaits your taking on administration. What would be Master's priority?' The Master replied, 'Certainly – rectifying names!' ... If names are not rectified then language will not flow. If language does not flow, then affairs cannot be completed. If affairs are not completed, ritual and music will not flourish. If ritual and music do not flourish, punishments and penalties will miss their mark. When punishments and penalties miss their mark, people lack the wherewithal to control hand and foot. Hence a gentleman's words must be acceptable to vocalize and his language must be acceptable as action. A gentleman's language lacks anything that misleads – period.
>
> (*Analects* 13:3)

The strategy of setting examples threatens a regress unless someone in the chain of models knows what example to set in some other way. Stopping the regress pushes Confucianism toward intuitionism. Confucius seemed to regard a mysterious quality, *ren* (humanity), as the key to correct practical interpretation of the *li* (ritual). 'Humanity' is a moral insight that guides the attribution of terms in following circumstances.

One does not rectify by consulting definitions: no Chinese accounts of language generate or point to anything like the concept 'meaning'. The model of the language–world relation is political. Social authorities tag things for ethical purposes. This tagging facilitates guiding discourse. Two theories of Confucian tagging emerge: one determined by traditional training and one by innate moral intuition.

Classical Chinese grammar reflects this model of language–world relations in its topic–comment structure. In the place of sentences, literary Chinese makes 'comments' on contextually indexed 'stuff'. Classical sentences required no subject. Language appeared as far more context dependent than in modern Western thought, with its focus on the subject-predicate sentence and 'complete thought'.

Implicit cognitive theory also mirrored this topic–comment structure. Western philosophy focused on propositional belief, a mental state that represents a fact, and knowledge. However, ancient Chinese grammar had neither propositional belief nor knowledge structures. Chinese grammar suggests a person tending to deem some real object (X) as P (the comment). Knowing is correctly deeming or assigning P to X (or knowing X's being deemed P). Literary Chinese used adjectives, one-place verbs and even nouns as two-place predicates in situations where we would use propositional belief structures: one P's some X. An alternative structure uses the Daoist concept of *wei* ('deem–act', the *wei* of *wuwei*, 'lack deeming action'). One, with regard to X, 'deems–acts' it P.

For these reasons (along with the absence of functional inflection, an ideographic conception of writing and the close grammatical similarity of proper and common nouns, adjectives and even verbs), Chinese linguistic theory focused on the question of what term to assign to things rather than on the propositional units so central to Western theory of language and logic (see LANGUAGE, PHILOSOPHY OF). The dominant conception was that a word had a scope or range of application, rather than that of referring to individuals or objects. This tendency reflects the fact that Chinese nouns resemble mass-nouns in having cumulative reference, in lacking both grammatical number and articles, and in being associated with various ways of individuating. The use of sortals for individuation became regularized for Chinese nouns at the end of the classical period.

2 Mozi: language utilitarianism

The natural development of this model in Mozi's early work (and the subsequent elaboration in later Mohism) focuses on *bian* (distinction/dispute) (see MOHIST PHILOSOPHY; MOZI). A term's use involves an 'is this/right' (*shi*) and an 'is not this/wrong' (*fei*). To learn the term is to learn to 'is this/is not this' appropriately with it. Mozi argued that society should use the pre-conventional or natural 'will' toward benefit (and against harm). This contrast guides the assignment of 'is this/is not this' to words used in social discourse. This interpretive proposal flowed imperceptibly into a proposal to order guiding dialogues differently, to change Confucius' traditional 'guiding discourse'.

The clearest example is Mozi's argument about spirits and fate. General utility dictates that social discourse should include the string 'lack spirits' and 'have spirits'. He represents this conclusion as an example of knowing the *dao* of *you–wu* (have–lack) (see YOU–WU). That means making a 'is this/is not this' (*li–hai*) distinction for each of these terms using the standard of 'benefit–harm'. We use either 'have' or 'lack' of things when so doing will lead to general utility.

The implication was initially anti-realistic. Mozi advocated three standards of language use. The first recognized the historical, conventional aspect of language. Language should conform to the guidance intentions of the ancient sage-kings. Second, language standards should be applicable by ordinary people using their 'eyes and ears'. Mozi's favourite examples of *fa* (standards) are measurements: a plumb line, a compass, a square and stakes for plotting where the sun rises and sets (see FA). Finally, we should use words in ways that maximize general utility. For Mozi, these standards pull in essentially the same direction. He assumed the people's good motivated the sage kings and he repeatedly likened the 'will of nature' to an objective utility measurement.

These standards govern the content and practice of discourse, regulations, injunctions, maxims and slogans. Including any string in the approved discourse was 'making it constant'. The ideal was a discourse *dao* that could consistently (reliably) and correctly (objectively) guide society. Mozi identified that *dao* as the one that resulted in the greatest utility for the country and its people. Thus, description or assignment of names is a handmaiden to ethics.

To count as the constant *dao*, Mozi's 'benefit harm' standard must itself be 'constant'; it should be a reliable, unambiguous and objectively correct, unchanging standard. He argued that in fact it was, since it came from *tian* (nature) rather than from society, convention or contingent history (see TIAN).

Mozi's attack on conventional guiding discourse led MENCIUS to defend Confucianism by postulating an innate moral intuition. Mencius argued that language should not manipulate or guide human action. Guidance should only come from the innate patterns or dispositions in the heart-mind; these include an innate ability to 'is this/is not this' (see XIN)). The heart-mind selects the appropriate 'is this/is not this' assignment and thus the appropriate action in real contexts. Society should not distort or reshape those natural moral inclinations. Mencius believed that, left to itself, everyone's heart-

mind would innately select the 'correct' action for them.

Laozi pointed in a similar direction but undermined Mencius' optimism. Indeed, we should resist the conventional socialization that comes with language. Learning names both constrains natural spontaneity and creates new and disruptive competitive desires. However, Laozi portrayed natural behaviour as being much more 'primitive' than did Mencius. The realm of social concern would extend no further than the local agrarian village. Laozi also emphasized the anti-language aspect of intuitive guidance more than did Mencius. He hinted that Mencius' idea that some particular moral values were intuitive or innate was a result of confusing the unconscious result of learning a guiding language with innate intuition. Learning names involves training in how to make distinctions and how to 'desire' with them. The names, distinctions, desires and actions are linked distortions of natural spontaneity. Laozi's conclusion is his opening line: no guidance in discourse form is constant (see DAOIST PHILOSOPHY §2).

3 Rediscovery of later Mohist theory

Before discussing the later Mohists, let us glance at the textual explanation of the loss and recovery of the Mohist Canons. The current 'best' textual theory says the Mohists wrote two 'Canons' (I and II). Each consisted of a series of short maxims; the first half of each Canon was written vertically across the top of a standard-sized book of bamboo strips, and the second half on the bottom. The terse analytic theorems were then keyed to another bamboo book containing longer explanations, examples or arguments for them. The second set of bamboo books was indexed by putting the first character of the claim alongside the first character of the explanation.

When scribes later copied each strip of the canons straight through, they turned this clever system into a puzzle. With no understanding of linguistic theory, they treated the whole corpus as a set of consecutive essays. Since classical Chinese had no punctuation or grammatical inflection, this textual disaster obscured the slogans, jumbled the order and shrouded the indexing principle. The scribes absorbed the indexing character as part of the text of the now orphaned explications.

Given the philosophical sophistication and difficulty of the text, the Mohist school's obliteration at the beginning of China's philosophical Dark Age (roughly 200 BC–1000 AD) and the placement of the Canons in the middle of the most vociferous anti-Confucian classical text, the medieval Confucian orthodoxy had little motivation to tackle the puzzle until the late Qing dynasty. Sun Yirang (1848–1908) found the essential clue to unzipping and analysing the content in a phrase in the middle which read, 'read these horizontally'. Other Chinese scholars tried different reconstructions and this work still goes on. Angus Graham's *Later Mohist Logic, Ethics and Science* first delivered a version of the reconstructed text to Western sinologists in 1978 (Graham 1978).

As his title suggests, Graham shared the common view that the subject matter was logic. He assumed Mohists intended the text as a deductively connected set of definitions and propositions. The statements, however, do not resemble definitions. Genus–species form is infrequent and the slogans fit into a theory of use, not of meaning. They are far from forming a deductive set. Still, Graham's assumption guided his reconstruction in ways that made the content accessible to analysis. Many problems and obscurities remain, but Graham's reconstruction reveals a systematic and reasonably coherent theory of language.

The maxims do deal with central philosophical concepts and, like Chinese dictionaries, frequently give lists of substitution characters or a range of examples. Some slogans are metaphors which the explications exploit; others are helpful ways of re-thinking and reflecting on a familiar concept. In addition to theory of language, intelligible sections of the Canon present fragments of epistemological, geometrical, optical and economic theory.

4 Later Mohists: names and distinctions

The School of Names was technically not a school (see MOHIST PHILOSOPHY §5). Traditional scholars gave the name to individual thinkers who analysed names in conflicting ways; their motivations reflect the differing trends in pre-analytic political thinking. The later Mohists developed Mozi's pragmatic, reality-based approach to naming. Gongsun Long defended the Confucian ideal of an unambiguous guiding scheme of names (the one produced by rectifying names). This principle, he presumed, dictated a goal of one-name-one-thing. Hui Shi raised sceptical problems designed to show that language 'constancy' across all situations was impossible (a Daoist conclusion).

The later Mohists spoke of four 'objects' of *zhi* (knowing): names, 'stuff', union and deeming-action (see ZHI). Mozi used an example that helps us fix the relevant concept of 'knowing'. Blind people can 'know-to' produce utterances like 'black like coal' or 'white as snow' but cannot distinguish things when placed in front of them. They know names, but not 'stuff' or union. Thus they cannot use the names to guide their actions.

The Mohists, as we noted above, lacked a doctrine of 'belief'. 'Knowing union' meant competently assigning terms and descriptions to objects. The Mohists accepted that 'knowing names' was conventional knowledge. They stressed, however, that we apply conventions to an external reality, known independently of language. The goal of knowledge remained practical guidance, not representation or picturing. Once conventionally attached to some reality, the inherent similarities and differences determined a term's application. Conventions presuppose a world-guided way to mark distinctions. Mohists portray name–object relations mereologically: a name applies to a scattered reality determined by *tong–yi* (same–different).

The Mohist terms for 'reference' – *ju* (pick out) and *qu* (choose) – had a practical tone. A name picks out some 'stuff' from the background. Convention determines which similarities and differences mark the boundary between *shi* ('is this', what a name picks out) and *fei* ('is not this', what it excludes). In using a name, we commit ourselves to go to some real limit and then stop.

The Mohists argued against the one-name-one-reality principle of rectifying names. Names, the Mohists argued, could be very general (like 'thing' itself), or based on similarity classes (like 'horse') or applied to only one thing (like 'John'). They saw no objection in principle to having overlapping scopes and even two names for the same thing (like 'puppy' and 'dog').

Elaboration and defence of this account of *bian* (distinction) led to complications. How should we expand the account to explain what a string of two *ming* ('names', characters) picks out? The model used was the string *niu–ma* (ox–horse). The Mohist took this to pick out a compound stuff, the sum of the range of the two component terms ('draft animals'). They called the unit a *jian* (whole) and its parts *ti* (substantive parts). This analysis of compounds made them analogous to general terms. However, this treatment raised several questions. In what sense is a compound really two things? Could we not view anything as a compound of more basic stuffs? Is there any fundamental kind of 'substantive part'?

These questions lead to another: are there any basic *tong–yi* (same–different)? The Mohists gave no clear answer. They noticed many senses in which things can be 'same – different'; some realities might be different only in being called by different names. Being 'two' was necessarily differentiated even though called by one name. Realities could also be the same in the sense of being included in some compound object.

Conversely, they could be different in not being included in some 'substantial part': they could be the same or different in being in the same place or not, and finally they could be same or different in belonging to the same *lei* (kind) (see MOHIST PHILOSOPHY §5).

However, the Mohists analysed *lei* in a loose way. Having that with which *tong* (same) was the criteria of being *tonglei* (same kind). Not having 'same' was the criteria of not being of a 'kind'. Although they might initially have intended to limit 'kind' to natural kinds, the account generalized it to almost any similarity based grouping of stuffs. Thus the Mohists could refer to oxen and horses as the same 'kind'. The only clear examples of not-'kind' are things so unlike they are not comparable. 'Which is longer, wood or night?' they suggest, is an unintelligible question because it compares two different 'kinds'.

The looseness of this account of classifying buttressed the sceptic's position (see §§8–9) that the world offered no reliable basis for fundamental distinctions. The Mohists seemed vaguely aware of the difficulty and did condemn *kuangju* ('wild picking out', where we use irrelevant 'same' or 'different' to classify or distinguish). They gave no account, however, of what marks a 'wild' or irrelevant way of grouping 'stuff'.

5 Semantic paradoxes and compound terms

The central term of assessment in the Mohist study was *ke* (assertible). They used it in several related ways. An expression may be described as 'assertible' of some object. If this object is introduced by another term, then 'assertible' became a way of exploring semantic relations between terms (see SEMANTICS). Mohists asked whether we can sometimes, always or never describe things picked out by term *X* as *Y*.

The analysis, although in terms of assertibility rather than truth, yielded a familiar and important conclusion against certain forms of relativism (see RELATIVISM). The Mohists argued that in any dispute involving 'distinctions', there will be a 'winner'. If one disputant claimed it was ox and the other that it was not ox, one would be correct. When one disputant claimed the object was ox and the other that it was horse, they did not count that as a distinction dispute. This was merely a formal result, but the Mohists took it as confirming that the world, not conventions, determined the right designation. The winner is the one whose description *dang* (hit on) it.

Another result was a distant cousin of 'All sentences are false'. Unlike the classic liar paradox (see SEMANTIC PARADOXES AND THEORIES OF TRUTH), the universal sentence does have a consistent truth value: it is always false. The Mohist conceptual tools, however, lacked two concepts, namely 'sentence' and 'truth'. Instead they construct the following replacement: with regard to language, deeming it exhaustively inadmissible is inadmissible. They explain this result as arising from one's own language and suggest the proposer try harder to find acceptable words.

This result undermines the anti-language positions, notably those of Mencius and Laozi. It invalidates any claim that language distorts 'guidance'. Two similar results undermine different formulations of similar points. One version decries distinctions. To make a distinction is to regard something as 'is not this', and to say 'distinctions are wrong' is to make a distinction. The Mohists say, 'to *fei* "*fei*" is perverse' (that is, to say 'saying "wrong" is wrong' is wrong). To recommend making no distinctions is to make a distinction (between making and not-making) and thus the recommender violates his own recommendation. Similarly, the Mohists observe, to teach that teaching lacks use, lacks use.

The analysis of compound terms produced some of the most striking evidence of the different conceptual structure. The Mohists ask what was assertible of the things picked out by compound terms. One standard case was 'ox–horse'. The Mohists note that 'not-ox' is assertable of 'ox–horse' on the same grounds that 'ox' is. The explanation goes that part of ox-horse is non-ox, so 'non-ox' is 'assertible'. We can understand the idea by reflecting on another example. We may ask someone how many children they have by asking how many 'boys girls' they have. Suppose the answer is 'three'. Now we may ask how many are boys. The answer may come back, 'none'. This would be a case in which we could say 'their boy–girls are not boys'.

However, the Mohists seems to have something stronger in mind. Even if the answer was 'two girls and a boy', the Mohists would argue that it would be right to say that (some of) their boy–girls were non-boy. Thus the Mohist concludes that, although we cannot say ox is non-ox or horse is non-horse, we can say intelligibly that ox–horse is non-ox-non-non-horse. The Mohists explain this result as arising from the fact that ox–horse 'does not interpenetrate'. In any compound that is ox–horse, the minimal parts will be either ox or horse, but not both. They term it a 'separable' compound.

The contrast is hard–white. This is also a compound term but, in this case, the components are inseparable. Wherever you go in that which is appropriately called hard–white, you get both. This is the kind of compound term more familiar in Western languages, the intersection compound (see LANGUAGE, PHILOSOPHY OF). The scope of the combined term is an intersection of the scopes of the two component terms. Ox–horse, by contrast, is a sum compound. The scope of the combined term is the union of the scopes of the two component terms.

The Mohists do not give us any rule for distinguishing intersection compounds from union compounds beyond the metaphysical feature of 'penetrating' or 'excluding'. They do not explicitly use the language of scope. They also characterize compounds as 'inseparable' and 'separable'. This curious result arises partly because they treat both nouns and adjectives as 'names'. Both pick out or distinguish one part of reality from the rest. This leaves us with the impression of arbitrariness in how names form compounds, which Mohists explain via metaphysical 'penetrability' or its opposite.

6 Phrase matching

Although the Mohists proposed a realist theory of reference, they embedded this in a further theory that we are guided by language. Thus the fourth object is knowing how to 'deem act'. The Mohists viewed the object of combining names as guiding action. Thus names pick out 'stuff', while strings or *ci* (phrases) convey intentions. This led them to analyse mainly ethical compounds. The other study, of 'ox–horse' and 'hard–white' compounds (see §5), construed them merely as complex names (though it gave no consistent principle for determining their conventional scope). In the long intact section of this text, the Mohists pursued a different analysis, one that can take a superficially logical form:

Premise: X is Y (white horse is horse)

Conclusion: KX is KY (ride white horse is ride horse)

They called this 'matching phrases', and argued that it was not reliable. Success would be as follows: whenever the version with simple terms was positive (an 'is this' phrase), then the parallel with compound terms should be positive (a *ran* ('so') phrase). Conversely, a negative base (X is not Y: a 'not this' phrase) should yield a negative result (KX is not KY: a 'not so' phrase).

The Mohists list the different kinds breakdowns:

- Sometimes an 'is this' yields a not-'so';
- Sometimes a 'not this' yields a 'so';
- Sometimes a reference is comprehensive and sometimes not;
- Sometimes one reference is 'is this' and another one is 'not this'

The rest of the essay consists of examples that illustrate the respective outcomes.

Graham, drawing on a part-of-speech analysis of 'is this' (subject) and 'so' (verb), treated this chapter as evidence that the Mohists discovered the subject-predicate sentence. He translated the procedure as 'matching sentences' and treated it as a discussion of logical form. The first two models do rely on syntactic complexes ($X\ Y\ ke$) which resemble syllogistic premises, but the latter two do not.

Classical Chinese uses no articles and has no 'is' verb. Expressions ending with the particle *ye* (assert) mark descriptive uses of referring expressions (noun-phrases). This signals that one is applying a descriptive term to a contextually selected object, not using the term to pick out the object. Translators typically render such structures in English as '(X) is Y'. In Chinese comments, the topic term (the X) is optional. The comment functions the same when the string is simply 'Y assert' and context supplies the topic. The 'assert', in other words, does not link two terms, it links a term to an object.

The *shi-ran* (is this-so) analysis given by the Mohists does fit the examples in a way consistent with the topic–comment analysis. If, on the other hand, we focus on the examples as sentences and treat the pattern as a form of inference, then the Mohist analysis will resemble a kind of algebraic logic. However, consistent with a topic–comment analysis, it may be better to regard it as extending the analysis of the conventional semantic effects of combining 'names' to form 'phrases'.

That the analysis rests on conventional semantics of terms rather than logic of sentences sheds a new light on how the examples work. The Mohists do not use the model to correct conventional reasoning errors; rather, they use what we would conventionally say to determine whether a result is a 'so' or a not-'so'. The most thoroughly illustrated breakdowns are those where an 'is this' base produces a not-'so'. The examples are:

- Someone's parents are people; one's serving one's parents is not one's serving the people;
- One's younger brother is a handsome man; one's loving one's younger brother is not one's loving a handsome man;
- A carriage is wood; riding a carriage is not riding wood;
- A boat is wood; entering a boat is not entering wood;
- Robbers are people; abounding in robbers is not abounding in people; lacking robbers is not lacking people.

The Mohists expand on the last example in a way that signals both the ethical importance of the analysis and the nature of the alleged breakdown in parallelism:

- Disliking the abundance of robbers is not disliking the abundance of people.
- Desiring to be without robbers is not desiring to be without people.
- Everyone would agree with these so they should not object if we say 'robbers are people but killing robbers is not killing people'.

We guess, following Graham, that the Mohists are defending their inherited doctrine of universal love by arguing that it is consistent with the (presumed) practice in Mohist communities of executing thieves.

What the denial amounts to is that, even if naming is objectively constant and reliable, the use of names in descriptions of actions or intentions does not reliably take one from an 'is this' to a 'so'. An execution is not murder. Loving a brother is morally required, loving a handsome man is (presumably) shameful. Serving one's parents is one kind of duty and serving the people another. One does not fulfil the latter in merely doing the former.

What emerges is an alternative strategy for dealing with the problem that Confucius addressed via rectifying names (see §1). The Mohists resist the implication that in executing thieves they must deny that thieves are people. They deny instead that executing thieves is murdering people. Rectifying takes place at the 'phrase' or 'so' level rather than at the 'name' level.

The next set of examples illustrate the converse case, those where we start with a 'not this' base and the result is a 'so':

- To read books is not books; to like reading book is to like book.
- Cockfights are not cocks; to like cockfights is to like cocks.
- About to fall in a well is not falling in a well. To stop one about to fall in a well is to stop one falling in a well.

This time the Mohists are expanding on fatalism: 'That there is fate is not fated; to deny that there is fate is to deny fate'. It is harder to reconstruct a problem that is plausibly solved by this analysis.

The algebraic form is abandoned in illustrating the next two breakdowns in parallelism. The first is 'part comprehensive; part not':

- 'Loving people' depends on comprehensively loving people. 'Not loving people' does not.
- 'Rides horses' does not depend on comprehensively riding horses. To have ridden on horses is enough to count as riding horses.

These examples highlight the mass-substantive structure of reasoning about reference. In one phrase the term-reference is implicitly comprehensive, in the other it is not.

Finally, we come to the examples of one 'is this' and one is 'not this':

- Fruit of a peach is a peach, fruit of a bramble is not a bramble.
- Asking about a person's illness is asking about the person. Disliking the person's illness is not disliking the person.
- A person's ghost is not the person. Your brother's ghost is your brother. Offering to a ghost is not offering to a person. Offering to your brother's ghost is offering to your brother.
- If the indicated horse's eyes are blind, then we call the horse blind. The horses eyes are large yet we do not call the horse large.
- If the indicated oxen's hairs are brown, then we call the oxen brown. The indicated oxen's hairs are many yet we do not call the oxen many.
- One horse is horse; two horses are horse. Saying 'horses are four footed things' is a case of one horse and four feet, not a pair of horses and four feet. Saying 'horses are partly white' is two horses and some white, not one horse and partly white.

There is no further analysis or summing up. The moral, we assume, is a negative one. Had we treated the first algebraic model as a kind of logic, the Mohists' argument by example would still show that it was invalid; it is not a reliable form in the sense that a true premise formally guarantees a true conclusion. However, the essay is not about sentences and truth at all. It is about whether there are reliable parallels developing from terms to longer (guiding) phrases.

The implicit answer is 'no'. The Mohists offer no constant or consistent principles guiding the construction of longer 'phrases' out of terms even when the terms are consistently applied to external realities. They offer no way to systematically rationalize the conventional patterns of use. They retreat implicitly from Mozi's goal of replacing convention with a constant *dao* (guide). If there is such a 'guide', then it is not a product of any simple projection from term reference. Moral guidance cannot derive from knowledge of natural kinds; it requires conventional, creative human social activity. Dialectically, the negative result gives ammunition to the Daoists who argue that no constant 'guide' exists (see DAOIST PHILOSOPHY §2).

7 Gongsun Long: one name, one thing

Against the Mohist background, we can now make some sense of the previously obscure writings of Gongsun Long. The text that bears his name consists of a few dialogues. Each is introduced by a counter-intuitive paradox followed by a discussion or chain of reasoning. Graham argued that at least two of these were forged out of misunderstood fragments of the Mohist writings. They apparently copied the phrases after the Canons had been zipped together and the indexing characters mixed into the text.

Two of the remaining dialogues: 'White Horse' and 'Referring and Things', serve as useful examples. They pose difficult puzzles, to which scholars have offered speculative, controversial and mutually inconsistent interpretations. The various interpretations flow partly from different principles used in selecting interpretive theories or 'translation manuals'. A couple of interpretations are given here, serving both to illustrate that point and to allow us to locate and discuss alternative views of Gongsun Long's theory.

In a (perhaps spurious) preface to the dialogues, Gongsun Long explains his motivation. He cites an example of Confucius rectifying names (see §1) and alleges that he is defending that view. Confucians mostly reject the affiliation, but it makes formal sense. If rectifying is to remove ambiguity from guidance, then it requires that only one name in a guidance situation can refer to the object. I either regard the male before me as 'father' or as 'ruler' or as 'person'. Supposing he is all three, if I am to extract guidance from codified rules, I must decide which rule to use. That means deciding which term is relevant to this action situation. The Mohist attack on that policy rejected any one-name-one-thing principle.

The Mohist account of compounding had negative implications from this point of view. Separable or sum compounds, such as 'ox–horse', conform to the one-name-one-thing principle. The scope of each term remains constant when we combine the terms. The combination names a sum of the two. Hard–white compounding, by contrast, violates the principle of strict clarity and consistency in naming. The scopes change when we compound the terms.

Other sources record Gongsun Long as defending two theses: 'separating the inseparable' and 'separating hard–white'. Since Graham argued that the dialogue on 'Hard–White' was forged, we cannot rely on it for an explanation. Still, we can confidently interpret the slogan since 'hard–white' is the Mohist example of an 'inseparable' or 'interpenetrating' compound. To 'separate' them would be to treat them as 'excluding each other' and the compound as a sum compound. Gongsun Long thus objects to the hard–white model.

The phrase 'white horse' selects one term from each type of compound. The White Horse dialogue begins with a question in the canonical analytic form: 'Is "white horse not horse" assertible?' followed by the answer, 'assertible'. The rest is generally agreed to be a discussion between the sophist defending the answer and an 'other' who raises objections. The first defence is that 'white' names a colour and 'horse' names a shape. Shape and colour are different, so a combination of shape and colour is not merely a shape.

The other most cited argument is 'if you ask for a horse, both a black or yellow horse can arrive. If you ask for a white horse, a black horse or yellow horse will not arrive.' This illustrates an argument thread that 'X is not Y' follows from 'X is different or distinguishable from Y'. The linking theme is that 'white horse' is a combination of two things and this requires that 'white horse not horse' be 'assertible'. A Mohist might respond that 'asking for a white horse' is indeed different from 'asking for a horse', but a white horse is still a horse.

One line of interpretation treats the term 'horse' as referring to the abstract object 'horseness', and thus 'white horse' to 'white-horseness'. The opening sentence thus states the *true* proposition that the two abstract concepts are distinct entities. Since the connected terms are logically singular, the 'not this' represents 'non-identity'. This line of interpretation is motivated by the principle of charity and undermined by the principle of humanity. It makes the puzzling sentence true (by Western lights) but does not explain how the sophist would have had access to the concepts involved. It does not apply to the two terms when used in the supporting arguments, all of which refer to concrete horses.

An alternative interpretation, that 'horse' refers to horse-stuff, can exploit the 'distinct-hence-different' line of argument and still consistently interpret the concrete references in the rest of the dialogue. If we similarly regard white as the mass-substantive – white stuff – rather than the abstract 'whiteness', we can see a connection to the Mohist theory of compound names. Gongsun Long regards 'intersection' or 'inter-penetrating' compounds as contrary to the one-name-one-thing principle. If white horse consists of two names, each should consistently name (scattered) things. Used in combination, their 'naming' should remain consistent. Thus, they should name the sum of the two stuffs and, as in the case of 'ox–horse', 'not-horse' would be assertable of it.

Alternatively, we may either deny that 'white horse' consists of two names or that they are the same names as when used separately. 'White horse' must be thought of as having no essential relation to 'horse' but as a *sui generis* term for a new stuff. We might then say 'white horse is horse' is not analytically true. Its truth is an accident of usage which *could have been otherwise*. Thus, 'white horse not horse' is assertible.

Gongsun Long's argument then becomes a dilemma. Either we regard 'white–horse' as a sum-compound term – in which case the 'ox–horse' result follows – or we regard it as a *sui generis* non-compound name – in which case the conventions of its use could tie it to anything at all; it need not necessarily be horse. The assumption must be that a name is the same only if it has the same scope (names the same thing). Since 'horse' in 'white horse' does not have that scope it is not the same name and its use in the compound constitutes an arbitrary new term.

The other dialogue poses, if possible, even more daunting barriers to interpretation. The first sentence seems to be an explicit contradiction: everything under heaven is *zhi* (pointing), and yet 'pointing' is not 'pointing'. The rest of the dialogue is content-thin and teeters repeatedly on the edge of pure syntactic contradiction. The only nouns are the puzzling *zhi* (pointing) along with *wu* (thing-kind) and *tianxia* (the world). Most interpreters take the issue to be the meaning of 'pointing' (a rare, mild consensus), and most treat it as semantic reference or meaning.

There are reasons for worry: as we saw, the Mohists focused on 'picking out' 'stuff' from its surroundings. There is no evidence of the semantic concept of 'meaning'; 'reference' is a more plausible evolution of that theory. Using 'meaning,' however, makes this dialogue mesh better with the abstract interpretation of the 'White Horse' thesis. Otherwise, it is hard to find any evidence of a sense–reference distinction or find any indication that it is individual objects rather than mereological wholes or types that we 'point to' (see SENSE AND REFERENCE; MEREOLOGY).

One speculative interpretation exploiting the 'reference' interpretation is both philosophically interesting and relevant to issues that emerge in theory of language and metaphysics. Graham treats the crucial first phrase as meaning that although one can refer to each thing, one cannot refer to 'everything' because in that reference one does not refer to one's own act of referring. Zhuangzi later makes a similar argument against assertions of absolute monism: to say everything is one is to have the one and the saying, which makes two. Tempting as it is, the interpretation has little theoretical connection to the White–Horse thesis. Graham treats both dialogues as dealing with the principle that whole is different from the part. The principle in question needs both careful formulation and plausible motivation.

8 Hui Shi: relativism and monism

We have even less direct textual evidence of the philosophical views of Hui Shi. All that remains are ten paradoxical sayings recorded in the *Zhuangzi* and some stories of his playing as Zhuangzi's 'debating companion'. Still, we can be confident of his position because plausible motivations for the sayings are more intuitive and are plausibly reflected in Zhuangzi's Daoism (see ZHUANGZI).

Hui Shi focuses on such distinctions as large/small, thick/thin, high/low, south/north and today/yesterday. The common feature is the variability in which term from each pair we can assert of some object. Most of his paradoxes make sense as contrary comments about the same thing, made from different points of view, such as these examples from *Zhuangzi* 33:

- Heaven is as low as the earth; mountains are level with marshes.
- The sun from one perspective is in the middle from another declining.
- Natural kinds are from one perspective living and from one dying.
- I go to Yue today and arrive yesterday.

The most important one for theory of language purpose strikes at the Achilles heel of Mohist realism, the construction of similarity classes:

- The ten thousand thing-kinds are ultimately alike and ultimately different. This is called the great similarity–difference.

As the *Zhuangzi* develops this insight, it suggests that we can find a difference between any two things no matter how alike, and a similarity between any two things no matter how different. So, even if there are objective similarities and differences, they do not justify any particular way of distinguishing between thing kinds. For every category and name, we could have had conventions that just as consistently and with equal 'world-guidedness' divide things differently.

However, the list of Hui Shi's sayings begins and ends with seeming absolutes. He seems to take a classic, so-called Daoist metaphysical view of an undifferentiated single totality:

- The ultimately great which has nothing outside it – call it the Great One!
- The ultimately small has nothing inside it – call it the Small One!
- Universally love the ten thousand thing-kinds; the cosmos is one 'substantive part'.

The concluding statement echoes the Mohists' ethical doctrine and one of their technical terms. We do not have Hui Shi's reasoning, but a plausible explanation is that normally taken by interpreters of Zhuangzi. It is the familiar inference of absolutism from relativism. If all distinctions are relative to some perspective, then we can conclude that reality has no distinctions. All distinctions are false: reality is an undifferentiated total one.

The *Zhuangzi* presentation of Hui Shi's views notes: 'He had many perspectives and his library would fill five carts, but his doctrine was self-contradictory and his language did not hit the target: the intent to make sense of things' (*Zhuangzi* 33). Zhuangzi presumably understood the incoherence of denying distinctions and, if we accept Graham's speculation about pointing and things, also the notion of an ultimate one – an 'everything' concept. Whether or not Gongsun Long rejected the inference, Zhuangzi clearly did. Zhuangzi almost paraphrases Hui Shi:

> 'The cosmos and I were born together, the ten-thousand things and I are one.' Now, having already constructed a 'one' is it possible to say something about it? Having already called it a 'one' can we fail to say something about it? 'One' and saying it make two. Two and one make three and going from here, even a skilled calculator can't keep up with us, let alone an ordinary man.
>
> (*Zhuangzi* 2)

Zhuangzi displays an immense fondness for Hui Shi alongside a dismissive, almost belittling attitude toward the result of his 'distinction-dispute'. Traditional accounts have reckoned this as a mystic's haughty disdain for logic. However, when we grasp that Hui Shi's doctrines have nothing to do with logic and everything to do with theory of language, a different view of the dynamic emerges. It pairs an erudite, enthusiastic and loquacious but somewhat wooly-minded semantic dilettante (Hui Shi) and a language theorist *par excellence* (Zhuangzi). This is not a case of mysticism versus logic, it is a case of clear versus befuddled theory of language. Zhuangzi enjoyed debating with Hui Shi because he was one of the few with enough learning to be worth refuting, even though he was a relatively easy target for a dialectician of Zhuangzi's calibre.

9   Zhuangzi: Sceptical perspectivalism

ZHUANGZI develops perspectivalism in a more consistent direction. He does not reject language (as perhaps Laozi did). Naturalism, taking the point of view of 'nature', does not require abandoning language. Human language, from the empty greetings and small talk to the disputes of philosophers, is another natural 'noise'. We are all 'pipes of nature' (*Zhuangzi* 2).

Zhuangzi grants the Mohist point that language has 'aboutness': 'Language is not blowing breath; there is language for language. That which it languages, however, is radically underdetermined' (*Zhuangzi* 2). He develops this claim with the aid of Hui Shi's relativism and his own analysis of the indexicality of all distinctions, and starts by asking to what does 'this' or 'that' refer? Is there anything that cannot be a 'this' or a 'that'? These terms do not have a rigid, naming relation to an external reality; they trace our changing relations to the realities. Zhuangzi's perspectival pluralism is not a version of Western subjectivity. He does not assign any special perspective to the individual consciousness or internal representations. The kinds of perspective Zhuangzi discusses range from the ways people who speak different languages or accept different moral theories constitute a perspective. At the other extreme, each of us takes different perspectives at different times in our lives – or for that matter, different times of the day.

The Mohists' *ke* (assertible) is also relative to perspective, the changing conventions of usage and principles within disputing factions and schools. Any language that actually is spoken is 'assertible'. Zhuangzi says the appearance of right and wrong in language is a function of elaboration and embellishment of a way of speaking. So the disputes between Mohists and Confucians amount to different elaborated ways of assigning 'is this' and 'not this'.

Zhuangzi calls his 'perspective' on the relativity of language *ming* (clarity). It is a perspective from which we can project backward to an 'axis' of linguistic guidance systems. From that 'axis' there would be no limit to what could be treated as 'is this' or 'not this'; a *dao* (guide) is merely the path one takes from that axis. Thing-kinds are made so by our classifications.

Lacking any limit on possible systems of naming and guiding, we lack any limit on know-how. No matter how much we advance and promote a way of dealing with things, there are things at which we will be deficient. To have any developed perspective is to leave something out. This, however, is not a reason to avoid language and a perspective; it is simply the inevitable result of limitless knowledge and limited lives.

'Sages' project their perspectives and prejudices on 'nature' and 'those who have arrived' know to deem everything as one. Zhuangzi does not recommend we use that attitude. Instead of trying to transcend and abandon the usual or conventional ways of speaking, we should treat them as useful. They enable us to communicate and get things done. That is all it is intelligible to ask of them.

Beyond the usefulness of our language, we don't know the way things are in themselves. We may dub our lack of that metaphysical knowledge as *dao*. To tax our minds by trying to treat everything as 'one' differs from that admission of ignorance only in the emotion that accompanies it. In the end, neither scepticism nor monistic mysticism allows us to say anything about ultimate reality. They merely exhibit different attitudes towards saying ... nothing.

10 Xunzi: Confucian conventionalism

The final chapter in Chinese language theory comes in the 'Rectifying Names' chapter of the *Xunzi*. XUNZI focuses on language because he wants to reassert that 'ritual' is the only standard of correct behaviour. He rejected Mencian intuitionism and gleaned insights from Zhuangzi and the dialecticians. The apparent moral he drew was that, since reality cannot be a standard of language correctness, the default standard must be convention.

Appeal to the usage of the sage-kings determines correct name use. The correct account of that usage is a historical tradition, by which Xunzi means the judgment of Confucian scholar-gentlemen. Thus Confucianism is vindicated by the weakness Mozi had exposed. Xunzi then goes on to construct an explicitly conventionalist theory of language which carries political implications.

Xunzi introduced an important clarification. He distinguished between two kinds of 'distinctions': *gui–jian* (noble–base) and *tong–yi* (same–different). The former correspond roughly to value distinctions and the latter to empirical or descriptive distinctions. The latter are the basis for interaction with other cultures, and a king is entitled to change these 'miscellaneous' terms. Even a king, however, cannot change conventional evaluative distinctions (ranks, titles, punishments or anything in the *li* (ritual)). For these we rely on the sage-kings' *dao* (guide) via the scholar-gentlemen's interpretation. Xunzi regards moral terms as conventional 'artifice' arising from thought, not from nature.

Political authorities rectify names for the original Confucian purposes (order and obedience). Xunzi treats the positions and paradoxes of the dialecticians solely in political terms. Philosophy of language causes social instability by undermining the public guiding language. Philosophers confuse the conventional relations of names and make 'is this/not this' unclear. This we must stop: we must have but one standard of terminology. The king, not disputing philosophers and warring schools, will govern introduction of new descriptive terms.

The king should keep three things in mind as he creates names:

(1) the reason for having names: the reason for having names is coordinating social behaviour and achieving social order. Hence, value terms govern how we assign descriptive terms.
(2) the basis of classifying as similar and different: we classify by taking the distinctions delivered by sense organs and using them according to the dictates of a heart imbued with the correct evaluative distinctions.
(3) the essentials of regulating names: the basis of regulating names is social order and the preservation of a stable, traditional scheme of language.

Xunzi's account of classifying similar and different takes a markedly empirical (epistemological) turn. Unlike the Mohists, Xunzi did not rely on claims that reality presented objective similarities and differences. Zhuangzi had argued that human standards of 'is this/not this' were no more natural than the opposing ones of other animals. Taking Zhuangzi's hint, Xunzi focused on human sense reactions to reality. Indeed, no neutral, inter-species ways of distinguishing things as similar and different exist. Still, while the senses of one species work differently from those of another, those of any one species makes similar distinctions.

All humans sense and respond to approximately the same range of natural distinctions (see SENSE-DATA). The eyes of humans distinguish the same range and bands of colours, the mouth the same classifications of taste, the ears the same range and discriminations of pitch and so on. The shared nature of intra-species distinction-making underwrites the possibility of community and language. Thus, we abandon any appeal to cosmic nature and rely on what is pragmatically possible for humans in achieving natural human goals.

Our language conventionally clusters some sensible differences and ignores others. Historical, conventional standards dictate how it does this. These norms are transmitted into the cultured gentleman's heart when he masters the transmitted, sage-king's scheme of values. The heart rules the sense organs (as it did for MENCIUS). It determines what range of sensible discriminants counts as categories for moral purposes. Thus the categories mesh with the moral system of the sage-kings and match the clustering they originated.

It is clear that Xunzi absorbed a good deal of his contemporary theory of language. It is less clear if he understood the arguments and motivation. He deals with the problem of compound terms by ignoring it: 'If a single term is sufficient to convey the intent then use that and otherwise use a compound term.' The intent, presumably, is the conventionally understood intent. Xunzi does accept the Mohist view of names with varying scopes, and disowns the one-name-one-thing ideal. The only important kind of clarity or consistency is the constancy of convention.

Xunzi treats a number of related problems about names in sensitive fashion. He saw that spatial separation was a basis of describing two things of the same kind as two 'stuffs'. He then defines 'change' as being when a thing's spatial position does not change (exhibits characteristic continuity) and its type does. We then treat the thing as the same thing that has changed characteristics. This discussion of metamorphosis is the closest approximation of the classical Western problem of change (see CHANGE).

Whether or not Xunzi understood the theories behind the paradoxes he criticizes, he clearly did not appreciate them. He exhibits no philosophical fascination with solving conceptual puzzles for their own sake or using them to drive theory. He criticizes paradoxical statements on primarily political grounds, namely the deleterious social effects of asserting their conclusions. Each upsets conventional ways of using terms. Xunzi's solution is political rather intellectual: ban them.

Xunzi classifies the paradoxes into three groups, which vaguely suggests the line of thought leading to them. Each, he argues, violates one of the three insights into names. The reason for naming is coordinating behaviour, so paradoxes which 'use names to confuse names' include the Mohist's claim that 'killing thieves is not killing men'. This uses a theory of names to yield a conclusion that sounds unconventional. So, we forbid saying them.

The second set 'use reality to confuse names', and the central examples are like Hui Shi's relativity paradoxes. These ignore the shared human empirical basis for assigning similarity and difference and use the fact that having different perspectives on reality might lead us to saying unconventional things about size and shape. So, the king will forbid saying them.

The final group use names to confuse reality and includes 'white horse not horse'. Xunzi's analysis does not help resolve the interpretive puzzles about the line of reasoning since it addresses only the pragmatic consequences of allowing such theorizing. His solution, once again, is for the king to avoid and prevent such distracting sophistry.

11 The aftermath: death of philosophy

One of Xunzi's students, HAN FEIZI, was a minor royal in one of the Warring States, who became a central figure of the Legalist school. He had learned a smattering of Chinese theory of language, and he exaggerated the threat of interpretative anarchy to justify repressing philosophy and language creativity. He followed Xunzi's argument that the ruler should enforce uniformity in language but rejected using a scholarly tradition as the norm. His theory of regulation and punishment was based on a crude argument about shape and name which takes us back to the unexplained Confucian notion that names by themselves guide action. An official post is a capsule description of functions (duties) the holder should perform. In the light of recent discoveries, this doctrine appears to be an application of the doctrine of a cult of ruler worship (Huang–Lao) which taught that the 'guide' was in nature and names were embedded in natural shapes.

Legalism became the official doctrine of the repressive Qin empire, which brought the classical period of Chinese philosophy to an abrupt halt (see LEGALIST PHILOSOPHY, CHINESE). In the aftermath, the insights of Chinese theory of language slipped into obscurity. Huang–Lao became the dominant theory surviving during China's philosophical dark age until the importation of Buddhist theory. The early medieval Daoist interpreters argued that we can have names only for things we see. Suppression had worked its magic.

See also: CHINESE PHILOSOPHY; CONFUCIAN PHILOSOPHY, CHINESE; DAOIST PHILOSOPHY; LANGUAGE, PHILOSOPHY OF; MOHIST PHILOSOPHY; MOZI; XUNZI; ZHUANGZI

References and further reading

Fung Yu-lan (1952) *History of Chinese Philosophy*, trans. D. Bodde, Princeton, NJ: Princeton University Press. (A classic account that highlights the abstract interpretation of the 'White Horse' dialogue. Good for general purposes.)

* Graham, A. (1978) *Later Mohist Logic, Ethics and Science*, Hong Kong: The Chinese University Press, and London: School of Oriental and African Studies. (The only source in English for the Later Mohist text. Difficult: understanding Graham virtually requires knowledge of classical Chinese.)

* —— (1981) *Chuang-tzu: The Inner Chapters*, London: Allen & Unwin. (A translation of the *Zhuangzi*, including the summary of Hui Shi's paradoxes.)

—— (1989) *Disputers of the Tao: Philosophical Argument in Ancient China*, La Salle, IL: Open Court. (An easier but less detailed treatment in the context of Graham's account of ancient Chinese thought.)

Hansen, C. (1983) *Language and Logic in Ancient China*, Ann Arbor, MI: University of Michigan Press. (Difficult, based on Graham's reconstruction. A philosophical argument for a radically different interpretation of the linguistic doctrines.)

—— (1992) *A Daoist Theory of Chinese Thought*, New York: Oxford University Press. (An easier and more extended treatment in an account of ancient Chinese philosophy that emphasizes language.)

Thompson, K.O. (1995) 'When a "White Horse" is not a "Horse"', *Philosophy East and West* 45 (4): 481–99. (A definitive view of Gongsun Long's most important dialogue.)

CHAD HANSEN

LOGIC IN ISLAMIC PHILOSOPHY

Islamic logic was inspired primarily by Aristotle's logical corpus, the Organon (which according to a late Greek taxonomy also included the Rhetoric *and* Poetics*). Islamic authors were also familiar with some elements in Stoic logic and linguistic theory, and their logical sources included not only Aristotle's own works but also the works of the late Greek Aristotelian commentators, the Isagōgē of Porphyry and the logical writings of Galen. However, most of the logical work of the Islamic philosophers remained squarely within the tradition of Aristotelian logic, and most of their writings in this area were in the form of commentaries on Aristotle.*

For the Islamic philosophers, logic included not only the study of formal patterns of inference and their validity but also elements of the philosophy of language and even of epistemology and metaphysics. Because of territorial disputes with the Arabic grammarians, Islamic philosophers were very interested in working out the relationship between logic and language, and they devoted much discussion to the question of the subject matter and aims of logic in relation to reasoning and speech. In the area of formal logical analysis, they elaborated upon the theory of terms, propositions and syllogisms as formulated in Aristotle's Categories, De interpretatione *and* Prior Analytics. *In the spirit of Aristotle, they considered the syllogism to be the form to which all rational argumentation could be reduced, and they regarded syllogistic theory as the focal point of logic. Even poetics was considered as a syllogistic art in some fashion by most of the major Islamic Aristotelians.*

Since logic was viewed as an organon *or* instrument *by which to acquire knowledge, logic in the Islamic world also incorporated a general theory of argumentation focused upon epistemological aims. This element of Islamic logic centred upon the theory of demonstration found in Aristotle's* Posterior Analytics, *since demonstration was considered the ultimate goal sought by* *logic. Other elements of the theory of argumentation, such as dialectics and rhetoric, were viewed as secondary to demonstration, since it was held that these argument forms produced cognitive states inferior in certitude and stability to demonstration. The philosopher's aim was ultimately to demonstrate necessary and certain truth; the use of dialectical and rhetorical arguments was accounted for as preparatory to demonstration, as defensive of its conclusions, or as aimed at communicating its results to a broader audience.*

1   **The subject matter and aims of logic**
2   **Logic, language and grammar**
3   **Conceptualization and assent**
4   **Predicables, categories and propositions**
5   **Theory of argumentation**

1   The subject matter and aims of logic

As was their custom in discussing all the branches of philosophy, the Islamic philosophers devoted considerable attention to identifying the subject matter studied by logic and the aims at which logical studies are directed. AL-FARABI, whose logical and linguistic writings comprise the majority of his philosophical output, epitomizes the approach to logic that is characteristic of Islamic Aristotelianism. In his *Ihsa' al-'ulum* (Enumeration of the Sciences), he defines logic as an instrumental, rule-based science aimed at directing the intellect towards the truth and safeguarding it from error in its acts of reasoning. He defends the need for such a science of reasoning on the grounds that it is possible for the mind to err in at least some of its acts, for example, in those in which the intelligibles sought are not innate, but are rather attained discursively and empirically 'through reflection and contemplation'. Al-Farabi compares logic to tools such as rulers and compasses, which are used to ensure exactness when we measure physical objects subject to the errors of sensation. Like these tools, logical measures can be employed by their users to verify both their own acts of reasoning and the arguments of others. Indeed, logic is especially useful and important to guide the intellect when it is faced with the need to adjudicate between opposed and conflicting opinions and authorities.

Al-Farabi's view of logic as a rule-based science which governs the mind's operations over intelligibles is repeated in many of his introductory logical works, and it formed the foundation for Ibn Sina's later refinements (see IBN SINA). In the opening chapters of his *al-Madkhal* (Introduction), the first logical book of his encyclopaedic work *al-Shifa'* (Healing), Ibn Sina describes the purpose of logic as one of enabling the intellect to acquire 'knowledge of the unknown from the known'. Like al-Farabi, he defends the need for logic by arguing that the innate capacities of reasoning are insufficient to ensure the attainment of this purpose, and thus they require the aid of an art. While there may be some cases in which innate intelligence is sufficient to ensure the attainment of true knowledge, such cases are haphazard at best; he compares them to someone who manages to hit a target on occasion without being a true marksman. The most important and influential innovation that Ibn Sina introduces into the characterization of logic is his identification of its subject matter as 'second intentions' or 'secondary concepts', in contrast to 'first intentions'. This distinction is closely linked in Ibn Sina's philosophy to his important metaphysical claim that essence or quiddity can be distinguished from existence, and that existence in turn can be considered in either of its two modes: existence in concrete, singular things in the external world; or conceptual existence in one of the soul's sensible or intellectual faculties (see EXISTENCE).

In *al-Madkhal*, Ibn Sina argues that logic differs from the other sciences because it considers not conceptual existence as such (this would be psychology), but rather the accidents or properties that belong to any quiddity by virtue of its being conceptualized by the mind. These properties, according to Ibn Sina, include such things as essential and accidental predication, being a subject or being a predicate, and being a premise or a syllogism (see LOGICAL FORM §1). It is these properties that allow the mind to connect concepts together in order to acquire knowledge of the unknown; they provide the foundation for the rules of reasoning and inference that logic studies. They are moreover formal properties in the sense that, as properties belonging to all concepts in virtue of their mental mode of existence, they are entirely independent of the content of the thought itself; they are indifferent to the intrinsic natures of the quiddities which they serve to link together.

In the *Ilahiyyat* (*Metaphysics*) of *al-Shifa'*, Ibn Sina introduces the terminology of first and second 'intentions' or concepts in order to express the relation between the concepts of these quiddities themselves – which are studied in the theoretical sciences – and the concepts of the states and accidents of their mental existence which logic studies: 'As you know, the subject matter of logical science is second, intelligible intentions (*al-ma'ani al-ma'qula al-tha-niyya*) which are dependent upon the primary intelligible intentions with respect to some property by which they lead from the known to the unknown' (*Ilahiyyat* Book 1, ch. 2, in Anawati and Zayed 1960:

10–11). For example, the second intentions of 'being a subject' and 'being a predicate' are studied in logic independently of whatever first intentions function as the subject and predicate terms in a given proposition, for example, 'human being' and 'rational animal' in the proposition 'a human being is a rational animal'. The logical second intentions depend upon the first intentions because the first intentions are the conceptual building blocks of the new knowledge which second intentions link together: but logic studies the second intentions in abstraction from whatever particular first intentions the logical relations depend upon in any given case.

2 Logic, language and grammar

The attention that Ibn Sina and al-Farabi devote to the proper characterization of the subject matter of logic stems in part from a concern to distinguish logic from grammar. In the ancient and medieval traditions, the study of logic was closely tied to the philosophical consideration of language (see LANGUAGE, MEDIEVAL THEORIES OF; LOGIC, ANCIENT; LOGIC, MEDIEVAL), and for this reason many Arabic grammarians – whose linguistic theories were developed to a high degree of complexity and sophistication – were contemptuous of the philosophers for importing Greek logic, which they saw as a foreign linguistic tradition, into the Arabic milieu. This attitude toward Greek logic is epitomized in a famous debate reported to have taken place in Baghdad in 932 between the grammarian Abu Sa'id al-Sirafi and Abu Bishr Matta, a Syriac Christian who translated some of Aristotle's works into Arabic and is purported to have been one of al-Farabi's teachers. The extant account of the debate is heavily biased towards al-Sirafi, who attacks logical formalism and denies the ability of logic to act as a measure of reasoning over and above the innate capacities of the intellect itself. His principal claims are that philosophical logic is nothing but Greek grammar warmed over, that it is inextricably tied to the idiom of the Greek language and that it has nothing to offer speakers of another language such as Arabic.

It is against the background of such attacks that the discussions of the relations between logic, language and grammar by al-Farabi, Ibn Sina and al-Farabi's pupil Yahya IBN 'ADI (also a Syriac Christian and translator), are to be understood. Al-Farabi and Yahya both present essentially the same perspective on the relations between logic and language, a moderate perspective which Ibn Sina later rejects. In the *Ihsa' al-'ulum*, al-Farabi argues that logic and grammar both have some legitimate interest in language, but whereas grammatical rules primarily govern the use of language, logical rules primarily govern the use of intelligibles:

> And this art [of logic] is analogous to the art of grammar, in that the relation of the art of logic to the intellect and the intelligibles is like the relation of the art of grammar to language and expressions. That is, to every rule for expressions which the science of grammar provides us, there is a corresponding [rule] for intelligibles which the science of logic provides us.
>
> (*Ihsa' al-'ulum*, in Amin 1968: 68)

More precisely, al-Farabi explains that although grammar and logic share a mutual concern with expressions, grammar provides rules that govern the correct use of expressions in a given language, but logic provides rules that govern the use of any language whatsoever in so far as it signifies intelligibles. Thus, logic will have some of the characteristics of a universal grammar, attending to the common features of all languages that reflect their underlying intelligible content. Some linguistic features will be studied in both logic and grammar, but logic will study them as they are common, and grammar in so far as they are idiomatic. On the basis of this comparison with grammar, then, al-Farabi is able to complete his characterization of the subject matter of logic as follows: 'The subject-matters of logic are the things for which [logic] provides the rules, namely, intelligibles in so far as they are signified by expressions, and expressions in so far as they signify intelligibles' (*Ihsa' al-'ulum*, in Amin 1968: 74).

Like al-Farabi, Yahya ibn 'Adi, in a treatise entitled *Maqala fi tabyin al-fasl bayna sina'atay al-mantiq al-falsafi wa-al-nahw al-'arab* (On the Difference Between Philosophical Logic and Arabic Grammar), makes his case for the independence of logic from grammar based upon the differences between the grammar of a particular nation and the universal science of logic. He argues that the subject matter of grammar is mere expressions (*al-alfaz*), which it studies from the limited perspective of their correct articulation and vocalization according to Arabic conventions. The grammarian is especially concerned with language as an oral phenomenon; the logician alone is properly concerned with 'expressions in so far as they signify meanings' (*al-alfaz al-dalla 'ala al-ma'ani*) (*Maqala fi tabyin*, in Endress 1978: 188). To support this claim, Yahya points out that changing grammatical inflections do not affect the basic signification of a word: if in one sentence a word occurs in the nominative case, with the appropriate vocalization, its signification remains unchanged when it is used in another sentence in the accusative case and with a different vocal ending.

In Ibn Sina's view, however, such accounts of the logician's interest in language and its differences from that of the grammarian did not go far enough. In keeping with his own understanding of logic as the science which studies second intentions, Ibn Sina criticized such earlier attempts to introduce linguistic concerns into the subject matter of logic. In *al-Madkhal*, Ibn Sina labels as 'stupid' those who say that 'the subject matter of logic is speculation concerning expressions in so far as they signify meanings (*ma'ani*)'. However, Ibn Sina does not deny that the logician is sometimes or even often required to consider linguistic matters; his objection is to the inclusion of language as an essential constituent of the subject matter of logic. The logician is only incidentally concerned with language because of the constraints of human thought and the practical exigencies of learning and communication. Ibn Sina goes so far as to claim that, 'if logic could be learned through pure thought so that meanings alone could be attended to in it, then it would dispense entirely with expressions'; but since this is not in fact possible, 'the art of logic is compelled to have some of its parts come to consider the states of expressions' (*al-Madkhal*, in Anawati *et al.* 1952: 22–3). For Ibn Sina, then, logic is a purely rational art whose purpose is entirely captured by its goal of leading the mind from the known to the unknown; only accidentally and secondarily can it be considered a linguistic art.

3   Conceptualization and assent

While the close links between logic and linguistic studies emerge in the Islamic philosophers' consideration of the subject matter of logic, the links between logic and epistemology come to the fore in the consideration of the divisions within logic and the order of the books within Aristotle's Organon. All the principal Islamic Aristotelians organize their understanding of the divisions of logic around the epistemological couplet of *tasawwur* (conceptualization), and *tasdiq* (assent), which constitute for them the two states of knowledge that logic aims to produce in the intellect.

Conceptualization is the act of the mind by which it grasps singular (though not necessarily simple) essences or quiddities, such as the concept of 'human being'. Assent, by contrast, is the act of the intellect whereby it makes a determinate judgment to which a truth-value can be assigned; in fact, conceptualization is defined in Islamic philosophy principally by contrast with assent. Thus, any act of knowledge that does not entail the assignment of a truth-value to the proposition that corresponds to it will be an act of conceptualization alone, not assent. More specifically, the Islamic philosophers link assent to the affirmation or denial of the existence of the thing conceived, or to the judgment that it exists in a certain state, with certain properties. Thus, assent presupposes some prior act of conceptualization, although conceptualization does not presuppose assent.

One of the purposes of including a consideration of the *tasawwur–tasdiq* dichotomy in introductory discussions of the purpose of logic is to provide an epistemological foundation for the two focal points of Aristotelian logic, the definition and the syllogism (see LOGICAL FORM §1). The purpose of the definition is identified as the production of an act of conceptualization, and the purpose of the syllogism is identified as causing assent to the truth of a proposition. However, since the definition and the syllogism are both considered in the *Prior* and *Posterior Analytics* and the works that come after them in the Organon, the study of the ways of producing conceptualization and assent presupposes as its foundation the study of single terms and propositions in the *Categories* and *De interpretatione*.

4 Predicables, categories and propositions

In keeping with the ancient Greek tradition, the Islamic philosophers considered the books of the Organon to be an ordered series which begins with the study of the signification of simple terms in the *Categories* and then proceeds to the study of propositions in the *De interpretatione*. In addition to these two Aristotelian texts, a work of the Neoplatonist PORPHYRY, known as the *Isagōgē* (Introduction), was appended to the beginning of this series as an introduction to the study of the *Categories* (see ARISTOTLE §7). It was concerned with the five predicables: genus, species, difference, property and accident. While all of the Islamic Aristotelians wrote commentaries on the *Isagōgē* and utilized its grouping of the predicables, not all were convinced of its utility as an introduction to Aristotle. IBN RUSHD openly expresses such doubts in the introduction to his *Talkhis kitab al-maqulat* (Middle Commentary on the Categories), where he indicates that his original intention was to omit the *Isagōgē* entirely from his series of middle commentaries on the Organon. At the end of his work on the *Isagōgē* itself, he explains bluntly that he does not believe that Porphyry's text is a helpful introduction to the study of logic and questions whether it is really a logical text at all. His sole reason for completing the commentary, he tells us, was to comply with a request made by his friends.

The logical character of the *Categories* presented a related problem for other Islamic philosophers. In the introduction to his *Sharh al-'ibarah (Great Commen-*

tary on the De interpretatione), al-Farabi rehearses some of the controversies inherited from the Greek tradition over the relations between the *Categories* and the *De interpretatione*. As al-Farabi points out, the *De interpretatione* can be understood quite well without a prior knowledge of the *Categories*, and the former work makes no explicit references to the latter. Moreover, the *De interpretatione* is principally concerned with the formal relations amongst propositions, such as contradiction and contrariety, whereas the *Categories* is concerned with the signification or meaning of terms as such. Furthermore, in its opening chapters, the *De interpretatione* considers in formal terms the simple parts of which propositions are composed, that is, the noun and the verb. Despite these concerns, however, al-Farabi opts for the traditional ordering of these books on the grounds that the *Categories* is relevant to the whole of logic, since it studies 'the simplest of the subject matters in which logic actualizes itself'. In his *Falsafa Aristutalis* (Philosophy of Aristotle), al-Farabi opts for a similar solution to the logical status of the Categories, explaining that it comprises an investigation and classification of 'the instances of being from which the first premises are compounded', which are 'the primary significations of the expressions generally accepted by all' (*Falsafa Aristutalis*, in Mahdi 1969: 82–3).

Al-Farabi's misgivings in both of these texts stem from the largely ontological focus of the Aristotelian *Categories*, which calls into question its placement within the Organon. This concern was echoed later by Ibn Sina, who points out that many of the discussions in the *Categories* would be better placed in metaphysics or psychology, since they pertain to the study of expressions as directly signifying external or mental beings, in other words, to first rather than to second intentions. But since the *Categories* is useful in instructing us how to formulate definitions – which is one of the principal goals of logic – its placement in the Organon can be justified on practical grounds.

Islamic philosophers viewed *De interpretatione* as a study of the composition and truth-values of categorical propositions. Thus al-Farabi, in his great commentary on this text, explains that the term 'interpretation' used in the title of the work means 'complete statement' (*al-qawl al-tamm*). A complete statement, according to al-Farabi, must be one which causes a complete understanding in the mind; in other words, one in which assent occurs along with conceptualization. This is achieved principally by a simple, predicative, categorical statement (*al-qawl al-jazim al-hamli al-basit*) which affirms or denies a predicate of its subject.

5 Theory of argumentation

For the entire Islamic tradition, the crowning glory of Aristotelian logic is the syllogistic theory outlined in the *Prior* and *Posterior Analytics*, especially the latter. The purpose of logic is to provide the means whereby knowledge is to be acquired, and the most valuable type of knowledge is that which is certain and necessary, that is, knowledge gained according to the paradigm of demonstrative science laid out in the *Posterior Analytics*. This part of logic, in the words of al-Farabi's *Ihsa' al-'ulum*, is 'the strongest and pre-eminent in dignity and authority. Logic seeks its primary aim in this part alone, and the rest of its parts are only for its sake' (*Ihsa' al-'ulum*, in Amin 1968: 89). Even the formal study of the syllogism itself is primarily undertaken for the sake of its employment in demonstrations.

In their formal syllogistic theory, the Islamic Aristotelians mainly follow Aristotle's *Prior Analytics*. While they are aware of the fourth figure traditionally ascribed to GALEN, the tendency is to dismiss this figure as superfluous and intuitively implausible, as Ibn Sina does in the seventh method of his *al-Isharat wa-'l-tanbihat* (Remarks and Admonitions); or to ignore it entirely, as al-Farabi does in his *Kitab al-qiyas* (Book on the Syllogism). Similarly, the Arabic philosophers knew of the alternative propositional logic of the Stoics and incorporated elements of it in their discussions of conditional or hypothetical (*shartiyyah*) syllogisms (see LOGIC, ANCIENT). However, they did not accept the Stoic inference schemata, nor did they treat conditional connectives as truth-functional, since they did not consider the parts of conditional statements to be complete propositions in their own right. Moreover, for the Islamic logicians 'conditional' was a generic term which included both 'conjunctive' (*al-muttasilat*) conditionals (of the form, 'if . . . then') and 'disjunctive' (*al-munfasilat*) conditionals (of the form, 'either . . . or'). Conditional syllogisms of both sorts were viewed as relying upon a process of 'reiteration' or 'repetition' (*istithna'*), a term which referred to the repetition of the antecedent or the consequent, or one of the two disjuncts, in so far as it formed the second premise of a syllogism. Thus in the conjunctive conditional syllogism, 'If it is daytime, then it is light; but it is daytime, therefore it is light', 'it is daytime' would be labelled the *mustathna'* or reiterated premise, since it is by its restatement that the syllogism reaches its conclusion.

When we turn to the specific application of syllogistic theory to particular types of argumentation, the epistemological concerns of Islamic logic surface once more. In particular, the Islamic philoso-phers explained the primacy of demonstration, and the ancillary role of dialectical, rhetorical, poetic and sophistical syllogisms, by reference to the epistemic status of the premises used in each type of syllogism, and the type of assent they could produce to the conclusion of the syllogisms in which they were employed. The classification of syllogisms and their premises according to the nature of their assent is found in the logical writings of all the major Islamic philosophers, but the most complete and systematic classification of premises occurs in three of Ibn Sina's works, *al-Burhan* (Demonstration), in *al-Shifa'*, *al-Najah* (Deliverance) and *al-Isharat wa-'l-tanbihat* (Remarks and Admonitions). Although these three accounts differ somewhat in the number and variety of the premises listed in each, generally they present a single and consistent theory. Demonstrative syllogisms are composed of premises which necessitate assent and include self-evident first principles as well as sensible, empirically evident propositions. Dialectical syllogisms are based upon generally accepted beliefs (*al-mashhurat*), which are equivalent to the *endoxa* of Aristotle's Topics; on premises granted for the purposes of dialectical debate; and in general, on all premises assented to because they are universally accepted by all people, or by people deemed author-itative. Rhetorical syllogisms are similar to dialectical ones, except that they are accepted unreflectively and on the basis of a more limited authority, relative, for example, to a particular group or sect; as such, they are only supposed or presumed to be 'generally-accepted beliefs'. Sophistical premises are those accepted because of some misleading resemblance to another type of premise, and poetic premises are those that produce a motion in the faculty of imagination (*al-takhyil*), not an act of intellectual assent.

The inclusion of rhetorical and poetical syllogisms in this enumeration reflects a common assumption among Islamic philosophers that Aristotle's *Rhetoric* and *Poetics* are parts of his logical Organon. This assumption was inherited by the Islamic tradition from the Greek commentators, and it was used by them in part to account for the differences between philosophical and popular modes of discourse and argumentation, particularly in the context of discussions of the relations between philosophy and religion. The Islamic philosophers held that whereas philosophers rely principally upon demonstrative and dialectical syllogisms, religious leaders and theologians generally use rhetorical and poetical syllogisms to persuade the general populace. Religion is thus viewed as an image or reflection of philosophical, demonstrative truth propounded in language and argument-forms that can be easily understood by the mass of humanity.

The place of dialectic within the theory of argumentation is perhaps the most ambivalent in Islamic logic. While dialectic is seen as inferior to demonstration, its importance for philosophy is none the less recognized. A good example of this is found in al-Farabi's enumeration in his *Kitab al-jadal* (Book on Dialectic) of the ways in which dialectic serves philosophers. According to al-Farabi, dialectic hones argumentative skills, introduces the principles of the special demonstrative sciences, alerts the mind to the self-evident principles of demonstration, helps to develop communicative skills and provides the means for refuting sophistry. Of these five uses, only the fourth is external to the proper aims of philosophy and closer to the tasks usually reserved to theology and religion. The other four pertain to the learning or acquisition of truly philosophical skills, even if they lie outside the strictly demonstrative aims that are the ultimate end of philosophy.

In the case of the theory of demonstration itself, Islamic logicians organized their commentaries on the *Posterior Analytics* around the definition and the demonstrative syllogism as the means by which both conceptualization and assent are most perfectly attained. Al-Farabi's *Kitab al-burhan* (Book on Demonstration) offers an excellent summary of the standard approach taken by Islamic philosophers to theory of demonstration and its epistemological aims. Just as he identified the categorical statement as the embodiment of perfect assent on the propositional level, here al-Farabi identifies demonstrative certitude as complete or perfect assent on the level of syllogistic inference. Moreover, certitude is defined by al-Farabi in terms of what we would now label 'second-order' knowledge:

> Certitude is for us to believe, concerning the truth to which we have assented, that it is not possible at all for what we believe about this matter to be different from what we believe it to be; and in addition to this for us to believe, concerning our belief, that another belief is not possible – in the sense that whenever some belief about the first belief is formed, it is impossible for it to be otherwise, and so on *ad infinitum*.
>
> (*Kitab al-burhan*,
> in al-'Ajam and Fakhry 1986–7, 4: 20)

Certitude requires not just knowledge of a conclusion, *p*, but knowing that we know *p*. This sort of certitude al-Farabi calls 'necessary certitude'. However, he also allows for non-necessary certitude, which holds 'only at a particular time', and thus can be applied to propositions about merely contingent beings: 'Necessary certitude and necessary existence are convertible in entailment, for what is verified as

necessarily certain is necessarily existent' (*Kitab al-burhan*, in al-'Ajam and Fakhry 1986–7, 4: 22). While al-Farabi recognizes both of these varieties of certitude to be forms of perfect assent, in his view necessary certitude alone fulfils the strict conditions of Aristotelian demonstration, since it alone will pertain to objects which cannot be other than they are.

Al-Farabi's remarks on the utility of dialectic, combined with his extension of the notion of perfect assent beyond the confines of strict and necessary demonstration, illustrate the overall breadth of the Islamic philosophers' theories of argumentation. Despite their professions of the primacy of the demonstrative paradigm within philosophy, the Islamic Aristotelians recognized a broad range of legitimate and useful argument forms and acknowledged their importance as philosophical tools leading to knowledge of the unknown.

See also: ARISTOTELIANISM IN ISLAMIC PHILOSOPHY; ARISTOTLE; AL-FARABI; IBN SINA; LOGICAL FORM; LOGIC, ANCIENT; LOGIC, MEDIEVAL; LOGIC, PHILOSOPHY OF; MEANING IN ISLAMIC PHILOSOPHY; SYNTAX

References and further reading

Abed, S.B. (1991) *Aristotelian Logic and the Arabic Language in Al-Farabi*, Albany, NY: State University of New York Press. (An excellent consideration of the central issues in al-Farabi's linguistic philosophy.)

Black, D.L. (1990) *Logic and Aristotle's 'Rhetoric' and 'Poetics' in Medieval Arabic Philosophy*, Leiden: Brill. (Discusses the interpretation of these Aristotelian texts as works of logic.)

* Al-Farabi (*c.*870–950) *Ihsa' al-'ulum* (Enumeration of the Sciences), ed. U. Amin, Cairo: Librairie Anglo-Égyptienne, 3rd edn, 1968. (Al-Farabi's major work, in which he investigates in detail different forms of knowledge.)

* —— (*c.*870–950) *Kitab al-burhan* (Book on Demonstration), in R. al-'Ajam and M. Fakhry (eds) *al-Mantiq 'inda al-Farabi*, Beirut: Dar el-Mashreq, 1986–7, 4 vols. (*Al-Mantiq* is a collection of al-Farabi's writings on logic.)

* —— (*c.*870–950) *Falsafah Aristutalis* (Philosophy of Aristotle), trans. M. Mahdi in *Alfarabi's Philosophy of Plato and Aristotle*, Ithaca, NY: Cornell University Press, 1969. (The *Falsafah Aristutalis* contains al-Farabi's account of the Organon.)

* —— (*c.*870–950) *Sharh al-'ibarah* (Great Commentary on *De interpretatione*), trans. F.W. Zimmerman, *Al-Farabi's Commentary and Short Treatise on Aristotle's 'De Interpretatione'*, Oxford: Oxford

University Press, 1981. (Very learned introduction which sets al-Farabi's text against the background of the Greek and Arabic traditions in logic.)

—— (c.870–950) Commentary on the *Isagōgē*, ed. and trans. D.M. Dunlop, 'Al-Farabi's *Eisagoge*', *Islamic Quarterly* 3, 1956: 117–38. (Excellent translation of this crucial logical text, given the significance of the *Isagōgē* for this period of logic.)

—— (c.870–950) *Risalah* on Logic, ed. and trans. D.M. Dunlop, 'Al-Farabi's Introductory *Risalah* on Logic', *Islamic Quarterly* 3, 1957: 224–35. (A brief but influential summary of his views on logic.)

—— (c.870–950) Introductory Sections on Logic, ed. and trans. D.M. Dunlop, 'Al-Farabi's Introductory Sections on Logic', *Islamic Quarterly* 2, 1955: 264–82. (Another translation of a section on logic, designed by al-Farabi as a propaedeutic to the study of philosophy itself.)

—— (c.870–950) Paraphrase on the *Categories*, ed. and trans. D.M. Dunlop, 'Al-Farabi's Paraphrase of the *Categories* of Aristotle', *Islamic Quarterly* 4, 1958–9: 168–97; 5, 1958–9: 21–54. (A short summary of what al-Farabi took the main points of the *Categories* to be.)

—— (c.870–950) Commentary on the *Prior Analytics*, trans. N. Rescher, *Al-Farabi's Short Commentary on Aristotle's 'Prior Analytics'*, Pittsburgh, PA: Pittsburgh University Press, 1963. (Another of al-Farabi's Aristotelian commentaries.)

Galston, M. (1981) 'Al-Farabi on Aristotle's Theory of Demonstration', in P. Morewedge (ed.) *Islamic Philosophy and Mysticism*, Delmar, NY: Caravan Books, 23–34. (Clear account of how al-Farabi developed Aristotle's notion of demonstrative reasoning, the best form of argumentation.)

Gyekye, D. (1971) 'The Terms *Prima intentio* and *Secunda intentio* in Arabic Logic', *Speculum* 46: 32–48. (Explanation of two key logical terms, linking them to their Greek and Latin equivalents and explaining how they are used in al-Farabi's logic.)

* Ibn 'Adi, Yahya (893–974) *Maqalah fi tabyin al-fasl bayna sina'atay al-mantiq al-falsafi wa-al-nahw al-'arab* (Treatise on the Difference between the Arts of Philosophical Logic and of Arabic Grammar), ed. G. Endress, *Journal of the History of Arabic Science* 2, 1978: 192–81. (Influential work from the early years when the divisions between logic and language were still highly controversial.)

Ibn Rushd (c.1170) Short Commentaries on Aristotle, ed. and trans. C.E. Butterworth, *Averroes' Three Short Commentaries on Aristotle's 'Topics', 'Rhetoric', and 'Poetics'*, Albany, NY: State University of New York Press, 1977. (Ibn Rushd's short commentaries on areas of thought which he thought were

less strongly logical than demonstrative and dialectical reasoning, yet which still embody logical techniques in some form.)

—— (c.1174) Middle Commentary on the *Isagōgē*, trans. H.A. Davidson, *Averroes' Middle Commentary on Porphyry's 'Isagoge' and on Aristotle's 'Categoriae'*, Cambridge, MA: Mediaeval Academy of America, 1969. (A middle commentary on a crucial logical text by Porphyry, which was important in linking Ibn Rushd's use of logical language with that of his Islamic predecessors.)

* —— (c.1174) Middle Commentaries on *Categories* and *De interpretatione*, trans. C.E. Butterworth, *Averroes' Middle Commentary on Aristotle's 'Categories' and 'De interpretatione'*, Princeton, NJ: Princeton University Press, 1983. (Ibn Rushd's middle commentaries on two Aristotelian texts which are important for what they show of how he developed some of the key terms of his philosophical logic.)

* Ibn Sina (980–1037) *al-Isharat wa-'l-tanbihat* (Remarks and Admonitions), Part One trans. S.C. Inati, *Remarks and Admonitions, Part One: Logic*, Toronto: Pontifical Institute of Mediaeval Studies, 1984. (The logic portion of *al-Isharat wa'l-tanbihat*.)

* —— (c.1014–20) *al-Shifa'* (Healing), *al-Ilahiyyat* (Theology), vol. 1 (Books 1–5) ed. G. Anawati and S. Zayed; vol. 2 (Books 6–10) ed. S. Dunya, M.Y. Moussa, and S. Zayed, Cairo: Organisation Générale des Imprimerie Gouvernementales, 1960. (The part of *al-Shifa'* which deals with theological issues.)

* —— (c.1014–20) *al-Shifa'* (Healing), *al-Madkhal (Isagōgē)*, ed. G. Anawati, M. El-Khodeiri and F. al-Ahwani, rev. I. Madkour, Cairo: Al-Matba'ah al-Amiriyyah, 1952. (Ibn Sina's account of Porphyry's *Isagōgē*, giving him the opportunity to specify the meaning he gives to logical language.)

Inati, S. (1996) 'Logic', in S.H. Nasr and O. Leaman, *History of Islamic Philosophy*, London: Routledge, ch. 48, 802–23. (Analysis of the main concepts in Islamic logic, and the role of logic itself in philosophy.)

Lameer, J. (1994) *Al-Farabi and Aristotelian Syllogistics: Greek Theory and Islamic Practice*, Leiden: Brill. (A thorough study of al-Farabi's logical writings and their ancient sources.)

Madkour, I. (1969) *L'organon d'Aristote dans le monde arabe* (The Organon of Aristotle in the Arab World), 2nd edn, Paris: Vrin. (A useful overview of the logic portions of Ibn Sina's Shifa'.)

Mahdi, M. (1970) 'Language and Logic in Classical Islam', in G.E. von Grunebaum (ed.) *Logic in Classical Islamic Culture*, Wiesbaden: Harrasowitz,

51–83. (An account of the debate between al-Sirafi and Abu Bishr Matta.)

Margoliouth, D.S. (1905) 'The Discussion Between Abu Bishr Matta and Abu Sa'id al-Sirafi on the Merits of Logic and Grammar', *Journal of the Royal Asiatic Society*: 79–129. (A translation of the famous debate; for a fuller account see also Mahdi 1970.)

Marmura, M.E. (1963) *Studies in the History of Arabic Logic*, Pittsburgh, PA: University of Pittsburgh Press. (An uneven collection of studies and translations but with some useful items.)

—— (1975) 'Ghazali's Attitude to the Secular Sciences and Logic', in G.F. Hourani (ed.) *Essays on Islamic Philosophy*, Albany, NY: State University of New York Press.

Rescher, N. (1964) *The Development of Arabic Logic*, Pittsburgh, PA: University of Pittsburgh Press. (Demonstration that in spite of his opposition to philosophy, al-Ghazali was an enthusiastic supporter of logic. Somewhat dated but still useful.)

—— (1980) 'Avicenna on the Division of the Sciences in the *Isagoge* of his *Shifa*', *Journal for the History of Arabic Science* 4: 239–50. (Very clear analysis of the text.)

Sabra, A.I. (1980) 'Avicenna on the Subject Matter of Logic', *Journal of Philosophy* 77: 757–64. (Excellent analysis of Ibn Sina's approach to logic.)

Wolfson, H.A. (1973) 'The Terms *Tasawwur* and *Tasdiq* in Arabic Philosophy and Their Greek, Latin and Hebrew Equivalents', in I. Twersky and G.H. Williams (eds) *Studies in the History and Philosophy of Religion*, Cambridge, MA: Harvard University Press, vol. 1, 478–92. (Important analysis of this critical distinction in Islamic logic, with discussions of its origins in wider philosophy.)

Zimmermann, F.W. (1972) 'Some Observations on al-Farabi and the Logical Tradition', in S.M. Stern *et al.* (eds) *Islamic Philosophy and the Classical Tradition*, Oxford: Oxford University Press, 517–46. (Discussion of the role which al-Farabi played in establishing the notion of logic as a separate theoretical inquiry.)

DEBORAH L. BLACK

LOGIC IN JAPAN

'Logic' became an explicit topic in Japanese philosophy only in the twentieth century. Most effort has been directed to developing a dialectical logic in a Hegelian mode rather than a symbolic system. The Japanese term coined for logic in this sense is ronri *(the 'principles of discourse or argument'). The term* ronrigaku *(*ronri *+ *-ology*) is the more common term for formal, symbolic logic. In the twentieth century two Japanese philosophers, Nishida Kitarō (1870–1945) and Tanabe Hajime (1885–1962), developed distinctive dialectical logics that drew on key assumptions from traditional Japanese thought, but followed a Western style of analysis and articulation.*

Nishida's logic of basho *(place,* topos, *field) located the contextual premises of empirical and idealist judgments within a trans-judgmental domain called the 'acting-intuiting'. He related this to his logic of the predicate, which rejected the Aristotelian priority of the grammatical subject as signifier of substance, instead making the subject the qualifier of the predicate, the signifier of the event. Tanabe criticized Nishida's system as ahistorical and transcultural. His logic of species gave priority to the specificity of cultural and historical embededness, the middle ground between the universal ought and individual freedom.*

1   **Dialectical logic**
2   **Nishida's logic of *basho* and logic of the predicate**
3   **Tanabe's logic of species**

1   Dialectical logic

To appreciate the development of logic in modern Japan, it is useful to bear in mind three tendencies from traditional Japanese philosophy. First, Japanese thought has tended to emphasize internal rather than external relations. That is, in a relationship the two relatents, *a* and *b*, are generally understood to be not separate entities that have been connected by a relating principle, but to be two overlapping entities: part of *a* is *b* and part of *b* is *a*. Traditional Buddhist philosophy assumes no entity ever exists independently as a discrete substance; it is always in flux and depends for its existence on some other entity (see BUDDHIST PHILOSOPHY, JAPANESE).

The second point in traditional Japanese thought is the application of internal relations to the part/whole model (see MEREOLOGY). In esoteric, Tendai and Kegon Buddhism, the whole has typically not been understood as simply the sum of the parts. Because the whole and parts are internally related, the part (as in a recursive set) always reflects in some way the whole.

The third point about traditional Japanese thought is that even opposites are often understood as being internally related. If, therefore, *a* and not-*a* overlap in some way, that suggests that *a* can only be fully *a* insofar as it contains something of not-*a*. At the least, in defining an entity, it is typically distinguished from and therefore related to its opposite. In East Asian texts, such as the translation of the Indian Buddhist *Perfection of Wisdom* texts, the Sino-Japanese term *soku* is commonly used to express this identity within difference: *a soku* not-*a*. The term *soku* can be used as a special kind of copula or can be used as a phrase meaning something like 'that is to say'. English translations (not completely successfully) tend to capture this sense by using the Latinate phrases '*a qua* not-*a*' or '*a sive* not-*a*' (see KYOTO SCHOOL §3).

When Western philosophy entered Japan in the latter half of the nineteenth century, Japanese philosophers became aware that the dominant Western modes of logical expression could not adequately express the premodern tendencies just explained. Among Western systems, Hegel's dialectical logic (see HEGEL, G.W.F.) seemed to most resemble the *soku* way of relating opposites and many Japanese philosophers studied it intensely in the early twentieth century. In the end, however, most Japanese philosophers found it unacceptable. In fact, it seemed almost the mirror image of the kind of dialectical logic sought by the Japanese. First, Hegelian logic is grounded in being, whereas traditional Asian (especially Buddhist and Daoist) philosophy gave more primacy to nonbeing or nothingness. Second, the Hegelian system of dialectic expresses how static beings are transformed into events of becoming. In Japanese thought, however, events are the starting point and logical analysis is used to abstract from it discrete beings within the becoming. Third, the Hegelian dialectic is progressive. It shows the development of thought through time into what it is becoming. In Japanese thought, however, the dialectical process is more commonly used regressively to understand how thought comes about and out of what it is formed. Therefore, although modern Japanese philosophers have continued to use the term 'dialectic' (*benshōhō*), except for Marxists and certain other neo-Hegelians, the term usually refers to a distinctively Japanese logic of dialectic.

Two of the best known dialectical Japanese logics were developed by NISHIDA KITARŌ (1870–1945) and TANABE HAJIME (1885–1962). Both figures were trained in mathematics (in fact, in his younger days, Tanabe was Japan's most renowned philosopher of mathematics and science), well versed in Hegelianism and steeped in Buddhism (Nishida was a Zen Buddhist, Tanabe a Pure Land Buddhist). Both belonged to what is often called the Kyoto School of Japanese philosophy.

2 Nishida's logic of *basho* and logic of the predicate

Nishida attacked Western paradigms of logic from two directions, epistemological and metaphysical/syntactical. When taking the former approach he generally spoke of his logic as the 'logic of *basho*'. *Basho* is an ordinary Japanese word meaning 'place' that can serve as an equivalent for the technical terms *topos* or 'field'. Nishida understood the philosophical construction of reality to take place within three experiential domains or *basho*: empiricism, idealism and what he called the 'acting-intuiting'. The empiricist speaks from out of the '*basho* of being'; that is, the empiricist judges the world of physical entities (see EMPIRICISM). The idealist, on the other hand, judges the world of psychological entities, showing their role in the construction of our experience of physical entities (see IDEALISM). This is the realm of consciousness, experience, self and the transcendent ego. Sometimes the Kyoto School refers to this as the '*basho* of relative nothingness', because from the standpoint of the empiricist this psychological world is considered so transparent as to be omitted from the discussion of what is. Relative to empirical reality, it is a place of nothingness.

The third *basho* is supposedly less commonly articulated in the West, although Nishida found suggestive references to it in William JAMES, BERGSON, some neo-Kantians and some religiously or aesthetically oriented philosophers. The third *basho* is where knowing and doing are virtually a single act. It occurs when a person responds spontaneously without deliberation to the information being intuited, or when their intake of information is the same act as going out and gathering information. Nishida calls that immediacy the single event of 'acting-intuiting'. This realm is unknown to the categories of both the empiricist's material world and the idealist's inner world. In fact, in its immediacy and oneness, it cannot be analysed in any systematic way at all. Therefore, it can be called the '*basho* of absolute nothingness' (see BUDDHIST CONCEPT OF EMPTINESS).

In themselves, these three realms may constitute the contents of kinds of knowing, but Nishida argues there is a formal connection among them: there is a hierarchical 'logic of *basho*'. His analysis of the hierarchy is based in his evaluation of how the *basho* are implicated in each other through the logical analysis of the conditions of judgment. Consider an empirical judgment such as 'The cat is black'. Nishida asks in what place, in what *basho*, one is standing when making that judgment. He argues that for such an empirical judgment to be made, one must have an experience of perceiving that black cat. In other words, one assumes there is a perceiver and a perception that makes the judgment possible. Once we recognize this fact, we realize that judgments within the *basho* of being are logically dependent on experience within the *basho* of relative being, the idealist's world of consciousness and perception. In turn, I may ask about the judgment of 'I see that the cat is black'. That judgment of the *basho* of relative nothingness is itself only possible as a reflection and abstraction out of an experience of the acting-intuiting. So, the *basho* of relative nothingness has as its logical precondition experience within the *basho* of absolute nothingness. The acting-intuiting, being immediate and unitary, is not itself capable of making judgments; yet at the same time, it is the totality out of which reflection can generate the judgments of either idealism or empiricism. For Nishida, it is the universal that becomes concrete through the mediation of the other two *basho*. In this way Nishida's dialectic takes us from the simplest of truths, the empirical judgment, to show regressively its logical basis in the immediacy of absolute nothingness.

Nishida also attacked the Western bias of the ontology of being over nonbeing, of substance over event and of the grammatical subject over the grammatical predicate (see BEING; SUBSTANCE; EVENTS; SYNTAX). Instead of the Aristotelian model in which the sentential subject is correlated with the metaphysical substance and the predicate with the attribute, Nishida proposed a 'logic of the predicate'. In his logic, the primary unit of reality is the event, and only through abstraction do we separate out of that event the sentential subject or the ontological substance. The predicate is a universal whose function becomes concrete and specified through the sentential subject. In doing so, Nishida has in effect made the substance into an attribute of the event. By changing the metaphysical priority from substance to event and the logical or syntactic priority from subject to predicate, Nishida's Buddhism-inspired logic is grounded in change or process rather than stasis or essence. When merged with the threefold model of the logic of *basho*, Nishida attempted to develop a comprehensive philosophical system including a metaphysics, a phenomenology, an epistemology and an analysis of judgment. His system was at once intelligible to Western analysis, yet simultaneously continuous with the premodern Japanese intellectual tradition.

3 Tanabe's logic of species

Tanabe criticized Nishida's logic of *basho*, proposing two qualifications or fundamental modifications. First, he questioned the implicit assumption that a totally unmediated experience (the acting-intuiting) is possible. Second, he believed Nishida's system was too simplistic in postulating a direct relation between the individual and the universal without the media-

tion of culture or society. He believed that without taking account of ethnicity and nationality, we cannot truly understand the dialectical development of thought and value through history. The arena of human activity is the social realm, not the unmediated realm of the acting-intuiting, nor the abstracted realm of intellectual philosophical positions like idealism and empiricism.

Tanabe referred to the level of the transcendent universal (that is, not conceptually particularized) totality as the level of 'genus' Below it is the level of 'species', and below that the level of the 'individual'. In social terms, the logic of genus applies to humankind as a whole, the source of absolute values for ethics and the spiritual basis for the state. The logic of the individual, on the other hand, applies to epistemological judgment and the basis of personal creativity. Between the two lies the logic of species that applies to particularized ethnic, cultural and national values. Without that mediated middle realm, the actual lived experience of human action cannot be explained.

Tanabe began to develop his logic of species during the 1930s, but as he observed developments in Japan during the militarist period, he began to build into the system a more explicit mechanism of self-criticism. He did not feel free to publish his revisions until after the Second World War, however, at which point he emphasized the self-critical moment in his system by developing the philosophical concept of *range*. He himself translated this term as 'metanoia', a philosophical and personal sense of repentance and conversion that leads one to question the absoluteness of any philosophical system one has devised. Essentially, the dynamic of the logic of species is to be the dialectical mediation between the totalitarianism of the genus and the liberalism of individual. From the genus, the species derives the sense of absolute transcendent values applicable to all mankind; from the individual, the species derives the pragmatic concerns of working toward the particular benefit of one's fellow individuals. The nation, indeed the collective or personal activity of any human endeavour, can therefore never speak with the authority of the absolute; on the other hand, no such endeavour can ever be truly individual either, because all expression is enmeshed in the social. Once again, the realm of human activity is not that of fixed being, but that of Buddhist mediation, interdependence and a dialectical tension that deconstructs any system as soon as it makes it claim to be either absolute or individualistic.

References and further reading

Carter, R.E. (1989) *The Nothingness Beyond God: An Introduction to the Philosophy of Nishida Kitarō*, New York: Paragon House. (An introductory text emphasizing religious and ethical issues; Chapter 2 is a discussion of the logic of *basho*.)

Dilworth, D. (trans.) (1970) *Fundamental Problems of Philosophy*, Tokyo: Sophia University Press. (Translation of six of Nishida Kitarō's essays related to his logic of *basho*.)

—— (1987) *Last Writings: Nothingness and the Religious Worldview*, Honolulu, HI: University of Hawaii Press. (Translation of Nishida Kitarō's last essays with Dilworth's analysis of Nishida's logic in a comparative context.)

Dilworth, D. and Satō Taira (trans.) (1969) 'The Logic of the Species as Dialectics', *Monumenta Nipponica* 24 (3): 273–88. (Translation of Chapter 1 of Tanabe Hajime's *Shu no ronri no benshōhō* (Dialectic of the Logic of Species).)

Nishida Kitarō (1911–45) *Nishida Kitarō zenshū* (Collected works of Nishida Kitarō), ed. Watsuji Tetsurō *et al.*, Tokyo: Iwanami Shoten, 1978, 19 vols. (Standard edition of original works.)

Piovesan, G.K. (1968) *Contemporary Japanese Philosophical Thought*, New York: St. John's University Press. (Good survey of modern Japanese philosophy including a chapter on Nishida Kitarō and a section on Tanabe Hajime's logic of species.)

Tanabe Hajime (1910–61) *Tanabe Hajime zenshū* (Collected Works of Tanabe Hajime), ed. Nishitani Keiji *et al.*, Tokyo: Chikuma Shobō, 1963, 15 vols. (Standard edition of original works with vols 6 and 7 being the locus of many of Tanabe's central essays on the logic of species.)

—— (1946) *Zangedō to shite no tetsugaku*, trans. Takeuchi Yoshinori, *Philosophy as Metanoetics*, Berkeley, CA: University of California Press, 1986. (Translation of one of Tanabe Hajime's major work dealing with metanoia.)

Unno Taitetsu and Heisig, J.W. (eds) (1990) *The Religious Philosophy of Tanabe Hajime*, Berkeley, CA: Asian Humanities Press. (Good collection of essays on Tanabe's philosophy, several of which refer to the logic of species and its differences from Nishida's logic of *basho*.)

Wargo, R.J.J. (1972) *The Logic of Basho and the Concept of Nothingness in the Philosophy of Nishida Kitarō*, Ann Arbor, MI: University Microfilms. (A dissertation, this work has never been surpassed as the best Western treatment of Nishida's logic. It includes a translation of the 'General Summary' from Nishida's *Ippansha no jikakuteki taikei* (System of Self-consciousness of the Universal).)

THOMAS P. KASULIS

LOGIC IN THE 17th AND 18th CENTURIES

Logic in the seventeenth century was characterized by attempts to reconcile older viewpoints, such as those of Ramus and Melanchthon, and by criticism of the nature and scope of traditional logic. F. Bacon indicated induction, rather than deduction, as the object of logic, thus opening the way for a logic of the empirical sciences. Descartes proposed to replace the complicated precepts of old logic by simple rules of method. However, even the authors of the Port-Royal Logic, who were influenced by Descartes, could not follow him all the way and continued to teach traditional doctrines, albeit with a new attention to the doctrine of ideas. Other logicians, following Locke, tried to modernize logic by concentrating on an analysis of human cognitive faculties, of the idea–word relation and of other than certain knowledge, thus broadening the scope of logic so as to account for probability. Another suggestion for the improvement of logic came from those who thought that logic should assume mathematics as an example either for its axiomatic-deductive method or for the inventive techniques of algebra. The last of these suggestions prompted research in the area of logical calculi. But this kind of research benefited from the doctrines devised by non-mathematically oriented authors who thus provided the logical framework in which algebraic techniques would be tried. This general background accounts not only for the exceptional logic of Leibniz, but also for some logical calculi worked out in the eighteenth century.

1 **Seventeenth-century eclecticism**
2 **Criticism of the syllogism**
3 **Logic after Descartes**
4 **The emergence of a logic of cognitive faculties**
5 **Logic and mathematics**
6 **Leibniz and the emergence of logical calculi**
7 **Logical calculi in the eighteenth century**

1 Seventeenth-century eclecticism

Seventeenth-century logic was conditioned by the debate of the previous two centuries for and against Aristotelianism and scholasticism, both of which had a quasi-autonomous life until well into the eighteenth century, so that differences of opinion persisted.

However, followers of Aristotle's defender Philipp MELANCHTHON and of the anti-Aristotelian Petrus RAMUS merged to form a Philippo-Ramist or Semi-Ramist school (see LOGIC, RENAISSANCE §5). They restored the parts of Aristotelian logic left out by Ramus (conversion, the square of opposition, categories, demonstration, fallacies), but also attended to Ramist doctrines (for example, definition and division). The Philippo-Ramist B. KECKERMANN published a *Systema Logicum* (1600) in which he assigned to logic the aim of being systematic, that is, of being a first science directing the human mind; hence the additional name of Systematics given to his followers, such as J.H. Alsted, author of *Clavis Artis Lullianae* (A Key to Lull's Art) (1609) and *Logicae Systema Harmonicum* (1614), and R. Sanderson, who wrote a *Logicae Artis Compendium* (1618).

Eclecticism also characterized followers of the sixteenth-century logician J. ZABARELLA, according to whom Aristotle had provided an analytic method of discovery ('regressus') for mathematical demonstrations. Many seventeenth-century Zabarellists endorsed Ramist and scholastic doctrines, including F. Burgersdijck, whose *Institutionum logicarum libri duo* (Two Books of Logical Institutions, 1626) became the standard handbook in the Netherlands.

Another eclectic, J. JUNGIUS, was one of the outstanding logicians of the century. He was acquainted with Philippo-Ramist dialectic and with the then recent scholasticism of Fonseca and Suarez. He also had Systematic and Zabarellist teachers and admired the *logistica* of Viète. In his *Logica Hamburgensis* (1635) he dealt with a logic of relations, non-syllogistic inferences, contraposition and special syllogisms.

2 Criticism of the syllogism

However, some of the major philosophers of the seventeenth century persisted in criticizing traditional logic, in particular the syllogism. In his *Instauratio magna* (1620) Francis BACON, while acknowledging the cogency of the syllogism, observed that it cannot guarantee that the ideas occurring in it are abstracted from reality and defined correctly. Since induction presides over the abstraction and definition of ideas, he indicated induction, rather than deduction, as the object of logical research, thus opening the way for a logic of the empirical sciences.

DESCARTES repeated the sceptical argument that the syllogism, apart from being sterile, begs the question and has no more claim to certainty than non-inferential truths. As is clear from his *Regulae*

(1628), for him the problem of inference was not how to infer (since we do this naturally), but how to infer with certainty. Descartes' solution to this problem rests on an analysis of our scientific knowledge which singles out two cognitive operations: intuition and deduction. Intuition is the basic operation because it makes us certain of simple propositions, whereas deduction is just a chain of successive intuitions. Having found this solution, Descartes saw little use for a complicated logic: indeed, he considered it detrimental to the natural light of reason. As a substitute he listed, in the *Discours de la méthode* (1637), some rules of method meant as mere guidelines for the cognitive operations whose certainty he claimed to have explained.

3 Logic after Descartes

So limited a scope for logic was by no means universally accepted. For example, H. Fabri [Mosnerius] in the first tome of his *Philosophia* (1646) joined late medieval doctrines to mathematics and devised a combinatory calculus of 576 syllogistic moods in all figures. He also introduced truth tables based on three truth-values: truth, falsity and partial falsity. Later in the century independent research was pursued at a higher level in the *Logica demonstrativa* (1697) of G. Saccheri. He emphasized the demonstrative role of the so-called 'consequentia mirabilis' showing that 'If not p then p' entails 'p'.

But even scholars who accepted Descartes' rules of method as the core of logic had to account for traditional doctrines. This is clear from the *Logica vetus et nova* (Old and New Logic) (1654) of Clauberg; and even more from the *Logica restituta* (1662) of the independent Cartesian A. Geulincx, who revived medieval doctrines, related disjunction, conjunction and negation by means of their truth-conditions and devised a 'logical cube' whose faces represented logical axioms and forms of argumentation.

Old and new doctrines were also adopted in *La Logique ou l'art de penser* (1662), known as 'The Port-Royal Logic', by A. Arnauld and P. Nicole. The authors referred to Descartes' views (the 1664 edition mentions the manuscript of Descartes' *Regulae* (1628), and showed appreciation of Pascal's theory of definition, probability and method (they included a special section on method, imitated by many subsequent logics), and of Augustine's theory of language, from which their attentiveness to the idea–word relation was derived. As for traditional instruction, their syllogistic was more accurate than might be expected of a Cartesian logic. For they devised a combinatory calculus of possible moods with rules to choose the valid ones, and correctly warned against confusing the fourth figure and the first figure with transposed premises. None the less, the Port-Royal logicians agreed with Descartes that deduction has a derivative importance as compared with judgment. And given that they defined judgment as a comparison of ideas, they paid great attention to the ideas themselves. The Port-Royal doctrine of ideas revolves around the notions of comprehension (later, 'intension') and extension. The comprehension of an idea consists of the attributes it comprises in itself that cannot be removed from it without destroying it; the extension of an idea consists of the subjects with which the idea agrees. Comprehension and extension stand in inverse relation: the greater the comprehension of an idea, the smaller its extension, and vice versa. This relation regulated all other relations between ideas and operations (for example, abstraction and composition) performable on them.

The influence of Port-Royal doctrines upon French logic was evident right up to the end of the eighteenth century, for example from the *Logique* (1780) and the *Langue des calculs* (Language of Calculi, 1798) of É.B. DE CONDILLAC. In England the Port-Royal *Logic* was acknowledged even by scholars of a declared Aristotelian disposition, such as J. Wallis, who, in his *Institutio logicae* (1687), rejected Ramist syllogisms with singular terms and classified syllogistic figures competently. H. Aldrich, too, though mostly concerned with his valuable presentation of syllogistic, mentioned Port-Royal doctrines when discussing methodology and the history of logic in his *Artis Logicae Compendium* (1691).

4 The emergence of a logic of cognitive faculties

Towards the end of the seventeenth century, logic began to centre increasingly on an analysis of cognitive faculties. Such an analysis, introduced by Descartes, was carried further in the *Essay concerning Human Understanding* (1690) of John LOCKE and was the stepping-stone to what has been called 'facultative logic'. In this kind of logic the content of ideas is as important as their form, and equally important are the signs designating ideas. This not only explains why Locke equated logic with semiotics, but also gives an insight into the origins of the importance of language for later philosophy and logic.

The logic of cognitive faculties was promoted by the success of Locke's philosophy which, especially in Germany (for example, in the 1752 *Vernunftlehre* (Doctrine of Reason) of G.F. Meier), was often preferred to Descartes' because of its avoidance of innate ideas and its applicability to other than certain knowledge (which later brought the study of probability within its scope). The influence of Locke's philosophy is evident in England in both the *Logick* (1725) and the *Improvement of the Mind* (1741) of I. Watts, who proposed a mixture of Locke with Port-Royal, as well as in the *Elements of Logick* (1748) of W. Duncan and the *Logicae compendium* (1759) of F. Hutcheson. Locke also influenced the *Système de réflexions* (1712) of the Swiss J.P. de Crousaz.

5 Logic and mathematics

At almost the same time as the birth of the logic of cognitive faculties, another image of the discipline began to emerge. It was born of the conviction that logic compared unfavourably with mathematics.

Some ascribed the superiority of mathematics to its axiomatic-deductive method. Indeed, Descartes' rules of method were interpreted as recommendations to start with a few simple and acknowledged notions (axioms) and thence to proceed to unknown ones (theorems). The supporters of such an interpretation maintained that the axiomatic-deductive method should replace logic and be the model for the right conduct of understanding. A prime example of this view is the *Medicina mentis* (1687) of VON TSCHIRN-HAUS, who indicated the mathematical method as a therapy in all fields of knowledge and practical life.

Some attributed the superiority of mathematics to the problem-solving and inventive techniques of algebra. The search for equations relating unknown elements with given elements, exemplified in Descartes' *Géométrie* (1637), was considered the true Cartesian logic and was absorbed into the tradition which viewed mathematics as a universal science of invention (*mathesis universalis*).

This assessment of the merits of algebra outlived the imitation of the mathematical method: the latter was either reduced to a mere synthetic order of exposition, or restricted to mathematics because its wider use was held responsible for the degeneration of Cartesianism into Spinozism. Algebraic tools, on the other hand, were fitted for use in the construction of logical calculi. Despite this, the calculi which were actually or tentatively constructed at the time are not comparable to the later algebra of logic, mainly because they were still bound to the quantitative interpretation of algebra.

6 Leibniz and the emergence of logical calculi

Leibniz's logical calculus is connected with his project of an '*ars characteristica combinatoria*', whose accomplishment required (1) an alphabet of thoughts and appropriate symbols for it, (2) a rational grammar common to all languages, (3) an encyclopedia of the sciences and (4) a universal science by which the contents of all sciences would be ordered systematically and combined so as to discover new truths. This last requirement, in its turn, demanded a logical calculus.

LEIBNIZ could not achieve his entire project, but none the less he wrote several incomplete versions of a logical calculus in papers dating from 1679 to the early 1690s (see Leibniz 1966). Common to all versions – which were related to Leibniz's many logical interests (syllogistic, logic of relations, modality and so on), as well as to his monadology – is the idea that a *'calculus ratiocinator'* is a mechanical procedure for drawing conclusions. It is based on: a universal mathematics similar to algebra; symbols standing for concepts or for propositions; and substitution rules governed by the principle that what is concluded with certain variable letters can be concluded equally with other letters satisfying the same conditions.

For all its exceptionality and complexity Leibniz's calculus represents a development of logic that can also be found in others' work which came soon after. This did not depend on Leibniz's direct influence because his calculus remained unpublished until the nineteenth century. The likely explanation is the existence of certain favourable conditions: the reputation of algebra as a universal means of discovery (see §5); and the existence of doctrines of ideas such as that of Port-Royal and the emerging logic of cognitive faculties (see §§3, 4 above). In this respect Cartesian logic and the logic of cognitive faculties were only apparently disconnected from logical calculi: the former provided the latter with a logical field of application. Indeed Locke, who belittled syllogistic, hoped for an algebra of logic. Admittedly, he did not construct a logical calculus and nor did HOBBES, despite his statement in *De Corpore* (1655) that ratiocination is computation. But an early attempt made by Jakob Bernoulli to establish a *Parallelismus ratiocinii logici et algebraici* (1685), while ending in admitted failure, was demonstrably based on a comparison of algebra with the Port-Royal doctrine of ideas.

7 Logical calculi in the eighteenth century

Between the 1740s and the 1760s progress both in the study of ideas and in algebra prompted a number of logical calculi by German-speaking authors.

The theory of ideas had been much developed in Germany due to the influence of A. Rüdiger. In his *De sensu veri et falsi* (1709) he maintained that all syllogism can be a means of discovery provided that, given a premise, we connect one of its terms with a new concept that stands in one of a set of well-defined idea-relations with the other term. For example, by connecting the predicate-term of a universal affirmative premise with any concept subordinated to the subject-term, we establish enthymematically the conclusion of a 'synthetic syllogism'. In general, Rüdiger's point was that if the syllogism can be used to discover truths, then logic does not have to be given a mathematical formulation in order for it to be inventive.

Taking the contrary viewpoint, Christian WOLFF supported a mathematical view of logic maintaining that all mathematical demonstrations consist of chains of syllogisms in the first figure. Therefore in his *Vernünfftige Gedanken von den Kräfften des menschlichen Verstandes* (Rational Thoughts on the Powers of the Human Understanding) (1713) and his *Philosophia rationalis* (1728) he considered it futile to advocate the mathematical method as a substitute for logic or to charge traditional logic with being sterile and nugatory.

In the 1730s a number of authors, strengthened by the confidence in the value of logic characterizing the then dominant Wolffism, resumed logical work even along lines unforeseen by Wolff. In particular, J.P. Reusch in his *Systema logicum* (1734) gave a description of judgments and inferences as based on a set of idea-relations (reminiscent of Rüdiger) and on a principle of substitutivity for ideas.

But Reusch did not take the further step of building a calculus of idea-relations. This step was taken by J.A. Segner in his *Specimen logicae universaliter demonstratae* (An Example of a Universally Demonstrated Logic, 1740). By using the notion of containment in intension and by an accurate employment of negative terms, he classified, assigned symbols to, and subjected to a set of rules the five idea-relations later known as the Gergonne relations. This produced a rare and beautiful example of a calculus applicable to syllogistic and to some non-syllogistic inferences.

An extensional perspective was chosen by G. Ploucquet in his *Fundamenta philosophiae speculativae* (1759). In his syllogistic calculus all concepts, including predicates, are quantified and there is a single general rule stating that concepts must retain in the conclusion of an argument the quantity they have in the premises.

Many topics were treated by J.H. Lambert in his *Neues Organon* (1764), ranging from probabilistic inference to symbolic knowledge to a theory of truth and error. In it he also represented the A, E, I, O propositions and syllogisms extensionally by means of straight lines. Such diagrams were independent of but served the same purpose as the circles used by Euler in his *Lettres à une Princesse d'Allemagne sur divers sujets de physique et de philosophie* (Letters to a German Princess on Various Subjects of Physics and Philosophy, 1760–2). Circles, lines and other figures had also been used by J.C. Sturm (*Universalia Euclidea*, 1661), J.C. Lange (*Nucleus logicae Weisianae*, 1712), Ploucquet and the then unpublished Leibniz. But Lambert's most interesting contribution to logic is a calculus he worked out in letters and in some of his *Logische und philosophische Abhandlungen* (Logical and Philosophical Essays, 1782–7) which were published after his death. He based it on concepts, their mutual interrelationships, and on the similarities between logical and algebraic operations. This calculus – which allowed for a tentative logic of relations and was capable of expressing composite propositions – was intensional. This feature was criticized by the Ploucquetian G.J. Holland in a letter (1765) to Lambert in which he sketched his own, extensional calculus. (For a comparison of Lambert's and Ploucquet's calculi see Bök (1766).)

Interest in logical calculi faded in the later part of the eighteenth century due, in all likelihood, to the influence of Kant's ideas on logic. In his *Nova dilucidatio* (New Exposition, 1755) KANT had maintained that Leibniz's *combinatoria* was far from being a genuine '*ars inveniendi*' but apparently did not deny that an *ars inveniendi* based on an algebraic calculus of concepts could be achieved. However, in his *Critique of Pure Reason* (1781) and in his *Logik* (1800), he developed a conception according to which an application of algebra to non-mathematical concepts would have no inventive power. Algebra is synthetic a priori, hence inventive and absolutely certain only on condition that its symbols stand for mathematical concepts. The latter are the only concepts whose objects can be exhibited a priori in intuition, which gives algebraic proofs heuristic advantages and freedom from error. Kant's separation of logic from mathematics was counterbalanced by his rejection of the conception of a logic of the cognitive faculties that he had originally favoured. His mature view was that pure logic, as opposed to transcendental logic, is a formal science – a view not lightly to be dismissed.

See also: LOGIC MACHINES AND DIAGRAMS; LOGICAL AND MATHEMATICAL TERMS, GLOSSARY OF; PORT-ROYAL; UNIVERSAL LANGUAGE

References and further reading

This bibliography gives details only of editions of primary sources referred to in the text which are not listed in Risse's *Bibliographia Logica* (1965).

Arndt, H.W. (1971) *Methodo scientifica pertractatum: Mos geometricus und Kalkülbegriff in der philosophischen Theorienbildung des 17. und 18. Jahrhunderts* (Treated with the Scientific Method: The Geometric Way and the Concept of Calculus in the Construction of Philosophical Theories in the 17th and 18th Centuries), Berlin and New York: De Gruyter. (A good guide to appreciate the importance of mathematics for philosophy and logic in the seventeenth and eighteenth centuries.)

Ashworth, E.J. (1967) 'Joachim Jungius (1587–1657) and the Logic of Relations', *Archiv für Geschichte der Philosophie*, 49: 72–85. (A brief outline of Jungius' views on relations.)

—— (1974) *Language and Logic in the Post-Medieval Period*, Dordrecht and Boston, MA: Reidel. (A classic guide to logic 1500–1650.)

Auroux, S. (1993) *La logique des idées*, Montreal, Que., and Paris: Bellarmin-Vrin. (A discussion of the Port-Royal Logic. It also contains a good bibliography of logical works in French 1700–1800.)

Blanché, R. (1970) *La logique et son histoire, d'Aristote à Russell*, Paris: Colin. (An introductory book on the history of logic.)

Bocheński, I.M. (1956) *Formale Logik*, Freiburg and Munich: Alber; trans. and ed. I. Thomas, *A History of Formal Logic*, Notre Dame, IN: University of Notre Dame Press, 1961; repr. New York: Chelsea, 1970. (An introductory book on the history of logic with several excerpts from original texts.)

Buickerood, J.G. (1985) 'The Natural History of the Understanding: Locke and the Rise of Facultative Logic in the Eighteenth Century', *History and Philosophy of Logic* 6: 157–90. (This work introduced the term 'facultative logic' in the history of logic.)

Capozzi, M. (1987) 'Kant on Logic, Language and Thought', in D. Buzzetti and M. Ferriani (eds) *Speculative Grammar, Universal Grammar and Philosophical Analysis of Language*, Amsterdam and Philadelphia, PA: Benjamin, 97–147. (Gives an insight in the evolution of Kant's conception of logic.)

—— (1994) 'Algebra e logica in Jakob Bernoulli', in *Atti del Congresso 'Logica e filosofia della scienza: problemi e prospettive', Lucca 7–10 gennaio 1993*, Pisa: ETS, 55–74. (Considers one of the first attempts to establish the relations between algebra and logic.)

Daston, L. (1988) *Classical Probability in the Enlightenment*, Princeton, NJ: Princeton University Press. (An important contribution to the subject.)

* Descartes, R. (1628) *Regulae ad directionem ingenii*, 1701; trans. 'Rules for the Direction of our Native Intelligence', in *The Philosophical Writings of*

Descartes, vol. 1, ed. J. Cottingham, R. Stoothoff and D. Murdoch, Cambridge: Cambridge University Press, 1984–5. (An incomplete work which was first published posthumously in 1701. However, the Port-Royal logicians read the manuscript in 1644 and the cultivated public knew its contents thanks to a Dutch translation of 1684.)

* —— (1637) *La Géométrie*; repr. and trans. in *The Geometry of René Descartes*, ed. D.E. Smith and M.L. Latham, LaSalle, IL: Open Court, 1925; repr. New York: Dover, 1954. (Marks the beginning of analytic geometry.)

* Euler, L. (1760–2) *Lettres à une Princesse d'Allemagne sur divers sujets de physique et de philosophie* (Letters to a German Princess on Various Subjects of Physics and Philosophy), St. Petersburg, 1768–72; repr. in *Leonhardi Euleri opera omnia*, Leipzig: Teubner, 1911. (In a few pages the famous mathematician Euler gives a clear representation, by means of circles, of the basic categorical propositions entering simple syllogisms.)

Gardner, M. (1958) *Logic Machines and Diagrams*; 2nd edn with foreword by D. Michie, Brighton: Harvester, 1983. (An outline of the development of mechanically induced inference.)

Gaukroger, S. (1989) *Cartesian Logic: An Essay on Descartes's Conception of Inference*, Oxford: Clarendon Press. (A clear and well-argued introduction to the topic.)

Hacking, I. (1975) *Why Does Language Matter to Philosophy?*, Cambridge: Cambridge University Press. (The origins of the importance of language for philosophy are traced back to the doctrines of ideas of Locke and Port-Royal.)

Hamilton, W. (1860–9) *Lectures on Metaphysics and Logic*, ed. H.L. Mansel and J. Veitch, Edinburgh and London: Blackwood, vol. 2, appendix. (Hamilton gives an account of the logic of many seventeenth- and eighteenth-century authors, with special attention to early attempts at a quantification of predicates.)

* Holland, G.J. (1765) 'Letter to Lambert (9 April 1765)', in J.H. Lambert, *Philosophische Schriften*, vol. 9.1, Hildesheim: Olms, 1968, 17–20. (In this letter Holland is critical of Lambert's intensional calculus and sketches his own, extensional one.)

Hoorman, C.F.A., Jr (1976) 'A Further Examination of Saccheri's Use of "*Consequentia Mirabilis*"', *Notre Dame Journal of Formal Logic* 17: 239–47. (This paper takes into account modern literature on the subject.)

Howell, W.S. (1956) *Logic and Rhetoric in England, 1500–1700*, Princeton, NJ: Princeton University Press. (Though sometimes inaccurate, this book is taken into account by most writers on the subject.)

—— (1971) *Eighteenth Century British Logic and Rhetoric*, Princeton, NJ: Princeton University Press. (Shares the defects of Howell (1956). However, this is still the only comprehensive introduction to eighteenth-century British logic.)

* Kant, I. (1755) *Principiorum primorum cognitionis metaphysicae nova dilucidatio* (A New Exposition of the First Principles of Metaphysical Knowledge); repr. in *Gesammelte Schriften*, Berlin: De Gruyter, 1902–10, vol. 1, 389; trans. F.E. England, in *Kant's Conception of God: A Critical Exposition of its Metaphysical Development Together with a Translation of the 'Nova Dilucidatio'*, London: Allen & Unwin, 1929. (With this dissertation Kant was granted the right to give university lectures on many subjects, in particular on logic, a subject he continued to teach for forty years.)

Kneale, W. and Kneale, M. (1962) *The Development of Logic*, Oxford: Clarendon Press, 1984. (The most comprehensive introduction to the history of logic.)

* Leibniz, G.W. (1966) *Logical Papers: A Selection*, trans. and ed. G.H.R. Parkinson, Oxford: Clarendon Press. (Collected papers on logic from 1679 to the early 1690s.)

Lewis, C.I. (1918) *A Survey of Symbolic Logic*, Berkeley, CA: University of California Press; revised edn, New York: Dover, 1960. (An early attempt to give an outline of the development of logic.)

Nuchelmans, G. (1983) *Judgement and Proposition: from Descartes to Kant*, Amsterdam: North Holland. (A very important contribution to the subject.)

—— (1991) *Dilemmatic Arguments: Towards a History of Their Logic and Rhetoric*, Amsterdam: North Holland. (A history of the subject ranging from Greek logic and rhetoric to the seventeenth century, with special attention to the '*consequentia mirabilis*' and Geulincx.)

Ong, W. (1958) *Ramus, Method, and the Decay of Dialogue*, Cambridge, MA, and London: Harvard University Press. (A general history of Ramism and of sixteenth-century logic.)

Risse, W. (1964–70) *Die Logik der Neuzeit* (The Logic of the Modern Age), Stuttgart and Bad Cannstatt: Frommann (Holzboog), 2 vols. (The first comprehensive account of logic 1500–1780. It contains extensive quotations from almost all the authors it cites.)

—— (1965) *Bibliographia Logica: Verzeichnis der Druckschriften zur Logik mit Angabe ihre Fundorte* (Logical Bibliography: Catalogue of Printed Works on Logic with Information about where They can be Found), Hildesheim: Olms, vol. 1, 1472–1800. (An invaluable bibliographical source.)

Roncaglia, G. (1996) *Palaestra rationis. Discussioni su natura della copula e modalità nella filosofia 'scolastica' tedesca del XVII secolo*, Florence: Olschki. (Includes a detailed exposition and evaluation of modal theories discussed in German universities 1600–70.)

Rossi, P. (1968) *Francis Bacon: From Magic to Science*, trans. S. Rabinovitch, London: Routledge. (Still to be recommended because it connects Bacon with the logical and methodological trends of his time.)

Schepers, H. (1959) *Andreas Rüdigers Methodologie und ihre Voraussetzungen* (The Methodology of Andreas Rüdiger and its Presuppositions), Kant-Studien, Ergänzungsheft 78, Cologne: Kölner Universitäts-Verlag. (An exemplary account of Rüdiger's philosophy and logic.)

Scholz, H. (1931) *Geschichte der Logik*, Berlin; repr. as *Abriß der Geschichte der Logik*, Freiburg: Alber, 1959; trans. K.F. Leidecker, *Concise History of Logic*, New York: Philosophical Library, 1961. (An early attempt to sketch the development of mathematical logic.)

Styazhkin, N.I. (1964) *History of Mathematical Logic from Leibniz to Peano*, trans., Cambridge, MA, and London: MIT Press, 1969. (An outline of the development of mathematical logic.)

Venn, J. (1881) *Symbolic Logic*, London: Macmillan, 2nd edn, 1894; repr. New York: Chelsea, 1979. (A book that has created an interest in the history of logic of the seventeenth and eighteenth centuries.)

Yolton, J. (1986) 'Schoolmen, Logic and Philosophy', in T.H. Aston (ed.) *The History of the University of Oxford*, ed. L.S. Sutherland and L.G. Mitchell, Oxford: Clarendon Press, 565–91. (Especially concerns Locke and his influence on English logicians such as Watts and Duncan.)

MIRELLA CAPOZZI

LOGIC IN THE 19th CENTURY

The nineteenth century was one of the most active periods for logic in Western philosophy. It is regarded foremost as being the first time logic became 'symbolic' and 'mathematical'.

There was tremendous diversity and conflict in logic in this period – indeed there were substantial debates over whether there even is a subject called 'formal logic' and over what the most basic logical forms were. There was an explicit discussion in the early part of the century of whether logic should be extensional or intensional, opinion eventually settling on a purely extensional conception. By the end of the century, many of these debates had been resolved or had withered away, and the most widespread conception and practice of logic coalesced in the early twentieth century into a view we now identify with the works of Frege, Russell and Whitehead.

The nineteenth century brought, for the first time, from Boole and Frege, distinct proposals on how to symbolize logic that were both extensively developed and had widespread influence. Boole is correctly regarded as the father of modern symbolic logic. Frege shared two concerns of many nineteenth-century mathematicians – avoiding incorrect derivations and providing rigorous and clear foundations for the infinitesimal and derivative calculus – and therefore sought to develop a very clear notion of mathematical 'proof'. His notation has not been taken up but his influence, especially on the move towards symbolization, has been considerable.

De Morgan was the first logician extensively and symbolically to discuss the logic of relations. However, a systematic algebraic notation for relations was provided only later by Peirce, and developed also by Schröder.

1   **Major movements and themes**
2   **Purpose and scope of logic**
3   **Logic and mathematics: Boole**
4   **Logic and mathematics: Frege**
5   **Relations**
6   **Main discoveries of nineteenth-century logic**

1   Major movements and themes

Among the main topics in nineteenth-century logic were (1) the purpose or scope of logic, (2) the extent to which logic can usefully be symbolized or diagrammed, (3) the organization or codification of basic and derivative logical principles, such as in an axiomatization, (4) the relationship of logic to mathematics, (5) the relationship of types of logic, such as deductive and inductive, to each other, and to other ideal forms of reasoning, such as the scientific method, (6) how far logic should depart from the account of quantification in Aristotle's theory of the categorical syllogism, (7) the relationship of types of deductive logic, especially of categorical to propositional logic (usually called 'hypothetical logic' in the nineteenth century), and (8) the extent to which logic needs to treat relations in a special way.

There was little discussion of modal logics; of what we now call 'deviant' logic, such as discussions of nonstandard connectives (including the non-material conditional); or of the relationship of logic and natural language. There was an explicit discussion only in the early part of the nineteenth century (and in Schröder 1890–1905, vol. 1) of whether logic should be 'extensional' or 'intensional', opinion eventually settling on a purely extensional conception. Extensional logic treats terms only according to the concrete entities to which they refer; intensional logic treats terms according to their 'meaning', variously called intension, comprehension or connotation (see INTENSIONAL LOGICS §1). C.I. Lewis (1918) advanced the thesis that the extensive symbolic development of logic required this extensional conception.

An already existing English (nominalistic) penchant for a logic of individual, concrete things was further solidified in works by Whately, Boole, Mill, De Morgan, Venn and Peirce; W.S. Jevons (1864) is unusual for his intensional theory of logic. German logic, owing to its often-noted idealist tendencies, had traditionally gravitated towards the approach that logic deals with concepts, not with 'things'. But works by Hermann Grassmann (1844) and Schröder (1877, and the monumental *Vorlesungen* of 1890–1905) had reversed this course. The works of Frege fall squarely within the older German intensional tradition, but this feature was virtually ignored by his English popularizers, such as Russell, and was later conflated with the firmly extensionalist, set-theoretic views of Dedekind and Cantor that arose contemporaneously in mathematics.

2 Purpose and scope of logic

Early modern philosophy, from the Renaissance to the late eighteenth century, had bequeathed numerous candidates for what was to be identified as the purpose or goal of 'logic'. The Renaissance Reform movement in logic, begun by Ramus and continuing through the Port-Royal logicians, modified and simplified the Aristotelian conception of logic, and augmented it with a study of 'method' – which included inductive logic, for example. The English textbook movement, associated with works by figures such as Isaac Watts in the eighteenth, and Richard Whately and J.S. Mill in the nineteenth centuries, adopted standard Reformist topics, but were less interested in a philosophical theory of logic than in improving the reasoning of their student-readers. (Many twentieth-century textbooks unwittingly follow the Reformist topics and the pedagogical approach.)

Several issues in the very characterization of logic itself emerge. Was logic to cover all forms of reasoning, or only deductive reasoning? Was logic to be a theoretical account of the patterns of valid inference, or a practical, 'how-to' manual to help readers reason better or identify the faulty reasoning of others? The

Reform and English-textbook traditions included treatments of deductive and inductive logic, together with other types of reasoning (analogy, causation, or scientific reasoning). This broad scope, together with an overriding pedagogical purpose, usually kept writing at a fairly superficial level, simply summarizing earlier views. The influential and subtle text of Richard Whately (1826) and the popular text of Mill (1843) fall squarely within this tradition. Even Augustus De Morgan (1847) treated 'the Calculus of Inference, Necessary and Probable'. The works of George Boole and Charles S. Peirce are also devoted to both deductive and inductive logics. (Only Peirce seems to have had a fully integrated and original theory of reasoning of all sorts; other authors simply followed the Reform syllabus.) Presumably because of a long-standing interest in a priori sentences and forms of inference going back to Leibniz, German logic was always focused exclusively on deductive logic. This included authors as diverse as Kant, Moritz Drobisch, Ernst Schröder and Frege.

Kant's views had considerable impact on German logic in the early nineteenth century and sharpened the tension between traditional, narrower conceptions of logic and a 'psychological' logic about the way humans must reason (see Kant 1800). Kant's conception of logic as the science of a priori judgments of all sorts, popularized by William Hamilton, led many English writers (Boole, Alexander Bain, Mill) to speak of the 'laws of thought'. In Germany, psychological theories and philosophical theories of logic were more thoroughly mixed by Wilhelm Wundt, Wilhelm Schuppe, Otto Külpe and – under the additional influence of Hegel – Christoff Sigwart and R.H. Lotze (and F.H. Bradley and B. Bosanquet) and many other psychologist-philosophers. These unholy mixtures brought fulminations from Frege that have been widely repeated in the twentieth century, often to suggest a fatal empirical taint to all of nineteenth-century logic. They are, however, rather 'laws' in the sense of how human beings 'must' (Kant) or 'should' (Peirce) reason; this is at worst a transcendental or normative theory of judgment and reasoning, rather than being simply empirical psychology.

Georg Hegel (1812) attacked what had been the often underdescribed guiding concept of most previous theories of logic, namely the idea of 'logical form', arguing that the distinction between 'form' and 'content' (of judgments or thoughts) was illegitimate. His own conception of logic defies simple summary, but vastly extended the Kantian conception. The extensions and critiques of Kant and Hegel drove early nineteenth-century German logic away from traditional logic. German logic as a philosophical discipline survived in the works of several anti-Kantian (and anti-Hegelian) logicians, among them Solomon Maimon, Moritz Drobisch (1838) and Bernard Bolzano, and was renewed through the later historical reappraisal of Leibniz and Aristotle by F.A. Trendelenburg (1847–67). Its true resurrection was, however, almost entirely due to professional mathematicians – Schröder and Frege, then Hilbert – who had little understanding of, or sympathy with, traditional philosophical logic.

3   Logic and mathematics: Boole

The idea of an 'algebra of logic' is a very old one, going back at least to observations by Jakob Bernoulli in 1685 (see LOGIC IN THE 17TH AND 18TH CENTURIES), with developed theories in unpublished manuscripts by Leibniz, and in published works by Lambert, Ploucquet, Euler and Grassmann (1844). George BOOLE then could modestly be credited only with the 'rediscovery' of the algebra of logic (1847, 1854). (Boole was apparently unaware of all these precedents, but was perhaps influenced by English views that were creeping towards a notion of an 'abstract' algebra, such as George Peacock's.) Nevertheless, his was an extensional theory of logic, was more developed than previous theories, occurred at a time when logic was ripe for a new and more mathematical approach and so had a sustained impact (direct or indirect) on all later symbolic theories (except Frege's). Boole is for these reasons correctly counted as the founder of modern symbolic logic.

However, Boole's logic had four features that were widely perceived as shortcomings. First, it had no account of relations. C.S. PEIRCE (1867–90) merged Boole's theory with De Morgan's work on relations to develop the 'algebra of relations' (see §5 below). Second, Boole treated propositional logic as a different interpretation of terms (as classes of 'occasions' or of 'times', rather than of concrete things). This reduction seemed unproblematic to Booleans but became suspect as Hugh MacColl (in a series of articles, 'The Calculus of Equivalent Statements', 1877–80) and Frege drew attention to what we now think of as propositional logic. Third, particular statements (using 'Some...', that is, I or O propositions) were enduringly problematic, and eventually pointed the way towards the generally inadequate handling of quantification by Booleans. Boole would indicate that some A's are B's by writing $A = vB$, where 'v' can be thought of as an operator that forms an arbitrary non-empty subset. Peirce and Schröder eventually introduced quantifier-like class operators, Π and Σ, to form classes with, respectively, all

individuals and some individuals having a given logical attribute. The intersection of two classes, which we indicate by $A \cap B$, might then be written as $\Pi i\, A i \times B i$ – the class of all i's that are both A and B – as well as by the simpler $A \times B$.

Finally, Boole's symbol, '+', as described unambiguously in his more influential work of 1854, which can mean class union or propositional disjunction, was notoriously non-inclusive: '$A + B$' is interpretable only when A and B are mutually exclusive. Boole was not without his reasons for this troublesome requirement – it greatly simplifies the calculation of joint probabilities in inductive logic, permits an inverse operation to '+', and gets rids of the odd '$1 + 1 = 1$' (Lambert's reasoning as well) – but as a feature of deductive logic, it was widely regarded as merely cumbersome. An inclusive interpretation was proposed by Jevons and Peirce in 1867, and this was widely adopted among Booleans. John Venn (1881) held on to the exclusive interpretation – presumably because of his joint concern for inductive logic.

Boole's earlier work (1847) is in some ways a remarkable, subtle and little-understood work: it does not discuss 'classes' and instead gives a theory of what Boole calls 'elective symbols'. These behave like subset-forming operators on the universe, 1.

Although Boole was paid homage by Peirce and Schröder as the founder (for Schröder, with Grassmann) of the algebra of logic, there are nevertheless respects in which they moved considerably beyond him. They thoroughly revised his handling of quantification, increasingly using quantifier-like operators. They were more interested in the algebra of relations, regarding the simple algebra of logic as somewhat trivial. And finally, they eventually moved away from Boole's 'equational' style of presentation. That is, rather than using a primary symbol of class identity, '=', they used a symbol of class subsumption ('subset'): Peirce's '—<' and Schröder's '⊆'.

A deeper difficulty was with Boole's apparent reasoning why we should want to turn logic into algebra at all. He seems to have had the idea that doing so would make logic-learning easier and, since many people had algebraic symbol-manipulating abilities, logical reasoning could then rely upon these. He did not articulate deep or philosophical reasons why logic really 'is' an algebra; it was convenient and helpful to think this way. (In largely unpublished works of the early 1880s) Frege extensively criticized the underlying motivations for this connection between algebra and logic as superficial and philosophically casual.

The works of Peirce and Schröder in the late nineteenth century moved in a direction compatible with Frege's critiques. Namely, they became less and less algebraic: no longer equational, and with the introduction of quantifiers, they contained variable-binding operators that disallow context-free algebraic-style substitutions. They also ceased pointing out parallels between logic and numerical algebra, and substantive uses of '1' and '0' disappeared.

4 Logic and mathematics: Frege

FREGE speaks only briefly of his conception of the purpose of logic: it is to use a '*Begriffsschrift*' ('conceptual notation' – Trendelenburg's translation of a concept used in discussing Leibniz's twin goals of a '*calculus ratiocinator*' and a '*characteristica universalis*'). That is, Frege's goal in his notation is to display in a perspicuous way the relationships between concepts and propositions (and presumably not merely those that are usefully similar to relationships in mathematics). The goal of the whole of logic is to demonstrate the correctness of deductions without gaps between premises and conclusions, using acknowledged formal and precise rules of inference. Frege's focus seems initially to have been on determining the correctness (and hence non-synthetic, a priori nature) of mathematical proofs, rather than examining reasoning of all sorts, as had traditionally been the subject of logic. Logic before Frege had not devoted itself only, or even extensively, to reasoning in mathematics; mathematicians were thought to be those least in need of help. Frege seems to have shared two concerns of many nineteenth-century mathematicians: avoiding incorrect derivations, like many faulty 'proofs' of the parallel postulate from other axioms and postulates in Euclidean geometry; and providing rigorous and clear foundations for the infinitesimal and derivative calculus ('analysis' – see ANALYSIS, PHILOSOPHICAL ISSUES IN §§1–2). His solution was, in essence, to develop a very clear notion of what counts as a mathematical 'proof'.

One might then guess that Frege was importantly involved in the axiomatic movements of the late nineteenth century, which first occurred in geometry (Hilbert and Veblen), then extended to the axiomatization of number theory (Peirce, Dedekind and Peano), set theory (Zermelo) and logic itself (R.A. Bernstein and Hilbert). This is not precisely correct, for Frege does not have a theory of axiomatics; certainly he had a general desire for care and precision, and developed reasons for this care and clarity, but his own demonstrations are neither more nor less likely to be flawed than those of Boole, Peirce, or Schröder, and are not axiomatic in any definite sense. Furthermore, Frege's notational system was so unusual and cumbersome that even Peano insisted that Frege's formulas be translated into his own notation before he would consider them. Our present notation for quantificational logic derives primarily from that of Whitehead and Russell's *Principia Mathematica*, which they in turn borrowed from Peano (see Peano 1973) – and these symbolisms were taken from original works by Peirce and Schröder's notational devices.

Frege's contribution lay elsewhere. He developed the first theory of quantification. The Boolean quantifiers of Peirce and Schröder were typically only class abstraction operators, with implicit rules given for their use. Frege also gave a very careful account of propositional logic (using notational devices for the material conditional and for negation) and made it the core of his theory – whereas for Aristotelians and Booleans, propositional logic was dependent on the logic of categorical statements, understood as a theory of classes. Furthermore, in later works, Frege was to use this theory to develop an account of the nature of numbers (1893, 1903) that was to have an enormous impact on Russell, and on the philosophy of mathematics. Finally, Frege contributed a great many concepts that have become part of the philosophy of logic: what we now call predicates and propositional functions; the use of 'functions' in logic; the distinction between sense and reference (see SENSE AND REFERENCE §§1–2); and many others.

Logic can be 'mathematical' in several distinct senses. It can simply use mathematical symbols and rules governing them; this is the method of Boole. It can be developed in the methodical, non-circular, clear way that was epitomized in Euclid's axioms and postulates for geometry, but had rarely been applied to other branches of mathematics, or to logic until the very late nineteenth century. It can be an independent discipline that is applied to mathematics, to give an analysis of concepts such as number or proof; this is closer to Frege's methodology. Finally, it can use mathematical techniques – of diagrams, demonstrations and proofs, and careful descriptions of mathematical structures. This is the modern and popular sense in which logic is sometimes said to be 'mathematical'. Peirce and Schröder might have understood and appreciated a claim, for example, that propositional logic defines a distributive lattice – a certain abstract algebraic structure – but Boole probably would not have understood such a claim and Frege would not have thought it insightful.

5 Relations

De Morgan is famous in logic for an often-repeated sentence he never wrote, roughly to the effect that all of Aristotelian logic was helpless to show the validity of the inference 'Since every horse is an animal, every head of a horse is the head of an animal'. The spirit is De Morgan's (except that he was surprisingly sympathetic to Aristotelian logic), but the example was Jevons'. The greatest logical and philosophical minds had long been aware of difficulties with relations, although they had often treated relational arguments as a marginal phenomenon. Plato and Aristotle were keenly aware of issues with regard to relations, and the medievals developed many theories of them (in supposition theory and in the theory of 'oblique' syllogisms – see LOGIC, MEDIEVAL §§5, 7). Joachim Jung, the Port-Royal logicians and Leibniz were all aware of this literature – as were De Morgan and Peirce.

With the exception of the remarkable treatment of functions by Lambert in the mid-eighteenth century, De Morgan (1860) deserves credit for being the first logician extensively and symbolically to discuss the logic of relations. He briefly surveys the history of relations (starting with Aristotle), argues for the importance of relations in common thought, and for the centrality of relations in mathematics. He argues that traditional logic had only treated the relations 'identity' and 'non-identity'. De Morgan emphasizes the formal properties of identity that form the basis of inferential operations, namely transitivity and 'convertibility' (what we would now call symmetry or commutativity). He then proposes a notation for relations (or at least for identity), but demurs from a systematic algebraic notation, later to be provided by Peirce.

Peirce first made his proposals in a rambling essay of 1870. They were presented in a more succinct manner in papers of 1882 and 1883. He published his most successful axiomatic-like presentation of the non-relational and relational algebra of logic (extensively using the quantifier-like Σ and Π operators) in 1885 (see Peirce 1867–90). His logic of relations, unlike many logical proposals, was woven into his more general philosophical system, into his philosophy of mathematics, and into his theory of infinity. (Peirce, following a hint from De Morgan, defines infinite classes as those in which certain relational arguments are invalid, although they are valid for finite ones: this is the theory of the 'transposed' syllogism.) Peirce used his system extensively, proved a number of results in the logic of relations, invented a number of technical tools (such as 'prenex' form, in which all quantifiers occur first and with global scope), and suggested Church's theorem: that there is no general mechanical routine for determining the validity or invalidity of an argument once relations and quantifiers are permitted.

In 1895, in the third volume of his *Vorlesungen*, Schröder presented the algebraic theory of relations in a lengthy but highly organized fashion, including the proofs of hundreds of theorems. He uses Peirce's notation and theory, adding some notational variants – he is notably careful about the distinct universes of discourse (Boole's '1') for two- and higher-place relations, and, more fastidious still, proposes distinct empty classes (Boole's '0'). Schröder uses Peirce's quantifier-like Σ and Π expressions, but presents both relational logic (1895: vol. 3) and non-relational logic (1890: vol. 1) in a less axiomatic-like way than Peirce had in 1885. He connects the logic of relations to various matrix, numerical and geometric representations, sometimes using these as what we would now describe as 'models'. Bertrand Russell in 1910, already familiar with Frege's and especially Peano's notations, pronounced the algebra of logic 'cumbersome'.

The Peirce–Schröder notation and theory with relations was used, mainly in German-language logical work, until about 1920 (and in Skolem's work for slightly longer). An overview is presented in English in Whitehead's work of 1897, but otherwise no translation of Schröder's *Vorlesungen* has ever appeared in English or French. (Although reprinted in 1966, it runs to over 2,000 pages and lacks an index.) Peirce's work was buried in American mathematics journals of the 1870s and 1880s, at least until the publication of his *Collected Papers* from 1931 on. He published no book summarizing his logic. Consequently, since the 1920s, the algebra and logic of relations as a distinct field has been known only to scholars of the history of logic and mathematics, or to those fluent in German. Interestingly, no conclusive proof has ever been printed that the algebra of logic, particularly when enriched with its quantifier-like expressions or with relations, is inadequate in any technical respects. (Tarski claimed in 1941 that there were formulas of first-order predicate logic it could not express, but did not offer a complete demonstration.)

Frege stands curiously outside of the history of attempts to deal with the logic of relations. This is because he seems to have been completely unaware of the history of the logic of relations, and because his own theory was developed so independently of the other efforts to address the problem (that is, he was unaware of the works of De Morgan and Peirce, while Schröder's work on relations appeared after Frege's system was already formulated). His own theory, even in the early *Begriffsschrift* (1879), can obviously express everything that the algebraic theories could. Propositional functions (predicates) can have one or more argument places (1879: §10), but Frege does not draw attention to the difference between one-place functions (monadic predicates such as 'is a cat') and those with two or more places (relational predicates, such as 'is smaller than'). He seems unaware of or uninterested in the different logical and philosophical behaviour of properties and relations.

6 Main discoveries of nineteenth-century logic

In terms of successful influences, systematic symbolizations comprise the most obvious logical heritage of the nineteenth century. This is a tradition that clearly began with Boole, was modified and extended by Peirce (and to a lesser extent by Schröder), and then slightly reformed by Peano. Frege had little influence on notation now in common use, but considerable influence on the impetus to use symbolization. The linking of logic with mathematics had enormous impact on twentieth-century logic, but there are many distinct such links: the exact connections seen by De Morgan, Boole, Peirce and Frege are thoroughly different, ranging from the view that both logic and mathematics can and should use similarly behaving symbolic systems, to views that mathematics 'is' logic (Frege, and perhaps Peano), or that logic 'is' mathematics (Boole, De Morgan, certainly Peirce). A further influence was the use of variable-binding operators, like those seen in mathematics (especially in the calculus). Finally, logic of both the Boolean and Fregean sort regarded a treatment of relational predicates as necessary, and not a marginal phenomenon – although this view is only implicit in Frege.

Both Peirce and Schröder used something quite similar to truth tables, a discovery usually credited to Wittgenstein. They also occasionally used models to show the independence of logical principles, a technique that was rediscovered and applied to logic in the 1920s; models themselves were suggested by the 'interpretations' and 'universes of discourse' of Boole and De Morgan. A clear notion of the 'completeness' of a logical system was absent, although they understood notions of independence and consistency; Peirce had some idea of decidability.

The value of studying nineteenth-century logic today, for other than its historical value, might include: algebraic – or at any rate 'mathematical' – structures inherent in logic as a theory of idealized thought or of the world; a reconsideration of the special structures and features to be found in the logic of relations; a perspective of the relationship of logic and mathematics that is closer to De Morgan's and Peirce's than to Frege's or Russell's; a return to an intensional conception of logic that once dominated logic and was rediscovered by Church in the 1950s and 1960s in the works of Frege; and conceptions of collective entities, and infinite collections, that retreat from the ornate and perplexing 'sets' of the twentieth century to something closer to the 'classes' of Boole, Peirce and Schröder – or perhaps to the concepts of Frege.

See also: DE MORGAN, A.; LOGIC MACHINES AND DIAGRAMS; LOGICAL AND MATHEMATICAL TERMS, GLOSSARY OF; MILL, J.S. §§2–3

References and further reading

* Boole, G. (1847) *The Mathematical Analysis of Logic, Being an Essay Towards a Calculus of Deductive Reasoning*, London: G. Bell & Sons; repr. in *Studies in Logic and Probability*, ed. R. Rhees, London: Watts, and LaSalle, IL: Open Court, 1952; also repr. in *An Investigation of the Laws of Thought*, New York: Dover, 1973. (Boole's first and in some ways best attempt at a symbolic calculus; far less influential than the *Laws of Thought* (1854) but philosophically far more interesting and exact.)

* —— (1854) *An Investigation of the Laws of Thought, on which are Founded the Mathematical Theories of Logic and Probabilities*, London: Walton & Maberley; repr. in *An Investigation of the Laws of Thought*, New York: Dover, 1973. (Boole's most famous work, and arguably the most influential work in the history of symbolic logic. Some, including Peirce, have nevertheless considered it to be inferior to his 1847 work.)

Boyer, C.B. and Merzbach, U.C. (1968) *A History of Mathematics*, New York and London: Wiley; 2nd edn, 1989, repr. 1991. (A standard work in the history of mathematics, with useful discussion of the intertwined histories of abstract algebra and 'Boolean' logic, and of the mathematization of logic in the late nineteenth century.)

* De Morgan, A. (1847) *Formal Logic: Or, The Calculus of Inference, Necessary and Probable*, London: Open Court, 1926. (A careful work from the same year as Boole's first major logical work; it had less influence than it deserved because of De Morgan's resistance to algebraic-style symbolizations.)

* —— (1860) 'On the Syllogism IV and on the Logic of Relations', in *On the Syllogism and Other Logical Writings*, ed. P. Heath, New Haven, CT: Yale University Press, 1966. (The first major work solely on the logic of relations, this had an enormous influence on Peirce, and through him on Schröder and others. De Morgan continued to resist an algebraic-style symbolization but was nevertheless highly rigorous.)

Dipert, R.R. (1990–1) 'The Life and Work of Ernst Schröder' and 'Individuals and Extensional Logic in Schröder's *Vorlesungen über die Algebra der Logik*', in V. Peckhaus (ed.) *Schröder*, special issue of *Modern Logic* 1 (2/3). (The only extensive works in English on Schröder's life and work.)

* Drobisch, M. (1838) *Neue Darstellung der Logik nach ihren einfachsten Verhältnissen*, Leipzig: Voss; 3rd revised edn, 1863. (Perhaps the most important and influential logic book in German before Frege, and probably known by him; experiments with notations and diagrams, and shows some independence from the then-dominant Aristotelian and Kantian/Hegelian approaches.)

* Frege, G. (1879) *Begriffsschrift, eine der arithmetischen nachgebildete Formelsprache des reinen Denkens*, Halle: Nebert; trans. 'Begriffsschrift, a Formula Language, Modelled Upon That of Arithmetic, for Pure Thought', in J. van Heijenoort (ed.) *From Frege to Gödel: A Source Book in Mathematical Logic, 1879–1931*, Cambridge, MA: Harvard University Press, 1967, 1–82. (The first major work of logic in a modern, twentieth-century, non-algebraic calculus; a remarkable and much-praised work but with little direct influence on later developments.)

* —— (1893, 1903) *Grundgesetze der Arithmetik: begriffsschriftlich abgeleitet*, Jena: Pohle, 2 vols; part 1 of vol. 1 trans. M. Furth, *Basic Laws of Arithmetic: An Exposition of the System*, Berkeley, CA: University of California Press, 1964. (A difficult work of enormous importance and influence, especially on Russell and for logicism: that mathematics was really logic.)

* Grassmann, H. (1844) *Die lineale Ausdehnungslehre, ein neuer Zweig der Mathematik*, Leipzig: Otto Wigand, 2nd edn, 1862; repr. in *Gesammelte mathematische und physikalische Werke*, ed. F. Engel, New York: Chelsea, 1969; trans. L.C. Kannenberg, 'The Linear Theory of Extension: A New Branch of Mathematics', in *A New Branch of Mathematics: The 'Ausdehnungslehre' of 1844, and Other Works*, La Salle, IL: Open Court, 1995. (A strikingly idiosyncratic symbolic work. Grassmann proposes a theory of all extension [one-dimensional quantities] including logic; predates Boole but was well-known only in the German-speaking world, with the exception of Peano.)

Hailperin, T. (1976) *Boole's Logic and Probability: A Critical Exposition from the Standpoint of Contemporary Algebra, Logic and Probability Theory*, Amsterdam and New York: North Holland; 2nd edn, 1986. (Perhaps the best secondary monograph on Boole's logic; unusually sensitive to the integrated aspects of his deductive and inductive logics; possibly the first edition is superior.)

* Hegel, G.W.F. (1812–16) *Science of Logic*, trans. A.V. Miller, London: Allen & Unwin, 1969. (A work whose major thesis is that there is no distinction between form and matter in judgments, this work had a huge and negative impact on philosophical formal logic in nineteenth-century Germany.)

* Jevons, W.S. (1864, 1869) 'Pure Logic' and 'The Substitution of Similars', in *Pure Logic and Other Minor Works*, London: Macmillan, 1890. (Jevons' early works were, with a less influential essay of Peirce's (1867), the major English symbolic works to advocate an 'exclusive' approach to the or/union operator.)

—— (1873) *The Principles of Science: A Treatise on Logic and Scientific Method*, New York: Dover, 1958. (An important English logic text, and one of the few that is intensional.)

Kant, I. (1781/1787) *Critique of Pure Reason*, trans. N. Kemp Smith, New York: St Martin's Press, and London: Macmillan, 1965. (A major work with little apparent concern for logic; its extension of a priori to include some synthetic judgments, as well as the 'Table of Categories', nevertheless altered nineteenth-century logic.)

* —— (1800) *Logic*, ed. G.B. Jäsche, repr., together with lecture notes taken by Kant's logic students c.1770–90, in *Lectures on Logic*, trans. J.M. Young, Cambridge: Cambridge University Press, 1992. (A 'minor' work of Kant, it nevertheless shows the influence of his philosophy and had considerable impact on later German logicians.)

Kneale, W. and Kneale, M. (1962) *The Development of Logic*, Oxford: Clarendon Press, 1984. (The standard but now dated work in the history of logic; has usable discussions of the nineteenth century, adequate discussions of major figures such as Boole and Frege, but thin and unphilosophical discussions of other figures and important issues such as relations.)

* Lewis, C.I. (1918) *A Survey of Symbolic Logic*, doctoral dissertation, Berkeley, CA: University of California Press; revised edn, New York: Dover, 1960. (Quite a dated work in many ways, but one of the few historical works in the field with a single, well-developed, unifying and enlightening thesis: the rise of extensional logic, and its separation from intensional logics.)

MacHale, D. (1985) *George Boole: His Life and Work*, Dublin: Boole Press. (The only extensive discussion of Boole's life, including some of his non-logical work – such as his work in calculus.)

Merrill, D.D. (1990) *Augustus De Morgan and the Logic of Relations*, Boston, MA: Kluwer. (The only major work on either De Morgan or the early history of relations.)

* Mill, J.S. (1843) *System of Logic: Ratiocinative and Inductive*, in *Collected Works of John Stuart Mill*, vols 7 and 8, London: Routledge, 1991. (Sometimes

said to be the most-published logic book ever (perhaps since surpassed by Copi's *Introduction to Logic*); an accessible, well-organized work often lamented for its lack of rigour, poor sense of history, and undeserved influence.)

* Peano, G. (1973) *Selected Works of Giuseppe Peano*, trans. and ed. H. Kennedy, Toronto, Ont.: University of Toronto Press. (A good selection in English of the works of Peano, whose notation and conception of logic were probably more influential than any other nineteenth-century logician; a very small collection.)

* Peirce, C.S. (1867–90) 'On an Improvement in Boole's Calculus of Logic' and other important logical papers, in *Collected Papers*, vol. 3, ed. C. Hartshorne, P. Weiss and A.W. Burks, Cambridge, MA: Harvard University Press, 1933; and in *Writings of Charles S. Peirce: A Chronological Edition*, ed. M. Fisch *et al.*, Bloomington, IN: Indiana University Press, 1982–. (The *Collected Writings* includes the more carefully edited versions – at least of works up to 1886.)

* Schröder, E. (1877) *Der Operationskreis des Logikkalküls*, Leipzig: Teubner. (Schröder's first, brief and elegant work on logic; shows familiarity with works by Boole and Grassmann, but not yet with works by Peirce or De Morgan, or with the theory of relations.)

* —— (1890–1905) *Vorlesungen über die Algebra der Logik* (Lectures on the Algebra of Logic), Leipzig: Teubner, 3 vols; repr. New York: Chelsea, 1966. (The monumental *locus classicus* of the algebra of logic, including relations; a highly systematic work that totals thousands of pages and hundreds of theorems; unindexed, it remains untranslated and has probably been read in its entirety by only a handful of German-speaking readers. See Dipert (1990–1) for discussion.)

Styazhkin, N.I. (1964) trans. *History of Mathematical Logic from Leibniz to Peano*, Cambridge, MA, and London: MIT Press, 1969. (A briefer treatment of nineteenth-century logic than Kneale and Kneale (1962), but often more insightful and knowledgeable in its discussions of symbolisms, of German logic in the eighteenth and nineteenth centuries, and of Russian figures such as Poretskii.)

* Trendelenburg, F.A. (1847–67) *Historische Beiträge zur Philosophie*, Berlin: Bethge. (Together with his *Logische Untersuchungen* and editions of Aristotle's *Prior Analytics*, this book began interest in the logics of Leibniz and Aristotle in the German-speaking world; probably read in part by Frege.)

* Venn, J. (1881) *Symbolic Logic*, London: Macmillan, 2nd edn, 1894; repr. New York: Chelsea, 1979. (By the time it appeared, this work was unoriginal, but usefully summarized Boolean logic in a book-length form more readable than Boole's own works; the first Boolean 'textbook'.)

* Whately, R. (1826) *Elements of Logic*, Delmar, NY: Scholars' Facsimiles and Reprints, 1975. (A highly intelligent, succinct, non-symbolic work that represents the high-water mark of the non-symbolic English 'logic textbook' tradition.)

RANDALL R. DIPERT

LOGIC IN THE EARLY 20th CENTURY

The creation of modern logic is one of the most stunning achievements of mathematics and philosophy in the twentieth century. Modern logic – sometimes called logistic, symbolic logic or mathematical logic – makes essential use of artificial symbolic languages.

Since Aristotle, logic has been a part of philosophy. Around 1850 the mathematician Boole began the modern development of symbolic logic. During the twentieth century, logic continued in philosophy departments, but it began to be seriously investigated and taught in mathematics departments as well. The most important examples of the latter were, from 1905 on, Hilbert at Göttingen and then, during the 1920s, Church at Princeton.

As the twentieth century began, there were several distinct logical traditions. Besides Aristotelian logic, there was an active tradition in algebraic logic initiated by Boole in the UK and continued by C.S. Peirce in the USA and Schröder in Germany. In Italy, Peano began in the Boolean tradition, but soon aimed higher: to express all major mathematical theorems in his symbolic logic. Finally, from 1879 to 1903, Frege consciously deviated from the Boolean tradition by creating a logic strong enough to construct the natural and real numbers. The Boole–Schröder tradition culminated in the work of Löwenheim (1915) and Skolem (1920) on the existence of a countable model for any first-order axiom system having a model.

Meanwhile, in 1900, Russell was strongly influenced by Peano's logical symbolism. Russell used this as the basis for his own logic of relations, which led to his logicism: pure mathematics is a part of logic. But his discovery of Russell's paradox in 1901 required him to build a new basis for logic. This culminated in his masterwork, Principia Mathematica, *written with Whitehead, which offered the theory of types as a solution.*

Hilbert came to logic from geometry, where models were used to prove consistency and independence results. He brought a strong concern with the axiomatic method and a rejection of the metaphysical goal of determining what numbers 'really' are. In his view, any objects that satisfied the axioms for numbers were numbers. He rejected the genetic method, favoured by Frege and Russell, which emphasized constructing numbers rather than giving axioms for them. In his 1917 lectures Hilbert was the first to introduce first-order logic as an explicit subsystem of all of logic (which, for him, was the theory of types) without the infinitely long formulas found in Löwenheim. In 1923 Skolem, directly influenced by Löwenheim, also abandoned those formulas, and argued that first-order logic is all of logic.

Influenced by Hilbert and Ackermann (1928), Gödel proved the completeness theorem for first-order logic (1929) as well as incompleteness theorems for arithmetic in first- order and higher-order logics (1931). These results were the true beginning of modern logic.

1 **What is modern logic?**
2 **Logic in 1900**
3 **The algebraic tradition of Boole and Schröder**
4 **Peano's tradition**
5 **Russell's response to Peano and Frege**
6 **Hilbert, the geometric tradition and the American postulate theorists**
7 ***Principia Mathematica***
8 **The emergence of first-order logic**
9 **The definitive metatheorems: Gödel on completeness and incompleteness**
10 **The prehistory of infinitary logic**
11 **A glance past Gödel: recursion theory, model theory, set theory**
12 **Coda: what is modern logic?**

1 What is modern logic?

Modern logic crystallized gradually during the period 1850–1950. It was not created by any one person or school, but evolved from the work of several. We now recognize that the following features were needed for its mature development:

(a) There is a formal language whose symbols separate it from ordinary language.

(b) In the formal language, *L*, the syntax is clearly separated from the semantics. The syntax is like the grammar of a natural language, specifying which sequences of symbols (called 'formulas') are permissible. Meaning does not occur in the syntax but in the semantics. Thus logical concepts such as sentence, axiom, formal proof and consistency are part of the syntax. Concepts such as truth, satisfiability and definability are part of the semantics. Formal proofs can be checked effectively and do not depend on the meaning of the terms in them.

(c) Within the syntax of *L*, the logical symbols are clearly separated from the non-logical symbols. The logical symbols include connectives such as 'and', 'not', 'if...then...'. The meaning of the non-logical symbols changes with different interpretations, while that of the logical symbols does not. The non-logical symbols may include individual constants, which, in the semantics, are interpreted as specific individuals. There may also be function constants and relation constants, which are interpreted as specific functions and relations. Besides the logical and non-logical symbols, there are variables, which may be free or bound.

(d) The syntax gives a recursive definition for the formulas of *L*.

(e) There is a clear distinction between the object language *L*, in which our formulas occur, and the metalanguage, in which we speak about *L*. Within the metalanguage, we must define what truth means in *L*. Theorems in the metalanguage are called metatheorems.

(f) Usually there will be levels within our symbolic logic. The lowest level (called propositional logic) is that of the connectives 'and', 'not', and so on. The next level will have individual variables *x* and quantifiers ('for all *x*', 'there exists an *x*') over those variables. If that is the highest level, then we have first-order logic. But there may also be function variables (or relation variables) and quantifiers over them, giving second-order logic (see SECOND- AND HIGHER-ORDER LOGICS). In the simple theory of types, there are individual variables, function variables, variables for functions of functions, and so on, and this is sometimes called ω-order logic. We must decide which order our logic will have.

(g) We must also specify other matters. Will the semantics of our logic have only two truth-values, 'true' and 'false', as in traditional logic, or will it have three or more truth-values (see MANY-VALUED LOGICS)? Will our logic be 'classical' (in which the law of the excluded middle holds) or 'intuitionistic' (in which that law fails; see INTUITIONISM)? Will our logic be finitary (like all the logics discussed above) or will it be infinitary (that is, have infinitely long formulas, or have variable-binding operators that give the same effect, or have rules of inference with infinitely many premises; see INFINITARY LOGICS)?

(h) Finally, we must study the metatheory of *L*, that is, what general results can be proved, in the metalanguage, to be true of *L*. This includes the consistency and independence of the logical axioms for *L* as well as whether *L* is 'complete' (that is, whether every true sentence of *L* is provable in *L*).

2 Logic in 1900

In 1900 there were five main approaches to logic. The first of these was traditional Aristotelian logic, in which the syllogism was central. It had split into several branches, encompassing the idealist logic of Bradley and the pragmatist logic of Dewey. The remaining approaches differed from the first by using symbols in a fundamental way.

The second approach was that of Boole. In 1854 Boole had introduced a logical calculus, whose symbols were borrowed from mathematics, and given his calculus three interpretations: propositions, classes and probability. Around 1900, Boole's active successors were Peirce and Schröder. During the 1880s Peirce had modified Boole's logic by introducing quantifiers and relations. The second approach was regarded as trivial by certain Oxford logicians who espoused the traditional one (see Passmore 1968: 156, 240).

The third approach originated in Italy. There Peano began his work on logic (1888) within the Boolean tradition, influenced by Schröder (1877). To avoid confusing Schröder's logical symbols '·' and '+' (for 'and' and 'or', respectively) with the corresponding arithmetical symbols for addition and multiplication, Peano replaced them with his own, derived from Hermann Grassmann: '∩' and '∪'. Peano retained a Boolean ambiguity by interpreting '∩' and '∪' not only as 'and' and 'or' between propositions but also as 'intersection' and 'union' of classes. (In 1906 Russell removed this ambiguity by keeping '∩' and '∪' for 'intersection' and 'union' while introducing a new symbol '∨' for 'or' and using a dot for 'and'; nevertheless, like Frege, he had no non-logical symbols and so did not satisfy requirement (c) above.) Peano went beyond the Boolean tradition by symbolizing much of mathematics.

The fourth approach, that of Frege, was isolated from the others. Frege proposed a second-order symbolic language for treating mathematics – particularly the real and complex numbers – in his *Begriffsschrift* (1879). There he replaced the traditional logical notions of subject and predicate by the more mathematical ones of function and argument. In the culmination of his work (*Grundgesetze der Arithmetik*, 1893 and 1903), he attempted to establish that all truths of arithmetic (but not geometry) can be proved from logic alone (see LOGICISM). To do so, he used a very strong logic, which in 1902 turned out to be inconsistent. No doubt his daunting two-dimensional symbolism partly accounts for his limited influence at the time. But Frege was also isolated by his explicit refusal to work in the Boolean tradition,

as well as by his many innovations and his severe criticisms of other logicians.

The fifth approach to logic, that of Hilbert, was rooted in the foundations of geometry. In 1899 he gave axioms for Euclidean geometry that were purely formal, although not yet expressed in symbols. He proposed three main tasks for such an axiom system: establishing its consistency, independence and completeness. (At that time, 'completeness' was imprecise and required only that the axioms imply all known theorems of geometry.)

So at the turn of the century there was no unified tradition in logic and no common view of what logic is and what its goals are; at the same time, it was generally agreed that there is only one correct logic. This fragmented situation continued until at least 1930 (although the Boole–Schröder tradition was strong until the 1920s), when the theory of types became increasingly important. After 1930, first-order logic gradually replaced the theory of types.

3 The algebraic tradition of Boole and Schröder

During the 1890s Schröder continued the Boolean tradition (see §2 above). Schröder's logic began with his 'identical calculus' or lattice theory (1890: 161); it was related to a calculus of classes, one of domains and one of propositions. In 1895, his calculus of relations elaborated that of Peirce.

Although a critic of Frege, Schröder too regarded arithmetic as a part of deductive logic (1890: v) and later went beyond Frege's version of logicism by stating that 'I consider pure Mathematics to be only one branch of general Logic' (1898: 46).

The Boole–Schröder tradition culminated in the work of Löwenheim and Skolem. Löwenheim's most important paper (1915), on Schröder's calculus of relations, distinguished between first-order and second-order logic while retaining elements of infinitary logic (see §10 below). Löwenheim's semantic theorem was that if a first-order formula is true in all countable domains, then it is true in all domains. Löwenheim was well aware that this result failed in his full logic, which was a kind of infinitary second-order logic.

In 1920 Skolem extended Löwenheim's theorem, and in this form it is known as the 'Löwenheim–Skolem theorem': if a countable set of first-order formulas has a model, it has a countable model. This was the first major metatheorem for first-order logic.

4 Peano's tradition

The most important of Peano's logical accomplishments was to invent a clear symbolism. Much of it –

such as $\in$ for class membership and $\supset$ for material implication – continues today, thanks to its adoption by Russell. By contrast, the logical symbolisms of Frege and Schröder are all but extinct.

In 1891 Peano believed that he could express any logical relation by using seven primitive symbols: $\in$ ('is'), $=$ ('is equal'), $\supset$ ('implies'), $\cap$ ('and'), $\cup$ ('or'), $-$ ('not') and $\wedge$ ('absurd'). He was mistaken, as Frege remarked. Partly under Frege's influence, Peano used nine kinds of primitive symbol in 1897: the old signs $\in$, $\supset$, $\cap$, $-$, together with the signs K ('class'), (x, y) ('ordered pair'), $=_{\text{Df}}$ ('definition'), parentheses and variables. Yet both Frege and Peano accepted the principle of comprehension (that is every predicate determines the class of those things satisfying the predicate), which eventually led to the paradoxes.

Peano tried to render mathematics completely unambiguous by expressing it in his symbolism. He first used his symbolism in geometry (1888), next in his postulates for the natural numbers (1889), and then he applied it to differential equations (1890). He assembled a group of Italian collaborators to create the encyclopedic *Formulaire de mathématiques* (1894–1908), which aimed to symbolize all major mathematical theorems.

Among those collaborators was Alessandro Padoa, who investigated the undefinability of a term from other terms in a given axiom system (1901). Padoa emphasized that the notion 'definable' was not absolute but depended on the particular axiom system and its primitive symbols. This insight was overlooked when the paradoxes of definability, such as Richard's paradox, were discovered soon afterward (see PARADOXES OF SET AND PROPERTY §6).

5 Russell's response to Peano and Frege

In 1900, before he discovered the paradoxes, Russell adopted Peano's symbolism and used it to develop his own logic of relations. Russell was particularly impressed by Peano's distinction between the membership relation $\in$ and the relation $\supset$ construed as inclusion. Peano did not distinguish, however, between the implication $p \supset q$ and the inference 'From the proposition p infer the proposition q', although this distinction had already been made by Frege (1879). The deduction theorem – a metatheorem showing the correct relation between the two – was only proved by Tarski in about 1921.

For Russell, symbolic logic had three parts: the calculi of propositions, of classes and of relations. In the *Principles of Mathematics*, he gave primacy to the propositional calculus over the calculus of classes (1903: 12), and also proposed his logicism, which went beyond Frege's by including geometry and parts

of mechanics: all mathematical concepts are definable from the basic concepts of logic, and all mathematical theorems are provable from the axioms of logic.

In 1903, after finishing the *Principles*, Russell shifted from an analysis of logic in the spirit of Peano to one in the spirit of Frege. Peano had given the universal quantifier only in the form $\phi x \supset_x \psi x$, that is, 'For every x, ϕx implies ψx'. Russell introduced a new notation for an idea that he took from Frege: $(x)\phi x$, that is, 'For every x, ϕx'. Likewise, Peano had been able to express an existential quantifier only in the form $\exists a$, that is, 'The class a is non-empty'. Russell introduced a Fregean existential quantifier: $(\exists x)\phi x$, that is, 'There is an x such that ϕx'. Russell's notation later became standard. It had the virtue of disentangling quantifiers from the quantifier-free part of a formula and of disentangling logical formulas from the notion of class. Finally, Russell adopted Frege's assertion sign, '$\vdash$'. Thus, for Russell, $\vdash (x)\phi x$ meant 'It is true that $(x)\phi x$'. (Nowadays $\vdash$ does not mean 'it is true that' but rather, 'it is provable that', and indicates a theorem of logic; see Church (1956: 82).)

6 Hilbert, the geometric tradition and the American postulate theorists

Hilbert's interest in logic stemmed from his devotion to the axiomatic method, which he first exploited to give a definitive form to the axioms of Euclidean geometry in 1899. Here he continued the geometric tradition by using models to establish the consistency and independence of his axioms. Yet he distanced himself from the traditional philosophical concern with what points or numbers 'really' are by treating them as unspecified 'things', defined only by the axioms. As long as the 'things' satisfied the axioms, he insisted, it did not matter if they were points, lines and planes, or tables, chairs and mugs. In accordance with requirement (b) in §1 above, the syntax was separated clearly from the semantics.

At that time Hilbert corresponded with Frege on the foundations of geometry. Frege held the traditional view that the geometric axioms express intuitions, while Hilbert supported the modern view that an axiom system at most determines the 'things' mentioned up to isomorphism (see Nagel 1939). Frege insisted that the only way to prove the consistency of an axiom system was to give a model, while Hilbert believed that the consistency of a system yields the existence of a model in which it is 'true' (see Frege 1980: 39). Brouwer disputed Hilbert's claim in 1929. Around 1930, Gödel proved this claim for first-order logic, but, using incompleteness, refuted it for second-order logic (see §9).

From 1900 until 1940, the axiomatic method, as

formulated by Hilbert and Peano, was used by a group of mathematicians sometimes called the American postulate theorists (see Scanlan 1991) to axiomatize a variety of mathematical systems – including the complex numbers, Boolean algebra, and fields – and to prove the consistency and independence of the axioms. This group included Huntington, Veblen and E.H. Moore. In 1902, while giving an axiomatization for the real numbers, Huntington isolated the idea that this system has, up to isomorphism, only one model. Such a system is 'categorical' (to use the name that Veblen gave it in 1904). A year later, Huntington conjectured that every categorical system S is deductively complete, that is, every sentence expressible in S is provable or refutable in S. It was not until Gödel's incompleteness theorems that Huntington was proved wrong. Moreover, in first-order logic, any system having an infinite model is not categorical (see §8).

7 *Principia Mathematica*

Between 1902 and 1913 Russell and Whitehead wrote rincipia Mathematica (1910–13), which aimed to give strong evidence for logicism by axiomatizing logic (via the theory of types) and deducing much of pure mathematics from it. In doing so, Russell was particularly concerned to avoid the paradoxes of logic. He also shared with Peano a desire to minimize the number of axioms and primitive concepts.

Principia Mathematica strongly influenced the development of logic, but most of that influence did not come until the 1920s. When its second edition appeared in 1925, Russell considered the most important improvement to logic to be the reduction by Sheffer of the primitive concepts of propositional logic from two ('or' and 'not') to one ('neither... nor') and the reduction by Nicod of its axioms from five to one. (Ironically, later logical research hardly used such reductions.) But in that edition Russell did not mention a more important advance made by Wiener (1914) and known to Russell: the definition of ordered pair (and hence of relation) in terms of classes.

Not everyone accepted the theory of types. Veblen argued that 'formal logic has to be taken over by mathematicians.... There does not exist an adequate logic at the present time, and unless the mathematicians create one, no one else is likely to do so' (1925: 141).

Already in the *Principles* (1903: §17) Russell believed it impossible to establish the independence of one axiom of logic from the others. In *Principia Mathematica*, Whitehead and Russell retained this conviction (1910: 95). For Russell, as for Frege, one cannot stand outside of logic, and so it is not surprising that *Principia Mathematica* lacked a metalanguage. This notion of metalanguage originated with Hilbert (1922), from whom it was adopted by Tarski (1930) and Carnap (1934). It was natural when a system of logic was viewed as simply another mathematical system. (Russell (1922) independently considered levels of language.) Nowadays, the most important theorems of logic are metatheorems, that is, theorems in the metalanguage about the system of logic, and they involve the sort of notions that Hilbert used in his theorems about geometry: consistency, independence and completeness.

8 The emergence of first-order logic

By 1955, first-order logic was dominant among logicians who were mathematicians (though the theory of types remained important among philosophers). However, first-order logic was slow in coming. It first clearly emerged as a 'subsystem' of logic in Hilbert's lectures of 1917, published in Hilbert and Ackermann (1928). (Löwenheim had separated a subsystem of logic from his full system in 1915, but his subsystem allowed quantifiers to be expanded into infinitely long formulas, and so was richer than first-order logic, in which all formulas have finite length.)

Hilbert, unlike Löwenheim, was very careful to specify his syntax, and gave, for the first time, a recursive definition of first-order formula (see (d) in §1 above). Hilbert also stated axioms for first-order logic. While he had borrowed his axioms for propositional logic from *Principia Mathematica*, first-order logic was his own. Moreover, he differed from Russell by posing the metamathematical questions of the consistency, independence and completeness of his axioms. He proved the consistency of both propositional and first-order logic, but was unable to answer the other questions. Hilbert wanted to give axiomatizations for various theories within logic, whereas Russell wanted a strong logic in which to deduce those theories from his logical axioms. Hilbert's long-term goal was to prove the consistency of all of classical mathematics by finitary means (see HILBERT'S PROGRAMME AND FORMALISM.)

In 1917 Hilbert persuaded Bernays to work with him on logic. Bernays' first results (1918, published only in 1926) established the independence and completeness of propositional logic. Meanwhile, Post had independently found and published them (1921).

Also in 1917, Hilbert emphasized the 'Entscheidungsproblem': to find a decision procedure for every mathematical problem. Within the Schröderian tradition, decision procedures had already been studied by Löwenheim (1915), who solved the *Entscheidungsproblem* for monadic predicates within first-order logic, a solution improved by Skolem (1919). Within Hilbert's school, Bernays gave a decision procedure for propositional logic in 1918, and in 1928 argued that the *Entscheidungsproblem* was the central problem of logic (see PROOF THEORY §2). Work on the *Entscheidungsproblem* consisted of finding a decision procedure for more and more complicated classes of first-order sentences in prenex normal form (that is, consisting of a quantifier-free matrix preceded by a string of quantifiers), where the complexity of the class was measured by the number of quantifiers in the prefix.

Meanwhile, in 1923, Skolem abandoned the infinitely long formulas adopted from Schröder and Löwenheim, and began working explicitly in first-order logic. Skolem made the radical proposal that the membership relation '∈' of set theory be treated, not as a part of logic in the way that Peano and Russell had done, but like any other relation (that is, as a non-logical symbol). In logic, such relations could be given various interpretations, and so should '∈'. This proposal resulted in the so-called 'Skolem paradox' of first-order logic: set theory has a countable model although it contains uncountable sets (see PARADOXES OF SET AND PROPERTY §9).

In France, Herbrand (1930) made a major contribution to the relation between propositional logic and first-order logic.

9 The definitive metatheorems: Gödel on completeness and incompleteness

The most important person influenced by Hilbert's logic was Gödel, whose doctoral dissertation (1929) solved Hilbert and Ackermann's problem of showing, for countable languages, the completeness of first-order logic: every valid first-order formula is provable. In fact, Gödel proved the stronger result that every consistent set of first-order formulas has a model (1929).

When Gödel's completeness theorem was published in 1930, he included as a corollary the 'compactness theorem': a set of first-order formulas has a model if every finite subset has a model. The importance of this theorem was only appreciated later by Maltsev (1936) and Henkin (1947) when they introduced uncountable languages.

Even more important were Gödel's incompleteness theorems (1931). His first incompleteness theorem stated that if a 'decidable' set Σ of formulas implies the axioms for the natural numbers with addition and multiplication, then there is a sentence in the language of Σ that is neither provable nor refutable. (Here 'decidable' means that there is a mechanical procedure for determining whether a formula is in Σ.) The

second incompleteness theorem stated that such an axiom system Σ cannot prove its own consistency (see GÖDEL'S THEOREMS).

The incompleteness theorems were devastating. They refuted Russell's logicism by showing that there are true mathematical sentences which cannot be proved in the theory of types. Likewise, they refuted Hilbert's programme, since the consistency of number theory cannot be established except by a stronger theory. Church soon established that there is no decision procedure for first-order logic. Finally, the incompleteness theorems led to attempts, by Carnap and Zermelo, to circumvent them by introducing an infinitary logic (see §10).

10 The prehistory of infinitary logic

Peirce and Schröder treated quantifiers in a way that differs from the modern one. If we fix a finite set with n elements $a_1, a_2, \ldots, a_n$ as our universe D of discourse and let Px mean that x has the property P, then in D we can express 'All x have property P' by 'Pa_1 and Pa_2 and ... and Pa_n'. If D is infinite and its elements are $a_1, a_2, \ldots, a_n, \ldots$, then Peirce and Schröder still treat 'All x have property P' as equivalent to 'Pa_1 and Pa_2 and ... and Pa_n and ...'. (An analogous statement holds in D for 'Some x has P' and 'Pa_1 or Pa_2 or ... or Pa_n or ...'.) Thus a quantifier could be expanded as an infinite conjunction or disjunction. This was the beginning of an infinitary logic, but one that was not yet formulated as a distinct kind of logic.

Here we see two distinct ways of treating quantifiers: (1) 'For all x, Px' and (2) the infinitely long conjunction 'Pa_1 and Pa_2 and ... and Pa_n and ...'. Frege, Peano and Russell used quantifiers only in the first way. By contrast, Peirce and Schröder used both ways interchangeably. Hilbert (1905) was influenced by Schröder to define quantifiers in the second way when the universe D was the natural numbers. In his mature work (1923), Hilbert still viewed quantifiers as going beyond the finitary.

Meanwhile, within the Schröderian tradition, Löwenheim used not only such infinitely long conjunctions and disjunctions but also infinite strings of quantifiers, in his paper proving Löwenheim's theorem. Skolem continued to use this infinitary logic when in 1920 he extended Löwenheim's theorem to a countable set of first-order formulas, but by 1923 he abandoned infinitary logic in favour of first-order logic.

Infinitary logic arose, independently, in Zermelo's paper (1931) reacting against first-order logic and specifically against Skolem's argument that there is a countable model for set theory (see PARADOXES OF SET AND PROPERTY §9). Zermelo formulated a strong infinitary logic in which, he hoped, the Löwenheim–Skolem theorem was false. Soon he had a second reason to propose an infinitary logic, namely to avoid Gödel's incompleteness theorems and to have every valid sentence be provable. But Zermelo's logic was adopted by no one.

Hilbert, Tarski and Zermelo each formulated a different version of an infinitary rule of inference, now known as the ω-rule. (Influenced by Hilbert and Tarski, Carnap also used the ω-rule.) This rule requires the language of logic to have infinitely many names, one for each natural number n. If a formula $\phi(a_n)$ has been proved for the name a_n of each natural number n, the ω-rule infers 'For every x, $\phi(x)$'. Without the ω-rule, an axiomatization of the natural numbers could be ω-inconsistent, that is, prove $\phi(a_n)$ for each natural number n but also prove 'There is some x such that not $\phi(x)$'. Unlike Carnap, Hilbert and Zermelo, all of whom supported this rule, Tarski was occasionally sceptical of it.

Only in 1955 were infinitely long formulas accepted as a legitimate part of mathematical logic – thanks to Henkin, Tarski and Karp – in apparent ignorance of earlier work on such formulas by Zermelo and others. By this time, first-order logic was firmly established as the logical framework for mathematics, and those infinitary formulas were considered within various extensions of first-order logic. A different kind of extension was proposed by Mostowski (1957): generalized quantifiers. One such quantifier was 'there exist uncountably many'. For that quantifier, Mostowski asked if it is possible to prove a completeness theorem analogous to that for first-order logic. Later the answer turned out to be 'yes'.

11 A glance past Gödel: recursion theory, model theory, set theory

Modern logic began with Gödel's completeness and incompleteness theorems. Today they are the goal of most introductory logic courses. From his incompleteness theorems, recursion theory emerged during the 1930s, when the notion of 'computable' was made precise by the Gödel–Herbrand notion of recursive function and, equivalently, by Turing machines (see COMPUTABILITY THEORY).

Model theory emerged as a distinct part of logic around 1950, although its first important result (Löwenheim's theorem) dates back to 1915. One fundamental notion – relational structure – was already vaguely present in Hilbert (1899). A relational structure is an ordered pair consisting of a set and a family of relations on that set; such structures include groups, fields and Boolean algebras, but not topologies. Model theory began to develop into its modern

form through the discovery that the strong completeness theorem for first-order logic (that is, any consistent set of first-order sentences has a model) implies results about structures. Connected with this was Henkin's use of languages with uncountably many symbols (1947) and Tarski's classification (1952) of structures up to 'elementary equivalence' (that is, being indistinguishable in first-order logic).

Meanwhile, set theory developed much closer ties with logic. In 1938 Gödel used first-order logic to prove the important result that if the usual axioms of set theory are consistent, they remain so when the axiom of choice and the generalized continuum hypothesis are assumed (see AXIOM OF CHOICE; SET THEORY). Gödel's idea was to consider, not all sets, but only those sets first-order definable from sets of previous levels (see CONSTRUCTIBLE UNIVERSE). And in 1963 first-order logic was essential to Cohen's proof that the axiom of choice and the generalized continuum hypothesis are independent of the usual axioms of set theory (see FORCING).

12 Coda: what is modern logic?

Until about 1850, it was fairly easy to say what logic was. Today it is much harder, although classical first-order logic remains dominant. After 1920, many-valued logics (that is, those having three or more truth-values) were investigated by Post and Łukasiewicz. Likewise, modal logic was seriously studied, thanks to C.I. Lewis (1918; see MODAL LOGIC). And during the 1950s infinitary logic crystallized. Finally, there are now many specialized logics (see, for example, QUANTUM LOGIC).

During the 1970s first-order logic was characterized by 'Lindström's theorem': first-order logic is the strongest logic that contains propositional logic and for which the compactness theorem and the Löwenheim–Skolem theorem hold. Thus any logic which extends first-order logic must violate the compactness theorem or the Löwenheim–Skolem theorem. An idea of the wide range of modern logic can be obtained by consulting Barwise (1977), Barwise and Feferman (1985), and Gabbay and Guenthner (1983–9).

See also: LOGICAL AND MATHEMATICAL TERMS, GLOSSARY OF

References and further reading

* Barwise, J. (ed.) (1977) *Handbook of Mathematical Logic*, Amsterdam: North Holland. (An excellent survey of modern logic.)
* Barwise, J. and Feferman, S. (eds) (1985) *Model-*

Theoretic Logics, New York: Springer. (The best survey of infinitary logic.)

* Bernays, P. (1918) 'Beiträge zur axiomatischen Behandlung des Logik-Kalküls' (Contributions to the Axiomatic Treatment of the Logical Calculus), unpublished *Habilitationsschrift*, Göttingen University; published in much revised form, 'Axiomatische Untersuchung des Aussagen-Kalküls der *Principia Mathematica*' (Axiomatic Investigation of the Propositional Calculus of Principia Mathematica), *Mathematische Zeitschrift* 25: 305–20, 1926. (First proof of the completeness of propositional logic; compare with Post (1921).)

* Carnap, R. (1934) *Logische Syntax der Sprache*, Vienna: Springer; revised and trans. A. Smeaton, *The Logical Syntax of Language*, London: Kegan Paul, and New York: Harcourt Brace, 1937. (A precise version of the theory of types and the ω-rule.)

* Church, A. (1956) *Introduction to Mathematical Logic*, Princeton, NJ: Princeton University Press. (An erudite but useful introduction to modern logic.)

* Frege, G. (1879) *Begriffsschrift, eine der arithmetischen nachgebildete Formelsprache des reinen Denkens*, Halle: Nebert; trans. '*Begriffsschrift*, a Formula Language, Modelled Upon That of Arithmetic, for Pure Thought', in J. van Heijenoort (ed.) *From Frege to Gödel: A Source Book in Mathematical Logic, 1879–1931*, Cambridge, MA: Harvard University Press, 1967, 1–82. (Frege's first, ground-breaking work.)

* —— (1893, 1903) *Grundgesetze der Arithmetik: begriffsschriftlich abgeleitet*, Jena: Pohle, 2 vols; repr. as *Grundgesetze der Arithmetik*, Hildesheim: Olms, 1966; Part 1 of vol. 1 trans. M. Furth, *Basic Laws of Arithmetic: An Exposition of the System*, Berkeley, CA: University of California Press, 1964; extracts from vol. 2, including 'Frege on Russell's Paradox', in *Translations from the Philosophical Writings of Gottlob Frege*, trans. and ed. P.T. Geach and M. Black, Oxford: Blackwell, 3rd edn, 1980. (Volume 1 gives a detailed development of his system of logic. Volume 2 has Frege's reaction to Russell's paradox.)

* —— (1980) *Philosophical and Mathematical Correspondence*, trans. H. Kaal, ed. G. Gabriel *et al*, Chicago, IL: University of Chicago Press. (Translation of Frege's letters. The correspondence with Hilbert and Russell is especially interesting.)

* Gabbay, D. and Guenthner, F. (eds) (1983–9) *Handbook of Philosophical Logic*, Dordrecht: Reidel, 4 vols. (A standard modern source on classical and non-classical logics.)

* Gödel, K. (1929) 'Über die Vollständigkeit des Logikkalküls', doctoral dissertation, University of Vienna; trans. 'On the Completeness of the Logical Calculus', in *Collected Works*, vol. 1, *Publications 1929–1936*, ed. S. Feferman, J.W. Dawson Jr, S.C. Kleene, G.H. Moore, R.M. Solovay, and J. van Heijenoort, New York and Oxford: Oxford University Press, 1986, 44–101. (First proof of the completeness theorem for first-order logic.)

* —— (1930) 'Die Vollständigkeit der Axiome des logischen Funktionenkalküls', *Monatshefte für Mathematik und Physik* 37: 349–60; trans. 'The Completeness of the Axioms of the Functional Calculus of Logic', in *Collected Works*, vol. 1, *Publications 1929–1936*, ed. S. Feferman, J.W. Dawson Jr, S.C. Kleene, G.H. Moore, R.M. Solovay, and J. van Heijenoort, New York and Oxford: Oxford University Press, 1986, 102–23; and in J. van Heijenoort (ed.) *From Frege to Gödel: A Source Book in Mathematical Logic, 1879–1931*, Cambridge, MA: Harvard University Press, 1967, 582–91. (First published proof of the completeness of first-order logic, together with the compactness theorem.)

* —— (1931) 'Über formal unentscheidbare Sätze der *Principia Mathematica* und verwandter Systeme I', *Monatshefte für Mathematik und Physik* 38: 173–98; trans. 'On Formally Undecidable Propositions of *Principia Mathematica* and Related Systems', in *Collected Works*, vol. 1, *Publications 1929–1936*, ed. S. Feferman, J.W. Dawson Jr, S.C. Kleene, G.H. Moore, R.M. Solovay, and J. van Heijenoort, New York and Oxford: Oxford University Press, 1986, 126–95; and in J. van Heijenoort (ed.) *From Frege to Gödel: A Source Book in Mathematical Logic, 1879–1931*, Cambridge, MA: Harvard University Press, 1967, 592–617. (First proof of Gödel's incompleteness theorems.)

Grattan-Guinness, I. (1981) 'On the Development of Logics between the Two World Wars', *American Mathematical Monthly* 88: 495–509. (Overview of logic from 1920 to 1940.)

—— (1985) 'Russell's Logicism versus Oxbridge Logics, 1890–1925: A Contribution to the Real History', *Russell: The Journal of the Bertrand Russell Archives*, new series, 5: 101–31. (Traditional logic versus the symbolic logic of Peano and Russell.)

Heijenoort, J. van (ed.) (1967) *From Frege to Gödel: A Source Book in Mathematical Logic, 1879–1931*, Cambridge, MA: Harvard University Press. (Includes translations of many relevant articles.)

* Henkin, L. (1947) 'The Completeness of Formal Systems', unpublished doctoral dissertation, Princeton University. (First proof of the completeness theorem for uncountable languages.)

* Herbrand, J. (1930) 'Recherches sur la théorie de la démonstration', *Prace Towarzystwa Naukowego Warszawskiego*, Wydzial 3, no. 33; trans. 'Researches on Proof Theory', in J. van Heijenoort (ed.) *From Frege to Gödel: A Source Book in Mathematical Logic, 1879–1931*, Cambridge, MA: Harvard University Press, 1967, 525–81. (Herbrand's theorem.)

* Hilbert, D. (1899) *Grundlagen der Geometrie*, Leipzig: Teubner, 7th edn, 1930; 2nd edn trans. L. Unger and P. Bernays, *Foundations of Geometry*, La Salle, IL: Open Court, 1971. (Consistency and independence results in geometry; the modern axiomatic method.)

* —— (1905) 'Über die Grundlagen der Logik und der Arithmetik', in A. Krazer (ed.) *Verhandlungen des dritten internationalen Mathematiker-Kongresses in Heidelberg vom 8. bis 13. August 1904*, Leipzig: Teubner, 174–85; trans. 'On the Foundations of Logic and Arithmetic', in J. van Heijenoort (ed.) *From Frege to Gödel: A Source Book in Mathematical Logic, 1879–1931*, Cambridge, MA: Harvard University Press, 1967, 129–38. (Hilbert's first attempt to prove the consistency of arithmetic.)

* —— (1922) 'Neubegründung der Mathematik. Erste Mitteilung' (New Foundations of Mathematics. First Communication), *Abhandlungen aus dem mathematischen Seminar der Hamburgischen Universität* 1: 157–77; trans. 'The New Grounding of Mathematics', in W.B. Ewald (ed). *From Kant to Hilbert: A Source Book in the Foundation of Mathematics*, vol. 2, Oxford: Clarendon Press, 1996, 1115–34. (His first explicit use of 'metamathematics'.)

* —— (1923) 'Die logischen Grundlagen der Mathematik' (The Logical Foundations of Mathematics), *Mathematische Annalen* 88: 151–65; trans. 'The Logical Foundations of Mathematics', in W.B. Ewald (ed.) *From Kant to Hilbert: A Source Book in the Foundations of Mathematics*, vol. 2, Oxford: Clarendon Press, 1996, 1134–48. (His mature work on proof theory.)

* Hilbert, D. and Ackermann, W. (1928) *Grundzüge der theoretischen Logik*, Berlin: Springer, 2nd edn, 1938; trans. L.M. Hammond, G.G. Leckie and F. Steinhardt, *Principles of Mathematical Logic*, ed. R.E. Luce, New York: Chelsea, 1950. (First modern textbook in mathematical logic.)

* Lewis, C.I. (1918) *A Survey of Symbolic Logic*, Berkeley, CA: University of California Press; revised edn, New York: Dover, 1960. (A historical account of modern logic, together with an axiomatization of modal logic.)

* Löwenheim, L. (1915) 'Über Möglichkeiten im Relativkalkül', *Mathematische Annalen* 76: 447–70; trans. S. Bauer-Mengelberg, 'On Possibilities in the Calculus of Relatives', in J. van Heijenoort (ed.) *From Frege to Gödel: A Source Book in Mathematical Logic, 1879–1931*, Cambridge, MA: Harvard University Press, 1967, 232–51. (First important results on the semantics of first-order and infinitary logic.)

* Maltsev, A.I. (1936) 'Untersuchungen aus dem Gebiete der mathematischen Logik', *Matematicheskii Sbornik*, new series, 1: 323–36; trans. 'Investigations in the Area of Mathematical Logic', in B. Wells (ed.) *The Metamathematics of Algebraic Systems: Collected Papers, 1936–1967*, Amsterdam: North Holland, 1971. (First use of the compactness theorem for uncountable first-order languages.)

Moore, G.H. (1980) 'Beyond First-Order Logic: The Historical Interplay Between Mathematical Logic and Axiomatic Set Theory', *History and Philosophy of Logic* 1: 95–137. (The influence of logic on set theory, and vice versa.)

—— (1988) 'The Emergence of First-Order Logic', in W. Aspray and P. Kitcher (eds) *History and Philosophy of Modern Mathematics*, Minneapolis, MN: University of Minnesota Press, 95–135. (How first-order logic emerged from richer logics, including higher-order and infinitary logics.)

—— (1997) 'The Prehistory of Infinitary Logic: 1885–1955', in *Tenth International Congress of Logic, Methodology, and Philosophy of Science, Florence, August 1995*, vol. 2, M.L. dalla Chiara, K. Doets, D. Mundici and J. van Benthem (eds) *Structures and Norms in Science*, Dordrecht: Kluwer, 105–23. (The early history of infinitary logics from Peirce through Löwenheim and Skolem to Novikov and Bochvar.)

* Mostowski, A. (1957) 'On a Generalization of Quantifiers', *Fundamenta Mathematicae* 44: 12–36. (Introduces 'generalized' quantifiers as an extension of first-order logic.)

* Nagel, E. (1939) 'The Formation of Modern Conceptions of Formal Logic in the Development of Geometry', *Osiris* 7: 142–224; repr. in *Teleology Revisited and Other Essays in the Philosophy and History of Science*, New York: Columbia University Press, 1982, 195–259. (The influence of geometry on modern logic.)

* Padoa, A. (1901) 'Essai d'une théorie algébrique des nombres entiers, précédé d'une introduction logique à une théorie déductive quelconque', in *Premier Congrès International de Philosophie*, vol. 3, *Logique et Histoire des Sciences*, Paris: Armand Colin, 309–65; partial trans. in van Heijenoort (1967), 118–23. (Method for showing a term to be indefinable.)

* Passmore, J. (1968) *A Hundred Years of Philosophy*,

Baltimore, MD: Penguin. (A general history emphasizing logic, especially good on Oxbridge logicians.)

* Peano, G. (1888) *Calcolo geometrico*, Turin: Bocca. (Includes Peano's first contribution to logic, which was used in geometry.)

* —— (1889) *Arithmetices principia, nova methodo exposita*, Turin: Bocca; partial trans. 'The Principles of Arithmetic', in J. van Heijenoort (1967), 83–97. (Includes the Peano postulates for the natural numbers.)

* —— (1890) 'Démonstration de l'intégrabilité des équations différentielles ordinaires', *Mathematische Annalen* 37: 182–228. (First use of logical symbolism outside of arithmetic and geometry.)

* —— (1891) 'Principii di logica matematica', *Revista di matematica* 1: 1–10; trans. 'Principles of Mathematical Logic', in *Selected Works of Giuseppe Peano*, Toronto, Ont.: University of Toronto Press, 1973, 153–61. (Peano's first full logical system.)

* —— (1897) 'Logique mathématique', in *Formulaire de mathématiques*, Turin: Bocca, vol. 2, §1. (Peano's revised logical system.)

* Post, E.L. (1921) 'Introduction to a General Theory of Elementary Propositions', *American Journal of Mathematics* 43: 163–85; repr. in J. van Heijenoort (ed.) *From Frege to Gödel: A Source Book in Mathematics, 1879–1931*, Cambridge, MA: Harvard University Press, 1967, 264–83. (First published proof of the completeness of propositional logic; compare with Bernays (1918).)

* Russell, B.A.W. (1903) *The Principles of Mathematics*, Cambridge: Cambridge University Press; 2nd edn, London: Allen & Unwin, 1937; repr. London: Routledge, 1992. (First publication of Russell's paradox and his logicism.)

* —— (1906) 'The Theory of Implication', *American Journal of Mathematics* 28: 159–202. (His full development of propositional logic.)

* —— (1922) 'Introduction', in L.J.J. Wittgenstein, *Tractatus Logico-Philosophicus*, trans. C.K. Ogden and F.P. Ramsey, London: Routledge; trans. D.F. Pears and B.F. McGuinness, London: Routledge, 1961. (Russell's introduction of a hierarchy of metalanguages.)

* Scanlan, M. (1991) 'Who Were the American Postulate Theorists?', *Journal of Symbolic Logic* 56: 981–1,002. (Early American axiomatic theory.)

* Schröder, E. (1877) *Der Operationskreis des Logikkalküls*, Leipzig: Teubner. (Schröder's first logical system.)

* —— (1890) *Vorlesungen über die Algebra der Logik (Exakte Logik)* (Lectures on the Algebra of Logic (Exact Logic)), vol. 1, Leipzig: Teubner; repr. New York: Chelsea, 1966. (Summary of the Boolean tradition in logic.)

* —— (1898) 'On Pasigraphy: Its Present State and the Pasigraphic Movement in Italy', *The Monist* 9: 44–62. (Schröder's logicism.)

* Tarski, A. (1930) 'Über einige fundamentale Begriffe der Metamathematik', *Comptes rendus des séances de la Société des Sciences et des Lettres de Varsovie* 23: 22–29; trans. J.H. Woodger (1956), 'On Some Fundamental Concepts of Mathematics', in *Logic, Semantics, Metamathematics: Papers from 1923 to 1938*, ed. J. Corcoran, Indianapolis, IN: Hackett Publishing Company, 2nd edn, 1983. (Tarski's first venture into metalogic.)

* —— (1952) 'Some Notions and Methods on the Borderline of Algebra and Metamathematics', in *Proceedings of the International Congress of Mathematicians, Cambridge, Massachusetts*, Providence, RI: American Mathematical Society, vol. 1, 705–20. (Beginnings of modern model theory.)

—— (1956) *Logic, Semantics, Metamathematics: Papers from 1923 to 1938*, trans. and ed. J.H. Woodger, Oxford: Clarendon Press; repr. and ed. J. Corcoran, Indianapolis, IN: Hackett Publishing Company, 2nd edn, 1983. (Translations of his papers on logic.)

* Veblen, O. (1925) 'Remarks on the Foundations of Geometry', *Bulletin of the American Mathematical Society* 31: 121–41. (Veblen's plea for involving mathematicians with logic.)

* Whitehead, A.N. and Russell, B.A.W. (1910) *Principia Mathematica*, vol. 1, Cambridge: Cambridge University Press; 2nd edn, 1925; repr. London: Routledge, 1994. (Their full development of the theory of types.)

* Wiener, N. (1914) 'A Simplification of the Logic of Relations', *Proceedings of the Cambridge Philosophical Society* 17: 387–90. (Shows that ordered pairs, and hence relations, can be defined in the theory of types.)

GREGORY H. MOORE

LOGIC, INTENSIONAL
see INTENSIONAL LOGICS

LOGIC, INTUITIONISTIC AND ANTIREALISM
see INTUITIONISTIC LOGIC AND ANTIREALISM

LOGIC, LINEAR *see* LINEAR LOGIC

LOGIC MACHINES AND DIAGRAMS

By 'logical diagrams' we generally mean any two-dimensional representations of logical relationships, such as of class inclusion or consequence. One usually also means representations using non-typographical symbols or geometric figures. Such diagrams were first used in the seventeenth and eighteenth centuries, but gained wide currency only in the nineteenth; the best known are the Euler and Venn diagrams. It is an open question whether logical diagrams are useful only as elementary pedagogical devices, or have implications for advanced logical research.

The conception of an organism, the mind, or of the universe as 'machine' was not really attractive and useful until machines were widespread, complex and able to perform interesting tasks. This occurred first in the late Renaissance, and initiated ways of thinking that dominated the seventeenth and eighteenth centuries. It was also becoming evident that machines could be used to perform some complex, repetitive or difficult tasks more reliably or faster than human beings.

The very idea of machines that can perform 'symbolic' tasks, such as mathematical, logical or, eventually, linguistic ones required first a symbolism. For this reason, the idea of computers for mathematical or logical tasks, and systems of mathematical and logical notation, are strongly intertwined: one must have efficient ways of feeding information into a machine, and interpreting the results.

1   **Logical notation**
2   **Philosophies of logical notation**
3   **Euler and Venn diagrams**
4   **Frege's *Begriffsschrift***
5   **Peirce's existential graphs and conceptual graphs**
6   **Early logic machines and mechanical machines for Aristotelian logic**
7   **Electrical machines and the twentieth century**

1   Logical notation

Among the higher-level purposes for any symbolism in logic are: to abbreviate or simplify the writing or the display; to highlight strictly logical relationships without non-logical distractions (roughly Leibniz's *lingua philosophica* or his *characteristica universalis*); or to facilitate insights into the ways these representations may be manipulated, such as through inference

(roughly Leibniz's *calculus ratiocinator*, 'calculus of reason').

It is customary to divide notational devices between those that represent substantive (often called 'categorematic') terms and those that represent logical relations or properties (often called 'syncategorematic' terms). Symbols for categorematic terms can stand for determinate individual or abstract entities, such as '*c*' for Julius Caesar, '*a*' for the class of apples, '*A*' for the property of being an apple, or '*P*' for the sentence 'All apples are red'. Symbols may also stand for arbitrary, non-specific examples of such terms, such as in the example, 'Consider a class of objects, *c*, or a proposition, *P*'. These are usually called variables, schemata or place-holders.

Perhaps the earliest use of abbreviations for categorematic terms was by Aristotle, who occasionally used single letters to stand for non-specific categorical terms in his *Prior Analytics*. While many later Aristotelian logicians occasionally used letters to represent categorical terms, only in the late medieval and early modern period do we find any use of special symbols, other than Latin or other 'natural language' expressions, for syncategorematic (logical) notions. One of the first of these was Luis Vives' use in the first half of the sixteenth century of a V-shaped symbol to represent term inclusion:

$$
\begin{array}{llll}
(1) & A & (2) & A \\
& \text{v} & & \text{v} \\
& B & & B \\
& & & \text{v} \\
& & & C
\end{array}
$$

Diagram (1) represents that the term *A* is wholly included in *B*. ('All *A*'s are *B*'s.') Diagram (2) indicates that *A* is included in *B*, *B* is included in *C*, and, implicitly, *A* is (thus) included in *C*.

2   Philosophies of logical notation

The final goal of any logical notation is presumably to best allow one to carry out and communicate logical work. With Vives' and later notations, we begin to see four intermediate goals concerning how logical notation can achieve this final goal:

(1) The use of linear linguistic symbols, primarily deriving from natural language or other common usage (such as mathematics) and used mainly as abbreviations. Polish notation is an extreme example of this phenomenon, using, for example, '*Kpq*' for *p* & *q*. (We might also include here mnemonic aids: for example, 'K' for Konjunktion – alas, only for speakers of some languages.)

(2) The use of special symbols chosen mainly for their distinctness from natural language symbols.

(3) The use of special symbols or notations that are 'ideographic' (Styazhkin) or 'iconic' (Peirce): properties of the symbols themselves are intended to mirror attributes of the represented logical relationship.

(4) Two- (or higher) dimensional notational systems using elements of 1, 2, or 3; that is, diagrams.

Observe that (1) and (4) may clash: achieving (1) may aid writers, printers and proof-readers, while achieving (4) may aid readers of the notational system. Similarly, (1) obviously clashes with (2) and perhaps with (3), if the natural language symbols are not fortuitously iconic ('and' is a non-palindrome although conjunction is symmetric).

Leibniz was fascinated by ideographic notations (owing to a passing interest in Chinese pictograms), but it was C.S. Peirce who first seems to have consciously chosen and systematically discussed symbolisms according to their iconic characteristics. One of his points is that to represent a non-symmetric logical relationship, one should use a visually non-symmetric symbol. That is, since $A \supset B$ does not always have the same truth-conditions as $B \supset A$, then one should use an asymmetric symbol, such as $\supset$, $>$ or his own $\multimap<$. Such considerations have been at work implicitly in the choice of virtually all logical symbols for conjunction, disjunction and so on (except those chosen in line with (1), such as 'K' and '$\&$').

Various symbols that came into widespread use in algebra and calculus in the sixteenth, seventeenth and eighteenth centuries, such as '$=$' and '$+$', involved similar (implicit) considerations, and hark back to suggestions by Viète, Descartes and Leibniz. The 'algebra of logic', such as we see in works by Leibniz, Lambert and, especially, Boole, borrows symbols already in use from algebraic notation (and thus is a species of goal (1)), but capitalizes upon their original iconic character in mathematics – goal (3). Both Peirce and Schröder later gave up the use of symbols for logical constants that were simply borrowed from algebra, using considerations from both (2) and (3), while preserving the algebraic (substitutional) character of many operations. (See LOGIC IN THE 19TH CENTURY.)

While the use of parentheses as indicating priority or scope of operations is of long-standing mathematical use, many of the other symbols now in use derive from the work of Giuseppe Peano. (These were sometimes inspired by earlier works in the algebra of logic, and were later injected into the mainstream of logic by Russell, Whitehead and others.) These symbols were primarily chosen by Peano according to

consideration (2) – distinctiveness – and according to their suggestive, or etymological character: '$\in$' for the Greek 'esti'; '$\supset$', a backward 'C', for the converse of 'containment', and so on. He seems not to have considered the 'iconic' arguments of Leibniz and Peirce, and forcefully rejected the more original two-dimensional proposals of Frege.

3 Euler and Venn diagrams

The two most widely used styles of logical diagrams are usually referred to as 'Euler' and as 'Venn' diagrams. Both are primarily used to represent inclusion or subsumption of classes or terms in Aristotelian logic. There are two main distinctions between these diagrams. Euler's method involves placing circles of various sizes in various patterns; Venn's uses circles of uniform size in fixed positions, which are then modified by other markings. Euler's method does not have any unambiguous way of indicating the existence of individuals satisfying a certain description, other than implicitly by the spacing of the circles. Venn has such techniques.

Leonhard Euler developed his method in his *Lettres à une Princesse d'Allemagne sur divers sujets de physique et de philosophie* (Letters to a German Princess on Various Subjects of Physics and Philosophy) in 1761, published in 1772 (see LOGIC IN THE 17TH AND 18TH CENTURIES §5). The method was later adapted by Gergonne, Maimon and others, and was frequently given an intensional as well as the original extensional interpretation. The following diagrams exhibit the method:

Euler Diagrams

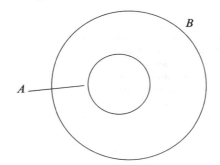

1. *A*-statement

Intensional reading: all the properties in concept *A* are included in the concept of *B*; all *A*'s are *B*'s. Extensional reading: all of the *A*-type things fall in the class of *B*-type things; all *A*'s are *B*'s.

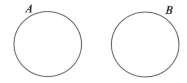

2.   *E*-statement

Intensional reading: concepts *A* and *B* share no properties. Extensional reading: no individual is both *A* and *B*.

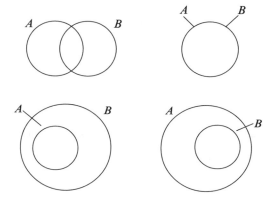

3.   *I*-statement

Intensional reading: concepts *A* and *B* share some properties. Extensional reading: there are individuals that are both *A* and *B*. (Alternatives classified by Gergonne.)

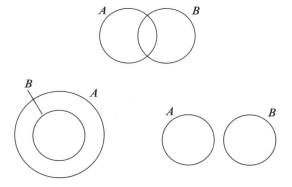

4.   *O*-statement

Intensional reading: there are properties in concept *A* that are not in concept *B*. Extensional reading: there are individuals that are *A* but not *B*. (Alternatives classified by Gergonne.)

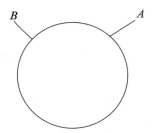

5.   Identity

Intensional reading: *A* and *B* share all their properties. Extensional reading: the individuals that are *A* are the same as those that are *B*.

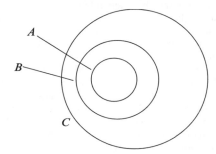

6.   'Barbara' syllogism

All *A*'s are *B*'s, all *B*'s are *C*'s, so all *A*'s are *C*'s, extensionally interpreted.

Observe that the intensional and extensional reading of the *A*-statement are 'reversed': to say that all apples are fruit is to say that all components of the concept of fruit (come from a plant, contain a seed, are edible, and so on) are included in the more numerous components of the concept of 'apple'. Observe also that there is an overlap in the alternative diagrams of the *O*- and *A*-statements (made explicit by Gergonne). Such an observation led to William Hamilton's (and George Bentham's) notorious doctrine of the 'quantification of the predicate', although similar ideas were common in the eighteenth and nineteenth centuries: we should distinguish between 'All *A*'s are some *B*'s' (1, 3, and 4) and 'All *A*'s are all *B*'s' (5).

The method of using movable, usually intensionally interpreted, circles was first suggested in published works by J.C. Sturm in 1661, and in unpublished writings of Leibniz. Contemporaneous with Euler, J.H. Lambert (1764) developed a method of using overlapping lines, also extensionally interpreted:

1.   *A*: __*B*: _____

2. *A*:__*B*: __

3. *A*:__*B*: __ or ⎺ or ⎺ or ⎯⎯
                        __   ⎯⎯   ⎯

4. *A*:__*B*: __ or ⎯⎯ or ⎺
                        __   ⎯

5. *A*:___*B*:___

6. *A*:____*B*: ___*C*: __

This method had also been anticipated by Leibniz in unpublished notes. In fact, the uses of circles or lines iconically to represent logical relationships reappears so often, and apparently independently, in the history of logic since the seventeenth century that one can count the idea – like that of an 'algebra' of logic – as more or less obvious to anyone who thought much about logic.

Venn diagrams are usually credited to John Venn in an article of 1880, and then more extensively developed in his *Symbolic Logic* (1881). This method was anticipated by similarly extensional diagrams of the German logician Moritz Drobisch in his 1838 *Neue Darstellung der Logik* (New Conception of Logic) (see LOGIC IN THE 19TH CENTURY §2). After a decline in usage in the early twentieth century, Venn diagrams have reappeared in many introductory logic texts of the second half of the twentieth century.

Venn Diagrams
Statements are interpreted extensionally: points in an area indicate individuals having certain properties. What properties individuals have (or what classes they belong to) is indicated by inclusion in a circle: if they lack a property, they fall outside of that circle. The non-existence of individuals with a certain description is indicated by shading the corresponding area. The existence of an individual with certain properties (or lacking certain properties) is shown by an 'x' if it is fully determinate what properties it has, or by a line across two or more areas if it is not determinate.

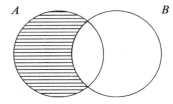

All *A*'s are *B*'s.

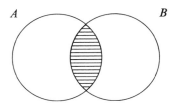

No *A*'s are *B*'s.

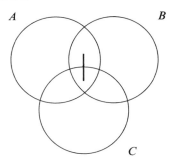

Some *A*'s are *B*'s: maybe they are *C*'s, maybe not.

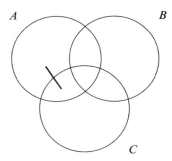

Some *A*'s are not *B*'s.

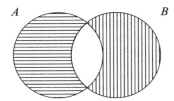

All *A*'s are *B*'s, and all *B*'s are *A*'s.

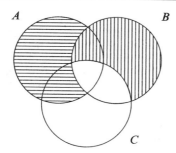

All *A*'s are *B*'s.
All *B*'s are *C*'s.
So, all *A*'s are *C*'s.

The details of this interpretation are suggested by Drobisch and Venn, but carefully stated by Schröder in his *Vorlesungen* (1890–1905). Other diagrammatic methods in the nineteenth century included a system of triangles used by William Hamilton, and the use of matrices or tables by Allan Marquand and Lewis Carroll. Still other methods in the twentieth century include Veitch diagrams (see Veitch 1952) and Karnaugh maps. All of these methods, with the exceptions of the methods of Peirce and Frege, are versatile enough only for Aristotelian (monadic predicate) or propositional logic, and not for full first-order predicate logic.

4 Frege's *Begriffsschrift*

Gottlob Frege's notation, the famous '*Begriffsschrift*' ('conceptual notation'; see FREGE, G.), is partly diagrammatic. He draws the material conditional in a two-dimensional way, writing $P \supset Q$ as follows.

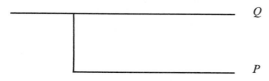

The only specifically two-dimensional feature seems to be intended to highlight a feature of *modus ponens*, the main rule of inference using the material conditional – namely, the condition (antecedent) 'drops away'. The use of the negation line and the descending vertical line (negation stroke) in the material conditional was clearly intended to suggest the interpretation of the material conditional $P \supset Q$ as $-P \lor Q$. Frege stubbornly stuck to his own notational system throughout his life, in spite of the difficulty it presented for typographers, criticism from Peano (and Schröder), its non-iconic and ahistorical character, and the fact that even admirers such as Russell and, later, Wittgenstein and Hilbert, never

adopted it. Nevertheless, something of what motivated Frege, namely a concern for displaying features of *inferences* in a two-dimensional way, rather than the logical content or 'sense' of individual sentences, leads one to helpful formats for displaying mathematical or logical demonstrations ('proofs'), such as the later 'natural deduction' methods of Gerhard Gentzen. (See NATURAL DEDUCTION, TABLEAU AND SEQUENT SYSTEMS §1.)

5 Peirce's existential graphs and conceptual graphs

There is little suggestion in any of these proposals that diagrams have any point much beyond a heuristic value, being 'suggestive', and helping to learn logic at the introductory level. No one seems to have proposed that diagrams have a serious, advanced use for professional logicians, or represent more accurately an underlying metaphysical reality. A notable exception is Charles S. Peirce's 'existential graphs' (see PEIRCE, C.S. §8). Peirce, a historian of logic and a careful reader of his contemporaries, knew about the diagrammatic methods of Euler, Lambert and Venn. In the 1890s he developed three sophisticated systems of logical diagrams that he called the alpha, beta and gamma existential graphs. (His choice of 'graph' for these diagrams is somewhat unfortunate, since they are not graphs in the technical sense first used by J.J. Sylvester in 1878, now in wide use, and which Peirce would have known.) Both graph theory and Peirce's graphs were inspired, interestingly, by chemical diagrams. Furthermore, other chemical metaphors occur in both the works of Frege ('saturated') and Peirce. Alpha graphs are similar to Venn diagrams, and can be used for either categorical logic or for what we would call propositional logic. Beta graphs can be used to represent any quantified relational sentence or set of sentences, and are thus a fully general method for diagramming sentences in first-order predicate logic – the first such method in the history of logic. Gamma graphs are used for the representation of modal statements. All three graph systems are 'iconic' in a sense of which Peirce was explicitly aware; he was also interested in enhancing their calculational usefulness for producing new inferences ('forward inference'), or for identifying the correctness of given conclusions from given premises ('backward inference').

Furthermore, the graphs are not just employed for their usefulness in some narrow sense, but grew out of views he had developed much earlier: his 'philosophy of notation' of 1885. This was the first statement of what became a large, developed theory of signs (his semiotics) and a philosophy of mind – of thoughts themselves, at least in all a priori disciplines, being 'diagrammatic'. (Peirce's views are reminiscent of the better-known 'picture theory' of Wittgenstein's *Tractatus*.) Peirce believed that our visual notations should match or facilitate, as much as possible, the best possible mental diagrams, and this means that the notational system should exhibit useful logical relationships. In earlier, algebraic-style writings, this was developed within a standard linear sequence of symbols; in later writings, he seems to have believed that two-dimensional representations were required for the properly 'iconic' display of some logical relationships, especially once relations are introduced.

Peirce's ideas about existential graphs were not much noticed until the 1960s, and have not had a noticeable impact, except as a curiosity, until the 1980s. In computer science and artificial intelligence, Peirce's ideas have been put forward as 'conceptual graphs' (by John Sowa 1991) and have found a wider audience. This is in part because there had existed in artificial intelligence a prior interest in using 'semantic networks' for representations of the meaning of natural language sentences. In cognitive science and learning theory, there is also a resurgence of interest in optimizing the display of information to native human cognitive processes, and thus of presenting complex relational information through visual images.

6 Early logic machines and mechanical machines for Aristotelian logic

Interestingly, the very first speculations about or design of machines that performed conceptual tasks – one hesitates to call them exactly 'logic' – were inspired not by arithmetic calculators, but by a strange mixture of medieval magic and theology. This was the fantastic *Ars Magna* ('Great Art' or 'Technique') of the Spanish (Majorcan) mystic and tinkerer RAMON LLULL (§2). Llull was interested in the way the various concepts (God, evil, . . .) could be combined. To this end, he designed various notations, as well as 'machines' that used labelled, movable, concentric wheels to show these combinations. Although his views were respected by a variety of later thinkers such as Bruno and Swift, his greatest impact was on the development of the combinatoric theory by Pascal and Leibniz in the late seventeenth century.

Not surprisingly, the thought occurred to Pascal, Leibniz and others of using the combinatoric wheels of Llull, but labelling them with numerals, and gearing them so that they could do various arithmetic calculations. There are thus two conceptual steps that were necessary to produce the idea of logic machines. First, one must be able to think of machines as being able to perform calculations – to compute. (This in turn requires a notation and machines of some complexity and accuracy, that is, many finely machined parts.) Second, one must be able to think of reasoning and inference as a type of 'mechanical' calculation: this was the contribution of Llull, refined by Pascal and Leibniz, and explicitly stated by Leibniz as the *calculus ratiocinator*.

Both Pascal and Leibniz designed and had constructed for them geared arithmetic calculators. Leibniz also proposed, perhaps for the first time, the idea of a logic machine, and left some suggestions about how this might be done – but never developed precise designs nor constructed an actual machine.

The first reasonably successful logic machine was probably the eighteenth-century 'Demonstrator' of Charles Stanhope. It used a notation system that anticipated William Hamilton's variant of Aristotelian logic, and could also perform elementary arithmetic and probabilistic calculations. The Demonstrator was constructed from a block into which two moving slides were inserted, one of grey wood and the other of red glass; the positions of these slides served as the input premises and the extent of their overlap, visible in a small square in the block, represented the strongest possible conclusion validly derivable from these premises. That is, the Demonstrator was a 'forward inference' machine that actually generated a conclusion, rather than determining the validity or invalidity of a given conclusion with given premises. The use of the Demonstrator for deductive logic was limited to categorical logic with two premises.

The high-water mark of mechanical logic machines was reached by William Stanley Jevons' machine, usually called the 'Logical Piano', from the appearance of its keyboard. While restricted to categorical logic, this 1870 machine represented a vast improvement over Stanhope's Demonstrator, both logically and mechanically. Consisting of a keyboard for inputting premises and, above it, connected by pulleys and levers, a display of terms, the Jevons machine could accommodate up to four terms, and thus arguments with more than two premises ('sorites'), with designs for machines with up to ten terms. It could also handle 'or' terms in either subject or predicate terms (understood inclusively), such as 'All fruit are apples or oranges'. It used a Boolean equational system, and thus could also be considered the first algebra machine, since it essentially solved systems of equations. Like the Demonstrator, one did not input a conclusion to determine its validity given a set of input premises, but instead the machine output all valid conclusions with the input premises in the logical system.

7 Electrical machines and the twentieth century

A slight improvement in Jevons' design was made by Allan Marquand, who had been a logic student of Peirce and later became a professor of art history at Princeton. He called his a 'New Logical Machine' (1885). It was not logically more sophisticated than Jevons' machine, but had a better display, consisting of a grid of rotary indicators, looking something like a water or gas meter. Marquand also sketched designs for the first electrical logic machine, using relays and switches. (The very first electrical circuit diagram to be used for logic or interpreted logically was proposed in a letter from Peirce to Marquand.) Nothing really came of these proposals, and they, like Babbage's ideas for a general-purpose symbolic manipulator, were historical curiosities that had no discernible influence on electrical and electronic computers of the mid- and late twentieth century.

While there were a number of authors who developed mechanical logic machines in the late nineteenth and early twentieth centuries, mostly in imitation of Jevons' device, the collapse of the Aristotelian approach to logic made most of these techniques obsolete. Indeed, the logic of Frege, Russell and Whitehead, which permits quantifiers and relations, and which we know as predicate logic, makes the very idea of logic machines a daunting task. Expressions no longer consist of certain restricted combinations of terms. Furthermore, as Church's theorem was later to suggest, it may be that certain logical tasks in this framework are mechanically impossible. Similarly, the idea of allowing a machine to reason whatever it can from given premises – forward inference, imitative of human reasoning – becomes extremely problematic. Designs for electrical logic machines appeared again shortly after the Second World War, first with work by two students of W.V. Quine, William Burkhart and Theodore Kalin in 1947, a number of machines in the late 1940s and early 1950s, and culminating in the 'Logic Theory Machine' of Allen Newell and Herbert Simon in 1956. (During the Second World War, Claude Shannon had developed his influential logical interpretation of electrical circuitry, thus rediscovering the observations of Peirce and Marquand.) Significantly, all these machines were restricted to propositional logic, and thus also fell far short of the expressivity and complexity of quantificational logic. Logic machines and computer programs in the twentieth century have been largely focused on 'backward' inference: confirming that a given conclusion does, or does not, validly follow from a given set of premises.

The history of logic machines grew distinct, after the early days of Leibniz and Pascal, from the history of machines to perform arithmetic calculations. There were enormous economic pressures to develop numerical calculators (for accounting and also for navigational tables), and few incentives to develop machines that reasoned using logic. Another line of development that was initially distinct from that of logic machines was the development of general purpose, programmable computers. Most early calculating and logic machines of all sorts were one-purpose and 'hard-wired'. Charles Babbage is the originator of the conception of a general-purpose 'computer', but the approach was rediscovered in the twentieth century, and intensively developed in mechanical, electrical and electronic implementations during and after the Second World War. In this approach, we build a 'computer' so that it can be 'programmed' to perform any task of symbolic manipulation that is capable of algorithmic description. Although the idea of such a general-purpose symbol-manipulator is an old one, going back to Babbage in the early nineteenth century, no one seems to have thought of programming such machines to perform logical tasks until Turing, nor succeeded until the Logic Theory Machine. Today, virtually all computational projects in logic are performed on general-purpose computers, and thus in an important sense the idea of dedicated 'logic machines' is obsolete. It is the software (programming), not the hardware, that is designed to perform logical tasks. Starting in the 1960s and accelerating rapidly in the 1970s and 1980s, a large amount of computer software (including 'mechanical theorem provers') now exists that performs a variety of logical tasks in various logical systems, including first- and second-order predicate logic, 'deviant' logics and modal logics.

See also: COMPUTABILITY AND INFORMATION; COMPUTABILITY THEORY; LOGICAL AND MATHEMATICAL TERMS, GLOSSARY OF

References and further reading

Cajori, F. (1952) *A History of Mathematical Notations*, La Salle, IL: Open Court; repr. New York: Dover, 1993. (A classic book – and the only one – on a monumentally important topic in intellectual history; nevertheless dated and much in need of a treatment using recent historical, logical and cognitive-science research.)

Eames, C. and Eames, R. (1990) *A Computer Perspective: Background to the Computer Age*, ed. G. Fleck, Cambridge, MA: Harvard University Press, new edn. (A pictorial and well-researched history of computers that includes pictures, diagrams and facsimiles of Stanhope's, Jevons' and

Marquand's logic machines, Peirce's circuit diagrams, and some post-Second World War work.)

Gardner, M. (1982) *Logic Machines and Diagrams*, Chicago, IL: University of Chicago Press, 2nd edn. (A classic discussion of the topic, and the only monograph, but somewhat elementary and superficial.)

Goldstine, H. (1972) *The Computer from Pascal to von Neumann*, Princeton, NJ: Princeton University Press, 1993. (The history of arithmetic and general-purpose computers, including some 'logic' machines.)

Kneale, W. and Kneale, M. (1962) *The Development of Logic*, Oxford: Clarendon Press, 1984. (Standard but now dated work in the history of logic, with some brief discussions of notations and diagrams, and mention of some logic machines.)

* Lambert, J.H. (1764) *Neues Organon oder Gedanken über die Erforschung und Bezeichnung des Wahren und dessen Unterscheidung vom Irrthum und Schein* (New Organon or Thoughts on the Investigation and Designation of the True and its Distinction from Error and Appearance), Leipzig, vol. 1, part 1, 109–33; repr. in *Philosophische Schriften*, vols 1–2, ed. H.W. Arndt, Hildesheim: Olms, 1965. (Introduces the diagrams sometimes known as 'Lambert lines'; also referred to in later works by Venn and John Neville Keynes in the nineteenth century.)

Peano, G. (1973) *Selected Works of Giuseppe Peano*, trans. and ed. H. Kennedy, Toronto, Ont.: University of Toronto Press. (A small collection of Peano's huge output, this includes some of his important writings on logical and mathematical notations, and his visionary proposals for a new universal language, 'Latin without inflections'.)

Peirce, C.S. (1931–58) *Collected Papers*, ed. C. Hartshorne, P. Weiss and A.W. Burks, Cambridge, MA: Harvard University Press, 8 vols; and *Writings of Charles S. Peirce: A Chronological Edition*, ed. M. Fisch *et al.*, Bloomington, IN: Indiana University Press, 1982–. (Important logical papers of 1867–86 appear in volume 3 of the *Collected Papers*; other volumes include some writings on the existential graphs and iconicity.)

Roberts, D.D. (1973) *The Existential Graphs of Charles S. Peirce*, The Hague: Mouton. (The only book-length work in English on Peirce's existential graphs; more accessible than Peirce's own works.)

* Schröder, E. (1890–1905) *Vorlesungen über die Algebra der Logik*, Leipzig: Teubner, 3 vols; repr. New York: Chelsea, 1966. (The monumental *locus classicus* of the algebra of logic, including relations; extensive discussions of diagrams, various notations, and philosophical aspects of them.)

Shin, S.J. (1990) *The Logical Status of Diagrams*, Cambridge: Cambridge University Press. (Situation theory is used to provide a precise analysis of reasoning with Venn diagrams.)

* Sowa, J. (ed.) (1991) *Principles of Semantic Networks*, San Mateo, CA: Morgan Kaufmann. (Discussions of various network and graph formalisms in cognitive science, including the Peirce-inspired conceptual graphs.)

Styazhkin, N.I. (1964) *History of Mathematical Logic from Leibniz to Peano*, Cambridge, MA, and London: MIT Press, 1969. (Often more useful discussions of diagrams than Kneale and Kneale (1962), including Lambert lines.)

* Veitch, E.W. (1952) 'A Chart Method for Simplifying Truth Functions', *Proceedings of the Association for Computing Machinery* 1952: 127–33. (An exposition of what have come to be known as 'Veitch diagrams'.)

* Venn, J. (1881) *Symbolic Logic*, London: Macmillan, 2nd edn, 1894; repr. New York: Chelsea, 1979. (By the time it appeared, this work was unoriginal, but introduced in textbook fashion the now-popular Venn diagrams.)

RANDALL R. DIPERT

LOGIC, MANY-VALUED

see MANY-VALUED LOGICS, PHILOSOPHICAL ISSUES IN

LOGIC, MEDIEVAL

Medieval logic is crucial to the understanding of medieval philosophy, for every educated person was trained in logic, as well as in grammar, and these disciplines provided techniques of analysis and a technical vocabulary that permeate philosophical, scientific and theological writing. At the practical level, logic provided the training necessary for participation in the disputations that were a central feature of medieval instruction, and whose structure – with arguments for and against a thesis, followed by a resolution – is reflected in many written works. At the theoretical level, logic, like other subjects, involved the study of written texts through lectures and written commentaries. The core of the logic curriculum from the twelfth century onwards was provided by the logical works of Aristotle. These provided the material for the study of types of predication, the analysis of simple propositions and their relations of inference and equivalence, the analysis of modal propositions, categorical and modal syllogisms, fallacies, dialectical Topics, and scientific reasoning as captured in the demonstrative syllogism. Comprehensive as this list might seem, medieval logicians realized that other logical subjects needed to be investigated, and, again from the twelfth century onward, new techniques and new genres of writing appeared. The main new technique involved the use of 'sophismata', or puzzling cases intended to draw attention to weaknesses and difficulties in logical definitions and rules. The new genres of writing especially included works on 'supposition theory', which concerned the types of reference that the subjects and predicates of propositions have in different contexts, and works on 'syncategoremata', which concerned the effect on sense and reference produced by the presence and placing of such logical terms as 'all', 'some', 'not', 'if... then', 'except', and so on. Other important topics for investigation include 'insolubles', or semantic paradoxes, and 'consequences', or valid inference forms. These new developments were seen as providing a supplement to Aristotelian logic, rather than an alternative. The only context in which people occasionally suggested that Aristotelian logic was inapplicable was that of Trinitarian theology, and the only logician who deliberately set out to reform logic as a whole was Ramon Llull.

The study of medieval logic involves two kinds of difficulty. In the first place, few texts are available in translation, and indeed, many are not even available in printed form. In the second place, there is a problem of interpretation. For a very long time, the specifically medieval contributions to logic were ignored or despised, and when people began to take them more seriously, there was a strong tendency to look at them through the spectacles of modern formal logic. More recently, scholars have come to realize that medieval interests cannot be mapped precisely onto modern interests, and that any attempt, for example, to make a sharp distinction between propositional and quantificational logic is misleading. The first task of the modern reader is to try to understand what the medieval logician was really concerned with.

1 Background

The story of medieval logic is the story of logic in western Europe after the split of the Roman Empire into the Latin-speaking, Catholic west and the Greek-speaking, Orthodox east (see BYZANTINE PHILOSOPHY §3). Because this split was followed by barbarian invasions and constant upheaval, very little happened between 550 and 1000, and learning was mainly kept alive in Benedictine monasteries. However, it is important to consider the Latin texts that were transmitted, for they formed part of the basis for later developments. One very important early source is the *Peri Hermeneias* by Apuleius of Madaura which dates from the second century AD. It discusses the proposition and the categorical syllogism, and it was influential until the late twelfth century. It was the main source for Martianus Capella (early fifth century), author of *De nuptiis Philologiae et Mercurii* (The Marriage of Philology and Mercury), Cassiodorus (sixth century), author of *Institutiones*, and Isidore of Seville (seventh century), author of *Etymologies*, all of whose encyclopedic works include sections on logic (see ENCYCLOPEDISTS, MEDIEVAL §§4, 6, 7). Other early works include Marius Victorinus on definitions and a work attributed to Augustine, the *Categoriae decem* (The Ten Categories), which is from the fourth-century circle of Themistius and was the most intensely studied logical work in the ninth and tenth centuries.

Most important of all are the works of Boethius. He seems to have been responsible for translating all of Aristotle's Organon (that is, his six works on logic) into Latin, and all but the *Posterior Analytics* survive. He also translated Porphyry's *Isagoge* (Introduction), and wrote commentaries on some of Aristotle's logic, on Porphyry and on the *Topics* of Cicero. In addition he composed monographs of his own on Division, on Topics, on categorical syllogisms and on hypothetical syllogisms, that is, on conditional propositions and arguments built up from them (see BOETHIUS, A.M.S. §§2–3). At first, little attention was paid to this body of writing, but signs of revival first appear at Charlemagne's court, for which Alcuin (d.804) wrote a little work on dialectic (see CAROLINGIAN RENAISSANCE §2). The first outstanding figure is GERBERT OF AURILLAC, who taught in the cathedral school at Reims from about 972 before becoming a bishop and finally Pope. He taught the *Logica vetus* (Old Logic) (that is, Porphyry's *Isagoge*, Aristotle's *Categories* and *On Interpretation*), Cicero's *Topics* and a good deal of Boethius.

As western Europe became more settled, so educational institutions began to flourish. Better monastic schools (for example, Bec, where Anselm taught) and cathedral schools (see CHARTRES, SCHOOL OF) developed, and in the twelfth century, especially in Paris, schools grew up around individual masters such as Abelard and Adam of Balsham [Parvipontanus]. The monographs and commentaries of Boethius had been largely recovered by the beginning of the eleventh century and, with the *Logica vetus*, became the focus of attention. The *Liber sex principiorum* (Book of Six Principles) (that is, the last six categories, about which Aristotle had had less to say), attributed to Gilbert of Poitiers, became part of the *Logica vetus*. At the same time the philosophical study of grammar became important, with a focus on the *Institutiones grammaticae* (Institutions of Grammar) of Priscian (see LANGUAGE, MEDIEVAL THEORIES OF §1). Anselm's important discussion of the reference of the word '*grammaticus*' ('expert in grammar' or 'literate') shows an attempt to harmonize Aristotle's and Priscian's doctrines (see ANSELM §5). By far the most outstanding figure, and the first really original logician, was Peter ABELARD (§§2, 4). Unfortunately, his own turbulent life and the important events of the later twelfth century combined to diminish any influence his logical work may have had.

2 After 1150: a general survey

Logic after 1150 is shaped by four interrelated developments: the recovery of the rest of Aristotle's logical works, along with other texts; the foundation of universities and the *studia* of the new religious orders; the development of 'sophismata', a new technique for handling logical problems; and the development of new areas of logic.

New translations. Aristotle's *Topics* and *Sophistical Refutations* were known by the 1130s and the entire *Logica nova*, including the *Prior* and *Posterior Analytics*, was known by 1159 when John of Salisbury referred to them in his *Metalogicon*. All circulated in translations by Boethius, with the exception of the *Posterior Analytics*, which was translated by James of Venice in the twelfth century. Both the *Topics* (see Alexander NECKHAM) and the *Sophistical Refutations* were used in the twelfth century, but most especially the latter, and the *Prior Analytics* gradually displaced Boethius' works on the categorical syllogism. The *Posterior Analytics* was absorbed more slowly. The first known complete commentary is that by GROSSETESTE (§1), dating from the early 1220s.

In the second half of the twelfth century Arabic logic began to appear. The first part of Avicenna's *Logic* (see IBN SINA §1), dealing with the *Isagoge*, was translated by Gundissalinus, as was Farabi's *Catalogue of Sciences*, whose second chapter dealt with

logic. The *Logic* of Ghazali was also translated. In the 1230s the logic commentaries of Averroes on the *Categories*, *On Interpretation* and the *Prior* and *Posterior Analytics* were translated, though they were less successful than the Arab works translated earlier. Some Greek commentators were also translated. Themistius' *Paraphrase of the Posterior Analytics* and some extracts from Philoponus on the *Posterior Analytics* became known in the late twelfth century. Much later William of Moerbeke translated Simplicius on the *Categories* (1266) and Ammonius on *On Interpretation* (1268). The frequently cited but now lost commentary by 'Alexander' on *Sophistical Refutations* was probably the translation of a work by Michael of Ephesus (*c*.1130). Other Greek works on logic were not translated until the Renaissance. The important thing about all these texts is not just their content but the fact that they provide a full curriculum for an organized institution. (See ARISTOTELIANISM, MEDIEVAL §3 for the twelfth-century reception of translations.)

New institutions. By the beginning of the thirteenth century the Universities of Oxford, Paris and Bologna were taking shape as organized institutions. Gradually other universities were founded, along with the *studia* of the new teaching orders, especially the Dominicans (at whose Cologne *studium* Albert the Great taught) and the Franciscans (at whose London *studium* Ockham taught), and all these institutions offered a training in the liberal arts (see ENCYCLOPEDISTS, MEDIEVAL §1). Two things should be noted. First, a degree from the arts faculty was required for all advanced (graduate) study in theology, medicine and law (though especially in Italy, medicine and law, unlike theology, could be pursued at the undergraduate level). Second, logic formed a very large part of the arts curriculum, especially during the first two years. One reason for its importance was the large place given to disputation at all levels of university teaching: logic clearly offers training in the techniques of debate, and inculcates quickness in analysing and responding to arguments. However, university teaching also involved the close study of texts, especially the texts of Aristotle, and many commentaries, as well as original textbooks, were written by medieval logicians. (See NATURAL PHILOSOPHY, MEDIEVAL §5 for teaching practices.)

Sophismata: a new technique. Medieval logic is characterized by a new technique, the analysis and solution of sophismata. The word 'sophisma' covers two phenomena. First, there is the sophisma sentence itself, which is a logical puzzle intended to introduce or illustrate a difficulty, a concept, or a general problem. The origin of these sentences seems to lie in the twelfth-century use of '*instantiae*', or counter-examples. Second, there is the technique of the sophismatic disputation, which is used to show that the very same reasoning which supported a plausible thesis could also be used to establish something implausible. By the end of the twelfth century the sophisma was established in different genres of logical and grammatical writing. These genres included treatises on syncategoremata, that is, those words which perform a function in a sentence by negating, conjoining, disjoining and so on (see §8), and treatises on sophismata themselves. The relationship between these treatises was very close. Typically, a treatise on syncategoremata would start with a syncategorematic term and then appeal to sophismata to illustrate the difficulties its use might cause. A treatise on sophismata would start with a sophisma and, using disputational techniques, appeal to facts about a syncategorematic term or to logical distinctions to solve it, or to show that different truth-values were possible according to different senses of the sophisma sentence. Various types of sophismata and treatises on sophismata survive. It seems that in Paris the sophisma was an element of teaching, and had to be debated in the schools, that is, within a fairly formal setting. Very elaborate sophismata survive from the latter part of the thirteenth century which were given solutions by the teaching masters, for example, BOETHIUS OF DACIA, and which were often used as a vehicle for the straightforward discussion of interesting logical problems. On the face of it, Oxford sophismata seem to have been quite different. They were the subject of live debate, but this debate was at a strictly undergraduate level, and was part of the practical training in logical disputation. They were not primarily a vehicle for discussing doctrine, and they seem to disappear as a genre when the curriculum changes. Fourteenth-century Oxford sophismata had two special features. First, they exhibit a new emphasis on the 'casus', or initial hypothesis about the context of the sophisma-sentence, which might itself be identified as the source of the problems in determining the truth-value of that sentence. This notion of casus played a key role in treatises on insolubles (see §10) and obligations (see §11), which are both closely linked to sophismata. Second, many of them are about natural philosophy, and introduce mathematical considerations and calculatory techniques (see OXFORD CALCULATORS §§2, 4).

Among the surviving fourteenth-century treatises on sophismata are important works by Richard KILVINGTON, William HEYTESBURY, John Buridan and Albert of Saxony. In the fifteenth century, PAUL OF VENICE wrote on sophismata, as well as using them extensively in other works. Both the technique

and the genre of writing disappeared early in the sixteenth century.

3 After 1150: new logical writings

While the writings of Aristotle were central to the logic curriculum, there were matters that he did not discuss, which left room for a considerable number of new developments. The most prominent is the so-called 'logica moderna' or 'modernorum' (a label coined by twentieth-century authors). Also known as 'terminist logic', this includes supposition theory and its ramifications (see §7). Treatises on supposition theory deal with the reference of subject and predicate terms in propositions, and they have as a corollary the treatises on syncategoremata, which deal with all the other terms in propositions. The material dealt with in treatises on syncategoremata was also dealt with in treatises on sophismata (see §2 above), but in the fourteenth century much of it also appeared in treatises on the 'proofs of terms' (see §8). Three more important developments are found in treatises on consequences (see §9), insolubles (see §10) and obligations (see §11).

While supposition theory constitutes the most important new development, it was not always privileged. Paris in the second half of the thirteenth century, and Bologna and Erfurt at the beginning of the fourteenth century, were centres of 'modist logic', and tended not to use supposition theory. Modist logicians (for example, PETER OF AUVERGNE) were more interested in the sense than the reference of terms, and they made much use of the relationships between the modi essendi (modes of being) of things, the modi intelligendi (modes of understanding) and the modi significandi (modes of signifying) of words. They were also characterized by their lengthy discussions of the rational nature of logic and its relation to second intentions (see §4). Another rival to supposition theory as a tool of analysis was provided by 'proofs of terms', which were particularly important in the later fourteenth century.

Another new form of writing was the comprehensive textbook. At least six survive from the thirteenth century, including those by William of Sherwood, Peter of Spain and Roger Bacon. In the fourteenth century we find those by William Ockham, John Buridan and Albert of Saxony. Some universities, especially Oxford and Cambridge, preferred to use loose collections of brief treatises on various topics, and a good example of such a collection is the Logica parva of Paul of Venice.

There are three things to note about these new writings. First, they were not officially part of the curriculum at most universities, but that did not prevent their being used. Second, because Latin was the common language of instruction in western Europe, a text written in one place could be used anywhere else. Peter of Spain's text was generally the most popular, but Buridan was particularly important in Poland, and in late fourteenth- and fifteenth-century Italy short texts from England were heavily used. Third, there is no genuine division between the authors of Aristotle commentaries and the authors of the new texts. To take just one example, John Buridan wrote a comprehensive textbook, commentaries on parts of Aristotle's Organon, and separate treatises on consequences and sophismata, the last containing a noteworthy treatment of insolubles.

4 The nature of logic

The purpose of logic had nothing to do with the setting up of formal systems or the metalogical analysis of formal structures. Instead, it had a straightforwardly cognitive orientation. Everyone accepted the view that logic is about discriminating the true from the false by means of argument. This is why logic was essential to the speculative sciences, since it provided the instruments for finding truth and for proceeding from the known to the unknown.

The first problem with logic was what to call it. The name 'dialectica' was most prevalent until the thirteenth century, when 'logica' gained the upper hand. Both words have various associations. 'Dialectica' in the broad sense just is logic, but the word also has three narrower senses: dialectic as the art of debate; dialectic as the art of finding material for arguments; and dialectic as a kind of reasoning which falls between demonstrative and sophistical reasoning. The first sense was appealed to by Roger Bacon when he said that logic as an art has to do with disputation. The second sense is associated with the discussion of Topics, the headings under which the material for arguments can be sorted. Because the study of Topics also included maxims, or self-evidently true generalizations, which could provide the warrant for different types of argument, there is a close link between Topics and argumentation. Hence, the third and most usual sense of dialectica had to do with topical or dialectical syllogisms as a part of logic. Medieval logicians treated Aristotle's distinction between dialectical and demonstrative syllogisms as an epistemological one concerning the status of their premises, so that dialectical syllogisms had the same formally valid structure as demonstrative syllogisms.

The problems associated with the word 'logica' have to do with whether logic is a linguistic or a rational pursuit. Isidore of Seville noted that 'logica' comes from the Greek word 'logos' which can mean 'sermo' (word) or 'ratio' (reason). As a result logic could be called either a scientia sermocinalis (linguistic science) or a scientia rationalis (rational science). There were considerations supporting both titles. On the one hand, the Stoics had divided philosophy into natural, moral and rational, and the last was equated with logic which could then, as Boethius pointed out, be seen as both an instrument and a part of philosophy (see STOICISM). On the other hand, logic was one of the liberal arts (see ENCYCLOPEDISTS, MEDIEVAL §1) and belonged to the trivium, along with rhetoric and grammar, which made it seem a linguistic science. This emphasis was intensified by the discovery of Arab logicians who included Aristotle's Rhetoric and Poetics in the Organon, or logical works, a classification accepted by Albert the Great and Aquinas, among others. Some logicians, such as William of Sherwood, preferred to call logic just a linguistic science, but many others in the thirteenth century, including Robert Kilwardby and St Bonaventure, called it both linguistic and rational.

In the late thirteenth and fourteenth centuries the notion of logic as a rational science only became predominant. This move was partly associated with the rediscovery of the Posterior Analytics, the new emphasis on demonstrative science, and the increased importance of the classification of science into practical and speculative, along with the associated division of speculative science into natural philosophy, mathematics and divine science. Unlike the Stoic classification, this one offered no obvious place for logic. Some later logicians, including Ockham, Buridan and Albert of Saxony, classified logic as a practical science, but most preferred to think of it as speculative (though of course with practical applications). People then called logic a supporting science (scientia adminiculativa), subordinated to the three important sciences. The notion that logic was a tool directing reason in the acquisition of knowledge was one reason for calling it rational.

However, the most important reason for calling logic rational had to do with views about its subject matter, and here the influence of Avicenna is crucial, for it was Avicenna who had said that logic was about second intentions. Second intentions, often identified with beings of reason (entia rationis), are those higher level concepts we use to classify our concepts of things in the world, and they include such notions as genus, species, subject, predicate and syllogism. There were obvious ontological difficulties here, for one could argue that second intentions pick out special common objects including both universals and logical structures, and one could also argue that second intentions are just mental constructs reached through reflection on individual things and on actual pieces of discourse or writing. Nominalists and realists obviously disagreed on ontology, but this did not prevent such nominalists as Ockham from agreeing that logic deals with second intentions, and that the syllogism the logician considers is neither a thing in the world, nor a piece of writing or speaking. Some people preferred to say that logic was about things in the world as they fall under second intentions, and other people preferred to pick out some special second intention such as argumentation or the syllogism as the subject of logic, but there was still a strong consensus that the objects of logic are rational objects.

These remarks have to be balanced by the obvious fact that people reason in ordinary language, and that ordinary locutions are often vague, ambiguous or misleading. Medieval logicians spent an enormous amount of time on the analysis of ordinary Latin, not because they thought that logic was theoretically concerned with ordinary language, but because this was the only way to avoid fallacious reasoning. Indeed, the avoidance of fallacy is at the heart of all the new types of logical writing.

5 Syllogistic

Despite the new forms of logical writing, syllogistic remained basic, and the syllogism was generally regarded as the central form of argumentation, to which all other forms could be reduced. This view is a lot less restrictive than one might imagine, because of the general way in which 'syllogism' was defined. Following Aristotle, logicians wrote: 'A syllogism is an expression in which, when certain things have been asserted, something else must occur by means of the things which were asserted' (Peter of Spain, in Kretzmann and Stump 1988: 217). This definition encompassed modal syllogisms, syllogisms with singular terms (called 'expository syllogisms'), tensed syllogisms with past and future verbs, syllogisms with 'oblique' (or inflected) terms such as genitives (for example, 'Every man's donkeys are running, Brownie (the donkey) is a man's, therefore Brownie is running'), and syllogisms containing such exponible terms (see §8) as 'only' and 'except'.

The standard core of syllogistic included immediate inference as captured by the square of opposition, the rules of equipollence (for example, 'Not every man is running' is equivalent to 'Some man is not running'), the laws of conversion and contraposition, and the categorical syllogism itself, together with the laws of reduction which allow one to prove non-first-figure syllogisms on the basis of the first-figure syllogisms, treated as axioms, and some other rules including conversion. (For details, see LOGIC, ANCIENT.) The main medieval contribution here was the provision of

mnemonic devices, particularly the verse 'Barbara, Celarent, . . . ', which accounts for nineteen valid categorical syllogisms, together with detailed rules of reduction (see Peter of Spain, in Kretzmann and Stump 1988: 224–5).

One topic of discussion was whether a fourth figure should be recognized. This question relates to the ways in which the major and minor terms can be defined. From the sixteenth century onward, it became more usual to adopt the definition of Philoponus and to say that the major term is the predicate of the conclusion, while the minor term is the subject of the conclusion. This definition gives four figures which represent four possible arrangements of the major, minor and middle terms in two differentiated premises. Alternatively, if one adopts the standard medieval definition, whereby the major term is the term that appears with the middle term in the first premise, one can still speak of four figures with differentiated premises but it turns out that each figure also has indirect modes, in which the major term is the subject of the conclusion. The normal medieval account encompassed just the direct and indirect modes of the first figure, and the direct modes of the second and third figures. People argued that the fourth figure is just the first indirect figure with transposed premises, and they did not count this as involving a genuinely different disposition of the middle term. John Buridan seems to have been the first to realize (in rather brief remarks) that on the medieval account, one will still have four distinct figures, and that the direct modes of the first figure will count as the indirect modes of the fourth figure in just the same way as the direct modes of the fourth figure count as the indirect modes of the first.

Another subject of discussion concerned the relation of perfect and imperfect syllogisms. 'Perfect' syllogisms were first-figure syllogisms whose necessity was obvious, and so needed no proof in terms of simpler argument forms, though they can be said to be founded on the regulative principles *dici de omni* (which 'occurs when nothing is to be subsumed under the subject of which the predicate is not said') and *dici de nullo* (which 'occurs when nothing is to be subsumed under the subject from which the predicate is not removed': Peter of Spain, in Kretzmann and Stump 1988: 217). Links between *dici de omni* and the Topic of quantitative whole were occasionally mentioned in the thirteenth century, but the general view was that perfect syllogisms do not need to be justified by appeal to Topics. Other syllogisms, however, are imperfect, and need to be justified by the rules of reduction, which involve the use of the laws of conversion. This immediately raises the problem of circularity, for if all arguments are reducible to the syllogism, it seems to follow that the laws of conversion are themselves reducible. There was considerable uncertainty on this point, and Burley, in his early treatise on consequences, says both that everything is reducible to the syllogism and that the laws of conversion are not. One way out of the impasse was to see the syllogism itself as just one among many forms of consequence (see §9), but although this is the approach taken by the later Burley and by Buridan, followed by Albert of Saxony, it is less prevalent than has often been suggested. Nor is there any reason to suppose that Burley or Buridan regarded themselves as showing that quantificational logic is based on propositional logic when they suggested that general inferences with unanalysed parts have some kind of priority.

The laws of contraposition raised an interesting semantic issue, which was discussed by Buridan and by various other logicians up to the early sixteenth century. It was commonly held that affirmative sentences with a non-referring subject were false, and the corresponding negative sentences true. But if one accepts term-negation while holding that sentences with term-negation (and no other) are affirmative, contraposition of the sort 'All men are beings, therefore all non-beings are non-men' will be invalid, given that there are no non-beings. Buridan and other late medieval logicians responded by claiming that the laws of contraposition could hold only when an extra existential premise was supplied. It is important to note a corollary of their view. In classical quantificational logic, the standard interpretation of sentences with non-referring terms is that universal sentences (formulated with 'if... then') are true, and particular ones (formulated with 'and') are false. As a result, quantificational formulations of the simple inferences 'All As are B, therefore some As are B' and 'No A is B, therefore some As are not B' are rejected as invalid, as are the quantificational formulations of syllogisms with universal premises and particular conclusions. When medieval logicians had to decide on a uniform way of treating sentences with non-referring terms they decided not to draw a line between universal and particular sentences, but between affirmative and negative ones. As a result, the simple inferences captured in the square of opposition, the laws of equipollence, the laws of conversion and the standard categorical syllogisms remain valid. It is only the laws of contraposition that need reformulation.

6 Compounded and divided senses; modal logic

The discussion of modal logic is in part parallel to the discussion of categorical syllogistic. In general introductions to logic the discussion of modal propositions was followed by the discussion of simple modal inferences and equivalences as captured in a square of modal opposition, modal conversion and, finally, modal syllogisms. Buridan is noteworthy for the large number of modal equivalences he considered, and Ockham for his thorough exploration of different kinds of modal syllogism. Modal logic also figures in treatises on consequences, on proofs of terms, and on compounded and divided senses. The central modal notions employed were 'necessary', 'impossible', 'possible' and 'contingent', of which the last two need some explication. In the earlier period such logicians as Peter of Spain followed Boethius in treating 'possible' as equivalent to 'contingent', but later logicians, such as Buridan, made a careful distinction between 'possible' as compatible with 'necessary' but not with 'impossible', and 'contingent' as incompatible with both 'necessary' and 'impossible'.

A full understanding of modal logic requires a consideration both of the basic tool of analysis, the distinction between compounded and divided senses, and also of the general theory of modality.

The distinction between compounded and divided senses has its origin in Aristotle's discussion of the fallacy of composition and division, to which Abelard was one of the first to pay careful attention. The basic point concerns two ways of reading the sentence 'A seated man can walk'. Interpreted according to its compounded sense, this proposition is *de dicto* (about a dictum or 'that' clause – see DE RE/DE DICTO §1) and means 'That-a-seated-man-walk (that is, while seated) is possible'. Interpreted according to its divided sense, the proposition is *de re* (about a *res* or thing), and means 'A seated man has the power or ability to walk'. The proposition is false in the first sense, but true in the second. It became standard when considering modal inferences in general and modal syllogisms in particular to distinguish between the compounded and divided senses of premises and conclusion, and to work out the logical results of these different readings.

In the fourteenth century the distinction between the compounded and divided senses was very widely used, as can be seen from the work of William HEYTESBURY, the first to devote a complete treatise to this topic. He listed nine types of logical problems which could be solved by paying attention to the distinction. These problems were signalled by the presence of modal words but also, for example, by the presence of future tense verbs, verbs producing confused supposition (see §7), terms such as 'infinite' which could be taken both categorematically and syncategorematically (see OXFORD CALCULATORS §§2, 4), and words about acts of will and intellect. This last case ties in with epistemic logic, as a branch of applied modal logic. For instance, Heytesbury cites the inference 'Your father you believe to be a donkey; therefore, you believe your father to be a donkey' (Kretzmann and Stump 1988: 426–7), and remarks that it is invalid because the antecedent is taken in the divided sense ('Your father happens to be the thing [at a distance] that you take to be a donkey': true) and the consequent is to be taken in the compounded sense ('You believe that your father is a donkey': false).

The general theory of modality underwent interesting changes during the Middle Ages. In the earlier period, there were two possible approaches. On one approach, the interpretation of modalities is straightforwardly ontological and possibility is seen as a potency, an aspect of beings and events to be discussed in the context of change and motion. A second interpretation of modalities is the so-called statistical interpretation. On this account, to say that an object or state of affairs is necessary is to say that it occurs at all times, to say that it is possible is to say that it occurs at some but not all times, and to say that it is impossible is to say that it never occurs. For both these views, to talk about modalities is just to talk about what exists or occurs at various times, and modality is not some feature of the world over and above what there is. Moreover, they are tied to the principle of the necessity of the present, that is, that if P is true at time t, then it is not possible for not-P to be true at time t. An alternative model of possibility was at first confined to purely theological contexts, but in the twelfth century such authors as Gilbert of Poitiers and Abelard began to take a new approach, and in the fourteenth century Duns Scotus worked out the full philosophical implications of the alternative model, the so-called synchronic interpretation. On this model, possibility involves reference, not just to the present state of affairs, or to the potentialities of objects, but to states of affairs or worlds which are here and now alternative to the present world. There is no necessity of the present, and the basic notion is that of conceptual consistency. This new view leads to more complete and satisfactory formulations of the relations between modal sentences, especially when they are taken in the divided sense.

7 Supposition theory

The most notable new theory that took shape in the twelfth century was supposition theory and its ramifications, particularly ampliation and restriction. In the early period, *suppositio* was taken to be a property of a substantive term, while *copulatio* was a property of an adjectival term, and *appellatio* a property of a term that referred to actual existents.

Later, the term *copulatio* was dropped, and *appellatio* acquired a totally new meaning (see below). Roughly speaking, supposition theory concerned what a categorical term (the subject or predicate of a proposition) can be taken to stand for in a particular context, and it was used to diagnose fallacies and test inferences.

The three main types of supposition were material, simple and personal. A term was said to have 'material' supposition when it stood for itself or its equiforms, as in 'Man is a noun'. Material supposition took the place of twentieth-century quotation devices, and gave rise to the same sorts of problems. A term was said to have 'simple' supposition when it stood for a universal, as in 'Man is a species', but this type was controversial, and not only because the question of the nature of universals is itself highly controversial. Peter of Spain suggested that nouns used as predicates, such as 'animal' in 'Every man is an animal', had simple supposition, and William Arnaud in the late thirteenth century suggested that singular terms, such as 'Socrates' in 'Socrates is an individual', had simple supposition. These views were not generally accepted. Finally, a term has 'personal' supposition when it is taken for its normal referents, as when 'man' is taken for Socrates, Plato and so on.

Some logicians distinguished accidental personal supposition from natural supposition which allowed a term to have pre-propositional reference to all its referents, past, present and future, while others insisted that supposition must be purely propositional and contextual. This debate in turn affects the doctrines of 'ampliation', whereby the reference of a term can be extended, and 'restriction' (the opposite). Parisian logicians, such as Jean le Page (writing *c.*1235), tended to accept natural supposition, and to say (like Buridan in the fourteenth century) that terms had natural supposition in scientific propositions – that is, universal necessary truths – so that no ampliation was necessary. As a corollary, in non-scientific propositions the supposition of terms was restricted in various ways. For English logicians in the thirteenth century, all supposition was contextual, and the notion of ampliation had to be used when the subject of a proposition was to extend beyond present existent things. Both groups agreed that modal terms were particularly apt to produce ampliation. For instance, in 'A man can run', 'man' is ampliated to supposit for present and future men (Lambert of Lagny, mistakenly called 'of Auxerre', in Kretzmann and Stump 1988: 117).

The three types of personal supposition most often appealed to are determinate, purely confused (*confuse tantum*), and confused and distributive. These types were normally illustrated by means of the descent to singulars. For instance, to say that the subject of a particular affirmative proposition, 'Some A is B', has 'determinate' supposition is to say that one can infer the disjunction of singular propositions, 'This A is B, or that A is B, or the other A is B, ...'. To say that the predicate of a universal affirmative proposition, 'Every A is B', has 'purely confused' supposition is to say that one can infer a proposition with a disjoint predicate, 'Every A is this B or that B or the other B, ...'. To say that the subject of a universal affirmative proposition has 'confused and distributive' supposition is to say that one can infer a conjunction of propositions, 'This A is B, and that A is B, and the other A is B, ...'.

Some people distinguished between mobile and immobile cases. For instance, no descent is possible from 'Only every A is B', and so A has 'immobile' supposition. A fourth type of supposition is 'collective' supposition, as in 'Every man is hauling a boat', given that they are doing it together. Here any descent will involve a conjoint subject, as in 'This man and that man and the other man ... are all hauling a boat'.

The theory of personal supposition was used to solve a variety of problems. Some involved tense (for example, how to convert the proposition 'No old man will be a boy'); some involved multiple quantification (for example, how to distinguish 'Every donkey of some man is running' from 'Some donkey of every man is running', to take an early sixteenth-century example); and some involved such verbs as 'promise', as in 'I promise you a horse'. How such sentences should be analysed, and what kinds of inferences they could figure in, elicited a variety of complex solutions. The positions adopted included these: Heytesbury took it that 'horse' had purely confused supposition; Paul of Venice added that the supposition was immobile; and Buridan appealed to the new doctrine of appellation, according to which some verbs appellate a form, that is, bring into play the notion of something coming under a certain description. Ockham preferred to replace the sentence by a more complex sentence, 'You will have one horse by means of my gift'. This solution is closer to the type found in treatises on the proofs of terms, which focused, not on the reference of the term 'horse', but on the analysis of the word 'promise' in terms of giving a right to an object.

8 Syncategoremata; proofs of terms

Supposition theory concerned the reference of the subject and predicate terms in propositions; treatises on syncategoremata dealt with all the other terms, such as 'all', 'some', 'not', which appear in a proposition and exercise some logical function. The two areas of investigation were very closely associated. Not only are there terms such as 'infinite' which can be interpreted both as categorematic and as syncategorematic, but some terms were dealt with in each type of treatise. For instance, in the first half of the thirteenth century the word 'all' or 'every' (*omnis*) was discussed in the tracts on distribution associated with supposition theory in the textbooks of Jean le Page, Peter of Spain and Nicholas of Paris, but in the treatises on syncategoremata by the Englishmen William of Sherwood and Robert Bacon. Peter of Spain and Nicholas of Paris both wrote treatises on syncategoremata in which '*omnis*' is not discussed. As was noted above (§2) these works were very closely associated with those on sophismata.

Treatises on syncategoremata were most prominent in the thirteenth century, and they did not altogether disappear in the fourteenth. For instance, the late-fourteenth-century English logician, Richard Lavenham, wrote one. However, two other forms of writing come to the fore. First, there are a lot of short treatises on particular syncategorematic terms, including 'know' (*scire*), 'begins' (*incipit*) and 'ceases' (*desinit*), and terms with the power of producing purely confused supposition. Second, and most important, are the treatises on the proofs of terms (or proofs of propositions), whose best-known example is the *Speculum puerorum* of Richard Billingham, an Oxford author of the mid-fourteenth century.

In this context, a proof seems to be a method of clarifying a sentence containing a particular sort of term, or of showing how one might justify that sentence. There were three groups of terms. 'Resoluble' terms are those whose presence calls for explanation or clarification through ostensive reference, as captured in an expository syllogism (that is, one with singular terms). Thus 'A man runs' is resolved into the expository syllogism 'This runs; and this is a man; therefore a man runs'. 'Exponible' terms are those whose presence calls for exposition of the sentence in terms of a set of equivalent sentences. For instance, the sentence 'Only a man is running', which contains the exclusive term 'only', is expounded as 'A man is running and nothing other than a man is running'. Other exponible terms are exceptives, such as 'except', reduplicatives, such as 'inasmuch as', 'begins' and 'ceases', 'infinite', and so on. In fact, they are the terms which had figured prominently in treatises on syncategoremata. Finally, there are 'official' (*officiales*) or 'officiable' (*officiabiles*) terms, so called because they performed a function (*officium*). These included any term that governed a whole sentence or that treated a whole sentence as modifiable, such as modal terms, and such terms as 'know', 'believe', 'promise', 'desire' and 'owe'. Analysis of sentences containing such terms shows why they are referentially opaque when taken in the compounded sense.

Treatises on proofs of terms were very popular during the late fourteenth and fifteenth centuries, but they were joined by treatises which dealt with exponible terms alone. Pierre d'Ailly wrote one such treatise, and several were written in the early sixteenth century.

9 Consequences

The notion of '*consequentia*' was already discussed in the context of conditional statements by Garlandus Compotista, who wrote in the eleventh century, and was heavily influenced by Boethius' work on hypothetical syllogisms and on Topics. However, it was not until the beginning of the fourteenth century that consequences became the subject of separate studies, one of the very earliest being written by Walter Burley around 1300. The origin of these treatises is controversial. It has been argued that consequences grew out of the study of Topics, especially topical maxims (see §4), but there is no sign of a theory of consequences in thirteenth-century works on Topics, and very little in thirteenth-century commentaries on the *Prior Analytics* or the *Sophistical Refutations*, both places where discussion might be expected. There is some evidence of relevant discussion in treatises on syncategorematic terms, especially under '*si*' (if... then), but it seems most likely that ordered treatment grew out of the English desire to produce lists of rules for use in disputations about sophismata. This ties in with the strong orientation of many fourteenth-century English treatises towards syncategorematic terms. A small group of authors, including Ockham and the later Burley, did produce treatises between about 1325 and 1340 which are more oriented towards Topics, but these constitute a minority treatment. The rare Continental treatises, such as that of John Buridan (c. 1335), had more to do with syllogistic than with syncategoremata. English treatises, especially those by such later fourteenth-century authors as Ralph Strode and Richard Ferribrigge, were used and commented on in the fifteenth century in Germany and Italy.

One problem to do with consequences is the relationship between a *consequentia* and a conditional statement. Unlike modern logicians who make sharp distinctions between syntax (what the rules allow one to infer) and semantics (validity), and between language (statements) and metalanguage (statements about statements), medieval logicians seem to have been indifferent about whether to present conse-

quences as rules of inference, as arguments which may be valid or invalid, or as conditional statements. Buridan, for instance, defined a consequence as a hypothetical (that is, compound) proposition, and said that a good consequence could be called true or valid. The standard remark that all true conditionals are necessary, and all false ones impossible, strengthened the tendency to equate consequences and conditionals, as did the use of 'antecedent' to refer to the conjunction of the members of the set of premises and 'consequent' to refer to the conclusion of a consequence.

Another problem concerns the definition of validity. The claim that a consequence is valid if and only if it is impossible for the consequent to be false when the antecedent is true was questioned for two reasons. In the first place, the propositions involved were taken to be occurrent items, whether written, spoken or mental. They could fail to exist, in which case there is nothing to carry a truth-value. Alternatively, their meaning could be at odds with their actual expression, as in 'Every proposition is affirmative, therefore no proposition is negative'. Such problems were discussed at length, for example, by Buridan, who solved them by substituting a definition in terms of signification, that is, that a consequence is valid if and only if it is impossible for it to be as signified by the antecedent without its being as signified by the consequent.

The presence of 'if and only if' raises the second problem. The truth definition (or Buridan's substitute) may provide a necessary condition for validity, but is it sufficient? If it is sufficient, then we must accept the paradoxes of strict implication, that is, that anything follows from an impossible proposition, and a necessary proposition follows from anything. The debate about these paradoxes began in the twelfth century, and there was a series of attempts to provide a second condition which, with the first, would be sufficient for validity. Abelard had a containment principle by which the dictum of the antecedent should contain the dictum of the consequent (see ABELARD, P. §4), and Robert Kilwardby in the next century, like Strode in mid-fourteenth-century Oxford, said that the consequent had to be understood in the antecedent. Some people in the thirteenth century focused on reality, and argued that a consequence must capture a causal relation, and that as a result the antecedent must be about a state of affairs that can at least be supposed to be possible. None of these people could accept the paradoxes as formally valid. On the other hand, the Parvipontani or Adamites (followers of Adam of Balsham) in the twelfth century and Buridan in the fourteenth were happy to accept the first clause as offering both necessary and sufficient conditions for validity, with all that that implied for the acceptance of the paradoxes.

One favourite division of consequences, found in such authors as William of Sherwood and Robert Kilwardby, was into natural and accidental (or non-natural) consequences. A natural consequence met the two-clause condition for validity, and an accidental one did not. The paradoxes could then be classified as accidental consequences. Later authors tended to make a division into formal and material consequences, but we have to be careful here, as there were two approaches to the notion of material consequence. For some, a material consequence involved the independence of antecedent and consequent, and just was the two paradoxes. For others, such as Buridan, a materially valid consequence is defined as one which does not hold for all terms arranged in the same way, and includes such enthymemes as 'If all animals are running, then all humans are running'.

Another division of consequences is into those valid absolutely (*simpliciter*) and those valid as of now (*ut nunc*). This division, which appears in Ockham, has been much discussed, though it is in fact relatively rare, at least in fourteenth-century English treatises. Consequences valid *ut nunc* have been thought to correspond to the modern material conditional, but this is not so, as modal notions are definitely involved. Given that Socrates may not exist, and given that sentences with non-existent subjects are held to be false, 'If all men are running, then Socrates is running' is not generally valid. However, if Socrates does exist, then it is impossible for the antecedent to be true and the conclusion false, and we have a consequence which is valid as of now.

The question of the paradoxes also leads us to the question of the relationship between consequences and propositional logic, as discussion of the paradoxes provided one of the main occasions for sequences of rules to be used in a proof. The typical sequence was as follows: from the contradiction '*P* and not-*P*' we can infer *P*, and from *P* we can infer '*P* or *Q*'. From '*P* and not-*P*' we can also infer not-*P*, and from '*P* or *Q* and not-*P*' we can infer *Q*. Hence, from '*P* and not-*P*' we can infer *Q*. This sequence is found in the twelfth-century theologian Alexander Neckham, and it reappears through the centuries. But the explanations given differ widely. In his treatise on syncategoremata, Peter of Spain appealed to topical maxims, and claimed more generally that we need topical maxims as a foundation for consequences. On the other hand, in Pseudo-Scotus, writing c.1350, we get an appeal to what seem to be straightforward rules of propositional logic.

It has been claimed that later treatments of consequences showed that medieval logicians grasped that quantificational logic is founded on propositional logic, but this is anachronistic. Texts on consequences contain a mixture of rules (from the point of view of the modern logician, that is). Some are general ('If *A* is the antecedent of *B*, and *B* is the antecedent of *C*, then *A* is the antecedent of *C*'). Some are propositional and truth-functional ('Since a conjunction is true if and only if its conjuncts are true, from "*A* and *B*" we may infer *A*'). *Modus ponens*, *modus tollens* and De Morgan's rules are given. Other rules are syllogistic; yet others are modal. Medieval logicians had no interest in classifying rules according to different formal systems, since they did not operate with the notion of a formal system in the first place.

10 Insolubles

'Insolubles' (*insolubilia*), so-called, it was claimed, because they are difficult to solve rather than completely insoluble, are semantic paradoxes. The simplest version is the liar paradox, 'What I am saying is false', given the *casus* or initial situation that this is all that is said, but complex versions with hypothetical propositions ('God exists, and some conjunctive proposition is false') or sequences of mutually referring propositions ('Suppose that Socrates says "Plato says something false", and Plato says "Socrates says something true"' – Albert of Saxony, in Kretzmann and Stump 1988: 357, 349) were also discussed. In the twentieth century such paradoxes have been used to cast doubt on the very foundations of semantic theory, and have led to elaborate distinctions between levels of language and metalanguage. Medieval logicians, however, showed no signs of such a crisis mentality, and while they did employ certain restrictions on self-reference, and make certain distinctions between language and metalanguage, these techniques were generally limited to the problem in hand.

A very early formulation of the liar paradox is found in Adam of Balsham, writing in 1132, and later in the twelfth century Alexander Neckham gives a formulation. Full discussion seems to have started at least by the second half of the twelfth century, and continued until the sixteenth century. In the early period insolubles seem to have been discussed in the framework of Aristotle's *Sophistical Refutations*, and after that, within the general framework of a sophismatic disputation. From about 1320 to 1350 there was a period of intense and sophisticated activity, during which new solutions were given, and the framework of an obligational disputation was used (see §11). After 1350 some authors, such as John

Wyclif and Pierre d'Ailly, still had original solutions to offer, but most authors, including Paul of Venice, merely elaborated previous ones.

The early solutions to the paradox include 'restriction', which forbids self-reference, either by saying that a part ('false') cannot supposit for a whole ('I say what is false'), or by saying that 'I say' cannot refer to the present moment; and 'cassatio', according to which a paradox says nothing at all. The first major new solution was that of Thomas Bradwardine (c.1320–4). Bradwardine claims that propositions signify whatever follows from them and that insolubles signify that they are true. As a result, an insoluble signifies that it is true, but it is true if and only if it is both true and false. This cannot be, so it is false. John BURIDAN (§2) and Albert of Saxony both follow Bradwardine. Roger Swyneshed was author of another popular solution. He said that truth requires not just correspondence with reality but also absence of self-falsification, and Paul of Venice gives a version of this solution in his *Logica Magna*.

11 Obligations

Treatises on 'obligations' discussed the rules for obligational disputations, which were logical exercises for students. They got their title because of the rules obliging one to answer in a certain way. Obligational terminology is found in the late twelfth century, and the theory was already well-advanced in Paris by 1240–50. In 1302 Walter Burley wrote a treatise which summarized much previous material, and laid the foundations for later developments. Other important treatises were by Roger Swyneshed (1330–5), Ralph Strode and Marsilius of Inghen. The terminology of obligational disputation, including the use of a *casus* or description of the initial situation, permeated much fourteenth-century writing, including theology.

Various types of obligational disputation were discussed. One classification, which has thirteenth-century origins and was popularized by Marsilius of Inghen in the second half of the fourteenth century, related to the three legitimate ways of responding: '*concedo*' or 'I grant it'; '*nego*' or 'I deny it'; and '*dubito*' or 'I doubt it'. Walter Burley had six types, including '*impositio*', in which words and sentences were given new meanings for the duration of the disputation.

The most important of the different types of obligational disputation was '*positio*'. In this type of disputation, the opponent began the game by positing a proposition which the respondent had to grant, provided that it was logically possible. This *positum* was normally false, and it was usually trivial in content. Next the opponent had to propose a series of

other propositions, which could be either true or false. In replying to these, the respondent had to follow the rules of the game. If a proposition followed from the set formed by the *positum*, the propositions already granted and the negations of propositions already denied, it had to be granted. If a proposition was inconsistent with the set so determined, it had to be denied. If a proposition was such that neither it nor its negation followed from the set so determined, it was called *impertinens* or irrelevant, and the respondent had to reply to it according to his current state of knowledge. The task of the opponent in this game was to lead the respondent to the point of accepting an inconsistent set, either by granting and denying the same proposition, or by granting a proposition whose negation would follow from the set of propositions already granted. The task of the respondent, of course, was to avoid falling into these traps. In order to be successful, the respondent needed an excellent grasp of the logical relations between propositions and also an excellent memory. This is why obligational disputations could serve as valuable exercises for young logicians.

Some changes are reflected in the treatises. In the early period, impossible *positio* was very important, and still occurs in Ockham, though very rarely afterwards. In this kind of disputation, one begins with an impossible proposition which can at least be conceived to be true, a condition which excluded the use of explicit contradictions. Another change related to developments in modal logic. In the thirteenth century, the respondent had to deny that the actual 'now' of disputation was the instant at which the false but possible *positum* is treated as true, and as a result the replies to irrelevant propositions were related to actual time, while the replies to relevant propositions were related to an imaginary time. Once the notion of synchronic alternatives to the actual world had been adopted, all replies could be related to the same time. In the later period, Roger Swyneshed altered the relationship between irrelevant propositions and the *positum*. In the usual rules, once an irrelevant proposition had been admitted into the sequence, it (or its negation) became relevant. For Swyneshed, relevance was strictly a matter of a relation between the *positum* and those propositions that follow from or are incompatible with it alone. This produces two separate sets of responses, one involving relevant propositions, and one involving irrelevant propositions. As a result, one can deny a conjunction both of whose parts have been granted, and grant a disjunction both of whose parts have been denied. This view generated a good deal of discussion in the fourteenth and fifteenth centuries, and was usually rejected.

The biggest problem presented by treatises on

obligations has to do with their purpose. They were certainly closely connected with consequences, insolubles and sophismata. Equally certainly they were closely connected with undergraduate training. Among other possibilities, it has been suggested that they also presented theories of counter-factual conditionals, or that they represented thought-experiments in which retrospective construction of a possible world takes place.

See also: LANGUAGE, MEDIEVAL THEORIES OF; LOGIC, RENAISSANCE; LOGICAL AND MATHEMATICAL TERMS, GLOSSARY OF

References and further reading

Ashworth, E.J. (1978) *The Tradition of Medieval Logic and Speculative Grammar from Anselm to the End of the Seventeenth Century: A Bibliography from 1836 Onwards*, Toronto, Ont.: Pontifical Institute of Mediaeval Studies. (Annotated bibliography with full indexes.)

Ashworth, E.J. and Spade, P.V. (1992) 'Logic in Late Medieval Oxford', in J.I. Catto and R. Evans (eds) *The History of the University of Oxford*, vol. 2, *Late Medieval Oxford*, Oxford: Clarendon Press, 35–64. (Detailed account of the period 1330–1500 when English logicians were influential throughout Europe.)

Broadie, A. (1993) *Introduction to Medieval Logic*, Oxford: Clarendon Press, 2nd edn. (A brief, readable introduction to some parts of medieval logic. The first edition should not be used.)

Buzzetti, D., Ferriani, M. and Tabarroni, A. (eds) (1992) *L'Insegnamento della Logica a Bologna nel XIV Secolo* (Logic Teaching at Bologna in the Fourteenth Century), Bologna: L'Istituto per la Storia dell'Università. (A useful collection of Italian studies and Latin texts related to logic teaching at an important Italian university.)

Green-Pedersen, N.J. (1984) *The Tradition of the Topics in the Middle Ages: The Commentaries on Aristotle's and Boethius' 'Topics'*, Munich and Vienna: Philosophia. (The standard study of Topics; from Aristotle to the sixteenth century.)

Jacobi, K. (1988) 'Logic (ii): The Later Twelfth Century', in P. Dronke (ed.) *A History of Twelfth-Century Western Philosophy*, Cambridge: Cambridge University Press, 227–51. (Excellent introduction to the debates in the twelfth-century schools of logic.)

—— (ed.) (1993) *Argumentationstheorie: scholastische Forschungen zu den logischen und semantischen Regeln korrekten Folgerns* (Theory of Argumentation: Scholastic Researches into the Logical and Semantic Rules of Correct Inference), Leiden, New York and Cologne: Brill. (A collection of 35 studies, 25 in English, on inference in various parts of medieval logic, with full introductions to the different sections in both German and English. An excellent source, with a full bibliography.)

Knuuttila, S. (1993) *Modalities in Medieval Philosophy*, London and New York: Routledge. (A difficult but rewarding study of modal logic and how it was employed.)

Kretzmann, N., Kenny, A. and Pinborg, J. (eds) (1982) *The Cambridge History of Later Medieval Philosophy*, Cambridge: Cambridge University Press. (Much of this volume is devoted to logic between 1200 and 1350; the best single source on this period available.)

* Kretzmann, N. and Stump, E. (trans.) (1988) *The Cambridge Translations of Medieval Philosophical Texts*, vol. 1, *Logic and the Philosophy of Language*, Cambridge: Cambridge University Press. (An invaluable collection of translations of authors from Boethius to Albert of Saxony; designed to supplement the *Cambridge History* (Kretzmann, Kenny and Pinborg 1982).)

Lewry, P.O. (1984) 'Grammar, Logic and Rhetoric 1220–1320', in J.I. Catto (ed.) *The History of the University of Oxford*, vol. 1, *The Early Oxford Schools*, Oxford: Clarendon Press, 401–33. (A lot of useful material about logic and logic teaching.)

Libera, A. de (1985–92) 'Bulletin d'histoire de la logique médiévale', *Revue des sciences philosophiques et théologiques* 69: 273–309, 71: 590–634, 76: 640–66. (A detailed, critical discussion of recent literature, with mini-introductions to a number of topics, including deontic logic and obligations.)

Maierù, A. (1994) *University Training in Medieval Europe*, trans. and ed. D.N. Pryds, Leiden: Brill. (This work, by a leading historian of logic, focuses particularly on how logic was taught, and its place in the curriculum, not just in universities, but in the *studia* of the religious orders.)

Pinborg, J. (1984) *Medieval Semantics: Selected Studies on Medieval Logic and Grammar*, London: Variorum. (A collection of seminal articles, published between 1969 and 1981.)

Read, S. (ed.) (1993) *Sophisms in Medieval Logic and Grammar: Acts of the Ninth European Symposium for Medieval Logic and Semantics, held at St Andrews, June 1990*, Dordrecht, Boston, MA, and London: Kluwer. (A very useful collection of articles.)

Rijk, L.M. de (1962–7) *Logica Modernorum: A Contribution to the History of Early Terminist Logic*, Assen: Van Gorcum, 2 vols in 3 parts. (A seminal collection of mainly twelfth-century texts with discussion. The source of much subsequent research, especially on supposition theory.)

Spade, P.V. (1988) *Lies, Language and Logic in the Late Middle Ages*, London: Variorum. (Articles on insolubles, Ockham's semantics, and obligations, by a leading historian of logic.)

Stump, E. (1989) *Dialectic and Its Place in the Development of Medieval Logic*, Ithaca, NY, and London: Cornell University Press. (A very readable collection of studies, and an excellent introduction to dialectic. Some of the material on consequences and obligations needs updating.)

Tweedale, M. (1988) 'Logic (i): From the Late Eleventh Century to the Time of Abelard', in P. Dronke (ed.) *A History of Twelfth-Century Western Philosophy*, Cambridge: Cambridge University Press, 196–226. (A good account of the early period, including Abelard.)

E.J. ASHWORTH

LOGIC, MULTIPLE-CONCLUSION *see* MULTIPLE-CONCLUSION LOGIC

LOGIC OF ETHICAL DISCOURSE

Logic, as a discipline, is largely concerned with discovering principles and methods for evaluating the evidential strength between the premises and conclusions of arguments. Because the meanings of terms (and the concepts they express) that occur in arguments bear importantly on questions about evidential relations, much of the work on the topic of logic and ethics has been preoccupied with questions about the meanings of moral terms and concepts, and with the correct linguistic analysis of sentences that contain them. Taking logic to include issues about meaning (which has commonly been done by those who refer to the so-called 'logic of moral discourse') is to construe the subject broadly. But the field of logic is often construed quite narrowly to refer to the study of formal languages whose syntax, axioms and inference rules are sufficiently determinate to allow decisions about what counts as the theorem in such a language. On the narrower understanding of logic, the intersection of logic and ethics has mainly to do with work in deontic logic. This article takes up issues concerning the intersection of ethics and logic broadly construed. The

intersection of logic and ethics concerns questions about the nature of moral reasoning. Some philosophers have attempted to deduce substantive moral conclusions from factual statements – in particular, to derive 'ought' statements from 'is' statements. If one can successfully carry out such deductions, then moral reasoning is guided properly by consideration of nonmoral facts from which moral conclusions can be derived. However, the eighteenth-century philosopher David Hume is often credited with arguing that no such deductions are correct; that there is a gap between factual 'is' statements and moral 'ought' statements. There is disagreement over whether or not Hume's negative claim is correct; but even if it is, there may still be logical features of moral concepts that impose constraints on proper moral reasoning.

One such widely discussed constraint is the thesis of universalizability, according to which relevantly similar cases must receive the same moral evaluation. One implication of this thesis is that moral judgments about particular cases entail universal moral principles and so some have argued that all correct moral reasoning must be understood in terms of subsuming particular cases under general moral principles. Although many philosophers have accepted this subsumptive model of moral reasoning, it has come under attack by philosophers who argue that proper moral reasoning is primarily a matter of sensitively discerning the morally relevant details of a case under consideration and rendering a moral judgment about it without the guidance of principles.

1 The is/ought question and Hume's law
2 Searle's challenge
3 Some implications of accepting Hume's law
4 Universalizability and the role of principles
5 Basic moral principles and the universality of reasons thesis
6 Particularism, reasons holism, and the rejection of moral principles

1 The is/ought question and Hume's law

In a famous passage (1739/40), David Hume complains that writers on morality often move almost 'imperceptibly' from factual statements about what is the case to conclusions about what ought to be the case, and do so without adequately explaining or justifying this transition from 'is' to 'ought' (see HUME, D. §4). Hume then demands that 'a reason should be given, for what seems altogether inconceivable, how this new relation can be a deduction from others, which are entirely different from it' (1739/40: 469). What has come to be called 'Hume's law' is the claim that the sort of 'deduction' Hume calls for cannot be negotiated successfully, hence the maxim, 'No "ought" from an "is"'. (Whether Hume actually held this maxim is the subject of some scholarly debate.) The alleged is/ought gap is often used to support the claim that ethics is logically autonomous in the sense that no moral statements can be correctly inferred from any set of nonmoral premises (a thesis which, as we shall see in §4, is much stronger than Hume's law).

Although questions about the relation between 'is' statements and (moral) 'ought' statements has generated a great deal of philosophical discussion, the problems and issues they involve are part of a more general issue about the relation between factual statements and normative statements (in particular moral statements of all types, including statements about value or goodness) (see MORAL REALISM). However, most of what follows will focus on the is/ought issue.

To understand the debate surrounding the alleged is/ought gap, more must be said about Hume's law and its philosophical presuppositions. The law presupposes that a useful distinction can be made between factual ('is') statements and moral (specifically, 'ought') statements, though, of course, many moral statements (such as 'Keeping one's promises is right' and 'Lying for personal gain is something one ought not do') contain the word 'is'. If we take for granted an understanding of specifically moral uses of such terms as 'right', 'good' and 'ought', then, intuitively, moral statements are statements in which some moral term like 'right', 'good' or 'ought' is predicated of some object of evaluation (whether or not the statement contains the word 'is'). Nonmoral statements are all those statements in which moral terms are not predicated of some object of evaluation. Factual statements represent a proper subset of nonmoral statements which purport to assert the existence of, or describe (using vocabulary other than terms like 'right', 'good' and 'ought'), things, events, states of affairs or whatever. Now the root idea behind Hume's law is that it is not possible to infer validly an 'ought' statement from a set of factual statements, since, as Hume puts it, 'this *ought*, or *ought not*, expresses some new relation or affirmation' (1739/40: 469; original emphasis) not contained in the premises. In order, that is, for a moral 'ought' statement to be inferred validly from a set of factual statements, the latter would have to entail the former; but there is no such entailment relation since factual claims do not include any moral terms and, in particular, they do not include any use of the term 'ought'. So, for example, from the factual claim of the form (F) one cannot infer validly a moral claim of the form (M):

(F) All or most people do, or would upon reflection, approve of such and such type of action being performed.

(M) Such and such type of action ought to be performed.

Obviously, one way to refute Hume's law and overcome the alleged is/ought gap would be to include among the set of factual premises what can be called 'moral bridge principles' that would link moral terms with nonmoral terms and thus allow for the valid deduction of moral conclusions. So, for instance, if we add to (F) a bridge principle of the form (B), then statements of the form (M) can be inferred validly by canons of ordinary logic:

(B) If all or most people do, or would upon reflection, approve of such and such type of action, then actions of that type ought to be performed.

Granted, (B) together with (F) jointly entail (M), but this does not disprove Hume's law unless a case can be made for claiming that (B) is a nonmoral, factual claim. And this in turn depends on how we interpret it. Traditionally (and this is another presupposition of the philosophical debate over Hume's law) any claim (if true) is either an analytic truth, in which case it is true simply in virtue of the meanings of its constituent terms, or a synthetic truth, in which case its truth does not depend simply on the meanings of its constituent terms (see ANALYTICITY). If construed properly as a synthetic truth, then any instance of (B) has the status of a substantive moral claim, and hence adding it to an appropriate instance of (F) to derive an instance of (M) will not count as a violation of Hume's law – in fact such a derivation tends to confirm that law. However, if we can find an appropriate moral bridge principle that is construed properly as an analytic truth, then, since in general such truths simply report conceptual or linguistic truths about language, such a principle would simply describe a nonmoral fact about proper linguistic usage. So it would appear that if the is/ought gap is to be negotiated successfully, there must be analytic bridge principles that link moral terms and concepts with nonmoral terms and concepts. Moreover, although linking moral terms and concepts analytically with any sort of nonmoral, descriptive terms and concepts would serve to bridge the gap, most serious philosophical efforts to find any such analytic connections represent versions of ethical naturalism (see NATURALISM IN ETHICS). Ethical naturalism (at least in its traditional form) involves the attempt to define basic moral terms and concepts by terms and concepts that describe or refer to the sorts of natural properties and relations that are the subject of scientific inquiry. Thus, those who wanted to defend Hume's law were particularly concerned to refute versions of ethical naturalism.

One of the most forceful defences of Hume's law was offered by G.E. Moore (1903), who claimed that all attempts to define moral terms and concepts using naturalistic terms and concepts commit the 'naturalistic fallacy' (see MOORE, G.E. §1). To expose this fallacy, Moore noted that for any genuine definition of a moral term like 'good' by some naturalistic term, N, the question, 'Entity E has property N, but is it good?', should be a closed question, that is, a question the answer to which anyone would know to be affirmative simply on the basis of understanding it. But he pointed out with a great deal of plausibility that all such questions were 'open questions', indicating that no such proposed definitions were genuine.

2 Searle's challenge

In 1964, John Searle published what became a much discussed paper, 'How to Derive "Ought" from "Is"', in which he challenges Hume's law by offering a deduction of an 'ought' statement from a set of factual statements. Here are the basic steps in his alleged deduction:

(1) Jones uttered the words, 'I hereby promise to pay you, Smith, five dollars.'

(2) Jones promised to pay Smith five dollars.

(3) Jones placed himself under (undertook) an obligation to pay Smith five dollars.

(4) Jones is under an obligation to pay Smith five dollars.

(5) Jones ought to pay Smith five dollars.

Searle argues that philosophers have generally failed to recognize that in addition to 'brute facts', such as 'John is six feet tall', there are 'institutional facts', facts that presuppose certain institutions like marriage, promises and private property. These institutions are defined by systems of rules – constitutive rules – and some of these rules, like the ones characteristic of the institution of promising, involve obligations, permissions and responsibilities. Searle's deduction, then, is supposed to work by appealing to an institutional fact (Jones made a promise), which, given the constitutive rules that define what a promise is, allows one to infer something about what Jones ought to do.

Searle's deduction works only if he is right in claiming that the full-blown argument (including the supplementary premises) does not represent or presuppose any evaluative and specifically moral claims. Searle's critics doubt that his deduction is successful on this count.

3 Some implications of accepting Hume's law

But what if Hume's law is correct? What are the implications for the logic of moral argument? Here are three observations. (1) We have noted that Hume's law prohibits any *deduction* of moral statements from factual premises, but this leaves open the possibility that moral statements can be inferred correctly from factual premises by some *nondeductive* mode of inference, perhaps inductively. (2) Moreover, even if Hume's law is correct, the so-called 'autonomy of ethics' thesis does not, strictly speaking, follow. Recall that, according to this thesis, moral discourse is autonomous in the sense that moral claims cannot be deduced from a set of nonmoral premises (see AUTONOMY, ETHICAL §5). But, even granting Hume's law, it might still be possible to derive moral conclusions from nonmoral normative (and hence nonfactual) premises. For instance, some philosophers have wanted to derive substantive moral conclusions from normative claims about rationality (where there is no attempt to construe rationality claims as a type of factual claim) (see PRACTICAL REASON AND ETHICS §3). So, the truth of Hume's law does not establish the autonomy of ethics. (3) Even if there are no bridge principles directly linking moral concepts with nonmoral concepts by means of some analytic definition, there might still be bridge principles, expressing what some have called 'synthetic definitions' of moral terms, patterned after the sorts of definitions that are offered in science (see Brink 1989; Boyd 1988).

These remarks make clear that Hume's law can be strengthened in two ways: by prohibiting inductive as well as deductive inference from the factual to the moral, and by prohibiting transition from any sort of nonmoral claims, including nonmoral normative claims, to moral claims. Presumably, many defenders of Hume's law would also want to defend a strengthened version of the law that would prohibit the possibilities just mentioned for negotiating the is/ought gap. If these philosophers are right, where does that leave things with our main question about the logic of moral argumentation?

4 Universalizability and the role of principles

Some philosophers, who accept Hume's law in both its original and its strengthened versions, claim that the meanings of moral terms and concepts impose special consistency constraints on proper moral argumentation. One such widely discussed consistency constraint stems from the alleged *universalizability* of moral statements (see UNIVERSALISM IN ETHICS). The basic idea is that any two or more relevantly similar objects being morally evaluated must receive the same moral evaluation. Thus, if Jane's lying to Fred on some occasion was morally permissible, then the same moral evaluation holds for any relevantly similar action. Of course, everything depends on how 'relevantly similar' is interpreted.

The most influential recent treatment of universalizability is owing to R.M. HARE, as presented in *Freedom and Reason* (1963). For Hare, one situation is relevantly similar to the first if it shares with the first all of those qualitative properties, P^1–P^n, that served as the basis (namely, one's reasons) for the original judgment. For example, if Peter judges that Paul's action was wrong because it was a case of misleading a customer about the quality of a product in order to make a sale, then Peter is bound, on pain of logical contradiction, to judge of any other action having these features that it too is wrong, or else withdraw his original moral judgment. One immediate implication of Hare's thesis of universalizability is that moral judgments entail universal moral principles. The moral judgment that action A is wrong because it has properties P^1–P^n commits one to the moral principle, 'Any action having properties P^1–P^n is wrong'. Thus, on Hare's view, even if there are no nonmoral bridge principles that would link moral concepts to nonmoral concepts, correct moral reasoning and argumentation about the morality of specific cases nevertheless exemplify the *subsumptive* model of reasoning: particular objects of moral evaluation are subsumed under a moral principle which governs a range of relevantly similar cases.

Hare's universalism, and in particular his use of the thesis of universalizability, is apparently open to certain counterexamples. If, for example, one judges that some particular action performed on some particular occasion was wrong because in that situation properties P^1, P^2 and P^3 were present, then even if in some new situation the same properties are present, there may be some other property which, in the new situation but not in the original situation, defeats the reasons in favour of judging the action to be wrong. Of course, the defender of universalizability will reply that the two cases are not relevantly similar because in addition to all of those features that count in favour of some particular moral evaluation, we must also recognize any features that count against that same evaluation. The second case, then, is not relevantly similar to the first one and we have no violation of the principle of universalizability. Thus, the defender of universalizability is moved to broaden

the universalizability base (and hence the account of relevant similarity) to include not only those properties taken as reasons in favour of a particular moral evaluation, but also those properties taken as reasons against a particular moral evaluation. But this manoeuvre is not entirely satisfactory since, in addition to both positive and negative reasons regarding some moral evaluation of a situation, there are all sorts of potentially relevant defeaters whose absence is a condition of the correct moral evaluation about the particular case. For example, if a man stops to help a woman whose car has broken down, our reasons for moral approval include obvious facts about the situation (one person needing help, another stopping to render aid, and so on). But there are all sorts of possible defeaters whose absence is required for our positive moral evaluation of the man's actions, including, for instance, that his motive is not to seduce or in any way harm the woman. So in addition to properties that figure among a person's reasons there are other relevant aspects including the absence of certain defeaters that affect moral judgments about particular cases. And so the defender of universalizability seems forced to broaden the universalizability base even further. But once one begins to broaden the universalizability base in this way so that any aspect of a situation (including both properties instantiated in the situation and those potential defeaters that are not instantiated) counts as part of what makes two situations relevantly similar, what started out as an interesting thesis yielding interesting moral principles approaches triviality. That is, broadening the universalizability base in this way tends to reduce the thesis to the claim that any two exactly similar objects of moral evaluation must be judged in the same way. But then, the sorts of moral principles yielded by the thesis of universalizability tend to become less useful in constraining moral argumentation – they do not apply to a very interesting range of cases.

But apart from problems for Hare's notion of universalizability, there remains the idea that correct moral reasoning proceeds by way of subsumption under moral principles. As we shall see, however, the subsumption model is not without its problems. To understand the problems we need to say a bit more about moral principles.

5 Basic moral principles and the universality of reasons thesis

Many moral philosophers have supposed that underlying all right and wrong actions is some nonmoral feature or property (or perhaps small set of them) whose presence makes all right actions right and whose absence makes all wrong actions wrong. One traditional aim of moral theory has been to discover such features or properties, which can then be expressed as basic moral principles – principles that tell us what, ultimately, makes an action right or wrong. Some philosophers have been *ethical monists*: they suppose that there is some single ultimate feature whose presence makes right actions right and whose absence makes wrong actions wrong. For example, according to hedonistic versions of act utilitarianism, facts about how much pleasure and pain would be experienced by persons (and perhaps other sentient creatures) were some action to be performed determine in every case whether or not the action if morally right (see UTILITARIANISM; HEDONISM). In contrast, *ethical pluralists*, such as W.D. Ross (1930), insist that there is no such single ultimate feature, but rather a small set of irreducible ultimate features whose presence or absence tends to make actions either right or wrong (depending on the feature in question), even though the presence or absence of any one such feature may not be decisive in determining whether or not an action is (all things considered) right (see MORAL PLURALISM). Despite their disagreement over the number of ultimate features, both monists and pluralists are united in accepting what can be called the *universality of reasons* thesis: there is at least one ultimate right/wrong-making feature of actions such that for it (1) it is morally relevant whenever they are present and (2) it always counts in the same way – either as a right-making feature or as a wrong-making feature. And so, for both camps, correct moral reasoning proceeds by way of subsuming particular cases calling for moral evaluation under basic moral principles.

The universality of reasons thesis is challenged by so-called moral particularists who then reject the subsumptive model of moral reasoning and argumentation.

6 Particularism, reasons holism, and the rejection of moral principles

Moral particularism rejects the universality of reasons thesis in favour of what some call *reasons holism*, according to which what counts as a reason in some particular case, and how it counts, is a matter of the details of the particular situation. Reasons holism finds intuitive support by reflecting on common examples. For instance, normally the fact that I borrowed a book from you is a reason for me to return it to you. But if I learn that you have stolen the book, then the fact that I borrowed it from you is no reason at all to return it to you; in fact it seems to be a reason against doing so.

For our purposes, the important thing to notice is

that reasons holism amounts to a rejection of basic moral principles (at least a rejection of the idea that such principles are required for making sense of moral reasoning and the difference between correct and incorrect moral argumentation) since such principles, as usually interpreted, presuppose that the properties featured in them are always morally relevant and relevant in the same way. But if basic moral principles are not (or need not be) involved in correct moral argumentation, what does the particularist have to say about such argumentation? Furthermore, since in ordinary moral reasoning and argumentation we often do appeal to moral generalizations, principles or rules in defending our moral views about particular cases, how can the particularist accommodate this phenomenon?

In response to the first question, the particularist insists that correct moral reasoning and argumentation, instead of being a matter of subsuming particular cases under general principles, proceeds by examining the details of particular cases and making judgments based on one's moral discernment about the case at hand. The particularist accepts the idea that relevantly similar cases must be judged in the same way, but insists (contra universalists) that because of the potential complexity of particular cases and the fact that what counts as a reason is a contextually sensitive matter, there are no useful moral principles that force one, on pain of logical contradiction, to come to some particular moral conclusion about the case in hand. Rather, instead of relying on moral principles to guide proper moral reasoning and argumentation, the particularist insists on the use of trained moral perception which allows one to discern the morally relevant features in a particular case and then assess their bearing on the morality of the case. In response to the second question, particularists can allow that a moral principle can serve as a useful heuristic, reminding us of the sort of importance a property can have in particular circumstances. But as mere heuristic devices, moral principles are not cast in the role of premises in moral arguments guiding us to make judgments about present cases that are consistent with past moral judgments (see MORAL PARTICULARISM).

The particularist mounts a fairly strong case against certain allegedly ultimate properties conforming to the universality of reasons thesis, as the borrowed book example and other such examples make clear. However, it is harder to imagine cases in which the fact that someone's action would be a case of knowingly causing the death of a normal human being is not morally relevant or indeed counts in favour of performing the act. The same can be said for actions in which one knowingly causes others to experience significant pain. If this speculation is correct, then perhaps universalism can survive the objections of the particularist.

The ethical naturalists and some anti-naturalists like Hare agree that correct moral reasoning and argumentation is subject to constraints of logical consistency imposed on such reasoning and argumentation by universal moral principles. Thus, both subscribe to a subsumptive model of moral reasoning and argumentation, according to which proper judgments about particular cases are subsumed under universal moral principles. The main difference between Hare and the naturalists is over the status of such principles. In sharp contrast to the universalists, the particularists reject the universalist assumption about moral reasons and consequently reject the subsumptive model of moral reasoning and argumentation. Instead, the particularist argues that correct moral reasoning and argumentation can rely on trained moral perception of the morally relevant details of particular cases as a way of coming to have correct or at least justified moral beliefs about particular cases.

See also: ANALYTIC ETHICS; DEONTIC LOGIC; PRESCRIPTIVISM

References and further reading

Altham, J.E.J. (1985) 'Wicked Promises', in I. Hacking (ed.) *Exercises in Analysis*, Cambridge: Cambridge University Press, 1–21. (An example of opposition to Searle's purported derivation of 'ought' from 'is'.)

* Boyd, R. (1988) 'How to be a Moral Realist', in G. Sayre-McCord (ed.) *Essays on Moral Realism*, Ithaca, NY: Cornell University Press. (A fairly advanced discussion and defence of ethical naturalism.)

* Brink, D.O. (1989) *Moral Realism and the Foundations of Ethics*, Cambridge: Cambridge University Press. (A defender of ethical naturalism who construes moral principles as synthetic necessary truths.)

Dancy, J. (1993) *Moral Reasons*, Oxford: Blackwell, chaps 4–7. (A critic of ethical universalism (generalism) and a defender of particularism.)

* Hare, R.M. (1963) *Freedom and Reason*, Oxford: Oxford University Press. (A defender of ethical universalism.)

Hudson, W.D. (1969) *The Is/Ought Question*, London: Macmillan. (A collection of important essays on the is/ought controversy.)

Horgan, T. and Timmons, M. (1992) 'Troubles for New Wave Moral Semantics: The "Open Question Argument" Revised', *Philosophical Papers* 21: 153–29. (The authors are critical of the sort of semantic view needed to support the version of ethical naturalism defended by Brink and Boyd.)

* Hume, D. (1739/40) *A Treatise of Human Nature*, ed. L.A. Selby-Bigge, revised by P.H. Nidditch, Oxford: Clarendon Press, 2nd edn, 1978. (Contains the original statement of 'Hume's law' – the claim that it is not possible to derive an 'ought' statement from a set of 'is' statements.)

* Moore, G.E. (1903) *Principia Ethica*, Cambridge: Cambridge University Press, chaps 1–2. (Contains Moore's attack on ethical naturalism.)

Prior, A.N. (1949) *Logic and the Basis of Ethics*, Oxford: Oxford University Press. (Contains a historical survey of various attempts to derive 'ought' statements from factual statements as well as a discussion of the naturalistic fallacy.)

* Ross, W.D. (1930) *The Right and the Good*, Oxford: Oxford University Press, ch. 2. (Contains a defence of ethical pluralism.)

* Searle, J. (1964) 'How to Derive "Ought" from "Is"', *Philosophical Review* 73: 43–58; repr. in W.D. Hudson (ed.) *The Is/Ought Question*, London: Macmillan, 1969. (Contains Searle's attempt to derive 'ought' statements from 'is' statements.)

MARK TIMMONS

LOGIC, PARACONSISTENT
see PARACONSISTENT LOGIC

LOGIC, PHILOSOPHY OF

Philosophy of logic can be roughly characterized as those philosophical topics which have emerged either from the technical development of symbolic (mathematical) logic, or from the motivations that logicians have offered for their technical pursuits. In settling on a list of subjects to classify as philosophy of logic, therefore, there is a certain degree of arbitrariness, since the issues which emerge from the technical development of logic can equally well be assigned to such areas as semantics, philosophy of language, philosophy of mathematics, epistemology, and even ethics (see SEMANTICS; LANGUAGE, PHILOSOPHY OF; MATHEMATICS, FOUNDATIONS OF).

1 The impact of modal logic

In the broad area of mathematical logic, the biggest

philosophical punch is packed by modal logic, including tense logic (see MODAL LOGIC; MODAL LOGIC, PHILOSOPHICAL ISSUES IN; TENSE AND TEMPORAL LOGIC). Modal logic has been important since Aristotle (see LOGIC, ANCIENT; LOGIC IN THE 17TH AND 18TH CENTURIES; LOGIC IN THE 19TH CENTURY; LOGIC IN THE EARLY 20TH CENTURY) but has only been put on a rigorous footing in the second half of the twentieth century, by such figures as Hintikka, Kanger, Prior, and most especially Kripke (see SEMANTICS, POSSIBLE WORLDS). The most important philosophical outgrowth of this mathematical work is contained in Kripke's three lectures from January 1970 published as 'Naming and Necessity', in which Kripke draws out some ways in which possible worlds semantics is in tension with then-prevailing orthodoxies in the philosophy of language and mind. Some of Kripke's views have become new orthodoxies since (see ESSENTIALISM; PROPER NAMES; REFERENCE §§2–4; for related work by David Lewis, Robert Stalnaker, David Kaplan and others that uses the possible worlds framework, see COUNTERFACTUAL CONDITIONALS; DEMONSTRATIVES AND INDEXICALS; DESCRIPTIONS).

To give some flavour of developments here, consider the familiar Fregean view that the relation of *reference* which holds between a name and its bearer is sustained by the relation of *presentation* which holds between the *sense* of the name and the bearer of the name: the name refers to such-and-such an object precisely because it expresses a sense which presents that object (see FREGE, G. §3; SENSE AND REFERENCE). When pressed for an explanation of what the senses of names are like, the natural Fregean response is to specify them, as Frege himself did in some cases, using definite descriptions (see DESCRIPTIONS). So, for instance, the sense of the name 'Aristotle' might be 'the pupil of Plato who taught Alexander'. However, though it may well in fact have been Aristotle who taught Alexander, there are many ways things might have gone (many 'possible worlds') in which someone other than Aristotle is taught by Plato and teaches Alexander: suppose Aristotle had got the appointment but been killed in an accident before he could take it up, and had been replaced at Philip's insistence by another pupil of Plato. The description 'the pupil of Plato who taught Alexander' is therefore 'non-rigid', in Kripke's terminology. That is, it can pick out different individuals in different possible worlds, and in some worlds may pick out no one (Philip for some reason comes to distrust Platonic pedagogy and fails to conduct an equal opportunity search). But it is clear from the formal semantics for modal logic that there is conceptual 'room' for a category of expression which is 'rigid', in the sense

that it picks out the same object in every possible world, or at least in every possible world where it picks out any object at all. So the formal semantics prompts the question whether names in natural language behave as if their reference is determined by a sense which presents different individuals at different worlds, or whether they behave as if they are rigid designators. With a series of brilliant examples Kripke demonstrates that names are rigid designators and therefore do not express reference-determining senses which are non-rigid (see PROPER NAMES).

The idea that a formal semantics for a kind of logic provides an account of a possible semantics for a category of natural-language expression, opening the door to debate on whether it is the right account or not, also captures some of the philosophical bearing of kinds of logic other than modal logic. Thus free logic shows how name-like expressions can function without standard existential commitment (see FREE LOGICS, PHILOSOPHICAL ISSUES IN); intuitionistic logic and many-valued logic show how a language can have a compositional semantics even if its sentences are not used to make statements with verification-transcendent truth-conditions which always either obtain or fail to obtain (see COMPOSITIONALITY; INTUITIONISTIC LOGIC AND ANTIREALISM; MANY-VALUED LOGICS, PHILOSOPHICAL ISSUES IN; PRESUPPOSITION). And second-order logic offers a particular way of understanding the semantic import of a range of puzzling locutions, such as plural quantifiers (see SECOND-ORDER LOGIC, PHILOSOPHICAL ISSUES IN). In all these cases the formal semantics for the logical system prompts debates about how well the semantics carries over to natural language.

2 Logic and language

There is also a collection of long-established topics discussion of which can be much improved, in rigour at least, in the light of the development of modern logic. For example, a distinction between propositions (or statements, or sentential contexts) which are *de dicto* and propositions (and so on) which are *de re* originates in medieval philosophy. But only contemporary modal logic affords the tools for a precise characterization of this distinction, although it must be granted that the distinction remains a puzzle in *epistemic* contexts (see DE RE/DE DICTO; DESCRIPTIONS §2; PROPOSITIONAL ATTITUDE STATEMENTS). Other topics which can be classified in this way include ESSENTIALISM, EXISTENCE, IDENTITY, INDICATIVE CONDITIONALS, MODAL OPERATORS, QUANTIFIERS and VAGUENESS. Again, to give some of the flavour of this kind of work, consider the *de re/de dicto* contrast. There is an evident syntactic difference between 'It is necessary that parents have children' and 'Parents are such that it is necessary that they have children', but just because there is a syntactic difference, it does not follow that there is any interesting difference in meaning. But the difference can be brought out quite precisely in possible worlds semantics. To say that it is necessary that parents have children is to say that in every possible world, the people who are parents *in that world* have children in that world; and this is an obvious truth. On the other hand, to say that parents are such that it is necessary that they have children is to say that the people who are parents *in the actual world* are such that they have children in every possible world. This is clearly false, even putting aside contingency of existence of actual parents. For given anyone who is actually a parent, there is a way things could have gone – a possible world – in which that person is childless, hence not a parent (see QUANTIFIERS, SUBSTITUTIONAL AND OBJECTUAL; MODAL OPERATORS).

When a formal semantics for a system of logic is applied to a fragment of natural language, a very precise account of the literal content of sentences in that fragment is given. But there may be aspects of the meanings of those sentences which are omitted. Philosophical views may then divide over whether the formal semantics has been shown to be wanting as an account of the semantics of the fragment, or whether instead the aspects of meaning not captured have been shown not to belong to literal content (see PRESUPPOSITION). In the case of indicative conditionals, for instance, the formal semantics that is relevant is the simplest possible kind, namely, the truth-functional account of 'if...then...'. According to this account, 'If p then q' is true if p is false or if q is true, regardless of the actual meanings of p and q. So in particular, any indicative conditional with a true consequent is true; examples would include 'If lead floats in water then lead sinks in water' and 'If the solar system has nine planets then the Conservative Party lost the British elections in 1997'. Barring an astrological justification of the latter, both these conditionals look decidedly odd. But oddness is one thing, falsity another. The idea that such conditionals are false is based on the thought that if a conditional is true, then in establishing it in the most direct manner, non-redundant use has to be made of the antecedent. Spelling this out leads to relevance logic (see RELEVANCE LOGIC AND ENTAILMENT; INDICATIVE CONDITIONALS). On the other hand, if we say the conditionals are merely odd, we are led to some theory of communication to explain the oddness (see GRICE, H.P.; IMPLICATURE).

But we should not take away the impression that the traffic is all one way, from logic to language or from pure mathematics to pure philosophy. There is a two-way street here, with the above comments on conditionals representing a common phenomenon; that of a concern in the philosophy of language giving rise to a formal development which in turn feeds back into philosophy. For example, the idea that for a conditional to be true, the most direct way of establishing it must make non-redundant use of its antecedent seems clear enough on the face of it, but familiarity with logic of conditionals literature may well lead one to reconsider. This kind of dialectical interplay should continue to be a fruitful source of philosophical research for the foreseeable future.

See also: ADVERBS; AMBIGUITY; ANAPHORA; DUMMETT, M.A.E.; FALLACIES; FORMAL AND INFORMAL LOGIC; IDENTITY OF INDISCERNIBLES; IMPERATIVE LOGIC; INDIRECT DISCOURSE; INTENSIONAL ENTITIES; INTENSIONALITY; KRIPKE, S.A.; LINEAR LOGIC; LOGIC IN CHINA; LOGIC IN ISLAMIC PHILOSOPHY; LOGIC IN JAPAN; LOGICAL AND MATHEMATICAL TERMS, GLOSSARY OF; LOGICAL CONSTANTS; LOGICAL FORM; LOGICAL LAWS; MASS TERMS; NECESSARY TRUTH AND CONVENTION; ONTOLOGICAL COMMITMENT; PREDICATION; PRIOR, A.N.; PROPOSITIONS, SENTENCES AND STATEMENTS; QUANTIFICATION AND INFERENCE; QUANTIFIERS, GENERALIZED; QUESTIONS; QUINE, W.V.O.; RUSSELL, B.A.W.; SCOPE; TYPE/TOKEN DISTINCTION; USE/MENTION DISTINCTION AND QUOTATION; VAGUENESS

References and further reading

Hughes, R.I.G. (ed.) (1993) *A Philosophical Companion to First-Order Logic*, Indianapolis, IN: Hackett Publishing Company. (New and reprinted papers of varying levels of difficulty.)

Tomberlin, J.E. (ed.) (1994) *Logic and Language*, Philosophical Perspectives 8, Atascadero, CA: Ridgeview. (A collection of new papers on relevant topics.)

GRAEME FORBES

LOGIC, POLISH *see* POLISH LOGIC

LOGIC, QUANTUM *see* QUANTUM LOGIC

LOGIC, RENAISSANCE

Renaissance logic is often identified with humanist logic, which is in some ways closer to rhetoric than to the study of formal argumentation. This is a mistake, for although changes did take place, a hard core of logical teaching remained the same throughout the medieval and Renaissance periods and into the eighteenth century. Logic was embedded in the educational system as the main study of beginning undergraduates, and although institutional changes had an effect on the presentation and use of logic texts, the study of valid arguments was always central.

There are two obvious differences between medieval texts and their sixteenth-century successors. The first is a new emphasis on following the order and material of Aristotle's Organon, with the consequent emphasis on the categorical syllogism as the central type of argument. Such medieval material as survived was strictly subordinated to this end; and even though the humanist logicians Agricola and Ramus had tried to ignore Aristotelian syllogistic and the doctrines propaedeutic to it (such as conversion and opposition), their omissions were rapidly remedied by subsequent textbook writers.

The second difference has to do with language and style. Medieval writers treated Latin as a technical, almost artificial language. They were deeply concerned with the effects that different word-orders and the addition of extra logical particles had on both meaning and reference, and they made heavy use of sophismata, *deliberately constructed problematic or puzzling sentences. Although Latin remained the language of instruction, the approach of a Renaissance logician, whether humanist or Aristotelian, commentator or textbook writer, is totally different. Sophismata have completely disappeared, and so too has any attempt to treat Latin as a technical language in which different word-orders represent different logical structures. The propositions used for such operations as syllogistic conversion are presented in an already fully standardized form, and they are always relatively simple.*

Why these changes came about is a difficult question. Humanism coexisted too long with medieval logic for humanism to be the sole explanation, and the fact that Renaissance logicians returned to the commentaries of Averroes and Aquinas on the Organon shows that mere revolt against anything medieval is not a sufficient explanation either. Changes in grammar teaching, changes in the relation of logic to the study of natural science, and changes in other parts of the university curriculum presumably have a good deal to do with the appearance of a new style of logic. In particular, the humanist emphasis on logic as a tool for analysing discourse focused attention on the use of logic

in literature, history and biblical studies, and demanded a combination of simplicity and literary elegance, rather than any genuine formal innovation. There was no concurrent move to relate logic to the new developments in mathematics, and logic was not to be seen as a formal system linked with other formal systems until the nineteenth century.

1   The nature and divisions of logic

One of the features distinguishing sixteenth-century textbooks, whatever their orientation, from their medieval predecessors was their approach to the nature and divisions of logic. Medieval authors had asked whether logic is more properly a linguistic discipline directed towards spoken words (*scientia sermocinalis*) or a rational discipline directed towards concepts (*scientia rationalis*), and this question did not disappear (see LOGIC, MEDIEVAL §4). However, its presentation was to some extent altered. The influence of the humanists, especially AGRICOLA, gave general popularity to Cicero's definition (*Topics* II 6) of logic as an art of discourse (or *ratio disserendi*) (see CICERO §2), and this notion is also found in such scholastic authors as TOLETUS and FONSECA. At the same time, logic was frequently said to have as its subject either conceptual entities (beings of reason: *entia rationis*) (see JOHN OF ST THOMAS §2; LANGUAGE, RENAISSANCE PHILOSOPHY OF §3), or second intentions (see ZABARELLA, J. §2). Toletus denied a distinction between these two notions in this context, on the grounds that to talk about the kind of conceptual entity which has no existence independently of the mind is just to talk about those second-order logical concepts or intentions (genus, species, syllogism and so on) which we use to organize first-order concepts, those which apply directly to things in the world.

One issue which was the subject of lively debate concerned the very use of the word *logica* as opposed to *dialectica*. It was a medieval commonplace that *dialectica* could be used in two senses, a broad sense which equated dialectic with logic, and a narrow sense, in which dialectic was the kind of probable argumentation discussed in Aristotle's *Topics* (see §4) (see FONSECA, P. DA §2). In the sixteenth century, RAMUS argued in his *Scholae* (Lectures) that the division of logic into demonstrative, dialectical and sophistical reasoning is baseless, and that all logic is dialectic (see §4). Zabarella, on the other hand, believed that 'dialectic' did name a distinct part of logic, and should be reserved for that part alone.

Another issue which reflects the impact of humanism concerned the way in which logic was divided. Perhaps the most important division was that into invention and judgment, invention being the part of logic which finds the subject matter for argumentation, and judgment being the part which organizes the subject matter. This division came principally from Cicero (*Topics* II 6) and was well known to medieval logicians, before it was further popularized by Agricola, MELANCHTHON and Ramus. A mark of Ramist textbooks was that they began with invention, but Melanchthon, followed by various authors including John Seton (see §5) put judgment first. Another way of organizing which was to become especially popular in the seventeenth century (see JOHN OF ST THOMAS §2; LOGIC IN THE 17TH AND 18TH CENTURIES §1) was a division in accordance with the three acts of mind, the apprehension of simples (terms), composition and division (propositions), and reasoning (arguments). Like the division into invention and judgment, this division has a long history.

2 The medieval inheritance

Although Aristotle served as a focal point for the study of logic during the Middle Ages and Renaissance (see §3), one of the main features of medieval logic was the production of independent texts on particular topics, some of which had no reference to Aristotelian logic. The most important of these texts were the so-called *parva logicalia*, or treatises dealing with the properties of terms, including their reference in various contexts. Here we find tracts on supposition, on relative terms, on ampliation, appellation, restriction and distribution (see LOGIC, MEDIEVAL §7). These core treatises were supplemented in various ways, particularly by treatises about exponible terms, those logical particles such as 'except' and 'only' whose presence calls for the analysis of an apparently simple categorical proposition into several conjoined propositions.

A second major group of treatises consisted of the 'three tracts of the moderns', which concern propositions and the relations between them. Here we find treatises on consequences, obligations and insolubles. Treatises on consequences covered all types of argumentation, beginning with a general discussion of what constitutes a formally valid inference, and including a good deal of propositional logic. The syllogism often appeared as a special example of one kind of argumentation. Treatises on obligations dealt with the rules to be followed in a certain kind of disputation which was specifically designed to test the logical skills of undergraduates, and which deliberately confined itself to exploring the logical consequences of affirming an often bizarre falsehood. Treatises on insolubles dealt with semantic paradoxes, such as the standard liar paradox, 'What I am now saying to you is false', and they explored in some depth the semantic presuppositions of language (see SEMANTIC PARADOXES AND THEORIES OF TRUTH).

During the fifteenth century much of this medieval material was used throughout Europe, and Italy was particularly enthusiastic about the products of fourteenth-century Oxford logicians, such as HEYTESBURY and Ralph Strode. *Summulae* or general textbooks from the earlier period were also used. The best known is by PETER OF SPAIN, and it gives a fairly complete outline of Aristotelian logic as well as the *parva logicalia*. However, it would be a mistake to think that only Peter of Spain was used, for in some places (such as England) he was never used, and in other places only parts of his work were used. BURIDAN (§2), ALBERT OF SAXONY and PAUL OF VENICE were the authors of other popular textbooks. Indeed, the first medieval logic text known to have been printed is Paul's *Logica parva*, printed in 1472 (and still being reprinted in Venice as late as 1614).

At the beginning of the sixteenth century, particularly in Paris, there was a strong revival of the medieval tradition. Separate treatises on supposition theory, exponibles, consequences, insolubles and obligations continued to be written (see MAJOR, J. §2), and to these were added new treatises on such matters as terms and opposed propositions. At the same time, new commentaries on Peter of Spain were being published in Paris, Germany and Spain. The 1529 edition of Domingo de Soto's *Summulae* included commentary on the first and fourth books of Peter of Spain along with treatises dealing with terms and supposition theory, exponibles, insolubles, and obligations (see SOTO, D. DE).

Outside Spain, this activity came to an abrupt halt around 1530. No new independent treatises on Peter of Spain were written; the publication of works written during the first three decades of the sixteenth century ceased, and the publication of such medieval authors as Buridan and Heytesbury also ceased. Only in Spain and its colonies did authors continue to produce commentaries on Peter of Spain, such as that by Alonso de la Vera Cruz, first published in Mexico in 1554, or that by Tomás Mercado, published in Seville in 1571 (see LATIN AMERICA, COLONIAL THOUGHT IN §3; MEXICO, PHILOSOPHY IN §1).

By the end of the sixteenth century those parts of medieval material which could not easily be integrated with Aristotelian logic simply disappeared, at best being the subject of stray and often unflattering references. Insolubles were no longer discussed, obligations were replaced by a discussion of ordinary disputations in which truth was the main issue, and many of the topics connected with supposition theory were dropped. But exponibles, consequences and the central part of supposition theory remained in truncated and simplified form (see §6).

3 Aristotle and Aristotelianism

At least in principle, Aristotle's Organon played a central role throughout the medieval and Renaissance period (see ARISTOTLE §4), though not all parts were studied with equal fervour. For instance, the *Topics* was sometimes omitted altogether, and sometimes only certain of its books were assigned. The text of the Organon was accompanied by explanation and commentary, and the invention of printing brought the wide dissemination of some of the medieval commentaries on Aristotle's logical works, including those by Walter BURLEY and PAUL OF VENICE. Later there was a return to commentaries by the great theologians of the thirteenth and early fourteenth centuries. Thus, the commentaries of Aquinas on *De interpretatione* and *Posterior Analytics* reached a peak of popularity in the mid-sixteenth century, and the commentaries by or attributed to ALBERT THE GREAT (§2), GILES OF ROME and John Duns Scotus were also published (see ARISTOTELIANISM, MEDIEVAL §5). The great Giunta edition of Aristotle with the commentaries of Averroes (1550–2) should also be mentioned.

The impact of humanist classical studies on Renaissance logic is particularly important in two respects: first, the edition and translation of Greek commentators on Aristotle, only some of whom had been known during the Middle Ages; and second, the edition and translation of Aristotle himself. During the fifteenth century the Byzantine humanist and philosopher Johannes Argyropoulos (c. 1415–87) had produced new Latin translations, but as the Greek text became better known, more and more dissatisfaction was felt with former translations, including those of Argyropoulos. A good example of the new Greek-based texts is the Organon edition of Giulio Pace first published in 1584. In it we find the Greek text side-by-side with a new translation designed not only to read well but also to capture the philosophical significance of Aristotle's words. In the margins there is a commentary dealing with difficult points both of theory and of translation. However, the old translations did not disappear, because they provided much

of the standard vocabulary in philosophy, and the work of surviving medieval commentators was keyed to them (see HUMANISM, RENAISSANCE).

So far as content is concerned, there were few developments within Aristotelian logic. There was considerable discussion of scientific method (see §7), and there was also some lively debate about the acceptability of the fourth figure of the syllogism, particularly inspired by ZABARELLA. Otherwise, Aristotelianism's main achievement was its successful stand against attempts such as those by Lorenzo VALLA (§4) and Petrus RAMUS to replace basic Aristotelian notions. This achievement was mainly due to the felt need for formal content in logic teaching (see §5) (see ARISTOTELIANISM, RENAISSANCE §1).

4 Humanist logic and the topics

To understand humanist logic, one must consider the relations between dialectic, the topics, and rhetoric. 'Dialectic' is a term with various meanings. For those who did not use it as a mere synonym for logic, at least three approaches were possible. One could present dialectic as the study of debate or disputation; one could present dialectic as the study of the topics (roughly speaking, headings under which material could be gathered); or one could present dialectic as the study of probable argumentation.

The last two approaches are closely related to the concerns of rhetoric, and there is a tendency in the literature to speak as if humanist logic was the result of subordinating logic to rhetoric. However, while it is true that rhetoric texts featured the invention or finding of topics, and that rhetoric, as the art of persuasion, could be construed as dealing with arguments about probabilities, the three standard works about topics had always been firmly part of the logic syllabus. These were Aristotle's *Topics*, together with Boethius' two works, *De topicis differentiis* (On Topical Differences) and *In Ciceronis Topica* (On Cicero's *Topics*) (see BOETHIUS, A.M.S. §3). Boethius' first work was more important in the medieval period, though in the fourteenth century it was largely replaced by the account of topics given by Peter of Spain in his *Summulae*. In the sixteenth century Boethius' second work became popular again, as did Cicero's original text. Agricola himself was well-acquainted with both Aristotle and Boethius.

The notion that dialectic is concerned with probable argumentation comes from Aristotle's *Topics*, which opens with a distinction between demonstrative reasoning, said to deal with certainties, and dialectical reasoning, said to deal with probabilities. However, there are two ways of reading the distinction. One way involves two types of logic, a logic of formally valid deductive arguments, and a logic of informal arguments or strategies. The other way of reading Aristotle's distinction is to assume that 'argument' or 'reasoning' in the Topics refers only to the syllogism as described in the *Prior Analytics*, namely a particular kind of formally valid deductive structure. This second reading led medieval logicians to interpret Aristotle's distinction between demonstrative reasoning and dialectical reasoning as an epistemic one. Thus, demonstrative reasoning involves formal syllogisms with premises that are certainly true, and dialectical reasoning involves the same formal syllogisms with premises that are only probably true. It was this epistemic reading that led Ramus to argue that dialectic and logic are the same, since the same patterns of argumentation appear in both. In Agricola, on the other hand, we find a somewhat greater awareness of the possibility of a properly non-formal logic.

The general failure of humanist logicians, including Agricola, to pursue dialectic as an informal logic of probabilities was closely associated with their treatment of the other aspect of dialectic, dialectic as a topics-logic, or means of finding the material for arguments. In Boethius, the notion of a topic had covered two things. First, a topic was a maxim (or 'maximal proposition'), a self-evidently true universal generalization which could either be inserted into an argument as a premise or which could be appealed to as providing a warrant for an argument. Some of these maxims were themselves turned into formal deductive arguments by medieval logicians, who had a tendency to absorb invention into judgment, but others were not easily formalized. As such, they provide the perfect nucleus for a developed informal logic. The second sense of topic for Boethius was the topic as the *differentia* of a maximal proposition, that is, the characteristic that enables us to classify maximal propositions into groups. To list the topics in this second sense is simply to list the headings under which material can be gathered: 'definition', 'genus', 'cause', 'opposite', 'similar' and so on.

What we find in AGRICOLA (§2) is a deliberate rejection of the maxims, and of material that might belong to judgment rather than invention. He argued that the purpose of any maxim is simply to present a necessary argument, and that they are quite inappropriate for all the cases in which we are dealing with probabilities. We should note here that Agricola is clearly talking not just of the epistemological status of the premises of an argument, but of a probabilistic and informal relationship between premises and conclusion. He also claimed that maxims were too restrictive, for they represent an attempt to force a

wide range of material into a narrow compass; and that they are of no use to someone who really understands the nature of topics. What we are left with, then, is the topics solely as headings under which material can be organized. Their most obvious link with argumentation, both formal and informal, has been broken.

In the hands of Agricola's later follower, Petrus RAMUS (§2), we find the topics presented in an Agricolan way, without maxims, but with a new theoretical foundation. They are not merely useful headings for gathering material, but they represent the mind's natural organization of data. As such, topics function as categories; and, indeed, Ramus emphasized that his topics are more useful and more natural than Aristotle's ten categories (see CATE-GORIES §1). If we are asked to discuss war, peace, or the state, it is no use to think in terms of the category of substance. Instead we must appeal to such topics as cause, event and opposites.

The result of these reforms was a subordination of rhetoric to logic (rather than the reverse), in three respects. First, the topics were now to be confined to dialectic, and rhetorical topics, which had covered material of a more particular kind, were to be reduced to dialectical topics. Second, rhetoric's *dispositio* is introduced into the dialectic text through the discussion of method as a way of ordering discourse. Third, we find that rhetoric, at least in the eyes of the humanist logician, was to be confined to the business of ornamenting discourse, and discussing only those persuasive devices which did not involve argumentation.

5 Humanist and Ramist textbooks

The needs of the university curriculum meant that humanist insights and changes were only partially reflected in logic teaching. Thus Agricola's seminal *De inventione dialectica* (see AGRICOLA §2) was often used in conjunction with a little Aristotelian handbook by GEORGE OF TREBIZOND. The very popular textbooks of MELANCHTHON provide another good example. He enjoyed the Agricolan emphasis on clarity of style and the use of literary allusions; he accepted the importance of the topics and the part of logic called invention; and he discussed method. At the same time, he remained a convinced Aristotelian, who believed that students needed to be taught some formal logic. The formal techniques he used were those of syllogistic, and his work included a discussion of the other standard Aristotelian logical subjects, including the categories and the square of opposition for propositions.

Another example from the first part of the

sixteenth century is John Seton's *Dialectica*, first published in England in 1545, and later to appear with annotations by Peter Carter. Seton explained in his introduction that he had written the work because of the absence of a suitable text for the instruction of the young. Aristotle was too difficult, Agricola had deliberately restricted himself to the subject of invention, and Melanchthon's style was not suited to elementary teaching. He makes frequent references to Agricola, as well as to CICERO, Quintilian and ERASMUS. He included the bulk of traditional Aristotelian logic from the categories to the syllogism, which he described as the most important part of judgment, and he also retained the strictly medieval doctrine of the supposition of terms, though in a considerably truncated form.

In the second part of the century the most important textbook writer was Petrus RAMUS (§2), the most notorious logician of the period. He is known both for his attacks on Aristotle and for the simplified logic presented in his *Dialectique* of 1555, and in a variety of Latin versions. The *Dialectique* had two parts. The first, on invention, covered the topics, and the second, on judgment, presented a deliberately simplified version of the syllogism followed by an account of method as a means of ordering in the arts and sciences. No reference was made to such standard material as the categories, the square of opposition, conversion, demonstration and fallacies. On the other hand, the work is rich with quotations from the poetry and prose of classical authors, which must have strengthened the impression among students that logic was both easy and fun.

The book had a remarkable publishing history, but it is not clear how much impact it actually had on the university scene. In England, Ramus certainly enjoyed some popularity at Cambridge but was less well received at Oxford. Even in Germany, where 151 editions appeared, university teachers of logic soon found serious deficiencies in Ramus' book, and in the 1590s a new school of textbook writers known as the Philippo-Ramists appeared in Germany. Their aim was to combine what was best in Ramus with what was best in the more Aristotelian work of Philipp Melanchthon. As a result, they tended to restore those parts of Aristotelian logic that Ramus had deliberately omitted, and the syllogism was once more presented as central to formal logic (see LOGIC IN THE 17TH AND 18TH CENTURIES §1).

6 Late scholastic textbooks

If England and Germany saw the production of slim textbooks exemplifying the marriage between humanism and a simplified Aristotelianism, Spain and Italy were the scene of a much more substantial textbook production. Two important texts, both recommended by the Jesuit *Ratio Studiorum* of 1599, and thus possibly studied by Descartes at La Flèche, were the *Introductio in dialecticam Aristotelis* (Introduction to the Dialectic of Aristotle) of Franciscus TOLETUS (§3) and the *Institutionum dialecticarum* (Dialectical Instructions) of Pedro da FONSECA (§2). Toletus' book was first published in Rome in 1560, and the last of its eighteen editions appeared in Milan in 1621. Fonseca's work was first published in Lisbon in 1564, and the last of its fifty-two editions appeared in Lyons in 1625. The works were fairly similar in content. The Organon is very much central but medieval material is used to supplement Aristotle in various places. Exponibles are discussed, albeit in a simplified form; some non-syllogistic consequences dealing with truth and modality are listed, and material about supposition and related doctrines is presented as an aid to understanding fallacies.

The most important English text of this type was Robert Sanderson's *Logicae Artis Compendium* which appeared at Oxford in 1615 and was to remain a standard text there until well into the eighteenth century. This, too, contains a full account of strictly Aristotelian logic, together with brief discussions of the medieval doctrines of supposition, exponibles and consequences, and a full discussion of method as a way of ordering discourse.

7 The discussion of method

A particular feature of textbooks, especially in the second part of the sixteenth century, was the discussion of method. First, and most important, is the study of scientific method, which is particularly characteristic of Italian universities. These had always been distinguished from Northern European universities by their strong emphasis on law and medicine, combined with a relatively slight emphasis on theology. The faculties of arts at such places as Padua provided studies leading to a degree in arts and medicine, and as a result the main emphasis was placed on logic and natural philosophy, as propaedeutic to medicine. In the fifteenth century works stemming from Oxford and Paris on such topics as the intension and remission of forms were particularly important (see NATURAL PHILOSOPHY, MEDIEVAL §6), but after about 1520 these works fell into sudden oblivion. By the mid-sixteenth century the focus of attention was on the Greek commentators and on Averroes (see IBN RUSHD), especially his *Physics* commentary. The main Aristotelian text studied was the *Posterior Analytics*. From Cajetan of Thiene (Gaetano da Thiene) (1387–1465) to NIFO there was a gradual refinement of writings on demonstration and scientific method which culminated in the work of Jacopo ZABARELLA (§4). His discussions of the methods of resolution, composition, and the so-called *regressus* (a method for uniting resolution and composition) were summarized in many later textbooks, often in uneasy alliance with two other types of method.

A second notion of method presents it as a way of organizing discourse, a method fully discussed by AGRICOLA (§2). Agricola showed how argumentative and expository passages from classical literature could be analysed, a method which brought the logical text very close to the new humanist curriculum of many institutions (see HUMANISM, RENAISSANCE §7). Agricola's approach was picked up and further popularized by MELANCHTHON (§2).

A third type of method is that of RAMUS (§3), which is particularly directed towards the presentation of a subject, and best known for its presentation through diagrammed dichotomies. This too could be and was adapted to the analysis of literary and biblical texts.

See also: LOGIC, ANCIENT; ARISTOTELIANISM, MEDIEVAL; ARISTOTELIANISM, RENAISSANCE; ARISTOTLE; HUMANISM, RENAISSANCE; LANGUAGE, MEDIEVAL THEORIES OF; LANGUAGE, RENAISSANCE PHILOSOPHY OF; LOGIC, MEDIEVAL

References and further reading

Ashworth, E.J. (1974) *Language and Logic in the Post-Medieval Period*, Dordrecht and Boston, MA: Reidel. (A comprehensive account, thematically arranged, and making use of the techniques of modern symbolic logic.)

—— (1978) *The Tradition of Medieval Logic and Speculative Grammar from Anselm to the End of the Seventeenth Century: A Bibliography from 1836 Onwards*, Toronto, Ont.: Pontifical Institute of Mediaeval Studies. (Annotated bibliography with full indexes.)

—— (1985) *Studies in Post-Medieval Semantics*, London: Variorum. (A collection including studies of supposition theory, insolubles and exponibles.)

—— (1988) 'Traditional Logic', in *The Cambridge History of Renaissance Philosophy*, ed. C.B. Schmitt, Q. Skinner and E. Kessler, Cambridge: Cambridge University Press, 143–72. (A useful general account with plenty of references.)

Jardine, L. (1988) 'Humanistic Logic', in *The Cambridge History of Renaissance Philosophy*, ed. C.B. Schmitt, Q. Skinner and E. Kessler, Cambridge: Cambridge University Press, 173–98. (A useful general account, though controversial on Valla; shows how humanist logic was used in textual exegesis.)

Lohr, C.H. (1988) *Latin Aristotle Commentaries II. Renaissance Authors*, Florence: Olschki. (Alphabetically organized list of Renaissance Aristotelians, with biographies and bibliographies of primary and secondary sources.)

Mack, P. (1993) *Renaissance Argument: Valla and Agricola in the Traditions of Rhetoric and Dialectic*, Leiden, New York and Cologne: Brill. (Excellent account of humanist logic, including Melanchthon and Ramus.)

Risse, W. (1964) *Die Logik der Neuzeit. I Band. 1500–1640* (The Logic of the Modern Period), Stuttgart and Bad Cannstatt: Frommann. (A dense, scholarly account, without much awareness of the medieval background, and with no awareness of twentieth-century logical developments.)

—— (1965) *Bibliographia Logica. Verzeichnis der Druckschriften zur Logik mit Angabe ihrer Fundorte. Band I. 1472–1800* (Bibliography of Logic: List of Printed Works on Logic with Details of their Location), Hildesheim: Olms. (The bibliography organized chronologically but it is fully indexed.)

* Sanderson, R. (1618) *Logicae Artis Compendium*, ed. E.J. Ashworth, Bologna: Editrice CLUEB. (This book contains a facsimile of the 1618 edition of Sanderson's work (referred to in §6), together with indexes and a lengthy introduction which gives full information about English logic in the sixteenth century, including a discussion of John Seton (referred to in §5).)

Vasoli, C. (1968) *La dialettica e la retorica dell'Umanesimo. 'Invenzione' e 'Metodo' nella cultura del XV e XVI secolo* (Humanist Dialectic and Rhetoric: 'Invention' and 'Method' in the Culture of the 15th and 16th Centuries), Milan: Feltrinelli. (Dated but classic account of humanist logic.)

Wallace, W.A. (1995) 'Circularity and the Paduan *Regressus*: From Pietro d'Abano to Galileo Galilei', *Vivarium* 33: 76–97. (Outline of Paduan discussions of scientific method.)

E.J. ASHWORTH

LOGICAL ATOMISM

The name 'logical atomism' refers to a network of theses about the parts and structure of the world and the means by which language represents the world. Wittgenstein, in his Tractatus Logico-Philosophicus, *expounds a version of logical atomism developed by him around the time of the First World War, as does Russell in works published contemporaneously. It is no accident that their work on logical atomism shares a common surface description since it resulted from their mutual influence at Cambridge. The common theme is that the meaning of our sentences is rooted in a primitive relation between simple expressions and their simple worldly bearers, the logical atoms. In a logically perfect language, atomic sentences describe configurations of these atoms, and complex sentences are combinations of the atomic sentences. But sentences of ordinary language may have a misleading surface form which is revealed as such by analysis. The common theme masks considerable differences of doctrine. In particular, there are differences in the nature of logical atoms and in the arguments for the existence of these atoms.*

1 **Wittgenstein's logical atomism**
2 **Russell's logical atomism**

1 Wittgenstein's logical atomism

Wittgenstein's logical atomism is expounded in his *Tractatus Logico-Philosophicus* (1921) in which he explores the structure of the world and the structure of any language fit to represent the world (see WITTGENSTEIN, L. §5). The unit of sentential representation is the atomic sentence, and Wittgenstein claims that every sentence can be analysed into a combination of atomic sentences which describe atomic states of affairs. Each atomic sentence has exactly one of the two truth-values, true and false, and there are no necessarily true or necessarily false atomic sentences. If an atomic sentence is true, then the state of affairs it describes exists, the existent atomic state of affairs being called 'an atomic fact'. If an atomic sentence is false, then the state of affairs it describes does not exist (see FACTS §1; TRUTH, CORRESPONDENCE THEORY OF).

An atomic sentence is structurally isomorphic to the atomic state of affairs described. It consists of an arrangement of names, and these names have simple objects as their meanings. The atomic state of affairs described by the atomic sentence consists of the named objects arranged in a way which corresponds to the arrangement of the names in the sentence. The objects named in atomic sentences and featuring in atomic states of affairs are Wittgenstein's logical atoms.

The atomic sentences form a system which is fit to represent any possible world. A possible world is represented by an assignment of truth-values to the atomic sentences. Atomic sentences are independent in the sense that there are no logical relations between them which rule out certain assignments of truth-

values to the atomic sentences. The actual world is completely described by the atomic sentences which are true and false in it. So the actual world is the totality of atomic facts, the existent states of affairs described by the true atomic sentences.

Atomic sentences form the basis for Wittgenstein's analysis of the sentences of ordinary language. Any sentence of ordinary language has a unique translation into a sentence which is a truth-functional combination of atomic sentences. This is the principle of extensionality. A complex sentence is a truth-functional combination of atomic sentences just in case the truth-value of the complex sentence is entirely determined by the truth-values of its constituent atomic sentences. The sentential connectives of the propositional calculus, such as '&', yield truth-functional combinations of atomic sentences.

Some truth-functional combinations of atomic sentences yield sentences which are true no matter what truth-values are assigned to the constituent atomic sentences, and sentences which are false no matter what truth-values are assigned to the constituent atomic sentences. These are the tautologies (such as 'P or not-P') and the contradictions (such as 'P & not-P'), respectively. Wittgenstein claims that all necessary truths are tautologies and all necessary falsehoods are contradictions.

Sentences of ordinary language may appear to be atomic, but analysis can reveal them to be complex. The aim of analysis is thus to uncover the accurate representations of the world which lie behind the misleading surface forms of ordinary language. The unit of sentential representation is the atomic sentence, but an atomic sentence is itself compounded out of names which have simple objects as their meanings. Hence, the meaning of every sentence of our language is grounded in this primitive meaning relation holding between names and the simple objects which they name. But the more familiar entities of ordinary discourse, such as tables and chairs, are complex. So a sentence about a complex entity is bound to be analysed as a combination of atomic sentences, these sentences describing the arrangements of the simple objects which are the parts of the complex entity. Here we have the idea of analysis as the decomposition of complex entities into arrangements of their simple parts.

Why should there be simple objects at all? Why can complex objects not divide for ever and ever into less complex parts? Wittgenstein argues a priori from the possibility of representation to the existence of his simple objects using a *reductio ad absurdum*. First, he assumes that there is an atomic sentence featuring an expression standing for a complex entity. Second, he brings in a background assumption that sense be determinate, that is, every sentence has exactly one of the two truth-values in any possible world. As an illustration, suppose that the sentence 'the broom is to the left of the cupboard' is an atomic sentence. It features the expression 'the broom' which stands for a complex entity. The broom exists only if its parts exist and are arranged in the right way. Consider a possible world in which the broom does not exist – our sentence is not true in this world. But neither can it be false. For the sentence is atomic and thus does not contain as part of its meaning a condition which determines that the sentence is false when the broom does not exist. But every sentence must be either true or false in any possible world. So an atomic sentence must contain only expressions which stand for simple objects.

This shows that simple objects must exist but does not tell us what they are like. It appears that Wittgenstein thought that this was not a logician's job. Early interpreters of the *Tractatus*, taking their cue from Russell's logical atomism and Wittgenstein's examples, took the simples to be the units of perceptual experience, in other words sense-data. But the independence of atomic sentences precludes such an interpretation. 'This sense-datum is red' and 'this (same) sense-datum is green' would be atomic sentences but they cannot both be true.

Wittgenstein later came to think that his model of the relationship between language and the world was radically misconceived. His most immediate criticism was to reject the independence of atomic sentences, which he did by considering sentences featuring colour predicates. This was at the same time the denial that all necessary truths and falsehoods are tautologies and contradictions, respectively. For the necessary falsehood 'this sense-datum is red and green' is not a contradiction. In the first part of his *Philosophical Investigations* (1953) Wittgenstein mounts a sustained attack against the pivotal claims that the meaning of sentences is rooted in the relationship between name and bearer and that the sense of sentences is determinate. Thus the justification for the existence of logical atoms is overturned.

2 Russell's logical atomism

Russell developed his logical atomism over two decades, beginning with 'On Denoting' (1905) and ending with 'Logical Atomism'(1924) (see RUSSELL, B. §11). During this time he continually revised his ideas. (This section sketches the version of logical atomism he expounds in the eight 1918 lectures entitled *The Philosophy of Logical Atomism*.) Russell had originally coined the phrase 'logical atomism' to distinguish his picture of the world as containing many separate things from the opposing picture advocated by the British Idealists, such as F.H. BRADLEY, according to whom the world is an indivisible whole. His logical atomism justifies his method of analysis, for this method aims to reduce ordinary sentences to complex combinations of atomic sentences, sentences which feature expressions standing for Russell's many separate things.

Wittgenstein and Russell disagree about the structure of atomic sentences. For Russell, atomic sentences consist of simple symbols which divide into proper names and predicates. Simple symbols have simple things (Russell's logical atoms) as their meanings. The mark of a simple symbol is that understanding it consists in being acquainted with its meaning. Russell held that one cannot be acquainted with an ordinary object such as a chair, but only with the perceptual experiences, the sense-data, one has in perceiving the chair, such as the visual experience of a brown rectangular patch and the tactile experience of a rough and hard surface. He also allowed that one can be acquainted with the meanings of predicates, properties and relations. So atomic sentences feature proper names standing for sense-data, and predicates standing for properties and relations of sense-data. For example, 'this is red' is an atomic sentence in which the proper name 'this' stands for a sense-datum and the predicate '...is red' stands for a property ascribed to the sense-datum.

If an atomic sentence is true, it is made true by a corresponding atomic fact which contains the meanings of the simple symbols of the atomic sentence. For example, 'This is red' is made true by the fact consisting of the sense-datum named by 'this' having the property redness. But Russell's inventory of facts far exceeds Wittgenstein's totality of atomic facts. He also has negative facts which make false sentences false. 'This is red' is made false by the negative fact that the sense-datum is not red. Further, Russell has general facts corresponding to true general sentences such as 'All men are mortal' and 'Some man is mortal'.

Whereas Wittgenstein remains silent about the nature of his simple objects, Russell claims that his simples are sense-data and their properties and relations. This entails that Russell cannot hold that atomic sentences are independent, because two atomic sentences ascribing different colours to a given sense-datum cannot both be true. Russell is more specific about his simples because his argument for their existence turns on an epistemic condition, the principle of acquaintance. This principle holds that the understanding of any sentence consists in acquaintance with the meaning units from which the meaning of the whole sentence is compounded. The principle is satisfied by an atomic sentence because understanding such a sentence consists in acquaintance with the meanings of its simple symbols. A non-atomic sentence must be completely analysed into a sentence which consists entirely of simple symbols standing for objects with which we are acquainted. Analysis thus provides a route whereby the analysed sentence can be understood. The surface form of an ordinary sentence is not a reliable guide to the underlying meaning units which make up the meaning of the sentence. For example, 'Socrates is snub-nosed' seems to feature a proper name, 'Socrates', standing for a person. But Russell claims that the analysis of such a sentence reveals that 'Socrates' is not really a proper name but a descriptive phrase picking out a complicated logical construction from sense-data.

Sense-data and their properties and relations are thus not only the fundamental units of meaning, but also the ultimate constituents of reality. Socrates and his properties and relations are reduced to logical constructions from these ultimate constituents. This reduction has the epistemological advantage embodied in Ockham's razor. By taking Socrates to be a logical construction from sense-data, one reduces the risk of error because beliefs about sense-data and constructions from sense-data are supposed to be more secure than beliefs about objects which stand behind the sense-data.

Russell's logical atomism was well-received by the logical positivists who confused it with Wittgenstein's logical atomism (see LOGICAL POSITIVISM §3). They fixed on Russell's reductionist programme for translating empirical sentences into sentences about sense-data. This programme is fraught with difficulties both of principle and detail. One chief difficulty, promoted by Wittgenstein in his *Philosophical Investigations*, is the alleged incoherence of a private language consisting of reports of a single person's sense-data (see PRIVATE LANGUAGE ARGUMENT).

See also: KNOWLEDGE BY ACQUAINTANCE AND DESCRIPTION; PLURALISM

References and further reading

Anscombe, G.E.M. (1959) *An Introduction to Wittgenstein's Tractatus*, London: Hutchinson. (Chapter 1 argues against the view that Wittgenstein's logical atoms are sense-data.)

Griffin, J.P. (1964) *Wittgenstein's Logical Atomism*, Oxford: Clarendon Press. (A clear account of Wittgenstein's logical atomism, emphasizing the influence of Hertz's ideas about models in natural science.)

Pears, D.F. (1967) *Bertrand Russell & the British Tradition in Philosophy*, London: Fontana. (A detailed exposition of the development of Russell's logical atomism.)

* Russell, B. (1905) 'On Denoting', in *Logic and Knowledge*, ed. R.C. Marsh, London: Allen & Unwin, 1956, 41–56. (Introduces the Russellian theory of definite descriptions which lies at the heart of Russell's logical atomism.)

—— (1911) 'Knowledge by Acquaintance and Knowledge by Description', in *Mysticism and Logic*, London: Longman, 1918, 209–32. (States the principle of acquaintance.)

—— (1914) *Our Knowledge of the External World*, London: Allen & Unwin. (Chapters 1–4 contain the rudiments of the metaphysics of facts and logical constructions from sense-data.)

* —— (1918) 'The Philosophy of Logical Atomism', in *Logic and Knowledge*, ed. R.C. Marsh, London: Allen & Unwin, 1956, 177–281. (The version of Russell's logical atomism sketched in this entry.)

* —— (1924) 'Logical Atomism', in *Logic and Knowledge*, ed. R.C. Marsh, London: Allen & Unwin, 1956, 323–43. (A review of the principles of Russell's logical atomism in which sense-data drop out of the picture.)

Urmson, J.O. (1956) *Philosophical Analysis*, Oxford: Clarendon Press. (An example of the conflation of Russell's and Wittgenstein's logical atomism, but useful for tracing the influence of logical atomism on the logical positivists.)

* Wittgenstein, L. (1921) *Tractatus Logico-Philosophicus*, trans. D.F. Pears and B.F. McGuinness, London: Routledge & Kegan Paul, 1974. (Wittgenstein's statement of his logical atomism.)

—— (1929) 'Some Remarks on Logical Form', supplement to *Proceedings of the Aristotelian Society* 9: 162–71. (Rejection of the independence of atomic sentences.)

* —— (1953) *Philosophical Investigations*, trans. G.E.M. Anscombe, Oxford: Blackwell. (Paragraphs 1–242 undermine the fundamental principles of 'the author of the *Tractatus*'.)

ALEX OLIVER

LOGICAL CONSTANTS

A fundamental problem in the philosophy of logic is to characterize the concepts of 'logical consequence' and 'logical truth' in such a way as to explain what is semantically, metaphysically or epistemologically distinctive about them. One traditionally says that a sentence p is a logical consequence of a set S of sentences in a language L if and only if (1) the truth of the sentences of S in L guarantees the truth of p and (2) this guarantee is due to the 'logical form' of the sentences of S and the sentence p. A sentence is said to be logically true if its truth is guaranteed by its logical form (for example, '2 is even or 2 is not even'). There are three problems presented by this picture: to explicate the notion of logical form or structure; to explain how the logical forms of sentences give rise to the fact that the truth of certain sentences guarantees the truth of others; and to explain what such a guarantee consists in.

The logical form of a sentence may be exhibited by replacing nonlogical expressions with a schematic letter. Two sentences have the same logical form when they can be mapped onto the same schema using this procedure ('2 is even or 2 is not even' and '3 is prime or 3 is not prime' have the same logical form: 'p or not-p'). If a sentence is logically true then each sentence sharing its logical form is true. Any characterization of logical consequence, then, presupposes a conception of logical form, which in turn assumes a prior demarcation of the logical constants. Such a demarcation yields an answer to the first problem above; the goal is to generate the demarcation in such a way as to enable a solution of the remaining two.

Approaches to the characterization of logical constants and logical consequence are affected by developments in mathematical logic. One way of viewing logical constanthood is as a semantic property; a property that an expression possesses by virtue of the sort of contribution it makes to determining the truth conditions of sentences containing it. Another way is proof-theoretical: appealing to aspects of cognitive or operational role as the defining characteristics of logical expressions. Broadly, proof-theoretic accounts go naturally with the conception of logic as a theory of formal deductive inference; model-theoretic accounts complement a conception of logic as an instrument for the characterization of structure.

1   **The Tarskian paradigm**
2   **Extensions of elementary logic**
3   **Notions of invariance**
4   **Syntactic characterizations of logical notions**

1   The Tarskian paradigm

Suppose we are given a theory of truth for a language L, a theory which explains how the truth-conditions of sentences of L are determined by their construction from the semantic properties of a set of primitive expressions. A semantic characterization of logical consequence and logical truth for L appeals to the idea of an 'interpretation' of L, that is, roughly, an assignment of semantic properties of the appropriate sort to the nonlogical (or 'lexical') primitive expressions of L, properties which, once assigned, determine a (unique) truth-value for each sentence in L. If p is a sentence and S a set of sentences of L, then p is said to be a logical consequence of S if p is true on each interpretation of L rendering every sentence of S true, and p is logically true if it is true on each interpretation of L.

The technical implementation of this idea for elementary logic goes back to Löwenheim (1915), but its full significance was appreciated only in the 1930s; it receives an important exposition in Tarski's 1936 paper 'Über den Begriff der logischen Folgerung' ('On the Concept of Logical Consequence'). Let L be an elementary first-order language. The logical constants of L are given by enumeration as the four connectives '¬' (negation), '&' (conjunction), '∨' (disjunction), '→' (material conditional) and the two quantifiers '∀' (universal quantifier) and '∃' (existential quantifier). In some cases, the identity symbol '=' is also distinguished as a logical constant. The formulas of L arise in the following three ways: (1) by applying any primitive n-place predicate symbol R to n terms $t_1, \ldots, t_n$ to obtain a formula $R(t_1, \ldots, t_n)$; (2) by applying connectives to given formulas; and (3) where $x_0, x_1, \ldots$ is a fixed set of individual variables, by applying the quantifiers '∀' and '∃' to a variable x_n and formula p to give formulas $(\forall x_n)p$ and $(\exists x_n)p$. An interpretation of L consists, first, of a non-empty set D, its domain or universe; second, of an assignment of relations and functions of the appropriate type over D to the predicate and function symbols of L; and third, of an assignment of objects in D to each individual constant (or name) in L. If the identity predicate is treated as a logical constant, it is understood that the interpretation assigns to it the identity relation over D, that is, the set $\{\langle a, a \rangle : a \in D\}$.

If J is an interpretation of L, the meanings of the logical expressions determine, for each formula of L, when the formula is true on J relative to an assignment of objects in D to the individual variables of L. Such an assignment may be represented by a sequence over D, that is, a function mapping the natural numbers $\{0, 1, 2, \ldots\}$ into D. A sequence s then expresses the assignment to each variable x_n of the object $s(n)$ from D. A formula which is true on J with respect to an assignment s is said to be 'satisfied' by s in J. The sequences which satisfy a given formula on J are determined by those which satisfy its component formulas (subformulas). Thus, for example, a sequence satisfies the conjunction of two formulas on J when it satisfies both conjuncts, and satisfies the negation of a formula when it fails to satisfy the formula. Finally, if $q = (\exists x_n)p$, a sequence s

satisfies q on J if and only if there exists an assignment s' differing from s only in the value assigned to the variable x_n such that s' satisfies p in J. This expresses the idea that q should be true on an assignment if it is possible to vary the object assigned to the quantified variable in such a way as to make p true. An analogous clause may be given for the universal quantifier. The interpretation J is said to be a 'model' of a set S of formulas with respect to an assignment if each formula in the set is true in J with respect to that assignment; S is said to be 'consistent' if it has a model. Tarski then says that a formula p is a logical consequence of a set S of formulas if and only if for any interpretation J of L and assignment s in J, if J is a model of S with respect to s, then p is true in J with respect to s; equivalently, p is a logical consequence of S if the result of adding $\neg p$ to S is inconsistent. A formula is logically true if it is true in each interpretation of L with respect to each assignment; and two formulas are said to be logically equivalent when they are true in just the same interpretations relative to just the same assignments (see TARSKI, A.; MODEL THEORY; TARSKI'S DEFINITION OF TRUTH).

2 Extensions of elementary logic

It is fair to say that the account of logical consequence and logical truth we have just sketched for elementary logic has set the standard for semantic accounts of these notions in other contexts. Typical of these are extensions of elementary logic that arise by treating additional quantifiers as logical constants.

A first-order quantifier Q may be regarded as describing a relation between a universe D (any non-empty set) and the subsets E of D such that the sentence $(Qx)(Ax)$ is true on an interpretation that assigns E to $A(x)$ over the universe D. Consider, for example, the quantifier symbol Q_0, read 'for infinitely many'. The sentence $(Q_0x)A(x)$ holds in an interpretation J if $A(x)$ holds in J relative to infinitely many values for the variable x. In effect, then, Q_0 describes the relation between a universe and its infinite subsets. Similarly, the quantifier Q_1 describes the relation between a universe and its uncountable subsets (if any), where a set is called 'countable' if it can be put into a one-to-one correspondence with a subset of the natural numbers. Q_0 and Q_1 are examples of 'generalized quantifiers' (see QUANTIFIERS, GENERALIZED).

Elementary logic is characterized by three properties which are focal points of any evaluation of its extensions. The 'completeness theorem' for elementary logic states that if a formula p is a logical consequence of a set S of formulas in elementary

logic, then p is in fact provable from S within the deductive systems for elementary logic usually considered. Combined with the soundness theorem, which states the converse property, this result has the effect of saying that the logical consequence relation for an elementary language can be represented syntactically: the consequences of any set are precisely the formulas that stand to that set in a syntactically characterized relation of deducibility. The 'compactness property' holds for a relation of logical consequence just in case a formula is a consequence of an infinite set S of formulas only if it is a consequence of some finite subset of S. Finally, the (downward) Löwenheim–Skolem theorem for elementary logic states that if a set of formulas has a model, then it has a model with a countable universe. The quantifiers Q_0 and Q_1 properly extend elementary logic in rather different ways: the consequence relation that arises by adding Q_0 to elementary logic has the Löwenheim–Skolem property but not the compactness or completeness properties; while the corresponding relation derived from Q_1 has both the completeness and compactness properties, but not the Löwenheim–Skolem property (see Keisler 1971). Other extensions of elementary logic have neither property. An example is second-order logic, which extends elementary logic by allowing quantification into predicate places (see LÖWENHEIM–SKOLEM THEOREMS AND NONSTANDARD MODELS; SECOND-ORDER LOGIC, PHILOSOPHICAL ISSUES IN).

3 Notions of invariance

In a model-theoretic definition of logical consequence, the logical constants are given simply by a list. The choice of one such list over another may seem, to some extent, ungrounded. Thus, Tarski wrote in 1936 that 'no objective grounds are known to me which would permit us to draw a sharp boundary between the two groups of terms', that is, to solve the demarcation problem. However, in later years Tarski was led to a less sceptical attitude towards the demarcation problem (see Tarski 1966). The solution he suggested consisted of a very general condition – it is satisfied, in fact, by all of the generalized quantifiers usually considered – but one strong enough to exclude many of the expressions which are generally regarded as nonlogical. Let us formulate the requirement for the case of a quantifier symbol Q that applies to a formula $A(x)$ and variable x to yield a sentence $(Qx)(Ax)$. (The generalization of this constraint to other classes of expressions is straightforward and may be found in the literature – see McCarthy (1981: §3) and Sher (1991: ch. 4).) The meaning of Q must determine, for each chosen universe D and each interpretation of $A(x)$ over D, a truth-value for the sentence $(Qx)(Ax)$ over D. Now consider any one-to-one function mapping D on to an alternative universe D^*. Such a function fixes an interpretation for $A(x)$ over D^*, consisting precisely of the images under the function of the items in the given interpretation of $A(x)$ over D. The requirement is then that the two interpretations assign the same truth-value to $(Qx)(Ax)$. Such a function is said to constitute an 'isomorphism' of the one interpretation with the other; and so a succinct statement of the indicated condition is that the behaviour of a logical constant must be 'invariant under isomorphism of interpretations'. Tarski's suggestion is that the boundary between logical and nonlogical notions coincides with the boundary between the expressions which satisfy the present invariance condition and those which do not.

What is the significance of the invariance requirement? Interpretations are 'isomorphic' when they share the same structure, so the invariance condition says roughly that the semantic result of applying a logical constant should depend only on the structure of the interpretation of the expressions to which it is applied, independently of properties and relations specific to objects in any particular interpretation. This requirement may be used to confer a clear sense on one very traditional thesis about logical notions, namely that they are 'topic-neutral' concepts. Tarski noticed that this sort of topic-neutrality is related to a unifying idea behind certain generalizations of the notion of a 'geometry', an idea developed by the German mathematician Felix Klein (1872). Klein viewed a space S as being given by a set with a certain geometric structure. Consider a collection G of one-to-one transformations mapping this set onto itself. Geometric structures can in many cases be described by families of such transformations. For example, consider the collection of all transformations that can be defined in terms of rotations and linear motions (translations). Then the properties of (plane) Euclidean geometry are characterized by the fact that they are 'invariant under transformations of this type', in the sense that any such transformation maps a set S of points on to a set congruent to S and, conversely, any set congruent to S can be obtained from S by a transformation of this type. Similarly, topology, a generalized geometry, may be viewed as the study of those properties which are preserved by one-to-one transformations mapping a space 'continuously' (intuitively, without breaking or tearing it) onto itself. Tarski's idea was to use the limiting case of this situation to characterize logic: logic is the study of those properties of a 'space' (that is, a set or universe)

which are preserved by *any* one-to-one transformation mapping that space onto itself or, more generally, onto some other set. The indicated invariance requirement for Q may be seen as the special case of Tarski's constraint where we focus on relations of a universe and its subsets of the sort described by quantifiers.

The invariance condition is generally regarded as necessary for logical status. The question we must now consider is whether it is also sufficient. One difficulty faced by an affirmative answer concerns the necessitation requirement: that it is not possible – in a strong, uniquely logical sense of 'possible' – that each member of a set of sentences is true and one of its logical consequences is false. The difficulty is that there appear to be expressions which are counted as logical by the invariance criterion which lead to consequence relations violating this requirement. For example, let P represent a fixed contingently false sentence of English, for example, 'The French Revolution failed'. Consider a quantifier symbol Q interpreted as follows: in any interpretation J, $(Qx)(Ax)$ holds in J if P and $A(x)$ holds for some member of J, or not-P and $A(x)$ fails for each member of J. Since P is in fact false, if Q were a logical constant then $(Qx)(Ax)$ would be logically equivalent to $(\forall x)\neg A(x)$. This is a violation of the necessitation requirement, since in a logically possible world in which P is true, $(Qx)(x = x)$ is true, but $(\forall x)\neg(x = x)$ is false.

However, it may be that the lesson to be learned from examples such as the one just considered is not that the invariance constraint fails to underwrite the necessitation requirement, but that the invariance requirement has been understood too narrowly (see Sher 1991; McCarthy 1987). The example would not arise if that requirement were understood 'rigidly', that is, in such a way as to apply to the interpretation of Q 'across all logically possible worlds'. For consider a world w_1 in which P is true containing the same objects as a world w_2 in which P is false. Then the transformation that associates each object with itself will map the interpretation of the formula x = x in w_1 on to its interpretation in w_2 (both are the whole universe), but the sentence $(Qx)(x = x)$ is true in w_1 and false in w_2, which shows that the invariance condition for Q breaks down if that condition is applied to the interpretation of Q across all logically possible worlds. Let us say that an expression satisfying this stronger invariance condition is 'rigidly invariant'. The suggestion is then that rigid invariance be taken as the defining property of the logical constants. The problem created by this proposal lies in a threat of circularity: we would require a characterization of the notion of logical possibility, sufficient for a demarcation of the logically possible worlds, not dependent upon a prior demarcation of the logical constants.

4 Syntactic characterizations of logical notions

An alternative approach to the demarcation problem locates the distinctive feature of the logical constants in the role that they play in deductive arguments. On this view, a logical expression is one whose meaning can be characterized by a set of rules of inference of a certain sort. These rules may be formulated in different ways; for example, in terms of a sequent calculus, or a natural deduction system (see NATURAL DEDUCTION, TABLEAU AND SEQUENT SYSTEMS). Each formulation will incorporate in some way a distinction between rules that license the introduction of a logical expression in an inference (introduction rules), and those which describe the conditions under which it can be eliminated (elimination rules). Thus, for example, the introduction condition for conjunction may be given by the rule

$$A, B/A \& B,$$

and its elimination conditions by the rules

$$A \& B/A, \quad A \& B/B.$$

A rule of the form

$$X_1, \ldots, X_n/Z$$

is to be read as an inference-licence, saying that if $X_1, \ldots, X_n$ have been inferred, then it is permissible to infer Z. The existential quantifier may be similarly characterized by the rules

$$A(t)/(\exists x)A(x), \quad (\exists x)A(x)/A(c),$$

where in the first rule t is any term and in the second c is a constant subject to the restriction that it not appear previously in the inference in question (the 'non-occurrence restriction'). Analogous rules characterize the other notions of classical quantification theory.

The most straightforward reading of the syntactic view is that an expression counts as logical if and only if it is possible to write a set of introduction and elimination rules for it. Arthur Prior criticized this idea by means of a simple counterexample (1960). In the absence of substantive restrictions governing the interaction of introduction and elimination rules, it would seem that we could characterize a connective 'tonk' by means of the following pair of rules:

$$A/A \text{ TONK } B, \quad A \text{ TONK } B/B,$$

from which we obtain the schema A/B, licensing the inference of any sentence from any other, as a derived

rule of inference! In order to avoid this sort of pathology, Belnap (1961) imposed the requirement that adding a logical constant to a given deductive system S by reference to a set of rules of inference result in a 'conservative' extension of S; one in which no formula in the notation of S is provable that is not already provable in S.

Even thus amended, however, the syntactic conception of what it is to be a logical constant would appear to be too liberal. Let S be a standard system of proof for elementary logic, and suppose that P represents a fixed nonlogical predicate. Consider the quantifier Q such that $(Qx)(Ax)$ holds in any interpretation J if and only if some object falling under P satisfies $A(x)$ in J. (Thus, for example, if P represents '...is a bird', the quantificational expression Q means 'For some bird...'.) Let S^+ result from S by adding the following introduction and elimination rules for Q:

$$A(t), P(t)/(Qx)A(x) \quad (Qx)A(x)/A(c), P(c),$$

where in the second rule c is an individual constant subject to the non-occurrence requirement. It may be shown that S^+ is a conservative extension of S, but the expression Q thus characterized is not a logical constant.

Belnap's requirement may be seen as a by-product of a later viewpoint on syntactic characterizations of logical notions developed by Ian Hacking (1979). On this view, the fundamental rules of inference associated with the logical constants implicitly define their semantic interpretation. The three rules given above for conjunction determine its semantic interpretation in the following sense: there is precisely one truth table for '&' with respect to which these rules are sound. The introduction and elimination rules for the existential quantifier can similarly be shown to characterize its semantic interpretation. It is clear that the indicated rules for Q do not thus characterize its semantic role, for its interpretation over any set varies with the interpretation assigned to P. Of course, to speak of a set of rules of inference as 'characterizing' the interpretation of a connective or a quantifier symbol presupposes that such an expression is to have an interpretation of the indicated (classical) sort; the justification of this assumption must be given in other terms. The idea is that in ascribing such an interpretation to an expression we look for the one – or *a* one – that makes the introduction and elimination rules associated with the expression truth-preserving; the expression counts as logical if over any universe there is only one such interpretation.

What is the relation between the semantic and syntactic solutions to the demarcation problem? One answer is that they correspond to two broad conceptions of the nature of logic (see Tharp 1975). On the first conception, logic is a theory of a certain type of deductive inference. On this view, what is distinctive about logical notions is their role in deductive inference, and logical consequence consists in a (perhaps idealized) type of deducibility. The syntactic view (on which, under very general conditions, a completeness result links a relation of logical consequence to the deductive system that characterizes the logical constants) provides a natural interpretation of this conception. An alternative conception, of more modern vintage, sees logic as an instrument for the characterization of structure. A logic (that is, a choice of logical constants) may be said to 'characterize' a structure if there is a set S of sentences in the logic such that any model of S exemplifies that structure. On this conception, the invariance criterion would seem to be very natural, for the behaviour of logical notions should be preserved under 'structure-preserving' transformations of any subject matter to which they are applied. From this point of view, there will be no particular premium on completeness, and the Löwenheim–Skolem property is an anomaly. Elementary logic is a paradigm of the first conception of logic and second-order logic typifies the second.

See also: LOGICAL AND MATHEMATICAL TERMS, GLOSSARY OF; LOGICAL FORM; LOGICAL LAWS; PROOF THEORY

References and further reading

Barwise, J. and Feferman, S. (1985) *Model-Theoretic Logics*, Berlin: Springer. (An excellent sourcebook in generalized model theory, containing detailed treatments of all the technical issues touched on in this entry.)

* Belnap, N. (1961) 'Tonk, Plonk, and Plink', *Analysis* 22: 130–4. (Addresses problems with syntactic criteria for interpreting logical constants in terms of introduction and elimination rules.)

Etchemendy, J. (1990) *The Concept of Logical Consequence*, Cambridge, MA: Harvard University Press. (An important critical evaluation of the Tarskian paradigm, emphasizing problems pertaining to the necessitation requirement.)

* Hacking, I. (1979) 'What is Logic?', *Journal of Philosophy* 76 (6): 499–523. (Develops a sophisticated proof-theoretic account of the nature of logical constants.)

Harman, G. (1986) 'The Meaning of Logical Constants', in E. LePore (ed.) *Truth and Interpretation: Perspectives on the Philosophy of Donald Davidson*, Oxford and New York: Blackwell, 125–34. (Explains the meaning of logical constants in terms of 'immediate implications' and 'immediate incompatibilities'.)

* Keisler, H.J. (1971) 'Logic with the Quantifier "there exist uncountably many"', *Annals of Mathematical Logic* 1: 1–93. (Gives a completeness result for logic with the 'uncountability' quantifier, by means of a particularly nice axiomatization.)

* Klein, F. (1872) *Vergleichende Betrachtungen über neuere geometrische Forschungen*, Erlangen: Deichert; repr. in *Gesammelte mathematische Adhandlungen*, Berlin: Springer, 1921, vol. 1, 460–97; trans. M.W. Haskell, 'A Comparative Review of Recent Geometric Researches', *Bulletin of the New York Mathematical Society* 2: 215–49, 1993. (The inspiration for Tarski 1966; of considerable interest in itself.)

Lindström, P. (1969) 'On Extensions of Elementary Logic', *Theoria* 31: 1–11. (A seminal article in generalized model theory, establishing that elementary logic is characterized by the completeness, compactness and Löwenheim–Skolem properties.)

* Löwenheim, L. (1915) 'Über Möglichkeiten im Relativkalkül', *Mathematische Annalen* 76: 447–70; trans. S. Bauer-Mengelberg, 'On Possibilities in the Calculus of Relatives', in J. van Heijenoort, *From Frege to Gödel: A Sourcebook in Mathematical Logic*, Cambridge, MA: Harvard University Press, 1967. (A seminal paper in the theory of models, giving the first statement and proof of the Löwenheim–Skolem theorem for elementary logic.)

* McCarthy, T. (1981) 'The Idea of a Logical Constant', *Journal of Philosophy* 78 (9): 499–523. (Discusses the invariance criterion and its problems, and includes an extension of the criterion to intensional logics.)

* —— (1987) 'Modality, Invariance, and Logical Truth', *Journal of Philosophical Logic* 16: 423–43. (Establishes a general result saying that on weak assumptions if a set of notions is invariant across a class of possible worlds, then a logic based on those notions will satisfy a necessitation requirement with respect to that class.)

Peacocke, C. (1987) 'Understanding Logical Constants', *Proceedings of the British Academy* 83: 153–200. (Explains what is special about logical constants in terms of the way they are understood.)

* Prior, A. (1960) 'The Runabout Inference-Ticket', *Analysis* 21: 38–9. (Criticizes the thesis that logical constants are generally characterized in terms of introduction and elimination rules.)

Sher, G. (1989) 'A Tarskian Conception of Logic', *Pacific Philosophical Quarterly* 70: 341–68. (An illuminating discussion of Tarski's later views on the demarcation problem.)

* —— (1991) *The Bounds of Logic*, Cambridge, MA: MIT Press/Bradford. (A general discussion of problems in the philosophy of classical logic from a model-theoretic point of view.)

* Tarski, A. (1936) 'Über den Begriff der logischen Folgerung', *Actes du Congrès International de Philosophie Scientifique* 7: 1–11; repr. 'On the Concept of Logical Consequence', in *Logic, Semantics, Metamathematics*, trans. and ed. J.H. Woodger, Oxford: Oxford University Press, 2nd edn, 1983. (An early important informal discussion of the semantic conception of logical consequence.)

* —— (1966) 'What are Logical Notions?', ed. and with intro. by J. Corcoran, *History and Philosophy of Logic* 7: 143–54. (An illuminating discussion of notions of invariance in relation to logic.)

* Tharp, L. (1975) 'Which Logic is the Right Logic?', *Synthese* 31: 1–21. (An excellent introduction to the problems treated in this entry.)

TIMOTHY McCARTHY

LOGICAL FORM

Consider the following argument: All men are mortal; Socrates is a man; therefore, Socrates is mortal. Intuitively, what makes this a valid argument has nothing to do with Socrates, men or mortality. Rather, each sentence in the argument exhibits a certain 'logical form' and those forms, taken together, constitute a pattern that guarantees the truth of the conclusion given the truth of the premises. More generally, the logical form of a sentence of natural language is what determines both its logical properties and its logical relations to other sentences.

The logical form of a sentence of natural language is typically represented in a theory of logical form by a well-formed formula in a 'logically pure' language whose only meaningful symbols are expressions with fixed, distinctly logical meanings (for example, quantifiers). Thus, the logical forms of the sentences in the above argument would be represented in a theory based on pure predicate logic by the formulas '$\forall x(Fx \rightarrow Gx)$', '$Fy$' and '$Gy$', respectively, where 'F' and 'G' are free predicate variables and 'y' a free individual variable. The argument's intuitive validity is then explained by the fact that the logical forms of the premises formally entail the logical form of the conclusion. The primary goal of a theory of logical form is to explain as broad a range of such intuitive logical phenomena as possible in terms of the logical forms that it assigns to sentences of natural language.

1   **Logical form in Aristotelian logic**
2   **A general characterization of logical form**
3   **Comparing theories of logical form**

1   Logical form in Aristotelian logic

Broadly speaking, the 'logical form' of a sentence of natural language is what determines both its logical properties and its logical relations to other sentences. Most notably, the logical form of a sentence *S* determines whether or not it is logically true, and the logical forms of the sentences in a set *K* together with the logical form of *S* jointly determine whether or not the latter is a logical consequence of the former.

Although particularly prominent in the twentieth century, due especially to the influence of Bertrand Russell, the idea of logical form can be traced back to Aristotle. In the so-called 'traditional logic' that stems from Aristotle's work in the *Prior Analytics*, the central form of argument is the 'syllogism', that is, an argument consisting of two premises and a conclusion. For example:

(1)   Every whale is a mammal.

       Some carnivore is a whale.

     ∴ Some carnivore is a mammal.

Aristotle was the first to recognize explicitly that the validity of a syllogism (that is, its conclusion being a logical consequence of its premises) is entirely independent of the common noun phrases, or 'terms', in its constituent sentences. Rather, each sentence in a valid syllogism such as (1) above exhibits a certain form and, taken together, those forms constitute a pattern that, of itself, guarantees the truth of the conclusion given the truth of the premises.

To capture this idea systematically, Aristotle first restricted his attention to syllogisms the constituent sentences of which exhibit any of four basic sentential forms, known traditionally as *A*, *E*, *I* and *O*, respectively: 'Every α is a β', 'No α is a β', 'Some α is a β' and 'Some α is not a β', where 'α' and 'β' represent the roles of the subject and predicate terms in such sentences. Thus, the first premise of (1) is of the sentential form *A*, and both the second premise and the conclusion are of the form *I*. These sentential forms alone, however, are not enough to characterize the pattern that (1) exhibits. A further logically relevant feature of (1) is the way in which the terms occur in its constituent sentences: 'carnivore', for instance, is the subject term of both the second premise and the conclusion but does not occur at all in the first premise. To capture this feature generally, Aristotle introduced schematic variables *F, G, H, ...*

Call the result of replacing the terms in a sentence that exhibits one of the basic sentential forms with distinct schematic variables a 'schematic' form. The pattern exhibited by a given syllogism can then be represented by replacing its constituent sentences with schematic forms that preserve the arrangement of terms in the syllogism. For example, (1) exhibits the following pattern:

(2)   Every F is a G.

   Some H is an F.

   Some H is a G.

By sole means of representations such as (2), Aristotle proved, for each possible syllogistic pattern, whether or not it is valid; that is, for Aristotle, whether or not it is impossible for the premises of any instance of the pattern to be true and the conclusion false. Thus, the schematic forms of its premises and conclusion (relative to a given choice of schematic variables) completely determine the validity or invalidity of each pattern. Aristotle's schematic forms are thus paradigms of logical forms.

The central goal of a theory of logical form is to explain the logical properties of (and relations between) the members of a broad class K of sentences of natural language in terms of the logical forms that the theory assigns to those sentences. With only four general types of logical form to choose from – the four basic sentential forms, the scope of Aristotle's account as it stands is far too limited to count as a fully fledged theory of logical form. However, a perusal of any modern text with a section on traditional logic yields a variety of techniques for translating sentences with entirely different grammatical forms into instances of Aristotle's four basic sentential forms. For example, a simple individual assertion such as

(3)   Matthew is a politician

is obviously not an instance of any of the basic sentential forms, since it does not begin with one of the quantifiers 'Every', 'Some' and 'No'. But by introducing a term that picks out a class containing only Matthew, (3) can be translated into the intuitively equivalent, albeit somewhat stilted, sentence

(4)   Every person identical to Matthew is a politician,

which exhibits the sentential form A. Again, a sentence such as

(5)   Someone gave *The Brothers Karamazov* to Andrea,

which involves a transitive verb, can be put into the appropriate sentential form by replacing the verb with its nominal '-er' counterpart followed by the preposition 'of', to produce a term that picks out exactly the class of individuals to which the original predicate applies. (5) then gives way to

(6)   Some person is a giver of *The Brothers Karamazov* to Andrea.

Supplemented by such techniques, Aristotle's logic has a considerably broader application, as a much larger class of sentences can be assigned logical forms than would initially appear to be the case. So supplemented, then, Aristotle's account is plausibly taken to be the first genuine theory of logical form (see LOGIC, ANCIENT §§1–3).

2   A general characterization of logical form

Although differing considerably in content and detail, the basic components and characteristics of Aristotle's theory of logical form (in this somewhat anachronistic rendering) are essentially the same as in contemporary accounts deriving from Bertrand RUSSELL. In this section, these components and characteristics are made explicit.

In general, the notion of logical form is always relative to a theory T of logical form which is directed towards some broad class K of sentences of natural language. Call K the 'target class' of the theory. The logical forms of the members of K are represented by formulas in a 'logically pure' canonical language; that is, a language that contains (perhaps in addition to punctuation) only variables and logical constants – expressions with fixed and, according to the theory, distinctly logical meanings (see LOGICAL CONSTANTS §1). For Aristotle, this is the language of schematic forms the logical constants of which are 'Every', 'Some', 'No', 'is a' and 'is not a'; and for Russell and his followers it is generally (some variant of) the language of *Principia Mathematica* (1910–13), with its now familiar quantifiers and propositional connectives.

The route from the sentences of the target class K to their logical forms according to T consists of two steps. First, and most important, is the translation of the members of K into an 'impure' hybrid language that consists of the canonical language supplemented by nonlogical constants: for Aristotle, ordinary terms such as 'carnivore' and also stilted terms such as 'person identical with Matthew'; for Russellians, individual constants such as 'Socrates' and n-place predicates such as 'mortal' (or perhaps abbreviations thereof such as 's' and 'M'). These nonlogical constants carry the same meaning as their informal counterparts and are used to construct the hybrid language translations of the sentences in which those counterparts occur. The translation of a sentence of K into a hybrid language is typically known as its 'analysis'. (Sentences such as 'Every boy danced with a girl', which are logically ambiguous, should of course receive a distinct analysis for each possible reading.) The analysis of a sentence is a paraphrase of the sentence which displays its logical form overtly in its surface grammatical structure. Thus, (3) and (5) are translated as (4) and (6), respectively, while for the Russellian, (7), for example, is translated as (8):

(7)   If every man is mortal and Socrates is a man, then Socrates is mortal.

(8) $(\forall y(\text{man}(y) \rightarrow \text{mortal}(y))$ & $\text{man}(\text{Socrates})) \rightarrow$ $\text{mortal}(\text{Socrates})$.

In the second step of the process, the logical forms for the sentences of K are derived simply by uniformly replacing all the nonlogical constants in the analyses of those sentences with variables of the appropriate type. So, for example (assuming a choice of replacement variables for the nonlogical constants), the sentences in (1) – which in this case are identical with their analyses – yield the logical forms in (2), and (8) likewise yields (9) as the logical form of (7):

(9) $(\forall y(Fy \rightarrow Gy)$ & $Fx) \rightarrow Gx$.

As noted, the primary goal of a theory T of logical form is to account for the logical properties of the sentences in its target class K in terms of their logical forms. This is accomplished by means of a logical theory for the canonical language of T in which formal correlates of the ordinary logical notions – logical truth, logical consequence and so on – are defined for the formulas of the language. The apparent logical properties of the members of K are then explained (or explained away) by virtue of the fact that the formal correlates of those properties hold (or fail to hold) among the logical forms of the members of K. Thus, once again, the intuitive validity of (1) is explained by the formal validity of (2). Similarly, for the Russellian, the intuitive logical truth of (7) is explained by the formal logical truth of (9) – typically understood as truth in any domain under any interpretation (relative to that domain) of the free variables 'F', 'G' and 'x', following the work of Tarski (1933; see MODEL THEORY). In either case, the actual meanings of the nonlogical expressions in the natural language sentences in question play no role in determining the logical properties of those sentences. Rather, as the theories demonstrate, the logical properties are determined by their logical forms alone.

3   Comparing theories of logical form

The central principle for comparing theories of logical form is the following:

CP T' is preferable (*prima facie*) to T if T' explains a greater range of logical behaviour than T without appeal to extralogical principles (or, 'meaning postulates').

To illustrate, intuitively (10) follows directly from (5):

(10)   Someone gave something to Andrea.

And yet, in Aristotle's theory, as noted, (5) must be analysed along the lines of (6) and (10) along the lines of (11):

(11)   Some person is a giver of something to Andrea.

However, then the analyses (6) and (11) exhibit only the obviously invalid argument pattern

(12)   Some A is a B.
Some A is a C.

To capture the original entailment, (12) must be treated as enthymematic: that is, there is a suppressed premise with the logical form 'Every B is a C', namely

(13)   Every giver of *The Brothers Karamazov* to Andrea is a giver of something to Andrea.

Aristotle's logic, therefore, explains the relation between (5) and (10) by introducing an extralogical principle linking the two predicate terms, in effect reducing it to an instance of the argument pattern (2).

By contrast, represented in predicate logic, the logical forms of (5) and (10) constitute the valid pattern

(14) $\exists x Hxyz$
$\exists y \exists x Hxyz$

Hence, that (10) is a consequence of (5) is explained on the basis of their logical forms alone, without appeal to any extralogical principles. So, *prima facie*, a theory based on predicate logic is preferable to Aristotle's theory.

The '*prima facie*' qualification in CP marks the influence of other factors besides extent of explanatory range that are relevant to an evaluation of competing theories of logical form. Two particularly influential principles can be observed in recent debates over the logical forms of one or another class of sentences: logical conservatism and ontological conservatism.

The shift from Aristotle to Russell exhibits a typical way in which one theory T' of logical form can broaden the explanatory range of another T;

namely, by extending or otherwise subsuming the canonical language and logic of T. In such cases, the language of T' is able to provide logical forms for all sentences in the target class of T. In addition, the language of T' includes logical constants and classes of complex expressions not present in the language of T that enable T' to construct logical forms not available to T. Appropriate logical principles for its new forms then enable T' to explain logical phenomena that are left unexplained (without extralogical principles) in T, for example, (10)'s being a logical consequence of (5). The principle of logical conservatism stipulates that supplementation to a given canonical language should be kept to a minimum. More exactly, let T and T' be theories with roughly equal target classes and let L be a background logical theory (first-order logic, for example) that is common to both T and T'; then

LC T' is preferable (*prima facie*) to T if T' requires fewer extensions to L than T.

The increase in explanatory range of predicate logic, of course, is far too vast for LC to override CP in the choice between Aristotle and Russell. A better example is found in recent well-known work on the logical form of action sentences with adverbial modifiers. For example:

(15) April kissed Jonathan tenderly.

It is intuitively clear that (15) entails

(16) April kissed Jonathan.

Typical predicate logic analyses of these sentences represent 'kissed' and 'kissed tenderly' as distinct two-place predicates. The entailment is then explained by means of a meaning postulate to the effect that if A kisses B tenderly, then A kisses B. As with Aristotle's explanation of the relation between (5) and (10), then, in this explanation the apparent entailment is actually enthymematic. However, the entailment can be explained directly by treating an adverb such as 'tenderly' as an adverbial operator t that, when prefixed to an n-place predicate F (such as 'kissed'), yields a new n-place predicate $[tF]$ ('tenderly kissed') (see ADVERBS §1). The logic of these new constructions is then characterized generally by the principle that

(17) $[\alpha\Pi]x_1 \ldots x_n \to \Pi x_1 \ldots x_n$, for any adverbial operator α and n-place predicate Π.

The logical forms of (15) and (16), then, on this approach, are (18) and (19), respectively:

(18) $[tF]xy$

(19) Fxy

and so by the new logical principle (17), (16) follows from (15) directly in virtue of their logical forms.

Most philosophers would probably agree that this increase in explanatory range is significant enough to override LC and warrant the added apparatus. However, Davidson (1967) proposed a logically more conservative analysis which avoids the new apparatus. Specifically, for Davidson, the proper analysis of action sentences takes the structure of an action verb such as 'kissed' to involve an implicit parameter for an event. Thus, (15) is to be analysed as

(20) $\exists x$ (kissing-of(April, Jonathan, x) & tender(x))

(read, roughly, as 'There is an event x such that x is a kissing of Jonathan by April and x is tender'), and (16) as

(21) $\exists x$ (kissing-of(April, Jonathan, x))

The entailment from (15) to (16) is then explained by standard logical principles governing conjunction and the existential quantifier, and the apparently hasty introduction of new constructions and unfamiliar logical principles is avoided. Since their explanatory ranges are the same, then, CP provides no support for the adverbial operator account over Davidson's, and so, by LC, Davidson's account is to be preferred (see ADVERBS).

As Davidson's account illustrates, however, conservatism with regard to logic is often accompanied by liberalism with regard to ontology – in this case, the postulation of events. The 'ontological commitments' of a theory T of logical form consist of the kinds of things that must exist if the analyses that T assigns to the sentences of its target class are to be meaningful (see ONTOLOGICAL COMMITMENT). The second principle – ontological conservatism – is that such commitments are to be kept to a minimum; that is, more exactly, where again T and T' have roughly equal target classes,

OC T' is preferable (*prima facie*) to T if T' has fewer ontological commitments than T.

Unlike LC, this principle favours the operator account of adverbial modification over Davidson's more ontologically permissive account. The choice between the two thus turns on one's preferred brand of conservatism.

LC tends to be overridden by CP when they conflict, as additional apparatus is usually viewed as a small price to pay for greater explanatory range. However, more is often at stake in conflicts between CP and OC, as theories of logical form that have great explanatory range often exact a high price in ontological commitment: possibilia (that is, possible but non-actual objects) are introduced to explain sentences involving modality (see MODAL LOGIC, PHILOSOPHICAL ISSUES IN §§1–2), intensional entities to explain the logic of attitude verbs (see PROPOSITIONAL ATTITUDE STATEMENTS §§1–2) and so on. One must either choose between the two or offer a competing account with the same explanatory range but fewer ontological commitments. Since Russell first formulated his theory of descriptions (see DESCRIPTIONS) to counter what he saw as Meinong's ontological excesses, the development of competing theories of logical form has been, and largely remains, the primary tool for metaphysical discovery and the central approach to metaphysical debate in the twentieth century (see ANALYTICAL PHILOSOPHY).

See also: LOGICAL AND MATHEMATICAL TERMS, GLOSSARY OF; MONTAGUE, R.M.; QUINE, W.V.O.

References and further reading

* Aristotle (*c.*350s–330s BC) *Prior Analytics*, trans. and with commentary by R. Smith, Indianapolis, IN: Hackett Publishing Company, 1989, esp. I.1–7. (Referred to in §1. The primary source for Aristotle's formal logic.)
* Davidson, D. (1967) 'The Logical Form of Action Sentences', in N. Rescher (ed.) *The Logic of Decision and Action*, Pittsburgh, PA: University of Pittsburgh Press, 81–95; repr. with replies to critics in D. Davidson, *Essays on Actions and Events*, Oxford: Clarendon Press, 1980, esp. 137–46. (The source of Davidson's account of action sentences with adverbial modifiers; discussed in §3.)
  Harman, G. (1972) 'Logical Form', *Foundations of Language* 9: 38–65; repr. in D. Davidson and G. Harman (eds) *The Logic of Grammar*, Encino, CA: Dickenson, 1975, 289–307. (A fine discussion of theories of logical form on which the comparative principles in §3 are based.)
  Russell, B.A.W. (1914) 'Logic as the Essence of Philosophy', in *Our Knowledge of the External World*, London: Allen & Unwin, 33–53; London: Routledge, 1993. (Perhaps Russell's strongest statement of his view of the role of logical form in logic and philosophy.)
  —— (1919) *An Introduction to Mathematical Philosophy*, London: Routledge, 1993. (An engaging if not always wholly clear account of the basic issues in philosophical logic and the philosophy of mathematics. Chapter 16 is a classic account of Russell's theory of definite descriptions; chapter 18 includes a lengthy discussion of logical form.)
* Tarski, A. (1933) *Pojęcie prawdy w językach nauk dedukcyjnych*, Warsaw; trans. J.H. Woodger (1956), 'On the Concept of Truth in Formalized Languages', in *Logic, Semantics, Metamathematics*, ed. J. Corcoran, Indianapolis, IN: Hackett Publishing Company, 2nd edn, 1983, 152–278. (Referred to in §2. The classic work of model-theoretic semantics.)
* Whitehead, A.N. and Russell, B.A.W. (1910–13) *Principia Mathematica*, Cambridge: Cambridge University Press, 3 vols; 2nd edn, 1925–7. (Referred to in §2. Probably the most influential work in logic in the twentieth century; extremely technical.)
  Wittgenstein, L.J.J. (1922) *Tractatus Logico-Philosophicus*, trans. C.K. Ogden and F.P. Ramsey, London: Routledge; trans. D.F. Pears and B.F. McGuinness, London: Routledge, 1975. (A unique, highly influential work by Russell's most famous student in which a very interesting, somewhat eccentric notion of logical form plays a prominent role.)

CHRISTOPHER MENZEL

LOGICAL LAWS

There are at least three different kinds of answer to the question 'What is a logical law?' One establishes what it means for something to be a logical law. This answers the semantic question: What is the meaning of 'logical law'? The second explains what makes something a logical law. This answers the metaphysical question: What is the ground of logical law? The third tells you what the logical laws are. This answers the question: What is the extension of 'logical law'?

Even though logic is often seen as a complete science, the answers to all three questions are disputed. For example, there are at least three different conceptions of what it means for something to be a law of logic. Different conceptions account for logic in terms of necessity, truth in all models, and proof.

There are also different answers to the metaphysical question. If truth-preservation is central to logic, then the ground of logic depends on the metaphysics of truth. If logic is a matter of the meanings of terms, then the metaphysics of meaning is important for logic. Unfortunately, there is no widespread agreement on the metaphysics of meaning or truth.

Finally, there is no widespread agreement as to what the logical laws are. There are two general disputes here. First, it is not clear what notions count as logical. Does logic contain laws about identity, second-order quantification or modality? Second, given agreement on the scope of logic, there are still questions about the logical laws in that area. Intuitionists, quantum logicians, relevance and paraconsistent logicians each reject things taken as laws by others, even in the language of 'and', 'or' and 'not'.

1   **The semantic question**
2   **The metaphysical question**
3   **The question of extension**

1   The semantic question

When we claim that something is a logical law, what do we mean? Sometimes we use 'logical law' to mean 'theorem of a formal system'. Depending on taste, we might call theorems of first-order classical logic, or some other formal system, laws of logic. This is a derivative use of the phrase, akin to calling the claims of a particular scientific theory laws of nature. The propositions of a theory may be laws of nature, but only if the theory 'gets it right'. The theory must describe the world in the right way for its claims to be laws of nature. Similarly, theorems of a formal system are only logical laws if they 'get it right' in some appropriate way. The interest consists in elaborating what it means for a theory to 'get it right'. So, by 'logical law' we do not simply mean 'theorem in a particular formal system'.

Another non-answer to this question is that logical laws are the ways we cannot help but think. Anyone familiar with the history of logic in the twentieth century will be aware that almost any principle that some take to be a logical law, others reject as invalid. If a logical law is something to which no one can help but assent, nothing counts as a logical law. No purely psychological answer, in terms of 'laws of thought', will give us logical laws.

Now to a more plausible account. The goal in the study of logic is an account of deductively valid inferences: these are the logical laws. A deductively valid inference is one in which necessarily, if the premises are true, so is the conclusion. Laws of logic are those inferences that are necessarily truth-preserving. This conception goes back to Aristotle (see LOGIC, ANCIENT §§1–3).

> A syllogism is a form of words in which when certain assumptions are made, something other than what has been assumed necessarily follows from the fact that the assumptions are such.
>
> (*Prior Analytics*: 24b18)

We are interested in necessarily truth-preserving inferences because given these, and given true premises from which to infer, we will never (and in fact, *can* never) deduce falsehood. Given our concern for finding truth and avoiding falsehood, it is easy to see why logical laws are interesting, on this picture. It is also clear how logic can be normative. Given that we have the goal of gaining truth and avoiding falsehood, we *ought* to deduce validly. (Which is not to say that we ought not reason in other ways as well.)

We have one answer to our semantic question: a logical law is a necessarily truth-preserving inference. However, many have found this answer unsatisfactory. The main reason for dissatisfaction with this account is the reliance upon the intensional notion of necessity. Some have sought to give an account of logical laws that has no recourse to necessity, or to any other intensional notion.

There are two important analyses of logical consequence which, at least at first glance, avoid using the notion of necessity. One was given its canonical exposition by TARSKI in his 1936 essay 'Über den Begriff der logischen Folgerung' (On the Concept of Logical Consequence), though it was prefigured by BOLZANO in 1837. Tarski wrote 'The sentence *X follows logically* from the sentences of the class *K* if and only if every model of the class *K* is also a model of the sentence *X* ([1936] 1956: 417; original emphasis).

There are no modal notions here, provided that there is an adequate non-modal explanation of what it is to be a model. There are a number of ways to do this, and there is no need for us to consider them in detail. Suffice to say that models are structures in which each of the non-logical constants in a language is given an interpretation in terms of the objects in the model, and the logical constants have a fixed interpretation in each model (see LOGICAL CONSTANTS §1; MODEL THEORY).

Model-theoretic notions of consequence do not, as they stand, make any appeal to modality. However, they do not give a modal-free account of necessary truth-preservation.

For example, the model-theoretic account needs a collection of logical terms. If *all* terms are logical, then the interpretation of each term is fixed, and there is only one model. This would make logical truth vacuous, as Tarski realized (1936). Now suppose that the terms 'blue' and 'coloured' are not counted as logical terms. The deduction 'My car is blue; therefore my car is coloured' fails to be valid on the model-theoretic account, because we can assign disjoint extensions to the predicates 'blue' and 'coloured'. In contrast, the inference is necessarily truth-preserving. In this way, necessary truth-preservation and model-theoretic validity come apart. (For a detailed account of how the notions differ, see Etchemendy's *The Concept of Logical Consequence* (1990).)

These two approaches to analysing logical validity differ quite sharply from a third account. According to the proof-theoretic account of validity, an argument is valid just when there is a proof of the conclusion from the premises. This approach is championed by Prawitz (1974) with many other constructivists, and Wagner (1987) (a non-constructivist) who sees this view in the work of Gottlob FREGE. The proof-theoretic account grounds validity in the meanings of the logical constants. These meanings determine the validity of simple deductions (such as conjunction elimination: from $p \& q$ to derive q). An argument is valid if and only if there are simple deductions from the premises to the conclusion (see PROOF THEORY).

On this account, logical validity is analytic, and the epistemic function of logic (as a calculus for ideal justification) is obvious. As with model theory, a proof-theoretic account of validity depends on the choice of logical particles, and the rules that govern them.

The proof-theoretic account differs from the other two approaches. If validity is ultimately proof-theoretic, then the class of logical validities is recursively enumerable. If we can list the basic rules, we can list the valid deductions (provided that proofs are finite). Similarly, validity is compact (if K follows from X, then K must follow from some finite subset of X). Neither of these properties is essential to the other conceptions of logical validity.

Without doubt, each of these conceptions has a place in the study of logical law. It is harder to discern how they are to be related. My tentative proposal is this. Validity is a matter of necessary truth-preservation. Model-theoretic validity is important, because models can represent possibilities (however ontological commitment to possibilities is to be analysed). Sometimes, models do not represent real possibilities (as when the extension of 'blue' is not a subset of the extension of 'coloured') so, model-theoretic validity can differ from actual validity. Similarly, proof-theoretic validity can coincide with actual validity. Although analytic truth and necessary truth may not coincide in all cases, simple deductions involving logical particles are instances of necessary truth-preserving inferences. Perhaps these simple deductions will capture all of the necessary truth-preserving inferences in the language. In this case, the proof procedure is complete. On the other hand, the validities in the language may not be recursively enumerable, as in the case of second-order logic. In these cases, no recursive proof-theoretic account will capture all of the validities.

2 The metaphysical question

Even if we have decided what we mean when we call something a logical law, the issue of the *ground* of logical law remains. If validity is necessary truth-

preservation, an account has to be given of necessity and of truth. Similarly for the model-theoretic approach. If models are to bear any resemblance to the world, truth-in-a-model ought to have the same structure as truth *simpliciter*. In these cases, doctrines of truth are relevant to the outcome of logical theory. For example, intuitionists have claimed that, at least in the domain of mathematics, truth comes by way of construction or verification. This claim has resulted in disagreement about logical laws (see INTUITIONISTIC LOGIC AND ANTIREALISM). The case is similar with quantum logic. Given a particular reading of the correspondence theory of truth (in which propositions correspond to subspaces of the Hilbert spaces of quantum physics), quantum logic seems to follow naturally (see QUANTUM LOGIC). On the other hand, the correspondence, coherence or pragmatist theories of truth do not seem to dictate a particular theory of logic. Metaphysical doctrines of truth are relevant to an account of logic, but they need not determine that account.

Some take it that logical validity is independent of any particular account of truth, because logical laws are purely a matter of convention. Clearly convention has a large part to play in language, but it is much more than this to say that logical laws are simply true by convention. For example, it is clear that it is a matter of convention that 'snow is white or snow is not white' is used to express a truth (and hence, a logical truth). It is also a matter of convention that 'snow is white' refers to snow. In this case it would be very strange to say that the whiteness of snow is *purely* a matter of convention. Similarly, 'snow is white or snow is not white' is not true solely by convention, but also by the way the world is (see NECESSARY TRUTH AND CONVENTION).

Convention in logic is more at home in the view of logic as proof theory. Here, validity is a matter of the meanings of logical particles. Terms get meanings by convention. However, this does not exempt us from the difficult matters of semantics. Logic depends on the meanings of individual particles such as 'not'.

Is the meaning of 'not' a matter of its truth-functionality, and does this yield classical negation? Or is negation to be analysed inferentially, with intuitionists? The analysis of meaning undergirds the proof-theoretic account of validity. No account of logical validity exempts the practitioner from the difficult task of giving an account of the ground of logical law. This is essentially a matter of metaphysics and semantics.

3 The question of extension

Even given answers to the semantic and metaphysical

questions, we are not at an end. We have yet to give an account of which inferences qualify as logical truths. Logicians have a ready supply of formal systems designed to do just this: there is a whole wealth of different formal systems designed to give an account of valid inference in different languages. These systems differ from each other in a number of ways. They can contain the truth-functional connectives, quantifiers for objects (both the standard existential and universal quantifiers, and perhaps more exotic quantifiers), quantifiers of higher order, the identity relation, modalities of various sorts, and so on. If validity is construed as necessary truth-preservation, there is no need to make a principled choice of logical constants, because any term may be relevant in determining validities. The only choice is a pragmatic one, of which laws are worth studying. The way is open for a logic of colour, a logic of perception sentences, a logic of action, or a logic of all three. These 'logics' will be partial accounts of validity, just as a theory of electromagnetism is a partial account of physical law.

On the other accounts of validity, a distinction must be made between logical and non-logical terms, in order for there to be a univocal sense of logical validity. This is not an easy task, because there are no principled criteria that something must satisfy in order for it to be a logical constant. People disagree over whether generalized quantifiers of objects (such as 'uncountably many') and second-order quantifiers ought to feature in logic (see QUANTIFIERS, GENERALIZED; SECOND-ORDER LOGIC, PHILOSOPHICAL ISSUES IN).

Second, formal systems may differ in terms of their results, even if they have the same language. For example, intuitionistic logic and classical logic disagree about double negation elimination (not-not-p; therefore p) provided that you take intuitionistic logic and classical logic to have the same vocabulary. There is a subtlety here. It is obvious that two different formal systems can be reconciled by treating them as modelling different things. Then intuitionistic logic and classical logic can be seen as not disagreeing, because they have different negations. Quine said as much when he claimed that changing a logic amounted to changing the subject (1970).

However, this is not the whole story. Classical logic and intuitionistic logic can disagree as to the validity of real arguments. Given a particular argument in natural language, an intuitionist and a classical logician may disagree about its validity. If there is a fact of the matter as to whether the argument is valid, then classical logic and intuitionistic logic can be seen to disagree about this fact. The change of logic does not involve a change of subject when the subject (in

this case, natural language arguments) is fixed in advance. Given a particular instance of the natural language 'not', classical logic and intuitionistic logic are different accounts of the valid arguments involving this fragment of natural language. The natural language particle is *prior* to its formalizations, which are intended to capture the meaning of the particle. These formalizations can capture the meaning well, or not well, and hence these formalizations can disagree.

With intuitionistic logic, the locus of disagreement is the conception of truth or, alternatively, the meanings of the logical particles. Given a verificationist or constructivist view of truth, you have a reason to be an intuitionist with regard to the standard logical particles. However, if you disagree with constructivism, and you do not analyse the meanings of logical terms in constructivist terms, you can use intuitionistic logic as a logic of necessary provability preservation. Disagreement about intuitionism can only be resolved by agreeing on theories of truth and meaning. The case is similar with quantum logic, as we saw before.

Disagreement becomes more subtle when we consider paraconsistency (permitting contradictions in some way to hold) and relevance. According to most logics, the argument from p & not-p to q is valid, but according to paraconsistent logics (including all logics of relevance – see Anderson and Belnap 1975; Anderson, Belnap and Dunn 1992), it is not. In this disagreement no doctrines of truth or meaning stand out as motivating the peculiar features of the logics. Instead, there seem to be two major reasons that proponents of these systems can have for analysing validity in this way.

The first is quite simple. If a contradiction were true, or even possibly true, it would be clear that the inference from p & not-p to q would be invalid. While many doubt the coherence of this supposition, enough work has been done in the field of paraconsistent logic to show that the approach is coherent (see PARACONSISTENT LOGIC; Priest, Routley and Norman 1989).

If we admit the need to be able to deduce in inconsistent situations (whether they are epistemic situations, possible situations or actual situations), a logic without the inference from p & not-p to q is necessary. Note that this does not involve any particular doctrine about the nature of truth (correspondence, pragmatic or coherence), but simply the view that it is possible that a contradiction be true. Resolving such disagreements is a matter of examining the arguments for and against the truth of contradictions.

The second motivation for the view that the argument from p & not-p to q is invalid is quite different. On this view you need not hold that it is possible that a contradiction be true. Instead, you maintain that for an argument to be valid, and for a conditional to be true, its antecedent must be relevant to its consequent. If this is the case, then there may be a reason to reject the inference (see RELEVANCE LOGIC AND ENTAILMENT). Again, this disagreement is not about a particular doctrine of the nature of truth. Instead, it is a disagreement about the relationship between relevance on the one hand, and validity and conditionality on the other. Opponents can trade intuitions about the validity or otherwise of individual arguments, but this kind of discussion is rarely fruitful. A saner approach might go as follows: if the relevantist can develop a coherent theory of validity, which models our valid argument at least as well as can be done otherwise, and which, in addition, gives an account of phenomena that cannot be modelled otherwise, then, clearly, the relevantist position is viable and valuable. If it cannot, it will not succeed as a theory of validity.

In all of these considerations, we have seen that logic is quite similar to other sciences. The practitioners have some idea of what the subject matter is (valid inferences) but there is debate about its exact nature. The task is to model the subject matter, and there is no wide consensus about how this is to be done. However, as in other sciences, this does not mean that the study is not worthwhile, nor that it will not enrich our knowledge of the way things are.

See also: LOGICAL AND MATHEMATICAL TERMS, GLOSSARY OF; LOGICAL FORM

References and further reading

* Anderson, A.R. and Belnap, N.D., Jr (1975) *Entailment: The Logic of Relevance and Necessity*, vol. 1, Princeton, NJ: Princeton University Press. (Together with volume 2, this gives the canonical exposition of much of the work on logics of relevance implication and entailment.)
* Anderson, A.R., Belnap, N.D., Jr and Dunn, J.M. (1992) *Entailment: The Logic of Relevance and Necessity*, vol. 2, Princeton, NJ: Princeton University Press. (Both volumes together give the canonical exposition of much of the work on logics of relevance implication and entailment. Volume 2 also includes an interesting discussion of different approaches to relevance validity.)
* Aristotle (*c.* mid 4th century BC) *Prior Analytics*, trans. Richard McKeon, in *The Basic Works of Aristotle*, New York: Random House, 1941. (Aristotle's work on the syllogism.)
Boolos, G. (1975) 'On Second Order Logic', *Journal of Philosophy* 72: 509–27. (Defence of second-order logic as *logic*.)
* Etchemendy, J. (1990) *The Concept of Logical Consequence*, Cambridge, MA: Harvard University Press. (Critique of the model-theoretic account of validity.)
* Prawitz, D. (1974) 'On the Idea of a General Proof Theory', *Synthese* 27: 63–77. (Exposition and defence of the proof-theoretic account of validity.)
* Priest, G., Routley, R. and Norman, J. (1989) *Paraconsistent Logic: Essays on the Inconsistent*, Munich: Philosophia. (Essays on paraconsistent logic.)
* Quine, W.V. (1970) *Philosophy of Logic*, Englewood Cliffs, NJ: Prentice Hall. (Exposition and defence of the model-theoretic account of validity, with a discussion of the scope of logic, and 'deviant' logics.)
Shapiro, S. (1991) *Foundations Without Foundationalism*, Oxford: Oxford University Press. (Defence and applications of second-order logic.)
Sher, G. (1991) *The Bounds of Logic*, Cambridge, MA: MIT Press. (Discussion of first-order quantification and the scope of logic, from the perspective of model theory.)
* Tarski, A. (1936) 'Über den Begriff der logischen Folgerung', *Actes du Congrès International de Philosophie Scientifique* 7: 1–11; trans. J.H. Woodger, 'On the Concept of Logical Consequence', in *Logic, Semantics, Metamathematics: Papers from 1923 to 1938*, Oxford: Clarendon Press, 1956. (The classic exposition of the model-theoretic account of validity.)
* Wagner, S. (1987) 'The Rationalist Conception of Logic', *Notre Dame Journal of Formal Logic* 28: 3–35. (Exposition and defence of the proof-theoretic account of validity, and first-order logic.)

GREG RESTALL

LOGICAL POSITIVISM

Logical positivism (logical empiricism, neo-positivism) originated in Austria and Germany in the 1920s. Inspired by late nineteenth- and early twentieth-century revolutions in logic, mathematics and mathematical physics, it aimed to create a similarly revolutionary scientific philosophy purged of the endless controversies of traditional metaphysics. Its most important representatives were members of the Vienna Circle who gathered around Moritz Schlick at the University of Vienna (including Rudolf Carnap, Herbert Feigl, Kurt Gödel, Hans Hahn, Karl Menger, Otto Neurath and

Friedrich Waismann) and those of the Society for Empirical Philosophy who gathered around Hans Reichenbach at the University of Berlin (including Walter Dubislav, Kurt Grelling and Carl Hempel). Although not officially members of either group, the Austrian philosophers Ludwig Wittgenstein and Karl Popper were, at least for a time, closely associated with logical positivism.

The logical positivist movement reached its apogee in Europe in the years 1928–34, but the rise of National Socialism in 1933 marked the effective end of this phase. Thereafter, however, many of its most important representatives emigrated to the USA. Here logical positivism found a receptive audience among such pragmatically, empirically and logically minded American philosophers as Charles Morris, Ernest Nagel and W.V. Quine. Thus transplanted to the English-speaking world of 'analytic' philosophy it exerted a tremendous influence – particularly in philosophy of science and the application of logical and mathematical techniques to philosophical problems more generally. This influence began to wane around 1960, with the rise of a pragmatic form of naturalism due to Quine and a historical-sociological approach to the philosophy of science due mainly to Thomas Kuhn. Both of these later trends, however, developed in explicit reaction to the philosophy of logical positivism and thereby attest to its enduring significance.

1   **Historical background**
2   **Relativistic physics**
3   **Logic and the foundations of mathematics**
4   **The Vienna Circle**
5   **Emigration, influence, aftermath**

1   Historical background

Immanuel KANT, in the positivists' eyes, had made a lasting contribution to scientific philosophy – particularly in his rejection of the possibility of supersensible metaphysical knowledge and his reorientation of theoretical philosophy around the two questions 'how is pure mathematics possible?' and 'how is pure natural science possible?' In answering these questions Kant developed his famous defence of synthetic a priori knowledge – knowledge independent of sensible experience yet nonetheless substantively applicable to the empirical world. For Kant, the mathematical physics of Newton paradigmatically exemplified such synthetic a priori knowledge through its reliance on Euclidean geometry and fundamental laws of motion such as the law of inertia. Kant's theory of a priori faculties of the mind – the faculty of pure intuition or sensibility and the faculty of pure understanding – was then intended to explain the origin of synthetic a priori knowledge and thus make philosophically comprehensible the possibility of Newtonian mathematical physics.

After the intervening dominance of post-Kantian idealism, a number of German-speaking philosophers renewed the call for a scientific, epistemological and non-metaphysical form of philosophy. But these Neo-Kantian philosophers also had to face an important new challenge to the Kantian synthetic a priori: the nineteenth-century development of non-Euclidean geometry by Gauss, Bolyai, Lobachevskii, Riemann and Klein (see GEOMETRY, PHILOSOPHICAL ISSUES IN §§1, 3). Although some Neo-Kantians attempted to defend the uniqueness and apriority of Euclidean geometry nonetheless, others – especially those of the Marburg School such as Paul Natorp and Ernst Cassirer – aimed to generalize the synthetic a priori beyond its particular embodiment in classical Euclidean–Newtonian mathematical physics (see NEO-KANTIANISM). This latter tendency was similar in important respects to ideas the logical positivists were to elaborate.

But the most important nineteenth-century predecessors of logical positivism were Hermann von HELMHOLTZ, Ernst MACH and Henri POINCARÉ. Through their efforts to comprehend the radical changes sweeping through nineteenth-century science, these three thinkers initiated a new style of scientific philosophy later taken up and systematized by the positivists. The changes in question included the rise of non-Euclidean geometry, the formulation of the conservation of energy and general thermodynamics, and the beginnings of scientific physiology and psychology. Helmholtz made fundamental contributions to all three areas. He based geometry on the postulate of 'free mobility' of rigid bodies, and, since all classical geometries of constant curvature – negative, positive or zero (Euclidean) – satisfy this postulate, he opposed the Kantian commitment to the aprioricity of geometry: whether space is Euclidean or non-Euclidean is an empirical question about the actual behaviour of rigid bodies. In physiology, Helmholtz articulated a general principle of psychophysical correlation whereby our sensations correspond to – but are in no way pictures or images of – processes in the external physical world. These processes consist, in the end, of microscopic atoms interacting via central forces, and, on this basis, Helmholtz developed his famous interpretation of the conservation of energy.

Mach and Poincaré can be seen as reacting, in diverse ways, to Helmholtz. Mach attacked especially atomism and the idea of a psychophysical correlation between two incommensurable realms, and he advanced a programme for the unity of science based on immediately perceptible 'elements' or 'sensations'. The task of science consists solely in seeking correlations among such elements (as in phenomenological thermodynamics), and all dualistic and atomistic tendencies are to be purged as metaphysical via historico-critical analysis. This Machian empiricism exerted a decisive influence on the logical positivists. Poincaré, on the other hand, influenced the positivists primarily through his philosophy of geometry. He agreed with Helmholtz's emphasis on the free mobility of rigid bodies but disagreed with Helmholtz's empiricism. According to Poincaré, the idea of a rigid body is an idealization that cannot be straightforwardly instantiated in the physical world. By freely choosing one of the three classical geometries as, so to speak, a definition of rigidity, we then first make it possible to carry out empirical investigations with real physical bodies. Physical geometry is thus neither synthetic a priori nor empirical: it is 'conventional' (see CONVENTIONALISM).

2 Relativistic physics

Albert Einstein's special (1905) and general (1916) theories of relativity entered this volatile intellectual situation as a revelation (see EINSTEIN, A.; GENERAL RELATIVITY, PHILOSOPHICAL RESPONSES TO; RELATIVITY THEORY, PHILOSOPHICAL SIGNIFICANCE OF). And the relativistic revolution in physics directly stimulated SCHLICK, REICHENBACH and CARNAP to initiate a parallel revolution in scientific philosophy. All three thinkers agreed that relativity – especially through the general relativistic description of gravitation via a (four-dimensional) geometry of variable curvature – definitively refutes the Kantian idea that Euclidean geometry is synthetic a priori. Moreover, relativity arises from critical reflection on the empirical significance of spatiotemporal concepts in physics (in particular, the concept of simultaneity and the concept of motion) and thus demonstrates the fruitfulness of Mach's basic point of view. At the same time, however, through its use of sophisticated abstract mathematics, relativity also illustrates the limitations of Machian empiricism (according to which even mathematical concepts have an empirical origin). All three thinkers therefore attempted to formulate an intermediate position that would do justice to both Machian empiricism and the continued importance of a priori mathematical elements in physics. Poincaré's concept of convention came to play a central role.

Schlick, Reichenbach and Carnap first pursued rather different paths. Whereas Schlick emphasized from the outset that the Kantian synthetic a priori has no place at all in the new relativistic context,

Reichenbach and Carnap initially attempted to salvage important aspects of Kantianism. Reichenbach began by distinguishing the idea of necessary and unrevisable truth from the idea of necessary presupposition of a given scientific conceptualization of nature. For Reichenbach, relativity refuted the former but embodied the latter. Kant was right that the necessary presuppositions of Newtonian physics included Euclidean geometry and the laws of motion. In moving to relativistic physics, however, these are replaced by fundamentally new presuppositions. We thus end up with a relativized version of the Kantian a priori (as constituting the presuppositions of a particular theory). Carnap, by contrast, began by distinguishing metrical from topological features of physical space. The latter are indeed synthetic a priori as Kant thought (they even depend on a kind of pure intuition), but the former – as general relativity has shown – essentially involve the behaviour of empirically given bodies. We thus end up with a weakening of the Kantian a priori (from metrical to topological features).

These early attempts to salvage aspects of the synthetic a priori did not survive, however. For Schlick's view that relativity is simply incompatible with Kant eventually won the day. Although the distinction between Poincaré's conventionalism and Helmholtzian empiricism was not entirely clear (and Reichenbach, in particular, preferred to associate his later viewpoint with Helmholtz rather than Poincaré), both Reichenbach and Carnap soon came to replace the Kantian notion of the a priori with Poincaré's concept of convention. Yet this form of conventionalism (unlike Poincaré's) was forged in the crucible of a revolutionary new physics and thus demonstrated the vitality and relevance of a new philosophy.

3 Logic and the foundations of mathematics

Whereas the positivists appealed to Poincaré's concept of convention (as realized, so they thought, in relativistic physics) to give a new answer to Kant's question concerning the possibility of pure natural science, they appealed to modern developments in logic and the foundations of mathematics to give a new answer to Kant's question concerning the possibility of pure mathematics. There were in fact two distinguishable sets of developments here. The formal point of view, typified by David Hilbert's logically rigorous axiomatization of geometry, freed geometry from any reference at all to intuitively spatial forms and instead portrayed its subject matter as consisting of any things whatever that satisfy the relevant axioms (see GEOMETRY, PHILOSOPHICAL ISSUES IN §2; HILBERT'S PROGRAMME AND FORMALISM). Geometry is rigorously and a priori true, not because it reflects the structure of an intuitively given space, but rather because it 'implicitly defines' its subject matter via purely logical – but otherwise entirely undetermined – formulas. Mathematical truth, on this view, is identified with logical consistency. The 'logicism' of Gottlob Frege and Bertrand RUSSELL, by contrast, aimed to construct particular mathematical disciplines (especially arithmetic) within an all-embracing system of logic. On this view mathematical disciplines (like arithmetic) indeed have a definite subject matter about which they express truths: namely, the subject matter of logic itself (propositions, classes, and so on). As thus purely logical, however, such pure mathematical disciplines express merely analytic truths and are not synthetic a priori (see LOGICISM).

Hilbert's formal point of view was pursued especially by Schlick, who in a sense made the notion of implicit definition, together with the associated distinction between undetermined form and determinate (given) content, the centrepiece of his philosophy. The logicist point of view, by contrast, was pursued especially by Carnap, who studied with Frege and then was decisively influenced by Russell. Indeed, Carnap was inspired by Russell's conception of 'logic as the essence of philosophy' to reconceive philosophy itself on the model of the logicist construction of arithmetic. He began, in *Der logische Aufbau der Welt* (1928), by developing a 'rational reconstruction' of empirical knowledge – an epistemology – within the logical framework of Russell and Whitehead's *Principia Mathematica* (1910–13). By defining or 'constituting' all concepts of empirical science within this logic from a basis of subjective 'elementary experiences', Carnap's reconstruction was to show, among other things, that the dichotomy between empirical truth and analytic/definitional truth is indeed exhaustive.

Yet the logic of *Principia Mathematica* was afflicted with serious technical difficulties: the need for special existential axioms such as the axioms of infinity and choice. Partly in response to such difficulties, Ludwig Wittgenstein asserted in his *Tractatus Logico-Philosophicus* (1922) that logic has no subject matter after all: the propositions of logic are entirely tautological or empty of content (see WITTGENSTEIN, L.J. §§3–7). Carnap eagerly embraced this idea, but he also attempted to adapt it to the new, post-*Principia* technical situation – which involved the articulation of the 'intuitionist' or 'constructivist' point of view by L.E.J. Brouwer and the development of meta-mathematics by Hilbert and Kurt Gödel (see INTUITIONISM §§2–3; LOGIC IN THE EARLY 20TH CENTURY §§6–9; MATHEMATICS, FOUNDATIONS OF). In *Logische Syntax der Sprache* (1934) Carnap formulated his mature theory of formal languages

and put forward his famous 'Principle of Tolerance' – according to which logic has no business at all looking for true or 'correct' principles. The task of logic is rather to investigate the structure of any and all formal languages – 'the boundless ocean of unlimited possibilities' – so as to map out and explore their infinitely diverse logical structures. Indeed, the construction and logical investigation of such formal languages became, for Carnap, the new task of philosophy. The concept of analyticity thereby took on an even more important role. For this concept characterizes logical as opposed to empirical investigation and thus now expresses the distinctive character of philosophy itself.

4 The Vienna Circle

Otto NEURATH, Hans Hahn, and the physicist Philipp Frank initiated a discussion group in Vienna, beginning in 1907, in which they considered a combination of Machian empiricism with Poincaré's new insights into the conventional character of physical geometry. Deeply impressed by Schlick's work on relativity theory, they arranged (apparently with Einstein's help) to bring Schlick to the University of Vienna in 1922 to take over the Chair in Philosophy of the Inductive Sciences previously held by Mach. What we now know as the Vienna Circle quickly took shape. Reichenbach, who had become acquainted with Carnap through their common interest in relativity, introduced him to Schlick in 1924. In 1925 Carnap lectured to the Circle in Vienna on his new 'constitutional theory of experience' and became assistant professor under Schlick in 1926. The Circle then engaged in intensive discussions of Carnap's epistemology and Wittgenstein's *Tractatus*. Wittgenstein's view that all propositions are truth-functions of 'elementary propositions' was combined with Carnap's constitution of scientific concepts from a basis of 'elementary experiences' so as to create a new, logically rigorous form of empiricism according to which all meaningful – scientific – propositions are reducible to propositions about immediately given experience. And this was articulated as the 'official' philosophy of the Vienna Circle in the famous manifesto *Wissenschaftliche Weltauffassung* in 1929.

Neurath was the driving force in thus turning the Vienna Circle into a public philosophical movement. Trained in economics and the social sciences, Neurath was extremely active politically as a scientific neo-Marxist. In particular, he took the community of natural scientists as the model for a rationally organized human society, and, on this basis, he advocated a reorganization of both intellectual and social life from which all non-rational, 'metaphysical' elements would be definitively purged. In this sense, Neurath saw the philosophical work of the Vienna Circle as a reflection of the wider movement for a *neue Sachlichkeit* then current in Weimar culture – as typified, for example, by the Dessau Bauhaus. As in the wider culture, this movement stood in philosophy for a rejection of individualism in favour of the cooperative, piecemeal, and 'technological' approach to problems exemplified in the sciences, and it was therefore particularly hostile to what was perceived as a return to the metaphysical system-building of post-Kantian idealism by influential German philosophers such as Martin Heidegger. Carnap was especially sympathetic to Neurath's broader philosophical-political vision and clearly expresses this vision in the Preface to the *Aufbau*. Schlick, by contrast, preferred a more individualistic model of philosophy and resisted the idea of a 'movement'.

This divergence between a 'left wing' and a 'right wing' of the Circle emerged in the sphere of epistemology in a debate over 'protocol-sentences' in the years 1930–4. At issue was the status of the basic propositions or protocols in which the results of scientific observation are recorded. It had initially appeared, in Carnap's constitutional system of the *Aufbau*, that such propositions must express private, subjective sense-experience. For Neurath, however, this view was inconsistent with the publicity and intersubjectivity required by science. He therefore advocated a more naturalistic conception of protocols as sentences accepted by the scientific community as recording the results of observation at a given time (see NATURALIZED PHILOSOPHY OF SCIENCE). These sentences must thus be expressible within the public and 'physicalistic' language of unified science and hence, like all other sentences, are in principle revisable. Schlick was deeply shocked by Neurath's view – which he took to represent an abandonment of empiricism in favour of the coherence theory of truth (see TRUTH, COHERENCE THEORY OF). Carnap attempted, in typical fashion, to mediate the dispute: at issue was simply a choice between two different languages in which to formulate or rationally reconstruct the results of unified science. Although Neurath's thoroughly intersubjective 'physicalistic' language (where, as Karl Popper emphasized especially, every sentence is revisable) was clearly preferable on pragmatic grounds, Carnap held that this choice – like every other choice of formal language – is in the end conventional (see POPPER, K.R. §3). Empiricism, in Carnap's hands, is itself framed by conventional and hence non-empirical choices (see VIENNA CIRCLE).

5 Emigration, influence, aftermath

The rise of the Nazi regime set off a wholesale migration of logical positivists to the English-speaking world. Carnap, who had become professor at Prague in 1931, moved in 1936 to the University of Chicago. Reichenbach, who had fled to Istanbul in 1933, moved in 1938 to the University of California at Los Angeles. (After Reichenbach's death in 1953 Carnap took over his position at UCLA, beginning in 1954.) Neurath, after leaving Vienna for The Hague in 1934, fled to England in 1940 – where he worked in Oxford until his death in 1945. Friedrich Waismann fled for England as well, where he lectured at Oxford from 1939. Philip Frank emigrated to the USA (also from Prague) in 1938 and settled at Harvard in 1939. Karl Menger took up a position at Notre Dame in 1937, and Kurt Gödel became a member of the Institute for Advanced Study at Princeton in 1940. Herbert Feigl went first to the University of Iowa in 1933 and then to the University of Minnesota in 1940, where he founded the influential Minnesota Center for the Philosophy of Science in 1953. Carl HEMPEL joined Carnap at the University of Chicago in 1939 and, after teaching at Queens College and Yale, settled at Princeton in 1955. (Schlick was murdered by a deranged student at the University of Vienna in 1936.)

The growth of philosophy of science in the USA was decisively shaped by the work of Carnap, Reichenbach and Hempel. Reichenbach influenced especially the development of philosophy of physics through his work on geometry, relativity and the direction of time (see RELATIVITY THEORY, PHILOSOPHICAL SIGNIFICANCE OF §3). Hempel published extraordinarily influential papers on the logical analysis of explanation and confirmation and thereby furthered the ideal of scientific philosophy first articulated by Carnap (see EXPLANATION; CONFIRMATION THEORY). Carnap himself continued the construction of formal languages in which such concepts as testability, modality and probability could be rationally reconstructed or 'explicated' and thus contributed further to the same ideal. Indeed, Carnap's explication of concepts through the construction of formal languages influenced the English-speaking world of analytic philosophy far beyond the borders of philosophy of science. Developments in formal semantics and philosophy of language, in particular, rested on Carnap's initial work on modality (see SEMANTICS §2).

The Carnapian ideal of explication is based on a sharp distinction between logical and empirical investigation, analytic and synthetic truth. In his *Logical Syntax of Language* (1934) Carnap had attempted a general explication of the concept of analyticity itself – a general formal method for distinguishing, within the context of any given formal language, the analytic from the synthetic sentences of that language. After accepting Alfred Tarski's semantical conception of truth in 1935, however, Carnap abandoned the approach of *Logical Syntax* and frankly admitted that (although explications for various particular languages could still be constructed) he now had no generally applicable explication of the concept of analyticity. After studying with Carnap in the early 1930s, W.V. Quine then exploited this situation to attack the concept of analyticity as such and, on this basis, to attack the Carnapian ideal of logical explication as well (see QUINE, W.V. §§2, 4). Philosophy, for Quine, is itself a kind of empirical science – a branch of human psychology or 'naturalized epistemology' (see NATURALIZED EPISTEMOLOGY). Moreover, at the same time that Quine was articulating this new philosophical vision, Thomas KUHN published *The Structure of Scientific Revolutions* (1962) in the *International Encyclopedia of Unified Science* edited by Carnap and Charles Morris. Whereas Carnap had relegated the (conventional) choice of scientific language to the limbo of pragmatics, Kuhn concentrated on those factors – especially social factors – which, in a scientific revolution, determine precisely this kind of choice. These ideas, in harmony with Quine's more general naturalistic point of view, then led to historical and sociological approaches to the study of science and thus, in the end, to the decline of logical analyses of scientific language in the Carnapian style.

See also: ANALYSIS, PHILOSOPHICAL ISSUES IN; ANALYTICITY; BRIDGMAN, P.W.; EMOTIVISM; EMPIRICISM; LOGICAL ATOMISM; MEANING AND VERIFICATION; OPERATIONALISM; POSITIVISM IN THE SOCIAL SCIENCES; THEORIES, SCIENTIFIC; UNITY OF SCIENCE

References and further reading

Ayer, A. (ed.) (1959) *Logical Positivism*, New York: Free Press. (Very useful short collection. Contains, in particular, some of the most important papers from the 'protocol-sentence' debate discussed in §4.)

Carnap, R. (1922) *Der Raum: Ein Beitrag zur Wissenschaftslehre*, Berlin: Reuther & Reichard. (Carnap's early analysis of relativity theory. Discussed in §2.)

* —— (1928) *Der logische Aufbau der Welt*, Berlin: Weltkreis; trans. R. George, *The Logical Structure of the World*, Berkeley, CA: University of California Press, 1967. (Referred to in §§3, 4.)

* —— (1934) *Logische Syntax der Sprache*, Vienna: Springer; trans. A. Smeaton, *The Logical Syntax of Language*, London: Routledge & Kegan Paul, 1937. (Referred to in §§3, 5. English version contains important material not appearing in the original.)

—— (1947) *Meaning and Necessity*, Chicago, IL: University of Chicago Press. (Carnap's most influential post-war contribution to logic and philosophy of language. Second edition appearing in 1956 contains important supplementary material.)

—— (1950) *Logical Foundations of Probability*, Chicago, IL: University of Chicago Press. (Carnap's fundamental analysis of 'logical probability' and the concept of degree of confirmation.)

—— (1963) 'Intellectual Autobiography', in P. Schilpp (ed.) *The Philosophy of Rudolf Carnap*, La Salle, IL: Open Court. (Contains detailed information about the historical development of the logical positivist movement.)

Coffa, A. (1991) *The Semantic Tradition from Kant to Carnap*, Cambridge: Cambridge University Press. (Most extensive scholarly treatment of the background to and evolution of logical positivism.)

Creath, R. (ed.) (1990) *Dear Carnap, Dear Van: The Quine–Carnap Correspondence and Related Work*, Berkeley, CA: University of California Press. (Excellent source for the Quine–Carnap debate on analyticity discussed in §5.)

Feigl, H. (1969) 'The Wiener Kreis in America', in D. Fleming and B. Bailyn (eds) *The Intellectual Migration*, Cambridge, MA: Harvard University Press. (Discussion of the positivists' migration to America by a participant.)

Frank P. (1949) *Modern Science and its Philosophy*, Cambridge, MA: Harvard University Press. (Classic discussion of the positivist movement by a participant. Contains, in particular, good discussions of the influence of Mach and Poincaré.)

Haller, R. (1993) *Neopositivism*, Darmstadt: Wissenschaftliche Buchgesellschaft. (Special attention to Neurath.)

Hempel, C. (1965) *Aspects of Scientific Explanation*, New York: Free Press. (Collection of Hempel's classic papers which decisively shaped philosophy of science in the USA.)

Kraft, V. (1950) *Der Wiener Kreis*, Vienna: Springer; trans. A. Pap, *The Vienna Circle*, New York: Philosophical Library, 1953. (Good discussion of how Carnap's *Aufbau* and Wittgenstein's *Tractatus* were combined by the Vienna Circle.)

* Kuhn, T. (1962) *The Structure of Scientific Revolutions*, Chicago, IL: University of Chicago Press. (Referred to in §5. Extraordinarily influential reaction to logical positivist philosophy of science.)

Neurath, O. (1981) *Gesammelte philosophische und methodologische Schriften*, eds R. Haller and H. Rutte, Vienna: Hölder-Pichler-Tempsky. (Most extensive collection of Neurath's philosophical works in the original. Contains the manifesto *Wissenschaftliche Weltauffassung* on pages 299–336.)

—— (1983) *Philosophical Papers 1913–1946*, ed. and trans. R. Cohen and M. Neurath. (Most extensive collection of Neurath's philosophical works in English.)

Popper, K. (1935) *Logik der Forschung*, Berlin: Springer; *The Logic of Scientific Discovery*, London: Hutchinson, 1958. (Popper's extraordinarily influential discussion of scientific method – partly in the spirit of, but also partly explicitly opposed to, logical positivism.)

Reichenbach, H. (1920) *Relativitätstheorie und Erkenntnis Apriori*, Berlin: Springer; trans. M. Reichenbach, *The Theory of Relativity and A Priori Knowledge*, Berkeley, CA: University of California Press, 1965. (Reichenbach's earliest analysis of relativity theory. Discussed in §2.)

—— (1928) *Philosophie der Raum-Zeit-Lehre*, Berlin: de Gruyter; trans. M. Reichenbach and J. Freund, *The Philosophy of Space and Time*, New York: Dover, 1958. (Reichenbach's most influential analysis of geometry and relativity theory.)

—— (1951) *The Rise of Scientific Philosophy*, Berkeley, CA: University of California Press. (Widely read popularization.)

—— (1978) *Selected Writings, 1909–1953*, ed. M. Reichenbach and R. Cohen, Dordrecht: Reidel. (English collection of Reichenbach's most important papers.)

* Russell, B. and Whitehead, A. (1910–13) *Principia Mathematica*, Cambridge: Cambridge University Press. (Referred to in §3. Monumental presentation of modern mathematical logic. Exerted a profound influence on logical positivism.)

Schlick, M. (1917) *Raum und Zeit in der gegenwärtigen Physik*, Berlin: Springer; trans. H. Brose, *Space and Time in Contemporary Physics*, Oxford: Oxford University Press, 1920. (Schlick's widely read and influential treatment of relativity theory. Discussed in §2.)

—— (1918) *Allgemeine Erkenntnislehre*, Berlin: Springer; trans. H. Feigl and A. Blumberg, *General Theory of Knowlege*, La Salle, IL: Open Court, 1974. (Schlick's major epistemological work. Contains, in particular, the general theory of 'implicit definition' discussed in §3. Second edition appearing in 1925 – on which the English translation is based – is significantly revised.)

—— (1938) *Gesammelte Aufsätze*, Vienna: Gerold. (Collection of papers, 1926–36.)

—— (1979) *Philosophical Papers*, eds H. Mülder and B. van de Velde-Schlick, Dordrecht: Reidel. (Most extensive collection of Schlick's works in English. Contains, in particular, the Brose translation of Schlick 1917.)

Uebel, T. (1992) *Overcoming Logical Positivism from Within*, Amsterdam: Rodopoi. (Most extensive treatment – with special emphasis on Neurath's role – of the 'protocol-sentence' debate discussed in §4.)

Waismann, F. (1967) *Wittgenstein und der Wiener Kreis*, Frankfurt: Suhrkamp; trans. J. Schulte and B. McGuiness, *Wittgenstein and the Vienna Circle*, Oxford: Blackwell, 1979. (Very useful material on Wittgenstein's special influence.)

* Wittgenstein, L. (1922) *Tractatus Logico-Philosophicus*, trans. C. Ogden with an introduction by B. Russell, London: Routledge & Kegan Paul. (Referred to in §§3, 4. Although Wittgenstein himself was not officially a member, this work and Carnap's *Aufbau* constitute the two most central texts of the logical positivist movement. New translation D. Pears and B. McGuinness, 1961.)

MICHAEL FRIEDMAN

LOGICAL AND MATHEMATICAL TERMS, GLOSSARY OF

Algorithm. Basic concept in mathematics and, especially, computability theory. Generally, an algorithm is a calculatory procedure given by a finite set of instructions for computing solutions to a class of mathematical problems. In computability theory, algorithms, also called 'effective procedures', are finitary rules for computing functions, to be executed mechanically on relevant inputs. In this sense, algorithmic calculation cannot rely upon any special mathematical insight (for example, constructing proofs for unsolved mathematical problems) or upon the outcomes of random processes (for example, rolls of a die). Example: the rules, learned in primary school, for finding sums of columns of figures represent an algorithm, in either sense, for number addition.

Analytic (judgment or proposition). Notion of modern logic. A judgment or proposition of subject–predicate form is analytic if the predicate (concept) is 'contained in' the subject (concept). Kant's way of putting this was to say that in an analytic judgment

795

Table of logical symbols

Set theory

$\{x: Px\}$ $\{x\mid Px\}$ $\hat{x}Px$	Set abstraction (read: 'the set of things x such that x has P')
$x \in A$	Membership ('x is an element of A')
$A \subseteq B$ $A \subset B$	Subset ('A is a subset of B')
$A \subset B$ $A \subsetneq B$	Proper subset
$A \supseteq B$ $A \supset B$	Superset ('A is a superset of B')
$A \supset B$ $A \supsetneq B$	Proper superset
$\bar{A}$ A' $-A$	Complement of A
$A_1 \times \ldots \times A_n$	Cartesian product of $A_1, \ldots, A_n$
$A - B$ $A \setminus B$	Difference of A and B
$A \oplus B$ $A \triangle B$	Symmetric difference of A and B
$A \cap B$ AB	Intersection (meet, logical product) of A and B
$\cap_\gamma$ $\cap_{\alpha \in \gamma} \alpha$	Intersection of the family of sets γ
$A \cup B$ $A + B$	Union (join, logical sum) of A and B
$\cup_\gamma$ $\cup_{\alpha \in \gamma} \alpha$	Union of the family of sets γ
$\mathbf{V}$ 1	The universal set
Λ 0 $\emptyset$	The empty set
(a,b) $\langle a,b \rangle$	Ordered pair of a and b
$\{a,b\}$	Unordered pair of a and b

$A \simeq B$	Equipollence ('A is equipollent to B')
$A \upharpoonright R$	Relation R with its domain restricted to A
$R \upharpoonright A$	Relation R with its converse domain restricted to A
$R \restriction A$	Relation R with its field restricted to A
$\breve{R}$ R^{-1}	Converse (inverse) of relation R

Propositional and predicate logic

$\forall x$ (x) Πx $\wedge x$	Universal quantifier ('for all $x \ldots$')
$\exists x$ (Ex) Σx $\vee x$	Existential quantifier ('there exists $x \ldots$')
$\imath x$	Definite description operator ('the unique $x \ldots$')
$p \rightarrow q$ $p \supset q$ Cpq	Conditional ('p implies q')
$p \leftarrow q$ Bpq	Inverse conditional
$p \leftrightarrow q$ $p \equiv q$ Epq $p \sim q$	Biconditional ('p if and only if q')
$\neg p$ $\sim p$ Np $-p$ p' $\bar{p}$	Negation ('not p')
$p \,\&\, q$ $p \wedge q$ Kpq pq $p.q$	Conjunction ('p and q')

$p \lor q$ Apq	Disjunction (inclusive) ('p or q [or both]')
$p \veebar q$ Jpq	Disjunction (exclusive) ('p or q [but not both]')
$p \downarrow q$ Xpq	Joint denial ('neither p nor q')
$p \mid q$ Dpq	Alternative denial (Sheffer stroke) ('not both p and q')
$\top$	Verum (the constant true truth-function)
$\bot$	Falsum (the constant false truth-function)
$=$	Identity (a logical constant)
$\neq$	Difference
$\therefore$ $/$	Therefore

Modal logic

$\Box p$ Np Lp	Necessity ('it is necessary that p')
$\Diamond p$ Mp	Possibility ('it is possible that p')
$p \rightarrow q$	Strict implication ('p strictly implies q')
$p \circ q$	Compossibility ('p and q are jointly possible')

Metalogic

$\Gamma \vdash A$	A is formally deducible from the set of sentences Γ
$\vdash A$	A is a logical theorem
$\Gamma \models A$	A is a logical consequence of the set of sentences Γ
$\models A$	A is a logical truth
$\models_M A$	A is true in structure (model) M
$A \Rightarrow B$	Implication (used informally) ('A implies B')

the predicate is *thought* in (the very act of) *thinking* the subject. Analytic judgments are opposed to *synthetic* judgments, which are defined as judgments in which thinking the subject does not entail thinking the predicate (though the two may legitimately be associated by other means). In more recent philosophy the term 'analytic' is generally applied to propositions that are true by dint of their forms or the meanings of their constituent terms.

Argument. Basic notion of logic. The simplest argument is a set of propositions divided into two parts: (1) a set of propositions referred to collectively as the *premises*, and (2) a single proposition referred to as the *conclusion*. Complex arguments are built up by suitably arranging a number of simple arguments or steps. The premises, taken together, are supposed to provide a reason for believing the conclusion in this sense: their joint truth is supposed either to guarantee (in the case of deductive, non-ampliative or demonstrative arguments) or to support to some lesser extent (in the case of inductive, ampliative or non-demonstrative arguments) the truth of the conclusion.

Axiom. Term of traditional and modern logic. An axiom is a proposition of a theory that is treated as fundamental or not admitting of proof. Traditionally, axioms were also treated as epistemically basic in various senses (for example, as being self-evident or as not requiring proof for their acceptance). In modern axiomatic systems, *logical* axioms are the propositions that are fundamental in presenting the underlying logic of the theory (for example, the law of the excluded middle), and *proper* axioms are the propositions that are fundamental in presenting the non-logical or substantive truths of the theory (for example, in usual axiomatizations of the arithmetic of the natural numbers, the law that 0 has no predecessor).

Axiom of choice. Controversial principle of set theory used implicitly in the nineteenth century and formulated explicitly by Zermelo in 1904 for use in his proof of the well-ordering theorem. Also known as the multiplicative axiom. There are different versions of the axiom of choice in modern set theory. In its most familiar statement, it is understood to guarantee, for every set A of non-empty sets, a choice set, which is a set containing exactly one member from each x in A. It is essential to proofs of standard mathematical results concerning the transfinite. It is also equivalent to other noteworthy principles, among them Zorn's lemma. Thanks to celebrated theorems of Gödel and of Paul Cohen, we know that it is neither refutable nor provable from standard axioms for sets, such as those of Zermelo–Fraenkel set theory,

797

provided that they are consistent. See AXIOM OF
CHOICE; *Zorn's lemma*.

Axiom of infinity. Principle of set or type theory,
variously formulated, requiring the existence of an
infinite number of objects of the theory. In the type
theory of *Principia Mathematica* (1910), Whitehead
and Russell introduced an axiom of infinity to
guarantee infinitely many individuals; items of lowest
type. In set theories, axioms of infinity assert the
existence of infinite collections. Zermelo included one
formulation among his 1908 axioms for Cantor's set
theory. In Zermelo's version the axiom states that
there is a set Z of which $\emptyset$ (the empty set) is an
element and which contains, for each of its elements e,
the further element $\{e\}$.

Axiom of separation. Principle of set theory included
by Zermelo in his 1908 axioms for set theory, later
reformulated by Skolem. It permits one to separate
off those elements of a given set which satisfy a given
property. Stated more formally, it says that whenever
A is a set and P is a well-defined property of A, the
collection of precisely those members of A possessing
P is also a set.

Axiom schema. Term of modern logic. An axiom
schema is an expression which employs schematic
'letters' (metalinguistic variables) and which determines an infinity of particular axioms, one for each
substitution of a definite expression of the appropriate sort for the schematic letters. A classic example
is the axiom schema of induction in first-order
arithmetic. It is formulated as

$$(\phi(0) \mathbin{\&} \forall x(\phi x \rightarrow \phi x')) \rightarrow \forall x \phi x,$$

where ϕ is schematic for well-formed formulas of the
language. When such an expression is substituted for
ϕ, we get an axiom of first-order arithmetic.

Axiomatic theory. Basic concept of modern logic. A
theory T (conceived of as a set of sentences) is said to
be *axiomatized* by a set of sentences A (its axioms)
when the sentences making up T are precisely the
sentences provable from A (that is, the sentences
making up T are the deductive closure of A). It is said
to be *axiomatizable* just in case it is the deductive
closure of some subset of its theorems. It is said to be
recursively axiomatizable just in case it is the deductive
closure of some recursive subset of its theorems. It is
said to be *finitely axiomatizable* just in case it is the
deductive closure of some finite subset of its
theorems.

Biconditional. Term of propositional logic. A biconditional is a sentence-forming operator which, given
two sentences, produces a sentence that is true just in

case the given sentences have the same truth-value.
The word can also refer to the compound sentence
formed using a biconditional operator. The typical
example in English is the operator 'if and only if'.

Bijection. Term of set theory and mathematics generally. A function is said to be a bijection when it is
both one-one and onto (in other words, when it is
both an *injection* and a *surjection*). If $f : A \rightarrow B$ is a
bijection then for any b in B there is exactly one a in A
such that $f(a) = b$.

Bound (occurrence of a) variable. See *Variable*.

Cantor's theorem. Basic result in set theory, proved by
Cantor in 1892. It states that the power set $\wp(A)$ of a
set A (that is, the set of all subsets of A) is always of
greater size or cardinality than A. Indeed, if A has
cardinality α, then $\wp(A)$ has cardinality 2^α. See
CANTOR'S THEOREM.

Cardinality (cardinal number). Concept of set theory.
Two sets A and B have the same cardinality if and
only if there is a bijection from A to B. When sets are
of the same cardinality they are often treated as
having the same size. Cardinal numbers measure
cardinality. Hence, two sets have the same cardinal
number just in case they have the same cardinality.
Example: Cantor showed that the sets of natural
numbers and integers have the same cardinal number,
$\aleph_0$ ('aleph-nought'). See SET THEORY.

Categorical proposition. Basic notion of traditional
logic. A categorical proposition is a subject–predicate
sentence consisting of a quantifier, two terms (the
minor or *subject* term and the *major* or *predicate* term)
and a copula (negated or not). (The name comes from
the Greek '*katēgoreīn*', 'to predicate'.) Two possible
quantifiers ('all', 'some') and two copulas ('are', 'are
not') yield four categorical forms, universal or
particular in quantity, affirmative or negative in
quality (sign of the copula). In the Middle Ages they
came to be called by the first four vowels:

A	All A are B (universal affirmative);
E	No A are B (universal negative);
I	Some A are B (particular affirmative);
O	Some A are not B (particular negative).

In *De interpretatione* Aristotle recognizes also 'indefinite' categorical propositions, which lack a
quantifier. Their precise interpretation remains a
matter of dispute.

Categorical syllogism. See *Syllogism, categorical*.

Categorical theory. Important model-theoretic property of formal theories. A theory is categorical (or has

the categoricity property) whenever it has a model and all of its models are isomorphic. Equivalently, a theory is categorical if it has, up to isomorphism, a unique model. Example: full second-order Peano arithmetic (that is, the second-order Peano axioms under full second-order logical consequences) is categorical.

Church's theorem. A major result in the metamathematics of first-order logic, proved by Church in 1936. Church's theorem asserts that validity in full first-order logic is undecidable; equivalently, that there is no decision procedure for determining whether or not an arbitrary formula in full first-order predicate logic is a theorem. In fact, it is possible to show that validity is undecidable for any first-order language containing at least one binary predicate symbol. Church's theorem yields a definitive negative solution to Hilbert's *Entscheidungsproblem* (decision problem) for elementary logic. See CHURCH'S THEOREM AND THE DECISION PROBLEM; *Decidability*.

Church's thesis. Also known as the Church–Turing thesis. A claim which is foundational for abstract computability and recursion theory, first put forward by Church. Church's thesis maintains that a mathematical function is computable mechanically by intuitive algorithm just in case it is Turing computable or, equivalently, is recursive. Church's thesis is widely thought not to admit of definitive proof, although certain forms of evidence for it can be adduced. See CHURCH'S THESIS; *Turing machine*.

Closure (deductive, logical). Term of metalogic. A set *A* of sentences of a language *L* is deductively closed just in case every sentence of *L* that is deducible from *A* is an element of *A*. The deductive closure of a set *A* is the set of all sentences deducible from *A*. *Deductive* closure is a syntactic notion. *Logical* closure is a semantic notion which obtains when a set *A* of sentences of *L* contains every sentence of *L* that follows validly from *A*.

Compactness. Semantic property of formal systems in modern logic and a leading idea in model theory. A formal system is compact just in case the semantic consistency or satisfiability of every set of formulas is finitely determined; that is, a set is satisfiable whenever all its finite subsets are. Equivalently, a system is compact if whenever a sentence *S* is a logical consequence of a set of sentences Γ, *S* is a logical consequence of some finite subset of Γ. Classical propositional logic and first-order logic are both compact (as proved by Gödel and Maltsev), the latter fact being of crucial import in the model theory of first-order languages. Classical second-order logic, however, is not compact. See *Satisfaction*.

Completeness (of a logical calculus). Term of metalogic. A logical calculus is *weakly* complete if every logical truth is a logical theorem. If one is interested in formalizing the more general notion of logical consequence, then one will require that the calculus is also *strongly* complete, that is, whenever a sentence *S* is a logical consequence of a set of premises Γ, there is a derivation of *S* from Γ. The name 'completeness theorem' is used for the theorem, first proved by Gödel in 1930, that every consistent set of sentences of a first-order calculus has a model. From this it follows that the calculus is both weakly and strongly complete. See *Soundness (of a logical calculus)*.

Completeness (of a theory). Notion of metamathematics. A theory *T* is said to be complete with respect to a given semantical property *P* (for example, classical validity, classical truth) when all sentences of the language of *T* that have *P* are theorems of *T*. Thus, if *P* is the classical truth (viz. a notion of truth according to which every sentence is either true or false), *T* is complete if, for every sentence *A* of the language of *T*, either *A* or the denial of *A* is a theorem of *T*. (This completeness property is sometimes referred to as 'negation completeness'.) Examples: the formal system known as first-order Peano arithmetic (PA) is incomplete; full second-order Peano arithmetic (that is, the full set of second-order logical consequences of the second-order Peano axioms), however, is complete with respect to classical truth. See *Theory*.

Computable function. Essential notion in abstract computability theory. A mathematical function *f* is computable whenever there is an algorithm or finitary mechanical procedure which will accept any *x* for which *f* is defined and, after a finite series of steps, produce the appropriate value $f(x)$ of the function on *x*. Computable functions are also called 'effectively computable', 'effectively calculable' or 'algorithmic' functions. Since the early 1930s, a variety of mathematically rigorous explications of computable function have been offered, among them Turing computable function and recursive function.

Conditional, counterfactual. Term of philosophical logic. Also known as 'contrary to fact conditionals' or 'subjunctive conditionals', these are any of a variety of conditional or 'If... then...' statements in which the 'if' clause or *antecedent* states a condition which the speaker assumes to be unsatisfied. Example: 'If Oswald hadn't killed Kennedy, someone else would have'. (Contrast 'If Oswald didn't kill Kennedy, someone else did'.) Counterfactual conditionals are neither truth-functional nor strict conditionals and the issue of proper logical rules and

799

semantics to govern them continues to spark debate in philosophical logic.

Conditional, material. Term of logic. Sometimes also known as the Philonian conditional. It is a statement which places a condition (called the *antecedent*) on the obtaining of another statement (called the *consequent*). A material conditional is false when the antecedent is true and the consequent false. Otherwise, it is true. 'If..., then ___', '___ if...' and '...only if ___' are expressions in English that are often used to express material conditionals. In each of these, the antecedent is the sentence that goes in the place of '...', and the consequent the sentence that goes in the place of '___'.

Conditional proof. Term of logic and mathematics. It signifies a type of proof in which one deduces a conclusion C from a list of assumed premises $P_1, \ldots, P_n$ and asserts on the basis of this the conditional proposition 'If P_1 and P_2 and...and P_n, then C'.

Connective. See *Propositional operator/connective.*

Conservative extension. Notion of metalogic. A theory U is a conservative extension of theory T whenever every theorem of U which is stable in the vocabulary of T is also a theorem of T. Example: first-order arithmetic with addition and multiplication is a conservative extension of first-order arithmetic with addition only. See *Theory.*

Consistency. Basic notion of metalogic. In the *syntactic* sense, a set Γ of sentences or propositions is said to be consistent (satisfiable) just in case there is no sentence S such that both S and $\neg S$ are derivable from Γ. In the *semantic* sense, Γ is consistent just in case there is no proposition S such that both S and $\neg S$ are logically implied by Γ.

Constant. In mathematics and science generally, a quantity or linguistic expression having, in the context, a fixed, determinate value, such as π or the acceleration of gravity, g. In logic, constants represent, syntactically, those places and patterns in a formal expression not open to government by a quantifier or other binding operator. Semantically, contants are those elements of an expression which do not range over various values after an interpretation of the language has been fixed. *Logical* constants are those formal items which never permit re-interpretation; standardly, these include connectives and quantifiers. Predicate and individual constants are those which, under a given interpretation, are assigned fixed subsets of or elements from the domain of interpretation.

Continuum hypothesis. Problem of set theory first raised by Cantor in 1878. The smallest infinite class is that of the natural numbers $0, 1, 2, \ldots$, whose size is denoted by $\aleph_0$. The continuum (the class of real numbers) is isomorphic to the power set of the natural numbers so, by Cantor's theorem, the continuum is larger than the class of natural numbers. The continuum *problem* is the problem of determining whether the continuum is the very next largest size (cardinality) of infinite class after that of the natural numbers or whether there are infinite classes of intermediate size. Cantor conjectured that there are not. This conjecture has come to be known as the continuum hypothesis (in symbols, $\aleph_1 = 2^{\aleph_0}$). The *generalized* continuum hypothesis is the conjecture that this same structure holds for the entire increasing series of infinite class sizes: that is, for every size of infinite class $\aleph_\alpha$, one obtains the next largest cardinal $\aleph_{\alpha+1}$ by forming the power set of a set of cardinality $\aleph_\alpha$. See *Cantor's theorem*; CONTINUUM HYPOTHESIS.

Contraction. Term of modern logic. A type of structural rule in sequent systems. Roughly it signifies a modification of a valid argument or inference in which repetition of premises is eliminated or diminished.

Contradiction. Basic notion of logic. A proposition is said to be a contradiction when it is logically impossible that it be true or, equivalently, when it is logically necessary that it be false. Example: any proposition of the form 'p and not p' is a contradiction.

Contraposition. Basic notion of logic. In *sentential* logic, turning a sentence 'If p then q' around to 'If not-q then not-p' (called the contrapositive of the original sentence) is contraposition. This is valid in most logics of conditionals. In *Aristotelian* logic, contraposition refers to the valid immediate inference forms 'All A are B; therefore all non-B are non-A' and 'Some A are not B; therefore some non-B are not non-A' and their converses.

Converse (of a relation). Term of logic and set theory. The converse (also called the inverse) of a relation R is the relation $\breve{R}$ such that $\breve{R}xy$ if and only if Ryx.

Countable. Term of set theory. A set is countable (or denumerable) when it is either empty or can be exhaustively listed using the natural numbers. Equivalently, a set is countable when it is either finite or in one-one correspondence with the set of natural numbers. Any set which is not countable is uncountable.

Counterfactual (conditional). See *Conditional, counterfactual.*

Cut-elimination theorems. A class of crucial results in the proof theory of formal logics, the first theorem of which was stated and proved in 1934 by Gerhard Gentzen (though anticipated by Jacques Herbrand). Gentzen's cut-elimination theorem is also known as the '*Hauptsatz*' (main theorem). When formulated as a sequent calculus (that is, as a system representing logical consequence immediately) first-order predicate logic naturally contains a 'cut rule' for eliminating extra hypotheses. In a simple case, such a rule states, 'If *A* derives *B* or *C*, while *A* and *C* derives *D*, then *A* derives *B* or *D*', hence cutting the extra hypothesis *C*. Gentzen showed how to convert every proof in his system into a (possibly much longer) cut-free proof. Cut-elimination theorems have been formulated and proved for a wide variety of formal systems, including arithmetic and predicative analysis, and shed considerable light on issues of provability and consistency.

De Morgan's laws. Theorems of propositional logic and Boolean algebra known, in effect, to medieval logicians but named for De Morgan (1806–71) who stated them as laws for class operations. In propositional logic, De Morgan's laws assert that not-(*A* and *B*) is equivalent to (not-*A* or not-*B*) and that not-(*A* or *B*) is equivalent to (not-*A* and not-*B*) for statements *A* and *B*.

De relde dicto. Important distinction in modal and intensional logics. An epistemic or modal expression such as 'possibly' or 'it is known that' is used *de dicto* just in case it is taken as modifying an entire sentence or proposition (dictum). It is used *de re* when it is understood as attributing an epistemic or modal characteristic to some particular items or features (res) mentioned in the sentence. The distinction, which played an implicit role in Greek logic and an explicit role in medieval logic, has received various formulations over the centuries. Examples: when we construe 'It is possible that everyone is married' as putting forward the statement that everyone is married as possibly true, 'it is possible' is used *de dicto*. If we understand 'It is possible that everyone is married' to mean, of each individual person, that they are possibly married, then that possibility is ascribed *de re*. See DE RE/DE DICTO.

Decidability. Basic notion of computability theory and metamathematics. A *set* (for example, of numbers or of formulas in some formal language) is decidable if there is a decision procedure for membership in it, that is, an algorithm which determines for any suitable item (number, formula and so on) whether it is a member of the set. A set is said to be semi-decidable if there is a procedure which reliably confirms when presented with a member of the set that it is a member, but which need not produce an answer at all when presented with a non-member. A *property* is said to be decidable or semi-decidable if the set of items having the property is. A *sentence S* is decidable by or in a theory *T* just in case either *S* or ¬*S* is provable in *T*. Examples: the truth-table method provides a decision procedure for classical propositional logic and shows that the set of propositional tautologies is decidable. The set of valid sentences of predicate logic, on the other hand, is only semi-decidable. See *Algorithm*.

Deducibility. In a formal system *F* consisting of a language *L*, axioms and/or rules of inference, a formula *φ* of *L* is said to be deducible from a set of formulas *A* of *L* just in case there is a finite sequence of formulas $\phi_1, \ldots, \phi_n$ of *L* such that ϕ_n is *φ* and each ϕ_i, $i < n$, is either an element of *A*, an axiom of *F* or follows from preceding elements of $\phi_1, \ldots, \phi_n$ by a rule of inference of *F*. In an informal sense, a sentence is said to be deducible from a set of sentences just in case it follows from them by deductive means of reasoning.

Deduction theorem. A theorem apparently first proved by Tarski in 1921 and first published by Herbrand in 1930. It states that if a formula *B* can be derived from a set of formulas Γ and a single formula *A* (that is, if $\Gamma, A \vdash B$), then the sentence $A \rightarrow B$ can be derived from Γ (that is, $\Gamma \vdash A \rightarrow B$).

Derivation. Notion of metalogic. A derivation (or deduction) is a syntactic entity which corresponds to an argument, proof or inference in a given formal system of inference or proof. Typically, it is a finite sequence of sentences of a formal language in which the first is an axiom or assumption of some sort and each succeeding element is either an axiom or assumption or follows from previous elements via the rules of inference of the system. The conclusion of the derivation is the last element of the sequence. In such a system, a sentence *S* is said to be derivable if there is a derivation whose last element is *S*.

Distributed term (of a syllogism). Notion of traditional logic which signifies the way in which a term is used in a categorical proposition. Historically, a distributed term is one that refers to or stands for all members of its extension. One common rule for distribution is that universal (that is, *A* and *E*) propositions distribute their subject terms and *negative* (that is, *E* and *O*) propositions distribute their predicate terms. Another common rule, however, teaches that universal propositions distribute their subjects and that *particular* propositions distribute their predicates. This illustrates the lack of clarity of the central notion of the traditional characterization; namely, that of a terms 'referring to' the elements of its extension.

Duality. Important property of equational laws in Boolean algebra and logical equivalences in classical logic. In Boolean algebra, the duality theorem asserts that an equation expresses a law of Boolean algebra just in case its dual also does. Here, the dual of a Boolean equation results from interchanging the symbol for meet (intersection) with that of join (union), and 0 with 1 throughout the equation. In a language for propositional logic in which disjunction, conjunction and negation are primitives, the dual of a formula is obtained by replacing disjunction by conjunction and conversely. In this case, whenever two formulas are logically equivalent, so are their duals. The concept was also prominent in early nineteenth-century geometry, where it was noticed that many theorems in plane geometry had duals obtainable by interchanging the term 'line' with the term 'point'.

Effective procedure. See *Algorithm*.

Enthymeme. Term of logic. In modern logic, it signifies any argument which, taken literally, is invalid, but which becomes valid when certain propositions thought too obvious or apparent to require explicit statement are taken as implicit premises. In traditional logic it referred broadly to a syllogism having a missing premise that the reader was supposed to supply.

Entscheidungsproblem. Problems highly influential in the development of metamathematics and computability theory, first set by David Hilbert. To construct a positive solution to the Entscheidungsproblem or decision problem for a formal system is to describe a decision procedure or algorithm for determining the provability or unprovability of arbitrary statements in the system. The work of Church and Turing in 1935 and 1936 showed definitively that there can be no such procedures for full first-order logic and for elementary arithmetic. See *Church's theorem*.

Equinumerosity/equipollence. Term of set theory. Sets are said to be equipollent, or equinumerous, whenever they have the same number of members. More precisely, sets are equipollent whenever there is a bijection between them. Equipollence is a foundational notion for Cantor's treatment of transfinite cardinal numbers. See *Cardinality (cardinal number)*.

Equivalence relation. Term of mathematics. A binary relation is an equivalence relation if it is reflexive, symmetric and transitive in its field. Example: being parallel. See *Relations (properties of)*.

Existential generalization. Rule governing the logic of the existential quantifier. It permits one to conclude that there is something that has the property P from a premise which asserts of some particular thing that it has the property P.

Existential instantiation. Rule governing the logic of the existential quantifier. It permits one to conclude a proposition of the form '*o* has *P*', where '*o*' is the name of an object, from the premise that 'There is at least one thing that has *P*'. In using this inference in a proof, however, one cannot choose '*o*' to be the name of any object about which one has additional information. Hence, the inference is tantamount to giving a mere name (that is, a tag which carries no descriptive information with it) to that which is said to exist.

Existential quantifier. See *Quantifier*.

Fallacy. Term of logic. A fallacy is an (often unnoticed) error or flaw in an argument which prevents it from fulfilling its task of rational persuasion; also an argument featuring such an error. A fallacy is *formal* when its invalidity is discernible from the argument's structure alone. Otherwise, the fallacy counts as *informal*. See FALLACIES.

Figure (of a categorical syllogism). Term of traditional logic. Signifies the relationship in which the *middle term* of a syllogism stands to its *major* and *minor terms*. Aristotle gave three figures (also called schemata). In the first, the middle term is the predicate of one of the premises and the subject of the other. In the second it is the predicate of both premises. In the third it is the subject of both. Some medievals and most moderns divided the first figure into two to get four rather than three figures. The first of these is one in which the middle term is the predicate of the minor term in one of the premises and the subject of the major term in the other. In the other, the middle term is the subject of the minor term in one of the premises and the predicate of the major term in the other.

First-order/higher-order. Notions of metalogic. A first-order variable ranges over individuals (that is, the elements of the domain of an interpreting structure). A second-order variable ranges over sets of (or properties of or relations between) individuals, and a third-order variable ranges over sets of sets of (or properties of properties of, ...) individuals, and so on. Logic of order *n* is the logic of systems whose variables are of order at most *n*. See *Variable*.

Forcing. Semantic method for extending models of set theory. Forcing was first introduced in 1963 by Paul Cohen in his celebrated proofs of the independence from Zermelo–Fraenkel set theory of the axiom of choice and Cantor's continuum hypothesis. Since Cohen's initial results, elaborations and simplifications of forcing have been applied to obtain consistency and independence results in many branches of higher mathematics, including topology and algebra. See FORCING.

Formal language. Basic notion of metalogic. A formal language is constituted by a finite vocabulary of symbols, together with formation rules for determining which strings of symbols are grammatically well formed (in particular, which are sentences). The crucial requirement is that it be effectively decidable whether a string of symbols is a well formed expression or not. See FORMAL LANGUAGES AND SYSTEMS.

Formal proof (derivation). See *Formal system.*

Formal system. Basic notion of metalogic. Also known as a *logistic system* or *calculus*. It is a system of proof based on a formal language. The distinction between the finite sequences of words of the language that are *proofs* or *derivations* and those that are not is effectively decidable. No appeal to the meaning of any symbol is thus required in order to determine of a finite sequence of words whether or not it is a derivation. It is purely a mechanical decision based upon the *forms* or *shapes* of the symbols involved and the orders of their combinations. The *theorems* of a formal system are those words for which there is a derivation. Because the derivations form an effectively decidable set, the theorems form an effectively enumerable or (assuming Church's Thesis) *recursively enumerable* set. See *Formal language.*

Free (occurrence of a) variable. See *Variable.*

Function. Term of set theory and mathematics generally. Also called a mapping. A function is an operation which takes elements from one set and produces elements of another (or the same) set. If f is a function from A to B (in symbols, $f : A \rightarrow B$), A is called the *domain* of f and B the *range* or *codomain*. The elements a of A are called the *arguments* or *inputs* of f, and the element $f(a)$ of B produced by applying f to a is called the *value* or *output* or *image* of f at a. A *total* function from A to B is a function which is defined for every element of A. Otherwise it is a *partial* function. In set-theoretic terms, a function signifies a many-one *relation* (that is, a relation that associates with each appropriate sequence of elements of its field a unique single element of its field). An n-ary function f is an $n+1$-ary relation R_f such that for all $a_1, \ldots, a_n, c, d$ in the field of R_f, if $R_f(a_1, \ldots, a_n, c)$

(that is, $f(a_1, \ldots, a_n) = c$) and $R_f(a_1, \ldots, a_n, d)$, then $c = d$.

Halting problem. Basic undecidability result in computability theory. It is provable that the halting problem does not admit of general solution. To solve the halting problem would be to construct a general computer program (more precisely, a Turing machine or register machine) which will correctly determine, of an arbitrary program or machine P in the same language and an arbitrary potential input n, whether P's computation will ever halt once n is actually input to P. Part of the import of the halting problem lies in the fact that there are many natural, mathematical problems which can be shown unsolvable by comparison with it.

Homomorphism. Term of algebra and model theory. In mathematics generally, a homomorphism is (1) a function from the domain or universe of a structure A into the domain of a structure B of the same type or signature which (2) preserves structural features relevant to the signature. More specifically, a homomorphism maps the distinguished elements, relations and operations of A into corresponding elements, relations and operations of B. In formal logic, a homomorphism is a structure-preserving function between similar models.

Identity of indiscernibles. Principle enunciated by Leibniz (*Discourse on Metaphysics*, §9). It states that two substances may not be exactly alike in all qualitative respects and differ only numerically. Stated contrapositively and in more modern terms, it says that for all individuals x and y, if, for every property P, x has P if and only if y has P, then x is identical to y.

Impredicative definition. Term of metalogic. An impredicative definition of an object or class is any definition that refers to a collection of which that object or class is an element. The use of impredicative definitions in mathematics was forsworn by Russell in his vicious-circle principle. The enforcement of this principle was the primary motive of his theory of types.

Incompleteness theorems. Common name for two theorems first published by Gödel in 1931. The first of these says (roughly) that, if T is a consistent, recursively axiomatizable theory that includes an elementary fragment of arithmetic, then there is a sentence G of the language of T such that neither G nor $\neg G$ is provable in T. The second says (roughly) that, if T is a consistent, recursively axiomatizable theory that includes an elementary fragment of arithmetic, then there is a formula Con_T of the language of T which expresses the idea that T is consistent and which is not provable in T. See GÖDEL'S THEOREMS.

Independence. Basic notion of logic and axiomatics. Typically, a proposition p is said to be independent of a set of propositions A just in case p is not logically implied by A. A set of sentences may then be said to be independent (or its elements mutually independent) if none of its elements is logically implied by the remaining elements. Independence in this sense has commonly been identified as a virtue of an axiomatic system by modern foundational thinkers. In another sense of independence, a proposition p is said to be independent of a set of propositions A just in case neither p nor $\neg p$ is logically implied by A.

Indirect proof. See *Reductio ad absurdum*.

Indiscernibility of identicals. Converse of Leibniz's principle of the identity of indiscernibles formulated in such famous texts of modern logic as Frege's *Begriffsschrift* (1879). It states that for all individuals x and y, if x and y are identical, then, for every property P, x has P if and only if y has P. A first-order version not quantifying over properties can be written in symbolic notation as

$$\forall x \forall y (x = y \rightarrow (Px \leftrightarrow Py)).$$

Induction, mathematical. Fundamental principle or form of mathematical reasoning for the natural numbers, variants of which apply to other well-ordered or recursively defined collections. For the natural numbers, induction allows one to conclude that every number has a property P from the premises that 0 has P and that, whenever a number has P, so does its successor. A variant, known as 'complete induction' or 'course-of-values' or *strong* induction, allows one to conclude that every number has a property P from the premise that any number is such that it has P whenever all its predecessors do. See *Axiom schema*; *Transfinite induction*.

Injection. See *One-one correspondence*.

Interpretation. Term of mathematical logic and linguistics. Logicians use the term 'interpretation' for a variety of distinct conceptions. First, in semantics, an interpretation of a formal language is a function (or other mathematical setting) sufficient to determine meanings or denotations for all grammatically correct expressions of the language. For formal propositional logic, a semantic interpretation is an assignment of truth-values to atomic formulas extendible recursively to all formulas in accordance with the truth tables for the connectives. In quantifier logics, interpretations in this sense are functions assigning denotations to each of the nonlogical symbols of the language. Alterna-

tively, 'interpretation' sometimes refers to assignments of truth-conditions to all formulas of a language. It is also sometimes used in a syntactic sense to describe mappings of one formal language (or of one formal theory) into another that preserve certain of their important characteristics.

Isomorphism. Term of set theory, model theory and mathematics generally. An isomorphism between two structures A and B of the same type or signature is a bijection $f : A \rightarrow B$ from the domain (or universe) of A to the domain of B which preserves structure. If $R_A xy$ for elements x, y of A, then $R_B f(x) f(y)$, where R_B is the relation in B which corresponds to the relation R_A in A and $f(x)$ and $f(y)$ the elements of B which correspond to x and y. And if $g_A : A \rightarrow A$ and $g_B : B \rightarrow B$ are corresponding functions defined on A and B, respectively, then $f(g_A(a)) = g_B(f(a))$ for all a in A. In formal logic, an isomorphism is such a correspondence between similar models. Example: the function 'multiplication by 2' is an isomorphism between the structure of the natural numbers $\{0, 1, 2, \ldots\}$ together with the operation of addition, and the set $\{0, 2, 4, \ldots\}$ with the same operation. This function is one-one because every number in the set $\{0, 2, 4, \ldots\}$ corresponds to a unique natural number (found by dividing by 2). It is onto because every number in the set $\{0, 2, 4, \ldots\}$ is the image of some natural number. And it is structure-preserving because it maps the zero element of the natural numbers to the zero element of the set $\{0, 2, 4, \ldots\}$ and for all natural numbers n, m, $2(n + m) = 2n + 2m$.

Laws of thought. Term of traditional logic used to refer to a family of principles that were taken to be laws according to which valid inference proceeds regardless of the subject matter involved. The three principles most commonly identified as belonging to this family are: *the law of identity* (taken as stating (1) that every thing is identical to itself or (2) that every proposition implies itself), *the law of contradiction* (taken as stating (1) that nothing both has and lacks a given attribute or (2) that no proposition is both true and false), and *the law of the excluded middle* (taken as stating (1) that every thing either has or lacks a given property or (2) that every proposition is either true or false).

Liar paradox. Attributed to Eubulides (4th century BC). A man says, 'What I am saying is false'. If what he says is true then it is false, and if it is false then it is true. Assuming that it is either true or false, it follows that it must be both, which is absurd. The *strengthened* liar is a variant designed to rule out the alternative that what he says is meaningless, by having him say 'What I am saying is either false or meaningless'. See PARADOXES OF SET AND PROPERTY.

Logical implication. Basic term of logic. A set of propositions *A* is said to logically imply a proposition *p* just in case it is impossible that all the elements of *A* be true and *p* be false.

Logistic system. See *Formal system*.

Löwenheim–Skolem theorem(s). Basic theorem proved by Löwenheim in 1915 and Skolem in 1919, showing that any theory in first-order logic (with identity) that has a model has a countable model. Tarski (1928) later showed that every such theory that has an infinite model has a model of every infinite cardinality. The original theorem shows that some theories (for example, set theory and the theory of real numbers) have unexpectedly small models and is therefore sometimes referred to as the *downward* Löwenheim–Skolem theorem. The theorem proved by Tarski indicates that theories with infinite models have unexpectedly large models and is sometimes called the *upward* Löwenheim–Skolem theorem.

Major term (of a syllogism). Term of traditional logic. The predicate term of the conclusion of a categorical syllogism. See *Syllogism, categorical*.

Mapping. See *Function*.

Maximal consistent set. Notion of metalogic. If *A* is a set of sentences of a language *L*, *A* is said to be maximal consistent just in case (1) *A* is consistent, and (2) no further sentence of *L* can be added to *A* to form a consistent set.

Middle term (of a syllogism). Term of traditional logic. The term that appears in each of the premises but not in the conclusion of a categorical syllogism. See *Syllogism, categorical*.

Minor term (of a syllogism). Term of traditional logic. The subject term of the conclusion of a categorical syllogism. See *Syllogism, categorical*.

Mnemonics, syllogistic. The mnemonic names for the syllogistic moods (valid forms of syllogism) were established by the early thirteenth century. An early fairly complete list is given by Peter of Spain (*Summulae logicales* 4.17). The names encode the way to reduce the syllogisms to the first figure. The significant letters in the mnemonics are the initial consonant, the first three vowels and 's', 'p', 'm' and 'c'. Syllogisms whose names begin with 'B' reduce to Barbara; with 'C' to Celarent; with 'D' to Darii; and with 'F' to Ferio. The vowels 'a', 'e', 'i' and 'o' denote the four forms of categorical proposition. The consonant 's' after a vowel indicates a *simple* conversion of the corresponding first-figure proposition; 'p' indicates conversion *per accidens*, which presupposes existential import; 'm' indicates *mutatio*

praemissarum, that is, interchange of the premises; and 'c' indicates indirect proof, *per contradictionem*. (Subalternation, a mode of immediate inference recognized by Aristotle that also presupposes existential import, is not indicated, for the so-called subaltern moods were codified only later.) Example: to reduce a second-figure syllogism in the mood Camestrop to the first-figure mood Celarent, we interchange the premises (*m*), convert the *E*-premise simply (*s*), and convert the *E*-conclusion *per accidens* (*p*) to the desired *O*-conclusion. See *Categorical proposition*; *Figure (of a categorical syllogism)*; *Mood (of a categorical syllogism)*.

Model. See *Structure*.

Modus ponens. Term of traditional logic and modern logic (in full, *modus ponendo ponens*). Traditionally, *modus ponens* is one of the basic forms or moods of the mixed hypothetical syllogism; namely, that in which the minor premise is the antecedent of the major premise and the conclusion its consequent. In other words, it is the following argument form: 'If *p* then *q*. *p* ∴ *q*'. It is also used as the name for the rule of inference which allows one to infer '*q*' from the two propositions 'If *p* then *q*' and '*p*'.

Modus tollens. Term of traditional logic (in full, *modus tollendo tollens*). *Modus tollens* signifies the basic form or mood of the mixed hypothetical syllogism in which the minor premise is the denial of the consequent of the major premise and whose conclusion is the denial of its antecedent. In other words, it is the following argument form: 'If *p* then *q*. Not *q* ∴ not *p*'. It is also used as the name for the rule of inference which allows one to infer 'not *p*' from the two propositions 'If *p* then *q*' and 'Not *q*'.

Mood (of a categorical syllogism). Term of traditional logic. The moods are the different valid syllogistic forms that are available within a given figure through variation of the quantities (universal or particular) and qualities (affirmative or negative) of the premises and conclusion. As an example, consider the figure '*A* is *B*, *C* is *A* ∴ *C* is *B*' (where *B* is the major, *C* the minor and *A* the middle term). It has the following moods: (1) 'Every *A* is *B*, every *C* is *A* ∴ every *C* is *B*', (2) 'No *A* is *B*, every *C* is *A* ∴ no *C* is *B*', (3) 'Every *A* is *B*, some *C* is *A* ∴ some *C* is *B*' and (4) 'No *A* is *B*, some *C* is *A* ∴ some *C* is not *B*'. In the first figure, then, (1) is in the mood *AAA* (Barbara), (2) in the mood *EAE* (Celarent), (3) in the mood *AII* (Darii) and (4) in the mood *EIO* (Ferio). See *Categorical proposition*; *Figure (of a categorical syllogism)*; *Mnemonics, syllogistic*.

Normal form (conjunctive). Notion of metalogic. A

formula is in conjunctive normal form if it is a conjunction of disjunctions of atomic formulas and negations of atomic formulas. In classical propositional logic, every formula is logically equivalent to one in conjunctive normal form.

Normal form (disjunctive). Notion of metalogic. A formula is in disjunctive normal form if it is a disjunction of conjunctions of atomic formulas and negations of atomic formulas. In classical propositional logic, every formula is logically equivalent to one in disjunctive normal form.

Normal form (prenex). Notion of metalogic. A formula is said to be in prenex normal form if it consists of a (possibly empty) string of quantifiers (called its quantifier prefix) followed by a formula (called its matrix) that contains no quantifiers. Every formula of a first-order language is logically equivalent to a first-order formula in prenex normal form.

Omega-completeness. Notion of metamathematics. A theory T in an arithmetic language L is said to be omega-complete (usually written 'ω-complete') just in case for every formula ϕx of L, if every formula of the form ϕn (where 'n' is a numeral) is provable in T, then so is the formula $\forall x \phi x$.

Omega-consistency. Notion of metamathematics. A theory T in an arithmetic language L is said to be omega-consistent (usually written 'ω-consistent') if there is no formula ϕx of L such that each formula of the form ϕn (where 'n' is a numeral) is provable in T and T also proves $\neg \forall x \phi x$. Gödel used ω-consistency as a condition on the theories for which he proved his incompleteness theorems. Rosser later showed how to prove the first incompleteness theorem using just consistency (a weaker condition than omega-consistency). See *Consistency*.

One-one correspondence. Term of set theory and mathematics generally. Also called a one-to-one correspondence and an injection. A one-one (or 1-1) correspondence between two sets A and B is a function $f : A \rightarrow B$ which maps every element of A to an element of B and never maps distinct elements of A into the same element of B: for all x, y in A, if $f(x) = f(y)$, then $x = y$.

Onto function. Term of set theory and mathematics generally. Also called a surjection. A function $f : A \rightarrow B$ is said to be *onto* B when every element of B is the value of f for some element of A: for all b in B, $b = f(a)$ for some a in A.

Opposition. Term of traditional logic. Aristotle used 'opposition' as a general term for the different ways in which categorical propositions could be at odds with

one another. He delineated three species of opposition: contradictories, contraries and subcontraries. Contradictories cannot both be true and cannot both be false. Contraries cannot both be true but can both be false. Subcontraries cannot both be false but can both be true. These relations were captured in the famous *square of opposition*, a post-Aristotelian device which arranged the A, E, I and O propositions as follows. The proposition-types in the top row (that is, A and E) are contraries, the proposition-types of the bottom row (that is, I and O) subcontraries, and the diagonal pairs (that is, A and O, and E and I) are contradictories.

Universal affirmative (A)	Universal negative (E)
All A are B.	No A are B.

Particular affirmative (I)	Particular negative (O)
Some A are B.	Some A are not B.

Ordering. Term of set theory and mathematics generally. An ordering (or order) is a relation defined on a set which allows at least certain elements of that set to be arranged in order. A relation R defined on a set A yields a *partial* ordering if it is reflexive, antisymmetric and transitive on A. R is said to be a *total* ordering, a *linear* ordering or simply an ordering of A if it is connected, irreflexive and transitive in A. Example: the 'subset of' relation gives a partial order on the power set of a set. The 'less than' relation is a total order of the natural numbers. See *Relations (properties of)*.

Ordinal (number). Term of set theory and mathematics generally. The cardinal number of a collection is concerned only with its 'size', but the ordinal is concerned also with the relationship of its elements. The ordinal numbers are generally defined as the order types of the well-ordered sets, two orders having the same order type if there is an isomorphism between them. Intuitively, ordinals measure the size of a collection by determining how far into a given 'indexing' set one has to go in order to count its members. Cantor pointed out that the differences between these two ways of measuring class size become significant when one is dealing with infinite or transfinite sets. See SET THEORY.

Peano postulates (Peano arithmetic). System of axioms for the arithmetic of the natural numbers. Dedekind introduced an equivalent system in 1888, but it was Peano's system introduced a year later that became widely used. In its early form, the system comprises five postulates:

(1) 0 is a natural number.
(2) Any successor of a natural number is a natural number.
(3) 0 is not the successor of any natural number.
(4) If two successors are identical, then the numbers of which they are successors are identical.
(5) For any property P, if (a) 0 has P and (b) for any natural number x, if x has P, then so does the successor of x, then (c) every natural number has P.

Formulated in this way, with a quantifier over properties in axiom (5) (the induction postulate), Peano arithmetic is a second-order system. A first-order system is obtained by treating induction not as an axiom but as an axiom schema.

Power set. Term of set theory. The power set $\wp(A)$ of a set A is the set of all subsets of A.

Proposition. From the Middle Ages to the nineteenth century, a proposition was understood as (1) a declarative sentence considered together with its meaning or content; or as the one or the other in particular contexts. In the early twentieth century, 'proposition' came to be used in two overlapping senses: (2) the intension or meaning of a (possible) sentence; and (3) the fully determinate circumstance or content capable of being asserted or expressed by a particular utterance of a sentence. A proposition in sense (3) is the sort of thing that can be an object of belief. Sense (2) is often explicated, following Carnap, as a set of 'indices' (or a function from indices to truth-values), where an index is a possible world, a state description, a context of use, or the like. But it is not clear that this explication is adequate for all the uses to which (2) is put, for example, as what synonymous sentences have in common. See *Categorical proposition*; *Singular proposition*.

Propositional operator/connective. Basic notion of propositional logic. In its most general sense, a propositional operator/connective is any operator or expression of a language that forms sentences from sentences (for example, 'and', 'or', 'It is not the case that', 'Wilbur believes that'). Some of these operators are *truth-functional* in character; that is, sentences formed using them are such that their truth-values are uniquely determined by the truth-values of the component sentences. In most of their usages, the first three English operators named above are truth-functional; the fourth is not.

Quantifier. Basic notion of logic. Classically, it referred to those syncategorematic expressions in categorical propositions (for example, 'all', 'some', 'none') that indicate the *quantity* of the proposition.

In modern logic, it refers to any of a variety of operators that are capable of binding occurrences of variables so as to turn term-like expressions into terms, or propositional functions into propositions. A *universal* quantifier attached to a proposition 'A are B' asserts that every element of A (or everything having the property A) is an element of (or has the property) B. An *existential* quantifier attached to a proposition 'A are B' asserts that there is at least one element of A (or at least one object having the property A) that is an element of (or has the property) B. See *Categorical proposition*; QUANTIFIERS; *Variable*.

Recursive function. Term of computability theory. A function on the natural numbers is recursive if it is one of the following:

(1) the identity function, a constant function, the successor function or a projection function;
(2) definable by composition of recursive functions;
(3) definable from recursive functions by recursion;
(4) definable in terms of a given recursive function ϕ as the least natural number such that ϕ takes the value zero.

A function is *primitive recursive* if it is definable using only (1)–(3). A primitive recursive function must be *total*, that is, defined for every natural number (or n-tuple, for appropriate n) as input. Moreover, the function which gives the number of steps required to calculate the value for any input is computable as a function of the input. A recursive funtion need not be total since the recursive function in terms of which it is defined in (4) above might never take the value zero. It is not in general decidable whether a given recursive function is total; even if it is total, there need not be any computable bound to the number of steps required to calculate its value. The recursive functions can be proved to coincide with the Turing computable functions, and with those computable by register machines. Church's thesis is the claim that these classes of functions coincide with those which are computable algorithmically. See COMPUTABILITY THEORY.

Recursive set. Term of computability theory. A set of natural numbers is said to be recursive if the characteristic function of the set, that is, the function which maps the members of the set to 1 and all other numbers to 0, is total recursive. Church's thesis claims that the recursive sets are just the decidable ones. See *Decidability*; *Recursive function*.

Recursively enumerable set. Term of computability theory. A set of natural numbers is recursively enumerable if it is the range (or codomain) of a recursive function or, equivalently, if it is the domain

807

of a partial recursive function. If Church's thesis holds, the recursively enumerable sets are just the semi-decidable ones. See *Decidability*; *Recursive function*.

Reductio ad absurdum. Term of logic. This is the rule, valid in most systems of logic, that if you can deduce a contradictory pair of sentences q, not-q from an assumption p, then p must be false and not-p (the contradictory of p) follows. When p is itself negative, the rule is also called indirect proof. *Reductio ad absurdum* (or *reductio ad impossibile*) was a mode of immediate inference in Aristotle's syllogistic.

Register machine. Concept of computability theory. A register machine is a type of automaton or idealized computing device characterizing computable functions, closely related to the notion of an abacus machine. It consists of an infinite array of abstract memory locations or registers and a finite set of simple instructions for the stepwise manipulation of data stored in these registers. A numerical function is register computable just in case there is a register program which computes its outputs correctly from its inputs using the set of registers. It is provable that a function is register computable precisely when it is Turing computable or, equivalently, recursive.

Relation. Notion of logic and set theory. In the first systematic treatment, De Morgan defined a proposition to be the presentation of two names under a relation, and took its general form to be 's is in relation R to p', with R acting as a copula between the subject s and the predicate p. He treated relational expressions as having both *intensions* and *extensions*. He also saw a general theory of relations as having to allow for relational expressions with any finite number of terms or *arguments*. Modern logic takes the extension of an n-termed relational expression to be a set of n-tuples of elements of a the set on which the relation is defined, known as the *field* of the relation. See LOGIC IN THE 19TH CENTURY.

Relations (properties of). Let R be a relation on a set A. Then

R is *connected* (or *complete*) in A iff any two distinct elements of A are R-related: for any x, y in A, then Rxy (read: 'x bears R to y') or Ryx or $x = y$.

R is *dense* iff whenever R relates two elements of A there is a third which relates to both of them as follows: if Rxy, there is a z in A such that Rxz and Rzy.

R is *reflexive* iff R relates every element of A to itself: Rxx for every x in A.

R is *irreflexive* iff no element of A is R-related to itself: if Rxy then $x \neq y$.

R is *symmetric* iff R and its converse coincide: for all x, y in A, if Rxy, then Ryx.

R is *anti-symmetric* iff no two distinct elements of A are in both R and its converse: if Rxy and Ryx then $x = y$.

R is *transitive* iff whenever R relates x to y and y to z, then it relates x directly to z: if Rxy and Ryz, then Rxz.

R is *linear* (or *simple* or *total*) in A iff R is anti-symmetric, connected, reflexive and transitive in A.

R is *well-founded* iff every non-empty subset of A has a least element under R; or there are no infinite descending chains of R-related elements.

See *Converse (of a relation)*; *Ordering*; *Well-ordering*.

Russell's paradox. The most celebrated of the set-theoretic paradoxes. Let A be the set of all sets which do not belong to themselves. If A belongs to itself, it must satisfy the condition for membership of A, that is, it must not belong to itself. This is absurd. So A does not belong to itself, in which case it satisfies the condition for membership of itself, which is also absurd. We have therefore to conclude that A does not exist. (Note that the derivation of the absurdity makes no use of the law of the excluded middle.) See PARADOXES OF SET AND PROPERTY.

Satisfaction. Basic concept of model theory and formal semantics, introduced by Tarski in order to define truth for languages with quantifiers. It signifies a three-place relation between (a) formulae of a formal language L, (b) interpretations or structures M for L, and (c) sequences of items from the domain of M. Intuitively, a sequence satisfies a formula under an interpretation just in case the formula, so interpreted, holds of the items of the sequence taken in the order in which the sequence arranges them. Thus, for example, if m_1 and m_2 are elements of the domain of M and 'Rxy' is a formula of L, the sequence $\langle m_1, m_2 \rangle$ satisfies 'Rxy' under M just in case $\langle m_1, m_2 \rangle$ is in the extension (i.e. the set of ordered pairs of elements of the domain of M) assigned to 'Rxy' by M. Sentences (i.e. formulas containing no occurrences of free variables) turn out to be satisfied by all sequences under M if they are satisfied by any. A sentence that is satisfied by all (some) sequences under M is said to be true-in-M. A set S of sentences of L is said to be satisfiable (or simultaneously satisfiable) just in case there is at least one structure M for L that makes all the sentences in S true. See *Interpretation*; MODEL THEORY; *Structure*.

Sentence. Term of logic. In a formal language, a formula is said to be a sentence if it contains no free occurrences of variables. See *Variable*.

Signature. Notion of model theory. The signature of a structure or model M is specified by giving (1) the set of individual constants to which M assigns elements of its domain, (2) for each $n > 0$, the set of n-ary relation symbols to which M assigns sets of n-tuples of elements of its domain as extensions, and (3) for each $n > 0$, the set of n-ary function symbols to which M assigns sets of $n + 1$-tuples of elements of its domain as extensions. 'Signature' is another term for what model theorists often refer to as a 'language', by which they mean not a whole formal language (complete with logical symbols, such devices as parentheses and a grammar), but rather those elements of a formal language whose different interpretation serves to differentiate models or structures that have the same domain.

Singular proposition. Term of logic. Traditionally, a singular proposition is a categorical proposition with a proper name as subject term. No express quantifier is present, but William of Ockham construed the proper name as a universally quantified term of unit extension, thereby rendering singular propositions tractable in syllogistic. In modern logic a singular proposition is a simple sentence consisting of nothing but a predicate and the appropriate number of singular terms, as 'Fa' or 'Rxy'.

Sophism. Term used by Aristotle (*Topics*, 162a14) to describe an argument that is not valid but may misleadingly appear to be so.

Sorites paradox. Term of logic and linguistics. Also known as the 'paradox of the heap', *soros* being Greek for heap. This refers to any of a number of paradoxical arguments related to gradual or continuous change. The most famous such argument concludes that no amount of sand constitutes a heap. This is because (1) a single grain of sand does not constitute a heap and (2) if n grains of sand do not make a heap, then $n + 1$ grains do not make a heap. By mathematical induction, no number of grains of sand yields a heap. Typically, sorites paradoxes are thought symptomatic of the vagueness of such predicates as 'heap', 'bald' and 'red'. See FUZZY LOGIC; VAGUENESS.

Soundness (of a logical calculus). Term of metalogic. A logical calculus is *weakly* sound if every one of its theorems is a logical truth. If one is interested in formalizing the more general notion of logical consequence, then one may require that the calculus is also *strongly* sound, that is, whenever a sentence S can be derived from a set of premises Γ, S is a logical consequence of Γ. See *Completeness (of a logical calculus)*.

Soundness (of a theory). Term of metamathematics. A theory is sound if each of its theorems is true in the intended structure. Example: every theorem of first-order Peano arithmetic is true in the intended structure of the natural numbers. See *Theory*.

Soundness (of an argument). Term of basic logic. An argument is said to be sound when it is valid and all its premises are true.

Square of opposition. See *Opposition*.

Structure. Central notion of model theory. A structure M for a language (or signature) L is a pair $\langle D, I \rangle$, where D is a set referred to as the domain of M (sometimes also called the universe of discourse of M or the carrier of M) and I (called the interpretation function of M) is a function which maps each individual constant of L to an element of D, each n-ary relation symbol of L to a set of n-tuples of elements of D, and each m-ary function of L to a mapping of the m-tuples of elements of D to the elements of D. A structure is a *model* of a theory (that is, a set of sentences) T when it makes every element of T true. Classically, D is required to be non-empty, though this requirement is no longer enforced as a general requirement in model-theoretic work. See *Interpretation*; MODEL THEORY; *Satisfaction*.

Surjection. See *Onto function*.

Syllogism, categorical. A valid form of argument in the oldest known system of formal logic in the West, presented by Aristotle at the beginning of his *Prior Analytics*. A syllogistic argument has a major premise, a minor premise and a conclusion, all of them categorical propositions. (Hence the name 'categorical syllogism'; hypothetical syllogisms consist of compound propositions.) See *Categorical proposition*.

Syllogism, disjunctive. Originally, this referred to either of the two valid argument forms 'p or q; p; therefore not q' (the 'fourth indemonstrable' of Stoic logic) or 'p or q; not p; therefore q' (the 'fifth indemonstrable'), or the same but with the major premise commuted. The 'or' here was exclusive. The disjunctive syllogism was considered a species of hypothetical syllogism. Now 'disjunctive syllogism' is used only for the second form (corresponding to the fifth indemonstrable), but with 'or' taken inclusively. It fails in certain relevance logics.

Syllogism, hypothetical. Originally, this referred to a valid two-premise argument from conditionals; later, involving various connectives. Aristotle's syllogisms consist of categorical propositions but he also spoke of 'syllogisms from hypotheses'. Theophrastus was credited with formulating hypothetical syllogisms, particularly 'thoroughly hypothetical syllogisms', such as 'If *A* then *B*; if *B* then *C*; so if *A* then *C*'. This is what is called 'hypothetical syllogism' today. (By the time of Boethius, the term had been extended to Stoic two-premise arguments in general.)

Syllogism, modal. A two-premise argument made up of modalized and unmodalized categorical propositions. For Aristotle the modalization typically affected the predicate term: for example, 'All *A* are necessarily-*B*'. Thus the modality was *de re*. He recognized both one-sided possibility ('not impossible') and two-sided possibility (contingency). His most curious form of modalized categorical proposition was 'All possibly-*A* are possibly-*B*', and similarly for other quantities and qualities (two-sided possibility). Theophrastus interpreted the modalities *de dicto*, which gave much clearer results. Ultimately, the two systems complement each other. Example: 'All men are necessarily animals; all Greeks are men; so all Greeks are necessarily animals'. See *Categorical proposition*.

Symbols See table on pages 796–797.

Tautology, tautological implication. Basic notions of logic. A proposition is said to be a tautology when its truth is logically necessary or, equivalently, when its negation is a contradiction. A sentence built up by means of truth-functional operators is a tautology if it is true under every assignment of truth-values to the atomic sentences. A set of premises tautologically imply a conclusion if every assignment of truth-values to the atomic sentences that make all the premises true also makes the conclusion true. Examples: '$p \vee \neg p$' is a tautology; 'p' and '$p \to q$' tautologically imply 'q'.

Theory. Term of metamathematics. A (formal) theory is a set T of sentences (or formulas) of a formal language that is closed under logical consequence, that is, T is such that everything that follows from members of T is also in T. The elements of T are its *theorems*. Examples: a set of axioms together with all their consequences is a theory. The set of all the sentences true in a structure M is a theory.

Transfinite induction. Concept of set theory. Transfinite induction, a generalization of ordinary, finite mathematical induction, is one or another principle of inductive proof as applied to an ordinal number or well-ordered set which is larger than that of the natural numbers. Generally, transfinite induction on a well-ordered set A shows that every element of A has a property P by proving that, whenever all the order predecessors of an element x in A have P, then so does x. See *Induction, mathematical*.

Truth table. Basic notion of propositional logic. A truth table is a diagram displaying, for a propositional formula or argument, the truth-values of the whole formula or argument as determined by each possible combination of the truth-values of its ultimate constituents (frequently referred to as 'base components' or 'atomic sentences'). In a logic with k different basic truth-values, a proposition made up of n atomic sentences, or an n-ary truth-function, is given by a truth table that has n input columns and one output column, each of k^n rows. Example:

A	B	$A \wedge B$
T	T	T
T	F	F
F	T	F
F	F	F

See MANY-VALUED LOGICS; *Truth-value*.

Truth-function. Term of formal propositional logic. A truth-function takes (lists of) truth-values into truth-values. In classical, two-valued logic, a truth-function takes n-tuples of elements of the set $\{T, F\}$ to the set $\{T, F\}$. In many-valued logics, truth-functions take their arguments and values from larger sets. Generally speaking, if there are k different basic truth-values, there are k^{k^n} n-ary truth-functions. See MANY-VALUED LOGICS; *Truth-value*.

Truth-value. Term of formal propositional logic. In classical, two-valued logic, the members of the set $\{T, F\}$, 'true' and 'false', are conventionally adopted as truth-values, that is, objects over which propositional formulas are interpreted. For nonclassical and many-valued logics, other sets of truth-values provide objects for interpretation. Sometimes, elements of Boolean algebras or open sets from topological spaces serve as useful sets of truth-values.

-Tuple. Term of set theory denoting a sequence or ordered set. An n-tuple is an ordered set of n elements.

Turing machine. Notion fundamental to computability theory. Devised by Turing as a characterization of the notion of computable function or mechanical calculation, a Turing machine is an abstract automaton or idealized computing device which consists of a program – a finite set of simple instructions – to be carried out on a one-dimensional recording tape by a reading-writing device with a memory restricted in capacity. A numerical function f is said to be computed by a Turing machine or to be Turing computable just in case there is a program which, when implemented, mimics on its tape the input-output behaviour of f. Turing computability can be proved to be equivalent to register computability and to a function's being recursive. See TURING MACHINES.

Universal generalization. Rule governing the logic of the universal quantifier. It permits one to conclude that everything has the property *P* from a premise to the effect that an arbitrarily selected object *o* has *P*. In saying that *o* is arbitrarily selected, we mean that one has no information about it that could serve to distinguish it from any other object. It thus functions as a kind of generic object.

Universal instantiation. Rule governing the logic of the universal quantifier. It permits one to conclude of any object *o* that it has the property *P* from the premise that everything has *P*.

Universal quantifier. See *Quantifier*.

Validity. Basic notion of logic. In modern usage, it is applied both to arguments or inferences and to individual propositions. It is also traditionally divided into two types, *deductive* and *inductive*, although some would reserve it for the deductive case alone. In the deductive case, an *argument* is valid if it is impossible that all the premises be true and the conclusion false; a *proposition* is valid if it is impossible that the proposition be false. In the inductive case, an argument is valid if the premises' being true makes it likely (to some implied degree) that the conclusion is true.

Valuation. Term of mathematical logic and formal semantics. Generally, a valuation for a formal language, given a semantic domain *D*, is any function which assigns appropriate semantic values over *D* to chosen expressions of the language. In predicate logic, 'valuation' often refers to functions (also called 'assignments') from the set of variables of a language into the universe of a structure *D*. Occasionally, 'valuation' is used as a synonym for 'interpretation'. See *Interpretation*.

Variable. Term of logic. A variable is a linguistic expression, typically a letter of the alphabet, having, in the context, no fixed, determined value but capable of adopting any of a range of values. Variables are often said to 'range over' items in those domains in which they are assigned values. In many formalisms, not all appearances of variables in a well-formed expression need be attached to a binding operator (for example, a quantifier); those which are are called 'bound' (Russell: 'apparent'), and those which are not are called 'free' (Russell: 'real'). Types in a hierarchy of systems or languages are often distinguished by the order of the variables available. See *First-order/higher-order*; *Sentence*.

Well-ordering. Term of set theory and mathematics generally. A set *A* is well-ordered by a relation *R* (equivalently, *R* is a well-ordering of *A*) just in case *R* is an ordering of *A* and every non-empty subset of *A* has an *R*-least element. See *Ordering*; *Relations (properties of)*.

Zorn's lemma. A noted maximality principle of set theory first introduced by Hausdorff in 1909; rediscovered by Zorn in 1933. Zorn's lemma asserts that a non-empty partially ordered set has a maximal element provided that each totally ordered subcollection of its members is bounded above. Zorn's lemma is provably equivalent to the axiom of choice in standard set theories and is extremely useful in a wide variety of formal contexts, among them proofs for completeness. See *Axiom of choice*; *Ordering*.

MICHAEL DETLEFSEN
DAVID CHARLES McCARTY
JOHN B. BACON

LOGICISM

The term 'logicism' refers to the doctrine that mathematics is a part of (deductive) logic. It is often said that Gottlob Frege and Bertrand Russell were the first proponents of such a view; this is inaccurate, in that Frege did not make such a claim for all of mathematics. On the other hand, Richard Dedekind deserves to be mentioned among those who first expressed the conviction that arithmetic *is a branch of logic.*

The logicist claim has two parts: that our knowledge of mathematical theorems is grounded fully in logical demonstrations from basic truths of logic; and that the concepts involved in such theorems, and the objects whose existence they imply, are of a purely logical nature. Thus Frege maintained that arithmetic requires no assumptions besides those of logic; that the concept of number is a concept of pure logic; and that numbers themselves are, as he put it, logical objects.

This view of mathematics would not have been possible without a profound transformation of logic that occurred in the late nineteenth century – most especially through the work of Frege. Before that time, actual mathematical reasoning could not be carried out under the recognized logical forms of argument: this circumstance lent considerable plausibility to Immanuel Kant's teaching that mathematical reasoning is not 'purely discursive', but relies upon 'constructions' grounded in intuition. The new logic, however, made it possible to represent standard mathematical reasoning in the form of purely logical derivations – as Frege, on the one hand, and Russell, in collaboration with Whitehead, on the other, undertook to show in detail.

It is now generally held that logicism has been undermined by two developments: first, the discovery that the principles assumed in Frege's major work are inconsistent, and the more or less unsatisfying character (or so it is claimed) of the systems devised to remedy this defect; second, the epoch-making discovery by Kurt Gödel that the 'logic' that would be required for derivability of all mathematical truths can in principle not be 'formalized'. Whether these considerations 'refute' logicism will be considered further below.

1   **Preliminary discussion**
2   **Connection with developments in arithmetic, algebra and analysis**
3   **The logicist foundations of arithmetic**
4   **Extension to other mathematical domains**
5   **The setbacks; a brief evaluation**

1   Preliminary discussion

Although the thesis that arithmetic is a part of logic was stated quite explicitly by FREGE (1884, 1893, 1903) and by RUSSELL (1903), it is surprisingly difficult to determine the exact content of this thesis; and, indeed, to determine whether it should be understood to mean the same thing to each of them. For the obvious question presents itself: exactly what are we to understand by 'logic'? How do we tell whether a certain basic assumption, or a certain basic concept, properly belongs to logic, or not? And, since an important part of the thesis is its epistemological aspect – the claim that mathematical knowledge is purely logical in nature – one would naturally expect an account of the grounding of our knowledge of logic. On the first of these questions – how to tell what belongs to logic – Frege has little to say (although he acknowledges the importance of the issue for his philosophy, and does provide a few pregnant suggestions); Russell has some lengthy considerations, which have proved not to be very satisfactory. On the second question, Frege and Russell appear to disagree sharply. Both regard the thesis as being in opposition to Kant; but whereas Frege, in denying that arithmetic is based upon any Kantian 'pure intuition' and maintaining that it is entirely grounded in logic, concludes that Kant was wrong to consider arithmetical propositions synthetic, and holds by contrast that, as propositions of logic, they are analytic (roughly speaking: known to be true by 'analysis' of their meanings alone), Russell denies the latter, and holds that logic itself is synthetic in character:

Kant never doubted for a moment that the

propositions of logic are analytic, whereas he rightly perceived that those of mathematics are synthetic. It has since appeared that logic is just as synthetic as all other kinds of truth; but this is a purely philosophical question, which I shall here pass by.

(1903: 457)

Yet even here the issue is not so clearly drawn; for one must still ask whether Frege, in affirming that logic is analytic and not synthetic, and Russell, in affirming the opposite, understood the words 'analytic' and 'synthetic' in the same way – in particular, whether their opposite formulations might none the less have expressed the same opinions. The possibility is lent some weight by the fact that in certain late writings Frege refers to a 'logical source of knowledge' as a distinct knowledge-source (alongside 'sense perception' and 'the geometrical source of knowledge') ([1924–5] 1979: 267, 278–9). Russell's view that logical truth is synthetic may be essentially identical with Frege's view that knowledge of such truth requires a 'knowledge-source'.

2   Connection with developments in arithmetic, algebra and analysis

The thesis that mathematics is a part of logic could not have been maintained before logic had undergone the deep transformation which took place in the late nineteenth century, most especially through the work of Frege. Before that time, actual mathematical reasoning could not be carried out under the recognized logical forms of argument. The new logic, however, made it possible to represent standard mathematical reasoning in the form of purely logical derivations. It is equally true that no such claim could have been made except for a deep transformation that had taken place in mathematics itself during the nineteenth century; and a brief consideration of this may help to shed some light on a plausible way to construe the logicist thesis.

From the time of Aristotle, it had been usual to regard mathematics as concerned with 'discrete' and 'continuous' quantity: whole numbers on the one hand; continuous magnitudes on the other. In the seventeenth and early eighteenth centuries it was generally supposed that our knowledge of mathematical truths was exclusively concerned with 'relations of ideas', and that – even if these ideas were obtained by some process of abstraction from empirical things' – this character explained how it is that the knowledge in question is certain and independent of experienced 'facts' (such a view was common, for instance, to the rationalist Leibniz and the empiricist Hume). Kant had presented arguments to subvert this position: he argued, rather convincingly, not just that logic (as it then existed) was insufficient to warrant the reasoning of mathematicians, but also that such reasoning demanded attention to more than 'ideas', or (rather) concepts – that a kind of mental visualization of the objects falling under mathematical concepts was an indispensable ingredient.

Among mathematicians – although within a fairly small circle – confidence in *either* the Kantian *or* the pre-Kantian traditional view of the nature of mathematical knowledge was disturbed by the development, in the early nineteenth century, of new forms of geometry: these seemed to show that neither mere consideration of 'relations of ideas' (that is, of such concepts as 'point', 'line', 'distance' and so on), nor the appeal to 'intuition', could decide the truth of propositions of geometry (see GEOMETRY, PHILOSOPHICAL ISSUES IN). At the same time, attempts were begun to work out new foundations for analysis – that is, the theory of the real (and complex) numbers, functions thereof, and limiting processes – that should be independent of any 'extrinsic' appeal to an 'intuition' of continuous magnitude. Again, in parallel (and partly in connection) with the preceding, systematic procedures were developed for the introduction of 'new objects' – or 'ideal objects' – in several branches of mathematics: for example, 'infinitely distant points' and 'points with imaginary coordinates' in geometry; real and imaginary numbers (alongside the rational numbers) in analysis; and, perhaps most decisively for our subject, 'ideal factors' of algebraic integers in the newly developing subject of algebraic number theory. In this last context in particular, Dedekind achieved fundamental new results with the help of concepts that involved the treatment of *classes* of (already introduced) objects as new objects ('modules', 'ideals', 'orders', 'number fields', among others) which could themselves be made subject both to general mathematical investigation and to actual calculation.

With all of this work in the background, Dedekind was led to examine the foundations of the theory of the whole numbers themselves; and he arrived at the conviction that this theory, together with algebra and analysis which are further derived from it, is 'a part of logic' – in saying which, he tells us, 'I mean to imply that I consider the number-concept entirely independent of the notions or intuitions of space and time, that I consider it *an immediate result from the laws of thought*' ([1888] 1901: 31; emphasis added). The way he develops his theory allows us to conclude that he regards both the concept of number and the theorems of arithmetic, as well as the concepts and theorems of the other mathematical theories he mentions, as

resulting from certain fundamental abilities of the mind: the ability to form classes (his word is 'systems') of objects of thought (which themselves then have the status of such objects); to correlate or map such systems onto one another; and to 'create' new objects to 'represent' ones already present ('to relate things to things, to let a thing correspond to a thing, or to represent a thing by a thing'); and he tells us that without this ability, 'no thinking is possible'.

This version of the logicist thesis – namely, that mathematics (or that part of it which is claimed to belong to logic) requires no other source, either of its concepts or of its knowledge, than what is presupposed by all systematic thought – may be taken as applicable to the doctrines of all who have made that claim, whatever epistemological or metaphysical differences may attach to their further elaboration of what those 'presuppositions of all thought' might be.

3 The logicist foundations of arithmetic

The fundamental problem for the logicist theory of the arithmetic of the ordinary whole numbers was to show how (1) the general concept of such numbers, (2) the individual numbers themselves, and (3) the modes of reasoning that suffice for the mathematical demonstrations of their properties, can all be derived from principles of logic. It will be convenient here to consider first the solution offered by Frege (1884), with which Russell's substantially coincides; a brief comparison with Dedekind's rather different approach will be made later.

Frege set about creating an entirely systematic and universally applicable formal system codifying all logical concepts and processes: his *Begriffsschrift*, or 'concept writing', which he characterized as 'a formula language... for pure thought' (1879). He therefore faced the task of making explicit, within the framework of such a formal system, how the cardinal numbers could be defined.

Now for Frege, as for Dedekind, a central logical role was played by a notion of 'class' – Dedekind's 'system', characterized by him in the following way:

'Such a system *S*... is completely determined when with respect to every thing it is determined whether it is an element of *S* or not. The system *S* is hence the same as the system *T*... when every element of *S* is also an element of *T*, and every element of *T* is also an element of *S*'

([1888] 1901: 45)

(Compare with 'extensionality' in SET THEORY, DIFFERENT SYSTEMS OF.) However, in Frege's opinion, such notions as that of a system or class, and that of a 'correspondence' ('a thing belongs to a thing') are 'not usual in logic and are not reduced [by Dedekind] to acknowledged logical notions' ([1893] 1964: 4). Frege therefore relies, for the *logical* ground of the notions of class and correspondence, upon the 'acknowledged' logical notions of a 'concept' (which when it is unary corresponds to a property, and when binary, ternary, . . . , to a two-place, three-place, . . . relation) and of the 'extension' of such a concept (in particular, the extension of a unary concept is a class). The existence of such an extension for every concept, satisfying the principle that two concepts have the same extension if and only if every object falling under either also falls under the other (see Dedekind's characterization of 'system' above), is a fundamental principle of the logic on which Frege bases arithmetic.

To avoid certain verbal complexities, we now follow Russell in formulating the arithmetic notions in terms of classes. Two classes A, B are said to be 'equinumerous' if, for some relation R: (1) for every element x of A there is an element y of B such that x has the relation R to y, but to no other element of B; and (2) for every element y of B there is an element x of A such that x, but no other element of A, has the relation R to y. One says that R is a one-to-one relation between A and B. 'Equinumerous', as just defined, is a binary relation that holds between certain classes. Being equinumerous with a given class A is, then, a property which holds of certain classes. In Frege's usage, the extension of this property [or concept] – and thus, the class of all such classes – is called 'the number of the class A'; thus we have succeeded, according to the premises of this whole procedure, in defining the individual numbers as 'objects', in purely logical terms. As to the general concept of number, that is now easy: 'n is a number' means that there is some class A such that n is the number of the class A.

A most crucial step remains to be taken. We have defined the concept of number – allegedly at least – in purely logical terms; but this is too wide a concept to serve as the basis for ordinary arithmetic. Indeed, ordinary arithmetic has to do with the non-negative integers, and these, in the present context, are numbers of *finite* sets. But no such restriction appears in our definition of number: we have defined 'the number of the set A' for arbitrary sets – for example, for the set of all the points on a given line. At the same time – what at first will seem a quite unrelated issue – we have yet to show how all arithmetical reasoning can be carried out by purely logical argumentation concerning the number-concept.

The two issues have in fact a deep connection; and it is one of Frege's great accomplishments (also achieved independently by Dedekind) to have perceived the connection and found in it the simulta-

neous solution to both of them. A characteristic feature of reasoning in arithmetic is the 'argument from n to $n+1$', or the principle of mathematical induction:

> If a certain property P holds of the number 0, and if whenever P holds of a number n it holds also of the number $n+1$, then P holds of all the whole numbers.

(Of course, to formulate this principle at all, one must have defined the process of adding 1 to a given number; but that is a detail, easily accomplished.) The chief problem for placing the argumentation of arithmetic on a 'purely logical' footing was to find a logical justification for this principle. But, speaking 'intuitively', it is clear that the principle in question cannot apply except to finite numbers (for the property of being finite holds of 0, and holds of $n+1$ whenever it holds of n; but of course holds only of finite numbers). This 'intuitive' argument can of course have no systematic standing so long as the notion of finite number has not been defined. Frege's idea, however, was to use this 'intuitive' insight as the basis for a purely logical definition of the concept of finite number:

> A number x is said to be 'finite' if and only if x belongs to every class C such that: (1) 0 belongs to C; and (2) whenever a number n belongs to C, so does $n+1$.

With this definition, not only are the finite numbers singled out, but all the remaining concepts of traditional number theory can be introduced, and the reasoning of traditional number theory can be carried out within the framework of Frege's extended logic.

4 Extension to other mathematical domains

The extension of these results to the arithmetic of the rational, real and complex numbers offers no new fundamental difficulties, after the pioneering work that had already been done by mathematicians (see NUMBERS §7).

A difficulty does arise in the theory of functions: namely, the need – first brought to prominent notice by Zermelo (1904), who characterized it as a 'logical principle' – for what has come to be called the 'axiom of choice'; this says, in effect, that if f is a function defined on a domain A, such that, for each x in A, $f(x)$ is a non-empty set, then there is a function g, also defined on A, such that, for each x in A, $g(x)$ is an element of $f(x)$.

An interesting point arises when we come to geometry. Frege never extended the thesis of logicism to geometry; but, in a rather polemical exchange with Hilbert concerning the latter's path-breaking work on the foundations of geometry (see Frege 1980), Frege actually came near to formulating the point of view from which this extension can – and, indeed, so far as logicism is viable at all, *should* – be made: namely, one regards geometric theory – or, rather, *a* geometric theory (for there are infinitely many) – as concerned with a species of structure (of any one of which there may be many exemplars), characterized – indeed, defined – by the 'axioms' of that geometry; the theorems deduced from those axioms are then demonstrated 'by pure logic' to hold of any exemplar of the species so defined. That is the view maintained by Whitehead and Russell in the projected treatment of geometry in their major work, *Principia Mathematica* (1910–13). And it is the view that had already been expressed, in effect, by Dedekind and still earlier by Riemann (see Stein 1988: 244, 251–3). What is also noteworthy is that Dedekind, in contrast to Frege and to Russell and Whitehead, adopts the same point of view concerning even the system of the whole numbers: that is, he characterizes the *structure* a system must have to serve as that of the whole numbers, in explicit preference to identifying those numbers with any 'objects' specified in other than those structural terms.

5 The setbacks; a brief evaluation

The first of the setbacks for the logicist view was the discovery of a contradiction in Frege's logic (see PARADOXES OF SET AND PROPERTY §2), which arises from the assumption, already noted, that every concept has an extension – a very strong form of what has come, in the theory of sets, to be called a 'comprehension principle'. Frege himself was eventually led to abandon his logicist view of arithmetic, and to suggest instead that arithmetic is not only – as Kant thought – synthetic a priori, but is actually to be grounded in the 'geometric knowledge-source' ([1924–5] 1979: 276–80). Others, however – notably Russell ([1903] 1937: introduction), Ramsey (1925) and Carnap (1931) – felt no need to abandon the logicist thesis, but reconciled themselves to a modified view of logic, designed to circumvent the contradiction and still allow the essential modes of reasoning. Most celebrated among logicians as such a modified logic is Russell's 'theory of types'; but the axiomatic theory of sets, which has proved most serviceable as a medium for mathematics, could perfectly well also claim to be a form of 'logic' (see the characterization quoted from Zermelo, the pioneer of axiomatic set theory, in §4 above).

The second setback is more profound. Frege's own

invention of a way of rendering logic purely formal made it possible to apply modes of mathematical reasoning to the formal linguistic structures of logical systems themselves. The undertaking of such application was a fundamental contribution of Hilbert. This process has further revolutionized our way of looking at logic itself. Among the most basic results of this examination are two theorems of Gödel (1930, 1931), one of which tells us that 'elementary logic' – or first-order logic – can be formulated so that every proposition that deserves to be considered logically true can be derived by 'purely formal', or 'mechanical', means (for example, these propositions can be generated by a computer program); whereas the other tells us that no such thing can be achieved for a system – whether a higher-order logic (of which the theory of types is an example), or a first-order axiomatized theory (of which set theory is an example) – that is strong enough to generate the theorems of elementary arithmetic.

With Gödel's theorems there should be mentioned a discovery that preceded them by several years: the Löwenheim–Skolem theorem (see Löwenheim 1915 and, for clearer and more adequate proofs, Skolem 1920, 1923). This theorem implies that any theory axiomatized in first-order logic that has an infinite model (domain that satisfies the axioms) has a countably infinite model (one whose domain can be placed in one-to-one correspondence with the natural numbers). In a very remarkable paper, Skolem (1923) invoked this theorem (and other considerations) to cast grave doubt on the view that set theory could be 'a satisfactory ultimate foundation for mathematics'. Indeed (restricting attention here to the implications of the Löwenheim–Skolem theorem), it is, for example, a fundamental proposition of classical analysis that the set of all the real numbers is uncountably infinite. The existence of a model for the allegedly foundational theory containing only countably many elements seems, then, prima facie to show that the foundational attempt has failed: that, in particular, the assertion within the theory that a certain set is uncountable has not captured what ought to be the genuine meaning of the term 'uncountable'. The issue is both deep and subtle; here, it must suffice to remark that both Gödel's theorems and the Löwenheim–Skolem theorem lead to the notion of nonstandard models – the theory of which has since become an important part of logic (see LÖWENHEIM–SKOLEM THEOREMS AND NONSTANDARD MODELS).

These results may be summed up by saying that *there is not, and in principle cannot be, a 'completely formalized' logic within which all mathematically statable questions are correctly answerable.* Whether

815

one chooses to call this a refutation of logicism, or an unexpected result about the 'uncompletable' nature of logic itself, the result is unquestionably a deep and interesting one simultaneously concerning mathematics and logic; and, for its discovery, a great debt is owed to those who advanced the thesis of logicism.

See also: ARITHMETIC, PHILOSOPHICAL ISSUES IN §4; HILBERT'S PROGRAMME AND FORMALISM; INTUITIONISM §1; LOGICAL AND MATHEMATICAL TERMS, GLOSSARY OF

References and further reading

* Carnap, R. (1931) 'Die logizistische Grundlegung der Mathematik', *Erkenntnis* 2: 91–105; trans. E. Putnam and G. Massey, 'The Logicist Foundations of Mathematics', in P. Benacerraf and H. Putnam (eds) *Philosophy of Mathematics: Selected Readings*, Cambridge: Cambridge University Press, 2nd edn, 1983, 41–52. (A classic account of logicism. Referred to in §5.)
—— (1939) *Foundations of Logic and Mathematics*, Chicago, IL: University of Chicago Press. (A lucid account of Carnap's view of the relation of logic to the analysis of language, and of how mathematics – a part of the purely logical aspect of language – acquires relevance for the formulation of propositions of empirical science.)
* Dedekind, R. (1888) *Was sind und was sollen die Zahlen?*, Braunschweig: Vieweg; repr. in *Gesammelte mathematische Werke* (Collected Mathematical Works), ed. R. Fricke, E. Noether and Ö. Ore, Braunschweig: Vieweg, 1932, vol. 3, 335–90; trans. W.W. Beman (1901), 'The Nature and Meaning of Numbers', in *Essays on the Theory of Numbers*, New York: Dover, 1963. (Dedekind's theory of the natural numbers. Referred to in §§2–4.)
* Frege, G. (1879) *Begriffsschrift, eine der arithmetischen nachgebildete Formelsprache des reinen Denkens*, Halle: Nebert; repr. Hildesheim: Olms, 1964; trans. S. Bauer-Mengelberg, '*Begriffsschrift*, a Formula Language, Modelled Upon That of Arithmetic, for Pure Thought', in van Heijenoort (1967), 5–82. (Includes the first formulation of Frege's system of logic. Referred to in §3.)
* —— (1884) *Die Grundlagen der Arithmetik: eine logisch-mathematische Untersuchung über den Begriff der Zahl*, Breslau: Koebner; repr. and trans. J.L. Austin, *The Foundations of Arithmetic: A Logico-Mathematical Enquiry into the Concept of Number*, Evanston, IL: Northwestern University Press, 2nd edn, 1980. (An extended philosophical essay which culminates in Frege's definitions of number and finite number, and his analysis of mathematical induction; referred to in §3.)
* —— (1893, 1903) *Grundgesetze der Arithmetik: begriffsschriftlich abgeleitet*, Jena: Pohle, 2 vols; repr. Hildesheim: Olms, 1966; part 1 of vol. 1 trans. M. Furth, *Basic Laws of Arithmetic: An Exposition of the System*, Berkeley, CA: University of California Press, 1964. (The first two volumes of Frege's projected complete systematic treatment of arithmetic, including the theory of the real numbers, on an explicitly logical foundation. In consequence of Russell's discovery of a contradiction in the system, the third volume was never written. Referred to in §§1, 3.)
* —— (1924–5) 'Erkenntnisquellen der Mathematik und der mathematischen Naturwissenschaften', 'Zahlen und Arithmetik' and 'Versuch einer neuen Begründung für die Arithmetik', in *Nachgelassene Schriften und Wissenschaftlicher Briefwechsel*, vol. 1, ed. H. Hermes, F. Kambartel and F. Kaulbach, Hamburg: Meiner, 1969; trans. P. Long and R. White, 'Sources of Knowledge of Mathematics and the Mathematical Natural Sciences', 'Numbers and Arithmetic' and 'A New Attempt at a Foundation for Arithmetic', in *Posthumous Writings*, ed. H. Hermes, F. Kambartel and F. Kaulbach, Chicago, IL: University of Chicago Press, 1979. (Three very late brief manuscripts, giving Frege's final thoughts on the foundations of mathematics. Referred to in §§1, 5.)
* —— (1980) *Philosophical and Mathematical Correspondence*, ed. B. McGuinness, Chicago, IL: University of Chicago Press, 34–48. (Frege's correspondence with Hilbert on the latter's *Foundations of Geometry*. Referred to in §4.)
* Gödel, K. (1930) 'Die Vollständigkeit der Axiome des logischen Funktionenkalküls', *Monatshefte für Mathematik und Physik* 37: 349–60; trans. S. Bauer-Mengelberg, 'The Completeness of the Axioms of the Functional Calculus of Logic', in van Heijenoort (1967), 582–91. (Gödel's proof of the completeness of first-order logic; referred to in §5.)
* —— (1931) 'Über formal unentscheidbare Sätze der *Principia Mathematica* und verwandter Systeme I', *Monatshefte für Mathematik und Physik* 38: 173–98; trans. J. van Heijenoort, 'On Formally Undecidable Propositions of *Principia Mathematica* and Related Systems', in van Heijenoort (1967), 592–617. (Gödel's celebrated incompleteness theorems, the first of which is referred to in §5.)
Heijenoort, J. van (ed.) (1967) *From Frege to Gödel: A Source Book in Mathematical Logic, 1879–1931*, Cambridge, MA: Harvard University Press.

(Includes translations of several of the works discussed in this article, with introductions.)

* Löwenheim, L. (1915) 'Über Möglichkeiten im Relativkalkül', *Mathematische Annalen* 76: 447–70; trans. S. Bauer-Mengelberg, 'On Possibilities in the Calculus of Relatives', in van Heijenoort (1967), 232–51. (Löwenheim's original proof – difficult, and couched in now unfamiliar notation – of the Löwenheim–Skolem theorem; van Heijenoort's introduction is very helpful. Referred to in §5.)

* Ramsey, F.P. (1925) The Foundations of Mathematics, *Proceedings of the London Mathematical Society*, series 2, 25(5): 338–84; repr. in *The Foundations of Mathematics and Other Logical Essays*, ed. R.B. Braithwaite, London: Routledge, 1931. (Referred to in §5. The posthumous collection, of both previously published and unpublished works, in which this essay appears includes important discussions of the theory of types, the axiom of choice and (a point not discussed in the text above) Russell and Whitehead's axiom of infinity – needed in their version of a logicist theory in order to obtain a complete system of arithmetic.)

* Russell, B.A.W. (1903) *The Principles of Mathematics*, Cambridge: Cambridge University Press; 2nd edn, London: Allen & Unwin, 1937; repr. London: Routledge, 1992. (A historically important work, of substantial difficulty; quoted in §1.)

* Skolem, T. (1920) 'Logisch-kombinatorische Untersuchungen über die Erfüllbarkeit oder Beweisbarkeit mathematischer Sätze nebst einem Theorem über dichte Mengen', *Videnskapsselskapets skrifter, I. Matematisk-naturvidenskabelig klasse* 4; §1 trans. S. Bauer-Mengelberg, 'Logico-Combinatorial Investigations in the Satisfiability or Provability of Mathematical Propositions: A Simplified Proof of a Theorem by L. Löwenheim and Generalizations of the Theorem', in van Heijenoort (1967), 254–63. (Skolem's more satisfactory proof, and strengthening, of Löwenheim's theorem on countable models; referred to in §5.)

* —— (1923) 'Einige Bemerkungen zur axiomatischen Begründung der Mengenlehre', in *Matematikerkongressen i Helsingfors den 4–7 Juli 1922, Den femte skandinaviska matematikerkongressen, Redogörelse*, Helsinki: Akademiska Bokhandeln, 217–32; trans. S. Bauer-Mengelberg, 'Some Remarks on Axiomatized Set Theory', in van Heijenoort (1967), 291–301. (A brief, remarkably clear and very deep discussion of a series of issues concerning the foundations of mathematics. Referred to in §5.)

* Stein, H. (1988) 'Logos, Logic, and Logistiké: Some Philosophical Remarks on the Nineteenth-Century Transformation of Mathematics', in W. Aspray and P. Kitcher (eds) *History and Philosophy of Modern Mathematics*, Minneapolis, MN: University of Minnesota Press, 238–59. (Includes a discussion of some of the nineteenth-century developments that form the mathematical background to the logicist thesis referred to in §2; and gives an indication of the views of Riemann and Dedekind on geometry, referred to in §4.)

* Whitehead, A.N. and Russell, B.A.W. (1910–13) *Principia Mathematica*, Cambridge: Cambridge University Press, 3 vols; 2nd edn, 1925–7. (Referred to in §4.)

* Zermelo, E. (1904) 'Beweis, daß jede Menge wohlgeordnet werden kann', *Mathematische Annalen* 59: 514–16; trans. S. Bauer-Mengelberg, 'Proof that Every Set can be Well-Ordered', in van Heijenoort (1967), 139–41. (The article that brought prominently to the attention of mathematicians the axiom of choice – here 'the assumption that coverings exist'; referred to in §4.)

HOWARD STEIN

LOGICS, FREE see FREE LOGICS; FREE LOGICS, PHILOSOPHICAL ISSUES IN

LOGICS, INFINITARY
see INFINITARY LOGICS

LOGICS, ORDINAL see ORDINAL LOGICS

LOGOS

The noun logos *derives from the Greek verb* legein, *meaning 'to say' something significant. Logos developed a wide variety of senses, including 'description', 'theory' (sometimes as opposed to 'fact'), 'explanation', 'reason', 'reasoning power', 'principle', 'ratio', 'prose'.*

Logos emerges as a philosophical term with Heraclitus (c.540–c.480 BC), for whom it provided the link between rational discourse and the world's rational structure. It was freely used by Plato and Aristotle and especially by the Stoics, who interpreted the rational world order as immanent deity. Platonist philosophers gave pre-eminence to nous, *the intuitive intellect expressed in* logos. *To Philo of Alexandria and subsequently to Christian theologians it meant 'the Word', a derivative divine power, at first seen as subordinate but eventually coordinated with the Father.*

1 Greek philosophy
2 Christian theology: antecedents and developments

1 Greek philosophy

Logos became an important term in almost all philosophical schools. It emerged about 700 BC as the accepted term for discourse at any length, though seldom if ever naming a single word; it displaced the older terms *epos* and *mythos*, which survived only with specialized meanings.

HERACLITUS expounded a highly original philosophy in enigmatic phrases. *Logos* apparently means his own account of the world, which is 'common' but rarely grasped (frs 1, 2); it also suggests the everlasting cosmic order whose contrasting aspects or phases disclose an underlying unity (fr. 51). All phenomena spring from a basic element, fire, and return to it in regular 'measures' (*logoi*); earth exchanges with sea in the same proportion, *logos* (frs 30, 31, 90). This could suggest that changing phenomena can be known; but Heraclitus was seldom credited with this view.

The SOPHISTS of the fifth century BC who *inter alia* taught the art of public speaking, naturally emphasized the power of *logos*, which GORGIAS in his *Encomium of Helen* personifies as 'a great potentate who brings truly godlike things to pass' and Isocrates represents as the foundation of human culture.

PLATO uses the term *logos* in almost all the senses mentioned above, though without giving it exclusive emphasis as compared with other cognate words (especially *dialektikē*, 'dialectic'); moreover, the general term *nous* for intellect, thought or intelligence is basic to his philosophy (see NOUS); *logos*, and sometimes *dianoia*, 'thinking' (*Republic* 533d), stand for its expression. Both are contrasted with sense-experience (for example, *Republic* 509d) which Plato associates with instability and untruth; immunity from change is a precondition of real knowledge. In *Timaeus* 27–28 he contrasts unchanging being with change: 'the one is apprehended by thought (*noēsis*) with discourse (*logos*), being ever self-same; the other grasped by belief and unreasoned sensation'. Since mathematics expounds unchanging truths, Plato gave it an important place in his educational system.

He presents Socrates as initiating discussions which lead towards a 'true and certain and comprehensible *logos*' of ethical concepts and so promote right action, ignoring the body and its sensations as well as unsound *logoi* which lead to contradictions (*Phaedo* 90). Distrust of sense-experience is not always expressed; the *Seventh Letter* (344) states that knowledge calls for a combination of nomenclature, *logos* (definition), sensation and civilized discussion. The *Theaetetus* presents some attempts to define knowledge: it cannot be mere sensation, nor mere true belief, which might arise by accident; one must be able to give an account of it (*logon dounai*); but no satisfactory definition of *logos* is found. Discussion is necessary since written words can mislead (*Phaedrus* 275); its aim is to 'ignore all the senses [!] and press on through *logos* towards the essential reality of each thing' (*Republic* 532), its Idea or Form. Discussion (*dialektikē*) seeks a classification of all such Forms, showing their dependence on the Form of the Good, though this itself is an 'unpostulated' or absolute source, *anhypothetos archē* (*Republic* 510) (see ARCHĒ), 'beyond being in dignity and power' (509b).

Aristotle defines *logos* as a composite 'significant utterance', *phonē semantikē* (*De Interpretatione* 4 16b26), but actually uses it in a wide variety of senses. It often deputizes for more specific terms, and thus traverses useful distinctions, for example, sentence/treatise, or proposition/syllogism. It often occurs in Aristotle's logical works, but the term 'logic' is a later coinage; Aristotle speaks of 'analytics'. His ethics prescribes following reason, or 'right reason' (*orthos logos*), sometimes conceived mathematically as a mean between two extremes. In his metaphysics *logos* indicates, and sometimes equates with, the substance, form or essence of things (*ousia, eidos, to ti ēn einai*). Its relation to *nous*, pure intelligence, is left unexplained; but the intelligence moving the cosmos is always designated by *nous*, not *logos*. (See ARISTOTLE §16.)

The Stoics held that only material things were fully real; but they were not, in the ordinary sense, materialists (see STOICISM §§3, 5). They held that the universe embodied a *logos* as its supreme directive principle. Natural objects, plants and animals have their own increasingly complex patterns of behaviour, culminating in the human reason, itself a lower analogue of the universal *logos*. This principle could thus be named in material terms as *pneuma* (spirit, breath; see PNEUMA), in functional terms as *logos*, reason, and in valuational terms as *theos*, god. They did not, however, discard the common use of *logos* to denote purely human reason, or specialized forms of it ('argument', 'experience'); they accepted the common designation of animals as unreasoning, *aloga*.

Passions were commonly described as 'impulses contrary to *logos*' (see STOICISM §19); but were occasionally ascribed to, or identified with, 'a bad and licentious *logos*', and described as 'decisions', *kriseis*. But since *logos* could also mean 'the world order', conformity to *logos* could imply 'accepting the predetermined order of events', so that moral freedom was interpreted as resignation.

2 Christian theology: antecedents and developments

The Israelites came to believe that God's name, though revealed, should not be uttered; they used periphrases, for example, 'heaven', and ascribed divine action to intermediate agencies, including God's Word (*logos*) and his Wisdom (*sophia*). These are prominent in PHILO OF ALEXANDRIA, who held that the best Greek thought can be found, by appropriate exegesis, in the Jewish scriptures.

Philo echoes the 'dogmatic' Platonism reconstituted by ANTIOCHUS, with some Stoic elements, and Pythagorean ideas stemming probably from fellow-Alexandrian Eudorus (see NEO-PYTHAGOREANISM; PLATONISM, EARLY AND MIDDLE §§4, 8–9). He is our first extant source for the view that the Platonic Ideas are thoughts in God's mind. He describes the Logos as the 'Idea of Ideas' (*Migration* 103), the 'intelligible world' (*Creation* 24–), the 'divider' (*tomeus*) who arranged the pattern of Ideas for creation; indeed as 'a second God' (*Allegories* 1.32–), rightly honoured by those (Stoics?) unable to grasp the supreme reality. Stoic influence appears in his description of the Logos as 'fiery' (*Cherubim* 28) and 'physically pervasive' (*The Heir* 217). In *Immutable* 31 the Logos is God's elder son, the world his younger (compare the Platonist triad of God, the Ideas and matter?). Sophia is described in comparable terms; once only (*Flight* 109) she appears as 'mother' of the Logos, associated with God in a triadic divine family.

The New Testament appears as indifferent or even hostile to philosophy (*Colossians* 2:8). Exceptions are the hints of an 'argument from design' (*Acts* 17:22–29, *Romans* 1:20) and the prologue to the Fourth Gospel, apparently aimed at readers with philosophical interests, where the Logos appears as God's associate, a source of light or enlightenment, who in due course took human form. The title Logos suggests the Jewish theology of God's Word (*memra*) as developed in the biblical *Wisdom of Solomon* and Philo; it also expresses the Christian claim that Jesus is God's accredited representative and agent, appointed as his Son (see *Romans* 1:1–4, *Hebrews* 1–), the title which became dominant in the Gospel and the New Testament in general. The Christian Trinity of Father, Son and Spirit (2 *Corinthians* 13; 14, *c.* AD 55) – with the alternatives Logos and Sophia – can hardly derive from the very differently formulated triadic theology attributed to Moderatus (*c.*50–100), though later Christians could claim the support of philosophers such as NUMENIUS. (PLOTINUS, who sees *nous* as the first derivative power, was little known to Christians before Augustine.)

Ignatius (*c.* AD 35–107) describes Jesus as God's Word (*logos*) 'proceeding from silence' (*Magnesians* 8.2). Justin Martyr (*c.*100–65) inaugurated a distinctive Logos-theology, which although retaining the Trinitarian confession emphasized the Logos, with philosophical echoes, as God's agent and interpreter at the expense of the Holy Spirit. Origen (*c.*185–*c.*254) was the most important exponent of this theology, which was superseded by the Council of Nicaea in 325.

See also: ANTISTHENES

References and further reading

Armstrong, A.H. (ed.) (1967) *The Cambridge History of Later Greek and Early Medieval Philosophy*, Cambridge: Cambridge University Press. (Comprehensive survey from Plato to Anselm.)

Dillon, J. (1977) *The Middle Platonists*, London: Duckworth. (Indispensable guide to Platonic tradition to *c.* AD 200.)

Kahn, C.H. (1979) *The Art and Thought of Heraclitus*, Cambridge: Cambridge University Press. (Authoritative study with texts and translations.)

Kittel, G. (1967) 'Logos', in *Theological Dictionary of the New Testament*, Grand Rapids, MI: Eerdmans, vol. 4, 71–136. (Comprehensive; fullest on biblical usage.)

Sandbach, F.H. (1975) *The Stoics*, London: Chatto & Windus. (Well-written introductory account.)

Stead, G.C. (1991) 'Logos', in *Theologische Realenzyklopädie*, Berlin: de Gruyter, vol. 21, 432–44. (Includes Hellenic, biblical and Christian usage.)

—— (1994) *Philosophy in Christian Antiquity*, Cambridge: Cambridge University Press. (Introductory: Thales to Augustine.)

CHRISTOPHER STEAD

LOISY, ALFRED (1857–1940)

Loisy was a French biblical exegete who worked in the tradition of biblical criticism whose earlier members included D.F. Strauss and Ernest Renan. His critical views involved a sharp separation between the Jesus of history and the Christ of Catholic faith, and he came to regard the doctrine of the incarnation of God in Jesus Christ, a central Christian doctrine, as merely metaphorical and symbolic. He has been called the father of Catholic modernism.

Alfred Loisy was born in Ambrières, Marne, and was

ordained a Catholic priest in 1879. He became Professor of Hebrew at the Catholic Institute in Paris in 1881, where he attended Ernest Renan's lectures from 1882 to 1885. He was made Professor of Biblical Exegesis in 1889, but was removed from his position in 1893 after publishing criticism of Catholic seminaries for not taking account of contemporary critical scholarship. From 1893 to 1899 he taught religion in Neuilly, and from 1901 to 1904 he was a lecturer in the École Pratique des Hautes Études in Paris. In 1909 he became Professor of the History of Religion in the Collège de France and also, after 1927, in the École des Hautes Études. Loisy came to describe his own views as pantheistic and positivistic, and was excommunicated in 1908.

Loisy's work was in the critical tradition of D.F. STRAUSS and Ernest Renan. In a series of works, he recorded and practised what the Church regarded as radical biblical and historical criticism. One example of this is his treatment of the fourth Gospel. (It is traditional in New Testament studies to refer to the Gospels of Matthew, Mark and Luke as the Synoptic Gospels, as distinct from that of John, the fourth Gospel.) In *Le Quatrième Évangile* (The Fourth Gospel, 1903), Loisy argued that the fourth Gospel is the coherent work of a single great theological genius, a symbolic description of Christian belief, a foundation stone of Christian truth, but not a trustworthy account of the life and teaching of Jesus Christ. The Synoptic Gospels, he held, are almost impersonal works which collect traditional reminiscences concerning Jesus, and have a greater historical value than the Gospel of John. More theologian than historian, still more an apologist or defender of the Christian faith, the author of the Gospel of John, according to Loisy, offers a brilliant history of Christianity since the resurrection of Jesus. But the Gospel does not deal with the times and events with which it ostensibly deals, namely what Jesus did and taught during his life and ministry. The author was unable to distinguish between what he received from tradition and what he found in the depths of his own imagination and conviction.

The fourth Gospel was intended, Loisy maintained, to support the legitimacy of Christianity in the context of contemporary Judaism. Its author manifests a supreme indifference to history, selecting from the traditional materials available what suits his purpose, and altering it as his purpose requires. That purpose is the construction of allegorical pictures that convey a wholly mystical and spiritual Christ, who is not subject to the conditions of historical human existence. The language used is figurative and ambiguous; it concerns a Christ who lives in the Church, and has scant connection with the Jesus who

called disciples and was crucified. History belongs to the Synoptic Gospels, and the facts that they refer to receive theological and transcendental interpretation in the Gospel of John. But the difference in the worlds of thought occupied by the Synoptics and John is so great that the standard practice of weaving texts and themes from both sources into a single portrayal of the life and teaching of Jesus is undermined. This laid the foundation for a sharp distinction between the Jesus of history and the Christ of Catholic faith. Loisy saw in the author of the Gospel of John the first Christian mystic, for whom history is swallowed up in his mysticism.

Loisy's views, of course, were and are controversial, even setting aside the doctrinal implications that he drew from his critical work. Both his dismissal of the Gospel of John as a historical source and his treatment of that Gospel as theologically oriented in a manner different in kind from the other Gospels are challengeable.

List of works

Loisy, A. (1902) *L'Évangile et l'église*, Paris: E. Nourry, 5th edn, 1930; *The Gospel and the Church*, New York: Prometheus Books, 1988. (Reply to A. Harnack's *The Essence of Christianity*; a defence of Loisy's Catholicism.)
—— (1903) *Le Quatrième Évangile* (The Fourth Gospel), Paris: Vrin. (An important example of Loisy's radical approach to biblical texts.)
—— (1924) *My Duel with the Vatican*, New York: Greenwood Press, 1968. (Loisy presents his side of the story.)
—— (1933) *La Naissance du christianisme*, trans. L.P. Jacks, *The Birth of the Christian Religion*, London: Allen & Unwin, 1948. (Loisy's account of the origins of Christianity.)

References and further reading

Hoskyns, Sir E. (1957) *The Fourth Gospel*, revised edn, ed. F.N. Davey, London: Faber & Faber. (A commentary on the Gospel of John which discusses the history of its interpretation; see chapter 2.)
Kummel, W.G. (1970) *Das Neue Testament: Geschichte der Erforschung seiner Probleme*, Verlag Karl Alber; trans. S. McLean Gilmour and H.C. Kee, *The New Testament: The History of the Investigation of its Problems*, Nashville, TN: Abington Press, 1972. (This is a comprehensive study of the history of New Testament criticism, with copious quotations from critics.)

KEITH E. YANDELL

LOKAYĀTA *see* MATERIALISM, INDIAN SCHOOL OF

LOMBARD, PETER (1095/1100–1160)

Peter Lombard's philosophical views are important given the formative role his Sent0entiae in IV libris distinctae *(Four Books of Sentences) played in the education of university theologians in the high Middle Ages, many of whom were also philosophers. Peter staunchly opposes theologies, cosmologies and anthropologies of a Platonic or Neoplatonic type. While conversant with new trends in logic in his day, he is disinclined to treat theological issues as illustrations of the rules of formal logic or natural philosophy, preferring to view them from a metaphysical perspective. In his doctrine of God he deliberately eschews terminology associated with any one philosophical school. In his anthropology and sacramental theology he shows a marked preference for Aristotelianism. The hospitability of his theology to Aristotelianism and to a philosophical treatment of a range of theological questions made his* Sentences *elastic enough to accommodate the reception of Greco-Arabic thought and to serve as a pedagogical framework usable by philosophers of every persuasion during the succeeding three centuries.*

Born in the Novara region of Italy, Peter left no traces on the historical record until he was noticed by BERNARD OF CLAIRVAUX in the mid-1130s. With Bernard's advice and help, he went to France to study theology, first at the cathedral school at Rheims and then, in 1136, at Paris, probably under HUGH OF ST VICTOR. His earliest works were commentaries on the Psalms, written before 1138, and the Pauline epistles (first rescension 1139–41). He had become a recognized master by 1142. In 1145 Peter became a canon of Notre Dame, an unusual honour for a foreigner, teaching there until 1159 when he was elected bishop of Paris, a post he held until his death in 1160. His major work, the *Sententiae in IV libris distinctae* (Four Books of Sentences), sums up his systematic theology. The final version of this work was completed in 1155–7.

For Peter, not all branches or schools of philosophy are equally pertinent to theology. He is uninterested in natural philosophy and says less about it than do the patristic authorities on whom he relies for his account of creation. He is familiar with the logicians' debates over universals. Without taking a personal stand on the priority or posteriority of universals to concepts standing for individuals, he refers to them in glossing 'all creation' (Romans 8: 19), which, he states, is a universal collecting all aspects of the human nature that is to be saved. Peter applies the contemporary nominalist view of the unitary signification of nouns and verbs and their consignification in oblique cases or past and future tenses, using this principle against Peter Abelard's argument that God could do otherwise or better than he does, in a defence of divine omniscience and omnipotence that contributes to the development of the distinction between God's absolute and ordained power (see ABELARD, P.; NOMINALISM; OMNIPOTENCE).

Peter rejects any kind of emanationist, exemplarist or immanentalist understanding of God and his relationship to creation, as well as the equation made in some quarters during his time of the Platonic One, Nous and World Soul with the Trinity (see NEOPLATONISM). In glossing Romans 1: 20, he agrees with MARIUS VICTORINUS that the Neoplatonic triad of being, life and thought is apposite to the Trinity but his appreciation of the Platonic tradition stops there. Sometimes he favours a philosophical vocabulary neutral enough to shoulder its theological duties, unconstrained by the denotations which particular schools impose on key terms. At other points he opts for Aristotelianism. Opposing the Platonic notion of the human being as a soul using a body, he joins the Aristotelians in defining it as an integral union of body and soul. This principle undergirds his treatment of the creation of mankind, the fall and its consequences, Christ's human nature, the redemption, ethics and the sacraments. While he accents inner intentionality in ethics, he thinks that good intentions should be expressed in appropriate external actions, and while he holds that it is consent that makes a marriage, he regards the physical as well as the spiritual union of spouses as sacramental. He calls the present consent of spouses the efficient cause of marriage, and the ends of marriage (fidelity, lifelong commitment and offspring) its final cause. He applies 'substance' and 'accidents' in their Aristotelian sense to the change in the eucharistic elements at the time of consecration.

In other areas, Peter's use of Aristotelianism is muted by his felt need for a more neutral lexicon or because he wants to emphasize something else. He offers four proofs for God's existence, including Aristotle's argument from motion to a prime mover. His other proofs move from physical to metaphysical arguments in accenting the idea that the deity is the ground of being of the creation, rather than the idea that he is the cause of effects in the phenomenal world (see GOD, ARGUMENTS FOR THE EXISTENCE OF). In treating the deity, Peter prefers a generic definition of 'substance' as referring simply to an entity's basic nature, because the Aristotelian understanding of 'substance' as referring to composite created beings is inapposite to God. Similarly, he rejects the Aristotelian definition of 'relation' as an accident when he discusses the mutual relations that name the persons of the Trinity. In another case, his doctrine of conscience as the spark of reason not extinguished even in the worst of sinners, Peter draws on an idea ultimately Stoic in provenance which he is the first medieval thinker to revive (see STOICISM).

More generally, Peter's acknowledgement of natural reason as a real epistemic state and his positive use of it in theology in opposition to Neoplatonic negative theology, his resolutely metaphysical approach to the deity and to the unmanifested Trinity as the supreme objects of knowledge that reason can address, and his interest in human nature as such, before the fall, open up zones for philosophical reflection which later scholastics could and did develop, whatever their philosophical proclivities. While issuing Aristotelians a warning concerning the appositeness of 'substance' and 'relation' to the divine nature, he provides notable support for that school. At the same time, he throws down the gauntlet to defenders of a more thoroughgoing Platonism.

See also: ARISTOTELIANISM, MEDIEVAL; GOD, CONCEPTS OF; PLATONISM, MEDIEVAL; TRINITY

List of works

Peter Lombard (1139–41) *Collectanea in omnes d. Pauli Epistolas*, ed. J.P. Migne, Patrologia Latina cursus completus, vols 191–92, Paris, 1880. (Peter's commentary on the Pauline epistles. Material of philosophical interest is found primarily in gloss on Romans.)

—— (final recension 1155–7) *Sententiae in IV libris distinctae* (Four Books of Sentences), ed. I.C. Brady, 3rd revised edn, Grottaferrata: Collegi S. Bonaventurae ad Claras Aquas, 1971, 2 vols. (Text of the *Sentences*, Peter's major work, excellently introduced and annotated by editor.)

References and further reading

Bertola, E. (1956) 'Il problema di Dio in Pier Lombardo' (The Problem of God in Peter Lombard), *Rivista di filosofia neo-scolastica* 48: 135–50. (Places Peter's doctrine of God in its contemporary context.)

Bertola, E. (1959) 'La dottrina lombardiana dell'anima nella storia delle dottrine psicologiche

del XII secolo' (Lombard's Doctrine of the Soul in the History of Psychological Doctrine in the Twelfth Century), *Pier Lombardo* 3 (1): 3–18. (Only brief study of Lombardian psychology in contemporary context.)

Colish, M.L. (1990) 'Gilbert, the Early Porretans, and Peter Lombard: Semantics and Theology', in J. Jolivet and A. de Libera (eds) *Gilbert de Poitiers et ses contemporaines: Aux origines de la logica modernorum*, Naples: Bibliopolis, 229–50. (Peter's theological language and the influence, positive and negative, of Gilbert of Poitiers and his early disciples on him.)

—— (1992) 'Peter Lombard and Abelard: The *Opinio Nominalium* and Divine Transcendence', *Vivarium* 30: 139–56. (Contrasts use of the theory of the unitary signification of nouns and verbs in Abelard and Lombard.)

—— (1994) *Peter Lombard*, Leiden: Brill, 2 vols. (The only full length modern study, covering all aspects of Peter's thought, with extensive bibliography.)

Delhaye, P. (1961) *Pierre Lombard: Sa vie, ses oeuvres, sa morale* (Peter Lombard: His Life, His Works, His Ethics), Montreal, Ont.: Institut d'Études Médiévales. (The only monographic treatment of Peter's ethics.)

Gilson, E. (1945) 'Pierre Lombard et les théologies d'essence' (Peter Lombard and the Theologies of Essence), *Revue du moyen âge latin* 1: 173–6. (Good if brief study correctly noting Peter's emphasis on divine transcendence.)

MARCIA L. COLISH

LONERGAN, BERNARD JOSEPH FRANCIS (1904–84)

The Canadian philosopher and theologian Bernard Lonergan approached the problems of philosophy by inviting his readers to attend to the mental acts in which they engage when they come to know anything. He claimed that these acts are of three fundamental kinds: 'experience' of the data of sensation, feeling or mental activity; 'understanding' possible explanations of that experience; and 'judgment' that one such explanation is in each case certainly or probably so. Denial that we engage in these three types of mental activity is actually self-destructive, since we have to engage in them in the very act of justifying such denial. In getting to grips with what it is to come to know, we also gain a vital clue as to the overall nature of the world which is to be known; and light is thrown on the relation between the natural and the human sciences, and on the questions of ethics and religion.

1 **The nature of knowledge**
2 **Science and metaphysics**
3 **Human science, ethics and religion**

1 The nature of knowledge

Bernard Joseph Francis Lonergan was born in 1904, in Buckingham, Quebec. He entered the Jesuit Order in 1922, and studied at Heythrop College, England, and the Gregorian University in Rome. After some years as professor of theology at Jesuit seminaries in Montreal and Toronto, he was appointed to the faculty of the Gregorian University in 1953. In 1965 he returned to Canada, after a serious illness; later he taught at Harvard Divinity School, and finally at Boston College.

'Thoroughly understand what it is to understand, and not only will you understand the broad lines of all there is to be understood but you will possess a fixed base, an invariant pattern, opening upon all further developments of understanding' (Lonergan 1957: xxviii, 748). The main object of Lonergan's most substantial philosophical book, *Insight: A Study of Human Understanding*, is to get readers to take possession of their own rational self-consciousness; once this is done the philosophy which he calls 'critical realism' will show itself to be the only one which does justice both to human knowledge and to the world which is to be known by it. The true judgments of which human knowledge consists are to be arrived at by putting two kinds of question to the data of experience. I may inquire with respect to any phenomenon what it may be, or why it may occur; and having thought of an answer, I may ask another sort of question with respect to that, 'Is it so or not so?' The first kind of question, which culminates in an act of understanding or 'insight', Lonergan terms 'a question for intelligence'; the second, which issues in a judgment that something is the case or not the case, 'a question for reflection'. Questions for reflection, as opposed to those for intelligence, may properly be answered 'Yes' or 'No'. 'What sort of a rose is that?', or 'What is the cause of the unpleasant smell in this room?', cannot be answered in such a way; but 'Is it a rugosa?', or 'Is it the fish we threw into the garbage yesterday?', may certainly be so. Examples of the two kinds of question, and of the answers which may be given to them, are readily to be found in the most ordinary circumstances of life, as well as in the further reaches of theoretical science and scholarship. After *Insight*, Lonergan refers to the 'transcendental precepts' – 'be attentive, be intelligent, be reasonable' –

which correspond respectively to experience, understanding and judgment; and claims that these precepts are relevant to the acquisition of knowledge of every kind.

It might be asked whether the claim that we perform such acts is not mere 'mentalism' or folk psychology, destined to disappear before the march of science. The answer is, that I cannot deny that I am at least to some extent really attentive, intelligent and reasonable, without thereby disqualifying myself from saying anything at all which is worth taking seriously. I can hardly argue soundly for a conclusion which implies that I am incapable of soundly arguing for a conclusion. And all such argument is a matter of being attentive, intelligent and reasonable – in other words, of attending to relevant evidence in experience, of envisaging possibilities which may account for that experience, and of affirming with more or less certainty the possibility which does seem best to account for it. Lonergan refers to the method underlying his philosophy as 'generalized empirical method', since it is based on our awareness not only of our sense-experience and feeling, but also of the mental acts (of questioning, hypothesizing, marshalling evidence, judging and so on) which we apply to these.

2 Science and metaphysics

With the advance of the sciences, it has become more and more clear that the possibilities which may be envisaged to explain what is observable are not themselves couched in terms of what is observable. Mass, valency and electrical charge are not direct objects of sight or hearing; but they have been intelligently conceived and reasonably affirmed as constitutive of the best available explanation of a huge range of observable phenomena. 'Experiential conjugates' are properties of things in relation to our senses. 'Pure conjugates', as progressively discovered by scientific inquiry, are properties of things as related to one another. The moral, that knowledge can reach beyond experience, is also applicable to the notorious problem of other minds. Though I cannot have experience of your thoughts and feelings, I can certainly conceive that you may be thinking and feeling in a certain way, and verify the judgment that you are actually doing so on the evidence of my experience.

Does scientific realism commit one to determinism? (see DETERMINISM AND INDETERMINISM; SCIENTIFIC REALISM AND ANTIREALISM). Modern physics seems to demand statistical laws to explain such phenomena as radioactive decay; there appears to be no adequate reason to suppose that these laws are a mere cloak for ignorance of underlying classical laws. The application within the universe of statistical as well as classical laws is to be grasped by what is called an 'inverse insight' to the effect that a whole familiar body of assumptions and strategy of questioning are wrong. (It is by inverse insight that one grasps that the square root of two cannot be the quotient of two whole numbers, however large, that one might have expected; or the crucial point of the special theory of relativity, that the common-sense notion of absolute rest is without application (see RELATIVITY THEORY, PHILOSOPHICAL SIGNIFICANCE OF).) The world-order turns out to be constituted by 'schemes of recurrence' each characterized by a set of classical laws, and each with certain probabilities of emergence and of survival which are determined by statistical laws. These schemes of recurrence form a hierarchy corresponding to the different sciences (physics, chemistry, biology, sensitive psychology and so on).

Metaphysics, on Lonergan's account, is to be based on the theory of knowledge; the nature and structure of knowing determines the overall nature and structure of what is to be known. Reality is not the object of naïve extroverted consciousness, as we seem biased towards believing; it is nothing other than what is to be known so far as we exercise our attentiveness, intelligence and reasonableness to the full. 'Positions' in epistemology, metaphysics, ethics and so on, which are consistent with being intelligently conceived and reasonably affirmed, are to be distinguished from 'counter-positions', which are not so. Behaviourism in psychology is a fair example of a counter-position; since it follows inevitably from it that human beings, including behaviourists, never believe what they do because it is intelligent and reasonable for them to do so. Erroneous metaphysical doctrines are due largely to mistaking one part of the business of coming to know for the whole. Empiricism is 'a bundle of blunders', based on the fundamental error that 'what is obvious in knowing', that is, experience, 'is what knowing obviously is' (see EMPIRICISM). Idealism rightly attends to the creative acts of intelligence which are essential in knowing; but does not take sufficient account of the fact that hypotheses concocted by intelligence may be verified or otherwise as obtaining in the actual world (see IDEALISM). The 'critical realism' which is for Lonergan the correct metaphysical stance takes account of the fact that knowledge is to be had in judgments as to what is so, in which experience and understanding both play their part. While taking full account of the 'turn to the subject' characteristic of philosophy since Descartes, critical realism reaffirms central elements in the philosophies of Aristotle and Aquinas.

3 Human science, ethics and religion

While the methods of the human sciences cannot be reduced to those of the natural sciences, it should not be inferred that a kind of divination is necessary to grasp the meanings implicit in human speech and action. In getting to know what Isaiah was about in propounding his oracles, or Churchill in pursuing his foreign policy, just as in the case of inquiries into the carbon cycle or the drift of the continents, I have to be attentive, intelligent and reasonable; the difference is that in the case of what is studied by the human sciences, the object as well as the subject of inquiry is to be understood as applying, at least to some extent, the same mental capacities. To envisage a fully 'scientific' account of human beings which would dispense with such 'primitive' and 'mentalistic' explanation is self-destructive for the reasons already given. All normally endowed human beings have experience, understand and judge; but it is one thing to do so, another to attend to the fact that one does so, another still to work out the consequences in an adequate philosophy. Throughout most of history, human worldviews have been dominated by myth, where thought on issues not immediately affected by practice is directed by emotion-laden images rather than by rational self-consciousness.

Value judgments, like (other) judgments of fact, may be due to more or less attentiveness, intelligence and reasonableness; they have to be distinguished sharply from direct response to experienced inclination or aversion. I may want a good breakfast, and act accordingly; but I may also conceive and work for an economic order where as many people as possible get a good breakfast. Of course, it is one thing to make a value judgment, another thing to act in accordance with it. To complete our account of the transition from knowing what is true to knowing and doing what is good, a fourth kind of mental act, that of 'decision', has to be invoked; and a corresponding fourth 'transcendental precept', 'be responsible'. Of course, it is generally taken for granted that seeking for the truth is an aspect of being good; and, sure enough, following the evidence where it leads is apt to involve a responsible decision – especially when one's peers or paymasters have an interest in one's failing to do so.

The arguments of HUME and KANT against rational theism are to be contested as due to an inadequate theory of knowledge. In accordance with a fully worked-out critical realism, one conceives and affirms an 'unrestricted act of understanding' (God) which understands all possible worlds, and wills the one which actually obtains; such a being must exist if the intelligibility of the world is to be adequately explained. Given the notorious fact of moral evil and human deficiency in general, one might have expected God to act in such a manner as to remedy the situation; attention to human history indicates that God has actually done so. However far rational self-consciousness is developed, the human emotional needs apt to give rise to myth remain; the remedy takes the form of an actual human history which provides humankind with the emotion-laden symbols of myth without its falsifications.

See also: RELIGION AND SCIENCE

List of works

Lonergan, B.J.F. (1957) *Insight. A Study of Human Understanding*, Toronto, Ont.: Toronto University Press, 1992. (Lonergan's most complete exposition of his philosophy.)
—— (1967) *Collection*, London: Darton, Longman & Todd. (Includes useful introductions to aspects of Lonergan's thought.)
—— (1968) *Verbum. Word and Idea in Aquinas*, London: Darton, Longman & Todd. (Relates Lonergan's principles to the philosophies of Aristotle and Aquinas.)

References and further reading

Crowe, F.C. (1992) *Lonergan*, London: Chapman. (A general introduction to Lonergan's thought, against the background of his life.)
McShane, P. (ed.) (1972) *Language, Truth and Meaning: Papers from the International Lonergan Congress 1970*, Dublin: Gill & Macmillan. (A collection of appreciations and criticisms, and comparisons with other philosophical positions.)
Meynell, H. (1976) *An Introduction to the Philosophy of Bernard Lonergan*, London: Macmillan; 2nd edn, 1992. (An exposition and evaluation of the arguments of *Insight*.)
Sala, G.B. (1994) *Lonergan and Kant. Five Essays on Human Knowledge*, Toronto, Ont.: University of Toronto Press. (Compares Lonergan's *Insight* with Kant's *Critique of Pure Reason*, concentrating especially on the role of the a priori in the work of the two thinkers.)

HUGO MEYNELL

LORENZEN, PAUL (1915–95)

Paul Lorenzen, German philosopher of mathematics and sciences, programmatically set about implementing mathematical constructivism in wider philosophical contexts. Trained as a mathematician, he spent the greater part of his teaching career at the University of Erlangen, Germany. Here he assembled what came to be known as the 'Erlangen school', which included Wilhelm Kamlah, Kuno Lorenz, Jürgen Mittelstraß, Peter Janich, Oswald Schwemmer and others. In its heyday, the school also influenced work at the universities of Konstanz and Marburg, and was one of the main alternatives to 'traditional' philosophies such as hermeneutics.

The school's interests embraced mathematical logic, the major thinkers of the idealist and hermeneutic traditions (though not Heidegger), and a high level of philological expertise in classical philosophy. Regrettably, though, its encyclopedic initiative has remained incomplete, and the school has largely disbanded in the face of increasing polarization between straight analytical philosophy and a tougher response by existing traditions. To some extent, Lorenzen's own express interest in left-wing political traditions became a liability in view of the sobriety and retrenchment that characterized the 1980s.

1   **Lorenzen's constructivism**
2   **Counting and other operations**
3   **Ortholanguage and dialogical logic**
4   **Conclusion**

1   Lorenzen's constructivism

Lorenzen's work articulates concerns brought on by the fate of philosophy under National Socialism. He distrusted instrumentalist refusals to engage with foundational issues in epistemology, since this had (it appeared) contributed to the nationalism of the cultural sciences, the positivism of jurisprudence, and the racism of those philosophers of science who proclaimed such fantasies as 'Aryan physics'. Lorenzen's 'constructivism', by contrast, starts from the insistence that it is possible to establish a firm bridgehead in reality by a version of operationalism: we know what we have created, and to the extent that we repeatably create external things we are by that token entering reality. So while we may be unable to describe 'reality' *tout court*, we can say as much as we want about those parts that we can reproduce at will by means of effective procedures.

Lorenzen contends that all knowledge is derived from privileged practices and 'operations', that there is no knowledge that is not in some sense practical knowledge, and that it is precisely active intervention that constitutes our rational being in the world. There are two major steps in Lorenzen's arguments. The first is the determination of knowledge-constituting activities: where do deliberate human practice and intelligible reality coincide as perfectly as operationalist epistemology envisages? The second step extends this epistemological principle to issues in moral philosophy.

2 Counting and other operations

Traditionally, counting, as represented by the natural numbers and arithmetic, was the constructivists' favoured 'operation', as shown in Brouwer's contention that mathematics 'is more an activity than a doctrine'. Despite supplying the basis of the most refined structures the mind is capable of conceiving, counting is a practice common to all rational beings, and one whose practical effectiveness is vindicated by repeated application in all the concerns of human life. The philosophical challenge was to show that complex mathematical instruments such as analysis – or, failing that, equivalent substitutes for them – could be derived, 'constructively', from basic intuitive operations like counting. Non-constructive steps in the argument (such as the *tertium non datur*) had to be excluded, or interpreted in terms of some additional constructive principle. This is the area from which Lorenzen's own earlier work grew.

But counting is only a single, restricted 'operation'. In particular, it does not suffice to ground other branches of mathematics, such as geometry or mechanics, which require some account of spatial and temporal elements. To obtain these, Lorenzen turned to the work of Hugo Dingler (Dingler was an opponent of the Vienna Circle; discussion of his ideas can be found in early issues of *Erkenntnis*). Dingler had argued that a Euclidean geometry could be reconstructed by reference to certain intuitive practical activities. In particular, the production of plane surfaces was something for which lens grinders had an eminently effective procedure (they grind three objects together until one designated surface of each is exactly congruent with the designated surfaces of both others). Once plane surfaces have been effectively derived, other elements (straight lines, points) could be derived by further intuitive manipulation (a straight line is the intersection of two plane surfaces, a point is the intersection of two straight lines). Just as constructivist mathematics rejected the use of non-constructive elements in justifying maths (because they interrupted the chain of derivation from assured reality), so also Dingler rejected non-Euclidean approaches because they could not be intuitively grounded (see Dingler 1987).

The attempt to provide 'operative' foundations for mechanics – and hence for physics – has been extended into chronometry and stochastics in the so-called 'protophysics' of Lorenzen's pupil Janich. The central feature of this broadened constructivism is the attempt to find procedures that are repeatable under contextual invariance. Counting has this effect: whether you count apples or sheep, the results of this procedure (natural numbers) have the same properties in either case. In principle at least, Dingler's lens-grinding procedure in every case produces something (a plane surface) with the same properties. Clearly, few procedures satisfy this requirement of contextual invariance. Baking depends for the properties of its results on 'contextual' elements such as the ingredients I use; running depends on where I start from; and so on. But to the extent that we can find procedures that are contextually invariant, we have discovered operations that *are generally constitutive of intelligible reality*.

The most satisfactory examples of such procedures are in the schemata by which we conceptualize reality. Counting, as we have seen, is one of those. Lorenzen made two attempts, however, to extend this into the philosophy of language (see CONSTRUCTIVISM; CONSTRUCTIVISM IN MATHEMATICS; OPERATIONALISM).

3 Ortholanguage and dialogical logic

One attempt consisted in the development of a so-called 'ortholanguage' (with Oswald Schwemmer). This was based on an inversion of the 'classical' priority of syntax over semantics. Although the constructivist interpretation of counting as a general procedure already abandons the set-theoretic model of the universe, a general prioritization of semantics requires more. The ortholanguage attempted to supply this by specifying absolutely general *pragmatic* features of speech. In its details this project was not very successful and seems to have been abandoned (the basic semantic 'procedure' was giving orders, which does not entirely commend itself!). None the less it formed part of a wider project which produced the *Logical Propaedeutics* (1973), which became the Erlangen school's most widely influential text. It is best described as a constructivist introduction to philosophical logic.

Logical Propaedeutics, apart from setting out in general terms a derivation of the principles of rational communication from certain foundational pragmatic interests, provides an interpretation of the logical constants. This is perhaps the most interesting and enduring of Lorenzen's contributions. He calls it 'dialogical logic'. The classical approach to philosophical logic, Lorenzen argues, rests on metaphors derived from set theory. The assumption is that intelligible statements about the world are reducible to elementary propositions about whether objects are or are not elements of sets. A classical approach can then interpret the logical constants – or at least the connectives – in terms of these depictions of states of affairs. Wittgenstein's use of truth tables in the *Tractatus* is a celebrated example (see WITTGENSTEIN, L.J.J.). (Lorenzen also calls this approach 'semantic'.) Unless the system is to be disengaged from ontology and treated instrumentally, however, problems with 'difficult' sets (non-finite sets, self-membership and so on) have to be faced. In particular, truth tables presuppose that the truth-values of all the elementary propositions are determinate. But this raises difficulties, for example, in the case of the universal quantifier, and is by no means as intuitive as its proponents claim.

Lorenzen's constructivism supplies an answer. The logical constants are now interpreted as strategies in two-person games. They indicate a certain procedure in an argument; and the truth-values of elementary propositions are then presented no longer as pre-existing states of affairs, but as matters which might (or might not) fall for determination in the course of the strategy pursued. It might be, for example, that dialogue partner P puts forward a conditional sentence, $p \rightarrow q$. While the truth table interprets this as a collection of fixed assertions about p and q, the dialogue interpretation says it is no more than an offer to negotiate in certain determinate ways. If, for example, the opponent O challenges with the statement 'p', then, in order to make good the initial claim, P will affirm 'q'. If P cannot do that, O will win. If, on the other hand, O challenges with '$\neg q$', P will have to affirm '$\neg p$'; and so on. For certain affirmations there is always a winning strategy, and such formulations correspond to the 'logical truths' or 'tautologies' of the classical interpretation.

The advantage of this becomes more obvious in the case of the quantifiers. A universal quantifier is now not to be interpreted as a statement about some actual (and possibly infinite) totality of states of affairs, but as an offer to negotiate on the basis that the assertor challenges their opponent to find a counterexample – or, after a completed dialogue, that the challenge was made and not successfully taken up.

This idea has a precursor in Gentzen's 'natural deduction', and to a degree it has a rival in similar 'games' devised by J. Hintikka (1983). The core of Lorenzen's approach, however, is its strong constructivism, which is most evident in its insistence on the concrete temporality of the dialogue. As Lorenzen points out, much depends on the dialogical rules adopted for these exchanges, for they determine which statements are to be tautologies, and it is over the question of what is to be a tautology and what is not that, for example, constructivists and classical logi-

cians part company. These rules relate largely to the number of times each participant may respond to statements by an opponent (by attacking affirmations or defending themselves against attacks). If these rules are completely liberalized, and each side may continue attacking and defending until they have covered everything, then central classical tautologies (*tertium non datur, reductio ad absurdum*) become universally defensible strategies. These are excluded once the rules are tightened, for example, by specifying that P – the person making the original declaration – may *attack* any statement made by O, but may only *defend* himself or herself against the last attack.

Of course, the problem now arises over how such rule-making decisions may themselves be justified 'constructively'. Ideally, one would wish to do this by showing that the dialogue rules were intuitively more satisfactory than, say, the ontological insinuations of truth tables. This is not easy. Lorenzen seems to offer two responses. One assumes that the tighter rules are the intuitive ones. However, we need most of classical logic (including *reductio*) to be able to reason at all. We therefore have to enrich our original dialogical intuition with liberalization. In other words (interpreting this) we need tolerance in order to do science.

The other response does not really follow from the dialogical interpretation, but recurs to constructivism's ontological conviction that future facts (or otherwise unavailable facts) are not facts and hence do not fit into truth tables. This justifies rules excluding *tertium non datur*, and vindicates dialogues as part of the dynamic by means of which human beings construct their own future facts (see DIALOGICAL LOGIC).

4 Conclusion

Lorenzen is a transcendental pragmatist: that is to say, he thinks that certain activities provide direct access to reality, and that the conditions of such activities are thereby in some sense transcendental conditions of knowledge in general. The problem lies in identifying these activities. Counting is one possibility, and has done useful service for classical intuitionism. It is limited, however; and other attempts to extend the range of foundational activities within physics (Dingler, operationalism generally) have not been entirely convincing. The most widely canvassed transcendental activity – by Apel, HABERMAS and others as well as by Lorenzen – is language itself. But, as Wittgenstein asked in the *Philosophical Investigations*, to what extent is 'language' a single activity? The various transcendental-pragmatic attempts to determine precisely what this activity is have usually led to suggestions that are unconvincing or trite or both. In particular, the recurring suggestion (in Lorenzen, Habermas and elsewhere) that speaking somehow presupposes tolerance and openness, and thus has a natural telos in good behaviour, seems ultimately specious.

Despite any reservations one may have about the system eventually generated by Lorenzen and his followers, their work combines deep scholarship with breadth of interest and a properly philosophical emphasis on the moral and political aspects of reason.

List of works

Lorenzen, P. (1955) *Einführung in die operative Logik und Mathematik* (Introduction to Operative Logic and Mathematics), Berlin: de Gruyter. (An early, and technical, account of Lorenzen's constructivist philosophy of mathematics.)

Lorenzen, P. and Kamlah, W. (1973) *Logische Propädeutik; Vorschule des vernünftigen Redens* (Logical Propaedeutics: Rudiments of Rational Discourse), Mannheim: Bibliographisches Institut. (Written with his colleague Wilhelm Kamlah, this 'constructivist' introduction to philosophical logic popularized the 'Erlangen Circle'.)

Lorenzen, P. and Schwemmer, O. (1973) *Konstruktive Logik; Ethik und Wissenschaftstheorie* (Constructive logic, ethics and philosophy of science), Mannheim: Bibliographisches Institut. (The mature presentation of Lorenzen's work.)

Lorenzen, P. (1974) *Konstruktive Wissenschaftstheorie* (Constructive Epistemology), Frankfurt: Suhrkamp. (A collection of more popular papers.)

—— (1978) *Theorie der technischen und politischen Vernunft* (The Theory of Technical and Political Reason), Stuttgart: Philipp Reclam. (A collection of popular essays.)

Lorenzen, P. and Lorenz, K. (1978) *Dialogische Logik* (Dialogical Logic), Darmstadt: Wissenschaftliche Buchgesellschaft. (A more technical collection of essays by Lorenzen and his pupil Lorenz.)

Lorenzen, P. (1980) *Methodisches Denken* (Methodical Thinking), Frankfurt: Suhrkamp. (A collection of popular essays.)

—— (1987) 'Critique of Political and Technical Reason', *Synthese* 71 (2): 127–218. (The Evert Willem Beth Lectures of 1980. Written in English, this series of lectures was Lorenzen's last exposition of his work.)

References and further reading

* Dingler, H. (1987) *Aufsätze zur methodik* (Essays on Method), ed. U. Weiss, Hamburg: Felix Meiner.

(This selection includes Dingler's seminal 1936 attempt at an operationalist grounding of natural science.)

Felscher, W. (1986) 'Dialogues as a Foundation for Intuitionistic Logic', in Gabbay and Guenther (eds) *Handbook of Philosophical Logic*, Dordrecht: Reidel, vol. 3. (A useful review of the Erlangen school's dialogical logic.)

* Hintikka, J. (1983) 'Semantical Games and Transcendental Arguments', in J. Hintikka and J. Kulas, *The Game of Language*, Dordrecht: Reidel, 33–46. (Hintikka's semantical games are an alternative to Lorenzen's; this is an account.)

Janich, P. (ed.) (1992) *Entwicklungen der methodischen philosophie* (Developments in Methodical Philosophy), Frankfurt: Suhrkamp. (Recent essays on the Erlangen school; includes extended discussion of Dingler's influence.)

Roberts, J. (1992) *The Logic of Reflection*, New Haven, CT: Yale University Press. (Relates Lorenzen to Frege, Wittgenstein, Husserl and Habermas.)

JULIAN ROBERTS

LOSEV, ALEKSEI FËDOROVICH (1893–1988)

A leading Russian philosopher, religious thinker and classical scholar of the twentieth century, Losev made important contributions to the theory of language, myth and symbol, as well as to the understanding of ancient Greek thought and culture. He strongly resisted central aspects of modernization, in particular the spread of what he saw as 'bourgeois' and 'philistine' secularism, positivism, materialism, atheism, selfish individualism and 'machine civilization'.

A scholar of staggering erudition with a lifelong passion for the ancient world, especially the thought of Plato, Losev could be a fierce, sometimes abusive polemicist. His relation to the Soviet regime ranged from open defiance in the late 1920s (which led to prison and the gulag for almost three years) to at least pro forma *acceptance of certain key elements of Marxist ideology and philosophy in the period between 1953 and 1988.*

1   Philosophy of language, myth and symbol
2   Philosophy of history and critique of contemporary culture
3   Philosophy of religion and philosophical theology

1 Philosophy of language, myth and symbol

Aleksei Fëdorovich Losev was born in Novocherkassk. While studying at that city's classical gymnasium, from which he graduated in 1911, he made his first acquaintance with the works of Plato and Vladimir Solov'ëv, both of whom were to remain at the centre of his intellectual interest for the rest of his long life. He graduated from Moscow University in 1915 in both philosophy and classics. Among his teachers were L.M. Lopatin, G.I. Chelpanov and G.G. SHPET. Boris Pasternak was a university classmate.

In 1914 the university authorities sent Losev to Berlin to do research in medieval philosophy in preparation for a university career in Russia. His stay was cut short by the outbreak of war, and he never again travelled outside Russia. In 1919 he was named a professor at the University of Nizhny Novgorod. From 1921 he taught the history of aesthetics at the Moscow Conservatory and then, with the rank of professor from 1923, taught a variety of subjects at various institutions of higher education. From 1942 until his death (in Moscow) he was a professor of classics at the Lenin Pedagogical Institute in Moscow. As a result of his trying experiences in the gulag in the early 1930s he was judged in 1947 to be clinically blind. His prodigious scholarly output during his final four decades (a lifetime total of some 400 scholarly works, including thirty monographs) was made possible by his second wife, A.A. Takho-Godi, a classicist and his former student, as well as by various polyglot secretaries.

When between 1927 and 1930 Losev was publishing his first eight, 'privately printed', volumes – what Khoruzhii has called his 'Octateuch' (*Vos'miknizhie*) – he used three techniques to confuse the Soviet censors: (1) misleading titles, especially for his 900-page *Ocherki antichnogo simvolizma i mifologii* (Essays in Ancient Symbolism and Mythology) (1930a), which in fact consists of an extended monograph on Plato's theory of ideas and shorter monographs on Plato's social philosophy and Aristotle's ethics and aesthetics; (2) a ponderous technical terminology with many Greek-based terms and a dense and difficult philosophical style – especially prominent in *Filosofiia imeni* (The Philosophy of the Name) (1927b); (3) careful avoidance of the words 'God' or 'Deity' in what are clearly theological discussions (again, most in evidence in Filosofiia imeni). It was not until his final book of the series, *Dialektika mifa* (The Dialectic of Myth) (1930b) that Losev ventured to use the word 'God' – which in fact occurs frequently in the final chapters of that work.

Losev is unique among Russian thinkers in combining close scholarship in several languages – including the translating of, and commenting on, key classical and medieval texts – with bold and sometimes fanciful speculation. His translations of works of Aristotle, Plotinus, Proclus, Sextus Empiricus and Nicholas of Cusa have been widely praised, as has the splendid four-volume translation of Plato (1968–72) that he co-edited with V.F. ASMUS.

Although Losev's Russian Orthodox convictions can be read between the lines in several of his works published in the late 1920s, he managed to avoid public censure, except for one attack by A.M. Deborin in 1929. Perhaps partly as a result of this relative impunity, he was emboldened to make his criticisms of Soviet ideology and practice sharper and more explicit, and his religious views much more open, in two works published in 1930. In *Ocherki antichnogo simvolizma i mifologii* he declared that a proletarian state cannot permit the existence of free art or science; if it does, such science may begin to refute Darwin's theory. 'It is necessary to forbid the refutation of Darwin and to devote major resources to the refutation of Einstein' ([1930a: 822] 1993: 837). As he admitted to a Western visitor in the 1960s, this was meant ironically; but the Soviet censors took it with deadly seriousness. And they were outraged by his claim that "dialectical materialism" is a scandalous absurdity, the total flaunting of all dialectic and a most typical abstract bourgeois metaphysics' (1930b: 147; 1994: 123).

The axe fell promptly, with denunciations in *Pravda* and *Izvestia*, and a diatribe delivered to the 16th Party Congress (1930) by L.M. Kaganovich. Losev was arrested in April 1930 and spent eighteen months in prison (four of them in solitary confinement) under interrogation. He was sentenced to ten years in the gulag, and his wife to five years, but both were released in 1933 on grounds of failing health. Losev was able to continue teaching but forbidden to publish (except one or two translations) until 1953, when, by joining in the universal praise of Stalin's pamphlet *Marxism and Problems of Linguistics*, he was able to resume publication, mainly in the field of classical philology.

In a letter of 30 January 1923 to his mentor and friend Fr. Pavel FLORENSKII, first published in 1990, Losev made clear that his interest in the philosophy of the name and the theory of language and symbolism generally, had theological roots. He sided with Florenskii in defending the controversial claims concerning *imiaslavie* ('glorification of the name [of God]'). His ontological model – widely applied in a variety of fields of thought and culture – is that of an essence (*sushchnost'*) and its 'energies' (*energii*). An 'energy' for Losev is not an Aristotelian *energeia*, in other words, the actualization (of a potentiality), but rather the 'manifestation' or 'expression' of an essence. As he wrote to Florenskii: 'The name of God is an energy of God's essence'. But, wishing to avoid the pantheism with which many defenders of *imiaslavie* had been charged, Losev added: 'The name of God is God Himself, but God Himself is not a name; God is above every name' (*Kontekst 1990*: 15). The theological implications of this position will be explored (briefly) in §3.

Losev envisages a hierarchy of essence-energy relations: *eidos* (Platonic Form) is manifested in myth, myth is manifested in symbol, and symbol is manifested in the person. Losev's dialectical phenomenology – as Zenkovsky aptly called it – is more dialectical than phenomenological, more indebted to PLATO, PLOTINUS and HEGEL than to Husserl. As both Zenkovsky and Khoruzhii (1994) have noted, Losev always enriched his Husserlian analysis of the structure of meanings with a very un-Husserlian intuition of inclusive 'total-unity' (*vseedinstvo*) inspired by Vladimir SOLOV'ËV. This is evident in his theory of dialectic and of language. Dialectic, he insists, 'is the sole method capable of grasping living reality as a [dynamic] whole'. And words – especially proper names – have a 'magical power'; they are instruments of 'living communion' of human beings with one another and with nature. A person for whom words were only sounds, devoid of meanings, would live in a 'deaf-and-dumb' universe, plunged in 'gloom and madness', an 'eternal prisoner of himself, . . . antisocial, uncommunicative, non-conciliar [*nesoboren*]' (1927b: 47; 1993: 642).

By 1927 Losev knew the first two volumes (1923, 1925) of Cassirer's seminal work, *The Philosophy of Symbolic Forms*. He found much that was congenial there, and was astonished to discover that Cassirer's view of myth and mythical time was very close to his own view of music and musical time. But he rejected Cassirer's sharp contrast between myth and science and asserted, against Cassirer, that myth has its own 'mythical truth' and 'mythical authenticity [*dostovernost'*]'. Furthermore, Losev insisted that mythical consciousness is an essential accompaniment of every culture, including our own, rather than an early, now superseded stage of cultural development, as many theorists of myth assumed (see CASSIRER, E.).

2 Philosophy of history and critique of contemporary culture

Losev's views of European history exhibit an intriguing parallel with those of Konstantin LEONT'EV. For both thinkers the high point of West European cultural and religious development came with the Middle Ages, permeated as it was by religious values and at the social level by *sobornost'* ('conciliarity' or 'organic spiritual togetherness'). (A significant difference is that Losev did not follow Leont'ev in looking to contemporary Greece and Turkey as models of effective resistance to the modernization that was sweeping Russia.) Since the Renaissance the cultural and spiritual movement of Europe has been retrograde: the Enlightenment, the French Revolution and the development of an influential bourgeoisie have resulted in social atomization, a self-centred individualism and the flattening and emptying of cultural and spiritual values in the movements of secularism, liberalism, technologism, positivism, atheism, a materialist ontology and an abstractly rationalistic, non-dialectical metaphysics – what Hegel had called *Verstandesmetaphysik*. When Zenkovsky said that Losev in his early works had developed a 'metaphysics of the name' he meant this as a compliment. Losev would have taken it as an insult, insisting that Zenkovsky use the word 'ontology' if he meant simply a general theory of being.

Like Leont'ev, Losev was often abusive in his criticism of the various aspects of modernity just enumerated. Thus he spoke of the 'nightmare of Kantian subjectivism and dualism', branding Kant's philosophy a 'synthesis of a prison [the human self alone with its 'hallucinations'] and nihilism' ('Veshch' i imia' (1993: 860)). In praising Husserl for repudiating the naturalistic philosophy of his time, Losev went on to call it 'a naturalistically-decadent [or 'corrupt' – *rastlennaia*] philosophy' ([1930a] 1993). In 1962 he turned his abuse towards Husserl himself, accusing him of a 'monstrous nihilism' and of being a 'most dreadful illustration of the period of disintegration [*raspad*] of bourgeois philosophy'.

Losev's repudiation of high technology is even more idiosyncratic than Leont'ev's, and somewhat differently motivated. For Leont'ev trains, the telegraph and the telephone were destroying the independence of national and ethnic cultures; in Losev's view machinery of every kind, along with electric light and power, are obtrusive, vulgar and destructive of high culture generally and spiritual values in particular. One can sympathize with his claim that 'Gothic architecture is more beautiful than the latest barracks-like buildings', and one can understand his statements that 'Platonism is more beautiful than materialism' and that the 'ringing of [church] bells is more beautiful than the howling of automobiles'. But one is at a loss when Losev adds: 'burning people at the stake is more beautiful than executing them by shooting' (1930b). And his diatribe against electric light (which has a less hysterical prototype in a BERDIAEV text of 1916) is simply baffling. For Losev electric light is 'dead, mechanical', and exhibits the 'limitation and emptiness of Americanism and machine production'. It is 'lacking in Grace,...banal, and boring'. *Human* actions, like praying or making love, cannot be performed by electric light, but only inhuman and dehumanizing actions, such as examining a victim of torture or presenting a promissory note for collection. It is an act of 'nihilism' for a Russian Orthodox believer, Losev asserts, to replace a 'living, trembling candle flame' by the 'trivial abstraction...of vulgar electric light'. He concludes: 'Apartments in which there is no living flame – in a stove, in candles, or icon-lamps – are dreadful places' (1930b: 63–4; 1994: 53–4).

There is a certain historical irony in the fact that Losev's mentor and friend, Fr. Pavel Florenskii, no less devoutly Orthodox than Losev, was at this very time working conscientiously as a scientist and engineer to bring electricity to Soviet factories, offices and homes.

3   Philosophy of religion and philosophical theology

A key fact of Losev's biography, not mentioned in §1, is directly relevant to his views on religion. For nearly six decades he had kept from the world, including his friends, associates and students, the fact that in 1929 he and his first wife had secretly taken monastic vows, that he was the monk Andronik. To his friends, even though many of them were aware that in his final two or three years Losev had taken to wearing a Russian Orthodox cross, this was a stunning revelation, first made public five years after his death at the Losev centennial conference in Moscow (October 1993). They might have been less stunned if they had paid closer attention to the several eloquent passages in *Dialektika mifa* celebrating the simple and devout lives of Russian Orthodox monks and nuns – their fasting, prayers and spiritual discipline.

Claims by such commentators as Nakhov (see 'The Life and Thought of Aleksei Losev' (1996)) that 1953–88 was Losev's sincerely neo-Marxist period tend to be undercut by the fact that he was a Russian Orthodox monk throughout that period. This fact also focuses a clear new light on many of the discussions of religion in Losev's works – both early and late – that had appeared on the surface to be either ambiguous or insufficiently explicit. And it throws a fresh, though not necessarily reassuring, light on Losev's troubling statements (in his 1990 book on Vladimir Solov'ëv) about the 'ghastly historical satanism' of such 'amoral' thinkers as Leont'ev, ROZANOV and NIETZSCHE.

In his first published essay (1916) Losev had declared that 'Plato's thought, which was...unillu-minated by the Light of [Christian] Truth', had nevertheless managed to attain 'almost Christian revelations', even though in Plato's time the 'world did not yet know the Word of God'. During the 1920s Losev spoke not of God (until the final chapters of *Dialektika mifa* in 1930) but of the 'Primordial One' (*Pervo-Edinoe*) or 'Primordial Essence' (*Pervo-Sushchnost'*). He reinterpreted the Platonic ideas as 'radiant symbols' which involve a 'dialectical self-disclosure of the Primordial One'. His theology at this point is both apophatic (negative) and mystical: the Primordial Essence is knowable not in Itself but only through its 'energies'. The name of that Essence 'glows in the immaculate splendour of sempiternal light...having overcome the darkness of the *meon* (non-being)'. For Losev the cosmos is a complex system of 'magical' and 'miraculous' words and meanings, all of which are grounded in the Primordial Essence, a Being – here Losev's language became quite biblical – from whose 'womb' there 'pours the inexhaustible stream of Its life and Its ever-new determinations' (1927b: 163; 1993: 732).

In his 1923 letter to Florenskii (see §1) Losev set out the last of his 'theses' concerning *imiaslavie* in these words:

> a person's energy is nothing more than the Divine energies as received by that person. In mystery and miracle God Himself, and He alone, acts authentically in His names, and the person becomes no more than a vessel of God's name.
>
> (*Kontekst 1990*: 17)

Losev would doubtless be willing to have these words stand as the valediction of the devout and learned, if sometimes irascible, monk Andronik.

List of works

Losev's main philosophical ideas are presented in eight works – ranging in length from fewer than 200 pages to more than 900 pages – privately printed between 1927 and 1930:

Losev, A. (1927a) *Antichnyi kosmos i sovremennaia nauka* (The Ancient Cosmos and Contemporary Science), Moscow. (A close study of ancient Greek dialectic, including such principles as being and becoming and such categories as rest and motion, identity and difference, and space and time.)

—— (1927b) *Filosofiia imeni* (The Philosophy of the Name), Moscow. (A phenomenological investigation, inspired by *imiaslavie* or onomatodoxy – the glorification of the name of God – of the objective and pre-objective structures of the name in their relation to *eidos*, *logos* and *meon*.)

—— (1927c) *Dialektika khudozhestvennoi formy* (The Dialectic of Artistic Form), Moscow. (A highly theoretical discussion of such topics as the categorial structure of the *eidos*, essence and its 'energies', the antinomies of myth and meaning, and a typology of artistic forms.)

—— (1927d) *Muzyka kak predmet logiki* (Music as a Subject of Logic), Moscow. (A phenomenology of pure or absolute music, a comparison of music and mathematics, and a close discussion of musical time, rhythm, melody, harmony and so on.)

—— (1928) *Dialektika chisla u Plotina* (Plotinus' Dialectic of Number). (A Russian translation, with extensive commentary, of Plotinus' discussion of number in *Enneads* VI, 6.)

—— (1929) *Kritika platonizma u Aristotelia* (Aristotle's Critique of Platonism). (A Russian translation, with detailed commentary, of Books 13 and 14 of Aristotle's *Metaphysics*.)

—— (1930a) *Ocherki antichnogo simvolizma i mifologii* (Essays in Ancient Symbolism and Mythology), Moscow: Mysl'; 2nd edn 1993, with additional annotations. (Shorter essays on ancient symbolism and certain of the pre-Socratic philosophers, an extended monograph on Plato's theory of ideas, and shorter monographs on Aristotle's ethics and aesthetics and Plato's social philosophy.)

—— (1930b) *Dialektika mifa* (The Dialectic of Myth), Moscow. This work is currently being translated into English by V. Marchenkov. A portion of this translation was published in *Symposion* 1, 1996. (Negative and positive definitions of myth; the 'dialectical' relation of contemporary mythology to science, religion and politics; and the distinction between 'relative' and 'absolute' mythology.)

—— (1963–94) *Istoriia antichnoi èstetiki* (A History of Ancient Aesthetics), Moscow: various publishers, 8 vols. (Losev's work in ancient thought and culture is perhaps best represented by this monumental work, the second volume of which (Moscow: Iskusstvo, 1969, 145–677) contains a magisterial study of Plato's views of art and aesthetics.)

—— (1990) *Vladimir Solov'ëv i ego vremia (Vladimir Solov'ëv and His Times)*, Moscow: Progress. (Losev's work in the history of Russian philosophy is best represented by this posthumously published volume.)

The following posthumously published volumes, together with the reprint of 1930a, collect all of the eight volumes of 1927–30.

—— (1993) *Bytie. Imia. Kosmos* (Existence. Name. Cosmos), Moscow: Mysl'. (Includes 1927a and 1927b, along with Losev's 1916 essay 'Eros u Platona' (Eros in Plato) and a previously unpublished article 'Veshch' i imia' (Thing and Name).)

—— (1994) *Mif. Chislo. Sushchnost'* (Myth. Number. Essence), Moscow: Mysl'. (Includes 1928, 1929 and 1930b, and several previously unpublished texts.)

—— (1995) *Forma. Stil'. Vyrazhenie* (Form. Style. Expression), Moscow: Mysl'. (Includes 1927c and 1927d as well as several shorter works.)

—— (1996) *Mifologiia grekov i rimlian* (The Mythology of the Greeks and Romans), Moscow: Mysl'. (Includes two extended works: *Antichnaia mifologiia v ee istoricheskom razvitii* (Ancient Mythology in its Historical Development), first published in 1957, and a previously unpublished work, *Teogoniia i kosmogoniia* (Theogony and Cosmogony).)

Several of Losev's shorter essays on language, symbolism and poetry are translated, by J. Hellie, in the special Losev issue of *Soviet Studies in Literature*, vol. 20 no. 2–3 (1984).

References and further reading

Averintsev, S. (1990) 'Pamiati uchitelia' (In Memory of my Teacher), in *Kontekst 1990*, 3–5. (A moving personal statement by a leading Russian intellectual.)

—— (1994) '"Mirovozzrencheskii stil'": podstupy k iavleniiu Loseva' (The Style of a Worldview: Approaches to the Losev Phenomenon), in *Nachala* no. 2–4: 76–87. (A perceptive discussion of Losev's 'love–hate' relation to such historical figures as Scriabin and Plato and such historical phenomena as the Renaissance and Soviet totalitarianism.)

Ehlen, P. (1996) 'A.F. Losevs personalistische Ontologie' (A.F. Losev's Personalistic Ontology), in *Studies in East European Thought* 48: 83–108. (Stresses the personalist, as opposed to the symbolist, elements in Losev's early ontology.)

Haardt, A. (1993) *Husserl in Rußland: Phänomenologie der Sprache und Kunst bei Gustav Shpet und Aleksej Losev* (Husserl in Russia: The Phenomenology of Language and Art in Gustav Shpet and Aleksei Losev), Munich: Fink. (Part 2 contains a careful examination of the Husserlian influences on Losev's philosophy of language and theory of art.)

* Khoruzhii, S. (1994) 'Ar'ergardnyi boi' (A Rearguard Action) in *Posle pereryva: Puti russkoi filosofii* (After the Interruption: The Paths of Russian Philosophy), St Petersburg: Aleteiia, 209–53. (A lucid and informed account which stresses Losev's position in the 1920s as an embattled Russian Orthodox thinker. Originally published as 'Ar'ergardnyi boi: Mysl' i mif Alekseia Loseva' (A

Rearguard Action: The Thought and Myth of Aleksei Losev), in *Voprosy filosofii* (1992) no. 10.)

Kline, G.L. (1990) 'La Philosophie en Union Soviétique autour de 1930', in *Histoire de la littérature russe: Le XXe siècle, Gels et dégels*, Paris: Payard, 256–8, 259–63, 964–6. (An examination of Losev's early work in the light of Gustav Shpet's and in opposition to the position of A.M. Deborin, leading Marxist-Leninist philosopher of the period.)

—— (1994) 'Vospominaniia ob A.F. Loseve' (Reminiscences of A.F. Losev), in *Nachala* no. 2–4: 63–73. (Recollections of half a dozen conversations with Losev in Moscow between 1956 and 1968.)

Scanlan, J.P. (1984) 'A.F. Losev and the Rebirth of Soviet Aesthetics After Stalin', in J.J. O'Rourke *et al* (eds) *Contemporary Marxism: Essays in Honour of J.M. Bochenski*, Dordrecht: Reidel, 221–35. (An informative account of Losev's aesthetic views, which draws on such early works as *Dialektika khudozhestvennoi formy* (1927c) and such later works as *Problema simvola i realisticheskoe iskusstvo* (The Problem of the Symbol and Realist Art) (1976).)

—— (1994) 'A.F. Losev and Mysticism in Russian Philosophy', in *Studies in East European Thought*, 46: 263–86. (A detailed study of Losev's changing views concerning the place of mysticism in the history of Russian thought.)

* 'The Life and Thought of Aleksei Losev' (1996) A special issue of *Russian Studies in Philosophy* 35: 3–91. (Includes L. Gogotishvili, 'The Early Losev' (1989), S. Khoruzhii, 'The Idea of Total-Unity from Heraclitus to Losev' (1994), I. Nakhov, 'Losev and Marxism' (1991), and Fr. V.V. Mokhov, 'Aleksei Fëdorovich Losev and Orthodoxy' (1993). Referred to in §3.)

* Zenkovsky, V.V. (1950) Istoriia russkoi filosofii, Paris: YMCA-Press, vol. 2, 372–8; trans. G.L. Kline, *A History of Russian Philosophy*, London: Routledge & Kegan Paul and New York: Columbia University Press, 1953, vol. 2, 833–9. (A compact and thoughtful analysis of Losev's early works – except for Dialektika mifa – in their relation to Plato, Hegel, Husserl and Solov'ëv. Referred to in §§1 and 2.)

GEORGE L. KLINE

LOSSKY, NICHOLAS ONUFRIEVICH (1870–1965)

In 1922, the Russian neo-Leibnizian idealist Nicholas Onufrievich Lossky, one of his country's most distinguished professional philosophers, was banished from Russia along with more than a hundred other non-Marxist intellectuals whose influence the communist authorities feared. A prolific writer before his exile, Lossky continued to write and publish widely abroad, becoming not only the dean of the Russian émigré philosophical community but a thinker well known in Europe and the English-speaking world through many translations of his works.

The systematic structure and rationalistic tone of Lossky's philosophizing set him apart from most of his fellow Russian idealists, but like them he proceeded in his thinking from a strong conviction of the truth of Christianity; he wrote of his commitment to 'working out a system of metaphysics necessary for a Christian interpretation of the world' (1951: 266). He adhered to a radical form of theism according to which the created natural order has nothing in common ontologically with the divine order that created it.

Lossky is best known for a set of interrelated views in epistemology and metaphysics connected with what he considered his fundamental philosophical insight – the principle that 'everything is immanent in everything'. According to his doctrine of 'intuitivism' in epistemology, all cognition is intuitive; there is an 'epistemological co-ordination' of subject and object such that any object, whether sensory, intellectual or mystical, is immediately present in the mind of the knower. As the heir to a Leibnizian tradition in Russian metaphysics represented before him by Aleksei Kozlov and others, Lossky advanced a theory of 'hierarchical personalism' in which Leibniz's monads became interacting 'substantival agents' existing at various levels of development; the choices of these ideal beings generate the material world (hence Lossky's term 'ideal realism' for his ontology) and their reconfigurations and reincarnations move the cosmic process towards the perfection of the Kingdom of God. In his 'ontological theory of values' Lossky affirms a metaphysical basis for absolute values and attributes all evil – including diseases and natural disasters – to the misuse of free will by substantival agents, both human and subhuman.

1   **Life and neo-Leibnizian system**
2   **Intuitivism**
3   **Theism**
4   **Hierarchical personalism and ideal realism**
5   **The ontological theory of values**

1 Life and neo-Leibnizian system

Lossky was born into a petty nobility family of Polish origin residing in the province of Vitebsk in western Russia. He received his philosophical education mainly at St Petersburg University (1891–8), studying under the noted Neo-Kantian Aleksandr Ivanovich Vvedenskii (1856–1925); subsequently (1901–3) Lossky also had periods of study in Germany with Wilhelm Windelband, Wilhelm Wundt and Georg Müller. He began teaching at St Petersburg University in 1900, and in 1916, by then a major figure in Russian philosophical circles, he was appointed to a chair of philosophy at the University.

A professed atheist and social radical in his youth, as an adult Lossky returned to his family's Russian Orthodox faith – a 'conversion' prompted in part by studying the thought of his religiously minded compatriots Tolstoi, Dostoevskii and Solov'ëv. At the time of the Russian revolution Lossky was active in the Constitutional Democratic Party. An opponent of the Bolsheviks both politically and philosophically, he was dismissed from his university position in 1921 and expelled from the country in November 1922.

Lossky's professorial career abroad was spent mostly in Czechoslovakia, where he taught at universities in Prague, Brno and Bratislava over the period 1922–45. In 1946 he moved to the United States, and in 1947 he was named professor at the St Vladimir Theological Seminary in New York. He retired from teaching in 1950. A frequent visitor to France in his later years, Lossky died near Paris on 24 January 1965.

The only Russian predecessor whose philosophical influence Lossky explicitly acknowledged was Aleksei Aleksandrovich Kozlov (1831–1901), a professor of philosophy at Kiev University from 1876 until illness forced him to retire in 1887, when he settled in St Petersburg. Thereafter developing his views in the private journal *Svoë slovo* (A Personal Word) (1888–98), Kozlov is credited with initiating a Leibnizian movement in Russian philosophy that was continued not only by Lossky but by Lev Mikhailovich Lopatin (1855–1920), who became professor of philosophy at Moscow University and president of the Moscow Psychological Society; by Kozlov's son, Sergei Alekseevich Askol'dov (1870–1945), who was a fellow student of Lossky's at St Petersburg University and is known particularly for his works in epistemology; and by a number of other less prominent thinkers.

The Russian Leibnizians all subscribed to a form of pluralistic idealism or personalism that was inspired by Leibniz's monadology (see LEIBNIZ §§4–7). They saw in the monadology a conceptual framework for establishing the reality and independence of the individual person without abrogating the principle of the organic unity of the cosmic order. Even Leibniz's supposedly 'windowless' monads (see LEIBNIZ §4), these thinkers pointed out, already contained the stamp of the entire universe within each of them; the only thing needed for a fully interpenetrating, organic cosmos is to release the monads from their causal isolation and allow them to interact. This step was taken by Kozlov, who elaborated a metaphysical system called 'panpsychism', according to which individual conscious spirits are both substances and agents; Kozlov also, like Lossky after him, developed an intuitionistic epistemology. Lopatin, too, emphasized the agency of the spiritual entities that comprise reality, attributing to them the 'creative causality' from which all spatiotemporal causality is derived. A defender of free will, Lopatin was the first of this group of thinkers to devote close attention to questions of ethics. The Russian Leibnizians regarded the material world as a product of the activity of individual spirits and advanced theories of reincarnation based on Leibniz's concept of metamorphosis.

Lossky, the longest-lived and most productive member of the group, developed a worldview that was unusual in the history of Russian philosophy for its deliberately systematic character and its rationalistic elaboration. It was also an unusually comprehensive system, incorporating logic, philosophical psychology, epistemology, metaphysics, philosophy of religion, ethics and aesthetics – to each of which fields Lossky devoted at least one major book. The only traditional philosophical discipline that Lossky largely avoided was social and political philosophy – a surprising omission for a Russian philosopher.

In the sections that follow, Lossky's system is examined under the various labels that he himself employed to identify its principal elements.

2 Intuitivism

Lossky's intuitionist epistemology was sketched in his first book (1903) before its formal presentation in *Obosnovanie intuitivizma* (The Intuitive Basis of Knowledge) (1906). Its inspiration, however, dates from about 1898, as Lossky explains in an autobiographical passage in a subsequent work. He relates that, driving through St Petersburg in a cab one foggy autumn evening, sunk in solipsistic doubt,

> I was thinking that there are no sharp boundaries between things, when suddenly the thought flashed into my head: 'Everything is immanent in everything'. I sensed at once that the riddle was solved, that the elaboration of this idea would provide the

answer to all the questions that disturbed me.... From that time on the idea of an all-pervading cosmic unity became my guiding thought. Developing it led me to *intuitivism* in epistemology, and to *the organic worldview* in metaphysics.

(1938: 157; original emphases)

Lossky believed that this insight (dubbed the doctrine of 'absolute immanentism' by the eminent historian of Russian philosophy, V.V. Zenkovsky) pointed the way to overcoming what he called the 'epistemological individualism' of philosophers in the Cartesian tradition. These philosophers, according to Lossky, typically hold that because the only content of consciousness is subjective states, the knowing subject and the object of knowledge are separated from each other and can be connected only causally. Efforts to specify the causal relation invariably result in some form of subordination, he argues – subordination either of subject to object (materialism) or of object to subject (spiritualism). But if immanence is mutual, subject and object are immanent in each other and neither is subordinate, so that the correct conception is what Lossky calls the 'epistemological co-ordination' of subject and object. The cognized object itself is present in consciousness and is grasped as it is in itself (not as a copy, image or other representation). This immediate grasp of the object in itself is what Lossky means by 'intuition'.

Furthermore, the 'absolute' character of immanence entails that *all* objects of consciousness, of whatever sort, are immanent in consciousness, so that every object is directly 'given'; epistemologically, there is no root difference between sense perception and the spiritual contemplation of God. Hence Lossky affirms that all cognition is grounded in intuition, although he concedes that the establishment of *knowledge* on this ground requires further acts of attention, discrimination, and the like. In his book *Chuvstvennaia, intellektual'naia i misticheskaia intuitsiia* (Sensory, Intellectual and Mystical Intuition) (1938), Lossky identifies three varieties of intuition, which he differentiates not epistemologically but according to the ontology of their objects: sensory intuition has as its object 'real being' – being with spatiotemporal existence; intellectual intuition is addressed to 'ideal being' – abstract entities conceived on the model of Platonic ideas; mystical intuition, finally, is intuition of 'metalogical being' – being that transcends the laws of identity, noncontradiction, and excluded middle, such as God. Lossky considered philosophical discourse a form of intellectual intuition, and thus held that rational, discursive thinking, rather than standing opposed to intuition, is one of its species.

The prominence of intuition in Lossky's philosophy suggests comparisons with his French contemporary, Henri BERGSON. Lossky knew Bergson's work well and spoke highly of some of his views, especially the analysis of the physiology of perception and the theory of dream memory advanced in *Matter and Memory* (1896). At the same time, Lossky believed that there was a profound difference between his intuitionism and that of Bergson: for the latter, intuition discloses a conceptually unarticulated, irrational reality, whereas intellectual intuition as Lossky understood it displays the thoroughly rational and systematic structure of ideal being.

Zenkovsky criticizes Lossky's statement of his theory of intuitivism on the grounds that it supposedly contains no actual intuitions; he finds in Lossky no 'radiance of truth', but only 'ordinary theoretical *constructions* or *hypotheses*' ([1948–50] 1953: 660–1; original emphases). But if we accept Lossky's view of rational philosophical discourse as proceeding through the intuition of ideal being ('intellectual intuition'), then 'ordinary theoretical constructions' do not exclude but rather presuppose the presence of intuitions. Moreover, Lossky's initial consciousness of universal immanence (the sudden thought that 'everything is immanent in everything') seems a classic instance of the 'radiance of truth', on a par with the intuitive sense of 'the oneness of being' found in many mystical philosophies through the ages.

A more weighty criticism voiced by Zenkovsky has to do with Lossky's apparent inability to explain the possibility of radical cognitive error. Lossky is willing to acknowledge no more than a partial deviation from truth in the epistemological process whereby intuition becomes knowledge; 'like the other forms of intuition', he writes, 'mystical intuition cannot lead to ideas and concepts that are completely erroneous' (1938: 198). In Lossky's epistemology the fundamental coincidence of idea and reality is guaranteed by the mutual immanence of subject and object; indeed, if intuition is the ground of all cognition, and if in intuition the object *itself* is present in consciousness, it is difficult to understand how even a partial cognitive failure can occur. Yet surely, as Zenkovsky points out ([1948–50] 1953: 673), our ideas are at times radically erroneous. The reality of error requires us to assume a disjunction between subject and object that Lossky's philosophy of 'absolute immanentism' cannot admit.

3 Theism

The 'organic worldview' to which Lossky subscribes in metaphysics is a view of the 'world' or cosmic order, but it does not describe the relation between God and that world. In Lossky's metaphysics (best expounded in his book, *Mir kak organicheskoe tseloe* (*The World as an Organic Whole*) (1917)), the cosmic order within which organic unity prevails is a realm of being utterly different from the supernatural realm to which it owes its existence. Arguing that a world system cannot contain the ground of its own existence, Lossky contends that its ground can only be a Supracosmic Principle that transcends all systems. This is the realm of 'metalogical being' – a realm to which such cosmic categories as 'reason' and 'person' do not apply. Lossky holds, however, that in religious experience we recognize this Supracosmic Principle as God, as a Person, as Triune and the like, but he cautions that all such designations are based on 'metalogical analogy'. Even the relation between the two realms requires analogical language: it can and should be called 'creation out of nothing', but 'creation' must be understood noncausally, because a causal relation requires some degree of ontological homogeneity, which does not exist in the relation between these two realms.

This dualism distinguished Lossky's outlook from the monistic current, inspired by Vladimir Solov'ëv, that was more prevalent among Russian idealist philosophers of the early twentieth century (see SOLOV'ËV §§1–2, 5). Solov'ëv's concept of 'total-unity' (*vseedinstvo*) incorporates Creator and created in a comprehensive organic whole with no ontological gulf between them. Whereas for this reason Solov'ëv and his followers are sometimes charged with pantheism, Lossky recommends his own view as the antithesis of pantheism, 'the purest form of theism' (1951: 265). Lossky does profess adherence to the doctrine of 'Sophiology' developed by Solov'ëv and other Russian idealists (see SOLOV'ËV §2), but he insists that Sophia is not an aspect or element of the Deity but is a purely created spirit, standing at the head of all creation ('next to Christ as His closest co-worker') and receiving earthly incarnation in the form of the Virgin Mary.

4 Hierarchical personalism and ideal realism

In its treatment of the created order, Lossky's metaphysics marked the culmination of the neo-Leibnizian movement of ontological pluralism or personalism in late nineteenth- and early twentieth-century Russia. Agreeing with Kozlov that the myriad ontological units that comprise the cosmic order are not isolated or 'windowless', as Leibniz had conceived them, Lossky calls his interacting monads 'substantival agents'. He regards them as ideal (that is, non-spatiotemporal), active entities that are created by God as free agents and that ground the reality of every individual thing in the universe, from the

smallest subatomic particle to complex objects at all levels of development. Even the simplest of these entities has the ability to 'choose' to subordinate itself to others to form a molecule, a cell or an organism. Indeed each substantival agent can rise to become eventually a human person, defined by Lossky as an ideal being capable of acknowledging absolute values and recognizing the duty to implement them; at still higher levels of development stand such 'persons' as tribes, states, heavenly bodies and the universe as a whole. On this basis, Lossky calls his outlook 'hierarchical personalism', with the qualification that lower, less developed substantival agents are merely potential rather than actual persons.

But what, then, of the spatiotemporal form assumed by these ideal agents in the material world? According to Lossky it is a by-product of their own free choices. To the extent that substantival agents, created by God, reject the Divine Principle and strive 'egoistically' to set themselves apart from the supraempirical Kingdom of God, their 'struggle' and 'acts of attraction and repulsion' produce the phenomenon of materiality. Thus space, time and matter are not God's creations. God creates only substantival agents, and he creates them radically free and indeterminate; hence he is not responsible for what each substantival agent makes of itself. Because on this view 'real' (spatiotemporal) being is a result of choices made by 'ideal' being in the form of substantival agents, Lossky calls his ontology 'ideal realism'.

It is not easy to square Lossky's conception of the indeterminate nature of substantival agents with the confidence he simultaneously exhibits in the progressive, teleological character of cosmic development, expressed in such statements as 'the ultimate universal victory of the good is guaranteed by the structure of the world' (1941: 79). Although on the one hand each substantival agent is said to forge its own destiny freely from the moment of its creation, on the other hand it would appear that the 'freedom' of the agent is limited by a direction (from the simple to the complex) and a goal (the production of human life) that are inherent in cosmic evolution. Thus Lossky wrote in one of his more imaginative passages:

The human self is an agent that perhaps led the life of a proton billions of years ago. Then, gathering around itself a few electrons, it assumed the type of life of oxygen. Making its body still more complex, it then raised itself to the type of life of, say, a droplet of water. After that it made the transition to the type of life of a unicellular animal. After a series of reincarnations – or better, a series of metamorphoses, to use Leibniz's term – it became a human self.

(1941: 33)

More tellingly, Lossky contended that through continued reincarnation 'all agents sooner or later overcome their selfishness' and enter into the Kingdom of God. He introduces the term 'normal [normative] evolution' for 'the line of development which leads straight to the threshold of the Kingdom of God' (1951: 264). To account for this benign tendency on the part of free agents, Lossky can only appeal to a principle of 'the inseparability of existence and value' that he says exists unconsciously as an ideal in every individual (1941: 51). But if individuals do harbour such an ideal, they are not fully indeterminate.

Questions of consistency aside, Lossky's doctrines of the voluntaristic character of evolution (even inorganic evolution) and of reincarnation as an evolutionary mechanism generated much controversy among his fellow Russian religious philosophers. Zenkovsky dismisses the doctrines as 'the most fantastic hypotheses' ([1948–50] 1953: 663).

5 The ontological theory of values

Lossky's conception (cited in §4) of a fully developed person as a substantival agent capable of acknowledging absolute values presupposes that such values exist. In his ethical works (the most important of which are his 1931 and 1949 books), Lossky criticizes ethical relativism and elaborates what he calls his 'ontological theory of values', according to which absolute values are found in 'the fullness of being' that is God, as known through religious experience. In accordance with this conception, everything existing is valued from the point of view of its participation in and communion with the divine 'fullness of being': 'Existence that brings us nearer to the absolute fullness of life is a positive value, and that which draws us away from it is a negative value' (1951: 258).

Because spatiotemporal being results, as we have seen, from the wilful self-assertion of free substantival agents, the material world is truly a 'fallen' realm for Lossky; to call it an incarnation of evil would be redundant, for incarnation in itself is evil: 'The whole [of] nature consists of entities which would have been members of the Kingdom of God had they not entered the path of egoism' (1951: 262–3). The 'path of egoism' or self-assertion is thus the source of all evil, natural as well as humanly produced. Unlike some other religious thinkers, who attribute humanly caused evil to the misuse of free will but have no comparable explanation of diseases and natural

disasters such as earthquakes, Lossky ascribes the latter evils as well to immoral choices (presumably by subhuman agents such as molecules, cells and tectonic plates): all are 'kinds of derivative evil necessarily connected with the relative separation of agents from one another and leading to ruptures and dissolution' (1951: 262). Natural evils will be eliminated (along with humanly created evils) only when nature itself ceases to exist – as it indisputably will when all agents have attained the path of divine righteousness.

But if the explanation of natural evil presents Lossky with no special difficulty, on another level he is faced with the more general problem of explaining why there is evil at all, natural or human. He holds that evil at every stage of evolutionary complexity is produced by the will of substantival agents – specifically, by their will to elevate themselves above God. But what is there in the nature of these ideal beings as they come from the hands of God to induce them to make such bizarre and ultimately self-defeating choices – especially since, as we have seen, they come equipped with an inborn sense of ideal value? In the words of Natalie Duddington, Lossky's first and principal English translator, 'How could beings so admirably fitted by their Creator for a life of blissful intercommunion with Him suddenly conceive the impious thought of putting themselves in his place?' (1968: 10). Duddington justifiably concludes that in Lossky's account of the cosmic order as originally created by God there is nothing to explain the initial and continuing presence of evil.

Thus the problem of accounting for cognitive error, noted in Lossky's epistemology in §2, is echoed in his ethics by the problem of accounting for moral error.

List of works

Lossky, N.O. (1903) *Osnovnye ucheniia psikhologii s tochki zreniia voliuntarizma* (Basic Doctrines of Psychology from the Standpoint of Voluntarism), St Petersburg: St Petersburg University Press.

—— (1906) *Obosnovanie intuitivizma*, St Petersburg: M.M. Stasiulevich; trans. N. Duddington, *The Intuitive Basis of Knowledge: An Epistemological Inquiry*, London: Macmillan, 1919.

—— (1917) *Mir kak organicheskoe tseloe*, Moscow: Leman & Sakharov; trans. N. Duddington, *The World as an Organic Whole*, London: Oxford, 1928.

—— (1922) *Logika* (Logic), Petrograd: Nauka i shkola, 2 vols.

—— (1927) *Svoboda voli*, Paris: YMCA-Press; trans. N. Duddington, *Freedom of Will*, London: Williams & Norgate, 1932.

—— (1931) *Tsennost' i bytie*, Paris: YMCA-Press; trans. S. Vinokooroff as Part I of N.O. Lossky and

J.S. Marshall, *Value and Existence*, London: Allen & Unwin, 1935.

—— (1934) *Dialekticheskii materializm v S.S.S.R.* (Dialectical Materialism in the USSR), Paris: YMCA-Press.

—— (1938) *Chuvstvennaia, intellektual'naia i misticheskaia intuitsiia* (Sensory, Intellectual and Mystical Intuition), Paris: YMCA-Press.

—— (1941) *Bog i mirovoe zlo: Osnovy teoditsei* (God and Worldly Evil: Principles of a Theodicy), Berlin: Za Tser'kov'.

—— (1949a) *Usloviia absoliutnogo dobra* (Conditions of the Absolute Good), Paris: YMCA-Press. (First circulated in mimeographed form in Bratislava in 1944.)

—— (1949b) 'Absolute Criterion of Truth', in *The Review of Metaphysics* 2 (8): 47–96. (The original Russian text of this work was first published posthumously under the title 'Intuitivism' in *Grani* (1970) 77: 144–70; 78: 212–40.)

—— (1951) *History of Russian Philosophy*, New York: International Universities Press. (Includes Lossky's summary of his own philosophy and that of the other Russian neo-Leibnizians, 158–62, 251–66, 381–83.)

—— (1961) 'Smysl istorii' (The Meaning of History), in *Vol'naia mysl'* 3 (September), Buenos Aires; repr. in *Zapiski russkoi akademicheskoi gruppy v S.Sh.A.* 19: 95–105. (This article is a good late statement of Lossky's 'hierarchical personalism'.)

—— (1968) *Vospominaniia: Zhizn' i filosofskii put'* (Memoirs: Life and Philosophical Journey), Munich: Wilhelm Fink; repr. St Petersburg: St Petersburg University Press, 1994.

—— (1991) *Izbrannoe* (Selected Works), Moscow: Pravda. (Includes the complete Russian text of the 1906, 1917 and 1927 works listed above.)

—— (1996) *Mir kak osushchestvlenie krasoty: Osnovy estetiki* (The World as the Manifestation of Beauty: Principles of Aesthetics), Moscow: Progress Publishers. (The first publication of this work, long thought to have been left unfinished but actually completed by Lossky before his death.)

References and further reading

Askol'dov, S. (1912) *Aleksei Aleksandrovich Kozlov*, Moscow: A.I. Mamontov. (A study of the life and work of the originator of Russian neo-Leibnizianism by his son and follower.)

—— (1914) *Mysl' i deistvitel'nost'* (Thought and Reality), Moscow: Put'. (Askol'dov's best work on problems of epistemology.)

* Duddington, N. (1968) 'Epistemology and Metaphysics: Lossky, Frank, and Others', Conference on Idealist Philosophy in Russia, Aix-en-Provence, France, 25–29 March (mimeographed). (Referred to in §5.)

Kohanski, A.S. (1936) *Lossky's Theory of Knowledge*, Nashville, TN: Vanderbilt University. (An exposition and analysis of Lossky's epistemology and its metaphysical implications; contains bibliographies of works by and about Lossky.)

* Kozlov, A. (1888–98) *Svoë slovo* (A Personal Word), St Petersburg: A. Kozlov, 5 vols. (Referred to in §1. Kozlov's mature exposition of his philosophy.)

Lopatin, L.M. (1911) *Filosofskie kharakteristiki i rechi* (Philosophical Characterizations and Addresses), Moscow: Put'. (Essays on Leibniz and other Western philosophers as well as several Russian philosophers by a prominent neo-Leibnizian.)

—— (1886–91) *Polozhitel'nye zadachi filosofii* (The Positive Tasks of Philosophy), Moscow: Lisner & Roman, 2 vols. (Lopatin's basic work in metaphysics and epistemology.)

Lossky, B. and Lossky, N. (1978) *Bibliographie des oeuvres de Nicolas Lossky*, Paris: Institut d'Études Slaves. (An excellent complete bibliography of works by N.O. Lossky and translations of his works, prefaced by a detailed chronology of his life.)

Jakovenko, B., ed. (1932) *Festschrift N. O. Losskij zum 60. Geburtstage* (A Festschrift for N.O. Lossky on His Sixtieth Birthday), Bonn: Friedrich Cohen. (Contains a bibliography of Lossky's works up to 1932.)

* Zenkovsky, V.V. (1948–50) *Istoriia russkoi filosofii*, Paris: YMCA-Press, 2 vols; 2nd edn 1989; trans. G.L. Kline, *A History of Russian Philosophy*, vol. 2, London: Routledge & Kegan Paul and New York: Columbia University Press, 1953, 630–76. (Referred to in §2 and §4. Exposition and critique of the philosophies of Lossky and the other Russian neo-Leibnizians by the authoritative historian of Russian philosophy.)

JAMES P. SCANLAN

LOTTERY PARADOX

see PARADOXES, EPISTEMIC

LOTZE, RUDOLPH HERMANN (1817–81)

Lotze was among the pre-eminent figures in German academic philosophy between the demise of Absolute Idealism and the rise of Neo-Kantianism proper. He sought to avoid two extremes: first, that of an idealism which seeks to deduce the world from a single, general principle; and, second, that of a realism which, by divorcing reality from the mind, splits the world into two utterly separate spheres. The search for knowledge should be tempered by a recognition of the results of natural science and sobered by the awareness that reality will, by necessity, always outstrip thought. Furthermore, our mental life cannot be reduced to purely intellectual functions: feelings and evaluations, for example, are also an integral part of human existence. While there can be no a priori deduction of a metaphysical system, a teleological interpretation, which elucidates the ultimate value of man and the world, must supplement purely naturalistic explanation. The universe has the significance of an unfolding plan, where things are subject to the general laws of order, expressing spiritual import. In this way, Lotze combined a kind of respect for the findings of scientific research with his own peculiar idealistic programme.

1   **Philosophy of biology**
2   **Logic**
3   **Epistemology**
4   **Metaphysics**

1   Philosophy of biology

Hermann Lotze was born in Bautzen and attended the Gymnasium at Zittau. At the University of Leipzig he studied medicine and philosophy. In 1844 he was nominated at Göttingen as the successor to Herbart in the chair of philosophy. Here he remained until the call to Berlin in 1881. His work after the 'materialism controversy' (from the convention at Göttingen in 1854) made clear his anti-naturalism and his affinities with the epistemological bent of early Neo-Kantianism (see NEO-KANTIANISM §2). A quasi-systematic philosopher, Lotze none the less eschewed the presumptions of German Idealism while preserving its ethical imperative.

As a student of Christian Hermann Weisse, Lotze fell under the sway of his teacher's post-Hegelian view of idealism (so-called *Spätidealismus*). Yet as a medical scientist he came to reject key aspects of the idealist and Romantic philosophy of nature, most notably, its dependence upon the notion of 'vital force' (*Lebenskraft*) (see NATURPHILOSOPHIE). After

Kant there had quickly arisen an acceptance, within biological thought, of a special vital force, indicative of an organizing principle of organic bodies. Lotze presented a series of arguments designed to correct false applications of this concept. He reiterated Kant's warning that the assumption of purposive organization could only be a regulative (not a constitutive) principle. As part of an organizing principle of merely subjective validity, the concept of vital force must not be hypostatized: that is, such force ought not to be treated as a material *cause* of organic phenomena.

Therefore, while inquiry must begin with the assumption of a purposive organization, no conclusion should be drawn which identifies vital force as an actual causal principle in the biological realm. On the other hand, this assumption does not imply that mechanistic explanation may be precluded. Teleology and mechanism are mutually compatible, not competing, investigative procedures. Lotze rejects the notion of a special force as superfluous for the scientific side of the investigation. Yet the formal constraint of 'order' or 'purpose' remains a necessary presupposition: mechanism should be understood as the way in which purpose realizes itself in our world.

As some concept of finality is required to fill the 'metaphysical vacuum' left by the intrusion of mechanistic procedures (not only in life science, but in the human sciences as well), an idealistic *Weltanschauung* is combined with a clear recognition of the power of scientific explanation. This requirement harks back to Fichte's imperative to determine what *is* on the basis of what *ought* to be, but with an important difference: this ethical requirement, in Lotze's hands, was translated into a new language of 'values'. The terminology of 'is' and 'ought' is replaced by that of 'existence' and 'meaning': science may be allowed to determine what actually exists, but philosophy is required to expound what this existence means. These early convictions are retained in the mature expositions of Lotze's thought, found in his *Mikrokosmus* (Microcosmos) (1858–64) and *System der Philosophie* (System of Philosophy). Of the latter, which was intended as a three-volume work, only two volumes had been published at his death: *Logik* (Logic) (1874) and *Metaphysik* (Metaphysics) (1879).

2   Logic

The first book of the first volume of Lotze's *System* begins with 'pure logic'. He starts by affirming that our mental life – the 'current of ideas' – essentially involves 'connection': ideas appear in relations of succession or simultaneity. But does this connection denote real coherence or mere coincidence? That is, are the associative connections found in the current of ideas sufficient for objective knowledge or indicative only of subjective error and illusion? Lotze concludes that coherence is distinguished from mere conjunction only by reference to a ground (or basis) for such coherence. And this investigation is the province of 'thought' proper.

Hence to logic, and not to psychology, belongs the discovery of the bases of justification. The dog can associate the raised stick (in the hand of its master) with pain, but only human thought can relate the identical matter in inferential terms, in virtue of logical consequence. The peculiar nature of thought thus lies in the supplement that it provides over and above the mere current of ideas: the addition of a justificatory ground (or rationale) for the connection. This, in turn, depends critically upon the capacity of thought to impose logical form. To provide for a firm structure of truth, it must arrange its building stones precisely. This foundation must, further, be of a form suitable for thought; so there must exist some process by which thought logically apprehends the sensory manifold.

Lotze believed that concept-formation belongs to thought proper and not to the psychological processes of abstraction or synthesis. This principle is to be established by a careful determination of the different stages involved in the refining of ideation into thought. The first step in the creation of logical building stones is the conversion of 'impressions' into 'ideas'. This takes place by naming: in the process of designation one separates out objective 'content' from subjective 'act'. The logical objectification (of what initially appears as subjective) proceeds through the categorization effected by the recognized parts of speech. In meaning (as opposed to mere venting) one calls upon the formal, grammatical categories of substantive, adjective or verb. These are mirrored in (or are shadows of) the logical categories of object, property and relation. While thought is not dependent upon language *per se*, it does depend upon some such inward articulation that respects these fixed logical categories; by contrast, the musical scale is an articulated structure, but not one which can support propositional thought.

Lotze proposed few formal innovations in logic. Among them was that found in his insistence that the coordination of part-concepts (*Merkmale*) in the intention of a given concept be expressed not in simple additive relations but rather in a functional representation. Instead of a simple equation, such as $S = a + b + c + \ldots$, a functional notation, such as $S = F(a, b, c, \ldots)$, indicates that the relations of dependence among the part-concepts must be determined according to a general rule or law. (The constant reference to rules and laws furnishes a leitmotiv of Lotze's entire philosophical endeavour.)

3 Epistemology

Among Lotze's best-known contributions to the theory of knowledge, found in the third book of his *Logic* (1874), is his reinterpretation of Platonism: the construal of metaphysical objectivity as epistemic validity. Lotze argued that Plato had been fundamentally misunderstood. In specifying that the Ideas were non-spatial, Plato had intended to imply that they were not 'things' at all. (Here 'Idea' invokes thought-*content*, not an *act* of ideation.) These contents are to be understood as having an existence completely different from the type of existence associated with objects or things. While physical objects can possess 'being' in the strict sense and events merely 'occur', such contents have 'validity'. This implies a kind of epistemological realism: there are thoughts (or propositions) which are true or false and which are true or false independently of and antecedent to our judgment of them.

Such epistemic realism is sharply distinguished from any metaphysical variety. The latter view holds that these thought-contents must exist (or subsist) in some particular place. It may entail a false hypostatization that seems to follow from the correct emphasis we give to the independence of our thoughts from us. To assert the 'objective significance' of thought-contents is, hence, not to ascribe to them any sort of 'real' existence. Our apprehension of a thought seems to presuppose its existence in a preordained 'place'; yet this can be nothing other than its setting within the inferential relations which hold between different thoughts and their meaningful components. As such, it is part of 'a whole': what Lotze calls the world of the 'thinkable'. It is thus that the apprehension of a thought-content, as part of a larger system, may appear to be analogous to the perception of a physical object.

This picture affects the approach to epistemic justification that emerges in Lotze's views on the validity of the Euclidean axioms. Even if our spatial perception depended upon some cognitive capacity such as 'intuition', Lotze argued, this fact alone could not account for our taking these axioms and their derivable theorems to constitute justified belief. Lotze tried to detach the concept of the a priori (as justificatory) from that of the innate (as genesis or source). Any sense in which one might speak of the innateness of Euclidean geometry only indicates causal or psychological origin and is irrelevant to the question of justification. Instead, Lotze characterized a priori truths as those rooted in 'truths of universal validity, and thus prior to the particular instances in the sense of being rules by which they are determined' ([1874] 1887 2: 131). Yet this exhibition of truth must not be confused with the panlogicist attempt to discover truth by means of an a priori deduction. Rather, it is 'reduction' (or the regressive method) which makes possible the apprehension of the ultimate presuppositions of thought.

4 Metaphysics

Lotze also affirmed the centrality of 'law' in his conception of metaphysics. While metaphysics has a role in his system, it is a limited one: namely, to delimit not the thinkable, but the 'actual' – that is, what can be conceived of as actually existing or occurring without pain of contradiction. This constraint brings him to attack Herbart's theory of being in the first book of the *Metaphysics* (1879). The Herbartian view is indicated in the notion of 'pure being' as *Setzung*: that 'what we call the true Being should be found only in the pure "position", void of relation'. In fact, on this view, it is only because pure being lacks relations that existing things are able to enter into relations at all. Herbart concludes that reality is composed of something plural, simple and indestructible: what he called 'the Reals'. Since reality is compounded of substances that can suffer no change, and are hence immutable, the relations (into which things 'enter in') must be utterly external and accidental (see HERBART, J.F.).

Lotze's polemic stands in sharp opposition to this. He proceeds with an eye to the possible contradictions inherent in such an approach. On Lotze's account, relations 'between' things are impossible: therefore such relations must be internal. This relatedness is characteristic of being, yet not essentially so: what being *means* is something indefinable. Yet, the reality of being is ultimately exhausted by the reality of its relations. Being must be portrayed as part and parcel of a determinate and interconnected 'whole'. Hence, it is inconceivable that one might arrive at pure being through abstraction, by an attempt to negate all relations. This activity could only empty the concept of 'position' of all possible content.

Lotze also questions the view which makes the being of things (*qua* self-subsistent things) equivalent to a substantival notion of the Real. He points out that since 'real' can be used as an adjective, it may indicate a property of things. So the term 'real' cannot be used to characterize the being of things any more than the term 'position' can. Since what is real must be seen as part of an ordered system, its 'essence is only to be found in a law'. This points the way toward an interpretation of both the individual thing and the larger cosmos as systematic wholes, not as accidental juxtapositions of qualities or entities. All must be recognized as the ultimate workings of some Good, which orders and gives purpose to our reality.

While Lotze formed no school, he influenced, most notably, W. Dilthey, R. Eucken, C. Stumpf, W. Windelband, G. Frege, E. Husserl, H. Rickert and B. Bauch. Abroad, his readers and admirers included Josiah Royce and F.H. Bradley. Lotze was a figure who marked the transition from the classical era of Goethe and Hegel to a more scientifically informed philosophy. An original thinker in his own right – and despite his wide-ranging influence – today Lotze remains in relative obscurity.

List of works

Lotze, R.H. (1841) *Metaphysik* (Metaphysics), Leipzig: Weidmann. (The 'lesser' metaphysics, published while Lotze was a *Docent* at Leipzig.)
—— (1843) *Logik* (Logic), Leipzig: Weidmann. (The 'lesser' logic.)
—— (1852) *Medicinische Psychologie, oder Physiologie der Seele* (Medical psychology, or physiology of the soul), Leipzig: Weidmann. (Lotze's physiological psychology, notable for its discussion of his theory of 'local signs'.)
—— (1856–8, 1858–64) *Mikrokosmus, Ideen zur Naturgeschichte und Geschichte der Menschheit, Versuch einer Anthropologie*, Leipzig: S. Hirzel, 3rd edn, 1876–80; trans. E. Hamilton and E.E.C. Jones *Microcosmos: An Essay Concerning Man and his Relation to the World*, Edinburgh: T.&T. Clark, 1885. (Lotze's popular exposition of his views on human nature and on the meaning of human existence.)
—— (1857) *Streitschriften* (Polemical writings), Leipzig: S. Hirzel. (A reply to criticism by I.H. Fichte, a 'late-idealist'.)
—— (1868) *Geschichte der Aesthetik in Deutschland* (History of aesthetics in Germany), Munich: J.G. Cotta. (A three-part work, containing a detailed review of prior German aesthetic theory.)
—— (1874) *Logik, Drei Bücher vom Denken, vom Untersuchen und vom Erkennen*, Leipzig: S. Hirzel, 2nd edn, 1880; *Logik, Erstes Buch, vom Denken*, and *Logik, Drittes Buch, vom Erkennen*, ed. G. Gabriel, Hamburg: Felix Meiner, 1989; trans. and ed. B. Bosanquet, *Logic, in Three Books: Ontology, Cosmology and Psychology*, Oxford: Clarendon Press, 1884; 2nd edn, 1887. (The first volume of Lotze's incompleted *System der Philosophie*. The new German edition, in two volumes for Books One and Three, contains both valuable introductory essays and extensive bibliographies.)

841

—— (1879) *Metaphysik, Drei Bücher der Ontologie, Kosmologie und Psychologie*, Leipzig: S. Hirzel; trans. and ed. B. Bosanquet, *Metaphysics in Three Books: Ontology, Cosmology and Psychology*, Oxford: Clarendon Press, 1884; 2nd edn, 1887. (The second volume of Lotze's incompleted *System der Philosophie*.)

—— (1885–91) *Kleine Schriften* (Lesser writings), ed. D. Peipers, Leipzig: S. Hirzel. (A posthumous collection including, *inter alia*, short essays and book reviews.)

—— (1989) *Kleine Schriften zur Psychologie* (Lesser writings on psychology), ed. R. Pester, Berlin: Springer. (A recent collection of original source texts with additional material and commentary.)

References and further reading

Besoli, S. (1992) *Il valore della verità* (The value of truth), Florence: Ponte Alle Grazie. (A detailed examination of Lotze's logic and of his epistemology.)

Morgan, M.J. (1977) *Molyneux's Question: Vision, Touch, And The Philosophy Of Perception*, Cambridge and New York: Cambridge University Press. (An idiosyncratic work containing an extended discussion of Lotze's 'theory of local signs'.)

Orth, E.W. (1986) 'Rudolf Hermann Lotze: Das Ganze unseres Welt-und Selbstverständnisses' (Rudolf Hermann Lotze: the Systematic Understanding of Self And World), in *Grundprobleme der grossen Philosophen. Philosophie der Neuzeit IV* (Basic Problems of the Great Philosophers. Modern Philosophy IV), ed. J. Speck, Göttingen: Vandenhoeck & Ruprecht. (An important survey article which divides Lotze's work into three phases of development and contains detailed biographical information.)

Santayana, G. (1971) *Lotze's System of Philosophy*, ed. P.G. Kuntz, Bloomington, IN, and London: Indiana University Press. (Santayana's 1889 doctoral dissertation at Harvard, under J. Royce, transcribed with an extensive introduction and exhaustive bibliography supplied by the editor.)

Schnädelbach, H. (1984) *Philosophy in Germany, 1831–1933*, trans. E. Matthews Cambridge: Cambridge University Press. (An important general reference work, which also contains a chapter largely devoted to Lotze's theory of value.)

Wagner, G. (1987) *Geltung und normativer Zwang* (Validity and normative force), Freiburg and Munich: Verlag Karl Alber. (A study of the development of Neo-Kantianism which also situates Lotze's metaphysics in its historical context-

Willard, D. (1984) *Logic and the Objectivity of Knowledge*, Athens, OH: Ohio University Press. (While devoted to the early history of Husserl and phenomenology, this work also contains many references to Lotze and his influence.)

Woodward, W.R. (1999) *From Mechanism to Value. Hermann Lotze: Physician, Philosopher, Psychologist 1817–1881*, Cambridge and New York: Cambridge University Press. (This book promises to be the definitive study of Lotze in English to date.)

DAVID SULLIVAN

LOVE

Love is usually understood to be a powerful emotion involving an intense attachment to an object and a high evaluation of it. On some understandings, however, love does not involve emotion at all, but only an active interest in the wellbeing of the object. On other accounts, love is essentially a relationship involving mutuality and reciprocity, rather than an emotion. Moreover, there are many varieties of love, including erotic/romantic love, friendly love, and love of humanity. Different cultures also recognize different types of love. Love has, as well, a complicated archaeology: because it has strong links with early experiences of attachment, it can exist in the personality at different levels of depth and articulateness, posing special problems for self-knowledge. It is a mistake to try to give too unified an account of such a complex set of phenomena.

Love has been understood by many philosophers to be a source of great richness and energy in human life. But even those who praise its contribution have seen it as a potential threat to virtuous living. Philosophers in the Western tradition have therefore been preoccupied with proposing accounts of the reform or 'ascent' of love, in order to demonstrate that there are ways of retaining the energy and beauty of this passion while removing its bad consequences.

1 **Love: emotion, relationship, action**
2 **Types of love**
3 **Cultural variation**
4 **Love and human development**
5 **Love and human good: the ascent of love**

1 Love: emotion, relationship, action

Love is frequently understood to be a powerful emotion. It seems to involve both intense attachment to an object and a high appraisal of the value of the object. Often, though not always, the object is seen as something one needs in one's own life; for this reason love is often connected with projects of possession or incorporation, and with jealous emotions towards the object seen as separate and capable of frustrating the lover's needs. Spinoza (1677) argued that love involves an awareness of the object as promoting one's own wellbeing (see SPINOZA, B. DE §9). Since all particular objects are, in virtue of their separateness from the self, also capable of frustrating wellbeing, all love, he concluded, is essentially ambivalent, mixed with anger and even hate. One may, however, hold that love is an emotion or emotions while insisting that these emotions can be free from jealousy and possessive desire. Thus Plato, in the *Phaedrus*, imagines love as a powerful response to beauty and value that is linked closely, in good people, to reverence and awe; it thus respects the separateness of the object and seeks its good. These accounts describe different experiences, both of which can be real (as Plato, unlike Spinoza, recognized).

Love is not just an emotion: it can also be a type of relationship. Aristotle, in *Nicomachean Ethics*, insisted that (friendly) love always involves mutual awareness and mutual good will (see FRIENDSHIP; ARISTOTLE §25). While any account of love needs to make room for loves that are unrequited, or directed at objects which cannot reciprocate (infants, some animals) or do not do so clearly (God), Aristotle's insistence on interaction and mutuality provides an important ingredient for a normative account of many types of human love, both friendly and romantic/erotic. Indeed, the refusal to conceive of love in relational terms is a central defect in many instances of erotic love, in which the loved object is indeed treated as an object, to be possessed and immobilized. Although Proust believed that such projects were essential to erotic love, one might doubt this.

Some loves may not involve strong emotion at all. Kant (1797) insisted that 'pathological love' (love involving passive emotion) was inferior to 'practical love', an active attachment to the good of others, including emotions of respect and concern. Whether or not we agree, we should acknowledge that this active practical commitment is one type of love: the love of humanity, for example, may be best understood this way. The Greek Stoics believed that even erotic love could be reimagined in a way that rendered it compatible with the *apatheia*, emotionlessness, proper to the wise (see STOICISM §19). It would be an active enthusiasm about the good of the object, without the currents of agonizing passivity that usually characterize erotic attachment.

2 Types of love

English, like Latin, has only a single term for a large family of different experiences. Other languages, such as ancient Greek and modern Japanese, disambiguate the varieties from the start by the use of different terms. But even in English and Latin, we may distinguish different species of love. Erotic/romantic love is linked closely to sexual desire, while friendly love apparently is not. The love of parents for children and children for parents is frequently thought in the modern era to have an erotic dimension; but this was not the view of most earlier cultures, nor is it likely to be true in cultures where well-off parents rarely saw their children. Ancient Greek culture thought of *eros* as sexual, concerned with possession, and potentially destructive; *philia*, which could obtain between either friends or relations, was seen as mutual and reciprocal, concerned with benefit, and a positive cultural force. Christian *agape* is distinguished from both of these loves by its essentially selfless character; its paradigm is Christ's gift of his life for the redemption of sinful humanity (see CHARITY).

We may also categorize loves by their object-type. We love other people, and it is reasonable to expect that these loves will involve some reciprocity and mutuality. People's loves of animals may be very intense; they vary greatly in the type of reciprocity they offer. People also intensely love inanimate objects such as works of art and natural beauty. Such loves cannot be reciprocal. Love may also take as its object a moral abstraction, such as social justice, or the good of humanity. This type of love is especially well explained on the Stoic/Kantian model, as involving active commitment more than emotion.

The love of God or gods has been understood in many different ways. The Stoics thought that loving God was loving the rational purpose that animates the universe; such a love was best understood as a form of active thought, without any emotional receptivity. Spinoza's *amor intellectualis dei* follows this paradigm. Augustine, criticizing Stoic *apatheia*, insisted that a strongly emotional form of love, mingled with fear, guilt and mourning, is most appropriate to a Christian life (see MORALITY AND EMOTIONS §5). Many Christian thinkers follow his lead. Jewish conceptions of the love of God tend to stress proper action, both ritual and ethical (see RITUAL §§2–3). Modern religious thought continues these debates.

3 Cultural variation

Most societies contain many different types and conceptions of love. But cross-cultural variation also complicates analysis. Societies vary (a) in the behaviour they deem fitting in a relationship of love; thus modern American lovers behave publicly in ways that would have been unthinkable in nineteenth-century India. Variation is also present (b) in the norms societies teach concerning appropriate objects of love; thus fifth-century BC Athens taught young men that it was to be expected that they would have strong erotic desires for both males and females; many modern cultures do not convey this impression. Societies also vary (c) in their normative evaluations of different species of love itself – differing, for example, about whether erotic love is something noble or shameful, good or bad. All these variations can be expected to shape not only concepts but also the experience of love itself.

Most interestingly, societies also vary (d) in the precise taxonomy of types of love their language and form of life display and perpetuate. For example, ancient Greek *eros* is imagined as a terrible power that seizes the personality and causes it to fix on an object with overwhelming intensity. Its goal is taken to be the possession of the object. Medieval courtly love, by contrast, stresses the ideal purity and remoteness of its object and associates love with a tender and refined attention to that object. Those who nowadays have lost the beliefs and forms of life that grounded courtly love cannot experience exactly that passion.

Differences in taxonomy are often revealed and further shaped by differences in terminology: thus the fact that ancient Greeks distinguished *eros* from *philia* and Romans used only the single word *amor* probably shaped thought and experience to at least some extent, although Romans clearly did recognize different varieties of *amor*. (Similarly in the modern world, the fact that Japanese has several distinct words for what English calls 'love' probably reveals some real difference in experience, although these differences should not be overestimated.) In the modern world, understanding of cultural variation is complicated by inter-cultural contact and the translation of formative texts: thus the fact that Japanese *ai* is used to translate biblical *agape* no doubt shapes the evolution of that concept as applied to experience.

4 Love and human development

People begin to have strong emotions before they can move or speak. A human infant's combination of cognitive maturity with physical helplessness gives rise to a complex and ambivalent emotional life, as it sees that the very objects it needs for comfort and survival are also separate and ungovernable. Spinoza's profound conjecture about the relationship between love and anger has by now received much clinical and experimental confirmation. One task of human development is to manage and even surmount this ambivalence, which will exist in many different forms

in different lives, as love is powerfully shaped by the individual identity of the early objects of attachment.

The early experiences that shape the pattern of a person's loves are remembered imperfectly, if at all; even to put them into words is to change them. And yet it seems likely that they shadow one's later experiences. Proust plausibly suggested that when an adult embraces a lover, he or she is at the same time embracing the shadow of an earlier object. Thus Albertine is also the mother whose goodnight kiss the small boy so eagerly awaited. And yet it is difficult to grasp these aspects of oneself; even to the extent that one does, one alters the past by making it definite and articulate. So people's self-knowledge in love is likely to be very imperfect.

5 Love and human good: the ascent of love

Love is generally acknowledged to be a source of beauty and value in life. No philosopher, therefore, has proposed its complete removal. But it is also judged to involve various difficulties for a person aiming at a good and virtuous life. One concern is that love entails partiality: by focusing intensely on the value of a single object, one loses sight of the legitimate claims of other objects and goals (see IMPARTIALITY). A second concern is with excessive neediness: by allowing a single object to become central to one's life, lovers put themselves at the mercy of events that they cannot control, thus sacrificing their dignity and agency. Finally, partly because of this passivity, love is often linked with anger and revenge, whether against the loved object or a rival, or both. A society that wants to reduce anger and violence therefore may have reasons to discourage love.

Philosophers in the Western tradition have therefore been preoccupied with the project of constructing a reform or 'ascent' of love that would enable us to retain its mystery and beauty while purifying it of deforming excesses. For Diotima in Plato's *Symposium*, the ascent centrally involves the idea of an abstract object. Once one understands that the real object of one's love is not a body or even a whole person, but the beauty that is seated in that body or person, then one can begin a process of reform, compared to climbing a ladder, through which one eventually comes to love all the beauty in the universe, and, beyond that, to contemplate the deathless form of the beautiful itself in all its unity. In this way, lovers become invulnerable to life's vicissitudes: the object of their love will never betray or disappoint them.

Christian proponents of a 'ladder' of love tend to criticize the Platonist programme for its goal of personal self-sufficiency. Proper humility requires that one retain a continual awareness of one's incompleteness and neediness. Christian writers also attempt to retain the love of particular individuals as part of purified love.

Spinoza returned to a Platonic proposal for the contemplative reform of love: by focusing on the mind's freedom from external contingencies, one ultimately comes to love the deterministic structure of the entire universe, and one's mind is freed from the passivity and ambivalence that characterize human attachments.

A remarkable modern interpretation of the Platonic tradition can be found in Proust's *À la recherche du temps perdu* (*Remembrance of Things Past*) (1914–27), which asserts that each of a writer's loves is like a step in a ladder that leads him upwards to general forms, in which, alone, his intellect finds comfort and delight. By using one's past experiences of pain and vulnerability as raw material for a creative work of art, one surmounts vulnerability and achieves a kind of freedom from time and death.

None of these reformers likes real human beings very much. This tradition therefore gives rise to a counter-tradition that tries to restore human beings to a greater acceptance of their loves as they are, seeing the interest in ascent as itself a disease that needs curing. Much of this tradition lies outside philosophy. A salient example is Joyce's *Ulysses* (1922), which playfully turns Diotima's ladder upside down, indicating that it is only in the inconstant and flawed emotion of daily life that real love is to be found. By linking religious idealism with anti-Semitism and Bloom's love of the body with a general love of humanity, Joyce indicates, too, that the ascent tradition may be a cause of social hatreds, rather than their cure.

See also: ABRAVANEL, I.; EMOTIONS, NATURE OF; EMOTIONS, PHILOSOPHY OF; FAMILY, ETHICS AND THE; SEXUALITY, PHILOSOPHY OF

References and further reading

* Aristotle (*c.* mid 4th century BC) *Nicomachean Ethics*, trans. with notes by T. Irwin, Indianapolis, IN: Hackett Publishing Company, 1985, books VIII, IX. (On friendly love.)

Augustine (397–401) *Confessionum libri tredecim* (Confessions), trans. F.J. Sheed, Indianapolis, IN: Hackett Publishing Company, 1993. (Argues that highly emotional love is most appropriate to a Christian life.)

—— (413–27) *De civitate Dei* (The City of God), trans. P. Levine, Loeb Classical Library, Cambridge, MA: Harvard University Press, 1966. (Discusses the emotions proper to a Christian life.)

Bowlby, J. (1982) *Attachment and Loss*, New York: Basic Books, 3 vols, 2nd edn. (Important psychological study of development of love in children.)

Cavell, S. (1969) 'The Avoidance of Love: a Reading of King Lear', in *Must We Mean What We Say?*, Cambridge: Cambridge University Press; repr. 1976. (Influential discussion of people's reasons for avoiding love.)

Dante (1313–21) *Divina Commedia*, trans. J. Ciardi, *The Divine Comedy*, New York: E.P. Dutton, 3 vols, 1989. (The most influential medieval Christian account of love, combining theoretical views of Aquinas with insights drawn from the tradition of courtly love.)

Hume, D. (1739/40) *A Treatise of Human Nature*, ed. L.A. Selby-Bigge, revised by P.H. Nidditch, Oxford: Clarendon Press, 2nd edn, 1978. (Important discussions of love and hate.)

* Joyce, J. (1922) *Ulysses*, New York: Modern Library, 1961. (Suggests that real love is to be found only in the flawed emotion of daily life.)

* Kant, I. (1797) *Metaphysische Anfangsgründe der Tugendlehre*, trans. J.W. Ellington, *Metaphysical Principles of Virtue*, Indianapolis, IN: Hackett Publishing Company, 1964. (Discussion of the relationship between love as passion and love as active commitment.)

Klein, M. (1921–45) *Love, Guilt, and Reparation and Other Works, 1921–45*, London: Tavistock, 1985. (Important psychoanalytic treatment of love, envy, guilt.)

Murdoch, I. (1993) *Metaphysics as a Guide to Morals*, New York: Allen Lane, The Penguin Press. (Novelist-philosopher discusses the relationship between love and a vision of the good.)

Nussbaum, M. (1995) '*Eros* and the Wise: The Stoic Response to a Cultural Dilemma', *Oxford Studies in Ancient Philosophy* 13: 231–67. (Discusses the Stoic project of having erotic love without need and vulnerability.)

* Plato (*c.*386–380 BC) *Symposium*, trans. A. Nehamas and P. Woodruff, Indianapolis, IN: Hackett Publishing Company, 1989. (Proposes the ascent of love to contemplation of ideal beauty.)

* —— (*c.*366–360 BC) *Phaedrus*, trans. A. Nehamas and P. Woodruff, Indianapolis, IN: Hackett Publishing Company, 1995. (An account of erotic passion mingled with reverence and awe.)

Price, A. (1989) *Love and Friendship in Plato and Aristotle*, Oxford: Clarendon Press. (Excellent treatment of the texts, with subtle insights about the topic.)

* Proust, M. (1914–27) *À la recherche du temps perdu*, trans. C.K. Scott Moncrieff and T. Kilmartin, *Remembrance of Things Past*, New York: Random

House, Vintage, 1981. (Great philosophical novel analysing love's relation to need, jealousy and artistic creativity.)

* Spinoza, B. (1677) *Ethica Ordine Geometrico Demonstrata* (Ethics Demonstrated in a Geometrical Manner), trans. E. Curley, *Ethics*, Harmondsworth: Penguin, 1996. (Analyses the ambivalent character of human emotion and proposes a process by which we may be freed from bondage to emotion, in favour of the intellectual love of God.)

Vlastos, G. (1973) 'The Individual as Object of Love in Plato's Dialogues', in *Platonic Studies*, Princeton, NJ: Princeton University Press. (Important analysis and criticism of ancient views of love.)

MARTHA C. NUSSBAUM

LÖWENHEIM–SKOLEM THEOREMS AND NON-STANDARD MODELS

Sometimes we specify a structure by giving a description and counting anything that satisfies the description as just another model of it. But at other times we start from a conception we try to articulate, and then our articulation may fail to pin down what we had in mind. Sets seem to have had such a fate. For millennia sets lay fallow in logic, but when cultivated by mathematics in the nineteenth century, they seemed to bear both a foundation and a theory of the infinite. The paradoxes of set theory seemed to threaten this promise. With an eye to proving freedom from paradox, versions of set theory were articulated rigorously. But around 1920, Löwenheim and Skolem proved that no such formalized set theory can come out true only in the hugely infinite world it seemed to reveal, for if it is true in such a world, it will also be true in a world of the smallest infinite size. (Versions of this remain true even if we augment the standard expressive devices used to formalize set theory.) But then, Skolem inferred, we cannot articulate sets determinately enough for them to constitute a firm foundation for mathematics.

1   Background

To see how a model could fail to be standard, one first needs some idea of what a model is supposed to be. The basic distinction here is that between words and the world, signs and things. If the extension (denotation, reference) of each sign in a sentence or collection of sentences is held utterly fixed, and no reinterpretation is allowed at all, then what that sentence or collection commits us to should also be fixed. In that case there is little point in trying to distinguish various ways those sentences might come out true, that is, various models for them. If, in contrast, the extensions of none of the signs are in any way constrained, then just about anything could be gerrymandered into a way of making those sentences come out true. In this case too it seems unlikely that there will be interesting distinctions among the models. So the interest in models for a collection of sentences depends on holding the extensions for some but not all of the signs in those sentences fixed. (See MODEL THEORY.)

In modern algebra, a group is defined as a nonempty set G and a function ∘ such that:

(a) whenever *a*, *b* are in G, so is $a \circ b$;
(b) whenever *a*, *b*, *c* are in G, then $a \circ (b \circ c) = (a \circ b) \circ c$;
(c) there is a member e of G such that $a \circ e = e \circ a = a$ for each a in G; and
(d) for each a in G there is a member a^{-1} of G such that $a \circ a^{-1} = a^{-1} \circ a = e$.

The integers under addition constitute a group. The one-to-one correspondences between a set and itself also form a group under composition of those correspondences. Note that any model for the axioms is a group; there is no question of any groups being somehow standard, and others not. (On the other hand, because addition of integers commutes, that is, $a + b = b + a$, while composition of one-to-one correspondences need not, composition of correspondences illustrates groups in general better than addition of integers.)

If we put the second axiom of groups into the notation of quantification theory, we get

$$(\forall a, b, c)(a, b, c \in G \rightarrow a \circ (b \circ c) = (a \circ b) \circ c).$$

Any choice of a non-empty set for G and a binary function on G for ∘ is a candidate for a structure or interpretation making this axiom true. In this way, the extensions of the signs 'G' and '∘' are allowed a huge range of variation. But those of '∀', '∈', '→' and '=' are held fixed; they must be taken as universal quantification, membership, the conditional, and identity. This mixture of variation and constancy is part of what gives groups an interesting structure.

Modern algebra was a nineteenth-century development, and groups are an artifact of that growth. There was no favoured or intended group to begin with; it is instead the general group structure that proved to be of interest. So there is no distinction between standard and non-standard models of the group axioms.

We think of groups as given by their axioms; they have no life prior to their characterization that would distinguish intended models of that description from unintended ones. But sets probably began life among us as extensions of predicates. On the one side there are predicates like 'is a lion.' On the other, there are the lions. One way words and things link up is that all and only the lions are members of the extension of the predicate 'is a lion.' We take the extension of a predicate as the collection, set or class of all and only the things of which that predicate is true. Disguised as extensions sets led fairly inactive, boring lives in logic for ages.

But around the turn of the nineteenth century, reliance on geometric intuition led analysis, the theory growing out of differential and integral calculus, into paradox; intuition is not always trustworthy on infinitary processes. So a movement arose in nineteenth-century mathematics to replace geometry with arithmetic. We had learned in analytic geometry to individuate a point in the plane by an ordered pair of numbers, the point's abscissa and ordinate. Now we could rethink a literal curve passing (for example, continuously) through such points as some sort of arithmetical law, or even equation, relating the abscissas of such points to their ordinates. This rethinking of analysis is called its arithmetization.

The arithmetization of analysis focused attention on the kind of numbers used as coordinates of points on the plane. Nowadays we call these real numbers; they are the numbers used for lengths, temperatures and many other natural quantities, and given by decimals. Arithmetizing analysis calls for a clear view of the reals and their laws. To those with a taste for abstraction or essence, it even raises the question of what a real number is. Later on in the nineteenth century, Richard Dedekind showed how to answer this question by taking reals as (roughly) certain sets of rational numbers. (One can think of rationals as quotients of integers in lowest terms.) The details to one side, the idea is to rethink reals as certain constructions out of rationals using sets to do the constructing. Such constructions can be shown to satisfy the laws of reals needed to do analysis (see DEDEKIND, J.W.R.).

At that point we seem to be on to something. Reals are constructed from rationals using sets. It is a lot easier to construct rationals from integers (positive, negative and zero) using sets and to construct integers from natural numbers (non-negative whole numbers)

using sets. Then Frege and Cantor seem independently to have got the idea of constructing natural numbers out of sets alone (at least that is how we in hindsight might put it). Sets seem to be becoming the basic stuff of mathematics, so if these sets are the same old extensions of logic, then perhaps, as Frege claimed, mathematics is reducible to logic (see CANTOR, G.; FREGE, G.).

The basic idea was to begin with the as-many-as relation. One set A has as many members as another set B precisely in case there is a binary relation R such that (1) for each $a \in A$ there is exactly one $b \in B$ such that aRb; (2) R matches different members of A with different members of B, and; (3) for each $b \in B$ there is an $a \in A$ such that aRb. Beyond set-membership, only notions of logic (all, some, identity, and so on) are needed for this exposition of as-many-as. But with it, Cantor and Frege could take the number N_A of members of a set A as the set of all sets B with as many members as A, and a number as the number of members of some set (see LOGICISM).

But there is more. Mathematics had always looked to be about things like numbers, of which there are infinitely many, and triangles, of which there are infinitely many and in each of which there are infinitely many points. But mathematics lacked a good general account of the infinite *per se*. Dedekind provided one; a set is infinite precisely in case it has exactly as many members as one of its proper subsets (that is, a set included in but not exhausting the original set). Dedekind's account might have been only a curiosity had Cantor not proved that for each set, even infinite, there is a strictly larger set. At a single stroke, Cantor revealed a wealth of different infinite sizes, and thus a realm of transfinite arithmetic, which Hilbert called Cantor's paradise. Set theory looked to promise both a foundation for mathematics and a whole new mathematics of the infinite (see SET THEORY; CANTOR'S THEOREM; CONTINUUM HYPOTHESIS).

But there were serpents in paradise. Most philosophers have seen Russell's paradox. Cantor's starts from a predicate like 'is a thing' which is true of everything. Every set would have to be a subset of U, the extension of this predicate, and so be no larger than U. But by Cantor's result cited in the previous paragraph, there is a set strictly larger than U. This contradiction together with Russell's and a third due to Burali-Forti constitute the paradoxes of set theory, and around the turn of the twentieth century some regarded these paradoxes as a crisis in the foundation of mathematics (see PARADOXES OF SET AND PROPERTY).

One response to this crisis was to formulate the mathematics at issue with unprecedented rigour. We would be utterly explicit about exactly which signs (i.e., marks) may be written, how these marks may be concatenated, and how such strings may be manipulated. This idea of a formal system had been implicit in Frege, but it acquires a new prominence in Hilbert's programme for responding to the crisis in the foundation of mathematics. For once we have such a formal system we can ask whether anything with the shape of a contradiction can be cranked out by its rules of manipulation. Here we might prescind from all questions about how these marks might be interpreted and focus instead only on which finite combinations of them the rules for their manipulation permit. This latter inquiry sounds like very elementary mathematics indeed. Hilbert's programme might look to show how to use only the most concrete and trustworthy mathematics, combinatorics, to prove the consistency of, and so to that extent legitimate trust in, the most basic (and so most powerful), set theory, at least as formalized (see FORMAL LANGUAGES AND SYSTEMS; HILBERT'S PROGRAMME AND FORMALISM).

But now we have come back to a distinction between words and the world. On the one side, in the world, we have the sets. These are not just any old sets; they are to be a foundation for all of mathematics and to embody a new mathematics of the infinite. We have expectations of these sets; there are, for example, to be enormously many sets, many more than there are natural numbers or even real numbers. So much was promised by Cantor's theorem long before set theory got formalized, or even axiomatized. On the other side, in language, we have formalized set theory. To formalize it means to give its primitive marks and the rules for their manipulation just in terms of their shapes without a thought for how these marks might be assigned things in the world as extensions or interpretations. We want that purely formal presentation in hopes of as concrete and combinatorial a consistency proof for the system as possible. One might have other aims in formalizing, but Hilbert wanted a consistency proof as a *laissez-passer* back into Cantor's paradise. But having made this distinction between words and the world, one then can see the possibility of the words having an interpretation in the world quite different from what was intended.

2 One proof of the Löwenheim–Skolem Theorem

In 1915 Leopold Löwenheim, a secondary school teacher, published a claim that a formula in the calculus of relatives that comes out true under an interpretation in an infinite domain also comes out true under an interpretation in a domain of the smallest infinite size. This size is that of the natural numbers, and domains of that size are called countably infinite. We might now describe the formulas in which Löwenheim was interested as those in which only the truth functional connectives and the quantifiers are interpreted uniformly across domains, that is, non-empty sets; the other signs, that is, constants, function letters and predicate letters, may be interpreted by any member of, or function or relation (of suitable polyadicity) on, any such domain. The consensus nowadays is that Löwenheim failed to prove his claim.

But after the First World War, the Norwegian logician Thoralf Skolem gave two rather different but equally correct proofs of Löwenheim's claim; this is the origin of the Löwenheim–Skolem theorem. Nowadays, one of these arguments is usually presented with a proof of the completeness of quantification theory (first order logic). To show completeness, we start from a valid formula, that is, one true under all interpretations in all non-empty domains, and we must show that it has a proof by the rules of quantification theory. Equivalently by contraposition, we must show that a formula without such a proof fails in some interpretation. For this it suffices to show that any formula that yields no explicit contradiction by the rules is true in some interpretation. We can in fact show that the domain of such an interpretation need be no larger than countably infinite. But any formula true in some hugely infinite domain cannot yield a contradiction by the rules, and so by our result is true in an at most countably infinite domain.

Skolem not only proved Löwenheim's claim: he also strengthened it. For example, the claim holds not just for single formulas, but for countably infinite sets of formulas. Now remember our precisely formalized set theory. As standardly presented, this can be taken as a countably infinite set of sentences in which, over and above logic (which may be taken to include identity), there is only a single binary predicate (intended for the membership relation). Replace this binary predicate by a dyadic predicate letter allowed to be interpreted by any two-place relation on any non-empty domain. We get a set of formulas to which Skolem's strengthening of Löwenheim's result applies. Call this set of formulas the logical skeleton of set theory. It has lost its meat, the real extension of the predicate originally intended for the membership relation. It can be taken as the set of formulas that would be true were the predicate interpreted as intended, not just the theorems of some axiomatization of set theory. If set theory as standardly presented is, interpreted as intended, true, then because of Cantor's result on different infinite sizes, this set of formulas is true in a hugely infinite domain, namely, the world; and so by the Löwenheim–Skolem theorem, it is also true in an at most countably infinite domain. Indeed, since a countable model always has an isomorphic copy in the natural numbers, that countable model can be taken as one on the natural numbers. Hence the logical skeleton of set theory cannot come out true only when it is interpreted as intended in set theory. One might begin to worry whether the laws of sets pin them down determinately enough for them to be a firm foundation for mathematics.

But raising this worry, as we have, with a spotlight on the logical skeleton of set theory suggests a way to assuage it. Surely parallel evolution could result in two very different animals whose skeletons are none the less indistinguishable. If so, an animal's skeleton need not individuate it. Similarly, the wealth of sets comes not from the logical form of (first order) truths about membership, but rather from the nature of membership. For by the Löwenheim–Skolem theorem, the logical forms of the first order truths of set theory come out true in a world vastly smaller than the real world of sets. So those forms alone fail to pin down the full nature of the membership relation, which is what makes the real world so big. That nature cannot be isolated just by the logical form of first order truths about it. Note in this connection that the proof of the Löwenheim–Skolem theorem sketched above makes no use of the huge model it supposes except to infer simple consistency; it constructs the small model from the merely consistent theory alone. Perhaps it is not surprising that with the meat thrown away, bones no longer carry its tang.

3   Another proof of the theorem

But Skolem also proved the theorem in another way that makes much more intimate use of the huge original model. To get the gist, we need the idea of a Skolem function, which is another way of taking a quantifier in a model. A formula, perhaps with free variables, is in prenex form when all its truth functional connectives lie in the scopes of all its quantifiers. There are mechanical routines for finding prenex equivalents of formulas. Take prenex forms for each of the formulas in the logical skeleton T of set theory. Let these formulas be interpreted as intended in a huge domain D of sets on which E is the membership relation, the intended extension of the binary predicate letter that is the only extra-logical sign in T. (There may be a problem here. For model theory to be a theory, the domains of models should be objects we know how to handle. For that reason, they are usually required to be sets. But the standard response to paradoxes like Cantor's is nowadays to

deny that there is a set of all sets. So if D is to be treated by the laws of all sets (as it is), then it had better not exhaust the sets, in which case E cannot be *the* membership relation.) Next we glance at orderings of D. A linear ordering of D is a 2-place relation that arranges its elements as in a straight line; picture the relation of being-to-the-right-of. A well ordering of D is a linear ordering R of D such that every non-empty subset of D has an R-least member, which then by linearity is unique. Being-to-the-right-of is not a well ordering of the points on a line. But an equivalent of the axiom of choice of set theory says there is a well-ordering R of D (see AXIOM OF CHOICE). Pick an arbitrary member d of D for don't-care cases. Let

$$(\forall x)(\exists y)M(x,y,z)$$

be one of our prenex forms, where M is a quantifier free truth functional compound in which only x, y and z are variables. Skolem functions come from existential quantifiers in such prenexes. The existential quantifier binding y lies in the scope of one universal quantifier binding x and in a formula in which z occurs free. So the Skolem function for this quantifier is a two-place function f of the arguments x and z. For any members x and z of D, the value of f at x and z is the R-least member a of D such that $M(x,a,z)$ if there is any such a at all, but d otherwise (the don't-care case). Skolem functions are a little more complex in general, but that is the basic idea.

Take one prenex form for each formula in T. That is a countable infinity of forms, each of which has only finitely many existential quantifiers in its prenex. So there is only a countable infinity of Skolem functions. Pick any countable subset A of D, but toss d into it. Let A_o be A, and for each natural number n, let A_{n+1} be A_n together with all the values of all the Skolem functions on members of A_n. We can show that for each n, A_n is countable, and thus that $D' = A_o \cup A_1 \cup \ldots$ is also countable. D' is also closed under all Skolem functions; that is, if f is a k-adic Skolem function and $d_1, \ldots, d_k \in D'$, then $f(d_1, \ldots, d_k)$ is also in D'. This last is crucial; it comes from the fact that any prenex of any formula is finitely long, which comes from the fact that formulas are of finite size. Now let E' be E cut down to Dr; that is, $aE'b$ if and only if aEb, and a, b are both in Dr. The relation Er on the domain Dr constitutes our new small model of T; it is called the Skolem hull of our huge old model.

A definition of satisfaction converts the extension Er of T's only extra-logical sign into extensions in Dr for each of its formulas. (See TARSKI'S DEFINITION OF TRUTH.) It is only for members of Dr that there is much point in asking whether they do or do not belong to these extensions. Satisfaction also converts

E into extensions in D for formulas of T, and we can compare how these extensions treat objects from the overlap of their domains, namely Dr. Let F be a formula of T in which the variables $x_1, \ldots, x_k$ occur free and let $d_1, \ldots, d_k$ be members of Dr. Then we can show that $d_1, \ldots, d_k$ satisfy F as interpreted by E in D if and only if they satisfy it as interpreted by Er in Dr. The two interpretations agree where both make sense. This includes all sentences of T, so the same sentences of T are true in both. All the truths of set theory were to hold in the big interpretation, so they hold in the smaller one, even the formalization of Cantor's theorem.

This time around Er has been carved directly out of E. All that has been pared away is whatever in D was unnecessary to make the formulas of T true when interpreted by E. But that turns out to be almost all of D. In particular, although a formula of T was intended under E to say that there are more than countably many things (in D), and though E' has enough of E for both to satisfy the same formulas in Dr, that formula intended to assert uncountability is true in Dr even though Dr is countable.

In 1922 Skolem wrote:

> *axiomatizing set theory leads to a relativity of set theoretic notions, and this relativity is inseparably bound up with every thoroughgoing axiomatization. . . .* In order to obtain something absolutely non-denumerable, we would have to have either an absolutely non-denumerably infinite number of axioms or an axiom that could yield an absolutely non-denumerable number of first-order propositions. But this would in all cases lead to a circular introduction of the higher infinites; that is, on an axiomatic basis higher infinites exist only in a relative sense.
>
> (Skolem 1922)

These words are the origin of what has come to be called Skolem's paradox. It is pretty cut and dried what Russell's paradox is, but not Skolem's. Just what distinction between absoluteness and relativity did Skolem intend? Was it to be the same for notions as for existence? How does it line up with the countable/uncountable distinction? Do his results rule axiomatic set theory out as a foundation for mathematics?

These questions might lead us in many directions, but we have space only to gesture in one. When, then, might formulas capture, express or pin down a notion? One fairly evident idea is that they do so just in case all and only the models for those formulas exemplify the notion. In this way, the axioms for a group pin down the notion of a group because the groups are, not surprisingly, the models for those axioms. Perhaps formulas catch a notion absolutely if

all and only the models for those formulas exemplify the notion. Then we note that uncountability is exemplified by some but not all models for T, so T does not capture uncountability absolutely but only, Skolem may have meant, at best relatively. (Maybe, but now there seem to be many things he might have meant.) Any first order theory with uncountable models also has countable models, so no first order theory guarantees that its models are countable, and thus satisfaction of a first order theory does not guarantee the existence of an uncountable infinity. But satisfaction of the axioms of a group does guarantee the existence of a group. Some such contrast may be what Skolem meant by calling the existence of uncountable infinities relative.

4   One try at a solution to the paradox

Skolem seems to have had it in for set theory. But maybe the Löwenheim–Skolem theorem reveals not so much flaws in axiomatic set theory as limitations in the expressive powers of first order logical notation. Skolem's words above hint that only a somehow question begging uncountable infinity of notations could guarantee uncountability in models of those notations. The circle is too faint. Is it vicious to use ink to describe ink, or to describe finitude in finitely many words? The hint seems suspect. Add to the notation a new quantifier 'Ux' such that '$(Ux)Fx$' is true only in a domain with uncountably many members that satisfy F, and count as models only interpretations that verify '$(Ux)(x = x)$'. Would limiting ourselves to such models be any more circular than limiting ourselves to models without non-self-identical members?

Second order quantification is quantification into the positions of predicates, rather than singular terms, in sentences. (See SECOND-ORDER LOGIC, PHILOSOPHICAL ISSUES IN.) Such quantification might seem less obtrusive than uncountable individual quantification, but it also lets us say that there are uncountably many things, though framing the claim calls for a bit more ingenuity. But if the domains of models for formulas with quantifiers of either sort must be sets, then discourse with either sort of quantifier is subject to generalized versions of Löwenheim–Skolem. Formal languages are usually distinguished by choices among countable infinities of individual constants, predicate letters and function signs. If so, there are only as many such languages as there are reals, and though there are lots of reals, they make up a set. So there are only that many theories, and thus satisfiable theories, too. To each such satisfiable theory assign the least cardinal that is the size of the domain of a model of the theory; all sets have cardinals, so if domains must be sets, this assignment works. Then (by the axiom of replacement) there is a set of all these least cardinals, and so a smallest cardinal greater than all of them. Whether we allow uncountable individual or second order quantification, this cardinal is to those theories as the cardinal next after that of the natural numbers is to first order theories according to the Löwenheim–Skolem theorem. For each is a size smaller than that of the intended world of set theory, yet each is a size larger than that of a world in which set theory comes out true. So long as the domains of models must be sets and languages distinguished by choices from a set of primitives, some such result seems inevitable whatever expressive devices we allow our languages; but if the domains need not be sets, it is unclear what they might be and how we might handle them.

See also: LOGICAL AND MATHEMATICAL TERMS, GLOSSARY OF

References and further reading

Chang, C.C. and Keisler, H.J. (1973) *Model Theory*, Amsterdam: North Holland, 3rd edn, 1990, 141–2. (The authors present a quick but contemporary version of Skolem functions and hulls.)

Fraassen, B.C. van (1971) *Formal Semantics and Logic*, New York: Macmillan, 122–5. (The author presents a tidy exposition of Skolem hulls.)

Hart, W.D. (1970) 'Skolem's Promises and Paradoxes', *Journal of Philosophy* (1970), 98–109. (An exposition and discussion of the paradox from a Platonist perspective.)

Quine, W.V. (1976) 'Ontological Reduction and the World of Numbers', in *The Ways of Paradox and Other Essays*, revised edn, Cambridge, MA: Harvard University Press, esp. 212–20. (Unlike Skolem, Quine worries about whether the theorem shows that Pythagoras was right and only numbers exist.)

Skolem, T. (1920) 'Logico-Combinatorial Investigations in the Satisfiability or Provability of Mathematical Propositions', in J. van Heijenoort (ed.) *From Frege to Gödel: A Source Book in Mathematical Logic, 1879–1931*, Cambridge, MA: Harvard University Press, 1967, 252–63. (Skolem proves the version of the theorem using the axiom of choice.)

* —— (1922) 'Some Remarks on Axiomatized Set Theory', in J. van Heijenoort (ed.) *From Frege to Gödel: A Source Book in Mathematical Logic, 1879–1931*, Cambridge, MA: Harvard University Press, 1967, 290–310. (Skolem proves the version of the theorem without the axiom of choice. This paper contains his original presentation of his paradox.)

Tarski, A. and Vaught, R. (1956) 'Arithmetical Extensions of Relational Systems', *Compositio Mathematica* (1956), 81–102. (The authors set out the basics of the contemporary understanding of how Skolem functions and hulls work.)

W.D. HART

LU HSIANG-SHAN
see LU XIANGSHAN

LU XIANGSHAN (1139–93)

A leading Chinese philosopher of the twelfth century, Lu Xiangshan was the founder of that dimension of neo-Confucian thought known as the learning of the heart-and-mind. Lu emphasized the necessity for personal responsibility and action in everyday affairs, as opposed to the search for moral understanding through classical texts.

Lu Xiangshan (named Jiuyuan, styled Zijing and popularly called Xiangshan) was a leading thinker of the Song dynasty (960–1279) philosophical movement commonly called neo-Confucianism (see NEO-CONFUCIAN PHILOSOPHY). He is considered the founder of that dimension of neo-Confucianism known as the learning of the heart-and-mind (see XIN) and was an important rival of ZHU XI, the pre-eminent twelfth-century philosopher and advocate of the learning of principle. Lu came from a large, multi-generational, elite family in south China that engaged in a medicinal drug trade, farming, local defence, social welfare projects and Confucian education. He attained the highest degree, served briefly but vigorously in office, and was famous for his teaching. His few writings, recorded sayings and biography are collected in the *Xiangshan quanji* (The Complete Works of Lu Xiangshan).

Critical of contemporary scholars' preoccupation with the civil service examinations and speculative ontological thought concerning *li* (principle(s) or pattern(s) of things) and *qi* (matter–energy) (see LI; QI), Lu focused on actual human experience. Reflecting the importance of the *Yijing* (Book of Changes) (see YIJING) and MENCIUS in his thought, his primary concerns were the principles ordering the world (human society and nature) and the necessity for assuming personal responsibility for moral-social action.

Lu maintained that there is only one principle in

(and one ordering source of) the universe. Shared by the 'three ultimates' of heaven, earth and humanity, this principle orders all things and affairs. It is the Way, the heart-and-mind, and human nature, and (as *qi*) does not exist apart from the world. Lu summarized his position in such claims as 'the heart-and-mind is principle' and 'my heart-and-mind and the universe are one'. This principle is public-mindedness and moral rightness, in contrast to selfishness and private profit.

Lu stressed the necessity to take responsibility for one's actions and to pursue Confucian learning in order to develop and implement one's moral-social nature. Emphasizing inner, natural capacities over outer, textual knowledge, Lu taught people to distinguish between morality and selfishness and to establish their aim. Echoing Mencius, he called this effort 'establishing one's greater part' (that is, the heart-and-mind). This kind of knowing was completed by moral-social action. In addition, a person should engage in constant self-examination and self-correction, while seeking help from reading and teachers and friends.

Scholars disagree about the interpretation of Lu's thought. Although some describe it as monism and subjective idealism, these Western labels are highly misleading because Lu was not concerned with the kinds of philosophical questions they imply, such as fundamental substances of being, objective–subjective reality, mind as consciousness and the unreliability of sensory knowledge.

See also: NEO-CONFUCIAN PHILOSOPHY; SELF-CULTIVATION IN CHINESE PHILOSOPHY

List of works

Lu Xiangshan (*c.*1150–90) *[Lu] Xiangshan [xiansheng] quanji* (Complete Works of Master Lu Jiuyuan). (Collected writings in 34 chapters published in 1212, recorded sayings in 2 chapters published in 1237, complete works in 36 chapters pub. in 1521 and 1559. There are three modern 'editions', the Sibu beiyao edition, the Sibu congkan edition and the Guoxue jiben congshu edition.

References and further reading

de Bary, W.T., Chan Wing-tsit and Watson, B. (1960) *Sources of Chinese Tradition*, New York: Columbia University Press, vol. 1, ch. 18, 509–14. (Selected translations with an emphasis on universal mind and intuition, in contrast to Zhu Xi.)

Cady, L. (1939) 'The Philosophy of Lu Hsiang-shan,

A Neo-Confucian Monistic Idealist', unpublished Ph.D. dissertation, Union Theological Seminary. (Numerous translations, a comprehensive discussion of life, thought and contexts, with Lu viewed as a monistic idealist.)

Chan Wing-tsit (1963) *A Source Book in Chinese Philosophy*, Princeton, NJ: Princeton University Press, ch. 33, 572–87. (Selected translations and brief comments; Lu is viewed as an idealist, in contrast to Zhu Xi.)

—— (1989) *Chu Hsi: New Studies*, Honolulu, HI: University of Hawaii Press, ch. 26, 435–61. (Discussion of Zhu and Lu's personal relationship.)

Chang, C. (1957) *The Development of Neo-Confucian Thought*, New York: Bookman Associates, vol. 1, ch. 13, 285–307; 2nd edn, 1962. (Summary of Lu's life and thought, selected translations and the debate with Zhu Xi; Lu is viewed here as an idealist.)

Ching, J. (1974) 'The Goose Lake Monastery Debate (1175)', *Journal of Chinese Philosophy* 1 (2): 161–78. (Translations and discussion of Zhu and Lu's meeting.)

Foster, R.W. (1987) 'Differentiating Rightness from Profit: The Life and Thought of Lu Jiuyuan (1139–1193)', unpublished PhD. dissertation, Harvard University. (Examination of Lu's ethical philosophy and its political application.)

Fung Yu-lan (1952–3) *A History of Chinese Philosophy*, trans. D. Bodde, Princeton, NJ: Princeton University Press, vol. 2, ch. 14, 572–92. (Discussion and selected translations, giving an idealist and subjective interpretation of Lu's thought.)

Huang, S. (1944) *Lu Hsiang-shan: A Twelfth Century Chinese Idealist Philosopher*, New Haven, CN: American Oriental Society. (General introduction to Lu's thought, context and influence; he is viewed here as a monistic idealist.)

Hymes, R. (1989) 'Lu Chiu-yuan, Academies, and the Problem of the Local Community', in W.T. de Bary and J.W. Chaffee (eds) *Neo-Confucian Education: The Formative Stage*, Berkeley, CA: University of California Press, ch. 16, 432–56. (Discussion of Lu in the context of social institutions.)

Kim, O.C. (1980) 'Chu Hsi and Lu Hsiang-shan: A Study of Philosophical Achievements and Controversy in Neo-Confucianism', unpublished Ph.D. dissertation, University of Iowa. (Emphasis on the this-worldly focus of Lu's thought and contexts, rejects idealist and monistic interpretations; good bibliography.)

Tillman, H.C. (1992) *Confucian Discourse and Chu Hsi's Ascendancy*, Honolulu, HI: University of Hawaii Press, 187–234. (Discussion of life and thought from historical perspective, rejecting interpretation of extreme philosophical subjectivism, and also describes Zhu and Lu's debates; good bibliography.)

ANNE D. BIRDWHISTELL

LUCIAN (*c.* AD 120–80)

Lucian of Samosata (in ancient Syria) was one of the most original and engaging figures of post-classical Greek culture. He produced a diverse and influential corpus comparable in size to that of Plato (consisting of seventy-six authentic libelli). Formally the dialogue (in both Platonic and Cynic forms) dominates (thirty-six of seventy-three prose works), but there are also satiric narratives, tall tales (for example, A True Story*), 'Cynic' diatribes (for example,* On Mourning*), and multifarious lectures, or essays (for example,* The Master of Rhetoric*) in his singular* oeuvre.

Like other Greek writers in the Empire, Lucian is difficult to classify generically or ideologically. Who was this jester from the East, who dared ape the classics and yet succeeded in persuading posterity that he was, in the words of Macaulay, 'the last great master of Attic eloquence and Attic wit' (Macaulay)? A Hellenized Syrian of the Christian era who made Greek culture come to life as if were contemporary (Duncan 1979), Lucian was, none the less, not an absolute traditionalist: he parodied the classicizing literary fashions of Greeks in the Empire (such as 'Atticism' in *Lexiphanes*) and treated Greek ethnocentrism and the easy idealization of the classical past as targets ripe for satire (see for example, *Anacharsis, and Philosophers for Sale!*). Although long associated with philosophy, he was not a philosopher but a sophist, satirist and parodist, who, following Plato, the Cynics (for example, Menippus), and the Old Comic poets (for example, Aristophanes), took philosophers and their discourse as one of his principal subjects in a lengthy career as a writer and performer giving public readings of his work throughout the Roman Empire.

Lucian's work is philosophically significant in at least three senses. First, it is a source of ostensibly 'eye-witness' accounts of contemporary philosophical and religious figures, such as, the Cynic/Socratic Demonax of Cyprus, whom Lucian claimed as a teacher (in his *Life of Demonax*), the notorious Cynic Peregrinus of Parium and the 'false-prophet' Alexander of Abonoteichus, all of whom were extremely influential figures in their day and were, as such, mercilessly anatomized by Lucian in satiric

narratives (*On the Death of Peregrinus, Alexander or the False-Prophet*) in which Democritus and Epicurus provide the philosophical armature. Second, he provides a general commentary on and evaluation of the reception of classical philosophical traditions in the polyglot cultural landscape of the Roman Empire. Lucian is suspicious of the inflated value of tradition(s) in a classicizing culture; accordingly, two works satirize the experience of 'conversion' to classical philosophical traditions (to Platonism in the *Nigrinus*, to Stoicism in the *Hermotimus* (compare *The Cynic*)). Similarly, the hilarious *Philosophers for Sale!*, in which the founding fathers of Greek philosophy are auctioned off as slaves, uses parody and caricature to satirize *all* the idols of the philosophers' tribe. (Lucian takes no prisoners: neither Diogenes the Cynic nor Pyrrho the Sceptic is spared satiric scrutiny, despite their own credentials as critics of philosophy.) The philosophical import of texts in these first two categories is more or less overt and explicit. Third, there are the philosophical implications of his practice as a seriocomic (*spoudogeloios*) writer of dialogue, satire and parody, which are generally Cynical or Sceptical in tendency. For example, in the *Anacharsis* two legendary sages (Solon the Athenian and Anacharsis the Scythian) engage in dialogue but, instead of generating philosophical insight, seem to speak past each other, unable to inhabit a culturally alien point of view. Similarly, in his *Symposium* Lucian constructs an ironic counter-image to the myth of philosophy as an ascent to timeless wisdom memorialized by Plato in his own *Symposium*.

While Lucian's parodic treatment of philosophers and their discourse makes him indispensable reading for any student of the history of philosophy, the value of good parody resists summary by its very form, as does a literary repertoire of over 170 characters. Lucian's own philosophical stance is consequently elusive and is never stated directly (even in the *Demonax*). If we consider his *oeuvre* as a whole, however, there are clear patterns of aversion and affinity. Lucian is attracted to Epicureanism for its rational hedonism and critique of religious ideology (see EPICUREANISM); to Cynics for their courageous practice of *parrhēsia* ('free speech') – the moral basis of satire – and their unflinchingly satiric perspective on the *ancien régime* (see CYNICS); to Pyrrhonism for its 'suspension of judgment' on such questions as the value of philosophy as an activity or an institution (see PYRRHONISM). It makes sense, therefore, that Lucian has been of most interest to satirists (for example, Rabelais, Jonson, Swift, Voltaire), sceptics (for example, HUME) and highly literary thinkers of sceptical tendency (for example, MONTAIGNE,

DIDEROT) who do not fit easily into the history of philosophy. Lucian was taken up as a model of the witty, erudite cultural critic by Renaissance Humanists and is historically significant for transmitting Cynic and Sceptic tradition to Europe (see HUMANISM, RENAISSANCE §6). David Hume is said to have read Lucian's comic *Dialogues of the Gods* on his deathbed. In an age as awash in parody, cynicism and religious entrepreneurs as it is alienated from its own traditions, Lucian is finding new audiences.

See also: CYNICS §4

List of works

Lucian (*c.* AD 140–80) Works, trans. A.M. Harmon, K. Kilburn and M.D. Macleod, Loeb Classical Library, Cambridge, MA: Harvard University Press and London: Heinemann, 1913–17, 8 vols; trans. H.W. Fowler and F.G. Fowler, Oxford: Clarendon Press, 1905, 4 vols. (The former includes parallel Greek text and English translation; the latter is an almost complete English translation by two masters of English prose.)

References and further reading

Branham, R.B. (1989) *Unruly Eloquence: Lucian and the Comedy of Traditions*, Cambridge, MA: Harvard University Press. (Analyses Lucian's use of literary and philosophical traditions focusing on the idea of the seriocomic or *spoudogeloios.*)

Clay, D. (1992) 'Lucian of Samosata: Four Philosophical Lives (Nigrinus, Demonax, Peregrinus, Alexander Pseudomantis)', in W. Haase (ed.) *Aufstieg und Niedergang der römischen Welt*, Berlin: de Gruyter, II 36: 5, 3406–50. (Analyses Lucian's *Nigrinus, Demonax, Peregrinus,* and *Alexander.*)

* Duncan, D. (1979) *Ben Jonson and the Lucianic Tradition*, Cambridge: Cambridge University Press. (Studies Lucian's reception in Renaissance England.)

Jones, C.P. (1986) *Culture and Society in Lucian*, Cambridge, MA: Harvard University Press. (Places Lucian in his historical context.)

Niehues-Pröbsting, H. (1979) *Der Kynismus des Diogenes und der Begriff des Zynismus* (The Cynicism of Diogenes and the [Modern] Concept of Cynicism), Munich: Wilhelm Fink. (The best account of the whole Cynic tradition (ancient and modern) in one volume; contains a brilliant analysis of Lucian's *Peregrinus* and of the relation of ancient Cynicism to modern cynicism.)

Relihan, J.C. (1992) *Ancient Menippean Satire*, Baltimore, MD: Johns Hopkins University Press.

(The best history of the genre; includes close readings of Lucian's Menippean pieces.)

Robinson, C. (1979) *Lucian and his Influence in Europe*, Chapel Hill, NC: University of North Carolina Press. (Surveys Lucian's reception in Europe.)

Sloterdijk, P. (1988) *Critique of Cynical Reason*, trans. M. Eldred, London: Verso. (An influential interpretation of Cynicism focusing on the relation of ancient Cynicism to modern cynicism; includes a discussion of Lucian's *Peregrinus.*)

R. BRACHT BRANHAM

LUCRETIUS (*c.*94–*c.*55 BC)

Titus Lucretius Carus was a Roman Epicurean philosopher and poet. About his life and personality little can be said with certainty, yet his only known work, 'On the Nature of Things' (De rerum natura), is of considerable size and one of the most brilliant achievements of Latin poetry. A didactic poem in six books, it expounds Epicurean physics. Its manifesto is to abolish the fear of gods and of death by demonstrating that the soul is mortal and the world not governed by gods but by mechanical laws.

The two main biographical sources – St Jerome, and the *Life of Virgil* attributed to Donatus – are unreliable and often inconsistent. The one near-contemporary reference to Lucretius is a letter of Cicero's written in 54 BC, revealing that he and his brother had read and admired the poem. All that we can say with confidence about Lucretius' life is that he lived in the earlier half of the first century BC. He was probably a member of the aristocratic family the Lucretii. Some take the cognomen Carus as testimony that he was a freedman or a slave. However, the dedication of his poem to one Memmius is strong evidence that he was, or aspired to be, a friend of C. Memmius, the wealthy patron of the poets Cinna and Catullus. Much more suspect is Jerome's story of Lucretius' madness caused by a love potion, and of his eventual suicide. Although now rightly rejected, the story was influential in Lucretian criticism, confirming for some the poet's profound pessimism.

The strongest evidence that at Lucretius' death the poem had not received its final revision is V 155, where he makes a promise, nowhere redeemed, of a full treatment of the nature of the gods. Whether other features, such as repeated lines and passages, are also evidence of its unfinished state is more disputed. But since Lucretius states at VI 92–5 that Book VI is to conclude the work, the poem cannot be substantially incomplete.

Lucretius writes as what the Romans called a 'learned poet'. He was a highly educated writer, whose sources of inspiration lay largely in Greek literature. The poem itself belongs to the tradition of didactic poetry, which stemmed from Hesiod's *Works and Days*, although a more direct model is the physical poem of Empedocles, *On Nature* (see HESIOD; EMPEDOCLES). He also shows debts to satire, epic and tragedy. Although complaining about the 'poverty' of the Latin language, Lucretius shows skill in adapting existing words to new concepts. His poetical expressions include archaism and periphrasis, but also formal expository devices based on Epicurean methods of argumentation.

The poem is divided into three pairs of books. Books I and II analyse the infinite universe into its microscopic components, atoms and void, refute rival theories of the elements, and show how atoms combine to produce the familiar phenomenal world. The next pair moves up to the human level. Book III covers the soul and its mortality, culminating in an eloquent denunciation of the fear of death. Book IV explains cognitive and other vital functions, ending with a diatribe against sexual passion. Finally, Books V and VI seek to demystify the world as a whole. The former explains its origin and future destruction, its structure and early human history. The latter accounts naturalistically for a comprehensive series of phenomena, from earthquakes to magnets.

In a pair of famous metaphors, Lucretius describes himself as 'traversing the pathless haunts of the Pierides [that is, Muses], where no one's foot has trodden before' (I 921–50), and as planting his feet in the precise tracks which Epicurus has marked for him (III 3–4). In short, he regards himself a faithful Epicurean, but as breaking new ground in his use of poetry. A central question of Lucretian criticism has long been the relationship between poetry and philosophy. It has been doubted whether strict Epicurean philosophy approved of poetry, but the evidence for this is inconclusive at best. Lucretius himself regards his subject matter as off-puttingly obscure, yet essential to human happiness. He therefore compares his use of poetry to the honey which doctors smear on the lip of a cup of bitter medicine in order to trick children into drinking it, for their own greater good. Epicurus is the saviour of mankind, whose philosophy alone can free us from the shackles of religion and from terror at the prospect of death. Both the formal addressee Memmius and the intended wider readership are novices in Epicureanism. Lucretius attracts them in at the beginning with a traditional hymn to Venus, then proceeds to lead them systematically through his arguments about the world's nature and structure. But at the end he confronts them with a disturbing account of the great plague at Athens, which might be regarded as a final test.

Lucretius' poem concentrates on physics, but important ethical statements are made in the proems to several books and in the concluding parts of Books III, IV and V. He makes many notable contributions to our understanding and appreciation of Epicureanism. For instance, at II 216–93 he offers the only detailed surviving argument for the 'swerve' of atoms, which in Epicureanism underpins free will. Book III's concluding diatribe against the unacknowledged source of most human misery, the fear of death, is especially celebrated. And the history of early human civilization in Book V has been much admired, especially for its reconstructions of the origins of society, language and justice.

In the world of Latin Christianity, Lucretius became the leading voice of Epicureanism, much quoted and vilified as an enemy of religion. He was widely read and studied in the Renaissance, with a tendency to Christianization of his thought (see RENAISSANCE PHILOSOPHY). He remains a primary source for our knowledge of Epicurean physics.

See also: ATOMISM, ANCIENT

List of works

Lucretius (c.55 BC) *On the Nature of Things*, ed. C. Bailey, *Titi Lucreti Cari De rerum natura libri sex*, Oxford: Oxford University Press, 3 vols, 1947; trans. R.E. Latham, revised by J. Godwin, *Lucretius On the Nature of the Universe*. London: Penguin, 1994; trans. W.H.D. Rouse, revised M.F. Smith, *Lucretius, De rerum natura*, Loeb Classical Library, Cambridge, MA: Harvard University Press and London: Heinemann, 1975. (Bailey is the monumental standard edition, with text, translation and commentary, still highly informative and not fully superseded; Latham offers a serviceable English translation; Rouse/Smith a conservative text with good facing English translation.)

References and further reading

Boyancé, P. (1963) *Lucrèce et l'épicurisme*, Paris: Presses Universitaires de France. (A classic study of Lucretius as poet and philosopher.)

Clay, D. (1983) *Lucretius and Epicurus*, Ithaca, NY, and London: Cornell University Press. (One of the best-integrated philosophical studies of Lucretius' poetry.)

Erler, M. (1994), 'Epikur; Die Schule Epikurs;

Lukrez' (Epicurus; The School of Epicurus; Lucretius), in H. Flashar (ed.) *Die Philosophie der Antike, Band 4: Die Hellenische Philosophie*, Basle: Schwabe, 381–490. (Informative about Lucretius and his philosophy, with extensive bibliography.)

Long, A.A. and Sedley, D.N. (1987) *The Hellenistic Philosophers*, Cambridge: Cambridge University Press, 2 vols. (Discussion of various passages of Lucretius in their philosophical context.)

Segal, C. (1990) *Lucretius on Death and Anxiety*, Princeton, NJ: Princeton University Press. (A study of Lucretius' poetry and thought, centred on Book III.)

MICHAEL ERLER

LUKÁCS, GEORG (1885–1971)

Lukács' Geschichte und Klassenbewusstsein (History and Class Consciousness) (1923) is, for both its intrinsic merits and its enormous influence, the most important work of Marxist philosophy to have appeared in the twentieth century. It sought to render explicit the dependence of Marx's thought on Hegel's dialectic as a means of elucidating both the distinctive character of historical materialism as a form of theoretical inquiry and its revolutionary rejection of the modes of thinking prevailing in capitalist society. Lukács' general aim had been shared by the authors of the first philosophical reflections on Marx's project – Engels and Plekhanov, for example, had stressed its debt to Hegel. Lukács, however, sought to draw Marx into that broad current of twentieth-century Continental thought which has drawn a sharp distinction between the methods of the physical sciences, suitable at best for analysing inanimate nature, and those of the human sciences, whose aim is to interpret human actions in the light of the thoughts which move them. Thus Lukács sees Marx as the theorist, not of the laws of the dialectic or of inevitable social transformation, but of revolutionary subjectivity, of the proletariat as 'the identical subject– object' of history. This was a version of Marxism which suited the times, in the immediate aftermath of the Russian Revolution of October 1917. As the revolutionary tides receded, Lukács found philosophical and political reasons for retreating to a more orthodox historical materialism which laid much greater stress on objective constraints and processes than his version of the early 1920s had. Yet the force of its overall argument and the quality of its individual analyses have made History and Class Consciousness *a constant reference-point in subsequent discussions of Marxist theory.*

1 Life
2 *History and Class Consciousness*
3 Lukács as an orthodox communist

1 Life

Lukács is perhaps the only major Marxist philosopher to have had a significant intellectual career prior to his becoming a Marxist. He later described his youthful views as 'romantic anti-capitalism' – a rejection of existing society based on nostalgia for a past believed to be less fragmented and individualist than the present. The sources of this outlook are no doubt connected to the tensions in Lukács' own background. He was born in Budapest on 13 April 1885, the son of a successful self-made Jewish banker. The predominantly Jewish business class were outsiders in a Hungary still dominated by the gentry, a fact which perhaps helps to explain what Lukács was to call his 'passionate rejection of the order then existing in Hungary', expressed, for example, in an enthusiasm for the revolutionary poetry of Endre Ady. The prime philosophical influences on Lukács were, however, German. He took part in the Heidelberg Circle which Max Weber gathered around him between 1906 and 1918 (see WEBER, M. §1). Lukács' pre-Marxist writings, of which the most notable was *Die Theorie des Romans* (The Theory of the Novel) (1916), are permeated by the ideas of members of the circle such as Georg SIMMEL. They combine a strongly critical attitude towards a modernity conceived as rationalized and soulless with a Neo-Kantian insistence on sharply distinguishing between facts and values, so that authentic values are held to be incapable of achieving practical realization.

Lukács' decision to join the new Hungarian communist party in December 1918 and his participation in its abortive attempt to take power at the beginning of 1919 reflected the belief that this 'tragic' antinomy could after all be overcome, that socialist revolution could bring into being a society which would not suffer from the disharmonies characteristic of modern capitalism. Exiled after the failure of the 1919 Revolution, Lukács was for the rest of his life a leading figure in the international communist movement, indeed he was a party functionary until he took up academic positions after his return to Hungary in 1945.

Controversy, however, dogged his career as a communist. Initially, he was a 'left communist', on the wing of the communist international which demanded an unremitting revolutionary offensive against capitalism. *Geschichte und Klassenbewusstsein* (History and Class Consciousness) (1923), Lukács' masterwork, is arguably still infused with the Messianic hopes which inspired his original adhesion to communism. Its hostile reception in the communist press was, however, one sign of the consolidation of a new 'Leninist' orthodoxy to which Lukács progressively adapted himself. Although *History and Class Consciousness* had an enormous impact on German intellectual life under the Weimar republic (to the extent that Lukács' admirer Lucien Goldmann claimed that Heidegger's *Being and Time* (1927) was, in part, a response), Lukács soon began to distance himself from his book. He always insisted that his reasons for doing so were philosophical (see §3). Certainly, he stuck by the views which he first formulated in the mid-1920s – which involved, in stark contrast to his youthful writings, an emphasis on the positive virtues of bourgeois civilization and on the continuities between them and those of a socialist society – even when it was politically dangerous to do so. Lukács' participation in Imre Nagy's government during the Hungarian Revolution of 1956 nearly cost him his life. Some commentators, however, believe that, in the very last years before his death on 4 June 1971, Lukács, under the impact of the student revolts in the West and in reaction to the 1968 invasion of Czechoslovakia, was returning to the more revolutionary Marxism of his youth.

2 *History and Class Consciousness*

History and Class Consciousness may be seen as the most powerful philosophical expression of a general revolt against the dominant form of Marxism in the Second International (1889–1914). Antonio GRAMSCI called the Bolshevik Revolution of October 1917 'The Revolution against *Capital*'; the victory of socialist revolution in a backward country overturned the Marxist orthodoxy formulated by theorists such as Karl KAUTSKY and Georgii PLEKHANOV according to which history proceeded by natural necessity according to deterministic economic laws. Both Lukács and Gramsci were influenced by Georges SOREL, for whom revolution was an act of collective will.

However, rather than abandon Marxism as Sorel did, Lukács sought to reformulate it in terms consistent with this conception of revolution. This involved, in the first place, an identification of orthodoxy with method. Marxism could not be equated with any specific theoretical proposition, even the claim that production provides social life with its foundation. Famously Lukács took this to the extreme of asserting that 'if recent research had disproved once and for all every one of MARX's individual theses' (1923: 1), the truth of Marxism itself would be unaffected.

The distinctive feature of the Marxist method,

according to Lukács, is that it conceives the different elements of social life, not as isolated fragments, but as aspects of an integrated whole. '*The primacy of the category of totality is the bearer of the principle of revolution in science*' (1923: 27; original emphasis). This assertion is a variation on HEGEL's declaration that 'the True is the whole'. Lukács further took from Hegel the idea that it is possible to know the totality only because the subject and object of knowledge are identical: 'consciousness here is not the knowledge of an opposed object but is the self-consciousness of the object' (1923: 178). Therefore, 'reality can only be understood and penetrated as a totality, and only a subject which is itself a totality is capable of this penetration' (1923: 39).

Lukács' appropriation of Hegel provides the basis of the critique of bourgeois thought and society which forms the leitmotif of the central essay in *History and Class Consciousness*, 'Reification and the Consciousness of the Proletariat'. Capitalism is precisely a form of society which operates as if it were not a totality. Taking over and integrating into a Marxist framework the ideas of Weber and Simmel, Lukács depicts a society in which quantity increasingly drives out quality and where instrumental rationality reigns: individual aspects of social life may be modernized and subjected to bureaucratic procedures, but the relationships which bind these together into a whole are incomprehensible. But whereas Weber conceived this process of rationalization as an inescapable consequence of the triumph of modernity, Lukács treats it as a developed form of what Marx in *Capital* calls commodity fetishism (see MARX, K. §10). It is distinctive of capitalism, Marx argues, that social relationships among human beings take on the form of relationships between things. The exchange of commodities on the market rules people's lives, setting a price on their labour power and, in times of economic crisis, perhaps condemning them to unemployment and poverty. Lukács takes over this idea and develops it into the idea of a process of 'reification' permeating the whole of social life. Even the most advanced forms of modern philosophy from Descartes to Kant are scarred by commodity fetishism, and in particular by their inability to grasp society as a whole. Hegel alone recognized that the social totality could only be understood as and by a total subject, but expressed this thought in the mystified form of the concept of Absolute Spirit.

Lukács' solution to what he calls 'the antinomies of bourgeois thought' involved, once again, making strategic use of Marx's *Capital*. Capitalist exploitation depends, according to Marx, on the transformation of labour power, or the ability to work, into a commodity bought and sold for the market. For

Marx the chief interest of this state of affairs lies in the way that it makes possible, he believes, the extraction of surplus value from the worker. For Lukács, however, it is of significance chiefly as the limit-point of reification: the workers – that is, the bulk of humanity – are transformed into saleable objects. But, since the exploitation that follows is the presupposition of the entire network of commodity relationships constituting capitalist society, the worker is the pivot of this society. It follows, Lukács believes, that only the working class is in a position to comprehend capitalist society as a totality. For 'the worker can only become conscious of his existence in society when he becomes aware of himself as a commodity'. Therefore, 'his consciousness is *the self-consciousness of the commodity*; or in other words it is the self-knowledge, the self-revelation of the capitalist society founded upon the production and exchange of commodities' (1923: 168; original emphasis).

The proletariat is thus the total subject required to understand society as a totality, because knowing its own position involves knowing the set of relations of which, as absolute commodity, it is the source. It is, therefore, 'the identical subject–object of the social and historical processes of evolution'. Further, it is this peculiar status of the working class which makes historical materialism possible. Marx and his successors theoretically articulated the self-understanding of the proletariat. They were able to do so, despite their usually not being workers themselves, because this self-understanding depends on the objective position of the proletariat in capitalist society. There is, in principle, a distinction between the class consciousness that can be imputed to workers on the basis of this position and their actual beliefs and desires. Moreover, the process through which workers become aware of their real situation in society is primarily an intellectual one. None the less, 'the consciousness of the proletariat must become deed' (1923: 178). Lukács believes that this is partly because workers becoming self-aware will have practical consequences: '*the act of consciousness overthrows the objective form of its object*' (1923: 178; original emphasis). At the same time, the very process of class struggle in which workers are compelled to engage by their economic circumstances will transform their consciousness. In this way the reified structures of capitalist society will be broken up.

History and Class Consciousness is undeniably a philosophical *tour de force*. Lukács skilfully draws on the resources of German classical idealism and a close reading of Marx's works to offer a version of Marxism which is, primarily, a theory of revolutionary subjectivity. It is, however, easy to see why later Marxists, such as the Frankfurt School, were more influenced by Lukács' analysis of reification than by his theory of class consciousness (see FRANKFURT SCHOOL §1). He himself later called the book 'an attempt to out-Hegel Hegel', with the proletariat as a sociological version of Absolute Spirit. If this self-criticism is hard to fault, some of the charges made by others seem less fair. The concept of imputed class consciousness, for example, has been seen as an anticipation of Stalinism, since it seems to allow the revolutionary party to tell the working class what the latter 'objectively' thinks. In fact, the idea of a party hardly figures in the key 'Reification' essay; it appears mainly in the two final chapters of *History and Class Consciousness*, which engage much more directly, and empirically, with historical and social realities than the rest of the book.

3 Lukács as an orthodox communist

For Lukács to come to terms with a communist movement which by the mid-1920s was becoming increasingly Stalinist in any case involved abandoning the main positions of *History and Class Consciousness*. The decisive step in this transition was taken in 'Moses Hess and the Problem of the Idealist Dialectics' (1926). Here he defends the later Hegel's 'reconciliation with reality', most famously expressed in the Preface to the *Philosophy of Right* (1821). Lukács praises 'Hegel's magnificent realism, his rejection of all utopias, his concern to conceive philosophy *as the conceptual expression of history itself* and not as philosophy *about* history' (1972: 188), and denounces his left Hegelian critics, such as Hess, for regressing to the subjective idealism of Kant and Fichte. The same stance – an identification with the unfolding historical process, warts and all – informs Lukács' later philosophical writings, for example, *Der junge Hegel* (*The Young Hegel*) (1948). In Moscow in the late 1920s he was among the first to study Marx's *Economic and Philosophic Manuscripts of 1844*. This led him to seek to reformulate the dialectic of subject and object at work in *History and Class Consciousness* as the interaction of man and nature, mediated by labour. This forms the leading idea of the posthumously published *Zur Ontologie des gesellschaftlichen Seins* (*Ontology of Social Being*) (1971).

Lukács' later 'reconciliation with reality' involved a strongly positive appraisal of classical bourgeois culture, especially of nineteenth-century literary realism. Indeed Michael Löwy calls 'Lukács' political and intellectual career from 1928 onwards... a consistent attempt to "reconcile" Stalinism with bourgeois-democratic culture' (1979: 204). Certainly there was a marked change from Lukács' pre-Marxist years, when he had been influenced by Dostoevskii's novels, works which arguably anticipate many of the formal innovations of modernism. Lukács' voluminous aesthetic writings from the 1930s onwards wage constant war on the modernism of Joyce and Kafka, which, he argues, marks a regression from the pinnacle of bourgeois cultural achievement, the classical realist novel. Writers such as Tolstoi and Mann, despite their bourgeois limitations, anticipate the future achievements of socialist realism. Never a time-server (he greeted Solzhenitsyn as a socialist realist novelist). Lukács certainly became a cultural conservative, at odds with Marxist champions of modernism such as Brecht and Adorno. Subsequently, however, Fredric Jameson (1981) sought to develop a version of Lukácsian Marxism in which there is a place for modernism, and even for postmodernism.

List of works

Lukács, G. (1916) *Die Theorie des Romans*, Berlin: Paul Cassirer, 1920; trans. A. Bostock, *The Theory of the Novel*, London: Merlin, 1978. (Lukács' most important pre-Marxist work, expressing what he came to regard as a romantic rebellion against, rather than a materialist critique of capitalism.)

—— (1923) *Geschichte und Klassenbewusstsein*, Berlin: Malik-Verlag; trans. R. Livingstone, *History and Class Consciousness*, London: Merlin, 1971. (The most important single work of twentieth-century Marxist philosophy; the English edition contains a highly self-critical preface written in 1967.)

—— (1924) *Lenin*, Berlin: Malik-Verlag; trans. N. Jacobs, *Lenin*, London: New Left Books, 1970. (Written immediately after Lenin's death, and offering an interpretation of the unity of his thought around the theme of 'the actuality of the revolution'.)

—— (1948) *Der junge Hegel*, Zurich and Vienna: Europa Verlag, 2 vols; trans. R. Livingstone, *The Young Hegel*, London: Merlin, 1975. (A detailed discussion of the development of Hegel's thought up to *The Phenomenology of Spirit* (1807), stressing its sociopolitical content and the theme of labour, and anticipating in many respects the later *Ontology of Social Being*.)

—— (1954) *Die Zerstorung der Vernunft*, Berlin: Aufbau-Verlag; trans. P. Palmer, *The Destruction of Reason*, London: Merlin, 1980. (A wide-ranging assault on what Lukács regarded as the German irrationalist tradition culminating in Heidegger.)

—— (1957) *Il significato attuale del realismo critico*, Turin: Einaudi; trans. J. Mander and N. Mander, *The Meaning of Contemporary Realism*, London:

Merlin, 1963. (A succinct polemical statement of Lukács' views on realism and modernism.)

—— (1963) *Die Eigenart des Asthetischen* (The Specificity of the Aesthetic), Neuwied: Luchterhand, 2 vols. (The magnum opus of Lukács' later years.)

—— (1971) *Zur Ontologie des gesellschaftlichen Seins*, Neuwied: Luchterhand; selections trans. D. Fernbach as *The Ontology of Social Being*, London: Merlin, vol.1, *Hegel* (1978), vol. 2, *Marx* (1978), vol. 3, *Labour* (1978). (An attempt to restate the concept of Being starting from an analysis of labour as the mediating activity uniting subject (humankind) and object (nature).)

—— (1972) *Political Writings, 1919–1929*, trans. M. McColgan, London: New Left Books. (Includes, along with many more directly political texts reflecting mainly Lukács' 'left communist' period, 'Moses Hess and the Problem of the Idealist Dialectics' (1926), in which he announced his conversion to a more right Hegelian 'realism'.)

References and further reading

Arato, A., and Breines, P. (1979) *The Young Lukács and the Origins of Western Marxism*, London: Pluto. (Particularly good at reconstructing Lukács' German intellectual context and exploring the debate provoked by *History and Class Consciousness*.)

Bloch, E. *et al.* (1977) *Aesthetics and Politics*, London: New Left Books. (The main texts of the controversy among Marxists over modernism, including an important exchange between Lukács and Brecht.)

* Jameson, F. (1981) *The Political Unconscious*, London: Methuen. (An ambitious attempt at a new synthesis by a cultural theorist heavily influenced by Lukács.)

Kadarkay, A. (1991) *George Lukács*, Oxford: Blackwell. (An informative if philosophically weak biography.)

* Lowy, M. (1979) *George Lukács – From Romanticism to Bolshevism*, London: New Left Books. (A careful, politically shrewd account of Lukács' formation as an intellectual, culminating in *History and Class Consciousness*, but also dealing briefly with his later career.)

Stedman Jones, G. (1971) 'The Marxism of the Early Lukács', *New Left Review* 70: 27–64. (Incisive and highly influential critique of *History and Class Consciousness*, written from a standpoint sympathetic to Althusser.)

ALEX CALLINICOS

859

ŁUKASIEWICZ, JAN (1878–1956)

Before 1918, Łukasiewicz's interests centred on logic (in the broad sense) and philosophy, and he worked on induction and probability. He also wrote an important historical book on the principle of contradiction in Aristotle. After 1918, Łukasiewicz concentrated almost entirely on mathematical logic and was the main organizer of the Warsaw School of Logic. The discovery of many-valued systems of logic is perhaps the most important result he achieved. He also invented an ingenious logical symbolism in which brackets (or other punctuation signs) are not necessary (bracket-free or Polish notation). Propositional calculi became a favourite topic of Łukasiewicz's logical investigations. The history of logic was another subject in which Łukasiewicz achieved important results.

1 Life

Jan Łukasiewicz was born on 21 December 1878 in Lwów. In 1896 he began to study law at the University of Lwów, but in the next year he changed his mind and decided to study philosophy under Kazimierz TWARDOWSKI. He obtained his Ph.D. on the basis of a thesis on the theory of induction. In 1904–5 he studied in Berlin, with Karl Stumpf, and in Louvain, with the cardinal Mercier. In 1906 he obtained his habilitation degree on the basis of a dissertation on the concept of cause. In the same year he became a *Privatdozent* at the University of Lwów and began courses in logic. His course in 1906 was the first in mathematical logic in Poland. In 1909 Łukasiewicz went to Graz, where he participated in Meinong's seminars (see MEINONG, A.). In 1911 he was appointed an extraordinary professor in Lwów. When the University of Warsaw reopened in 1915 (it had been closed by the Tsarist government in the nineteenth century), Łukasiewicz was invited to assume the full professorship there. In 1918 he briefly left to become Minister of Religious Denominations and Public Education in Paderewski's government, but returned in 1920 when the university established a special position for him as professor of philosophy at the Faculty of Mathematics and Science; in fact, it was a position in mathematical logic. As a professor,

Łukasiewicz began a very intensive research and teaching programme with the aim of establishing a logical school in Poland. He fully succeeded and, together with Stanisław LEŚNIEWSKI and the Warsaw mathematicians (Siperpiński, Mazurkiewicz, Kuratowski), he trained a group of brilliant logicians, including Alfred TARSKI (who soon after became the third leader of the Warsaw Logic Group). In the interwar period Łukasiewicz was twice elected the Rector of Warsaw University; he was also awarded an honorary degree by the University of Münster. In 1943–4 he taught in the clandestine University in Warsaw, but he left Poland in 1944 and spent the last months of the Second World War in Germany. In 1946 he became the professor of mathematical logic at the Royal Irish Academy in Dublin, which awarded him an honorary degree in 1955. He died in Dublin on 3 February 1956.

2 Early writings

Induction and probability were the favourite subjects of Łukasiewicz's research in the period 1902–13. At first, he tried to develop the inverse theory of induction proposed by the nineteenth-century logicians Jevons and Sigwart. At the same time, Łukasiewicz was always sceptical about the possibility of evaluating inductive conclusions by probability. He argued that if we have an empirical hypothesis referring to the infinite domain, then its initial (a priori) probability approaches zero and no finite empirical evidence can change this situation. This argument anticipates Popper's basic tenets of anti-inductivism (see POPPER, K.R. §2). Łukasiewicz maintained this scepticism about the value of induction in his later writings (1929); he argued that induction had no scientific value, because science is basically deductive and creative.

While working on induction, Łukasiewicz encountered the problem of the logical foundations of probability (1913). In line with his scepticism about induction, he held that probability has no use in the logical evaluation of sentences which are either true or false. On the other hand, formulas with free variables ('indefinite proposition' is his term) can be characterized by their logical probability. Let D be a domain consisting of a finite number of objects and let Fx be a formula with x as a free variable. Assume that n is the number of objects in D and m is the number of those objects which satisfy the formala Fx. Under these assumptions, the ratio m/n expresses the probability of Fx. The finite case is extensible to infinite domains by means of the mathematical theory of probability.

During this period Łukasiewicz also produced important work on the liar paradox. For Łukasiewicz

(1915), the sentence 'This sentence is false' cannot be a value of variables representing sentences. Thus, it does not fall under general logical rules including itself. However, Łukasiewicz did not explain why the sentence cannot be a value of a variable. Tarski carried this out later, developing Łukasiewicz's ideas and arguing that the liar paradox arises because the sentence confuses object-language and metalanguage (see SEMANTIC PARADOXES AND THEORIES OF TRUTH §1).

O zasadzie sprzeczności u Arystotelesa (On the Principle of Contradiction in Aristotle) (1910) is Łukasiewicz's most important work of the period 1902–17. This book has two objectives: a contribution to the history of philosophy by providing an original interpretation of the principle of contradiction in Aristotle, and an evaluation of arguments in its favour (see ARISTOTLE §5). According to Łukasiewicz, we can find three meanings of the principle in Aristotle: first, the logical principle that no proposition and its negation can be true together; second, the ontological principle that no object can have and not have the same property at the same time; and third, the psychological principle that one cannot have contradictory beliefs. Now, the psychological principle of contradiction is plainly false. Since one can prove the equivalence of the logical and ontological principles of contradiction, there remains the problem of providing a justification for one of them; Łukasiewicz argues that Aristotle's justification is not convincing. His main thesis is that we can give a justification for the principle (it follows from the definition of 'being an object'), but that it is not thereby shown to be among the axioms of logic. Hence the reason that we accept it is ethical rather than logical: we need some means of distinguishing truths from falsehoods.

3 Many-valued logic

Łukasiewicz's doubts about the principle of contradiction clearly set him on the path of many-valued logic. Before leaving the university in 1918 for his post in the government, he announced his discovery of a non-Aristotelian logic, then presented the idea in two talks in Lwów in 1920. Łukasiewicz's first motivation for many-valued logic was ethical. He believed that creativity, freedom and responsibility require a special ontology in which determinism fails. For this reason, he introduced a third logical value: possibility, which can be ascribed to sentences about future events. Łukasiewicz was also guided by the ancient question of what truth-value, if any, statements about the future have. However, he soon began to describe his system as 'many-valued logic' instead of 'non-Aristotelian logic'. For it is not clear that Aristotle himself

considered the law of the excluded middle to be universally valid; there are statements in Aristotle's writings which suggest that this principle does not apply to sentences about the future. Furthermore, it was CHRYSIPPUS, a Stoic, who argued very strongly for the universality of the excluded middle. Thus Łukasiewicz called many-valued logic 'non-Chrysippean' rather than non-Aristotelian. However, on his final view, the issue does not lie in the acceptability of certain principles of logic, the law of contradiction or the law of the excluded middle, for example. Since logic is based on metalogical assumptions, the difference between two-valued and many-valued logic ultimately depends on whether one accepts the principle of bivalence: that every sentence is either true or false.

From the formal point of view, Łukasiewicz first elaborated a three-valued logic. Let the fraction $\frac{1}{2}$ denote the third value. If p has this value, its negation not-p has the same value. A disjunction always has the value of the 'greater or equal' disjuncts, a conjunction has that of the 'smaller or equal' conjuncts, and an implication has the third value, if its antecedent is 'third' and its consequent false or its antecedent is true and its consequent 'third'; in all other cases an implication is true, except where it has a true antecedent and a false consequent, in which case it is false. So the truth-tables for cases in which only truth and falsity are involved remain the same as usual. Łukasiewicz then generalized many-valued logic to systems with an arbitrary, finite or infinite, number of values. The conditional 'If p, then q' is true if $p \leqslant q$, and has a value given by the formula $1 - p + q$ if $p > q$. The value of not-p is always calculated as $1 - p$. Łukasiewicz also considered the axiomatization of many-valued logic. For example, he and Wajsberg established that many-valued logic with a countable infinite number of values is axiomatized by the formulas (in Łukasiewicz's notation; see §4 below): $CpCqp$, $CCpqCCqrCpr$, $CCCpqqCCqpp$, $CCCpqCqpCqp$, $CCNpNqCqp$.

Many-valued logic became a basis for Łukasiewicz's treatment of modality. He wanted to have a modal logic with the following principles: (1) if it is not possible that p, then not-p, (2) if not-p, then it is not possible that p and (3) for some p, it is possible that p and it is possible that not-p (Aristotle's principle). Łukasiewicz proved that (1)–(3) cannot be represented together in two-valued logic. Tarski suggested to him that possibility could be defined within three-valued logic by the formula 'If not-p, then p'. However, Łukasiewicz did not complete his modal logic before the Second World War. He returned to this question after 1945 and offered several systems of modal logic (see MODAL LOGIC §1).

A historical question remains: who discovered many-valued logic? There are anticipations in antiquity and the Middle Ages. One can also find several hints in Peirce's work and in that of the Russian philosopher Vasiliev. However, it is evident that Łukasiewicz first elaborated many-valued logic as a mature formal system along with its intuitive motivation (see MANY-VALUED LOGICS §1).

4 Propositional calculi

Łukasiewicz invented a special notation for logic. This notation, often called 'Polish' notation, ensures that punctuation signs (brackets, dots and so on) are dispensable. The principle is that functors are always written before arguments. For example, the formulas $(p > \rightarrow \neg p) \rightarrow q$ and $p \rightarrow (\neg p \rightarrow q)$ have respectively '$CCpNpq$' and 'as their 'Polish' counterparts $CpCNpq$' ('C' stands for implication, 'N' for negation). It can be proved that the succession of letters in the Polish notation uniquely determines the structure of expressions.

Łukasiewicz achieved several results in propositional calculi. For example, he axiomatized the classical propositional calculus by the following set of axioms: $CCpqCCqrCpr$, $CCNppp$, $CpCNpq$. He also investigated partial propositional calculi, that is, calculi in which there occur only some of the propositional functors, such as systems with equivalence or implication as sole functors. Giving the most economic axiomatic bases for propositional calculi was his favourite subject-matter. For example, he proved that the sole axiom for the equivalential propositional calculus must have at least ten letters. Łukasiewicz also investigated intuitionistic logic.

5 The history of logic

Łukasiewicz had a deep understanding of the history of logic and proposed a study of it from the point of view of modern mathematical logic. The result was very striking. Łukasiewicz, recognizing that there is a basic difference between the propositional calculus and syllogistic logic which had been overlooked before mathematical logic arose, discovered that the ancient Stoics had elaborated a propositional calculus and thus had a system of logic which differed fundamentally from that of Aristotle (see LOGIC, ANCIENT §5; STOICISM §10). Łukasiewicz also found interesting examples of propositional logic in the Middle Ages (see LOGIC, MEDIEVAL §9). But Aristotle remained Łukasiewicz's favourite philosopher. Even before 1939 he began research on Aristotelian logic which resulted in an extensive reconstruction of syllogistic logic from the point of view of modern

logic. In his book *Aristotle's Syllogistic from the Standpoint of Modern Formal Logic* (1951) he brought this work together, while displaying his new methodology for the history of logic.

6 Philosophy of logic

Many-valued logic leads to the question of which logic is 'right'. At first, Łukasiewicz advocated the ontological conception of logic: logic is a description of reality. Hence, one and only one system from the family of rivals is true in the real world. He believed that the infinite many-valued logic is right. However, after 1945 he took a more conventionalist route: logics are devices of our thinking, and when we decide which tool is to be chosen, we must take into account various factors, such as simplicity. Łukasiewicz regarded logic as an independent science which is the servant neither of philosophy nor of mathematics. However, he always maintained that logic is of the utmost significance for philosophy. In particular, he demanded that philosophy should be axiomatized.

See also: POLISH LOGIC §2

List of works

Łukasiewicz, J. (1970) *Selected Works*, ed. L. Borkowski, Amsterdam and Warsaw: North Holland and PWN. (A selection of the most important logical and philosophical papers of Łukasiewicz.)

—— (1903) 'O indukcji jako inwersji dedukcji' (On Induction as Inversion of Deduction), *Przegląd Filozoficzny* 6: 9–24; 138–52. (Łukasiewicsz's Ph.D. thesis; an attempt to develop the inversion theory of induction.)

—— (1906) 'Analiza i konstrukcja pojęcia przyczyny' (An Analysis and Construction of the Concept of Cause), *Przegląd Filzoficzny* 9: 105–79. (Łukasiewicz's *Habilitation* dissertation; an attempt to define causality as a logical relation.)

—— (1909) 'O prawdopodobieństwie wniosków indukcyjnych' (On the Probability of Inductive Conclusions), *Przegląd Filozoficzny* 12: 209–10. (Łukasiewicz's arguments against the probabilistic justification of induction)

—— (1910) *O zasadzie sprzeczności u Arystotelesa*, Cracow: Polska Akademia Umiejętności; partly trans. V. Wedlin in 'On the Principle of Contradiction in Aristotle', *Review of Metaphysics* 24: 485–509. (An extensive treatment of Aristotle's views on the principles of contradiction, together with its interpretation in the framework of algebra of logic.)

—— (1913) *Die logischen Grundlagen der Wahrschein-*

lichkeitsrechnung (The Logical Foundations of Probability), Cracow: Polska Akademia Umiejętności; partly trans. O. Wojtasiewicz in *Selected Works*, Borkowski, 1970. (An attempt to formulate the logical foundations of probability.)

—— (1915) 'O nauce' (On Science), in *Poradnik dla samouków* (A Guide for Autodidacts), Warsaw: Heflich i Michalski, XV–XXXIX. (Contains Łukasiewicz's treatment of the liar paradox.)

—— (1918) *Wykład pożegnalny w Uniwłersytetu Warszawskiego, 7 marca 1918* (Farewell Lecture in the University Hall of the University of Warsaw, 7 March 1918), Warsaw; trans. O. Wojtasiewicz in *Selected Works*, Borkowski, 1970. (The first public announcement of many-valued logic and motives behind it.)

—— (1920a) 'O pojęciu możliwości' (On the Concept of Possibility), *Ruch Filzoficzny* 6: 169–70; trans. O. Wojtasiewicz in *Selected Works*, Borkowski, 1970. (Łukasiewicz's first talk on many-valued logic, given in Lwów in 1920; contains formal details of many-valued logic.)

—— (1920b) 'O logice trójwartościowej' (On Three-Valued Logic), *Ruch Filzoficzny* 6: 170–1; trans. O. Wojtasiewicz in *Selected Works*, Borkowski, 1970. (The second talk on many-valued logic in Lwów in 1920; a continuation of 1920a.)

—— (1929) *Elementy logiki matematycznej*, Warsaw: PWN; trans. O. Wojtasiewicz, *Elements of Mathematical Logic*, Oxford: Pergamon Press, 1963. (Lecture notes of Łukasiewicz; contain an exposition of Polish notation, a system of propositional logic, various metalogical results, information on many-valued logic, plus a brief formal treatment of syllogistic.)

—— (1930) 'Philosophische Bemerkungen zu mehrwertigen Systemen des Aussagenkalküls', *Compt. Rend. Soc. d. Sc. Let. Varsovie, Cl. III* 23: 51–77; trans. H. Weber in *Selected Works*, Borkowski, 1970. (A systematic exposition of intuitions and formal problems of many-valued logic.)

—— (1951) *Aristotle's Syllogistic from the Standpoint of Modern Formal Logic*, Oxford: Oxford University Press; 2nd enlarged edition, 1957. (A systematic modern treatment of Aristotelian syllogistic; the second edition contains chapters on modal syllogistic.)

References and further reading

Bolc, L. and Borowik, P. (1992) *Many-valued Logics, 1, Theoretical Foundations*, Springer-Verlag. (An extensive monograph on many-valued logics, including a survey of Łukasiewiczian logics.)

Borkowski, L. and Słupecki, J. (1958) 'The Logical Works of Jan Łukasiewicz', *Studia Logica* 8: 7–56. (Contains a presentation of all Łukasiewicz's works in logic, including his ideas in philosophy of science.)

Kwiatkowski, T. (1981) 'Jan Łukasiewicz – A Historian of Logic', *Organon* 16/17: 169–88. (A survey of Łukasiewicz's works in the history of logic.)

Malinowski, G. (1993) *Many-valued Logics*, Oxford: Oxford University Press. (A concise survey of many-valued logics from the contemporary point of view.)

Rescher, N. (1967) *Many-valued Logic*, New York: McGraw-Hill. (A extensive historical and systematic survey of many-valued logics with a very useful bibliography.)

Seddon, F.A. (1996) *Aristotle and Łukasiewicz on the Principle of Contradiction*, Ames, IA: Modern Logic Publishing. (A critical analysis of Łukasiewicz's treatment of the principle of contradiction in Aristotle; however, Seddon bases his criticism on Łukasiewicz (1971), which is only a summary of Łukasiewicz (1910).)

Sobociński, B. (1957) '*In Memoriam* Jan Łukasiewicz', *Philosophical Studies* (Maynooth, Ireland) 6: 3–49. (A detailed presentation of Łukasiewicz's logical ideas; this paper also includes Łukasiewicz's short autobiography.)

Woleński, J. (1989) *Logic and Philosophy in the Lvov-Warsaw School*, Dordrecht: Kluwer. (Chapters 1, 3, 5, 6 and 10 contain information about Łukasiewicz's views in philosophy as well as his works in logic and philosophy of science.)

—— (1994) 'Jan Łukasiewicz on the Liar Paradox, Logical Consequence, Truth, and Induction', *Modern Logic* 4: 392–400. (Contains a summary of Łukasiewicz 's views on the liar paradox, logical consequence, truth and induction.)

Wójcicki, R. and Czelakowski, J. (eds) (1977) *Selected Papers on Łukasiewicz Sentential Calculi*, Wrocław: Ossolineum. (A collection on Łukasiewiczian logics from the contemporary perspective.)

JAN WOLEŃSKI

LULL, RAMON *see* LLULL, RAMON

LUNYU *see* CONFUCIUS

LUSHI CHUNQIU

The Lushi chunqiu *(Spring and Autumn Annals of Master Lu Buwei), composed 241–238 BC, marks a firm beginning for the eclectic movement in Qin and Han philosophy. It embraces various pre-Qin philosophies such as Lao–Zhuang and Huang–Lao Daoism, Confucianism, Mozi, Legalism, the logicians, the military arts, Agriculturalists, Yang Zhu, Zou Yen and Story Tellers. As a compendium of classical knowledge, the* Lushi chunqiu *contains cultural and philosophical material on the art of rulership.*

The *Lushi chunqiu*, or *Lü-shih Ch'un-ch'iu* (Spring and Autumn Annals of Master Lu Buwei) was completed between 241 and 238 BC by guest scholars at the estate of Lu Buwei during his appointment as Prime Minister of Qin (249–237 BC). It is divided into three sections: the Twelve Chronicles (*shi'erji*), containing twelve subsections with five chapters each and a postscript; the Eight Observations (*balan*), divided into eight subsections of eight chapters each (the first subsection is missing a chapter); and the Six Discussions (*liulun*), divided into six subsections with six chapters apiece. These numbers possibly had symbolic significance, representing the Three Powers, heaven, earth and humans.

The lead chapter of each Chronicle, arranged according to the months of the four seasons, gives instructions on the monthly court ritual, also found in the 'Monthly Commands' chapter of the *Liji* (Book of Rites). The remaining chapters in each Chronicle discuss numerous concerns of rulership from an eclectic perspective, loosely arranged under a seasonal programme. The spring section contains Yang Zhu and Daoist-like advice on self-cultivation; the summer presents Confucian approaches to education and music; the autumn focuses on military affairs; and the winter focuses on frugal funerals and administering state personnel.

The text is eclectic, and one ought to be wary of scholars who contend that *Lushi chunqiu* as a whole advocates one particular philosophy or argues exclusively against one. Although the postscript claims that the Twelve Chronicles relate the Yellow Emperor's Daoist teachings and the spring Chronicles are Daoist-like, it would be misleading to say that the text is chiefly Daoist because other chapters are clearly Confucian, Mohist and Legalist. Some contend that the text is anti-Legalist; however, the chapter 'Examining the Present' (*chajin*) advocates the Legalist doctrine of not following the standards of the early kings, and some of this material appears in edicts written later by the notorious Legalist Prime

Minister of Qin, Li Si. The *Lushi chunqiu* is in fact drawn from various pre-Qin philosophers.

Some of the Daoist ideas in the *Lushi chunqiu* concern the ruler's self-cultivation and ruling by nonaction (*wuwei*) (see SELF-CULTIVATION IN CHINESE PHILOSOPHY). The ruler practises non-action while the ministers perform their duties. The ruler is warned against overindulgence in sensual gratification, and to carefully guard and protect life; it is the ministers who must sacrifice their lives for the king. The ruler is encouraged to govern with public spiritedness; political factions and selfish exploits are to be avoided. The ruler is expected to be obscure and unknown. His self-cultivation generates harmony with nature, which maintains political order.

The Confucian teachings in the text also deal with the ruler's self-cultivation and rulership. Court ritual and music are emphasized; the *Lushi chunqiu* contains the most extensive extant pre-Qin material on ritual music. Analogies are drawn between musical and political harmony. Following the teachings of CONFUCIUS and MENCIUS, some passages delineate the importance of governing by moral virtue, following the example of the early sage-kings. Other passages resemble the heavy-handed teachings of XUNZI, emphasizing rewards and punishments and the need for the ruler to heed the remonstrance of teachers and ministers.

Mohist ideas are present as well. Many of the chapters, like MOZI, advocate a practical approach to rulership, especially learning from past historical errors. The Mohist material in the *Lushi chunqiu* advocates the value of keeping the people happy and not squandering the state treasury on royal funerals; the latter counters Confucian practice.

The text of Zou Yen and his Five Phases (*wuxing*) philosophy is lost, but passages in the *Lushi chunqiu* represent those teachings. One such passage narrates how past rulers established their respective dynasties by following the cosmic changes of the Five Phases. For example, King Wen founded the Zhou dynasty by complying with the Fire Phase. It further states that water will conquer fire; the King of Qin used this cosmology to justify his unification of the empire in 221 BC. The *Lushi chunqiu*'s Militarist chapters reject disarmament, and advocate maintaining troops to fight a just war. A virtuous ruler ought to attack an immoral king who oppresses his people.

The *Lushi chunqiu* contains most of the extant pre-Qin Agriculturalist philosophy. Details on farming practices and the importance of bountiful harvests to maintain political order and attract immigrants are discussed. The Agriculturalists, like the Confucian ritualists, emphasize that the ruler should take timely action to create and maintain cosmic and political harmony. Finally, the Story Tellers, the masters of rhetoric, contribute a vast number of interesting, sometimes humorous, illustrative stories to elucidate various philosophical points in the *Lushi chunqiu*. Some of their practical guidelines are applicable to our age. For example, the various discussions on the relationship between humans and nature are relevant to environmental ethics. Some of the ideas on governing and employment of the masses are pertinent to modern politics. The advice given for the ruler's self-cultivation can be applied by anyone.

See also: CHINESE PHILOSOPHY; CONFUCIAN PHILOSOPHY, CHINESE; DAOIST PHILOSOPHY; LEGALIST PHILOSOPHY, CHINESE; MOHIST PHILOSOPHY; SELF-CULTIVATION IN CHINESE PHILOSOPHY; YANGZHU

References and further readings

Bodde, D. (1967) *China's First Unifier, A Study in the Ch'in Dynasty as seen in the Life of Li Ssu*, Hong Kong: Hong Kong University Press. (A valuable source for understanding the Qin (Ch'in) dynasty.)

Carson, M.F. (1985) *A Concordance to Lü-shih ch'un-ch'iu*, Taipei: Chinese Material Center. (Contains material on the structure and history of the text; required for a comprehensive study of specific characters.)

Fung Yu-lan (1952) *A History of Chinese Philosophy*, trans. D. Bodde, Princeton, NJ: Princeton University Press. 2 vols. (Volume 1 makes extensive use of *Lushi chunqiu* to explicate the philosophy of the Hundred Schools, especially Yang Zhu and Zou Yen.)

Graham, A.C. (1989) *Disputers of the Tao*, La Salle, IL: Open Court. (Proposes that Yangism is at the core of the text, and describes its cosmology.)

Hsiao Kung-ch'üan (1979) *A History of Chinese Political Thought*, trans F. Mote, Princeton, NJ: Princeton University Press. (Part 2, Section 3 develops the idea that the text is anti-Legalist.)

Louton, J. (1984) 'Concepts of Comprehensiveness and Historical Change on the *Lü-shih ch'un-ch'iu*', in H. Rosemont, Jr (ed.) *Explorations in Early Chinese Cosmology*, Chico, CA: Scholars Press, 105–18. (Argues that its authors understood historical change to be a product of the interaction of humans and nature.)

Lushi chunqiu (241–238 BC), trans. R. Wilhelm, *Frühling und Herbst des Lü Bu We*, Düsseldorf: Eugen Diederichs Verlag, 1979. (The first complete translation of the *Lushi chunqiu* in a Western language.)

Needham, J. (1956) *Science and Civilisation in China*, vol. 2, *History of Scientific Thought*, Cambridge: Cambridge University Press. (Provides an insightful survey of pre-Qin philosophy. Many of the later volumes cite passages from the *Lushi chunqiu* to illustrate Chinese science.)

Sellman, J. (1983) 'On Mobilizing the Military: Arguments for a Just War Theory from the *Lü-shih ch'un-ch'iu*', *Asian Culture Quarterly* 11 (4): 26–43. (Contains a translation of the relevant portion of the text.)

—— (1985) 'The *Lü-shih ch'un-ch'iu*'s Proposal of Governing by Filial Piety', *Asian Culture Quarterly* 13 (1): 43–62. (Explicates the philosophical arguments, and provides a translation of one chapter.)

—— (1990) 'Seasonality in the Achievement of *Hsing* in the *Lü-shih ch'un-ch'iu*', *Asian Culture Quarterly* 18 (2): 42–68. (Explicates the eclectic understanding of human nature.)

Watson, B. (1962) *Early Chinese Literature*, New York: Columbia University Press, 186–9. (Provides a critical review and a translation of one chapter.)

JAMES D. SELLMANN

LÜ-SHIH CH'UN-CH'IU
see LUSHI CHUNQIU